Collins
Italian
Dictionary
& Grammar

HarperCollins Publishers
Westerhill Road
Bishopbriggs
Glasgow
G64 2QT

Third Edition 2014

10 9 8 7 6 5 4 3 2

© HarperCollins Publishers 2008, 2010, 2014

ISBN 978-0-00-748437-9
Collins Italian Concise Dictionary
US 6th Edition
ISBN 978-0-06-241015-3

Collins® is a registered trademark of
HarperCollins Publishers Limited

www.collinsdictionary.com
www.collins.co.uk

A catalogue record for this book is
available from the British Library

Typeset by Davidson Publishing Solutions

Printed and bound in India by
Thomson Press India Ltd.

Acknowledgements
We would like to thank those authors
and publishers who kindly gave
permission for copyright material to be
used in the Collins Corpus. We would also
like to thank Times Newspapers Ltd for
providing valuable data.

EDITOR
Susie Beattie

CONTRIBUTORS
Phyllis Buchanan
Francesca Logi
Janice McNeillie
Helen Newstead

TECHNICAL SUPPORT
Thomas Callan
Agnieszka Urbanowicz
Dave Wark

FOR THE PUBLISHER
Gerry Breslin
Catherine Love
Evelyn Sword

Contributors to the previous edition
Gaëlle Amiot-Cadey, Gabriella Bacchelli,
Donatella Boi, Michela Clari, Daphne Day,
Genevieve Gerrard, Angela Jack,
Joyce Littlejohn, Val McNulty,
Elizabeth Potter, Maggie Seaton,
Caroline Smart, Rachel Smith,
Jill Williams

Indice

Contents

I MARCHI REGISTRATI

I termini che a nostro parere costituiscono un marchio registrato sono stati designati come tali. In ogni caso, né la presenza né l'assenza di tale designazione implicano alcuna valutazione del loro reale stato giuridico.

NOTE ON TRADEMARKS

Words which we have reason to believe constitute trademarks have been designated as such. However, neither the presence nor the absence of such designation should be regarded as affecting the legal status of any trademark.

Introduzione

Se desiderate imparare l'inglese o approfondire le conoscenze già acquisite, se volete leggere o redigere dei testi in inglese, oppure conversare con interlocutori di madrelingua inglese, se siete studenti, turisti, uomini o donne d'affari avete scelto il compagno di viaggio ideale per esprimervi e comunicare in inglese sia a voce che per iscritto. Strumento pratico e moderno, il vostro dizionario dà largo spazio al linguaggio quotidiano in campi quali l'attualità, gli affari, la gestione d'ufficio, l'informatica e il turismo. Come in tutti i nostri dizionari, grande importanza è stata data alla lingua contemporanea e alle espressioni idiomatiche.

Come usare il dizionario

Troverete qui di seguito alcune spiegazioni sul modo in cui le informazioni sono state presentate nel testo. L'obiettivo del dizionario è quello di darvi il maggior numero possibile di informazioni senza tuttavia sacrificare la chiarezza all'interno delle voci.

Le voci

Qui di seguito verranno descritti i vari elementi di cui si compone una voce tipo del vostro dizionario.

La trascrizione fonetica

Come regola generale è stata data la pronuncia di tutte le parole inglesi e quella delle parole italiane che potevano presentare qualche difficoltà per il parlante inglese. Nella parte inglese-italiano, tuttavia, per la pronuncia di nomi composti formati da due parole non unite dal trattino si dovrà cercare la trascrizione di ciascuna di queste parole alla rispettiva posizione alfabetica. La pronuncia si trova tra parentesi quadre, subito dopo il lemma. Come nella maggior parte dei dizionari moderni è stato adottato il sistema noto come "alfabeto fonetico internazionale". Troverete qui di seguito, a pagina xiii e xiv, un elenco completo dei caratteri utilizzati in questo sistema.

Le categorie grammaticali

Tutte le parole appartengono ad una categoria grammaticale, cioè possono essere sostantivi, verbi, aggettivi, avverbi, pronomi, articoli o congiunzioni.

I sostantivi possono essere singolari o plurali, sia in italiano che in inglese, e maschili o femminili in italiano. I verbi possono essere transitivi o intransitivi in entrambe le lingue, ma anche riflessivi o impersonali in italiano; nella sezione italiano-inglese, i verbi sono seguiti da un numero in grassetto che rimanda alle tavole dei verbi nelle pagine xviii-xxii. La categoria grammaticale appare in maiuscoletto subito dopo la pronuncia ed eventuali informazioni di tipo morfologico (plurali irregolari ecc.).

Numerose voci sono state suddivise in varie categorie grammaticali. Per esempio la parola italiana **bene** può essere sia un avverbio che un aggettivo o un sostantivo, e la parola inglese **sneeze** può essere sia un sostantivo ("starnuto") che un verbo intransitivo ("starnutire"). Analogamente il verbo italiano **correre** può essere usato sia come verbo intransitivo ("correre alla stazione") che come transitivo ("correre un rischio"). Per presentare la voce con maggiore chiarezza e permettervi di trovare rapidamente la traduzione che cercate, è stato introdotto un triangolino nero ▶ per contrassegnare il passaggio da una categoria grammaticale ad un'altra.

Suddivisioni semantiche

La maggior parte delle parole ha più di un significato. Per esempio, la parola **fiocco** può essere sia un'annodatura di un nastro che una falda di neve. Molte parole si traducono in modo diverso a seconda del contesto in cui sono usate: per esempio **scala** si tradurrà in inglese con "staircase" o "stairs" se si tratta di una scala con gradini, con "ladder" se è una scala a pioli. Per permettervi di scegliere la traduzione giusta per ciascuno dei contesti in cui la parola si può trovare, le voci sono state suddivise in categorie di significato. Ciascuna suddivisione è introdotta da un "indicatore d'uso" tra parentesi in *corsivo*. Le voci **fiocco** e **scala** compariranno quindi nel testo nel modo seguente:

> **fi'occo, -chi** SM (*di nastro*) bow; (*di stoffa, lana*)
> flock; (*di neve*) flake; ...

> **'scala** SF (*a gradini ecc*) staircase, stairs pl;
> (*a pioli, di corda*) ladder; ...

Per segnalare la traduzione appropriata sono stati introdotti anche degli indicatori d'ambito d'uso in *corsivo* con la prima lettera maiuscola, tra parentesi, spesso in forma abbreviata, come per esempio nel caso della voce **tromba**:

> **'tromba** SF (*Mus*) trumpet; (*Aut*) horn; ...

L'elenco completo delle abbreviazioni adottate nel dizionario è riportato alle pagine xiii e xiv.

Le traduzioni

Per la maggior parte delle parole inglesi ed italiane ci sono traduzioni precise a seconda del significato o del contesto, come risulta dagli esempi riportati fin qui. A volte, tuttavia, le parole non hanno un preciso equivalente nella lingua d'arrivo: in questi casi è stato fornito un equivalente approssimativo, preceduto dal segno ≈, come ad esempio per l'abbreviazione **RAC**, per cui è stato dato l'equivalente italiano "A.C.I.", dato che le due associazioni svolgono nei due paesi funzioni analoghe:

> **RAC** N ABBR (*BRIT*: = *Royal Automobile Club*)
> ≈ A.C.I. m (= *Automobile Club d'Italia*)

A volte è persino impossibile trovare un equivalente approssimativo. Questo è il caso, per esempio, di piatti tipici di un certo paese, come ad esempio **pandoro**:

> **pan'doro** SM *type of sponge cake eaten at* Christmas

In questi casi, al posto della traduzione, che non esiste, comparirà una spiegazione: per maggiore chiarezza, questa spiegazione o glossa è stata messa in *corsivo*.

Molto spesso la traduzione di una parola può non funzionare all'interno di una data locuzione. Ad esempio alla voce **dare**, verbo spesso tradotto con "to give" in inglese, troviamo varie locuzioni per alcune delle quali la traduzione fornita all'inizio della voce non si può utilizzare: **quanti anni mi dai?** "how old do you think I am?" **danno ancora quel film?** "is that film still showing?", **dare per certo qc** "to consider sth certain", e così via. Ed è proprio in questi casi che potrete verificare l'utilità e la completezza del dizionario, che contiene una ricca gamma di composti, locuzioni e frasi idiomatiche.

Il registro linguistico

In italiano sapete istintivamente scegliere l'espressione corretta da usare a seconda del contesto in cui vi esprimete. Per esempio saprete quando dire **Non me ne importa!** e quando invece potete dire **Chi se ne frega?** Più difficile sarà farlo in inglese, dove avete minore consapevolezza delle sfumature di registro linguistico. Per questo motivo nella parte inglese-italiano le parole ed espressioni inglesi di uso più familiare sono segnalate dall'abbreviazione (*col*), mentre (*col!*) segnala le parole ed espressioni volgari. Nella parte italiano-inglese (*!*) dopo una traduzione segnala che si tratta di una parola od espressione volgare.

Parole chiave

Come vedrete, ad alcune voci è stato riservato un trattamento particolare sia dal punto di vista grafico che da quello linguistico. Si tratta di voci come **essere** o **fare**, o dei loro equivalenti inglesi **be** e **do**, che per la loro importanza e complessità meritano una strutturazione più articolata ed un maggior numero di locuzioni illustrative. Queste voci sono strutturate in diverse categorie di significato contrassegnate da numeri, e le costruzioni sintattiche e locuzioni che illustrano quel particolare significato sono riportate all'interno della relativa categoria.

Informazioni culturali

Le voci affiancate da una sbarra verticale digradante approfondiscono aspetti della cultura italiana o di quella dei paesi di lingua inglese in argomenti quali la politica, la scuola, i mass media e le festività nazionali.

Introduction

You may be starting to learn Italian, or you may wish to extend your knowledge of the language. Perhaps you want to read and study Italian books, newspapers and magazines, or perhaps simply have a conversation with Italian speakers. Whatever the reason, whether you're a student, a tourist or want to use Italian for business, this is the ideal book to help you understand and communicate. This modern, user-friendly dictionary gives priority to everyday vocabulary and the language of current affairs, business and tourism. As in all Collins dictionaries, the emphasis is firmly placed on contemporary language and expressions.

How to use the dictionary
Below you will find an outline of how information is presented in your dictionary. Our aim is to give you the maximum amount of detail in the clearest and most helpful way.

Entries
A typical entry in your dictionary will be made up of the following elements:

Phonetic transcription
Phonetics appear in square brackets immediately after the headword. They are shown using the International Phonetic Alphabet (IPA), and a complete list of the symbols used in this system can be found on pages xiii and xiv.

Grammatical information
All words belong to one of the following parts of speech: noun, verb, adjective, adverb, pronoun, article, conjunction, preposition.

Nouns can be singular or plural and, in Italian, masculine or feminine. Verbs can be transitive, intransitive, reflexive or impersonal: on the Italian side, each verb is followed by a number in bold, which corresponds to verb tables on pages xvi-xix. Parts of speech appear in SMALL CAPS immediately after the phonetic spelling of the headword.

Often a word can have more than one part of speech. Just as the English word **chemical** can be an adjective or a noun, the Italian word **fondo** can be an adjective ("deep") or a masculine noun ("bottom"). In the same way the verb **to walk** is sometimes transitive, ie it takes an object ("to walk the dog") and sometimes intransitive, ie it doesn't take an object ("to walk to school"). To help you find the meaning you are looking for quickly and for clarity of presentation, the different part of speech categories are separated by a solid black triangle ▶.

Meaning divisions

Most words have more than one meaning. Take, for example, **punch** which can be, amongst other things, a blow with the fist or an object used for making holes. Other words are translated differently depending on the context in which they are used. The transitive verb **to roll up**, for example, can be translated by "arrotolare" or "rimboccare" depending on what it is you are rolling up. To help you select the most appropriate translation in every context, entries are divided according to meaning. Each different meaning is introduced by an "indicator" in *italics* and in brackets. Thus, the examples given above will be shown as follows:

> **punch** [pʌntʃ] N (*blow*) pugno; (*fig: force*) forza; (*tool*) punzone *m*; ...

> ▸ **roll up** VI (*col: arrive*) arrivare ▸ VT (*carpet, cloth, map*) arrotolare; (*sleeves*) rimboccare ...

Likewise, some words can have a different meaning when used to talk about a specific subject area or field. For example, **bishop**, which is generally used to mean a high-ranking clergyman, is also the name of a chess piece. To show English speakers which translation to use, we have added "subject field labels" in *italics*, starting with a capital letter, and in brackets, in this case (*Chess*):

> **bishop** ['bɪʃəp] N vescovo; (*Chess*) alfiere *m*

Field labels are often shortened to save space. You will find a complete list of abbreviations used in the dictionary on pages xi and xii.

Translations

Most English words have a direct translation in Italian and vice versa, as shown in the examples given above. Sometimes, however, no exact equivalent exists in the target language. In such cases we have given an approximate equivalent, indicated by the sign ≈. Such is the case of **National Insurance**, the Italian equivalent of which is "Previdenza Sociale". This is not an exact translation since the systems of the two countries in question are quite different:

> **National Insurance** N (*BRIT*) ≈ Previdenza Sociale

On occasion it is impossible to find even an approximate equivalent. This may be the case, for example, with the names of types of food:

> **cottage pie** N *piatto a base di carne macinata in sugo e purè di patate*

Here the translation (which doesn't exist) is replaced by an explanation. For increased clarity the explanation, or "gloss", is shown in *italics*.

It is often the case that a word, or a particular meaning of a word, cannot be translated in isolation. The translation of **Dutch**, for example, is "olandese". However, the phrase **to go Dutch** is rendered by "fare alla romana". Even an expression as simple as **washing powder** needs a separate translation since it translates as "detersivo (in polvere)", not "polvere per lavare". This is where your dictionary will prove to be particularly informative and useful since it contains an abundance of compounds, phrases and idiomatic expressions.

Levels of formality and familiarity

In English you instinctively know when to say **I'm broke** or **I'm a bit short of cash** and when to say **I don't have any money**. When you are trying to understand someone who is speaking Italian, however, or when you yourself try to speak Italian, it is important to know what is polite and what is less so, and what you can say in a relaxed situation but not in a formal context. To help you with this, on the Italian-English side we have added the label (*col*) to show that an Italian word or expression is colloquial, while those words or expressions which are vulgar are given an exclamation mark (*col!*), warning you they can cause serious offence. Note also that on the English-Italian side, translations which are vulgar are followed by an exclamation mark in brackets.

Keywords

Words labelled in the text as KEYWORDS, such as **be** and **do** or their Italian equivalents **essere** and **fare**, have been given special treatment because they form the basic elements of the language. This extra help will ensure that you know how to use these complex words with confidence.

Cultural information

Entries which appear next to a fading vertical bar explain aspects of culture in Italy and English-speaking countries. Subject areas covered include politics, education, media and national festivals.

Abbreviazioni

Abbreviations

abbreviazione	ABBR	abbreviation
aggettivo	ADJ, AG	adjective
amministrazione	*Admin*	administration
avverbio	ADV	adverb
aeronautica, viaggi aerei	*Aer*	flying, air travel
aggettivo	AG	adjective
agricoltura	*Agr*	agriculture
amministrazione	*Amm*	administration
anatomia	*Anat*	anatomy
architettura	*Archit*	architecture
astronomia, astrologia	*Astr*	astronomy, astrology
l'automobile	*Aut*	the motor car and motoring
verbo ausiliare	AUX VB	auxiliary verb
avverbio	AV	adverb
aeronautica, viaggi aerei	*Aviat*	flying, air travel
biologia	*Biol*	biology
botanica	*Bot*	botany
inglese della Gran Bretagna	BRIT	British English
consonante	C	consonant
chimica	*Chim, Chem*	chemistry
familiare (! da evitare)	*col(!)*	colloquial usage (! particularly offensive)
commercio, finanza, banca	*Comm*	commerce, finance, banking
informatica	*Comput*	computing
congiunzione	CONG	conjunction
congiunzione	CONJ	conjunction
edilizia	*Constr*	building
sostantivo usato come aggettivo, non può essere usato nè come attributo, nè dopo il sostantivo qualificato	CPD	compound element: noun used as adjective and which cannot follow the noun it qualifies
cucina	*Cus, Culin*	cookery
davanti a	*dav*	before
determinante: articolo, aggettivo dimostrativo o indefinito etc	DET	determiner: article, demonstrative etc
diritto	*Dir*	law
economia	*Econ*	economics
edilizia	*Edil*	building
elettricità, elettronica	*Elettr, Elec*	electricity, electronics
esclamazione, interiezione	*escl, excl*	exclamation, interjection
specialmente	*esp*	especially
femminile	*f*	feminine
ferrovia	*Ferr*	railways
figurato	*fig*	figurative use
fisiologia	*Fisiol*	physiology
fotografia	*Fot*	photography
(verbo inglese) la cui particella è inseparabile dal verbo	VT FUS	(phrasal verb) where the particle cannot be separated from main verb
nella maggior parte dei sensi; generalmente	*gen*	in most or all senses; generally
geografia, geologia	*Geo*	geography, geology
geometria	*Geom*	geometry
impersonale	*impers*	impersonal
informatica	*Inform*	computing
insegnamento, sistema scolastico e universitario	*Ins*	schooling, schools and universities

invariabile	*inv*	invariable
irregolare	*irreg*	irregular
grammatica, linguistica	*Ling*	grammar, linguistics
maschile	*m*	masculine
matematica	*Mat(h)*	mathematics
termine medico, medicina	*Med*	medical term, medicine
il tempo, meteorologia	*Meteor*	the weather, meteorology
maschile o femminile	*m/f*	either masculine or feminine depending on sex
esercito, linguaggio militare	*Mil*	military matters
musica	*Mus*	music
sostantivo	N	noun
nautica	*Naut*	sailing, navigation
sostantivo che non si usa al plurale	*no pl*	uncountable noun: not used in the plural
numerale (aggettivo, sostantivo)	NUM	numeral adjective or noun
	o.s.	oneself
peggiorativo	*peg, pej*	derogatory, pejorative
fotografia	*Phot*	photography
fisiologia	*Physiol*	physiology
plurale	*pl*	plural
politica	*Pol*	politics
participio passato	*pp*	past participle
preposizione	PREP	preposition
pronome	PRON	pronoun
psicologia, psichiatria	*Psic, Psych*	psychology, psychiatry
tempo passato	*pt*	past tense
qualcosa	*qc*	
qualcuno	*qn*	
religione, liturgia	*Rel*	religions, church service
sostantivo	s	noun
	sb	somebody
insegnamento, sistema scolastico e universitario	*Scol*	schooling, schools and universities
singolare	*sg*	singular
soggetto (grammaticale)	*sog*	(grammatical) subject
	sth	something
congiuntivo	*sub*	subjunctive
soggetto (grammaticale)	*subj*	(grammatical) subject
termine tecnico, tecnologia	*Tecn, Tech*	technical term, technology
telecomunicazioni	*Tel*	telecommunications
tipografia	*Tip*	typography, printing
televisione	TV	television
tipografia	*Typ*	typography, printing
inglese degli Stati Uniti	US	American English
vocale	*v*	vowel
verbo (ausiliare)	VB (AUS)	(auxiliary) verb
verbo o gruppo verbale con funzione intransitiva	VI	verb or phrasal verb used intransitively
verbo riflessivo	VR	reflexive verb
verbo o gruppo verbale con funzione transitiva	VT	verb or phrasal verb used transitively
zoologia	*Zool*	zoology
marchio registrato	®	registered trademark
introduce un'equivalenza culturale	≈	introduces a cultural equivalent

Trascrizione fonetica

Consonanti		Consonants
NB.**p, b, t, d, k, g** sono seguite da un'aspirazione in inglese.		NB.**p, b, t, d, k, g** are not aspirated in Italian.
padre	p	puppy
bambino	b	baby
tutto	t	tent
dado	d	daddy
cane che	k	cork kiss chord
gola ghiro	g	gag guess
sano	s	so rice kiss
svago esame	z	cousin buzz
scena	ʃ	sheep sugar
	ʒ	pleasure beige
pece lanciare	tʃ	church
giro gioco	dʒ	judge general
afa faro	f	farm raffle
vero bravo	v	very rev
	θ	thin maths
	ð	that other
letto ala	l	little ball
gli	ʎ	
rete arco	r	rat brat
ramo madre	m	mummy comb
no fumante	n	no ran
gnomo	ɲ	
	ŋ	singing bank
	h	hat reheat
buio piacere	j	yet
uomo guaio	w	wall bewail
	x	loch

Varie		Miscellaneous
per l'inglese: la "r" finale viene pronunciata se seguita da una vocale	ͬ	
precede la sillaba accentata	'	precedes the stressed syllable

Come regola generale, in tutte le voci la trascrizione fonetica in parentesi quadra segue il termine cui si riferisce. Tuttavia, nella parte inglese-italiano del dizionario, per la pronuncia di composti che sono formati da più parole non unite da trattino che appaiono comunque nel dizionario, si veda la trascrizione fonetica di ciascuna di queste parole alla rispettiva posizione alfabetica.

Phonetic transcription

NB. L'associazione di certi suoni indica solo una rassomiglianza approssimativa.

NB. The pairing of some vowel sounds only indicates approximate equivalence.

Vocali	IPA	Vowels
vino idea	i i:	heel bead
	ɪ	hit pity
stella edera	e	
epoca eccetto	ɛ	set tent
mamma amore	a æ	apple bat
	ɑ:	after car calm
	ʌ	fun cousin
	ə	over above
	ə:	urn fern work
rosa occhio	ɔ	wash pot
	ɔ:	born cork
ponte ognuno	o	
utile zucca	u	full soot
	u:	boon lewd

Dittonghi / Diphthongs

IPA	Diphthongs
ɪə	beer tier
ɛə	tear fair there
eɪ	date plaice day
aɪ	life buy cry
au	owl foul now
əu	low no
ɔɪ	boil boy oily
uə	poor tour

In general, we give the pronunciation of each entry in square brackets after the word in question. However, on the English-Italian side, where the entry is composed of two or more unhyphenated words, each of which is given elsewhere in this dictionary, you will find the pronunciation of each word in its alphabetical position.

Italian pronunciation

Vowels

Where the vowel **e** or the vowel **o** appears in a stressed syllable it can be either open [ɛ], [ɔ] or closed [e], [o]. As the open or closed pronunciation of these vowels is subject to regional variation, the distinction is of little importance to the user of this dictionary. Phonetic transcription for headwords containing these vowels will therefore only appear where other pronunciation difficulties are present.

Consonants

c before "e" or "i" is pronounced *tch*.

ch is pronounced like the "k" in "kit".

g before "e" or "i" is pronounced like the "j" in "jet".

gh is pronounced like the "g" in "get".

gl before "e" or "i" is normally pronounced like the "lli" in "million", and in a few cases only like the "gl" in "glove".

gn is pronounced like the "ny" in "canyon".

sc before "e" or "i" is pronounced *sh*.

z is pronounced like the "ts" in "stetson", or like the "d's" in "bird's eye".

Headwords containing the above consonants and consonantal groups have been given full phonetic transcription in this dictionary.

NB. All double written consonants in Italian are fully sounded: e.g. the *tt* in "tutto" is pronounced as in "hat trick".

Italian verbs

a Gerund b Past participle c Present d Imperfect e Past historic f Future g Conditional
h Present subjunctive i Imperfect subjunctive j Imperative

1 **abbattere e** abbattei, abbattesti *(doesn't
  have alternative forms* -etti, -ette, -ettero)
2 **accendere b** acceso **e** accesi, accendesti
3 **accludere b** accluso **e** acclusi,
  accludesti
4 **accorgersi b** accorto **e** mi accorsi, ti
  accorgesti
5 **aggiungere b** aggiunto **e** aggiunsi,
  aggiungesti
6 **andare c** vado, vai, va, andiamo,
  andate, vanno **f** andrò *etc.* **h** vada **j** va'!,
  vada!, andate!, vadano!
7 **apparire b** apparso **c** appaio, appari *or*
  apparisci, appare *or* apparisce, appaiono
  or appariscono **e** apparvi *or* apparsi,
  apparisti, apparve *or* apparì *or* apparse,
  apparvero *or* apparirono *or* apparsero
  h appaia *or* apparisca
8 **appendere b** appeso **e** appesi,
  appendesti
9 **aprire b** aperto **c** apro **e** aprii, apristi
  h apra
10 **ardere b** arso **e** arsi, ardesti
11 **assistere b** assistito **e** assistei *or*
  assistetti, assistesti
12 **assumere b** assunto **e** assunsi,
  assumesti
13 **AVERE c** ho, hai, ha, abbiamo, avete,
  hanno **e** ebbi, avesti, ebbe, avemmo,
  aveste, ebbero **f** avrò *etc.* **h** abbia *etc.*
  j abbi!, abbia!, abbiate!, abbiano!
14 **baciare***when the ending begins with* -e,
  the i *is dropped* → bacerò *(not* bacierò)
15 **bagnare c** bagniamo, bagniate
  h bagniamo, bagniate *(not* bagnamo,
  bagnate)
16 **bere a** bevendo **b** bevuto **c** bevo *etc.*
  d bevevo *etc.* **e** bevvi *or* -bevetti, bevesti
  f berrò *etc.* **h** beva *etc.* **i** bevessi *etc.*
17 **bollire c** bollo *or* bollisco, bolli *or* bollisci
  etc.
18 **cadere e** caddi, cadesti **f** cadrò *etc.*
19 **cambiare***drops the i of the root if the ending

starts with* i (cambi, cambino *not* cambii,
cambiino *(cf.* inviare)
20 **caricare***when c in the root is -followed by* -i
  or -e *an* h *should be inserted (ie* carichi,
  carichiamo, caricherò)
21 **chiedere b** chiesto **e** chiesi, chiedesti
22 **chiudere b** chiuso **e** chiusi, -chiudesti
23 **cogliere b** colto **c** colgo, colgono
  e colsi, cogliesti **h** colga
24 **compiere b** compiuto **e** compii,
  compisti
25 **confondere b** confuso **e** confusi,
  confondesti
26 **conoscere b** conosciuto **e** conobbi,
  conoscesti
27 **consigliare***when the ending begins with* -i,
  the i *of the root is dropped* → consigli *(not*
  consiglii)
28 **correre b** corso **e** corsi, corresti
29 **CREDERE a** credendo **b** creduto
  c credo, credi, crede, crediamo, credete,
  credono **d** credevo, -credevi, credeva,
  credevamo, -credevate, credevano
  e credei *or* credetti, credesti, credé *or*
  -credette, credemmo, credeste,
  crederono *or* credettero **f** crederò,
  crederai, crederà, crederemo, crederete,
  crederanno **g** crederei, crederesti,
  crederebbe, -crederemmo, credereste,
  -crederebbero **h** creda, creda, creda,
  crediamo, crediate, credano **i** credessi,
  credessi, -credesse, credessimo,
  credeste, credessero **j** credi!, creda!,
  -credete!, credano!
30 **crescere b** cresciuto **e** crebbi, crescesti
31 **cucire***when c or g in the root is -followed by*
  -o *or* -a *an* i *should be inserted (ie* cucio,
  cucia)
32 **cuocere b** cotto **c** cuocio, -cociamo,
  cuociono **e** cossi, -cocesti
33 **dare b** do, dai, dà, diamo, date, danno
  e diedi *or* detti, desti **f** darò *etc.* **h** dia *etc.*
  i dessi *etc.* **j** da'!, dai!, date!, diano!

34 decidere **b** deciso **e** decisi, decidesti
35 deludere **b** deluso **e** delusi, -deludesti
36 difendere **b** difeso **e** difesi, -difendesti
37 dipingere **b** dipinto **e** dipinsi, dipingesti
38 dire **a** dicendo **b** detto **c** dico, dici, dice, diciamo, dite, dicono **d** dicevo *etc.* **e** dissi, dicesti **f** dirò *etc.* **h** dica, diciamo, diciate, dicano **i** dicessi *etc.* **j** di'!, dica!, dite!, dicano!
39 dirigere **b** diretto **e** diressi, dirigesti
40 discutere **b** discusso **e** discussi, discutesti
41 disfare *like* fare *but* **c** disfo, dis' *etc.* **f** disferò, disferai *etc.* **i** dis', dis' *etc.* *(regular forms)*
42 distinguere **b** distinto **e** distinsi, distinguesti
43 dividere **b** diviso **e** divisi, dividesti
44 dolere **c** dolgo, duoli, duole, -dolgono **e** dolsi, dolesti **f** dorrò *etc.* **h** dolga
45 DORMIRE **a** dormendo **b** dormito **c** dormo, dormi, dorme, -dormiamo, dormite, dormono **d** dormivo, dormivi, dormiva, dormivamo, dormivate, -dormivano **e** dormii, dormisti, dormì, dormimmo, dormiste, dormirono **f** dormirò, dormirai, dormirà, dormiremo, dormirete, dormiranno **g** dormirei, dormiresti, dormirebbe, dormiremmo, dormireste, dormirebbero **h** dorma, dorma, dorma, dormiamo, dormiate, -dormano **i** dormissi, dormissi, dormisse, dormissimo, dormiste, dormissero **j** dormi!, dorma!, -dormite!, dormano!
46 dovere **c** devo *or* debbo, devi, deve, dobbiamo, dovete, devono *or* debbono **f** dovrò *etc.* **h** debba, dobbiamo, dobbiate, devano *or* debbano
47 esigere **b** esatto *(not common)* **e** esigei *or* esigetti, esigesti
48 espellere **b** espulso **e** espulsi, espellesti
49 esplodere **b** esploso **e** esplosi, esplodesti
50 esprimere **b** espresso **e** espressi, esprimesti

51 ESSERE **b** stato **c** sono, sei, è, siamo, siete, sono **d** ero, eri, era, eravamo, eravate, erano **e** fui, fosti, fu, fummo, foste, furono **f** sarò *etc.* **h** sia *etc.* **i** fossi, fossi, fosse, fossimo, foste, fossero **j** sii!, sia!, siate!, siano!
52 evadere **b** evaso **e** evasi, evadesti
53 fare **a** facendo **b** fatto **c** faccio, fai, fa, facciamo, fate, fanno **d** facevo *etc.* **e** feci, facesti **f** farò *etc.* **h** faccia *etc.* **i** facessi *etc.* **j** fa'!, faccia!, fate!, facciano!
54 fingere **b** 'nto **e** 'nsi, 'ngesti
55 FINIRE **a** 'nendo **b** 'nito **c** 'nisco, 'nisci, 'nisce, 'niamo, 'nite, 'niscono **d** 'nivo, 'nivi, 'niva, 'nivamo, 'nivate, 'nivano **e** 'nii, 'nisti, 'nì, 'nimmo, 'niste, 'nirono **f** 'nirò, 'nirai, 'nirà, 'niremo, 'nirete, 'niranno **g** 'nirei, 'niresti, 'nirebbe, -'niremmo, 'nireste, 'nirebbero **h** 'nisca, 'nisca, 'nisca, 'niamo, 'niate, 'niscano **i** 'nissi, 'nissi, 'nisse, 'nissimo, 'niste, 'nissero **j** 'nisci!, 'nisca!, 'nite!, 'niscano!
56 friggere **b** fritto **e** frissi, friggesti
57 giacere **b** giaciuto **e** giacqui, giacesti
58 godere **f** godrò, godrai *etc.* **g** godrei, godresti *etc.*
59 immergere **b** immerso **e** immersi, immergesti
60 inviare **c** (tu) invii **f** (essi) inviino
61 leggere **b** letto **e** lessi, leggesti
62 mangiare *when the ending begins with* -e, *the* i *is dropped* → mangerò *(not* mangierò*)*
63 mettere **b** messo **e** misi, mettesti
64 mordere **b** morso **e** morsi, mordesti
65 morire **b** morto **c** muoio, muori, muore, moriamo, morite, muoiono **f** morirò *or* morrò *etc.* **h** muoia
66 muovere **b** mosso **e** mossi, muovesti
67 nascere **b** nato **e** nacqui, nascesti
68 nascondere **b** nascosto **e** nascosi, nascondesti
69 nuocere **b** nuociuto **c** nuoccio, nuoci, nuoce, nociamo *or* -nuociamo, nuocete, nuocciono **d** nuocevo *etc.* **e** nocqui, nuocesti **f** nuocerò *etc.* **g** nuoccia
70 offrire **b** offerto **c** offro **e** offersi *or* offrii, offristi **h** offra

71 parere **b** parso **c** paio, paiamo, paiono
e parvi *or* parsi, paresti **f** parrò *etc.*
h paia, paiamo, paiate, paiano
72 PARLARE **a** parlando **b** parlato **c** parlo,
parli, parla, parliamo, -parlate, parlano
d parlavo, parlavi, parlava, parlavamo,
parlavate, parlavano **e** parlai, -parlasti,
parlò, parlammo, -parlaste, parlarono
f parlerò, -parlerai, parlerà, parleremo,
-parlerete, parleranno **g** parlerei,
parleresti, parlerebbe, -parleremmo,
parlereste, -parlerebbero **h** parli, parli,
parli, parliamo, parliate, parlino
i parlassi, parlassi, parlasse,
-parlassimo, parlaste, parlassero
j parla!, parli!, parlate!, parlino!
73 perdere **b** perso *or* perduto **e** persi,
perdesti
74 piacere **b** piaciuto **c** piaccio,
-piacciamo, piacciono **e** piacqui,
piacesti **h** piaccia *etc.*
75 piangere **b** pianto **e** piansi, piangesti
76 piovere **b** piovuto **e** piovve
77 porre **a** ponendo **b** posto **c** pongo,
poni, pone, poniamo, ponete, pongono
d ponevo *etc.* **e** posi, ponesti **f** porrò *etc.*
h ponga, -poniamo, poniate, pongano
i ponessi *etc.*
78 potere **c** posso, puoi, può, -possiamo,
potete, possono **f** potrò *etc.* **h** possa,
possiamo, possiate, possano
79 prefiggersi **b** pre'sso **e** mi -pre'ssi, ti
pre'ggesti
80 pregare *when* g *in the root is* -followed by -i
or -e *an* h *should be inserted* (*ie* preghi,
preghiamo, pregherò)
81 prendere **b** preso **e** presi, -prendesti
82 prevedere *like* vedere *but* **f** prevederò,
prevederai *etc.* **g** prevederei *etc.*
83 proteggere **b** protetto **e** protessi,
proteggesti
84 pungere **b** punto **e** punsi, pungesti
85 radere **b** raso **e** rasi, radesti
86 redimere **b** redento **e** redensi,
redimesti
87 reggere **b** retto **e** ressi, reggesti
88 rendere **b** reso **e** resi, rendesti

89 ridere **b** riso **e** risi, ridesti
90 ridurre **a** riducendo **b** ridotto **c** riduco
etc. **d** riducevo *etc.* **e** ridussi, riducesti
f ridurrò *etc.* **h** riduca *etc.* **i** riducessi *etc.*
91 riempire **a** riempiendo **c** riempio,
riempi, riempie, riempiono
92 riflettere **b** ri,ettuto *or* ri,esso
93 rimanere **b** rimasto **c** rimango,
rimangono **e** rimasi, rimanesti
f rimarrò *etc.* **h** rimanga
94 risolvere **b** risolto **e** risolsi, risolvesti
95 rispondere **b** risposto **e** risposi,
rispondesti
96 rivolgere **b** rivolto **e** rivolsi, -rivolgesti
97 rompere **b** rotto **e** ruppi, rompesti
98 salire **c** salgo, sali, salgono **h** salga
99 sapere **c** so, sai, sa, sappiamo, sapete,
sanno **e** seppi, sapesti **f** saprò *etc.*
h sappia *etc.* **j** sappi!, sappia!, sappiate!,
sappiano!
100 scegliere **b** scelto **c** scelgo, scegli,
sceglie, scegliamo, -scegliete, scelgono
e scelsi, -scegliesti **h** scelga, scegliamo,
scegliate, scegliano **j** scegli!, -scelga!,
scegliamo!, scegliete!, scelgano!
101 scendere **b** sceso **e** scesi, -scendesti
102 scindere **b** scisso **e** scissi, scindesti
103 sciogliere **b** sciolto **c** sciolgo, sciogli,
scioglie, sciogliamo, sciogliete,
sciolgono **e** sciolsi, sciogliesti
h sciolga, sciogliamo, sciogliate,
sciolgano **j** sciogli!, -sciolga!,
sciogliamo!, sciogliete!, sciolgano!
104 sconfiggere **b** scon'tto **e** scon'ssi,
scon'ggesti
105 scrivere **b** scritto **e** scrissi, scrivesti
106 scuotere **b** scosso **e** scossi, scuotesti
107 sedere **c** siedo, siedi, siede, siedono
h sieda
108 solere **b** solito **e** soglio, suoli, suole,
sogliamo, solete, sogliono **h** soglia
(*regular imperfect, gerund, past participle; no*
other verb forms)
109 sorgere **b** sorto **e** sorse, sorsero
110 spandere **b** spanto **e** spansi,
spandesti
111 spargere **b** sorto **e** sorse, sorsero

112 sparire **e** sparii, sparisti

113 spegnere **b** spento **c** spengo, spengono **e** spensi, spegnesti **h** spenga

114 spingere **b** spinto **e** spinsi, spingesti

115 sporgere **b** sporto **e** sporsi, sporgesti

116 stare **b** stato **c** sto, stai, sta, -stiamo, state, stanno **e** stetti, stesti **f** starò *etc.* **h** stia *etc.* **i** stessi *etc.* **j** sta'!, stia!, state!, stiano!

117 stringere **b** stretto **e** strinsi, stringesti

118 succedere **b** successo **e** successi, succedesti

119 tacere **b** taciuto **c** taccio, -tacciono **e** tacqui, tacesti **h** taccia

120 tendere **b** teso **e** tesi, tendesti

121 tenere **c** tengo, tieni, tiene, -tengono **e** tenni, tenesti **f** terrò *etc.* **h** tenga

122 togliere **b** tolto **c** tolgo, togli, toglie, togliamo, togliete, tolgono **e** tolsi,

togliesti **h** tolga **j** togli!, tolga!, togliamo!, togliete!, -tolgano!

123 trarre **a** traendo **b** tratto **c** traggo, trai, trae, traiamo, traete, traggono **d** traevo *etc.* **e** trassi, traesti **f** trarrò *etc.* **h** tragga **i** traessi *etc.*

124 udire **c** odo, odi, ode, odono **h** oda

125 uscire **c** esco, esci, esce, escono **h** esca

126 valere **b** valso **c** valgo, valgono **e** valsi, valesti **f** varrò *etc.* **h** valga

127 vedere **b** visto *or* veduto **e** vidi, vedesti **f** vedrò *etc.*

128 venire **b** venuto **c** vengo, vieni, viene, vengono **e** venni, venisti **f** verrò *etc.* **h** venga

129 vincere **b** vinto **e** vinsi, vincesti

130 vivere **b** vissuto **e** vissi, vivesti

131 volere **c** voglio, vuoi, vuole, vogliamo, volete, vogliono **e** volli, volesti **f** vorrò *etc.* **h** voglia *etc.* **j** *not common*

For additional information on Italian verb formation, see pp6–125 of the Grammar section.

Verbi inglesi

PRESENT	PT	PP	PRESENT	PT	PP
arise	arose	arisen	drink	drank	drunk
awake	awoke	awoken	drive	drove	driven
be (am, is, are; being)	was, were	been	dwell	dwelt	dwelt
			eat	ate	eaten
bear	bore	born(e)	fall	fell	fallen
beat	beat	beaten	feed	fed	fed
become	became	become	feel	felt	felt
befall	befell	befallen	fight	fought	fought
begin	began	begun	find	found	found
behold	beheld	beheld	flee	fled	fled
bend	bent	bent	fling	flung	flung
beset	beset	beset	fly	flew	flown
bet	bet, betted	bet, betted	forbid	forbad(e)	forbidden
bid (at auction, cards)	bid	bid	forecast	forecast	forecast
			forget	forgot	forgotten
bid (say)	bade	bidden	forgive	forgave	forgiven
bind	bound	bound	forsake	forsook	forsaken
bite	bit	bitten	freeze	froze	frozen
bleed	bled	bled	get	got	got, (US) gotten
blow	blew	blown			
break	broke	broken	give	gave	given
breed	bred	bred	go (goes)	went	gone
bring	brought	brought	grind	ground	ground
build	built	built	grow	grew	grown
burn	burnt, burned	burnt, burned	hang	hung	hung
			hang (execute)	hanged	hanged
burst	burst	burst	have	had	had
buy	bought	bought	hear	heard	heard
can	could	(been able)	hide	hid	hidden
cast	cast	cast	hit	hit	hit
catch	caught	caught	hold	held	held
choose	chose	chosen	hurt	hurt	hurt
cling	clung	clung	keep	kept	kept
come	came	come	kneel	knelt, kneeled	knelt, kneeled
cost	cost	cost			
cost (work out price of)	costed	costed	know	knew	known
			lay	laid	laid
creep	crept	crept	lead	led	led
cut	cut	cut	lean	leant, leaned	leant, leaned
deal	dealt	dealt			
dig	dug	dug	leap	leapt, leaped	leapt, leaped
do (3rd person: he/she/ it does)	did	done			
			learn	learnt, learned	learnt, learned
draw	drew	drawn	leave	left	left
dream	dreamed, dreamt	dreamed, dreamt	lend	lent	lent
			let	let	let

PRESENT	PT	PP	PRESENT	PT	PP
lie (lying)	lay	lain	sow	sowed	sown, sowed
light	lit, lighted	lit, lighted	speak	spoke	spoken
lose	lost	lost	speed	sped, speeded	sped, speeded
make	made	made	spell	spelt, spelled	spelt, spelled
may	might	—			
mean	meant	meant	spend	spent	spent
meet	met	met	spill	spilt, spilled	spilt, spilled
mistake	mistook	mistaken			
mow	mowed	mown, mowed	spin	spun	spun
			spit	spat	spat
must	(had to)	(had to)	spoil	spoiled, spoilt	spoiled, spoilt
pay	paid	paid			
put	put	put	spread	spread	spread
quit	quit, quitted	quit, quitted	spring	sprang	sprung
			stand	stood	stood
read	read	read	steal	stole	stolen
rid	rid	rid	stick	stuck	stuck
ride	rode	ridden	sting	stung	stung
ring	rang	rung	stink	stank	stunk
rise	rose	risen	stride	strode	stridden
run	ran	run	strike	struck	struck
saw	sawed	sawed, sawn	strive	strove	striven
			swear	swore	sworn
say	said	said	sweep	swept	swept
see	saw	seen	swell	swelled	swollen, swelled
seek	sought	sought			
sell	sold	sold	swim	swam	swum
send	sent	sent	swing	swung	swung
set	set	set	take	took	taken
sew	sewed	sewn	teach	taught	taught
shake	shook	shaken	tear	tore	torn
shear	sheared	shorn, sheared	tell	told	told
			think	thought	thought
shed	shed	shed	throw	threw	thrown
shine	shone	shone	thrust	thrust	thrust
shoot	shot	shot	tread	trod	trodden
show	showed	shown	wake	woke, waked	woken, waked
shrink	shrank	shrunk			
shut	shut	shut	wear	wore	worn
sing	sang	sung	weave	wove	woven
sink	sank	sunk	weave(wind)	weaved	weaved
sit	sat	sat	wed	wedded, wed	wedded, wed
slay	slew	slain			
sleep	slept	slept	weep	wept	wept
slide	slid	slid	win	won	won
sling	slung	slung	wind	wound	wound
slit	slit	slit	wring	wrung	wrung
smell	smelt, smelled	smelt, smelled	write	wrote	written

I numeri

Numbers

uno(a)	1	one
due	2	two
tre	3	three
quattro	4	four
cinque	5	five
sei	6	six
sette	7	seven
otto	8	eight
nove	9	nine
dieci	10	ten
undici	11	eleven
dodici	12	twelve
tredici	13	thirteen
quattordici	14	fourteen
quindici	15	fifteen
sedici	16	sixteen
diciassette	17	seventeen
diciotto	18	eighteen
diciannove	19	nineteen
venti	20	twenty
ventuno	21	twenty-one
ventidue	22	twenty-two
ventitré	23	twenty-three
ventotto	28	twenty-eight
trenta	30	thirty
quaranta	40	forty
cinquanta	50	fifty
sessanta	60	sixty
settanta	70	seventy
ottanta	80	eighty
novanta	90	ninety
cento	100	a hundred, one hundred
centouno	101	a hundred and one
duecento	200	two hundred
mille	1 000	a thousand, one thousand
milleduecentodue	1 202	one thousand two hundred and two
cinquemila	5 000	five thousand .
un milione	1 000 000	a million, one million

I numeri

primo(a), 1°
secondo(a), 2°
terzo(a), 3°
quarto(a)
quinto(a)
sesto(a)
settimo(a)
ottavo(a)
nono(a)
decimo(a)
undicesimo(a)
dodicesimo(a)
tredicesimo(a)
quattordicesimo(a)
quindicesimo(a)
sedicesimo(a)
diciassettesimo(a)
diciottesimo(a)
diciannovesimo(a)
ventesimo(a)
ventunesimo(a)
ventiduesimo(a)
ventitreesimo(a)
ventottesimo(a)
trentesimo(a)
centesimo(a)
centunesimo(a)
millesimo(a)
milionesimo(a)

Numbers

first, 1st
second, 2nd
third, 3rd
fourth, 4th
fifth, 5th
sixth, 6th
seventh
eighth
ninth
tenth
eleventh
twelfth
thirteenth
fourteenth
fifteenth
sixteenth
seventeenth
eighteenth
nineteenth
twentieth
twenty-first
twenty-second
twenty-third
twenty-eighth
thirtieth
hundredth
hundred-and-first
thousandth
millionth

L'ora

che ora è ?, che ore sono?
è ..., sono ...
mezzanotte
l'una (del mattino)
l'una e cinque
l'una e dieci
l'una e un quarto, l'una e quindici
l'una e venticinque
l'una e mezzo *o* mezza, l'una e trenta
l'una e trentacinque
le due meno venti, l'una e quaranta
le due meno un quarto, l'una e
   quarantacinque
le due meno dieci, l'una e cinquanta
mezzogiorno
le tre (del pomeriggio), le quindici
le sette (di sera), le diciannove

a che ora?
a mezzanotte
alle sette
fra venti minuti
venti minuti fa

The time

what time is it?
it's ...
midnight
one o'clock (in the morning), one (am)
five past one
ten past one
a quarter past one, one fifteen
twenty-five past one, one twenty-five
half past one, one thirty
twenty-five to two, one thirty-five
twenty to two, one forty
a quarter to two, one forty-five

ten to two, one fifty
twelve o'clock, midday, noon
three o'clock (in the afternoon), three (pm)
seven o'clock (in the evening), seven (pm)

at what time?
at midnight
at seven o'clock
in twenty minutes
twenty minutes ago

La data

oggi
domani
dopodomani
ieri
l'altro ieri
il giorno prima
il giorno dopo
la mattina
la sera
stamattina
stasera
questo pomeriggio

The date

today
tomorrow
the day after tomorrow
yesterday
the day before yesterday
the day before, the previous day
the next *or* following day
morning
evening
this morning
this evening
this afternoon

ieri mattina	yesterday morning
ieri sera	yesterday evening
domani mattina	tomorrow morning
domani sera	tomorrow evening
nella notte tra sabato e domenica	during Saturday night, during the night of Saturday to Sunday
viene sabato	he's coming on Saturday
il sabato	on Saturdays
tutti i sabati	every Saturday
sabato scorso, lo scorso sabato	last Saturday
il prossimo sabato	next Saturday
fra due sabati	a week on Saturday
fra tre sabati	a fortnight or two weeks on Saturday
da lunedì a sabato	from Monday to Saturday
tutti i lunedì	every day
una volta alla settimana	once a week
una volta al mese	once a month
due volte alla settimana	twice a week
una settimana fa	a week ago
quindici giorni fa	a fortnight or two weeks ago
l'anno scorso or passato	last year
fra due giorni	in two days
fra una settimana	in a week
fra quindici giorni	in a fortnight or two weeks
il mese prossimo	next month
l'anno prossimo	next year

che giorno è oggi? **what day is it?**

il primo/24 ottobre 2013	the 1st/24th of October 2013, October 1st/24th 2013
nel 2013	in 2013
il millenovecentonovantacinque	nineteen ninety-five
44 a.C.	44 BC
14 d.C.	14 AD
nel diciannovesimo secolo, nel XIX secolo, nell'Ottocento	in the nineteenth century
negli anni trenta	in the thirties
c'era una volta ...	once upon a time ...

ITALIANO–INGLESE

ITALIAN–ENGLISH

Aa

A, a [a] SM O F INV (*lettera*) A, a; **A come Ancona** = A for Andrew (*BRIT*), ≈ A for Able (*US*); **dalla a alla z** from a to z

A ABBR (= *altezza*) h; (= *area*) A; (= *autostrada*) ≈ M (*BRIT*)

(**PAROLA CHIAVE**)

a (*a + il* = **al**, *a + lo* = **allo**, *a + l'* = **all'**, *a + la* = **alla**, *a + i* = **ai**, *a + gli* = **agli**, *a + le* = **alle**) PREP **1** (*stato in luogo*) at; (: *in*) in; **essere alla stazione** to be at the station; **essere a casa/a scuola/a Roma** to be at home/at school/in Rome; **è a 10 km da qui** it's 10 km from here, it's 10 km away; **restare a cena** to stay for dinner

2 (*moto a luogo*) to; **andare a casa/a scuola/ alla stazione** to go home/to school/to the station; **andare a Roma/al mare** to go to Rome/to the seaside

3 (*tempo*) at; (: *epoca, stagione*) in; **alle cinque** at five (o'clock); **a mezzanotte/Natale** at midnight/Christmas; **al mattino** in the morning; **a maggio/primavera** in May/ spring; **a cinquant'anni** at fifty (years of age); **a domani!** see you tomorrow!; **a lunedì!** see you on Monday!; **a giorni** within (a few) days

4 (*complemento di termine*) to; **dare qc a qn** to give sb sth, give sth to sb; **l'ho chiesto a lui** I asked him

5 (*mezzo, modo*) with, by; **a piedi/cavallo** on foot/horseback; **viaggiare a 100 km all'ora** to travel at 100 km an *o* per hour; **alla televisione/radio** on television/the radio; **fatto a mano** made by hand, handmade; **una barca a motore** a motorboat; **una stufa a gas** a gas heater; **a uno a uno** one by one; **a fatica** with difficulty; **all'italiana** the Italian way, in the Italian fashion

6 (*rapporto*) a, per; (: *con prezzi*) at; **due volte al giorno/mese** twice a day/month; **prendo 2000 euro al mese** I get 2000 euro a *o* per month; **pagato a ore** paid by the hour; **vendere qc a 2 euro il chilo** to sell sth at 2 euros a *o* per kilo; **cinque a zero** (*punteggio*) five nil

AA SIGLA = **Alto Adige**

AAST SIGLA F = **Azienda Autonoma di Soggiorno e Turismo**

AA.VV. ABBR = **autori vari**

ab. ABBR = **abitante**

a'bate SM abbot

abbacchi'ato, -a [abbak'kjato] AG downhearted, in low spirits

abbacin'are [abbatʃi'nare] /**72**/ VT to dazzle

abbagli'ante [abbaʎ'ʎante] AG dazzling; **abbaglianti** SMPL (*Aut*): **accendere gli abbaglianti** to put one's headlights on full (*BRIT*) *o* high (*US*) beam

abbagli'are [abbaʎ'ʎare] /**27**/ VT to dazzle; (*illudere*) to delude

ab'baglio [ab'baʎʎo] SM blunder; **prendere un ~** to blunder, make a blunder

abbai'are /**19**/ VI to bark

abba'ino SM dormer window; (*soffitta*) attic room

abbando'nare /**72**/ VT to leave, abandon, desert; (*trascurare*) to neglect; (*rinunciare a*) to abandon, give up; **abbandonarsi** VPR to let o.s. go; **~ il campo** (*Mil*) to retreat; **~ la presa** to let go; **abbandonarsi a** (*ricordi, vizio*) to give o.s. up to

abbando'nato, -a AG (*casa*) deserted; (*miniera*) disused; (*trascurato: terreno, podere*) neglected; (: *bambino*) abandoned

abban'dono SM abandoning; neglecting; (*stato*) abandonment; neglect; (*Sport*) withdrawal; (*fig*) abandon; **in ~** (*edificio, giardino*) neglected

abbarbi'carsi /**61**/ VPR: **~ (a)** (*anche fig*) to cling (to)

abbassa'mento SM lowering; (*di pressione, livello dell'acqua*) fall; (*di prezzi*) reduction; **~ di temperatura** drop in temperature

abbas'sare /**72**/ VT to lower; (*radio*) to turn down; **abbassarsi** VPR (*chinarsi*) to stoop; (*livello, sole*) to go down; (*fig: umiliarsi*) to demean o.s.; **~ i fari** (*Aut*) to dip (*BRIT*) *o* dim (*US*) one's lights; **~ le armi** (*Mil*) to lay down one's arms

ab'basso ESCL: **~ il re!** down with the king!
abbas'tanza [abbas'tantsa] AV (*a sufficienza*)
enough; (*alquanto*) quite, rather, fairly; **non
è ~ furbo** he's not shrewd enough; **un vino
~ dolce** quite a sweet wine, a fairly sweet
wine; **averne ~ di qn/qc** to have had enough
of sb/sth
ab'battere /**1**/ VT (*muro, casa, ostacolo*) to knock
down; (*albero*) to fell; (: *vento*) to bring down;
(*bestie da macello*) to slaughter; (*cane, cavallo*) to
destroy, put down; (*selvaggina, aereo*) to shoot
down; (*fig: malattia, disgrazia*) to lay low;
abbattersi VPR (*avvilirsi*) to lose heart;
abbattersi a terra o **al suolo** to fall to the
ground; **abbattersi su** (*maltempo*) to beat
down on; (*disgrazia*) to hit, strike
abbatti'mento SM knocking down; felling;
(*di casa*) demolition; (*prostrazione: fisica*)
exhaustion; (: *morale*) despondency
abbat'tuto, -a AG (*fig*) despondent,
depressed
abba'zia [abbat'tsia] SF abbey
abbece'dario [abbetʃe'darjo] SM primer
abbelli'mento SM embellishment
abbel'lire /**55**/ VT to make beautiful; (*ornare*)
to embellish
abbeve'rare /**72**/ VT to water; **abbeverarsi**
VPR to drink
abbevera'toio SM drinking trough
'abbi VB *vedi* **avere**
'abbia VB *vedi* **avere**
abbi'amo VB *vedi* **avere**
'abbiano VB *vedi* **avere**
abbi'ate VB *vedi* **avere**
abbiccì [abbit'tʃi] SM INV alphabet; (*sillabario*)
primer; (*fig*) rudiments *pl*
abbi'ente AG well-to-do, well-off; **abbienti**
SMPL: **gli abbienti** the well-to-do
abbi'etto, -a AG = **abietto**
abbiezi'one [abbjet'tsjone] SF = **abiezione**
abbiglia'mento [abbiʎʎa'mento] SM dress *no
pl*; (*indumenti*) clothes *pl*; (*industria*) clothing
industry
abbigli'are [abbiʎ'ʎare] /**27**/ VT to dress up
abbina'mento SM combination; linking;
matching
abbi'nare /**72**/ VT: **~ (con** o **a)** (*gen*) to combine
(with); (*nomi*) to link (with); **~ qc a qc** (*colori
ecc*) to match sth with sth
abbindo'lare /**72**/ VT (*fig*) to cheat, trick
abbocca'mento SM (*colloquio*) talks *pl*,
meeting; (*Tecn: di tubi*) connection
abboc'care /**20**/ VT (*tubi, canali*) to connect,
join up ▶ VI (*pesce*) to bite; (*tubi*) to join;
~ (all'amo) (*fig*) to swallow the bait
abboc'cato, -a AG (*vino*) sweetish
abbona'mento SM subscription; (*alle ferrovie
ecc*) season ticket; **in ~** for subscribers only;
for season ticket holders only; **fare l'~ (a)** to

take out a subscription (to); to buy a season
ticket (for)
abbo'nare /**72**/ VT (*cifra*) to deduct; (*fig:
perdonare*) to forgive; **abbonarsi** VPR:
abbonarsi a un giornale to take out a
subscription to a newspaper; **abbonarsi al
teatro/alle ferrovie** to take out a season
ticket for the theatre/the train
abbo'nato, -a SM/F subscriber; season-
ticket holder; **elenco degli abbonati**
telephone directory
abbon'dante AG abundant, plentiful; (*giacca*)
roomy
abbon'danza [abbon'dantsa] SF abundance;
plenty
abbon'dare /**72**/ VI to abound, be plentiful;
~ in o **di** to be full of, abound in
abbor'dabile AG (*persona*) approachable;
(*prezzo*) reasonable
abbor'dare /**72**/ VT (*nave*) to board; (*persona*) to
approach; (*argomento*) to tackle; **~ una curva**
to take a bend
abbotto'nare /**72**/ VT to button up, do up;
abbottonarsi VPR to button (up)
abbotto'nato, -a AG (*camicia ecc*) buttoned
(up); (*fig*) reserved
abbottona'tura SF buttons *pl*; **questo
cappotto ha l'~ da uomo/da donna** this
coat buttons on the man's/woman's side
abboz'zare [abbot'tsare] /**72**/ VT to sketch,
outline; (*Scultura*) to rough-hew; **~ un
sorriso** to give a hint of a smile
ab'bozzo [ab'bottso] SM sketch, outline; (*Dir*)
draft
abbracci'are [abbrat'tʃare] /**14**/ VT to
embrace; (*persona*) to hug, embrace;
(*professione*) to take up; (*contenere*) to include;
abbracciarsi VPR to hug o embrace (one
another)
ab'braccio [ab'brattʃo] SM hug, embrace
abbrevi'are /**19**/ VT to shorten; (*parola*) to
abbreviate, shorten
abbreviazi'one [abbrevjat'tsjone] SF
abbreviation
abbron'zante [abbron'dzante] AG tanning,
sun *cpd*
abbron'zare [abbron'dzare] /**72**/ VT (*pelle*) to
tan; (*metalli*) to bronze; **abbronzarsi** VPR to
tan, get a tan
abbron'zato, -a [abbron'dzato] AG
(sun)tanned
abbronza'tura [abbrondza'tura] SF tan,
suntan
abbrusto'lire /**55**/ VT (*pane*) to toast; (*caffè*) to
roast; **abbrustolirsi** VPR to toast; (*fig: al sole*)
to soak up the sun
abbruti'mento SM exhaustion; degradation
abbru'tire /**55**/ VT (*snervare, stancare*) to
exhaust; (*degradare*) to degrade; **essere**

abbrutito dall'alcool to be ruined by drink

abbuffarsi /**72**/ VPR (*col*): ~ **(di qc)** to stuff o.s. (with sth)

abbuffata SF (*col*) nosh-up; (*fig*) binge; **farsi un'~** to stuff o.s.

abbuo'nare /**72**/ VT = **abbonare**

abbu'ono SM (*Comm*) allowance, discount; (*Sport*) handicap

abdi'care /**20**/ VI to abdicate; ~ **a** to give up, renounce

abdicazi'one [abdikat'tsjone] SF abdication

aberrazi'one [aberrat'tsjone] SF aberration

abe'taia SF fir wood

a'bete SM fir (tree); ~ **bianco** silver fir; ~ **rosso** spruce

abi'etto, -a AG despicable, abject

abiezi'one [abjet'tsjone] SF abjection

'**abile** AG (*idoneo*): ~ **(a qc/a fare qc)** fit (for sth/ to do sth); (*capace*) able; (*astuto*) clever; (*accorto*) skilful; ~ **al servizio militare** fit for military service

abilità SF INV ability; cleverness; skill

abili'tante AG qualifying; **corsi abilitanti** (*Ins*) ≈ teacher training *sg*

abili'tare /**72**/ VT: ~ **qn a qc/a fare qc** to qualify sb for sth/to do sth; **è stato abilitato all'insegnamento** he has qualified as a teacher

abili'tato, -a AG qualified; (*Tel*) which has an outside line

abilitazi'one [abilitat'tsjone] SF qualification

abis'sale AG abysmal; (*fig: senza limiti*) profound

abis'sino, -a AG, SM/F Abyssinian

a'bisso SM abyss, gulf

abitabilità SF: **licenza di** ~ *document stating that a property is fit for habitation*

abi'tacolo SM (*Aer*) cockpit; (*Aut*) inside; (*di camion*) (driver's) cab

abi'tante SMF inhabitant

abi'tare /**72**/ VT to live in, dwell in ▶ VI: ~ **in campagna/a Roma** to live in the country/in Rome; **dove abita?** where do you live?

abi'tato, -a AG inhabited; lived in ▶ SM (*anche*: **centro abitato**) built-up area

abitazi'one [abitat'tsjone] SF residence; house

'**abito** SM dress *no pl*; (*da uomo*) suit; (*da donna*) dress; (*abitudine, disposizione, Rel*) habit; **abiti** SMPL (*vestiti*) clothes; **in ~ da cerimonia** in formal dress; **in ~ da sera** in evening dress; "**è gradito l'~ scuro**" "dress formal"; ~ **mentale** way of thinking

abitu'ale AG usual, habitual; (*cliente*) regular

abitual'mente AV usually, normally

abitu'are /**72**/ VT: ~ **qn a** to get sb used o accustomed to; **abituarsi a** to get used to, accustom o.s. to

abitudi'nario, -a AG of fixed habits ▶ SM/F creature of habit

abi'tudine SF habit; **aver l'~ di fare qc** to be in the habit of doing sth; **d'~** usually; **per** ~ from o out of habit

abiu'rare /**72**/ VT to renounce

abla'tivo SM ablative

abnegazi'one [abnegat'tsjone] SF (self-) abnegation, self-denial

ab'norme AG (*enorme*) extraordinary; (*anormale*) abnormal

abo'lire /**55**/ VT to abolish; (*Dir*) to repeal

abolizi'one [abolit'tsjone] SF abolition; repeal

abomi'nevole AG abominable

abo'rigeno [abo'ridʒeno] SM aborigine

abor'rire /**17**/ VT to abhor, detest

abor'tire /**55**/ VI (*Med: accidentalmente*) to miscarry, have a miscarriage; (: *deliberatamente*) to have an abortion; (*fig*) to miscarry, fail

abor'tista, -i, -e AG pro-choice, pro-abortion ▶ SM/F pro-choicer

a'borto SM miscarriage; abortion; (*fig*) freak; ~ **clandestino** backstreet abortion

abrasi'one SF abrasion

abra'sivo, -a AG, SM abrasive

abro'gare /**80**/ VT to repeal, abrogate

abrogazi'one [abrogat'tsjone] SF repeal

abruz'zese [abrut'tsese] AG of (o from) the Abruzzi

A'bruzzo [a'bruttso] SM: **l'~**, **gli Abruzzi** the Abruzzi

ABS [abi'esse] SIGLA M (= *Anti-Blockier System*) ABS (= *anti-lock braking system*)

'**abside** SF apse

'**Abu 'Dhabi** SF Abu Dhabi

a'bulico, -a, -ci, -che AG lacking in willpower

abu'sare /**72**/ VI: ~ **di** to abuse, misuse; (*approfittare, violare*) to take advantage of; ~ **dell'alcool/dei cibi** to drink/eat to excess

abusi'vismo SM (*anche*: **abusivismo edilizio**) unlawful building, building without planning permission (BRIT)

abu'sivo, -a AG unauthorized, unlawful; (**occupante**) ~ (*di una casa*) squatter

a'buso SM abuse, misuse; excessive use; **fare** ~ **di** (*stupefacenti, medicine*) to abuse

a.C. ABBR (= *avanti Cristo*) BC

a'cacia, -cie [a'katʃa] SF (*Bot*) acacia

'**acca** SF letter H; **non capire un'~** not to understand a thing

ac'cadde VB *vedi* **accadere**

acca'demia SF (*società*) learned society; (*scuola: d'arte, militare*) academy; **A~ di Belle Arti** art school

acca'demico, -a, -ci, -che AG academic ▶ SM academician

acca'dere /**18**/ VB IMPERS to happen, occur

3

acca'duto SM event; **raccontare l'~** to describe what has happened

accalappia'cani SM INV dog-catcher

accalappi'are /19/ VT to catch; (*fig*) to trick, dupe

accal'care /20/ VT, **accal'carsi** VPR to crowd, throng

accal'darsi /61/ VPR to grow hot

accal'dato, -a AG hot

accalo'rarsi /61/ VPR (*fig*) to get excited

accampa'mento SM camp

accam'pare /72/ VT to encamp; (*fig*) to put forward, advance; **accamparsi** VPR to camp; **~ scuse** to make excuses

accani'mento SM fury; (*tenacia*) tenacity, perseverance

acca'nirsi /55/ VPR (*infierire*) to rage; (*ostinarsi*) to persist

accanita'mente AV fiercely; assiduously

acca'nito, -a AG (*odio, gelosia*) fierce, bitter; (*lavoratore*) assiduous; (*giocatore, fumatore*) inveterate; (*tifoso, sostenitore*) keen; **fumatore ~** chain smoker

ac'canto AV near, nearby; **~ a** prep near, beside, close to; **la casa ~** the house next door

accanto'nare /72/ VT (*problema*) to shelve; (*somma*) to set aside

accaparra'mento SM (*Comm*) cornering, buying up

accapar'rare /72/ VT (*Comm*) to corner, buy up; (*versare una caparra*) to pay a deposit on; **accaparrarsi** VPR: **accaparrarsi qc** (*fig: simpatia, voti*) to secure sth (for o.s.)

accapigli'arsi [akkapiʎ'ʎarsi] /27/ VPR to come to blows; (*fig*) to quarrel

accappa'toio SM bathrobe

accappo'nare /72/ VI: **far ~ la pelle a qn** (*fig*) to bring sb out in goosepimples

accarez'zare [akkaret'tsare] /72/ VT to caress, stroke, fondle; (*fig*) to toy with

accartocci'are [akkartot'tʃare] /14/ VT (*carta*) to roll up, screw up; **accartocciarsi** VPR (*foglie*) to curl up

acca'sarsi /27/ VPR to set up house; to get married

accasci'arsi [akkaʃ'ʃarsi] /14/ VPR to collapse; (*fig*) to lose heart

accatas'tare /72/ VT to stack, pile

accatto'naggio [akkatto'naddʒo] SM begging

accat'tone, -a SM/F beggar

accaval'lare /72/ VT (*gambe*) to cross; **accavallarsi** VPR (*sovrapporsi*) to overlap; (*addensarsi*) to gather

acce'care [attʃe'kare] /20/ VT to blind ▶ VI to go blind

ac'cedere [at'tʃɛdere] /29/ VI: **~ a** to enter; (*richiesta*) to grant, accede to; (*fonte*) to gain access to

accele'rare [attʃele'rare] /72/ VT to speed up ▶ VI (*Aut*) to accelerate; **~ il passo** to quicken one's pace

accele'rato, -a [attʃele'rato] AG quick, rapid ▶ SM (*Ferr*) local train, stopping train

accelera'tore [attʃelera'tore] SM (*Aut*) accelerator

accelerazi'one [attʃelerat'tsjone] SF acceleration

ac'cendere [at'tʃɛndere] /2/ VT (*fuoco, sigaretta*) to light; (*luce, televisione*) to put o switch o turn on; (*Aut: motore*) to switch on; (*Comm: conto*) to open; (: *debito*) to contract; (: *ipoteca*) to raise; (*fig: suscitare*) to inflame, stir up; **accendersi** VPR (*luce*) to come o go on; (*legna*) to catch fire, ignite; (*fig: lotta, conflitto*) to break out

accen'dino [attʃen'dino], **accendi'sigaro** [attʃendi'sigaro] SM (*cigarette*) lighter

accen'nare [attʃen'nare] /72/ VT to indicate, point out; (*Mus*) to pick out the notes of; to hum ▶ VI: **~ a** (*fig: alludere a*) to hint at; (: *far atto di*) to make as if; **~ un saluto** (*con la mano*) to make as if to wave; (*col capo*) to half nod; **~ un sorriso** to half smile; **accenna a piovere** it looks as if it's going to rain

ac'cenno [at'tʃenno] SM (*cenno*) sign; nod; (*allusione*) hint

accensi'one [attʃen'sjone] SF (*vedi accendere*) lighting; switching on; opening; (*Aut*) ignition

accen'tare [attʃen'tare] /72/ VT (*parlando*) to stress; (*scrivendo*) to accent

accentazi'one [attʃentat'tsjone] SF accentuation; stressing

ac'cento [at'tʃento] SM accent; (*Fonetica, fig*) stress; (*inflessione*) tone (of voice)

accentra'mento [attʃentra'mento] SM centralization

accen'trare [attʃen'trare] /72/ VT to centralize

accentra'tore, -'trice [attʃentra'tore] AG (*persona*) unwilling to delegate; **politica accentratrice** policy of centralization

accentu'are [attʃentu'are] /72/ VT to stress, emphasize; **accentuarsi** VPR to become more noticeable

accerchi'are [attʃer'kjare] /19/ VT to surround, encircle

accerta'mento [attʃerta'mento] SM check; assessment

accer'tare [attʃer'tare] /72/ VT to ascertain; (*verificare*) to check; (*reddito*) to assess; **accertarsi** VPR: **accertarsi (di qc/che)** to make sure (of sth/that)

ac'ceso, -a [at'tʃeso] PP *di* **accendere** ▶ AG lit; on; open; (*colore*) bright; **~ di** (*ira, entusiasmo ecc*) burning with

acces'sibile [attʃes'sibile] AG (*luogo*)

accessible; (*persona*) approachable; (*prezzo*) reasonable; (*idea*): ~ **a qn** within the reach of sb

ac'cesso [at'tʃɛsso] SM (*anche* Inform) access; (*Med*) attack, fit; (*impulso violento*) fit, outburst; **programmi dell'~** (*TV*) educational programmes; **tempo di ~** (*Inform*) access time; ~ **casuale/seriale/sequenziale** (*Inform*) random/serial/sequential access

accessori'ato, -a [attʃesso'rjato] AG with accessories

acces'sorio, -a [attʃes'sɔrjo] AG secondary, of secondary importance; **accessori** SMPL accessories

ac'cetta [at'tʃetta] SF hatchet

accet'tabile [attʃet'tabile] AG acceptable

accet'tare [attʃet'tare] /**72**/ VT to accept; ~ **di fare qc** to agree to do sth

accettazi'one [attʃettat'tsjone] SF acceptance; (*locale di servizio pubblico*) reception; ~ **bagagli** (*Aer*) check-in (desk); ~ **con riserva** qualified acceptance

ac'cetto, -a [at'tʃetto] AG (*persona*) welcome; **(ben)~ a tutti** well-liked by everybody

accezi'one [attʃet'tsjone] SF meaning

acchiap'pare [akkjap'pare] /**72**/ VT to catch; (*afferrare*) to seize

ac'chito [ak'kito] SM: **a primo ~** at first sight

acciac'cato, -a [attʃak'kato] AG (*persona*) full of aches and pains; (*abito*) crushed

acci'acco, -chi [at'tʃakko] SM ailment; **acciacchi** SMPL aches and pains

acciaie'ria [attʃaje'ria] SF steelworks *sg*

acci'aio [at'tʃajo] SM steel; ~ **inossidabile** stainless steel

acciden'tale [attʃiden'tale] AG accidental

accidental'mente [attʃidental'mente] AV (*per caso*) by chance; (*non deliberatamente*) accidentally, by accident

acciden'tato, -a [attʃiden'tato] AG (*terreno ecc*) uneven

acci'dente [attʃi'dɛnte] SM (*caso imprevisto*) accident; (*disgrazia*) mishap; **accidenti!** (*col: per rabbia*) damn (it)!; (: *per meraviglia*) good heavens!; **accidenti a lui!** damn him!; **non vale un ~** it's not worth a damn; **non capisco un ~** it's as clear as mud to me; **mandare un ~ a qn** to curse sb

ac'cidia [at'tʃidja] SF (*Rel*) sloth

accigli'ato, -a [attʃiʎ'ʎato] AG frowning

ac'cingersi [at'tʃindʒersi] /**54**/ VPR: ~ **a fare** to be about to do

acciotto'lato [attʃotto'lato] SM cobbles *pl*

acciuffare [attʃuf'fare] /**72**/ VT to seize, catch

acci'uga, -ghe [at'tʃuga] SF anchovy; **magro come un'~** as thin as a rake

accla'mare /**72**/ VT (*applaudire*) to applaud; (*eleggere*) to acclaim

acclamazi'one [akklamat'tsjone] SF applause; acclamation

acclima'tare /**72**/ VT to acclimatize; **acclimatarsi** VPR to become acclimatized

acclimatazi'one [akklimatat'tsjone] SF acclimatization

ac'cludere /**3**/ VT to enclose

ac'cluso, -a PP *di* **accludere** ▸ AG enclosed

accocco'larsi /**72**/ VPR to crouch

acco'darsi /**72**/ VPR to follow, tag on (behind)

accogli'ente [akkoʎ'ʎɛnte] AG welcoming, friendly

accogli'enza [akkoʎ'ʎɛntsa] SF reception; welcome; **fare una buona ~ a qn** to welcome sb

ac'cogliere [ak'kɔʎʎere] /**23**/ VT (*ricevere*) to receive; (*dare il benvenuto*) to welcome; (*approvare*) to agree to, accept; (*contenere*) to hold, accommodate

ac'colgo *etc* VB *vedi* **accogliere**

accol'lare /**72**/ VT: ~ **qc a qn** (*fig*) to force sth on sb; **accollarsi** VPR: **accollarsi qc** to take sth upon o.s., shoulder sth

accol'lato, -a AG (*vestito*) high-necked

ac'colsi *etc* VB *vedi* **accogliere**

accol'tellare /**72**/ VT to knife, stab

ac'colto, -a PP *di* **accogliere**

accoman'dita SF (*Dir*) limited partnership

accomia'tare /**72**/ VT to dismiss; **accomiatarsi** VPR: **accomiatarsi (da)** to take one's leave (of)

accomoda'mento SM agreement, settlement

accomo'dante AG accommodating

accomo'dare /**72**/ VT (*aggiustare*) to repair, mend; (*riordinare*) to tidy; (*sistemare: questione, lite*) to settle; **accomodarsi** VPR (*sedersi*) to sit down; (*fig: risolversi: situazione*) to work out; **si accomodi!** (*venga avanti*) come in!; (*si sieda*) take a seat!

accompagna'mento [akkompaɲɲa'mento] SM (*Mus*) accompaniment; (*Comm*): **lettera di ~** accompanying letter

accompa'gnare [akkompaɲ'ɲare] /**15**/ VT to accompany, come *o* go with; (*Mus*) to accompany; (*unire*) to couple; **accompagnarsi** VPR (*armonizzarsi*) to go well together; ~ **qn a casa** to see sb home; ~ **qn alla porta** to show sb out; ~ **un regalo con un biglietto** to put in *o* send a card with a present; ~ **qn con lo sguardo** to follow sb with one's eyes; ~ **la porta** to close the door gently; **accompagnarsi a** (*frequentare*) to frequent; (*colori*) to go with, match; (*cibi*) to go with

accompagna'tore, -'trice [akkompaɲɲa'tore] SM/F companion, escort; (*Mus*) accompanist; (*Sport*) team manager; ~ **turistico** courier; tour guide

accomu'nare /**72**/ vt to pool, share; (*avvicinare*) to unite

acconcia'tura [akkontʃa'tura] sf hairstyle

accondiscen'dente [akkondiʃʃen'dɛnte] AG affable

accondi'scendere [akkondiʃʃendere] /**101**/ vi: ~ **a** to agree o consent to

accondi'sceso, -a [akkondiʃʃeso] PP *di* **accondiscendere**

acconsen'tire /**17**/ vi: ~ **(a)** to agree o consent (to); **chi tace acconsente** silence means consent

acconten'tare /**72**/ vt to satisfy; **accontentarsi** vpr: **accontentarsi di** to be satisfied with, content o.s. with; **chi si accontenta gode** there's no point in complaining

ac'conto sm part payment; **pagare una somma in** ~ to pay a sum of money as a deposit; ~ **di dividendo** interim dividend

accoppia'mento sm pairing off; mating; (*Elettr, Inform*) coupling

accoppi'are /**19**/ vt to couple, pair off; (*Biol*) to mate; **accoppiarsi** vpr to pair off; to mate

accoppia'tore sm (*Tecn*) coupler; ~ **acustico** (*Inform*) acoustic coupler

acco'rato, -a AG heartfelt

accorci'are [akkor'tʃare] /**14**/ vt to shorten; **accorciarsi** vpr to become shorter; (*vestiti: nel lavaggio*) to shrink

accor'dare /**72**/ vt to reconcile; (*colori*) to match; (*Mus*) to tune; (*Ling*): ~ **qc con qc** to make sth agree with sth; (*Dir*) to grant; **accordarsi** vpr to agree, come to an agreement; (*colori*) to match

ac'cordo sm agreement; (*armonia*) harmony; (*Mus*) chord; **essere d'~** to agree; **andare d'~** to get on well together; **d'~!** all right!, agreed!; **mettersi d'~ (con qn)** to agree o come to an agreement (with sb); **prendere accordi con** to reach an agreement with; ~ **commerciale** trade agreement; **A~ generale sulle tariffe ed il commercio** General Agreement on Tariffs and Trade, GATT

ac'corgersi [ak'kɔrdʒersi] /**4**/ vpr: ~ **di** to notice; (*fig*) to realize

accorgi'mento [akkordʒi'mento] sm shrewdness *no pl*; (*espediente*) trick, device

ac'correre /**28**/ vi to run up

ac'corsi vb *vedi* **accorgersi; accorrere**

ac'corso, -a PP *di* **accorrere**

accor'tezza [akkor'tettsa] sf (*avvedutezza*) good sense; (*astuzia*) shrewdness

ac'corto, -a PP *di* **accorgersi** ▶ AG shrewd; **stare** ~ to be on one's guard

accosta'mento sm (*di colori ecc*) combination

accos'tare /**72**/ vt (*avvicinarsi a*) to approach; (*socchiudere: imposte*) to half-close; (: *porta*) to leave ajar ▶ vi: ~ **(a)** (*Naut*) to come alongside; (*Aut*) to draw up (at); **accostarsi** vpr: **accostarsi a** to draw near, approach; (*somigliare*) to be like, resemble; (*fede, religione*) to turn to; (*idee politiche*) to come to agree with; ~ **qc a** (*avvicinare*) to bring sth near to, put sth near to; (*colori, stili*) to match sth with; (*appoggiare: scala ecc*) to lean sth against

accovacci'arsi [akkovat'tʃarsi] /**14**/ vpr to crouch

accoz'zaglia [akkot'tsaʎʎa] sf (*peg: di idee, oggetti*) jumble, hotchpotch; (: *di persone*) odd assortment

ac'crebbi *etc* vb *vedi* **accrescere**

accredi'tare /**72**/ vt (*notizia*) to confirm the truth of; (*Comm*) to credit; (*diplomatico*) to accredit; **accreditarsi** vpr (*fig*) to gain credit

ac'credito sm (*Comm: atto*) crediting; (: *effetto*) credit

ac'crescere [ak'kreʃʃere] /**30**/ vt to increase; **accrescersi** vpr to increase, grow

accresci'mento [akkreʃʃi'mento] sm increase, growth

accresci'tivo, -a [akkreʃʃi'tivo] AG, sm (*Ling*) augmentative

accresci'uto, -a [akkreʃʃuto] PP *di* **accrescere**

accucci'arsi [akkut'tʃarsi] /**14**/ vpr (*cane*) to lie down; (*persona*) to crouch down

accu'dire /**55**/ vi: ~ **a** to attend to ▶ vt to look after

acculturazi'one [akkulturat'tsjone] sf (*Sociologia*) integration

accumu'lare /**72**/ vt to accumulate; **accumularsi** vpr to accumulate; (*Finanza*) to accrue

accumula'tore sm (*Elettr*) accumulator

accumulazi'one [akkumulat'tsjone] sf accumulation

ac'cumulo sm accumulation

accurata'mente AV carefully

accura'tezza [akkura'tettsa] sf care; accuracy

accu'rato, -a AG (*diligente*) careful; (*preciso*) accurate

ac'cusa sf accusation; (*Dir*) charge; **l'~, la pubblica** ~ (*Dir*) the prosecution; **mettere qn sotto** ~ to indict sb; **in stato di** ~ committed for trial

accu'sare /**72**/ vt (*sentire: dolore*) to feel; ~ **qn di qc** to accuse sb of sth; (*Dir*) to charge sb with sth; ~ **ricevuta di** (*Comm*) to acknowledge receipt of; ~ **la fatica** to show signs of exhaustion; **ha accusato il colpo** (*anche fig*) you could see that he had felt the blow

accusa'tivo sm accusative

accu'sato, -a sm/f accused

accusa'tore, -'trice AG accusing ▶ sm/f accuser ▶ sm (*Dir*) prosecutor

a'cerbo, -a [a'tʃɛrbo] AG bitter; (*frutta*) sour,

unripe; (*persona*) immature

'**acero** ['atʃero] SM maple

a'**cerrimo, -a** [a'tʃɛrrimo] AG very fierce

ace'**tato** [atʃe'tato] SM acetate

a'**ceto** [a'tʃeto] SM vinegar; **mettere sotto ~** to pickle

ace'**tone** [atʃe'tone] SM nail varnish remover

'**A.C.I.** ['atʃi] SIGLA M (= *Automobile Club d'Italia*) ≈ AA (BRIT), ≈ AAA (US)

aci'**dità** [atʃidi'ta] SF acidity; sourness; **~ (di stomaco)** heartburn

'**acido, -a** ['atʃido] AG (*sapore*) acid, sour; (*Chim, colore*) acid ▶ SM (*Chim*) acid

a'**cidulo, -a** [a'tʃidulo] AG slightly sour, slightly acid

'**acino** ['atʃino] SM berry; **~ d'uva** grape

'**ACLI** SIGLA FPL (= *Associazioni Cristiane dei Lavoratori Italiani*) Christian Trade Union Association

'**acme** SF (*fig*) acme, peak; (*Med*) crisis

'**acne** SF acne

ACNUR SIGLA M (= *Alto Commissariato delle Nazioni Unite per i Rifugiati*) UNHCR

'**acqua** SF water; (*pioggia*) rain; **acque** SFPL (*di mare, fiume ecc*) waters; **fare ~** (*Naut*) to leak, take in water; **essere con** o **avere l'~ alla gola** to be in great difficulty; **tirare ~ al proprio mulino** to feather one's own nest; **navigare in cattive acque** (*fig*) to be in deep water; **~ in bocca!** mum's the word!; **~ corrente** running water; **~ dolce** fresh water; **~ di mare** sea water; **~ minerale** mineral water; **~ ossigenata** hydrogen peroxide; **~ piovana** rain water; **~ potabile** drinking water; **~ salata** o **salmastra** salt water; **~ tonica** tonic water

acqua'**forte** (*pl* **acqueforti**) SF etching

a'**cquaio** SM sink

acqua'**ragia** [akkwa'radʒa] SF turpentine

a'**cquario** SM aquarium; **A~** Aquarius; **essere dell'A~** to be Aquarius

acquartie'**rare** /**72**/ VT (*Mil*) to quarter

acqua'**santa** SF holy water

acquas'**cooter** [akkwas'kuter] SM INV Jet Ski®

a'**cquatico, -a, -ci, -che** AG aquatic; (*sport, sci*) water *cpd*

acquat'**tarsi** /**72**/ VPR to crouch (down)

acqua'**vite** SF brandy

acquaz'**zone** [akkwat'tsone] SM cloudburst, heavy shower

acque'**dotto** SM aqueduct; waterworks *pl*, water system

'**acqueo, -a** AG: **vapore ~** water vapour (BRIT) o vapor (US); **umore ~** aqueous humour (BRIT) o humor (US)

acque'**rello** SM watercolour (BRIT), watercolor (US)

acque'**rugiola** [akkwe'rudʒola] SF drizzle

acquie'**tare** /**72**/ VT to appease; (*dolore*) to ease; **acquietarsi** VPR to calm down

acqui'**rente** SMF purchaser, buyer

acqui'**sire** /**55**/ VT to acquire

acquisizi'**one** [akkwizit'tsjone] SF acquisition

acquis'**tare** /**72**/ VT to purchase, buy; (*fig*) to gain ▶ VI to improve; **~ in bellezza** to become more beautiful; **ha acquistato in salute** his health has improved

a'**cquisto** SM purchase; **fare acquisti** to go shopping; **ufficio acquisti** (*Comm*) purchasing department; **~ rateale** instalment purchase, hire purchase (BRIT)

acqui'**trino** SM bog, marsh

acquo'**lina** SF: **far venire l'~ in bocca a qn** to make sb's mouth water

a'**cquoso, -a** AG watery

'**acre** AG acrid, pungent; (*fig*) harsh, biting

a'**credine** SF (*fig*) bitterness

a'**crilico, -a, -ci, -che** AG, SM acrylic

a'**critico, -a, -ci, -che** AG uncritical

a'**crobata, -i, -e** SM/F acrobat

acro'**batico, -a, -ci, -che** AG (*ginnastica*) acrobatic; (*Aer*) aerobatic ▶ SF acrobatics *sg*

acroba'**zia** [akrobat'tsia] SF acrobatic feat; **acrobazie aeree** aerobatics

a'**cronimo** SM acronym

a'**cropoli** SF INV: **l'A~** the Acropolis

acu'**ire** /**55**/ VT to sharpen; **acuirsi** VPR (*gen*) to increase; (*crisi*) to worsen

a'**culeo** SM (*Zool*) sting; (*Bot*) prickle

a'**cume** SM acumen, perspicacity

acumi'**nato, -a** AG sharp

a'**custico, -a, -ci, -che** AG acoustic ▶ SF (*scienza*) acoustics *sg*; (*di una sala*) acoustics *pl*; **apparecchio ~** hearing aid; **cornetto ~** ear trumpet

acu'**tezza** [aku'tettsa] SF sharpness; shrillness; acuteness; high pitch; intensity; keenness

acutiz'**zare** [akutid'dzare] /**72**/ VT (*fig*) to intensify; **acutizzarsi** VPR (*fig*: *crisi, malattia*) to become worse, worsen

a'**cuto, -a** AG (*appuntito*) sharp, pointed; (*suono, voce*) shrill, piercing; (*Mat, Ling, Med*) acute; (*Mus*) high-pitched; (*fig*: *dolore, desiderio*) intense; (: *perspicace*) acute, keen ▶ SM (*Mus*) high note

ad PREP (*dav V*) = **a**

adagi'**are** [ada'dʒare] /**62**/ VT to lay o set down carefully; **adagiarsi** VPR to lie down, stretch out

a'**dagio** [a'dadʒo] AV slowly ▶ SM (*Mus*) adagio; (*proverbio*) adage, saying

ada'**mitico, -a, -ci, -che** AG: **in costume ~** in one's birthday suit

adat'**tabile** AG adaptable

adattabi'**lità** SF adaptability

adatta'mento SM adaptation; **avere spirito di ~** to be adaptable

adat'tare /72/ VT to adapt; (*sistemare*) to fit; **adattarsi** VPR: **adattarsi (a)** (*ambiente, tempi*) to adapt (to); (*essere adatto*) to be suitable (for); **adattarsi a qc/a fare qc** (*accontentarsi*) to make the best of sth/of doing sth

adatta'tore SM (*Elettr*) adapter, adaptor

a'datto, -a AG: **~ (a)** suitable (for), right (for)

addebi'tare /72/ VT: **~ qc a qn** to debit sb with sth; (*fig: incolpare*) to blame sb for sth

ad'debito SM (*Comm*) debit

addensa'mento SM thickening; gathering

adden'sare /72/ VT to thicken; **addensarsi** VPR to thicken; (*nuvole*) to gather

adden'tare /72/ VT to bite into

adden'trarsi /72/ VPR: **~ in** to penetrate, go into

ad'dentro AV (*fig*): **essere molto ~ in qc** to be well-versed in sth

addestra'mento SM training; **~ aziendale** company training

addes'trare /72/ VT, **addes'trarsi** VPR to train; **addestrarsi in qc** to practise (*BRIT*) o practice (*US*) sth

ad'detto, -a AG: **~ a** (*persona*) assigned to; (*oggetto*) intended for ▶ SM employee; (*funzionario*) attaché; **~ commerciale/stampa** commercial/press attaché; **~ al telex** telex operator; **gli addetti ai lavori** authorized personnel; (*fig*) those in the know; **"vietato l'ingresso ai non addetti ai lavori"** "authorized personnel only"

addì AV (*Amm*): **~ 3 luglio 1989** on the 3rd of July 1989 (*BRIT*), on July 3rd 1989 (*US*)

addi'accio [ad'djattʃo] SM (*Mil*) bivouac; **dormire all'~** to sleep in the open

addi'etro AV (*indietro*) behind; (*nel passato, prima*) before, ago

ad'dio SM, ESCL goodbye, farewell

addirit'tura AV (*veramente*) really, absolutely; (*perfino*) even; (*direttamente*) directly, right away

ad'dirsi /38/ VPR: **~ a** to suit, be suitable for

'Addis A'beba SF Addis Ababa

addi'tare /72/ VT to point out; (*fig*) to expose

addi'tivo SM additive

addizio'nale [addittsjo'nale] AG additional ▶ SF (*anche*: **imposta addizionale**) surtax

addizio'nare [addittsjo'nare] /72/ VT (*Mat*) to add (up)

addizi'one [addit'tsjone] SF addition

addob'bare /72/ VT to decorate

ad'dobbo SM decoration

addol'cire [addol'tʃire] /55/ VT (*caffè ecc*) to sweeten; (*acqua, fig: carattere*) to soften; **addolcirsi** VPR (*fig*) to mellow, soften; **~ la pillola** (*fig*) to sugar the pill

addolo'rare /72/ VT to pain, grieve;

addolorarsi VPR: **addolorarsi (per)** to be distressed (by)

addolo'rato, -a AG distressed, upset; **l'Addolorata** (*Rel*) Our Lady of Sorrows

ad'dome SM abdomen

addomesti'care /20/ VT to tame

addomi'nale AG abdominal; **(muscoli) addominali** stomach muscles

addormen'tare /72/ VT to put to sleep; **addormentarsi** VPR to fall asleep, go to sleep

addormen'tato, -a AG sleeping, asleep; (*fig: tardo*) stupid, dopey

addos'sare /72/ VT (*appoggiare*): **~ qc a qc** to lean sth against sth; (*fig*): **~ la colpa a qn** to lay the blame on sb; **addossarsi** VPR: **addossarsi qc** (*responsabilità ecc*) to shoulder sth

ad'dosso AV (*sulla persona*) on; **~ a** prep (*sopra*) on; (*molto vicino*) right next to; **mettersi ~ il cappotto** to put one's coat on; **andare** (*o* **venire**) **~ a** (*Aut: altra macchina*) to run into; (*: pedone*) to run over; **non ho soldi ~** I don't have any money on me; **stare ~ a qn** (*fig*) to breathe down sb's neck; **dare ~ a qn** (*fig*) to attack sb; **mettere gli occhi ~ a qn/qc** to take quite a fancy to sb/sth; **mettere le mani ~ a qn** (*picchiare*) to hit sb; (*catturare*) to seize sb; (*molestare: donna*) to touch sb up

ad'dotto, -a PP *di* **addurre**

ad'duco *etc* VB *vedi* **addurre**

ad'durre /90/ VT (*Dir*) to produce; (*citare*) to cite

ad'dussi *etc* VB *vedi* **addurre**

adegu'are /72/ VT: **~ qc a** to adjust sth to; **adeguarsi** VPR to adapt

adegua'tezza [adegwa'tettsa] SF adequacy; suitability; fairness

adegu'ato, -a AG adequate; (*conveniente*) suitable; (*equo*) fair

a'dempiere /24/ VT to fulfil (*BRIT*), fulfill (*US*), carry out; (*comando*) to carry out

adempi'mento SM fulfilment (*BRIT*), fulfillment (*US*); carrying out; **nell'~ del proprio dovere** in the performance of one's duty

adem'pire /17/ VT = **adempiere**

'Aden: **il golfo di ~** *sm* the Gulf of Aden

ade'noidi SFPL adenoids

a'depto SM disciple, follower

ade'rente AG adhesive; (*vestito*) close-fitting ▶ SMF follower

ade'renza [ade'rentsa] SF adhesion; **aderenze** SFPL (*fig*) connections, contacts

ade'rire /55/ VI (*stare attaccato*) to adhere, stick; **~ a** to adhere to, stick to; (*fig: società, partito*) to join (*: opinione*) to support; (*richiesta*) to agree to

ades'care /20/ VT (*attirare*) to lure, entice; (*Tecn: pompa*) to prime

adesi'one SF adhesion; (*fig: assenso*) agreement, acceptance; (*appoggio*) support

ade'sivo, -a AG, SM adhesive

a'desso AV (*ora*) now; (*or ora, poco fa*) just now; (*tra poco*) any moment now; **da ~ in poi** from now on; **per ~** for the moment, for now

adia'cente [adja'tʃente] AG adjacent

adi'bire /**55**/ VT (*usare*): **~ qc a** to turn sth into

'Adige ['adidʒe] SM: **l'~** the Adige

'adipe SM fat

adi'poso, -a AG (*tessuto, zona*) adipose

adi'rarsi /**72**/ VPR: **~ (con** o **contro qn per qc)** to get angry (with sb over sth)

adi'rato, -a AG angry

a'dire /**55**/ VT (*Dir*): **~ le vie legali** to take legal proceedings; **~ un'eredità** to take legal possession of an inheritance

'adito SM: **dare ~ a** (*sospetti*) to give rise to

adocchi'are [adok'kjare] /**19**/ VT (*scorgere*) to catch sight of; (*occhieggiare*) to eye

adole'scente [adoleʃʃente] AG, SMF adolescent

adole'scenza [adoleʃʃentsa] SF adolescence

adolescenzi'ale [adoleʃʃen'tsjale] AG adolescent

adom'brarsi /**72**/ VPR (*cavallo*) to shy; (*persona*) to grow suspicious; (: *aversene a male*) to be offended

adope'rare /**72**/ VT to use; **adoperarsi** VPR to strive; **adoperarsi per qn/qc** to do one's best for sb/sth

ado'rabile AG adorable

ado'rare /**72**/ VT to adore; (*Rel*) to adore, worship

adorazi'one [adorat'tsjone] SF adoration; worship

ador'nare /**72**/ VT to adorn

a'dorno, -a AG: **~ (di)** adorned (with)

adot'tare /**72**/ VT to adopt; (*decisione, provvedimenti*) to pass

adot'tivo, -a AG (*genitori*) adoptive; (*figlio, patria*) adopted

adozi'one [adot'tsjone] SF adoption; **~ a distanza** child sponsorship

adrena'linico, -a, -ci, -che AG (*fig: vivace, eccitato*) charged-up

adri'atico, -a, -ci, -che AG Adriatic ▶ SM: **l'A~, il mare A~** the Adriatic, the Adriatic Sea

ADSL SIGLA M ADSL (= *asymmetric digital subscriber line*)

adu'lare /**72**/ VT to flatter

adula'tore, -'trice SM/F flatterer

adula'torio, -a AG flattering

adulazi'one [adulat'tsjone] SF flattery

adulte'rare /**72**/ VT to adulterate

adul'terio SM adultery

a'dultero, -a AG adulterous ▶ SM/F adulterer (adulteress)

a'dulto, -a AG adult; (*fig*) mature ▶ SM adult, grown-up

adu'nanza [adu'nantsa] SF assembly, meeting

adu'nare /**72**/ VT, **adu'narsi** VPR to assemble, gather

adu'nata SF (*Mil*) parade, muster

a'dunco, -a, -chi, -che AG hooked

aerazi'one [aerat'tsjone] SF ventilation; (*Tecn*) aeration

a'ereo, -a AG air *cpd*; (*radice*) aerial ▶ SM aerial; (*aeroplano*) plane; **~ da caccia** fighter (plane); **~ di linea** airliner; **~ a reazione** jet (plane)

ae'robica SF aerobics *sg*

aerodi'namico, -a, -ci, -che AG aerodynamic; (*affusolato*) streamlined ▶ SF aerodynamics *sg*

aeromo'dello SM model aircraft

aero'nautica SF (*scienza*) aeronautics *sg*; **~ militare** air force

aerona'vale AG (*forze, manovre*) air and sea *cpd*

aero'plano SM (aero)plane (*BRIT*), (air)plane (*US*)

aero'porto SM airport

aeroportu'ale AG airport *cpd*

aeros'calo SM airstrip

aero'sol SM INV aerosol

aerospazi'ale [aerospat'tsjale] AG aerospace

aeros'tatico, -a, -ci, -che AG aerostatic; **pallone ~** air balloon

ae'rostato SM aerostat

A.F. ABBR (= *alta frequenza*) HF; (*Amm*) = **assegni familiari**

'afa SF sultriness

affabile AG affable

affabilità SF affability

affaccen'darsi [affattʃen'darsi] /**72**/ VPR: **~ intorno a qc** to busy o.s. with sth

affaccen'dato, -a [affattʃen'dato] AG (*persona*) busy

affacci'arsi [affat'tʃarsi] /**14**/ VPR: **~ (a)** to appear (at); **~ alla vita** to come into the world

affa'mato, -a AG starving; (*fig*): **~ (di)** eager (for)

affan'nare /**72**/ VT to leave breathless; (*fig*) to worry; **affannarsi** VPR: **affannarsi per qn/qc** to worry about sb/sth

affanno SM breathlessness; (*fig*) anxiety, worry

affannosa'mente AV with difficulty; anxiously

affan'noso, -a AG (*respiro*) difficult; (*fig*) troubled, anxious

af'fare SM (*faccenda*) matter, affair; (*Comm*) piece of business, (business) deal; (*occasione*) bargain; (*Dir*) case; (*col: cosa*) thing; **affari** SMPL (*Comm*) business *sg*; **~ fatto!** done!, it's a deal!; **sono affari miei** that's my business;

bada agli affari tuoi! mind your own business!; **uomo d'affari** businessman; **ministro degli Affari Esteri** Foreign Secretary (*Brit*), Secretary of State (*US*)

affa'rista, -i sm profiteer, unscrupulous businessman

affasci'nante [affaʃʃi'nante] AG fascinating

affasci'nare [affaʃʃi'nare] /**72**/ VT to bewitch; (*fig*) to charm, fascinate

affatica'mento sm tiredness

affati'care /**20**/ VT to tire; **affaticarsi** VPR (*durar fatica*) to tire o.s. out

affati'cato, -a AG tired

affatto AV completely; **non ... ~** not ... at all; **niente ~** not at all

affer'mare /**72**/ VI (*dire di sì*) to say yes ▶ VT (*dichiarare*) to maintain, affirm; **affermarsi** VPR to assert o.s., make one's name known

affermativa'mente AV in the affirmative, affirmatively

afferma'tivo, -a AG affirmative

affer'mato, -a AG established, well-known

affermazi'one [affermat'tsjone] SF affirmation, assertion; (*successo*) achievement

affer'rare /**72**/ VT to seize, grasp; (*fig: idea*) to grasp; **afferrarsi** VPR: **afferrarsi a** to cling to

Aff. Est. ABBR = **Affari Esteri**

affet'tare /**72**/ VT (*tagliare a fette*) to slice; (*ostentare*) to affect

affet'tato, -a AG sliced; affected ▶ SM sliced cold meat

affetta'trice [affetta'tritʃe] SF meat slicer

affettazi'one [affetta't'tsjone] SF affectation

affet'tivo, -a AG emotional, affective

af'fetto, -a AG: **essere ~ da** to suffer from ▶ SM affection; **gli affetti familiari** one's nearest and dearest

affettuosa'mente AV affectionately; (*nelle lettere*): (**ti saluto**) **~, Maria** love, Maria

affettuosità SF INV affection ▶ SFPL (*manifestazioni*) demonstrations of affection

affettu'oso, -a AG affectionate

affezio'narsi [affettsjo'narsi] /**72**/ VPR: **~ a** to grow fond of

affezio'nato, -a [affettsjo'nato] AG: **~ a qn/qc** fond of sb/sth; (*attaccato*) attached to sb/sth

affezi'one [affet'tsjone] SF (*affetto*) affection; (*Med*) ailment, disorder

affian'care /**20**/ VT to place side by side; (*Mil*) to flank; (*fig*) to support; **~ qc a qc** to place sth next to o beside sth; **affiancarsi** VPR: **affiancarsi a qn** to stand beside sb

affiata'mento SM understanding

affia'tato, -a AG: **essere affiatati** to work well together o get on; **formano una squadra affiatata** they make a good team

affibbi'are /**19**/ VT to buckle, do up; (*fig: dare*) to give

affi'dabile AG reliable

affidabilità SF reliability

affida'mento SM (*Dir: di bambino*) custody; (*fiducia*): **fare ~ su qn** to rely on sb; **non dà nessun ~** he's not to be trusted

affi'dare /**72**/ VT: **~ qc o qn a qn** to entrust sth o sb to sb; **affidarsi** VPR: **affidarsi a** to place one's trust in

affievo'lirsi /**55**/ VPR to grow weak

af'figgere [af'fiddʒere] /**104**/ VT to stick up, post up

affi'lare /**72**/ VT to sharpen

affi'lato, -a AG (*gen*) sharp; (*volto, naso*) thin

affili'are /**19**/ VT to affiliate; **affiliarsi** VPR: **affiliarsi a** to become affiliated to

affi'nare /**72**/ VT to sharpen

affinché [affin'ke] CONG in order that, so that

af'fine AG similar

affinità SF INV affinity

affio'rare /**72**/ VI to emerge

af'fissi etc VB vedi **affiggere**

affissi'one SF billposting

af'fisso, -a PP di **affiggere** ▶ SM bill, poster; (*Ling*) affix

affitta'camere SM INV/F INV landlord (landlady)

affit'tare /**72**/ VT (*dare in affitto*) to let, rent (out); (*prendere in affitto*) to rent

af'fitto SM rent; (*contratto*) lease; **dare in ~** to rent (out), let; **prendere in ~** to rent

affittu'ario SM lessee

af'fliggere [af'fliddʒere] /**104**/ VT to torment; **affliggersi** VPR to grieve

af'flissi etc VB vedi **affliggere**

af'flitto, -a PP di **affliggere**

afflizi'one [afflit'tsjone] SF distress, torment

afflosci'arsi [affloʃ'ʃarsi] /**14**/ VPR to go limp; (*frutta*) to go soft

afflu'ente SM tributary

afflu'enza [afflu'entsa] SF flow; (*di persone*) crowd

afflu'ire /**55**/ VI to flow; (*fig: merci, persone*) to pour in

af'flusso SM influx

affo'gare /**80**/ VT, VI to drown; **affogarsi** VPR to drown; (*deliberatamente*) to drown o.s.

affo'gato, -a AG drowned; (*Cuc: uova*) poached

affolla'mento SM crowding; (*folla*) crowd

affol'lare /**72**/ VT, **affol'larsi** VPR to crowd

affol'lato, -a AG crowded

affonda'mento SM (*di nave*) sinking

affon'dare /**72**/ VT to sink

affran'care /**20**/ VT to free, liberate; (*Amm*) to redeem; (*lettera*) to stamp; (: *meccanicamente*) to frank (*Brit*), meter (*US*); **affrancarsi** VPR to free o.s.

affranca'trice [affranka'tritʃe] SF franking machine (*Brit*), postage meter (*US*)

affranca'tura SF (*di francobollo*) stamping; franking (BRIT), metering (US); (*tassa di spedizione*) postage; **~ a carico del destinatario** postage paid

affranto, -a AG (*esausto*) worn out; (*abbattuto*) overcome

affresco, -schi SM fresco

affret'tare /**72**/ VT to quicken, speed up; **affrettarsi** VPR to hurry; **affrettarsi a fare qc** to hurry o hasten to do sth

affret'tato, -a AG (*veloce: passo, ritmo*) quick, fast; (*frettoloso: decisione*) hurried, hasty; (: *lavoro*) rushed

affron'tare /**72**/ VT (*pericolo ecc*) to face; (*assalire: nemico*) to confront; **affrontarsi** VPR (*reciproco*) to confront each other

affronto SM affront, insult; **fare un ~ a qn** to insult sb

affumi'care /**20**/ VT to fill with smoke; to blacken with smoke; (*alimenti*) to smoke

affumi'cato, -a AG (*prosciutto, aringa ecc*) smoked

affuso'lato, -a AG tapering

afgano, -a AG, SM/F Afghan

Afghanistan [afˈganistan] SM: **l'~** Afghanistan

afghano, -a AG, SM/F = **afgano**

afo'risma, -i SM aphorism

a'foso, -a AG sultry, close

'Africa SF: **l'~** Africa

afri'cano, -a AG, SM/F African

afroasi'atico, -a, -ci, -che AG Afro-Asian

afrodi'siaco, -a, -ci, -che AG, SM aphrodisiac

AG SIGLA = **Agrigento**

a'genda [aˈdʒɛnda] SF diary; **~ tascabile/da tavolo** pocket/desk diary

a'gente [aˈdʒɛnte] SM agent; **~ di cambio** stockbroker; **~ di custodia** prison officer; **~ marittimo** shipping agent; **~ di polizia** police officer; **~ segreto** secret agent; **~ provocatore** agent provocateur; **~ delle tasse** tax inspector; **~ di vendita** sales agent; **resistente agli agenti atmosferici** weather-resistant

agen'zia [adʒenˈtsia] SF agency; (*succursale*) branch; **~ di collocamento** employment agency; **~ immobiliare** estate agent's (office) (BRIT), real estate office (US); **A~ Internazionale per l'Energia Atomica** International Atomic Energy Agency; **~ matrimoniale** marriage bureau; **~ pubblicitaria** advertising agency; **~ di stampa** press agency; **~ viaggi** travel agency

agevo'lare [adʒevoˈlare] /**72**/ VT to facilitate, make easy

agevolazi'one [adʒevolatˈtsjone] SF (*facilitazione economica*) facility; **~ di pagamento** payment on easy terms; **agevolazioni creditizie** credit facilities;

agevolazioni fiscali tax concessions

a'gevole [aˈdʒevole] AG easy; (*strada*) smooth

aggan'ci'are [aggan'tʃare] /**14**/ VT to hook up; (*Ferr*) to couple; **agganciarsi** VPR: **agganciarsi a** to hook up to; (*fig: pretesto*) to seize on

ag'gancio [agˈgantʃo] SM (*Tecn*) coupling; (*fig: conoscenza*) contact

ag'geggio [adˈdʒeddʒo] SM gadget, contraption

agget'tivo [addʒetˈtivo] SM adjective

agghiacci'ante [aggjatˈtʃante] AG (*fig*) chilling

agghiacci'are [aggjatˈtʃare] /**14**/ VT to freeze; (*fig*) to make one's blood run cold; **agghiacciarsi** VPR to freeze

agghin'darsi [aggin'darsi] /**61**/ VPR to deck o.s. out

aggiorna'mento [addʒorna'mento] SM updating; revision; postponement; **corso di ~** refresher course

aggior'nare [addʒor'nare] /**72**/ VT (*opera, manuale*) to bring up-to-date; (: *rivedere*) to revise; (*listino*) to maintain, up-date; (*seduta ecc*) to postpone; **aggiornarsi** VPR to bring (o keep) o.s. up-to-date

aggior'nato, -a [addʒor'nato] AG up-to-date

aggio'taggio [addʒo'taddʒo] SM (*Econ*) rigging the market

aggi'rare [addʒi'rare] /**72**/ VT to go round; (*fig: ingannare*) to trick; **aggirarsi** VPR to wander about; **il prezzo s'aggira sul milione** the price is around the million mark

aggiudi'care [addʒudi'kare] /**20**/ VT to award; (*all'asta*) to knock down; **aggiudicarsi qc** to win sth

aggi'ungere [ad'dʒundʒere] /**5**/ VT to add; (*Inform*): **grazie per avermi aggiunto (come amico)** thanks for the add

aggi'unsi *etc* [ad'dʒunsi] VB *vedi* **aggiungere**

aggi'unto, -a [ad'dʒunto] PP *di* **aggiungere** ▶ AG assistant *cpd* ▶ SM assistant ▶ SF addition; **sindaco ~** deputy mayor; **in aggiunta ...** what's more ...

aggius'tare [addʒus'tare] /**72**/ VT (*accomodare*) to mend, repair; (*riassettare*) to adjust; (*fig: lite*) to settle; **aggiustarsi** VPR (*arrangiarsi*) to make do; (*con senso reciproco*) to come to an agreement; **ti aggiusto io!** I'll fix you!

agglome'rato SM (*di rocce*) conglomerate; (*di legno*) chipboard; **~ urbano** built-up area

aggrap'parsi /**72**/ VPR: **~ a** to cling to

aggrava'mento SM worsening

aggra'vante AG (*Dir*) aggravating ▶ SF aggravation

aggra'vare /**72**/ VT (*aumentare*) to increase; (*appesantire: anche fig*) to weigh down, make heavy; (*fig: pena*) to make worse; **aggravarsi** VPR (*fig*) to worsen, become worse

ag'gravio SM: ~ **di costi** increase in costs

aggrazi'ato, -a [aggrat'tsjato] AG graceful

aggre'dire /55/ VT to attack, assault

aggre'gare /8o/ VT: ~ **qn a qc** to admit sb to sth; **aggregarsi** VPR to join; **aggregarsi a** to join, become a member of

aggre'gato, -a AG associated ▶ SM aggregate; ~ **urbano** built-up area

aggressi'one SF aggression; (atto) attack, assault; ~ **a mano armata** armed assault

aggressività SF aggressiveness

aggres'sivo, -a AG aggressive

aggres'sore SM aggressor, attacker

aggrot'tare /72/ VT: ~ **le sopracciglia** to frown

aggrovigli'are [aggroviʎ'ʎare] /27/ VT to tangle; **aggrovigliarsi** VPR (fig) to become complicated

agguan'tare /72/ VT to catch, seize

aggu'ato SM trap; (imboscata) ambush; **tendere un ~ a qn** to set a trap for sb

agguer'rito, -a AG (sostenitore, nemico) fierce

agia'tezza [adʒa'tettsa] SF prosperity

agi'ato, -a [a'dʒato] AG (vita) easy; (persona) well-off, well-to-do

'agile ['adʒile] AG agile, nimble

agilità [adʒili'ta] SF agility, nimbleness

'agio ['adʒo] SM ease, comfort; **agi** SMPL comforts; **mettersi a proprio ~** to make o.s. at home o comfortable; **dare ~ a qn di fare qc** to give sb the chance of doing sth

a'gire [a'dʒire] /55/ VI to act; (esercitare un'azione) to take effect; (Tecn) to work, function; ~ **contro qn** (Dir) to take action against sb

agi'tare [adʒi'tare] /72/ VT (bottiglia) to shake; (mano, fazzoletto) to wave; (fig: turbare) to disturb; (: incitare) to stir (up); (: dibattere) to discuss; **agitarsi** VPR (mare) to be rough; (malato, dormitore) to toss and turn; (bambino) to fidget; (emozionarsi) to get upset; (Pol) to agitate

agi'tato, -a [adʒi'tato] AG rough; restless; fidgety; upset, perturbed

agita'tore, -'trice [adʒita'tore] SM/F (Pol) agitator

agitazi'one [adʒitat'tsjone] SF agitation; (Pol) unrest, agitation; **mettere in ~ qn** to upset o distress sb

'agli ['aʎʎi] PREP + DET vedi **a**

'aglio ['aʎʎo] SM garlic

a'gnello [aɲ'ɲɛllo] SM lamb

a'gnostico, -a, -ci, -che [aɲ'ɲɔstiko] AG, SM/F agnostic

'ago (pl **aghi**) SM needle; ~ **da calza** knitting needle

ago. ABBR (= agosto) Aug.

ago'nia SF agony

ago'nistico, -a, -ci, -che AG athletic; (fig) competitive

agoniz'zante [agonid'dzante] AG dying

agoniz'zare [agonid'dzare] /72/ VI to be dying

agopun'tura SF acupuncture

agorafo'bia SF agoraphobia

a'gosto SM August; vedi anche **luglio**

a'grario, -a AG agrarian, agricultural; (riforma) land cpd ▶ SM landowner ▶ SF agriculture

a'gricolo, -a AG agricultural, farm cpd

agricol'tore SM farmer

agricol'tura SF agriculture, farming

agri'foglio [agri'fɔʎʎo] SM holly

agrimen'sore SM land surveyor

agritu'rismo SM farm holidays pl

agritu'ristico, -a, -ci, -che AG farm holiday cpd

'agro, -a AG sour, sharp

agro'dolce [agro'doltʃe] AG bittersweet; (salsa) sweet and sour

agrono'mia SF agronomy

a'gronomo SM agronomist

a'grume SM (spesso al pl: pianta) citrus; (: frutto) citrus fruit

agru'meto SM citrus grove

aguz'zare [agut'tsare] /72/ VT to sharpen; ~ **gli orecchi** to prick up one's ears; ~ **l'ingegno** to use one's wits

aguz'zino, -a [agud'dzino] SM/F jailer; (fig) tyrant

a'guzzo, -a [a'guttso] AG sharp

'ahi ESCL (dolore) ouch!

ahimè ESCL alas!

'ai PREP + DET vedi **a**

'Aia SF: **L'~** The Hague

'aia SF threshing floor

AIDDA SIGLA F (= Associazione Imprenditrici Donne Dirigenti d'Azienda) association of women entrepreneurs and managers

AIDS ['aids] ABBR M/ABBR F AIDS

AIE SIGLA F (= Associazione Italiana degli Editori) publishers' association

AIEA SIGLA F = **Agenzia Internazionale per l'Energia Atomica**

AIED SIGLA F (= Associazione Italiana Educazione Demografica) ≈ FPA (= Family Planning Association)

AIG SIGLA F (= Associazione Italiana Alberghi per la Gioventù) ≈ YHA (BRIT)

ai'ola SF = **aiuola**

airbag SM INV air bag

AIRC ABBR F = **Associazione Italiana per la Ricerca sul Cancro**

ai'rone SM heron

ai'tante AG robust

aiu'ola SF flower bed

aiu'tante SMF assistant ▶ SM (Mil) adjutant; (Naut) master-at-arms; ~ **di campo** aide-de-camp

aiu'tare /72/ VT to help; ~ **qn (a fare)** to help sb (to do); **aiutarsi** VPR to help each other;

~ **qn in qc/a fare qc** to help sb with sth/ to do sth; **può aiutarmi?** can you help me?

ai'uto SM help, assistance, aid; (*aiutante*) assistant; **venire in ~ di qn** to come to sb's aid; ~ **chirurgo** assistant surgeon

aiz'zare [ait'tsare] /**72**/ VT to incite; ~ **i cani contro qn** to set the dogs on sb

al PREP + DET *vedi* **a**

a.l. ABBR = **anno luce**

'ala (*pl* **ali**) SF wing; **fare ~** to fall back, make way; ~ **destra/sinistra** (*Sport*) right/left wing

ala'bastro SM alabaster

'alacre AG quick, brisk

alacrità SF promptness, speed

alam'bicco, -chi SM still (*Chim*)

a'lano SM Great Dane

a'lare AG wing *cpd*; **alari** SMPL firedogs

A'laska SF: **l'~** Alaska

a'lato, -a AG winged

'alba SF dawn; **all'~** at dawn

alba'nese AG, SMF Albanian

Alba'nia SF: **l'~** Albania

al'batro SM albatross

albeggi'are [albed'dʒare] /**72**/ VI, VB IMPERS to dawn

albe'rato, -a AG (*viale, piazza*) lined with trees, tree-lined

albera'tura SF (*Naut*) masts *pl*

alber'gare /**80**/ VT (*dare albergo*) to accommodate ▶ VI (*poetico*) to dwell

alberga'tore, -'trice SM/F hotelier, hotel owner

alberghi'ero, -a [alber'gjɛro] AG hotel *cpd*

al'bergo, -ghi SM hotel; ~ **diurno** *public toilets with washing and shaving facilities etc*; ~ **della gioventù** youth hostel

'albero SM tree; (*Naut*) mast; (*Tecn*) shaft; ~ **a camme** camshaft; ~ **genealogico** family tree; ~ **a gomiti** crankshaft; ~ **maestro** mainmast; ~ **di Natale** Christmas tree; ~ **di trasmissione** transmission shaft

albi'cocca, -che SF apricot

albi'cocco, -chi SM apricot tree

al'bino, -a AG, SM/F albino

'albo SM (*registro*) register, roll; (*Amm*) notice board

'album SM INV album; ~ **da disegno** sketch book

al'bume SM albumen; (*bianco d'uovo*) egg white

albu'mina SF albumin

'alce ['altʃe] SM elk

al'chimia [al'kimja] SF alchemy

alchi'mista, -i [alki'mista] SM alchemist

'alcol SM INV = **alcool**

alcolicità [alkolitʃi'ta] SF alcohol(ic) content

al'colico, -a, -ci, -che AG alcoholic ▶ SM alcoholic drink

alco'lismo SM alcoholism

alco'lista, -i, -e SM/F alcoholic

alcoliz'zato, -a [alkolid'dzato] SM/F alcoholic

'alcool SM INV alcohol; ~ **denaturato** methylated spirits *pl* (*BRIT*), wood alcohol (*US*); ~ **etilico** ethyl alcohol; ~ **metilico** methyl alcohol

alco'olico *etc vedi* **alcolico** *ecc*

alco'test SM INV Breathalyser® (*BRIT*), Breathalyzer® (*US*)

al'cova SF alcove

al'cuno, -a DET (*dav sm:* **alcun** + C, V, **alcuno** + *s impura, gn, pn, ps, x, z; dav sf:* **alcuna** + C, **alcun'** + V: *nessuno*): **non ...** ~ no, not any; **alcuna**, **alcun'** + V: **nessuno**): **non ...** ~ no, not any; **alcuni, e** DET PL, PRON PL some, a few; **non c'è alcuna fretta** there's no hurry, there isn't any hurry; **senza alcun riguardo** without any consideration

aldilà SM INV: **l'~** the next life, the after-life

alea'torio, -a AG (*incerto*) uncertain

aleggi'are [aled'dʒare] /**62**/ VI (*fig: profumo, sospetto*) to be in the air

Ales'sandria SF (*anche:* **Alessandria d'Egitto**) Alexandria

a'letta SF (*Tecn*) fin; tab

alet'tone SM (*Aer*) aileron

Aleu'tine SFPL: **le isole ~** the Aleutian Islands

alfa'betico, -a, -ci, -che AG alphabetical

alfa'beto SM alphabet

alfanu'merico, -a, -ci, -che AG alphanumeric

alfi'ere SM standard-bearer; (*Scacchi*) bishop

al'fine AV finally, in the end

'alga, -ghe SF seaweed *no pl*, alga

'algebra ['aldʒebra] SF algebra

Al'geri [al'dʒeri] SF Algiers

Alge'ria [aldʒe'ria] SF: **l'~** Algeria

alge'rino, -a [aldʒe'rino] AG, SM/F Algerian

algo'ritmo SM algorithm

ALI SIGLA F (= *Associazione Librai Italiani*) *booksellers' association*

ali'ante SM (*Aer*) glider

'alibi SM INV alibi

a'lice [a'litʃe] SF anchovy

alie'nare /**72**/ VT (*Dir*) to transfer; (*rendere ostile*) to alienate; **alienarsi qn** to alienate sb

alie'nato, -a AG alienated; transferred; (*fuor di senno*) insane ▶ SM lunatic, insane person

alienazi'one [aljenat'tsjone] SF alienation; transfer; insanity

ali'eno, -a AG (*avverso*): ~ (**da**) opposed (to), averse (to) ▶ SM/F alien

alimen'tare /**72**/ VT to feed; (*Tecn*) to feed, supply; (*fig*) to sustain ▶ AG food *cpd*; **alimentari** SMPL foodstuffs; (*anche:* **negozio di alimentari**) grocer's shop; **regime ~** diet

alimenta'tore SM (*Elettr*) feeder

alimentazi'one [alimentat'tsjone] SF

feeding; supplying; sustaining; (*cibi*) diet;
~ **di fogli** (*Inform*) sheet feed

ali'mento SM food; **alimenti** SMPL food *sg*;
(*Dir*) alimony

a'liquota SF share; ~ **d'imposta** tax rate;
~ **minima** (*Fisco*) basic rate

alis'cafo SM hydrofoil

'alito SM breath

all. ABBR (= *allegato*) enc., encl.

'alla PREP + DET *vedi* **a**

allaccia'mento [allattʃa'mento] SM (*Tecn*)
connection

allacci'are [allat'tʃare] /**14**/ VT (*scarpe*) to tie,
lace (up); (*cintura*) to do up, fasten; (*due
località*) to link; (*luce, gas*) to connect;
(*amicizia*) to form; **allacciarsi** VPR (*vestito*) to
fasten; ~ *o* **allacciarsi la cintura** to fasten
one's belt

allaccia'tura [allattʃa'tura] SF fastening

allaga'mento SM flooding *no pl*; flood

alla'gare /**80**/ VT, **alla'garsi** VPR to flood

allampa'nato, -a AG lanky

allar'gare /**80**/ VT to widen; (*vestito*) to let out;
(*aprire*) to open; (*fig: dilatare*) to extend;
allargarsi VPR (*gen*) to widen; (*scarpe,
pantaloni*) to stretch; (*fig: problema, fenomeno*) to
spread

allar'mare /**72**/ VT to alarm; **allarmarsi** VPR to
become alarmed

al'larme SM alarm; **mettere qn in** ~ to alarm
sb; ~ **aereo** air-raid warning

allar'mismo SM scaremongering

allar'mista, -i, -e SM/F scaremonger,
alarmist

allat'tare /**72**/ VT (*donna*) to (breast-)feed;
(: *animale*) to suckle; ~ **artificialmente** to
bottle-feed

'alle PREP + DET *vedi* **a**

alle'anza [alle'antsa] SF alliance; **A~
Democratica** (*Pol*) *moderate centre-left party*;
A~ Nazionale (*Pol*) *party on the far right*

alle'arsi /**72**/ VPR to form an alliance

alle'ato, -a AG allied ▶ SM/F ally

alleg. ABBR = **all.**

alle'gare /**80**/ VT (*accludere*) to enclose; (*Dir:
citare*) to cite, adduce; (*denti*) to set on edge

alle'gato, -a AG enclosed ▶ SM enclosure; (*di
e-mail*) attachment; **in** ~ enclosed; **in** ~ **Vi
inviamo ...** please find enclosed ...

allegge'rire [alledd ʒe'rire] /**55**/ VT to lighten,
make lighter; (*fig: sofferenza*) to alleviate,
lessen; (: *lavoro, tasse*) to reduce

allego'ria SF allegory

alle'gorico, -a, -ci, -che AG allegorical

alle'gria SF gaiety, cheerfulness

al'legro, -a AG cheerful, merry; (*un po' brillo*)
merry, tipsy; (*vivace: colore*) bright ▶ SM (*Mus*)
allegro

allena'mento SM training

alle'nare /**72**/ VT, **alle'narsi** VPR to train

allena'tore SM (*Sport*) trainer, coach

allen'tare /**72**/ VT to slacken; (*disciplina*) to
relax; **allentarsi** VPR to become slack;
(*ingranaggio*) to work loose

aller'gia, -'gie [aller'dʒia] SF allergy

al'lergico, -a, -ci, -che [al'lεrdʒiko] AG
allergic

allesti'mento SM preparation, setting up; **in**
~ in preparation

alles'tire /**55**/ VT (*cena*) to prepare; (*esercito,
nave*) to equip, fit out; (*spettacolo*) to stage

allet'tante AG attractive, alluring

allet'tare /**72**/ VT to lure, entice

alleva'mento SM breeding, rearing; (*luogo*)
stock farm; **pollo d'**~ battery hen

alle'vare /**72**/ VT (*animale*) to breed, rear;
(*bambino*) to bring up

alleva'tore SM breeder

allevi'are /**19**/ VT to alleviate

alli'bire /**55**/ VI to turn pale; (*essere turbato*) to
be disconcerted

alli'bito, -a AG pale; disconcerted; astounded

allibra'tore SM bookmaker

allie'tare /**72**/ VT to cheer up, gladden

alli'evo SM pupil; (*apprendista*) apprentice;
~ **ufficiale** cadet

alliga'tore SM alligator

allinea'mento SM alignment

alline'are /**72**/ VT (*persone, cose*) to line up; (*Tip*)
to align; (*fig: economia, salari*) to adjust, align;
allinearsi VPR to line up; (*fig: a idee*)
allinearsi a to come into line with

alline'ato, -a AG aligned, in line; **paesi non
allineati** (*Pol*) non-aligned countries

'allo PREP + DET *vedi* **a**

allo'care /**20**/ VT to allocate

al'locco, -a, -chi, -che SM/F oaf ▶ SM tawny
owl

allocuzi'one [allokut'tsjone] SF address,
solemn speech

al'lodola SF (sky)lark

alloggi'are [allod'dʒare] /**62**/ VT to
accommodate ▶ VI to live

al'loggio [al'lɔddʒo] SM lodging,
accommodation (*Brit*), accommodations
(*US*); (*appartamento*) flat (*Brit*), apartment (*US*)

allontana'mento SM removal; dismissal;
estrangement

allonta'nare /**72**/ VT to send away, send off;
(*impiegato*) to dismiss; (*pericolo*) to avert,
remove; (*estraniare*) to alienate; **allontanarsi**
VPR: **allontanarsi (da)** to go away (from);
(*estraniarsi*) to become estranged (from)

al'lora AV (*in quel momento*) then ▶ CONG (*in
questo caso*) well then; (*dunque*) well then, so;
la gente d'~ people then *o* in those days; **da
~ in poi** from then on; **e ~?** (*che fare?*) what
now?; (*e con ciò?*) so what?

allor'ché [allor'ke] CONG (formale) when, as soon as

al'loro SM laurel; **riposare** o **dormire sugli allori** to rest on one's laurels

'alluce ['allutʃe] SM big toe

alluci'nante [allutʃi'nante] AG (scena, spettacolo) awful, terrifying; (col: incredibile) amazing

alluci'nato, -a [allutʃi'nato] AG terrified; (fuori di sé) bewildered, confused

allucinazi'one [allutʃinat'tsjone] SF hallucination

al'ludere /35/ VI: ~ **a** to allude to, hint at

allu'minio SM aluminium (BRIT), aluminum (US)

allu'naggio [allu'naddʒo] SM moon landing

allu'nare /72/ VI to land on the moon

allun'gare /80/ VT to lengthen; (distendere) to prolong, extend; (diluire) to water down; **allungarsi** VPR to lengthen; (ragazzo) to stretch, grow taller; (sdraiarsi) to lie down, stretch out; ~ **le mani** (rubare) to pick pockets; **gli allungò uno schiaffo** he took a swipe at him

al'lusi etc VB vedi **alludere**

allusi'one SF hint, allusion

al'luso, -a PP di **alludere**

alluvi'one SF flood

alma'nacco, -chi SM almanac

al'meno AV at least ▶ CONG: **(se)** ~ if only; **(se)** ~ **piovesse!** if only it would rain!

a'logeno, -a [a'lɔdʒeno] AG: **lampada alogena** halogen lamp

a'lone SM halo

al'pestre AG (delle alpi) alpine; (montuoso) mountainous

'Alpi SFPL: **le** ~ the Alps

alpi'nismo SM mountaineering, climbing

alpi'nista, -i, -e SM/F mountaineer, climber

al'pino, -a AG Alpine; mountain cpd; **alpini** SMPL (Mil) Italian Alpine troops

al'quanto AV rather, a little ▶ DET: ~(-a) a certain amount of, some ▶ PRON a certain amount, some; **alquanti, e** DET PL, PRON PL several, quite a few

Al'sazia [al'sattsja] SF Alsace

alt ESCL halt!, stop! ▶ SM: **dare l'**~ to call a halt

alta'lena SF (a funi) swing; (in bilico, anche fig) seesaw

alta'mente AV extremely, highly

al'tare SM altar

alte'rare /72/ VT to alter, change; (cibo) to adulterate; (registro) to falsify; (persona) to irritate; **alterarsi** VPR to alter; (cibo) to go bad; (persona) to lose one's temper

alterazi'one [alterat'tsjone] SF alteration, change; adulteration; falsification; annoyance

al'terco, -chi SM altercation, wrangle

alter'nanza [alter'nantsa] SF alternation; (Agr) rotation

alter'nare /72/ VT, **alter'narsi** VPR to alternate

alterna'tivo, -a AG alternative ▶ SF alternative; **non abbiamo alternative** we have no alternative

alter'nato, -a AG alternate; (Elettr) alternating

alterna'tore SM alternator

al'terno, -a AG alternate; **a giorni alterni** on alternate days, every other day; **circolazione a targhe alterne** (Aut) system of restricting vehicle use to odd/even registrations on alternate days

al'tero, -a AG proud

al'tezza [al'tettsa] SF (di edificio, persona) height; (di tessuto) width, breadth; (di acqua, pozzo) depth; (di suono) pitch; (Geo) latitude; (titolo) highness; (fig: nobiltà) greatness; **essere all'**~ **di** to be on a level with; (fig) to be up to o equal to; **all'**~ **della farmacia** near the chemist's

altez'zoso, -a [altet'tsoso] AG haughty

al'ticcio, -a, -ci, -ce [al'tittʃo] AG tipsy

altipi'ano SM = **altopiano**

altiso'nante AG (fig) high-sounding, pompous

alti'tudine SF altitude

'alto, -a AG high; (persona) tall; (tessuto) wide, broad; (sonno, acque) deep; (suono) high (-pitched); (Geo) upper; (: settentrionale) northern ▶ SM top (part) ▶ AV high; (parlare) aloud, loudly; **il palazzo è** ~ **20 metri** the building is 20 metres high; **il tessuto è** ~ **70 cm** the material is 70 cm wide; **ad alta voce** aloud; **a notte alta** in the dead of night; **in** ~ up, upwards; at the top; **mani in** ~! hands up!; **dall'**~ **in** o **al basso** up and down; **degli alti e bassi** (fig) ups and downs; **andare a testa alta** (fig) to carry one's head high; **essere in** ~ **mare** (fig) to be far from a solution; **alta fedeltà** high fidelity, hi-fi; **alta finanza/società** high finance/society; **alta moda** haute couture; **l'A**~ **Medioevo** the Early Middle Ages; **l'**~ **Po** the upper reaches of the Po; **alta velocità** (Ferr) high speed rail system

altoate'sino, -a AG of (o from) the Alto Adige

alto'forno SM blast furnace

altolo'cato, -a AG of high rank, highly placed

altopar'lante SM loudspeaker

altopi'ano (pl **altipiani**) SM upland plain, plateau

'Alto 'Volta SM: **l'**~ Upper Volta

altret'tanto, -a AG, PRON as much; (pl) as many ▶ AV equally; **tanti auguri! — grazie,** ~ all the best! — thank you, the same to you

'altri PRON INV (*qualcuno*) somebody; (: *in espressioni negative*) anybody; (*un'altra persona*) another (person)

altri'menti AV otherwise

PAROLA CHIAVE

'altro, -a DET **1** (*diverso*) other, different; **questa è un'altra cosa** that's another *o* a different thing; **passami l'altra penna** give me the other pen

2 (*supplementare*) other; **prendi un altro cioccolatino** have another chocolate; **hai avuto altre notizie?** have you had any more *o* any other news?; **hai altro pane?** have you got any more bread?

3 (*nel tempo*): **l'altro giorno** the other day; **l'altr'anno** last year; **l'altro ieri** the day before yesterday; **domani l'altro** the day after tomorrow; **quest'altro mese** next month

4: **d'altra parte** on the other hand

▶ PRON **1** (*persona: cosa diversa o supplementare*): **un altro, un'altra** another (one); **lo farà un altro** someone else will do it; **altri, e** others; **gli altri** (*la gente*) others, other people; **l'uno e l'altro** both (of them); **aiutarsi l'un l'altro** to help one another; **prendine un altro** have another (one); **da un giorno all'altro** from day to day; (*nel giro di 24 ore*) from one day to the next; (*da un momento all'altro*) any day now

2 (*sostantivato: solo maschile*) something else; (: *in espressioni interrogative*) anything else; **non ho altro da dire** I have nothing else *o* I don't have anything else to say; **desidera altro?** do you want anything else?; **più che altro** above all; **se non altro** if nothing else, at least; **tra l'altro** among other things; **ci mancherebbe altro!** that's all we need!; **non faccio altro che lavorare** I do nothing but work; **contento? — altro che!** are you pleased? — I certainly am!; *vedi anche* **senza**; **noialtri; voialtri; tutto**

altroché [altro'ke] ESCL certainly!, and how!

al'tronde AV: **d'~** on the other hand

al'trove AV elsewhere, somewhere else

al'trui AG INV other people's ▶ SM: **l'~** other people's belongings *pl*

altru'ismo SM altruism

altru'ista, -i, -e AG altruistic ▶ SM/F altruist

al'tura SF (*rialto*) height, high ground; (*alto mare*) open sea; **pesca d'~** deep-sea fishing

a'lunno, -a SM/F pupil

alve'are SM hive

'alveo SM riverbed

alzabandi'era [altsaban'djera] SM INV (*Mil*): **l'~** the raising of the flag

al'zare [al'tsare] **/72/** VT to raise, lift; (*issare*) to hoist; (*costruire*) to build, erect; **alzarsi** VPR to rise; (*dal letto*) to get up; (*crescere*) to grow tall (*o* taller); **~ le spalle** to shrug one's shoulders; **~ le carte** to cut the cards; **~ il gomito** to drink too much; **~ le mani su qn** to raise one's hand to sb; **~ i tacchi** to take to one's heels; **alzarsi in piedi** to stand up, get to one's feet; **alzarsi col piede sbagliato** to get out of bed on the wrong side

al'zata [al'tsata] SF lifting, raising; **un'~ di spalle** a shrug

A.M. ABBR = **Aeronautica Militare**

a'mabile AG lovable; (*vino*) sweet

'AMAC SIGLA F = **Aeronautica Militare-Aviazione Civile**

a'maca, -che SF hammock

amalga'mare **/72/** VT, **amalga'marsi** VPR to amalgamate

a'mante AG: **~ di** (*musica ecc*) fond of ▶ SM F lover (mistress)

amara'mente AV bitterly

ama'ranto SM (*Bot*) love-lies-bleeding ▶ AG INV: **color ~** reddish purple

a'mare **/72/** VT to love; (*amico, musica, sport*) to like; **amarsi** VPR to love each other

amareggi'are [amared'dʒare] **/62/** VT to sadden, upset; **amareggiarsi** VPR to get upset; **amareggiarsi la vita** to make one's life a misery

amareggi'ato, -a [amared'dʒato] AG upset, saddened

ama'rena SF sour black cherry

ama'retto SM (*dolce*) macaroon; (*liquore*) bitter liqueur made with almonds

ama'rezza [ama'rettsa] SF bitterness

a'maro, -a AG bitter ▶ SM bitterness; (*liquore*) bitters *pl*

ama'rognolo, -a [ama'roɲɲolo] AG slightly bitter

a'mato, -a AG beloved, loved, dear ▶ SM/F loved one

ama'tore, -'trice SM/F (*amante*) lover; (*intenditore: di vini ecc*) connoisseur; (*dilettante*) amateur

a'mazzone [a'maddzone] SF (*Mitologia*) Amazon; (*cavallerizza*) horsewoman; (*abito*) riding habit; **cavalcare all'~** to ride sidesaddle; **il Rio delle Amazzoni** the (river) Amazon

Amaz'zonia [amad'dzonja] SF Amazonia

amaz'zonico, -a, -ci, -che [amad'dzoniko] AG Amazonian; Amazon *cpd*

ambasce'ria [ambaʃʃe'ria] SF embassy

ambasci'ata [ambaʃ'ʃata] SF embassy; (*messaggio*) message

ambascia'tore, -'trice [ambaʃʃa'tore] SM/F ambassador (ambassadress)

ambe'due AG INV: **~ i ragazzi** both boys ▶ PRON INV both

ambi'destro, -a AG ambidextrous

ambien'tale AG (*temperatura*) ambient *cpd*; (*problemi, tutela*) environmental

ambienta'lismo SM environmentalism

ambienta'lista, -i, -e AG environmental ▶ SM/F environmentalist

ambien'tare /**72**/ VT to acclimatize; (*romanzo, film*) to set; **ambientarsi** VPR to get used to one's surroundings

ambientazi'one [ambjentat'tsjone] SF setting

ambi'ente SM environment; (*fig: insieme di persone*) milieu; (*stanza*) room

ambiguità SF INV ambiguity

am'biguo, -a AG ambiguous; (*persona*) shady

am'bire /**55**/ VT (*anche: vi: ambire a*) to aspire to; **un premio molto ambito** a much sought-after prize

'ambito SM sphere, field

ambiva'lente AG ambivalent; **questo apparecchio è ~** this is a dual-purpose device

ambizi'one [ambit'tsjone] SF ambition

ambizi'oso, -a [ambit'tsjoso] AG ambitious

'ambo AG INV both ▶ SM (*al gioco*) double

'ambra SF amber; **~ grigia** ambergris

ambu'lante AG travelling, itinerant ▶ SM peddler

ambu'lanza [ambu'lantsa] SF ambulance; **chiamate un'~** call an ambulance

ambulatori'ale AG (*Med*) outpatients *cpd*; **operazione ~** operation as an outpatient; **visita ~** visit to the doctor's surgery (BRIT) *o* office (US)

ambula'torio SM (*studio medico*) surgery (BRIT), doctor's office (US)

'AMDI SIGLA F = **Associazione Medici Dentisti Italiani**

a'meba SF amoeba (BRIT), ameba (US)

amenità SF INV pleasantness *no pl*; (*facezia*) pleasantry

a'meno, -a AG pleasant; (*strano*) funny, strange; (*spiritoso*) amusing

A'merica SF: **l'~** America; **l'~ latina** Latin America; **l'~ del sud** South America

america'nata SF (*peg*): **le Olimpiadi sono state una vera ~** the Olympics were a typically vulgar American extravaganza

america'nismo SM Americanism; (*ammirazione*) love of America

ameri'cano, -a AG, SM/F American

ame'tista SF amethyst

ami'anto SM asbestos

a'mica SF *vedi* **amico**

ami'chevole [ami'kevole] AG friendly

ami'cizia [ami'tʃittsja] SF friendship; **amicizie** SFPL (*amici*) friends; **fare ~ con qn** to make friends with sb

a'mico, -a, -ci, -che SM/F friend; (*amante*) boyfriend (girlfriend); **~ del cuore** *o* **intimo** bosom friend; **~ d'infanzia** childhood friend; **aggiungere come ~** (*Internet*) to friend

'amido SM starch

ammac'care /**20**/ VT (*pentola*) to dent; (*persona*) to bruise; **ammaccarsi** VPR to bruise

ammacca'tura SF dent; bruise

ammaes'trare /**72**/ VT (*animale*) to train; (*persona*) to teach

ammai'nare /**72**/ VT to lower, haul down

amma'larsi /**72**/ VPR to fall ill

amma'lato, -a AG ill, sick ▶ SM/F sick person; (*paziente*) patient

ammali'are /**19**/ VT (*fig*) to enchant, charm

ammalia'tore, -'trice SM/F enchanter (enchantress)

am'manco, -chi SM (*Econ*) deficit

ammanet'tare /**72**/ VT to handcuff

ammani'cato, -a, ammanigli'ato, -a [ammaniʎ'ʎato] AG (*fig*) with friends in high places

amman'sire /**55**/ VT (*animale*) to tame; (*fig: persona*) to calm down, placate

amman'tarsi /**72**/ VPR: **~ di** (*persona*) to wrap o.s. in; (*fig: prato ecc*) to be covered in

amma'raggio [amma'raddʒo] SM (*sea*) landing; splashdown

amma'rare /**72**/ VI (*Aer*) to make a sea landing; (*astronave*) to splash down

ammas'sare /**72**/ VT (*ammucchiare*) to amass; (*raccogliere*) to gather together; **ammassarsi** VPR to pile up; to gather

am'masso SM mass; (*mucchio*) pile, heap; (*Econ*) stockpile

ammat'tire /**55**/ VI to go mad

ammaz'zare [ammat'tsare] /**72**/ VT to kill; **ammazzarsi** VPR (*uccidersi*) to kill o.s.; (*rimanere ucciso*) to be killed; **ammazzarsi di lavoro** to work o.s. to death

am'menda SF amends *pl*; (*Dir, Sport*) fine; **fare ~ di qc** to make amends for sth

am'messo, -a PP *di* **ammettere** ▶ CONG: **~ che** supposing that

am'mettere /**63**/ VT to admit; (*riconoscere: fatto*) to acknowledge, admit; (*permettere*) to allow, accept; (*supporre*) to suppose; **ammettiamo che ...** let us suppose that ...

ammez'zato [ammed'dzato] SM (*anche:* **piano ammezzato**) entresol, mezzanine

ammic'care /**20**/ VI: **~ (a)** to wink (at)

amminis'trare /**72**/ VT to run, manage; (*Rel, Dir*) to administer

amministra'tivo, -a AG administrative

amministra'tore SM administrator; (*di condominio*) flats manager; (*Comm*) director; **~ aggiunto** associate director; **~ delegato** managing director; **~ fiduciario** trustee; **~ unico** sole director

amministrazi'one [amministrat'tsjone] SF management; administration; **consiglio d'~** board of directors; **l'~ comunale** local government; **~ fiduciaria** trust

ammi'raglia [ammi'raʎʎa] SF flagship

ammiragli'ato [ammiraʎ'ʎato] SM admiralty

ammi'raglio [ammi'raʎʎo] SM admiral

ammi'rare /72/ VT to admire

ammira'tore, -'trice SM/F admirer

ammirazi'one [ammirat'tsjone] SF admiration

am'misi etc VB vedi **ammettere**

ammis'sibile AG admissible, acceptable

ammissi'one SF admission; (approvazione) acknowledgment

Amm.ne ABBR = **amministrazione**

ammobili'are /19/ VT to furnish

ammobili'ato, -a AG (camera, appartamento) furnished

ammoder'nare /72/ VT to modernize

am'modo, a 'modo AV properly ▶ AG INV respectable, nice

ammogli'are [ammoʎ'ʎare] /27/ VT to find a wife for; **ammogliarsi** VPR to marry, take a wife

am'mollo SM: **lasciare in ~** to leave to soak

ammo'niaca SF ammonia

ammoni'mento SM warning; admonishment

ammo'nire /55/ VT (avvertire) to warn; (rimproverare) to admonish; (Dir) to caution

ammonizi'one [ammonit'tsjone] SF (monito: anche Sport) warning; (rimprovero) reprimand; (Dir) caution

ammon'tare /72/ VI: **~ a** to amount to ▶ SM (total) amount

ammonticchi'are [ammontik'kjare] /19/ VT to pile up, heap up

ammor'bare /72/ VT (diffondere malattia) to infect; (odore) to taint, foul

ammorbi'dente SM fabric softener

ammorbi'dire /55/ VT to soften

ammorta'mento SM redemption; amortization; **~ fiscale** capital allowance

ammor'tare /72/ VT (Finanza: debito) to pay off, redeem; (: spese d'impianto) to write off

ammortiz'zare [ammortid'dzare] /72/ VT (Finanza) to pay off, redeem; (: spese d'impianto) to write off; (Aut, Tecn) to absorb, deaden

ammortizza'tore [ammortiddza'tore] SM (Aut, Tecn) shock absorber

ammucchi'are [ammuk'kjare] /19/ VT, **ammucchi'arsi** VPR to pile up, accumulate

ammuf'fire /55/ VI to go mouldy (BRIT) o moldy (US)

ammutina'mento SM mutiny

ammuti'narsi /72/ VPR to mutiny

ammuti'nato, -a AG mutinous ▶ SM mutineer

ammuto'lire /55/ VI to be struck dumb

amne'sia SF amnesia

amnis'tia SF amnesty

'amo SM (Pesca) hook; (fig) bait

amo'rale AG amoral

a'more SM love; **amori** SMPL love affairs; **il tuo bambino è un ~** your baby's a darling; **fare l'~** o **all'~** to make love; **andare d'~ e d'accordo con qn** to get on like a house on fire with sb; **per ~ o per forza** by hook or by crook; **amor proprio** self-esteem, pride

amoreggi'are [amored'dʒare] /62/ VI to flirt

amo'revole AG loving, affectionate

a'morfo, -a AG amorphous; (fig: persona) lifeless

amo'rino SM cupid

amo'roso, -a AG (affettuoso) loving, affectionate; (d'amore: sguardo) amorous; (: poesia, relazione) love cpd

am'pere [ã'pɛr] SM INV amp(ère)

ampi'ezza [am'pjettsa] SF width, breadth; spaciousness; (fig: importanza) scale, size; **~ di vedute** broad-mindedness

'ampio, -a AG wide, broad; (spazioso) spacious; (abbondante: vestito) loose; (: gonna) full; (: spiegazione) ample, full

am'plesso SM (sessuale) intercourse

amplia'mento SM (di strada) widening; (di aeroporto) expansion; (fig) broadening

ampli'are /19/ VT (ingrandire) to enlarge; (allargare) to widen; (fig: discorso) to enlarge on; **ampliarsi** VPR to grow, increase; **~ la propria cultura** to broaden one's mind

amplifi'care /20/ VT to amplify; (magnificare) to extol

amplifica'tore SM (Tecn, Mus) amplifier

amplificazi'one [amplifikat'tsjone] SF amplification

am'polla SF (vasetto) cruet

ampol'loso, -a AG bombastic, pompous

ampu'tare /72/ VT (Med) to amputate

amputazi'one [amputat'tsjone] SF amputation

'Amsterdam SF Amsterdam

amu'leto SM lucky charm

AN SIGLA = **Ancona**

A.N. SIGLA F (Pol) = **Alleanza Nazionale**

anabbagli'ante [anabbaʎ'ʎante] AG (Aut) dipped (BRIT), dimmed (US); **anabbaglianti** SMPL dipped or dimmed headlights

anaboliz'zante [anabolid'dzante] SM anabolic steroid ▶ AG anabolic

anacro'nismo SM anachronism

a'nagrafe SF (registro) register of births, marriages and deaths; (ufficio) registry office (BRIT), office of vital statistics (US)

ana'grafico, -a, -ci, -che AG (Amm): **dati**

anagrafici personal data; **comune di residenza anagrafica** district where resident

ana'gramma, -i SM anagram

anal'colico, -a, -ci, -che AG non-alcoholic ▶ SM soft drink; **bevanda analcolica** soft drink

a'nale AG anal

analfa'beta, -i, -e AG, SM/F illiterate

analfabe'tismo SM illiteracy

anal'gesico, -a, -ci, -che [anal'dʒɛziko] AG, SM analgesic

a'nalisi SF INV analysis; (*Med: esame*) test; **in ultima ~** in conclusion, in the final analysis; **~ grammaticale** parsing; **~ del sangue** blood test; **~ dei sistemi/costi** systems/cost analysis

ana'lista, -i, -e SM/F analyst; (*Psic*) (psycho)analyst; **~ finanziario** financial analyst; **~ di sistemi** systems analyst

ana'litico, -a, -ci, -che AG analytic(al)

analiz'zare [analid'dzare] /**72**/ VT to analyse (*BRIT*), analyze (*US*); (*Med*) to test

analo'gia, -'gie [analo'dʒia] SF analogy

ana'logico, -a, -ci, -che [ana'lɔdʒiko] AG analogical; (*calcolatore, orologio*) analog(ue)

a'nalogo, -a, -ghi, -ghe AG analogous

'ananas SM INV pineapple

anar'chia [anar'kia] SF anarchy

a'narchico, -a, -ci, -che [a'narkiko] AG anarchic(al) ▶ SM/F anarchist

anarco-insurreziona'lista [anarko,insurrettsjona'lista] AG anarcho-revolutionary

'A.N.A.S. SIGLA F (= *Azienda Nazionale Autonoma delle Strade*) national roads department

ana'tema, -i SM anathema

anato'mia SF anatomy

ana'tomico, -a, -ci, -che AG anatomical; (*sedile*) contoured

'anatra SF duck; **~ selvatica** mallard

ana'troccolo SM duckling

'ANCA SIGLA F = **Associazione Nazionale Cooperative Agricole**

'anca, -che SF (*Anat*) hip; (*Zool*) haunch

ANCC SIGLA F = **Associazione Nazionale Carabinieri**

'anche ['anke] CONG (*inoltre, pure*) also, too; (*perfino*) even; **vengo anch'io!** I'm coming too!; **~ se** even if; **~ volendo, non finiremmo in tempo** even if we wanted to, we wouldn't finish in time

ancheggi'are [anked'dʒare] /**62**/ VI to wiggle (one's hips)

anchilo'sato, -a [ankilo'zato] AG stiff

'ANCI ['antʃi] SIGLA F (= *Associazione Nazionale dei Comuni Italiani*) national confederation of local authorities

ancone'tano, -a AG of (*o* from) Ancona

an'cora[1] AV still; (*di nuovo*) again; (*di più*) some more; (*persino*): **~ più forte** even stronger; **non ~** not yet; **~ una volta** once more, once again; **~ un po'** a little more; (*di tempo*) a little longer

'ancora[2] SF anchor; **gettare/levare l'~** to cast/weigh anchor; **~ di salvezza** (*fig*) last hope

anco'raggio [anko'raddʒo] SM anchorage

anco'rare /**72**/ VT, **anco'rarsi** VPR to anchor

ANCR SIGLA F (= *Associazione Nazionale Combattenti e Reduci*) servicemen's and ex-servicemen's association

Andalu'sia SF: **l'~** Andalusia

anda'luso, -a AG, SM/F Andalusian

anda'mento SM (*di strada, malattia*) course; (*del mercato*) state

an'dante AG (*corrente*) current; (*di poco pregio*) cheap, second-rate ▶ SM (*Mus*) andante

an'dare /**6**/ SM: **a lungo ~** in the long run; **con l'andar del tempo** with the passing of time; **racconta storie a tutto ~** she's forever talking rubbish ▶ VI (*gen*) to go; **~ a** (*essere adatto*) to suit; **il suo comportamento non mi va** (*piace*) I don't like the way he behaves; **ti va di ~ al cinema?** do you feel like going to the cinema?; **~ a cavallo** to ride; **~ in macchina/aereo** to go by car/plane; **~ a fare qc** to go and do sth; **~ a pescare/sciare** to go fishing/skiing; **andarsene** to go away; **questa camicia va lavata** this shirt needs a wash *o* should be washed; **vado e vengo** I'll be back in a minute; **~ per i 50** (*età*) to be getting on for 50; **~ a male** to go bad; **~ fiero di qc/qn** to be proud of sth/sb; **~ perduto** to be lost; **come va?** (*lavoro, progetto*) how are things?; **come va? — bene, grazie!** how are you? — fine, thanks!; **va fatto entro oggi** it's got to be done today; **ne va della nostra vita** our lives are at stake; **se non vado errato** if I'm not mistaken; **le mele vanno molto** apples are selling well; **va da sé** (*è naturale*) it goes without saying; **per questa volta vada** let's say no more about it this time

an'data SF going; (*viaggio*) outward journey; **biglietto di sola ~** single (*BRIT*) *o* one-way ticket; **biglietto di ~ e ritorno** return (*BRIT*) *o* round-trip (*US*) ticket

anda'tura SF (*modo di andare*) walk, gait; (*Sport*) pace; (*Naut*) tack

an'dazzo [an'dattso] SM (*peg*): **prendere un brutto ~** to take a turn for the worse

'Ande SFPL: **le ~** the Andes

an'dino, -a AG Andean

andirivi'eni SM INV coming and going

'andito SM corridor, passage

An'dorra SF Andorra

andrò *etc* VB *vedi* **andare**

an'drone SM entrance hall

a'neddoto SM anecdote

ane'lare /72/ VI: **~ a** (fig) to long for, yearn for

a'nelito SM (fig): **~ di** longing o yearning for

a'nello SM ring; (di catena) link; **anelli** SMPL (Ginnastica) rings

ane'mia SF anaemia (BRIT), anemia (US)

a'nemico, -a, -ci, -che AG anaemic (BRIT), anemic (US)

a'nemone SM anemone

aneste'sia SF anaesthesia (BRIT), anesthesia (US)

aneste'sista, -i, -e SM/F anaesthetist (BRIT), anesthetist (US)

anes'tetico, -a, -ci, -che AG, SM anaesthetic (BRIT), anesthetic (US)

anestetiz'zare [anestetid'dzare] /72/ VT to anaesthetize (BRIT), anesthetize (US)

anfeta'mina SF amphetamine

anfeta'minico, -a, -ci, -che AG (fig) hyper

an'fibio, -a AG amphibious ▶ SM amphibian; (Aut) amphibious vehicle

anfite'atro SM amphitheatre (BRIT), amphitheater (US)

anfitri'one SM host

'anfora SF amphora

an'fratto SM ravine

an'gelico, -a, -ci, -che [an'dʒɛliko] AG angelic(al)

'angelo ['andʒelo] SM angel; **~ custode** guardian angel; **l'~ del focolare** (fig) the perfect housewife

anghe'ria [ange'ria] SF vexation

an'gina [an'dʒina] SF tonsillitis; **~ pectoris** angina

angli'cano, -a AG Anglican

angli'cismo [angli'tʃizmo] SM anglicism

an'glofilo, -a AG anglophilic ▶ SM/F anglophile

anglo'sassone AG Anglo-Saxon

An'gola SF: **l'~** Angola

ango'lano, -a AG, SM/F Angolan

ango'lare AG angular

angolazi'one [angolat'tsjone] SF (di angolo) angulation; (Fot, Cine, TV, fig) angle

'angolo SM corner; (Mat) angle; **~ cottura** (di appartamento ecc) cooking area; **fare ~ con** (strada) to run into; **dietro l'~** (anche fig) round the corner

ango'loso, -a AG (oggetto) angular; (volto, corpo) angular, bony

'angora SF: **lana d'~** angora

an'goscia, -sce [an'goʃʃa] SF deep anxiety, anguish no pl

angosci'are [angoʃ'ʃare] /14/ VT to cause anguish to; **angosciarsi** VPR: **angosciarsi (per)** (preoccuparsi) to become anxious (about); (provare angoscia) to get upset (about o over)

angosci'oso, -a [angoʃ'ʃoso] AG (d'angoscia) anguished; (che dà angoscia) distressing, painful

angu'illa SF eel

an'guria SF watermelon

an'gustia SF (ansia) anguish, distress; (povertà) poverty, want

angusti'are /19/ VT to distress; **angustiarsi** VPR: **angustiarsi (per)** to worry (about)

an'gusto, -a AG (stretto) narrow; (fig) mean, petty

'anice ['anitʃe] SM (Cuc) aniseed; (Bot) anise; (liquore) anisette

ani'dride SF (Chim): **~ carbonica/solforosa** carbon/sulphur dioxide

'anima SF soul; (abitante) inhabitant; **~ gemella** soul mate; **un'~ in pena** (anche fig) a tormented soul; **non c'era ~ viva** there wasn't a living soul; **volere un bene dell'~ a qn** to be extremely fond of sb; **rompere l'~ a qn** to drive sb mad; **il nonno buon'~ ...** Grandfather, God rest his soul ...

ani'male SM, AG animal; **~ domestico** pet

anima'lesco, -a, -schi, -sche AG (gesto, atteggiamento) animal-like

anima'lista, -i, -e AG animal rights cpd ▶ SM/F animal rights activist

ani'mare /72/ VT to give life to, liven (up); (incoraggiare) to encourage; **animarsi** VPR to become animated, come to life

ani'mato, -a AG animate; (vivace) lively, animated; (: strada) busy

anima'tore, -'trice SM/F guiding spirit; (Cine) animator; (di festa) life and soul

animazi'one [animat'tsjone] SF liveliness; (di strada) bustle; (Cine) animation; **~ teatrale** amateur dramatics

'animo SM (mente) mind; (cuore) heart; (coraggio) courage; (disposizione) character, disposition; **avere in ~ di fare qc** to intend o have a mind to do sth; **farsi ~** to pluck up courage; **fare qc di buon/mal ~** to do sth willingly/unwillingly; **perdersi d'~** to lose heart

animosità SF animosity

A'NITA SIGLA F = **Associazione Naturista Italiana**

'anitra SF = **anatra**

'Ankara SF Ankara

ANM SIGLA F (= Associazione Nazionale dei Magistrati) national association of Magistrates

anna'cquare /72/ VT to water down, dilute

annaffi'are /19/ VT to water

annaffia'toio SM watering can

an'nali SMPL annals

annas'pare /72/ VI (nell'acqua) to flounder; (fig: nel buio, nell'incertezza) to grope

an'nata SF year; (importo annuo) annual amount; **vino d'~** vintage wine

annebbi'are/19/ VT (*fig*) to cloud;
annebbiarsiVPR to become foggy; (*vista*) to
become dim

annega'mento SM drowning

anne'gare/80/ VT, VI to drown; **annegarsi**
VPR (*accidentalmente*) to drown;
(*deliberatamente*) to drown o.s.

anne'rire/55/ VT to blacken ▶ VI to become
black

annessi'one SF (*Pol*) annexation

an'nesso, -a PP *di* **annettere** ▶ AG attached;
(*Pol*) annexed; **... e tutti gli annessi e
connessi** ... and so on and so forth

an'nettere/63/ VT (*Pol*) to annex; (*accludere*) to
attach

annichi'lire [anniki'lire] **/55/** VT to annihilate

anni'darsi/72/ VPR to nest

annienta'mento SM annihilation,
destruction

annien'tare/72/ VT to annihilate, destroy

anniver'sario SM anniversary; **~ di
matrimonio** wedding anniversary

'anno SM year; **quanti anni hai? — ho 40
anni** how old are you? — I'm 40 (years old);
gli anni 20 the 20s; **porta bene gli anni** she
doesn't look her age; **porta male gli anni**
she looks older than she is; **~ commerciale**
business year; **~ giudiziario** legal year;
~ luce light year; **gli anni di piombo** *the
Seventies in Italy, characterized by terrorist attacks
and killings*

anno'dare/72/ VT to knot, tie; (*fig: rapporto*) to
form

annoi'are/19/ VT to bore; (*seccare*) to annoy;
annoiarsiVPR to be bored; to be annoyed

an'noso, -a AG (*albero*) old; (*fig: problema ecc*)
age-old

anno'tare/72/ VT (*registrare*) to note, note
down (BRIT); (*commentare*) to annotate

annotazi'one [annotat'tsjone] SF note;
annotation

annove'rare/72/ VT to number

annu'ale AG annual

annual'mente AV annually, yearly

annu'ario SM yearbook

annu'ire/55/ VI to nod; (*acconsentire*) to agree

annulla'mento SM annihilation,
destruction; cancellation; annulment;
quashing

annul'lare/72/ VT to annihilate, destroy;
(*contratto, francobollo*) to cancel; (*matrimonio*) to
annul; (*sentenza*) to quash; (*risultati*) to
declare void

annunci'are [annun'tʃare] **/14/** VT to
announce; (*dar segni rivelatori*) to herald

annuncia'tore, -'trice[annuntʃa'tore] SM/F
(*Radio, TV*) announcer

Annunciazi'one [annuntʃat'tsjone] SF (*Rel*):
l'~ the Annunciation

an'nuncio [an'nuntʃo] SM announcement;
(*fig*) sign; **~ pubblicitario** advertisement;
annunci economici classified
advertisements, small ads; **piccoli annunci**
small ads, classified ads; **annunci
mortuari** (*colonna*) obituary column

'annuo, -a AG annual, yearly

annu'sare/72/ VT to sniff, smell; **~ tabacco**
to take snuff

annuvola'mento SM clouding (over)

annuvo'lare/72/ VT to cloud; **annuvolarsi**
VPR to become cloudy, cloud over

'ano SM anus

'anodo SM anode

anoma'lia SF anomaly

,**a'nomalo, -a** AG anomalous

anoni'mato SM anonymity; **conservare l'~**
to remain anonymous

a'nonimo, -a AG anonymous ▶ SM (*autore*)
anonymous writer (*o painter etc*); **un tipo ~**
(*peg*) a colourless (BRIT) *o* colorless (US)
character; **società anonima** (*Comm*) joint
stock company

anores'sia SF anorexia; **~ nervosa** anorexia
nervosa

ano'ressico, -a, -ci, -che AG anorexic

anor'male AG abnormal ▶ SMF subnormal
person; (*eufemismo*) homosexual

anormalità SF INV abnormality

'ANSA SIGLA F (= *Agenzia Nazionale Stampa
Associata*) national press agency

'ansa SF (*manico*) handle; (*di fiume*) bend, loop

an'sante AG out of breath, panting

'ANSEA SIGLA F (= *Associazione delle Nazioni del
Sud-Est asiatico*) ASEAN

'ansia SF anxiety; **stare in ~ (per qn/qc)** to be
anxious (about sb/sth)

ansietà SF anxiety

ansi'mare/72/ VI to pant

ansi'oso, -a AG anxious

'anta SF (*di finestra*) shutter; (*di armadio*) door

antago'nismo SM antagonism

antago'nista, -i, -e SM/F antagonist

an'tartico, -a, -ci, -che AG Antarctic ▶ SM:
l'A~ the Antarctic

An'tartide SF: **l'~** Antarctica

ante'bellico, -a, -ci, -che AG prewar *cpd*

antece'dente [antetʃe'dɛnte] AG preceding,
previous

ante'fatto SM previous events *pl*; previous
history

ante'guerra SM pre-war period

ante'nato SM ancestor, forefather

an'tenna SF (*Radio, TV*) aerial; (*Zool*) antenna,
feeler; (*Naut*) yard; **rizzare le antenne** (*fig*)
to prick up one's ears; **~ parabolica** (*TV*)
satellite dish

ante'porre/77/ VT: **~ qc a qc** to place *o* put sth
before sth

ante'posto, -a PP *di* **anteporre**

ante'prima SF preview; **~ di stampa** (*Inform*) print preview

anteri'ore AG (*ruota, zampa*) front *cpd*; (*fatti*) previous, preceding

antesi'gnano [antesiɲ'ɲano] SM (*Storia*) standard-bearer; (*fig*) forerunner

antiade'rente AG non-stick

antia'ereo, -a AG anti-aircraft *cpd*

antial'lergico, -a [antial'lɛrdʒiko] AG, SM hypoallergenic

antia'tomico, -a, -ci, -che AG anti-nuclear; **rifugio ~** fallout shelter

antibi'otico, -a, -ci, -che AG, SM antibiotic

anti'caglia [anti'kaʎʎa] SF junk *no pl*

antical'care AG (*prodotto, detersivo*) anti-limescale

anti'camera SF anteroom; **fare ~** to be kept waiting; **non mi passerebbe neanche per l'~ del cervello** it wouldn't even cross my mind

anti'carie AG INV which fights tooth decay

antichità [antiki'ta] SF INV antiquity; (*oggetto*) antique

antici'clone [antitʃi'klone] SM anticyclone

antici'pare [antitʃi'pare] /**72**/ VT (*consegna, visita*) to bring forward, anticipate; (*somma di denaro*) to pay in advance; (*notizia*) to disclose ▶ VI to be ahead of time

antici'pato, -a [antitʃi'pato] AG (*prima del previsto*) early; **pagamento ~** payment in advance

anticipazi'one [antiʃipat'tsjone] SF anticipation; (*di notizia*) advance information; (*somma di denaro*) advance

an'ticipo [an'titʃipo] SM anticipation; (*di denaro*) advance; **in ~** early, in advance; **con un sensibile ~** well in advance

anti'clan AG INV (*magistrato, processo*) anti-Mafia

an'tico, -a, -chi, -che AG (*quadro, mobili*) antique; (*dell'antichità*) ancient; **all'antica** old-fashioned

anticoncezio'nale [antikontʃettsjo'nale] SM contraceptive

anticonfor'mista, -i, -e AG, SM/F nonconformist

anticonge'lante [antikondʒe'lante] AG, SM antifreeze

anticongiuntu'rale [antikondʒuntu'rale] AG (*Econ*): **misure anticongiunturali** measures to remedy the economic situation

anti'corpo SM antibody

anticostituzio'nale [antikostituttsjo'nale] AG unconstitutional

antidepres'sivo, -a AG, SM antidepressant

antidiluvi'ano, -a AG (*fig: antiquato*) ancient

antidolo'rifico, -ci SM painkiller

anti'doping SM INV (*Sport*) dope test ▶ AG INV

drug testing; **test ~** drugs (*BRIT*) o drug (*US*) test

an'tidoto SM antidote

anti'droga AG INV anti-drugs *cpd*

antie'stetico, -a, -ci, -che AG unsightly

an'tifona SF (*Mus, Rel*) antiphon; **capire l'~** (*fig*) to take the hint

anti'forfora AG INV anti-dandruff

anti'furto SM anti-theft device

anti'gelo [anti'dʒelo] AG INV antifreeze *cpd* ▶ SM (*per motore*) antifreeze; (*per cristalli*) de-icer

an'tigene [an'tidʒene] SM antigen

antigi'enico, -a, -ci, -che [anti'dʒɛniko] AG unhygienic

antiglobalizza'zione [antiglobaliddza'tsjone] AG anti-globalization

An'tille SFPL: **le ~** the West Indies

an'tilope SF antelope

anti'mafia AG INV anti-mafia *cpd*

antin'cendio [antin'tʃendjo] AG INV fire *cpd*; **bombola ~** fire extinguisher

anti'nebbia SM INV (*anche:* **faro antinebbia**: *Aut*) fog lamp

antine'vralgico, -a, -ci, -che [antine'vraldʒiko] AG painkilling ▶ SM painkiller

antin'fiammatorio, -a AG, SM anti-inflammatory

antio'rario AG: **in senso ~** in an anticlockwise (*BRIT*) o counterclockwise (*US*) direction, anticlockwise, counterclockwise

anti'pasto SM hors d'œuvre

antipa'tia SF antipathy, dislike

anti'patico, -a, -ci, -che AG unpleasant, disagreeable

anti'placca AG INV (*dentifricio*) anti-plaque

an'tipodi SMPL: **essere agli ~** (*fig: di idee opposte*) to be poles apart

antipro'iettile AG INV bulletproof

antiquari'ato SM antique trade; **un pezzo d'~** an antique

anti'quario SM antique dealer

anti'quato, -a AG antiquated, old-fashioned

antirici'claggio [antiritʃi'kladdʒo] AG INV (*attività, operazioni*) anti-laundering

antiri'flesso AG INV (*schermo*) non-glare *cpd*

anti'ruggine [anti'ruddʒine] AG INV anti-rust *cpd* ▶ SM INV rust-preventer

anti'rughe [anti'ruge] AG INV (*crema, prodotto*) anti-wrinkle

antise'mita, -i, -e AG anti-semitic

antisemi'tismo SM anti-semitism

anti'settico, -a, -ci, -che AG, SM antiseptic

antista'minico, -a, -ci, -che AG, SM antihistamine

anti'stante AG opposite

anti'tartaro AG INV anti-tartar

antiterro'rismo SM anti-terrorist measures *pl*
an'titesi SF antithesis
antitraspi'rante AG antiperspirant
anti'vipera AG INV: **siero ~** remedy for snake bites
antivi'rale AG antiviral
anti'virus [anti'virus] SM INV antivirus software *no pl* ▶ AG INV antivirus
antolo'gia, -'gie [antolo'dʒia] SF anthology
antono'masia SF antonomasia; **per ~** par excellence
antra'cite [antra'tʃite] SF anthracite
'antro SM cavern
antro'pofago, -gi SM cannibal
antropolo'gia [antropolo'dʒia] SF anthropology
antropo'logico, -a, -ci, -che [antropo'lɔdʒiko] AG anthropological
antro'pologo, -a, -gi, -ghe SM/F anthropologist
anu'lare AG ring *cpd* ▶ SM ring finger
An'versa SF Antwerp
'anzi ['antsi] AV (*invece*) on the contrary; (*o meglio*) or rather, or better still
anzianità [antsjani'ta] SF old age; (*Amm*) seniority
anzi'ano, -a [an'tsjano] AG old; (*Amm*) senior ▶ SM/F old person; senior member
anziché [antsi'ke] CONG rather than
anzi'tempo [antsi'tɛmpo] AV (*in anticipo*) early
anzi'tutto [antsi'tutto] AV first of all
AO SIGLA = **Aosta**
a'orta SF aorta
aos'tano, -a AG of (*o* from) Aosta
AP SIGLA = **Ascoli Piceno**
apar'titico, -a, -ci, -che AG (*Pol*) non-party *cpd*
apa'tia SF apathy, indifference
a'patico, -a, -ci, -che AG apathetic, indifferent
a.p.c. ABBR = **a pronta cassa**
'ape SF bee
aperi'tivo SM apéritif
aperta'mente AV openly
a'perto, -a PP *di* **aprire** ▶ AG open ▶ SM: **all'~** in the open (air); **rimanere a bocca aperta** (*fig*) to be taken aback
aper'tura SF opening; (*ampiezza*) width, spread; (*Pol*) approach; (*Fot*) aperture; **~ alare** wing span; **~ mentale** open-mindedness; **~ di credito** (*Comm*) granting of credit
API SIGLA F = **Associazione Piccole e Medie Industrie**
'apice ['apitʃe] SM apex; (*fig*) height
apicol'tore SM beekeeper
apicol'tura SF beekeeping
ap'nea SF: **immergersi in ~** to dive without breathing apparatus

apoca'lisse SF apocalypse
apo'geo [apo'dʒɛo] SM (*Astr*) apogee; (*fig: culmine*) zenith
a'polide AG stateless
apo'litico, -a, -ci, -che AG (*neutrale*) nonpolitical; (*indifferente*) apolitical
apolo'gia, -gie [apolo'dʒia] SF (*difesa*) apologia; (*esaltazione*) praise; **~ di reato** attempt to defend criminal acts
apoples'sia SF (*Med*) apoplexy
apop'lettico, -a, -ci, -che AG apoplectic; **colpo ~** apoplectic fit
a'postolo SM apostle
apostro'fare/72/ VT (*parola*) to write with an apostrophe; (*persona*) to address
a'postrofo SM apostrophe
app. ABBR (= *appendice*) app.
appaga'mento SM satisfaction; fulfilment
appa'gare/80/ VT to satisfy; (*desiderio*) to fulfil; **appagarsi** VPR: **appagarsi di** to be satisfied with
appa'gato, -a AG satisfied
appai'are/19/ VT to couple, pair
ap'paio *etc* VB *vedi* **apparire**
appallotto'lare/72/ VT (*carta, foglio*) to screw into a ball; **appallottolarsi** VPR (*gatto*) to roll up into a ball
appalta'tore SM contractor
ap'palto SM (*Comm*) contract; **dare/prendere in ~ un lavoro** to let out/undertake a job on contract
appan'naggio [appan'naddʒo] SM (*compenso*) annuity; (*fig*) privilege, prerogative
appan'nare/72/ VT (*vetro*) to mist; (*metallo*) to tarnish; (*vista*) to dim; **appannarsi** VPR to mist over; to tarnish; to grow dim
appa'rato SM equipment, machinery; (*Anat*) apparatus; **~ scenico** (*Teat*) props *pl*
apparecchi'are [apparek'kjare] /19/ VT to prepare; (*tavola*) to set ▶ VI to set the table
apparecchia'tura [apparekkja'tura] SF equipment; (*macchina*) machine, device
appa'recchio [appa'rekkjo] SM piece of apparatus, device; (*aeroplano*) aircraft *inv*; **apparecchi sanitari** bathroom *o* sanitary appliances; **~ acustico** hearing aid; **~ televisivo/telefonico** television set/telephone
appa'rente AG apparent
apparente'mente AV apparently
appa'renza [appa'rɛntsa] SF appearance; **in *o* all'~** apparently, to all appearances
appa'rire/7/ VI to appear; (*sembrare*) to seem, appear
appari'scente [appariʃ'ʃɛnte] AG (*colore*) garish, gaudy; (*bellezza*) striking
apparizi'one [apparit'tsjone] SF apparition
ap'parso, -a PP *di* **apparire**
apparta'mento SM flat (BRIT), apartment (US)

appar'tarsi /**72**/ VPR to withdraw

appar'tato, -a AG (*luogo*) secluded

apparte'nenza [apparte'nɛntsa] SF: ~ **(a)** (*gen*) belonging (to); (*a un partito, club*) membership (of)

apparte'nere /**121**/ VI: ~ **a** to belong to

ap'parvi *etc* VB *vedi* **apparire**

appassio'nante AG thrilling, exciting

appassio'nare /**72**/ VT to thrill; (*commuovere*) to move; **appassionarsi** VPR: **appassionarsi a qc** to take a great interest in sth; to be deeply moved by sth

appassio'nato, -a AG passionate; (*entusiasta*): ~ **(di)** keen (on)

appas'sire /**55**/ VI to wither

appas'sito, -a AG dead

appel'larsi /**72**/ VPR (*ricorrere*): ~ **a** to appeal to; (*Dir*) ~ **contro** to appeal against

ap'pello SM roll-call; (*implorazione, Dir*) appeal; (*sessione d'esame*) exam session; **fare ~ a** to appeal to; **fare l'~** (*Ins*) to call the register *o* roll; (*Mil*) to call the roll

ap'pena AV (*a stento*) hardly, scarcely; (*solamente, da poco*) just ▶ CONG as soon as; **(non)** ~ **furono arrivati …** as soon as they had arrived …; ~ **… che** *o* **quando** no sooner … than; **basta ~ a sfamarli** it's scarcely enough to feed them; **ho ~ finito** I've just finished

ap'pendere /**8**/ VT to hang (up)

appendi'abiti SM INV hook, peg; (*mobile*) hall stand (*BRIT*), hall tree (*US*)

appen'dice [appen'ditʃe] SF appendix; **romanzo d'~** popular serial

appendi'cite [appendi'tʃite] SF appendicitis

appen'dino SM (coat) hook

Appen'nini SMPL: **gli ~** the Apennines

appesan'tire /**55**/ VT to make heavy; **appesantirsi** VPR to grow stout

ap'peso, -a PP *di* **appendere**

appe'tito SM appetite

appeti'toso, -a AG appetising; (*fig*) attractive, desirable

appezza'mento [appettsa'mento] SM (*anche*: **appezzamento di terreno**) plot, piece of ground

appia'nare /**72**/ VT to level; (*fig*) to smooth away, iron out; **appianarsi** VPR (*divergenze*) to be ironed out

appiat'tire /**55**/ VT to flatten; **appiattirsi** VPR to become flatter; (*farsi piatto*) to flatten o.s.; **appiattirsi al suolo** to lie flat on the ground

appic'care /**20**/ VT: ~ **il fuoco a** to set fire to, set on fire

appicci'care [appittʃi'kare] /**20**/ VT to stick; (*fig*): ~ **qc a qn** to palm sth off on sb; **appiccicarsi** VPR to stick; (*fig: persona*) to cling

appiccica'ticcio, -a, -ci, -ce [appittʃika'tittʃo], **appicci'coso, -a**

[appittʃi'koso] AG sticky; (*fig: persona*): **essere ~** to cling like a leech

appie'dato, -a AG: **rimanere ~** to be left without means of transport

appi'eno AV fully

appigli'arsi [appiʎ'ʎarsi] /**27**/ VPR: ~ **a** (*afferrarsi*) to take hold of; (*fig*) to cling to

ap'piglio [ap'piʎʎo] SM hold; (*fig*) pretext

appiop'pare /**72**/ VT: ~ **qc a qn** (*nomignolo*) to pin sth on sb; (*compito difficile*) to saddle sb with sth; **gli ha appioppato un pugno sul muso** he punched him in the face

appiso'larsi /**72**/ VPR to doze off

applau'dire /**45**/ VT, VI to applaud

ap'plauso SM applause *no pl*

appli'cabile AG: ~ **(a)** applicable (to)

appli'care /**20**/ VT to apply; (*regolamento*) to enforce; **applicarsi** VPR to apply o.s.

appli'cato, -a AG (*arte, scienze*) applied ▶ SM (*Amm*) clerk

applica'tore SM applicator

applicazi'one [applikat'tsjone] SF application; enforcement; ~ **per il cellulare** mobile app; **applicazioni tecniche** (*Ins*) practical subjects

appoggi'are [appod'dʒare] /**62**/ VT (*fig: sostenere*) to support; ~ **qc a qc** (*mettere contro*) to lean *o* rest sth against sth; **appoggiarsi** VPR: **appoggiarsi a** to lean against; (*fig*) to rely upon

ap'poggio [ap'pɔddʒo] SM support

appollai'arsi /**72**/ VPR (*anche fig*) to perch

ap'pongo, ap'poni *etc* VB *vedi* **apporre**

ap'porre /**77**/ VT to affix

appor'tare /**72**/ VT to bring

ap'porto SM (*gen, Finanza*) contribution

ap'posi *etc* VB *vedi* **apporre**

apposita'mente AV (*apposta*) on purpose; (*specialmente*) specially

ap'posito, -a AG appropriate

ap'posta AV on purpose, deliberately; **neanche a farlo ~, …** by sheer coincidence, …

appos'tarsi /**72**/ VPR to lie in wait

ap'posto, -a PP *di* **apporre**

ap'prendere /**81**/ VT (*imparare*) to learn; (*comprendere*) to grasp

apprendi'mento SM learning

appren'dista, -i, -e SM/F apprentice

apprendi'stato SM apprenticeship

apprensi'one SF apprehension

appren'sivo, -a AG apprehensive

ap'preso, -a PP *di* **apprendere**

ap'presso AV (*accanto, vicino*) close by, near; (*dietro*) behind; (*dopo, più tardi*) after, later ▶ AG INV (*dopo*): **il giorno ~** the next day; ~ **a** *prep* (*vicino a*) near, close to

appres'tare /**72**/ VT to prepare, get ready; **apprestarsi** VPR: **apprestarsi a fare qc** to prepare *o* get ready to do sth

ap'pretto SM starch

apprez'zabile [appret'tsabile] AG (*notevole*) noteworthy, significant; (*percepibile*) appreciable

apprezza'mento [apprettsa'mento] SM appreciation; (*giudizio*) opinion; (*commento*) comment

apprez'zare [appret'tsare] /**72**/ VT to appreciate

ap'proccio [ap'prɔttʃo] SM approach

appro'dare /**72**/ VI (*Naut*) to land; (*fig*): **non ~ a nulla** to come to nothing

ap'prodo SM landing; (*luogo*) landing place

approfit'tare /**72**/ VI: **~ di** (*situazione*) to make the most of; (*persona*) to take advantage of; (*occasione, opportunità*) to make the most of, profit by

approfon'dire /**55**/ VT to deepen; (*fig*) to study in depth; **approfondirsi** VPR (*gen, fig*) to deepen; (*peggiorare*) to get worse

appron'tare /**72**/ VT to prepare, get ready

appropri'arsi /**19**/ VPR: **~ di qc** to appropriate sth, take possession of sth; **~ indebitamente di** to embezzle

appropri'ato, -a AG appropriate

appropriazi'one [approprjat'tsjone] SF appropriation; **~ indebita** (*Dir*) embezzlement

approssi'mare /**72**/ VT (*cifra*): **~ per eccesso/ per difetto** to round up/down; **approssimarsi** VPR: **approssimarsi a** to approach, draw near

approssima'tivo, -a AG approximate, rough; (*impreciso*) inexact, imprecise

approssimazi'one [approssimat'tsjone] SF approximation; **per ~** approximately, roughly

appro'vare /**72**/ VT (*condotta, azione*) to approve of; (*candidato*) to pass; (*progetto di legge*) to approve

approvazi'one [approvat'tsjone] SF approval

approvvigiona'mento [approvvidʒona'mento] SM supplying; stocking up; **approvvigionamenti** SMPL (*Mil*) supplies

approvvigio'nare [approvvidʒo'nare] /**72**/ VT to supply; **approvvigionarsi** VPR to lay in provisions, stock up; **~ qn di qc** to supply sb with sth

appunta'mento SM appointment; (*amoroso*) date; **darsi ~** to arrange to meet (one another); **ho un ~ con...** I have an appointment with...; **vorrei prendere un ~** I'd like to make an appointment

appun'tare /**72**/ VT (*rendere aguzzo*) to sharpen; (*fissare*) to pin, fix; (*annotare*) to note down

appun'tato SM (*Carabinieri*) corporal

appun'tino AV perfectly

appun'tire /**55**/ VT to sharpen

ap'punto SM note; (*rimprovero*) reproach; (*Inform*): **Appunti** Clipboard *sg* ▶ AV (*proprio*) exactly, just; **per l'~!, ~!** exactly!

appu'rare /**72**/ VT to check, verify

apr. ABBR (= *aprile*) Apr.

apribot'tiglie [apribot'tiʎʎe] SM INV bottle opener

a'prile SM April; **pesce d'~!** April Fool!; *vedi anche* **luglio**

a'prire /**9**/ VT to open; (*via, cadavere*) to open up; (*gas, luce, acqua*) to turn on ▶ VI to open; **aprirsi** VPR to open; **~ le ostilità** (*Mil*) to start up *o* begin hostilities; **~ una sessione** (*Inform*) to log on; **aprirsi a qn** to confide in sb, open one's heart to sb; **mi si è aperto lo stomaco** I feel rather peckish; **apriti cielo!** heaven forbid!

apris'catole SM INV tin (*Brit*) *o* can opener

APT SIGLA F (= *Azienda di Promozione*) ≈ tourist board

AQ SIGLA = **L'Aquila**

aquagym [akwa'dʒim] SF aquarobics

a'quario SM = **acquario**

'aquila SF (*Zool*) eagle; (*fig*) genius

aqui'lino, -a AG aquiline

aqui'lone SM (*giocattolo*) kite; (*vento*) North wind

AR SIGLA = **Arezzo**

A/R ABBR (= *andata e ritorno: biglietto*) return (ticket) (*Brit*), round-trip ticket (*US*)

ara'besco, -schi SM (*decorazione*) arabesque

A'rabia Sau'dita SF: **l'~** Saudi Arabia

a'rabico, -a, -ci, -che AG: **il Deserto ~** the Arabian Desert

a'rabile AG arable

'arabo, -a AG, SM/F Arab ▶ SM (*Ling*) Arabic; **parlare ~** (*fig*) to speak double Dutch (*Brit*)

a'rachide [a'rakide] SF peanut

ara'gosta SF crayfish; spiny lobster

a'raldica SF heraldry

a'raldo SM herald

aran'ceto [aran'tʃeto] SM orange grove

a'rancia, -ce [a'rantʃa] SF orange

aranci'ata [aran'tʃata] SF orangeade

a'rancio [a'rantʃo] SM (*Bot*) orange tree; (*colore*) orange ▶ AG INV (*colore*) orange; **fiori di ~** orange blossom *sg*

aranci'one [aran'tʃone] AG INV: **(color) ~** bright orange

a'rare /**72**/ VT to plough (*Brit*), plow (*US*)

ara'tore SM ploughman (*Brit*), plowman (*US*)

a'ratro SM plough (*Brit*), plow (*US*)

ara'tura SF ploughing (*Brit*), plowing (*US*)

a'razzo [a'rattso] SM tapestry

arbi'traggio [arbi'traddʒo] SM (*Sport*) refereeing; umpiring; (*Dir*) arbitration; (*Comm*) arbitrage

arbi'trare /**72**/ VT (*Sport*) to referee; to umpire; (*Dir*) to arbitrate

arbi'trario, -a AG arbitrary

arbi'trato SM arbitration

ar'bitrio SM will; (*abuso, sopruso*) arbitrary act

'arbitro SM arbiter, judge; (*Dir*) arbitrator; (*Sport*) referee; (: *Tennis, Cricket*) umpire

ar'busto SM shrub

'arca, -che SF (*sarcofago*) sarcophagus; **l'~ di Noè** Noah's ark

ar'caico, -a, -ci, -che AG archaic

arca'ismo SM (*Ling*) archaism

ar'cangelo [arˈkandʒelo] SM archangel

ar'cano, -a AG arcane, mysterious ▶ SM mystery

ar'cata SF (*Archit, Anat*) arch; (*ordine di archi*) arcade

archeolo'gia [arkeoloˈdʒia] SF arch(a)eology

archeo'logico, -a, -ci, -che [arkeoˈlɔdʒiko] AG arch(a)eological

arche'ologo, -a, -gi, -ghe [arkeˈɔlogo] SM/F arch(a)eologist

ar'chetipo [arˈkɛtipo] SM archetype

ar'chetto [arˈketto] SM (*Mus*) bow

architet'tare [arkitetˈtare] /**72**/ VT (*fig: ideare*) to devise; (: *macchinare*) to plan, concoct

archi'tetto [arkiˈtetto] SM architect

architet'tonico, -a, -ci, -che [arkitetˈtɔniko] AG architectural

architet'tura [arkitetˈtura] SF architecture

archivi'are [arkiˈvjare] /**19**/ VT (*documenti*) to file; (*Dir*) to dismiss

archiviazi'one [arkivjatˈtsjone] SF filing; dismissal

ar'chivio [arˈkivjo] SM archives pl; (*Inform*) file; **~ principale** (*Inform*) master file

archi'vista, -i, -e [arkiˈvista] SM/F (*Amm*) archivist; (*in ufficio*) filing clerk

'ARCI [ˈartʃi] SIGLA F (= *Associazione Ricreativa Culturale Italiana*) *cultural society*

arci'duca, -chi [artʃiˈduka] SM archduke

arci'ere [arˈtʃɛre] SM archer

ar'cigno, -a [arˈtʃiɲɲo] AG grim, severe

arci'pelago, -ghi [artʃiˈpɛlago] SM archipelago

arci'vescovo [artʃiˈveskovo] SM archbishop

'arco, -chi SM (*arma, Mus*) bow; (*Archit*) arch; (*Mat*) arc; **nell'~ di 3 settimane** within the space of 3 weeks; **~ costituzionale** *political parties involved in formulating Italy's post-war constitution*

arcoba'leno SM rainbow

arcu'ato, -a AG curved, bent; **dalle gambe arcuate** bow-legged

ar'dente AG burning; (*fig*) burning, ardent

'ardere /**10**/ VT, VI to burn; **legna da ~** firewood

ar'desia SF slate

ardi'mento SM daring

ar'dire /**55**/ VI to dare ▶ SM daring

ar'dito, -a AG brave, daring, bold; (*sfacciato*) bold

ar'dore SM blazing heat; (*fig*) ardour, fervour

'arduo, -a AG arduous, difficult

'area SF area; (*Edil*) land, ground; **nell'~ dei partiti di sinistra** among the parties of the left; **~ fabbricabile** building land; **~ di rigore** (*Sport*) penalty area; **~ di servizio** (*Aut*) service area

a'rena SF arena; (*per corride*) bullring; (*sabbia*) sand

are'naria SF sandstone

are'narsi /**72**/ VPR to run aground; (*fig: trattative*) to come to a standstill

areo'plano SM = **aeroplano**

are'tino, -a AG of (*o* from) Arezzo

'argano SM winch

argen'tato, -a [ardʒenˈtato] AG silver-plated; (*colore*) silver, silvery; (*capelli*) silver(-grey)

ar'genteo, -a [arˈdʒenteo] AG silver, silvery

argente'ria [ardʒenteˈria] SF silverware, silver

Argen'tina [ardʒenˈtina] SF: **l'~** Argentina

argen'tino, -a [ardʒenˈtino] AG, SM/F (*dell'Argentina*) Argentinian ▶ SF crewneck sweater

ar'gento [arˈdʒɛnto] SM silver; **~ vivo** quicksilver; **avere l'~ (vivo) addosso** (*fig*) to be fidgety

ar'gilla [arˈdʒilla] SF clay

argil'loso, -a [ardʒilˈloso] AG (*contenente argilla*) clayey; (*simile ad argilla*) clay-like

argi'nare [ardʒiˈnare] /**72**/ VT (*fiume, acque*) to embank; (: *con diga*) to dyke up; (*fig: inflazione, corruzione*) to check; (: *spese*) to limit

'argine [ˈardʒine] SM embankment, bank; (*diga*) dyke, dike; **far ~ a, porre un ~ a** (*fig*) to check, hold back

argomen'tare /**72**/ VI to argue

argo'mento SM argument; (*motivo*) motive; (*materia, tema*) subject; **tornare sull'~** to bring the matter up again

argu'ire /**55**/ VT to deduce

ar'guto, -a AG sharp, quick-witted; (*spiritoso*) witty

ar'guzia [arˈguttsja] SF wit; (*battuta*) witty remark

'aria SF air; (*espressione, aspetto*) air, look; (*Mus: melodia*) tune; (: *di opera*) aria; **all'~ aperta** in the open (air); **manca l'~** it's stuffy; **andare all'~** (*piano, progetto*) to come to nothing; **mandare all'~ qc** to ruin *o* upset sth; **darsi delle arie** to put on airs and graces; **ha la testa per ~** his head is in the clouds; **che ~ tira?** (*fig: atmosfera*) what's the atmosphere like?

aridità SF aridity, dryness; (*fig*) lack of feeling

'arido, -a AG arid

arieggi'are [arjedˈdʒare] /**62**/ VT (*cambiare aria*)

to air; (*imitare*) to imitate
ari'ete SM ram; (*Mil*) battering ram; **A~** Aries;
  essere dell'A~ to be Aries
a'ringa, -ghe SF herring *inv*; **~ affumicata**
  smoked herring, kipper; **~ marinata** pickled
  herring
ari'oso, -a AG (*ambiente, stanza*) airy; (*Mus*)
  ariose
'arista SF (*Cuc*) chine of pork
aristo'cratico, -a, -ci, -che AG aristocratic
aristocra'zia [aristokrat'tsia] SF aristocracy
arit'metica SF arithmetic
arit'metico, -a, -ci, -che AG arithmetical
arlec'chino [arlek'kino] SM harlequin
'arma, -i SF weapon, arm; (*parte dell'esercito*)
  arm; **alle armi!** to arms!; **chiamare alle
  armi** to call up (*BRIT*), draft (*US*); **sotto le
  armi** in the army (*o forces*); **combattere ad
  armi pari** (*anche fig*) to fight on equal terms;
  essere alle prime armi (*fig*) to be a novice;
  passare qn per le armi to execute sb; **~ a
  doppio taglio** (*anche fig*) double-edged
  weapon; **~ atomica/nucleare** atomic/
  nuclear weapon; **~ da fuoco** firearm; **armi
  convenzionali/non convenzionali**
  conventional/unconventional weapons;
  armi di distruzione di massa weapons of
  mass destruction
arma'dietto SM (*di medicinali*) medicine
  cabinet; (*in palestra ecc*) locker; (*in cucina*)
  (kitchen) cupboard
ar'madio SM cupboard; (*per abiti*) wardrobe;
  ~ a muro built-in cupboard
armamen'tario SM equipment,
  instruments *pl*
arma'mento SM (*Mil*) armament; (: *materiale*)
  arms *pl*, weapons *pl*; (*Naut*) fitting out;
  manning; **la corsa agli armamenti** the
  arms race
ar'mare /**72**/ VT to arm; (*arma da fuoco*) to cock;
  (*Naut*: *nave*) to rig, fit out; to man; (*Edil*: *volta,
  galleria*) to prop up, shore up; **armarsi** VPR to
  arm o.s.; (*Mil*) to take up arms
ar'mato, -a AG: **~ (di)** (*anche fig*) armed (with)
  ▶ SF (*Mil*) army; (*Naut*) fleet; **rapina a mano
  armata** armed robbery
arma'tore SM shipowner
arma'tura SF (*struttura di sostegno*) framework;
  (*impalcatura*) scaffolding; (*Storia*) armour *no pl*
  (*BRIT*), armor *no pl* (*US*), suit of armour
armeggi'are [armed'dʒare] /**62**/ VI
  (*affaccendarsi*): **~ (intorno a qc)** to mess about
  (with sth)
ar'meno, -a AG, SM/F Armenian
arme'ria SF (*deposito*) armoury (*BRIT*), armory
  (*US*); (*collezione*) collection of arms
armis'tizio [armis'tittsjo] SM armistice
armo'nia SF harmony
ar'monico, -a, -ci, -che AG harmonic;

(*fig*) harmonious ▶ SF (*Mus*) harmonica;
  armonica a bocca mouth organ
armoni'oso, -a AG harmonious
armoniz'zare [armonid'dzare] /**72**/ VT
  to harmonize; (*colori, abiti*) to match
  ▶ VI to be in harmony; to match
ar'nese SM tool, implement; (*oggetto
  indeterminato*) thing, contraption; **male in ~**
  (*malvestito*) badly dressed; (*di salute malferma*)
  in poor health; (*di condizioni economiche*)
  down-at-heel
'arnia SF hive
a'roma, -i SM aroma; fragrance; **aromi** SMPL
  (*Cuc*) herbs and spices; **aromi naturali/
  artificiali** natural/artificial flavouring *sg*
  (*BRIT*) *o* flavoring *sg* (*US*)
aromatera'pia SF aromatherapy
aro'matico, -a, -ci, -che AG aromatic; (*cibo*)
  spicy
aromatiz'zare [aromatid'dzare] /**72**/ VT to
  season, flavour (*BRIT*), flavor (*US*)
'arpa SF (*Mus*) harp
ar'peggio [ar'peddʒo] SM (*Mus*) arpeggio
ar'pia SF (*anche fig*) harpy
arpi'one SM (*gancio*) hook; (*cardine*) hinge;
  (*Pesca*) harpoon
arrabat'tarsi /**72**/ VPR to do all one can, strive
arrabbi'are /19/ VI (*cane*) to be affected with
  rabies; **arrabbiarsi** VPR (*essere preso dall'ira*) to
  get angry, fly into a rage
arrabbi'ato, -a AG (*cane*) rabid, with rabies;
  (*persona*) furious, angry
arrabbia'tura SF: **prendersi un'~ (per qc)**
  to become furious (over sth)
arraffare /72/ VT to snatch, seize; (*sottrarre*)
  to pinch
arrampi'carsi /20/ VPR to climb (up); **~ sui
  vetri** *o* **sugli specchi** (*fig*) to clutch at straws
arrampi'cata SF climb
arrampica'tore, -'trice SM/F (*gen, Sport*)
  climber; **~ sociale** (*fig*) social climber
arran'care /20/ VI to limp, hobble; (*fig*) to
  struggle along
arrangia'mento [arrandʒa'mento] SM (*Mus*)
  arrangement
arran'giare [arran'dʒare] /**62**/ VT to arrange;
  arrangiarsi VPR to manage, do the best one
  can
arre'care /20/ VT to bring; (*causare*) to cause
arreda'mento SM (*studio*) interior design;
  (*mobili ecc*) furnishings *pl*
arre'dare /72/ VT to furnish
arreda'tore, -'trice SM/F interior designer
ar'redo SM fittings *pl*, furnishings *pl*; **~ per
  uffici** office furnishings
arrem'baggio [arrem'baddʒo] SM (*Naut*)
  boarding
ar'rendersi /88/ VPR to surrender;
  ~ all'evidenza (dei fatti) to face (the) facts

arren'devole AG (*persona*) yielding, compliant

arrendevo'lezza [arrendevo'lettsa] SF compliancy

ar'reso, -a PP *di* **arrendersi**

arres'tare /**72**/ VT (*fermare*) to stop, halt; (*catturare*) to arrest; **arrestarsi** VPR (*fermarsi*) to stop

arres'tato, -a SM/F person under arrest

ar'resto SM (*cessazione*) stopping; (*fermata*) stop; (*cattura, Med*) arrest; (*Comm: in produzione*) stoppage; **subire un ~** to come to a stop *o* standstill; **mettere agli arresti** to place under arrest; **arresti domiciliari** (*Dir*) house arrest *sg*

arre'trare /**72**/ VT, VI to withdraw

arre'trato, -a AG (*lavoro*) behind schedule; (*paese, bambino*) backward; (*numero di giornale*) back *cpd*; **arretrati** SMPL arrears; **gli arretrati dello stipendio** back pay *sg*

arricchi'mento [arrikki'mento] SM enrichment

arric'chire [arrik'kire] /**55**/ VT to enrich; **arricchirsi** VPR to become rich

arric'chito, -a [arrik'kito] SM/F nouveau riche

arricci'are [arrit'tʃare] /**14**/ VT to curl; **~ il naso** to turn up one's nose

ar'ridere /**89**/ VI: **~ a qn** (*fortuna, successo*) to smile on sb

ar'ringa, -ghe SF harangue; (*Dir*) address by counsel

arrischi'are [arris'kjare] /**19**/ VT to risk; **arrischiarsi** VPR to venture, dare

arrischi'ato, -a [arris'kjato] AG risky; (*temerario*) reckless, rash

ar'riso, -a PP *di* **arridere**

arri'vare /**72**/ VI to arrive; (*avvicinarsi*) to come; (*accadere*) to happen, occur; **~ a** (*livello, grado ecc*) to reach; **lui arriva a Roma alle 7** he gets to *o* arrives at Rome at 7; **~ a fare qc** to manage to do sth, succeed in doing sth; **non ci arrivo** I can't reach it; (*fig: non capisco*) I can't understand it

arri'vato, -a AG (*persona: di successo*) successful ▶ SM/F: **essere un ~** to have made it; **nuovo ~** newcomer; **ben ~!** welcome!; **non sono l'ultimo ~!** (*fig*) I'm no fool!

arrive'derci [arrive'dertʃi] ESCL goodbye!

arrive'derla ESCL (*forma di cortesia*) goodbye!

arri'vismo SM (*ambizione*) ambitiousness; (*sociale*) social climbing

arri'vista, -i, -e SM/F go-getter

ar'rivo SM arrival; (*Sport*) finish, finishing line

arro'gante AG arrogant

arro'ganza [arro'gantsa] SF arrogance

arro'gare /**80**/ VT: **arrogarsi il diritto di fare qc** to assume the right to do sth; **arrogarsi il merito di qc** to claim credit for sth

arrossa'mento SM reddening

arros'sare /**72**/ VT (*occhi, pelle*) to redden, make red; **arrossarsi** VPR to go *o* become red

arros'sire /**55**/ VI (*per vergogna, timidezza*) to blush; (*per gioia*) to flush, blush

arros'tire /**55**/ VT to roast; (*pane*) to toast; (*ai ferri*) to grill

ar'rosto SM, AG INV roast; **~ di manzo** roast beef

arro'tare /**72**/ VT to sharpen; (*investire con un veicolo*) to run over

arro'tino SM knife-grinder

arroto'lare /**72**/ VT to roll up

arroton'dare /**72**/ VT (*forma, oggetto*) to round; (*stipendio*) to add to; (*somma*) to round off

arrovel'larsi /**72**/ VPR (*anche:* **arrovellarsi il cervello**) to rack one's brains

arroven'tato, -a AG red-hot

arruf'fare /**72**/ VT to ruffle; (*fili*) to tangle; (*fig: questione*) to confuse

arruggi'nire [arruddʒi'nire] /**55**/ VT to rust; **arrugginirsi** VPR to rust; (*fig*) to become rusty

arruggi'nito, -a [arruddʒin'nito] AG rusty

arruola'mento SM (*Mil*) enlistment

arruo'lare /**72**/ VT (*Mil*) to enlist; **arruolarsi** VPR to enlist, join up

arse'nale SM (*Mil*) arsenal; (*cantiere navale*) dockyard

ar'senico SM arsenic

'arsi VB *vedi* **ardere**

'arso, -a PP *di* **ardere** ▶ AG (*bruciato*) burnt; (*arido*) dry

ar'sura SF (*calore opprimente*) burning heat; (*siccità*) drought

art. ABBR (= *articolo*) art.

'arte SF art; (*abilità*) skill; **a regola d'~** (*fig*) perfectly; **senz'~ né parte** penniless and out of a job; **arti figurative** visual arts

arte'fatto, -a AG (*stile, modi*) affected; (*cibo*) adulterated

ar'tefice [ar'tefitʃe] SMF craftsman(-woman); (*autore*) author

ar'teria SF artery; **~ stradale** main road

arterioscle'rosi SF arteriosclerosis, hardening of the arteries

arteri'oso, -a AG arterial

'artico, -a, -ci, -che AG Arctic ▶ SM: **l'A~** the Arctic; **il Circolo polare ~** the Arctic Circle; **l'Oceano ~** the Arctic Ocean

artico'lare /**72**/ AG (*Anat*) of the joints, articular ▶ VT to articulate; (*suddividere*) to divide, split up; **articolarsi** VPR: **articolarsi in** (*discorso, progetto*) to be divided into

artico'lato, -a AG (*linguaggio*) articulate; (*Aut*) articulated

articolazi'one [artikolat'tsjone] SF (*Anat, Tecn*) joint; (*di voce, concetto*) articulation

ar'ticolo SM article; **~ di fondo** (*Stampa*) leader, leading article; **articoli di marca**

branded goods; **un bell'~** (*fig*) a real character

'**Artide** SM: **l'~** the Arctic

artifici'ale [artifi'tʃale] AG artificial

artifici'ere [artifi'tʃere] SM (*Mil*) artificer; (: *per disinnescare bombe*) bomb-disposal expert

arti'ficio [arti'fitʃo] SM (*espediente*) trick, artifice; (*ricerca di effetto*) artifice;

artifici'oso, -a [artifi'tʃoso] AG cunning; (*non spontaneo*) affected

artigia'nale [artidʒa'nale] AG craft *cpd*

artigia'nato [artidʒa'nato] SM craftsmanship; craftsmen *pl*

artigi'ano, -a [arti'dʒano] SM/F craftsman(-woman)

artigli'ere [artiʎ'ʎere] SM artilleryman

artiglie'ria [artiʎʎe'ria] SF artillery

ar'tiglio [ar'tiʎʎo] SM claw; (*di rapaci*) talon; **sfoderare gli artigli** (*fig*) to show one's claws

ar'tista, -i, -e SM/F artist; **un lavoro da ~** (*fig*) a professional piece of work

ar'tistico, -a, -ci, -che AG artistic

'**arto** SM (*Anat*) limb

ar'trite SF (*Med*) arthritis

ar'trosi SF osteoarthritis

arzigogo'lato, -a [ardzigogo'lato] AG tortuous

ar'zillo, -a [ar'dzillo] AG lively, sprightly

a'scella [aʃ'ʃella] SF (*Anat*) armpit

ascen'dente [aʃʃen'dɛnte] SM ancestor; (*fig*) ascendancy; (*Astr*) ascendant

a'scendere [aʃ'ʃendere] /**101**/ VI: **~ al trono** to ascend the throne

ascensi'one [aʃʃen'sjone] SF (*Alpinismo*) ascent; (*Rel*): **l'A~** the Ascension; **isola dell'A~** Ascension Island

ascen'sore [aʃʃen'sore] SM lift

a'scesa [aʃ'ʃesa] SF ascent; (*al trono*) accession; (*al potere*) rise

a'scesi [aʃ'ʃezi] SF asceticism

a'sceso, -a [aʃ'ʃeso] PP *di* **ascendere**

a'scesso [aʃ'ʃesso] SM (*Med*) abscess

a'sceta, -i [aʃ'ʃeta] SM ascetic

'**ascia** ['aʃʃa] (*pl* **asce**) SF axe

asciugaca'pelli [aʃʃugaka'pelli] SM INV hair dryer

asciuga'mano [aʃʃuga'mano] SM towel

asciu'gare [aʃʃu'gare] /**80**/ VT to dry; **asciugarsi** VPR to dry o.s.; (*diventare asciutto*) to dry

asciuga'trice [aʃʃuga'tritʃe] SF spin-dryer

asciut'tezza [aʃʃut'tettsa] SF dryness; leanness; curtness

asci'utto, -a [aʃ'ʃutto] AG dry; (*fig: magro*) lean; (: *burbero*) curt ▶ SM: **restare all'~** (*fig*) to be left penniless; **restare a bocca asciutta** (*fig*) to be disappointed

asco'lano, -a AG of (*o* from) Ascoli

ascol'tare /**72**/ VT to listen to; **~ il consiglio di qn** to listen to *o* heed sb's advice

ascolta'tore, -'trice SM/F listener

as'colto SM: **essere** *o* **stare in ~** to be listening; **dare** *o* **prestare ~ (a)** to pay attention (to); **indice di ~** (*TV, Radio*) audience rating

AS. COM. SIGLA F = **Associazione Commercianti**

as'critto, -a PP *di* **ascrivere**

as'crivere /**105**/ VT (*attribuire*): **~ qc a qn** to attribute sth to sb; **~ qc a merito di qn** to give sb credit for sth

a'settico, -a, -ci, -che AG aseptic

asfal'tare /**72**/ VT to asphalt

as'falto SM asphalt

asfis'sia SF asphyxia, asphyxiation

asfissi'ante AG (*gas*) asphyxiating; (*fig: calore, ambiente*) stifling, suffocating; (: *persona*) tiresome

asfissi'are /**19**/ VT to asphyxiate, suffocate; (*fig: opprimere*) to stifle; (: *infastidire*) to get on sb's nerves ▶ VI to suffocate, asphyxiate

'**Asia** SF: **l'~** Asia

asi'atico, -a, -ci, -che AG, SM/F Asiatic, Asian

a'silo SM refuge, sanctuary; **~ (d'infanzia)** nursery(-school); **~ nido** day nursery, crèche (*for children aged o to 3*); **~ politico** political asylum

asim'metrico, -a, -ci, -che AG asymmetric(al)

'**asino** SM donkey, ass; **la bellezza dell'~** (*fig: di ragazza*) the beauty of youth; **qui casca l'~!** there's the rub!

ASL [azl] SIGLA F (= *Azienda Sanitaria Locale*) local health centre

'**asma** SF asthma

as'matico, -a, -ci, -che AG, SM/F asthmatic

asoci'ale [aso'tʃale] AG antisocial

'**asola** SF buttonhole

as'parago, -gi SM asparagus *no pl*

as'pergere [as'pɛrdʒere] /**59**/ VT: **~ (di** *o* **con)** to sprinkle (with)

asperità SF INV roughness *no pl*; (*fig*) harshness *no pl*

as'persi *etc* VB *vedi* **aspergere**

as'perso, -a PP *di* **aspergere**

aspet'tare /**72**/ VT to wait for; (*anche Comm*) to await; (*aspettarsi*) to expect; (*essere in serbo: notizia, evento ecc*) to be in store for, lie ahead of ▶ VI to wait; **aspettarsi qc** to expect sth; **~ un bambino** to be expecting (a baby); **questo non me l'aspettavo** I wasn't expecting this; **me l'aspettavo!** I thought as much!

aspetta'tiva SF expectation; **inferiore all'~** worse than expected; **essere/mettersi in ~** (*Amm*) to be on/take leave of absence

as'petto SM (*apparenza*) aspect, appearance,

look; (*punto di vista*) point of view; **di bell'~** good-looking

aspi'rante AG (*attore ecc*) aspiring ▶ SMF candidate, applicant

aspira'polvere SM INV vacuum cleaner

aspi'rare /72/ VT (*respirare*) to breathe in, inhale; (*apparecchi*) to suck (up) ▶ VI: **~ a** to aspire to

aspira'tore SM extractor fan

aspirazi'one [aspirat'tsjone] SF (*Tecn*) suction; (*anelito*) aspiration

aspi'rina SF aspirin

aspor'tare /72/ VT (*anche Med*) to remove, take away

as'prezza [as'prettsa] SF sourness, tartness; pungency; harshness; roughness; rugged nature

'**aspro, -a** AG (*sapore*) sour, tart; (*odore*) acrid, pungent; (*voce, clima, fig*) harsh; (*superficie*) rough; (*paesaggio*) rugged

Ass. ABBR = **assicurazione; assicurato; assegno**

assaggi'are [assad'dʒare] /**62**/ VT to taste

assag'gini [assad'dʒini] SMPL (*Cuc*) selection of first courses

as'saggio [as'saddʒo] SM tasting; (*piccola quantità*) taste; (*campione*) sample

as'sai AV (*molto*) a lot, much; (: *con ag*) very; (*a sufficienza*) enough ▶ AG INV (*quantità*) a lot of, much; (*numero*) a lot of, many; **~ contento** very pleased

as'salgo *etc* VB *vedi* **assalire**

assa'lire /98/ VT to attack, assail

assali'tore, -'trice SM/F attacker, assailant

assal'tare /72/ VT (*Mil*) to storm; (*banca*) to raid; (*treno, diligenza*) to hold up

as'salto SM attack, assault; **prendere d'~** (*fig: negozio, treno*) to storm; (: *personalità*) to besiege; **d'~** (*editoria, giornalista ecc*) aggressive

assapo'rare /72/ VT to savour (*BRIT*), savor (*US*)

assassi'nare /72/ VT to murder; (*Pol*) to assassinate; (*fig*) to ruin

assas'sinio SM murder; assassination

assas'sino, -a AG murderous ▶ SM/F murderer; assassin

'**asse** SM (*Tecn*) axle; (*Mat*) axis ▶ SF board; **~ da stiro** ironing board

assecon'dare /72/ VT: **~ qn (in qc)** to go along with sb (in sth); **~ i desideri di qn** to go along with sb's wishes; **~ i capricci di qn** to give in to sb's whims

assedi'are /19/ VT to besiege

as'sedio SM siege

asse'gnare [assen'ɲare] /**15**/ VT to assign, allot; (*premio*) to award

assegna'tario [assenɲa'tarjo] SM (*Dir*) assignee; (*Comm*) recipient; **l'~ del premio** the person awarded the prize

assegnazi'one [assenɲat'tsjone] SF (*di casa, somma*) allocation; (*di carica*) assignment; (*di premio, borsa di studio*) awarding

as'segno [as'senɲo] SM allowance; (*anche:* **assegno bancario**) cheque (*BRIT*), check (*US*); **contro ~** cash on delivery; **~ circolare** bank draft; **~ di malattia** *o* **di invalidità** sick pay/ disability benefit; **~ post-datato** post-dated cheque; **~ sbarrato** crossed cheque; **~ non sbarrato** uncrossed cheque; **~ di studio** study grant; "**~ non trasferibile**" "account payee only"; **~ di viaggio** travel(l)er's cheque; **~ a vuoto** dud cheque; **assegni alimentari** alimony *sg*; **assegni familiari** ≈ child benefit *sg*

assem'blaggio [assem'bladdʒo] SM (*Industria*) assembly

assem'blare /72/ VT to assemble

assem'blea SF assembly; (*raduno, adunanza*) meeting

assembra'mento SM public gathering; **divieto di ~** ban on public meetings

assen'nato, -a AG sensible

as'senso SM assent, consent

assen'tarsi /72/ VPR to go out

as'sente AG absent; (*fig*) faraway, vacant ▶ SMF absentee

assente'ismo SM absenteeism

assente'ista, -i, -e SM/F (*dal lavoro*) absentee

assen'tire /45/ VI: **~ (a)** to agree (to), assent (to)

as'senza [as'sɛntsa] SF absence

asse'rire /55/ VT to maintain, assert

asserragli'arsi [asserraʎ'ʎarsi] /**27**/ VPR: **~ (in)** to barricade o.s. (in)

asser'vire /55/ VT to enslave; (*fig: animo, passioni*) to subdue; **asservirsi** VPR: **asservirsi (a)** to submit (to)

asserzi'one [asser'tsjone] SF assertion

assesso'rato SM councillorship

asses'sore SM councillor

assesta'mento SM (*sistemazione*) arrangement; (*Edil, Geo*) settlement

asses'tare /72/ VT (*mettere in ordine*) to put in order, arrange; **assestarsi** VPR to settle in; (*Geo*) to settle; **~ un colpo a qn** to deal sb a blow

asse'tato, -a AG thirsty, parched

as'setto SM order, arrangement; (*Naut, Aer*) trim; **in ~ di guerra** on a war footing; **~ territoriale** country planning

assicu'rare /72/ VT (*accertare*) to ensure; (*infondere certezza*) to assure; (*fermare, legare*) to make fast, secure; (*fare un contratto di assicurazione*) to insure; **assicurarsi** VPR: **assicurarsi (di)** (*accertarsi*) to make sure (of); **assicurarsi (contro)** (*il furto ecc*) to insure o.s. (against)

assicu'rato, -a AG insured ▶ SF (*anche:* **lettera assicurata**) registered letter

assicura'tore, -'trice AG insurance *cpd* ▶ SM/F insurance agent; **società assicuratrice** insurance company

assicurazi'one [assikurat'tsjone] SF assurance; insurance; ~ **multi-rischio** comprehensive insurance

assidera'mento SM exposure

asside'rare /**72**/ VT to freeze; **assiderarsi** VPR to freeze; **morire assiderato** to die of exposure

as'siduo, -a (*costante*) assiduous; (*regolare*) regular

assi'eme AV (*insieme*) together ▶ PREP: ~ **a** (together) with

assil'lante AG (*dubbio, pensiero*) nagging; (*creditore*) pestering

assil'lare /**72**/ VT to pester, torment

as'sillo SM (*fig*) worrying thought

assimi'lare /**72**/ VT to assimilate

assimilazi'one [assimilat'tsjone] SF assimilation

assi'oma, -i SM axiom

assio'matico, -a, -ci, -che AG axiomatic

as'sise SFPL (*Dir*) assizes (*BRIT*); **corte d'~** court of assizes, ≈ crown court (*BRIT*); *vedi anche* **corte**

assis'tente SMF assistant; ~ **sociale** social worker; ~ **universitario** (assistant) lecturer; ~ **di volo** (*Aer*) steward (stewardess)

assis'tenza [assis'tɛntsa] SF assistance; ~ **legale** legal aid; ~ **ospedaliera** free hospital treatment; ~ **sanitaria** health service; ~ **sociale** welfare services *pl*

assistenzi'ale [assisten'tsjale] AG (*ente, organizzazione*) welfare *cpd*; (*opera*) charitable

assistenzia'lismo [assistentsja'lizmo] SM (*peg*) excessive state aid

as'sistere /**11**/ VT (*aiutare*) to assist, help; (*curare*) to treat ▶ VI: ~ **a qc** (*essere presente*) to be present (at sth), attend (sth)

assis'tito, -a PP *di* **assistere**

'asso SM ace; **piantare qn in** ~ to leave sb in the lurch

associ'are [asso'tʃare] /**14**/ VT to associate; (*rendere partecipe*): ~ **qn a** (*affari*) to take sb into partnership in; (*partito*) to make sb a member of; **associarsi** VPR to enter into partnership; **associarsi a** to become a member of, join; (*dolori, gioie*) to share in; ~ **qn alle carceri** to take sb to prison

associazi'one [assotʃat'tsjone] SF association; (*Comm*) association, society; ~ **di categoria** trade association; ~ **a** *o* **per delinquere** (*Dir*) criminal association; **A~ Europea di Libero Scambio** European Free Trade Association, EFTA; ~ **in partecipazione** (*Comm*) joint venture

asso'dare /**72**/ VT (*muro, posizione*) to strengthen; (*fatti, verità*) to ascertain

asso'dato, -a AG well-founded

assogget'tare [assoddʒet'tare] /**72**/ VT to subject, subjugate; **assoggettarsi** VPR: **assoggettarsi a** to submit to

asso'lato, -a AG sunny

assol'dare /**72**/ VT to recruit

as'solsi *etc* VB *vedi* **assolvere**

as'solto, -a PP *di* **assolvere**

assoluta'mente AV absolutely

asso'luto, -a AG absolute

assoluzi'one [assolut'tsjone] SF (*Dir*) acquittal; (*Rel*) absolution

as'solvere /**94**/ VT (*Dir*) to acquit; (*Rel*) to absolve; (*adempiere*) to carry out, perform

assomigli'are [assomiʎ'ʎare] /**27**/ VI: ~ **a** to resemble, look like; **assomigliarsi** VPR to look alike; (*nel carattere*) to be alike

asson'nato, -a AG sleepy

asso'pirsi /**55**/ VPR to doze off

assor'bente AG absorbent ▶ SM: ~ **igienico/esterno** sanitary towel; ~ **interno** tampon

assor'bire /**17**/ VT to absorb; (*fig: far proprio*) to assimilate

assor'dante AG (*rumore, musica*) deafening

assor'dare /**72**/ VT to deafen

assorti'mento SM assortment

assor'tire /**55**/ VT (*disporre*) to arrange

assor'tito, -a AG assorted; (*colori*) matched, matching

as'sorto, -a AG absorbed, engrossed

assottigli'are [assottiʎ'ʎare] /**27**/ VT to make thin, thin; (*aguzzare*) to sharpen; (*ridurre*) to reduce; **assottigliarsi** VPR to grow thin; (*fig: ridursi*) to be reduced

assue'fare /**41**/ VT to accustom; **assuefarsi** VPR: **assuefarsi a** to get used to, accustom o.s. to

assue'fatto, -a PP *di* **assuefare**

assuefazi'one [assuefat'tsjone] SF (*Med*) addiction

as'sumere /**12**/ VT (*impiegato*) to take on, engage; (*responsabilità*) to assume, take upon o.s.; (*contegno, espressione*) to assume, put on; (*droga*) to consume

as'sunsi *etc* VB *vedi* **assumere**

as'sunto, -a PP *di* **assumere** ▶ SM (*tesi*) proposition

assunzi'one [assun'tsjone] SF (*di impiegati*) employment, engagement; (*Rel*): **l'A~** the Assumption

assurdità SF INV absurdity; **dire delle** ~ to talk nonsense

as'surdo, -a AG absurd

'asta SF pole; (*modo di vendita*) auction

as'tante SM bystander

astan'teria SF casualty department

as'temio, -a AG teetotal ▶ SM/F teetotaller

aste'nersi /**121**/ VPR: ~ **(da)** to abstain (from), refrain (from); (*Pol*) to abstain (from)

astensi'one SF abstention

astensio'nista, -i, -e SM/F (Pol) abstentionist

aste'risco, -schi SM asterisk

aste'roide SM asteroid

'astice ['astit∫e] SM lobster

astigi'ano, -a [asti'dʒano] AG of (o from) Asti

astig'matico, -a, -ci, -che AG astigmatic

asti'nenza [asti'nɛntsa] SF abstinence;
essere in crisi di ~ to suffer from
withdrawal symptoms

'astio SM rancour, resentment

asti'oso, -a AG resentful

astrat'tismo SM (Arte) abstract art

as'tratto, -a AG abstract

astrin'gente [astrin'dʒɛnte] AG, SM
astringent

'astro SM star

'astro PREFISSO astro

astrolo'gia [astrolo'dʒia] SF astrology

astro'logico, -a, -ci, -che [astro'lɔdʒiko] AG
astrological

as'trologo, -a, -ghi, -ghe SM/F astrologer

astro'nauta, -i, -e SM/F astronaut

astro'nautica SF astronautics sg

astro'nave SF space ship

astrono'mia SF astronomy

astro'nomico, -a, -ci, -che AG
astronomic(al)

as'tronomo SM astronomer

as'truso, -a AG (discorso, ragionamento) abstruse

as'tuccio [as'tuttʃo] SM case, box, holder

as'tuto, -a AG astute, cunning, shrewd

as'tuzia [as'tuttsja] SF astuteness,
shrewdness; (azione) trick

AT SIGLA = **Asti**

ATA SIGLA F = **Associazione Turistica
Albergatori**

a'tavico, -a, -ci, -che AG atavistic

ate'ismo SM atheism

atelier [atə'lje] SM INV (laboratorio) workshop;
(studio) studio; (sartoria) fashion house

A'tene SF Athens

ate'neo SM university

ateni'ese AG, SMF Athenian

'ateo, -a AG, SM/F atheist

a'tipico, -a, -ci, -che AG atypical

at'lante SM atlas; **i Monti dell'A~** the Atlas
Mountains

at'lantico, -a, -ci, -che AG Atlantic ▶ SM:
l'A~, l'Oceano A~ the Atlantic, the Atlantic
Ocean

at'leta, -i, -e SM/F athlete

at'letica SF athletics sg; **~ leggera** track and
field events pl; **~ pesante** weightlifting and
wrestling

atmos'fera SF atmosphere

atmos'ferico, -a, -ci, -che AG atmospheric

a'tollo SM atoll

a'tomico, -a, -ci, -che AG atomic;
(nucleare) atomic, atom cpd, nuclear

atomizza'tore [atomiddza'tore] SM (di acqua,
lacca) spray; (di profumo) atomizer

'atomo SM atom

'atono, -a AG (Fonetica) unstressed

'atrio SM entrance hall, lobby

a'troce [a'trotʃe] AG (che provoca orrore)
dreadful; (terribile) atrocious

atrocità [atrotʃi'ta] SF INV atrocity

atro'fia SF atrophy

attacca'brighe [attakka'brige] SM INV/F INV
quarrelsome person

attacca'mento SM (fig) attachment,
affection

attac'cante SMF (Sport) forward

attacca'panni SM hook, peg; (mobile) hall
stand

attac'care /20/ VT (unire) to attach; (cucire) to
sew on; (far aderire) to stick (on); (appendere) to
hang (up); (assalire: anche fig) to attack;
(iniziare) to begin, start; (fig: contagiare) to pass
on ▶ VI to stick, adhere; **attaccarsi** VPR to
stick, adhere; (trasmettersi per contagio) to be
contagious; (afferrarsi) **attaccarsi (a)** to cling
(to); (fig: affezionarsi) **attaccarsi (a)** to become
attached (to); **~ discorso** to start a
conversation; **con me non attacca!** that
won't work with me!

attac'ticcio, -a, -ci, -ce [attakka'tittʃo] AG
sticky

attacca'tura SF (di manica) join; **~ (dei
capelli)** hairline

at'tacco, -chi SM (azione offensiva: anche fig)
attack; (Med) attack, fit; (Sci) binding; (Elettr)
socket; **~ informatico** cyber attack

attanagli'are [attanaʎ'ʎare] /27/ VT (anche fig)
to grip

attar'darsi /72/ VPR: **~ a fare qc** (fermarsi) to
stop to do sth; (stare più a lungo) to stay behind
to do sth

attec'chire [attek'kire] /55/ VI (pianta) to take
root; (fig) to catch on

atteggia'mento [atteddʒa'mento] SM
attitude

atteggi'arsi [atted'dʒarsi] /62/ VPR: **~ a** to
pose as

attem'pato, -a AG elderly

atten'dente SM (Mil) orderly, batman

at'tendere /120/ VT to wait for, await ▶ VI: **~ a**
to attend to

atten'dibile AG (scusa, storia) credible; (fonte,
testimone, notizia) reliable; (persona)
trustworthy

atte'nersi /121/ VPR: **~ a** to keep o stick to

atten'tare /72/ VI: **~ a** to make an attempt on

atten'tato SM attack; **~ alla vita di qn**
attempt on sb's life

attenta'tore, -'trice SM/F bomber; **~ suicida**
suicide bomber

at'tento, -a AG attentive; (*accurato*) careful, thorough ▶ ESCL be careful!; **stare ~ a qc** to pay attention to sth; **attenti!** (*Mil*) attention!; **attenti al cane** beware of the dog

attenu'ante SF (*Dir*) extenuating circumstance

attenu'are /**72**/ VT to alleviate, ease; (*diminuire*) to reduce; **attenuarsi** VPR to ease, abate

attenuazi'one [attenuat'tsjone] SF alleviation; easing; reduction

attenzi'one [atten'tsjone] SF attention ▶ ESCL watch out!, be careful!; **attenzioni** SFPL (*premure*) attentions; **fare ~ a** to watch out for; **coprire qn di attenzioni** to lavish attention on sb

atter'raggio [atter'raddʒo] SM landing; **~ di fortuna** emergency landing

atter'rare /**72**/ VT to bring down ▶ VI to land

atter'rire /**55**/ VT to terrify

at'tesa SF waiting; (*tempo trascorso aspettando*) wait; **essere in ~ di qc** to be waiting for sth; **in ~ di una vostra risposta** (*Comm*) awaiting your reply; **restiamo in ~ di Vostre ulteriori notizie** (*Comm*) we look forward to hearing (further) from you

at'tesi *etc* VB *vedi* **attendere**

at'teso, -a PP *di* **attendere**

attes'tare /**72**/ VT: **~ qc/che** to testify to sth/ (to the fact) that

attes'tato SM certificate

attestazi'one [attestat'tsjone] SF (*certificato*) certificate; (*dichiarazione*) statement

'attico, -ci SM attic

at'tiguo, -a AG adjacent, adjoining

attil'lato, -a AG (*vestito*) close-fitting, tight; (*persona*) dressed up

'attimo SM moment; **in un ~** in a moment

atti'nente AG: **~ a** relating to, concerning

atti'nenza [atti'nentsa] SF connection

at'tingere [at'tindʒere] /**37**/ VT: **~ a o da** (*acqua*) to draw from; (*denaro, notizie*) to obtain from

at'tinto, -a PP *di* **attingere**

atti'rare /**72**/ VT to attract; **attirarsi delle critiche** to incur criticism

atti'tudine SF (*disposizione*) aptitude; (*atteggiamento*) attitude

atti'vare /**72**/ VT to activate; (*far funzionare*) to set going, start

atti'vista, -i, -e SM/F activist

attività SF INV activity; (*Comm*) assets *pl*; **~ liquide** (*Comm*) liquid assets

at'tivo, -a AG active; (*Comm*) profit-making, credit *cpd* ▶ SM (*Comm*) assets *pl*; **in ~** in credit; **chiudere in ~** to show a profit; **avere qc al proprio ~** (*fig*) to have sth to one's credit

attiz'zare [attit'tsare] /**72**/ VT (*fuoco*) to poke; (*fig*) to stir up

attizza'toio [attittsa'tojo] SM poker

'atto, -a AG: **~ a** fit for, capable of ▶ SM act; (*azione, gesto*) action, act, deed; (*Dir: documento*) deed, document; **atti** SMPL (*di congressi ecc*) proceedings; **essere in ~** to be under way; **mettere in ~** to put into action; **fare ~ di fare qc** to make as if to do sth; **all'~ pratico** in practice; **dare ~ a qn di qc** to give sb credit for sth; **~ di nascita/morte** birth/ death certificate; **~ di proprietà** title deed; **~ pubblico** official document; **~ di vendita** bill of sale; **atti osceni (in luogo pubblico)** (*Dir*) indecent exposure; **atti verbali** transactions

at'tonito, -a AG dumbfounded, astonished

attorcigli'are [attortʃiʎ'ʎare] /**27**/ VT, **attorcigli'arsi** VPR to twist

at'tore, -'trice SM/F actor (actress)

attorni'are /**19**/ VT (*circondare*) to surround; **attorniarsi** VPR: **attorniarsi di** to surround o.s. with

at'torno AV round, around, about ▶ PREP: **~ a** round, around, about

attrac'care /**20**/ VT, VI (*Naut*) to dock, berth

at'tracco, -chi SM (*Naut: manovra*) docking, berthing; (: *luogo*) berth

at'trae *etc* VB *vedi* **attrarre**

attra'ente AG attractive

at'traggo *etc* VB *vedi* **attrarre**

at'trarre /**123**/ VT to attract

at'trassi *etc* VB *vedi* **attrarre**

attrat'tiva SF attraction, charm

at'tratto, -a PP *di* **attrarre**

attraversa'mento SM crossing; **~ pedonale** pedestrian crossing

attraver'sare /**72**/ VT to cross; (*città, bosco, fig: periodo*) to go through; (*fiume*) to run through

attra'verso PREP through; (*da una parte all'altra*) across

attrazi'one [attrat'tsjone] SF attraction

attrez'zare [attret'tsare] /**72**/ VT to equip; (*Naut*) to rig

attrezza'tura [attrettsa'tura] SF equipment *no pl*; rigging; **attrezzature per uffici** office equipment

at'trezzo [at'trettso] SM tool, instrument; (*Sport*) piece of equipment

attribu'ire /**55**/ VT: **~ qc a qn** (*assegnare*) to give o award sth to sb; (*quadro ecc*) to attribute sth to sb

attri'buto SM attribute

at'trice [at'tritʃe] SF *vedi* **attore**

at'trito SM (*anche fig*) friction

attu'abile AG feasible

attuabilità SF feasibility

attu'ale AG (*presente*) present; (*di attualità*) topical; (*che è in atto*) actual

attualità SF INV topicality; (*avvenimento*) current event; **notizie d'~** (*TV*) the news *sg*

attualiz'zare [attualid'dzare] /**72**/ VT to update, bring up to date

attual'mente AV at the moment, at present

attu'are /**72**/ VT to carry out; **attuarsi** VPR to be realized

attuazi'one [attuat'tsjone] SF carrying out

attu'tire /**55**/ VT to deaden, reduce; **attutirsi** VPR to die down

A.U. ABBR = **allievo ufficiale**

au'dace [au'datʃe] AG audacious, daring, bold; (*provocante*) provocative; (*sfacciato*) impudent, bold

au'dacia [au'datʃa] SF audacity, daring; boldness; provocativeness; impudence

'audio SM (*TV, Radio, Cine*) sound

audiocas'setta SF (*audio*) cassette

audio'leso, -a SM/F person who is hard of hearing

audiovi'sivo, -a AG audiovisual

audi'torio SM, **audi'torium** SM INV auditorium

audizi'one [audit'tsjone] SF hearing; (*Mus*) audition

'auge ['audʒe] SF (*della gloria, carriera*) height, peak; **essere in ~** to be at the top

augu'rale AG: **messaggio ~** greeting; **biglietto ~** greetings card

augu'rare /**72**/ VT to wish; **augurarsi qc** to hope for sth

au'gurio SM (*presagio*) omen; (*voto di benessere ecc*) (good) wish; **essere di buon/cattivo ~** to be of good omen/be ominous; **auguri** SMPL best wishes; **fare gli auguri a qn** to give sb one's best wishes; **tanti auguri!** best wishes!; (*per compleanno*) happy birthday!

'aula SF (*scolastica*) classroom; (*universitaria*) lecture theatre; (*di edificio pubblico*) hall; **~ magna** main hall; **~ del tribunale** courtroom

aumen'tare /**72**/ VT, VI to increase; **~ di peso** (*persona*) to put on weight; **la produzione è aumentata del 50%** production has increased by 50%

au'mento SM increase

'aureo, -a AG (*di oro*) gold *cpd*; (*fig: colore, periodo*) golden

au'reola SF halo

au'rora SF dawn

ausili'are AG, SM F auxiliary

au'silio SM aid

auspi'cabile AG desirable

auspi'care /**20**/ VT to call for, express a desire for

aus'picio [aus'pitʃo] SM omen; (*protezione*) patronage; **sotto gli auspici di** under the auspices of; **è di buon ~** it augurs well

austerità SF INV austerity

aus'tero, -a AG austere

aus'trale AG southern

Aus'tralia SF: **l'~** Australia

australi'ano, -a AG, SM/F Australian

'Austria SF: **l'~** Austria

aus'triaco, -a, -ci, -che AG, SM/F Austrian

au'tarchico, -a, -ci, -che [au'tarkiko] AG (*sistema*) self-sufficient, autarkic; (*prodotto*) home *cpd*, home-produced

'aut 'aut SM INV ultimatum

autenti'care /**20**/ VT to authenticate

autenticità [autentitʃi'ta] SF authenticity

au'tentico, -a, -ci, -che AG (*quadro, firma*) authentic, genuine; (*fatto*) true, genuine

au'tista, -i SM driver; (*personale*) chauffeur

'auto SF INV car; **~ blu** official car

autoabbron'zante AG self-tanning

autoade'sivo, -a AG self-adhesive ▶ SM sticker

autoartico'lato SM articulated lorry (BRIT), semi (trailer) (US)

autobiogra'fia SF autobiography

autobio'grafico, -a, -ci, -che AG autobiographic(al)

auto'blinda SF armoured (BRIT) o armored (US) car

auto'bomba SF INV car carrying a bomb; **l'~ si trovava a pochi metri** the car bomb was a few metres away

auto'botte SF tanker

'autobus SM INV bus

autocari'cabile AG: **scheda ~** top-up card

auto'carro SM lorry (BRIT), truck

autocertificazi'one [autotʃertifikat'tsjone] SF self-declaration

autocis'terna [autotʃis'terna] SF tanker

autoco'lonna SF convoy

autocon'trollo SM self-control

autocopia'tivo, -a AG: **carta autocopiativa** carbonless paper

autocorri'era SF coach, bus

auto'cratico, -a, -ci, -che AG autocratic

auto'critica, -che SF self-criticism

au'toctono, -a AG, SM/F native

autodemolizi'one [autodemolit'tsjone] SF breaker's yard (BRIT)

autodi'datta, -i, -e SM/F autodidact, self-taught person

autodi'fesa SF self-defence

autodistrut'tivo, -a AG self-destructive

autoferrotranvi'ario, -a AG public transport *cpd*

autogesti'one [autodʒes'tjone] SF worker management

autoges'tito, -a [autodʒes'tito] AG under worker management

auto'gol SM INV own goal

au'tografo, -a AG, SM autograph

auto'grill® SM INV motorway café (BRIT), roadside restaurant (US)

autoim'mune AG autoimmune

autolesio'nismo SM (fig) self-destruction; (Med) self-harm

auto'linea SF bus route

au'toma, -i SM automaton

auto'matico, -a, -ci, -che AG automatic ▶ SM (bottone) snap fastener; (fucile) automatic; **selezione automatica** (Tel) direct dialling

automazi'one [automat'tsjone] SF: **~ delle procedure d'ufficio** office automation

automedicazi'one [automedikat'tsjone] SF (medicine, farmaci): **medicinale di ~** self-medication

auto'mezzo [auto'mɛddzo] SM motor vehicle

auto'mobile SF (motor) car; **~ da corsa** racing car (BRIT), race car (US)

automobi'lismo SM (gen) motoring; (Sport) motor racing

automobi'lista, -i, -e SM/F motorist

automobi'listico, -a, -ci, -che AG car cpd (BRIT), automobile cpd (US); (sport) motor cpd

autono'leggio [autono'leddʒo] SM car hire (BRIT), car rental

autono'mia SF autonomy; (di volo) range

au'tonomo, -a AG autonomous; (sindacato, pensiero) independent

auto'parco, -chi SM (parcheggio) car park (BRIT), parking lot (US); (insieme di automezzi) transport fleet

auto'pompa SF fire engine

autop'sia SF post-mortem (examination), autopsy

auto'radio SF INV (apparecchio) car radio; (autoveicolo) radio car

au'tore, -'trice SM/F author; **l'~ del furto** the person who committed the robbery; **diritti d'~** copyright sg; (compenso) royalties

autoreg'gente [autored'dʒɛnte] AG: **calze autoreggenti** hold ups

autoregolamentazi'one [autoregolamentat'tsjone] SF self-regulation

auto'revole AG authoritative; (persona) influential

autoricari'cabile AG: **scheda ~** top-up card

autori'messa SF garage

autorità SF INV authority

autori'tratto SM self-portrait

autoriz'zare [autorid'dzare] /72/ VT (permettere) to authorize, give permission for; (giustificare) to allow, sanction

autorizzazi'one [autoriddzat'tsjone] SF authorization; **~ a procedere** (Dir) authorization to proceed

autos'catto SM (Fot) timer

autos'contro SM dodgem car (BRIT), bumper car (US)

autoscu'ola SF driving school

autosno'dato SM articulated vehicle

autos'tima SF self-esteem

autos'top SM hitchhiking

autostop'pista, -i, -e SM/F hitchhiker

autos'trada SF motorway (BRIT), highway (US); **~ informatica** information superhighway

> You have to pay to use Italian motorways. They are indicated by an A followed by a number on a green sign. The speed limit on Italian motorways is 130 kph.

autosuffici'ente [autosuffi'tʃɛnte] AG self-sufficient

autosuffici'enza [autosuffi'tʃɛntsa] SF self-sufficiency

auto'treno SM articulated lorry (BRIT), semi (trailer) (US)

autove'icolo SM motor vehicle

auto'velox® SM INV (police) speed camera

autovet'tura SF (motor) car

autun'nale AG (di autunno) autumn cpd; (da autunno) autumnal

au'tunno SM autumn

AV SIGLA = **Avellino**

aval'lare /72/ VT (Finanza) to guarantee; (fig: sostenere) to back; (: confermare) to confirm

a'vallo SM (Finanza) guarantee

avam'braccio [avam'brattʃo] (pl(f) **avambraccia**) SFPL forearm

avam'posto SM (Mil) outpost

A'vana SF: **l'~** Havana

a'vana SM INV (sigaro) Havana (cigar); (colore) Havana brown

avangu'ardia SF vanguard; (Arte) avant-garde

avansco'perta SF (Mil) reconnaissance; **andare in ~** to reconnoitre

a'vanti AV (stato in luogo) in front; (moto: andare, venire) forward; (tempo: prima) before ▶ PREP (luogo): **~ a** before, in front of; (tempo) **~ Cristo** before Christ ▶ ESCL (entrate) come (o go) in!; (Mil) forward!; (coraggio) come on! ▶ SM INV (Sport) forward; **il giorno ~** the day before; **~ e indietro** backwards and forwards; **andare ~** to go forward; (continuare) to go on; (precedere) to go (on) ahead; (orologio) to be fast; **essere ~ negli studi** to be well advanced with one's studies; **mandare ~ la famiglia** to provide for one's family; **mandare ~ un'azienda** to run a business; **~ il prossimo!** next please!

avan'treno SM (Aut) front chassis

avanza'mento [avantsa'mento] SM (gen) advance; (fig) progress; promotion

avan'zare [avan'tsare] /72/ VT (spostare in avanti) to move forward, advance; (domanda) to put forward; (promuovere) to promote; (essere creditore): **~ qc da qn** to be owed sth by sb ▶ vɪ (*andare avanti*) to move forward, advance; (*fig: progredire*) to make progress; (*essere d'avanzo*) to be left, remain; **basta e avanza** that's more than enough

avan'zato, -a [avan'tsato] ᴀɢ (*teoria, tecnica*) advanced ▶ sꜰ (*Mil*) advance; **in età avanzata** advanced in years, up in years

a'vanzo [a'vantso] sᴍ (*residuo*) remains *pl*, left-overs *pl*; (*Mat*) remainder; (*Comm*) surplus; (*eccedenza di bilancio*) profit carried forward; **averne d'~ di qc** to have more than enough of sth; **~ di cassa** cash in hand; **~ di galera** (*fig*) jailbird

ava'ria sꜰ (*guasto*) damage; (*: meccanico*) breakdown

avari'ato, -a ᴀɢ (*merce*) damaged; (*cibo*) off

ava'rizia [ava'rittsja] sꜰ avarice; **crepi l'~!** to hang with the expense!

a'varo, -a ᴀɢ avaricious, miserly ▶ sᴍ miser

a'vena sꜰ oats *pl*

──────────────
(PAROLA CHIAVE)
──────────────

a'vere /**13**/ sᴍ (*Comm*) credit; **gli averi** (*ricchezze*) wealth *sg*, possessions

▶ vᴛ **1** (*possedere*) to have; **ha due bambini/una bella casa** she has (got) two children/a lovely house; **ha i capelli lunghi** he has (got) long hair; **non ho da mangiare/bere** I've (got) nothing to eat/drink, I don't have anything to eat/drink

2 (*indossare*) to wear, have on; **aveva una maglietta rossa** he was wearing *o* he had on a red T-shirt; **ha gli occhiali** he wears *o* has glasses

3 (*ricevere*) to get; **hai avuto l'assegno?** did you get *o* have you had the cheque?

4 (*età, dimensione*) to be; **la stanza ha 3 metri di lunghezza** the room is 3 metres in length; **ha 9 anni** he is 9 (years old); *vedi* **fame; paura; sonno** *ecc*

5 (*tempo*): **quanti ne abbiamo oggi?** what's the date today?; **ne hai per molto?** will you be long?

6 (*fraseologia*): **avercela con qn** to be angry with sb; **cos'hai?** what's wrong *o* what's the matter (with you)?; **non ha niente a che vedere** *o* **fare con me** it's got nothing to do with me

▶ vʙ ᴀᴜx **1** to have; **aver bevuto/mangiato** to have drunk/eaten; **l'ho già visto** I have seen it already; **l'ho visto ieri** I saw it yesterday; **ci ha creduto?** did he believe it?

2 (+ *da* + *infinito*): **avere da fare qc** to have to do sth; **non ho niente da dire** I have nothing to say; **non hai che da chiederlo** you only have to ask him

avi'ario, -a ᴀɢ bird *cpd*; **influenza aviaria** bird flu

avia'tore, -'trice sᴍ/ꜰ aviator, pilot

aviazi'one [avjat'tsjone] sꜰ aviation; (*Mil*) air force; **~ civile** civil aviation

avicol'tura sꜰ bird breeding; (*di pollame*) poultry farming

avidità sꜰ eagerness; greed

'avido, -a ᴀɢ eager; (*peg*) greedy

avi'ere sᴍ (*Mil*) airman

avitami'nosi sꜰ vitamin deficiency

'avo sᴍ (*antenato*) ancestor; **i nostri avi** our ancestors

avo'cado sᴍ avocado

a'vorio sᴍ ivory

a'vulso, -a ᴀɢ: **parole avulse dal contesto** words out of context; **~ dalla società** (*fig*) cut off from society

Avv. ᴀʙʙʀ = **avvocato**

avva'lersi /**126**/ vᴘʀ: **~ di** to avail o.s. of

avvalla'mento sᴍ sinking *no pl*; (*effetto*) depression

avvalo'rare /**72**/ vᴛ to confirm

avvantaggi'are [avvantad'dʒare] /**62**/ vᴛ to favour (*Brit*), favor (*US*); **avvantaggiarsi** vᴘʀ (*trarre vantaggio*): **avvantaggiarsi di** to take advantage of; **avvantaggiarsi negli affari/sui concorrenti** (*prevalere*) to get ahead in business/of one's competitors

avve'dersi /**127**/ vᴘʀ: **~ di qn/qc** to notice sb/sth

avve'duto, -a ᴀɢ (*accorto*) prudent; (*scaltro*) astute

avvelena'mento sᴍ poisoning

avvele'nare /**72**/ vᴛ to poison

avve'nente ᴀɢ attractive, charming

avve'nenza [avve'nentsa] sꜰ good looks *pl*

av'vengo *etc* vʙ *vedi* **avvenire**

avveni'mento sᴍ event

avve'nire /**128**/ vɪ, vʙ ɪᴍᴘᴇʀs to happen, occur ▶ sᴍ future

av'venni *etc* vʙ *vedi* **avvenire**

avven'tarsi /**72**/ vᴘʀ: **~ su** *o* **contro qn/qc** to hurl o.s. *o* rush at sb/sth

avven'tato, -a ᴀɢ rash, reckless

avven'tizio, -a [avven'tittsjo] ᴀɢ (*impiegato*) temporary; (*guadagno*) casual

av'vento sᴍ advent, coming; (*Rel*): **l'A~** Advent

avven'tore sᴍ customer

avven'tura sꜰ adventure; (*amorosa*) affair; **avere spirito d'~** to be adventurous

avventu'rarsi /**72**/ vᴘʀ to venture

avventuri'ero, -a sᴍ/ꜰ adventurer (*adventuress*)

avventu'roso, -a ᴀɢ adventurous

avve'nuto, -a ᴘᴘ *di* **avvenire**

avve'rarsi /**72**/ vᴘʀ to come true

av'verbio sᴍ adverb

avverrò *etc* vʙ *vedi* **avvenire**

avver'sare /**72**/ vᴛ to oppose

avver'sario, -a AG opposing ▶ SM opponent, adversary

avversi'one SF aversion

avversità SF INV adversity, misfortune

av'verso, -a AG (*contrario*) contrary; (*sfavorevole*) unfavourable (BRIT), unfavorable (US)

avver'tenza [avver'tɛntsa] SF (*ammonimento*) warning; (*cautela*) care; (*premessa*) foreword; **avvertenze** SFPL (*istruzioni per l'uso*) instructions

avverti'mento SM warning

avver'tire /45/ VT (*avvisare*) to warn; (*rendere consapevole*) to inform, notify; (*percepire*) to feel

av'vezzo, -a [av'vettso] AG: ~ **a** used to

avvia'mento SM (*atto*) starting; (*effetto*) start; (*Aut*) starting; (: *dispositivo*) starter; (*Comm*) goodwill

avvi'are /60/ VT (*mettere sul cammino*) to direct; (*impresa, trattative*) to begin, start; (*motore*) to start; **avviarsi** VPR to set off, set out

avvicenda'mento [avvitʃenda'mento] SM alternation; (*Agr*) rotation; **c'è molto ~ di personale** there is a high turnover of staff

avvicen'dare [avvitʃen'dare] /72/ VT, **avvicen'darsi** VPR to alternate

avvicina'mento [avvitʃina'mento] SM approach

avvici'nare [avvitʃi'nare] /72/ VT to bring near; (*trattare con: persona*) to approach; **avvicinarsi** VPR: **avvicinarsi (a qn/qc)** to approach (sb/sth), draw near (to sb/sth); (*somigliare*) to be similar (to sb/sth), be close (to sb/sth)

avvi'lente AG (*umiliante*) humiliating; (*scoraggiante*) discouraging, disheartening

avvili'mento SM humiliation; disgrace; discouragement

avvi'lire /55/ VT (*umiliare*) to humiliate; (*degradare*) to disgrace; (*scoraggiare*) to dishearten, discourage; **avvilirsi** VPR (*abbattersi*) to lose heart

avvi'lito, -a AG discouraged

avvilup'pare /72/ VT (*avvolgere*) to wrap up; (*ingarbugliare*) to entangle

avvinaz'zato, -a [avvinat'tsato] AG drunk

avvin'cente [avvin'tʃɛnte] AG (*film, racconto*) enthralling

av'vincere [av'vintʃere] /129/ VT to charm, enthral

avvinghi'are [avvin'gjare] /19/ VT to clasp; **avvinghiarsi** VPR: **avvinghiarsi a** to cling to

av'vinsi etc VB vedi **avvincere**

av'vinto, -a PP di **avvincere**

av'vio SM start, beginning; **dare l'~ a qc** to start sth off; **prendere l'~** to get going, get under way

avvi'saglia [avvi'zaʎʎa] SF (*sintomo: di temporale ecc*) sign; (*di malattia*) manifestation, sign, symptom; (*scaramuccia*) skirmish

avvi'sare /72/ VT (*far sapere*) to inform; (*mettere in guardia*) to warn

avvisa'tore SM (*apparecchio d'allarme*) alarm; **~ acustico** horn; **~ d'incendio** fire alarm

av'viso SM warning; (*annuncio*) announcement; (*affisso*) notice; (*inserzione pubblicitaria*) advertisement; **a mio ~** in my opinion; **mettere qn sull'~** to put sb on their guard; **fino a nuovo ~** until further notice; **~ di chiamata** (*servizio*) call waiting; (*segnale*) call waiting signal; **~ di consegna/ spedizione** (*Comm*) delivery/consignment note; **~ di garanzia** (*Dir*) notification (*of impending investigation and of the right to name a defence laywer*); **~ di pagamento** (*Comm*) payment advice

avvista'mento SM sighting

avvis'tare /72/ VT to sight

avvi'tare /72/ VT to screw down (*o* in)

avviz'zire [avvit'tsire] /55/ VI to wither

avvo'cato, -'essa SM/F (*Dir*) barrister (BRIT), lawyer; (*fig*) defender, advocate; **~ del diavolo, fare l'~ del diavolo** to play devil's advocate; **~ difensore** counsel for the defence; **~ di parte civile** counsel for the plaintiff

av'volgere [av'vɔldʒere] /96/ VT to roll up; (*bobina*) to wind up; (*avviluppare*) to wrap up; **avvolgersi** VPR (*avvilupparsi*) to wrap o.s. up

avvol'gibile [avvol'dʒibile] SM roller blind (BRIT), blind

avvolgi'mento [avvoldʒi'mento] SM winding

av'volsi etc VB vedi **avvolgere**

av'volto, -a PP di **avvolgere**

avvol'toio SM vulture

aza'lea [addza'lea] SF azalea

Azerbaigi'an [addzɛrbai'dʒan] SM Azerbaijan

azerbaigi'ano, -a [addzɛrbai'dʒano] AG Azerbaijani ▶ SM/F (*abitante*) Azerbaijani ▶ SM (*Ling*) Azerbaijani

a'zero, -a [ad'dzɛro] SM/F Azeri

azi'enda [ad'dzjɛnda] SF business, firm, concern; **~ agricola** farm; **~ (autonoma) di soggiorno** tourist board; **~ a partecipazione statale** *business in which the State has a financial interest*; **aziende pubbliche** public corporations

azien'dale [addzjen'dale] AG company *cpd*; **organizzazione ~** business administration

azio'nare [attsjo'nare] /72/ VT to activate

azio'nario, -a [attsjo'narjo] AG share *cpd*; **capitale ~** share capital; **mercato ~** stock market

azi'one [at'tsjone] SF action; (*Comm*) share; **~ sindacale** industrial action; **azioni**

37

preferenziali preference shares (*Brit*), preferred stock *sg* (*US*)

azio'nista, -i, -e [attsjo'nista] sm/f (*Comm*) shareholder

a'zoto [ad'dzɔto] sm nitrogen

az'teco, -a, -ci, -che [as'tɛko] ag, sm/f Aztec

azzan'nare [attsan'nare] /**72**/ vt to sink one's teeth into

azzar'dare [addzar'dare] /**72**/ vt (*soldi, vita*) to risk, hazard; (*domanda, ipotesi*) to hazard, venture; **azzardarsi** vpr: **azzardarsi a fare** to dare (to) do

azzar'dato, -a [addzar'dato] ag (*impresa*) risky; (*risposta*) rash

az'zardo [ad'dzardo] sm risk; **gioco d'~** game of chance

azzec'care [attsek'kare] /**20**/ vt (*bersaglio*) to hit, strike; (*risposta, pronostico*) to get right; (*fig: indovinare*) to guess

azzera'mento [addzera'mento] sm (*Inform*) reset

azze'rare [addze'rare] /**72**/ vt (*Mat, Fisica*) to make equal to zero, reduce to zero; (*Tecn: strumento*) to (re)set to zero

'azzimo, -a ['addzimo] ag unleavened ▶ sm unleavened bread

azzop'pare [attsop'pare] /**72**/ vt to lame, make lame

Az'zorre [ad'dzorre] sfpl: **le ~** the Azores

azzuffarsi [attsuf'farsi] /**72**/ vpr to come to blows

az'zurro, -a [ad'dzurro] ag blue ▶ sm (*colore*) blue; **gli azzurri** (*Sport*) the Italian national team

azzur'rognolo, -a [addzur'roɲɲolo] ag bluish

Bb

B, b [bi] SM O F INV (*lettera*) B, b; **B come
Bologna** ≈ B for Benjamin (*BRIT*), ≈ B for
Baker (*US*)

BA SIGLA = **Bari**

ba'bau SM INV ogre, bogey man

bab'beo SM simpleton

'babbo SM (*col*) dad, daddy; **B~ Natale** Father
Christmas

bab'buccia, -ce [bab'buttʃa] SF slipper;
(*per neonati*) bootee

babbu'ino SM baboon

babilo'nese AG, SMF Babylonian

Babi'lonia SF Babylonia

ba'bordo SM (*Naut*) port side

baby'sitter ['beɪbɪsɪtəʳ] SM INV/F INV
baby-sitter

ba'cato, -a AG worm-eaten, rotten; (*fig:
mente*) diseased; (: *persona*) corrupt

'bacca, -che SF berry

baccalà SM dried salted cod; (*fig: peg*) dummy

bac'cano SM din, clamour (*BRIT*), clamor (*US*)

bac'cello [bat'tʃello] SM pod

bac'chetta [bak'ketta] SF (*verga*) stick, rod;
(*di direttore d'orchestra*) baton; (*di tamburo*)
drumstick; **comandare a ~** to rule with a
rod of iron; **~ magica** magic wand

ba'checa, -che [ba'kɛka] SF (*mobile*)
showcase, display case; (*Università, in ufficio*)
notice board (*BRIT*), bulletin board (*US*)

bacia'mano [batʃa'mano] SM: **fare il ~ a qn**
to kiss sb's hand

baci'are [ba'tʃare] /14/ VT to kiss; **baciarsi** VPR
to kiss (one another)

ba'cillo [ba'tʃillo] SM bacillus, germ

baci'nella [batʃi'nella] SF basin

ba'cino [ba'tʃino] SM basin; (*Mineralogia*)
field, bed; (*Anat*) pelvis; (*Naut*) dock;
~ carbonifero coalfield; **~ di carenaggio** dry
dock; **~ petrolifero** oilfield; **~ d'utenza**
catchment area

'bacio ['batʃo] SM kiss

'baco, -chi SM worm; **~ da seta** silkworm

'bada SF: **tenere qn a ~** (*tener d'occhio*) to keep
an eye on sb; (*tenere a distanza*) to hold sb at bay

ba'dante SMF care worker

ba'dare /72/ VI (*fare attenzione*) to take care, be
careful; **~ a** (*occuparsi di*) to look after, take
care of; (*dar ascolto*) to pay attention to; **è un
tipo che non bada a spese** money is no
object to him; **bada ai fatti tuoi!** mind your
own business!

ba'dia SF abbey

ba'dile SM shovel

'baffi SMPL moustache *sg*, mustache *sg* (*US*);
(*di animale*) whiskers; **leccarsi i ~** to lick
one's lips; **ridere sotto i ~** to laugh up one's
sleeve

bagagli'aio [bagaʎ'ʎajo] SM luggage van
(*BRIT*) o car (*US*); (*Aut*) boot (*BRIT*), trunk (*US*)

ba'gaglio [ba'gaʎʎo] SM luggage *no pl*,
baggage *no pl*; **fare/disfare i bagagli** to
pack/unpack; **~ a mano** hand luggage

bagat'tella SF trifle, trifling matter

Bag'dad SF Baghdad

baggia'nata [baddʒa'nata] SF foolish action;
dire baggianate to talk nonsense

bagli'ore [baʎ'ʎore] SM flash, dazzling light;
un ~ di speranza a (sudden) ray of hope

ba'gnante [baɲ'ɲante] SMF bather

ba'gnare [baɲ'ɲare] /15/ VT to wet; (*inzuppare*)
to soak; (*innaffiare*) to water; (*fiume*) to flow
through; (: *mare*) to wash, bathe; (*brindare*) to
drink to, toast; **bagnarsi** VPR to get wet; (*al
mare*) to go swimming o bathing; (*in vasca*) to
have a bath

ba'gnato, -a [baɲ'ɲato] AG wet; **era come un
pulcino ~** he looked like a drowned rat

ba'gnino [baɲ'ɲino] SM lifeguard

'bagno ['baɲɲo] SM bath; (*locale*) bathroom;
(*toilette*) toilet; **bagni** SMPL (*stabilimento*)
baths; **fare il ~** to have a bath; (*nel mare*) to go
swimming o bathing; **fare il ~ a qn** to give
sb a bath; **mettere a ~** to soak

bagnoma'ria [baɲɲoma'ria] SM: **cuocere a ~**
to cook in a double saucepan (*BRIT*) o double
boiler (*US*)

bagnoschi'uma [baɲɲo'skjuma] SM INV
bubble bath

Ba'hama [ba'ama] SFPL: **le ~** the Bahamas

Bah'rein [ba'rein] SM: **il ~** Bahrain o Bahrein

'baia SF bay

baio'netta SF bayonet

'baita SF mountain hut

balaus'trata SF balustrade

balbet'tare /72/ VI to stutter, stammer; (*bimbo*) to babble ▶ VT to stammer out

bal'buzie [bal'buttsje] SF stammer

balbuzi'ente [balbut'tsjɛnte] AG stuttering, stammering

Bal'cani SMPL: **i ~** the Balkans

bal'canico, -a, -ci, -che AG Balkan

bal'cone SM balcony

baldac'chino [baldak'kino] SM canopy; **letto a ~** four-poster (bed)

bal'danza [bal'dantsa] SF self-confidence; boldness

'baldo, -a AG bold, daring

bal'doria SF: **fare ~** to have a riotous time

Bale'ari SFPL: **le isole ~** the Balearic Islands

ba'lena SF whale

bale'nare /72/ VB IMPERS: **balena** there's lightning ▶ VI to flash; **mi balenò un'idea** an idea flashed through my mind

baleni'era SF (*per la caccia*) whaler, whaling ship

ba'leno SM flash of lightning; **in un ~** in a flash

ba'lera SF (*locale*) dance hall; (*pista*) dance floor

ba'lestra SF crossbow

'balia¹ SF wet-nurse; **~ asciutta** nanny

ba'lia² SF: **in ~ di** at the mercy of; **essere lasciato in ~ di se stesso** to be left to one's own devices

ba'lilla SM INV (*Storia*) *member of Fascist youth group*

ba'listico, -a, -ci, -che AG ballistic ▶ SF ballistics *sg*; **perito ~** ballistics expert

'balla SF (*di merci*) bale; (*fandonia*) (tall) story

bal'labile SM dance number, dance tune

bal'lare /72/ VT, VI to dance

bal'lata SF ballad

balla'toio SM (*terrazzina*) gallery

balle'rina SF dancer; ballet dancer; (*scarpa*) pump, ballet shoe; **~ di rivista** chorus girl

balle'rino SM dancer; ballet dancer

bal'letto SM ballet

'ballo SM dance; (*azione*) dancing *no pl*; **~ in maschera** o **mascherato** fancy-dress ball; **essere in ~** (*fig: persona*) to be involved; (: *cosa*) to be at stake; **tirare in ~ qc** to bring sth up, raise sth

ballot'taggio [ballot'taddʒo] SM (*Pol*) second ballot

balne'are AG seaside *cpd*; (*stagione*) bathing

ba'locco, -chi SM toy

ba'lordo, -a AG stupid, senseless

bal'samico, -a, -ci, -che AG (*aria, brezza*) balmy; **pomata balsamica** balsam

'balsamo SM (*aroma*) balsam; (*lenimento, fig*) balm; (*per capelli*) conditioner

'baltico, -a, -ci, -che AG Baltic; **il (mar) B~** the Baltic (Sea)

balu'ardo SM bulwark

'balza ['baltsa] SF (*dirupo*) crag; (*di stoffa*) frill

bal'zano, -a [bal'tsano] AG (*persona, idea*) queer, odd

bal'zare [bal'tsare] /72/ VI to bounce; (*lanciarsi*) to jump, leap; **la verità balza agli occhi** the truth of the matter is obvious

'balzo ['baltso] SM bounce; jump, leap; (*del terreno*) crag; **prendere la palla al ~** (*fig*) to seize one's opportunity

bam'bagia [bam'badʒa] SF (*ovatta*) cotton wool (BRIT), absorbent cotton (US); (*cascame*) cotton waste; **tenere qn nella ~** (*fig*) to mollycoddle sb

bam'bina SF *vedi* **bambino**

bambi'naia SF nanny, nurse(maid)

bam'bino, -a SM/F child; **fare il ~** to behave childishly

bam'boccio [bam'bɔttʃo] SM plump child; (*pupazzo*) rag doll

'bambola SF doll

bambo'lotto SM male doll

bambù SM bamboo

ba'nale AG banal, commonplace

banalità SF INV banality

ba'nana SF banana

ba'nano SM banana tree

'banca, -che SF bank; **~ d'affari** merchant bank; **~ (di) dati** data bank

banca'rella SF stall

ban'cario, -a AG banking, bank *cpd* ▶ SM bank clerk

banca'rotta SF bankruptcy; **fare ~** to go bankrupt

bancarotti'ere SM bankrupt

ban'chetto [ban'ketto] SM banquet

banchi'ere [ban'kjɛre] SM banker

ban'china [ban'kina] SF (*di porto*) quay; (*per pedoni, ciclisti*) path; (*di stazione*) platform; **~ cedevole** (*Aut*) soft verge (BRIT) o shoulder (US); **~ spartitraffico** (*Aut*) central reservation (BRIT), median (strip) (US)

ban'chisa [ban'kiza] SF pack ice

'banco, -chi SM bench; (*di negozio*) counter; (*di mercato*) stall; (*di officina*) (work)bench; (*Geo, banca*) bank; **sotto ~** under the counter; **tenere il ~** (*nei giochi*) to be (the) banker; **tener ~** (*fig*) to monopolize the conversation; **medicinali da ~** over-the-counter medicines; **~ di chiesa** pew; **~ di corallo** coral reef; **~ degli imputati** dock; **~ del Lotto** lottery-ticket office; **~ di prova** (*fig*) testing ground; **~ dei testimoni** witness

box (BRIT) o stand (US); ~ **dei pegni**
pawnshop; ~ **di nebbia** bank of fog

banco'giro [banko'dʒiro] SM credit transfer

'Bancomat® SM INV automated banking;
(tessera) cash card; (sportello automatico)
cashpoint

banco'nota SF banknote

'banda SF band; (di stoffa) band, stripe; (lato,
parte) side; (di calcolatore) tape; ~ **larga**
broadband; ~ **perforata** punch tape

banderu'ola SF (Meteor) weathercock,
weathervane; **essere una ~** (fig) to be fickle

bandi'era SF flag, banner; **battere ~ italiana**
(nave ecc) to fly the Italian flag; **cambiare ~**
(fig) to change sides; ~ **di comodo** flag of
convenience

ban'dire /55/ VT to proclaim; (esiliare) to exile;
(fig) to dispense with

ban'dito SM outlaw, bandit

bandi'tore SM (di aste) auctioneer

'bando SM proclamation; (esilio) exile,
banishment; **mettere al ~ qn** to exile sb;
(fig) to freeze sb out; ~ **alle ciance!** that's
enough talk!; ~ **di concorso** announcement
of a competition

'bandolo SM (di matassa) end; **trovare il ~
della matassa** (fig) to find the key to the
problem

Bang'kok [ban'kɔk] SF Bangkok

Bangla'desh [bangla'dɛʃ] SM: **il ~** Bangladesh

bar SM INV bar

'bara SF coffin

ba'racca, -che SF shed, hut; (peg) hovel;
mandare avanti la ~ to keep things going;
piantare ~ e burattini to throw everything up

barac'cato, -a SM/F person living in temporary
camp

barac'chino [barak'kino] SM (chiosco) stall;
(apparecchio) CB radio

barac'cone SM booth, stall; **baracconi** SMPL
(luna park) funfair sg (BRIT), amusement park;
fenomeno da ~ circus freak

barac'copoli SF INV shanty town

bara'onda SF hubbub, bustle

ba'rare /72/ VI to cheat

'baratro SM abyss

barat'tare /72/ VT: ~ **qc con** to barter sth for,
swap sth for

ba'ratto SM barter

ba'rattolo SM (di latta) tin; (di vetro) jar; (di
coccio) pot

'barba SF beard; **farsi la ~** to shave; **farla in ~
a qn** (fig) to do sth to sb's face; **servire qn di
~ e capelli** (fig) to teach sb a lesson; **che ~!**
what a bore!

barbabi'etola SF beetroot (BRIT), beet (US);
~ **da zucchero** sugar beet

Bar'bados SF Barbados

bar'barico, -a, -ci, -che AG (invasione)
barbarian; (usanze, metodi) barbaric

bar'barie SF barbarity

'barbaro, -a AG barbarous ▶ SM barbarian;
i Barbari the Barbarians

'barbecue ['ba:bikju:] SM INV barbecue

barbi'ere SM barber

barbi'turico, -a, -ci, -che AG barbituric
▶ SM barbiturate

bar'bone SM (cane) poodle; (vagabondo) tramp

bar'buto, -a AG bearded

'barca, -che SF boat; **una ~ di** (fig) heaps of,
tons of; **mandare avanti la ~** (fig) to keep
things going; ~ **a motore** motorboat; ~ **a
remi** rowing boat (BRIT), rowboat (US); ~ **a
vela** sailing boat (BRIT), sailboat (US)

barcai'olo SM boatman

barcame'narsi /72/ VPR (nel lavoro) to get by;
(a parole) to beat about the bush

Barcel'lona [bartʃel'lona] SF Barcelona

barcol'lare /72/ VI to stagger

bar'cone SM (per ponti di barche) pontoon

ba'rella SF (lettiga) stretcher

'Barents: il mar di ~ SM the Barents Sea

ba'rese AG of (o from) Bari

bari'centro [bari'tʃentro] SM centre (BRIT) o
center (US) of gravity

ba'rile SM barrel, cask

ba'rista, -i, -e SM/F barman (barmaid);
(proprietario) bar owner

ba'ritono SM baritone

bar'lume SM glimmer, gleam

'baro SM (Carte) cardsharp

ba'rocco, -a, -chi, -che AG, SM baroque

ba'rometro SM barometer

ba'rone SM baron; **i baroni della medicina**
(fig: peg) the top brass in the medical faculty

baro'nessa SF baroness

'barra SF bar; (Naut) helm; (linea grafica) line,
stroke

bar'rare /72/ VT to bar

barri'care /20/ VT to barricade; **barricarsi** VPR
to barricade o.s.

barri'cata SF barricade; **essere dall'altra
parte della ~** (fig) to be on the other side of
the fence

barri'era SF barrier; (Geo) reef; **la Grande B~
Corallina** the Great Barrier Reef

bar'roccio [bar'rɔttʃo] SM cart

ba'ruffa SF scuffle; **fare ~** to squabble

barzel'letta [bardzel'letta] SF joke, funny story

basa'mento SM (parte inferiore, piedestallo) base;
(Tecn) bed, base plate

ba'sare /72/ VT to base, found; **basarsi** VPR:
basarsi su (fatti, prove) to be based o founded
on; (persona) to base one's arguments on

'basco, -a, -schi, -sche AG Basque ▶ SM/F
Basque ▶ SM (lingua) Basque; (copricapo) beret

bas'culla SF weighing machine,
weighbridge

'**base** SF base; (fig: fondamento) basis; (Pol) rank and file; **di** ~ basic; **in** ~ **a** on the basis of, according to; **in** ~ **a ciò** ... on that basis ...; **a** ~ **di caffè** coffee-based; **essere alla** ~ **di qc** to be at the root of sth; **gettare le basi per qc** to lay the basis o foundations for sth; **avere buone basi** (Ins) to have a sound educational background

'**baseball** ['beisbɔ:l] SM baseball

ba'**setta** SF sideburn

basi'**lare** AG basic, fundamental

Basi'lea SF Basle

ba'**silica, -che** SF basilica

ba'**silico** SM basil

'**basket** ['basket] SM basketball

bas'**sezza** [bas'settsa] SF (d'animo, di sentimenti) baseness; (azione) base action

bas'**sista, -i, -e** SM/F bass player

'**basso, -a** AG low; (di statura) short; (meridionale) southern ▶ SM bottom, lower part; (Mus) bass; **a occhi bassi** with eyes lowered; **a** ~ **prezzo** cheap; **scendere da** ~ to go downstairs; **cadere in** ~ (fig) to come down in the world; **la bassa Italia** southern Italy; **il** ~ **Medioevo** the late Middle Ages

basso'**fondo** (pl **bassifondi**) SM (Geo) shallows pl; **i bassifondi (della città)** the seediest parts of the town

bassorili'**evo** SM bas-relief

bas'**sotto, -a** AG squat ▶ SM (cane) dachshund

'**basta** ESCL (that's) enough!, that will do!

bas'**tardo, -a** AG (animale, pianta) hybrid, crossbreed; (persona) illegitimate, bastard (peg) ▶ SM/F illegitimate child, bastard (peg); (cane) mongrel

bas'**tare** /72/ VI, VB IMPERS to be enough, be sufficient; ~ **a qn** to be enough for sb; ~ **a se stesso** to be self-sufficient; **basta chiedere** o **basta chieda a un vigile** you have only to o need only ask a policeman; **basti dire che** ... suffice it to say that ...; **basta!** that's enough!, that will do!; **basta così?** (al bar ecc) will that be all?; **basta così, grazie** that's enough, thanks; **punto e basta!** and that's that!

basti'**an** SM: ~ **contrario** awkward customer

basti'**mento** SM ship, vessel

basti'**one** SM bastion

basto'**nare** /72/ VT to beat, thrash; **avere l'aria di un cane bastonato** to look crestfallen

basto'**nata** SF blow (with a stick); **prendere qn a bastonate** to give sb a good beating

baston'**cino** [baston'tʃino] SM (piccolo bastone) small stick; (Tecn) rod; (Sci) ski pole; **bastoncini di pesce** (Cuc) fish fingers (BRIT), fish sticks (US)

bas'**tone** SM stick; **bastoni** SMPL (Carte) suit in Neapolitan pack of cards; ~ **da passeggio** walking stick; **mettere i bastoni fra le ruote a qn** to put a spoke in sb's wheel

bat'**tage** [ba'taʒ] SM INV: ~ **promozionale** o **pubblicitario** publicity campaign

bat'**taglia** [bat'taʎʎa] SF battle; fight

bat'**taglio** [bat'taʎʎo] SM (di campana) clapper; (di porta) knocker

battagli'**one** [battaʎ'ʎone] SM battalion

bat'**tello** SM boat

bat'**tente** SM (imposta: di porta) wing, flap; (: di finestra) shutter; (batacchio: di porta) knocker; (: di orologio) hammer; **chiudere i battenti** (fig) to shut up shop

'**battere** /1/ VT to beat; (grano) to thresh; (percorrere) to scour; (rintoccare: le ore) to strike ▶ VI (bussare) to knock; (pioggia, sole) to beat down; (cuore) to beat; (Tennis) to serve; (urtare): ~ **contro** to hit o strike against; **battersi** VPR to fight; ~ **le mani** to clap; ~ **i piedi** to stamp one's feet; ~ **su un argomento** to hammer home an argument; ~ **a macchina** to type; ~ **bandiera italiana** to fly the Italian flag; ~ **il marciapiede** (peg) to walk the streets, be on the game; ~ **un rigore** (Calcio) to take a penalty; ~ **in testa** (Aut) to knock; **in un batter d'occhio** in the twinkling of an eye; **senza** ~ **ciglio** without batting an eyelid; **battersela** to run off

batte'**ria** SF battery; (Mus) drums pl; ~ **da cucina** pots and pans pl

bat'**terio** SM bacterium; **batteri** SMPL bacteria

batteriolo'**gia** [batterjolo'dʒia] SF bacteriology

batte'**rista, -i, -e** SM/F drummer

bat'**tesimo** SM (sacramento) baptism; (rito) baptism; christening; **tenere qn a** ~ to be godfather (o godmother) to sb

battez'**zare** [batted'dzare] /72/ VT to baptize; to christen

battiba'**leno** SM: **in un** ~ in a flash

batti'**becco, -chi** SM squabble

batticu'**ore** SM palpitations pl; **avere il** ~ to be frightened to death

bat'**tigia** [bat'tidʒa] SF water's edge

batti'**mano** SM applause

batti'**panni** SM INV carpet-beater

battis'**tero** SM baptistry

battis'**trada** SM INV (di pneumatico) tread; (di gara) pacemaker

battitap'**peto** SM INV upright vacuum cleaner

'**battito** SM beat, throb; ~ **cardiaco** heartbeat; ~ **della pioggia/dell'orologio** beating of the rain/ticking of the clock

batti'**tore** SM (Cricket) batsman; (Baseball) batter; (Caccia) beater

batti'**tura** SF (anche: **battitura a macchina**) typing (del grano) threshing

bat'tuta SF blow; (*di macchina da scrivere*) stroke; (*Mus*) bar; beat; (*Teat*) cue; (*frase spiritosa*) witty remark; (*di caccia*) beating; (*Polizia*) combing, scouring; (*Tennis*) service; **fare una ~** to crack a joke, make a witty remark; **aver la ~ pronta** (*fig*) to have a ready answer; **è ancora alle prime battute** it's just started
ba'tuffolo SM wad
ba'ule SM trunk; (*Aut*) boot (BRIT), trunk (US)
bau'xite [bauk'site] SF bauxite
'bava SF (*di animale*) slaver, slobber; (*di lumaca*) slime; (*di vento*) breath
bava'glino [bavaʎ'ʎino] SM bib
ba'vaglio [ba'vaʎʎo] SM gag
bava'rese AG, SMF Bavarian
'bavero SM collar
Bavi'era SF Bavaria
ba'zar [bad'dzar] SM INV bazaar
baz'zecola [bad'dzekola] SF trifle
bazzi'care [battsi'kare] /20/ VT (*persona*) to hang about with; (*posto*) to hang about with ▶ VI: **~ in/con** to hang about/hang about with
BCE SIGLA F (= *Banca centrale europea*) ECB
be'arsi /72/ VPR: **~ di qc/a fare qc** to delight in sth/in doing sth; **~ alla vista di** to enjoy looking at
beati'tudine SF bliss
be'ato, -a AG blessed; (*fig*) happy; **~ te!** lucky you!
bebè SM INV baby
bec'caccia, -ce [bek'kattʃa] SF woodcock
bec'care /20/ VT to peck; (*fig: raffreddore*) to catch, pick up; **beccarsi** VPR (*fig*) to squabble; **beccarsi qc** to catch sth
bec'cata SF peck
beccheggi'are [bekked'dʒare] /62/ VI to pitch
becche'rò etc [bekke'rɔ] VB vedi **beccare**
bec'chime [bek'kime] SM birdseed
bec'chino [bek'kino] SM gravedigger
'becco, -chi SM beak, bill; (*di caffettiera ecc*) spout; lip; (*fig: col*) cuckold; **mettere ~** (*col*) to butt in; **chiudi il ~!** (*col*) shut your mouth!, shut your trap!; **non ho il ~ di un quattrino** (*col*) I'm broke
Be'fana SF old woman who, according to legend, brings children their presents at the Epiphany; (*Epifania*) Epiphany; (*donna brutta*): **befana** hag, witch; *see note*

> Marking the end of the traditional 12 days of Christmas on 6 January, the *Befana*, or the feast of the Epiphany, is a national holiday in Italy. It is named after the old woman who, legend has it, comes down the chimney the night before, bringing gifts to children who have been good during the year and leaving lumps of coal for those who have not.

'beffa SF practical joke; **farsi ~ o beffe di qn** to make a fool of sb
bef'fardo, -a AG scornful, mocking
bef'fare /72/ VT (*anche:* **beffarsi di**) to make a fool of, mock
'bega, -ghe SF quarrel
'begli ['beʎʎi], **'bei** AG vedi **bello**
beige [bɛʒ] AG INV beige
Bei'rut SF Beirut
bel AG vedi **bello**
be'lare /72/ VI to bleat
be'lato SM bleating
'belga, -gi, -ghe AG, SM/F Belgian
'Belgio ['bɛldʒo] SM: **il ~** Belgium
Bel'grado SF Belgrade
'bella SF (*Sport*) decider; *vedi* **bello**
bel'lezza [bel'lettsa] SF beauty; **chiudere** o **finire qc in ~** to finish sth with a flourish; **che ~!** fantastic!; **ho pagato la ~ di 300 euro** I paid 300 euro, no less
belli'coso, -a AG warlike
bellige'rante [bellidʒe'rante] AG belligerent
bellim'busto SM dandy

(PAROLA CHIAVE)

'bello, -a (*ag: dav sm* **bel** + C, **bell'** + V, **bello** + *s impura, gn, pn, ps, x, z, pl* **bei** + C, **begli** + *s impura ecc o* V) AG **1** (*oggetto, donna, paesaggio*) beautiful, lovely; (*uomo*) handsome; (*tempo*) beautiful, fine, lovely; **farsi bello di qc** to show off about sth; **fare la bella vita** to have an easy life; **le belle arti** fine arts
2 (*quantità*): **una bella cifra** a considerable sum of money; **un bel niente** absolutely nothing
3 (*rafforzativo*): **è una truffa bella e buona!** it's a real fraud!; **oh bella!, anche questa è bella!** (*ironico*) that's nice!; **è bell'e finito** it's already finished
▶ SM/F (*innamorato*) sweetheart
▶ SM **1** (*bellezza*) beauty; (*tempo*) fine weather
2: adesso viene il bello now comes the best bit; **sul più bello** at the crucial point; **cosa fai di bello?** are you doing anything interesting?
▶ SF **1** (*anche:* **bella copia**) fair copy
2 (*Sport, Carte*) decider
▶ AV: **fa bello** the weather is fine, it's fine; **alla bell'e meglio** somehow or other

bellu'nese AG of (o from) Belluno
'belva SF wild animal
belve'dere SM INV panoramic viewpoint
benché [ben'ke] CONG although
'benda SF bandage; (*per gli occhi*) blindfold
ben'daggio [ben'daddʒo] SM bandages; **fare un ~ a qc** to bandage sth up; **~ gastrico** gastric band surgery
ben'dare /72/ VT to bandage; to blindfold

bendis'posto, -a AG: ~ **a qn/qc** well disposed towards sb/sth

'**bene** AV well; *(completamente, affatto)*: **è ben difficile** it's very difficult ▶ AG INV: **gente ~** well-to-do people ▶ SM good; *(Comm)* asset; **beni** SMPL *(averi)* property *sg*, estate *sg*; **io sto ~/poco ~** I'm well/not very well; **va ~** all right; **ben più lungo/caro** much longer/more expensive; **lo spero ~** I certainly hope so; **volere un ~ dell'anima a qn** to love sb very much; **un uomo per ~** a respectable man; **fare ~** to do the right thing; **fare ~ a** *(salute)* to be good for; **fare del ~ a qn** to do sb a good turn; **di ~ in meglio** better and better; **beni ambientali** environmental assets; **beni di consumo** consumer goods; **beni di consumo durevole** consumer durables; **beni culturali** cultural heritage; **beni immateriali** immaterial *o* intangible assets; **beni patrimoniali** fixed assets; **beni privati** private property *sg*; **beni pubblici** public property *sg*; **beni reali** tangible assets

bene'detto, -a PP *di* **benedire** ▶ AG blessed, holy

bene'dire /38/ VT to bless; to consecrate; **l'ho mandato a farsi ~** *(fig)* I told him to go to hell

benedizi'one [benedit'tsjone] SF blessing

benedu'cato, -a AG well-mannered

benefat'tore, -'trice SM/F benefactor (benefactress)

benefi'cenza [benefi'tʃɛntsa] SF charity

benefici'are [benefi'tʃare] **/14/** VI: ~ **di** to benefit by, benefit from

benefici'ario, -a [benefi'tʃarjo] AG, SM/F beneficiary

bene'ficio [bene'fitʃo] SM benefit; **con ~ d'inventario** *(fig)* with reservations

be'nefico, -a, -ci, -che AG beneficial; charitable

'**Benelux** SM: **il ~** Benelux, the Benelux countries

beneme'renza [beneme'rɛntsa] SF merit

bene'merito, -a AG meritorious

bene'placito [bene'platʃito] SM *(approvazione)* approval; *(permesso)* permission

be'nessere SM well-being

benes'tante AG well-to-do

benes'tare SM consent, approval

benevo'lenza [benevo'lɛntsa] SF benevolence

be'nevolo, -a AG benevolent

ben'godi SM land of plenty

benia'mino, -a SM/F favourite (BRIT), favorite (US)

be'nigno, -a [be'niɲɲo] AG kind, kindly; *(critica ecc)* favourable (BRIT), favorable (US); *(Med)* benign

benintenzio'nato, -a [benintentsjo'nato] AG well-meaning

benin'teso AV of course; ~ **che** *cong* provided that

benpen'sante SMF conformist

benser'vito SM: **dare il ~ a qn** *(sul lavoro)* to give sb the sack, fire sb; *(fig)* to send sb packing

bensì CONG but (rather)

benve'nuto, -a AG, SM welcome; **dare il ~ a qn** to welcome sb

ben'visto, -a AG: **essere ~ (da)** to be well thought of (by)

benvo'lere /131/ VT: **farsi ~ da tutti** to win everybody's affection; **prendere a ~ qn/qc** to take a liking to sb/sth

ben'zina [ben'dzina] SF petrol (BRIT), gas (US); **fare ~** to get petrol *o* gas; **rimanere senza ~** to run out of petrol *o* gas; ~ **verde** unleaded petrol, lead-free petrol

benzi'naio [bendzi'najo] SM petrol (BRIT) *o* gas (US) pump attendant

be'one SM heavy drinker

'**bere /16/** VT to drink; *(assorbire)* to soak up; **darla a ~ a qn** *(fig)* to fool sb; **questa volta non me la dai a ~!** I won't be taken in this time!

berga'masco, -a, -schi, -sche AG of *(o* from*)* Bergamo

'**Bering** ['beriŋ]: **il mar di ~** *sm* the Bering Sea

ber'lina SF *(Aut)* saloon (car) (BRIT), sedan (US); **mettere alla ~** *(fig)* to hold up to ridicule

Ber'lino SF Berlin; ~ **est/ovest** East/West Berlin

Ber'muda SFPL: **le ~** Bermuda *sg*

ber'muda SMPL *(calzoncini)* Bermuda shorts

'**Berna** SF Bern

ber'noccolo SM bump; *(inclinazione)* flair

ber'retto SM cap

berrò *etc* VB *vedi* **bere**

bersagli'are [bersaʎ'ʎare] **/27/** VT to shoot at; *(colpire ripetutamente, fig)* to bombard; **bersagliato dalla sfortuna** dogged by ill fortune

bersagli'ere [bersaʎ'ʎɛre] SM *member of rifle regiment in Italian army*

ber'saglio [ber'saʎʎo] SM target

bescia'mella [beʃʃa'mɛlla] SF béchamel sauce

bes'temmia SF curse; *(Rel)* blasphemy

bestemmi'are /19/ VI to curse, swear; to blaspheme ▶ VT to curse, swear at; to blaspheme; ~ **come un turco** to swear like a trooper

'**bestia** SF animal; **lavorare come una ~** to work like a dog; **andare in ~** *(fig)* to fly into a rage; **una ~ rara** *(fig: persona)* an oddball; ~ **da soma** beast of burden

besti'ale AG beastly; animal *cpd*; *(col)*: **fa un**

caldo ~ it's terribly hot; **fa un freddo** ~ it's bitterly cold

bestialità SF INV (*qualità*) bestiality; **dire/ fare una** ~ **dopo l'altra** to say/do one idiotic thing after another

besti'ame SM livestock; (*bovino*) cattle *pl*

Bet'lemme SF Bethlehem

betoni'era SF cement mixer

'bettola SF (*peg*) dive

be'tulla SF birch

be'vanda SF drink, beverage; ~ **energetica** energy drink

bevi'tore, -'trice SM/F drinker

'bevo *etc* VB *vedi* **bere**

be'vuto, -a PP *di* **bere** ▶ SF drink

'bevvi *etc* VB *vedi* **bere**

BG SIGLA = **Bergamo**

BI SIGLA F = **Banca d'Italia** ▶ SIGLA = **Biella**

bi'ada SF fodder

bianche'ria [bjanke'ria] SF linen; ~ **intima** underwear; ~ **da donna** ladies' underwear, lingerie; ~ **femminile** lingerie

bi'anco, -a, -chi, -che AG white; (*non scritto*) blank ▶ SM white; (*intonaco*) whitewash ▶ SM/F white, white man(-woman); **in ~** (*foglio, assegno*) blank; **in ~ e nero** (TV, *Fot*) black and white; **mangiare in ~** to follow a bland diet; **pesce in ~** boiled fish; **andare in ~** (*non riuscire*) to fail; (*in amore*) to be rejected; **notte bianca** *o* **in ~** sleepless night; **voce bianca** (*Mus*) treble (voice); **votare scheda bianca** to return a blank voting slip; ~ **dell'uovo** egg-white

bianco'segno [bjanko'seɲɲo] SM signature to a blank document

biancos'pino SM hawthorn

biasci'care [bjaʃʃi'kare] /**20**/ VT to mumble

biasi'mare /**72**/ VT to disapprove of, censure

bi'asimo SM disapproval, censure

'bibbia SF (*anche fig*) bible

bibe'ron SM INV feeding bottle

'bibita SF (*soft*) drink

bibliogra'fia SF bibliography

biblio'teca, -che SF library; (*mobile*) bookcase

bibliote'cario, -a SM/F librarian

bicame'rale AG (*Pol*) two-chamber *cpd*

bicarbo'nato SM: ~ **(di sodio)** bicarbonate (of soda)

bicchi'ere [bik'kjɛre] SM glass; **è (facile) come bere un bicchier d'acqua** it's as easy as pie

bici'cletta [bitʃi'kletta] SF bicycle; **andare in** ~ to cycle

bi'cipite [bi'tʃipite] SM bicep

bidè SM INV bidet

bi'dello, -a SM/F (*Ins*) janitor

bi'det SM INV = **bidè**

bidirezio'nale [bidirettsjo'nale] AG bidirectional

bido'nare /**72**/ VT (*col: piantare in asso*) to let down; (: *imbrogliare*) to cheat, swindle

bido'nata SF (*col*) swindle

bi'done SM drum, can; (*anche:* **bidone dell'immondizia**) (dust)bin; (*col: truffa*) swindle; **fare un ~ a qn** (*col*) to let sb down; to cheat sb

bidon'ville [bidɔ'vil] SF INV shanty town

bi'eco, -a, -chi, -che AG sinister

bi'ella SF (*Tecn*) connecting rod

Bielo'russia SF Belarus, Belorussia

bielo'russo, -a AG, SM/F Belarussian, Belorussian

bien'nale AG biennial ▶ SF: **la B~ di Venezia** the Venice Arts Festival; *see note*

> Dating back to 1895, the *Biennale di Venezia* is an international festival of the contemporary arts. It takes place every two years in the *Giardini Pubblici*. The various countries taking part each put on exhibitions in their own pavilions. There is a section dedicated to the work of young artists, as well as a special exhibition organized around a specific theme for that year.

bi'ennio SM period of two years

bi'erre SM F *member of the Red Brigades*

bi'etola SF beet

bifami'liare AG (*villa, casetta*) semi-detached

bifo'cale AG bifocal

bi'folco, -a, -chi, -che SM/F (*peg*) bumpkin

'bifora SF (*Archit*) mullioned window

bifor'carsi /**20**/ VPR to fork

biforcazi'one [biforkat'tsjone] SF fork

bifor'cuto, -a AG (*anche fig*) forked

biga'mia SF bigamy

'bigamo, -a AG bigamous ▶ SM/F bigamist

bighello'nare [bigello'nare] /**72**/ VI to loaf (about)

bighel'lone, -a [bigel'lone] SM/F loafer

bigiotte'ria [bidʒotte'ria] SF costume jewellery (BRIT) *o* jewelry (US); (*negozio*) jeweller's (shop) (BRIT) *o* jewelry store (US: *selling only costume jewellery*)

bigli'ardo [biʎ'ʎardo] SM = **biliardo**

bigliet'taio, -a [biʎʎet'tajo] SM/F (*nei treni*) ticket inspector; (*in autobus ecc*) conductor (conductress); (*Cine, Teat*) box-office attendant

bigliette'ria [biʎʎette'ria] SF (*di stazione*) ticket office; booking office; (*di teatro*) box office

bigli'etto [biʎ'ʎetto] SM (*per viaggi, spettacoli ecc*) ticket; (*cartoncino*) card; ~ **di banca** (bank)note; (*anche:* **biglietto d'auguri/da visita**) greetings/visiting card; ~ **di andata e ritorno** return (BRIT) *o* round-trip (US) ticket; ~ **di sola andata** single (ticket); ~ **elettronico** e-ticket; ~ **omaggio** complimentary ticket

45

bignè [biɲˈɲɛ] SM INV cream puff
bigo'dino SM roller, curler
bi'gotto, -a AG over-pious ▶ SM/F church fiend
bi'kini SM INV bikini
bi'lancia, -ce [biˈlantʃa] SF (*pesa*) scales *pl*; (: *di precisione*) balance; **B~** Libra; **essere della B~** to be Libra; **~ commerciale/dei pagamenti** balance of trade/payments
bilanci'are [bilanˈtʃare] /**14**/ VT (*pesare*) to weigh; (: *fig*) to weigh up; **~ le uscite e le entrate** (*Comm*) to balance expenditure and revenue
bi'lancio [biˈlantʃo] SM (*Comm*) balance (sheet); (*statale*) budget; **far quadrare il ~** to balance the books; **chiudere il ~ in attivo/ passivo** to make a profit/loss; **fare il ~ di** (*fig*) to assess; **~ consolidato** consolidated balance; **~ consuntivo** (final) balance; **~ preventivo** budget; **~ pubblico** national budget; **~ di verifica** trial balance
bilate'rale AG bilateral
'bile SF bile; (*fig*) rage, anger
biliar'dino SM pinball
bili'ardo SM billiards *sg*; (*tavolo*) billiard table
'bilico, -chi SM: **essere in ~** to be balanced; (*fig*) to be undecided; **tenere qn in ~** to keep sb in suspense
bi'lingue AG bilingual
bili'one SM (*mille milioni*) thousand million, billion (US); (*milione di milioni*) billion (BRIT), trillion (US)
bilo'cale SM two-room flat (BRIT) *o* apartment (US)
'bimbo, -a SM/F little boy (girl)
bimen'sile AG fortnightly
bimes'trale AG two-monthly, bimonthly
bi'mestre SM two-month period; **ogni ~** every two months
bi'nario, -a AG (*sistema*) binary ▶ SM (railway) track *o* line; (*piattaforma*) platform; **~ morto** dead-end track
bi'nocolo SM binoculars *pl*
bio... PREFISSO bio
biocarbu'rante SM biofuel
bio'chimica [bioˈkimika] SF biochemistry
biodegra'dabile AG biodegradable
bio'diesel [bioˈdizel] SM INV biodiesel
biodi'namico, -a, -ci, -che AG biodynamic
biodiversità SF biodiversity
bio'etica SF bioethics *sg*
bio'etico, -a, -ci, -che AG bioethical
bio'fabbrica SF *factory producing biological control agents*
bio'fisica SF biophysics *sg*
biogra'fia SF biography
bio'grafico, -a, -ci, -che AG biographical
bi'ografo, -a SM/F biographer
biolo'gia [biologˈdʒia] SF biology

bio'logico, -a, -ci, -che [bioˈlɔdʒiko] AG (*scienze, fenomeni ecc*) biological; (*agricoltura, prodotti*) organic; **guerra biologica** biological warfare
bi'ologo, -a, -ghi, -ghe SM/F biologist
bi'ondo, -a AG blond, fair
bi'onico, -a, -ci, -che AG bionic
biop'sia SF biopsy
bio'ritmo SM biorhythm
bios'fera SF biosphere
biotecnolo'gia [bioteknoloˈdʒia] SF biotechnology
bipar'tito, -a AG (*Pol*) two-party *cpd* ▶ SM (*Pol*) two-party alliance
'birba SF rascal, rogue
bir'bante SM rascal, rogue
birbo'nata SF naughty trick
bir'bone, -a AG (*bambino*) naughty ▶ SM/F little rascal
biri'chino, -a [biriˈkino] AG mischievous ▶ SM/F scamp, little rascal
bi'rillo SM skittle (BRIT), pin (US); **birilli** SMPL (*gioco*) skittles *sg* (BRIT), bowling *no pl* (US)
Bir'mania SF: **la ~** Burma
bir'mano, -a AG, SM/F Burmese (*inv*)
'biro® SF INV biro®
'birra SF beer; **~ chiara/scura** lager/stout; **a tutta ~** (*fig*) at top speed
birre'ria SF (*locale*) ≈ bierkeller; (*fabbrica*) brewery
bis ESCL, SM INV encore ▶ AG INV (*treno, autobus*) relief *cpd* (BRIT), additional; (*numero*) **12** = 12a
bi'saccia, -ce [biˈzattʃa] SF knapsack
Bi'sanzio [biˈzantsjo] SF Byzantium
bis'betico, -a, -ci, -che AG ill-tempered, crabby
bisbigli'are [bizbiʎˈʎare] /**27**/ VT, VI to whisper
bis'biglio[1] [bizˈbiʎʎo] SM whisper; (*notizia*) rumour (BRIT), rumor (US)
bisbi'glio[2] [bizbiʎˈʎio] SM whispering
bis'boccia, -ce [bizˈbɔttʃa] SF binge, spree; **fare ~** to have a binge
'bisca, -sche SF gambling house
Bis'caglia [bisˈkaʎʎa] SF: **il golfo di ~** the Bay of Biscay
'bischero [ˈbiskero] SM (*Mus*) peg; (*col: toscano*) fool, idiot
'biscia, -sce [ˈbiʃʃa] SF snake; **~ d'acqua** water snake
biscot'tato, -a AG crisp; **fette biscottate** rusks
bis'cotto SM biscuit
bisessu'ale AG, SMF bisexual
bises'tile AG: **anno ~** leap year
bisezi'one [bisetˈtsjone] SF dichotomy
bis'lacco, -a, -chi, -che AG odd, weird
bis'lungo, -a, -ghi, -ghe AG oblong
bis'nonno, -a SM/F great grandfather/ grandmother

biso'gnare [bizoɲ'ɲare] /**15**/ vʙ ɪᴍᴘᴇʀꜱ: **bisogna che tu parta/lo faccia** you'll have to go/do it; **bisogna parlargli** we'll (o I'll) have to talk to him ▶ vɪ (*esser utile*) to be necessary

bi'sogno [bi'zoɲɲo] ꜱᴍ need; **bisogni** ꜱᴍᴘʟ (*necessità corporali*): **fare i propri bisogni** to relieve o.s.; **avere ~ di qc/di fare qc** to need sth/to do sth; **ha ~ di qualcosa?** do you need anything?; **al ~**, **in caso di ~** if need be

biso'gnoso, -a [bizoɲ'ɲoso] ᴀɢ needy, poor; **~ di** in need of, needing

bi'sonte ꜱᴍ (*Zool*) bison

bis'tecca, -che ꜱꜰ steak, beefsteak; **~ al sangue/ai ferri** rare/grilled steak

bisticci'are [bistit'tʃare] /**14**/ vɪ to quarrel, bicker; **bisticciarsi** vᴘʀ to quarrel, bicker

bis'ticcio [bis'tittʃo] ꜱᴍ quarrel, squabble; (*gioco di parole*) pun

bistrat'tare /**72**/ vᴛ to maltreat

'bisturi ꜱᴍ ɪɴᴠ scalpel

bi'sunto, -a ᴀɢ very greasy

bi'torzolo [bi'tortsolo] ꜱᴍ (*sulla testa*) bump; (*sul corpo*) lump

'bitter ꜱᴍ ɪɴᴠ bitters *pl*

bi'tume ꜱᴍ bitumen

bivac'care /**20**/ vɪ (*Mil*) to bivouac; (*fig*) to bed down

bi'vacco, -chi ꜱᴍ bivouac

'bivio ꜱᴍ fork; (*fig*) dilemma

bizan'tino, -a [biddzan'tino] ᴀɢ Byzantine

'bizza ['biddza] ꜱꜰ tantrum; **fare le bizze** to throw a tantrum

biz'zarro, -a [bid'dzarro] ᴀɢ bizarre, strange

biz'zeffe [bid'dzɛffe]: **a ~** *av* in plenty, galore

BL ꜱɪɢʟᴀ = **Belluno**

blan'dire /**55**/ vᴛ to soothe; to flatter

'blando, -a ᴀɢ mild, gentle

blas'femo, -a ᴀɢ blasphemous ▶ ꜱᴍ/ꜰ blasphemer

bla'sone ꜱᴍ coat of arms

blate'rare /**72**/ vɪ to chatter

'blatta ꜱꜰ cockroach

blin'dare /**72**/ vᴛ to armour (*Brit*), armor (*US*)

blin'data ꜱꜰ (*macchina*) armoured car o limousine

blin'dato, -a ᴀɢ armoured (*Brit*), armored (*US*); **camera blindata** strongroom; **mezzo ~** armoured vehicle; **porta blindata** reinforced door; **vita blindata** life amid maximum security; **vetro ~** bulletproof glass

bloc'care /**20**/ vᴛ to block; (*isolare*) to isolate, cut off; (*porto*) to blockade; (*prezzi, beni*) to freeze; (*meccanismo*) to jam; **bloccarsi** vᴘʀ (*motore*) to stall; (*freni, porta*) to jam, stick; (*ascensore*) to get stuck, stop; **ha bloccato la macchina** (*Aut*) he jammed on the brakes

bloccas'terzo [blokkas'tɛrtso] ꜱᴍ (*Aut*) steering lock

blocche'rò *etc* [blokke'rɔ] vʙ *vedi* **bloccare**

bloc'chetto [blok'ketto] ꜱᴍ notebook; (*di biglietti*) book

'blocco, -chi ꜱᴍ block; (*Mil*) blockade; (*dei fitti*) restriction; (*quadernetto*) pad; (*fig: unione*) coalition; (*il bloccare*) blocking; isolating, cutting-off; blockading; freezing; jamming; **in ~** (*nell'insieme*) as a whole; (*Comm*) in bulk; **~ cardiaco** cardiac arrest; **~ stradale** road block

bloc-'notes [blɔk'nɔt] ꜱᴍ ɪɴᴠ notebook, notepad

blog [blog] ꜱᴍ ɪɴᴠ blog

'bloggare /**80**/ vɪ to blog

blogos'fera [blogos'fɛra] ꜱꜰ blogosphere

blu ᴀɢ ɪɴᴠ, ꜱᴍ ɪɴᴠ dark blue

bluff [blɛf] ꜱᴍ ɪɴᴠ bluff

bluf'fare /**72**/ vɪ (*anche fig*) to bluff

'blusa ꜱꜰ (*camiciotto*) smock; (*camicetta*) blouse

BN ꜱɪɢʟᴀ = **Benevento**

BO ꜱɪɢʟᴀ = **Bologna**

'boa ꜱᴍ ɪɴᴠ (*Zool*) boa constrictor; (*sciarpa*) feather boa ▶ ꜱꜰ buoy

bo'ato ꜱᴍ rumble, roar

bob [bob] ꜱᴍ ɪɴᴠ bobsleigh

bo'bina ꜱꜰ reel, spool; (*di pellicola*) spool; (*di film*) reel; (*Elettr*) coil

'bocca, -che ꜱꜰ mouth; **essere di buona ~** to be a hearty eater; (*fig*) to be easily satisfied; **essere sulla ~ di tutti** (*persona, notizia*) to be the talk of the town; **rimanere a ~ asciutta** to have nothing to eat; (*fig*) to be disappointed; **in ~ al lupo!** good luck!; **~ di leone** (*Bot*) snapdragon

boc'caccia, -ce [bok'kattʃa] ꜱꜰ (*malalingua*) gossip; (*smorfia*): **fare le boccacce** to pull faces

boc'caglio [bok'kaʎʎo] ꜱᴍ (*Tecn*) nozzle; (*di respiratore*) mouthpiece

boc'cale ꜱᴍ jug; **~ da birra** tankard

bocca'scena [bokkaʃ'ʃɛna] ꜱᴍ ɪɴᴠ proscenium

boc'cata ꜱꜰ mouthful; (*di fumo*) puff; **prendere una ~ d'aria** to go out for a breath of (fresh) air

boc'cetta [bot'tʃetta] ꜱꜰ small bottle

boccheggi'are [bokked'dʒare] /**62**/ vɪ to gasp

boc'chino [bok'kino] ꜱᴍ (*di sigaretta, sigaro: cannella*) cigarette-holder; cigar-holder; (*di pipa, strumenti musicali*) mouthpiece

'boccia, -ce ['bottʃa] ꜱꜰ bottle; (*da vino*) decanter, carafe; (*palla di legno, metallo*) bowl; **gioco delle bocce** bowls *sg*

bocci'are [bot'tʃare] /**14**/ vᴛ (*proposta, progetto*) to reject; (*Ins*) to fail; (*Bocce*) to hit

boccia'tura [bottʃa'tura] ꜱꜰ failure

bocci'olo [bot'tʃolo] ꜱᴍ bud

'**boccolo** SM curl

boccon'cino [bokkon'tʃino] SM (*pietanza deliziosa*) delicacy

boc'cone SM mouthful, morsel; **mangiare un ~** to have a bite to eat

boc'coni AV face downwards

Bo'emia SF Bohemia

bo'emo, -a AG, SM/F Bohemian

bofonchi'are [bofon'kjare] **/19/** VI to grumble

Bogotá SF Bogotá

'**boia** SM INV executioner; hangman; **fa un freddo ~** (*col*) it's cold as hell; **mondo ~!**, **~ d'un mondo ladro!** (*col*) damn!, blast!

boi'ata SF botch

boicot'taggio [boikot'taddʒo] SM boycott

boicot'tare /72/ VT to boycott

'**bolgia, -ge** ['boldʒa] SF (*fig*): **c'era una tale ~ al cinema** the cinema was absolutely mobbed

'**bolide** SM (*Astr*) meteor; (*macchina: da corsa*) racing car (*BRIT*), race car (*US*); (*: elaborata*) performance car; **come un ~** like a flash, at top speed; **entrare/uscire come un ~** to charge in/out

Bo'livia SF: **la ~** Bolivia

bolivi'ano, -a AG, SM/F Bolivian

'**bolla** SF bubble; (*Med*) blister; (*Comm*) bill, receipt; **finire in una ~ di sapone** (*fig*) to come to nothing; **~ di accompagnamento** waybill; **~ di consegna** (*Comm*) delivery note; **~ papale** papal bull

bol'lare /72/ VT to stamp; (*fig*) to brand

bol'lente AG boiling; boiling hot; **calmare i bollenti spiriti** to sober up, calm down

bol'letta SF bill; (*ricevuta*) receipt; **essere in ~** to be hard up; **~ di consegna** delivery note; **~ doganale** clearance certificate; **~ di trasporto aereo** air waybill

bollet'tino SM bulletin; (*Comm*) note; **~ meteorologico** weather forecast; **~ di ordinazione** order form; **~ di spedizione** consignment note

bolli'cina [bolli'tʃina] SF bubble; **acqua con le ~** fizzy water

bol'lire /17/ VT, VI to boil; **qualcosa bolle in pentola** (*fig*) there's something brewing

bol'lito SM (*Cuc*) boiled meat

bolli'tore SM (*Tecn*) boiler; (*Cuc: per acqua*) kettle; (*: per latte*) milk pan

bolli'tura SF boiling

'**bollo** SM stamp; **imposta di ~** stamp duty; **~ auto** road tax; **~ per patente** driving licence tax; **~ postale** postmark

bol'lore SM: **dare un ~ a qc** to bring sth to the boil (*BRIT*) o a boil (*US*); **i bollori della gioventù** youthful enthusiasm *sg*

Bo'logna [bo'lɔɲɲa] SF Bologna

bolo'gnese [boloɲ'nese] AG Bolognese; **spaghetti alla ~** spaghetti bolognese

'**bomba** SF bomb; **tornare a ~** (*fig*) to get back to the point; **sei stato una ~!** you were tremendous!; **~ atomica** atom bomb; **~ a mano** hand grenade; **~ ad orologeria** time bomb

bombarda'mento SM bombardment; bombing

bombar'dare /72/ VT to bombard; (*da aereo*) to bomb

bombardi'ere SM bomber

bom'betta SF bowler (hat) (*BRIT*), derby (*US*)

'**bombola** SF cylinder; **~ del gas** gas cylinder

bombo'letta SF spray can

bomboni'era SF box of sweets (*as souvenir at weddings, first communions etc*)

bo'naccia, -ce [bo'nattʃa] SF dead calm

bonacci'one, -a [bonat'tʃone] AG good-natured ▶ SM/F good-natured sort

bo'nario, -a AG good-natured, kind

bo'nifica, -che SF reclamation; reclaimed land

bo'nifico, -ci SM (*riduzione, abbuono*) discount; (*versamento a terzi*) credit transfer

Bonn SF Bonn

bontà SF goodness; (*cortesia*) kindness; **aver la ~ di fare qc** to be good o kind enough to do sth

'**bonus-'malus** SM INV ≈ no-claims bonus

bor'bonico, -a, -ci, -che AG Bourbon; (*fig*) backward, out of date

borbot'tare /72/ VI to mumble; (*stomaco*) to rumble

borbot'tio, -ii SM mumbling; rumbling

'**borchia** ['borkja] SF stud

borda'tura SF (*Sartoria*) border, trim

bor'deaux [bor'dɔ] AG INV maroon ▶ SM INV (*colore*) burgundy, maroon; (*vino*) Bordeaux

bor'dello SM brothel

'**bordo** SM (*Naut*) ship's side; (*orlo*) edge; (*striscia di guarnizione*) border, trim; **a ~ di** (*nave, aereo*) aboard, on board; (*macchina*) in; **sul ~ della strada** at the roadside; **persona d'alto ~** VIP

bor'dura SF border

bor'gata SF hamlet; (*a Roma*) working-class suburb

bor'ghese [bor'geze] AG (*spesso peg*) middle-class; bourgeois; **abito ~** civilian dress; **poliziotto in ~** plainclothes policeman

borghe'sia [borge'zia] SF middle classes *pl*; bourgeoisie

'**borgo, -ghi** SM (*paesino*) village; (*quartiere*) district; (*sobborgo*) suburb

'**boria** SF self-conceit, arrogance

bori'oso, -a AG arrogant

bor'lotto SM kidney bean

'**Borneo** SM: **il ~** Borneo

boro'talco SM talcum powder

bor'raccia, -ce [bor'rattʃa] SF canteen, water-bottle

'borsa SF bag; (anche: **borsa da signora**) handbag; (Econ) **la B~ (valori)** the Stock Exchange; **~ dell'acqua calda** hot-water bottle; **B~ merci** commodity exchange; **~ nera** black market; **~ della spesa** shopping bag; **~ di studio** grant

borsai'olo SM pickpocket

bor'seggio [bor'seddʒo] SM pickpocketing

borsel'lino SM purse

bor'sello SM gent's handbag

bor'setta SF handbag

bor'sista, -i, -e SM/F (Econ) speculator; (Ins) grant-holder

bos'caglia [bos'kaʎʎa] SF woodlands pl

boscai'olo, boscaiu'olo SM woodcutter; forester

bos'chetto [bos'ketto] SM copse, grove

'bosco, -schi SM wood

bos'coso, -a AG wooded

bos'niaco, -a, -ci, -che AG, SM/F Bosnian

'Bosnia-Erze'govina ['bɔsnja erdze'govina] SF: **la ~** Bosnia-Herzegovina

'bossolo SM cartridge case

Bot, bot SIGLA M INV (= buono ordinario del Tesoro) short-term Treasury bond

bo'tanico, -a, -ci, -che AG botanical ▶ SM botanist ▶ SF botany

'botola SF trap door

Bots'wana [bots'vana] SM: **il ~** Botswana

'botta SF blow; (rumore) bang; **dare (un sacco di) botte a qn** to give sb a good thrashing; **~ e risposta** (fig) cut and thrust

'botte SF barrel, cask; **essere in una ~ di ferro** (fig) to be as safe as houses; **volere la ~ piena e la moglie ubriaca** to want to have one's cake and eat it

bot'tega, -ghe SF shop; (officina) workshop; **stare a ~ da qn** to serve one's apprenticeship (with sb); **le Botteghe Oscure** headquarters of the DS, Italian left-wing party

botte'gaio, -a SM/F shopkeeper

botte'ghino [botte'gino] SM ticket office; (del lotto) public lottery office

bot'tiglia [bot'tiʎʎa] SF bottle

bottiglie'ria [bottiʎʎe'ria] SF wine shop

bot'tino SM (di guerra) booty; (di rapina, furto) loot; **fare ~ di qc** (anche fig) to make off with sth

'botto SM bang; crash; **di ~** suddenly; **d'un ~** (col) in a flash

bot'tone SM button; (Bot) bud; **stanza dei bottoni** control room; (fig) nerve centre; **attaccare (un) ~ a qn** to buttonhole sb

bo'vino, -a AG bovine; **bovini** SMPL cattle

box [bɔks] SM INV (per cavalli) horsebox; (per macchina) lock-up; (per macchina da corsa) pit; (per bambini) playpen

boxe [bɔks] SF boxing

'boxer ['bɔkser] SM INV (cane) boxer ▶ SMPL (mutande): **un paio di ~** a pair of boxer shorts

'bozza ['bɔttsa] SF draft; (Tip) proof; **~ di stampa/impaginata** galley/page proof

boz'zetto [bot'tsetto] SM sketch

'bozzolo ['bɔttsolo] SM cocoon

BR SIGLA FPL = **Brigate Rosse** ▶ SIGLA = **Brindisi**

b

'braca, -che SF (gamba di pantalone) trouser leg; **brache** SFPL (col) trousers, pants (US); (mutandoni) drawers; **calare le brache** (fig: col) to chicken out

brac'care /20/ VT to hunt

brac'cetto [brat'tʃetto] SM: **a ~** arm in arm

bracche'rò etc [brakke'rɔ] VB vedi **braccare**

bracci'ale [brat'tʃale] SM bracelet; (per nuotare, anche distintivo) armband

braccia'letto [brattʃa'letto] SM bracelet, bangle

bracci'ante [brat'tʃante] SM (Agr) day labourer

bracci'ata [brat'tʃata] SF armful; (nel nuoto) stroke

'braccio (Anat pl(f) **braccia**, di gru, fiume pl(m) **bracci**) ['brattʃo] SM arm; (di edificio) wing; **camminare sotto ~** to walk arm in arm; **è il suo ~ destro** he's his right-hand man; **~ di ferro** (anche fig) trial of strength; **~ di mare** sound

bracci'olo [brat'tʃolo] SM (appoggio) arm

'bracco, -chi SM hound

bracconi'ere SM poacher

'brace ['bratʃe] SF embers pl

braci'ere [bra'tʃɛre] SM brazier

braci'ola [bra'tʃɔla] SF (Cuc) chop

'bradipo SM (Zool) sloth

'brado, -a AG: **allo stato ~** in the wild o natural state

'brama SF: **~ (di/di fare)** longing (for/to do), yearning (for/to do)

bra'mare /72/ VT: **~ (qc/di fare qc)** to long (for sth/to do sth), yearn (for sth/to do sth)

bramo'sia SF: **~ (di)** longing (for), yearning (for)

'branca, -che SF branch

'branchia ['brankja] SF (Zool) gill

'branco, -chi SM (di cani, lupi) pack; (di uccelli, pecore) flock; (peg: di persone) gang, pack

branco'lare /72/ VI to grope, feel one's way

'branda SF camp bed

bran'dello SM scrap, shred; **a brandelli** in tatters, in rags; **fare a brandelli** to tear to shreds

bran'dina SF camp bed (BRIT), cot (US)

bran'dire /55/ VT to brandish

'brano SM piece; (di libro) passage

bra'sare /72/ VT to braise

bra'sato SM braised beef

Bra'sile sm: **il** ~ Brazil
Bra'silia sf Brasilia
brasili'ano, -a ag, sm/f Brazilian
bra'vata sf (*azione spavalda*) act of bravado
'bravo, -a ag (*abile*) clever, capable, skilful; (*buono*) good, honest; (: *bambino*) good; (*coraggioso*) brave; **~!** well done!; (*al teatro*) bravo!; **su da ~!** (*col*) there's a good boy!; **mi sono fatto le mie brave 8 ore di lavoro** I put in a full 8 hours' work
bra'vura sf cleverness, skill
'breccia, -ce ['brettʃa] sf breach; **essere sulla ~** (*fig*) to be going strong; **fare ~ nell'animo** o **nel cuore di qn** to find the way to sb's heart
'Brema sf Bremen
bre'saola sf *kind of dried salted beef*
bresci'ano, -a [breʃʃano] ag (*o from*) Brescia
Bre'tagna [bre'taɲɲa] sf: **la ~** Brittany
bre'tella sf (*Aut*) link; **bretelle** sfpl (*di calzoni*) braces
'bret(t)one ag, smf Breton
'breve ag brief, short; **in ~** in short; **per farla ~** to cut a long story short; **a ~** (*Comm*) short-term
brevet'tare /72/ vt to patent
bre'vetto sm patent; **~ di pilotaggio** pilot's licence (Brit) o license (US)
brevità sf brevity
'brezza ['breddza] sf breeze
'bricco, -chi sm jug; **~ del caffè** coffeepot
bricco'nata sf mischievous trick
bric'cone, -a sm rogue, rascal
'briciola ['britʃola] sf crumb
'briciolo ['britʃolo] sm (*fig*) bit
bridge [bridʒ] sm bridge
'briga, -ghe sf (*fastidio*) trouble, bother; **attaccar ~** to start a quarrel; **pigliarsi la ~ di fare qc** to take the trouble to do sth
brigadi'ere sm (*dei carabinieri ecc*) ≈ sergeant
bri'gante sm bandit
bri'gata sf (*Mil*) brigade; (*gruppo*) group, party; **le Brigate Rosse** (*Pol*) the Red Brigades
briga'tismo sm *phenomenon of the Red Brigades*
briga'tista, -i, -e sm/f (*Pol*) member of the Red Brigades
'briglia ['briʎʎa] sf rein; **a ~ sciolta** at full gallop; (*fig*) at full speed
bril'lante ag bright; (*anche fig*) brilliant; (*che luccica*) shining ▸ sm diamond
brillan'tina sf brilliantine
bril'lare /72/ vi to shine; (*mina*) to blow up ▸ vt (*mina*) to set off
'brillo, -a ag merry, tipsy
'brina sf hoarfrost
brin'dare /72/ vi: **~ a qn/qc** to drink to o toast sb/sth

'brindisi sm inv toast
'brio sm liveliness, go
bri'oche [bri'ɔʃ] sf inv brioche (bun)
bri'oso, -a ag lively
'briscola sf *type of card game*; (*seme vincente*) trump(s); (*carta*) trump card
bri'tannico, -a, -ci, -che ag British ▸ sm/f Briton; **i Britannici** the British *pl*
'brivido sm shiver; (*di ribrezzo*) shudder; (*fig*) thrill; **racconti del ~** suspense stories
brizzo'lato, -a [brittso'lato] ag (*persona*) going grey; (*barba, capelli*) greying
'brocca, -che sf jug
broc'cato sm brocade
'broccoli smpl broccoli *sg*
bro'daglia [bro'daʎʎa] sf (*peg*) dishwater
'brodo sm broth; (*per cucinare*) stock; **~ ristretto** consommé; **lasciare (cuocere) qn nel suo ~** to let sb stew (in his own juice); **tutto fa ~** every little bit helps
'broglio ['brɔʎʎo] sm: **~ elettorale** gerrymandering; **brogli** smpl (*Dir*) malpractices
'bromo sm (*Chim*) bromine
bron'chite [bron'kite] sf (*Med*) bronchitis
'broncio ['brontʃo] sm sulky expression; **tenere il ~** to sulk
'bronco, -chi sm bronchial tube
bronto'lare /72/ vi to grumble; (*tuono, stomaco*) to rumble
bronto'lio sm grumbling, mumbling
bronto'lone, -a ag grumbling ▸ sm/f grumbler
bron'zina [bron'dzina] sf (*Tecn*) bush
'bronzo ['brondzo] sm bronze; **che faccia di ~!** what a brass neck!
bross. abbr = **in brossura**
bros'sura sf: **in ~** (*libro*) limpback
'browser ['brauzer] sm inv (*Inform*) browser
bru'care /20/ vt to browse on, nibble at
brucherà *etc* [bruke'ra] vb *vedi* **brucare**
bruciacchi'are [brutʃak'kjare] /19/ vt to singe, scorch; **bruciacchiarsi** vpr to become singed o scorched
brucia'pelo [brutʃa'pelo]: **a ~** av point-blank
bruci'are [bru'tʃare] /14/ vt to burn; (*scottare*) to scald ▸ vi to burn; **bruciarsi** vpr to burn o.s.; (*fallire*) to ruin one's chances; **~ gli avversari** (*Sport, fig*) to leave the rest of the field behind; **~ le tappe** o **i tempi** (*Sport, fig*) to shoot ahead; **bruciarsi la carriera** to put an end to one's career
brucia'tore [brutʃa'tore] sm burner
brucia'tura [brutʃa'tura] sf (*atto*) burning *no pl*; (*segno*) burn; (*scottatura*) scald
bruci'ore [bru'tʃore] sm burning o smarting sensation
'bruco, -chi sm grub; (*di farfalla*) caterpillar
'brufolo sm pimple, spot

brughi'era [bru'gjɛra] SF heath, moor

bruli'care /**20**/ VI to swarm

bruli'chio, -ii [bruli'kio] SM swarming

'brullo, -a AG bare, bleak

'bruma SF mist

'bruno, -a AG brown, dark; (*persona*) dark(-haired)

brusca'mente AV (*frenare, fermarsi*) suddenly; (*rispondere, reagire*) sharply

'brusco, -a, -schi, -sche AG (*sapore*) sharp; (*modi, persona*) brusque, abrupt; (*movimento*) abrupt, sudden

bru'sio SM buzz, buzzing

bru'tale AG brutal

brutalità SF INV brutality

'bruto, -a AG (*forza*) brute *cpd* ▶ SM brute

'brutta SF *vedi* **brutto**

brut'tezza [brut'tettsa] SF ugliness

'brutto, -a AG ugly; (*cattivo*) bad; (*malattia, strada, affare*) nasty, bad ▶ SM: **guardare qn di ~** to give sb a nasty look ▶ SF rough copy, first draft; **~ tempo** bad weather; **passare un ~ quarto d'ora** to have a nasty time of it; **vedersela brutta** (*per un attimo*) to have a nasty moment; (*per un periodo*) to have a bad time of it

brut'tura SF (*cosa brutta*) ugly thing; (*sudiciume*) filth; (*azione meschina*) mean action

Bru'xelles [bry'sɛl] SF Brussels

BS SIGLA = **Brescia**

BSE [biesse'e] SIGLA F BSE (= *bovine spongiform encephalopathy*)

B.T. ABBR (= *bassa tensione*) LT ▶ SIGLA M INV = **buono del Tesoro**

btg ABBR = **battaglione**

Btp SIGLA M = **buono del Tesoro poliennale**; *vedi* **buono**

bub'bone SM swelling

'buca, -che SF hole; (*avvallamento*) hollow; **~ delle lettere** letterbox

buca'neve SM INV snowdrop

bu'care /**20**/ VT (*forare*) to make a hole (*o* holes) in; (*pungere*) to pierce; (*biglietto*) to punch; **bucarsi** VPR (*con eroina*) to mainline; **~ una gomma** to have a puncture; **avere le mani bucate** (*fig*) to be a spendthrift

Bucarest SF Bucharest

bu'cato SM (*operazione*) washing; (*panni*) wash, washing

'buccia, -ce ['buttʃa] SF skin, peel; (*corteccia*) bark

bucherel'lare [bukerel'lare] /**72**/ VT to riddle with holes

bucherò *etc* [buke'rɔ] VB *vedi* **bucare**

'buco, -chi SM hole; **fare un ~ nell'acqua** to fail, draw a blank; **farsi un ~** (*col: drogarsi*) to have a fix; **~ nero** (*anche fig*) black hole

'Budapest SF Budapest

'Budda SM INV Buddha

bud'dismo SM Buddhism

bu'dello SM intestine; (*fig: tubo*) tube; (*vicolo*) alley; **budella** SFPL bowels, guts

bu'dino SM pudding

'bue (*pl* **buoi**) SM ox; (*anche:* **carne di bue**) beef; **uovo all'occhio di ~** fried egg

Bu'enos 'Aires SF Buenos Aires

'bufalo SM buffalo

bu'fera SF storm

buf'fetto SM flick

'buffo, -a AG funny; (*Teat*) comic

buffo'nata SF (*azione*) prank, jest; (*parola*) jest

buf'fone SM buffoon

bugge'rare [buddʒe'rare] /**72**/ VT to swindle, cheat

bu'gia, -'gie [bu'dʒia] SF lie; (*candeliere*) candleholder; **dire una ~** to tell a lie

bugi'ardo, -a [bu'dʒardo] AG lying, deceitful ▶ SM/F liar

bugi'gattolo [budʒi'gattolo] SM poky little room

'buio, -a AG dark ▶ SM dark, darkness; **fa ~ pesto** it's pitch-dark

'bulbo SM (*Bot*) bulb; **~ oculare** eyeball

Bulga'ria SF: **la ~** Bulgaria

'bulgaro, -a AG, SM/F Bulgarian

buli'mia SF bulimia

bu'limico, -a, -ci, -che AG bulimic

bul'lismo [bul'lizmo] SM bullying

'bullo SM (*persona*) tough

bul'lone SM bolt

bu'oi SMPL *di* **bue**

buona'fede SF good faith

buon'anima SF = **buon'anima**; *vedi* **anima**

buona'notte ESCL good night! ▶ SF: **dare la ~ a** to say good night to

buona'sera ESCL good evening!

buoncos'tume SM public morality; **la (squadra del) ~** (*Polizia*) the vice squad

buondì ESCL hello!

buongi'orno [bwon'dʒorno] ESCL good morning (*o* afternoon)!

buon'grado AV: **di ~** willingly

buongus'taio, -a SM/F gourmet

buon'gusto SM good taste

(**PAROLA CHIAVE**)

bu'ono, -a (*ag: dav sm* **buon** + C *o* V, **buono** + *s impura, gn, pn, ps, z; dav sf* **buon'** + V) AG **1** (*gen*) good; **un buon pranzo/ristorante** a good lunch/restaurant; (**stai**) **buono!** behave!; **che buono!** (*cibo*) this is nice!

2 (*benevolo*): **buono (con)** good (to), kind (to)

3 (*giusto, valido*) right; **al momento buono** at the right moment

4 (*adatto*): **buono a/da** fit for/to; **essere buono a nulla** to be no good *o* use at anything

5 (*auguri*): **buon anno!** happy New Year!; **buon appetito!** enjoy your meal!; **buon**

compleanno! happy birthday!; **buon divertimento!** have a nice time!; **buona fortuna!** good luck!; **buon riposo!** sleep well!; **buon viaggio!** bon voyage!, have a good trip!
6: **ad ogni buon conto** in any case; **tante buone cose!** all the best!; **di buon cuore** (*persona*) goodhearted; **di buon grado** willingly; **le buone maniere** good manners; **di buon mattino** early in the morning; **a buon mercato** cheap; **di buon'ora** early; **mettere una buona parola** to put in a good word; **di buon passo** at a good pace; **buon pro ti faccia!** much good may it do you!; **buon senso** common sense; **la buona società** the upper classes; **una buona volta** once and for all; **alla buona** *ag* simple
▶ AV in a simple way, without any fuss; **un tipo alla buona** an easy-going sort
▶ SM/F: **essere un buono/una buona** to be a good person; **buono a nulla** good for nothing; **i buoni e i cattivi** (*in storia, film*) the goodies and the baddies; **accetterà con le buone o con le cattive** one way or another he's going to agree to it
▶ SM 1 (*bontà*) goodness, good
2 (*Comm*) voucher, coupon; **buono d'acquisto** credit note; **buono di cassa** cash voucher; **buono di consegna** delivery note; **buono fruttifero** interest-bearing bond; **buono ordinario del Tesoro** short-term Treasury bond; **buono postale fruttifero** interest-bearing bond (*issued by Italian Post Office*); **buono del Tesoro** Treasury bill

buon'senso SM = **buon senso**
buontem'pone, -a SM/F jovial person
buonu'scita [bwonuʃʃita] SF (*Industria*) golden handshake; (*di affitti*) sum paid for the relinquishing of tenancy rights

buratti'naio SM puppeteer, puppet master
burat'tino SM puppet
'burbero, -a AG surly, gruff
'burla SF prank, trick
bur'lare /72/ VT: ~ **qc/qn, burlarsi di qc/qn** to make fun of sth/sb
bu'rocrate SM bureaucrat
buro'cratico, -a, -ci, -che AG bureaucratic
burocra'zia [burokrat'tsia] SF bureaucracy
bur'rasca, -sche SF storm
burras'coso, -a AG stormy
'burro SM butter
bur'rone SM ravine
bus'care /20/ VT (*raffreddore: anche:* **buscarsi**) to get, catch; **buscarle** (*col*) to get a hiding
buscheròetc [buske'rɔ] VB *vedi* **buscare**
bus'sare /72/ VI to knock; ~ **a quattrini** (*fig*) to ask for money
'bussola SF compass; **perdere la ~** (*fig*) to lose one's bearings
'busta SF (*da lettera*) envelope; (*astuccio*) case; **in ~ aperta/chiusa** in an unsealed/sealed envelope; ~ **paga** pay packet
busta'rella SF bribe, backhander
bus'tina SF (*piccola busta*) envelope; (*di cibi, farmaci*) sachet; (*Mil*) forage cap; ~ **di tè** tea bag
'busto SM bust; (*indumento*) corset, girdle; **a mezzo ~** (*fotografia, ritratto*) half-length
bu'tano SM butane
but'tare /72/ VT to throw; (*anche:* **buttare via**) to throw away; **buttarsi** VPR (*saltare*) to jump; ~ **giù** (*scritto*) to scribble down, dash off; (*cibo*) to gulp down; (*edificio*) to pull down, demolish; (*pasta, verdura*) to put into boiling water; **ho buttato là una frase** I mentioned it in passing; **buttiamoci!** (*saltiamo*) let's jump!; (*rischiamo*) let's have a go!; **buttarsi dalla finestra** to jump out of the window
'buzzo ['buddzo] SM (*col: pancia*) belly, paunch; **di ~ buono** (*con impegno*) with a will
byte ['bait] SM INV byte

Cc

C

C, c [tʃi] SM O F INV (*lettera*) C, c ▶ ABBR (*Geo*)
= **capo**; (= *Celsius, centigrado*) C; (= *conto*) a/c;
C come Como = C for Charlie

CA SIGLA = **Cagliari**

c.a. ABBR (*Elettr*) *vedi* **corrente alternata**;
(*Comm*) = **corrente anno**

caba'ret [kaba'rɛ] SM INV cabaret

ca'bina SF (*di nave*) cabin; (*da spiaggia*) beach
hut; (*di autocarro, treno*) cab; (*di aereo*) cockpit;
(*di ascensore*) cage; ~ **di pilotaggio** cockpit;
~ **di proiezione** (*Cine*) projection booth; ~ **di
registrazione** recording booth;
~ **telefonica** callbox, (tele)phone box *o* booth

cabi'nato SM cabin cruiser

ca'blaggio [ka'bladdʒo] SM wiring

cablo'gramma SM cable(gram)

ca'cao SM cocoa

'cacca SF (*col: anche fig*) shit (*!*)

'caccia ['kattʃa] SF hunting; (*con fucile*)
shooting; (*inseguimento*) chase; (*cacciagione*)
game ▶ SM INV (*aereo*) fighter; (*nave*)
destroyer; **andare a ~** to go hunting;
andare a ~ di guai to be asking for trouble;
~ **grossa** big-game hunting; ~ **all'uomo**
manhunt

cacciabombardi'ere [kattʃabombar'djɛre]
SM fighter-bomber

cacciagi'one [kattʃa'dʒone] SF game

cacci'are [kat'tʃare] /**14**/ VT to hunt; (*mandar
via*) to chase away; (*ficcare*) to shove, stick
▶ VI to hunt; **cacciarsi** VPR (*col: mettersi*):
cacciarsi tra la folla to plunge into the
crowd; ~ **fuori qc** to whip *o* pull sth out;
~ **un urlo** to let out a yell; **dove s'è cacciata
la mia borsa?** where has my bag got to?;
cacciarsi nei guai to get into trouble

caccia'tora [kattʃa'tora] SF (*giacca*) hunting
jacket; (*Cuc*): **pollo** *etc* **alla ~** chicken *etc*
chasseur

caccia'tore [kattʃa'tore] SM hunter; ~ **di
frodo** poacher; ~ **di dote** fortune-hunter

cacciatorpedini'ere [kattʃatorpedi'njɛre]
SM destroyer

caccia'vite [kattʃa'vite] SM INV screwdriver

cache'mire [kaʃ'mir] SM INV cashmere

ca'chet [ka'ʃɛ] SM (*Med*) capsule; (*: compressa*)
tablet; (*compenso*) fee; (*colorante per capelli*) rinse

'cachi ['kaki] SM INV (*albero, frutto*) persimmon;
(*colore*) khaki ▶ AG INV khaki

'cacio ['katʃo] SM cheese; **essere come il ~
sui maccheroni** (*fig*) to turn up at the right
moment

'cactus SM INV cactus

ca'davere SM (dead) body, corpse

cada'verico, -a, -ci, -che AG (*fig*) deathly pale

'caddie *etc* VB *vedi* **cadere**

ca'dente AG falling; (*casa*) tumbledown;
(*persona*) decrepit

ca'denza [ka'dɛntsa] SF cadence; (*andamento
ritmico*) rhythm; (*Mus*) cadenza

ca'dere/18/ VI to fall; (*denti, capelli*) to fall out;
(*tetto*) to fall in; **questa gonna cade bene**
this skirt hangs well; **lasciar ~** (*anche fig*) to
drop; ~ **dal sonno** to be falling asleep on
one's feet; ~ **ammalato** to fall ill; ~ **dalle
nuvole** (*fig*) to be taken aback

ca'detto SM cadet

cadrò *etc* VB *vedi* **cadere**

ca'duta SF fall; **la ~ dei capelli** hair loss

ca'duto, -a AG (*morto*) dead ▶ SM dead soldier
▶ SF fall; **monumento ai caduti** war
memorial; **caduta di temperatura** drop in
temperature; **la caduta dei capelli** hair
loss; **caduta del sistema** (*Inform*) system
failure

caffè SM INV coffee; (*locale*) café; ~ **corretto**
coffee with liqueur; ~ **in grani** coffee beans;
~ **macchiato** coffee with a dash of milk;
~ **macinato** ground coffee

caffe'ina SF caffeine

caffel'latte SM INV white coffee

caffette'ria SF coffee shop

caffetti'era SF coffeepot

ca'fone SM (*contadino*) peasant; (*peg*) boor

cagio'nare [kadʒo'nare] /**72**/ VT to cause, be
the cause of

cagio'nevole [kadʒo'nevole] AG delicate,
weak

cagli'are [kaʎ'ʎare] /**27**/ vi to curdle

cagliari'tano, -a [kaʎʎari'tano] AG of (o from) Cagliari

'**cagna** ['kaɲɲa] SF (Zool, peg) bitch

ca'gnara [kaɲ'ɲara] SF (fig) uproar

ca'gnesco, -a, -schi, -sche [kaɲ'ɲesko] AG (fig): **guardare qn in ~** to scowl at sb

CAI SIGLA M = **Club Alpino Italiano**

'**Cairo** SM: **il ~** Cairo

cala'brese AG, SMF Calabrian

cala'brone SM hornet

Cala'hari [kala'ari]: **il Deserto di ~** sm the Kalahari Desert

cala'maio SM inkpot; inkwell

cala'maro SM squid

cala'mita SF magnet

calamità SF INV calamity, disaster; **~ naturale** natural disaster

ca'lare /**72**/ VT (far discendere) to lower; (Maglia) to decrease ▶ VI (discendere) to go (o come) down; (tramontare) to set, go down; **~ di peso** to lose weight

ca'lata SF (invasione) invasion

'**calca** SF throng, press

cal'cagno [kal'kaɲɲo] SM heel

cal'care /**20**/ SM limestone; (incrostazione) (lime)scale ▶ VT (premere coi piedi) to tread, press down; (premere con forza) to press down; (mettere in rilievo) to stress; **~ la mano** to overdo it, exaggerate; **~ le scene** (fig) to be on the stage; **~ le orme di qn** (fig) to follow in sb's footsteps

'**calce** ['kaltʃe] SM: **in ~** at the foot of the page ▶ SF lime; **~ viva** quicklime

calces'truzzo [kaltʃes'truttso] SM concrete

cal'cetto [kal'tʃetto] SM (calcio-balilla) table football; (calcio a cinque) five-a-side (football)

calcherò etc [kalke'rɔ] VB vedi **calcare**

calci'are [kal'tʃare] /**14**/ VT, VI to kick

calcia'tore [kaltʃa'tore] SM footballer (BRIT), (football) player

cal'cina [kal'tʃina] SF (lime) mortar

calci'naccio [kaltʃi'nattʃo] SM flake of plaster

'**calcio** ['kaltʃo] SM (pedata) kick; (sport) football, soccer; (di pistola, fucile) butt; (Chim) calcium; **~ d'angolo** (Sport) corner (kick); **~ di punizione** (Sport) free kick; **~ di rigore** penalty

'**calco, -chi** SM (Arte) casting, moulding (BRIT), molding (US); cast, mo(u)ld

calco'lare /**72**/ VT to calculate, work out, reckon; (ponderare) to weigh (up)

calcola'tore, -'trice AG calculating ▶ SM calculator; (fig) calculating person ▶ SF (anche: **macchina calcolatrice**) calculator; **~ digitale** digital computer; **~ elettronico** computer; **~ da tavolo** desktop computer

calcola'trice SF calculator

'**calcolo** SM (anche Mat) calculation; (infinitesimale ecc) calculus; (Med) stone; **fare il ~ di qc** to work sth out; **fare i propri calcoli** (fig) to weigh the pros and cons; **per ~** out of self-interest

cal'daia SF boiler

caldar'rosta SF roast chestnut

caldeggi'are [kalded'dʒare] /**62**/ VT to support

'**caldo, -a** AG warm; (molto caldo) hot; (fig: appassionato) keen; hearty ▶ SM heat; **ho ~** I'm warm; I'm hot; **fa ~** it's warm; it's hot; **non mi fa né ~ né freddo** I couldn't care less; **a ~** (fig) in the heat of the moment

caleidos'copio SM kaleidoscope

calen'dario SM calendar

ca'lende SFPL calends; **rimandare qc alle ~ greche** to put sth off indefinitely

ca'lesse SM gig

'**calibro** SM (di arma) calibre, bore; (Tecn) callipers pl; (fig) calibre; **di grosso ~** (fig) prominent

'**calice** ['kalitʃe] SM goblet; (Rel) chalice

Cali'fornia SF California

californi'ano, -a AG Californian

ca'ligine [ka'lidʒine] SF fog; (mista con fumo) smog

calligra'fia SF (scrittura) handwriting; (arte) calligraphy

'**callo** SM callus; (ai piedi) corn; **fare il ~ a qc** to get used to sth

'**calma** SF calm; **faccia con ~** take your time

cal'mante SM sedative, tranquillizer

cal'mare /**72**/ VT to calm; (lenire) to soothe; **calmarsi** VPR to grow calm, calm down; (vento) to abate; (dolori) to ease

calmi'ere SM controlled price

'**calmo, -a** AG calm, quiet

'**calo** SM (Comm: di prezzi) fall; (: di volume) shrinkage; (: di peso) loss

ca'lore SM warmth; (intenso, Fisica) heat; **essere in ~** (Zool) to be on heat

calo'ria SF calorie

calo'rifero SM radiator

calo'roso, -a AG warm; **essere ~** not to feel the cold

calpes'tare /**72**/ VT to tread on, trample on; **"è vietato ~ l'erba"** "keep off the grass"

ca'lunnia SF slander; (scritta) libel

calunni'are /**19**/ VT to slander

cal'vario SM (fig) affliction, cross

cal'vizie [kal'vittsje] SF baldness

'**calvo, -a** AG bald

'**calza** ['kaltsa] SF (da donna) stocking; (da uomo) sock; **fare la ~** to knit; **calze di nailon** nylons, (nylon) stockings

calza'maglia [kaltsa'maʎʎa] SF tights pl; (per danza, ginnastica) leotard

cal'zare [kal'tsare] /**72**/ VT (scarpe, guanti:

mettersi) to put on; (: *portare*) to wear ▶ VI to fit;
~ **a pennello** to fit like a glove
calza'tura [kaltsa'tura] SF footwear
calzaturi'ficio [kaltsaturi'fitʃo] SM shoe o
footwear factory
cal'zetta [kal'tsetta] SF ankle sock; **una
mezza ~** (*fig*) a nobody
calzet'tone [kaltset'tone] SM heavy
knee-length sock
cal'zino [kal'tsino] SM sock
calzo'laio [kaltso'lajo] SM shoemaker; (*che
ripara scarpe*) cobbler
calzole'ria [kaltsole'ria] SF (*negozio*) shoe
shop; (*arte*) shoemaking
calzon'cini [kaltson'tʃini] SMPL shorts; ~ **da
bagno** (swimming) trunks
cal'zone [kal'tsone] SM trouser leg; (*Cuc*)
savoury turnover made with pizza dough; **calzoni**
SMPL (*pantaloni*) trousers (BRIT), pants (US)
camale'onte SM chameleon
cambi'ale SF bill (of exchange); (*pagherò
cambiario*) promissory note; ~ **di comodo** o **di
favore** accommodation bill
cambia'mento SM change; **cambiamenti
climatici** climate change *sg*
cambi'are/19/ VT to change; (*modificare*) to
alter, change; (*barattare*): ~ **(qc con qn/qc)** to
exchange (sth with sb/for sth) ▶ VI to
change, alter; **cambiarsi** VPR (*variare abito*) to
change; ~ **casa** to move (house); ~ **idea** to
change one's mind; ~ **treno** to change
trains; ~ **le carte in tavola** (*fig*) to change
one's tune; ~ **(l')aria in una stanza** to air a
room; **è ora di ~ aria** (*andarsene*) it's time to
move on
cambiava'lute SM INV exchange office
'**cambio** SM change; (*modifica*) alteration,
change; (*scambio, Comm*) exchange; (*corso dei
cambi*) rate (of exchange); (*Tecn, Aut*) gears *pl*;
in ~ di in exchange for; **dare il ~ a qn** to take
over from sb; **fare il** o **un ~** to change (over);
~ **a termine** (*Comm*) forward exchange
'**Cambital** SIGLA M = **Ufficio Italiano dei
Cambi**
Cam'bogia [kam'bɔdʒa] SF: **la ~** Cambodia
cambogi'ano, -a [kambo'dʒano] AG, SM/F
Cambodian
cam'busa SF storeroom
'**camera** SF room; (*anche*: **camera da letto**)
bedroom; (*Pol*) chamber, house; ~ **ardente**
mortuary chapel; ~ **d'aria** inner tube; (*di
pallone*) bladder; ~ **blindata** strongroom; **C~
di Commercio** Chamber of Commerce; **C~
dei Deputati** Chamber of Deputies, ≈ House
of Commons (BRIT), ≈ House of
Representatives (US); *see note*; ~ **a gas** gas
chamber; ~ **del lavoro** trades union centre
(BRIT), labor union center (US); ~ **a un
letto/a due letti/matrimoniale** single/

twin-bedded/double room; ~ **oscura** (*Fot*)
dark room; ~ **da pranzo** dining room

▍ The *Camera dei deputati* is the lower house
▍ of the Italian Parliament and is presided
▍ over by the *Presidente della Camera* who is
▍ chosen by the *deputati*. Elections to the
▍ Chamber are normally held every 5 years.
▍ Since the electoral reform of 1993
▍ members have been voted in via a
▍ system which combines a first-past-
▍ the-post element with proportional
▍ representation. See also *Parlamento*.

came'rata, -i, -e SM/F companion, mate
▶ SF dormitory
camera'tismo SM comradeship
cameri'era SF (*domestica*) maid; (*che serve a
tavola*) waitress; (*che fa le camere*)
chambermaid
cameri'ere SM (man)servant; (*di ristorante*)
waiter
came'rino SM (*Teat*) dressing room
'**Camerun** SM: **il ~** Cameroon
'**camice** ['kamitʃe] SM (*Rel*) alb; (*per medici ecc*)
white coat
cami'cetta [kami'tʃetta] SF blouse
ca'micia, -cie [ka'mitʃa] SF (*da uomo*) shirt;
(*da donna*) blouse; **nascere con la ~** (*fig*) to be
born lucky; **sudare sette camicie** (*fig*) to
have a hell of a time; ~ **di forza** straitjacket;
~ **da notte** (*da donna*) nightdress; (*da uomo*)
nightshirt; **C~ nera** (*fascista*) Blackshirt
camici'aio, -a [kami'tʃajo] SM/F (*sarto*)
shirtmaker; (*che vende camicie*) shirtseller
camici'ola [kami'tʃɔla] SF vest
camici'otto [kami'tʃɔtto] SM casual shirt;
(*per operai*) smock
cami'netto SM hearth, fireplace
ca'mino SM chimney; (*focolare*) fireplace,
hearth
'**camion** SM INV lorry (BRIT), truck (US)
camion'cino [kamjon'tʃino] SM van
camio'netta SF jeep
camio'nista, -i SM lorry driver (BRIT), truck
driver (US)
'**camma** SF cam; **albero a camme** camshaft
cam'mello SM (*Zool*) camel; (*tessuto*) camel
hair
cam'meo SM cameo
cammi'nare/72/ VI to walk; (*funzionare*) to
work, go; ~ **a carponi** o **a quattro zampe** to
go on all fours
cammi'nata SF walk; **fare una ~** to go for a
walk
cam'mino SM walk; (*sentiero*) path; (*itinerario,
direzione, tragitto*) way; **mettersi in ~** to set o
start off; **cammin facendo** on the way;
riprendere il ~ to continue on one's way
camo'milla SF camomile; (*infuso*)
camomile tea

C

ca'morra SF Camorra; (fig) racket

camor'rista, -i, -e SM/F member of the Camorra; (fig) racketeer

ca'moscio [ka'moʃʃo] SM chamois; **di ~** (scarpe, borsa) suede cpd

cam'pagna [kam'paɲɲa] SF country, countryside; (Pol, Comm, Mil) campaign; **in ~** in the country; **andare in ~** to go to the country; **fare una ~** to campaign; **~ promozionale vendite** sales campaign; **~ pubblicitaria** advertising campaign

campa'gnolo, -a [kampaɲ'ɲɔlo] AG country cpd ▶ SF (Aut) cross-country vehicle

cam'pale AG field cpd; (fig): **una giornata ~** a hard day

cam'pana SF bell; (anche: **campana di vetro**) bell jar; **sordo come una ~** as deaf as a doorpost; **sentire l'altra ~** (fig) to hear the other side of the story; **~ (per la raccolta del vetro)** bottle bank

campa'nella SF small bell; (di tenda) curtain ring

campa'nello SM (all'uscio, da tavola) bell

campa'nile SM bell tower, belfry

campani'lismo SM parochialism

cam'pano, -a AG of (o from) Campania

cam'pare /72/ VI to live; (tirare avanti) to get by, manage; **~ alla giornata** to live from day to day

cam'pato, -a AG: **~ in aria** unsound, unfounded

campeggi'are [kampedd'dʒare] /62/ VI to camp; (risaltare) to stand out

campeggia'tore, -'trice [kampeddʒa'tore] SM/F camper

cam'peggio [kam'peddʒo] SM camping; (terreno) camp site; **fare (del) ~** to go camping

camper ['kamper] SM INV motor caravan (BRIT), motor home (US)

cam'pestre AG country cpd, rural; **corsa ~** cross-country race

Campi'doglio [kampi'dɔʎʎo] SM: **il ~** the Capitol; see note

▌ The Campidoglio, one of the Seven Hills of Rome, is the home of the Comune di Roma.

'camping ['kæmpiŋ] SM INV camp site

campiona'mento SM sampling

campio'nario, -a AG: **fiera campionaria** trade fair ▶ SM collection of samples

campio'nato SM championship

campiona'tura SF (Comm) production of samples; (Statistica) sampling

campi'one, -'essa SM/F (Sport) champion ▶ SM (Comm) sample; **~ gratuito** free sample; **prelievi di ~** product samples

'campo SM (gen) field; (Mil) field; (: accampamento) camp; (spazio delimitato: sportivo ecc) ground; field; (di quadro)

background; **i campi** (campagna) the countryside; **padrone del ~** (fig) victor; **~ da aviazione** airfield; **~ di battaglia** (Mil, fig) battlefield; **~ di concentramento** concentration camp; **~ di golf** golf course; **~ profughi** refugee camp; **~ sportivo** sports ground; **~ lungo** (Cine, TV, Fot) long shot; **~ nomadi** travellers' camp; **~ da tennis** tennis court; **~ visivo** field of vision

campobas'sano, -a AG of (o from) Campobasso

campo'santo (pl **campisanti**) SM cemetery

camuf'fare /72/ VT to disguise; **camuffarsi** VPR: **camuffarsi (da)** to disguise o.s. (as); (per ballo in maschera) to dress up (as)

CAN ABBR (= Costo, Assicurazione e Nolo) CIF

Can. ABBR (Geo) = **canale**

'Canada SM: **il ~** Canada

cana'dese AG, SM/F Canadian ▶ SF (anche: **tenda canadese**) ridge tent

ca'naglia [ka'naʎʎa] SF rabble, mob; (persona) scoundrel, rogue

ca'nale SM (anche fig) channel; (artificiale) canal

'canapa SF hemp; **~ indiana** (droga) cannabis

Ca'narie SFPL: **le (isole) ~** the Canary Islands, the Canaries

cana'rino SM canary

Can'berra SF Canberra

cancel'lare [kantʃel'lare] /72/ VT (con la gomma) to rub out, erase; (con la penna) to strike out; (annullare) to annul, cancel; (disdire) to cancel

cancel'lata [kantʃel'lata] SF railing(s) pl

cancelle'ria [kantʃelle'ria] SF chancery; (quanto necessario per scrivere) stationery

cancelli'ere [kantʃel'ljɛre] SM chancellor; (di tribunale) clerk of the court

can'cello [kan'tʃello] SM gate

cance'rogeno, -a [kantʃe'rɔdʒeno] AG carcinogenic ▶ SM carcinogen

cance'rologo, -a, -gi, -ghe [kantʃe'rɔlogo] SM/F cancer specialist

cance'roso, -a [kantʃe'roso] AG cancerous ▶ SM/F cancer patient

can'crena SF gangrene

'cancro SM (Med) cancer; **C~** Cancer; **essere del C~** to be Cancer

candeggi'are [kanded'dʒare] /62/ VT to bleach

candeg'gina [kanded'dʒina] SF bleach

can'deggio [kan'deddʒo] SM bleaching

can'dela SF candle; **~ (di accensione)** (Aut) spark(ing) plug; **una lampadina da 100 candele** (Elettr) a 100 watt bulb; **a lume di ~** by candlelight; **tenere la ~** (fig) to play gooseberry (BRIT), act as chaperone

cande'labro SM candelabra

candeli'ere SM candlestick

cande'lotto SM candle; **~ di dinamite** stick of dynamite; **~ lacrimogeno** tear gas grenade

candi'dare/72/ VT to present as candidate; **candidarsi** VPR to present o.s. as candidate

candi'dato, -a SM/F candidate; (*aspirante a una carica*) applicant

candida'tura SF candidature; application

'candido, -a AG white as snow; (*puro*) pure; (*sincero*) sincere, candid

can'dito, -a AG candied

can'dore SM brilliant white; purity; sincerity, candour (BRIT), candor (US)

'cane SM dog; (*di pistola, fucile*) cock; **fa un freddo ~** it's bitterly cold; **non c'era un ~** there wasn't a soul; **quell'attore è un ~** he's a rotten actor; **~ da caccia** hunting dog; **~ da guardia** guard dog; **~ lupo** alsatian; **~ da salotto** lap dog; **~ da slitta** husky; **~ pastore** sheepdog

ca'nestro SM basket; **fare un ~** (*Sport*) to shoot a basket

'canfora SF camphor

cangi'ante [kan'dʒante] AG iridescent; **seta ~** shot silk

can'guro SM kangaroo

ca'nicola SF scorching heat

ca'nile SM kennel; (*di allevamento*) kennels *pl*; **~ municipale** dog pound

ca'nino, -a AG, SM canine

'canna SF (*pianta*) reed; (*: indica, da zucchero*) cane; (*bastone*) stick, cane; (*di fucile*) barrel; (*di organo*) pipe; (*col: Droga*) joint; **~ fumaria** chimney flue; **~ da pesca** (fishing) rod; **~ da zucchero** sugar cane

can'nella SF (*Cuc*) cinnamon; (*di conduttura, botte*) tap

cannel'loni SMPL *pasta tubes stuffed with sauce and baked*

can'neto SM bed of reeds

can'nibale SM cannibal

cannocchi'ale [kannok'kjale] SM telescope

canno'nata SF: **è una vera ~!** (*fig*) it's (*o* he's *etc*) fantastic!

can'none SM (*Mil*) gun; (*: Storia*) cannon; (*tubo*) pipe, tube; (*piega*) box pleat; (*fig*) ace; **donna ~** fat woman

cannoni'ere SM (*Naut*) gunner; (*Calcio*) goal scorer

can'nuccia, -ce [kan'nuttʃa] SF (drinking) straw

ca'noa SF canoe

'canone SM canon, criterion; (*mensile, annuo*) rent; fee; **legge dell'equo ~** fair rent act

ca'nonica, -che SF presbytery

ca'nonico, -ci SM (*Rel*) canon

canoniz'zare [kanonid'dzare] /72/ VT to canonize

ca'noro, -a AG (*uccello*) singing, song *cpd*

ca'notta SF vest

canot'taggio [kanot'taddʒo] SM rowing

canot'tiera SF vest (BRIT), undershirt (US)

ca'notto SM small boat, dinghy; canoe

cano'vaccio [kano'vattʃo] SM (*tela*) canvas; (*strofinaccio*) duster; (*trama*) plot

can'tante SMF singer

can'tare/72/ VT, VI to sing; **~ vittoria** to crow; **fare ~ qn** (*fig*) to make sb talk

cantas'torie SM INV/F INV storyteller

cantau'tore, -'trice SM/F singer-composer

canterel'lare/72/ VT, VI to hum, sing to o.s.

canticchi'are [kantik'kjare] /19/ VT, VI to hum, sing to o.s.

canti'ere SM (*Edil*) (building) site; (*anche*: **cantiere navale**) shipyard

canti'lena SF (*filastrocca*) lullaby; (*fig*) singsong voice

can'tina SF (*locale*) cellar; (*bottega*) wine shop; **~ sociale** cooperative winegrowers' association

'canto SM song; (*arte*) singing; (*Rel*) chant; chanting; (*Poesia*) poem, lyric; (*parte di una poesia*) canto; (*parte, lato*): **da un ~** on the one hand; **d'altro ~** on the other hand

canto'nata SF (*di edificio*) corner; **prendere una ~** (*fig*) to blunder

can'tone SM (*in Svizzera*) canton

cantoni'era AG: (**casa**) **~** road inspector's house

can'tuccio [kan'tuttʃo] SM corner, nook

ca'nuto, -a AG white, whitehaired

canzo'nare [kantso'nare] /72/ VT to tease

canzona'tura [kantsona'tura] SF teasing; (*beffa*) joke

can'zone [kan'tsone] SF song; (*Poesia*) canzone

canzoni'ere [kantso'njɛre] SM (*Mus*) songbook; (*Letteratura*) collection of poems

'caos SM INV chaos

ca'otico, -a, -ci, -che AG chaotic

CAP SIGLA M = **codice di avviamento postale**

cap. ABBR (= *capitolo*) ch.

ca'pace [ka'patʃe] AG able, capable; (*ampio, vasto*) large, capacious; **sei ~ di farlo?** can you *o* are you able to do it?; **~ d'intendere e di volere** (*Dir*) in full possession of one's faculties

capacità [kapatʃi'ta] SF INV ability; (*Dir, di recipiente*) capacity; **~ produttiva** production capacity

capaci'tarsi [kapatʃi'tarsi] /72/ VPR: **~ di** to make out, understand

ca'panna SF hut

capan'nello SM knot (of people)

ca'panno SM (*di cacciatori*) hide; (*da spiaggia*) bathing hut

capan'none SM (*Agr*) barn; (*fabbricato industriale*) (factory) shed

caparbietà SF stubbornness

ca'parbio, -a AG stubborn

ca'parra SF deposit, down payment

capa'tina SF: **fare una ~ da qn/in centro** to pop in on sb/into town

capeggi'are [kaped'dʒare] /**62**/ VT (*rivolta ecc*) to head, lead

ca'pello SM hair; **capelli** SMPL (*capigliatura*) hair *sg*; **averne fin sopra i capelli di qc/qn** to be fed up to the (back) teeth with sth/sb; **mi ci hanno tirato per i capelli** (*fig*) they dragged me into it; **tirato per i capelli** (*spiegazione*) far-fetched

capel'lone, -a SM/F hippie

capel'luto, -a AG: **cuoio ~** scalp

capez'zale [kapet'tsale] SM bolster; (*fig*) bedside

ca'pezzolo [ka'pettsolo] SM nipple

capi'ente AG capacious

capi'enza [ka'pjɛntsa] SF capacity

capiglia'tura [kapiʎʎa'tura] SF hair

capil'lare AG (*fig*) detailed ▶ SM (*Anat: anche:* **vaso capillare**) capillary

ca'pire /**55**/ VT to understand; **~ al volo** to catch on straight away; **si capisce!** (*certamente!*) of course!, certainly!

capi'tale AG (*mortale*) capital; (*fondamentale*) main *cpd*, chief *cpd* ▶ SF (*città*) capital ▶ SM (*Econ*) capital; **~ azionario** equity capital, share capital; **~ d'esercizio** working capital; **~ fisso** capital assets, fixed capital; **~ immobile** real estate; **~ liquido** cash assets *pl*; **~ mobile** movables *pl*; **~ di rischio** risk capital; **~ sociale** (*di società*) authorized capital; (*di club*) funds *pl*; **~ di ventura** venture capital, risk capital

capita'lismo SM capitalism

capita'lista, -i, -e AG, SM/F capitalist

capitaliz'zare [kapitalid'dzare] /**72**/ VT to capitalize

capitalizzazi'one [kapitaliddzat'tsjone] SF capitalization

capita'nare /**72**/ VT to lead; (*Calcio*) to captain

capitane'ria SF: **~ (di porto)** port authorities *pl*

capi'tano SM captain; **~ di lungo corso** master mariner; **~ di ventura** (*Storia*) mercenary leader

capi'tare /**72**/ VI (*giungere casualmente*) to happen to go, find o.s.; (*accadere*) to happen; (*presentarsi: cosa*) to turn up, present itself ▶ VB IMPERS to happen; **~ a proposito/bene/male** to turn up at the right moment/at a good time/at a bad time; **mi è capitato un guaio** I've had a spot of trouble

capi'tello SM (*Archit*) capital

capito'lare /**72**/ VI to capitulate

capitolazi'one [kapitolat'tsjone] SF capitulation

ca'pitolo SM chapter; **capitoli** SMPL (*Comm*) items; **non ho voce in ~** (*fig*) I have no say in the matter

capi'tombolo SM headlong fall, tumble

'capo SM (*Anat*) head; (*persona*) head, leader; (*: in ufficio*) head, boss; (*: in tribù*) chief; (*estremità: di tavolo, scale*) head, top; (*: di filo*) end; (*Geo*) cape; **andare a ~** to start a new paragraph; **"punto a ~"** "full stop — new paragraph"; **da ~** over again; **in ~ a** (*tempo*) within; **da un ~ all'altro** from one end to the other; **fra ~ e collo** (*all'improvviso*) out of the blue; **un discorso senza né ~ né coda** a senseless *o* meaningless speech; **~ d'accusa** (*Dir*) charge; **~ di bestiame** head *inv* of cattle; **C~ di Buona Speranza** Cape of Good Hope; **~ di vestiario** item of clothing

capo'banda (*pl* **capibanda**) SM (*Mus*) bandmaster; (*di malviventi, fig*) gang leader

ca'poccia [ka'pɔttʃa] SM INV (*di lavoranti*) overseer; (*peg: capobanda*) boss

capo'classe (*mpl* **capiclasse**, *fpl* **~**) SM/F (*Ins*) ≈ form captain (BRIT), class president (US)

capocu'oco, -chi SM head cook

Capo'danno SM New Year

capofa'miglia [kapofa'miʎʎa] (*mpl* **capifamiglia**, *fpl* **~**) SM/F head of the family

capo'fitto: **a ~** *av* headfirst, headlong

capo'giro [kapo'dʒiro] SM dizziness *no pl*; **da ~** (*fig*) astonishing, staggering

capo'gruppo (*mpl* **capigruppo**, *fpl* **~**) SM/F group leader

capola'voro, -i SM masterpiece

capo'linea (*pl* **capilinea**) SM terminus; (*fig*) end of the line

capo'lino SM: **far ~** to peep out (*o* into *etc*)

capo'lista (*mpl* **capilista**, *fpl* **~**) SM/F (*Pol*) top candidate on electoral list

capolu'ogo (**capoluoghi**, *pl* **capiluoghi**) SM chief town, administrative centre (BRIT) *o* center (US)

capo'mastro (**capomastri**, *pl* **capimastri**) SM master builder

capo'rale SM (*Mil*) lance corporal (BRIT), private first class (US)

capore'parto (*mpl* **capireparto**, *fpl* **~**) SM/F (*di operai*) foreman; (*di ufficio, negozio*) head of department

capo'sala SF INV (*Med*) ward sister

capo'saldo (*pl* **capisaldi**) SM stronghold; (*fig: fondamento*) basis, cornerstone

capo'squadra (*pl* **capisquadra**) SM (*di operai*) foreman, ganger; (*Mil*) squad leader; (*Sport*) team captain

capostazi'one [kapostat'tsjone] (*pl* **capistazione**) SM station master

capos'tipite SM progenitor; (*fig*) earliest example

capo'tavola (*mpl* **capitavola**, *fpl* **~**) SM/F
(*persona*) head of the table; **sedere a ~** to sit at
the head of the table

ca'pote [ka'pɔt] SF INV (*Aut*) hood (*Brit*), soft
top

capo'treno (**capitreno**, *pl* **capotreni**) SM
guard

capouf'ficio [kapouf'fitʃo] SM INV/F INV head
clerk

'Capo 'Verde SM: **il ~** Cape Verde

capo'verso SM (*di verso, periodo*) first line; (*Tip*)
indent; (*paragrafo*) paragraph; (*Dir: comma*)
section

capo'volgere [kapo'voldʒere] /**96**/ VT to
overturn; (*fig*) to reverse; **capovolgersi** VPR
to overturn; (*barca*) to capsize; (*fig*) to be
reversed

capovolgi'mento [kapovoldʒi'mento] SM
(*fig*) reversal, complete change

capo'volto, -a PP *di* **capovolgere** ▶ AG upside
down; (*barca*) capsized

'cappa SF (*mantello*) cape, cloak; (*del camino*)
hood

cap'pella SF (*Rel*) chapel

cappel'lano SM chaplain

cap'pello SM hat; **Tanto di ~!** (*fig*) I take my
hat off to you!; **~ a bombetta** bowler (hat),
derby (*US*); **~ a cilindro** top hat; **~ di paglia**
straw hat

'cappero SM caper

cap'pone SM capon

cappot'tare /**72**/ VI (*Aut*) to overturn

cap'potto SM (over)coat

cappuc'cino [kapput'tʃino] SM (*frate*)
Capuchin monk; (*bevanda*) cappuccino

cap'puccio [kap'puttʃo] SM (*copricapo*) hood;
(*della biro*) cap

'capra SF (she-)goat

ca'prese AG from (*o* of) Capri

ca'pretto SM kid

ca'priccio [ka'prittʃo] SM caprice, whim;
(*bizza*) tantrum; **fare i capricci** to be very
naughty; **~ della sorte** quirk of fate

capricci'oso, -a [kaprit'tʃoso] AG capricious,
whimsical; naughty

Capri'corno SM Capricorn; **essere del ~** (*dello
zodiaco*) to be Capricorn

capri'foglio [kapri'fɔʎʎo] SM honeysuckle

capri'ola SF somersault

capri'olo SM roe deer

'capro SM billy-goat; **~ espiatorio** (*fig*)
scapegoat

ca'prone SM billy-goat

'capsula SF capsule; (*di arma, per bottiglie*) cap

cap'tare /**72**/ VT (*Radio, TV*) to pick up;
(*cattivarsi*) to gain, win

CAR SIGLA M = **Centro Addestramento
Reclute**

cara'bina SF rifle

carabini'ere SM *member of Italian military police
force*; *see note*

> Originally part of the armed forces,
> the *Carabinieri* are police who now have
> civil as well as military duties, such as
> maintaining public order. They include
> paratroop units and mounted divisions
> and report to either the Minister of the
> Interior or the Minister of Defence,
> depending on the function they are
> performing.

Ca'racas SF Caracas

ca'raffa SF carafe

Ca'raibi SMPL: **il mar dei ~** the Caribbean
(Sea)

cara'ibico, -a, -ci, -che AG Caribbean

cara'mella SF sweet

cara'mello SM caramel

ca'rato SM (*di oro, diamante ecc*) carat

ca'rattere SM character; (*caratteristica*)
characteristic, trait; **avere un buon ~** to be
good-natured; **informazione di ~ tecnico/
confidenziale** information of a technical/
confidential nature; **essere in ~ con qc**
(*intonarsi*) to be in harmony with sth; **~ jolly**
wild card

caratte'rino SM difficult nature *o* character

caratte'ristico, -a, -ci, -che AG
characteristic ▶ SF characteristic, feature,
trait; **segni caratteristici** (*su passaporto ecc*)
distinguishing marks

caratteriz'zare [karatterid'dzare] /**72**/ VT to
characterize, distinguish

carboi'drato SM carbohydrate

carbo'naio SM (*chi fa carbone*) charcoal-burner;
(*commerciante*) coalman, coal merchant

car'bone SM coal; **~ fossile** (pit) coal; **essere
o stare sui carboni ardenti** to be like a cat
on hot bricks

car'bonio SM (*Chim*) carbon

carboniz'zare [karbonid'dzare] /**72**/ VT (*legna*)
to carbonize; (*: parzialmente*) to char; **morire
carbonizzato** to be burned to death

carbu'rante SM (*motor*) fuel

carbura'tore SM carburettor

car'cassa SF carcass; (*fig: peg: macchina ecc*)
(old) wreck

carce'rato, -a [kartʃe'rato] SM/F prisoner

'carcere ['kartʃere] SM prison; (*pena*)
imprisonment; **~ di massima sicurezza**
top-security prison

carceri'ere, -a [kartʃe'rjere] SM/F (*anche fig*)
jailer

carci'ofo [kar'tʃɔfo] SM artichoke

cardel'lino SM goldfinch

car'diaco, -a, -ci, -che AG cardiac, heart *cpd*

cardi'nale AG, SM cardinal

'cardine SM hinge

cardiolo'gia [kardjolo'dʒia] SF cardiology

cardi'ologo, -gi SM heart specialist, cardiologist

'**cardo** SM thistle

ca'rente AG: ~ **di** lacking in

ca'renza [ka'rɛntsa] SF lack, scarcity; (*vitaminica*) deficiency

cares'tia SF famine; (*penuria*) scarcity, dearth

ca'rezza [ka'rettsa] SF caress; **dare** o **fare una ~ a** (*persona*) to caress; (*animale*) to stroke, pat

carez'zare [karet'tsare] /**20**/ VT to caress, stroke, fondle

carez'zevole [karet'tsevole] AG sweet, endearing

'**cargo, -ghi** SM (*nave*) cargo boat, freighter; (*aereo*) freighter

cari'are /**20**/ VT, **cari'arsi** VPR (*denti*) to decay

'**carica** SF *vedi* **carico**

caricabatte'ria SM INV (*Elettr*) battery charger

cari'care /**20**/ VT (*merce*) to load; (*aggravare: anche fig*) to weigh down; (*orologio*) to wind up; (*batteria, Mil*) to charge; (*Inform*) to load; **caricarsi** VPR: **caricarsi di** to burden o load o.s. with; (*fig: di responsabilità, impegni*) to burden o.s. with

carica'tura SF caricature

'**carico, -a, -chi, -che** AG (*fucile*) loaded; (*orologio*) wound up; (*batteria*) charged; (*colore*) deep; (*caffè, tè*) strong; **~ di** (*che porta un peso*) loaded o laden with ▶ SM (*il caricare*) loading; (*ciò che si carica*) load; (*Comm*) shipment; (*fig: peso*) burden, weight ▶ SF (*mansione ufficiale*) office, position; (*Mil, Tecn, Elettr*) charge; **~ di debiti** up to one's ears in debt; **persona a ~** dependent; **essere a ~ di qn** (*spese ecc*) to be charged to sb; (*accusa, prova*) to be against sb; **testimone a ~** witness for the prosecution; **farsi ~ di** (*problema, responsabilità*) to take on; **a ~ del cliente** at the customer's expense; **~ di lavoro** (*di ditta, reparto*) workload; **~ utile** payload; **capacità di ~** cargo capacity; **entrare/essere in carica** to come into/be in office; **ricoprire** o **rivestire una carica** to hold a position; **uscire di carica** to leave office; **dare la carica a** (*orologio*) to wind up; (*fig: persona*) to back up; **tornare alla carica** (*fig*) to insist, persist; **ha una forte carica di simpatia** he's very likeable

'**carie** SF (*dentaria*) decay

ca'rino, -a AG (*grazioso*) lovely, pretty, nice; (*simpatico*) nice

ca'risma [ka'rizma] SM charisma

caris'matico, -a, -ci, -che AG charismatic

carità SF charity; **per ~!** (*escl di rifiuto*) good heavens, no!

carita'tevole AG charitable

carnagi'one [karna'dʒone] SF complexion

car'nale AG (*amore*) carnal; (*fratello*) blood *cpd*

'**carne** SF flesh; (*bovina, ovina ecc*) meat; **in ~ e ossa** in the flesh, in person; **essere (bene) in ~** to be well padded, be plump; **non essere né ~ né pesce** (*fig*) to be neither fish nor fowl; **~ di manzo/maiale/pecora** beef/pork/mutton; **~ in scatola** tinned o canned meat; **~ tritata** o **macinata** mince (BRIT), hamburger meat (US), minced (BRIT) o ground (US) meat

car'nefice [kar'nefitʃe] SM executioner; hangman

carnefi'cina [karnefi'tʃina] SF carnage; (*fig*) disaster

carne'vale SM carnival; **C~** *see note*

> *Carnevale* is the name given to the period between Epiphany (6 January) and the beginning of Lent, when people throw parties, put on processions with spectacular floats, build bonfires in the *piazze* and dress up in fabulous costumes and masks. Building to a peak just before Lent, *Carnevale* culminates in the festivities of *Martedì grasso* (Shrove Tuesday).

car'nivoro, -a AG carnivorous

car'noso, -a AG fleshy; (*pianta, frutto, radice*) pulpy; (*labbra*) full

'**caro, -a** AG (*amato*) dear; (*costoso*) dear, expensive; **se ti è cara la vita** if you value your life; **è troppo ~** it's too expensive

ca'rogna [ka'roɲɲa] SF carrion; (*fig: col*) swine

caro'sello SM merry-go-round

ca'rota SF carrot

caro'vana SF caravan

caro'vita SM high cost of living

'**carpa** SF carp

Car'pazi [kar'patsi] SMPL: **i ~** the Carpathian Mountains

carpente'ria SF carpentry

carpenti'ere SM carpenter

car'pire /**55**/ VT: **~ qc a qn** (*segreto ecc*) to get sth out of sb

car'poni AV on all fours

car'rabile AG suitable for vehicles; **"passo ~"** "keep clear"

car'raio, -a AG: **passo ~** vehicle entrance

carré SM (*acconciatura*) bob

carreggi'ata [karred'dʒata] SF carriageway (BRIT), roadway; **rimettersi in ~** (*fig: recuperare*) to catch up; **tenersi in ~** (*fig*) to keep to the right path

carrel'lata SF (*Cine, TV: tecnica*) tracking; (: *scena*) running shot; **~ di successi** medley of hit tunes

car'rello SM trolley; (*Aer*) undercarriage; (*Cine*) dolly; (*di macchina da scrivere*) carriage; (*Internet*) shopping basket (BRIT), shopping cart (US)

car'retta SF: **tirare la ~** (fig) to plod along
car'retto SM handcart
carri'era SF career; **fare ~** to get on; **ufficiale di ~** (Mil) regular officer; **a gran ~** at full speed
carri'ola SF wheelbarrow
'carro SM cart, wagon; **il Gran/Piccolo C~** (Astr) the Great/Little Bear; **mettere il ~ avanti ai buoi** (fig) to put the cart before the horse; **~ armato** tank; **~ attrezzi** (Aut) breakdown van (BRIT), tow truck (US); **~ funebre** hearse; **~ merci/bestiame** (Ferr) goods/animal wagon
car'roccio [kar'rɔtʃo] SM (Pol): **il C~** symbol of Lega Nord
car'rozza [kar'rɔttsa] SF carriage, coach; **~ letto** (Ferr) sleeper; **~ ristorante** (Ferr) dining car
carroz'zella [karrot'tsɛlla] SF (per bambini) pram (BRIT), baby carriage (US); (per invalidi) wheelchair
carrozze'ria [karrottse'ria] SF body, coachwork (BRIT); (officina) coachbuilder's workshop (BRIT), body shop
carrozzi'ere [karrot'tsjɛre] SM (Aut: progettista) car designer; (: meccanico) coachbuilder
carroz'zina [karrot'tsina] SF pram (BRIT), baby carriage (US)
carroz'zone [karrot'tsone] SM (da circo, di zingari) caravan
car'rucola SF pulley
'carta SF paper; (al ristorante) menu; (Geo) map; plan; (documento) card; (costituzione) charter; **carte** SFPL (documenti) papers, documents; **alla ~** (al ristorante) à la carte; **cambiare le carte in tavola** (fig) to shift one's ground; **fare carte false** (fig) to go to great lengths; **~ assegni** bank card; **~ assorbente** blotting paper; **~ bollata** o **da bollo** (Amm) official stamped paper; **~ (da gioco)** playing card; **~ di credito** credit card; **~ di debito** cash card; **~ fedeltà** loyalty card; **~ (geografica)** map; **~ d'identità** identity card; **~ igienica** toilet paper; **~ d'imbarco** (Aer, Naut) boarding card, boarding pass; **~ da lettere** writing paper; **~ libera** (Amm) unstamped paper; **~ stradale** road map; **~ millimetrata** graph paper; **~ oleata** waxed paper; **~ da pacchi, ~ da imballo** wrapping paper, brown paper; **~ da parati** wallpaper; **~ verde** (Aut) green card; **~ vetrata** sandpaper; **~ da visita** visiting card
cartacar'bone (pl **cartecarbone**) SF carbon paper
car'taccia, -ce [kar'tattʃa] SF waste paper
cartamo'dello SM (Cucito) paper pattern
cartamo'neta SF paper money

carta'pecora SF parchment
carta'pesta SF papier-mâché
cartas'traccia [kartas'trattʃa] SF waste paper
car'teggio [kar'teddʒo] SM correspondence
car'tella SF (scheda) card; (custodia: di cartone, Inform) folder; (: di uomo d'affari ecc) briefcase; (: di scolaro) schoolbag, satchel; **~ clinica** (Med) case sheet
cartel'lino SM (etichetta) label; (su porta) notice; (scheda) card; **timbrare il ~** (all'entrata) to clock in; (all'uscita) to clock out; **~ di presenza** clock card, timecard
car'tello SM sign; (pubblicitario) poster; (stradale) sign, signpost; (in dimostrazioni) placard; (Econ) cartel; **~ stradale** sign
cartel'lone SM (della tombola) scoring frame; (Teat) playbill; **tenere il ~** (spettacolo) to have a long run; **~ pubblicitario** advertising poster
carti'era SF paper mill
carti'lagine [karti'ladʒine] SF cartilage
car'tina SF (Aut, Geo) map
car'toccio [kar'tɔttʃo] SM paper bag; **cuocere al ~** (Cuc) to bake in tinfoil
cartogra'fia SF cartography
carto'laio, -a SM/F stationer
cartolarizzazi'one [kartolariddza'tsjone] SF securitization
cartole'ria SF stationer's (shop (BRIT))
carto'lina SF postcard; **~ di auguri** greetings card; **~ precetto** o **rosa** (Mil) call-up card; **~ postale** ready-stamped postcard; **~ virtuale** e-card
carto'mante SMF fortune-teller (using cards)
carton'cino [karton'tʃino] SM (materiale) thin cardboard; (biglietto) card; **~ della società** compliments slip
car'tone SM cardboard; (del latte, dell'aranciata) carton; (Arte) cartoon; **cartoni animati** (Cine) cartoons
car'tuccia, -ce [kar'tuttʃa] SF cartridge; **~ a salve** blank cartridge; **mezza ~** (fig: persona) good-for-nothing
'casa SF house; (specialmente la propria casa) home; (Comm) firm, house; **essere a ~** to be at home; **vado a ~ mia/tua** I'm going home/to your house; **~ di correzione** ≈ community home (BRIT), reformatory (US); **vino della ~** house wine; **~ di cura** nursing home; **~ editrice** publishing house; **C~ delle Libertà** House of Liberties, centre-right coalition; **~ di riposo** old people's) home, care home; **~ dello studente** student hostel; **~ di tolleranza, ~ d'appuntamenti** brothel; **case popolari** ≈ council houses (o flats) (BRIT), ≈ public housing units (US)
ca'sacca, -che SF military coat; (di fantino) blouse

ca'sale SM (*gruppo di case*) hamlet; (*casa di campagna*) farmhouse

casa'lingo, -a, -ghi, -ghe AG household, domestic; (*fatto a casa*) home-made; (*semplice*) homely; (*amante della casa*) home-loving ▶ SF housewife; **casalinghi** SMPL (*oggetti*) household articles; **cucina casalinga** plain home cooking

ca'sata SF family lineage

ca'sato SM family name

casca'morto SM woman-chaser; **fare il** ~ to chase women

cas'care /20/ VI to fall; ~ **bene/male** (*fig*) to land lucky/unlucky; ~ **dalle nuvole** (*fig*) to be taken aback; ~ **dal sonno** to be falling asleep on one's feet; **caschi il mondo** no matter what; **non cascherà il mondo se …** it won't be the end of the world if …

cas'cata SF fall; (*d'acqua*) cascade, waterfall

cascherò etc [kaske'rɔ] VB *vedi* **cascare**

ca'scina [kaʃʃina] SF farmstead

casci'nale [kaʃʃi'nale] SM (*casolare*) farmhouse; (*cascina*) farmstead

'casco (*pl* **caschi**) SM helmet; (*del parrucchiere*) hair-dryer; (*di banane*) bunch; ~ **blu** (*Mil*) blue helmet (*UN soldier*)

caseggi'ato [kased'dʒato] SM (*edificio*) large block of flats (*BRIT*) o apartment building (*US*); (*gruppo di case*) group of houses

casei'ficio [kazei'fitʃo] SM creamery

ca'sella SF pigeonhole; ~ **email** mailbox; ~ **di posta elettronica** mailbox; ~ **postale** post office box

casel'lario SM (*mobile*) filing cabinet; (*raccolta di pratiche*) files *pl*; ~ **giudiziale** court records *pl*; ~ **penale** police files *pl*

ca'sello SM (*di autostrada*) tollgate

case'reccio, -a, -ci, -ce [kase'rettʃo] AG home-made

ca'serma SF barracks

caser'tano, -a AG of (*o from*) Caserta

ca'sino SM (*col: confusione*) row, racket; (*casa di prostituzione*) brothel

casinò SM INV casino

ca'sistica SF (*Med*) record of cases; **secondo la ~ degli incidenti stradali** according to road accident data

'caso SM chance; (*fatto, vicenda*) event, incident; (*possibilità*) possibility; (*Med, Ling*) case; **a ~** at random; **per ~** by chance, by accident; **in ogni ~, in tutti i casi** in any case, at any rate; **in ~ contrario** otherwise; **al ~** should the opportunity arise; **nel ~ che** in case; ~ **mai** if by chance; **far ~ a qc/qn** to pay attention to sth/sb; **fare** o **porre** o **mettere il ~ che** to suppose that; **fa proprio al ~ nostro** it's just what we need; **guarda ~ …** strangely enough …; **è il ~ che ce ne andiamo** we'd better go; ~ **limite** borderline case

caso'lare SM cottage

'Caspio SM: **il mar ~** the Caspian Sea

'caspita ESCL (*di sorpresa*) good heavens!; (*di impazienza*) for goodness' sake!

'cassa SF case, crate, box; (*bara*) coffin; (*mobile*) chest; (*involucro: di orologio ecc*) case; (*macchina*) cash register, till; (*luogo di pagamento*) cash desk, checkout (counter); (*fondo*) fund; (*istituto bancario*) bank; **battere ~** (*fig*) to come looking for money; ~ **automatica prelievi** automatic telling machine, cash dispenser; ~ **continua** night safe; **mettere in ~ integrazione** ≈ to lay off; **C~ del Mezzogiorno** *development fund for the South of Italy*; ~ **mutua** o **malattia** health insurance scheme; ~ **di risonanza** (*Mus*) soundbox; (*fig*) platform; ~ **di risparmio** savings bank; ~ **rurale e artigiana** credit institution (*serving farmers and craftsmen*); ~ **toracica** (*Anat*) chest

cassa'forte (*pl* **casseforti**) SF safe

cassa'panca (*pl* **cassapanche** o **cassepanche**) SF settle

casseru'ola, casse'rola SF saucepan

cas'setta SF box; (*per registratore*) cassette; (*Cine, Teat*) box-office takings *pl*; **pane** a o **in ~** toasting loaf; **film di ~** (*commerciale*) box-office draw; **far ~** to be a box-office success; ~ **delle lettere** letterbox; ~ **di sicurezza** strongbox

cas'setto SM drawer

casset'tone SM chest of drawers

cassi'ere, -a SM/F cashier; (*di banca*) teller

cassinte'grato, -a SM/F *person who has been laid off*

cas'sone SM (*cassa*) large case, large chest

casso'netto SM wheelie-bin

'casta SF caste

cas'tagna [kas'taɲɲa] SF chestnut; **prendere qn in ~** (*fig*) to catch sb in the act

cas'tagno [kas'taɲɲo] SM chestnut (tree)

cas'tano, -a AG chestnut (brown)

cas'tello SM castle; (*Tecn*) scaffolding

casti'gare /80/ VT to punish

casti'gato, -a AG (*casto, modesto*) pure, chaste; (*emendato: prosa, versione*) expurgated, amended

cas'tigo, -ghi SM punishment; **mettere/essere in ~** to punish/be punished

castità SF chastity

'casto, -a AG chaste, pure

cas'toro SM beaver

cas'trante AG frustrating

cas'trare /72/ VT to castrate; to geld; to doctor (*BRIT*), fix (*US*); (*fig: iniziativa*) to frustrate

castrone'ria SF (*col*): **dire castronerie** to talk rubbish

casu'ale AG chance *cpd*; (*Inform*) random *cpd*

ca'supola SF simple little cottage

catac'lisma, -i SM (*fig*) catastrophe

cata'comba SF catacomb

cata'fascio [kata'faʃʃo] SM: **andare a ~** to collapse; **mandare a ~** to wreck

cata'litico, -a, -ci, -che AG: **marmitta catalitica** (*Aut*) catalytic converter

cataliz'zare [katalid'dzare] /**72**/ VT (*fig*) to act as a catalyst (up)on

cataliz'zato, -a [katalid'dzato] AG (*Aut*) with catalytic converter

catalizza'tore [kataliddza'tore] SM (*anche fig*) catalyst; (*Aut*) catalytic converter

Cata'logna [kata'loɲɲa] SF: **la ~** Catalonia

ca'talogo, -ghi SM catalogue; **~ dei prezzi** price list

cata'nese AG of (*o* from) Catania

catanza'rese [katandza'rese] AG of (*o* from) Catanzaro

cata'pecchia [kata'pekkja] SF hovel

cata'pulta SF catapult

catarifran'gente [katarifran'dʒɛnte] SM (*Aut*) reflector

ca'tarro SM catarrh

ca'tarsi SF INV catharsis

ca'tasta SF stack, pile

ca'tasto SM land register; land registry office

ca'tastrofe SF catastrophe, disaster

catas'trofico, -a, -ci, -che AG (*evento*) catastrophic; (*persona, previsione*) pessimistic

catastro'fista, -i, -e AG, SM/F doom-monger; **non fare il ~** don't be so pessimistic

cate'chismo [kate'kizmo] SM catechism

catego'ria SF category; (*di albergo*) class

cate'gorico, -a, -ci, -che AG categorical

ca'tena SF chain; **reazione a ~** chain reaction; **susseguirsi a ~** to happen in quick succession; **~ alimentare** food chain; **~ di montaggio** assembly line; **~ montuosa** mountain range; **catene da neve** (*Aut*) snow chains

cate'naccio [kate'nattʃo] SM bolt

cate'nella SF (*ornamento*) chain; (*di orologio*) watch chain; (*di porta*) door chain

cate'nina SF (*gioiello*) (thin) chain

cate'ratta SF cataract; (*chiusa*) sluice gate

ca'terva SF (*di cose*) loads *pl*, heaps *pl*; (*di persone*) horde

cate'tere SM (*Med*) catheter

cati'nella SF: **piovere a catinelle** to pour, rain cats and dogs

ca'tino SM basin

ca'todico, -a, -ci, -che AG: **tubo a raggi catodici** cathode-ray tube

ca'torcio [ka'tɔrtʃo] SM (*peg*) old wreck

ca'trame SM tar

'cattedra SF teacher's desk; (*di università*) chair; **salire** *o* **montare in ~** (*fig*) to pontificate

catte'drale SF cathedral

catte'dratico, -a, -ci, -che AG (*insegnamento*) university *cpd*; (*ironico*) pedantic ▶ SM/F professor

catti'veria SF (*qualità*) wickedness, malice; (*di bambino*) naughtiness; (*azione*) spiteful act; (*parole*) malicious *o* spiteful remark; **fare una ~** to do something wicked; to be naughty

cattività SF captivity

cat'tivo, -a AG bad; (*malvagio*) bad, wicked; (*turbolento: bambino*) bad, naughty; (: *mare*) rough; (*odore, sapore*) nasty, bad ▶ SM/F bad *o* wicked person; **farsi ~ sangue** to worry, get in a state; **farsi un ~ nome** to earn o.s. a bad reputation; **i cattivi** (*nei film*) the baddies (*BRIT*), the bad guys (*US*)

cattocomu'nista, -i, -e AG combining Catholic and communist ideas

cattoli'cesimo [kattoli'tʃezimo] SM Catholicism

cat'tolico, -a, -ci, -che AG, SM/F (Roman) Catholic

cat'tura SF capture

cattu'rare /**72**/ VT to capture

cau'casico, -a, -ci, -che AG, SM/F Caucasian

'Caucaso SM: **il ~** the Caucasus

caucciù [kaut'tʃu] SM rubber

'causa SF cause; (*Dir*) lawsuit, case, action; **a ~ di, per ~ di** because of; **per ~ sua** because of him; **fare** *o* **muovere ~ a qn** to take legal action against sb; **parte in ~** litigant

cau'sale AG (*Ling*) causal ▶ SF cause, reason

cau'sare /**72**/ VT to cause

'caustico, -a, -ci, -che AG caustic

cau'tela SF caution, prudence

caute'lare /**72**/ VT to protect; **cautelarsi** VPR: **cautelarsi (da** *o* **contro)** to take precautions (against)

'cauto, -a AG cautious, prudent

cauzio'nare [kauttsjo'nare] /**72**/ VT to guarantee

cauzi'one [kaut'tsjone] SF security; (*Dir*) bail; **rilasciare dietro ~** to release on bail

cav. ABBR = **cavaliere**

'cava SF quarry

caval'care /**20**/ VT (*cavallo*) to ride; (*muro*) to sit astride; (*ponte*) to span

caval'cata SF ride; (*gruppo di persone*) riding party

cavalca'via SM INV flyover

cavalci'oni [kaval'tʃoni]: **a ~ di** *prep* astride

cavali'ere SM rider; (*feudale, titolo*) knight; (*soldato*) cavalryman; (*al ballo*) partner

cavalleg'gero [kavalled'dʒɛro] SM (*Mil*) light cavalryman

cavalle'resco, -a, -schi, -sche AG chivalrous

cavalle'ria SF chivalry; (*milizia a cavallo*) cavalry

cavalle'rizzo, -a [kavalle'rittso] SM/F riding
instructor; circus rider

caval'letta SF grasshopper; (*dannosa*) locust

caval'letto SM (*Fot*) tripod; (*da pittore*) easel

caval'lina SF (*Ginnastica*) horse; (*gioco*)
leap-frog; **correre la ~** (*fig*) to sow one's wild
oats

ca'vallo SM horse; (*Scacchi*) knight; (*Aut:
anche*: **cavallo vapore**) horsepower; (*dei
pantaloni*) crotch; **a ~** on horseback; **a ~ di**
astride, straddling; **siamo a ~** (*fig*) we've
made it; **da ~** (*fig: dose*) drastic; (: *febbre*)
raging; **vivere a ~ tra due periodi** to
straddle two periods; **~ di battaglia** (*Teat*)
tour de force; (*fig*) hobbyhorse; **~ da corsa**
racehorse; **~ a dondolo** rocking horse; **~ da
sella** saddle horse; **~ da soma** packhorse

ca'vare /72/ VT (*togliere*) to draw out, extract,
take out; (: *giacca, scarpe*) to take off; (: *fame,
sete, voglia*) to satisfy; **cavarsi** VPR: **cavarsi da**
(*guai, problemi*) to get out of; **cavarsela** to get
away with it; to manage, get on all right;
non ci caverà un bel nulla you'll get
nothing out of it (*o* him *etc*)

cava'tappi SM INV corkscrew

ca'verna SF cave

caver'noso, -a AG (*luogo*) cavernous; (*fig: voce*)
deep; (: *tosse*) raucous

ca'vezza [ka'vettsa] SF halter

'cavia SF guinea pig

cavi'ale SM caviar

ca'viglia [ka'viʎʎa] SF ankle

cavil'lare /72/ VI to quibble

ca'villo SM quibble

cavil'loso, -a AG quibbling, hair-splitting

cavità SF INV cavity

'cavo, -a AG hollow ▶ SM (*Anat*) cavity; (*grossa
corda*) rope, cable; (*Elettr, Tel*) cable

cavo'lata SF (*col*) stupid thing

cavo'letto SM: **~ di Bruxelles** Brussels sprout

cavolfi'ore SM cauliflower

'cavolo SM cabbage; **non m'importa un ~**
(*col*) I don't give a hoot; **che ~ vuoi?** (*col*)
what the heck do you want?

caz'zata [kat'tsata] SF (!: *stupidaggine*) stupid
thing, something stupid

'cazzo ['kattso] SM (!: *pene*) prick (!); **non
gliene importa un ~** (*fig: !*) he doesn't give a
damn about it; **fatti i cazzi tuoi** (*fig: !*) mind
your own damn business

caz'zotto [kat'tsɔtto] SM punch; **fare a
cazzotti** to have a punch-up

cazzu'ola [kat'tswɔla] SF trowel

CB SIGLA = **Campobasso**

CC ABBR = **Carabinieri**

cc ABBR (= *centimetro cubico*) cc

C.C. ABBR = **codice civile**

c.c. ABBR (= *conto corrente*) c/a, a/c; (*Elettr*) *vedi*
corrente continua

c/c ABBR (= *conto corrente*) c/a, a/c

C.C.D. SIGLA M (*Pol*: = *Centro Cristiano
Democratico*) *party originating from Democrazia
Cristiana*

CCI SIGLA F (= *Camera di Commercio Internazionale*)
ICC (= *International Chamber of Commerce*)

CCIAA ABBR = **Camera di Commercio
Industria, Agricoltura e Artigianato**

CCT SIGLA M = **certificato di credito del
Tesoro**

C.D. ABBR (= *Corpo Diplomatico*) CD ▶ SM INV
(= *compact disc*) CD; (*lettore*) CD player

c.d. ABBR = **cosiddetto**

C.d.A. ABBR = **Consiglio di Amministrazione**

c.d.d. ABBR (= *come dovevasi dimostrare*) QED
(= *quod erat demonstrandum*)

C.d.M. ABBR = **Cassa del Mezzogiorno**

CD-Rom [tʃidi'rɔm] SIGLA M INV (= *Compact
Disc Read Only Memory*) CD-Rom

C.d.U. [tʃidi'u] SIGLA M (= *Cristiano Democratici
Uniti*) United Christian Democrats (*Italian
centre-right political party*)

CE SIGLA = **Caserta**

ce [tʃe] PRON, AV *vedi* **ci**

C.E. SIGLA = **Consiglio d'Europa**

cec'chino [tʃek'kino] SM sniper; (*Pol*) *member
of parliament who votes against his own party*

'cece ['tʃetʃe] SM chickpea, garbanzo (*US*)

Ce'cenia [tʃe'tʃenja] SF Chechnya

ce'ceno, -a [tʃe'tʃeno] AG, SM/F Chechen

cecità [tʃetʃi'ta] SF blindness

'ceco, -a, -chi, -che ['tʃɛko] AG, SM/F, SM
Czech; **la Repubblica Ceca** the Czech
Republic

Cecoslo'vacchia [tʃekozlo'vakkja] SF (*Storia*):
la ~ Czechoslovakia

cecoslo'vacco, -a, -chi, -che
[tʃekozlo'vakko] AG, SM/F (*Storia*)
Czechoslovakian

CED [tʃɛd] SIGLA M = **centro elaborazione
dati**

'cedere ['tʃedere] /29/ VT (*concedere: posto*) to
give up; (*Dir*) to transfer, make over ▶ VI
(*cadere*) to give way, subside; **~ (a)** to
surrender (to), yield (to), give in (to); **~ il
passo (a qn)** to let (sb) pass in front; **~ il
passo a qc** (*fig*) to give way to sth; **~ la
parola (a qn)** to hand over (to sb)

ce'devole [tʃe'devole] AG (*terreno*) soft; (*fig*)
yielding

ce'dola ['tʃedola] SF (*Comm*) coupon; voucher

ce'drata [tʃe'drata] SF citron juice

'cedro ['tʃedro] SM cedar; (*albero da frutto,
frutto*) citron

'CEE ['tʃee] SIGLA F = **Comunità Economica
Europea**

'ceffo ['tʃɛffo] SM (*peg*) ugly mug

ceffone [tʃef'fone] SM slap, smack

'ceko, -a ['tʃɛko] AG, SM/F = **ceco**

ce'lare [tʃe'lare] /**72**/ vt to conceal; **celarsi** vpr to hide

cele'brare [tʃele'brare] /**72**/ vt to celebrate; (*cerimonia*) to hold; **~ le lodi di qc/qn** to sing the praises of sth/sb

celebrazi'one [tʃelebrat'tsjone] sf celebration

'celebre ['tʃelebre] ag famous, celebrated

celebrità [tʃelebri'ta] sf inv fame; (*persona*) celebrity

'celere ['tʃɛlere] ag fast, swift; (*corso*) crash *cpd* ▶ sf (*Polizia*) riot police

ce'leste [tʃe'leste] ag celestial; heavenly; (*colore*) sky-blue

'celia [tʃɛlja] sf joke; **per ~** for a joke

celi'bato [tʃeli'bato] sm celibacy

'celibe ['tʃɛlibe] ag single, unmarried ▶ sm bachelor

'cella ['tʃɛlla] sf cell; **~ di rigore** punishment cell; **~ frigorifera** cold store

cello'phane® [sɛlo'fan] sm cellophane®

'cellula ['tʃɛllula] sf (*Biol, Elettr, Pol*) cell

cellu'lare [tʃellu'lare] ag cellular ▶ sm (*furgone*) police van; (*telefono*) cellphone; **segregazione ~** (*Dir*) solitary confinement

cellu'lite [tʃellu'lite] sf cellulite

'celta ['tʃɛlta] smf Celt

'celtico, -a, -ci, -che ['tʃɛltiko] ag, sm Celtic

'cembalo ['tʃembalo] sm (*Mus*) harpsichord

cemen'tare [tʃemen'tare] /**72**/ vt (*anche fig*) to cement

ce'mento [tʃe'mento] sm cement; **~ armato** reinforced concrete

'cena ['tʃena] sf dinner; (*leggera*) supper

ce'nacolo [tʃe'nakolo] sm (*circolo*) coterie, circle; (*Rel, dipinto*) Last Supper

ce'nare [tʃe'nare] /**72**/ vi to dine, have dinner

'cencio ['tʃentʃo] sm piece of cloth, rag; (*per spolverare*) duster; **essere bianco come un ~** to be as white as a sheet

'cenere ['tʃenere] sf ash

Cene'rentola [tʃene'rɛntola] sf (*anche fig*) Cinderella

'cenno ['tʃenno] sm (*segno*) sign, signal; (*gesto*) gesture; (*col capo*) nod; (*con la mano*) wave; (*allusione*) hint, mention; (*breve esposizione*) short account; **far ~ di sì/no** to nod (one's head)/shake one's head; **~ d'intesa** sign of agreement; **cenni di storia dell'arte** an outline of the history of art

censi'mento [tʃensi'mento] sm census

cen'sire [tʃen'sire] /**55**/ vt to take a census of

'CENSIS ['tʃensis] sigla m (= *Centro Studi Investimenti Sociali*) *independent institute carrying out research on Italy's social and cultural welfare*

cen'sore [tʃen'sore] sm censor

cen'sura [tʃen'sura] sf censorship; censor's office; (*fig*) censure

censu'rare [tʃensu'rare] /**72**/ vt to censor; to censure

cent. abbr = **centesimo**

centelli'nare [tʃentelli'nare] /**72**/ vt to sip; (*fig*) to savour (brit), savor (us)

cente'nario, -a [tʃente'narjo] ag (*che ha cento anni*) hundred-year-old; (*che ricorre ogni cento anni*) centennial, centenary *cpd* ▶ sm/f centenarian ▶ sm centenary

cen'tesimo, -a [tʃen'tɛzimo] ag, sm hundredth; (*di euro, dollaro*) cent; **essere senza un ~** to be penniless

cen'tigrado, -a [tʃen'tigrado] ag centigrade; **20 gradi centigradi** 20 degrees centigrade

cen'tilitro [tʃen'tilitro] sm centilitre

cen'timetro [tʃen'timetro] sm centimetre (brit), centimeter (us); (*nastro*) measuring tape (*in centimetres*)

centi'naio [tʃenti'najo] (*pl(f)* **centinaia**) sm: **un ~ (di)** a hundred; about a hundred

'cento ['tʃento] num a hundred, one hundred; **per ~** per cent; **al ~ per ~** a hundred per cent; **~ di questi giorni!** many happy returns (of the day)!

centodi'eci [tʃento'djɛtʃi] num one hundred and ten; **~ e lode** (*Università*) ≈ first-class honours

cento'mila [tʃento'mila] num a o one hundred thousand; **te l'ho detto ~ volte** (*fig*) I've told you a thousand times

Cen'trafrica [tʃen'trafrika] sm: **il ~** the Central African Republic

cen'trale [tʃen'trale] ag central ▶ sf: **~ elettrica** electric power station; **~ eolica** wind farm; **~ del latte** dairy; **~ di polizia** police headquarters *pl*; **~ telefonica** (telephone) exchange; **sede ~** head office

centrali'nista [tʃentrali'nista] smf operator

centra'lino [tʃentra'lino] sm (telephone) exchange; (*di albergo ecc*) switchboard

centraliz'zare [tʃentralid'dzare] /**72**/ vt to centralize

centraliz'zato, -a [tʃentralid'dzato] ag central

cen'trare [tʃen'trare] /**72**/ vt to hit the centre (brit) o center (us) of; (*Tecn*) to centre; **~ una risposta** to get the right answer; **ha centrato il problema** you've hit the nail on the head

centra'vanti [tʃentra'vanti] sm inv centre forward

cen'trifuga [tʃen'trifuga] sf spin-dryer

centrifu'gare [tʃentrifu'gare] /**80**/ vt (*Tecn*) to centrifuge; (*biancheria*) to spin-dry

'centro ['tʃentro] sm centre (brit), center (us); **fare ~** to hit the bull's eye; (*Calcio*) to score; (*fig*) to hit the nail on the head; **~ balneare** seaside resort; **~ civico** civic centre; **~ commerciale** shopping centre; (*città*) commercial centre; **~ di costo** cost centre; **~ elaborazione dati** data-processing unit; **~ ospedaliero** hospital complex; **~ di permanenza temporanea** reception centre; **~ sociale** community centre; **centri vitali** (*anche fig*) vital organs

centro'destra [tʃentro'dɛstra] SM (*Pol*) centre right

centromedi'ano [tʃentrome'djano] SM (*Calcio*) centre half

centrosi'nistra [tʃentrosi'nistra] SM (*Pol*) centre left

'**ceppo** ['tʃeppo] SM (*di albero*) stump; (*pezzo di legno*) log

'**cera** ['tʃera] SF wax; (*aspetto*) appearance, look; **~ per pavimenti** floor polish

cera'lacca [tʃera'lakka] SF sealing wax

ce'ramica [tʃe'ramika] (*pl* **ceramiche**) SF ceramic; (*Arte*) ceramics *sg*

cerbi'atto [tʃer'bjatto] SM (*Zool*) fawn

'**cerca** ['tʃerka] SF: **in** *o* **alla ~ di** in search of

cercaper'sone [tʃerkaper'sone] SM INV bleeper

cer'care [tʃer'kare] /**20**/ VT to look for, search for ▶ VI: **~ di fare qc** to try to do sth

cercherò *etc* [tʃerke'rɔ] VB *vedi* **cercare**

'**cerchia** ['tʃerkja] SF circle

cerchi'ato, -a [tʃer'kjato] AG: **occhiali cerchiati d'osso** horn-rimmed spectacles; **avere gli occhi cerchiati** to have dark rings under one's eyes

cer'chietto [tʃer'kjetto] SM (*per capelli*) hairband

'**cerchio** ['tʃerkjo] SM circle; (*giocattolo, di botte*) hoop; **dare un colpo al ~ e uno alla botte** (*fig*) to keep two things going at the same time

cerchi'one [tʃer'kjone] SM (wheel)rim

cere'ale [tʃere'ale] SM cereal

cere'brale [tʃere'brale] AG cerebral

ceri'monia [tʃeri'mɔnja] SF ceremony; **senza tante cerimonie** (*senza formalità*) informally; (*bruscamente*) unceremoniously, without so much as a by-your-leave

cerimoni'ale [tʃerimo'njale] SM etiquette; ceremonial

cerimoni'ere [tʃerimo'njɛre] SM master of ceremonies

cerimoni'oso, -a [tʃerimo'njoso] AG formal, ceremonious

ce'rino [tʃe'rino] SM wax match

CERN [tʃɛrn] SIGLA M (= *Comitato Europeo di Ricerche Nucleari*) CERN

'**cernia** ['tʃɛrnja] SF (*Zool*) stone bass

cerni'era [tʃer'njɛra] SF hinge; **~ lampo** zip (fastener) (*BRIT*), zipper (*US*)

'**cernita** ['tʃɛrnita] SF selection; **fare una ~ di** to select

'**cero** ['tʃero] SM (church) candle

ce'rone [tʃe'rone] SM (*trucco*) greasepaint

ce'rotto [tʃe'rɔtto] SM sticking plaster

certa'mente [tʃerta'mente] AV certainly, surely

cer'tezza [tʃer'tettsa] SF certainty

certifi'care [tʃertifi'kare] /**20**/ VT to certify

certifi'cato [tʃertifi'kato] SM certificate; **~ medico/di nascita/di morte** medical/birth/death certificate; **~ di credito del Tesoro** treasury bill

certificazi'one [tʃertifikat'tsjone] SF certification; **~ di bilancio** (*Comm*) external audit

'**certo, -a** ['tʃɛrto] AG (*sicuro*): **certo (di/che)** certain *o* sure (of/that)
▶ DET **1** (*tale*) certain; **un certo signor Smith** a (certain) Mr Smith
2 (*qualche: con valore intensivo*) some; **dopo un certo tempo** after some time; **un fatto di una certa importanza** a matter of some importance; **di una certa età** past one's prime, not so young
▶ PRON: **certi, e** (*pl*) some
▶ AV (*certamente*) certainly; (*senz'altro*) of course; **di certo** certainly; **no (di) certo!**, **certo che no!** certainly not!; **sì certo** yes indeed, certainly

certo'sino [tʃerto'zino] SM Carthusian monk; (*liquore*) chartreuse; **è un lavoro da ~** it's a pernickety job

cer'tuni [tʃer'tuni] PRON PL some (people)

ce'rume [tʃe'rume] SM (ear) wax

'**cerva** ['tʃɛrva] SF (female) deer, doe

cer'vello [tʃer'vɛllo] (*pl* **cervelli**, *pl*(*f*) **cervella**, *pl*(*f*) **cervelle**) SM (*Anat*) brain; **~ elettronico** computer; **avere il** *o* **essere un ~ fino** to be sharp-witted; **è uscito di ~, gli è dato di volta il ~** he's gone off his head

cervi'cale [tʃervi'kale] AG cervical

'**cervo, -a** ['tʃɛrvo] SM/F stag (hind) ▶ SM deer; **~ volante** stag beetle

cesel'lare [tʃezel'lare] /**72**/ VT to chisel; (*incidere*) to engrave

ce'sello [tʃe'zɛllo] SM chisel

ce'soie [tʃe'zoje] SFPL shears

ces'puglio [tʃes'puʎʎo] SM bush

ces'sare [tʃes'sare] /**72**/ VI, VT to stop, cease; **~ di fare qc** to stop doing sth; **"cessato allarme"** "all clear"

ces'sate il fu'oco [tʃes'sate-] SM ceasefire

cessazi'one [tʃessat'tsjone] SF cessation; (*interruzione*) suspension

cessi'one [tʃes'sjone] SF transfer

'**cesso** ['tʃɛsso] SM (*col: gabinetto*) bog

'**cesta** ['tʃesta] SF (large) basket

ces'tello [tʃes'tɛllo] SM (per bottiglie) crate; (di lavatrice) drum

cesti'nare [tʃesti'nare] /72/ VT to throw away; (fig: proposta) to turn down; (: romanzo) to reject

ces'tino [tʃes'tino] SM basket; (per la carta straccia) wastepaper basket; (Inform) recycle bin; ~ **da viaggio** (Ferr) packed lunch (o dinner)

'cesto ['tʃesto] SM basket

'cesura [tʃe'zura] SF caesura

ce'taceo [tʃe'tatʃeo] SM sea mammal

'ceto ['tʃeto] SM (social) class

'cetra ['tʃetra] SF zither; (fig: di poeta) lyre

cetrio'lino [tʃetrio'lino] SM gherkin

cetri'olo [tʃetri'ɔlo] SM cucumber

Cf., Cfr. ABBR (= confronta) cf.

CFC [tʃiɛffe'tʃi] ABBR MPL (= clorofluorocarburi) CFC

Cfr. ABBR (= confronta) cf

CFS SIGLA M (= Corpo Forestale dello Stato) body responsible for the planting and management of forests

cg ABBR (= centigrammo) cg

C.G.I.L. [tʃidʒi'ɛlle] SIGLA F (= Confederazione Generale Italiana del Lavoro) trades union organization

CH SIGLA = **Chieti**

cha'let [ʃa'lɛ] SM INV chalet

cham'pagne [ʃã'paɲ] SM INV champagne

chance [ʃãs] SF INV chance

charme [ʃarm] SM charm

'charter ['tʃa:tər] AG INV (volo) charter cpd; (aereo) chartered ▶ SM INV chartered plane

chat'line [tʃæt'laen] SF INV chat room

chat'tare [tʃat'tare] /72/ VI to chat; (online) to chat

chat'tata [tʃat'tata] SF chat

(PAROLA CHIAVE)

che [ke] PRON **1** (relativo: persona: soggetto) who; (: oggetto) whom, that; (: cosa, animale) which, that; **il ragazzo che è venuto** the boy who came; **l'uomo che io vedo** the man (whom) I see; **il libro che è sul tavolo** the book which o that is on the table; **il libro che vedi** the book (which o that) you see; **la sera che ti ho visto** the evening I saw you
2 (interrogativo, esclamativo) what; **che (cosa) fai?** what are you doing?; **a che (cosa) pensi?** what are you thinking about?; **non sa che (cosa) fare** he doesn't know what to do; **sai di che si tratta?** do you know what it's about?; **che (cosa) succede?** what's happening?; **ma che dici!** what are you saying!
3 (indefinito): **quell'uomo ha un che di losco** there's something suspicious about that man; **un certo non so che** an indefinable

something; **non è un gran che** it's nothing much
▶ DET **1** (interrogativo: tra tanti) what; (: tra pochi) which; **che tipo di film preferisci?** what sort of film do you prefer?; **che vestito ti vuoi mettere?** what (o which) dress do you want to put on?
2 (esclamativo: seguito da aggettivo) how; (: seguito da sostantivo) what; **che buono!** how delicious!; **che bel vestito!** what a lovely dress!; **che macchina!** what a car!
▶ CONG **1** (con proposizioni subordinate) that; **credo che verrà** I think he'll come; **voglio che tu studi** I want you to study; **so che tu c'eri** I know (that) you were there; **non che sia sbagliato, ma ...** not that it's wrong, but ...
2 (finale) so that; **vieni qua, che ti veda** come here, so (that) I can see you; **stai attento che non cada** mind it doesn't fall
3 (temporale): **arrivai che eri già partito** you had already left when I arrived; **sono anni che non lo vedo** I haven't seen him for years
4 (in frasi imperative, concessive): **che venga pure!** let him come by all means!; **che tu sia benedetto!** may God bless you!; **che tu venga o no partiamo lo stesso** we're going whether you come or not
5 (comparativo: con più, meno) than; **è più lungo che largo** it's longer than it's wide; **più bella che mai** more beautiful than ever vedi anche **più; meno**
6 vedi anche **così** ecc

'checca, -che ['kekka] SF (col: omosessuale) fairy

chef [ʃɛf] SM INV chef

chemiotera'pia [kemjotera'pia] SF chemotherapy

chero'sene [kero'zɛne] SM kerosene

cheru'bino [keru'bino] SM cherub

che'tare [ke'tare] /72/ VT to hush, silence; chetarsi VPR to quieten down, fall silent

cheti'chella [keti'kɛlla] SF: **alla ~** av stealthily, unobtrusively; **andarsene alla ~** to slip away

'cheto, -a ['keto] AG quiet, silent

(PAROLA CHIAVE)

chi [ki] PRON **1** (interrogativo: soggetto) who; (: oggetto) who, whom; **chi è?** who is it?; **di chi è questo libro?** whose book is this?, whose is this book?; **con chi parli?** who are you talking to?; **a chi pensi?** who are you thinking about?; **chi di voi?** which of you?; **non so a chi rivolgermi** I don't know who to ask
2 (relativo) whoever, anyone who; **dillo a chi vuoi** tell whoever you like; **portate chi**

volete bring anyone you like; **so io di chi parlo** I know who I'm talking about; **lo riferirò a chi di dovere** I'll pass it on to the relevant person
3 (*indefinito*): **chi ... chi ...** some ... others ...; **chi dice una cosa, chi dice un'altra** some say one thing, others say another

chiacchie'rare [kjakkje'rare] **/72/** VI to chat; (*discorrere futilmente*) to chatter; (*far pettegolezzi*) to gossip

chiacchie'rata [kjakkje'rata] SF chat; **farsi una ~** to have a chat

chi'acchiere ['kjakkjere] SFPL chatter *no pl*; gossip *no pl*; **fare due** *o* **quattro ~** to have a chat; **perdersi in ~** to waste time talking

chiacchie'rone, -a [kjakkje'rone] AG talkative, chatty gossipy ▶ SM/F chatterbox; gossip

chia'mare [kja'mare] **/72/** VT to call; (*rivolgersi a qn*) to call (in), send for; **chiamarsi** VPR (*aver nome*) to be called; **come ti chiami?** what's your name?; **mi chiamo Paolo** my name is Paolo, I'm called Paolo; **mandare a ~ qn** to send for sb, call sb in; **~ alle armi** to call up; **~ in giudizio** to summon; **~ qn da parte** to take sb aside

chia'mata [kja'mata] SF (*Tel*) call; (*Mil*) call-up; **~ interurbana** long-distance call; **~ con preavviso** person-to-person call; **~ alle urne** (*Pol*) election

chi'appa ['kjappa] SF (*col: natica*) cheek; **chiappe** SFPL bottom *sg*

chi'ara ['kjara] SF egg white

chia'rezza [kja'rettsa] SF clearness; clarity

chiarifi'care [kjarifi'kare] **/20/** VT (*anche fig*) to clarify

chiarificazi'one [kjarifikat'tsjone] SF clarification

chiari'mento [kjari'mento] SM clarification *no pl*, explanation

chia'rire [kja'rire] **/55/** VT to make clear; (*fig: spiegare*) to clear up, explain; **chiarirsi** VPR to become clear; **si sono chiariti** they've sorted things out

chi'aro, -a ['kjaro] AG clear; (*luminoso*) clear, bright; (*colore*) pale, light ▶ AV (*parlare, vedere*) clearly; **si sta facendo ~** the day is dawning; **sia chiara una cosa** let's get one thing straight; **mettere in ~ qc** (*fig*) to clear sth up; **parliamoci ~** let's be frank; **trasmissione in ~** (*TV*) uncoded broadcast

chia'rore [kja'rore] SM (diffuse) light

chiaroveg'gente [kjaroved'dʒɛnte] SMF clairvoyant

chi'asso ['kjasso] SM uproar, row; **far ~** to make a din; (*fig*) to make a fuss (: *notizia*) to cause a stir

chias'soso, -a [kjas'soso] AG noisy, rowdy; (*vistoso*) showy, gaudy

'chiatta ['kjatta] SF barge

chi'ave ['kjave] SF key ▶ AG INV key *cpd*; **chiudere a ~** to lock; **~ d'accensione** (*Aut*) ignition key; **~ a forcella** fork spanner; **~ inglese** monkey wrench; **in ~ politica** in political terms; **~ di volta** (*anche fig*) keystone; **chiavi in mano** (*contratto*) turn-key *cpd*; **prezzo chiavi in mano** (di *macchina*) on-the-road price; **~ hardware** (*Inform*) dongle; **~ USB** (*Inform*) USB key

chiavis'tello [kjavis'tɛllo] SM bolt

chi'azza ['kjattsa] SF stain, splash

chiaz'zare [kjat'tsare] **/72/** VT to stain, splash

chic [ʃik] AG INV chic, elegant

chicches'sia [kikkes'sia] PRON anyone, anybody

'chicco, -chi ['kikko] SM (di cereale, riso) grain; (di caffè) bean; **~ di grandine** hailstone; **~ d'uva** grape

chi'edere ['kjɛdere] **/21/** VT (per sapere) to ask; (per avere) to ask for ▶ VI: **~ di qn** to ask after sb; (al telefono) to ask for *o* want sb; **chiedersi** VPR: **chiedersi (se)** to wonder (whether); **~ qc a qn** to ask sb sth; to ask sb for sth; **~ scusa a qn** to apologize to sb; **~ l'elemosina** to beg; **non chiedo altro** that's all I want

chieri'chetto [kjeri'ketto] SM altar boy

chi'erico, -ci ['kjɛriko] SM cleric; altar boy

chi'esa ['kjɛza] SF church

chi'esi *etc* ['kjɛzi] VB *vedi* **chiedere**

chi'esto, -a ['kjɛsto] PP *di* **chiedere**

'Chigi ['kidʒi]: **palazzo ~** SM (*Pol*) offices of the Italian Prime Minister

'chiglia ['kiʎʎa] SF keel

'chilo ['kilo] SM kilo

chilo'grammo [kilo'grammo] SM kilogram(me)

chilome'traggio [kilome'traddʒo] SM (*Aut*) ≈ mileage

chilo'metrico, -a, -ci, -che [kilo'mɛtriko] AG kilometric; (*fig*) endless

chi'lometro [ki'lɔmetro] SM kilometre (*BRIT*), kilometer (*US*)

'chimico, -a, -ci, -che ['kimiko] AG chemical ▶ SM/F chemist ▶ SF chemistry

chi'mono [ki'mɔno] SM INV kimono

'china ['kina] SF (pendio) slope, descent; (*Bot*) cinchona; (**inchiostro di**) **~** Indian ink; **risalire la ~** (fig) to be on the road to recovery

chi'nare [ki'nare] **/72/** VT to lower, bend; **chinarsi** VPR to stoop, bend

chincaglie'ria [kinkaʎʎe'ria] SF fancy-goods shop; **chincaglierie** SFPL fancy goods, knick-knacks

chi'nino [ki'nino] SM quinine

'chino, -a ['kino] AG: **a capo ~**, **a testa china**

head bent o bowed

chi'occia, -ce ['kjɔttʃa] SF brooding hen

chi'occio, -a, -ci, -ce ['kjɔttʃo] AG (voce) clucking

chi'occiola ['kjɔttʃola] SF snail; (di indirizzo e-mail) at (symbol); **scala a ~** spiral staircase

chi'odo ['kjɔdo] SM nail; (fig) obsession; **~ scaccia ~** (proverbio) one problem drives away another; **roba da chiodi!** it's unbelievable!; **~ di garofano** (Cuc) clove

chi'oma ['kjɔma] SF (capelli) head of hair; (di albero) foliage

chi'osco, -schi ['kjɔsko] SM kiosk, stall

chi'ostro ['kjɔstro] SM cloister

chiro'mante [kiro'mante] SMF palmist; (indovino) fortune-teller

chirur'gia [kirur'dʒia] SF surgery; **~ estetica** cosmetic surgery

chi'rurgico, -a, -ci, -che [ki'rurdʒiko] AG (anche fig) surgical

chi'rurgo, -ghi, -gi [ki'rurgo] SM surgeon

chissà [kis'sa] AV who knows, I wonder

chi'tarra [ki'tarra] SF guitar

chitar'rista, -i, -e [kitar'rista] SM/F guitarist, guitar player

chi'udere ['kjudere] /22/ VT to close, shut; (luce, acqua) to put off, turn off; (definitivamente: fabbrica) to close down, shut down; (strada) to close; (recingere) to enclose; (porre termine a) to end ▶ VI to close, shut; to close down, shut down, to end; **chiudersi** VPR to shut, close; (ritirarsi: anche fig) to shut o.s. away; (ferita) to close up; **~ un occhio su** (fig) to turn a blind eye to; **chiudi la bocca!** o **il becco!** (col) shut up!

chi'unque [ki'unkwe] PRON (relativo) whoever; (indefinito) anyone, anybody; **~ sia** whoever it is

'chiusi etc ['kjusi] VB vedi **chiudere**

chi'uso, -a ['kjuso] PP di chiudere ▶ AG (porta) shut, closed; (: a chiave) locked; (senza uscita: strada ecc) blocked off; (: rubinetto) off; (: persona) uncommunicative; (: ambiente, club) exclusive ▶ SM: **stare al ~** (fig) to be shut up ▶ SF (di corso d'acqua) sluice, lock; (recinto) enclosure; (di discorso ecc) conclusion, ending; **"~"** (negozio ecc) "closed"; **"~ al pubblico"** "no admittance to the public"

chiu'sura [kju'sura] SF closing; shutting; closing o shutting down; enclosing; putting o turning off; ending; (dispositivo) catch; fastening; fastener; **orario di ~** closing time; **~ lampo®** zip (fastener) (BRIT), zipper (US)

(PAROLA CHIAVE)

ci [tʃi] (dav lo, la, li, le, ne diventa **ce**) PRON **1** (personale: complemento oggetto) us; (: a noi: complemento di termine) (to) us; (: riflessivo)

ourselves; (: reciproco) each other, one another; (: impersonale): **ci si veste** we get dressed; **ci ha visti** he's seen us; **non ci ha dato niente** he gave us nothing; **ci vestiamo** we get dressed; **ci amiamo** we love one another o each other; **ci siamo divertiti** we had a good time

2 (dimostrativo: di ciò, su ciò, in ciò ecc) about (o on o of) it; **non ci capisco nulla** I can't make head nor tail of it; **non so cosa farci** I don't know what to do about it; **che ci posso fare?** what can I do about it?; **che c'entro io?** what have I got to do with it?; **ci puoi giurare** you can bet on it; **ci puoi contare** you can depend on it; **ci sei?** (sei pronto?) are you ready?; (hai capito?) are you with me?

▶ AV (qui) here; (lì) there; (moto attraverso luogo): **ci passa sopra un ponte** a bridge passes over it; **non ci passa più nessuno** nobody comes this way any more; **qui ci abito da un anno** I've been living here for a year; **esserci** vedi **essere**

C.I. ABBR = **carta d'identità**

CIA ['tʃia] SIGLA F (= Central Intelligence Agency) CIA

C.ia ABBR (= compagnia) Co

cia'batta [tʃa'batta] SF mule, slipper; (pane) ciabatta

ciabat'tino [tʃabat'tino] SM cobbler

ciac [tʃak] SM (Cine) clapper board; **~, si gira!** action!

Ci'ad [tʃad] SM: **il ~** Chad

ci'alda ['tʃalda] SF (Cuc) wafer

cial'trone [tʃal'trone] SM good-for-nothing

ciam'bella [tʃam'bɛlla] SF (Cuc) ring-shaped cake; (salvagente) rubber ring

ci'ancia, -ce ['tʃantʃa] SF gossip no pl, tittle-tattle no pl

cianfru'saglie [tʃanfru'zaʎʎe] SFPL bits and pieces

ci'anuro [tʃa'nuro] SM cyanide

ci'ao ['tʃao] ESCL (all'arrivo) hello!; (alla partenza) cheerio! (BRIT), bye!

ciar'lare [tʃar'lare] /72/ VI to chatter; (peg) to gossip

ciarla'tano [tʃarla'tano] SM charlatan

cias'cuno, -a [tʃas'kuno] (dav sm: **ciascun** + C, V, **ciascuno** + s impura, gn, pn, ps, x, z; dav sf: **ciascuna** + C, **ciascun'** + V) DET every, each; (ogni) every ▶ PRON each (one); (tutti) everyone, everybody

ci'bare [tʃi'bare] /72/ VT to feed; **cibarsi** VPR: **cibarsi di** to eat

ci'barie [tʃi'barje] SFPL foodstuffs

ciber'nauta, -i, -e [tʃiber'nauta] SM/F Internet surfer

ciber'netica [tʃiber'nɛtika] SF cybernetics sg

ciberspazio [tʃiber'spattsjo] SM cyberspace

'**cibo** ['tʃibo] SM food
ci'cala [tʃi'kala] SF cicada
cica'trice [tʃika'tritʃe] SF scar
cicatriz'zarsi [tʃikatrid'dzarsi] /**72**/ VPR to form a scar, heal (up)
'**cicca, -che** ['tʃikka] SF cigarette end; (col: sigaretta) fag; **non vale una ~** (fig) it's worthless
'**ciccia** ['tʃittʃa] SF (col: carne) meat; (grasso umano) fat, flesh
cicci'one, -a [tʃit'tʃone] SM/F (col) fatty
cice'rone [tʃitʃe'rone] SM guide
cicla'mino [tʃikla'mino] SM cyclamen
ci'clismo [tʃi'klizmo] SM cycling
ci'clista, -i, -e [tʃi'klista] SM/F cyclist
'**ciclo** ['tʃiklo] SM cycle; (di malattia) course
ciclomo'tore [tʃiklomo'tore] SM moped
ci'clone [tʃi'klone] SM cyclone
ciclos'tile [tʃiklos'tile] SM cyclostyle (BRIT)
ci'cogna [tʃi'koɲɲa] SF stork
ci'coria [tʃi'kɔrja] SF chicory
ci'eco, -a, -chi, -che ['tʃɛko] AG blind ► SM/F blind man(-woman); **alla cieca** (anche fig) blindly
ciel'lino, -a [tʃiel'lino] SM/F (Pol) member of CL movement
ci'elo ['tʃɛlo] SM sky; (Rel) heaven; **toccare il ~ con un dito** (fig) to walk on air; **per amor del ~!** for heavens' sake!
'**cifra** ['tʃifra] SF (numero) figure, numeral; (somma di denaro) sum, figure; (monogramma) monogram, initials pl; (codice) code, cipher
ci'frare [tʃi'frare] /**72**/ VT (messaggio) to code; (lenzuola ecc) to embroider with a monogram
'**ciglio** ['tʃiʎʎo] SM (margine) edge, verge; (pl(f) **ciglia**: delle palpebre) (eye)lash; (eye)lid; (sopracciglio) eyebrow; **non ha battuto ~** (fig) he didn't bat an eyelid
'**cigno** ['tʃiɲɲo] SM swan
cigo'lante [tʃigo'lante] AG squeaking, creaking
cigo'lare [tʃigo'lare] /**72**/ VI to squeak, creak
'**Cile** ['tʃile] SM: **il ~** Chile
ci'lecca [tʃi'lekka] SF: **far ~** to fail
ci'leno, -a [tʃi'leno] AG, SM/F Chilean
cili'egia, -gie, -ge [tʃi'ljɛdʒa] SF cherry
cilie'gina [tʃilje'dʒina] SF glacé cherry; **la ~ sulla torta** (fig) the icing o cherry on the cake
cili'egio [tʃi'ljɛdʒo] SM cherry tree
cilin'drata [tʃilin'drata] SF (Aut) (cubic) capacity; **una macchina di grossa ~** a big-engined car
ci'lindro [tʃi'lindro] SM cylinder; (cappello) top hat
CIM [tʃim] SIGLA M = **centro d'igiene mentale**
'**cima** ['tʃima] SF (sommità) top; (di monte) top, summit; (estremità) end; (fig: persona) genius;

in ~ a at the top of; **da ~ a fondo** from top to bottom; (fig) from beginning to end
ci'melio [tʃi'mɛljo] SM relic
cimen'tarsi [tʃimen'tarsi] /**72**/ VPR: **~ in** (atleta, concorrente) to try one's hand at
'**cimice** ['tʃimitʃe] SF (Zool) bug; (puntina) drawing pin (BRIT), thumbtack (US)
cimini'era [tʃimi'njɛra] SF chimney; (di nave) funnel
cimi'tero [tʃimi'tɛro] SM cemetery
ci'murro [tʃi'murro] SM (di cani) distemper
'**Cina** ['tʃina] SF: **la ~** China
cin'cin, cin cin [tʃin'tʃin] ESCL cheers!
cincischi'are [tʃintʃis'kjare] /**19**/ VI to mess about
'**cine** ['tʃine] SM INV (col) cinema
cine'asta, -i, -e [tʃine'asta] SM/F person in the film industry; film-maker
cinegior'nale [tʃinedʒor'nale] SM newsreel
'**cinema** ['tʃinema] SM INV cinema; **~ muto** silent films; **~ d'essai** (locale) avant-garde cinema, experimental cinema
cinemato'grafico, -a, -ci, -che [tʃinemato'grafiko] AG (attore, critica) movie cpd, film cpd; (festival) film cpd; **sala cinematografica** cinema; **successo ~** box-office success
cinema'tografo [tʃinema'tɔgrafo] SM cinema
cine'presa [tʃine'presa] SF cine-camera
ci'nese [tʃi'nese] AG, SM/F, SM Chinese inv
cine'teca, -che [tʃine'tɛka] SF (collezione) film collection; (locale) film library
ci'netico, -a, -ci, -che [tʃi'nɛtiko] AG kinetic
'**cingere** ['tʃindʒere] /**54**/ VT (attorniare) to surround, encircle; **~ la vita con una cintura** to put a belt round one's waist; **~ d'assedio** to besiege, lay siege to
'**cinghia** ['tʃingja] SF strap; (cintura, Tecn) belt; **tirare la ~** (fig) to tighten one's belt
cinghi'ale [tʃin'gjale] SM wild boar
cinguet'tare [tʃingwet'tare] /**72**/ VI to twitter
'**cinico, -a, -ci, -che** ['tʃiniko] AG cynical ► SM/F cynic
ci'nismo [tʃi'nizmo] SM cynicism
cin'quanta [tʃin'kwanta] NUM fifty
cinquante'nario [tʃinkwante'narjo] SM fiftieth anniversary
cinquan'tenne [tʃinkwan'tɛnne] SMF fifty-year-old man/woman
cinquan'tesimo, -a [tʃinkwan'tɛzimo] NUM fiftieth
cinquan'tina [tʃinkwan'tina] SF (serie): **una ~ (di)** about fifty; (età) **essere sulla ~** to be about fifty
'**cinque** ['tʃinkwe] NUM five; **avere ~ anni** to be five (years old); **il ~ dicembre 2008** the fifth of December 2008; **alle ~** (ora) at five (o'clock); **siamo in ~** there are five of us

cinquecen'tesco, -a, -schi, -sche
[tʃinkwetʃen'tesko] AG sixteenth-century

cinque'cento [tʃinkwe'tʃento] NUM five
hundred ▶ SM: **il C~** the sixteenth century

cinque'mila [tʃinkwe'mila] NUM five
thousand

'**cinsi** etc ['tʃinsi] VB vedi **cingere**

'**cinta** ['tʃinta] SF (anche: **cinta muraria**) city
walls pl; **muro di ~** (di giardino ecc)
surrounding wall

cin'tare [tʃin'tare] /**72**/ VT to enclose

'**cinto, -a** ['tʃinto] PP di **cingere**

'**cintola** ['tʃintola] SF (cintura) belt; (vita) waist

cin'tura [tʃin'tura] SF belt; **~ di salvataggio**
lifebelt (BRIT), life preserver (US); **~ di
sicurezza** (Aut, Aer) safety o seat belt

cintu'rino [tʃintu'rino] SM strap;
~ dell'orologio watch strap

CIO SIGLA M (= Comitato Internazionale Olimpico)
IOC (= International Olympic Committee)

ciò [tʃɔ] PRON this; that; **~ che** what;
~ nonostante o **nondimeno** nevertheless,
in spite of that; **con tutto ~** for all that, in
spite of everything

ci'occa, -che ['tʃɔkka] SF (di capelli) lock

ciocco'lata [tʃokko'lata] SF chocolate;
(bevanda) (hot) chocolate; **~ al latte/
fondente** milk/plain chocolate

cioccola'tino [tʃokkola'tino] SM chocolate

ciocco'lato [tʃokko'lato] SM chocolate

cio'è [tʃo'ɛ] AV that is (to say)

ciondo'lare [tʃondo'lare] /**72**/ VT (far dondolare)
to dangle, swing ▶ VI to dangle; (fig) to loaf
(about)

ci'ondolo ['tʃondolo] SM pendant;
~ portafortuna charm

ciondo'loni [tʃondo'loni] AV: **con le braccia/
gambe ~** with arms/legs dangling

cionono'stante [tʃononos'tante] AV
nonetheless, nevertheless

ci'otola ['tʃotola] SF bowl

ci'ottolo ['tʃɔttolo] SM pebble; (di strada)
cobble(stone)

C.I.P. [tʃip] SIGLA M = **comitato
interministeriale prezzi**; vedi **comitato**

Cipe ['tʃipe] SIGLA M = **comitato
interministeriale per la programmazione
economica**; vedi **comitato**

'**Cipi** ['tʃipi] SIGLA M = **comitato
interministeriale per lo sviluppo
industriale**; vedi **comitato**

ci'piglio [tʃi'piʎʎo] SM frown

ci'polla [tʃi'polla] SF onion; (di tulipano ecc)
bulb

cipol'lina [tʃipol'lina] SF onion; **cipolline
sottaceto** pickled onions; **cipolline
sottolio** baby onions in oil

ci'presso [tʃi'prɛsso] SM cypress (tree)

'**cipria** ['tʃiprja] SF (face) powder

cipri'ota, -i, -e [tʃipri'ɔta] AG, SM/F Cypriot

'**Cipro** ['tʃipro] SM Cyprus

'**circa** ['tʃirka] AV about, roughly ▶ PREP about,
concerning; **a mezzogiorno ~** about midday

'**circo, -chi** ['tʃirko] SM circus

circo'lare [tʃirko'lare] /**72**/ VI to circulate;
(Aut) to drive (along), move (along) ▶ AG
circular ▶ SF (Amm) circular; (di autobus)
circle (line); **circola voce che ...** there is a
rumour going about that ...; **assegno ~**
banker's draft

circolazi'one [tʃirkolat'tsjone] SF
circulation; (Aut): **la ~** (the) traffic; **libretto
di ~** log book, registration book; **tassa di ~**
road tax; **~ a targhe alterne** see note

> Circolazione a targhe alterne was introduced
> by some town councils to combat the
> increase in traffic and pollution in town
> centres. It stipulates that on days with an
> even date, only cars whose number plate
> ends in an even number or a zero may be
> on the road; on days with an odd date,
> only cars with odd registration numbers
> may be used. Public holidays are
> generally, but not always, exempt.

'**circolo** ['tʃirkolo] SM circle; **entrare in ~**
(Anat) to enter the bloodstream

circoncisi'one [tʃirkontʃi'zjone] SF
circumcision

circon'dare [tʃirkon'dare] /**72**/ VT to
surround; **circondarsi** VPR: **circondarsi di**
to surround o.s. with

circondari'ale [tʃirkonda'rjale] AG: **casa di
pena ~** district prison

circon'dario [tʃirkon'darjo] SM (Dir)
administrative district; (zona circostante)
neighbourhood (BRIT), neighborhood (US)

circonfe'renza [tʃirkonfe'rɛntsa] SF
circumference

circonvallazi'one [tʃirkonvallat'tsjone] SF
ring road (BRIT), beltway (US); (per evitare una
città) by-pass

circos'critto, -a [tʃirkos'kritto] PP di
circoscrivere

circos'crivere [tʃirkos'krivere] /**105**/ VT to
circumscribe; (fig) to limit, restrict

circoscrizi'one [tʃirkoskrit'tsjone] SF (Amm)
district, area; **~ elettorale** constituency

circos'petto, -a [tʃirkos'pɛtto] AG
circumspect, cautious

circos'tante [tʃirkos'tante] AG surrounding,
neighbouring (BRIT), neighboring (US)

circos'tanza [tʃirkos'tantsa] SF
circumstance; (occasione) occasion; **parole
di ~** words suited to the occasion

circu'ire [tʃirku'ire] /**55**/ VT (fig) to fool, take in

cir'cuito [tʃir'kuito] SM circuit; **andare in** o
fare corto ~ to short-circuit; **~ integrato**
integrated circuit

cirillico – cleptomane

ci'rillico, -a, -ci, -che [tʃi'rilliko] AG Cyrillic
cir'rosi [tʃir'rɔzi] SF: ~ **epatica** cirrhosis (of the liver)
'C.I.S.A.L. ['tʃizal] SIGLA F (= *Confederazione Italiana Sindacati Autonomi dei Lavoratori*) trades union organization
C.I.S.L. [tʃizl] SIGLA F (= *Confederazione Italiana Sindacati Lavoratori*) trades union organization
'C.I.S.N.A.L. ['tʃiznal] SIGLA F (= *Confederazione Italiana Sindacati Nazionali dei Lavoratori*) trades union organization
'ciste ['tʃiste] SF = **cisti**
cis'terna [tʃis'tɛrna] SF tank, cistern
'cisti ['tʃisti] SF INV cyst
cis'tite [tʃis'tite] SF cystitis
cit. ABBR = **citato**; (= *citata*) cit.
C.I.T. [tʃit] SIGLA F = **Compagnia Italiana Turismo**
ci'tare [tʃi'tare] /**72**/ VT (*Dir*) to summon; (*autore*) to quote; (*a esempio, modello*) to cite; ~ **qn per danni** to sue sb
citazi'one [tʃitat'tsjone] SF summons *sg*; quotation; (*di persona*) mention
ci'tofono [tʃi'tɔfono] SM entry phone; (*in uffici*) intercom
cito'logico, -a, -ci, -che [tʃito'lɔdʒiko] AG: **esame** ~ test for detection of cancerous cells
'citrico, -a, -ci, -che ['tʃitriko] AG citric
città [tʃit'ta] SF INV town; (*importante*) city; ~ **giardino** garden city; ~ **mercato** shopping centre, mall; ~ **universitaria** university campus; **C~ del Capo** Cape Town
citta'della [tʃitta'dɛlla] SF citadel, stronghold
cittadi'nanza [tʃittadi'nantsa] SF citizens *pl*, inhabitants *pl* of a town (*o* city); (*Dir*) citizenship
citta'dino, -a [tʃitta'dino] AG town *cpd*; city *cpd* ▶ SM/F (*di uno Stato*) citizen; (*abitante di città*) town dweller, city dweller
ci'uccio ['tʃuttʃo] SM (*col*) comforter, dummy (*BRIT*), pacifier (*US*)
ci'uco, -a, -chi, -che ['tʃuko] SM/F ass
ci'uffo ['tʃuffo] SM tuft
ci'urma ['tʃurma] SF (*di nave*) crew
ci'vetta [tʃi'vetta] SF (*Zool*) owl; (*fig: donna*) coquette, flirt ▶ AG INV: **auto/nave** ~ decoy car/ship; **fare la** ~ **con qn** to flirt with sb
civet'tare [tʃivet'tare] /**72**/ VT to flirt
civette'ria [tʃivette'ria] SF coquetry, coquettishness
civettu'olo, -a [tʃivet'twɔlo] AG flirtatious
'civico, -a, -ci, -che ['tʃiviko] AG civic; (*museo*) municipal, town *cpd*; city *cpd*; **guardia civica** town policeman; **senso** ~ public spirit
ci'vile [tʃi'vile] AG civil; (*non militare*) civilian; (*nazione*) civilized ▶ SM civilian; **stato** ~ marital status; **abiti civili** civvies

civi'lista, -i, -e [tʃivi'lista] SM/F (*avvocato*) civil lawyer; (*studioso*) expert in civil law
civiliz'zare [tʃivilid'dzare] /**72**/ VT to civilize
civilizzazi'one [tʃiviliddzat'tsjone] SF civilization
civiltà [tʃivil'ta] SF civilization; (*cortesia*) civility
ci'vismo [tʃi'vizmo] SM public spirit
CL [tʃi'elle] SIGLA F (*Pol*: = *Comunione e Liberazione*) Catholic youth movement ▶ SIGLA = **Caltanissetta**
cl ABBR (= *centilitro*) cl
'clacson SM INV (*Aut*) horn
cla'more SM (*frastuono*) din, uproar, clamour (*BRIT*), clamor (*US*); (*fig*) outcry
clamo'roso, -a AG noisy; (*fig*) sensational
clan SM INV clan
clandestinità SF (*di attività*) secret nature; **vivere nella** ~ to live in hiding; (*ricercato politico*) to live underground
clandes'tino, -a AG clandestine; (*Pol*) underground, clandestine; (*immigrato*) illegal ▶ SM/F stowaway; (*anche*: **immigrato clandestino**) illegal immigrant
clari'netto SM clarinet
'classe SF class; **di** ~ (*fig*) with class; of excellent quality; ~ **operaia** working class; ~ **turistica** (*Aer*) economy class
classi'cismo [klassi'tʃizmo] SM classicism
'classico, -a, -ci, -che AG classical; (*tradizionale: moda*) classic(al) ▶ SM classic; classical author; (*anche*: **liceo classico**) secondary school with emphasis on the humanities
clas'sifica, -che SF classification; (*Sport*) placings *pl*; (*di dischi*) charts *pl*, hit parade
classifi'care /**20**/ VT to classify; (*candidato, compito*) to grade; **classificarsi** VPR to be placed
classifica'tore SM filing cabinet
classificazi'one [klassifikat'tsjone] SF classification; grading
clas'sista, -i, -e AG class-conscious ▶ SM/F class-conscious person
claudi'cante AG (*zoppo*) lame; (*fig: prosa*) halting
'clausola SF (*Dir*) clause
claustro'fobico, -a, -ci, -che AG claustrophobic
clau'sura SF (*Rel*): **monaca di** ~ nun belonging to an enclosed order; **fare una vita di** ~ (*fig*) to lead a cloistered life
'clava SF club
clavi'cembalo [klavi'tʃembalo] SM harpsichord
cla'vicola SF (*Anat*) collarbone
cle'mente AG merciful; (*clima*) mild
cle'menza [kle'mentsa] SF mercy, clemency; mildness
clep'tomane SMF kleptomaniac

cleri'cale AG clerical

'clero SM clergy

cles'sidra SF (*a sabbia*) hourglass; (*ad acqua*) water clock

clic'care /20/ VI (*Inform*): ~ **su** to click on

cliché [kli'ʃe] SM INV (*Tip*) plate; (*fig*) cliché

cli'ente SMF customer, client

clien'tela SF customers *pl*, clientèle

cliente'lismo SM: ~ **politico** political nepotism

'clima, -i SM climate

cli'matico, -a, -ci, -che AG climatic; **stazione climatica** health resort

climatizza'tore [klimatiddza'tore] SM air conditioner

climatizzazi'one [klimatiddzat'tsjone] SF air conditioning

'clinico, -a, -ci, -che AG clinical ► SM (*medico*) clinician ► SF (*scienza*) clinical medicine; (*casa di cura*) clinic, nursing home; (*settore d'ospedale*) clinic; **quadro** ~ anamnesis; **avere l'occhio** ~ (*fig*) to have an expert eye

clis'tere SM (*Med*) enema; (: *apparecchio*) *device used to give an enema*

clo'aca, -che SF sewer

cloche [klɔʃ] SF INV control stick, joystick; **cambio a** ~ (*Aut*) floor-mounted gear lever

clo'nare /72/ VT to clone

clona'zione [klonat'tsjone] SF (*Biol, fig*) cloning

'cloro SM chlorine

cloro'filla SF chlorophyll

cloro'formio SM chloroform

cloud computing [klaud kom'pjutin] SM INV cloud computing

club SM INV club

cm ABBR (= *centimetro*) cm

c.m. ABBR (= *corrente mese*) inst.

CN SIGLA = **Cuneo**

c/n ABBR = **conto nuovo**

CNEN SIGLA M (= *Comitato Nazionale per l'Energia Nucleare*) = AEA (*BRIT*), AEC (*US*)

CNIOP SIGLA M = **Centro Nazionale per l'Istruzione e l'Orientamento Professionale**

CNR SIGLA M (= *Consiglio Nazionale delle Ricerche*) *science research council*

CNRN SIGLA M = **Comitato Nazionale Ricerche Nucleari**

CO SIGLA = **Como**

Co. ABBR (= *compagnia*) Co.

c/o ABBR (= *care of*) c/o

coabi'tare /72/ VI to live together, live under the same roof

coagu'lare /72/ VT to coagulate ► VI (*anche*: **coagularsi**) to coagulate; (: *latte*) to curdle

coalizi'one [koalit'tsjone] SF coalition

co'atto, -a AG (*Dir*) compulsory, forced; **condannare al domicilio** ~ to place under house arrest

'COBAS SIGLA MPL (= *Comitati di base*) *independent trades unions*

'cobra SM INV cobra

'coca SF (*bibita*) Coke®; (*droga*) cocaine

'coca 'cola® SF coca cola®

coca'ina SF cocaine

coc'carda SF cockade

cocchi'ere [kok'kjɛre] SM coachman

'cocchio ['kɔkkjo] SM (*carrozza*) coach; (*biga*) chariot

cocci'nella [kottʃi'nɛlla] SF ladybird (*BRIT*), ladybug (*US*)

'coccio ['kɔttʃo] SM earthenware; (*vaso*) earthenware pot; **cocci** SMPL fragments (of pottery)

cocciu'taggine [kottʃu'taddʒine] SF stubbornness, pig-headedness

cocci'uto, -a [kot'tʃuto] AG stubborn, pigheaded

'cocco, -chi SM (*pianta*) coconut palm; (*frutto*): **noce di** ~ coconut ► SM/F (*col*) darling; **è il ~ della mamma** he's mummy's darling

cocco'drillo SM crocodile

cocco'lare /72/ VT to cuddle, fondle

co'cente [ko'tʃɛnte] AG (*anche fig*) burning

cocerò *etc* [kotʃe'rɔ] VB *vedi* **cuocere**

co'comero SM watermelon

co'cuzzolo [ko'kuttsolo] SM top; (*di capo, cappello*) crown

cod. ABBR = **codice**

'coda SF tail; (*fila di persone, auto*) queue (*BRIT*), line (*US*); (*di abiti*) train; **con la ~ dell'occhio** out of the corner of one's eye; **mettersi in ~** to queue (up) (*BRIT*), line up (*US*); to join the queue *o* line; ~ **di cavallo** (*acconciatura*) ponytail; **avere la ~ di paglia** (*fig*) to have a guilty conscience; ~ **di rospo** (*Cuc*) frogfish tail

codar'dia SF cowardice

co'dardo, -a AG cowardly ► SM/F coward

co'desto, -a AG, PRON (*poetico*) this; that

'codice ['kɔditʃe] SM code; (*manoscritto antico*) codex; ~ **di avviamento postale** postcode (*BRIT*), zip code (*US*); ~ **a barre** bar code; ~ **civile** civil code; ~ **fiscale** tax code; ~ **penale** penal code; ~ **segreto** (*di tessera magnetica*) PIN (number); ~ **della strada** highway code

co'difica SF codification; (*Inform*: *di programma*) coding

codifi'care /20/ VT (*Dir*) to codify; (*cifrare*) to code

codificazi'one [kodifikat'tsjone] SF coding

coercizi'one [koertʃit'tsjone] SF coercion

coe'rente AG coherent

coe'renza [koe'rentsa] SF coherence

coesi'one SF cohesion

coe'sistere /11/ VI to coexist

coe'taneo, -a AG, SM/F contemporary; **essere ~ di qn** to be the same age as sb

cofa'netto SM casket; **~ dei gioielli** jewel case

'**cofano** SM (Aut) bonnet (BRIT), hood (US); (forziere) chest

'**coffa** SF (Naut) top

'**cogli** ['kɔʎʎi] PREP + DET vedi **con**

'**cogliere** ['kɔʎʎere] /**23**/ VT (fiore, frutto) to pick, gather; (sorprendere) to catch, surprise; (bersaglio) (!); (fig: momento opportuno ecc) to grasp, seize, take; (: capire) to grasp; **~ l'occasione (per fare)** to take the opportunity (to do); **~ sul fatto** o **in flagrante/alla sprovvista** to catch red-handed/unprepared; **~ nel segno** (fig) to hit the nail on the head

cogli'one [koʎ'ʎone] SM (!: testicolo): **coglioni** balls (!); (fig: persona sciocca) jerk; **rompere i coglioni a qn** to get on sb's tits (!)

co'gnac [kɔ'ɲak] SM INV cognac

co'gnato, -a [koɲ'ɲato] SM/F brother-in-law(-sister-in-law)

cogni'tivo, -a [koɲɲi'tivo] AG cognitive

cognizi'one [koɲɲit'tsjone] SF knowledge; **con ~ di causa** with full knowledge of the facts

co'gnome [koɲ'ɲome] SM surname

'**coi** PREP + DET vedi **con**

coi'bente AG insulating

coinci'denza [kointʃi'dentsa] SF coincidence; (Ferr, Aer, di autobus) connection

coin'cidere [koin'tʃidere] /**34**/ VI to coincide

coin'ciso, -a [koin'tʃizo] PP di **coincidere**

coinqui'lino SM fellow tenant

cointeres'senza [kointeres'sɛntsa] SF (Comm): **avere una ~ in qc** to own shares in sth; **~ dei lavoratori** profit-sharing

coin'volgere [koin'vɔldʒere] /**96**/ VT: **~ in** to involve in

coinvolgi'mento [koinvoldʒi'mento] SM involvement

coin'volto, -a PP di **coinvolgere**

col PREP + DET vedi **con**

Col. ABBR (= colonnello) Col.

colà AV there

cola'brodo SM INV strainer

cola'pasta SM INV colander

co'lare /**72**/ VT (liquido) to strain; (pasta) to drain; (oro fuso) to pour ▶ VI (sudore) to drip; (botte) to leak; (cera) to melt; **~ a picco** vt (nave) to sink

co'lata SF (di lava) flow; (Industria) casting

colazi'one [kolat'tsjone] SF (anche: **prima colazione**) breakfast; (anche: **seconda colazione**) lunch; **fare ~** to have breakfast (o lunch); **~ di lavoro** working lunch

Coldi'retti ABBR F (= Confederazione nazionale coltivatori diretti) federation of Italian farmers

co'lei PRON vedi **colui**

co'lera SM (Med) cholera

coleste'rolo SM cholesterol

colf ABBR F = **collaboratrice familiare**

'**colgo** etc VB vedi **cogliere**

colibrì SM hummingbird

'**colica** SF (Med) colic

co'lino SM strainer

'**colla** PREP + DET vedi **con** ▶ SF glue; (di farina) paste

collabo'rare /**72**/ VI to collaborate; (con la polizia) to co-operate; **~ a** to collaborate on; (giornale) to contribute to

collabora'tore, -'trice SM/F collaborator; (di giornale, rivista) contributor; **~ esterno** freelance; **collaboratrice familiare** home help; **~ di giustizia** = **pentito**

collaborazi'one [kollaborat'tsjone] SF collaboration; contribution

col'lana SF necklace; (collezione) collection, series

col'lant [kɔ'lã] SM INV tights pl

col'lare SM collar

col'lasso SM (Med) collapse

collate'rale AG collateral; **effetti collaterali** side effects

collau'dare /**72**/ VT to test, try out

col'laudo SM testing no pl; test

'**colle** PREP + DET vedi **con** ▶ SM hill

col'lega, -ghi, -ghe SM/F colleague

collega'mento SM connection; (Mil) liaison; (Radio) link(-up); (Inform) link; **ufficiale di ~** liaison officer; **~ ipertestuale** hyperlink

colle'gare /**80**/ VT to connect, join, link; **collegarsi** VPR (Radio, TV) to link up; **collegarsi con** (Tel) to get through to

collegi'ale [kolle'dʒale] AG (riunione, decisione) collective; (Ins) boarding school cpd ▶ SMF boarder; (fig: persona timida e inesperta) schoolboy(-girl)

col'legio [kol'lɛdʒo] SM college; (convitto) boarding school; **~ elettorale** (Pol) constituency

'**collera** SF anger; **andare in ~** to get angry

col'lerico, -a, -ci, -che AG quick-tempered, irascible

col'letta SF collection

collettività SF community

collet'tivo, -a AG collective; (interesse) general, everybody's; (biglietto, visita ecc) group cpd ▶ SM (Pol) (political) group; **società in nome ~** (Comm) partnership

col'letto SM collar; **colletti bianchi** (fig) white-collar workers

collezio'nare [kollettsjo'nare] /**72**/ VT to collect

collezi'one [kollet'tsjone] SF collection

collezio'nista [kollettsjo'nista] SMF collector

colli'mare /**72**/ VI to correspond, coincide

col'lina SF hill

colli'nare AG hill *cpd*

col'lirio SM eyewash

collisi'one SF collision

'**collo** PREP + DET *vedi* **con** ▸ SM neck; (*di abito*) neck, collar; (*pacco*) parcel; **~ del piede** instep

colloca'mento SM (*impiego*) employment; (*disposizione*) placing, arrangement; **ufficio di ~** ≈ Jobcentre (*BRIT*), state (*o* federal) employment agency (*US*); **~ a riposo** retirement

collo'care /20/ VT (*libri, mobili*) to place; (*persona: trovare un lavoro per*) to find a job for, place; (*Comm: merce*) to find a market for; **~ qn a riposo** to retire sb

collocazi'one [kollokat'tsjone] SF placing; (*di libro*) classification

colloqui'ale AG (*termine ecc*) colloquial; (*tono*) informal

col'loquio SM conversation, talk; (*ufficiale, per un lavoro*) interview; (*Ins*) preliminary oral exam; **avviare un ~ con qn** (*Pol ecc*) to start talks with sb

col'loso, -a AG sticky

col'lottola SF nape *o* scruff of the neck; **afferrare qn per la ~** to grab sb by the scruff of the neck

collusi'one SF (*Dir*) collusion

colluttazi'one [kolluttat'tsjone] SF scuffle

col'mare /72/ VT: **~ di** (*anche fig*) to fill with; (*dare in abbondanza*) to load *o* overwhelm with; **~ un divario** (*fig*) to bridge a gap

'**colmo, -a** AG: **~ (di)** full (of) ▸ SM summit, top; (*fig*) height; **al ~ della disperazione** in the depths of despair; **è il ~!** it's the last straw!; **e per ~ di sfortuna ...** and to cap it all ...

co'lomba SF *vedi* **colombo**

Co'lombia SF: **la ~** Colombia

colombi'ano, -a AG, SM/F Colombian

co'lombo, -a SM/F dove; pigeon; **colombi** (*fig: col*) lovebirds

Co'lonia SF Cologne

co'lonia SF colony; (*per bambini*) holiday camp; **(acqua di) ~** (eau de) cologne

coloni'ale AG colonial ▸ SMF colonist, settler

co'lonico, -a, -ci, -che AG: **casa colonica** farmhouse

coloniz'zare [kolonid'dzare] /72/ VT to colonize

co'lonna SF column; **~ sonora** (*Cine*) sound track; **~ vertebrale** spine, spinal column

colon'nello SM colonel

co'lono SM (*coltivatore*) tenant farmer

colo'rante SM colouring (*BRIT*), coloring (*US*)

colo'rare /72/ VT to colour (*BRIT*), color (*US*); (*disegno*) to colour in

co'lore SM colour (*BRIT*), color (*US*); (*Carte*) suit; **a colori** in colour, colour *cpd*; **la gente di ~** coloured people; **diventare di tutti i colori** to turn scarlet; **farne di tutti i colori** to get up to all sorts of mischief; **passarne di tutti i colori** to go through all sorts of problems

colo'rito, -a AG coloured (*BRIT*), colored (*US*); (*viso*) rosy, pink; (*linguaggio*) colourful (*BRIT*), colorful (*US*) ▸ SM (*tinta*) colour (*BRIT*), color (*US*); (*carnagione*) complexion

co'loro PRON PL *vedi* **colui**

colos'sale AG colossal, enormous

co'losso SM colossus

'**colpa** SF fault; (*biasimo*) blame; (*colpevolezza*) guilt; (*azione colpevole*) offence; (*peccato*) sin; **di chi è la ~?** whose fault is it?; **è ~ sua** it's his fault; **per ~ di** through, owing to; **senso di ~** sense of guilt; **dare la ~ a qn di qc** to blame sb for sth

col'pevole AG guilty

colpevoliz'zare [kolpevolid'dzare] /72/ VT: **~ qn** to make sb feel guilty

col'pire /55/ VT to hit, strike; (*fig*) to strike; **rimanere colpito da qc** to be amazed *o* struck by sth; **è stato colpito da ordine di cattura** there is a warrant out for his arrest; **~ nel segno** (*fig*) to hit the nail on the head, be spot on (*BRIT*)

'**colpo** SM (*urto*) knock; (*fig: affettivo*) blow, shock; (: *aggressivo*) blow; (*di pistola*) shot; (*Med*) stroke; (*furto*) raid; **di ~, tutto d'un ~** suddenly; **fare ~** to make a strong impression; **il motore perde colpi** the engine is misfiring; **è morto sul ~** he died instantly; **mi hai fatto venire un ~!** what a fright you gave me!; **ti venisse un ~!** (*col*) drop dead!; **~ d'aria** chill; **~ in banca** bank job *o* raid; **~ basso** (*Pugilato, fig*) punch below the belt; **~ di fulmine** love at first sight; **~ di grazia** coup de grâce; (*fig*) finishing blow; **a ~ d'occhio** at a glance; **~ di scena** (*Teat*) coup de théâtre; (*fig*) dramatic turn of events; **~ di sole** sunstroke; **colpi di sole** (*nei capelli*) highlights; **~ di Stato** coup d'état; **~ di telefono** phone call; **~ di testa** (sudden) impulse *o* whim; **~ di vento** gust (of wind)

col'poso, -a AG: **omicidio ~** manslaughter

'**colsi** *etc* VB *vedi* **cogliere**

coltel'lata SF stab

col'tello SM knife; **avere il ~ dalla parte del manico** (*fig*) to have the whip hand; **~ a serramanico** clasp knife

colti'vare /72/ VT to cultivate; (*verdura*) to grow, cultivate

coltiva'tore SM farmer; **~ diretto** small independent farmer

coltivazi'one [koltivat'tsjone] SF cultivation; growing; **~ intensiva** intensive farming

'colto, -a PP di **cogliere** ▶ AG (*istruito*) cultured, educated

'coltre SF blanket

col'tura SF cultivation; **~ alternata** crop rotation

co'lui (f **colei**, pl **coloro**) PRON the one; **~ che parla** the one o the man o the person who is speaking; **colei che amo** the one o the woman o the person (whom) I love

com. ABBR = **comunale**; **commissione**

'coma SM INV coma

comanda'mento SM (*Rel*) commandment

coman'dante SM (*Mil*) commander, commandant; (*di reggimento*) commanding officer; (*Naut*, *Aer*) captain

coman'dare /72/ VI to be in command ▶ VT to command; (*imporre*) to order, command; **~ a qn di fare** to order sb to do

co'mando SM (*ingiunzione*) order, command; (*autorità*) command; (*Tecn*) control; **~ generale** general headquarters pl; **~ a distanza** remote control

co'mare SF (*madrina*) godmother; (*donna pettegola*) gossip

co'masco, -a, -schi, -sche AG of (o from) Como

combaci'are [komba'tʃare] /14/ VI to meet; (*fig*: *coincidere*) to coincide, correspond

combat'tente AG fighting ▶ SM combatant; **ex-~** ex-serviceman

com'battere /1/ VT to fight; (*fig*) to combat, fight against ▶ VI to fight

combatti'mento SM fight; fighting no pl; (*di pugilato*) match; **mettere fuori ~** to knock out

combat'tivo, -a AG pugnacious

combat'tuto, -a AG (*incerto*: *persona*) uncertain, undecided; (*gara*, *partita*) hard fought

combi'nare /72/ VT to combine; (*organizzare*) to arrange; (*col*: *fare*) to make, cause ▶ VI (*corrispondere*): **~ (con)** to correspond (with)

combinazi'one [kombinat'tsjone] SF combination; (*caso fortuito*) coincidence; **per ~** by chance

com'briccola SF (*gruppo*) party; (*banda*) gang

combus'tibile AG combustible ▶ SM fuel

combusti'one SF combustion

com'butta SF (*peg*) gang; **in ~** in league

PAROLA CHIAVE

'come AV **1** (*alla maniera di*) like; **ti comporti come lui** you behave like him o like he does; **bianco come la neve** (as) white as snow; **come se** as if, as though; **com'è vero Dio!** as God is my witness!

2 (*in qualità di*) as a; **lavora come autista** he works as a driver

3 (*interrogativo*) how; **come ti chiami?** what's your name?; **come sta?** how are you?; **com'è il tuo amico?** what is your friend like?; **come?** (*prego?*) pardon?, sorry?; **come mai?** how come?; **come mai non ci hai avvertiti?** how come you didn't warn us?

4 (*esclamativo*): **come sei bravo!** how clever you are!; **come mi dispiace!** I'm terribly sorry!

▶ CONG **1** (*in che modo*) how; **mi ha spiegato come l'ha conosciuto** he told me how he met him; **non so come sia successo** I don't know how it happened; **attento a come parli!** watch your mouth!

2 (*correlativo*) as; (: *con comparativi di maggioranza*) than; **non è bravo come pensavo** he isn't as clever as I thought; **è meglio di come pensassi** it's better than I thought

3 (*quasi se*) as; **è come se fosse ancora qui** it's as if he was still here; **come se niente fosse** as if nothing had happened; **come non detto!** let's forget it!

4 (*appena che*, *quando*) as soon as; **come arrivò, iniziò a lavorare** as soon as he arrived, he set to work

5 *vedi anche* **così**; **oggi**; **ora**; **tanto**

'COMECON ABBR M (= *Consiglio di Mutua Assistenza Economica*) COMECON

come'done SM blackhead

co'meta SF comet

'comico, -a, -ci, -che AG (*Teat*) comic; (*buffo*) comical ▶ SM (*attore*) comedian, comic actor; (*comicità*) comic spirit, comedy

co'mignolo [ko'miɲɲolo] SM chimney top

cominci'are [komin'tʃare] /14/ VT, VI to begin, start; **~ a fare/col fare** to begin to do/by doing; **cominciamo bene!** (*ironico*) we're off to a fine start!

comi'tato SM committee; **~ direttivo** steering committee; **~ di gestione** works council; **~ interministeriale prezzi** interdepartmental committee on prices; **~ interministeriale per la programmazione economica** interdepartmental committee for economic planning; **~ interministeriale per lo sviluppo industriale** interdepartmental committee for industrial development

comi'tiva SF party, group

co'mizio [ko'mittsjo] SM (*Pol*) meeting, assembly; **~ elettorale** election rally

'comma, -i SM (*Dir*) subsection

com'mando SM INV commando (squad)

com'media SF comedy; (*opera teatrale*) play; (: *che fa ridere*) comedy; (*fig*) playacting no pl

commedi'ante SMF (*peg*) third-rate actor(-actress); (: *fig*) sham

commedi'ografo, -a SM/F (*autore*) comedy writer

commemo'rare /72/ vt to commemorate

commemorazi'one [kommemorat'tsjone] sf commemoration

commenda'tore sm *official title awarded for services to one's country*

commen'sale smf table companion

commen'tare /72/ vt to comment on; (*testo*) to annotate; (*Radio*, TV) to give a commentary on

commenta'tore, -'trice sm/f commentator

com'mento sm comment; (*a un testo*, *Radio*, TV) commentary; ~ **musicale** (*Cine*) background music

commerci'ale [kommer'tʃale] ag commercial, trading; (*peg*) commercial

commercia'lista, -i, -e [kommertʃa'lista] sm/f (*laureato*) graduate in economics and commerce; (*consulente*) business consultant

commercializ'zare [kommertʃalid'dzare] /72/ vt to market

commercializzazi'one [kommertʃaliddzat'tsjone] sf marketing

commerci'ante [kommer'tʃante] smf trader, dealer; (*negoziante*) shopkeeper; ~ **all'ingrosso** wholesaler; ~ **in proprio** sole trader

commerci'are [kommer'tʃare] /14/ vi: ~ **in** to deal *o* trade in ▶ vt to deal *o* trade in

com'mercio [kom'mertʃo] sm trade, commerce; **essere in** ~ (*prodotto*) to be on the market *o* on sale; **essere nel** ~ (*persona*) to be in business; ~ **all'ingrosso/al dettaglio** wholesale/retail trade

com'messo, -a pp *di* **commettere** ▶ sm/f shop assistant (*BRIT*), sales clerk (*US*) ▶ sm (*impiegato*) clerk ▶ sf (*Comm*) order; ~ **viaggiatore** commercial traveller

commes'tibile ag edible; **commestibili** smpl foodstuffs

com'mettere /63/ vt to commit; (*ordinare*) to commission, order

commi'ato sm leave-taking; **prendere ~ da qn** to take one's leave of sb

commi'nare /72/ vt (*Dir*) to make provision for

commise'rare /72/ vt to sympathize with, commiserate with

commiserazi'one [kommizerat'tsjone] sf commiseration

com'misi *etc* vb *vedi* **commettere**

commissaria'mento sm temporary receivership

commissari'are /19/ vt to put under temporary receivership

commissari'ato sm (*Amm*) commissionership; (*: sede*) commissioner's office; (*: di polizia*) police station

commis'sario sm commissioner; (*di pubblica sicurezza*) ≈ (police) superintendent (*BRIT*),

≈ (police) captain (*US*); (*Sport*) steward; (*membro di commissione*) member of a committee *o* board; **alto** ~ high commissioner; ~ **di bordo** (*Naut*) purser; ~ **d'esame** member of an examining board; ~ **di gara** race official; ~ **tecnico** (*Sport*) national coach

commissio'nare /72/ vt to order, place an order for

commissio'nario sm (*Comm*) agent, broker

commissi'one sf (*incarico*) errand; (*comitato, percentuale*) commission; (*Comm: ordinazione*) order; **commissioni** sfpl (*acquisti*) shopping sg; ~ **d'esame** examining board; ~ **d'inchiesta** committee of enquiry; ~ **permanente** standing committee; **commissioni bancarie** bank charges

commit'tente smf (*Comm*) purchaser, customer

com'mosso, -a pp *di* **commuovere**

commo'vente ag moving

commozi'one [kommot'tsjone] sf emotion, deep feeling; ~ **cerebrale** (*Med*) concussion

commu'overe /66/ vt to move, affect; **commuoversi** vpr to be moved

commu'tare /72/ vt (*pena*) to commute; (*Elettr*) to change *o* switch over

commutazi'one [kommutat'tsjone] sf (*Dir*, *Elettr*) commutation

comò sm inv chest of drawers

como'dino sm bedside table

comodità sf inv comfort; convenience

'comodo, -a ag comfortable; (*facile*) easy; (*conveniente*) convenient; (*utile*) useful, handy ▶ sm comfort; convenience; **con** ~ at one's convenience *o* leisure; **fare il proprio** ~ to do as one pleases; **far** ~ to be useful *o* handy; **stia ~!** don't bother to get up!

'compact disc sm inv compact disc

compae'sano, -a sm/f fellow-countryman(-woman); person from the same town

com'pagine [kom'padʒine] sf (*squadra*) team

compa'gnia [kompaɲ'ɲia] sf company; (*gruppo*) gathering; **fare ~ a qn** to keep sb company; **essere di ~** to be sociable

com'pagno, -a [kom'paɲɲo] sm/f (*di classe, gioco*) companion; (*Pol*) comrade; ~ **di lavoro** workmate; ~ **di scuola** schoolfriend; ~ **di viaggio** fellow traveller

com'paio *etc* vb *vedi* **comparire**

compa'rare /72/ vt to compare

compara'tivo, -a ag, sm comparative

comparazi'one [komparat'tsjone] sf comparison

com'pare sm (*padrino*) godfather; (*complice*) accomplice; (*col: amico*) old pal, old mate

compa'rire /7/ vi to appear; ~ **in giudizio** (*Dir*) to appear before the court

to establish responsibilities

comparizi'one [komparit'tsjone] SF (Dir) appearance; **mandato di** ~ summons sg

com'parso, -a PP di **comparire** ▶ SF appearance; (Teat) walk-on; (Cine) extra

comparteci'pare [kompartetʃi'pare] /**72**/ VI (Comm): ~ **a** to have a share in

compartecipazi'one [kompartetʃipat'tsjone] SF sharing; (quota) share; ~ **agli utili** profit-sharing; **in** ~ jointly

comparti'mento SM compartment; (Amm) district

com'parvi etc vedi **comparire**

compas'sato, -a AG (persona) composed; **freddo e** ~ cool and collected

compassi'one SF compassion, pity; **avere** ~ **di qn** to feel sorry for sb, pity sb; **fare** ~ to arouse pity

compassio'nevole AG compassionate

com'passo SM (pair of) compasses pl; callipers pl

compa'tibile AG (scusabile) excusable; (conciliabile, Inform) compatible

compati'mento SM compassion; indulgence; **con aria di** ~ with a condescending air

compa'tire /**55**/ VT (aver compassione di) to sympathize with, feel sorry for; (scusare) to make allowances for

compatri'ota, -i, -e SM/F compatriot

compat'tezza [kompat'tettsa] SF (solidità) compactness; (fig: unità) solidarity

com'patto, -a AG compact; (roccia) solid; (folla) dense; (fig: gruppo, partito) united, close-knit

com'pendio SM summary; (libro) compendium

compen'sare /**72**/ VT (equilibrare) to compensate for, make up for; **compensarsi** VPR (reciproco) to balance each other out; ~ **qn di** (rimunerare) to pay o remunerate sb for; (risarcire) to pay compensation to sb for; (fig: fatiche, dolori) to reward sb for

compen'sato SM (anche: **legno compensato**) plywood

com'penso SM compensation; payment, remuneration; reward; **in** ~ (d'altra parte) on the other hand

'compera SF purchase; **fare le compere** to do the shopping

compe'rare /**72**/ VT = **comprare**

'compere SFPL: **fare** ~ to do the shopping

compe'tente AG competent; (mancia) apt, suitable; (capace) qualified; **rivolgersi all'ufficio** ~ to apply to the office concerned

compe'tenza [kompe'tentsa] SF competence; (Dir: autorità) jurisdiction; (Tecn, Comm) expertise; **competenze** SFPL (onorari) fees; **definire le competenze**

to establish responsibilities

com'petere /**45**/ VI to compete, vie; (Dir): (spettare) ~ **a** to lie within the competence of

competitività SF INV competitiveness

competi'tivo, -a AG competitive

competi'tore, -'trice SM/F competitor

competizi'one [kompetit'tsjone] SF competition; **spirito di** ~ competitive spirit

compia'cente [kompja'tʃɛnte] AG courteous, obliging

compia'cenza [kompja'tʃɛntsa] SF courtesy

compia'cere [kompja'tʃere] /**74**/ VI: ~ **a** to gratify, please ▶ VT to please; **compiacersi** VPR: **compiacersi di** o **per qc** (provare soddisfazione) to be delighted at sth; **compiacersi con qn** (rallegrarsi) to congratulate sb; **compiacersi di fare** (degnarsi) to be so good as to do

compiaci'mento [kompjatʃi'mento] SM satisfaction

compiaci'uto, -a [kompja'tʃuto] PP di **compiacere**

compi'angere [kom'pjandʒere] /**75**/ VT to sympathize with, feel sorry for

compi'anto, -a PP di **compiangere** ▶ AG: **il** ~ **presidente** the late lamented president ▶ SM mourning, grief

'compiere /**24**/ VT (concludere) to finish, complete; (adempiere) to carry out, fulfil; **compiersi** VPR (avverarsi) to be fulfilled, come true; ~ **gli anni** to have one's birthday

compi'lare /**72**/ VT to compile; (modulo) to complete, fill in (BRIT), fill out (US)

compila'tore, -'trice SM/F compiler

compilazi'one [kompilat'tsjone] SF compilation; completion

compi'mento SM (termine, conclusione) completion, fulfilment; **portare a** ~ **qc** to conclude sth, bring sth to a conclusion

com'pire /**92**/ VB = **compiere**

'compito¹ SM (incarico) task, duty; (dovere) duty; (Ins) exercise; (: a casa) piece of homework; **fare i compiti** to do one's homework

com'pito², -a AG well-mannered, polite

compiu'tezza [kompju'tettsa] SF (completezza) completeness; (perfezione) perfection

compi'uto, -a PP di **compiere** ▶ AG: **a 20 anni compiuti** at 20 years of age, at age 20; **un fatto** ~ a fait accompli

comple'anno SM birthday

complemen'tare AG complementary; (Ins: materia) subsidiary

comple'mento SM complement; (Mil) reserve (troops); ~ **oggetto** (Ling) direct object

comples'sato, -a AG, SM/F: **essere (un)** ~ to be full of complexes o hang-ups (col)

complessità SF complexity
complessiva'mente AV (*nell'insieme*) on the whole; (*in tutto*) altogether
comples'sivo, -a AG (*globale*) comprehensive, overall; (*totale: cifra*) total; **visione complessiva** overview
com'plesso, -a AG complex ▶ SM (*Psic, Edil*) complex; (*Mus: corale*) ensemble; (: *orchestrina*) band; (: *di musica pop*) group; **in** *o* **nel** ~ on the whole; ~ **alberghiero** hotel complex; ~ **edilizio** building complex; ~ **vitaminico** vitamin complex
completa'mente AV completely
completa'mento SM completion
comple'tare /72/ VT to complete
com'pleto, -a AG complete; (*teatro, autobus*) full ▶ SM suit; **al** ~ full; **essere al** ~ (*teatro*) to be sold out; ~ **da sci** ski suit
compli'care /20/ VT to complicate; **complicarsi** VPR to become complicated
complicazi'one [komplikat'tsjone] SF complication; **salvo complicazioni** unless any difficulties arise
'**complice** ['kɔmplitʃe] SMF accomplice
complicità [komplitʃi'ta] SF INV complicity; **un sorriso/uno sguardo di** ~ a knowing smile/look
complimen'tarsi /72/ VPR: ~ **con** to congratulate
compli'mento SM compliment; **complimenti** SMPL (*cortesia eccessiva*) ceremony *sg*; (*ossequi*) regards, compliments; **complimenti!** congratulations!; **senza complimenti!** don't stand on ceremony!; make yourself at home!; help yourself!
complot'tare /72/ VI to plot, conspire
com'plotto SM plot, conspiracy
com'pone *etc* VB *vedi* **comporre**
compo'nente SMF member ▶ SM component
com'pongo *etc* VB *vedi* **comporre**
compo'nibile AG (*mobili, cucina*) fitted
componi'mento SM (*Dir*) settlement; (*Ins*) composition; (*poetico, teatrale*) work
com'porre /77/ VT (*musica, testo*) to compose; (*mettere in ordine*) to arrange; (*Dir: lite*) to settle; (*Tip*) to set; (*Tel*) to dial; **comporsi** VPR: **comporsi di** to consist of, be composed of
comportamen'tale AG behavioural (*BRIT*), behavioral (*US*)
comporta'mento SM behaviour (*BRIT*), behavior (*US*); (*di prodotto*) performance
compor'tare /72/ VT (*implicare*) to involve, entail; (*consentire*) to permit, allow (of); **comportarsi** VPR (*condursi*) to behave
com'posi *etc* VB *vedi* **comporre**
composi'tore, -'trice SM/F composer; (*Tip*) compositor, typesetter
composizi'one [kompozit'tsjone] SF composition; (*Dir*) settlement

com'posta SF *vedi* **composto**
compos'tezza [kompos'tettsa] SF composure; decorum
com'posto, -a PP *di* **comporre** ▶ AG (*persona*) composed, self-possessed; (: *decoroso*) dignified; (*formato da più elementi*) compound *cpd* ▶ SM compound; (*Cuc ecc*) mixture ▶ SF (*Cuc*) stewed fruit *no pl*; (*Agr*) compost
com'prare /72/ VT to buy; (*corrompere*) to bribe
compra'tore, -'trice SM/F buyer, purchaser
compra'vendita SF (*Comm*) (contract of) sale; **un atto di** ~ a deed of sale
com'prendere /81/ VT (*contenere*) to comprise, consist of; (*capire*) to understand
compren'donio SM: **essere duro di** ~ to be slow on the uptake
compren'sibile AG understandable
comprensi'one SF understanding
compren'sivo, -a AG (*prezzo*): ~ **di** inclusive of; (*indulgente*) understanding
compren'sorio SM area, territory; (*Amm*) district
com'preso, -a PP *di* **comprendere** ▶ AG (*incluso*) included; **tutto** ~ all included, all-in (*BRIT*)
com'pressa SF *vedi* **compresso**
compressi'one SF compression
com'presso, -a PP *di* **comprimere** ▶ AG (*vedi comprimere*) pressed; compressed; repressed ▶ SF (*Med: garza*) compress; (: *pastiglia*) tablet
compres'sore SM compressor; (*anche:* **rullo compressore**) steamroller
compri'mario, -a SM/F (*Teat*) supporting actor(-actress)
com'primere /50/ VT (*premere*) to press; (*Fisica*) to compress; (*fig*) to repress
compro'messo, -a PP *di* **compromettere** ▶ SM compromise
compro'mettere /63/ VT to compromise; **compromettersi** VPR to compromise o.s.
comproprietà SF (*Dir*) joint ownership
compro'vare /72/ VT to confirm
com'punto, -a AG contrite; **con fare** ~ with a solemn air
compunzi'one [kompun'tsjone] SF contrition; solemnity
compu'tare /72/ VT to calculate; (*addebitare*): ~ **qc a qn** to debit sb with sth
com'puter [kəm'pju:tər] SM INV computer
computeriz'zato, -a [komputerid'dzato] AG computerized
computerizzazi'one [komputeriddzat'tsjone] SF computerization
compute'ria SF accounting, book-keeping
'**computo** SM calculation; **fare il** ~ **di** to count
comu'nale AG municipal, town *cpd*; **consiglio/palazzo** ~ town council/hall;

è un impiegato ~ he works for the local council

Co'mune SM (*Amm*) town council; (*sede*) town hall; *see note*

> The *Comune* is the smallest autonomous political and administrative unit. It keeps records of births, marriages and deaths and has the power to levy taxes and vet proposals for public works and town planning. It is run by a *Giunta comunale*, which is elected by the *Consiglio Comunale*. The *Comune* is headed by the *sindaco* (mayor) who since 1993 has been elected directly by the citizens.

co'mune AG common; (*consueto*) common, everyday; (*di livello medio*) average; (*ordinario*) ordinary ▶ SF (*di persone*) commune; **fuori del ~** out of the ordinary; **avere in ~** to have in common, share; **mettere in ~** to share; **un nostro ~ amico** a mutual friend of ours; **fare cassa ~** to pool one's money

comuni'care/20/ VT (*notizia*) to pass on, convey; (*malattia*) to pass on; (*ansia ecc*) to communicate; (*trasmettere: calore ecc*) to transmit, communicate; (*Rel*) to administer communion to ▶ VI to communicate; **comunicarsi** VPR (*propagarsi*): **comunicarsi a** to spread to; (*Rel*) to receive communion

comunica'tivo, -a AG (*sentimento*) infectious; (*persona*) communicative ▶ SF communicativeness

comuni'cato SM communiqué; **~ stampa** press release

comunicazi'one [komunikat'tsjone] SF communication; (*annuncio*) announcement; (*Tel*): **~ (telefonica)** (telephone) call; **dare la ~ a qn** to put sb through; **ottenere la ~** to get through; **salvo comunicazioni contrarie da parte Vostra** unless we hear from you to the contrary

comuni'one SF communion; **~ dei beni** (*Dir: tra coniugi*) joint ownership of property

comu'nismo SM communism

comu'nista, -i, -e AG, SM/F communist

comunità SF INV community; **C~ Economica Europea** European Economic Community; **~ terapeutica** *rehabilitation centre run by voluntary organizations for people with drug, alcohol etc dependency*

comuni'tario, -a AG community *cpd*

co'munque CONG however, no matter how ▶ AV (*in ogni modo*) in any case; (*tuttavia*) however, nevertheless

con PREP (*nei seguenti casi* **con** *può fondersi con l'articolo definito:* con + il = **col**, con + la = **colla**, con + gli = **cogli**, con + I = **coi**, con + le = **colle**) with; **partire col treno** to leave by train; **~ mio grande stupore** to my great astonishment; **~ la forza** by force; **~ questo freddo** in this

cold weather; **~ il 1° di ottobre** as of October 1st; **~ tutto ciò** in spite of that, for all that; **~ tutto che era arrabbiato** even though he was angry, in spite of the fact that he was angry; **e ~ questo?** so what?

co'nato SM: **~ di vomito** retching

'conca, -che SF (*Geo*) valley

concate'nare/72/ VT to link up, connect; **concatenarsi** VPR to be connected

'concavo, -a AG concave

con'cedere [kon'tʃɛdere] /**29**/ VT (*accordare*) to grant; (*ammettere*) to admit, concede; **concedersi qc** to treat o.s. to sth, allow o.s. sth

concentra'mento [kontʃentra'mento] SM concentration

concen'trare [kontʃen'trare] /**72**/ VT, **concen'trarsi** VPR to concentrate

concen'trato [kontʃen'trato] SM concentrate; **~ di pomodoro** tomato purée

concentrazi'one [kontʃentrat'tsjone] SF concentration; **~ orizzontale/verticale** (*Econ*) horizontal/vertical integration

con'centrico, -a, -ci, -che [kon'tʃɛntriko] AG concentric

conce'pibile [kontʃe'pibile] AG conceivable

concepi'mento [kontʃepi'mento] SM conception

conce'pire [kontʃe'pire] /**55**/ VT (*bambino*) to conceive; (*progetto, idea*) to conceive (of); (*metodo, piano*) to devise; (*situazione*) to imagine, understand

con'cernere [kon'tʃɛrnere] /**45**/ VT to concern; **per quanto mi concerne** as far as I'm concerned

concer'tare [kontʃer'tare] /**72**/ VT (*Mus*) to harmonize; (*ordire*) to devise, plan; **concertarsi** VPR to agree

concer'tista, -i, -e [kontʃer'tista] SM/F (*Mus*) concert performer

con'certo [kon'tʃɛrto] SM (*Mus*) concert; (*: componimento*) concerto

con'cessi etc [kon'tʃɛssi] VB *vedi* **concedere**

concessio'nario [kontʃessjo'narjo] SM (*Comm*) agent, dealer; **~ esclusivo (di)** sole agent (for)

concessi'one [kontʃes'sjone] SF concession

con'cesso, -a [kon'tʃɛsso] PP *di* **concedere**

con'cetto [kon'tʃetto] SM (*pensiero, idea*) concept; (*opinione*) opinion; **è un impiegato di ~ ~** he's a white-collar worker

concezi'one [kontʃet'tsjone] SF conception; (*idea*) view, idea

con'chiglia [kon'kiʎʎa] SF shell

'concia ['kontʃa] SF (*di pelli*) tanning; (*di tabacco*) curing; (*sostanza*) tannin

conci'are [kon'tʃare] /**14**/ VT (*pelli*) to tan; (*tabacco*) to cure; (*fig: ridurre in cattivo stato*) to beat up; **conciarsi** VPR (*sporcarsi*) to get in a mess; (*vestirsi male*) to dress badly; **ti hanno conciato male** *o* **per le feste!** they've really beaten you up!

concili'abile [kontʃi'ljabile] AG compatible

concili'abolo [kontʃi'ljabolo] SM secret meeting

concili'ante [kontʃi'ljante] AG conciliatory

concili'are [kontʃi'ljare] /**19**/ VT to reconcile; (*contravvenzione*) to pay on the spot; (*favorire: sonno*) to be conducive to, induce; (*procurare: simpatia*) to gain; **conciliarsi qc** to gain *o* win sth (for o.s.); **conciliarsi qn** to win sb over; **conciliarsi con** to be reconciled with

conciliazi'one [kontʃiljat'tsjone] SF reconciliation; (*Dir*) settlement; **la C~** (*Storia*) the Lateran Pact

con'cilio [kon'tʃiljo] SM (*Rel*) council

conci'mare [kontʃi'mare] /**72**/ VT to fertilize; (*con letame*) to manure

con'cime [kon'tʃime] SM manure; (*chimico*) fertilizer

concisi'one [kontʃi'zjone] SF concision, conciseness

con'ciso, -a [kon'tʃizo] AG concise, succinct

conci'tato, -a [kontʃi'tato] AG excited, emotional

concitta'dino, -a [kontʃitta'dino] SM/F fellow citizen

con'clave SM conclave

con'cludere /**3**/ VT to conclude; (*portare a compimento*) to conclude, finish, bring to an end; (*operare positivamente*) to achieve ▶ VI (*essere convincente*) to be conclusive; **concludersi** VPR to come to an end, close

conclusi'one SF conclusion; (*risultato*) result

conclu'sivo, -a AG conclusive; (*finale*) final

con'cluso, -a PP *di* **concludere**

concomi'tanza [konkomi'tantsa] SF (*di circostanze, fatti*) combination

concor'danza [konkor'dantsa] SF (*anche Ling*) agreement

concor'dare /**72**/ VT (*prezzo*) to agree on; (*Ling*) to make agree ▶ VI to agree; **~ una tregua** to agree to a truce

concor'dato SM agreement; (*Rel*) concordat

con'corde AG (*d'accordo*) in agreement; (*simultaneo*) simultaneous

con'cordia SF harmony, concord

concor'rente AG competing; (*Mat*) concurrent ▶ SMF (*Sport, Comm*) competitor; (*Ins*) candidate; (*a un concorso di bellezza*) contestant

concor'renza [konkor'rentsa] SF competition; **~ sleale** unfair competition; **a prezzi di ~** at competitive prices

concorrenzi'ale [konkorren'tsjale] AG competitive

con'correre /**28**/ VI: **~ (in)** (*Mat*) to converge *o*

meet (in); **~ (a)** (*competere*) to compete (for); (*Ins: a una cattedra*) to apply (for); (*partecipare: a un'impresa*) to take part (in), contribute (to)

con'corso, -a PP *di* **concorrere** ▶ SM competition; (*esame*) competitive examination; **~ di bellezza** beauty contest; **~ di circostanze** combination of circumstances; **~ di colpa** (*Dir*) contributory negligence; **un ~ ippico** a showjumping event; **~ in reato** (*Dir*) complicity in a crime; **~ per titoli** competitive examination for qualified candidates

con'creto, -a AG concrete ▶ SM: **in ~** in reality

concu'bina SF concubine ▶ SM: **sono concubini** they are living together

concussi'one SF (*Dir*) extortion

con'danna SF condemnation; sentence; conviction; **~ a morte** death sentence

condan'nare /**72**/ VT (*disapprovare*) to condemn; (*Dir*): **~ a** to sentence to; **~ per** to convict of

condan'nato, -a SM/F convict

con'densa SF condensation

conden'sare /**72**/ VT, **conden'sarsi** VPR to condense

condensa'tore SM capacitor

condensazi'one [kondensat'tsjone] SF condensation

condi'mento SM seasoning; dressing

con'dire /**55**/ VT to season; (*insalata*) to dress

condiscen'dente [kondiʃʃen'dɛnte] AG obliging; compliant

condiscen'denza [kondiʃʃen'dɛntsa] SF (*disponibilità*) obligingness; (*arrendevolezza*) compliance

condi'scendere [kondiʃʃendere] /**101**/ VI: **~ a** to agree to

condi'sceso, -a [kondiʃʃeso] PP *di* **condiscendere**

condi'videre /**43**/ VT to share

condi'viso, -a PP *di* **condividere**

condizio'nale [kondittsjo'nale] AG conditional ▶ SM (*Ling*) conditional ▶ SF (*Dir*) suspended sentence

condiziona'mento [kondittsjona'mento] SM conditioning; **~ d'aria** air conditioning

condizio'nare [kondittsjo'nare] /**72**/ VT to condition; **ad aria condizionata** air-conditioned

condiziona'tore [kondittsjona'tore] SM air conditioner

condizi'one [kondit'tsjone] SF condition; **condizioni** SFPL (*di pagamento ecc*) terms, conditions; **a ~ che** on condition that, provided that; **a nessuna ~** on no account; **condizioni a convenirsi** terms to be arranged; **condizioni di lavoro** working conditions; **condizioni di vendita** sales terms

condogli'anze [kondoʎ'ʎantse] SFPL condolences

condomini'ale AG: **riunione** ~ residents' meeting; **spese condominialei** common charges

condo'minio SM joint ownership; (*edificio*) jointly-owned building

con'domino SM joint owner

condo'nare/72/ VT (*Dir*) to remit

con'dono SM remission; ~ **fiscale** *conditional amnesty for people evading tax*

con'dotta SF *vedi* **condotto**

con'dotto, -a PP *di* **condurre** ▶ AG: **medico** ~ local authority doctor (*in country district*) ▶ SM (*canale, tubo*) pipe, conduit; (*Anat*) duct ▶ SF (*modo di comportarsi*) conduct, behaviour (*BRIT*), behavior (*US*); (*di un affare ecc*) handling; (*di acqua*) piping; (*incarico sanitario*) *country medical practice controlled by a local authority*

condu'cente [kondu'tʃɛnte] SM driver

con'ducoetc VB *vedi* **condurre**

con'durre/90/ VT to conduct; (*azienda*) to manage; (*accompagnare: bambino*) to take; (: *automobile*) to drive; (*trasportare: acqua, gas*) to convey, conduct; (*fig*) to lead ▶ VI to lead; **condursi**VPR to behave, conduct o.s.; ~ **a termine** to conclude

con'dussietc VB *vedi* **condurre**

condut'tore, -'trice AG: **filo** ~ (*fig*) thread; **motivo** ~ leitmotiv ▶ SM (*di mezzi pubblici*) driver; (*Fisica*) conductor

condut'tura SF (*gen*) pipe; (*di acqua, gas*) main

conduzi'one [kondut'tsjone] SF (*di affari, ditta*) management; (*Dir: locazione*) lease; (*Fisica*) conduction

confabu'lare/72/ VI to confab

confa'cente [konfa'tʃɛnte] AG: ~ **a qn/qc** suitable for sb/sth; **clima ~ alla salute** healthy climate

CONFAGRICOL'TURA ABBR F (= *Confederazione generale dell'Agricoltura Italiana*) *confederation of Italian farmers*

CON'FAPI SIGLA F = **Confederazione Nazionale della Piccola Industria**

con'farsi/53/ VPR: ~ **a** to suit, agree with

CONFARTIGIA'NATO [konfartidʒa'nato] ABBR F = **Confederazione Generale dell'Artigianato Italiano**

con'fatto, -a PP *di* **confarsi**

CONFCOM'MERCIO [konfkom'mɛrtʃo] ABBR F = **Confederazione Generale del Commercio**

confederazi'one [konfederat'tsjone] SF confederation; ~ **imprenditoriale** employers' association

confe'renza [konfe'rɛntsa] SF (*discorso*) lecture; (*riunione*) conference; ~ **stampa** press conference

conferenzi'ere, -a [konferen'tsjɛre] SM/F lecturer

conferi'mento SM conferring, awarding

confe'rire/55/ VT: ~ **qc a qn** to give sth to sb, confer sth on sb ▶ VI to confer

con'ferma SF confirmation

confer'mare/72/ VT to confirm

confes'sare/72/ VT, **confes'sarsi**VPR to confess; **andare a confessarsi** (*Rel*) to go to confession

confessio'nale AG, SM confessional

confessi'one SF confession; (*setta religiosa*) denomination

con'fesso, -a AG: **essere reo** ~ to have pleaded guilty

confes'sore SM confessor

con'fetto SM sugared almond; (*Med*) pill

confet'tura SF (*gen*) jam; (*di arance*) marmalade

confezio'nare [konfettsjo'nare] /72/ VT (*vestito*) to make (up); (*merci, pacchi*) to package

confezi'one [konfet'tsjone] SF (*di abiti: da uomo*) tailoring; (: *da donna*) dressmaking; (*imballaggio*) packaging; ~ **regalo** gift pack; ~ **risparmio** economy size; ~ **da viaggio** travel pack; **confezioni per signora** ladies' wear *no pl*; **confezioni da uomo** menswear *no pl*

confic'care/20/ VT: ~ **qc in** to hammer o drive sth into; **conficcarsi**VPR to stick

confi'dare/72/ VI: ~ **in** to confide in, rely on ▶ VT to confide; **confidarsi con qn** to confide in sb

confi'dente SMF (*persona amica*) confidant (*confidante*); (*informatore*) informer

confi'denza [konfi'dɛntsa] SF (*familiarità*) intimacy, familiarity; (*fiducia*) trust, confidence; (*rivelazione*) confidence; **prendersi (troppe) confidenze** to take liberties; **fare una ~ a qn** to confide something to sb

confidenzi'ale [konfiden'tsjale] AG familiar, friendly; (*segreto*) confidential; **in via ~** confidentially

configu'rare/72/ VT (*Inform*) to set; **configurarsi**VPR: **configurarsi a** to assume the shape o form of

configurazi'one [konfigurat'tsjone] SF configuration; (*Inform*) setting

confi'nante AG neighbouring (*BRIT*), neighboring (*US*)

confi'nare/72/ VI: ~ **con** to border on ▶ VT (*Pol*) to intern; (*fig*) to confine; **confinarsi**VPR (*isolarsi*): **confinarsi** to shut o.s. up in

confi'nato, -a AG interned ▶ SM/F internee

CONFIN'DUSTRIA SIGLA F (= *Confederazione Generale dell'Industria Italiana*) *employers' association*, ≈ CBI (*BRIT*)

con'fine SM boundary; (*di paese*) border, frontier; **territorio di ~** border zone

con'fino SM internment

con'fisca SF confiscation

confis'care /20/ VT to confiscate

conflagrazi'one [konflagrat'tsjone] SF conflagration

con'flitto SM conflict; **essere in ~ con qc** to clash with sth; **essere in ~ con qn** to be at loggerheads with sb; **~ d'interessi** conflict of interests

conflittu'ale AG: **rapporto ~** relationship based on conflict

conflittualità SF conflicts pl

conflu'enza [konflu'entsa] SF (di fiumi) confluence; (di strade) junction

conflu'ire /55/ VI (fiumi) to flow into each other, meet; (strade) to meet

con'fondere /25/ VT to mix up, confuse; (imbarazzare) to embarrass; **confondersi** VPR (mescolarsi) to mingle; (turbarsi) to be confused; (sbagliare) to get mixed up; **~ le idee a qn** to mix sb up, confuse sb

confor'mare /72/ VT (adeguare): **~ a** to adapt o conform to; **conformarsi** VPR: **conformarsi (a)** to conform (to)

con'forme AG: **~ a** (simile) similar to; (corrispondente) in keeping with

conforme'mente AV accordingly; **~ a** in accordance with

confor'mismo SM conformity

confor'mista, -i, -e SM/F conformist

conformità SF conformity; **in ~ a** in conformity with

confor'tare /72/ VT to comfort, console

confor'tevole AG (consolante) comforting; (comodo) comfortable

con'forto SM (consolazione, sollievo) comfort, consolation; (conferma) support; **a ~ di qc** in support of sth; **i conforti (religiosi)** the last sacraments

confra'ternita SF brotherhood

confron'tare /72/ VT to compare; **confrontarsi** VPR (scontrarsi) to have a confrontation

con'fronto SM comparison; (Dir, Mil, Pol) confrontation; **in** o **a ~ di** in comparison with, compared to; **nei miei** (o **tuoi** etc) **confronti** towards me (o you etc)

con'fusi etc VB vedi **confondere**

confusi'one SF confusion; (imbarazzo) embarrassment; **far ~** (disordine) to make a mess; (chiasso) to make a racket; (confondere) to confuse things

con'fuso, -a PP di **confondere** ▸ AG (vedi confondere) confused; embarrassed

confu'tare /72/ VT to refute

conge'dare [kondʒe'dare] /72/ VT to dismiss; (Mil) to demobilize; **congedarsi** VPR to take one's leave

con'gedo [kon'dʒedo] SM (anche Mil) leave;

prendere ~ da qn to take one's leave of sb; **~ assoluto** (Mil) discharge

conge'gnare [kondʒeɲ'ɲare] /15/ VT to construct, put together

con'gegno [kon'dʒeɲɲo] SM device, mechanism

congela'mento [kondʒela'mento] SM (gen) freezing; (Med) frostbite; **~ salariale** wage freeze

conge'lare [kondʒe'lare] /72/ VT, **conge'larsi** VPR to freeze

congela'tore [kondʒela'tore] SM freezer

con'genito, -a [kon'dʒɛnito] AG congenital

con'gerie [kon'dʒɛrje] SF INV (di oggetti) heap; (di idee) muddle, jumble

congestio'nare [kondʒestjo'nare] /72/ VT to congest; **essere congestionato** (persona, viso) to be flushed; (zona: per traffico) to be congested

congesti'one [kondʒes'tjone] SF congestion

conget'tura [kondʒet'tura] SF conjecture, supposition

con'giungere [kon'dʒundʒere] /5/ VT, **con'giungersi** VPR to join (together)

congiunti'vite [kondʒunti'vite] SF conjunctivitis

congiun'tivo [kondʒun'tivo] SM (Ling) subjunctive

congi'unto, -a [kon'dʒunto] PP di **congiungere** ▸ AG (unito) joined ▸ SM/F (parente) relative

congiun'tura [kondʒun'tura] SF (giuntura) junction, join; (Anat) joint; (circostanza) juncture; (Econ) economic situation

congiuntu'rale [kondʒuntu'rale] AG of the economic situation; **crisi ~** economic crisis

congiunzi'one [kondʒun'tsjone] SF (Ling) conjunction

congi'ura [kon'dʒura] SF conspiracy

congiu'rare [kondʒu'rare] /72/ VI to conspire

conglome'rato SM (Geo) conglomerate; (fig) conglomeration; (Edil) concrete

'Congo SM: **il ~** the Congo

congo'lese AG, SMF Congolese inv

congratu'larsi /72/ VPR: **~ con qn per qc** to congratulate sb on sth

congratulazi'oni [kongratulat'tsjoni] SFPL congratulations

con'grega, -ghe SF band, bunch

congregazi'one [kongregat'tsjone] SF congregation

congres'sista, -i, -e SM/F participant at a congress

con'gresso SM congress

'congruo, -a AG (prezzo, compenso) adequate, fair; (ragionamento) coherent, consistent

conguagli'are [kongwaʎ'ʎare] /27/ VT to balance; (stipendio) to adjust

congu'aglio [kon'gwaʎʎo] SM balancing; adjusting; (somma di denaro) balance;

fare il ~ di to balance; to adjust

C.O.N.I. SIGLA M (= *Comitato Olimpico Nazionale Italiano*) Italian Olympic Games Committee

coni'are/19/ VT to mint, coin; (*fig*) to coin

coniazi'one [konjat'tsjone] SF mintage

'**conico, -a, -ci, -che** AG conical

co'nifere SFPL conifers

conigli'era [koniʎ'ʎɛra] SF (*gabbia*) rabbit hutch; (*più grande*) rabbit run

conigli'etta [koniʎ'ʎetta] SF bunny girl

conigli'etto [koniʎ'ʎetto] SM bunny

co'niglio [ko'niʎʎo] SM rabbit; **sei un ~!** (*fig*) you're chicken!

coniu'gale AG (*amore, diritti*) conjugal; (*vita*) married, conjugal

coniu'gare/80/ VT to combine; (*Ling*) to conjugate; **coniugarsi** VPR to get married

coniu'gato, -a AG (*Amm*) married

coniugazi'one [konjugat'tsjone] SF (*Ling*) conjugation

'**coniuge** ['kɔnjudʒe] SMF spouse

connatu'rato, -a AG inborn

connazio'nale [konnattsjo'nale] SMF fellow-countryman(-woman)

connessi'one SF connection

con'nesso, -a PP *di* **connettere**

con'nettere/63/ VT to connect, join ▶ VI (*fig*) to think straight

connet'tore SM (*Elettr*) connector

conni'vente AG conniving

conno'tati SMPL distinguishing marks; **rispondere ai ~** to fit the description; **cambiare i ~ a qn** (*col*) to beat sb up

con'nubio SM (*matrimonio*) marriage; (*fig*) union

'**cono** SM cone; **~ gelato** ice-cream cone

co'nobbi *etc* VB *vedi* **conoscere**

cono'scente [konoʃʃente] SMF acquaintance

cono'scenza [konoʃʃentsa] SF (*il sapere*) knowledge *no pl*; (*persona*) acquaintance; (*facoltà sensoriale*) consciousness *no pl*; **essere a ~ di qc** to know sth; **portare qn a ~ di qc** to inform sb of sth; **per vostra ~** for your information; **fare la ~ di qn** to make sb's acquaintance; **perdere ~** to lose consciousness; **~ tecnica** know-how

co'noscere [ko'noʃʃere] /26/ VT to know; **ci siamo conosciuti a Firenze** we (first) met in Florence; **conoscersi** VPR to know o.s.; (*reciproco*) to know each other; (*incontrarsi*) to meet; **~ qn di vista** to know sb by sight; **farsi ~** (*fig*) to make a name for o.s.

conosci'tore, -'trice [konoʃʃi'tore] SM/F connoisseur

conosci'uto, -a [konoʃʃuto] PP *di* **conoscere** ▶ AG well-known

con'quista SF conquest

conquis'tare/72/ VT to conquer; (*fig*) to gain, win

conquista'tore, -'trice SM/F (*in guerra*) conqueror ▶ SM (*seduttore*) lady-killer

cons. ABBR = **consiglio**

consa'crare/72/ VT (*Rel*) to consecrate; (: *sacerdote*) to ordain; (*dedicare*) to dedicate; (*fig: uso ecc*) to sanction; **consacrarsi a** to dedicate o.s. to

consangu'ineo, -a SM/F blood relation

consa'pevole AG **~ di** aware of

consapevo'lezza [konsapevo'lettsa] SF awareness, consciousness

conscia'mente [konʃa'mente] AV consciously

'**conscio, -a, -sci, -sce** ['kɔnʃo] AG **~ di** aware o conscious of

consecu'tivo, -a AG consecutive; (*successivo*: *giorno*) following, next

con'segna [kon'seɲɲa] SF delivery; (*merce consegnata*) consignment; (*custodia*) care, custody; (*Mil: ordine*) orders *pl*; (: *punizione*) confinement to barracks; **alla ~** on delivery; **dare qc in ~ a qn** to entrust sth to sb; **passare le consegne a qn** to hand over to sb; **~ a domicilio** home delivery; **~ in contrassegno, pagamento alla ~** cash on delivery; **~ sollecita** prompt delivery

conse'gnare [konseɲ'ɲare] /15/ VT to deliver; (*affidare*) to entrust, hand over; (*Mil*) to confine to barracks

consegna'tario [konseɲɲa'tarjo] SM consignee

consegu'ente AG consequent

conseguente'mente AV consequently

consegu'enza [konse'gwɛntsa] SF consequence; **per o di ~** consequently

consegui'mento SM (*di scopo, risultato ecc*) achievement, attainment; **al ~ della laurea** on graduation

consegu'ire/17/ VT to achieve ▶ VI to follow, result; **~ la laurea** to graduate, obtain one's degree

con'senso SM approval, consent; **~ informato** informed consent

consensu'ale AG (*Dir*) by mutual consent

consen'tire/45/ VI: **~ a** to consent o agree to ▶ VT to allow, permit; **mi si consenta di ringraziare ...** I would like to thank ...

consenzi'ente [konsen'tsjɛnte] AG (*gen, Dir*) consenting

con'serto, -a AG: **a braccia conserte** with one's arms folded

con'serva SF (*Cuc*) preserve; **~ di frutta** jam; **~ di pomodoro** tomato purée; **conserve alimentari** tinned (o canned o bottled) foods

conser'vante SM (*per alimenti*) preservative

conser'vare/72/ VT (*Cuc*) to preserve; (*custodire*) to keep; (: *dalla distruzione ecc*) to preserve, conserve; **conservarsi** VPR to keep

conserva'tore, -'trice AG, SM/F (*Pol*) conservative

conserva'torio SM (*di musica*) conservatory

conservato'rismo SM (*Pol*) conservatism

conservazi'one [konservat'tsjone] SF preservation; conservation; **istinto di ~** instinct for self-preservation; **a lunga ~** (*latte, panna*) long-life *cpd*

con'sesso SM (*assemblea*) assembly; (*riunione*) meeting

conside'rabile AG worthy of consideration

conside'rare/72/ VT to consider; (*reputare*) to consider, regard; **~ molto qn** to think highly of sb; **considerarsi** VPR to consider o.s.

conside'rato, -a AG (*prudente*) cautious, careful; (*stimato*) highly thought of, esteemed

considerazi'one [konsiderat'tsjone] SF (*esame, riflessione*) consideration; (*stima*) regard, esteem; (*pensiero, osservazione*) observation; **prendere in ~** to take into consideration

conside'revole AG considerable

consigli'abile [konsiʎ'ʎabile] AG advisable

consigli'are [konsiʎ'ʎare] /27/ VT (*persona*) to advise; (*metodo, azione*) to recommend, advise, suggest; **consigliarsi** VPR: **consigliarsi con qn** to ask sb for advice

consigli'ere, -a [konsiʎ'ʎɛre] SM/F adviser ▶ SM: **~ d'amministrazione** board member; **~ comunale** town councillor; **~ delegato** (*Comm*) managing director

con'siglio [kon'siʎʎo] SM (*suggerimento*) advice *no pl*, piece of advice; (*assemblea*) council; **~ d'amministrazione** board; **C~ d'Europa** Council of Europe; **~ di fabbrica** works council; **il C~ dei Ministri** (*Pol*) ≈ the Cabinet; **C~ di stato** *advisory body to the Italian government on administrative matters and their legal implications*; **C~ superiore della magistratura** *state body responsible for judicial appointments and regulations; see note*

> The *Consiglio dei Ministri*, the Italian Cabinet, is headed by the *Presidente del Consiglio*, the Prime Minister, who is the leader of the Government. The *Consiglio superiore della Magistratura*, the magistrates' governing body, ensures their autonomy and independence as enshrined in the Constitution. Chaired by the *Presidente della Repubblica*, it mainly deals with appointments and transfers, and can take disciplinary action as required. Of the 30 magistrates elected to the *Consiglio* for a period of four years, 20 are chosen by their fellow magistrates and 10 by Parliament. The *Presidente della Repubblica* and the *Vicepresidente* are ex-officio members.

con'simile AG similar

consis'tente AG thick; solid; (*fig*) sound, valid

consis'tenza [konsis'tɛntsa] SF (*di impasto*) consistency; (*di stoffa*) texture; **senza ~** (*sospetti, voci*) ill-founded, groundless; **~ di cassa/di magazzino** cash/stock in hand; **~ patrimoniale** financial solidity

con'sistere/11/ VI: **~ in** to consist of

consis'tito, -a PP *di* **consistere**

'CONSOB SIGLA F (= *Commissione nazionale per le società e la borsa*) *regulatory body for the Italian Stock Exchange*

consoci'arsi [konso'tʃarsi] /14/ VPR to go into partnership

consociati'vismo [konsotʃati'vizmo] SM (*Pol*) pact-building

consocia'tivo, -a [konsotʃa'tivo] AG (*Pol: democrazia*) based on pacts

consoci'ato, -a [konso'tʃato] AG associated ▶ SM/F associate

conso'lante AG consoling, comforting

conso'lare/72/ AG consular ▶ VT (*confortare*) to console, comfort; (*rallegrare*) to cheer up; **consolarsi** VPR to be comforted; to cheer up

conso'lato SM consulate

consolazi'one [konsolat'tsjone] SF consolation, comfort

'console[1] SM consul

console[2] [kɔ̃'sɔl] SF (*quadro di comando*) console

consolida'mento SM strengthening; consolidation

consoli'dare/72/ VT to strengthen, reinforce; (*Mil, terreno*) to consolidate; **consolidarsi** VPR to consolidate

consolidazi'one [konsolidat'tsjone] SF strengthening; consolidation

consommé [kɔ̃sɔ'me] SM INV consommé

conso'nante SF consonant

conso'nanza [konso'nantsa] SF consonance

'consono, -a AG: **~ a** consistent with, consonant with

con'sorte SMF consort

con'sorzio [kon'sɔrtsjo] SM consortium; **~ agrario** farmers' cooperative; **~ di garanzia** (*Comm*) underwriting syndicate

con'stare/72/ VI: **~ di** to consist of ▶ VB IMPERS: **mi consta che** it has come to my knowledge that, it appears that; **a quanto mi consta** as far as I know

consta'tare/72/ VT to establish, verify; (*notare*) to notice, observe

constatazi'one [konstatat'tsjone] SF observation; **~ amichevole** (*in incidenti*) *jointly-agreed statement for insurance purposes*

consu'eto, -a AG habitual, usual ▶ SM: **come di ~** as usual

consuetudi'nario, -a AG: **diritto ~** (*Dir*) common law

consue'tudine SF habit; (*usanza*) custom

consu'lente SMF consultant; **~ aziendale/tecnico** management/technical consultant

consu'lenza [konsu'lɛntsa] SF consultancy; **~ medica/legale** medical/legal advice; **ufficio di ~ fiscale** tax consultancy office; **~ tecnica** technical consultancy o advice

consul'tare /**72**/ VT to consult; **consultarsi** VPR: **consultarsi con qn** to seek the advice of sb

consultazi'one [konsultat'tsjone] SF consultation; **consultazioni** SFPL (Pol) talks, consultations; **libro di ~** reference book

consul'tivo, -a AG consultative

consul'torio SM: **~ familiare** family planning clinic; **~ matrimoniale** marriage guidance centre; **~ pediatrico** children's clinic

consu'mare /**72**/ VT (logorare: abiti, scarpe) to wear out; (usare) to consume, use up; (mangiare, bere) to consume; (Dir) to consummate; **consumarsi** VPR to wear out; to be used up; (anche fig) to be consumed; (combustibile) to burn out

consu'mato, -a AG (vestiti, scarpe, tappeto) worn; (persona: esperto) accomplished

consuma'tore SM consumer

consumazi'one [konsumat'tsjone] SF (bibita) drink; (spuntino) snack; (Dir) consummation

consu'mismo SM consumerism

con'sumo SM consumption; wear; use; **generi** o **beni di ~** consumer goods; **beni di largo ~** basic commodities; **imposta sui consumi** tax on consumer goods

consun'tivo SM (Econ) final balance

con'sunto, -a AG worn-out; (viso) wasted

'conta SF (nei giochi): **fare la ~** to see who is going to be "it"

con'tabile AG accounts cpd, accounting ▶ SMF accountant

contabilità SF (attività, tecnica) accounting, accountancy; (insieme dei libri ecc) books pl, accounts pl; **(ufficio) ~** accounts department; **~ finanziaria** financial accounting; **~ di gestione** management accounting

contachi'lometri [kontaki'lɔmetri] SM INV ≈ mileometer

conta'dino, -a SM/F countryman(-woman); farm worker; (peg) peasant

contagi'are [konta'dʒare] /**62**/ VT to infect

con'tagio [kon'tadʒo] SM infection; (per contatto diretto) contagion; (epidemia) epidemic

contagi'oso, -a [konta'dʒoso] AG infectious; contagious

conta'giri [konta'dʒiri] SM INV (Aut) rev counter

conta'gocce [konta'gottʃe] SM INV (Med) dropper

contami'nare /**72**/ VT to contaminate

contaminazi'one [kontaminat'tsjone] SF contamination

con'tante SM cash; **pagare in contanti** to pay cash; **non ho contanti** I haven't got any cash

con'tare /**72**/ VT to count; (considerare) to consider ▶ VI to count, be of importance; **~ su qn** to count o rely on sb; **~ di fare qc** to intend to do sth; **ha i giorni contati, ha le ore contate** his days are numbered; **la gente che conta** people who matter

contas'catti SM INV telephone meter

conta'tore SM meter

contat'tare /**72**/ VT to contact

con'tatto SM contact; **essere in ~ con qn** to be in touch with sb; **fare ~** (Elettr: fili) to touch

'conte SM count

con'tea SF (Storia) earldom; (Amm) county

conteggi'are [konted'dʒare] /**62**/ VT to charge, put on the bill

con'teggio [kon'teddʒo] SM calculation

con'tegno [kon'teɲɲo] SM (comportamento) behaviour (BRIT), behavior (US); (atteggiamento) attitude; **darsi un ~** (ostentare disinvoltura) to act nonchalant; (ricomporsi) to pull o.s. together

conte'gnoso, -a [konteɲ'ɲoso] AG reserved, dignified

contem'plare /**72**/ VT to contemplate, gaze at; (Dir) to make provision for

contempla'tivo, -a AG contemplative

contemplazi'one [kontemplat'tsjone] SF contemplation

con'tempo SM: **nel ~** meanwhile, in the meantime

contemporanea'mente AV simultaneously; at the same time

contempo'raneo, -a AG, SM/F contemporary

conten'dente SMF opponent, adversary

con'tendere /**120**/ VI (competere) to compete; (litigare) to quarrel ▶ VT: **~ qc a qn** to contend with o be in competition with sb for sth

conte'nere /**121**/ VT to contain; **contenersi** VPR to contain o.s.

conteni'tore SM container

conten'tabile AG: **difficilmente ~** difficult to please

conten'tare /**72**/ VT to please, satisfy; **contentarsi** VPR: **contentarsi di** to be satisfied with, content o.s. with; **si contenta di poco** he is easily satisfied

conten'tezza [konten'tettsa] SF contentment

conten'tino SM sop

con'tento, -a AG pleased, glad; **~ di** pleased with

conte'nuto AG (ira, entusiasmo) restrained, suppressed; (forza) contained ▶ SM contents pl; (argomento) content

contenzi'oso, -a [konten'tsɔso] AG (*Dir*) contentious ▶ SM (*Amm: ufficio*) legal department

con'teso, -a PP *di* **contendere** ▶ SF dispute, argument

con'tessa SF countess

contes'tare/72/ VT (*Dir*) to notify; (*fig*) to dispute; **~ il sistema** to protest against the system

contesta'tore, -'trice AG anti-establishment ▶ SM/F protester

contestazi'one [kontestat'tsjone] SF (*Dir: disputa*) dispute; (: *notifica*) notification; (*Pol*) anti-establishment activity; **in caso di ~** if there are any objections

con'testo SM context

con'tiguo, -a AG: **~ (a)** adjacent (to)

continen'tale AG, SMF continental

conti'nente AG continent ▶ SM (*Geo*) continent; (: *terra ferma*) mainland

conti'nenza [konti'nɛntsa] SF continence

contin'gente [kontin'dʒɛnte] AG contingent ▶ SM (*Comm*) quota; (*Mil*) contingent

contin'genza [kontin'dʒɛntsa] SF circumstance; (**indennità di**) **~** cost-of-living allowance

continua'mente AV (*senza interruzione*) continuously, nonstop; (*ripetutamente*) continually

continu'are/72/ VT to continue (with), go on with ▶ VI to continue, go on; **~ a fare qc** to go on o continue doing sth; **continua a nevicare/a fare freddo** it's still snowing/cold

continua'tivo, -a AG (*occupazione*) permanent; (*periodo*) consecutive

continuazi'one [kontinuat'tsjone] SF continuation

continuità SF continuity

con'tinuo, -a AG (*numerazione*) continuous; (*pioggia*) continual, constant; (*Elettr: corrente*) direct; **di ~** continually

'conto SM (*calcolo*) calculation; (*Comm, Econ*) account; (*di ristorante, albergo*) bill; (*fig: stima*) consideration, esteem; **avere un ~ in sospeso (con qn)** to have an outstanding account (with sb); (*fig*) to have a score to settle (with sb); **fare i conti con qn** to settle one's account with sb; **fare ~ su qn** to count o rely on sb; **fare ~ che** (*supporre*) to suppose that; **rendere ~ a qn di qc** to be accountable to sb for sth; **rendersi ~ di qc/che** to realize sth/that; **tener ~ di qn/qc** to take sb/sth into account; **tenere qc da ~** to take great care of sth; **ad ogni buon ~** in any case; **di poco/nessun ~** of little/no importance; **per ~ di** on behalf of; **per ~ mio** as far as I'm concerned; (*da solo*) on my own; **a conti fatti**, **in fin dei conti** all things considered;

mi hanno detto strane cose sul suo **~** I've heard some strange things about him; **~ capitale** capital account; **~ cifrato** numbered account; **~ corrente** current account (*BRIT*), checking account (*US*); **~ corrente postale** Post Office account; **~ economico** profit and loss account; **~ in partecipazione** joint account; **~ passivo** account payable; **~ profitti e perdite** profit and loss account; **~ alla rovescia** countdown; **~ valutario** foreign currency account

con'torcere [kon'tɔrtʃere] **/106/** VT to twist; (*panni*) to wring (out); **contorcersi** VPR to twist, writhe

contor'nare/72/ VT to surround; **contornarsi** VPR: **contornarsi di** to surround o.s. with

con'torno SM (*linea*) outline, contour; (*ornamento*) border; (*Cuc*) vegetables *pl*; **fare da ~ a** to surround

contorsi'one SF contortion

con'torto, -a PP *di* **contorcere**

contrabban'dare/72/ VT to smuggle

contrabbandi'ere, -a SM/F smuggler

contrab'bando SM smuggling, contraband; **merce di ~** contraband, smuggled goods *pl*

contrab'basso SM (*Mus*) (double) bass

contraccambi'are/19/ VT (*favore ecc*) to return; **vorrei ~** I'd like to show my appreciation

contraccet'tivo, -a [kontrattʃet'tivo] AG, SM contraceptive

contrac'colpo SM rebound; (*di arma da fuoco*) recoil; (*fig*) repercussion

con'trada SF street; district; *vedi anche* **palio**

contrad'detto, -a PP *di* **contraddire**

contrad'dire/38/ VT to contradict; **contraddirsi** VPR to contradict o.s.; (*uso reciproco: persone*) to contradict each other o one another; (: *testimonianze ecc*) to be contradictory

contraddis'tinguere/42/ VT (*merce*) to mark; (*fig: atteggiamento, persona*) to distinguish

contraddis'tinto, -a PP *di* **contraddistinguere**

contraddit'torio, -a AG contradictory; (*sentimenti*) conflicting ▶ SM (*Dir*) cross-examination

contraddizi'one [kontraddit'tsjone] SF contradiction; **cadere in ~** to contradict o.s.; **essere in ~** (*tesi, affermazioni*) to contradict one another; **spirito di ~** argumentativeness

con'trae *etc* VB *vedi* **contrarre**

contra'ente SM contractor

contra'erea SF (*Mil*) anti-aircraft artillery

contra'ereo, -a AG anti-aircraft

contraf'fare/41/ VT (*persona*) to mimic; (*alterare: voce*) to disguise; (: *firma*) to forge, counterfeit

contraf'fatto, -a PP *di* **contraffare** ▸ AG
counterfeit

contraffazi'one [kontraffat'tsjone] SF
mimicking *no pl*; disguising *no pl*; forging *no
pl*; (*cosa contraffatta*) forgery

contraf'forte SM (*Archit*) buttress; (*Geo*) spur

con'traggo *etc* VB *vedi* **contrarre**

con'tralto SM (*Mus*) contralto

contrap'pello SM (*Mil*) second roll call

contrappe'sare /72/ VT to counterbalance;
(*fig: decisione*) to weigh up

contrap'peso SM counterbalance,
counterweight

contrap'porre /77/ VT: ~ **qc a qc** to counter
sth with sth; (*paragonare*) to compare sth
with sth; **contrapporsi** VPR: **contrapporsi a
qc** to contrast with sth, be opposed to sth

contrap'posto, -a PP *di* **contrapporre**

contraria'mente AV: ~ **a** contrary to

contrari'are /19/ VT (*contrastare*) to thwart,
oppose; (*irritare*) to annoy, bother;
contrariarsi VPR to get annoyed

contrari'ato, -a AG annoyed

contrarietà SF adversity; (*fig*) aversion

con'trario, -a AG opposite; (*sfavorevole*)
unfavourable (BRIT), unfavorable (US) ▸ SM
opposite; **essere ~ a qc** (*persona*) to be against
sth; **al ~** on the contrary; **in caso ~**
otherwise; **avere qualcosa in ~** to have
some objection; **non ho niente in ~** I have
no objection

con'trarre /123/ VT (*malattia, debito*) to
contract; (*muscoli*) to tense; (*abitudine, vizio*) to
pick up; (*accordo, patto*) to enter into;
contrarsi VPR to contract; ~ **matrimonio** to
marry

contrasse'gnare [kontrassep'ɲare] /15/ VT to
mark

contras'segno [kontras'seɲɲo] SM (*distintivo*)
distinguishing mark; **spedire in ~** (*Comm*)
to send COD

con'trassi *etc* VB *vedi* **contrarre**

contras'tante AG contrasting

contras'tare /72/ VT (*avversare*) to oppose;
(*impedire*) to bar; (*negare: diritto*) to contest,
dispute ▸ VI: ~ (**con**) (*essere in disaccordo*) to
contrast (with); (*lottare*) to struggle (with)

con'trasto SM contrast; (*conflitto*) conflict;
(*litigio*) dispute

contrat'tacco SM counterattack; **passare al
~** (*fig*) to fight back

contrat'tare /72/ VT, VI to negotiate

contrat'tempo SM hitch

con'tratto, -a PP *di* **contrarre** ▸ SM contract;
~ **di acquisto** purchase agreement; ~ **di
affitto**, ~ **di locazione** lease; ~ **collettivo di
lavoro** collective agreement; ~ **di lavoro**
contract of employment; ~ **a termine**
forward contract

contrattu'ale AG contractual; **forza ~**
(*di sindacato*) bargaining power

contravve'nire /128/ VI: ~ **a** (*legge*) to
contravene; (*obbligo*) to fail to meet

contravven'tore, -'trice SM/F offender

contravve'nuto, -a PP *di* **contravvenire**

contravvenzi'one [kontravven'tsjone] SF
contravention; (*ammenda*) fine

contrazi'one [kontrat'tsjone] SF
contraction; (*di prezzi ecc*) reduction

contribu'ente SMF taxpayer; ratepayer
(BRIT), property tax payer (US)

contribu'ire /55/ VI to contribute

contribu'tivo, -a AG contributory

contri'buto SM contribution; (*sovvenzione*)
subsidy, contribution; (*tassa*) tax;
contributi previdenziali ≈ national
insurance (BRIT) *o* welfare (US)
contributions; **contributi sindacali**
trade union dues

con'trito, -a AG contrite, penitent

'contro PREP against; ~ **di me/lui** against
me/him; **pastiglie ~ la tosse** throat
lozenges; ~ **pagamento** (*Comm*) on
payment; ~ **ogni mia aspettativa**
contrary to my expectations; **per ~** on the
other hand

contro'battere /1/ VT (*fig: a parole*) to answer
back; (: *confutare*) to refute

controbilanci'are [kontrobilan'tʃare] /14/ VT
to counterbalance

controcor'rente AV: **andare ~** (*anche fig*) to
swim against the tide

controcul'tura SF counterculture

contro'esodo SM return from holiday

contro'fax SM INV reply to a fax

controffen'siva SF counteroffensive

controfi'gura SF (*Cine*) double

controfir'mare /72/ VT to countersign

control'lare /72/ VT (*accertare*) to check;
(*sorvegliare*) to watch, control; (*tenere nel proprio
potere, fig: dominare*) to control; **controllarsi**
VPR to control o.s.

control'lato, -a AG (*persona*) self-possessed;
(*reazioni*) controlled ▸ SF (*Comm: società*)
associated company

con'trollo SM check; watch; control; **base di
~** (*Aer*) ground control; **telefono sotto ~**
tapped telephone; **visita di ~** (*Med*) checkup;
~ **doganale** customs inspection; ~ **di
gestione** management control; ~ **delle
nascite** birth control; ~ **di qualità** quality
control

control'lore SM (*Ferr, Aut*) (ticket) inspector;
~ **di volo** *o* **del traffico aereo** air traffic
controller

contro'luce [kontro'lutʃe] SF INV (*Fot*) backlit
shot ▸ AV: (**in**) ~ against the light; (*fotografare*)
into the light

contro'mano AV: **guidare ~** to drive on the wrong side of the road; (in un senso unico) to drive the wrong way up a one-way street

contropar'tita SF (fig: compenso): **come ~** in return

contropi'ede SM (Sport): **azione di ~** sudden counter-attack; **prendere qn in ~** (fig) to catch sb off his (o her) guard

controprodu'cente [kontroprodu'tʃɛnte] AG counterproductive

con'trordine SM counter-order; **salvo ~** unless I (o you etc) hear to the contrary

contro'senso SM (contraddizione) contradiction in terms; (assurdità) nonsense

controspio'naggio [kontrospio'naddʒo] SM counterespionage

controva'lore SM equivalent (value)

contro'vento AV against the wind; **navigare ~** (Naut) to sail to windward

contro'versia SF controversy; (Dir) dispute; **~ sindacale** industrial dispute

contro'verso, -a AG controversial

contro'voglia [kontro'vɔʎʎa] AV unwillingly

contu'mace [kontu'matʃe] AG (Dir): **rendersi ~** to default, fail to appear in court ▶ SMF (Dir) defaulter

contu'macia [kontu'matʃa] SF (Dir) default

contun'dente AG: **corpo ~** blunt instrument

contur'bante AG (sguardo, bellezza) disturbing

contur'bare/72/ VT to disturb, upset

contusi'one SF (Med) bruise

convale'scente [konvaleʃ'ʃɛnte] AG, SMF convalescent

convale'scenza [konvaleʃ'ʃɛntsa] SF convalescence

con'valida SF (Dir) confirmation; (di biglietto) stamping

convali'dare/72/ VT (Amm) to validate; (fig: sospetto, dubbio) to confirm

con'vegno [kon'veɲɲo] SM (incontro) meeting; (congresso) convention, congress; (luogo) meeting place

conve'nevoli SMPL civilities

conveni'ente AG suitable; (vantaggioso) profitable; (: prezzo) cheap

conveni'enza [konve'njɛntsa] SF suitability; advantage; cheapness; **convenienze** SFPL social conventions

conve'nire/128/ VT to agree upon ▶ VI (riunirsi) to gather, assemble; (concordare) to agree; (tornare utile) to be worthwhile ▶ VB IMPERS: **conviene fare questo** it is advisable to do this; **conviene andarsene** we should go; **ne convengo** I agree; **come convenuto** as agreed; **in data da ~** on a date to be agreed; **come (si) conviene ad una signorina** as befits a young lady

conven'ticola SF (cricca) clique; (riunione) secret meeting

con'vento SM (di frati) monastery; (di suore) convent

conve'nuto, -a PP di **convenire** ▶ SM (cosa pattuita) agreement ▶ SM/F (Dir) defendant; **i convenuti** (i presenti) those present

convenzio'nale [konventsjo'nale] AG conventional

convenzio'nato, -a [konventsjo'nato] AG (ospedale, clinica) providing free health care, ≈ National Health Service cpd (BRIT)

convenzi'one [konven'tsjone] SF (Dir) agreement; (nella società) convention; **le convenzioni (sociali)** social conventions

conver'gente [konver'dʒɛnte] AG convergent

conver'genza [konver'dʒɛntsa] SF convergence

con'vergere [kon'vɛrdʒere] /59/ VI to converge

con'versa SF (Rel) lay sister

conver'sare/72/ VI to have a conversation, converse

conversazi'one [konversat'tsjone] SF conversation; **fare ~** (chiacchierare) to chat, have a chat

conversi'one SF conversion; **~ ad U** (Aut) U-turn

con'verso, -a PP di **convergere**; **per ~** conversely

conver'tire/45/ VT (trasformare) to change; (Inform, Pol, Rel) to convert; **convertirsi** VPR: **convertirsi (a)** to be converted (to)

conver'tito, -a SM/F convert

converti'tore SM (Elettr) converter

con'vesso, -a AG convex

convin'cente [konvin'tʃɛnte] AG convincing

con'vincere [kon'vintʃere] /129/ VT to convince; **convincersi** VPR: **convincersi (di qc)** to convince o.s. (of sth); **~ qn di qc** to convince sb of sth; (Dir) to prove sb guilty of sth; **~ qn a fare qc** to persuade sb to do sth

con'vinto, -a PP di **convincere** ▶ AG: **reo ~** (Dir) convicted criminal

convinzi'one [konvin'tsjone] SF conviction, firm belief

convis'suto, -a PP di **convivere**

convi'tato, -a SM/F guest

con'vitto SM (Ins) boarding school

convi'vente SMF common-law husband/wife

convi'venza [konvi'vɛntsa] SF living together; (Dir) cohabitation

con'vivere/130/ VI to live together

convivi'ale AG convivial

convo'care/20/ VT to call, convene; (Dir) to summon

convocazi'one [konvokat'tsjone] SF meeting; summons sg; **lettera di ~** (letter of) notification to appear o attend

convogli'are [konvoʎ'ʎare] /**27**/ vt to convey; (*dirigere*) to direct, send

con'voglio [kon'vɔʎʎo] sm (*di veicoli*) convoy; (*Ferr*) train; ~ **funebre** funeral procession

convo'lare /**72**/ vi: ~ **a (giuste) nozze** (*scherzoso*) to tie the knot

convulsi'one sf convulsion

con'vulso, -a ag (*pianto*) violent, convulsive; (*attività*) feverish

COOP abbr f = **cooperativa**

coope'rare /**72**/ vi: ~ **(a)** to cooperate (in)

coopera'tiva sf cooperative

cooperazi'one [kooperat'tsjone] sf cooperation

coordina'mento sm coordination

coordi'nare /**72**/ vt to coordinate

coordi'nato, -a ag (*movimenti*) coordinated ▶ sf (*Ling, Geo, Mat*) coordinate ▶ smpl: **coordinati** (*Moda*) coordinates

coordinazi'one [koordinat'tsjone] sf coordination

co'perchio [ko'pɛrkjo] sm cover; (*di pentola*) lid

co'perta sf cover; (*di lana*) blanket; (*da viaggio*) rug; (*Naut*) deck

coper'tina sf (*Stampa*) cover, jacket

co'perto, -a pp di **coprire** ▶ ag covered; (*cielo*) overcast ▶ sm place setting; (*posto a tavola*) place; (*al ristorante*) cover charge; ~ **di** covered in o with

coper'tone sm (*telo impermeabile*) tarpaulin; (*Aut*) rubber tyre

coper'tura sf (*anche Econ, Mil*) cover; (*di edificio*) roofing; **fare un gioco di** ~ (*Sport*) to play a defensive game; ~ **assicurativa** insurance cover

'copia sf copy; (*Fot*) print; **brutta/bella** ~ rough/final copy; ~ **conforme** (*Dir*) certified copy; ~ **omaggio** presentation copy

copi'are /**19**/ vt to copy

copia'trice [kopja'tritʃe] sf copier, copying machine

copincol'lare /**72**/ vt to copy and paste

copin'collo sm copy and paste

copi'one sm (*Cine, Teat*) script

'coppa sf (*bicchiere*) goblet; (*per frutta, gelato*) dish; (*trofeo*) cup, trophy; **coppe** sfpl (*Carte*) suit in Neapolitan pack of cards; ~ **dell'olio** oil sump (*Brit*) o pan (*US*)

'coppia sf (*di persone*) couple; (*di animali, Sport*) pair

cop'rente ag (*colore, cosmetico*) covering; (*calze*) opaque

copri'capo sm headgear; (*cappello*) hat

coprifu'oco, -chi sm curfew

copri'letto sm bedspread

copripiu'mino sm inv duvet cover

co'prire /**9**/ vt to cover; (*occupare: carica, posto*) to hold; **coprirsi** vpr (*cielo*) to cloud over; (*vestirsi*) to wrap up, cover up; (*Econ*) to cover o.s.; **coprirsi di** (*macchie, muffa*) to become covered in; ~ **qn di baci** to smother sb with kisses; ~ **le spese** to break even; **coprirsi le spalle** (*fig*) to cover o.s.

coque [kɔk] sf: **uovo alla** ~ boiled egg

co'raggio [ko'raddʒo] sm courage, bravery; ~! (*forza!*) come on!; (*animo!*) cheer up!; **farsi** ~ to pluck up courage; **hai un bel** ~! (*sfacciataggine*) you've got a nerve o a cheek!

coraggi'oso, -a [korad'dʒoso] ag courageous, brave

co'rale ag choral; (*approvazione*) unanimous

co'rallo sm coral; **il mar dei Coralli** the Coral Sea

Co'rano sm (*Rel*) Koran

co'razza [ko'rattsa] sf armour (*Brit*), armor (*US*); (*di animali*) carapace, shell; (*Mil*) armour(-plating)

coraz'zato, -a [korat'tsato] ag (*Mil*) armoured (*Brit*), armored (*US*) ▶ sf battleship

corazzi'ere [korat'tsjɛre] sm (*Storia*) cuirassier; (*guardia presidenziale*) carabiniere of the President's guard

corbelle'ria sf stupid remark; **corbellerie** sfpl (*sciocchezze*) nonsense no pl

'corda sf cord; (*fune*) rope; (*spago, Mus*) string; **dare ~ a qn** (*fig*) to let sb have his (o her) way; **tenere sulla ~ qn** (*fig*) to keep sb on tenterhooks; **tagliare la ~** (*fig*) to slip away, sneak off; **essere giù di ~** to feel down; **corde vocali** vocal cords

cor'data sf (*Alpinismo*) roped party; (*fig*) alliance system in financial and business world

cordi'ale ag cordial, warm ▶ sm (*bevanda*) cordial

cordialità sf inv warmth, cordiality ▶ sfpl (*saluti*) best wishes

'cordless ['kɔːdlɪs] sm inv cordless phone

cor'doglio [kor'dɔʎʎo] sm grief; (*lutto*) mourning

cor'done sm cord, string; (*linea: di polizia*) cordon; ~ **ombelicale** umbilical cord; ~ **sanitario** quarantine line

Co'rea sf: **la** ~ Korea; **la** ~ **del Nord/Sud** North/South Korea

core'ano, -a ag, sm/f Korean

coreogra'fia sf choreography

core'ografo, -a sm/f choreographer

cori'aceo, -a [ko'rjatʃeo] ag (*Bot, Zool*) coriaceous; (*fig*) tough

cori'andolo sm (*Bot*) coriander; **coriandoli** smpl (*per carnevale ecc*) confetti no pl

cori'care /**20**/ vt to put to bed; **coricarsi** vpr to go to bed

coricherò etc [korike'rɔ] vb vedi **coricare**

Co'rinto sf Corinth

co'rista, -i, -e sm/f (*Rel*) choir member, chorister; (*Teat*) member of the chorus '**corna** SFPL *vedi* **corno**

cor'nacchia [kor'nakkja] SF crow

corna'musa SF bagpipes *pl*

'**cornea** SF (*Anat*) cornea

'**corner** SM INV (*Calcio*) corner (kick);
  salvarsi in ~ (*fig: in gara, esame ecc*) to get
  through by the skin of one's teeth

cor'netta SF (*Mus*) cornet; (*Tel*) receiver

cor'netto SM (*Cuc*) croissant; (*gelato*) cone;
  ~ acustico ear trumpet

cor'nice [kor'nitʃe] SF frame; (*fig*)
  background, setting

cornici'one [korni'tʃone] SM (*di edificio*) ledge;
  (*Archit*) cornice

'**corno** SM (*pl(f)* **corna**: *Zool*) horn; (*pl(m)*
  corni; *Mus*) horn; (*col*) **fare le corna a qn**
  to be unfaithful to sb; **dire peste e corna
  di qn** to call sb every name under the sun;
  un ~! not on your life!

Corno'vaglia [korno'vaʎʎa] SF: **la ~**
  Cornwall

cor'nuto, -a AG (*con corna*) horned; (*col: marito*)
  cuckolded ► SM (*col*) cuckold; (*: insulto*)
  bastard (*!*)

'**coro** SM chorus; (*Rel*) choir

corol'lario SM corollary

co'rona SF crown; (*di fiori*) wreath

corona'mento SM (*di impresa*) completion; (*di
  carriera*) crowning achievement; **il ~ dei
  propri sogni** the fulfilment of one's dreams

coro'nare /72/ VT to crown

coro'naria SF coronary artery

'**corpo** SM body; (*cadavere*) (dead) body;
  (*militare, diplomatico*) corps *inv*; (*di opere*) corpus;
  prendere ~ to take shape; **darsi anima e ~ a**
  to give o.s. heart and soul to; **a ~ a ~**
  hand-to-hand; **~ d'armata** army corps; **~ di
  ballo** corps de ballet; **~ dei carabinieri**
  ≈ police force; **~ celeste** heavenly body; **~ di
  guardia** (*soldati*) guard; (*locale*) guardroom;
  ~ insegnante teaching staff; **~ del reato**
  material evidence

corpo'rale AG bodily; (*punizione*) corporal

corpora'tura SF build, physique

corporazi'one [korporat'tsjone] SF
  corporation

cor'poreo, -a AG bodily, physical

cor'poso, -a AG (*vino*) full-bodied

corpu'lento, -a AG stout, corpulent

corpu'lenza [korpu'lɛntsa] SF stoutness,
  corpulence

cor'puscolo SM corpuscle

corre'dare /72/ VT: **~ di** to provide *o* furnish
  with; **domanda corredata dai seguenti
  documenti** application accompanied by the
  following documents

cor'redo SM equipment; (*di sposa*) trousseau

cor'reggere [kor'rɛddʒere] /87/ VT to correct;
  (*compiti*) to correct, mark

cor'rente AG (*fiume*) flowing; (*acqua del
  rubinetto*) running; (*moneta, prezzo*) current;
  (*comune*) everyday ► SM: **essere al ~ (di)** to be
  well-informed (about) ► SF (*movimento di
  liquido*) current, stream; (*spiffero*) draught;
  (*Elettr, Meteor*) current; (*fig*) trend, tendency;
  mettere al ~ (di) to inform (of); **la vostra
  lettera del 5 ~ mese** (*in lettere commerciali*)
  in your letter of the 5th inst.; **articoli di
  qualità ~** average-quality products;
  ~ alternata alternating current; **~ continua**
  direct current

corrente'mente AV (*comunemente*)
  commonly; **parlare una lingua ~** to speak a
  language fluently

corren'tista, -i, -e SM/F (current (BRIT) *o*
  checking (US)) account holder

cor'reo, -a SM/F (*Dir*) accomplice

'**correre** /28/ VI to run; (*precipitarsi*) to rush;
  (*partecipare a una gara*) to race, run; (*fig:
  diffondersi*) to go round ► VT (*Sport: gara*) to
  compete in; (*: rischio*) to run; (*: pericolo*) to face;
  ~ dietro a qn to run after sb; **corre voce che
  ...** it is rumoured that ...

corresponsabilità SF joint responsibility;
  (*Dir*) joint liability

corresponsi'one SF payment

cor'ressi *etc* VB *vedi* **correggere**

corret'tezza [korret'tettsa] SF (*di
  comportamento*) correctness; (*Sport*) fair play

cor'retto, -a PP *di* **correggere** ► AG
  (*comportamento*) correct, proper; **caffè ~ al
  cognac** coffee laced with brandy

corret'tore, -'trice SM/F: **~ di bozze**
  proofreader ► SM: (*liquido*) **~ correction
  fluid**

correzi'one [korret'tsjone] SF correction;
  marking; **~ di bozze** proofreading

cor'rida SF bullfight

corri'doio SM corridor; (*in aereo, al cinema*)
  aisle; **manovre di ~** (*Pol*) lobbying *sg*

corri'dore SM (*Sport*) runner; (*: su veicolo*) racer

corri'era SF coach (BRIT), bus

corri'ere SM (*diplomatico, di guerra, postale*)
  courier; (*spedizioniere*) carrier

corri'mano SM handrail

corrispet'tivo SM amount due; **versare a qn
  il ~ di una prestazione** to pay sb the
  amount due for his (*o* her) services

corrispon'dente AG corresponding ► SMF
  correspondent

corrispon'denza [korrispon'dɛntsa] SF
  correspondence; **~ in arrivo/partenza**
  incoming/outgoing mail

corris'pondere /95/ VI (*equivalere*): **~ (a)** to
  correspond (to); (*per lettera*): **~ con** to
  correspond with ► VT (*stipendio*) to pay; (*fig:
  amore*) to return

corris'posto, -a PP *di* **corrispondere**

corrobo'rare /**72**/ VT to strengthen, fortify; (*fig*) to corroborate, bear out

cor'rodere /**49**/ VT, **cor'rodersi** VPR to corrode

cor'rompere /**97**/ VT to corrupt; (*comprare*) to bribe

corrosi'one SF corrosion

corro'sivo, -a AG corrosive

cor'roso, -a PP *di* **corrodere**

corrotta'mente AV corruptly

cor'rotto, -a PP *di* **corrompere** ▶ AG corrupt

corrucci'arsi [korrut'tʃarsi] /**14**/ VPR to grow angry *o* vexed

corru'gare /**80**/ VT to wrinkle; ~ **la fronte** to knit one's brows

cor'ruppi *etc* VB *vedi* **corrompere**

corrut'tela SF corruption, depravity

corruzi'one [korrut'tsjone] SF corruption; bribery; ~ **di minorenne** (*Dir*) corruption of a minor

'**corsa** SF running *no pl*; (*gara*) race; (*di autobus, taxi*) journey, trip; **fare una** ~ to run, dash; (*Sport*) to run a race; **andare** *o* **essere di** ~ to be in a hurry; ~ **automobilistica/ciclistica** motor/cycle race; ~ **campestre** cross-country race; ~ **ad ostacoli** (*Ippica*) steeplechase; (*Atletica*) hurdles race

cor'saro, -a AG: **nave corsara** privateer ▶ SM privateer

'**corsi** *etc* VB *vedi* **correre**

cor'sia SF (*Aut, Sport*) lane; (*di ospedale*) ward; ~ **di emergenza** (*Aut*) hard shoulder; ~ **preferenziale** = bus lane; (*fig*) fast track; ~ **di sorpasso** (*Aut*) overtaking lane

'**Corsica** SF: **la** ~ Corsica

cor'sivo SM cursive (writing); (*Tip*) italics *pl*

'**corso, -a** PP *di* **correre** ▶ AG, SM/F Corsican ▶ SM course; (*strada cittadina*) main street; (*di unità monetaria*) circulation; (*di titoli, valori*) rate, price; **dar libero** ~ **a** to give free expression to; **in** ~ in progress, under way; (*annata*) current; ~ **d'acqua** river; stream; (*artificiale*) waterway; ~ **d'aggiornamento** refresher course; ~ **serale** evening class; **aver** ~ **legale** to be legal tender

'**corte** SF (*court*)yard; (*Dir, regale*) court; **fare la** ~ **a qn** to court sb; ~ **d'appello** court of appeal; ~ **di cassazione** final court of appeal; **C**~ **dei Conti** *State audit court*; **C**~ **Costituzionale** *special court dealing with constitutional and ministerial matters*; ~ **marziale** court-martial; *see note*

> The *Corte d'Appello* hears appeals against sentences passed by courts in both civil and criminal cases and can modify sentences where necessary. The *Corte d'Assise* tries serious crimes such as manslaughter and murder; its judges include both legal professionals and members of the public. Similar in structure, the *Corte d'Assise d'Appello* hears appeals imposed by these two courts. The *Corte di Cassazione* is the highest judicial authority and ensures that the law is correctly applied by the other courts; it may call for a re-trial if required. The politically independent *Corte Costituzionale* decides whether laws comply with the principles of the Constitution, and has the power to impeach the "Presidente della Repubblica". The *Corte dei Conti* ensures the Government's compliance with the law and the Constitution. Reporting directly to Parliament, it oversees the financial aspects of the state budget.

cor'teccia, -ce [kor'tettʃa] SF bark

corteggia'mento [korteddʒa'mento] SM courtship

corteggi'are [korted'dʒare] /**62**/ VT to court

corteggia'tore [korteddʒa'tore] SM suitor

cor'teo SM procession; ~ **funebre** funeral cortège

cor'tese AG courteous

corte'sia SF courtesy; **fare una** ~ **a qn** to do sb a favour; **per** ~, **dov'è …?** excuse me, please, where is …?

cortigi'ano, -a [korti'dʒano] SM/F courtier ▶ SF courtesan

cor'tile SM (court)yard

cor'tina SF curtain; (*anche fig*) screen

corti'sone SM cortisone

'**corto, -a** AG short ▶ AV: **tagliare** ~ to come straight to the point; **essere a** ~ **di qc** to be short of sth; **essere a** ~ **di parole** to be at a loss for words; **la settimana corta** the 5-day week; ~ **circuito** short-circuit

cortocir'cuito [kortotʃir'kuito] SM = **corto circuito**

cortome'traggio [kortome'traddʒo] SM short (feature film)

cor'vino, -a AG (*capelli*) jet-black

'**corvo** SM raven

'**cosa** SF thing; (*faccenda*) affair, matter, business *no pl*; (*che*) ~? what?; (*che*) **cos'è?** what is it?; **a** ~ **pensi?** what are you thinking about?; **tante belle cose!** all the best!; **ormai è** ~ **fatta!** (*positivo*) it's in the bag!; (*negativo*) it's done now!; **a cose fatte** when it's all over

'**Cosa 'Nostra** SF Cosa Nostra

'**cosca, -sche** SF (*di mafiosi*) clan

'**coscia, -sce** ['kɔʃʃa] SF thigh; ~ **di pollo** (*Cuc*) chicken leg

cosci'ente [koʃʃente] AG conscious; ~ **di** conscious *o* aware of

cosci'enza [koʃʃentsa] SF conscience; (*consapevolezza*) consciousness; ~ **politica** political awareness

coscienzi'oso, -a [koʃʃen'tsjoso] AG
conscientious
cosci'otto [koʃʃɔtto] SM (*Cuc*) leg
cos'critto SM (*Mil*) conscript
coscrizi'one [koskrit'tsjone] SF conscription

PAROLA CHIAVE

così AV **1** (*in questo modo*) like this, (in) this
way; (*in tal modo*) so; **le cose stanno così** this
is the way things stand; **non ho detto così!**
I didn't say that!; **come stai? — (e) così** how
are you? — so-so; **e così via** and so on; **per
così dire** so to speak; **così sia** amen
2 (*tanto*) so; **così lontano** so far away; **un
ragazzo così intelligente** such an
intelligent boy
▶ AG INV (*tale*): **non ho mai visto un film
così** I've never seen such a film
▶ CONG **1** (*perciò*) so, therefore; **e così ho
deciso di lasciarlo** so I decided to leave him
2: **così ... come** as ... as; **non è così bravo
come te** he's not as good as you; **così ... che**
so ... that

cosicché [kosik'ke] CONG so (that)
cosid'detto, -a AG so-called
cos'mesi SF (*scienza*) cosmetics *sg*; (*prodotti*)
cosmetics *pl*; (*trattamento*) beauty treatment
cos'metico, -a, -ci, -che AG, SM cosmetic
'cosmico, -a, -ci, -che AG cosmic
'cosmo SM cosmos
cosmo'nauta, -i, -e SM/F cosmonaut
cosmopo'lita, -i, -e AG cosmopolitan
'coso SM (*col: oggetto*) thing, thingumajig;
(*aggeggio*) contraption; (*persona*) what's his
name, thingumajig
cos'pargere [kos'pardʒere] /**111**/ VT: **~ di** to
sprinkle with
cos'parso, -a PP *di* **cospargere**
cos'petto SM: **al ~ di** in front of; in the
presence of
cospicuità SF vast quantity
cos'picuo, -a AG considerable, large
cospi'rare /**72**/ VI to conspire
cospira'tore, -'trice SM/F conspirator
cospirazi'one [kospirat'tsjone] SF
conspiracy
'cossi *etc* VB *vedi* **cuocere**
Cost. ABBR = **costituzione**
'costa SF (*tra terra e mare*) coast(line); (*litorale*)
shore; (*pendio*) slope; (*Anat*) rib; **navigare
sotto ~** to hug the coast; **la C~ Azzurra** the
French Riviera; **la C~ d'Avorio** the Ivory
Coast; **velluto a coste** corduroy
costà AV there
cos'tante AG constant; (*persona*) steadfast
▶ SF constant
cos'tanza [kos'tantsa] SF (*gen*) constancy;
(*fermezza*) constancy, steadfastness; **il Lago**

di C~ Lake Constance
cos'tare /**72**/ VI, VT to cost; **~ caro** to be
expensive, cost a lot; **~ un occhio della
testa** to cost a fortune; **costi quel che costi**
no matter what
'Costa 'Rica SF: **la ~** Costa Rica
cos'tata SF (*Cuc: di manzo*) large chop
cos'tato SM (*Anat*) ribs *pl*
costeggi'are [kosted'dʒare] /**62**/ VT to be
close to; to run alongside
cos'tei PRON *vedi* **costui**
costellazi'one [kostellat'tsjone] SF
constellation
coster'nare /**72**/ VT to dismay
coster'nato, -a AG dismayed
costernazi'one [kosternat'tsjone] SF
dismay, consternation
costi'ero, -a AG coastal, coast *cpd* ▶ SF stretch
of coast
costi'pato, -a AG (*stitico*) constipated
costitu'ire /**55**/ VT (*comitato, gruppo*) to set up,
form; (*collezione*) to put together, build up;
(*elementi, parati: comporre*) to make up,
constitute; (*rappresentare*) to constitute; (*Dir*)
to appoint; **costituirsi** VPR: **costituirsi (alla
polizia)** to give o.s. up (to the police);
costituirsi parte civile (*Dir*) *to associate in an
action with the public prosecutor for damages*; **il
fatto non costituisce reato** this is not a
crime
costitu'tivo, -a AG constituent, component;
atto ~ (*Dir: di società*) memorandum of
association
costituzio'nale [kostituttsjo'nale] AG
constitutional
costituzi'one [kostitut'tsjone] SF setting up;
building up; constitution
'costo SM cost; **sotto ~** for less than cost
price; **a ogni** o **qualunque ~**, **a tutti i costi**
at all costs; **costi di esercizio** running
costs; **costi fissi** fixed costs; **costi di
gestione** operating costs; **costi di
produzione** production costs
'costola SF (*Anat*) rib; **ha la polizia alle
costole** the police are hard on his heels
costo'letta SF (*Cuc*) cutlet
cos'toro PRON PL *vedi* **costui**
cos'toso, -a AG expensive, costly
cos'tretto, -a PP *di* **costringere**
cos'tringere [kos'trindʒere] /**117**/ VT: **~ qn a
fare qc** to force sb to do sth
costrit'tivo, -a AG coercive
costrizi'one [kostrit'tsjone] SF coercion
costru'ire /**55**/ VT to construct, build
costrut'tivo, -a AG (*Edil*) building *cpd*; (*fig*)
constructive
costruzi'one [kostrut'tsjone] SF
construction, building; **di ~ inglese**
British-made

C

cos'tui (*f* **costei**, *pl* **costoro**) PRON (*soggetto*) he (she); (*pl*) they; (*complemento*) him (her); (*pl*) them; **si può sapere chi è ~?** (*peg*) just who is that fellow?

cos'tume SM (*uso*) custom; (*foggia di vestire, indumento*) costume; **il buon ~** public morality; **donna di facili costumi** woman of easy morals; **~ da bagno** bathing *o* swimming costume (BRIT), swimsuit; (*da uomo*) bathing *o* swimming trunks *pl*

costu'mista, -i, -e SM/F costume maker, costume designer

co'tenna SF bacon rind

co'togna [ko'toɲɲa] SF quince

coto'letta SF (*di maiale, montone*) chop; (*di vitello, agnello*) cutlet

coto'nare /**72**/ VT (*capelli*) to backcomb

co'tone SM cotton; **~ idrofilo** cotton wool (BRIT), absorbent cotton (US)

cotoni'ficio [kotoni'fitʃo] SM cotton mill

'cotta SF (*Rel*) surplice; (*col: innamoramento*) crush

'cottimo SM: **lavorare a ~** to do piecework

'cotto, -a PP *di* **cuocere** ▶ AG cooked; (*col: innamorato*) head-over-heels in love ▶ SM brickwork; **~ a puntino** cooked to perfection; **dirne di cotte e di crude a qn** to call sb every name under the sun; **farne di cotte e di crude** to get up to all kinds of mischief; **mattone di ~** fired brick; **pavimento in ~** tile floor; **ben ~** (*carne*) well done

cot'tura SF cooking; (*in forno*) baking; (*in umido*) stewing; **~ a fuoco lento** simmering; **angolo (di) ~** cooking area

co'vare /**72**/ VT to hatch; (*fig: malattia*) to be sickening for; (: *odio, rancore*) to nurse ▶ VI (*fuoco, fig*) to smoulder (BRIT), smolder (US)

co'vata SF (*anche fig*) brood

'covo SM den; **~ di terroristi** terrorist base

co'vone SM sheaf

'cozza ['kɔttsa] SF mussel

coz'zare [kot'tsare] /**72**/ VI: **~ contro** to bang into, collide with

'cozzo ['kɔttso] SM collision

C.P. ABBR (= *cartolina postale*) pc; (*Posta*) *vedi* **casella postale**; (*Naut*) = **capitaneria (di porto)**; (*Dir*) = **codice penale**

CPT SIGLA M INV = **Centro di Permanenza Temporanea**

crac'care /**20**/ VT (*Inform*) to crack

crack SM INV (*droga*) crack

Cra'covia SF Cracow

'crampo SM cramp; **ho un ~ alla gamba** I've got cramp in my leg

'cranio SM skull

cra'tere SM crater

cra'vatta SF tie; **~ a farfalla** bow tie

cravat'tino SM bow tie

cre'anza [kre'antsa] SF manners *pl*; **per buona ~** out of politeness

cre'are /**72**/ VT to create

creativi'tà SF creativity

cre'ato SM creation

crea'tore, -'trice AG creative ▶ SM/F creator; **un ~ di alta moda** fashion designer; **andare al C~** to go to meet one's maker

crea'tura SF creature; (*bimbo*) baby, infant

creazi'one [kreat'tsjone] SF creation; (*fondazione*) foundation, establishment

'crebbi *etc* VB *vedi* **crescere**

cre'dente SMF (*Rel*) believer

cre'denza [kre'dɛntsa] SF belief; (*armadio*) sideboard

credenzi'ali [kreden'tsjali] SFPL credentials

'credere /**29**/ VT to believe ▶ VI: **~ in, ~ a** to believe in; **~ qn onesto** to believe sb (to be) honest; **~ che** to believe *o* think that; **credersi furbo** to think one is clever; **lo credo bene!** I can well believe it!; **fai quello che credi** *o* **come credi** do as you please

cre'dibile AG credible, believable

credibili'tà SF credibility

credi'tizio, -a [kredi'tittsjo] AG credit

'credito SM (*anche Comm*) credit; (*reputazione*) esteem, repute; **comprare a ~** to buy on credit; **~ agevolato** easy credit terms; **~ d'imposta** tax credit

credi'tore, -'trice SM/F creditor

'credo SM INV creed

'credulo, -a AG credulous

credu'lone, -a SM/F simpleton, sucker (*col*)

'crema SF cream; (*con uova, zucchero ecc*) custard; **~ idratante** moisturizing cream; **~ pasticciera** confectioner's custard; **~ solare** sun cream

cre'mare /**72**/ VT to cremate

crema'torio SM crematorium

cremazi'one [kremat'tsjone] SF cremation

'cremisi AG INV, SM INV crimson

Crem'lino SM: **il ~** the Kremlin

cremo'nese AG of (*o* from) Cremona

cre'moso, -a AG creamy

'crepa SF crack

cre'paccio [kre'pattʃo] SM large crack, fissure; (*di ghiacciaio*) crevasse

crepacu'ore SM broken heart

crepa'pelle AV: **ridere a ~** to split one's sides laughing

cre'pare /**72**/ VI (*col: morire*) to snuff it (BRIT), kick the bucket; **~ dalle risa** to split one's sides laughing; **~ dall'invidia** to be green with envy

crêpe [krɛp] SF INV pancake

crepi'tare /**72**/ VI (*fuoco*) to crackle; (*pioggia*) to patter

crepi'tio, -ii SM crackling; pattering

cre'puscolo SM twilight, dusk

cre'scendo [kreʃʃendo] SM (Mus) crescendo

cre'scente [kreʃʃente] AG (gen) growing, increasing; (luna) waxing

'crescere ['kreʃʃere] **/30/** VI to grow ▶ VT (figli) to raise

cre'scione [kreʃʃone] SM watercress

'crescita ['kreʃʃita] SF growth

cresci'uto, -a [kreʃʃuto] PP di **crescere**

'cresima SF (Rel) confirmation

cresi'mare /72/ VT to confirm

'crespo, -a AG (capelli) frizzy; (tessuto) puckered ▶ SM crêpe

'cresta SF crest; (di polli, uccelli) crest, comb; **alzare la ~** (fig) to become cocky; **abbassare la ~** (fig) to climb down; **essere sulla ~ dell'onda** (fig) to be riding high

'Creta SF Crete

'creta SF (gesso) chalk; (argilla) clay

cre'tese AG, SMF Cretan

creti'nata SF (col): **dire/fare una ~** to say/do a stupid thing

cre'tino, -a AG stupid ▶ SM/F idiot, fool

CRI SIGLA F = **Croce Rossa Italiana**

cric SM INV (Tecn) jack

'cricca, -che SF clique

'cricco, -chi SM = **cric**

cri'ceto [kri'tʃeto] SM hamster

crimi'nale AG, SMF criminal

criminalità SF crime; **~ organizzata** organized crime

'Criminalpol ABBR = **polizia criminale**

'crimine SM (Dir) crime

criminolo'gia [kriminolo'dʒia] SF criminology

crimi'noso, -a AG criminal

cri'nale SM ridge

'crine SM horsehair

crini'era SF mane

'cripta SF crypt

crip'tare /72/ VT (TV: programma) to encrypt

crip'tato, -a AG (programma, messaggio) encrypted

crisan'temo SM chrysanthemum; vedi anche **giorno**

'crisi SF INV crisis; (Med) attack, fit; **essere in ~** (partito, impresa ecc) to be in a state of crisis; **~ energetica** energy crisis; **~ di nervi** attack o fit of nerves

cristalle'ria SF (fabbrica) crystal glassworks sg; (oggetti) crystalware

cristal'lino, -a AG (Mineralogia) crystalline; (fig: suono, acque) crystal clear ▶ SM (Anat) crystalline lens

cristalliz'zare [kristallid'dzare] **/72/** VI, **cristalliz'zarsi** VPR to crystallize; (fig) to become fossilized

cris'tallo SM crystal; **cristalli liquidi** liquid crystals

cristia'nesimo SM Christianity

cristianità SF Christianity; (i cristiani) Christendom

cristi'ano, -a AG, SM/F Christian; **un povero ~** (fig) a poor soul o beggar; **comportarsi da ~** (fig) to behave in a civilized manner

'cristo SM: **C~** Christ; **(un) povero ~** (a) poor beggar

cri'terio SM criterion; (buon senso) (common) sense

'critica, -che SF vedi **critico**

criti'care /20/ VT to criticize

'critico, -a, -ci, -che AG critical ▶ SM critic ▶ SF criticism; **la critica** (attività) criticism; (persone) the critics pl

criti'cone, -a SM/F faultfinder

crivel'lare /72/ VT: **~ (di)** to riddle (with)

cri'vello SM riddle

cro'ato, -a AG, SM/F Croatian, Croat

Cro'azia [kro'attsja] SF: **la ~** Croatia

croc'cante AG crisp, crunchy ▶ SM (Cuc) almond crunch

'crocchia ['krɔkkja] SF chignon, bun

'crocchio ['krɔkkjo] SM (di persone) small group, cluster

'croce ['krotʃe] SF cross; **in ~** (di traverso) crosswise; (fig) on tenterhooks; **mettere in ~** (anche fig: criticare) to crucify (: tormentare) to nag to death; **la C~ Rossa** the Red Cross; **~ uncinata** swastika

croce'figgere etc [krotʃe'fiddʒere] = **crocifiggere** ecc

croceros'sina [krotʃeros'sina] SF Red Cross nurse

croce'via [krotʃe'via] SM INV crossroads sg

croci'ato, -a [kro'tʃato] AG cross-shaped ▶ SM (anche fig) crusader ▶ SF crusade

cro'cicchio [kro'tʃikkjo] SM crossroads sg

croci'era [kro'tʃera] SF (viaggio) cruise; (Archit) transept; **altezza di ~** (Aer) cruising height; **velocità di ~** (Aer, Naut) cruising speed

croci'figgere [krotʃi'fiddʒere] **/104/** VT to crucify

crocifissi'one [krotʃifis'sjone] SF crucifixion

croci'fisso, -a [krotʃi'fisso] PP di **crocifiggere** ▶ SM crucifix

crogio'larsi [krodʒo'larsi] **/72/** VPR: **~ al sole** to bask in the sun

crogi'olo [kro'dʒolo], **crogiu'olo** [kro'dʒwɔlo] SM crucible; (fig) melting pot

crol'lare /72/ VI to collapse

'crollo SM collapse; (di prezzi) slump, sudden fall; **~ in Borsa** slump in prices on the Stock Exchange

'croma SF (Mus) quaver (BRIT), eighth note (US)

cro'mato, -a AG chromium-plated

'cromo SM chrome, chromium

cromo'soma, -i SM chromosome

'cronaca, -che SF chronicle; (*Stampa*) news *sg*; (: *rubrica*) column; (*TV, Radio*) commentary; **fatto** *o* **episodio di** ~ news item; ~ **nera** crime news *sg*; crime column

'cronico, -a, -ci, -che AG chronic

cro'nista, -i SM (*Stampa*) reporter, columnist

cronis'toria SF chronicle; (*fig: ironico*) blow-by-blow account

cro'nografo SM (*strumento*) chronograph

cronolo'gia [kronolo'dʒia] SF chronology

crono'metro SM chronometer; (*a scatto*) stopwatch

cronome'trare /**72**/ VT to time

'crosta SF crust; (*Med*) scab; (*Zool*) shell; (*di ghiaccio*) layer; (*fig: peg: quadro*) daub

cros'tacei [kros'tatʃei] SMPL shellfish

cros'tata SF (*Cuc*) tart

cros'tino SM (*Cuc*) croûton; (: *da antipasto*) canapé

crowd'sourcing [kraud'sursin(g)] SM crowdsourcing

crucci'are [krut'tʃare] /**14**/ VT to torment, worry; **crucciarsi** VPR: **crucciarsi per** to torment o.s. over

'cruccio ['kruttʃo] SM worry, torment

cruci'ale [kru'tʃale] AG crucial

cruci'verba [krutʃi'vɛrba] SM INV crossword (puzzle)

cru'dele AG cruel

crudeltà SF cruelty

'crudo, -a AG (*non cotto*) raw; (*aspro*) harsh, severe

cru'ento, -a AG bloody

cru'miro SM (*peg*) blackleg (BRIT), scab

'cruna SF eye (of a needle)

'crusca SF bran

crus'cotto SM (*Aut*) dashboard

CS SIGLA = **Cosenza**

c.s. ABBR = **come sopra**

CSI [tʃi'esse'i] SIGLA F (= *Comunità di Stati Indipendenti*) CIS

CSM [tʃiɛsse'emme] SIGLA M (= *consiglio superiore della magistratura*) Magistrates' Board of Supervisors

CT SIGLA = **Catania**

c.t. ABBR = **commissario tecnico**

'Cuba SF Cuba

cu'bano, -a AG, SM/F Cuban

cu'betto SM (small) cube; ~ **di ghiaccio** ice cube

'cubico, -a, -ci, -che AG cubic

cu'bista, -i, -e AG (*Arte*) Cubist ▶ SF podium dancer, *dancer who performs on stage in a club*

'cubo, -a AG cubic ▶ SM cube; **elevare al** ~ (*Mat*) to cube

cuc'cagna [kuk'kaɲɲa] SF: **paese della** ~ land of plenty; **albero della** ~ greasy pole (*fig*)

cuc'cetta [kut'tʃetta] SF (*Ferr*) couchette; (*Naut*) berth

cucchiai'ata [kukkja'jata] SF spoonful; tablespoonful

cucchia'ino [kukkja'ino] SM teaspoon; coffee spoon

cucchi'aio [kuk'kjajo] SM spoon; (*da tavola*) tablespoon; (*cucchiaiata*) spoonful; tablespoonful

'cuccia, -ce ['kuttʃa] SF dog's bed; **a** ~! down!

cuccio'lata [kuttʃo'lata] SF litter

'cucciolo ['kuttʃolo] SM cub; (*di cane*) puppy

cu'cina [ku'tʃina] SF (*locale*) kitchen; (*arte culinaria*) cooking, cookery; (*le vivande*) food, cooking; (*apparecchio*) cooker; **di** ~ (*libro, lezione*) cookery cpd; ~ **componibile** fitted kitchen; ~ **economica** kitchen range

cuci'nare [kutʃi'nare] /**72**/ VT to cook

cuci'nino [kutʃi'nino] SM kitchenette

cu'cire [ku'tʃire] /**31**/ VT to sew, stitch; ~ **la bocca a qn** (*fig*) to shut sb up

cu'cito, -a [ku'tʃito] SM sewing; (*Ins*) sewing, needlework

cuci'trice [kutʃi'tritʃe] SF (*Tip: per libri*) stitching machine; (*per fogli*) stapler

cuci'tura [kutʃi'tura] SF sewing, stitching; (*costura*) seam

cucù SM INV, cu'culo SM cuckoo

'cuffia SF bonnet, cap; (*da infermiera*) cap; (*da bagno*) (bathing) cap; (*per ascoltare*) headphones *pl*, headset

cu'gino, -a [ku'dʒino] SM/F cousin

(PAROLA CHIAVE)

'cui PRON **1** (*nei complementi indiretti: persona*) whom; (: *oggetto, animale*) which; **la persona/ le persone a cui accennavi** the person/ people you were referring to *o* to whom you were referring; **la penna con cui scrivo** the pen I'm writing with; **il paese da cui viene** the country he comes from; **i libri di cui parlavo** the books I was talking about *o* about which I was talking; **parla varie lingue, fra cui l'inglese** he speaks several languages, including English; **il quartiere in cui abito** the district where I live; **visto il modo in cui ti ha trattato** ... considering how he treated you ...; **la ragione per cui** the reason why; **per cui non so più che fare** that's why I don't know what to do

2 (*inserito tra articolo e sostantivo*) whose; **la donna i cui figli sono scomparsi** the woman whose children have disappeared; **il signore, dal cui figlio ho avuto il libro** the man from whose son I got the book

culi'naria SF cookery

culi'nario, -a AG culinary

'culla SF cradle

cul'lare /72/ VT to rock; (*fig: idea, speranza*) to cherish; **cullarsi** VPR (*gen*) to sway; **cullarsi in vane speranze** (*fig*) to cherish fond hopes; **cullarsi nel dolce far niente** (*fig*) to sit back and relax

culmi'nante AG: **posizione ~** (*Astr*) highest point; **punto** *o* **momento ~** (*fig*) climax

culmi'nare /72/ VI: **~ in** *o* **con** to culminate in

'culmine SM top, summit

'culo SM (*col*) arse (BRIT !), ass (*US* !); (: *fig: fortuna*): **aver ~** to have the luck of the devil; **prendere qn per il ~** to take the piss out of sb (!)

'culto SM (*religione*) religion; (*adorazione*) worship, adoration; (*venerazione: anche fig*) cult

cul'tura SF (*gen*) culture; (*conoscenza*) education, learning; **di ~** (*persona*) cultured; (*istituto*) cultural, of culture; **~ generale** general knowledge; **~ di massa** mass culture

cultu'rale AG cultural

cultu'rismo SM body-building

cumu'lare /72/ VT to accumulate, amass

cumula'tivo, -a AG cumulative; (*prezzo*) inclusive; (*biglietto*) group *cpd*

'cumulo SM (*mucchio*) pile, heap; (*Meteor*) cumulus; **~ dei redditi** (*Fisco*) combined incomes; **~ delle pene** (*Dir*) consecutive sentences

'cuneo SM wedge

cu'netta SF (*di strada ecc*) bump; (*scolo: nelle strade di città*) gutter; (: *di campagna*) ditch; (*avvallamento*) dip

cu'nicolo SM (*galleria*) tunnel; (*di miniera*) pit, shaft; (*di talpa*) hole

cu'oca SF *vedi* **cuoco**

cu'ocere ['kwɔtʃere] /32/ VT (*alimenti*) to cook; (*mattoni ecc*) to fire ▶ VI to cook; **~ in umido/a vapore/in padella** to stew/steam/fry; **~ al forno** (*pane*) to bake; (*arrosto*) to roast

cu'oco, -a, -chi, -che SM/F cook; (*di ristorante*) chef

cuoi'ame SM leather goods *pl*

cu'oio SM leather; **~ capelluto** scalp; **tirare le cuoia** (*col*) to kick the bucket

cu'ore SM heart; **cuori** SMPL (*Carte*) hearts; **avere buon ~** to be kind-hearted; **stare a ~ a qn** to be important to sb; **un grazie di ~** heartfelt thanks; **ringraziare di ~** to thank sincerely; **nel profondo del ~** in one's heart of hearts; **avere la morte nel ~** to be sick at heart; **club dei cuori solitari** lonely hearts club

cupi'digia [kupi'didʒa] SF greed, covetousness

'cupo, -a AG dark; (*suono*) dull; (*fig*) gloomy, dismal

'cupola SF dome; (*più piccola*) cupola; (*fig*) Mafia high command

'cura SF care; (*Med: trattamento*) (course of) treatment; **aver ~ di** (*occuparsi di*) to look after; **a ~ di** (*libro*) edited by; **fare una ~** to follow a course of treatment; **~ dimagrante** diet

cu'rabile AG curable

cu'rante AG: **medico ~** doctor (in charge of a patient)

cu'rare /72/ VT (*malato, malattia*) to treat; (: *guarire*) to cure; (*aver cura di*) to take care of; (*testo*) to edit; **curarsi** VPR to take care of o.s.; (*Med*) to follow a course of treatment; **curarsi di** to pay attention to; (*occuparsi di*) to look after

cu'rato SM parish priest; (*protestante*) vicar, minister

cura'tore, -'trice SM/F (*Dir*) trustee; (*di antologia ecc*) editor; **~ fallimentare** (official) receiver

'curdo, -a AG Kurdish ▶ SM/F Kurd

'curia SF (*Rel*): **la ~ romana** the Roman curia; **~ notarile** notaries' association *o* guild

curio'saggine [kurjo'saddʒine] SF nosiness

curio'sare /72/ VI to look round, wander round; (*tra libri*) to browse; **~ nei negozi** to look *o* wander round the shops; **~ nelle faccende altrui** to poke one's nose into other people's affairs

curiosità SF INV curiosity; (*cosa rara*) curio, curiosity

curi'oso, -a AG (*che vuol sapere*) curious, inquiring; (*ficcanaso*) curious, inquisitive; (*bizzarro*) strange, curious ▶ SM/F busybody, nosy parker; **essere ~ di** to be curious about; **una folla di curiosi** a crowd of onlookers

cur'riculum SM INV: **~ (vitae)** curriculum vitae

cur'sore SM (*Inform*) cursor

'curva SF curve; (*stradale*) bend, curve

cur'vare /72/ VT to bend ▶ VI (*veicolo*) to take a bend; (*strada*) to bend, curve; **curvarsi** VPR to bend; (*legno*) to warp

'curvo, -a AG curved; (*piegato*) bent

CUS SIGLA M = **Centro Universitario Sportivo**

cusci'netto [kuʃʃi'netto] SM pad; (*Tecn*) bearing ▶ AG INV: **stato ~** buffer state; **~ a sfere** ball bearing

cu'scino [kuʃʃino] SM cushion; (*guanciale*) pillow

'cuspide SF (*Archit*) spire

cus'tode SMF (*di museo*) keeper, custodian; (*di parco*) warden; (*di casa*) concierge; (*di fabbrica, carcere*) guard

cus'todia SF care; (*Dir*) custody; (*astuccio*) case, holder; **avere qc in ~** to look after sth; **dare qc in ~ a qn** to entrust sth to sb's care;

agente di ~ prison warder; **~ delle carceri** prison security; **~ cautelare** (*Dir*) remand
custo'dire /**55**/ VT (*conservare*) to keep; (*assistere*) to look after, take care of; (*fare la guardia*) to guard
customiz'zare [kustomid'dzare] /**72**/ VT (*Inform*) to customize
'**cute** SF (*Anat*) skin
cu'ticola SF cuticle

C.V. ABBR (= *cavallo vapore*) h.p.
c.v.d. ABBR (= *come volevasi dimostrare*) QED (= *quod erat demonstrandum*)
c.vo ABBR = **corsivo**
cyberca'ffè [tʃiberka'fe] SM INV cybercafé
cyber'nauta, -i, -e SM/F Internet surfer
cyber'spazio SM cyberspace
cy'clette® [si'klɛt] SF INV exercise bike
CZ SIGLA = **Catanzaro**

Dd

D¹, d [di] SM O F INV (*lettera*) D, d; **D come
Domodossola** ≈ D for David (*BRIT*), D for Dog
(*US*)

D² ABBR (= *destra*) R; (*Ferr*) = **diretto**

[PAROLA CHIAVE]

da (*da + il* = **dal**, *da + lo* = **dallo**, *da + l'* = **dall'**, *da + la*
= **dalla**, *da + i* = **dai**, *da + gli* = **dagli**, *da + le* = **dalle**)
PREP **1** (*agente*) by; **dipinto da un grande
artista** painted by a great artist
2 (*causa*) with; **tremare dalla paura** to
tremble with fear
3 (*stato in luogo*) at; **abito da lui** I'm living at
his house *o* with him; **sono dal giornalaio**
I'm at the newsagent's; **era da Francesco**
she was at Francesco's (house)
4 (*moto a luogo*) to; (*moto per luogo*) through;
vado da Pietro/dal giornalaio I'm going to
Pietro's (house)/to the newsagent's; **sono
passati dalla finestra** they came in
through the window
5 (*provenienza, allontanamento*) from; **da ... a**
from ... to; **arrivare/partire da Milano** to
arrive/depart from Milan; **scendere dal
treno/dalla macchina** to get off the train/
out of the car; **viene da una famiglia
povera** he comes from a poor background;
viene dalla Scozia he comes from Scotland;
ti chiamo da una cabina I'm phoning from
a call box; **si trova a 5 km da qui** it's 5 km
from here
6 (*tempo: durata*) for; (: *a partire da: nel passato*)
since; (: *nel futuro*) from; **vivo qui da un anno**
I've been living here for a year; **è dalle 3 che
ti aspetto** I've been waiting for you since
3 (o'clock); **da mattina a sera** from morning
till night; **da oggi in poi** from today
onwards; **da bambino** as a child, when I
(*o* he *etc*) was a child
7 (*modo, maniera*) like; **comportarsi da uomo**
to behave like a man; **l'ho fatto da me** I did
it (by) myself; **non è da lui** it's not like him
8 (*descrittivo*): **una macchina da corsa** a
racing car; **è una cosa da poco** it's nothing

special; **una ragazza dai capelli biondi**
a girl with blonde hair; **sordo da un
orecchio** deaf in one ear; **abbigliamento
da uomo** menswear; **un vestito da 100 euro**
a 100 euro dress; **qualcosa da bere/mangiare**
something to drink/eat

dà VB *vedi* **dare**
dab'bene AG INV honest, decent
'Dacca SF Dacca
dac'capo, da 'capo AV (*di nuovo*) (once) again;
(*dal principio*) all over again, from the
beginning
dacché [dak'ke] CONG since
'dado SM (*da gioco*) dice *o* die; (*Cuc*) stock cube
(*BRIT*), bouillon cube (*US*); (*Tecn*) (screw) nut;
dadi SMPL (game of) dice; **giocare a dadi** to
play dice
daf'fare, da 'fare SM work, toil; **avere un
gran ~** to be very busy
'dagli ['daʎʎi], **'dai** PREP + DET *vedi* **da**
'daino SM (fallow) deer *inv*; (*pelle*) buckskin
Da'kar SF Dakar
dal¹ PREP + DET *vedi* **da**
dal² ABBR (= *decalitro*) dal
dall', 'dalla, 'dalle, 'dallo PREP + DET *vedi* **da**
dal'tonico, -a, -ci, -che AG colour-blind
(*BRIT*), colorblind (*US*)
dam ABBR (= *decametro*) dam
'dama SF lady; (*nei balli*) partner; (*gioco*)
draughts *sg* (*BRIT*), checkers *sg* (*US*); **far ~**
(*nel gioco*) to make a crown; **~ di compagnia**
lady's companion; **~ di corte** lady-in-
waiting
Da'masco SF Damascus
dami'gella [dami'dʒɛlla] SF (*Storia*) damsel;
(: *titolo*) mistress; **~ d'onore** (*di sposa*)
bridesmaid
damigi'ana [dami'dʒana] SF demijohn
dam'meno AG INV: **per non essere ~ di qn** so
as not to be outdone by sb
DAMS SIGLA M: **Discipline delle Arti, della
Musica, dello Spettacolo** *study of the
performing arts*

da'naro SM = **denaro**

dana'roso, -a AG wealthy

da'nese AG Danish ▶ SM/F Dane ▶ SM (*Ling*) Danish

Dani'marca SF: **la ~** Denmark

dan'nare /72/ VT (*Rel*) to damn; **dannarsi** VPR: **dannarsi per** (*fig: tormentarsi*) to be worried to death (by); **far ~ qn** to drive sb mad; **dannarsi l'anima per qc** (*affannarsi*) to work o.s. to death for sth; (*tormentarsi*) to worry o.s. to death over sth

dan'nato, -a AG damned

dannazi'one [dannat'tsjone] SF damnation

danneggi'are [danned'dʒare] /62/ VT to damage; (*rovinare*) to spoil; (*nuocere*) to harm; **la parte danneggiata** (*Dir*) the injured party

'danno VB *vedi* **dare** ▶ SM damage; (*a persona*) harm, injury; **danni** SMPL (*Dir*) damages; **a ~ di qn** to sb's detriment; **chiedere/risarcire i danni** to sue for/pay damages

dan'noso, -a AG: **~ (a o per)** harmful (to), bad (for)

dan'tesco, -a, -schi, -sche AG Dantesque; **l'opera dantesca** Dante's work

Da'nubio SM: **il ~** the Danube

'danza ['dantsa] SF: **la ~** dancing; **una ~** a dance

dan'zante [dan'tsante] AG dancing; **serata ~** dance

dan'zare [dan'tsare] /72/ VT, VI to dance

danza'tore, -'trice [dantsa'tore] SM/F dancer

dapper'tutto AV everywhere

dap'poco AG INV inept; worthless

dap'prima AV at first

Darda'nelli SMPL: **i ~** the Dardanelles

'dardo SM dart

'dare /33/ SM (*Comm*) debit ▶ VT to give; (*produrre: frutti, suono*) to produce ▶ VI (*guardare*): **~ su** to look (out) onto; **darsi** VPR: **darsi a** to dedicate o.s. to; **quanti anni mi dai?** how old do you think I am?; **danno ancora quel film?** is that film still showing?; **~ da mangiare a qn** to give sb something to eat; **~ per certo qc** to consider sth certain; **~ ad intendere a qn che ...** to lead sb to believe that ...; **~ per morto qn** to give sb up for dead; **~ qc per scontato** to take sth for granted; **darsi ammalato** to report sick; **darsi alla bella vita** to have a good time; **darsi al bere** to take to drink; **darsi al commercio** to go into business; **darsi da fare per fare qc** to go to a lot of bother to do sth; **darsi per vinto** to give in; **può darsi** maybe, perhaps; **si dà il caso che ...** it so happens that ...; **darsela a gambe** to take to one's heels; **il ~ e l'avere** (*Econ*) debits and credits *pl*

Dar-es-Sa'laam SF Dar-es-Salaam

'darsena SF dock

'data SF date; **in ~ da destinarsi** on a date still to be announced; **in ~ odierna** as of today; **amicizia di lunga o vecchia ~** long-standing friendship; **~ di emissione** date of issue; **~ di nascita** date of birth; **~ di scadenza** expiry date; **~ limite d'utilizzo o di consumo** (*Comm*) best-before date

da'tare /72/ VT to date ▶ VI: **~ da** to date from

da'tato, -a AG dated

da'tivo SM dative

'dato, -a AG (*stabilito*) given ▶ SM datum; **dati** SMPL data *pl*; **~ che** given that; **in dati casi** in certain cases; **è un ~ di fatto** it's a fact; **dati sensibili** sense data

da'tore, -'trice SM/F: **~ di lavoro** employer

'dattero SM date (*Bot*)

dattilogra'fare /72/ VT to type

dattilogra'fia SF typing

datti'lografo, -a SM/F typist

dattilos'critto SM typescript

da'vanti AV in front; (*dirimpetto*) opposite ▶ AG INV front ▶ SM front; **~ a** *prep* in front of; (*dirimpetto a*) facing, opposite; (*in presenza di*) before, in front of

davan'zale [davan'tsale] SM windowsill

da'vanzo, d'a'vanzo [da'vantso] AV more than enough

dav'vero AV really, indeed; **dico ~** I mean it

dazi'ario, -a [dat'tsjarjo] AG excise *cpd*

'dazio ['dattsjo] SM (*somma*) duty; (*luogo*) customs *pl*; **~ d'importazione** import duty

db ABBR (= *decibel*) dB

DC SIGLA F (*former political party*) = **la Democrazia Cristiana**

d.C. ABBR (= *dopo Cristo*) A.D.

D.D.T. ABBR M (= *dicloro-difenil-tricloroetano*) D.D.T.

'dea SF goddess

'debbo *etc* VB *vedi* **dovere**

debel'lare /72/ VT to overcome, conquer

debili'tare /72/ VT to debilitate

debita'mente AV duly, properly

'debito, -a AG due, proper ▶ SM debt; (*Comm: dare*) debit; **a tempo ~** at the right time; **portare a ~ di qn** to debit sb with; **~ consolidato** consolidated debt; **~ d'imposta** tax liability; **~ pubblico** national debt

debi'tore, -'trice SM/F debtor

'debole AG weak, feeble; (*suono*) faint; (*luce*) dim ▶ SM weakness

debo'lezza [debo'lettsa] SF weakness

debut'tante SM/F (*gen*) beginner, novice; (*Teat*) actor (actress) (*at the beginning of his (or her) career*)

debut'tare /72/ VI to make one's début

de'butto SM début

'decade SF period of ten days

deca'dente AG decadent

deca'denza [deka'dɛntsa] SF decline; (*Dir*) loss, forfeiture

deca'dere /**18**/ VI to decline

deca'duto, -a AG (*persona*) impoverished; (*norma*) lapsed

decaffei'nato, -a AG decaffeinated

de'calogo SM (*fig*) rulebook

de'cano SM (*Rel*) dean

decan'tare /**72**/ VT (*virtù, bravura ecc*) to praise; (*persona*) to sing the praises of

decapi'tare /**72**/ VT to decapitate, behead

decappot'tabile AG, SF convertible

dece'duto, -a [detʃe'duto] AG deceased

decele'rare [detʃele'rare] /**72**/ VT, VI to decelerate, slow down

decen'nale [detʃen'nale] AG (*che dura 10 anni*) ten-year *cpd*; (*che ricorre ogni 10 anni*) ten-yearly, every ten years ▶ SM (*ricorrenza*) tenth anniversary

de'cenne [de'tʃɛnne] AG: **un bambino ~** a ten-year-old child, a child of ten

de'cennio [de'tʃɛnnjo] SM decade

de'cente [de'tʃɛnte] AG decent, respectable, proper; (*accettabile*) satisfactory, decent

decentraliz'zare [detʃentralid'dzare] /**72**/ VT (*Amm*) to decentralize

decentra'mento [detʃentra'mento] SM decentralization

decen'trare [detʃen'trare] /**72**/ VT to decentralize, move out of *o* away from the centre

de'cenza [de'tʃɛntsa] SF decency, propriety

de'cesso [de'tʃɛsso] SM death; **atto di ~** death certificate

de'cidere [de'tʃidere] /**34**/ VI to decide, make up one's mind ▶ VT: **~ qc** to decide on sth; (*questione, lite*) to settle sth; **decidersi** VPR: **decidersi (a fare)** to decide (to do), make up one's mind (to do); **~ di fare/che** to decide to do/that; **~ di qc** (*cosa*) to determine sth

deci'frare [detʃi'frare] /**72**/ VT to decode; (*fig*) to decipher, make out

de'cilitro [de'tʃilitro] SM decilitre (*BRIT*), deciliter (*US*)

deci'male [detʃi'male] AG decimal

deci'mare [detʃi'mare] /**72**/ VT to decimate

de'cimetro [de'tʃimetro] SM decimetre

'decimo, -a ['dɛtʃimo] NUM tenth

de'cina [de'tʃina] SF ten; (*circa dieci*): **una ~ (di)** about ten

de'cisi etc [de'tʃizi] VB *vedi* **decidere**

decisio'nale [detʃizjo'nale] AG decision-making *cpd*

decisi'one [detʃi'zjone] SF decision; **prendere una ~** to make a decision; **con ~** decisively, resolutely

deci'sivo, -a [detʃi'zivo] AG (*gen*) decisive; (*fattore*) deciding

de'ciso, -a [de'tʃizo] PP *di* **decidere** ▶ AG (*persona, carattere*) determined; (*tono*) firm, resolute

declas'sare /**72**/ VT to downgrade; to lower in status; **1ª declassata** (*Ferr*) first-class carriage which may be used by second-class passengers

decli'nare /**72**/ VI (*pendio*) to slope down; (*fig: diminuire*) to decline; (: *tramontare*) to set, go down ▶ VT to decline; **~ le proprie generalità** (*fig*) to give one's particulars; **~ ogni responsabilità** to disclaim all responsibility

declinazi'one [deklinat'tsjone] SF (*Ling*) declension

de'clino SM decline

de'clivio SM (*downward*) slope

decodifi'care /**20**/ VT to decode

decodifica'tore SM (*Tel*) decoder

decol'lare /**72**/ VI (*Aer*) to take off

décolleté [dekol'te] AG INV (*abito*) low-necked, low-cut ▶ SM (*di abito*) low neckline; (*di donna*) cleavage

de'collo SM take-off

decolo'rare /**72**/ VT to bleach

decom'porre /**77**/ VT, **decomporsi** VPR to decompose

decomposizi'one [dekompozit'tsjone] SF decomposition

decom'posto, -a PP *di* **decomporre**

decompressi'one SF decompression

deconge'lare [dekondʒe'lare] /**72**/ VT to defrost

decongestio'nare [dekondʒestjo'nare] /**72**/ VT (*Med, traffico*) to relieve congestion in

deco'rare /**72**/ VT to decorate

decora'tivo, -a AG decorative

decora'tore, -'trice SM/F (interior) decorator

decorazi'one [dekorat'tsjone] SF decoration

de'coro SM decorum

deco'roso, -a AG decorous, dignified

decor'renza [dekor'rɛntsa] SF: **con ~ da** (as) from

de'correre /**28**/ VI to pass, elapse; (*avere effetto*) to run, have effect

de'corso, -a PP *di* **decorrere** ▶ SM (*evoluzione: anche Med*) course

de'crebbi etc VB *vedi* **decrescere**

de'crepito, -a AG decrepit

de'crescere [de'kreʃʃere] /**30**/ VI (*diminuire*) to decrease, diminish; (*acque*) to subside, go down; (*prezzi*) to go down

decresci'uto, -a [dekreʃʃuto] PP *di* **decrescere**

decre'tare /**72**/ VT (*norma*) to decree; (*mobilitazione*) to order; **~ lo stato d'emergenza** to declare a state of emergency; **~ la nomina di qn** to decide on the appointment of sb

de'creto SM decree; **~ legge** *decree with the force of law*; **~ di sfratto** eviction order

decrip'tare [dekrip'tare] vt to decrypt

decur'tare /**72**/ vt (*debito, somma*) to reduce

decurtazi'one [dekurtat'tsjone] sf reduction

'dedalo sm maze, labyrinth

'dedica, -che sf dedication

dedi'care /**20**/ vt to dedicate; **dedicarsi** vpr: **dedicarsi a** (*votarsi*) to devote o.s. to

dedicherò etc [dedike'rɔ] vb vedi **dedicare**

'dedito, -a ag: ~ **a** (*studio ecc*) dedicated o devoted to; (*vizio*) addicted to

de'dotto, -a pp di **dedurre**

de'duco etc vb vedi **dedurre**

de'durre /**90**/ vt (*concludere*) to deduce; (*defalcare*) to deduct

de'dussi etc vb vedi **dedurre**

deduzi'one [dedut'tsjone] sf deduction

defal'care /**20**/ vt to deduct

defenes'trare /**72**/ vt to throw out of the window; (*fig*) to remove from office

defe'rente ag respectful, deferential

defe'rire /**55**/ vt (*Dir*): ~ **a** to refer to

defezi'one [defet'tsjone] sf defection, desertion

defici'ente [defi'tʃɛnte] ag (*insufficiente*) insufficient; ~ **di** (*mancante*) deficient in ▶ smf mental defective; (*peg: cretino*) idiot

defici'enza [defi'tʃɛntsa] sf deficiency; (*carenza*) shortage; (*fig: lacuna*) weakness

'deficit ['dɛfitʃit] sm inv (*Econ*) deficit

defi'nire /**55**/ vt to define; (*risolvere*) to settle; (*questione*) to finalize

defini'tivo, -a ag definitive, final ▶ sf: **in definitiva** (*dopotutto*) when all is said and done; (*dunque*) hence

defi'nito, -a ag definite; **ben** ~ clear, clear cut

definizi'one [definit'tsjone] sf (*gen*) definition; (*di disputa, vertenza*) settlement; (*di tempi, obiettivi*) establishment

deflagrazi'one [deflagrat'tsjone] sf explosion

deflazi'one [deflat'tsjone] sf (*Econ*) deflation

deflet'tore sm (*Aut*) quarterlight (*Brit*), deflector (*US*)

deflu'ire /**55**/ vi: ~ **da** (*liquido*) to flow away from; (*fig: capitali*) to flow out of

de'flusso sm (*della marea*) ebb

defor'mare /**72**/ vt (*alterare*) to put out of shape; (*corpo*) to deform; (*pensiero, fatto*) to distort; **deformarsi** vpr to lose its shape

deformazi'one [deformat'tsjone] sf (*Med*) deformation; **questa è ~ professionale!** that's force of habit because of your (*o his etc*) job!

de'forme ag deformed; disfigured

deformità sf inv deformity

defrau'dare /**72**/ vt: ~ **qn di qc** to defraud sb of sth, cheat sb out of sth

de'funto, -a ag late *cpd* ▶ sm/f deceased

degene'rare [dedʒene'rare] /**72**/ vi to degenerate

degenerazi'one [dedʒenerat'tsjone] sf degeneration

de'genere [de'dʒɛnere] ag degenerate

de'gente [de'dʒɛnte] smf bedridden person; (*ricoverato in ospedale*) in-patient

de'genza [de'dʒɛntsa] sf confinement to bed; ~ **ospedaliera** period in hospital

'degli ['deʎʎi] prep + det vedi **di**

deglu'tire /**55**/ vt to swallow

de'gnare [deɲ'ɲare] /**15**/ vt: ~ **qn della propria presenza** to honour sb with one's presence; **degnarsi** vpr: **degnarsi di fare qc** to deign o condescend to do sth; **non mi ha degnato di uno sguardo** he wouldn't even look at me

'degno, -a ['deɲɲo] ag dignified; ~ **di** worthy of; ~ **di lode** praiseworthy

degra'dare /**72**/ vt (*Mil*) to demote; (*privare della dignità*) to degrade; **degradarsi** vpr to demean o.s

de'grado sm: ~ **urbano** urban decline

degus'tare /**72**/ vt to sample, taste

degustazi'one [degustat'tsjone] sf sampling, tasting; ~ **di vini** (*locale*) specialist wine bar; ~ **di caffè** (*locale*) specialist coffee shop

'dei smpl di **dio** ▶ prep + det vedi **di**

del prep + det vedi **di**

dela'tore, -'trice sm/f police informer

delazi'one [delat'tsjone] sf informing

'delega, -ghe sf (*procura*) proxy; **per ~ notarile** ≈ through a solicitor (*Brit*) o lawyer

dele'gare /**80**/ vt to delegate

dele'gato sm delegate

delegazi'one [delegat'tsjone] sf delegation

delegherò etc [delege'rɔ] vb vedi **delegare**

dele'terio, -a ag damaging; (*per salute ecc*) harmful

del'fino sm (*Zool*) dolphin; (*Storia*) dauphin; (*fig*) probable successor

'Delhi ['dɛli] sf Delhi

de'libera sf decision

delibe'rare /**72**/ vt to come to a decision on ▶ vi (*Dir*): ~ **(su qc)** to rule (on sth)

delica'tezza [delika'tettsa] sf delicacy; frailty; thoughtfulness; tactfulness

deli'cato, -a ag delicate; (*salute*) delicate, frail; (*fig: gentile*) thoughtful, considerate; (: *che dimostra tatto*) tactful

delimi'tare /**72**/ vt (*anche fig*) to delimit

deline'are /**72**/ vt to outline; **delinearsi** vpr to be outlined; (*fig*) to emerge

delin'quente smf criminal, delinquent; ~ **abituale** regular offender, habitual offender

delin'quenza [delin'kwɛntsa] sf criminality, delinquency; ~ **minorile** juvenile delinquency de'liquio SM (Med) swoon; **cadere in ~ to** swoon

deli'rante AG (Med) delirious; (fig: folla) frenzied; (: discorso, mente) insane

deli'rare /**72**/ VI to be delirious, rave; (fig) to rave

de'lirio SM delirium; (ragionamento insensato) raving; (fig): **andare/mandare in ~ to go/** send into a frenzy

de'litto SM crime; **~ d'onore** crime committed to avenge one's honour

delittu'oso, -a AG criminal

de'lizia [de'littsja] SF delight

delizi'are [delit'tsjare] /**19**/ VT to delight; **deliziarsi** VPR: **deliziarsi di qc/a fare qc to** take delight in sth/in doing sth

delizi'oso, -a [delit'tsjoso] AG delightful; (cibi) delicious

dell', 'della, 'delle, 'dello PREP + DET vedi di

'delta SM INV delta

delta'plano SM hang-glider; **volo col ~** hang-gliding

delucidazi'one [delutʃidat'tsjone] SF clarification no pl

delu'dente AG disappointing

de'ludere /**35**/ VT to disappoint

delusi'one SF disappointment

de'luso, -a PP di **deludere** ▶ AG disappointed

dema'gogico, -a, -ci, -che [dema'ɡɔdʒiko] AG popularity-seeking, demagogic

dema'gogo, -ghi SM demagogue

de'manio SM state property

de'mente AG (Med) demented, mentally deranged; (fig) crazy, mad

de'menza [de'mentsa] SF dementia; madness; **~ senile** senile dementia

demenzi'ale [demen'tsjale] AG (fig) off-the-wall

'demmo VB vedi **dare**

demo'cratico, -a, -ci, -che AG democratic

democra'zia [demokrat'tsia] SF democracy; **la D~ Cristiana** the Christian Democrat Party

democristi'ano, -a AG, SM/F Christian Democrat

demogra'fia SF demography

demo'grafico, -a, -ci, -che AG demographic; **incremento ~** increase in population

demo'lire /**55**/ VT to demolish

demolizi'one [demolit'tsjone] SF demolition

'demone SM demon

de'monio SM demon, devil; **il D~** the Devil

demoniz'zare [demonid'dzare] /**72**/ VT to make a monster of

demonizzazi'one [demoniddzat'tsjone] SF demonizing, demonization

demoraliz'zare [demoralid'dzare] /**72**/ VT to demoralize; **demoralizzarsi** VPR to become demoralized

de'mordere /**64**/ VI: **non ~ (da)** to refuse to give up

demoti'vare /**72**/ VT: **~ qn** to take away sb's motivation

demoti'vato, -a AG unmotivated, lacking motivation

de'naro SM money; **denari** SMPL (Carte) suit in Neapolitan pack of cards

denatu'rato, -a AG vedi **alcool**

deni'grare /**72**/ VT to denigrate, run down

denomi'nare /**72**/ VT to name; **denominarsi** VPR to be named o called

denomina'tore SM (Mat) denominator

denominazi'one [denominat'tsjone] SF name; denomination; **~ di origine controllata** label guaranteeing the quality and origin of a wine

deno'tare /**72**/ VT to denote, indicate

densità SF INV density; (di nebbia) thickness, denseness; **ad alta/bassa ~ di popolazione** densely/sparsely populated

'denso, -a AG thick, dense

den'tale AG dental

den'tario, -a AG dental

denta'tura SF set of teeth, teeth pl; (Tecn: di ruota) serration

'dente SM tooth; (di forchetta) prong; (Geo: cima) jagged peak; **al ~** (Cuc: pasta) al dente; **mettere i denti** to teethe; **mettere qc sotto i denti** to have a bite to eat; **avere il ~ avvelenato contro** o **con qn** to bear sb a grudge; **~ di leone** (Bot) dandelion; **denti del giudizio** wisdom teeth; **denti da latte** milk teeth

'dentice ['dentitʃe] SM (Zool) sea bream

denti'era SF (set of) false teeth pl

denti'fricio [denti'fritʃo] SM toothpaste

den'tista, -i, -e SM/F dentist

'dentro AV inside; (in casa) indoors; (fig: nell'intimo) inwardly ▶ PREP: **~ (a)** in; **piegato in ~** folded over; **qui/là ~** in here/ there; **~ di sé** (pensare, brontolare) to oneself; **tenere tutto ~** to keep everything bottled up (inside o.s.); **darci ~** (fig: col) to slog away, work hard

denuclearizz'zato, -a [denuklearid'dzato] AG denuclearized, nuclear-free

denu'dare /**72**/ VT (persona) to strip; (parte del corpo) to bare; **denudarsi** VPR to strip

de'nuncia [de'nuntʃa] (pl **-ce** o **-cie**), de'nunzia [de'nuntsja] SF denunciation; declaration; **fare una ~** o **sporgere ~ contro qn** (Dir) to report sb to the police; **~ del reddito** (income) tax return

denunci'are [denun'tʃare] /**14**/, denunzi'are [denun'tsjare] VT to denounce; (dichiarare) to declare; **~ qn/qc (alla polizia)** to report sb/ sth to the police

denu'trito, -a AG undernourished

denutrizi'one [denutrit'tsjone] SF
malnutrition

deodo'rante SM deodorant

deontolo'gia [deontolo'dʒia] SF (*professionale*)
professional code of conduct

depenalizzazi'one [depenaliddzat'tsjone]
SF decriminalization

dépen'dance [depã'dãs] SF INV outbuilding

depe'ribile AG perishable; **merce ~**
perishables *pl*, perishable goods *pl*

deperi'mento SM (*di persona*) wasting away;
(*di merci*) deterioration

depe'rire /55/ VI to waste away

depi'lare /72/ VT to depilate; **depilarsi** VPR:
depilarsi (le gambe) (*con rasoio*) to shave
(one's legs); (*con ceretta*) to wax (one's legs)

depila'torio, -a AG hair-removing *cpd*,
depilatory ► SM hair remover, depilatory

depilazi'one [depilat'tsjone] SF hair
removal, depilation

depis'taggio [depis'taddʒo] SM diversion

depis'tare /72/ VT to set on the wrong track

dépli'ant [depli'ã] SM INV leaflet; (*opuscolo*)
brochure

deplo'rare /72/ VT to deplore; to lament

deplo'revole AG deplorable

de'pone, de'pongo *etc* VB *vedi* **deporre**

de'porre /77/ VT (*depositare*) to put down;
(*rimuovere: da una carica*) to remove; (: *re*) to
depose; (*Dir*) to testify; ~ **le armi** (*Mil*) to lay
down arms; ~ **le uova** to lay eggs

depor'tare /72/ VT to deport

depor'tato, -a SM/F deportee

deportazi'one [deportat'tsjone] SF
deportation

de'posi *etc* VB *vedi* **deporre**

deposi'tante SM (*Comm*) depositor

deposi'tare /72/ VT (*gen, Geo, Econ*) to deposit;
(*lasciare*) to leave; (*merci*) to store; **depositarsi**
VPR (*sabbia, polvere*) to settle

deposi'tario SM (*Comm*) depository

de'posito SM deposit; (*luogo*) warehouse;
depot; (: *Mil*) depot; ~ **bagagli** left-luggage
office; ~ **di munizioni** ammunition dump

deposizi'one [depozit'tsjone] SF deposition;
(*da una carica*) removal; **rendere una falsa ~**
to perjure o.s.

de'posto, -a PP *di* **deporre**

depra'vare /72/ VT to corrupt, pervert

depra'vato, -a AG depraved ► SM/F
degenerate

depre'care /20/ VT to deprecate, deplore

depre'dare /72/ VT to rob, plunder

depressi'one SF depression; **area** *o* **zona di ~**
(*Meteor*) area of low pressure; (*Econ*)
depressed area

de'presso, -a PP *di* **deprimere** ► AG depressed

deprezza'mento [deprettsa'mento] SM
depreciation

deprez'zare [depret'tsare] /72/ VT (*Econ*) to
depreciate

depri'mente AG depressing

de'primere /50/ VT to depress

depu'rare /72/ VT to purify

depura'tore SM: ~ **d'acqua** water purifier;
~ **di gas** scrubber

depu'tato, -a SM/F (*Pol*) deputy, ≈ Member of
Parliament (*BRIT*), ≈ Congressman(-woman)
(*US*); *vedi anche* **Camera dei Deputati**

deputazi'one [deputat'tsjone] SF
deputation; (*Pol*) position of deputy,
≈ parliamentary seat (*BRIT*), ≈ seat in
Congress (*US*)

deraglia'mento [deraʎʎa'mento] SM
derailment

deragli'are [deraʎ'ʎare] /27/ VI to be derailed;
far ~ to derail

dera'pare /72/ VI (*veicolo*) to skid; (*Sci*) to
sideslip

derattizzazi'one [derattiddzat'tsjone] SF
rodent control

deregolamen'tare /72/ VT to deregulate

deregolamentazi'one
[deregolamentat'tsjone] SF deregulation

dere'litto, -a AG derelict

dere'tano SM (*col*) bottom, buttocks *pl*

de'ridere /89/ VT to mock, deride

de'risi *etc* VB *vedi* **deridere**

derisi'one SF derision, mockery

de'riso, -a PP *di* **deridere**

deri'sorio, -a AG (*gesto, tono*) mocking

de'riva SF (*Naut, Aer*) drift; (*dispositivo: Aer*) fin;
(: *Naut*) centre-board (*BRIT*), centerboard (*US*);
andare alla ~ (*anche fig*) to drift

deri'vare /72/ VI: ~ **da** to derive from ► VT to
derive; (*corso d'acqua*) to divert

deri'vato, -a AG derived ► SM (*Chim, Ling*)
derivative; (*prodotto*) by-product

derivazi'one [derivat'tsjone] SF derivation,
diversion

derma'tite SF dermatitis

dermatolo'gia [dermatolo'dʒia] SF
dermatology

derma'tologo, -a, -gi, -ghe SM/F
dermatologist

dermoprotet'tivo, -a AG (*crema, azione*)
protecting the skin

'deroga, -ghe SF (special) dispensation;
in ~ a as a (special) dispensation to

dero'gare /80/ VI: ~ **a** (*Dir*) to repeal in part

der'rate SFPL commodities; ~ **alimentari**
foodstuffs

deru'bare /72/ VT to rob

des'critto, -a PP *di* **descrivere**

des'crivere /105/ VT to describe

descrizi'one [deskrit'tsjone] SF description

de'serto, -a AG deserted ► SM (*Geo*) desert;
isola deserta desert island

deside'rabile AG desirable

deside'rare /**72**/ VT to want, wish for; (*sessualmente*) to desire; **~ fare/che qn faccia** to want *o* wish to do/sb to do; **desidera fare una passeggiata?** would you like to go for a walk?; **farsi ~** (*fare il prezioso*) to play hard to get; (*farsi aspettare*) to take one's time; **lascia molto a ~** it leaves a lot to be desired

desi'derio SM wish; (*più intenso, carnale*) desire

deside'roso, -a AG: **~ di** longing *o* eager for

desi'gnare [desiɲ'ɲare] /**15**/ VT to designate, appoint; (*data*) to fix; **la vittima designata** the intended victim

designazi'one [desiɲɲat'tsjone] SF designation, appointment

desi'nare /**72**/ VI to dine, have dinner ▶ SM dinner

desi'nenza [dezi'nɛntsa] SF (*Ling*) ending, inflexion

de'sistere /**11**/ VI: **~ da** to give up, desist from

desis'tito, -a PP *di* **desistere**

deso'lante AG distressing

deso'lato, -a AG (*paesaggio*) desolate; (*persona: spiacente*) sorry

desolazi'one [dezolat'tsjone] SF desolation

'despota, -i SM despot

'dessi *etc* VB *vedi* **dare**

destabiliz'zare [destabilid'dzare] /**72**/ VT to destabilize

des'tare /**72**/ VT to wake (up); (*fig*) to awaken, arouse; **destarsi** VPR to wake (up)

'deste *etc* VB *vedi* **dare**

desti'nare /**72**/ VT to destine; (*assegnare*) to appoint, assign; (*indirizzare*) to address; **~ qc a qn** to intend to give sth to sb, intend sb to have sth

destina'tario, -a SM/F (*di lettera*) addressee; (*di merce*) consignee; (*di mandato*) payee

destinazi'one [destinat'tsjone] SF destination; (*uso*) purpose

des'tino SM destiny, fate

destitu'ire /**55**/ VT to dismiss, remove

destituzi'one [destitut'tsjone] SF dismissal, removal

'desto, -a AG (wide) awake

'destra SF *vedi* **destro**

destreggi'arsi [destred'dʒarsi] /**62**/ VPR to manoeuvre (*BRIT*), maneuver (*US*)

des'trezza [des'trettsa] SF skill, dexterity

'destro, -a AG right, right-hand; (*abile*) skilful (*BRIT*), skillful (*US*), adroit ▶ SF (*mano*) right hand; (*parte*) right (side); (*Pol*) right ▶ SM (*Pugilato*) right; **a destra** (*essere*) on the right; (*andare*) to the right; **tenere la destra** to keep to the right

de'sumere /**12**/ VT (*dedurre*) to infer, deduce; (*trarre: informazioni*) to obtain

de'sunto, -a PP *di* **desumere**

detas'sare /**72**/ VT to remove the duty (*o* tax) from

dete'nere /**121**/ VT (*incarico, primato*) to hold; (*proprietà*) to have, possess; (*in prigione*) to detain, hold

de'tengo, de'tenni *etc* VB *vedi* **detenere**

deten'tivo, -a AG: **mandato ~** imprisonment order; **pena detentiva** prison sentence

deten'tore, -'trice SM/F (*di titolo, primato ecc*) holder

dete'nuto, -a SM/F prisoner

detenzi'one [deten'tsjone] SF holding; possession; detention

deter'gente [deter'dʒɛnte] AG (*crema, latte*) cleansing ▶ SM cleanser

de'tergere [de'tɛrdʒere] /**111**/ VT (*gen*) to clean; (*pelle, viso*) to cleanse; (*sudore*) to wipe (away)

deteriora'mento SM: **~ (di)** deterioration (in)

deterio'rare /**72**/ VT to damage; **deteriorarsi** VPR to deteriorate

deteri'ore AG (*merce*) second-rate; (*significato*) pejorative; (*tradizione letteraria*) lesser, minor

determi'nante AG decisive, determining

determi'nare /**72**/ VT to determine

determina'tivo, -a AG determining; **articolo ~** (*Ling*) definite article

determi'nato, -a AG (*gen*) certain; (*particolare*) specific; (*risoluto*) determined, resolute

determinazi'one [determinat'tsjone] SF determination; (*decisione*) decision

deter'rente AG, SM deterrent

deter'rò *etc* VB *vedi* **detenere**

deter'sivo SM detergent; (*per bucato: in polvere*) washing powder (*BRIT*), soap powder

de'terso, -a PP *di* **detergere**

detes'tare /**72**/ VT to detest, hate

deti'ene *etc* VB *vedi* **detenere**

deto'nare /**72**/ VI to detonate

detona'tore SM detonator

detonazi'one [detonat'tsjone] SF (*di esplosivo*) detonation, explosion; (*di arma*) bang; (*di motore*) pinking (*BRIT*), knocking

de'trae, de'traggo *etc* VB *vedi* **detrarre**

de'trarre /**123**/ VT: **~ (da)** to deduct (from), take away (from)

de'trassi *etc* VB *vedi* **detrarre**

de'tratto, -a PP *di* **detrarre**

detrazi'one [detrat'tsjone] SF deduction; **~ d'imposta** tax allowance

detri'mento SM detriment, harm; **a ~ di** to the detriment of

de'trito SM (*Geo*) detritus

detroniz'zare [detronid'dzare] /**72**/ VT to dethrone

'detta SF: **a ~ di** according to

dettagli'ante [detta'ʎʎante] SMF (*Comm*) retailer

dettagli'are [dettaʎ'ʎare] /**27**/ VT to detail, give full details of

dettagliata'mente [dettaʎʎata'mente] AV in detail

det'taglio [det'taʎʎo] SM detail; (*Comm*): **il ~** retail; **al ~** (*Comm*) retail; separately

det'tame SM dictate, precept

det'tare /**72**/ VT to dictate; **~ legge** (*fig*) to lay down the law

det'tato SM dictation

detta'tura SF dictation

'detto, -a PP *di* **dire** ▶ AG (*soprannominato*) called, known as; (*già nominato*) above-mentioned ▶ SM saying; **~ fatto** no sooner said than done; **presto ~!** it's easier said than done!

detur'pare /**72**/ VT to disfigure; (*moralmente*) to sully

devas'tante AG (*anche fig*) devastating

devas'tare /**72**/ VT to devastate; (*fig*) to ravage

devastazi'one [devastat'tsjone] SF devastation, destruction

devi'are /**19**/ VI: **~ (da)** to turn off (from) ▶ VT to divert

devi'ato, -a AG (*fig: persona, organizzazione*) corrupt, bent (*col*)

deviazi'one [devjat'tsjone] SF (*anche Aut*) diversion; **fare una ~** to make a detour

'devo *etc* VB *vedi* **dovere**

devo'luto, -a PP *di* **devolvere**

devoluzi'one [devolut'tsjone] SF (*Dir*) devolution, transfer

de'volvere /**94**/ VT (*Dir*) to transfer, devolve; **~ qc in beneficenza** to give sth to charity

de'voto, -a AG (*Rel*) devout, pious; (*affezionato*) devoted

devozi'one [devot'tsjone] SF devoutness; (*anche Rel*) devotion

dezip'pare [dedzip'pare] /**72**/ VT (*Inform*) to unzip

dg ABBR (= *decigrammo*) dg

(**PAROLA CHIAVE**)

di (*di* + *il* = **del**, *di* + *lo* = **dello**, *di* + *l'* = **dell'**, *di* + *la* = **della**, *di* + *i* = **dei**, *di* + *gli* = **degli**, *di* + *le* = **delle**) PREP **1** (*possesso, specificazione*) of; (*composto da, scritto da*) by; **la macchina di Paolo/di mio fratello** Paolo's/my brother's car; **un amico di mio fratello** a friend of my brother's, one of my brother's friends; **la grandezza della casa** the size of the house; **le foto delle vacanze** the holiday photos; **la città di Firenze** the city of Florence; **il nome di Maria** the name Mary; **un quadro di Botticelli** a painting by Botticelli

2 (*caratterizzazione, misura*) of; **una casa di mattoni** a brick house, a house made of bricks; **un orologio d'oro** a gold watch; **un bimbo di 3 anni** a child of 3, a 3-year-old child; **una trota di un chilo** a trout weighing a kilo; **una strada di 10 km** a road 10 km long; **un quadro di valore** a valuable picture

3 (*causa, mezzo, modo*) with; **tremare di paura** to tremble with fear; **morire di cancro** to die of cancer; **spalmare di burro** to spread with butter

4 (*argomento*) about, of; **discutere di sport** to talk about sport; **parlare di politica/lavoro** to talk about politics/work

5 (*luogo: provenienza*) from; **essere di Roma** to be from Rome; out of; **uscire di casa** to come out of *o* leave the house

6 (*tempo*) in; **d'estate/d'inverno** in (the) summer/winter; **di notte** by night, at night; **di mattina/sera** in the morning/evening; **di lunedì** on Mondays; **di ora in ora** by the hour

7 (*partitivo*) of; **alcuni di voi/noi** some of you/us; **il più bravo di tutti** the best of all; **il migliore del mondo** the best in the world; **non c'è niente di peggio** there's nothing worse

8 (*paragone*) than; **più veloce di me** faster than me; **guadagna meno di me** he earns less than me

▶ DET (*una certa quantità di*) some; (: *negativo*) any; (: *interrogativo*) any; some; **del pane** (some) bread; **delle caramelle** (some) sweets; **degli amici miei** some friends of mine; **vuoi del vino?** do you want some *o* any wine?

dì SM day; **buon dì!** hallo!; **a dì = addì**

DIA SIGLA F = **Direzione investigativa antimafia**

dia'bete SM diabetes *sg*

dia'betico, -a, -ci, -che AG, SM/F diabetic

dia'bolico, -a, -ci, -che AG diabolical

di'acono SM (*Rel*) deacon

dia'dema, -i SM diadem; (*di donna*) tiara

di'afano, -a AG (*trasparente*) diaphanous; (*pelle*) transparent

dia'framma, -i SM (*divisione*) screen; (*Anat, Fot: contraccettivo*) diaphragm

di'agnosi [di'aɲɲozi] SF diagnosis *sg*

diagnosti'care [diaɲɲosti'kare] /**20**/ VT to diagnose

dia'gnostico, -a, -ci, -che [diaɲ'nɔstiko] AG diagnostic; **aiuti diagnostici** (*Inform*) debugging aids

diago'nale AG, SF diagonal

dia'gramma, -i SM diagram; **~ a barre** bar chart; **~ di flusso** flow chart

dialet'tale AG dialectal; **poesia ~** poetry in dialect

dia'letto SM dialect

di'alisi SF dialysis *sg*

dialo'gante AG: **unità ~** (*Inform*) interactive terminal

dialo'gare /80/ VI: **~ (con)** to have a dialogue (with); (*conversare*) to converse (with) ▶ VT (*scena*) to write the dialogue for

di'alogo, -ghi SM dialogue

dia'mante SM diamond

di'ametro SM diameter

di'amine ESCL: **che ~ ...?** what on earth ...?

diapo'rama [djapo'rama] SM INV slide show

diaposi'tiva SF transparency, slide

di'aria SF daily (expense) allowance

di'ario SM diary; **~ di bordo** (*Naut*) log(book); **~ di classe** (*Ins*) class register; **~ degli esami** (*Ins*) exam timetable

diar'rea SF diarrhoea

dia'triba SF diatribe

diavole'ria SF (*azione*) act of mischief; (*aggeggio*) weird contraption

di'avolo SM devil; **è un buon ~** he's a good sort; **avere un ~ per capello** to be in a foul temper; **avere una fame/un freddo del ~** to be ravenously hungry/frozen stiff; **mandare qn al ~** (*col*) to tell sb to go to hell; **fare il ~ a quattro** to kick up a fuss

di'battere /1/ VT to debate, discuss; **dibattersi** VPR to struggle

dibatti'mento SM (*dibattito*) debate, discussion; (*Dir*) hearing

di'battito SM debate, discussion

dic. ABBR (= *dicembre*) Dec

dicas'tero SM ministry

'dice ['ditʃe] VB *vedi* **dire**

di'cembre [di'tʃɛmbre] SM December; *vedi anche* **luglio**

dice'ria [ditʃe'ria] SF rumour (*Brit*), rumor (*US*), piece of gossip

dichia'rare [dikja'rare] **/72/** VT to declare; **dichiararsi** VPR to declare o.s.; (*innamorato*) to declare one's love; **si dichiara che ...** it is hereby declared that ...; **dichiararsi vinto** to admit defeat

dichia'rato, -a [dikja'rato] AG (*nemico, ateo*) avowed

dichiarazi'one [dikjarat'tsjone] SF declaration; **~ dei redditi** statement of income; (*modulo*) tax return

dician'nove [ditʃan'nɔve] NUM nineteen

dicianno'venne [ditʃanno'vɛnne] AG, SMF nineteen-year-old

dicias'sette [ditʃas'sɛtte] NUM seventeen

diciasset'tenne [ditʃasset'tɛnne] AG, SMF seventeen-year-old

diciot'tenne [ditʃot'tɛnne] AG, SMF eighteen-year-old

dici'otto [di'tʃɔtto] NUM eighteen ▶ SM INV (*Ins*) *minimum satisfactory mark awarded in Italian universities*

dici'tura [ditʃi'tura] SF words *pl*, wording

'dico *etc* VB *vedi* **dire**

didasca'lia SF (*di illustrazione*) caption; (*Cine*) subtitle; (*Teat*) stage directions *pl*

di'dattico, -a, -ci, -che AG didactic; (*metodo, programma*) teaching; (*libro*) educational ▶ SF didactics *sg*; teaching methodology

di'dentro AV inside, indoors

didi'etro AV behind ▶ AG INV (*ruota, giardino*) back, rear *cpd* ▶ SM (*di casa*) rear; (*col: sedere*) backside

di'eci ['djɛtʃi] NUM ten

dieci'mila [djɛtʃi'mila] NUM ten thousand

die'cina [dje'tʃina] SF = **decina**

di'edi *etc* VB *vedi* **dare**

di'eresi SF dieresis *sg*

'diesel ['di:zəl] SM INV diesel engine

dies'sino, -a AG (*Pol*) of o belonging to the Democrats of the Left (*Italian left-wing party*) ▶ SM/F *member of the DS political party*

di'eta SF diet; **essere a ~** to be on a diet

die'tetica SF dietetics *sg*

die'tologo, -a, -gi, -ghe SM/F dietician

di'etro AV behind; (*in fondo*) at the back ▶ PREP behind; (*tempo: dopo*) after ▶ SM (*di foglio, giacca*) back; (*di casa*) back, rear ▶ AG INV back *cpd*; **le zampe di ~** the hind legs; **~ ricevuta** against receipt; **~ richiesta** on demand; (*scritta*) on application; **andare ~ a** (*anche fig*) to follow; **stare ~ a qn** (*sorvegliare*) to keep an eye on sb; (*corteggiare*) to hang around sb; **portarsi ~ qn/qc** to bring sb/sth with one, bring sb/sth along; **gli hanno riso/parlato ~** they laughed at/talked about him behind his back

di'etro 'front ESCL about turn! (*Brit*), about face! (*US*) ▶ SM (*Mil*) about-turn, about-face; (*fig*) volte-face, about-turn, about-face; **fare ~** (*Mil, fig*) to about-turn, about-face; (*tornare indietro*) to turn round

di'fatti CONG in fact, as a matter of fact

di'fendere /36/ VT to defend; **difendersi** VPR (*cavarsela*) to get by; **difendersi da/contro** to defend o.s. from/against; **difendersi dal freddo** to protect o.s. from the cold; **sapersi ~** to know how to look after o.s.

difen'sivo, -a AG defensive ▶ SF: **stare sulla difensiva** (*anche fig*) to be on the defensive

difen'sore, -a SM/F defender; **avvocato ~** counsel for the defence (*Brit*) o defense (*US*)

di'fesa SF *vedi* **difeso**

di'fesi *etc* VB *vedi* **difendere**

di'feso, -a PP *di* **difendere** ▶ SF defence (*Brit*), defense (*US*); **prendere le difese di qn** to defend sb, take sb's part

difet'tare /72/ VI to be defective; **~ di** to be lacking in, lack

difet'tivo, -a AG defective

di'fetto SM (*mancanza*): **~ di** lack of; shortage of; (*di fabbricazione*) fault, flaw, defect; (*morale*) fault, failing, defect; (*fisico*) defect; **far ~** to be lacking; **in ~** at fault; in the wrong

difet'toso, -a AG defective, faulty

diffa'mare /**72**/ VT (*a parole*) to slander; (*per iscritto*) to libel

diffama'torio, -a AG slanderous; libellous

diffamazi'one [diffamat'tsjone] SF slander; libel

diffe'rente AG different

diffe'renza [diffe'rɛntsa] SF difference; **a ~ di** unlike; **non fare ~ (tra)** to make no distinction (between)

differenzi'ale [differen'tsjale] AG, SM differential; **classi differenziali** (*Ins*) special classes (*for backward children*)

differenzi'are [differen'tsjare] /**19**/ VT to differentiate; **differenziarsi da** to differentiate o.s. from; to differ from

diffe'rire /**55**/ VT to postpone, defer ▶ VI to be different

diffe'rita SF: **in ~** (*trasmettere*) prerecorded

dif'ficile [dif'fitʃile] AG difficult; (*persona*) hard to please, difficult (to please); (*poco probabile*): **è ~ che sia libero** it is unlikely that he'll be free ▶ SMF: **fare il(la) ~** to be difficult, be awkward ▶ SM difficult part; difficulty; **essere ~ nel mangiare** to be fussy about one's food

difficil'mente [diffitʃil'mente] AV (*con difficoltà*) with difficulty; **~ verrà** he's unlikely to come

difficoltà SF INV difficulty

difficol'toso, -a AG (*compito*) difficult, hard; (*persona*) difficult, hard to please; **digestione difficoltosa** poor digestion

dif'fida SF (*Dir*) warning, notice

diffi'dare /**72**/ VI: **~ di** to be suspicious o distrustful of ▶ VT (*Dir*) to warn; **~ qn dal fare qc** to warn sb not to do sth, caution sb against doing sth

diffi'dente AG suspicious, distrustful

diffi'denza [diffi'dɛntsa] SF suspicion, distrust

dif'fondere /**25**/ VT (*luce, calore*) to diffuse; (*notizie*) to spread, circulate; **diffondersi** VPR to spread

dif'fusi *etc* VB *vedi* **diffondere**

diffusi'one SF diffusion; spread; (*anche di giornale*) circulation; (*Fisica*) scattering

dif'fuso, -a PP *di* **diffondere** ▶ AG (*Fisica*) diffuse; (*fenomeno, notizia, malattia ecc*) widespread; **è opinione diffusa che ...** it's widely held that ....

difi'lato AV (*direttamente*) straight, directly; (*subito*) straight away

difte'rite SF diphtheria

'diga, -ghe SF dam; (*portuale*) breakwater

dige'rente [didʒe'rɛnte] AG (*apparato*) digestive

dige'rire [didʒe'rire] /**55**/ VT to digest

digesti'one [didʒes'tjone] SF digestion

diges'tivo, -a [didʒes'tivo] AG digestive ▶ SM (after-dinner) liqueur

Digi'one [di'dʒone] SF Dijon

digi'tale [didʒi'tale] AG digital; (*delle dita*) finger *cpd*, digital ▶ SF (*Bot*) foxglove

digi'tare [didʒi'tare] /**72**/ VT (*dati*) to key (in); (*tasto*) to press

digiu'nare [didʒu'nare] /**72**/ VI to starve o.s.; (*Rel*) to fast

digi'uno, -a [di'dʒuno] AG: **essere ~** not to have eaten ▶ SM fast; **a ~** on an empty stomach

dignità [diɲɲi'ta] SF INV dignity

digni'tario [diɲɲi'tarjo] SM dignitary

digni'toso, -a [diɲɲi'toso] AG dignified

'DIGOS SIGLA F (= *Divisione Investigazioni Generali e Operazioni Speciali*) *police department dealing with political security*

digressi'one SF digression

digri'gnare [digriɲ'ɲare] /**15**/ VT: **~ i denti** to grind one's teeth

dila'gare /**80**/ VI to flood; (*fig*) to spread

dilani'are /**19**/ VT to tear to pieces

dilapi'dare /**72**/ VT to squander, waste

dila'tare /**72**/ VT to dilate; (*gas*) to cause to expand; (*passaggio, cavità*) to open (up); **dilatarsi** VPR to dilate; (*Fisica*) to expand

dilatazi'one [dilatat'tsjone] SF (*Anat*) dilation; (*di gas, metallo*) expansion

dilazio'nare [dilattsjo'nare] /**72**/ VT to delay, defer

dilazi'one [dilat'tsjone] SF deferment

dileggi'are [diled'dʒare] /**62**/ VT to mock, deride

dilegu'are /**72**/ VI, **dilegu'arsi** VPR to vanish, disappear

di'lemma, -i SM dilemma

dilet'tante SMF dilettante; (*anche Sport*) amateur

dilet'tare /**72**/ VT to give pleasure to, delight; **dilettarsi** VPR: **dilettarsi di** to take pleasure in, enjoy

dilet'tevole AG delightful

di'letto, -a AG dear, beloved ▶ SM pleasure, delight

dili'gente [dili'dʒɛnte] AG (*scrupoloso*) diligent; (*accurato*) careful, accurate

dili'genza [dili'dʒɛntsa] SF diligence; care; (*carrozza*) stagecoach

dilu'ire /**55**/ VT to dilute

dilun'garsi /**80**/ VPR (*fig*): **~ su** to talk at length on o about

diluvi'are /**19**/ VB IMPERS to pour (down)

di'luvio SM downpour; (*inondazione, fig*) flood; **il ~ universale** the Flood

dima'grante AG slimming *cpd*

dima'grire /**55**/ VI to get thinner, lose weight

dime'nare /**72**/ VT to wave, shake; **dimenarsi**
VPR to toss and turn; (fig) to struggle; ~ **la
coda** (cane) to wag its tail
dimensi'one SF dimension; (grandezza) size;
**considerare un discorso nella sua ~
politica** to look at a speech in terms of its
political significance
dimenti'canza [dimenti'kantsa] SF
forgetfulness; (errore) oversight, slip; **per ~**
inadvertently
dimenti'care /**20**/ VT to forget; **dimenticarsi**
VPR: **dimenticarsi di qc** to forget sth
dimentica'toio SM (scherzoso): **cadere/
mettere nel ~** to sink into/consign to
oblivion
di'mentico, -a, -chi, -che AG: ~ **di** (che non
ricorda) forgetful of; (incurante) oblivious of,
unmindful of
di'messo, -a PP di **dimettere** ▸ AG (voce)
subdued; (uomo, abito) modest, humble
dimesti'chezza [dimesti'kettsa] SF
familiarity
di'mettere /**63**/ VT: ~ **qn da** to dismiss sb
from; (dall'ospedale) to discharge sb from;
dimettersi VPR: **dimettersi (da)** to resign
(from)
dimez'zare [dimed'dzare] /**72**/ VT to halve
diminu'ire /**55**/ VT to reduce, diminish;
(prezzi) to bring down, reduce ▸ VI to
decrease, diminish; (rumore) to die down, die
away; (prezzi) to fall, go down
diminu'tivo, -a AG, SM diminutive
diminuzi'one [diminut'tsjone] SF
decreasing, diminishing; **in ~** on the
decrease; ~ **della produttività** fall in
productivity
di'misi etc VB vedi **dimettere**
dimissio'nario, -a AG outgoing, resigning
dimissi'oni SFPL resignation sg; **dare** o
presentare le ~ to resign, hand in one's
resignation
di'mora SF residence; **senza fissa ~** of no
fixed address o abode
dimo'rare /**72**/ VI to reside
dimos'trante SMF (Pol) demonstrator
dimos'trare /**72**/ VT to demonstrate, show;
(provare) to prove, demonstrate;
dimostrarsi VPR: **dimostrarsi molto
abile** to show o.s. o prove to be very clever;
non dimostra la sua età he doesn't look
his age; **dimostra 30 anni** he looks about
30 (years old)
dimostra'tivo, -a AG (anche Ling)
demonstrative
dimostrazi'one [dimostrat'tsjone] SF
demonstration; proof
di'namico, -a, -ci, -che AG dynamic ▸ SF
dynamics sg
dina'mismo SM dynamism

dinami'tardo, -a AG: **attentato ~** dynamite
attack ▸ SM/F dynamiter
dina'mite SF dynamite
'dinamo SF INV dynamo
di'nanzi [di'nantsi]: ~ **a** prep in front of
dinas'tia SF dynasty
dini'ego, -ghi SM (rifiuto) refusal; (negazione)
denial
dinocco'lato, -a AG lanky; **camminare ~**
to walk with a slouch
dino'sauro SM dinosaur
din'torno AV round, (round) about;
dintorni SMPL outskirts; **nei dintorni di**
in the vicinity o neighbourhood of
'dio (pl **dei**) SM god; **D~** God; **gli dei** the gods;
si crede un ~ he thinks he's wonderful;
D~ mio! my God!; **D~ ce la mandi buona**
let's hope for the best; **D~ ce ne scampi e
liberi!** God forbid!
di'ocesi [di'ɔtʃezi] SF INV diocese
dios'sina SF dioxin
dipa'nare /**72**/ VT (lana) to wind into a ball;
(fig) to disentangle, sort out
diparti'mento SM department
dipen'dente AG dependent ▸ SMF employee;
~ **statale** state employee
dipen'denza [dipen'dɛntsa] SF dependence;
essere alle dipendenze di qn to be
employed by sb o in sb's employ
di'pendere /**8**/ VI: ~ **da** to depend on;
(finanziariamente) to be dependent on; (derivare)
to come from, be due to
di'pesi etc VB vedi **dipendere**
di'peso, -a PP di **dipendere**
di'pingere [di'pindʒere] /**37**/ VT to paint
di'pinsi etc VB vedi **dipingere**
di'pinto, -a PP di **dipingere** ▸ SM painting
di'ploma, -i SM diploma
diplo'mare /**72**/ VT to award a diploma to,
graduate (US) ▸ VI to obtain a diploma,
graduate (US)
diplo'matico, -a, -ci, -che AG diplomatic
▸ SM diplomat
diplo'mato, -a AG qualified ▸ SM/F qualified
person, holder of a diploma
diploma'zia [diplomat'tsia] SF diplomacy
di'porto SM: **imbarcazione da ~** pleasure
craft
dira'dare /**72**/ VT to thin (out); (visite) to
reduce, make less frequent; **diradarsi** VPR to
disperse; (nebbia) to clear (up)
dira'mare /**72**/ VT to issue ▸ VI (strade: anche:
diramarsi) to branch
'dire /**38**/ VT to say; (segreto, fatto) to tell; ~ **qc
a qn** to tell sb sth; ~ **a qn di fare qc** to tell sb
to do sth; ~ **di sì/no** to say yes/no; **si dice
che ...** they say that ...; **mi si dice che ...**
I am told that ...; **si direbbe che ...** it looks
(o sounds) as though ...; **dica, signora?**

(*in un negozio*) yes, Madam, can I help you?;
sa quello che dice he knows what he's
talking about; **lascialo ~** (*esprimersi*) let him
have his say; (*ignoralo*) just ignore him; **come
sarebbe a ~?** what do you mean?; **che ne
diresti di andarcene?** how about leaving?;
chi l'avrebbe mai detto! who would have
thought it!; **si dicono esperti** they say they
are experts; **per così ~** so to speak; **a dir
poco** to say the least; **non c'è che ~** there's
no doubt about it; **non dico di no** I can't
deny it; **il che è tutto ~** need I say more?

di'ressi *etc* VB *vedi* **dirigere**

di'retta SF: **in ~** (*trasmettere*) live; **un incontro
di calcio in ~ a** live football match; *vedi*
diretto

diretta'mente AV (*immediatamente*) directly,
straight; (*personalmente*) directly; (*senza
intermediari*) direct, straight

diret'tissima SF (*tragitto*) most direct route;
(*Dir*): **processo per ~** summary trial

diret'tissimo SM (*Ferr*) fast (through) train

diret'tivo, -a AG (*Pol, Amm*) executive; (*Comm*)
managerial, executive ▶ SM leadership,
leaders *pl* ▶ SF directive, instruction

di'retto, -a PP *di* **dirigere** ▶ AG direct ▶ SM
(*Ferr*) through train ▶ SF: **in (linea) diretta**
(*Radio, TV*) live; **il mio ~ superiore** my
immediate superior

diret'tore, -'trice SM/F (*di azienda*) director,
manager (manageress); (*di scuola elementare*)
head (teacher) (BRIT), principal (US);
~ amministrativo company secretary (BRIT),
corporate executive secretary (US); **~ del
carcere** prison governor (BRIT) *o* warden
(US); **~ di filiale** branch manager;
~ d'orchestra conductor; **~ di produzione**
(*Cine*) producer; **~ sportivo** team manager;
~ tecnico (*Sport*) trainer, coach; **~ vendite**
sales director *o* manager

direzi'one [diret'tsjone] SF board of directors;
management; (*senso: anche fig*) direction;
(*conduzione: gen*) running; (: *di partito*)
leadership; (: *di società*) management; (: *di
giornale*) editorship; (*direttori*) management;
in ~ di in the direction of, towards

diri'gente [diri'dʒɛnte] AG managerial ▶ SMF
executive; (*Pol*) leader ▶ AG: **classe ~** ruling
class

diri'genza [diri'dʒɛntsa] SF management;
(*Pol*) leadership

dirigenzi'ale [diridʒen'tsjale] AG managerial

di'rigere [di'ridʒere] /**39**/ VT to direct;
(*impresa*) to run, manage; (*Mus*) to conduct;
dirigersi VPR: **dirigersi verso** *o* **a** to make *o*
head for; **~ i propri passi verso** to make
one's way towards; **il treno era diretto a
Pavia** the train was heading for Pavia

diri'gibile [diri'dʒibile] SM airship

dirim'petto AV opposite; **~ a** *prep* opposite,
facing

di'ritto, -a AG straight; (*onesto*) straight,
upright ▶ AV straight, directly ▶ SM right
side; (*Tennis*) forehand; (*Maglia*) plain stitch,
knit stitch; (*prerogativa*) right; (*leggi, scienza*):
il ~ law; **diritti** SMPL (*tasse*) duty *sg*; **stare ~** to
stand up straight; **aver ~ a qc** to be entitled
to sth; **punto ~** plain (stitch); **andare ~** to go
straight on; **a buon ~** quite rightly; **diritti
(d'autore)** royalties; **~ di successione** right
of succession

dirit'tura SF (*Sport*) straight; (*fig*) rectitude

diroc'cato, -a AG tumbledown, in ruins

dirom'pente AG (*anche fig*) explosive

dirotta'mento SM: **~ (aereo)** hijack

dirot'tare /**72**/ VT (*nave, aereo*) to change the
course of; (*aereo: sotto minaccia*) to hijack;
(*traffico*) to divert ▶ VI (*nave, aereo*) to change
course

dirotta'tore, -'trice SM/F hijacker

di'rotto, -a AG (*pioggia*) torrential; (*pianto*)
unrestrained; **piovere a ~** to pour, rain
cats and dogs; **piangere a ~** to cry one's
heart out

di'rupo SM crag, precipice

di'sabile SMF disabled person ▶ AG disabled;
i disabili the disabled

disabi'tato, -a AG uninhabited

disabitu'arsi /**72**/ VPR: **~ a** to get out of the
habit of

disac'cordo SM disagreement

disadat'tato, -a AG (*Psic*) maladjusted

disa'dorno, -a AG plain, unadorned

disaffezi'one [dizaffet'tsjone] SF
disaffection

disa'gevole [disa'dʒevole] AG (*scomodo*)
uncomfortable; (*difficile*) difficult

disagi'ato, -a [diza'dʒato] AG poor, needy;
(*vita*) hard

di'sagio [di'zadʒo] SM discomfort; (*disturbo*)
inconvenience; (*fig: imbarazzo*)
embarrassment; **disagi** SMPL hardship *sg*,
poverty *sg*; **essere a ~** to be ill at ease

di'samina SF close examination

disappro'vare /**72**/ VT to disapprove of

disapprovazi'one [dizapprovat'tsjone] SF
disapproval

disap'punto SM disappointment

disarcio'nare [dizartʃo'nare] /**72**/ VT to
unhorse

disar'mante AG (*fig*) disarming

disar'mare /**72**/ VT, VI to disarm

di'sarmo SM (*Mil*) disarmament

di'sastro SM disaster

disas'troso, -a AG disastrous

disat'tento, -a AG inattentive

disattenzi'one [dizatten'tsjone] SF
carelessness, lack of attention

disatti'vare /**72**/ VT (*bomba*) to de-activate, defuse

disa'vanzo [diza'vantso] SM (*Econ*) deficit

disavven'tura SF misadventure, mishap

dis'brigo, -ghi SM (*prompt*) clearing up *o* settlement

dis'capito SM: **a ~ di** to the detriment of

dis'carica, -che SF (*di rifiuti*) rubbish tip *o* dump

discen'dente [diʃʃen'dɛnte] AG descending ▶ SMF descendant

di'scendere [diʃʃendere] /**101**/ VT to go (*o* come) down ▶ VI to go (*o* come) down; (*strada*) to go down; (*smontare*) to get off; **~ da** (*famiglia*) to be descended from; **~ dalla macchina/dal treno** to get out of the car/out of *o* off the train; **~ da cavallo** to dismount, get off one's horse

di'scepolo, -a [diʃʃepolo] SM/F disciple

di'scernere [diʃʃɛrnere] /**29**/ VT to discern

discerni'mento [diʃʃerni'mento] SM discernment

di'scesa SF descent; (*pendio*) slope; **in ~** (*strada*) downhill *cpd*, sloping; **~ libera** (*Sci*) downhill (race)

disce'sista [diʃʃe'sista] SMF downhill skier

di'sceso, -a [diʃʃeso] PP di **discendere** ▶ SF descent; (*pendio*) slope; **in discesa** (*strada*) downhill *cpd*, sloping; **discesa libera** (*Sci*) downhill race

dischi'udere [dis'kjudere] /**22**/ VT (*aprire*) to open; (*fig: rivelare*) to disclose, reveal

dischi'usi *etc* [dis'kjusi] VB *vedi* **dischiudere**

dischi'uso, -a [dis'kjuso] PP di **dischiudere**

di'scinto, -a [diʃʃinto] AG (*anche:* **in abiti discinti**) half-undressed

disci'ogliere [diʃʃɔʎʎere] /**103**/ VT, **disci'ogliersi** VPR to dissolve; (*fondere*) to melt

disci'plina [diʃʃi'plina] SF discipline

discipli'nare [diʃʃipli'nare] /**72**/ AG disciplinary ▶ VT to discipline

'disco, -schi SM disc, disk; (*Sport*) discus; (*fonografico*) record; (*Inform*) disk; **~ magnetico** (*Inform*) magnetic disk; **~ orario** (*Aut*) parking disc; **~ rigido** (*Inform*) hard disk; **~ volante** flying saucer

discogra'fia SF (*tecnica*) recording, record-making; (*industria*) record industry

disco'grafico, -a, -ci, -che AG record *cpd*, recording *cpd* ▶ SM record producer; **casa discografica** record(ing) company

'discolo, -a AG (*bambino*) undisciplined, unruly ▶ SM/F rascal

discol'pare /**72**/ VT to clear of blame; **discolparsi** VPR to clear o.s., prove one's innocence; (*giustificarsi*) to excuse o.s.

disco'noscere [disko'noʃʃere] /**26**/ VT (*figlio*) to disown; (*meriti*) to ignore, disregard

disconosci'uto, -a [diskonoʃʃuto] PP di **disconoscere**

discon'tinuo, -a AG (*linea*) broken; (*rendimento, stile*) irregular; (*interesse*) sporadic

dis'corde AG conflicting, clashing

dis'cordia SF discord; (*dissidio*) disagreement, clash

dis'correre /**28**/ VI: **~ (di)** to talk (about)

dis'corso, -a PP di **discorrere** ▶ SM speech; (*conversazione*) conversation, talk

dis'costo, -a AG faraway, distant ▶ AV far away; **~ da** *prep* far from

disco'teca, -che SF (*raccolta*) record library; (*luogo di ballo*) disco(theque)

dis'count [dis'kaunt] SM INV (*supermercato*) cut-price supermarket

discre'panza [diskre'pantsa] SF discrepancy

dis'creto, -a AG discreet; (*abbastanza buono*) reasonable, fair

discrezi'one [diskret'tsjone] SF discretion; (*giudizio*) judgment, discernment; **a ~ di** at the discretion of

discrimi'nante AG (*fattore, elemento*) decisive ▶ SF (*Dir*) extenuating circumstance

discrimi'nare /**72**/ VT to discrimate

discriminazi'one [diskriminat'tsjone] SF discrimination

dis'cussi *etc* VB *vedi* **discutere**

discussi'one SF discussion; (*litigio*) argument; **mettere in ~** to bring into question; **fuori ~** out of the question

dis'cusso, -a PP di **discutere**

dis'cutere /**40**/ VT to discuss, debate; (*contestare*) to question, dispute ▶ VI (*litigare*) to argue; (*conversare*): **~ (di)** to discuss

discu'tibile AG questionable

disde'gnare [dizdeɲ'ɲare] /**15**/ VT to scorn

dis'degno [diz'deɲɲo] SM scorn, disdain

disde'gnoso, -a [dizdeɲ'ɲoso] AG disdainful, scornful

dis'detto, -a PP di **disdire** ▶ SF (*di prenotazione ecc*) cancellation; (*sfortuna*) bad luck

disdi'cevole [dizdi'tʃevole] AG improper, unseemly

dis'dire /**38**/ VT (*prenotazione*) to cancel; **~ un contratto d'affitto** (*Dir*) to give notice (to quit)

dise'gnare [diseɲ'ɲare] /**15**/ VT to draw; (*progettare*) to design; (*fig*) to outline

disegna'tore, -'trice [diseɲɲa'tore] SM/F designer

di'segno [di'zeɲɲo] SM drawing; (*su stoffa ecc*) design; (*fig: schema*) outline; **~ industriale** industrial design; **~ di legge** (*Dir*) bill

diser'bante SM weedkiller

disere'dare /**72**/ VT to disinherit

diser'tare /**72**/ VT, VI to desert

diser'tore SM (*Mil*) deserter

diserzi'one [dizer'tsjone] SF (*Mil*) desertion

disfaci'mento [disfatʃi'mento] SM (*di cadavere*) decay; (*fig: di istituzione, impero, società*) decline, decay; **in** ~ in decay

dis'fare /41/ VT to undo; (*valigie*) to unpack; (*meccanismo*) to take to pieces; (*lavoro, paese*) to destroy; (*neve*) to melt; **disfarsi** VPR to come undone; (*neve*) to melt; ~ **il letto** to strip the bed; **disfarsi di qn** (*liberarsi*) to get rid of sb

dis'fatta SF *vedi* **disfatto**

disfat'tista, -i, -e SM/F defeatist

dis'fatto, -a PP *di* **disfare** ▶ AG (*gen*) undone, untied; (*letto*) unmade; (*persona: sfinito*) exhausted, worn-out; (: *addolorato*) grief-stricken ▶ SF (*sconfitta*) rout

disfunzi'one [disfun'tsjone] SF (*Med*) dysfunction; ~ **cardiaca** heart trouble

disge'lare [dizdʒe'lare] **/72/** VT, VI, **disge'larsi** VPR to thaw

dis'gelo [diz'dʒɛlo] SM thaw

dis'grazia [diz'grattsja] SF (*sventura*) misfortune; (*incidente*) accident, mishap

disgrazi'ato, -a [dizgrat'tsjato] AG unfortunate ▶ SM/F wretch

disgre'gare /80/ VT, **disgre'garsi** VPR to break up

disgu'ido SM hitch; ~ **postale** error in postal delivery

disgus'tare /72/ VT to disgust; **disgustarsi** VPR: **disgustarsi di** to be disgusted by

dis'gusto SM disgust

disgus'toso, -a AG disgusting

disidra'tare /72/ VT to dehydrate

disidra'tato, -a AG dehydrated

disil'ludere /35/ VT to disillusion, disenchant

disillusi'one SF disillusion, disenchantment

disimpa'rare /72/ VT to forget

disimpe'gnare [dizimpeɲ'ɲare] **/15/** VT (*oggetto dato in pegno*) to redeem, get out of pawn; ~ **da** (*persona: da obblighi*) to release from; **disimpegnarsi** VPR: **disimpegnarsi da** (*obblighi*) to release o.s. from, free o.s. from

disincagli'are [dizinkaʎ'ʎare] **/27/** VT (*barca*) to refloat; **disincagliarsi** VPR to get afloat again

disincan'tato, -a AG disenchanted, disillusioned

disincenti'vare [dizintʃenti'vare] **/72/** VT to discourage

disinfes'tare /72/ VT to disinfest

disinfestazi'one [dizinfestat'tsjone] SF disinfestation

disinfet'tante AG, SM disinfectant

disinfet'tare /72/ VT to disinfect

disinfezi'one [dizinfet'tsjone] SF disinfection

disingan'nare /72/ VT to disillusion

disin'ganno SM disillusion

disini'bito, -a AG uninhibited

disinnes'care /20/ VT to defuse

disinnes'tare /72/ VT (*marcia*) to disengage

disinqui'nare /72/ VT to free from pollution

disinstal'lare /72/ VT (*software*) to uninstall

disinte'grare /72/ VT, VI to disintegrate; **disintegrarsi** VPR to disintegrate

disinteres'sarsi /72/ VPR: ~ **di** to take no interest in

disinte'resse SM indifference; (*generosità*) unselfishness

disintossi'care /20/ VT (*alcolizzato, drogato*) to treat for alcoholism (*o drug addiction*); **disintossicarsi** VPR to clear out one's system; (*alcolizzato, drogato*) to be treated for alcoholism (*o drug addiction*)

disintossicazi'one [dizintossikat'tsjone] SF treatment for alcoholism (*o drug addiction*)

disin'volto, -a AG casual, free and easy

disinvol'tura SF casualness, ease

disles'sia SF dyslexia

disli'vello SM difference in height; (*fig*) gap

dislo'care /20/ VT to station, position

dismi'sura SF excess; **a** ~ to excess, excessively

disobbe'dire *etc* = **disubbidire** *ecc*

disoccu'pato, -a AG unemployed ▶ SM/F unemployed person

disoccupazi'one [dizokkupat'tsjone] SF unemployment

disonestà SF dishonesty

diso'nesto, -a AG dishonest

disono'rare /45/ VT to dishonour (BRIT), dishonor (US), bring disgrace upon

diso'nore SM dishonour (BRIT), dishonor (US), disgrace

di'sopra AV (*con contatto*) on top; (*senza contatto*) above; (*al piano superiore*) upstairs ▶ AG INV (*superiore*) upper ▶ SM INV top, upper part; **la gente** ~ the people upstairs; **il piano** ~ the floor above

disordi'nare /72/ VT to mess up, disarrange; (*Mil*) to throw into disorder

disordi'nato, -a AG untidy; (*privo di misura*) irregular, wild

di'sordine SM (*confusione*) disorder, confusion; (*sregolatezza*) debauchery; **disordini** SMPL (*Pol ecc*) disorder *sg*; (*tumulti*) riots

disor'ganico, -a, -ci, -che AG incoherent, disorganized

disorganiz'zato, -a [dizorganid'dzato] AG disorganized

disorienta'mento SM (*fig*) confusion, bewilderment

disorien'tare /72/ VT to disorientate; **disorientarsi** VPR (*fig*) to get confused, lose one's bearings

disorien'tato, -a AG disorientated

disos'sare /72/ VT (*Cuc*) to bone

di'sotto AV below, underneath; (*in fondo*) at the bottom; (*al piano inferiore*) downstairs

► AG INV (*inferiore*) lower; bottom *cpd* ► SM INV (*parte inferiore*) lower part; bottom; **la gente ~** the people downstairs; **il piano ~** the floor below

dis'paccio [dis'pattʃo] SM dispatch

dispa'rato, -a AG disparate

'**dispari** AG INV odd, uneven

disparità SF INV disparity

dis'parte: in ~ av (*da lato*) aside, apart; **tenersi** *o* **starsene in ~** to keep to o.s., hold aloof

dis'pendio SM (*di denaro, energie*) expenditure; (: *spreco*) waste

dispendi'oso, -a AG expensive

dis'pensa SF pantry, larder; (*mobile*) sideboard; (*Dir*) exemption; (*Rel*) dispensation; (*fascicolo*) number, issue

dispen'sare /**72**/ VT (*elemosine, favori*) to distribute; (*esonerare*) to exempt

dispe'rare /**72**/ VI: **~ (di)** to despair (of); **disperarsi** VPR to despair

dispe'rato, -a AG (*persona*) in despair; (*caso, tentativo*) desperate

disperazi'one [disperat'tsjone] SF despair

dis'perdere /**73**/ VT (*disseminare*) to disperse; (*Mil*) to scatter, rout; (*fig: consumare*) to waste, squander; **disperdersi** VPR to disperse; to scatter

dispersi'one SF dispersion, dispersal; (*Fisica, Chim*) dispersion

disper'sivo, -a AG (*lavoro ecc*) disorganized

dis'perso, -a PP di **disperdere** ► SM/F missing person; (*Mil*) missing soldier

dis'petto SM spite *no pl*, spitefulness *no pl*; **fare un ~ a qn** to play a (nasty) trick on sb; **a ~ di** in spite of; **con suo grande ~** much to his annoyance

dispet'toso, -a AG spiteful

dispia'cere [dispja'tʃere] /**74**/ SM (*rammarico*) regret, sorrow; (*dolore*) grief ► VI: **~ a** to displease ► VB IMPERS: **mi dispiace (che)** I am sorry (that); **le dispiace se...?** do you mind if ...?; **dispiaceri** SMPL (*preoccupazioni*) troubles, worries; **se non le dispiace, me ne vado adesso** if you don't mind, I'll go now

dispiaci'uto, -a [dispja'tʃuto] PP di **dispiacere** ► AG sorry

dis'pone, dis'pongo etc VB vedi **disporre**

dispo'nibile AG available; (*persona: solerte, gentile*) helpful

disponibilità SF INV availability; (*solerzia, gentilezza*) helpfulness ► SFPL (*economiche*) resources

dis'porre /**77**/ VT (*sistemare*) to arrange; (*preparare*) to prepare; (*Dir*) to order; (*persuadere*): **~ qn a** to incline *o* dispose sb towards ► VI (*decidere*) to decide; (*usufruire*): **~ di** to use, have at one's disposal; (*essere dotato*): **~ di** to have; **disporsi** VPR (*ordinarsi*) to

place o.s., arrange o.s.; **disporsi a fare** to get ready to do; **disporsi all'attacco** to prepare for an attack; **disporsi in cerchio** to form a circle

dis'posi etc VB vedi **disporre**

disposi'tivo SM (*meccanismo*) device; (*Dir*) pronouncement; **~ di controllo** *o* **di comando** control device; **~ di sicurezza** (*gen*) safety device; (*di arma da fuoco*) safety catch

disposizi'one [dispozit'tsjone] SF arrangement, layout; (*stato d'animo*) mood; (*tendenza*) bent, inclination; (*comando*) order; (*Dir*) provision, regulation; **a ~ di qn** at sb's disposal; **per ~ di legge** by law; **~ testamentaria** provisions of a will

dis'posto, -a PP di **disporre** ► AG (*incline*): **~ a fare** disposed *o* prepared to do

dis'potico, -a, -ci, -che AG despotic

dispo'tismo SM despotism

disprez'zare [dispret'tsare] /**72**/ VT to despise

dis'prezzo [dis'prɛttso] SM contempt; **con ~ del pericolo** with a total disregard for the danger involved

'**disputa** SF dispute, quarrel

dispu'tare /**72**/ VT (*contendere*) to dispute, contest; (*Sport: partita*) to play; (: *gara*) to take part in ► VI to quarrel; **~ di** to discuss; **disputarsi qc** to fight for sth

disqui'sire /**55**/ VI to discourse on

disquisizi'one [diskwizit'tsjone] SF detailed analysis

dissa'crare /**72**/ VT to desecrate

dissangua'mento SM loss of blood

dissangu'are /**72**/ VT (*fig: persona*) to bleed white; (: *patrimonio*) to suck dry; **dissanguarsi** VPR (*Med*) to lose blood; (*fig*) to ruin o.s.; **morire dissanguato** to bleed to death

dissa'pore SM slight disagreement

'**disse** VB vedi **dire**

disse'care /**20**/ VT to dissect

dissec'care /**20**/ VT, **dissec'carsi** VPR to dry up

dissemi'nare /**72**/ VT to scatter; (*fig: notizie*) to spread

dissenna'tezza [dissenna'tettsa] SF foolishness

dis'senso SM dissent; (*disapprovazione*) disapproval

dissente'ria SF dysentery

dissen'tire /**45**/ VI: **~ (da)** to disagree (with)

disseppel'lire /**55**/ VT (*esumare: cadavere*) to disinter, exhume; (*dissotterrare: anche fig*) to dig up, unearth; (*rancori*) to resurrect

dissertazi'one [dissertat'tsjone] SF dissertation

disser'vizio [disser'vittsjo] SM inefficiency

disses'tare /**72**/ VT (*Econ*) to ruin

disses'tato, -a AG (*fondo stradale*) uneven; (*economia, finanze*) shaky; **"strada dissestata"**

(*per lavori in corso*) "road up" (BRIT), "road
out" (US)

dis'sesto SM (financial) ruin

disse'tante AG refreshing

disse'tare /72/ VT to quench the thirst of;
dissetarsi VPR to quench one's thirst

dissezi'bne [disset'tsjone] SF dissection

'dissi VB *vedi* **dire**

dissi'dente AG, SMF dissident

dis'sidio SM disagreement

dis'simile AG different, dissimilar

dissimu'lare /72/ VT (*fingere*) to dissemble;
(*nascondere*) to conceal

dissimula'tore, -'trice SM/F dissembler

dissimulazi'one [dissimulat'tsjone] SF
dissembling; concealment

dissi'pare /72/ VT to dissipate; (*scialacquare*) to
squander, waste

dissipa'tezza [dissipa'tettsa] SF dissipation

dissi'pato, -a AG dissolute, dissipated

dissipazi'one [dissipat'tsjone] SF
squandering

dissoci'are [disso'tʃare] /14/ VT to dissociate

dis'solto, -a PP *di* **dissolvere**

disso'lubile AG soluble

dissolu'tezza [dissolu'tettsa] SF
dissoluteness

dissolu'tivo, -a AG (*forza*) divisive; **processo ~**
(*anche fig*) process of dissolution

disso'luto, -a PP *di* **dissolvere** ▶ AG dissolute,
licentious

dissol'venza [dissol'vɛntsa] SF (*Cine*)
fading

dis'solvere /94/ VT to dissolve; (*neve*) to melt;
(*fumo*) to disperse; **dissolversi** VPR to
dissolve; to melt; to disperse

disso'nante AG discordant

disso'nanza [disso'nantsa] SF (*fig: di opinioni*)
clash

dissotter'rare /72/ VT (*cadavere*) to disinter,
exhume; (*tesori, rovine*) to dig up, unearth;
(*fig: sentimenti, odio*) to bring up again,
resurrect

dissu'adere /88/ VT: **~ qn da** to dissuade sb
from

dissuasi'one SF dissuasion

dissu'aso, -a PP *di* **dissuadere**

dissua'sore SM: **~ di velocità** (*Aut*) speed
bump

distacca'mento SM (*Mil*) detachment

distac'care /20/ VT to detach, separate;
(*Sport*) to leave behind; **distaccarsi** VPR to
be detached; (*fig*) to stand out; **distaccarsi da**
(*fig: allontanarsi*) to grow away from

dis'tacco, -chi SM (*separazione*) separation;
(*fig: indifferenza*) detachment; (*Sport*): **vincere
con un ~ di ...** to win by a distance of ...

dis'tante AV far away ▶ AG distant, far away;
essere ~ (da) to be a long way (from); **è ~ da**

qui? is it far from here?; **essere ~ nel tempo**
to be in the distant past

dis'tanza [dis'tantsa] SF distance; **comando
a ~** remote control; **a ~ di 2 giorni** 2 days later;
tener qn a ~ to keep sb at arm's length;
prendere le distanze da qc/qn to dissociate
o.s. from sth/sb; **tenere o mantenere le
distanze** to keep one's distance; **~ focale**
focal length; **~ di sicurezza** safe distance;
(*Aut*) braking distance; **~ di tiro** range; **~ di
visibilità** visibility

distanzi'are [distan'tsjare] /19/ VT to space
out, place at intervals; (*Sport*) to outdistance;
(*fig: superare*) to outstrip, surpass

dis'tare /72/ VI: **distiamo pochi chilometri
da Roma** we are only a few kilometres
(away) from Rome; **dista molto da qui?** is it
far (away) from here?; **non dista molto** it's
not far (away); **quanto dista il centro da
qui?** how far is the town centre?

dis'tendere /120/ VT (*coperta*) to spread out;
(*gambe*) to stretch (out); (*mettere a giacere*) to
lay; (*rilassare: muscoli, nervi*) to relax;
distendersi VPR (*rilassarsi*) to relax; (*sdraiarsi*)
to lie down

distensi'one SF stretching; relaxation; (*Pol*)
détente

disten'sivo, -a AG (*gen*) relaxing, restful;
(*farmaco*) tranquillizing; (*Pol*) conciliatory

dis'teso, -a PP *di* **distendere** ▶ AG (*allungato:
persona, gamba*) stretched out; (*rilassato:
persona, atmosfera*) relaxed ▶ SF expanse,
stretch; **avere un volto ~** to look relaxed

distil'lare /72/ VT to distil

distil'lato SM distillate

distillazi'one [distillat'tsjone] SF distillation

distille'ria SF distillery

dis'tinguere /42/ VT to distinguish;
distinguersi VPR (*essere riconoscibile*) to be
distinguished; (*emergere*) to stand out, be
conspicuous, distinguish o.s.; **un vino
che si distingue per il suo aroma** a wine
with a distinctive bouquet

dis'tinguo SM INV distinction

dis'tinta SF (*nota*) note; (*elenco*) list; **~ di
pagamento** receipt; **~ di versamento**
pay-in slip

distin'tivo, -a AG distinctive; distinguishing
▶ SM badge

dis'tinto, -a PP *di* **distinguere** ▶ AG (*dignitoso ed
elegante*) distinguished; **distinti saluti** (*in
lettera*) yours faithfully

distinzi'one [distin'tsjone] SF distinction;
non faccio distinzioni (*tra persone*) I don't
discriminate; (*tra cose*) it's all one to me;
senza ~ di razza/religione ... no matter
what one's race/creed ...

dis'togliere [dis'tɔʎʎere] /122/ VT: **~ da** to take
away from; (*fig*) to dissuade from

dis'tolto, -a PP *di* **distogliere**

dis'torcere [dis'tɔrtʃere] **/106/** VT to twist; *(fig)* to twist, distort; **distorcersi** VPR *(contorcersi)* to twist

distorsi'one SF *(Med)* sprain; *(Fisica, Ottica)* distortion

dis'torto, -a PP *di* **distorcere**

dis'trarre **/123/** VT to distract; *(divertire)* to entertain, amuse; **distrarsi** VPR *(non fare attenzione)* to be distracted, let one's mind wander; *(svagarsi)* to amuse o enjoy o.s.; **~ lo sguardo** to look away; **non distrarti!** pay attention!

distratta'mente AV absent-mindedly, without thinking

dis'tratto, -a PP *di* **distrarre** ▶ AG absent-minded; *(disattento)* inattentive

distrazi'one [distrat'tsjone] SF absent-mindedness; inattention; *(svago)* distraction, entertainment; **errori di ~** careless mistakes

dis'tretto SM district

distribu'ire **/55/** VT to distribute; *(Carte)* to deal (out); *(consegnare: posta)* to deliver; *(: lavoro)* to allocate, assign; *(ripartire)* to share out

distribu'tore SM *(di benzina)* petrol (BRIT) o gas (US) pump; *(Aut, Elettr)* distributor; *(automatico)* vending machine

distribuzi'one [distribut'tsjone] SF distribution; allocation; assignment; sharing out

distri'care **/20/** VT to disentangle, unravel; **districarsi** VPR *(tirarsi fuori)*: **districarsi da** to get out of, disentangle o.s. from; *(fig: cavarsela)* to manage, get by

dis'truggere [dis'truddʒere] **/83/** VT to destroy

distrut'tivo, -a AG destructive

dis'trutto, -a PP *di* **distruggere**

distruzi'one [distrut'tsjone] SF destruction

distur'bare **/72/** VT to disturb, trouble; *(sonno, lezioni)* to disturb, interrupt; **disturbarsi** VPR to put o.s. out; **non si disturbi** please don't bother

dis'turbo SM trouble, bother, inconvenience; *(indisposizione)* (slight) disorder, ailment; **disturbi** SMPL *(Radio, TV)* static *sg*; **~ della quiete pubblica** *(Dir)* disturbance of the peace; **disturbi di stomaco** stomach trouble *sg*

disubbidi'ente AG disobedient

disubbidi'enza [dizubbi'djɛntsa] SF disobedience; **~ civile** civil disobedience

disubbi'dire **/55/** VI: **~ (a qn)** to disobey (sb)

disuguagli'anza [dizugwaʎ'ʎantsa] SF inequality

disugu'ale AG unequal; *(diverso)* different; *(irregolare)* uneven

disumanità SF inhumanity

disu'mano, -a AG inhuman; **un grido ~** a terrible cry

disuni'one SF disunity

disu'nire **/55/** VT to divide, disunite

di'suso SM: **andare** o **cadere in ~** to fall into disuse

'dita SFPL *di* **dito**

di'tale SM thimble

di'tata SF *(colpo)* jab (with one's finger); *(segno)* fingermark

'dito *(pl(f)* **dita)** SM finger; *(misura)* finger, finger's breadth; **~ (del piede)** toe; **mettersi le dita nel naso** to pick one's nose; **mettere il ~ sulla piaga** *(fig)* to touch a sore spot; **non ha mosso un ~ (per aiutarmi)** he didn't lift a finger (to help me); **ormai è segnato a ~** everyone knows about him now

'ditta SF firm, business; **macchina della ~** company car

dit'tafono SM Dictaphone®

ditta'tore SM dictator

ditta'tura SF dictatorship

dit'tongo, -ghi SM diphthong

di'urno, -a AG day *cpd*, daytime *cpd*; **ore diurne** daytime *sg*; **spettacolo ~** matinee; **turno ~** day shift; *vedi anche* **albergo**

'diva SF *vedi* **divo**

diva'gare **/80/** VI to digress

divagazi'one [divagat'tsjone] SF digression; **divagazioni sul tema** variations on a theme

divam'pare **/72/** VI to flare up, blaze up

di'vano SM sofa; *(senza schienale)* divan; **~ letto** bed settee, sofa bed

divari'care **/20/** VT to open wide

di'vario SM difference

di'vengo *etc* VB *vedi* **divenire**

dive'nire **/128/** VI = **diventare**

di'venni *etc* VB *vedi* **divenire**

diven'tare **/72/** VI to become; **~ famoso/ professore** to become famous/a teacher; **~ vecchio** to grow old; **c'è da ~ matti** it's enough to drive you mad

dive'nuto, -a PP *di* **divenire**

di'verbio SM altercation

diver'gente [diver'dʒɛnte] AG divergent

diver'genza [diver'dʒɛntsa] SF divergence; **~ d'opinioni** difference of opinion

di'vergere [di'vɛrdʒere] **/59/** VI to diverge

diverrò *etc* VB *vedi* **divenire**

diversa'mente AV *(in modo differente)* differently; *(altrimenti)* otherwise; **~ da quanto stabilito** contrary to what had been decided

diversifi'care **/20/** VT to diversify, vary; to differentiate; **diversificarsi** VPR: **diversificarsi (per)** to differ (in)

diversificazi'one [diversifikat'tsjone] SF
diversification; difference

diversi'one SF diversion

diversità SF INV difference, diversity; (*varietà*)
variety

diver'sivo, -a AG diversionary ▶ SM
diversion, distraction; **fare un'azione
diversiva** to create a diversion

di'verso, -a AG (*differente*): ~ **(da)** different
(from) ▶ SM (*omosessuale*) homosexual;
diversi, e DET PL, PRON PL several, various;
(*Comm*) sundry; several people, many
(people)

diver'tente AG amusing

diverti'mento SM amusement, pleasure;
(*passatempo*) pastime, recreation; **buon ~!**
enjoy yourself!, have a nice time!

diver'tire /45/ VT to amuse, entertain;
divertirsi VPR to amuse o enjoy o.s.;
divertiti! enjoy yourself, have a good time!;
divertirsi alle spalle di qn to have a laugh
at sb's expense

diver'tito, -a AG amused

divi'dendo SM dividend

di'videre /43/ VT (*anche Mat*) to divide;
(*distribuire, ripartire*) to divide (up), split (up);
dividersi VPR (*persone*) to separate, part;
(*coppia*) to separate; (*ramificarsi*) to fork;
dividersi (in) (*scindersi*) to divide (into), split
up (into); **è diviso dalla moglie** he's
separated from his wife; **si divide tra casa
e lavoro** he divides his time between home
and work

divi'eto SM prohibition; **"~ di accesso"** "no
entry"; **"~ di caccia"** "no hunting"; **"~ di
parcheggio"** "no parking"; **"~ di sosta"**
(*Aut*) "no waiting"

divinco'larsi /72/ VPR to wriggle, writhe

divinità SF INV divinity

di'vino, -a AG divine

di'visa SF (*Mil ecc*) uniform; (*Comm*) foreign
currency

di'visi *etc* VB *vedi* **dividere**

divisi'one SF division; **~ in sillabe** syllable
division; (*a fine riga*) hyphenation

di'vismo SM (*esibizionismo*) playing to the
crowd

di'viso, -a PP *di* **dividere**

divi'sorio, -a AG (*siepe, muro esterno*) dividing;
(*muro interno*) dividing, partition *cpd* ▶ SM (*in
una stanza*) partition

'divo, -a SM/F star; **come una diva** like a
prima donna

divo'rare /72/ VT to devour; **~ qc con gli occhi**
to eye sth greedily

divorzi'are [divor'tsjare] /19/ VI: **~ (da qn)** to
divorce (sb)

divorzi'ato, -a [divor'tsjato] AG divorced
▶ SM/F divorcee

di'vorzio [di'vɔrtsjo] SM divorce

divul'gare /80/ VT to divulge, disclose;
(*rendere comprensibile*) to popularize;
divulgarsi VPR to spread

divulgazi'one [divulgat'tsjone] SF (*vedi vb*)
disclosure; popularization; spread

dizio'nario [dittsjo'narjo] SM dictionary

dizi'one [dit'tsjone] SF diction;
pronunciation

DJ [di'dʒei] SIGLA M/SIGLA F (= *Disc Jockey*) DJ

Dja'karta [dʒa'karta] SF Djakarta

dl ABBR (= *decilitro*) dl

dm ABBR (= *decimetro*) dm

DNA [di'ennɛa] SIGLA M (*Biol*: = *acido
deossiribonucleico*) DNA ▶ SIGLA F = **direzione
nazionale antimafia**

do SM (*Mus*) C; (: *solfeggiando la scala*) do(h)

dobbi'amo VB *vedi* **dovere**

doc. ABBR = **documento**

D.O.C. [dɔk] SIGLA (= *denominazione di origine
controllata*) label guaranteeing the quality of wine

'doccia, -ce ['dottʃa] SF (*bagno*) shower;
(*condotto*) pipe; **fare la ~** to have a shower;
~ fredda (*fig*) slap in the face

docciaschi'uma [dottʃas'kjuma] SM INV
shower gel

do'cente [do'tʃɛnte] AG teaching ▶ SMF
teacher; (*di università*) lecturer; **personale
non ~** non-teaching staff

do'cenza [do'tʃɛntsa] SF university teaching
o lecturing; **ottenere la libera ~** to become
a lecturer

D.O.C.G. SIGLA (= *denominazione di origine
controllata e garantita*) label guaranteeing the
quality and origin of a wine

'docile ['dɔtʃile] AG docile

docilità [dotʃili'ta] SF docility

documen'tare /72/ VT to document;
documentarsi VPR: **documentarsi (su)** to
gather information o material (about)

documen'tario, -a AG, SM documentary

documentazi'one [dokumentat'tsjone] SF
documentation

docu'mento SM document; **documenti** SMPL
(*d'identità ecc*) papers

Dodecan'neso SM: **le Isole del ~** the
Dodecanese Islands

dodi'cenne [dodi'tʃenne] AG, SMF twelve-
year-old

dodi'cesimo, -a [dodi'tʃezimo] NUM twelfth

'dodici ['doditʃi] NUM twelve

do'gana SF (*ufficio*) customs *pl*; (*tassa*)
(customs) duty; **passare la ~** to go through
customs

doga'nale AG customs *cpd*

dogani'ere SM customs officer

'doglie ['dɔʎʎe] SFPL (*Med*) labour *sg* (BRIT),
labor *sg* (US), labour pains

'dogma, -i SM dogma

dog'matico, -a, -ci, -che AG dogmatic

'dolce ['doltʃe] AG sweet; (*colore*) soft; (*carattere, persona*) gentle, mild; (*fig: mite: clima*) mild; (*non ripido: pendio*) gentle ► SM (*sapore dolce*) sweetness, sweet taste; (*Cuc: portata*) sweet, dessert; (: *torta*) cake; **il ~ far niente** sweet idleness

dolcemente AV (*baciare, trattare*) gently; (*sorridere, cantare*) sweetly; (*parlare*) softly

dol'cezza [dol'tʃettsa] SF sweetness; softness; mildness; gentleness

dolci'ario, -a[dol'tʃarjo] AG confectionery *cpd*

dolci'astro, -a[dol'tʃastro] AG (*sapore*) sweetish

dolcifi'cante [doltʃifi'kante] AG sweetening ► SM sweetener

dolci'umi [dol'tʃumi] SMPL sweets

do'lente AG sorrowful, sad

do'lere/44/ VI to be sore, hurt, ache; **dolersi** VPR to complain; (*essere spiacente*) **dolersi di** to be sorry for; **mi duole la testa** my head aches, I've got a headache

'dolgoetc VB vedi **dolere**

'dollaro SM dollar

'dolo SM (*Dir*) malice; (*frode*) fraud, deceit

Dolo'miti SFPL: **le ~** the Dolomites

dolo'rante AG aching, sore

do'lore SM (*fisico*) pain; (*morale*) sorrow, grief; **se lo scoprono sono dolori!** if they find out there'll be trouble!

dolo'roso, -a AG painful; sorrowful, sad

do'loso, -a AG (*Dir*) malicious; **incendio ~** arson

'dolsietc VB vedi **dolere**

dom. ABBR (= *domenica*) Sun

do'manda SF (*interrogazione*) question; (*richiesta*) demand; (: *cortese*) request; (*Dir: richiesta scritta*) application; (*Econ*): **la ~** demand; **fare una ~ a qn** to ask sb a question; **fare ~ (per un lavoro)** to apply (for a job); **far regolare ~ (di qc)** to apply through the proper channels (for sth); **fare ~ all'autorità giudiziaria** to apply to the courts; **~ di divorzio** divorce petition; **~ di matrimonio** proposal

doman'dare/72/ VT (*per avere*) to ask for; (*per sapere*) to ask; (*esigere*) to demand; **domandarsi**VPR to wonder; to ask o.s.; **~ qc a qn** to ask sb for sth; to ask sb sth

do'mani AV tomorrow ► SM (*l'indomani*) the next day, the following day; **il ~** (*il futuro*) the future; (*il giorno successivo*) the next day; **un ~** some day; **~ l'altro** the day after tomorrow; **~ (a) otto** tomorrow week, a week tomorrow; **a ~!** see you tomorrow!

do'mare/72/ VT to tame

doma'tore, -'trice SM/F (*gen*) tamer; **~ di cavalli** horsebreaker; **~ di leoni** lion tamer

domat'tina AV tomorrow morning

do'menica, -che SF Sunday; **di** o **la ~** on Sundays; vedi anche **martedì**

domeni'cale AG Sunday *cpd*

domeni'cano, -a AG, SM/F Dominican

do'mestica, -che SF vedi **domestico**

do'mestico, -a, -ci, -che AG domestic ► SM/F servant, domestic; **le pareti domestiche** one's own four walls; **animale ~** pet; **una domestica a ore** a daily (woman)

domicili'are[domitʃi'ljare] AG vedi **arresto**

domicili'arsi[domitʃi'ljarsi] /**19**/ VPR to take up residence

domi'cilio [domi'tʃiljo] SM (*Dir*) domicile, place of residence; (~ *Med*) house call; **"recapito a ~"** "deliveries"; **violazione di ~** (*Dir*) breaking and entering

domi'nante AG (*colore, nota*) dominant; (*opinione*) prevailing; (*idea*) main *cpd*, chief *cpd*; (*posizione*) dominating *cpd*; (*classe, partito*) ruling *cpd*

domi'nare/72/ VT to dominate; (*fig: sentimenti*) to control, master ► VI to be in the dominant position; **dominarsi**VPR (*controllarsi*) to control o.s.; **~ su** (*fig*) to surpass, outclass

domina'tore, -'trice AG ruling *cpd* ► SM/F ruler

dominazi'one [dominat'tsjone] SF domination

domini'cano, -a AG: **la Repubblica Dominicana** the Dominican Republic

do'minio SM dominion; (*fig: campo*) field, domain; **domini coloniali** colonies; **essere di ~ pubblico** (*notizia ecc*) to be common knowledge

don SM (*Rel*) Father

do'nare/72/ VT to give, present; (*per beneficenza ecc*) to donate ► VI (*fig*): **~ a** to suit, become; **~ sangue** to give blood

dona'tore, -'trice SM/F donor; **~ di sangue/ di organi** blood/organ donor

donazi'one [donat'tsjone] SF donation; **atto di ~** (*Dir*) deed of gift

'donde AV (*poetico*) whence

dondo'lare/72/ VT (*cullare*) to rock; **dondolarsi**VPR to swing, sway

'dondolo SM: **sedia/cavallo a ~** rocking chair/horse

dongio'vanni [dondʒo'vanni] SM Don Juan, ladies' man

'donna SF woman; (*titolo*) Donna; (*Carte*) queen; **figlio di buona ~!** (*col*) son of a bitch!; **~ di casa** housewife; home-loving woman; **~ a ore** daily (help o woman); **~ delle pulizie** cleaning lady, cleaner; **~ di servizio** maid; **~ di vita** o **di strada** prostitute, streetwalker

donnai'olo SM ladykiller

'donnola SF weasel

'dono SM gift

'doping SM doping

'dopo AV (*tempo*) afterwards; (: *più tardi*) later; (*luogo*) after, next ▶ PREP after ▶ CONG (*temporale*): ~ **aver studiato** after having studied ▶ AG INV: **il giorno** ~ the following day; ~ **mangiato va a dormire** after having eaten o after a meal he goes for a sleep; **un anno** ~ a year later; ~ **di me/lui** after me/him; ~, **a** ~! see you later!; ~ **che** = **dopoché**

dopo'barba SM INV after-shave

dopoché [dopo'ke] CONG after, when

dopodiché [dopodi'ke] AV after which

dopodo'mani AV the day after tomorrow

dopogu'erra SM postwar years *pl*

dopola'voro SM recreational club

dopo'pranzo [dopo'prandzo] AV after lunch (o dinner)

doposcì [dopoʃ'ʃi] SM INV après-ski outfit

doposcu'ola SM INV *school club offering extra tuition and recreational facilities*

dopo'sole SM INV, AG INV: (**lozione/crema**) ~ aftersun (lotion/cream)

dopo'tutto AV (*tutto considerato*) after all

doppi'aggio [dop'pjaddʒo] SM (*Cine*) dubbing

doppi'are /19/ VT (*Naut*) to round; (*Sport*) to lap; (*Cine*) to dub

doppia'tore, -'trice SM/F dubber

doppi'etta SF (*fucile*) double-barrelled (BRIT) o double-barreled (US) shotgun; (*sparo*) shot from both barrels; (*Calcio*) double; (*Pugilato*) one-two; (*Aut*) double-declutch (BRIT), double-clutch (US)

doppi'ezza [dop'pjettsa] SF (*fig: di persona*) duplicity, double-dealing

'doppio, -a AG double; (*fig: falso*) double-dealing, deceitful ▶ SM (*quantità*): **il** ~ (**di**) twice as much (o many), double the amount (o number) of; (*Sport*) doubles *pl* ▶ AV double; **battere una lettera in doppia copia** to type a letter with a carbon copy; **fare il** ~ **gioco** (*fig*) to play a double game; **chiudere a doppia mandata** to double-lock; ~ **senso** double entendre; **frase a** ~ **senso** sentence with a double meaning; **un utensile a** ~ **uso** a dual-purpose utensil

doppio'fondo SM (*di valigia*) false bottom; (*Naut*) double hull

doppi'one SM duplicate (copy)

doppio'petto SM double-breasted jacket

dop'pista SMF (*Tennis*) doubles player

do'rare /72/ VT to gild; (*Cuc*) to brown; ~ **la pillola** (*fig*) to sugar the pill

do'rato, -a AG golden; (*ricoperto d'oro*) gilt, gilded

dora'tura SF gilding

dormicchi'are [dormik'kjare] /19/ VI to doze

dormi'ente AG sleeping ▶ SMF sleeper

dormigli'one, -a [dormiʎ'ʎone] SM/F sleepyhead

dor'mire /45/ VI to sleep; **andare a** ~ to go to bed; (*essere addormentato*) to be asleep, be sleeping; **il caffè non mi fa** ~ coffee keeps me awake; ~ **come un ghiro** to sleep like a log; ~ **della grossa** to sleep soundly, be dead to the world; ~ **in piedi** (*essere stanco*) to be asleep on one's feet

dor'mita SF: **farsi una** ~ to have a good sleep

dormi'torio SM dormitory; ~ **pubblico** doss house (BRIT) o flophouse (US: *run by local authority*)

dormi'veglia [dormi'veʎʎa] SM drowsiness

dorrò *etc* VB *vedi* **dolere**

dor'sale AG: **spina** ~ backbone, spine

'dorso SM back; (*di montagna*) ridge, crest; (*di libro*) spine; (*Nuoto*) backstroke; **a** ~ **di cavallo** on horseback

do'saggio [do'zaddʒo] SM (*atto*) measuring out; **sbagliare il** ~ to get the proportions wrong

do'sare /72/ VT to measure out; (*Med*) to dose

'dose SF quantity, amount; (*Med*) dose

dossi'er [do'sje] SM INV dossier, file

'dosso SM (*rilievo*) rise; (: *di strada*) bump; (*dorso*): **levarsi di** ~ **i vestiti** to take one's clothes off; **levarsi un peso di** ~ (*fig*) to take a weight off one's mind

do'tare /72/ VT: ~ **di** to provide o supply with; (*fig*) to endow with

do'tato, -a AG: ~ **di** (*attrezzature*) equipped with; (*bellezza, intelligenza*) endowed with; **un uomo** ~ a gifted man

dotazi'one [dotat'tsjone] SF (*insieme di beni*) endowment; (*di macchine ecc*) equipment; **dare qc in** ~ **a qn** to issue sb with sth, issue sth to sb; **i macchinari in** ~ **alla fabbrica** the machinery in use in the factory

'dote SF (*di sposa*) dowry; (*assegnata a un ente*) endowment; (*fig*) gift, talent

Dott. ABBR (= *dottore*) Dr

'dotto, -a AG (*colto*) learned ▶ SM (*sapiente*) scholar; (*Anat*) duct

dotto'rato SM degree; ~ **di ricerca** doctorate, doctor's degree

dot'tore, -'essa SM/F doctor

In Italy, anyone who has a degree in any subject can use the title *dottore*. Thus a person who is addressed as *dottore* is not necessarily a doctor of medicine.

dot'trina SF doctrine

Dott.ssa ABBR (= *dottoressa*) Dr

double-'face [dubl'fas] AG INV reversible

'dove AV (*gen*) where; (*in cui*) where, in which; (*dovunque*) wherever ▶ CONG (*mentre, laddove*) whereas ▶ SM: **per ogni** ~ everywhere; ~ **sei?/vai?** where are you?/are you going?; **dimmi dov'è** tell me where it is; **di dov'è?** where are you from?; **da** ~ **abito vedo tutta la città** I can see the whole city from where

I live; **per ~ si passa?** which way should we go?; **le dò una mano fin ~ posso** I'll help you as much as I can; **la città ~ abito** the town where o in which I live; **siediti ~ vuoi** sit wherever you like

do'vere/46/ SM (*obbligo*) duty ▸ VT (*essere debitore*): **~ qc (a qn)** to owe (sb) sth ▸ VI (*seguito dall'infinito: obbligo*) to have to; **devo partire domani** (*intenzione*) I'm (due) to leave tomorrow; **dev'essere tardi** (*probabilità*) it must be late; **lui deve farlo** he has to do it, he must do it; **quanto le devo?** how much do I owe you?; **è dovuto partire** he had to leave; **ha dovuto pagare** he had to pay; **doveva accadere** it was bound to happen; **avere il senso del ~** to have a sense of duty; **rivolgersi a chi di ~** to apply to the appropriate authority o person; **a ~** (*bene*) properly; (*debitamente*) as he (o she *etc*) deserves; **come si deve** (*bene*) properly; (*meritatamente*) properly, as he (o she *etc*) deserves; **una persona come si deve** a respectable person

dove'roso, -a AG (right and) proper
do'vizia [do'vittsja] SF abundance
dovrò*etc* VB *vedi* **dovere**
do'vunque AV (*in qualunque luogo*) wherever; (*dappertutto*) everywhere; **~ io vada** wherever I go

dovuta'mente AV (*debitamente: redigere, compilare*) correctly; (*: rimproverare*) as he (o she *etc*) deserves

do'vuto, -a AG (*causato*): **~ a** due to ▸ SM due; **nel modo ~** in the proper way; **ho lavorato più del ~** I worked more than was necessary
doz'zina [dod'dzina] SF dozen; **una ~ di uova** a dozen eggs; **di** o **da ~** (*scrittore, spettacolo*) second-rate
dozzi'nale [doddzi'nale] AG cheap, second-rate

DP SIGLA F (= *Democrazia Proletaria*) political party
'draga, -ghe SF dredger
dra'gare/80/ VT to dredge
dragherò*etc* [drage'rɔ] VB *vedi* **dragare**
'drago, -ghi SM dragon; (*fig: col*) genius
'dramma, -i SM drama; **fare un ~ di qc** to make a drama out of sth
dram'matico, -a, -ci, -che AG dramatic
drammatiz'zare [drammatid'dzare] /72/ VT to dramatize
dramma'turgo, -ghi SM playwright
drappeggi'are [drapped'dʒare] /62/ VT to drape
drap'peggio [drap'peddʒo] SM (*tessuto*) drapery; (*di abito*) folds
drap'pello SM (*Mil*) squad; (*gruppo*) band, group
'drappo SM cloth
'drastico, -a, -ci, -che AG drastic

dre'naggio [dre'naddʒo] SM drainage
dre'nare/72/ VT to drain
'Dresda SF Dresden
drib'blare/72/ VI (*Calcio*) to dribble ▸ VT (*avversario*) to dodge, avoid
'dritto, -a AG, AV = **diritto** ▸ SM/F (*col: furbo*): **è un ~** he's a crafty o sly one ▸ SF (*destra*) right, right hand; (*Naut*) starboard; **a dritta e a manca** (*fig*) on all sides, right, left and centre
driz'zare [drit'tsare] /72/ VT (*far tornare diritto*) to straighten; (*volgere: sguardo, occhi*) to turn, direct; (*innalzare: antenna, muro*) to erect; **drizzarsi**VPR to stand up; **~ le orecchie** to prick up one's ears; **drizzarsi in piedi** to rise to one's feet; **drizzarsi a sedere** to sit up
'droga, -ghe SF (*sostanza aromatica*) spice; (*stupefacente*) drug; **droghe pesanti/leggere** hard/soft drugs
dro'gare/80/ VT to drug, dope; **drogarsi**VPR to take drugs
dro'gato, -a SM/F drug addict
droghe'ria [droge'ria] SF grocer's (shop) (BRIT), grocery (store) (US)
drogherò*etc* [droge'rɔ] VB *vedi* **drogare**
droghi'ere, -a[dro'gjɛre] SM/F grocer
drome'dario SM dromedary
DS [di'ɛsse] SMPL (= *Democratici di Sinistra*) Democrats of the Left (*Italian left-wing party*)
'dubbio, -a AG (*incerto*) doubtful, dubious; (*ambiguo*) dubious ▸ SM (*incertezza*) doubt; **avere il ~ che** to be afraid that, suspect that; **essere in ~ fra** to hesitate between; **mettere in ~ qc** to question sth; **nutrire seri dubbi su qc** to have grave doubts about sth; **senza ~** doubtless, no doubt
dubbi'oso, -a AG doubtful, dubious
dubi'tare/72/ VI: **~ di** (*onestà*) to doubt; (*risultato*) to be doubtful of; **~ di qn** to mistrust sb; **~ di sé** to be unsure of o.s.
Du'blino SF Dublin
'duca, -chi SM duke
'duce ['dutʃe] SM (*Storia*) captain; (*: del fascismo*) duce
du'chessa [du'kessa] SF duchess
'due NUM two; **a ~ a ~** two at a time, two by two; **dire ~ parole** to say a few words; **ci metto ~ minuti** I'll have it done in a jiffy
duecen'tesco, -a, -schi, -sche [duetʃen'tesko] AG thirteenth-century
due'cento [due'tʃento] NUM two hundred ▸ SM: **il D~** the thirteenth century
duel'lare/72/ VI to fight a duel
du'ello SM duel
due'mila NUM two thousand ▸ SM INV: **il ~** the year two thousand
due'pezzi [due'pɛttsi] SM (*costume da bagno*) two-piece swimsuit; (*abito femminile*) two-piece suit

du'etto SM duet

'dulcis in 'fundo ['dultʃisin'fundo] AV to cap it all

'duna SF dune

'dunque CONG (perciò) so, therefore; (riprendendo il discorso) well (then) ▶ SM INV: **venire al ~** to come to the point

'duo SM INV (Mus) duet; (Teat, Cine, fig) duo

du'ole etc VB vedi **dolere**

du'omo SM cathedral

'duplex SM INV (Tel) party line

dupli'cato SM duplicate

'duplice ['duplitʃe] AG double, twofold; **in ~ copia** in duplicate

duplicità [duplitʃi'ta] SF (fig) duplicity

du'rante PREP during; **vita natural ~** for life

du'rare /72/ VI to last; **non può ~!** this can't go on any longer!; **~ fatica a** to have difficulty in; **~ in carica** to remain in office

du'rata SF length (of time); duration; **per tutta la ~ di** throughout; **~ media della vita** life expectancy

dura'turo, -a AG, du'revole AG (ricordo) lasting; (materiale) durable

du'rezza [du'rettsa] SF hardness; stubbornness; harshness; toughness

'duro, -a AG (pietra, lavoro, materasso, problema) hard; (persona: ostinato) stubborn, obstinate; (: severo) harsh, hard; (voce) harsh; (carne) tough ▶ SM/F hardness; (difficoltà) hard part; (persona) tough one ▶ AV: **tener ~** (resistere) to stand firm, hold out; **avere la pelle dura** (fig: persona) to be tough; **fare il ~** to act tough; **~ di comprendonio** slow-witted; **~ d'orecchi** hard of hearing

du'rone SM hard skin

'duttile AG (sostanza) malleable; (fig: carattere) docile, biddable; (: stile) adaptable

DVD [divu'di] SM INV DVD; (lettore) DVD player

Ee

E, e [e] SM O F INV (*lettera*) E, e; **E come Empoli** ≈ E for Edward (*Brit*), E for Easy (*US*)

E ABBR (= *est*) E; (*Aut*) = **itinerario europeo**

e(*dav V spesso* **ed**) CONG and; (*avversativo*) but; (*eppure*) and yet; **e lui?** what about him?; **e compralo!** well buy it then!

è VB *vedi* **essere**

E.A.D. SIGLA F = **elaborazione automatica dei dati**

ebaniste'ria SF cabinet-making; (*negozio*) cabinet-maker's shop

'ebano SM ebony

eb'bene CONG well (then)

'ebbietc VB *vedi* **avere**

eb'brezza [eb'brettsa] SF intoxication

'ebbro, -a AG drunk; **~ di** (*gioia ecc*) beside o.s. *o* wild with

'ebete AG stupid, idiotic

ebe'tismo SM stupidity

ebollizi'one [ebollit'tsjone] SF boiling; **punto di ~** boiling point

e'braico, -a, -ci, -che AG Hebrew, Hebraic ▶ SM (*Ling*) Hebrew

e'breo, -a AG Jewish ▶ SM/F Jewish person, Jew (Jewess)

'Ebridi SFPL: **le (isole) ~** the Hebrides

e'burneo, -a AG ivory *cpd*

EC ABBR (= *Eurocity*) *fast train connecting Western European cities*

E/C ABBR = **estratto conto**

eca'tombe SF (*strage*) slaughter, massacre

ecc. ABBR (= *eccetera*) etc

ecce'dente [ettʃe'dɛnte] SM surplus

ecce'denza [ettʃe'dɛntsa] SF excess, surplus; (*Inform*) overflow

ec'cedere [et'tʃɛdere] /29/ VT to exceed ▶ VI to go too far; **~ nel bere/mangiare** to indulge in drink/food to excess

eccel'lente [ettʃel'lɛnte] AG excellent; (*cadavere, arresto*) of a prominent person

eccel'lenza [ettʃe'lɛntsa] SF excellence; (*titolo*): **Sua E~** His Excellency

ec'cellere [et'tʃɛllere] /45/ VI: **~ (in)** to excel (at); **~ su tutti** to surpass everyone

ec'celso, -a[et'tʃɛlso] PP *di* **eccellere** ▶ AG (*cima, montagna*) high; (*fig: ingegno*) great, exceptional

ec'centrico, -a, -ci, -che[et'tʃɛntriko] AG eccentric

ecces'sivo, -a[ettʃes'sivo] AG excessive

ec'cesso [et'tʃɛsso] SM excess; **all'~** (*gentile, generoso*) to excess, excessively; **dare in eccessi** to fly into a rage; **~ di velocità** (*Aut*) speeding; **~ di zelo** overzealousness

ec'cetera [et'tʃɛtera] AV et cetera, and so on

ec'cetto [et'tʃɛtto] PREP except, with the exception of; **~ che** *cong* except, other than; **~ che (non)** unless

eccettu'are [ettʃettu'are] /72/ VT to except; **eccettuati i presenti** present company excepted

eccezio'nale [ettʃettsjo'nale] AG exceptional; **in via del tutto ~** in this instance, exceptionally

eccezi'one [ettʃet'tsjone] SF exception; (*Dir*) objection; **a ~ di** with the exception of, except for; **d'~** exceptional; **fare un'~ alla regola** to make an exception to the rule

ec'chimosi [ek'kimozi] SF INV bruise

ec'cidio [et'tʃidjo] SM massacre

ecci'tante [ettʃi'tante] AG (*gen*) exciting; (*sostanza*) stimulating ▶ SM stimulant

ecci'tare [ettʃi'tare] /72/ VT (*curiosità, interesse*) to excite, arouse; (*folla*) to incite; **eccitarsi** VPR to get excited; (*sessualmente*) to become aroused

eccitazi'one [ettʃitat'tsjone] SF excitement

ecclesi'astico, -a, -ci, -che AG ecclesiastical, church *cpd*; clerical ▶ SM ecclesiastic

'ecco AV (*per dimostrare*): **~ il treno!** here's *o* here comes the train!; (*dav pronome*) **eccomi!** here I am!; **eccone uno!** here's one (of them)!; (*dav pp*) **~ fatto!** there, that's it done!

ec'come AV rather; **ti piace? — ~!** do you like it? — I'll say! *o* and how! *o* rather! (*Brit*)

ECG SIGLA M = **elettrocardiogramma**

echeggi'are [eked'dʒare] /62/ VI to echo

e'clettico, -a, -ci, -cheAG, SM/F eclectic

eclet'tismo SM eclecticism

eclis'sare /72/ VT to eclipse; (*fig*) to eclipse, overshadow; **eclissarsi** VPR (*persona: scherzoso*) to slip away

e'clisse SF eclipse

e'clissi SF eclipse

'eco (*pl(m)* **echi**) SM O F echo; **suscitò** *o* **ebbe una profonda ~** it caused quite a stir

ecogra'fia SF (*Med*) ultrasound

ecolo'gia [ekolo'dʒia] SF ecology

eco'logico, -a, -ci, -che [eko'lɔdʒiko] AG ecological

ecolo'gista, -i, -e [ekolo'dʒista] AG ecological ▶ SM/F ecologist, environmentalist

e'cologo, -a, -gi, -ghe SM/F ecologist

eco'mafia SF *mafia involved in crimes related to the environment, in particular the illegal disposal of waste*

econo'mato SM (*Ins*) bursar's office

econo'mia SF economy; (*scienza*) economics *sg*; (*risparmio: azione*) saving; **fare ~** to economize, make economies; **l'~ sommersa** the black (*BRIT*) *o* underground (*US*) economy; **~ di mercato** market economy; **~ pianificata** planned economy

eco'nomico, -a, -ci, -che AG economic; (*poco costoso*) economical; **edizione economica** economy edition

econo'mista, -i SM economist

economiz'zare [ekonomid'dzare] /72/ VT, VI to save

e'conomo, -a AG thrifty ▶ SM/F (*Ins*) bursar

ecosis'tema, -i SM ecosystem

eco'tassa [eko'tassa] SF green tax

'ecstasy ['ɛkstasi] SF INV ecstasy

'Ecuador SM: **l'~** Ecuador

ecu'menico, -a, -ci, -che AG ecumenical

ec'zema [ek'dzɛma] SM eczema

ed CONG *vedi* **E**

Ed. ABBR = **editore**

ed. ABBR = **edizione**

'edera SF ivy

e'dicola SF newspaper kiosk *o* stand (*US*)

edico'lante SMF news vendor (*in kiosk*)

edifi'cante AG edifying

edifi'care /20/ VT to build; (*fig: teoria, azienda*) to establish; (*indurre al bene*) to edify

edi'ficio [edi'fitʃo] SM building; (*fig*) structure

e'dile AG building *cpd*

edi'lizio, -a [edi'littsjo] AG building *cpd* ▶ SF building, building trade

Edim'burgo SF Edinburgh

'edito, -a AG published

edi'tore, -'trice AG publishing *cpd* ▶ SM/F publisher

edito'ria SF publishing

editori'ale AG publishing *cpd* ▶ SM (*articolo di fondo*) editorial, leader

e'ditto SM edict

edizi'one [edit'tsjone] SF edition; (*tiratura*) printing; **~ a tiratura limitata** limited edition; **~ straordinaria** special edition

edo'nismo SM hedonism

e'dotto, -a AG informed; **rendere qn ~ su qc** to inform sb about sth

edu'canda SF boarder

edu'care /20/ VT to educate; (*gusto, mente*) to train; **~ qn a fare** to train sb to do

educa'tivo, -a AG educational

edu'cato, -a AG polite, well-mannered

educazi'one [edukat'tsjone] SF education; (*familiare*) upbringing; (*comportamento*) (good) manners *pl*; **per ~** out of politeness; **questa è pura mancanza d'~!** this is sheer bad manners!; **~ fisica** (*Ins*) physical training *o* education

educherò *etc* [eduke'rɔ] VB *vedi* **educare**

E.E.D. SIGLA F = **elaborazione elettronica dei dati**

EEG SIGLA M = **elettroencefalogramma**

e'felide SF freckle

effemi'nato, -a AG effeminate

effe'rato, -a AG brutal, savage

efferve'scente [efferveʃ'ʃɛnte] AG effervescent

effettiva'mente AV (*in effetti*) in fact; (*a dire il vero*) really, actually

effet'tivo, -a AG (*reale*) real, actual; (*impiegato, professore*) permanent; (*Mil*) regular ▶ SM (*Mil*) strength; (*di patrimonio ecc*) sum total

ef'fetto SM effect; (*Comm: cambiale*) bill; (*fig: impressione*) impression; **far ~** (*medicina*) to take effect, (start to) work; **cercare l'~** to seek attention; **in effetti** in fact, actually; **effetti attivi** (*Comm*) bills receivable; **effetti passivi** (*Comm*) bills payable; **effetti personali** personal effects, personal belongings; **~ serra** greenhouse effect; **effetti speciali** (*Cine*) special effects

effettu'are /72/ VT to effect, carry out

effi'cace [effi'katʃe] AG effective

effi'cacia [effi'katʃa] SF effectiveness

effici'ente [effi'tʃɛnte] AG efficient

efficien'tismo [effitʃen'tizmo] SM maximum efficiency

effici'enza [effi'tʃɛntsa] SF efficiency

effigi'are [effi'dʒare] /62/ VT to represent, portray

ef'figie [ef'fidʒe] SF INV effigy

ef'fimero, -a AG ephemeral

ef'fluvio SM (*anche peg, ironico*) scent, perfume

effusi'one SF effusion

e.g. ABBR (= *exempli gratia*) e.g.

egemo'nia [edʒemo'nia] SF hegemony

E'geo [e'dʒɛo] SM: **l'~, il mare ~** the Aegean (Sea)

'egida ['ɛdʒida] SF: **sotto l'~ di** under the aegis of

E'gitto [e'dʒitto] SM: **l'~** Egypt
egizi'ano, -a [edʒit'tsjano] AG, SM/F Egyptian
e'gizio, -a [e'dʒittsjo] AG, SM/F (ancient) Egyptian
'egli ['eʎʎi] PRON he; **~ stesso** he himself
'ego SM INV (Psic) ego
ego'centrico, -a, -ci, -che [ego'tʃɛntriko] AG egocentric(al) ▶ SM/F self-centred (BRIT) o self-centered (US) person
egocen'trismo [egotʃen'trizmo] SM egocentricity
ego'ismo SM selfishness, egoism
ego'ista, -i, -e AG selfish, egoistic ▶ SM/F egoist
ego'istico, -a, -ci, -che AG egoistic, selfish
ego'tismo SM egotism
ego'tista, -i, -e AG egotistic ▶ SM/F egotist
Egr. ABBR = **egregio**
e'gregio, -a, -gi, -gie [e'grɛdʒo] AG distinguished; (nelle lettere): **E~ Signore** Dear Sir
eguagli'anza etc [egwaʎ'ʎantsa] vedi **uguaglianza** ecc
eguali'tario, -a AG, SM/F egalitarian
E.I. ABBR = **Esercito Italiano**
eiaculazi'one [ejakulat'tsjone] SF ejaculation; **~ precoce** premature ejaculation
elabo'rare /72/ VT (progetto) to work out, elaborate; (dati) to process; (digerire) to digest
elabora'tore SM (Inform): **~ elettronico** computer
elaborazi'one [elaborat'tsjone] SF elaboration; processing; digestion; **~ automatica dei dati** (Inform) automatic data processing; **~ elettronica dei dati** (Inform) electronic data processing; **~ testi** (Inform) text processing
elar'gire [elar'dʒire] /55/ VT to hand out
elargizi'one [elardʒit'tsjone] SF donation
elasticiz'zato, -a [elastitʃid'dzato] AG (tessuto) stretch cpd
e'lastico, -a, -ci, -che AG elastic; (fig: andatura) springy; (: decisione, vedute) flexible ▶ SM (gommino) rubber band; (per il cucito) elastic no pl
ele'fante SM elephant
ele'gante AG elegant
ele'ganza [ele'gantsa] SF elegance
e'leggere [e'lɛddʒere] /61/ VT to elect
elemen'tare AG elementary; **le (scuole) elementari** sfpl primary (BRIT) o grade (US) school; **prima ~** first year of primary school, ≈ infants' class (BRIT), ≈ 1st grade (US)
ele'mento SM element; (parte componente) element, component, part; **elementi** SMPL (della scienza ecc) elements, rudiments
ele'mosina SF charity, alms pl; **chiedere l'~** to beg

elemosi'nare /72/ VT to beg for, ask for ▶ VI to beg
elen'care /20/ VT to list
elencherò etc [elenke'rɔ] VB vedi **elencare**
e'lenco, -chi SM list; **~ nominativo** list of names; **~ telefonico** telephone directory
e'lessi etc VB vedi **eleggere**
elet'tivo, -a AG (carica ecc) elected
e'letto, -a PP di **eleggere** ▶ SM/F (nominato) elected member
eletto'rale AG electoral, election cpd
eletto'rato SM electorate
elet'tore, -'trice SM/F voter, elector
elet'trauto SM INV workshop for car electrical repairs; (tecnico) car electrician
elettri'cista, -i [elettri'tʃista] SM electrician
elettricità [elettritʃi'ta] SF electricity
e'lettrico, -a, -ci, -che AG electric(al)
elettrifi'care /20/ VT to electrify
elettriz'zante [elettrid'dzante] AG (fig) electrifying, thrilling
elettriz'zare [elettrid'dzare] /72/ VT to electrify; **elettrizzarsi** VPR to become charged with electricity; (fig: persona) to be thrilled
e'lettro... PREFISSO electro...
elettrocardio'gramma, -i SM electrocardiogram
e'lettrodo SM electrode
elettrodo'mestico, -a, -ci, -che AG: **apparecchi elettrodomestici** domestic (electrical) appliances
elettroencefalo'gramma, -i [elettroentʃefalo'gramma] SM electroencephalogram
elet'trogeno, -a [elet'trɔdʒeno] AG: **gruppo ~** generator
elet'trolisi SF electrolysis
elettroma'gnetico, -a, -ci, -che [elettromaɲ'nɛtiko] AG electromagnetic
elettromo'trice [elettromo'tritʃe] SF electric train
elet'trone SM electron
elet'tronico, -a, -ci, -che AG electronic ▶ SF electronics sg
elettro'shock [elettroʃ'ʃɔk] SM INV (electro)shock treatment
elettro'tecnico, -a, -ci, -che AG electrotechnical ▶ SM electrical engineer
ele'vare /72/ VT to raise; (edificio) to erect; (multa) to impose; **~ un numero al quadrato** to square a number
eleva'tezza [eleva'tettsa] SF (altezza) elevation; (di animo, pensiero) loftiness
ele'vato, -a AG (gen) high; (cime) high, lofty; (fig: stile, sentimenti) lofty
elevazi'one [elevat'tsjone] SF elevation; (l'elevare) raising

elezi'one [elet'tsjone] SF election; **elezioni** SFPL (Pol) election(s); **patria d'~** chosen country

'**elica, -che** SF propeller

eli'cottero SM helicopter

e'lidere /89/ VT (Fonetica) to elide; **elidersi** VPR (forze) to cancel each other out, neutralize each other

elimi'nare /72/ VT to eliminate

elimina'toria SF eliminating round

eliminazi'one [eliminat'tsjone] SF elimination

'**elio** SM helium

eli'porto SM heliport

elisabetti'ano, -a AG Elizabethan

eli'sir SM INV elixir

e'liso, -a PP di **elidere**

elisoc'corso SM helicopter ambulance

eli'tario, -a AG elitist

é'lite [e'lit] SF INV élite

'**ella** PRON she; (forma di cortesia) you; **~ stessa** she herself; you yourself

el'lisse SF ellipse

el'littico, -a, -ci, -che AG elliptic(al)

el'metto SM helmet

'**elmo** SM helmet

elogi'are [elo'dʒare] /62/ VT to praise

elogia'tivo, -a [elodʒa'tivo] AG laudatory

e'logio [e'lɔdʒo] SM (discorso, scritto) eulogy; (lode) praise; **~ funebre** funeral oration

elo'quente AG eloquent; **questi dati sono eloquenti** these facts speak for themselves

elo'quenza [elo'kwɛntsa] SF eloquence

e'loquio SM speech, language

elucu'brare /72/ VT to ponder about o over

elucubrazi'oni [elukubrat'tsjoni] SFPL (anche ironico) cogitations, ponderings

e'ludere /35/ VT to evade

e'lusi etc VB vedi **eludere**

elusi'one SF: **~ d'imposta** tax evasion

elu'sivo, -a AG evasive

e'luso, -a PP di **eludere**

el'vetico, -a, -ci, -che AG Swiss

emaci'ato, -a [ema'tʃato] AG emaciated

e-'mail, email [e'mɛil] SF INV (messaggio, sistema) e-mail ▸ AG INV email; **indirizzo ~** email address

ema'nare /72/ VT to send out, give off; (fig: leggi) to promulgate; (: decreti) to issue ▸ VI: **~ da** to come from

emanazi'one [emanat'tsjone] SF (di raggi, calore) emanation; (di odori) exhalation; (di legge) promulgation; (di ordine, circolare) issuing

emanci'pare [emantʃi'pare] /72/ VT to emancipate; **emanciparsi** VPR (fig) to become liberated o emancipated

emancipazi'one [emantʃipat'tsjone] SF emancipation

emargi'nare [emardʒi'nare] /72/ VT (fig: socialmente) to cast out

emargi'nato, -a [emardʒi'nato] SM/F outcast

emarginazi'one [emardʒinat'tsjone] SF marginalization

ematolo'gia [ematolo'dʒia] SF haematology (BRIT), hematology (US)

ema'toma, -i SM haematoma (BRIT), hematoma (US)

em'blema, -i SM emblem

emble'matico, -a, -ci, -che AG emblematic; (fig: atteggiamento, parole) symbolic

embo'lia SF embolism

embrio'nale, -i, -i AG embryonic, embryo cpd; **allo stadio ~** at the embryo stage

embri'one SM embryo

emenda'mento SM amendment

emen'dare /72/ VT to amend

emer'gente [emer'dʒɛnte] AG emerging

emer'genza [emer'dʒɛntsa] SF emergency; **in caso di ~** in an emergency

e'mergere [e'mɛrdʒere] /59/ VI to emerge; (sommergibile) to surface; (fig: distinguersi) to stand out

e'merito, -a AG (insigne) distinguished; **è un ~ cretino!** he's a complete idiot!

e'mersi etc VB vedi **emergere**

e'merso, -a PP di **emergere** ▸ AG (Geo): **terre emerse** lands above sea level

e'messo, -a PP di **emettere**

e'mettere /63/ VT (suono, luce) to give out, emit; (onde radio) to send out; (assegno, francobollo, ordine) to issue; (fig: giudizio) to express, voice; **~ la sentenza** (Dir) to pass sentence

emi'crania SF migraine

emi'grante AG, SMF emigrant

emi'grare /72/ VI to emigrate

emi'grato, -a AG emigrant ▸ SM/F emigrant; (Storia) émigré

emigrazi'one [emigrat'tsjone] SF emigration

emili'ano, -a AG of (o from) Emilia

emi'nente AG eminent, distinguished

emi'nenza [emi'nɛntsa] SF eminence; **~ grigia** (fig) éminence grise

emi'rato SM emirate; **gli Emirati Arabi Uniti** the United Arab Emirates

e'miro SM emir

emis'fero SM hemisphere; **~ boreale/ australe** northern/southern hemisphere

e'misi etc VB vedi **emettere**

emis'sario SM (Geo) outlet, effluent; (inviato) emissary

emissi'one SF (vedi emettere) emission; sending out; issue; (Radio) broadcast

emit'tente AG (banca) issuing; (Radio) broadcasting, transmitting ▸ SF (Radio) transmitter

emofi'lia SF haemophilia (BRIT), hemophilia (US)

emofi'liaco, -a, -ci, -che AG, SM/F haemophiliac (BRIT), hemophiliac (US)

emoglo'bina SF haemoglobin (BRIT), hemoglobin (US)

emolli'ente AG soothing

emorra'gia, -'gie [emorra'dʒia] SF haemorrhage (BRIT), hemorrhage (US)

emor'roidi SFPL haemorrhoids pl (BRIT), hemorrhoids pl (US)

emos'tatico, -a, -ci, -che AG haemostatic (BRIT), hemostatic (US); **laccio ~** tourniquet; **matita emostatica** styptic pencil

emotività SF emotionalism

emo'tivo, -a AG emotional

emozio'nante [emottsjo'nante] AG exciting, thrilling

emozio'nare [emottsjo'nare] /72/ VT (appassionare) to excite, thrill; (commuovere) to move; (agitare) to make nervous; (innervosire) to upset; **emozionarsi** VPR to be excited; to be moved; to be nervous; to be upset

emozionato, -a [emottsjo'nato] AG (commosso) moved; (agitato) nervous; (elettrizzato) excited

emozi'one [emot'tsjone] SF emotion; (agitazione) excitement

'empio, -a AG (sacrilego) impious; (spietato) cruel, pitiless; (malvagio) wicked, evil

em'pirico, -a, -ci, -che AG empirical

em'porio SM general store

emu'lare /72/ VT to emulate

'emulo, -a SM/F imitator

emulsi'one SF emulsion

EN SIGLA = **Enna**

en'ciclica, -che [en'tʃiklika] SF (Rel) encyclical

enciclope'dia [entʃiklope'dia] SF encyclop(a)edia

encomi'abile AG commendable, praiseworthy

encomi'are /19/ VT to commend, praise

en'comio SM commendation; **~ solenne** (Mil) mention in dispatches

endove'noso, -a AG (Med) intravenous ► SF intravenous injection

E'NEA SIGLA F = **Comitato nazionale per la ricerca e lo sviluppo dell'Energia Nucleare e delle Energie Alternative**

'E.N.E.L. SIGLA M (= Ente Nazionale per l'Energia Elettrica) national electricity company

ener'getico, -a, -ci, -che [ener'dʒɛtiko] AG (risorse, crisi) energy cpd; (sostanza, alimento) energy-giving

ener'gia, -'gie [ener'dʒia] SF (Fisica) energy; (fig) energy, strength, vigour (BRIT), vigor (US); **~ eolica** wind power; **~ solare** solar energy, solar power

e'nergico, -a, -ci, -che [e'nɛrdʒiko] AG energetic, vigorous

'enfasi SF emphasis; (peg) bombast, pomposity

en'fatico, -a, -ci, -che AG emphatic; pompous

enfatiz'zare [enfatid'dzare] /72/ VT to emphasize, stress

enfi'sema SM emphysema

'ENI SIGLA M = **Ente Nazionale Idrocarburi**

e'nigma, -i SM enigma

enig'matico, -a, -ci, -che AG enigmatic

'ENIT SIGLA M (= Ente Nazionale Italiano per il Turismo) Italian tourist authority

en'nesimo, -a AG (Mat, fig) nth; **per l'ennesima volta** for the umpteenth time

enolo'gia [enolo'dʒia] SF oenology (BRIT), enology (US)

e'nologo, -gi SM wine expert

e'norme AG enormous, huge

enormità SF INV enormity, huge size; (assurdità) absurdity; **non dire ~!** don't talk nonsense!

eno'teca, -che SF (negozio) wine bar

'E.N.P.A. SIGLA M (= Ente Nazionale Protezione Animali) ≈ RSPCA (BRIT), ≈ SPCA (US)

'E.N.P.A.S. SIGLA M (= Ente Nazionale di Previdenza e Assistenza per i Dipendenti Statali) welfare organization for State employees

'ente SM (istituzione) body, board, corporation; (Filosofia) being; **~ locale** local authority (BRIT), local government (US); **~ pubblico** public body; **~ di ricerca** research organization

ente'rite SF enteritis

entità SF INV (Filosofia) entity; (di perdita, danni, investimenti) extent; (di popolazione) size; **di molta/poca ~** (avvenimento, incidente) of great/little importance

en'trambi, -e PRON PL both (of them) ► AG PL: **~ i ragazzi** both boys, both of the boys

en'trante AG (prossimo: mese, anno) next, coming

en'trare /72/ VI to enter, go (o come) in; **~ in** (luogo) to enter, go (o come) into; (trovar posto, poter stare) to fit into; (essere ammesso a: club ecc) to join, become a member of; **~ in automobile** to get into the car; **far ~ qn** (visitatore ecc) to show sb in; **~ in società/in commercio con qn** to go into partnership/business with sb; **questo non c'entra** (fig) that's got nothing to do with it

en'trata SF entrance, entry; **dov'è l'~?** where's the entrance?; **entrate** SFPL (Comm) receipts, takings; (Econ) income sg; **"~ libera"** "admission free"; **con l'~ in vigore dei nuovi provvedimenti …** once the new measures come into effect …; **entrate tributarie** tax revenue sg '**entro** PREP (*temporale*) within; ~ **domani** by tomorrow; ~ **e non oltre il 25 aprile** no later than 25th April

entro'terra SM INV hinterland

entusias'mante AG exciting

entusias'mare /**72**/ VT to excite, fill with enthusiasm; **entusiasmarsi** VPR: **entusiasmarsi (per qc/qn)** to become enthusiastic (about sth/sb)

entusi'asmo SM enthusiasm

entusi'asta, -i, -e AG enthusiastic ▶ SM/F enthusiast

entusi'astico, -a, -ci, -che AG enthusiastic

enucle'are /**72**/ VT (*formale: chiarire*) to explain

enume'rare /**72**/ VT to enumerate, list

enunci'are [enun't∫are] /**14**/ VT (*teoria*) to enunciate, set out

en'zima, -i SM enzyme

e'olico, -a, -chi, -che AG wind; **energia eolica** wind power

e'patico, -a, -ci, -che AG hepatic; **cirrosi epatica** cirrhosis of the liver

epa'tite SF hepatitis

'**epico, -a, -ci, -che** AG epic

epide'mia SF epidemic

epi'dermico, -a, -ci, -che AG (*Anat*) skin *cpd*; (*fig: interesse, impressioni*) superficial

epi'dermide SF skin, epidermis

Epifa'nia SF Epiphany

e'pigono SM imitator

e'pigrafe SF epigráph; (*su libro*) dedication

epiles'sia SF epilepsy

epi'lettico, -a, -ci, -che AG, SM/F epileptic

e'pilogo, -ghi SM conclusion

epi'sodico, -a, -ci, -che AG (*romanzo, narrazione*) episodic; (*fig: occasionale*) occasional

epi'sodio SM episode; **sceneggiato a episodi** serial

e'pistola SF epistle

episto'lare AG epistolary; **essere in rapporto** *o* **relazione ~ con qn** to correspond *o* be in correspondence with sb

e'piteto SM epithet

'**epoca, -che** SF (*periodo storico*) age, era; (*tempo*) time; (*Geo*) age; **mobili d'~** period furniture; **fare ~** (*scandalo*) to cause a stir; (*cantante, moda*) to mark a new era

epo'pea SF (*anche fig*) epic

ep'pure CONG and yet, nevertheless

EPT SIGLA M (= *Ente Provinciale per il Turismo*) district tourist bureau

epu'rare /**72**/ VT (*Pol*) to purge

equ'anime AG (*imparziale*) fair, impartial

equa'tore SM equator

equazi'one [ekwat'tsjone] SF (*Mat*) equation

e'questre AG equestrian

equi'latero, -a AG equilateral

equili'brare /**72**/ VT to balance

equili'brato, -a AG (*carico, fig: giudizio*) balanced; (*vita*) well-regulated; (*persona*) stable, well-balanced

equi'librio SM balance, equilibrium; **perdere l'~** to lose one's balance; **stare in ~ su** (*persona*) to balance on; (*oggetto*) to be balanced on

equili'brismo SM tightrope walking; (*fig*) juggling

e'quino, -a AG horse *cpd*, equine

equi'nozio [ekwi'nɔttsjo] SM equinox

equipaggia'mento [ekwipaddʒa'mento] SM (*operazione: di nave*) equipping, fitting out; (: *di spedizione, esercito*) equipping, kitting out; (*attrezzatura*) equipment

equipaggi'are [ekwipad'dʒare] /**62**/ VT (*di persone*) to man; (*di mezzi*) to equip; **equipaggiarsi** VPR to equip o.s.

equi'paggio [ekwi'paddʒo] SM crew

equipa'rare /**72**/ VT to make equal

é'quipe [e'kip] SF (*Sport, gen*) team

equità SF equity, fairness

equitazi'one [ekwitat'tsjone] SF (horse-) riding

equiva'lente AG, SM equivalent

equiva'lenza [ekwiva'lentsa] SF equivalence

equiva'lere /**126**/ VI: ~ **a** to be equivalent to; **equivalersi** VPR (*forze ecc*) to counterbalance each other; (*soluzioni*) to amount to the same thing; **equivale a dire che ...** that is the same as saying that ...

equi'valso, -a PP *di* **equivalere**

equivo'care /**20**/ VI to misunderstand

e'quivoco, -a, -ci, -che AG equivocal, ambiguous; (*sospetto*) dubious ▶ SM misunderstanding; **a scanso di equivoci** to avoid any misunderstanding; **giocare sull'~** to equivocate

'**equo, -a** AG fair, just

'**era** SF era

'**era** *etc* VB *vedi* **essere**

erari'ale AG: **ufficio ~** ≈ tax office; **imposte erariali** revenue taxes; **spese erariali** public expenditure *sg*

e'rario SM: **l'~** ≈ the Treasury

'**erba** SF grass; **in ~** (*fig*) budding; **fare di ogni ~ un fascio** (*fig*) to lump everything (*o* everybody) together; **erbe aromatiche** herbs; ~ **medica** lucerne

er'baccia, -ce [er'battʃa] SF weed

er'bivoro, -a AG herbivorous ▶ SM/F herbivore

erbo'rista, -i, -e SM/F herbalist

erboriste'ria SF (*scienza*) study of medicinal herbs; (*negozio*) herbalist's (shop)

er'boso, -a AG grassy

e'rede SMF heir(-ess); ~ **legittimo** heir-at-law

eredità SF (*Dir*) inheritance; (*Biol*) heredity; **lasciare qc in ~ a qn** to leave o bequeath sth to sb

eredi'tare /**72**/ VT to inherit

eredi'tario, -a AG hereditary

erediti'era SF heiress

ere'mita, -i SM hermit

eremi'taggio [eremi'taddʒo] SM hermitage

'eremo SM hermitage; (*fig*) retreat

ere'sia SF heresy

e'ressi *etc* VB *vedi* **erigere**

e'retico, -a, -ci, -che AG heretical ▶ SM/F heretic

e'retto, -a PP *di* **erigere** ▶ AG erect, upright

erezi'one [eret'tsjone] SF (*Fisiol*) erection

ergasto'lano, -a SM/F prisoner serving a life sentence, lifer (*col*)

er'gastolo SM (*Dir: pena*) life imprisonment; (: *luogo di pena*) prison (*for those serving life sentences*)

ergono'mia SF ergonomics *sg*

ergo'nomico, -a, -ci, -che AG ergonomic(al)

'erica SF heather

e'rigere [e'ridʒere] /**39**/ VT to erect, raise; (*fig: fondare*) to found

eri'tema SM (*Med*) inflammation, erythema; **~ solare** sunburn

Eri'trea SF Eritrea

ermel'lino SM ermine

er'metico, -a, -ci, -che AG hermetic

'ernia SF (*Med*) hernia; **~ del disco** slipped disc

'ero VB *vedi* **essere**

e'rodere /**49**/ VT to erode

e'roe SM hero

ero'gare /**80**/ VT (*somme*) to distribute; (*gas, servizi*) to supply

erogazi'one [erogat'tsjone] SF distribution; supply

e'roico, -a, -ci, -che AG heroic

ero'ina SF heroine; (*droga*) heroin

ero'ismo SM heroism

'eros SM Eros

erosi'one SF erosion

e'roso, -a PP *di* **erodere**

e'rotico, -a, -ci, -che AG erotic

ero'tismo SM eroticism

'erpete SM herpes *sg*

'erpice ['erpitʃe] SM (*Agr*) harrow

er'rare /**72**/ VI (*vagare*) to wander, roam; (*sbagliare*) to be mistaken

er'rato, -a AG wrong

er'roneo, -a AG erroneous, wrong

er'rore SM error, mistake; (*morale*) error; **per ~** by mistake; **ci dev'essere un ~** there must be some mistake; **~ giudiziario** miscarriage of justice

'erto, -a AG (very) steep ▶ SF steep slope; **stare all'erta** to be on the alert

eru'dire /**55**/ VT to teach, educate

eru'dito, -a AG learned, erudite

erut'tare /**72**/ VT (*vulcano*) to throw out, belch

eruzi'one [erut'tsjone] SF eruption; (*Med*) rash

es. ABBR (= *esempio*) e.g.

E.S. SIGLA M (= *elettroshock*) ECT

E.S.A. ['eza] SIGLA M (= *European Space Agency*) ESA

esacer'bare [ezatʃer'bare] /**72**/ VT to exacerbate

esage'rare [ezadʒe'rare] /**72**/ VT to exaggerate ▶ VI to exaggerate; (*eccedere*) to go too far; **senza ~** without exaggeration

esage'rato, -a [ezadʒe'rato] AG (*notizia, proporzioni*) exaggerated; (*curiosità, pignoleria*) excessive; (*prezzo*) exorbitant ▶ SM/F: **sei il solito ~** you are exaggerating as usual

esagerazi'one [esadʒerat'tsjone] SF exaggeration

esago'nale AG hexagonal

e'sagono SM hexagon

esa'lare /**72**/ VT (*odori*) to give off ▶ VI: **~ (da)** to emanate (from); **~ l'ultimo respiro** (*fig*) to breathe one's last

esalazi'one [ezalat'tsjone] SF (*emissione*) exhalation; (*odore*) fumes *pl*

esal'tante AG exciting

esal'tare /**72**/ VT to exalt; (*entusiasmare*) to excite, stir; **esaltarsi** VPR: **esaltarsi (per qc)** to grow excited (about sth)

esal'tato, -a SM/F fanatic

esaltazi'one [ezaltat'tsjone] SF (*elogio*) extolling, exalting; (*nervosa*) intense excitement; (*mistica*) exaltation

e'same SM examination; (*Ins*) exam, examination; **fare** o **dare un ~** to take an exam; **fare un ~ di coscienza** to search one's conscience; **~ di guida** driving test; **~ del sangue** blood test

esami'nare /**72**/ VT to examine

e'sangue AG bloodless; (*fig: pallido*) pale, wan; (: *privo di vigore*) lifeless

e'sanime AG lifeless

esaspe'rare /**72**/ VT to exasperate; (*situazione*) to exacerbate; **esasperarsi** VPR to become annoyed o exasperated

esasperazi'one [ezasperat'tsjone] SF exasperation

esatta'mente AV exactly; accurately, precisely

esat'tezza [ezat'tettsa] SF exactitude, accuracy, precision; **per l'~** to be precise

e'satto, -a PP *di* **esigere** ▶ AG (*calcolo, ora*) correct, right, exact; (*preciso*) accurate, precise; (*puntuale*) punctual

esat'tore SM (*di imposte ecc*) collector

esatto'ria SF: **~ comunale** district rates office (*BRIT*) o assessor's office (*US*)

esau'dire /55/ VT to grant, fulfil (BRIT), fulfill (US)

esauri'ente AG exhaustive

esauri'mento SM exhaustion; **~ nervoso** nervous breakdown; **svendita (fino) ad ~ della merce** clearance sale

esau'rire /55/ VT (stancare) to exhaust, wear out; (provviste, miniera) to exhaust; **esaurirsi** VPR to exhaust o.s., wear o.s. out; (provviste) to run out

esau'rito, -a AG exhausted; (merci) sold out; (libri) out of print; **essere ~** (persona) to be run down; **registrare il tutto ~** (Teat) to have a full house

e'sausto, -a AG exhausted

esauto'rare /72/ VT (dirigente, funzionario) to deprive of authority

esazi'one [ezat'tsjone] SF collection (of taxes)

'esca (pl **esche**) SF bait

escamo'tage [ɛskamɔ'taʒ] SM subterfuge

escande'scenza [eskandeʃʃentsa] SF: **dare in escandescenze** to lose one's temper, fly into a rage

'esce ['ɛʃʃe] VB vedi **uscire**

eschi'mese [eski'mese] AG, SMF, SM Eskimo

'esci ['ɛʃʃi] VB vedi **uscire**

escl. ABBR (= escluso) excl

escla'mare /72/ VI to exclaim, cry out

esclama'tivo, -a AG: **punto ~** exclamation mark

esclamazi'one [esklamat'tsjone] SF exclamation

es'cludere /3/ VT to exclude

es'clusi etc VB vedi **escludere**

esclusi'one SF exclusion; **a ~ di**, **fatta ~ per** except (for), apart from; **senza ~ (alcuna)** without exception; **procedere per ~** to follow a process of elimination; **senza ~ di colpi** (fig) with no holds barred; **~ sociale** social exclusion

esclu'siva SF vedi **esclusivo**

esclusiva'mente AV exclusively, solely

esclu'sivo, -a AG exclusive ▶ SF (Dir, Comm) exclusive o sole rights pl

es'cluso, -a PP di **escludere** ▶ AG: **nessuno ~** without exception; **IVA esclusa** excluding VAT, exclusive of VAT

'esco VB vedi **uscire**

escogi'tare [eskodʒi'tare] /72/ VT to devise, think up

'escono VB vedi **uscire**

escoriazi'one [eskorjat'tsjone] SF abrasion, graze

escre'menti SMPL excrement sg, faeces

escursi'one SF (gita) excursion, trip; (: a piedi) hike, walk; (Meteor): **~ termica** temperature range

escursio'nista, -i, -e SM/F (gitante) (day) tripper; (a piedi) hiker, walker

ese'crare /72/ VT to loathe, abhor

esecu'tivo, -a AG, SM executive

esecu'tore, -'trice SM/F (Mus) performer; (Dir) executor

esecuzi'one [ezekut'tsjone] SF execution, carrying out; (Mus) performance; **~ capitale** execution

ese'geta, -i [eze'dʒɛta] SM commentator

esegu'ire /45/ VT to carry out, execute; (Mus) to perform, execute

e'sempio SM example; **per ~** for example, for instance; **fare un ~** to give an example

esem'plare AG exemplary ▶ SM example; (copia) copy; (Bot, Zool, Geo) specimen

esemplifi'care /20/ VT to exemplify

esen'tare /72/ VT: **~ qn/qc da** to exempt sb/sth from

esen'tasse AG INV tax-free

e'sente AG: **~ da** (dispensato da) exempt from; (privo di) free from

esenzi'one [ezen'tsjone] SF exemption

e'sequie SFPL funeral rites; funeral service sg

eser'cente [ezer'tʃente] SMF trader, dealer; shopkeeper

eserci'tare [ezertʃi'tare] /72/ VT (professione) to practise (BRIT), practice (US); (allenare: corpo, mente) to exercise, train; (: diritto) to exercise; (: influenza, pressione) to exert; **esercitarsi** VPR to practise; **esercitarsi nella guida** to practise one's driving

esercitazi'one [ezertʃitat'tsjone] SF (scolastica, militare) exercise; **esercitazioni di tiro** target practice sg

e'sercito [e'zertʃito] SM army

eser'cizio [ezer'tʃittsjo] SM practice; (compito, movimento) exercise; (azienda) business, concern; exercising; (fisico: di matematica) exercise; (Econ): **~ finanziario** financial year; **in ~** (medico ecc) practising (BRIT), practicing (US); **nell'~ delle proprie funzioni** in the execution of one's duties

esfoli'ante SM exfoliator

esi'bire /55/ VT to exhibit, display; (documenti) to produce, present; **esibirsi** VPR (attore) to perform; (fig) to show off

esibizi'one [ezibit'tsjone] SF exhibition; (di documento) presentation; (spettacolo) show, performance

esibizio'nista, -i, -e [ezibittsjo'nista] SM/F exhibitionist

esi'gente [ezi'dʒɛnte] AG demanding

esi'genza [ezi'dʒɛntsa] SF demand, requirement

e'sigere [e'zidʒere] /47/ VT (pretendere) to demand; (richiedere) to demand, require; (imposte) to collect

esi'gibile [ezi'dʒibile] AG payable

e'siguo, -a AG small, slight

esila'rante AG hilarious; **gas ~** laughing gas

'**esile** AG (*persona*) slender, slim; (*stelo*) thin; (*voce*) faint

esili'are /**19**/ VT to exile

esili'ato, -a AG exiled ▶ SM/F exile

e'silio SM exile

e'simere /**29**/ VT: ~ **qn/qc da** to exempt sb/sth from; **esimersi** VPR: **esimersi da** to get out of

esis'tente AG existing; (*attuale*) present, current

esis'tenza [ezis'tɛntsa] SF existence

esistenzia'lismo [ezistɛntsja'lizmo] SM existentialism

e'sistere /**11**/ VI to exist; **esiste più di una versione dell'opera** there is more than one version of the work; **non esiste!** (*col*) no way!

esis'tito, -a PP *di* **esistere**

esi'tante AG hesitant; (*voce*) faltering

esi'tare /**72**/ VI to hesitate

esitazi'one [ezitat'tsjone] SF hesitation

'**esito** SM result, outcome

'**eskimo** SM (*giaccone*) parka

'**esodo** SM exodus

e'sofago, -gi SM oesophagus (BRIT), esophagus (US)

esone'rare /**72**/ VT: ~ **qn da** to exempt sb from

esorbi'tante AG exorbitant, excessive

esor'cismo [ezor'tʃizmo] SM exorcism

esor'cista, -i [ezor'tʃista] SM exorcist

esorciz'zare [ezortʃid'dzare] /**72**/ VT to exorcize

esordi'ente SMF beginner

e'sordio SM debut

esor'dire /**55**/ VI (*nel teatro*) to make one's debut; (*fig*) to start out, begin (one's career); **esordì dicendo che ...** he began by saying (that) ...

esor'tare /**72**/ VT: ~ **qn a fare** to urge sb to do

esortazi'one [ezortat'tsjone] SF exhortation

e'soso, -a AG (*prezzo*) exorbitant; (*persona: avido*) grasping

eso'terico, -a, -ci, -che AG esoteric

e'sotico, -a, -ci, -che AG exotic

es'pandere /**110**/ VT to expand; (*confini*) to extend; (*influenza*) to extend, spread; **espandersi** VPR to expand

espansi'one SF expansion; ~ **di memoria** (*Inform*) memory upgrade

espansività SF expansiveness

espan'sivo, -a AG expansive, communicative

es'panso, -a PP *di* **espandere**

espatri'are /**19**/ VI to leave one's country

es'patrio SM expatriation; **permesso di ~** authorization to leave the country

espedi'ente SM expedient; **vivere di espedienti** to live by one's wits

es'pellere /**48**/ VT to expel

esperi'enza [espe'rjɛntsa] SF experience; (*Sci: prova*) experiment; **parlare per ~** to speak from experience

esperi'mento SM experiment; **fare un ~** to carry out *o* do an experiment

es'perto, -a AG, SM/F expert

espi'anto SM (*Med*) removal

espi'are /**60**/ VT to atone for

espiazi'one [espiat'tsjone] SF: ~ **(di)** expiation (of), atonement (for)

espi'rare /**72**/ VT, VI to breathe out

espleta'mento SM (*Amm*) carrying out

esple'tare /**72**/ VT (*Amm*) to carry out

espli'care /**20**/ VT (*attività*) to carry out, perform

esplica'tivo, -a AG explanatory

es'plicito, -a [es'plitʃito] AG explicit

es'plodere /**49**/ VI (*anche fig*) to explode ▶ VT to fire

esplo'rare /**72**/ VT to explore

esplora'tore, -'trice SM/F explorer; (*anche:* **giovane esploratore**) (boy) scout/(girl) guide (BRIT) *o* scout (US) ▶ SM (*Naut*) scout (ship)

esplorazi'one [esplorat'tsjone] SF exploration; **mandare qn in ~** (*Mil*) to send sb to scout ahead

esplosi'one SF (*anche fig*) explosion

esplo'sivo, -a AG, SM explosive

es'ploso, -a PP *di* **esplodere**

es'pone *etc* VB *vedi* **esporre**

espo'nente SMF (*rappresentante*) representative

esponenzi'ale [esponen'tsjale] AG (*Mat*) exponential

es'pongo, es'poni *etc* VB *vedi* **esporre**

es'porre /**77**/ VT (*merci*) to display; (*quadro*) to exhibit, show; (*fatti, idee*) to explain, set out; (*porre in pericolo, Fot*) to expose; **esporsi** VPR: **esporsi a** (*sole, pericolo*) to expose o.s. to; (*critiche*) to lay o.s. open to

espor'tare /**72**/ VT to export

esporta'tore, -'trice AG exporting ▶ SM exporter

esportazi'one [esportat'tsjone] SF (*azione*) exportation, export; (*insieme di prodotti*) exports *pl*

es'pose *etc* VB *vedi* **esporre**

espo'simetro SM exposure meter

esposizi'one [espozit'tsjone] SF displaying; exhibiting; setting out; (*anche Fot*) exposure; (*mostra*) exhibition; (*narrazione*) explanation, exposition

es'posto, -a PP *di* **esporre** ▶ AG: ~ **a nord** facing north, north-facing ▶ SM (*Amm*) statement, account; (: *petizione*) petition

espressi'one SF expression

espres'sivo, -a AG expressive

es'presso, -a PP di **esprimere** ▶ AG express
▶ SM (lettera) express letter; (anche: **treno espresso**) express train; (anche: **caffè espresso**) espresso
es'primere /**50**/ VT to express; **esprimersi** VPR to express o.s.
espropri'are /**19**/ VT (terreni, edifici) to place a compulsory purchase order on; (persona) to dispossess
espropriazi'one [esproprjat'tsjone] SF, **es'proprio** SM expropriation; ~ **per pubblica utilità** compulsory purchase
espu'gnare [espuɲ'ɲare] /**15**/ VT to take by force, storm
es'pulsi etc VB vedi **espellere**
espulsi'one SF expulsion
es'pulso, -a PP di **espellere**
'essa PRON F (pl **esse**) vedi **esso**
es'senza [es'sɛntsa] SF essence
essenzi'ale [essen'tsjale] AG essential; (stile, linea) simple ▶ SM: **l'~** the main o most important thing

(**PAROLA CHIAVE**)

'essere /**51**/ SM being; **essere umano** human being
▶ VB COPULATIVO **1** (con attributo, sostantivo) to be; **sei giovane/simpatico** you are o you're young/nice; **è medico** he is o he's a doctor
2 (+ di: appartenere) to be; **di chi è la penna?** whose pen is it?; **è di Carla** it is o it's Carla's, it belongs to Carla
3 (+ di: provenire) to be; **è di Venezia** he is o he's from Venice
4 (data, ora): **è il 15 agosto** it is o it's the 15th of August; **è lunedì** it is o it's Monday; **che ora è?, che ore sono?** what time is it?; **è l'una** it is o it's one o'clock; **sono le due** it is o it's two o'clock
5 (costare): **quant'è?** how much is it?; **sono 20 euro** it's 20 euros
▶ VB AUS **1** (attivo): **essere arrivato/venuto** to have arrived/come; **è già partita** she has already left
2 (passivo) to be; **essere fatto da** to be made by; **è stata uccisa** she has been killed
3 (riflessivo): **si sono lavati** they washed, they got washed
4 (+ da + infinito): **è da farsi subito** it must be done o is to be done immediately
▶ VI **1** (esistere, trovarsi) to be; **sono a casa** I'm at home; **essere in piedi/seduto** to be standing/sitting
2 (succedere): **sarà quel che sarà** what will be will be; **sia quel che sia, io me ne vado** come what may, I'm going now
3: **esserci**: **c'è** there is; **ci sono** there are; **che c'è?** what's the matter?, what is it?; **non c'è niente da fare** there's nothing we

can do; **c'è da sperare che ...** one can only hope that ...; **ci sono!** (sono pronto) I'm ready; (ho capito) I get it!
▶ VB IMPERS: **è tardi/Pasqua** it's late/Easter; **è mezzanotte** it's midnight; **è bello/caldo/freddo** it's nice/hot/cold; **è possibile che venga** he may come; **è così** that's the way it is

'essi PRON MPL vedi **esso**
essic'care /**20**/ VT (gen) to dry; (legname) to season; (cibi) to desiccate; (bacino, palude) to drain; **essiccarsi** VPR (fiume, pozzo) to dry up; (vernice) to dry (out)
'esso, -a PRON it; (riferito a persona: soggetto) he (she); (: complemento) him (her); **essi, e** PRON PL (soggetto) they; (complemento) them
est SM east; **i paesi dell'E~** the Eastern bloc sg
'estasi SF ecstasy
estasi'are /**19**/ VT to send into raptures; **estasiarsi** VPR: **estasiarsi (davanti a)** to go into ecstasies (over), go into raptures (over)
es'tate SF summer
es'tatico, -a, -ci, -che AG ecstatic
estempo'raneo, -a AG (discorso) extempore, impromptu; (brano musicale) impromptu
es'tendere /**120**/ VT to extend; **estendersi** VPR (diffondersi) to spread; (territorio, confini) to extend
estensi'one SF extension; (di superficie) expanse; (di voce) range
estenu'ante AG wearing, tiring
estenu'are /**72**/ VT (stancare) to wear out, tire out
esteri'ore AG outward, external
esteriorità SF INV outward appearance
esterioriz'zare [esterjorid'dzare] /**72**/ VT (gioia ecc) to show
ester'nare /**72**/ VT to express; **~ un sospetto** to voice a suspicion
es'terno, -a AG (porta, muro) outer, outside; (scala) outside; (alunno, impressione) external ▶ SM outside, exterior ▶ SM/F (allievo) day pupil; **esterni** SMPL (Cine) location shots; **"per uso ~"** "for external use only"; **all'~** outside; **gli esterni sono stati girati a Glasgow** the location shots were taken in Glasgow
es'tero, -a AG foreign ▶ SM: **all'~** abroad; **Ministero degli Esteri, gli Esteri** Ministry for Foreign Affairs, ≈ Foreign Office (BRIT), ≈ State Department (US)
esterofi'lia SF excessive love of foreign things
esterre'fatto, -a AG (costernato) horrified; (sbalordito) astounded
es'tesi etc VB vedi **estendere**
es'teso, -a PP di **estendere** ▶ AG extensive, large; **scrivere per ~** to write in full

estetica'mente AV aesthetically

es'tetico, -a, -ci, -che AG aesthetic ▶ SF (disciplina) aesthetics sg; (bellezza) attractiveness; **chirurgia estetica** cosmetic surgery; **cura estetica** beauty treatment

este'tista, -i, -e SM/F beautician

'estimo SM valuation; (disciplina) surveying

es'tinguere /42/ VT to extinguish, put out; (debito) to pay off; (conto) to close; **estinguersi** VPR to go out; (specie) to become extinct

es'tinsi etc VB vedi **estinguere**

es'tinto, -a PP di **estinguere**

estin'tore SM (fire) extinguisher

estinzi'one [estin'tsjone] SF putting out; (di specie) extinction; (di debito) payment; (di conto) closing

estir'pare /72/ VT (pianta) to uproot, pull up; (dente) to extract; (tumore) to remove; (fig: vizio) to eradicate

es'tivo, -a AG summer cpd

'estone AG, SMF, SM Estonian

Es'tonia SF: **l'~** Estonia

es'torcere [es'tɔrtʃere] **/106/** VT: **~ qc (a qn)** to extort sth (from sb)

estorsi'one SF extortion

es'torto, -a PP di **estorcere**

estra'dare /72/ VT to extradite

estradizi'one [estradit'tsjone] SF extradition

es'trae, es'traggo etc VB vedi **estrarre**

es'traneo, -a AG foreign; (discorso) extraneous, unrelated ▶ SM/F stranger; **rimanere ~ a qc** to take no part in sth; **sentirsi ~ a** (famiglia, società) to feel alienated from; **"ingresso vietato agli estranei"** "no admittance to unauthorized personnel"

estrani'arsi /19/ VPR: **~ (da)** to cut o.s. off (from)

es'trarre /123/ VT to extract; (minerali) to mine; (sorteggiare) to draw; **~ a sorte** to draw lots

es'trassi etc VB vedi **estrarre**

es'tratto, -a PP di **estrarre** ▶ SM extract; (di documento) abstract; **~ conto** (bank) statement; **~ di nascita** birth certificate

estrazi'one [estrat'tsjone] SF extraction; mining; drawing no pl; draw

estrema'mente AV extremely

estre'mismo SM extremism

estre'mista, -i, -e SM/F extremist

estremità SF INV extremity, end ▶ SFPL (Anat) extremities

es'tremo, -a AG extreme; (ultimo: ora, tentativo) final, last ▶ SM extreme; (di pazienza, forza) limit, end; **estremi** SMPL (Amm: dati essenziali) details, particulars; **l'E~ Oriente** the Far East

estrinse'care /20/ VT to express, show

'estro SM (capriccio) whim, fancy; (ispirazione creativa) inspiration

estro'messo, -a PP di **estromettere**

estro'mettere /63/ VT: **~ (da)** (partito, club ecc) to expel (from); (discussione) to exclude (from)

estromissi'one SF expulsion

es'troso, -a AG whimsical, capricious; inspired

estro'verso, -a AG, SM extrovert

estu'ario SM estuary

esube'rante AG exuberant; (Comm) redundant (BRIT)

esube'ranza [ezube'rantsa] SF (di persona) exuberance; **~ di personale** (Comm) overmanning (BRIT), over-staffing (US)

e'subero SM: **~ di personale** surplus staff; **in ~** redundant, due to be laid off

esu'lare /72/ VI: **~ da** (competenza) to be beyond; (compiti) not to be part of

'esule SMF exile

esul'tanza [ezul'tantsa] SF exultation

esul'tare /72/ VI to exult

esu'mare /72/ VT (salma) to exhume, disinter; (fig) to unearth

età SF INV age; **all'~ di 8 anni** at the age of 8, at 8 years of age; **ha la mia ~** he (o she) is the same age as me o as I am; **di mezza ~** middle-aged; **raggiungere la maggiore ~** to come of age; **essere in ~ minore** to be under age; **in ~ avanzata** advanced in years

eta'nolo SM ethanol

etc. ABBR etc.

'etere SM ether; **via ~** on the airwaves

e'tereo, -a AG ethereal

eternità SF eternity

e'terno, -a AG eternal; (interminabile: lamenti, attesa) never-ending; **in ~** for ever, eternally

etero'geneo, -a [etero'dʒɛneo] AG heterogeneous

eterosessu'ale AG, SMF heterosexual

'etica SF vedi **etico**

eti'chetta [eti'ketta] SF label; (cerimoniale): **l'~** etiquette

'etico, -a, -ci, -che AG ethical ▶ SF ethics sg

eti'lometro SM Breathalyzer®

etimolo'gia, -'gie [etimolo'dʒia] SF etymology

etimo'logico, -a, -ci, -che [etimo'lɔdʒiko] AG etymological

e'tiope AG, SMF Ethiopian

Eti'opia SF: **l'~** Ethiopia

eti'opico, -a, -ci, -che AG, SM (Ling) Ethiopian

'Etna SM: **l'~** Etna

'etnico, -a, -ci, -che AG ethnic

e'trusco, -a, -schi, -sche AG, SM/F Etruscan

'ettaro SM hectare (10,000 m²)

'etto ABBR M (= ettogrammo) 100 grams

etto'grammo SM hectogram(me) (= 100 grams)

etto'litro SM hectolitre (BRIT), hectoliter (US)

et'tometro SM hectometre

EU ABBR = **Europa**

euca'lipto SM eucalyptus

Eucaris'tia SF: **l'**~ the Eucharist
eufe'mismo SM euphemism
eufe'mistico, -a, -ci, -che AG euphemistic
eufo'ria SF euphoria
eu'forico, -a, -ci, -che AG euphoric
Eu'rasia SF Eurasia
eurasi'atico, -a, -ci, -che AG, SM/F Eurasian
Eura'tom SIGLA F (= *Comunità Europea dell'Energia Atomica*) Euratom
eu'ristico, -a, -ci, -che AG heuristic
'euro SM INV (*divisa*) euro
euro'corpo SM European force
eurodepu'tato SM Euro MP
eurodi'visa SF Eurocurrency
euro'dollaro SM Eurodollar
Euro'landia SF Euroland
euromer'cato SM Euromarket
euro'missile SM Euro-missile
Eu'ropa SF: **l'**~ Europe
europarlamen'tare SMF Member of the European Parliament, MEP
euro'peo, -a AG, SM/F European
euro'scettico, -a, -ci, -che [euroʃʃettiko] SM/F Euro-sceptic
eutana'sia SF euthanasia
E.V. ABBR = **Eccellenza Vostra**
evacu'are /**72**/ VT to evacuate
evacuazi'one [evakuat'tsjone] SF evacuation
e'vadere /**52**/ VI (*fuggire*): ~ **da** to escape from ▶ VT (*sbrigare*) to deal with, dispatch; (*tasse*) to evade
evan'gelico, -a, -ci, -che [evan'dʒɛliko] AG evangelical
evange'lista, -i [evandʒe'lista] SM evangelist
evapo'rare /**72**/ VI to evaporate
evaporazi'one [evaporat'tsjone] SF evaporation
e'vasi etc VB vedi **evadere**
evasi'one SF (*vedi* evadere) escape; dispatch; **dare** ~ **ad un ordine** to carry out o execute an order; **letteratura d'**~ escapist literature; ~ **fiscale** tax evasion
eva'sivo, -a AG evasive
e'vaso, -a PP di **evadere** ▶ SM escapee
eva'sore SM: ~ (**fiscale**) tax evader
eveni'enza [eve'njɛntsa] SF: **nell'**~ **che ciò succeda** should that happen; **essere pronto ad ogni** ~ to be ready for anything o any eventuality
e'vento SM event
eventu'ale AG possible

eventualità SF INV eventuality, possibility; **nell'**~ **di** in the event of
eventual'mente AV if need be, if necessary
'Everest SM: **l'**~, **il Monte** ~ (Mount) Everest
eversi'one SF subversion
ever'sivo, -a AG subversive
evi'dente AG evident, obvious
evidente'mente AV evidently; (*palesemente*) obviously, evidently
evi'denza [evi'dɛntsa] SF obviousness; **mettere in** ~ to point out, highlight; **tenere in** ~ **qc** to bear sth in mind
evidenzi'are [eviden'tsjare] /**19**/ VT (*sottolineare*) to emphasize, highlight; (*con evidenziatore*) to highlight
evidenzia'tore [evidentsja'tore] SM (*penna*) highlighter
evi'rare /**72**/ VT to castrate
evi'tabile AG avoidable
evi'tare /**72**/ VT to avoid; ~ **di fare** to avoid doing; ~ **qc a qn** to spare sb sth
'evo SM age, epoch
evo'care /**20**/ VT to evoke
evoca'tivo, -a AG evocative
evocherò etc [evoke'rɔ] VB vedi **evocare**
evolu'tivo, -a AG (*gen*, *Biol*) evolutionary; (*Med*) progressive
evo'luto, -a PP di **evolversi** ▶ AG (*popolo, civiltà*) (highly) developed, advanced; (*persona: emancipato*) independent; (: *senza pregiudizi*) broad-minded
evoluzi'one [evolut'tsjone] SF evolution
e'volversi /**94**/ VPR to evolve; **con l'**~ **della situazione** as the situation develops
ev'viva ESCL hurrah!; ~ **il re!** long live the king!, hurrah for the king!
ex PREFISSO ex-, former ▶ SM INV/F INV ex-boyfriend/girlfriend
ex 'aequo [ɛg'zɛkwo] AV: **classificarsi primo** ~ to come joint first, come equal first
'extra AG INV first-rate; top-quality ▶ SM INV extra
extracomuni'tario, -a AG non-EU ▶ SM/F non-EU citizen (*often referred to non-European immigrant*)
extraconiu'gale AG extramarital
extraparlamen'tare AG extraparliamentary
extrasensori'ale AG: **percezione** ~ extrasensory perception
extrater'restre AG, SMF extraterrestrial
extraur'bano, -a AG suburban

Ff

F, f ['ɛffe] SM O F INV (*lettera*) F, f; **F come Firenze** = F for Frederick (BRIT), F for Fox (US)
F ABBR (= *Fahrenheit*) F
F. ABBR (= *fiume*) R
fa VB *vedi* **fare** ▶ SM INV (*Mus*) F; (: *solfeggiando la scala*) fa ▶ AV: **10 anni fa** 10 years ago
fabbi'sogno [fabbi'zoɲɲo] SM needs *pl*, requirements *pl*; **il ~ nazionale di petrolio** the country's oil requirements; **~ del settore pubblico** public sector borrowing requirement (BRIT), government debt borrowing (US)
'fabbrica SF factory
fabbri'cante SM manufacturer, maker
fabbri'care/20/ VT to build; (*produrre*) to manufacture, make; (*fig*) to fabricate, invent
fabbri'cato SM building
fabbricazi'one [fabbrikat'tsjone] SF building, fabrication; making, manufacture, manufacturing
'fabbro SM (black)smith
fac'cenda [fat'tʃɛnda] SF matter, affair; (*cosa da fare*) task, chore; **le faccende domestiche** the housework *sg*
faccendi'ere [fattʃen'djɛre] SM wheeler-dealer, (shady) operator
fac'cetta [fat'tʃetta] SF (*di pietra preziosa*) facet
fac'chino [fak'kino] SM porter
'faccia, -ce ['fattʃa] SF face; (*di moneta, medaglia*) side; **~ a ~** face to face; **di ~ a** opposite, facing; **avere la ~ (tosta) di dire/ fare qc** to have the cheek o nerve to say/do sth; **fare qc alla ~ di qn** to do sth to spite sb; **leggere qc in ~ a qn** to see sth written all over sb's face
facci'ata [fat'tʃata] SF façade; (*di pagina*) side
fac'cina [fat'tʃina] SF (*Inform*) emoticon
'faccioetc ['fattʃo] VB *vedi* **fare**
Facebook® ['feisbuk] SM Facebook®
fa'cente [fa'tʃente]: **~ funzione** *sm* (*Amm*) deputy
fa'cessietc [fa'tʃessi] VB *vedi* **fare**
fa'ceto, -a[fa'tʃeto] AG witty, humorous
fa'cevoetc [fa'tʃevo] VB *vedi* **fare**

fa'cezia [fa'tʃettsja] SF witticism, witty remark
fa'chiro [fa'kiro] SM fakir
'facile ['fatʃile] AG easy; (*affabile*) easy-going; (*disposto*): **~ a** inclined to, prone to; (*probabile*): **è ~ che piova** it's likely to rain; **donna di facili costumi** woman of easy virtue, loose woman
facili'tà [fatʃili'ta] SF easiness; (*disposizione, dono*) aptitude
facili'tare [fatʃili'tare] **/72/** VT to make easier
facilitazi'one [fatʃilitat'tsjone] SF (*gen*) facilities *pl*; **facilitazioni di pagamento** easy terms, credit facilities
facil'mente [fatʃil'mente] AV (*gen*) easily; (*probabilmente*) probably
faci'lone, -a[fatʃi'lone] SM/F (*peg*) happy-go-lucky person
facino'roso, -a[fatʃino'roso] AG violent
facol'tà SF INV faculty; (*Chim*) property; (*autorità*) power
facolta'tivo, -a AG optional; (*fermata d'autobus*) request *cpd*
facol'toso, -a AG wealthy, rich
fac'simile SM facsimile
'faggio ['faddʒo] SM beech
fagi'ano [fa'dʒano] SM pheasant
fagio'lino [fadʒo'lino] SM French (BRIT) o string bean
fagi'olo [fa'dʒɔlo] SM bean; **capitare a ~** to come at the right time
fagoci'tare [fagotʃi'tare] **/72/** VT (*fig: industria ecc*) to absorb, swallow up; (*scherzoso: cibo*) to devour
fa'gotto SM bundle; (*Mus*) bassoon; **far ~** (*fig*) to pack up and go
'Fahrenheit ['fa:rənheit] SM Fahrenheit
'fai VB *vedi* **fare**
'faida SF feud
'fai-da-'te SM INV DIY, do-it-yourself
fa'ina SF (*Zool*) stone marten
fa'lange [fa'landʒe] SF (*Anat, Mil*) phalanx
fal'cata SF stride

'falce ['faltʃe] SF scythe; **~ e martello** (*Pol*) hammer and sickle

fal'cetto [fal'tʃetto] SM sickle

falci'are [fal'tʃare] /**14**/ VT to cut; (*fig*) to mow down

falcia'trice [faltʃa'tritʃe] SF (*per fieno*) reaping machine; (*per erba*) mowing machine

'falco, -chi SM (*anche fig*) hawk

fal'cone SM falcon

'falda SF (*Geo*) layer, stratum; (*di cappello*) brim; (*di cappotto*) tails pl; (*di monte*) lower slope; (*di tetto*) pitch; (*di neve*) flake; **abito a falde** tails pl

fale'gname [falen'ɲame] SM joiner

fa'lena SF (*Zool*) moth

'Falkland ['fɔːlklənd] SFPL: **le isole ~** the Falkland Islands

fal'lace [fal'latʃe] AG misleading, deceptive

'fallico, -a, -ci, -che AG phallic

fallimen'tare AG (*Comm*) bankruptcy cpd; **bilancio ~** negative balance, deficit; **diritto ~** bankruptcy law

falli'mento SM failure; bankruptcy

fal'lire /**55**/ VI (*Dir*) to go bankrupt; (*non riuscire*): **~ (in)** to fail (in) ▶ VT (*colpo, bersaglio*) to miss

fal'lito, -a AG unsuccessful; bankrupt ▶ SM/F bankrupt

'fallo SM error, mistake; (*imperfezione*) defect, flaw; (*Sport*) foul; fault; (*Anat*) phallus; **senza ~** without fail; **cogliere qn in ~** to catch sb out; **mettere il piede in ~** to slip

fal'locrate SM male chauvinist

falò SM INV bonfire

fal'sare /**72**/ VT to distort, misrepresent

falsa'riga, -ghe SF lined page, ruled page; **sulla ~ di ...** (*fig*) along the lines of ...

fal'sario SM forger; counterfeiter

falsifi'care /**20**/ VT to forge; (*monete*) to forge, counterfeit

falsità SF INV (*di persona, notizia*) falseness; (*bugia*) falsehood, lie

'falso, -a AG false; (*errato*) wrong; (*falsificato*) forged; fake; (: *oro, gioielli*) imitation cpd ▶ SM forgery; **essere un ~ magro** to be heavier than one looks; **giurare il ~** to commit perjury; **~ in atto pubblico** forgery (of a legal document)

'fama SF fame; (*reputazione*) reputation, name

'fame SF hunger; **aver ~** to be hungry; **fare la ~** (*fig*) to starve, exist at subsistence level

fa'melico, -a, -ci, -che AG ravenous

famige'rato, -a [famidʒe'rato] AG notorious, ill-famed

fa'miglia [fa'miʎʎa] SF family

famili'are AG (*della famiglia*) family cpd; (*ben noto*) familiar; (*rapporti, atmosfera*) friendly; (*Ling*) informal, colloquial ▶ SM F relative, relation; **una vettura ~** a family car

familiarità SF familiarity; friendliness; informality

familiariz'zare [familjarid'dzare] /**72**/ VI: **~ con qn** to get to know sb; **abbiamo familiarizzato subito** we got on well together from the start

fa'moso, -a AG famous, well-known

fa'nale SM (*Aut*) light, lamp (BRIT); (*luce stradale, Naut*) light; (*di faro*) beacon

fa'natico, -a, -ci, -che AG fanatical; (*del teatro, calcio ecc*): **~ di o per** mad o crazy about ▶ SM/F fanatic; (*tifoso*) fan

fana'tismo SM fanaticism

fanciul'lezza [fantʃul'lettsa] SF childhood

fanci'ullo, -a [fan'tʃullo] SM/F child

fan'donia SF tall story; **fandonie** SFPL nonsense sg

fan'fara SF brass band; (*musica*) fanfare

fanfa'rone SM braggart

fan'ghiglia [fan'giʎʎa] SF mire, mud

'fango, -ghi SM mud; **fare i fanghi** (*Med*) to take a course of mud baths

fan'goso, -a AG muddy

'fanno VB *vedi* **fare**

fannul'lone, -a SM/F idler, loafer

fantasci'enza [fantaʃʃentsa] SF science fiction

fanta'sia SF fantasy, imagination; (*capriccio*) whim, caprice ▶ AG INV: **vestito ~** patterned dress

fantasi'oso, -a AG (*dotato di fantasia*) imaginative; (*bizzarro*) fanciful, strange

fan'tasma, -i SM ghost, phantom

fantasti'care /**20**/ VI to daydream

fantastiche'ria [fantastike'ria] SF daydream

fan'tastico, -a, -ci, -che AG fantastic; (*potenza, ingegno*) imaginative

'fante SM infantryman; (*Carte*) jack, knave (BRIT)

fante'ria SF infantry

fan'tino SM jockey

fan'toccio [fan'tɔttʃo] SM puppet

fanto'matico, -a, -ci, -che AG (*nave, esercito*) phantom cpd; (*personaggio*) mysterious

FAO SIGLA F (= *Food and Agriculture Organization*) FAO

fara'butto SM crook

fara'ona SF guinea fowl

fara'one SM (*Storia*) Pharaoh

fara'onico, -a, -ci, -che AG of the Pharaohs; (*fig*) enormous, huge

far'cire [far'tʃire] /**55**/ VT (*carni, peperoni ecc*) to stuff; (*torte*) to fill

fard [far] SM INV blusher

far'dello SM bundle; (*fig*) burden

'fare /53/ SM **1** (*modo di fare*): **con fare distratto** absent-mindedly; **ha un fare simpatico** he has a pleasant manner **2**: **sul far del giorno/della notte** at daybreak/nightfall

▶ VT **1** (*fabbricare, creare*) to make; (: *casa*) to build; (: *assegno*) to make out; **fare un pasto/ una promessa/un film** to make a meal/ promise/a film; **fare rumore** to make a noise

2 (*effettuare: lavoro, attività, studi*) to do; (: *sport*) to play; **cosa fa?** (*adesso*) what are you doing?; (*di professione*) what do you do?; **fare psicologia/italiano** (*Ins*) to do psychology/ Italian; **fare tennis** to play tennis; **fare un viaggio** to go on a trip *o* journey; **fare una passeggiata** to go for a walk; **fare la spesa** to do the shopping

3 (*funzione*) to be; (: *Teat*) to play, be; **fare il medico** to be a doctor; **fare il malato** (*fingere*) to act the invalid

4 (*suscitare: sentimenti*): **fare paura a qn** to frighten sb; **mi fa rabbia** it makes me angry; **(non) fa niente** (*non importa*) it doesn't matter

5 (*ammontare*): **3 più 3 fa 6** 3 and 3 are *o* make 6; **fanno 6 euro** that's 6 euros; **Roma fa oltre 2.000.000 di abitanti** Rome has over 2,000,000 inhabitants; **che ora fai?** what time do you make it?

6 (+ *infinito*): **far fare qc a qn** (*obbligare*) to make sb do sth; (*permettere*) to let sb do sth; **fare piangere/ridere qn** to make sb cry/ laugh; **fare venire qn** to send for sb; **fammi vedere** let me see; **far partire il motore** to start (up) the engine; **far riparare la macchina/costruire una casa** to get *o* have the car repaired/a house built

7: **farsi**: **farsi una gonna** to make o.s. a skirt; **farsi un nome** to make a name for o.s.; **farsi la permanente** to get a perm; **farsi notare** to get o.s. noticed; **farsi tagliare i capelli** to get one's hair cut; **farsi operare** to have an operation

8 (*fraseologia*): **farcela** to succeed, manage; **non ce la faccio più** I can't go on; **ce la faremo** we'll make it; **me l'hanno fatta!** (*imbrogliare*) I've been done!; **lo facevo più giovane** I thought he was younger; **fare sì/ no con la testa** to nod/shake one's head

▶ VI **1** (*agire*) to act, do; **fate come volete** do as you like; **fare presto** to be quick; **fare da** to act as; **non c'è niente da fare** it's no use; **saperci fare con qn/qc** to know how to deal with sb/sth; **ci sa fare** she's very good at it; **faccia pure!** go ahead!

2 (*dire*) to say; **"davvero?" fece** "really?" he said

3: **fare per** (*essere adatto*) to be suitable for;

fare per fare qc to be about to do sth; **fece per andarsene** he made as if to leave

4: **farsi**: **si fa così** you do it like this, this is the way it's done; **non si fa così!** (*rimprovero*) that's no way to behave!; **la festa non si fa** the party is off

5: **fare a gara con qn** to compete with sb; **fare a pugni** to come to blows; **fare in tempo a fare** to be in time to do

▶ VB IMPERS: **fa bel tempo** the weather is fine; **fa caldo/freddo** it's hot/cold; **fa notte** it's getting dark

▶ VPR **1** (*diventare*) to become; **farsi prete** to become a priest; **farsi grande/vecchio** to grow tall/old

2 (*spostarsi*): **farsi avanti/indietro** to move forward/back; **fatti più in là** move along a bit

3 (*col: drogarsi*) to be a junkie

fa'retra SF quiver
far'falla SF butterfly
farfugli'are [farfuʎ'ʎare] /27/ VT, VI to mumble, mutter
fa'rina SF flour; **~ gialla** maize (*BRIT*) *o* corn (*US*) flour; **~ integrale** wholemeal (*BRIT*) *o* whole-wheat (*US*) flour; **questa non è ~ del tuo sacco** (*fig*) this isn't your own idea (*o* work)
fari'nacei [fari'natʃei] SMPL starches
fa'ringe [fa'rindʒe] SF (*Anat*) pharynx
farin'gite [farin'dʒite] SF pharyngitis
fari'noso, -a AG (*patate*) floury; (*neve, mela*) powdery
farma'ceutico, -a, -ci, -che [farma'tʃeutiko] AG pharmaceutical
farma'cia, -'cie [farma'tʃia] SF pharmacy; (*negozio*) chemist's (shop) (*BRIT*), pharmacy
farma'cista, -i, -e [farma'tʃista] SM/F chemist (*BRIT*), pharmacist
'farmaco, -ci, -chi (SM drug, medicine
farneti'care /20/ VI to rave, be delirious
'faro SM (*Naut*) lighthouse; (*Aer*) beacon; (*Aut*) headlight, headlamp (*BRIT*)
farragi'noso, -a [farradʒi'noso] AG (*stile*) muddled, confused
'farsa SF farce
far'sesco, -a, -schi, -sche AG farcical
fasc. ABBR = **fascicolo**
'fascia, -sce ['faʃʃa] SF band, strip; (*Med*) bandage; (*di sindaco, ufficiale*) sash; (*parte di territorio*) strip, belt; (*di contribuenti ecc*) group, band; **essere in fasce** (*anche fig*) to be in one's infancy; **~ oraria** time band
fasci'are [faʃ'ʃare] /14/ VT to bind; (*Med*) to bandage; (*bambino*) to put a nappy (*BRIT*) *o* diaper (*US*) on
fascia'tura [faʃʃa'tura] SF (*azione*) bandaging; (*fascia*) bandage

fa'scicolo [faʃʃikolo] SM (*di documenti*) file, dossier; (*di rivista*) issue, number; (*opuscolo*) booklet, pamphlet

'fascino ['faʃʃino] SM charm, fascination

'fascio ['faʃʃo] SM bundle, sheaf; (*di fiori*) bunch; (*di luce*) beam; (*Pol*): **il F~** the Fascist Party

fa'scismo [faʃʃizmo] SM fascism

fa'scista, -i, -e [faʃʃista] AG, SM/F fascist

'fase SF phase; (*Tecn*) stroke; **in ~ di espansione** in a period of expansion; **essere fuori ~** (*motore*) to be rough (BRIT), run roughly; (*fig*) to feel rough (BRIT) *o* rotten

fas'tidio SM bother, trouble; **dare ~ a qn** to bother *o* annoy sb; **sento ~ allo stomaco** my stomach's upset; **avere fastidi con la polizia** to have trouble *o* bother with the police

fastidi'oso, -a AG annoying, tiresome; (*schifiltoso*) fastidious

'fasto SM pomp, splendour (BRIT), splendor (US)

fas'toso, -a AG sumptuous, lavish

fa'sullo, -a AG (*gen*) fake; (*dichiarazione, persona*) false; (*pretesto*) bogus

'fata SF fairy

fa'tale AG fatal; (*inevitabile*) inevitable; (*fig*) irresistible

fata'lismo SM fatalism

fatalità SF INV inevitability; (*avversità*) misfortune; (*fato*) fate, destiny

fa'tato, -a AG (*spada, chiave*) magic; (*castello*) enchanted

fa'tica, -che SF hard work, toil; (*sforzo*) effort; (*di metalli*) fatigue; **a ~** with difficulty; **respirare a ~** to have difficulty (in) breathing; **fare ~ a fare qc** to find it difficult to do sth; **animale da ~** beast of burden

fati'caccia, -ce [fati'kattʃa] SF: **fu una ~** it was hard work, it was a hell of a job (*col*)

fati'care /20/ VI to toil; **~ a fare qc** to have difficulty doing sth

fati'cata SF hard work

fa'tichi *etc* [fa'tiki] VB *vedi* **faticare**

fati'coso, -a AG (*viaggio, camminata*) tiring, exhausting; (*lavoro*) laborious

fa'tidico, -a, -ci, -che AG fateful

'fato SM fate, destiny

Fatt. ABBR (= *fattura*) inv

fat'taccio [fat'tattʃo] SM foul deed

fat'tezze [fat'tettse] SFPL features

fat'tibile AG feasible, possible

fattis'pecie [fattis'pɛtʃe] SF: **nella** *o* **in ~** in this case *o* instance

'fatto, -a PP *di* **fare** ▶ AG: **un uomo ~** a grown man ▶ SM fact; (*azione*) deed; (*avvenimento*) event, occurrence; (*di romanzo, film*) action, story; **~ a mano/in casa** hand-/home-made;

è ben fatta she has a nice figure; **cogliere qn sul ~** to catch sb red-handed; **il ~ sta** *o* **è che** the fact remains *o* is that; **in ~ di** as for, as far as ... is concerned; **fare i fatti propri** to mind one's own business; **è uno che sa il ~ suo** he knows what he's about; **gli ho detto il ~ suo** I told him what I thought of him; **porre qn di fronte al ~ compiuto** to present sb with a fait accompli; **coppia/unione di ~** long-standing relationship

fat'tore SM (*Agr*) farm manager; (*Mat: elemento costitutivo*) factor; **~ di protezione** (*di lozione solare*) factor

fatto'ria SF farm; (*casa*) farmhouse

fatto'rino SM errand boy; (*di ufficio*) office boy; (*d'albergo*) porter

fattucchi'era [fattuk'kjera] SF witch

fat'tura SF (*Comm*) invoice; (*di abito*) tailoring; (*malia*) spell; **pagamento contro presentazione ~** payment on invoice

fattu'rare /72/ VT (*Comm*) to invoice; (*prodotto*) to produce; (*vino*) to adulterate

fattu'rato SM (*Comm*) turnover

fatturazi'one [fatturat'tsjone] SF billing, invoicing

'fatuo, -a AG vain, fatuous; **fuoco ~** (*anche fig*) will-o'-the-wisp

'fauci ['fautʃi] SFPL (*di leone ecc*) jaws; (*di vulcano*) mouth *sg*

'fauna SF fauna

'fausto, -a AG (*formale*) happy; **un ~ presagio** a good omen

fau'tore, -'trice SM/F advocate, supporter

'fava SF broad bean

fa'vella SF speech

fa'villa SF spark

'favo SM (*di api*) honeycomb

'favola SF (*fiaba*) fairy tale; (*d'intento morale*) fable; (*fandonia*) yarn; **essere la ~ del paese** (*oggetto di critica*) to be the talk of the town; (*zimbello*) to be a laughing stock

favo'loso, -a AG fabulous; (*incredibile*) incredible

fa'vore SM favour (BRIT), favor (US); **per ~** please; **prezzo/trattamento di ~** preferential price/treatment; **condizioni di ~** (*Comm*) favo(u)rable terms; **fare un ~ a qn** to do sb a favour; **col ~ delle tenebre** under cover of darkness

favoreggia'mento [favoreddʒa'mento] SM (*Dir*) aiding and abetting

favo'revole AG favourable (BRIT), favorable (US)

favo'rire /55/ VT to favour (BRIT), favor (US); (*il commercio, l'industria, le arti*) to promote, encourage; **vuole ~?** won't you help yourself?; **favorisca in salotto** please come into the sitting room; **mi favorisca i documenti** please may I see your papers?

favori'tismo SM favouritism (BRIT), favoritism (US)

favo'rito, -a AG, SM/F favourite (BRIT), favorite (US)

fax SM INV fax; **mandare qc via** ~ to fax sth

fa'xare /72/ VT to fax

fazi'one [fat'tsjone] SF faction

faziosità [fattsjosi'ta] SF sectarianism

fazzo'letto [fattso'letto] SM handkerchief; (_per la testa_) (head)scarf; ~ **di carta** tissue

F.B.I. SIGLA F (= _Federal Bureau of Investigation_) FBI

F.C. ABBR = **fuoricorso**

f.co ABBR = **franco**

FE SIGLA = **Ferrara**

febb. ABBR (= _febbraio_) Feb

feb'braio SM February; _vedi anche_ **luglio**

'febbre SF fever; **aver la** ~ to have a high temperature; ~ **da fieno** hay fever

feb'brile AG (_anche fig_) feverish

'feccia, -ce ['fettʃa] SF dregs _pl_

'feci ['fɛtʃi] SFPL faeces, excrement _sg_

'feci _etc_ ['fɛtʃi] VB _vedi_ **fare**

'fecola SF potato flour

fecon'dare /72/ VT to fertilize

fecondazi'one [fekondat'tsjone] SF fertilization; ~ **artificiale** artificial insemination

fecondità SF fertility

fe'condo, -a AG fertile

'Fedcom SIGLA M = **Fondo Europeo di Cooperazione Monetaria**

'fede SF (_credenza_) belief, faith; (_Rel_) faith; (_fiducia_) faith, trust; (_fedeltà_) loyalty; (_anello_) wedding ring; (_attestato_) certificate; **aver ~ in qn** to have faith in sb; **tener ~ a** (_ideale_) to remain loyal to; (_giuramento, promessa_) to keep; **in buona/cattiva** ~ in good/bad faith; **"in ~"** (_Dir_) "in witness whereof"

fe'dele AG (_leale, veritiero_) true, accurate; ~ **(a)** faithful (to) ▶ SMF follower; **i fedeli** (_Rel_) the faithful

fedeltà SF faithfulness; (_coniugale_) fidelity; (_esattezza: di copia, traduzione_) accuracy; **alta ~** (_Radio_) high fidelity

'federa SF pillowslip, pillowcase

fede'rale AG federal

federa'lismo SM (_Pol_) federalism

federa'lista, -i, -e AG, SM/F (_Pol_) federalist

federazi'one [federat'tsjone] SF federation

Feder'caccia [feder'kattʃa] ABBR F (= _Federazione Italiana della Caccia_) hunting federation

Feder'calcio [feder'kaltʃo] ABBR M (= _Federazione Italiana Gioco Calcio_) Italian football association

Federcon'sorzi [federkon'sɔrtsi] ABBR F (= _Federazione Italiana dei Consorzi Agrari_) federation of farmers' cooperatives

fe'difrago, -a, -ghi, -ghe AG faithless, perfidious

fe'dina SF (_Dir_): ~ **(penale)** record; **avere la ~ penale sporca** to have a police record

'fegato SM liver; (_fig_) guts _pl_, nerve; **mangiarsi** o **rodersi il** ~ to be consumed with rage

'felce ['feltʃe] SF fern

fe'lice [fe'litʃe] AG happy; (_fortunato_) lucky

felicità [felitʃi'ta] SF happiness

felici'tarsi [felitʃi'tarsi] /72/ VPR (_congratularsi_): ~ **con qn per qc** to congratulate sb on sth

felicitazi'oni [felitʃitat'tsjoni] SFPL congratulations

fe'lino, -a AG, SM feline

'felpa SF sweatshirt

fel'pato, -a AG (_tessuto_) brushed; (_passo_) stealthy; **con passo** ~ stealthily

'feltro SM felt

'femmina SF (_Zool, Tecn_) female; (_figlia_) girl, daughter; (_spesso peg_) woman

femmi'nile AG feminine; (_sesso_) female; (_lavoro, giornale_) woman's, women's; (_moda_) women's ▶ SM (_Ling_) feminine

femminilità SF femininity

femmi'nismo SM feminism

femmi'nista, -i, -e AG, SM/F feminist

'femore SM thighbone, femur

'fendere /36/ VT to cut through

fendi'nebbia SM (_Aut_) fog lamp

fendi'tura SF (_gen_) crack; (_di roccia_) cleft, crack

fe'nomeno SM phenomenon

'feretro SM coffin

feri'ale AG: **giorno** ~ weekday, working day

'ferie SFPL holidays (BRIT), vacation _sg_ (US); **andare in** ~ to go on holiday o vacation; **25 giorni di** ~ **pagate** 25 days' holiday o vacation with pay

feri'mento SM wounding

fe'rire /55/ VT to injure; (_deliberatamente: Mil ecc_) to wound; (_colpire_) to hurt; **ferirsi** VPR to hurt o.s., injure o.s.

fe'rito, -a SM/F wounded o injured man/woman ▶ SF injury; wound

feri'toia SF slit

'ferma SF (_Mil_) (period of) service; (_Caccia_): **cane da** ~ pointer

ferma'carte SM INV paperweight

fermacra'vatta SM INV tiepin (BRIT), tie tack (US)

fer'maglio [fer'maʎʎo] SM clasp; (_gioiello_) brooch; (_per documenti_) clip

ferma'mente AV firmly

fer'mare /72/ VT to stop, halt; (_Polizia_) to detain, hold; (_bottone ecc_) to fasten, fix ▶ VI to stop; **fermarsi** VPR to stop, halt; **fermarsi a fare qc** to stop to do sth

fer'mata SF stop; ~ **dell'autobus** bus stop

fermen'tare /72/ vı to ferment; (fig) to be in a ferment

fermentazi'one [fermentat'tsjone] sf fermentation

fer'mento sm (anche fig) ferment; (lievito) yeast; **fermenti lattici** probiotics, probiotic bacteria

fer'mezza [fer'mettsa] sf (fig) firmness, steadfastness

'fermo, -a AG still, motionless; (veicolo) stationary; (orologio) not working; (saldo: anche fig) firm; (voce, mano) steady ▶ ESCL stop!; keep still! ▶ sm (chiusura) catch, lock; (Dir): ~ **di polizia** police detention; ~ **restando che ...** it being understood that ...

'fermo 'posta AV, sm ınv poste restante (Brıt), general delivery (US)

fe'roce [fe'rɔtʃe] AG (animale) wild, fierce, ferocious; (persona) cruel, fierce; (fame, dolore) raging; **le bestie feroci** wild animals

fe'rocia, -cie [fe'rɔtʃa] sf ferocity

Ferr. ABBR = **ferrovia**

fer'raglia [fer'raʎʎa] sf scrap iron

ferra'gosto sm (festa) feast of the Assumption; (periodo) August holidays pl (Brıt) o vacation (US); see note

> Ferragosto, 15 August, is a national holiday. Marking the feast of the Assumption, its origins are religious but in recent years it has simply become the most important public holiday of the summer season. Most people take some extra time off work and head out of town to the holiday resorts. Consequently, most of industry and commerce grinds to a standstill.

ferra'menta sFPL ironmongery sg (Brıt), hardware sg; **negozio di** ~ ironmonger's (Brıt), hardware shop o store (US)

fer'rare /72/ vт (cavallo) to shoe

fer'rato, -a AG (Ferr): **strada ferrata** railway line (Brıt), railroad line (US); (fig) **essere** ~ **in** (materia) to be well up in

ferra'vecchio [ferra'vɛkkjo] sm scrap merchant

'ferreo, -a AG iron cpd

ferri'era sf ironworks inv

'ferro sm iron; **una bistecca ai ferri** a grilled steak; **mettere a** ~ **e fuoco** to put to the sword; **essere ai ferri corti** (fig) to be at daggers drawn; **tocca** ~**!** touch wood!; ~ **battuto** wrought iron; ~ **di cavallo** horseshoe; ~ **da stiro** iron; **ferri da calza** knitting needles; **i ferri del mestiere** the tools of the trade

ferrotranvi'ario, -a AG public transport cpd

Ferrotranvi'eri ABBR F (= Federazione Nazionale Lavoratori Autoferrotranvieri e Internavigatori) transport workers' union

ferro'vecchio [ferro'vɛkkjo] sm = **ferravecchio**

ferro'via sf railway (Brıt), railroad (US)

ferrovi'ario, -a AG railway cpd (Brıt), railroad cpd (US)

ferrovi'ere sm railwayman (Brıt), railroad man (US)

'fertile AG fertile

fertilità sf fertility

fertiliz'zante [fertilid'dzante] sm fertilizer

fertiliz'zare [fertilid'dzare] /72/ vт to fertilize

fer'vente AG fervent, ardent

'fervere /29/ vı: **fervono i preparativi per ...** they are making feverish preparations for ...

'fervido, -a AG fervent, ardent

fer'vore sm fervour (Brıt), fervor (US), ardour (Brıt), ardor (US); (punto culminante) height

'fesa sf (Cuc) rump of veal

fesse'ria sf stupidity; **dire fesserie** to talk nonsense

'fesso, -a PP di **fendere** ▶ AG (col: sciocco) crazy, cracked

fes'sura sf crack, split; (per gettone, moneta) slot

'festa sf (religiosa) feast; (pubblica) holiday; (compleanno) birthday; (onomastico) name day; (ricevimento) celebration, party; **far** ~ to have a holiday; (far baldoria) to live it up; **far** ~ **a qn** to give sb a warm welcome; **essere vestito a** ~ to be dressed up to the nines; ~ **comandata** (Rel) holiday of obligation; **la** ~ **della mamma/del papà** Mother's/Father's Day; **la F~ della Repubblica** see note

> The Festa della Repubblica, 2 June, celebrates the founding of the Italian Republic after the fall of the monarchy and the subsequent referendum in 1946. It is marked by military parades and political speeches.

festeggia'menti [festeddʒa'menti] sMPL celebrations

festeggi'are [fested'dʒare] /62/ vт to celebrate; (persona) to have a celebration for

fes'tino sm party; (con balli) ball

fes'tivo, -a AG (atmosfera) festive; **giorno** ~ holiday

fes'toso, -a AG merry, joyful

fe'tente AG (puzzolente) fetid; (comportamento) disgusting ▶ smF (col) stinker, rotter (Brıt)

fe'ticcio [fe'tittʃo] sm fetish

'feto sm foetus (Brıt), fetus (US)

fe'tore sm stench, stink

'fetta sf slice

fet'tuccia, -ce [fet'tuttʃa] sf tape, ribbon

fettuc'cine [fettut'tʃine] sFPL (Cuc) ribbon-shaped pasta

feu'dale AG feudal

'feudo sm (Storia) fief; (fig) stronghold

ff ABBR (Amm) = **facente funzione**; (= fogli) pp

FF.AA ABBR = **forze armate**

FF.SS. ABBR = **Ferrovie dello Stato**

FG SIGLA = **Foggia**

FI SIGLA = **Firenze** ▶ ABBR (= *Forza Italia*) Italian centre-right political party

fi'aba SF fairy tale

fia'besco, -a, -schi, -sche AG fairy-tale *cpd*

fi'acca SF weariness; (*svogliatezza*) listlessness; **battere la ~** to shirk

fiac'care /20/ VT to weaken

fiaccherò *etc* [fjakke'rɔ] VB *vedi* **fiaccare**

fi'acco, -a, -chi, -che AG (*stanco*) tired, weary; (*svogliato*) listless; (*debole*) weak; (*mercato*) slack

fi'accola SF torch

fiacco'lata SF torchlight procession

fi'ala SF phial

fi'amma SF flame; (*Naut*) pennant

fiam'mante AG (*colore*) flaming; **nuovo ~** brand new

fiam'mata SF blaze

fiammeggi'are [fjammed'dʒare] **/62/** VI to blaze

fiam'mifero SM match

fiam'mingo, -a, -ghi, -ghe AG Flemish ▶ SM/F Fleming ▶ SM (*Ling*) Flemish; (*Zool*) flamingo; **i Fiamminghi** the Flemish

fian'cata SF (*di nave ecc*) side; (*Naut*) broadside

fiancheggi'are [fjanked'dʒare] **/62/** VT to border; (*fig*) to support, back (up); (*Mil*) to flank

fi'anco, -chi SM side; (*di persona*) hip; (*Mil*) flank; **di ~** sideways, from the side; **a ~ a ~** side by side; **prestare il proprio ~ alle critiche** to leave o.s. open to criticism; **~ destr/sinistr!** (*Mil*) right/left turn!

Fi'andre SFPL: **le ~** Flanders *sg*

fiaschette'ria [fjaskette'ria] SF wine shop

fi'asco, -schi SM flask; (*fig*) fiasco; **fare ~ to fail**

fia'tare /72/ VI (*fig: parlare*): **senza ~** without saying a word

fi'ato SM breath; (*resistenza*) stamina; **fiati** SMPL (*Mus*) wind instruments; **avere il ~ grosso** to be out of breath; **prendere ~** to catch one's breath; **bere qc tutto d'un ~** to drink sth in one go *o* gulp

'fibbia SF buckle

'fibra SF fibre, fiber (*US*); (*fig*) constitution; **~ ottica** optical fibre; **~ di vetro** fibreglass (*BRIT*), fiberglass (*US*)

ficca'naso (*mpl* **ficcanasi,** *fpl* **~**) SM/F busybody, nos(e)y parker

fic'care /20/ VT to push, thrust, drive; **ficcarsi** VPR (*andare a finire*) to get to; **~ il naso negli affari altrui** (*fig*) to poke *o* stick one's nose into other people's business; **ficcarsi nei pasticci** *o* **nei guai** to get into hot water *o* a fix

ficcherò *etc* [fikke'rɔ] VB *vedi* **ficcare**

fiche [fiʃ] SF INV (*nei giochi d'azzardo*) chip

'fico, -chi SM (*pianta*) fig tree; (*frutto*) fig; **~ d'India** prickly pear; **~ secco** dried fig

fiction ['fikʃon] SF INV TV drama

fidanza'mento [fidantsa'mento] SM engagement

fidan'zarsi [fidan'tsarsi] **/72/** VPR to get engaged

fidan'zato, -a [fidan'tsato] SM/F fiancé (fiancée)

fi'darsi /72/ VPR: **~ di** to trust; **~ è bene non ~ è meglio** (*proverbio*) better safe than sorry

fi'dato, -a AG reliable, trustworthy

fide'ismo SM unquestioning belief

fide'istico, -a, -ci, -che AG (*atteggiamento, posizione*) totally uncritical

fideius'sore SM (*Dir*) guarantor

fideliz'zare [fidelid'dzare] **/72/** VT: **~ la clientela** to build customer loyalty; **fidelizzarsi** VPR to stay loyal

'fido, -a AG faithful, loyal ▶ SM (*Comm*) credit

fi'ducia [fi'dutʃa] SF confidence, trust; **incarico di ~** position of trust, responsible position; **persona di ~** reliable person; **è il mio uomo di ~** he is my right-hand man; **porre la questione di ~** (*Pol*) to ask for a vote of confidence

fiduci'oso, -a [fidu'tʃoso] AG trusting

fi'ele SM (*Med*) bile; (*fig*) bitterness

fie'nile SM barn; hayloft

fi'eno SM hay

fi'era SF fair; (*animale*) wild beast; **~ di beneficenza** charity bazaar; **~ campionaria** trade fair

fie'rezza [fje'rettsa] SF pride

fi'ero, -a AG proud; (*crudele*) fierce, cruel; (*audace*) bold

fi'evole AG (*luce*) dim; (*suono*) weak

'fifa SF (*col*): **aver ~** to have the jitters

F.I.F.A. SIGLA F (= *Fédération Internationale de Football Association*) FIFA

fi'fone, -a SM/F (*col, scherzoso*) coward

fig. ABBR (= *figura*) fig

FIGC SIGLA F (= *Federazione Italiana Gioco Calcio*) *Italian football association*

'Figi ['fidʒi] SFPL: **le isole ~** Fiji, the Fiji Islands

'figlia ['fiʎʎa] SF daughter; (*Comm*) counterfoil (*BRIT*), stub

figli'are [fiʎ'ʎare] **/27/** VI to give birth

figli'astro, -a [fiʎ'ʎastro] SM/F stepson(-daughter)

'figlio ['fiʎʎo] SM son; (*senza distinzione di sesso*) child; **~ d'arte**: **essere ~ d'arte** to come from a theatrical (*o* musical *etc*) family; **~ di puttana** (!) son of a bitch (!); **~ di papà** spoilt, wealthy young man; **~ unico** only child

139

figli'occio, -a, -ci, -ce [fiʎˈʎɔttʃo] SM/F godchild, godson(-daughter)

figli'ola [fiʎˈʎɔla] SF daughter; (*fig: ragazza*) girl

figli'olo [fiʎˈʎɔlo] SM (*anche fig: ragazzo*) son

fi'gura SF figure; (*forma, aspetto esterno*) form, shape; (*illustrazione*) picture, illustration; **far ~** to look smart; **fare una brutta ~** to make a bad impression; **che ~!** how embarrassing!

figu'raccia, -ce [figuˈrattʃa] SF: **fare una ~** to create a bad impression

figu'rare /72/ VI to appear ▶ VT: **figurarsi qc** to imagine sth; **figurarsi** VPR: **figurati!** imagine that!; **ti do noia? — ma figurati!** am I disturbing you? — not at all!

figura'tivo, -a AG figurative

figu'rina SF (*statuetta*) figurine; (*cartoncino*) picture card

figuri'nista, -i, -e SM/F dress designer

figu'rino SM fashion sketch

fi'guro SM: **un losco ~** a suspicious character

figu'rone SM: **fare un ~** (*persona, oggetto*) to look terrific; (*persona: con un discorso ecc*) to make an excellent impression

'fila SF row, line; (*coda*) queue; (*serie*) series, string; **di ~** in succession; **fare la ~** to queue; **in ~ indiana** in single file

fila'mento SM filament

fi'lanca® SF *stretch material*

fi'landa SF spinning mill

fi'lante AG: **stella ~** (*stella cadente*) shooting star; (*striscia di carta*) streamer

filantro'pia SF philanthropy

filan'tropico, -a, -ci, -che AG philanthropic(al)

fi'lantropo SM philanthropist

fi'lare /72/ VT to spin; (*Naut*) to pay out ▶ VI (*baco, ragno*) to spin; (*formaggio fuso*) to go stringy; (*liquido*) to trickle; (*discorso*) to hang together; (*col: amoreggiare*) to go steady; (*muoversi a forte velocità*) to go at full speed; (*andarsene lestamente*) to make o.s. scarce ▶ SM (*di alberi ecc*) row, line; **~ diritto** (*fig*) to toe the line; **~ via** to dash off

filar'monico, -a, -ci, -che AG philharmonic

filas'trocca, -che SF nursery rhyme

fila'telia SF philately, stamp collecting

fi'lato, -a AG spun ▶ SM yarn ▶ AV: **vai dritto ~ a casa** go straight home; **3 giorni filati** 3 days running *o* on end

fila'tura SF spinning; (*luogo*) spinning mill

file 'sharing [failˈʃerin(g)] SM (*Inform*) file sharing

fi'letto SM (*ornamento*) braid, trimming; (*di vite*) thread; (*di carne*) fillet

fili'ale AG filial ▶ SF (*di impresa*) branch

filibusti'ere SM pirate; (*fig*) adventurer

fili'grana SF (*in oreficeria*) filigree; (*su carta*) watermark

fi'lippica SF invective

Filip'pine SFPL: **le ~** the Philippines

filip'pino, -a AG, SM/F Filipino

film SM INV film

fil'mare /72/ VT to film

fil'mato SM short film

fil'mina SF film strip

'filo SM (*anche fig*) thread; (*filato*) yarn; (*metallico*) wire; (*di lama, rasoio*) edge; **con un ~ di voce** in a whisper; **un ~ d'aria** (*fig*) a breath of air; **dare del ~ da torcere a qn** to create difficulties for sb, make life difficult for sb; **fare il ~ a qn** (*corteggiare*) to be after sb, chase sb; **per ~ e per segno** in detail; **~ d'erba** blade of grass; **~ interdentale** dental floss; **~ di perle** string of pearls; **~ di Scozia** fine cotton yarn; **~ spinato** barbed wire

filoameri'cano, -a AG pro-American

'filobus SM INV trolley bus

filodiffusi'one SF rediffusion

filodram'matico, -a, -ci, -che AG: **(compagnia) filodrammatica** amateur dramatic society ▶ SM/F amateur actor (actress)

filon'cino [filonˈtʃino] SM ≈ French stick

fi'lone SM (*di minerali*) seam, vein; (*pane*) ≈ Vienna loaf; (*fig*) trend

filoso'fia SF philosophy

filo'sofico, -a, -ci, -che AG philosophical

fi'losofo, -a SM/F philosopher

filosovi'etico, -a, -ci, -che AG pro-Soviet

filo'via SF (*linea*) trolley line; (*bus*) trolley bus

fil'trare /72/ VT, VI to filter

'filtro SM filter; (*pozione*) potion; **~ dell'olio** (*Aut*) oil filter

'filza [ˈfiltsa] SF (*anche fig*) string

FIN SIGLA F = **Federazione Italiana Nuoto**

fin AV, PREP = **fino**

fi'nale AG final ▶ SM (*di libro, film*) end, ending; (*Mus*) finale ▶ SF (*Sport*) final

fina'lista, -i, -e SM/F finalist

finalità SF (*scopo*) aim, purpose

finaliz'zare [finalidˈdzare] /72/ VT: **~ a** to direct towards

final'mente AV finally, at last

fi'nanza [fiˈnantsa] SF finance; **finanze** SFPL (*di individuo, Stato*) finances; **(Guardia di) ~** (*di frontiera*) ≈ Customs and Excise (BRIT), ≈ Customs Service (US); **(Intendenza di) ~** ≈ Inland Revenue (BRIT), ≈ Internal Revenue Service (US); **Ministro delle finanze** Minister of Finance, ≈ Chancellor of the Exchequer (BRIT), ≈ Secretary of the Treasury (US)

finanzia'mento [finantsjaˈmento] SM (*azione*) financing; (*denaro fornito*) funds *pl*

finanzi'are [finanˈtsjare] /19/ VT to finance, fund

finanzi'ario, -a [finan'tsjarjo] AG financial ▶ *anche:* **società finanziaria**) investment company; (*anche:* **legge finanziaria**) finance act, ≈ budget (BRIT)

finanzia'tore, -'trice AG: **ente ~** backer ▶ SM/F backer

finanzi'ere [finan'tsjɛre] SM financier; (*guardia di finanza: doganale*) customs officer; (: *tributaria*) Inland Revenue official (BRIT), Internal Revenue official (US)

finché [fin'ke] CONG (*per tutto il tempo che*) as long as; (*fino al momento in cui*) until; **~ vorrai** as long as you like; **aspetta ~ non esca** wait until he goes (*o* comes) out; **aspetta ~ io (non) sia ritornato** wait until I get back

'fine AG (*lamina, carta*) thin; (*capelli, polvere*) fine; (*vista, udito*) keen, sharp; (*persona: raffinata*) refined, distinguished; (*osservazione*) subtle ▶ SF end ▶ SM aim, purpose; (*esito*) result, outcome; **in *o* alla ~** in the end, finally; **alla fin ~** at the end of the day, in the end; **che ~ ha fatto?** what became of him?; **buona ~ e buon principio!** (*augurio*) happy New Year!; **a fin di bene** with the best of intentions; **al ~ di fare qc** (in order) to do sth; **condurre qc a buon ~** to bring sth to a successful conclusion; **secondo ~** ulterior motive

'fine setti'mana SM *o* F INV weekend

fi'nestra SF window

fines'trino SM (*di treno, auto*) window

fi'nezza [fi'nettsa] SF thinness; fineness; keenness, sharpness; refinement; subtlety

'fingere ['findʒere] /**54**/ VT to feign; (*supporre*) to imagine, suppose; **fingersi** VPR: **fingersi ubriaco/pazzo** to pretend to be drunk/crazy; **~ di fare** to pretend to do

fini'menti SMPL (*di cavallo ecc*) harness *sg*

fini'mondo SM pandemonium

fi'nire /**55**/ VT to finish ▶ VI to finish, end ▶ SM: **sul ~ della festa** towards the end of the party; **~ di fare** (*compiere*) to finish doing; (*smettere*) to stop doing; **~ in galera** to end up *o* finish up in prison; **farla finita** (*con la vita*) to put an end to one's life; **farla finita con qc** to have done with sth; **com'è andata a ~?** what happened in the end?; **finiscila!** stop it!

fini'tura SF finish

finlan'dese AG Finnish ▶ SMF Finn ▶ SM (*Ling*) Finnish

Fin'landia SF: **la ~** Finland

'fino, -a AG (*capelli, seta*) fine; (*oro*) pure; (*fig: acuto*) shrewd ▶ AV (*spesso troncato in fin: pure, anche*) even ▶ PREP (*spesso troncato in fin*): **fin quando?** till when?; **fin qui** as far as here; **~ a** (*tempo*) until, till; (*luogo*) as far as, (up) to; **fin da domani** from tomorrow onwards;

fin da ieri since yesterday; **fin dalla nascita** from *o* since birth

fi'nocchio [fi'nɔkkjo] SM fennel; (*col, peg: omosessuale*) queer

fi'nora AV up till now

'finsi *etc* VB *vedi* **fingere**

'finto, -a PP *di* **fingere** ▶ AG (*capelli, dente*) false; (*fiori*) artificial; (*cuoio, pelle*) imitation *cpd*; (*fig: simulato: pazzia ecc*) feigned, sham ▶ SF pretence (BRIT), pretense (US), sham; (*Sport*) feint; **far finta (di fare)** to pretend (to do); **l'ho detto per finta** I was only pretending; (*per scherzo*) I was only kidding

finzi'one [fin'tsjone] SF pretence (BRIT), pretense (US), sham

fioc'care /**20**/ VI (*neve*) to fall; (*fig: insulti ecc*) to fall thick and fast

fi'occo, -chi SM (*di nastro*) bow; (*di stoffa, lana*) flock; (*di neve*) flake; (*Naut*) jib; **coi fiocchi** (*fig*) first-rate; **fiocchi di avena** oatflakes; **fiocchi di granoturco** cornflakes

fi'ocina ['fjɔtʃina] SF harpoon

fi'oco, -a, -chi, -che AG faint, dim

fi'onda SF catapult

fio'raio, -a SM/F florist

fiorda'liso SM (*Bot*) cornflower

fi'ordo SM fjord

fi'ore SM flower; **fiori** SMPL (*Carte*) clubs; **nel ~ degli anni** in one's prime; **a fior d'acqua** on the surface of the water; **a fior di labbra** in a whisper; **aver i nervi a fior di pelle** to be on edge; **fior di latte** cream; **è costato fior di soldi** it cost a pretty penny; **il fior ~ della società** the cream of society; **~ all'occhiello** feather in the cap; **fiori di campo** wild flowers

fio'rente AG (*industria, paese*) flourishing; (*salute*) blooming; (*petto*) ample

fioren'tino, -a AG, SM/F Florentine ▶ SF (*Cuc*) T-bone steak

fio'retto SM (*Scherma*) foil

fio'rino SM florin

fio'rire /**55**/ VI (*rosa*) to flower; (*albero*) to blossom; (*fig*) to flourish

fio'rista, -i, -e SM/F florist

fiori'tura SF (*di pianta*) flowering, blooming; (*di albero*) blossoming; (*fig: di commercio, arte*) flourishing; (*insieme dei fiori*) flowers *pl*; (*Mus*) fioritura

fi'otto SM (*di lacrime*) flow, flood; (*di sangue*) gush, spurt

'FIPE SIGLA F = **Federazione Italiana Pubblici Esercizi**

Fi'renze [fi'rɛntse] SF Florence

'firma SF signature; (*reputazione*) name

firma'mento SM firmament

fir'mare /**72**/ VT to sign; **un abito firmato** a designer suit

firma'tario, -a SM/F signatory

fisar'monica, -che SF accordion

fis'cale AG fiscal, tax *cpd*; (*meticoloso*) punctilious; **medico** ~ *doctor employed by Social Security to verify cases of sick leave*

fisca'lista, -i, -e SM/F tax consultant

fiscaliz'zare [fiskalid'dzare] /**72**/ VT to exempt from taxes

fischi'are [fis'kjare] /**19**/ VI to whistle ▶ VT to whistle; (*attore*) to boo, hiss; **mi fischian le orecchie** my ears are singing; (*fig*) my ears are burning

fischiet'tare [fiskjet'tare] /**72**/ VI, VT to whistle

fischi'etto [fis'kjetto] SM (*strumento*) whistle

'fischio ['fiskjo] SM whistle; **prendere fischi per fiaschi** to get hold of the wrong end of the stick

'fisco SM tax authorities *pl*, ≈ Inland Revenue (BRIT), ≈ Internal Revenue Service (US)

'fisica SF *vedi* **fisico**

fisica'mente AV physically

'fisico, -a, -ci, -che AG physical ▶ SM/F physicist ▶ SM physique ▶ SF physics *sg*

'fisima SF fixation

fisiolo'gia [fizjolo'dʒia] SF physiology

fisiono'mia SF face, physiognomy

fisiotera'pia SF physiotherapy

fisiotera'pista SMF physiotherapist

fis'saggio [fis'saddʒo] SM (*Fot*) fixing

fis'sante AG (*spray, lozione*) holding

fis'sare /**72**/ VT to fix, fasten; (*guardare intensamente*) to stare at; (*data, condizioni*) to fix, establish, set; (*prenotare*) to book; **fissarsi** VPR: **fissarsi su** (*sguardo, attenzione*) to focus on; (*fig: idea*) to become obsessed with

fissazi'one [fissat'tsjone] SF (*Psic*) fixation

fissi'one SF fission

'fisso, -a AG fixed; (*stipendio, impiego*) regular ▶ AV: **guardare** ~ **qn/qc** to stare at sb/sth; **avere un ragazzo** ~ to have a steady boyfriend; **senza fissa dimora** of no fixed abode; **telefono** ~ landline

fitoterma'lismo SM herbal hydrotherapy

'fitta SF *vedi* **fitto**

fit'tavolo SM tenant

fit'tizio, -a [fit'tittsjo] AG fictitious, imaginary

'fitto, -a AG thick, dense; (*pioggia*) heavy ▶ SM depths *pl*, middle; (*affitto, pigione*) rent ▶ SF sharp pain; **una fitta al cuore** (*fig*) a pang of grief; **nel** ~ **del bosco** in the heart o depths of the wood

fiu'mana SF torrent; (*fig*) stream, flood

fi'ume SM river ▶ AG INV: **processo** ~ long-running trial; **scorrere a fiumi** (*acqua, sangue*) to flow in torrents

fiu'tare /**72**/ VT to smell, sniff; (*animale*) to scent; (*fig: inganno*) to get wind of, smell; ~ **tabacco** to take snuff; ~ **cocaina** to snort cocaine

fi'uto SM (sense of) smell; (*fig*) nose

'flaccido, -a ['flattʃido] AG flabby

fla'cone SM bottle

flagel'lare [fladʒel'lare] /**72**/ VT to flog, scourge; (*onde*) to beat against

fla'gello [fla'dʒello] SM scourge

fla'grante AG flagrant; **cogliere qn in** ~ to catch sb red-handed

fla'nella SF flannel

flash [flaʃ] SM INV (*Fot*) flash; (*giornalistico*) newsflash

flau'tista, -i SM/F flautist

'flauto SM flute

'flebile AG faint, feeble

fle'bite SF phlebitis

'flemma SF (*calma*) coolness, phlegm; (*Med*) phlegm

flem'matico, -a, -ci, -che AG phlegmatic, cool

fles'sibile AG pliable; (*fig: che si adatta*) flexible

flessibili'tà SF (*anche fig*) flexibility

flessi'one SF (*gen*) bending; (*Ginnastica: a terra*) sit-up; (*: in piedi*) forward bend; (*: sulle gambe*) knee-bend; (*diminuzione*) slight drop, slight fall; (*Ling*) inflection; **fare una** ~ to bend; **una** ~ **economica** a downward trend in the economy

'flesso, -a PP *di* **flettere**

flessu'oso, -a AG supple, lithe; (*andatura*) flowing, graceful

'flettere /**92**/ VT to bend

'flipper ['flipper] SM INV pinball machine

flirt [fləːt] SM INV brief romance, flirtation

flir'tare /**72**/ VI to flirt

F.lli ABBR (= *fratelli*) Bros

'flora SF flora

flo'rido, -a AG flourishing; (*fig*) glowing with health

'floscio, -a, -sci, -sce ['floʃʃo] AG (*cappello*) floppy, soft; (*muscoli*) flabby

'flotta SF fleet

flot'tante SM (*Econ*): **titoli a largo** ~ blue chips, stocks on the market

'fluido, -a AG, SM fluid

flu'ire /**55**/ VI to flow

fluore'scente [fluoreʃ'ʃente] AG fluorescent

flu'oro SM fluorine

fluo'ruro SM fluoride

'flusso SM flow; (*Fisica, Med*) flux; ~ **e riflusso** ebb and flow; ~ **di cassa** (*Comm*) cash flow

'flutti SMPL waves

fluttu'are /**72**/ VI to rise and fall; (*Econ*) to fluctuate

fluvi'ale AG river *cpd*, fluvial

FM ABBR *vedi* **modulazione di frequenza**

FMI SIGLA M (= *Fondo Monetario Internazionale*) IMF

FO SIGLA = **Forlì**

fo'bia SF phobia

'foca, -che SF (Zool) seal

fo'caccia, -ce [fo'kattʃa] SF kind of pizza; (dolce) bun; **rendere pan per** ~ to get one's own back, give tit for tat

fo'cale AG focal

focaliz'zare [fokalid'dzare] /**72**/ VT (Fot: immagine) to get into focus; (fig: situazione) to get into perspective; ~ **l'attenzione su** to focus one's attention on

'foce ['fotʃe] SF (Geo) mouth

fo'chista, -i [fo'kista] SM (Ferr) stoker, fireman

foco'laio SM (Med) centre (BRIT) o center (US) of infection; (fig) hotbed

foco'lare SM hearth, fireside; (Tecn) furnace

fo'coso, -a AG fiery; (cavallo) mettlesome, fiery

'fodera SF (di vestito) lining; (di libro, poltrona) cover

fode'rare /**72**/ VT to line; to cover

'fodero SM (di spada) scabbard; (di pugnale) sheath; (di pistola) holster

'foga SF enthusiasm, ardour (BRIT), ardor (US)

'foggia, -ge ['fɔddʒa] SF (maniera) style; (aspetto) form, shape; (moda) fashion, style

foggi'are [fod'dʒare] /**62**/ VT to shape; to style

'foglia ['fɔʎʎa] SF leaf; **ha mangiato la** ~ (fig) he's caught on; ~ **d'argento/d'oro** silver/gold leaf

fogli'ame [foʎ'ʎame] SM foliage, leaves pl

fogli'etto [foʎ'ʎetto] SM (piccolo foglio) slip of paper, piece of paper; (manifestino) leaflet, handout

'foglio ['fɔʎʎo] SM (di carta) sheet (of paper); (di metallo) sheet; (documento) document; (banconota) (bank)note; ~ **di calcolo** (Inform) spreadsheet; ~ **rosa** (Aut) provisional licence; ~ **di via** (Dir) expulsion order; ~ **volante** pamphlet

'fogna ['foɲɲa] SF drain, sewer

fogna'tura [foɲɲa'tura] SF drainage, sewerage

föhn [fø:n] SM INV hair-dryer

fo'lata SF gust

fol'clore SM folklore

folclo'ristico, -a, -ci, -che AG folk cpd

folgo'rare /**72**/ VT (fulmine) to strike down; (: alta tensione) to electrocute

folgorazi'one [folgorat'tsjone] SF electrocution; **ebbe una** ~ (fig: idea) he had a brainwave

'folgore SF thunderbolt

folksono'mia SF (Inform) folksonomy

'folla SF crowd, throng

'folle AG mad, insane; (Tecn) idle; **in** ~ (Aut) in neutral

folleggi'are [folled'dʒare] /**62**/ VI (divertirsi) to paint the town red

fol'letto SM elf

fol'lia SF folly, foolishness; foolish act; (pazzia) madness, lunacy; **amare qn alla** ~ to love sb to distraction; **costare una** ~ to cost the earth

'folto, -a AG thick

fomen'tare /**72**/ VT to stir up, foment

fon SM INV = **föhn**

fon'dale SM (del mare) bottom; (Teat) backdrop; **il** ~ **marino** the sea bed

fondamen'tale AG fundamental, basic

fondamenta'lista, -i, -e AG, SM/F (Rel) fundamentalist

fonda'mento SM foundation; **fondamenta** SFPL (Edil) foundations

fon'dare /**72**/ VT to found; (fig: dar base): ~ **qc su** to base sth on; **fondarsi** VPR (teorie): **fondarsi (su)** to be based (on)

fonda'tezza [fonda'tettsa] SF (di ragioni) soundness; (di dubbio, sospetto) basis in fact

fon'dato, -a AG (ragioni) sound; (dubbio, sospetto) well-founded

fondazi'one [fondat'tsjone] SF foundation

fon'dente AG: **cioccolato** ~ plain o dark chocolate

'fondere /**25**/ VT (neve) to melt; (metallo) to fuse, melt; (fig: colori) to merge, blend; (: imprese, gruppi) to merge ▶ VI to melt; **fondersi** VPR to melt; (fig: partiti, correnti) to unite, merge

fonde'ria SF foundry

fondi'ario, -a AG land cpd

fon'dina SF (piatto fondo) soup plate; (portapistola) holster

'fondo, -a AG deep ▶ SM (di recipiente, pozzo) bottom; (di stanza) back; (quantità di liquido che resta, deposito) dregs pl; (sfondo) background; (unità immobiliare) property, estate; (somma di denaro) fund; (Sport) long-distance race; **fondi** SMPL (denaro) funds; **a notte fonda** at dead of night; **in** ~ **a** at the bottom of; at the back of; (strada) at the end of; **laggiù in** ~ (lontano) over there; (in profondità) down there; **in** ~ (fig) after all, all things considered; **andare fino in** ~ **a** (fig) to examine thoroughly; **andare a** ~ (nave) to sink; **conoscere a** ~ to know inside out; **dar** ~ **a** (provviste, soldi) to use up; **toccare il** ~ (fig) to plumb the depths; **a** ~ **perduto** (Comm) without security; ~ **comune di investimento** investment trust; **F~ Monetario Internazionale** International Monetary Fund; ~ **di previdenza** social insurance fund; ~ **di riserva** reserve fund; ~ **urbano** town property; **fondi di caffè** coffee grounds; **fondi d'esercizio** working capital sg; **fondi liquidi** ready money sg,

liquid assets; **fondi di magazzino** old o unsold stock sg; **fondi neri** slush fund sg
fondo'tinta sm inv (cosmetico) foundation
fo'nema sm phoneme
fo'netica sf phonetics sg
fo'netico, -a, -ci, -che ag phonetic
fon'tana sf fountain
fonta'nella sf drinking fountain
'fonte sf spring, source; (fig) source ▶ sm: **~ battesimale** (Rel) font; **~ energetica** source of energy
fon'tina sm full fat hard, sweet cheese
'footing ['futin] sm jogging
forag'giare [forad'dʒare] /62/ vt (cavalli) to fodder; (fig: partito ecc) to bankroll
fo'raggio [fo'raddʒo] sm fodder, forage
fo'rare /72/ vt to pierce, make a hole in; (pallone) to burst; (pneumatico) to puncture; (biglietto) to punch; **forarsi** vpr (gen) to develop a hole; (Aut, pallone, timpano) to burst; **~ una gomma** to burst a tyre (Brit) o tire (US)
fora'tura sf piercing; bursting; puncturing; punching
'forbici ['forbitʃi] sfpl scissors
forbi'cina [forbi'tʃina] sf earwig
for'bito, -a ag (stile, modi) polished
'forca, -che sf (Agr) fork, pitchfork; (patibolo) gallows sg
for'cella [for'tʃella] sf (Tecn) fork; (di monte) pass
for'chetta [for'ketta] sf fork; **essere una buona ~** to enjoy one's food
for'cina [for'tʃina] sf hairpin
'forcipe ['fortʃipe] sm forceps pl
for'cone sm pitchfork
fo'rense ag (linguaggio) legal; **avvocato ~** barrister (Brit), lawyer
fo'resta sf forest; **la F~ Nera** the Black Forest
fores'tale ag forest cpd; **guardia ~** forester
foreste'ria sf (di convento, palazzo ecc) guest rooms pl, guest quarters pl
foresti'ero, -a ag foreign ▶ sm/f foreigner
for'fait [for'fε] sm inv: **(prezzo a) ~** fixed price, set price; **dichiarare ~** (Sport) to withdraw; (fig) to give up
forfe'tario, -a ag: **prezzo ~** (da pagare) fixed o set price; (da ricevere) lump sum
'forfora sf dandruff
'forgia, -ge ['fordʒa] sf forge
forgi'are [for'dʒare] /62/ vt to forge
'forma sf form; (aspetto esteriore) form, shape; (Dir: procedura) procedure; (per calzature) last; (stampo da cucina) mould (Brit), mold (US); **forme** sfpl (del corpo) figure, shape; **le forme** (convenzioni) appearances; **errori di ~** stylistic errors; **essere in ~** to be in good shape; **mantenersi in ~** to keep fit; **in ~ ufficiale/privata** officially/privately; **una ~ di formaggio** a (whole) cheese

formag'gino [formad'dʒino] sm processed cheese
for'maggio [for'maddʒo] sm cheese
for'male ag formal
formalità sf inv formality
formaliz'zare [formalid'dzare] /72/ vt to formalize
for'mare /72/ vt to form, shape, make; (numero di telefono) to dial; (fig: carattere) to form, mould (Brit), mold (US); **formarsi** vpr to form, take shape; **il treno si forma a Milano** the train starts from Milan
for'mato sm format, size
format'tare /72/ vt (Inform) to format
formattazi'one [formattat'tsjone] sf (Inform) formatting
formazi'one [format'tsjone] sf formation; (fig: educazione) training; **~ continua** continuing education; **~ permanente** lifelong learning; **~ professionale** vocational training
for'mica¹, -che sf ant
for'mica²® ['fɔrmika] sf (materiale) Formica®
formi'caio sm anthill
formico'lare /72/ vi (gamba, braccio) to tingle; (brulicare: anche fig): **~ di** to be swarming with; **mi formicola la gamba** I've got pins and needles in my leg, my leg's tingling
formico'lio sm pins and needles pl; swarming
formi'dabile ag powerful, formidable; (straordinario) remarkable
for'moso, -a ag shapely
'formula sf formula; **~ di cortesia** (nelle lettere) letter ending
formu'lare /72/ vt to formulate; to express
for'nace [for'natʃe] sf (per laterizi ecc) kiln; (per metalli) furnace
for'naio sm baker
for'nello sm (elettrico, a gas) ring; (di pipa) bowl
for'nire /55/ vt: **~ qn di qc, ~ qc a qn** to provide o supply sb with sth, supply sth to sb; **fornirsi** vpr: **fornirsi di** (procurarsi) to provide o.s. with
for'nito, -a ag: **ben ~** (negozio) well-stocked
forni'tore, -'trice ag: **ditta fornitrice di ...** company supplying ... ▶ sm/f supplier
forni'tura sf supply
'forno sm (di cucina) oven; (panetteria) bakery; (Tecn: per calce ecc) kiln; (: per metalli) furnace; **fare i forni** (Med) to undergo heat treatment; **~ a microonde** microwave oven
'foro sm (buco) hole; (Storia) forum; (tribunale) (law) court
'forse av perhaps, maybe; (circa) about; **essere in ~** to be in doubt
forsen'nato, -a ag mad, crazy, insane
'forte ag strong; (suono) loud; (spesa) considerable, great; (passione, dolore) great,

deep ▶ AV strongly; (*velocemente*) fast; (*a voce alta*) loud(ly); (*violentemente*) hard ▶ SM (*edificio*) fort; (*specialità*) forte, strong point; **piatto ~** (*Cuc*) main dish; **avere un ~ mal di testa/raffreddore** to have a bad headache/cold; **essere ~ in qc** to be good at sth; **farsi ~ di qc** to make use of sth; **dare man ~ a qn** to back sb up, support sb; **usare le maniere forti** to use strong-arm tactics

for'tezza [for'tettsa] SF (*morale*) strength; (*luogo fortificato*) fortress

fortifi'care /20/ VT to fortify, strengthen

for'tuito, -a AG fortuitous, chance *cpd*

for'tuna SF (*destino*) fortune, luck; (*buona sorte*) success, fortune; (*eredità, averi*) fortune; **per ~** luckily, fortunately; **di ~** makeshift, improvised; **atterraggio di ~** emergency landing

fortu'nale SM storm

fortunata'mente AV luckily, fortunately

fortu'nato, -a AG lucky, fortunate; (*coronato da successo*) successful

fortu'noso, -a AG (*vita*) eventful; (*avvenimento*) unlucky

fo'runcolo SM (*Med*) boil

forvi'are /19/ VT, VI = **fuorviare**

'forza ['fɔrtsa] SF strength; (*potere*) power; (*Fisica*) force ▶ ESCL come on!; **forze** SFPL (*fisiche*) strength *sg*; (*Mil*) forces; **per ~** against one's will; (*naturalmente*) of course; **per ~ di cose** by force of circumstances; **a viva ~** by force; **a ~ di** by dint of; **farsi ~** (*coraggio*) to pluck up one's courage; **bella ~!** (*ironico*) how clever of you (*o him etc*)!; **~ lavoro** work force, manpower; **per causa di ~ maggiore** (*Dir*) by reason of an act of God; (*per estensione*) due to circumstances beyond one's control; **la ~ pubblica** the police *pl*; **forze dell'ordine** the forces of law and order; **~ di pace** peacekeeping force; **~ di vendita** (*Comm*) sales force; **~ di volontà** willpower; **le forze armate** the armed forces; **F~ Italia** (*Pol*) moderate right-wing party

for'zare [for'tsare] /72/ VT to force; (*cassaforte, porta*) to force (open); (*voce*) to strain; **~ qn a fare** to force sb to do

for'zato, -a [for'tsato] AG forced ▶ SM (*Dir*) prisoner sentenced to hard labour (*BRIT*) *o* labor (*US*)

forzi'ere [for'tsjɛre] SM strongbox; (*di pirati*) treasure chest

for'zista, -i, -e [for'tsista] AG of Forza Italia ▶ SM/F member (*o* supporter) of Forza Italia

for'zuto, -a [for'tsuto] AG big and strong

fos'chia [fos'kia] SF mist, haze

'fosco, -a, -schi, -sche AG dark, gloomy; **dipingere qc a tinte fosche** (*fig*) to paint a gloomy picture of sth

fos'fato SM phosphate

fosfore'scente [fosforeʃʃɛnte] AG phosphorescent; (*lancetta dell'orologio ecc*) luminous

'fosforo SM phosphorous

'fossa SF pit; (*di cimitero*) grave; **~ comune** mass grave; **~ biologica** septic tank

fos'sato SM ditch; (*di fortezza*) moat

fos'setta SF dimple

'fossi *etc* VB *vedi* **essere**

'fossile AG, SM fossil (*cpd*)

'fosso SM ditch; (*Mil*) trench

'foste *etc* VB *vedi* **essere**

'foto SF INV photo ▶ PREFISSO: **~ ricordo** souvenir photo; **~ tessera** passport(-type) photo

foto... PREFISSO photo...

foto'camera SF: **~ digitale** digital camera

fotocomposi'tore SM filmsetter

fotocomposizi'one [fotokompozit'tsjone] SF film setting

foto'copia SF photocopy

fotocopi'are /19/ VT to photocopy

fotocopia'trice [fotokopja'tritʃe] SF photocopier

fotocopiste'ria SF photocopy shop

fotofo'nino SM camera phone

foto'genico, -a, -ci, -che [foto'dʒɛniko] AG photogenic

fotogra'fare /72/ VT to photograph

fotogra'fia SF (*procedimento*) photography; (*immagine*) photograph; **fare una ~** to take a photograph; **una ~ a colori/in bianco e nero** a colour/black and white photograph

foto'grafico, -a, -ci, -che AG photographic; **macchina fotografica** camera

fo'tografo, -a SM/F photographer

foto'gramma, -i SM (*Cine*) frame

fotomo'dello, -a SM/F fashion model

fotomon'taggio [fotomon'taddʒo] SM photomontage

fotore'porter SM INV/F INV newspaper (*o* magazine) photographer

foto'manzo [fotoro'mandzo] SM romantic picture story

foto'sintesi SF photosynthesis

fotovol'taico, -a, -ci, -che AG photovoltaic; **pannelli fotovoltaici** solar panels

'fottere /1/ VT (!: *avere rapporti sessuali*) to fuck (!), screw (!); (*rubare*) to pinch, swipe; (*fregare*): **mi hanno fottuto** they played a dirty trick on me; **vai a farti ~!** fuck off! (!)

fot'tuto, -a AG (!) bloody, fucking (!)

fou'lard [fu'lar] SM INV scarf

FR SIGLA = **Frosinone**

fra PREP = **tra**

fracas'sare /72/ VT to shatter, smash; **fracassarsi** VPR to shatter, smash; (*veicolo*) to crash

145

fra'casso SM smash; crash; (*baccano*) din, racket

'fradicio, -a, -ci, -ce['fradit∫o] AG (*guasto*) rotten; (*molto bagnato*) soaking (wet); **ubriaco** ~ blind drunk

'fragile ['fradʒile] AG fragile; (*fig: salute*) delicate; (*nervi, vetro*) brittle

fragilità [fradʒili'ta] SF (*vedi ag*) fragility; delicacy; brittleness

'fragola SF strawberry

fra'gore SM (*di cascate, carro armato*) roar; (*di tuono*) rumble

frago'roso, -a AG deafening; **ridere in modo** ~ to roar with laughter

fra'grante AG fragrant

frain'tendere/120/ VT to misunderstand

fraintendi'mento SM misunderstanding

frain'teso, -a PP *di* **fraintendere**

fram'mento SM fragment

fram'misto, -a AG: ~ **a** interspersed with

'frana SF landslide; (*fig: persona*): **essere una** ~ to be useless, be a walking disaster area

fra'nare/72/ VI to slip, slide down

franca'mente AV frankly

fran'cese [fran't∫eze] AG French ▶ SMF Frenchman(-woman) ▶ SM (*Ling*) French; **i Francesi** the French

fran'chezza [fran'kettsa] SF frankness, openness

fran'chigia, -gie[fran'kidʒa] SF (*Amm*) exemption; (*Dir*) franchise; (*Naut*) shore leave; ~ **doganale** exemption from customs duty

'Francia ['frant∫a] SF: **la** ~ France

'franco, -a, -chi, -che AG (*Comm*) free; (*sincero*) frank, open, sincere ▶ SM (*moneta*) franc; **farla franca** (*fig*) to get off scot-free; ~ **a bordo** free on board; ~ **di dogana** duty-free; ~ **a domicilio** delivered free of charge; ~ **fabbrica** ex factory, ex works; **prezzo** ~ **fabbrica** ex-works price; ~ **magazzino** ex warehouse; ~ **di porto** carriage free; ~ **vagone** free on rail; ~ **tiratore** sniper (*Pol*) member of parliament who votes against his own party

franco'bollo SM (postage) stamp

franco-cana'dese AG, SMF French Canadian

Franco'forte SF Frankfurt

fran'gente [fran'dʒente] SM (*onda*) breaker; (*scoglio emergente*) reef; (*circostanza*) situation, circumstance

'frangia, -ge['frandʒa] SF fringe

frangi'flutti [frandʒi'flutti] SM INV breakwater

frangi'vento [frandʒi'vɛnto] SM windbreak

fran'toio SM (*Agr*) olive press; (*Tecn*) crusher

frantu'mare/72/ VT, **frantu'marsi**VPR to break into pieces, shatter

fran'tumi SMPL pieces, bits; (*schegge*) splinters; **andare in** ~, **mandare in** ~ to shatter, smash to pieces o smithereens

frappé SM (*Cuc*) milk shake

fra'sario SM (*gergo*) vocabulary, language

'frasca, -sche SF (leafy) branch; **saltare di palo in** ~ to jump from one subject to another

'frase SF (*Ling*) sentence; (*locuzione, espressione, Mus*) phrase; ~ **fatta** set phrase

fraseolo'gia [frazeolo'dʒia] SF phraseology

'frassino SM ash (tree)

frastagli'ato, -a[frasta∥'∥ato] AG (*costa*) indented, jagged

frastor'nare/72/ VT (*intontire*) to daze; (*confondere*) to bewilder, befuddle

frastor'nato, -a AG dazed; bewildered

frastu'ono SM hubbub, din

'frate SM friar, monk

fratel'lanza [fratel'lantsa] SF brotherhood; (*associazione*) fraternity

fratel'lastro SM stepbrother; (*con genitore in comune*) half brother

fra'tello SM brother; **fratelli**SMPL brothers; (*nel senso di fratelli e sorelle*) brothers and sisters

fra'terno, -a AG fraternal, brotherly

fratri'cida, -i, -e[fratri't∫ida] AG fratricidal ▶ SM/F fratricide; **guerra** ~ civil war

frat'taglie [frat'ta∥∥e] SFPL (*Cuc: gen*) offal *sg*; (: *di pollo*) giblets

frat'tanto AV in the meantime, meanwhile

frat'tempo SM: **nel** ~ in the meantime, meanwhile

frat'tura SF fracture; (*fig*) split, break

frattu'rare/72/ VT to fracture

fraudo'lento, -a AG fraudulent

fraziona'mento [frattsjona'mento] SM division, splitting up

frazio'nare [frattsjo'nare] /**72**/ VT to divide, split up

frazi'one [frat'tsjone] SF fraction; (*anche:* **frazione di comune**) hamlet

'freccia, -ce['frett∫a] SF arrow; ~ **di direzione** (*Aut*) indicator

frec'ciata [fret't∫ata] SF: **lanciare una** ~ to make a cutting remark

fred'dare/72/ VT to shoot dead

fred'dezza [fred'dettsa] SF coldness

'freddo, -a AG, SM cold; **fa** ~ it's cold; **aver** ~ to be cold; **soffrire il** ~ to feel the cold; **a** ~ (*fig*) deliberately

freddo'loso, -a AG sensitive to the cold

fred'dura SF pun

'freezer ['frizer] SM INV fridge-freezer

fre'gare/80/ VT to rub; (*col: truffare*) to take in, cheat; (: *rubare*) to swipe, pinch; **fregarsene** (*col*): **chi se ne frega?** who gives a damn (about it)?

fre'gata SF rub; (*col*) swindle; (*Naut*) frigate

frega'tura SF (col: imbroglio) rip-off; (: delusione) let-down

fregherò etc [frege'rɔ] VB vedi **fregare**

'fregio ['fredʒo] SM (Archit) frieze; (ornamento) decoration

'fremere /29/ VI: ~ **di** to tremble o quiver with; ~ **d'impazienza** to be champing at the bit

'fremito SM tremor, quiver

fre'nare /72/ VT (veicolo) to slow down; (cavallo) to rein in; (lacrime) to restrain, hold back ▶ VI to brake; **frenarsi** VPR (fig) to restrain o.s., control o.s.

fre'nata SF: **fare una** ~ to brake

frene'sia SF frenzy

fre'netico, -a, -ci, -che AG frenetic

'freno SM brake; (morso) bit; **tenere a** ~ (passioni ecc) to restrain; **tenere a** ~ **la lingua** to hold one's tongue; ~ **a disco** disc brake; ~ **a mano** handbrake

'freon ® SM INV (Chim) Freon®

frequen'tare /72/ VT (scuola, corso) to attend; (locale, bar) to go to, frequent; (persone) to see (often)

frequen'tato, -a AG (locale) busy

fre'quente AG frequent; **di** ~ frequently

fre'quenza [fre'kwɛntsa] SF frequency; (Ins) attendance

fre'sare /72/ VT (Tecn) to mill

fres'chezza [fres'kettsa] SF freshness

'fresco, -a, -schi, -sche AG fresh; (temperatura) cool; (notizia) recent, fresh ▶ SM: **godere il** ~ to enjoy the cool air; ~ **di bucato** straight from the wash, newly washed; **stare** ~ (fig) to be in for it; **mettere al** ~ to put in a cool place; (fig: in prigione) to put inside o in the cooler

fres'cura SF cool

'fresia SF freesia

'fretta SF hurry, haste; **in** ~ in a hurry; **in** ~ **e furia** in a mad rush; **aver** ~ to be in a hurry; **far** ~ **a qn** to hurry sb

frettolosa'mente AV hurriedly, in a rush

fretto'loso, -a AG (persona) in a hurry; (lavoro ecc) hurried, rushed

fri'abile AG (terreno) friable; (pasta) crumbly

'friggere ['friddʒere] /56/ VT to fry ▶ VI (olio ecc) to sizzle; **vai a farti** ~! (col) get lost!

frigidità [fridʒidi'ta] SF frigidity

'frigido, -a ['fridʒido] AG (Med) frigid

fri'gnare [friɲ'ɲare] /15/ VI to whine, snivel

fri'gnone, -a [friɲ'ɲone] SM/F whiner, sniveller

'frigo, -ghi SM fridge

frigo'bar SM INV minibar

frigo'rifero, -a AG refrigerating ▶ SM refrigerator; **cella frigorifera** cold store

fringu'ello SM chaffinch

'frissi etc VB vedi **friggere**

frit'tata SF omelet(te); **fare una** ~ (fig) to make a mess of things

frit'tella SF (Cuc) pancake; (: ripiena) fritter

'fritto, -a PP di **friggere** ▶ AG fried ▶ SM fried food; **ormai siamo fritti!** (fig: col) now we've had it!; **è un argomento – e rifritto** that's old hat; ~ **misto** mixed fry

frit'tura SF (cibo) fried food; ~ **di pesce** mixed fried fish

friu'lano, -a AG of (o from) Friuli

frivo'lezza [frivo'lettsa] SF frivolity

'frivolo, -a AG frivolous

frizi'one [frit'tsjone] SF friction; (di pelle) rub, rub-down; (Aut) clutch

friz'zante [frid'dzante] AG (anche fig) sparkling

'frizzo ['friddzo] SM witticism

fro'dare /72/ VT to defraud, cheat

'frode SF fraud; ~ **fiscale** tax evasion

'frodo SM: **di** ~ illegal, contraband; **pescatore di** ~, **cacciatore di** ~ poacher

'frogia, -gie ['frɔdʒa] SF (di cavallo ecc) nostril

'frollo, -a AG (carne) tender; (: selvaggina) high; (fig: persona) soft; **pasta frolla** short(crust) pastry

'fronda SF (leafy) branch; (di partito politico) internal opposition; **fronde** SFPL (di albero) foliage sg

fron'tale AG frontal; (scontro) head-on

'fronte SF (Anat) forehead; (di edificio) front, façade ▶ SM (Mil, Pol, Meteor) front; **a** ~, **di** ~ facing, opposite; **di** ~ **a** (posizione) opposite, facing, in front of; (a paragone di) compared with; **far** ~ **a** (nemico, problema) to confront; (responsabilità) to face up to; (spese) to cope with

fronteggi'are [fronted'dʒare] /62/ VT (avversari, difficoltà) to face, stand up to; (spese) to cope with

frontes'pizio [frontes'pittsjo] SM (Archit) frontispiece; (di libro) title page

fronti'era SF border, frontier

fron'tone SM pediment

'fronzolo ['frondzolo] SM frill

'frotta SF crowd; **in** ~, **a frotte** in their hundreds, in droves

'frottola SF fib; **raccontare un sacco di frottole** to tell a pack of lies

fru'gale AG frugal

fru'gare /80/ VI to rummage ▶ VT to search

frugherò etc [fruge'rɔ] VB vedi **frugare**

frui'tore SM user

fruizi'one [fruit'tsjone] SF use

frul'lare /72/ VT (Cuc) to whisk ▶ VI (uccelli) to flutter; **cosa ti frulla in mente?** what is going on in that mind of yours?

frul'lato SM (Cuc) milk shake; (: con solo frutta) fruit drink

frulla'tore SM electric mixer

f

frul'lino SM whisk

fru'mento SM wheat

frusci'are [fruʃʃare] /**14**/ VI to rustle

fru'scio [fruʃʃio] SM rustle; rustling; (di acque) murmur

'frusta SF whip; (Cuc) whisk

frus'tare/72/ VT to whip

frus'tata SF lash

frus'tino SM riding crop

frus'trare/72/ VT to frustrate

frus'trato, -a AG frustrated

frustrazi'one [frustrat'tsjone] SF frustration

'frutta SF fruit; (portata) dessert; ~ **candita/ secca** candied/dried fruit

frut'tare/72/ VI (investimenti, deposito) to bear dividends, give a return; **il mio deposito in banca (mi) frutta il 10%** my bank deposits bring (me) in 10%; **quella gara gli fruttò la medaglia d'oro** he won the gold medal in that competition

frut'teto SM orchard

frutticol'tura SF fruit growing

frut'tifero, -a AG (albero ecc) fruit-bearing; (fig: che frutta) fruitful, profitable; **deposito ~** interest-bearing deposit

frutti'vendolo, -a SM/F greengrocer (BRIT), produce dealer (US)

'frutto SM fruit; (fig: risultato) result(s); (Econ: interesse) interest; (: reddito) income; **è ~ della tua immaginazione** it's a figment of your imagination; **frutti di mare** seafood sg; **frutti di bosco** berries

fruttu'oso, -a AG fruitful, profitable

FS ABBR (= Ferrovie dello Stato) Italian railways

f.t. ABBR = **fuori testo**

f.to ABBR (= firmato) signed

fu VB vedi **essere** ▶ AG INV: **il fu Paolo Bianchi** the late Paolo Bianchi

fuci'lare [futʃi'lare] /**72**/ VT to shoot

fuci'lata [futʃi'lata] SF rifle shot

fucilazi'one [futʃilat'tsjone] SF execution (by firing squad)

fu'cile [fu'tʃile] SM rifle, gun; (da caccia) shotgun, gun; **~ a canne mozze** sawn-off shotgun

fu'cina [fu'tʃina] SF forge

'fuco, -chi SM drone

'fucsia SF fuchsia

'fuga, -ghe SF escape, flight; (di gas, liquidi) leak; (Mus) fugue; **mettere qn in ~** to put sb to flight; **~ di cervelli** brain drain

fu'gace [fu'gatʃe] AG fleeting, transient

fu'gare/80/ VT (dubbi, incertezze) to dispel, drive out

fug'gevole [fud'dʒevole] AG fleeting

fuggi'asco, -a, -schi, -sche [fud'dʒasko] AG, SM/F fugitive

fuggi'fuggi [fuddʒi'fuddʒi] SM scramble, stampede

fug'gire [fud'dʒire] /**31**/ VI to flee, run away; (fig: passar veloce) to fly ▶ VT to avoid

fuggi'tivo, -a [fuddʒi'tivo] SM/F fugitive, runaway

'fui VB vedi **essere**

'fulcro SM (Fisica) fulcrum; (fig: di teoria, questione) central o key point

ful'gore SM brilliance, splendour (BRIT), splendor (US)

fu'liggine [fu'liddʒine] SF soot

fulmi'nare/72/ VT (elettricità) to electrocute; (con arma da fuoco) to shoot dead; **fulminarsi** VPR (lampadina) to go, blow; (fig: con lo sguardo) **mi fulminò (con uno sguardo)** he looked daggers at me

'fulmine SM bolt of lightning; **fulmini** SMPL lightning sg; **~ a ciel sereno** bolt from the blue

ful'mineo, -a AG (fig: scatto) rapid; (: minaccioso) threatening

'fulvo, -a AG tawny

fumai'olo SM (di nave) funnel; (di fabbrica) chimney

fu'mante AG (piatto ecc) steaming

fu'mare/72/ VI to smoke; (emettere vapore) to steam ▶ VT to smoke

fu'mario, -a AG: **canna fumaria** flue

fu'mata SF (segnale) smoke signal; **farsi una ~** to have a smoke; **~ bianca/nera** (in Vaticano) signal that a new pope has/has not been elected

fuma'tore, -'trice SM/F smoker

fu'metto SM comic strip; **giornale a fumetti** comic

'fummo VB vedi **essere**

'fumo SM smoke; (vapore) steam; (il fumare tabacco) smoking; **fumi** SMPL (industriali ecc) fumes; **vendere ~** to deceive, cheat; **è tutto ~ e niente arrosto** it has no substance to it; **i fumi dell'alcool** (fig) the after-effects of drink; **~ passivo** passive smoking

fu'mogeno, -a [fu'mɔdʒeno] AG (candelotto) smoke cpd ▶ SM smoke bomb; **cortina fumogena** smoke screen

fu'moso, -a AG smoky; (fig) muddled

fu'nambolo, -a SM/F tightrope walker

'fune SF rope, cord; (più grossa) cable

'funebre AG (rito) funeral; (aspetto) gloomy, funereal

fune'rale SM funeral

fu'nesto, -a AG (incidente) fatal; (errore, decisione) fatal, disastrous; (atmosfera) gloomy, dismal

'fungere ['fundʒere] /**5**/ VI: **~ da** to act as

'fungo, -ghi SM fungus; (commestibile) mushroom; **~ velenoso** toadstool; **crescere come i funghi** (fig) to spring up overnight

funico'lare SF funicular railway

funi'via SF cable railway

'funsietc VB vedi **fungere**
'funto, -a PP di **fungere**
funzio'nare [funtsjo'nare] /**72**/ VI to work, function; (fungere): ~ **da** to act as
funzio'nario [funtsjo'narjo] SM official; ~ **statale** civil servant
funzi'one [fun'tsjone] SF function; (carica) post, position; (Rel) service; **in** ~ (meccanismo) in operation; **in ~ di** (come) as; **vive in ~ dei figli** he lives for his children; **far ~ di** to act as; **fare la ~ di qn** (farne le veci) to take sb's place
fu'oco, -chi SM fire; (fornello) ring; (Fot, Fisica) focus; **dare ~ a qc** to set fire to sth; **far ~** (sparare) to fire; **prendere ~** to catch fire; **al ~!** fire!; ~ **d'artificio** firework; ~ **di paglia** flash in the pan; ~ **sacro** o **di Sant'Antonio** (Med: col) shingles sg
fuorché [fwor'ke] CONG, PREP except
FU'ORI SIGLA M (= Fronte Unitario Omosessuale Rivoluzionario Italiano) gay liberation movement
fu'ori AV outside; (all'aperto) outdoors, outside; (fuori di casa, Sport) out; (esclamativo) get out! ▶ PREP: ~ **(di)** out of, outside ▶ SM outside; **essere in** ~ (sporgere) to stick out; **lasciar ~ qc/qn** to leave sth/sb out; **far ~** (col: soldi) to spend; (: cioccolatini) to eat up; (: rubare) to nick; **far ~ qn** (col) to kill sb, do sb in; **essere tagliato ~** (da un gruppo, ambiente) to be excluded; **essere ~ di sé** to be beside oneself; ~ **luogo** (inopportuno) out of place, uncalled for; ~ **mano** out of the way, remote; ~ **pasto** between meals; ~ **pericolo** out of danger; ~ **dai piedi!** get out of the way!; ~ **servizio** out of order; ~ **stagione** out of season; **illustrazione ~ testo** (Stampa) plate; ~ **uso** old-fashioned; obsolete
fuori'bordo SM INV speedboat (with outboard motor); outboard motor
fuori'busta SM INV unofficial payment
fuori'classe SM INV/F INV (undisputed) champion
fuori'corso AG INV (moneta) no longer in circulation; (Ins): **(studente)** ~ undergraduate who has not completed a course in due time
fuorigi'oco [fwori'dʒɔko] SM offside
fuori'legge [fwori'leddʒe] SM INV/F INV outlaw
fuoriprog'ramma SM INV (TV, Radio) unscheduled programme; (fig) change of plan o programme
fuori'serie AG INV (auto ecc) custom-built ▶ SF custom-built car

fuoris'trada SM (Aut) cross-country vehicle
fuoru'scito, -a [fworuʃ'ʃito], **fuoriu'scito, -a** [fworiuʃ'ʃito] SM/F exile ▶ SF (di gas) leakage, escape; (di sangue, linfa) seepage
fuorvi'are/60/ VT to mislead; (fig) to lead astray ▶ VI to go astray
furbacchi'one, -a [furbak'kjone] SM/F cunning old devil
fur'bizia [fur'bittsja] SF (vedi ag) cleverness; cunning; **una ~** a cunning trick
'furbo, -a AG clever, smart; (peg) cunning ▶ SM/F: **fare il ~** to (try to) be clever o smart; **fatti ~!** show a bit of sense!
fu'rente AG: ~ **(contro)** furious (with)
fure'ria SF (Mil) orderly room
fu'retto SM ferret
fur'fante SM rascal, scoundrel
furgon'cino [furgon'tʃino] SM small van
fur'gone SM van
'furia SF (ira) fury, rage; (fig: impeto) fury, violence; (: fretta) rush; **a ~ di** by dint of; **andare su tutte le furie** to fly into a rage
furi'bondo, -a AG furious
furi'ere SM quartermaster
furi'oso, -a AG furious; (mare, vento) raging
'furono VB vedi **essere**
fu'rore SM fury; (esaltazione) frenzy; **far ~** to be all the rage
furtiva'mente AV furtively
fur'tivo, -a AG furtive
'furto SM theft; ~ **con scasso** burglary
'fusa SF PL: **fare le ~** to purr
fu'scello [fuʃ'ʃello] SM twig
fu'seaux SM PL leggings
'fusietc VB vedi **fondere**
fu'sibile SM (Elettr) fuse
fusi'one SF (di metalli) fusion, melting; (colata) casting; (Comm) merger; (fig) merging
'fuso, -a PP di **fondere** ▶ SM (Filatura) spindle; **diritto come un ~** as stiff as a ramrod; ~ **orario** time zone
fusoli'era SF (Aer) fusillage
fus'tagno [fus'taɲɲo] SM corduroy
fus'tella SF (su scatola di medicinali) tear-off tab
fusti'gare/80/ VT (frustare) to flog; (fig: costumi) to censure, denounce
fus'tino SM (di detersivo) tub
'fusto SM stem; (Anat, di albero) trunk; (recipiente) drum, can; (col) he-man
'futile AG vain, futile
futilità SF INV futility
futu'rismo SM futurism
fu'turo, -a AG, SM future

Gg

G, g [dʒi] SM O F INV (*lettera*) G, g; **G come
  Genova** ≈ G for George
g ABBR (= *grammo*) g
G8 [dʒi'otto] SM (= *Gruppo degli Otto*) G8
G20 [dʒi'venti] SM (= *Gruppo dei Venti*) G20
gabar'dine [gabar'din] SM (*tessuto*)
  gabardine; (*soprabito*) gabardine raincoat
gab'bare /72/ VT to take in, dupe; **gabbarsi**
  VPR: **gabbarsi di qn** to make fun of sb
'**gabbia** SF cage; (*Dir*) dock; (*da imballaggio*)
  crate; **la ~ degli accusati** (*Dir*) the dock;
  ~ dell'ascensore lift (*BRIT*) o elevator (*US*)
  shaft; **~ toracica** (*Anat*) rib cage
gabbi'ano SM (sea)gull
gabi'netto SM (*Med ecc*) consulting room;
  (*Pol*) ministry; (*di decenza*) toilet, lavatory;
  (*Ins: di fisica ecc*) laboratory
Ga'bon SM: **il ~** Gabon
ga'elico, -a, -ci, -che AG, SM Gaelic
gaffe [gaf] SF INV blunder, boob (*col*)
gagli'ardo, -a [gaʎ'ʎardo] AG strong, vigorous
gai'ezza [ga'jettsa] SF gaiety, cheerfulness
'**gaio, -a** AG cheerful
'**gala** SF (*sfarzo*) pomp; (*festa*) gala
ga'lante AG gallant, courteous; (*avventura,
  poesia*) amorous
galante'ria SF gallantry
galantu'omo (*pl* **galantuomini**) SM
  gentleman
Ga'lapagos SFPL: **le (isole) ~** the Galapagos
  Islands
ga'lassia SF galaxy
gala'teo SM (good) manners *pl*, etiquette
gale'otto SM (*rematore*) galley slave; (*carcerato*)
  convict
ga'lera SF (*Naut*) galley; (*prigione*) prison
'**galla** SF: **a ~** afloat; **venire a ~** to surface,
  come to the surface; (*fig: verità*) to come out
galleggia'mento [galleddʒa'mento] SM
  floating; **linea di ~** (*di nave*) waterline
galleggi'ante [galled'dʒante] AG floating
  ▶ SM (*natante*) barge; (*di pescatore, lenza, Tecn*)
  float
galleggi'are [galled'dʒare] /62/ VI to float

galle'ria SF (*traforo*) tunnel; (*Archit, d'arte*)
  gallery; (*Teat*) circle; (*strada coperta con negozi*)
  arcade; **~ del vento** o **aerodinamica** (*Aer*)
  wind tunnel
'**Galles** SM: **il ~** Wales
gal'lese AG Welsh ▶ SMF Welshman(-woman)
  ▶ SM (*Ling*) Welsh; **i Gallesi** the Welsh
gal'letta SF cracker; (*Naut*) ship's biscuit
gal'letto SM young cock, cockerel; (*fig*) cocky
  young man; **fare il ~** to play the gallant
'**Gallia** SF: **la ~** Gaul
gal'lina SF hen; **andare a letto con le
  galline** to go to bed early
gal'lismo SM machismo
'**gallo** SM cock; **al canto del ~** at daybreak, at
  cockcrow; **fare il ~** to play the gallant
gal'lone SM piece of braid; (*Mil*) stripe; (*unità
  di misura*) gallon
galop'pare /72/ VI to gallop
galop'pino SM errand boy; (*Pol*) canvasser
ga'loppo SM gallop; **al** o **di ~** at a gallop
galvaniz'zare [galvanid'dzare] /72/ VT to
  galvanize
'**gamba** SF leg; (*asta: di lettera*) stem; **in ~**
  (*in buona salute*) well; (*bravo, sveglio*) bright,
  smart; **prendere qc sotto ~** (*fig*) to treat sth
  too lightly; **scappare a gambe levate** to
  take to one's heels; **gambe!** scatter!
gam'bale SM legging
gambe'retto SM shrimp
'**gambero** SM (*di acqua dolce*) crayfish; (*di mare*)
  prawn
'**Gambia** SF: **la ~** the Gambia
gambiz'zare [gambid'dzare] /72/ VT to kneecap
'**gambo** SM stem; (*di frutta*) stalk
ga'mella SF mess tin
'**gamma** SF (*Mus*) scale; (*di colori, fig*) range;
  ~ di prodotti product range
ga'nascia, -sce [ga'naʃʃa] SF jaw; **ganasce
  del freno** (*Aut*) brake shoes
'**gancio** ['gantʃo] SM hook
'**Gange** ['gandʒe] SM: **il ~** the Ganges
'**gangheri** ['gangeri] SMPL: **uscire dai ~** (*fig*)
  to fly into a temper

gan'grena SF = **cancrena**

'gara SF competition; (*Sport*) competition; contest; match; (: *corsa*) race; **fare a ~** to compete, vie; **~ d'appalto** (*Comm*) tender

ga'rage [ga'raʒ] SM INV garage

ga'rante SMF guarantor

garan'tire/55/ VT to guarantee; (*debito*) to stand surety for; (*dare per certo*) to assure

garan'tismo SM protection of civil liberties

garan'tista, -i, -e AG concerned with civil liberties

garan'zia [garan'tsia] SF guarantee; (*pegno*) security; **in ~** under guarantee

gar'bare/72/ VI: **non mi garba** I don't like it (*o him etc*)

garba'tezza [garba'tettsa] SF courtesy, politeness

gar'bato, -a AG courteous, polite

'garbo SM (*buone maniere*) politeness, courtesy; (*di vestito ecc*) grace, style

gar'buglio [gar'buʎʎo] SM tangle; (*fig*) muddle, mess

gareggi'are [gared'dʒare] /**62**/ VI to compete

garga'nella SF: **a ~** from the bottle

garga'rismo SM gargle; **fare i gargarismi** to gargle

ga'ritta SF (*di caserma*) sentry box

ga'rofano SM carnation; **chiodo di ~** clove

gar'retto SM hock

gar'rire/55/ VI to chirp

'garrulo, -a AG (*uccello*) chirping; (*persona: loquace*) garrulous, talkative

'garza ['gardza] SF (*per bende*) gauze

gar'zone [gar'dzone] SM (*di negozio*) boy

gas SM INV gas; **a tutto ~** at full speed; **dare ~** (*Aut*) to accelerate; **~ lacrimogeno** tear gas; **~ naturale** natural gas

ga'sare etc /**72**/ = **gassare** etc

ga'sato, -a SM/F (*col: persona*) freak

gas'dotto SM gas pipeline

ga'solio SM diesel (oil)

ga's(s)are/72/ VT to aerate, carbonate; (*asfissiare*) to gas; **gas(s)arsi** VPR (*col*) to get excited

ga's(s)ato, -a AG (*bibita*) aerated, fizzy

gas'soso, -a AG gaseous; gassy ▶ SF fizzy drink

'gastrico, -a, -ci, -che AG gastric

gast'rite SF gastritis

gastroente'rite SF gastroenteritis

gastrono'mia SF gastronomy

gas'tronomo, -a SM/F gourmet, gastronome

G.A.T.T. SIGLA M (= *General Agreement on Tariffs and Trade*) GATT

'gatta SF cat, she-cat; **una ~ da pelare** (*col*) a thankless task; **qui ~ ci cova!** I smell a rat!, there's something fishy going on here!

gatta'buia SF (*col, scherzoso: prigione*) clink

gat'tino SM kitten

'gatto SM cat, tomcat; **~ delle nevi** (*Aut, Sci*) snowcat; **~ a nove code** cat-o'-nine-tails; **~ selvatico** wildcat

gatto'pardo SM: **~ africano** serval; **~ americano** ocelot

gat'tuccio [gat'tuttʃo] SM dogfish

gau'dente SMF pleasure-seeker

'gaudio SM joy, happiness

ga'vetta SF (*Mil*) mess tin; **venire dalla ~** (*Mil, fig*) to rise from the ranks

'gazza ['gaddza] SF magpie

gaz'zarra [gad'dzarra] SF racket, din

gaz'zella [gad'dzɛlla] SF gazelle; (*dei carabinieri*) (high-speed) police car

gaz'zetta [gad'dzetta] SF news sheet; **G~ Ufficiale** *official publication containing details of new laws*

gaz'zoso, -a [gad'dzoso] AG = **gassoso**

Gazz. Uff. ABBR = **Gazzetta Ufficiale**

GB SIGLA (= *Gran Bretagna*) GB

G.C. ABBR = **genio civile**

G.d.F. ABBR = **guardia di finanza**

GE SIGLA = **Genova**

gel [dʒɛl] SM INV gel

ge'lare [dʒe'lare] /**72**/ VT, VI, VB IMPERS to freeze; **mi ha gelato il sangue** (*fig*) it made my blood run cold

ge'lata [dʒe'lata] SF frost

gela'taio, -a [dʒela'tajo] SM/F ice-cream vendor

gelate'ria [dʒelate'ria] SF ice-cream shop

gela'tina [dʒela'tina] SF gelatine; **~ esplosiva** gelignite; **~ di frutta** fruit jelly

gelati'noso, -a [dʒelati'noso] AG gelatinous, jelly-like

ge'lato, -a [dʒe'lato] AG frozen ▶ SM ice cream

'gelido, -a ['dʒɛlido] AG icy, ice-cold

'gelo ['dʒɛlo] SM (*temperatura*) intense cold; (*brina*) frost; (*fig*) chill

ge'lone [dʒe'lone] SM chilblain

gelo'sia [dʒelo'sia] SF jealousy

ge'loso, -a [dʒe'loso] AG jealous

'gelso ['dʒɛlso] SM mulberry (tree)

gelso'mino [dʒelso'mino] SM jasmine

gemel'laggio [dʒemel'laddʒo] SM twinning

gemel'lare [dʒemel'lare] /**72**/ AG twin *cpd* ▶ VT (*città*) to twin

ge'mello, -a [dʒe'mɛllo] AG, SM/F twin; **gemelli** SMPL (*di camicia*) cufflinks; **Gemelli** Gemini *sg*; **essere dei Gemelli** to be Gemini

'gemere ['dʒemere] /**29**/ VI to moan, groan; (*cigolare*) to creak; (*gocciolare*) to drip, ooze

'gemito ['dʒemito] SM moan, groan

'gemma ['dʒemma] SF (*Bot*) bud; (*pietra preziosa*) gem

Gen. ABBR (*Mil*: = *generale*) Gen

gen. ABBR (= *generale, generalmente*) gen

gen'darme [dʒen'darme] SM policeman; (*fig*) martinet

151

'gene ['dʒɛne] SM gene

genealo'gia, -'gie [dʒenealo'dʒia] SF genealogy

genea'logico, -a, -ci, -che [dʒenea'lɔdʒiko] AG genealogical; **albero** ~ family tree

gene'rale [dʒene'rale] AG, SM general; **in** ~ (*per sommi capi*) in general terms; (*di solito*) usually, in general; **a** ~ **richiesta** by popular request

generalità [dʒenerali'ta] SFPL (*dati d'identità*) particulars

generaliz'zare [dʒeneralid'dzare] /**72**/ VT, VI to generalize

generalizzazi'one [dʒeneraliddzat'tsjone] SF generalization

general'mente [dʒeneral'mente] AV generally

gene'rare [dʒene'rare] /**72**/ VT (*dar vita*) to give birth to; (*produrre*) to produce; (*causare*) to arouse; (*Tecn*) to produce, generate

genera'tore [dʒenera'tore] SM (*Tecn*) generator

generazi'one [dʒenerat'tsjone] SF generation

'genere ['dʒenere] SM kind, type, sort; (*Biol*) genus; (*merce*) article, product; (*Ling*) gender; (*Arte, Letteratura*) genre; **in** ~ generally, as a rule; **cose del** *o* **di questo** ~ such things; **il** ~ **umano** mankind; **generi alimentari** foodstuffs; **generi di consumo** consumer goods; **generi di prima necessità** basic essentials

ge'nerico, -a, -ci, -che [dʒe'nɛriko] AG generic; (*vago*) vague, imprecise; **medico** ~ general practitioner

'genero ['dʒenero] SM son-in-law

generosità [dʒenerosi'ta] SF generosity

gene'roso, -a [dʒene'roso] AG generous

'genesi ['dʒenezi] SF genesis

ge'netico, -a, -ci, -che [dʒe'nɛtiko] AG genetic ▶ SF genetics *sg*

gen'giva [dʒen'dʒiva] SF (*Anat*) gum

ge'nia [dʒe'nia] SF (*peg*) mob, gang

geni'ale [dʒe'njale] AG (*persona*) of genius; (*idea*) ingenious, brilliant

'genio ['dʒɛnjo] SM genius; (*attitudine, talento*) talent, flair, genius; **andare a** ~ **a qn** to be to sb's liking, appeal to sb; ~ **civile** civil engineers *pl*; **il** ~ **(militare)** the Engineers

geni'tale [dʒeni'tale] AG genital; **genitali** SMPL genitals

geni'tore [dʒeni'tore] SM parent, father *o* mother; **genitori** SMPL parents

genn. ABBR (= *gennaio*) Jan

gen'naio [dʒen'najo] SM January; *vedi anche* **luglio**

geno'cidio [dʒeno'tʃidjo] SM genocide

'Genova ['dʒɛnova] SF Genoa

geno'vese [dʒeno'vese] AG, SMF Genoese (*pl inv*)

gen'taglia [dʒen'taʎʎa] SF (*peg*) rabble

'gente ['dʒɛnte] SF people *pl*

gentil'donna [dʒentil'dɔnna] SF lady

gen'tile [dʒen'tile] AG (*persona, atto*) kind; (: *garbato*) courteous, polite; (*nelle lettere*): **G~ Signore** Dear Sir; **G~ Signor Fernando Villa** (*sulla busta*) Mr Fernando Villa

genti'lezza [dʒenti'lettsa] SF kindness; courtesy, politeness; **per** ~ (*per favore*) please

gentilu'omo [dʒenti'lwɔmo] (*pl* **gentiluomini**) SM gentleman

genuflessi'one [dʒenufles'sjone] SF genuflection

genu'ino, -a [dʒenu'ino] AG (*prodotto*) natural; (*persona, sentimento*) genuine, sincere

geogra'fia [dʒeogra'fia] SF geography

geo'grafico, -a, -ci, -che [dʒeo'grafiko] AG geographical

ge'ografo, -a [dʒe'ɔgrafo] SM/F geographer

geolo'gia [dʒeolo'dʒia] SF geology

geo'logico, -a, -ci, -che [dʒeo'lɔdʒiko] AG geological

ge'ometra, -i, -e [dʒe'ɔmetra] SM/F (*professionista*) surveyor

geome'tria [dʒeome'tria] SF geometry

geo'metrico, -a, -ci, -che [dʒeo'mɛtriko] AG geometric(al)

geopo'litico, -a, -ci, -che [dʒeopo'litiko] AG geopolitical

Ge'orgia [dʒe'ɔrdʒa] SF Georgia

geor'giano, -a [dʒeor'dʒano] AG, SM/F Georgian

ge'ranio [dʒe'ranjo] SM geranium

ge'rarca, -chi [dʒe'rarka] SM (*Storia: nel fascismo*) party official

gerar'chia [dʒerar'kia] SF hierarchy

ge'rarchico, -a, -ci, -che [dʒe'rarkiko] AG hierarchical

ge'rente [dʒe'rɛnte] SMF manager (manageress)

ge'renza [dʒe'rɛntsa] SF management

ger'gale [dʒer'gale] AG slang *cpd*

'gergo, -ghi ['dʒergo] SM jargon; slang

geria'tria [dʒerja'tria] SF geriatrics *sg*

geri'atrico, -a, -ci, -che [dʒe'rjatriko] AG geriatric

'gerla ['dʒɛrla] SF conical wicker basket

Ger'mania [dʒer'manja] SF: **la** ~ Germany; **la** ~ **occidentale/orientale** West/East Germany

'germe ['dʒɛrme] SM germ; (*fig*) seed

germinazi'one [dʒerminat'tsjone] SF germination

germogli'are [dʒermoʎ'ʎare] /**27**/ VI (*emettere germogli*) to sprout; (*germinare*) to germinate

ger'moglio [dʒer'mɔʎʎo] SM shoot; (*gemma*) bud

gero'glifico, -ci [dʒero'glifiko] SM hieroglyphic

geron'tologo, -a, -gi, -ghe [dʒeron'tɔlogo] SM/F specialist in geriatrics

ge'rundio [dʒe'rundjo] SM gerund
Gerusa'lemme [dʒeruza'lemme] SF Jerusalem
'gesso ['dʒɛsso] SM chalk; (*Scultura, Med, Edil*) plaster; (*statua*) plaster figure; (*minerale*) gypsum
'gesta ['dʒɛsta] SFPL (*letterario*) deeds, feats
ges'tante [dʒes'tante] SF expectant mother
gestazi'one [dʒestat'tsjone] SF gestation
gestico'lare [dʒestiko'lare] /**72**/ VI to gesticulate
gestio'nale [dʒestjo'nale] AG administrative, management *cpd*
gesti'one [dʒes'tjone] SF management; **~ di magazzino** stock control; **~ patrimoniale** investment management
ges'tire [dʒes'tire] /**55**/ VT to run, manage
'gesto ['dʒɛsto] SM gesture
ges'tore [dʒes'tore] SM manager
Gesù [dʒe'zu] SM Jesus; **~ bambino** the Christ Child
gesu'ita, -i [dʒezu'ita] SM Jesuit
get'tare [dʒet'tare] /**72**/ VT to throw; (*anche*: **gettare via**) to throw away o out; (*Scultura*) to cast; (*Edil*) to lay; (*acqua*) to spout; (*grido*) to utter; **gettarsi** VPR: **gettarsi in** (*impresa*) to throw o.s. into; (*mischia*) to hurl o.s. into; (*fiume*) to flow into; **~ uno sguardo su** to take a quick look at
get'tata [dʒet'tata] SF (*di cemento, gesso, metalli*) cast; (*diga*) jetty
'gettito ['dʒettito] SM revenue
'getto ['dʒetto] SM (*di gas, liquido, Aer*) jet; (*Bot*) shoot; **a ~ continuo** uninterruptedly; **di ~** (*fig*) straight off, in one go
get'tone [dʒet'tone] SM token; (*per giochi*) counter; (*: roulette ecc*) chip; **~ di presenza** attendance fee; **~ telefonico** telephone token
gettoni'era [dʒetto'njɛra] SF telephone-token dispenser
'geyser ['gaizə] SM INV geyser
'Ghana ['gana] SM: **il ~** Ghana
'ghenga, -ghe ['gɛnga] SF (*col*) gang, crowd
ghe'pardo [ge'pardo] SM cheetah
gher'mire [ger'mire] /**55**/ VT to grasp, clasp, clutch
'ghetta ['getta] SF (*gambale*) gaiter
ghettiz'zare [gettid'dzare] /**72**/ VT to segregate
'ghetto ['getto] SM ghetto
ghiacci'aia [gjat'tʃaja] SF (*anche fig*) icebox
ghiacci'aio [gjat'tʃajo] SM glacier
ghiacci'are [gjat'tʃare] /**14**/ VT to freeze; (*fig*): **~ qn** to make sb's blood run cold ▶ VI to freeze, ice over
ghiacci'ato, -a [gjat'tʃato] AG frozen; (*bevanda*) ice-cold
ghi'accio ['gjattʃo] SM ice

ghiacci'olo [gjat'tʃolo] SM icicle; (*tipo di gelato*) ice lolly (BRIT), popsicle (US)
ghi'aia ['gjaja] SF gravel
ghi'anda ['gjanda] SF (*Bot*) acorn
ghi'andola ['gjandola] SF gland
ghiando'lare [gjando'lare] AG glandular
ghigliot'tina [giʎʎot'tina] SF guillotine
ghi'gnare [giɲ'ɲare] /**15**/ VI to sneer
'ghigno ['giɲɲo] SM (*espressione*) sneer; (*risata*) mocking laugh
'ghingheri ['gingeri] SMPL: **in ~** all dolled up; **mettersi in ~** to put on one's Sunday best
ghi'otto, -a ['gjotto] AG greedy; (*cibo*) delicious, appetizing
ghiot'tone, -a [gjot'tone] SM/F glutton
ghiotto'neria [gjotto'ria] SF greed, gluttony; (*cibo*) delicacy, titbit (BRIT), tidbit (US)
ghiri'goro [giri'goro] SM scribble, squiggle
ghir'landa [gir'landa] SF garland, wreath
'ghiro ['giro] SM dormouse
'ghisa ['giza] SF cast iron
G.I. ABBR = **giudice istruttore**
già [dʒa] AV already; (*ex, in precedenza*) formerly ▶ ESCL of course!, yes indeed!; **~ che ci sei ...** while you are at it ...
gi'acca, -che ['dʒakka] SF jacket; **~ a vento** windcheater (BRIT), windbreaker (US)
giacché [dʒak'ke] CONG since, as
giac'chetta [dʒak'ketta] SF (light) jacket
'giaccio etc ['dʒattʃo] VB vedi **giacere**
giac'cone [dʒak'kone] SM heavy jacket
gia'cenza [dʒa'tʃɛntsa] SF: **merce in ~** goods in stock; **capitale in ~** uninvested capital; **giacenze di magazzino** unsold stock
gia'cere [dʒa'tʃere] /**57**/ VI to lie
giaci'mento [dʒatʃi'mento] SM deposit
gia'cinto [dʒa'tʃinto] SM hyacinth
giaci'uto, -a [dʒa'tʃuto] PP di **giacere**
gi'acqui etc ['dʒakkwi] VB vedi **giacere**
gi'ada ['dʒada] SF jade
giaggi'olo [dʒad'dʒolo] SM iris
giagu'aro [dʒa'gwaro] SM jaguar
gial'lastro, -a [dʒal'lastro] AG yellowish; (*carnagione*) sallow
gi'allo ['dʒallo] AG yellow; (*carnagione*) sallow ▶ SM yellow; (*anche*: **romanzo giallo**) detective novel; (*anche*: **film giallo**) detective film; **~ dell'uovo** yolk; **il mar G~** the Yellow Sea
gial'lognolo, -a [dʒal'loɲɲolo] AG yellowish, dirty yellow
Gia'maica [dʒa'maika] SF: **la ~** Jamaica
giamai'cano, -a [dʒamai'kano] AG, SM/F Jamaican
giam'mai [dʒam'mai] AV never
Giap'pone [dʒap'pone] SM: **il ~** Japan
giappo'nese [dʒappo'nese] AG, SMF, SM Japanese *inv*
gi'ara ['dʒara] SF jar

giardi'naggio [dʒardi'naddʒo] SM gardening

giardi'netta [dʒardi'netta] SF estate car (BRIT), station wagon (US)

giardini'ere, -a [dʒardi'njɛre] SM/F gardener ▶ SF (misto di sottaceti) mixed pickles pl; (automobile) = **giardinetta**

giar'dino [dʒar'dino] SM garden; ~ **d'infanzia** nursery school; ~ **pubblico** public gardens pl, (public) park; ~ **zoologico** zoo

giarretti'era [dʒarret'tjɛra] SF garter

Gi'ava ['dʒava] SF Java

giavel'lotto [dʒavel'lɔtto] SM javelin

gib'boso, -a [dʒib'boso] AG (superficie) bumpy; (naso) crooked

Gibil'terra [dʒibil'tɛrra] SF Gibraltar

giga SM INV (Inform) gig

giga'byte [dʒiga'bait] SM INV gigabyte

gi'gante, -'essa [dʒi'gante] SM/F giant ▶ AG giant, gigantic; (Comm) giant-size

gigan'tesco, -a, -schi, -sche [dʒigan'tesko] AG gigantic

gigantogra'fia [dʒigantogra'fia] SF (Fot) blow-up

'giglio ['dʒiʎʎo] SM lily

gilè [dʒi'lɛ] SM INV waistcoat

gin [dʒin] SM INV gin

gin'cana [dʒin'kana] SF gymkhana

ginecolo'gia [dʒinekolo'dʒia] SF gynaecology (BRIT), gynecology (US)

gine'cologo, -a, -gi, -ghe [dʒine'kɔlogo] SM/F gynaecologist (BRIT), gynecologist (US)

gi'nepro [dʒi'nepro] SM juniper

gi'nestra [dʒi'nɛstra] SF (Bot) broom

Gi'nevra [dʒi'nevra] SF Geneva; **il Lago di ~** Lake Geneva

gingil'larsi [dʒindʒil'larsi] /**72**/ VPR to fritter away one's time; (giocare): ~ **con** to fiddle with

gin'gillo [dʒin'dʒillo] SM plaything

gin'nasio [dʒin'nazjo] SM the 4th and 5th year of secondary school in Italy

gin'nasta, -i, -e [dʒin'nasta] SM/F gymnast

gin'nastica [dʒin'nastika] SF gymnastics sg; (esercizio fisico) keep-fit exercises pl; (Ins) physical education

'ginnico, -a, -ci, -che ['dʒinnko] AG gymnastic

gi'nocchio [dʒi'nɔkkjo] (pl(m) **ginocchi**, pl(f) **ginocchia**) SM knee; **stare in ~** to kneel, be on one's knees; **mettersi in ~** to kneel (down)

ginocchi'oni [dʒinok'kjoni] AV on one's knees

gio'care [dʒo'kare] /**20**/ VT to play; (scommettere) to stake, wager, bet; (ingannare) to take in ▶ VI to play; (a roulette ecc) to gamble; (fig) to play a part, be important; (Tecn: meccanismo) to be loose; ~ **a** (gioco, sport) to play; (cavalli) to bet on; ~ **d'astuzia** to be

crafty; **giocarsi la carriera** to put one's career at risk; **giocarsi tutto** to risk everything; **a che gioco giochiamo?** what are you playing at?

gioca'tore, -'trice [dʒoka'tore] SM/F player; gambler

gio'cattolo [dʒo'kattolo] SM toy

giocherel'lare [dʒokerel'lare] /**72**/ VI: ~ **con** (giocattolo) to play with; (distrattamente) to fiddle with

giocherò etc [dʒoke'rɔ] VB vedi **giocare**

gio'chetto [dʒo'ketto] SM (gioco) game; (tranello) trick; (fig): **è un ~** it's child's play

gi'oco, -chi ['dʒɔko] SM game; (divertimento, Tecn) play; (al casinò) gambling; (Carte) hand; (insieme di pezzi ecc necessari per un gioco) set; **per ~** for fun; **fare il doppio ~ con qn** to double-cross sb; **prendersi ~ di qn** to pull sb's leg; **stare al ~ di qn** to play along with sb; **è in ~ la mia reputazione** my reputation is at stake; ~ **d'azzardo** game of chance; ~ **della palla** ball game; ~ **degli scacchi** chess set; **i Giochi Olimpici** the Olympic Games

gioco'forza [dʒoko'fɔrtsa] SM: **essere ~** to be inevitable

giocoli'ere [dʒoko'ljɛre] SM juggler

gio'coso, -a [dʒo'koso] AG playful, jesting

gio'gaia [dʒo'gaja] SF (Geo) range of mountains

gi'ogo, -ghi ['dʒogo] SM yoke

gi'oia ['dʒoja] SF joy, delight; (pietra preziosa) jewel, precious stone

gioielle'ria [dʒojelle'ria] SF jeweller's (BRIT) o jeweler's (US) craft; (negozio) jewel(l)er's (shop)

gioielli'ere, -a [dʒojel'ljɛre] SM/F jeweller (BRIT), jeweler (US)

gioi'ello [dʒo'jello] SM jewel, piece of jewellery (BRIT) o jewelry (US); **gioielli** SMPL (anelli, collane ecc) jewellery sg; **i miei gioielli** my jewels o jewellery; **i gioielli della Corona** the crown jewels

gioi'oso, -a [dʒo'joso] AG joyful

Gior'dania [dʒor'danja] SF: **la ~** Jordan

Gior'dano [dʒor'dano] SM: **il ~** the Jordan

gior'dano, -a [dʒor'dano] AG, SM/F Jordanian

giorna'laio, -a [dʒorna'lajo] SM/F newsagent (BRIT), newsdealer (US)

gior'nale [dʒor'nale] SM (news)paper; (diario) journal, diary; (Comm) journal; ~ **di bordo** (Naut) ship's log; ~ **radio** radio news sg

giorna'letto [dʒorna'letto] SM (children's) comic

giornali'ero, -a [dʒorna'ljero] AG daily; (che varia: umore) changeable ▶ SM day labourer (BRIT) o laborer (US)

giorna'lino [dʒorna'lino] SM children's comic

giorna'lismo [dʒorna'lizmo] SM journalism

giorna'lista, -i, -e [dʒorna'lista] SM/F
journalist

giorna'listico, -a, -ci, -che [dʒorna'listiko]
AG journalistic; **stile ~** journalese

giornal'mente [dʒornal'mente] AV daily

gior'nata [dʒor'nata] SF day; (paga) day's
wages, day's pay; **durante la ~ di ieri**
yesterday; **fresco di ~** (uovo) freshly laid;
vivere alla ~ to live from day to day;
~ lavorativa working day

gi'orno ['dʒorno] SM day; (opposto alla notte)
day, daytime; (luce del giorno) daylight; **al ~**
per day; **di ~** by day; **~ per ~** day by day; **al ~**
d'oggi nowadays; **tutto il santo ~** all day
long; **il G~ dei Morti** see note

> Il Giorno dei Morti, All Souls' Day, falls on
> 2 November. At this time of year people
> visit cemeteries to lay flowers on the
> graves of their loved ones.

gi'ostra ['dʒostra] SF (per bimbi) merry-go-
round; (torneo storico) joust

gios'trare [dʒos'trare] /**72**/ VI (Storia) to joust,
tilt; **giostrarsi** VPR to manage

giov. ABBR (= giovedì) Thur(s)

giova'mento [dʒova'mento] SM benefit,
help

gi'ovane ['dʒovane] AG young; (aspetto)
youthful ▶ SM youth, young man ▶ SF girl,
young woman; **i giovani** young people;
è ~ del mestiere he's new to the job

giova'netto, -a [dʒova'netto] SM/F young
man(-woman)

giova'nile [dʒova'nile] AG youthful; (scritti)
early; (errore) of youth

giova'notto [dʒova'notto] SM young man

gio'vare [dʒo'vare] /**72**/ VI: **~ a** (essere utile) to be
useful to; (far bene) to be good for ▶ VB IMPERS
(essere bene, utile) to be useful; **giovarsi** VPR:
giovarsi di qc to make use of sth; **a che**
giova prendersela? what's the point of
getting upset?

Gi'ove ['dʒove] SM (Mitologia) Jove; (Astr)
Jupiter

giovedì [dʒove'di] SM INV Thursday; **di** o **il ~**
on Thursdays; vedi anche **martedì**

gio'venca, -che [dʒo'vɛnka] SF heifer

gioventù [dʒoven'tu] SF (periodo) youth;
(i giovani) young people pl, youth

giovi'ale [dʒo'vjale] AG jovial, jolly

giovi'nastro [dʒovi'nastro] SM young thug

giovin'cello [dʒovin'tʃɛllo] SM young lad

giovi'nezza [dʒovi'nettsa] SF youth

gip [dʒip] SIGLA M INV (= giudice per le indagini
preliminari) judge for preliminary enquiries

gira'dischi [dʒira'diski] SM INV record player

gi'raffa [dʒi'raffa] SF giraffe; (TV, Cine, Radio)
boom

gira'mento [dʒira'mento] SM: **~ di testa** fit
of dizziness

gira'mondo [dʒira'mondo] SM INV/F INV
globetrotter

gi'randola [dʒi'randola] SF (fuoco d'artificio)
Catherine wheel; (giocattolo) toy windmill;
(banderuola) weather vane, weathercock

gi'rante [dʒi'rante] SMF (di assegno) endorser

gi'rare [dʒi'rare] /**72**/ VT (far ruotare) to turn;
(percorrere, visitare) to go round; (Cine) to shoot;
(: film: come regista) to make; (Comm) to
endorse ▶ VI to turn; (più veloce) to spin;
(andare in giro) to wander, go around; **girarsi**
VPR to turn; **~ attorno a** to go round; to
revolve round; **si girava e rigirava nel**
letto he tossed and turned in bed; **far ~ la**
testa a qn to make sb dizzy; (fig) to turn
sb's head; **gira al largo** keep your
distance; **girala come ti pare** (fig) look at
it whichever way you like; **gira e rigira ...**
after a lot of driving (o walking) about ...;
(fig) whichever way you look at it; **cosa ti**
gira? (col) what's got into you?; **mi ha fatto**
~ le scatole (col) he drove me crazy

girar'rosto [dʒirar'rosto] SM (Cuc) spit

gira'sole [dʒira'sole] SM sunflower

gi'rata [dʒi'rata] SF (passeggiata) stroll; (con
veicolo) drive; (Comm) endorsement

gira'tario, -a [dʒira'tarjo] SM/F endorsee

gira'volta [dʒira'volta] SF twirl, turn; (curva)
sharp bend; (fig) about-turn

gi'rello [dʒi'rello] SM (di bambino) Babywalker®
(BRIT), go-cart (US); (taglio di carne) topside
(BRIT), top round (US)

gi'retto [dʒi'retto] SM (passeggiata) walk, stroll;
(: in macchina) drive, spin; (: in bicicletta) ride

gi'revole [dʒi'revole] AG revolving, turning

gi'rino [dʒi'rino] SM tadpole

'giro ['dʒiro] SM (circuito, cerchio) circle; (di
chiave, manovella) turn; (viaggio) tour,
excursion; (passeggiata) stroll, walk; (in
macchina) drive; (in bicicletta) ride; (Sport: della
pista) lap; (di denaro) circulation; (Carte) hand;
(Tecn) revolution; **fare un ~** to go for a walk
(o a drive o a ride); **fare il ~ di** (parco, città) to
go round; **andare in ~** (a piedi) to go about,
walk around; **guardarsi in ~** to look around;
prendere in ~ qn (fig) to take sb for a ride; **a**
stretto ~ di posta by return of post; **nel ~ di**
un mese in a month's time; **essere nel ~**
(fig) to belong to a circle (of friends);
~ d'affari (viaggio) business tour; (Comm)
turnover; **~ di parole** circumlocution; **~ di**
prova (Aut) test drive; **~ turistico**
sightseeing tour; **~ vita** waist measurement

giro'collo [dʒiro'kollo] SM: **a ~** crewneck cpd

giro'conto [dʒiro'konto] SM (Econ) credit
transfer

gi'rone [dʒi'rone] SM (Sport) series of games;
~ di andata/ritorno (Calcio) first/second half
of the season

gironzo'lare [dʒirondzo'lare] /**72**/ VI to stroll about

giro'tondo [dʒiro'tondo] SM ring-a-ring-o'-roses (BRIT), ring-around-the-rosey (US); **in ~** in a circle

girova'gare [dʒirova'gare] /**80**/ VI to wander about

gi'rovago, -a, -ghi, -ghe [dʒi'rɔvago] SM/F (vagabondo) tramp; (venditore) peddler; **una compagnia di girovaghi** (attori) a company of strolling actors

'gita ['dʒita] SF excursion, trip; **fare una ~** to go for a trip, go on an outing

gi'tano, -a [dʒi'tano] SM/F gipsy

gi'tante [dʒi'tante] SMF member of a tour

giù [dʒu] AV down; (dabbasso) downstairs; **in ~** downwards, down; **la mia casa è un po' più in ~** my house is a bit further on; **~ di lì** (pressappoco) thereabouts; **bambini dai 6 anni in ~** children aged 6 and under; **~ per, cadere ~ per le scale** to fall down the stairs; **~ le mani!** hands off!; **essere ~** (fig: di salute) to be run down; (: di spirito) to be depressed; **quel tipo non mi va ~** I can't stand that guy

gi'ubba ['dʒubba] SF jacket

giub'botto [dʒub'bɔtto] SM jerkin; **~ antiproiettile** bulletproof vest; **~ salvagente** life jacket

giubi'lare [dʒubi'lare] /**72**/ VI to rejoice

gi'ubilo ['dʒubilo] SM rejoicing

giudi'care [dʒudi'kare] /**20**/ VT to judge; (accusato) to try; (lite) to arbitrate in; **~ qn/qc bello** to consider sb/sth (to be) beautiful

giudi'cato [dʒudi'kato] SM (Dir): **passare in ~** to pass final judgment

gi'udice ['dʒuditʃe] SM judge; **~ collegiale** member of the court; **~ conciliatore** justice of the peace; **~ istruttore** examining (BRIT) o committing (US) magistrate; **~ popolare** member of a jury

giudizi'ale [dʒudit'tsjale] AG judicial

giudizi'ario, -a [dʒudit'tsjarjo] AG legal, judicial

giu'dizio [dʒu'dittsjo] SM judgment; (opinione) opinion; (Dir) judgment, sentence; (: processo) trial; (: verdetto) verdict; **aver ~** to be wise o prudent; **essere in attesa di ~** to be awaiting trial; **citare in ~** to summons; **l'imputato è stato rinviato a ~** the accused has been committed for trial

giudizi'oso, -a [dʒudit'tsjoso] AG prudent, judicious

gi'uggiola ['dʒuddʒola] SF: **andare in brodo di giuggiole** (col) to be over the moon

gi'ugno ['dʒuɲɲo] SM June; vedi anche **luglio**

giu'livo, -a [dʒu'livo] AG merry

giul'lare [dʒul'lare] SM jester

giu'menta [dʒu'menta] SF mare

gi'unco, -chi ['dʒunko] SM (Bot) rush

gi'ungere ['dʒundʒere] /**5**/ VI to arrive ▸ VT (mani ecc) to join; **~ a** to arrive at, reach; **~ nuovo a qn** to come as news to sb; **~ in porto** to reach harbour; (fig) to be brought to a successful outcome

gi'ungla ['dʒungla] SF jungle

gi'unsi etc ['dʒunsi] VB vedi **giungere**

gi'unto, -a ['dʒunto] PP di **giungere** ▸ SM (Tecn) coupling, joint ▸ SF addition; (organo esecutivo, amministrativo) council, board; **per giunta** into the bargain, in addition; **giunta militare** military junta; vedi anche **Comune; Provincia; Regione**

giun'tura [dʒun'tura] SF joint

giuo'care [dʒwo'kare] /**20**/ VT, VI = **giocare**

giu'oco ['dʒwɔko] SM = **gioco**

giura'mento [dʒura'mento] SM oath; **~ falso** perjury

giu'rare [dʒu'rare] /**72**/ VT to swear ▸ VI to swear, take an oath; **gliel'ho giurata** I swore I would get even with him

giu'rato, -a [dʒu'rato] AG: **nemico ~** sworn enemy ▸ SM/F juror, juryman(-woman)

giu'ria [dʒu'ria] SF jury

giu'ridico, -a, -ci, -che [dʒu'ridiko] AG legal

giurisdizi'one [dʒurizdit'tsjone] SF jurisdiction

giurispru'denza [dʒurispru'dɛntsa] SF jurisprudence

giu'rista, -i, -e [dʒu'rista] SM/F jurist

giustap'porre [dʒustap'porre] /**77**/ VT to juxtapose

giustapposizi'one [dʒustappozit'tsjone] SF juxtaposition

giustap'posto, -a [dʒustap'posto] PP di **giustapporre**

giustifi'care [dʒustifi'kare] /**20**/ VT to justify; **giustificarsi** VPR: **giustificarsi di** o **per qc** to justify o excuse o.s. for sth

giustifica'tivo, -a [dʒustifika'tivo] AG (Amm): **nota** o **pezza giustificativa** receipt

giustificazi'one [dʒustifikat'tsjone] SF justification; (Ins) (note of) excuse

gius'tizia [dʒus'tittsja] SF justice; **farsi ~ (da sé)** (vendicarsi) to take the law into one's own hands

giustizi'are [dʒustit'tsjare] /**19**/ VT to execute, put to death

giustizi'ere [dʒustit'tsjɛre] SM executioner

gi'usto, -a ['dʒusto] AG (equo) fair, just; (vero) true, correct; (adatto) right, suitable; (preciso) exact, correct ▸ AV (esattamente) exactly, precisely; (per l'appunto, appena) just; **arrivare ~** to arrive just in time; **ho ~ bisogno di te** you're just the person I need

'glabro, -a ['glabro] AG hairless

glaci'ale [gla'tʃale] AG glacial

gla'diolo SM gladiolus

'glandola ['glandola] SF = **ghiandola**

'**glassa** SF (*Cuc*) icing
glau'coma SM glaucoma
gli [ʎi] DET MPL (*dav V, s impura, gn, pn, ps, x, z*) the
▶ PRON (*a lui*) to him; (*a esso*) to it; (*in coppia con lo, la, li, le, ne: a lui, a lei, a loro ecc*): **gliele do** I'm giving them to him (*o her o them*); **gliene ho parlato** I spoke to him (*o her o them*) about it; *vedi anche* **il**
glice'mia [glitʃe'mia] SF glycaemia
glice'rina [glitʃe'rina] SF glycerine
'**glicine** ['glitʃine] SM wistaria
gli'ela *etc* ['ʎela] *vedi* **gli**
glo'bale AG overall; (*vista*) global
'**globo** SM globe
'**globulo** SM (*Anat*): ~ **rosso/bianco** red/white corpuscle
glocalizzazi'one [glokaliddza'tsjone] SF glocalization
'**gloria** SF glory; **farsi ~ di qc** to pride o.s. on sth, take pride in sth
glori'arsi /**72**/ VPR: ~ **di qc** to pride o.s. on sth, glory *o* take pride in sth
glorifi'care /**20**/ VT to glorify
glori'oso, -a AG glorious
glos'sario SM glossary
glu'cosio SM glucose
'**gluteo** SM gluteus; **glutei** SMPL buttocks
GM ABBR = **genio militare**
'**gnocchi** ['ɲɔkki] SMPL (*Cuc*) small dumplings *made of semolina pasta or potato*
'**gnomo** ['ɲɔmo] SM gnome
'**gnorri** ['ɲɔrri] SM INV/F INV: **non fare lo ~!** stop acting as if you didn't know anything about it!
GO SIGLA = **Gorizia**
'**goal** ['goul] SM INV (*Sport*) goal
'**gobba** SF (*Anat*) hump; (*protuberanza*) bump
'**gobbo, -a** AG hunchbacked; (*ricurvo*) round-shouldered ▶ SM/F hunchback
'**Gobi** SMPL: **il Deserto dei ~** the Gobi Desert
'**goccia, -ce** ['gottʃa] SF drop; ~ **di rugiada** dewdrop; **somigliarsi come due gocce d'acqua** to be as like as two peas in a pod; **è la ~ che fa traboccare il vaso!** it's the last straw!
'**goccio** ['gottʃo] SM drop, spot
goccio'lare [gottʃo'lare] /**72**/ VI, VT to drip
goccio'lio [gottʃo'lio] SM dripping
go'dere /**58**/ VI: ~ (**di**) (*compiacersi*) to be delighted (at), rejoice (at); ~ **di** (*trarre vantaggio*) to enjoy, to benefit from ▶ VT to enjoy; **godersi la vita** to enjoy life; **godersela** to have a good time, enjoy o.s.
godi'mento SM enjoyment
godrò *etc* VB *vedi* **godere**
goffaggine [gof'faddʒine] SF clumsiness
'**goffo, -a** AG clumsy, awkward
'**gogna** ['goɲɲa] SF pillory
'**gol** [gɔl] SM INV (*Sport*) = **goal**

'**gola** SF (*Anat*) throat; (*golosità*) gluttony, greed; (*di camino*) flue; (*di monte*) gorge; **fare ~** (*anche fig*) to tempt; **ricacciare il pianto** *o* **le lacrime in ~** to swallow one's tears
go'letta SF (*Naut*) schooner
golf SM INV (*Sport*) golf; (*maglia*) cardigan
'**golfo** SM gulf
goli'ardico, -a, -ci, -che AG (*canto, vita*) student *cpd*
go'loso, -a AG greedy
'**golpe** SM INV (*Pol*) coup
gomi'tata SF: **dare una ~ a qn** to elbow sb; **farsi avanti a** (**forza** *o* **furia di**) **gomitate** to elbow one's way through; **fare a gomitate per qc** to fight to get sth
'**gomito** SM elbow; (*di strada ecc*) sharp bend
go'mitolo SM ball
'**gomma** SF rubber; (*colla*) gum; (*per cancellare*) rubber, eraser; (*di veicolo*) tyre (BRIT), tire (US); ~ **da masticare** chewing gum; ~ **a terra** flat tyre
gommapi'uma® SF foam rubber
gom'mino SM rubber tip; (*rondella*) rubber washer
gom'mista, -i, -e SM/F tyre (BRIT) *o* tire (US) specialist; (*rivenditore*) tyre *o* tire merchant
gom'mone SM rubber dinghy
gom'moso, -a AG rubbery
'**gondola** SF gondola
gondoli'ere SM gondolier
gonfa'lone SM banner
gonfi'are /**19**/ VT (*pallone*) to blow up, inflate; (*dilatare, ingrossare*) to swell; (*fig: notizia*) to exaggerate; **gonfiarsi** VPR to swell; (*fiume*) to rise
'**gonfio, -a** AG swollen; (*stomaco*) bloated; (*palloncino, gomme*) inflated, blown up; (*con pompa*) pumped up; (*vela*) full; **occhi gonfi di pianto** eyes swollen with tears; ~ **di orgoglio** (*persona*) puffed up (with pride); **avere il portafoglio ~** to have a bulging wallet
gonfi'ore SM swelling
gongo'lare /**72**/ VI to look pleased with o.s.; ~ **di gioia** to be overjoyed
'**gonna** SF skirt; ~ **pantalone** culottes *pl*
'**gonzo** ['gondzo] SM simpleton, fool
goo'glare [gu'glare] /**72**/ VT (*Inform*) to google
gorgheggi'are [gorged'dʒare] /**62**/ VI to warble; to trill
gor'gheggio [gor'geddʒo] SM (*Mus, di uccello*) trill
'**gorgo, -ghi** SM whirlpool
gorgogli'are [gorgoʎ'ʎare] /**27**/ VI to gurgle
gorgo'glio [gorgoʎ'ʎio] SM gurgling
go'rilla SM INV gorilla; (*guardia del corpo*) bodyguard
'**Gotha** SM INV (*del cinema, letteratura, industria*) leading lights *pl*

g

'gotico, -a, -ci, -che AG, SM Gothic

'gotta SF gout

gover'nante SMF ruler ▶ SF (di bambini) governess; (donna di servizio) housekeeper

gover'nare /72/ VT (stato) to govern, rule; (pilotare, guidare) to steer; (bestiame) to tend, look after

governa'tivo, -a AG (politica, decreto) government cpd, governmental; (stampa) pro-government

governa'tore SM governor

go'verno SM government; **~ ombra** shadow cabinet

'gozzo ['gottso] SM (Zool) crop; (Med) goitre; (fig: col) throat

gozzovigli'are [gottsoviʎ'ʎare] /27/ VI to make merry, carouse

GPL [dʒipi'elle] SIGLA M (= Gas di Petrolio Liquefatto) LPG (= Liquefied Petroleum Gas)

gpm ABBR (= giri per minuto) rpm

GPS [dʒipi'ɛsse] SIGLA M GPS (= Global Positioning System)

GR [dzi'erre] SIGLA = **Grosseto** ▶ SIGLA M (= giornale radio) radio news

gracchi'are [grak'kjare] /19/ VI to caw

graci'dare [gratʃi'dare] /72/ VI to croak

graci'dio, -ii [gratʃi'dio] SM croaking

'gracile ['gratʃile] AG frail, delicate

gra'dasso SM boaster

grada'mente AV gradually, by degrees

gradazi'one [gradat'tsjone] SF (sfumatura) gradation; **~ alcolica** alcoholic content, strength

gra'devole AG pleasant, agreeable

gradi'mento SM pleasure, satisfaction; **essere di mio** (o **tuo** etc) **~** to be to my (o your etc) liking

gradi'nata SF flight of steps; (in teatro, stadio) tiers pl

gra'dino SM step; (Alpinismo) foothold

gra'dire /55/ VT (accettare con piacere) to accept; (desiderare) to wish, like; **gradisce una tazza di tè?** would you like a cup of tea?

gra'dito, -a AG welcome

'grado SM (Mat, Fisica ecc) degree; (stadio) degree, level; (Mil, sociale) rank; **essere in ~ di fare** to be in a position to do; **di buon ~** willingly; **per gradi** by degrees; **un cugino di primo/secondo ~** a first/second cousin; **subire il terzo ~** (anche fig) to be given the third degree

gradu'ale AG gradual

gradu'are /72/ VT to grade

gradu'ato, -a AG (esercizi) graded; (scala, termometro) graduated ▶ SM (Mil) non-commissioned officer

gradua'toria SF (di concorso) list; (per la promozione) order of seniority

'graffa SF (gancio) clip; (segno grafico) brace

graf'fetta SF paper clip

graffi'are /19/ VT to scratch; **graffiarsi** VPR to get scratched; (con unghie) to scratch o.s.

graffia'tura SF scratch

'graffio SM scratch

graf'fiti SMPL graffiti

gra'fia SF spelling; (scrittura) handwriting

'grafico, -a, -ci, -che AG graphic ▶ SM graph; (persona) graphic designer ▶ SF graphic arts pl; **~ a torta** pie chart

gra'migna [gra'miɲɲa] SF weed; couch grass

gram'matica, -che SF grammar

grammati'cale AG grammatical

'grammo SM gram(me)

gram'mofono SM gramophone

'gramo, -a AG (vita) wretched

gran AG vedi **grande**

'grana SF (granello, di minerali, corpi spezzati) grain; (col: seccatura) trouble; (: soldi) cash ▶ SM INV cheese similar to Parmesan

gra'naglie [gra'naʎʎe] SFPL corn sg, seed sg

gra'naio SM granary, barn

gra'nata SF (frutto) pomegranate; (pietra preziosa) garnet; (proiettile) grenade

granati'ere SM (Mil) grenadier; (fig) fine figure of a man

Gran Bre'tagna [granbre'taɲɲa] SF: **la ~** Great Britain

gran'cassa SF (Mus) bass drum

'granchio ['grankjo] SM crab; (fig) blunder; **prendere un ~** (fig) to blunder

grandango'lare SM wide-angle lens sg

gran'dangolo SM (Fot) wide-angle lens sg

'grande (qualche volta **gran** + C, **grand'** + V) AG (grosso, largo, vasto) big, large; (alto) tall; (lungo) long; (in sensi astratti) great ▶ SMF (persona adulta) adult, grown-up; (chi ha ingegno e potenza) great man(-woman); **mio fratello più ~** my big o older brother; **il gran pubblico** the general public; **di gran classe** (prodotto) high-class; **cosa farai da ~?** what will you be o do when you grow up?; **fare le cose in ~** to do things in style; **fare il ~** (strafare) to act big; **una gran bella donna** a very beautiful woman; **non è una gran cosa** o **un gran che** it's nothing special; **non ne so gran che** I don't know very much about it

grandeggi'are [granded'dʒare] /62/ VI (emergere per grandezza): **~ su** to tower over; (darsi arie) to put on airs

gran'dezza [gran'dettsa] SF (dimensione) size; magnitude; (fig) greatness; **in ~ naturale** lifesize; **manie di ~** delusions of grandeur

grandi'nare /72/ VB IMPERS to hail

'grandine SF hail

grandi'oso, -a AG grand, grandiose

gran'duca, -chi SM grand duke

grandu'cato SM grand duchy

grandu'chessa [grandu'kessa] SF grand
  duchess
gra'nello SM (di cereali, uva) seed; (di frutta) pip;
  (di sabbia, sale ecc) grain
gra'nita SF kind of water ice
gra'nito SM granite
'grano SM (in quasi tutti i sensi) grain; (frumento)
  wheat; (di rosario, collana) bead; **~ di pepe**
  peppercorn
gran'turco SM maize
'granulo SM granule; (Med) pellet
'grappa SF rough, strong brandy
'grappolo SM bunch, cluster
'graspo SM bunch (of grapes)
gras'setto SM (Tip) bold (type) (BRIT), bold
  face
'grasso, -a AG fat; (cibo) fatty; (pelle) greasy;
  (terreno) rich; (fig: guadagno, annata) plentiful;
  (: volgare) coarse, lewd ▶ SM (di persona, animale)
  fat; (sostanza che unge) grease
gras'soccio, -a, -ci, -ce [gras'sɔttʃo] AG
  plump
gras'sone, -a SM/F (col: persona) dumpling
'grata SF grating
gra'ticcio [gra'tittʃo] SM trellis; (stuoia) mat
gra'ticola SF grill
gra'tifica, -che SF bonus; **~ natalizia**
  Christmas bonus
gratificazi'one [gratifikat'tsjone] SF
  (soddisfazione) satisfaction, reward
grati'nare /72/ VT (Cuc) to cook au gratin
'gratis AV free, for nothing
grati'tudine SF gratitude
'grato, -a AG grateful; (gradito) pleasant,
  agreeable
gratta'capo SM worry, headache
grattaci'elo [gratta'tʃɛlo] SM skyscraper
gratta e 'sosta SM INV scratch card used to pay
  for parking
gratta e 'vinci [grattae'vintʃi] SM (lotteria)
  lottery; (biglietto) scratchcard
grat'tare /72/ VT (pelle) to scratch; (raschiare)
  to scrape; (pane, formaggio, carote) to grate;
  (col: rubare) to pinch ▶ VI (stridere) to grate;
  (Aut) to grind; **grattarsi** VPR to scratch o.s.;
  grattarsi la pancia (fig) to twiddle one's
  thumbs
grat'tata SF scratch; **fare una ~** (Aut: col) to
  grind the gears
grat'tugia [grat'tudʒa], **-gie** SF grater
grattugi'are [grattu'dʒare] **/62/** VT to grate;
  pane grattugiato breadcrumbs pl
gratuità SF (fig) gratuitousness
gra'tuito, -a AG free; (fig) gratuitous
gra'vame SM tax; (fig) burden, weight
gra'vare /72/ VT to burden ▶ VI: **~ su** to
  weigh on
'grave AG (danno, pericolo, peccato ecc) grave,
  serious; (responsabilità) heavy, grave;

(contegno) grave, solemn; (voce, suono) deep,
low-pitched; (Ling): **accento ~** grave accent
▶ SM (Fisica) (heavy) body; **un malato ~** a
person who is seriously ill
grave'mente AV (ammalato, ferito) seriously
gravi'danza [gravi'dantsa] SF pregnancy
'gravido, -a AG pregnant
gravità SF seriousness; (anche Fisica) gravity
gravi'tare /72/ VI (Fisica): **~ intorno a** to
  gravitate round
gra'voso, -a AG heavy, onerous
'grazia ['grattsja] SF grace; (favore) favour
  (BRIT), favor (US); (Dir) pardon; **di ~** (ironico)
  if you please; **troppa ~!** (ironico) you're too
  generous!; **quanta ~ di Dio!** what
  abundance!; **entrare nelle grazie di qn**
  to win sb's favour; **Ministero di G~ e
  Giustizia** Ministry of Justice, ≈ Lord
  Chancellor's Office (BRIT), ≈ Department of
  Justice (US)
grazi'are [grat'tsjare] **/19/** VT (Dir) to pardon
'grazie ['grattsje] ESCL thank you!; **~ mille!** o
  tante! o **infinite!** thank you very much!;
  ~ a thanks to
grazi'oso, -a [grat'tsjoso] AG charming,
  delightful; (gentile) gracious
'Grecia ['gretʃa] SF: **la ~** Greece
'greco, -a, -ci, -che AG, SM/F, SM Greek
gre'gario SM (Ciclismo) supporting rider
'gregge ['greddʒe] (pl(f) **greggi**) SM flock
'greggio, -a, -gi, -ge ['greddʒo] AG raw,
  unrefined; (diamante) rough, uncut; (tessuto)
  unbleached ▶ SM (anche: **petrolio greggio**)
  crude (oil)
grembi'ule SM apron; (sopravveste) overall
'grembo SM lap; (ventre della madre) womb
gre'mito, -a AG: **~ (di)** packed o crowded
  (with)
'greto SM (exposed) gravel bed of a river
'gretto, -a AG mean, stingy; (fig) narrow-
  minded
'greve AG heavy
'grezzo, -a ['greddzo] AG = **greggio**
gri'dare /72/ VI (per chiamare) to shout, cry
  (out); (strillare) to scream, yell ▶ VT to shout
  (out), yell (out); **~ aiuto** to cry o shout for
  help
'grido (pl(m) **gridi**, pl(f) **grida**) SM shout, cry;
  scream, yell; (di animale) cry; **di ~** famous;
  all'ultimo ~ in the latest style
'grigio ['gridʒo], **-a, -gi, -gie** AG, SM grey
  (BRIT), gray (US)
'griglia ['griʎʎa] SF (per arrostire) grill; (Elettr)
  grid; (inferriata) grating; **alla ~** (Cuc) grilled
grigli'ata [griʎ'ʎata] SF (Cuc) grill
gril'letto SM trigger
'grillo SM (Zool) cricket; (fig) whim; **ha dei
  grilli per la testa** his head is full of
  nonsense

g

'grimal'dello SM picklock

'grinfia SF: **cadere nelle grinfie di qn** (*fig*) to fall into sb's clutches

'grinta SF grim expression; (*Sport*) fighting spirit; **avere molta** ~ to be very determined

grintoso, -a AG forceful

'grinza ['grintsa] SF crease, wrinkle; (*ruga*) wrinkle; **il tuo ragionamento non fa una ~** your argument is faultless

grin'zoso, -a [grin'tsoso] AG wrinkled; creased

grip'pare /72/ VI (*Tecn*) to seize

gris'sino SM bread-stick

groenlan'dese AG Greenland *cpd* ▶ SMF Greenlander

Groen'landia SF: **la** ~ Greenland

'gronda SF eaves *pl*

gron'daia SF gutter

gron'dante AG dripping

gron'dare /72/ VI to pour; (*essere bagnato*): **~ di** to be dripping with ▶ VT to drip with

'groppa SF (*di animale*) back, rump; (*col: dell'uomo*) back, shoulders *pl*

'groppo SM tangle; **avere un ~ alla gola** (*fig*) to have a lump in one's throat

'grossa SF (*unità di misura*) gross

gros'sezza [gros'settsa] SF size; thickness

gros'sista, -i, -e SM/F (*Comm*) wholesaler

'grosso, -a AG big, large; (*di spessore*) thick; (*grossolano: anche fig*) coarse; (*grave, insopportabile*) serious, great; (*tempo, mare*) rough ▶ SM: **il ~ di** the bulk of; **un pezzo ~** (*fig*) a VIP, a bigwig; **farla grossa** to do something very stupid; **dirle grosse** to tell tall stories (*BRIT*) *o* tales (*US*); **questa è grossa!** that's a good one!; **sbagliarsi di ~** to be completely wrong; **dormire della grossa** to sleep like a log

grossolanità SF coarseness

grosso'lano, -a AG rough, coarse; (*fig*) coarse, crude; (*: errore*) stupid

grosso'modo AV roughly

'grotta SF cave; grotto

grot'tesco, -a, -schi, -sche AG grotesque

grovi'era SM *o* F gruyère (cheese)

gro'viglio [gro'viλλo] SM tangle; (*fig*) muddle

gru SF INV crane

'gruccia, -ce ['gruttʃa] SF (*per camminare*) crutch; (*per abiti*) coat-hanger

gru'gnire [grun'ɲire] /55/ VI to grunt

gru'gnito [grun'ɲito] SM grunt

'grugno ['gruɲɲo] SM snout; (*col: faccia*) mug

'grullo, -a AG silly, stupid

'grumo SM (*di sangue*) clot; (*di farina ecc*) lump

gru'moso, -a AG lumpy

'gruppo SM group; **~ sanguigno** blood group

gruvi'era SM *o* F = **groviera**

'gruzzolo ['gruttsolo] SM (*di denaro*) hoard

GSM SIGLA M (= *Global System for Mobile Communication*) GSM

GT ABBR (*Aut*: = *gran turismo*) GT

G.U. ABBR = **Gazzetta Ufficiale**

guada'gnare [gwadaɲ'ɲare] /15/ VT (*ottenere*) to gain; (*soldi, stipendio*) to earn; (*vincere*) to win; (*raggiungere*) to reach; **tanto di guadagnato!** so much the better!

gua'dagno [gwa'daɲɲo] SM earnings *pl*; (*Comm*) profit; (*vantaggio, utile*) advantage, gain; **~ di capitale** capital gains *pl*; **~ lordo/ netto** gross/net earnings *pl*

gu'ado SM ford; **passare a ~** to ford

gu'ai ESCL: **~ a te** (*o lui etc*)! woe betide you (*o him etc*)!

gua'ina SF (*fodero*) sheath; (*indumento per donna*) girdle

gu'aio SM trouble, mishap; (*inconveniente*) trouble, snag

gua'ire /55/ VI to whine, yelp

gua'ito SM (*di cane*) yelp, whine; (*il guaire*) yelping, whining

gu'ancia, -ce ['gwantʃa] SF cheek

guanci'ale [gwan'tʃale] SM pillow; **dormire fra due guanciali** (*fig*) to sleep easy, have no worries

gu'anto SM glove; **trattare qn con i guanti** (*fig*) to handle sb with kid gloves; **gettare/ raccogliere il ~** (*fig*) to throw down/take up the gauntlet

guan'tone SM boxing glove

guarda'boschi [gwarda'bɔski] SM INV forester

guarda'caccia [gwarda'kattʃa] SM INV gamekeeper

guarda'coste SM INV coastguard; (*nave*) coastguard patrol vessel

guarda'linee SM INV (*Sport*) linesman

guarda'macchine [gwarda'makkine] SM INV/F INV car-park (*BRIT*) *o* parking lot (*US*) attendant

guar'dare /72/ VT (*con lo sguardo: osservare*) to look at; (*: film, televisione*) to watch; (*custodire*) to look after, take care of ▶ VI to look; (*badare*): **~ a** to pay attention to; (*luoghi: esser orientato*): **~ a** to face; **guardarsi** VPR to look at o.s.; **~ di** to try to; **guardarsi da** (*astenersi*) to refrain from; (*stare in guardia*) to beware of; **guardarsi dal fare** to take care not to do; **guarda di non sbagliare** try not to make a mistake; **ma guarda un po'!** good heavens!; **e guarda caso …** as if by coincidence …; **~ qn dall'alto in basso** to look down on sb; **non ~ in faccia a nessuno** (*fig*) to have no regard for anybody; **~ di traverso** to scowl *o* frown at; **~ a vista qn** to keep a close watch on sb

guarda'roba SM INV wardrobe; (*locale*) cloakroom

guardarobi'ere, -a SM/F cloakroom attendant

guardasi'gilli [gwardasi'dʒilli] SM INV ≈ Lord Chancellor (BRIT), ≈ Attorney General (US)

gu'ardia SF (*individuo, corpo*) guard; (*sorveglianza*) watch; **fare la ~ a qc/qn** to guard sth/sb; **stare in ~** (*fig*) to be on one's guard; **il medico di ~** the doctor on call; **il fiume ha raggiunto il livello di ~** the river has reached the high-water mark; **~ carceraria** (*prison*) warder (BRIT) o guard (US); **~ del corpo** bodyguard; **~ di finanza** (*corpo*) customs pl; (*persona*) customs officer; *see note*; **~ forestale** forest ranger; **~ giurata** security guard; **~ medica** emergency doctor service; **~ municipale** town policeman; **~ notturna** night security guard; **~ di pubblica sicurezza** policeman

> The *Guardia di Finanza* is a military body which deals with infringements of the laws governing income tax and monopolies. It reports to the Ministers of Finance, Justice or Agriculture, depending on the function it is performing.

guardia'caccia [gwardja'kattʃa] SM INV = **guardacaccia**

guardi'ano, -a SM/F (*di carcere*) warder (BRIT), guard (US); (*di villa ecc*) caretaker; (*di museo*) custodian; (*di zoo*) keeper; **~ notturno** night watchman

guar'dina SF cell

guar'dingo, -a, -ghi, -ghe AG wary, cautious

guardi'ola SF porter's lodge; (*Mil*) look-out tower

guarigi'one [gwari'dʒone] SF recovery

gua'rire /55/ VT (*persona, malattia*) to cure; (*ferita*) to heal ▶ VI to recover, be cured; to heal (up)

guarnigi'one [gwarni'dʒone] SF garrison

guar'nire /55/ VT (*ornare: abiti*) to trim; (*Cuc*) to garnish

guarnizi'one [gwarnit'tsjone] SF trimming; garnish; (*Tecn*) gasket

guas'tare /72/ VT to spoil, ruin; (*meccanismo*) to break; **guastarsi** VPR (*cibo*) to go bad; (*meccanismo*) to break down; (*tempo*) to change for the worse; (*amici*) to quarrel, fall out

gu'asto, -a AG (*non funzionante*) broken; (: *telefono ecc*) out of order; (*andato a male*) bad, rotten; (: *dente*) decayed, bad; (*fig: corrotto*) depraved ▶ SM breakdown; (*avaria*) failure; **~ al motore** engine failure

Guate'mala SM: **il ~** Guatemala

guatemal'teco, -a, -ci, -che AG, SM/F Guatemalan

gu'ercio, -a, -ci, -ce ['gwertʃo] AG cross-eyed

gu'erra SF war; (*tecnica: atomica, chimica ecc*) warfare; **fare la ~ (a)** to wage war (against); **la ~ fredda** the Cold War; **~ mondiale** world war; **~ preventiva** preventive war; **la prima/seconda ~ mondiale** the First/Second World War

guerrafon'daio SM warmonger

guerreggi'are [gwerred'dʒare] /62/ VI to wage war

guer'resco, -a, -schi, -sche AG (*di guerra*) war cpd; (*incline alla guerra*) warlike

guerri'ero, -a AG warlike ▶ SM warrior

guer'riglia [gwer'riʎʎa] SF guerrilla warfare

guerrigli'ero [gwerriʎ'ʎɛro] SM guerrilla

'gufo SM owl

'guglia ['guʎʎa] SF (*Archit*) spire; (*di roccia*) needle

Gui'ana SF: **la ~ francese** French Guiana

gu'ida SF (*persona*) guide; (*libro*) guide(book); (*comando, direzione*) guidance, direction; (*Aut*) driving; (: *sterzo*) steering; (*tappeto: di tenda, cassetto*) runner; **~ a destra/sinistra** (*Aut*) right-/left-hand drive; **essere alla ~ di** (*governo*) to head; (*spedizione, paese*) to lead; **far da ~ a qn** (*mostrare la strada*) to show sb the way; (*in una città*) to show sb (a)round; **~ telefonica** telephone directory; **~ turistica** tourist guide

gui'dare /72/ VT to guide; (*squadra, rivolta*) to lead; (*auto*) to drive; (*aereo, nave*) to pilot; **sa ~?** can you drive?

guida'tore, -'trice SM/F (*conducente*) driver

Gui'nea SF: **la Repubblica di ~** the Republic of Guinea; **la ~ Equatoriale** Equatorial Guinea

guin'zaglio [gwin'tsaʎʎo] SM leash, lead

gu'isa SF: **a ~ di** like, in the manner of

guiz'zare [gwit'tsare] /72/ VI to dart; to flicker; to leap; **~ via** (*fuggire*) to slip away

gu'izzo ['gwittso] SM (*di animali*) dart; (*di fulmine*) flash

'guru SM INV (*Rel, anche fig*) guru

guscio ['guʃʃo] SM shell

gus'tare /72/ VT (*cibi*) to taste; (: *assaporare con piacere*) to enjoy, savour (BRIT), savor (US); (*fig*) to enjoy, appreciate ▶ VI: **~ a** to please; **non mi gusta affatto** I don't like it at all

gusta'tivo, -a AG: **papille gustative** taste buds

'gusto SM (*senso*) taste; (*sapore*) taste, flavour (BRIT), flavor (US); (*godimento*) enjoyment; **al ~ di fragola** strawberry-flavoured; **di ~ barocco** in the baroque style; **mangiare di ~** to eat heartily; **prenderci ~: ci ha preso ~** he's acquired a taste for it, he's got to like it

gus'toso, -a AG tasty; (*fig*) agreeable

guttu'rale AG guttural

Gu'yana [gu'jana] SF: **la ~** Guyana

Hh

H, h ['akka] SM O F INV (*lettera*) H, h ▶ ABBR
(= *ora*) hr; (= *etto, altezza*) h; **H come hotel** =
H for Harry (BRIT), H for How (US)
ha¹, 'hai [a, ai] VB *vedi* **avere**
ha² ABBR (= *ettaro*) ha
ha'cker ['haker] SM INV hacker
Ha'iti [a'iti] SF Haiti
haiti'ano, -a [ai'tjano] AG, SM/F Haitian
hall [hɔːl] SF INV hall, foyer
ham'burger [am'burger] SM INV (*carne*)
hamburger; (*panino*) burger
'handicap ['handikap] SM INV handicap
handicap'pato, -a [andikap'pato] AG
handicapped ▶ SM/F handicapped person,
disabled person
'hanno ['anno] VB *vedi* **avere**
hard dis'count [ardis'kaunt] SM INV
discount supermarket
hard 'disk [ar'disk] SM INV hard disk
'hardware ['ardwer] SM INV hardware
ha'scisc, hascisch [aʃʃiʃ] SM hashish
'hashtag ['aʃtag] SM INV (*Inform*) hashtag
hawai'ano, -a [ava'jano] AG, SM/F Hawaiian
Ha'waii [a'vai] SFPL: **le ~** Hawaii *sg*
help [ɛlp] SM INV (*Inform*) help

help' desk [ɛlp'dɛsk] SM INV (*Inform*) help desk
'Helsinki ['ɛlsinki] SF Helsinki
'herpes ['ɛrpes] SM (*Med*) herpes *sg*; **~ zoster**
shingles *sg*
hg ABBR (= *ettogrammo*) hg
'hi-fi ['haifai] SM INV, AG INV hi-fi
Hima'laia [ima'laja] SM: **l'~** the Himalayas *pl*
hl ABBR (= *ettolitro*) hl
ho [ɔ] VB *vedi* **avere**
'hobby ['hɔbi] SM INV hobby
'hockey ['hɔki] SM hockey; **~ su ghiaccio** ice
hockey
'holding ['houldiŋ] SF INV holding company
'home page ['hɔm'pɛidʒ] SF INV home page
Hon'duras [on'duras] SM Honduras
'Hong Kong ['ɔkɔ̃g] SF Hong Kong
Hono'lulu [ono'lulu] SF Honolulu
'hostess ['houstis] SF INV air hostess (BRIT) o
stewardess
'hot dog ['hɔtdɔg] SM INV hot dog
ho'tel [o'tɛl] SM INV hotel
'humour ['jumor] SM INV (sense of) humour
'humus SM humus
'husky ['aski] SM INV (*cane*) husky
Hz ABBR (= *hertz*) Hz

I i

I, i [i] SM O F INV (*lettera*) I, i; **I come Imola** ≈
I for Isaac (BRIT), I for Item (US)

i DET MPL the; *vedi anche* **il** ¯

IACP SIGLA M (= *Istituto Autonomo per le Case
Popolari*) public housing association

i'ato SM hiatus

i'berico, -a, -ci, -che AG Iberian; **la Penisola
Iberica** the Iberian Peninsula

iber'nare /72/ VI to hibernate ▶ VT (*Med*) to
induce hypothermia in

ibernazi'one [ibernat'tsjone] SF hibernation

ibid. ABBR (= *ibidem*) ib(id)

'ibrido, -a AG, SM hybrid

IC ABBR (= *Intercity*) Intercity

'ICE ['itʃe] SIGLA M (= *Istituto nazionale per il
Commercio Estero*) overseas trade board

'ICI ['itʃi] SIGLA F (= *Imposta Comunale sugli
Immobili*) ≈ Council Tax

i'cona SF (*Rel, Inform, anche fig*) icon

id ABBR (= *idem*) do.

Id'dio SM God

i'dea SF idea; (*opinione*) opinion, view; (*ideale*)
ideal; **avere le idee chiare** to know one's
mind; **cambiare ~** to change one's mind;
dare l' ~ di to seem, look like; **neanche** o
neppure per ~! certainly not!, no way!;
~ fissa obsession

ide'ale AG, SM ideal

idea'lismo SM idealism

idea'lista, -i, -e SM/F idealist

idea'listico, -a, -ci, -che AG idealistic

idealiz'zare [idealid'dzare] /72/ VT to idealize

ide'are /72/ VT (*immaginare*) to think up,
conceive; (*progettare*) to plan

idea'tore, -'trice SM/F author

i'dentico, -a, -ci, -che AG identical

identifi'care /20/ VT to identify; **identificarsi**
VPR: **identificarsi (con)** to identify o.s. (with)

identificazi'one [identifikat'tsjone] SF
identification

identità SF INV identity

ideolo'gia, -'gie [ideolo'dʒia] SF ideology

ideo'logico, -a, -ci, -che [ideo'lɔdʒiko] AG
ideological

idil'liaco, -a, -ci, -che AG = **idillico**

i'dillico, -a, -ci, -che AG idyllic

i'dillio SM idyll; **tra di loro è nato un ~**
they have fallen in love

idi'oma, -i SM idiom, language

idio'matico, -a, -ci, -che AG idiomatic;
frase idiomatica idiom

idiosincra'sia SF idiosyncrasy

idi'ota, -i, -e AG idiotic ▶ SM/F idiot

idio'zia [idjot'tsia] SF idiocy; (*atto, discorso*)
idiotic thing to do (*o say*)

ido'latra, -i, -e AG idolatrous ▶ SM/F idolater

idola'trare /72/ VT to worship; (*fig*) to idolize

idola'tria SF idolatry

'idolo SM idol

idoneità SF suitability; **esame di ~**
qualifying examination

i'doneo, -a AG: **~ a** suitable for, fit for; (*Mil*) fit
for; (*qualificato*) qualified for

i'drante SM hydrant

idra'tante AG (*crema*) moisturizing ▶ SM
moisturizer

idra'tare /72/ VT (*pelle*) to moisturize

idratazi'one [idratat'tsjone] SF moisturizing

i'draulico, -a, -ci, -che AG hydraulic ▶ SM
plumber ▶ SF hydraulics *sg*

'idrico, -a, -ci, -che AG water *cpd*

idrocar'buro SM hydrocarbon

idroe'lettrico, -a, -ci, -che AG hydroelectric

i'drofilo, -a AG: **cotone ~** cotton wool (BRIT),
absorbent cotton (US)

idrofo'bia SF rabies *sg*

i'drofobo, -a AG rabid; (*fig*) furious

i'drogeno [i'drɔdʒeno] SM hydrogen

idroli'pidico, -a, -ci, -che AG hydrolipid

idro'porto SM (*Aer*) seaplane base

idrorepel'lente AG water-repellent

idros'calo SM = **idroporto**

idrovo'lante SM seaplane

i'ella SF bad luck

iel'lato, -a AG plagued by bad luck

i'ena SF hyena

ie'ratico, -a, -ci, -che AG (*Rel: scrittura*)
hieratic; (*fig: atteggiamento*) solemn

i'eri AV, SM yesterday; **il giornale di ~** yesterday's paper; **~ l'altro** the day before yesterday; **~ sera** yesterday evening

ietta'tore, -'trice SM/F jinx

igi'ene [i'dʒɛne] SF hygiene; **norme d'~** sanitary regulations; **ufficio d'~** public health office; **~ mentale** mental health; **~ pubblica** public health

igi'enico, -a, -ci, -che [i'dʒɛniko] AG hygienic; (salubre) healthy

igloo [i'glu] SM INV igloo; (tenda) dome tent

IGM SIGLA M (= Ispettorato Generale della Motorizzazione) road traffic inspectorate

i'gnaro, -a [iɲ'ɲaro] AG: **~ di** unaware of, ignorant of

i'gnifugo, -a, -ghi, -ghe [iɲ'ɲifugo] AG flame-resistant, fireproof

i'gnobile [iɲ'ɲɔbile] AG despicable, vile

igno'minia [iɲɲo'minja] SF ignominy

igno'rante [iɲɲo'rante] AG ignorant

igno'ranza [iɲɲo'rantsa] SF ignorance

igno'rare [iɲɲo'rare] /72/ VT (non sapere, conoscere) to be ignorant o unaware of, not to know; (fingere di non vedere, sentire) to ignore

i'gnoto, -a [iɲ'ɲɔto] AG unknown ▶ SM/F: **figlio di ignoti** child of unknown parentage; **il Milite I~** the Unknown Soldier

┌─────────────────┐
│ PAROLA CHIAVE │
└─────────────────┘

il (pl(m) **i**; diventa **lo** (pl **gli**) davanti a s impura, gn, pn, ps, x, z; f **la** (pl **le**)) DET M **1** the; **il libro/lo studente/l'acqua** the book/the student/the water; **gli scolari** the pupils

2 (astrazione): **il coraggio/l'amore/la giovinezza** courage/love/youth

3 (tempo): **il mattino/la sera** in the morning/evening; **il venerdì** (abitualmente) on Fridays; (quel giorno) on (the) Friday; **la settimana prossima** next week

4 (distributivo) a, an; **2 euro il chilo/paio** 2 euros a o per kilo/pair

5 (partitivo) some, any; **hai messo lo zucchero?** have you added sugar?; **hai comprato il latte?** did you buy (some o any) milk?

6 (possesso): **aprire gli occhi** to open one's eyes; **rompersi la gamba** to break one's leg; **avere i capelli neri/il naso rosso** to have dark hair/a red nose; **mettiti le scarpe** put your shoes on

7 (con nomi propri): **il Petrarca** Petrarch; **il Presidente Bush** President Bush; **dov'è la Francesca?** where's Francesca?

8 (con nomi geografici): **il Tevere** the Tiber; **l'Italia** Italy; **il Regno Unito** the United Kingdom; **l'Everest** Everest

'ilare AG cheerful

ilarità SF hilarity, mirth

ill. ABBR = **illustrazione**; (= illustrato) ill.

illangui'dire /55/ VI to grow weak o feeble

illazi'one [illat'tsjone] SF inference, deduction

il'lecito, -a [il'letʃito] AG illicit

ille'gale AG illegal

illegalità SF illegality

illeg'gibile [illed'dʒibile] AG illegible

illegittimità [illedʒittimi'ta] SF illegitimacy

ille'gittimo, -a [ille'dʒittimo] AG illegitimate

il'leso, -a AG unhurt, unharmed

illette'rato, -a AG illiterate

illiba'tezza [illiba'tettsa] SF (di donna) virginity

illi'bato, -a AG: **donna illibata** virgin

illimi'tato, -a AG boundless; unlimited

illivi'dire /55/ VI (volto, mani) to turn livid; (cielo) to grow leaden

ill.mo ABBR = **illustrissimo**

il'logico, -a, -ci, -che [il'lɔdʒiko] AG illogical

il'ludere /35/ VT to deceive, delude; **illudersi** VPR to deceive o.s., delude o.s.

illumi'nare /72/ VT to light up, illuminate; (fig) to enlighten; **illuminarsi** VPR to light up; **~ a giorno** (con riflettori) to floodlight

illumi'nato, -a AG (fig: sovrano, spirito) enlightened

illuminazi'one [illuminat'tsjone] SF lighting; illumination; floodlighting; (fig) flash of inspiration

illumi'nismo SM (Storia): **l'I~** the Enlightenment

il'lusi etc VB vedi **illudere**

illusi'one SF illusion; **farsi delle illusioni** to delude o.s.; **~ ottica** optical illusion

illusio'nismo SM conjuring

illusio'nista, -i, -e SM/F conjurer

il'luso, -a PP di **illudere**

illu'sorio, -a AG illusory

illus'trare /72/ VT to illustrate

illustra'tivo, -a AG illustrative

illustrazi'one [illustrat'tsjone] SF illustration

il'lustre AG eminent, renowned

illus'trissimo, -a AG (negli indirizzi) very revered

'ILOR SIGLA F = **imposta locale sui redditi**

IM SIGLA = **Imperia**

imbacuc'care /20/ VT, imbacuc'carsi VPR to wrap up

imbaldan'zire [imbaldan'tsire] /55/ VT to give confidence to; **imbaldanzirsi** VPR to grow bold

imbal'laggio [imbal'laddʒo] SM packing no pl

imbal'lare /72/ VT to pack; (Aut) to race; **imballarsi** VPR (Aut) to race

imbalsa'mare /72/ VT to embalm

imbalsa'mato, -a AG embalmed

imbambo'lato, -a AG (sguardo, espressione) vacant, blank

imban'dire /55/ VT: **~ un banchetto** to prepare a lavish feast

imban'dito, -a AG: **tavola imbandita** lavishly o sumptuously decked table

imbaraz'zante [imbarat'tsante] AG embarrassing, awkward

imbaraz'zare [imbarat'tsare] /72/ VT (*mettere a disagio*) to embarrass; (*ostacolare: movimenti*) to hamper; (: *stomaco*) to lie heavily on; **imbarazzarsi** VPR to become embarrassed

imbaraz'zato, -a [imbarat'tsato] AG embarrassed; **avere lo stomaco ~** to have an upset stomach

imba'razzo [imba'rattso] SM (*disagio*) embarrassment; (*perplessità*) puzzlement, bewilderment; **essere o trovarsi in ~** to be in an awkward situation o predicament; **mettere in ~** to embarrass; **~ di stomaco** indigestion

imbarbari'mento SM (*di civiltà, costumi*) barbarization

imbarca'dero SM landing stage

imbar'care /20/ VT (*passeggeri*) to embark; (*merci*) to load; **imbarcarsi** VPR: **imbarcarsi su** to board; **imbarcarsi per l'America** to sail for America; **imbarcarsi in** (*fig: affare*) to embark on

imbarcazi'one [imbarkat'tsjone] SF (small) boat, (small) craft *inv*; **~ di salvataggio** lifeboat

im'barco, -chi SM embarkation; loading; boarding; (*banchina*) landing stage; **carta d'~** boarding pass (BRIT), boarding card

imbastar'dire /55/ VT to bastardize, debase; **imbastardirsi** VPR to degenerate, become debased

imbas'tire /55/ VT (*cucire*) to tack; (*fig: abbozzare*) to sketch, outline

im'battersi /72/ VPR: **~ in** (*incontrare*) to bump o run into

imbat'tibile AG unbeatable, invincible

imbavagli'are [imbavaʎ'ʎare] /27/ VT to gag

imbec'care /20/ VT (*uccelli*) to feed; (*fig*) to prompt, put words into sb's mouth

imbec'cata SF (*Teat*) prompt; **dare l'~ a qn** to prompt sb; (*fig*) to give sb their cue

imbe'cille [imbe'tʃille] AG idiotic ▶ SM/F idiot; (*Med*) imbecile

imbecillità [imbetʃilli'ta] SF INV (*Med, fig*) imbecility, idiocy; **dire ~** to talk nonsense

imbellet'tare /72/ VT (*viso*) to make up, put make-up on; **imbellettarsi** VPR to make o.s. up, put on one's make-up

imbel'lire /55/ VT to adorn, embellish ▶ VI to grow more beautiful

im'berbe AG beardless; **un giovanotto ~** a callow youth

imbestia'lire /55/ VT to infuriate; **imbestialirsi** VPR to become infuriated, fly into a rage

im'bevere /16/ VT to soak; **imbeversi** VPR: **imbeversi di** to soak up, absorb

imbe'vuto, -a AG: **~ (di)** soaked (in)

imbian'care /20/ VT to whiten; (*muro*) to whitewash ▶ VI to become o turn white

imbianca'tura SF (*di muro: con bianco di calce*) whitewashing; (: *con altre pitture*) painting

imbian'chino [imbjan'kino] SM (house) painter, painter and decorator

imbion'dire /55/ VT (*capelli*) to lighten; (*Cuc: cipolla*) to brown; **imbiondirsi** VPR (*capelli*) to lighten, go blonde, go fair; (*messi*) to turn golden, ripen

imbizzar'rirsi [imbiddzar'rirsi] /55/ VPR (*cavallo*) to become frisky

imboc'care /20/ VT (*bambino*) to feed; (*entrare: strada*) to enter, turn into ▶ VI: **~ in** (*strada*) to lead into (: *fiume*) to flow into

imbocca'tura SF mouth; (*di strada, porto*) entrance; (*Mus, del morso*) mouthpiece

im'bocco, -chi SM entrance

imboni'tore SM (*di spettacolo, circo*) barker

imborghe'sire [imborge'zire] /55/ VI, **imborghe'sirsi** VPR to become bourgeois

imbos'care /20/ VT to hide; **imboscarsi** VPR (*Mil*) to evade military service

imbos'cata SF ambush

imbos'cato SM draft dodger (*US*)

imboschi'mento [imboski'mento] SM afforestation

imbottigli'are [imbottiʎ'ʎare] /27/ VT to bottle; (*Naut*) to blockade; (*Mil*) to hem in; **imbottigliarsi** VPR to be stuck in a traffic jam

imbot'tire /55/ VT to stuff; (*giacca*) to pad; **imbottirsi** VPR (*rimpinzarsi*): **imbottirsi di** to stuff o.s. with

imbot'tito, -a AG stuffed; (*sedia*) upholstered; (*giacca*) padded ▶ SF quilt; **panino ~** filled roll

imbotti'tura SF stuffing; padding

imbracci'are [imbrat'tʃare] /14/ VT (*fucile*) to shoulder; (*scudo*) to grasp

imbra'nato, -a AG clumsy, awkward ▶ SM/F clumsy person

imbratta'carte SMF (*peg*) scribbler

imbrat'tare /72/ VT to dirty, smear, daub; **imbrattarsi** VPR: **imbrattarsi (di)** to dirty o.s. (with)

imbratta'tele SMF (*peg*) dauber

imbrigli'are [imbriʎ'ʎare] /27/ VT to bridle

imbroc'care /20/ VT (*fig*) to guess correctly

imbrogli'are [imbroʎ'ʎare] /27/ VT to mix up; (*fig: raggirare*) to deceive, cheat; (: *confondere*) to confuse, mix up; **imbrogliarsi** VPR to get tangled; (*fig*) to become confused

im'broglio [im'brɔʎʎo] SM (*groviglio*) tangle; (*situazione confusa*) mess; (*truffa*) swindle, trick

imbrogli'one, -a [imbroʎ'ʎone] SM/F cheat, swindler

imbronci'ato, -a [imbron'tʃato] AG (*persona*) sulky; (*cielo*) cloudy, threatening

imbru'nire /55/ VI, VB IMPERS to grow dark; **all'~** at dusk

imbrut'tire /**55**/ vt to make ugly ▶ vi to become ugly
imbu'care /**20**/ vt to post
imbur'rare /**72**/ vt to butter
imbuti'forme AG funnel-shaped
im'buto SM funnel
I.M.C.T.C. SIGLA (= *Ispettorato Generale della Motorizzazione Civile e dei Trasporti in Concessione*) ≈ DVLA
i'mene SM hymen
imi'tare /**72**/ vt to imitate; (*riprodurre*) to copy; (*assomigliare*) to look like
imita'tore, -'trice SM/F (*gen*) imitator; (*Teat*) impersonator, impressionist
imitazi'one [imitat'tsjone] SF imitation
immaco'lato, -a AG spotless; immaculate
immagazzi'nare [immagaddzi'nare] /**72**/ vt to store
immagi'nabile [immadʒi'nabile] AG imaginable
immagi'nare [immadʒi'nare] /**72**/ vt to imagine; (*supporre*) to suppose; (*inventare*) to invent; **s'immagini!** don't mention it!, not at all!
immagi'nario, -a [immadʒi'narjo] AG imaginary
immagina'tiva [immadʒina'tiva] SF imagination
immaginazi'one [immadʒinat'tsjone] SF imagination; (*cosa immaginata*) fancy
im'magine [im'madʒine] SF image; (*rappresentazione grafica, mentale*) picture
immagi'noso, -a [immadʒi'noso] AG (*linguaggio, stile*) fantastic
immalinco'nire /**55**/ vt to sadden, depress; **immalinconirsi** VPR to become depressed, become melancholy
imman'cabile AG certain; unfailing
immancabil'mente AV without fail, unfailingly
im'mane AG (*smisurato*) huge; (*spaventoso, inumano*) terrible
imma'nente AG (*Filosofia*) inherent, immanent
immangi'abile [imman'dʒabile] AG inedible
immatrico'lare /**72**/ vt to register; **immatricolarsi** VPR (*Ins*) to matriculate, enrol
immatricolazi'one [immatrikolat'tsjone] SF registration; matriculation; enrolment
immaturità SF immaturity
imma'turo, -a AG (*frutto*) unripe; (*persona*) immature; (*prematuro*) premature
immedesi'marsi /**72**/ VPR: **~ in** to identify with
immediata'mente AV immediately, at once
immedia'tezza [immedja'tettsa] SF immediacy
immedi'ato, -a AG immediate
immemo'rabile AG immemorial; **da tempo ~** from time immemorial

im'memore AG: **~ di** forgetful of
immensità SF immensity
im'menso, -a AG immense
im'mergere [im'merdʒere] /**59**/ vt to immerse, plunge; **immergersi** VPR to plunge; (*sommergibile*) to dive, submerge; (*dedicarsi a*) **immergersi in** to immerse o.s. in
immeri'tato, -a AG undeserved
immeri'tevole AG undeserving, unworthy
immersi'one SF immersion; (*di sommergibile*) submersion, dive; (*di palombaro*) dive; **linea di ~** (*Naut*) water line
im'merso, -a PP *di* **immergere**
im'messo, -a PP *di* **immettere**
im'mettere /**63**/ vt: **~ (in)** to introduce (into); **~ dati in un computer** to enter data on a computer
immi'grante AG, SMF immigrant
immi'grare /**72**/ vi to immigrate
immi'grato, -a SM/F immigrant
immigrazi'one [immigrat'tsjone] SF immigration
immi'nente AG imminent
immi'nenza [immi'nentsa] SF imminence
immischi'are [immis'kjare] /**19**/ vt: **~ qn in** to involve sb in; **immischiarsi** VPR: **immischiarsi in** to interfere *o* meddle in
immiseri'mento SM impoverishment
immise'rire /**55**/ vt to impoverish
immis'sario SM (*Geo*) affluent, tributary
immissi'one SF (*gen*) introduction; (*di aria, gas*) intake; **~ di dati** (*Inform*) data entry
im'mobile AG motionless, still; (**beni**) **immobili** real estate *sg*
immobili'are AG (*Dir*) property *cpd*; **patrimonio ~** real estate; **società ~** property company
immobi'lismo SM inertia
immobilità SF immobility
immobiliz'zare [immobilid'dzare] /**72**/ vt to immobilize; (*Econ*) to lock up
immobi'lizzo [immobi'liddzo] SM: **spese d'~** capital expenditure
immo'destia SF immodesty
immo'desto, -a AG immodest
immo'lare /**72**/ vt to sacrifice
immondez'zaio [immondet'tsajo] SM rubbish dump
immon'dizia [immon'dittsja] SF dirt, filth; (*spesso al pl: spazzatura, rifiuti*) rubbish *no pl*, refuse *no pl*
immo'rale AG immoral
immoralità SF immorality
immorta'lare /**72**/ vt to immortalize
immor'tale AG immortal
immortalità SF immortality
im'mune AG (*esente*) exempt; (*Med, Dir*) immune
immunità SF immunity; **~ diplomatica** diplomatic immunity; **~ parlamentare** parliamentary privilege

immuniz'zare [immunid'dzare] /**72**/ vt (*Med*) to immunize

immunizzazi'one [immuniddzat'tsjone] sf immunization

immunodefi'cienza [immunodefi'tʃɛntsa] sf: ~ **acquisita** acquired immunodeficiency

immuno'logico, -a, -ci, -che [immuno'lɔdʒiko] ag immunological

immu'tabile ag immutable; unchanging

impac'care /**20**/ vt to pack

impacchet'tare [impakket'tare] /**72**/ vt to pack up

impacci'are [impat'tʃare] /**14**/ vt to hinder, hamper

impacci'ato, -a [impat'tʃato] ag awkward, clumsy; (*imbarazzato*) embarrassed

im'paccio [im'pattʃo] sm obstacle; (*imbarazzo*) embarrassment; (*situazione imbarazzante*) awkward situation

im'pacco, -chi sm (*Med*) compress

impadro'nirsi /**55**/ vpr: ~ **di** to seize, take possession of; (*fig: apprendere a fondo*) to master

impa'gabile ag priceless

impagi'nare [impadʒi'nare] /**72**/ vt (*Tip*) to paginate, page (up)

impaginazi'one [impadʒinat'tsjone] sf pagination

impagli'are [impaʎ'ʎare] /**27**/ vt to stuff (with straw)

impa'lato, -a ag (*fig*) stiff as a board

impalca'tura sf scaffolding; (*anche fig*) framework

impalli'dire /**55**/ vi to turn pale; (*fig*) to fade

impalli'nare /**72**/ vt to riddle with shot

impal'pabile ag impalpable

impa'nare /**72**/ vt (*Cuc*) to dip (*o* roll) in breadcrumbs, bread (*US*)

impa'nato, -a ag (*Cuc*) coated in breadcrumbs

impanta'narsi /**72**/ vpr to sink (in the mud); (*fig*) to get bogged down

impape'rarsi /**72**/ vpr to stumble over a word

impappi'narsi /**72**/ vpr to stammer, falter

impa'rare /**72**/ vt to learn; **così impari!** that'll teach you!

impara'ticcio [impara'tittʃo] sm half-baked notions *pl*

impareggi'abile [impared'dʒabile] ag incomparable

imparen'tarsi /**72**/ vpr: ~ **con** (*famiglia*) to marry into

'impari ag inv (*disuguale*) unequal; (*dispari*) odd

impar'tire /**55**/ vt to bestow, give

imparzi'ale [impar'tsjale] ag impartial, unbiased

imparzialità [impartsjali'ta] sf impartiality

impas'sibile ag impassive

impas'tare /**72**/ vt (*pasta*) to knead; (*colori*) to mix

impastic'carsi /**20**/ vpr to pop pills

im'pasto sm (*l'impastare: di pane*) kneading; (: *di cemento*) mixing; (*pasta*) dough; (*anche fig*) mixture

im'patto sm impact; ~ **ambientale** impact on the environment

impau'rire /**55**/ vt to scare, frighten ▶ vi (*anche:* **impaurirsi**) to become scared *o* frightened

im'pavido, -a ag intrepid, fearless

impazi'ente [impat'tsjɛnte] ag impatient

impazi'enza [impat'tsjɛntsa] sf impatience

impaz'zata [impat'tsata] sf: **all'~** (*precipitosamente*) at breakneck speed; (*colpire*) wildly

impaz'zire [impat'tsire] /**55**/ vi to go mad; ~ **per qn/qc** to be crazy about sb/sth

impec'cabile ag impeccable

impedi'mento sm obstacle, hindrance

impe'dire /**55**/ vt (*vietare*): ~ **a qn di fare** to prevent sb from doing; (*ostruire*) to obstruct; (*impacciare*) to hamper, hinder

impe'gnare [impeɲ'ɲare] /**15**/ vt (*dare in pegno*) to pawn; (*onore ecc*) to pledge; (*prenotare*) to book, reserve; (*obbligare*) to oblige; (*occupare*) to keep busy; (*Mil: nemico*) to engage; **impegnarsi** vpr (*vincolarsi*): **impegnarsi a fare** to undertake to do; (*mettersi risolutamente*): **impegnarsi in qc** to devote o.s. to sth; **impegnarsi con qn** (*accordarsi*) to come to an agreement with sb

impegna'tivo, -a [impeɲɲa'tivo] ag binding; (*lavoro*) demanding, exacting

impe'gnato, -a [impeɲ'ɲato] ag (*occupato*) busy; (*fig: romanzo, autore*) committed, engagé

im'pegno [im'peɲɲo] sm (*obbligo*) obligation; (*promessa*) promise, pledge; (*zelo*) diligence, zeal; (*compito: d'autore*) commitment; **impegni di lavoro** business commitments

impego'larsi /**72**/ vpr (*fig*): ~ **in** to get heavily involved in

impela'garsi /**80**/ vpr = **impegolarsi**

impel'lente ag pressing, urgent

impene'trabile ag impenetrable

impen'narsi /**72**/ vpr (*cavallo*) to rear up; (*Aer*) to go into a climb; (*fig*) to bridle

impen'nata sf (*di cavallo*) rearing up; (*di aereo*) climb, nose-up; (*fig: scatto d'ira*) burst of anger; (: *di prezzi ecc*) sudden increase

impen'sabile ag (*inaccettabile*) unthinkable; (*difficile da concepire*) inconceivable

impen'sato, -a ag unforeseen, unexpected

impensie'rirsi /**55**/ vt to worry; **impensierirsi** vpr to worry

impe'rante ag prevailing

impe'rare /**72**/ vi (*anche fig*) to reign, rule

impera'tivo, -a ag, sm imperative

impera'tore, -'trice sm/f emperor (empress)

impercet'tibile [impertʃet'tibile] ag imperceptible

imperdo'nabile AG unforgivable, unpardonable

imper'fetto, -a AG imperfect ▶ SM (Ling) imperfect (tense)

imperfezi'one [imperfet'tsjone] SF imperfection

imperi'ale AG imperial

imperia'lismo SM imperialism

imperia'lista, -i, -e AG imperialist

imperi'oso, -a AG (persona) imperious; (motivo, esigenza) urgent, pressing

imperi'turo, -a AG everlasting

impe'rizia [impe'rittsja] SF lack of experience

imperma'lirsi /55/ VPR to take offence

imperme'abile AG waterproof ▶ SM raincoat

imperni'are /19/ VT: **~ qc su** to hinge sth on; (fig: discorso, relazione ecc) to base sth on; **imperniarsi** VPR (fig): **imperniarsi su** to be based on

im'pero SM empire; (forza, autorità) rule, control

imperscru'tabile AG inscrutable

imperso'nale AG impersonal

imperso'nare /72/ VT to personify; (Teat) to play, act (the part of); **impersonarsi** VPR: **impersonarsi in un ruolo** to get into a part, live a part

imper'territo, -a AG unperturbed, undaunted; impassive

imperti'nente AG impertinent

imperti'nenza [imperti'nɛntsa] SF impertinence

impertur'babile AG imperturbable

imperver'sare /72/ VI to rage

im'pervio, -a AG (luogo) inaccessible; (strada) impassable

'impeto SM (moto, forza) force, impetus; (assalto) onslaught; (fig: impulso) impulse; (: slancio) transport; **con ~** (parlare) forcefully, energetically; vehemently

impet'tito, -a AG stiff, erect; **camminare ~** to strut

impetu'oso, -a AG (vento) strong, raging; (persona) impetuous

impian'tare /72/ VT (motore) to install; (azienda, discussione) to establish, start

impian'tistica SF plant design and installation

impi'anto SM (installazione) installation; (apparecchiature) plant; (sistema) system; **~ elettrico** wiring; **~ di riscaldamento** heating system; **~ sportivo** sports complex; **impianti di risalita** (Sci) ski lifts

impias'trare /72/, **impiastricci'are** [impjastrit'tʃare] VT to smear, dirty

impi'astro SM poultice; (fig: col: persona) nuisance

impiccagi'one [impikka'dʒone] SF hanging

impic'care /20/ VT to hang; **impiccarsi** VPR to hang o.s.

impicci'are [impit'tʃare] /**14**/ VT to hinder, hamper; **impicciarsi** VPR (immischiarsi): **impicciarsi (in)** to meddle (in), interfere (in); **impicciati degli affari tuoi!** mind your own business!

im'piccio [im'pittʃo] SM (ostacolo) hindrance; (seccatura) trouble, bother; (affare imbrogliato) mess; **essere d' ~** to be in the way; **cavare o togliere qn dagli impicci** to get sb out of trouble

impicci'one, -a [impit'tʃone] SM/F busybody

impie'gare /80/ VT (usare) to use, employ; (assumere) to employ, take on; (spendere: denaro, tempo) to spend; (investire) to invest; **impiegarsi** VPR to get a job, obtain employment; **impiego un quarto d'ora per andare a casa** it takes me o I take a quarter of an hour to get home

impiega'tizio, -a [impjega'tittsjo] AG clerical, white-collar cpd; **lavoro/ceto ~** clerical o white-collar work/workers pl

impie'gato, -a SM/F employee; **~ statale** state employee

impi'ego, -ghi SM (uso) use; (occupazione) employment; (posto di lavoro) (regular) job, post; (Econ) investment; **~ pubblico** job in the public sector

impieto'sire /55/ VT to move to pity; **impietosirsi** VPR to be moved to pity

impie'toso, -a AG pitiless, cruel

impie'trire /55/ VT (anche fig) to petrify

impigli'are [impiʎ'ʎare] /**27**/ VT to catch, entangle; **impigliarsi** VPR to get caught up o entangled

impi'grire /55/ VT to make lazy ▶ VI (anche: **impigrirsi**) to grow lazy

impingu'are /72/ VT (maiale ecc) to fatten; (fig: tasche, casse dello Stato) to stuff with money

impiom'bare /72/ VT (pacco) to seal (with lead); (dente) to fill

impla'cabile AG implacable

implemen'tare /72/ VT to implement

impli'care /20/ VT to imply; (coinvolgere) to involve; **implicarsi** VPR: **implicarsi (in)** to become involved (in)

implicazi'one [implikat'tsjone] SF implication

im'plicito, -a [im'plitʃito] AG implicit

implo'rare /72/ VT to implore; (pietà ecc) to beg for

implorazi'one [implorat'tsjone] SF plea, entreaty

impolli'nare /72/ VT to pollinate

impollinazi'one [impollinat'tsjone] SF pollination

impolve'rare /72/ VT to cover with dust; **impolverarsi** VPR to get dusty

impoma'tare /72/ VT (pelle) to put ointment on; (capelli) to pomade; (baffi) to wax; **impomatarsi** VPR (col) to get spruced up

imponde'rabile AG imponderable

im'pone etc VB vedi **imporre**

impo'nente AG imposing, impressive

im'pongo etc VB vedi **imporre**

impo'nibile AG taxable ▶ SM taxable income

impopo'lare AG unpopular

impopolarità SF unpopularity

im'porre /77/ VT to impose; (costringere) to force, make; (far valere) to impose, enforce; **imporsi** VPR (persona) to assert o.s.; (cosa: rendersi necessario) to become necessary; (aver successo: moda, attore) to become popular; **~ a qn di fare** to force sb to do, make sb do

impor'tante AG important

impor'tanza [impor'tantsa] SF importance; **dare ~ a qc** to attach importance to sth; **darsi ~** to give o.s. airs

impor'tare /72/ VT (introdurre dall'estero) to import ▶ VI to matter, be important ▶ VB IMPERS (essere necessario) to be necessary; (interessare) to matter; **non importa!** it doesn't matter!; **non me ne importa!** I don't care!

importa'tore, -'trice AG importing ▶ SM/F importer

importazi'one [importat'tsjone] SF importation; (merci importate) imports pl

im'porto SM (total) amount

importu'nare /72/ VT to bother

impor'tuno, -a AG irksome, annoying

im'posi etc VB vedi **imporre**

imposizi'one [impozit'tsjone] SF imposition; (ordine) order, command; (onere, imposta) tax

imposses'sarsi /72/ VPR: **~ di** to seize, take possession of

impos'sibile AG impossible; **fare l'~** to do one's utmost, do all one can

impossibilità SF impossibility; **essere nell'~ di fare qc** to be unable to do sth

impossibili'tato, -a AG: **essere ~ a fare qc** to be unable to do sth

im'posta SF (di finestra) shutter; (tassa) tax; **~ indiretta sui consumi** excise duty o tax; **~ locale sui redditi (ILOR)** tax on unearned income; **~ patrimoniale** property tax; **~ sul reddito** income tax; **~ sul reddito delle persone fisiche** personal income tax; **~ di successione** capital transfer tax (BRIT), inheritance tax (US); **~ sugli utili** tax on profits; **~ sul valore aggiunto** value added tax (BRIT), sales tax (US)

impos'tare /72/ VT (imbucare) to post; (servizio, organizzazione) to set up; (lavoro) to organize, plan; (resoconto, rapporto) to plan; (problema) to set out, formulate; (avviare) to begin, start off; (Tip: pagina) to lay out; **~ la voce** (Mus) to pitch one's voice

impostazi'one [impostat'tsjone] SF (di lettera) posting (BRIT), mailing (US); (di problema, questione) formulation, statement; (di lavoro) organization, planning; (di attività) setting up; (Mus: di voce) pitch; **impostazioni** SFPL (di computer) settings

im'posto, -a PP di **imporre**

impos'tore, -a SM/F impostor

impo'tente AG weak, powerless; (anche Med) impotent

impo'tenza [impo'tɛntsa] SF weakness, powerlessness; impotence

impove'rire /55/ VT to impoverish ▶ VI (anche: **impoverirsi**) to become poor

imprati'cabile AG (strada) impassable; (campo da gioco) unplayable

imprati'chire [imprati'kire] /55/ VT to train; **impratichirsi** VPR: **impratichirsi in qc** to practise (BRIT) o practice (US) sth

impre'care /20/ VI to curse, swear; **~ contro** to hurl abuse at

imprecazi'one [imprekat'tsjone] SF abuse, curse

impreci'sato, -a [impretʃi'zato] AG (non preciso: quantità, numero) indeterminate

imprecisi'one [impretʃi'zjone] SF imprecision; inaccuracy

impre'ciso, -a [impre'tʃizo] AG imprecise, vague; (calcolo) inaccurate

impre'gnare [impreɲ'ɲare] /15/ VT: **~ (di)** (imbevere) to soak o impregnate (with); (riempire: anche fig) to fill (with)

imprendi'tore SM (industriale) entrepreneur; (appaltatore) contractor; **piccolo ~** small businessman

imprendito'ria SF enterprise; (imprenditori) entrepreneurs pl

imprenditori'ale AG (ceto, classe) entrepreneurial

imprepa'rato, -a AG: **~ (a)** (gen) unprepared (for); (lavoratore) untrained (for); **cogliere qn ~** to catch sb unawares

impreparazi'one [impreparat'tsjone] SF lack of preparation

im'presa SF (iniziativa) enterprise; (azione) exploit; (azienda) firm, concern; **~ familiare** family firm; **~ pubblica** state-owned enterprise

impre'sario SM (Teat) manager, impresario; **~ di pompe funebri** funeral director

imprescin'dibile [impreʃʃin'dibile] AG not to be ignored

im'pressi etc VB vedi **imprimere**

impressio'nante AG impressive; upsetting

impressio'nare /72/ VT to impress; (turbare) to upset; (Fot) to expose; **impressionarsi** VPR to be easily upset

impressi'one SF impression; (fig: sensazione) sensation, feeling; (stampa) printing; **fare ~** (colpire) to impress; (turbare) to frighten, upset; **fare buona/cattiva ~ a** to make a good/bad impression on

im'presso, -a PP di **imprimere**

impres'tare /**72**/ VT: ~ qc a qn to lend sth to sb

impreve'dibile AG unforeseeable; (persona) unpredictable

imprevi'dente AG lacking in foresight

imprevi'denza [imprevi'dɛntsa] SF lack of foresight

impre'visto, -a AG unexpected, unforeseen
▶ SM unforeseen event; **salvo imprevisti** unless anything unexpected happens

imprezio'sire [imprettsjo'sire] /**55**/ VT: ~ **di** to embellish with

imprigiona'mento [impridʒona'mento] SM imprisonment

imprigio'nare [impridʒo'nare] /**72**/ VT to imprison

im'primere /**50**/ VT (anche fig) to impress, stamp; (comunicare: movimento) to transmit, give

impro'babile AG improbable, unlikely

'improbo, -a AG (fatica, lavoro) hard, laborious

improdut'tivo, -a AG (investimento) unprofitable; (terreno) unfruitful; (fig: sforzo) fruitless

im'pronta SF imprint, impression, sign; (di piede, mano) print; (fig) mark, stamp; ~ **di carbonio** carbon footprint; ~ **digitale** fingerprint; **rilevamento delle impronte genetiche** genetic fingerprinting

impro'perio SM insult

impropo'nibile AG which cannot be proposed o suggested

im'proprio, -a AG improper; **arma impropria** offensive weapon

improro'gabile AG (termine) that cannot be extended

improvvisa'mente AV suddenly; unexpectedly

improvvi'sare /**72**/ VT to improvise; improvvisarsi VPR: **improvvisarsi cuoco** to (decide to) act as cook

improvvi'sata SF (pleasant) surprise

improvvisazi'one [improvvizat'tsjone] SF improvisation; **spirito d'~** spirit of invention

improv'viso, -a AG (imprevisto) unexpected; (subitaneo) sudden; **all'~** unexpectedly; suddenly

impru'dente AG foolish, imprudent; (osservazione) unwise, rash

impru'denza [impru'dɛntsa] SF foolishness, imprudence; **è stata un'~** that was a foolish o an imprudent thing to do

impu'dente AG impudent

impu'denza [impu'dɛntsa] SF impudence

impudi'cizia [impudi'tʃittsja] SF immodesty

impu'dico, -a, -chi, -che AG immodest

impu'gnare [impuɲ'ɲare] /**15**/ VT to grasp, grip; (Dir) to contest

impugna'tura [impuɲɲa'tura] SF grip, grasp; (manico) handle; (: di spada) hilt

impulsività SF impulsiveness

impul'sivo, -a AG impulsive

im'pulso SM impulse; **dare un ~ alle vendite** to boost sales

impune'mente AV with impunity

impunità SF impunity

impun'tarsi /**72**/ VPR to stop dead, refuse to budge; (fig) to be obstinate

impun'tura SF stitching

impurità SF INV impurity

im'puro, -a AG impure

impu'tare /**72**/ VT (ascrivere): ~ **qc a** to attribute sth to; (Dir: accusare) ~ **qn di** to charge sb with, accuse sb of

impu'tato, -a SM/F (Dir) accused, defendant

imputazi'one [imputat'tsjone] SF (Dir) charge; (di spese) allocation

imputri'dire /**55**/ VI to rot

PAROLA CHIAVE

in (in + il = **nel**, in + lo = **nello**, in + l' = **nell'**, in + la = **nella**, in + i = **nei**, in + gli = **negli**, in + le = **nelle**) PREP **1** (stato in luogo) in; **vivere in Italia/ città** to live in Italy/town; **essere in casa/ ufficio** to be at home/the office; **è nel cassetto/in salotto** it's in the drawer/in the sitting room; **se fossi in te** if I were you
2 (moto a luogo) to; (: dentro) into; **andare in Germania/città** to go to Germany/town; **andare in ufficio** to go to the office; **entrare in macchina/casa** to get into the car/go into the house
3 (tempo) in; **nel 1989** in 1989; **in giugno/ estate** in June/summer; **l'ha fatto in sei mesi** he did it in six months; **in gioventù, io …** when I was young, I …
4 (modo, maniera) in; **in silenzio** in silence; **parlare in tedesco** to speak (in) German; **in abito da sera** in evening dress; **in guerra** at war; **in vacanza** on holiday; **Maria Bianchi in Rossi** Maria Rossi née Bianchi
5 (mezzo) by; **viaggiare in autobus/treno** to travel by bus/train
6 (materia) made of; **in marmo** made of marble, marble cpd; **una collana in oro** a gold necklace
7 (misura) in; **siamo in quattro** there are four of us; **in tutto** in all
8 (fine): **dare in dono** to give as a gift; **spende tutto in alcool** he spends all his money on drink; **in onore di** in honour of

i'nabile AG: ~ **a** incapable of; (fisicamente, Mil) unfit for

inabilità SF: ~ **(a)** unfitness (for)

inabis'sare /**72**/ VT (nave) to sink; **inabissarsi** VPR to go down

inabi'tabile AG uninhabitable

inabi'tato, -a AG uninhabited

inacces'sibile [inattʃes'sibile] AG (*luogo*) inaccessible; (*persona*) unapproachable; (*mistero*) unfathomable

inaccet'tabile [inattʃet'tabile] AG unacceptable

inacer'bire [inatʃer'bire] /**55**/ VT to exacerbate; **inacerbirsi** VPR (*persona*) to become embittered

inaci'dire [inatʃi'dire] /**55**/ VT (*persona, carattere*) to embitter; **inacidirsi** VPR (*latte*) to go sour; (*fig: persona, carattere*) to become sour, become embittered

ina'datto, -a AG: ~ **(a)** unsuitable *o* unfit (for)

inadegu'ato, -a AG inadequate

inadempi'ente AG defaulting ▶ SMF defaulter

inadempi'enza [inadem'pjɛntsa] SF: ~ **a un contratto** non-fulfilment of a contract; **dovuto alle inadempienze dei funzionari** due to negligence on the part of the officials

inadempi'mento SM non-fulfilment

inaffer'rabile AG elusive; (*concetto, senso*) difficult to grasp

inaffi'dabile AG unreliable

'INAIL SIGLA M (= *Istituto Nazionale per l'Assicurazione contro gli Infortuni sul Lavoro*) state body providing sickness benefit in the event of accidents at work

ina'lare /**72**/ VT to inhale

inala'tore SM inhaler

inalazi'one [inalat'tsjone] SF inhalation

inalbe'rare /**72**/ VT (*Naut*) to hoist, raise; **inalberarsi** VPR (*fig*) to flare up, fly off the handle

inalte'rabile AG unchangeable; (*colore*) fast, permanent; (*affetto*) constant

inalte'rato, -a AG unchanged

inami'dare /**72**/ VT to starch

inami'dato, -a AG starched

inammis'sibile AG inadmissible

inani'mato, -a AG inanimate; (*senza vita: corpo*) lifeless

inappa'gabile AG insatiable

inappel'labile AG (*decisione*) final, irrevocable; (*Dir*) final, not open to appeal

inappe'tenza [inappe'tɛntsa] SF (*Med*) lack of appetite

inappun'tabile AG irreproachable, flawless

inar'care /**20**/ VT (*schiena*) to arch; (*sopracciglia*) to raise; **inarcarsi** VPR to arch

inaridi'mento SM (*anche fig*) drying up

inari'dire /**55**/ VT to make arid, dry up ▶ VI (*anche:* **inaridirsi**) to dry up, become arid

inarres'tabile AG (*processo*) irreversible; (*emorragia*) that cannot be stemmed; (*corsa del tempo*) relentless

inascol'tato, -a AG unheeded, unheard

inaspettata'mente AV unexpectedly

inaspet'tato, -a AG unexpected

inas'prire /**55**/ VT (*disciplina*) to tighten up, make harsher; (*carattere*) to embitter; (*rapporti*) to make worse; **inasprirsi** VPR to become harsher; to become bitter; to become worse

inattac'cabile AG (*anche fig*) unassailable; (*alibi*) cast-iron

inatten'dibile AG unreliable

inat'teso, -a AG unexpected

inat'tivo, -a AG inactive, idle; (*Chim*) inactive

inattu'abile AG impracticable

inau'dito, -a AG unheard of

inaugu'rale AG inaugural

inaugu'rare /**72**/ VT to inaugurate, open; (*monumento*) to unveil

inaugurazi'one [inaugurat'tsjone] SF inauguration; unveiling

inavve'duto, -a AG careless, inadvertent

inavver'tenza [inavver'tentsa] SF carelessness, inadvertence

inavvertita'mente AV inadvertently, unintentionally

inavvici'nabile [inavvitʃi'nabile] AG unapproachable

'Inca AG INV, SM INV/F INV Inca

incagli'are [inkaʎ'ʎare] /**27**/ VI (*Naut: anche:* **incagliarsi**) to run aground

incalco'labile AG incalculable

incal'lito, -a AG calloused; (*fig*) hardened, inveterate; (: *insensibile*) hard

incal'zante [inkal'tsante] AG urgent, insistent; (*crisi*) imminent

incal'zare [inkal'tsare] /**72**/ VT to follow *o* pursue closely; (*fig*) to press ▶ VI (*urgere*) to be pressing; (*essere imminente*) to be imminent

incame'rare /**72**/ VT (*Dir*) to expropriate

incammi'nare /**72**/ VT (*fig: avviare*) to start up; **incamminarsi** VPR to set off

incana'lare /**72**/ VT (*anche fig*) to channel; **incanalarsi** VPR (*folla*): **incanalarsi verso** to converge on

incancre'nire /**55**/ VI, **incancre'nirsi** VPR to become gangrenous

incande'scente [inkandeʃ'ʃɛnte] AG incandescent, white-hot

incan'tare /**72**/ VT to enchant, bewitch; **incantarsi** VPR (*rimanere intontito*) to be spellbound; to be in a daze; (*meccanismo: bloccarsi*) to jam

incanta'tore, -'trice AG enchanting, bewitching ▶ SM/F enchanter (enchantress)

incan'tesimo SM spell, charm

incan'tevole AG charming, enchanting

in'canto SM spell, charm, enchantment; (*asta*) auction; **come per** ~ as if by magic; **ti sta d'~!** (*vestito ecc*) it really suits you!; **mettere all'**~ to put up for auction

incanu'tire /**55**/ VI to go white

inca'pace [inka'patʃe] AG incapable

171

incapacità [inkapatʃi'ta] SF inability; (*Dir*) incapacity; ~ **d'intendere e di volere** diminished responsibility

incapo'nirsi /55/ VPR to be stubborn, be determined

incap'pare /72/ VI: ~ **in qc/qn** (*anche fig*) to run into sth/sb

incappucci'are [inkapput'tʃare] /14/ VT to put a hood on; **incappucciarsi** VPR (*persona*) to put on a hood

incapricci'arsi [inkaprit'tʃarsi] /14/ VPR: ~ **di** to take a fancy to o for

incapsu'lare /72/ VT (*dente*) to crown

incarce'rare [inkartʃe'rare] /72/ VT to imprison

incari'care /20/ VT: ~ **qn di fare** to give sb the responsibility of doing; **incaricarsi** VPR: **incaricarsi di** to take care o charge of

incari'cato, -a AG: ~ **(di)** in charge (of), responsible (for) ▶ SM/F delegate, representative; **docente** ~ (*di università*) lecturer without tenure; ~ **d'affari** (*Pol*) chargé d'affaires

in'carico, -chi SM task, job; (*Ins*) temporary post

incar'nare /72/ VT to embody; **incarnarsi** VPR to be embodied; (*Rel*) to become incarnate

incarnazi'one [inkarnat'tsjone] SF incarnation; (*fig*) embodiment

incarta'mento SM dossier, file

incartapeco'rito, -a AG (*pelle*) wizened, shrivelled (*BRIT*), shriveled (*US*)

incar'tare /72/ VT to wrap (in paper)

incasel'lare /72/ VT (*posta*) to sort; (*fig: nozioni*) to pigeonhole

incas'sare /72/ VT (*merce*) to pack (in cases); (*gemma: incastonare*) to set; (*Econ: riscuotere*) to collect; (*Pugilato: colpi*) to take, stand up to

in'casso SM cashing, encashment; (*introito*) takings *pl*

incasto'nare /72/ VT to set

incastona'tura SF setting

incas'trare /72/ VT to fit in, insert; (*fig: intrappolare*) to catch; **incastrarsi** VPR (*combaciare*) to fit together; (*restare bloccato*) to become stuck

in'castro SM slot, groove; (*punto di unione*) joint; **gioco a** ~ interlocking puzzle

incate'nare /72/ VT to chain up

incatra'mare /72/ VT to tar

incatti'vire /55/ VT to make wicked; **incattivirsi** VPR to turn nasty

in'cauto, -a AG imprudent, rash

inca'vare /72/ VT to hollow out

inca'vato, -a AG hollow; (*occhi*) sunken

in'cavo SM hollow; (*solco*) groove

incavo'larsi /72/ VPR (*col*) to lose one's temper, get annoyed

incaz'zarsi [inkat'tsarsi] /72/ VPR (*col*) to get steamed up

in'cedere [in'tʃɛdere] /29/ VI (*poetico*) to advance solemnly ▶ SM solemn gait

incendi'are [intʃen'djare] /19/ VT to set fire to; **incendiarsi** VPR to catch fire, burst into flames

incendi'ario, -a [intʃen'djarjo] AG incendiary ▶ SM/F arsonist

in'cendio [in'tʃɛndjo] SM fire

incene'rire [intʃene'rire] /55/ VT to burn to ashes, incinerate; (*cadavere*) to cremate; **incenerirsi** VPR to be burnt to ashes

inceneri'tore [intʃeneri'tore] SM incinerator

in'censo [in'tʃɛnso] SM incense

incensu'rato, -a [intʃensu'rato] AG (*Dir*): **essere** ~ to have a clean record

incenti'vare [intʃenti'vare] /72/ VT (*produzione, vendite*) to boost; (*persona*) to motivate

incen'tivo [intʃen'tivo] SM incentive

incen'trarsi [intʃen'trarsi] /72/ VPR: ~ **su** (*fig*) to centre (*BRIT*) o center (*US*) on

incep'pare [intʃep'pare] /72/ VT to obstruct, hamper; **incepparsi** VPR to jam

ince'rata [intʃe'rata] SF (*tela*) tarpaulin; (*impermeabile*) oilskins *pl*

incer'tezza [intʃer'tettsa] SF uncertainty

in'certo, -a [in'tʃɛrto] AG uncertain; (*irresoluto*) undecided, hesitating ▶ SM uncertainty; **gli incerti del mestiere** the risks of the job

incespi'care [intʃespi'kare] /20/ VI: ~ **(in qc)** to trip (over sth)

inces'sante [intʃes'sante] AG incessant

in'cesto [in'tʃɛsto] SM incest

incestu'oso, -a [intʃestu'oso] AG incestuous

in'cetta [in'tʃetta] SF buying up; **fare** ~ **di qc** to buy up sth

inchi'esta [in'kjɛsta] SF investigation, inquiry

inchi'nare [inki'nare] /72/ VT to bow; **inchinarsi** VPR to bend down; (*per riverenza*) to bow; (*: donna*) to curtsy

in'chino [in'kino] SM bow; curtsy

inchio'dare [inkjo'dare] /72/ VT to nail (down); ~ **la macchina** (*Aut*) to jam on the brakes

inchi'ostro [in'kjɔstro] SM ink; ~ **simpatico** invisible ink

inciam'pare [intʃam'pare] /72/ VI to trip, stumble

inci'ampo [in'tʃampo] SM obstacle; **essere d'~ a qn** (*fig*) to be in sb's way

inciden'tale [intʃiden'tale] AG incidental

incidental'mente [intʃidental'mente] AV (*per caso*) by chance; (*per inciso*) incidentally, by the way

inci'dente [intʃi'dɛnte] SM accident; (*episodio*) incident; **e con questo l'~ è chiuso** and that is the end of the matter; ~ **automobilistico** o **d'auto** car accident; ~ **diplomatico** diplomatic incident

inci'denza [intʃi'dɛntsa] SF incidence; **avere una forte ~ su qc** to affect sth greatly

in'cidere [in'tʃidere] /**34**/ vi: ~ **su** to bear upon, affect ▶ vt (*tagliare incavando*) to cut into; (*Arte*) to engrave; to etch; (*canzone*) to record

in'cinta [in'tʃinta] AG F pregnant

incipi'ente [intʃi'pjɛnte] AG incipient

incipri'are [intʃi'prjare] /**19**/ vt to powder; **incipriarsi** VPR to powder one's face

in'circa [in'tʃirka] AV: **all'**~ more or less, very nearly

in'cisi *etc* [in'tʃizi] vB *vedi* **incidere**

incisi'one [intʃi'zjone] SF cut; (*disegno*) engraving; etching; (*registrazione*) recording; (*Med*) incision

inci'sivo, -a [intʃi'zivo] AG incisive; (*Anat*): **(dente)** ~ incisor

in'ciso, -a [in'tʃizo] PP *di* **incidere** ▶ SM: **per** ~ incidentally, by the way

inci'sore [intʃi'zore] SM (*Arte*) engraver

incita'mento [intʃita'mento] SM incitement

inci'tare [intʃi'tare] /**72**/ vt to incite

inci'vile [intʃi'vile] AG uncivilized; (*villano*) impolite

incivi'lire [intʃivi'lire] /**55**/ vt to civilize

incivil'tà [intʃivil'ta] SF (*di popolazione*) barbarism; (*fig: di trattamento*) barbarity; (: *maleducazione*) incivility, rudeness

incl. ABBR (= *incluso*) encl.

incle'mente AG (*giudice, sentenza*) severe, harsh; (*fig: clima*) harsh; (: *tempo*) inclement

incle'menza [inkle'mɛntsa] SF severity; harshness; inclemency

incli'nabile AG (*schienale*) reclinable

incli'nare /**72**/ vt to tilt ▶ vi (*fig*): ~ **a qc/a fare** to incline towards sth/doing; to tend towards sth/to do; **inclinarsi** VPR (*barca*) to list; (*aereo*) to bank

incli'nato, -a AG sloping

inclinazi'one [inklinat'tsjone] SF slope; (*fig*) inclination, tendency

in'cline AG: ~ **a** inclined to

in'cludere /**3**/ vt to include; (*accludere*) to enclose

inclusi'one SF inclusion

inclu'sivo, -a AG: ~ **di** inclusive of

in'cluso, -a PP *di* **includere** ▶ AG included; enclosed

incoe'rente AG incoherent; (*contraddittorio*) inconsistent

incoe'renza [inkoe'rɛntsa] SF incoherence; inconsistency

in'cognito, -a [in'kɔɲɲito] AG unknown ▶ SM: **in** ~ incognito ▶ SF (*Mat, fig*) unknown quantity

incol'lare /**72**/ vt to glue, gum; (*unire con colla*) to stick together; ~ **gli occhi addosso a qn** (*fig*) to fix one's eyes on sb

incolla'tura SF (*Ippica*): **vincere/perdere di un'**~ to win/lose by a head

incolon'nare /**72**/ vt to draw up in columns

inco'lore AG colourless (BRIT), colorless (US)

incol'pare /**72**/ vt: ~ **qn di** to charge sb with

in'colto, -a AG (*terreno*) uncultivated; (*trascurato: capelli*) neglected; (*persona*) uneducated

in'colume AG safe and sound, unhurt

incolumità SF safety

incom'bente AG (*pericolo*) imminent, impending

incom'benza [inkom'bɛntsa] SF duty, task

in'combere /**29**/ vi (*sovrastare minacciando*): ~ **su** to threaten, hang over

incominci'are [inkomin'tʃare] /**14**/ vi, vt to begin, start

incomo'dare /**72**/ vt to trouble, inconvenience; **incomodarsi** VPR to put o.s. out

in'comodo, -a AG uncomfortable; (*inopportuno*) inconvenient ▶ SM inconvenience, bother

incompa'rabile AG incomparable

incompa'tibile AG incompatible

incompatibilità SF incompatibility; ~ **di carattere** (mutual) incompatibility

incompe'tente AG incompetent

incompe'tenza [inkompe'tɛntsa] SF incompetence

incompi'uto, -a AG unfinished, incomplete

incom'pleto, -a AG incomplete

incompren'sibile AG incomprehensible

incomprensi'one SF incomprehension

incom'preso, -a AG not understood; misunderstood

inconce'pibile [inkontʃe'pibile] AG inconceivable

inconcili'abile [inkontʃi'ljabile] AG irreconcilable

inconclu'dente AG inconclusive; (*persona*) ineffectual

incondizio'nato, -a [inkondittsjo'nato] AG unconditional

inconfes'sabile AG (*pensiero, peccato*) unmentionable

inconfon'dibile AG unmistakable

inconfu'tabile AG irrefutable

incongru'ente AG inconsistent

incongru'enza [inkongru'ɛntsa] SF inconsistency

in'congruo, -a AG incongruous

inconsa'pevole AG: ~ **di** unaware of, ignorant of

inconsapevo'lezza [inkonsapevo'lettsa] SF ignorance, lack of awareness

in'conscio, -a, -sci, -sce [in'kɔnʃo] AG unconscious ▶ SM (*Psic*): **l'**~ the unconscious

inconsis'tente AG (*patrimonio*) insubstantial; (*dubbio*) unfounded; (*ragionamento, prove*) tenuous, flimsy

inconsis'tenza [inkonsis'tɛntsa] SF insubstantial nature; lack of foundation; flimsiness

inconso'labile AG inconsolable
inconsu'eto, -a AG unusual
incon'sulto, -a AG rash
inconte'nibile AG (*rabbia*) uncontrollable; (*entusiasmo*) irrepressible
inconten'tabile AG (*desiderio, avidità*) insatiable; (*persona: capriccioso*) hard to please, very demanding
incontes'tabile AG incontrovertible, indisputable
incontes'tato, -a AG undisputed
inconti'nenza [inkonti'nɛntsa] SF incontinence
incon'trare /72/ VT to meet; (*difficoltà*) to meet with; **incontrarsi** VPR to meet
incon'trario AV: **all'~** (*sottosopra*) upside down; (*alla rovescia*) back to front; (*all'indietro*) backwards; (*nel senso contrario*) the other way round
incontras'tabile AG incontrovertible, indisputable
incontras'tato, -a AG (*successo, vittoria, verità*) uncontested, undisputed
in'contro AV: **~ a** (*verso*) towards ▶ SM meeting; (*Sport*) match; meeting; (*fortuito*) encounter; **venire ~ a** (*richieste, esigenze*) to comply with; **~ di calcio** football match (BRIT), soccer game (US)
incontrol'labile AG uncontrollable
inconveni'ente SM drawback, snag
incoraggia'mento [inkoraddʒa'mento] SM encouragement; **premio d'~** consolation prize
incoraggi'are [inkorad'dʒare] /62/ VT to encourage
incor'nare /72/ VT to gore
incornici'are [inkorni'tʃare] /14/ VT to frame
incoro'nare /72/ VT to crown
incoronazi'one [inkoronat'tsjone] SF coronation
incorpo'rare /72/ VT to incorporate; (*fig: annettere*) to annex
incorreg'gibile [inkorred'dʒibile] AG incorrigible
in'correre /28/ VI: **~ in** to meet with, run into
incorrut'tibile AG incorruptible
in'corso, -a PP *di* **incorrere**
incosci'ente [inkoʃʃɛnte] AG (*inconscio*) unconscious; (*irresponsabile*) reckless, thoughtless
incosci'enza [inkoʃʃɛntsa] SF unconsciousness; recklessness, thoughtlessness
incos'tante AG (*studente, impiegato*) inconsistent; (*carattere*) fickle, inconstant; (*rendimento*) sporadic
incos'tanza [inkos'tantsa] SF inconstancy, fickleness

incostituzio'nale [inkostituttsjo'nale] AG unconstitutional
incre'dibile AG incredible, unbelievable
incredulità SF incredulity
in'credulo, -a AG incredulous, disbelieving
incremen'tare /72/ VT to increase; (*dar sviluppo a*) to promote
incre'mento SM (*sviluppo*) development; (*aumento numerico*) increase, growth
incresci'oso, -a [inkreʃ'ʃoso] AG (*spiacevole*) unpleasant; (*incidente ecc*) regrettable
incres'pare /72/ VT (*capelli*) to curl; (*acque*) to ripple; **incresparsi** VPR (*vedi vt*) to curl; to ripple
incrimi'nare /72/ VT (*Dir*) to charge
incriminazi'one [inkriminat'tsjone] SF (*atto d'accusa*) indictment, charge
incri'nare /72/ VT to crack; (*fig: rapporti, amicizia*) to cause to deteriorate; **incrinarsi** VPR to crack; to deteriorate
incrina'tura SF crack; (*fig*) rift
incroci'are [inkro'tʃare] /14/ VT to cross; (*incontrare*) to meet ▶ VI (*Naut, Aer*) to cruise; **incrociarsi** VPR (*strade*) to cross, intersect; (*persone, veicoli*) to pass each other; **~ le braccia/le gambe** to fold one's arms/cross one's legs
incrocia'tore [inkrotʃa'tore] SM cruiser
in'crocio [in'krotʃo] SM (*anche Ferr*) crossing; (*di strade*) crossroads
incrol'labile AG (*fede*) unshakeable, firm
incros'tare /72/ VT to encrust; **incrostarsi** VPR: **incrostarsi di** to become encrusted with
incrostazi'one [inkrostat'tsjone] SF encrustation; (*di calcare*) scale; (*nelle tubature*) fur (BRIT), scale
incru'ento, -a AG (*battaglia*) without bloodshed, bloodless
incuba'trice [inkuba'tritʃe] SF incubator
incubazi'one [inkubat'tsjone] SF incubation
'incubo SM nightmare
in'cudine SF anvil; **trovarsi** *o* **essere tra l'~ e il martello** (*fig*) to be between the devil and the deep blue sea
incul'care /20/ VT: **~ qc in** to inculcate sth into, instill sth into
incune'are /72/ VT to wedge
incu'pire /55/ VT (*rendere scuro*) to darken; (*fig: intristire*) to fill with gloom ▶ VI (*vedi vt*) to darken; to become gloomy
incu'rabile AG incurable
incu'rante AG: **~ (di)** heedless (of), careless (of)
in'curia SF negligence
incurio'sire /55/ VT to make curious; **incuriosirsi** VPR to become curious
incursi'one SF raid
incur'vare /72/ VT to bend, curve; **incurvarsi** VPR to bend, curve

in'cusso, -a PP *di* **incutere**
incusto'dito, -a AG unguarded, unattended; **passaggio a livello ~** unmanned level crossing
in'cutere /40/ VT to arouse; **~ timore/ rispetto a qn** to strike fear into sb/ command sb's respect
'indaco SM indigo
indaffa'rato, -a AG busy
inda'gare /80/ VT to investigate
indaga'tore, -'trice AG (*sguardo, domanda*) searching; (*mente*) inquiring
in'dagine [in'dadʒine] SF investigation, inquiry; (*ricerca*) research, study; **~ di mercato** market survey
indebita'mente AV (*immeritatamente*) undeservedly; (*erroneamente*) wrongfully
indebi'tare /72/ VT: **~ qn** to get sb into debt; **indebitarsi** VPR to run o get into debt
in'debito, -a AG undeserved; wrongful
indeboli'mento SM weakening; (*debolezza*) weakness
indebo'lire /55/ VT, VI (*anche*: **indebolirsi**) to weaken
inde'cente [inde'tʃɛnte] AG indecent
inde'cenza [inde'tʃɛntsa] SF indecency; **è un'~!** (*vergogna*) it's scandalous!, it's a disgrace!
indeci'frabile [indetʃi'frabile] AG indecipherable
indecisi'one [indetʃi'zjone] SF indecisiveness; indecision
inde'ciso, -a [inde'tʃizo] AG indecisive; (*irresoluto*) undecided
indeco'roso, -a AG (*comportamento*) indecorous, unseemly
inde'fesso, -a AG untiring, indefatigable
indefi'nibile AG indefinable
indefi'nito, -a AG (*anche Ling*) indefinite; (*impreciso, non determinato*) undefined
indefor'mabile AG crushproof
in'degno, -a [in'deɲɲo] AG (*atto*) shameful; (*persona*) unworthy
inde'lebile AG indelible
indelica'tezza [indelika'tettsa] SF tactlessness
indeli'cato, -a AG (*domanda*) indiscreet, tactless
indemoni'ato, -a AG possessed (by the devil)
in'denne AG unhurt, uninjured
indennità SF INV (*rimborso: di spese*) allowance; (*: di perdita*) compensation, indemnity; **~ di contingenza** cost-of-living allowance; **~ di fine rapporto** severance payment (*on retirement, redundancy or when taking up other employment*); **~ di trasferta** travel expenses *pl*
indenniz'zare [indennid'dzare] /72/ VT to compensate
inden'nizzo [inden'niddzo] SM (*somma*) compensation, indemnity

indero'gabile AG binding
indescri'vibile AG indescribable
indeside'rabile AG undesirable
indeside'rato, -a AG unwanted
indetermina'tezza [indetermina'tettsa] SF vagueness
indetermina'tivo, -a AG (*Ling*) indefinite
indetermi'nato, -a AG indefinite, indeterminate
in'detto, -a PP *di* **indire**
'India SF: **l'~** India; **le Indie occidentali** the West Indies
indi'ano, -a AG Indian ▸ SM/F (*d'India*) Indian; (*d'America*) Native American, (American) Indian; **l'Oceano I~** the Indian Ocean
indiavo'lato, -a AG possessed (by the devil); (*vivace, violento*) wild
indi'care /20/ VT (*mostrare*) to show, indicate; (*: col dito*) to point to, point out; (*consigliare*) to suggest, recommend
indica'tivo, -a AG indicative ▸ SM (*Ling*) indicative (mood)
indi'cato, -a AG (*consigliato*) advisable; (*adatto*): **~ per** suitable for, appropriate for
indica'tore, -'trice AG indicating ▸ SM (*elenco*) guide; directory; (*Tecn*) gauge; indicator; **cartello ~** sign; **~ della benzina** petrol (BRIT) o gas (US) gauge, fuel gauge; **~ di velocità** (*Aut*) speedometer; (*Aer*) airspeed indicator
indicazi'one [indikat'tsjone] SF indication; (*informazione*) piece of information; **indicazioni per l'uso** instructions for use
'indice ['inditʃe] SM (*Anat: dito*) index finger, forefinger; (*lancetta*) needle, pointer; (*fig: indizio*) sign; (*Tecn, Mat, nei libri*) index; **~ azionario** share index; **~ di gradimento** (*Radio, TV*) popularity rating; **~ dei prezzi al consumo** ≈ retail price index
indicherò *etc* [indike'rɔ] VB *vedi* **indicare**
indi'cibile [indi'tʃibile] AG inexpressible
indiciz'zare [inditʃid'dzare] /72/ VT: **~ al costo della vita** to index-link (BRIT), index (US)
indiciz'zato, -a [inditʃid'dzato] AG (*polizza, salario ecc*) index-linked (BRIT), indexed (US)
indicizzazi'one [inditʃiddzat'tsjone] SF indexing
indietreggi'are [indjetred'dʒare] /62/ VI to draw back, retreat
indi'etro AV back; (*guardare*) behind, back; (*andare, cadere: anche*: **all'indietro**) backwards; **rimanere ~** to be left behind; **essere ~** (*col lavoro*) to be behind; (*orologio*) to be slow; **rimandare qc ~** to send sth back; **non vado né avanti né ~** (*fig*) I'm not getting anywhere, I'm getting nowhere
indi'feso, -a AG (*città, confine*) undefended; (*persona*) defenceless (BRIT), defenseless (US), helpless

indiffe'rente AG indifferent ▶ SM: **fare l'~**
to pretend to be indifferent, be *o* act casual;
(*fingere di non vedere o sentire*) to pretend not to
notice

indiffe'renza [indiffe'rɛntsa] SF indifference

in'digeno, -a [in'didʒeno] AG indigenous,
native ▶ SM/F native

indi'gente [indi'dʒɛnte] AG poverty-stricken,
destitute

indi'genza [indi'dʒɛntsa] SF extreme poverty

indigesti'one [indidʒes'tjone] SF indigestion

indi'gesto, -a [indi'dʒɛsto] AG indigestible

indi'gnare [indiɲ'ɲare] /**15**/ VT to fill with
indignation; **indignarsi** VPR to be (*o* get)
indignant

indignazi'one [indiɲɲat'tsjone] SF
indignation

indimenti'cabile AG unforgettable

'indio, -a AG, SM/F (South American) Indian

indipen'dente AG independent

indipendente'mente AV independently;
~ dal fatto che gli piaccia o meno, verrà!
he's coming, whether he likes it or not!

indipen'denza [indipen'dɛntsa] SF
independence

in'dire /**38**/ VT (*concorso*) to announce; (*elezioni*)
to call

indi'retto, -a AG indirect

indiriz'zare [indirit'tsare] /**72**/ VT (*dirigere*) to
direct; (*mandare*) to send; (*lettera*) to address;
~ la parola a qn to address sb

indiriz'zario [indirit'tsarjo] SM mailing list

indi'rizzo [indi'rittso] SM address; (*direzione*)
direction; (*avvio*) trend, course; **~ assoluto**
(*Inform*) absolute address

indisci'plina [indiʃʃi'plina] SF indiscipline

indiscipli'nato, -a [indiʃʃipli'nato] AG
undisciplined, unruly

indis'creto, -a AG indiscreet

indiscrezi'one [indiskret'tsjone] SF
indiscretion

indiscrimi'nato, -a AG indiscriminate

indis'cusso, -a AG unquestioned

indiscu'tibile AG indisputable,
unquestionable

indispen'sabile AG indispensable, essential

indispet'tire /**55**/ VT to irritate, annoy ▶ VI
(*anche*: **indispettirsi**) to get irritated *o* annoyed

indispo'nente AG irritating, annoying

indis'porre /**77**/ VT to antagonize

indisposizi'one [indispozit'tsjone] SF
(*slight*) indisposition

indis'posto, -a PP *di* **indisporre** ▶ AG
indisposed, unwell

indisso'lubile AG indissoluble

indissolubil'mente AV indissolubly

indistinta'mente AV (*senza distinzioni*)
indiscriminately, without exception; (*in
modo indefinito*: *vedere, sentire*) vaguely, faintly

indis'tinto, -a AG indistinct

indistrut'tibile AG indestructible

in'divia SF endive

individu'ale AG individual

individua'lismo SM individualism

individua'lista, -i, -e SM/F individualist

individualità SF individuality

individual'mente AV individually

individu'are /**72**/ VT (*dar forma distinta a*) to
characterize; (*determinare*) to locate;
(*riconoscere*) to single out

indi'viduo SM individual

indivi'sibile AG indivisible; **quei due sono
indivisibili** (*fig*) those two are inseparable

indizi'are [indit'tsjare] /**19**/ VT: **~ qn di qc**
to cast suspicion on sb for sth

indizi'ato, -a [indit'tsjato] AG suspected
▶ SM/F suspect

in'dizio [in'dittsjo] SM (*segno*) sign,
indication; (*Polizia*) clue; (*Dir*) piece of
evidence

Indo'cina [indo'tʃina] SF: **l'~** Indochina

'indole SF nature, character

indo'lente AG indolent

indo'lenza [indo'lɛntsa] SF indolence

indolen'zire [indolen'tsire] /**55**/ VT (*gambe,
braccia ecc*) to make stiff, cause to ache;
(: *intorpidire*) to numb; **indolenzirsi** VPR to
become stiff; to go numb

indolen'zito, -a [indolen'tsito] AG stiff,
aching; (*intorpidito*) numb

indo'lore AG (*anche fig*) painless

indo'mani SM: **l'~** the next day, the following
day

Indo'nesia SF: **l'~** Indonesia

indonesi'ano, -a AG, SM/F, SM Indonesian

indo'rare /**72**/ VT (*rivestire in oro*) to gild; (*Cuc*) to
dip in egg yolk; **~ la pillola** (*fig*) to sugar the pill

indos'sare /**72**/ VT (*mettere indosso*) to put on;
(*avere indosso*) to have on

indossa'tore, -'trice SM/F model

in'dotto, -a PP *di* **indurre**

indottri'nare /**72**/ VT to indoctrinate

indovi'nare /**72**/ VT (*scoprire*) to guess;
(*immaginare*) to imagine, guess; (*il futuro*) to
foretell; **tirare a ~** to make a shot in the
dark

indovi'nato, -a AG successful; (*scelta*)
inspired

indovi'nello SM riddle

indo'vino, -a SM/F fortuneteller

indù AG, SMF Hindu

indubbia'mente AV undoubtedly

in'dubbio, -a AG certain, undoubted

in'duco *etc* VB *vedi* **indurre**

indugi'are [indu'dʒare] /**62**/ VI to take one's
time, delay

in'dugio [in'dudʒo] SM (*ritardo*) delay; **senza ~**
without delay

indul'gente [indul'dʒɛnte] AG indulgent; (*giudice*) lenient

indul'genza [indul'dʒɛntsa] SF indulgence; leniency

in'dulgere [in'duldʒere] /**54**/ VI: ~ **a** (*accondiscendere*) to comply with; (*abbandonarsi*) to indulge in

in'dulto, -a PP *di* **indulgere** ▶ SM (*Dir*) pardon

indu'mento SM article of clothing, garment; **indumenti** SMPL (*vestiti*) clothes; **indumenti intimi** underwear *sg*

induri'mento SM hardening

indu'rire /**55**/ VT to harden ▶ VI (*anche*: **indurirsi**) to harden, become hard

in'durre /**90**/ VT: ~ **qn a fare qc** to induce *o* persuade sb to do sth; ~ **qn in errore** to mislead sb; ~ **in tentazione** to lead into temptation

in'dussi *etc* VB *vedi* **indurre**

in'dustria SF industry; **la piccola/grande** ~ small/big business

industri'ale AG industrial ▶ SM industrialist

industrializ'zare [industrjalid'dzare] /**72**/ VT to industrialize

industrializzazi'one [industrjaliddzat'tsjone] SF industrialization

industri'arsi /**19**/ VPR to do one's best, try hard

industri'oso, -a AG industrious, hard-working

induzi'one [indut'tsjone] SF induction

inebe'tito, -a AG dazed, stunned

inebri'are /**19**/ VT (*anche fig*) to intoxicate; **inebriarsi** VPR to become intoxicated

inecce'pibile [inettʃe'pibile] AG unexceptionable

i'nedia SF starvation

i'nedito, -a AG unpublished

ineffabile AG ineffable

ineffi'cace [ineffi'katʃe] AG ineffective

ineffi'cacia [ineffi'katʃa] SF inefficacy, ineffectiveness

ineffici'ente [ineffi'tʃɛnte] AG inefficient

ineffici'enza [ineffi'tʃɛntsa] SF inefficiency

ineguagli'abile [inegwaʎ'ʎabile] AG incomparable, matchless

ineguagli'anza [inegwaʎ'ʎantsa] SF (*sociale*) inequality; (*di superficie, livello*) unevenness

inegu'ale AG unequal; (*irregolare*) uneven

inelut'tabile AG inescapable

ineluttabilità SF inescapability

inenar'rabile AG unutterable

inequivo'cabile AG unequivocal

ine'rente AG: ~ **a** concerning, regarding

i'nerme AG unarmed, defenceless (BRIT), defenseless (US)

inerpi'carsi /**72**/ VPR: ~ (**su**) to clamber (up)

i'nerte AG inert; (*inattivo*) indolent, sluggish

i'nerzia [i'nɛrtsja] SF inertia; indolence, sluggishness

inesat'tezza [inezat'tettsa] SF inaccuracy

ine'satto, -a AG (*impreciso*) inaccurate, inexact; (*erroneo*) incorrect; (*Amm: non riscosso*) uncollected

inesau'ribile AG inexhaustible

inesis'tente AG non-existent

ineso'rabile AG inexorable, relentless

inesorabil'mente AV inexorably

inesperi'enza [inespe'rjɛntsa] SF inexperience

ines'perto, -a AG inexperienced

inespli'cabile AG inexplicable

inesplo'rato, -a AG unexplored

ines'ploso, -a AG unexploded

inespres'sivo, -a AG (*viso*) expressionless, inexpressive

ines'presso, -a AG unexpressed

inespri'mibile AG inexpressible

inespu'gnabile [inespuɲ'ɲabile] AG (*fortezza, torre ecc*) impregnable

ineste'tismo SM beauty problem

inesti'mabile AG inestimable; (*valore*) incalculable

inestir'pabile AG ineradicable

inestri'cabile AG (*anche fig*) impenetrable

inetti'tudine SF ineptitude

i'netto, -a AG (*incapace*) inept; (*che non ha attitudine*): ~ (**a**) unsuited (to)

ine'vaso, -a AG (*ordine, corrispondenza*) outstanding

inevi'tabile AG inevitable

inevitabil'mente AV inevitably

i'nezia [i'nɛttsja] SF trifle, thing of no importance

infagot'tare /**72**/ VT to bundle up, wrap up; **infagottarsi** VPR to wrap up

infal'libile AG infallible

infallibilità SF infallibility

infa'mante AG (*accusa*) defamatory, slanderous

infa'mare /**72**/ VT to defame

in'fame AG infamous; (*fig: cosa, compito*) awful, dreadful

in'famia SF infamy

infan'gare /**80**/ VT (*sporcare*) to cover with mud; (*fig: nome, reputazione*) to sully; **infangarsi** VPR to get covered in mud; to be sullied

infan'tile AG child *cpd*; childlike; (*adulto, azione*) childish; **letteratura** ~ children's books *pl*

in'fanzia [in'fantsja] SF childhood; (*bambini*) children *pl*; **prima** ~ babyhood, infancy

infari'nare /**72**/ VT to cover with (*o* sprinkle with *o* dip in) flour; ~ **di zucchero** to sprinkle with sugar

infarina'tura SF (*fig*) smattering

in'farto SM (*Med*): ~ **(cardiaco)** coronary

infasti'dire /55/ VT to annoy, irritate;
infastidirsi VPR to get annoyed *o* irritated

infati'cabile AG tireless, untiring

in'fatti CONG as a matter of fact, in fact,
actually

infatu'arsi /72/ VPR: ~ **di** *o* **per** to become
infatuated with, fall for

infatuazi'one [infatuat'tsjone] SF
infatuation

in'fausto, -a AG unpropitious, unfavourable
(*BRIT*), unfavorable (*US*)

infecondità SF infertility

infe'condo, -a AG infertile

infe'dele AG unfaithful

infedeltà SF infidelity

infe'lice [infe'litʃe] AG unhappy; (*sfortunato*)
unlucky, unfortunate; (*inopportuno*)
inopportune, ill-timed; (*mal riuscito: lavoro*)
bad, poor

infelicità [infelitʃi'ta] SF unhappiness

infel'trire /55/ VI, **infeltrirsi** VPR (*lana*) to
become matted

infe'renza [infe'rentsa] SF inference

inferi'ore AG lower; (*per intelligenza, qualità*)
inferior ▶ SMF inferior; ~ **a** (*numero, quantità*)
less *o* smaller than; (*meno buono*) inferior to;
~ **alla media** below average

inferiorità SF inferiority

infe'rire /55/ VT (*dedurre*) to infer, deduce

inferme'ria SF infirmary; (*di scuola, nave*) sick
bay

infermi'ere, -a SM/F nurse

infermità SF INV illness; infirmity;
~ **mentale** mental illness; (*Dir*) insanity

in'fermo, -a AG (*ammalato*) ill; (*debole*) infirm;
~ **di mente** mentally ill

infer'nale AG infernal; (*proposito, complotto*)
diabolical; **un tempo** ~ (*col*) hellish weather

in'ferno SM hell; **soffrire le pene dell'** ~ (*fig*)
to go through hell

infero'cire [infero'tʃire] /55/ VT to make fierce
▶ VI (*anche*: **inferocirsi**) to become fierce

inferri'ata SF grating

infervo'rare /72/ VT to arouse enthusiasm in;
infervorarsi VPR to get excited, get carried
away

infes'tare /72/ VT to infest

infet'tare /72/ VT to infect; **infettarsi** VPR to
become infected

infet'tivo, -a AG infectious

in'fetto, -a AG infected; (*acque*) polluted,
contaminated

infezi'one [infet'tsjone] SF infection

infiac'chire [infjak'kire] /55/ VT to weaken
▶ VI (*anche*: **infiacchirsi**) to grow weak

infiam'mabile AG inflammable

infiam'mare /72/ VT to set alight; (*fig, Med*) to
inflame; **infiammarsi** VPR to catch fire;

(*Med*) to become inflamed; (*fig*)
infiammarsi di to be fired with

infiammazi'one [infjammat'tsjone] SF
(*Med*) inflammation

infias'care /20/ VT to bottle

infici'are [infi'tʃare] /14/ VT (*Dir: atto,
dichiarazione*) to challenge

in'fido, -a AG unreliable, treacherous

infie'rire /55/ VI: ~ **su** (*fisicamente*) to attack
furiously; (*verbalmente*) to rage at; (*epidemia*)
to rage over

in'figgere [in'fiddʒere] /104/ VT: ~ **qc in** to
thrust *o* drive sth into

infi'lare /72/ VT (*ago*) to thread; (*mettere: chiave*)
to insert; (: *vestito*) to slip *o* put on; (*strada*) to
turn and take; **infilarsi** VPR: **infilarsi in** to
slip into; (*indossare*) to slip on; ~ **un anello al
dito** to slip a ring on one's finger; ~ **l'uscio**
to slip in; to slip out; **infilarsi la giacca** to
put on one's jacket

infil'trarsi /72/ VPR to penetrate, seep
through; (*Mil*) to infiltrate

infil'trato, -a SM/F infiltrator

infiltrazi'one [infiltrat'tsjone] SF
infiltration

infil'zare [infil'tsare] /72/ VT (*infilare*) to string
together; (*trafiggere*) to pierce

'infimo, -a AG lowest; **un albergo di** ~ **ordine**
a third-rate hotel

in'fine AV finally; (*insomma*) in short

infin'gardo, -a AG lazy ▶ SM/F slacker

infinità SF infinity; (*in quantità*): **un'** ~ **di** an
infinite number of

infinitesi'male AG infinitesimal

infi'nito, -a AG infinite; (*Ling*) infinitive ▶ SM
infinity; (*Ling*) infinitive; **all'** ~ (*senza fine*)
endlessly; (*Ling*) in the infinitive

infinocchi'are [infinok'kjare] /19/ VT (*col*) to
hoodwink

infiore'scenza [infjoreʃʃentsa] SF
inflorescence

infir'mare /72/ VT (*Dir*) to invalidate

infischi'arsi [infis'kjarsi] /19/ VPR: ~ **di** not
to care about

in'fisso, -a PP *di* **infiggere** ▶ SM fixture; (*di
porta, finestra*) frame

infit'tire /55/ VT, VI (*anche*: **infittirsi**) to
thicken

inflazio'nare [inflattsjo'nare] /72/ VT to
inflate

inflazi'one [inflat'tsjone] SF inflation

inflazio'nistico, -a, -ci, -che
[inflattsjo'nistiko] AG inflationary

infles'sibile AG inflexible; (*ferreo*) unyielding

inflessi'one SF inflexion

in'fliggere [in'fliddʒere] /104/ VT to inflict

in'flissi *etc* VB *vedi* **infliggere**

in'flitto, -a PP *di* **infliggere**

influ'ente AG influential

influ'enza [influ'ɛntsa] SF influence; (Med) influenza, flu; **~ aviaria** bird flu; **~ suina** swine flu

influen'zare [influen'tsare] /**72**/ VT to influence, have an influence on

influ'ire /**55**/ VI: **~ su** to influence

in'flusso SM influence

INFN SIGLA M = **Istituto Nazionale di Fisica Nucleare**

info'cato, -a AG = **infuocato**

info'gnarsi [infoɲ'ɲarsi] /**15**/ VPR (col) to get into a mess; **~ in un mare di debiti** to be up to one's o the eyes in debt

infol'tire /**55**/ VT, VI to thicken

infon'dato, -a AG unfounded, groundless

in'fondere /**25**/ VT: **~ qc in qn** to instill sth in sb; **~ fiducia in qn** to inspire sb with confidence

infor'care /**20**/ VT to fork (up); (bicicletta, cavallo) to get on; (occhiali) to put on

infor'male AG informal

infor'mare /**72**/ VT to inform, tell; **informarsi** VPR: **informarsi (di o su)** to inquire (about); **tenere informato qn** to keep sb informed

infor'matico, -a, -ci, -che AG (settore) computer cpd ▶ SF computer science

informa'tivo, -a AG informative; **a titolo ~** for information only

informatiz'zare [informatid'dzare] /**72**/ VT to computerize

infor'mato, -a AG informed; **tenersi ~** to keep o.s. (well-)informed

informa'tore SM informer

informazi'one [informat'tsjone] SF piece of information; **informazioni** SFPL information sg; **chiedere un'~** to ask for (some) information; **~ di garanzia** (Dir) = **avviso di garanzia**

in'forme AG shapeless

informico'larsi /**72**/, **informico'lirsi** VPR: **mi si è informicolata una gamba** I've got pins and needles in my leg

infor'nare /**72**/ VT to put in the oven

infor'nata SF (anche fig) batch

infortu'narsi /**72**/ VPR to injure o.s., have an accident

infortu'nato, -a AG injured, hurt ▶ SM/F injured person

infor'tunio SM accident; **~ sul lavoro** industrial accident, accident at work

infortu'nistica SF study of (industrial) accidents

infos'sarsi /**72**/ VPR (terreno) to sink; (guance) to become hollow

infos'sato, -a AG hollow; (occhi) deep-set; (: per malattia) sunken

infradici'are [infradi'tʃare] /**14**/ VT (inzuppare) to soak, drench; (marcire) to rot; **infradiciarsi** VPR to get soaked, get drenched; to rot

infra'dito SM INV (calzatura) flip flop (BRIT), thong (US)

in'frangere [in'frandʒere] /**37**/ VT to smash; (fig: legge, patti) to break; **infrangersi** VPR to smash, break

infran'gibile [infran'dʒibile] AG unbreakable

in'franto, -a PP di **infrangere** ▶ AG broken

infra'rosso, -a AG, SM infrared

infrasettima'nale AG midweek cpd

infrastrut'tura SF infrastructure

infrazi'one [infrat'tsjone] SF: **~ a** breaking of, violation of

infredda'tura SF slight cold

infreddo'lito, -a AG cold, chilled

infre'quente AG infrequent, rare

infrol'lire /**55**/ VI, **infrol'lirsi** VPR (selvaggina) to become high

infruttu'oso, -a AG fruitless

infuo'cato, -a AG (metallo) red-hot; (sabbia) burning; (fig: discorso) heated, passionate

infu'ori AV out; **all'~** outwards; **all'~ di** (eccetto) except, with the exception of

infuri'are /**19**/ VI to rage; **infuriarsi** VPR to fly into a rage

infusi'one SF infusion

in'fuso, -a PP di **infondere** ▶ AG: **scienza infusa** (anche ironico) innate knowledge ▶ SM infusion; **~ di camomilla** camomile tea

Ing. ABBR = **ingegnere**

ingabbi'are /**19**/ VT to (put in a) cage

ingaggi'are [ingad'dʒare] /**62**/ VT (assumere con compenso) to take on, hire; (Sport) to sign on; (Mil) to engage

in'gaggio [in'gaddʒo] SM hiring; signing on

ingagliar'dire [ingaʎʎar'dire] /**55**/ VT to strengthen, invigorate ▶ VI (anche: **ingagliardirsi**) to grow stronger

ingan'nare /**72**/ VT to deceive; (coniuge) to be unfaithful to; (fisco) to cheat; (eludere) to dodge, elude; (fig: tempo) to while away ▶ VI (apparenza) to be deceptive; **ingannarsi** VPR to be mistaken, be wrong

inganna'tore, -'trice AG deceptive; (persona) deceitful

ingan'nevole AG deceptive

in'ganno SM deceit, deception; (azione) trick; (menzogna, frode) cheat, swindle; (illusione) illusion

ingarbugli'are [ingarbuʎ'ʎare] /**27**/ VT to tangle; (fig) to confuse, muddle; **ingarbugliarsi** VPR to become confused o muddled

ingarbu'gliato, -a [ingarbuʎ'ʎato] AG tangled; confused, muddled

inge'gnarsi [indʒeɲ'ɲarsi] /**15**/ VPR to do one's best, try hard; **~ per vivere** to live by one's wits; **basta ~ un po'** you just need a bit of ingenuity

inge'gnere [indʒeɲ'ɲɛre] SM engineer; **~ civile/navale** civil/naval engineer

ingegne'ria [indʒeɲɲe'ria] SF engineering;
~ **genetica** genetic engineering

in'gegno [in'dʒeɲɲo] SM (*intelligenza*)
intelligence, brains pl; (*capacità creativa*)
ingenuity; (*disposizione*) talent

ingegnosità [indʒeɲɲosi'ta] SF ingenuity

inge'gnoso, -a [indʒeɲ'ɲoso] AG ingenious,
clever

ingelo'sire [indʒelo'sire] /**55**/ VT to make
jealous ▶ VI (*anche*: **ingelosirsi**) to become
jealous

in'gente [in'dʒɛnte] AG huge, enormous

ingenti'lire [indʒenti'lire] /**55**/ VT to refine,
civilize; **ingentilirsi** VPR to become more
refined, become more civilized

ingenuità [indʒenui'ta] SF ingenuousness

in'genuo, -a [in'dʒɛnuo] AG naïve

inge'renza [indʒe'rɛntsa] SF interference

inge'rire [indʒe'rire] /**55**/ VT to ingest

inges'sare [indʒes'sare] /**72**/ VT (*Med*) to put
in plaster

ingessa'tura [indʒessa'tura] SF plaster

Inghil'terra [ingil'tɛrra] SF: l'~ England

inghiot'tire [ingjot'tire] /**17**/ VT to swallow

in'ghippo [in'gippo] SM trick

ingial'lire [indʒal'lire] /**55**/ VI to go yellow

ingigan'tire [indʒigan'tire] /**55**/ VT to
enlarge, magnify ▶ VI to become gigantic o
enormous

inginocchi'arsi [indʒinok'kjarsi] /**19**/ VPR to
kneel (down)

inginocchia'toio [indʒinokkja'tojo] SM
prie-dieu

ingioiel'lare [indʒojel'lare] /**72**/ VT to bejewel,
adorn with jewels

ingiù [in'dʒu] AV down, downwards

ingi'ungere [in'dʒundʒere] /**5**/ VT: ~ **a qn di
fare qc** to enjoin o order sb to do sth

ingi'unto, -a [in'dʒunto] PP *di* **ingiungere**

ingiunzi'one [indʒun'tsjone] SF injunction,
command; ~ **di pagamento** final demand

ingi'uria [in'dʒurja] SF insult; (*fig: danno*)
damage

ingiuri'are [indʒu'rjare] /**19**/ VT to insult,
abuse

ingiuri'oso, -a [indʒu'rjoso] AG insulting,
abusive

ingiusta'mente [indʒusta'mente] AV
unjustly

ingiustifi'cabile [indʒustifi'kabile] AG
unjustifiable

ingiustifi'cato, -a [indʒustifi'kato] AG
unjustified

ingius'tizia [indʒus'tittsja] SF injustice

ingi'usto, -a [in'dʒusto] AG unjust, unfair

in'glese AG English ▶ SMF
Englishman(-woman) ▶ SM (*Ling*) English;
gli Inglesi the English; **andarsene** o **filare
all'~** to take French leave

inglori'oso, -a AG inglorious

ingob'bire /**55**/ VI, **ingob'birsi** VPR to become
stooped

ingoi'are /**19**/ VT to gulp (down); (*fig*) to
swallow (up); **ha dovuto ~ il rospo** (*fig*) he
had to accept the situation

ingol'fare /**72**/ VT, **ingol'farsi** VPR (*motore*) to
flood

ingolo'sire /**55**/ VT: ~ **qn** to make sb's mouth
water; (*fig*) to attract sb ▶ VI (*anche*:
ingolosirsi): ~ (**di**) (*anche fig*) to become
greedy (for)

ingom'brante AG cumbersome

ingom'brare /**72**/ VT (*strada*) to block; (*stanza*)
to clutter up

in'gombro, -a AG: ~ **di** (*strada*) blocked by;
(*stanza*) cluttered up with ▶ SM obstacle;
essere d'~ to be in the way; **per ragioni di ~**
for reasons of space

ingor'digia [ingor'didʒa] SF: ~ (**di**) greed (for);
avidity (for)

in'gordo, -a AG: ~ **di** greedy for; (*fig*) greedy o
avid for ▶ SM/F glutton

ingor'gare /**80**/ VT to block; **ingorgarsi** VPR
to be blocked up, be choked up

in'gorgo, -ghi SM blockage, obstruction;
(*anche*: **ingorgo stradale**) traffic jam

ingoz'zare [ingot'tsare] /**72**/ VT (*animali*) to
fatten; (*fig: persona*) to stuff; **ingozzarsi** VPR:
ingozzarsi (di) to stuff o.s. (with)

ingra'naggio [ingra'naddʒo] SM (*Tecn*) gear;
(*di orologio*) mechanism; **gli ingranaggi
della burocrazia** the bureaucratic
machinery

ingra'nare /**72**/ VI to mesh, engage ▶ VT to
engage; ~ **la marcia** to get into gear

ingrandi'mento SM enlargement;
extension; magnification; growth;
expansion

ingran'dire /**55**/ VT (*anche Fot*) to enlarge;
(*estendere*) to extend; (*Ottica, fig*) to magnify
▶ VI (*anche*: **ingrandirsi**) to become larger o
bigger; (: *aumentare*) to grow, increase;
(: *espandersi*) to expand

ingrandi'tore SM (*Fot*) enlarger

ingras'saggio [ingras'saddʒo] SM greasing

ingras'sare /**72**/ VT to make fat; (*animali*) to
fatten; (*Agr: terreno*) to manure; (*lubrificare*) to
oil, lubricate ▶ VI (*anche*: **ingrassarsi**) to get
fat, put on weight

ingrati'tudine SF ingratitude

in'grato, -a AG ungrateful; (*lavoro*) thankless,
unrewarding

ingrazi'are [ingrat'tsjare] /**19**/ VT:
ingraziarsi qn to ingratiate o.s. with sb

ingredi'ente SM ingredient

in'gresso SM (*porta*) entrance; (*atrio*) hall;
(*l'entrare*) entrance, entry; (*facoltà di entrare*)
admission; **"~ libero"** "admission free";

~ principale main entrance; **~ di servizio** tradesmen's entrance

ingros'sare/**72**/ vt to increase; (folla, livello) to swell ▶ vi (anche: **ingrossarsi**) to increase; to swell

in'grosso av: **all'~** (Comm) wholesale; (all'incirca) roughly, about

ingru'gnato, -a[ingruɲ'ɲato] AG grumpy

inguai'arsi/**19**/ vpr to get into trouble

inguai'nare/**72**/ vt to sheathe

ingual'cibile [ingwal'tʃibile] AG crease-resistant

ingua'ribile AG incurable

'inguine sm (Anat) groin

ingurgi'tare [ingurdʒi'tare] /**72**/ vt to gulp down

ini'bire/**55**/ vt to forbid, prohibit; (Psic) to inhibit; **inibirsi**vpr to restrain o.s.

ini'bito, -a AG inhibited ▶ sm/f inhibited person

inibi'torio, -a AG (Psic) inhibitory, inhibitive; (provvedimento, misure) restrictive

inibizi'one [inibit'tsjone] sf prohibition; inhibition

iniet'tare/**72**/ vt to inject; **iniettarsi**vpr: **iniettarsi di sangue** (occhi) to become bloodshot

iniet'tore sm injector

iniezi'one [injet'tsjone] sf injection

inimi'care/**20**/ vt to alienate, make hostile; **inimicarsi**vpr: **inimicarsi con qn** to fall out with sb; **si è inimicato gli amici di un tempo** he has alienated his old friends

inimi'cizia [inimi'tʃittsja] sf animosity

inimi'tabile AG inimitable

inimmagi'nabile [inimmadʒi'nabile] AG unimaginable

ininfiam'mabile AG non-flammable

inintelli'gibile [inintelli'dʒibile] AG unintelligible

ininterrotta'mente av non-stop, continuously

ininter'rotto, -a AG (fila) unbroken; (rumore) uninterrupted

iniquità sf INV iniquity; (atto) wicked action

i'niquo, -a AG iniquitous

inizi'ale [init'tsjale] AG, sf initial

inizializ'zare [inittsjalid'dzare] /**72**/ vt (Inform) to boot

inizial'mente [inittsjal'mente] av initially, at first

inizi'are [init'tsjare] /**19**/ vi, vt to begin, start; **~ qn a** to initiate sb into; (pittura ecc) to introduce sb to; **~ a fare qc** to start doing sth

inizia'tiva [inittsja'tiva] sf initiative; **~ privata** private enterprise

inizia'tore, -'trice[inittsja'tore] sm/f initiator

i'nizio [i'nittsjo] sm beginning; **all'~** at the beginning, at the start; **dare ~ a qc** to start

sth, get sth going; **essere agli inizi** (progetto, lavoro ecc) to be in the initial stages

innaffi'areetc = **annaffiare** ecc

innal'zare [innal'tsare] /**72**/ vt (sollevare, alzare) to raise; (rizzare) to erect; **innalzarsi** vpr to rise

innamora'mento sm falling in love

innamo'rare/**72**/ vt to enchant, charm; **innamorarsi**vpr: **innamorarsi (di qn)** to fall in love (with sb)

innamo'rato, -a AG: **~ (di)** (che nutre amore) in love (with); **~ di** (appassionato) very fond of ▶ sm/f lover; (anche scherzoso) sweetheart

in'nanzi [in'nantsi] av (stato in luogo) in front, ahead; (moto a luogo) forward, on; (tempo: prima) before ▶ prep (prima) before; **~ a** in front of; **d'ora ~** from now on; **farsi ~** to step forward; **~ tempo** ahead of time

innanzi'tutto [innantsi'tutto] av above all; (per prima cosa) first of all

in'nato, -a AG innate

innatu'rale AG unnatural

inne'gabile AG undeniable

inneggi'are [inned'dʒare] /**62**/ vi: **~ a** to sing hymns to; (fig) to sing the praises of

innervo'sire/**55**/ vt: **~ qn** to get on sb's nerves; **innervosirsi**vpr to get irritated o upset

innes'care/**20**/ vt to prime

in'nesco, -schi sm primer

innes'tare/**72**/ vt (Bot, Med) to graft; (Tecn) to engage; (inserire: presa) to insert

in'nesto sm graft; grafting no pl; (Tecn) clutch; (Elettr) connection

'inno sm hymn; **~ nazionale** national anthem

inno'cente [inno'tʃente] AG innocent

inno'cenza [inno'tʃentsa] sf innocence

in'nocuo, -a AG innocuous, harmless

innomi'nato, -a AG unnamed

inno'vare/**72**/ vt to change, make innovations in

innova'tivo, -a AG innovative

innovazi'one [innovat'tsjone] sf innovation

innume'revole AG innumerable

inocu'lare/**72**/ vt (Med) to inoculate

ino'doro, -a AG odourless (BRIT), odorless (US)

inoffen'sivo, -a AG harmless

inol'trare/**72**/ vt (Amm) to pass on, forward; **inoltrarsi**vpr (addentrarsi) to advance, go forward

inol'trato, -a AG: **a notte inoltrata** late at night; **a primavera inoltrata** late in the spring

i'noltre av besides, moreover

i'noltro sm (Amm) forwarding

inon'dare/**72**/ vt to flood

inondazi'one [inondat'tsjone] sf flooding no pl; flood

inope'roso, -a AG inactive, idle

inopi'nato, -a AG unexpected

inoppor'tuno, -a AG untimely, ill-timed; (*poco adatto*) inappropriate; (*momento*) inopportune

inoppu'gnabile [inoppuɲ'ɲabile] AG incontrovertible

inor'ganico, -a, -ci, -che AG inorganic

inorgo'glire [inorgoʎ'ʎire] **/55/** VT to make proud ▶ VI (*anche*: **inorgoglirsi**) to become proud; **inorgoglirsi di qc** to pride o.s. on sth

inorri'dire /55/ VT to horrify ▶ VI to be horrified

inospi'tale AG inhospitable

inosser'vante AG: **essere ~ di** to fail to comply with

inosser'vato, -a AG (*non notato*) unobserved; (*non rispettato*) not observed, not kept; **passare ~** to go unobserved, escape notice

inossi'dabile AG stainless

INPS SIGLA M (= *Istituto Nazionale Previdenza Sociale*) social security service

inqua'drare /72/ VT (*foto, immagine*) to frame; (*fig*) to situate, set

inquadra'tura AG (*Cine, Fot: atto*) framing; (: *immagine*) shot; (: *sequenza*) sequence

inqualifi'cabile AG unspeakable

inquie'tante AG disturbing, worrying

inquie'tare /72/ VT (*turbare*) to disturb, worry; **inquietarsi** VPR to worry, become anxious; (*impazientirsi*) to get upset

inqui'eto, -a AG restless; (*preoccupato*) worried, anxious

inquie'tudine SF anxiety, worry

inqui'lino, -a SM/F tenant

inquina'mento SM pollution

inqui'nare /72/ VT to pollute

inqui'rente AG (*Dir*): **magistrato ~** examining (*BRIT*) *o* committing (*US*) magistrate; **commissione ~** commission of inquiry

inqui'sire /55/ VT, VI to investigate

inqui'sito, -a AG (*persona*) under investigation

inquisi'tore, -'trice AG (*sguardo*) inquiring

inquisizi'one [inkwizit'tsjone] SF inquisition

insabbia'mento SM (*fig*) shelving

insabbi'are /19/ VT (*fig: pratica*) to shelve; **insabbiarsi** VPR (*arenarsi: barca*) to run aground; (*fig: pratica*) to be shelved

insac'care /20/ VT (*grano, farina ecc*) to bag, put into sacks; (*carne*) to put into sausage skins

insac'cati SMPL (*Cuc*) sausages

insa'lata SF salad; (*pianta*) lettuce; **~ mista** mixed salad; **~ russa** (*Cuc*) Russian salad (*comprised of cold diced cooked vegetables in mayonnaise*)

insalati'era SF salad bowl

insa'lubre AG unhealthy

insa'nabile AG (*piaga*) which cannot be healed; (*situazione*) irremediable; (*odio*) implacable

insangui'nare /72/ VT to stain with blood

in'sania SF insanity

in'sano, -a AG (*pazzo, folle*) insane

insapo'nare /72/ VT to soap; **insaponarsi le mani** to soap one's hands

insapo'nata SF: **dare un'~ a qc** to give sth a (quick) soaping

insapo'rire /55/ VT to flavour (*BRIT*), flavor (*US*); (*con spezie*) to season; **insaporirsi** VPR to acquire flavo(u)r

insa'poro, -a AG tasteless, insipid

insa'puta SF: **all'~ di qn** without sb knowing

insazi'abile [insat'tsjabile] AG insatiable

inscato'lare /72/ VT (*frutta, carne*) to can

insce'nare [inʃe'nare] **/72/** VT (*Teat*) to stage, put on; (*fig*) to stage

inscin'dibile [inʃin'dibile] AG (*fattori*) inseparable; (*legame*) indissoluble

insec'chire [insek'kire] **/55/** VT (*seccare*) to dry up; (: *piante*) to wither ▶ VI to dry up, become dry; to wither

insedia'mento SM (*Amm: in carica, ufficio*) installation; (*villaggio, colonia*) settlement

insedi'are /19/ VT (*Amm*) to install; **insediarsi** VPR (*Amm*) to take up office; (*colonia, profughi ecc*) to settle; (*Mil*) to take up positions

in'segna [in'seɲɲa] SF sign; (*emblema*) sign, emblem; (*bandiera*) flag, banner; **insegne** SFPL (*decorazioni*) insignia *pl*

insegna'mento [inseɲɲa'mento] SM teaching; **trarre ~ da un'esperienza** to learn from an experience, draw a lesson from an experience; **che ti serva da ~** let this be a lesson to you

inse'gnante [inseɲ'ɲante] AG teaching ▶ SMF teacher; **~ di sostegno** teaching assistant

inse'gnare [inseɲ'ɲare] **/15/** VT, VI to teach; **~ a qn qc** to teach sb sth; **~ a qn a fare qc** to teach sb (how) to do sth; **come lei ben m'insegna …** (*ironico*) as you will doubtless be aware …

insegui'mento SM pursuit, chase; **darsi all'~ di qn** to give chase to sb

insegu'ire /45/ VT to pursue, chase

insegui'tore, -'trice SM/F pursuer

insel'lare /72/ VT to saddle

inselvati'chire [inselvati'kire] **/55/** VT (*persona*) to make unsociable ▶ VI (*anche*: **inselvatichirsi**) to grow wild; (: *persona*) to become unsociable

inseminazi'one [inseminat'tsjone] SF insemination

insena'tura SF inlet, creek

insen'sato, -a AG senseless, stupid

insen'sibile AG (*anche fig*) insensitive

insensibilità SF insitivity, insensibility
insepa'rabile AG inseparable
inse'polto, -a AG unburied
inseri'mento SM (gen) insertion; **problemi di** ~ (di persona) adjustment problems
inse'rire /55/ VT to insert; (Elettr) to connect; (allegare) to enclose; (annuncio) to put in, place; **inserirsi** VPR (fig): **inserirsi in** to become part of; ~ **un annuncio sul giornale** to put o place an advertisement in the newspaper
in'serto SM (pubblicazione) insert; ~ **filmato** (film) clip
inser'vibile AG useless
inservi'ente SMF attendant
inserzi'one [inser'tsjone] SF insertion; (avviso) advertisement; **fare un'~ sul giornale** to put an advertisement in the newspaper
inserzio'nista, -i, -e [insertsjo'nista] SM/F advertiser
insetti'cida, -i [insetti'tʃida] SM insecticide
in'setto SM insect
insicu'rezza [insiku'rettsa] SF insecurity
insi'curo, -a AG insecure
in'sidia SF snare, trap; (pericolo) hidden danger; **tendere un'~ a qn** to lay o set a trap for sb
insidi'are /19/ VT (Mil) to harass; ~ **la vita di qn** to make an attempt on sb's life
insidi'oso, -a AG insidious
insi'eme AV together; (contemporaneamente) at the same time ▶ PREP: ~ **a** o **con** together with ▶ SM whole; (Mat, servizio, assortimento) set; (Moda) ensemble, outfit; **tutti** ~ all together; **tutto** ~ all together; (in una volta) at one go; **nell'~** on the whole; **d'~** (veduta ecc) overall
in'signe [in'siɲɲe] AG (persona) famous, distinguished, eminent; (città, monumento) notable
insignifi'cante [insiɲɲifi'kante] AG insignificant
insi'gnire [insiɲ'ɲire] /55/ VT: ~ **qn di** to honour (BRIT) o honor (US) sb with, decorate sb with
insin'cero, -a [insin'tʃero] AG insincere
insinda'cabile AG unquestionable
insinu'ante AG (osservazione, sguardo) insinuating; (maniere) ingratiating
insinu'are /72/ VT (fig) to insinuate, imply; ~ **qc in** (introdurre) to slip o slide sth into; **insinuarsi** VPR: **insinuarsi in** to seep into; (fig) to creep into; to worm one's way into
insinuazi'one [insinuat'tsjone] SF (fig) insinuation
in'sipido, -a AG insipid
insis'tente AG insistent; (pioggia, dolore) persistent

insistente'mente AV repeatedly
insis'tenza [insis'tɛntsa] SF insistence; persistence
in'sistere /11/ VI: ~ **su qc** to insist on sth; ~ **in qc/a fare** (perseverare) to persist in sth/in doing
insis'tito, -a PP di **insistere**
'insito, -a AG: ~ **(in)** inherent (in)
insoddis'fatto, -a AG dissatisfied
insoddisfazi'one [insoddisfat'tsjone] SF dissatisfaction
insoffe'rente AG intolerant
insoffe'renza [insoffe'rɛntsa] SF impatience
insolazi'one [insolat'tsjone] SF (Med) sunstroke
inso'lente AG insolent
insolen'tire /55/ VI to grow insolent ▶ VT to insult, be rude to
inso'lenza [inso'lɛntsa] SF insolence
in'solito, -a AG unusual, out of the ordinary
inso'lubile AG insoluble
inso'luto, -a AG (non risolto) unsolved; (non pagato) unpaid, outstanding
insol'vente AG (Dir) insolvent
insol'venza [insol'vɛntsa] SF (Dir) insolvency
insol'vibile AG insolvent
in'somma AV (in breve, in conclusione) in short; (dunque) well ▶ ESCL for heaven's sake!
inson'dabile AG unfathomable
in'sonne AG sleepless
in'sonnia SF insomnia, sleeplessness
insonno'lito, -a AG sleepy, drowsy
insonorizzazi'one [insonoriddzat'tsjone] SF soundproofing
insoppor'tabile AG unbearable
insoppri'mibile AG insuppressible
insor'genza [insor'dʒentsa] SF (di malattia) onset
in'sorgere [in'sordʒere] /109/ VI (ribellarsi) to rise up, rebel; (apparire) to come up, arise
insormon'tabile AG (ostacolo) insurmountable, insuperable
in'sorsi etc VB vedi **insorgere**
in'sorto, -a PP di **insorgere** ▶ SM/F rebel, insurgent
insospet'tabile AG (al di sopra di ogni sospetto) above suspicion; (inatteso) unsuspected
insospet'tire /55/ VT to make suspicious ▶ VI (anche: **insospettirsi**) to become suspicious
insoste'nibile AG (posizione, teoria) untenable; (dolore, situazione) intolerable, unbearable; **le spese di manutenzione sono insostenibili** the maintenance costs are excessive
insostitu'ibile AG (persona) irreplaceable; (aiuto, presenza) invaluable
insoz'zare [insot'tsare] /72/ VT (pavimento) to make dirty; (fig: reputazione, memoria) to tarnish, sully; **insozzarsi** VPR to get dirty

inspe'rabile AG: **la guarigione/salvezza era
~** there was no hope of a cure/of rescue;
abbiamo ottenuto risultati insperabili
the results we achieved were far better than
we had hoped

inspe'rato, -a AG unhoped-for

inspie'gabile AG inexplicable

inspi'rare /**72**/ VT to breathe in, inhale

in'stabile AG (carico, indole) unstable; (tempo)
unsettled; (equilibrio) unsteady

instabilità SF instability; (di tempo)
changeability

instal'lare /**72**/ VT to install; **installarsi** VPR
(sistemarsi): **installarsi in** to settle in

installazi'one [installat'tsjone] SF
installation

instan'cabile AG untiring, indefatigable

instau'rare /**72**/ VT to establish, introduce

instaurazi'one [instaurat'tsjone] SF
establishment

instil'lare /**72**/ VT to instil

instra'dare /**72**/ VT = **istradare**

insù AV up, upwards; **guardare all'~** to
look up o upwards; **naso all'~** turned-up
nose

insubordinazi'one [insubordinat'tsjone] SF
insubordination

insuc'cesso [insut'tʃɛsso] SM failure, flop

insudici'are [insudi'tʃare] /**14**/ VT to dirty;
insudiciarsi VPR to get dirty

insuffici'ente [insuffi'tʃɛnte] AG
insufficient; (compito, allievo) inadequate

insuffici'enza [insuffi'tʃɛntsa] SF
insufficiency; inadequacy; (Ins) fail; **~ di
prove** (Dir) lack of evidence; **~ renale** renal
insufficiency

insu'lare AG insular

insu'lina SF insulin

in'sulso, -a AG (sciocco) inane, silly; (persona)
dull, insipid

insul'tare /**72**/ VT to insult, affront

in'sulto SM insult, affront

insupe'rabile AG (ostacolo, difficoltà)
insuperable, insurmountable; (eccellente:
qualità, prodotto) unbeatable; (: persona,
interpretazione) unequalled

insuper'bire /**55**/ VT to make proud, make
arrogant; **insuperbirsi** VPR to become
arrogant

insurrezi'one [insurret'tsjone] SF revolt,
insurrection

insussis'tente AG non-existent

intac'care /**20**/ VT (fare tacche) to cut into;
(corrodere) to corrode; (fig: cominciare ad usare:
risparmi) to break into; (: ledere) to damage

intagli'are [intaʎ'ʎare] /**27**/ VT to carve

intaglia'tore, -'trice [intaʎʎa'tore] SM/F
engraver

in'taglio [in'taʎʎo] SM carving

intan'gibile [intan'dʒibile] AG (bene,
patrimonio) untouchable; (fig: diritto)
inviolable

in'tanto AV (nel frattempo) meanwhile, in the
meantime; (per cominciare) just to begin with;
~ che cong while

intarsi'are /**19**/ VT to inlay

in'tarsio SM inlaying no pl, marquetry no pl;
inlay

intasa'mento SM (ostruzione) blockage,
obstruction; (Aut: ingorgo) traffic jam

inta'sare /**72**/ VT to choke (up), block (up);
(Aut) to obstruct, block; **intasarsi** VPR to
become choked o blocked

intas'care /**20**/ VT to pocket

in'tatto, -a AG intact; (puro) unsullied

intavo'lare /**72**/ VT to start, enter into

inte'gerrimo, -a [inte'dʒɛrrimo] AG honest,
upright

inte'grale AG complete; (pane, farina)
wholemeal (BRIT), wholewheat (US); **film in
versione ~** uncut version of a film; **calcolo ~**
(Mat) integral calculus; **edizione ~**
unabridged edition

inte'grante AG: **parte ~** integral part

inte'grare /**72**/ VT to complete; (Mat) to
integrate; **integrarsi** VPR (persona) to become
integrated

integra'tivo, -a AG (assegno) supplementary;
(Ins): **esame ~** assessment test sat when changing
schools

integra'tore SM: **integratori alimentari**
nutritional supplements

integrazi'one [integrat'tsjone] SF
integration

integrità SF integrity

'integro, -a AG (intatto, intero) complete,
whole; (retto) upright

intelaia'tura SF frame; (fig) structure,
framework

intel'letto SM intellect

intellettu'ale AG, SMF intellectual

intellettua'loide (peg) AG pseudo-
intellectual ▸ SMF pseudo-intellectual,
would-be intellectual

intelli'gente [intelli'dʒɛnte] AG intelligent

intelli'genza [intelli'dʒɛntsa] SF intelligence

intelli'ghenzia [intelli'gɛntsja] SF
intelligentsia

intelli'gibile [intelli'dʒibile] AG intelligible

inteme'rato, -a AG (persona, vita) blameless,
irreproachable; (coscienza) clear; (fama)
unblemished

intempe'rante AG intemperate, immoderate

intempe'ranza [intempe'rantsa] SF
intemperance; **intemperanze** SFPL (eccessi)
excesses

intem'perie SFPL bad weather sg

intempes'tivo, -a AG untimely

inten'dente SM: ~ **di Finanza** inland (BRIT) o internal (US) revenue officer

inten'denza [inten'dɛntsa] SF: ~ **di Finanza** inland (BRIT) o internal (US) revenue office

in'tendere/120/ VT (*comprendere*) to understand; (*udire*) to hear; (*significare*) to mean; (*avere intenzione*): ~ **fare qc** to intend o mean to do sth; **intendersi**VPR (*conoscere*): **intendersi di** to know a lot about, be a connoisseur of; (*accordarsi*) to get on (well); **intendersi con qn su qc** to come to an agreement with sb about sth; **intendersela con qn** (*avere una relazione amorosa*) to have an affair with sb; **mi ha dato a ~ che …** he led me to believe that …; **non vuole ~ ragione** he won't listen to reason; **s'intende!** naturally!, of course!; **intendiamoci** let's get it quite clear; **ci siamo intesi?** is that clear?, is that understood?

intendi'mento SM (*intelligenza*) understanding; (*proposito*) intention

intendi'tore, -'trice SM/F connoisseur, expert; **a buon intenditor poche parole** (*proverbio*) a word is enough to the wise

intene'rire/55/ VT (*fig*) to move (to pity); **intenerirsi**VPR (*fig*) to be moved

intensifi'care/20/ VT, **intensifi'carsi**VPR to intensify

intensità SF intensity; (*del vento*) force, strength

inten'sivo, -a AG intensive

in'tenso, -a AG (*luce, profumo*) strong; (*colore*) intense, deep

inten'tare/72/ VT (*Dir*): ~ **causa contro qn** to start o institute proceedings against sb

inten'tato, -a AG: **non lasciare nulla d'~** to leave no stone unturned, try everything

in'tento, -a AG (*teso, assorto*): ~ **(a)** intent (on), absorbed (in) ▶ SM aim, purpose; **fare qc con l'~ di** to do sth with the intention of; **riuscire nell'~** to achieve one's aim

intenzio'nale [intentsjo'nale] AG intentional; (*Dir: omicidio*) premeditated; **fallo ~** (*Sport*) deliberate foul

intenzio'nato, -a[intentsjo'nato] AG: **essere ~ a fare qc** to intend to do sth, have the intention of doing sth; **ben ~** well-meaning, well-intentioned; **mal ~** ill-intentioned

intenzi'one [inten'tsjone] SF intention; (*Dir*) intent; **avere ~ di fare qc** to intend to do sth, have the intention of doing sth

intera'gire [intera'dʒire] /55/ VI to interact

intera'mente AV entirely, completely

interat'tivo, -a AG interactive

interazi'one [interat'tsjone] SF interaction

interca'lare/72/ SM pet phrase, stock phrase ▶ VT to insert

interca'pedine SF gap, cavity

inter'cedere [inter'tʃedere] /29/ VI to intercede

intercessi'one [intertʃes'sjone] SF intercession

intercetta'mento [intertʃetta'mento] SM = **intercettazione**

intercet'tare [intertʃet'tare] /72/ VT to intercept

intercettazi'one [intertʃettat'tsjone] SF: ~ **telefonica** telephone tapping

intercity [inter'siti] SM INV (*Ferr*) ≈ intercity (train)

intercon'nettere/63/ VT to interconnect

inter'correre/28/ VI (*esserci*) to exist; (*passare: tempo*) to elapse

inter'corso, -a PP *di* **intercorrere**

inter'detto, -a PP *di* **interdire** ▶ AG forbidden, prohibited; (*sconcertato*) dumbfounded ▶ SM (*Rel*) interdict; **rimanere ~** to be taken aback

inter'dire/38/ VT to forbid, prohibit, ban; (*Rel*) to interdict; (*Dir*) to deprive of civil rights

interdizi'one [interdit'tsjone] SF prohibition, ban

interessa'mento SM interest; (*intervento*) intervention, good offices *pl*

interes'sante AG interesting; **essere in stato ~** to be expecting (a baby)

interes'sare/72/ VT to interest; (*concernere*) to concern, be of interest to; (*far intervenire*): ~ **qn a** to draw sb's attention to ▶ VI: ~ **a** to interest, matter to; **interessarsi**VPR (*mostrare interesse*): **interessarsi a** to take an interest in, be interested in; (*occuparsi*): **interessarsi di** to take care of; **precipitazioni che interessano le regioni settentrionali** rainfall affecting the north; **si è interessato di farmi avere quei biglietti** he took the trouble to get me those tickets

interes'sato, -a AG (*coinvolto*) interested, involved; (*peg*): **essere ~** to act out of pure self-interest ▶ SM/F (*coinvolto*) person concerned; **a tutti gli interessati** to all those concerned, to all interested parties

inte'resse SM (*anche Comm*) interest; (*tornaconto*): **fare qc per ~** to do sth out of self-interest; ~ **maturato** (*Econ*) accrued interest; ~ **privato in atti di ufficio** (*Amm*) abuse of public office

interes'senza [interes'sɛntsa] SF (*Econ*) profit-sharing

inter'faccia, -ce[inter'fattʃa] SF (*Inform*) interface; ~ **utente** user interface

interfacci'are [interfat'tʃare] /14/ VT (*Inform*) to interface

interfe'renza [interfe'rɛntsa] SF interference

interfe'rire/55/ VI to interfere

inter'fono SM intercom; (*apparecchio*) internal phone

interiezi'one [interjet'tsjone] SF exclamation, interjection '**interim** SM INV (*periodo*) interim, interval; (*incarico*) temporary appointment; **ministro ad** ~ acting o interim minister

interi'nale AG: **lavoro** ~ temporary work (*through an agency*); **lavoratore** ~ temporary worker

interi'ora SFPL entrails

interi'ore AG inner *cpd*; **parte** ~ inside

interiorità SF inner being

interioriz'zare [interjorid'dzare] /**72**/ VT to internalize

inter'linea SF (*Dattilografia*) spacing; (*Tip*) leading; **doppia** ~ double spacing

interlocu'tore, -'trice SM/F speaker

interlocu'torio, -a AG interlocutory

inter'ludio SM (*Mus*) interlude

intermedi'ario, -a AG, SM/F intermediary

intermediazi'one [intermedjat'tsjone] SF mediation

inter'medio, -a AG intermediate

inter'mezzo [inter'meddzo] SM (*intervallo*) interval; (*breve spettacolo*) intermezzo

intermi'nabile AG interminable, endless

intermit'tente AG intermittent

intermit'tenza [intermit'tentsa] SF: **ad** ~ intermittent

interna'mento SM internment; confinement (to a mental hospital)

inter'nare /**72**/ VT (*arrestare*) to intern; (*Med*) to commit (to a mental institution)

inter'nato, -a AG interned; confined (to a mental hospital) ▶ SM/F internee; inmate (of a mental hospital) ▶ SM (*collegio*) boarding school; (*Med*) period as a houseman (*BRIT*) o an intern (*US*)

inter'nauta SMF Internet user

internazio'nale [internattsjo'nale] AG international

'**Internet** ['internet] SF Internet; **in** ~ on the Internet

inter'nista, -i, -e SM/F specialist in internal medicine

in'terno, -a AG (*di dentro*) internal, interior, inner; (: *mare*) inland; (*nazionale*) domestic; (*allievo*) boarding ▶ SM inside, interior; (*di paese*) interior; (*fodera*) lining; (*di appartamento*) flat (*BRIT*) o apartment (*US*) (number); (*Tel*) extension ▶ SM/F (*Ins*) boarder; **interni** SMPL (*Cine*) interior shots; **commissione interna** (*Ins*) internal examination board; **"per uso ~"** (*Med*) "to be taken internally"; **all'**~ inside; **Ministero degli Interni** Ministry of the Interior, ≈ Home Office (*BRIT*), ≈ Department of the Interior (*US*); **notizie dall'**~ (*Stampa*) home news

in'tero, -a AG (*integro, intatto*) whole, entire; (*completo, totale*) complete; (*numero*) whole; (*non ridotto: biglietto*) full; (*latte*) full-cream

interpel'lanza [interpel'lantsa] SF: **presentare un'**~ (*Pol*) to ask a (parliamentary) question; ~ **parlamentare** interpellation

interpel'lare /**72**/ VT to consult; (*Pol*) to question

INTER'POL SIGLA F (= *International Criminal Police Organization*) INTERPOL

inter'porre /**77**/ VT (*influenza*) to use; (*ostacolo*): ~ **qc a qc** to put sth in the way of sth; **interporsi** VPR to intervene; ~ **appello** (*Dir*) to appeal; **interporsi fra** (*mettersi in mezzo*) to come between

inter'posto, -a PP *di* **interporre**

interpre'tare /**72**/ VT (*spiegare, tradurre*) to interpret; (*Mus, Teat*) to perform; (*personaggio, sonata*) to play; (*canzone*) to sing

interpretari'ato SM interpreting

interpretazi'one [interpretat'tsjone] SF interpretation

in'terprete SMF interpreter; (*Teat*) actor (actress), performer; (*Mus*) performer; **farsi** ~ **di** to act as a spokesman for

interpunzi'one [interpun'tsjone] SF punctuation; **segni di** ~ punctuation marks

inter'rare /**72**/ VT (*seme, pianta*) to plant; (*tubature ecc*) to lay underground; (*Mil*: *pezzo d'artiglieria*) to dig in; (*riempire di terra: canale*) to fill in

interregio'nale [interreddʒo'nale] SM *train that travels between two or more regions of Italy*

interro'gare /**80**/ VT to question; (*Ins*) to test

interroga'tivo, -a AG (*occhi, sguardo*) questioning, inquiring; (*Ling*) interrogative ▶ SM question; (*fig*) mystery

interroga'torio, -a AG interrogatory, questioning ▶ SM (*Dir*) questioning *no pl*

interrogazi'one [interrogat'tsjone] SF questioning *no pl*; (*Ins*) oral test; (*Pol*): ~ **(parlamentare)** question

inter'rompere /**97**/ VT to interrupt; (*studi, trattative*) to break off, interrupt; **interrompersi** VPR to break off, stop

inter'rotto, -a PP *di* **interrompere**

interrut'tore SM switch

interruzi'one [interrut'tsjone] SF (*vedi interrompere*) interruption; break; ~ **di gravidanza** termination of pregnancy

interse'care /**20**/ VT, **interse'carsi** VPR to intersect

inter'stizio [inter'stittsjo] SM interstice, crack

interur'bano, -a AG inter-city; (*Tel: chiamata, telefono*) long-distance ▶ SF long-distance call

inter'vallo SM interval; (*spazio*) space, gap; ~ **pubblicitario** (*TV*) commercial break

interve'nire /**128**/ VI (*partecipare*): ~ **a** to take part in; (*intromettersi: anche Pol*) to intervene; (*Med: operare*) to operate

interven'tista, -i, -e AG, SM/F interventionist
inter'vento SM participation; (*intromissione*) intervention; (*Med*) operation; (*breve discorso*) speech; **fare un ~ nel corso di** (*dibattito, programma*) to take part in
interve'nuto, -a PP *di* **intervenire** ▶ SM: **gli intervenuti** those present
inter'vista SF interview
intervis'tare /72/ VT to interview
intervista'tore, -'trice SM/F interviewer
in'teso, -a PP *di* **intendere** ▶ AG agreed ▶ SF understanding; (*accordo*) agreement, understanding; **resta ~ che ...** it is understood that ...; **non darsi per ~ di qc** to take no notice of sth; **uno sguardo d'intesa** a knowing look
intes'sere /1/ VT to weave together; (*fig: trama, storia*) to weave
intes'tare /72/ VT (*lettera*) to address; (*proprietà*): **~ a** to register in the name of; **~ un assegno a qn** to make out a cheque to sb
intesta'tario, -a SM/F holder
intestato, -a AG (*proprietà, casa, conto*) in the name of; (*assegno*) made out to; **carta intestata** headed paper
intestazi'one [intestat'tsjone] SF heading; (*su carta da lettere*) letterhead; (*registrazione*) registration
intesti'nale AG intestinal
intes'tino, -a AG (*lotte*) internal, civil ▶ SM (*Anat*) intestine
intiepi'dire /55/ VT (*riscaldare*) to warm (up); (*raffreddare*) to cool (down); (*fig: amicizia ecc*) to cool; **intiepidirsi** VPR to warm (up); to cool (down); to cool
Inti'fada SF Intifada
intima'mente AV intimately; **sono ~ convinto che ...** I'm firmly o deeply convinced that ...; **i due fatti sono ~ connessi** the two events are closely connected
inti'mare /72/ VT to order, command; **~ la resa a qn** (*Mil*) to call upon sb to surrender
intimazi'one [intimat'tsjone] SF order, command
intimida'torio, -a AG threatening
intimidazi'one [intimidat'tsjone] SF intimidation
intimi'dire /55/ VT to intimidate ▶ VI (*anche:* **intimidirsi**) to grow shy
intimità SF intimacy; privacy; (*familiarità*) familiarity
'intimo, -a AG intimate; (*affetti, vita*) private; (*fig: profondo*) inmost ▶ SM (*persona*) intimate o close friend; (*dell'animo*) bottom, depths *pl*; **parti intime** (*Anat*) private parts; **rapporti intimi** (*sessuali*) intimate relations
intimo'rire /55/ VT to frighten; **intimorirsi** VPR to become frightened

in'tingere [in'tindʒere] /37/ VT to dip
in'tingolo SM sauce; (*pietanza*) stew
in'tinto, -a PP *di* **intingere**
intiriz'zire [intirid'dzire] /55/ VT to numb ▶ VI (*anche:* **intirizzirsi**) to go numb
intiriz'zito, -a [intirid'dzito] AG numb (with cold)
intito'lare /72/ VT to give a title to; (*dedicare*) to dedicate; **intitolarsi** VPR (*libro, film*) to be called
intolle'rabile AG intolerable
intolle'rante AG intolerant
intolle'ranza [intolle'rantsa] SF intolerance
intona'care /20/ VT to plaster
in'tonaco (**intonaci** *o pl* **intonachi**) SM plaster
into'nare /72/ VT (*canto*) to start to sing; (*armonizzare*) to match; **intonarsi** VPR (*colori*) to go together; **intonarsi a** (*carnagione*) to suit; (*abito*) to go with, match
intonazi'one [intonat'tsjone] SF intonation
inton'tire /55/ VT to stun, daze ▶ VI (*anche:* **intontirsi**) to be stunned o dazed
inton'tito, -a AG stunned, dazed; **~ dal sonno** stupid with sleep
in'toppo SM stumbling block, obstacle
intorbi'dire /55/ VT (*liquido*) to make turbid; (*mente*) to cloud; **~ le acque** (*fig*) to muddy the waters
in'torno AV around; **~ a** prep (*attorno a*) around; (*riguardo, circa*) about
intorpi'dire /55/ VT to numb; (*fig*) to make sluggish ▶ VI (*anche:* **intorpidirsi**) to grow numb; (*: fig*) to become sluggish
intossi'care /20/ VT to poison
intossicazi'one [intossikat'tsjone] SF poisoning
intradu'cibile [intradu'tʃibile] AG untranslatable
intralci'are [intral'tʃare] /14/ VT to hamper, hold up
in'tralcio [in'traltʃo] SM hitch
intrallaz'zare [intrallat'tsare] /72/ VI to intrigue, scheme
intral'lazzo [intral'lattso] SM (*Pol*) intrigue, manoeuvre (*BRIT*), maneuver (*US*); (*traffico losco*) racket
intramon'tabile AG timeless
intramusco'lare AG intramuscular
'Intranet ['intranet] SF Intranet
intransi'gente [intransi'dʒɛnte] AG intransigent, uncompromising
intransi'genza [intransi'dʒɛntsa] SF intransigence
intransi'tivo, -a AG, SM intransitive
intrappo'lare /72/ VT to trap; **rimanere intrappolato** to be trapped; **farsi ~** to get caught
intrapren'dente AG enterprising, go-ahead; (*con le donne*) forward, bold

intrapren'denza [intrapren'dɛntsa] SF
audacity, initiative; *(con le donne)* boldness

intra'prendere /81/ VT to undertake; *(carriera)*
to embark (up)on

intra'preso, -a PP *di* intraprendere

intrat'tabile AG intractable

intratte'nere /121/ VT *(divertire)* to entertain;
(chiacchierando) to engage in conversation;
(rapporti) to have, maintain; **intrattenersi**
VPR to linger; **intrattenersi su qc** to dwell
on sth

intratteni'mento SM entertainment

intrave'dere /127/ VT to catch a glimpse of;
(fig) to foresee

intrecci'are [intret'tʃare] /14/ VT *(capelli)* to
plait, braid; *(intessere: anche fig)* to weave,
interweave, intertwine; **intrecciarsi** VPR to
intertwine, become interwoven; **~ le mani**
to clasp one's hands; **~ una relazione
amorosa** *(fig)* to begin an affair

in'treccio [in'trettʃo] SM *(fig: trama)* plot, story

in'trepido, -a AG fearless, intrepid

intri'care /20/ VT *(fili)* to tangle; *(fig: faccenda)*
to complicate; **intricarsi** VPR to become
tangled; to become complicated

in'trico, -chi SM *(anche fig)* tangle

intri'gante AG scheming ▶ SMF schemer,
intriguer

intri'gare /80/ VI to manoeuvre *(BRIT)*,
maneuver *(US)*, scheme

in'trigo, -ghi SM plot, intrigue

in'trinseco, -a, -ci, -che AG intrinsic

in'triso, -a AG: **~ (di)** soaked (in)

intris'tire /55/ VI *(persona: diventare triste)* to
grow sad; *(pianta)* to wilt

intro'dotto, -a PP *di* introdurre

intro'durre /90/ VT to introduce; *(chiave ecc)*:
~ qc in to insert sth into; *(persona: far entrare)*
to show in; **introdursi** VPR *(moda, tecniche)* to
be introduced; **introdursi in** *(persona:
penetrare)* to enter; *(: entrare furtivamente)* to
steal *o* slip into

introduzi'one SF introduction

in'troito SM income, revenue

intro'messo, -a PP *di* intromettersi

intro'mettersi /63/ VPR to interfere, meddle;
(interporsi) to intervene

intromissi'one SF interference, meddling;
intervention

introspezi'one [introspet'tsjone] SF
introspection

intro'vabile AG *(persona, oggetto)* who *(o* which)
cannot be found; *(libro ecc)* unobtainable

intro'verso, -a AG introverted ▶ SM/F
introvert

intrufo'larsi /72/ VPR: **~ (in)** *(stanza)* to sneak
(into), slip (into); *(conversazione)* to butt in
(on)

in'truglio [in'truʎʎo] SM concoction

intrusi'one SF intrusion; interference

in'truso, -a SM/F intruder

intu'ire /55/ VT to perceive by intuition;
(rendersi conto) to realize

in'tuito SM intuition; *(perspicacia)*
perspicacity

intuizi'one [intuit'tsjone] SF intuition

inturgi'dire [inturdʒi'dire] /55/ VI,
inturgi'dirsi VPR to swell

inumanità SF INV inhumanity

inu'mano, -a AG inhuman

inu'mare /72/ VT *(seppellire)* to bury, inter

inumazi'one [inumat'tsjone] SF burial,
interment

inumi'dire /55/ VT to dampen, moisten;
inumidirsi VPR to become damp *o* wet

inurba'mento SM urbanization

inusi'tato, -a AG unusual

i'nutile AG useless; *(superfluo)* pointless,
unnecessary; **è stato tutto ~!** it was all in
vain!

inutilità SF uselessness; pointlessness

inutiliz'zabile [inutilid'dzabile] AG unusable

inutil'mente AV *(senza risultato)* in vain;
(senza utilità, scopo) unnecessarily, needlessly;
l'ho cercato ~ I looked for him in vain; **ti
preoccupi ~** there's nothing for you to
worry about, there's no need for you to
worry

inva'dente AG *(fig)* interfering, nosey

inva'denza [inva'dɛntsa] SF intrusiveness

in'vadere /52/ VT to invade; *(affollare)* to
swarm into, overrun; *(acque)* to flood

invadi'trice [invadi'tritʃe] AG F *vedi* invasore

inva'ghirsi [inva'girsi] /55/ VPR: **~ di** to take a
fancy to

invali'cabile AG *(montagna)* impassable

invali'dare /72/ VT to invalidate

invalidità SF infirmity; disability; *(Dir)*
invalidity

in'valido, -a AG *(infermo)* infirm, invalid; *(al
lavoro)* disabled; *(Dir: nullo)* invalid ▶ SM/F
invalid; disabled person; **~ di guerra**
disabled ex-serviceman; **~ del lavoro**
industrially disabled person

in'valso, -a AG *(diffuso)* established

in'vano AV in vain

invari'abile AG invariable

invari'ato, -a AG unchanged

inva'sare /72/ VT *(pianta)* to pot

inva'sato, -a AG possessed (by the devil)
▶ SM/F person possessed by the devil; **urlare
come un ~** to shout like a madman

invasi'one SF invasion

in'vaso, -a PP *di* invadere

inva'sore, invadi'trice [invadi'tritʃe] AG
invading ▶ SMF invader

invecchia'mento [invekkja'mento] SM
growing old; ageing; **questo whisky ha**

un ~ di 12 anni this whisky has been matured for 12 years

invecchi'are [invek'kjare] **/19/** VI (*persona*) to grow old; (*vino, popolazione*) to age; (*moda*) to become dated ▶ VT to age; (*far apparire più vecchio*) to make look older; **lo trovo invecchiato** I find he has aged

in'vece [in'vetʃe] AV instead; (*al contrario*) on the contrary; **~ di** *prep* instead of

inve'ire **/55/** VI: **~ contro** to rail against

invele'nire **/55/** VT to embitter; **invelenirsi** VPR to become bitter

inven'duto, -a AG unsold

inven'tare **/72/** VT to invent; (*pericoli, pettegolezzi*) to make up, invent

inventari'are **/19/** VT to make an inventory of, inventory

inven'tario SM inventory; (*Comm*) stocktaking *no pl*

inven'tivo, -a AG inventive ▶ SF inventiveness

inven'tore, -'trice SM/F inventor

invenzi'one [inven'tsjone] SF invention; (*bugia*) lie, story

invere'condia SF shamelessness, immodesty

inver'nale AG winter *cpd*; (*simile all'inverno*) wintry

in'verno SM winter; **d'~** in (the) winter

invero'simile AG unlikely ▶ SM: **ha dell'~** it's hard to believe, it's incredible

inversi'one SF inversion; reversal; **"divieto d'~"** (*Aut*) "no U-turns"

in'verso, -a AG opposite; (*Mat*) inverse ▶ SM contrary, opposite; **in senso ~** in the opposite direction; **in ordine ~** in reverse order

inverte'brato, -a AG, SM invertebrate

inver'tire **/45/** VT to invert, reverse; (*disposizione, posti*) to change; (*ruoli*) to exchange; **~ la marcia** (*Aut*) to do a U-turn; **~ la rotta** (*Naut*) to go about; (*fig*) to do a U-turn

inver'tito, -a SM/F homosexual

investi'gare **/80/** VT, VI to investigate

investiga'tivo, -a AG: **squadra investigativa** detective squad

investiga'tore, -'trice SM/F investigator, detective; **~ privato** private investigator

investigazi'one [investigat'tsjone] SF investigation, inquiry

investi'mento SM (*Econ*) investment; (*di veicolo*) crash, collision; (*di pedone*) knocking down

inves'tire **/45/** VT (*denaro*) to invest; (*veicolo: pedone*) to knock down; (: *altro veicolo*) to crash into; (*apostrofare*) to assail; (*incaricare*): **~ qn di** to invest sb with; **investirsi** VPR (*fig*): **investirsi di una parte** to enter thoroughly into a role

investi'tore, -'trice SM/F driver responsible for an accident

investi'tura SF investiture

invete'rato, -a AG inveterate

invet'tiva SF invective

invi'are **/60/** VT to send

invi'ato, -a SM/F envoy; (*Stampa*) correspondent; **~ speciale** (*Pol*) special envoy; (*di giornale*) special correspondent

in'vidia SF envy; **fare ~ a qn** to make sb envious

invidi'abile AG enviable

invidi'are **/19/** VT: **~ qn (per qc)** to envy sb (for sth); **~ qc a qn** to envy sb sth; **non aver nulla da ~ a nessuno** to be as good as the next one

invidi'oso, -a AG envious

invin'cibile [invin'tʃibile] AG invincible

in'vio, -'vii SM sending; (*insieme di merci*) consignment; (*tasto*) Return (key), Enter (key)

invio'labile AG inviolable

invio'lato, -a AG (*diritto, segreto*) inviolate; (*foresta*) virgin *cpd*; (*montagna, vetta*) unscaled

invipe'rire **/55/** VI, **invipe'rirsi** VPR to become furious, fly into a temper

invipe'rito, -a AG furious

invis'chiare [invis'kjare] **/19/** VT (*fig*): **~ qn in qc** to involve sb in sth, mix sb up in sth; **invischiarsi** VPR: **invischiarsi (con qn/in qc)** to get mixed up o involved (with sb/in sth)

invi'sibile AG invisible

in'viso, -a AG: **~ a** unpopular with

invi'tante AG (*proposta, odorino*) inviting; (*sorriso*) appealing, attractive

invi'tare **/72/** VT to invite; **~ qn a fare** to invite sb to do

invi'tato, -a SM/F guest

in'vito SM invitation; **dietro ~ del sig. Rossi** at Mr Rossi's invitation

invo'care **/20/** VT (*chiedere: aiuto, pace*) to cry out for; (*appellarsi: la legge, Dio*) to appeal to, invoke

invogli'are [invoʎ'ʎare] **/27/** VT: **~ qn a fare** to tempt sb to do, induce sb to do

involon'tario, -a AG (*errore*) unintentional; (*gesto*) involuntary

invol'tino SM (*Cuc*) roulade

in'volto SM (*pacco*) parcel; (*fagotto*) bundle

in'volucro SM cover, wrapping

involu'tivo, -a AG: **subire un processo ~** to regress

invo'luto, -a AG involved, intricate

involuzi'one [involut'tsjone] SF (*di stile*) convolutedness; (*regresso*): **subire un'~** to regress

invulne'rabile AG invulnerable

inzacche'rare [intsakke'rare] **/72/** VT to spatter with mud; **inzaccherarsi** VPR to get muddy

inzup'pare [intsup'pare] /**72**/ VT to soak; **inzupparsi** VPR to get soaked; **inzuppò i biscotti nel latte** he dipped the biscuits in the milk

'**io** PRON I ▶ SM INV: **l'io** the ego, the self; **io stesso(a)** I myself; **sono io** it's me

i'odio SM iodine

i'ogurt SM INV = **yogurt**

i'one SM ion

I'onio SM: **lo ~, il mar ~** the Ionian (Sea)

ionizza'tore [joniddza'tore] SM ioniser

'**iosa**: **a ~** av in abundance, in great quantity

'**IPAB** SIGLA FPL (= *Istituzioni pubbliche di Assistenza e Beneficenza*) charitable institutions

iPad® [ai'pad] SM INV iPad®

i'perbole SF (*Letteratura*) hyperbole; (*Mat*) hyperbola

iper'bolico, -a, -ci, -che AG (*Letteratura, Mat*) hyperbolic(al); (*fig: esagerato*) exaggerated

ipermer'cato SM hypermarket

ipersen'sibile AG (*persona*) hypersensitive; (*Fot: lastra, pellicola*) hypersensitized

ipertecno'logico, -a, -ci, -che [ipertekno'lɔdʒiko] AG hi-tech

ipertensi'one SF high blood pressure, hypertension

iper'testo SM hypertext

ipertestu'ale AG (*Inform*): **collegamento** *o* **link ~** hyperlink

iPhone® [ai'fon] SM INV iPhone®

ip'nosi SF hypnosis

ip'notico, -a, -ci, -che AG hypnotic

ipno'tismo SM hypnotism

ipnotiz'zare [ipnotid'dzare] /**72**/ VT to hypnotize

ipoaller'genico, -a, -ci, -che [ipoaller'dʒeniko] AG hypoallergenic

ipocon'dria SF hypochondria

ipocon'driaco, -a, -ci, -che AG, SM/F hypochondriac

ipocri'sia SF hypocrisy

i'pocrita, -i, -e AG hypocritical ▶ SM/F hypocrite

ipo'sodico, -a, -ci, -che AG low sodium *cpd*

ipo'teca, -che SF mortgage

ipote'care /**20**/ VT to mortgage

ipote'nusa SF hypotenuse

i'potesi SF INV hypothesis; **facciamo l'~ che ...**, **ammettiamo per ~ che ...** let's suppose *o* assume that ...; **nella peggiore/migliore delle ~** at worst/best; **nell'~ che venga** should he come, if he comes; **se per ~ io partissi ...** just supposing I were to leave ....

ipo'tetico, -a, -ci, -che AG hypothetical

ipotiz'zare [ipotid'dzare] /**72**/ VT: **~ che** to form the hypothesis that

'**ippico, -a, -ci, -che** AG horse *cpd* ▶ SF horseracing

ippocas'tano SM horse chestnut

ip'podromo SM racecourse

ippo'potamo SM hippopotamus

'**ipsilon** SM O F INV (*lettera*) Y, y; (: *dell'alfabeto greco*) epsilon

IP'SOA SIGLA M (= *Istituto Post-Universitario per lo Studio dell'Organizzazione Aziendale*) postgraduate institute of business administration

IR ABBR (*Ferr*: = *Interregionale*) long distance train which stops frequently

IRA SIGLA F (= *Irish Republican Army*) IRA

'**ira** SF anger, wrath

ira'cheno, -a [ira'kɛno] AG, SM/F Iraqi

l'ran SM: **l'~** Iran

irani'ano, -a AG, SM/F Iranian

l'raq SM: **l'~** Iraq

iras'cibile [iraʃʃibile] AG quick-tempered

'**IRCE** ['irtʃe] SIGLA M = **Istituto per le relazioni culturali con l'Estero**

'**IRI** SIGLA M (= *Istituto per la Ricostruzione Industriale*) state-controlled industrial investment office

'**iride** SF (*arcobaleno*) rainbow; (*Anat, Bot*) iris

'**iris** SM INV iris

Ir'landa SF: **l'~** Ireland; **l'~ del Nord** Northern Ireland, Ulster; **la Repubblica d'~** Eire, the Republic of Ireland; **il mar d'~** the Irish Sea

irlan'dese AG Irish ▶ SMF Irishman(-woman); **gli Irlandesi** the Irish

iro'nia SF irony

i'ronico, -a, -ci, -che AG ironic(al)

ironiz'zare [ironid'dzare] /**72**/ VT, VI: **~ su** to be ironical about

i'roso, -a AG (*sguardo, tono*) angry, wrathful; (*persona*) irascible

'**IRPEF** SIGLA F = **imposta sul reddito delle persone fisiche**

ir'pino, -a AG of (*o* from) Irpinia

irradi'are /**19**/ VT to radiate; (*raggi di luce: illuminare*) to shine on ▶ VI (*diffondersi: anche:* **irradiarsi**) to radiate

irradiazi'one [irradjat'tsjone] SF radiation

irraggiun'gibile [irraddʒun'dʒibile] AG unreachable; (*fig: meta*) unattainable

irragio'nevole [irradʒo'nevole] AG (*privo di ragione*) irrational; (*fig: persona, pretese, prezzo*) unreasonable

irrazio'nale [irrattsjo'nale] AG irrational

irre'ale AG unreal

irrealiz'zabile [irrealid'dzabile] AG (*sogno, desiderio*) unattainable, unrealizable; (*progetto*) unworkable, impracticable

irrealtà SF unreality

irrecupe'rabile AG (*gen*) irretrievable; (*fig: persona*) irredeemable

irrecu'sabile AG (*offerta*) not to be refused; (*prova*) irrefutable

irreden'tista, -i, -e AG, SM/F (*Storia*) Irredentist

irrefre'nabile AG uncontrollable

irrefu'tabile AG irrefutable

irrego'lare AG irregular; (*terreno*) uneven

irregolarità SF INV irregularity; unevenness *no pl*

irremo'vibile AG (*fig*) unshakeable, unyielding

irrepa'rabile AG irreparable; (*fig*) inevitable

irrepe'ribile AG nowhere to be found

irrepren'sibile AG irreproachable

irrequi'eto, -a AG restless

irresis'tibile AG irresistible

irreso'luto, -a AG irresolute

irrespi'rabile AG (*aria*) unbreathable; (*fig: opprimente*) stifling, oppressive; (: *malsano*) unhealthy

irrespon'sabile AG irresponsible

irrestrin'gibile [irrestrin'dʒibile] AG unshrinkable, non-shrink (BRIT)

irre'tire /55/ VT to seduce

irrever'sibile AG irreversible

irrevo'cabile AG irrevocable

irricono'scibile [irrikonoʃʃibile] AG unrecognizable

irridu'cibile [irridu'tʃibile] AG irreducible; (*fig*) unshakeable

irrifles'sivo, -a AG thoughtless

irri'gare /80/ VT (*annaffiare*) to irrigate; (*fiume ecc*) to flow through

irrigazi'one [irrigat'tsjone] SF irrigation

irrigidi'mento [irridʒidi'mento] SM stiffening; hardening; tightening

irrigi'dire [irridʒi'dire] /55/ VT to stiffen; (*disciplina*) to tighten; **irrigidirsi** VPR to stiffen; (*posizione, atteggiamento*) to harden

irriguar'doso, -a AG disrespectful

irrile'vante AG (*trascurabile*) insignificant

irrimedi'abile AG: **un errore ~** a mistake which cannot be rectified; **non è ~!** we can do something about it!

irrinunci'abile [irrinun'tʃabile] AG vital; which cannot be abandoned

irripe'tibile AG unrepeatable

irri'solto, -a AG (*problema*) unresolved

irri'sorio, -a AG derisory

irrispet'toso, -a AG disrespectful

irri'tabile AG irritable

irri'tante AG (*atteggiamento*) irritating, annoying; (*Med*) irritant

irri'tare /72/ VT (*mettere di malumore*) to irritate, annoy; (*Med*) to irritate; **irritarsi** VPR (*stizzirsi*) to become irritated o annoyed; (*Med*) to become irritated

irritazi'one [irritat'tsjone] SF irritation; annoyance

irrive'rente AG irreverent

irrobus'tire /55/ VT (*persona*) to make stronger, make more robust; (*muscoli*) to strengthen; **irrobustirsi** VPR to become stronger

ir'rompere /97/ VI: **~ in** to burst into

irro'rare /72/ VT to sprinkle; (*Agr*) to spray

ir'rotto, -a PP *di* **irrompere**

irru'ente AG (*fig*) impetuous, violent

irru'enza [irru'ɛntsa] SF impetuousness; **con ~** impetuously

ir'ruppi *etc* VB *vedi* **irrompere**

irruvi'dire /55/ VT to roughen ▶ VI (*anche*: **irruvidirsi**) to become rough

irruzi'one [irrut'tsjone] SF: **fare ~ in** to burst into; (*polizia*) to raid

ir'suto, -a AG (*petto*) hairy; (*barba*) bristly

'irto, -a AG bristly; **~ di** bristling with

Is. ABBR (= *isola*) I

ISBN ABBR (= *International Standard Book Number*) ISBN

is'crissi *etc* VB *vedi* **iscrivere**

is'critto, -a PP *di* **iscrivere** ▶ SM/F member; **gli iscritti alla gara** the competitors; **per** o **in ~** in writing

is'crivere /105/ VT to register, enter; (*persona*): **~ (a)** to register (in), enrol (in); **iscriversi** VPR: **iscriversi (a)** (*club, partito*) to join; (*università*) to register o enrol (at); (*esame, concorso*) to register o enter (for)

iscrizi'one [iskrit'tsjone] SF (*epigrafe ecc*) inscription; (*a scuola, società ecc*) enrolment, registration; (*registrazione*) registration

'ISEF SIGLA M = **Istituto Superiore di Educazione Fisica**

Is'lam SM: **l'~** Islam

is'lamico, -a, -ci, -che AG Islamic

Is'landa SF: **l'~** Iceland

islan'dese AG Icelandic ▶ SMF Icelander ▶ SM (*Ling*) Icelandic

'isola SF island; **~ pedonale** (*Aut*) pedestrian precinct

isola'mento SM isolation; (*Tecn*) insulation; **essere in cella di ~** to be in solitary confinement; **~ acustico** soundproofing; **~ termico** thermal insulation

iso'lano, -a AG island *cpd* ▶ SM/F islander

iso'lante AG insulating ▶ SM insulator

iso'lare /72/ VT to isolate; (*Tecn*) to insulate; (: *acusticamente*) to soundproof; **isolarsi** VPR to isolate o.s.

iso'lato, -a AG isolated; insulated ▶ SM (*edificio*) block

isolazio'nismo [isolattsjo'nismo] SM isolationism

i'sotopo SM isotope

ispessi'mento SM thickening

ispes'sire /55/ VT to thicken; **ispessirsi** VPR to get thicker, thicken

ispet'torato SM inspectorate

ispet'tore, -'trice SM/F inspector; (*Comm*) supervisor; **~ di zona** (*Comm*) area supervisor o manager; **~ di reparto** shop walker (BRIT), floor walker (US)

ispezio'nare [ispettsjo'nare] /**72**/ VT to inspect

ispezi'one [ispet'tsjone] SF inspection

'ispido, -a AG bristly, shaggy

ispi'rare /**72**/ VT to inspire; **ispirarsi** VPR: **ispirarsi a** to draw one's inspiration from; (conformarsi) to be based on; **l'idea m'ispira** the idea appeals to me

ispira'tore, -'trice AG inspiring ▶ SM/F inspirer; (di ribellione) instigator

ispirazi'one [ispirat'tsjone] SF inspiration; **secondo l'~ del momento** according to the mood of the moment

Isra'ele SM: **l'~** Israel

israeli'ano, -a AG, SM/F Israeli

israe'lita, -i, -e SM/F Jew (Jewess); (Storia) Israelite

israe'litico, -a, -ci, -che AG Jewish

is'sare /**72**/ VT to hoist; **~ l'ancora** to weigh anchor

'Istanbul SF Istanbul

istan'taneo, -a AG instantaneous ▶ SF (Fot) snapshot

is'tante SM instant, moment; **all'~, sull'~** instantly, immediately

is'tanza [is'tantsa] SF petition, request; **giudice di prima ~** (Dir) judge of the court of first instance; **giudizio di seconda ~** judgment on appeal; **in ultima ~** (fig) finally; **~ di divorzio** petition for divorce

'ISTAT SIGLA M = **Istituto Centrale di Statistica**

'ISTEL SIGLA F = **Indagine sull'ascolto delle televisioni in Italia**

is'terico, -a, -ci, -che AG hysterical

isteri'lire /**55**/ VT (terreno) to render infertile; (fig: fantasia) to dry up; **isterilirsi** VPR to become infertile; to dry up

iste'rismo SM hysteria

isti'gare /**80**/ VT to incite

istigazi'one [istigat'tsjone] SF instigation; **~ a delinquere** (Dir) incitement to crime

istin'tivo, -a AG instinctive

is'tinto SM instinct

istitu'ire /**55**/ VT (fondare) to institute, found; (porre: confronto) to establish; (intraprendere: inchiesta) to set up

isti'tuto SM institute; (di università) department; (ente, Dir) institution; **~ di bellezza** beauty salon; **~ di credito** bank, banking institution; **~ di ricerca** research institute; **~ tecnico commerciale** ≈ commercial college; **~ tecnico industriale statale** ≈ technical college

istitu'tore, -'trice SM/F (fondatore) founder; (precettore) tutor, governess

istituzi'one [istitut'tsjone] SF institution; **istituzioni** SFPL (Dir) institutes; **lotta alle istituzioni** struggle against the Establishment

'istmo SM (Geo) isthmus

isto'gramma, -i SM histogram

istra'dare /**72**/ VT (fig: persona): **~ (a/verso)** to direct (to/towards)

istri'ano, -a AG, SM/F Istrian

'istrice ['istritʃe] SM porcupine

istri'one SM (peg) ham (actor)

istru'ire /**55**/ VT (insegnare) to teach; (ammaestrare) to train; (informare) to instruct, inform; (Dir) to prepare

istru'ito, -a AG educated

istrut'tivo, -a AG instructive

istrut'tore, -'trice SM/F instructor ▶ AG: **giudice ~** examining (BRIT) o committing (US) magistrate

istrut'toria SF (Dir) (preliminary) investigation and hearing; **formalizzare un'~** to proceed to a formal hearing

istruzi'one [istrut'tsjone] SF (gen) training; (Ins, cultura) education; (direttiva) instruction; (Dir) = **istruttoria**; **istruzioni** SFPL (norme) instructions; **Ministero della Pubblica I-** Ministry of Education; **istruzioni di spedizione** forwarding instructions; **istruzioni per l'uso** instructions (for use); **~ obbligatoria** (Ins) compulsory education

istupi'dire /**55**/ VT (colpo) to stun, daze; (droga, stanchezza) to stupefy; **istupidirsi** VPR to become stupid

'ISVE SIGLA M (= Istituto di Studi per lo Sviluppo Economico) institute for research into economic development

l'talia SF: **l'~** Italy

itali'ano, -a AG Italian ▶ SM/F Italian ▶ SM (Ling) Italian; **gli Italiani** the Italians

ITC SIGLA M = **istituto tecnico commerciale**

'iter SM passage, course; **l'~ burocratico** the bureaucratic process

itine'rante AG wandering, itinerant; **mostra ~** touring exhibition; **spettacolo ~** travelling (BRIT) o traveling (US) show, touring show

itine'rario SM itinerary

'ITIS SIGLA M = **istituto tecnico industriale statale**

itte'rizia [itte'rittsja] SF (Med) jaundice

'ittico, -a, -ci, -che AG fish cpd; fishing cpd

IUD SIGLA M INV (= intra-uterine device) IUD

Iugos'lavia SF = **Jugoslavia**

iugos'lavo, -a AG, SM/F = **jugoslavo**

i'uta SF jute

'I.V.A. SIGLA F (= imposta sul valore aggiunto) VAT

'ivi AV (formale, poetico) therein; (nelle citazioni) ibid

Jj

J, j [i'lunga] SM O F INV (*lettera*) J, j;
  J come Jersey ≈ J for Jack (*BRIT*),
  J for Jig (*US*)
jazz [dʒaz] SM jazz
jaz'zista, -i [dʒad'dzista] SM jazz player
jeans [dʒinz] SMPL jeans
jeep® [dʒip] SF INV jeep
'jersey ['dʒɛrzi] SM INV jersey (cloth)
'jockey ['dʒɔki] SM INV (*Carte*) jack; (*fantino*)
  jockey

'jogging ['dʒɔgiŋ] SM jogging; **fare ~**
  to go jogging
'jolly ['dʒɔli] SM INV joker
joys'tick [dʒɔis'tik] SM INV joystick
jr. ABBR (= *junior*) Jr., jr.
ju'do· [dʒu'dɔ] SM judo
Jugos'lavia [jugoz'lavja] SF (*Storia*): **la ~**
  Yugoslavia; **la ex-~** former Yugoslavia
jugos'lavo, -a AG, SM/F (*Storia*) Yugoslav(ian)
'juke 'box ['dʒuk'bɔks] SM INV jukebox

K k

K, k ['kappa] SM O F INV (*lettera*) K, k ▶ ABBR
(= *kilo-, chilo-*) k; (*Inform*) K; **K come Kursaal**
≈ K for King
kami'kaze [kami'kaddze] SM INV kamikaze
Kam'pala SF Kampala
kara'oke [kara'oke] SM INV karaoke
karatè [kara'tɛ] SM karate
'Kashmir ['kaʃmir] SM: **il** ~ Kashmir
ka'yak [ka'jak] SM INV kayak
Ka'zakistan [ka'dzakistan] SM
Kazakhstan
ka'zako, -a [ka'dzako] AG, SM/F Kazakh
'Kenia ['kenja] SM: **il** ~ Kenya
keni'ano, -a AG, SM/F Kenyan
keni'ota, -i, -e AG, SM/F Kenyan
'Kenya ['kenja] SM: **il** ~ Kenya
kero'sene [kero'zɛne] SM = **cherosene**
kg ABBR (= *chilogrammo*) kg
kib'butz [kib'buts] SM INV kibbutz
Kilimangi'aro [kiliman'dʒaro] SM: **il** ~
Kilimanjaro

'killer ['killer] SM INV gunman, hired gun
'kilo = **chilo** *ecc*
kilt [kilt] SM INV kilt
ki'mono [ki'mɔno] SM = **chimono**
Kindle® ['kindœl] SM INV Kindle®
kir'ghiso, -a [kir'gizo] AG, SM/F Kyrgyz
Kir'ghizistan [kir'gidzistan] SM Kyrgyzstan
kitsch [kitʃ] SM kitsch
'kiwi ['kiwi] SM INV kiwi (fruit)
km ABBR (= *chilometro*) km
kmq ABBR (= *chilometro quadrato*) km²
K.'O. [kappa'o] SM INV knockout
ko'ala [ko'ala] SM INV koala (bear)
koso'varo, -a AG, SM/F Kosovan
'Kosovo SM Kosovo
KR SIGLA = **Crotone**
'krapfen ['krapfən] (*Cuc*) SM INV doughnut
Ku'ala Lum'par SF Kuala Lumpur
Ku'wait [ku'vait] SM: **il** ~ Kuwait
kW ABBR (= *kilowatt, chilowatt*) kW
kWh ABBR (= *kilowattora*) kW/h

L l

L, l ['ɛlle] SM O F INV (*lettera*) L, l ▶ ABBR (= *lira*) L; **L come Livorno** = L for Lucy (BRIT), L for Love (US)

l ABBR (= *litro*) l

l' DET *vedi* **la; lo**

la DET F (*dav* V **l'**) the ▶ PRON (*dav* V **l'**: *oggetto: persona*) her; (: *cosa*) it; (: *forma di cortesia*) you ▶ SM INV (*Mus*) A; (: *solfeggiando la scala*) la; *vedi anche* **il**

là AV there; **di là** (*da quel luogo*) from there; (*in quel luogo*) in there; (*dall'altra parte*) over there; **di là di** beyond; **per di là** that way; **più in là** further on; (*tempo*) later on; **fatti in là** move up; **là dentro/sopra/sotto** in/up *o* on/under there; **là per là** (*sul momento*) there and then; **essere in là con gli anni** to be getting on (in years); **essere più di là che di qua** to be more dead than alive; **va' là!** come off it!; **stavolta è andato troppo in là** this time he's gone too far; *vedi anche* **quello**

'labbro SM (*Anat: pl(f)* **labbra**) lip

'labile AG fleeting, ephemeral

labi'rinto SM labyrinth, maze

labora'torio SM (*di ricerca*) laboratory; (*di arti, mestieri*) workshop; **~ linguistico** language laboratory

labori'oso, -a AG (*faticoso*) laborious; (*attivo*) hard-working

labu'rista, -i, -e AG Labour *cpd* (BRIT) ▶ SM/F Labour Party member (BRIT)

'lacca, -che SF lacquer; (*per unghie*) nail varnish (BRIT), nail polish

lac'care/20/ VT (*mobili*) to varnish, lacquer

'laccio ['lattʃo] SM noose; (*legaccio, tirante*) lasso; (*di scarpa*) lace; **~ emostatico** (*Med*) tourniquet

lace'rante [latʃe'rante] AG (*suono*) piercing, shrill

lace'rare [latʃe'rare] /72/ VT to tear to shreds, lacerate; **lacerarsi** VPR to tear

lacerazi'one [latʃerat'tsjone] SF (*anche Med*) tear

'lacero, -a ['latʃero] AG (*logoro*) torn, tattered; (*Med*) lacerated; **ferita ~-contusa** injury with lacerations and bruising

la'conico, -a, -ci, -che AG laconic, brief

'lacrima SF tear; (*goccia*) drop; **in lacrime** in tears

lacri'mare/72/ VI to water

lacri'mevole AG heartrending, pitiful

lacri'mogeno, -a [lakri'mɔdʒeno] AG: **gas ~** tear gas

lacri'moso, -a AG tearful

la'cuna SF (*fig*) gap

la'custre AG lake *cpd*

lad'dove CONG whereas

'ladro SM thief; **al ~!** stop thief!

ladro'cinio [ladro'tʃinjo] SM theft, robbery

la'druncolo, -a SM/F petty thief

laggiù [lad'dʒu] AV down there; (*di là*) over there

'lagna ['laɲɲa] SF (*col: persona, cosa*) drag, bore; **fare la ~** to whine, moan

la'gnanza [laɲ'ɲantsa] SF complaint

la'gnarsi [laɲ'ɲarsi] /15/ VPR: **~ (di)** to complain (about)

'lago, -ghi SM lake

'Lagos ['lagos] SF Lagos

'lagrima *etc* = **lacrima** *ecc*

la'guna SF lagoon

lagu'nare AG lagoon *cpd*

'laico, -a, -ci, -che AG (*apostolato*) lay; (*vita*) secular; (*scuola*) non-denominational ▶ SM/F layman(-woman) ▶ SM lay brother

'laido, -a AG filthy, foul; (*fig: osceno*) obscene, filthy

'lama SF blade ▶ SM INV (*Zool*) llama; (*Rel*) lama

lambic'care/20/ VT to distil; **lambiccarsi il cervello** to rack one's brains

lam'bire/55/ VT (*fig: fiamme*) to lick; (*acqua*) to lap

lam'bretta® SF scooter

la'mella SF (*di metallo ecc*) thin sheet, thin strip; (*di fungo*) gill

lamen'tare/72/ VT to lament; **lamentarsi** VPR (*emettere lamenti*) to moan, groan; (*rammaricarsi*) **lamentarsi (di)** to complain (about)

lamen'tela SF complaining *no pl*
lamen'tevole AG (*voce*) complaining, plaintive; (*stato*) lamentable, pitiful
la'mento SM moan, groan; (*per la morte di qn*) lament
lamen'toso, -a AG plaintive
la'metta SF razor blade
lami'era SF sheet metal
'**lamina** SF (*lastra sottile*) thin sheet (*o* layer *o* plate); ~ **d'oro** gold leaf; gold foil
lami'nare /**72**/ VT to laminate
lami'nato, -a AG laminated; (*tessuto*) lamé
▶ SM laminate
'**lampada** SF lamp; ~ **a petrolio/a gas** oil/gas lamp; ~ **a spirito** blowlamp (BRIT), blowtorch; ~ **a stelo** standard lamp (BRIT), floor lamp; ~ **da tavolo** table lamp
lampa'dario SM chandelier
lampa'dina SF light bulb; ~ **tascabile** pocket torch (BRIT), flashlight (US)
lam'pante AG (*fig: evidente*) crystal clear, evident
lam'para SF fishing lamp; (*barca*) boat for fishing by lamplight (*in Mediterranean*)
lampeggi'are [lamped'dʒare] /**62**/ VI (*luce, fari*) to flash ▶ VB IMPERS: **lampeggia** there's lightning
lampeggia'tore [lampeddʒa'tore] SM (*Aut*) indicator
lampi'one SM street light *o* lamp (BRIT)
'**lampo** SM (*Meteor*) flash of lightning; (*di luce, fig*) flash ▶ AG INV: **cerniera ~** zip (fastener) (BRIT), zipper (US); **guerra ~** blitzkrieg; **lampi** SMPL (*Meteor*) lightning *no pl*; **passare come un ~** to flash past *o* by
lam'pone SM raspberry
'**lana** SF wool; ~ **d'acciaio** steel wool; **pura ~ vergine** pure new wool; ~ **di vetro** glass wool
lan'cetta [lan'tʃetta] SF (*indice*) pointer, needle; (*di orologio*) hand
'**lancia, -ce** ['lantʃa] SF (*arma*) lance; (: *picca*) spear; (*di pompa antincendio*) nozzle; (*imbarcazione*) launch; **partire ~ in resta** (*fig*) to set off ready for battle; **spezzare una ~ in favore di qn** (*fig*) to come to sb's defence; ~ **di salvataggio** lifeboat
lancia'bombe [lantʃa'bombe] SM INV (*Mil*) mortar
lanciafi'amme [lantʃa'fjamme] SM INV flamethrower
lancia'missili [lantʃa'missili] AG INV missile-launching ▶ SM INV missile launcher
lancia'razzi [lantʃa'raddzi] AG INV rocket-launching ▶ SM INV rocket launcher
lanci'are [lan'tʃare] /**14**/ VT to throw, hurl, fling; (*Sport*) to throw; (*far partire: automobile*) to get up to full speed; (*bombe*) to drop; (*razzo,*

prodotto, moda) to launch; (*emettere: grido*) to give out; **lanciarsi** VPR: **lanciarsi contro/su** to throw *o* hurl *o* fling o.s. against/on; **lanciarsi in** (*fig*) to embark on; ~ **un cavallo** to give a horse his head; ~ **il disco** (*Sport*) to throw the discus; ~ **il peso** (*Sport*) to put the shot; **lanciarsi all'inseguimento di qn** to set off in pursuit of sb; **lanciarsi col paracadute** to parachute
lanci'ato, -a [lan'tʃato] AG (*affermato: attore, prodotto*) well-known, famous; (: *veicolo*) speeding along, racing along
lanci'nante [lantʃi'nante] AG (*dolore*) shooting, throbbing; (*grido*) piercing
'**lancio** ['lantʃo] SM throwing *no pl*; throw; dropping *no pl*; drop; launching *no pl*; launch; ~ **del disco** (*Sport*) throwing the discus; ~ **del peso** (*Sport*) putting the shot
'**landa** SF (*Geo*) moor
'**languido, -a** AG (*fiacco*) languid, weak; (*tenero, malinconico*) languishing
langu'ire /**17**/ VI to languish; (*conversazione*) to flag
langu'ore SM weakness, languor
lani'ero, -a AG wool *cpd*, woollen (BRIT), woolen (US)
lani'ficio [lani'fitʃo] SM woollen (BRIT) *o* woolen (US) mill
lano'lina SF lanolin(e)
la'noso, -a AG woolly
lan'terna SF lantern; (*faro*) lighthouse
lanter'nino SM: **cercarsele col ~** to be asking for trouble
la'nugine [la'nudʒine] SF down
'**Laos** SM Laos
lapalissi'ano, -a AG self-evident
La 'Paz [la'pas] SF La Paz
lapi'dare /**72**/ VT to stone
lapi'dario, -a AG (*fig*) terse
'**lapide** SF (*di sepolcro*) tombstone; (*commemorativa*) plaque
la'pin [la'pɛ̃] SM INV coney
'**lapis** SM INV pencil
'**lappone** AG, SMF, SM Lapp
Lap'ponia SF: **la ~** Lapland
'**lapsus** SM INV slip
'**laptop** ['læp tɔp] SM INV laptop (computer)
'**lardo** SM bacon fat, lard
lar'ghezza [lar'gettsa] SF width; breadth; looseness; generosity; ~ **di vedute** broad-mindedness
lar'gire [lar'dʒire] /**55**/ VT to give generously
'**largo, -a, -ghi, -ghe** AG wide; broad; (*maniche*) wide; (*abito: troppo ampio*) loose; (*fig*) generous ▶ SM width; breadth; (*mare aperto*): **il ~** the open sea ▶ SF: **stare** *o* **tenersi alla larga (da qn/qc)** to keep one's distance (from sb/sth), keep away (from sb/sth); ~ **due metri** two metres wide; ~ **di spalle**

broad-shouldered; **di larghe vedute**
broad-minded; **in larga misura** to a great o
large extent; **su larga scala** on a large scale;
di manica larga generous, open-handed;
al ~ di Genova off (the coast of) Genoa;
farsi ~ tra la folla to push one's way
through the crowd
'**larice** ['laritʃe] SM (*Bot*) larch
la'ringe [la'rindʒe] SF larynx
larin'gite [larin'dʒite] SF laryngitis
laringoi'atra, -i, -e SM/F (*medico*) throat
specialist
'**larva** SF larva; (*fig*) shadow
la'sagne [la'zaɲɲe] SFPL lasagna *sg*
lasciapas'sare [laʃʃapas'sare] SM INV pass,
permit
lasci'are [laʃʃare] /**14**/ VT to leave;
(*abbandonare*) to leave, abandon, give up;
(*cessare di tenere*) to let go of ▶ VB AUS: **~ qn fare
qc** to let sb do sth ▶ VI: **~ di fare** (*smettere*) to
stop doing; **lasciarsi**VPR (*persone*) to part;
(*coppia*) to split up; **~ andare** o **correre** o
perdere to let things go their own way;
~ stare qc/qn to leave sth/sb alone; **~ qn
erede** to make sb one's heir; **~ la presa** to
lose one's grip; **~ il segno (su qc)** to leave a
mark (on sth); (*fig*) to leave one's mark (on
sth); **~ (molto) a desiderare** to leave much
to be desired; **ci ha lasciato la vita** it cost
him his life; **lasciarsi andare/truffare** to
let o.s. go/be cheated
'**lascito** ['laʃʃito] SM (*Dir*) legacy
la'scivia [laʃʃivja] SF lust, lasciviousness
la'scivo, -a[laʃʃivo] AG lascivious
'**laser** ['lazer] AG, SM INV: **(raggio) ~** laser (beam)
lassa'tivo, -a AG, SM laxative
las'sismo SM laxity
'**lasso** SM: **~ di tempo** interval, lapse of time
lassù AV up there
'**lastra** SF (*di pietra*) slab; (*di metallo, Fot*) plate;
(*di ghiaccio, vetro*) sheet; (*radiografica*) X-ray
(plate)
lastri'care/20/ VT to pave
lastri'cato SM paving
'**lastrico**(*pl* **lastrici** o **lastrichi**) SM paving;
essere sul ~ (*fig*) to be penniless; **gettare qn
sul ~** (*fig*) to leave sb destitute
las'trone SM (*Alpinismo*) sheer rock face
la'tente AG latent
late'rale AG lateral, side *cpd*; (*uscita, ingresso
ecc*) side *cpd* ▶ SM (*Calcio*) half-back
lateral'mente AV sideways
late'rizio [late'rittsjo] SM (perforated) brick
latifon'dista, -i, -e SM/F large agricultural
landowner
lati'fondo SM large estate
la'tino, -a AG, SM Latin
la'tinoameri'cano, -a AG, SM/F Latin-
American

lati'tante AG: **essere ~** to be on the run ▶ SMF
fugitive (from justice)
lati'tanza [lati'tantsa] SF: **darsi alla ~** to go
into hiding
lati'tudine SF latitude
'**lato, -a** AG (*fig*) wide, broad; **in senso ~**
broadly speaking ▶ SM side; (*fig*) aspect,
point of view; **d'altro ~** (*d'altra parte*) on the
other hand
la'trare/72/ VI to bark
la'trato SM howling
la'trina SF public lavatory
latro'cinio [latro'tʃinjo] SM = **ladrocinio**
'**latta** SF tin (plate); (*recipiente*) tin, can
lat'taio, -a SM/F (*distributore*)
milkman(-woman); (*commerciante*)
dairyman(-woman)
lat'tante AG unweaned ▶ SMF breast-fed
baby
'**latte** SM milk; **fratello di ~** foster brother;
avere ancora il ~ alla bocca (*fig*) to be still
wet behind the ears; **tutto ~ e miele** (*fig*)
all smiles; **~ detergente** cleansing milk
o lotion; **~ intero** full-cream milk; **~ a
lunga conservazione** UHT milk,
long-life milk; **~ magro** o **scremato**
skimmed milk; **~ secco** o **in polvere**
dried o powdered milk; **~ solare** suntan
lotion
'**latteo, -a** AG milky; (*dieta, prodotto*) milk *cpd*
latte'ria SF dairy
latti'cini [latti'tʃini] SMPL dairy o milk products
lat'tina SF (*di birra ecc*) can
lat'tuga, -ghe SF lettuce
'**laurea** SF degree; **~ in ingegneria**
engineering degree; **~ in lettere** ≈ arts
degree; **~ breve** *university degree awarded at the
end of a three-year course*; **avere una ~ in
chimica** to have a degree in chemistry o a
chemistry degree; *see note*

> The *laurea* is awarded to students who
> successfully complete their degree
> courses. Traditionally, this takes
> between four and six years; a major
> element of the final examinations is
> the presentation and discussion of a
> dissertation. A shorter, more vocational
> course of study, taking from two to three
> years, is also available; at the end of this
> time students receive a diploma called
> the *laurea breve*.

laure'ando, -a SM/F final-year student
laure'are/72/ VT to confer a degree on;
laurearsiVPR to graduate
laure'ato, -a AG, SM/F graduate
'**lauro** SM laurel
'**lauto, -a** AG (*pranzo, mancia*) lavish; **lauti
guadagni** handsome profits
'**lava** SF lava

lavabianche'ria [lavabjanke'ria] SF INV washing machine

la'vabo SM washbasin

la'vaggio [la'vaddʒo] SM washing no pl; **~ del cervello** brainwashing no pl; **~ a secco** dry-cleaning

la'vagna [la'vaɲɲa] SF (Geo) slate; (di scuola) blackboard; **~ interattiva** interactive whiteboard; **~ luminosa** overhead projector

la'vanda SF (anche Med) wash; (Bot) lavender; **fare una ~ gastrica a qn** to pump sb's stomach

lavan'daia SF washerwoman

lavande'ria SF (di ospedale, caserma ecc) laundry; **~ automatica** launderette; **~ a secco** dry-cleaner's

lavan'dino SM sink; (del bagno) washbasin

lavapi'atti SM O F INV dishwasher

la'vare /72/ VT to wash; **lavarsi** VPR to wash, have a wash; **~ a secco** to dry-clean; **~ i panni sporchi in pubblico** (fig) to wash one's dirty linen in public; **lavarsi le mani/i denti** to wash one's hands/clean one's teeth

lava'secco SM O F INV dry-cleaner's

lavasto'viglie [lavasto'viʎʎe] SM O F INV (macchina) dishwasher

la'vata SF wash; (fig): **dare una ~ di capo a qn** to give sb a good telling-off

lava'tivo SM (clistere) enema; (buono a nulla) good-for-nothing, idler

lava'toio SM (public) washhouse

lava'trice [lava'tritʃe] SF washing machine

lava'tura SF washing no pl; **~ di piatti** dishwater

la'vello SM (kitchen) sink

la'vina SF snowslide

lavo'rante SMF worker

lavo'rare /72/ VI to work; (fig: bar, studio ecc) to do good business ▸ VT to work; **~ a** to work on; **~ a maglia** to knit; **~ di fantasia** (suggestionarsi) to imagine things; (fantasticare) to let one's imagination run free; **lavorarsi qn** (fig: convincere) to work on sb

lavora'tivo, -a AG working

lavora'tore, -'trice SM/F worker ▸ AG working

lavorazi'one [lavorat'tsjone] SF (gen) working; (di legno, pietra) carving; (di film) making; (di prodotto) manufacture; (modo di esecuzione) workmanship

lavo'rio SM intense activity

la'voro SM work; (occupazione) job, work no pl; (opera) piece of work, job; (Econ) labour (BRIT), labor (US); **che ~ fa?** what do you do?; **Ministero del L~** Department of Employment (BRIT), Department of Labor (US); **(fare) i lavori di casa** (to do) the housework sg; **lavori forzati** hard labour sg;

i lavori del parlamento the parliamentary session sg; **lavori pubblici** public works; **~ interinale** o **in affitto** temporary work

lazi'ale [lat'tsjale] AG of (o from) Lazio

lazza'retto [laddza'retto] SM leper hospital

lazza'rone [laddza'rone] SM scoundrel

'lazzo ['laddzo] SM jest

LC SIGLA = **Lecco**

LE SIGLA = **Lecce**

le DET FPL the ▸ PRON (oggetto) them; (a lei, a essa) (to) her; (forma di cortesia) (to) you; vedi anche **il**

le'ale AG loyal; (sincero) sincere; (onesto) fair

lea'lista, -i, -e SM/F loyalist

lealtà SF loyalty; sincerity; fairness

'leasing ['li:ziŋ] SM leasing, lease

'lebbra SF leprosy

'lecca 'lecca SM INV lollipop

leccapi'edi SMF (peg) toady, bootlicker

lec'care /20/ VT to lick; (gatto: latte ecc) to lick o lap up; (fig) to flatter; **leccarsi** VPR (fig) to preen o.s.; **leccarsi i baffi** to lick one's lips

lec'cato, -a AG affected ▸ SF lick

leccherò etc [lekke'rɔ] VB vedi **leccare**

'leccio ['lettʃo] SM holm oak, ilex

leccor'nia SF titbit, delicacy

'lecito, -a ['lɛtʃito] AG permitted, allowed; **se mi è** ~ if I may; **mi sia ~ far presente che ...** may I point out that ...

'ledere /81/ VT to damage, injure; **~ gli interessi di qn** to be prejudicial to sb's interests

'lega, -ghe SF (anche Pol) league; (di metalli) alloy; **metallo di bassa ~** base metal; **gente di bassa ~** common o vulgar people; **L~ Nord** (Pol) federalist party

le'gaccio [le'gattʃo] SM string, lace

le'gale AG legal ▸ SM lawyer; **corso ~ delle monete** official exchange rate; **medicina ~** forensic medicine; **studio ~** lawyer's office

legalità SF legality, lawfulness

legaliz'zare [legalid'dzare] /72/ VT to legalize; (documento) to authenticate

legalizzazi'one [legaliddzat'tsjone] SF (vedi vt) legalization; authentication

le'game SM (corda, fig: affettivo) tie, bond; (nesso logico) link, connection; **~ di sangue** o **di parentela** family tie

lega'mento SM (Anat) ligament

le'gare /80/ VT (prigioniero, capelli, cane) to tie (up); (libro) to bind; (Chim) to alloy; (fig: collegare) to bind, join ▸ VI (far lega) to unite; (fig) to get on well; **è pazzo da ~** (col) he should be locked up

lega'tario, -a SM/F (Dir) legatee

le'gato SM (Rel) legate; (Dir) legacy, bequest

lega'toria SF (attività) bookbinding; (negozio) bookbinder's

lega'tura SF (di libro) binding; (Mus) ligature

legazi'one [legat'tsjone] SF legation

le'genda [le'dʒɛnda] SF (di carta geografica ecc) = **leggenda**

'**legge** ['leddʒe] SF law; **~ procedurale** procedural law

leg'genda [le'dʒɛnda] SF (narrazione) legend; (di carta geografica ecc) key, legend

leggen'dario, -a [leddʒen'darjo] AG legendary

'**leggere** ['leddʒere] /61/ VT, VI to read; **~ il pensiero di qn** to read sb's mind o thoughts

legge'rezza [leddʒe'rettsa] SF lightness; thoughtlessness; fickleness

leg'gero, -a [led'dʒero] AG light; (agile, snello) nimble, agile, light; (tè, caffè) weak; (fig: non grave, piccolo) slight; (: spensierato) thoughtless; (: incostante) fickle; free and easy; **una ragazza leggera** (fig) a flighty girl; **alla leggera** thoughtlessly

leggi'adro, -a [led'dʒadro] AG pretty, lovely; (movimenti) graceful

leg'gibile [led'dʒibile] AG legible; (libro) readable, worth reading

leg'gio, -'gii [led'dʒio] SM lectern; (Mus) music stand

legherò etc [lege'rɔ] VB vedi **legare**

le'ghismo [le'gismo] SM political movement with federalist tendencies

le'ghista, -i, -e [le'gista] AG (Pol) of a "lega" (especially Lega Nord) ▶ SM/F member (o supporter) of a "lega" (especially Lega Nord)

legife'rare [ledʒife'rare] /72/ VI to legislate

legio'nario [ledʒo'narjo] SM (romano) legionary; (volontario) legionnaire

legi'one [le'dʒone] SF legion; **~ straniera** foreign legion

legisla'tivo, -a [ledʒizla'tivo] AG legislative

legisla'tore [ledʒizla'tore] SM legislator

legisla'tura [ledʒizla'tura] SF legislature

legislazi'one [ledʒizlat'tsjone] SF legislation

legitti'mare [ledʒitti'mare] /72/ VT (figlio) to legitimize; (comportamento ecc) to justify

legittimità [ledʒittimi'ta] SF legitimacy

le'gittimo, -a [le'dʒittimo] AG legitimate; (fig: giustificato, lecito) justified, legitimate; **legittima difesa** (Dir) self-defence (BRIT), self-defense (US)

'**legna** ['leɲɲa] SF firewood

le'gnaia [leɲ'ɲaja] SF woodshed

legnai'olo [leɲɲa'jɔlo] SM woodcutter

le'gname [leɲ'ɲame] SM wood, timber

le'gnata [leɲ'ɲata] SF blow with a stick; **dare a qn un sacco di legnate** to give sb a good hiding

'**legno** ['leɲɲo] SM wood; (pezzo di legno) piece of wood; **di ~** wooden; **~ compensato** plywood

le'gnoso, -a [leɲ'ɲoso] AG (di legno) wooden; (come il legno) woody; (carne) tough

le'gume SM (Bot) pulse; **legumi** SMPL (fagioli, piselli ecc) pulses

'**lei** PRON (soggetto) she; (oggetto: per dare rilievo, con preposizione) her; (forma di cortesia: anche: **Lei**) you ▶ SF INV: **la mia ~** my beloved ▶ SM: **dare del ~ a qn** to address sb as "lei"; **~ stessa** she herself; you yourself; **è ~** it's her

> lei is the third person singular pronoun. It is used in Italian to address an adult whom you do not know or with whom you are on formal terms.

'**lembo** SM (di abito, strada) edge; (striscia sottile: di terra) strip

'**lemma, -i** SM headword

'**lemme 'lemme** AV (very) very slowly

'**lena** SF (fig) energy, stamina; **di buona ~** (lavorare, camminare) at a good pace

Lenin'grado SF Leningrad

le'nire/55/ VT to soothe

lenta'mente AV slowly

'**lente** SF (Ottica) lens sg; **~ d'ingrandimento** magnifying glass; **lenti** (occhiali) lenses; **lenti a contatto, lenti corneali** contact lenses; **lenti (a contatto) morbide/rigide** soft/hard contact lenses

len'tezza [len'tettsa] SF slowness

len'ticchia [len'tikkja] SF (Bot) lentil

len'tiggine [len'tiddʒine] SF freckle

'**lento, -a** AG slow; (molle: fune) slack; (non stretto: vite, abito) loose ▶ SM (ballo) slow dance

'**lenza** ['lentsa] SF fishing line

lenzu'olo [len'tswɔlo] SM sheet; **lenzuola** SFPL pair of sheets; **~ funebre** shroud

leon'cino [leon'tʃino] SM lion cub

le'one SM lion; **L~** Leo; **essere del L~** to be Leo

leo'pardo SM leopard

lepo'rino, -a AG: **labbro ~** harelip

'**lepre** SF hare

'**lercio, -a, -ci, -ce** ['lɛrtʃo] AG filthy

lerci'ume [ler'tʃume] SM filth

'**lesbico, -a, -ci, -che** AG, SF lesbian

'**lesi** etc VB vedi **ledere**

lesi'nare /72/ VT to be stingy with ▶ VI: **~ (su)** to skimp (on), be stingy (with)

lesi'one SF (Med) lesion; (Dir) injury, damage; (Edil) crack

le'sivo, -a AG: **~ (di)** damaging (to), detrimental (to)

'**leso, -a** PP di **ledere** ▶ AG (offeso) injured; **parte lesa** (Dir) injured party; **lesa maestà** lese-majesty

Le'sotho [le'soto] SM Lesotho

les'sare /72/ VT (Cuc) to boil

'**lessi** etc VB vedi **leggere**

lessi'cale AG lexical

'**lessico, -ci** SM vocabulary; (dizionario) lexicon

lessicogra'fia SF lexicography

lessi'cografo, -a SM/F lexicographer

'lesso, -a AG boiled ▶ SM boiled meat

'lesto, -a AG quick; (*agile*) nimble; **~ di mano** (*per rubare*) light-fingered; (*per picchiare*) free with one's fists

lesto'fante SM swindler, con man

le'tale AG lethal; fatal

leta'maio SM dunghill

le'tame SM manure, dung

le'targo, -ghi SM lethargy; (*Zool*) hibernation

le'tizia [le'tittsja] SF joy, happiness

'letta SF: **dare una ~ a qc** to glance *o* look through sth

'lettera SF letter; **lettere** SFPL (*letteratura*) literature *sg*; (*studi umanistici*) arts (subjects); **alla ~** literally; **in lettere** in words, in full; **diventar ~ morta** (*legge*) to become a dead letter; **restar ~ morta** (*consiglio, invito*) to go unheeded; **~ di accompagnamento** accompanying letter; **~ assicurata** registered letter; **~ di cambio** (*Comm*) bill of exchange; **~ di credito** (*Comm*) letter of credit; **~ di intenti** letter of intent; **~ di presentazione** *o* **raccomandazione** letter of introduction; **~ raccomandata** recorded delivery (*BRIT*) *o* certified (*US*) letter; **~ di trasporto aereo** (*Comm*) air waybill

lette'rale AG literal

letteral'mente AV literally

lette'rario, -a AG literary

lette'rato, -a AG well-read, scholarly

lettera'tura SF literature

let'tiga, -ghe SF (*portantina*) litter; (*barella*) stretcher

let'tino SM cot (*BRIT*), crib (*US*); (*per il sole*) sun lounger; **~ solare** sunbed

'letto, -a PP *di* **leggere** ▶ SM bed; **andare a ~** to go to bed; **~ a castello** bunk beds *pl*; **~ a una piazza/a due piazze** *o* **matrimoniale** single/double bed

'lettone AG, SMF Latvian ▶ SM (*Ling*) Latvian, Lettish

Let'tonia SF: **la ~** Latvia

lettorato SM (*Ins*) lectorship, assistantship; (*Rel*) lectorate

let'tore, -'trice SM/F reader; (*Ins*) (foreign language) assistant (*BRIT*), (foreign) teaching assistant (*US*) ▶ SM (*Tecn*): **~ ottico (di caratteri)** optical character reader; **~ CD/DVD** CD/DVD player; **~ MP3/MP4** MP3/MP4 player

let'tura SF reading

leuce'mia [leutʃe'mia] SF leukaemia

'leva SF lever; (*Mil*) conscription; **far ~ su qn** to work on sb; **essere di ~** to be due for call-up; **~ del cambio** (*Aut*) gear lever

le'vante SM east; (*vento*) East wind; **il L~** the Levant

le'vare /72/ VT (*occhi, braccio*) to raise; (*sollevare, togliere: tassa, divieto*) to lift; (: *indumenti*) to take

off, remove; (*rimuovere*) to take away; (: *dal di sopra*) to take off; (: *dal di dentro*) to take out; **levarsi** VPR to get up; (*sole*) to rise; **~ le tende** (*fig*) to pack up and leave; **levarsi il pensiero** to put one's mind at rest; **levati di mezzo** *o* **di lì** *o* **di torno!** get out of my way!

le'vata SF (*di posta*) collection

leva'taccia, -ce [leva'tattʃa] SF early rise

leva'toio, -a AG: **ponte ~** drawbridge

leva'trice [leva'tritʃe] SF midwife

leva'tura SF intelligence, mental capacity

levi'gare /80/ VT to smooth; (*con carta vetrata*) to sand

levi'gato, -a AG (*superficie*) smooth; (*fig: stile*) polished; (: *viso*) flawless

levità SF lightness

levri'ere SM greyhound

lezi'one [let'tsjone] SF lesson; (*all'università, sgridata*) lecture; **fare ~** to teach; to lecture; **dare una ~ a qn** to teach sb a lesson; **lezioni private** private lessons

lezi'oso, -a [let'tsjoso] AG affected; simpering

'lezzo ['leddzo] SM stench, stink

LI SIGLA = **Livorno**

li PRON PL (*oggetto*) them

lì AV there; **di** *o* **da lì** from there; **per di lì** that way; **di lì a pochi giorni** a few days later; **lì per lì** there and then; at first; **essere lì (lì) per fare** to be on the point of doing, be about to do; **lì dentro** in there; **lì sotto** under there; **lì sopra** on there; up there; **tutto lì** that's all; *vedi anche* **quello**

libagi'one [liba'dʒone] SF libation

liba'nese AG, SMF Lebanese *inv*

Li'bano SM: **il ~** the Lebanon

'libbra SF (*peso*) pound

li'beccio [li'bettʃo] SM south-west wind

li'bello SM libel

li'bellula SF dragonfly

libe'rale AG, SMF liberal

liberaliz'zare [liberalid'dzare] /72/ VT to liberalize

libe'rare /72/ VT (*rendere libero: prigioniero*) to release; (: *popolo*) to free, liberate; (*sgombrare: passaggio*) to clear; (: *stanza*) to vacate; (*produrre: energia*) to release; **liberarsi** VPR: **liberarsi di qc/qn** to get rid of sth/sb

libera'tore, -'trice AG liberating ▶ SM/F liberator

liberazi'one [liberat'tsjone] SF (*di prigioniero*) release, freeing; (*di popolo*) liberation; rescuing; **che ~!** what a relief!; **la L~** *see note*

▌ The *Liberazione* is a national holiday which falls on 25 April. It commemorates the liberation of Italy in 1945 from German forces and Mussolini's government and marks the end of the war on Italian soil.

li'bercolo SM (*peg*) worthless book

Li'beria SF: **la ~** Liberia

liberi'ano, -a AG, SM/F Liberian

libe'rismo SM (*Econ*) laissez-faire

'libero, -a AG free; (*strada*) clear; (*non occupato: posto ecc*) vacant; free; not taken; empty; (*: Tel*) not engaged; ~ **di fare qc** free to do sth; ~ **da** free from; **una donna di liberi costumi** a woman of loose morals; **avere via libera** to have a free hand; **dare via libera a qn** to give sb the go-ahead; **via libera!** all clear!; ~ **arbitrio** free will; ~ **professionista** self-employed professional person; ~ **scambio** free trade; **libera uscita** (*Mil*) leave

liberoscam'bismo SM (*Econ*) free trade

liber'tà SF INV freedom; (*tempo disponibile*) free time ▶ SFPL (*licenza*) liberties; **essere in ~ provvisoria/vigilata** to be released without bail/be on probation; ~ **di riunione** right to hold meetings

liber'tario, -a AG libertarian

liber'tino, -a AG, SM/F libertine

'liberty ['liberti] AG INV, SM art nouveau

'Libia SF: **la ~** Libya

'libico, -a, -ci, -che AG, SM/F Libyan

li'bidine SF lust

libidi'noso, -a AG lustful, libidinous

li'bido SF libido

li'braio SM bookseller

li'brario, -a AG book *cpd*

li'brarsi/72/ VPR to hover

libre'ria SF (*bottega*) bookshop; (*stanza*) library; (*mobile*) bookcase

li'bretto SM booklet; (*taccuino*) notebook; (*Mus*) libretto; ~ **degli assegni** chequebook (BRIT), checkbook (US); ~ **di circolazione** (*Aut*) logbook; ~ **di deposito** (bank) deposit book; ~ **di risparmio** (savings) bankbook, passbook; ~ **universitario** student's report book

'libro SM book; ~ **bianco** (*Pol*) white paper; ~ **di cassa** cash book; ~ **di consultazione** reference book; ~ **mastro** ledger; ~ **paga** payroll; ~ **tascabile** paperback; ~ **di testo** textbook; **libri contabili** (account) books; **libri sociali** company records

li'cantropo SM werewolf

lice'ale [litʃe'ale] AG secondary school *cpd* (BRIT), high school *cpd* (US) ▶ SMF secondary school *o* high school pupil

li'cenza [li'tʃεntsa] SF (*permesso*) permission, leave; (*di pesca, caccia, circolazione*) permit, licence (BRIT), license (US); (*Ins*) school-leaving certificate; (*libertà*) liberty; licence; (*sfrenatezza*) licentiousness; **andare in ~** (*Mil*) to go on leave; **su ~ di ...** (*Comm*) under licence from ...; ~ **di esportazione** export licence; ~ **di fabbricazione** manufacturer's licence; ~ **poetica** poetic licence

licenzia'mento [litʃentsja'mento] SM dismissal

licenzi'are [litʃen'tsjare] /**19**/ VT (*impiegato*) to dismiss; (*Comm: per eccesso di personale*) to make redundant; (*Ins*) to award a certificate to; **licenziarsi** VPR (*impiegato*) to resign, hand in one's notice; (*Ins*) to obtain one's school-leaving certificate

licenziosità [litʃentsjosi'ta] SF licentiousness

licenzi'oso, -a [litʃen'tsjoso] AG licentious

li'ceo [li'tʃεo] SM (*Ins*) secondary (BRIT) *o* high (US) school (*for 14- to 19-year-olds*); ~ **classico/scientifico** secondary or high school specializing in classics/scientific subjects

li'chene [li'kεne] SM (*Bot*) lichen

'lido SM beach, shore

'Liechtenstein ['liktənstain] SM: **il ~** Liechtenstein

li'eto, -a AG happy, glad; "**molto ~**" (*nelle presentazioni*) "pleased to meet you"; **a ~ fine** with a happy ending

li'eve AG light; (*di poco conto*) slight; (*sommesso: voce*) faint, soft

lievi'tare/72/ VI (*anche fig*) to rise ▶ VT to leaven

li'evito SM yeast; ~ **di birra** brewer's yeast

'ligio, -a, -gi, -gie ['lidʒo] AG faithful, loyal

li'gnaggio [liɲ'naddʒo] SM descent, lineage

'ligure AG Ligurian; **la Riviera L~** the Italian Riviera

Li'kud [li'kud] SM Likud

'lilla, lillà SM INV lilac

'Lima SF Lima

'lima SF file; ~ **da unghie** nail file

limacci'oso, -a [limat'tʃoso] AG slimy; muddy

li'mare/72/ VT to file (down); (*fig*) to polish

'limbo SM (*Rel*) limbo

li'metta SF nail file

limi'tare/72/ VT to limit, restrict; (*circoscrivere*) to bound, surround; **limitarsi** VPR: **limitarsi nel mangiare** to limit one's eating; **limitarsi a qc/a fare qc** to limit o.s. to sth/ to doing sth

limitata'mente AV to a limited extent; ~ **alle mie possibilità** in so far as I am able

limi'tato, -a AG limited, restricted

limitazi'one [limitat'tsjone] SF limitation, restriction

'limite SM limit; (*confine*) border, boundary ▶ AG INV: **caso ~** extreme case; **al ~** if the worst comes to the worst (BRIT), if worst comes to worst (US); ~ **di velocità** speed limit

li'mitrofo, -a AG neighbouring (BRIT), neighboring (US)

'limo SM mud, slime; (*Geo*) silt

limo'nata SF lemonade (BRIT), (lemon) soda (US); (spremuta) lemon squash (BRIT), lemonade (US)

li'mone SM (pianta) lemon tree; (frutto) lemon

limpi'dezza [limpi'dettsa] SF clearness; (di discorso) clarity

'limpido, -a AG (acqua) limpid, clear; (cielo) clear; (fig: discorso) clear, lucid

'lince ['lintʃe] SF lynx

linci'aggio [lin'tʃaddʒo] SM lynching

linci'are [lin'tʃare] /**14**/ VT to lynch

'lindo, -a AG tidy, spick and span; (biancheria) clean

'linea SF (gen) line; (di mezzi pubblici di trasporto: itinerario) route; (: servizio) service; (di prodotto: collezione) collection; (: stile) style; **a grandi linee** in outline; **mantenere la ~** to look after one's figure; **è caduta la ~** (Tel) I (o you etc) have been cut off; **di ~, aereo di ~** airliner; **nave di ~** liner; **volo di ~** scheduled flight; **in ~ diretta da** (TV, Radio) coming to you direct from; **~ aerea** airline; **~ continua** solid line; **~ di partenza/d'arrivo** (Sport) starting/finishing line; **~ punteggiata** dotted line; **~ di tiro** line of fire

linea'menti SMPL features; (fig) outlines

line'are AG linear; (fig) coherent, logical

line'etta SF (trattino) dash; (d'unione) hyphen

'linfa SF (Bot) sap; (Anat) lymph; **~ vitale** (fig) lifeblood

lin'gotto SM ingot, bar

'lingua SF (Anat, Cuc) tongue; (idioma) language; **mostrare la ~** to stick out one's tongue; **di ~ italiana** Italian-speaking; **~ madre** mother tongue; **una ~ di terra** a spit of land

lingu'accia [lin'gwattʃa] SF (fig) spiteful gossip

linguacci'uto, -a [lingwat'tʃuto] AG gossipy

lingu'aggio [lin'gwaddʒo] SM language; **~ giuridico** legal language; **~ macchina** (Inform) machine language; **~ di programmazione** (Inform) programming language

lingu'etta SF (di strumento) reed; (di scarpa, Tecn) tongue; (di busta) flap

lingu'ista, -i, -e SM/F linguist

lingu'istico, -a, -ci, -che AG linguistic ▶ SF linguistics sg

lini'mento SM liniment

'lino SM (pianta) flax; (tessuto) linen

li'noleum SM INV linoleum, lino

liofiliz'zare [liofilid'dzare] /**72**/ VT to freeze-dry

liofiliz'zati [liofilid'dzati] SMPL freeze-dried foods

Li'one SF Lyons

liposuzi'one [liposut'tsjone] SF liposuction

'LIPU SIGLA F (= Lega Italiana Protezione Uccelli) society for the protection of birds

liqu'ame SM liquid sewage

lique'fare /**41**/ VT (render liquido) to liquefy; (fondere) to melt; **liquefarsi** VPR to liquefy; to melt

lique'fatto, -a PP di **liquefare**

liqui'dare /**72**/ VT (società, beni, persona: uccidere) to liquidate; (persona: sbarazzarsene) to get rid of; (conto, problema) to settle; (Comm: merce) to sell off, clear

liquidazi'one [likwidat'tsjone] SF (di società, persona) liquidation; (di conto) settlement; (di problema) settling; (Comm: di merce) clearance sale; (Amm) severance pay (on retirement, redundancy, or when taking up other employment)

liquidità SF liquidity

'liquido, -a AG, SM liquid; **denaro ~** cash, ready money; **~ per freni** brake fluid

liqui'gas® SM INV Calor gas® (BRIT), butane

liqui'rizia [likwi'rittsja] SF liquorice

li'quore SM liqueur

liquo'roso, -a AG: **vino ~** dessert wine

'lira SF (unità monetaria) lira; (Mus) lyre; **~ sterlina** pound sterling

'lirico, -a, -ci, -che AG lyric(al); (Mus) lyric ▶ SF (poesia) lyric poetry; (componimento poetico) lyric; (Mus) opera; **cantante/teatro ~** opera singer/house

li'rismo SM lyricism

Lis'bona SF Lisbon

'lisca, -sche SF (di pesce) fishbone

lisci'are [liʃʃare] /**14**/ VT to smooth; (fig) to flatter; **lisciarsi i capelli** to straighten one's hair

'liscio, -a, -sci, -sce ['liʃʃo] AG smooth; (capelli) straight; (mobile) plain; (bevanda alcolica) neat; (fig) straightforward, simple ▶ AV: **andare ~** to go smoothly; **passarla liscia** to get away with it

'liso, -a AG worn out, threadbare

'lista SF (striscia) strip; (elenco) list; **~ elettorale** electoral roll; **~ delle spese** shopping list; **~ dei vini** wine list; **~ delle vivande** menu

lis'tare /**72**/ VT: **~ (di)** to edge (with), border (with)

lis'tato SM (Inform) list, listing

lis'tino SM list; **~ di borsa** the Stock Exchange list; **~ dei cambi** (foreign) exchange rate; **~ dei prezzi** price list

lita'nia SF litany

'lite SF quarrel, argument; (Dir) lawsuit

liti'gare /**80**/ VI to quarrel; (Dir) to litigate

li'tigio [li'tidʒo] SM quarrel

litigi'oso, -a [liti'dʒoso] AG quarrelsome; (Dir) litigious

litogra'fia SF (sistema) lithography; (stampa) lithograph

lito'grafico, -a, -ci, -che AG lithographic
lito'rale AG coastal, coast *cpd* ▶ SM coast
lito'raneo, -a AG coastal
'litro SM litre (*BRIT*), liter (*US*)
lit'torio, -a AG (*Storia*) lictorial; **fascio ~** fasces *pl*
Litu'ania SF: **la ~** Lithuania
litu'ano, -a AG, SM/F, SM Lithuanian
litur'gia, -'gie [litur'dʒia] SF liturgy
li'uto SM lute
li'vella SF level; **~ a bolla d'aria** spirit level
livel'lare /72/ VT to level, make level; **livellarsi** VPR to become level; (*fig*) to level out, balance out
livella'trice [livella'tritʃe] SF steamroller
li'vello SM level; (*fig*) level, standard; **ad alto ~** (*fig*) high-level; **a ~ mondiale** world-wide; **a ~ di confidenza** confidentially; **~ di magazzino** stock level; **~ del mare** sea level; **sul ~ del mare** above sea level; **~ occupazionale** level of employment; **~ retributivo** salary level
'livido, -a AG livid; (*per percosse*) bruised, black and blue; (*cielo*) leaden ▶ SM bruise
li'vore SM malice, spite
Li'vorno SF Livorno, Leghorn
li'vrea SF livery
'lizza ['littsa] SF lists *pl*; **essere in ~ per** (*fig*) to compete for; **scendere in ~** (*anche fig*) to enter the lists
LO SIGLA = **Lodi**
lo DET M (*dav s impura, gn, pn, ps, x, z; dav V* **l'**) the ▶ PRON (*dav V* **l'**: *oggetto: persona*) him; (: *cosa*) it; **lo sapevo** I knew it; **lo so** I know; **sii buono, anche se lui non lo è** be good, even if he isn't; *vedi anche* **il**
lob'bista, -i, -e SM/F lobbyist
'lobby SF INV lobby
'lobo SM lobe; **~ dell'orecchio** ear lobe
lo'cale AG local ▶ SM room; (*luogo pubblico*) premises *pl*; **~ notturno** nightclub
località SF INV locality
localiz'zare [lokalid'dzare] /72/ VT (*circoscrivere*) to confine, localize; (*accertare*) to locate, place
lo'canda SF inn
locandi'ere, -a SM/F innkeeper
locan'dina SF (*Teat*) poster
lo'care /20/ VT (*casa*) to rent out, let; (*macchina*) to hire out (*BRIT*), rent (out)
loca'tario, -a SM/F tenant
loca'tivo, -a AG (*Dir*) rentable
loca'tore, -'trice SM/F landlord (lady)
locazi'one [lokat'tsjone] SF (*da parte del locatario*) renting *no pl*; (*da parte del locatore*) renting out *no pl*, letting *no pl*; (**contratto di**) **~** lease; (**canone di**) **~** rent; **dare in ~** to rent out, let
locomo'tiva SF locomotive

locomo'tore SM electric locomotive
locomot'rice [lokomo'tritʃe] SF = **locomotore**
locomozi'one [lokomot'tsjone] SF locomotion; **mezzi di ~** vehicles, means of transport
'loculo SM burial recess
lo'custa SF locust
locuzi'one [lokut'tsjone] SF phrase, expression
lo'dare /72/ VT to praise
'lode SF praise; (*Ins*): **laurearsi con 110 e ~** ≈ to graduate with first-class honours (*BRIT*), ≈ to graduate summa cum laude (*US*)
'loden SM INV (*stoffa*) loden; (*cappotto*) loden overcoat
lo'devole AG praiseworthy
loga'ritmo SM logarithm
log'garsi /72/ VPR (*Inform*) to log in
'loggia, -ge ['lɔddʒa] SF (*Archit*) loggia; (*circolo massonico*) lodge
loggi'one [lod'dʒone] SM (*di teatro*): **il ~** the Gods *sg*
logica'mente [lodʒika'mente] AV naturally, obviously
logicità [lodʒitʃi'ta] SF logicality
'logico, -a, -ci, -che ['lɔdʒiko] AG logical ▶ SF logic
lo'gistica [lo'dʒistika] SF logistics *sg*
'logo SM INV logo
logora'mento SM (*di vestiti ecc*) wear
logo'rante AG exhausting
logo'rare /72/ VT to wear out; (*sciupare*) to waste; **logorarsi** VPR to wear out; (*fig*) to wear o.s. out
logo'rio SM wear and tear; (*fig*) strain
'logoro, -a AG (*stoffa*) worn out, threadbare; (*persona*) worn out
'Loira SF: **la ~** the Loire
lom'baggine [lom'baddʒine] SF lumbago
Lombar'dia SF: **la ~** Lombardy
lom'bardo, -a AG, SM/F Lombard
lom'bare AG (*Anat, Med*) lumbar
lom'bata SF (*taglio di carne*) loin
'lombo SM (*Anat*) loin
lom'brico, -chi SM earthworm
londi'nese AG London *cpd* ▶ SM/F Londoner
'Londra SF London
lon'ganime AG forbearing
longevità [londʒevi'ta] SF longevity
lon'gevo, -a [lon'dʒevo] AG long-lived
longi'lineo, -a [londʒi'lineo] AG long-limbed
longi'tudine [londʒi'tudine] SF longitude
lontana'mente AV remotely; **non ci pensavo neppure ~** it didn't even occur to me
lonta'nanza [lonta'nantsa] SF distance; absence
lon'tano, -a AG (*distante*) distant, faraway; (*assente*) absent; (*vago: sospetto*) slight,

remote; (*tempo: remoto*) far-off, distant; (*parente*) distant, remote ▶ AV far; **è lontana la casa?** is it far to the house?, is the house far from here?; **è ~ un chilometro** it's a kilometre away *o* a kilometre from here; **più ~** farther; **da** *o* **di ~** from a distance; **~ da** a long way from; **è molto ~ da qui?** is it far from here?; **alla lontana** slightly, vaguely

'**lontra** SF otter

lo'quace [lo'kwatʃe] AG talkative, loquacious; (*fig: gesto ecc*) eloquent

loquacità [lokwatʃi'ta] SF talkativeness, loquacity

'**lordo, -a** AG dirty, filthy; (*peso, stipendio*) gross; **~ d'imposta** pre-tax

Lo'rena SF (*Geo*) Lorraine

'**loro** PRON PL (*oggetto, con preposizione*) them; (*complemento di termine*) to them; (*soggetto*) they; (*forma di cortesia: anche:* **Loro**) you; to you; **il (la) ~, i (le) ~** *det* their; (*forma di cortesia: anche:* **Loro**) your ▶ PRON theirs; (*forma di cortesia: anche:* **Loro**) yours ▶ SM INV: **il ~** their (*o* your) money ▶ SF INV: **la ~** (*opinione*) their (*o* your) view; **i ~** (*famiglia*) their (*o* your) family; (*amici ecc*) their (*o* your own) people; **un ~ amico** a friend of theirs; **è dalla ~** he's on their (*o* your) side; **ne hanno fatto un'altra delle ~** they've (*o* you've) done it again; **~ stessi(e)** they themselves; you yourselves

lo'sanga, -ghe SF diamond, lozenge

Lo'sanna SF Lausanne

'**losco, -a, -schi, -sche** AG (*fig*) shady, suspicious

'**lotta** SF struggle, fight; (*Sport*) wrestling; **essere in ~ (con)** to be in conflict (with); **fare la ~ (con)** to wrestle (with); **~ armata** armed struggle; **~ di classe** (*Pol*) class struggle; **~ libera** (*Sport*) all-in wrestling (*BRIT*), freestyle

lot'tare /**72**/ VI to fight, struggle; to wrestle

lotta'tore, -'trice SM/F wrestler

lotte'ria SF lottery; (*di gara ippica*) sweepstake

lottiz'zare [lottid'dzare] /**72**/ VT to divide into plots; (*fig*) to share out

lottizzazi'one [lottiddzat'tsjone] SF division into plots; (*fig*) share-out

'**lotto** SM (*gioco*) (state) lottery; (*parte*) lot; (*Edil*) site; **vincere un terno al ~** (*anche fig*) to hit the jackpot

> The *Lotto* is an official lottery run by the Italian Finance Ministry. It consists of a weekly draw of numbers and is very popular.

lozi'one [lot'tsjone] SF lotion

LT SIGLA = **Latina**

LU SIGLA = **Lucca**

lubrifi'cante SM lubricant

lubrifi'care /**20**/ VT to lubricate

lu'cano, -a AG of (*o* from) Lucania

luc'chetto [luk'ketto] SM padlock

lucci'care [luttʃi'kare] /**20**/ VI to sparkle; (*oro*) to glitter; (*stella*) to twinkle; (*occhi*) to glisten

lucci'chio [luttʃi'kio] SM sparkling; glittering; twinkling; glistening

lucci'cone [luttʃi'kone] SM: **avere i lucciconi agli occhi** to have tears in one's eyes

'**luccio** ['luttʃo] SM (*Zool*) pike

'**lucciola** ['luttʃola] SF (*Zool*) firefly; glow-worm; (*col: fig: prostituta*) girl (*o* woman) on the game

'**luce** ['lutʃe] SF light; (*finestra*) window; **alla ~ di** by the light of; **fare qc alla ~ del sole** (*fig*) to do sth in the open; **dare alla ~** (*bambino*) to give birth to; **fare ~ su qc** (*fig*) to shed *o* throw light on sth; **~ del sole/della luna** sun/moonlight

lu'cente [lu'tʃente] AG shining

lucen'tezza [lutʃen'tettsa] SF shine

lu'cerna [lu'tʃerna] SF oil lamp

lucer'nario [lutʃer'narjo] SM skylight

lu'certola [lu'tʃertola] SF lizard

luci'dare [lutʃi'dare] /**72**/ VT to polish; (*ricalcare*) to trace

lucida'trice [lutʃida'tritʃe] SF floor polisher

lucidità [lutʃidi'ta] SF lucidity

'**lucido, -a** ['lutʃido] AG shining, bright; (*lucidato*) polished; (*fig*) lucid ▶ SM shine, lustre (*BRIT*), luster (*US*); (*per scarpe ecc*) polish; (*disegno*) tracing

lu'cignolo [lu'tʃiɲɲolo] SM wick

lucrare /**72**/ VT to make money out of

lucra'tivo, -a AG lucrative; **a scopo ~** for gain

'**lucro** SM profit, gain; **a scopo di ~** for gain; **organizzazione senza scopo di ~** non-profit-making (*BRIT*) *o* non-profit (*US*) organization

lu'croso, -a AG lucrative, profitable

luculli'ano, -a AG (*pasto*) sumptuous

lu'dibrio SM mockery *no pl*; (*oggetto di scherno*) laughing stock

'**lue** SF syphilis

'**luglio** ['luʎʎo] SM July; **nel mese di ~** in July, in the month of July; **il primo ~** the first of July; **arrivare il 2 ~** to arrive on the 2nd of July; **all'inizio/alla fine di ~** at the beginning/at the end of July; **durante il mese di ~** during July; **a ~ del prossimo anno** in July of next year; **ogni anno a ~** every July; **che fai a ~?** what are you doing in July?; **ha piovuto molto a ~ quest'anno** July was very wet this year

'**lugubre** AG gloomy

'**lui** PRON (*soggetto*) he; (*oggetto: per dare rilievo, con preposizione*) him ▶ SM INV: **il mio ~** my beloved; **~ stesso** he himself; **è ~** it's him

lu'maca, -che SF slug; (*chiocciola*) snail

luma'cone SM (large) slug; (*fig*) slowcoach (*BRIT*), slowpoke (*US*) '**lume** SM light; (*lampada*) lamp; ~ **a olio** oil lamp; **chiedere lumi a qn** (*fig*) to ask sb for advice; **a ~ di naso** (*fig*) by rule of thumb

lumi'cino [lumi'tʃino] SM small *o* faint light; **essere (ridotto) al ~** (*fig*) to be at death's door

lumi'era SF chandelier

lumi'nare SM luminary

lumi'naria SF (*per feste*) illuminations *pl*

lumine'scente [lumineʃʃɛnte] AG luminescent

lu'mino SM small light; ~ **da notte** night-light; ~ **per i morti** candle for the dead

luminosità SF brightness; (*fig: di sorriso, volto*) radiance

lumi'noso, -a AG (*che emette luce*) luminous; (*cielo, colore, stanza*) bright; (*sorgente*) of light, light *cpd*; (*fig: sorriso*) bright, radiant; **insegna luminosa** neon sign

lun. ABBR (= *lunedì*) Mon.

'**luna** SF moon; ~ **nuova/piena** new/full moon; **avere la ~** to be in a bad mood; ~ **di miele** honeymoon

'**luna park** SM INV amusement park, funfair

lu'nare AG lunar, moon *cpd*

lu'nario SM almanac; **sbarcare il ~** to make ends meet

lu'natico, -a, -ci, -che AG whimsical, temperamental

lunedì SM INV Monday; **di** *o* **il ~** on Mondays; *vedi anche* **martedì**

lun'gaggine [lun'gaddʒine] SF slowness; **lungaggini della burocrazia** red tape

lunga'mente AV (*a lungo*) for a long time; (*estesamente*) at length

lun'garno SM embankment along the Arno

lun'ghezza [lun'gettsa] SF length; ~ **d'onda** (*Fisica*) wavelength

'**lungi** ['lundʒi]: ~ **da** *prep* far from

lungimi'rante [lundʒimi'rante] AG far-sighted

'**lungo, -a, -ghi, -ghe** AG long; (*lento: persona*) slow; (*diluito: caffè, brodo*) weak, watery, thin ▶ SM length ▶ PREP along; ~ **3 metri** 3 metres long; **avere la barba lunga** to be unshaven; **a ~** for a long time; **a ~ andare** in the long run; **di gran lunga** (*molto*) by far; **andare in ~** *o* **per le lunghe** to drag on; **saperla lunga** to know what's what; **in ~ e in largo** far and wide, all over; ~ **il corso dei secoli** throughout the centuries; **navigazione di ~ corso** ocean-going navigation

lungofi'ume SM embankment

lungo'lago SM road round a lake

lungo'mare SM promenade

lungome'traggio [lungome'traddʒo] SM (*Cine*) feature film

lungo'tevere SM embankment along the Tiber

lu'notto SM (*Aut*) rear *o* back window; ~ **termico** heated rear window

lu'ogo, -ghi SM place; (*posto: di incidente ecc*) scene, site; (*punto, passo di libro*) passage; **in ~ di** instead of; **in primo ~** in the first place; **aver ~** to take place; **dar ~ a** to give rise to; ~ **comune** commonplace; ~ **del delitto** scene of the crime; ~ **geometrico** locus; ~ **di nascita** birthplace; (*Amm*) place of birth; ~ **di pena** prison, penitentiary; ~ **di provenienza** place of origin

luogote'nente SM (*Mil*) lieutenant

lupacchi'otto [lupak'kjɔtto] SM (*Zool*) (wolf) cub

lu'para SF sawn-off shotgun

lu'petto SM (*Zool*) (wolf) cub; (*negli scouts*) cub scout

'**lupo, -a** SM/F wolf/she-wolf; **cane ~** alsatian (dog) (BRIT), German shepherd (dog); **tempo da lupi** filthy weather

'**luppolo** SM (*Bot*) hop

'**lurido, -a** AG filthy

luri'dume SM filth

lu'singa, -ghe SF (*spesso al pl*) flattery *no pl*

lusin'gare /**80**/ VT to flatter

lusinghi'ero, -a [luzin'gjɛro] AG flattering, gratifying

lus'sare /**72**/ VT (*Med*) to dislocate

lussazi'one [lussat'tsjone] SF (*Med*) dislocation

lussembur'ghese [lussembur'gese] AG of (*o* from) Luxembourg ▶ SMF native (*o* inhabitant) of Luxembourg

Lussem'burgo SM (*stato*): **il ~** Luxembourg ▶ SF (*città*) Luxembourg

'**lusso** SM luxury; **di ~** luxury *cpd*

lussu'oso, -a AG luxurious

lussureggi'are [lussured'dʒare] /**62**/ VI to be luxuriant

lus'suria SF lust

lussuri'oso, -a AG lascivious, lustful

lus'trare /**72**/ VT to polish, shine

lustras'carpe SM INV/F INV shoeshine

lus'trino SM sequin

'**lustro, -a** AG shiny; (*pelliccia*) glossy ▶ SM shine, gloss; (*fig*) prestige, glory; (*quinquennio*) five-year period

lute'rano, -a AG, SM/F Lutheran

'**lutto** SM mourning; **essere in/portare il ~** to be in/wear mourning

Mm

M, m ['ɛmme] SM O F INV (*lettera*) M, m;
M come Milano M for Mary (BRIT), M for
Mike (US)

m. ABBR = **mese; metro; miglia; monte**

ma CONG but; **ma insomma!** for goodness
sake!; **ma no!** of course not!

'**macabro, -a** AG gruesome, macabre

ma'caco, -chi SM (*Zool*) macaque

macché [mak'ke] ESCL not at all!, certainly
not!

macche'roni [makke'roni] SMPL macaroni *sg*

'**macchia** ['makkja] SF stain, spot; (*chiazza di
diverso colore*) spot, splash, patch; (*tipo di
boscaglia*) scrub; **~ d'inchiostro** ink stain;
estendersi a ~ d'olio (*fig*) to spread rapidly;
darsi/vivere alla ~ (*fig*) to go into/live in
hiding

macchi'are [mak'kjare] /**19**/ VT (*sporcare*) to
stain, mark; **macchiarsi** VPR (*persona*) to get
o.s. dirty; (*stoffa*) to stain; to get stained *o*
marked; **macchiarsi di un delitto** to be
guilty of a crime

macchi'ato, -a [mak'kjato] AG (*pelle, pelo*)
spotted; **~ di** stained with; **caffè ~** coffee
with a dash of milk

macchi'etta [mak'kjetta] SF (*disegno*) sketch,
caricature; (*Teat*) caricature; (*fig: persona*)
character

'**macchina** ['makkina] SF machine; (*motore,
locomotiva*) engine; (*automobile*) car; (*fig:
meccanismo*) machinery; **andare in ~** (*Aut*) to
go by car; (*Stampa*) to go to press; **salire in ~**
to get into the car; **venire in ~** to come by
car; **sala macchine** (*Naut*) engine room;
~ da cucire sewing machine; **~ fotografica**
camera; **~ da presa** cine *o* movie camera;
~ da scrivere typewriter; **~ utensile**
machine tool; **~ a vapore** steam engine

macchinal'mente [makkinal'mente] AV
mechanically

macchi'nare [makki'nare] /**72**/ VT to plot

macchi'nario [makki'narjo] SM machinery

macchinazi'one [makkinat'tsjone] SF plot,
machination

macchi'netta [makki'netta] SF (*col:
caffettiera*) percolator; (: *accendino*) lighter

macchi'nista, -i [makki'nista] SM (*di treno*)
engine-driver; (*di nave*) engineer; (*Teat, TV*)
stagehand

macchi'noso, -a [makki'noso] AG complex,
complicated

ma'cedone [ma'tʃɛdone] AG, SMF Macedonian

Mace'donia [matʃe'dɔnja] SF Macedonia

mace'donia [matʃe'dɔnja] SF fruit salad

macel'laio [matʃel'lajo] SM butcher

macel'lare [matʃel'lare] /**72**/ VT to slaughter,
butcher

macellazi'one [matʃellat'tsjone] SF
slaughtering, butchering

macelle'ria [matʃelle'ria] SF butcher's (shop)

ma'cello [ma'tʃɛllo] SM (*mattatoio*)
slaughterhouse, abattoir (BRIT); (*fig*)
slaughter, massacre; (: *disastro*) shambles *sg*

mace'rare [matʃe'rare] /**72**/ VT to macerate;
(*Cuc*) to marinate; **macerarsi** VPR to waste
away; (*fig*) **macerarsi in** to be consumed
with

macerazi'one [matʃerat'tsjone] SF
maceration

ma'cerie [ma'tʃɛrje] SFPL rubble *sg*, debris *sg*

'**macero** ['matʃero] SM (*operazione*) pulping;
(*stabilimento*) pulping mill; **carta da ~** paper
for pulping

machia'vellico, -a, -ci, -che [makja'vɛlliko]
AG (*anche fig*) Machiavellian

ma'cigno [ma'tʃiɲɲo] SM (*masso*) rock,
boulder

maci'lento, -a [matʃi'lɛnto] AG emaciated

'**macina** ['matʃina] SF (*pietra*) millstone;
(*macchina*) grinder

macinacaffè [matʃinakaf'fɛ] SM INV coffee
grinder

macina'pepe [matʃina'pepe] SM INV
peppermill

maci'nare [matʃi'nare] /**72**/ VT to grind;
(*carne*) to mince (BRIT), grind (US)

maci'nato [matʃi'nato] SM meal, flour;
(*carne*) minced (BRIT) *o* ground (US) meat

maci'nino [matʃi'nino] SM (per caffè) coffee grinder; (per pepe) peppermill; (scherzoso: macchina) old banger (BRIT), clunker (US)

maciul'lare [matʃul'lare] **/72/** VT (canapa, lino) to brake; (fig: braccio ecc) to crush

'macro ... PREFISSO macro...

macrobi'otico, -a AG macrobiotic ▶ SF macrobiotics sg

macu'lato, -a AG (pelo) spotted

Ma'dama : **palazzo ~** SM (Pol) seat of the Italian Chamber of Senators

made in Italy [meɪdɪ'nɪtəlɪ] SM: **il ~** Italian exports pl (especially fashion goods)

Ma'dera SF (Geo) Madeira ▶ SM INV (vino) Madeira

'madido, -a AG: **~ (di)** wet o moist (with)

Ma'donna SF (Rel) Our Lady

mador'nale AG enormous, huge

'madre SF mother; (matrice di bolletta) counterfoil ▶ AG INV mother cpd; **ragazza ~** unmarried mother; **scena ~** (Teat) principal scene; (fig) terrible scene

madre'lingua SF mother tongue, native language

madre'patria SF mother country, native land

madre'perla SF mother-of-pearl

Ma'drid SF Madrid

madri'gale SM madrigal

madri'leno, -a AG of (o from) Madrid ▶ SM/F person from Madrid

ma'drina SF godmother

maestà SF INV majesty; **Sua M~ la Regina** Her Majesty the Queen

maestosità SF majesty

maes'toso, -a AG majestic

ma'estra SF vedi **maestro**

maes'trale SM north-west wind, mistral

maes'tranze [maes'trantse] SFPL workforce sg

maes'tria SF mastery, skill

ma'estro, -a SM/F (Ins: anche: **maestro di scuola** o **elementare**) primary (BRIT) o grade school (US) teacher; (esperto) expert ▶ SM (artigiano, fig: guida) master; (Mus) maestro ▶ AG (principale) main; (di grande abilità) masterly, skilful (BRIT), skillful (US); **un colpo da ~** (fig) a masterly move; **muro ~** main wall; **strada maestra** main road; **maestra d'asilo** nursery teacher; **~ di ballo** dancing master; **~ di cerimonie** master of ceremonies; **~ d'orchestra** conductor, director (US); **~ di scherma** fencing master; **~ di sci** ski instructor

'mafia SF Mafia

mafi'oso SM member of the Mafia

'maga, -ghe SF sorceress

ma'gagna [ma'gaɲɲa] SF defect, flaw, blemish; (noia, guaio) problem

ma'gari ESCL (esprime desiderio): **~ fosse vero!** if only it were true!; **ti piacerebbe andare in Scozia? — ~!** would you like to go to Scotland? — I certainly would! ▶ AV (anche) even; (forse) perhaps

magazzi'naggio [magaddzi'naddʒo] SM: **(spese di) ~** storage charges pl, warehousing charges pl

magazzini'ere [magaddzi'njɛre] SM warehouseman

magaz'zino [magad'dzino] SM warehouse; **grande ~** department store; **~ doganale** bonded warehouse

'maggio ['maddʒo] SM May; vedi anche **luglio**

maggio'rana [maddʒo'rana] SF (Bot) (sweet) marjoram

maggio'ranza [maddʒo'rantsa] SF majority; **nella ~ dei casi** in most cases

maggio'rare [maddʒo'rare] **/72/** VT to increase, raise

maggiorazi'one [maddʒorat'tsjone] SF (Comm) rise, increase

maggior'domo [maddʒor'dɔmo] SM butler

maggi'ore [mad'dʒore] AG (comparativo: più grande) bigger, larger; taller; greater; (: più vecchio: sorella, fratello) older, elder; (: di grado superiore) senior; (: più importante: Mil, Mus) major; (superlativo) biggest, largest; tallest; greatest; oldest, eldest ▶ SMF (di grado) superior; (di età) elder; (Mil) major; (: Aer) squadron leader; **la maggior parte** the majority; **andare per la ~** (cantante, attore ecc) to be very popular, be "in"

maggio'renne [maddʒo'rɛnne] AG of age ▶ SMF person who has come of age

maggiori'tario, -a [maddʒori'tarjo] AG majority cpd; (Pol: anche: **sistema maggioritario**) first-past-the-post system

maggior'mente [maddʒor'mente] AV much more; (con senso superlativo) most

ma'gia [ma'dʒia] SF magic

'magico, -a, -ci, -che ['madʒiko] AG magic; (fig) fascinating, charming, magical

'magio ['madʒo] SM (Rel): **i re Magi** the Magi, the Three Wise Men

magis'tero [madʒis'tɛro] SM teaching; (fig: maestria) skill; (Ins): **Facoltà di M~** ≈ teacher training college

magis'trale [madʒis'trale] AG primary (BRIT) o grade school (US) teachers', primary (BRIT) o grade school (US) teaching; (abile) skilful (BRIT), skillful (US); **istituto ~** secondary school for the training of primary teachers

magis'trato [madʒis'trato] SM magistrate

magistra'tura [madʒistra'tura] SF magistrature; (magistrati): **la ~** the Bench

'maglia ['maʎʎa] SF stitch; (lavoro ai ferri) knitting no pl; (tessuto, Sport) jersey; (maglione) jersey, sweater; (di catena) link; (di rete) mesh; **avviare/diminuire le maglie** to cast on/ cast off; **lavorare a ~, fare la ~** to knit; **~ diritta/rovescia** plain/purl

maglie'ria [maʎʎe'ria] SF knitwear; (negozio) knitwear shop; **macchina per ~** knitting machine

magli'etta [maʎ'ʎetta] SF (canottiera) vest; (tipo camicia) T-shirt

magli'ficio [maʎʎi'fitʃo] SM knitwear factory

ma'glina [maʎ'ʎina] SF (tessuto) jersey

'maglio ['maʎʎo] SM mallet; (macchina) power hammer

magli'one [maʎ'ʎone] SM jumper, sweater

'magma SM magma; (fig) mass

ma'gnaccia [maɲ'ɲattʃa] SM INV (peg) pimp

magnanimità [maɲɲanimi'ta] SF magnanimity

ma'gnanimo, -a [maɲ'ɲanimo] AG magnanimous

ma'gnate [maɲ'ɲate] SM tycoon, magnate

ma'gnesia [maɲ'ɲɛzja] SF (Chim) magnesia

ma'gnesio [maɲ'ɲɛzjo] SM (Chim) magnesium; **al ~** (lampada, flash) magnesium cpd

ma'gnete [maɲ'ɲɛte] SM magnet

ma'gnetico, -a, -ci, -che [maɲ'ɲɛtiko] AG magnetic

magne'tismo [maɲɲe'tizmo] SM magnetism

magnetiz'zare [maɲɲetid'dzare] /**72**/ VT (Fisica) to magnetize; (fig) to mesmerize

magne'tofono [maɲɲe'tɔfono] SM tape recorder

magnifica'mente [maɲɲifika'mente] AV magnificently, extremely well

magnifi'cenza [maɲɲifi'tʃentsa] SF magnificence, splendour (BRIT), splendor (US)

ma'gnifico, -a, -ci, -che [maɲ'ɲifiko] AG magnificent, splendid; (ospite) generous

'magno, -a ['maɲɲo] AG: **aula magna** main hall

ma'gnolia [maɲ'ɲɔlja] SF magnolia

'mago, -ghi SM (stregone) magician, wizard; (illusionista) magician

ma'grezza [ma'grettsa] SF thinness

'magro, -a AG (very) thin, skinny; (carne) lean; (formaggio) low-fat; (fig: scarso, misero) meagre (BRIT), meager (US), poor; (: meschino: scusa) poor, lame; **mangiare di ~** not to eat meat

'mai AV (nessuna volta) never; (talvolta) ever; **non ... ~** never; **~ più** never again; **come ~?** why (o how) on earth?; **chi/dove/quando ~?** whoever/wherever/whenever?

mai'ale SM (Zool) pig; (carne) pork

mail ['meil] SF INV = **e-mail**

mai'olica SF majolica

maio'nese SF mayonnaise

Mai'orca SF Majorca

'mais SM maize (BRIT), corn (US)

mai'uscolo, -a AG (lettera) capital; (fig) enormous, huge ▶ SF capital letter ▶ SM capital letters pl; (Tip) upper case; **scrivere tutto (in) ~** to write everything in capitals o in capital letters

mal AV, SM vedi **male**

'mala SF (gergo) underworld

malac'corto, -a AG rash, careless

mala'fede SF bad faith

malaf'fare: di ~ ag (gente) shady, dishonest; **donna di ~** prostitute

mala'gevole [mala'dʒevole] AG difficult, hard

mala'grazia [mala'grattsja] SF: **con ~** with bad grace, impolitely

mala'lingua (pl **malelingue**) SF gossip (person)

mala'mente AV badly; (sgarbatamente) rudely

malan'dato, -a AG (persona: di salute) in poor health; (: di condizioni finanziarie) badly off; (trascurato) shabby

ma'lanimo SM ill will, malevolence; **di ~** unwillingly

ma'lanno SM (disgrazia) misfortune; (malattia) ailment

mala'pena SF: **a ~** hardly, scarcely

ma'laria SF (Med) malaria

ma'larico, -a, -ci, -che AG malarial

mala'sorte SF bad luck

mala'ticcio, -a [mala'tittʃo] AG sickly

ma'lato, -a AG ill, sick; (gamba) bad; (pianta) diseased ▶ SM/F sick person; (in ospedale) patient; **darsi ~** (sul lavoro ecc) to go sick

malat'tia SF (infettiva ecc) illness, disease; (cattiva salute) illness, sickness; (di pianta) disease; **mettersi in ~** to go on sick leave; **fare una ~ di qc** (fig: disperarsi) to get in a state about sth

malaugu'rato, -a AG ill-fated, unlucky

malau'gurio SM bad o ill omen; **uccello del ~** bird of ill omen

mala'vita SF underworld

malavi'toso, -a SM/F gangster

mala'voglia [mala'vɔʎʎa]: **di ~** av unwillingly, reluctantly

Ma'lawi [ma'lavi] SM: **il ~** Malawi

Mala'ysia SF Malaysia

malaysi'ano, -a AG, SM/F Malaysian

malcapi'tato, -a AG unlucky, unfortunate ▶ SM/F unfortunate person

mal'concio, -a, -ci, -ce [mal'kontʃo] AG in a sorry state

malcon'tento SM discontent

malcos'tume SM immorality

mal'destro, -a AG (inabile) inexpert, inexperienced; (goffo) awkward

maldi'cente [maldi'tʃente] AG slanderous

maldi'cenza [maldi'tʃentsa] SF malicious gossip

maldis'posto, -a AG: **~ (verso)** ill-disposed (towards)

Mal'dive SFPL: **le ~** the Maldives

'male AV badly ▶ SM *(ciò che è ingiusto, disonesto)* evil; *(danno, svantaggio)* harm; *(sventura)* misfortune; *(dolore fisico, morale)* pain, ache; **sentirsi ~** to feel ill; **aver mal di cuore/fegato** to have a heart/liver complaint; **aver mal di denti/d'orecchi/di testa** to have toothache/earache/a headache; **aver mal di gola** to have a sore throat; **aver ~ ai piedi** to have sore feet; **far ~** *(dolere)* to hurt; **far ~ alla salute** to be bad for one's health; **far del ~ a qn** to hurt *o* harm sb; **parlar ~ di qn** to speak ill of sb; **restare** *o* **rimanere ~** to be sorry; to be disappointed, to be hurt; **trattar ~ qn** to ill-treat sb; **andare a ~** to go off *o* bad; **come va? — non c'è ~** how are you? — not bad; **di ~ in peggio** from bad to worse; **per ~ che vada** however badly things go; **non avertene a ~**, **non prendertela a ~** don't take it to heart; **mal comune mezzo gaudio** *(proverbio)* a trouble shared is a trouble halved; **mal d'auto** carsickness; **mal di mare** seasickness

male'detto, -a PP *di* **maledire** ▶ AG cursed, damned; *(fig: col)* damned, blasted

male'dire /38/ VT to curse

maledizi'one [maledit'tsjone] SF curse; **~!** damn it!

maledu'cato, -a AG rude, ill-mannered

maleducazi'one [maledukat'tsjone] SF rudeness

male'fatta SF misdeed

male'ficio [male'fitʃo] SM witchcraft

ma'lefico, -a, -ci, -che AG *(aria, cibo)* harmful, bad; *(influsso, azione)* evil

ma'lese AG, SMF Malay(an) ▶ SM *(Ling)* Malay

Ma'lesia SF Malaya

ma'lessere SM indisposition, slight illness; *(fig)* uneasiness

malevo'lenza [malevo'lɛntsa] SF malevolence

ma'levolo, -a AG malevolent

malfa'mato, -a AG notorious

mal'fatto, -a AG *(persona)* deformed; *(oggetto)* badly made; *(lavoro)* badly done

malfat'tore, -'trice SM/F wrongdoer

mal'fermo, -a AG unsteady, shaky; *(salute)* poor, delicate

malformazi'one [malformat'tsjone] SF malformation

'malga, -ghe SF Alpine hut

malgo'verno SM maladministration

mal'grado PREP in spite of, despite ▶ CONG although; **mio** *o* **tuo** *etc* **~** against my *(o* your *etc)* will

ma'lia SF spell; *(fig: fascino)* charm

mali'ardo, -a AG *(occhi, sorriso)* bewitching ▶ SF enchantress

maligna'mente [maliɲɲa'mente] AV maliciously

mali'gnare [maliɲ'ɲare] /15/ VI: **~ su** to malign, speak ill of

malignità [maliɲɲi'ta] SF INV *(qualità)* malice, spite; *(osservazione)* spiteful remark; **con ~** spitefully, maliciously

ma'ligno, -a [ma'liɲɲo] AG *(malvagio)* malicious, malignant; *(Med)* malignant

malinco'nia SF melancholy, gloom

malin'conico, -a, -ci, -che AG melancholy

malincu'ore: a ~ *av* reluctantly, unwillingly

malinfor'mato, -a AG misinformed

malintenzio'nato, -a [malintentsjo'nato] AG ill-intentioned

malin'teso, -a AG misunderstood; *(riguardo, senso del dovere)* mistaken, wrong ▶ SM misunderstanding; **c'è stato un ~** there's been a misunderstanding

ma'lizia [ma'littsja] SF *(malignità)* malice; *(furbizia)* cunning; *(espediente)* trick

malizi'oso, -a [malit'tsjoso] AG malicious; cunning; *(vivace, birichino)* mischievous

malle'abile AG malleable

mal'loppo SM *(col: refurtiva)* loot

malme'nare /72/ VT to beat up; *(fig)* to ill-treat

mal'messo, -a AG shabby

malnu'trito, -a AG undernourished

malnutrizi'one [malnutrit'tsjone] SF malnutrition

'malo, -a AG: **in ~ modo** badly

ma'locchio [ma'lɔkkjo] SM evil eye

ma'lora SF *(col)*: **andare in ~** to go to the dogs; **va in ~!** go to hell!

ma'lore SM *(sudden)* illness

malri'dotto, -a AG *(abiti, scarpe, persona)* in a sorry state; *(casa, macchina)* dilapidated, in a poor state of repair

mal'sano, -a AG unhealthy

malsi'curo, -a AG unsafe

'Malta SF Malta

'malta SF *(Edil)* mortar

mal'tempo SM bad weather

'malto SM malt

mal'tolto SM ill-gotten gains *pl*

maltratta'mento SM ill treatment

maltrat'tare /72/ VT to ill-treat

malu'more SM bad mood; *(irritabilità)* bad temper; *(discordia)* ill feeling; **di ~** in a bad mood

'malva SF *(Bot)* mallow ▶ AG, SM INV mauve

mal'vagio, -a, -gi, -gie [mal'vadʒo] AG wicked, evil

malvagità [malvadʒi'ta] SF INV *(qualità)* wickedness; *(azione)* wicked deed

malva'sia SF Italian dessert wine

malversazi'one [malversat'tsjone] SF *(Dir)* embezzlement

malves'tito, -a AG badly dressed, ill-clad

mal'visto, -a AG: **~ (da)** disliked (by), unpopular (with)

m

malvi'vente SM criminal
malvolenti'eri AV unwillingly, reluctantly
malvo'lere/131/ VT: **farsi ~ da qn** to make o.s.
unpopular with sb ▶ SM: **prendere qn a ~**
to take a dislike to sb
'**malware** ['malwer] SM INV (*Inform*) malware
(program)
'**mamma** SF mum(my) (*BRIT*), mom (*US*);
~ mia! my goodness!
mam'mario, -a AG (*Anat*) mammary
mam'mella SF (*Anat*) breast; (*di vacca, capra
ecc*) udder
mam'mifero SM mammal
mam'mismo SM *excessive attachment to one's
mother*
'**mammola** SF (*Bot*) violet
'**manager** ['mænidʒə] SM INV manager
manageri'ale [manadʒe'rjale] AG
managerial
ma'nata SF (*colpo*) slap; (*quantità*) handful
'**manca** SF left (hand); **a destra e a ~** left,
right and centre, on all sides
manca'mento SM (*di forze*) (feeling of)
faintness, weakness
man'canza [man'kantsa] SF lack; (*carenza*)
shortage, scarcity; (*fallo*) fault; (*imperfezione*)
failing, shortcoming; **per ~ di tempo**
through lack of time; **in ~ di meglio** for lack
of anything better; **sentire la ~ di qc/qn** to
miss sth/sb
man'care/20/ VI (*essere insufficiente*) to be
lacking; (*venir meno*) to fail; (*sbagliare*) to be
wrong, make a mistake; (*non esserci*) to be
missing, not to be there; (*essere lontano*):
~ (da) to be away (from) ▶ VT to miss; **~ di**
to lack; **~ a** (*promessa*) to fail to keep; **tu mi
manchi** I miss you; **mancò poco che
morisse** he very nearly died; **mancano
ancora 10 sterline** we're still £10 short;
manca un quarto alle 6 it's a quarter to 6;
non mancherò I won't forget, I'll make
sure I do; **ci mancherebbe altro!** of course I
(*o you etc*) will!; **~ da casa** to be away from
home; **~ di rispetto a** *o* **verso qn** to be
lacking in respect towards sb, be
disrespectful towards sb; **~ di parola** not to
keep one's word, go back on one's word;
sentirsi ~ to feel faint
man'cato, -a AG (*tentativo*) unsuccessful;
(*artista*) failed
manche [mãʃ] SF INV (*Sport*) heat
mancherò*etc* [manke'tɔ] VB *vedi* **mancare**
man'chevole [man'kevole] AG (*insufficiente*)
inadequate, insufficient
manchevo'lezza [mankevo'lettsa] SF
(*scorrettezza*) fault, shortcoming
'**mancia, -ce** ['mantʃa] SF tip; **~ competente**
reward
manci'ata [man'tʃata] SF handful

man'cino, -a [man'tʃino] AG (*braccio*) left;
(*persona*) left-handed; (*fig*) underhand
'**manco** AV (*nemmeno*): **~ per sogno** *o* **per idea!**
not on your life!
man'dante SMF (*Dir*) principal; (*istigatore*)
instigator
manda'rancio [manda'rantʃo] SM
clementine
man'dare/72/ VT to send; (*far funzionare:
macchina*) to drive; (*emettere*) to send out;
(*: grido*) to give, utter, let out; **~ avanti**
(*persona*) to send ahead; (*fig: famiglia*) to
provide for; (*: ditta*) to look after, run;
(*: fabbrica*) to run, look after; (*: pratica*) to
attend to; **~ a chiamare qn** to send for sb;
~ giù to send down; (*anche fig*) to swallow;
~ in onda (*Radio, TV*) to broadcast; **~ in
rovina** to ruin; **~ via** to send away; (*licenziare*)
to fire
manda'rino SM mandarin (orange); (*cinese*)
mandarin
man'data SF (*quantità*) lot, batch; (*di chiave*)
turn; **chiudere a doppia ~** to double-lock
manda'tario SM (*Dir*) representative, agent
man'dato SM (*incarico*) commission; (*Dir:
provvedimento*) warrant; (*di deputato ecc*)
mandate; (*ordine di pagamento*) postal *o* money
order; **~ d'arresto, ~ di cattura** warrant for
arrest; **~ di comparizione** summons *sg*;
~ di perquisizione search warrant
man'dibola SF mandible, jaw
mando'lino SM mandolin(e)
'**mandorla** SF almond
mandor'lato SM nut brittle
'**mandorlo** SM almond tree
'**mandria** SF herd
mandri'ano SM cowherd, herdsman
man'drino SM (*Tecn*) mandrel
maneg'gevole [maned'dʒevole] AG easy to
handle
maneggi'are [maned'dʒare] **/62/** VT (*creta,
cera*) to mould (*BRIT*), mold (*US*), work, fashion;
(*arnesi, utensili*) to handle; (*: adoperare*) to use;
(*fig: persone, denaro*) to handle, deal with
ma'neggio [ma'neddʒo] SM moulding (*BRIT*),
molding (*US*); handling; use; (*intrigo*) plot,
scheme; (*per cavalli*) riding school
ma'nesco, -a, -schi, -sche AG free with
one's fists
ma'nette SFPL handcuffs
manga'nello SM club
manga'nese SM manganese
mange'reccio, -a, -ci, -ce [mandʒe'rettʃo] AG
edible
mangi'abile [man'dʒabile] AG edible, eatable
mangia'dischi [mandʒa'diski] SM INV record
player
mangia'nastri [mandʒa'nastri] SM INV
cassette-recorder

mangi'are [man'dʒare] /**62**/ VT to eat;
(*intaccare*) to eat into o away; (*Carte, Scacchi ecc*)
to take ▶ VI to eat ▶ SM eating; (*cibo*) food;
(*cucina*) cooking; **fare da ~** to do the cooking;
mangiarsi le parole to mumble;
mangiarsi le unghie to bite one's nails
mangia'soldi [mandʒa'sɔldi] AG INV (*col*):
macchinetta ~ one-armed bandit
mangia'toia [mandʒa'toja] SF feeding-
trough
man'gime [man'dʒime] SM fodder
mangiucchi'are [mandʒuk'kjare] /**19**/ VT to
nibble
'**mango, -ghi** SM mango
ma'nia SF (*Psic*) mania; (*fig*) obsession, craze;
avere la ~ di fare qc to have a habit of doing
sth; **~ di persecuzione** persecution complex
o mania
mania'cale AG (*Psic*) maniacal; (*fanatico*)
fanatical
ma'niaco, -a, -ci, -che AG suffering from a
mania; **~ (di)** obsessed (by), crazy (about)
'**manica, -che** SF sleeve; (*fig: gruppo*) gang,
bunch; (*Geo*): **la M~, il Canale della M~** the
(English) Channel; **senza maniche**
sleeveless; **essere in maniche di camicia** to
be in one's shirt sleeves; **essere di ~ larga/
stretta** to be easy-going/strict; **~ a vento**
(*Aer*) wind sock
manica'retto SM titbit (BRIT), tidbit (US)
mani'chetta [mani'ketta] SF (*Tecn*) hose
mani'chino [mani'kino] SM (*di sarto, vetrina*)
dummy
'**manico, -ci** SM handle; (*Mus*) neck; **~ di
scopa** broomstick
mani'comio SM mental hospital; (*fig*)
madhouse
mani'cotto SM muff; (*Tecn*) coupling; sleeve
mani'cure SM O F INV manicure ▶ SF INV
manicurist
mani'era SF way, manner; (*stile*) style,
manner; **maniere** SFPL (*comportamento*)
manners; **in ~ che** so that; **in ~ da** so as to;
alla ~ di in o after the style of; **in una ~ o
nell'altra** one way or another; **in tutte le
maniere** at all costs; **usare buone
maniere con qn** to be polite to sb; **usare
le maniere forti** to use strong-arm tactics
manie'rato, -a AG affected
mani'ero SM manor
manifat'tura SF (*lavorazione*) manufacture;
(*stabilimento*) factory
manifatturi'ero, -a AG manufacturing
manifes'tante SMF demonstrator
manifes'tare /**72**/ VT to show, display;
(*esprimere*) to express; (*rivelare*) to reveal,
disclose ▶ VI to demonstrate; **manifestarsi**
VPR to show o.s.; **manifestarsi amico** to
prove o.s. (to be) a friend

manifestazi'one [manifestat'tsjone] SF
show, display, expression; (*sintomo*) sign,
symptom; (*dimostrazione pubblica*)
demonstration; (*cerimonia*) event
manifes'tino SM leaflet
mani'festo, -a AG obvious, evident ▶ SM
poster, bill; (*scritto ideologico*) manifesto
ma'niglia [ma'niʎʎa] SF handle; (*sostegno:
negli autobus ecc*) strap
Ma'nila SF Manila
manipo'lare /**72**/ VT to manipulate; (*alterare:
vino*) to adulterate
manipolazi'one [manipolat'tsjone] SF
manipulation; adulteration
ma'nipolo SM (*drappello*) handful
manis'calco, -chi SM blacksmith, farrier
(BRIT)
'**manna** SF (*Rel*) manna
man'naia SF (*del boia*) (executioner's) axe o ax
(US); (*per carni*) cleaver
man'naro, -a AG: **lupo ~** werewolf
'**mano, -i** SF hand; (*strato: di vernice ecc*) coat;
a ~ by hand; **cucito a ~** hand-sewn; **fatto a ~**
handmade; **alla ~** (*persona*) easy-going;
fuori ~ out of the way; **di prima ~** (*notizia*)
first-hand; **di seconda ~** second-hand; **man
~ che** little by little, gradually; **man ~ che** as; **a
piene mani** (*fig*) generously; **avere le mani
bucate** to spend money like water; **aver le
mani in pasta** to be in the know; **avere qc
per le mani** (*progetto, lavoro*) to have sth in
hand; **dare una ~ a qn** to lend sb a hand;
dare una ~ di vernice a qc to give sth a coat
of paint; **darsi o stringersi la ~** to shake
hands; **forzare la ~** to go too far; **mettere ~
a qc** to have a hand in sth; **mettere le mani
avanti** (*fig*) to safeguard o.s.; **restare a mani
vuote** to be left empty-handed; **venire alle
mani** to come to blows; **mani in alto!** hands
up!; **mani pulite** *see note*

Mani pulite ("clean hands") is a term used
to describe the judicial operation of the
early 1990s to gather evidence against
politicians and industrialists who were
implicated in bribery and corruption
scandals.

mano'dopera SF labour (BRIT), labor (US)
mano'messo, -a PP *di* **manomettere**
ma'nometro SM gauge, manometer
mano'mettere /**63**/ VT (*alterare*) to tamper
with; (*aprire indebitamente*) to break open
illegally
manomissi'one SF (*di prove ecc*) tampering;
(*di lettera*) opening
ma'nopola SF (*dell'armatura*) gauntlet; (*guanto*)
mitt; (*di impugnatura*) hand-grip; (*pomello*)
knob
manos'critto, -a AG handwritten ▶ SM
manuscript

m

manova'lanza [manova'lantsa] SF unskilled workers pl

mano'vale SM labourer (BRIT), laborer (US)

mano'vella SF handle; (Tecn) crank

ma'novra SF manoeuvre (BRIT), maneuver (US); (Ferr) shunting; **manovre di corridoio** palace intrigues

mano'vrare/72/ VT (veicolo) to manoeuvre (BRIT), maneuver (US); (macchina, congegno) to operate; (fig: persona) to manipulate ▶ VI to manoeuvre

manro'vescio [manro'vɛʃʃo] SM (with back of hand) slap

man'sarda SF attic

mansi'one SF task, duty, job

mansu'eto, -a AG (animale) tame; (persona) gentle, docile

mansue'tudine SF tameness gentleness, docility

man'tello SM cloak; (fig: di neve ecc) blanket, mantle; (Tecn: involucro) casing, shell; (Zool) coat

mante'nere/121/ VT to maintain; (adempiere: promesse) to keep, abide by; (provvedere a) to support, maintain; **mantenersi**VPR: **mantenersi calmo/giovane** to stay calm/ young; **~ i contatti con qn** to keep in touch with sb

manteni'mento SM maintenance

mante'nuto, -a SM/F gigolo/kept woman

'mantice ['mantitʃe] SM bellows pl; (di carrozza, automobile) hood

'manto SM cloak; **~ stradale** road surface

'Mantova SF Mantua

manto'vano, -a AG of (o from) Mantua

manu'ale AG manual ▶ SM (testo) manual, handbook

manua'listico, -a, -ci, -che AG textbook cpd

manual'mente AV manually, by hand

ma'nubrio SM handle; (di bicicletta ecc) handlebars pl; (Sport) dumbbell

manu'fatto SM manufactured article; **manufatti**SMPL manufactured goods

manutenzi'one [manuten'tsjone] SF maintenance, upkeep; (d'impianti) maintenance, servicing

'manzo ['mandzo] SM (Zool) steer; (carne) beef

Mao'metto SM Mohammed

'mappa SF (Geo) map

mappa'mondo SM map of the world; (globo girevole) globe

ma'rasma, -i SM (fig) decay, decline

mara'tona SF marathon

'marca, -che SF mark; (bollo) stamp; (Comm: di prodotti) brand; (contrassegno, scontrino) ticket, check; **prodotti di (gran) ~** high-class products; **~ da bollo** official stamp

mar'care/20/ VT (munire di contrassegno) to

mark; (a fuoco) to brand; (Sport: gol) to score; (: avversario) to mark; (accentuare) to stress; **~ visita** (Mil) to report sick

mar'cato, -a AG (lineamenti, accento ecc) pronounced

'Marche ['marke] SFPL: **le ~** the Marches (region of central Italy)

marcheròetc [marke'rɔ] VB vedi **marcare**

mar'chese, -a[mar'keze] SM/F marquis o marquess/marchioness

marchi'ano, -a[mar'kjano] AG (errore) glaring, gross

marchi'are [mar'kjare] /19/ VT to brand

marchigi'ano, -a[marki'dʒano] AG of (o from) the Marches

'marchio ['markjo] SM (di bestiame: Comm: fig) brand; **~ depositato** registered trademark; **~ di fabbrica** trademark

'marcia, -ce['martʃa] SF (anche Mus, Mil) march; (funzionamento) running; (il camminare) walking; (Aut) gear; **mettere in ~** to start; **mettersi in ~** to get moving; **far ~ indietro** (Aut) to reverse; (fig) to back-pedal; **~ forzata** forced march; **~ funebre** funeral march

marciapi'ede [martʃa'pjɛde] SM (di strada) pavement (BRIT), sidewalk (US); (Ferr) platform

marci'are [mar'tʃare] /14/ VI to march; (andare: treno, macchina) to go; (funzionare) to run, work

'marcio, -a, -ci, -ce['martʃo] AG (frutta, legno) rotten, bad; (Med) festering; (fig) corrupt, rotten ▶ SM: **c'è del ~ in questa storia** (fig) there's something fishy about this business; **avere torto ~** to be utterly wrong

mar'cire [mar'tʃire] /55/ VI (andare a male) to go bad, rot; (suppurare) to fester; (fig) to rot, waste away

marci'ume [mar'tʃume] SM (parte guasta: di cibi ecc) rotten part, bad part; (: di radice, pianta) rot; (fig: corruzione) rottenness, corruption

'marco, -chi SM (unità monetaria) mark

'mare SM sea; **di ~** (brezza, acqua, uccelli, pesce) sea cpd; **in ~** at sea; **per ~** by sea; **sul ~** (barca) on the sea; (villaggio, località) by o beside the sea; **andare al ~** (in vacanza ecc) to go to the seaside; **il mar Caspio** the Caspian Sea; **il mar Morto** the Dead Sea; **il mar Nero** the Black Sea; **il ~ del Nord** the North Sea; **il mar Rosso** the Red Sea; **il mar dei Sargassi** the Sargasso Sea; **i mari del Sud** the South Seas

ma'rea SF tide; **alta/bassa ~** high/low tide

mareggi'ata [mared'dʒata] SF heavy sea

ma'remma SF (Geo) maremma, swampy coastal area

marem'mano, -a AG (zona, macchia) swampy; (della Maremma) of (o from) the Maremma

mare'moto SM seaquake

maresci'allo [mareʃʃallo] SM (Mil) marshal; (: sottufficiale) warrant officer

marez'zato, -a [mared'dzato] AG (seta ecc) watered, moiré; (legno) veined; (carta) marbled

marga'rina SF margarine

marghe'rita [marge'rita] SF (ox-eye) daisy, marguerite

margheri'tina [margeri'tina] SF daisy

margi'nale [mardʒi'nale] AG marginal

'margine ['mardʒine] SM margin; (di bosco, via) edge, border; **avere un buon ~ di tempo/denaro** to have plenty of time/money; **~ di guadagno** o **di utile** profit margin; **~ di sicurezza** safety margin

mariju'ana [mæri'wa:nə] SF marijuana

ma'rina SF navy; (costa) coast; (quadro) seascape; **~ mercantile** merchant navy (BRIT) o marine (US); **~ militare** ≈ Royal Navy (BRIT), ≈ Navy (US)

mari'naio SM sailor

mari'nare/72/ VT (Cuc) to marinate; **~ la scuola** to play truant

mari'naro, -a AG (tradizione, popolo) seafaring; (Cuc) with seafood; **alla marinara** (vestito, cappello) sailor cpd; **borgo ~** district where fishing folk live

mari'nata SF marinade

ma'rino, -a AG sea cpd, marine

mario'netta SF puppet

mari'tare/72/ VT to marry; **maritarsi** VPR: **maritarsi a** o **con qn** to marry sb, get married to sb

mari'tato, -a AG married

ma'rito SM husband; **prendere ~** to get married; **ragazza (in età) da ~** girl of marriageable age

ma'rittimo, -a AG maritime, sea cpd

mar'maglia [mar'maʎʎa] SF mob, riff-raff

marmel'lata SF jam; (di agrumi) marmalade

mar'mitta SF (recipiente) pot; (Aut) silencer; **~ catalitica** catalytic converter

'marmo SM marble

mar'mocchio [mar'mɔkkjo] SM (col) (little) kid

mar'motta SF (Zool) marmot

maroc'chino, -a [marok'kino] AG, SM/F Moroccan

Ma'rocco SM: **il ~** Morocco

ma'roso SM breaker

'marra SF hoe

Marra'kesh [marra'keʃ] SF Marrakesh

mar'rone AG INV brown ▶ SM (Bot) chestnut

mar'sala SM INV (vino) Marsala (wine)

Mar'siglia [mar'siʎʎa] SF Marseilles

mar'sina SF tails pl, tail coat

mar'supio SM (Zool) pouch, marsupium

mart. ABBR (= martedì) Tue(s)

'Marte SM (Astr, Mitologia) Mars

martedì SM INV Tuesday; **di** o **il ~** on Tuesdays; **oggi è ~ 3 aprile** (the date) today is Tuesday 3rd April; **~ stavo male** I wasn't well on Tuesday; **il giornale di ~** Tuesday's newspaper; **~ grasso** Shrove Tuesday

martel'lante AG (fig: dolore) throbbing

martel'lare/72/ VT to hammer ▶ VI (pulsare) to throb; (: cuore) to thump

martel'letto SM (di pianoforte) hammer; (di macchina da scrivere) typebar; (di giudice, nelle vendite all'asta) gavel; (Med) percussion hammer

mar'tello SM hammer; (di uscio) knocker; **suonare a ~** (fig: campane) to sound the tocsin; **~ pneumatico** pneumatic drill

marti'netto SM (Tecn) jack

martin'gala SF (di giacca) half-belt; (di cavallo) martingale

'martire SMF martyr

mar'tirio SM martyrdom; (fig) agony, torture

martori'are/19/ VT to torment, torture

mar'xismo SM Marxism

mar'xista, -i, -e AG, SM/F Marxist

marza'pane [martsa'pane] SM marzipan

marzi'ale [mar'tsjale] AG martial

'marzo ['martso] SM March; vedi **luglio**

marzo'lino, -a [martso'lino] AG March cpd

mascalzo'nata [maskaltso'nata] SF dirty trick

mascal'zone [maskal'tsone] SM rascal, scoundrel

mas'cara SM INV mascara

mascar'pone SM soft cream cheese often used in desserts

ma'scella [maʃʃɛlla] SF (Anat) jaw

'maschera ['maskera] SF mask; (travestimento) disguise; (per un ballo ecc) fancy dress; (Teat, Cine) usher/usherette; (personaggio del teatro) stock character; **in ~** (mascherato) masked; **ballo in ~** fancy-dress ball; **gettare la ~** (fig) to reveal o.s.; **~ antigas/subacquea** gas/diving mask; **~ di bellezza** face pack

masche'rare [maske'rare] **/72/** VT to mask; (travestire) to disguise; to dress up; (fig: celare) to hide, conceal; (Mil) to camouflage; **mascherarsi** VPR: **mascherarsi da** to disguise o.s. as; to dress up as; (fig) to masquerade as

masche'rina [maske'rina] SF (piccola maschera) mask; (di animale) patch; (di scarpe) toe-cap; (Aut) radiator grill

mas'chile [mas'kile] AG masculine; (sesso, popolazione) male; (abiti) men's; (per ragazzi: scuola) boys'

mas'chilista, -i, -e AG, SM/F (uomo) (male) chauvinist, sexist; (donna) sexist

'maschio, -a ['maskjo] AG (Biol) male; (virile) manly ▶ SM (anche Zool, Tecn) male; (uomo) man; (ragazzo) boy; (figlio) son

masco'lino, -a AG masculine

mas'cotte [mas'kɔt] SF INV mascot

maso'chismo [mazo'kizmo] SM masochism

maso'chista, -i, -e [mazo'kista] AG masochistic ▶ SM/F masochist

'massa SF mass; (di gente) mass, multitude; (Elettr) earth; **una ~ di** (di errori ecc) heaps of, masses of; **in ~** (Comm) in bulk; (tutti insieme) en masse; **adunata in ~** mass meeting; **manifestazione/cultura di ~** mass demonstration/culture; **produrre in ~** to mass-produce; **la ~ (del popolo)** the masses pl

massa'crante AG exhausting, gruelling

massa'crare /72/ VT to massacre, slaughter

mas'sacro SM massacre, slaughter; (fig) mess, disaster

massaggi'are [massad'dʒare] /62/ VT to massage

massaggia'tore, -'trice [massad̪dʒa'tore] SM/F masseur (masseuse)

mas'saggio [mas'saddʒo] SM massage; **~ cardiaco** cardiac massage

mas'saia SF housewife

masse'ria SF large farm

masse'rizie [masse'rittsje] SFPL (household) furnishings

massicci'ata [massit'tʃata] SF (di strada, ferrovia) ballast

mas'siccio, -a, -ci, -ce [mas'sittʃo] AG (oro, legno) solid; (palazzo) massive; (corporatura) stout ▶ SM (Geo) massif

'massima SF vedi **massimo**

massi'male SM maximum; (Comm) ceiling, limit

'massimo, -a AG, SM maximum ▶ SF (sentenza, regola) maxim; (Meteor) maximum temperature; **in linea di massima** generally speaking; **arrivare entro il tempo ~** to arrive within the time limit; **al ~** at (the) most; **sfruttare qc al ~** to make full use of sth; **arriverò al ~ alle 5** I'll arrive at 5 at the latest; **erano presenti le massime autorità** all the most important dignitaries were there; **il ~ della pena** (Dir) the maximum penalty

mas'sivo, -a AG (intervento) en masse; (emigrazione) mass; (emorragia) massive

'masso SM rock, boulder

mas'sone SM freemason

massone'ria SF freemasonry

mas'sonico, -a, -ci, -che AG masonic

mas'tello SM tub

masteriz'zare [masterid'dzare] /72/ VT (CD, DVD) to burn

masterizza'tore [masteriddza'tore] SM CD burner o writer

masti'care /20/ VT to chew

'mastice ['mastitʃe] SM mastic; (per vetri) putty

mas'tino SM mastiff

masto'dontico, -a, -ci, -che AG gigantic

mastur'barsi /72/ VPR to masturbate

masturbazi'one [masturbat'tsjone] SF masturbation

ma'tassa SF skein

mate'matico, -a, -ci, -che AG mathematical ▶ SM/F mathematician ▶ SF mathematics sg

materas'sino SM mat; **~ gonfiabile** air bed

mate'rasso SM mattress; **~ a molle** spring o interior-sprung mattress

ma'teria SF (Fisica) matter; (Tecn, Comm) material, matter no pl; (disciplina) subject; (argomento) subject matter, material; **in ~ di** (per quanto concerne) on the subject of; **prima di entrare in ~ ...** before discussing the matter in hand ...; **un esperto in ~ (di musica ecc)** an expert on the subject (of music etc); **sono ignorante in ~** I know nothing about it; **~ cerebrale** cerebral matter; **~ grassa** fat; **~ grigia** (anche fig) grey matter; **materie plastiche** plastics; **materie prime** raw materials

materi'ale AG material; (fig: grossolano) rough, rude ▶ SM material; (insieme di strumenti ecc) equipment no pl, materials pl; **~ da costruzione** building materials pl

materia'lista, -i, -e AG materialistic ▶ SM/F materialist

materializ'zarsi [materjalid'dzarsi] /72/ VPR to materialize

material'mente AV (fisicamente) materially; (economicamente) financially

maternità SF motherhood, maternity; (clinica) maternity hospital; (reparto) maternity ward; **in (congedo di) ~** on maternity leave

ma'terno, -a AG (amore, cura ecc) maternal, motherly; (nonno) maternal; (lingua, terra) mother cpd; vedi anche **scuola**

ma'tita SF pencil; **matite colorate** coloured pencils; **~ per gli occhi** eyeliner (pencil)

ma'trice [ma'tritʃe] SF matrix; (Comm) counterfoil; (fig: origine) background

ma'tricola SF (registro) register; (numero) registration number; (nell'università) freshman, fresher (BRIT col)

ma'trigna [ma'triɲɲa] SF stepmother

matrimoni'ale AG matrimonial, marriage cpd; **camera/letto ~** double room/bed

matri'monio SM marriage, matrimony; (durata) marriage, married life; (cerimonia) wedding

ma'trona SF (fig) matronly woman

matta'toio SM abattoir (BRIT), slaughterhouse

mat'tina SF morning; **la** o **alla** o **di ~** in the morning; **di prima ~, la ~ presto** early in the morning; **dalla ~ alla sera** (*continuamente*) from morning to night; (*improvvisamente: cambiare*) overnight

matti'nata SF morning; (*spettacolo*) matinée, afternoon performance; **in ~** in the course of the morning; **nella ~** in the morning; **nella tarda ~** at the end of the morning; **nella tarda ~ di sabato** late on Saturday morning

mattini'ero, -a AG: **essere ~** to be an early riser

mat'tino SM morning; **di buon ~** early in the morning

'matto, -a AG mad, crazy; (*fig: falso*) false, imitation; (*opaco*) matt, dull ▶ SM/F madman/woman; **avere una voglia matta di qc** to be dying for sth; **far diventare ~ qn** to drive sb mad o crazy; **una gabbia di matti** (*fig*) a madhouse

mat'tone SM brick; (*fig*): **questo libro/film è un ~** this book/film is heavy going

matto'nella SF tile

mattu'tino, -a AG morning *cpd*

matu'rare/72/ VI (*anche:* **maturarsi**: *frutta, grano*) to ripen; (*ascesso*) to come to a head; (*fig: persona, idea, Econ*) to mature ▶ VT to ripen, to (make) mature; **~ una decisione** to come to a decision

maturità SF maturity; (*di frutta*) ripeness, maturity; (*Ins*) school-leaving examination, ≈ GCE A-levels (*BRIT*)

ma'turo, -a AG mature; (*frutto*) ripe, mature

ma'tusa SM INV/F INV (*scherzoso*) old fogey

Mauri'tania SF: **la ~** Mauritania

Mau'rizio [mau'rittsjo] SF: **(l'isola di) ~** Mauritius

mauso'leo SM mausoleum

max. ABBR (= *massimo*) max

'maxi... PREFISSO maxi...

maxipro'cesso [maksipro'tʃɛsso] SM *see note*

> A *maxiprocesso* is a criminal trial which is characterized by the large number of co-defendants. These people are usually members of terrorist or criminal organizations. The trials are often lengthy and many witnesses may be called to give evidence.

maxis'chermo [maksis'kermo] SM giant screen

'mazza ['mattsa] SF (*bastone*) club; (*martello*) sledge-hammer; (*Sport: da golf*) club; (: *da baseball, cricket*) bat

maz'zata [mat'tsata] SF (*anche fig*) heavy blow

maz'zetta [mat'tsetta] SF (*di banconote ecc*) bundle; (*fig*) rake-off

'mazzo ['mattso] SM (*di fiori, chiavi ecc*) bunch; (*di carte da gioco*) pack

MC SIGLA = **Macerata**

m.c.d. ABBR (= *minimo comune denominatore*) lcd

m.c.m. ABBR (= *minimo comune multiplo*) lcm

ME SIGLA = **Messina**

me PRON me; **me stesso, me stessa** myself; **sei bravo quanto me** you are as clever as I (am) o as me

me'andro SM meander

M.E.C. [mɛk] ABBR M = **Mercato Comune Europeo**

'Mecca SF (*anche fig*): **La ~** Mecca

meccanica'mente AV mechanically

mec'canico, -a, -ci, -che AG mechanical ▶ SM mechanic ▶ SF mechanics *sg*; (*attività tecnologica*) mechanical engineering; (*meccanismo*) mechanism; **officina meccanica** garage

mecca'nismo SM mechanism

meccaniz'zare [mekkanid'dzare] /72/ VT to mechanize

meccanizzazi'one [mekkaniddzat'tsjone] SF mechanization

meccanogra'fia SF (*mechanical*) data processing

meccano'grafico, -a, -ci, -che AG: **centro ~** data processing department

mece'nate [metʃe'nate] SM patron

mèche [mɛʃ] SF INV streak; **farsi le ~** to have one's hair streaked

me'daglia [me'daʎʎa] SF medal; **~ d'oro** (*oggetto*) gold medal; (*persona*) gold medallist (*BRIT*) o medalist (*US*)

medagli'one [medaʎ'ʎone] SM (*Archit*) medallion; (*gioiello*) locket

me'desimo, -a AG same; (*in persona*): **io ~** I myself

'media SF *vedi* **medio**

media'mente AV on average

medi'ano, -a AG median; (*valore*) mean ▶ SM (*Calcio*) half-back

medi'ante PREP by means of

medi'are/19/ VT (*fare da mediatore*) to act as mediator in; (*Mat*) to average

medi'ato, -a AG indirect

media'tore, -'trice SM/F mediator; (*Comm*) middle man, agent; **fare da ~ fra** to mediate between

mediazi'one [medjat'tsjone] SF mediation; (*Comm: azione, compenso*) brokerage

medica'mento SM medicine, drug

medi'care/20/ VT to treat; (*ferita*) to dress

medi'cato, -a AG (*garza, shampoo*) medicated

medicazi'one [medikat'tsjone] SF treatment, medication dressing; **fare una ~ a qn** to dress sb's wounds

medi'cina [medi'tʃina] SF medicine; **~ legale** forensic medicine

medici'nale [meditʃi'nale] AG medicinal ▶ SM drug, medicine

'**medico, -a, -ci, -che** AG medical ▶ SM doctor;
~ **di bordo** ship's doctor; ~ **di famiglia**
family doctor; ~ **fiscale** *doctor who examines
patients signed off sick for a lengthy period by their
private doctor*; ~ **generico** general
practitioner, GP

medie'vale AG medieval

'**medio, -a** AG average; (*punto, ceto*) middle;
(*altezza, statura*) medium ▶ SM (*dito*) middle
finger ▶ SF average; (*Mat*) mean; (*Ins: voto*)
end-of-term average; **medie** SFPL *vedi* **scuola
media**; **licenza media** *leaving certificate
awarded at the end of 3 years of secondary
education*; **in media** on average; **al di
sopra/sotto della media** above/below
average; **viaggiare ad una media di ...**
to travel at an average speed of ...; **il M~
Oriente** the Middle East

medi'ocre AG (*gen*) mediocre; (*qualità, stipendio*)
poor

mediocrità SF mediocrity; poorness

medioe'vale AG = **medievale**

Medio'evo SM Middle Ages *pl*

medita'bondo, -a AG thoughtful

medi'tare /72/ VT to ponder over, meditate
on; (*progettare*) to plan, think out ▶ VI to
meditate

medi'tato, -a AG (*gen*) meditated; (*parole*)
carefully-weighed; (*vendetta*) premeditated;
ben ~ (*piano*) well worked-out, neat

meditazi'one [meditat'tsjone] SF
meditation

mediter'raneo, -a AG Mediterranean;
il (mare) M~ the Mediterranean (Sea)

'**medium** SM INV/F INV medium

me'dusa SF (*Zool*) jellyfish

mega SM INV (*Inform*) meg

mega'byte SM INV (*Inform*) megabyte

me'gafono SM megaphone

mega'lomane AG, SMF megalomaniac

me'gera [me'dʒɛra] SF (*peg: donna*) shrew

'**meglio** ['mɛʎʎo] AV, AG INV better; (*con senso
superlativo*) best ▶ SM (*la cosa migliore*): **il ~** the
best (thing); **faresti ~ ad andartene** you
had better leave; **alla ~** as best one can;
andar di bene in ~ to get better and better;
fare del proprio ~ to do one's best; **per il ~**
for the best; **aver la ~ su qn** to get the
better of sb

'**mela** SF apple; ~ **cotogna** quince

mela'grana SF pomegranate

melan'zana [melan'dzana] SF aubergine
(*BRIT*), eggplant (*US*)

me'lassa SF molasses *sg*, treacle

melato'nina SF melatonin

me'lenso, -a AG dull, stupid

me'lissa SF (*Bot*) balm

mel'lifluo, -a AG (*peg*) sugary, honeyed

'**melma** SF mud, mire

'**melo** SM apple tree

melo'dia SF melody

me'lodico, -a, -ci, -che AG melodic

melodi'oso, -a AG melodious

melo'dramma, -i SM melodrama

me'lone SM (musk) melon

'**membra** SFPL *vedi* **membro**

mem'brana SF membrane

'**membro** SM (*pl(m)* **membri**: *person*) member;
(*pl(f)* **membra**: *arto*) limb

memo'rabile AG memorable

memo'randum SM INV memorandum

'**memore** AG: ~ **di** (*ricordando*) mindful of;
(*riconoscente*) grateful for

me'moria SF (*anche Inform*) memory;
memorie SFPL (*opera autobiografica*) memoirs;
a ~ (*imparare, sapere*) by heart; **a ~ d'uomo**
within living memory; ~ **di sola lettura**
(*Inform*) read-only memory; ~ **tampone**
(*Inform*) buffer

memori'ale SM (*raccolta di memorie*) memoirs
pl; (*Dir*) memorial

memoriz'zare [memorid'dzare] /72/ VT (*gen*)
to memorize; (*Inform*) to store

memorizzazi'one [memoriddzat'tsjone] SF
memorization; storage

'**mena** SF scheme

mena'dito : a ~ *av* perfectly, thoroughly;
sapere qc a ~ to have sth at one's fingertips

mena'gramo SM INV/F INV jinx, Jonah

me'nare /72/ VT to lead; (*picchiare*) to hit, beat;
(*dare: colpi*) to deal; ~ **la coda** (*cane*) to wag
its tail; ~ **qc per le lunghe** to drag sth out;
~ **il can per l'aia** (*fig*) to beat about (*BRIT*) o
around (*US*) the bush

mendi'cante SMF beggar

mendi'care /20/ VT to beg for ▶ VI to beg

menefre'ghismo [menefre'gizmo] SM (*col*)
couldn't-care-less attitude

me'ninge [me'nindʒe] SF (*Med*) meninx;
spremersi le meningi to rack one's brains

menin'gite [menin'dʒite] SF meningitis

me'nisco SM (*Anat, Mat, Fisica*) meniscus

(**PAROLA CHIAVE**)

'**meno** AV **1** (*in minore misura*) less; **dovresti
mangiare meno** you should eat less, you
shouldn't eat so much; **è sempre meno
facile** it's getting less and less easy; **ne
voglio di meno** I don't want so much
2 (*comparativo*): **meno ... di** not as ... as, less ...
than; **sono meno alto di te** I'm not as tall
as you (are), I'm less tall than you (are);
meno ... che not as ... as, less ... than; **meno
che mai** less than ever; **è meno
intelligente che ricco** he's more rich than
intelligent; **meno fumo più mangio** the
less I smoke the more I eat; **meno di quanto
pensassi** less than I thought

3 (*superlativo*) least; **il meno dotato degli studenti** the least gifted of the students; **è quello che compro meno spesso** it's the one I buy least often

4 (*Mat*) minus; **8 meno 5** 8 minus 5, 8 take away 5; **sono le 8 meno un quarto** it's a quarter to 8; **meno 5 gradi** 5 degrees below zero, minus 5 degrees; **mille euro in meno** a thousand euros less; **ha preso 6 meno** (*a scuola*) he scraped a pass; **cento euro meno le spese** a hundred euros minus *o* less expenses

5 (*fraseologia*): **quanto meno poteva telefonare** he could at least have phoned; **non so se accettare o meno** I don't know whether to accept or not; **non essere da meno di** not to be outdone by; **fare a meno di qc/qn** to do without sth/sb; **non potevo fare a meno di ridere** I couldn't help laughing; **meno male!** thank goodness!; **meno male che sei arrivato** it's a good job that you've come

▶ AG INV (*tempo, denaro*) less; (*errori, persone*) fewer; **ha fatto meno errori di tutti** he made fewer mistakes than anyone, he made the fewest mistakes of all

▶ SM INV **1: il meno** (*il minimo*) the least; **parlare del più e del meno** to talk about this and that; **era il meno che ti potesse succedere** it was the least you could have expected

2 (*Mat*) minus

▶ PREP (*eccetto*) except (for), apart from; **tutti meno lui** everybody apart from *o* except him; **a meno che, a meno di** unless; **a meno che non piova** unless it rains; **non posso, a meno di prendere ferie** I can't, unless I take some leave; *vedi anche* **più**

meno'mare/72/ VT (*danneggiare*) to maim, disable

meno'mato, -a AG (*persona*) disabled ▶ SM/F disabled person

menomazi'one [menomat'tsjone] SF disablement

meno'pausa SF menopause

'mensa SF (*locale*) canteen; (: *Mil*) mess; (: *nelle università*) refectory

men'sile AG monthly ▶ SM (*periodico*) monthly (magazine); (*stipendio*) monthly salary

mensil'mente AV (*ogni mese*) every month; (*una volta al mese*) monthly

'mensola SF bracket; (*ripiano*) shelf; (*Archit*) corbel

'menta SF mint; (*anche*: **menta piperita**) peppermint; (: *bibita*) peppermint cordial; (: *caramella*) mint, peppermint

men'tale AG mental

mentalità SF INV mentality

mental'mente AV mentally

'mente SF mind; **imparare/sapere qc a ~** to learn/know sth by heart; **avere in ~ qc** to have sth in mind; **avere in ~ di fare qc** to intend to do sth; **fare venire in ~ qc a qn** to remind sb of sth; **mettersi in ~ di fare qc** to make up one's mind to do sth; **passare di ~ a qn** to slip sb's mind; **tenere a ~ qc** to bear sth in mind; **a ~ fredda** objectively; **lasciami fare ~ locale** let me think

mente'catto, -a AG half-witted ▶ SM/F halfwit, imbecile

men'tire/17/ VI to lie

men'tito, -a AG: **sotto mentite spoglie** under false pretences (*BRIT*) *o* pretenses (*US*)

'mento SM chin; **doppio ~** double chin

men'tolo SM menthol

'mentre CONG (*temporale*) while; (*avversativo*) whereas ▶ SM: **in quel ~** at that very moment

menù SM INV (set) menu; **~ turistico** set *o* tourists' menu

menzio'nare [mentsjo'nare] /**72**/ VT to mention

menzi'one [men'tsjone] SF mention; **fare ~ di** to mention

men'zogna [men'tsɔɲɲa] SF lie

menzo'gnero, -a[mentsoɲ'ɲɛro] AG false, untrue

mera'viglia [mera'viʎʎa] SF amazement, wonder; (*persona, cosa*) marvel, wonder; **a ~** perfectly, wonderfully

meravigli'are [meraviʎ'ʎare] /**27**/ VT to amaze, astonish; **meravigliarsi**VPR: **meravigliarsi (di)** to marvel (at); (*stupirsi*) to be amazed (at), be astonished (at); **mi meraviglio di te!** I'm surprised at you!; **non c'è da meravigliarsi** it's not surprising

meravigli'oso, -a[meraviʎ'ʎoso] AG wonderful, marvellous (*BRIT*), marvelous (*US*)

merc. ABBR (= *mercoledì*) Wed

mer'cante SM merchant; **~ d'arte** art dealer; **~ di cavalli** horse dealer

mercanteggi'are [merkanted'dʒare] /**62**/ VT (*onore, voto*) to sell ▶ VI to bargain, haggle

mercan'tile AG commercial, mercantile; (*nave, marina*) merchant *cpd* ▶ SM (*nave*) merchantman

mercan'zia [merkan'tsia] SF merchandise, goods *pl*

merca'tino SM (*rionale*) local street market; (*Econ*) unofficial stock market

mer'cato SM market; **di ~** (*economia, prezzo, ricerche*) market *cpd*; **mettere** *o* **lanciare qc sul ~** to launch sth on the market; **a buon ~** cheap; **~ dei cambi** exchange market; **M~ Comune (Europeo)** (European) Common Market; **~ del lavoro** labour market, job market; **~ nero** black market; **~ al rialzo/al ribasso** (*Borsa*) sellers'/buyers' market

'**merce** ['mɛrtʃe] SF goods *pl*, merchandise; **~ deperibile** perishable goods *pl*

mercè [mer'tʃe] SF mercy; **essere alla ~ di qn** to be at sb's mercy

merce'nario, -a [mertʃe'narjo] AG, SM mercenary

merce'ria [mertʃe'ria] SF (*articoli*) haberdashery (BRIT), notions *pl* (US); (*bottega*) haberdasher's shop (BRIT), notions store (US)

mercoledì SM INV Wednesday; **di** *o* **il ~ on** Wednesdays; **~ delle Ceneri** Ash Wednesday; *see notevedi anche* **martedì**

> In the Catholic church, *Mercoledì delle Ceneri* signals the beginning of Lent. Churchgoers are marked on the forehead with ash from the burning of the olive branch. Ash Wednesday is traditionally a day of fasting, abstinence and repentance.

mer'curio SM mercury

'**merda** SF (*col*) shit (!)

me'renda SF afternoon snack

meren'dina SF snack

meridi'ano, -a AG (*di mezzogiorno*) midday *cpd*, noonday ▶ SM meridian ▶ SF (*orologio*) sundial

meridio'nale AG southern ▶ SMF southerner

meridi'one SM south

me'ringa, -ghe SF (*Cuc*) meringue

meri'tare /**72**/ VT to deserve, merit ▶ VB IMPERS (*valere la pena*): **merita andare** it's worth going; **non merita neanche parlarne** it's not worth talking about; **per quel che merita** for what it's worth

meri'tevole AG worthy

'**merito** SM merit; (*valore*) worth; **dare ~ a qn di** to give sb credit for; **finire a pari ~** to finish joint first (*o* second *etc*); to tie; **in ~ a** as regards, with regard to; **entrare nel ~ di una questione** to go into a matter; **non so niente in ~** I don't know anything about it

meritocra'zia [meritokrat'tsia] SF meritocracy

meri'torio, -a AG praiseworthy

mer'letto SM lace

'**merlo** SM (*Zool*) blackbird; (*Archit*) battlement

mer'luzzo [mer'luttso] SM (*Zool*) cod

'**mescere** ['meʃʃere] /**29**/ VT to pour (out)

meschinità [meskini'ta] SF wretchedness; meagreness; meanness, narrow-mindedness

mes'chino, -a [mes'kino] AG wretched; (*scarso*) meagre (BRIT), meager (US), scanty, poor; (*persona: gretta*) mean; (: *limitata*) narrow-minded, petty; **fare una figura meschina** to cut a poor figure

'**mescita** ['meʃʃita] SF wine shop

mesci'uto, -a [meʃ'ʃuto] PP *di* **mescere**

mesco'lanza [mesko'lantsa] SF mixture

mesco'lare /**72**/ VT to mix; (*vini, colori*) to blend; (*mettere in disordine*) to mix up, muddle up; (*carte*) to shuffle; **mescolarsi** VPR to mix; to blend; to get mixed up; (*fig*) **mescolarsi in** to get mixed up in, meddle in

'**mese** SM month; **il ~ scorso** last month; **il corrente ~** this month

'**messa** SF (*Rel*) mass; (*il mettere*): **~ a fuoco** focusing; **~ in moto** starting; **~ in piega** (*acconciatura*) set; **~ a punto** (*Tecn*) adjustment; (*Aut*) tuning; (*fig*) clarification; **~ in scena** = **messinscena**

messagge'rie [messaddʒe'rie] SFPL (*ditta: di distribuzione*) distributors; (: *di trasporto*) freight company

messag'gero [messad'dʒero] SM messenger

messaggiare [messa'dzare] VI (*col*) to message ▶ VT to message; **~ con qn** to message sb; **~ qn su Facebook** to facebook sb

messaggi'arsi [messad'dʒarsi] /**72**/ VPR to text; **messaggiamoci** we'll text each other

messag'gino [messad'dʒino] SM (*di telefonino*) text (message)

mes'saggio [mes'saddʒo] SM message; **~ istantaneo** instant message

messag'gistica [messad'dʒistika] SF: **~ immediata** (*Inform*) instant messaging; **programma di ~ immediata** instant messenger

mes'sale SM (*Rel*) missal

'**messe** SF harvest

Mes'sia SM INV (*Rel*): **il ~** the Messiah

messi'cano, -a AG, SM/F Mexican

'**Messico** SM: **il ~** Mexico; **Città del ~** Mexico City

messin'scena [messin'ʃena] SF (*Teat*) production

'**messo, -a** PP *di* **mettere** ▶ SM messenger

mestie'rante SMF (*peg*) money-grubber; (: *scrittore*) hack

mesti'ere SM (*professione*) job; (*artigianale*) craft; (*manuale*) trade; (*fig: abilità nel lavoro*) skill, technique; **di ~** by *o* trade; **essere del ~** to know the tricks of the trade

mes'tizia [mes'tittsja] SF sadness, melancholy

'**mesto, -a** AG sad, melancholy

'**mestolo** SM (*Cuc*) ladle

mestru'ale AG menstrual

mestruazi'one [mestruat'tsjone] SF menstruation; **avere le mestruazioni** to have one's period

'**meta** SF destination; (*fig*) aim, goal

metà SF INV half; (*punto di mezzo*) middle; **dividere qc a** *o* **per ~** to divide sth in half, halve sth; **fare a ~ (di qc con qn)** to go halves (with sb in sth); **a ~ prezzo** at half price; **a ~ settimana** midweek; **a ~ strada** halfway; **verso la ~ del mese** halfway through the month, towards the middle of the month; **dire le cose a ~** to leave some things unsaid; **fare le cose a ~** to leave things half-done; **la mia dolce ~** (col, scherzoso) my better half

metabo'lismo SM metabolism

meta'done SM methadone

meta'fisica SF metaphysics sg

me'tafora SF metaphor

meta'forico, -a, -ci, -che AG metaphorical

me'tallico, -a, -ci, -che AG (di metallo) metal cpd; (splendore, rumore ecc) metallic

metalliz'zato, -a [metallid'dzato] AG (verniciatura) metallic

me'tallo SM metal; **di ~** metal cpd

metallur'gia [metallur'dʒia] SF metallurgy

metalmec'canico, -a, -ci, -che AG engineering cpd ▶ SM engineering worker

meta'morfosi SF metamorphosis

me'tano SM methane

me'teora SF meteor

meteo'rite SM meteorite

meteorolo'gia [meteorolo'dʒia] SF meteorology

meteoro'logico, -a, -ci, -che [meteoro'lɔdʒiko] AG meteorological, weather cpd

meteo'rologo, -a, -ghi, -ghe SM/F meteorologist

me'ticcio, -a, -ci, -ce [me'tittʃo] SM/F half-caste, half-breed

meticolosità SF meticulousness

metico'loso, -a AG meticulous

me'todico, -a, -ci, -che AG methodical

'metodo SM method; (manuale) tutor (BRIT), manual; **far qc con/senza ~** to do sth methodically/unmethodically

me'traggio [me'traddʒo] SM (Sartoria) length; (Cine) footage; **film a lungo ~** feature film; **film a corto ~** short film

metra'tura SF length

'metrico, -a, -ci, -che AG metric; (Poesia) metrical ▶ SF metrics sg

'metro SM metre (BRIT), meter (US); (nastro) tape measure; (asta) (metre) rule

metrò SM INV underground (BRIT), subway (US)

metro'notte SM INV night security guard

me'tropoli SF metropolis

metropoli'tano, -a AG metropolitan ▶ SF underground (BRIT), subway (US); **metropolitana leggera** metro (mainly on the surface)

metroses'suale AG metrosexual

'mettere /63/ VT to put; (abito) to put on; (: portare) to wear; (installare: telefono) to put in;

~ fame/allegria a qn (fig: provocare) to make sb hungry/happy; (supporre): **mettiamo che ...** let's suppose o say that ...; **mettersi** VPR (persona) to put o.s.; (oggetto) to go; (disporsi: faccenda) to turn out; **mettersi a** (cominciare) to begin to, start to; **mettersi a piangere/ridere** to start crying/laughing, start o begin to cry/laugh; **mettersi a sedere** to sit down; **mettersi al lavoro** to set to work; **mettersi a letto** to get into bed; (per malattia) to take to one's bed; **mettersi il cappello** to put on one's hat; **mettersi sotto** to get down to things; **mettersi in società** to set up in business; **si sono messi insieme** (coppia) they've started going out together (BRIT) o dating (US); **mettersi con qn** (in società) to team up with sb; (in coppia) to start going out with sb; **mettterci: mettterci molta cura/molto tempo** to take a lot of care/a lot of time; **mettercela tutta** to do one's best; **ci ho messo 3 ore per venire** it's taken me 3 hours to get here; **~ un annuncio sul giornale** to place an advertisement in the paper; **~ a confronto** to compare; **~ in conto** (somma ecc) to put on account; **~ in luce** (problemi, errori) to stress, highlight; **~ a tacere qn/qc** to keep sb/sth quiet; **~ su casa** to set up house; **~ su un negozio** to start a shop; **~ su peso** to put on weight; **~ via** to put away

mez'zadro [med'dzadro] SM (Agr) sharecropper

mezza'luna [meddza'luna] (pl **mezzelune**) SF half-moon; (dell'islamismo) crescent; (coltello) (semicircular) chopping knife

mezza'nino [meddza'nino] SM mezzanine (floor)

mez'zano, -a [med'dzano] AG (medio) average, medium; (figlio) middle cpd ▶ SM/F (intermediario) go-between; (ruffiano) pimp

mezza'notte [meddza'nɔtte] SF midnight

'mezzo, -a ['mɛddzo] AG half; **un ~ litro/panino** half a litre/roll ▶ AV half-; **~ morto** half-dead ▶ SM (metà) half; (parte centrale: di strada ecc) middle; (per raggiungere un fine) means sg; (veicolo) vehicle; (nell'indicare l'ora): **le nove e ~** half past nine; **mezzogiorno e ~** half past twelve ▶ SF: **la mezza** half-past twelve (in the afternoon); **mezzi** SMPL (possibilità economiche) means; **di mezza età** middle-aged; **aver una mezza idea di fare qc** to have half a mind to do sth; **è stato un ~ scandalo** it almost caused a scandal; **un soprabito di mezza stagione** a spring (o autumn) coat; **a mezza voce** in an undertone; **una volta e ~ più grande** one and a half times bigger; **di ~** middle, in the middle; **andarci di ~** (patir danno) to suffer; **esserci di ~** (ostacolo) to be in the way;

levarsi o **togliersi di** ~ to get out of the way; **mettersi di** ~ to interfere; **togliere di** ~ (*persona, cosa*) to get rid of; (*col: uccidere*) to bump off; **non c'è una via di** ~ there's no middle course; **in** ~ **a** in the middle of; **nel bel** ~ **(di)** right in the middle (of); **per** o **a** ~ **di** by means of; **a** ~ **corriere** by carrier; **mezzi di comunicazione di massa** mass media *pl*; **mezzi pubblici** public transport *sg*; **mezzi di trasporto** means of transport

mezzogi'orno [meddzo'dʒorno] SM midday, noon; (*Geo*) south; **a** ~ at 12 (o'clock) o midday o noon; **il** ~ **d'Italia** southern Italy

mezz'ora [med'dzora] SF half-hour, half an hour

MI SIGLA = **Milano**

mi PRON (*dav lo, la, li, le, ne diventa* **me**: *oggetto*) me; (*complemento di termine*) (to) me; (*riflessivo*) myself ▶ SM (*Mus*) E; (: *solfeggiando la scala*) mi; **mi aiuti?** will you help me?; **me ne ha parlato** he spoke to me about it, he told me about it; **mi servo da solo** I'll help myself

'mia *vedi* **mio**

miago'lare /**72**/ VI to miaow, mew

Mib SIGLA M, AG (= *indice borsa Milano*) Milan Stock Exchange Index

'mica SF (*Chim*) mica ▶ AV (*col*): **non ...** ~ not ... at all; **non sono** ~ **stanco** I'm not a bit tired; **non sarà** ~ **partito?** he wouldn't have left, would he?; ~ **male** not bad

'miccia, -ce ['mittʃa] SF fuse

micidi'ale [mitʃi'djale] AG fatal; (*dannosissimo*) deadly

'micio, -a, -ci, -cie ['mitʃo] SM/F pussy (cat)

microbiolo'gia [mikrobiolo'dʒia] SF microbiology

micro'blog [mikro'blɔg] SM INV microblog

'microbo SM microbe

microcir'cuito [mikrotʃir'kuito] SM microcircuit

micro'fibra SF microfibre

micro'film SM INV microfilm

mi'crofono SM microphone

microinfor'matica SF microcomputing

micro'onda SF microwave

microproces'sore [mikroprotʃes'sore] SM microprocessor

micros'copico, -a, -ci, -che AG microscopic

micros'copio SM microscope

micro'solco, -chi SM (*solco*) microgroove; (*disco: a 33 giri*) long-playing record, LP; (: *a 45 giri*) extended-play record, EP

micros'pia SF hidden microphone, bug (*col*)

mi'dollo (*pl(f)* **midolla**) SM (*Anat*) marrow; ~ **spinale** spinal cord; ~ **osseo** bone marrow

'mie *vedi* **mio**

mi'ele SM honey

mi'etere /**29**/ VT (*Agr*) to reap, harvest; (*fig: vite*) to take, claim

mietitrebbia'trice [mjetitrebbja'tritʃe] SF combine harvester

mieti'trice [mjeti'tritʃe] SF (*macchina*) harvester

mieti'tura SF (*raccolto*) harvest; (*lavoro*) harvesting; (*tempo*) harvest-time

'miglia ['miʎʎa] SFPL *di* **miglio¹**

migli'aio [miʎ'ʎajo] (*pl(f)* **migliaia**) SM thousand; **un** ~ **(di)** about a thousand; **a migliaia** by the thousand, in thousands

'miglio¹ ['miʎʎo] (*pl(f)* **miglia**) SM (*unità di misura*) mile; ~ **marino** o **nautico** nautical mile

'miglio² ['miʎʎo] SM (*Bot*) millet

migliora'mento [miʎʎora'mento] SM improvement

miglio'rare [miʎʎo'rare] /**72**/ VT, VI to improve

migli'ore [miʎ'ʎore] AG (*comparativo*) better; (*superlativo*) best ▶ SM: **il** ~ the best (thing) ▶ SMF: **il (la)** ~ the best (person); **il miglior vino di questa regione** the best wine in this area; **i migliori auguri** best wishes

miglio'ria [miʎʎo'ria] SF improvement

mignolo ['miɲɲolo] SM (*Anat*) little finger, pinkie; (: *dito del piede*) little toe

mi'grare /**72**/ VI to migrate

migrazi'one [migrat'tsjone] SF migration

'mila PL *di* **mille**

mila'nese AG Milanese ▶ SMF person from Milan; **i milanesi** the Milanese; **cotoletta alla** ~ (*Cuc*) Wiener schnitzel; **risotto alla** ~ (*Cuc*) risotto with saffron

Mi'lano SF Milan

miliar'dario, -a AG, SM/F millionaire

mili'ardo SM thousand million (*BRIT*), billion (*US*)

mili'are AG: **pietra** ~ milestone

milio'nario, -a AG, SM/F millionaire

mili'one SM million; **un** ~ **di euro** a million euros

mili'tante AG, SMF militant

mili'tanza [mili'tantsa] SF militancy

mili'tare /**72**/ VI (*Mil*) to be a soldier, serve; (*fig: in un partito*) to be a militant ▶ AG military ▶ SM serviceman; **fare il** ~ to do one's military service; ~ **di carriera** regular (soldier)

milita'resco, -a, -schi, -sche AG (*portamento*) military *cpd*

'milite SM soldier

mi'lizia [mi'littsja] SF (*corpo armato*) militia

milizi'ano [milit'tsjano] SM militiaman

millanta'tore, -'trice SM/F boaster

millante'ria SF (*qualità*) boastfulness

'mille (*pl* **mila**) NUM a o one thousand; **diecimila** ten thousand; ~ **euro** one thousand euros

mille'foglie [mille'fɔʎʎe] SM INV (*Cuc*) cream o vanilla slice

mil'lennio SM millennium
millepi'edi SM INV centipede
mil'lesimo, -a AG, SM thousandth
milli'grammo SM milligram(me)
mil'lilitro SM millilitre (BRIT), milliliter (US)
mil'limetro SM millimetre (BRIT), millimeter (US)
'milza ['miltsa] SF (Anat) spleen
mi'metico, -a, -ci, -che AG (arte) mimetic; **tuta mimetica** (Mil) camouflage
mime'tismo SM camouflage
mimetiz'zare [mimetid'dzare] /**72**/ VT to camouflage; **mimetizzarsi** VPR to camouflage o.s.
'mimica SF (arte) mime
'mimo SM (attore, componimento) mime
mi'mosa SF mimosa
min. ABBR (= minuto, minimo) min
'mina SF (esplosiva) mine; (di matita) lead
mi'naccia, -ce [mi'nattʃa] SF threat; **sotto la ~ di** under threat of
minacci'are [minat'tʃare] /**14**/ VT to threaten; **~ qn di morte** to threaten to kill sb; **~ di fare qc** to threaten to do sth; **minaccia di piovere** it looks like rain
minacci'oso, -a [minat'tʃoso] AG threatening
mi'nare /**72**/ VT (Mil) to mine; (fig) to undermine
mina'tore SM miner
mina'torio, -a AG threatening
minchi'one, -a [min'kjone] AG (col) idiotic ▶ SM/F idiot
mine'rale AG, SM mineral
mineralo'gia [mineralo'dʒia] SF mineralogy
mine'rario, -a AG (delle miniere) mining; (dei minerali) ore cpd
mi'nestra SF soup; **~ in brodo** noodle soup; **~ di verdura** vegetable soup
mines'trone SM thick vegetable and pasta soup
mingher'lino, -a [minger'lino] AG thin, slender
'mini AG INV mini ▶ SF INV miniskirt
minia'tura SF miniature
mini'bar SM INV minibar
minielabora'tore SM minicomputer
mini'era SF mine; **~ di carbone** coalmine; (impresa) colliery (BRIT), coalmine
mini'gonna SF miniskirt
minima'lista, -i, -e AG, SM/F minimalist
minimiz'zare [minimid'dzare] /**72**/ VT to minimize
'minimo, -a AG minimum, least, slightest; (piccolissimo) very small, slight; (il più basso) lowest, minimum ▶ SM minimum; **al ~** at least; **girare al ~** (Aut) to idle; **il ~ indispensabile** the bare minimum; **il ~ della pena** the minimum sentence

minis'tero SM (Pol, Rel) ministry; (governo) government; (Dir): **Pubblico M~** State Prosecutor; **M~ delle Finanze** Ministry of Finance, ≈ Treasury
mi'nistro SM (Pol, Rel) minister; **M~ delle Finanze** Minister of Finance, ≈ Chancellor of the Exchequer (BRIT)
mino'ranza [mino'rantsa] SF minority; **essere in ~** to be in the minority
mino'rato, -a AG handicapped ▶ SM/F physically (o mentally) handicapped person
minorazi'one [minorat'tsjone] SF handicap
Mi'norca SF Minorca
mi'nore AG (comparativo) less; (più piccolo) smaller; (numero) lower; (inferiore) lower, inferior; (meno importante) minor; (più giovane) younger; (superlativo) least; smallest; lowest, least important, youngest ▶ SM/F
= minorenne; in misura ~ to a lesser extent; **questo è il male ~** this is the lesser evil
mino'renne AG under age ▶ SM/F minor, person under age
mino'rile AG juvenile; **carcere ~** young offenders' institution; **delinquenza ~** juvenile delinquency
minori'tario, -a AG minority cpd
mi'nuscolo, -a AG (scrittura, carattere) small; (piccolissimo) tiny ▶ SF small letter ▶ SM small letters pl; (Tip) lower case; **scrivere tutto (in) ~** to write everything in small letters
mi'nuta SF rough copy, draft
mi'nuto, -a AG tiny, minute; (pioggia) fine; (corporatura) delicate, fine; (lavoro) detailed ▶ SM (unità di misura) minute; **al ~** (Comm) retail; **avere i minuti contati** to have very little time
mi'nuzia [mi'nuttsja] SF (cura) meticulousness; (particolare) detail
minuziosa'mente [minuttsjosa'mente] AV meticulously; in minute detail
minuzi'oso, -a [minut'tsjoso] AG (persona, descrizione) meticulous; (esame) minute
'mio, 'mia, mi'ei, 'mie DET: **il ~, la mia** etc my ▶ PRON: **il ~, la mia** etc mine ▶ SM: **ho speso del ~** I spent my own money ▶ SF: **la mia** (opinione) my view; **i miei** my family; **un ~ amico** a friend of mine; **per amor ~** for my sake; **è dalla mia** he is on my side; **anch'io ho avuto le mie** (disavventure) I've had my problems too; **ne ho fatta una delle mie!** (sciocchezze) I've done it again!; **cerco di stare sulle mie** I try to keep myself to myself
'miope AG short-sighted
mio'pia SF short-sightedness, myopia; (fig) short-sightedness
'mira SF (anche fig) aim; **avere una buona/ cattiva ~** to be a good/bad shot; **prendere la ~** to take aim; **prendere di ~ qn** (fig) to pick on sb

m

mi'rabile AG admirable, wonderful

mi'racolo SM miracle

miraco'loso, -a AG miraculous

mi'raggio [mi'radd3o] SM mirage

mi'rare /72/ VI: **~ a** to aim at

mi'rato, -a AG targeted

mi'riade SF myriad

mi'rino SM (Tecn) sight; (Fot) viewer, viewfinder

mir'tillo SM bilberry (BRIT), blueberry (US), whortleberry

'**mirto** SM myrtle

mi'santropo, -a SM/F misanthropist

mi'scela [miʃʃela] SF mixture; (di caffè) blend

miscel'lanea [miʃʃel'lanea] SF miscellany

'**mischia** ['miskja] SF scuffle; (Rugby) scrum, scrummage

mischi'are [mis'kjare] /19/ VT, **mischi'arsi** VPR to mix, blend

misco'noscere [misko'noʃʃere] /26/ VT (qualità, coraggio ecc) to fail to appreciate

miscre'dente AG (Rel) misbelieving; (: incredulo) unbelieving ▸ SMF misbeliever; unbeliever

mis'cuglio [mis'kuʎʎo] SM mixture, hotchpotch, jumble

'**mise** VB vedi **mettere**

mise'rabile AG (infelice) miserable, wretched; (povero) poverty-stricken; (di scarso valore) miserable

mi'seria SF extreme poverty; (infelicità) misery; **miserie** SFPL (del mondo ecc) misfortunes, troubles; **costare una ~** to cost next to nothing; **piangere ~** to plead poverty; **ridursi in ~** to be reduced to poverty; **porca ~!** (col) (bloody) hell!

miseri'cordia SF mercy, pity

misericordi'oso, -a AG merciful

'**misero, -a** AG miserable, wretched; (povero) poverty-stricken; (insufficiente) miserable

mis'fatto SM misdeed, crime

'**misi** VB vedi **mettere**

mi'sogino [mi'zɔdʒino] SM misogynist

'**missile** SM missile; **~ cruise** o **di crociera** cruise missile; **~ terra-aria** surface-to-air missile

missio'nario, -a AG, SM/F missionary

missi'one SF mission

misteri'oso, -a AG mysterious

mis'tero SM mystery; **fare ~ di qc** to make a mystery out of sth; **quanti misteri!** why all the mystery?

'**mistico, -a, -ci, -che** AG mystic(al) ▸ SM mystic

mistifi'care /20/ VT to fool, bamboozle

'**misto, -a** AG mixed; (scuola) mixed, coeducational ▸ SM mixture; **un tessuto in ~ lino** a linen mix

mis'tura SF mixture

mi'sura SF measure; (misurazione, dimensione) measurement; (taglia) size; (provvedimento) measure, step; (moderazione) moderation; (Mus) time; (: divisione) bar; (fig: limite) bounds pl, limit; **in ~ di** in accordance with, according to; **nella ~ in cui** inasmuch as, insofar as; **in giusta ~** moderately; **oltre ~** beyond measure; **su ~** made to measure; **in ugual ~** equally, in the same way; **a ~ d'uomo** on a human scale; **passare la ~** to overstep the mark, go too far; **prendere le misure a qn** to take sb's measurements, measure sb; **prendere le misure di qc** to measure sth; **ho preso le mie misure** I've taken the necessary steps; **non ha il senso della ~** he doesn't know when to stop; **~ di lunghezza/capacità** measure of length/capacity; **misure di sicurezza/prevenzione** safety/precautionary measures

misu'rare /72/ VT (ambiente, stoffa) to measure; (terreno) to survey; (abito) to try on; (pesare) to weigh; (fig: parole ecc) to weigh up; (: spese, cibo) to limit ▸ VI to measure; **misurarsi** VPR: **misurarsi con qn** to have a confrontation with sb; (competere) to compete with sb

misu'rato, -a AG (ponderato) measured; (prudente) cautious; (moderato) moderate

misurazi'one [mizurat'tsjone] SF measuring; (di terreni) surveying

'**mite** AG mild; (prezzo) moderate, reasonable

'**mitico, -a, -ci, -che** AG mythical

miti'gare /80/ VT to mitigate, lessen; (lenire) to soothe, relieve; **mitigarsi** VPR (odio) to subside; (tempo) to become milder

'**mitilo** SM mussel

'**mito** SM myth

mitolo'gia, -'gie [mitolo'dʒia] SF mythology

mito'logico, -a, -ci, -che [mito'lɔdʒiko] AG mythological

'**mitra** SF (Rel) mitre (BRIT), miter (US) ▸ SM INV (arma) sub-machine gun

mitragli'are [mitraʎ'ʎare] /27/ VT to machine-gun

mitraglia'tore, -'trice [mitraʎʎa'tore] AG: **fucile ~** sub-machine gun ▸ SF machine gun

mitteleuro'peo, -a AG Central European

mit'tente SMF sender

ml ABBR (= millilitro) ml

MLD SIGLA M = **Movimento per la Liberazione della Donna**

MM ABBR = **Metropolitana Milanese**

mm ABBR (= millimetro) mm

M.M. ABBR = **marina militare**

mms SIGLA M INV (= multimedia messaging service) (servizio) MMS (= multimedia messaging service); (messaggio) MMS message

MN SIGLA = **Mantova**

M/N, m/n ABBR (= *motonave*) MV

MO SIGLA = **Modena**

mo' SM: **a ~di** like; **a ~di esempio** by way of example

M.O. ABBR = **Medio Oriente**

'**mobile** AG mobile; (*parte di macchina*) moving; (*Dir: bene*) movable, personal ▶ SM (*arredamento*) piece of furniture; **mobili** SMPL (*mobilia*) furniture *sg*

mo'bilia SF furniture

mobili'are AG (*Dir*) personal, movable

mo'bilio SM = **mobilia**

mobilità SF mobility

mobili'tare /**72**/ VT to mobilize; ~ **l'opinione pubblica** to rouse public opinion

mobilitazi'one [mobilitat'tsjone] SF mobilization

mocas'sino SM moccasin

mocci'oso, -a [mot'tʃoso] SM/F (*bambino piccolo*) little kid; (*peg*) snotty-nosed kid

'**moccolo** SM (*di candela*) candle end; (*col: bestemmia*) oath; (: *moccio*) snot; **reggere il ~** to play gooseberry (BRIT), act as chaperon(e)

'**moda** SF fashion; **alla ~, di ~** fashionable, in fashion

modalità SF INV formality; **seguire attentamente le ~ d'uso** to follow the instructions carefully; ~ **giuridiche** legal procedures; ~ **di pagamento** method of payment

mo'della SF model

model'lare /**72**/ VT (*creta*) to model, shape; **modellarsi** VPR: **modellarsi su** to model o.s. on

mo'dello SM model; (*stampo*) mould (BRIT), mold (US) ▶ AG INV model *cpd*

'**modem** SM INV modem

mode'nese AG of (*o from*) Modena

mode'rare /**72**/ VT to moderate; **moderarsi** VPR to restrain o.s.; ~ **la velocità** to reduce speed; ~ **i termini** to weigh one's words

mode'rato, -a AG moderate

modera'tore, -'trice SM/F moderator

moderazi'one [moderat'tsjone] SF moderation

moderniz'zare [modernid'dzare] /**72**/ VT to bring up to date, modernize; **modernizzarsi** VPR to get up to date

mo'derno, -a AG modern

mo'destia SF modesty; ~ **a parte ...** in all modesty ..., though I say it myself ...

mo'desto, -a AG modest

'**modico, -a, -ci, -che** AG reasonable, moderate

mo'difica, -che SF modification; **subire delle modifiche** to undergo some modifications

modifi'cabile AG modifiable

modifi'care /**20**/ VT to modify, alter; **modificarsi** VPR to alter, change

mo'dista SF milliner

'**modo** SM way, manner; (*mezzo*) means, way; (*occasione*) opportunity; (*Ling*) mood; (*Mus*) mode; **modi** SMPL (*maniere*) manners; **a suo ~, a ~ suo** in his own way; **ad o in ogni ~** anyway; **di o in ~ che** so that; **in ~ da** so as to; **in tutti i modi** at all costs; (*comunque sia*) anyway; (*in ogni caso*) in any case; **in un certo qual ~** in a way, in some ways; **in qualche ~** somehow or other; **oltre ~** extremely; ~ **di dire** turn of phrase; **per ~ di dire** so to speak; **fare a ~ proprio** to do as one likes; **fare le cose a ~** to do things properly; **una persona a ~** a well-mannered person; **c'è ~ e ~ di farlo** there's a right way and a wrong way of doing it

modu'lare /**72**/ VT to modulate ▶ AG modular

modulazi'one [modulat'tsjone] SF modulation; ~ **di frequenza** frequency modulation

'**modulo** SM (*modello*) form; (*Archit: lunare, di comando*) module; ~ **di domanda** application form; ~ **d'iscrizione** enrolment form; ~ **di versamento** deposit slip

Moga'discio [moga'diʃʃo] SM Mogadishu

'**mogano** SM mahogany

'**mogio, -a, -gi, -gie** ['mɔdʒo] AG down in the dumps, dejected

'**moglie** ['moʎʎe] SF wife

mo'hair [mɔ'ɛr] SM mohair

mo'ine SFPL cajolery *sg*; (*leziosità*) affectation *sg*; **fare le ~ a qn** to cajole sb

'**mola** SF millstone; (*utensile abrasivo*) grindstone

mo'lare /**72**/ VT to grind ▶ AG (*pietra*) mill *cpd* ▶ SM (*dente*) molar

'**mole** SF mass; (*dimensioni*) size; (*edificio grandioso*) massive structure; **una ~ di lavoro** masses (BRIT) *o* loads of work

mo'lecola SF molecule

moles'tare /**72**/ VT to bother, annoy

mo'lestia SF annoyance, bother; **recar ~ a qn** to bother sb; **molestie sessuali** sexual harassment *sg*

mo'lesto, -a AG annoying

moli'sano, -a AG of (*o from*) Molise

'**molla** SF spring; **molle** SFPL (*per camino*) tongs; **prendere qn con le molle** to treat sb with kid gloves

mol'lare /**72**/ VT to release, let go; (*Naut*) to ease; (*fig: ceffone*) to give ▶ VI (*cedere*) to give in; ~ **gli ormeggi** (*Naut*) to cast off; ~ **la presa** to let go

'**molle** AG soft; (*muscoli*) flabby; (*fig: debole*) weak, feeble

molleggi'ato, -a [molled'dʒato] AG (*letto*) sprung; (*auto*) with good suspension

mol'leggio [mol'leddʒo] SM (*per veicoli*) suspension; (*elasticità*) springiness; (*Ginnastica*) knee-bends *pl*

mol'letta SF (*per capelli*) hairgrip; (*per panni stesi*) clothes peg (BRIT) *o* pin (US); **mollette** SFPL (*per zucchero*) tongs

mol'lezza [mol'lettsa] SF softness flabbiness weakness, feebleness; **mollezze** SFPL: **vivere nelle mollezze** to live in the lap of luxury

mol'lica, -che SF crumb, soft part

mol'liccio, -a, -ci, -ce [mol'littʃo] AG (*terreno, impasto*) soggy; (*frutta*) soft; (*floscio: mano*) limp; (: *muscolo*) flabby

mol'lusco, -schi SM mollusc

'molo SM breakwater; jetty, pier

mol'teplice [mol'teplitʃe] AG (*formato di più elementi*) complex; **molteplici** PL (*svariati: interessi, attività*) numerous, various

molteplicità [molteplitʃi'ta] SF multiplicity

moltipli'care/20/ VT to multiply; **moltiplicarsi** VPR to multiply; (*richieste*) to increase in number

moltiplicazi'one [moltiplikat'tsjone] SF multiplication

molti'tudine SF multitude; **una ~ di** a vast number *o* a multitude of

---

(PAROLA CHIAVE)

'molto, -a DET (*quantità*) a lot of, much; (*numero*) a lot of, many; **molto pane/carbone** a lot of bread/coal; **molta gente** a lot of people, many people; **molti libri** a lot of books, many books; **non ho molto tempo** I haven't got much time; **per molto (tempo)** for a long time; **ci vuole molto (tempo)?** will it take long?; **arriverà fra non molto** he'll arrive soon; **ne hai per molto?** will you be long?

▶ AV **1** a lot, (very) much; **viaggia molto** he travels a lot; **non viaggia molto** he doesn't travel much *o* a lot

2 (*intensivo: con aggettivi, avverbi*) very; (: *con participio passato*) (very) much; **molto buono** very good; **molto migliore, molto meglio** much *o* a lot better

▶ PRON much, a lot; **molti, e** (*pl*) many, a lot; **molti pensano che ...** many (people) think that ...; **molte sono rimaste a casa** a lot of them stayed at home; **c'era gente, ma non molta** there were people there, but not many

---

momentanea'mente AV at the moment, at present

momen'taneo, -a AG momentary, fleeting

mo'mento SM moment; **da un ~ all'altro** at any moment; (*all'improvviso*) suddenly; **al ~ di fare** just as I was (*o* you were *o* he was *etc*) doing; **a momenti** (*da un momento all'altro*) any time *o* moment now; (*quasi*) nearly; **per il ~** for the time being; **dal ~ che** ever since; (*dato che*) since; **~ culminante** climax

'monaca, -che SF nun

'Monaco SF Monaco; **~ (di Baviera)** Munich

'monaco, -ci SM monk

mo'narca, -chi SM monarch

monar'chia [monar'kia] SF monarchy

mo'narchico, -a, -ci, -che [mo'narkiko] AG (*stato, autorità*) monarchic; (*partito, fede*) monarchist ▶ SM/F monarchist

monas'tero SM (*di monaci*) monastery; (*di monache*) convent

mo'nastico, -a, -ci, -che AG monastic

'monco, -a, -chi, -che AG maimed; (*fig*) incomplete; **~ d'un braccio** one-armed

mon'cone SM stump

mon'dana SF prostitute

mondanità SF (*frivolezza*) worldliness; **le ~** (*piaceri*) the pleasures of the world

mon'dano, -a AG (*anche fig*) worldly; (*dell'alta società*) society *cpd*; fashionable

mon'dare/72/ VT (*frutta, patate*) to peel; (*piselli*) to shell; (*pulire*) to clean

mondez'zaio [mondet'tsajo] SM rubbish (BRIT) *o* garbage (US) dump

mondi'ale AG (*campionato, popolazione*) world *cpd*; (*influenza*) world-wide; **di fama ~** world famous

'mondo SM world; (*grande quantità*): **un ~ di** lots of, a host of; **il gran *o* bel ~** high society; **per niente al ~, per nessuna cosa al ~** not for all the world; **da che ~ è ~** since time *o* the world began; **mandare qn all'altro ~** to kill sb; **mettere/venire al ~** to bring/come into the world; **vivere fuori dal ~** to be out of touch with the real world; (**sono**) **cose dell'altro ~**! it's incredible!; **com'è piccolo il ~**! it's a small world!

mone'gasco, -a, -schi, -sche AG, SM/F Monegasque

monelle'ria SF prank, naughty trick

mo'nello, -a SM/F street urchin; (*ragazzo vivace*) scamp, imp

mo'neta SF coin; (*Econ: valuta*) currency; (*denaro spicciolo*) (small) change; **~ estera** foreign currency; **~ legale** legal tender

mone'tario, -a AG monetary

mongol'fiera SF hot-air balloon

Mon'golia SF: **la ~** Mongolia

mon'golico, -a, -ci, -che AG Mongolian

mongo'lismo SM Down's syndrome

'mongolo, -a AG Mongolian ▶ SM/F, SM Mongol, Mongolian

mongo'loide AG, SM F (*Med*) mongol

'monito SM warning

'monitor SM INV (*Tecn, TV*) monitor

monito'raggio [monito'raddʒo] SM monitoring

monito'rare /**72**/ VT to monitor

mo'nocolo SM (*lente*) monocle, eyeglass

monoco'lore AG (*Pol*): **governo** ~ one-party government

monoga'mia SF monogamy

mo'nogamo, -a AG monogamous ▶ SM monogamist

monogra'fia SF monograph

mono'gramma, -i SM monogram

mono'lingue AG monolingual

monolo'cale SM ≈ studio flat

mo'nologo, -ghi SM monologue

mono'pattino SM scooter

mono'polio SM monopoly; ~ **di stato** government monopoly

monopoliz'zare [monopolid'dzare] /**72**/ VT to monopolize

mono'sillabo, -a AG monosyllabic ▶ SM monosyllable

monoto'nia SF monotony

mo'notono, -a AG monotonous

mono'uso AG INV disposable

monovo'lume SF INV (*anche*: **automobile monovolume**) people carrier, MPV

Mons. ABBR (= *Monsignore*) Mgr

monsi'gnore [monsiɲ'ɲore] SM (*Rel*: *titolo*) Your (*o* His) Grace

mon'sone SM monsoon

monta'carichi [monta'kariki] SM INV hoist, goods lift

mon'taggio [mon'taddʒo] SM (*Tecn*) assembly; (*Cine*) editing

mon'tagna [mon'taɲɲa] SF mountain; (*zona montuosa*): **la** ~ the mountains *pl*; **andare in** ~ to go to the mountains; **aria/strada di** ~ mountain air/road; **casa di** ~ house in the mountains; **montagne russe** roller coaster *sg*, big dipper *sg* (BRIT)

monta'gnoso, -a [montaɲ'ɲoso] AG mountainous

monta'naro, -a AG mountain *cpd* ▶ SM/F mountain dweller

mon'tano, -a AG mountain *cpd*; alpine

mon'tante SM (*di porta*) jamb; (*di finestra*) upright; (*Calcio*: *palo*) post; (*Pugilato*) upper cut; (*Comm*) total amount

mon'tare /**72**/ VT to go (*o* come) up; (*cavallo*) to ride; (*apparecchiatura*) to set up, assemble; (*Cuc*) to whip; (*Zool*) to cover; (*incastonare*) to mount, set; (*Cine*) to edit; (*Fot*) to mount ▶ VI to go (*o* come) up; (*aumentare di livello, volume*) to rise; (*a cavallo*): ~ **bene/male** to ride well/badly; **montarsi** VPR to become big-headed; ~ **qc** to exaggerate sth; ~ **qn** *o* **la testa a qn** to turn sb's head; **montarsi la testa** to become big-headed; ~ **in bicicletta/ macchina/treno** to get on a bicycle/ into a car/on a train; ~ **a cavallo** to get on *o* mount a horse; ~ **la guardia** (*Mil*) to mount guard

monta'tura SF assembling *no pl*; (*di occhiali*) frames *pl*; (*di gioiello*) mounting, setting; (*fig*): ~ **pubblicitaria** publicity stunt

montavi'vande SM INV dumbwaiter

'monte SM mountain; **a** ~ upstream; **andare a** ~ (*fig*) to come to nothing; **mandare a** ~ **qc** (*fig*) to upset sth, cause sth to fail; **il M~ Bianco** Mont Blanc; **il M~ Everest** Mount Everest; ~ **di pietà** pawnshop; ~ **premi** prize

Monteci'torio [montetʃi'torjo] SM: **palazzo** ~ (*Pol*) seat of the Italian Chamber of Deputies

montene'grino, -a AG, SM/F Montenegrin

Monte'negro SM Montenegro

mont'gomery [mənt'gʌməri] SM INV duffel coat

mon'tone SM (*Zool*) ram; (*anche*: **giacca di montone**) sheepskin (jacket); **carne di** ~ mutton

montuosità SF mountainous nature

montu'oso, -a AG mountainous

monu'mento SM monument

mo'quette [mɔ'kɛt] SF fitted carpet

'mora SF (*del rovo*) blackberry; (*del gelso*) mulberry; (*Dir*) delay; (: *somma*) arrears *pl*

mo'rale AG moral ▶ SF (*scienza*) ethics *sg*, moral philosophy; (*complesso di norme*) moral standards *pl*, morality; (*condotta*) morals *pl*; (*insegnamento morale*) moral ▶ SM morale; **la** ~ **della favola** the moral of the tale; **essere giù di** ~ to be feeling down; **aver il** ~ **alto/a terra** to be in good/low spirits

mora'lista, -i, -e AG moralistic ▶ SM/F moralist

moralità SF morality; (*condotta*) morals *pl*

moraliz'zare [moralid'dzare] /**72**/ VT (*costumi, vita pubblica*) to set moral standards for

moralizzazi'one [moraliddzat'tsjone] SF setting of moral standards

mora'toria SF (*Dir*) moratorium

morbi'dezza [morbi'dettsa] SF softness; smoothness; tenderness

'morbido, -a AG soft; (*pelle*) soft, smooth; (*carne*) tender

mor'billo SM (*Med*) measles *sg*

'morbo SM disease

mor'boso, -a AG (*fig*) morbid

'morchia ['mɔrkja] SF (*residuo grasso*) dregs *pl*; oily deposit

mor'dente SM (*fig*: *di satira, critica*) bite; (: *di persona*) drive

'mordere /**64**/ VT to bite; (*addentare*) to bite into; (*corrodere*) to eat into

mordicchi'are [mordik'kjare] /**19**/ VT (*gen*) to chew at

mo'rente AG dying ▶ SMF dying man/woman

mor'fina SF morphine

mo'ria SF high mortality

mori'bondo, -a AG dying, moribund

morige'rato, -a [moridʒe'rato] AG of good morals

mo'rire/65/ VI to die; (*abitudine, civiltà*) to die out; **~ di dolore** to die of a broken heart; **~ di fame** to die of hunger; (*fig*) to be starving; **~ di freddo** to freeze to death; (*fig*) to be frozen; **~ d'invidia** to be green with envy; **~ di noia/paura** to be bored/scared to death; **~ dalla voglia di fare qc** to be dying to do sth; **fa un caldo da ~** it's terribly hot

mormo'rare/72/ VI to murmur; (*brontolare*) to grumble; **si mormora che ...** it's rumoured (*BRIT*) o rumored (*US*) that ...; **la gente mormora** people are talking

mormo'rio SM murmuring; grumbling

'moro, -a AG dark(-haired), dark(-complexioned); **i Mori** SMPL (*Storia*) the Moors

mo'roso, -a AG in arrears ▶ SM/F (*col: innamorato*) sweetheart

'morsa SF (*Tecn*) vice (*BRIT*), vise (*US*); (*fig: stretta*) grip

mor'setto SM (*Tecn*) clamp; (*Elettr*) terminal

morsi'care/20/ VT to nibble (at), gnaw (at); (*insetto*) to bite

'morso, -a PP di **mordere** ▶ SM bite; (*di insetto*) sting; (*parte della briglia*) bit; **dare un ~ a qc/qn** to bite sth/sb; **i morsi della fame** pangs of hunger

morta'della SF (*Cuc*) mortadella (*type of salted pork meat*)

mor'taio SM mortar

mor'tale AG, SM mortal

mortalità SF mortality; (*Statistica*) mortality, death rate

'morte SF death; **in punto di ~** at death's door; **ferito a ~** (*soldato*) mortally wounded; (*in incidente*) fatally injured; **essere annoiato a ~** to be bored to death o to tears; **avercela a ~ con qn** to be bitterly resentful of sb; **avere la ~ nel cuore** to have a heavy heart

mortifi'care/20/ VT to mortify

'morto, -a PP di **morire** ▶ AG dead ▶ SM/F dead man/woman; **i morti** the dead; **fare il ~** (*nell'acqua*) to float on one's back; **il Mar M~** the Dead Sea; **un ~ di fame** (*fig peg*) a down-and-out; **le campane suonavano a ~** the funeral bells were tolling; *vedi anche* **il Giorno dei Morti**

mor'torio SM (*anche fig*) funeral

mo'saico, -ci SM mosaic; **l'ultimo tassello del ~** (*fig*) the last piece of the puzzle

'Mosca SF Moscow

'mosca, -sche SF fly; **rimanere** o **restare con un pugno di mosche** (*fig*) to be left empty-handed; **non si sentiva volare una ~** (*fig*) you could have heard a pin drop; **~ cieca** blind-man's buff

mos'cato SM muscatel (wine)

mosce'rino [moʃʃe'rino] SM midge, gnat

mos'chea [mos'kea] SF mosque

mos'chetto [mos'ketto] SM musket

moschet'tone [mosket'tone] SM (*gancio*) spring clip; (*Alpinismo*) karabiner, snaplink

moschi'cida, -i, -e [moski'tʃida] AG fly *cpd*; **carta ~** flypaper

'moscio, -a, -sci, -sce ['moʃʃo] AG (*fig*) lifeless; **ha la "r" moscia** he can't roll his "r"s

mos'cone SM (*Zool*) bluebottle; (*barca*) pedalo; (*: a remi*) *kind of pedalo with oars*

mosco'vita, -i, -e AG, SM/F Muscovite

'mossa SF movement; (*nel gioco*) move; **darsi una ~** (*fig*) to give o.s. a shake; **prendere le mosse da qc** to come about as the result of sth

'mossi *etc* VB *vedi* **muovere**

'mosso, -a PP di **muovere** ▶ AG (*mare*) rough; (*capelli*) wavy; (*Fot*) blurred; (*ritmo, prosa*) animated

mos'tarda SF mustard; **~ di Cremona** pickled fruit with mustard

'mosto SM must

'mostra SF exhibition, show; (*ostentazione*) show; **in ~** on show; **far ~ di** (*fingere*) to pretend; **far ~ di sé** to show off; **mettersi in ~** to draw attention to o.s.

mos'trare/72/ VT to show ▶ VI: **~ di fare** to pretend to do; **mostrarsi** VPR to appear; **~ la lingua** to stick out one's tongue

'mostro SM monster

mostru'oso, -a AG monstrous

mo'tel SM INV motel

moti'vare/72/ VT (*causare*) to cause; (*giustificare*) to justify, account for

motivazi'one [motivat'tsjone] SF justification; (*Psic*) motivation

mo'tivo SM (*causa*) reason, cause; (*movente*) motive; (*letterario*) (central) theme; (*disegno*) motif, design, pattern; (*Mus*) motif; **per quale ~?** why?, for what reason?; **per motivi di salute** for health reasons, on health grounds; **motivi personali** personal reasons

'moto SM (*anche Fisica*) motion; (*movimento, gesto*) movement; (*esercizio fisico*) exercise; (*sommossa*) rising, revolt; (*commozione*) feeling, impulse ▶ SF INV (*motocicletta*) motorbike; **fare del ~** to take some exercise; **un ~ d'impazienza** an impatient gesture; **mettere in ~** to set in motion; (*Aut*) to start up; **~ d'acqua** Jet Ski®

moto'carro SM three-wheeler van

motoci'cletta [mototʃi'kletta] SF motorcycle

motoci'clismo [mototʃi'klizmo] SM motorcycling, motorcycle racing

motoci'clista, -i, -e [mototʃi'klista] SM/F motorcyclist

moto'nave SF motor vessel

motopesche'reccio [motopeske'rettʃo] SM
motor fishing vessel

mo'tore, -'trice AG motor; (Tecn) driving
▶ SM engine, motor ▶ SF (Tecn) engine,
motor; **albero ~** drive shaft; **forza motrice**
driving force; **a ~** motor cpd, power-driven;
~ a combustione interna/a reazione
internal combustion/jet engine; **~ di
ricerca** (Inform) search engine

moto'rino SM moped; **~ di avviamento** (Aut)
starter

motoriz'zato, -a [motorid'dzato] AG (truppe)
motorized; (persona) having a car o transport

motorizzazi'one [motoriddzat'tsjone] SF
(ufficio tecnico e organizzativo): **(ufficio della) ~**
road traffic office

motos'cafo SM motorboat

motove'detta SF motor patrol vessel

mo'trice [mo'tritʃe] SF vedi **motore**

mot'teggio [mot'teddʒo] SM banter

motto SM (battuta scherzosa) witty remark;
(frase emblematica) motto, maxim

mountain bike SF INV mountain bike

'mouse ['maus] SM INV (Inform) mouse

mo'vente SM motive

mo'venza [mo'ventsa] SF movement

movimen'tare /**72**/ VT to liven up

movimen'tato, -a AG (festa, partita) lively;
(riunione) animated; (strada, vita) busy;
(soggiorno) eventful

movi'mento SM movement; (fig) activity,
hustle and bustle; (Mus) tempo, movement;
essere sempre in ~ to be always on the go;
fare un po' di ~ (esercizio fisico) to take some
exercise; **c'è molto ~ in città** the town is
very busy; **~ di capitali** movement of
capital; **M~ per la Liberazione della
Donna** Women's Movement

movi'ola SF moviola; **rivedere qc ~** to
see an action (BRIT) o instant (US) replay of
sth

Mozam'bico [moddzam'biko] SM: **il ~**
Mozambique

mozi'one [mot'tsjone] SF (Pol) motion;
~ d'ordine (Pol) point of order

mozzafi'ato [mottsa'fjato] AG INV
breathtaking

moz'zare [mot'tsare] /**72**/ VT to cut off; (coda)
to dock; **~ il fiato** o **il respiro a qn** (fig) to
take sb's breath away

mozza'rella [mottsa'rella] SF mozzarella

mozzi'cone [mottsi'kone] SM stub, butt,
end; (anche: **mozzicone di sigaretta**)
cigarette end

'mozzo[1] ['mɔddzo] SM (Meccanica) hub

'mozzo[2] ['mottso] SM (Naut) ship's boy;
~ di stalla stable boy

mq ABBR (= metro quadro) sq.m

MS SIGLA = **Massa Carrara**

M.S.I. SIGLA M (= Movimento Sociale Italiano)
former right-wing political party

Mti ABBR = **monti**

'mucca, -che SF cow; **~ pazza** BSE; **(morbo
della) ~ pazza** mad cow disease, BSE;
l'emergenza ~ pazza the mad cow crisis

'mucchio ['mukkjo] SM pile, heap; (fig): **un ~
di** lots of, heaps of

mucil'lagine [mutʃil'ladʒine] SF (Bot)
mucilage (green slime produced by plants growing
in water)

'muco, -chi SM mucus

mu'cosa SF mucous membrane

'muesli ['mjusli] SM muesli

'muffa SF mould (BRIT), mold (US), mildew;
fare la ~ to go mouldy (BRIT) o moldy (US)

mugghi'are [mug'gjare] /**19**/ VI (fig: mare,
tuono) to roar; (: vento) to howl

mug'gire [mud'dʒire] /**55**/ VI (vacca) to low,
moo; (toro) to bellow; (fig) to roar

mug'gito [mud'dʒito] SM moo; bellow; roar

mu'ghetto [mu'getto] SM lily of the valley

mu'gnaio, -a [muɲ'ɲajo] SM/F miller

mugo'lare /**72**/ VI (cane) to whimper, whine;
(fig: persona) to moan

mugu'gnare [muguɲ'ɲare] /**15**/ VI (col) to
mutter, mumble

mulatti'era SF mule track

mu'latto, -a AG, SM/F mulatto

muli'nare /**72**/ VI to whirl, spin round
(and round)

muli'nello SM (moto vorticoso) eddy, whirl;
(di canna da pesca) reel; (Naut) windlass

mu'lino SM mill; **~ a vento** windmill

'mulo SM mule

'multa SF fine

mul'tare /**72**/ VT to fine

multico'lore AG multicoloured (BRIT),
multicolored (US)

multi'etnico, -a, -ci, -che AG multiethnic

multi'forme AG (paesaggio, attività, interessi)
varied; (ingegno) versatile

multimedi'ale AG multimedia cpd

multinazio'nale [multinattsjo'nale] AG, SF
multinational; **forza ~ di pace**
multinational peace-keeping force

'multiplo, -a AG, SM multiple

multiraz'ziale [multirat'tsjale] AG
multiracial

multi'sala AG INV multiscreen

multiu'tenza [multiu'tentsa] SF (Inform)
time sharing

multivitami'nico, -a, -ci, -che AG:
complesso ~ multivitamin

'mummia SF mummy

'mungere ['mundʒere] /**5**/ VT (anche fig)
to milk

mungi'tura [mundʒi'tura] SF milking

munici'pale [munitʃi'pale] AG (gen)

m

municipal; town *cpd*; **palazzo** ~ town hall;
autorità municipali local authorities
(BRIT), local government *sg*
muni'cipio [muni't∫ipjo] SM town council,
corporation; (*edificio*) town hall; **sposarsi
in** ~ ≈ to get married in a registry office
(BRIT), have a civil marriage
munifi'cenza [munifi't∫entsa] SF munificence
mu'nifico, -a, -ci, -che AG munificent,
generous
mu'nire/55/ VT: ~ **qc/qn di** to equip sth/sb
with; ~ **di firma** (*documento*) to sign
munizi'oni [munit'tsjoni] SFPL (*Mil*)
ammunition *sg*
'**munsi**etc VB *vedi* **mungere**
'**munto, -a** PP *di* **mungere**
mu'oioetc VB *vedi* **morire**
mu'overe/66/ VT to move; (*ruota, macchina*)
to drive; (*sollevare: questione, obiezione*) to raise,
bring up; (: *accusa*) to make, bring forward;
muoversiVPR to move; ~ **causa a qn** (*Dir*) to
take legal action against sb; ~ **a
compassione** to move to pity; ~ **guerra a**
o **contro qn** to wage war against sb; ~ **mari
e monti** to move heaven and earth; ~ **al
pianto** to move to tears; ~ **i primi passi** to
take one's first steps; (*fig*) to be starting out;
muoviti! hurry up!, get a move on!
'**mura** SFPL *vedi* **muro**
mu'raglia [mu'raλλa] SF (high) wall
mu'rale AG wall *cpd*; mural
mu'rare/72/ VT (*persona, porta*) to wall up
mu'rario, -a AG building *cpd*; **arte muraria**
masonry
mura'tore SM (*con pietre*) mason; (*con mattoni*)
bricklayer
mura'tura SF (*lavoro murario*) masonry; **casa
in** ~ (*di pietra*) stonebuilt house; (*di mattoni*)
brick house
'**muro** SM wall; **mura**SFPL (*cinta cittadina*)
walls; **a** ~ wall *cpd*; (*armadio ecc*) built-in;
mettere al ~ (*fucilare*) to shoot o execute (by
firing squad); ~ **di cinta** surrounding wall;
~ **divisorio** dividing wall; ~ **del suono**
sound barrier
'**musa** SF muse
'**muschio** ['muskjo] SM (*Zool*) musk; (*Bot*)
moss
musco'lare AG muscular, muscle *cpd*
muscola'tura SF muscle structure

'**muscolo** SM (*Anat*) muscle
musco'loso, -a AG muscular
mu'seo SM museum
museru'ola SF muzzle
'**musica** SF music; ~ **da ballo/camera** dance/
chamber music
musi'cale AG musical
musicas'setta SF (pre-recorded) cassette
musi'cista, -i, -e[muzi't∫ista] SM/F musician
musi'comane SMF music lover
'**müsli** ['mysli] SM muesli
'**muso** SM muzzle; (*di auto, aereo*) nose; **tenere
il** ~ to sulk
mu'sone, -a SM/F sulky person
mussola SF muslin
mus(s)ul'mano, -a AG, SM/F Muslim,
Moslem
'**muta** SF (*di animali*) moulting (BRIT), molting
(US); (*di serpenti*) sloughing; (*per immersioni
subacquee*) diving suit; (*gruppo di cani*) pack
mu'tabile AG changeable
muta'mento SM change
mu'tande SFPL (*da uomo*) (under)pants
mutan'dine SFPL (*da donna, bambino*) pants
(BRIT), briefs; ~ **di plastica** plastic pants
mu'tare/72/ VT, VI to change, alter
mutazi'one [mutat'tsjone] SF change,
alteration; (*Biol*) mutation
mu'tevole AG changeable
muti'lare/72/ VT to mutilate, maim; (*fig*) to
mutilate, deface
muti'lato, -a SM/F disabled person; (*through
loss of limbs*): ~ **di guerra** disabled ex-
serviceman (BRIT) o war veteran (US)
mutilazi'one [mutilat'tsjone] SF mutilation
mu'tismo SM (*Med*) mutism; (*atteggiamento*)
(stubborn) silence
'**muto, -a** AG (*Med*) dumb; (*emozione, dolore:
Cine*) silent; (*Ling*) silent, mute; (*carta
geografica*) blank; ~ **per lo stupore** *etc*
speechless with amazement *etc*; **ha fatto
scena muta** he didn't utter a word
'**mutua** SF (*anche:* **cassa mutua**) health
insurance scheme; **medico della** ~
≈ National Health Service doctor (BRIT)
mutu'are/72/ VT (*fig*) to borrow
mutu'ato, -a SM/F member of a health
insurance scheme
'**mutuo, -a** AG (*reciproco*) mutual ▶ SM (*Econ*)
(long-term) loan; ~ **ipotecario** mortgage

Nn

N, n ['ɛnne] SM O F (*lettera*) N, n; **N come Napoli** = N for Nellie (BRIT), N for Nan (US)

N ABBR (= *nord*) N

n ABBR (= *numero*) no.

NA SIGLA = **Napoli**

na'babbo SM (*anche fig*) nabob

'nacchere ['nakkere] SFPL castanets

NAD SIGLA M = **nucleo anti-droga**

na'dir SM (*Astr*) nadir

'nafta SF naphtha; (*per motori diesel*) diesel oil

nafta'lina SF (*Chim*) naphthalene; (*tarmicida*) mothballs *pl*

'naia SF (*Zool*) cobra; (*Mil*) *slang term for national service*

na'ïf [na'if] AG INV naïve

'nailon SM = **nylon**

Nai'robi SF Nairobi

'nanna SF (*linguaggio infantile*): **andare a ~** to go to beddy-byes

'nano, -a AG, SM/F dwarf

napole'tano, -a AG, SM/F Neapolitan ▶ SF (*macchinetta da caffè*) Neapolitan coffee pot

'Napoli SF Naples

'nappa SF tassel

nar'ciso [nar'tʃizo] SM narcissus

narco'dollari SMPL drug money *sg*

'narcos SM INV (*colombiano*) Colombian drug trafficker

nar'cosi SF general anaesthesia, narcosis

nar'cotico, -ci SM narcotic

narcotraffi'cante SMF drug trafficker

narco'traffico SM drug trade

na'rice [na'ritʃe] SF nostril

nar'rare /72/ VT to tell the story of, recount

narra'tivo, -a AG narrative ▶ SF (*branca*) fiction

narra'tore, -'trice SM/F narrator

narrazi'one [narrat'tsjone] SF narration; (*racconto*) story, tale

N.A.S.A. ['naza] SIGLA F (= *National Aeronautics and Space Administration*) NASA

na'sale AG nasal

na'scente [naʃʃente] AG (*sole, luna*) rising

'nascere ['naʃʃere] /67/ VI (*bambino*) to be born; (*pianta*) to come o spring up; (*fiume*) to rise, have its source; (*sole*) to rise; (*dente*) to come through; (*fig: derivare, conseguire*): **~ da** to arise from, be born out of; **è nata nel 1952** she was born in 1952; **da cosa nasce cosa** one thing leads to another

'nascita ['naʃʃita] SF birth

nasci'turo, -a [naʃʃi'turo] SM/F future child; **come si chiamerà il ~?** what's the baby going to be called?

nas'condere /68/ VT to hide, conceal; **nascondersi** VPR to hide

nascon'diglio [naskon'diʎʎo] SM hiding place

nascon'dino SM (*gioco*) hide-and-seek

nas'cosi *etc* VB *vedi* **nascondere**

nas'costo, -a PP *di* **nascondere** ▶ AG hidden; **di ~** secretly

na'sello SM (*Zool*) hake

'naso SM nose

Nas'sau SF Nassau

'nastro SM ribbon; (*magnetico, isolante: Sport*) tape; **~ adesivo** adhesive tape; **~ trasportatore** conveyor belt

nas'turzio [nas'turtsjo] SM nasturtium

na'tale AG of one's birth ▶ SM (*Rel*): **N~** Christmas; (*giorno della nascita*) birthday; **natali** SMPL: **di illustri/umili natali** of noble/humble birth

natalità SF birth rate

nata'lizio, -a [nata'littsjo] AG (*del Natale*) Christmas *cpd*

na'tante SM craft *inv*, boat

'natica, -che SF (*Anat*) buttock

na'tio, -a, -tii, -tie AG native

Nativi'tà SF (*Rel*) Nativity

na'tivo, -a AG, SM/F native

'nato, -a PP *di* **nascere** ▶ AG: **un attore ~** a born actor; **nata Pieri** née Pieri

'N.A.T.O. SIGLA F NATO (= *North Atlantic Treaty Organization*)

na'tura SF nature; **pagare in ~** to pay in kind; **~ morta** still life

natu'rale AG natural ▶ SM: **al ~** (*alimenti*) served plain; (*ritratto*) life-size; (**ma**) **è ~!** (*in risposte*) of course!; **a grandezza ~** life-size; **acqua ~** spring water

natura'lezza [natura'lettsa] SF naturalness

natura'lista, -i, -e SM/F naturalist

naturaliz'zare [naturalid'dzare] /**72**/ VT to naturalize

natural'mente AV naturally; (*certamente, sì*) of course

natu'rismo SM naturism, nudism

natu'rista, -i, -e AG, SM/F naturist, nudist

naufra'gare /**80**/ VI (*nave*) to be wrecked; (*persona*) to be shipwrecked; (*fig*) to fall through

nau'fragio [nau'fradʒo] SM shipwreck; (*fig*) ruin, failure

'naufrago, -ghi SM castaway, shipwreck victim

'nausea SF nausea; **avere la ~** to feel sick (BRIT) o ill (US); **fino alla ~** ad nauseam

nausea'bondo, -a AG, **nause'ante** AG (*sapore*) disgusting; nauseating, sickening

nause'are /**72**/ VT to nauseate, make (feel) sick (BRIT) o ill (US)

'nautico, -a, -ci, -che AG nautical ▶ SF (art of) navigation; **salone ~** (*mostra*) boat show

na'vale AG naval; **battaglia ~** naval battle; (*gioco*) battleships pl

na'vata SF (*anche:* **navata centrale**) nave; (*anche:* **navata laterale**) aisle

'nave SF ship, vessel; **~ da carico** cargo ship, freighter; **~ cisterna** tanker; **~ da guerra** warship; **~ di linea** liner; **~ passeggeri** passenger ship; **~ portaerei** aircraft carrier; **~ spaziale** spaceship

na'vetta SF shuttle; (*servizio di collegamento*) shuttle (service)

navi'cella [navi'tʃella] SF (*di aerostato*) gondola; **~ spaziale** spaceship

navi'gabile AG navigable

navi'gante SM sailor, seaman

navi'gare /**80**/ VI to sail; **~ in cattive acque** (*fig*) to be in deep water; **~ in Internet** to surf the Net

navi'gato, -a AG (*fig: esperto*) experienced

naviga'tore, -'trice SM: **~ satellitare** sàtnav, satellite navigator ▶ SM/F (*gen*) navigator; **~ solitario** single-handed sailor

navigazi'one [navigat'tsjone] SF navigation; **dopo una settimana di ~** after a week at sea

na'viglio [na'viʎʎo] SM fleet, ships pl; (*canale artificiale*) canal; **~ da pesca** fishing fleet

nazio'nale [nattsjo'nale] AG national ▶ SF (*Sport*) national team

naziona'lismo [nattsjona'lizmo] SM nationalism

naziona'lista, -i, -e [nattsjona'lista] AG, SM/F nationalist

nazionalità [nattsjonali'ta] SF INV nationality

nazionaliz'zare [nattsjonalid'dzare] /**72**/ VT to nationalize

nazionalizzazi'one [nattsjonaliddzat'tsjone] SF nationalization

nazi'one [nat'tsjone] SF nation

naziskin ['nɑ:tsiskin] SM INV Nazi skinhead

na'zismo [nat'tsizmo] SM Nazism

na'zista, -i, -e [nat'tsista] AG, SM/F Nazi

NB ABBR (= *nota bene*) NB

N.d.A. ABBR (= *nota dell'autore*) author's note

N.d.D. ABBR = **nota della direzione**

N.d.E. ABBR (= *nota dell'editore*) publisher's note

N.d.R. ABBR (= *nota della redazione*) editor's note

'nd'rangheta [nd'rangeta] SF Calabrian Mafia

N.d.T. ABBR (= *nota del traduttore*) translator's note

(**PAROLA CHIAVE**)

ne PRON **1** (*di lui, lei, loro*) of him/her/them; about him/her/them; **ne riconosco la voce** I recognize his (o her) voice

2 (*di questa, quella cosa*) of it; about it; **ne voglio ancora** I want some more (of it o them); **non parliamone più!** let's not talk about it any more!

3 (*da ciò*) from this; **ne deduco che l'avete trovato** I gather you've found it; **ne consegue che ...** it follows therefore that ...

4 (*con valore partitivo*): **hai dei libri? — sì, ne ho** have you any books? — yes, I have (some); **hai del pane? — no, non ne ho** have you any bread? — no, I haven't any; **quanti anni hai? — ne ho 17** how old are you? — I'm 17

▶ AV (*moto da luogo: da lì*) from there; **ne vengo ora** I've just come from there

né CONG: **né ... né** neither ... nor; **né l'uno né l'altro lo vuole** neither of them wants it; **né più né meno** no more no less; **non parla né l'italiano né il tedesco** he speaks neither Italian nor German, he doesn't speak either Italian or German; **non piove né nevica** it isn't raining or snowing

N.E. ABBR (= *nordest*) NE

ne'anche [ne'anke] AV, CONG not even; **non ... ~** not even; **~ se volesse potrebbe venire** he couldn't come even if he wanted to; **non l'ho visto — neanch'io** I didn't see him — neither did I o I didn't either; **~ per idea** o **sogno!** not on your life!; **non ci penso ~!** I wouldn't dream of it!; **~ a pagarlo lo farebbe** he wouldn't do it even if you paid him

'nebbia SF fog; (*foschia*) mist

nebbi'oso, -a AG foggy; misty

nebulizza'tore [nebuliddza'tore] SM atomizer

nebu'losa SF nebula

nebulosità SF haziness

nebu'loso, -a AG (*atmosfera, cielo*) hazy; (*fig*) hazy, vague

néces'saire [nesɛ'sɛr] SM INV: **~ da viaggio** overnight case o bag

necessaria'mente [netʃessarja'mente] AV necessarily

neces'sario, -a [netʃes'sarjo] AG necessary ▶ SM: **fare il ~** to do what is necessary; **lo stretto ~** the bare essentials *pl*

necessità [netʃessi'ta] SF INV necessity; (*povertà*) need, poverty; **trovarsi nella ~ di fare qc** to be forced o obliged to do sth, have to do sth

necessi'tare [netʃessi'tare] /**72**/ VT to require ▶ VI (*aver bisogno*): **~ di** to need

necro'logio [nekro'lɔdʒo] SM obituary notice; (*registro*) register of deaths

ne'fando, -a AG infamous, wicked

ne'fasto, -a AG inauspicious, ill-omened

ne'gare /80/ VT to deny; (*rifiutare*) to deny, refuse; **~ di aver fatto/che** to deny having done/that

negativa'mente AV negatively; **rispondere ~** to give a negative response

nega'tivo, -a AG, SF, SM negative

negazi'one [negat'tsjone] SF negation

negherò *etc* [nege'rɔ] VB *vedi* **negare**

ne'gletto, -a [ne'glɛtto] AG (*trascurato*) neglected

'negli ['neʎʎi] PREP + DET *vedi* **in**

négli'gé [negli'ʒe] SM INV negligee

negli'gente [negli'dʒɛnte] AG negligent, careless

negli'genza [negli'dʒɛntsa] SF negligence, carelessness

negozi'abile [negot'tsjabile] AG negotiable

negozi'ante [negot'tsjante] SMF trader, dealer; (*bottegaio*) shopkeeper (BRIT), storekeeper (US)

negozi'are [negot'tsjare] /**19**/ VT to negotiate ▶ VI: **~ in** to trade o deal in

negozi'ato [negot'tsjato] SM negotiation

negozia'tore, -'trice [negottsja'tore] SM/F negotiator

ne'gozio [ne'gɔttsjo] SM (*locale*) shop (BRIT), store (US); (*affare*) (piece of) business *no pl*; (*Dir*): **~ giuridico** legal transaction

negri'ere, -a, negri'ero, -a SM/F slave trader; (*fig*) slave driver

'negro, -a AG, SM/F Negro

negro'mante SMF necromancer

negroman'zia [negroman'tsia] SF necromancy

'nei, nel, nell', 'nella, 'nelle, 'nello PREP + DET *vedi* **in**

'nembo SM (*Meteor*) nimbus

ne'mico, -a, -ci, -che AG hostile; (*Mil*) enemy *cpd* ▶ SM/F enemy; **essere ~ di** to be strongly averse o opposed to

nem'meno AV, CONG = **neanche**

'nenia SF dirge; (*motivo monotono*) monotonous tune

'neo SM mole; (*fig*) (slight) flaw

'neo... PREFISSO neo...

neofa'scista, -i, -e [neofaʃ'ʃista] SM/F neofascist

neolo'gismo [neolo'dʒizmo] SM neologism

'neon SM (*Chim*) neon

neo'nato, -a AG newborn ▶ SM/F newborn baby

neozelan'dese [neoddzelan'dese] AG New Zealand *cpd* ▶ SMF New Zealander

Ne'pal SM: **il ~** Nepal

nepo'tismo SM nepotism

nep'pure AV, CONG = **neanche**

ner'bata SF (*colpo*) blow; (*sferzata*) whiplash

'nerbo SM lash; (*fig*) strength, backbone

nerbo'ruto, -a AG muscular; robust

ne'retto SM (*Tip*) bold type

'nero, -a AG black; (*scuro*) dark ▶ SM black; **nella miseria più nera** in utter o abject poverty; **essere di umore ~, essere ~** to be in a filthy mood; **mettere qc su bianco** to put sth down in black and white; **vedere tutto ~** to look on the black side (of things); **il Mar N~** the Black Sea

nero'fumo SM lampblack

nerva'tura SF (*Anat*) nervous system; (*Bot*) veining; (*Archit, Tecn*) rib

'nervo SM (*Anat*) nerve; (*Bot*) vein; **avere i nervi** to be on edge; **dare sui nervi a qn** to get on sb's nerves; **tenere/avere i nervi saldi** to keep/be calm; **che nervi!** damn (it)!

nervo'sismo SM (*Psic*) nervousness; (*irritazione*) irritability

ner'voso, -a AG nervous; (*irritabile*) irritable ▶ SM (*col*): **far venire il ~ a qn** to get on sb's nerves; **farsi prendere dal ~** to let o.s. get irritated

'nespola SF (*Bot*) medlar; (*fig*) blow, punch

'nespolo SM medlar tree

'nesso SM connection, link

PAROLA CHIAVE

nes'suno, -a (*det: dav sm* **nessun** + C, V, **nessuno** + *s impura, gn, pn, ps, x, z; dav sf* **nessuna** + C, **nessun'** + V) DET **1** (*non uno*) no **2** (*espressione negativa*) + *any*; **non c'è nessun libro** there isn't any book, there is no book; **nessun altro** no one else, nobody else; **nessun'altra cosa** nothing else; **in nessun luogo** nowhere

3 (*qualche*) any; **hai nessuna obiezione?** do you have any objections?
▶ PRON **1** (*non uno*) no one, nobody; (*espressione negativa*) any(one); **nessuno è venuto, non è venuto nessuno** nobody came
2 (*cosa: espressione negativa*) none; (: *espressione negativa*) any
3 (*qualcuno*) anyone, anybody; **ha telefonato nessuno?** did anyone phone?

netta'mente AV clearly
net'tare¹ VT to clean
'**nettare²** ['nɛttare] SM nectar
net'tezza [net'tettsa] SF cleanness, cleanliness; **~ urbana** cleansing department (*BRIT*), department of sanitation (*US*)
'**netto, -a** AG (*pulito*) clean; (*chiaro*) clear, clear-cut; (*deciso*) definite; (*Econ*) net; **tagliare qc di ~** to cut sth clean off; **taglio ~ col passato** (*fig*) clean break with the past
nettur'bino SM dustman (*BRIT*), garbage collector (*US*)
'**neuro...** PREFISSO neuro...
neurochirur'gia [neurokirur'dʒia] SF neurosurgery
neurolo'gia [neurolo'dʒia] SF neurology
neuro'logico, -a, -ci, -che [neuro'lɔdʒiko] AG neurological
neu'rologo, -a, -gi, -ghe SM/F neurologist
neu'rosi SF INV **= nevrosi**
neu'trale AG neutral
neutralità SF neutrality
neutraliz'zare [neutralid'dzare] /**72**/ VT to neutralize
'**neutro, -a** AG neutral; (*Ling*) neuter ▶ SM (*Ling*) neuter
neu'trone SM neutron
ne'vaio SM snowfield
'**neve** SF snow; **montare a ~** (*Cuc*) to whip up; **~ carbonica** dry ice
nevi'care /**20**/ VB IMPERS to snow
nevi'cata SF snowfall
ne'vischio [ne'viskjo] SM sleet
ne'voso, -a AG snowy; snow-covered
nevral'gia [nevral'dʒia] SF neuralgia
ne'vralgico, -a, -ci, -che [ne'vraldʒiko] AG: **punto ~** (*Med*) nerve centre; (*fig*) crucial point
nevras'tenico, -a, -ci, -che AG (*Med*) neurasthenic; (*fig*) hot-tempered ▶ SM/F neurasthenic; hot-tempered person
ne'vrosi SF INV neurosis
ne'vrotico, -a, -ci, -che AG, SM/F (*anche fig*) neurotic
Nia'gara SM: **le cascate del ~** the Niagara Falls
'**nibbio** SM (*Zool*) kite
Nica'ragua SM: **il ~** Nicaragua
nicaragu'ense AG, SMF Nicaraguan

'**nicchia** ['nikkja] SF niche; (*naturale*) cavity, hollow; **~ di mercato** (*Comm*) niche market
nicchi'are [nik'kjare] /**19**/ VI to shilly-shally, hesitate
'**nichel** ['nikel] SM nickel
nichi'lismo [niki'lizmo] SM nihilism
Nico'sia SF Nicosia
nico'tina SF nicotine
nidi'ata SF (*di uccelli: anche fig: di bambini*) brood; (*di altri animali*) litter
nidifi'care /**20**/ VI to nest
'**nido** SM nest ▶ AG INV: **asilo ~** day nursery, crèche (*for children aged 0 to 3*); **a ~ d'ape** (*tessuto ecc*) honeycomb *cpd*

ni'ente PRON **1** (*nessuna cosa*) nothing; **niente può fermarlo** nothing can stop him; **niente di niente** absolutely nothing; **grazie! — di niente!** thank you! — not at all!; **nient'altro** nothing else; **nient'altro che** nothing but, just, only; **niente affatto** not at all, not in the least; **come se niente fosse** as if nothing had happened; **cose da niente** trivial matters; **per niente** (*gratis, invano*) for nothing; **non per niente, ma ...** not for any particular reason, but ...; **poco o niente** next to nothing; **un uomo da niente** a man of no consequence
2 (*qualcosa*): **hai bisogno di niente?** do you need anything?
3: **non ... niente** nothing; (*espressione negativa*) + anything; **non ho visto niente** I saw nothing, I didn't see anything; **non può farci niente** he can't do anything about it; (**non**) **fa niente** (*non importa*) it doesn't matter; **non ho niente da dire** I have nothing *o* haven't anything to say
▶ AG INV: **niente paura!** never fear!; **e niente scuse!** and I don't want to hear excuses!
▶ SM nothing; **un bel niente** absolutely nothing; **basta un niente per farla piangere** the slightest thing is enough to make her cry; **finire in niente** to come to nothing
▶ AV (*in nessuna misura*): **non ... niente** not ... at all; **non è** (**per**) **niente buono** it isn't good at all; **non ci penso per niente** (*non ne ho nessuna intenzione*) I wouldn't think of it; **niente male!** not bad at all!

nientedi'meno, niente'meno AV actually, even ▶ ESCL really!, I say!
'**Niger** ['nidʒer] SM: **il ~** Niger; (*fiume*) the Niger
Ni'geria [ni'dʒɛrja] SF: **la ~** Nigeria
nigeri'ano, -a [nidʒe'rjano] AG, SM/F Nigerian
'**Nilo** SM: **il ~** the Nile
'**nimbo** SM halo

'ninfa SF nymph

nin'fea SF water lily

nin'fomane SF nymphomaniac

ninna'nanna SF lullaby

'ninnolo SM (balocco) plaything; (gingillo) knick-knack

ni'pote SMF (di zii) nephew (niece); (di nonni) grandson (daughter), grandchild

nip'ponico, -a, -ci, -che AG Japanese

niti'dezza [niti'dettsa] SF (gen) clearness; (di stile) clarity; (Fot, TV) sharpness

'nitido, -a AG clear; (immagine) sharp; (specchio) bright

ni'trato SM nitrate

'nitrico, -a, -ci, -che AG nitric

ni'trire/55/ VI to neigh

ni'trito SM (di cavallo) neighing no pl; neigh; (Chim) nitrite

nitroglice'rina [nitroglitʃe'rina] SF nitroglycerine

'niveo, -a AG snow-white

'Nizza ['nittsa] SF Nice

nn ABBR (= numeri) nos

NO SIGLA = **Novara**

no AV (risposta) no; **vieni o no?** are you coming or not?; **come no!** of course!, certainly!; **perché no?** why not?; **lo conosciamo? — tu no ma io sì** do we know him? — you don't but I do; **verrai, no?** you'll come, won't you?

N.O. ABBR (= nordovest) NW

nobil'donna SF noblewoman

'nobile AG noble ▶ SMF noble, nobleman/woman

nobili'are AG noble

nobili'tare/72/ VT (anche fig) to ennoble; **nobilitarsi** VPR (rendersi insigne) to distinguish o.s.

nobiltà SF nobility; (di azione ecc) nobleness

nobilu'omo (pl **nobiluomini**) SM nobleman

'nocca, -che (Anat) knuckle

'noccioetc ['nɔttʃo] VB vedi **nuocere**

nocci'ola [not'tʃɔla] SF hazelnut ▶ AG INV (anche: **color nocciola**) hazel, light brown

noccio'lina [nottʃo'lina] SF (anche: **nocciolina americana**) peanut

'nocciolo¹ [nɔt'tʃolo] SM (di frutto) stone; (fig) heart, core

nocci'olo² [not'tʃolo] SM (albero) hazel

'noce ['notʃe] SM (albero) walnut tree ▶ SF (frutto) walnut; **una ~ di burro** (Cuc) a knob of butter (BRIT), a dab of butter (US); **~ di cocco** coconut; **~ moscata** nutmeg

noce'pesca, -sche [notʃe'pɛska] SF nectarine

no'cevoetc [no'tʃevo] VB vedi **nuocere**

noci'uto [no'tʃuto] PP di **nuocere**

no'civo, -a [no'tʃivo] AG harmful, noxious

'nocqui VB vedi **nuocere**

'nodo SM (di cravatta, legname, Naut) knot; (Aut, Ferr) junction; (Med, Astr, Bot) node; (fig: legame) bond, tie; (: punto centrale) heart, crux; **avere un ~ alla gola** to have a lump in one's throat; **tutti i nodi vengono al pettine** (proverbio) your sins will find you out

no'doso, -a AG (tronco) gnarled

'nodulo SM (Anat, Bot) nodule

no-'global [no-'global] SMF anti-globalization protester ▶ AG (movimento, manifestante) anti-globalization

'noi PRON (soggetto) we; (oggetto: per dare rilievo, con preposizione) us; **~ stessi(e)** we ourselves; (oggetto) ourselves; **da ~** (nel nostro paese) in our country, where we come from; (a casa nostra) at our house

'noia SF boredom; (disturbo, impaccio) bother no pl, trouble no pl; **avere qn/qc a ~** not to like sb/sth; **mi è venuto a ~** I'm tired of it; **dare ~ a** to annoy; **avere delle noie con qn** to have trouble with sb

noi'altri PRON we

noi'oso, -a AG boring; (fastidioso) annoying, troublesome

noleggi'are [noled'dʒare] /62/ VT (prendere a noleggio) to hire (BRIT), rent; (dare a noleggio) to hire out (BRIT), rent out; (aereo, nave) to charter

noleggia'tore, -'trice [noleddʒa'tore] SM/F hirer (BRIT), renter; charterer

no'leggio [no'leddʒo] SM hire (BRIT), rental; charter

no'lente AG: **volente o ~** whether one likes it or not, willy-nilly

'nolo SM hire (BRIT), rental charter; (per trasporto merci) freight; **prendere/dare a ~ qc** to hire/hire out sth (BRIT), rent/rent out sth

'nomade AG nomadic ▶ SMF nomad

noma'dismo SM nomadism

'nome SM name; (Ling) noun; **in** o **a ~ di** in the name of; **di** o **per ~** (chiamato) called, named; **conoscere qn di ~** to know sb by name; **fare il ~ di qn** to name sb; **faccia pure il mio ~** feel free to mention my name; **~ d'arte** stage name; **~ di battesimo** Christian name; **~ depositato** trade name; **~ di famiglia** surname; **~ da ragazza** maiden name; **~ da sposata** married name; **~ utente** login

no'mea SF notoriety

nomencla'tura SF nomenclature

nomenkla'tura SF (di partito, stato) nomenklatura

no'mignolo [no'miɲɲolo] SM nickname

'nomina SF appointment

nomi'nale AG nominal; (Ling) noun cpd

nomi'nare /72/ VT to name; (eleggere) to appoint; (citare) to mention; **non l'ho mai sentito ~** I've never heard of it (o him)

nomination [nomi'neʃʃon] SF INV (in reality show) nomination

nomina'tivo, -a AG (*intestato: titolo*) registered; (: *libretto*) personal; (*Ling*) nominative ▶ SM (*Amm: nome*) name; (*Ling*) nominative; **elenco ~** list of names

non AV not ▶ PREFISSO non-; **grazie — ~ c'è di che** thank you — don't mention it; **i ~ credenti** the unbelievers; **~ autosufficiente** (*persona anziana*) needing care; *vedi anche* **affatto**; **appena** *ecc*

nonché [non'ke] CONG (*tanto più, tanto meno*) let alone; (*e inoltre*) as well as

nonconfor'mista, -i, -e AG, SM/F nonconformist

noncu'rante AG: **~ (di)** careless (of), indifferent (to); **con fare ~** with a nonchalant air

noncu'ranza [nonku'rantsa] SF carelessness, indifference; **un'aria di ~** a nonchalant air

nondi'meno CONG (*tuttavia*) however; (*nonostante*) nevertheless

'nonno, -a SM/F grandfather/mother; (*in senso più familiare*) grandma/grandpa; **nonni** SMPL grandparents

non'nulla SM INV: **un ~** nothing, a trifle

'nono, -a NUM ninth

nonos'tante PREP in spite of, notwithstanding ▶ CONG although, even though

non plus 'ultra SM INV: **il ~ (di)** the last word (in)

nontiscordardimé SM INV (*Bot*) forget-me-not

nord SM north ▶ AG INV north; (*regione*) northern; **verso ~** north, northwards; **l'America del N~** North America; **il Mare del N~** the North Sea

nor'dest SM north-east

'nordico, -a, -ci, -che AG nordic, northern European

nor'dista, -i, -e AG, SM/F Yankee

nor'dovest SM north-west

Norim'berga SF Nuremberg

'norma SF (*principio*) norm; (*regola*) regulation, rule; (*consuetudine*) custom, rule; **di ~** normally; **a ~ di legge** according to law, as laid down by law; **al di sopra della ~** above average, above the norm; **per sua ~ e regola** for your information; **proporsi una ~ di vita** to set o.s. rules to live by; **norme di sicurezza** safety regulations; **norme per l'uso** instructions for use

nor'male AG normal; standard *cpd*

normalità SF normality

normaliz'zare [normalid'dzare] /72/ VT to normalize, bring back to normal

normal'mente AV normally

Norman'dia SF: **la ~** Normandy

nor'manno, -a AG, SM/F Norman

norma'tivo, -a AG normative ▶ SF regulations *pl*

norve'gese [norve'dʒese] AG, SMF, SM Norwegian

Nor'vegia [nor'vɛdʒa] SF: **la ~** Norway

noso'comio SM hospital

nostal'gia [nostal'dʒia] SF (*di casa, paese*) homesickness; (*del passato*) nostalgia

nos'talgico, -a, -ci, -che [nos'taldʒiko] AG homesick; nostalgic ▶ SM/F (*Pol*) person who hopes for the return of Fascism

nos'trano, -a AG local; national; (*pianta, frutta*) home-produced

'nostro, -a DET: **il (la) ~(nostra)** *etc* our ▶ PRON: **il (la) ~(nostra)** *etc* ours ▶ SM: **il ~** our money; our belongings ▶ SF: **la nostra** (*opinione*) our view; **abbiamo speso del ~** we spent our own money; **i nostri** our family; our own people; **è dei nostri** he's one of us; **è dalla nostra** (*parte*) he's on our side; **anche noi abbiamo avuto le nostre** (*disavventure*) we've had our problems too; **alla nostra!** (*brindisi*) to us!

nos'tromo SM boatswain

'nota SF (*segno*) mark; (*comunicazione scritta: Mus*) note; (*fattura*) bill; (*elenco*) list; **prendere ~ di qc** to note sth, make a note of sth, write sth down; (*fig: fare attenzione*) to note sth, take note of sth; **degno di ~** noteworthy, worthy of note; **note caratteristiche** distinguishing marks o features; **note a piè di pagina** footnotes

no'tabile AG notable; (*persona*) important ▶ SM prominent citizen

no'taio SM notary

no'tare /72/ VT (*segnare: errori*) to mark; (*registrare*) to note (down), write down; (*rilevare, osservare*) to note, notice; **farsi ~** to get o.s. noticed

nota'rile AG: **atto ~** legal document (*authorized by a notary*); **studio ~** notary's office

notazi'one [notat'tsjone] SF (*Mus*) notation

no'tevole AG (*talento*) notable, remarkable; (*peso*) considerable

no'tifica, -che SF notification

notifi'care /2o/ VT (*Dir*): **~ qc a qn** to notify sb of sth, give sb notice of sth

notificazi'one [notifikat'tsjone] SF notification

no'tizia [no'tittsja] SF (*piece of*) news *sg*; (*informazione*) piece of information; **notizie** SFPL news *sg*; information *sg*

notizi'ario [notit'tsjarjo] SM (*Radio, TV, Stampa*) news *sg*

'noto, -a AG (*well-*)known

notorietà SF fame; notoriety

no'torio, -a AG well-known; (*peg*) notorious

not'tambulo, -a SM/F night-bird (*fig*)

not'tata SF night

'notte SF night; **di ~** at night; (*durante la notte*) in the night, during the night; **questa ~**

(*passata*) last night; (*che viene*) tonight; **nella ~ dei tempi** in the mists of time; **come va? — peggio che andar di ~** how are things? — worse than ever; **~ bianca** sleepless night

notte'tempo AV at night; during the night

'nottola SF (*Zool*) noctule

not'turno, -a AG nocturnal; (*servizio, guardiano*) night *cpd* ▶ SF (*Sport*) evening fixture (BRIT) o match

nov. ABBR (= *novembre*) Nov

no'vanta NUM ninety

novan'tenne AG, SMF ninety-year-old

novan'tesimo, -a NUM ninetieth

novan'tina SF: **una ~ (di)** about ninety

'nove NUM nine

novecen'tesco, -a, -schi, -sche [novet∫en'tesko] AG twentieth-century

nove'cento [nove't∫ento] NUM nine hundred ▶ SM: **il N~** the twentieth century

no'vella SF (*Letteratura*) short story

novel'lino, -a AG (*pivello*) green, inexperienced

novel'lista, -i, -e SM/F short-story writer

novel'listica SF (*arte*) short-story writing; (*insieme di racconti*) short stories *pl*

no'vello, -a AG (*piante, patate*) new; (*insalata, verdura*) early; (*sposo*) newly-married

no'vembre SM November; *vedi anche* **luglio**

novem'brino, -a AG November *cpd*

nove'mila NUM nine thousand

noven'nale AG (*che dura 9 anni*) nine-year *cpd*; (*ogni 9 anni*) nine-yearly

novi'lunio SM (*Astr*) new moon

novità SF INV novelty; (*innovazione*) innovation; (*cosa originale, insolita*) something new; (*notizia*) (piece of) news *sg*; **le ~ della moda** the latest fashions

novizi'ato [novit'tsjato] SM (*Rel*) novitiate; (*tirocinio*) apprenticeship

no'vizio, -a [no'vittsjo] SM/F (*Rel*) novice; (*tirocinante*) beginner, apprentice

nozi'one [not'tsjone] SF notion, idea; **nozioni** SFPL (*rudimenti*) basic knowledge *sg*, rudiments

nozio'nismo [nottsjo'nizmo] SM superficial knowledge

nozio'nistico, -a, -ci, -che [nottsjo'nistiko] AG superficial

'nozze ['nɔttse] SFPL wedding *sg*, marriage *sg*; **~ d'argento/d'oro** silver/golden wedding *sg*

ns . ABBR (*Comm*) = **nostro**

NU SIGLA = **Nuoro**

N.U. SIGLA (= *Nazioni Unite*) UN

'nube SF cloud

nubi'fragio [nubi'fradʒo] SM cloudburst

'nubile AG (*donna*) unmarried, single

'nuca, -che SF nape of the neck

nucle'are AG nuclear ▶ SM: **il ~** nuclear energy

'nucleo SM nucleus; (*gruppo*) team, unit, group; (*Mil, Polizia*) squad; **~ antidroga** anti-drugs squad; **il ~ familiare** the family unit

nu'dismo SM nudism

nu'dista, -i, -e SM/F nudist

nudità SF INV nudity, nakedness; (*di paesaggio*) bareness ▶ SFPL (*parti nude del corpo*) nakedness *sg*

'nudo, -a AG (*persona*) bare, naked, nude; (*membra*) bare, naked; (*montagna*) bare ▶ SM (*Arte*) nude; **a occhio ~** to the naked eye; **a piedi nudi** barefoot; **mettere a ~** (*cuore, verità*) to lay bare; **gli ha detto ~ e crudo che …** he told him bluntly that …

'nugolo SM: **un ~ di** a whole host of

'nulla PRON, AV = **niente** ▶ SM: **il ~** nothing; **svanire nel ~** to vanish into thin air; **basta un ~ per farlo arrabbiare** he gets annoyed over the slightest thing

nulla'osta SM INV authorization

nullate'nente AG: **essere ~** to own nothing ▶ SMF person with no property

nullità SF INV nullity; (*persona*) nonentity

'nullo, -a AG useless, worthless; (*Dir*) null (and void); (*Sport*): **incontro ~** draw

nume'rale AG, SM numeral

nume'rare /72/ VT to number

numera'tore SM (*Mat*) numerator; (*macchina*) numbering device

numerazi'one [numerat'tsjone] SF numbering; (*araba, decimale*) notation

nu'merico, -a, -ci, -che AG numerical

'numero SM number; (*romano, arabo*) numeral; (*di spettacolo*) act, turn; **dare i numeri** (*farneticare*) not to be all there; **tanto per fare ~ invitiamo anche lui** why don't we invite him to make up the numbers?; **ha tutti i numeri per riuscire** he's got what it takes to succeed; **che ~ tuo fratello!** your brother is a real character!; **~ civico** house number; **~ chiuso** (*Università*) selective entry system; **~ doppio** (*di rivista*) issue with supplement; **~ di scarpe** shoe size; **~ di telefono** telephone number; **~ verde** (*Tel*) ≈ Freephone®

nume'roso, -a AG numerous, many; (*folla, famiglia*) large

numis'matica SF numismatics *sg*, coin collecting

'nunzio ['nuntsjo] SM (*Rel*) nuncio

nu'occio *etc* ['nwɔtt∫o] VB *vedi* **nuocere**

nu'ocere ['nwɔt∫ere] /69/ VI: **~ a** to harm, damage; **il tentar non nuoce** (*proverbio*) there's no harm in trying

nuoci'uto, -a [nwo't∫uto] PP *di* **nuocere**

nu'ora SF daughter-in-law

nuo'tare /72/ VI to swim; (*galleggiare: oggetti*) to float; **~ a rana/sul dorso** to do the breast stroke/backstroke

n

235

nuo'tata sf swim

nuota'tore, -'trice sm/f swimmer

nu'oto sm swimming

nu'ova sf vedi **nuovo**

nuova'mente av again

Nu'ova York sf New York

Nu'ova Ze'landa [-dze'landa] sf: **la** ~ New Zealand

nu'ovo, -a ag new ▶ sf (notizia) (piece of) news sg; **come** ~ as good as new; **di** ~ again; **fino a** ~ **ordine** until further notice; **il suo volto non mi è** ~ I know his face; **rimettere a** ~ (cosa, macchina) to do up like new; **anno** ~, **vita nuova!** it's time to turn over a new leaf!; ~ **fiammante** o **di zecca** brand-new; **la Nuova Guinea** New Guinea; **la Nuova Inghilterra** New England; **la Nuova Scozia** Nova Scotia

nu'trice [nu'tritʃe] sf wet nurse

nutri'ente ag nutritious, nourishing; (crema, balsamo) nourishing

nutri'mento sm food, nourishment

nu'trire /**45**/ vt to feed; (fig: sentimenti) to harbour (BRIT), harbor (US), nurse; **nutrirsi** vpr: **nutrirsi di** to feed on, to eat

nutri'tivo, -a ag nutritional; (alimento) nutritious

nu'trito, -a ag (numeroso) large; (fitto) heavy; **ben/mal** ~ well/poorly fed

nutrizi'one [nutrit'tsjone] sf nutrition

'nuvolo, -a ag cloudy ▶ sf cloud

nuvolosità sf cloudiness

nuvo'loso, -a ag cloudy

nuzi'ale [nut'tsjale] ag nuptial; wedding cpd

'nylon ['nailən] sm nylon

Oo

O, o [ɔ] SM O F INV (*lettera*) O, o; **O come
Otranto** ≈ O for Oliver (BRIT), O for Oboe (US)
o CONG (*dav V spesso*): **od** or; **o … o** either … or;
o l'uno o l'altro either (of them); **o meglio**
or rather
O. ABBR (= *ovest*) W
'oasi SF INV oasis
obbedi'ente *etc vedi* **ubbidiente** *ecc*
obbiet'tare *etc vedi* **obiettare** *ecc*
obbli'gare /**80**/ VT (*Dir*) to bind; (*costringere*):
~ qn a fare to force *o* oblige sb to do;
obbligarsi VPR: **obbligarsi a fare** to
undertake to do; **obbligarsi per qn** (*Dir*) to
stand surety for sb, act as guarantor for sb
obbliga'tissimo, -a AG (*ringraziamento*): **~!**
much obliged!
obbli'gato, -a AG (*costretto, grato*) obliged;
(*percorso, tappa*) set, fixed; **passaggio ~** (*fig*)
essential requirement
obbliga'torio, -a AG compulsory, obligatory
obbligazi'one [obbligat'tsjone] SF
obligation; (*Comm*) bond, debenture; **~ dello
Stato** government bond; **obbligazioni
convertibili** convertible loan stock,
convertible debentures
obbligazio'nista, -i, -e [obbligattsjo'nista]
SM/F bond-holder
'obbligo, -ghi SM obligation; (*dovere*) duty;
avere l'~ di fare, essere nell'~ di fare to be
obliged to do; **essere d'~** (*discorso, applauso*) to
be called for; **avere degli obblighi con *o*
verso qn** to be under an obligation to sb, be
indebted to sb; **le formalità d'~** the
necessary formalities
obb.mo ABBR = **obbligatissimo**
ob'brobrio SM disgrace; (*fig*) mess, eyesore
obe'lisco, -schi SM obelisk
obe'rato, -a AG: **~ di** (*lavoro*) overloaded *o*
overburdened with; (*debiti*) crippled with
obesità SF obesity
o'beso, -a AG obese
obiet'tare /**72**/ VT: **~ che** to object that; **~ su
qc** to object to sth, raise objections
concerning sth

obiettiva'mente AV objectively
obiettività SF objectivity
obiet'tivo, -a AG objective ▶ SM (*Ottica, Fot*)
lens *sg*, objective; (*Mil, fig*) objective
obiet'tore SM objector; **~ di coscienza**
conscientious objector
obiezi'one [objet'tsjone] SF objection
obi'torio SM morgue
o'bliquo, -a AG oblique; (*inclinato*) slanting;
(*fig*) devious, underhand; **sguardo ~**
sidelong glance
oblite'rare /**72**/ VT (*francobollo*) to cancel;
(*biglietto*) to stamp
oblitera'trice [oblitera'tritʃe] SF (*anche:
macchina obliteratrice*) cancelling
machine; stamping machine
oblò SM INV porthole
o'blungo, -a, -ghi, -ghe AG oblong
'oboe SM (*Mus*) oboe
'obolo SM (*elemosina*) (small) offering, mite
obsole'scenza [obsoleʃʃɛntsa] SF (*Econ*)
obsolescence
obso'leto, -a AG obsolete
OC ABBR (= *onde corte*) SW
'oca (*pl* **oche**) SF goose
o'caggine [o'kaddʒine] SF silliness, stupidity
occasio'nale AG (*incontro*) chance; (*cliente,
guadagni*) casual, occasional
occasi'one SF (*caso favorevole*) opportunity;
(*causa, motivo, circostanza*) occasion; (*Comm*)
bargain; **all'~** should the need arise; **alla
prima ~** at the first, opportunity; **d'~** (*a buon
prezzo*) bargain *cpd*; (*usato*) secondhand
occhi'aia [ok'kjaja] SF eye socket; **occhiaie**
SFPL (*sotto gli occhi*) shadows (under the eyes);
avere le occhiaie to have shadows under
one's eyes
occhi'ali [ok'kjali] SMPL glasses, spectacles;
~ da sole/da vista sunglasses/(prescription)
glasses
occhi'ata [ok'kjata] SF look, glance; **dare
un'~ a** to have a look at
occhieggi'are [okkjed'dʒare] /**62**/ VI (*apparire
qua e là*) to peep (out)

occhi'ello [ok'kjɛllo] sᴍ buttonhole; (asola) eyelet

'**occhio** ['ɔkkjo] sᴍ eye; ~! careful!, watch out!; **a ~ nudo** with the naked eye; **a quattr'occhi** privately, tête-à-tête, in private; **avere ~** to have a good eye; **chiudere un ~ (su)** (fig) to turn a blind eye (to), shut one's eyes (to); **costare un ~ della testa** to cost a fortune; **dare all'~ o nell'~ a qn** to catch sb's eye; **fare l'~ a qc** to get used to sth; **tenere d'~ qn** to keep an eye on sb; **vedere di buon/mal ~ qc** to look favourably/unfavourably on sth

occhio'lino [okkjo'lino] sᴍ: **fare l'~ a qn** to wink at sb

occiden'tale [ottʃiden'tale] ᴀɢ western ▸ sᴍꜰ Westerner

occi'dente [ottʃi'dɛnte] sᴍ west; (Pol): **l'O~** the West; **a ~** in the west

oc'cipite [ot'tʃipite] sᴍ back of the head, occiput (Anat)

oc'cludere /3/ ᴠᴛ to block

occlusi'one sꜰ blockage, obstruction

oc'cluso, -a ᴘᴘ di occludere

occor'rente ᴀɢ necessary ▸ sᴍ all that is necessary

occor'renza [okkor'rɛntsa] sꜰ necessity, need; **all'~** in case of need

oc'correre /28/ ᴠɪ to be needed, be required ▸ ᴠʙ ɪᴍᴘᴇʀs: **occorre farlo** it must be done; **occorre che tu parta** you must leave, you'll have to leave; **mi occorrono i soldi** I need the money

oc'corso, -a ᴘᴘ di occorrere

occulta'mento sᴍ concealment

occul'tare /72/ ᴠᴛ to hide, conceal

oc'culto, -a ᴀɢ hidden, concealed; (scienze, forze) occult

occu'pante sᴍꜰ (di casa) occupier, occupant; **~ abusivo** squatter

occu'pare /72/ ᴠᴛ to occupy; (manodopera) to employ; (ingombrare) to occupy, take up; **occuparsi** ᴠᴘʀ to occupy o.s., keep o.s. busy; (impiegarsi) to get a job; **occuparsi di** (interessarsi) to take an interest in; (prendersi cura di) to look after, take care of

occu'pato, -a ᴀɢ (Mil, Pol) occupied; (persona: affaccendato) busy; (posto, sedia) taken; (toilette, Tel) engaged; **la linea è occupata** the line's engaged

occupazio'nale [okkupattsjo'nale] ᴀɢ employment cpd, of employment

occupazi'one [okkupat'tsjone] sꜰ occupation; (impiego, lavoro) job; (Econ) employment

Oce'ania [otʃe'anja] sꜰ: **l'~** Oceania

o'ceano [o'tʃɛano] sᴍ ocean

'**ocra** sꜰ ochre

'**OCSE** sɪɢʟᴀ ꜰ (= Organizzazione per la Cooperazione e lo Sviluppo Economico) OECD (= Organization for Economic Cooperation and Development)

ocu'lare ᴀɢ ocular, eye cpd; **testimone ~** eye witness

ocula'tezza [okula'tettsa] sꜰ caution; shrewdness

ocu'lato, -a ᴀɢ (attento) cautious, prudent; (accorto) shrewd

ocu'lista, -i, -e sᴍ/ꜰ eye specialist, oculist

od ᴄᴏɴɢ vedi **o**

'**ode** sꜰ ode

'**ode** etc ᴠʙ vedi **udire**

odi'are /19/ ᴠᴛ to hate, detest

odi'erno, -a ᴀɢ today's, of today; (attuale) present; **in data odierna** (formale) today

'**odio** sᴍ hatred; **avere in ~ qc/qn** to hate o detest sth/sb

odi'oso, -a ᴀɢ hateful, odious; **rendersi ~ (a)** to make o.s. unpopular (with)

'**odo** etc ᴠʙ vedi **udire**

odontoi'atra, -i, -e sᴍ/ꜰ dentist, dental surgeon

odontoia'tria sꜰ dentistry

odonto'tecnico, -ci sᴍ dental technician

odo'rare /72/ ᴠᴛ (annusare) to smell; (profumare) to perfume, scent ▸ ᴠɪ: **~ (di)** to smell (of)

odo'rato sᴍ sense of smell

o'dore sᴍ smell; **gli odori** (Cuc) (aromatic) herbs; **sentire ~ di qc** to smell sth; **morire in ~ di santità** (Rel) to die in the odour (BRIT) o odor (US) of sanctity

odo'roso, -a ᴀɢ sweet-smelling

offendere /36/ ᴠᴛ to offend; (violare) to break, violate; (insultare) to insult; (ferire) to hurt; **offendersi** ᴠᴘʀ (con senso reciproco) to insult one another; (risentirsi) **offendersi (di)** to take offence (at), be offended (by)

offen'sivo, -a ᴀɢ, sꜰ offensive

offen'sore sᴍ offender; (Mil) aggressor

offe'rente sᴍ (in aste): **al migliore ~** to the highest bidder

offerto, -a ᴘᴘ di offrire ▸ sꜰ offer; (donazione: anche Rel) offering; (in gara d'appalto) tender; (in aste) bid; (Econ) supply; **fare un'offerta** to make an offer; (per appalto) to tender; (ad un'asta) to bid; **offerta pubblica d'acquisto** takeover bid; **offerta pubblica di vendita** public offer for sale; **offerta reale** tender; **"offerte d'impiego"** (Stampa) "situations vacant" (BRIT), "help wanted" (US); **offerta speciale** special offer

offeso, -a ᴘᴘ di offendere ▸ ᴀɢ offended; (fisicamente) hurt, injured ▸ sᴍ/ꜰ offended party ▸ sꜰ insult, affront; (Mil) attack; (Dir) offence (BRIT), offense (US); **essere ~ con qn** to be annoyed with sb; **parte offesa** (Dir) plaintiff

offi'ciare [offi'tʃare] /14/ ᴠɪ (Rel) to officiate

offi'cina [offi'tʃina] sꜰ workshop

of'frire /7o/ VT to offer; **offrirsi** VPR (*proporsi*) to offer (o.s.), volunteer; (*occasione*) to present itself; (*esporsi*) **offrirsi a** to expose o.s. to; **ti offro da bere** I'll buy you a drink; **"offresi posto di segretaria"** "secretarial vacancy", "vacancy for secretary"; **"segretaria offresi"** "secretary seeks post"

offus'care /20/ VT to obscure, darken; (*fig: intelletto*) to dim, cloud; (*: fama*) to obscure, overshadow; **offuscarsi** VPR to grow dark; to cloud, grow dim; to be obscured

of'talmico, -a, -ci, -che AG ophthalmic

oggettività [oddʒettivi'ta] SF objectivity

ogget'tivo, -a [oddʒet'tivo] AG objective

og'getto [od'dʒetto] SM object; (*materia, argomento*) subject (matter); (*in lettere commerciali*): ~ ... re ...; **essere ~ di** (*critiche, controversia*) to be the subject of; (*odio, pietà ecc*) to be the object of; **essere ~ di scherno** to be a laughing stock; **in ~ a quanto detto** (*in lettere*) as regards the matter mentioned above; **oggetti preziosi** valuables, articles of value; **oggetti smarriti** lost property *sg* (BRIT), lost and found *sg* (US)

'oggi ['ɔddʒi] AV, SM today; ~ **stesso** today, this very day; ~ **come** ~ at present, as things stand; **dall'** ~ **al domani** from one day to the next; **a tutt'**~ up till now, till today; **le spese a tutt'**~ **sono** ... expenses to date are ...; ~ **a otto** a week today

oggigi'orno [oddʒi'dʒorno] AV nowadays

o'giva [o'dʒiva] SF ogive, pointed arch

OGM [ɔdʒi'ɛmme] SIGLA MPL (= *organismi geneticamente modificati*) GMO (= *genetically modified organisms*)

'ogni ['oɲɲi] DET every, each; (*tutti*) all; (*con valore distributivo*) every; ~ **uomo è mortale** all men are mortal; **viene ~ due giorni** he comes every two days; ~ **cosa** everything; **ad ~ costo** at all costs, at any price; **in ~ luogo** everywhere; ~ **tanto** every so often; ~ **volta che** every time that

Ognis'santi [oɲɲis'santi] SM All Saints' Day

o'gnuno [oɲ'ɲuno] PRON everyone, everybody

'ohi ESCL oh!; (*esprimente dolore*) ow!

ohi'mè ESCL oh dear!

'OIL SIGLA F (= *Organizzazione Internazionale del Lavoro*) ILO

OL ABBR (= *onde lunghe*) LW

O'landa SF: l'~ Holland

olan'dese AG Dutch ▶ SM (*Ling*) Dutch ▶ SMF Dutchman/woman; **gli Olandesi** the Dutch

ole'andro SM oleander

ole'ato, -a AG: **carta oleata** greaseproof paper (BRIT), wax paper (US)

oleo'dotto SM oil pipeline

ole'oso, -a AG oily; (*che contiene olio*) oil *cpd*, oil-yielding

o'lezzo [o'leddzo] SM fragrance

ol'fatto SM sense of smell

oli'are /19/ VT to oil

olia'tore SM oil can, oiler

oli'era SF oil cruet

oligar'chia [oligar'kia] SF oligarchy

Olim'piadi SFPL Olympic Games

o'limpico, -a, -ci, -che AG Olympic

'olio SM oil; (*Pittura*): **un (quadro a)** ~ an oil painting; **sott'**~ (*Cuc*) in oil; **oli essenziali** essential oils; ~ **di fegato di merluzzo** cod liver oil; ~ **d'oliva** olive oil; ~ **santo** holy oil; ~ **di semi** vegetable oil; ~ **solare** suntan oil; **oli essenziali** essential oils

o'liva SF olive

oli'vastro, -a AG olive(-coloured) (BRIT), olive(-colored) (US); (*carnagione*) sallow

oli'veto SM olive grove

o'livo SM olive tree

'olmo SM elm

olo'causto SM holocaust

OLP SIGLA F (= *Organizzazione per la Liberazione della Palestina*) PLO

oltraggi'are [oltrad'dʒare] /62/ VT to offend, insult

ol'traggio [ol'traddʒo] SM outrage; offence (BRIT), offense (US), insult; (*Dir*): ~ **a pubblico ufficiale** insulting a public official; (*Dir*): ~ **al pudore** indecent behaviour (BRIT) o behavior (US); ~ **alla corte** contempt of court

oltraggi'oso, -a [oltrad'dʒoso] AG offensive

ol'tralpe AV beyond the Alps

ol'tranza [ol'trantsa] SF: **a** ~ to the last, to the bitter end; **sciopero ad** ~ all-out strike

oltran'zismo [oltran'tsizmo] SM (*Pol*) extremism

oltran'zista, -i, -e [oltran'tsista] SM/F (*Pol*) extremist

'oltre AV (*più in là*) further; (*di più: aspettare*) longer, more ▶ PREP (*di là da*) beyond, over, on the other side of; (*più di*) more than, over; (*in aggiunta a*) besides; (*eccetto*): ~ **a** except, apart from; ~ **a tutto** on top of all that

oltrecor'tina AV behind the Iron Curtain; **paesi d'**~ Iron Curtain countries

oltre'manica AV across the Channel

oltre'mare AV overseas

oltre'modo AV extremely, greatly

oltreo'ceano [oltreo'tʃeano] AV overseas ▶ SM: **paesi d'**~ overseas countries

oltrepas'sare /72/ VT to go beyond, exceed

oltre'tomba SM INV: l'~ the hereafter

OM ABBR (= *onde medie*) MW; (*Mil*) = **ospedale militare**

o'maggio [o'maddʒo] SM (*dono*) gift; (*segno di rispetto*) homage, tribute; **omaggi** SMPL (*complimenti*) respects; **in** ~ (*copia, biglietto*) complimentary; **rendere** ~ **a** to pay homage

O

o tribute to; **presentare i propri omaggi a
qn** (*formale*) to pay one's respects to sb

'**Oman** SM: l'~ Oman

ombeli'cale AG umbilical

ombe'lico, -chi SM navel

'**ombra** SF (*zona non assolata, fantasma*) shade;
(*sagoma scura*) shadow ▸ AG INV: **bandiera ~**
flag of convenience; **governo ~** (*Pol*) shadow
cabinet; **sedere all'~** to sit in the shade;
nell'~ (*tramare, agire*) secretly; **restare nell'~**
(*fig: persona*) to remain in obscurity; **senza ~
di dubbio** without the shadow of a doubt

ombreggi'are [ombred'dʒare] /**62**/ VT to
shade

om'brello SM umbrella; **~ da sole** parasol,
sunshade

ombrel'lone SM beach umbrella

om'bretto SM eyeshadow

om'broso, -a AG shady, shaded; (*cavallo*)
nervous, skittish; (*persona*) touchy, easily
offended

O.M.C. SIGLA F (= *Organizzazione Mondiale del
Commercio*) WTO

ome'lette [ɔmə'lɛt] SF INV omelet(te)

ome'lia SF (*Rel*) homily, sermon

ome'opata SMF hom(o)eopath

omeopa'tia SF hom(o)eopathy

omeo'patico, -a, -ci, -che AG
hom(o)eopathic ▸ SM hom(o)eopath

omertà SF conspiracy of silence

o'messo, -a PP *di* **omettere**

o'mettere/63/ VT to omit, leave out; **~ di fare**
to omit *o* fail to do

omi'cida, -i, -e [omi'tʃida] AG homicidal,
murderous ▸ SM/F murderer (murderess)

omi'cidio [omi'tʃidjo] SM murder; **~ colposo**
(*Dir*) culpable homicide; **~ premeditato** (*Dir*)
murder

o'misi *etc* VB *vedi* **omettere**

omissi'one SF omission; **reato d'~** criminal
negligence; **~ di atti d'ufficio** negligence;
~ di denuncia failure to report a crime;
~ di soccorso (*Dir*) failure to stop and give
assistance

omogeneiz'zato [omodʒeneid'dzato] SM
baby food

omo'geneo, -a [omo'dʒɛneo] AG
homogeneous

omolo'gare/80/ VT (*Dir*) to approve,
recognize; (*ratificare*) to ratify

omologazi'one [omologat'tsjone] SF
approval; ratification

o'mologo, -a, -ghi, -ghe AG homologous,
corresponding ▸ SM/F opposite number

o'monimo, -a SM/F namesake ▸ SM (*Ling*)
homonym

omosessu'ale AG, SMF homosexual

O.M.S. SIGLA F = **Organizzazione Mondiale
della Sanità**

On. ABBR (*Pol*) = **onorevole**

'**oncia, -ce** ['ontʃa] SF ounce

'**onda** SF wave; **mettere** *o* **mandare
in ~** (*Radio, TV*) to broadcast; **andare in ~**
(*Radio, TV*) to go on the air; **onde corte/
medie/lunghe** short/medium/long
wave *sg*; **l'~ verde** (*Aut*) synchronized
traffic lights *pl*

on'data SF wave, billow; (*fig*) wave, surge;
a ondate in waves; **~ di caldo** heatwave;
~ di freddo cold spell *o* snap

'**onde** CONG (*affinché: con il congiuntivo*) so that,
in order that; (: *con l'infinito*) so as to, in
order to

ondeggi'are [onded'dʒare] /**62**/ VI (*acqua*) to
ripple; (*muoversi sulle onde: barca*) to rock, roll;
(*fig: muoversi come le onde, barcollare*) to sway;
(*essere incerto*) to waver

on'doso, -a AG (*moto*) of the waves

ondu'lato, -a AG (*capelli*) wavy; (*terreno*)
undulating; **cartone ~** corrugated paper;
lamiera ondulata sheet of corrugated iron

ondula'torio, -a AG undulating; (*Fisica*)
undulatory, wave *cpd*

ondulazi'one [ondulat'tsjone] SF
undulation; (*acconciatura*) wave

one'rato, -a AG: **~ di** burdened with, loaded
with

'**onere** SM burden; **~ finanziario** financial
charge; **oneri fiscali** taxes

one'roso, -a AG (*fig*) heavy, onerous

onestà SF honesty

onesta'mente AV honestly; fairly,
virtuously; (*in verità*) honestly, frankly

o'nesto, -a AG (*probo, retto*) honest; (*giusto*) fair;
(*casto*) chaste, virtuous

ONG SIGLA F INV (= *Organizzazione Non
Governativa*) NGO

'**onice** ['ɔnitʃe] SF onyx

o'nirico, -a, -ci, -che AG dreamlike, dream *cpd*

onnipo'tente AG omnipotent

onnipre'sente AG omnipresent; (*scherzoso*)
ubiquitous

onnisci'ente [onniʃʃɛnte] AG omniscient

onniveg'gente [onnived'dʒɛnte] AG
all-seeing

ono'mastico, -ci SM name day

onomato'pea SF onomatopoeia

onomato'peico, -a, -ci, -che AG
onomatopoeic

ono'ranze [ono'rantse] SFPL honours (*Brit*),
honors (*US*)

ono'rare/72/ VT to honour (*Brit*), honor (*US*);
(*far onore a*) to do credit to; **onorarsi** VPR:
onorarsi di qc/di fare to feel hono(u)red by
sth/to do

ono'rario, -a AG honorary ▸ SM fee

onora'tissimo, -a AG (*in presentazioni*): **~!**
delighted to meet you!

ono'rato, -a AG (*reputazione, famiglia, carriera*) distinguished; **essere ~ di fare qc** to have the honour to do sth *o* of doing sth; **~ di conoscerla!** (it is) a pleasure to meet you!

o'nore SM honour (*BRIT*), honor (*US*); **in ~ di** in hono(u)r of; **fare gli onori di casa** to play host (*o* hostess); **fare ~ a** to honour; (*pranzo*) to do justice to; (*famiglia*) to be a credit to; **farsi ~** to distinguish o.s.; **posto d'~** place of honour; **a onor del vero ...** to tell the truth ...

ono'revole AG honourable (*BRIT*), honorable (*US*) ▸ SM/F (*Pol*) ≈ Member of Parliament (*BRIT*), ≈ Congressman/woman (*US*)

onorifi'cenza [onorifi'tʃentsa] SF honour (*BRIT*), honor (*US*); decoration

ono'rifico, -a, -ci, -che AG honorary

'onta SF shame, disgrace; **ad ~ di** despite, notwithstanding

on'tano SM (*Bot*) alder

'O.N.U. SIGLA F (= *Organizzazione delle Nazioni Unite*) UN, UNO

'OPA SIGLA F = **offerta pubblica d'acquisto**

o'paco, -a, -chi, -che AG (*vetro*) opaque; (*metallo*) dull, matt

o'pale SM O F opal

'O.P.E.C. SIGLA F (= *Organization of Petroleum Exporting Countries*) OPEC

'opera SF (*gen*) work; (*azione rilevante*) action, deed, work; (*Mus*) work, opus; (: *melodramma*) opera; (: *teatro*) opera house; (*ente*) institution, organization; **per ~ sua** thanks to him; **fare ~ di persuasione presso qn** to try to convince sb; **mettersi/essere all'~** to get down to/be at work; **~ d'arte** work of art; **~ buffa** comic opera; **~ lirica** (grand) opera; **~ pia** religious charity; **opere pubbliche (OO.PP.)** public works; **opere di restauro/di scavo** restoration/excavation work *sg*

ope'raio, -a AG working-class; workers'; (*Zool*: *ape, formica*) worker *cpd* ▸ SM/F worker; **classe operaia** working class; **~ di fabbrica** factory worker; **~ a giornata** day labourer (*BRIT*) *o* laborer (*US*); **~ specializzato** *o* **qualificato** skilled worker; **~ non specializzato** semi-skilled worker

ope'rare /72/ VT to carry out, make; (*Med*) to operate on ▸ VI to operate, work; (*rimedio*) to act, work; (*Med*) to operate; **operarsi** VPR to occur, take place; (*Med*) to have an operation; **operarsi d'appendicite** to have one's appendix out; **~ qn d'urgenza** to perform an emergency operation on sb

opera'tivo, -a AG operative, operating; **piano ~** (*Mil*) plan of operations

ope'rato SM (*comportamento*) actions *pl*

opera'tore, -'trice SM/F operator; (*TV, Cine*) cameraman; **aperto solo agli operatori** (*Comm*) open to the trade only; **~ di borsa** dealer on the stock exchange; **~ ecologico** refuse collector; **~ economico** agent, broker; **~ del suono** sound recordist; **~ turistico** tour operator

opera'torio, -a AG (*Med*) operating

operazi'one [operat'tsjone] SF operation

ope'retta SF (*Mus*) operetta, light opera

operosità SF industry

ope'roso, -a AG industrious, hard-working

opi'ficio [opi'fitʃo] SM factory, works *pl*

opi'nabile AG (*discutibile*) debatable, questionable; **è ~** it is a matter of opinion

opini'one SF opinion; **avere il coraggio delle proprie opinioni** to have the courage of one's convictions; **l'~ pubblica** public opinion

opinio'nista, -i, -e SM/F (political) columnist

op là ESCL (*per far saltare*) hup!; (*a bimbo che è caduto*) upsy-daisy!

'oppio SM opium

oppi'omane SM/F opium addict

oppo'nente AG opposing ▸ SM/F opponent

op'pongo *etc* VB *vedi* **opporre**

op'porre /77/ VT to oppose; **opporsi** VPR: **opporsi (a qc)** to oppose (sth); to object (to sth); **~ resistenza/un rifiuto** to offer resistance/to refuse

opportu'nista, -i, -e SM/F opportunist

opportunità SF INV opportunity; (*convenienza*) opportuneness, timeliness

oppor'tuno, -a AG timely, opportune; (*giusto*) right, appropriate; **a tempo ~** at the right *o* the appropriate time

op'posi *etc* VB *vedi* **opporre**

opposi'tore, -'trice SM/F opposer, opponent

opposizi'one [oppozit'tsjone] SF opposition; (*Dir*) objection; **essere in netta ~** (*idee, opinioni*) to clash, be in complete opposition; **fare ~ a qn/qc** to oppose sb/sth

op'posto, -a PP *di* **opporre** ▸ AG opposite; (*opinioni*) conflicting ▸ SM opposite, contrary; **all'~** on the contrary

oppressi'one SF oppression

oppres'sivo, -a AG oppressive

op'presso, -a PP *di* **opprimere**

oppres'sore SM oppressor

oppri'mente AG (*caldo, noia*) oppressive; (*persona*) tiresome; (*deprimente*) depressing

op'primere /50/ VT (*premere, gravare*) to weigh down; (*estenuare*: *caldo*) to suffocate, oppress; (*tiranneggiare*: *popolo*) to oppress

oppu'gnare [oppuɲ'ɲare] /15/ VT (*fig*) to refute

op'pure CONG or (else)

op'tare /72/ VI: **~ per** (*scegliere*) to opt for, decide upon; (*Borsa*) to take (out) an option on

'optimum SM INV optimum

o

opu'lento, -a AG (*ricco*) rich, wealthy, affluent; (*arredamento ecc*) opulent

opu'lenza [opu'lɛntsa] SF (*vedi ag*) richness, wealth, affluence; opulence

o'puscolo SM booklet, pamphlet

OPV SIGLA F = **offerta pubblica di vendita**

opzio'nale [optsjo'nale] AG optional

opzi'one [op'tsjone] SF option

OR SIGLA = **Oristano**

'**ora** SF (*60 minuti*) hour; (*momento*) time ► AV (*adesso*) now; (*tra poco*) presently, in a minute; **è uscito proprio ~** (*poco fa*) he's just gone out; **~ ... ~** (*correlativo*) now ... now; **che – è?**, **che ore sono?** what time is it?; **domani a quest'~** this time tomorrow; **non veder l'~ di fare** to long to do, look forward to doing; **fare le ore piccole** to stay up till the early hours (of the morning) *o* the small hours; **è – di partire** it's time to go; **di buon' ~** early; **alla buon'~!** at last!; **~ legale** *o* **estiva** summer time (BRIT), daylight saving time (US); **~ di cena** dinner time; **~ locale** local time; **~ di pranzo** lunchtime; **~ di punta** (*Aut*) rush hour; **d'~ in avanti** *o* **poi** from now on; **or ~** just now, a moment ago; **~ come ~** right now, at present; **10 anni or sono** 10 years ago

o'racolo SM oracle

'**orafo** SM goldsmith

o'rale AG, SM oral

oral'mente AV orally

ora'mai AV = **ormai**

o'rario, -a AG hourly; (*fuso, segnale*) time *cpd*; (*velocità*) per hour ► SM timetable, schedule; (*di ufficio, visite ecc*) hours *pl*; time(s); **~ di apertura/chiusura** opening/closing time; **~ di apertura degli sportelli** bank opening hours; **~ elastico** *o* **flessibile** (*Industria*) flexitime; **~ ferroviario** railway timetable; **~ di lavoro/d'ufficio** working/office hours; **in ~** on time

o'rata SF (*Zool*) sea bream

ora'tore, -'trice SM/F speaker; orator

ora'torio, -a AG oratorical ► SM (*Rel*) oratory; (*Mus*) oratorio ► SF (*arte*) oratory

orazi'one [orat'tsjone] SF (*Rel*) prayer; (*discorso*) speech, oration

or'bene CONG so, well (then)

'**orbita** SF (*Astr, Fisica*) orbit; (*Anat*) (eye-)socket

orbi'tare/72/ VI to orbit

'**orbo, -a** AG blind

'**Orcadi** SFPL: **le (isole) ~** the Orkney Islands, the Orkneys

or'chestra [or'kɛstra] SF orchestra

orches'trale [orkes'trale] AG orchestral ► SMF orchestra player

orches'trare [orkes'trare] /72/ VT to orchestrate; (*fig*) to stage-manage

orchi'dea [orki'dɛa] SF orchid

'**orcio** ['ortʃo] SM jar

'**orco, -chi** SM ogre

'**orda** SF horde

or'digno [or'diɲɲo] SM: **~ esplosivo** explosive device

ordi'nale AG, SM ordinal

ordina'mento SM order, arrangement; (*regolamento*) regulations *pl*, rules *pl*; **~ scolastico/giuridico** education/legal system

ordi'nanza [ordi'nantsa] SF (*Dir, Mil*) order; (*Amm: decreto*) decree; (*persona: Mil*) orderly, batman; **d'~** (*Mil*) regulation *cpd*; **ufficiale d'~** orderly; **~ municipale** by(e)-law

ordi'nare/72/ VT (*mettere in ordine*) to arrange, organize; (*Comm*) to order; (*prescrivere: medicina*) to prescribe; (*comandare*) **~ a qn di fare qc** to order *o* command sb to do sth; (*Rel*) to ordain

ordi'nario, -a AG (*comune*) ordinary; everyday; standard; (*grossolano*) coarse, common ► SM ordinary; (*Ins: di università*) full professor

ordina'tivo, -a AG regulating, governing ► SM (*Comm*) order

ordi'nato, -a AG tidy, orderly

ordinazi'one [ordinat'tsjone] SF (*Comm*) order; (*Rel*) ordination; **fare un'~ di qc** to put in an order for sth, order sth; **eseguire qc su ~** to make sth to order

'**ordine** SM order; (*carattere*): **d'~ pratico** of a practical nature; **all'~** (*Comm: assegno*) to order; **di prim'~** first-class; **fino a nuovo ~** until further notice; **essere in ~** (*documenti*) to be in order; (*persona, stanza*) to be tidy; **mettere in ~** to put in order, tidy (up); **richiamare all'~** to call to order; **le forze dell'~** the forces of law and order; **~ d'acquisto** purchase order; **l'~ degli avvocati** = the Bar; **~ del giorno** (*di seduta*) agenda; (*Mil*) order of the day; **l'~ dei medici** = the Medical Association; **~ di pagamento** standing order (BRIT), automatic payment (US); (*Comm*) order for payment; **l'~ pubblico** law and order; **ordini (sacri)** (*Rel*) holy orders

or'dire/55/ VT (*fig*) to plot, scheme

or'dito SM (*di tessuto*) warp

orecchi'abile [orek'kjabile] AG (*canzone*) catchy

orec'chino [orek'kino] SM earring

o'recchio [o'rekkjo] (*pl(f)* **orecchie**) SM (*Anat*) ear; **avere ~** to have a good ear (for music); **venire all'~ di qn** to come to sb's attention; **fare orecchie da mercante (a)** to turn a deaf ear (to)

orecchi'oni [orek'kjoni] SMPL (*Med*) mumps *sg*

o'refice [o'refitʃe] SM goldsmith; jeweller (BRIT), jeweler (US)

orefice'ria [orefitʃe'ria] SF (arte) goldsmith's art; (negozio) jeweller's (shop) (BRIT), jewelry store (US)

'**orfano, -a** AG orphan(ed) ▶ SM/F orphan; ~ **di padre/madre** fatherless/motherless

orfano'trofio SM orphanage

orga'netto SM barrel organ; (col: armonica a bocca) mouth organ; (: fisarmonica) accordion

or'ganico, -a, -ci, -che AG organic ▶ SM personnel, staff

organi'gramma, -i SM organization chart; (Inform) computer flow chart

orga'nismo SM (Biol) organism; (Anat, Amm) body, organism

orga'nista, -i, -e SM/F organist

organiz'zare [organid'dzare] /72/ VT to organize; **organizzarsi** VPR to get organized

organizza'tivo, -a [organiddza'tivo] AG organizational

organizza'tore, -'trice [organiddza'tore] AG organizing ▶ SM/F organizer

organizzazi'one [organiddzat'tsjone] SF (azione) organizing, arranging; (risultato) organization; **O~ Mondiale della Sanità** World Health Organization

'**organo** SM organ; (di congegno) part; (portavoce) spokesman/woman, mouthpiece; **organi di trasmissione** (Tecn) transmission (unit) sg

or'gasmo SM (Fisiol) orgasm; (fig) agitation, anxiety

'**orgia, -ge** ['ɔrdʒa] SF orgy

or'goglio [or'goʎʎo] SM pride

orgogli'oso, -a [orgoʎ'ʎoso] AG proud

orien'tabile AG adjustable

orien'tale AG (paese, regione) eastern; (tappeti, lingua, civiltà) oriental; east

orienta'mento SM positioning; orientation; direction; **senso di ~** sense of direction; **perdere l'~** to lose one's bearings; **~ professionale** careers guidance

orien'tare /72/ VT (situare) to position; (carta, bussola) to orientate; (fig) to direct; **orientarsi** VPR to find one's bearings; (fig: tendere) to tend, lean; (indirizzarsi) **orientarsi verso** to take up, go in for

orienta'tivo, -a AG indicative, for guidance; **a scopo ~** for guidance

ori'ente SM east; **l'O~** the East, the Orient; **il Medio/l'Estremo O~** the Middle/Far East; **a ~** in the east

ori'ficio [ori'fitʃo], **ori'fizio** [ori'fittsjo] SM (apertura) opening; (di tubo) mouth; (Anat) orifice

o'rigano SM oregano

origi'nale [oridʒi'nale] AG original; (bizzarro) eccentric ▶ SM original

originalità [oridʒinali'ta] SF originality; eccentricity

origi'nare [oridʒi'nare] /72/ VT to bring about, produce ▶ VI: ~ **da** to arise o spring from

origi'nario, -a [oridʒi'narjo] AG original; **essere ~ di** to be a native of; (provenire da) to originate from; (animale, pianta) to be native to, be indigenous to

o'rigine [o'ridʒine] SF origin; **all'~** originally; **d'~ inglese** of English origin; **avere ~ da** to originate from; **dare ~ a** to give rise to

origli'are [oriʎ'ʎare] /27/ VI: ~ **(a)** to eavesdrop (on)

o'rina SF urine

ori'nale SM chamberpot

ori'nare /72/ VI to urinate ▶ VT to pass

orina'toio SM (public) urinal

ori'undo, -a AG: **essere ~ di Milano** etc to be of Milanese etc extraction o origin ▶ SM/F person of foreign extraction o origin

orizzon'tale [oriddzon'tale] AG horizontal

oriz'zonte [orid'dzonte] SM horizon

ORL SIGLA F (Med: = otorinolaringoiatria) ENT

or'lare /72/ VT to hem

orla'tura SF (azione) hemming no pl; (orlo) hem

'**orlo** SM edge, border; (di recipiente) rim, brim; (di vestito ecc) hem; **pieno fino all'~** full to the brim, brimful; **sull'~ della pazzia/della rovina** on the brink o verge of madness/ruin; ~ **a giorno** hemstitch

'**orma** SF (di persona) footprint; (di animale) track; (impronta, traccia) mark, trace; **seguire** o **calcare le orme di qn** to follow in sb's footsteps

or'mai AV by now, by this time; (adesso) now; (quasi) almost, nearly

ormeggi'are [ormed'dʒare] /62/ VT, **ormeggi'arsi** VPR (Naut) to moor

or'meggio [or'meddʒo] SM (atto) mooring no pl; (luogo) moorings pl; **posto d'~** berth

ormo'nale AG hormonal; (disfunzione, cura) hormone cpd; **terapia ~** hormone therapy

or'mone SM hormone

ornamen'tale AG ornamental, decorative

orna'mento SM ornament, decoration

or'nare /72/ VT to adorn, decorate; **ornarsi** VPR: **ornarsi (di)** to deck o.s. (out) (with)

or'nato, -a AG ornate

ornitolo'gia [ornitolo'dʒia] SF ornithology

orni'tologo, -a, -gi, -ghe SM/F ornithologist

'**oro** SM gold; **d'~, in ~** gold cpd; **d'~** (colore, occasione) golden; (persona) marvellous (BRIT), marvelous (US); **un affare d'~** a real bargain; **prendere qc per ~ colato** to take sth as gospel (truth); ~ **nero** black gold; ~ **zecchino** pure gold

orologe'ria [orolodʒe'ria] SF watchmaking no pl; watchmaker's (shop), clockmaker's (shop); **bomba a ~** time bomb

orologi'aio [orolo'dʒajo] SM watchmaker; clockmaker

o

oro'logio [oro'lɔdʒo] SM clock; (*da tasca, da polso*) watch; **~ biologico** biological clock; **~ da polso** wristwatch; **~ al quarzo** quartz watch; **~ a sveglia** alarm clock

o'roscopo SM horoscope

or'rendo, -a AG (*spaventoso*) horrible, awful; (*bruttissimo*) hideous

or'ribile AG horrible

'orrido, -a AG fearful, horrid

orripi'lante AG hair-raising, horrifying

or'rore SM horror; **avere in ~ qn/qc** to loathe *o* detest sb/sth; **mi fanno ~** I loathe *o* detest them

orsacchi'otto [orsak'kjɔtto] SM teddy bear

'orso SM bear; **~ bruno/bianco** brown/polar bear

orsù ESCL come now!

or'taggio [or'taddʒo] SM vegetable

or'tensia SF hydrangea

or'tica, -che SF (stinging) nettle

orti'caria SF nettle rash

orticol'tura SF horticulture

'orto SM vegetable garden, kitchen garden; (*Agr*) market garden (*BRIT*), truck farm (*US*); **~ botanico** botanical garden(s)

orto'dosso, -a AG orthodox

ortofrut'ticolo, -a AG fruit and vegetable *cpd*

ortogo'nale AG perpendicular

ortogra'fia SF spelling

orto'lano, -a SM/F (*venditore*) greengrocer (*BRIT*), produce dealer (*US*)

ortope'dia SF orthopaedics *sg* (*BRIT*), orthopedics *sg* (*US*)

orto'pedico, -a, -ci, -che AG orthopaedic (*BRIT*), orthopedic (*US*) ▶ SM orthopaedic specialist (*BRIT*), orthopedist (*US*)

orzai'olo [ordza'jɔlo], **orzaiu'olo** [ordza'jwɔlo] SM (*Med*) stye

or'zata [or'dzata] SF barley water

'orzo ['ɔrdzo] SM barley

'OSA SIGLA F (= *Organizzazione degli Stati Americani*) OAS (= *Organization of American States*)

o'sare/72/ VT, VI to dare; **~ fare** to dare (to) do; **come osi?** how dare you?

oscenità [oʃʃeni'ta] SF INV obscenity

o'sceno, -a [oʃ'ʃɛno] AG obscene; (*ripugnante*) ghastly

oscil'lare [oʃʃil'lare] /72/ VI (*pendolo*) to swing; (*dondolare: al vento ecc*) to rock; (*variare*) to fluctuate; (*Tecn*) to oscillate; (*fig*): **~ fra** to waver *o* hesitate between

oscillazi'one [oʃʃillat'tsjone] SF oscillation; (*di prezzi, temperatura*) fluctuation

oscura'mento SM darkening; obscuring; (*in tempo di guerra*) blackout

oscu'rare/72/ VT to darken, obscure; (*fig*) to obscure; **oscurarsi** VPR (*cielo*) to darken, cloud over; (*persona*) **si oscurò in volto** his face clouded over

oscurità SF (*vedi ag*) darkness; obscurity, gloominess

os'curo, -a AG dark; (*fig: incomprensibile*) obscure; (*umile: vita, natali*) humble, lowly, obscure; (*triste: pensiero*) gloomy, sombre ▶ SM: **all'~** in the dark; **tenere qn all'~ di qc** to keep sb in the dark about sth

'Oslo SF Oslo

ospe'dale SM hospital

ospedali'ero, -a AG hospital *cpd*

ospi'tale AG hospitable

ospitalità SF hospitality

ospi'tare/72/ VT to give hospitality to; (*albergo*) to accommodate

'ospite SMF (*persona che ospita*) host/hostess; (*persona ospitata*) guest

os'pizio [os'pittsjo] SM (*per vecchi ecc*) home

'ossa SF PL *vedi* **osso**

os'sario SM (*Mil*) war memorial (*with burial place*)

ossa'tura SF (*Anat*) skeletal structure, frame; (*Tecn: fig*) framework

'osseo, -a AG bony; (*tessuto ecc*) bone *cpd*

osse'quente AG: **~ alla legge** law-abiding

os'sequio SM deference, respect; **ossequi** SM PL (*saluto*) respects, regards; **porgere i propri ossequi a qn** (*formale*) to pay one's respects to sb; **ossequi alla signora!** (give my) regards to your wife!

ossequi'oso, -a AG obsequious

osser'vanza [osser'vantsa] SF observance

osser'vare/72/ VT to observe, watch; (*esaminare*) to examine; (*notare, rilevare*) to notice, observe; (*Dir: la legge*) to observe, respect; (*mantenere: silenzio*) to keep, observe; **far ~ qc a qn** to point sth out to sb

osserva'tore, -'trice AG observant, perceptive ▶ SM/F observer

osserva'torio SM (*Astr*) observatory; (*Mil*) observation post

osservazi'one [osservat'tsjone] SF observation; (*di legge ecc*) observance; (*considerazione critica*) observation, remark; (*rimprovero*) reproof; **in ~** under observation; **fare un'~** to make a remark; to raise an objection; **fare un'~ a qn** to criticize sb

ossessio'nare/72/ VT to obsess, haunt; (*tormentare*) to torment, harass

ossessi'one SF obsession; (*seccatura*) nuisance

osses'sivo, -a AG obsessive, haunting troublesome

os'sesso, -a AG (*spiritato*) possessed

os'sia CONG that is, to be precise

ossi'buchi [ossi'buki] SM PL *di* **ossobuco**

ossi'dare/72/ VT, **ossi'darsi** VPR to oxidize

ossidazi'one [ossidat'tsjone] SF oxidization, oxidation

'ossidoSM oxide; **~ di carbonio** carbon monoxide

ossige'nare[ossidʒe'nare] /**72**/ VT to oxygenate; (*decolorare*) to bleach; **acqua ossigenata** hydrogen peroxide

os'sigeno[os'sidʒeno] SM oxygen

'ossoSM (*pl(f)* **ossa**: *Anat*) bone; **d'~** (*bottone ecc*) of bone, bone *cpd*; **avere le ossa rotte** to be dead *o* dog tired; **bagnato fino all'~** soaked to the skin; **essere ridotto all'~** (*fig: magro*) to be just skin and bone; (: *senza soldi*) to be in dire straits; **rompersi l'~ del collo** to break one's neck; **rimetterci l'~ del collo** (*fig*) to ruin o.s., lose everything; **un ~ duro** (*persona, impresa*) a tough number; **~ di seppia** cuttlebone

osso'buco(*pl* **ossibuchi**) SM (*Cuc*) marrowbone; (*piatto*) stew made with knuckle of veal in tomato sauce

os'suto, -aAG bony

ostaco'lare/**72**/ VT to block, obstruct

os'tacoloSM obstacle; (*Equitazione*) hurdle, jump; **essere di ~ a qn/qc** (*fig*) to stand in the way of sb/sth

os'taggio[os'taddʒo] SM hostage

'oste, ostessaSM/F innkeeper

osteggi'are[osted'dʒare] /**62**/ VT to oppose, be opposed to

os'telloSM hostel; **~ della gioventù** youth hostel

osten'sorioSM (*Rel*) monstrance

osten'tare/**72**/ VT to make a show of, flaunt

ostentazi'one[ostentat'tsjone] SF ostentation, show

oste'riaSF inn

os'tessaSF *vedi* **oste**

os'tetrico, -a, -ci, -cheAG obstetric ▶ SM obstetrician ▶ SF midwife

'ostiaSF (*Rel*) host; (*per medicinali*) wafer

'ostico, -a, -ci, -cheAG (*fig*) harsh; difficult, tough; unpleasant

os'tileAG hostile

ostilitàSF hostility ▶ SFPL (*Mil*) hostilities

osti'narsi/**72**/ VPR to insist, dig one's heels in; **~ a fare** to persist (obstinately) in doing

osti'nato, -aAG (*caparbio*) obstinate; (*tenace*) persistent, determined

ostinazi'one[ostinat'tsjone] SF obstinacy; persistence

ostra'cismo[ostra'tʃizmo] SM ostracism

'ostrica, -cheSF oyster

ostru'ire/**55**/ VT to obstruct, block

ostruzi'one[ostrut'tsjone] SF obstruction, blockage

ostruzio'nismo[ostruttsjo'nizmo] SM (*Pol*) obstructionism; (*Sport*) obstruction; **fare dell'~ a** (*progetto, legge*) to obstruct; **~ sindacale** work-to-rule (*BRIT*), slowdown (*US*)

o'titeSF ear infection

oto'rino(laringoi'atra), -i, -eSM/F ear, nose and throat specialist

'otreSM (*recipiente*) goatskin

ott.ABBR (= *ottobre*) Oct

ottago'naleAG octagonal

ot'tagonoSM octagon

ot'tanoSM octane; **numero di ottani** octane rating

ot'tantaNUM eighty

ottan'tenneAG eighty-year-old ▶ SMF octogenarian

ottan'tesimo, -aNUM eightieth

ottan'tinaSF: **una ~ (di)** about eighty

ot'tavo, -aNUM eighth ▶ SF octave

ottempe'ranza[ottempe'rantsa] SF: **in ~ a** (*Amm*) in accordance with, in compliance with

ottempe'rare/**72**/ VI: **~ a** to comply with, obey

ottene'brare/**72**/ VT to darken; (*fig*) to cloud

otte'nere/**121**/ VT to obtain, get; (*risultato*) to achieve, obtain

'ottico, -a, -ci, -cheAG (*della vista: nervo*) optic; (*dell'ottica*) optical ▶ SM optician ▶ SF (*scienza*) optics *sg*; (*Fot: lenti, prismi ecc*) optics *pl*

otti'maleAG optimal, optimum

ottima'menteAV excellently, very well

otti'mismoSM optimism

otti'mista, -i, -eSM/F optimist

ottimiz'zare[ottimid'dzare] /**72**/ VT to optimize

ottimizzazi'one[ottimiddzat'tsjone] SF optimization

'ottimo, -aAG excellent, very good

'ottoNUM eight

ot'tobreSM October; *vedi anche* **luglio**

otto'brino, -aAG October *cpd*

ottocen'tesco, -a, -schi, -sche [ottotʃen'tesko] AG nineteenth-century

otto'cento[otto'tʃento] NUM eight hundred ▶ SM: **l'O~** the nineteenth century

otto'milaNUM eight thousand

ot'toneSM brass; **gli ottoni** (*Mus*) the brass

ottuage'nario, -a[ottuadʒe'narjo] AG, SM/F octogenarian

ot'tundere/**34**/ VT (*fig*) to dull

ottu'rare/**72**/ VT to close (up); (*dente*) to fill; **otturarsi**/VPR to become *o* get blocked up

ottura'toreSM (*Fot*) shutter; (*nelle armi*) breechblock

otturazi'one[otturat'tsjone] SF closing (up); (*dentaria*) filling

ottusitàSF (*vedi ag*) obtuseness; dullness

ot'tuso, -aPP *di* **ottundere** ▶ AG (*Mat: fig*) obtuse; (*suono*) dull

o'vaiaSF, **o'vaio**SM (*Anat*) ovary

o'valeAG, SM oval

o'varico, -aAG ovarian

O

o'vatta SF cotton wool; (*per imbottire*) padding, wadding

ovat'tare /**72**/ VT (*imbottire*) to pad; (*fig: smorzare*) to muffle

ovazi'one [ovat'tsjone] SF ovation

'ovest SM west; **a ~ (di)** west (of); **verso ~** westward(s)

o'vile SM pen, enclosure; **tornare all'~** (*fig*) to return to the fold

o'vino, -a AG sheep *cpd*, ovine

'O.V.N.I. SIGLA M (= *oggetto volante non identificato*) UFO

ovulazi'one [ovulat'tsjone] SF ovulation

'ovulo SM (*Fisiol*) ovum

o'vunque AV = **dovunque**

ov'vero CONG (*ossia*) that is, to be precise; (*oppure*) or (else)

ovvi'are /**19**/ VI: **~ a** to obviate

'ovvio, -a AG obvious

ozi'are [ot'tsjare] /**19**/ VI to laze around, idle

'ozio ['ɔttsjo] SM idleness; (*tempo libero*) leisure; **ore d'~** leisure time; **stare in ~** to be idle

ozi'oso, -a [ot'tsjoso] AG idle

o'zono [od'dzɔno] SM ozone; **lo strato d'~** the ozone layer

ozonos'fera [oddzonos'fɛra] SF ozone layer

Pp

P, p [pi] SM O F INV (*lettera*) P, p; **P come Padova** ≈ P for Peter

P ABBR (= *peso*) WT; (= *parcheggio*) P; (*Aut:* = *principiante*) L

p. ABBR (= *pagina*) p

P2 ABBR F (= *la* (*loggia*) P2) the P2 masonic lodge

PA SIGLA = **Palermo**

P.A. ABBR = **pubblica amministrazione**

pa'care/20/ VT to calm; **pacarsi** VPR (*tempesta, disordini*) to subside

paca'tezza [paka'tettsa] SF quietness, calmness

pa'cato, -a AG quiet, calm

'pacca, -che SF slap

pac'chetto [pak'ketto] SM packet; **~ applicativo** (*Inform*) applications package; **~ azionario** (*Finanza*) shareholding; **~ software** (*Inform*) software package; **~ turistico** package holiday (BRIT) o tour

pacchi'ano, -a [pak'kjano] AG (*colori*) garish; (*abiti, arredamento*) vulgar, garish

'pacco, -chi SM parcel; (*involto*) bundle; **~ postale** parcel

paccot'tiglia [pakkot'tiʎʎa] SF trash, junk

'pace ['patʃe] SF peace; **darsi ~** to resign o.s.; **fare (la) ~ con qn** to make it up with sb

pachis'tano, -a [pakis'tano] AG, SM/F Pakistani

pacifi'care [patʃifi'kare] /20/ VT (*riconciliare*) to reconcile, make peace between; (*mettere in pace*) to pacify

pacificazi'one [patʃifikat'tsjone] SF (*vedi vt*) reconciliation; pacification

pa'cifico, -a, -ci, -che [pa'tʃifiko] AG (*persona*) peaceable; (*vita*) peaceful; (*fig: indiscusso*) indisputable; (: *ovvio*) obvious, clear ▸ SM: **il P~, l'Oceano P~** the Pacific (Ocean)

paci'fismo [patʃi'fizmo] SM pacifism

paci'fista, -i, -e [patʃi'fista] SM/F pacifist

PACS [paks] SIGLA MPL civil partnerships

pa'dano, -a AG of the Po; **la pianura padana** the Lombardy plain

pa'della SF frying pan; (*per infermi*) bedpan

padigli'one [padiʎ'ʎone] SM pavilion

'Padova SF Padua

pado'vano, -a AG of (o from) Padua

'padre SM father; **padris** MPL (*antenati*) forefathers

Padre'terno SM: **il ~** God the Father

pa'drino SM godfather

padro'nale AG (*scala, entrata*) main, principal; **casa ~** country house

padro'nanza [padro'nantsa] SF command, mastery

padro'nato SM: **il ~** the ruling class

pa'drone, -a SM/F master/mistress; (*proprietario*) owner; (*datore di lavoro*) employer; **essere ~ di sé** to be in control of o.s.; **~/padrona di casa** master/mistress of the house; (*per gli inquilini*) landlord/lady

padroneggi'are [padroned'dʒare] /62/ VT (*fig: sentimenti*) to master, control; (*materia*) to master, know thoroughly; **padroneggiarsi** VPR to control o.s.

pae'saggio [pae'zaddʒo] SM landscape

paesag'gista, -i, -e [paezad'dʒista] SM/F (*pittore*) landscape painter

pae'sano, -a AG country *cpd* ▸ SM/F villager, countryman/woman

pa'ese SM (*nazione*) country, nation; (*terra*) country, land; (*villaggio*) village; **~ di provenienza** country of origin; **i Paesi Bassi** the Netherlands

paf'futo, -a AG chubby, plump

'paga, -ghe SF pay, wages *pl*; **giorno di ~** pay day

pa'gabile AG payable; **~ alla consegna/a vista** payable on delivery/on demand

pa'gaia SF paddle

paga'mento SM payment; **~ anticipato** payment in advance; **~ alla consegna** payment on delivery; **~ all'ordine** cash with order; **la TV a ~** pay TV

pa'gano, -a AG, SM/F pagan

pa'gare/80/ VT to pay; (*acquisto, fig, colpa*) to pay for; (*contraccambiare*) to repay, pay back ▸ VI to pay; **quanto l'ha pagato?** how much did you pay for it?; **~ con carta di credito**

to pay by credit card; **~ in contanti** to pay cash; **~ di persona** (fig) to suffer the consequences; **l'ho pagata cara** (fig) I paid dearly for it

pa'gella [pa'dʒɛlla] SF (Ins) report card

'paggio ['paddʒo] SM page(boy)

pagherò [page'rɔ] VB vedi **pagare** ▶ SM INV acknowledgement of a debt, IOU; **~ cambiario** promissory note

'pagina ['padʒina] SF page; **Pagine bianche** phone book, telephone directory; **Pagine Gialle®** Yellow Pages®

'paglia ['paʎʎa] SF straw; **avere la coda di ~** (fig) to have a guilty conscience; **fuoco di ~** (fig) flash in the pan

pagliac'cetto [paʎʎat'tʃetto] SM (per bambini) rompers pl

pagliac'ciata [paʎʎat'tʃata] SF farce

pagli'accio [paʎ'ʎattʃo] SM clown

pagli'aio [paʎ'ʎajo] SM haystack

paglie'riccio [paʎʎe'rittʃo] SM straw mattress

paglie'rino, -a [paʎʎe'rino] AG: **giallo ~** pale yellow

pagli'etta [paʎ'ʎetta] SF (cappello per uomo) (straw) boater; (per tegami ecc) steel wool

pagli'uzza [paʎ'ʎuttsa] SF (blade of) straw; (d'oro ecc) tiny particle, speck

pa'gnotta [paɲ'ɲɔtta] SF round loaf

'pago, -a, -ghi, -ghe AG: **~ (di)** satisfied (with)

pa'goda SF pagoda

pail'lette [pa'jet] SF INV sequin

'paio (pl(f) **paia**) SM pair; **un ~ di** (alcuni) a couple of; **un ~ di occhiali** a pair of glasses; **è un altro ~ di maniche** (fig) that's another kettle of fish

'paio etc VB vedi **parere**

pai'olo, paiu'olo SM (copper) pot

'Pakistan SM: **il ~** Pakistan

pakis'tano, -a AG, SM/F = **pachistano**

pal. ABBR = **palude**

'pala SF shovel; (di remo, ventilatore, elica) blade; (di ruota) paddle

palan'drana SF (scherzoso: abito lungo e largo) tent

pa'lata SF shovelful; **fare soldi a palate** to make a mint

pala'tale AG (Anat, Ling) palatal

pa'lato SM palate

pa'lazzo [pa'lattso] SM (reggia) palace; (edificio) building; **~ di giustizia** courthouse; **~ dello sport** sports stadium; see note

Several of the Roman palazzi now have political functions. The sixteenth-century Palazzo Chigi, in Piazza Colonna, was acquired by the state in 1919 and became the seat of the Ministry of Foreign Affairs; since 1961 it has housed the Prime Minister's office and hosted Cabinet meetings. Palazzo Madama, another sixteenth-century building which was originally built for the Medici family, has been the home of the Senate since 1871. Palazzo di Montecitorio, completed in 1694, has housed the Camera dei deputati since 1870.

pal'chetto [pal'ketto] SM shelf

'palco, -chi SM (Teat) box; (tavolato) platform, stand; (ripiano) layer

palco'scenico, -ci [palkoʃ'ʃɛniko] SM (Teat) stage

palermi'tano, -a AG of (o from) Palermo ▶ SM/F person from Palermo

Pa'lermo SF Palermo

pale'sare /72/ VT to reveal, disclose; **palesarsi** VPR to reveal o show o.s.

pa'lese AG clear, evident

Pales'tina SF: **la ~** Palestine

palesti'nese AG, SM/F Palestinian

pa'lestra SF gymnasium; (esercizio atletico) exercise, training; (fig) training ground, school

paletot [pal'to] SM INV overcoat

pa'letta SF spade; (per il focolare) shovel; (del capostazione) signalling disc

pa'letto SM stake, peg; (spranga) bolt

palin'sesto SM (Storia) palimpsest; (TV, Radio) programme (BRIT) o program (US) schedule

'palio SM (gara): **il P~** horse race run at Siena; **mettere qc in ~** to offer sth as a prize; see note

The Palio is a horse race which takes place in a number of Italian towns, the most famous being the Palio di Siena. The Tuscan race dates back to the thirteenth century; nowadays it is usually held twice a year, on 2 July and 16 August, in the Piazza del Campo. 10 of the 17 city districts or contrade take part; the winner is the first horse to complete the course, whether or not it still has its rider. The race is preceded by a procession of contrada members in historical dress.

palis'sandro SM rosewood

paliz'zata [palit'tsata] SF palisade

'palla SF ball; (pallottola) bullet; **~ di neve** snowball; **~ ovale** rugby ball

pallaca'nestro SF basketball

palla'mano [palla'mano] SF handball

pallanu'oto SF water polo

palla'volo SF volleyball

palleggi'are [palled'dʒare] /62/ VI (Calcio) to practise (BRIT) o practice (US) with the ball; (Tennis) to knock up

pallia'tivo SM palliative; (fig) stopgap measure

'pallido, -a AG pale

pal'lina SF (bilia) marble

pal'lino SM (*Biliardo*) cue ball; (*Bocce*) jack; (*proiettile*) pellet; (*pois*) dot; **bianco a pallini blu** white with blue dots; **avere il ~ di** (*fig*) to be crazy about

pallon'cino [pallon'tʃino] SM balloon; (*lampioncino*) Chinese lantern

pal'lone SM (*palla*) ball; (*Calcio*) football; (*aerostato*) balloon; **gioco del ~** football

pal'lore SM pallor, paleness

pal'lottola SF pellet; (*proiettile*) bullet

'palma SF (*Anat*) = **palmo**; (*Bot, simbolo*) palm; **~ da datteri** date palm

pal'mato, -a AG (*Zool: piede*) webbed; (*Bot*) palmate

pal'mipede AG web-footed

pal'mizio [pal'mittsjo] SM (*palma*) palm tree; (*ramo*) palm

'palmo SM (*Anat*) palm; **essere alto un ~** (*fig*) to be tiny; **restare con un ~ di naso** (*fig*) to be badly disappointed

'palo SM (*legno appuntito*) stake; (*sostegno*) pole; **fare da** *o* **il ~** (*fig*) to act as look-out; **saltare di ~ in frasca** (*fig*) to jump from one topic to another

palom'baro SM diver

pa'lombo SM (*pesce*) dogfish

pal'pare/72/ VT to feel, finger

'palpebra SF eyelid

palpi'tare/72/ VI (*cuore, polso*) to beat; (*più forte*) to pound, throb; (*fremere*) to quiver

palpitazi'one [palpitat'tsjone] SF palpitation

'palpito SM (*del cuore*) beat; (*fig: d'amore ecc*) throb

pal'tò SM INV overcoat

pa'lude SF marsh, swamp

palu'doso, -a AG marshy, swampy

pa'lustre AG marsh *cpd*, swamp *cpd*

'pampino SM vine leaf

pana'cea [pana'tʃɛa] SF panacea

'Panama SF Panama; **il canale di ~** the Panama Canal

pana'mense AG, SMF Panamanian

'panca, -che SF bench

pancar'rè SM sliced bread

pan'cetta [pan'tʃetta] SF (*Cuc*) bacon

pan'chetto [pan'ketto] SM stool; footstool

pan'china [pan'kina] SF garden seat; (*di giardino pubblico*) (park) bench

'pancia, -ce ['pantʃa] SF belly, stomach; **mettere** *o* **fare ~** to be getting a paunch; **avere mal di ~** to have stomach ache *o* a sore stomach

panci'era [pan'tʃɛra] SF corset

panci'olle [pan'tʃɔlle] AV: **stare in ~** to lounge about (*BRIT*) *o* around

panci'otto [pan'tʃɔtto] SM waistcoat

panci'uto, -a [pan'tʃuto] AG (*persona*) potbellied; (*vaso, bottiglia*) rounded

'pancreas SM INV pancreas

'panda SM INV panda

pande'mia SF pandemic

pande'monio SM pandemonium

pan'doro SM *type of sponge cake eaten at Christmas*

'pane SM bread; (*pagnotta*) loaf (of bread); (*forma*): **un ~ di burro/cera** *etc* a pat of butter/bar of wax *etc*; **guadagnarsi il ~** to earn one's living; **dire ~ al ~, vino al vino** (*fig*) to call a spade a spade; **rendere pan per focaccia** (*fig*) to give tit for tat; **~ casereccio** homemade bread; **~ a cassetta** sliced bread; **~ integrale** wholemeal bread; **~ di segale** rye bread; **~ di Spagna** sponge cake; **~ tostato** toast

pane'girico [pane'dʒiriko] SM (*fig*) panegyric

panette'ria SF (*forno*) bakery; (*negozio*) baker's (shop), bakery

panetti'ere, -a SM/F baker

panet'tone SM *a kind of spiced brioche with sultanas (eaten at Christmas)*

'panfilo SM yacht

pan'forte SM *Sienese nougat-type delicacy*

pangrat'tato SM breadcrumbs *pl*

'panico, -a, -ci, -che AG, SM panic; **essere in preda al ~** to be panic-stricken; **lasciarsi prendere dal ~** to panic

pani'ere SM basket

panifica'tore, -trice SM/F bread-maker, baker

pani'ficio [pani'fitʃo] SM (*forno*) bakery; (*negozio*) baker's (shop), bakery

pa'nino SM roll; **~ caldo** toasted sandwich; **~ imbottito** filled roll; sandwich

panino'teca, -che SF sandwich bar

'panna SF (*Cuc*) cream; (*Aut*) = **panne**; **~ da cucina** cooking cream; **~ montata** whipped cream

'panne [pan] SF INV (*Aut*) breakdown; : **essere in ~** to have broken down

pan'nello SM panel; **~ di controllo** control panel; **~ solare** solar panel

'panno SM cloth; **panni** SMPL (*abiti*) clothes; **mettiti nei miei panni** (*fig*) put yourself in my shoes

pan'nocchia [pan'nɔkkja] SF (*di mais ecc*) ear

panno'lino SM (*per bambini*) nappy (*BRIT*), diaper (*US*)

panno'lone SM incontinence pad

pano'rama, -i SM panorama

pano'ramico, -a, -ci, -che AG panoramic; **strada panoramica** scenic route

pantacol'lant SMPL leggings

panta'loni SMPL trousers (*BRIT*), pants (*US*), pair *sg* of trousers *o* pants

pan'tano SM bog

pan'tera SF panther

'pantheon ['panteon] SM INV pantheon

pan'tofola SF slipper
panto'mima SF pantomime
pan'zana [pan'tsana] SF fib, tall story
pao'nazzo, -a [pao'nattso] AG purple
'papa, -i SM pope
papà SM INV dad(dy); **figlio di ~** spoilt young man
pa'pale AG papal
pa'pato SM papacy
pa'pavero SM poppy
'papero, -a SM/F (Zool) gosling ▶ SF (fig) slip of the tongue, blunder
papi'llon [papi'jõ] SM INV bow tie
pa'piro SM papyrus
'pappa SF baby cereal; **~ reale** royal jelly
pappa'gallo SM parrot; (fig: uomo) Romeo, wolf
pappa'gorgia, -ge [pappa'gɔrdʒa] SF double chin
pappar'della SF (fig) rigmarole
pap'pare /72/ VT (col: anche: **papparsi**) to gobble up
par. ABBR (= paragrafo) par
'para SF: **suole di ~** crepe soles
parà ABBR M INV (= paracadutista) para
pa'rabola SF (Mat) parabola; (Rel) parable
para'bolico, -a, -ci, -che AG (Mat) parabolic; vedi anche **antenna**
para'brezza [para'breddza] SM INV (Aut) windscreen (BRIT), windshield (US)
paracadu'tare /72/ VT, **paracadu'tarsi** VPR to parachute
paraca'dute SM INV parachute
paracadu'tismo SM parachuting
paracadu'tista, -i, -e SM/F parachutist; (Mil) paratrooper
para'carro SM kerbstone (BRIT), curbstone (US)
paradi'siaco, -a, -ci, -che AG heavenly
para'diso SM paradise; **~ fiscale** tax haven
parados'sale AG paradoxical
para'dosso SM paradox
para'fango, -ghi SM mudguard
paraf'fina SF paraffin, paraffin wax
parafra'sare /72/ VT to paraphrase
pa'rafrasi SF INV paraphrase
para'fulmine SM lightning conductor
pa'raggi [pa'raddʒi] SMPL: **nei ~** in the vicinity, in the neighbourhood (BRIT) o neighborhood (US)
parago'nare /72/ VT: **~ con/a** to compare with/to
para'gone SM comparison; (esempio analogo) analogy, parallel; **reggere al ~** to stand comparison
pa'ragrafo SM paragraph
paraguai'ano, -a AG, SM/F Paraguayan
Paragu'ay [para'gwai] SM: **il ~** Paraguay
pa'ralisi SF INV paralysis

para'litico, -a, -ci, -che AG, SM/F paralytic
paraliz'zare [paralid'dzare] /72/ VT to paralyze
paralle'lamente AV in parallel
paralle'lismo SM (Mat) parallelism; (fig: corrispondenza) similarities pl
paral'lelo, -a AG parallel ▶ SM (Geo) parallel; (comparazione): **fare un ~ tra** to draw a parallel between ▶ SF parallel (line); **parallele** SFPL (attrezzo ginnico) parallel bars
para'lume SM lampshade
para'medico, -a, -ci, -che AG paramedical
para'menti SMPL (Rel) vestments
pa'rametro SM parameter
paramili'tare AG paramilitary
pa'ranco, -chi SM hoist
para'noia SF paranoia; **andare/mandare in ~** (col) to freak/be freaked out
para'noico, -a, -ci, -che AG, SM/F paranoid; (col: angosciato) freaked (out)
paranor'male AG paranormal
para'occhi [para'ɔkki] SMPL blinkers (BRIT), blinders (US)
paraolim'piadi SFPL paralympics
para'petto SM parapet
para'piglia [para'piʎʎa] SM commotion
parapsicolo'gia [parapsikolo'dʒia] SF parapsychology
pa'rare /72/ VT (addobbare) to adorn, deck; (proteggere) to shield, protect; (scansare: colpo) to parry; (Calcio) to save ▶ VI: **dove vuole andare a ~?** what are you driving at?; **pararsi** VPR (presentarsi) to appear, present o.s.
parasco'lastico, -a, -ci, -che AG (attività) extracurricular
para'sole SM INV parasol, sunshade
paras'sita, -i SM parasite
parassi'tario, -a AG parasitic
parasta'tale AG state-controlled
paras'tato SM employees in the state-controlled sector
pa'rata SF (Sport) save; (Mil) review, parade
pa'rati SMPL hangings pl; **carta da ~** wallpaper
para'tia SF (di nave) bulkhead
para'urti SM INV (Aut) bumper
para'vento SM folding screen; **fare da ~ a qn** (fig) to shield sb
par'cella [par'tʃɛlla] SF account, fee (of lawyer etc)
parcheggi'are [parked'dʒare] /62/ VT to park
parcheggia'tore, -'trice [parkeddʒa'tore] SM/F parking attendant
par'cheggio [par'keddʒo] SM parking no pl; (luogo) car park (BRIT), parking lot (US); (singolo posto) parking space; **~ di interscambio** park and ride
par'chimetro [par'kimetro] SM parking meter

'parco¹, -chi SM park; (*spazio per deposito*) depot; (*complesso di veicoli*) fleet

'parco², -a, -chi, -che AG: ~ **(in)** (*sobrio*) moderate (in); (*avaro*) sparing (with)

par'cometro SM (*Aut*) (Pay and Display) ticket machine

pa'recchio, -a [pa'rekkjo] DET quite a lot of; (*tempo*) quite a lot of, a long ▶ PRON quite a lot, quite a bit; (*tempo*) quite a while, a long time ▶ AV (*con ag*) quite, rather; (*con vb*) quite a lot, quite a bit; **parecchi,** ●DET PL, PRON PL quite a lot of, several; quite a lot, several

pareggi'are [pared'dʒare] **/62/** VT to make equal; (*terreno*) to level, make level; (*bilancio, conti*) to balance ▶ VI (*Sport*) to draw

pa'reggio [pa'reddʒo] SM (*Econ*) balance; (*Sport*) draw

paren'tado SM relatives *pl*, relations *pl*

pa'rente SMF relative, relation

paren'tela SF (*vincolo di sangue, fig*) relationship; (*insieme dei parenti*) relations *pl*, relatives *pl*

pa'rentesi SF (*segno grafico*) bracket, parenthesis; (*frase incisa*) parenthesis; (*digressione*) parenthesis, digression; **tra** ~ in brackets; (*fig*) incidentally

pa'rere/71/ SM (*opinione*) opinion; (*consiglio*) advice, opinion; **a mio** ~ in my opinion ▶ VI to seem, appear ▶ VB IMPERS: **pare che** it seems o appears that, they say that; **mi pare che** it seems to me that; **mi pare di sì/no** I think so/don't think so; **fai come ti pare** do as you like; **che ti pare del mio libro?** what do you think of my book?

pa'rete SF wall

'pargolo, -a SM/F child

'pari AG INV (*uguale*) equal, same; (*in giochi*) equal, drawn, tied; (*Mat*) even ▶ SM INV (*Pol: di Gran Bretagna*) peer ▶ SM O F INV peer, equal; **copiato** ~ ~ copied word for word; **siamo** ~ (*fig*) we are quits o even; **alla** ~ on the same level; (*Borsa*) at par; **ragazza alla** ~ au pair (girl); **mettersi alla** ~ **con** to place o.s. on the same level as; **mettersi in** ~ **con** to catch up with; **andare di** ~ **passo con qn** to keep pace with sb

parifi'care /20/ VT (*scuola*) to recognize officially

parifi'cato, -a AG: **scuola parificata** *officially recognized private school*

Pa'rigi [pa'ridʒi] SF Paris

pari'gino, -a [pari'dʒino] AG, SM/F Parisian

pa'riglia [pa'riʎʎa] SF pair; **rendere la** ~ to give tit for tat

parità SF parity, equality; (*Sport*) draw, tie

pari'tetico, -a, -ci, -che AG: **commissione paritetica** joint committee; **rapporto** ~ equal relationship

parlamen'tare/72/ AG parliamentary ▶ SM/F ≈ Member of Parliament (BRIT), ≈ Congressman/woman (US) ▶ VI to negotiate, parley

parla'mento SM parliament; *see note*

> The Italian constitution, which came into force on 1 January 1948, states that the *Parlamento* has legislative power. It is made up of two chambers, the *Camera dei deputati* and the *Senato*. Parliamentary elections are held every 5 years.

parlan'tina SF (*col*) talkativeness; **avere** ~ to have the gift of the gab

par'lare/72/ VI to speak, talk; (*confidare cose segrete*) to talk ▶ VT to speak; ~ **(a qn) di** to speak o talk (to sb) about; ~ **chiaro** to speak one's mind; ~ **male di qn/qc** to speak ill of sb/sth; ~ **del più e del meno** to talk of this and that; **ne ho sentito** ~ I have heard it mentioned; **non parliamone più** let's just forget about it; **i dati parlano** (*fig*) the facts speak for themselves

par'lata SF (*dialetto*) dialect

parla'tore, -'trice SM/F speaker

parla'torio SM (*di carcere ecc*) visiting room; (*Rel*) parlour (BRIT), parlor (US)

parlot'tare/72/ VI to mutter

parmigi'ano, -a [parmi'dʒano] AG Parma *cpd* of (o from) Parma ▶ SM (*grana*) Parmesan (cheese); **alla parmigiana** (*Cuc*) with Parmesan cheese

paro'dia SF parody

parodi'are/19/ VT to parody

pa'rola SF word; (*facoltà*) speech; **parole** SFPL (*chiacchiere*) talk *sg*; **chiedere la** ~ to ask permission to speak; **dare la** ~ **a qn** to call on sb to speak; **dare la propria** ~ **a qn** to give sb one's word; **mantenere la** ~ to keep one's word; **mettere una buona** ~ **per qn** to put in a good word for sb; **passare dalle parole ai fatti** to get down to business; **prendere la** ~ to take the floor; **rimanere senza parole** to be speechless; **rimangiarsi la** ~ to go back on one's word; **non ho parole per ringraziarla** I don't know how to thank you; **rivolgere la** ~ **a qn** to speak to sb; **non è detta l'ultima** ~ that's not the end of the matter; **è una persona di** ~ he is a man of his word; **in parole povere** in plain English; ~ **d'onore** word of honour; ~ **d'ordine** (*Mil*) password; **parole incrociate** crossword (puzzle) *sg*

paro'laccia, -ce [paro'lattʃa] SF bad word, swearword

paros'sismo SM paroxysm

par'quet [par'kɛ] SM parquet (flooring)

parrò *etc* VB *vedi* **parere**

par'rocchia [par'rɔkkja] SF parish; (*chiesa*) parish church

parrocchi'ano, -a [parrok'kjano] SM/F parishioner

'parroco, -ci SM parish priest

par'rucca, -che SF wig

parrucchi'ere, -a [parruk'kjɛre] SM/F hairdresser ▶ SM barber

parruc'cone SM (peg) old fogey

parsi'monia SF frugality, thrift

parsimoni'oso, -a AG frugal, thrifty

'parso, -a PP di **parere**

'parte SF part; (lato) side; (quota spettante a ciascuno) share; (direzione) direction; (Pol) party; faction; (Dir) party; **a ~ ag** separate ▶ AV separately; **scherzi a ~** joking aside; **a ~ ciò** apart from that; **inviare a ~** (campioni ecc) to send under separate cover; **da ~** (in disparte) to one side, aside; **mettere/ prendere da ~** to put/take aside; **d'altra ~** on the other hand; **da ~ di** (per conto di) on behalf of; **da ~ mia** as far as I'm concerned, as for me; **da ~ di madre** on his (o her etc) mother's side; **essere dalla ~ della ragione** to be in the right; **da ~ a ~** right through; **da qualche ~** somewhere; **da nessuna ~** nowhere; **da questa ~** (in questa direzione) this way; **da ogni ~** on all sides, everywhere; (moto da luogo) from all sides; **fare ~ di qc** to belong to sth; **prendere ~ a qc** to take part in sth; **prendere le parti di qn** to take sb's side; **mettere qn a ~ di qc** to inform sb of sth; **costituirsi ~ civile contro qn** (Dir) to associate in an action with the public prosecutor against sb; **la ~ lesa** (Dir) the injured party; **le parti in causa** the parties concerned; **parti sociali** representatives of workers and employers

parteci'pante [partetʃi'pante] SMF: **~ (a)** (a riunione, dibattito) participant (in); (a gara sportiva) competitor (in); (a concorso) entrant (to)

parteci'pare [partetʃi'pare] /72/ VI: **~ a** to take part in, participate in; (spese ecc) to contribute to; (dolore, successo di qn) ▸ to share (in) ▶ VT: **~ le nozze (a)** to announce one's wedding (to)

partecipazi'one [partetʃipat'tsjone] SF participation; sharing; (Econ) interest; **~ a banda armata** (Dir) belonging to an armed gang; **~ di maggioranza/ minoranza** controlling/minority interest; **~ agli utili** profit-sharing; **partecipazioni di nozze** wedding announcement card; **ministro delle Partecipazioni statali** minister responsible for companies in which the state has a financial interest

par'tecipe [par'tetʃipe] AG participating; **essere ~ di** to take part in, participate in; (gioia, dolore) to share (in); (consapevole) to be aware of

parteggi'are [parted'dʒare] /62/ VI: **~ per** to side with, be on the side of

par'tenza [par'tɛntsa] SF departure; (Sport) start; **essere in ~** to be about to leave, be leaving; **passeggeri in ~ per** passengers travelling (BRIT) o traveling (US) to; **siamo tornati al punto di ~** (fig) we are back where we started; **falsa ~** (anche fig) false start

parti'cella [parti'tʃɛlla] SF particle

parti'cipio [parti'tʃipjo] SM participle

partico'lare AG (specifico) particular; (proprio) personal, private; (speciale) special, particular; (caratteristico) distinctive, characteristic; (fuori dal comune) peculiar ▶ SM detail, particular; **in ~** in particular, particularly; **entrare nei particolari** to go into details

particolareggi'ato, -a [partikolared'dʒato] AG (extremely) detailed

particolarità SF INV (carattere eccezionale) peculiarity; (dettaglio) particularity, detail; (caratteristica) characteristic, feature

partigi'ano, -a [parti'dʒano] AG partisan ▶ SM (fautore) supporter, champion; (Mil) partisan

par'tire /45/ VI to go, leave; (allontanarsi) to go (o drive etc) away o off; (petardo, colpo) to go off; (fig: avere inizio, Sport) to start; **sono partita da Roma alle 7** I left Rome at 7; **il volo parte da Ciampino** the flight leaves from Ciampino; **a ~ da** from; **la seconda a ~ da destra** the second from the right; **~ in quarta** to drive off at top speed; (fig) to be very enthusiastic

par'tita SF (Comm) lot, consignment; (Econ: registrazione) entry, item; (Carte, Sport: gioco) game; (: competizione) match, game; **~ di caccia** hunting party; **numero di ~ IVA** VAT registration number; **~ semplice/ doppia** (Comm) single-/double-entry book-keeping

par'tito SM (Pol) party; (decisione) decision, resolution; (persona da maritare) match; **per ~ preso** on principle; **mettere la testa a ~** to settle down

partitocra'zia [partitokrat'tsia] SF hijacking of institutions by the party system

parti'tura SF (Mus) score

'parto SM (Med) labour (BRIT), labor (US), delivery, (child)birth; **sala ~** labo(u)r room; **morire di ~** to die in childbirth

partori'ente SF woman in labour (BRIT) o labor (US)

parto'rire /55/ VT to give birth to; (fig) to produce

par'venza [par'vɛntsa] SF semblance

'parvi etc VB vedi **parere**

parzi'ale [par'tsjale] AG (limitato) partial; (non obiettivo) biased, partial

parzialità [partsjali'ta] SF: ~ **a favore di** partiality (for), bias (towards); ~ **contro** bias (against)

'**pascere** ['paʃʃere] /**29**/ VI to graze ▶ VT (*brucare*) to graze on; (*far pascolare*) to graze, pasture

pasci'uto, -a [paʃʃuto] PP *di* **pascere** ▶ AG: **ben** ~ plump

pasco'lare /**72**/ VT, VI to graze

'**pascolo** SM pasture

'**Pasqua** SF Easter; **isola di** ~ Easter Island

pas'quale AG Easter *cpd*

Pasqu'etta SF Easter Monday

pas'sabile AG fairly good, passable

pas'saggio [pas'saddʒo] SM passing *no pl*, passage; (*traversata*) crossing *no pl*, passage; (*luogo, prezzo della traversata, brano di libro ecc*) passage; (*su veicolo altrui*) lift (BRIT), ride; (*Sport*) pass; **di** ~ (*persona*) passing through; ~ **pedonale/a livello** pedestrian/level (BRIT) *o* grade (US) crossing; ~ **di proprietà** transfer of ownership

passamane'ria SF braid, trimming

passamon'tagna [passamon'taɲɲa] SM INV balaclava

pas'sante SMF passer-by ▶ SM loop

passa'porto SM passport

pas'sare /**72**/ VI (*andare*) to go; (*veicolo, pedone*) to pass (by), go by; (*fare una breve sosta: postino ecc*) to come, call; (: *amico: per fare una visita*) to call *o* drop in; (*sole, aria, luce*) to get through; (*trascorrere: giorni, tempo*) to pass, go by; (*fig: proposta di legge*) to be passed; (: *dolore*) to go away; (*Carte*) to pass ▶ VT (*attraversare*) to cross; (*trasmettere: messaggio*): ~ **qc a qn** to pass sth on to sb; (*dare*): ~ **qc a qn** to pass sth to sb, give sb sth; (*trascorrere: tempo*) to spend; (*superare: esame*) to pass; (*triturare: verdura*) to strain; (*approvare*) to pass, approve; (*oltrepassare, sorpassare: anche fig*) to go beyond, pass; (*fig: subire*) to go through; ~ **da ... a** to pass from ... to; ~ **di padre in figlio** to be handed down *o* to pass from father to son; ~ **per** (*anche fig*) to go through; ~ **per stupido/un genio** to be taken for a fool/a genius; ~ **sopra** (*anche fig*) to pass over; ~ **attraverso** (*anche fig*) to go through; ~ **ad altro** to change the subject; (*in una riunione*) to discuss the next item; ~ **in banca/ufficio** to call (in) at the bank/office; ~ **alla storia** to pass into history; ~ **a un esame** to go up (to the next class) after an exam; ~ **inosservato** to go unnoticed; ~ **di moda** to go out of fashion; ~ **a prendere qc/qn** to call and pick sth/sb up; **le passo il Signor X** (*al telefono*) here is Mr X; I'm putting you through to Mr X; **farsi** ~ **per** to pass o.s. off as, pretend to be; **lasciar** ~ **qn/qc** to let sb/ sth through; **col** ~ **degli anni** (*riferito al presente*) as time goes by; (*riferito al passato*) as time passed *o* went by; **il peggio è passato** the worst is over; **30 anni e passa** well over 30 years ago; ~ **una mano di vernice su qc** to give sth a coat of paint; **passarsela, come te la passi?** how are you getting on *o* along?

pas'sata SF: **dare una** ~ **di vernice a qc** to give sth a coat of paint; **dare una** ~ **al giornale** to have a look at the paper, skim through the paper

passa'tempo SM pastime, hobby

pas'sato, -a AG (*scorso*) last; (*finito: gloria, generazioni*) past; (*usanze*) out of fashion; (*sfiorito*) faded ▶ SM past; (*Ling*) past (tense); **l'anno** ~ last year; **nel corso degli anni passati** over the past years; **nei tempi passati** in the past; **sono le 8 passate** it's past *o* after 8 o'clock; **è acqua passata** (*fig*) it's over and done with; ~ **prossimo** (*Ling*) present perfect; ~ **remoto** (*Ling*) past historic; ~ **di verdura** (*Cuc*) vegetable purée

passa'tutto, passaver'dura SM INV vegetable mill

passeg'gero, -a [passed'dʒero] AG passing ▶ SM/F passenger

passeggi'are [passed'dʒare] /**62**/ VI to go for a walk; (*in veicolo*) to go for a drive

passeggi'ata [passed'dʒata] SF walk; drive; (*luogo*) promenade; **fare una** ~ to go for a walk (*o* drive)

passeg'gino [passed'dʒino] SM pushchair (BRIT), stroller (US)

pas'seggio [pas'seddʒo] SM walk, stroll; (*luogo*) promenade; **andare a** ~ to go for a walk *o* a stroll

passe'rella SF footbridge; (*di nave, aereo*) gangway; (*pedana*) catwalk

'**passero** SM sparrow

pas'sibile AG: ~ **di** liable to

passio'nale AG (*temperamento*) passionate; **delitto** ~ crime of passion

passi'one SF passion

passività SF (*qualità*) passivity, passiveness; (*Comm*) liability

pas'sivo, -a AG passive ▶ SM (*Ling*) passive; (*Econ*) debit; (*complesso dei debiti*) liabilities *pl*

'**passo** SM step; (*andatura*) pace; (*rumore*) (foot)step; (*orma*) footprint; (*passaggio, fig: brano*) passage; (*valico*) pass; **a** ~ **d'uomo** at walking pace; (*Aut*) dead slow; ~ **(a)** ~ step by step; **fare due** *o* **quattro passi** to go for a walk *o* a stroll; **andare al** ~ **coi tempi** to keep up with the times; **di questo** ~ (*fig*) at this rate; **fare i primi passi** (*anche fig*) to take one's first steps; **fare il gran** ~ (*fig*) to take the plunge; **fare un** ~ **falso** (*fig*) to make the wrong move; **tornare sui propri passi** to retrace one's steps; **"~ carraio"** "vehicle entrance — keep clear"

'pasta SF (*Cuc*) dough; (: *impasto per dolce*) pastry; (*anche:* **pasta alimentare**) pasta; (*massa molle di materia*) paste; (*fig: indole*) nature; **paste** SFPL (*pasticcini*) pastries; ~ **in brodo** noodle soup; ~ **sfoglia** puff pastry *o* paste (*US*)

pastascì'utta [pastaʃʃutta] SF pasta

pasteggi'are [pasted'dʒare] /**62**/ VI: ~ **a vino/ champagne** to have wine/champagne with one's meal

pas'tella SF batter

pas'tello SM pastel

pas'tetta SF (*Cuc*) = **pastella**

pas'ticca, -che SF = **pastiglia**

pasticce'ria [pastittʃe'ria] SF (*pasticcini*) pastries *pl*, cakes *pl*; (*negozio*) cake shop; (*arte*) confectionery

pasticci'are [pastit'tʃare] /**14**/ VT to mess up, make a mess of ► VI to make a mess

pasticci'ere, -a [pastit'tʃere] SM/F pastrycook; confectioner

pastic'cino [pastit'tʃino] SM petit four

pas'ticcio [pas'tittʃo] SM (*Cuc*) pie; (*lavoro disordinato, imbroglio*) mess; **trovarsi nei pasticci** to get into trouble

pasti'ficio [pasti'fitʃo] SM pasta factory

pas'tiglia [pas'tiʎʎa] SF pastille, lozenge

pas'tina SF *small pasta shapes used in soup*

pasti'naca, -che SF parsnip

'pasto SM meal; **vino da** ~ table wine

pas'toia SF (*fig*): ~ **burocratica** red tape

pas'tone SM (*per animali*) mash; (*peg*) overcooked stodge

pasto'rale AG pastoral

pas'tore SM shepherd; (*Rel*) pastor, minister; (*anche:* **cane pastore**) sheepdog; ~ **scozzese** (*Zool*) collie; ~ **tedesco** (*Zool*) Alsatian (dog) (*BRIT*) German shepherd (dog)

pasto'rizia [pasto'rittsja] SF sheep-rearing, sheep farming

pastoriz'zare [pastorid'dzare] /**72**/ VT to pasteurize

pas'toso, -a AG doughy; pasty; (*fig: voce, colore*) mellow, soft

pas'trano SM greatcoat

pa'tacca, -che SF (*distintivo*) medal, decoration; (*fig: macchia*) grease spot, grease mark; (*articolo scadente*) bit of rubbish

pa'tata SF potato; **patate fritte** chips (*BRIT*), French fries

pata'tine SFPL (*potato*) crisps (*BRIT*) *o* chips (*US*); ~ **fritte** chips

pata'trac SM (*crollo: anche fig*) crash

pâté [pa'te] SM INV pâté; ~ **di fegato d'oca** pâté de foie gras

pa'tella SF (*Zool*) limpet

pa'tema, -i SM anxiety, worry

paten'tato, -a AG (*munito di patente*) licensed, certified; (*fig: scherzoso: qualificato*) utter, thorough

pa'tente SF licence (*BRIT*), license (*US*); (*anche:* **patente di guida**) driving licence (*BRIT*), driver's license (*US*); ~ **a punti** *driving licence with penalty points*

paten'tino SM temporary licence (*BRIT*) *o* license (*US*)

paterna'lismo SM paternalism

paterna'lista SM paternalist

paterna'listico, -a, -ci, -che AG paternalistic

paternità SF paternity, fatherhood

pa'terno, -a AG (*affetto, consigli*) fatherly; (*casa, autorità*) paternal

pa'tetico, -a, -ci, -che AG pathetic; (*commovente*) moving, touching

'pathos ['patos] SM pathos

pa'tibolo SM gallows *sg*, scaffold

pati'mento SM suffering

'patina SF (*su rame ecc*) patina; (*sulla lingua*) fur, coating

pa'tire /**55**/ VT, VI to suffer

pa'tito, -a SM/F enthusiast, fan, lover

patolo'gia [patolo'dʒia] SF pathology

pato'logico, -a, -ci, -che [pato'lɔdʒiko] AG pathological

pa'tologo, -a, -gi, -ghe SM/F pathologist

'patria SF homeland; **amor di** ~ patriotism

patri'arca, -chi SM patriarch

pa'trigno [pa'triɲɲo] SM stepfather

patrimoni'ale AG (*rendita*) from property ► SF (*anche:* **imposta patrimoniale**) property tax

patri'monio SM estate, property; (*fig*) heritage; **mi è costato un** ~ (*fig*) it cost me a fortune, I paid a fortune for it; ~ **spirituale/culturale** spiritual/cultural heritage; ~ **ereditario** (*fig*) hereditary characteristics *pl*; ~ **pubblico** public property

'patrio, -a, -ii, -ie AG (*di patria*) native *cpd*, of one's country; (*Dir*): **patria potestà** parental authority; **amor** ~ love of one's country

patri'ota, -i, -e SM/F patriot

patri'ottico, -a, -ci, -che AG patriotic

patriot'tismo SM patriotism

patroci'nare [patrotʃi'nare] /**72**/ VT (*Dir: difendere*) to defend; (*sostenere*) to sponsor, support

patro'cinio [patro'tʃinjo] SM defence (*BRIT*), defense (*US*); support, sponsorship

patro'nato SM patronage; (*istituzione benefica*) charitable institution *o* society

pa'trono SM (*Rel*) patron saint; (*socio di patronato*) patron; (*Dir*) counsel

'patta SF flap; (*dei pantaloni*) fly

patteggia'mento [patteddʒa'mento] SM (*Dir*) plea bargaining

patteggi'are [patted'dʒare] /**62**/ VT, VI to negotiate; (*Dir*) to plea-bargain

patti'naggio [patti'naddʒo] SM skating; ~ **a rotelle/sul ghiaccio** roller-/ice-skating

patti'nare /**72**/ vi to skate; **~ sul ghiaccio** to ice-skate

pattina'tore, -'trice sm/f skater

'pattino¹ sm skate; (*di slitta*) runner; (*Aer*) skid; (*Tecn*) sliding block; **pattini (da ghiaccio)** (ice) skates; **pattini in linea** rollerblades®; **pattini a rotelle** roller skates

pat'tino² sm (*barca*) kind of pedalo with oars

pat'tista, -i, -e ag (*Pol*) of Patto per l'Italia ► sm/f (*Pol*) member (*o* supporter) of Patto per l'Italia

'patto sm (*accordo*) pact, agreement; (*condizione*) term, condition; **a ~ che** on condition that; **a nessun ~** under no circumstances; **venire *o* scendere a patti (con)** to come to an agreement (with); **P~ per l'Italia** (*Pol*) centrist party

pat'tuglia [pat'tuʎʎa] sf (*Mil*) patrol

pattugli'are [pattuʎ'ʎare] /**27**/ vt to patrol

pattu'ire /**55**/ vt to reach an agreement on

pattumi'era sf (dust)bin (*Brit*), ashcan (*US*)

pa'ura sf fear; **aver ~ di/di fare/che** to be frightened *o* afraid of/of doing/that; **far ~ a** to frighten; **per ~ di/che** for fear of/that; **ho ~ di sì/no** I am afraid so/not

pau'roso, -a ag (*che fa paura*) frightening; (*che ha paura*) fearful, timorous

'pausa sf (*sosta*) break; (*nel parlare: Mus*) pause

paven'tato, -a ag much-feared

pa'vese ag of (*o* from) Pavia

'pavido, -a ag (*letterario*) fearful

pavimen'tare /**72**/ vt (*stanza*) to floor; (*strada*) to pave

pavimentazi'one [pavimentat'tsjone] sf flooring; paving

pavi'mento sm floor

pa'vone sm peacock

pavoneggi'arsi [pavoned'dʒarsi] /**62**/ vpr to strut about, show off

'paywall ['peiwol] sm inv paywall

pazien'tare [pattsjen'tare] /**72**/ vi to be patient

pazi'ente [pat'tsjɛnte] ag, smf patient

pazi'enza [pat'tsjɛntsa] sf patience; **perdere la ~** to lose (one's) patience

pazza'mente [pattsa'mente] av madly; **essere ~ innamorato** to be madly in love

paz'zesco, -a, -schi, -sche [pat'tsesko] ag mad, crazy

paz'zia [pat'tsia] sf (*Med*) madness, insanity; (*di azione, decisione*) madness, folly; **è stata una ~!** it was sheer madness!

'pazzo, -a ['pattso] ag (*Med*) mad, insane; (*strano*) wild, mad ► sm/f madman/woman; **~ di** (*gioia, amore ecc*) mad *o* crazy with; **~ per qc/qn** mad *o* crazy about sth/sb; **essere ~ da legare** to be raving mad *o* a raving lunatic

PC sigla = **Piacenza** ► sigla m inv [pi'tʃi] (= *personal computer*) PC; **PC portatile** laptop

p.c. abbr = **per condoglianze**; **per conoscenza**

p.c.c. abbr (= *per copia conforme*) cc

P.C.I. sigla m (= *Partito Comunista Italiano*) former political party

PCUS sigla m = **Partito Comunista dell'Unione Sovietica**

PD sigla = **Padova**

P.D. abbr = **partita doppia**

PE sigla = **Pescara**

'pecca, -che sf defect, flaw, fault

peccami'noso, -a ag sinful

pec'care /**20**/ vi to sin; (*fig*) to err

pec'cato sm sin; **è un ~ che** it's a pity that; **che ~!** what a shame *o* pity!; **un ~ di gioventù** (*fig*) a youthful error *o* indiscretion

pecca'tore, -'trice sm/f sinner

pecche'rò etc [pekke'rɔ] vb vedi **peccare**

'pece ['petʃe] sf pitch

pechi'nese [peki'nese] ag, smf Pekin(g)ese inv ► sm (*anche*: **cane pechinese**) Pekin(g)ese inv, Peke

Pe'chino [pe'kino] sf Beijing, Peking

'pecora sf sheep; **~ nera** (*fig*) black sheep

peco'raio sm shepherd

peco'rella sf lamb; **la ~ smarrita** the lost sheep; **cielo a pecorelle** (*fig: nuvole*) mackerel sky

peco'rino sm sheep's milk cheese

pecu'lato sm (*Dir*) embezzlement

peculi'are ag: **~ di** peculiar to

peculiarità sf peculiarity

pecuni'ario, -a ag financial, money *cpd*

pe'daggio [pe'daddʒo] sm toll

pedago'gia [pedago'dʒia] sf pedagogy, educational methods *pl*

peda'gogico, -a, -ci, -che [peda'gɔdʒiko] ag pedagogic(al)

peda'gogo, -a, -ghi, -ghe sm/f pedagogue

peda'lare /**72**/ vi to pedal; (*andare in bicicletta*) to cycle

pe'dale sm pedal

pe'dana sf footboard; (*Sport: nel salto*) springboard; (: *nella scherma*) piste

pe'dante ag pedantic ► smf pedant

pedante'ria sf pedantry

pe'data sf (*impronta*) footprint; (*colpo*) kick; **prendere a pedate qn/qc** to kick sb/sth

pede'rasta, -i sm pederast

pe'destre ag prosaic, pedestrian

pedi'atra, -i, -e sm/f paediatrician (*Brit*), pediatrician (*US*)

pedia'tria sf paediatrics *sg* (*Brit*), pediatrics *sg* (*US*)

pedi'atrico, -a, -ci, -che ag pediatric

pedi'cure sm inv/f inv chiropodist (*Brit*), podiatrist (*US*)

pedigree sm inv pedigree

pedi'luvio sm footbath

pe'dina SF (*della dama*) draughtsman (BRIT), draftsman (US); (*fig*) pawn

pedi'nare /**72**/ VT to shadow, tail

pe'dofilo, -a AG, SM/F paedophile

pedo'nale AG pedestrian

pe'done, -a SM/F pedestrian ▶ SM (*Scacchi*) pawn

peeling ['piling] SM INV (*Cosmesi*) facial scrub

'**peggio** ['pɛddʒo] AV, AG INV worse ▶ SM O F: **il** *o* **la** ~ the worst; **cambiare in** ~ to get *o* become worse; **alla** ~ at worst, if the worst comes to the worst; **tirare avanti alla meno** ~ to get along as best one can; **avere la** ~ to come off worse, get the worst of it

peggiora'mento [peddʒora'mento] SM worsening

peggio'rare [peddʒo'rare] /**72**/ VT to make worse, worsen ▶ VI to grow worse, worsen

peggiora'tivo, -a [peddʒora'tivo] AG pejorative

peggi'ore [ped'dʒore] AG (*comparativo*) worse; (*superlativo*) worst ▶ SM F: **il (la)** ~ the worst (person); **nel** ~ **dei casi** if the worst comes to the worst

'**pegno** ['peɲɲo] SM (*Dir*) security, pledge; (*nei giochi di società*) forfeit; (*fig*) pledge, token; **dare in** ~ **qc** to pawn sth; **in** ~ **d'amicizia** as a token of friendship; **banco dei pegni** pawnshop

pelapa'tate SM INV potato peeler

pe'lare /**72**/ VT (*spennare*) to pluck; (*spellare*) to skin; (*sbucciare*) to peel; (*fig*) to make pay through the nose; **pelarsi** VPR to go bald

pe'lato, -a AG (*sbucciato*) peeled; (*calvo*) bald; **(pomodori) pelati** peeled tomatoes

pel'lame SM skins *pl*, hides *pl*

'**pelle** SF skin; (*di animale*) skin, hide; (*cuoio*) leather; **essere** ~ **ed ossa** to be skin and bone; **avere la** ~ **d'oca** to have goose pimples *o* goose flesh; **avere i nervi a fior di** ~ to be edgy; **non stare più nella** ~ **dalla gioia** to be beside o.s. with delight; **lasciarci la** ~ to lose one's life; **amici per la** ~ firm *o* close friends

pellegri'naggio [pellegri'naddʒo] SM pilgrimage

pelle'grino, -a SM/F pilgrim

pelle'rossa (*pl* **pellerosse**) SM/F (*peg*) Red Indian (*peg*)

pellette'ria SF (*articoli*) leather goods *pl*; (*negozio*) leather goods shop

pelli'cano SM pelican

pellicce'ria [pellittʃe'ria] SF (*negozio*) furrier's (shop); (*quantità di pellicce*) furs *pl*

pel'liccia, -ce [pel'littʃa] SF (*mantello di animale*) coat, fur; (*indumento*) fur coat; ~ **ecologica** fake fur

pellicci'aio [pellit'tʃajo] SM furrier

pel'licola SF (*membrana sottile*) film, layer; (*Fot, Cine*) film

pelli'rossa SM F = **pellerossa**

'**pelo** SM hair; (*pelame*) coat, hair; (*pelliccia*) fur; (*di tappeto*) pile; (*di liquido*) surface; **per un** ~: **per un** ~ **non ho perduto il treno** I very nearly missed the train; **c'è mancato un** ~ **che affogasse** he narrowly escaped drowning; **cercare il** ~ **nell'uovo** (*fig*) to pick holes, split hairs; **non aver peli sulla lingua** (*fig*) to speak one's mind

pe'loso, -a AG hairy

'**peltro** SM pewter

pe'luche [pə'lyʃ] SM plush; **giocattoli di** ~ soft toys

pe'luria SF down

'**pelvi** SF INV pelvis

pelvico, -a, -ci, -che AG pelvic

'**pena** SF (*Dir*) sentence; (*punizione*) punishment; (*sofferenza*) sadness *no pl*, sorrow; (*fatica*) trouble *no pl*, effort; (*difficoltà*) difficulty; **far** ~ to be pitiful; **mi fai** ~ I feel sorry for you; **essere** *o* **stare in** ~ (**per qc/qn**) to worry *o* be anxious (about sth/sb); **prendersi** *o* **darsi la** ~ **di fare** to go to the trouble of doing; **vale la** ~ **farlo** it's worth doing, it's worth it; **non ne vale la** ~ it's not worth the effort, it's not worth it; ~ **di morte** death sentence; ~ **pecuniaria** fine

pe'nale AG penal ▶ SF (*anche*: **clausola penale**) penalty clause; **causa** ~ criminal trial; **diritto** ~ criminal law; **pagare la** ~ to pay the penalty

pena'lista, -i, -e SM/F (*avvocato*) criminal lawyer

penalità SF INV penalty

penaliz'zare [penalid'dzare] /**72**/ VT (*Sport*) to penalize

penalizzazi'one [penaliddzat'tsjone] SF (*Sport*) penalty

pe'nare /**72**/ VI (*patire*) to suffer; (*faticare*) to struggle

pen'dente AG hanging; leaning ▶ SM (*ciondolo*) pendant; (*orecchino*) drop earring

pen'denza [pen'dɛntsa] SF slope, slant; (*grado d'inclinazione*) gradient; (*Econ*) outstanding account

pendere /**8**/ VI (*essere appeso*): ~ **da** to hang from; (*essere inclinato*) to lean; (*fig: incombere*) ~ **su** to hang over

pen'dice [pen'ditʃe] SF (*di monte*) slope

pen'dio, -ii SM slope, slant; (*luogo in pendenza*) slope

'**pendola** SF pendulum clock

pendo'lare AG pendulum *cpd*, pendular ▶ SM F commuter

pendola'rismo SM commuting

pendo'lino SM high-speed train

'pendolo SM (*peso*) pendulum; (*anche:* **orologio a pendolo**) pendulum clock

'pene SM penis

pene'trante AG piercing, penetrating

pene'trare /**72**/ VI to come *o* get in ▶ VT to penetrate; **~ in** to enter; (*proiettile*) to penetrate; (: *acqua, aria*) to go *o* come into

penetrazi'one [penetrat'tsjone] SF penetration

penicil'lina [penitʃil'lina] SF penicillin

peninsu'lare AG peninsular; **l'Italia ~** mainland Italy

pe'nisola SF peninsula

peni'tente SMF penitent

peni'tenza [peni'tɛntsa] SF penitence; (*punizione*) penance

penitenzi'ario [peniten'tsjarjo] SM prison

'penna SF (*di uccello*) feather; (*per scrivere*) pen; **penne** SFPL (*Cuc*) quills (*type of pasta*); **~ a feltro/stilografica/a sfera** felt-tip/fountain/ballpoint pen

pen'nacchio [pen'nakkjo] SM (*ornamento*) plume; **un ~ di fumo** (*fig*) a plume *o* spiral of smoke

penna'rello SM felt(-tip) pen

pennel'lare /**72**/ VI to paint

pennel'lata SF brushstroke

pen'nello SM brush; (*per dipingere*) (paint)brush; **a ~** (*perfettamente*) to perfection, perfectly; **~ per la barba** shaving brush

pen'netta SF: **~ USB** memory stick

Pen'nini SMPL: **i ~** the Pennines

pen'nino SM nib

pen'none SM (*Naut*) yard; (*stendardo*) banner, standard

pen'nuto SM bird

pe'nombra SF half-light, dim light

pe'noso, -a AG painful, distressing; (*faticoso*) tiring, laborious

pen'sare /**72**/ VI to think ▶ VT to think; (*inventare, escogitare*) to think out; **~ a** to think of; (*amico, vacanze*) to think of *o* about; (*problema*) to think about; **~ di fare qc** to think of doing sth; **~ bene/male di qn** to think well/badly of sb, have a good/bad opinion of sb; **penso di sì** I think so; **penso di no** I don't think so; **a pensarci bene ...** on second thoughts (*Brit*) *o* thought (*US*)...; **non voglio nemmeno pensarci** I don't even want to think about it; **ci penso io** I'll see to *o* take care of it

pen'sata SF (*trovata*) idea, thought

pensa'tore, -'trice SM/F thinker

pensie'rino SM (*dono*) little gift; (*pensiero*): **ci farò un ~** I'll think about it

pensi'ero SM thought; (*modo di pensare, dottrina*) thinking *no pl*; (*preoccupazione*) worry, care, trouble; **darsi ~ per qc** to worry about

sth; **stare in ~ per qn** to be worried about sb; **un ~ gentile** (*anche fig*: *dono ecc*) a kind thought

pensie'roso, -a AG thoughtful

'pensile AG hanging ▶ SM (*in cucina*) wall cupboard

pensi'lina SF (*in stazione*) platform roof

pensiona'mento SM retirement; **~ anticipato** early retirement

pensio'nante SMF (*presso una famiglia*) lodger; (*di albergo*) guest

pensio'nato, -a SM/F pensioner ▶ SM (*istituto*) hostel

pensi'one SF (*al prestatore di lavoro*) pension; (*vitto e alloggio*) board and lodging; (*albergo*) boarding house; **andare in ~** to retire; **mezza ~** half board; **~ completa** full board; **~ d'invalidità** disablement pension; **~ per la vecchiaia** old-age pension

pensio'nistico, -a, -ci, -che AG pension *cpd*

pen'soso, -a AG thoughtful, pensive, lost in thought

pen'tagono SM pentagon; **il P~** the Pentagon

penta'gramma, -i SM (*Mus*) staff, stave

pentapar'tito SM (*Pol*) five-party coalition government

'pentathlon ['pɛntatlon] SM (*Sport*) pentathlon

Pente'coste SF Pentecost, Whit Sunday (*Brit*)

penti'mento SM repentance, contrition

pen'tirsi /**45**/ VPR: **~ di** to repent of; (*rammaricarsi*) to regret, be sorry for

penti'tismo SM *confessions from terrorists and members of organized crime rackets; see note*

> The practice of *pentitismo* first emerged in Italy during the 1970s, a period marked by major terrorist activity. Once arrested, some members of terrorist groups would collaborate with the authorities by providing information in return for a reduced sentence, or indeed for their own reasons. In recent years it has become common practice for members of Mafia organizations to become *pentiti*, and special legislation has had to be introduced to provide for the sentencing and personal protection of these informants.

pen'tito, -a SM/F ≈ supergrass (*Brit*), *terrorist/ criminal who turns police informer*

'pentola SF pot; **~ a pressione** pressure cooker

pe'nultimo, -a AG last but one (*Brit*), next to last, penultimate

pe'nuria SF shortage

penzo'lare [pendzo'lare] /**72**/ VI to dangle, hang loosely

penzo'loni [pendzo'loni] AV dangling, hanging down; **stare ~** to dangle, hang down

pe'pato, -a AG (condito con pepe) peppery, hot; (fig: pungente) sharp

'pepe SM pepper; **~ macinato/in grani/nero** ground/whole/black pepper

pepero'nata SF stewed peppers, tomatoes and onions

peperon'cino [peperon'tʃino] SM chilli pepper

pepe'rone SM: **~ (rosso)** red pepper, capsicum; **~ (verde)** green pepper, capsicum; (piccante) chili; **rosso come un ~** as red as a beetroot (BRIT), fire-engine red (US); **peperoni ripieni** stuffed peppers

pe'pita SF nugget

(PAROLA CHIAVE)

per PREP **1** (moto attraverso luogo) through; **i ladri sono passati per la finestra** the thieves got in (o out) through the window; **l'ho cercato per tutta la casa** I've searched the whole house o all over the house for it **2** (moto a luogo) for, to; **partire per la Germania/il mare** to leave for Germany/the sea; **il treno per Roma** the Rome train, the train for o to Rome; **proseguire per Londra** to go on to London **3** (stato in luogo): **seduto/sdraiato per terra** sitting/lying on the ground **4** (tempo) for; **per anni/lungo tempo** for years/a long time; **per tutta l'estate** throughout the summer, all summer long; **lo rividi per Natale** I saw him again at Christmas; **lo faccio per lunedì** I'll do it for Monday **5** (mezzo, maniera) by; **per lettera/ferrovia/ via aerea** by letter/rail/airmail; **prendere qn per un braccio** to take sb by the arm **6** (causa, scopo) for; **assente per malattia** absent because of o through o owing to illness; **ottimo per il mal di gola** excellent for sore throats; **per abitudine** out of habit, from habit **7** (limitazione) for; **è troppo difficile per lui** it's too difficult for him; **per quel che mi riguarda** as far as I'm concerned; **per poco che sia** however little it may be; **per questa volta ti perdono** I'll forgive you this time **8** (prezzo, misura) for; (distributivo) a, per; **venduto per 3 milioni** sold for 3 million; **la strada continua per 3 km** the street goes on for 3 km; **15 euro per persona** 15 euros o a o per person; **uno per volta** one at a time; **uno per uno** one by one; **giorno per giorno** day by day; **due per parte** two either side; **5 per cento** 5 per cent; **3 per 4 fa 12** 3 times 4 equals 12; **dividere/moltiplicare**

12 per 4 to divide/multiply 12 by 4 **9** (in qualità di) as; (al posto di) for; **avere qn per professore** to have sb as a teacher; **ti ho preso per Mario** I mistook you for Mario, I thought you were Mario; **dare per morto qn** to give sb up for dead; **lo prenderanno per pazzo** they'll think he's crazy **10** (seguito da vb: finale): **per fare qc** (so as) to do sth, in order to do sth; (: causale): **per aver fatto qc** for having done sth; **studia per passare l'esame** he's studying in order to o (so as) to pass his exam; **l'hanno punito per aver rubato i soldi** he was punished for having stolen the money; (: consecutivo): **è abbastanza grande per andarci da solo** he's big enough to go on his own

---

'pera SF pear

pe'raltro AV moreover, what's more

per'bacco ESCL by Jove!

per'bene AG INV respectable, decent ▶ AV (con cura) properly, well

perbe'nismo SM (so-called) respectability

percentu'ale [pertʃentu'ale] SF percentage; (commissione) commission

perce'pire [pertʃe'pire] /**55**/ VT (sentire) to perceive; (ricevere) to receive

percet'tibile [pertʃet'tibile] AG perceptible

percezi'one [pertʃet'tsjone] SF perception

(PAROLA CHIAVE)

perché [per'ke] AV why; **perché no?** why not?; **perché non vuoi andarci?** why don't you want to go?; **spiegami perché l'hai fatto** tell me why you did it ▶ CONG **1** (causale) because; **non posso uscire perché ho da fare** I can't go out because o as I've a lot to do **2** (finale) in order that, so that; **te lo do perché tu lo legga** I'm giving it to you so (that) you can read it **3** (consecutivo): **è troppo forte perché si possa batterlo** he's too strong to be beaten ▶ SM INV reason; **il perché di** the reason for; **non c'è un vero perché** there's no real reason for it

---

perciò [per'tʃɔ] CONG so, for this o that reason

per'correre /**28**/ VT (luogo) to go all over; (paese) to travel up and down, go all over; (distanza) to cover

percor'ribile AG (strada) which can be followed

per'corso, -a PP di **percorrere** ▶ SM (tragitto) journey; (tratto) route

per'cosso, -a PP di **percuotere** ▶ SF blow

percu'otere /**106**/ VT to hit, strike

percussi'one SF percussion; **strumenti a ~** (Mus) percussion instruments

per'dente AG losing ▶ SM F loser

'**perdere** /73/ VT to lose; (*lasciarsi sfuggire*) to miss; (*sprecare: tempo, denaro*) to waste; (*mandare in rovina: persona*) to ruin ▶ VI to lose; (*serbatoio ecc*) to leak; **perdersi** VPR (*smarrirsi*) to get lost; (*svanire*) to disappear, vanish; **saper ~** to be a good loser;•**lascia ~!** forget it!, never mind!; **non ho niente da ~** (*fig*) I've got nothing to lose; **è un'occasione da non ~** it's a marvellous opportunity; (*affare*) it's a great bargain; **è fatica persa** it's a waste of effort; **~ al gioco** to lose money gambling; **~ di vista qn** (*anche fig*) to lose sight of sb; **perdersi di vista** to lose sight of each other; (*fig*) to lose touch; **perdersi alla vista** to disappear from sight; **perdersi in chiacchiere** to waste time talking

perdifi'ato: a ~ av (*correre*) at breathtaking speed; (*gridare*) at the top of one's voice

perdigi'orno [perdi'dʒorno] SM INV/F INV idler, waster

'**perdita** SF loss; (*spreco*) waste; (*fuoriuscita*) leak; **siamo in ~** (*Comm*) we are running at a loss; **a ~ d'occhio** as far as the eye can see

perdi'tempo SM INV/F INV waster, idler

perdizi'one [perdit'tsjone] SF (*Rel*) perdition, damnation; **luogo di ~** place of ill repute

perdo'nare /72/ VT to pardon, forgive; (*scusare*) to excuse, pardon; **per farsi ~** in order to be forgiven; **perdona la domanda ...** if you don't mind my asking ...; **vogliate ~ il (mio) ritardo** my apologies for being late; **un male che non perdona** an incurable disease

per'dono SM forgiveness; (*Dir*) pardon; **chiedere ~ a qn (per)** to ask for sb's forgiveness (for); (*scusarsi*) to apologize to sb (for)

perdu'rare /72/ VI to go on, last; (*perseverare*) to persist

perduta'mente AV desperately, passionately

per'duto, -a PP di **perdere** ▶ AG (*gen*) lost; **sentirsi** *o* **vedersi ~** (*fig*) to realize the hopelessness of one's position; **una donna perduta** (*fig*) a fallen woman

peregri'nare /72/ VI to wander, roam

pe'renne AG eternal, perpetual, perennial; (*Bot*) perennial

peren'torio, -a AG peremptory; (*definitivo*) final

perfetta'mente AV perfectly; **sai ~ che ...** you know perfectly well that ...

per'fetto, -a AG perfect ▶ SM (*Ling*) perfect (tense)

perfeziona'mento [perfettsjona'mento] SM: **~ (di)** improvement (in), perfection (of); **corso di ~** proficiency course

perfezio'nare [perfettsjo'nare] /72/ VT to improve, perfect; **perfezionarsi** VPR to improve

perfezi'one [perfet'tsjone] SF perfection

perfezio'nismo [perfettsjo'nizmo] SM perfectionism

perfezio'nista, -i, -e [perfettsjo'nista] SM/F perfectionist

per'fidia SF perfidy

'**perfido, -a** AG perfidious, treacherous

per'fino AV even

perfo'rare /72/ VT to pierce; (*Med*) to perforate, to punch a hole (*o* holes) in; (*banda, schede*) to punch; (*trivellare*) to drill

perfora'tore, -'trice SM/F punch-card operator ▶ SM (*utensile*) punch; (*Inform*): **~ di schede** card punch ▶ SF (*Tecn*) boring *o* drilling machine; (*Inform*) card punch

perforazi'one [perforat'tsjone] SF piercing; perforation; punching drilling

perga'mena SF parchment

'**pergola** SF pergola

pergo'lato SM pergola

perico'lante AG precarious

pe'ricolo SM danger; **essere fuori ~** to be out of danger; (*Med*) to be off the danger list; **mettere in ~** to endanger, put in danger

perico'loso, -a AG dangerous

perife'ria SF (*anche fig*) periphery; (*di città*) outskirts *pl*

peri'ferico, -a, -ci, -che AG (*Anat, Inform*) peripheral; (*zona*) outlying

pe'rifrasi SF INV circumlocution

pe'rimetro SM perimeter

peri'odico, -a, -ci, -che AG periodic(al); (*Mat*) recurring ▶ SM periodical

pe'riodo SM period; **~ contabile** accounting period; **~ di prova** trial period

peripe'zie [peripet'tsie] SFPL ups and downs, vicissitudes

'**periplo** SM circumnavigation

pe'rire /55/ VI to perish, die

peris'copio SM periscope

pe'rito, -a AG expert, skilled ▶ SM/F expert; (*agronomo, navale*) surveyor; **un ~ chimico** a qualified chemist

perito'nite SF peritonitis

pe'rizia [pe'rittsja] SF (*abilità*) ability; (*giudizio tecnico*) expert opinion; expert's report; **~ psichiatrica** psychiatrist's report

peri'zoma, -i [peri'dzoma] SM G-string

'**perla** SF pearl

per'lina SF bead

perli'nato SM matchboarding

perlo'meno AV (*almeno*) at least

perlopiù AV (*quasi sempre*) in most cases, usually

perlus'trare /72/ VT to patrol

P

perlustrazi'one [perlustrat'tsjone] SF patrol, reconnaissance; **andare in** ~ to go on patrol

perma'loso, -a AG touchy

perma'nente AG permanent ▶ SF permanent wave, perm

perma'nenza [perma'nɛntsa] SF permanence; (*soggiorno*) stay; **buona ~!** enjoy your stay!

perma'nere /93/ VI to remain

per'mango VB *vedi* **permanere**

per'masi *etc* VB *vedi* **permanere**

perme'abile AG permeable

perme'are /72/ VT to permeate

per'messo, -a PP *di* **permettere** ▶ SM (*autorizzazione*) permission, leave; (*dato a militare, impiegato*) leave; (*licenza*) licence (BRIT), license (US), permit; (*Mil: foglio*) pass; **~?, è ~?** (*posso entrare?*) may I come in?; (*posso passare?*) excuse me; **~ di lavoro/pesca** work/fishing permit; **~ di soggiorno** residence permit

per'mettere /63/ VT to allow, permit; **~ a qn qc/di fare qc** to allow sb sth/to do sth; **permettersi** VPR: **permettersi qc/di fare qc** (*concedersi*) to allow o.s. sth/to do sth; (*avere la possibilità*) to afford sth/to do sth; **permettete che mi presenti** let me introduce myself, may I introduce myself?; **mi sia permesso di sottolineare che ...** may I take the liberty of pointing out that ...

per'misi *etc* VB *vedi* **permettere**

permis'sivo, -a AG permissive

'permuta SF (*Dir*) transfer; (*Comm*) trade-in; **accettare qc in ~** to take sth as a trade-in; **valore di ~** (*di macchina ecc*) trade-in value

permu'tare /72/ VT to exchange; (*Mat*) to permute

per'nacchia [per'nakkja] SF (*col*): **fare una ~** to blow a raspberry

per'nice [per'nitʃe] SF partridge

'perno SM pivot

pernotta'mento SM overnight stay

pernot'tare /72/ VI to spend the night, stay overnight

'pero SM pear tree

però CONG (*ma*) but; (*tuttavia*) however, nevertheless

pero'rare /72/ VT (*Dir: fig*): **~ la causa di qn** to plead sb's case

perpendico'lare AG, SF perpendicular

perpen'dicolo SM: **a ~** perpendicularly

perpe'trare /72/ VT to perpetrate

perpetu'are /72/ VT to perpetuate

per'petuo, -a AG perpetual

perplessità SF INV perplexity

per'plesso, -a AG perplexed, puzzled; uncertain

perqui'sire /55/ VT to search

perquisizi'one [perkwizit'tsjone] SF (police) search; **mandato di ~** search warrant

'perse *etc* VB *vedi* **perdere**

persecu'tore SM persecutor

persecuzi'one [persekut'tsjone] SF persecution

persegu'ibile AG (*Dir*): **essere ~ per legge** to be liable to prosecution

persegu'ire /45/ VT to pursue; (*Dir*) to prosecute

persegui'tare /72/ VT to persecute

persevel'rante AG persevering

perseve'ranza [perseve'rantsa] SF perseverance

perseve'rare /72/ VI to persevere

'persi *etc* VB *vedi* **perdere**

'Persia SF: **la ~** Persia

persi'ano, -a AG, SM/F Persian ▶ SF shutter; **persiana avvolgibile** roller blind

'persico, -a, -ci, -che AG: **il golfo P~** the Persian Gulf; **pesce ~** perch

per'sino AV = **perfino**

persis'tente AG persistent

persis'tenza [persis'tɛntsa] SF persistence

per'sistere /11/ VI to persist; **~ a fare** to persist in doing

persis'tito, -a PP *di* **persistere**

'perso, -a PP *di* **perdere** ▶ AG (*smarrito: anche fig*) lost; (*sprecato*) wasted; **fare qc a tempo ~** to do sth in one's spare time; **~ per ~** I've (*o we've etc*) got nothing further to lose

per'sona SF person; (*qualcuno*): **una ~** someone, somebody; (*espressione*) anyone *o* anybody; **persone** SFPL people *pl*; **non c'è ~ che ...** there's nobody who ..., there isn't anybody who ...; **in ~**, **di ~** in person; **per interposta ~** through an intermediary *o* a third party; **~ giuridica** (*Dir*) legal person

perso'naggio [perso'naddʒo] SM (*persona ragguardevole*) personality, figure; (*tipo*) character, individual; (*Letteratura*) character

perso'nale AG personal ▶ SM staff; personnel; (*figura fisica*) build ▶ SF (*mostra*) one-man *o* one-woman exhibition

personalità SF INV personality

personaliz'zare [personalid'dzare] **/72/** VT (*arredamento, stile*) to personalize; (*adattare*) to customize

personaliz'zato, -a [personalid'dzato] AG personalized

personal'mente AV personally

personifi'care /20/ VT to personify; (*simboleggiare*) to embody

personificazi'one [personifikat'tsjone] SF (*vedi vb*) personification; embodiment

perspi'cace [perspi'katʃe] AG shrewd, discerning

perspi'cacia [perspi'katʃa] SF perspicacity, shrewdness

persu'adere/88/ VT: ~ **qn (di qc/a fare)** to persuade sb (of sth/to do)

persuasi'one SF persuasion

persua'sivo, -a AG persuasive

persu'aso, -a PP di **persuadere**

per'tanto CONG (quindi) so, therefore

'pertica, -che SF pole

perti'nace [perti'natʃe] AG determined; persistent

perti'nente AG: ~ **(a)** relevant (to), pertinent (to)

perti'nenza [perti'nɛntsa] SF (attinenza) pertinence, relevance; (competenza): **essere di ~ di qn** to be sb's business

per'tosse SF whooping cough

per'tugio [per'tudʒo] SM hole, opening

pertur'bare/72/ VT to disrupt; (persona) to disturb, perturb

perturbazi'one [perturbat'tsjone] SF disruption; disturbance; ~ **atmosferica** atmospheric disturbance

Perù SM: **il ~** Peru

peru'gino, -a [peru'dʒino] AG of (o from), Perugia

peruvi'ano, -a AG, SM/F Peruvian

per'vadere/52/ VT to pervade

per'vaso, -a PP di **pervadere**

perve'nire/128/ VI: ~ **a** to reach, arrive at, come to; (venire in possesso) **gli pervenne una fortuna** he inherited a fortune; **far ~ qc a** to have sth sent to

perve'nuto, -a PP di **pervenire**

perversi'one SF perversion

perversità SF perversity

per'verso, -a AG perverted; perverse

perver'tire/55/ VT to pervert

perver'tito, -a SM/F pervert

pervi'cace [pervi'katʃe] AG stubborn, obstinate

pervi'cacia [pervi'katʃa] SF stubbornness, obstinacy

per'vinca, -che SF periwinkle ▶ SM INV (colore) periwinkle (blue)

p.es. ABBR (= per esempio) e.g.

'pesa SF weighing no pl weighbridge

pe'sante AG heavy; (fig: noioso) dull, boring

pesan'tezza [pesan'tettsa] SF (anche fig) heaviness; **avere ~ di stomaco** to feel bloated

pesaper'sone AG INV: **(bilancia) ~** (weighing) scales pl; (automatica) weighing machine

pe'sare/72/ VT to weigh ▶ VI (avere un peso) to weigh; (essere pesante) to be heavy; (fig) to carry weight; ~ **su** (fig) to lie heavy on; to influence; to hang over; **mi pesa sgridarlo** I find it hard to scold him; **tutta la responsabilità pesa su di lui** all the responsibility rests on his shoulders; **è una situazione che mi pesa** it's a difficult

situation for me; **il suo parere pesa molto** his opinion counts for a lot; ~ **le parole** to weigh one's words

'pesca (pl **pesche**) SF (frutto) peach; (il pescare) fishing; **andare a ~** to go fishing; ~ **di beneficenza** (lotteria) lucky dip; ~ **con la lenza** angling; ~ **subacquea** underwater fishing

pes'caggio [pes'kaddʒo] SM (Naut) draught (BRIT), draft (US)

pes'care/20/ VT (pesce) to fish for; to catch; (qc nell'acqua) to fish out; (fig: trovare) to get hold of, find; **andare a ~** to go fishing

pesca'tore SM fisherman; (con lenza) angler

'pesce ['peʃʃe] SM fish gen inv; **Pesci** (dello zodiaco) Pisces; **essere dei Pesci** to be Pisces; **non saper che pesci prendere** (fig) not to know which way to turn; ~ **d'aprile!** April Fool!; see note; ~ **martello** hammerhead; ~ **rosso** goldfish; ~ **spada** swordfish

> Il pesce d'aprile is a sort of April Fool's joke, played on 1 April. Originally it took its name from a paper fish which was secretly attached to a person's back but nowadays all sorts of practical jokes are popular.

pesce'cane [peʃʃe'kane] SM shark

pesche'reccio [peske'rettʃo] SM fishing boat

pesche'ria [peske'ria] SF fishmonger's (shop) (BRIT), fish store (US)

pescheròetc [peske'rɔ] VB vedi **pescare**

peschi'era [pes'kjɛra] SF fishpond

pesci'vendolo, -a [peʃʃi'vendolo] SM/F fishmonger (BRIT), fish merchant (US)

'pesco, -schi SM peach tree

pes'coso, -a AG teeming with fish

pe'seta SF peseta

'peso SM weight; (Sport) shot; **dar ~ a qc** to attach importance to sth; **essere di ~ a qn** (fig) to be a burden to sb; **rubare sul ~** to give short weight; **lo portarono via di ~** they carried him away bodily; **avere due pesi e due misure** (fig) to have double standards; ~ **lordo/netto** gross/net weight; ~ **piuma/mosca/gallo/medio/massimo** (Pugilato) feather/fly/bantam/middle/heavyweight

pessi'mismo SM pessimism

pessi'mista, -i, -e AG pessimistic ▶ SM/F pessimist

'pessimo, -a AG very bad, awful; **di pessima qualità** of very poor quality

pes'tare/72/ VT to tread on, trample on; (sale, pepe) to grind; (uva, aglio) to crush; (fig: picchiare): ~ **qn** to beat sb up; ~ **i piedi** to stamp one's feet; ~ **i piedi a qn** (anche fig) to tread on sb's toes

'peste SF plague; (persona) nuisance, pest

pes'tello SM pestle

pesti'cida, -i [pesti'tʃida] SM pesticide

pes'tifero, -a AG (*anche fig*) pestilential, pestiferous; (*odore*) noxious

pesti'lenza [pesti'lɛntsa] SF pestilence; (*fetore*) stench

'pesto, -a AG: **c'è buio ~** it's pitch dark ▶ SM (*Cuc*) sauce made with basil, garlic, cheese and oil; **occhio ~** black eye

'petalo SM (*Bot*) petal

pe'tardo SM firecracker, banger (*BRIT*)

petizi'one [petit'tsjone] SF petition; **fare una ~ a** to petition

'peto SM (*!*) fart (*!*)

petro'dollaro SM petrodollar

petrol'chimica [petrol'kimika] SF petrochemical industry

petroli'era SF (*nave*) oil tanker

petroli'ere SM (*industriale*) oilman; (*tecnico*) worker in the oil industry

petroli'ero, -a AG oil *cpd*

petro'lifero, -a AG oil *cpd*

pe'trolio SM oil, petroleum; (*per lampada, fornello*) paraffin (*BRIT*), kerosene (*US*); **lume a ~** oil *o* paraffin *o* kerosene lamp; **~ grezzo** crude oil

pettego'lare /**72**/ VI to gossip

pettego'lezzo [pettego'leddzo] SM gossip *no pl*; **fare pettegolezzi** to gossip

pet'tegolo, -a AG gossipy ▶ SM/F gossip

petti'nare /**72**/ VT to comb (the hair of); **pettinarsi** VPR to comb one's hair

pettina'tura SF (*acconciatura*) hairstyle

'pettine SM comb; (*Zool*) scallop

petti'rosso SM robin

'petto SM chest; (*seno*) breast, bust; (*Cuc: di carne bovina*) brisket; (: *di pollo ecc*) breast; **prendere qn/qc di ~** to face up to sb/sth; **a doppio ~** (*abito*) double-breasted

petto'rale AG pectoral

petto'rina SF (*di grembiule*) bib

petto'ruto, -a AG broad-chested; full-breasted

petu'lante AG insolent

pe'tunia SF petunia

'pezza ['pɛttsa] SF piece of cloth; (*toppa*) patch; (*cencio*) rag, cloth; (*Amm*): **~ d'appoggio** *o* **giustificativa** voucher; **trattare qn come una ~ da piedi** to treat sb like a doormat

pez'zato, -a [pet'tsato] AG piebald

pez'zente [pet'tsɛnte] SMF beggar

'pezzo ['pɛttso] SM (*gen*) piece; (*brandello, frammento*) piece, bit; (*di macchina, arnese ecc*) part; (*Stampa*) article; **aspettare un ~** to wait quite a while *o* some time; **in** *o* **a pezzi** in pieces; **andare a pezzi** to break into pieces; **essere a pezzi** (*oggetto*) to be in pieces *o* bits; (*fig: persona*) to be shattered; **un bel ~ d'uomo** a fine figure of a man; **abito a due pezzi** two-piece suit; **essere tutto d'un ~**

(*fig*) to be a man (*o* woman) of integrity; **~ di cronaca** (*Stampa*) report; **~ grosso** (*fig*) bigwig; **~ di ricambio** spare part

PG SIGLA = **Perugia**

P.G. ABBR = **procuratore generale**

pH [pi'akka] SM INV (*Chim*) pH

PI SIGLA = **Pisa**

P.I. ABBR = **Pubblica Istruzione**

pi'accio *etc* ['pjattʃo] VB *vedi* **piacere**

pia'cente [pja'tʃɛnte] AG attractive, pleasant

pia'cere [pja'tʃere] /**74**/ VI to please ▶ SM pleasure; (*favore*) favour (*BRIT*), favor (*US*); **una ragazza che piace** (*piacevole*) a likeable girl; (*attraente*) an attractive girl; **mi piace** I like it; **quei ragazzi non mi piacciono** I don't like those boys; **gli piacerebbe andare al cinema** he would like to go to the cinema; **il suo discorso è piaciuto molto** his speech was well received; **"~!"** (*nelle presentazioni*) "pleased to meet you!"; **~ (di conoscerla)** nice to meet you; **con ~** certainly, with pleasure; **per ~** please; **fare un ~ a qn** to do sb a favour; **mi fa ~ per lui** I am pleased for him; **mi farebbe ~ rivederlo** I would like to see him again

pia'cevole [pja'tʃevole] AG pleasant, agreeable

piaci'mento [pjatʃi'mento] SM: **a ~** (*a volontà*) as much as one likes, at will; **lo farà a suo ~** he'll do it when it suits him

piaci'uto, -a [pja'tʃuto] PP *di* **piacere**

pi'acqui *etc* VB *vedi* **piacere**

pi'aga, -ghe SF (*lesione*) sore; (*ferita: anche fig*) wound; (*fig: flagello*) scourge, curse; (: *persona*) pest, nuisance

piagnis'teo [pjaɲɲis'tɛo] SM whining, whimpering

piagnuco'lare [pjaɲɲuko'lare] /**72**/ VI to whimper

piagnuco'lio, -ii [pjaɲɲuko'lio] SM whimpering

piagnuco'loso, -a [pjaɲɲuko'loso] AG whiny, whimpering, moaning

pi'alla SF (*arnese*) plane

pial'lare /**72**/ VT to plane

pialla'trice [pjalla'tritʃe] SF planing machine

pi'ana SF stretch of level ground; (*più esteso*) plain

pianeggi'ante [pjaned'dʒante] AG flat, level

piane'rottolo SM landing

pia'neta SM (*Astr*) planet

pi'angere ['pjandʒere] /**75**/ VI to cry, weep; (*occhi*) to water ▶ VT to cry, weep; (*lamentare*) to bewail, lament; **~ la morte di qn** to mourn sb's death

pianifi'care /**20**/ VT to plan

pianificazi'one [pjanifikat'tsjone] SF (*Econ*) planning; **~ aziendale** corporate planning

pia'nista, -i, -e SM/F pianist

pi'ano, -a AG (*piatto*) flat, level; (*Mat*) plane; (*facile*) straightforward, simple; (*chiaro*) clear, plain ▶ AV (*adagio*) slowly; (*a bassa voce*) softly; (*con cautela*) slowly, carefully ▶ SM (*Mat*) plane; (*Geo*) plain; (*livello*) level, plane; (*di edificio*) floor; (*programma*) plan; (*Mus*) piano; **pian ~** very slowly; (*poco a poco*) little by little; **una casa di 3 piani** a 3-storey (*BRIT*) *o* 3-storied (*US*) house; **al ~ di sopra/di sotto** on the floor above/below; **all'ultimo ~** on the top floor; **al ~ terra** on the ground floor; **in primo/secondo ~** (*Fot*, *Cine ecc*) in the foreground/background; **fare un primo ~** (*Fot*, *Cine*) to take a close-up; **di primo ~** (*fig*) prominent, high-ranking; **un fattore di secondo ~** a secondary *o* minor factor; **passare in secondo ~** to become less important; **mettere tutto sullo stesso ~** to lump everything together, give equal importance to everything; **tutto secondo i piani** all according to plan; **~ di lavoro** (*superficie*) worktop; (*programma*) work plan; **~ regolatore** (*Urbanistica*) town-planning scheme; **~ stradale** road surface

piano'forte SM piano, pianoforte
piano'terra SM INV = **piano terra**
pi'ansietc VB vedi **piangere**
pi'anta SF (*Bot*) plant; (*Anat: anche*: **pianta del piede**) sole (of the foot); (*grafico*) plan; (*cartina topografica*) map; **ufficio a ~ aperta** open-plan office; **in ~ stabile** on the permanent staff; **~ stradale** street map, street plan
piantagi'one [pjanta'dʒone] SF plantation
pianta'grane SM INV/F INV troublemaker
pian'tare /**72**/ VT to plant; (*conficcare*) to drive *o* hammer in; (*tenda*) to put up, pitch; (*fig: lasciare*) to leave, desert; **piantarsi** VPR: **piantarsi davanti a qn** to plant o.s. in front of sb; **~ qn in asso** to leave sb in the lurch; **~ grane** (*fig*) to cause trouble; **piantala!** (*col*) cut it out!
pian'tato, -a AG: **ben ~** (*persona*) well-built
pianta'tore SM planter
pianter'reno SM ground floor
pian'tina SF (*di edificio, città*) (small) map; (*Bot*) (small) plant
pi'anto, -a PP *di* **piangere** ▶ SM tears *pl*, crying
pianto'nare /**72**/ VT to guard, watch over
pian'tone SM (*vigilante*) sentry, guard; (*soldato*) orderly; (*Aut*) steering column
pia'nura SF plain
pi'astra SF plate; (*di pietra*) slab; (*di fornello*) hotplate; **panino alla ~** ≈ toasted sandwich; **~ di registrazione** tape deck
pias'trella SF tile
piastrel'lare /**72**/ VT to tile
pias'trina SF (*Anat*) platelet; (*Mil*) identity disc (*BRIT*) *o* tag (*US*)

piatta'forma SF (*anche fig*) platform; **~ continentale** (*Geo*) continental shelf; **~ girevole** (*Tecn*) turntable; **~ di lancio** (*Mil*) launching pad *o* platform; **~ rivendicativa** *document prepared by the unions in an industry, setting out their claims*
piat'tello SM clay pigeon; **tiro al ~** clay-pigeon shooting (*BRIT*), trapshooting
piat'tino SM (*di tazza*) saucer
pi'atto, -a AG flat; (*fig: scialbo*) dull ▶ SM (*recipiente, vivanda*) dish; (*portata*) course; (*parte piana*) flat (part); **piatti** SMPL (*Mus*) cymbals; **un ~ di minestra** a plate of soup; **~ fondo** soup dish; **~ forte** main course; **~ del giorno** dish of the day, plat du jour; **~ del giradischi** turntable; **piatti già pronti** (*Cuc*) ready-cooked dishes; **~ piano** dinner plate
pi'azza ['pjattsa] SF square; (*Comm*) market; (*letto, lenzuolo*): **a una ~** single; **a due piazze** double; **far ~ pulita** to make a clean sweep; **mettere in ~** (*fig: rendere pubblico*) to make public; **scendere in ~** (*fig*) to take to the streets, demonstrate; **~ d'armi** (*Mil*) parade ground
piazza'forte [pjattsa'forte] (*pl* **piazzeforti**) SF (*Mil*) stronghold
piaz'zale [pjat'tsale] SM (large) square
piazza'mento [pjattsa'mento] SM (*Sport*) place, placing
piaz'zare [pjat'tsare] /**72**/ VT to place; (*Comm*) to market, sell; **piazzarsi** VPR (*Sport*) to be placed; **piazzarsi bene** to finish with the leaders *o* in a good position
piaz'zista, -i [pjat'tsista] SM (*Comm*) commercial traveller
piaz'zola [pjat'tsola] SF (*Aut*) lay-by (*BRIT*), (roadside) stopping place; (*di tenda*) pitch
'picca, -che SF pike; **picche** SFPL (*Carte*) spades; **rispondere picche a qn** (*fig*) to give sb a flat refusal
pic'cante AG hot, pungent; (*fig*) racy; biting
pic'carsi /**20**/ VPR: **~ di fare** to pride o.s. on one's ability to do; **~ per qc** to take offence (*BRIT*) *o* offense (*US*) at sth
picchet'taggio [pikket'taddʒo] SM picketing
picchet'tare [pikket'tare] /**72**/ VT to picket
pic'chetto [pik'ketto] SM (*Mil*, *di scioperanti*) picket; (*di tenda*) peg
picchi'are [pik'kjare] /**19**/ VT (*persona: colpire*) to hit, strike; (: *prendere a botte*) to beat (up); (*battere*) to beat; (*sbattere*) to bang ▶ VI (*bussare*) to knock; (: *con forza*) to bang; (*colpire*) to hit, strike; (*sole*) to beat down
picchi'ata [pik'kjata] SF knock; bang; blow; (*percosse*) beating, thrashing; (*Aer*) dive; **scendere in ~** to (nose-)dive
picchiet'tare [pikkjet'tare] /**72**/ VT (*punteggiare*) to spot, dot; (*colpire*) to tap
'picchio ['pikkjo] SM woodpecker

pic'cino, -a [pit'tʃino] AG tiny, very small

picci'olo [pit'tʃɔlo] SM (*Bot*) stalk

piccio'naia [pittʃo'naja] SF pigeon-loft; (*Teat*): **la ~** the gods *sg* (BRIT), the gallery

picci'one [pit'tʃone] SM pigeon; **pigliare due piccioni con una fava** (*fig*) to kill two birds with one stone

'picco, -chi SM peak; **a ~** vertically; **colare a ~** (*Naut, fig*) to sink

picco'lezza [pikko'lettsa] SF (*dimensione*) smallness; (*fig*: *grettezza*) meanness, pettiness; (*inezia*) trifle

'piccolo, -a AG small; (*oggetto, mano, di età*: *bambino*) small, little; (*dav sostantivo*: *di breve durata*: *viaggio*) short; (*fig*) mean, petty ▶ SM/F child, little one ▶ SM: **nel mio ~** in my own small way; **piccoli** SMPL (*di animale*) young *pl*; **in ~** in miniature; **la piccola borghesia** the lower middle classes; (*peg*) the petty bourgeoisie

pic'cone SM pick(-axe)

pic'cozza [pik'kɔttsa] SF ice-axe

pic'nic SM INV picnic; **fare un ~** to have a picnic

pidies'sino, -a AG (*Pol*) of P.D.S ▶ SM/F member (*o supporter*) of P.D.S

pi'docchio [pi'dɔkkjo] SM louse

pidocchi'oso, -a [pidok'kjoso] AG (*infestato*) lousy; (*fig*: *taccagno*) mean, stingy, tight

pidu'ista, -i, -e AG P2 *cpd* (*masonic lodge*) ▶ SM member of the P2 masonic lodge

piè SM INV: **a ogni ~ sospinto** (*fig*) at every step; **saltare a ~ pari** (*omettere*) to skip; **a ~ di pagina** at the foot of the page; **note a ~ di pagina** footnotes

pi'ede SM foot; (*di mobile*) leg; **in piedi** standing; **a piedi** on foot; **a piedi nudi** barefoot; **su due piedi** (*fig*) at once; **mettere qc in piedi** (*azienda ecc*) to set sth up; **prendere ~** (*fig*) to gain ground, catch on; **puntare i piedi** (*fig*) to dig one's heels in; **sentirsi mancare la terra sotto i piedi** to feel lost; **non sta in piedi** (*persona*) he can't stand; (*fig*: *scusa ecc*) it doesn't hold water; **tenere in piedi** (*persona*) to keep on his (*o* her) feet; (*fig*: *ditta ecc*) to keep going; **a ~ libero** (*Dir*) on bail; **sul ~ di guerra** (*Mil*) ready for action; **~ di porco** crowbar

piedipi'atti SM INV (*peg*: *poliziotto*) cop

piedis'tallo, piedes'tallo SM pedestal

pi'ega, -ghe SF (*piegatura, Geo*) fold; (*di gonna*) pleat; (*di pantaloni*) crease; (*grinza*) wrinkle, crease; **prendere una brutta** *o* **cattiva ~** (*fig*: *persona*) to get into bad ways; (: *situazione*) to take a turn for the worse; **non fa una ~** (*fig*: *ragionamento*) it's faultless; **non ha fatto una ~** (*fig*: *persona*) he didn't bat an eye(lid) (BRIT) *o* an eye(lash) (US)

piega'mento SM folding; bending; **~ sulle gambe** (*Ginnastica*) kneebend

pie'gare /**80**/ VT to fold; (*braccia, gambe, testa*) to bend ▶ VI to bend; **piegarsi** VPR to bend; (*fig*) **piegarsi (a)** to yield (to), submit (to)

piega'tura SF folding *no pl*; bending *no pl*; fold bend

pieghe'rò *etc* [pjege'rɔ] VB *vedi* **piegare**

pieghet'tare [pjeget'tare] /**72**/ VT to pleat

pie'ghevole [pje'gevole] AG pliable, flexible; (*porta*) folding; (*fig*) yielding, docile

Pie'monte SM: **il ~** Piedmont

piemon'tese AG, SM F Piedmontese

pi'ena SF *vedi* **pieno**

pie'nezza [pje'nettsa] SF fullness

pi'eno, -a AG full; (*muro, mattone*) solid ▶ SM (*colmo*) height, peak; (*carico*) full load ▶ SF (*di fiume*) flood, spate; (*gran folla*) crowd, throng; **~ di** full of; **a piene mani** abundantly; **a tempo ~** full-time; **a pieni voti** (*eleggere*) unanimously; **laurearsi a pieni voti** *to graduate with full marks*; **in ~ giorno** in broad daylight; **in ~ inverno** in the depths of winter; **in piena notte** in the middle of the night; **in piena stagione** at the height of the season; **in ~** (*completamente*: *sbagliare*) completely; (*colpire, centrare*) bang *o* right in the middle; **avere pieni poteri** to have full powers; **nel ~ possesso delle sue facoltà** in full possession of his faculties; **fare il ~ (di benzina)** to fill up (with petrol)

pie'none SM: **c'era il ~ al cinema/al teatro** the cinema/the theatre was packed

'piercing ['pirsing] SM: **farsi il ~ all'ombelico** to have one's navel pierced

pietà SF pity; (*Rel*) piety; **senza ~** (*agire*) ruthlessly; (*persona*) pitiless, ruthless; **avere ~ di** (*compassione*) to pity, feel sorry for; (*misericordia*) to have pity *o* mercy on; **far ~** to arouse pity; (*peg*) to be terrible

pie'tanza [pje'tantsa] SF dish, course

pie'toso, -a AG (*compassionevole*) pitying, compassionate; (*che desta pietà*) pitiful

pi'etra SF stone; **mettiamoci una ~ sopra** (*fig*) let bygones be bygones; **~ preziosa** precious stone, gem; **~ dello scandalo** (*fig*) cause of scandal

pie'traia SF (*terreno*) stony ground

pietrifi'care /**20**/ VT to petrify; (*fig*) to transfix, paralyze

piet'rina SF (*per accendino*) flint

pie'trisco, -schi SM crushed stone, road metal

pi'eve SF parish church

'piffero SM (*Mus*) pipe

pigi'ama [pi'dʒama] SM pyjamas *pl*

'pigia 'pigia ['pidʒa'pidʒa] SM crowd, press

pigi'are [pi'dʒare] /**62**/ VT to press

pigia'trice [pidʒa'tritʃe] SF (*macchina*) wine press

pigi'one [pi'dʒone] SF rent
pigli'are [piʎ'ʎare] /**27**/ VT to take, grab; (*afferrare*) to catch
'piglio ['piʎʎo] SM look, expression
pig'mento SM pigment
pig'meo, -a SM/F pygmy
'pigna ['piɲɲa] SF pine cone
pignole'ria [piɲɲole'ria] SF fastidiousness, fussiness
pi'gnolo, -a [piɲ'ɲɔlo] AG pernickety
pigno'rare [piɲɲo'rare] /**72**/ VT (*Dir*) to distrain
pigo'lare /**72**/ VI to cheep, chirp
pigo'lio SM cheeping, chirping
pigra'mente AV lazily
pi'grizia [pi'grittsja] SF laziness
'pigro, -a AG lazy; (*fig: ottuso*) slow, dull
PIL SIGLA M (= *prodotto interno lordo*) GDP
'pila SF (*catasta, di ponte*) pile; (*Elettr*) battery; (*col: torcia*) torch (BRIT), flashlight; **a ~, a pile** battery-operated
pi'lastro SM pillar
'pile ['pail] SM INV fleece
'pillola SF pill; **prendere la ~** (*contraccettivo*) to be on the pill; **~ del giorno dopo** morning-after pill
pi'lone SM (*di ponte*) pier; (*di linea elettrica*) pylon
pi'lota, -i, -e SM/F pilot; (*Aut*) driver ▶ AG INV pilot *cpd*; **~ automatico** automatic pilot
pilo'taggio [pilo'taddʒo] SM: **cabina di ~** flight deck
pilo'tare /**72**/ VT to pilot; to drive
piluc'care /**20**/ VT to nibble at
pi'mento SM pimento, allspice
pim'pante AG lively, full of beans
pinaco'teca, -che SF art gallery
pi'neta SF pinewood
ping-'pong [pɪŋ'pɔŋ] SM table tennis
'pingue AG fat, corpulent
pingu'edine SF corpulence
pingu'ino SM (*Zool*) penguin
'pinna SF fin; (*di cetaceo, per nuotare*) flipper
pin'nacolo SM pinnacle
'pino SM pine (tree)
pi'nolo SM pine kernel
'pinta SF pint
'pinza ['pintsa] SF pliers *pl*; (*Med*) forceps *pl*; (*Zool*) pincer
pinzette [pin'tsette] SFPL tweezers
'pio, -a, -'pii, -'pie AG pious; (*opere, istituzione*) charitable, charity *cpd*
piogge'rella [pjoddʒe'rɛlla] SF drizzle
pi'oggia, -ge ['pjɔddʒa] SF rain; (*fig: di regali, fiori*) shower; (*di insulti*) hail; **sotto la ~** in the rain; **~ acida** acid rain
pi'olo SM peg; (*di scala*) rung
piom'bare /**72**/ VI to fall heavily; (*gettarsi con impeto*): **~ su** to fall upon, assail ▶ VT (*dente*) to fill

piomba'tura SF (*di dente*) filling
piom'bino SM (*sigillo*) (lead) seal; (*del filo a piombo*) plummet; (*Pesca*) sinker
pi'ombo SM (*Chim*) lead; (*sigillo*) (lead) seal; (*proiettile*) (lead) shot; **a ~** (*cadere*) straight down; (*muro ecc*) plumb; **andare con i piedi di ~** (*fig*) to tread carefully; **senza ~** (*benzina*) unleaded; **anni di ~** (*fig*) era of terrorist outrages
pioni'ere, -a SM/F pioneer
pi'oppo SM poplar
pio'vano, -a AG: **acqua piovana** rainwater
pi'overe /**76**/ VB IMPERS to rain ▶ VI (*fig: scendere dall'alto*) to rain down; (*affluire in gran numero*): **~ in** to pour into; **non ci piove sopra** (*fig*) there's no doubt about it
pioviggi'nare [pjoviddʒi'nare] /**72**/ VB IMPERS to drizzle
piovosità SF rainfall
pio'voso, -a AG rainy
pi'ovra SF octopus
pi'ovve *etc* VB *vedi* **piovere**
'pipa SF pipe
pipì SF (*col*): **fare ~** to have a wee (wee)
pipis'trello SM (*Zool*) bat
pi'ramide SF pyramid
pi'ranha SM INV piranha
pi'rata, -i SM pirate; **~ informatico** hacker; **~ della strada** hit-and-run driver
Pire'nei SMPL: **i ~** the Pyrenees
pi'retro SM pyrethrum
'pirico, -a, -ci, -che AG: **polvere pirica** gunpowder
pi'rite SF pyrite
piro'etta SF pirouette
pi'rofilo, -a AG heat-resistant ▶ SF heat-resistant glass; (*tegame*) heat-resistant dish
pi'roga, -ghe SF dug-out canoe
pi'romane SMF pyromaniac; arsonist
pi'roscafo SM steamer, steamship
'Pisa SF Pisa
pi'sano, -a AG Pisan
pisci'are [piʃ'ʃare] /**14**/ VI (*col*) to piss (!), pee (!)
pi'scina [piʃ'ʃina] SF (swimming) pool
pi'sello SM pea
piso'lino SM nap; **fare un ~** to have a nap
'pista SF (*traccia*) track, trail; (*di stadio*) track; (*di pattinaggio*) rink; (*da sci*) run; (*Aer*) runway; (*di circo*) ring; **~ da ballo** dance floor; **~ ciclabile** cycle lane; **~ di lancio** launch(ing) pad; **~ di rullaggio** (*Aer*) taxiway; **~ di volo** (*Aer*) runway
pis'tacchio [pis'takkjo] SM pistachio (tree); pistachio (nut)
pis'tillo SM (*Bot*) pistil
pis'tola SF pistol, gun; **~ a spruzzo** spray gun; **~ a tamburo** revolver
pis'tone SM piston
pi'tocco, -chi SM skinflint, miser
pi'tone SM python

'**pittima** SF (*fig*) bore
pit'tore, -'trice SM/F painter
pitto'resco, -a, -schi, -sche AG picturesque
pit'torico, -a, -ci, -che AG of painting, pictorial
pit'tura SF painting; **~ fresca** wet paint
pittu'rare /**72**/ VT to paint

(PAROLA CHIAVE)

più AV **1** (*in maggiore quantità*) more; **più del solito** more than usual; **in più, di più** more; **ne voglio di più** I want some more; **ci sono 3 persone in** *o* **di più** there are 3 more *o* extra people; **costa di più** it's more expensive; **una volta di più** once more; **più o meno** more or less; **né più né meno** no more, no less; **per di più** (*inoltre*) what's more, moreover; **è sempre più difficile** it is getting more and more difficult; **chi più chi meno hanno tutti contribuito** everybody made a contribution of some sort; **più dormo e più dormirei** the more I sleep the more I want to sleep
2 (*comparativo*) more; (: *se monosillabo, spesso*) + ...er; **più ... di/che** more ... than; **più intelligente di lui** more intelligent than him; **più furbo di te** smarter than you; **più tardi di ...** later than ...; **lavoro più di te/di Paola** I work harder than you/than Paola; **è più intelligente che ricco** he's more intelligent than rich; **è più fortunato che bravo** he is lucky rather than skilled; **più di quanto pensassi** more than I thought; **più che altro** mainly; **più che mai** more than ever
3 (*superlativo*) most; (: *se monosillabico, spesso*) + ...est; **il più grande/intelligente** the biggest/most intelligent; **è quello che compro più spesso** that's the one I buy most often; **al più presto** as soon as possible; **al più tardi** at the latest
4 (*negazione*): **non ... più** no more, no longer; **non ho più soldi** I've got no more money, I don't have any more money; **non lavoro più** I'm no longer working, I don't work any more; **non ce n'è più** there isn't any left; **non c'è più nessuno** there's no one left; **non c'è più niente da fare** there's nothing more to be done; **a più non posso** (*gridare*) at the top of one's voice; (*correre*) as fast as one can
5 (*Mat*) plus; **4 più 5 fa 9** 4 plus 5 equals 9; **più 5 gradi** 5 degrees above freezing, plus 5; **6 più** (*a scuola*) just above a pass
▶ PREP plus; **500 più le spese** 500 plus expenses; **siamo in quattro più il nonno** there are four of us plus grandpa
▶ AG INV **1**: **più ... (di)** more ... (than); **più denaro/tempo** more money/time;

più persone di quante ci aspettassimo more people than we expected
2 (*numerosi, diversi*) several; **l'aspettai per più giorni** I waited for it for several days
▶ SM **1** (*la maggior parte*): **il più è fatto** most of it is done; **il più delle volte** more often than not, generally; **parlare del più e del meno** to talk about this and that
2 (*Mat*) plus (sign)
3: **i più** the majority

piuccheper'fetto [pjukkeper'fɛtto] SM (*Ling*) pluperfect, past perfect
pi'uma SF feather; **piume** SFPL down *sg*; (*piumaggio*) plumage *sg*, feathers
piu'maggio [pju'maddʒo] SM plumage, feathers *pl*
piu'mino SM (eider)down; (*per letto*) eiderdown; (: *tipo danese*) duvet, continental quilt; (*giacca*) quilted jacket (*with goose-feather padding*); (*per cipria*) powder puff; (*per spolverare*) feather duster
piut'tosto AV rather; **~ che** (*anziché*) rather than
'**piva** SF: **con le pive nel sacco** (*fig*) empty-handed
pi'vello, -a SM/F greenhorn
'**pizza** ['pittsa] SF (*Cuc*) pizza; (*Cine*) reel
pizze'ria [pittse'ria] SF *place where pizzas are made, sold or eaten*
pizzi'cagnolo, -a [pittsi'kaɲɲolo] SM/F specialist grocer
pizzi'care [pittsi'kare] /**20**/ VT (*stringere*) to nip, pinch; (*pungere*) to sting; to bite; (*Mus*) to pluck ▶ VI (*prudere*) to itch, be itchy; (*cibo*) to be hot *o* spicy
pizziche'ria [pittsike'ria] SF delicatessen (shop)
'**pizzico, -chi** ['pittsiko] SM (*pizzicotto*) pinch, nip; (*piccola quantità*) pinch, dash; (*d'insetto*) sting; bite
pizzi'cotto [pittsi'kɔtto] SM pinch, nip
'**pizzo** ['pittso] SM (*merletto*) lace; (*barbetta*) goatee beard; (*tangente*) protection money
pla'care /**20**/ VT to placate, soothe; **placarsi** VPR to calm down
'**placca, -che** SF plate; (*con iscrizione*) plaque; (*anche*: **placca dentaria**) (dental) plaque
plac'care /**20**/ VT to plate; **placcato in oro/ argento** gold-/silver-plated
pla'centa [pla'tʃɛnta] SF placenta
placidità [platʃidi'ta] SF calm, peacefulness
'**placido, -a** ['platʃido] AG placid, calm
plafoni'era SF ceiling light
plagi'are [pla'dʒare] /**62**/ VT (*copiare*) to plagiarize; (*Dir: influenzare*) to coerce
'**plagio** ['pladʒo] SM plagiarism; (*Dir*) duress
plaid [plɛd] SM INV (travelling) rug (*BRIT*), lap robe (*US*)

pla'nare /**72**/ vi (Aer) to glide

'**plancia, -ce** ['plantʃa] sf (Naut) bridge; (Aut: cruscotto) dashboard

'**plancton** sm inv plankton

plane'tario, -a ag planetary ▶ sm (locale) planetarium

planis'fero sm planisphere

plan'tare sm arch support

'**plasma** sm plasma

plas'mare /**72**/ vt to mould (BRIT), mold (US), shape

'**plastico, -a, -ci, -che** ag plastic ▶ sm (rappresentazione) relief model; (esplosivo): **bomba al ~** plastic bomb ▶ sf (arte) plastic arts pl; (Med) plastic surgery; (sostanza) plastic; **plastica facciale** face lift; **in materiale ~** plastic

plasti'lina® sf plasticine®

'**platano** sm plane tree

pla'tea sf (Teat) stalls pl (BRIT), orchestra (US)

plate'ale ag (gesto, atteggiamento) theatrical

plateal'mente av theatrically

'**platino** sm platinum

pla'tonico, -a, -ci, -che ag platonic

plau'dire /**45**/ vi: **~ a** to applaud

plau'sibile ag plausible

'**plauso** sm (fig) approval

'**playback** ['plei bæk] sm: **cantare in ~** to mime

'**playboy** ['pleibɔi] sm inv playboy

'**playmaker** ['pleimeikəʳ] sm inv/f inv (Sport) playmaker

'**play-off** ['pleiɔf] sm inv (Sport) play-off

ple'baglia [ple'baʎʎa] sf (peg) rabble, mob

'**plebe** sf common people

ple'beo, -a ag plebeian; (volgare) coarse, common

plebi'scito [plebiʃ'ʃito] sm plebiscite

ple'nario, -a ag plenary

pleni'lunio sm full moon

plenipotenzi'ario, -a [plenipoten'tsjarjo] ag plenipotentiary

'**plenum** sm inv plenum

'**plettro** sm plectrum

'**pleura** sf (Anat) pleura

pleu'rite sf pleurisy

P.L.I. SIGLA M (= Partito Liberale Italiano) former political party

'**plico, -chi** sm (pacco) parcel; **in ~ a parte** (Comm) under separate cover

plissé [pli'se] ag inv plissé cpd ▶ sm inv (anche: **tessuto plissé**) plissé

plisset'tato, -a ag plissé cpd

plo'tone sm (Mil) platoon; **~ d'esecuzione** firing squad

plug-in [pla'gin] ag inv, sm inv (Inform) plug-in

'**plumbeo, -a** ag leaden

plu'rale ag, sm plural

plura'lismo sm pluralism

plurali'tà sf plurality; (maggioranza) majority

plusva'lenza [pluzva'lɛntsa] sf capital gain

plusva'lore sm (Econ) surplus

plu'tonio sm plutonium

pluvi'ale ag rain cpd

pluvi'ometro sm rain gauge

pm ABBR = **peso molecolare**

P.M. ABBR (Pol) = **Pubblico Ministero**; (= Polizia Militare) MP (= Military Police)

PMI SIGLA FPL (= Piccole e Medie Imprese) SME (= Small and Medium-sized Enterprises)

PN SIGLA = **Pordenone**

pneu'matico, -a, -ci, -che ag inflatable; (Tecn) pneumatic ▶ sm (Aut) tyre (BRIT), tire (US)

PNL SIGLA M = **prodotto nazionale lordo**

PO SIGLA = **Prato**

Po SM: **il Po** the Po

po' AV, SM vedi **poco**

P.O. ABBR = **posta ordinaria**

po'chezza [po'kettsa] sf insufficiency, shortage; (fig: meschinità) meanness, smallness

(**PAROLA CHIAVE**)

'**poco, -a, -chi, -che** ag (quantità) little, not much; (numero) few, not many; **poco pane/denaro/spazio** little o not much bread/money/space; **con poca spesa** without spending much; **a poco prezzo** at a low price, cheap; **poco (tempo) fa** a short time ago; **poche persone/idee** few o not many people/ideas; **è un tipo di poche parole** he's a man of few words; **ci vediamo tra poco** (sottinteso: tempo) see you soon

▶ AV **1** (in piccola quantità) little, not much **2** (numero limitato) few, not many; **guadagna poco** he doesn't earn much, he earns little **3** (con ag, av) (a) little, not very; **è poco più vecchia di lui** she's a little o slightly older than him; **è poco socievole** he's not very sociable; **sta poco bene** he isn't very well **4** (tempo): **poco dopo/prima** shortly afterwards/before; **il film dura poco** the film doesn't last very long; **ci vediamo molto poco** we don't see each other very often, we hardly ever see each other **5**: **un po'** a little, a bit; **è un po' corto** it's a little o a bit short; **arriverà fra un po'** he'll arrive shortly o in a little while **6**: **a dir poco** to say the least; **a poco a poco** little by little; **per poco non cadevo** I nearly fell; **è una cosa da poco** it's nothing, it's of no importance; **una persona da poco** a worthless person

▶ PRON (a) little; **pochi, poche** pl (persone) few (people); (cose) few; **ci vediamo tra poco** see you soon; **pochi lo sanno** not many

people know it; **ci vuole tempo ed io ne ho poco** it takes time, and I haven't got much to spare
▶ SM **1** little; **vive del poco che ha** he lives on the little he has
2: un po' a little; **un po' di zucchero** a little sugar; **un bel po' di denaro** quite a lot of money; **un po' per ciascuno** a bit each

podcast ['pɔdkast] SM podcast
po'dere SM (*Agr*) farm
pode'roso, -a AG powerful
podestà SM INV (*nel fascismo*) podestà, mayor
'podio SM dais, platform; (*Mus*) podium
po'dismo SM (*Sport: marcia*) walking; (: *corsa*) running
po'dista, -i, -e SM/F walker; runner
po'ema, -i SM poem
poe'sia SF (*arte*) poetry; (*componimento*) poem
po'eta, -'essa SM/F poet (poetess)
poe'tare /**72**/ VI to write poetry
po'etico, -a, -ci, -che AG poetic(al)
poggi'are [pod'dʒare] /**62**/ VT to lean, rest; (*posare*) to lay, place
poggia'testa [poddʒa'tɛsta] SM INV (*Aut*) headrest
'poggio ['pɔddʒo] SM hillock, knoll
poggi'olo [pod'dʒɔlo] SM balcony
'poi AV then; (*alla fine*) finally, at last ▶ SM: **pensare al ~** to think of the future; **e ~** (*inoltre*) and besides; **questa ~ (è bella)!** (*ironico*) that's a good one!; **d'ora in ~** from now on; **da domani in ~** from tomorrow onwards
poi'ana SF buzzard
poiché [poi'ke] CONG since, as
pois [pwa] SM INV spot, (polka) dot; **a ~** spotted, polka-dot *cpd*
'poker SM poker
po'lacco, -a, -chi, -che AG Polish ▶ SM/F Pole
po'lare AG polar
polariz'zare [polarid'dzare] /**72**/ VT (*anche fig*) to polarize
'polca, -che SF polka
po'lemico, -a, -ci, -che AG polemical, controversial ▶ SF controversy; **fare polemiche** to be contentious
polemiz'zare [polemid'dzare] /**72**/ VI: ~ (**su qc**) to argue (about sth)
po'lenta SF (*Cuc*) sort of thick porridge made with maize flour
polen'tone, -a SM/F slowcoach (*BRIT*), slowpoke (*US*)
pole'sano, -a AG of (*o* from) Polesine (*area between the Po and the Adige*)
POL'FER ABBR F = **Polizia Ferroviaria**
'poli... PREFISSO poly...
poliambula'torio SM (*Med*) health clinic
poli'clinico, -ci SM general hospital, polyclinic

poli'edro SM polyhedron
poli'estere SM polyester
poliga'mia SF polygamy
polig'lotta, -i, -e AG, SM/F polyglot
po'ligono SM polygon; ~ **di tiro** rifle range
Poli'nesia SF: **la ~** Polynesia
polinesi'ano, -a AG, SM/F Polynesian
polio(mielite) SF polio(myelitis)
'polipo SM polyp
polisti'rolo SM polystyrene
poli'tecnico, -ci SM postgraduate technical college
po'litica, -che SF *vedi* **politico**
politica'mente AV politically; ~ **corretto** politically correct
politi'cante SMF (*peg*) petty politician
politiciz'zare [politritʃid'dzare] /**72**/ VT to politicize
po'litico, -a, -ci, -che AG political ▶ SM/F politician ▶ SF politics *sg*; (*linea di condotta*) policy; **elezioni politiche** parliamentary (*BRIT*) *o* congressional (*US*) election(s); **uomo ~** politician; **darsi alla politica** to go into politics; **fare politica** (*militante*) to be a political activist; (*come professione*) to be in politics; **la politica del governo** the government's policies; **politica aziendale** company policy; **politica estera** foreign policy; **politica dei prezzi** prices policy; **politica dei redditi** incomes policy
poliva'lente AG multi-purpose
poli'zia [polit'tsia] SF police; ~ **giudiziaria** ≈ Criminal Investigation Department (CID) (*BRIT*), Federal Bureau of Investigation (FBI) (*US*); ~ **sanitaria/tributaria** health/tax inspectorate; ~ **stradale** traffic police; ~ **di stato** *see note*

> The remit of the *polizia di stato* is to maintain public order, to uphold the law, and to prevent and investigate crime. This is a civilian branch of the police force; male and female officers perform similar duties. The *polizia di stato* reports to the Minister of the Interior.

polizi'esco, -a, -schi, -sche [polit'tsjesko] AG police *cpd*; (*film, romanzo*) detective *cpd*
polizi'otto [polit'tsjɔtto] SM policeman; **cane ~** police dog; **donna ~** policewoman; ~ **di quartiere** local police officer
'polizza ['pɔlittsa] SF (*Comm*) bill; ~ **di assicurazione** insurance policy; ~ **di carico** bill of lading
pol'laio SM henhouse
pollai'olo, -a SM/F poulterer (*BRIT*), poultryman
pol'lame SM poultry
pol'lastra SF pullet; (*fig: ragazza*) chick, wench
pol'lastro SM (*Zool*) cockerel

'pollice ['pɔllitʃe] SM thumb; *(unità di)* inch

'polline SM pollen

'pollo SM chicken; **far ridere i polli** *(situazione, persona)* to be utterly ridiculous

polmo'nare AG lung *cpd*, pulmonary

pol'mone SM lung; **~ d'acciaio** *(Med)* iron lung

polmo'nite SF pneumonia; **~ atipica** SARS

'Polo SM *(Pol) centre-right coalition*

'polo SM *(Geo, Fisica)* pole; *(gioco)* polo ▶ SF INV *(maglia)* polo shirt; **il ~ sud/nord** the South/North Pole

Po'lonia SF: **la ~** Poland

'polpa SF flesh, pulp; *(carne)* lean meat

pol'paccio [pol'pattʃo] SM *(Anat)* calf

polpas'trello SM fingertip

pol'petta SF *(Cuc)* meatball

polpet'tone SM *(Cuc)* meatloaf

'polpo SM octopus

pol'poso, -a AG fleshy

pol'sino SM cuff

'polso SM *(Anat)* wrist; *(pulsazione)* pulse; *(fig: forza)* drive, vigour (BRIT), vigor (US); **avere ~** *(fig)* to be strong; **un uomo di ~** a man of nerve

pol'tiglia [pol'tiʎʎa] SF *(composto)* mash, mush; *(di fango e neve)* slush

pol'trire /55/ VI to laze about

pol'trona SF armchair; *(Teat: posto)* seat in the front stalls (BRIT) o the orchestra (US)

poltron'cina [poltron'tʃina] SF *(Teat)* seat in the back stalls (BRIT) o the orchestra (US)

pol'trone AG lazy, slothful

'polvere SF dust; *(sostanza ridotta minutissima)* powder, dust; **caffè in ~** instant coffee; **latte in ~** dried o powdered milk; **sapone in ~** soap powder; **~ d'oro** gold dust; **~ pirica** o **da sparo** gunpowder; **polveri sottili** particulates

polveri'era SF powder magazine

polve'rina SF *(gen, Med)* powder; *(gergo: cocaina)* snow

polveriz'zare [polverid'dzare] **/72/** VT to pulverize; *(nebulizzare)* to atomize; *(fig)* to crush, pulverize; *(record)* to smash

polve'rone SM thick cloud of dust

polve'roso, -a AG dusty

po'mata SF ointment, cream

po'mello SM knob

pomeridi'ano, -a AG afternoon *cpd*; **nelle ore pomeridiane** in the afternoon

pome'riggio [pome'riddʒo] SM afternoon; **nel primo/tardo ~** in the early/late afternoon

'pomice ['pomitʃe] SF pumice

pomici'are [pomi'tʃare] **/14/** VI *(col)* to neck

'pomo SM *(mela)* apple; *(ornamentale)* knob; *(di sella)* pommel; **~ d'Adamo** *(Anat)* Adam's apple

pomo'doro SM tomato; **pomodori pelati** skinned tomatoes

'pompa SF pump; *(sfarzo)* pomp (and ceremony); **~ antincendio** fire hose; **~ di benzina** petrol (BRIT) o gas (US) pump; *(distributore)* filling o gas (US) station; **impresa di pompe funebri** funeral parlour *sg* (BRIT), undertaker's *sg*, mortician's (US)

pom'pare **/72/** VT to pump; *(trarre)* to pump out; *(gonfiare d'aria)* to pump up

pompei'ano, -a AG of (o from) Pompei

pom'pelmo SM grapefruit

pompi'ere SM fireman

pom'pon [pom'pɔn] SM INV pompom, pompon

pom'poso, -a AG pompous

ponde'rare **/72/** VT to ponder over, consider carefully

ponde'roso, -a AG *(anche fig)* weighty

po'nente SM west

'pongo VB *vedi* **porre**

'poni VB *vedi* **porre**

'ponte SM bridge; *(di nave)* deck; *(anche:* **ponte di comando***)* bridge; *(impalcatura)* scaffold; **vivere sotto i ponti** to be a tramp; **fare il ~** *(fig)* to take the extra day off *(between 2 public holidays)*; **governo ~** interim government; **~ aereo** airlift; **~ di barche** *(Mil)* pontoon bridge; **~ di coperta** *(Naut)* upper deck; **~ levatoio** drawbridge; **~ radio** radio link; **~ sospeso** suspension bridge

pon'tefice [pon'tefitʃe] SM *(Rel)* pontiff

ponti'cello [ponti'tʃello] SM *(di occhiali: Mus)* bridge

pontifi'care **/20/** VI *(anche fig)* to pontificate

pontifi'cato SM pontificate

ponti'ficio, -a, -ci, -cie [ponti'fitʃo] AG papal; **Stato P~** Papal State

pon'tile SM jetty

'pony ['pɔni] SM INV pony

pool [pu:l] SM INV *(consorzio)* consortium; *(organismo internazionale)* pool; *(di esperti, ricercatori)* team; *(antimafia, antidroga)* working party

pop [pɔp] AG INV pop *cpd*

'popcorn ['pɔpkɔ:n] SM INV popcorn

'popeline ['pɔpelin] SM poplin

popò SM INV *(sedere)* botty

popo'lano, -a AG popular, of the people ▶ SM/F man/woman of the people

popo'lare **/72/** AG popular; *(quartiere, clientela)* working-class; *(Pol)* of P.P.I. ▶ SM/F *(Pol)* member *(o* supporter) of P.P.I. ▶ VT *(rendere abitato)* to populate; **popolarsi** VPR to fill with people, get crowded; **manifestazione ~** mass demonstration; **repubblica ~** people's republic

popolarità SF popularity

popolazi'one [popolat'tsjone] SF population

'popolo SM people

popo'loso, -a AG densely populated

po'pone SM melon

'poppa SF (*di nave*) stern; (*col: mammella*) breast; **a ~** aft, astern

pop'pante SMF unweaned infant; (*fig*) whippersnapper

pop'pare /72/ VT to suck

pop'pata SF (*allattamento*) feed

poppa'toio SM (*feeding*) bottle

popu'lista, -i, -e AG populist

por'caio SM (*anche fig*) pigsty

por'cata SF (*libro, film ecc*) load of rubbish; **fare una ~ a qn** to play a dirty trick on sb

porcel'lana [portʃelˈlana] SF porcelain, china; (*oggetto*) piece of porcelain

porcel'lino, -a [portʃelˈlino] SM/F piglet; **~ d'India** guinea pig

porche'ria [porkeˈria] SF filth, muck; (*fig: oscenità*) obscenity; (: *azione disonesta*) dirty trick; (: *cosa mal fatta*) rubbish

por'chetta [porˈketta] SF roast sucking pig

por'cile [porˈtʃile] SM pigsty

por'cino, -a [porˈtʃino] AG of pigs, pork *cpd* ▶ SM (*fungo*) *type of edible mushroom*

'porco, -ci SM pig; (*carne*) pork

porcos'pino SM porcupine

'porfido SM porphyry

'porgere [ˈpɔrdʒere] /115/ VT to hand, give; (*tendere*) to hold out

'porno AG INV porn, porno

pornogra'fia SF pornography

porno'grafico, -a, -ci, -che AG pornographic

'poro SM pore

po'roso, -a AG porous

'porpora SF purple

'porre /77/ VT (*mettere*) to put; (*collocare*) to place; (*posare*) to lay (down), put (down); (*fig: supporre*): **poniamo (il caso) che ...** let's suppose that ...; **porsi** VPR (*mettersi*): **porsi a sedere/in cammino** to sit down/, set off; **~ le basi di** (*fig*) to lay the foundations of, establish; **~ una domanda a qn** to ask sb a question, put a question to sb; **~ la propria fiducia in** to place one's trust in sb; **~ fine** *o* **termine a qc** to put an end *o* a stop to sth; **posto che ...** supposing that ..., on the assumption that ...; **porsi in salvo** to save o.s.

'porro SM (*Bot*) leek; (*Med*) wart

'porsi *etc* VB *vedi* **porgere; porsi**

'porta SF door; (*Sport*) goal; (*Inform*) port; **porte** SFPL (*di città*) gates; **mettere qn alla ~** to throw sb out; **sbattere** *o* **chiudere la ~ in faccia a qn** (*anche fig*) to slam the door in sb's face; **trovare tutte le porte chiuse** (*fig*) to find the way barred; **a porte chiuse** (*Dir*) in camera; **l'inverno è alle porte** (*fig*) winter is upon us; **vendita ~ a ~** door-to-door selling; **~ di servizio** tradesmen's entrance; **~ di sicurezza** emergency exit; **~ stagna** watertight door

portaba'gagli [portabaˈgaʎʎi] SM INV (*facchino*) porter; (*Aut, Ferr*) luggage rack

portabandi'era SM INV standard bearer

porta'borse SM INV (*peg*) lackey

portabot'tiglie [portabotˈtiʎʎe] SM INV bottle rack

porta-'CD [portatʃiˈdi] SM INV (*mobile*) CD rack; (*astuccio*) CD holder

porta'cenere [portaˈtʃenere] SM INV ashtray

portachi'avi [portaˈkjavi] SM INV keyring

porta'cipria [portaˈtʃiprja] SM INV powder compact

porta'erei SF INV (*nave*) aircraft carrier ▶ SM INV (*aereo*) aircraft transporter

portafi'nestra (*pl* **portefinestre**) SF French window

porta'foglio [portaˈfɔʎʎo] SM (*busta*) wallet; (*cartella*) briefcase; (*Pol, Borsa*) portfolio; **~ titoli** investment portfolio

portafor'tuna SM INV lucky charm; mascot

portagi'oie [portaˈdʒɔje], **portagioi'elli** [portadʒoˈjɛlli] SM INV jewellery (*Brit*) *o* jewelry (*US*) box

por'tale SM (*di chiesa, Inform*) portal

porta'lettere SM INV/F INV postman/woman (*Brit*), mailman/woman (*US*)

porta'mento SM carriage, bearing

portamo'nete SM INV purse

por'tante AG (*muro ecc*) supporting, load-bearing

portan'tina SF sedan chair; (*per ammalati*) stretcher

portaog'getti [portaodˈdʒetti] AG INV: **vano ~** (*in macchina*) glove compartment

portaom'brelli SM INV umbrella stand

porta'pacchi [portaˈpakki] SM INV (*di moto, bicicletta*) luggage rack

porta'penne [portaˈpenne] SM INV pen holder; (*astuccio*) pencil case

por'tare /72/ VT (*sostenere, sorreggere: peso, bambino, pacco*) to carry; (*indossare: abito, occhiali*) to wear; (: *capelli lunghi*) to have; (*avere: nome, titolo*) to have, bear; (*recare*): **~ qc a qn** to take (*o* bring) sth to sb; (*fig: sentimenti*) to bear; **portarsi** VPR (*recarsi*) to go; **~ avanti** (*discorso, idea*) to pursue; **~ via** to take away; (*rubare*) to take; **~ i bambini a spasso** to take the children for a walk; **~ fortuna** to bring good luck; **~ qc alla bocca** to lift *o* put sth to one's lips; **porta bene i suoi anni** he's wearing well; **dove porta questa strada?** where does this road lead?, where does this road take you?; **il documento porta la tua firma** the document has *o* bears your signature; **non gli porto rancore** I don't bear him a grudge; **la polizia si è portata**

sul luogo del disastro the police went to the scene of the disaster

portarit'ratti SM INV photo(graph) frame

portari'viste SM INV magazine rack

portasa'pone SM INV soap dish

portasiga'rette SM INV cigarette case

portas'pilli SM INV pincushion

por'tata SF (*vivanda*) course; (*Aut*) carrying (*o* loading) capacity; (*di arma*) range; (*volume d'acqua*) (rate of) flow; (*fig: limite*) scope, capability; (*: importanza*) impact, import; **alla ~ di tutti** (*conoscenza*) within everybody's capabilities; (*prezzo*) within everybody's means; **a/fuori ~ (di)** within/out of reach (of); **a ~ di mano** within (arm's) reach; **di grande ~** of great importance

por'tatile AG portable

por'tato, -a AG (*incline*): **~ a** inclined *o* apt to

porta'tore, -'trice SM/F (*anche Comm*) bearer; (*Med*) carrier; **pagabile al ~** payable to the bearer; **~ di handicap** disabled person

portatovagli'olo [portatovaʎ'ʎɔlo] SM napkin ring

portau'ovo SM INV eggcup

porta'voce [porta'votʃe] SM O F INV spokesman/woman

por'tello SM (*di portone*) door; (*Naut*) hatch

portel'lone SM (*Naut, Aer*) hold door

por'tento SM wonder, marvel

porten'toso, -a AG wonderful, marvellous (*BRIT*), marvelous (*US*)

porti'cato SM portico

'portico, -ci SM portico; (*riparo*) lean-to

porti'era SF (*Aut*) door

porti'ere SM (*portinaio*) concierge, caretaker; (*di hotel*) porter; (*nel calcio*) goalkeeper

porti'naio, -a SM/F concierge, caretaker

portine'ria SF caretaker's lodge

'porto, -a PP *di* **porgere** ▶ SM (*Naut*) harbour (*BRIT*), harbor (*US*), port; (*spesa di trasporto*) carriage ▶ SM INV port (wine); **andare** *o* **giungere in ~** (*fig*) to come to a successful conclusion; **condurre qc in ~** to bring sth to a successful conclusion; **~ d'armi** gun licence (*BRIT*) *o* license (*US*); **~ fluviale** river port; **~ franco** free port; **~ marittimo** seaport; **~ militare** naval base; **~ pagato** carriage paid, post free *o* paid; **~ di scalo** port of call

Porto'gallo SM: **il ~** Portugal

porto'ghese [porto'gese] AG, SMF, SM Portuguese *inv*

por'tone SM main entrance, main door

portori'cano, -a AG, SM/F Puerto Rican

Porto'rico SF Puerto Rico

portu'ale AG harbour *cpd* (*BRIT*), harbor *cpd* (*US*), port *cpd* ▶ SM dock worker

porzi'one [por'tsjone] SF portion, share; (*di cibo*) portion, helping

'posa SF (*Fot*) exposure; (*atteggiamento, di modello*) pose; (*riposo*) pose; **lavorare senza ~** to work without a break; **mettersi in ~** to pose; **teatro di ~** photographic studio

posa'cenere [posa'tʃenere] SM INV ashtray

po'sare /**72**/ VT to put (down), lay (down) ▶ VI (*ponte, edificio, teoria*): **~ su** to rest on; (*Fot: atteggiarsi*) to pose; **posarsi** VPR (*ape, aereo*) to land; (*uccello*) to alight; (*sguardo*) to settle

po'sata SF piece of cutlery; **posate** SFPL cutlery *sg*

posa'tezza [posa'tettsa] SF (*di persona*) composure; (*di discorso*) balanced nature

po'sato, -a AG steady; (*discorso*) balanced

pos'critto SM postscript

'posi *etc* VB *vedi* **porre**

positiva'mente AV positively; (*rispondere*) in the affirmative, affirmatively

posi'tivo, -a AG positive

posizi'one [pozit'tsjone] SF position; **farsi una ~** to make one's way in the world; **prendere ~** (*fig*) to take a stand; **luci di ~** (*Aut*) sidelights

posolo'gia, -'gie [pozolo'dʒia] SF dosage, directions *pl* for use

pos'porre /**77**/ VT to place after; (*differire*) to postpone, defer

pos'posto, -a PP *di* **posporre**

posse'dere /**107**/ VT to own, possess; (*qualità, virtù*) to have, possess; (*conoscere a fondo: lingua ecc*) to have a thorough knowledge of; (*ira ecc*) to possess

possedi'mento SM possession

pos'sente AG strong, powerful

posses'sivo, -a AG possessive

pos'sesso SM ownership *no pl*; possession; **essere in ~ di** to be in possession of sth; **prendere ~** to take possession of sth; **entrare in ~** to come into one's inheritance

posses'sore SM owner

pos'sibile AG possible ▶ SM: **fare tutto il ~** to do everything possible; **nei limiti del ~** as far as possible; **al più tardi ~** as late as possible; **vieni prima ~** come as soon as possible

possibi'lista, -i, -e AG: **essere ~** to keep an open mind

possibilità SF INV possibility ▶ SFPL (*mezzi*) means; **aver la ~ di fare** to be in a position to do; to have the opportunity to do; **nei limiti delle nostre ~** in so far as we can

possibil'mente AV if possible

possi'dente SMF landowner

possi'edo *etc* VB *vedi* **possedere**

'posso *etc* VB *vedi* **potere**

post ... PREF*ISSO* post...

'posta SF (*servizio*) post, postal service; (*corrispondenza*) post, mail; (*ufficio postale*) post office; (*nei giochi d'azzardo*) stake; (*Caccia*) hide

P

(*Brit*), blind (*US*); **poste** SFPL (*amministrazione*) post office; **fare la ~ a qn** (*fig*) to lie in wait for sb; **la ~ in gioco è troppo alta** (*fig*) there's too much at stake; **a bella ~** (*apposta*) on purpose; **piccola ~** (*su giornale*) letters to the editor, letters page; **~ aerea** airmail; **~ elettronica** E-mail, e-mail, electronic mail; **~ in arrivo** inbox; **~ inviata** sent items; **~ in uscita** outbox; **~ ordinaria** ≈ second-class mail; **~ prioritaria** first class (post); **Poste e Telecomunicazioni** *postal and telecommunications service*; **ministro delle Poste e Telecomunicazioni** Postmaster General

posta'giro [posta'dʒiro] SM post office cheque (*Brit*) *o* check (*US*), postal giro (*Brit*)

pos'tale AG postal, post office *cpd* ▸ SM (*treno*) mail train; (*nave*) mail boat; (*furgone*) mail van; (*timbro*) postmark

postazi'one [postat'tsjone] SF (*Mil*) emplacement

post'bellico, -a, -ci, -che AG postwar

postda'tare /72/ VT to postdate

posteggi'are [posted'dʒare] /62/ VT, VI to park

posteggia'tore, -'trice [posteddʒa'tore] SM/F car-park attendant (*Brit*), parking-lot attendant (*US*)

pos'teggio [pos'teddʒo] SM car park (*Brit*), parking lot (*US*); (*di taxi*) rank (*Brit*), stand (*US*)

postelegra'fonico, -a, -ci, -che AG postal and telecommunications *cpd*

'poster SM INV poster

'posteri SMPL posterity *sg*; **i nostri ~** our descendants

posteri'ore AG (*dietro*) back; (*dopo*) later ▸ SM (*col: sedere*) behind

posteri'ori: a posteri'ori *ag inv* after the event ▸ AV (*dopo sostantivo*) looking back

pos'ticcio, -a, -ci, -ce [pos'tittʃo] AG false ▸ SM hairpiece

postici'pare [postitʃi'pare] /72/ VT to defer, postpone

pos'tilla SF marginal note

pos'tino SM postman (*Brit*), mailman (*US*)

'posto, -a PP *di* **porre** ▸ SM (*sito, posizione*) place; (*impiego*) job; (*spazio libero*) room, space; (*di parcheggio*) space; (*sedile: al teatro, in treno ecc*) seat; (*Mil*) post; **a ~** (*in ordine*) in place, tidy; (*fig*) settled (*: persona*) reliable; **mettere a ~** (*riordinare*) to tidy (up), put in order; (*faccende: sistemare*) to sort out; **prender ~** to take a seat; **al ~ di** in place of; **sul ~** on the spot; **~ di blocco** roadblock; **~ di lavoro** job; **~ di polizia** police station; **~ telefonico pubblico** public telephone; **~ di villeggiatura** holiday (*Brit*) *o* tourist spot; **posti in piedi** (*Teat, in autobus*) standing room

postopera'torio, -a AG (*Med*) postoperative

pos'tribolo SM brothel

post'scriptum SM INV postscript

'postumo, -a AG posthumous; (*tardivo*) belated; **postumi** SMPL (*conseguenze*) after-effects, consequences

po'tabile AG drinkable; **acqua ~** drinking water

po'tare /72/ VT to prune

po'tassio SM potassium

pota'tura SF pruning

po'tente AG (*nazione*) strong, powerful; (*veleno, farmaco*) potent, strong

poten'tino, -a AG of (*o* from) Potenza

Po'tenza [po'tentsa] SF Potenza

po'tenza [po'tentsa] SF power; (*forza*) strength; **all'ennesima ~** to the nth degree; **le Grandi Potenze** the Great Powers; **~ militare** military might *o* strength

potenzi'ale [poten'tsjale] AG, SM potential

potenzia'mento [potentsja'mento] SM development

potenzi'are [poten'tsjare] /19/ VT to develop

(PAROLA CHIAVE)

po'tere /78/ SM power; **al potere** (*partito ecc*) in power; **potere d'acquisto** purchasing power; **potere esecutivo** executive power; **potere giudiziario** legal power; **potere legislativo** legislative power

▸ VB AUS **1** (*essere in grado di*) can, be able to; **non ha potuto ripararlo** he couldn't *o* he wasn't able to repair it; **non è potuto venire** he couldn't *o* he wasn't able to come; **spiacente di non poter aiutare** sorry not to be able to help

2 (*avere il permesso*) can, may, be allowed to; **posso entrare?** can *o* may I come in?; **posso chiederti, dove sei stato?** where, may I ask, have you been?

3 (*eventualità*) may, might, could; **potrebbe essere vero** it might *o* could be true; **può aver avuto un incidente** he may *o* might *o* could have had an accident; **può darsi** perhaps; **può darsi** *o* **può essere che non venga** he may *o* might not come

4 (*augurio*): **potessi almeno parlargli!** if only I could speak to him!

5 (*suggerimento*): **potresti almeno scusarti!** you could at least apologize!

▸ VT can, be able to; **può molto per noi** he can do a lot for us; **non ne posso più** (*per stanchezza*) I'm exhausted; (*per rabbia*) I can't take any more

potestà SF (*potere*) power; (*Dir*) authority

potrò *etc* VB *vedi* **potere**

pove'raccio, -a, -ci, -ce [pove'rattʃo] SM/F poor devil

'povero, -a AG poor; (*disadorno*) plain, bare ▶ SM/F poor man/woman; **i poveri** the poor; ~ **di** lacking in, having little; **minerale ~ di ferro** ore with a low iron content; **paese ~ di risorse** country short of *o* lacking in resources

povertà SF poverty; ~ **energetica** fuel poverty

pozi'one [pot'tsjone] SF potion

'pozza ['pottsa] SF pool

poz'zanghera [pot'tsangera] SF puddle

'pozzo ['pottso] SM well; (*cava: di carbone*) pit; (*di miniera*) shaft; ~ **nero** cesspit; ~ **petrolifero** oil well

pp. ABBR (= *pagine*) pp

p.p. ABBR (= *per procura*) pp

P.P.I. SIGLA M (*Pol: Partito Popolare Italiano*) party originating from D.C.

PP.TT. ABBR = **Poste e Telecomunicazioni**

PR SIGLA = **Parma** ▶ SIGLA M (*Pol*) = **Partito Radicale**

P.R. ABBR = **piano regolatore; procuratore della Repubblica**

P.R.A. [pra] SIGLA M (= *Pubblico Registro Automobilistico*) ≈ DVLA

'Praga SF Prague

prag'matico, -a, -ci, -che AG pragmatic

pram'matica SF custom; **essere di ~** to be customary

pranotera'pia SF pranotherapy

pran'zare [pran'dzare] /**72**/ VI to dine, have dinner, to lunch, have lunch

'pranzo ['prandzo] SM dinner; (*a mezzogiorno*) lunch

'prassi SF usual procedure

'pratica, -che SF practice; (*esperienza*) experience; (*conoscenza*) knowledge, familiarity; (*tirocinio*) training, practice; (*Amm: affare*) matter, case; (: *incartamento*) file, dossier; **in ~** (*praticamente*) in practice; **mettere in ~** to put into practice; **fare le pratiche per** (*Amm*) to do the paperwork for; ~ **restrittiva** restrictive practice; **pratiche illecite** dishonest practices

prati'cabile AG (*progetto*) practicable, feasible; (*luogo*) passable, practicable

pratica'mente AV (*in modo pratico*) in a practical way, practically; (*quasi*) practically, almost

prati'cante SMF apprentice, trainee; (*Rel*) (regular) churchgoer

prati'care /**20**/ VT to practise (BRIT), practice (US); (*Sport: tennis ecc*) to play; (: *nuoto, scherma ecc*) to go in for; (*eseguire: apertura, buco*) to make; ~ **uno sconto** to give a discount

praticità [pratitʃi'ta] SF practicality, practicalness; **per ~** for practicality's sake

'pratico, -a, -ci, -che AG practical; ~ **di** (*esperto*) experienced *o* skilled in; (*familiare*) familiar with; **all'atto ~** in practice; **è ~ del mestiere** he knows his trade; **mi è più ~ venire di pomeriggio** it's more convenient for me to come in the afternoon

'prato SM meadow; (*di giardino*) lawn

preal'larme SM warning (signal)

Pre'alpi SFPL: **le ~** (the) Pre-Alps

preal'pino, -a AG of the Pre-Alps

pre'ambolo SM preamble; **senza tanti preamboli** without beating about (BRIT) *o* around (US) the bush

preannunci'are [preannun'tʃare] /**14**/, **preannunzi'are** [preannun'tsjare] VT to give advance notice of

preavvi'sare /**72**/ VT to give advance notice of

preav'viso SM notice; **telefonata con ~** personal *o* person to person call

pre'bellico, -a, -ci, -che AG prewar *cpd*

precari'ato SM temporary employment

precarietà SF precariousness

pre'cario, -a AG precarious; (*Ins*) temporary, without tenure

precauzio'nale [prekauttsjo'nale] AG precautionary

precauzi'one [prekaut'tsjone] SF caution, care; (*misura*) precaution; **prendere precauzioni** to take precautions

prece'dente [pretʃe'dente] AG previous ▶ SM precedent; **il discorso/film ~** the previous *o* preceding speech/film; **senza precedenti** unprecedented; **precedenti penali** (*Dir*) criminal record *sg*

precedente'mente [pretʃedente'mente] AV previously

prece'denza [pretʃe'dɛntsa] SF priority, precedence; (*Aut*) right of way; **dare ~ assoluta a qc** to give sth top priority

pre'cedere [pre'tʃedere] /**29**/ VT to precede, go *o* (come) before

precet'tare [pretʃet'tare] /**72**/ VT (*lavoratori*) to order back to work (*via an injunction*)

precettazi'one [pretʃettat'tsjone] SF (*di lavoratori*) order to resume work

pre'cetto [pre'tʃɛtto] SM precept; (*Mil*) call-up notice

precet'tore [pretʃet'tore] SM (private) tutor

precipi'tare [pretʃipi'tare] /**72**/ VI (*cadere*) to fall headlong; (*fig: situazione*) to get out of control ▶ VT (*gettare dall'alto in basso*) to hurl, fling; (*fig: affrettare*) to rush; **precipitarsi** VPR (*gettarsi*) to hurl *o* fling o.s.; (*affrettarsi*) to rush

precipi'tato, -a [pretʃipi'tato] AG hasty ▶ SM (*Chim*) precipitate

precipitazi'one [pretʃipitat'tsjone] SF (*Meteor*) precipitation; (*fig*) haste

precipi'toso, -a [pretʃipi'toso] AG (*caduta, fuga*) headlong; (*fig: avventato*) rash, reckless; (: *affrettato*) hasty, rushed

preci'pizio [pretʃi'pittsjo] SM precipice; **a ~** (fig: correre) headlong

pre'cipuo, -a [pre'tʃipuo] AG principal, main

precisa'mente [pretʃiza'mente] AV (gen) precisely; (con esattezza) exactly

preci'sare [pretʃi'zare] /**72**/ VT to state, specify; (spiegare) to explain (in detail); **vi preciseremo la data in seguito** we'll let you know the exact date later; **tengo a ~ che ...** I must point out that ...

precisazi'one [pretʃizat'tsjone] SF clarification

precisi'one [pretʃi'zjone] SF precision; accuracy; **strumenti di ~** precision instruments

pre'ciso, -a [pre'tʃizo] AG (esatto) precise; (accurato) accurate, precise; (deciso: idea) precise, definite; (uguale): **2 vestiti precisi** 2 dresses exactly the same; **sono le 9 precise** it's exactly 9 o'clock

pre'cludere /**3**/ VT to block, obstruct

pre'cluso, -a PP di **precludere**

pre'coce [pre'kɔtʃe] AG early; (bambino) precocious; (vecchiaia) premature

precocità [prekotʃi'ta] SF (di morte) untimeliness; (di bambino) precociousness

precon'cetto, -a [prekon'tʃetto] AG preconceived ▶ SM preconceived idea, prejudice

pre'correre /**28**/ VT to anticipate; **~ i tempi** to be ahead of one's time

precorri'tore, -'trice SM/F precursor, forerunner

pre'corso, -a PP di **precorrere**

precur'sore SM forerunner, precursor

'preda SF (bottino) booty; (animale, fig) prey; **essere ~ di** to fall prey to; **essere in ~ a** to be prey to

pre'dare /**72**/ VT to plunder

preda'tore SM predator

predeces'sore, -a [predetʃes'sore] SM/F predecessor

pre'della SF platform, dais, altar-step

predesti'nare /**72**/ VT to predestine

predestinazi'one [predestinat'tsjone] SF predestination

pre'detto, -a PP di **predire** ▶ AG aforesaid, aforementioned

'predica, -che SF sermon; (fig) lecture, talking-to

predi'care /**20**/ VT, VI to preach

predica'tivo, -a AG predicative

predi'cato SM (Ling) predicate

predi'letto, -a PP di **prediligere** ▶ AG, SM/F favourite (BRIT), favorite (US)

predilezi'one [predilet'tsjone] SF fondness, partiality; **avere una ~ per qc/qn** to be partial to sth/fond of sb

predi'ligere [predi'lidʒere] /**117**/ VT to prefer, have a preference for

pre'dire /**38**/ VT to foretell, predict

predis'porre /**77**/ VT to get ready, prepare; **~ qn a qc** to predispose sb to sth

predisposizi'one [predispozit'tsjone] SF (Med) predisposition; (attitudine) bent, aptitude; **avere ~ alla musica** to have a bent for music

predis'posto, -a PP di **predisporre**

predizi'one [predit'tsjone] SF prediction

predomi'nante AG predominant

predomi'nare /**72**/ VI (prevalere) to predominate; (eccellere) to excel

predo'minio SM predominance; supremacy

preesis'tente AG pre-existent

pree'sistere /**11**/ VI to pre-exist

preesis'tito, -a PP di **preesistere**

prefabbri'cato, -a AG (Edil) prefabricated

prefazi'one [prefat'tsjone] SF preface, foreword

prefe'renza [prefe'rɛntsa] SF preference; **a ~ di** rather than; **di ~** preferably, by preference; **non ho preferenze** I have no preferences either way, I don't mind

preferenzi'ale [preferen'tsjale] AG preferential; **corsia ~** (Aut) bus and taxi lane

prefe'ribile AG: **~ (a)** preferable (to), better (than); **sarebbe ~ andarsene** it would be better to go

preferibil'mente AV preferably

prefe'rire /**55**/ VT to prefer, like better; **~ il caffè al tè** to prefer coffee to tea, like coffee better than tea

pre'fetto SM prefect

prefet'tura SF prefecture

pre'figgersi [pre'fiddʒersi] /**79**/ VPR: **~ uno scopo** to set o.s. a goal

prefigu'rare /**72**/ VT (simboleggiare) to foreshadow; (prevedere) to foresee

pre'fisso, -a PP di **prefiggersi** ▶ SM (Ling) prefix; (Tel) dialling (BRIT) o dial (US) code

Preg. ABBR = **pregiatissimo**

pre'gare /**80**/ VI to pray ▶ VT (Rel) to pray to; (implorare) to beg; (chiedere): **~ qn di fare** to ask sb to do; **farsi ~** to need coaxing o persuading

pre'gevole [pre'dʒevole] AG valuable

pregheròetc [prege'rɔ] VB vedi **pregare**

preghi'era [pre'gjɛra] SF (Rel) prayer; (domanda) request

pregi'arsi [pre'dʒarsi] /**62**/ VPR: **mi pregio di farle sapere che ...** I am pleased to inform you that ...

pregia'tissimo, -a [predʒa'tissimo] AG (in lettere): **~ Signor G. Agnelli** G. Agnelli Esquire

pregi'ato, -a [pre'dʒato] AG (opera) valuable; (tessuto) fine; (valuta) strong; **vino ~** vintage wine

'pregio ['prɛdʒo] SM (*stima*) esteem, regard; (*qualità*) (good) quality, merit; (*valore*) value, worth; **il ~ di questo sistema è ...** the merit of this system is ...; **oggetto di ~** valuable object

pregiudi'care [predʒudi'kare] /**20**/ VT to prejudice, harm, be detrimental to

pregiudi'cato, -a [predʒudi'kato] SM/F (*Dir*) previous offender

pregiu'dizio [predʒu'dittsjo] SM (*idea errata*) prejudice; (*danno*) harm *no pl*

preg'nante [preɲ'ɲante] AG (*fig*) pregnant, meaningful

'pregno, -a ['preɲɲo] AG (*saturo*): **~ di** full of, saturated with

'prego ESCL (*a chi ringrazia*) don't mention it!; (*invitando qn ad accomodarsi*) please sit down!; (*invitando qn ad andare prima*) after you!

pregus'tare /**72**/ VT to look forward to

preis'toria SF prehistory

preis'torico, -a, -ci, -che AG prehistoric

pre'lato SM prelate

prela'vaggio [prela'vaddʒo] SM pre-wash

prelazi'one [prelat'tsjone] SF (*Dir*) pre-emption; **avere il diritto di ~ su qc** to have the first option on sth

preleva'mento SM (*Banca*) withdrawal; (*di merce*) picking up, collection

prele'vare /**72**/ VT (*denaro*) to withdraw; (*campione*) to take; (*merce*) to pick up, collect; (*polizia*) to take, capture

preli'evo SM (*Banca*) withdrawal; (*Med*): **fare un ~ (di)** to take a sample (of); **fare un ~ di sangue** to take a blood sample

prelimi'nare AG preliminary; **preliminari** SMPL preliminary talks; preliminaries

pre'ludere /**35**/ VI: **~ a** (*preannunciare: crisi, guerra, temporale*) to herald, be a sign of; (*introdurre: dibattito ecc*) to introduce, be a prelude to

pre'ludio SM prelude

pre'luso, -a PP *di* **preludere**

pre-ma'man [prema'mã] SM INV maternity dress

prematrimoni'ale AG premarital

prema'turo, -a AG premature

premedi'tare /**72**/ VT to premeditate, plan

premeditazi'one [premeditat'tsjone] SF (*Dir*) premeditation; **con ~** *ag* premeditated ▶ AV with intent

'premere /**29**/ VT to press ▶ VI: **~ su** to press down on; (*fig*) to put pressure on; **~ a** (*fig: importare*) to matter to; **~ il grilletto** to pull the trigger

pre'messo, -a PP *di* **premettere** ▶ SF introductory statement, introduction; **mancano le premesse per una buona riuscita** we lack the basis for a successful outcome

pre'mettere /**63**/ VT to put before; (*dire prima*) to start by saying, state first; **premetto che ...** I must say first of all that ...; **premesso che ...** given that ...; **ciò premesso ...** that having been said ...

premi'are /**19**/ VT to give a prize to; (*fig: merito, onestà*) to reward

premiazi'one [premjat'tsjone] SF prize giving

'premier ['prɛmjer] SM INV premier

premi'nente AG pre-eminent

'premio SM prize; (*ricompensa*) reward; (*Comm*) premium; (*Amm: indennità*) bonus; **in ~ per** as a prize (*o* reward) for; **~ d'ingaggio** (*Sport*) signing-on fee; **~ di produzione** productivity bonus

pre'misi *etc* VB *vedi* **premettere**

premoni'tore, -'trice AG premonitory

premonizi'one [premonit'tsjone] SF premonition

premu'nirsi /**55**/ VPR: **~ di** to provide o.s. with; **~ contro** to protect o.s. from, guard o.s. against

pre'mura SF (*fretta*) haste, hurry; (*riguardo*) attention, care; **premure** SFPL (*attenzioni, cure*) care *sg*; **aver ~** to be in a hurry; **far ~ a qn** to hurry sb; **usare ogni ~ nei riguardi di qn**, **circondare qn di premure** to be very attentive to sb

premu'roso, -a AG thoughtful, considerate

prena'tale AG antenatal

'prendere /**81**/ VT to take; (*andare a prendere*) to get, fetch; (*ottenere*) to get; (*guadagnare*) to get, earn; (*catturare: ladro, pesce*) to catch; (*: collaboratore, dipendente*) to take on; (*: passeggero*) to pick up; (*chiedere: somma, prezzo*) to charge, ask; (*trattare: persona*) to handle ▶ VI (*colla, cemento*) to set; (*pianta*) to take; (*fuoco: nel camino*) to catch; (*voltare*): **~ a destra** to turn (to the) right; **prendersi** VPR (*azzuffarsi*): **prendersi a pugni** to come to blows; **prende qualcosa?** (*da bere, da mangiare*) would you like something to eat (*o* drink)?; **prendo un caffè** I'll have a coffee; **~ a fare qc** to start doing sth; **~ qn/qc per** (*scambiare*) to take sb/sth for; **~ l'abitudine di** to get into the habit of; **~ fuoco** to catch fire; **~ le generalità di qn** to take down sb's particulars; **~ nota di** to take note of; **~ parte a** to take part in; **prendersi cura di qn/qc** to look after sb/sth; **prendersi un impegno** to take on a commitment; **prendersela** (*adirarsi*) to get annoyed; (*preoccuparsi*) to get upset, worry

prendi'sole SM INV sundress

preno'tare /**72**/ VT to book, reserve

prenotazi'one [prenotat'tsjone] SF booking, reservation

'prensile AG prehensile

P

preoccu'pante AG worrying

preoccu'pare/72/ VT to worry; to preoccupy; **preoccuparsi**VPR: **preoccuparsi di qn/qc** to worry about sb/sth; **preoccuparsi per qn** to be anxious for sb

preoccupazi'one [preokkupat'tsjone] SF worry, anxiety

preordi'nato, -a AG preordained

prepa'rare/72/ VT to prepare; (esame, concorso) to prepare for; **prepararsi**VPR (vestirsi) to get ready; **prepararsi a qc/a fare** to get ready o prepare (o.s.) for sth/to do; **~ da mangiare** to prepare a meal

prepara'tivi SMPL preparations

prepa'rato, -a AG (gen) prepared; (pronto) ready ▶ SM (prodotto) preparation

prepara'torio, -a AG preparatory

preparazi'one [preparat'tsjone] SF preparation; **non ha la necessaria ~ per svolgere questo lavoro** he lacks the qualifications necessary for the job

prepensiona'mento SM early retirement

preponde'rante AG predominant

pre'porre/77/ VT to place before; (fig) to prefer

preposizi'one [prepozit'tsjone] SF (Ling) preposition

pre'posto, -a PP di **preporre**

prepo'tente AG (persona) domineering, arrogant; (bisogno, desiderio) overwhelming, pressing ▶ SMF bully

prepo'tenza [prepo'tentsa] SF arrogance; (comportamento) arrogant behaviour (BRIT) o behavior (US)

pre'puzio [pre'puttsjo] SM (Anat) foreskin

preroga'tiva SF prerogative

'**presa** SF taking no pl; catching no pl; (di città) capture; (indurimento: di cemento) setting; (appiglio, Sport) hold; (di acqua, gas) (supply) point; (piccola quantità: di sale ecc) pinch; (Carte) trick; **~ (di corrente)** socket; (al muro) point; **far ~** (colla) to set; **ha fatto ~ sul pubblico** (fig) it caught the public's imagination; **a ~ rapida** (cemento) quick-setting; **di forte ~** (fig) with wide appeal; **essere alle prese con qc** (fig) to be struggling with sth; **macchina da ~** (Cine) cine camera (BRIT), movie camera (US); **~ d'aria** air inlet; **~ diretta** (Aut) direct drive; **~ in giro** leg-pull (BRIT), joke; **~ di posizione** stand

pre'sagio [pre'zadʒo] SM omen

presa'gire [preza'dʒire] /55/ VT to foresee

presa'lario SM (Ins) grant

'**presbite** AG long-sighted

presbiteri'ano, -a AG, SM/F Presbyterian

presbi'terio SM presbytery

pre'scindere [preʃʃindere] /102/ VI: **~ da** to leave out of consideration; **a ~ da** apart from

pre'scisso, -a[preʃʃisso] PP di **prescindere**

presco'lastico, -a, -ci, -che AG pre-school cpd

pres'critto, -a PP di **prescrivere**

pres'crivere/105/ VT to prescribe

prescrizi'one [preskrit'tsjone] SF (Med, Dir) prescription; (norma) rule, regulation; **cadere in ~** (Dir) to become statute-barred

'**prese**etc VB vedi **prendere**

presen'tare/72/ VT to present; (Amm: inoltrare) to submit; (far conoscere): **~ qn (a)** to introduce sb (to); **presentarsi**VPR (recarsi, farsi vedere) to present o.s., appear; (farsi conoscere) to introduce o.s.; (occasione) to arise; **~ qc in un'esposizione** to show o display sth at an exhibition; **~ qn in società** to introduce sb into society; **presentarsi come candidato** (Pol) to stand (BRIT) o run (US) as a candidate; **presentarsi bene/male** to have a good/poor appearance; **la situazione si presenta difficile** things aren't looking too good, things look a bit tricky

presentazi'one [prezentat'tsjone] SF presentation; introduction

pre'sente AG present; (questo) this ▶ SM present ▶ SF (lettera): **con la ~ vi comunico ...** this is to inform you that ... ▶ SMF person present; **i presenti** those present; **aver ~ qc/qn** to remember sth/sb; **essere ~ a una riunione** to be present at o attend a meeting; **tener ~ qn/qc** to keep sb/sth in mind; **esclusi i presenti** present company excepted

presenti'mento SM premonition

pre'senza [pre'zentsa] SF presence; (aspetto esteriore) appearance; **in ~ di** in (the) presence of; **di bella ~** of good appearance; **~ di spirito** presence of mind

presenzi'are [prezen'tsjare] /19/ VI: **~ a** to be present at, attend

pre'sepio, pre'sepe SM crib

preser'vare/72/ VT to protect; to save

preserva'tivo SM sheath, condom

'**presi**etc VB vedi **prendere**

'**preside** SMF (Ins) head (teacher) (BRIT), principal (US); (di facoltà universitaria) dean; **~ di facoltà** (Università) dean of faculty

presi'dente SM (Pol) president; (di assemblea, Comm) chairman; **il P~ della Camera** (Pol) ≈ the Speaker; **P~ del Consiglio (dei Ministri)** ≈ Prime Minister; **P~ della Repubblica** President of the Republic; see note

> The Presidente del Consiglio, the Italian Prime Minister, is the leader of the Government. He or she submits nominations for ministerial posts to the Presidente della Repubblica, who then appoints them if approved. The Presidente del Consiglio is appointed by the Presidente della Repubblica, in consultation with the

leaders of the parliamentary parties, former heads of state, the *Presidente della Camera* and the *Presidente del Senato*. The *Presidente della Repubblica* is the head of state. He or she must be an Italian citizen of at least 50 years of age, and is elected by Parliament and by three delegates from each of the Italian regions. He or she has the power to suspend the implementation of legislation and to dissolve one or both chambers of Parliament, and presides over the magistrates' governing body (the *Consiglio Superiore della Magistratura*).

presiden'tessa SF president; (*moglie*) president's wife; (*di assemblea, Comm*) chairwoman

presi'denza SF presidency; office of president; chairmanship; **assumere la ~** to become president; to take the chair; **essere alla ~** to be president (*o* chairman); **candidato alla ~** presidential candidate; candidate for the chairmanship

presidenzi'ale [presidɛn'tsjale] AG presidential

presidi'are/19/ VT to garrison

pre'sidio SM garrison

presi'edere/29/ VT to preside over ▶ VI: **~ a** to direct, be in charge of

'preso, -a PP *di* **prendere**

'pressa SF (*Tecn*) press

pres'sante AG (*bisogno, richiesta*) urgent, pressing

pressap'poco AV about, roughly, approximately

pres'sare/72/ VT (*anche fig*) to press; **~ qn con richieste** to pursue sb with demands

pressi'one SF pressure; **far ~ su qn** to put pressure on sb; **subire forti pressioni** to be under strong pressure; **~ sanguigna** blood pressure; **~ atmosferica** atmospheric pressure

'presso AV (*vicino*) nearby, close at hand ▶ PREP (*vicino a*) near; (*accanto a*) beside, next to; (*in casa di*): **~ qn** at sb's home; (*nelle lettere*) care of, c/o; (*alle dipendenze di*): **lavora ~ di noi** he works for *o* with us ▶ SMPL: **nei pressi di** near, in the vicinity of; **ha avuto grande successo ~ i giovani** it has been a hit with young people

pressoché [presso'ke] AV nearly, almost

pressuriz'zare [pressurid'dzare] /**72**/ VT to pressurize

prestabi'lire/55/ VT to arrange beforehand, arrange in advance

presta'nome SM INV/F INV (*peg*) figurehead

pres'tante AG good-looking

pres'tanza [pres'tantsa] SF (*robust*) good looks *pl*

pres'tare/72/ VT: **~ (qc a qn)** to lend (sb sth *o* sth to sb); **prestarsi** VPR (*offrirsi*): **prestarsi a fare** to offer to do; (*essere adatto*): **prestarsi a** to lend itself to, be suitable for; **~ aiuto** to lend a hand; **~ ascolto** *o* **orecchio** to listen; **~ attenzione** to pay attention; **~ fede a qc/ qn** to give credence to sth/sb; **~ giuramento** to take an oath; **la frase si presta a molteplici interpretazioni** the phrase lends itself to numerous interpretations

prestazi'one [prestat'tsjone] SF (*Tecn, Sport*) performance; **prestazioni** SFPL (*di persona: servizi*) services

prestigia'tore, -'trice [prestidʒa'tore] SM/F conjurer

pres'tigio [pres'tidʒo] SM (*potere*) prestige; (*illusione*): **gioco di ~** conjuring trick

prestigi'oso, -a [presti'dʒoso] AG prestigious

'prestito SM lending *no pl*; loan; **dar in ~** to lend; **prendere in ~** to borrow; **~ bancario** bank loan; **~ pubblico** public borrowing

'presto AV (*tra poco*) soon; (*in fretta*) quickly; (*di buon'ora*) early; **a ~** see you soon; **~ o tardi** sooner or later; **fare ~ a fare qc** to hurry up and do sth; (*non costare fatica*) to have no trouble doing sth; **si fa ~ a criticare** it's easy to criticize; **è ancora ~ per decidere** it's still too early *o* too soon to decide

pre'sumere/12/ VT to presume, assume

presu'mibile AG (*dati, risultati*) likely

pre'sunsi *etc* VB *vedi* **presumere**

pre'sunto, -a PP *di* **presumere** ▶ AG: **il ~ colpevole** the alleged culprit

presuntu'oso, -a AG presumptuous

presunzi'one [prezun'tsjone] SF presumption

presup'porre/77/ VT to suppose; to presuppose

presup'posto, -a PP *di* **presupporre** ▶ SM (*premessa*) supposition, premise; **partendo dal ~ che ...** assuming that ...; **mancano i presupposti necessari** the necessary conditions are lacking

'prete SM priest

preten'dente SMF pretender ▶ SM (*corteggiatore*) suitor

pre'tendere/120/ VT (*esigere*) to demand, require; (*sostenere*): **~ che** to claim that; **pretende di aver sempre ragione** he thinks he's always right

pretenzi'oso, -a [preten'tsjoso] AG pretentious

preterintenzio'nale [preterintentsjo'nale] AG (*Dir*): **omicidio ~** manslaughter

pre'teso, -a PP *di* **pretendere** ▶ SF (*esigenza*) claim, demand; (*presunzione, sfarzo*) pretentiousness ▶ AV unpretentiously; **avanzare una pretesa** to put forward a claim *o* demand; **senza pretese** *ag* unpretentious

P

pre'testo SM pretext, excuse; **con il ~ di** on the pretext of

pretestu'oso, -a AG (*data, motivo*) used as an excuse

pre'tore SM magistrate

pre'tura SF (*Dir: sede*) magistrate's court (BRIT); circuit o superior court (US); (: *magistratura*) magistracy

preva'lente AG prevailing

prevalente'mente AV mainly, for the most part

preva'lenza [preva'lɛntsa] SF predominance

preva'lere /126/ VI to prevail

pre'valso, -a PP *di* **prevalere**

prevari'care /20/ VI (*abusare del potere*) to abuse one's power

prevaricazi'one [prevarikat'tsjone] SF (*abuso di potere*) abuse of power

preve'dere /82/ VT (*indovinare*) to foresee; (*presagire*) to foretell; (*considerare*) to make provision for; **nulla lasciava ~ che ...** there was nothing to suggest o to make one think that ...; **come previsto** as expected; **spese previste** anticipated expenditure; **previsto per martedì** scheduled for Tuesday

prev'edibile AG predictable; **non era assolutamente ~ che ...** no one could have foreseen that ...

prevedibil'mente AV as one would expect

preve'nire /128/ VT (*anticipare: obiezione*) to forestall; (: *domanda*) to anticipate; (*evitare*) to avoid, prevent; (*avvertire*): **~ qn (di)** to warn sb (of); to inform sb (of)

preventi'vare /72/ VT (*Comm*) to estimate

preven'tivo, -a AG preventive ▶ SM (*Comm*) estimate; **fare un ~** to give an estimate; **bilancio ~** budget; **carcere ~** custody (*pending trial*)

preve'nuto, -a AG (*mal disposto*): **~ (contro qc/ qn)** prejudiced (against sth/sb)

prevenzi'one [preven'tsjone] SF prevention; (*preconcetto*) prejudice

previ'dente AG showing foresight; prudent

previ'denza [previ'dɛntsa] SF foresight; **istituto di ~** provident institution; **~ sociale** social security (BRIT), welfare (US)

pre'vidi *etc* VB *vedi* **prevedere**

previo, -a AG (*Comm*): **~ avviso** upon notice; **~ pagamento** upon payment

previsi'one SF forecast, prediction; **previsioni meteorologiche** o **del tempo** weather forecast *sg*

pre'visto, -a PP *di* **prevedere** ▶ SM: **piú/meno del ~** more/less than expected; **prima del ~** earlier than expected

prezi'oso, -a [pret'tsjoso] AG precious; (*aiuto, consiglio*) invaluable ▶ SM jewel; valuable

prez'zemolo [pret'tsemolo] SM parsley

'prezzo ['prɛttso] SM price; **a ~ di costo** at cost, at cost price (BRIT); **tirare sul ~** to bargain, haggle; **il ~ pattuito è di 1000 euro** the agreed price is 1000 euros; **~ d'acquisto/di vendita** purchase/selling price; **~ di fabbrica** factory price; **~ di mercato** market price; **~ scontato** reduced price; **~ unitario** unit price

P.R.I. SIGLA M (= *Partito Repubblicano Italiano*) *former political party*

prigi'one [pri'dʒone] SF prison

prigio'nia [pridʒo'nia] SF imprisonment

prigioni'ero, -a [pridʒo'njɛro] AG captive ▶ SM/F prisoner

'prima SF *vedi* **primo** ▶ AV before; (*in anticipo*) in advance, beforehand; (*per l'addietro*) at one time, formerly; (*più presto*) sooner, earlier; (*in primo luogo*) first ▶ CONG: **~ di fare/che parta** before doing/he leaves; **~ di** prep before; **~ o poi** sooner or later; **due giorni ~** two days before o earlier; **~ d'ora** before now

pri'mario, -a AG primary; (*principale*) chief, leading, primary ▶ SM/F (*medico*) head physician, chief physician

pri'mate SM (*Rel, Zool*) primate

prima'tista, -i, -e SM/F (*Sport*) record holder

pri'mato SM supremacy; (*Sport*) record

prima'vera SF spring

primave'rile AG spring *cpd*

primeggi'are [primed'dʒare] /62/ VI to excel, be one of the best

primi'tivo, -a AG (*gen*) primitive; (*significato*) original

pri'mizie [pri'mittsje] SFPL early produce *sg*

'primo, -a AG first; (*fig*) initial; basic; prime ▶ SM/F first (one) ▶ SM (*Cuc*) first course; (*in date*): **il ~ luglio** the first of July ▶ SF (*Teat*) first night; (*Cine*) première; (*Aut*) first (gear); **le prime ore del mattino** the early hours of the morning; **di prima mattina** early in the morning; **in prima pagina** (*Stampa*) on the front page; **ai primi freddi** at the first sign of cold weather; **ai primi di maggio** at the beginning of May; **i primi del Novecento** the early twentieth century; **viaggiare in prima** to travel first-class; **per prima cosa** firstly; **in ~ luogo** first of all, in the first place; **di prim'ordine** o **prima qualità** first-class, first-rate; **in un ~ tempo** o **momento** at first; **prima donna** leading lady; (*di opera lirica*) prima donna

primo'genito, -a [primo'dʒɛnito] AG, SM/F firstborn

pri'mordi SMPL beginnings

primordi'ale AG primordial

'primula SF primrose

princi'pale [printʃi'pale] AG main, principal ▶ SM manager, boss; **sede ~** head office

principal'mente [printʃipal'mente] AV mainly, principally

princi'pato [printʃi'pato] SM principality

'principe ['printʃipe] SM prince; **~ ereditario** crown prince

princi'pesco, -a, -schi, -sche [printʃi'pesko] AG *(anche fig)* princely

princi'pessa [printʃi'pessa] SF princess

principi'ante [printʃi'pjante] SMF beginner

principi'are [printʃi'pjare] **/19/** VT, VI to start, begin

prin'cipio [prin'tʃipjo] SM *(inizio)* beginning, start; *(origine)* origin, cause; *(concetto, norma)* principle; **principi** SMPL *(concetti fondamentali)* principles; **al** o **in ~** at first; **fin dal ~** right from the start; **per ~** on principle; **una questione di ~** a matter of principle; **~ attivo** active ingredient; **una persona di sani principi morali** a person of sound moral principles

pri'ore SM *(Rel)* prior

pri'ori: a pri'ori *ag inv* prior; a priori ▶ AV at first glance; initially; a priori

priorità SF priority; **avere la ~ (su)** to have priority (over)

priori'tario, -a AG of utmost importance; *(scelta)* first; *(interesse)* overriding; **posta prioritaria** first class (post)

'prisma, -i SM prism

pri'vare/72/ VT: **~ qn di** to deprive sb of; **privarsi** VPR: **privarsi di** to go o do without

priva'tiva SF *(Econ)* monopoly

privatiz'zare [privatid'dzare] **/72/** VT to privatize

privatizzazi'one [privatiddzat'tsjone] SF privatization

pri'vato, -a AG private ▶ SM/F *(anche: privato cittadino)* private citizen; **in ~** in private; **diritto ~** *(Dir)* civil law; **ritirarsi a vita privata** to withdraw from public life; **"non vendiamo a privati"** "wholesale only"

privazi'one [privat'tsjone] SF privation, hardship

privilegi'are [privile'dʒare] **/62/** VT to favour *(BRIT)*, favor *(US)*, to grant a privilege to

privilegi'ato, -a [privile'dʒato] AG *(individuo, classe)* privileged; *(trattamento, Comm: credito)* preferential; **azioni privilegiate** preference shares *(BRIT)*, preferred stock *(US)*

privi'legio [privi'lɛdʒo] SM privilege; **avere il ~ di fare** to have the privilege of doing, be privileged to do

'privo, -a AG: **~ di** without, lacking

pro PREP for, on behalf of ▶ SM INV *(utilità)* advantage, benefit; **a che ~?** what's the use?; **il ~ e il contro** the pros and cons

pro'babile AG probable, likely

probabilità SF INV probability; **con molta ~** very probably, in all probability

probabil'mente AV probably

pro'bante AG convincing

pro'blema, -i SM problem

proble'matico, -a, -ci, -che AG problematic; *(incerto)* doubtful ▶ SF problems *pl*

pro'boscide [pro'boʃʃide] SF *(di elefante)* trunk

procacci'are [prokat'tʃare] **/14/** VT to get, obtain

procaccia'tore [prokattʃa'tore] SM: **~ d'affari** sales executive

pro'cace [pro'katʃe] AG *(donna, aspetto)* provocative

pro'cedere [pro'tʃɛdere] **/29/** VI to proceed; *(comportarsi)* to behave; *(iniziare)*: **~ a** to start; **~ contro** *(Dir)* to start legal proceedings against; **~ oltre** to go on ahead; **prima di ~ oltre** before going any further; **gli affari procedono bene** business is going well; **bisogna ~ con cautela** we have to proceed cautiously; **non luogo a ~** *(Dir)* nonsuit

procedi'mento [protʃedi'mento] SM *(modo di condurre)* procedure; *(di avvenimenti)* course; *(Tecn)* process; **~ penale** *(Dir)* criminal proceedings *pl*

proce'dura [protʃe'dura] SF *(Dir)* procedure

proces'sare [protʃes'sare] **/72/** VT *(Dir)* to try

processi'one [protʃes'sjone] SF procession

pro'cesso [pro'tʃɛsso] SM *(Dir)* trial; proceedings *pl*; *(metodo)* process; **essere sotto ~** to be on trial; **mettere sotto ~** *(anche fig)* to put on trial; **~ di fabbricazione** manufacturing process; **~ di pace** peace process

processu'ale [protʃessu'ale] AG *(Dir)*: **atti processuali** records of a trial; **spese processuali** legal costs

Proc. Gen. ABBR = **procuratore generale**

pro'cinto [pro'tʃinto] SM: **in ~ di fare** about to do, on the point of doing

pro'clama, -i SM proclamation

procla'mare/72/ VT to proclaim

proclamazi'one [proklamat'tsjone] SF proclamation, declaration

procrasti'nare/72/ VT *(data)* to postpone; *(pagamento)* to defer

procre'are/72/ VT to procreate

pro'cura SF *(Dir)* proxy, power of attorney; *(ufficio)* attorney's office; **per ~** by proxy; **la P~ della Repubblica** the Public Prosecutor's Office

procu'rare/72/ VT: **~ qc a qn** *(fornire)* to get o obtain sth for sb; *(causare: noie ecc)* to bring o give sb sth

procura'tore, -'trice SM/F *(Dir)* ≈ solicitor; *(: chi ha la procura)* holder of power of attorney; **~ generale** *(in corte d'appello)* public prosecutor; *(in corte di cassazione)* Attorney General; **~ legale** ≈ solicitor *(BRIT)*, lawyer; **~ della Repubblica** *(in corte d'assise, tribunale)* public prosecutor

prodi'gare /8o/ VT to be lavish with;
prodigarsi VPR: **prodigarsi per qn** to do all
one can for sb

pro'digio [pro'didʒo] SM marvel, wonder;
(*persona*) prodigy

prodigi'oso, -a [prodi'dʒoso] AG prodigious;
phenomenal

'**prodigo, -a, -ghi, -ghe** AG lavish,
extravagant

pro'dotto, -a PP *di* **produrre** ▶ SM product;
~ **di base** primary product; ~ **finale** end
product; ~ **interno lordo** gross domestic
product; ~ **nazionale lordo** gross national
product; **prodotti agricoli** farm produce *sg*;
prodotti di bellezza cosmetics; **prodotti
chimici** chemicals

pro'duco *etc* VB *vedi* **produrre**

pro'durre /9o/ VT to produce

pro'dussi *etc* VB *vedi* **produrre**

produttività SF productivity

produt'tivo, -a AG productive

produt'tore, -'trice AG producing *cpd* ▶ SM/F
producer; **paese ~ di petrolio** oil-producing
country

produzi'one [produt'tsjone] SF production;
(*rendimento*) output; ~ **in serie** mass
production

pro'emio SM introduction, preface

Prof. ABBR (= *professore*) Prof

profa'nare /72/ VT to desecrate

pro'fano, -a AG (*mondano*) secular, profane;
(*sacrilego*) profane

profe'rire /55/ VT to utter

profes'sare /72/ VT to profess; (*medicina ecc*)
to practise (BRIT), practice (US)

professio'nale AG professional; **scuola ~**
training college

professi'one SF profession; **di ~** professional,
by profession; **libera ~** profession

professio'nista, -i, -e SM/F professional

profes'sore, -'essa SM/F (*Ins*) teacher;
(: *di università*) lecturer; (: *titolare di cattedra*)
professor; ~ **d'orchestra** member of an
orchestra

pro'feta, -i SM prophet

pro'fetico, -a, -ci, -che AG prophetic

profetiz'zare [profetid'dzare] /72/ VT to
prophesy

profe'zia [profet'tsia] SF prophecy

pro'ficuo, -a AG useful, profitable

profi'lare /72/ VT to outline; (*ornare: vestito*) to
edge; **profilarsi** VPR to stand out, be
silhouetted; to loom up

profi'lassi SF (*Med*) preventive treatment,
prophylaxis

profi'lattico, -a, -ci, -che AG prophylactic
▶ SM (*anticoncezionale*) sheath, condom

pro'filo SM profile; (*breve descrizione*) sketch,
outline; **di ~** in profile

profit'tare /72/ VI: ~ **di** (*trarre profitto*) to profit
by; (*approfittare*) to take advantage of

pro'fitto SM advantage, profit, benefit; (*fig:
progresso*) progress; (*Comm*) profit; **ricavare
un ~ da** to make a profit from *o* out of;
vendere con ~ to sell at a profit; **conto
profitti e perdite** profit and loss account

pro'fondere /25/ VT (*lodi*) to lavish; (*denaro*) to
squander; **profondersi** VPR: **profondersi in**
to be profuse in

profondità SF INV depth

pro'fondo, -a AG deep; (*rancore, meditazione*)
profound ▶ SM depth(s), bottom; ~ **8 metri** 8
metres deep

pro'forma AG routine *cpd* ▶ SM INV formality
▶ AV: **fare qc ~** to do sth as a formality

'**profugo, -a, -ghi, -ghe** SM/F refugee

profu'mare /72/ VT to perfume ▶ VI to be
fragrant; **profumarsi** VPR to put on perfume
o scent

profumata'mente AV: **pagare qc ~** to pay
through the nose for sth

profu'mato, -a AG (*fiore, aria*) fragrant;
(*fazzoletto, saponetta*) scented; (*pelle*)
sweet-smelling; (*persona*) with perfume on

profume'ria SF perfumery; (*negozio*) perfume
shop

pro'fumo SM (*prodotto*) perfume, scent;
(*fragranza*) scent, fragrance

profusi'one SF profusion; **a ~** in plenty

pro'fuso, -a PP *di* **profondere**

progeni'tore, -'trice [prodʒeni'tore] SM/F
ancestor

proget'tare [prodʒet'tare] /72/ VT to plan;
(*Tecn: edificio*) to plan, design; ~ **di fare qc** to
plan to do sth

progettazi'one [prodʒettat'tsjone] SF
planning; **in corso di ~** at the planning
stage

proget'tista, -i, -e [prodʒet'tista] SM/F
designer

pro'getto [pro'dʒetto] SM plan; (*idea*) plan,
project; **avere in ~ di fare qc** to be planning
to do sth; ~ **di legge** (*Pol*) bill

'**prognosi** ['proɲɲozi] SF (*Med*) prognosis;
essere in ~ riservata to be on the danger list

pro'gramma, -i SM programme (BRIT),
program (US); (*TV, Radio*) programmes *pl*;
(*Ins*) syllabus, curriculum; (*Inform*) program;
avere in ~ di fare qc to be planning to do sth;
~ **applicativo** (*Inform*) application program

program'mare /72/ VT (*TV, Radio*) to put on;
(*Inform*) to program; (*Econ*) to plan

programma'tore, -'trice SM/F (*Inform*)
computer programmer (BRIT) *o* programer
(US)

programmazi'one [programmat'tsjone] SF
programming (BRIT), programing (US);
planning

progre'dire/55/ VI to progress, make progress
progressi'one SF progression
progres'sista, -i, -e AG, SM/F progressive
progressiva'mente AV progressively
progres'sivo, -a AG progressive
pro'gresso SM progress *no pl*; **fare progressi** to make progress
proi'bire/55/ VT to forbid, prohibit; **~ a qn di fare qc** (*vietare*) to forbid sb to do sth; (*impedire*) to prevent sb from doing sth
proibi'tivo, -a AG prohibitive
proi'bito, -a AG forbidden; **"è ~ l'accesso"** "no admittance"; **"è ~ fumare"** "no smoking"
proibizi'one [proibit'tsjone] SF prohibition
proibizio'nismo [proibittsjo'nizmo] SM prohibition
proiet'tare/72/ VT (*gen, Geom, Cine*) to project; (*: presentare*) to show, screen; (*luce, ombra*) to throw, cast, project
proi'ettile SM projectile, bullet, shell *etc*
proiet'tore SM (*Cine*) projector; (*Aut*) headlamp; (*Mil*) searchlight
proiezi'one [projet'tsjone] SF (*Cine*) projection; showing
'prole SF children *pl*, offspring
proletari'ato SM proletariat
prole'tario, -a AG, SM/F proletarian
prolife'rare/72/ VI (*fig*) to proliferate
pro'lifico, -a, -ci, -che AG prolific
pro'lisso, -a AG verbose
'prologo, -ghi SM prologue
pro'lunga, -ghe SF (*di cavo elettrico ecc*) extension
prolunga'mento SM (*gen*) extension; (*di strada*) continuation
prolun'gare/80/ VT (*discorso, attesa*) to prolong; (*linea, termine*) to extend
prome'moria SM INV memorandum
pro'messa SF promise; **fare/mantenere una ~** to make/keep a promise
pro'messo, -a PP *di* **promettere**
promet'tente AG promising
pro'mettere/63/ VT to promise ▶ VI to be *o* look promising; **~ a qn di fare** to promise sb that one will do
promi'nente AG prominent
promi'nenza [promi'nɛntsa] SF prominence
promiscuità SF promiscuousness
pro'miscuo, -a AG: **matrimonio ~** mixed marriage; **nome ~** (*Ling*) common-gender noun
pro'misi *etc* VB *vedi* **promettere**
promon'torio SM promontory, headland
pro'mosso, -a PP *di* **promuovere**
promo'tore, -'trice SM/F promoter, organizer
promozio'nale [promottsjo'nale] AG promotional; **"vendita ~"** "special offer"

promozi'one [promot'tsjone] SF promotion; **~ delle vendite** sales promotion
promul'gare/80/ VT to promulgate
promulgazi'one [promulgat'tsjone] SF promulgation
promu'overe/66/ VT to promote
proni'pote SM F (*di nonni*) great-grandchild, great-grandson/granddaughter; (*di zii*) great-nephew/niece; **pronipotis** MPL (*discendenti*) descendants
pro'nome SM (*Ling*) pronoun
pronomi'nale AG pronominal
pronosti'care/20/ VT to foretell, predict
pro'nostico, -ci SM forecast
pron'tezza [pron'tettsa] SF readiness; quickness, promptness; **~ di riflessi** quick reflexes; **~ di spirito/mente** readiness of wit/mind
'pronto, -a AG ready; (*rapido*) fast, quick, prompt; **~!** (*Tel*) hello!; **essere ~ a fare qc** to be ready to do sth; **~ all'ira** quick-tempered; **a pronta cassa** (*Comm*) cash (*BRIT*) *o* collect (*US*) on delivery; **pronta consegna** (*Comm*) prompt delivery; **~ soccorso** (*trattamento*) first aid; (*reparto*) A&E (*BRIT*), ER (*US*)
prontu'ario SM manual, handbook
pro'nuncia [pro'nuntʃa] SF pronunciation
pronunci'are [pronun'tʃare] /14/ VT (*parola, sentenza*) to pronounce; (*dire*) to utter; (*discorso*) to deliver; **pronunciarsi** VPR to declare one's opinion; **pronunciarsi a favore di/contro** to pronounce o.s. in favour of/against; **non mi pronuncio** I'm not prepared to comment
pronunci'ato, -a [pronun'tʃato] AG (*spiccato*) pronounced, marked; (*sporgente*) prominent
pro'nunzia *etc* [pro'nuntsja] = **pronuncia** *ecc*
propa'ganda SF propaganda
propagan'dare/72/ VT (*idea*) to propagandize; (*prodotto, invenzione*) to push, plug (*col*)
propa'gare/80/ VT (*Fisica, Biol*) to propagate; (*notizia, idea, malattia*) to spread; **propagarsi** VPR to propagate; to spread
propagazi'one [propagat'tsjone] SF (*vedi vb*) propagation; spreading
prope'deutico, -a, -ci, -che AG (*corso, trattato*) introductory
pro'pendere/8/ VI: **~ per** to favour (*BRIT*), favor (*US*), lean towards
propensi'one SF inclination, propensity; **avere ~ a credere che ...** to be inclined to think that ...
pro'penso, -a PP *di* **propendere** ▶ AG: **essere ~ a qc** to be in favour (*BRIT*) *o* favor (*US*) of sth; **essere ~ a fare qc** to be inclined to do sth
propi'nare/72/ VT to administer
pro'pizio, -a [pro'pittsjo] AG favourable (*BRIT*), favorable (*US*)

P

pro'porre /77/ VT (*suggerire*): ~ **qc (a qn)** to suggest sth (to sb); (*candidato*) to put forward; (*legge, brindisi*) to propose; ~ **di fare** to suggest o propose doing; **proporsi di fare** to propose o intend to do; **proporsi una meta** to set o.s. a goal

proporzio'nale [proportsjo'nale] AG proportional; (**sistema**) ~ (*Pol*) proportional representation system

proporzio'nato, -a [proportsjo'nato] AG: ~ **a** proportionate to, proportional to; **ben ~** well-proportioned

proporzi'one [propor'tsjone] SF proportion; **in ~ a** in proportion to; **proporzioni** SFPL (*dimensioni*) proportions; **di vaste proporzioni** huge

pro'posito SM (*intenzione*) intention, aim; (*argomento*) subject, matter; **a ~ di** regarding, with regard to; **a questo ~** on this subject; **di ~** (*apposta*) deliberately, on purpose; **a ~** by the way; **capitare a ~** (*cosa, persona*) to turn up at the right time

proposizi'one [propozit'tsjone] SF (*Ling*) clause; (: *periodo*) sentence

pro'posto, -a PP di **proporre** ▶ SF proposal; (*suggerimento*) suggestion; **fare una proposta** to put forward a proposal; to make a suggestion; **proposta di legge** (*Pol*) bill

propria'mente AV (*correttamente*) properly, correctly; (*in modo specifico*) specifically; ~ **detto** in the strict sense of the word

proprietà SF INV (*ciò che si possiede*) property, estate; (*caratteristica*) property; (*correttezza*) correctness; **essere di ~ di qn** to belong to sb; ~ **edilizia** (developed) property; ~ **privata** private property

proprie'tario, -a SM/F owner; (*di albergo ecc*) proprietor, owner; (*per l'inquilino*) landlord/lady; ~ **terriero** landowner

'proprio, -a AG (*possessivo*) own; (: *impersonale*) one's; (*esatto*) exact, correct, proper; (*senso, significato*) literal; (*Ling: nome*) proper; (*particolare*): ~ **di** characteristic of, peculiar to ▶ AV (*precisamente*) just, exactly; (*davvero*) really; (*affatto*): **non ... ~** not ... at all ▶ SM (*Comm*): **mettersi in ~** to set up on one's own; **l'ha visto con i (suoi) propri occhi** he saw it with his own eyes

propu'gnare [propuɲ'ɲare] /15/ VT to support

propulsi'one SF propulsion; **a ~ atomica** atomic-powered

propul'sore SM (*Tecn*) propeller

'prora SF (*Naut*) bow(s), prow

'proroga, -ghe SF extension; postponement

proro'gare /80/ VT to extend; (*differire*) to postpone, defer

pro'rompere /97/ VI to burst out

pro'rotto, -a PP di **prorompere**

pro'ruppi etc VB vedi **prorompere**

'prosa SF prose; (*Teat*): **la stagione della ~** the theatre season; **attore di ~** theatre actor; **compagnia di ~** theatrical company

pro'saico, -a, -ci, -che AG (*fig*) prosaic, mundane

pro'sciogliere [proʃʃɔʎʎere] /103/ VT to release; (*Dir*) to acquit

prosciogli'mento [proʃʃoʎʎi'mento] SM acquittal

prosci'olto, -a [proʃ'ʃɔlto] PP di **prosciogliere**

prosciu'gare [proʃʃu'gare] /80/ VT (*terreni*) to drain, reclaim; **prosciugarsi** VPR to dry up

prosci'utto [proʃ'ʃutto] SM ham; ~ **cotto/crudo** cooked/cured ham

pro'scritto, -a PP di **proscrivere** ▶ SM/F exile; outlaw

pros'crivere /105/ VT to exile, banish

proscrizi'one [proskrit'tsjone] SF (*esilio*) banishment, exile

prosecuzi'one [prosekut'tsjone] SF continuation

prosegui'mento SM continuation; **buon ~!** all the best!; (*a chi viaggia*) enjoy the rest of your journey!

prosegu'ire /45/ VT to carry on with, continue ▶ VI to carry on, go on

pro'selito SM (*Rel, Pol*) convert

prospe'rare /72/ VI to thrive

prosperità SF prosperity

'prospero, -a AG (*fiorente*) flourishing, thriving, prosperous

prospe'roso, -a AG (*robusto*) hale and hearty; (*ragazza*) buxom

prospet'tare /72/ VT (*esporre*) to point out, show; (*ipotesi*) to advance; (*affare*) to outline; **prospettarsi** VPR to look, appear

prospet'tiva SF (*Arte*) perspective; (*veduta*) view; (*fig: previsione, possibilità*) prospect

pros'petto SM (*Disegno*) elevation; (*veduta*) view, prospect; (*facciata*) façade, front; (*tabella*) table; (*sommario*) summary

prospici'ente [prospi'tʃente] AG: ~ **qc** facing o overlooking sth

prossima'mente AV soon

prossimità SF nearness, proximity; **in ~ di** near (to), close to; **in ~ delle feste natalizie** as Christmas approaches

'prossimo, -a AG (*che viene subito dopo*) next; (*parente*) close; (*vicino*): ~ **a** near (to), close to ▶ SM neighbour (*Brit*), neighbor (*US*), fellow man; **nei prossimi giorni** in the next few days; **in un ~ futuro** in the near future; ~ **venturo (pv)** (*Amm*): **venerdì ~ venturo** next Friday

pro'stata SF prostate (gland)

prostitu'irsi /55/ VPR to prostitute o.s.

prosti'tuta SF prostitute

prostituzi'one [prostitut'tsjone] SF prostitution

pros'trare /72/ VT (*fig*) to exhaust, wear out; **prostrarsi** VPR (*fig*) to humble o.s.; **prostrato dal dolore** overcome *o* prostrate with grief

prostrazi'one [prostrat'tsjone] SF prostration

protago'nista, -i, -e SM/F protagonist

pro'teggere [pro'tɛddʒere] /83/ VT to protect

proteggi'slip [protɛddʒi'slip] SM INV panty liner

pro'teico, -a, -ci, -che AG protein *cpd*; **altamente ~** high in protein

prote'ina SF protein

pro'tendere /120/ VT to stretch out

'protesi SF INV (*Med*) prosthesis

pro'teso, -a PP *di* **protendere**

pro'testa SF protest

protes'tante AG, SMF Protestant

protes'tare /72/, VT, VI to protest; **protestarsi** VPR: **protestarsi innocente** *etc* to protest one's innocence *o* that one is innocent *etc*

pro'testo SM (*Dir*) protest; **mandare una cambiale in ~** to dishonour (BRIT) *o* dishonor (US) a bill

protet'tivo, -a AG protective

pro'tetto, -a PP *di* **proteggere**

protetto'rato SM protectorate

protet'tore, -'trice SM/F protector; (*sostenitore*) patron ▶ AG (*Rel*): **santo ~** patron saint; **società protettrice dei consumatori** consumer protection society

protezi'one [protet'tsjone] SF protection; (*patrocinio*) patronage; **misure di ~** protective measures; **~ civile** civil defence (BRIT) *o* defense (US)

protezio'nismo [protettsjo'nizmo] SM protectionism

protocol'lare /72/ VT to register ▶ AG formal; of protocol

proto'collo SM protocol; (*registro*) register of documents ▶ AG INV: **foglio ~** foolscap; **numero di ~** reference number

pro'tone SM proton

pro'totipo SM prototype

pro'trarre /123/ VT (*prolungare*) to prolong; **protrarsi** VPR to go on, continue

pro'tratto, -2o PP *di* **protrarre**

protube'ranza [protube'rantsa] SF protuberance, bulge

Prov. ABBR (= *provincia*) Prov

'prova SF (*esperimento, cimento*) test, trial; (*tentativo*) attempt, try; (*Mat*) proof *no pl*; (*Dir*) evidence *no pl*, proof *no pl*; (*Ins*) exam, test; (*Teat*) rehearsal; (*di abito*) fitting; **a ~ di** (*in testimonianza di*) as proof of; **a ~ di fuoco** fireproof; **assumere in ~** (*per lavoro*) to employ on a trial basis; **essere in ~** (*persona: per lavoro*) to be on trial; **mettere alla ~** to put to the test; **giro di ~** test *o* trial run; **fino a ~**

contraria until (it's) proved otherwise; **~ a carico/a discarico** (*Dir*) evidence for the prosecution/for the defence; **~ documentale** (*Dir*) documentary evidence; **~ generale** (*Teat*) dress rehearsal; **~ testimoniale** (*Dir*) testimonial evidence

pro'vare /72/ VT (*sperimentare*) to test; (*tentare*) to try, attempt; (*assaggiare*) to try, taste; (*sperimentare in sé*) to experience; (*sentire*) to feel; (*cimentare*) to put to the test; (*dimostrare*) to prove; (*abito*) to try on; **provarsi** VPR: **provarsi (a fare)** to try *o* attempt (to do); **~ a fare** to try *o* attempt to do

proveni'enza [prove'njentsa] SF origin, source

prove'nire /128/ VI: **~ da** to come from

pro'venti SMPL revenue *sg*

prove'nuto, -a PP *di* **provenire**

Pro'venza [pro'ventsa] SF: **la ~** Provence

proven'zale [proven'tsale] AG Provençal

pro'verbio SM proverb

pro'vetta SF test tube; **bambino in ~** test-tube baby

pro'vetto, -a AG skilled, experienced

pro'vider [pro'vaider] SM INV (*Inform*) service provider

pro'vincia [pro'vintʃa], **-ce** *o* **-cie** SF province; *see note*

A *Provincia* is the autonomous political and administrative unit which is on a level between a *Comune* and a *Regione*; there are 103 in the whole of Italy. The *Provincia* is responsible for public health and sanitation, for the maintenance of major roads and public buildings such as schools, and for agriculture and fisheries. Situated in the *capoluogo*, or chief town, each *Provincia* is run by a *Giunta provinciale*, which is elected by the *Consiglio Provinciale*; both of these bodies are presided over by a *Presidente*.

provinci'ale [provin'tʃale] AG provincial; (**strada**) **~** main road (BRIT), highway (US)

pro'vino SM (*Cine*) screen test; (*campione*) specimen

provo'cante AG (*attraente*) provocative

provo'care /2o/ VT (*causare*) to cause, bring about; (*eccitare: riso, pietà*) to arouse; (*irritare, sfidare*) to provoke

provoca'tore, -'trice SM/F agitator ▶ AG: **agente ~** agent provocateur

provoca'torio, -a AG provocative

provocazi'one [provokat'tsjone] SF provocation

provve'dere /82/ VI (*prendere un provvedimento*) to take steps, act; (*disporre*): **~ (a)** to provide (for) ▶ VT: **~ qc a qn** to supply sth to sb; **provvedersi** VPR: **provvedersi di** to provide o.s. with

provvedi'mento SM measure; (*di previdenza*) precaution; ~ **disciplinare** disciplinary measure

provvedito'rato SM (*Amm*): ~ **agli studi** divisional education offices *pl*

provvedi'tore SM (*Amm*): ~ **agli studi** divisional director of education

provvi'denza [provvi'dɛntsa] SF: **la ~** providence

provvidenzi'ale [provviden'tsjale] AG providential

provvigi'one [provvi'dʒone] SF (*Comm*) commission; **lavoro/stipendio a ~** job/salary on a commission basis

provvi'sorio, -a AG temporary; (*governo*) temporary, provisional

prov'vista SF (*riserva*) supply, stock; **fare ~ di** to stock up with

prov'visto, -a PP *di* **provvedere** ▶ SF provision, supply

pro'zia [prot'tsia] SF great-aunt

pro'zio, -zii [prot'tsio] SM great-uncle

'prua SF (*Naut*) bow(s), prow

pru'dente AG cautious, prudent; (*assennato*) sensible, wise

pru'denza [pru'dɛntsa] SF prudence, caution; wisdom; **per ~** as a precaution, to be on the safe side

'prudere /29/ VI to itch, be itchy

'prugna ['pruɲɲa] SF plum; ~ **secca** prune

prurigi'noso, -a [pruridʒi'noso] AG itchy

pru'rito SM itchiness *no pl*; itch

PS SIGLA = **Pesaro**

P.S. ABBR (= *postscriptum*) PS; (*Comm*) = **partita semplice** ▶ SIGLA F (*Polizia*) = **Pubblica Sicurezza**

P.S.D.I. SIGLA M (= *Partito Socialista Democratico Italiano*) *former political party*

pseu'donimo SM pseudonym

PSI SIGLA M (*Pol*) = **Partito Socialista Italiano**

psica'nalisi SF psychoanalysis

psicana'lista, -i, -e SM/F psychoanalyst

psicanaliz'zare [psikanalid'dzare] /72/ VT to psychoanalyse

'psiche ['psike] SF (*Psic*) psyche

psiche'delico, -a, -ci, -che [psike'dɛliko] AG psychedelic

psichi'atra, -i, -e [psi'kjatra] SM/F psychiatrist

psichia'tria [psikja'tria] SF psychiatry

psichi'atrico, -a, -ci, -che [psi'kjatriko] AG (*caso*) psychiatric; (*reparto, ospedale*) psychiatric, mental

'psichico, -a, -ci, -che ['psikiko] AG psychological

psico'farmaco, -ci SM (*Med*) *drug used in treatment of mental conditions*

psicolo'gia [psikolo'dʒia] SF psychology

psico'logico, -a, -ci, -che [psiko'lɔdʒiko] AG psychological

psi'cologo, -a, -gi, -ghe SM/F psychologist

psico'patico, -a, -ci, -che AG psychopathic ▶ SM/F psychopath

psi'cosi SF INV (*Med*) psychosis; (*fig*) obsessive fear

psicoso'matico, -a, -ci, -che AG psychosomatic

PT SIGLA = **Pistoia**

Pt. ABBR (*Geo*: = *punta*) Pt

P.T. ABBR (= *Posta e Telegrafi*) ≈ PO (= *Post Office*); (*Fisco*) = **polizia tributaria**

P.ta ABBR = **porta**

pubbli'care /20/ VT to publish

pubblicazi'one [pubblikat'tsjone] SF publication; ~ **periodica** periodical; **pubblicazioni (matrimoniali)** (marriage) banns

pubbli'cista, -i, -e [pubbli'tʃista] SM/F (*Stampa*) freelance journalist

pubblicità [pubblitʃi'ta] SF (*diffusione*) publicity; (*attività*) advertising; (*annunci nei giornali*) advertisements *pl*; **fare ~ a qc** to advertise sth

pubblici'tario, -a [pubblitʃi'tarjo] AG advertising *cpd*; (*trovata, film*) publicity *cpd* ▶ SM advertising agent; **annuncio** *o* **avviso ~** advertisement

'pubblico, -a, -ci, -che AG public; (*statale*: *scuola ecc*) state *cpd* ▶ SM public; (*spettatori*) audience; **in ~** in public; **la pubblica amministrazione** public administration; **un ~ esercizio** a catering (*o* hotel *o* entertainment) business; ~ **funzionario** civil servant; **Ministero della Pubblica Istruzione** ≈ Department of Education and Science (*BRIT*), ≈ Department of Health, Education and Welfare (*US*); **P~ Ministero** Public Prosecutor's Office; **la Pubblica Sicurezza** the police

'pube SM (*Anat*) pubis

pubertà SF puberty

'pudico, -a, -ci, -che AG modest

pu'dore SM modesty

puericul'tura SF infant care

pue'rile AG childish

pu'erpera SF *woman who has just given birth*

pugi'lato [pudʒi'lato] SM boxing

'pugile ['pudʒile] SM boxer

pugli'ese [puʎ'ʎese] AG of (*o* from) Puglia

pugna'lare [puɲɲa'lare] /72/ VT to stab

pu'gnale [puɲ'ɲale] SM dagger

'pugno ['puɲɲo] SM fist; (*colpo*) punch; (*quantità*) fistful; **avere qn in ~** to have sb in the palm of one's hand; **tenere la situazione in ~** to have control of the situation; **scrivere qc di proprio ~** to write sth in one's own hand '**pulce** ['pultʃe] SF flea

pul'cino [pul'tʃino] SM chick

pu'ledro, -a SM/F colt/filly

pu'leggia, -ge [pu'leddʒa] SF pulley

pu'lire /**55**/ VT to clean; (*lucidare*) to polish; **far ~ qc** to have sth cleaned; **~ a secco** to dry-clean

pu'lito, -a AG (*anche fig*) clean; (*ordinato*) neat, tidy ▸ SF quick clean; **avere la coscienza pulita** to have a clear conscience

puli'tura SF cleaning; **~ a secco** dry-cleaning

puli'zia [pulit'tsia] SF (*atto*) cleaning; (*condizione*) cleanness; **fare le pulizie** to do the cleaning, do the housework; **~ etnica** ethnic cleansing

'**pullman** SM INV coach (BRIT), bus

pul'lover SM INV pullover, jumper

pullu'lare /**72**/ VI to swarm, teem

pul'mino SM minibus

'**pulpito** SM pulpit

pul'sante SM (push-)button

pul'sare /**72**/ VI to pulsate, beat

pulsazi'one [pulsat'tsjone] SF beat

pul'viscolo SM fine dust; **~ atmosferico** specks pl of dust

'**puma** SM INV puma

pun'gente [pun'dʒɛnte] AG prickly; stinging; (*anche fig*) biting

'**pungere** ['pundʒere] /**84**/ VT to prick; (*insetto, ortica*) to sting; (*freddo*) to bite; **~ qn sul vivo** (*fig*) to cut sb to the quick

pungigli'one [pundʒiʎ'ʎone] SM sting

pungo'lare /**72**/ VT to goad

pu'nire /**55**/ VT to punish

puni'tivo, -a AG punitive

punizi'one [punit'tsjone] SF punishment; (*Sport*) penalty

'**punsi** etc VB vedi **pungere**

'**punta** SF point; (*parte terminale*) tip, end; (*di monte*) peak; (*di costa*) promontory; (*minima parte*) touch, trace; **in ~ di piedi** on tiptoe; **ore di ~** peak hours; **uomo di ~** (*Sport, Pol*) front-rank o leading man; **doppie punte** split ends

pun'tare /**72**/ VT (*piedi a terra, gomiti sul tavolo*) to plant; (*dirigere: pistola*) to point; (*scommettere*): **~ su** to bet on ▸ VI (*mirare*): **~ a** to aim at; (*avviarsi*): **~ su** to head o make for; (*fig: contare*): **~ su** to count o rely on

puntas'pilli SM INV = **portaspilli**

pun'tata SF (*gita*) short trip; (*scommessa*) bet; (*parte di opera*) instalment (BRIT), installment (US); **farò una ~ a Parigi** I'll pay a flying visit to Paris; **romanzo a puntate** serial

punteggi'are [punted'dʒare] /**62**/ VT to punctuate

punteggia'tura [punteddʒa'tura] SF (*Ling*) punctuation

pun'teggio [pun'teddʒo] SM score

puntel'lare /**72**/ VT to support

pun'tello SM prop, support

punteru'olo SM (*Tecn*) punch; (*per stoffa*) bodkin

pun'tiglio [pun'tiʎʎo] SM obstinacy, stubbornness

puntigli'oso, -a [puntiʎ'ʎoso] AG punctilious

pun'tina SF: **~ da disegno** drawing pin (BRIT), thumb tack (US); **puntine** SFPL (*Aut*) points

pun'tino SM dot; **fare qc a ~** to do sth properly; **arrivare a ~** to arrive just at the right moment; **cotto a ~** cooked to perfection; **mettere i puntini sulle "i"** (*fig*) to dot the i's and cross the t's

'**punto, -a** PP di **pungere** ▸ SM point; (*segno, macchiolina*) dot; (*Ling*) full stop; (*di indirizzo e-mail*) dot; (*posto*) spot; (*a scuola*) mark; (*nel cucire, nella maglia, Med*) stitch ▸ AV: **non ... ~** not ... at all; **due punti** (*inv: Ling*) colon; **ad un certo ~** at a certain point; **fino ad un certo ~** (*fig*) to a certain extent; **sul ~ di fare** (just) about to do; **fare il ~** (*Naut*) to take a bearing; **fare il ~ della situazione** (*analisi*) to take stock of the situation; (*riassunto*) to sum up the situation; **alle 6 in ~** at 6 o'clock sharp o on the dot; **essere a buon ~** to have reached a satisfactory stage; **mettere a ~** to adjust; (*motore*) to tune; (*cannocchiale*) to focus; (*fig*) to settle; **venire al ~** to come to the point; **vestito di tutto ~** all dressed up; **di ~ in bianco** point-blank; **~ d'arrivo** arrival point; **~ cardinale** point of the compass, cardinal point; **~ debole** weak point; **~ esclamativo/interrogativo** exclamation/question mark; **~ d'incontro** meeting place, meeting point; **~ morto** standstill; **~ nero** (*comedone*) blackhead; **~ nevralgico** (*anche fig*) nerve centre (BRIT) o center (US); **~ di partenza** (*anche fig*) starting point; **~ di riferimento** landmark; (*fig*) point of reference; **~ di vendita** retail outlet; **~ e virgola** semicolon; **~ di vista** (*fig*) point of view; **punti di sospensione** suspension points

puntu'ale AG punctual

puntualità SF punctuality

puntualiz'zare [puntualid'dzare] /**72**/ VT to make clear

puntual'mente AV (*gen*) on time; (*ironico: al solito*) as usual

pun'tura SF (*di ago*) prick; (*di insetto*) sting, bite; (*Med*) puncture; (*: iniezione*) injection; (*dolore*) sharp pain

punzecchi'are [puntsek'kjare] /**19**/ VT to prick; (*fig*) to tease

punzo'nare [puntso'nare] /**72**/ VT (*Tecn*) to stamp

pun'zone [pun'tsone] SM (*per metalli*) stamp, die

può VB *vedi* **potere**

puoi VB *vedi* **potere**

'**pupa** SF doll

pu'pazzo [pu'pattso] SM puppet

pu'pillo, -a SM/F (*Dir*) ward; (*prediletto*) favourite (BRIT), favorite (US), pet ▶ SF (*Anat*) pupil

purché [pur'ke] CONG provided that, on condition that

'**pure** CONG (*tuttavia*) and yet, nevertheless; (*anche se*) even if ▶ AV (*anche*) too, also; **pur di** (*al fine di*) just to; **faccia ~!** go ahead!, please do!

purè SM, **pu'rea** SF (*Cuc*) purée; (*di patate*) mashed potatoes *pl*

pu'rezza [pu'rettsa] SF purity

'**purga, -ghe** SF purging *no pl*; purge

pur'gante SM (*Med*) purgative, purge

pur'gare /**80**/ VT (*Med, Pol*) to purge; (*pulire*) to clean

purga'torio SM purgatory

purifi'care /**20**/ VT to purify; (*metallo*) to refine

purificazi'one [purifikat'tsjone] SF purification; refinement

puri'tano, -a AG, SM/F puritan

'**puro, -a** AG pure; (*acqua*) clear, limpid; (*vino*) undiluted; **di razza pura** thoroughbred;

per ~ caso by sheer chance, purely by chance

puro'sangue SM INV/F INV thoroughbred

pur'troppo AV unfortunately

pus SM pus

pusil'lanime AG cowardly

'**pustola** SF pimple

puta'caso AV just supposing, suppose

puti'ferio SM rumpus, row

putre'fare /**41**/ VI to putrefy, rot

putre'fatto, -a PP *di* **putrefare**

putrefazi'one [putrefat'tsjone] SF putrefaction

'**putrido, -a** AG putrid, rotten

put'tana SF (*col*) whore (!)

'**putto** SM cupid

'**puzza** ['puttsa] SF = **puzzo**

puz'zare [put'tsare] /**72**/ VI to stink; **la faccenda puzza (d'imbroglio)** the whole business stinks

'**puzzo** ['puttso] SM stink, foul smell

'**puzzola** ['puttsola] SF polecat

puzzo'lente [puttso'lɛnte] AG stinking

PV SIGLA = **Pavia**

PV ABBR = **prossimo venturo**

P.V.C. [pivi'tʃi] SIGLA M (= *polyvinyl chloride*) PVC

PZ SIGLA = **Potenza**

p.za ABBR = **piazza**

Qq

Q, q [ku] SM O F INV (*lettera*) Q, q; **Q come Quarto** ≈ Q for Queen

q ABBR (= *quintale*) q

Qa'tar [ka'tar] SM: **il ~** Qatar

q.b. ABBR (= *quanto basta*) as needed; (= *zucchero q.b.*) sugar to taste

Q.G. ABBR = **quartier generale**

Q.I. ABBR = **quoziente d'intelligenza**

qua AV here; **in ~** (*verso questa parte*) this way; **~ dentro/sotto** *etc* in/under here *etc*; **da un anno in ~** for a year now; **da quando in ~?** since when?; **per di ~** (*passare*) this way; **al di ~ di** (*fiume, strada*) on this side of; **~ dentro/fuori** *ecc* in/out here *ecc*; *vedi anche* **questo**

'quacchero, -a ['kwakkero] SM/F Quaker

qua'derno SM notebook; (*per scuola*) exercise book

qua'drangolo SM quadrangle

qua'drante SM quadrant; (*di orologio*) face

qua'drare /72/ VI (*bilancio*) to balance, tally; (*fig: corrispondere*): **~ (con)** to correspond (with) ▶ VT (*Mat*) to square; **far ~ il bilancio** to balance the books; **non mi quadra** I don't like it

qua'drato, -a AG square; (*fig: equilibrato*) level-headed, sensible; (*peg*) square ▶ SM (*Mat*) square; (*Pugilato*) ring; **5 al ~** 5 squared

quadret'tato, -a AG (*foglio*) squared; (*tessuto*) checked

qua'dretto SM: **a quadretti** (*tessuto*) checked; (*foglio*) squared

quadrien'nale AG (*che dura 4 anni*) four-year *cpd*; (*che avviene ogni 4 anni*) four-yearly

quadri'foglio [kwadri'fɔʎʎo] SM four-leaf clover

quadri'mestre SM (*periodo*) four-month period; (*Ins*) term

'quadro SM (*pittura*) painting, picture; (*quadrato*) square; (*tabella*) table, chart; (*Tecn*) board, panel; (*Teat*) scene; (*fig: scena, spettacolo*) sight; (*: descrizione*) outline, description; **quadri** SMPL (*Pol*) party organizers; (*Comm*) managerial staff; (*Mil*) cadres; (*Carte*) diamonds; **a quadri** (*disegno*) checked; **fare un ~ della situazione** to outline the situation; **~ clinico** (*Med*) case history; **~ di comando** control panel; **quadri intermedi** middle management *sg*

qua'drupede SM quadruped

quadrupli'care /20/ VT to quadruple

'quadruplo, -a AG, SM quadruple

quaggiù [kwad'dʒu] AV down here

'quaglia ['kwaʎʎa] SF quail

(PAROLA CHIAVE)

'qualche ['kwalke] DET **1** some, a few; (*in interrogative*) any; **ho comprato qualche libro** I've bought some *o* a few books; **qualche volta** sometimes; **hai qualche sigaretta?** have you any cigarettes?
2 (*uno*): **c'è qualche medico?** is there a doctor?; **in qualche modo** somehow
3 (*un certo, parecchio*) some; **un personaggio di qualche rilievo** a figure of some importance
4: **qualche cosa = qualcosa**

---

qualche'duno [kwalke'duno] PRON = **qualcuno**

qual'cosa PRON something; (*in espressioni interrogative*) anything; **qualcos'altro** something else; anything else; **~ di nuovo** something new; anything new; **~ da mangiare** something to eat; anything to eat; **c'è ~ che non va?** is there something *o* anything wrong?

qual'cuno PRON (*persona*) someone, somebody; (*: in espressioni interrogative*) anyone, anybody; (*alcuni*) some; **~ è favorevole a noi** some are on our side; **qualcun altro** someone *o* somebody else; anyone *o* anybody else

---

(PAROLA CHIAVE)

'quale (*spesso troncato in* **qual**) DET
1 (*interrogativo*) what; (*: scegliendo tra due o più cose o persone*) which; **quale uomo/denaro?**

what man/money?; which man/money?; **quali sono i tuoi programmi?** what are your plans?; **quale stanza preferisci?** which room do you prefer?
2 (*relativo: come*): **il risultato fu quale ci si aspettava** the result was as expected **3** (*in elenchi*) such as, like; **piante quali l'edera** plants such as *o* like ivy **4** (*esclamativo*) what; **quale disgrazia!** what bad luck!
5: **in un certo qual modo** in a way, in some ways; **per la qual cosa** for which reason
▶ PRON **1** (*interrogativo*) which; **quale dei due scegli?** which of the two do you want?
2 (*relativo*): **il (la) quale** (*persona: soggetto*) who; (: *oggetto, con preposizione*) whom; (*cosa*) which; (*possessivo*) whose; **suo padre, il quale è avvocato, ...** his father, who is a lawyer, ...; **a tutti coloro i quali fossero interessati ...** to whom it may concern ...; **il signore con il quale parlavo** the gentleman to whom I was speaking; **l'albergo al quale ci siamo fermati** the hotel where we stayed *o* which we stayed at; **la signora della quale ammiriamo la bellezza** the lady whose beauty we admire
▶ AV (*in qualità di, come*) as; **quale sindaco di questa città** as mayor of this town

qua'lifica, -che SF qualification; (*titolo*) title
qualifi'care /20/ VT to qualify; (*definire*): ~ **qn/ qc come** to describe sb/sth as; **qualificarsi** VPR (*Sport*) to qualify; **qualificarsi a un concorso** to pass a competitive exam
qualifica'tivo, -a AG qualifying
qualifi'cato, -a AG (*dotato di qualifica*) qualified; (*esperto, abile*) skilled; **non mi ritengo ~ per questo lavoro** I don't think I'm qualified for this job; **è un medico molto ~** he is a very distinguished doctor
qualificazi'one [kwalifikat'tsjone] SF qualification; **gara di ~** (*Sport*) qualifying event
qualità SF INV quality; **di ottima** *o* **prima ~** top quality; **in ~ di** in one's capacity as; **in ~ di amica** as a friend; **articoli di ogni ~** all sorts of goods; **controllo (di) ~** quality control; **prodotto di ~** quality product
qualita'tivo, -a AG qualitative
qua'lora CONG in case, if
qual'siasi, qua'lunque DET inv any; (*quale che sia*) whatever; (*discriminativo*) whichever; (*posposto: mediocre*) poor, indifferent; ordinary; **mettiti un vestito ~** put on any old dress; **~ cosa** anything; **~ cosa accada** whatever happens; **a ~ costo** at any cost, whatever the cost; **l'uomo ~** the man in the street; **~ persona** anyone, anybody

qualunqu'ista, -i, -e SM/F *person indifferent to politics*
'quando CONG, AV when; **~ sarò ricco** when I'm rich; **da ~** (*dacché*) since; (*interrogativo*) **da ~ sei qui?** how long have you been here?; **di ~ in ~** from time to time; **quand'anche** even if
quantifi'care /20/ VT to quantify
quantità SF INV quantity; **una ~ di** (*gran numero*) a great deal of; a lot of; **in grande ~** in large quantities
quantita'tivo, -a AG quantitative ▶ SM (*Comm: di merce*) amount, quantity

(PAROLA CHIAVE)

'quanto, -a DET **1** (*interrogativo: quantità*) how much; (: *numero*) how many; **quanto pane/ denaro?** how much bread/money?; **quanti libri/ragazzi?** how many books/boys?; **quanto tempo?** how long?; **quanti anni hai?** how old are you?
2 (*esclamativo*): **quante storie!** what a lot of nonsense!; **quanto tempo sprecato!** what a waste of time!
3 (*relativo: quantità*) as much ... as; (: *numero*) as many ... as; **ho quanto denaro mi occorre** I have as much money as I need; **prendi quanti libri vuoi** take as many books as you like
▶ PRON **1** (*interrogativo: quantità*) how much; (: *numero*) how many; (: *tempo*) how long; **quanto mi dai?** how much will you give me?; **quanti me ne hai portati?** how many did you bring me?; **quanto starai via?** how long will you be away (for)?; **da quanto sei qui?** how long have you been here?; **quanti ne abbiamo oggi?** what's the date today?
2 (*relativo: quantità*) as much as; (: *numero*) as many as; **farò quanto posso** I'll do as much as I can; **a quanto dice lui** according to him; **in risposta a quanto esposto nella sua lettera ...** in answer to the points raised in your letter; **possono venire quanti sono stati invitati** all those who have been invited can come
▶ AV **1** (*interrogativo: con ag, av*) how; (: *con vb*) how much; **quanto stanco ti sembrava?** how tired did he seem to you?; **quanto corre la tua moto?** how fast can your motorbike go?; **quanto costa?** how much does it cost?; **quant'è?** how much is it?
2 (*esclamativo: con ag, av*) how; (: *con vb*) how much; **quanto sono felice!** how happy I am!; **sapessi quanto abbiamo camminato!** if you knew how far we've walked!; **studierò quanto posso** I'll study as much as *o* all I can; **quanto prima** as soon as possible; **quanto più ... tanto meno** the

more … the less; **quanto più** … **tanto più** the more … the more

3: **in quanto** (*in qualità di*) as; (*perché, per il fatto che*) as, since; **in quanto legale della signora** as the lady's lawyer; **non è possibile in quanto non possiamo permettercelo** it isn't possible, since we can't afford it; **(in) quanto a** (*per ciò che riguarda*) as for, as regards; **(in) quanto a lui** as far as he's concerned

4: **per quanto** (*nonostante, anche se*) however; **per quanto si sforzi, non ce la farà** try as he may, he won't manage it; **per quanto sia brava, fa degli errori** however good she may be, she makes mistakes; **per quanto io sappia** as far as I know

quan'tunque CONG although, though
qua'ranta NUM forty
quaran'tena SF quarantine
quaran'tenne AG, SMF forty-year-old
quaran'tennio SM (period of) forty years
quaran'tesimo, -a NUM fortieth
quaran'tina SF: **una ~ (di)** about forty
quaran'totto SM INV forty-eight; **fare un ~** (*col*) to raise hell
Qua'resima SF: **la ~** Lent
'quarta SF *vedi* **quarto**
quar'tetto SM quartet(te)
quarti'ere SM district, area; (*Mil*) quarters *pl*; **~ generale** headquarters *pl*; **~ residenziale** residential area *o* district; **i quartieri alti** the smart districts
'quarto, -a AG fourth ▶ SM fourth; (*quarta parte*) quarter ▶ SF (*Aut*) fourth (gear); (*Ins: elementare*) fourth year of primary school; (: *superiore*) seventh year of secondary school; **un ~ di vino** a quarter-litre (BRIT) *o* quarter-liter (US) bottle of wine; **le 6 e un ~** a quarter past (BRIT) *o* after (US) 6; **~ d'ora** quarter of an hour; **tre quarti d'ora** three quarters of an hour; **le otto e tre quarti, le nove meno un ~** (a) quarter to (BRIT) *o* of (US) nine; **passare un brutto ~ d'ora** (*fig*) to have a bad *o* nasty time of it; **quarti di finale** (*Sport*) quarter finals
'quarzo ['kwartso] SM quartz
'quasi AV almost, nearly ▶ CONG (*anche:* **quasi che**) as if; **(non) … ~ mai** hardly ever; **~ ~ me ne andrei** I've half a mind to leave
quas'sù AV up here
'quatto, -a AG crouched, squatting; (*silenzioso*) silent; **~ ~** very quietly; stealthily
quattordi'cenne [kwattordi'tʃɛnne] AG, SMF fourteen-year-old
quat'tordici [kwat'torditʃi] NUM fourteen
quat'trini SMPL money *sg*, cash *sg*
'quattro NUM four; **in ~ e quattr'otto** in less than no time; **dirne ~ a qn** to give sb a piece

of one's mind; **fare il diavolo a ~** to kick up a rumpus; **fare ~ chiacchiere** to have a chat; **farsi in ~ per qn** to go out of one's way for sb, put o.s. out for sb; **~ per ~** four-by-four
quat'trocchi [kwat'trɔkki] SM INV (*fig*: *col*: *persona con occhiali*) four-eyes; **a ~** *av* (*tra 2 persone*) face to face; (*privatamente*) in private
quattrocen'tesco, -a, -schi, -sche [kwattrotʃen'tesko] AG fifteenth-century
quattro'cento [kwattro'tʃento] NUM four hundred ▶ SM: **il Q~** the fifteenth century
quattro'mila NUM four thousand

⸨**PAROLA CHIAVE**⸩

'quello, -a (*dav sm* **quel** + C, **quell'** + V, **quello** + *s impura, gn, pn, ps, x, z; pl* **quei** + C, **quegli** + V *o s impura, gn, pn, ps, x, z; dav sf* **quella** + C, **quell'** + V; *pl* **quelle**) DET that; *pl* those; **quella casa** that house; **quegli uomini** those men; **voglio quella camicia** (**lì** *o* **là**) I want that shirt; **quello è mio fratello** that's my brother
▶ PRON **1** (*dimostrativo*) that one; *pl* those ones; (*ciò*) that; **conosci quella?** do you know her?; **prendo quello bianco** I'll take the white one; **chi è quello?** who's that?; **prendiamo quello** (**lì** *o* **là**) let's take that one (there); **in quel di Milano** in the Milan area *o* region

2 (*relativo*): **quello(a) che** (*persona*) the one (who); (*cosa*) the one (which), the one (that); **quelli(e) che** (*persone*) those who; (*cose*) those which; **è lui quello che non voleva venire** he's the one who didn't want to come; **ho fatto quello che potevo** I did what I could; **è quella che ti ho prestato** that's the one I lent you; **è proprio quello che gli ho detto** that's exactly what I told him; **da quello che ho sentito** from what I've heard

'quercia, -ce ['kwertʃa] SF oak (tree); (*legno*) oak; **la Q~** (*Pol*) symbol of P.D.S.
que'rela SF (*Dir*) (legal) action
quere'lare /**72**/ VT to bring an action against
que'sito SM question, query; problem
'questi PRON (*poetico*) this person
questio'nario SM questionnaire
questi'one SF problem, question; (*controversia*) issue; (*litigio*) quarrel; **in ~** in question; **il caso in ~** the matter at hand; **la persona in ~** the person involved; **non voglio essere chiamato in ~** I don't want to be dragged into the argument; **fuor di ~** out of the question; **è ~ di tempo** it's a matter *o* question of time

⸨**PAROLA CHIAVE**⸩

'questo, -a DET **1** (*dimostrativo*) this; *pl* these; **questo libro** (**qui** *o* **qua**) this book; **io prendo questo cappotto, tu quello**

I'll take this coat, you take that one;
quest'oggi today; **questa sera** this evening
2 (*enfatico*): **non fatemi più prendere di
queste paure** don't frighten me like that
again
▶ PRON (*dimostrativo*) this (one); *pl* these
(ones); (*ciò*) this; **prendo questo (qui** *o* **qua)**
I'll take this one; **preferisci questi o
quelli?** do you prefer these (ones) or those
(ones)?; **questo intendevo io** this is what I
meant; **vengono Paolo e Luca: questo da
Roma, quello da Palermo** Paolo and Luca
are coming: the former from Palermo, the
latter from Rome; **questo non dovevi dirlo**
you shouldn't have said that; **e con questo?**
so what?; **e con questo se n'è andato** and
with that he left; **con tutto questo** in spite
of this, despite all this; **questo è quanto**
that's all

ques'tore SM *public official in charge of the police
in the provincial capital, reporting to the prefetto,*
≈ chief constable (*BRIT*), ≈ police
commissioner (*US*)
'**questua** SF collection (of alms)
ques'tura SF police headquarters *pl*
questu'rino SM (*col: poliziotto*) cop
qui AV here; **da** *o* **di ~** from here; **di ~ in
avanti** from now on; **di ~ a poco/una
settimana** in a little while/a week's time;
~ dentro/sopra/vicino in/up/near here; *vedi
anche* **questo**
quie'scenza [kwjeʃʃɛntsa] SF (*Amm*): **porre
qn in ~** to retire sb
quie'tanza [kwje'tantsa] SF receipt
quie'tare /**72**/ VT to calm, soothe
qui'ete SF quiet, quietness; calmness;
stillness; peace; **turbare la ~ pubblica** (*Dir*)
to disturb the peace
qui'eto, -a AG quiet; (*notte*) calm, still; (*mare*)
calm; **l'ho fatto per il ~ vivere** I did it for a
quiet life
'**quindi** AV then ▶ CONG therefore, so
quindi'cenne [kwindi'tʃɛnne] AG, SMF
fifteen-year-old
'**quindici** ['kwinditʃi] NUM fifteen; **~ giorni** a
fortnight (*BRIT*), two weeks

quindi'cina [kwindi'tʃina] SF (*serie*): **una ~
(di)** about fifteen; **fra una ~ di giorni** in a
fortnight (*BRIT*) *o* two weeks
quindici'nale [kwinditʃi'nale] AG fortnightly
(*BRIT*), semimonthly (*US*) ▶ SM (*rivista*)
fortnightly magazine (*BRIT*), semimonthly
(*US*)
quinquen'nale AG (*che dura 5 anni*) five-year
cpd; (*che avviene ogni 5 anni*) five-yearly
quin'quennio SM period of five years
quinta SF *vedi* **quinto**
quin'tale SM quintal (*100 kg*)
quin'tetto SM quintet(te)
'**quinto, -a** NUM fifth ▶ SF (*Aut*) fifth (gear);
(*Ins: elementare*) *fifth year of primary school*;
(*: superiore*) *final year of secondary school*; (*Teat*)
wing; **un ~ della popolazione** a fifth of
the population; **tre quinti** three fifths; **in
quinta pagina** on the fifth page, on page five
qui pro quo SM INV misunderstanding
Quiri'nale SM *see note*

> The *Quirinale* takes its name from one of
> the Seven Hills of Rome on which it
> stands. It is the official residence of the
> *Presidente della Repubblica*.

'**Quito** SF Quito
quiz [kwidz] SM INV (*domanda*) question;
(*anche: gioco a quiz*) quiz game
'**quorum** SM quorum
'**quota** SF (*parte*) quota, share; (*Aer*) height,
altitude; (*Ippica*) odds *pl*; **prendere/
perdere ~** (*Aer*) to gain/lose height *o*
altitude; **~ imponibile** taxable income;
~ d'iscrizione (*Ins*) enrolment fee; (*ad una
gara*) entry fee; (*ad un club*) membership fee;
~ di mercato market share; **quote rosa** (*Pol*)
quota for women
quo'tare /**72**/ VT (*Borsa*) to quote; (*valutare:
anche fig*) to value; **è un pittore molto
quotato** he is rated highly as a painter
quotazi'one [kwotat'tsjone] SF quotation
quotidiana'mente AV daily, every day
quotidi'ano, -a AG daily; (*banale*) everyday
▶ SM (*giornale*) daily (paper)
quozi'ente [kwot'tsjɛnte] SM (*Mat*) quotient;
~ di crescita zero zero growth rate;
~ d'intelligenza intelligence quotient, IQ

Rr

R, r ['ɛrre] SM O F (*lettera*) R, r; **R come Roma** ≈ R for Robert (BRIT), R for Roger (US)

R ABBR (*Posta*) = **raccomandato**; (*Ferr*) = **rapido**

RA SIGLA = **Ravenna**

ra'barbaro SM rhubarb

Ra'bat SF Rabat

rabberci'are [rabber'tʃare] /**14**/ VT (*anche fig*) to patch up

'rabbia SF (*ira*) anger, rage; (*accanimento, furia*) fury; (*Med: idrofobia*) rabies *sg*

rab'bino SM rabbi

rabbi'oso, -a AG angry, furious; (*facile all'ira*) quick-tempered; (*forze, acqua ecc*) furious, raging; (*Med*) rabid, mad

rabbo'nire /**55**/ VT, **rabbo'nirsi** VPR to calm down

rabbrivi'dire /**55**/ VI to shudder, shiver

rabbui'arsi /**19**/ VPR to grow dark

rabdo'mante SM water diviner

racc. ABBR (*Posta*) = **raccomandato**

raccapez'zarsi [rakkapet'tsarsi] /**72**/ VPR: **non ~** to be at a loss

raccapricci'ante [rakkaprit'tʃante] AG horrifying

racca'priccio [rakka'prittʃo] SM horror

raccatta'palle SM INV (*Sport*) ballboy

raccat'tare /**72**/ VT to pick up

rac'chetta [rak'ketta] SF (*per tennis*) racket; (*per ping-pong*) bat; **~ da neve** snowshoe; **~ da sci** ski stick

'racchio, -a ['rakkjo] AG (*col*) ugly

racchi'udere [rak'kjudere] /**22**/ VT to contain

racchi'uso, -a [rak'kjuso] PP *di* **racchiudere**

rac'cogliere [rak'koʎʎere] /**23**/ VT to collect; (*raccattare*) to pick up; (*frutti, fiori*) to pick, pluck; (*Agr*) to harvest; (*approvazione, voti*) to win; (*vele*) to furl; (*profughi*) to take in; (*capelli*) to put up; **raccogliersi** VPR to gather; (*fig*) to gather one's thoughts; to meditate; **non ha raccolto** (*allusione*) he didn't take the hint; (*frecciata*) he took no notice of it; **~ i frutti del proprio lavoro** (*fig*) to reap the benefits of one's work; **~ le idee** (*fig*) to gather one's thoughts

raccogli'mento [rakkoʎʎi'mento] SM meditation

raccogli'tore [rakkoʎʎi'tore] SM (*cartella*) folder, binder; **~ a fogli mobili** loose-leaf binder

rac'colta SF *vedi* **raccolto**

rac'colto, -a PP *di* **raccogliere** ▶ AG (*persona: pensoso*) thoughtful; (*luogo: appartato*) secluded, quiet ▶ SM (*Agr*) crop, harvest ▶ SF collecting *no pl*; collection; (*Agr*) harvesting *no pl*, gathering *no pl*; harvest, crop; (*adunata*) gathering; **fare la raccolta di qc** to collect sth; **chiamare a raccolta** to gather together; **raccolta differenziata** (*dei rifiuti*) *separate collection of different kinds of household waste*

raccoman'dabile AG (highly) commendable; **è un tipo poco ~** he is not to be trusted

raccoman'dare /**72**/ VT to recommend; (*affidare*) to entrust; **raccomandarsi** VPR: **raccomandarsi a qn** to commend o.s. to sb; **~ a qn di fare qc** to recommend that sb does sth; **~ a qn di non fare qc** to tell *o* warn sb not to do sth; **~ qn a qn/alle cure di qn** to entrust sb to sb/to sb's care; **mi raccomando!** don't forget!

raccoman'dato, -a AG (*lettera, pacco*) recorded-delivery (BRIT), certified (US); (*candidato*) recommended ▶ SM/F: **essere un(a) raccomandato(a) di ferro** to have friends in high places ▶ SF (*anche:* **lettera raccomandata**) recorded-delivery letter; **raccomandata con ricevuta di ritorno (Rr)** recorded-delivery letter with advice of receipt

raccomandazi'one [rakkomandat'tsjone] SF recommendation; **lettera di ~** letter of introduction

raccomo'dare /**72**/ VT (*riparare*) to repair, mend

raccon'tare /**72**/ VT: **~ (a qn)** (*dire*) to tell (sb); (*narrare*) to relate (to sb), tell (sb) about; **a me non la racconti** don't try and kid me; **cosa mi racconti di nuovo?** what's new?

r

rac'conto SM telling *no pl*, relating *no pl*; *(fatto raccontato)* story, tale; *(genere letterario)* short story; **racconti per bambini** children's stories

raccorci'are [rakkor'tʃare] /**14**/ VT to shorten

raccor'dare /**72**/ VT to link up, join

rac'cordo SM *(Tecn: giunzione)* connection, joint; *(Aut: di autostrada)* slip road *(BRIT)* entrance *(o exit)* ramp *(US)*; **~ anulare** *(Aut)* ring road *(BRIT)*, beltway *(US)*; **~ autostradale** slip road *(BRIT)*, entrance *(o exit)* ramp *(US)*; **~ ferroviario** siding; **~ stradale** link road

ra'chitico, -a, -ci, -che [ra'kitiko] AG suffering from rickets; *(fig)* scraggy, scrawny

rachi'tismo [raki'tizmo] SM *(Med)* rickets *sg*

racimo'lare [ratʃimo'lare] /**72**/ VT *(fig)* to scrape together, glean

'rada SF *(natural)* harbour *(BRIT)* o harbor *(US)*

'radar SM INV radar

raddol'cire [raddol'tʃire] /**55**/ VT *(persona, carattere)* to soften; **raddolcirsi** VPR *(tempo)* to grow milder; *(persona)* to soften, mellow

raddoppia'mento SM doubling

raddoppi'are /**19**/ VT, VI to double

rad'doppio SM *(gen)* doubling; *(Biliardo)* double; *(Equitazione)* gallop

raddriz'zare [raddrit'tsare] /**72**/ VT to straighten; *(fig: correggere)* to put straight, correct

'radere /**85**/ VT *(barba)* to shave off; *(mento)* to shave; *(fig: rasentare)* to graze; to skim; **radersi** VPR to shave (o.s.); **~ al suolo** to raze to the ground

radi'ale AG radial

radi'ante AG *(calore, energia)* radiant

radi'are /**19**/ VT to strike off

radia'tore SM radiator

radiazi'one [radjat'tsjone] SF *(Fisica)* radiation; *(cancellazione)* striking off

'radica SF *(Bot)*: **~ di noce** walnut (wood)

radi'cale AG radical ▸ SM *(Ling)* root; *(Mat, Pol)* radical; **radicali liberi** free radicals

radi'cato, -a AG *(pregiudizio, credenza)* deep-seated, deeply-rooted

ra'dicchio [ra'dikkjo] SM *variety of chicory*

ra'dice [ra'ditʃe] SF root; **segno di ~** *(Mat)* radical sign; **colpire alla ~** *(fig)* to strike at the root; **mettere radici** *(idee, odio ecc)* to take root; *(persona)* to put down roots; **~ quadrata** *(Mat)* square root

'radio SF INV radio ▸ SM *(Chim)* radium; **trasmettere per ~** to broadcast; **stazione/ ponte ~** radio station/link; **~ ricevente/ trasmittente** receiver/transmitter

radioabbo'nato, -a SM/F radio subscriber

radioama'tore, -'trice SM/F amateur radio operator, ham *(col)*

radioascolta'tore, -'trice SM/F *(radio)* listener

radioattività SF radioactivity

radioat'tivo, -a AG radioactive

radiocoman'dare /**72**/ VT to operate by remote control

radiocoman'dato, -a AG remote-controlled

radioco'mando SM remote control

radiocomunicazi'one [radjokomunikat'tsjone] SF radio message

radio'cronaca, -che SF radio commentary

radiocro'nista, -i, -e SM/F radio commentator

radiodiffusi'one SF *(radio)* broadcasting

radio'fonico, -a, -ci, -che AG radio *cpd*

radiogra'fare /**72**/ VT to X-ray

radiogra'fia SF radiography; *(foto)* X-ray photograph

radio'lina SF portable radio, transistor (radio)

radiolo'gia [radjolo'dʒia] SF radiology

radi'ologo, -a, -gi, -ghe SM/F radiologist

radiorice'vente [radjoritʃe'vɛnte] SF *(anche:* **apparecchio radioricevente)** receiver

radi'oso, -a AG radiant

radiostazi'one [radjostat'tsjone] SF radio station

radios'veglia [radjoz'veʎʎa] SF radio alarm

radio'taxi SM INV radio taxi

radio'tecnico, -a, -ci, -che AG radio engineering *cpd* ▸ SM radio engineer

radiotelegra'fista, -i, -e SM/F radiotelegrapher

radiotera'pia SF radiotherapy

radiotrasmit'tente AG *(radio)* broadcasting *cpd* ▸ SF *(radio)* broadcasting station

'rado, -a AG *(capelli)* sparse, thin; *(visite)* infrequent; **di ~** rarely; **non di ~** not uncommonly

radu'nare /**72**/ VT, **radu'narsi** VPR to gather, assemble

radu'nata SF *(Mil)* muster

ra'duno SM gathering, meeting

ra'dura SF clearing

'rafano SM horseradish

raffazzo'nare [raffattso'nare] /**72**/ VT to patch up

raf'fermo, -a AG stale

'raffica, -che SF *(Meteor)* gust (of wind); **~ di colpi** *(di fucile)* burst of gunfire

raffigu'rare /**72**/ VT to represent

raffigurazi'one [raffigurat'tsjone] SF representation, depiction

raffi'nare /**72**/ VT to refine

raffina'tezza [raffina'tettsa] SF refinement

raffi'nato, -a AG refined

raffinazi'one [raffinat'tsjone] SF *(di sostanza)* refining; **~ del petrolio** oil refining

raffine'ria SF refinery

raffor'zare [raffor'tsare] /**72**/ VT to reinforce

rafforza'tivo, -a [raffortsa'tivo] AG (*Ling*) intensifying ▸ SM (*Ling*) intensifier

raffredda'mento SM cooling

raffred'dare /**72**/ VT to cool; (*fig*) to dampen, have a cooling effect on; **raffreddarsi** VPR to grow cool *o* cold; (*prendere un raffreddore*) to catch a cold; (*fig*) to cool (off)

raffred'dato, -a AG (*Med*): **essere ~** to have a cold

raffred'dore SM (*Med*) cold

raffron'tare /**72**/ VT to compare

raf'fronto SM comparison

'rafia SF (*fibra*) raffia

'rafting ['rafting] SM white-water rafting

raga'nella SF (*Zool*) tree frog

ra'gazzo, -a [ra'gattso] SM/F boy/girl; (*col: fidanzato*) boyfriend/girlfriend; **ragazzi** SMPL (*figli*) kids; **nome da ragazza** maiden name; **ragazza madre** unmarried mother; **ragazza squillo** call girl; **ciao ragazzi!** (*gruppo*) hi guys!

ragge'lare [raddʒe'lare] /**72**/ VT, VI, **ragge'larsi** VPR to freeze

raggi'ante [rad'dʒante] AG radiant, shining; **~ di gioia** beaming *o* radiant with joy

raggi'era [rad'dʒɛra] SF (*di ruota*) spokes *pl*; **a ~** with a sunburst pattern

'raggio ['raddʒo] SM (*di sole ecc*) ray; (*Mat, distanza*) radius; (*di ruota ecc*) spoke; **nel ~ di 20 km** within a radius of 20 km *o* a 20-km radius; **a largo ~** (*esplorazione, incursione*) wide-ranging; **~ d'azione** range; **~ laser** laser beam; **raggi X** X-rays

raggi'rare [raddʒi'rare] /**72**/ VT to take in, trick

rag'giro [rad'dʒiro] SM trick

raggi'ungere [rad'dʒundʒere] /**5**/ VT to reach; (*persona: riprendere*) to catch up (with); (*bersaglio*) to hit; (*fig: meta*) to achieve; **~ il proprio scopo** to reach one's goal, achieve one's aim; **~ un accordo** to come to *o* reach an agreement

raggi'unto, -a [rad'dʒunto] PP *di* **raggiungere**

raggomito'larsi /**72**/ VPR to curl up

raggranel'lare /**72**/ VT to scrape together

raggrin'zare [raggrin'tsare] /**72**/ VT, VI (*anche: raggrinzarsi*) to wrinkle

raggrin'zire [raggrin'tsire] /**55**/ VT = **raggrinzare**

raggru'mare /**72**/ VT, **raggru'marsi** VPR (*sangue, latte*) to clot

raggruppa'mento SM (*azione*) grouping; (*gruppo*) group; (*Mil*) unit

raggrup'pare /**72**/ VT to group (together)

ragguagli'are [raggwaʎ'ʎare] /**27**/ VT (*paragonare*) to compare; (*informare*) to inform

raggu'aglio [rag'gwaʎʎo] SM comparison; (*informazione, relazione*) piece of information

ragguar'devole AG (*degno di riguardo*) distinguished, notable; (*notevole: somma*) considerable

'ragia ['radʒa] SF: **acqua ~** turpentine

ragiona'mento [radʒona'mento] SM reasoning *no pl*; arguing *no pl*; argument

ragio'nare [radʒo'nare] /**72**/ VI (*usare la ragione*) to reason; (*discorrere*): **~ (di)** to argue (about); **cerca di ~** try and be reasonable

ragi'one [ra'dʒone] SF reason; (*dimostrazione, prova*) argument, reason; (*diritto*) right; **aver ~** to be right; **aver ~ di qn** to get the better of sb; **dare ~ a qn** (*persona*) to side with sb; (*fatto*) to prove sb right; **farsi una ~ di qc** to accept sth, come to terms with sth; **in ~ di** at the rate of; to the amount of; according to; **a *o* con ~** rightly, justly; **perdere la ~** to become insane; (*fig*) to take leave of one's senses; **a ragion veduta** after due consideration; **per ragioni di famiglia** for family reasons; **~ di scambio** terms of trade; **~ sociale** (*Comm*) corporate name; **ragion di stato** reason of State

ragione'ria [radʒone'ria] SF accountancy; (*ufficio*) accounts department

ragio'nevole [radʒo'nevole] AG reasonable

ragioni'ere, -a [radʒo'njɛre] SM/F accountant

ragli'are [raʎ'ʎare] /**27**/ VI to bray

ragna'tela [raɲɲa'tela] SF cobweb, spider's web

'ragno ['raɲɲo] SM spider; **non cavare un ~ dal buco** (*fig*) to draw a blank

ragù SM INV (*Cuc*) meat sauce (*for pasta*); stew

RAI-TV [raiti'vu] SIGLA F (= *Radio televisione italiana*) *Italian Broadcasting Company*

rallegra'menti SMPL congratulations

ralle'grare /**72**/ VT to cheer up; **rallegrarsi** VPR to cheer up; (*provare allegrezza*) to rejoice; **rallegrarsi con qn** to congratulate sb

rallenta'mento SM slowing down; slackening

rallen'tare /**72**/ VT to slow down; (*fig*) to lessen, slacken ▸ VI to slow down; **~ il passo** to slacken one's pace

rallenta'tore SM (*Cine*) slow-motion camera; **al ~** (*anche fig*) in slow motion

raman'zina [raman'dzina] SF lecture, telling-off

ra'mare /**72**/ VT (*superficie*) to copper, coat with copper; (*Agr: vite*) to spray with copper sulphate

ra'marro SM green lizard

ra'mato, -a AG (*oggetto: rivestito di rame*) copper-coated, coppered; (*capelli, barba*) coppery, copper-coloured (BRIT), copper-colored (US)

'rame SM (*Chim*) copper; **di ~** copper *cpd*; **incisione su ~** copperplate

r

ramifi'care /**20**/ VI (*Bot*) to put out branches; **ramificarsi** VPR (*diramarsi*) to branch out; (*Med: tumore, vene*) to ramify; **ramificarsi in** (*biforcarsi*) to branch into

ramificazi'one [ramifikat'tsjone] SF ramification

ra'mingo, -a, -ghi, -ghe AG (*poetico*): **andare ~** to go wandering, wander

ra'mino SM (*Carte*) rummy

rammari'carsi /**20**/ VPR: **~ (di)** (*rincrescersi*) to be sorry (about), regret; (*lamentarsi*) to complain (about)

ram'marico, -chi SM regret

rammen'dare /**72**/ VT to mend; (*calza*) to darn

ram'mendo SM mending *no pl*; darning *no pl*; mend darn

rammen'tare /**72**/ VT to remember, recall; **rammentarsi** VPR: **rammentarsi (di qc)** to remember (sth); **~ qc a qn** to remind sb of sth

rammol'lire /**55**/ VT to soften ▶ VI (*anche*: **rammollirsi**) to go soft

rammol'lito, -a AG weak ▶ SM/F weakling

'ramo SM branch; (*di commercio*) field; **non è il mio ~** it's not my field *o* line

ramo'scello [ramoʃʃello] SM twig

'rampa SF flight (of stairs); **~ di lancio** launching pad

rampi'cante AG (*Bot*) climbing

ram'pino SM (*gancio*) hook; (*Naut*) grapnel

ram'pollo SM (*di acqua*) spring; (*Bot: germoglio*) shoot; (*fig: discendente*) descendant

ram'pone SM harpoon; (*Alpinismo*) crampon

'rana SF frog; **~ pescatrice** angler fish

'rancido, -a ['rantʃido] AG rancid

'rancio ['rantʃo] SM (*Mil*) mess; **ora del ~** mess time

ran'core SM rancour (*BRIT*), rancor (*US*), resentment; **portare ~ a qn, provare ~ per** *o* **verso qn** to bear sb a grudge

ran'dagio, -a, -gi, -gie *o* **-ge** [ran'dadʒo] AG (*gatto, cane*) stray

ran'dello SM club, cudgel

'rango, -ghi SM (*grado*) rank; (*condizione sociale*) station, social standing; **persone di ~ inferiore** people of lower standing; **uscire dai ranghi** to fall out; (*fig*) to step out of line

Ran'gun SF Rangoon

rannicchi'arsi [rannik'kjarsi] /**19**/ VPR to crouch, huddle

rannuvo'larsi /**72**/ VPR to cloud over, become overcast

ra'nocchio [ra'nɔkkjo] SM (edible) frog

ranto'lare /**72**/ VI to wheeze

ranto'lio SM (*il respirare affannoso*) wheezing; (*di agonizzante*) death rattle

'rantolo SM wheeze; death rattle

ra'nuncolo SM (*Bot*) buttercup

'rapa SF (*Bot*) turnip

ra'pace [ra'patʃe] AG (*animale*) predatory; (*fig*) rapacious, grasping ▶ SM bird of prey

ra'pare /**72**/ VT (*capelli*) to crop, cut very short

'rapida SF *vedi* **rapido**

rapida'mente AV quickly, rapidly

rapidità SF speed

'rapido, -a AG fast; (*esame, occhiata*) quick, rapid ▶ SM (*Ferr*) express (train) ▶ SF (*di fiume*) rapid

rapi'mento SM kidnapping; (*fig*) rapture

ra'pina SF robbery; **~ in banca** bank robbery; **~ a mano armata** armed robbery

rapi'nare /**72**/ VT to rob

rapina'tore, -'trice SM/F robber

ra'pire /**55**/ VT (*cose*) to steal; (*persone*) to kidnap; (*fig*) to enrapture, delight

ra'pito, -a AG (*persona*) kidnapped; (*fig: in estasi*): **ascoltare ~ qn** to be captivated by sb's words ▶ SM/F kidnapped person

rapi'tore, -'trice SM/F kidnapper

rappacifi'care [rappatʃifi'kare] /**20**/ VT (*riconciliare*) to reconcile; **rappacificarsi** VPR (*uso*) to be reconciled, make it up (*col*)

rappacificazi'one [rappatʃifikat'tsjone] SF reconciliation

rappez'zare [rappet'tsare] /**72**/ VT to patch

rappor'tare /**72**/ VT (*confrontare*) to compare; (*riprodurre*) to reproduce

rap'porto SM (*resoconto*) report; (*legame*) relationship; (*Mat, Tecn*) ratio; **rapporti** SMPL (*fra persone, paesi*) relations; **in ~ a quanto è successo** with regard to *o* in relation to what happened; **fare ~ a qn su qc** to report sth to sb; **andare a ~ da qn** to report to sb; **chiamare qn a ~** (*Mil*) to summon sb; **essere in buoni/cattivi rapporti con qn** to be on good/bad terms with sb; **~ d'affari, ~ di lavoro** business relations; **~ di compressione** (*Tecn*) pressure ratio; **~ coniugale** marital relationship; **~ di trasmissione** (*Tecn*) gear; **rapporti sessuali** sexual intercourse *sg*

rap'prendersi /**81**/ VPR to coagulate, clot; (*latte*) to curdle

rappre'saglia [rappre'saʎʎa] SF reprisal, retaliation

rappresen'tante SMF representative; **~ di commercio** sales representative, sales rep(*col*); **~ sindacale** union delegate *o* representative

rappresen'tanza [rapprezen'tantsa] SF delegation, deputation; (*Comm: ufficio, sede*) agency; **in ~ di qn** on behalf of sb; **spese di ~** entertainment expenses; **macchina di ~** official car; **avere la ~ di** to be the agent for; **~ esclusiva** sole agency; **avere la ~ esclusiva** to be sole agent

rappresen'tare /**72**/ VT to represent; (*Teat*) to perform; **farsi ~ dal proprio legale** to be represented by one's lawyer

rappresenta'tivo, -a AG representative ▶ SF (*di partito, sindacale*) representative group; (*Sport: squadra*) representative (team)

rappresentazi'one [rapprezentat'tsjone] SF representation; performing *no pl*; (*spettacolo*) performance; **prima ~ assoluta** world première

rap'preso, -a PP = **rapprendere**

rapso'dia SF rhapsody

'raptus SM INV: **~ di follia** fit of madness

rara'mente AV seldom, rarely

rare'fare /**41**/ VT, **rare'farsi** VPR to rarefy

rare'fatto, -a PP *di* **rarefare** ▶ AG rarefied

rarefazi'one [rarefat'tsjone] SF rarefaction

rarità SF INV rarity

'raro, -a AG rare

ra'sare /**72**/ VT (*barba ecc*) to shave off; (*siepi, erba*) to trim, cut; **rasarsi** VPR to shave (o.s.)

ra'sato, -a AG (*erba*) trimmed, cut; (*tessuto*) smooth; **avere la barba rasata** to be clean-shaven

rasa'tura SF shave

raschia'mento [raskja'mento] SM (*Med*) curettage; **~ uterino** D and C

raschi'are [ras'kjare] /**19**/ VT to scrape; (*macchia, fango*) to scrape off ▶ VI to clear one's throat

rasen'tare /**72**/ VT (*andar rasente*) to keep close to; (*sfiorare*) to skim along (*o over*); (*fig*) to border on

ra'sente PREP: **~ (a)** close to, very near

'raso, -a PP *di* **radere** ▶ AG (*barba*) shaved; (*capelli*) cropped; (*con misure di capacità*) level; (*pieno: bicchiere*) full to the brim ▶ SM (*tessuto*) satin; **~ terra** close to the ground; **volare ~ terra** to hedgehop; **un cucchiaio ~ a** level spoonful

ra'soio SM razor; **~ elettrico** electric shaver *o* razor

ras'pare /**72**/ VT (*levigare*) to rasp; (*grattare*) to scratch

'raspo SM (*di uva*) grape stalk

ras'segna [ras'senna] SF (*Mil*) inspection, review; (*esame*) inspection; (*resoconto*) review, survey; (*pubblicazione letteraria ecc*) review; (*mostra*) exhibition, show; **passare in ~** (*Mil, fig*) to review

rasse'gnare [rassen'nare] /**15**/ VT: **~ le dimissioni** to resign, hand in one's resignation; **rassegnarsi** VPR (*accettare*): **rassegnarsi (a qc/a fare)** to resign o.s. (to sth/to doing)

rassegnazi'one [rassennat'tsjone] SF resignation

rasse're'nare /**72**/ VT (*persona*) to cheer up; **rasserenarsi** VPR (*tempo*) to clear up

rasset'tare /**72**/ VT to tidy, put in order; (*aggiustare*) to repair, mend

rassicu'rante AG reassuring

rassicu'rare /**72**/ VT to reassure; **rassicurarsi** VPR to take heart, recover one's confidence

rassicurazi'one [rassikurat'tsjone] SF reassurance

rasso'dare /**72**/ VT to harden, stiffen; (*fig*) to strengthen, consolidate; **rassodarsi** VPR to harden, to strengthen

rassomigli'anza [rassomiʎ'ʎantsa] SF resemblance

rassomigli'are [rassomiʎ'ʎare] /**27**/ VI: **~ a** to resemble, look like

rastrella'mento SM (*Mil: di polizia*) (thorough) search

rastrel'lare /**72**/ VT to rake; (*fig: perlustrare*) to comb

rastrelli'era SF rack; (*per piatti*) dish rack

ras'trello SM rake

'rata SF (*quota*) instalment, installment (*US*); **pagare a rate** to pay by instal(l)ments *o* on hire purchase (*BRIT*); **comprare/vendere a rate** to buy/sell on hire purchase (*BRIT*) *o* on the installment plan (*US*)

rate'ale AG: **pagamento ~** payment by instal(l)ments; **vendita ~** hire purchase (*BRIT*), installment plan (*US*)

rate'are /**72**/ VT to divide into instal(l)ments

rateazi'one [rateat'tsjone] SF division into instal(l)ments

rateiz'zare [rateid'dzare] /**72**/ VT = **rateare**

'rateo SM (*Comm*) accrual

ra'tifica, -che SF ratification

ratifi'care /**20**/ VT (*Dir*) to ratify

'ratto SM (*Dir*) abduction; (*Zool*) rat

rattop'pare /**72**/ VT to patch

rat'toppo SM patching *no pl*; patch

rattrap'pire /**55**/ VT to make stiff; **rattrappirsi** VPR to be stiff

rattris'tare /**72**/ VT to sadden; **rattristarsi** VPR to become sad

rau'cedine [rau'tʃɛdine] SF hoarseness

'rauco, -a, -chi, -che AG hoarse

rava'nello SM radish

raven'nate AG *of* (*o from*) Ravenna

ravi'oli SMPL ravioli *sg*

ravve'dersi /**82**/ VPR to mend one's ways

ravvi'are /**60**/ VT (*capelli*) to tidy; **ravviarsi i capelli** to tidy one's hair

ravvicina'mento [ravvitʃina'mento] SM (*tra persone*) reconciliation; (*Pol: tra paesi ecc*) rapprochement

ravvici'nare [ravvitʃi'nare] /**72**/ VT (*avvicinare: oggetti*) to bring closer together; (*fig: persone*) to reconcile, bring together; **~ qc a** to bring sth nearer to; **ravvicinarsi** VPR to be reconciled

ravvi'sare /**72**/ VT to recognize

ravvi'vare /**72**/ VT to revive; (*fig*) to brighten up, enliven; **ravvivarsi** VPR to revive; to brighten up

r

Rawal'pindi [raval'pindi] SF Rawalpindi
razio'cinio [rattsjo'tʃinjo] SM reasoning *no pl*; reason; (*buon senso*) common sense
razio'nale [rattsjo'nale] AG rational
razionalità [rattsjonali'ta] SF rationality; (*buon senso*) common sense
razionaliz'zare [rattsjonalid'dzare] /**72**/ VT (*metodo, lavoro, programma*) to rationalize; (*problema, situazione*) to approach rationally
raziona'mento [rattsjona'mento] SM rationing
razio'nare [rattsjo'nare] /**72**/ VT to ration
razi'one [rat'tsjone] SF ration; (*porzione*) portion, share
'razza ['rattsa] SF race; (*Zool*) breed; (*discendenza, stirpe*) stock, race; (*sorta*) sort, kind
raz'zia [rat'tsia] SF raid, foray
razzi'ale [rat'tsjale] AG racial
raz'zismo [rat'tsizmo] SM racism, racialism
raz'zista, -i, -e [rat'tsista] AG, SM/F racist, racialist
'razzo ['raddzo] SM rocket; **~ di segnalazione** flare; **~ vettore** vector rocket
razzo'lare [rattso'lare] /**72**/ VI (*galline*) to scratch about
RC SIGLA = **Reggio Calabria**; (= *partito della Rifondazione Comunista*) left-wing Italian political party
RDT SIGLA F *vedi* **la Repubblica Democratica Tedesca**
RE SIGLA = **Reggio Emilia**
re SM INV (*sovrano*) king; (*Mus*) D; (: *solfeggiando la scala*) re; **i Re Magi** the Three Wise Men, the Magi
rea'gente [rea'dʒɛnte] SM reagent
rea'gire [rea'dʒire] /**55**/ VI to react
re'ale AG real; (*di, da re*) royal ▶ SM: **il ~** reality; **i Reali** the Royal family
rea'lismo SM realism
rea'lista, -i, -e SM/F realist; (*Pol*) royalist
rea'listico, -a, -ci, -che AG realistic
reality [ri'aliti] SM INV reality show
realiz'zare [realid'dzare] /**72**/ VT (*progetto ecc*) to realize, carry out; (*sogno, desiderio*) to realize, fulfil; (*scopo*) to achieve; (*Comm: titoli ecc*) to realize; (*Calcio ecc*) to score; **realizzarsi** VPR to be realized
realizzazi'one [realiddzat'tsjone] SF realization; fulfilment; achievement; **~ scenica** stage production
rea'lizzo [rea'liddzo] SM (*conversione in denaro*) conversion into cash; (*vendita forzata*) clearance sale
real'mente AV really, actually
realtà SF INV reality; **in ~** (*in effetti*) in fact; (*a dire il vero*) really
re'ame SM kingdom, realm; (*fig*) realm
re'ato SM offence (*BRIT*), offense (*US*)

reat'tore SM (*Fisica*) reactor; (*Aer: aereo*) jet; (: *motore*) jet engine
reazio'nario, -a [reattsjo'narjo] AG, SM/F (*Pol*) reactionary
reazi'one [reat'tsjone] SF reaction; **motore/aereo a ~** jet engine/plane; **forze della ~** reactionary forces; **~ a catena** (*anche fig*) chain reaction
'rebbio SM prong
'rebus SM INV rebus; (*fig*) puzzle; enigma
recapi'tare /**72**/ VT to deliver
re'capito SM (*indirizzo*) address; (*consegna*) delivery; **~ telefonico** phone number; **ha un ~ telefonico?** do you have a telephone number where you can be reached?; **~ a domicilio** home delivery (service)
re'care /**20**/ VT (*portare*) to bring; (*avere su di sé*) to carry, bear; (*cagionare*) to cause, bring; **recarsi** VPR to go; **~ danno a qn** to harm sb, cause harm to sb; **recarsi in città/a scuola** to go into town/to school
re'cedere [re'tʃedere] /**29**/ VI to withdraw
recensi'one [retʃen'sjone] SF review
recen'sire [retʃen'sire] /**55**/ VT to review
recen'sore, -a [retʃen'sore] SM/F reviewer
re'cente [re'tʃɛnte] AG recent; **di ~** recently; **più ~** latest, most recent
recente'mente [retʃɛnte'mente] AV recently
rece'pire [retʃe'pire] /**55**/ VT to understand, take in
recessi'one [retʃes'sjone] SF (*Econ*) recession
re'cesso [re'tʃɛsso] SM (*azione*) recession, receding; (*Dir*) withdrawal; (*luogo*) recess
recherò *etc* [reke'rɔ] VB *vedi* **recare**
re'cidere [re'tʃidere] /**34**/ VT to cut off, chop off
reci'divo, -a [retʃi'divo] SM/F (*Dir*) second (*o habitual*) offender, recidivist ▶ SF recidivism
recin'tare [retʃin'tare] /**72**/ VT to enclose, fence off
re'cinto [re'tʃinto] SM enclosure; (*ciò che recinge*) fence; surrounding wall
recinzi'one [retʃin'tsjone] SF (*azione*) enclosure, fencing-off; (*recinto: di legno*) fence; (: *di mattoni*) wall; (*reticolato*) wire fencing; (*a sbarre*) railings *pl*
recipi'ente [retʃi'pjɛnte] SM container
re'ciproco, -a, -ci, -che [re'tʃiproko] AG reciprocal
re'ciso, -a [re'tʃizo] PP *di* **recidere**
'recita ['rɛtʃita] SF performance
'recital ['rɛtʃital] SM INV recital
reci'tare [retʃi'tare] /**72**/ VT (*poesia, lezione*) to recite; (*dramma*) to perform; (*ruolo*) to play *o* act (the part of)
recitazi'one [retʃitat'tsjone] SF recitation; (*di attore*) acting; **scuola di ~** drama school

recla'mare /**72**/ VI to complain ▶ VT (*richiedere*)
to demand

ré'clame [re'klam] SF INV advertising *no pl*
advertisement, advert (BRIT), ad (*col*)

reclamiz'zare [reklamid'dzare] /**72**/ VT to
advertise

re'clamo SM complaint; **sporgere ~ a** to
complain to, make a complaint to

recli'nabile AG (*sedile*) reclining

recli'nare /**72**/ VT (*capo*) to bow, lower; (*sedile*)
to tilt

reclusi'one SF (*Dir*) imprisonment

re'cluso, -a SM/F prisoner

'recluta SF recruit

recluta'mento SM recruitment

reclu'tare /**72**/ VT to recruit

re'condito, -a AG secluded; (*fig*) secret,
hidden

'record AG INV record *cpd* ▶ SM INV record;
in tempo ~, a tempo di ~ in record time;
detenere il ~ di to hold the record for;
~ mondiale world record

recrimi'nare /**72**/ VI: **~ (su qc)** to complain
(about sth)

recriminazi'one [rekriminat'tsjone] SF
recrimination

recrude'scenza [rekrudeʃʃɛntsa] SF fresh
outbreak

recupe'rare *etc* = **ricuperare** *ecc*

redargu'ire /**55**/ VT to rebuke

re'dassi *etc* VB *vedi* **redigere**

re'datto, -a PP *di* **redigere**

redat'tore, -'trice SM/F (*Stampa*) editor;
(: *di articolo*) writer; (*di dizionario ecc*) compiler;
~ capo chief editor

redazi'one [redat'tsjone] SF editing;
writing; (*sede*) editorial office(s); (*personale*)
editorial staff; (*versione*) version

reddi'tizio, -a [reddi'tittsjo] AG profitable

'reddito SM income; (*dello Stato*) revenue;
(*di un capitale*) yield; **~ complessivo** gross
income; **~ disponibile** disposable income;
~ fisso fixed income; **~ imponibile/non
imponibile** taxable/non-taxable income;
~ da lavoro earned income; **~ nazionale**
national income; **~ pubblico** public revenue

re'densi *etc* VB *vedi* **redimere**

re'dento, -a PP *di* **redimere**

reden'tore SM: **il R~** the Redeemer

redenzi'one [reden'tsjone] SF redemption

re'digere [re'didʒere] /**47**/ VT to write;
(*contratto*) to draw up

re'dimere /**86**/ VT to deliver; (*Rel*) to redeem

'redini SFPL reins

redi'vivo, -a AG returned to life, reborn

'reduce ['rɛdutʃe] AG (*gen*): **~ da** returning
from, back from ▶ SMF survivor; (*veterano*)
veteran; **essere ~ da** (*esame, colloquio*) to have
been through; (*malattia*) to be just over

'refe SM thread

refe'rendum SM INV referendum

refe'renza [refe'rɛntsa] SF reference

re'ferto SM medical report

refet'torio SM refectory

refezi'one [refet'tsjone] SF (*Ins*) school meal

refrat'tario, -a AG refractory; (*fig*): **essere ~
alla matematica** to have no aptitude for
mathematics

refrige'rante [refridʒe'rante] AG (*Tecn*)
cooling, refrigerating; (*bevanda*) refreshing
▶ SM (*Chim: fluido*) coolant; (*Tecn: apparecchio*)
refrigerator

refrige'rare [refridʒe'rare] /**72**/ VT to
refrigerate; (*rinfrescare*) to cool, refresh

refrigerazi'one [refridʒerat'tsjone] SF
refrigeration; (*Tecn*) cooling; **~ ad acqua**
(*Aut*) water-cooling

refri'gerio [refri'dʒɛrjo] SM: **trovare ~** to find
somewhere cool

refur'tiva SF stolen goods *pl*

Reg. ABBR (= *reggimento*) Regt; (*Amm*)
= **regolamento**

rega'lare /**72**/ VT to give (as a present), make a
present of

re'gale AG regal

re'galo SM gift, present ▶ AG INV: **confezione
~** gift pack; **fare un ~ a qn** to give sb a
present; **"articoli da ~"** "gifts"

re'gata SF regatta

reg'gente [red'dʒɛnte] AG (*proposizione*) main;
(*sovrano*) reigning ▶ SMF regent; **principe ~**
prince regent

reg'genza [red'dʒɛntsa] SF regency

'reggere ['rɛddʒere] /**87**/ VT (*tenere*) to hold;
(*sostenere*) to support, bear, hold up; (*portare*)
to carry, bear; (*resistere*) to withstand;
(*dirigere: impresa*) to manage, run; (*governare*)
to rule, govern; (*Ling*) to take, be followed
by ▶ VI (*resistere*): **~ a** to stand up to, hold out
against; (*sopportare*): **~ a** to stand; (*durare*) to
last; (*fig: teoria ecc*) to hold water; **reggersi**
VPR (*stare ritto*) to stand; (*fig: dominarsi*) to
control o.s.; **reggersi sulle gambe** *o* **in
piedi** to stand up

'reggia, -ge ['rɛddʒa] SF royal palace

reggi'calze [reddʒi'kaltse] SM INV suspender
belt

reggi'mento [reddʒi'mento] SM (*Mil*)
regiment

reggi'petto [reddʒi'pɛtto], **reggi'seno**
[reddʒi'seno] SM bra

re'gia, -'gie [re'dʒia] SF (*TV, Cine ecc*) direction

re'gime [re'dʒime] SM (*Pol*) regime; (*Dir: aureo,
patrimoniale ecc*) system; (*Med*) diet; (*Tecn*)
(engine) speed; **~ di giri** (*di motore*) revs *pl* per
minute; **~ vegetariano** vegetarian diet

re'gina [re'dʒina] SF queen

'regio, -a, -gi, -gie ['rɛdʒo] AG royal

regionale – relazione

regio'nale [redʒo'nale] AG regional ▸ SM local train (*stopping frequently*)

regi'one [re'dʒone] SF (*gen*) region; (*territorio*) region, district, area; *see note*

> The *Regione* is the biggest administrative unit in Italy. Each of the 20 *Regioni* consists of a variable number of *Province*, which in turn are subdivided into *Comuni*. Each of the regions has a *capoluogo*, its chief province (for example, Florence is the chief province of the region of Tuscany). Five regions have special status and wider powers: Val d'Aosta, Friuli-Venezia Giulia, Trentino-Alto Adige, Sicily and Sardinia. A *Regione* is run by the *Giunta regionale*, which is elected by the *Consiglio regionale*; both are presided over by a *Presidente*. The *Giunta* has legislative powers within the region over the police, public health, schools, town planning and agriculture.

re'gista, -i, -e [re'dʒista] SM/F (*TV, Cine ecc*) director

regis'trare [redʒis'trare] /**72**/ VT (*Amm*) to register; (*Comm*) to enter; (*notare*) to report, note; (*canzone, conversazione, strumento di misura*) to record; (*mettere a punto*) to adjust, regulate; **~ i bagagli** (*Aer*) to check in one's luggage; **~ i freni** (*Tecn*) to adjust the brakes

registra'tore [redʒistra'tore] SM (*strumento*) recorder, register; (*magnetofono*) tape recorder; **~ di cassa** cash register; **~ a cassette** cassette recorder; **~ di volo** (*Aer*) flight recorder, black box (*col*)

registrazi'one [redʒistrat'tsjone] SF registration; entry; reporting recording adjustment; **~ bagagli** (*Aer*) check-in

re'gistro [re'dʒistro] SM register; (*Dir*) registry; (*Comm*): **~ (di cassa)** ledger; **ufficio del ~** registrar's office; **~ di bordo** logbook; **registri contabili** (account) books

re'gnante [reɲ'ɲante] AG reigning, ruling ▸ SMF ruler

re'gnare [reɲ'ɲare] /**15**/ VI to reign, rule; (*fig*) to reign

'regno ['reɲɲo] SM kingdom; (*periodo*) reign; (*fig*) realm; **il ~ animale/vegetale** the animal/vegetable kingdom; **il R~ Unito** the United Kingdom

'regola SF rule; **a ~ d'arte** duly; perfectly; **essere in ~** (*dipendente*) to be a registered employee; (*fig: essere pulito*) to be clean; **fare le cose in ~** to do things properly; **avere le carte in ~** (*gen*) to have one's papers in order; (*fig: essere adatto*) to be the right person; **per tua (norma e) ~** for your information; **un'eccezione alla ~** an exception to the rule

rego'labile AG adjustable

regolamen'tare /**72**/ AG (*distanza, velocità*) regulation *cpd*, proper; (*disposizione*) statutory ▸ VT (*gen*) to control; **entro il tempo ~** within the time allowed, within the prescribed time

regola'mento SM (*complesso di norme*) regulations *pl*; (*di debito*) settlement; **~ di conti** (*fig*) settling of scores

rego'lare /**72**/ AG regular; (*velocità*) steady; (*superficie*) even; (*passo*) steady, even; (*in regola: documento*) in order ▸ VT to regulate, control; (*apparecchio*) to adjust, regulate; (*questione, conto, debito*) to settle; **regolarsi** VPR (*comportarsi*) to behave, act; **regolarsi nel bere/nello spendere** (*moderarsi*) to control one's drinking/spending; **presentare ~ domanda** to apply through the proper channels; **~ i conti** (*fig*) to settle old scores

regolarità SF INV regularity; steadiness; evenness; (*nel pagare*) punctuality

regolariz'zare [regolarid'dzare] /**72**/ VT (*posizione*) to regularize; (*debito*) to settle

rego'lata SF: **darsi una ~** to pull o.s. together

regola'tezza [regola'tettsa] SF (*ordine*) orderliness; (*moderazione*) moderation

rego'lato, -a AG (*ordinato*) orderly; (*moderato*) moderate

regola'tore SM (*Tecn*) regulator; **~ di frequenza/di volume** frequency/volume control

'regolo SM ruler; **~ calcolatore** slide rule

regre'dire /**55**/ VI to regress

regressi'one SF regression

re'gresso SM (*fig: declino*) decline

rei'etto, -a SM/F outcast

reincarnazi'one [reinkarnat'tsjone] SF reincarnation

reinte'grare /**72**/ VT (*produzione*) to restore; (*energie*) to recover; (*dipendente*) to reinstate

reintegrazi'one [reintegrat'tsjone] SF (*di produzione*) restoration; (*di dipendente*) reinstatement

relativa'mente AV relatively

relatività SF relativity

rela'tivo, -a AG relative; (*attinente*) relevant; (*rispettivo*) respective; **~ a** (*che concerne*) relating to, concerning; (*proporzionato*) in proportion to

rela'tore, -'trice SM/F (*gen*) spokesman/woman; (*Ins: di tesi*) supervisor

re'lax [re'laks] SM relaxation

relazi'one [relat'tsjone] SF (*fra cose, persone*) relation(ship); (*resoconto*) report, account; **relazioni** SFPL (*conoscenze*) connections; **essere in ~** to be connected; **mettere in ~** (*fatti, elementi*) to make the connection between; **in ~ a quanto detto prima** with regard to what has already been said; **essere in buone relazioni con qn** to be on good terms with sb; **fare una** ~ to make a report, give an account; **relazioni pubbliche** public relations

rele'gare /**80**/ vt to banish; (*fig*) to relegate

religi'one [reli'dʒone] sf religion

religi'oso, -a [reli'dʒoso] ag religious ▶ sm/f monk/nun

re'liquia sf relic

re'litto sm wreck; (*fig*) down-and-out

re'mainder [ri'meində'] sm inv (*libro*) remainder

're'make** ['ri:'meik] sm inv (*Cine*) remake

re'mare /**72**/ vi to row

remini'scenze [reminiʃʃɛntse] sfpl reminiscences

remissi'one sf remission; (*deferenza*) submissiveness, compliance; ~ **del debito** remission of debt; ~ **di querela** (*Dir*) withdrawal of an action

remissività sf submissiveness

remis'sivo, -a ag submissive, compliant

're'mo** sm oar

'remora sf (*poetico: indugio*) hesitation

re'moto, -a ag remote

remune'rare *etc* = **rimunerare** *ecc*

'rena sf sand

re'nale ag kidney *cpd*

'rendere /**88**/ vt (*ridare*) to return, give back; (: *saluto ecc*) to return; (*produrre*) to yield, bring in; (*esprimere, tradurre*) to render; (*far diventare*): ~ **qc possibile** to make sth possible ▶ vi (*fruttare: ditta*) to be profitable; (: *investimento, campo*) to yield, be productive; ~ **grazie a qn** to thank sb; ~ **omaggio a qn** to honour sb; ~ **un servizio a qn** to do sb a service; ~ **una testimonianza** to give evidence; ~ **la visita** to pay a return visit; **non so se rendo l'idea** I don't know whether I'm making myself clear; **rendersi utile** to make o.s. useful; **rendersi conto di qc** to realize sth

rendi'conto sm (*rapporto*) report, account; (*Amm, Comm*) statement of account

rendi'mento sm (*reddito*) yield; (*di manodopera, Tecn*) efficiency; (*capacità*) output; (*di studenti*) performance

'rendita sf (*di individuo*) private *o* unearned income; (*Comm*) revenue; ~ **annua** annuity; ~ **vitalizia** life annuity

'rene sm kidney

'reni sfpl back *sg*

reni'tente ag reluctant, unwilling; ~ **ai consigli di qn** unwilling to follow sb's advice; **essere** ~ **alla leva** (*Mil*) to fail to report for military service

'renna sf reindeer *inv*

'Reno sm: **il** ~ the Rhine

'reo, -a sm/f (*Dir*) offender

re'parto sm department, section; (*Mil*) detachment; ~ **acquisti** purchasing office

repel'lente ag repulsive; (*Chim: insettifugo*): **liquido** ~ (liquid) repellent

repen'taglio [repen'taʎʎo] sm: **mettere a** ~ to jeopardize, risk

repen'tino, -a ag sudden, unexpected

repe'ribile ag available

repe'rire /**55**/ vt to find, trace

re'perto sm (*Archeologia*) find; (*Med*) report; (*anche:* **reperto giudiziario**) exhibit

reper'torio sm (*Teat*) repertory; (*elenco*) index, (alphabetical) list

'replica, -che sf repetition; reply, answer; (*obiezione*) objection; (*Teat, Cine*) repeat performance; (*copia*) replica

repli'care /**20**/ vt (*ripetere*) to repeat; (*rispondere*) to answer, reply

repor'tage [rəpɔr'taʒ] sm inv (*Stampa*) report

repressi'one sf repression

repres'sivo, -a ag repressive

re'presso, -a pp *di* **reprimere**

re'primere /**50**/ vt to suppress, repress

re'pubblica, -che sf republic; **la R~ Democratica Tedesca** the German Democratic Republic; **la R~ Federale Tedesca** the Federal Republic of Germany; **la Prima/la Seconda R~** *terms used to refer to Italy before and after the political changes resulting from the 1994 elections*; *vedi anche* **Festa della Repubblica**

repubbli'cano, -a ag, sm/f republican

repu'tare /**72**/ vt to consider, judge

reputazi'one [reputat'tsjone] sf reputation; **farsi una cattiva** ~ to get o.s. a bad name

'requie sf rest; **dare** ~ **a qn** to give sb some peace; **senza** ~ unceasingly

'requiem sm inv (*preghiera*) requiem, prayer for the dead; (*fig: ufficio funebre*) requiem

requi'sire /**55**/ vt to requisition

requi'sito sm requirement; **avere i requisiti necessari per un lavoro** to have the necessary qualifications for a job

requisi'toria sf (*Dir*) closing speech (for the prosecution)

requisizi'one [rekwizit'tsjone] sf requisition

'resa sf (*l'arrendersi*) surrender; (*restituzione, rendimento*) return; ~ **dei conti** rendering of accounts; (*fig*) day of reckoning

re'scindere [reʃʃindere] /**102**/ vt (*Dir*) to rescind, annul

re'scisso, -a [reʃʃisso] pp *di* **rescindere**

reset'tare /**72**/ vt (*Inform*) to reset

'resi *etc* vb *vedi* **rendere**

resi'dente ag resident

resi'denza [resi'dɛntsa] sf residence

residenzi'ale [residen'tsjale] ag residential

residu'ale ag residual

re'siduo, -a ag residual, remaining ▶ sm remainder; (*Chim*) residue; **residui industriali** industrial waste *sg*

r

'resina SF resin

resis'tente AG (*che resiste*): ~ **a** resistant to; (*forte*) strong; (*duraturo*) long-lasting, durable; ~ **all'acqua** waterproof; ~ **al caldo** heat-resistant; ~ **al fuoco** fireproof; ~ **al gelo** frost-resistant

resis'tenza [resis'tɛntsa] SF (*gen, Elettr*) resistance; (*di persona: fisica*) stamina, endurance; (: *mentale*) endurance, resistance; **opporre ~ (a)** to offer *o* put up resistance (to); (*decisione, scelta*) to show opposition (to); **la R~** *see note*

> The Italian *Resistenza* fought against both the Nazis and the Fascists during the Second World War. It was particularly active after the fall of the Fascist government on 25 July 1943, throughout the German occupation and during the period of Mussolini's Republic of Salò in northern Italy. Resistance members spanned the whole political spectrum and played a vital role in the Liberation and in the formation of the new democratic government.

re'sistere /**11**/ VI to resist; ~ **a** (*assalto, tentazioni*) ·to resist; (*dolore*) to withstand; (*non patir danno*) to be resistant to

resis'tito, -a PP *di* **resistere**

'reso, -a PP *di* **rendere**

reso'conto SM report, account

respin'gente [respin'dʒɛnte] SM (*Ferr*) buffer

res'pingere [res'pindʒere] /**114**/ VT to drive back, repel; (*rifiutare: pacco, lettera*) to return; (: *invito*) to refuse; (: *proposta*) to reject, turn down; (*Ins: bocciare*) to fail

res'pinto, -a PP *di* **respingere**

respi'rare /**72**/ VI to breathe; (*fig*) to get one's breath; to breathe again ▶ VT to breathe (in), inhale

respira'tore SM respirator

respira'torio, -a AG respiratory

respirazi'one [respirat'tsjone] SF breathing; ~ **artificiale** artificial respiration; ~ **bocca a bocca** mouth-to-mouth resuscitation, kiss of life (*col*)

res'piro SM breathing *no pl*; (*singolo atto*) breath; (*fig*) respite, rest; **mandare un ~ di sollievo** to give a sigh of relief; **trattenere il ~** to hold one's breath; **lavorare senza ~** to work non-stop; **di ampio ~** (*opera, lavoro*) far-reaching

respon'sabile AG responsible ▶ SMF person responsible; (*capo*) person in charge; ~ **di** responsible for; (*Dir*) liable for

responsabilità SF INV responsibility; (*legale*) liability; **assumere la ~ di** to take on the responsibility for; **affidare a qn la ~ di qc** to make sb responsible for sth; ~ **patrimoniale** debt liability; ~ **penale** criminal liability

responsabiliz'zare [responsabilid'dzare] /**72**/ VT: ~ **qn** to make sb feel responsible

res'ponso SM answer; (*Dir*) verdict

'ressa SF crowd, throng

'ressi *etc* VB *vedi* **reggere**

res'tare /**72**/ VI (*rimanere*) to remain, stay; (*avanzare*) to be left, remain; (*diventare*): ~ **orfano/cieco** to become *o* be left an orphan/become blind; (*trovarsi*): ~ **sorpreso** to be surprised; ~ **d'accordo** to agree; **non resta più niente** there's nothing left; **restano pochi giorni** there are only a few days left; **che resti tra di noi** this is just between ourselves; ~ **in buoni rapporti** to remain on good terms; ~ **senza parole** to be left speechless

restau'rare /**72**/ VT to restore

restaura'tore, -'trice SM/F restorer

restaurazi'one [restaurat'tsjone] SF (*Pol*) restoration

res'tauro SM (*di edifici ecc*) restoration; **in ~** under repair; **sotto ~** (*dipinto*) being restored; **chiuso per restauri** closed for repairs

res'tio, -a, -'tii, -'tie AG restive; (*persona*): ~ **a** reluctant to

restitu'ire /**55**/ VT to return, give back; (*energie, forze*) to restore

restituzi'one [restitut'tsjone] SF return; (*di soldi*) repayment

'resto SM remainder, rest; (*denaro*) change; (*Mat*) remainder; **resti** SMPL leftovers; (*di città*) remains; **del ~** moreover, besides; **tenga pure il ~** keep the change; **resti mortali** (mortal) remains

res'tringere [res'trindʒere] /**117**/ VT to reduce; (*vestito*) to take in; (*stoffa*) to shrink; (*fig*) to restrict, limit; **restringersi** VPR (*strada*) to narrow; (*stoffa*) to shrink

restrit'tivo, -a AG restrictive

restrizi'one [restrit'tsjone] SF restriction

resurrezi'one [resurret'tsjone] SF = **risurrezione**

resusci'tare [resuʃʃi'tare] /**72**/ VT, VI = **risuscitare**

re'tata SF (*Pesca*) haul, catch; **fare una ~ di** (*fig: persone*) to round up

'rete SF net; (*di recinzione*) wire netting; (*Aut, Ferr, di spionaggio ecc*) network; (*fig*) trap, snare; **segnare una ~** (*Calcio*) to score a goal; ~ **ferroviaria/stradale/di distribuzione** railway/road/distribution network; ~ **del letto** (sprung) bed base; ~ **da pesca** fishing net; ~ **sociale** social network; ~ (**televisiva**) (*sistema*) network; (*canale*) channel; **la R~** the web; **calze a ~** fishnet tights *o* stockings

reti'cente [reti'tʃɛnte] AG reticent

reti'cenza [reti'tʃɛntsa] SF reticence

retico'lato SM grid; (*rete metallica*) wire netting; (*di filo spinato*) barbed wire fence '**retina** SF (*Anat*) retina

re'torico, -a, -ci, -che AG rhetorical ▶ SF rhetoric

retribu'ire /**55**/ VT to pay; (*premiare*) to reward; **un lavoro mal retribuito** a poorly-paid job

retribu'tivo, -a AG pay *cpd*

retribuzi'one [retribut'tsjone] SF payment; reward

re'trivo, -a AG (*fig*) reactionary

'**retro** SM INV back ▶ AV (*dietro*): **vedi ~** see over(leaf)

retroattivi'tà SF retroactivity

retroat'tivo, -a AG (*Dir: legge*) retroactive; (*Amm: salario*) backdated

retrobot'tega, -ghe SF back shop

retro'cedere [retro'tʃedere] /**29**/ VI to withdraw ▶ VT (*Calcio*) to relegate; (*Mil*) to degrade; (*Amm*) to demote

retrocessi'one [retrotʃes'sjone] SF (*di impiegato*) demotion

retro'cesso, -a [retro'tʃɛsso] PP *di* **retrocedere**

retroda'tare /**72**/ VT (*Amm*) to backdate

re'trogrado, -a AG (*fig*) reactionary, backward-looking

retrogu'ardia SF (*anche fig*) rearguard

retro'marcia [retro'martʃa] SF (*Aut*) reverse; (: *dispositivo*) reverse gear

retro'scena [retro'ʃʃena] SF INV (*Teat*) backstage ▶ SM INV: **i ~** (*fig*) the behind-the-scenes activities

retrospet'tivo, -a AG retrospective ▶ SF (*Arte*) retrospective (exhibition)

retros'tante AG: **~ (a)** at the back (of)

retro'terra SM hinterland

retro'via SF (*Mil*) zone behind the front; **mandare nelle retrovie** to send to the rear

retrovi'sore SM (*Aut*) (rear-view) mirror

'**retta** SF (*Mat*) straight line; (*di convitto*) charge for bed and board; (*fig: ascolto*): **dar ~ a** to listen to, pay attention to

rettango'lare AG rectangular

ret'tangolo, -a AG right-angled ▶ SM rectangle

ret'tifica, -che SF rectification, correction

rettifi'care /**20**/ VT (*curva*) to straighten; (*fig*) to rectify, correct

'**rettile** SM reptile

retti'lineo, -a AG rectilinear

retti'tudine SF rectitude, uprightness

'**retto, -a** PP *di* **reggere** ▶ AG straight; (*onesto*) honest, upright; (*giusto, esatto*) correct, proper, right; **angolo ~** (*Mat*) right angle

ret'tore SM (*Rel*) rector; (*di università*) ≈ chancellor

re'tweet [ri'twit] SM INV (*su Twitter*) retweet

reuma'tismo SM rheumatism

Rev. ABBR (= *Reverendo*) Rev(d)

reve'rendo, -a AG: **il ~ padre Belli** the Reverend Father Belli

reve'rente AG = **riverente**

reve'renza [reve'rɛntsa] SF = **riverenza**

rever'sibile AG reversible

revisio'nare /**72**/ VT (*conti*) to audit; (*Tecn*) to overhaul, service; (*Dir: processo*) to review; (*componimento*) to revise

revisi'one SF auditing *no pl*; audit; servicing *no pl*; overhaul; review; revision; **~ di bilancio** audit; **~ di bozze** proofreading; **~ contabile interna** internal audit

revi'sore SM: **~ di conti/bozze** auditor/ proofreader

re'vival [ri'vaivəl] SM INV revival

'**revoca** SF revocation

revo'care /**20**/ VT to revoke

re'volver SM INV revolver

revolve'rata SF revolver shot

'**Reykjavik** ['reikjavik] SF Reykjavik

RFT SIGLA F *vedi* **la Repubblica Federale Tedesca**

ri'abbia *etc* VB *vedi* **riavere**

riabili'tare /**72**/ VT to rehabilitate; (*fig*) to restore to favour (BRIT) o favor (US)

riabilitazi'one [riabilitat'tsjone] SF rehabilitation

riac'cendere [riat'tʃɛndere] /**2**/ VT (*sigaretta, fuoco, gas*) to light again; (*luce, radio, TV*) to switch on again; (*fig: sentimenti, interesse*) to rekindle, revive; **riaccendersi** VPR (*fuoco*) to catch again; (*luce, radio, TV*) to come back on again; (*fig: sentimenti*) to revive, be rekindled

riac'ceso, -a [riat'tʃeso] PP *di* **riaccendere**

riacqui'stare /**72**/ VT (*gen*) to buy again; (*ciò che si era venduto*) to buy back; (*fig: buonumore, sangue freddo, libertà*) to regain; **~ la salute** to recover (one's health); **~ le forze** to regain one's strength

Ri'ad SF Riyadh

riaddormen'tare /**72**/ VT to put to sleep again; **riaddormentarsi** VPR to fall asleep again

riallac'ciare [riallat'tʃare] /**14**/ VT (*cintura, cavo ecc*) to refasten, tie up o fasten again; (*fig: rapporti, amicizia*) to resume, renew; **riallacciarsi** VPR: **riallacciarsi a** (*fig: a discorso, tema*) to resume, take up again

rial'zare [rial'tsare] /**72**/ VT to raise, lift; (*alzare di più*) to heighten, raise; (*aumentare: prezzi*) to increase, raise ▶ VI (*prezzi*) to rise, increase

rial'zato, -a [rial'tsato] AG: **piano ~** mezzanine, entresol

rial'zista, -i [rial'tsista] SM (*Borsa*) bull

ri'alzo [ri'altso] SM (*di prezzi*) increase, rise; (*sporgenza*) rise; **giocare al ~** (*Borsa*) to bull

rian'dare /**6**/ VI: **~ (in)**, **~ (a)** to go back (to), return (to)

riani'mare /**72**/ VT (*Med*) to resuscitate; (*fig: rallegrare*) to cheer up; (: *dar coraggio*) to give heart to; **rianimarsi** VPR to recover consciousness; to cheer up; to take heart

rianimazi'one [rianimat'tsjone] SF (Med) resuscitation; **centro di ~** intensive care unit

ria'perto, -a PP di **riaprire**

riaper'tura SF reopening

riappa'rire /7/ VI to reappear

riap'parso, -a PP di **riapparire**

riap'pendere /8/ VT to rehang; (Tel) to hang up

ria'prire /9/ VT, **ria'prirsi** VPR to reopen, open again

ri'armo SM (Mil) rearmament

ri'arso, -a AG (terreno) arid; (gola) parched; (labbra) dry

riasset'tare /72/ VT (vedi sm) to rearrange; to reorganize

rias'setto SM (di stanza ecc) rearrangement; (ordinamento) reorganization

rias'sumere /12/ VT (riprendere) to resume; (impiegare di nuovo) to re-employ; (sintetizzare) to summarize

rias'sunto, -a PP di **riassumere** ▶ SM summary

riattac'care /20/ VT (attaccare di nuovo): ~ **(a)** (manifesto, francobollo) to stick back (on); (bottone) to sew back (on); (quadro, chiavi) to hang back up (on); ~ **(il telefono o il ricevitore)** to hang up (the receiver)

riatti'vare /72/ VT to reactivate

ria'vere /13/ VT to have again; (avere indietro) to get back; (riacquistare) to recover; **riaversi** VPR to recover; (da svenimento, stordimento) to come round

riba'dire /55/ VT (fig) to confirm

ri'balta SF (sportello) flap; (Teat: proscenio) front of the stage; **luci della ~** footlights pl; (fig) limelight; **tornare alla ~** (personaggio) to make a comeback; (problema) to come up again

ribal'tabile AG (sedile) tip-up

ribal'tare /72/ VT, VI (anche: **ribaltarsi**) to turn over, tip over

ribas'sare /72/ VT to lower, bring down ▶ VI to come down, fall

ribas'sista, -i SM (Borsa) bear

ri'basso SM reduction, fall; **essere in ~** (azioni, prezzi) to be down; (fig: popolarità) to be on the decline; **giocare al ~** (Borsa) to bear

ri'battere /1/ VT (battere di nuovo) to beat again; (con macchina da scrivere) to type again; (palla) to return, hit back; (confutare) to refute; ~ **che** to retort that

ribattez'zare [ribatted'dzare] /72/ VT to rename

ribel'larsi /72/ VPR: ~ **(a)** to rebel (against)

ri'belle AG (soldati) rebel; (ragazzo) rebellious ▶ SMF rebel

ribelli'one SF rebellion

'ribes SM INV currant; ~ **nero** blackcurrant; ~ **rosso** redcurrant

ribol'lire /17/ VI (fermentare) to ferment; (fare bolle) to bubble, boil; (fig) to seethe

ri'brezzo [ri'breddzo] SM disgust, loathing; **far ~ a** to disgust

ribut'tante AG disgusting, revolting

ricacci'are [rikat'tʃare] /14/ VT (respingere) to drive back; ~ **qn fuori** to throw sb out

rica'dere /18/ VI to fall again; (scendere a terra: fig: nel peccato ecc) to fall back; (vestiti, capelli ecc) to hang (down); (riversarsi: fatiche: colpe): ~ **su** to fall on

rica'duta SF (Med) relapse

rical'care /20/ VT (disegni) to trace; (fig) to follow faithfully

ricalci'trare [rikaltʃi'trare] /72/ VI (cavalli, asini, muli) to kick

rica'mare /72/ VT to embroider

ricambi'are /19/ VT to change again; (contraccambiare) to return, repay

ri'cambio SM exchange, return; (Fisiol) metabolism; **ricambi** SMPL spare parts; **pezzi di ~** spare parts; ~ **della manodopera** labour turnover

ri'camo SM embroidery; **senza ricami** (fig) without frills

ricapitalizzazione [rikapitaliddza'tsjone] SF bailout

ricapito'lare /72/ VT to recapitulate, sum up

ricapitolazi'one [rikapitolat'tsjone] SF recapitulation, summary

ricari'care /20/ VT (arma, macchina fotografica) to reload; (penna, pipa) to refill; (orologio, giocattolo) to rewind; (Elettr) to recharge

ricat'tare /72/ VT to blackmail

ricatta'tore, -'trice SM/F blackmailer

ri'catto SM blackmail; **fare un ~ a qn** to blackmail sb; **subire un ~** to be blackmailed

rica'vare /72/ VT (estrarre) to draw out, extract; (ottenere) to obtain, gain

rica'vato SM (di vendite) proceeds pl

ri'cavo SM proceeds pl; (Contabilità) revenue

ric'chezza [rik'kettsa] SF wealth; (fig) richness; **ricchezze** SFPL (beni) wealth sg, riches; **ricchezze naturali** natural resources

'riccio, -a, -ci, -ce ['rittʃo] AG curly ▶ SM (Zool) hedgehog; (anche: **riccio di mare**) sea urchin

'ricciolo ['rittʃolo] SM curl

ricci'uto, -a [rit'tʃuto] AG curly

'ricco, -a, -chi, -che AG rich; (persona, paese) rich, wealthy ▶ SM/F rich man/woman; **i ricchi** the rich; ~ **di** (idee, illustrazioni ecc) full of; (risorse, fauna ecc) rich in

ri'cerca, -che [ri'tʃerka] SF search; (indagine) investigation, inquiry; (studio): **la ~** research; **una ~** a piece of research; **mettersi alla ~ di**

to go in search of, look o search o hunt for;
essere alla ~ di to be searching for, be
looking for; **~ di mercato** market research;
~ operativa operational research

ricer'care [ritʃer'kare] /**20**/ vt (*motivi, cause*) to
look for, try to determine; (*successo, piacere*) to
pursue; (*onore, gloria*) to seek

ricerca'tezza [ritʃerka'tettsa] sf (*raffinatezza*)
refinement; (*peg*) affectation

ricer'cato, -a [ritʃer'kato] AG (*apprezzato*)
much sought-after; (*affettato*) studied,
affected ▶ sм/ғ (*Polizia*) wanted man/woman

ricerca'tore, -'trice [ritʃerka'tore] sм/ғ (*Ins*)
researcher

ricetrasmit'tente [ritʃetrazmit'tɛnte] sf
two-way radio, transceiver

ri'cetta [ri'tʃetta] sf (*Med*) prescription; (*Cuc*)
recipe; (*fig: antidoto*): **~ contro** remedy for

ricet'tacolo [ritʃet'takolo] sм (*peg: luogo
malfamato*) den

ricet'tario [ritʃet'tarjo] sм (*Med*) prescription
pad; (*Cuc*) recipe book

ricetta'tore, -'trice [ritʃetta'tore] sм/ғ (*Dir*)
receiver (of stolen goods)

ricettazi'one [ritʃettat'tsjone] sf (*Dir*)
receiving (stolen goods)

ricet'tivo, -a [ritʃet'tivo] AG receptive

rice'vente [ritʃe'vente] AG (*Radio, TV*)
receiving ▶ sм/ғ (*Comm*) receiver

ri'cevere [ri'tʃevere] /**29**/ vt to receive;
(*stipendio, lettera*) to get, receive; (*accogliere:
ospite*) to welcome; (*vedere: cliente,
rappresentante ecc*) to see; **"confermiamo di
aver ricevuto tale merce"** (*Comm*) "we
acknowledge receipt of these goods"

ricevi'mento [ritʃevi'mento] sм receiving *no
pl*; (*trattenimento*) reception; **al ~ della merce**
on receipt of the goods

ricevi'tore [ritʃevi'tore] sм (*Tecn*) receiver;
~ delle imposte tax collector

ricevito'ria [ritʃevito'ria] sғ (*Fisco*): **~ (delle
imposte)** Inland Revenue(BRIT) Office,
Internal Revenue (US) Office; **~ del lotto**
lottery office

rice'vuta [ritʃe'vuta] sғ receipt; **accusare ~
di qc** (*Comm*) to acknowledge receipt of sth;
~ fiscale official receipt (for tax purposes);
~ di ritorno (*Posta*) advice of receipt; **~ di
versamento** receipt of payment

ricezi'one [ritʃet'tsjone] sғ (*Radio, TV*)
reception

richia'mare [rikja'mare] /**72**/ vt (*chiamare
indietro, ritelefonare*) to call back; (*ambasciatore,
truppe*) to recall; (*rimproverare*) to reprimand;
(*attirare*) to attract, draw; **richiamarsi** vpr:
richiamarsi a (*riferirsi a*) to refer to; **~ qn
all'ordine** to call sb to order; **desidero ~ la
vostra attenzione su ...** I would like to
draw your attention to ...

richi'amo [ri'kjamo] sм call; recall;
reprimand; attraction

richie'dente [rikje'dɛnte] sмғ applicant

richi'edere [ri'kjɛdere] /**21**/ vt to ask again
for; (*chiedere: per sapere*) to ask; (: *per avere*) to
ask for; (*Amm: documenti*) to apply for;
(*esigere*) to need, require; (*chiedere indietro*):
~ qc to ask for sth back; **essere molto
richiesto** to be in great demand

richi'esto, -a [ri'kjɛsto] PP *di* **richiedere** ▶ sf
(*domanda*) request; (*Amm*) application,
request; (*esigenza*) demand, request; **a
richiesta** on request

rici'claggio [ritʃi'kladdʒo] sм (*fig*)
laundering; **~ di materiale** recycling; **~ di
denaro sporco** money laundering

rici'clare [ritʃi'klare] /**72**/ vt (*vetro, carta,
bottiglie*) to recycle; (*fig: personale*) to retrain

'ricino ['ritʃino] sм: **olio di ~** castor oil

ricogni'tore [rikoɲɲi'tore] sм (*Aer*)
reconnaissance aircraft

ricognizi'one [rikoɲɲit'tsjone] sf (*Mil*)
reconnaissance; (*Dir*) recognition,
acknowledgement

ricolle'gare /**80**/ vt (*collegare nuovamente: gen*)
to join again, link again; (*connettere: fatti*):
~ (a, con) to connect (with); **ricollegarsi** vpr:
ricollegarsi a (*fatti: connettersi*) to be
connected to; (*persona: riferirsi*) to refer to

ri'colmo, -a AG: **~ (di)** (*bicchiere*) full to the
brim (with); (*stanza*) full (of)

ricominci'are [rikomin'tʃare] /**14**/ vt, vi to
start again, begin again; **~ a fare qc** to begin
doing o to do sth again, start doing o to do
sth again

ricom'pensa sf reward

ricompen'sare /**72**/ vt to reward

ricom'porsi /**77**/ vpr to compose o.s.,
regain one's composure

ricom'posto, -a PP *di* **ricomporsi**

riconcili'are [rikontʃi'ljare] /**19**/ vt to
reconcile; **riconciliarsi** vpr to be
reconciled

riconciliazi'one [rikontʃiliat'tsjone] sf
reconciliation

ricon'dotto, -a PP *di* **ricondurre**

ricon'durre /**90**/ vt to bring (o take) back

ricon'ferma sf reconfirmation

riconfer'mare /**72**/ vt to reconfirm

ricongiungi'mento [rikondʒundʒi'mento]
sм (*di famiglia, coniugi*) reconciliation;
~ familiare (*Dir: di immigrati*) family
reunification

ricono'scente [rikonoʃʃɛnte] AG grateful

ricono'scenza [rikonoʃʃɛntsa] sf gratitude

rico'noscere [riko'noʃʃere] /**26**/ vt to
recognize; (*Dir: figlio, debito*) to acknowledge;
(*ammettere: errore*) to admit, acknowledge;
~ qn colpevole to find sb guilty

r

riconosci'mento [rikonoʃʃi'mento] SM
recognition; acknowledgement;
(*identificazione*) identification; **come ~ dei
servizi resi** in recognition of services
rendered; **documento di ~** means of
identification; **segno di ~** distinguishing
mark; **programma per il ~ vocale** (*Inform*)
voice recognition program

riconosci'uto, -a [rikonoʃʃuto] PP *di*
riconoscere

riconquis'tare /72/ VT (*Mil*) to reconquer;
(*libertà, stima*) to win back

rico'perto, -a PP *di* **ricoprire**

ricopi'are /19/ VT to copy

rico'prire /9/ VT to re-cover; (*coprire*) to cover;
(*occupare: carica*) to hold

ricor'dare /72/ VT to remember, recall;
(*richiamare alla memoria*): **~ qc a qn** to remind
sb of sth; **ricordarsi** VPR: **ricordarsi (di)** to
remember; **ricordarsi di qc/di aver fatto** to
remember sth/having done

ri'cordo SM memory; (*regalo*) keepsake,
souvenir; (*di viaggio*) souvenir; **ricordi** SMPL
(*memorie*) memoirs

ricor'rente AG recurrent, recurring

ricor'renza [rikor'rentsa] SF recurrence;
(*festività*) anniversary

ri'correre /28/ VI (*ripetersi*) to recur; **~ a**
(*rivolgersi*) to turn to; (*Dir*) to appeal to;
(*servirsi di*) to have recourse to; **~ in appello**
to lodge an appeal

ri'corso, -a PP *di* **ricorrere** ▶ SM recurrence;
(*Dir*) appeal; **far ~ a = ricorrere a**

ricostitu'ente AG (*Med*): **cura ~** tonic
treatment, tonic ▶ SM (*Med*) tonic

ricostitu'ire /55/ VT (*società*) to build up again;
(*governo, partito*) to re-form; **ricostituirsi** VPR
(*gruppo ecc*) to re-form

ricostru'ire /55/ VT (*casa*) to rebuild; (*fatti*) to
reconstruct

ricostruzi'one [rikostrut'tsjone] SF
rebuilding *no pl*, reconstruction

ri'cotta SF *soft white unsalted cheese made from
sheep's milk*

ricove'rare /72/ VT to give shelter to; **~ qn in
ospedale** to admit sb to hospital

ricove'rato, -a SM/F patient

ri'covero SM shelter, refuge; (*Mil*) shelter;
(*Med*) admission (to hospital); **~ antiaereo**
air-raid shelter

ricre'are /72/ VT to recreate; (*rinvigorire*) to
restore; (*fig: distrarre*) to amuse

ricrea'tivo, -a AG recreational

ricreazi'one [rikreat'tsjone] SF recreation,
entertainment; (*Ins*) break

ri'credersi /29/ VPR to change one's mind

ricupe'rare /72/ VT (*rientrare in possesso di*) to
recover, get back; (*tempo perduto*) to make up
for; (*Naut*) to salvage; (*: naufraghi*) to rescue;

(*delinquente*) to rehabilitate; **~ lo svantaggio**
(*Sport*) to close the gap

ri'cupero SM (*gen*) recovery; (*di relitto ecc*)
salvaging; **capacità di ~** resilience

ricu'sare /72/ VT to refuse

ridacchi'are [ridak'kjare] /19/ VI to snigger

ri'dare /33/ VT to return, give back

'**ridda** SF (*di ammiratori ecc*) swarm; (*di pensieri*)
jumble

ri'dente AG (*occhi, volto*) smiling; (*paesaggio*)
delightful

'**ridere** /89/ VI to laugh; (*deridere, beffare*): **~ di**
to laugh at, make fun of; **non c'è niente
da ~, c'è poco da ~** it's not a laughing
matter

rides'tare /72/ VT (*fig: ricordi, passioni*) to
reawaken

ri'detto, -a PP *di* **ridire**

ridico'laggine [ridiko'laddʒine] SF (*di
situazione*) absurdity; (*cosa detta o fatta*)
nonsense *no pl*

ridicoliz'zare [ridikolid'dzare] /72/ VT to
ridicule

ri'dicolo, -a AG ridiculous, absurd ▶ SM:
cadere nel ~ to become ridiculous;
rendersi ~ to make a fool of o.s.

ridimensiona'mento SM reorganization;
(*di fatto storico*) reappraisal

ridimensio'nare /72/ VT to reorganize; (*fig*)
to see in the right perspective

ri'dire /38/ VT to repeat; (*criticare*) to find fault
with; to object to; **trova sempre qualcosa
da ~** he always manages to find fault

ridon'dante AG redundant

ri'dosso SM: **a ~ di** (*dietro*) behind; (*contro*)
against

ri'dotto, -a PP *di* **ridurre** ▶ AG (*biglietto*)
reduced; (*formato*) small

ri'duco *etc* VB *vedi* **ridurre**

ri'durre /90/ VT (*anche Chim, Mat*) to reduce;
(*prezzo, spese*) to cut, reduce; (*accorciare: opera
letteraria*) to abridge; (*Radio, TV*) to adapt;
ridursi VPR (*diminuirsi*) to be reduced, shrink;
ridursi a to be reduced to; **ridursi a pelle e
ossa** to be reduced to skin and bone

ri'dussi *etc* VB *vedi* **ridurre**

ridut'tore SM (*Tecn, Chim*) reducer; (*Elettr*)
adaptor

riduzi'one [ridut'tsjone] SF reduction;
abridgement; adaptation

ri'ebbi *etc* VB *vedi* **riavere**

riecheg'giare [rieked'dʒare] /62/ VI to
re-echo

riedu'care /20/ VT (*persona, arto*) to re-educate;
(*malato*) to rehabilitate

rieducazi'one [riedukat'tsjone] SF
re-education; rehabilitation; **centro di ~**
rehabilitation centre

rie'leggere [rie'lɛddʒere] /61/ VT to re-elect

rie'letto, -a PP di **rieleggere**

riempi'mento SM filling (up)

riem'pire /**91**/ VT (modulo) to fill in o out; **riempirsi** VPR to fill (up); (mangiare troppo) to stuff o.s.; **~ qc di** to fill sth (up) with

riempi'tivo, -a AG filling ▶ SM (anche fig) filler

rien'tranza [rien'trantsa] SF recess; indentation

rien'trare /**72**/ VI (entrare di nuovo) to go (o come) back in; (tornare) to return; (fare una rientranza) to go in, curve inwards; to be indented; (riguardare): **~ in** to be included among, form part of; **~ (a casa)** to get back home; **non rientriamo nelle spese** we are not within our budget

ri'entro SM (ritorno) return; (di astronave) re-entry; **è iniziato il grande ~** (estivo) people are coming back from their (summer) holidays

riepilo'gare /**80**/ VT to summarize ▶ VI to recapitulate

rie'pilogo, -ghi SM recapitulation; **fare un ~ di qc** to summarize sth

rie'same SM re-examination

riesami'nare /**72**/ VT to re-examine

ri'esco etc VB vedi **riuscire**

ri'essere /**51**/ VI: **ci risiamo!** (col) we're back to this again!

rievo'care /**20**/ VT (passato) to recall; (commemorare: figura, meriti) to commemorate

rievocazi'one [rievokat'tsjone] SF (vedi vt) recalling; commemoration

rifaci'mento [rifatʃi'mento] SM (di film) remake; (di opera letteraria) rehashing

ri'fare /**53**/ VT to do again; (ricostruire) to make again; (nodo) to tie again, do up again; (imitare) to imitate, copy; **rifarsi** VPR (risarcirsi): **rifarsi di** to make up for; (vendicarsi): **rifarsi di qc su qn** to get one's own back on sb for sth; (riferirsi): **rifarsi a** (periodo, fenomeno storico) to go back to; to follow; **~ il letto** to make the bed; **rifarsi una vita** to make a new life for o.s

ri'fatto, -a PP di **rifare**

riferi'mento SM reference; **in** o **con ~ a** with reference to; **far ~ a** to refer to

rife'rire /**55**/ VT (riportare) to report; (ascrivere): **~ qc a** to attribute sth to ▶ VI to do a report; **riferirsi** VPR: **riferirsi a** to refer to; **riferirò** I'll pass on the message

rifi'lare /**72**/ VT (tagliare a filo) to trim; (col: affibbiare): **~ qc a qn** to palm sth off on sb

rifi'nire /**55**/ VT to finish off, put the finishing touches to

rifini'tura SF finishing touch; **rifiniture** SFPL (di mobile, auto) finish sg

rifiu'tare /**72**/ VT to refuse; **~ di fare** to refuse to do

rifi'uto SM refusal; **rifiuti** SMPL (spazzatura) rubbish sg, refuse sg; **rifiuti solidi urbani** solid urban waste sg

riflessi'one SF (Fisica, meditazione) reflection; (il pensare) thought, reflection; (osservazione) remark

rifles'sivo, -a AG (persona) thoughtful, reflective; (Ling) reflexive

ri'flesso, -a PP di **riflettere** ▶ SM (di luce, allo specchio) reflection; (Fisiol) reflex; (su capelli) light; (fig) effect; **di** o **per ~** indirectly; **avere i riflessi pronti** to have quick reflexes

riflessolo'gia [riflessolo'dʒia] SF: **~ (plantare)** reflexology

ri'flettere /**92**/ VT to reflect ▶ VI to think; **riflettersi** VPR to be reflected; (ripercuotersi) **riflettersi su** to have repercussions on; **~ su** to think over

riflet'tore SM reflector; (proiettore) floodlight; (Mil) searchlight

ri'flusso SM flowing back; (della marea) ebb; **un'epoca di ~** an era of nostalgia

rifocil'larsi [rifotʃil'larsi] /**72**/ VPR (poetico) to take refreshment

rifondazi'one [rifondat'tsjone] SF (Pol): **R~ Comunista** hard left party, originating from former P.C.I.

ri'fondere /**25**/ VT (rimborsare) to refund, repay; **~ le spese a qn** to refund sb's expenses; **~ i danni a qn** to compensate sb for damages

ri'forma SF reform; (Mil) declaration of unfitness for service; discharge (on health grounds); **la R~** (Rel) the Reformation

rifor'mare /**72**/ VT to re-form; (cambiare, innovare) to reform; (Mil: recluta) to declare unfit for service; (: soldato) to invalid out, discharge

riforma'tore, -'trice AG reforming ▶ SM/F reformer

riforma'torio SM (Dir) community home (BRIT), reformatory (US)

rifor'mista, -i, -e AG, SM/F reformist

riforni'mento SM supplying, providing; restocking; (di carburante) refuelling; **rifornimenti** SMPL (provviste) supplies, provisions; **fare ~ di** (viveri) to stock up with; (benzina) to fill up with; **posto di ~** filling o gas (US) station

rifor'nire /**55**/ VT (fornire di nuovo: casa ecc) to restock; (provvedere): **~ di** to supply o provide with; **rifornirsi** VPR: **rifornirsi di qc** to stock up on sth

ri'frangere [ri'frandʒere] /**37**/ VT to refract

ri'fratto, -a PP di **rifrangere**

rifrazi'one [rifrat'tsjone] SF refraction

rifug'gire [rifud'dʒire] /**31**/ VI to escape again; (fig): **~ da** to shun

rifugi'arsi [rifu'dʒarsi] /**62**/ VPR to take refuge

rifugi'ato, -a [rifu'dʒato] SM/F refugee

ri'fugio [ri'fudʒo] sм refuge, shelter; (*in montagna*) shelter; ~ **antiaereo** air-raid shelter

ri'fuso, -a pp *di* **rifondere**

'riga, -ghe sF line; (*striscia*) stripe; (*di persone, cose*) line, row; (*regolo*) ruler; (*scriminatura*) parting; **mettersi in ~** to line up; **a righe** (*foglio*) lined; (*vestito*) striped; **buttare giù due righe** (*note*) to jot down a few notes; **mandami due righe appena arrivi** drop me a line as soon as you arrive

ri'gagnolo [ri'gaɲɲolo] sм rivulet

ri'gare/80/ vт (*foglio*) to rule ▶ vı: ~ **diritto** (*fig*) to toe the line

rigassifica'tore sм regasification terminal

riga'toni sмPL (*Cuc*) short, ridged pasta shapes

rigatti'ere sм junk dealer

riga'tura sF (*di pagina, quaderno*) lining, ruling; (*di fucile*) rifling

rigene'rare [ridʒene'rare] /72/ vт (*gen, Tecn*) to regenerate; (*forze*) to restore; (*gomma*) to retread; **rigenerarsi**vPR (*gen*) to regenerate; (*ramo, tumore*) to regenerate, grow again; **gomma rigenerata** retread

rigenerazi'one [ridʒenerat'tsjone] sF regeneration

riget'tare [ridʒet'tare] /72/ vт (*gettare indietro*) to throw back; (*fig: respingere*) to reject; (*vomitare*) to bring o throw up

ri'getto [ri'dʒɛtto] sм (*anche Med*) rejection

ri'ghello [ri'gɛllo] sм ruler

righeròetc [rige'rɔ] vв *vedi* **rigare**

rigi'dezza [ridʒi'dettsa], **rigidità** [ridʒidi'ta] sF rigidity, stiffness, severity, rigours pl (*BRIT*), rigors pl (*US*); strictness

'rigido, -a ['ridʒido] AG rigid, stiff; (*membra ecc*: *indurite*) stiff; (*Meteor*) harsh, severe; (*fig*) strict

rigi'rare [ridʒi'rare] /72/ vт to turn; **rigirarsi** vPR to turn round; (*nel letto*) to turn over; ~ **qc tra le mani** to turn sth over in one's hands; ~ **il discorso** to change the subject

'rigo, -ghi sм line; (*Mus*) staff, stave

rigogli'oso, -a [rigoʎ'ʎoso] AG (*pianta*) luxuriant; (*fig: commercio, sviluppo*) thriving

rigonfia'mento sм (*Anat*) swelling; (*su legno, intonaco ecc*) bulge

ri'gonfio, -a AG swollen; (*grembiule, sporta*): ~ **di** bulging with

ri'gore sм (*Meteor*) harshness, rigours pl (*BRIT*), rigors pl (*US*); (*fig*) severity, strictness; (*anche*: **calcio di rigore**) penalty; **di ~** compulsory; **"è di ~ l'abito da sera"** "evening dress"; **area di ~** (*Calcio*) penalty box (*BRIT*); **a rigor di termini** strictly speaking

rigorosità sF strictness; rigour (*BRIT*), rigor (*US*)

rigo'roso, -a AG (*severo: persona, ordine*) strict; (*preciso*) rigorous

rigover'nare/72/ vт to wash (up)

riguar'dare/72/ vт to look at again; (*considerare*) to regard, consider; (*concernere*) to regard, concern; **riguardarsi**vPR (*aver cura di sé*) to look after o.s.; **per quel che mi riguarda** as far as I'm concerned; **sono affari che non ti riguardano** it's none of your business

rigu'ardo sм (*attenzione*) care; (*considerazione*) regard, respect; ~ **a** concerning, with regard to; **per ~ a** out of respect for; **ospite/ persona di ~** very important guest/person; **non aver riguardi nell'agire/nel parlare** to act/speak freely

riguar'doso, -a AG (*rispettoso*) respectful; (*premuroso*) considerate, thoughtful

rigurgi'tare [rigurdʒi'tare] /72/ vı (*liquido*): ~ **da** to gush out from; (*recipiente: traboccare*) ~ **di** to overflow with

ri'gurgito [ri'gurdʒito] sм (*Med*) regurgitation; (*fig: ritorno, risveglio*) revival

rilanci'are [rilan'tʃare] /14/ vт (*lanciare di nuovo: gen*) to throw again; (: *moda*) to bring back; (: *prodotto*) to re-launch; ~ **un'offerta** (*asta*) to make a higher bid

ri'lancio [ri'lantʃo] sм (*Carte: di offerta*) raising

rilasci'are [rilaʃ'ʃare] /14/ vт (*rimettere in libertà*) to release; (*Amm: documenti*) to issue; (*intervista*) to give; ~ **delle dichiarazioni** to make a statement

ri'lascio [ri'laʃʃo] sм release; issue

rilassa'mento sм (*gen, Med*) relaxation

rilas'sare/72/ vт to relax; **rilassarsi**vPR to relax; (*fig: disciplina*) to become slack

rilassa'tezza [rilassa'tettsa] sF (*fig: di costumi, disciplina*) laxity

rilas'sato, -a AG (*persona, muscoli*) relaxed; (*disciplina, costumi*) lax

rile'gare/80/ vт (*libro*) to bind

rilega'tura sF binding

ri'leggere [ri'lɛddʒere] /61/ vт to reread, read again; (*rivedere*) to read over

ri'lento: a ~ av slowly

ri'letto, -a pp *di* **rileggere**

rilet'tura sF (*vedi vt*) rereading; reading over

rileva'mento sм (*topografico, statistico*) survey; (*Naut*) bearing

rile'vante AG considerable; important

rile'vanza [rile'vantsa] sF importance

rile'vare/72/ vт (*ricavare*) to find; (*notare*) to notice; (*mettere in evidenza*) to point out; (*venire a conoscere: notizia*) to learn; (*raccogliere: dati*) to gather, collect; (*Topografia*) to survey; (*Mil*) to relieve; (*Comm*) to take over

rilevazi'one [rilevat'tsjone] sF survey

rili'evo sм (*Arte, Geo*) relief; (*fig: rilevanza*) importance; (*osservazione*) point, remark; (*Topografia*) survey; **dar ~ a** o **mettere in ~ qc** (*fig*) to bring sth out, highlight sth; **di poco/**

nessun ~ (*fig*) of little/no importance; **un personaggio di** ~ an important person

rilut'tante AG reluctant

rilut'tanza [rilut'tantsa] SF reluctance

'**rima** SF rhyme; (*verso*) verse; **far** ~ **con** to rhyme with; **rispondere a qn per le rime** to give sb tit for tat

riman'dare /**72**/ VT to send again; (*restituire, rinviare*) to send back, return; ~ **qc (a)** (*differire*) to postpone sth o put sth off (till); ~ **qn a** (*fare riferimento*) to refer sb to; **essere rimandato** (*Ins*) to have to resit one's exams

ri'mando SM (*rinvio*) return; (*dilazione*) postponement; (*riferimento*) cross-reference

rimaneggi'are [rimaned'dʒare] /**62**/ VT (*testo*) to reshape, recast; (*Pol*) to reshuffle

rima'nente AG remaining ▶ SM rest, remainder; **i rimanenti** (*persone*) the rest of them, the others

rima'nenza [rima'nɛntsa] SF rest, remainder; **rimanenze** SFPL (*Comm*) unsold stock *sg*

rima'nere /**93**/ VI (*restare*) to remain, stay; (*avanzare*) to be left, remain; (*restare stupito*) to be amazed; **rimangono poche settimane a Pasqua** there are only a few weeks left till Easter; ~ **vedovo** to be left a widower; ~ **confuso/sorpreso** to be confused/surprised; **rimane da vedere se** it remains to be seen whether

rimangi'are [riman'dʒare] /**62**/ VT to eat again; **rimangiarsi la parola/una promessa** (*fig*) to go back on one's word/one's promise

ri'mango *etc* VB *vedi* **rimanere**

ri'mare /**72**/ VT, VI to rhyme

rimargi'nare [rimardʒi'nare] /**72**/ VT, VI (*anche*: **rimarginarsi**) to heal

ri'masto, -a PP *di* **rimanere**

rima'sugli [rima'suʎʎi] SMPL leftovers

rimbal'zare [rimbal'tsare] /**72**/ VI to bounce back, rebound; (*proiettile*) to ricochet

rim'balzo [rim'baltso] SM rebound; ricochet

rimbam'bire /**55**/ VI to be in one's dotage; (*rincretinire*) to grow foolish

rimbam'bito, -a AG senile, in one's dotage; (*col*): **un vecchio** ~ a doddering old man

rimbec'care /**20**/ VT (*persona*) to answer back; (*offesa*) to return

rimbecil'lire [rimbetʃil'lire] /**55**/ VI, **rimbecil'lirsi** VPR to become stupid

rimboc'care /**20**/ VT (*orlo*) to turn up; (*coperta*) to tuck in; (*maniche, pantaloni*) to turn o roll up

rimbom'bare /**72**/ VI to resound; (*artiglieria*) to boom; (*tuono*) to rumble

rim'bombo SM (*vedi vi*) boom; rumble

rimbor'sare /**72**/ VT to pay back, repay; ~ **qc a qn** to reimburse sb for sth

rim'borso SM repayment; (*di spese, biglietto*) refund; ~ **d'imposta** tax rebate

rimboschi'mento [rimboski'mento] SM reafforestation

rimbos'chire [rimbos'kire] /**55**/ VT to reafforest

rimbrot'tare /**72**/ VT to reproach

rim'brotto SM reproach

rimedi'are /**19**/ VI: ~ **a** to remedy ▶ VT (*col: procurarsi*) to get o scrape together; ~ **da vivere** to scrape a living

ri'medio SM (*medicina*) medicine; (*cura, fig*) remedy, cure; **porre** ~ **a qc** to remedy sth; **non c'è** ~ there's no way out, there's nothing to be done about it

rimesco'lare /**72**/ VT to mix well, stir well; (*carte*) to shuffle; **sentirsi** ~ **il sangue** (*per rabbia*) to feel one's blood boil

ri'messa SF (*locale: per veicoli*) garage; (*: per aerei*) hangar; (*Comm: di merce*) consignment; (*: di denaro*) remittance; (*Tennis*) return; (*Calcio: anche*: **rimessa in gioco**) throw-in

ri'messo, -a PP *di* **rimettere**

rimes'tare /**72**/ VT (*mescolare*) to mix well, stir well; (*fig: passato*) to drag up again

ri'mettere /**63**/ VT (*mettere di nuovo*) to put back; (*Comm: merci*) to deliver; (*: denaro*) to remit; (*vomitare*) to bring up; (*perdere: anche*: **rimetterci**) to lose; (*indossare di nuovo*): ~ **qc** to put sth back on, put sth on again; (*restituire*) to return, give back; (*affidare*) to entrust; (*decisione*) to refer; (*condonare*) to remit; **rimettersi** VPR: **rimettersi a** (*affidarsi*) to trust; ~ **a nuovo** (*casa ecc*) to do up (BRIT) o over (US); **rimetterci di tasca propria** to be out of pocket; **rimettersi al bello** (*tempo*) to clear up; **rimettersi in cammino** to set off again; **rimettersi al lavoro** to start working again; **rimettersi in salute** to get better, recover one's health

rimi'nese AG (*o from*) Rimini

ri'misi *etc* VB *vedi* **rimettere**

'**rimmel** ® SM INV mascara

rimoderna'mento SM modernization

rimoder'nare /**72**/ VT to modernize

ri'monta SF (*Sport: gen*) recovery

rimon'tare /**72**/ VT (*meccanismo*) to reassemble; (*tenda*) to put up again ▶ VI (*salire di nuovo*): ~ **in** (*macchina, treno*) to get back into; (*Sport*) to close the gap

rimorchi'are [rimor'kjare] /**19**/ VT to tow; (*fig: ragazza*) to pick up

rimorchia'tore [rimorkja'tore] SM (*Naut*) tug(boat)

ri'morchio [ri'mɔrkjo] SM tow; (*veicolo*) trailer; **andare a** ~ to be towed; **prendere a** ~ to tow; **cavo da** ~ towrope; **autocarro con** ~ articulated lorry (BRIT), semi(trailer) (US)

ri'morso SM remorse; **avere il** ~ **di aver fatto qc** to deeply regret having done sth

ri'mosso, -a PP *di* **rimuovere**

r

rimos'tranza [rimos'trantsa] SF protest, complaint; **fare le proprie rimostranze a qn** to remonstrate with sb

rimozi'one [rimot'tsjone] SF removal; (*da un impiego*) dismissal; (*Psic*) repression; **"~ forzata"** "illegally parked vehicles will be removed at owner's expense"

rimpas'tare /72/ VT (*Pol*: *ministero*) to reshuffle

rim'pasto SM (*Pol*) reshuffle; **~ ministeriale** cabinet reshuffle

rimpatri'are /19/ VI to return home ▶ VT to repatriate

rim'patrio SM repatriation

rimpi'angere [rim'pjandʒere] /75/ VT to regret; (*persona*) to miss; **~ di (non) aver fatto qc** to regret (not) having done sth

rimpi'anto, -a PP *di* **rimpiangere** ▶ SM regret

rimpiat'tino SM hide-and-seek

rimpiaz'zare [rimpjat'tsare] /72/ VT to replace

rimpiccio'lire [rimpittʃo'lire] /55/ VT to make smaller ▶ VI (*anche*: **rimpicciolirsi**) to become smaller

rimpin'zare [rimpin'tsare] /72/ VT: **~ di** to cram *o* stuff with; **rimpinzarsi** VPR: **rimpinzarsi (di qc)** to stuff o.s. (with sth)

rimprove'rare /72/ VT to rebuke, reprimand

rim'provero SM rebuke, reprimand; **di ~** (*tono, occhiata*) reproachful; (*parole*) of reproach

rimugi'nare [rimudʒi'nare] /72/ VT (*fig*) to turn over in one's mind

rimune'rare /72/ VT (*retribuire*) to remunerate; (*ricompensare*: *sacrificio ecc*) to reward; **un lavoro ben rimunerato** a well-paid job

rimunera'tivo, -a AG (*lavoro, attività*) remunerative, profitable

rimunerazi'one [rimunerat'tsjone] SF remuneration; (*premio*) reward

rimu'overe /66/ VT to remove; (*destituire*) to dismiss; (*fig*: *distogliere*) to dissuade

rinascimen'tale [rinaʃʃimen'tale] AG Renaissance *cpd*, of the Renaissance

Rinasci'mento [rinaʃʃi'mento] SM: **il ~** the Renaissance

ri'nascita [ri'naʃʃita] SF rebirth, revival

rincal'zare [rinkal'tsare] /72/ VT (*palo, albero*) to support, prop up; (*lenzuola*) to tuck in

rin'calzo [rin'kaltso] SM support, prop; (*rinforzo*) reinforcement; (*Sport*) reserve (player); **rincalzi** SMPL (*Mil*) reserves

rinca'rare /72/ VT to increase the price of ▶ VI to go up, become more expensive; **~ la dose** (*fig*) to pile it on

rin'caro SM: **~ (di)** (*prezzi, costo della vita*) increase (in); (*prodotto*) increase in the price (of)

rinca'sare /72/ VI to go home

rinchi'udere [rin'kjudere] /22/ VT to shut (*o lock*) up; **rinchiudersi** VPR: **rinchiudersi in** to shut o.s. up in; **rinchiudersi in se stesso** to withdraw into o.s.

rinchi'uso, -a [rin'kjuso] PP *di* **rinchiudere**

rincitrul'lirsi [rintʃitrul'lirsi] /55/ VPR to grow foolish

rin'correre /28/ VT to chase, run after

rin'corso, -a PP *di* **rincorrere** ▶ SF short run

rin'crescere [rin'kreʃʃere] /30/ VB IMPERS: **mi rincresce che/di non poter fare** I'm sorry that/I can't do, I regret that/being unable to do

rincresci'mento [rinkreʃʃi'mento] SM regret

rincresci'uto, -a [rinkreʃ'ʃuto] PP *di* **rincrescere**

rincu'lare /72/ VI to draw back; (*arma*) to recoil

rinfacci'are [rinfat'tʃare] /14/ VT (*fig*): **~ qc a qn** to throw sth in sb's face

rinfoco'lare /72/ VT (*fig*: *odio, passioni*) to rekindle; (: *risentimento, rabbia*) to stir up

rinfor'zare [rinfor'tsare] /72/ VT to reinforce, strengthen ▶ VI (*anche*: **rinforzarsi**) to grow stronger

rin'forzo [rin'fortso] SM: **mettere un ~ a** to strengthen; **rinforzi** SMPL (*Mil*) reinforcements; **di ~** (*asse, sbarra*) strengthening; (*esercito*) supporting; (*personale*) extra, additional

rinfran'care /20/ VT to encourage, reassure

rinfres'cante AG (*bibita*) refreshing

rinfres'care /20/ VT (*atmosfera, temperatura*) to cool (down); (*abito, pareti*) to freshen up ▶ VI (*tempo*) to grow cooler; **rinfrescarsi** VPR (*ristorarsi*) to refresh o.s.; (*lavarsi*) to freshen up; **~ la memoria a qn** to refresh sb's memory

rin'fresco, -schi SM (*festa*) party; **rinfreschi** SMPL (*cibi e bevande*) refreshments

rin'fusa SF: **alla ~** in confusion, higgledy-piggledy

ringhi'are [rin'gjare] /19/ VI to growl, snarl

ringhi'era [rin'gjɛra] SF railing; (*delle scale*) banister(s)

'ringhio ['ringjo] SM growl, snarl

ringhi'oso, -a [rin'gjoso] AG growling, snarling

ringiova'nire [rindʒova'nire] /55/ VT: **~ qn** (*vestito, acconciatura ecc*) to make sb look younger; (*vacanze ecc*) to rejuvenate sb ▶ VI (*anche*: **ringiovanirsi**) to become (*o* look) younger

ringrazia'mento [ringrattsja'mento] SM thanks *pl*; **lettera/biglietto di ~** thank you letter/card

ringrazi'are [ringrat'tsjare] /19/ VT to thank; **~ qn di qc** to thank sb for sth; **~ qn per aver fatto qc** to thank sb for doing sth

rinne'gare /80/ VT (*fede*) to renounce; (*figlio*) to disown, repudiate

rinne'gato, -a SM/F renegade

rinno'vabile AG (*contratto, energia*) renewable

rinnova'mento SM renewal; (*economico*) revival

rinno'vare/72/ VT to renew; (*ripetere*) to repeat, renew; **rinnovarsi** VPR (*fenomeno*) to be repeated, recur

rin'novo SM (*di contratto*) renewal; **"chiuso per ~ (dei) locali"** (*negozio*) "closed for alterations"

rinoce'ronte [rinotʃe'ronte] SM rhinoceros

rino'mato, -a AG renowned, celebrated

rinsal'dare/72/ VT to strengthen

rinsa'vire/55/ VI to come to one's senses

rinsec'chito, -a [rinsek'kito] AG (*vecchio, albero*) thin, gaunt

rinta'narsi/72/ VPR (*animale*) to go into its den; (*persona: nascondersi*) to hide

rintoc'care/20/ VI (*campana*) to toll; (*orologio*) to strike

rin'tocco, -chi SM toll

rintracci'are [rintrat'tʃare] /14/ VT to track down; (*persona scomparsa, documento*) to trace

rintro'nare/72/ VI to boom, roar ▶ VT (*assordare*) to deafen; (*stordire*) to stun

rintuz'zare [rintut'tsare] /72/ VT (*fig: sentimento*) to check, repress; (*: accusa*) to refute

ri'nuncia [ri'nuntʃa] SF renunciation; **~ a** (*carica*) resignation from; (*eredità*) relinquishment of; **~ agli atti del giudizio** (*Dir*) abandonment of a claim

rinunci'are [rinun'tʃare] /14/ VI: **~ a** to give up, renounce; **~ a fare qc** to give up doing sth

rinuncia'tario, -a [rinuntʃa'tarjo] AG defeatist

ri'nunzia*etc* [ri'nuntsja] = **rinuncia** *ecc*

rinveni'mento SM (*ritrovamento*) recovery; (*scoperta*) discovery; (*Metallurgia*) tempering

rinve'nire/128/ VT to find, recover; (*scoprire*) to discover, find out ▶ VI (*riprendere i sensi*) to come round; (*riprendere l'aspetto naturale*) to revive

rinve'nuto, -a PP *di* **rinvenire**

rinver'dire/55/ VI (*bosco, ramo*) to become green again

rinvi'are/60/ VT (*rimandare indietro*) to send back, return; **~ qc (a)** (*differire*) to postpone sth o put sth off (till) (*: seduta*) to adjourn sth (till); **~ qn a** (*fare un rimando*) to refer sb to; **~ a giudizio** (*Dir*) to commit for trial

rinvigo'rire/55/ VT to strengthen

rin'vio, -'vii SM (*rimando*) return; (*differimento*) postponement; (*: di seduta*) adjournment; (*in un testo*) cross-reference; **~ a giudizio** (*Dir*) indictment

riò*etc* VB *vedi* **riavere**

'Rio de Ja'neiro ['riodedʒa'neiro] SF Rio de Janeiro

rio'nale AG (*mercato, cinema*) local, district *cpd*

ri'one SM district, quarter

riordina'mento SM (*di ente, azienda*) reorganization

riordi'nare/72/ VT (*rimettere in ordine*) to tidy; (*riorganizzare*) to reorganize

riorganiz'zare [riorganid'dzare] /72/ VT to reorganize

riorganizzazi'one [riorganiddzat'tsjone] SF reorganization

ripa'gare/80/ VT to repay

ripa'rare/72/ VT (*proteggere*) to protect, defend; (*correggere: male, torto*) to make up for; (*: errore*) to put right; (*aggiustare*) to repair ▶ VI (*mettere rimedio*): **~ a** to make up for; **ripararsi** VPR (*rifugiarsi*) to take refuge o shelter

ripa'rato, -a AG (*posto*) sheltered

riparazi'one [riparat'tsjone] SF (*di un torto*) reparation; (*di guasto, scarpe*) repairing no pl; repair; (*risarcimento*) compensation; (*Ins*): **esame di ~** resit (*BRIT*), test retake (*US*)

ri'paro SM (*protezione*) shelter, protection; (*rimedio*) remedy; **al ~ da** (*sole, vento*) sheltered from; **mettersi al ~** to take shelter; **correre ai ripari** (*fig*) to take remedial action

ripar'tire/45/ VT (*dividere*) to divide up; (*distribuire*) to share out, distribute ▶ VI to set off again; to leave again; (*motore*) to start again

ripartizi'one [ripartit'tsjone] SF division sharing out, distribution; (*Amm: dipartimento*) department

ripas'sare/72/ VI to come (o go) back ▶ VT (*scritto, lezione*) to go over (again)

ri'passo SM (*di lezione*) revision (*BRIT*), review (*US*)

ripensa'mento SM second thoughts *pl* (*BRIT*), change of mind; **avere un ~** to have second thoughts, change one's mind

ripen'sare/72/ VI to think; (*cambiare idea*) to change one's mind; (*tornare col pensiero*): **~ a** to recall; **a ripensarci ...** on thinking it over ...

riper'correre/28/ VT (*itinerario*) to travel over again; (*strada*) to go along again; (*fig: ricordi, passato*) to go back over

riper'corso, -a PP *di* **ripercorrere**

riper'cosso, -a PP *di* **ripercuotersi**

ripercu'otersi/106/ VPR: **~ su** (*fig*) to have repercussions on

ripercussi'one SF (*fig*): **avere una ~ o delle ripercussioni su** to have repercussions on

ripes'care/20/ VT (*pesce*) to catch again; (*persona, cosa*) to fish out; (*fig: ritrovare*) to dig out

ripe'tente SMF student repeating the year, repeater (*US*)

ri'petere/1/ VT to repeat; (*ripassare*) to go over

ripeti'tore SM (*Radio, TV*) relay

r

ripetizi'one [ripetit'tsjone] SF repetition; (di lezione) revision; **ripetizioni** (Ins) private tutoring o coaching sg; **fucile a ~** repeating rifle

ripetuta'mente AV repeatedly, again and again

ripi'ano SM (Geo) terrace; (di mobile) shelf

ri'picca SF: **per ~** out of spite

'ripido, -a AG steep

ripiega'mento SM (Mil) retreat

ripie'gare /80/ VT to refold; (piegare più volte) to fold (up) ▶ VI (Mil) to retreat, fall back; (fig: accontentarsi): **~ su** to make do with; **ripiegarsi** VPR to bend

ripi'ego, -ghi SM expedient; **una soluzione di ~** a makeshift solution

ripi'eno, -a AG full; (Cuc) stuffed; (: panino) filled ▶ SM (Cuc) stuffing

ri'pone VB vedi **riporre**

ri'pongo etc VB vedi **riporre**

ri'porre /77/ VT (porre al suo posto) to put back, replace; (mettere via) to put away; (fiducia, speranza): **~ qc in qn** to place o put sth in sb

ripor'tare /72/ VT (portare indietro) to bring (o take) back; (riferire) to report; (citare) to quote; (ricevere) to receive, get; (vittoria) to gain; (successo) to have; (Mat) to carry; (Comm) to carry forward; **riportarsi** VPR: **riportarsi a** (anche fig) to go back to; (riferirsi a) to refer to; **~ danni** to suffer damage; **ha riportato gravi ferite** he was seriously injured

ri'porto SM amount carried over; amount carried forward

ripo'sante AG (gen) restful; (musica, colore) soothing

ripo'sare /72/ VT (bicchiere, valigia) to put down; (dare sollievo) to rest ▶ VI to rest; **riposarsi** VPR to rest; **qui riposa ...** (su tomba) here lies ...

ripo'sato, -a AG (viso, aspetto) rested; (mente) fresh

ri'posi etc VB vedi **riporre**

ri'poso SM rest; (Mil): **~!** at ease!; **a ~** (in pensione) retired; **giorno di ~** day off; **"oggi ~"** (Cine, Teat) "no performance today"; (ristorante) "closed today"

ripos'tiglio [ripos'tiʎʎo] SM lumber room (BRIT), storage room (US)

ri'posto, -a PP di **riporre** ▶ AG (fig: senso, significato) hidden

ri'prendere /81/ VT (prigioniero, fortezza) to recapture; (prendere indietro) to take back; (ricominciare: lavoro) to resume; (andare a prendere) to fetch, come back for; (assumere di nuovo: impiegati) to take on again, re-employ; (rimproverare) to tell off; (restringere: abito) to take in; (Cine) to shoot; **riprendersi** VPR to recover; (correggersi) to correct o.s.; **~ a fare qc** to start doing sth again; **~ il cammino** to set off again; **~ i sensi** to recover consciousness; **~ sonno** to go back to sleep

ripresen'tare /72/ VT (certificato) to submit again; (domanda) to put forward again; (persona) to introduce again; **ripresentarsi** VPR (ritornare: persona) to come back; (: occasione) to arise again; **ripresentarsi a** (esame) to sit (BRIT) o take (US) again; (concorso) to enter again; **ripresentarsi come candidato** (Pol) to stand (BRIT) o run (US) again (as a candidate)

ri'preso, -a PP di **riprendere** ▶ SF recapture; resumption; (economica, da malattia, emozione) recovery; (Aut) acceleration no pl; (Teat, Cine) rerun; (Cine: presa) shooting no pl; shot; (Sport) second half; (Pugilato) round; **a più riprese** on several occasions, several times; **ripresa cinematografica** shot

ripristi'nare /72/ VT to restore

ri'pristino SM (gen) restoration; (di tradizioni) revival

ripro'dotto, -a PP di **riprodurre**

ripro'durre /90/ VT to reproduce; **riprodursi** VPR (Biol) to reproduce; (riformarsi) to form again

riprodut'tivo, -a AG reproductive

riprodut'tore, -'trice AG (organo) reproductive ▶ SM: **~ acustico** pick-up; **~ a cassetta** cassette player

riproduzi'one [riprodut'tsjone] SF reproduction; **~ vietata** all rights reserved

ripro'messo, -a PP di **ripromettersi**

ripro'mettersi /63/ VT (aspettarsi): **~ qc da** to expect sth from; (intendere): **~ di fare qc** to intend to do sth

ripro'porre /77/ VT: **riproporsi di fare qc** to intend to do sth

ripro'posto, -a PP di **riproporre**

ri'prova SF confirmation; **a ~ di** as confirmation of

ripro'vare /72/ VT (provare di nuovo: gen) to try again; (: vestito) to try on again; (: sensazione) to experience again ▶ VI (tentare): **~ (a fare qc)** to try (to do sth) again; **riproverò più tardi** I'll try again later

ripro'vevole AG reprehensible

ripudi'are /19/ VT to repudiate, disown

ri'pudio SM repudiation, disowning

ripu'gnante [ripuɲ'ɲante] AG disgusting, repulsive

ripu'gnanza [ripuɲ'ɲantsa] SF repugnance, disgust

ripu'gnare [ripuɲ'ɲare] /15/ VI: **~ a qn** to repel o disgust sb

ripu'lire /55/ VT to clean up; (ladri) to clean out; (perfezionare) to polish, refine

ripulsi'one SF (Fisica, fig) repulsion

ri'quadro SM square; (Archit) panel

RIS [ris] SIGLA M (= *Reparto Investigazioni Scientifiche*) ≈ CID, *branch of the Carabinieri*

ri'sacca, -che SF backwash

ri'saia SF paddy field

risa'lire/98/ VI (*ritornare in su*) to go back up; ~ **a** (*ritornare con la mente*) to go back to; (*datare da*) to date back to, go back to

risa'lita SF: **mezzi di** ~ (*Sci*) ski lifts

risal'tare/72/ VI (*fig: distinguersi*) to stand out; (*Archit*) to project, jut out

ri'salto SM prominence; (*sporgenza*) projection; **mettere** o **porre in** ~ **qc** to make sth stand out

risana'mento SM (*economico*) improvement; (*bonifica*) reclamation; ~ **del bilancio** reorganization of the budget; ~ **edilizio** building improvement

risa'nare/72/ VT (*guarire*) to heal, cure; (*palude*) to reclaim; (*economia*) to improve; (*bilancio*) to reorganize

risa'pere/99/ VT: ~ **qc** to come to know of sth

risa'puto, -a AG: **è** ~ **che ...** everyone knows that ..., it's common knowledge that ...

risarci'mento [risartʃi'mento] SM: ~ **(di)** compensation (for); **aver diritto al** ~ **dei danni** to be entitled to damages

risar'cire [risar'tʃire] **/55/** VT (*cose*) to pay compensation for; (*persona*) ~ **qn di qc** to compensate sb for sth; ~ **i danni a qn** to pay sb damages

ri'sata SF laugh

riscalda'mento SM heating; ~ **centrale** central heating

riscal'dare/72/ VT (*scaldare*) to heat; (*: mani, persona*) to warm; (*: minestra*) to reheat; **riscaldarsi**VPR to warm up

ris'caldo SM (*col*) (slight) inflammation

riscat'tare/72/ VT (*prigioniero*) to ransom, pay a ransom for; (*Dir*) to redeem; **riscattarsi**VPR (*da disonore*) to redeem o.s.

ris'catto SM ransom; redemption

rischia'rare [riskja'rare] **/72/** VT (*illuminare*) to light up; (*colore*) to make lighter; **rischiararsi**VPR (*tempo*) to clear up; (*cielo*) to clear; (*fig: volto*) to brighten up; **rischiararsi la voce** to clear one's throat

rischi'are [ris'kjare] **/19/** VT to risk ▶ VI: ~ **di fare qc** to risk o run the risk of doing sth

'rischio ['riskjo] SM risk; **a** ~ (*zona, situazione*) at risk, vulnerable; **a proprio** ~ **e pericolo** at one's own risk; **correre il** ~ **di fare qc** to run the risk of doing sth; ~ **del mestiere** occupational hazard

rischi'oso, -a[ris'kjoso] AG risky, dangerous

risciac'quare [riʃʃak'kware] **/72/** VT to rinse

risci'acquo [riʃʃakkwo] SM rinse

riscon'trare/72/ VT (*confrontare: due cose*) to compare; (*esaminare*) to check, verify; (*rilevare*) to find

ris'contro SM comparison check, verification; (*Amm: lettera di risposta*) reply; **mettere a** ~ to compare; **in attesa di un vostro cortese** ~ we look forward to your reply

risco'perto, -a PP *di* **riscoprire**

risco'prire/9/ VT to rediscover

riscossi'one SF collection

ris'cosso, -a PP *di* **riscuotere** ▶ SF (*riconquista*) recovery, reconquest

riscri'vibile AG (CD, DVD) rewritable

riscu'otere/106/ VT (*ritirare una somma dovuta*) to collect; (*: stipendio*) to draw, collect; (*: assegno*) to cash; (*fig: successo ecc*) to win, earn; **riscuotersi**VPR: **riscuotersi (da)** to shake o.s. (out of), rouse o.s. (from); ~ **un assegno** to cash a cheque

'riseetc VB vedi **ridere**

risenti'mento SM resentment

risen'tire/45/ VT to hear again; (*provare*) to feel ▶ VI: ~ **di** to feel (o show) the effects of; **risentirsi**VPR: **risentirsi di** o **per** to take offence (BRIT) o offense (US) at, resent

risen'tito, -a AG resentful

ri'serbo SM reserve

ri'serva SF reserve; (*di caccia, pesca*) preserve; (*restrizione, di indigeni*) reservation; (*Calcio*) substitute; **fare** ~ **di** (*cibo*) to get in a supply of; **tenere di** ~ to keep in reserve; **con le dovute riserve** with certain reservations; **ha accettato con la** ~ **di potersi ritirare** he accepted with the proviso that he could pull out

riser'vare/72/ VT (*tenere in serbo*) to keep, put aside; (*prenotare*) to book, reserve; **riservarsi**VPR: **riservarsi di fare qc** to intend to do sth; **riservarsi il diritto di fare qc** to reserve the right to do sth

riserva'tezza [riserva'tettsa] SF reserve

riser'vato, -a AG (*prenotato: fig: persona*) reserved; (*confidenziale: lettera, informazione*) confidential

'risietc VB vedi **ridere**

ri'sibile AG laughable

risi'cato, -a AG (*vittoria ecc*) very narrow

risi'edere/29/ VI: ~ **a** o **in** to reside in

'risma SF (*di carta*) ream; (*fig*) kind, sort

'riso¹, -a PP *di* **ridere** ▶ SM (*pl(f)* **risa**) (*il ridere*): **un** ~ a laugh; **il** ~ laughter; **uno scoppio di risa** a burst of laughter

'riso² SM (*pianta*) rice

riso'lino SM snigger

risolle'vare/72/ VT (*sollevare di nuovo: testa*) to raise again, lift up again; (*fig: questione*) to raise again, bring up again; (*morale*) to raise; **risollevarsi**VPR (*da terra*) to rise again; (*fig: da malattia*) to recover; ~ **le sorti di qc** to improve the chances of sth

ri'solsietc VB vedi **risolvere**

ri'solto, -a PP *di* **risolvere**

risolu'tezza [risolu'tettsa] SF determination

risolu'tivo, -a AG (*determinante*) decisive; (*che risolve*): **arrivare ad una formula risolutiva** to come up with a formula to resolve a situation

riso'luto, -a AG determined, resolute

risoluzi'one [risolut'tsjone] SF solving *no pl*; (*Mat*) solution; (*decisione, di schermo, immagine*) resolution; (*Dir: di contratto*) annulment, cancellation

ri'solvere /**94**/ VT (*difficoltà, controversia*) to resolve; (*problema*) to solve; (*decidere*): **~ di fare** to resolve to do; **risolversi** VPR (*decidersi*): **risolversi a fare** to make up one's mind to do; (*andare a finire*): **risolversi in** to end up, turn out; **risolversi in nulla** to come to nothing

risol'vibile AG solvable

riso'nanza [riso'nantsa] SF resonance; **aver vasta ~** (*fig: fatto ecc*) to be known far and wide; **~ magnetica** magnetic resonance

riso'nare /**72**/ VT, VI = **risuonare**

ri'sorgere [ri'sordʒere] /**109**/ VI to rise again

risorgimen'tale [risordʒimen'tale] AG of the Risorgimento

risorgi'mento [risordʒi'mento] SM revival; **il R~** (*Storia*) the Risorgimento; *see note*

> The *Risorgimento*, the period stretching from the early nineteenth century to 1861 and the proclamation of the Kingdom of Italy, saw considerable upheaval and change. Political and personal freedom took on new importance as the events of the French Revolution unfolded. The *Risorgimento* paved the way for the unification of Italy in 1871.

ri'sorsa SF expedient, resort; **risorse** SFPL (*naturali, finanziarie ecc*) resources; **persona piena di risorse** resourceful person; **risorse umane** human resources

ri'sorsi *etc* VB *vedi* **risorgere**

ri'sorto, -a PP *di* **risorgere**

ri'sotto SM (*Cuc*) risotto

risparmi'are /**19**/ VT to save; (*non uccidere*) to spare ▶ VI to save; **~ qc a qn** to spare sb sth; **~ fatica/fiato** to save one's energy/breath; **risparmiati il disturbo** *o* **la fatica** (*anche ironico*) save yourself the trouble

risparmia'tore, -'trice SM/F saver

ris'parmio SM saving *no pl*; (*denaro*) savings *pl*; **risparmi** SMPL (*denaro*) savings

rispecchi'are [rispek'kjare] /**19**/ VT to reflect; **rispecchiarsi** VPR to be reflected

rispe'dire /**55**/ VT to send back; **~ qc a qn** to send sth back to sb

rispet'tabile AG respectable; (*considerevole: somma*) sizeable, considerable

rispet'tare /**72**/ VT to respect; (*legge*) to obey, comply with, abide by; (*promessa*) to keep; **farsi ~** to command respect; **~ le distanze** to keep one's distance; **~ i tempi** to keep to schedule; **ogni medico che si rispetti** every self-respecting doctor

rispettiva'mente AV respectively

rispet'tivo, -a AG respective

ris'petto SM respect; **rispetti** SMPL (*saluti*) respects, regards; **~ a** (*in paragone a*) compared to; (*in relazione a*) as regards, as for; **~ (di** *o* **per)** (*norme, leggi*) observance (of), compliance (with); **portare ~ a qn/qc** to have *o* feel respect for sb/sth; **mancare di ~ a qn** to be disrespectful to sb; **con ~ parlando** with respect, if you will excuse my saying so; **(porga) i miei rispetti alla signora** (give) my regards to your wife

rispet'toso, -a AG respectful

risplen'dente AG (*giornata, sole*) bright, shining; (*occhi*) sparkling

ris'plendere /**29**/ VI to shine

rispon'dente AG: **~ a** in keeping *o* conformity with

rispon'denza [rispon'dɛntsa] SF correspondence

ris'pondere /**95**/ VI to answer, reply; (*freni*) to respond; **~ a** (*domanda*) to answer, reply to; (*persona*) to answer; (*invito*) to reply to; (*provocazione, veicolo, apparecchio*) to respond to; (*corrispondere a*) to correspond to (: *speranze, bisogno*) to answer; **~ a qn di qc** (*essere responsabile*) to be answerable to sb for sth

rispo'sarsi /**72**/ VPR to get married again, remarry

ris'posto, -a PP *di* **rispondere** ▶ SF answer, reply; **in risposta a** in reply to; **dare una risposta** to give an answer; **diamo risposta alla vostra lettera del ...** in reply to your letter of ...

'rissa SF brawl

ris'soso, -a AG quarrelsome

rist. ABBR = **ristampa**

ristabi'lire /**55**/ VT to re-establish, restore; (*persona, riposo ecc*) to restore to health; **ristabilirsi** VPR to recover

rista'gnare [ristaɲ'ɲare] /**15**/ VI (*acqua*) to become stagnant; (*sangue*) to cease flowing; (*fig: industria*) to stagnate

ris'tagno [ris'taɲɲo] SM stagnation; **c'è un ~ delle vendite** business is slack

ris'tampa SF reprinting *no pl*; reprint

ristam'pare /**72**/ VT to reprint

risto'rante SM restaurant

risto'rare /**72**/ VT (*persona, forze*) to revive, refresh; **ristorarsi** VPR (*rifocillarsi*) to have something to eat and drink; (*riposarsi*) to rest, have a rest

ristora'tore, -'trice AG refreshing, reviving ► SM (*gestore di ristorante*) restaurateur

ris'toro SM (*bevanda, cibo*) refreshment; **posto di ~** (Ferr) buffet, snack bar; **servizio di ~** (Ferr) refreshments *pl*

ristret'tezza [ristret'tettsa] SF (*strettezza*) narrowness; (*fig: scarsezza*) scarcity, lack; (: *meschinità*) meanness; **ristrettezze** SFPL (*povertà*) poverty *sg*

ris'tretto, -a PP *di* **restringere** ► AG (*racchiuso*) enclosed, hemmed in; (*angusto*) narrow; (Cuc: *brodo*) thick; (: *caffè*) extra strong; **~ (a)** (*limitato*) restricted *o* limited (to)

ristruttu'rare /72/ VT (*azienda*) to reorganize; (*edificio*) to restore; (*appartamento*) to alter; (*crema, balsamo*) to repair

ristrutturazi'one [ristrutturat'tsjone] SF reorganization; restoration; alteration

risucchi'are [risuk'kjare] /19/ VT to suck in

ri'succhio [ri'sukkjo] SM (*di acqua*) undertow, pull; (*di aria*) suction

risul'tare /72/ VI (*dimostrarsi*) to prove (to be), turn out (to be); (*riuscire*): **~ vincitore** to emerge as the winner; **~ da** (*provenire*) to result from, be the result of; **mi risulta che ...** I understand that ..., as far as I know .; **(ne) risulta che ...** it follows that ...; **non mi risulta** not as far as I know

risul'tato SM result

risuo'nare /72/ VI (*rimbombare*) to resound

risurrezi'one [risurret'tsjone] SF (Rel) resurrection

risusci'tare [risuʃʃi'tare] /72/ VT to resuscitate, restore to life; (*fig*) to revive, bring back ► VI to rise (from the dead)

risvegli'are [rizveʎ'ʎare] /27/ VT (*gen*) to wake up, waken; (*fig: interesse*) to stir up, arouse; (: *curiosità*) to arouse; (: *dall'inerzia ecc*): **~ qn (da)** to rouse sb (from); **risvegliarsi** VPR to wake up, awaken; (*fig: interesse, curiosità*) to be aroused

ris'veglio [riz'veʎʎo] SM waking up; (*fig*) revival

ris'volto SM (*di giacca*) lapel; (*di pantaloni*) turn-up (BRIT), cuff (US); (*di manica*) cuff; (*di tasca*) flap; (*di libro*) inside flap; (*fig*) implication

ritagli'are [ritaʎ'ʎare] /27/ VT (*tagliar via*) to cut out

ri'taglio [ri'taʎʎo] SM (*di giornale*) cutting, clipping; (*di stoffa ecc*) scrap; **nei ritagli di tempo** in one's spare time

ritar'dare /72/ VI (*persona, treno*) to be late; (*orologio*) to be slow ► VT (*rallentare*) to slow down; (*impedire*) to delay, hold up; (*differire*) to postpone, delay; **~ il pagamento** to defer payment

ritarda'tario, -a SM/F latecomer

ritar'dato, -a AG (Psic) retarded

ri'tardo SM delay; (*di persona aspettata*) lateness *no pl*; (*fig: mentale*) backwardness; **in ~** late

ri'tegno [ri'teɲɲo] SM restraint

ritem'prare /72/ VT (*forze, spirito*) to restore

rite'nere /121/ VT (*trattenere*) to hold back; (: *somma*) to deduct; (*giudicare*) to consider, believe

ri'tengo VB *vedi* **ritenere**

ri'tenni *etc* VB *vedi* **ritenere**

riten'tare /72/ VT to try again, make another attempt at

rite'nuta SF (*sul salario*) deduction; **~ d'acconto** advance deduction of tax; **~ alla fonte** (*Fisco*) taxation at source

riterrò *etc* VB *vedi* **ritenere**

ritiene *etc* VB *vedi* **ritenere**

riti'rare /72/ VT to withdraw; (Pol: *richiamare*) to recall; (*andare a prendere: pacco ecc*) to collect, pick up; **ritirarsi** VPR to withdraw; (*da un'attività*) to retire; (*stoffa*) to shrink; (*marea*) to recede; **gli hanno ritirato la patente** they disqualified him from driving (BRIT), they took away his licence (BRIT) *o* license (US); **ritirarsi a vita privata** to withdraw from public life

riti'rata SF (Mil) retreat; (*latrina*) lavatory

riti'rato, -a AG secluded; **fare vita ritirata** to live in seclusion

ri'tiro SM (*di truppe, candidati, soldi*) withdrawal; (*di pacchi*) collection; (*di passaporto*) confiscation; (*da attività*) retirement; (*luogo appartato*) retreat

rit'mato, -a AG rhythmic(al)

'ritmico, -a, -ci, -che AG rhythmic(al)

'ritmo SM rhythm; (*fig*) rate; (: *della vita*) pace, tempo; **al ~ di** at a speed *o* rate of; **ballare al ~ di valzer** to waltz

'rito SM rite; **di ~** usual, customary

ritoc'care /20/ VT (*disegno, fotografia*) to touch up; (*testo*) to alter

ri'tocco, -chi SM touching up *no pl*; alteration

ri'torcere [ri'tɔrtʃere] /106/ VT (*filato*) to twist; (*fig: accusa, insulto*) to throw back; **ritorcersi** VPR (*tornare a danno di*): **ritorcersi contro** to turn against

ritor'nare /72/ VI to return, go (*o* come) back, get back; (*ripresentarsi*) to recur; (*ridiventare*): **~ ricco** to become rich again ► VT (*restituire*) to return, give back

ritor'nello SM refrain

ri'torno SM return; **durante il (viaggio di) ~** on the return trip, on the way back; **al ~** (*tornando*) on the way back; **essere di ~** to be back; **far ~** to return; **avere un ~ di fiamma** (Aut) to backfire; (*fig: persona*) to be back in love again

ritorsi'one SF (*rappresaglia*) retaliation

ri'torto, -a PP *di* **ritorcere** ► AG (*cotone, corda*) twisted

r

ri'trarre /123/ VT (*trarre indietro, via*) to withdraw; (*distogliere: sguardo*) to turn away; (*rappresentare*) to portray, depict; (*ricavare*) to get, obtain; **ritrarsi** VPR to move back

ritrat'tare /72/ VT (*disdire*) to retract, take back; (*trattare nuovamente*) to deal with again

ritrattazi'one [ritrattat'tsjone] SF withdrawal

ritrat'tista, -i, -e SM/F portrait painter

ri'tratto, -a PP *di* **ritrarre** ▶ SM portrait

ritro'sia SF (*riluttanza*) reluctance, unwillingness; (*timidezza*) shyness

ri'troso, -a AG (*restio*): ~ **(a)** reluctant (to); (*schivo*) shy; **andare a ~** to go backwards

ritrova'mento SM (*di cadavere, oggetto smarrito ecc*) finding; (*oggetto ritrovato*) find

ritro'vare /72/ VT to find; (*salute*) to regain; (*persona*) to find; to meet again; **ritrovarsi** VPR (*essere, capitare*) to find o.s.; (*raccapezzarsi*) to find one's way; (*con senso reciproco*) to meet (again)

ritro'vato SM discovery

ri'trovo SM meeting place; ~ **notturno** night club

'ritto, -a AG (*in piedi*) standing, on one's feet; (*levato in alto*) erect, raised; (: *capelli*) standing on end; (*posto verticalmente*) upright

ritu'ale AG, SM ritual

ritwit'tare [ritwit'tare] VT (*su Twitter*) to retweet

riuni'one SF (*adunanza*) meeting; (*riconciliazione*) reunion; **essere in ~** to be at a meeting

riu'nire /55/ VT (*ricongiungere*) to join (together); (*riconciliare*) to reunite, bring together (again); **riunirsi** VPR (*adunarsi*) to meet; (*tornare a stare insieme*) to be reunited; **siamo qui riuniti per festeggiare il vostro anniversario** we are gathered here to celebrate your anniversary

riu'scire [riuʃʃire] /125/ VI (*uscire di nuovo*) to go out again, go back out; (*aver esito: fatti, azioni*) to go, turn out; (*aver successo*) to succeed, be successful; (*essere, apparire*) to be, prove; (*raggiungere il fine*) to manage, succeed; ~ **a fare qc** to manage o be able to do sth; **questo mi riesce nuovo** this is new to me

riu'scita [riuʃʃita] SF (*esito*) result, outcome; (*buon esito*) success

riutiliz'zare [riutilid'dzare] /72/ VT to use again, re-use

'riva SF (*di fiume*) bank; (*di lago, mare*) shore; **in ~ al mare** on the (sea) shore

ri'vale AG rival *cpd* ▶ SMF rival; **non avere rivali** (*anche fig*) to be unrivalled

rivaleggi'are [rivaled'dʒare] /62/ VI to compete, vie

rivalità SF rivalry

ri'valsa SF (*rivincita*) revenge; (*risarcimento*) compensation; **prendersi una ~ su qn** to take revenge on sb

rivalu'tare /72/ VT (*Econ*) to revalue

rivalutazi'one [rivalutat'tsjone] SF (*Econ*) revaluation; (*fig*) re-evaluation

rivan'gare /80/ VT (*ricordi ecc*) to dig up (again)

rive'dere /127/ VT to see again; (*ripassare*) to revise; (*verificare*) to check

rivedrò *etc* VB *vedi* **rivedere**

rive'lare /72/ VT to reveal; (*divulgare*) to reveal, disclose; (*dare indizio*) to reveal, show; **rivelarsi** VPR (*manifestarsi*) to be revealed; **rivelarsi onesto** *etc* to prove to be honest *etc*

rivela'tore, -'trice AG revealing ▶ SM (*Tecn*) detector; (*Fot*) developer

rivelazi'one [rivelat'tsjone] SF revelation

ri'vendere /29/ VT (*vendere: di nuovo*) to resell, sell again; (: *al dettaglio*) to retail, sell retail

rivendi'care /20/ VT to claim, demand

rivendicazi'one [rivendikat'tsjone] SF claim; **rivendicazioni salariali** wage claims

ri'vendita SF (*bottega*) retailer's (shop); ~ **di tabacchi** tobacconist's (shop)

rivendi'tore, -'trice SM/F retailer; ~ **autorizzato** (*Comm*) authorized dealer

riverbe'rare /72/ VT to reflect

ri'verbero SM (*di luce, calore*) reflection; (*di suono*) reverberation

rive'rente AG reverent, respectful

rive'renza [rive'rɛntsa] SF reverence; (*inchino*) bow; curtsey

rive'rire /55/ VT (*rispettare*) to revere; (*salutare*) to pay one's respects to

river'sare /72/ VT (*anche fig*) to pour; **riversarsi** VPR (*fig: persone*) to pour out

rivesti'mento SM covering; coating

rives'tire /45/ VT to dress again; (*ricoprire*) to cover; (*con vernice*) to coat; (*fig: carica*) to hold; **rivestirsi** VPR to get dressed again, to change (one's clothes); ~ **di piastrelle** to tile

ri'vidi *etc* VB *vedi* **rivedere**

rivi'era SF coast; **la ~ italiana** the Italian Riviera

ri'vincita [ri'vintʃita] SF (*Sport*) return match; (*fig*) revenge; **prendersi la ~ (su qn)** to take o get one's revenge (on sb)

rivis'suto, -a PP *di* **rivivere**

ri'vista SF review; (*periodico*) magazine, review; (*Teat*) revue; variety show

ri'visto, -a PP *di* **rivedere**

rivitaliz'zante [rivitalid'dzante] AG revitalizing

rivitaliz'zare [rivitalid'dzare] /72/ VT to revitalize

ri'vivere /130/ VI (*riacquistare forza*) to come alive again; (*tornare in uso*) to be revived ▶ VT to relive

'**rivo** SM stream

ri'volgere [ri'vɔldʒere] /**96**/ VT (*attenzione, sguardo*) to turn, direct; (*parole*) to address; **rivolgersi** VPR to turn round; **rivolgersi a** (*fig: dirigersi per informazioni*) to go and see, go and speak to (: *ufficio*) to enquire at; ~ **un'accusa/una critica a qn** to accuse/ criticize sb; **rivolgersi all'ufficio competente** to apply to the office concerned

rivolgi'mento [rivoldʒi'mento] SM upheaval

ri'volsi etc VB vedi **rivolgere**

ri'volta SF revolt, rebellion

rivol'tante AG revolting, disgusting

rivol'tare /**72**/ VT to turn over; (*con l'interno all'esterno*) to turn inside out; (*disgustare: stomaco*) to upset, turn; (: *fig*) to revolt, disgust; **rivoltarsi** VPR (*ribellarsi*): **rivoltarsi (a)** to rebel (against)

rivol'tella SF revolver

ri'volto, -a PP di **rivolgere**

rivol'toso, -a AG rebellious ► SM/F rebel

rivoluzio'nare [rivoluttsjo'nare] /**72**/ VT to revolutionize

rivoluzio'nario, -a [rivoluttsjo'narjo] AG, SM/F revolutionary

rivoluzi'one [rivolut'tsjone] SF revolution

riz'zare [rit'tsare] /**72**/ VT to raise, erect; **rizzarsi** VPR to stand up; (*capelli*) to stand on end; **rizzarsi in piedi** to stand up, get to one's feet

RN SIGLA = **Rimini**

RNA SIGLA M RNA (= *ribonucleic acid*)

RO SIGLA = **Rovigo**

'**roba** SF stuff, things pl; (*possessi, beni*) belongings pl, things pl, possessions pl; ~ **da mangiare** things to eat, food; ~ **da matti!** it's sheer madness o lunacy!

robi'vecchi [robi'vɛkki] SM INV/F INV junk dealer

'**robot** SM INV robot

ro'botica SF robotics sg

robus'tezza [robus'tettsa] SF (*di persona, pianta*) robustness, sturdiness; (*di edificio, ponte*) soundness

ro'busto, -a AG robust, sturdy; (*solido: catena*) strong; (: *edificio, ponte*) sound, solid; (: *vino*) full-bodied

'**rocca, -che** SF fortress

rocca'forte SF stronghold

roc'chetto [rok'ketto] SM reel, spool

'**roccia, -ce** ['rɔttʃa] SF rock; **fare ~** (*Sport*) to go rock climbing

roccia'tore, -'trice [rottʃa'tore] SM/F rock climber

rocci'oso, -a [rot'tʃoso] AG rocky; **le Montagne Rocciose** the Rocky Mountains

'**roco, -a, -chi, -che** AG hoarse

ro'daggio [ro'daddʒo] SM running (BRIT) o breaking (US) in; **in ~** running o breaking in; **periodo di ~** (*fig*) period of adjustment

'**Rodano** SM: **il ~** the Rhone

ro'dare /**72**/ VT (*Aut, Tecn*) to run (BRIT) o break (US) in

ro'deo SM rodeo

rodere /**49**/ VT to gnaw (at); (*distruggere poco a poco*) to eat into

'**Rodi** SF Rhodes

rodi'tore SM (*Zool*) rodent

rodo'dendro SM rhododendron

'**rogito** ['rɔdʒito] SM (*Dir*) (notary's) deed

'**rogna** ['rɔɲɲa] SF (*Med*) scabies sg; (*di animale*) mange; (*fig*) bother, nuisance

ro'gnone [roɲ'ɲone] SM (*Cuc*) kidney

ro'gnoso, -a [roɲ'ɲoso] AG (*persona*) scabby; (*animale*) mangy; (*fig*) troublesome

'**rogo, -ghi** SM (*per cadaveri*) (funeral) pyre; (*supplizio*): **il ~** the stake

rol'lare /**72**/ VI (*Naut, Aer*) to roll

rol'lino SM = **rullino**

rol'lio SM roll(ing)

'**Roma** SF Rome

roma'gnolo, -a [romaɲ'ɲɔlo] AG of (o from) Romagna

roma'nesco, -a, -schi, -sche AG Roman ► SM Roman dialect

Roma'nia SF: **la ~** Romania

ro'manico, -a, -ci, -che AG Romanesque

ro'mano, -a AG, SM/F Roman; **fare alla romana** to go Dutch

romantiche'ria [romantike'ria] SF sentimentality

romanti'cismo [romanti'tʃizmo] SM romanticism

ro'mantico, -a, -ci, -che AG romantic

ro'manza [ro'mandza] SF (*Mus, Letteratura*) romance

roman'zare [roman'dzare] /**72**/ VT to romanticize

roman'zesco, -a, -schi, -sche [roman'dzesko] AG (*stile, personaggi*) fictional; (*fig*) storybook cpd

romanzi'ere [roman'dzjɛre] SM novelist

ro'manzo, -a [ro'mandzo] AG (*Ling*) romance cpd ► SM (*medievale*) romance; (*moderno*) novel; ~ **d'amore** love story; ~ **d'appendice** serial (story); ~ **cavalleresco** tale of chivalry; ~ **poliziesco**, ~ **giallo** detective story; ~ **rosa** romantic novel

rom'bare /**72**/ VI to rumble, thunder, roar

'**rombo** SM rumble, thunder, roar; (*Mat*) rhombus; (*Zool*) turbot; brill

ro'meno, -a AG, SM/F, SM = **rumeno**

'**rompere** /**97**/ VT to break; (*conversazione, fidanzamento*) to break off ► VI to break; **rompersi** VPR to break; **mi rompe le**

scatole (col) he (o she) is a pain in the neck; **rompersi un braccio** to break an arm
rompi'capo SM worry, headache; (indovinello) puzzle; (in enigmistica) brain-teaser
rompi'collo SM daredevil
rompighi'accio [rompi'gjattʃo] SM (Naut) icebreaker
rompis'catole SM O F INV (col) pest, pain in the neck
'ronda SF (Mil) rounds pl, patrol
ron'della SF (Tecn) washer
'rondine SF (Zool) swallow
ron'done SM (Zool) swift
ron'fare /72/ VI (russare) to snore
ron'zare [ron'dzare] /72/ VI to buzz, hum
ron'zino [ron'dzino] SM (peg: cavallo) nag
ron'zio, -ii [ron'dzio] SM buzzing, humming; ~ **auricolare** (Med) tinnitus sg
'rosa SF rose; (fig: gruppo): ~ **dei candidati** list of candidates ▶ AG INV, SM pink
ro'saio SM (pianta) rosebush, rose tree; (giardino) rose garden
ro'sario SM (Rel) rosary
ro'sato, -a AG pink, rosy ▶ SM (vino) rosé (wine)
ro'seo, -a AG (anche fig) rosy
ro'seto SM rose garden
ro'setta SF (diamante) rose-cut diamond; (rondella) washer
'rosi VB vedi **rodere**
rosicchi'are [rosik'kjare] /19/ VT to gnaw (at); (mangiucchiare) to nibble (at)
rosma'rino SM rosemary
'roso, -a PP di **rodere**
roso'lare /72/ VT (Cuc) to brown
roso'lia SF (Med) German measles sg, rubella
ro'sone SM rosette; (vetrata) rose window
'rospo SM (Zool) toad; **mandar giù** o **ingoiare un** o **il** ~ (fig) to swallow a bitter pill; **sputa il** ~**!** out with it!
ros'setto SM (per labbra) lipstick; (per guance) rouge
ros'siccio, -a, -ci, -ce [ros'sittʃo] AG reddish
'rosso, -a AG, SM, SM/F red; **diventare** ~ **(per la vergogna)** to blush o go red (with o for shame); **il mar R**~ the Red Sea; ~ **d'uovo** egg yolk
ros'sore SM flush, blush
rosticce'ria [rostittʃe'ria] SF shop selling roast meat and other cooked food
'rostro SM rostrum; (becco) beak
ro'tabile AG (percorribile): **strada** ~ roadway; (Ferr) **materiale** ~ rolling stock
ro'taia SF rut, track; (Ferr) rail
ro'tare /72/ VT, VI to rotate
rota'tivo, -a AG rotating, rotation cpd
rotazi'one [rotat'tsjone] SF rotation
rote'are /72/ VT, VI to whirl; ~ **gli occhi** to roll one's eyes

ro'tella SF small wheel; (di mobile) castor
roto'calco, -chi SM (Tip) rotogravure; (rivista) illustrated magazine
roto'lare /72/ VT, VI to roll; **rotolarsi** VPR to roll (about)
roto'lio SM rolling
'rotolo SM (di carta, stoffa) roll; (di corda) coil; **andare a rotoli** (fig) to go to rack and ruin; **mandare a rotoli** (fig) to ruin
ro'tondo, -a AG round ▶ SF rotunda
ro'tore SM rotor
'rotta SF (Aer, Naut) course, route; (Mil) rout; **a** ~ **di collo** at breakneck speed; **essere in** ~ **con qn** to be on bad terms with sb; **fare** ~ **su** o **per** o **verso** to head for o towards; **cambiare** ~ (anche fig) to change course; **in** ~ **di collisione** on a collision course; **ufficiale di** ~ navigator, navigating officer
rotta'mare /72/ VT to scrap old vehicles in return for incentives
rottama'zione [rottamat'tsjone] SF (come incentivo) the scrapping of old vehicles in return for incentives
rot'tame SM fragment, scrap, broken bit; **rottami** SMPL (di nave, aereo ecc) wreckage sg; **rottami di ferro** scrap iron sg
'rotto, -a PP di **rompere** ▶ AG broken; (calzoni) torn, split; (persona: pratico, resistente): ~ **a** accustomed o inured to ▶ SM: **per il** ~ **della cuffia** by the skin of one's teeth; **rotti** SMPL: **20 euro e rotti** 20-odd euros
rot'tura SF (azione) breaking no pl; break; (di rapporti) breaking off; (Med) fracture, break
rou'lotte [ru'lɔt] SF INV caravan
ro'vente AG red-hot
'rovere SM oak
ro'vescia [ro'veʃʃa] SF: **alla** ~ upside-down; inside-out; **oggi mi va tutto alla** ~ everything is going wrong (for me) today
rovesci'are [roveʃ'ʃare] /14/ VT (versare in giù) to pour; (: accidentalmente) to spill; (capovolgere) to turn upside down; (gettare a terra) to knock down; (fig: governo) to overthrow; (piegare all'indietro: testa) to throw back; **rovesciarsi** VPR (sedia, macchina) to overturn; (barca) to capsize; (liquido) to spill; (fig: situazione) to be reversed
ro'vescio, -sci [ro'veʃʃo] SM other side, wrong side; (della mano) back; (di moneta) reverse; (pioggia) sudden downpour; (fig) setback; (Maglia: anche: **punto rovescio**) purl (stitch); (Tennis) backhand (stroke); **a** ~ (sottosopra) upside-down; (con l'esterno all'interno) inside-out; **capire qc a** ~ to misunderstand sth; ~ **di fortuna** setback
ro'vina SF ruin; **rovine** SFPL (ruderi) ruins; **andare in** ~ (andare a pezzi) to collapse; (fig) to go to rack and ruin; **mandare qc/qn in** ~ to ruin sth/sb

rovi'nare /72/ vi to collapse, fall down ▶ vt (*far cadere giù: casa*) to demolish; (*danneggiare: fig*) to ruin; **rovinarsi** vpr (*persona*) to ruin o.s.; (*oggetto, vestito*) to be ruined

rovi'nato, -a ag ruined, damaged; (*fig: persona*) ruined

rovi'noso, -a ag ruinous

rovis'tare /72/ vt (*casa*) to ransack; (*tasche*) to rummage in (*o* through)

'rovo sm (*Bot*) blackberry *o* bramble bush

roz'zezza [rod'dzettsa] sf roughness, coarseness

'rozzo, -a ['roddzo] ag rough, coarse

RP sigla fpl *vedi* **relazioni pubbliche**

Rr abbr (*Posta*) = **raccomandata con ricevuta di ritorno**

R.R. abbr (*Posta*) = **ricevuta di ritorno**

RSVP abbr (= *répondez s'il vous plaît*) RSVP

'ruba sf: **andare a ~** to sell like hot cakes

rubacu'ori sm inv ladykiller

ru'bare /72/ vt to steal; **~ qc a qn** to steal sth from sb

rubi'condo, -a ag ruddy

rubi'netto sm tap, faucet (*US*)

ru'bino sm ruby

ru'bizzo, -a [ru'bittso] ag lively, sprightly

'rublo sm rouble

ru'brica, -che sf (*di giornale: colonna*) column; (*: pagina*) page; (*quadernetto*) index book; address book; **~ d'indirizzi** address book; **~ telefonica** list of telephone numbers

'rude ag tough, rough

'rudere sm (*rovina*) ruins *pl*

rudimen'tale ag rudimentary, basic

rudi'menti smpl rudiments; basic principles; basic knowledge *sg*

ruffi'ano sm pimp

'ruga, -ghe sf wrinkle

'ruggine ['ruddʒine] sf rust

rug'gire [rud'dʒire] /55/ vi to roar

rug'gito [rud'dʒito] sm roar

rugi'ada [ru'dʒada] sf dew

ru'goso, -a ag wrinkled; (*scabro: superficie ecc*) rough

rul'lare /72/ vi (*tamburo, nave*) to roll; (*aereo*) to taxi

rul'lino sm (*Fot*) (roll of) film, spool

rul'lio, -ii sm (*di tamburi*) roll

'rullo sm (*di tamburi*) roll; (*arnese cilindrico, Tip*) roller; **~ compressore** steam roller; **~ di pellicola** roll of film

rum sm rum

ru'meno, -a ag, sm/f, sm Romanian

rumi'nante sm (*Zool*) ruminant

rumi'nare /72/ vt (*Zool*) to ruminate; (*fig*) to ruminate on *o* over, chew over

ru'more sm: **un ~** a noise, a sound; **il ~** noise; **fare ~** to make a noise; **un ~ di passi** the sound of footsteps; **la notizia ha fatto molto ~** (*fig*) the news aroused great interest

rumoreggi'are [rumored'dʒare] /62/ vi (*tuono ecc*) to rumble; (*fig: folla*) to clamour (Brit), clamor (*US*)

rumo'roso, -a ag noisy

ru'olo sm (*Teat, fig*) role, part; (*elenco*) roll, register, list; **di ~** permanent, on the permanent staff; **professore di ~** (*Ins*) ≈ lecturer with tenure; **fuori ~** (*personale, insegnante*) temporary

ru'ota sf wheel; **a ~** (*forma*) circular; **~ anteriore/posteriore** front/back wheel; **andare a ~ libera** to freewheel; **parlare a ~ libera** (*fig*) to speak freely; **~ di scorta** spare wheel

ruo'tare /72/ vt, vi to rotate

'rupe sf cliff, rock

ru'pestre ag rocky

ru'pia sf rupee

'ruppi *etc* vb *vedi* **rompere**

ru'rale ag rural, country *cpd*

ru'scello [ruʃ'ʃɛllo] sm stream

'ruspa sf excavator

rus'pante ag (*pollo*) free-range

rus'sare /72/ vi to snore

'Russia sf: **la ~** Russia

'russo, -a ag, sm/f, sm Russian

'rustico, -a, -ci, -che ag country *cpd*, rural; (*arredamento*) rustic; (*fig*) rough, unrefined ▶ sm (*fabbricato: per attrezzi*) shed; (*: per abitazione*) farm labourer's (Brit) *o* farmhand's cottage

'ruta sf (*Bot*) rue

rut'tare /72/ vi to belch

'rutto sm belch

'ruvido, -a ag rough, coarse

ruzzo'lare [ruttso'lare] /72/ vi to tumble down

ruzzo'lone [ruttso'lone] sm tumble, fall

ruzzo'loni [ruttso'loni] av: **cadere ~** to tumble down; **fare le scale ~** to tumble down the stairs

r

Ss

S, s ['ɛsse] SM O F (*lettera*) S, s; **S come Savona** ≈ S for Sugar

s ABBR (= *secondo*) sec.

S. ABBR (= *sud*) S; (= *santo*) St

SA SIGLA = **Salerno** ▶ ABBR = **società anonima**

sa VB *vedi* **sapere**

sab. ABBR (= *sabato*) Sat.

'sabato SM Saturday; **di** *o* **il** ~ on Saturdays; *vedi anche* **martedì**

'sabbia SF sand; **sabbie mobili** quicksand(s *pl*)

sabbia'tura SF (*Med*) sand bath; (*Tecn*) sand-blasting; **fare le sabbiature** to take sand baths

sabbi'oso, -a AG sandy

sabo'taggio [sabo'taddʒo] SM sabotage

sabo'tare /**72**/ VT to sabotage

sabota'tore, -'trice SM/F saboteur

'sacca, -che SF bag; (*bisaccia*) haversack; (*insenatura*) inlet; ~ **d'aria** air pocket; ~ **da viaggio** travelling bag

sacca'rina SF saccharin(e)

sac'cente [sat'tʃɛnte] SMF know-all (BRIT), know-it-all (US)

saccheggi'are [sakked'dʒare] /**62**/ VT to sack, plunder

sac'cheggio [sak'keddʒo] SM sack(ing)

sac'chetto [sak'ketto] SM (small) bag; (small) sack; ~ **di carta/di plastica** paper/ plastic bag

'sacco, -chi SM bag; (*per carbone ecc*) sack; (*Anat, Biol*) sac; (*tela*) sacking; (*saccheggio*) sack(ing); (*fig: grande quantità*): **un ~ di** lots of, heaps of; **cogliere** *o* **prendere qn con le mani nel** ~ to catch sb red-handed; **vuotare il** ~ to confess, spill the beans; **mettere qn nel** ~ to cheat sb; **colazione al** ~ packed lunch; ~ **a pelo** sleeping bag; ~ **per i rifiuti** bin bag (BRIT), garbage bag (US)

sacer'dote [satʃer'dɔte] SM priest

sacer'dozio [satʃer'dɔttsjo] SM priesthood

'Sacra Co'rona U'nita SF *the mafia in Puglia*

sacra'mento SM sacrament

sa'crario SM memorial chapel

sacres'tano SM = **sagrestano**

sacres'tia SF = **sagrestia**

sacrifi'care /**20**/ VT to sacrifice; **sacrificarsi** VPR to sacrifice o.s.; (*privarsi di qc*) to make sacrifices

sacrifi'cato, -a AG sacrificed; (*non valorizzato*) wasted; **una vita sacrificata** a life of sacrifice

sacri'ficio [sakri'fitʃo] SM sacrifice

sacri'legio [sakri'ledʒo] SM sacrilege

sa'crilego, -a, -ghi, -ghe AG (*Rel*) sacrilegious

'sacro, -a AG sacred

sacro'santo, -a AG sacrosanct

'sadico, -a, -ci, -che AG sadistic ▶ SM/F sadist

sa'dismo SM sadism

sadomaso'chismo [sadomazo'kismo] SM sadomasochism

sa'etta SF arrow; (*fulmine: anche fig*) thunderbolt; flash of lightning

sa'fari SM INV safari

sa'gace [sa'gatʃe] AG shrewd, sagacious

sa'gacia [sa'gatʃa] SF sagacity, shrewdness

sag'gezza [sad'dʒettsa] SF wisdom

saggi'are [sad'dʒare] /**62**/ VT (*metalli*) to assay; (*fig*) to test

'saggio, -a, -gi, -ge ['saddʒo] AG wise ▶ SM (*persona*) sage; (*operazione sperimentale*) test; (: *dell'oro*) assay; (*fig: prova*) proof; (*campione indicativo*) sample; (*scritto: letterario*) essay; (: *Ins*) written test; **dare ~ di** to give proof of; **in ~** as a sample

sag'gistica [sad'dʒistika] SF ≈ non-fiction

Sagit'tario [sadʒit'tarjo] SM Sagittarius; **essere del** ~ to be Sagittarius

'sagoma SF (*profilo*) outline, profile; (*forma*) form, shape; (*Tecn*) template; (*bersaglio*) target; (*fig: persona*) character

'sagra SF festival

sa'grato SM churchyard

sagres'tano SM sacristan; sexton

sagres'tia SF sacristy; (*culto protestante*) vestry

Sa'hara [sa'ara] SM: **il (Deserto del)** ~ the Sahara (Desert)

sahari'ana [saa'rjana] SF bush jacket

'**sai** VB *vedi* **sapere**

'**saio** SM (*Rel*) habit

'**sala** SF hall; (*stanza*) room; (*Cine: di proiezione*) cinema; ~ **d'aspetto** waiting room; ~ **da ballo** ballroom; ~ **(dei) comandi** control room; ~ **per concerti** concert hall; ~ **per conferenze** (*Ins*) lecture hall; (*in aziende*) conference room; ~ **corse** betting shop; ~ **giochi** amusement arcade; ~ **da gioco** gaming room; ~ **macchine** (*Naut*) engine room; ~ **operatoria** (*Med*) operating theatre (*BRIT*) o room (*US*); ~ **da pranzo** dining room; ~ **per ricevimenti** banqueting hall; ~ **delle udienze** (*Dir*) courtroom

sa'lace [sa'latʃe] AG (*spinto, piccante*) salacious, saucy; (*mordace*) cutting, biting

sala'mandra SF salamander

sa'lame SM salami *no pl*, salami sausage

sala'moia SF (*Cuc*) brine

sa'lare /72/ VT to salt

salari'ale AG wage *cpd*, pay *cpd*; **aumento ~** wage o pay increase (*BRIT*) o raise (*US*)

salari'ato, -a SM/F wage-earner

sa'lario SM pay, wages *pl*; ~ **base** basic wage; ~ **minimo garantito** guaranteed minimum wage

salas'sare /72/ VT (*Med*) to bleed

sa'lasso SM (*Med*) bleeding, bloodletting; (*fig: forte spesa*) drain

sala'tino SM cracker, salted biscuit

sa'lato, -a AG (*sapore*) salty; (*Cuc*) salted, salt *cpd*; (*fig: discorso ecc*) biting, sharp; (: *prezzi*) steep, stiff

sal'dare /72/ VT (*congiungere*) to join, bind; (*parti metalliche*) to solder; (: *con saldatura autogena*) to weld; (*conto*) to settle, pay

salda'tore SM (*operaio*) solderer; welder; (*utensile*) soldering iron

salda'trice [salda'tritʃe] SF (*macchina*) welder, welding machine; ~ **ad arco** arc welder

salda'tura SF soldering; welding; (*punto saldato*) soldered joint; weld; ~ **autogena** welding; ~ **dolce** soft soldering

sal'dezza [sal'dettsa] SF firmness, strength

'**saldo, -a** AG (*resistente, forte*) strong, firm; (*fermo*) firm, steady, stable; (*fig*) firm, steadfast ▶ SM (*svendita*) sale; (*di conto*) settlement; (*Econ*) balance; **saldi** SMPL (*Comm*) sales; **pagare a ~** to pay in full; ~ **attivo** credit; ~ **passivo** deficit; ~ **da riportare** balance carried forward; **essere ~ nella propria fede** (*fig*) to stick to one's guns

'**sale** SM salt; (*fig*) wit; **sali** SMPL (*Med: da annusare*) smelling salts; **sotto ~** salted; **restare di ~** (*fig*) to be dumbfounded; **ha poco ~ in zucca** he doesn't have much sense; ~ **da cucina**, ~ **grosso** cooking salt; ~ **da tavola**, ~ **fino** table salt; **sali da bagno** bath salts; **sali minerali** mineral salts; **sali e tabacchi** tobacconist's (shop)

sal'gemma [sal'dʒɛmma] SM rock salt

'**salgo** *etc* VB *vedi* **salire**

'**salice** ['salitʃe] SM willow; ~ **piangente** weeping willow

sali'ente AG (*fig*) salient, main

sali'era SF salt cellar

sa'lino, -a AG saline ▶ SF saltworks *sg*

sa'lire /98/ VI to go (o come) up; (*aereo ecc*) to climb, go up; (*passeggero*) to get on; (*sentiero, prezzi, livello*) to go up, rise ▶ VT (*scale, gradini*) to go (o come) up; ~ **su** to climb (up); ~ **sul treno/sull'autobus** to board the train/the bus; ~ **in macchina** to get into the car; ~ **a cavallo** to mount; ~ **al potere** to rise to power; ~ **al trono** to ascend the throne; ~ **alle stelle** (*prezzi*) to rocket

sali'scendi [saliʃʃendi] SM INV latch

sa'lita SF climb, ascent; (*erta*) hill, slope; **in ~** *ag*, *av* uphill

sa'liva SF saliva

'**salma** SF corpse

sal'mastro, -a AG (*acqua*) salt *cpd*; (*sapore*) salty ▶ SM (*sapore*) salty taste; (*odore*) salty smell

salmì SM (*Cuc*) salmi; **lepre in ~** salmi of hare

'**salmo** SM psalm

sal'mone SM salmon

salmo'nella SF salmonella

Salo'mone: le isole ~ *sfpl* the Solomon Islands

sa'lone SM (*stanza*) sitting room, lounge; (*in albergo*) lounge; (*di ricevimento*) reception room; (*su nave*) lounge, saloon; (*mostra*) show, exhibition; (*negozio: di parrucchiere*) hairdresser's (salon); ~ **dell'automobile** motor show; ~ **di bellezza** beauty salon

salo'pette [salɔ'pɛt] SF INV dungarees *pl*

salotti'ero, -a AG mundane

sa'lotto SM lounge, sitting room; (*mobilio*) lounge suite

sal'pare /72/ VI (*Naut*) to set sail; (*anche:* **salpare l'ancora**) to weigh anchor

'**salsa** SF (*Cuc*) sauce; **in tutte le salse** (*fig*) in all kinds of ways; ~ **di pomodoro** tomato sauce

sal'sedine SF (*del mare, vento*) saltiness; (*incrostazione*) (dried) salt

sal'siccia, -ce [sal'sittʃa] SF pork sausage

salsi'era SF sauceboat (*BRIT*), gravy boat

'**salso** SM saltiness

sal'tare /72/ VI to jump, leap; (*esplodere*) to blow up, explode; (: *valvola*) to blow; (*venir via*) to pop off; (*non aver luogo: corso ecc*) to be cancelled ▶ VT to jump (over), leap (over); (*fig: pranzo, capitolo*) to skip, miss (out); (*Cuc*) to sauté; **far ~** to blow up; to burst open; (*serratura: forzare*) to break; **far ~ il banco** (*Gioco*) to break the bank; **farsi ~ le cervella** to blow one's brains out; **ma che ti salta in**

mente? what are you thinking of?; ~ **da un argomento all'altro** to jump from one subject to another; ~ **addosso a qn** (aggredire) to attack sb; ~ **fuori** to jump out, leap out; (venire trovato) to turn up; ~ **fuori con** (frase, commento) to come out with; ~ **giù da qc** to jump off sth, jump down from sth

saltel'lare /72/ vɪ to skip; to hop

sal'tello sᴍ hop, little jump

saltim'banco, -chi sᴍ acrobat

'**salto** sᴍ jump; (Sport) jumping; (dislivello) drop; **fare un ~** to jump, leap; **fare un ~ da qn** to pop over to sb's (place); ~ **in alto/ lungo** high/long jump; ~ **con l'asta** pole vaulting; ~ **mortale** somersault; **un ~ di qualità** (miglioramento) significant improvement

saltu'ario, -a ᴀɢ occasional, irregular

sa'lubre ᴀɢ healthy, salubrious

sa'lume sᴍ (Cuc) cured pork; **salumi** sᴍᴘʟ (insaccati) cured pork meats

salume'ria sF delicatessen

salumi'ere, -a sᴍ/F ≈ delicatessen owner

salumi'ficio [salumi'fitʃo] sᴍ cured pork meat factory

salu'tare /72/ ᴀɢ healthy; (fig) salutary, beneficial ▶ vᴛ (per dire buon giorno, fig) to greet; (per dire addio) to say goodbye to; (Mil) to salute; **mi saluti sua moglie** my regards to your wife

sa'lute sF health; ~! (a chi starnutisce) bless you!; (nei brindisi) cheers!; **bere alla ~ di qn** to drink (to) sb's health; **la ~ pubblica** public welfare; **godere di buona ~** to be healthy, enjoy good health

sa'luto sᴍ (gesto) wave; (parola) greeting; (Mil) salute; **gli ha tolto il ~** he no longer says hello to him; **cari saluti, tanti saluti** best regards; **vogliate gradire i nostri più distinti saluti** yours faithfully; **i miei saluti alla sua signora** my regards to your wife

'**salva** sF salvo

salvacon'dotto sᴍ (Mil) safe-conduct

salvada'naio sᴍ moneybox, piggy bank

salvado'regno, -a [salvado'reɲɲo] ᴀɢ, sᴍ/F Salvadorean

salva'gente [salva'dʒɛnte] sᴍ (Naut) lifebuoy; (pl inv: stradale) traffic island; ~ **a ciambella** lifebelt; ~ **a giubbotto** lifejacket (Bʀɪᴛ), life preserver (US)

salvaguar'dare /72/ vᴛ to safeguard

salvagu'ardia sF safeguard; **a ~ di** for the safeguard of

sal'vare /72/ vᴛ to save; (trarre da un pericolo) to rescue; (proteggere) to protect; **salvarsi** vᴘʀ to save o.s.; to escape; ~ **la vita a qn** to save sb's life; ~ **le apparenze** to keep up appearances; **si salvi chi può!** every man for himself!

salvas'chermo [salvas'kermo] sᴍ (Inform) screen saver

salva'slip® sᴍ ɪɴᴠ panty liner

salva'taggio [salva'taddʒo] sᴍ rescue

salva'tore, -'trice sᴍ/F saviour (Bʀɪᴛ), savior (US)

salvazi'one [salvat'tsjone] sF (Rel) salvation

'**salve** ᴇsᴄʟ (col) hi!

sal'vezza [sal'vettsa] sF salvation; (sicurezza) safety

'**salvia** sF (Bot) sage

salvi'etta sF napkin, serviette; ~ **umidificata** baby wipe

'**salvo, -a** ᴀɢ safe, unhurt, unharmed; (fuori pericolo) safe, out of danger ▶ sᴍ: **in ~** safe ▶ ᴘʀᴇᴘ (eccetto) except; ~ **che** cong (a meno che) unless; (eccetto che) except (that); **mettere qc in ~** to put sth in a safe place; **mettersi in ~** to reach safety; **portare qn in ~** to lead sb to safety; ~ **contrordini** barring instructions to the contrary; ~ **errori e omissioni** errors and omissions excepted; ~ **imprevisti** barring accidents

sam'buca sF (liquore) sambuca (type of anisette)

sam'buco sᴍ elder (tree)

sa'nare /72/ vᴛ to heal, cure; (economia) to put right

sana'toria sF (Dir) act of indemnity

sana'torio sᴍ sanatorium (Bʀɪᴛ), sanitarium (US)

san'cire [san'tʃire] /55/ vᴛ to sanction

'**sandalo** sᴍ (Bot) sandalwood; (calzatura) sandal

sang'ria [san'gria] sF (bibita) sangria

'**sangue** sᴍ blood; **farsi cattivo ~** to fret, get worked up; **all'ultimo ~** (duello, lotta) to the death; **non corre buon ~ tra di loro** there's bad blood between them; **buon ~ non mente!** blood will out!; ~ **freddo** (fig) sang-froid, calm; **a ~ freddo** in cold blood

sangu'igno, -a [san'gwiɲɲo] ᴀɢ blood cpd; (colore) blood-red

sangui'nante ᴀɢ bleeding

sangui'nare /72/ vɪ to bleed

sangui'nario, -a ᴀɢ bloodthirsty

sangui'noso, -a ᴀɢ bloody

sangui'suga, -ghe sF leech

sanità sF health; (salubrità) healthiness; **Ministero della S~** Department of Health; ~ **mentale** sanity; ~ **pubblica** public health

sani'tario, -a ᴀɢ health cpd; (condizioni) sanitary ▶ sᴍ (Amm) doctor; **Ufficiale S~** Health Officer; **sanitari** (impianti) bathroom o sanitary fittings

San Ma'rino sF: **la Repubblica di ~** the Republic of San Marino

'**sanno** vʙ vedi **sapere**

'**sano, -a** ᴀɢ healthy; (denti, costituzione) healthy, sound; (integro) whole, unbroken;

(*fig: politica, consigli*) sound; **~ di mente** sane; **di sana pianta** completely, entirely; **~ e salvo** safe and sound

San Silvestro [san sil'vestro] SM (*giorno*) New Year's Eve

Santi'ago SF: **~ (del Cile)** Santiago (de Chile)

santifi'care /20/ VT to sanctify; (*feste*) to observe

san'tino SM holy picture

san'tissimo, -a AG: **il S~ Sacramento** the Holy Sacrament; **il Padre S~** (*papa*) the Holy Father

santità SF sanctity; holiness; **Sua/Vostra ~** (*titolo di papa*) His/Your Holiness

'santo, -a AG holy; (*fig*) saintly; (*seguito da nome proprio: dav sm* **san** + C, **sant'** + V, **santo** + s *impura, gn, pn, ps, x, z; dav sf* **santa** + C, **sant'** + V) saint ▶ SM/F saint; **parole sante!** very true!; **tutto il ~ giorno** the whole blessed day, all day long; **non c'è ~ che tenga!** that's no excuse!; **la Santa Sede** the Holy See

san'tone SM holy man

santu'ario SM sanctuary

sanzio'nare [santsjo'nare] /**72**/ VT to sanction

sanzi'one [san'tsjone] SF sanction; (*penale, civile*) sanction, penalty; **sanzioni economiche** economic sanctions

sa'pere /99/ VT to know; (*essere capace di*): **so nuotare** I know how to swim, I can swim ▶ VI: **~ di** (*aver sapore*) to taste of; (*aver odore*) to smell of ▶ SM knowledge; **far ~ qc a qn** to inform sb about sth, let sb know sth; **venire a ~ qc** (*da qn*) to find out *o* hear about sth (from sb); **non ne vuole più ~ di lei** he doesn't want to have anything more to do with her; **mi sa che non sia vero** I don't think that's true; **non lo so** I don't know; **non so l'inglese** I don't speak English

sapi'ente AG (*dotto*) learned; (*che rivela abilità*) masterly ▶ SMF scholar

sapien'tone, -a SM/F (*peg*) know-all (BRIT), know-it-all (US)

sapi'enza [sa'pjɛntsa] SF wisdom

sa'pone SM soap; **~ da barba** shaving soap; **~ da bucato** washing soap; **~ liquido** liquid soap; **~ in scaglie** soapflakes *pl*

sapo'netta SF cake *o* bar *o* tablet of soap

sa'pore SM taste, flavour (BRIT), flavor (US)

sapo'rito, -a AG tasty; (*fig: arguto*) witty; (: *piccante*) racy

sappi'amo VB *vedi* **sapere**

saprò *etc* VB *vedi* **sapere**

sapu'tello, -a SM/F know-all (BRIT), know-it-all (US)

sarà *etc* VB *vedi* **essere**

sara'banda SF (*fig*) uproar

saraci'nesca, -sche [saratʃi'neska] SF (*serranda*) rolling shutter

sar'casmo SM sarcasm *no pl*; sarcastic remark

sar'castico, -a, -ci, -che AG sarcastic

sarchi'are [sar'kjare] /vb not found/ VT (*Agr*) to hoe

sar'cofago (*pl* **sarcofagi** *o* **sarcofaghi**) SM sarcophagus

Sar'degna [sar'deɲɲa] SF: **la ~** Sardinia

sar'dina SF sardine

'sardo, -a AG, SM/F Sardinian

sar'donico, -a, -ci, -che AG sardonic

sa'rei *etc* VB *vedi* **essere**

SARS SF (= *severe acute respiratory syndrome*) SARS

'sarta SF *vedi* **sarto**

'sartia SF (*Naut*) stay

'sarto, -a SM/F tailor/dressmaker; **~ d'alta moda** couturier

sarto'ria SF tailor's (shop); dressmaker's (shop); (*casa di moda*) fashion house; (*arte*) couture

sassai'ola SF hail of stones

sas'sata SF blow with a stone; **tirare una ~ contro** *o* **a qc/qn** to throw a stone at sth/sb

'sasso SM stone; (*ciottolo*) pebble; (*masso*) rock; **restare** *o* **rimanere di ~** to be dumbfounded

sassofo'nista, -i, -e SM/F saxophonist

sas'sofono SM saxophone

sas'sone AG, SMF, SM Saxon

sas'soso, -a AG stony; pebbly

'Satana SM Satan

sa'tanico, -a, -ci, -che AG satanic, fiendish

satelli'tare AG satellite *cpd*

sa'tellite SM, AG satellite

'satira SF satire

satireggi'are [satired'dʒare] /**62**/ VT to satirize ▶ VI (*fare della satira*) to be satirical; (*scrivere satire*) to write satires

sa'tirico, -a, -ci, -che AG satiric(al)

sa'tollo, -a AG full, replete

satu'rare /72/ VT to saturate

saturazi'one [saturat'tsjone] SF saturation

'saturo, -a AG saturated; (*fig*): **~ di** full of; **~ d'acqua** (*terreno*) waterlogged

'SAUB SIGLA F (= *Struttura Amministrativa Unificata di Base*) state welfare system

'sauna SF sauna; **fare la ~** to have *o* take a sauna

sa'vana SF savannah

'savio, -a AG wise, sensible ▶ SM wise man

Sa'voia SF: **la ~** Savoy

savoi'ardo, -a AG of Savoy, Savoyard ▶ SM (*biscotto*) sponge finger

sazi'are [sat'tsjare] /**19**/ VT to satisfy, satiate; **saziarsi** VPR (*riempirsi di cibo*): **saziarsi (di)** to eat one's fill (of); (*fig*): **saziarsi di** to grow tired *o* weary of

sazietà [sattsje'ta] SF satiety, satiation

'sazio, -a ['sattsjo] AG: **~ (di)** sated (with), full (of); (*fig: stufo*) fed up (with), sick (of); **sono ~** I'm full (up)

sbada'taggine [zbada'taddʒine] SF
(*sventatezza*) carelessness; (*azione*) oversight
sba'dato, -a AG careless, inattentive
sbadigli'are [zbadiʎ'ʎare] /**27**/ VI to yawn
sba'diglio [zba'diʎʎo] SM yawn; **fare uno ~**
to yawn
'sbafo SM: **a ~** at somebody else's expense
sbagli'are [zbaʎ'ʎare] /**27**/ VT to make a
mistake in, get wrong ▶ VI (*fare errori*) to
make a mistake (*o mistakes*), be mistaken;
(*ingannarsi*) to be wrong; (*operare in modo non
giusto*) to err; **sbagliarsi** VPR to make a
mistake, be mistaken, be wrong; **~ la
mira/strada** to miss one's target/take
the wrong road; **scusi, ho sbagliato
numero** (*Tel*) sorry, I've got the wrong
number; **non c'è da sbagliarsi** there can
be no mistake
sbagli'ato, -a [zbaʎ'ʎato] AG (*gen*) wrong;
(*compito*) full of mistakes; (*conclusione*)
erroneous
'sbaglio ['zbaʎʎo] SM mistake, error; (*morale*)
error; **fare uno ~** to make a mistake
sbales'trato, -a AG (*persona: scombussolato*)
unsettled
sbal'lare /**72**/ VT (*merce*) to unpack ▶ VI (*nel fare
un conto*) to overestimate; (*Droga: gergo*) to get
high
sbal'lato, -a AG (*calcolo*) wrong; (*col:
ragionamento, persona*) screwy
'sballo SM (*Droga: gergo*) trip
sballot'tare /**72**/ VT to toss (about)
sbalor'dire /**55**/ VT to stun, amaze ▶ VI to be
stunned, be amazed
sbalordi'tivo, -a AG amazing; (*prezzo*)
incredible, absurd
sbal'zare [zbal'tsare] /**72**/ VT to throw, hurl;
(*fig: da una carica*) to remove, dismiss ▶ VI
(*balzare*) to bounce; (*saltare*) to leap, bound
'sbalzo ['zbaltso] SM (*spostamento improvviso*)
jolt, jerk; **a sbalzi** jerkily; (*fig*) in fits and
starts; **uno ~ di temperatura** a sudden
change in temperature
sban'care /**20**/ VT (*nei giochi*) to break the bank
at (*o of*); (*fig*) to ruin, bankrupt
sbanda'mento SM (*Naut*) list; (*Aut*) skid;
(*fig: di persona*) confusion; **ha avuto un
periodo di ~** he went off the rails for a bit
sban'dare /**72**/ VI (*Naut*) to list; (*Aut*) to skid;
(*Aer*) to bank; **sbandarsi** VPR (*folla*) to
disperse; (*truppe*) to scatter; (*fig: famiglia*) to
break up
sban'data SF (*Aut*) skid; (*Naut*) list; **prendere
una ~ per qn** (*fig*) to fall for sb
sban'dato, -a SM/F mixed-up person
sbandie'rare /**72**/ VT (*bandiera*) to wave; (*fig*) to
parade, show off
'sbando SM: **essere allo ~** to drift
sbarac'care /**20**/ VT (*libri, piatti ecc*) to clear (up)

sbaragli'are [zbaraʎ'ʎare] /**27**/ VT (*Mil*) to
rout; (*in gare sportive ecc*) to beat, defeat
sba'raglio [zba'raʎʎo] SM rout; defeat;
gettarsi allo ~ (*soldato*) to throw o.s. into the
fray; (*fig*) to risk everything
sbaraz'zarsi [zbarat'tsarsi] /**72**/ VPR: **~ di** to
get rid of, rid o.s. of
sbaraz'zino, -a [zbarat'tsino] AG impish,
cheeky
sbar'bare /**72**/ VT, **sbar'barsi** VPR to shave
sbarba'tello SM novice, greenhorn
sbar'care /**20**/ VT (*passeggeri*) to disembark;
(*merci*) to unload ▶ VI to disembark
'sbarco SM disembarkation; unloading; (*Mil*)
landing
'sbarra SF bar; (*di passaggio a livello*) barrier;
(*Dir*): **mettere/presentarsi alla ~** to bring/
appear before the court
sbarra'mento SM (*stradale*) barrier; (*diga*)
dam, barrage; (*Mil*) barrage; (*Pol*) cut-off
point (*level of support below which a political party
is excluded from representation in Parliament*)
sbar'rare /**72**/ VT (*bloccare: strada ecc*) to block,
bar; (*cancellare: assegno*) to cross (BRIT); **~ il
passo** to bar the way; **~ gli occhi** to open
one's eyes wide
sbar'rato, -a AG (*porta*) barred; (*passaggio*)
blocked, barred; (*strada*) blocked,
obstructed; (*occhi*) staring; (*assegno*)
crossed (BRIT)
'sbattere /**1**/ VT (*porta*) to bang, slam; (*tappeti,
ali, Cuc*) to beat; (*urtare*) to knock, hit ▶ VI
(*porta, finestra*) to bang; (*agitarsi: ali, vele ecc*) to
flap; **~ qn fuori/in galera** to throw sb out/
into prison; **me ne sbatto!** (*col*) I don't give a
damn!
sbat'tuto, -a AG (*viso, aria*) dejected, worn out;
(*uovo*) beaten
sba'vare /**72**/ VI to dribble; (*colore*) to smear,
smudge
sbava'tura SF (*di persone*) dribbling; (*di
lumache*) slime; (*di rossetto, vernice*) smear
sbelli'carsi /**20**/ VPR: **~ dalle risa** to split one's
sides laughing
'sberla SF slap
sber'leffo SM: **fare uno ~ a qn** to make a face
at sb
sbia'dire /**55**/ VI (*anche:* **sbiadirsi**) to fade ▶ VT
to fade
sbia'dito, -a AG faded; (*fig*) colourless (BRIT),
colorless (US), dull
sbian'care /**20**/ VT to whiten; (*tessuto*) to
bleach ▶ VI (*impallidire*) to grow pale *o* white
sbi'eco, -a, -chi, -che AG (*storto*) squint,
askew; **di ~**, **guardare qn di ~** (*fig*) to look
askance at sb; **tagliare una stoffa di ~** to
cut material on the bias
sbigot'tire /**55**/ VT to dismay, stun ▶ VI
(*anche:* **sbigottirsi**) to be dismayed

sbilanci'are [zbilan'tʃare] /**14**/ VT to throw off balance; **sbilanciarsi** VPR (*perdere l'equilibrio*) to overbalance, lose one's balance; (*fig: compromettersi*) to compromise o.s.

sbi'lenco, -a, -chi, -che AG (*persona*) crooked, misshapen; (*fig: idea, ragionamento*) twisted

sbirci'are [zbir'tʃare] /**14**/ VT to cast sidelong glances at, eye

sbirci'ata [zbir'tʃata] SF: **dare una ~ a qc** to glance at sth, have a look at sth

'**sbirro** SM (*peg*) cop

sbizzar'rirsi [zbiddzar'rirsi] /**55**/ VPR to indulge one's whims

sbloc'care /**20**/ VT to unblock, free; (*freno*) to release; (*prezzi, affitti*) to free from controls; **sbloccarsi** VPR (*gen*) to become unblocked; (*passaggio, strada*) to clear, become unblocked; **la situazione si è sbloccata** things are moving again

'**sblocco, -chi** SM (*vedi vt*) unblocking, freeing; release

sboc'care /**20**/ VI: **~ in** (*fiume*) to flow into; (*strada*) to lead into; (*persona*) to come (out) into; (*fig: concludersi*) to end (up) in

sboc'cato, -a AG (*persona*) foul-mouthed; (*linguaggio*) foul

sbocci'are [zbot'tʃare] /**14**/ VI (*fiore*) to bloom, open (out)

'**sbocco, -chi** SM (*di fiume*) mouth; (*di strada*) end; (*di tubazione, Comm*) outlet; (*uscita: anche fig*) way out; **una strada senza ~** a dead end; **siamo in una situazione senza sbocchi** there's no way out of this for us

sbocconcel'lare [zbokkontʃel'lare] /**72**/ VT: **~ (qc)** to nibble (at sth)

sbollen'tare /**72**/ VT (*Cuc*) to parboil

sbol'lire /**55**/ VI (*fig*) to cool down, calm down

'**sbornia** SF (*col*): **prendersi una ~** to get plastered

sbor'sare /**72**/ VT (*denaro*) to pay out

sbot'tare /**72**/ VI: **~ in una risata/per la collera** to burst out laughing/explode with anger

sbotto'nare /**72**/ VT to unbutton, undo

sbra'cato, -a AG slovenly

sbracci'arsi [zbrat'tʃarsi] /**14**/ VPR to wave (one's arms about)

sbracci'ato, -a [zbrat'tʃato] AG (*camicia*) sleeveless; (*persona*) bare-armed

sbrai'tare /**72**/ VI to yell, bawl

sbra'nare /**72**/ VT to tear to pieces

sbricio'lare [zbritʃo'lare] /**72**/ VT, **sbricio'larsi** VPR to crumble

sbri'gare /**80**/ VT to deal with, get through; (*cliente*) to attend to, deal with; **sbrigarsi** VPR to hurry (up)

sbriga'tivo, -a AG (*persona, modo*) quick, expeditious; (*giudizio*) hasty

sbrina'mento SM defrosting

sbri'nare /**72**/ VT to defrost

sbrindel'lato, -a AG tattered, in tatters

sbrodo'lare /**72**/ VT to stain, dirty

'**sbronza** ['zbrontsa] (*col*) SF (*ubriaco*): **prendersi una ~** to get plastered

sbron'zarsi [zbron'tsarsi] /**72**/ VPR (*col*) to get plastered

sbruf'fone, -a SM/F boaster, braggart

sbu'care /**20**/ VI to come out, emerge; (*improvvisamente*) to pop out (*o up*)

sbucci'are [zbut'tʃare] /**14**/ VT (*arancia, patata*) to peel; (*piselli*) to shell; **sbucciarsi un ginocchio** to graze one's knee

sbucherò *etc* [zbuke'rɔ] VB *vedi* **sbucare**

sbudel'larsi /**72**/ VPR: **~ dalle risa** to split one's sides laughing

sbuf'fare /**72**/ VI (*persona, cavallo*) to snort; (*: ansimare*) to puff, pant; (*treno*) to puff

'**sbuffo** SM (*di aria, fumo, vapore*) puff; **maniche a ~** puff(ed) sleeves

sc. ABBR (*Teat: = scena*) SC.

'**scabbia** SF (*Med*) scabies *sg*

'**scabro, -a** AG rough, harsh; (*fig*) concise, terse

sca'broso, -a AG (*fig: difficile*) difficult, thorny; (*: imbarazzante*) embarrassing; (*: sconcio*) indecent

scacchi'era [skak'kjɛra] SF chessboard

scacchiere [skak'kjɛre] SM (*Mil*) sector; **S~** (*in Gran Bretagna*) Exchequer

scaccia'cani [skattʃa'kani] SM O F INV pistol with blanks

scacciapensi'eri [skattʃapen'sjɛri] SM INV (*Mus*) jew's-harp

scacci'are [skat'tʃare] /**14**/ VT to chase away *o* out, drive away *o* out; **~ qn di casa** to turn sb out of the house

'**scacco, -chi** SM (*pezzo del gioco*) chessman; (*quadretto di scacchiera*) square; (*fig*) setback, reverse; **scacchi** SMPL (*gioco*) chess *sg*; **a scacchi** (*tessuto*) check(ed); **subire uno ~** (*fig: sconfitta*) to suffer a setback

scacco'matto SM checkmate; **dare ~ a qn** (*anche fig*) to checkmate sb

'**scaddi** *etc* VB *vedi* **scadere**

sca'dente AG shoddy, of poor quality

sca'denza [ska'dɛntsa] SF (*di cambiale, contratto*) maturity; (*di passaporto*) expiry date; **a breve/lunga ~** short-/long-term; **data di ~** expiry date; **~ a termine** fixed deadline

sca'dere /**18**/ VI (*contratto ecc*) to expire; (*debito*) to fall due; (*valore, forze, peso*) to decline, go down

sca'fandro SM (*di palombaro*) diving suit; (*di astronauta*) spacesuit

scaffala'tura SF shelving, shelves *pl*

scaf'fale SM shelf; (*mobile*) set of shelves

sca'fista SM (*di immigrati*) people smuggler (*by boat*)

S

'scafo SM (*Naut, Aer*) hull

scagio'nare [skadʒo'nare] /**72**/ VT to exonerate, free from blame

'scaglia ['skaʎʎa] SF (*Zool*) scale; (*scheggia*) chip, flake

scagli'are [skaʎ'ʎare] /**27**/ VT (*lanciare: anche fig*) to hurl, fling; **scagliarsi** VPR: **scagliarsi su** *o* **contro** to hurl *o* fling o.s. at; (*fig*) to rail at

scagliona'mento [skaʎʎona'mento] SM (*Mil*) arrangement in echelons

scaglio'nare [skaʎʎo'nare] /**72**/ VT (*pagamenti*) to space out, spread out; (*Mil*) to echelon

scagli'one [skaʎ'ʎone] SM (*Mil*) echelon; (*Geo*) terrace; **a scaglioni** in groups

sca'gnozzo [skaɲ'ɲɔttso] SM (*peg*) lackey

'Scala : la ~ *see note*

Milan's *la Scala* first opened its doors in 1778 with a performance of Salieri's opera, "L'Europa riconosciuta". Built on the site of the church of Santa Maria della Scala, the theatre suffered serious damage in the bombing campaigns of 1943 but reopened in 1946 with a concert conducted by Toscanini. Enjoying world-wide renown for its opera, *la Scala* also has a famous school of classical dance.

'scala SF (*a gradini ecc*) staircase, stairs *pl*; (*a pioli, di corda*) ladder; (*Mus, Geo, di colori, valori, fig*) scale; **scale** SFPL (*scalinata*) stairs; **su larga** *o* **vasta** ~ on a large scale; **su piccola** ~, **su ~ ridotta** on a small scale; **su ~ nazionale/mondiale** on a national/worldwide scale; **in ~ di 1 a 100.000** on a scale of 1 cm to 1 km; **riproduzione in ~** reproduction to scale; **~ a chiocciola** spiral staircase; **~ a libretto** stepladder; **~ di misure** system of weights and measures; **~ mobile** escalator; (*Econ*) sliding scale; **~ mobile (dei salari)** index-linked pay scale; **~ di sicurezza** (*antincendio*) fire escape

sca'lare /**72**/ VT (*Alpinismo, muro*) to climb, scale; (*debito*) to scale down, reduce; **questa somma vi viene scalata dal prezzo originale** this sum is deducted from the original price

sca'lata SF scaling *no pl*, climbing *no pl*; (*arrampicata, fig*) climb; **dare la ~ a** (*fig*) to make a bid for

scala'tore, -'trice SM/F climber

scalca'gnato, -a [skalkaɲ'ɲato] AG (*logoro*) worn; (*persona*) shabby

scalci'are [skal'tʃare] /**14**/ VI to kick

scalci'nato, -a [skaltʃi'nato] AG (*fig: peg*) shabby

scalda'bagno [skalda'baɲɲo] SM water heater

scal'dare /**72**/ VT to heat; **scaldarsi** VPR to warm up, heat up; (*al fuoco, al sole*) to warm o.s.; (*fig*) to get excited; **~ la sedia** (*fig*) to twiddle one's thumbs

scaldavi'vande SM INV dish warmer

scal'dino SM (*per mani*) hand-warmer; (*per piedi*) foot-warmer; (*per letto*) bedwarmer

scal'fire /**55**/ VT to scratch

scalfit'tura SF scratch

scali'nata SF staircase

sca'lino SM (*anche fig*) step; (*di scala a pioli*) rung

scal'mana SF (hot) flush

scalma'narsi /**72**/ VPR (*affaticarsi*) to rush about, rush around; (*agitarsi, darsi da fare*) to get all hot and bothered; (*arrabbiarsi*) to get excited, get steamed up

scalma'nato, -a SM/F hothead

'scalo SM (*Naut*) slipway; (: *porto d'approdo*) port of call; (*Aer*) stopover; **fare ~ (a)** (*Naut*) to call (at), put in (at); (*Aer*) to land (at), make a stop (at); **volo senza ~** non-stop flight; **~ merci** (*Ferr*) goods (*BRIT*) *o* freight yard

sca'logna [ska'loɲɲa] SF (*col*) bad luck

scalo'gnato, -a [skaloɲ'ɲato] AG (*col*) unlucky

scalop'pina SF (*Cuc*) escalope

scal'pello SM chisel

scalpi'tare /**72**/ VI (*cavallo*) to paw the ground; (*persona*) to stamp one's feet

scal'pore SM noise, row; **far ~** (*notizia*) to cause a sensation *o* a stir

'scaltro, -a AG cunning, shrewd

scal'zare [skal'tsare] /**72**/ VT (*albero*) to bare the roots of; (*muro, fig: autorità*) to undermine

'scalzo, -a ['skaltso] AG barefoot

scambi'are /**19**/ VT to exchange; (*confondere*): **~ qn/qc per** to take *o* mistake sb/sth for; **mi hanno scambiato il cappello** they've given me the wrong hat; **scambiarsi** VPR (*auguri, confidenze, visite*) to exchange

scambi'evole AG mutual, reciprocal

'scambio SM exchange; (*Comm*) trade; (*Ferr*) points *pl*; **fare (uno) ~** to make a swap; **libero ~** free trade; **scambi con l'estero** foreign trade

scamosci'ato, -a [skamoʃ'ʃato] AG suede

scampa'gnata [skampaɲ'ɲata] SF trip to the country

scampa'nare /**72**/ VI to peal

scam'pare /**72**/ VT (*salvare*) to rescue, save; (*evitare: morte, prigione*) to escape ▶ VI: **~ (a qc)** to survive (sth), escape (sth); **scamparla bella** to have a narrow escape

'scampo SM (*salvezza*) escape; (*Zool*) prawn; **cercare ~ nella fuga** to seek safety in flight; **non c'è (via di) ~** there's no way out

'scampolo SM remnant

scanala'tura SF (*incavo*) channel, groove

scandagli'are [skandaʎ'ʎare] /**27**/ VT (*Naut*) to sound; (*fig*) to sound out; to probe

scanda'listico, -a, -ci, -che AG (*settimanale ecc*) sensational

scandaliz'zare [skandalid'dzare] /**72**/ VT to shock, scandalize; **scandalizzarsi** VPR to be shocked

'**scandalo** SM scandal; **dare ~** to cause a scandal

scanda'loso, -a AG scandalous, shocking

Scandi'navia SF: **la ~** Scandinavia

scandi'navo, -a AG, SM/F Scandinavian

scan'dire /**55**/ VT (*versi*) to scan; (*parole*) to articulate, pronounce distinctly; **~ il tempo** (*Mus*) to beat time

scan'nare /**72**/ VT (*animale*) to butcher, slaughter; (*persona*) to cut o slit the throat of

'**scanner** ['skanner] SM INV scanner

scanneriz'zare [skannerid'dzare] /**72**/ VT to scan

'**scanno** SM seat, bench

scansafa'tiche [skansafa'tike] SM O F INV idler, loafer

scan'sare /**72**/ VT (*rimuovere*) to move (aside), shift; (*schivare: schiaffo*) to dodge; (*sfuggire*) to avoid; **scansarsi** VPR to move aside

scan'sia SF shelves *pl*; (*per libri*) bookcase

'**scanso** SM: **a ~ di** in order to avoid, as a precaution against; **a ~ di equivoci** to avoid (any) misunderstanding

scanti'nato SM basement

scanto'nare /**72**/ VI to turn the corner; (*svignarsela*) to sneak off

scanzo'nato, -a [skantso'nato] AG easy-going

scapacci'one [skapat'tʃone] SM clout, slap

scapes'trato, -a AG dissolute

'**scapito** SM (*perdita*) loss; (*danno*) damage, detriment; **a ~ di** to the detriment of

'**scapola** SF shoulder blade

'**scapolo** SM bachelor

scappa'mento SM (*Aut*) exhaust

scap'pare /**72**/ VI (*fuggire*) to escape; (*andare via in fretta*) to rush off; **~ di prigione** to escape from prison; **~ di mano** (*oggetto*) to slip out of one's hands; **~ di mente a qn** to slip sb's mind; **lasciarsi ~** (*occasione, affare*) to let go by, miss; (*dettaglio*) to overlook; (*parola*) to let slip; (*prigioniero*) to let escape; **mi scappò detto** I let it slip

scap'pata SF quick visit o call

scappa'tella SF escapade

scappa'toia SF way out

scara'beo SM beetle

scarabocchi'are [skarabok'kjare] /**19**/ VT to scribble, scrawl

scara'bocchio [skara'bɔkkjo] SM scribble, scrawl

scara'faggio [skara'faddʒo] SM cockroach

scaraman'zia [skaraman'tsia] SF: **per ~** for luck

scara'muccia, -ce [skara'muttʃa] SF skirmish

scaraven'tare /**72**/ VT to fling, hurl; **scaraventarsi** VPR to fling o.s.

scarce'rare [skartʃe'rare] /**72**/ VT to release (from prison)

scarcerazi'one [skartʃerat'tsjone] SF release (from prison)

scardi'nare /**72**/ VT: **~ una porta** to take a door off its hinges

'**scarica, -che** SF (*di più armi*) volley of shots; (*di sassi, pugni*) hail, shower; (*Elettr*) discharge; **~ di mitra** burst of machine-gun fire

scari'care /**20**/ VT (*merci, camion ecc*) to unload; (*passeggeri*) to set down, put off; (*da Internet*) to download; (*arma*) to unload; (: *sparare, anche Elettr*) to discharge; (*corso d'acqua*) to empty, pour; (*fig: liberare da un peso*) to unburden, relieve; **scaricarsi** VPR (*orologio*) to run o wind down; (*batteria, accumulatore*) to go flat (BRIT) o dead; (*fig: rilassarsi*) to unwind; (: *sfogarsi*) to let off steam; **~ le proprie responsabilità su qn** to off-load one's responsibilities onto sb; **~ la colpa addosso a qn** to blame sb; **il fulmine si scaricò su un albero** the lightning struck a tree

scarica'tore SM loader; (*di porto*) docker

'**scarico, -a, -chi, -che** AG unloaded; (*orologio*) run down; (*batteria, accumulatore*) dead, flat (BRIT) ▶ SM (*di merci, materiali*) unloading; (*di immondizie*) dumping, tipping (BRIT); (: *luogo*) rubbish dump; (*Tecn: deflusso*) draining; (: *dispositivo*) drain; (*Aut*) exhaust; **~ del lavandino** waste outlet

scarlat'tina SF scarlet fever

scar'latto, -a AG scarlet

'**scarno, -a** AG thin, bony

'**scarpa** SF shoe; **fare le scarpe a qn** (*fig*) to double-cross sb; **scarpe da ginnastica** gym shoes; **scarpe coi tacchi (alti)** high-heeled shoes; **scarpe col tacco basso** low-heeled shoes; **scarpe senza tacco** flat shoes; **scarpe da tennis** tennis shoes

scar'pata SF escarpment

scarpi'era SF shoe rack

scar'pone SM boot; **scarponi da montagna** climbing boots; **scarponi da sci** ski-boots

scarroz'zare [skarrot'tsare] /**72**/ VT to drive around

scarseggi'are [skarsed'dʒare] /**62**/ VI to be scarce; **~ di** to be short of, lack

scar'sezza [skar'settsa] SF scarcity, lack

'**scarso, -a** AG (*insufficiente*) insufficient, meagre (BRIT), meager (US); (*povero: annata*) poor, lean; (*Ins: voto*) poor; **~ di** lacking in; **3 chili scarsi** just under 3 kilos, barely 3 kilos

scartabel'lare /**72**/ VT to skim through, glance through

scarta'faccio [skarta'fattʃo] SM notebook

scarta'mento SM (Ferr) gauge; **~ normale/ ridotto** standard/narrow gauge

scar'tare /**72**/ VT (pacco) to unwrap; (idea) to reject; (Mil) to declare unfit for military service; (carte da gioco) to discard; (Calcio) to dodge (past) ▶ VI to swerve

'scarto SM (cosa scartata, anche Comm) reject; (di veicolo) swerve; (differenza) gap, difference; **~ salariale** wage differential

scar'toffie SFPL (peg) papers pl

scas'sare /**72**/ VT (col: rompere) to wreck

scassi'nare /**72**/ VT to break, force

'scasso SM vedi **furto**

scate'nare /**72**/ VT (fig) to incite, stir up; **scatenarsi** VPR (temporale) to break; (rivolta) to break out; (persona: infuriarsi) to rage

scate'nato, -a AG wild

'scatola SF box; (di latta) tin (BRIT), can; **cibi in ~** tinned (BRIT) o canned foods; **una ~ di cioccolatini** a box of chocolates; **comprare qc a ~ chiusa** to buy sth sight unseen; **~ cranica** cranium

scato'lone SM (big) box

scat'tante AG quick off the mark; (agile) agile

scat'tare /**72**/ VT (fotografia) to take ▶ VI (congegno, molla ecc) to be released; (balzare) to spring up; (Sport) to put on a spurt; (fig: per l'ira) to fly into a rage; (legge, provvedimento) to come into effect; **~ in piedi** to spring to one's feet; **far ~** to release

'scatto SM (dispositivo) release; (: di arma da fuoco) trigger mechanism; (rumore) click; (balzo) jump, start; (Sport) spurt; (fig: di ira ecc) fit; (: di stipendio) increment; **di ~** suddenly; **serratura a ~** spring lock

scatu'rire /**55**/ VI to gush, spring

scaval'care /**20**/ VT (ostacolo) to pass (o climb) over; (fig) to get ahead of, overtake

sca'vare /**72**/ VT (terreno) to dig; (legno) to hollow out; (pozzo, galleria) to bore; (città sepolta ecc) to excavate

scava'trice [skava'tritʃe] SF (macchina) excavator

scavezza'collo [skavettsa'kɔllo] SM daredevil

'scavo SM excavating no pl; excavation

scazzot'tare [skattsot'tare] /**72**/ VT (col) to beat up, give a thrashing to

'scegliere ['ʃeʎʎere] /**100**/ VT (gen) to choose; (candidato, prodotto) to choose, select; **~ di fare** to choose to do

sce'icco, -chi [ʃe'ikko] SM sheik

'scelgo etc ['ʃelgo] VB vedi **scegliere**

scelle'rato, -a [ʃelle'rato] AG wicked, evil

scel'lino [ʃel'lino] SM shilling

'scelto, -a ['ʃelto] PP di **scegliere** ▶ AG (gruppo) carefully selected; (frutta, verdura) choice, top quality; (Mil: specializzato) crack cpd,

highly skilled ▶ SF choice; (selezione) selection, choice; **frutta o formaggi a scelta** choice of fruit or cheese; **fare una scelta** to make a choice, choose; **non avere scelta** to have no choice o option; **di prima scelta** top grade o quality

sce'mare [ʃe'mare] /**72**/ VT, VI to diminish

sce'menza [ʃe'mɛntsa] SF stupidity no pl; stupid thing (to do o say)

'scemo, -a ['ʃemo] AG stupid, silly

'scempio ['ʃempjo] SM slaughter, massacre; (fig) ruin; **far ~ di** (fig) to play havoc with, ruin

'scena ['ʃɛna] SF (gen) scene; (palcoscenico) stage; **le scene** (fig: teatro) the stage; **andare in ~** to be staged o put on o performed; **mettere in ~** to stage; **uscire di ~** to leave the stage; (fig) to leave the scene; **fare una ~** (fig) to make a scene; **ha fatto ~ muta** (fig) he didn't open his mouth

sce'nario [ʃe'narjo] SM scenery; (di film) scenario

sce'nata [ʃe'nata] SF row, scene

'scendere ['ʃendere] /**101**/ VI to go (o come) down; (strada, sole) to go down; (notte) to fall; (passeggero: fermarsi) to get out, alight; (fig: temperatura, prezzi) to fall, drop ▶ VT (scale, pendio) to go (o come) down; **~ dalle scale** to go (o come) down the stairs; **~ dal treno** to get off o out of the train; **~ dalla macchina** to get out of the car; **~ da cavallo** to dismount, get off one's horse; **~ ad un albergo** to put up o stay at a hotel

sceneggi'ato [ʃened'dʒato] SM television drama

sceneggia'tore, -'trice [ʃenedandʒa'tore] SM/F script-writer

sceneggia'tura [ʃenedandʒa'tura] SF (Teat) scenario; (Cine) screenplay, scenario

'scenico, -a, -ci, -che ['ʃeniko] AG stage cpd

scenogra'fia [ʃenogra'fia] SF (Teat) stage design; (Cine) set design; (elementi scenici) scenery

sce'nografo, -a [ʃe'nɔgrafo] SM/F set designer

sce'riffo [ʃe'riffo] SM sheriff

scervel'larsi [ʃervel'larsi] /**72**/ VPR: **~ (su qc)** to rack one's brains (over sth)

scervel'lato, -a [ʃervel'lato] AG featherbrained

'sceso, -a ['ʃeso] PP di **scendere**

scetti'cismo [ʃetti'tʃizmo] SM scepticism (BRIT), skepticism (US)

'scettico, -a, -ci, -che ['ʃettiko] AG sceptical (BRIT), skeptical (US)

'scettro ['ʃettro] SM sceptre (BRIT), scepter (US)

'scheda ['skɛda] SF (index) card; (TV, Radio) (brief) report; **~ audio** (Inform) sound card;

~ **bianca/nulla** (*Pol*) unmarked/spoiled ballot paper; ~ **a circuito stampato** printed-circuit board; ~ **elettorale** ballot paper; ~ **madre** (*Inform*) motherboard; ~ **di memoria** (*Inform*) memory card; ~ **perforata** punch card; ~ **ricaricabile** (*Tel*) top-up card; ~ **telefonica** phone card; ~ **video** (*Inform*) video card

sche'dare [ske'dare] **/72/** VT (*dati*) to file; (*libri*) to catalogue; (*registrare: anche Polizia*) to put on one's files

sche'dario [ske'darjo] SM file; (*mobile*) filing cabinet

sche'dato, -a [ske'dato] AG with a (police) record ▶ SM/F person with a (police) record

sche'dina [ske'dina] SF ≈ pools coupon (*BRIT*)

'**scheggia, -ge** ['skeddʒa] SF splinter, sliver; ~ **impazzita** (*fig*) maverick

sche'letrico, -a, -ci, -che [ske'lɛtriko] AG (*anche Anat*) skeletal; (*fig: essenziale*) skeleton *cpd*

'**scheletro** ['skɛletro] SM skeleton; **avere uno ~ nell'armadio** (*fig*) to have a skeleton in the cupboard

'**schema, -i** ['skɛma] SM (*diagramma*) diagram, sketch; (*progetto, abbozzo*) outline, plan; **ribellarsi agli schemi** to rebel against traditional values; **secondo gli schemi tradizionali** in accordance with traditional values

sche'matico, -a, -ci, -che [ske'matiko] AG schematic

schematiz'zare [skematid'dzare] **/72/** VT to schematize

'**scherma** ['skerma] SF fencing

scher'maglia [sker'maʎʎa] SF (*fig*) skirmish

scher'mata [sker'mata] SF screenshot

scher'mirsi [sker'mirsi] **/55/** VPR to defend o.s.

'**schermo** ['skermo] SM shield, screen; (*Cine, TV*) screen; **a ~ panoramico** (*TV*) widescreen

schermogra'fia [skermogra'fia] SF X-rays *pl*

scher'nire [sker'nire] **/55/** VT to mock, sneer at

'**scherno** ['skerno] SM mockery, derision; **farsi ~ di** to sneer at; **essere oggetto di ~** to be a laughing stock

scher'zare [sker'tsare] **/72/** VI to joke

'**scherzo** ['skertso] SM joke; (*tiro*) trick; (*Mus*) scherzo; **è uno ~!** (*una cosa facile*) it's child's play!, it's easy!; **per ~** in jest; for a joke *o* a laugh; **fare un brutto ~ a qn** to play a nasty trick on sb; **scherzi a parte** seriously, joking apart

scher'zoso, -a [sker'tsoso] AG (*tono, gesto*) playful; (*osservazione*) facetious; **è un tipo ~** he likes a joke

schiaccia'noci [skjattʃa'notʃi] SM INV nutcracker

schiacci'ante [skjat'tʃante] AG overwhelming

schiacci'are [skjat'tʃare] **/14/** VT (*dito*) to crush; (*noci*) to crack; ~ **un pisolino** to have a nap; **schiacciarsi** VPR (*appiattirsi*) to get squashed; (*frantumarsi*) to get crushed

schiaffeggi'are [skjaffed'dʒare] **/62/** VT to slap

schi'affo ['skjaffo] SM slap; **prendere qn a schiaffi** to slap sb's face; **uno ~ morale** a slap in the face, a rebuff

schiamaz'zare [skjamat'tsare] **/72/** VI to squawk, cackle

schia'mazzo [skja'mattso] SM (*fig: chiasso*) din, racket

schian'tare [skjan'tare] **/72/** VT to break, tear apart; **schiantarsi** VPR to break (up), shatter; **schiantarsi al suolo** (*aereo*) to crash (to the ground)

schi'anto ['skjanto] SM (*rumore*) crash; tearing sound; **è uno ~!** (*col*) it's (*o* he's *o* she's) terrific!; **di ~** all of a sudden

schia'rire [skja'rire] **/55/** VT to lighten, make lighter ▶ VI (*anche:* **schiarirsi**) to grow lighter; (*tornar sereno*) to clear, brighten up; **schiarirsi la voce** to clear one's throat

schia'rita [skja'rita] SF (*Meteor*) bright spell; (*fig*) improvement, turn for the better

schiat'tare [skjat'tare] **/72/** VI to burst; ~ **d'invidia** to be green with envy; ~ **di rabbia** to be beside o.s. with rage

schiavitù [skjavi'tu] SF slavery

schiaviz'zare [skjavid'dzare] **/72/** VT to enslave

schi'avo, -a ['skjavo] SM/F slave

schi'ena ['skjɛna] SF (*Anat*) back

schie'nale [skje'nale] SM (*di sedia*) back

schi'era ['skjɛra] SF (*Mil*) rank; (*gruppo*) group, band; **villette a ~** ≈ terraced houses

schiera'mento [skjera'mento] SM (*Mil, Sport*) formation; (*fig*) alliance

schie'rare [skje'rare] **/72/** VT (*esercito*) to line up, draw up, marshal; **schierarsi** VPR to line up; (*fig*) **schierarsi con** *o* **dalla parte di/ contro qn** to side with/oppose sb

schi'etto, -a ['skjɛtto] AG (*puro*) pure; (*fig*) frank, straightforward

schi'fare [ski'fare] **/72/** VT to disgust

schi'fezza [ski'fettsa] SF: **essere una ~** (*cibo, bibita ecc*) to be disgusting; (*film, libro*) to be dreadful

schifil'toso, -a [skifil'toso] AG fussy, difficult

'**schifo** ['skifo] SM disgust; **fare ~** (*essere fatto male, dare pessimi risultati*) to be awful; **mi fa ~** it makes me sick, it's disgusting; **quel libro è uno ~** that book's rotten

schi'foso, -a [ski'foso] AG disgusting, revolting; (*molto scadente*) rotten, lousy

S

schioc'care [skjok'kare] **/20/** VT (*frusta*) to crack; (*dita*) to snap; (*lingua*) to click; ~ **le labbra** to smack one's lips

schioppet'tata [skjoppet'tata] SF gunshot

schi'oppo ['skjɔppo] SM rifle, gun

schi'udere ['skjudere] **/22/** VT, **schi'udersi** VPR to open

schi'uma ['skjuma] SF foam; (*di sapone*) lather; (*di latte*) froth; (*fig: feccia*) scum

schiu'mare [skju'mare] **/72/** VT to skim ▶ VI to foam

schi'uso, -a ['skjuso] PP *di* **schiudere**

schi'vare [ski'vare] **/72/** VT to dodge, avoid

'schivo, -a ['skivo] AG (*ritroso*) stand-offish, reserved; (*timido*) shy

schizofre'nia [skiddzofre'nia] SF schizophrenia

schizo'frenico, -a, -ci, -che [skiddzo'freniko] AG schizophrenic

schiz'zare [skit'tsare] **/72/** VT (*spruzzare*) to spurt, squirt; (*sporcare*) to splash, spatter; (*fig: abbozzare*) to sketch ▶ VI to spurt, squirt; (*saltar fuori*) to dart up (*o off etc*); ~ **via** (*animale, persona*) to dart away; (*macchina, moto*) to accelerate away

schizzi'noso, -a [skittsi'noso] AG fussy, finicky

'schizzo ['skittso] SM (*di liquido*) spurt; splash, spatter; (*abbozzo*) sketch

sci [ʃi] SM INV (*attrezzo*) ski; (*attività*) skiing; ~ **di fondo** cross-country skiing, ski touring (*US*); ~ **d'acqua** *o* **nautico** water-skiing

'scia ['ʃia] (*pl* **scie**) SF (*di imbarcazione*) wake; (*di profumo*) trail

scià [ʃa] SM INV shah

sci'abola ['ʃabola] SF sabre (BRIT), saber (US)

scia'callo [ʃa'kallo] SM jackal; (*fig: peg: profittatore*) shark, profiteer; (: *ladro*) looter

sciac'quare [ʃak'kware] **/72/** VT to rinse

scia'gura [ʃa'gura] SF disaster, calamity; misfortune

sciagu'rato, -a [ʃagu'rato] AG unfortunate; (*malvagio*) wicked

scialac'quare [ʃalak'kware] **/72/** VT to squander

scia'lare [ʃa'lare] **/72/** VI to throw one's money around

sci'albo, -a ['ʃalbo] AG pale, dull; (*fig*) dull, colourless (BRIT), colorless (US)

sci'alle ['ʃalle] SM shawl

sci'alo ['ʃalo] SM squandering, waste

scia'luppa [ʃa'luppa] SF (*Naut*) sloop; (*anche*: **scialuppa di salvataggio**) lifeboat

scia'mare [ʃa'mare] **/72/** VI to swarm

sci'ame ['ʃame] SM swarm

scian'cato, -a [ʃan'kato] AG lame; (*mobile*) rickety

sci'are [ʃi'are] **/60/** VI to ski; **andare a** ~ to go skiing

sci'arpa ['ʃarpa] SF scarf; (*fascia*) sash

scia'tore, -'trice [ʃia'tore] SM/F skier

sciat'tezza [ʃat'tettsa] SF slovenliness

sci'atto, -a ['ʃatto] AG (*persona: nell'aspetto*) slovenly, unkempt; (: *nel lavoro*) sloppy, careless

'scibile ['ʃibile] SM knowledge

scien'tifico, -a, -ci, -che [ʃen'tifiko] AG scientific; **la (polizia) scientifica** the forensic department

sci'enza ['ʃentsa] SF science; (*sapere*) knowledge; **scienze** SFPL (*Ins*) science *sg*; **scienze naturali** natural sciences; **scienze politiche** political science *sg*

scienzi'ato, -a [ʃen'tsjato] SM/F scientist

'Scilly ['ʃilli]: **le isole** ~ *sfpl* the Scilly Isles

'scimmia ['ʃimmja] SF monkey

scimmiot'tare [ʃimmjot'tare] **/72/** VT to ape, mimic

scimpanzé [ʃimpan'tse] SM INV chimpanzee

scimu'nito, -a [ʃimu'nito] AG silly, idiotic

'scindere ['ʃindere] **/102/** VT, **'scindersi** VPR to split (up)

scin'tilla [ʃin'tilla] SF spark

scintil'lare [ʃintil'lare] **/72/** VI to spark; (*acqua, occhi*) to sparkle

scintil'lio [ʃintil'lio] SM sparkling

scioc'care [ʃok'kare] **/20/** VT to shock

scioc'chezza [ʃok'kettsa] SF stupidity *no pl*; stupid *o* foolish thing; **dire sciocchezze** to talk nonsense

sci'occo, -a, -chi, -che ['ʃɔkko] AG stupid, foolish

sci'ogliere ['ʃɔʎʎere] **/103/** VT (*nodo*) to untie; (*capelli*) to loosen; (*persona, animale*) to untie, release; (*nell'acqua: zucchero ecc*) to dissolve; (*fig: mistero*) to solve; (*porre fine a: contratto*) to cancel; (: *società, matrimonio*) to dissolve; (: *riunione*) to bring to an end; (*fig: persona*): ~ **da** to release from; (*neve*) to melt; **sciogliersi** VPR to loosen, come untied; to melt; to dissolve; (*assemblea, corteo, duo*) to break up; ~ **i muscoli** to limber up; ~ **il ghiaccio** (*fig*) to break the ice; ~ **le vele** (*Naut*) to set sail; **sciogliersi dai legami** (*fig*) to free o.s. from all ties

scioglilingua [ʃoʎʎi'lingwa] SM INV tongue-twister

sci'olgo *etc* ['ʃɔlgo] VB *vedi* **sciogliere**

sciol'tezza [ʃol'tettsa] SF agility; suppleness; ease

sci'olto, -a ['ʃɔlto] PP *di* **sciogliere** ▶ AG loose; (*agile*) agile, nimble; supple; (*disinvolto*) free and easy; **essere** ~ **nei movimenti** to be supple; **versi sciolti** (*Poesia*) blank verse

sciope'rante [ʃope'rante] SMF striker

sciope'rare [ʃope'rare] **/72/** VI to strike, go on strike

sci'opero ['ʃɔpero] SM strike; **fare** ~ to strike; **entrare in** ~ to go on *o* come out on strike;

~ **bianco** work-to-rule (BRIT), slowdown (US);
~ **della fame** hunger strike; ~ **selvaggio**
wildcat strike; ~ **a singhiozzo** on-off strike;
~ **di solidarietà** sympathy strike

scioriˈnare [ʃoriˈnare] /**72**/ VT (ostentare) to
show off, display

scioˈvia [ʃioˈvia] SF ski lift

scioviˈnismo [ʃoviˈnizmo] SM chauvinism

scioviˈnista, -i, -e [ʃoviˈnista] SM/F chauvinist

sciˈpito, -a [ʃiˈpito] AG insipid

scipˈpare [ʃipˈpare] /**72**/ VT: ~ **qn** to snatch
sb's bag

scippaˈtore [ʃippaˈtore] SM bag-snatcher

ˈscippo [ˈʃippo] SM bag-snatching

sciˈrocco [ʃiˈrɔkko] SM sirocco

sciˈroppo [ʃiˈrɔppo] SM syrup; ~ **per la tosse**
cough syrup, cough mixture

ˈscisma, -i [ˈʃizma] SM (Rel) schism

scissiˈone [ʃisˈsjone] SF (anche fig) split,
division; (Fisica) fission

ˈscisso, -a [ˈʃisso] PP di **scindere**

sciuˈpare [ʃuˈpare] /**72**/ VT (abito, libro, appetito)
to spoil, ruin; (tempo, denaro) to waste;
sciuparsi VPR to get spoilt o ruined; (rovinarsi
la salute) to ruin one's health

scivoˈlare [ʃivoˈlare] /**72**/ VI to slide o glide
along; (involontariamente) to slip, slide

ˈscivolo [ˈʃivolo] SM slide; (Tecn) chute

scivoˈloso, -a [ʃivoˈloso] AG slippery

scleˈrosi SF sclerosis

scocˈcare /**20**/ VT (freccia) to shoot ▶ VI
(guizzare) to shoot up; (battere: ora) to strike

scoccheˈrò etc [skokkeˈrɔ] VB vedi **scoccare**

scocciˈare [skotˈtʃare] /**14**/ VT to bother, annoy;
scocciarsi VPR to be bothered o annoyed

scocciaˈtore, -ˈtrice [skottʃaˈtore] SM/F
nuisance, pest (col)

scocciaˈtura [skottʃaˈtura] SF nuisance, bore

scoˈdella SF bowl

scodinzoˈlare [skodintsoˈlare] /**72**/ VI to wag
its tail

scogliˈera [skoʎˈʎɛra] SF reef; (rupe) cliff

ˈscoglio [ˈskɔʎʎo] SM (al mare) rock; (fig:
ostacolo) difficulty, stumbling block

scogliˈoso, -a [skoʎˈʎoso] AG rocky

scoiˈattolo SM squirrel

scolaˈpasta SM INV colander

scolapiˈatti SM INV drainer (for plates)

scoˈlare /**72**/ AG: **età** ~ school age ▶ VT to drain
▶ VI to drip

scolaˈresca SF schoolchildren pl, pupils pl

scoˈlaro, -a SM/F pupil, schoolboy(-girl)

scoˈlastico, -a, -ci, -che AG (gen) scholastic;
(libro, anno, divisa) school cpd

scolˈlare /**72**/ VT (staccare) to unstick; **scollarsi**
VPR to come unstuck

scolˈlato, -a AG (vestito) low-cut, low-necked;
(donna) wearing a low-cut dress (o blouse etc)

scollaˈtura SF neckline

scolleˈgare /**80**/ VT (fili, apparecchi) to
disconnect; **scollegarsi** VPR (da Internet) to
disconnect; (da chat-line) to log off

ˈscolo SM drainage; (sbocco) drain; (acqua)
waste water; **canale di** ~ drain; **tubo di** ~
drainpipe

scoloˈrire /**55**/ VT to fade; to discolour (BRIT),
discolor (US) ▶ VI (anche: **scolorirsi**) to fade; to
become discoloured; (impallidire) to turn pale

scolˈpire /**55**/ VT to carve, sculpt

scombiˈnare /**72**/ VT to mess up, upset

scombiˈnato, -a AG confused, muddled

scombussoˈlare /**72**/ VT to upset

scomˈmesso, -a PP di **scommettere** ▶ SF bet,
wager; **fare una scommessa** to bet

scomˈmettere /**63**/ VT, VI to bet

scomoˈdare /**72**/ VT to trouble, bother,
disturb; (fig: nome famoso) to involve, drag in;
scomodarsi VPR to put o.s. out; **scomodarsi
a fare** to go to the bother o trouble of doing

scomodità SF INV (di sedia, letto ecc)
discomfort; (di orario, sistemazione ecc)
inconvenience

ˈscomodo, -a AG uncomfortable; (sistemazione,
posto) awkward, inconvenient

scompagiˈnare [skompadʒiˈnare] /**72**/ VT to
upset, throw into disorder

scompagˈnato, -a [skompaɲˈɲato] AG (calzini,
guanti) odd

scompaˈrire /**7**/ VI (sparire) to disappear,
vanish; (fig) to be insignificant

scomˈparso, -a PP di **scomparire** ▶ SF
disappearance; (fig: morte) passing away,
death

scompartiˈmento SM (Ferr) compartment;
(sezione) division

scomˈparto SM compartment, division

scomˈpenso SM imbalance, lack of balance

scompigliˈare [skompiʎˈʎare] /**27**/ VT
(cassetto, capelli) to mess up, disarrange;
(fig: piani) to upset

scomˈpiglio [skomˈpiʎʎo] SM mess,
confusion

scomˈporre /**77**/ VT (parola, numero) to break
up; (Chim) to decompose; **scomporsi** VPR
(Chim) to decompose; (fig) to get upset, lose
one's composure; **senza scomporsi**
unperturbed

scomˈposto, -a PP di **scomporre** ▶ AG (gesto)
unseemly; (capelli) ruffled, dishevelled

scoˈmunica, -che SF excommunication

scomuniˈcare /**20**/ VT to excommunicate

sconcerˈtante [skontʃerˈtante] AG
disconcerting

sconcerˈtare [skontʃerˈtare] /**72**/ VT to
disconcert, bewilder

ˈsconcio, -a, -ci, -ce [ˈskontʃo] AG (osceno)
indecent, obscene ▶ SM (cosa riprovevole, mal
fatta) disgrace

sconclusio'nato, -a AG incoherent, illogical

sconfes'sare /**72**/ VT to renounce, disavow; to repudiate

scon'figgere [skon'fiddʒere] /**104**/ VT to defeat, overcome

sconfi'nare /**72**/ VI to cross the border; (*in proprietà privata*) to trespass; (*fig*): ~ **da** to stray o digress from

sconfi'nato, -a AG boundless, unlimited

scon'fitto, -a PP *di* **sconfiggere** ▶ SF defeat

sconfor'tante, -a AG discouraging, disheartening

sconfor'tare /**72**/ VT to discourage, dishearten; **sconfortarsi** VPR to become discouraged, become disheartened, lose heart

scon'forto SM despondency

sconge'lare [skondʒe'lare] /**72**/ VT to defrost

scongiu'rare [skondʒu'rare] /**72**/ VT (*implorare*) to beseech, entreat, implore; (*eludere: pericolo*) to ward off, avert

scongi'uro [skon'dʒuro] SM (*esorcismo*) exorcism; **fare gli scongiuri** to touch wood (BRIT), knock on wood (US)

scon'nesso, -a AG (*fig: discorso*) incoherent, rambling

sconosci'uto, -a [skonoʃʃu'to] AG unknown; new, strange ▶ SM/F stranger; unknown person

sconquas'sare /**72**/ VT to shatter, smash

scon'quasso SM (*danno*) damage; (*fig*) confusion

sconside'rato, -a AG thoughtless, rash

sconsigli'are [skonsiʎ'ʎare] /**27**/ VT: ~ **qc a qn** to advise sb against sth; ~ **qn dal fare qc** to advise sb not to do o against doing sth

sconso'lato, -a AG inconsolable; desolate

scon'tare /**72**/ VT (*Comm: detrarre*) to deduct; (: *debito*) to pay off; (: *cambiale*) to discount; (*pena*) to serve; (*colpa, errori*) to pay for, suffer for

scon'tato, -a AG (*previsto*) foreseen, taken for granted; (*prezzo, merce*) discounted, at a discount; **dare per ~ che** to take it for granted that

sconten'tare /**72**/ VT to displease, dissatisfy

sconten'tezza [skonten'tettsa] SF displeasure, dissatisfaction

scon'tento, -a AG: ~ **(di)** discontented o dissatisfied (with) ▶ SM discontent, dissatisfaction

'sconto SM discount; **fare** o **concedere uno ~** to give a discount; **uno ~ del 10%** a 10% discount

scon'trarsi /**72**/ VPR (*treni ecc*) to crash, collide; (*venire ad uno scontro: fig*) to clash; ~ **con** to crash into, collide with

scon'trino SM ticket; (*di cassa*) receipt

'scontro SM (*Mil, fig*) clash, encounter; (*di veicoli*) crash, collision; ~ **a fuoco** shoot-out

scon'troso, -a AG sullen, surly; (*permaloso*) touchy

sconveni'ente AG unseemly, improper

sconvol'gente [skonvol'dʒɛnte] AG (*notizia, brutta esperienza*) upsetting, disturbing; (*bellezza*) amazing; (*passione*) overwhelming

scon'volgere [skon'vɔldʒere] /**96**/ VT to throw into confusion, upset; (*turbare*) to shake, disturb, upset

scon'volto, -a PP *di* **sconvolgere** ▶ AG (*persona*) distraught, very upset

'scooter ['skuter] SM INV scooter

'scopa SF broom; (*Carte*) Italian card game

sco'pare /**72**/ VT to sweep; (!) to bonk (!)

sco'pata SF (!) bonk (!)

scoperchi'are [skoper'kjare] /**19**/ VT (*pentola, vaso*) to take the lid off, uncover; (*casa*) to take the roof off

sco'perto, -a PP *di* **scoprire** ▶ AG uncovered; (*capo*) uncovered, bare; (*macchina*) open; (*Mil*) exposed, without cover; (*conto*) overdrawn ▶ SF discovery ▶ SM: **allo ~** (*dormire ecc*) out in the open; **assegno ~** uncovered cheque; **avere un conto ~** to be overdrawn

'scopo SM aim, purpose; **a che ~?** what for?; **adatto allo ~** fit for its purpose; **allo ~ di fare qc** in order to do sth; **a ~ di lucro** for gain o money; **senza ~** (*fare, cercare*) pointlessly

scoppi'are /**19**/ VI (*spaccarsi*) to burst; (*esplodere*) to explode; (*fig*) to break out; ~ **in pianto** o **a piangere** to burst out crying; ~ **dalle risa** o **dal ridere** to split one's sides laughing; ~ **dal caldo** to be boiling; ~ **di salute** to be the picture of health

scoppiet'tare /**72**/ VI to crackle

'scoppio SM explosion; (*di tuono, arma ecc*) crash, bang; (*fig: di risa, ira*) fit; (*di pneumatico*) bang; (*fig: di guerra*) outbreak; **a ~ ritardato** delayed-action; **reazione a ~ ritardato** delayed o slow reaction; **uno ~ di risa** a burst of laughter; **uno ~ di collera** an explosion of anger

sco'prire /**9**/ VT to discover; (*liberare da ciò che copre*) to uncover; (: *monumento*) to unveil; **scoprirsi** VPR to put on lighter clothes; (*fig*) to give o.s. away

scopri'tore, -'trice SM/F discoverer

scoraggi'are [skorad'dʒare] /**62**/ VT to discourage; **scoraggiarsi** VPR to become discouraged, lose heart

scor'butico, -a, -ci, -che AG (*fig*) cantankerous

scorcia'toia [skortʃa'toja] SF short cut

'scorcio ['skortʃo] SM (*Arte*) foreshortening; (*di secolo, periodo*) end, close; ~ **panoramico** vista

scor'dare /**72**/ VT to forget; **scordarsi** VPR: **scordarsi di qc/di fare** to forget sth/to do
sco'reggia [sko'reddʒa] (!) SF fart (!)
scoreggi'are [skored'dʒare] /**62**/ (!) VI to fart (!)
'**scorgere** ['skɔrdʒere] /**59**/ VT to make out, distinguish, see
sco'ria SF (di metalli) slag; (vulcanica) scoria; **scorie radioattive** (Fisica) radioactive waste sg
'**scorno** SM ignominy, disgrace
scorpacci'ata [skorpat'tʃata] SF: **fare una ~ (di)** to stuff o.s. (with), eat one's fill (of)
scorpi'one SM scorpion; **S~** Scorpio; **essere dello S~** to be Scorpio
'**scorporo** SM (Pol) transfer of votes aimed at increasing the chances of representation for minority parties
scorraz'zare [skorrat'tsare] /**72**/ VI to run about
'**scorrere** /**28**/ VT (giornale, lettera) to run o skim through ▸ VI (liquido, fiume) to run, flow; (fune) to run; (cassetto, porta) to slide easily; (tempo) to pass (by)
scorre'ria SF raid, incursion
scorret'tezza [skorret'tettsa] SF incorrectness; lack of politeness, rudeness; unfairness; **commettere una ~** (essere sleale) to be unfair
scor'retto, -a AG (sbagliato) incorrect; (sgarbato) impolite; (sconveniente) improper; (sleale) unfair; (gioco) foul
scor'revole AG (porta) sliding; (fig: stile) fluent, flowing
scorri'banda SF (Mil) raid; (escursione) trip, excursion
'**scorsi** etc VB vedi **scorgere**
'**scorso, -a** PP di **scorrere** ▸ AG last ▸ SF quick look, glance; **lo ~ mese** last month
scor'soio, -a AG: **nodo ~** noose
'**scorta** SF (di personalità, convoglio) escort; (provvista) supply, stock; **sotto la ~ di due agenti** escorted by two policemen; **fare ~ di** to stock up with, get in a supply of; **di ~** (materiali) spare; **ruota di ~** spare wheel
scor'tare /**72**/ VT to escort
scor'tese AG discourteous, rude
scorte'sia SF discourtesy, rudeness; (azione) discourtesy
scorti'care /**20**/ VT to skin
'**scorto, -a** PP di **scorgere**
'**scorza** ['skɔrdza] SF (di albero) bark; (di agrumi) peel, skin
sco'sceso, -a [skoʃ'ʃeso] AG steep
'**scosso, -a** PP di **scuotere** ▸ AG (turbato) shaken, upset ▸ SF jerk, jolt, shake; (Elettr, fig) shock; **prendere la scossa** to get an electric shock; **scossa di terremoto** earth tremor

scos'sone SM: **dare uno ~ a qn** to give sb a shake; **procedere a scossoni** to jolt o jerk along
scos'tante AG (fig) off-putting (BRIT), unpleasant
scos'tare /**72**/ VT to move (away), shift; **scostarsi** VPR to move away
scostu'mato, -a AG immoral, dissolute
scotch [skɔtʃ] SM INV (whisky) Scotch®; (nastro adesivo) Scotch tape®, Sellotape®
scot'tante AG (fig: urgente) pressing; (: delicato) delicate
scot'tare /**72**/ VT (ustionare) to burn; (: con liquido bollente) to scald ▸ VI to burn; (caffè) to be too hot; **scottarsi** VPR to burn/scald o.s.; (fig) to have one's fingers burnt
scotta'tura SF burn; scald
'**scotto, -a** AG overcooked ▸ SM (fig): **pagare lo ~ (di)** to pay the penalty (for)
sco'vare /**72**/ VT to drive out, flush out; (fig) to discover
'**Scozia** ['skɔttsja] SF: **la ~** Scotland
scoz'zese [skot'tsese] AG Scottish ▸ SMF Scot
screan'zato, -a [skrean'tsato] AG ill-mannered ▸ SM/F boor
scredi'tare /**72**/ VT to discredit
'**screen saver** ['skriin'seivər] SM INV (Inform) screen saver
scre'mare /**72**/ VT to skim
scre'mato, -a AG skimmed; **parzialmente ~** semi-skimmed
screpo'lare /**72**/ VT, **screpo'larsi** VPR to crack
screpo'lato, -a AG (labbra) chapped; (muro) cracked
screpola'tura SF cracking no pl; crack
screzi'ato, -a [skret'tsjato] AG streaked
'**screzio** ['skrettsjo] SM disagreement
scribac'chino [skribak'kino] SM (peg: impiegato) penpusher; (: scrittore) hack
scricchio'lare [skrikkjo'lare] /**72**/ VI to creak, squeak
scricchio'lio [skrikkjo'lio] SM creaking
'**scricciolo** ['skrittʃolo] SM wren
'**scrigno** ['skriɲɲo] SM casket
scrimina'tura SF parting
'**scrissi** etc VB vedi **scrivere**
'**scritto, -a** PP di **scrivere** ▸ AG written ▸ SM writing; (lettera) letter, note ▸ SF inscription; **scritti** SMPL (letterari ecc) work(s), writings; **per** o **in ~** in writing
scrit'toio SM writing desk
scrit'tore, -'trice SM/F writer
scrit'tura SF writing; (Comm) entry; (contratto) contract; (Rel): **la Sacra S~** the Scriptures pl; **scritture** SFPL (Comm) accounts, books
scrittu'rare /**72**/ VT (Teat, Cine) to sign up, engage; (Comm) to enter
scriva'nia SF desk

S

331

scri'vano SM (*amanuense*) scribe; (*impiegato*) clerk

scri'vente SMF writer

'**scrivere** /**105**/ VT to write; **come si scrive?** how is it spelt?, how do you write it?; ~ **qc a qn** to write sth to sb; ~ **qc a macchina** to type sth; ~ **a penna/matita** to write in pen/pencil; ~ **qc maiuscolo/minuscolo** to write sth in capital/small letters

scroc'care /**20**/ VT (*col*) to scrounge, cadge

scroc'cone, -a SM/F scrounger

'**scrofa** SF (*Zool*) sow

scrol'lare /**72**/ VT to shake; **scrollarsi** VPR (*anche fig*) to give o.s. a shake; ~ **le spalle/il capo** to shrug one's shoulders/shake one's head; **scrollarsi qc di dosso** (*anche fig*) to shake sth off

scrol'lata SF shake; ~ **di spalle** shrug (of one's shoulders)

scrosci'ante [skroʃʃante] AG (*pioggia*) pouring; (*fig: applausi*) thunderous

scrosci'are [skroʃʃare] /**14**/ VI (*pioggia*) to pour down, pelt down; (*torrente, fig: applausi*) to thunder, roar

'**scroscio** ['skrɔʃʃo] SM pelting; thunder, roar; (*di applausi*) burst

scros'tare /**72**/ VT (*intonaco*) to scrape off, strip; **scrostarsi** VPR to peel off, flake off

'**scrupolo** SM scruple; (*meticolosità*) care, conscientiousness; **essere senza scrupoli** to be unscrupulous

scrupo'loso, -a AG scrupulous; conscientious

scru'tare /**72**/ VT to scrutinize; (*intenzioni, causa*) to examine, scrutinize

scruta'tore, -'trice SM/F (*Pol*) scrutineer

scruti'nare /**72**/ VT (*voti*) to count

scru'tinio SM (*votazione*) ballot; (*insieme delle operazioni*) poll; (*Ins*) meeting for assignment of marks at end of a term or year

scu'cire [sku'tʃire] /**31**/ VT (*orlo ecc*) to unpick, undo; **scucirsi** VPR to come unstitched

scude'ria SF stable

scu'detto SM (*Sport*) (championship) shield; (*distintivo*) badge

scu'discio [sku'diʃʃo] SM (riding) crop, (riding) whip

'**scudo** SM shield; **farsi ~ di** *o* **con qc** to shield o.s. with sth; ~ **aereo/missilistico** air/missile defence (BRIT) *o* defense (US); ~ **termico** heat shield

sculacci'are [skulat'tʃare] /**14**/ VT to spank

sculacci'one [skulat'tʃone] SM spanking

scul'tore, -'trice SM/F sculptor

scul'tura SF sculpture

scu'ola SF school; ~ **elementare** *o* **primaria** primary (BRIT) *o* grade (US) school (*for children from 6 to 11 years of age*); ~ **guida** driving school; ~ **materna** *o* **dell'infanzia** nursery school (*for children aged 3 to 6*); ~ **secondaria di**

primo grado *first 3 years of secondary school, for children from 11 to 14 years of age*; ~ **secondaria di secondo grado** secondary school (*for children aged 14 to 18*); ~ **media** secondary (BRIT) *o* high (US) school; ~ **dell'obbligo** compulsory education; ~ **privata/pubblica** private/state school; **scuole serali** evening classes, night school SG; ~ **tecnica** technical college; *see note*

Italian children first go to school at the age of three. They remain at the *scuola materna* until they are six, when they move on to the *scuola primaria* for another five years. After this come three years of *scuola secondaria di primo grado*. Students who wish to continue their schooling attend *scuola secondaria di secondo grado*, choosing between several types of institution which specialize in different subject areas.

scu'otere /**106**/ VT to shake; **scuotersi** VPR to jump, be startled; (*fig: muoversi*) to rouse o.s., stir o.s.; (: *turbarsi*) to be shaken

'**scure** SF axe, ax (US)

scu'rire /**55**/ VT to darken, make darker

'**scuro, -a** AG dark; (*fig: espressione*) grim ▶ SM darkness; dark colour (BRIT) *o* color (US); (*imposta*) (window) shutter; **verde/rosso** *etc* ~ dark green/red *etc*

scur'rile AG scurrilous

'**scusa** SF excuse; **scuse** SFPL apology SG, apologies; **chiedere ~ a qn (per)** to apologize to sb (for); **chiedo ~** I'm sorry; (*disturbando ecc*) excuse me; **vi prego di accettare le mie scuse** please accept my apologies

scu'sare /**72**/ VT to excuse; **scusarsi** VPR: **scusarsi (di)** to apologize (for); (**mi) scusi** I'm sorry; (*per richiamare l'attenzione*) excuse me

S.C.V. SIGLA = **Stato della Città del Vaticano**

sdebi'tarsi /**72**/ VPR: ~ **(con qn di** *o* **per qc)** (*anche fig*) to repay (sb for sth)

sde'gnare [zdeɲ'ɲare] /**15**/ VT to scorn, despise; **sdegnarsi** VPR (*adirarsi*) to get angry

sde'gnato, -a [zdeɲ'ɲato] AG indignant, angry

'**sdegno** ['zdeɲɲo] SM scorn, disdain

sdegnosa'mente [zdeɲɲosa'mente] AV scornfully, disdainfully

sde'gnoso, -a [zdeɲ'ɲoso] AG scornful, disdainful

sdilin'quirsi /**55**/ VPR (*illanguidirsi*) to become sentimental

sdoga'nare /**72**/ VT (*Comm*) to clear through customs

sdolci'nato, -a [zdoltʃi'nato] AG mawkish, oversentimental

sdoppia'mento SM (*Chim: di composto*) splitting; (*Psic*): ~ **della personalità** split personality

sdoppi'are /**19**/ VT (*dividere*) to divide o split in two

sdrai'arsi /**19**/ VPR to stretch out, lie down

'sdraio SM: **sedia a ~** deck chair

sdrammatiz'zare [zdrammatid'dzare] /**72**/ VT to play down, minimize

sdruccio'lare [zdruttʃo'lare] /**72**/ VI to slip, slide

sdruccio'levole [zdruttʃo'levole] AG slippery

sdru'cito, -a [zdru'tʃito] AG (*strappato*) torn; (*logoro*) threadbare

(PAROLA CHIAVE)

se PRON *vedi* **si**

▶ CONG **1** (*condizionale, ipotetica*) if; **se nevica non vengo** I won't come if it snows; **se fossi in te** if I were you; **sarei rimasto se me l'avessero chiesto** I would have stayed if they'd asked me; **non puoi fare altro se non telefonare** all you can do is phone; **se mai** if, if ever; **siamo noi se mai che le siamo grati** it is we who should be grateful to you; **se no** (*altrimenti*) or (else), otherwise; **se non** (*anzi*) if not; (*tranne*) except; **se non altro** if nothing else, at least; **se solo** o **solamente** if only

2 (*in frasi dubitative, interrogative indirette*) if, whether; **non so se scrivere o telefonare** I don't know whether o if I should write or phone

sé PRON (*gen*) oneself; (*esso, essa, lui, lei, loro*) itself; himself; herself; themselves; **sé stesso(a)** *pron* oneself; itself; himself; herself; **sé stessi(e)** (*pl*) themselves; **di per sé non è un problema** it's no problem in itself; **parlare tra sé e sé** to talk to oneself; **va da sé che ...** it goes without saying that ..., it's obvious that ..., it stands to reason that ...; **è un caso a sé** o **a sé stante** it's a special case; **un uomo che s'è fatto da sé** a self-made man

S.E. ABBR (= *sud-est*) SE; (= *Sua Eccellenza*) HE

S.E.A.T.O. SIGLA F (= *Southeast Asia Treaty Organization*) SEATO

seb'bene CONG although, though

'sebo SM sebum

sec. ABBR (= *secolo*) c.

'SECAM SIGLA M (= *séquentiel couleur à mémoire*) SECAM

'secca SF *vedi* **secco**

secca'mente AV (*rispondere, rifiutare*) sharply, curtly

sec'care /**20**/ VT to dry; (*prosciugare*) to dry up; (*fig: importunare*) to annoy, bother ▶ VI to dry; to dry up; **seccarsi** VPR to dry; to dry up; (*fig*) to grow annoyed; **si è seccato molto** he was very annoyed

sec'cato, -a AG (*fig: infastidito*) bothered, annoyed; (: *stufo*) fed up

secca'tore, -'trice SM/F nuisance, bother

secca'tura SF (*fig*) bother *no pl*, trouble *no pl*

seccherò *etc* [sekke'rɔ] VB *vedi* **seccare**

'secchia ['sekkja] SF bucket, pail

secchi'ello [sek'kjɛllo] SM (*per bambini*) bucket, pail; **~ del ghiaccio** ice bucket

'secchio ['sekkjo] SM bucket, pail; **~ della spazzatura** o **delle immondizie** dustbin (BRIT), garbage can (US)

'secco, -a, -chi, -che AG dry; (*fichi, pesce*) dried; (*foglie, ramo*) withered; (*magro: persona*) thin, skinny; (*fig: risposta, modo di fare*) curt, abrupt; (: *colpo*) clean, sharp ▶ SM (*siccità*) drought ▶ SF (*del mare*) shallows *pl*; **restarci ~** (*morire sul colpo*) to drop dead; **avere la gola secca** to feel dry, be parched; **lavare a ~** to dry-clean; **tirare a ~** (*barca*) to beach; **rimanere a ~** (*fig*) to be left in the lurch

secen'tesco, -a, -schi, -sche [setʃen'tesko] AG = **seicentesco**

se'cernere [se'tʃɛrnere] /**29**/ VT to secrete

seco'lare AG age-old, centuries-old; (*laico, mondano*) secular

'secolo SM century; (*epoca*) age

se'conda SF *vedi* **secondo**; **la S~ Repubblica** *see note*

> *Seconda Repubblica* is the term used, especially by the Italian media, to refer to the government and the country in general since the 1994 elections. This is when the old party system collapsed, following the *Tangentopoli* scandals. New political parties were set up and the electoral system was reformed, a first-past-the-post element being introduced side by side with proportional representation.

secondaria'mente AV secondly

secon'dario, -a AG secondary; **scuola/ istruzione secondaria** secondary school/ education

secon'dino SM prison officer, warder (BRIT)

se'condo, -a AG second ▶ SM second; (*di pranzo*) main course ▶ SF (*Aut*) second (gear); (*Ferr*) second class ▶ PREP according to; (*nel modo prescritto*) in accordance with; **seconda classe** second-class; **di seconda classe** second-class; **di seconda mano** second-hand; **viaggiare in seconda** to travel second-class; **comandante in seconda** second-in-command; **a seconda di** *prep* according to; in accordance with; **~ me** in my opinion, to my mind; **~ la legge/ quanto si era deciso** in accordance with the law/the decision taken

secondo'genito, -a [sekondo'dʒenito] SM/F second-born

S

secrezi'one [sekret'tsjone] SF secretion

'sedano SM celery

se'dare /**72**/ VT (*dolore*) to soothe; (*rivolta*) to put down, suppress

seda'tivo, -a AG, SM sedative

'sede SF (*luogo di residenza*) (place of) residence; (*di ditta: principale*) head office; (: *secondaria*) branch (office); (*di organizzazione*) headquarters pl; (*di governo, parlamento*) seat; (*Rel*) see; **in ~ di** (*in occasione di*) during; **in altra ~** on another occasion; **in ~ legislativa** in legislative sitting; **prendere ~** to take up residence; **un'azienda con diverse sedi in città** a firm with several branches in the city; **~ centrale** head office; **~ sociale** registered office

seden'tario, -a AG sedentary

se'dere /**107**/ VI to sit, be seated; **sedersi** VPR, SM to sit down; (*deretano*) bottom; **posto a ~** seat

'sedia SF chair; **~ elettrica** electric chair; **~ a rotelle** wheelchair

sedi'cenne [sedi'tʃɛnne] AG, SMF sixteen-year-old

sedi'cente [sedi'tʃɛnte] AG self-styled

sedi'cesimo, -a [sedi'tʃɛzimo] NUM sixteenth

'sedici ['seditʃi] NUM sixteen

se'dile SM seat; (*panchina*) bench

sedimen'tare /**72**/ VI to leave a sediment

sedi'mento SM sediment

sedizi'one [sedit'tsjone] SF revolt, rebellion

sedizi'oso, -a [sedit'tsjoso] AG seditious

se'dotto, -a PP di **sedurre**

sedu'cente [sedu'tʃɛnte] AG seductive; (*proposta*) very attractive

se'durre /**90**/ VT to seduce

se'duta SF session, sitting; (*riunione*) meeting; **essere in ~** to be in session, be sitting; **~ stante** (*fig*) immediately; **~ spiritica** seance

sedut'tore, -'trice SM/F seducer/seductress

seduzi'one [sedut'tsjone] SF seduction; (*fascino*) charm, appeal

SEeO ABBR (= *salvo errori e omissioni*) E & OE

'sega, -ghe SF saw; **~ circolare** circular saw; **~ a mano** handsaw

'segale SF rye

se'gare /**80**/ VT to saw; (*recidere*) to saw off

sega'tura SF (*residuo*) sawdust

'seggio ['sɛddʒo] SM seat; **~ elettorale** polling station

'seggiola ['sɛddʒola] SF chair

seggio'lino [seddʒo'lino] SM seat; (*per bambini*) child's chair; **~ di sicurezza** (*Aut*) child safety seat

seggio'lone [seddʒo'lone] SM (*per bambini*) highchair

seggio'via [seddʒo'via] SF chairlift

seghe'ria [sege'ria] SF sawmill

segherò etc [sege'rɔ] VB vedi **segare**

seghet'tato, -a [seget'tato] AG serrated

se'ghetto [se'getto] SM hacksaw

seg'mento SM segment

segna'lare [seɲɲa'lare] /**72**/ VT (*essere segno di*) to indicate, be a sign of; (*avvertire*) to signal; (*menzionare*) to indicate; (: *fatto, risultato, aumento*) to report; (: *errore, dettaglio*) to point out; (: *persona*) to single out; (*Aut*) to signal, indicate; **segnalarsi** VPR (*distinguersi*) to distinguish o.s.; **~ qn a qn** (*per lavoro ecc*) to bring sb to sb's attention

segnalazi'one [seɲɲalat'tsjone] SF (*azione*) signalling; (*segnale*) signal; (*annuncio*) report; (*raccomandazione*) recommendation

se'gnale [seɲ'ɲale] SM signal; (*cartello*): **~ stradale** road sign; **~ acustico** acoustic o sound signal; (*di segreteria telefonica*) tone; **~ d'allarme** alarm; (*Ferr*) communication cord; **~ di linea libera** (*Tel*) dialling (*Brit*) o dial (*US*) tone; **~ luminoso** light signal; **~ di occupato** (*Tel*) engaged tone (*Brit*), busy signal (*US*); **~ orario** (*Radio*) time signal

segna'letica [seɲɲa'letika] SF signalling, signposting; **~ stradale** road signs pl

segna'libro [seɲɲa'libro] SM (*anche Inform*) bookmark

segna'punti [seɲɲa'punti] SM INV/F INV scorer, scorekeeper

se'gnare [seɲ'ɲare] /**15**/ VT to mark; (*prendere nota*) to note; (*indicare*) to indicate, mark; (*Sport: goal*) to score; **segnarsi** VPR (*Rel*) to make the sign of the cross, cross o.s.

'segno ['seɲɲo] SM sign; (*impronta, contrassegno*) mark; (*limite*) limit, bounds pl; (*bersaglio*) target; **fare ~ di sì/no** to nod (one's head)/shake one's head; **fare ~ a qn di fermarsi** to motion (to) sb to stop; **cogliere o colpire nel ~** (*fig*) to hit the mark; **in o come ~ d'amicizia** as a mark o token of friendship; **"segni particolari"** (*su documento ecc*) "distinguishing marks"; **~ zodiacale** star sign

segre'gare /**80**/ VT to segregate, isolate

segregazi'one [segregat'tsjone] SF segregation

se'greta SF vedi **segreto**

segre'tario, -a SM/F secretary; **~ comunale** town clerk; **~ del partito** party leader; **S~ di Stato** Secretary of State

segrete'ria SF (*di ditta, scuola*) (secretary's) office; (*d'organizzazione internazionale*) secretariat; (*Pol ecc: carica*) office of Secretary; **~ telefonica** answering machine

segre'tezza [segre'tettsa] SF secrecy; **notizie della massima ~** confidential information; **in tutta ~** in secret; (*confidenzialmente*) in confidence

se'greto, -a AG secret ▶ SM secret; secrecy *no pl* ▶ SF dungeon; **in ~** in secret, secretly; **il ~ professionale** professional secrecy; **un ~ professionale** a professional secret

segu'ace [se'gwatʃe] SMF follower, disciple

segu'ente AG following, next; **nel modo ~** as follows, in the following way

se'gugio [se'gudʒo] SM hound, hunting dog; (*fig*) private eye, sleuth

segu'ire /45/ VT to follow; (*frequentare: corso*) to attend ▶ VI to follow; (*continuare: testo*) to continue; **~ i consigli di qn** to follow o to take sb's advice; **~ gli avvenimenti di attualità** to follow o keep up with current events; **come segue** as follows; **"segue"** "to be continued"

segui'tare /72/ VT to continue, carry on with ▶ VI to continue, carry on

'seguito SM (*scorta*) suite, retinue; (*discepoli*) followers *pl*; (*favore*) following; (*serie*) sequence, series *sg*; (*continuazione*) continuation; (*conseguenza*) result; **di ~** at a stretch, on end; **in ~** later on; **in ~ a, a ~ di** following; (*a causa di*) as a result of, owing to; **essere al ~ di qn** to be among sb's suite, be one of sb's retinue; **non aver ~** (*conseguenze*) to have no repercussions; **facciamo ~ alla lettera del ...** further to o in answer to your letter of ...

'sei VB *vedi* **essere** ▶ NUM six

Sei'celle [sei'tʃɛlle] SFPL: **le ~** the Seychelles

seicen'tesco, -a, -schi, -sche [seitʃen'tesko] AG seventeenth-century

sei'cento [sei'tʃɛnto] NUM six hundred ▶ SM: **il S~** the seventeenth century

sei'mila NUM six thousand

'selce ['seltʃe] SF flint, flintstone

selci'ato [sel'tʃato] SM cobbled surface

selet'tivo, -a AG selective

selet'tore SM (*Tecn*) selector

selezio'nare [selettsjo'nare] /72/ VT to select

selezi'one [selet'tsjone] SF selection; **fare una ~** to make a selection o choice

'sella SF saddle

sel'lare /72/ VT to saddle

sel'lino SM saddle

seltz SM INV soda (water)

'selva SF (*bosco*) wood; (*foresta*) forest

selvag'gina [selvad'dʒina] SF (*animali*) game

sel'vaggio, -a, -gi, -ge [sel'vaddʒo] AG wild; (*tribù*) savage, uncivilized; (*fig: brutale*) savage, brutal; (: *incontrollato: fenomeno, aumento ecc*) uncontrolled ▶ SM/F savage; **inflazione selvaggia** runaway inflation

sel'vatico, -a, -ci, -che AG wild

S.Em. ABBR (= *Sua Eminenza*) HE

se'maforo SM (*Aut*) traffic lights *pl*

se'mantico, -a AG semantic ▶ SF semantics *sg*

sembi'anza [sem'bjantsa] SF (*poetico: aspetto*) appearance; **sembianze** SFPL (*fig: lineamenti*) features; (*falsa apparenza*) semblance *sg*

sem'brare /72/ VI to seem ▶ VB IMPERS: **sembra che** it seems that; **mi sembra che** it seems to me that; (*penso che*) I think (that); **~ di essere** to seem to be; **non mi sembra vero!** I can't believe it!

'seme SM seed; (*sperma*) semen; (*Carte*) suit

se'mente SF seed

semes'trale AG (*che dura 6 mesi*) six-month *cpd*; (*che avviene ogni 6 mesi*) six-monthly

se'mestre SM half-year, six-month period

'semi ... PREFISSO semi ...

semi'cerchio [semi'tʃerkjo] SM semicircle

semicondut'tore SM semiconductor

semidetenzi'one [semideten'tsjone] SF *custodial sentence whereby individual must spend a minimum of 10 hours per day in prison*

semifi'nale SF semifinal

semi'freddo, -a AG (*Cuc*) chilled ▶ SM ice-cream dessert

semilibertà SF *custodial sentence which allows prisoner to study or work outside prison for part of the day*

'semina SF (*Agr*) sowing

semi'nare /72/ VT to sow

semi'nario SM seminar; (*Rel*) seminary

semi'nato SM: **uscire dal ~** (*fig*) to wander off the point

seminter'rato SM basement; (*appartamento*) basement flat (BRIT) o apartment (US)

semi'ologo, -a, -gi, -ghe SM/F semiologist

semi'otica SF semiotics *sg*

se'mitica, -a, -ci, -che AG semitic

semivu'oto, -a AG half-empty

sem'mai = **se mai**

'semola SF bran; **~ di grano duro** durum wheat

semo'lato AG: **zucchero ~** caster sugar

semo'lino SM semolina

'semplice ['semplitʃe] AG simple; (*di un solo elemento*) single; **è una ~ formalità** it's a mere formality

semplice'mente [semplitʃe'mente] AV simply

sempli'cistico, -a, -ci, -che [sempli'tʃistiko] AG simplistic

semplicità [semplitʃi'ta] SF simplicity

semplifi'care /20/ VT to simplify

semplificazi'one [semplifikat'tsjone] SF simplification; **fare una ~ di** to simplify

'sempre AV always; (*ancora*) still; **posso ~ tentare** I can always o still try; **da ~** always; **per ~** forever; **una volta per ~** once and for all; **~ che** *cong* as long as, provided (that); **~ più** more and more; **~ meno** less and less; **va ~ meglio** things are getting better and better; **è ~ più giovane** she gets younger

S

335

and younger; **è ~ meglio che niente** it's better than nothing; **è (pur) ~ tuo fratello** he is still your brother (however); **c'è ~ la possibilità che ...** there's still a chance that ..., there's always the possibility that ...

sempre'verde AG, SM O F (*Bot*) evergreen

Sen. ABBR (= *senatore*) Sen.

'**senape** SF (*Cuc*) mustard

se'nato SM senate; **il S~** *see note*

> The *Senato* is the upper house of the Italian parliament, with similar functions to the *Camera dei deputati*. Candidates must be at least 40 years of age and electors must be 25 or over. Elections are held every five years. Former heads of state become senators for life, as do five distinguished members of the public who are chosen by the head of state for their scientific, social, artistic or literary achievements. the chamber is presided over by the *Presidente del Senato*, who is elected by the senators.

sena'tore, -'trice SM/F senator

'**Senegal** SM: **il ~** Senegal

senega'lese AG, SMF Senegalese *inv*

se'nese AG OF (*o* from) Siena

se'nile AG senile

'**Senna** SF: **la ~** the Seine

'**senno** SM judgment, (common) sense; **col ~ di poi** with hindsight

sennò AV = **se no**

'**seno** SM (*Anat: petto, mammella*) breast; (: *grembo, anche fig*) womb; (: *cavità*) sinus; (*Geo*) inlet, creek; (*Mat*) sine; **in ~ al partito/all'organizzazione** within the party/the organization

sen'sale SM (*Comm*) agent

sensa'tezza [sensa'tettsa] SF good sense, good judgment

sen'sato, -a AG sensible

sensazio'nale [sensattsjo'nale] AG sensational

sensazi'one [sensat'tsjone] SF feeling, sensation; **fare ~** to cause a sensation, create a stir; **avere la ~ che** to have a feeling that

sen'sibile AG sensitive; (*ai sensi*) perceptible; (*rilevante, notevole*) appreciable, noticeable; **~ a** sensitive to

sensibilità SF sensitivity

sensibiliz'zare [sensibilid'dzare] /**72**/ VT (*fig*) to make aware, awaken

'**senso** SM (*Fisiol, istinto*) sense; (*impressione, sensazione*) feeling, sensation; (*significato*) meaning, sense; (*direzione*) direction; **sensi** SMPL (*coscienza*) consciousness *sg*; (*sensualità*) senses; **perdere/riprendere i sensi** to lose/regain consciousness; **avere ~ pratico** to be practical; **avere un sesto ~** to have a sixth sense; **fare ~ a** (*ripugnare*) to disgust, repel;

ciò non ha ~ that doesn't make sense; **senza** *o* **privo di ~** meaningless; **nel ~ che** in the sense that; **nel vero ~ della parola** in the true sense of the word; **nel ~ della lunghezza** lengthwise, lengthways; **nel ~ della larghezza** widthwise; **ho dato disposizioni in quel ~** I've given instructions to that end *o* effect; **~ comune** common sense; **~ del dovere** sense of duty; **in ~ opposto** in the opposite direction; **in ~ orario/antiorario** clockwise/anticlockwise; **~ dell'umorismo** sense of humour; **~ di colpa** sense of guilt; **a ~ unico** one-way; **"~ vietato"** (*Aut*) "no entry"

sensu'ale AG sensual; sensuous

sensualità SF sensuality; sensuousness

sen'tenza [sen'tentsa] SF (*Dir*) sentence; (*massima*) maxim

sentenzi'are [senten'tsjare] /**19**/ VI (*Dir*) to pass judgment

senti'ero SM path

sentimen'tale AG sentimental; (*vita, avventura*) love *cpd*

senti'mento SM feeling

senti'nella SF sentry

sen'tire /**45**/ VT (*percepire al tatto, fig*) to feel; (*udire*) to hear; (*ascoltare*) to listen to; (*odore*) to smell; (*avvertire con il gusto, assaggiare*) to taste ▶ VI: **~ di** (*avere sapore*) to taste of; (*avere odore*) to smell of; **sentirsi** VPR (*uso reciproco*) to be in touch; **sentirsi bene/male** to feel well/unwell *o* ill; **sentirsi di fare qc** (*essere disposto*) to feel like doing sth; **~ la mancanza di qn** to miss sb; **ho sentito dire che ...** I have heard that ...; **a ~ lui ...** to hear him talk ...; **fatti ~** keep in touch; **intendo ~ il mio legale/il parere di un medico** I'm going to consult my lawyer/a doctor

sentita'mente AV sincerely; **ringraziare ~** to thank sincerely

sen'tito, -a AG (*sincero*) sincere, warm; **per ~ dire** by hearsay

sen'tore SM rumour (*BRIT*), rumor (*US*), talk; **aver ~ di qc** to hear about sth

'**senza** ['sentsa] PREP, CONG without; **~ dir nulla** without saying a word; **~ dire che ...** not to mention the fact that ...; **~ contare che ...** without considering that ...; **fare ~ qc** to do without sth; **~ di me** without me; **~ che io lo sapessi** without me *o* my knowing; **~ amici** friendless; **senz'altro** of course, certainly; **~ dubbio** no doubt; **~ scrupoli** unscrupulous; **i ~ lavoro** the jobless, the unemployed; **i ~ tetto** the homeless

senza'tetto [sentsa'tetto] SM INV/F INV homeless person; **i ~** the homeless

sepa'rare /**72**/ VT to separate; (*dividere*) to divide; (*tenere distinto*) to distinguish;

separarsi VPR (*coniugi*) to separate, part; (*amici*) to part, leave each other; **separarsi da** (*coniuge*) to separate *o* part from; (*amico, socio*) to part company with; (*oggetto*) to part with

separata'mente AV separately

sepa'rato, -a AG (*letti, conto ecc*) separate; (*coniugi*) separated

separazi'one [separat'tsjone] SF separation; **~ dei beni** division of property

séparé [sepa're] SM INV screen

se'polcro SM sepulchre (BRIT), sepulcher (US)

se'polto, -a PP *di* **seppellire**

sepol'tura SF burial; **dare ~ a qn** to bury sb

seppel'lire /**55**/ VT to bury

'seppi *etc* VB *vedi* **sapere**

'seppia SF cuttlefish ▶ AG INV sepia

sep'pure CONG even if

se'quela SF (*di avvenimenti*) series, sequence; (*di offese, ingiurie*) string

se'quenza [se'kwentsa] SF sequence

sequenzi'ale [sekwen'tsjale] AG sequential

seques'trare /**72**/ VT (*Dir*) to impound; (*rapire*) to kidnap; (*costringere in un luogo*) to keep, confine

se'questro SM (*Dir*) impoundment; **~ di persona** kidnapping

se'quoia SF sequoia

'sera SF evening; **di ~** in the evening; **domani ~** tomorrow evening, tomorrow night; **questa ~** this evening, tonight

se'rale AG evening *cpd*; **scuola ~** evening classes *pl*, night school

se'rata SF evening; (*ricevimento*) party

ser'bare /**72**/ VT to keep; (*mettere da parte*) to put aside; **~ rancore/odio verso qn** to bear sb a grudge/hate sb

serba'toio SM tank; (*cisterna*) cistern

'Serbia SF: **la ~** Serbia

'serbo, -a AG Serbian ▶ SM/F Serbian, Serb ▶ SM (*Ling*) Serbian; (*il serbare*): **mettere/tenere** *o* **avere in ~ qc** to put/keep sth aside

serbocro'ato, -a AG, SM Serbo-Croat

serena'mente AV serenely, calmly

sere'nata SF (*Mus*) serenade

serenità SF serenity

se'reno, -a AG (*tempo, cielo*) clear; (*fig*) serene, calm ▶ SM (*tempo*) good weather; **un fulmine a ciel ~** (*fig*) a bolt from the blue

serg. ABBR (= *sergente*) Sgt.

ser'gente [ser'dʒɛnte] SM (*Mil*) sergeant

seri'ale AG (*Inform*) serial

seria'mente AV (*con serietà, in modo grave*) seriously; **lavorare ~** to take one's job seriously

'serie SF INV (*successione*) series *inv*; (*gruppo, collezione di chiavi ecc*) set; (*Sport*) division; league; (*Comm*): **modello di ~/fuori ~** standard/custom-built model; **in ~** in

quick succession; (*Comm*) mass *cpd*; **tutta una ~ di problemi** a whole string *o* series of problems

serietà SF seriousness; reliability

'serio, -a AG serious; (*impiegato*) responsible, reliable; (*ditta, cliente*) reliable, dependable; **sul ~** (*davvero*) really, truly; (*seriamente*) seriously, in earnest; **dico sul ~** I'm serious; **faccio sul ~** I mean it; **prendere qc/qn sul ~** to take sth/sb, seriously

seri'oso, -a AG (*persona, modi*): **un po' ~** a bit too serious

ser'mone SM sermon

'serpe SF snake; (*fig: peg*) viper

serpeggi'are [serped'dʒare] /**62**/ VI to wind; (*fig*) to spread

ser'pente SM snake; **~ a sonagli** rattlesnake

'serra SF greenhouse; hothouse; (*Geo*) sierra

serra'manico SM: **coltello a ~** jack-knife

ser'randa SF roller shutter

ser'rare /**72**/ VT to close, shut; (*a chiave*) to lock; (*stringere*) to tighten; (*premere: nemico*) to close in on; **~ i pugni/i denti** to clench one's fists/teeth; **~ le file** to close ranks

ser'rata SF (*Industria*) lockout

ser'rato, -a AG (*veloce*): **a ritmo ~** quickly, fast

serra'tura SF lock

'serva SF *vedi* **servo**

'server ['server] SM INV (*Inform*) server

ser'vigio [ser'vidʒo] SM favour (BRIT), favor (US), service

ser'vire /**45**/ VT to serve; (*clienti: al ristorante*) to wait on; (: *al negozio*) to serve, attend to; (*fig: giovare*) to aid, help; (*Carte*) to deal ▶ VI (*Tennis*) to serve; (*essere utile*): **~ a qn** to be of use to sb; **servirsi** VPR (*usare*): **servirsi di** to use; (*prendere: cibo*): **servirsi (di)** to help o.s. (to); (*essere cliente abituale*): **servirsi da** to be a regular customer at, go to; **non mi serve più** I don't need it any more; **non serve che lei vada** you don't need to go; **~ a qc/a fare** (*utensile ecc*) to be used for sth/for doing; **~ (a qn) da** to serve as (for sb); **serviti pure!** help yourself!

servitù SF servitude; slavery; (*personale di servizio*) servants *pl*, domestic staff

servizi'evole [servit'tsjevole] AG obliging, willing to help

ser'vizio [ser'vittsjo] SM service; (*al ristorante: sul cônto*) service (charge); (*Stampa, TV, Radio*) report; (*da tè, caffè ecc*) set, service; **servizi** SMPL (*di casa*) kitchen and bathroom; (*Econ*) services; **essere di ~** to be on duty; **fuori ~** (*telefono ecc*) out of order; **~ compreso/escluso** service included/not included; **entrata di ~** service *o* tradesman's (BRIT) entrance; **casa con doppi servizi** house with two bathrooms; **~ assistenza clienti** customer service; **~ civile** ≈ community service; **~ in diretta** (*TV, Radio*) live coverage; **~ fotografico** (*Stampa*) photo feature; **~ di posate** set of cutlery; **~ militare** military service; **~ d'ordine** (*Polizia*) police patrol; (*di manifestanti*) team of stewards (*responsible for crowd control*); **servizi segreti** secret service *sg*; **servizi di sicurezza** security forces

'**servo, -a** SM/F servant

servo'freno SM (*Aut*) servo brake

servos'terzo [servos'tɛrtso] SM (*Aut*) power steering

'**sesamo** SM (*Bot*) sesame

ses'santa NUM sixty

sessan'tenne AG, SMF sixty-year-old

sessan'tesimo, -a NUM sixtieth

sessan'tina SF: **una ~ (di)** about sixty

sessantot'tino, -a SM/F *a person who took part in the events of 1968*

sessan'totto SM *see note*

Sessantotto refers to the year 1968, the year of student protests. Originating in France, unrest soon spread to other industrialized countries including Italy. What began as a purely student concern gradually came to include other parts of society and led to major political and social change. Among the changes that resulted from the protests were reform of schools and universities and the referendum on divorce.

sessi'one SF session

'**sesso** SM sex; **il ~ debole/forte** the weaker/stronger sex

sessu'ale AG sexual, sex *cpd*

sessualità SF sexuality

sessu'ologo, -a, -gi, -ghe SM/F sexologist, sex specialist

ses'tante SM sextant

'**sesto, -a** NUM sixth ▶ SM: **rimettere in ~** (*aggiustare*) to put back in order; (*fig: persona*) to put back on his (*o* her) feet; **rimettersi in ~** (*riprendersi*) to recover, get well; (*riassettarsi*) to tidy o.s. up

'**seta** SF silk

setacci'are [setat'tʃare] /**14**/ VT (*farina ecc*) to sift, sieve; (*fig: zona*) to search, comb

se'taccio [se'tattʃo] SM sieve; **passare al ~** (*fig*) to search, comb

'**sete** SF thirst; **avere ~** to be thirsty; **~ di potere** thirst for power

seti'ficio [seti'fitʃo] SM silk factory

'**setola** SF bristle

sett. ABBR (= *settembre*) Sept.

'**setta** SF sect

set'tanta NUM seventy

settan'tenne AG, SMF seventy-year-old

settan'tesimo, -a NUM seventieth

settan'tina SF: **una ~ (di)** about seventy

set'tare/72/ VT (*Inform*) to set up

'**sette** NUM seven

settecen'tesco, -a, -schi, -sche [settetʃen'tesko] AG eighteenth-century

sette'cento [sette'tʃɛnto] NUM seven hundred ▶ SM: **il S~** the eighteenth century

set'tembre SM September; *vedi anche* **luglio**

sette'mila NUM seven thousand

settentrio'nale AG northern ▶ SMF northerner

settentri'one SM north

'**settico, -a, -ci, -che** AG (*Med*) septic

setti'mana SF week; **la ~ scorsa/prossima** last/next week; **a metà ~** in the middle of the week; **~ bianca** winter-sport holiday

Settimana bianca is the name given to a week-long winter-sports holiday taken by many Italians some time in the skiing season.

settima'nale AG, SM weekly

'**settimo, -a** NUM seventh

set'tore SM sector; **~ privato/pubblico** private/public sector; **~ terziario** service industries *pl*

Se'ul SF Seoul

severità SF severity

se'vero, -a AG severe

sevizi'are [sevit'tsjare] /**19**/ VT to torture

se'vizie [se'vittsje] SFPL torture *sg*

'**sexy** ['seksi] AG INV sexy

sez. ABBR = **sezione**

sezio'nare [settsjo'nare] /**72**/ VT to divide into sections; (*Med*) to dissect

sezi'one [set'tsjone] SF section; (*Med*) dissection

sfaccen'dato, -a [sfattʃen'dato] AG idle

sfacceta'tura [sfattʃetta'tura] SF (*azione*) faceting; (*parte sfaccettata, fig*) facet

sfacchi'nare [sfakki'nare] /**72**/ VI (*col*) to toil, drudge

sfacchi'nata [sfakki'nata] SF (*col*) chore, drudgery *no pl*

sfaccia'taggine [sfattʃa'taddʒine] SF insolence, cheek

sfacci'ato, -a [sfat'tʃato] AG (*maleducato*) cheeky, impudent; (*vistoso*) gaudy

sfa'celo [sfa'tʃɛlo] SM (*fig*) ruin, collapse

sfal'darsi/72/ VPR to flake (off)

sfal'sare/72/ VT to offset

sfa'mare/72/ VT (*nutrire*) to feed; (*cibo*) to fill; (*soddisfare la fame*): **~ qn** to satisfy sb's hunger; **sfamarsi**VPR to satisfy one's hunger, fill o.s. up

sfarfal'lio SM (*Cine, TV*) flickering

'**sfarzo** ['sfartso] SM pomp, splendour (*BRIT*), splendor (*US*)

sfar'zoso, -a [sfar'tsoso] AG splendid, magnificent

sfasa'mento SM (*Elettr*) phase displacement; (*fig*) confusion, bewilderment

sfa'sato, -a AG (*Elettr, motore*) out of phase; (*fig: persona*) confused, bewildered

sfasci'are [sfaʃʃare] /**14**/ VT (*ferita*) to unbandage; (*distruggere: porta*) to smash, shatter; **sfasciarsi** VPR (*rompersi*) to smash, shatter

sfa'tare /**72**/ VT (*leggenda*) to explode

sfati'cato, -a SM/F idler, loafer

'sfatto, -a AG (*letto*) unmade; (*orlo ecc*) undone; (*gelato, neve*) melted; (*frutta*) overripe; (*riso, pasta ecc*) overdone, overcooked; (*col: persona, corpo*) flabby

sfavil'lare /**72**/ VI to spark, send out sparks; (*risplendere*) to sparkle

sfa'vore SM disfavour (BRIT), disfavor (US), disapproval

sfavo'revole AG unfavourable (BRIT), unfavorable (US)

sfega'tato, -a AG fanatical

'sfera SF sphere

'sferico, -a, -ci, -che AG spherical

sfer'rare /**72**/ VT (*fig: colpo*) to land, deal; (: *attacco*) to launch

sfer'zante [sfer'tsante] AG (*critiche, parole*) stinging

sfer'zare [sfer'tsare] /**72**/ VT to whip; (*fig*) to lash out at

sfian'care /**20**/ VT to wear out, exhaust; **sfiancarsi** VPR to exhaust o.s., wear o.s. out

sfia'tare /**72**/ VI to allow air (*o gas etc*) to escape

sfiata'toio SM blowhole; (*Tecn*) vent

sfi'brante AG exhausting, energy-sapping

sfi'brare /**72**/ VT (*indebolire*) to exhaust, enervate

sfi'brato, -a AG exhausted, worn out

'sfida SF challenge

sfi'dante AG challenging ▶ SMF challenger

sfi'dare /**72**/ VT to challenge; (*fig*) to defy, brave; **~ qn a fare qc** to challenge sb to do sth; **~ un pericolo** to brave a danger; **sfido che ...** I dare say (that) ...

sfi'ducia [sfi'dutʃa] SF distrust, mistrust; **avere ~ in qn/qc** to distrust sb/sth

sfiduci'ato, -a [sfidu'tʃato] AG lacking confidence

sfi'gato, -a (*col*) AG: **essere ~** (*sfortunato*) to be unlucky ▶ SM/F (*fallito, sfortunato*) loser; (*fuori moda*) dork

sfigu'rare /**72**/ VT (*persona*) to disfigure; (*quadro, statua*) to deface ▶ VI (*far cattiva figura*) to make a bad impression

sfilacci'are [sfilat'tʃare] /**14**/ VT, VI, **sfilacci'arsi** VPR to fray

sfi'lare /**72**/ VT (*ago*) to unthread; (*abito, scarpe*) to slip off ▶ VI (*truppe*) to march past, parade; (*atleti*) to parade; (*manifestanti*) to march; **sfilarsi** VPR (*perle ecc*) to come unstrung; (*orlo, tessuto*) to fray; (*calza*) to run, ladder

sfi'lata SF (*Mil*) parade; (*di manifestanti*) march; **~ di moda** fashion show

'sfilza ['sfiltsa] SF (*di case*) row; (*di errori*) series *inv*

'sfinge ['sfindʒe] SF sphinx

sfini'mento SM exhaustion

sfi'nito, -a AG exhausted

sfio'rare /**72**/ VT to brush (against); (*argomento*) to touch upon; **~ la velocità di 150 km/h** to touch 150 km/h

sfio'rire /**55**/ VI to wither, fade

'sfitto, -a AG vacant, empty

sfo'cato, -a AG (*Fot*) out of focus

sfoci'are [sfo'tʃare] /**14**/ VI: **~ in** to flow into; (*fig: malcontento*) to develop into

sfode'rato, -a AG (*vestito*) unlined

sfo'gare /**80**/ VT to vent, pour out; **sfogarsi** VPR (*sfogare la propria rabbia*) to give vent to one's anger; (*confidarsi*) **sfogarsi (con)** to pour out one's feelings (to); **non sfogarti su di me!** don't take your bad temper out on me!

sfoggi'are [sfod'dʒare] /**62**/ VT, VI to show off

'sfoggio ['sfɔddʒo] SM show, display; **fare ~ di** to show off, display

sfogherò *etc* [sfoge'rɔ] VB *vedi* **sfogare**

'sfoglia ['sfɔʎʎa] SF sheet of pasta dough; **pasta ~** (*Cuc*) puff pastry

sfogli'are [sfoʎ'ʎare] /**27**/ VT (*libro*) to leaf through

'sfogo, -ghi SM outlet; (*eruzione cutanea*) rash; (*fig*) outburst; **dare ~ a** (*fig*) to give vent to

sfolgo'rante AG (*luce*) blazing; (*fig: vittoria*) brilliant

sfolgo'rare /**72**/ VI to blaze

sfolla'gente [sfolla'dʒɛnte] SM INV truncheon (BRIT), billy (US)

sfol'lare /**72**/ VT to empty, clear ▶ VI to disperse; **~ da** (*città*) to evacuate

sfol'lato, -a AG evacuated ▶ SM/F evacuee

sfol'tire /**55**/ VT, **sfol'tirsi** VPR to thin (out)

sfon'dare /**72**/ VT (*porta*) to break down; (*scarpe*) to wear a hole in; (*cesto, scatola*) to burst, knock the bottom out of; (*Mil*) to break through ▶ VI (*riuscire*) to make a name for o.s.

sfon'dato, -a AG (*scarpe*) worn out; (*scatola*) burst; (*sedia*) broken, damaged; **essere ricco ~** to be rolling in it

'sfondo SM background

sfo'rare /**72**/ VI to overrun

sfor'mare /**72**/ VT to put out of shape, knock out of shape; **sformarsi** VPR to lose shape, get out of shape

sfor'mato, -a AG (*che ha perso forma*) shapeless ▶ SM (*Cuc*) type of soufflé

sfor'nare /**72**/ VT (*pane*) to take out of the oven; (*fig*) to churn out

sfor'nito, -a AG: ~ **di** lacking in, without; (*negozio*) out of

sfor'tuna SF misfortune, ill luck *no pl*; **avere ~** to be unlucky; **che ~!** how unfortunate!

sfortu'nato, -a AG unlucky; (*impresa, film*) unsuccessful

sfor'zare [sfor'tsare] /**72**/ VT to force; (*voce, occhi*) to strain; **sforzarsi** VPR: **sforzarsi di** *o* **a** *o* **per fare** to try hard to do

'sforzo ['sfɔrtso] SM effort; (*tensione eccessiva*, Tecn) strain; **fare uno ~** to make an effort; **essere sotto ~** (*motore, macchina, fig: persona*) to be under stress

'sfottere /**1**/ VT (*col*) to tease

sfracel'lare [sfratʃel'lare] /**72**/ VT, **sfracel'larsi** VPR to smash

sfrat'tare /**72**/ VT to evict

'sfratto SM eviction; **dare lo ~ a qn** to give sb notice to quit

sfrecci'are [sfret'tʃare] /**14**/ VI to shoot *o* flash past

sfre'gare /**80**/ VT (*strofinare*) to rub; (*graffiare*) to scratch; **sfregarsi le mani** to rub one's hands; **~ un fiammifero** to strike a match

sfregi'are [sfre'dʒare] /**62**/ VT to slash, gash; (*persona*) to disfigure; (*quadro*) to deface

'sfregio ['sfredʒo] SM gash; scar; (*fig*) insult

sfre'nato, -a AG (*fig*) unrestrained, unbridled

sfron'dare /**72**/ VT (*albero*) to prune, thin out; (*fig: discorso, scritto*) to prune (down)

sfronta'tezza [sfronta'tettsa] SF impudence, cheek

sfron'tato, -a AG impudent, cheeky; shameless

sfrutta'mento SM exploitation

sfrut'tare /**72**/ VT (*terreno*) to overwork, exhaust; (*miniera*) to exploit, work; (*fig: operai, occasione, potere*) to exploit

sfrutta'tore, -'trice SM/F exploiter

sfug'gente [sfud'dʒɛnte] AG (*fig: sguardo*) elusive; (*mento*) receding

sfug'gire [sfud'dʒire] /**31**/ VI to escape; **~ a** (*custode*) to escape (from); (*morte*) to escape; **~ a qn** (*dettaglio, nome*) to escape sb; **~ di mano a qn** to slip out of sb's hand (*o* hands); **lasciarsi ~ un'occasione** to let an opportunity go by; **~ al controllo** (*macchina*) to go out of control; (*situazione*) to be no longer under control

sfug'gita [sfud'dʒita] SF: **di ~** (*rapidamente, in fretta*) in passing

sfu'mare /**72**/ VT (*colori, contorni*) to soften, shade off ▶ VI to shade (off), fade; (*fig: svanire*) to vanish, disappear; (: *speranze*) to come to nothing

sfuma'tura SF shading off *no pl*; (*tonalità*) shade, tone; (*fig*) touch, hint

sfuo'cato, -a AG = **sfocato**

sfuri'ata SF (*scatto di collera*) fit of anger; (*rimprovero*) sharp rebuke

'sfuso, -a AG (*caramelle ecc*) loose, unpacked; (*vino*) unbottled; (*birra*) draught (BRIT), draft (US)

sg. ABBR = **seguente**

sga'bello SM stool

sgabuz'zino [zgabud'dzino] SM lumber room

sgambet'tare /**72**/ VI to kick one's legs about

sgam'betto SM: **far lo ~ a qn** to trip sb up; (*fig*) to oust sb

sganasci'arsi [zganaʃʃarsi] /**14**/ VPR: **~ dalle risa** to roar with laughter

sganci'are [zgan'tʃare] /**14**/ VT to unhook; (*chiusura*) to unfasten, undo; (Ferr) to uncouple; (*bombe: da aereo*) to release, drop; (*fig: col: soldi*) to fork out; **sganciarsi** VPR to come unhooked; to come unfastened, come undone; to uncouple; (*fig*) **sganciarsi (da)** to get away (from)

sganghe'rato, -a [zgange'rato] AG (*porta*) off its hinges; (*auto*) ramshackle; (*riso*) wild, boisterous

sgar'bato, -a AG rude, impolite

'sgarbo SM: **fare uno ~ a qn** to be rude to sb

sgargi'ante [zgar'dʒante] AG gaudy, showy

sgar'rare /**72**/ VI (*persona*) to step out of line; (*orologio: essere avanti*) to gain; (: *essere indietro*) to lose

'sgarro SM inaccuracy

sgattaio'lare /**72**/ VI to sneak away *o* off

sge'lare [zdʒe'lare] /**72**/ VI, VT to thaw

'sghembo, -a ['zgembo] AG (*obliquo*) slanting; (*storto*) crooked

sghignaz'zare [zgiɲɲat'tsare] /**72**/ VI to laugh scornfully

sghignaz'zata [zgiɲɲat'tsata] SF scornful laugh

sgob'bare /**72**/ VI (*col: scolaro*) to swot; (: *operaio*) to slog

sgoccio'lare [zgottʃo'lare] /**72**/ VT (*vuotare*) to drain (to the last drop) ▶ VI (*acqua*) to drip; (*recipiente*) to drain

'sgoccioli ['zgottʃoli] SMPL: **essere agli ~** (*lavoro, provviste ecc*) to be nearly finished; (*periodo*) to be nearly over; **siamo agli ~** we've nearly finished, the end is in sight

sgo'larsi /**72**/ VPR to talk (*o* shout *o* sing) o.s. hoarse

sgombe'rare /**72**/, **sgomb'rare** VT (*tavolo, stanza*) to clear; (*andarsene da: stanza*) to vacate; (*evacuare: piazza, città*) to evacuate ▶ VI to move

'sgombero SM *vedi* **sgombro**

'sgombro, -a AG: **~ (di)** clear (of), free (from) ▶ SM (Zool) mackerel; (*anche:* **sgombero**) clearing; vacating; evacuation; (*trasloco*) removal

sgomen'tare /**72**/ VT to dismay; **sgomentarsi** VPR to be dismayed

sgo'mento, -a AG dismayed ▶ SM dismay, consternation

sgomi'nare/72/ VT (*nemico*) to rout; (*avversario*) to defeat; (*fig: epidemia*) to overcome

sgonfi'are/19/ VT to let down, deflate; **sgonfiarsi**VPR to go down

'**sgonfio, -a** AG (*pneumatico, pallone*) flat

'**sgorbio** SM blot; scribble

sgor'gare/80/ VI to gush (out)

sgoz'zare [zgot'tsare] /72/ VT to cut the throat of

sgra'devole AG unpleasant, disagreeable

sgra'dito, -a AG unpleasant, unwelcome

sgraffi'gnare [zgraffiɲ'ɲare] /15/ VT (*col*) to pinch, swipe

sgrammati'cato, -a AG ungrammatical

sgra'nare/72/ VT (*piselli*) to shell; **~ gli occhi** to open one's eyes wide

sgran'chirsi [zgran'kire] /55/ VT (*anche:* **sgranchirsi**) to stretch; **~ le gambe** to stretch one's legs

sgranocchi'are [zgranok'kjare] /19/ VT to munch

sgras'sare/72/ VT to remove the grease from

'**sgravio** SM: **~ fiscale** *o* **contributivo** tax relief

sgrazi'ato, -a[zgrat'tsjato] AG clumsy, ungainly

sgreto'lare/72/ VT to cause to crumble; **sgretolarsi**VPR to crumble

sgri'dare/72/ VT to scold

sgri'data SF scolding

sguai'ato, -a AG coarse, vulgar

sguai'nare/72/ VT to draw, unsheathe

sgual'cire [zgwal'tʃire] /55/ VT to crumple (up), crease

sgual'drina SF (*peg*) slut

sgu'ardo SM (*occhiata*) look, glance; (*espressione*) look (in one's eye); **dare uno ~ a qc** to glance at sth, cast a glance *o* an eye over sth; **alzare** *o* **sollevare lo ~** to raise one's eyes, look up; **cercare qc/qn con lo ~** to look around for sth/sb

'**sguattero, -a** SM/F scullery boy(-maid)

sguaz'zare [zgwat'tsare] /72/ VI (*nell'acqua*) to splash about; (*nella melma*) to wallow; **~ nell'oro** to be rolling in money

sguinzagli'are [zgwintsaʎ'ʎare] /27/ VT to let off the leash; (*fig: persona*): **~ qn dietro a qn** to set sb on sb

sgusci'are [zguʃ'ʃare] /14/ VT to shell ▶ VI (*sfuggire di mano*) to slip; **~ via** to slip *o* slink away

'**shaker** ['ʃeikəʳ] SM INV (cocktail) shaker

'**shampoo** ['ʃampo] SM INV shampoo

'**shiatzu** ['tʃiatsu] SM INV, AG INV shiatsu

shoc'care [ʃok'kare] /20/ VT = **shockare**

shock [ʃɔk] SM INV shock

shoc'kare [ʃok'kare] /72/ VT to shock

SI SIGLA = **Siena**

| PAROLA CHIAVE |

si(*dav lo, la, li, le, ne diventa* **se**) PRON **1** (*riflessivo: maschile*) himself; (*: femminile*) herself; (*: neutro*) itself; (*: impersonale*) oneself; *pl* themselves; **lavarsi** to wash (oneself); **si è tagliato** he has cut himself; **si credono importanti** they think a lot of themselves

2 (*riflessivo: con complemento oggetto*): **lavarsi le mani** to wash one's hands; **sporcarsi i pantaloni** to get one's trousers dirty; **si sta lavando i capelli** he (*o* she) is washing his (*o* her) hair

3 (*reciproco*) one another, each other; **si amano** they love one another *o* each other

4 (*passivo*): **si ripara facilmente** it is easily repaired; **affittasi camera** room to let

5 (*impersonale*): **si dice che ...** they *o* people say that ...; **si vede che è vecchio** one *o* you can see that it's old; **non si fa credito** we do not give credit; **ci si sbaglia facilmente** it's easy to make a mistake

6 (*noi*) we; **tra poco si parte** we're leaving soon

sì AV yes ▶ SM: **non mi aspettavo un sì** I didn't expect him (*o* her *etc*) to say yes; **per me è sì** I should think so, I expect so; **saranno stati sì e no in 20** there must have been about 20 of them; **uno sì e uno no** every other one; **un giorno sì e uno no** every other day; **dire di sì** to say yes; **spero/ penso di sì** I hope/think so; **fece di sì col capo** he nodded (his head); **e sì che ...** and to think that ...

'**sia¹** CONG: **~ ... ~**: (*o ... o*) **che lavori, ~ che non lavori** whether he works or not; (*tanto ... quanto*) **verranno ~ Luigi ~ suo fratello** both Luigi and his brother will be coming

'**sia²***etc* VB *vedi* **essere**

SIAE SIGLA F = **Società Italiana Autori ed Editori**

Si'am SM: **il ~** Siam

sia'mese AG, SMF siamese *inv*

si'amo VB *vedi* **essere**

Si'beria SF: **la ~** Siberia

siberi'ano, -a AG, SM/F Siberian

sibi'lare/72/ VI to hiss; (*fischiare*) to whistle

'**sibilo** SM hiss; whistle

si'cario SM hired killer

sicché [sik'ke] CONG (*perciò*) so (that), therefore; (*e quindi*) (and) so

siccità [sittʃi'ta] SF drought

sic'come CONG since, as

Si'cilia [si'tʃilja] SF: **la ~** Sicily

sicili'ano, -a[sitʃi'ljano] AG, SM/F Sicilian

sico'moro SM sycamore

'**siculo, -a** AG, SM/F Sicilian

S

si'cura SF (*di arma, spilla*) safety catch; (*Aut: di portiera*) safety lock

sicura'mente AV certainly

sicu'rezza [siku'rettsa] SF safety; security; confidence; certainty; **di ~** safety *cpd*; **la ~ stradale** road safety; **avere la ~ di qc** to be sure *o* certain of sth; **lo so con ~** I am quite certain; **ha risposto con molta ~** he answered very confidently; **~ informatica** cybersecurity

si'curo, -a AG safe; (*ben difeso*) secure; (*fiducioso*) confident; (*certo*) sure, certain; (*notizia, amico*) reliable; (*esperto*) skilled ▸ AV (*anche*: **di sicuro**) certainly ▸ SM: **andare sul ~** to play safe; **essere/mettere al ~** to be safe/put in a safe place; **~ di sé** self-confident, sure of o.s.; **sentirsi ~** to feel safe *o* secure; **essere ~ di/che** to be sure of/that; **da fonte sicura** from reliable sources

siderur'gia [siderur'dʒia] SF iron and steel industry

side'rurgico, -a, -ci, -che [side'rurdʒiko] AG iron and steel *cpd*

'sidro SM cider

si'edo *etc* VB *vedi* **sedere**

si'epe SF hedge

si'ero SM (*Med*) serum; **~ antivipera** snake bite serum; **~ del latte** whey

sieronegatività SF INV HIV-negative status

sieronega'tivo, -a AG HIV-negative ▸ SM/F HIV-negative person

sieropositività SF INV HIV-positive status

sieroposi'tivo, -a AG HIV-positive ▸ SM/F HIV-positive person

si'erra SF (*Geo*) sierra

Si'erra Le'one SF: **la ~** Sierra Leone

si'esta SF siesta, (afternoon) nap

si'ete VB *vedi* **essere**

si'filide SF syphilis

si'fone SM siphon

Sig. ABBR (= *signore*) Mr

siga'retta SF cigarette

'sigaro SM cigar

Sigg. ABBR (= *signori*) Messrs

sigil'lare [sidʒil'lare] /**72**/ VT to seal

si'gillo [si'dʒillo] SM seal

'sigla SF (*iniziali*) initials *pl*; (*abbreviazione*) acronym, abbreviation; **~ automobilistica** *abbreviation of province on vehicle number plate*; **~ musicale** signature tune

si'glare /**72**/ VT to initial

Sig.na ABBR (= *signorina*) Miss

signifi'care [siɲɲifi'kare] /**20**/ VT to mean; **cosa significa?** what does this mean?

significa'tivo, -a [siɲɲifika'tivo] AG significant

signifi'cato [siɲɲifi'kato] SM meaning

si'gnora [siɲ'ɲora] SF lady; **la ~ X** Mrs X; **buon giorno S~/Signore/Signorina** good morning; (*deferente*) good morning Madam/Sir/Madam; (*quando si conosce il nome*) good morning Mrs/Mr/Miss X; **Gentile S~/Signore/Signorina** (*in una lettera*) Dear Madam/Sir/Madam; **Gentile (o Cara) S~ Rossi** Dear Mrs Rossi; **Gentile S~ Anna Rossi** (*sulle buste*) Mrs Anna Rossi; **il signor Rossi e ~** Mr Rossi and his wife; **signore e signori** ladies and gentlemen; **le presento la mia ~** may I introduce my wife?

si'gnore [siɲ'ɲore] SM gentleman; (*padrone*) lord, master; (*Rel*): **il S~** the Lord; **il signor X** Mr X; **signor Presidente** Mr Chairman; **Gentile (o Caro) Signor Rossi** (*in lettere*) Dear Mr Rossi; **Gentile Signor Paolo Rossi** (*sulle buste*) Mr Paolo Rossi; **i signori Bianchi** (*coniugi*) Mr and Mrs Bianchi; *vedi anche* **signora**

signo'ria [siɲɲo'ria] SF (*Storia*) seignory, signoria; **S~ Vostra** (*Amm*) you

signo'rile [siɲɲo'rile] AG refined

signorilità [siɲɲorili'ta] SF (*raffinatezza*) refinement; (*eleganza*) elegance

signo'rina [siɲɲo'rina] SF young lady; **la ~ X** Miss X; **Gentile (o Cara) S~ Rossi** (*in lettere*) Dear Miss Rossi; **Gentile S~ Anna Rossi** (*sulle buste*) Miss Anna Rossi; *vedi anche* **signora**

signo'rino [siɲɲo'rino] SM young master

Sig.ra ABBR (= *signora*) Mrs

silenzia'tore [silentsja'tore] SM silencer

si'lenzio [si'lɛntsjo] SM silence; **fare ~** to be quiet, stop talking; **far passare qc sotto ~** to keep quiet about sth, hush sth up

silenzi'oso, -a [silen'tsjoso] AG silent, quiet

'silice ['silitʃe] SF silica

si'licio [si'litʃo] SM silicon; **piastrina di ~** silicon chip

sili'cone SM silicone

'sillaba SF syllable

silu'rare /**72**/ VT to torpedo; (*fig: privare del comando*) to oust

si'luro SM torpedo

SIM [sim] SIGLA F INV (*Tel*): **~ card** SIM card

simbi'osi SF (*Biol, fig*) symbiosis

simboleggi'are [simboled'dʒare] /**62**/ VT to symbolize

sim'bolico, -a, -ci, -che AG symbolic(al)

simbo'lismo SM symbolism

'simbolo SM symbol

simi'lare AG similar

'simile AG (*analogo*) similar; (*di questo tipo*): **un uomo ~** such a man, a man like this ▸ SM (*persona*) fellow man; **libri simili** such books; **~ a** similar to; **non ho mai visto niente di ~** I've never seen anything like that; **è insegnante o qualcosa di ~** he's a teacher or something like that; **vendono vasi e simili** they sell vases and things like that; **i suoi simili** one's fellow men; one's peers

simili'tudine SF (*Ling*) simile

simme'tria SF symmetry

sim'metrico, -a, -ci, -che AG symmetric(al)

simpa'tia SF (*qualità*) pleasantness; (*inclinazione*) liking; **avere ~ per qn** to like sb, have a liking for sb; **con ~** (*su lettera ecc*) with much affection

sim'patico, -a, -ci, -che AG (*persona*) nice, pleasant, likeable; (*casa, albergo ecc*) nice, pleasant

simpatiz'zante [simpatid'dzante] SMF sympathizer

simpatiz'zare [simpatid'dzare] /**72**/ VI: **~ con** to take a liking to

sim'posio SM symposium

simu'lacro SM (*monumento, statua*) image; (*fig*) semblance

simu'lare/**72**/ VT to sham, simulate; (*Tecn*) to simulate

simulazi'one [simulat'tsjone] SF shamming; simulation

simul'taneo, -a AG simultaneous

sin. ABBR (= *sinistra*) L

sina'goga, -ghe SF synagogue

since'ra'mente [sintʃera'mente] AV (*gen*) sincerely; (*francamente*) honestly, sincerely

since'rarsi [sintʃe'rarsi] /**72**/ VPR: **~ (di qc)** to make sure (of sth)

sincerità [sintʃeri'ta] SF sincerity

sin'cero, -a[sin'tʃero] AG (*genuino*) sincere; (*onesto*) genuine; heartfelt

'sincope SF syncopation; (*Med*) blackout

sincro'nia SF (*di movimento*) synchronism

sin'cronico, -a, -ci, -che AG synchronic

sincroniz'zare [sinkronid'dzare] /**72**/ VT to synchronize

sinda'cale AG (trade-)union *cpd*

sindaca'lista, -i, -e SM/F trade unionist

sinda'care/**20**/ VT (*controllare*) to inspect; (*fig: criticare*) to criticize

sinda'cato SM (*di lavoratori*) (trade) union; (*Amm, Econ, Dir*) syndicate, trust, pool; **~ dei datori di lavoro** employers' association

'sindaco, -ci SM mayor

'sindrome SF (*Med*) syndrome

siner'gia, -gie[siner'dʒia] SF (*anche fig*) synergy

sinfo'nia SF (*Mus*) symphony

sin'fonico, -a, -ci, -che AG symphonic; (*orchestra*) symphony *cpd*

singa'lese AG, SMF Sin(g)halese *inv*

Singa'pore SF Singapore

singhioz'zare [singjot'tsare] /**72**/ VI to sob; to hiccup

singhi'ozzo [sin'gjottso] SM (*di pianto*) sob; (*Med*) hiccup; **avere il ~** to have the hiccups; **a ~** (*fig*) by fits and starts

'single ['siŋgol] AG INV, SM O F INV single

singo'lare AG (*insolito*) remarkable, singular; (*Ling*) singular ▶ SM (*Ling*) singular; (*Tennis*): **~ maschile/femminile** men's(-women's) singles

singolar'mente AV (*separatamente*) individually, one at a time; (*in modo strano*) strangely, peculiarly, oddly

'singolo, -a AG single, individual ▶ SM (*persona*) individual; (*Tennis*) = **singolare**; **ogni ~ individuo** each individual; **camera singola** single room

sinis'trato, -a AG damaged ▶ SM/F disaster victim; **zona sinistrata** disaster area

si'nistro, -a AG left, left-hand; (*fig*) sinister ▶ SM (*incidente*) accident ▶ SF (*Pol*) left (wing); **a sinistra** on the left; (*direzione*) to the left; **a sinistra di** to the left of; **di sinistra** left-wing; **tenere la sinistra** to keep to the left; **guida a sinistra** left-hand drive

'sino PREP = **fino**

si'nonimo, -a AG synonymous ▶ SM synonym; **~ di** synonymous with

sin'tassi SF syntax

sin'tattico, -a, -ci, -che AG syntactic

'sintesi SF synthesis; (*riassunto*) summary, résumé; **in ~** in brief, in short

sin'tetico, -a, -ci, -che AG synthetic; (*conciso*) brief, concise

sintetiz'zare [sintetid'dzare] /**72**/ VT to synthesize; (*riassumere*) to summarize

sintetizza'tore [sintetiddza'tore] SM (*Mus*) synthesizer; **~ di voce** voice synthesizer

sinto'matico, -a, -ci, -che AG symptomatic

'sintomo SM symptom

sinto'nia SF (*Radio*) tuning; **essere in ~ con qn** (*fig*) to be on the same wavelength as sb

sintoniz'zare [sintonid'dzare] /**72**/ VT to tune (in); **sintonizzarsi**VPR: **sintonizzarsi su** to tune in to

sintonizza'tore [sintoniddza'tore] SM tuner

sinu'oso, -a AG (*strada*) winding

sinu'site SF sinusitis

SIP SIGLA F (= *Società Italiana per l'esercizio telefonico*) *former name of Italian telephone company*

si'pario SM (*Teat*) curtain

si'rena SF (*apparecchio*) siren; (*nella mitologia, fig*) mermaid; **~ d'allarme** (*per incendio*) fire alarm; (*per furto*) burglar alarm

'Siria SF: **la ~** Syria

siri'ano, -a AG, SM/F Syrian

si'ringa, -ghe SF syringe

'sisma, -i SM earthquake

'SISMI SIGLA M (= *Servizio per l'Informazione e la Sicurezza Militari*) *military security service*

'sismico, -a, -ci, -che AG seismic; (*zona*) earthquake *cpd*

sis'mografo SM seismograph

S

sissi'gnore [sissiɲ'ɲore] AV (*a un superiore*) yes, sir; (*enfatico*) yes indeed, of course

sis'tema, -i SM system; (*metodo*) method, way; **trovare il ~ per fare qc** to find a way to do sth; **~ decimale/metrico** decimal/metric system; **~ nervoso** nervous system; **~ operativo** (*Inform*) operating system; **~ solare** solar system; **~ di vita** way of life

siste'mare /**72**/ VT (*mettere a posto*) to tidy, put in order; (*risolvere: questione*) to sort out, settle; (*procurare un lavoro a*) to find a job for; (*dare un alloggio a*) to settle, find accommodation (*BRIT*) o accommodations (*US*) for; **sistemarsi** VPR (*problema*) to be settled; (*persona: trovare alloggio*) to find accommodation(s); (: *trovarsi un lavoro*) to get fixed up with a job; **ti sistemo io!** I'll soon sort you out!; **~ qn in un albergo** to fix sb up with a hotel

sistematica'mente AV systematically

siste'matico, -a, -ci, -che AG systematic

sistemazi'one [sistemat'tsjone] SF arrangement, order; settlement; employment; accommodation (*BRIT*), accommodations (*US*)

'sito, -a AG (*Amm*) situated ▶ SM (*letterario*) place; **~ Internet** website

situ'are /**72**/ VT to site, situate

situ'ato, -a AG: **~ a/su** situated at/on

situazi'one [situat'tsjone] SF situation; **vista la sua ~ familiare** given your family situation o circumstances; **nella sua ~** in your position o situation; **mi trovo in una ~ critica** I'm in a very difficult situation o position

'skai® SM Leatherette®

ski-lift [ski'lift] SM INV ski tow

ski pass [ski'pa:s] SM INV ski pass

slacci'are [zlat'tʃare] /**14**/ VT to undo, unfasten

slanci'arsi [zlan'tʃarsi] /**14**/ VPR to dash, fling o.s.

slanci'ato, -a [zlan'tʃato] AG slender

'slancio ['zlantʃo] SM dash, leap; (*fig*) surge; **in uno ~ d'affetto** in a burst o rush of affection; **di ~** impetuously

sla'vato, -a AG faded, washed out; (*fig: viso, occhi*) pale, colourless (*BRIT*), colorless (*US*)

sla'vina SF snowslide

'slavo, -a AG Slav(onic), Slavic

sle'ale AG disloyal; (*concorrenza ecc*) unfair

slealtà SF disloyalty; unfairness

sle'gare /**80**/ VT to untie

slip [zlip] SM INV (*mutandine*) briefs pl; (*da bagno: per uomo*) (swimming) trunks pl; (: *per donna*) bikini bottoms pl

'slitta SF sledge; (*trainata*) sleigh

slitta'mento SM slipping; skidding; postponement; **~ salariale** wage drift

slit'tare /**72**/ VI to slip, slide; (*Aut*) to skid; (*incontro, conferenza*) to be put off, be postponed

s.l.m. ABBR (= *sul livello del mare*) a.s.l.

slo'gare /**80**/ VT (*Med*) to dislocate; (: *caviglia, polso*) to sprain

sloga'tura SF dislocation; sprain

sloggi'are [zlod'dʒare] /**62**/ VT (*inquilino*) to turn out; (*nemico*) to drive out, dislodge ▶ VI to move out

Slo'vacchia [zlo'vakkja] SF Slovakia

slo'vacco, -a, -ci, -che AG, SM/F Slovak, Slovakian; **la Repubblica Slovacca** the Slovak Republic

Slo'venia SF Slovenia

slo'veno, -a AG, SM/F Slovene, Slovenian ▶ SM (*Ling*) Slovene

S.M. ABBR (*Mil*) = **Stato Maggiore**; (= *Sua Maestà*) HM

smac'cato, -a AG (*fig*) excessive

smacchi'are [zmak'kjare] /**19**/ VT to remove stains from

smacchia'tore [zmakkja'tore] SM stain remover

'smacco, -chi SM humiliating defeat

smagli'ante [zmaʎ'ʎante] AG brilliant, dazzling

smagli'are [zmaʎ'ʎare] /**27**/ VT, **smagli'arsi** VPR (*calza*) to ladder

smaglia'tura [zmaʎʎa'tura] SF (*su maglia, calza*) ladder (*BRIT*), run; (*Med: sulla pelle*) stretch mark

sma'grire /**55**/ VT to make thin ▶ VI to get o grow thin, lose weight

sma'grito, -a AG: **essere ~** to have lost a lot of weight

smalizi'ato, -a [zmalit'tsjato] AG shrewd, cunning

smal'tare /**72**/ VT to enamel; (*ceramica*) to glaze; (*unghie*) to varnish

smalti'mento SM (*di rifiuti*) disposal

smal'tire /**55**/ VT (*merce*) to sell off; (*rifiuti*) to dispose of; (*cibo*) to digest; (*peso*) to lose; (*rabbia*) to get over; **~ la sbornia** to sober up

'smalto SM (*anche di denti*) enamel; (*per ceramica*) glaze; **~ per unghie** nail varnish

smance'rie [zmantʃe'rie] SFPL mawkishness sg

'smania SF agitation, restlessness; (*fig*): **~ di** thirst for, craving for; **avere la ~ addosso** to have the fidgets; **avere la ~ di fare** to long o yearn to do

smani'are /**19**/ VI (*agitarsi*) to be restless o agitated; (*fig*): **~ di fare** to long o yearn to do

smantella'mento SM dismantling

smantel'lare /**72**/ VT to dismantle

smar'carsi /**20**/ VPR (*Sport*) to get free of marking

smargi'asso [zmar'dʒasso] SM show-off

smarri'mento SM loss; (*fig*) bewilderment; dismay

smar'rire/55/ VT to lose; (*non riuscire a trovare*) to mislay; **smarrirsi** VPR (*perdersi*) to lose one's way, get lost; (: *oggetto*) to go astray

smar'rito, -a AG (*oggetto*) lost; (*fig: confuso: persona*) bewildered, nonplussed; (: *sguardo*) bewildered; **ufficio oggetti smarriti** lost property office (BRIT), lost and found (US)

smasche'rare [zmaske'rare] **/72/** VT to unmask

SME ABBR = **Stato Maggiore Esercito** ▶ SIGLA M (= *Sistema Monetario Europeo*) EMS (= *European Monetary System*)

smem'brare/72/ VT (*gruppo, partito ecc*) to split; **smembrarsi** VPR to split up

smemo'rato, -a AG forgetful

smen'tire/55/ VT (*negare*) to deny; (*testimonianza*) to refute; (*reputazione*) to give the lie to; **smentirsi** VPR to be inconsistent

smen'tita SF denial; refutation

sme'raldo SM, AG INV emerald

smerci'are [zmer'tʃare] **/14/** VT (*Comm*) to sell; (: *svendere*) to sell off

'smercio ['zmɛrtʃo] SM sale; **avere poco/molto ~** to have poor/good sales

smerigli'ato, -a [zmeriʎ'ʎato] AG: **carta smerigliata** emery paper; **vetro ~** frosted glass

sme'riglio [zme'riʎʎo] SM emery

'smesso, -a PP *di* **smettere** ▶ AG: **abiti smessi** cast-offs

'smettere/63/ VT to stop; (*vestiti*) to stop wearing ▶ VI to stop, cease; **~ di fare** to stop doing

smidol'lato, -a AG spineless ▶ SM/F spineless person

smilitarizzazi'one [zmilitariddzat'tsjone] SF demilitarization

'smilzo, -a ['zmiltso] AG thin, lean

sminu'ire/72/ VT to diminish, lessen; (*fig*) to belittle; **~ l'importanza di qc** to play sth down

sminuz'zare [zminut'tsare] **/72/** VT to break into small pieces; to crumble

'smisi *etc* VB *vedi* **smettere**

smista'mento SM (*di posta*) sorting; (*Ferr*) shunting

smis'tare/72/ VT (*pacchi ecc*) to sort; (*Ferr*) to shunt

smisu'rato, -a AG boundless, immeasurable; (*grandissimo*) immense, enormous

smitiz'zare [zmitid'dzare] **/72/** VT to debunk

smobili'tare/72/ VT to demobilize

smobilitazi'one [zmobilitat'tsjone] SF demobilization

smobi'lizzo [zmobi'liddzo] SM (*Comm*) disinvestment

smo'dato, -a AG excessive, unrestrained

smode'rato, -a AG immoderate

smog [zmɔg] SM INV smog

'smoking ['smoukiŋ] SM INV dinner jacket (BRIT), tuxedo (US)

smon'tare/72/ VT (*mobile, macchina ecc*) to take to pieces, dismantle; (*fig: scoraggiare*) to dishearten ▶ VI (*scendere: da cavallo*) to dismount; (: *da treno*) to get off; (*terminare il lavoro*) to stop (work); **smontarsi** VPR to lose heart, to lose one's enthusiasm

'smorfia SF grimace; (*atteggiamento lezioso*) simpering; **fare smorfie** to make faces; to simper

smorfi'oso, -a AG simpering

'smorto, -a AG (*viso*) pale, wan; (*colore*) dull

smor'zare [zmor'tsare] **/72/** VT (*suoni*) to deaden; (*colori*) to tone down; (*luce*) to dim; (*sete*) to quench; (*entusiasmo*) to dampen; **smorzarsi** VPR (*suono, luce*) to fade; (*entusiasmo*) to dampen

'smosso, -a PP *di* **smuovere**

smotta'mento SM landslide

sms ['ɛsse'emme'esse] SM INV text (message)

'smunto, -a AG haggard, pinched

smu'overe/66/ VT to move, shift; (*fig: commuovere*) to move; (: *dall'inerzia*) to rouse, stir; **smuoversi** VPR to move, shift

smus'sare/72/ VT (*angolo*) to round off, smooth; (*lama ecc*) to blunt; **smussarsi** VPR to become blunt

s.n. ABBR = **senza numero**

snatu'rato, -a AG inhuman, heartless

snazionaliz'zare [znattsjonalid'dzare] **/72/** VT to denationalize

snelli'mento SM (*di traffico*) speeding up; (*di procedura*) streamlining

snel'lire/55/ VT (*persona*) to make slim; (*traffico*) to speed up; (*procedura*) to streamline; **snellirsi** VPR (*persona*) to (get) slim; (*traffico*) to speed up

'snello, -a AG (*agile*) agile; (*svelto*) slender, slim

sner'vante AG (*attesa, lavoro*) exasperating

sner'vare/72/ VT to enervate, wear out; **snervarsi** VPR to become enervated

sni'dare/72/ VT to drive out, flush out

sniffare [znif'fare] **/72/** VT (*col: cocaina*) to snort

snob'bare/72/ VT to snub

sno'bismo SM snobbery

snoccio'lare [znottʃo'lare] **/72/** VT (*frutta*) to stone; (*fig: orazioni*) to rattle off; (: *verità*) to blab; (: *col: soldi*) to shell out

sno'dabile AG (*lampada*) adjustable; (*tubo, braccio*) hinged; **rasoio con testina ~** swivel-head razor

sno'dare/72/ VT to untie, undo; (*rendere agile, mobile*) to loosen; **snodarsi** VPR to come loose; (*articolarsi*) to bend; (*strada, fiume*) to wind

sno'dato, -a AG (*articolazione, persona*) flexible; (*fune ecc*) undone

S

'snowboard ['znobord] SM INV (*tavola*)
snowboard; (*sport*) snowboarding; **fare ~**
to go snowboarding

SO SIGLA = **Sondrio**

so VB *vedi* **sapere**

S.O. ABBR (= *sudovest*) SW

so'ave AG (*voce, maniera*) gentle; (*volto*) delicate,
sweet; (*musica*) soft, sweet; (*profumo*) delicate

soavità SF gentleness; delicacy; sweetness;
softness

sobbal'zare [sobbal'tsare] /**72**/ VI to jolt, jerk;
(*trasalire*) to jump, start

sob'balzo [sob'baltso] SM jerk, jolt; jump,
start

sobbar'carsi /**20**/ VPR: **~ a** to take on,
undertake

sob'borgo, -ghi SM suburb

sobil'lare /**72**/ VT to stir up, incite

'sobrio, -a AG sober

Soc. ABBR (= *società*) Soc.

socchi'udere [sok'kjudere] /**22**/ VT (*porta*) to
leave ajar; (*occhi*) to half-close

socchi'uso, -a [sok'kjuso] PP *di*
socchiudere ▶ AG (*porta, finestra*) ajar; (*occhi*)
half-closed

soc'combere /**29**/ VI to succumb, give way

soc'correre /**28**/ VT to help, assist

soccorri'tore, -'trice SM/F rescuer

soc'corso, -a PP *di* **soccorrere** ▶ SM help, aid,
assistance; **soccorsi** SMPL relief *sg*, aid *sg*;
prestare ~ a qn to help *o* assist sb; **venire in
~ di qn** to help sb, come to sb's aid;
operazioni di ~ rescue operations;
~ stradale breakdown service

socialdemo'cratico, -a, -ci, -che
[sotʃaldemo'kratiko] SM/F Social Democrat

soci'ale [so'tʃale] AG social; (*di associazione*)
club *cpd*, association *cpd*

socia'lismo [sotʃa'lizmo] SM socialism

socia'lista, -i, -e [sotʃa'lista] AG, SM/F
socialist

socializ'zare [sotʃalid'dzare] /**72**/ VI to
socialize

società [sotʃe'ta] SF INV society; (*sportiva*)
club; (*Comm*) company; **in ~ con qn** in
partnership with sb; **mettersi in ~ con qn**
to go into business with sb; **l'alta ~** high
society; **~ anonima** ≈ limited (BRIT) *o*
incorporated (US) company; **~ per azioni**
joint-stock company; **~ di comodo** shell
company; **~ fiduciaria** trust company;
~ di mutuo soccorso friendly society (BRIT),
benefit society (US); **~ a responsabilità
limitata** *type of limited liability company*

soci'evole [so'tʃevole] AG sociable

socievo'lezza [sotʃevo'lettsa] SF sociableness

'socio ['sɔtʃo] SM (*Dir, Comm*) partner; (*membro
di associazione*) member

sociolo'gia [sotʃolo'dʒia] SF sociology

soci'ologo, -a, -gi, -ghe [so'tʃɔlogo] SM/F
sociologist

'soda SF (*Chim*) soda; (*acqua gassata*) soda (water)

soda'lizio [soda'littsjo] SM association,
society

soddisfa'cente [soddisfa'tʃɛnte] AG
satisfactory

soddis'fare /**41**/ VT, VI: **~ (a)** to satisfy;
(*impegno*) to fulfil; (*debito*) to pay off; (*richiesta*)
to meet, comply with; (*offesa*) to make
amends for

soddis'fatto, -a PP *di* **soddisfare** ▶ AG
satisfied, pleased; **essere ~ di** to be satisfied
o pleased with

soddisfazi'one [soddisfat'tsjone] SF
satisfaction

'sodio SM (*Chim*) sodium

'sodo, -a AG firm, hard; (*uovo*) hard-boiled
▶ SM: **venire al ~** to come to the point ▶ AV
(*picchiare, lavorare*) hard; **dormire ~** to sleep
soundly

sofà SM INV sofa

soffe'renza [soffe'rɛntsa] SF suffering;
(*Comm*): **in ~** unpaid

sof'ferto, -a PP *di* **soffrire** ▶ AG (*vittoria*)
hard-fought; (*distacco, decisione*) painful

soffi'are /**19**/ VT to blow; (*notizia, segreto*) to
whisper ▶ VI to blow; (*sbuffare*) to puff (and
blow); **soffiarsi il naso** to blow one's nose;
~ qc/qn a qn (*fig*) to pinch *o* steal sth/sb from
sb; **~ via qc** to blow sth away

soffi'ata SF (*col*) tip-off; **fare una ~ alla
polizia** to tip off the police

'soffice ['sɔffitʃe] AG soft

soffi'etto SM (*Mus, per fuoco*) bellows *pl*; **porta
a ~** folding door

'soffio SM (*di vento*) breath; (*di fumo*) puff;
(*Med*) murmur

soffi'one SM (*Bot*) dandelion

soffitta SF attic

soffitto SM ceiling

soffo'cante AG suffocating, stifling

soffo'care /**20**/ VI (*anche*: **soffocarsi**) to
suffocate, choke ▶ VT to suffocate, choke;
(*fig*) to stifle, suppress

soffocazi'one [soffokat'tsjone] SF
suffocation

sof'friggere [sof'friddʒere] /**56**/ VT to fry
lightly

sof'frire /**70**/ VT to suffer, endure; (*sopportare*)
to bear, stand ▶ VI to suffer; to be in pain;
~ (di) qc (*Med*) to suffer from sth

sof'fritto, -a PP *di* **soffriggere** ▶ SM (*Cuc*) fried
mixture of herbs, bacon and onions

sof'fuso, -a AG (*di luce*) suffused

So'fia SF (*Geo*) Sofia

sofisti'care /**20**/ VT (*vino, cibo*) to adulterate

sofisti'cato, -a AG sophisticated; (*vino*)
adulterated

sofisticazi'one [sofistikat'tsjone] SF
adulteration

'software ['softwɛa] SM: **~ applicativo**
applications package

sogget'tivo, -a [soddʒet'tivo] AG subjective

sog'getto, -a [sod'dʒɛtto] AG: **~ a** (sottomesso)
subject to; (esposto: a variazioni, danni ecc)
subject o liable to ▶ SM subject; **~ a tassa**
taxable; **recitare a ~** (Teat) to improvise

soggezi'one [soddʒet'tsjone] SF subjection;
(timidezza) awe; **avere ~ di qn** to stand in awe
of sb; to be ill at ease in sb's presence

sogghi'gnare [soggiɲ'ɲare] /15/ VI to sneer

sog'ghigno [sog'giɲɲo] SM sneer

soggia'cere [soddʒa'tʃere] /57/ VI: **~ a** to be
subjected to

soggio'gare [soddʒo'gare] /80/ VT to subdue,
subjugate

soggior'nare [soddʒor'nare] /72/ VI to stay

soggi'orno [sod'dʒorno] SM (permanenza) stay;
(stanza) living room

soggi'ungere [sod'dʒundʒere] /5/ VT to add

soggi'unto, -a [sod'dʒunto] PP di **soggiungere**

'soglia ['sɔʎʎa] SF doorstep; (anche fig)
threshold

'sogliola ['sɔʎʎola] SF (Zool) sole

so'gnante [soɲ'ɲante] AG dreamy

so'gnare [soɲ'ɲare] /15/ VT, VI to dream;
~ a occhi aperti to daydream

sogna'tore, -'trice [soɲɲa'tore] SM/F
dreamer

'sogno ['soɲɲo] SM dream

'soia SF (Bot) soya

sol SM (Mus) G; (: solfeggiando la scala) so(h)

so'laio SM (soffitta) attic

sola'mente AV only, just

so'lare AG solar, sun cpd

sol'care /20/ VT (terreno, fig: mari) to plough
(BRIT), plow (US)

'solco, -chi SM (scavo, fig: ruga) furrow; (incavo)
rut, track; (di disco) groove; (scia) wake

sol'dato SM soldier; **~ di leva** conscript;
~ semplice private

'soldo SM (fig): **non avere un ~** to be
penniless; : **non vale un ~** it's not worth a
penny; **soldi** SMPL (denaro) money sg; **non ho
soldi** I haven't got any money

'sole SM sun; (luce) sun(light); (tempo assolato)
sun(shine); **prendere il ~** to sunbathe;
il S~ che ride (Pol) symbol of the Italian
Green party

soleggi'ato, -a [soled'dʒato] AG sunny

so'lenne AG solemn

solennità SF solemnity; (festività) holiday,
feast day

so'lere /108/ VT: **~ fare qc** to be in the habit of
doing sth ▶ VB IMPERS: **come suole
accadere** as is usually the case, as usually
happens; **come si suol dire** as they say

so'lerte AG diligent

so'lerzia [so'lertsja] SF diligence

so'letta SF (per scarpe) insole

sol'fato SM sulphate (BRIT), sulfate (US)

sol'forico, -a, -ci, -che AG sulphuric (BRIT),
sulfuric (US); **acido ~** sulphuric o sulfuric
acid

sol'furo SM sulphur (BRIT), sulfur (US)

soli'dale AG in agreement; **essere ~ con qn**
(essere d'accordo) to be in agreement with sb;
(appoggiare) to be behind sb

solidarietà SF solidarity

solidifi'care /20/ VT, VI (anche: **solidificarsi**) to
solidify

solidità SF solidity

'solido, -a AG solid; (forte, robusto) sturdy, solid;
(fig: ditta) sound, solid ▶ SM (Mat) solid

soli'loquio SM soliloquy

so'lista, -i, -e AG solo ▶ SM/F soloist

solita'mente AV usually, as a rule

soli'tario, -a AG (senza compagnia) solitary,
lonely; (solo, isolato) solitary, lone; (deserto)
lonely ▶ SM (gioiello, gioco) solitaire

'solito, -a AG usual; **essere ~ fare** to be in the
habit of doing; **di ~** usually; **più tardi del ~**
later than usual; **come al ~** as usual; **siamo
alle solite!** (col) here we go again!

soli'tudine SF solitude

sollaz'zare [sollat'tsare] /72/ VT to entertain;
sollazzarsi VPR to amuse o.s.

sol'lazzo [sol'lattso] SM amusement

solleci'tare [solletʃi'tare] /72/ VT (lavoro) to
speed up; (persona) to urge on; (chiedere con
insistenza) to press for, request urgently;
(Tecn) to stress; (stimolare): **~ qn a fare** to urge
sb to do

sollecitazi'one [solletʃitat'tsjone] SF
entreaty, request; (fig) incentive; (Tecn)
stress; **lettera di ~** (Comm) reminder

sol'lecito, -a [sol'letʃito] AG prompt, quick
▶ SM (Comm) reminder; **~ di pagamento**
payment reminder

solleci'tudine [solletʃi'tudine] SF
promptness, speed

solleti'care /20/ VT to tickle

sol'letico SM tickling; **soffrire il ~** to be
ticklish

solleva'mento SM raising; lifting; (ribellione)
revolt; **~ pesi** (Sport) weight-lifting

solle'vare /72/ VT to lift, raise; (fig: persona:
alleggerire): **~ (da)** to relieve (of); (: dar conforto)
to comfort, relieve; (questione) to raise; (far
insorgere) to stir (to revolt); **sollevarsi** VPR to
rise; (fig: riprendersi) to recover; (: ribellarsi) to
rise up; **sollevarsi da terra** (persona) to get
up from the ground; (aereo) to take off;
sentirsi sollevato to feel relieved

solli'evo SM relief; (conforto) comfort; **con
mio grande ~** to my great relief

'solo, -a AG alone; *(in senso spirituale: isolato)* lonely; *(unico)*: **un ~ libro** only one book, a single book; *(con ag numerale)*: **veniamo noi tre soli** just *o* only the three of us are coming ▸ AV *(soltanto)* only, just; **~ che** *cong* but; **è il ~ proprietario** he's the sole proprietor; **l'incontrò due sole volte** he only met him twice; **non ~ ... ma anche** not only ... but also; **fare qc da ~** to do sth (all) by oneself; **vive (da) ~** he lives on his own; **possiamo vederci da soli?** can I see you in private?

sol'stizio [sol'stittsjo] SM solstice

sol'tanto AV only

so'lubile AG *(sostanza)* soluble; **caffè ~** instant coffee

soluzi'one [solut'tsjone] SF solution; **senza ~ di continuità** uninterruptedly

sol'vente AG, SM solvent; **~ per unghie** nail polish remover; **~ per vernici** paint remover

sol'venza [sol'vɛntsa] SF *(Comm)* solvency

'soma SF load, burden; **bestia da ~** beast of burden

So'malia SF: **la ~** Somalia

'somalo, -a AG, SM/F, SM Somali

so'maro SM ass, donkey

so'matico, -a, -ci, -che AG somatic

somigli'anza [somiʎ'ʎantsa] SF resemblance

somigli'are [somiʎ'ʎare] /**27**/ VI: **~ a** to be like, resemble; *(nell'aspetto fisico)* to look like; **somigliarsi** VPR to be *(o* look) alike

'somma SF *(Mat)* sum; *(di denaro)* sum (of money); *(complesso di varie cose)* whole amount, sum total; **tirare le somme** *(fig)* to sum up; **tirate le somme** *(fig)* all things considered

som'mare /**72**/ VT to add up; *(aggiungere)* to add; **tutto sommato** all things considered

som'mario, -a AG *(racconto, indagine)* brief; *(giustizia)* summary ▸ SM summary

som'mergere [som'mɛrdʒere] /**59**/ VT to submerge

sommer'gibile [sommer'dʒibile] SM submarine

som'merso, -a PP di **sommergere**

som'messo, -a AG *(voce)* soft, subdued

somminis'trare /**72**/ VT to give, administer

sommità SF INV summit, top; *(fig)* height

'sommo, -a AG highest; *(rispetto)* highest, greatest; *(poeta, artista)* great, outstanding ▸ SM *(fig)* height; **per sommi capi** in short, in brief

som'mossa SF uprising

sommozza'tore [sommottsa'tore] SM (deep-sea) diver; *(Mil)* frogman

so'naglio [so'naʎʎo] SM *(di mucche ecc)* bell; *(per bambini)* rattle

so'nante AG: **denaro** *o* **moneta ~** (ready) cash

so'nare *etc* = **suonare** *ecc*

'sonda SF *(Med, Meteor, Aer)* probe; *(Mineralogia)* drill ▸ AG INV: **pallone** *m* **~** weather balloon

son'daggio [son'daddʒo] SM sounding; probe; boring, drilling; *(indagine)* survey; **~ d'opinioni** opinion poll

son'dare /**72**/ VT *(Naut)* to sound; *(atmosfera, piaga)* to probe; *(Mineralogia)* to bore, drill; *(fig: opinione ecc)* to survey, poll

so'netto SM sonnet

son'nambulo, -a SM/F sleepwalker

sonnecchi'are [sonnek'kjare] /**19**/ VI to doze, nod

sonnel'lino SM nap

son'nifero SM sleeping drug *(o* pill)

'sonno SM sleep; **aver ~** to be sleepy; **prendere ~** to fall asleep

sonno'lento, -a AG sleepy, drowsy; *(movimenti)* sluggish

sonno'lenza [sonno'lɛntsa] SF sleepiness, drowsiness

'sono VB *vedi* **essere**

sonoriz'zare [sonorid'dzare] /**72**/ VT *(Ling)* to voice; *(Cine)* to add a sound-track to

so'noro, -a AG *(ambiente)* resonant; *(voce)* sonorous, ringing; *(onde, Cine)* sound *cpd* ▸ SM: **il ~** *(Cine)* the talkies *pl*

sontu'oso, -a AG sumptuous; lavish

so'pire /**55**/ VT *(fig: dolore, tensione)* to soothe

so'pore SM drowsiness

sopo'rifero, -a AG soporific

sop'palco, -chi SM mezzanine

soppe'rire /**55**/ VI: **~ a** to provide for; **~ alla mancanza di qc** to make up for the lack of sth

soppe'sare /**72**/ VT to weigh in one's hand(s), feel the weight of; *(fig)* to weigh up

soppian'tare /**72**/ VT to supplant

soppi'atto AV: **di ~** secretly; furtively

soppor'tabile AG tolerable, bearable

soppor'tare /**72**/ VT *(reggere)* to support; *(subire: perdita, spese)* to bear, sustain; *(soffrire: dolore)* to bear, endure; *(cosa: freddo)* to withstand; *(persona: freddo, vino)* to take; *(tollerare)* to put up with, tolerate

sopportazi'one [sopportat'tsjone] SF patience; **avere spirito di ~, avere capacità di ~** to be long-suffering

soppressi'one SF abolition; withdrawal; suppression; deletion; elimination, liquidation

sop'presso, -a PP di **sopprimere**

sop'primere /**50**/ VT *(carica, privilegi ecc)* to do away with, abolish; *(servizio)* to withdraw; *(pubblicazione)* to suppress; *(parola, frase)* to delete; *(uccidere)* to eliminate, liquidate

'sopra PREP *(gen)* on; *(al di sopra di, più in alto di)* above; over; *(riguardo a)* on, about ▸ AV on top;

(*attaccato, scritto*) on it; (*al di sopra*) above; (*al piano superiore*) upstairs; **donne ~ i 30 anni** women over 30 (years of age); **100 metri ~ il livello del mare** 100 metres above sea level; **5 gradi ~ lo zero** 5 degrees above zero; **abito di ~** I live upstairs; **essere al di ~ di ogni sospetto** to be above suspicion; **per i motivi ~ illustrati** for the above-mentioned reasons, for the reasons shown above; **dormirci ~** (*fig*) to sleep on it; **passar ~ a qc** (*anche fig*) to pass over sth

so'prabito SM overcoat

sopraccen'nato, -a [soprattʃen'nato] AG above-mentioned

soprac'ciglio [soprat'tʃiʎʎo] (*pl(f)* **sopracciglia**) SM eyebrow

sopracco'perta SF (*di letto*) bedspread; (*di libro*) jacket

soprad'detto, -a AG aforesaid

sopraffare /41/ VT to overcome, overwhelm

sopraffatto, -a PP *di* **sopraffare**

sopraffazi'one [sopraffat'tsjone] SF overwhelming, overpowering

sopraffino, -a AG (*pranzo, vino*) excellent; (*fig*) masterly

sopraggi'ungere [soprad'dʒundʒere] /5/ VI (*giungere all'improvviso*) to arrive (unexpectedly); (*accadere*) to occur (unexpectedly)

sopraggi'unto, -a [soprad'dʒunto] PP *di* **sopraggiungere**

soprallu'ogo, -ghi SM (*di esperti*) inspection; (*di polizia*) on-the-spot investigation

sopram'mobile SM ornament

soprannatu'rale AG supernatural

sopran'nome SM nickname

soprannomi'nare /72/ VT to nickname

sopran'numero AV: **in ~** in excess

so'prano, -a SM/F (*persona*) soprano ▶ SM (*voce*) soprano

soprappensi'ero AV lost in thought

soprappiù SM surplus, extra; **in ~** extra, surplus; (*per giunta*) besides, in addition

sopras'salto SM: **di ~** with a start, with a jump; suddenly

soprasse'dere /107/ VI: **~ a** to delay, put off

soprat'tassa SF surtax

soprat'tutto AV (*anzitutto*) above all; (*specialmente*) especially

sopravvalu'tare /72/ VT (*persona, capacità*) to overestimate

sopravve'nire /128/ VI to arrive, appear; (*fatto*) to occur

soprav'vento SM: **avere/prendere il ~ su qn** to have/get the upper hand over sb

sopravvis'suto, -a PP *di* **sopravvivere** ▶ SM/F survivor

sopravvi'venza [sopravvi'vɛntsa] SF survival

soprav'vivere /130/ VI to survive; (*continuare a vivere*): **~ (in)** to live on (in); **~ a** (*incidente ecc*) to survive; (*persona*) to outlive

soprele'vata SF (*di strada, ferrovia*) elevated section

soprinten'dente SMF supervisor; (*statale: di belle arti ecc*) keeper

soprinten'denza [soprinten'dɛntsa] SF supervision; (*ente*): **~ alle Belle Arti** government department responsible for monuments and artistic treasures

soprin'tendere /120/ VI: **~ a** to superintend, supervise

soprin'teso, -a PP *di* **soprintendere**

so'pruso SM abuse of power; **subire un ~** to be abused

soq'quadro SM: **mettere a ~** to turn upside-down

sor'betto SM sorbet, water ice (BRIT)

sor'bire /17/ VT to sip; (*fig*) to put up with

'sorcio ['sortʃo] SM mouse

'sordido, -a AG sordid; (*fig: gretto*) stingy

sor'dina SF: **in ~** softly; (*fig*) on the sly

sordità SF deafness

'sordo, -a AG deaf; (*rumore*) muffled; (*dolore*) dull; (*lotta*) silent, hidden; (*odio, rancore*) veiled ▶ SM/F deaf person

sordo'muto, -a AG deaf-and-dumb ▶ SM/F deaf-mute

so'rella SF sister

sorel'lastra SF stepsister; (*con genitore in comune*) half sister

sor'gente [sor'dʒɛnte] SF (*acqua che sgorga*) spring; (*di fiume, Fisica, fig*) source; **acqua di ~** spring water; **~ di calore** source of heat; **~ termale** thermal spring

'sorgere ['sordʒere] /109/ VI to rise; (*scaturire*) to spring, rise; (*fig: difficoltà*) to arise ▶ SM: **al ~ del sole** at sunrise

sori'ano, -a AG, SM/F tabby

sormon'tare /72/ VT (*fig*) to overcome, surmount

sorni'one, -a AG sly

sorpas'sare /72/ VT (*Aut*) to overtake; (*fig*) to surpass; (*: eccedere*) to exceed, go beyond; **~ in altezza** to be higher than; (*persona*) to be taller than

sorpas'sato, -a AG (*metodo, moda*) outmoded, old-fashioned; (*macchina*) obsolete

sor'passo SM (*Aut*) overtaking

sorpren'dente AG surprising; (*eccezionale, inaspettato*) astonishing, amazing

sor'prendere /81/ VT (*cogliere: in flagrante ecc*) to catch; (*stupire*) to surprise; **sorprendersi** VPR: **sorprendersi (di)** to be surprised (at)

sor'preso, -a PP *di* **sorprendere** ▶ SF surprise; **fare una sorpresa a qn** to give sb a surprise; **prendere qn di sorpresa** to take sb by surprise *o* unawares

S

sor'reggere [sor'rɛddʒere] /**87**/ ᴠᴛ to support, hold up; (*fig*) to sustain; **sorreggersi** ᴠᴘʀ (*tenersi ritto*) to stay upright

sor'retto, -a ᴘᴘ *di* **sorreggere**

sor'ridere /**89**/ ᴠɪ to smile

sor'riso, -a ᴘᴘ *di* **sorridere** ▶ sᴍ smile

sor'sata sꜰ gulp; **bere a sorsate** to gulp

sorseggi'are [sorsed'dʒare] /**62**/ ᴠᴛ to sip

'sorsi *etc* ᴠʙ *vedi* **sorgere**

'sorso sᴍ sip; **d'un ~**, **in un ~ solo** at one gulp

'sorta sꜰ sort, kind; **di ~** whatever, of any kind at all; **ogni ~ di** all sorts of; **di ogni ~** of every kind

'sorte sꜰ (*fato*) fate, destiny; (*evento fortuito*) chance; **tirare a ~** to draw lots; **tentare la ~** to try one's luck

sorteggi'are [sorted'dʒare] /**62**/ ᴠᴛ to draw for

sor'teggio [sor'teddʒo] sᴍ draw

sorti'legio [sorti'ledʒo] sᴍ witchcraft *no pl*; (*incantesimo*) spell; **fare un ~ a qn** to cast a spell on sb

sor'tire /**55**/ ᴠᴛ (*ottenere*) to produce

sor'tita sꜰ (*Mil*) sortie

'sorto, -a ᴘᴘ *di* **sorgere**

sorvegli'ante [sorveʎ'ʎante] sᴍꜰ (*di carcere*) guard, warder (Bʀɪᴛ); (*di fabbrica ecc*) supervisor

sorvegli'anza [sorveʎ'ʎantsa] sꜰ watch; supervision; (*Polizia, Mil*) surveillance

sorvegli'are [sorveʎ'ʎare] /**27**/ ᴠᴛ (*bambino, bagagli, prigioniero*) to watch, keep an eye on; (*malato*) to watch over; (*territorio, casa*) to watch o keep watch over; (*lavori*) to supervise

sorvo'lare /**72**/ ᴠᴛ (*territorio*) to fly over ▶ ᴠɪ: **~ su** (*fig*) to skim over

S.O.S. sɪɢʟᴀ ᴍ mayday, SOS

'sosia sᴍ ɪɴᴠ double

sos'pendere /**8**/ ᴠᴛ (*appendere*) to hang (up); (*interrompere, privare di una carica*) to suspend; (*rimandare*) to defer; (*appendere*) to hang; **~ un quadro al muro/un lampadario al soffitto** to hang a picture on the wall/a chandelier from the ceiling; **~ qn dal suo incarico** to suspend sb from office

sospensi'one sꜰ (*anche Chim, Aut*) suspension; deferment; **~ condizionale della pena** (*Dir*) suspended sentence

sos'peso, -a ᴘᴘ *di* **sospendere** ▶ ᴀɢ (*appeso*): **~ a** hanging on (*o* from); (*treno, autobus*) cancelled; **in ~** in abeyance; (*conto*) outstanding; **tenere in ~** (*fig*) to keep in suspense; **col fiato ~** with bated breath

sospet'tare /**72**/ ᴠᴛ to suspect ▶ ᴠɪ: **~ di** to suspect; (*diffidare*) to be suspicious of

sos'petto, -a ᴀɢ suspicious ▶ sᴍ suspicion; **destare sospetti** to arouse suspicion

sospet'toso, -a ᴀɢ suspicious

sos'pingere [sos'pindʒere] /**114**/ ᴠᴛ to drive, push

sos'pinto, -a ᴘᴘ *di* **sospingere**

sospi'rare /**72**/ ᴠɪ to sigh ▶ ᴠᴛ to long for, yearn for

sos'piro sᴍ sigh; **~ di sollievo** sigh of relief

'sosta sꜰ (*fermata*) stop, halt; (*pausa*) pause, break; **senza ~** non-stop, without a break

sostanti'vato, -a ᴀɢ (*Ling*): **aggettivo ~** adjective used as a noun

sostan'tivo sᴍ noun, substantive

sos'tanza [sos'tantsa] sꜰ substance; **sostanze** sꜰᴘʟ (*ricchezze*) wealth *sg*, possessions; **in ~** in short, to sum up; **la ~ del discorso** the essence of the speech

sostanzi'ale [sostan'tsjale] ᴀɢ substantial

sostanzi'oso, -a [sostan'tsjoso] ᴀɢ (*cibo*) nourishing, substantial

sos'tare /**72**/ ᴠɪ (*fermarsi*) to stop (for a while), stay; (*fare una pausa*) to take a break

sos'tegno [sos'teɲɲo] sᴍ support; **a ~ di** in support of; **muro di ~** supporting wall

soste'nere /**121**/ ᴠᴛ to support; (*prendere su di sé*) to take on, bear; (*resistere*) to withstand, stand up to; (*affermare*): **~ che** to maintain that; **sostenersi** ᴠᴘʀ to hold o.s. up, support o.s.; (*fig*) to keep up one's strength; **~ qn** (*moralmente*) to be a support to sb; (*difendere*) to stand up for sb, take sb's part; **~ gli esami** to sit exams; **~ il confronto** to bear *o* stand comparison

soste'nibile ᴀɢ (*tesi*) tenable; (*spese*) bearable; (*sviluppo*) sustainable

sosteni'tore, -'trice sᴍ/ꜰ supporter

sostenta'mento sᴍ maintenance, support; **mezzi di ~** means of support

soste'nuto, -a ᴀɢ (*stile*) elevated; (*velocità, ritmo*) sustained; (*prezzo*) high ▶ sᴍ/ꜰ: **fare il(la) ~(a)** to be standoffish, keep one's distance

sostitu'ire /**55**/ ᴠᴛ (*mettere al posto di*): **~ qn/qc a** to substitute sb/sth for; (*prendere il posto di*) to replace, take the place of

sostitu'tivo, -a ᴀɢ (*Amm: documento, certificato*) equivalent

sosti'tuto, -a sᴍ/ꜰ substitute; **~ procuratore della Repubblica** (*Dir*) deputy public prosecutor

sostituzi'one [sostitut'tsjone] sꜰ substitution; **in ~ di** as a substitute for, in place of

sotta'ceti [sotta'tʃeti] sᴍᴘʟ pickles

sot'tana sꜰ (*sottoveste*) underskirt; (*gonna*) skirt; (*Rel*) soutane, cassock

sot'tecchi [sot'tekki] ᴀᴠ: **guardare di ~** to steal a glance at

sotter'fugio [sotter'fudʒo] sᴍ subterfuge

sotter'raneo, -a ᴀɢ underground ▶ sᴍ cellar

sotter'rare /**72**/ ᴠᴛ to bury

sottigli'ezza [sottiʎ'ʎettsa] SF thinness; slimness; (fig: acutezza) subtlety; shrewdness; **sottigliezze** SFPL (pedanteria) quibbles

sot'tile AG thin; (figura, caviglia) thin, slim, slender; (fine: polvere, capelli) fine; (fig: leggero) light; (: vista) sharp, keen; (: olfatto) fine, discriminating; (: mente) subtle; shrewd ▶ SM: **non andare per il ~** not to mince matters

sottiliz'zare [sottilid'dzare] /72/ VI to split hairs

sottin'tendere /120/ VT (intendere qc non espresso) to understand; (implicare) to imply; **lasciare ~ che** to let it be understood that

sottin'teso, -a PP di **sottintendere** ▶ SM allusion; **parlare senza sottintesi** to speak plainly

'sotto PREP (gen) under; (più in basso di) below ▶ AV underneath, beneath; below; (al piano inferiore): **(al piano) di ~** downstairs; **~ il monte** at the foot of the mountain; **~ la pioggia/il sole** in the rain/sun(shine); **tutti quelli ~ i 18 anni** all those under 18 (years of age) (BRIT) o under age 18 (US); **~ il livello del mare** below sea level; **~ il chilo** under o less than a kilo; **ha 5 impiegati ~ di sé** he has 5 clerks under him; **siamo ~ Natale/Pasqua** it's nearly Christmas/Easter; **~ un certo punto di vista** in a sense; **~ forma di** in the form of; **~ falso nome** under a false name; **~ terra** underground; **~ voce** in a low voice; **chiuso ~ vuoto** vacuum packed

sotto'banco AV (di nascosto: vendere, comprare) under the counter; (: agire) in an underhand way

sottobicchi'ere [sottobik'kjere] SM mat, coaster

sotto'bosco, -schi SM undergrowth no pl

sotto'braccio [sotto'brattʃo] AV by the arm; **prendere qn ~** to take sb by the arm; **camminare ~ a qn** to walk arm in arm with sb

sottochi'ave [sotto'kjave] AV under lock and key

sottoco'perta AV (Naut) below deck

sotto'costo AV below cost (price)

sottocu'taneo, -a AG subcutaneous

sottoes'posto, -a AG (fotografia, pellicola) underexposed

sotto'fondo SM background; **~ musicale** background music

sotto'gamba AV: **prendere qc ~** not to take sth seriously

sotto'gonna SF underskirt

sottogo'verno SM political patronage

sotto'gruppo SM subgroup; (di partito) faction

sottoline'are /72/ VT to underline; (fig) to emphasize, stress

sot't'olio AV, AG INV in oil

sotto'mano AV (a portata di mano) within reach, to hand; (di nascosto) secretly

sottoma'rino, -a AG (flora) submarine; (cavo, navigazione) underwater ▶ SM (Naut) submarine

sotto'messo, -a PP di **sottomettere** ▶ AG submissive

sotto'mettere /63/ VT to subdue, subjugate; **sottomettersi** VPR to submit

sottomissi'one SF submission

sottopas'saggio [sottopas'saddʒo] SM (Aut) underpass; (pedonale) subway, underpass

sotto'porre /77/ VT (costringere) to subject; (fig: presentare) to submit; **sottoporsi** VPR to submit; **sottoporsi a** (subire) to undergo

sotto'posto, -a PP di **sottoporre**

sottopro'dotto SM by-product

sottoproduzi'one [sottoprodut'tsjone] SF underproduction

sottoproletari'ato SM: **il ~** the underprivileged class

sot'tordine AV: **passare in ~** to become of minor importance

sottos'cala SM INV (ripostiglio) cupboard (BRIT) o closet (US) under the stairs; (stanza) room under the stairs

sottos'critto, -a PP di **sottoscrivere** ▶ SM/F: **io ~, il ~** the undersigned

sottos'crivere /105/ VT to sign ▶ VI: **~ a** to subscribe to

sottoscrizi'one [sottoskrit'tsjone] SF signing; subscription

sottosegre'tario SM: **S~ di Stato** undersecretary of state (BRIT), assistant secretary of state (US)

sotto'sopra AV upside-down

sottos'tante AG (piani) lower; **nella valle ~** in the valley below

sottos'tare /116/ VI: **~ a** (assoggettarsi a) to submit to; (: richieste) to give in to; (subire: prova) to undergo

sottosu'olo SM subsoil

sottosvilup'pato, -a AG underdeveloped

sottosvi'luppo SM underdevelopment

sottote'nente SM (Mil) second lieutenant

sotto'terra AV underground

sotto'tetto SM attic

sotto'titolo SM subtitle

sottovalu'tare /72/ VT (persona, prova) to underestimate, underrate

sotto'vento AV (Naut) leeward(s) ▶ AG INV (lato) leeward, lee

sotto'veste SF underskirt

sotto'voce [sotto'votʃe] AV in a low voice

sottovu'oto AV: **confezionare ~** to vacuum-pack ▶ AG: **confezione** f **~** vacuum pack

S

sot'trarre /**123**/ VT (*Mat*) to subtract, take away; **sottrarsi** VPR: **sottrarsi a** (*sfuggire*) to escape; (*evitare*) to avoid; **~ qn/qc a** (*togliere*) to remove sb/sth from; (*salvare*) to save o rescue sb/sth from; **~ qc a qn** (*rubare*) to steal sth from sb; **sottratte le spese** once expenses have been deducted

sot'tratto, -a PP *di* **sottrarre**

sottrazi'one [sottrat'tsjone] SF (*Mat*) subtraction; (*furto*) removal

sottuffici'ale [sottuffi'tʃale] SM (*Mil*) non-commissioned officer; (*Naut*) petty officer

soufflé [su'fle] SM INV (*Cuc*) soufflé

souve'nir [suvə'nir] SM INV souvenir

so'vente AV often

soverchi'are [sover'kjare] /**19**/ VT to overpower, overwhelm

soverchie'ria [soverkje'ria] SF (*prepotenza*) abuse (of power)

sovi'etico, -a, -ci, -che AG Soviet ▶ SM/F Soviet citizen

sovrabbon'dante AG overabundant

sovrabbon'danza [sovrabbon'dantsa] SF overabundance; **in ~** in excess

sovraccari'care /**20**/ VT to overload

sovrac'carico, -a, -chi, -che AG: **~ (di)** overloaded (with) ▶ SM excess load; **~ di lavoro** extra work

sovraesposizi'one [sovraespozit'tsjone] SF (*Fot*) overexposure

sovraffol'lato, -a AG overcrowded

sovraimmagazzi'nare [sovraimmagaddzi'nare] /**72**/ VT to overstock

sovranità SF sovereignty; (*fig: superiorità*) supremacy

sovrannatu'rale AG = **soprannaturale**

so'vrano, -a AG sovereign; (*fig: sommo*) supreme ▶ SM/F sovereign, monarch

sovrappopolazi'one [sovrappopolat'tsjone] SF overpopulation

sovrap'porre /**77**/ VT to place on top of, put on top of; (*Fot, Geom*) to superimpose; **sovrapporsi** VPR (*fig: aggiungersi*) to be added; (*Fot*) to be superimposed

sovrapposizi'one [sovrapposit'tsjone] SF superimposition

sovrap'posto, -a PP *di* **sovrapporre**

sovrapproduzi'one [sovrapprodut'tsjone] SF overproduction

sovras'tante AG overhanging; (*fig*) imminent

sovras'tare /**72**/ VT (*vallata, fiume*) to overhang; (*fig*) to hang over, threaten

sovrastrut'tura SF superstructure

sovrecci'tare [sovrettʃi'tare] /**72**/ VT to overexcite

sovrimpressi'one SF (*Fot, Cine*) double exposure; **immagini in ~** superimposed images

sovrinten'dente *etc* = **soprintendente** *ecc*

sovru'mano, -a AG superhuman

sovve'nire /**128**/ VI (*venire in mente*): **~ a** to occur to

sovvenzio'nare [sovventsjo'nare] /**72**/ VT to subsidize

sovvenzi'one [sovven'tsjone] SF subsidy, grant

sovver'sivo, -a AG subversive

sovverti'mento SM subversion, undermining

sovver'tire /**45**/ VT (*Pol: ordine, stato*) to subvert, undermine

'sozzo, -a ['sottso] AG filthy, dirty

SP SIGLA = **La Spezia**

S.P. ABBR = **strada provinciale**; *vedi* **provinciale**

S.p.A. ABBR *vedi* **società per azioni**

spac'care /**20**/ VT to split, break; (*legna*) to chop; (*fig*) to divide; **spaccarsi** VPR to split, break

spacca'tura SF split

spaccherò *etc* [spakke'rɔ] VB *vedi* **spaccare**

spacci'are [spat'tʃare] /**14**/ VT (*vendere*) to sell (off); (*mettere in circolazione*) to circulate; (*droga*) to peddle, push; **spacciarsi** VPR: **spacciarsi per** (*farsi credere*) to pass o.s. off as, pretend to be

spacci'ato, -a [spat'tʃato] AG (*col: malato, fuggiasco*): **essere ~** to be done for

spaccia'tore, -'trice [spattʃa'tore] SM/F (*di droga*) pusher; (*di denaro falso*) dealer

'spaccio ['spattʃo] SM: **~ (di)** (*di merce rubata, droga*) trafficking (in); (*di denaro falso*) passing (of); (*vendita*) sale; (*bottega*) shop

'spacco, -chi SM (*fenditura*) split, crack; (*strappo*) tear; (*di gonna*) slit

spac'cone SM/F boaster, braggart

'spada SF sword

spadroneggi'are [spadroned'dʒare] /**62**/ VI to swagger

spae'sato, -a AG disorientated, lost

spaghet'tata [spaget'tata] SF spaghetti meal

spa'ghetti [spa'getti] SMPL (*Cuc*) spaghetti *sg*

'Spagna ['spaɲɲa] SF: **la ~** Spain

spa'gnolo, -a [spaɲ'ɲɔlo] AG Spanish ▶ SM/F Spaniard ▶ SM (*Ling*) Spanish; **gli Spagnoli** the Spanish

'spago, -ghi SM string, twine; **dare ~ a qn** (*fig*) to let sb have his (o her) way

spai'ato, -a AG (*calza, guanto*) odd

spalan'care /**20**/ VT, **spalan'carsi** VPR to open wide

spa'lare /**72**/ VT to shovel

'spalla SF shoulder; (*fig: Teat*) stooge; **spalle** SFPL (*dorso*) back; **di spalle** from behind; **seduto alle mie spalle** sitting behind me; **prendere/colpire qn alle spalle** to take/hit sb from behind; **mettere qn con le spalle al muro** (*fig*) to put sb with his (*o* her) back to the wall; **vivere alle spalle di qn** (*fig*) to live off sb

spal'lata SF (*urto*) shove *o* push with the shoulder; **dare una ~ a qc** to give sth a push *o* shove with one's shoulder

spalleggi'are [spalled'dʒare] /**62**/ VT to back up, support

spal'letta SF (*parapetto*) parapet

spalli'era SF (*di sedia ecc*) back; (*di letto: da capo*) head(board); (*: da piedi*) foot(board); (*Ginnastica*) wall bars *pl*

spal'lina SF (*Mil*) epaulette; (*di sottoveste, maglietta*) strap; (*imbottitura*) shoulder pad; **senza spalline** strapless

spal'mare /**72**/ VT to spread

'spalti SMPL (*di stadio*) terraces (*BRIT*), ≈ bleachers (*US*)

spamming ['spammiŋ] SM (*Internet*) spamming

'spandere /**110**/ VT to spread; (*versare*) to pour (out); **spandersi** VPR to spread; **~ lacrime** to shed tears

'spanto, -a PP *di* **spandere**

spa'rare /**72**/ VT to fire ▶ VI (*far fuoco*) to fire; (*tirare*) to shoot; **~ a qn/qc** to shoot sb/sth, fire at sb/sth

spa'rato SM (*di camicia*) dicky

spara'tore SM gunman

spara'toria SF exchange of shots

sparecchi'are [sparek'kjare] /**19**/ VT: **~ (la tavola)** to clear the table

spa'reggio [spa'reddʒo] SM (*Sport*) play-off

'spargere ['spardʒere] /**111**/ VT (*sparpagliare*) to scatter; (*versare: vino*) to spill; (*: lacrime, sangue*) to shed; (*diffondere*) to spread; (*emanare*) to give off (*o* out); **spargersi** VPR (*voce, notizia*) to spread; (*persone*) to scatter; **si è sparsa una voce sul suo conto** there is a rumour going round about him

spargi'mento [spardʒi'mento] SM scattering; spilling; shedding; **~ di sangue** bloodshed

spa'rire /**112**/ VI to disappear, vanish; **~ dalla circolazione** (*fig: col*) to lie low, keep a low profile

sparizi'one [sparit'tsjone] SF disappearance

spar'lare /**72**/ VI: **~ di** to run down, speak ill of

'sparo SM shot

sparpagli'are [sparpaʎ'ʎare] /**27**/ VT, **sparpagli'arsi** VPR to scatter

'sparso, -a PP *di* **spargere** ▶ AG scattered; (*sciolto*) loose; **in ordine ~** (*Mil*) in open order

sparti'acque SM (*Geo*) watershed

sparti'neve SM INV snowplough (*BRIT*), snowplow (*US*)

spar'tire /**55**/ VT (*eredità, bottino*) to share out; (*avversari*) to separate

spar'tito SM (*Mus*) score

sparti'traffico SM INV (*Aut*) central reservation (*BRIT*), median (strip) (*US*)

spartizi'one [spartit'tsjone] SF division

spa'ruto, -a AG (*viso ecc*) haggard

sparvi'ero SM (*Zool*) sparrowhawk

spasi'mante SM suitor

spasi'mare /**72**/ VI to be in agony; **~ di fare** (*fig*) to yearn to do; **~ per qn** to be madly in love with sb

'spasimo SM pang

'spasmo SM (*Med*) spasm

spas'modico, -a, -ci, -che AG (*angoscioso*) agonizing; (*Med*) spasmodic

spas'sarsela /**72**/ VI to enjoy o.s., have a good time

spassio'nato, -a AG dispassionate, impartial

'spasso SM (*divertimento*) amusement, enjoyment; **andare a ~** to go out for a walk; **essere a ~** (*fig*) to be out of work; **mandare qn a ~** (*fig*) to give sb the sack

spas'soso, -a AG amusing, entertaining

'spastico, -a, -ci, -che AG, SM/F spastic

'spatola SF spatula; (*di muratore*) trowel

spau'racchio [spau'rakkjo] SM scarecrow

spau'rire /**55**/ VT to frighten, terrify

spaval'deria SF boldness, arrogance

spa'valdo, -a AG arrogant, bold

spaventa'passeri SM INV scarecrow

spaven'tare /**72**/ VT to frighten, scare; **spaventarsi** VPR to become frightened, become scared; to get a fright

spa'vento SM fear, fright; **far ~ a qn** to give sb a fright

spaven'toso, -a AG frightening, terrible; (*fig: col*) tremendous, fantastic

spazi'ale [spat'tsjale] AG (*volo, nave, tuta*) space *cpd*; (*Archit, Geom*) spatial

spazia'tura [spattsja'tura] SF (*Tip*) spacing

spazien'tirsi [spattsjen'tirsi] /**55**/ VPR to lose one's patience

'spazio ['spattsjo] SM space; (*posto*) room, space; **fare ~ per qc/qn** to make room for sth/sb; **nello ~ di un'ora** within an hour, in the space of an hour; **dare ~ a** (*fig*) to make room for; **~ aereo** airspace

spazi'oso, -a [spat'tsjoso] AG spacious

spazzaca'mino [spattsaka'mino] SM chimney sweep

spazza'neve [spattsa'neve] SM INV (*spartineve, Sci*) snowplough (*BRIT*), snowplow (*US*)

spaz'zare [spat'tsare] /**72**/ VT to sweep; (*foglie ecc*) to sweep up; (*cacciare*) to sweep away

spazza'tura [spattsa'tura] SF sweepings *pl*; (*immondizia*) rubbish

spaz'zino [spat'tsino] SM street sweeper

'spazzola ['spattsola] SF brush; **capelli a ~** crew cut *sg*; **~ per abiti** clothesbrush; **~ da capelli** hairbrush

S

spazzo'lare [spattso'lare] /**72**/ vт to brush

spazzo'lino [spattso'lino] sм (small) brush;
~ da denti toothbrush

specchi'arsi [spek'kjarsi] /**19**/ vpr to look at
o.s. in a mirror; (*riflettersi*) to be mirrored, be
reflected

specchi'era [spek'kjɛra] sf large mirror;
(*mobile*) dressing table

specchi'etto [spek'kjetto] sм (*tabella*) table,
chart; **~ da borsetta** pocket mirror;
~ retrovisore (*Aut*) rear-view mirror

'specchio ['spɛkkjo] sм mirror; (*tabella*)
table, chart; **uno ~ d'acqua** a sheet of water

speci'ale [spe'tʃale] аg special; **in special
modo** especially; **inviato ~** (*Radio, TV,
Stampa*) special correspondent; **offerta ~**
special offer; **poteri/leggi speciali** (*Pol*)
emergency powers/legislation

specia'lista, -i, -e [spetʃa'lista] sм/ғ
specialist

specia'listico, -a, -ci, -che [spetʃa'listiko]
аg (*conoscenza, preparazione*) specialized

specialità [spetʃali'ta] sf inv speciality;
(*branca di studio*) special field, speciality

specializ'zare [spetʃalid'dzare] /**72**/ vт
(*industria*) to make more specialized;
specializzarsi vpr: **specializzarsi (in)** to
specialize (in)

specializ'zato, -a [spetʃalid'dzato] аg
(*manodopera*) skilled; **operaio non ~**
semiskilled worker; **essere ~ in** to be a
specialist in

specializzazi'one [spetʃaliddzat'tsjone] sf
specialization; **prendere la ~ in** to
specialize in

special'mente [spetʃal'mente] аv especially,
particularly

'specie ['spɛtʃe] sf inv (*Biol, Bot, Zool*) species
inv; (*tipo*) kind, sort ▶ аv especially,
particularly; **una ~ di** a kind of; **fare ~ a qn**
to surprise sb; **la ~ umana** mankind

spe'cifica, -che [spe'tʃifika] sf specification

specifi'care [spetʃifi'kare] /**20**/ vт to specify,
state

specificata'mente [spetʃifikata'mente] аv
in detail

spe'cifico, -a, -ci, -che [spe'tʃifiko] аg
specific

speck [ʃpɛk] sм inv *kind of smoked ham*

specu'lare /**72**/ vi: **~ su** (*Comm*) to speculate in;
(*sfruttare*) to exploit; (*meditare*) to speculate on

specula'tore, -'trice sм/ғ (*Comm*) speculator

speculazi'one [spekulat'tsjone] sf
speculation

spe'dire /**55**/ vт to send; (*Comm*) to dispatch,
forward; **~ per posta** to post (*BRIT*), mail
(*US*); **~ per mare** to ship

spedita'mente аv quickly; **camminare ~**
to walk at a brisk pace

spe'dito, -a аg (*gen*) quick; **con passo ~** at a
brisk pace

spedizi'one [spedit'tsjone] sf sending; (*collo*)
consignment; (*scientifica ecc*) expedition;
(*Comm*) forwarding; shipping; **fare una ~**
to send a consignment; **agenzia di ~**
forwarding agency; **spese di ~** postal
charges; (*Comm*) forwarding charges

spedizioni'ere [spedittsjo'njɛre] sм
forwarding agent, shipping agent

'spegnere ['spɛɲɲere] /**113**/ vт (*fuoco, sigaretta*)
to put out, extinguish; (*apparecchio elettrico*) to
turn o switch off; (*gas*) to turn off; (*fig: suoni,
passioni*) to stifle; (*debito*) to cancel; **spegnersi**
vpr to go out; to go off; (*morire*) to pass away;
puoi ~ la luce? could you switch off the
light?

speleolo'gia [speleolo'dʒia] sf (*studio*)
speleology; (*pratica*) potholing (*BRIT*),
speleology

spele'ologo, -a, -gi, -ghe sм/ғ speleologist;
potholer

spel'lare /**72**/ vт (*scuoiare*) to skin; (*scorticare*) to
graze; **spellarsi** vpr to peel

spendacci'one, -a [spendat'tʃone] sм/ғ
spendthrift

'spendere /**8**/ vт to spend; **~ una buona
parola per qn** (*fig*) to put in a good word
for sb

'spengo etc vв vedi **spegnere**

spen'nare /**72**/ vт to pluck

'spensi etc vв vedi **spegnere**

spensiera'tezza [spensjera'tettsa] sf
carefreeness, lightheartedness

spensie'rato, -a аg carefree

'spento, -a pp di **spegnere** ▶ аg (*suono*)
muffled; (*colore*) dull; (*sigaretta*) out; (*civiltà,
vulcano*) extinct

spe'ranza [spe'rantsa] sf hope; **nella ~ di
rivederti** hoping to see o in the hope of
seeing you again; **pieno di speranze**
hopeful; **senza ~** (*situazione*) hopeless; (*amare*)
without hope

speran'zoso, -a [speran'tsoso] аg hopeful

spe'rare /**72**/ vт to hope for ▶ vi: **~ in** to trust
in; **~ che/di fare** to hope that/to do; **lo
spero, spero di sì** I hope so; **tutto fa ~ per
il meglio** everything leads one to hope for
the best

sper'duto, -a аg (*isolato*) out-of-the-way;
(*persona: smarrita, a disagio*) lost

spergi'uro, -a [sper'dʒuro] sм/ғ perjurer
▶ sм perjury

sperico'lato, -a аg fearless, daring;
(*guidatore*) reckless

sperimen'tale аg experimental; **fare qc in
via ~** to try sth out

sperimen'tare /**72**/ vт to experiment with,
test; (*fig*) to test, put to the test

sperimentazi'one [sperimentat'tsjone] SF experimentation

'sperma, -i SM (*Biol*) sperm

spermato'zoo, -i [spermatod'dzɔo] SM spermatozoon

spe'rone SM spur

sperpe'rare /**72**/ VT to squander

'sperpero SM (*di denaro*) squandering, waste; (*di cibo, materiali*) waste

'spesa SF (*soldi spesi*) expense; (*costo*) cost; (*acquisto*) purchase; (*col: acquisto del cibo quotidiano*) shopping; **spese** SFPL expenses; (*Comm*) costs; charges; **ridurre le spese** (*gen*) to cut down; (*Comm*) to reduce expenditure; **fare la ~** to do the shopping; **fare le spese di qc** (*fig*) to pay the price for sth; **a spese di** (*a carico di*) at the expense of; **con la modica ~ di 200 euro** for the modest sum *o* outlay of 200 euros; **~ pubblica** public expenditure; **spese accessorie** incidental expenses; **spese generali** overheads; **spese di gestione** operating expenses; **spese d'impianto** initial outlay; **spese legali** legal costs; **spese di manutenzione**, **spese di mantenimento** maintenance costs; **spese postali** postage *sg*; **spese di sbarco e sdoganamento** landing charges; **spese di trasporto** handling charge; **spese di viaggio** travelling (*BRIT*) *o* traveling (*US*) expenses

spe'sare /**72**/ VT: **viaggio tutto spesato** all-expenses-paid trip

'speso, -a PP *di* **spendere**

'spesso, -a AG (*fitto*) thick; (*frequente*) frequent ▶ AV often; **spesse volte** frequently, often

spes'sore SM thickness; **ha uno ~ di 20 cm** it is 20 cm thick

Spett. ABBR *vedi* **spettabile**

spet'tabile AG (*in lettere: abbr Spett.*): **~ ditta X** Messrs X and Co; **avvertiamo la ~ clientela ...** we inform our customers ...

spettaco'lare AG spectacular

spet'tacolo SM (*rappresentazione*) performance, show; (*vista, scena*) sight; **dare ~ di sé** to make an exhibition *o* a spectacle of o.s.

spettaco'loso, -a AG spectacular

spet'tanza [spet'tantsa] SF (*competenza*) concern; **non è di mia ~** it's no concern of mine

spet'tare /**72**/ VI: **~ a** (*decisione*) to be up to; (*stipendio*) to be due to; **spetta a lei decidere** it's up to you to decide

spetta'tore, -'trice SM/F (*Cine, Teat*) member of the audience; (*di avvenimento*) onlooker, witness

spettego'lare /**72**/ VI to gossip

spetti'nare /**72**/ VT: **~ qn** to ruffle sb's hair; **spettinarsi** VPR to get one's hair in a mess

spetti'nato, -a AG dishevelled

spet'trale AG spectral, ghostly

'spettro SM (*fantasma*) spectre (*BRIT*), specter (*US*); (*Fisica*) spectrum

'spezie ['spettsje] SFPL (*Cuc*) spices

spez'zare [spet'tsare] /**72**/ VT (*rompere*) to break; (*fig: interrompere*) to break up; **spezzarsi** VPR to break

spezza'tino [spettsa'tino] SM (*Cuc*) stew

spez'zato, -a [spet'tsato] AG (*unghia, ramo, braccio*) broken ▶ SM (*abito maschile*) coordinated jacket and trousers (*BRIT*) *o* pants (*US*); **fare orario ~** to work a split shift

spezzet'tare [spettset'tare] /**72**/ VT to break up (*o* chop) into small pieces

spez'zino, -a [spet'tsino] AG of (*o* from) La Spezia

spez'zone [spet'tsone] SM (*Cine*) clip

'spia SF spy; (*confidente della polizia*) informer; (*Elettr*) indicating light; warning light; (*fessura*) peephole; (*fig: sintomo*) sign, indication; **~ dell'olio** (*Aut*) oil warning light

spiacci'care [spjattʃi'kare] /**20**/ VT to squash, crush

spia'cente [spja'tʃɛnte] AG sorry; **essere ~ di qc/di fare qc** to be sorry about sth/for doing sth; **siamo spiacenti di dovervi annunciare che ...** we regret to announce that ...

spia'cevole [spja'tʃevole] AG unpleasant, disagreeable

spi'aggia, -ge ['spjaddʒa] SF beach; **~ libera** public beach

spia'nare /**72**/ VT (*terreno*) to level, make level; (*edificio*) to raze to the ground; (*pasta*) to roll out; (*rendere liscio*) to smooth (out)

spi'ano SM: **a tutto ~** (*lavorare*) non-stop, without a break; (*spendere*) lavishly

spian'tato, -a AG penniless, ruined

spi'are /**60**/ VT to spy on; (*occasione ecc*) to watch *o* wait for

spi'ata SF tip-off

spiattel'lare /**72**/ VT (*col: verità, segreto*) to blurt out

spi'azzo ['spjattso] SM open space; (*radura*) clearing

spic'care /**20**/ VT (*assegno, mandato di cattura*) to issue ▶ VI (*risaltare*) to stand out; **~ il volo** to fly off; (*fig*) to spread one's wings; **~ un balzo** to jump, leap

spic'cato, -a AG (*marcato*) marked, strong; (*notevole*) remarkable

spiccherò *etc* [spikke'rɔ] VB *vedi* **spiccare**

'spicchio ['spikkjo] SM (*di agrumi*) segment; (*di aglio*) clove; (*parte*) piece, slice

spicci'are [spit'tʃare] /**14**/ VT (*faccenda, impegno*) to finish off; **spicciarsi** VPR (*fare in fretta*) to hurry up, get a move on

S

'spiccio, -a, -ci, -ce ['spittʃo] AG (modi, mezzi) quick; andare per le spicce to be quick off the mark, waste no time

spiccio'lata [spittʃo'lata] AV: alla ~ in dribs and drabs, a few at a time

'spicciolo, -a ['spittʃolo] AG: moneta spicciola (small) change; spiccioli SMPL (small) change

'spicco, -chi SM: fare ~ to stand out; di ~ outstanding, prominent; (tema) main, principal

spie'dino SM (utensile) skewer; (cibo) kebab

spi'edo SM (Cuc) spit; pollo allo ~ spit-roasted chicken

spiega'mento SM (Mil): ~ di forze deployment of forces

spie'gare /80/ VT (far capire) to explain; (tovaglia) to unfold; (vele) to unfurl; spiegarsi VPR to explain o.s., make o.s. clear; ~ qc a qn to explain sth to sb; il problema si spiega one can understand the problem; non mi spiego come ... I can't understand how ...

spiegazi'one [spjegat'tsjone] SF explanation; avere una ~ con qn to have it out with sb

spiegaz'zare [spjegat'tsare] /72/ VT to crease, crumple

spiegherò etc [spjege'rɔ] VB vedi spiegare

spie'tato, -a AG ruthless, pitiless

spiffe'rare /72/ VT (col) to blurt out, blab

'spiffero SM draught (BRIT), draft (US)

'spiga, -ghe SF (Bot) ear

spigli'ato, -a [spiʎ'ʎato] AG self-possessed, self-confident

spigo'lare /72/ VT (anche fig) to glean

'spigolo SM corner; (Geom) edge

spigo'loso, -a AG (mobile) angular; (persona, carattere) difficult

'spilla SF brooch; (da cravatta, cappello) pin; ~ di sicurezza o da balia safety pin

spil'lare /72/ VT (vino, fig) to tap; ~ denaro/ notizie a qn to tap sb for money/ information

'spillo SM pin; (spilla) brooch; tacco a ~ stiletto heel (BRIT), spike heel (US); ~ di sicurezza o da balia safety pin; ~ di sicurezza (Mil) (safety) pin

spilorce'ria [spilortʃe'ria] SF meanness, stinginess

spi'lorcio, -a, -ci, -ce [spi'lortʃo] AG mean, stingy

spilun'gone SMF beanpole

'spina SF (Bot) thorn; (Zool) spine, prickle; (di pesce) bone; (Elettr) plug; (di botte) bunghole; birra alla ~ draught beer; stare sulle spine (fig) to be on tenterhooks; ~ dorsale (Anat) backbone

spi'nacio [spi'natʃo] SM spinach no pl; (Cuc): spinaci spinach sg

spi'nale AG (Anat) spinal

spi'nato, -a AG (fornito di spine): filo ~ barbed wire; (tessuto) herringbone cpd

spi'nello SM (Droga: gergo) joint

'spingere ['spindʒere] /114/ VT to push; (condurre: anche fig) to drive; (stimolare): ~ qn a fare to urge o press sb to do; spingersi VPR (inoltrarsi) to push on, carry on; spingersi troppo lontano (anche fig) to go too far

'spino SM (Bot) thorn bush

spi'noso, -a AG thorny, prickly

'spinsi etc VB vedi spingere

spinte'rogeno [spinte'rɔdʒeno] SM (Aut) coil ignition

'spinto, -a PP di spingere ▶ SF (urto) push; (Fisica) thrust; (fig: stimolo) incentive, spur; (: appoggio) string-pulling no pl; dare una spinta a qn (fig) to pull strings for sb

spinto'nare /72/ VT to shove, push

spin'tone SM push, shove

spio'naggio [spio'naddʒo] SM espionage, spying

spion'cino [spion'tʃino] SM peephole

spi'one, -a SM/F (spia) informer; (ragazzino, collega) telltale, sneak

spio'nistico, -a, -ci, -che AG (organizzazione) spy cpd; rete spionistica spy ring

spi'overe /76/ VI (scorrere) to flow down; (ricadere) to hang down, fall

'spira SF coil

spi'raglio [spi'raʎʎo] SM (fessura) chink, narrow opening; (raggio di luce, fig) glimmer, gleam

spi'rale SF spiral; (contraccettivo) coil; a ~ spiral(-shaped); ~ inflazionistica inflationary spiral

spi'rare /72/ VI (vento) to blow; (morire) to expire, pass away

spiri'tato, -a AG possessed; (fig: persona, espressione) wild

spiri'tismo SM spiritualism

'spirito SM (Rel, Chim, disposizione d'animo, di legge ecc, fantasma) spirit; (pensiero, intelletto) mind; (arguzia) wit; (umorismo) humour, wit; in buone condizioni di ~ in the right frame of mind; è una persona di ~ he has a sense of humour (BRIT) o humor (US); battuta di ~ joke; ~ di classe class consciousness; non ha ~ di parte he never takes sides; lo S~ Santo the Holy Spirit o Ghost

spirito'saggine [spirito'saddʒine] SF witticism; (peg) wisecrack

spiri'toso, -a AG witty

spiritu'ale AG spiritual

splen'dente AG (giornata) bright, sunny; (occhi) shining; (pavimento) shining, gleaming

'splendere /29/ VI to shine

'**splendido, -a** AG splendid; (*splendente*) shining; (*sfarzoso*) magnificent, splendid

splen'dore SM splendour (BRIT), splendor (US); (*luce intensa*) brilliance, brightness

spodes'tare /**72**/ VT to deprive of power; (*sovrano*) to depose

'**spoglia** ['spɔʎʎa] SF *vedi* **spoglio**

spogli'are [spoʎ'ʎare] /**27**/ VT (*svestire*) to undress; (*privare, fig: depredare*): ~ **qn di qc** to deprive sb of sth; (*togliere ornamenti: anche fig*): ~ **qn/qc di** to strip sb/sth of; **spogliarsi** VPR to undress, strip; **spogliarsi di** (*ricchezze ecc*) to deprive o.s. of, give up; (*pregiudizi*) to rid o.s. of

spoglia'rello [spoʎʎa'rɛllo] SM striptease

spoglia'toio [spoʎʎa'tojo] SM dressing room; (*di scuola ecc*) cloakroom; (*Sport*) changing room

'**spoglio, -a** ['spɔʎʎo] AG (*pianta, terreno*) bare; (*privo*): ~ **di** stripped of; lacking in, without ▶ SM (*di voti*) counting ▶ SF (*Zool*) skin, hide; (*di rettile*) slough; **spoglie** SFPL (*salma*) remains; (*preda*) spoils, booty *sg*

'**spola** SF shuttle; (*bobina*) spool; **fare la ~ (fra)** to go to and fro *o* shuttle (between)

spo'letta SF (*Cucito: bobina*) spool; (*di bomba*) fuse

spol'pare /**72**/ VT to strip the flesh off

spolve'rare /**72**/ VT (*anche Cuc*) to dust; (*con spazzola*) to brush; (*con battipanni*) to beat; (*fig: mangiare*) to polish off ▶ VI to dust

spolve'rino SM (*soprabito*) dust coat

'**sponda** SF (*di fiume*) bank; (*di mare, lago*) shore; (*bordo*) edge

sponsoriz'zare [sponsorid'dzare] /**72**/ VT to sponsor

sponsorizzazi'one [sponsoriddzat'tsjone] SF sponsorship

spontanea'mente AV (*comportarsi*) naturally; (*agire*) spontaneously; (*reagire*) instinctively, spontaneously

spon'taneo, -a AG spontaneous; (*persona*) unaffected, natural; **di sua spontanea volontà** of his own free will

spopo'lare /**72**/ VT to depopulate ▶ VI (*attirare folla*) to draw the crowds; **spopolarsi** VPR to become depopulated

spo'radico, -a, -ci, -che AG sporadic

sporcacci'one, -a [sporkat'tʃone] SM/F (*peg*) pig, filthy person

spor'care /**20**/ VT to dirty, make dirty; (*fig*) to sully, soil; **sporcarsi** VPR to get dirty

spor'cizia [spor'tʃittsja] SF (*stato*) dirtiness; (*sudiciume*) dirt, filth; (*cosa sporca*) dirt *no pl*, something dirty; (*fig: cosa oscena*) obscenity

'**sporco, -a, -chi, -che** AG dirty, filthy; **avere la coscienza sporca** to have a guilty conscience

spor'genza [spor'dʒentsa] SF projection

'**sporgere** ['spɔrdʒere] /**115**/ VT to put out, stretch out ▶ VI (*venire in fuori*) to stick out; **sporgersi** VPR to lean out; ~ **querela contro qn** (*Dir*) to take legal action against sb

'**sporsi** *etc* VB *vedi* **sporgere**

sport SM INV sport

'**sporta** SF shopping bag

spor'tello SM (*di treno, auto ecc*) door; (*di banca, ufficio*) window, counter; ~ **automatico** (*Banca*) cash dispenser, automated telling machine

spor'tivo, -a AG (*gara, giornale*) sports *cpd*; (*persona*) sporty; (*abito*) casual; (*spirito, atteggiamento*) sporting ▶ SM/F sportsman(-woman); **campo** ~ playing field; **giacca sportiva** sports (BRIT) *o* sport (US) jacket

'**sporto, -a** PP *di* **sporgere**

'**sposa** SF bride; (*moglie*) wife; **abito** *o* **vestito da** ~ wedding dress

sposa'lizio [spoza'littsjo] SM wedding

spo'sare /**72**/ VT to marry; (*fig: idea, fede*) to espouse; **sposarsi** VPR to get married, marry; **sposarsi con qn** to marry sb, get married to sb

spo'sato, -a AG married

'**sposo** SM (bride)groom; (*marito*) husband; **gli sposi** the newlyweds

spos'sante AG exhausting

spossa'tezza [spossa'tettsa] SF exhaustion

spos'sato, -a AG exhausted, weary

sposta'mento SM movement, change of position

spos'tare /**72**/ VT to move, shift; (*cambiare: orario*) to change; **spostarsi** VPR to move; **hanno spostato la partenza di qualche giorno** they postponed *o* put off their departure by a few days

spot [spɔt] SM INV (*faretto*) spotlight, spot; (*TV*) advert, commercial, ad

'**spranga, -ghe** SF (*sbarra*) bar; (*catenaccio*) bolt

spran'gare /**80**/ VT to bar; to bolt

spray ['sprai] SM INV (*dispositivo, sostanza*) spray ▶ AG INV (*bombola, confezione*) spray *cpd*

'**sprazzo** ['sprattso] SM (*di sole ecc*) flash; (*fig: di gioia ecc*) burst

spre'care /**20**/ VT to waste; **sprecarsi** VPR (*persona*) to waste one's energy

'**spreco, -chi** SM waste

spre'gevole [spre'dʒevole] AG contemptible, despicable

'**spregio** ['spredʒo] SM scorn, disdain

spregiudi'cato, -a [spredʒudi'kato] AG unprejudiced, unbiased; (*peg*) unscrupulous

'**spremere** /**62**/ VT to squeeze; **spremersi le meningi** (*fig*) to rack one's brains

spremia'grumi SM INV lemon squeezer

spre'muta SF fresh fruit juice; ~ **d'arancia** fresh orange juice

S

sprez'zante [spret'tsante] AG scornful, contemptuous

'sprezzo ['sprɛttso] SM contempt, scorn, disdain

sprigio'nare [spridʒo'nare] /**72**/ VT to give off, emit; **sprigionarsi** VPR to emanate; (*uscire con impeto*) to burst out

spriz'zare [sprit'tsare] /**72**/ VT, VI to spurt; **~ gioia/salute** to be bursting with joy/ health

sprofon'dare /**72**/ VI to sink; (*casa*) to collapse; (*suolo*) to give way, subside; **sprofondarsi** VPR: **sprofondarsi in** (*poltrona*) to sink into; (*fig*) to become immersed *o* absorbed in

sproloqui'are /**19**/ VI to ramble on

spro'loquio SM rambling speech

spro'nare /**72**/ VT to spur (on)

'sprone SM (*sperone, fig*) spur

sproporzio'nato, -a [sproportsjo'nato] AG disproportionate, out of all proportion

sproporzi'one [spropor'tsjone] SF disproportion

sproposi'tato, -a AG (*lettera, discorso*) full of mistakes; (*fig: costo*) excessive, enormous

spro'posito SM blunder; **a ~** at the wrong time; (*rispondere, parlare*) irrelevantly

sprovve'duto, -a AG inexperienced, naïve

sprov'visto, -a AG (*mancante*): **~ di** lacking in, without; **ne siamo sprovvisti** (*negozio*) we are out of it (*o* them); **alla sprovvista** unawares

spruz'zare [sprut'tsare] /**72**/ VT (*a nebulizzazione*) to spray; (*aspergere*) to sprinkle; (*inzaccherare*) to splash

spruzza'tore [spruttsa'tore] SM (*per profumi*) spray, atomizer; (*per biancheria*) sprinkler, spray

'spruzzo ['spruttso] SM spray; splash; **verniciatura a ~** spray painting

spudora'tezza [spudora'tettsa] SF shamelessness

spudo'rato, -a AG shameless

'spugna ['spuɲɲa] SF (*Zool*) sponge; (*tessuto*) towelling

spu'gnoso, -a [spuɲ'ɲoso] AG spongy

spulci'are [spul'tʃare] /**14**/ VT (*animali*) to rid of fleas; (*fig: testo, compito*) to examine thoroughly

'spuma SF (*schiuma*) foam; (*bibita*) fizzy drink

spu'mante SM sparkling wine

spumeggi'ante [spumed'dʒante] AG (*vino, fig*) sparkling; (*birra, mare*) foaming

spu'mone SM (*Cuc*) mousse

spun'tare /**72**/ SM : **allo ~ del sole** at sunrise; : **allo ~ del giorno** at daybreak ▶ VT (*coltello*) to break the point of; (*capelli*) to trim; (*elenco*) to tick off (BRIT), check off (US) ▶ VI (*uscire: germogli*) to sprout; (: *capelli*) to begin to grow;

(: *denti*) to come through; (*apparire*) to appear (suddenly); **spuntarsi** VPR to become blunt, lose its point; **spuntarla** (*fig*) to make it, win through

spun'tino SM snack

'spunto SM (*Teat, Mus*) cue; (*fig*) starting point; **dare lo ~ a** (*fig*) to give rise to; **prendere ~ da qc** to take sth as one's starting point

spur'gare /**80**/ VT (*fogna*) to clean, clear; **spurgarsi** VPR (*Med*) to expectorate

spu'tare /**72**/ VT to spit out; (*fig*) to belch (out) ▶ VI to spit

'sputo SM spittle *no pl*, spit *no pl*

sputta'nare /**72**/ VT (*col*) to bad-mouth

spyware ['spaiwer] SM INV (*Inform*) spyware (program)

'squadra SF (*strumento*) (set) square; (*gruppo*) team, squad; (*di operai*) gang, squad; (*Mil*) squad; (: *Aer, Naut*) squadron; (*Sport*) team; **lavoro a squadre** teamwork; **~ mobile/del buon costume** (*Polizia*) flying/vice squad

squa'drare /**72**/ VT to square, make square; (*osservare*) to look at closely

squa'driglia [skwa'driʎʎa] SF (*Aer*) flight; (*Naut*) squadron

squa'drone SM squadron

squagli'arsi [skwaʎ'ʎarsi] /**27**/ VPR to melt; (*fig*) to sneak off

squa'lifica, -che SF disqualification

squalifi'care /**20**/ VT to disqualify

'squallido, -a AG wretched, bleak

squal'lore SM wretchedness, bleakness

'squalo SM shark

'squama SF scale

squa'mare /**72**/ VT to scale; **squamarsi** VPR to flake *o* peel (off)

squarcia'gola [skwartʃa'gola]: **a ~** AV at the top of one's voice

squarci'are [skwar'tʃare] /**14**/ VT (*muro, corpo*) to rip open; (*tessuto*) to rip; (*fig: tenebre, silenzio*) to split; (: *nuvole*) to pierce

'squarcio ['skwartʃo] SM (*ferita*) gash; (*in lenzuolo, abito*) rip; (*in un muro*) breach; (*in una nave*) hole; (*brano*) passage, excerpt; **uno ~ di sole** a burst of sunlight

squar'tare /**72**/ VT to quarter, cut up; (*cadavere*) to dismember

squattri'nato, -a AG penniless ▶ SM/F pauper

squili'brare /**72**/ VT to unbalance

squili'brato, -a AG (*Psic*) unbalanced ▶ SM/F deranged person

squi'librio SM (*differenza, sbilancio*) imbalance; (*Psic*) derangement

squil'lante AG (*suono*) shrill, sharp; (*voce*) shrill

squil'lare /**72**/ VI (*campanello, telefono*) to ring (out); (*tromba*) to blare

'squillo SM ring, ringing *no pl*; blare ▶ SF INV (*anche*: **ragazza squillo**) call girl

squi'sito, -a AG exquisite; (*cibo*) delicious; (*persona*) delightful

squit'tire /**55**/ VI (*uccello*) to squawk; (*topo*) to squeak

SR SIGLA = **Siracusa**

sradi'care /**20**/ VT to uproot; (*fig*) to eradicate

sragio'nare [zradʒo'nare] /**72**/ VI to talk nonsense, rave

sregola'tezza [zregola'tettsa] SF (*nel mangiare, bere*) lack of moderation; (*di vita*) dissoluteness, dissipation

srego'lato, -a AG (*senza ordine: vita*) disorderly; (*smodato*) immoderate; (*dissoluto*) dissolute

Sri 'Lanka [sri'lanka] SM: **lo ~** Sri Lanka

S.r.l. ABBR *vedi* **società a responsabilità limitata**

sroto'lare /**72**/ VT, **sroto'larsi** VPR to unroll

SS SIGLA = **Sassari**

S.S. ABBR (*Rel*) = **Sua Santità**; **Santa Sede**; **santi, santissimo**; (*Aut*) = **strada statale**; *vedi* **statale**

S.S.N. ABBR (= *Servizio Sanitario Nazionale*) ≈ NHS

sta *etc* VB *vedi* **stare**

'stabbio SM (*recinto*) pen, fold; (*di maiali*) pigsty; (*letame*) manure

'stabile AG stable, steady; (*tempo: non variabile*) settled; (*Teat: compagnia*) resident ▶ SM (*edificio*) building; **teatro ~** civic theatre

stabili'mento SM (*edificio*) establishment; (*fabbrica*) plant, factory; **~ balneare** bathing establishment; **~ tessile** textile mill

stabi'lire /**55**/ VT to establish; (*fissare: prezzi, data*) to fix; (*decidere*) to decide; **stabilirsi** VPR (*prendere dimora*) to settle; **resta stabilito che ...** it is agreed that ...

stabilità SF stability

stabiliz'zare [stabilid'dzare] /**72**/ VT to stabilize

stabilizza'tore [stabiliddza'tore] SM stabilizer; (*fig*) stabilizing force

stabilizzazi'one [stabiliddzat'tsjone] SF stabilization

stacano'vista, -i, -e SM/F (*ironico*) eager beaver

stac'care /**20**/ VT (*levare*) to detach, remove; (*separare: anche fig*) to separate, divide; (*strappare*) to tear off (*o* out); (*scandire: parole*) to pronounce clearly; (*Sport*) to leave behind; **staccarsi** VPR (*bottone ecc*) to come off; (*scostarsi*) **staccarsi (da)** to move away (from); (*fig: separarsi*) **staccarsi da** to leave; **non ~ gli occhi da qn** not to take one's eyes off sb; **~ la televisione/il telefono** to disconnect the television/the phone; **~ un assegno** to write a cheque

staccio'nata [stattʃo'nata] SF (*gen*) fence; (*Ippica*) hurdle

'stacco, -chi SM (*intervallo*) gap; (: *tra due scene*) break; (*differenza*) difference; (*Sport: nel salto*) takeoff

sta'dera SF lever scales *pl*

'stadio SM (*Sport*) stadium; (*periodo, fase*) phase, stage

'staffa SF (*di sella, Tecn*) stirrup; **perdere le staffe** (*fig*) to fly off the handle

staf'fetta SF (*messo*) dispatch rider; (*Sport*) relay race

stagflazi'one [stagflat'tsjone] SF (*Econ*) stagflation

stagio'nale [stadʒo'nale] AG seasonal ▶ SMF seasonal worker

stagio'nare [stadʒo'nare] /**72**/ VT (*legno*) to season; (*formaggi, vino*) to mature

stagio'nato, -a [stadʒo'nato] AG seasoned; matured; (*scherzoso: attempato*) getting on in years

stagi'one [sta'dʒone] SF season; **alta/bassa ~** high/low season

sta'gista, -i, -e [sta'dʒista] SM/F trainee, intern (*US*)

stagli'arsi [staʎ'ʎarsi] /**27**/ VPR to stand out, be silhouetted

sta'gnante [staɲ'ɲante] AG stagnant

sta'gnare [staɲ'ɲare] /**15**/ VT (*vaso, tegame*) to tin-plate; (*barca, botte*) to make watertight; (*sangue*) to stop ▶ VI to stagnate

sta'gnino [staɲ'ɲino] SM tinsmith

'stagno, -a ['staɲɲo] AG (*a tenuta d'acqua*) watertight; (*a tenuta d'aria*) airtight ▶ SM (*acquitrino*) pond; (*Chim*) tin

sta'gnola [staɲ'ɲɔla] SF tinfoil

stalag'mite SF stalagmite

stalat'tite SF stalactite

stali'nismo SM (*Pol*) Stalinism

'stalla SF (*per bovini*) cowshed; (*per cavalli*) stable

stalli'ere SM groom, stableboy

'stallo SM stall, seat; (*Scacchi*) stalemate; (*Aer*) stall; **situazione di ~** (*fig*) stalemate

stal'lone SM stallion

sta'mani, stamat'tina AV this morning

stam'becco, -chi SM ibex

stam'berga, -ghe SF hovel

stami'nale AG: **cellula ~** stem cell; **ricerca sulle cellule staminali** stem-cell research

'stampa SF (*Tip, Fot: tecnica*) printing; (*impressione, copia fotografica*) print; (*insieme di quotidiani, giornalisti ecc*): **la ~** the press; **andare in ~** to go to press; **mandare in ~** to pass for press; **errore di ~** printing error; **prova di ~** print sample; **libertà di ~** freedom of the press; **"stampe"** "printed matter"

stam'pante SF (*Inform*) printer; **~ seriale/termica** serial/thermal printer

stam'pare /**72**/ vt to print; (*pubblicare*) to publish; (*coniare*) to strike, coin; (*imprimere*: *anche fig*) to impress

stampa'tello sm block letters *pl*

stam'pato, -a ag printed ▶ sm (*opuscolo*) leaflet; (*modulo*) form; **stampati** smpl printed matter *sg*

stam'pella sf crutch

stampigli'are [stampiʎ'ʎare] /**27**/ vt to stamp

stampiglia'tura [stampiʎʎa'tura] sf (*atto*) stamping; (*marchio*) stamp

'**stampo** sm mould; (*fig: indole*) type, kind, sort

sta'nare /**72**/ vt to drive out

stan'care /**20**/ vt to tire, make tired; (*annoiare*) to bore; (*infastidire*) to annoy; **stancarsi** vpr to get tired, tire o.s. out; **stancarsi (di)** (*stufarsi*) to grow weary (of), grow tired (of)

stan'chezza [stan'kettsa] sf tiredness, fatigue

'**stanco, -a, -chi, -che** ag tired; **~ di** tired of, fed up with

stand [stand] sm inv (*in fiera*) stand

'**standard** ['standərd] sm inv (*livello*) standard

standardiz'zare [standardid'dzare] /**72**/ vt to standardize

stan'dista, -i, -e sm/f (*in una fiera ecc*) person responsible for a stand

'**stanga, -ghe** sm bar; (*di carro*) shaft

stan'gare /**80**/ vt (*fig: cliente*) to overcharge; (: *studente*) to fail

stan'gata sf (*colpo: anche fig*) blow; (*cattivo risultato*) poor result; (*Calcio*) shot

stan'ghetta [stan'getta] sf (*di occhiali*) leg; (*Mus, di scrittura*) bar

'**stanno** vb vedi **stare**

sta'notte av tonight; (*notte passata*) last night

'**stante** prep owing to, because of; **a sé ~** (*appartamento, casa*) independent, separate

stan'tio, -a, -'tii, -'tie ag stale; (*burro*) rancid; (*fig*) old

stan'tuffo sm piston

'**stanza** ['stantsa] sf room; (*Poesia*) stanza; **essere di ~ a** (*Mil*) to be stationed in; **~ da bagno** bathroom; **~ da letto** bedroom

stanzia'mento [stantsja'mento] sm allocation

stanzi'are [stan'tsjare] /**19**/ vt to allocate

stan'zino [stan'tsino] sm (*ripostiglio*) storeroom; (*spogliatoio*) changing room (Brit), locker room (US)

stap'pare /**72**/ vt to uncork; (*tappo a corona*) to uncap

star [star] sf (*attore, attrice ecc*) star

'**stare** /**116**/ vi (*restare in un luogo*) to stay, remain; (*abitare*) to stay, live; (*essere situato*) to be, be situated; (*anche*: **stare in piedi**) to stand; (*essere, trovarsi*) to be; (*seguito da gerundio*): **sta studiando** he's studying; **se stesse in me** if it were up to me, if it depended on me; **~ per fare qc** to be about to do sth; **starci** (*esserci spazio*): **nel baule non ci sta più niente** there's no more room in the boot; (*accettare*) to accept; **ci stai?** is that okay with you?; **~ a** (*attenersi a*) to follow, stick to; (*seguito dall'infinito*): **~ a sentire** to listen; **staremo a vedere** let's wait and see; **stiamo a discutere** we're talking; (*toccare a*): **sta a te giocare** it's your turn to play; **sta a te decidere** it's up to you to decide; **~ a qn** (*abiti ecc*) to fit sb; **queste scarpe mi stanno strette** these shoes are tight for me; **il rosso ti sta bene** red suits you; **come sta?** how are you?; **io sto bene/male** I'm very well/not very well; **~ fermo** to keep o stay still; **~ seduto** to sit, be sitting; **~ zitto** to keep quiet; **stando così le cose** given the situation; **stando a ciò che dice lui** according to him o to his version

starnaz'zare [starnat'tsare] /**72**/ vi to squawk

starnu'tire /**55**/ vi to sneeze

star'nuto sm sneeze

sta'sera av this evening, tonight

'**stasi** sf (*Med, fig*) stasis

sta'tale ag state *cpd*, government *cpd* ▶ smf state employee, local authority employee; (*nell'amministrazione*) ≈ civil servant; **bilancio ~** national budget; **strada ~** ≈ trunk (Brit) o main road

stataliz'zare [statalid'dzare] /**72**/ vt to nationalize, put under state control

'**statico, -a, -ci, -che** ag (*Elettr, fig*) static

sta'tista, -i sm statesman

sta'tistico, -a, -ci, -che ag statistical ▶ sf statistic; (*scienza*) statistics *sg*; **fare una statistica** to carry out a statistical examination

'**stato, -a** pp di **essere**; **stare** ▶ sm (*condizione*) state, condition; (*Pol*) state; (*Dir*) status; **essere in ~ d'accusa** (*Dir*) to be committed for trial; **essere in ~ d'arresto** (*Dir*) to be under arrest; **essere in ~ interessante** to be pregnant; **~ d'assedio/d'emergenza** state of siege/emergency; **~ civile** (*Amm*) marital status; **~ di famiglia** (*Amm*) *certificate giving details of a household and its dependents*; **~ d'animo** mood; **~ maggiore** (*Mil*) general staff; **~ patrimoniale** (*Comm*) statement of assets and liabilities; **gli Stati Uniti (d'America)** the United States (of America)

'**statua** sf statue

statuni'tense ag United States *cpd*, of the United States

sta'tura sf (*Anat*) height, stature; (*fig*) stature; **essere alto/basso di ~** to be tall/short o small

sta'tuto SM (*Dir*) statute; constitution; **regione a ~ speciale** *Italian region with political autonomy in certain matters*; **~ della società** (*Comm*) articles *pl* of association

sta'volta AV this time

staziona'mento [stattsjona'mento] SM (*Aut*) parking; (: *sosta*) waiting; **freno di ~** handbrake

stazio'nare [stattsjo'nare] /**72**/ VI (*veicoli*) to be parked

stazio'nario, -a [stattsjo'narjo] AG stationary; (*fig*) unchanged

stazi'one [stat'tsjone] SF station; (*balneare, invernale ecc*) resort; **~ degli autobus** bus station; **~ balneare** seaside resort; **~ climatica** health resort; **~ ferroviaria** railway (*BRIT*) *o* railroad (*US*) station; **~ invernale** winter sports resort; **~ di lavoro** work station; **~ di polizia** police station (*in small town*); **~ di servizio** service *o* petrol (*BRIT*) *o* filling station; **~ termale** spa; **~ radio base** mobile phone mast (*BRIT*), cell tower (*US*)

'stazza ['stattsa] SF tonnage

st. civ. ABBR = **stato civile**

'stecca, -che SF stick; (*di ombrello*) rib; (*di sigarette*) carton; (*Med*) splint; (*stonatura*): **fare una ~** to sing (*o* play) a wrong note

stec'cato SM fence

stec'chito, -a [stek'kito] AG dried up; (*persona*) skinny; **lasciar ~ qn** (*fig*) to leave sb flabbergasted; **morto ~** stone dead

'stella SF star; **~ alpina** (*Bot*) edelweiss; **~ cadente** *o* **filante** shooting star; **~ di mare** (*Zool*) starfish; **~ di Natale** (*Bot*) poinsettia

stel'lato, -a AG (*cielo, notte*) starry

'stelo SM stem; (*asta*) rod; **lampada a ~** standard lamp (*BRIT*), floor lamp

'stemma, -i SM coat of arms

'stemmo VB *vedi* **stare**

stempe'rare /**72**/ VT (*calce, colore*) to dissolve

stempi'ato, -a AG with a receding hairline

stempia'tura SF receding hairline

sten'dardo SM standard

'stendere /**120**/ VT (*braccia, gambe*) to stretch (out); (*tovaglia*) to spread (out); (*bucato*) to hang out; (*mettere a giacere*) to lay (down); (*spalmare: colore*) to spread; (*mettere per iscritto*) to draw up; **stendersi** VPR (*coricarsi*) to stretch out, lie down; (*estendersi*) to extend, stretch

stendibianche'ria [stendibjanke'ria] SM INV clotheshorse

stendi'toio SM (*locale*) drying room; (*stendibiancheria*) clotheshorse

stenodattilogra'fia SF shorthand typing (*BRIT*), stenography (*US*)

stenodatti'lografo, -a SM/F shorthand typist (*BRIT*), stenographer (*US*)

stenogra'fare /**72**/ VT to take down in shorthand

stenogra'fia SF shorthand

ste'nografo, -a SM/F stenographer

sten'tare /**72**/ VI: **~ a fare** to find it hard to do, have difficulty doing

sten'tato, -a AG (*compito, stile*) laboured (*BRIT*), labored (*US*); (*sorriso*) forced

'stento SM (*fatica*) difficulty; **stenti** SMPL (*privazioni*) hardship *sg*, privation *sg*; **a ~** *av* with difficulty, barely

'steppa SF steppe

'sterco SM dung

'stereo AG INV stereo ▶ SM INV (*impianto*) stereo

stereofo'nia SF stereophony

stereo('fonico), -a, -ci, -che AG stereo(phonic)

stereoti'pato, -a AG stereotyped

stere'otipo SM stereotype; **pensare per stereotipi** to think in clichés

'sterile AG sterile; (*terra*) barren; (*fig*) futile, fruitless

sterilità SF sterility

steriliz'zare [sterilid'dzare] /**72**/ VT to sterilize

sterilizzazi'one [steriliddzat'tsjone] SF sterilization

ster'lina SF pound (sterling)

stermi'nare /**72**/ VT to exterminate, wipe out

stermi'nato, -a AG immense; endless

ster'minio SM extermination, destruction; **campo di ~** death camp

'sterno SM (*Anat*) breastbone

ste'roide SM steroid

ster'paglia [ster'paʎʎa] SF brushwood

'sterpo SM dry twig

ster'rare /**72**/ VT to excavate

ster'zare [ster'tsare] /**72**/ VT, VI (*Aut*) to steer

'sterzo ['stertso] SM steering; (*volante*) steering wheel

'steso, -a PP *di* **stendere**

'stessi *etc* VB *vedi* **stare**

'stesso, -a AG same; (*rafforzativo: in persona, proprio*): **il re ~** the king himself *o* in person ▶ PRON: **lo(la) ~(a)** the same (one); **quello ~ giorno** that very day; **i suoi stessi avversari lo ammirano** even his enemies admire him; **fa lo ~** it doesn't matter; **parto lo ~** I'm going all the same; **per me è lo ~** it's all the same to me, it doesn't matter to me; *vedi* **io; tu** *ecc*

ste'sura SF (*azione*) drafting *no pl*, drawing up *no pl*; (*documento*) draft

stetos'copio SM stethoscope

'stetti *etc* VB *vedi* **stare**

'stia¹ SF hutch

'stia² *etc* VB *vedi* **stare**

'stigma, -i SM stigma

'stigmate SFPL (*Rel*) stigmata

sti'lare /**72**/ VT to draw up, draft

S

'stile SM style; (*classe*) style, class; (*Sport*): **~ libero** freestyle; **mobili in ~** period furniture; **in grande ~** in great style; **è proprio nel suo ~** (*fig*) it's just like him

sti'lismo SM concern for style

sti'lista, -i, -e SM/F designer

sti'listico, -a, -ci, -che AG stylistic

stiliz'zato, -a[stilid'dzato] AG stylized

stil'lare/72/ VI (*trasudare*) to ooze; (*gocciolare*) to drip

stilli'cidio [stilli't∫idjo] SM (*fig*) continual pestering (*o moaning etc*)

stilo'grafica, -che SF (*anche:* **penna stilografica**) fountain pen

Stim. ABBR = **stimata**

'stima SF esteem; valuation; assessment, estimate; **avere ~ di qn** to have respect for sb; **godere della ~ di qn** to enjoy sb's respect; **fare la ~ di qc** to estimate the value of sth

sti'mare/72/ VT (*persona*) to esteem, hold in high regard; (*terreno, casa ecc*) to value; (*stabilire in misura approssimativa*) to estimate, assess; (*ritenere*): **~ che** to consider that; **stimarsi fortunato** to consider o.s. (to be) lucky

Stim.ma ABBR = **stimatissima**

stimo'lante AG stimulating ▶ SM (*Med*) stimulant

stimo'lare/72/ VT to stimulate; (*incitare*): **~ qn (a fare)** to spur sb on (to do)

stimolazi'one [stimolat'tsjone] SF stimulation

'stimolo SM (*anche fig*) stimulus

'stinco, -chi SM shin; shinbone

'stingere ['stindʒere] /37/ VT, VI (*anche:* **stingersi**) to fade

'stinto, -a PP *di* **stingere**

sti'pare/72/ VT to cram, pack; **stiparsi**VPR (*accalcarsi*) to crowd, throng

stipendi'are/19/ VT (*pagare*) to pay (a salary to)

stipendi'ato, -a AG salaried ▶ SM/F salaried worker

sti'pendio SM salary

'stipite SM (*di porta, finestra*) jamb

stipu'lare/72/ VT (*redigere*) to draw up

stipulazi'one [stipulat'tsjone] SF (*di contratto: stesura*) drafting; (*: firma*) signing

stiracchi'are [stirak'kjare] /19/ VT (*fig: significato di una parola*) to stretch, force; **stiracchiarsi**VPR (*persona*) to stretch

stira'mento SM (*Med*) sprain

sti'rare/72/ VT (*abito*) to iron; (*distendere*) to stretch; (*strappare: muscolo*) to strain; **stirarsi** VPR (*col*) to stretch (o.s.)

stira'tura SF ironing

'stirpe SF birth, stock; descendants *pl*

stiti'chezza [stiti'kettsa] SF constipation

'stitico, -a, -ci, -che AG constipated

'stiva SF (*di nave*) hold

sti'vale SM boot

stiva'letto SM ankle boot

sti'vare/72/ VT to stow, load

'stizza ['stittsa] SF anger, vexation

stiz'zire [stit'tsire] /55/ VT to irritate ▶ VI (*anche:* **stizzirsi**) to become irritated, become vexed

stiz'zoso, -a[stit'tsoso] AG (*persona*) quick-tempered, irascible; (*risposta*) angry

stocca'fisso SM stockfish, dried cod

Stoc'carda SF Stuttgart

stoc'cata SF (*colpo*) stab, thrust; (*fig*) gibe, cutting remark

Stoc'colma SF Stockholm

stock [stɔk] SM INV (*Comm*) stock

'stoffa SF material, fabric; (*fig*): **aver la ~ di** to have the makings of; **avere della ~** to have what it takes

stoi'cismo [stoi't∫izmo] SM stoicism

'stoico, -a, -ci, -che AG stoic(al)

sto'ino SM doormat

'stola SF stole

stol'tezza [stol'tettsa] SF stupidity; (*azione*) foolish action

'stolto, -a AG stupid, foolish

'stomaco, -chi SM stomach; **dare di ~** to vomit, be sick

sto'nare/72/ VT to sing (*o play*) out of tune ▶ VI to be out of tune, sing (*o play*) out of tune; (*fig*) to be out of place, jar; (*: colori*) to clash

sto'nato, -a AG (*persona*) off-key; (*strumento*) off-key, out of tune

stona'tura SF (*suono*) false note

stop SM INV (*Telegrafia*) stop; (*Aut: cartello*) stop sign; (*: fanalino d'arresto*) brake-light (BRIT), stoplight

'stoppa SF tow

'stoppia SF (*Agr*) stubble

stop'pino SM (*di candela*) wick; (*miccia*) fuse

'storcere ['stɔrt∫ere] /106/ VT to twist; **storcersi**VPR to writhe, twist; **~ il naso** (*fig*) to turn up one's nose; **storcersi la caviglia** to twist one's ankle

stordi'mento SM (*gen*) dizziness; (*da droga*) stupefaction

stor'dire/55/ VT (*intontire*) to stun, daze; **stordirsi**VPR: **stordirsi col bere** to dull one's senses with drink

stor'dito, -a AG stunned; (*sventato*) scatterbrained, heedless

'storia SF (*scienza, avvenimenti*) history; (*racconto, bugia*) story; (*faccenda, questione*) business *no pl*; (*pretesto*) excuse, pretext; **storie**SFPL (*smancerie*) fuss *sg*; **passare alla ~** to go down in history; **non ha fatto storie** he didn't make a fuss

storicità [storit∫i'ta] SF historical authenticity

'storico, -a, -ci, -che AG historic(al) ▶ SM/F historian

storiogra'fia SF historiography

stori'one SM (Zool) sturgeon

stor'mire /55/ VI to rustle

'stormo SM (di uccelli) flock

stor'nare /72/ VT (Comm) to transfer

stor'nello SM kind of folk song

'storno SM starling

storpi'are /19/ VT to cripple, maim; (fig: parole) to mangle; (: significato) to twist

storpia'tura SF (fig: di parola) twisting, distortion

'storpio, -a AG crippled, maimed

'storsi etc VB vedi **storcere**

'storto, -a PP di **storcere** ▶ AG (chiodo) twisted, bent; (gamba, quadro) crooked; (fig: ragionamento) false, wrong ▶ SF (distorsione) sprain, twist; (recipiente) retort ▶ AV: **guardare ~ qn** (fig) to look askance at sb; **andar ~** to go wrong

sto'viglie [sto'viʎʎe] SFPL dishes pl, crockery sg

str. ABBR (Geo) = **stretto**

'strabico, -a, -ci, -che AG squint-eyed; (occhi) squint

strabili'ante AG astonishing, amazing

strabili'are /19/ VI to astonish, amaze

stra'bismo SM squinting

strabuz'zare [strabud'dzare] /72/ VT: **~ gli occhi** to open one's eyes wide

stra'carico, -a, -chi, -che AG overloaded

strac'chino [strak'kino] SM type of soft cheese

stracci'are [strat't∫are] /14/ VT to tear; **stracciarsi** VPR to tear

'straccio, -a, -ci, -ce ['strattʃo] AG: **carta straccia** waste paper ▶ SM rag; (per pulire) cloth, duster; **stracci** SMPL (indumenti) rags; **si è ridotto a uno ~** he's worn himself out; **non ha uno ~ di lavoro** he's not got a job of any sort

stracci'one, -a [strat't∫one] SM/F ragamuffin

stracci'vendolo [strattʃi'vendolo] SM ragman

'stracco, -a, -chi, -che AG: **~ (morto)** exhausted, dead tired

stra'cotto, -a AG overcooked ▶ SM (Cuc) beef stew

'strada SF road; (di città) street; (cammino, via, fig) way; **~ facendo** on the way; **tre ore di ~ (a piedi)/(in macchina)** three hours' walk/ drive; **essere sulla buona ~** (nella vita) to be on the right road o path; (con indagine ecc) to be on the right track; **essere fuori ~** (fig) to be on the wrong track; **fare ~ a qn** to show sb the way; **fare o farsi ~** (fig: persona) to get on in life; **portare qn sulla cattiva ~** to lead sb astray; **donna di ~** (fig: peg) streetwalker;

ragazzo di ~ (fig: peg) street urchin; **~ ferrata** railway (BRIT), railroad (US); **~ principale** main road; **~ senza uscita** dead end, cul-de-sac

stra'dale AG road cpd; (polizia, regolamento) traffic cpd

stra'dario SM street guide

stra'dino SM road worker

strafalci'one [strafal'tʃone] SM blunder, howler

stra'fare /53/ VI to overdo it

stra'fatto, -a PP di **strafare**

stra'foro : **di ~** AV (di nascosto) on the sly

strafot'tente AG: **è ~** he doesn't give a damn, he couldn't care less

strafot'tenza [strafot'tentsa] SF arrogance

'strage ['stradʒe] SF massacre, slaughter

stra'grande AG: **la ~ maggioranza** the overwhelming majority

stralci'are [stral't∫are] /14/ VT to remove

'stralcio ['stralt∫o] SM (Comm): **vendere in ~** to sell off (at bargain prices) ▶ AG INV: **legge ~** abridged version of an act

stralu'nato, -a AG (occhi) rolling; (persona) beside o.s., very upset

stramaz'zare [stramat'tsare] /72/ VI to fall heavily

strambe'ria SF eccentricity

'strambo, -a AG strange, queer

strampa'lato, -a AG odd, eccentric

strana'mente AV oddly, strangely; **e lui, ~, ha accettato** and surprisingly, he agreed

stra'nezza [stra'nettsa] SF strangeness

strango'lare /72/ VT to strangle; **strangolarsi** VPR to choke

strani'ero, -a AG foreign ▶ SM/F foreigner

stra'nito, -a AG dazed

'strano, -a AG strange, odd

straordi'nario, -a AG extraordinary; (treno ecc) special ▶ SM (lavoro) overtime

strapaz'zare [strapat'tsare] /72/ VT to ill-treat; **strapazzarsi** VPR to tire o.s. out, overdo things

strapaz'zato, -a [strapat'tsato] AG: **uova strapazzate** scrambled eggs

stra'pazzo [stra'pattso] SM strain, fatigue; **da ~** (fig) third-rate

strapi'eno, -a AG full to overflowing

strapi'ombo SM overhanging rock; **a ~** overhanging

strapo'tere SM excessive power

strappa'lacrime AG INV (col): **romanzo** (o **film** etc) **~** tear-jerker

strap'pare /72/ VT (gen) to tear, rip; (pagina ecc) to tear off, tear out; (sradicare) to pull up; (fig) to wrest sth from sb; (togliere): **~ qc a qn** to snatch sth from sb; **strapparsi** VPR (lacerarsi) to rip, tear; (rompersi) to break; **strapparsi un muscolo** to tear a muscle

S

strap'pato, -a AG torn, ripped

'strappo SM (*strattone*) pull, tug; (*lacerazione*) tear, rip; (*fig: col: passaggio*) lift (BRIT), ride (US); **fare uno ~ alla regola** to make an exception to the rule; **~ muscolare** torn muscle

strapun'tino SM jump *o* foldaway seat

strari'pare /**72**/ VI to overflow

Stras'burgo SF Strasbourg

strasci'care [straʃʃi'kare] /**20**/ VT to trail; (*piedi*) to drag; **~ le parole** to drawl

'strascico, -chi ['straʃʃiko] SM (*di abito*) train; (*conseguenza*) after-effect

strata'gemma, -i [strata'dʒɛmma] SM stratagem

stra'tega, -ghi SM strategist

strate'gia, -'gie [strate'dʒia] SF strategy

stra'tegico, -a, -ci, -che [stra'tɛdʒiko] AG strategic

'strato SM layer; (*rivestimento*) coat, coating; (*Geo, fig*) stratum; (*Meteor*) stratus; **~ d'ozono** ozone layer

strato'sfera SF stratosphere

strat'tone SM tug, jerk; **dare uno ~ a qc** to tug *o* jerk sth, give sth a tug *o* jerk

stravac'cato, -a AG sprawling

strava'gante AG odd, eccentric

strava'ganza [strava'gantsa] SF eccentricity

stra'vecchio, -a [stra'vɛkkjo] AG very old

strave'dere /**127**/ VI: **~ per qn** to dote on sb

stra'visto, -a PP di **stravedere**

stra'vizio [stra'vittsjo] SM excess

stra'volgere [stra'vɔldʒere] /**96**/ VT (*volto*) to contort; (*fig: animo*) to trouble deeply; (: *verità*) to twist, distort

stra'volto, -a PP di **stravolgere** ▶ AG (*persona: per stanchezza ecc*) in a terrible state; (: *per sofferenza*) distraught

strazi'ante [strat'tsjante] AG (*scena*) harrowing; (*urlo*) bloodcurdling; (*dolore*) excruciating

strazi'are [strat'tsjare] /**19**/ VT to torture, torment

'strazio ['strattsjo] SM torture; (*fig: cosa fatta male*): **essere uno ~** to be appalling; **fare ~ di** (*corpo, vittima*) to mutilate

'strega, -ghe SF witch

stre'gare /**80**/ VT to bewitch

stre'gone SM (*mago*) wizard; (*di tribù*) witch doctor

stregone'ria SF (*pratica*) witchcraft; **fare una ~** to cast a spell

'stregua SF: **alla ~ di** by the same standard as

stre'mare /**72**/ VT to exhaust

'stremo SM: **essere allo ~** to be at the end of one's tether

'strenna SF: **~ natalizia** (*regalo*) Christmas present; (*libro*) book published for the Christmas market

'strenuo, -a AG brave, courageous

strepi'tare /**72**/ VI to yell and shout

'strepito SM (*di voci, folla*) clamour (BRIT), clamor (US); (*di catene*) clanking, rattling

strepi'toso, -a AG clamorous, deafening; (*fig: successo*) resounding

stres'sante AG stressful

stres'sare /**72**/ VT to put under stress

stres'sato, -a AG under stress

stretch [stretʃ] AG INV stretch

'stretta SF vedi **stretto**

stretta'mente AV tightly; (*rigorosamente*) strictly

stret'tezza [stret'tettsa] SF narrowness; **strettezze** SFPL (*povertà*) poverty sg, straitened circumstances

'stretto, -a PP di **stringere** ▶ AG (*corridoio, limiti*) narrow; (*gonna, scarpe, nodo, curva*) tight; (*intimo: parente, amico*) close; (*rigoroso: osservanza*) strict; (*preciso: significato*) precise, exact ▶ SM (*braccio di mare*) strait ▶ SF (*di mano*) grasp; (*finanziaria*) squeeze; (*fig: dolore, turbamento*) pang; **a denti stretti** with clenched teeth; **lo ~ necessario** the bare minimum; **una stretta di mano** a handshake; **una stretta al cuore** a sudden sadness; **essere alle strette** to have one's back to the wall

stret'toia SF bottleneck; (*fig*) tricky situation

stri'ato, -a AG streaked

stria'tura SF (*atto*) streaking; (*effetto*) streaks pl

stric'nina SF strychnine

'strida SFPL screaming sg

stri'dente AG strident

stri'dere /**89**/ VI (*porta*) to squeak; (*animale*) to screech, shriek; (*colori*) to clash

'strido (*pl*(*f*) **strida**) SM screech, shriek

stri'dore SM screeching, shrieking

'stridulo, -a AG shrill

'striglia ['striʎʎa] SF currycomb

strigli'are [striʎ'ʎare] /**27**/ VT (*cavallo*) to curry

strigli'ata [striʎ'ʎata] SF (*di cavallo*) currying; (*fig*): **dare una ~ a qn** to give sb a scolding

stril'lare /**72**/ VT, VI to scream, shriek

'strillo SM scream, shriek

stril'lone SM newspaper seller

strimin'zito, -a [strimin'tsito] AG (*misero*) shabby; (*molto magro*) skinny

strimpel'lare /**72**/ VT (*Mus*) to strum

'stringa, -ghe SF lace; (*Inform*) string

strin'gare /**80**/ VT (*fig: discorso*) to condense

strin'gato, -a AG (*fig*) concise

'stringere ['strindʒere] /**117**/ VT (*avvicinare due cose*) to press (together), squeeze (together); (*tenere stretto*) to hold tight, clasp, clutch; (*pugno, mascella, denti*) to clench; (*labbra*) to compress; (*avvitare*) to tighten; (*abito*) to take in; (*scarpe*) to pinch, be tight for; (*fig: concludere: patto*) to make; (: *accelerare: passo*)

to quicken ▶ VI (*essere stretto*) to be tight;
(*tempo: incalzare*) to be pressing; **stringersi**
VPR (*accostarsi*): **stringersi a** to press o.s. up
against; ~ **la mano a qn** to shake sb's hand;
~ **gli occhi** to screw up one's eyes;
~ **amicizia con qn** to make friends with sb;
stringi stringi in conclusion; **il tempo**
stringe time is short

'**strinsi** *etc* VB *vedi* **stringere**

'**striscia, -sce** ['striʃʃa] SF (*di carta, tessuto ecc*)
strip; (*riga*) stripe; **strisce (pedonali)** zebra
crossing *sg*; **a strisce** striped

strisci'ante [striʃʃante] AG (*fig: peg*) unctuous;
(*Econ: inflazione*) creeping

strisci'are [striʃʃare] /**14**/ VT (*piedi*) to drag;
(*muro, macchina*) to graze ▶ VI to crawl, creep

'**striscio** ['striʃʃo] SM graze; (*Med*) smear;
colpire di ~ to graze

strisci'one [striʃʃone] SM banner

strito'lare /**72**/ VT to grind

striz'zare [strit'tsare] /**72**/ VT (*arancia*) to
squeeze; (*panni*) to wring (out); ~ **l'occhio**
to wink

striz'zata [strit'tsata] SF: **dare una** ~ **a qc** to
give sth a wring; **una** ~ **d'occhio** a wink

'**strofa** SF, '**strofe** SF INV strophe

strofi'naccio [strofi'nattʃo] SM duster, cloth;
(*per piatti*) dishcloth; (*per pavimenti*) floorcloth

strofi'nare /**72**/ VT to rub

stron'care /**20**/ VT to break off; (*fig: ribellione*)
to suppress, put down; (: *film, libro*) to tear to
pieces

'**stronzo** ['strontso] SM (*sterco*) turd; (*col:*
persona) shit (*!*)

stropicci'are [stropit'tʃare] /**14**/ VT to rub

stroz'zare [strot'tsare] /**72**/ VT (*soffocare*) to
choke, strangle; **strozzarsi** VPR to choke

strozza'tura [strottsa'tura] SF (*restringimento*)
narrowing; (*di strada ecc*) bottleneck

stroz'zino, -a [strot'tsino] SM/F (*usuraio*)
usurer; (*fig*) shark

struc'care /**20**/ VT to remove make-up from;
struccarsi VPR to remove one's make-up

'**struggere** ['struddʒere] /**39**/ VT (*fig*) to
consume; **struggersi** VPR (*fig*): **struggersi di**
to be consumed with

struggi'mento [struddʒi'mento] SM
(*desiderio*) yearning

strumen'tale AG (*Mus*) instrumental

strumentaliz'zare [strumentalid'dzare] /**72**/
VT to exploit, use to one's own ends

strumentalizzazi'one
[strumentaliddzat'tsjone] SF exploitation

strumentazi'one [strumentat'tsjone] SF
(*Mus*) orchestration; (*Tecn*) instrumentation

stru'mento SM (*arnese, fig*) instrument, tool;
(*Mus*) instrument; ~ **a corda** *o* **ad arco/a**
fiato string(ed)/wind instrument

'**strussi** *etc* VB *vedi* **struggere**

'**strutto** SM lard

strut'tura SF structure

struttu'rare /**72**/ VT to structure

'**struzzo** ['struttso] SM ostrich; **fare lo** ~,
fare la politica dello ~ to bury one's head
in the sand

stuc'care /**20**/ VT (*muro*) to plaster; (*vetro*) to
putty; (*decorare con stucchi*) to stucco

stucca'tore, -'trice SM/F plasterer; (*artista*)
stucco worker

stuc'chevole [stuk'kevole] AG nauseating;
(*fig*) tedious, boring

'**stucco, -chi** SM plaster; (*da vetri*) putty;
(*ornamentale*) stucco; **rimanere di** ~ (*fig*) to be
dumbfounded

stu'dente, -'essa SM/F student; (*scolaro*)
pupil, schoolboy(-girl)

studen'tesco, -a, -schi, -sche AG student *cpd*

studi'are /**19**/ VT to study; **studiarsi** VPR
(*sforzarsi*): **studiarsi di fare** to try *o*
endeavour (BRIT) *o* endeavor (US) to do

studi'ato, -a AG (*modi, sorriso*) affected

'**studio** SM studying; (*ricerca, saggio, stanza*)
study; (*di professionista*) office; (*di artista, Cine,*
TV, Radio) studio; (*di medico*) surgery (BRIT),
office (US); **studi** SMPL (*Ins*) studies; **alla fine**
degli studi at the end of one's course (of
studies); **secondo recenti studi, appare**
che ... recent research indicates that ...;
la proposta è allo ~ the proposal is under
consideration; ~ **legale** lawyer's office

studi'oso, -a AG studious, hardworking
▶ SM/F scholar

'**stufa** SF stove; ~ **elettrica** electric fire *o*
heater; ~ **a legna/carbone** wood-burning/
coal stove

stu'fare /**72**/ VT (*Cuc*) to stew; (*fig: col*) to
bore; **stufarsi** VPR (*col*): **stufarsi (di)** (*fig*)
to get fed up (with)

stu'fato SM (*Cuc*) stew

'**stufo, -a** AG (*col*): **essere** ~ **di** to be fed up
with, be sick and tired of

stu'oia SF màt

stu'olo SM crowd, host

stupefa'cente [stupefa'tʃɛnte] AG stunning,
astounding ▶ SM drug, narcotic

stupe'fare /**53**/ VT to stun, astound

stupe'fatto, -a PP *di* **stupefare**

stupefazi'one [stupefat'tsjone] SF
astonishment

stu'pendo, -a AG marvellous, wonderful

stupi'daggine [stupi'daddʒine] SF stupid
thing (to do *o* say)

stupidità SF stupidity

'**stupido, -a** AG stupid

stu'pire /**55**/ VT to amaze, stun ▶ VI (*anche:*
stupirsi): ~ **(di)** to be amazed (at), be stunned
(by); **non c'è da stupirsi** that's not
surprising

S

stu'pore SM amazement, astonishment
stu'prare /**72**/ VT to rape
stupra'tore SM rapist
'stupro SM rape
stu'rare /**72**/ VT (*lavandino*) to clear
stuzzica'denti [stuttsika'dɛnti] SM toothpick
stuzzi'cante [stuttsi'kante] AG (*gen*) stimulating; (*appetitoso*) appetizing
stuzzi'care [stuttsi'kare] /**20**/ VT (*ferita ecc*) to poke (at), prod (at); (*fig*) to tease; (: *appetito*) to whet; (: *curiosità*) to stimulate; ~ **i denti** to pick one's teeth

----

(**PAROLA CHIAVE**)

su (*su + il* = **sul**, *su + lo* = **sullo**, *su + l'* = **sull'**, *su + la* = **sulla**, *su + i* = **sui**, *su + gli* = **sugli**, *su + le* = **sulle**)
PREP **1** (*gen*) on; (*moto*) on(to); (*in cima a*) on (top of); **mettilo sul tavolo** put it on the table; **salire sul treno** to get on the train; **un paesino sul mare** a village by the sea; **è sulla destra** it's on the right; **cento metri sul livello del mare** a hundred metres above sea level; **fecero rotta su Palermo** they set out for Palermo; **sul vestito portava un golf rosso** she was wearing a red sweater over her dress
2 (*argomento*) about, on; **un libro su Cesare** a book on *o* about Caesar
3 (*circa*) about; **costerà sui 3 milioni** it will cost about 3 million; **una ragazza sui 17 anni** a girl of about 17 (years of age)
4: **su misura** made to measure; **su ordinazione** to order; **su richiesta** on request; **3 casi su dieci** 3 cases out of 10
▶ AV **1** (*in alto, verso l'alto*) up; **vieni su** come on up; **guarda su** look up; **andare su e giù** to go up and down; **su le mani!** hands up!; **in su** (*verso l'alto*) up(wards); (*in poi*) onwards; **vieni su da me?** are you going to come up?; **dai 20 anni in su** from the age of 20 onwards
2 (*addosso*) on; **cos'hai su?** what have you got on?
▶ ESCL come on!; **su avanti, muoviti!** come on, hurry up!; **su coraggio!** come on, cheer up!

'sua *vedi* **suo**
sua'dente AG persuasive
sub SM INV/F INV skin-diver
su'bacqueo, -a AG underwater ▶ SM skin-diver
subaffit'tare /**72**/ VT to sublet
subaf'fitto SM (*contratto*) sublet
subal'terno, -a AG, SM subordinate; (*Mil*) subaltern
subappal'tare /**72**/ VT to subcontract
subap'palto SM subcontract

sub'buglio [sub'buʎʎo] SM confusion, turmoil; **essere/mettere in** ~ to be in/ throw into a turmoil
sub'conscio, -a [sub'kɔnʃo] AG, SM subconscious
subcosci'ente [subkoʃʃɛnte] SM subconscious
'subdolo, -a AG underhand, sneaky
suben'trare /**72**/ VI: ~ **a qn in qc** to take over sth from sb; **sono subentrati altri problemi** other problems arose
su'bire /**55**/ VT to suffer, endure
subis'sare /**72**/ VT (*fig*): ~ **di** to overwhelm with, load with
subi'taneo, -a AG sudden
'subito AV immediately, at once, straight away
subli'mare /**72**/ VT (*Psic*) to sublimate; (*Chim*) to sublime
su'blime AG sublime
sublo'care /**20**/ VT to sublease
sublocazi'one [sublokat'tsjone] SF sublease
subnor'male AG subnormal ▶ SMF mentally handicapped person
subodo'rare /**72**/ VT (*insidia ecc*) to smell, suspect
subordi'nare /**72**/ VT to subordinate
subordi'nato, -a AG subordinate; (*dipendente*): ~ **a** dependent on, subject to
subordinazi'one [subordinat'tsjone] SF subordination
su'bordine SM: **in** ~ secondarily
sub'prime [sab'praim] AG INV subprime; **mutuo** ~ subprime mortgage ▶ SM subprime lending
subur'bano, -a AG suburban
succe'daneo [suttʃe'daneo] SM substitute
suc'cedere [sut'tʃɛdere] /**118**/ VI (*accadere*) to happen; ~ **a** (*prendere il posto di*) to succeed; (*venire dopo*) to follow; **succedersi** VPR to follow each other; ~ **al trono** to succeed to the throne; **sono cose che succedono** these things happen; **cos'è successo?** what happened?
successi'one [suttʃes'sjone] SF succession; **tassa di** ~ death duty (*Brit*), inheritance tax (*US*)
successiva'mente [suttʃessiva'mente] AV subsequently
succes'sivo, -a [suttʃes'sivo] AG successive; **il giorno** ~ the following day; **in un momento** ~ subsequently
suc'cesso, -a [sut'tʃɛsso] PP *di* **succedere** ▶ SM (*esito*) outcome; (*buona riuscita*) success; **di** ~ (*libro, personaggio*) successful; **avere** ~ (*persona*) to be successful; (*idea*) to be well received
succes'sore [suttʃes'sore] SM successor
succhi'are [suk'kjare] /**19**/ VT to suck (up)
succhi'otto [suk'kjɔtto] SM dummy (*Brit*), pacifier (*US*), comforter (*US*)

suc'cinto, -a [sut'tʃinto] AG (discorso) succinct; (abito) brief

'succo, -chi SM juice; (fig) essence, gist; **~ di frutta/pomodoro** fruit/tomato juice

suc'coso, -a AG juicy; (fig) pithy

'succube SMF victim; **essere ~ di qn** to be dominated by sb

succur'sale SF branch (office)

sud SM south ▶ AG INV south; (regione) southern; **verso ~** south, southwards; **l'Italia del S~** Southern Italy; **l'America del S~** South America

Su'dafrica SM: **il ~** South Africa

sudafri'cano, -a AG, SM/F South African

Suda'merica SM: **il ~** South America

sudameri'cano, -a AG, SM/F South American

Su'dan SM: **il ~** (the) Sudan

suda'nese AG, SMF Sudanese inv

su'dare /72/ VI to perspire, sweat; **~ freddo** to come out in a cold sweat

su'dato, -a AG (persona, mani) sweaty; (fig: denaro) hard-earned ▶ AG (anche fig) sweat; **una vittoria sudata** a hard-won victory; **ho fatto una bella sudata per finirlo in tempo** it was a real sweat to get it finished in time

sud'detto, -a AG above-mentioned

suddi'tanza [suddi'tantsa] SF subjection; (cittadinanza) citizenship

sud'dito, -a SM/F subject

suddi'videre /43/ VT to subdivide

suddivisi'one SF subdivision

suddi'viso, -a PP di **suddividere**

su'dest SM south-east; **vento di ~** south-easterly wind; **il ~ asiatico** South-East Asia

sudice'ria [suditʃe'ria] SF (qualità) filthiness, dirtiness; (cosa sporca) dirty thing

'sudicio, -a, -ci, -ce ['suditʃo] AG dirty, filthy

sudici'ume [sudi'tʃume] SM dirt, filth

su'doku SM INV sudoku

su'dore SM perspiration, sweat

su'dovest SM south-west; **vento di ~** south-westerly wind

'sue vedi **suo**

'Suez ['suez] SM: **il Canale di ~** the Suez Canal

suffici'ente [suffi'tʃɛnte] AG enough, sufficient; (borioso) self-important; (Ins) satisfactory

sufficiente'mente [suffitʃente'mente] AV sufficiently, enough; (guadagnare, darsi da fare) enough

suffici'enza [suffi'tʃɛntsa] SF self-importance; (Ins) pass mark; **con un'aria di ~** (fig) with a condescending air; **a ~** enough; **ne ho avuto a ~!** I've had enough of this!

suf'fisso SM (Ling) suffix

suffra'gare /80/ VT to support

suf'fragio [suf'fradʒo] SM (voto) vote; **~ universale** universal suffrage

suggel'lare [suddʒel'lare] **/72/** VT (fig) to seal

suggeri'mento [suddʒeri'mento] SM suggestion; (consiglio) piece of advice, advice no pl; **dietro suo ~** on his advice

sugge'rire [suddʒe'rire] **/55/** VT (risposta) to tell; (consigliare) to advise; (proporre) to suggest; (Teat) to prompt; **~ a qn di fare qc** to suggest to sb that he (o she) do sth

suggeri'tore, -'trice [suddʒeri'tore] SM/F (Teat) prompter

suggestio'nare [suddʒestjo'nare] **/72/** VT to influence

suggesti'one [suddʒes'tjone] SF (Psic) suggestion; (istigazione) instigation

sugges'tivo, -a [suddʒes'tivo] AG (paesaggio) evocative; (teoria) interesting, attractive

'sughero ['sugero] SM cork

'sugli ['suʎʎi] PREP + DET vedi **su**

'sugo, -ghi SM (succo) juice; (di carne) gravy; (condimento) sauce; (fig) gist, essence

su'goso, -a AG (frutto) juicy; (fig: articolo ecc) pithy

'sui PREP + DET vedi **su**

sui'cida, -i, -e [sui'tʃida] AG suicidal ▶ SMF suicide

suici'darsi [suitʃi'darsi] **/72/** VPR to commit suicide

sui'cidio [sui'tʃidjo] SM suicide

su'ino, -a AG: **carne suina** pork ▶ SM pig; **suini** SMPL swine pl

sul, sull', 'sulla, 'sulle, 'sullo PREP + DET vedi **su**

sulfa'midico, -a, -ci, -che AG, SM (Med) sulphonamide

sulta'nina SF: (uva) **~** sultana

sul'tano, -a SM/F sultan (sultana)

Su'matra SF Sumatra

'summit ['summit] SM INV summit

S.U.N.I.A. SIGLA M (= sindacato unitario nazionale inquilini e assegnatari) national association of tenants

sunnomi'nato, -a AG aforesaid cpd

'sunto SM summary

'suo (f **sua**, pl **sue**, **suoi**) DET: **il ~**, **la sua** etc (di lui) his; (di lei) her; (di esso) its; (con valore indefinito) one's, his/her; (forma di cortesia: anche: **Suo**) your ▶ PRON: **il ~**, **la sua** etc his; hers; yours ▶ SM: **ha speso del ~** he (o she etc) spent his (o her etc) own money ▶ SF: **la sua** (opinione) his (o her etc) view; **i suoi** (parenti) his (o her etc) family; **un ~ amico** a friend of his (o hers etc); **è dalla sua** he's on his (o her etc) side; **anche lui ha avuto le sue** (disavventure) he's had his problems too; **sta sulle sue** he keeps himself to himself

su'ocero, -a ['swɔtʃero] SM/F father-in-law (mother-in-law); **i suoceri** (pl) father- and mother-in-law

su'oi vedi **suo**

su'ola SF (*di scarpa*) sole

su'olo SM (*terreno*) ground; (*terra*) soil

suo'nare /72/ VT (*Mus*) to play; (*campana*) to ring; (*ore*) to strike; (*clacson, allarme*) to sound ▶ VI to play; (*telefono, campana*) to ring; (*ore*) to strike; (*clacson, fig: parole*) to sound

suo'nato, -a AG (*compiuto*): **ha cinquant'anni suonati** he is well over fifty

suona'tore, -'trice SM/F player; **~ ambulante** street musician

suone'ria SF (*di sveglia*) alarm; (*di telefono*) ringtone

su'ono SM sound

su'ora SF (*Rel*) nun; **Suor Maria** Sister Maria

'super AG INV: **(benzina) ~** ≈ four-star (petrol) (*BRIT*), ≈ premium (*US*)

supera'mento SM (*di ostacolo*) overcoming; (*di montagna*) crossing

supe'rare /72/ VT (*oltrepassare: limite*) to exceed, surpass; (*percorrere*) to cover; (*attraversare: fiume*) to cross; (*sorpassare: veicolo*) to overtake; (*fig: essere più bravo di*) to surpass, outdo; (: *difficoltà*) to overcome; (: *esame*) to get through; **~ qn in altezza/peso** to be taller/heavier than sb; **ha superato la cinquantina** he's over fifty (years of age); **~ i limiti di velocità** to exceed the speed limit; **stavolta ha superato se stesso** this time he has surpassed himself

supe'rato, -a AG outmoded

supe'rattico, -ci SM penthouse

su'perbia SF pride

su'perbo, -a AG proud; (*fig*) magnificent, superb

supercondut'tore SM superconductor

superena'lotto SM *Italian national lottery*

superfici'ale [superfi'tʃale] AG superficial

superficialità [superfitʃali'ta] SF superficiality

super'ficie, -ci [super'fitʃe] SF surface; **tornare in ~** (*a galla*) to return to the surface; (*fig: problemi ecc*) to resurface; **~ alare** (*Aer*) wing area; **~ velica** (*Naut*) sail area

su'perfluo, -a AG superfluous

superi'ora SF (*Rel: anche*: **madre superiora**) mother superior

superi'ore AG (*piano, arto, classi*) upper; (*più elevato: temperatura, livello*): **~ (a)** higher (than); (*migliore*): **~ (a)** superior (to) ▶ SFPL: **le superiori** (*Ins*) *vedi* **scuola media superiore**; **il corso ~ di un fiume** the upper reaches of a river; **scuola media ~** ≈ senior comprehensive school (*BRIT*), ≈ senior high (school) (*US*)

superiorità SF superiority

superla'tivo, -a AG, SM superlative

superla'voro SM overwork

super'market [super'market] SM INV = **supermercato**

supermer'cato SM supermarket

super'nova SF supernova

superpo'tenza [superpo'tentsa] SF (*Pol*) superpower

super'sonico, -a, -ci, -che AG supersonic

su'perstite AG surviving ▶ SMF survivor

superstizi'one [superstit'tsjone] SF superstition

superstizi'oso, -a [superstit'tsjoso] AG superstitious

super'strada SF ≈ expressway

supervisi'one SF supervision

supervi'sore SM supervisor

su'pino, -a AG supine; **accettazione supina** (*fig*) blind acceptance

suppel'lettile SF furnishings *pl*

suppergiù [supper'dʒu] AV more or less, roughly

suppl. ABBR (= *supplemento*) supp(l)

supplemen'tare AG extra; (*treno*) relief *cpd*; (*entrate*) additional

supple'mento SM supplement

sup'plente AG temporary; (*insegnante*) supply *cpd* (*BRIT*), substitute *cpd* (*US*) ▶ SMF temporary member of staff; supply (*o* substitute) teacher

sup'plenza [sup'plɛntsa] SF: **fare ~** to do supply (*BRIT*) *o* substitute (*US*) teaching

supple'tivo, -a AG (*gen*) supplementary; (*sessione d'esami*) extra

'supplica, -che SF (*preghiera*) plea; (*domanda scritta*) petition, request

suppli'care /20/ VT to implore, beseech

suppli'chevole [suppli'kevole] AG imploring

sup'plire /45/ VI: **~ a** to make up for, compensate for

sup'plizio [sup'plittsjo] SM torture

sup'pongo, sup'ponietc VB *vedi* **supporre**

sup'porre /77/ VT to suppose; **supponiamo che …** let's *o* just suppose that …

sup'porto SM (*sostegno*) support

supposizi'one [suppozit'tsjone] SF supposition

sup'posta SF (*Med*) suppository

sup'posto, -a PP *di* **supporre**

suppu'rare /72/ VI to suppurate

suprema'zia [supremat'tsia] SF supremacy

su'premo, -a AG supreme; **Suprema Corte (di Cassazione)** Supreme Court

surclas'sare /72/ VT to outclass

surge'lare [surdʒe'lare] /72/ VT to (deep-)freeze

surge'lato, -a [surdʒe'lato] AG (deep-)frozen ▶ SMPL: **i surgelati** frozen food *sg*

surme'nage [syrmə'naʒ] SM (*fisico*) overwork; (*mentale*) mental strain; (*Sport*) overtraining

sur'plus SM INV (*Econ*) surplus; **~ di manodopera** overmanning

surre'ale AG surrealistic

surriscalda'mento SM (gen, Tecn) overheating

surriscal'dare /**72**/ VT to overheat

surro'gato SM substitute

suscet'tibile [suʃʃet'tibile] AG (sensibile) touchy, sensitive; (soggetto): ~ **di miglioramento** that can be improved, open to improvement

suscettibilità [suʃʃettibili'ta] SF touchiness; **urtare la ~ di qn** to hurt sb's feelings

susci'tare [suʃʃi'tare] /**72**/ VT to provoke, arouse

su'sina SF plum

su'sino SM plum (tree)

sussegu'ire /**45**/ VT to follow; **susseguirsi** VPR to follow one another

sussidi'ario, -a AG subsidiary; (treno) relief cpd; (fermata) extra

sus'sidio SM subsidy; (aiuto) aid; **sussidi didattici/audiovisivi** teaching/audiovisual aids; **~ di disoccupazione** unemployment benefit (BRIT) o benefits (US); **~ per malattia** sickness benefit

sussi'ego SM haughtiness; **con aria di ~** haughtily

sussis'tenza [sussis'tentsa] SF subsistence

sus'sistere /**11**/ VI to exist; (essere fondato) to be valid o sound

sussul'tare /**72**/ VI to shudder

sus'sulto SM start

sussur'rare /**72**/ VT, VI to whisper, murmur; **si sussurra che …** it's rumoured (BRIT) o rumored (US) that …

sus'surro SM whisper, murmur

su'tura SF (Med) suture

sutu'rare /**72**/ VT to stitch up, suture

suv'via ESCL come on!

SV SIGLA = **Savona**

S.V. ABBR = **Signoria Vostra**

sva'gare /**80**/ VT (divertire) to amuse; (distrarre): **~ qn** to take sb's mind off things; **svagarsi** VPR to amuse o.s.; to take one's mind off things

sva'gato, -a AG (persona) absent-minded; (scolaro) inattentive

'svago, -ghi SM (riposo) relaxation; (ricreazione) amusement; (passatempo) pastime

svaligi'are [zvali'dʒare] /**62**/ VT to rob, burgle (BRIT), burglarize (US)

svaligia'tore, -'trice [zvalidʒa'tore] SM/F (di banca) robber; (di casa) burglar

svalu'tare /**72**/ VT (Econ) to devalue; (fig) to belittle; **svalutarsi** VPR (Econ) to be devalued

svalutazi'one [zvalutat'tsjone] SF devaluation

svam'pito, -a AG absent-minded ▶ SM/F absent-minded person

sva'nire /**55**/ VI to disappear, vanish

sva'nito, -a AG (fig: persona) absent-minded

svantaggi'ato, -a [zvantad'dʒato] AG at a disadvantage

svan'taggio [zvan'taddʒo] SM disadvantage; (inconveniente) drawback, disadvantage; **tornerà a suo ~** it will work against you

svantaggi'oso, -a [zvantad'dʒoso] AG disadvantageous; **è un'offerta svantaggiosa per me** it's not in my interest to accept this offer; **è un prezzo ~** it is not an attractive price

svapo'rare /**72**/ VI to evaporate

svapo'rato, -a AG (bibita) flat

vari'ato, -a AG (vario, diverso) varied; (numeroso) various

'svastica, -che SF swastika

sve'dese AG Swedish ▶ SMF Swede ▶ SM (Ling) Swedish

'sveglia ['zveʎʎa] SF waking up; (orologio) alarm (clock); **suonare la ~** (Mil) to sound the reveille; **~ telefonica** alarm call

svegli'are [zveʎ'ʎare] /**27**/ VT to wake up; (fig) to awaken, arouse; **svegliarsi** VPR to wake up; (fig) to be revived, reawaken

'sveglio, -a ['zveʎʎo] AG awake; (fig) alert, quick-witted

sve'lare /**72**/ VT to reveal

svel'tezza [zvel'tettsa] SF (gen) speed; (mentale) quick-wittedness

svel'tire /**55**/ VT (gen) to speed up; (procedura) to streamline

'svelto, -a AG (passo) quick; (mente) quick, alert; (linea) slim, slender; **alla svelta** quickly

'svendere /**29**/ VT to sell off, clear

'svendita SF (Comm) (clearance) sale

sve'nevole AG mawkish

'svengo etc VB vedi **svenire**

sveni'mento SM fainting fit, faint

sve'nire /**128**/ VI to faint

sven'tare /**72**/ VT to foil, thwart

sventa'tezza [zventa'tettsa] SF (distrazione) absent-mindedness; (mancanza di prudenza) rashness

sven'tato, -a AG (distratto) scatterbrained; (imprudente) rash

'sventola SF (colpo) slap; **orecchie a ~** sticking-out ears

svento'lare /**72**/ VT, VI to wave, flutter

sven'trare /**72**/ VT to disembowel

sven'tura SF misfortune

sventu'rato, -a AG unlucky, unfortunate

sve'nuto, -a PP di **svenire**

svergo'gnare [zvergoɲ'ɲare] /**15**/ VT to shame

svergo'gnato, -a [zvergoɲ'ɲato] AG shameless ▶ SM/F shameless person

sver'nare /**72**/ VI to spend the winter

sverrò etc VB vedi **svenire**

sves'tire /**45**/ VT to undress; **svestirsi** VPR to get undressed

'Svezia ['zvɛttsja] SF: **la ~** Sweden

svez'zare [zvet'tsare] /**72**/ VT to wean

svi'are /**60**/ VT to divert; (*fig*) to lead astray; **sviarsi** VPR to go astray

svico'lare /**72**/ VI to slip down an alley; (*fig*) to sneak off

svi'gnarsela [zviɲ'ɲarsela] /**72**/ VPR to slip away, sneak off

svili'mento SM debasement

svi'lire /**55**/ VT to debase

svilup'pare /**72**/ VT, **svilup'parsi** VPR to develop

sviluppa'tore, -trice SM/F (*Inform*) developer

svi'luppo SM development; (*di industria*) expansion; **in via di ~** in the process of development; **paesi in via di ~** developing countries

svinco'lare /**72**/ VT to free, release; (*merce*) to clear

'svincolo SM (*Comm*) clearance; (*stradale*) motorway (*BRIT*) *o* expressway (*US*) intersection

svisce'rare [zviʃʃe'rare] /**72**/ VT (*fig: argomento*) to examine in depth

svisce'rato, -a [zviʃʃe'rato] AG (*amore, odio*) passionate

'svista SF oversight

svi'tare /**72**/ VT to unscrew

'Svizzera ['zvittsera] SF: **la ~** Switzerland

'svizzero, -a ['zvittsero] AG, SM/F Swiss

svoglia'tezza [zvoʎʎa'tettsa] SF listlessness; indolence

svogli'ato, -a [zvoʎ'ʎato] AG listless; (*pigro*) lazy, indolent

svolaz'zare [zvolat'tsare] /**72**/ VI to flutter

'svolgere ['zvɔldʒere] /**96**/ VT to unwind; (*srotolare*) to unroll; (*fig: argomento*) to develop; (: *piano, programma*) to carry out; **svolgersi** VPR to unwind; to unroll; (*fig: aver luogo*) to take place; (: *procedere*) to go on; **tutto si è svolto secondo i piani** everything went according to plan

svolgi'mento [zvoldʒi'mento] SM development; carrying out; (*andamento*) course

'svolsi *etc* VB *vedi* **svolgere**

'svolta SF (*atto*) turning *no pl*; (*curva*) turn, bend; (*fig*) turning-point; **essere ad una ~ nella propria vita** to be at a crossroads in one's life

svol'tare /**72**/ VI to turn

'svolto, -a PP *di* **svolgere**

svuo'tare /**72**/ VT to empty (out)

'Swaziland ['swadziland] SM: **lo ~** Swaziland

Tt

T, t [ti] SM O F INV (*lettera*) T, t; **T come
Taranto** ≈ T for Tommy

T ABBR = **tabaccheria**

t ABBR = **tara; tonnellata**

TA SIGLA = **Taranto**

tabac'caio, -a SM/F tobacconist

tabacche'ria [tabakke'ria] SF tobacconist's
(shop)

> Tabaccherie sell cigarettes and tobacco
> and can easily be identified by their sign,
> a large white "T" on a black background.
> You can buy postage stamps and bus
> tickets at a *tabaccheria* and some also sell
> newspapers.

tabacchi'era [tabak'kjɛra] SF snuffbox

ta'bacco, -chi SM tobacco

ta'bella SF (*tavola*) table; (*elenco*) list; **~ di
marcia** schedule; **~ dei prezzi** price list

tabel'lone SM (*per pubblicità*) billboard; (*per
informazioni*) notice board (BRIT), bulletin
board (US); (: *in stazione*) timetable board

taber'nacolo SM tabernacle

tabù AG, SM INV taboo

'tabula 'rasa SF tabula rasa; **fare ~** (*fig*) to
make a clean sweep

tabu'lare /**72**/ VT to tabulate

tabu'lato SM (*Inform*) printout

tabula'tore SM tabulator

TAC SIGLA F (*Med*: = *Tomografia Assiale
Computerizzata*) CAT

'tacca, -che SF notch, nick; **di mezza ~** (*fig*)
mediocre

taccagne'ria [takkaɲɲe'ria] SF meanness,
stinginess

tac'cagno, -a [tak'kaɲɲo] AG mean, stingy

tac'cheggio [tak'keddʒo] SM shoplifting

tac'chino [tak'kino] SM turkey

'taccia, -ce ['tattʃa] SF bad reputation

tacci'are [tat'tʃare] /**14**/ VT: **~ qn di**
(*vigliaccheria ecc*) to accuse sb of

'taccio *etc* ['tattʃo] VB *vedi* **tacere**

'tacco, -chi SM heel; **tacchi a spillo** stiletto
heels

taccu'ino SM notebook

ta'cere [ta'tʃere] /**119**/ VI to be silent o quiet;
(*smettere di parlare*) to fall silent ▶ VT to keep to
oneself, say nothing about; **far ~ qn** to make
sb be quiet; (*fig*) to silence sb; **mettere a ~ qc**
to hush sth up

tachicar'dia [takikar'dia] SF (*Med*)
tachycardia

ta'chimetro [ta'kimetro] SM speedometer

'tacito, -a ['tatʃito] AG silent; (*sottinteso*) tacit,
unspoken

taci'turno, -a [tatʃi'turno] AG taciturn

taci'uto, -a [ta'tʃuto] PP *di* **tacere**

'tacqui *etc* VB *vedi* **tacere**

ta'fano SM horsefly

taffe'ruglio [taffe'ruʎʎo] SM brawl, scuffle

taffettà SM taffeta

'taglia ['taʎʎa] SF (*statura*) height; (*misura*)
size; (*riscatto*) ransom; (*ricompensa*) reward;
taglie forti (*Abbigliamento*) outsize

taglia'boschi [taʎʎa'bɔski] SM INV
woodcutter

taglia'carte [taʎʎa'karte] SM INV paperknife

taglia'legna [taʎʎa'leɲɲa] SM INV
woodcutter

tagli'ando [taʎ'ʎando] SM coupon

tagli'are [taʎ'ʎare] /**27**/ VT to cut; (*recidere,
interrompere*) to cut off; (*intersecare*) to cut
across, intersect; (*carne*) to carve; (*vini*) to
blend ▶ VI to cut; (*prendere una scorciatoia*) to
take a short-cut; **tagliarsi** VPR to cut o.s.;
~ la strada a qn to cut across in front of sb;
~ corto (*fig*) to cut short; **~ la corda** (*fig*) to
sneak off; **~ i ponti (con)** (*fig*) to break off
relations (with); **mi sono tagliato** I've cut
myself

taglia'telle [taʎʎa'tɛlle] SFPL tagliatelle *pl*

tagli'ato, -a [taʎ'ʎato] AG: **essere ~ per qc** (*fig*)
to be cut out for sth

taglia'trice [taʎʎa'tritʃe] SF (*Tecn*) cutter

taglia'unghie [taʎʎa'ungje] SM INV nail
clippers *pl*

taglieggi'are [taʎʎed'dʒare] /**62**/ VT to exact a
tribute from

tagli'ente [taʎ'ʎɛnte] AG sharp

t

tagli'ere [taʎ'ʎere] SM chopping board; (*per il pane*) bread board

'**taglio** ['taʎʎo] SM (*anche fig*) cut; (*azione*) cutting *no pl*; (*di carne*) piece; (*parte tagliente*) cutting edge; (*di abito*) cut, style; (*di stoffa*) length; (*di vini*) blending; **di ~** on edge, edgeways; **banconote di piccolo/grosso ~** notes of small/large denomination; **un bel ~ di capelli** a nice haircut *o* hairstyle; **pizza al ~** pizza by the slice; **~ cesareo** Caesarean section

tagli'ola [taʎ'ʎola] SF trap, snare

tagli'one [taʎ'ʎone] SM: **la legge del ~** the concept of an eye for an eye and a tooth for a tooth

tagliuz'zare [taʎʎut'tsare] /72/ VT to cut into small pieces

Ta'hiti [ta'iti] SF Tahiti

tailan'dese AG, SMF, SM Thai

Tai'landia SF: **la ~** Thailand

tai'lleur [ta'jœr] SM INV lady's suit

'**talamo** SM (*poetico*) marriage bed

'**talco** SM talcum powder

'**tale** DET **1** (*simile, così grande*) such; **un(a) tale ...** such a ...; **non accetto tali discorsi** I won't allow such talk; **è di una tale arroganza** he is so arrogant; **fa una tale confusione!** he makes such a mess!
2 (*persona o cosa indeterminata*) such-and-such; **il giorno tale all'ora tale** on such-and-such a day at such-and-such a time; **la tal persona** that person; **ha telefonato una tale Giovanna** somebody called Giovanna phoned
3 (*nelle similitudini*): **tale ... tale** like ... like; **tale padre tale figlio** like father, like son; **hai il vestito tale quale il mio** your dress is just *o* exactly like mine
▶ PRON (*indefinito: persona*): **un(a) tale** someone; **quel** (*o* **quella**) **tale** that person, that man (*o* woman); **il tal dei tali** what's-his-name

tale'bano SM Taliban

ta'lento SM talent

talis'mano SM talisman

talk-'show [tɔlk'ʃo] SM INV talk *o* chat show

tallo'nare /72/ VT to pursue; **~ il pallone** (*Calcio, Rugby*) to heel the ball

tallon'cino [tallon'tʃino] SM counterfoil (BRIT), stub; **~ del prezzo** (*di medicinali*) tear-off tag

tal'lone SM heel

tal'mente AV so

ta'lora AV = **talvolta**

'**talpa** SF (*Zool: anche fig*) mole

tal'volta AV sometimes, at times

tambu'rello SM tambourine

tambu'rino SM drummer boy

tam'buro SM drum; **freni a ~** drum brakes; **pistola a ~** revolver; **a ~ battente** (*fig*) immediately, at once

Ta'migi [ta'midʒi] SM: **il ~** the Thames

tampona'mento SM (*Aut*) collision; **~ a catena** pile-up

tampo'nare /72/ VT (*otturare*) to plug; (*urtare: macchina*) to crash *o* ram into

tam'pone SM (*Med*) wad, pad; (*per timbri*) ink-pad; (*respingente*) buffer; **~ assorbente** tampon

'**tamtam** SM INV (*fig*) grapevine

'**tana** SF lair, den; (*fig*) den, hideout

'**tanfo** SM (*di muffa*) musty smell; (*puzza*) stench

'**tanga** SM INV G-string

tan'gente [tan'dʒɛnte] AG (*Mat*): **~ a** tangential to ▶ SF tangent; (*quota*) share; (*denaro estorto*) rake-off (*col*), cut

tangen'topoli [tandʒɛn'tɔpoli] SF (*Pol, Media*) Bribesville; *see note*

> *Tangentopoli* refers to the corruption scandal of the early 1990s which involved a large number of politicians from all parties, including government ministers, as well as leading industrialists and business people. Subsequent investigations unearthed a complex series of illegal payments and bribes involving both public and private money. The scandal began in Milan, which came to be known as *Tangentopoli*, or "Bribesville".

tangenzi'ale [tandʒen'tsjale] SF (*strada*) bypass

'**Tangeri** ['tandʒeri] SF Tangiers

tan'gibile [tan'dʒibile] AG tangible

tangibil'mente [tandʒibilmente] AV tangibly

'**tango, -ghi** SM tango

'**tanica, -che** SF (*contenitore*) jerry can

tan'nino SM tannin

tan'tino: un ~ av (*un po'*) a little, a bit; (*alquanto*) rather

'**tanto, -a** DET **1** (*molto: quantità*) a lot of, much; (*: numero*) a lot of, many; **tanto pane/latte** a lot of bread/milk; **tanto tempo** a lot of time, a long time; **tanti auguri!** all the best!; **tante grazie** many thanks; **tanto persone** a lot of people, many people; **tante volte** many times, often; **ogni tanti chilometri** every so many kilometres
2 (*così tanto: quantità*) so much, such a lot of; (*: numero*) so many, such a lot of; **tanta fatica per niente!** a lot of trouble for nothing!;

ha tanto coraggio che ... he's got so much courage that ..., he's so brave that ...; **ho aspettato per tanto tempo** I waited so long *o* for such a long time
3: tanto ... quanto (*quantità*) as much ... as; (*numero*) as many ... as; **ho tanta pazienza quanta ne hai tu** I have as much patience as you have *o* as you; **ha tanti amici quanti nemici** he has as many friends as he has enemies
▶ PRON **1** (*molto*) much, a lot; (*così tanto*) so much, such a lot; **tanti/tante** many, a lot; so many; such a lot; **credevo ce ne fosse tanto** I thought there was (such) a lot, I thought there was plenty; **una persona come tante** a person just like any other; **è passato tanto** (*tempo*) it's been so long; **è tanto che aspetto** I've been waiting for a long time; **tanto di guadagnato!** so much the better!
2: tanto quanto (*denaro*) as much as; (*cioccolatini*) as many as; **ne ho tanto quanto basta** I have as much as I need; **due volte tanto** twice as much
3 (*indeterminato*) so much; **tanto per l'affitto, tanto per il gas** so much for the rent, so much for the gas; **costa un tanto al metro** it costs so much per metre; **di tanto in tanto**, **ogni tanto** every so often; **tanto vale che** ... I (*o* we *etc*) may as well ...; **tanto meglio!** so much the better!; **tanto peggio per lui!** so much the worse for him!; **se tanto mi dà tanto** if that's how things are; **guardare qc con tanto d'occhi** to gaze wide-eyed at sth
▶ AV **1** (*molto*) very; **vengo tanto volentieri** I'd be very glad to come; **non ci vuole tanto a capirlo** it doesn't take much to understand it
2 (*così tanto: con ag, av*) so; (: *con vb*) so much, such a lot; **è tanto bella!** she's so beautiful!; **non urlare tanto (forte)** don't shout so much; **sto tanto meglio adesso** I'm so much better now; **era tanto bella da non credere** she was incredibly beautiful; **tanto ... che** so ... (that); **tanto ... da** so ... as
3: tanto ... quanto as ... as; **conosco tanto Carlo quanto suo padre** I know both Carlo and his father; **non è poi tanto complicato quanto sembra** it's not as difficult as it seems; **è tanto bella quanto buona** she is as good as she is beautiful; **tanto più insisti, tanto più non mollerà** the more you insist, the more stubborn he'll be; **quanto più ... tanto meno** the more ... the less; **quanto più lo conosco tanto meno mi piace** the better I know him the less I like him

4 (*solamente*) just; **tanto per cambiare/scherzare** just for a change/a joke; **una volta tanto** for once
5 (*a lungo*) (for) long
▶ CONG after all; **non insistere, tanto è inutile** don't keep on, it's no use; **lascia stare, tanto è troppo tardi** forget it, it's too late

Tanza'nia [tandza'nia] SF: **la ~** Tanzania
tapi'oca SF tapioca
ta'piro SM (*Zool*) tapir
'tappa SF (*luogo di sosta, fermata*) stop, halt; (*parte di un percorso*) stage, leg; (*Sport*) lap; **a tappe** in stages; **bruciare le tappe** (*fig*) to be a whizz kid
tappa'buchi [tappa'buki] SM INV stopgap; **fare da ~** to act as a stopgap
tap'pare/72/ VT to plug, stop up; (*bottiglia*) to cork; **tapparsi** VPR: **tapparsi in casa** to shut o.s. up at home; **tapparsi la bocca** to shut up; **tapparsi il naso** to hold one's nose; **tapparsi le orecchie** to turn a deaf ear; **tapparsi gli occhi** to turn a blind eye
tappa'rella SF rolling shutter
tappe'tino SM (*per auto*) car mat; **~ antiscivolo** (*da bagno*) non-slip mat; **~ del mouse** mouse mat
tap'peto SM carpet; (*anche*: **tappetino**) rug; (*di tavolo*) cloth; (*Sport*): **andare al ~** to go down for the count; **mettere sul ~** (*fig*) to bring up for discussion
tappez'zare [tappet'tsare] /72/ VT (*con carta*) to paper; (*rivestire*): **~ qc (di)** to cover sth (with)
tappezze'ria [tappettse'ria] SF (*arredamento*) soft furnishings *pl*; (*tessuto*) tapestry; (*carta da parati*) wallpaper, wall covering; (*arte, di automobile*) upholstery; **far da ~** (*fig*) to be a wallflower
tappezzi'ere [tappet'tsjɛre] SM upholsterer
'tappo SM stopper; (*in sughero*) cork; **~ a corona** bottle top; **~ a vite** screw top
TAR SIGLA M = **Tribunale Amministrativo Regionale**
'tara SF (*peso*) tare; (*Med*) hereditary defect; (*difetto*) flaw
taran'tella SF tarantella
ta'rantola SF tarantula
ta'rare/72/ VT (*Comm*) to tare; (*Tecn*) to calibrate
ta'rato, -a AG (*Comm*) tared; (*Med*) with a hereditary defect
tara'tura SF (*Comm*) taring; (*Tecn*) calibration
tarchi'ato, -a [tar'kjato] AG stocky, thickset
tar'dare/72/ VI to be late ▶ VT to delay; **~ a fare** to delay doing
'tardi AV late; **più ~** later (on); **al più ~** at the latest; **sul ~** (*verso sera*) late in the day; **far ~**

to be late; (*restare alzato*) to stay up late; **è troppo ~** it's too late

tar'divo, -a AG (*primavera*) late; (*rimedio*) belated, tardy; (*fig: bambino*) retarded

'tardo, -a AG (*lento, fig: ottuso*) slow; (*tempo: avanzato*) late

tar'dona SF (*peg*): **essere una ~** to be mutton dressed as lamb

targa, -ghe SF plate; (*Aut*) number (BRIT) o license (US) plate; *vedi anche* **circolazione**

tar'gare /80/ VT (*Aut*) to register

targ'hetta [tar'getta] SF (*con nome: su porta*) nameplate; (*: su bagaglio*) name tag

ta'riffa SF (*gen*) rate, tariff; (*di trasporti*) fare; (*elenco*) price list; tariff; **la ~ in vigore** the going rate; **~ normale/ ridotta** standard/reduced rate; (*su mezzi di trasporto*) full/concessionary fare; **~ salariale** wage rate; **~ unica** flat rate; **tariffe doganali** customs rates o tariff; **tariffe postali/telefoniche** postal/telephone charges

tarif'fario, -ii AG: **aumento ~** increase in charges o rates ▶ SM tariff, table of charges

'tarlo SM woodworm

'tarma SF moth

tarmi'cida, -i [tarmi'tʃida] AG, SM moth-killer

ta'rocco, -chi SM tarot card; **tarocchi** SMPL (*gioco*) tarot *sg*

tar'pare /72/ VT (*fig*): **~ le ali a qn** to clip sb's wings

tartagli'are [tartaʎ'ʎare] /27/ VI to stutter, stammer

'tartaro, -a AG, SM (*in tutti i sensi*) tartar

tarta'ruga, -ghe SF tortoise; (*di mare*) turtle; (*materiale*) tortoiseshell

tartas'sare /72/ VT (*col*): **~ qn** to give sb the works; **~ qn a un esame** to give sb a grilling at an exam

tar'tina SF canapé

tar'tufo SM (*Bot*) truffle

'tasca, -sche SF pocket; **da ~** pocket *cpd*; **fare i conti in ~ a qn** (*fig*) to meddle in sb's affairs

tas'cabile AG (*libro*) pocket *cpd*

tasca'pane SM haversack

tas'chino [tas'kino] SM breast pocket

Tas'mania SF: **la ~** Tasmania

'tassa SF (*imposta*) tax; (*doganale*) duty; (*per iscrizione: a scuola ecc*) fee; **~ di circolazione/di soggiorno** road/tourist tax

tas'sametro SM taximeter

tas'sare /72/ VT to tax; to levy a duty on

tassa'tivo, -a AG peremptory

tassazi'one [tassat'tsjone] SF taxation; **soggetto a ~** taxable

tas'sello SM (*di legno, pietra*) plug; (*assaggio*) wedge

tassì SM INV = **taxi**

tas'sista, -i, -e SM/F taxi driver

'tasso SM (*di natalità, d'interesse ecc*) rate; (*Bot*) yew; (*Zool*) badger; **~ di cambio/d'interesse** rate of exchange/interest; **~ di crescita** growth rate

tas'tare /72/ VT to feel; **~ il terreno** (*fig*) to see how the land lies

tasti'era SF keyboard

tastie'rino SM: **~ numerico** numeric keypad

'tasto SM key; (*tatto*) touch, feel; **toccare un ~ delicato** (*fig*) to touch on a delicate subject; **toccare il ~ giusto** (*fig*) to strike the right note; **~ funzione** (*Inform*) function key; **~ delle maiuscole** (*su macchina da scrivere ecc*) shift key

tas'toni AV: **procedere (a) ~** to grope one's way forward

'tata SF (*linguaggio infantile*) nanny

'tattico, -a, -ci, -che AG tactical ▶ SF tactics *pl*

'tatto SM (*senso*) touch; (*fig*) tact; **duro al ~** hard to the touch; **aver ~** to be tactful, have tact

tatu'aggio [tatu'addʒo] SM tattooing; (*disegno*) tattoo

tatu'are /72/ VT to tattoo

tauma'turgico, -a, -ci, -che [tauma'turdʒiko] AG (*fig*) miraculous

TAV [tav] SM O F INV (= *treno alta velocità*) high-speed train; (*sistema*) high-speed rail system

ta'verna SF (*osteria*) tavern

'tavola SF table; (*asse*) plank, board; (*lastra*) tablet; (*quadro*) panel (painting); (*illustrazione*) plate; **~ calda** snack bar; **~ pieghevole** folding table; **~ rotonda** (*fig*) round table; **~ a vela** windsurfer

tavo'lata SF company at table

tavo'lato SM boarding; (*pavimento*) wooden floor

tavo'letta SF tablet, bar; **a ~** (*Aut*) flat out

tavo'lino SM small table; (*scrivania*) desk; **~ da tè/gioco** coffee/card table; **mettersi a ~** to get down to work; **decidere qc a ~** (*fig*) to decide sth on a theoretical level

'tavolo SM table; **~ da disegno** drawing board; **~ da lavoro** desk; (*Tecn*) workbench; **~ operatorio** (*Med*) operating table

tavo'lozza [tavo'lɔttsa] SF (*Arte*) palette

'taxi SM INV taxi

'tazza ['tattsa] SF cup; **~ da caffè/tè** coffee/ tea cup; **una ~ di caffè/tè** a cup of coffee/tea

taz'zina [tat'tsina] SF coffee cup

TBC ABBR F (= *tubercolosi*) TB

TCI SIGLA M = **Touring Club Italiano**

TE SIGLA = **Teramo**

te PRON (*soggetto: in forme comparative, oggetto*) you

tè SM INV tea; (*trattenimento*) tea party

tea'trale AG theatrical

te'atro SM theatre; ~ **comico** comedy; ~ **di posa** film studio

techno ['tɛkno] AG INV (*musica*) techno

'tecnico, -a, -ci, -che AG technical ▶ SM/F technician ▶ SF technique; (*tecnologia*) technology

tecnolo'gia [teknolo'dʒia] SF technology; **alta ~** high technology, hi-tech; **tecnologie ambientali** clean technology

tecno'logico, -a, -ci, -che [tekno'lɔdʒiko] AG technological

te'desco, -a, -schi, -sche AG, SM/F, SM German; ~ **orientale/occidentale** East/ West German

tedi'are /19/ VT (*infastidire*) to bother, annoy; (*annoiare*) to bore

'tedio SM tedium, boredom

tedi'oso, -a AG tedious, boring

te'game SM (*Cuc*) pan; **al ~** fried

'teglia ['teʎʎa] SF (*Cuc: per dolci*) (baking) tin (*BRIT*), cake pan (*US*); (: *per arrosti*) (roasting) tin

'tegola SF tile

Teh'ran SF Tehran

tei'era SF teapot

te'ina SF (*Chim*) theine

tel. ABBR (= *telefono*) tel.

'tela SF (*tessuto*) cloth; (*per vele, quadri*) canvas; (*dipinto*) canvas, painting; **di ~** (*calzoni*) (heavy) cotton *cpd*; (*scarpe, borsa*) canvas *cpd*; ~ **cerata** oilcloth; ~ **di ragno** spider's web

te'laio SM (*apparecchio*) loom; (*struttura*) frame

Tel A'viv SF Tel Aviv

tele... PREFISSO tele...

teleabbo'nato SM television licence holder

tele'camera SF television camera; ~ **TVCC** CCTV camera

telecoman'dare /72/ VT to operate by remote control

teleco'mando SM remote control; (*dispositivo*) remote-control device

telecomunicazi'oni [telekomunikat'tsjoni] SFPL telecommunications

teleconfe'renza SF teleconferencing

tele'cronaca, -che SF television report

telecro'nista, -i, -e SM/F (television) commentator

tele'ferica, -che SF cableway

tele'film SM INV television film

telefo'nare /72/ VI to telephone, ring; (*fare una chiamata*) to make a phone call ▶ VT to telephone; ~ **a qn** to phone o ring o call sb (up)

telefo'nata SF (telephone) call; ~ **urbana/ interurbana** local/long-distance call; ~ **a carico del destinatario** reverse charge (*BRIT*) o collect (*US*) call; ~ **con preavviso** person-to-person call

telefonica'mente AV by (tele)phone

tele'fonico, -a, -ci, -che AG (tele)phone *cpd*

telefo'nino SM (*cellulare*) mobile phone

telefo'nista, -i, -e SM/F telephonist; (*d'impresa*) switchboard operator

te'lefono SM telephone; **essere al ~** to be on the (tele)phone; ~ **a gettoni** ≈ pay phone; ~ **azzurro** ≈ Childline; ~ **fisso** landline; ~ **interno** internal phone; ~ **pubblico** public phone, call box (*BRIT*); ~ **rosa** ≈ rape crisis

telegior'nale [teledʒor'nale] SM television news (programme)

telegra'fare /41/ VT, VI to telegraph, cable

telegra'fia SF telegraphy

tele'grafico, -a, -ci, -che AG telegraph *cpd*, telegraphic

telegra'fista, -i, -e SM/F telegraphist, telegraph operator

te'legrafo SM telegraph; (*ufficio*) telegraph office

tele'gramma, -i SM telegram

telela'voro SM teleworking

tele'matica SF data transmission; telematics *sg*

teleno'vela SF soap opera

teleobiet'tivo SM telephoto lens *sg*

Tele'pass® SM INV *automatic payment card for use on Italian motorways*

telepa'tia SF telepathy

tele'quiz [tele'kwits] SM INV (*TV*) game show

teles'chermo [teles'kɛrmo] SM television screen

teles'copio SM telescope

telescri'vente SF teleprinter (*BRIT*), teletypewriter (*US*)

teleset'tivo, -a AG: **prefisso ~** dialling code (*BRIT*), dial code (*US*)

teleselezi'one [teleselet'tsjone] SF direct dialling

telespetta'tore, -'trice SM/F (television) viewer

tele'text SM INV teletext

tele'vendita [tele'vendita] SF teleshopping

tele'video SM *videotext service*

televisi'one SF television; *see note*

> Three state-owned channels, RAI 1, 2 and 3, and a large number of private companies broadcast television programmes in Italy. Some of the latter function at purely local level, while others are regional; some form part of a network, while others remain independent. As a public corporation, RAI reports to the Post and Telecommunications Ministry. Both RAI and the private-sector channels compete for advertising revenues.

televi'sore SM television set

'telex SM INV telex

'telo SM length of cloth

te'lone SM (*per merci ecc*) tarpaulin; (*sipario*) drop curtain

'tema, -i SM theme; (*Ins*) essay, composition

te'matica SF basic themes *pl*

teme'rario, -a AG rash, reckless

te'mere /**29**/ VT to fear, be afraid of; (*essere sensibile a: freddo, calore*) to be sensitive to ▶ VI to be afraid; (*essere preoccupato*): ~ **per** to worry about, fear for; ~ **di/che** to be afraid of/that

'tempera SF (*pittura*) tempera; (*dipinto*) painting in tempera

temperama'tite SM INV pencil sharpener

tempera'mento SM temperament

tempe'rante AG moderate

tempe'rare /**72**/ VT (*aguzzare*) to sharpen; (*fig*) to moderate, control, temper

tempe'rato, -a AG moderate, temperate; (*clima*) temperate

tempera'tura SF temperature; ~ **ambiente** room temperature

tempe'rino SM penknife

tem'pesta SF storm; ~ **di sabbia/neve** sand/snowstorm

tempes'tare /**72**/ VT (*percuotere*): ~ **qn di colpi** to rain blows on sb; (*bombardare*) ~ **qn di domande** to bombard sb with questions; (*ornare*) to stud

tempestività SF timeliness

tempes'tivo, -a AG timely

tempes'toso, -a AG stormy

'tempia SF (*Anat*) temple

'tempio SM (*edificio*) temple

tem'pismo SM sense of timing

tem'pistiche [tem'pistike] SFPL (*Comm*) time and motion

'tempo SM (*Meteor*) weather; (*cronologico*) time; (*epoca*) time, times *pl*; (*di film, gioco: parte*) part; (*Mus*) time; (*: battuta*) beat; (*Ling*) tense; **che ~ fa?** what's the weather like?; **un ~** once; **da ~** for a long time now; **~ fa** some time ago; **poco ~ dopo** not long after; **a ~ e luogo** at the right time and place; **ogni cosa a suo ~** we'll (*o* you'll *etc*) deal with it in due course; **al ~ stesso** *o* **a un ~** at the same time; **per ~** early; **per qualche ~** for a while; **trovare il ~ di fare qc** to find the time to do sth; **aver fatto il proprio ~** to have had its (*o* his *etc*) day; **primo/secondo ~** (*Teat*) first/second part; (*Sport*) first/second half; **rispettare i tempi** to keep to the timetable; **stringere i tempi** to speed things up; **con i tempi che corrono** these days; **in questi ultimi tempi** of late; **ai miei tempi** in my day; **~ di cottura** cooking time; **in ~ utile** in due time *o* course; **a ~ pieno** full-time; **~ libero** free time; **tempi di esecuzione** (*Comm*) time scale *sg*; **tempi di lavorazione** (*Comm*) throughput time *sg*; **tempi morti** (*Comm*) downtime *sg*, idle time *sg*

tempo'rale AG temporal ▶ SM (*Meteor*) (thunder)storm

tempora'lesco, -a, -schi, -sche AG stormy

tempo'raneo, -a AG temporary

temporeggi'are [tempored'dʒare] /**62**/ VI to play for time, temporize

'tempra SF (*Tecn: atto*) tempering, hardening; (*: effetto*) temper; (*fig: costituzione fisica*) constitution; (*: intellettuale*) temperament

tem'prare /**72**/ VT to temper

te'nace [te'natʃe] AG strong, tough; (*fig*) tenacious

te'nacia [te'natʃa] SF tenacity

te'naglie [te'naʎʎe] SFPL pincers *pl*

'tenda SF (*riparo*) awning; (*di finestra*) curtain; (*per campeggio ecc*) tent

ten'daggio [ten'daddʒo] SM curtaining, curtains *pl*, drapes *pl* (*US*)

ten'denza [ten'dɛntsa] SF tendency; (*orientamento*) trend; **avere ~ a** *o* **per qc** to have a bent for sth; **~ al rialzo/ribasso** (*Borsa*) upward/downward trend

tendenziosità [tendentsjosi'ta] SF tendentiousness

tendenzi'oso, -a [tenden'tsjoso] AG tendentious, bias(s)ed

'tendere /**120**/ VT (*allungare al massimo*) to stretch, draw tight; (*porgere: mano*) to hold out; (*fig: trappola*) to lay, set ▶ VI: ~ **a qc/a fare** to tend towards sth/to do; **tutti i nostri sforzi sono tesi a …** all our efforts are geared towards …; ~ **l'orecchio** to prick up one's ears; **il tempo tende al caldo** the weather is getting hot; **un blu che tende al verde** a greenish blue

ten'dina SF curtain

'tendine SM tendon, sinew

ten'done SM (*da circo*) big top

ten'dopoli SF INV (large) camp

'tenebre SFPL darkness *sg*

tene'broso, -a AG dark, gloomy

te'nente SM lieutenant

te'nere /**121**/ VT to hold; (*conservare, mantenere*) to keep; (*ritenere, considerare*) to consider; (*occupare: spazio*) to take up, occupy; (*seguire: strada*) to keep to; (*dare: lezione, conferenza*) to give ▶ VI to hold; (*colori*) to be fast; (*dare importanza*): ~ **a** to care about; ~ **a fare** to want to do, be keen to do; **tenersi** VPR (*stare in una determinata posizione*) to stand; (*stimarsi*) to consider o.s.; (*aggrapparsi*): **tenersi a** to hold on to; (*attenersi*): **tenersi a** to stick to; ~ **in gran conto** *o* **considerazione qn** to have a high regard for sb, think highly of sb; ~ **una conferenza** to give a lecture; ~ **conto di qc** to take sth into consideration; ~ **presente qc** to bear sth in mind; **non ci sono scuse che tengano** I'll take no excuses; **tenersi**

per la mano (*uso reciproco*) to hold hands;
tenersi in piedi to stay on one's feet
tene'rezza [tene'rettsa] SF tenderness
'tenero, -a AG tender; (*pietra, cera, colore*) soft;
(*fig*) tender, loving ▶ SM: **tra quei due c'è
del ~** there's a romance budding between
those two
'tengoetc VB vedi **tenere**
'tenia SF tapeworm
'tennietc VB vedi **tenere**
'tennis SM tennis; **~ da tavolo** table tennis
ten'nista, -i, -e SM/F tennis player
te'nore SM (*tono*) tone; (*Mus*) tenor; **~ di vita**
way of life; (*livello*) standard of living
tensi'one SF tension; **ad alta ~** (*Elettr*)
high-voltage *cpd*, high-tension *cpd*
tentaco'lare AG tentacular; (*fig: città*)
magnet-like
ten'tacolo SM tentacle
ten'tare/72/ VT (*indurre*) to tempt; (*provare*):
~ qc/di fare to attempt *o* try sth/to do;
~ la sorte to try one's luck
tenta'tivo SM attempt
tentazi'one [tentat'tsjone] SF temptation;
aver la ~ di fare to be tempted to do
tentenna'mento SM (*fig*) hesitation,
wavering; **dopo molti tentennamenti**
after much hesitation
tenten'nare/72/ VI to shake, be unsteady;
(*fig*) to hesitate, waver ▶ VT: **~ il capo** to
shake one's head
ten'toni AV: **andare a ~** (*anche fig*) to grope
one's way
'tenue AG (*sottile*) fine; (*colore*) soft; (*fig*)
slender, slight
te'nuta SF (*capacità*) capacity; (*divisa*)
uniform; (*abito*) dress; (*Agr*) estate; **a ~ d'aria**
airtight; **~ di strada** roadholding power; **in
~ da lavoro** in one's working clothes; **in ~ da
sci** in a skiing outfit
teolo'gia [teolo'dʒia] SF theology
teo'logico, -a, -ci, -che[teo'lɔdʒiko] AG
theological
te'ologo, -gi SM theologian
teo'rema, -i SM theorem
teo'ria SF theory; **in ~** in theory, theoretically
te'orico, -a, -ci, -che AG theoretic(al) ▶ SM
theorist, theoretician; **a livello ~, in linea
teorica** theoretically
teoriz'zare [teorid'dzare] /72/ VT to theorize
'tepido, -a AG = **tiepido**
te'pore SM warmth
'teppa SF mob, hooligans *pl*
tep'paglia [tep'paʎʎa] SF hooligans *pl*
tep'pismo SM hooliganism
tep'pista, -i SM hooligan
tera'peutico, -a, -ci, -che AG therapeutic
tera'pia SF therapy; **~ di gruppo** group
therapy; **~ intensiva** intensive care

tera'pista, -i, -e SM/F therapist
tergicris'tallo [terdʒikris'tallo] SM
windscreen (*BRIT*) *o* windshield (*US*) wiper
tergiver'sare [terdʒiver'sare] /72/ VI to
shilly-shally
'tergo SM: **a ~** behind; **vedi a ~** please turn
over
'terital® SM INV Terylene®
ter'male AG thermal; **stazione** *sf* ~ spa
'terme SFPL thermal baths
'termico, -a, -ci, -che AG thermal; **centrale
termica** thermal power station
termi'nale AG (*fase, parte*) final; (*Med*)
terminal ▶ SM terminal; **tratto ~** (*di fiume*)
lower reaches *pl*
termi'nare/72/ VT to end; (*lavoro*) to finish
▶ VI to end
terminazi'one [terminat'tsjone] SF (*fine*)
end; (*Ling*) ending; **terminazioni nervose**
(*Anat*) nerve endings
'termine SM term; (*fine, estremità*) end; (*di
territorio*) boundary, limit; **fissare un ~** to set
a deadline; **portare a ~ qc** to bring sth to a
conclusion; **contratto a ~** (*Comm*) forward
contract; **a breve/lungo ~** short-/long-term;
ai termini di legge by law; **in altri termini**
in other words; **parlare senza mezzi
termini** to talk frankly, not to mince one's
words
terminolo'gia [terminolo'dʒia] SF
terminology
'termite SF termite
termoco'perta SF electric blanket
ter'mometro SM thermometer
termonucle'are AG thermonuclear
'termos SM INV = **thermos**
termosi'fone SM radiator; (*riscaldamento
a*) ~ central heating
ter'mostato SM thermostat
'terna SF set of three; (*lista di tre nomi*) list of
three candidates
'terno SM (*al lotto ecc*) (set of) three winning
numbers; **vincere un ~ al lotto** (*fig*) to hit
the jackpot
'terra SF (*gen, Elettr*) earth; (*sostanza*) soil,
earth; (*opposto al mare*) land *no pl*; (*regione,
paese*) land; (*argilla*) clay; **terre**SFPL
(*possedimento*) lands, land *sg*; **a *o* per ~** (*stato*)
on the ground (*o* floor); (*moto*) to the ground,
down; **mettere a ~** (*Elettr*) to earth; **essere a
~** (*fig: depresso*) to be at rock bottom; **via ~**
(*viaggiare*) by land, overland; **strada in ~
battuta** dirt track; **~ di nessuno** no man's
land; **la T~ Santa** the Holy Land; **~ di Siena**
sienna; **~ ~** (*fig: persona, argomento*) prosaic,
pedestrian
'terra-'aria AG INV (*Mil*) ground-to-air
terra'cotta SF terracotta; **vasellame di ~**
earthenware

terra'ferma SF dry land, terra firma; (*continente*) mainland

ter'raglia [ter'raʎʎa] SF pottery; **terraglie** SFPL (*oggetti*) crockery *sg*, earthenware *sg*

Terra'nova SF: **la ~** Newfoundland

terrapi'eno SM embankment, bank

'terra-'terra AG INV (*Mil*) surface-to-surface

ter'razza [ter'rattsa] SF, **ter'razzo** [ter'rattso] SM terrace

terremo'tato, -a AG (*zona*) devastated by an earthquake ▶ SM/F earthquake victim

terre'moto SM earthquake

ter'reno, -a AG (*vita, beni*) earthly ▶ SM (*suolo, fig*) ground; (*Comm*) land *no pl*, plot (of land); site; (*Sport, Mil*) field; **perdere ~** (*anche fig*) to lose ground; **un ~ montuoso** a mountainous terrain; **~ alluvionale** (*Geo*) alluvial soil

'terreo, -a AG (*viso, colorito*) wan

ter'restre AG (*superficie*) of the earth, earth's; (*di terra: battaglia, animale*) land *cpd*; (*Rel*) earthly, worldly

ter'ribile AG terrible, dreadful

ter'riccio [ter'rittʃo] SM soil

terri'ero, -a AG: **proprietà terriera** landed property; **proprietario ~** landowner

terrifi'cante AG terrifying

ter'rina SF (*zuppiera*) tureen

territori'ale AG territorial

terri'torio SM territory

ter'rone, -a SM/F *derogatory term used by Northern Italians to describe Southern Italians*

ter'rore SM terror; **avere il ~ di qc** to be terrified of sth

terro'rismo SM terrorism

terro'rista, -i, -e SM/F terrorist

terroriz'zare [terrorid'dzare] /**72**/ VT to terrorize

'terso, -a AG clear

'terza ['tɛrtsa] SF *vedi* **terzo**

ter'zetto [ter'tsetto] SM (*Mus*) trio, terzetto; (*di persone*) trio

terzi'ario, -a [ter'tsjarjo] AG (*Geo, Econ*) tertiary

ter'zino [ter'tsino] SM (*Calcio*) fullback, back

'terzo, -a ['tɛrtso] AG third ▶ SM (*frazione*) third; (*Dir*) third party ▶ SF (*gen*) third; (*Aut*) third (gear); (*di trasporti*) third class; (*Ins: elementare*) third year at primary school; (: *media*) third year at secondary school; (: *superiore*) sixth year at secondary school; **terzi** SMPL (*altri*) others, other people; **agire per conto di terzi** to act on behalf of a third party; **assicurazione contro terzi** third-party insurance (BRIT), liability insurance (US); **la terza età** old age; **il ~ mondo** the Third World; **di terz'ordine** third rate; **la terza pagina** (*Stampa*) the Arts page

'tesa SF brim; **a larghe tese** wide-brimmed

'teschio ['tɛskjo] SM skull

'tesi¹ SF INV thesis; **~ di laurea** degree thesis

'tesi² *etc* VB *vedi* **tendere**

'teso, -a PP *di* **tendere** ▶ AG (*tirato*) taut, tight; (*fig*) tense

tesore'ria SF treasury

tesori'ere SM treasurer

te'soro SM treasure; **il Ministero del T~** the Treasury; **far ~ dei consigli di qn** to take sb's advice to heart

'tessera SF (*documento*) card; (*di abbonato*) season ticket; (*di giornalista*) pass; **ha la ~ del partito** he's a party member; **~ elettorale** ballot paper

tesse'rare /**72**/ VT (*iscrivere*) to give a membership card to

tesse'rato, -a SM/F (*di società sportiva ecc*) (fully paid-up) member; (*Pol*) (card-carrying) member

'tessere /**1**/ VT to weave; **~ le lodi di qn** (*fig*) to sing sb's praises

'tessile AG, SM textile

tessi'tore, -'trice SM/F weaver

tessi'tura SF weaving

tes'suto SM fabric, material; (*Biol*) tissue; (*fig*) web

'test ['tɛst] SM INV test

'testa SF head; (*di cose: estremità, parte anteriore*) head, front; **50 euro a ~** 50 euros apiece *o* a head *o* per person; **a ~ alta** with one's head held high; **a ~ bassa** (*correre*) headlong; (*con aria dimessa*) with head bowed; **di ~** *ag* (*vettura ecc*) front; **dare alla ~** to go to one's head; **fare di ~ propria** to go one's own way; **in ~** (*Sport*) in the lead; **essere in ~ alla classifica** (*corridore*) to be number one; (*squadra*) to be at the top of the league table; (*disco*) to be top of the charts, be number one; **essere alla ~ di qc** (*società*) to be the head of; (*esercito*) to be at the head of; **tenere ~ a qn** (*nemico ecc*) to stand up to sb; **una ~ d'aglio** a bulb of garlic; **~ o croce?** heads or tails?; **avere la ~ dura** to be stubborn; **~ di serie** (*Tennis*) seed, seeded player

'testa-'coda SM INV (*Aut*) spin

testamen'tario, -a AG (*Dir*) testamentary; **le sue disposizioni testamentarie** the provisions of his will

testa'mento SM (*atto*) will, testament; **l'Antico/il Nuovo T~** (*Rel*) the Old/New Testament; **~ biologico** living will

testar'daggine [testar'daddʒine] SF stubbornness, obstinacy

tes'tardo, -a AG stubborn, pig-headed

tes'tare /**72**/ VT to test

tes'tata SF (*parte anteriore*) head; (*intestazione*) heading; **missile a ~ nucleare** missile with a nuclear warhead

'teste SMF witness

tes'ticolo SM testicle

testi'era SF (*del letto*) headboard; (*di cavallo*) headpiece

testi'mone SMF (*Dir*) witness; **fare da ~ alle nozze di qn** to be a witness at sb's wedding; **~ oculare** eye witness

testimoni'anza [testimo'njantsa] SF (*atto*) deposition; (*effetto*) evidence; (*fig: prova*) proof; **accusare qn di falsa ~** to accuse sb of perjury; **rilasciare una ~** to give evidence

testimoni'are /19/ VT to testify; (*fig*) to bear witness to, testify to ▶ VI to give evidence, testify; **~ il vero** to tell the truth; **~ il falso** to perjure o.s.

tes'tina SF (*di giradischi, registratore*) head

'testo SM text; **fare ~** (*di autore*) to be authoritative; (*fig: dichiarazione*) to carry weight; **questo libro non fa ~** this book is not essential reading

testoste'rone SM testosterone

testu'ale AG textual; **le sue parole testuali** his (*o* her) actual words

tes'tuggine [tes'tuddʒine] SF tortoise; (*di mare*) turtle

'tetano SM (*Med*) tetanus

'tetro, -a AG gloomy

'tetta SF (*col*) boob, tit

tetta'rella SF teat

'tetto SM roof; **abbandonare il ~ coniugale** to desert one's family; **~ a cupola** dome

tet'toia SF roofing; canopy

tet'tuccio [tet'tuttʃo] SM: **~ apribile** (*Aut*) sunroof

'Tevere SM: **il ~** the Tiber

TG [tid'ʒi], **tg** ABBR M (= *telegiornale*) TV news *sg*

'thermos® ['tɛrmos] SM INV vacuum *o* Thermos® flask

'thriller ['θrilə], **'thrilling** ['θriliŋ] SM INV thriller

ti PRON (*dav lo, la, li, le, ne diventa* **te**: *oggetto*) you; (*complemento di termine*) (to) you; (*riflessivo*) yourself; **ti aiuto?** can I give you a hand?; **te lo ha dato?** did he give it to you?; **ti sei lavato?** have you washed?

ti'ara SF (*Rel*) tiara

'Tibet SM: **il ~** Tibet

tibe'tano, -a AG, SM/F Tibetan

'tibia SF tibia, shinbone

tic SM INV tic, (*nervous*) twitch; (*fig*) mannerism

ticchet'tio [tikket'tio] SM (*di macchina da scrivere*) clatter; (*di orologio*) ticking; (*della pioggia*) patter

'ticchio ['tikkjo] SM (*ghiribizzo*) whim; (*tic*) tic, (*nervous*) twitch

'ticket SM INV (*Med*) prescription charge (BRIT)

ti'ene *etc* VB *vedi* **tenere**

ti'epido, -a AG lukewarm, tepid

ti'fare /72/ VI: **~ per** to be a fan of; (*parteggiare*) to side with

'tifo SM (*Med*) typhus; (*fig*): **fare il ~ per** to be a fan of

tifoi'dea SF typhoid

ti'fone SM typhoon

ti'foso, -a SM/F (*Sport ecc*) fan

tight ['tait] SM INV morning suit

tigi [ti'dʒi] SM INV TV news

'tiglio ['tiʎʎo] SM lime (tree), linden (tree)

'tigna ['tiɲɲa] SF (*Med*) ringworm

ti'grato, -a AG striped

'tigre SF tiger

tilt SM: **andare in ~** (*fig*) to go haywire

tim'ballo SM (*strumento*) kettledrum; (*Cuc*) timbale

tim'brare /72/ VT to stamp; (*annullare: francobolli*) to postmark; **~ il cartellino** to clock in

'timbro SM stamp; (*Mus*) timbre, tone

timi'dezza [timi'dettsa] SF shyness, timidity

'timido, -a AG shy; timid

'timo SM thyme

ti'mone SM (*Naut*) rudder

timoni'ere SM helmsman

timo'rato, -a AG conscientious; **~ di Dio** God-fearing

ti'more SM (*paura*) fear; (*rispetto*) awe; **avere ~ di qc/qn** (*paura*) to be afraid of sth/sb

timo'roso, -a AG timid, timorous

'timpano SM (*Anat*) eardrum; (*Mus*): **timpani** kettledrums, timpani

'tinca, -che SF (*Zool*) tench

ti'nello SM small dining room

'tingere ['tindʒere] /37/ VT to dye

'tino SM vat

ti'nozza [ti'nɔttsa] SF tub

'tinsi *etc* VB *vedi* **tingere**

'tinta SF (*materia colorante*) dye; (*colore*) colour (BRIT), color (US), shade

tinta'rella SF (*col*) (sun)tan

tintin'nare /72/ VI to tinkle

tintin'nio SM tinkling

'tinto, -a PP *di* **tingere**

tinto'ria SF (*officina*) dyeworks *sg*; (*lavasecco*) dry cleaner's (shop)

tin'tura SF (*operazione*) dyeing; (*colorante*) dye; **~ di iodio** tincture of iodine

'tipico, -a, -ci, -che AG typical

'tipo SM type; (*genere*) kind, type; (*col*) chap, fellow; **che ~ di...?** what kind of ...?; **vestiti di tutti i tipi** all kinds of clothes; **sul ~ di questo** of this sort; **sei un bel ~!** you're a fine one!

tipogra'fia SF typography; (*procedimento*) letterpress (printing); (*officina*) printing house

tipo'grafico, -a, -ci, -che AG typographic(al)

ti'pografo SM typographer

t

tip 'tap [tip'tap] SM (*ballo*) tap dancing

T.I.R. SIGLA M (= *Transports Internationaux Routiers*) *International Heavy Goods Vehicle*

'tira e 'molla SM INV tug-of-war

ti'raggio [ti'raddʒo] SM (*di camino ecc*) draught (*BRIT*), draft (*US*)

Ti'rana SF Tirana

tiranneggi'are [tiranned'dʒare] /62/ VT to tyrannize

tiran'nia SF tyranny

ti'ranno, -a AG tyrannical ▶ SM tyrant

ti'rante SM (*Naut, di tenda ecc*) guy; (*Edil*) brace

tirapi'edi SM INV/F INV hanger-on

tira'pugni [tira'puɲɲi] SM INV knuckle-duster

ti'rare /72/ VT (*gen*) to pull; (*chiudere: tenda ecc*) to draw, pull; (*tracciare, disegnare*) to draw, trace; (*lanciare: sasso, palla*) to throw; (*stampare*) to print; (*pistola, freccia*) to fire; (*estrarre*): ~ **qc da** to take *o* pull sth out of; to get sth out of; to extract sth from ▶ VI (*pipa, camino*) to draw; (*vento*) to blow; (*abito*) to be tight; (*fare fuoco*) to fire; (*fare del tiro, Calcio*) to shoot; ~ **qn da parte** to take *o* draw sb aside; ~ **un sospiro (di sollievo)** to heave a sigh (of relief); ~ **a indovinare** to take a guess; ~ **sul prezzo** to bargain; ~ **avanti** vi to struggle on, to keep going; vt (*: famiglia*) to provide for; (*: ditta*) to look after; ~ **fuori** (*estrarre*) to take out, pull out; ~ **giù** to pull down; (*abbassare*) to bring down, to lower; (*da scaffale ecc*) to take down; ~ **su** to pull up; (*capelli*) to put up; (*fig: bambino*) to bring up; **tirar dritto** to keep right on going; ~ **via** (*togliere*) to take off; **tirarsi indietro** to move back; (*fig*) to back out; **tirarsi su** to pull o.s. up; (*fig*) to cheer o.s. up; **tirati su!** cheer up!

ti'rato, -a AG (*teso*) taut; (*fig: teso, stanco*) drawn

tira'tore SM gunman; **un buon** ~ a good shot; ~ **scelto** marksman

tira'tura SF (*azione*) printing; (*di libro*) (print) run; (*di giornale*) circulation

tirchie'ria [tirkje'ria] SF meanness, stinginess

'tirchio, -a ['tirkjo] AG mean, stingy

tiri'tera SF drivel, hot air

'tiro SM shooting *no pl*, firing *no pl*; (*colpo, sparo*) shot; (*di palla: lancio*) throwing *no pl*; throw; (*fig*) trick; **essere a** ~ to be in range; **giocare un brutto** ~ *o* **un** ~ **mancino a qn** to play a dirty trick on s.b.; **cavallo da** ~ draught (*BRIT*) *o* draft (*US*) horse; ~ **a segno** target shooting; (*luogo*) shooting range; ~ **con l'arco** archery

tiroci'nante [tirotʃi'nante] AG, SM F apprentice *cpd*; trainee *cpd*

tiro'cinio [tiro'tʃinjo] SM apprenticeship; (*professionale*) training

ti'roide SF thyroid (gland)

tiro'lese AG, SM F Tyrolean, Tyrolese *inv*

Ti'rolo SM: **il** ~ the Tyrol

tir'rennico, -a, -ci, -che AG Tyrrhenian

Tir'reno SM: **il (mar)** ~ the Tyrrhenian Sea

ti'sana SF herb tea

'tisi SF (*Med*) consumption

'tisico, -a, -ci, -che AG (*Med*) consumptive; (*fig: gracile*) frail ▶ SM/F consumptive (person)

ti'tanico, -a, -ci, -che AG gigantic, enormous

ti'tano SM (*Mitologia, fig*) titan

tito'lare AG appointed; (*sovrano*) titular ▶ SM F incumbent; (*proprietario*) owner; (*Calcio*) regular player

tito'lato, -a AG (*persona*) titled

'titolo SM title; (*di giornale*) headline; (*Comm*) security; (*: diploma*) qualification; (*: azione*) share; **a che ~?** for what reason?; **a ~ di amicizia** out of friendship; **a ~ di cronaca** for your information; **a ~ di premio** as a prize; ~ **di credito** share; ~ **obbligazionario** bond; ~ **al portatore** bearer bond; ~ **di proprietà** title deed; **titoli di stato** government securities; **titoli di testa** (*Cine*) credits

titu'bante AG hesitant, irresolute

tivù SF INV (*col*) telly (*BRIT*), TV

'tizio, -a ['tittsjo] SM/F fellow, chap

tiz'zone [tit'tsone] SM brand

T.M.G. ABBR (= *tempo medio di Greenwich*) GMT

TN SIGLA = **Trento**

TNT SIGLA M (= *trinitrotoluolo*) TNT

TO SIGLA = **Torino**

toast [toust] SM INV toasted sandwich (*generally with ham and cheese*)

toc'cante AG touching

toc'care /20/ VT to touch; (*tastare*) to feel; (*fig: riguardare*) to concern; (*commuovere*) to touch, move; (*pungere*) to hurt, wound; (*far cenno a: argomento*) to touch on, mention ▶ VI: ~ **a** (*accadere*) to happen to; (*spettare*) to be up to; **tocca a te difenderci** it's up to you to defend us; **a chi tocca?** whose turn is it?; **mi toccò pagare** I had to pay; ~ **il fondo** (*in acqua*) to touch the bottom; (*fig*) to touch rock bottom; ~ **con mano** (*fig*) to find out for o.s.; ~ **qn sul vivo** to cut sb to the quick

tocca'sana SM INV cure-all, panacea

tocche'rò *etc* [tokke'rɔ] VB *vedi* **toccare**

'tocco, -chi SM touch; (*Arte*) stroke, touch

toe'letta SF = **toilette**

'toga, -ghe SF toga; (*di magistrato, professore*) gown

'togliere ['tɔʎʎere] /122/ VT (*rimuovere*) to take away (*o* off), remove; (*riprendere, non concedere più*) to take away, remove; (*Mat*) to take away, subtract; (*liberare*) to free; ~ **qc a qn** to take sth (away) from sb; **ciò non toglie che ...** nevertheless ..., be that as it may ...; **togliersi il cappello** to take off one's hat

'Togo SM: **il** ~ Togo

toilette [twa'lɛt] SF INV (*gabinetto*) toilet; (*cosmesi*) make-up; (*abbigliamento*) gown, dress; (*mobile*) dressing table; **fare ~** to get made up, make o.s. beautiful

'Tokyo SF Tokyo

to'letta SF = **toilette**

'tolgo *etc* VB *vedi* **togliere**

tolle'rante AG tolerant

tolle'ranza [tolle'rantsa] SF tolerance; **casa di ~** brothel

tolle'rare /**72**/ VT to tolerate; **non tollero repliche** I won't stand for objections; **non sono tollerati i ritardi** lateness will not be tolerated

To'losa SF Toulouse

'tolsi *etc* VB *vedi* **togliere**

'tolto, -a PP *di* **togliere**

to'maia SF (*di scarpa*) upper

'tomba SF tomb

tom'bale AG: **pietra ~** tombstone, gravestone

tom'bino SM manhole cover

'tombola SF (*gioco*) tombola; (*ruzzolone*) tumble

'tomo SM volume

tomogra'fia SF (*Med*) tomography; **~ assiale computerizzata** computerized axial tomography

tonaca, -che SF (*Rel*) habit

to'nare /**72**/ VI = **tuonare**

'tondo, -a AG round

'tonfo SM splash; (*rumore sordo*) thud; (*caduta*): **fare un ~** to take a tumble

'tonico, -a, -ci, -che AG tonic ▶ SM tonic; (*cosmetico*) toner

tonifi'cante AG invigorating, bracing

tonifi'care /**20**/ VT (*muscoli, pelle*) to tone up; (*irrobustire*) to invigorate, brace

ton'nara SF tuna-fishing nets *pl*

ton'nato, -a AG (*Cuc*): **salsa tonnata** tuna fish sauce; **vitello ~** veal with tuna fish sauce

tonnel'laggio [tonnel'laddʒo] SM (*Naut*) tonnage

tonnel'lata SF ton

'tonno SM tuna (fish)

'tono SM (*gen*, *Mus*) tone; (: *di pezzo*) key; (*di colore*) shade, tone; **rispondere a ~** (*a proposito*) to answer to the point; (*nello stesso modo*) to answer in kind; (*per le rime*) to answer back

ton'silla SF tonsil

tonsil'lite SF tonsillitis

ton'sura SF tonsure

'tonto, -a AG dull, stupid ▶ SM/F blockhead, dunce; **fare il finto ~** to play dumb

top [tɔp] SM INV (*vertice, camicetta*) top

to'paia SF (*di topo*) mousehole; (*di ratto*) rat's nest; (*fig: casa ecc*) hovel, dump

to'pazio [to'pattsjo] SM topaz

topi'cida, -i [topi'tʃida] SM rat poison

'topless ['tɔplis] SM INV topless bathing costume

'topo SM mouse; **~ d'albergo** (*fig*) hotel thief; **~ di biblioteca** (*fig*) bookworm

topogra'fia SF topography

topog'rafico, -a, -ci, -che AG topographic, topographical

to'ponimo SM place name

'toppa SF (*serratura*) keyhole; (*pezza*) patch

to'race [to'ratʃe] SM chest

'torba SF peat

'torbido, -a AG (*liquido*) cloudy; (*fiume*) muddy; (*fig*) dark; troubled ▶ SM: **pescare nel ~** (*fig*) to fish in troubled waters

'torcere ['tɔrtʃere] /**106**/ VT to twist; (*biancheria*) to wring (out); **torcersi** VPR to twist, writhe; **dare del filo da ~ a qn** to make life *o* things difficult for sb

torchi'are [tor'kjare] /**19**/ VT to press

'torchio ['tɔrkjo] SM press; **mettere qn sotto il ~** (*fig: col: interrogare*) to grill sb; **~ tipografico** printing press

'torcia, -ce ['tɔrtʃa] SF torch; **~ elettrica** torch (BRIT), flashlight (US)

torci'collo [tortʃi'kɔllo] SM stiff neck

'tordo SM thrush

to'rero SM bullfighter, toreador

tori'nese AG of (*o* from) Turin ▶ SMF person from Turin

To'rino SF Turin

tor'menta SF snowstorm

tormen'tare /**72**/ VT to torment; **tormentarsi** VPR to fret, worry o.s.

tor'mento SM torment

torna'conto SM advantage, benefit

tor'nado SM tornado

tor'nante SM hairpin bend (BRIT) *o* curve (US)

tor'nare /**72**/ VI to return, go (*o* come) back; (*ridiventare: anche fig*) to become (again); (*riuscire giusto, esatto: conto*) to work out; (*risultare*) to turn out (to be), prove (to be); **~ al punto di partenza** to start again; **~ a casa** to go (*o* come) home; **i conti tornano** the accounts balance; **~ utile** to prove *o* turn out to be useful; **torno a casa martedì** I'm going home on Tuesday

torna'sole SM INV litmus

tor'neo SM tournament

'tornio SM lathe

tor'nire /**55**/ VT (*Tecn*) to turn (on a lathe); (*fig*) to shape, polish

tor'nito, -a AG (*gambe, caviglie*) well-shaped

'toro SM bull; **T~** Taurus; **essere del T~** to be Taurus

tor'pedine SF torpedo

torpedini'era SF torpedo boat

tor'pore SM torpor

'torre SF tower; (*Scacchi*) rook, castle; **~ di controllo** (*Aer*) control tower

torrefazi'one [torrefat'tsjone] SF roasting
torreggi'are [torred'dʒare] /**62**/ VI: ~ **(su)** to tower (over)
tor'rente SM torrent
torren'tizio, -a [torren'tittsjo] AG torrential
torrenzi'ale [torren'tsjale] AG torrential
tor'retta SF turret
'torrido, -a AG torrid
torri'one SM keep
tor'rone SM nougat
'torsi etc VB vedi **torcere**
torsi'one SF twisting; (Tecn) torsion
'torso SM torso, trunk; (Arte) torso; **a ~ nudo** bare-chested
'torsolo SM (di cavolo ecc) stump; (di frutta) core
'torta SF cake
tortel'lini SMPL (Cuc) tortellini
torti'era SF cake tin (BRIT), cake pan (US)
'torto, -a PP di **torcere** ▸ AG (ritorto) twisted; (storto) twisted, crooked ▸ SM (ingiustizia) wrong; (colpa) fault; **a ~** wrongly; **a ~ o a ragione** rightly or wrongly; **aver ~** to be wrong; **fare un ~ a qn** to wrong sb; **essere/passare dalla parte del ~** to be/put o.s. in the wrong; **lui non ha tutti i torti** there's something in what he says
'tortora SF turtle dove
tortu'oso, -a AG (strada) twisting; (fig) tortuous
tor'tura SF torture
tortu'rare /**72**/ VT to torture
'torvo, -a AG menacing, grim
tosa'erba SM O F INV (lawn)mower
to'sare /**72**/ VT (pecora) to shear; (cane) to clip; (siepe) to clip, trim
tosa'tura SF (di pecore) shearing; (di cani) clipping; (di siepi) trimming, clipping
Tos'cana SF: **la ~** Tuscany
tos'cano, -a AG, SM/F Tuscan ▸ SM (anche: **sigaro toscano**) strong Italian cigar
'tosse SF cough; **ho la ~** I've got a cough
tossicità [tossitʃi'ta] SF toxicity
'tossico, -a, -ci, -che AG toxic; (Econ): **titolo ~** toxic asset
tossicodipen'dente SMF drug addict
tossicodipen'denza [tossikodipen'dɛntsa] SF drug addiction
tossi'comane SMF drug addict
tossicoma'nia SF drug addiction
tos'sina SF toxin
tos'sire /**55**/ VI to cough
tosta'pane SM INV toaster
tos'tare /**72**/ VT to toast; (caffè) to roast
tosta'tura SF (di pane) toasting; (di caffè) roasting
'tosto, -a AG: **faccia tosta** cheek ▸ AV at once, immediately; **~ che** as soon as
to'tale AG, SM total
totalità SF: **la ~ di** all of, the total amount (o number) of; the whole (+n sg)

totali'tario, -a AG totalitarian; (totale) complete, total; **adesione totalitaria** complete support
totalita'rismo SM (Pol) totalitarianism
totaliz'zare [totalid'dzare] /**72**/ VT to total; (Sport: punti) to score
totalizza'tore [totaliddza'tore] SM (Tecn) totalizator; (Ippica) totalizator, tote (col)
to'tip SM gambling pool betting on horse racing
toto'calcio [toto'kaltʃo] SM gambling pool betting on football results, ≈ (football) pools pl (BRIT)
tou'pet [tu'pɛ] SM INV toupee
tour [tur] SM INV (giro) tour; (Ciclismo) tour de France
tour de 'force ['tur də 'fɔrs] SM INV (Sport: anche fig) tour de force
tour'née [tur'ne] SF tour; **essere in ~** to be on tour
to'vaglia [to'vaʎʎa] SF tablecloth
tovagli'olo [tovaʎ'ʎɔlo] SM napkin
'tozzo, -a ['tɔttso] AG squat ▸ SM: **~ di pane** crust of bread
TP SIGLA = **Trapani**
TR SIGLA = **Terni**
Tr ABBR (Comm) = **tratta**
tra PREP (di due persone, cose) between; (di più persone, cose) among(st); (tempo: entro) within, in; **prendere qn ~ le braccia** to take sb in one's arms; **litigano ~ (di) loro** they're fighting amongst themselves; **~ 5 giorni** in 5 days' time; **~ breve** o **poco** soon; **~ sé e sé** (parlare ecc) to oneself; **sia detto ~ noi ...** between you and me ...; **~ una cosa e l'altra** what with one thing and another
trabal'lante AG shaky
trabal'lare /**72**/ VI to stagger, totter
tra'biccolo SM (peg: auto) old banger (BRIT), jalopy
traboc'care /**20**/ VI to overflow
traboc'chetto [trabok'ketto] SM (fig) trap ▸ AG INV trap cpd; **domanda ~** trick question
traca'gnotto, -a [trakaɲ'ɲɔtto] AG dumpy ▸ SM/F dumpy person
tracan'nare /**72**/ VT to gulp down
'traccia, -ce ['trattʃa] SF (segno, striscia) trail, track; (orma) tracks pl; (residuo, testimonianza) trace, sign; (abbozzo) outline; **essere sulle tracce di qn** to be on sb's trail
tracci'are [trat'tʃare] /**14**/ VT to trace, mark (out); (disegnare) to draw; (fig: abbozzare) to outline; **~ un quadro della situazione** to outline the situation
tracci'ato [trat'tʃato] SM (grafico) layout, plan; **~ di gara** (Sport) race route
tra'chea [tra'kɛa] SF windpipe, trachea
tra'colla SF shoulder strap; **portare qc a ~** to carry sth over one's shoulder; **borsa a ~** shoulder bag

tra'collo SM (*fig*) collapse, ruin; ~ **finanziario** crash; **avere un** ~ (*Med*) to have a setback; (*Comm*) to collapse

traco'tante AG overbearing, arrogant

traco'tanza [trako'tantsa] SF arrogance

trad. ABBR = **traduzione**

tradi'mento SM betrayal; (*Dir, Mil*) treason; **a** ~ by surprise; **alto** ~ high treason

tra'dire/55/ VT to betray; (*coniuge*) to be unfaithful to; (*doveri: mancare*) to fail in; (*rivelare*) to give away, reveal; **ha tradito le attese di tutti** he let everyone down

tradi'tore, -trice SM/F traitor

tradizio'nale [tradittsjo'nale] AG traditional

tradizi'one [tradit'tsjone] SF tradition

tra'dotto, -a PP *di* **tradurre** ▶ SF (*Mil*) troop train

tra'durre/90/ VT to translate; (*spiegare*) to render, convey; (*Dir*): ~ **qn in carcere/ tribunale** to take sb to prison/court; ~ **in cifre** to put into figures; ~ **in atto** (*fig*) to put into effect

tradut'tore, -'trice SM/F translator

traduzi'one [tradut'tsjone] SF translation; (*Dir*) transfer

'trae VB *vedi* **trarre**

tra'ente SMF (*Econ*) drawer

trafe'lato, -a AG out of breath

traffi'cante SMF dealer; (*peg*) trafficker

traffi'care/20/ VI (*affaccendarsi*) to busy o.s.; (*commerciare*): ~ **(in)** to trade (in), deal (in) ▶ VT (*peg*) to traffic in

traffi'cato, -a AG (*strada, zona*) busy

'traffico, -ci SM traffic; (*commercio*) trade, traffic; ~ **aereo/ferroviario** air/rail traffic; ~ **di armi/droga** arms/drug trafficking; ~ **stradale** traffic

tra'figgere [tra'fiddʒere] **/104/** VT to run through, stab; (*fig*) to pierce

tra'fila SF procedure

trafi'letto SM (*di giornale*) short article

tra'fitto, -a PP *di* **trafiggere**

trafo'rare/72/ VT to bore, drill

tra'foro SM (*azione*) boring, drilling; (*galleria*) tunnel

trafu'gare/80/ VT to purloin

tra'gedia [tra'dʒɛdja] SF tragedy

'traggoetc VB *vedi* **trarre**

traghet'tare [traget'tare] **/72/** VT to ferry

tra'ghetto [tra'getto] SM crossing; (*barca*) ferry(boat)

tragicità [tradʒitʃi'ta] SF tragedy

'tragico, -a, -ci, -che ['tradʒiko] AG tragic ▶ SM (*autore*) tragedian; **prendere tutto sul** ~ (*fig*) to take everything far too seriously

tragi'comico, -a, -ci, -che [tradʒi'kɔmiko] AG tragicomic

tra'gitto [tra'dʒitto] SM (*passaggio*) crossing; (*viaggio*) journey

tragu'ardo SM (*Sport*) finishing line; (*fig*) goal, aim

'traietc VB *vedi* **trarre**

traiet'toria SF trajectory

trai'nante AG (*cavo, fune*) towing; (*fig: persona, settore*) driving

trai'nare/72/ VT to drag, haul; (*rimorchiare*) to tow

'training ['trɛiniŋ] SM INV training

'traino SM (*carro*) wagon; (*slitta*) sledge; (*carico*) load

tralasci'are [tralaʃ'ʃare] **/14/** VT (*studi*) to neglect; (*dettagli*) to leave out, omit

'tralcio ['traltʃo] SM (*Bot*) shoot

tra'liccio [tra'littʃo] SM (*tela*) ticking; (*struttura*) trellis; (*Elettr*) pylon

tram SM INV tram (*BRIT*), streetcar (*US*)

'trama SF (*filo*) weft, woof; (*fig: argomento, maneggio*) plot

traman'dare/72/ VT to pass on, hand down

tra'mare/72/ VT (*fig*) to scheme, plot

tram'busto SM turmoil

trames'tio SM bustle

tramez'zino [tramed'dzino] SM sandwich

tra'mezzo [tra'mɛddzo] SM partition

'tramite PREP through ▶ SM means *pl*; **agire/ fare da** ~ to act as/be a go-between

tramon'tana SF (*Meteor*) north wind

tramon'tare/72/ VI to set, go down

tra'monto SM setting; (*del sole*) sunset

tramor'tire/55/ VI to faint ▶ VT to stun

trampo'lino SM (*per tuffi*) springboard, diving board; (*per lo sci*) ski-jump

'trampolo SM stilt

tramu'tare/72/ VT: ~ **in** to change into

trance [tra:ns] SF INV (*di medium*) trance; **cadere in** ~ to fall into a trance

'trancia, -ce ['trantʃa] SF slice; (*cesoia*) shearing machine

tranci'are [tran'tʃare] **/14/** VT (*Tecn*) to shear

'trancio ['trantʃo] SM slice

tra'nello SM trap; **tendere un** ~ **a qn** to set a trap for sb; **cadere in un** ~ to fall into a trap

trangugi'are [trangu'dʒare] **/62/** VT to gulp down

'tranne PREP except (for), but (for); ~ **che** *cong* unless; **tutti i giorni** ~ **il venerdì** every day except o with the exception of Friday

tranquil'lante SM (*Med*) tranquillizer

tranquillità SF calm, stillness; quietness; peace of mind

tranquilliz'zare [trankwillid'dzare] **/72/** VT to reassure

tran'quillo, -a AG calm, quiet; (*bambino, scolaro*) quiet; (*sereno*) with one's mind at rest; **sta'** ~ don't worry

transat'lantico, -a, -ci, -che AG transatlantic ▶ SM transatlantic liner; (*Pol*) *corridor used as a meeting place by members of* *the lower chamber of the Italian Parliament*; *see note*

The *transatlantico* is a room in the Palazzo di Montecitorio which is used by *deputati* between parliamentary sessions for relaxation and conversation. It is also used for media interviews and press conferences.

tran'satto, -a PP *di* **transigere**

transazi'one [transat'tsjone] SF compromise; (*Dir*) settlement; (*Comm*) transaction, deal

tran'senna SF barrier

tran'setto SM transept

trans'genico, -a, -ci, -che [trans'dʒɛniko] AG genetically modified, GM; **pianta transgenica** GM crop; **cibo ~** GM food

transiberi'ano, -a AG trans-Siberian

tran'sigere [tran'sidʒere] /**47**/ VI (*Dir*) to reach a settlement; (*venire a patti*) to compromise, come to an agreement

tran'sistor SM INV, **transis'tore** SM transistor

transi'tabile AG passable

transi'tare /**72**/ VI to pass

transi'tivo, -a AG transitive

'transito SM transit; **di ~** (*merci*) in transit; (*stazione*) transit *cpd*; **"divieto di ~"** "no entry"; **"~ interrotto"** "road closed"

transi'torio, -a AG transitory, transient; (*provvisorio*) provisional

transizi'one [transit'tsjone] SF transition

tran'tran SM routine; **il solito ~** the same old routine

tran'via SF tramway (BRIT), streetcar line (US)

tranvi'ario, -a AG tram *cpd* (BRIT), streetcar *cpd* (US); **linea tranviaria** tramline, streetcar line

tranvi'ere SM (*conducente*) tram driver (BRIT), streetcar driver (US); (*bigliettaio*) tram *o* streetcar conductor

trapa'nare /**72**/ VT (*Tecn*) to drill

'trapano SM (*utensile*) drill; (*Med*) trepan

trapas'sare /**72**/ VT to pierce

trapas'sato SM (*Ling*) past perfect

tra'passo SM passage; **~ di proprietà** (*di case*) conveyancing; (*di auto ecc*) legal transfer

trape'lare /**72**/ VI to leak, drip; (*fig*) to leak out

tra'pezio [tra'pɛttsjo] SM (*Mat*) trapezium; (*attrezzo ginnico*) trapeze

trape'zista, -i, -e [trapet'tsista] SM/F trapeze artist

trapian'tare /**72**/ VT to transplant

trapi'anto SM transplanting; (*Med*) transplant; **~ cardiaco** heart transplant

'trappola SF trap

tra'punta SF quilt

'trarre /**123**/ VT to draw, pull; (*portare*) to take; (*prendere, tirare fuori*) to take (out), draw; (*derivare*) to obtain; **~ beneficio** *o* **profitto**

da qc to benefit from sth; **~ le conclusioni** to draw one's own conclusions; **~ esempio da qn** to follow sb's example; **~ guadagno** to make a profit; **~ qn d'impaccio** to get sb out of an awkward situation; **~ origine da qc** to have its origins *o* originate in sth; **~ in salvo** to rescue

trasa'lire /**55**/ VI to start, jump

trasan'dato, -a AG shabby

trasbor'dare /**72**/ VT to transfer; (*Naut*) to tran(s)ship ▶ VI (*Naut*) to change ship; (*Aer*) to change plane; (*Ferr*) to change (trains)

trascenden'tale [traʃʃenden'tale] AG transcendental

tra'scendere [traʃ'ʃendere] /**101**/ VT (*Filosofia, Rel*) to transcend; (*fig: superare*) to surpass, go beyond

tra'sceso, -a [traʃ'ʃeso] PP *di* **trascendere**

trasci'nare [traʃʃi'nare] /**72**/ VT to drag; **trascinarsi** VPR to drag o.s. along; (*fig*) to drag on

tras'correre /**28**/ VT (*tempo*) to spend, pass ▶ VI to pass

tras'corso, -a PP *di* **trascorrere** ▶ AG past ▶ SM mistake

tras'critto, -a PP *di* **trascrivere**

tras'crivere /**105**/ VT to transcribe

trascrizi'one [traskrit'tsjone] SF transcription

trascu'rare /**72**/ VT to neglect; (*non considerare*) to disregard

trascura'tezza [traskura'tettsa] SF carelessness, negligence

trascu'rato, -a AG (*casa*) neglected; (*persona*) careless, negligent

traseco'lato, -a AG astounded, amazed

trasferi'mento SM transfer; (*trasloco*) removal, move; **~ di chiamata** (*Tel*) call forwarding

trasfe'rire /**55**/ VT to transfer; **trasferirsi** VPR to move

tras'ferta SF transfer; (*indennità*) travelling expenses *pl*; (*Sport*) away game

trasfigu'rare /**72**/ VT to transfigure

trasfor'mare /**72**/ VT to transform, change; **trasformarsi** VPR to be transformed; **trasformarsi in qc** to turn into sth

trasforma'tore SM (*Elettr*) transformer

trasformazi'one [trasformat'tsjone] SF transformation

trasfusi'one SF (*Med*) transfusion

trasgre'dire /**55**/ VT to break, infringe; (*ordini*) to disobey, contravene

trasgressi'one SF breaking, infringement; disobeying

trasgres'sivo, -a AG (*personaggio, atteggiamento*) rule-breaking

trasgres'sore, trasgredi'trice [trazgredi'tritʃe] SM/F (*Dir*) transgressor

tras'lato, -a AG metaphorical, figurative

traslo'care /**20**/ VT to move, transfer; **traslocarsi** VPR to move

tras'loco, -chi SM removal

tras'messo, -a PP *di* **trasmettere**

tras'mettere /**63**/ VT (*passare*): ~ **qc a qn** to pass sth on to sb; (*mandare*) to send; (*Tecn, Tel, Med*) to transmit; (*TV, Radio*) to broadcast

trasmetti'tore SM transmitter

trasmissi'one SF (*gen, Fisica, Tecn*) transmission; (*passaggio*) transmission, passing on; (*TV, Radio*) broadcast

trasmit'tente SF transmitting *o* broadcasting station

traso'gnato, -a [trasoɲ'ɲato] AG dreamy

traspa'rente AG transparent

traspa'renza [traspa'rɛntsa] SF transparency; **guardare qc in ~** to look at sth against the light

traspa'rire /**112**/ VI to show (through)

tras'parso, -a PP *di* **trasparire**

traspi'rare /**72**/ VI to perspire; (*fig*) to come to light, leak out

traspirazi'one [traspirat'tsjone] SF perspiration

tras'porre /**77**/ VT to transpose

traspor'tare /**72**/ VT to carry, move; (*merce*) to transport, convey; **lasciarsi ~ (da qc)** (*fig*) to let o.s. be carried away (by sth)

tras'porto SM transport; (*fig*) rapture, passion; **con ~** passionately; **compagnia di ~** carriers *pl*; (*per strada*) hauliers *pl* (BRIT), haulers *pl* (US); **mezzi di ~** means of transport; **nave/aereo da ~** transport ship/ aircraft *inv*; **~ (funebre)** funeral procession; **~ marittimo/aereo** sea/air transport; **~ stradale** (road) haulage; **i trasporti pubblici** public transport

tras'posto, -a PP *di* **trasporre**

'trassi *etc* VB *vedi* **trarre**

trastul'lare /**72**/ VT to amuse; **trastullarsi** VPR to amuse o.s.

tras'tullo SM game

trasu'dare /**72**/ VI (*filtrare*) to ooze; (*sudare*) to sweat ▶ VT to ooze with

trasver'sale AG (*taglio, sbarra*) cross(-); (*retta*) transverse; running at right angles; **via ~** side street

trasvo'lare /**72**/ VT to fly over

'tratta SF (*Econ*) draft; **la ~ delle bianche** the white slave trade; **~ documentaria** documentary bill of exchange

tratta'mento SM treatment; (*servizio*) service; **ricevere un buon ~** (*cliente*) to get good service; **~ di bellezza** beauty treatment; **~ di fine rapporto** (*Comm*) severance pay

trat'tare /**72**/ VT (*gen*) to treat; (*commerciare*) to deal in; (*svolgere: argomento*) to discuss, deal with; (*negoziare*) to negotiate ▶ VI: ~ **di** to deal with; ~ **con** (*persona*) to deal with; **si tratta di ...** it's about ...; **si tratterebbe solo di poche ore** it would just be a matter of a few hours

tratta'tiva SF negotiation; **trattative** SFPL (*tra governi, stati*) talks; **essere in ~ con** to be in negotiation with

trat'tato SM (*testo*) treatise; (*accordo*) treaty; **~ commerciale** trade agreement; **~ di pace** peace treaty

trattazi'one [trattat'tsjone] SF treatment

tratteggi'are [tratted'dʒare] /**62**/ VT (*disegnare: a tratti*) to sketch, outline; (*: col tratteggio*) to hatch

trat'teggio [trat'teddʒo] SM hatching

tratte'nere /**121**/ VT (*far rimanere: persona*) to detain; (*intrattenere: ospiti*) to entertain; (*tenere, frenare, reprimere*) to hold back, keep back; (*astenersi dal consegnare*) to hold, keep; (*detrarre: somma*) to deduct; **trattenersi** VPR (*astenersi*) to restrain o.s., stop o.s.; (*soffermarsi*) to stay, remain; **sono stato trattenuto in ufficio** I was delayed at the office

tratteni'mento SM entertainment; (*festa*) party

tratte'nuta SF deduction

trat'tino SM dash; (*in parole composte*) hyphen

'tratto, -a PP *di* **trarre** ▶ SM (*di penna, matita*) stroke; (*parte*) part, piece; (*di strada*) stretch; (*di mare, cielo*) expanse; (*di tempo*) period (of time); **tratti** SMPL (*caratteristiche*) features; (*modo di*) ways, manners; **a un ~, d'un ~** suddenly

trat'tore SM tractor

tratto'ria SF (small) restaurant

'trauma, -i SM trauma; **~ cranico** concussion

trau'matico, -a, -ci, -che AG traumatic

traumatiz'zare [traumatid'dzare] /**72**/ VT (*Med*) to traumatize; (*fig: impressionare*) to shock

tra'vaglio [tra'vaʎʎo] SM (*angoscia*) pain, suffering; (*Med*) pains *pl*; **~ di parto** labour pains

trava'sare /**72**/ VT to pour; (*vino*) to decant

tra'vaso SM pouring; decanting

trava'tura SF beams *pl*

'trave SF beam

tra'veggole SFPL: **avere le ~** to be seeing things

tra'versa SF (*trave*) crosspiece; (*via*) sidestreet; (*Ferr*) sleeper (BRIT), (railroad) tie (US); (*Calcio*) crossbar

traver'sare /**72**/ VT to cross

traver'sata SF crossing; (*Aer*) flight, trip

traver'sie SFPL mishaps, misfortunes

traver'sina SF (*Ferr*) sleeper (BRIT), (railroad) tie (US)

t

tra'verso, -a AG oblique; **di ~** ag askew ▶ AV sideways; **andare di ~** (cibo) to go down the wrong way; **messo di ~** sideways on; **guardare di ~** to look askance at; **via traversa** side road; **ottenere qc per vie traverse** (fig) to obtain sth in an underhand way

travesti'mento SM disguise

traves'tire /**45**/ VT to disguise; **travestirsi** VPR to disguise o.s.

traves'tito SM transvestite

travi'are /**19**/ VT (fig) to lead astray

travi'sare /**72**/ VT (fig) to distort, misrepresent

travol'gente [travol'dʒɛnte] AG overwhelming

tra'volgere [tra'vɔldʒere] /**96**/ VT to sweep away, carry away; (fig) to overwhelm

tra'volto, -a PP di **travolgere**

trazi'one [trat'tsjone] SF traction; **~ anteriore/posteriore** (Aut) front-wheel/rear-wheel drive

tre NUM three

tre'alberi SM INV (Naut) three-master

'trebbia SF (Agr: operazione) threshing; (: stagione) threshing season

trebbi'are /**19**/ VT to thresh

trebbia'trice [trebbja'tritʃe] SF threshing machine

trebbia'tura SF threshing

'treccia, -ce ['trettʃa] SF plait, braid; **lavorato a trecce** (pullover ecc) cable-knit

trecen'tesco, -a, -schi, -sche [tretʃen'tesko] AG fourteenth-century

tre'cento [tre'tʃento] NUM three hundred ▶ SM: **il T~** the fourteenth century

tredi'cenne [tredi'tʃɛnne] AG, SMF thirteen-year-old

tredi'cesimo, -a [tredi'tʃɛzimo] NUM thirteenth ▶ SF Christmas bonus of a month's pay

'tredici ['treditʃi] NUM thirteen ▶ SM INV: **fare ~** (Totocalcio) to win the pools (BRIT)

'tregua SF truce; (fig) respite; **senza ~** non-stop, without stopping, uninterruptedly

tre'mante AG trembling, shaking

tre'mare /**72**/ VI to tremble, shake; **~ di** (freddo ecc) to shiver o tremble with; (paura, rabbia) to shake o tremble with

trema'rella SF shivers pl

tre'mendo, -a AG terrible, awful

tremen'tina SF turpentine

tre'mila NUM three thousand

'tremito SM trembling no pl; shaking no pl; shivering no pl

tremo'lare /**72**/ VI to tremble; (luce) to flicker; (foglie) to quiver

tremo'lio SM (vedi vi) tremble; flicker; quiver

tre'more SM tremor

'treno SM train; (Aut): **~ di gomme** set of tyres o (BRIT) o tires (US); **~ locale/diretto/**

espresso local/fast/express train; **~ merci** goods (BRIT) o freight train; **~ rapido** express (train) (for which supplement must be paid); **~ straordinario** special train; **~ viaggiatori** passenger train; see note

> There are several different types of train in Italy. Regionali and interregionali are local trains which stop at every small town and village; the former operate within regional boundaries, while the latter may cross them. Diretti are ordinary trains for which passengers do not pay a supplement; the main difference from espressi is that the latter are long-distance and mainly run at night. Intercity and eurocity are faster and entail a supplement. Rapidi only contain first-class seats, and the high-speed pendolino, which offers both first- and second-class travel, runs between the major cities.

'trenta NUM thirty ▶ SM INV (Ins): **~ e lode** full marks plus distinction o cum laude

tren'tenne AG, SMF thirty-year-old

tren'tennio SM period of thirty years

tren'tesimo, -a NUM thirtieth

tren'tina SF: **una ~ (di)** thirty or so, about thirty

tren'tino, -a AG of (o from) Trento

trepi'dante AG anxious

trepi'dare /**72**/ VI to be anxious; **~ per qn** to be anxious about sb

'trepido, -a AG anxious

treppi'ede SM tripod; (Cuc) trivet

tre'quarti SM INV three-quarter-length coat

'tresca, -sche SF (fig) intrigue; (: relazione amorosa) affair

'trespolo SM trestle

trevigi'ano, -a [trevi'dʒano] AG of (o from) Treviso

triango'lare AG triangular

tri'angolo SM triangle

tribo'lare /**72**/ VI (patire) to suffer; (fare fatica) to have a lot of trouble

tribolazi'one [tribolat'tsjone] SF suffering, tribulation

tri'bordo SM (Naut) starboard

tribù SF INV tribe

tri'buna SF (podio) platform; (in aule ecc) gallery; (di stadio) stand; **~ della stampa/riservata al pubblico** press/public gallery

tribu'nale SM; **presentarsi o comparire in ~** to appear in court; **~ militare** military tribunal; **~ supremo** supreme court

tribu'tare /**72**/ VT to bestow; **gli onori dovuti a qn** to pay tribute to sb

tribu'tario, -a AG (imposta) fiscal, tax cpd; (Geo): **essere ~ di** to be a tributary of

tri'buto SM tax; (fig) tribute
tri'checo, -chi [tri'kɛko] SM (Zool) walrus
tri'ciclo [tri'tʃiklo] SM tricycle
trico'lore AG three-coloured (BRIT), three-colored (US) ▶ SM tricolo(u)r; (bandiera italiana) Italian flag
tri'dente SM trident
trien'nale AG (che dura 3 anni) three-year cpd; (che avviene ogni 3 anni) three-yearly
tri'ennio SM period of three years
tries'tino, -a AG (o from) Trieste
tri'fase AG (Elettr) three-phase
tri'foglio [tri'fɔʎʎo] SM clover
trifo'lato, -a AG (Cuc) cooked in oil, garlic and parsley
'triglia ['triʎʎa] SF red mullet
trigonome'tria SF trigonometry
tril'lare /72/ VI (Mus) to trill
'trillo SM trill
tri'mestre SM period of three months; (Ins) term, quarter (US); (Comm) quarter
trimo'tore SM (Aer) three-engined plane
'trina SF lace
trin'cea [trin'tʃea] SF trench
trince'rare [trintʃe'rare] /72/ VT to entrench
trinci'are [trin'tʃare] /14/ VT to cut up
Trinidad SM: ~ **e Tobago** Trinidad and Tobago
Trinità SF (Rel) Trinity
'trio (pl **trii**) SM trio
trion'fale AG triumphal, triumphant
trion'fante AG triumphant
trion'fare /72/ VI to triumph, win; ~ **su** to triumph over, overcome
tri'onfo SM triumph
tripli'care /20/ VT to triple
'triplice ['triplitʃe] AG triple; **in ~ copia** in triplicate
'triplo, -a AG triple; treble ▶ SM: **il ~ (di)** three times as much (as); **la spesa è tripla** it costs three times as much
'tripode SM tripod
'Tripoli SF Tripoli
'trippa SF (Cuc) tripe
tri'pudio SM triumph, jubilation; (fig: di colori) galaxy
tris SM INV (Carte): ~ **d'assi/di re** etc three aces/kings etc
'triste AG sad; (luogo) dreary, gloomy
tris'tezza [tris'tettsa] SF sadness; gloominess
'tristo, -a AG (cattivo) wicked, evil; (meschino) sorry, poor
trita'carne SM INV mincer, grinder (US)
trita'ghiaccio [trita'gjattʃo] SM INV ice crusher
tri'tare /72/ VT to mince, grind (US)
trita'tutto SM INV mincer, grinder (US)
'trito, -a AG (tritàto) minced, ground (US); ~ **e ritrito** (idee, argomenti, frasi) trite, hackneyed
tri'tolo SM trinitrotoluene

tri'tone SM (Zool) newt
'trittico, -ci SM (Arte) triptych
tritu'rare /72/ VT to grind
tri'vella SF drill
trivel'lare /72/ VT to drill
trivellazi'one [trivellat'tsjone] SF drilling; **torre di ~** derrick
trivi'ale AG vulgar, low
trivialità SF INV (volgarità) coarseness, crudeness; (: osservazione) coarse o crude remark
tro'feo SM trophy
'trogolo SM (per maiali) trough
'troia SF (Zool) sow; (fig: peg) whore
troll [trɔl] SM INV (anche Internet) troll
'tromba SF (Mus) trumpet; (Aut) horn; ~ **d'aria** whirlwind; ~ **delle scale** stairwell
trombet'tista, -i, -e SM/F trumpeter, trumpet (player)
trom'bone SM trombone
trom'bosi SF thrombosis
tron'care /20/ VT to cut off; (spezzare) to break off
'tronco, -a, -chi, -che AG cut off; broken off; (Ling) truncated; (fig) cut short ▶ SM (Bot, Anat) trunk; (fig: tratto) section; (: pezzo: di lancia) stump; **licenziare qn in ~** (fig) to fire sb on the spot
troneggi'are [troned'dʒare] /62/ VI: ~ **(su)** to tower (over)
'tronfio, -a AG conceited
'trono SM throne
tropi'cale AG tropical
'tropico, -ci SM tropic; ~ **del Cancro/Capricorno** Tropic of Cancer/Capricorn; **i tropici** the tropics

PAROLA CHIAVE

'troppo, -a DET (in eccesso: quantità) too much; (: numero) too many; **ho messo troppo zucchero** I put too much sugar in; **c'era troppa gente** there were too many people; **fa troppo caldo** it's too hot
▶ PRON (in eccesso: quantità) too much; (: numero) too many; **ne hai messo troppo** you've put in too much; **meglio troppi che pochi** better too many than too few
▶ AV (eccessivamente: con ag, av) too; (: con vb) too much; **troppo amaro/tardi** too bitter/late; **lavora troppo** he works too much; **costa troppo** it costs too much; **troppo buono da parte tua!** (anche ironico) you're too kind!; **di troppo** too much; too many; **qualche tazza di troppo** a few cups too many; **5 euro di troppo** 5 euros too much; **essere di troppo** to be in the way

'trota SF trout
trot'tare /72/ VI to trot

trotterel'lare /72/ VI to trot along; (*bambino*) to toddle

'trotto SM trot

'trottola SF spinning top

tro'vare /72/ VT to find; (*giudicare*): **trovo che** I find *o* think that; **trovarsi** VPR (*reciproco: incontrarsi*) to meet; (*essere, stare*) to be; (*arrivare, capitare*) to find o.s.; **andare a ~ qn** to go and see sb; **~ qn colpevole** to find sb guilty; **trovo giusto/sbagliato che ...** I think/don't think it's right that ...; **trovarsi bene/male** (*in un luogo, con qn*) to get on well/badly; **trovarsi d'accordo con qn** to be in agreement with sb

tro'vata SF good idea; **~ pubblicitaria** advertising gimmick

trova'tello, -a SM/F foundling

truc'care /20/ VT (*falsare*) to fake; (*attore ecc*) to make up; (*travestire*) to disguise; (*Sport*) to fix; (*Aut*) to soup up; **truccarsi** VPR to make up (one's face)

trucca'tore, -'trice SM/F (*Cine, Teat*) make-up artist

'trucco, -chi SM trick; (*cosmesi*) make-up; **i trucchi del mestiere** the tricks of the trade

'truce ['trutʃe] AG fierce

truci'dare [trutʃi'dare] **/72/** VT to slaughter

'truciolo ['trutʃolo] SM shaving

'truffa SF fraud, swindle

truf'fare /72/ VT to swindle, cheat

truffa'tore, -'trice SM/F swindler, cheat

'truppa SF troop

TS SIGLA = **Trieste**

tu PRON you; **tu stesso(a)** you yourself; **dare del tu a qn** to address sb as "tu"; **trovarsi a tu per tu con qn** to find o.s. face to face with sb

'tua *vedi* **tuo**

'tuba SF (*Mus*) tuba; (*cappello*) top hat

tu'bare /72/ VI to coo

tuba'tura, tubazi'one [tubat'tsjone] SF piping *no pl*, pipes *pl*

tuberco'losi SF tuberculosis

'tubero SM (*Bot*) tuber

tu'betto SM tube

tu'bino SM (*cappello*) bowler (BRIT), derby (US); (*abito da donna*) sheath dress

'tubo SM tube; (*per conduttore*) pipe; **~ digerente** (*Anat*) alimentary canal, digestive tract; **~ di scappamento** (*Aut*) exhaust pipe

tubo'lare AG tubular ▶ SM tubeless tyre (BRIT) *o* tire (US)

'tue *vedi* **tuo**

tuf'fare /72/ VT to plunge; (*intingere*) to dip; **tuffarsi** VPR to plunge, dive

tuffa'tore, -'trice SM/F (*Sport*) diver

'tuffo SM dive; (*breve bagno*) dip

tu'gurio SM hovel

tuli'pano SM tulip

'tulle SM (*tessuto*) tulle

tume'fare /42/ VT to cause to swell; **tumefarsi** VPR to swell

'tumido, -a AG swollen

tu'more SM (*Med*) tumour (BRIT), tumor (US)

tumulazi'one [tumulat'tsjone] SF burial

tu'multo SM uproar, commotion; (*sommossa*) riot; (*fig*) turmoil

tumultu'oso, -a AG rowdy, unruly; (*fig*) turbulent, stormy

tungs'teno SM tungsten

'tunica, -che SF tunic

'Tunisi SF Tunis

Tuni'sia SF: **la ~** Tunisia

tuni'sino, -a AG, SM/F Tunisian

'tunnel SM INV tunnel

'tuo (*f* **tua**, *pl* **tue, tuoi**) DET: **il ~, la tua** *etc* your ▶ PRON: **il ~, la tua** *etc* yours ▶ SM: **hai speso del ~?** did you spend your own money? ▶ SF: **la tua** (*opinione*) your view; **i tuoi** (*genitori, famiglia*) your family; **una tua amica** a friend of yours; **è dalla tua** he is on your side; **alla tua!** (*brindisi*) your health!; **ne hai fatta una delle tue!** (*sciocchezze*) you've done it again!

tuo'nare /72/ VI to thunder; **tuona** it is thundering, there's some thunder

tu'ono SM thunder

tu'orlo SM yolk

tu'racciolo [tu'rattʃolo] SM cap, top; (*di sughero*) cork

tu'rare /72/ VT to stop, plug; (*con sughero*) to cork; **turarsi il naso** to hold one's nose

'turba SF (*folla*) crowd, throng; (: *peg*) mob; **turbe** SFPL disorder(s); **soffrire di turbe psichiche** to suffer from a mental disorder

turba'mento SM disturbance; (*di animo*) anxiety, agitation

tur'bante SM turban

tur'bare /72/ VT to disturb, trouble; **~ la quiete pubblica** (*Dir*) to disturb the peace

tur'bato, -a AG upset; (*preoccupato, ansioso*) anxious

tur'bina SF turbine

turbi'nare /72/ VI to whirl

'turbine SM whirlwind; **~ di neve** swirl of snow; **~ di polvere/sabbia** dust/sandstorm

turbi'noso, -a AG (*vento, danza ecc*) whirling

turbo'lento, -a AG turbulent; (*ragazzo*) boisterous, unruly

turbo'lenza [turbo'lentsa] SF turbulence

turboreat'tore SM turbojet engine

tur'chese [tur'kese] AG, SM, SF turquoise

Tur'chia [tur'kia] SF: **la ~** Turkey

tur'chino, -a [tur'kino] AG deep blue

'turco, -a, -chi, -che AG Turkish ▶ SM/F Turk (Turkish woman) ▶ SM (*Ling*) Turkish; **parlare ~** (*fig*) to talk double Dutch

'turgido, -a['turdʒido] AG swollen

tu'rismo SM tourism; tourist industry; **~ sessuale** sex tourism

tu'rista, -i, -e SM/F tourist

tu'ristico, -a, -ci, -che AG tourist *cpd*

tur'nista, -i, -e SM/F shift worker

'turno SM turn; (*di lavoro*) shift; **di ~** (*soldato, medico, custode*) on duty; **a ~** (*rispondere*) in turn; (*lavorare*) in shifts; **fare a ~ a fare qc** to take turns to do sth; **è il suo ~** it's your (*o his etc*) turn

'turpe AG filthy, vile

turpi'loquio SM obscene language

'tuta SF overalls *pl*; (*Sport*) tracksuit; **~ mimetica** (*Mil*) camouflage clothing; **~ spaziale** spacesuit; **~ subacquea** wetsuit

tu'tela SF (*Dir: di minore*) guardianship; (: *protezione*) protection; (*difesa*) defence (BRIT), defense (US); **~ dell'ambiente** environmental protection; **~ del consumatore** consumer protection

tute'lare/**72**/ VT to protect, defend ▶ AG (*Dir*): **giudice ~** *judge with responsibility for guardianship cases*

tutor ['tiutor] SM INV (*Aut*) speed monitoring system

tu'tore, -'trice SM/F (*Dir*) guardian

tutta'via CONG nevertheless, yet

(PAROLA CHIAVE)

'tutto, -a DET **1** (*intero*) all; **tutto il latte** all the milk; **tutta la notte** all night, the whole night; **tutto il libro** the whole book; **tutta una bottiglia** a whole bottle; **in tutto il mondo** all over the world

2 (*pl, collettivo*) all; every; **tutti i libri** all the books; **tutte le notti** every night; **tutti i venerdì** every Friday; **tutti gli uomini** all the men; (*collettivo*) all men; **tutto l'anno** all year long; **tutte le volte che** every time (that); **tutti e due** both *o* each of us (*o* them *o* you); **tutti e cinque** all five of us (*o* them *o* you)

3 (*completamente*): **era tutta sporca** she was

all dirty; **tremava tutto** he was trembling all over; **è tutta sua madre** she's just *o* exactly like her mother

4: **a tutt'oggi** so far, up till now; **a tutta velocità** at full *o* top speed

▶ PRON **1** (*ogni cosa*) everything, all; (*qualsiasi cosa*) anything; **ha mangiato tutto** he's eaten everything; **dimmi tutto** tell me all about it; **tutto compreso** all included, all-in (BRIT); **tutto considerato** all things considered; **con tutto che** (*malgrado*) although; **del tutto** completely; **100 euro in tutto** 100 euros in all; **in tutto eravamo 50** there were 50 of us in all; **in tutto e per tutto** completely; **il che è tutto dire** and that's saying a lot

2: **tutti, e** (*ognuno*) all, everybody; **vengono tutti** they are all coming, everybody's coming; **tutti sanno che** everybody knows that; **tutti quanti** all and sundry

▶ AV (*completamente*) entirely, quite; **è tutto il contrario** it's quite *o* exactly the opposite; **tutt'al più**: **saranno stati tutt'al più una cinquantina** there were about fifty of them at (the very) most; **tutt'al più possiamo prendere un treno** if the worst comes to the worst we can take a train; **tutt'altro** on the contrary; **è tutt'altro che felice** he's anything but happy; **tutt'intorno** all around; **tutt'a un tratto** suddenly

▶ SM: **il tutto** the whole lot, all of it; **il tutto si è svolto senza incidenti** it all went off without incident; **il tutto le costerà due milioni** the whole thing will cost you two million

tutto'fare AG INV: **domestica ~** general maid; **: ragazzo ~** office boy ▶ SM INV/F INV handyman(-woman)

tut'tora AV still

tutù SM INV tutu, ballet skirt

TV [ti'vu] SF INV (= *televisione*) TV ▶ SIGLA = **Treviso**

Uu

U, u [u] SM O F INV (*lettera*) U, u; **U come Udine** ≈ U for Uncle; **inversione ad U** U-turn

ub'bia SF (*letterario*) irrational fear

ubbidi'ente AG obedient

ubbidi'enza [ubbi'djɛntsa] SF obedience

ubbi'dire /**55**/ VI to obey; **~ a** to obey; (*veicolo, macchina*) to respond to

ubicazi'one [ubikat'tsjone] SF site, location

ubiquità SF: **non ho il dono dell'~** I can't be everywhere at once

ubria'care /**20**/ VT: **~ qn** to get sb drunk; (*alcool*) to make sb drunk; (*fig*) to make sb's head spin o reel; **ubriacarsi** VPR to get drunk; **ubriacarsi di** (*fig*) to become intoxicated with

ubria'chezza [ubria'kettsa] SF drunkenness

ubri'aco, -a, -chi, -che AG, SM/F drunk

ubria'cone SM drunkard

uccellagi'one [uttʃella'dʒone] SF bird catching

uccelli'era [uttʃel'ljɛra] SF aviary

uccel'lino [uttʃel'lino] SM baby bird, chick

uc'cello [ut'tʃɛllo] SM bird

uc'cidere [ut'tʃidere] /**34**/ VT to kill; **uccidersi** VPR (*suicidarsi*) to kill o.s.; (*perdere la vita*) to be killed

uccisi'one [uttʃi'zjone] SF killing

uc'ciso, -a [ut'tʃizo] PP di **uccidere**

ucci'sore [uttʃi'zore] SM killer

U'craina SF Ukraine

u'craino, -a AG, SM/F Ukrainian

UD SIGLA = **Udine**

U.D.C. SIGLA F (*Pol*: = *Unione di Centro*) centre party

u'dente SMF: **i non udenti** the hard of hearing

u'dibile AG audible

udi'enza [u'djɛntsa] SF audience; (*Dir*) hearing; **dare ~ (a)** to grant an audience (to); **~ a porte chiuse** hearing in camera

u'dire /**124**/ VT to hear

udi'tivo, -a AG auditory

u'dito SM (sense of) hearing

udi'tore, -'trice SM/F listener; (*Ins*) unregistered student (*attending lectures*)

udi'torio SM (*persone*) audience

UE SIGLA F (= *Unione Europea*) EU

U.E. ABBR = **uso esterno**

UEFA SIGLA F UEFA (= *Union of European Football Associations*)

UEM SIGLA F (= *Unione economica e monetaria*) EMU

'uffa ESCL tut!

uffici'ale [uffi'tʃale] AG official ▶ SM (*Amm*) official, officer; (*Mil*) officer; **pubblico ~** public official; **~ giudiziario** clerk of the court; **~ di marina** naval officer; **~ sanitario** health inspector; **~ di stato civile** registrar

ufficializ'zare [uffitʃalid'dzare] /**72**/ VT to make official

uf'ficio [uf'fitʃo] SM (*gen*) office; (*dovere*) duty; (*mansione*) task, function, job; (*agenzia*) agency, bureau; (*Rel*) service; **d'~** office *cpd*; official ▶ AV officially; **provvedere d'~** to act officially; **convocare d'~** (*Dir*) to summons; **difensore** o **avvocato d'~** (*Dir*) court-appointed counsel for the defence; **~ brevetti** patent office; **~ di collocamento** employment office; **~ informazioni** information bureau; **~ oggetti smarriti** lost property office (*BRIT*), lost and found (*US*); **~ postale** post office; **~ vendite/del personale** sales/personnel department

uffici'oso, -a [uffi'tʃoso] AG unofficial

'UFO SM INV (= *unidentified flying object*) UFO

'ufo: **a ~** av free, for nothing

U'ganda SF: **l'~** Uganda

'uggia ['uddʒa] SF (*noia*) boredom; (*fastidio*) bore; **avere/prendere qn in ~** to dislike/ take a dislike to sb

uggi'oso, -a [ud'dʒoso] AG tiresome; (*tempo*) dull

'ugola SF uvula

uguagli'anza [ugwaʎ'ʎantsa] SF equality

uguagli'are [ugwaʎ'ʎare] /**27**/ VT to make equal; (*essere uguale*) to equal, be equal to; (*livellare*) to level; **uguagliarsi** VPR:

uguagliarsi a *o* **con qn** (*paragonarsi*) to compare o.s. to sb

ugu'ale AG equal; (*identico*) identical, the same; (*uniforme*) level, even ▶ AV: **costano ~** they cost the same; **sono bravi ~** they're equally good

ugual'mente AV equally; (*lo stesso*) all the same

U.I. ABBR = **uso interno**

UIL SIGLA F (= *Unione Italiana del Lavoro*) *trade union federation*

'ulcera ['ultʃera] SF ulcer

ulcerazi'one [ultʃerat'tsjone] SF ulceration

u'liva *etc* = **oliva** *ecc*

U'livo SM (*Pol*) *centre-left coalition*

ulteri'ore AG further

ultima'mente AV lately, of late

ulti'mare /**72**/ VT to finish, complete

ulti'matum SM INV ultimatum

ulti'missime SFPL latest news *sg*

'ultimo, -a AG (*finale*) last; (*estremo*) farthest, utmost; (*recente: notizia, moda*) latest; (*fig: sommo, fondamentale*) ultimate ▶ SM/F last (one); **fino all'~** to the last, until the end; **da ~, in ~** in the end; **per ~** (*entrare, arrivare*) last; **abitare all'~ piano** to live on the top floor; **in ultima pagina** (*di giornale*) on the back page; **negli ultimi tempi** recently; **all'~ momento** at the last minute; **... la vostra lettera del 7 aprile ~ scorso** ... your letter of April 7th last; **in ultima analisi** in the final *o* last analysis; **in ~ luogo** finally

ultrà SMF ultra

ultrasi'nistra SF (*Pol*) extreme left

ultrasu'ono SM ultrasound

ultravio'letto, -a AG ultraviolet

ulu'lare /**72**/ VI to howl

ulu'lato SM howling *no pl*; howl

umana'mente AV (*con umanità*) humanely; (*nei limiti delle capacità umane*) humanly

uma'nesimo SM humanism

umanità SF humanity

umani'tario, -a AG humanitarian

umaniz'zare [umanid'dzare] /**72**/ VT to humanize

u'mano, -a AG human; (*comprensivo*) humane

umbi'lico SM = **ombelico**

'umbro, -a AG of (*o* from) Umbria

umet'tare /**72**/ VT to dampen, moisten

umi'diccio, -a, -ci, -ce [umi'dittʃo] AG (*terreno*) damp; (*mano*) moist, clammy

umidifi'care /**20**/ VT to humidify

umidifica'tore SM humidifier

umidità SF dampness; moistness; humidity

'umido, -a AG damp; (*mano, occhi*) moist; (*clima*) humid ▶ SM dampness, damp; **carne in ~** stew

'umile AG humble

umili'ante AG humiliating

umili'are /**19**/ VT to humiliate; **umiliarsi** VPR to humble o.s.

umiliazi'one [umiljat'tsjone] SF humiliation

umiltà SF humility, humbleness

u'more SM (*disposizione d'animo*) mood; (*carattere*) temper; **di buon/cattivo ~** in a good/bad mood

umo'rismo SM humour (BRIT), humor (US); **avere il senso dell'~** to have a sense of humour

umo'rista, -i, -e SM/F humorist

umo'ristico, -a, -ci, -che AG humorous, funny

un, un', una *vedi* **uno**

u'nanime AG unanimous

unanimità SF unanimity; **all'~** unanimously

'una 'tantum AG one-off *cpd* ▶ SF (*imposta*) one-off tax

unci'nato, -a [untʃi'nato] AG (*amo*) barbed; (*ferro*) hooked; **croce uncinata** swastika

unci'netto [untʃi'netto] SM crochet hook

un'cino [un'tʃino] SM hook

undi'cenne [undi'tʃenne] AG, SMF eleven-year-old

undi'cesimo, -a [undi'tʃezimo] AG eleventh

'undici ['unditʃi] NUM eleven

U'NESCO SIGLA F (= *United Nations Educational, Scientific and Cultural Organization*) UNESCO

'ungere ['undʒere] /**5**/ VT to grease, oil; (*Rel*) to anoint; (*fig*) to flatter, butter up; **ungersi** VPR (*sporcarsi*) to get covered in grease; **ungersi con la crema** to put on cream

unghe'rese [unge'rese] AG, SMF, SM Hungarian

Unghe'ria [unge'ria] SF: **l'~** Hungary

'unghia ['ungja] SF (*Anat*) nail; (*di animale*) claw; (*di rapace*) talon; (*di cavallo*) hoof; **pagare sull'~** (*fig*) to pay on the nail

unghi'ata [un'gjata] SF (*graffio*) scratch

ungu'ento SM ointment

unica'mente AV only

'UNICEF ['unitʃef] SIGLA M (= *United Nations International Children's Emergency Fund*) UNICEF

'unico, -a, -ci, -che AG (*solo*) only; (*ineguagliabile*) unique; (*singolo: binario*) single; **è figlio ~** he's an only child; **atto ~** (*Teat*) one-act play; **agente ~** (*Comm*) sole agent

uni'corno SM unicorn

unifi'care /**20**/ VT to unite, unify; (*sistemi*) to standardize

unificazi'one [unifikat'tsjone] SF uniting; unification; standardization

unifor'mare /**72**/ VT (*terreno, superficie*) to level; **uniformarsi** VPR: **uniformarsi a** to conform to; **~ qc a** to adjust *o* relate sth to

uni'forme AG uniform; (*superficie*) even ▶ SF (*divisa*) uniform; **alta ~** dress uniform

uniformità SF uniformity; evenness

unilate'rale AG one-sided; (*Dir, Pol*) unilateral

uninomi'nale AG (*Pol: collegio, sistema*) single-candidate *cpd*

uni'one SF union; (*fig: concordia*) unity, harmony; **l'U~** (*Pol*) *coalition of centre-left parties*; **U~ economica e monetaria** economic and monetary union; **U~ Europea** European Union; **ex U~ Sovietica** former Soviet Union

u'nire /55/ VT to unite; (*congiungere*) to join, connect; (*ingredienti, colori*) to combine; (*in matrimonio*) to unite, join together; **unirsi** VPR to unite; (*in matrimonio*) to be joined together; **~ qc a** to unite sth with; to join *o* connect sth with; to combine sth with; **unirsi a** (*gruppo, società*) to join

u'nisono SM: **all'~** in unison

unità SF INV (*unione, concordia*) unity; (*Mat, Mil, Comm, di misura*) unit; **~ centrale (di elaborazione)** (*Inform*) central processing unit; **~ disco** (*Inform*) disk drive; **~ monetaria** monetary unit; **~ di misura** unit of measurement

uni'tario, -a AG unitary; **prezzo ~** price per unit

u'nito, -a AG (*paese*) united; (*amici, famiglia*) close; **in tinta unita** plain, self-coloured (*Brit*), self-colored (*US*)

univer'sale AG universal; general

universalità SF universality

universal'mente AV universally

università SF INV university

universi'tario, -a AG university *cpd* ▶ SM/F (*studente*) university student; (*insegnante*) academic, university lecturer

uni'verso SM universe

u'nivoco, -a, -ci, -che AG unambiguous

(PAROLA CHIAVE)

'uno, -a (*dav sm* **un** + C, V, **uno** + s *impura, gn, pn, ps, x, z; dav sf* **un'** + V, **una** + C) DET **1** a; (*dav vocale*) an; **un bambino** a child; **una strada** a street; **uno zingaro** a gypsy

2 (*intensivo*): **ho avuto una paura!** I got such a fright!

▶ PRON **1** one; **ce n'è uno qui** there's one here; **prendine uno** take one (of them); **l'uno o l'altro** either (of them); **l'uno e l'altro** both (of them); **aiutarsi l'un l'altro** to help one another *o* each other; **sono entrati l'uno dopo l'altro** they came in one after the other; **a uno a uno** one by one; **metà per uno** half each

2 (*un tale*) someone, somebody; **ho incontrato uno che ti conosce** I met somebody who knows you

3 (*con valore impersonale*) one, you; **se uno vuole** if one wants, if you want; **cosa fa uno in quella situazione?** what does one do in that situation?

▶ NUM one; **una mela e due pere** one apple and two pears; **uno più uno fa due** one plus one equals two, one and one are two

▶ SF: **è l'una** it's one (o'clock)

'unsi *etc* VB *vedi* **ungere**

'unto, -a PP *di* **ungere** ▶ AG greasy, oily ▶ SM grease

untu'oso, -a AG greasy, oily

unzi'one [un'tsjone] SF: **l'Estrema U~** (*Rel*) Extreme Unction

u'omo (*pl* **uomini**) SM man; **da ~** (*abito, scarpe*) men's, for men; **a memoria d'~** since the world began; **a passo d'~** at walking pace; **~ d'affari** businessman; **~ d'azione** man of action; **~ di fiducia** right-hand man; **~ di mondo** man of the world; **~ di paglia** stooge; **~ politico** politician; **~ rana** frogman; **l'~ della strada** the man in the street

u'opo SM: **all'~** if necessary

u'ovo (*pl(f)* **uova**) SM egg; **cercare il pelo nell'~** (*fig*) to split hairs; **~ affogato** *o* **in camicia** poached egg; **~ bazzotto/sodo** soft-/hard-boiled egg; **~ alla coque** boiled egg; **~ di Pasqua** Easter egg; **~ al tegame** *o* **all'occhio di bue** fried egg; **uova strapazzate** scrambled eggs

ura'gano SM hurricane

U'rali SMPL: **gli ~, i Monti ~** the Urals, the Ural Mountains

u'ranio SM uranium; **~ impoverito** depleted uranium

urba'nista, -i, -e SM/F town planner

urba'nistica SF town planning

urbanità SF urbanity

ur'bano, -a AG urban, city *cpd*, town *cpd*; (*Tel: chiamata*) local; (*fig*) urbane

ur'gente [ur'dʒɛnte] AG urgent

ur'genza [ur'dʒɛntsa] SF urgency; **in caso d'~** (in case of) an emergency; **d'~** *ag* emergency; *av* urgently, as a matter of urgency; **non c'è ~** there's no hurry; **questo lavoro va fatto con ~** this work is urgent

'urgere [ur'dʒere] /5/ VI to be needed urgently

u'rina *etc* = **orina** *ecc*

ur'lare /72/ VI (*persona*) to scream, yell; (*animale, vento*) to howl ▶ VT to scream, yell

'urlo (*pl(m)* **urli**, *pl(f)* **urla**) SM scream, yell; howl

'urna SF urn; (*elettorale*) ballot box; **andare alle urne** to go to the polls

URP [urp] SIGLA M (= *Ufficio Relazioni con il Pubblico*) PR Office

urrà ESCL hurrah!

U.R.S.S. SIGLA F = **Unione delle Repubbliche Socialiste Sovietiche**; **l'U.R.S.S.** the USSR

ur'tare/72/ VT to bump into, knock against, crash into; (*fig: irritare*) to annoy ▶ VI: **~ contro** o **in** to bump into, knock against; (*fig: imbattersi*) to come up against; **urtarsi** VPR (*reciproco: scontrarsi*) to collide; (: *fig*) to clash; (*irritarsi*) to get annoyed

'urto SM (*colpo*) knock, bump; (*scontro*) crash, collision; (*fig*) clash; **terapia d'~** (*Med*) shock treatment

uruguai'ano, -a AG, SM/F Uruguayan

Urugu'ay SM: **l'~** Uruguay

u.s. ABBR = **ultimo scorso**

'USA SMPL: **gli ~** the USA

u'sanza [u'zantsa] SF custom; (*moda*) fashion

u'sare/72/ VT to use, employ ▶ VI (*essere di moda*) to be fashionable; (*servirsi*): **~ di** to use (*diritto*) to exercise; (*essere solito*): **~ fare** to be in the habit of doing, be accustomed to doing ▶ VB IMPERS: **qui usa così** it's the custom round here; **~ la massima cura nel fare qc** to exercise great care when doing sth

u'sato, -a AG used; (*consumato*) worn; (*di seconda mano*) used, second-hand ▶ SM second-hand goods pl

u'scente [uʃʃɛnte] AG (*Amm*) outgoing

usci'ere [uʃʃɛre] SM usher

'uscio ['uʃʃo] SM door

u'scire [uʃʃire] /125/ VI (*gen*) to come out; (*partire, andare a passeggio, a uno spettacolo ecc*) to go out; (*essere sorteggiato: numero*) to come up; **~ da** (*gen*) to leave; (*posto*) to go (o come) out of, leave; (*solco, vasca ecc*) to come out of; (*muro*) to stick out of; (*competenza ecc*) to be outside; (*infanzia, adolescenza*) to leave behind; (*famiglia nobile ecc*) to come from; **~ da** o **di casa** to go out; (*fig*) to leave home; **~ in automobile** to go out in the car, go for a drive; **~ di strada** (*Aut*) to go off o leave the road

u'scita [uʃʃita] SF (*passaggio, varco*) exit, way out; (*per divertimento*) outing; (*Econ: somma*) expenditure; (*Teat*) entrance; (*fig: battuta*) witty remark; **"vietata l'~"** "no exit"; **~ di sicurezza** emergency exit

user'name [juzer'neim] SM INV username

usi'gnolo [uziɲ'ɲɔlo] SM nightingale

'uso SM (*utilizzazione*) use; (*esercizio*) practice (BRIT), practise (US); (*abitudine*) custom; **fare ~ di qc** to use sth; **con l'~** with practice; **a ~ di** for (the use of); **d'~** (*corrente*) in use; **fuori ~** out of use; **essere in ~** to be in common o current use; **per ~ esterno** for external use only

ustio'nare/72/ VT to burn; **ustionarsi** VPR to burn o.s.

usti'one SF burn

usu'ale AG common, everyday

usufru'ire/55/ VI: **~ di** (*giovarsi di*) to take advantage of, make use of

usu'frutto SM (*Dir*) usufruct

u'sura SF usury; (*logoramento*) wear (and tear)

usu'raio SM usurer

usur'pare/72/ VT to usurp

usurpa'tore, -'trice SM/F usurper

uten'sile SM tool, implement ▶ AG: **macchina ~** machine tool; **utensili da cucina** kitchen utensils

utensile'ria SF (*utensili*) tools pl; (*reparto*) tool room

u'tente SMF user; (*di gas ecc*) consumer; (*del telefono*) subscriber; **~ finale** end user

'utero SM uterus, womb; **~ in affitto** host womb

'utile AG useful ▶ SM (*vantaggio*) advantage, benefit; (*Econ: profitto*) profit; **rendersi ~** to be helpful; **in tempo ~ per** in time for; **unire l'~ al dilettevole** to combine business with pleasure; **partecipare agli utili** (*Econ*) to share in the profits

utilità SF usefulness no pl; use; (*vantaggio*) benefit; **essere di grande ~** to be very useful

utili'tario, -a AG utilitarian ▶ SF (*Aut*) economy car

utiliz'zare [utilid'dzare] /72/ VT to use, make use of, utilize

utilizzazi'one [utiliddzat'tsjone] SF utilization, use

uti'lizzo [uti'liddzo] SM (*Amm*) utilization; (*Banca: di credito*) availment

util'mente AV usefully, profitably

uto'pia SF utopia; **è pura ~** that's sheer utopianism

uto'pistico, -a, -ci, -che AG utopian

UVA ABBR (= *ultravioletto prossimo*) UVA

'uva SF grapes pl; **~ passa** raisins pl; **~ spina** gooseberry

UVB ABBR (= *ultravioletto lontano*) UVB

Vv

V, v [vi, vu] SM O F INV (*lettera*) V, v; **V come Venezia** ≈ V for Victor

V ABBR (= *volt*) V

v. ABBR (= *vedi*) v.; (= *verso*) v.; (= *versetto*) v.

VA SIGLA = **Varese**

va, va' VB *vedi* **andare**

va'cante AG vacant

va'canza [va'kantsa] SF (*l'essere vacante*) vacancy; (*riposo, ferie*) holiday(s pl) (BRIT), vacation (US); (*giorno di permesso*) day off, holiday; **vacanze** SFPL (*periodo di ferie*) holidays, vacation sg; **essere/andare in ~** to be/go on holiday o vacation; **far ~** to have a holiday; **vacanze estive** summer holiday(s) o vacation; **vacanze natalizie** Christmas holidays o vacation

'vacca, -che SF COW

vacci'nare [vattʃi'nare] /**72**/ VT to vaccinate; **farsi ~** to have a vaccination, get vaccinated

vaccinazi'one [vattʃinat'tsjone] SF vaccination

vac'cino [vat'tʃino] SM (*Med*) vaccine

vacil'lante [vatʃil'lante] AG (*edificio, vecchio*) shaky, unsteady; (*fiamma*) flickering; (*salute, memoria*) shaky, failing

vacil'lare [vatʃil'lare] /**72**/ VI to sway, wobble; (*fiamma, luce*) to flicker; (*fig: memoria, coraggio*) to be failing, falter

'vacuo, -a AG (*fig*) empty, vacuous ▶ SM vacuum

'vado etc VB *vedi* **andare**

vagabon'daggio [vagabon'daddʒo] SM wandering, roaming; (*Dir*) vagrancy

vagabon'dare /**72**/ VI to roam, wander

vaga'bondo, -a SM/F tramp, vagrant; (*fannullone*) idler, loafer

va'gare /**80**/ VI to wander

vaggheggi'are [vaged'dʒare] /**62**/ VT to long for, dream of

vagherò etc [vage'rɔ] VB *vedi* **vagare**

va'ghezza [va'gettsa] SF vagueness

va'gina [va'dʒina] SF vagina

va'gire [va'dʒire] /**55**/ VI to whimper

va'gito [va'dʒito] SM cry, wailing

'vaglia ['vaʎʎa] SM INV money order; **~ cambiario** promissory note; **~ postale** postal order

vagli'are [vaʎ'ʎare] /**27**/ VT to sift; (*fig*) to weigh up

'vaglio ['vaʎʎo] SM sieve; **passare al ~** (*fig*) to examine closely

'vago, -a, -ghi, -ghe AG vague

va'gone SM (*Ferr: per passeggeri*) coach, carriage (BRIT), car (US); (: *per merci*) truck, wagon; **~ letto** sleeper, sleeping car; **~ ristorante** dining o restaurant car

'vai VB *vedi* **andare**

vai'olo SM smallpox

val. ABBR = **valuta**

va'langa, -ghe SF avalanche

va'lente AG able, talented

va'lenza [va'lentsa] SF (*fig: significato*) content; (*Chim*) valency

va'lere /**126**/ VI (*avere forza, potenza*) to have influence; (*essere valido*) to be valid; (*avere vigore, autorità*) to hold, apply; (*essere capace: poeta, studente*) to be good, be able ▶ VT (*prezzo, sforzo*) to be worth; (*corrispondere*) to correspond to; (*procurare*): **~ qc a qn** to earn sb sth; **valersi** VPR: **valersi di** to make use of, take advantage of; **far ~** (*autorità ecc*) to assert; **~ le proprie ragioni** to make o.s. heard; **farsi ~** to make o.s. appreciated o respected; **vale a dire** that is to say; **~ la pena** to be worth the effort o worth it; **l'uno vale l'altro** the one is as good as the other, they amount to the same thing; **non vale niente** it's worthless; **valersi dei consigli di qn** to take o act upon sb's advice

valeri'ana SF (*Bot, Med*) valerian

va'levole AG valid

'valgo etc VB *vedi* **valere**

vali'care /**20**/ VT to cross

'valico, -chi SM (*passo*) pass

validità SF validity

'valido, -a AG valid; (*rimedio*) effective; (*aiuto*) real; (*persona*) worthwhile; **essere di ~ aiuto a qn** to be a great help to sb

valige'ria [validʒe'ria] SF (*assortimento*) leather goods pl; (*fabbrica*) leather goods factory; (*negozio*) leather goods shop

vali'getta [vali'dʒɛtta] SF briefcase; ~ **ventiquattrore** overnight bag o case

va'ligia, -gie, -ge [va'lidʒa] SF (suit)case; **fare le valigie** to pack (up); ~ **diplomatica** diplomatic bag

val'lata SF valley

'valle SF valley; **a** ~ (*di fiume*) downstream; **scendere a** ~ to go downhill

val'letto SM valet

valligi'ano, -a [valli'dʒano] SM/F inhabitant of a valley

va'lore SM (*gen, Comm*) value; (*merito*) merit, worth; (*coraggio*) valour (BRIT), valor (US), courage; (*Finanza: titolo*) security; **valori** SMPL (*oggetti preziosi*) valuables; **crescere/ diminuire di** ~ to go up/down in value, gain/lose in value; **è di gran** ~ it's worth a lot, it's very valuable; **privo di** ~ worthless; ~ **contabile** book value; ~ **effettivo** real value; ~ **nominale** o **facciale** nominal value; ~ **di realizzo** break-up value; ~ **di riscatto** surrender value; **valori bollati** (*revenue*) stamps

valoriz'zare [valorid'dzare] /**72**/ VT (*terreno*) to develop; (*fig*) to make the most of

valo'roso, -a AG courageous

'valso, -a PP di **valere**

va'luta SF currency, money; (*Banca*): ~ **15 gennaio** interest to run from January 15th; ~ **estera** foreign currency

valu'tare /**72**/ VT (*casa, gioiello, fig*) to value; (*stabilire: peso, entrate, fig*) to estimate

valu'tario, -a AG (*Finanza: norme*) currency cpd

valutazi'one [valutat'tsjone] SF valuation; estimate

'valva SF (*Zool, Bot*) valve

'valvola SF (*Tecn, Anat*) valve; (*Elettr*) fuse; ~ **a farfalla del carburatore** (*Aut*) throttle; ~ **di sicurezza** safety valve

'valzer ['valtser] SM INV waltz

vam'pata SF (*di fiamma*) blaze; (*di calore*) blast; (: *al viso*) flush

vam'piro SM vampire

vana'gloria SF boastfulness

van'dalico, -a, -ci, -che AG vandal cpd; **atto** ~ act of vandalism

vanda'lismo SM vandalism

'vandalo SM vandal

vaneggia'mento [vaneddʒa'mento] SM raving, delirium

vaneggi'are [vaned'dʒare] /**62**/ VI to rave

va'nesio, -a AG vain, conceited

'vanga, -ghe SF spade

van'gare /**80**/ VT to dig

van'gelo [van'dʒɛlo] SM gospel

vanifi'care /**20**/ VT to nullify

va'niglia [va'niʎʎa] SF vanilla

vanigli'ato, -a [vaniʎ'ʎato] AG: **zucchero** ~ (*Cuc*) vanilla sugar

vanità SF vanity; (*di promessa*) emptiness; (*di sforzo*) futility

vani'toso, -a AG vain, conceited

'vanno VB vedi **andare**

'vano, -a AG vain ▶ SM (*spazio*) space; (*apertura*) opening; (*stanza*) room; **il** ~ **della porta** the doorway; **il** ~ **portabagagli** (*Aut*) the boot (BRIT), the trunk (US)

van'taggio [van'taddʒo] SM advantage; **trarre** ~ **da qc** to benefit from sth; **essere/portarsi in** ~ (*Sport*) to be in/take the lead

vantaggi'oso, -a [vantad'dʒoso] AG advantageous, favourable (BRIT), favorable (US)

van'tare /**72**/ VT to praise, speak highly of; **vantarsi** VPR: **vantarsi (di/di aver fatto)** to boast o brag (about/about having done)

vante'ria SF boasting

'vanto SM boasting; (*merito*) virtue, merit; (*gloria*) pride

'vanvera SF: **a** ~ haphazardly; **parlare a** ~ to talk nonsense

va'pore SM vapour (BRIT), vapor (US); (*anche:* **vapore acqueo**) steam; (*nave*) steamer; **a** ~ (*turbina ecc*) steam cpd; **al** ~ (*Cuc*) steamed

vapo'retto SM steamer

vapori'era SF (*Ferr*) steam engine

vaporiz'zare [vaporid'dzare] /**72**/ VT to vaporize

vaporizza'tore [vaporiddza'tore] SM spray

vaporizzazi'one [vaporiddzat'tsjone] SF vaporization

vapo'roso, -a AG (*tessuto*) filmy; (*capelli*) soft and full

va'rare /**72**/ VT (*Naut, fig*) to launch; (*Dir*) to pass

var'care /**20**/ VT to cross

'varco, -chi SM passage; **aprirsi un** ~ **tra la folla** to push one's way through the crowd

vare'china [vare'kina] SF bleach

vari'abile AG variable; (*tempo, umore*) changeable, variable ▶ SF (*Mat*) variable

vari'ante SF (*gen*) variation, change; (*di piano*) modification; (*Ling*) variant; (*Sport*) alternative route

vari'are /**19**/ VT, VI to vary; ~ **di opinione** to change one's mind

variazi'one [varjat'tsjone] SF variation, change; (*Mus*) variation; **una** ~ **di programma** a change of plan

va'rice [va'ritʃe] SF varicose vein

vari'cella [vari'tʃella] SF chickenpox

vari'coso, -a AG varicose

varie'gato, -a AG variegated

varietà SF INV variety ▶ SM INV variety show

V

'vario, -a AG varied; (*parecchi: col sostantivo al pl*) various; (*mutevole: umore*) changeable; **varie** SFPL: **varie ed eventuali** (*nell'ordine del giorno*) any other business

vario'pinto, -a AG multicoloured (BRIT), multicolored (US)

'varo SM (*Naut, fig*) launch; (*di leggi*) passing

varrò *etc* VB *vedi* **valere**

Var'savia SF Warsaw

va'saio SM potter

'vasca, -sche SF basin; (*anche:* **vasca da bagno**) bathtub, bath

va'scello [vaʃʃɛllo] SM (*Naut*) vessel, ship

vas'chetta [vas'ketta] SF (*per gelato*) tub; (*per sviluppare fotografie*) dish

vase'lina SF vaseline

vasel'lame SM (*stoviglie*) crockery; (*: di porcellana*) china; ~ **d'oro/d'argento** gold/silver plate

'vaso SM (*recipiente*) pot; (*: barattolo*) jar; (*: decorativo*) vase; (*Anat*) vessel; ~ **da fiori** vase; (*per piante*) flowerpot

vas'sallo SM vassal

vas'soio SM tray

vastità SF vastness

'vasto, -a AG vast, immense; **di vaste proporzioni** (*incendio*) huge; (*fenomeno, rivolta*) widespread; **su vasta scala** on a vast *o* huge scale

Vati'cano SM: **il ~** the Vatican; **la Città del ~** the Vatican City

VB SIGLA = **Vibo Valenza**

VC SIGLA = **Vercelli**

VE SIGLA = **Venezia** ▸ ABBR = **Vostra Eccellenza**

ve PRON, AV *vedi* **vi**

vecchi'aia [vek'kjaja] SF old age

'vecchio, -a ['vɛkkjo] AG old ▸ SM/F old man(-woman); **i vecchi** the old; **è un mio ~ amico** he's an old friend of mine; **è un uomo ~ stile** *o* **stampo** he's an old-fashioned man; **è ~ del mestiere** he's an old hand at the job

'vece ['vetʃe] SF: **in ~ di** in the place of, for; **fare le veci di qn** to take sb's place; **firma del padre o di chi ne fa le veci** signature of the father or guardian

ve'dere /**127**/ VT, VI to see; **vedersi** VPR to meet, see one another; ~ **di fare qc** to see (to it) that sth is done, make sure that sth is done; **avere a che ~ con** to have to do with; **far ~ qc a qn** to show sb sth; **farsi ~** to show o.s.; (*farsi vivo*) to show one's face; **vedi di non farlo** make sure *o* see you don't do it; **farsi ~ da un medico** to go and see a doctor; **modo di ~** outlook, view of things; **vedi pagina 8** (*rimando*) see page 8; **è da ~ se ...** it remains to be seen whether ...; **non vedo la ragione di farlo** I can't see any reason to do

it; **si era visto costretto a ...** he found himself forced to ...; **non (ci) si vede** (*è buio ecc*) you can't see a thing; **ci vediamo domani!** see you tomorrow!; **non lo posso ~** (*fig*) I can't stand him

ve'detta SF (*sentinella, posto*) look-out; (*Naut*) patrol boat

ve'dette [vɛ'dɛt] SF INV (*attrice*) star

'vedovo, -a SM/F widower (widow); **rimaner ~** to be widowed

vedrò *etc* VB *vedi* **vedere**

ve'duta SF view; **vedute** SFPL (*fig: opinioni*) views; **di larghe** *o* **ampie vedute** broad-minded; **di vedute limitate** narrow-minded

vee'mente AG (*discorso, azione*) vehement; (*assalto*) vigorous; (*passione*) overwhelming

vee'menza [vee'mɛntsa] SF vehemence; **con ~** vehemently

vege'tale [vedʒe'tale] AG, SM vegetable

vege'tare [vedʒe'tare] /**72**/ VI (*fig*) to vegetate

vegetari'ano, -a [vedʒeta'rjano] AG, SM/F vegetarian

vegeta'tivo, -a AG vegetative

vegetazi'one [vedʒetat'tsjone] SF vegetation

'vegeto, -a ['vɛdʒeto] AG (*pianta*) thriving; (*persona*) strong, vigorous

veg'gente [ved'dʒɛnte] SMF (*indovino*) clairvoyant

'veglia ['veʎʎa] SF wakefulness; (*sorveglianza*) watch; (*trattenimento*) evening gathering; **tra la ~ e il sonno** half awake; **fare la ~ a un malato** to watch over a sick person; ~ **funebre** wake

vegli'ardo, -a [veʎ'ʎardo] SM/F venerable old man/woman

vegli'are [veʎ'ʎare] /**27**/ VI to stay *o* sit up; (*stare vigile*) to watch; to keep watch ▸ VT (*malato, morto*) to watch over, sit up with

vegli'one [veʎ'ʎone] SM ball, dance; ~ **di Capodanno** New Year's Eve party

ve'icolo SM vehicle; ~ **spaziale** spacecraft *inv*

'vela SF (*Naut: tela*) sail; (*: sport*) sailing; **tutto va a gonfie vele** (*fig*) everything is going perfectly

ve'lare /**72**/ VT to veil; **velarsi** VPR (*occhi, luna*) to mist over; (*voce*) to become husky; **velarsi il viso** to cover one's face (with a veil)

ve'lato, -a AG veiled

vela'tura SF (*Naut*) sails *pl*

veleggi'are [veled'dʒare] /**62**/ VI to sail; (*Aer*) to glide

ve'leno SM poison

vele'noso, -a AG poisonous

ve'letta SF (*di cappello*) veil

veli'ero SM sailing ship

ve'lina SF: **carta ~** (*per imballare*) tissue paper; (*: per copie*) flimsy paper; (*copia*) carbon copy

ve'lista, -i, -e SM/F yachtsman(-woman)

ve'livolo SM aircraft

velleità SF INV vain ambition, vain desire

vellei'tario, -a AG unrealistic

'vello SM fleece

vellu'tato, -a AG (*stoffa, pesca, colore*) velvety; (*voce*) mellow

vel'luto SM velvet; **~ a coste** cord

'velo SM veil; (*tessuto*) voile

ve'loce [ve'lotʃe] AG fast, quick ▶ AV fast, quickly

velo'cista, -i, -e [velo'tʃista] SM/F (*Sport*) sprinter

velocità [velotʃi'ta] SF speed; **a forte ~** at high speed; **~ di crociera** cruising speed

ve'lodromo SM velodrome

ven. ABBR (= *venerdì*) Fri.

'vena SF (*gen*) vein; (*filone*) vein, seam; (*fig: ispirazione*) inspiration; (: *umore*) mood; **essere in ~ di qc** to be in the mood for sth

ve'nale AG (*prezzo, valore*) market *cpd*; (*fig*) venal; mercenary

venalità SF venality

ve'nato, -a AG (*marmo*) veined, streaked; (*legno*) grained

vena'torio, -a AG hunting; **la stagione venatoria** the hunting season

vena'tura SF (*di marmo*) vein, streak; (*di legno*) grain

ven'demmia SF (*raccolta*) grape harvest; (*quantità d'uva*) grape crop, grapes *pl*; (*vino ottenuto*) vintage

vendemmi'are /19/ VT to harvest ▶ VI to harvest the grapes

'vendere /29/ VT to sell; **~ all'ingrosso/al dettaglio** *o* **minuto** to sell wholesale/retail; **~ all'asta** to auction, sell by auction; **"vendesi"** "for sale"

ven'detta SF revenge

vendi'care /20/ VT to avenge; **vendicarsi** VPR: **vendicarsi (di)** to avenge o.s. (for); (*per rancore*) to take one's revenge (for); **vendicarsi su qn** to revenge o.s. on sb

vendica'tivo, -a AG vindictive

'vendita SF sale; **la ~** (*attività*) selling; (*smercio*) sales *pl*; **in ~** on sale; **mettere in ~** to put on sale; **in ~ presso** on sale at; **contratto di ~** sales agreement; **reparto vendite** sales department; **~ all'asta** sale by auction; **~ per telefono** telesales *sg*; **~ al dettaglio** *o* **minuto** retail; **~ all'ingrosso** wholesale

vendi'tore, -'trice SM/F seller, vendor; (*gestore di negozio*) trader, dealer

ven'duto, -a AG (*merce*) sold; (*fig: corrotto*) corrupt

ve'nefico, -a, -ci, -che AG poisonous

vene'rabile, vene'rando, -a AG venerable

vene'rare /72/ VT to venerate

venerazi'one [venerat'tsjone] SF veneration

venerdì SM INV Friday; **di** *o* **il ~** on Fridays; **V~ Santo** Good Friday; *vedi anche* **martedì**

'Venere SMF Venus

ve'nereo, -a AG venereal

'veneto, -a AG of (*o* from) the Veneto

'veneto-giuli'ano, -a ['vɛnetodʒu'ljano] AG of (*o* from) Venezia-Giulia

Ve'nezia [ve'nɛttsja] SF Venice

venezi'ano, -a [venet'tsjano] AG, SM/F Venetian

Venezu'ela [venettsu'ela] SM: **il ~** Venezuela

venezue'lano, -a [venettsue'lano] AG, SM/F Venezuelan

'vengo *etc* VB *vedi* **venire**

veni'ale AG venial

ve'nire /128/ VI to come; (*riuscire: dolce, fotografia*) to turn out; (*come ausiliare: essere*): **viene ammirato da tutti** he is admired by everyone; **~ da** to come from; **quanto viene?** how much does it cost?; **far ~** (*mandare a chiamare*) to send for; (*medico*) to call, send for; **~ a capo di qc** to unravel sth, sort sth out; **~ al dunque** *o* **nocciolo** *o* **fatto** to come to the point; **~ fuori** to come out; **~ giù** to come down; **~ meno** (*svenire*) to faint; **~ meno a qc** not to fulfil sth; **~ su** to come up; **~ via** to come away; **~ a sapere qc** to learn sth; **~ a trovare qn** to come and see sb; **negli anni a ~** in the years to come, in future; **è venuto il momento di ...** the time has come to ...

'venni *etc* VB *vedi* **venire**

ven'taglio [ven'taʎʎo] SM fan

ven'tata SF gust (of wind)

venten'nale AG (*che dura 20 anni*) twenty-year *cpd*; (*che ricorre ogni 20 anni*) which takes place every twenty years

ven'tenne AG: **una ragazza ~** a twenty-year-old girl, a girl of twenty ▶ SMF twenty-year-old

ven'tennio SM period of twenty years; **il ~ fascista** the Fascist period

ven'tesimo, -a NUM twentieth

'venti NUM twenty

venti'lare /72/ VT (*stanza*) to air, ventilate; (*fig: idea, proposta*) to air

venti'lato, -a AG (*camera, zona*) airy; **poco ~** airless

ventila'tore SM fan; (*su parete, finestra*) ventilator, fan

ventilazi'one [ventilat'tsjone] SF ventilation

ven'tina SF: **una ~ (di)** around twenty, twenty or so

ventiquattr'ore SFPL (*periodo*) twenty-four hours ▶ SF INV (*Sport*) twenty-four-hour race; (*valigetta*) overnight case

venti'sette NUM twenty-seven; **il ~** (*giorno di paga*) (monthly) pay day

V

397

ventitré NUM twenty-three ▶ SFPL: **portava il cappello sulle ~** he wore his hat at a jaunty angle

'**vento** SM wind; **c'è ~** it's windy; **un colpo di ~** a gust of wind; **contro ~** against the wind; **~ contrario** (Naut) headwind

'**ventola** SF (Aut, Tecn) fan

ven'tosa SF (Zool) sucker; (di gomma) suction pad

ven'toso, -a AG windy

ven'totto NUM twenty-eight

'**ventre** SM stomach

ven'triloquo SM ventriloquist

ven'tuno NUM twenty-one

ven'tura SF: **andare alla ~** to trust to luck; **soldato di ~** mercenary

ven'turo, -a AG next, coming

ve'nuto, -a PP di **venire** ▶ SM/F: **il(la) primo(a) ~(a)** the first person who comes along ▶ SF coming, arrival

ver. ABBR = **versamento**

'**vera** SF wedding ring

ve'race [ve'ratʃe] AG (testimone) truthful; (testimonianza) accurate; (cibi) real, genuine

vera'mente AV really

ve'randa SF veranda(h)

ver'bale AG verbal ▶ SM (di riunione) minutes pl; **accordo ~** verbal agreement; **mettere a ~** to place in the minutes o on record

'**verbo** SM (Ling) verb; (parola) word; (Rel): **il V~** the Word

ver'boso, -a AG verbose, wordy

ver'dastro, -a AG greenish

'**verde** AG, SM green; **~ bottiglia/oliva** (inv) bottle/olive green; **benzina ~** lead-free o unleaded petrol; **i Verdi** (Pol) the Greens; **essere al ~** (fig) to be broke

verdeggi'ante [verded'dʒante] AG green, verdant

verde'rame SM verdigris

ver'detto SM verdict

ver'dura SF vegetables pl

vere'condia SF modesty

vere'condo, -a AG modest

'**verga, -ghe** SF rod

ver'gato, -a AG (foglio) ruled

vergi'nale [verdʒi'nale] AG virginal

'**vergine** ['verdʒine] SF virgin; **V~** Virgo ▶ AG virgin; (ragazza): **essere ~** to be a virgin; **essere della V~** (dello zodiaco) to be Virgo; **pura lana ~** pure new wool; **olio ~ d'oliva** unrefined olive oil

vergi'nità [verdʒini'ta] SF virginity

ver'gogna [ver'goɲɲa] SF shame; (timidezza) shyness, embarrassment

vergo'gnarsi [vergoɲ'ɲarsi] /15/ VPR: **~ (di)** to be o feel ashamed (of); to be shy (about), be embarrassed (about)

vergo'gnoso, -a [vergoɲ'ɲoso] AG ashamed; (timido) shy, embarrassed; (causa di vergogna: azione) shameful

veridicità [veriditʃi'ta] SF truthfulness

ve'ridico, -a, -ci, -che AG truthful

ve'rifica, -che SF checking no pl; check; **fare una ~ di** (freni, testimonianza, firma) to check; **~ contabile** (Finanza) audit

verifi'care /20/ VT (controllare) to check; (confermare) to confirm, bear out; (Finanza) to audit

verità SF INV truth; **a dire la ~, per la ~** truth to tell, actually

veriti'ero, -a AG (che dice la verità) truthful; (conforme a verità) true

'**verme** SM worm

vermi'celli [vermi'tʃɛlli] SMPL vermicelli sg

ver'miglio [ver'miʎʎo] SM vermilion, scarlet

'**vermut** SM INV vermouth

ver'nacolo SM vernacular

ver'nice [ver'nitʃe] SF (colorazione) paint; (trasparente) varnish; (pelle) patent leather; **"~ fresca"** "wet paint"

vernici'are [verni'tʃare] /14/ VT to paint; to varnish

vernicia'tura [vernitʃa'tura] SF painting; varnishing

'**vero, -a** AG (veridico: fatti, testimonianza) true; (autentico) real ▶ SM (verità) truth; (realtà) (real) life; **un ~ e proprio delinquente** a real criminal, an out and out criminal; **tant'è ~ che …** so much so that …; **a onor del ~, a dire il ~** to tell the truth

Ve'rona SF Verona

vero'nese AG of (o from) Verona

vero'simile AG likely, probable

verrò etc VB vedi **venire**

ver'ruca, -che SF wart

versa'mento SM (pagamento) payment; (deposito di denaro) deposit

ver'sante SM slopes pl, side

ver'sare /72/ VT (fare uscire: vino, farina) to pour (out); (spargere: lacrime, sangue) to shed; (rovesciare) to spill; (Econ) to pay; (: depositare) to deposit, pay in ▶ VI: **~ in gravi difficoltà** to find o.s. with serious problems; **versarsi** VPR (rovesciarsi) to spill; (fiume, folla) **versarsi (in)** to pour (into)

versa'tile AG versatile

versatilità SF versatility

ver'sato, -a AG: **~ in** to be (well-)versed in

ver'setto SM (Rel) verse

versi'one SF version; (traduzione) translation

'**verso** SM (di poesia) verse, line; (di animale, uccello, venditore ambulante) cry; (direzione) direction; (modo) way; (di foglio di carta) verso; (di moneta) reverse; **versi** SMPL (poesia) verse sg ▶ PREP (in direzione di) toward(s); (nei pressi di) near, around (about); (in senso temporale) about, around; (nei confronti di) for; **per un ~ o**

per l'altro one way or another; **prendere qn/qc per il ~ giusto** to approach sb/sth the right wa; **rifare il ~ a qn** (*imitare*) to mimic sb; **non c'è ~ di persuaderlo** there's no way of persuading him, he can't be persuaded; **~ di me** towards me; **~ l'alto** upwards; **~ il basso** downwards; **~ sera** towards evening

'**vertebra** SF vertebra

verte'brale AG vertebral; **colonna ~** spinal column, spine

verte'brato, -a AG, SM vertebrate

ver'tenza [ver'tɛntsa] SF (*lite*) lawsuit, case; (*sindacale*) dispute

'**vertere** /vb not found/ VI: **~ su** to deal with, be about

verti'cale AG, SF vertical

'**vertice** ['vɛrtitʃe] SM summit, top; (*Mat*) vertex; **conferenza al ~** (*Pol*) summit conference

ver'tigine [ver'tidʒine] SF dizziness *no pl*; dizzy spell; (*Med*) vertigo; **avere le vertigini** to feel dizzy

vertigi'noso, -a [vertidʒi'noso] AG (*altezza*) dizzy; (*fig*) breathtakingly high (*o deep etc*)

'**verza** ['verdza] SF Savoy cabbage

ve'scica, -che [veʃ'ʃika] SF (*Anat*) bladder; (*Med*) blister

vesco'vile AG episcopal

'**vescovo** SM bishop

'**vespa** SF wasp; ® (*veicolo*) (motor) scooter

ves'paio SM wasps' nest; **suscitare un ~** (*fig*) to stir up a hornets' nest

vespasi'ano SM urinal

'**vespro** SM (*Rel*) vespers *pl*

ves'sare /72/ VT to oppress

vessazi'one [vessat'tsjone] SF oppression

ves'sillo SM standard; (*bandiera*) flag

ves'taglia [ves'taʎʎa] SF dressing gown, robe (*US*)

'**veste** SF garment; (*rivestimento*) covering; (*qualità, facoltà*) capacity; **vesti** SFPL clothes, clothing *sg*; **in ~ ufficiale** (*fig*) in an official capacity; **in ~ di** in the guise of, as; **~ da camera** dressing gown, robe (*US*); **~ editoriale** layout

vesti'ario SM wardrobe, clothes *pl*; **capo di ~** article of clothing, garment

ves'tibolo SM (*entrance*) hall

ves'tigia [ves'tidʒa] SFPL (*tracce*) vestiges, traces; (*rovine*) ruins, remains

ves'tire /45/ VT (*bambino, malato*) to dress; (*avere indosso*) to have on, wear; **vestirsi** VPR to dress, get dressed; **vestirsi da** (*negozio, sarto*) to buy *o* get one's clothes at

ves'tito, -a AG dressed ▶ SM garment; (*da donna*) dress; (*da uomo*) suit; **vestiti** SMPL (*indumenti*) clothes; **~ di bianco** dressed in white

Ve'suvio SM: **il ~** Vesuvius

vete'rano, -a AG, SM/F veteran

veteri'nario, -a AG veterinary ▶ SM veterinary surgeon (*BRIT*), veterinarian (*US*), vet ▶ SF veterinary medicine

'**veto** SM INV veto; **porre il ~ a qc** to veto sth

ve'traio SM glassmaker; (*per finestre*) glazier

ve'trato, -a AG (*porta, finestra*) glazed; (*che contiene vetro*) glass *cpd* ▶ SF glass door (*o* window); (*di chiesa*) stained glass window; **carta vetrata** sandpaper

vetre'ria SF (*stabilimento*) glassworks *sg*; (*oggetti di vetro*) glassware

ve'trina SF (*di negozio*) (shop) window; (*armadio*) display cabinet

vetri'nista, -i, -e SM/F window dresser

ve'trino SM slide

vetri'olo SM vitriol

'**vetro** SM glass; (*per finestra, porta*) pane (of glass); **~ blindato** bulletproof glass; **~ infrangibile** shatterproof glass; **~ di sicurezza** safety glass; **i vetri di Murano** Murano glassware *sg*

ve'troso, -a AG vitreous

'**vetta** SF peak, summit, top

vet'tore SM (*Mat, Fisica*) vector; (*chi trasporta*) carrier

vetto'vaglie [vetto'vaʎʎe] SFPL supplies

vet'tura SF (*carrozza*) carriage; (*Ferr*) carriage (*BRIT*), car (*US*); (*auto*) car (*BRIT*), automobile (*US*); **~ di piazza** hackney carriage

vettu'rino SM coach driver, coachman

vezzeggi'are [vettsed'dʒare] /62/ VT to fondle, caress

vezzeggia'tivo [vettsedd'ʒa'tivo] SM (*Ling*) term of endearment

'**vezzo** ['vettso] SM habit; **vezzi** SMPL (*smancerie*) affected ways; (*leggiadria*) charms

vez'zoso, -a [vet'tsoso] AG (*grazioso*) charming, pretty; (*lezioso*) affected

V.F. ABBR = **vigili del fuoco**

V.G. ABBR = **Vostra Grazia**

VI SIGLA = **Vicenza**

vi (*dav lo, la, li, le, ne diventa* **ve**) PRON (*oggetto*) you; (*complemento di termine*) (to) you; (*riflessivo*) yourselves; (*reciproco*) each other ▶ AV (*lì*) there; (*qui*) here; (*per questo/quel luogo*) through here/there; **vi è/sono** there is/are

'**via** SF (*gen*) way; (*strada*) street; (*sentiero, pista*) path, track; (*Amm: procedimento*) channels *pl* ▶ PREP (*passando per*) via, by way of ▶ AV away ▶ ESCL go away!; (*suvvia*) come on!; (*Sport*) go! ▶ SM (*Sport*) starting signal; **per ~ di** (*a causa di*) because of, on account of; **in ~ per ~** on the way; **in ~ di guarigione** (*fig*) on the road to recovery; **per ~ aerea** by air; (*lettere*) by airmail; **~ satellite** by satellite; **andare/ essere ~** to go/be away; **~ ~** (*pian piano*) gradually; **~ ~ che** (*a mano a mano*) as; **e ~ dicendo, e ~ di questo passo** and so on (and so forth); **dare il ~** (*Sport*) to give the starting signal; **dare il ~ a** (*fig*) to start; **dare il ~ a un progetto** to give the green light to a project; **hanno dato il ~ ai lavori** they've begun *o* started work; **in ~ amichevole** in a friendly manner; **comporre una disputa in ~ amichevole** (*Dir*) to settle a dispute out of court; **in ~ eccezionale** as an exception; **in ~ privata** *o* **confidenziale** (*dire ecc*) in confidence; **in ~ provvisoria** provisionally; **V~ lattea** (*Astr*) Milky Way; **~ di mezzo** middle course; **non c'è ~ di scampo** *o* **d'uscita** there's no way out; **vie di comunicazione** communication routes

viabilità SF (*di strada*) practicability; (*rete stradale*) roads *pl*, road network

via'dotto SM viaduct

viaggi'are [viad'dʒare] /**62**/ VI to travel; **le merci viaggiano via mare** the goods go by sea

viaggia'tore, -'trice [viaddʒa'tore] AG travelling (*BRIT*), traveling (*US*) ▶ SM traveller (*BRIT*), traveler (*US*), passenger

vi'aggio [vi'addʒo] SM travel(ling); (*tragitto*) journey, trip; **buon ~!** have a good trip!; **~ d'affari** business trip; **~ di nozze** honeymoon; **~ organizzato** package tour *o* holiday

vi'ale SM avenue

vian'dante SMF vagrant

vi'atico, -ci SM (*Rel*) viaticum; (*fig*) encouragement

via'vai SM coming and going, bustle

vi'brare /**72**/ VI to vibrate; (*agitarsi*): **~ (di)** to quiver (with)

vibra'tore SM vibrator

vibrazi'one [vibrat'tsjone] SF vibration

vi'cario SM (*apostolico ecc*) vicar

'vice ['vitʃe] SMF deputy ▶ PREFISSO vice

vice'console [vitʃe'kɔnsole] SM vice-consul

vicediret'tore, -'trice [vitʃediret'tore] SM/F assistant manager(-manageress); (*di giornale ecc*) deputy editor

vi'cenda [vi'tʃɛnda] SF event; **vicende** SFPL (*sorte*) fortunes; **a ~** in turn; **con alterne vicende** with mixed fortunes

vicen'devole [vitʃen'devole] AG mutual, reciprocal

vicen'tino, -a [vitʃen'tino] AG of (*o* from) Vicenza

vicepresi'dente [vitʃepresi'dɛnte] SM vice-president, vice-chairman

vice'versa [vitʃe'vɛrsa] AV vice versa; **da Roma a Pisa e ~** from Rome to Pisa and back

vi'chingo, -a, -ghi, -ghe [vi'kingo] AG, SM/F Viking

vici'nanza [vitʃi'nantsa] SF nearness, closeness; **vicinanze** SFPL (*paraggi*)

neighbourhood (*BRIT*), neighborhood (*US*), vicinity

vici'nato [vitʃi'nato] SM neighbourhood (*BRIT*), neighborhood (*US*); (*vicini*) neighbo(u)rs *pl*

vi'cino, -a [vi'tʃino] AG (*gen*) near; (*nello spazio*) near, nearby; (*accanto*) next; (*nel tempo*) near, close at hand ▶ SM/F neighbour (*BRIT*), neighbor (*US*) ▶ AV near, close; **da ~** (*guardare*) close up; (*esaminare, seguire*) closely; (*conoscere*) well, intimately; **~ a** prep near (to), close to; (*accanto a*) beside; **mi sono stati molto vicini** (*fig*) they were very supportive towards me; **~ di casa** neighbour

vicissi'tudini [vitʃissi'tudini] SFPL trials and tribulations

'vicolo SM alley; **~ cieco** blind alley

'video SM INV (*TV: schermo*) screen

video'camera SF camcorder

videocas'setta SF videocassette

videochia'mare [videokja'mare] /**72**/ VT to video call

video'clip [video'klip] SM INV videoclip

videodipen'dente SMF telly addict ▶ AG: **un pigrone ~** a couch potato

videofo'nino SM video mobile

videogi'oco, -chi [video'dʒɔko] SM video game

videono'leggio [videono'leddʒo] SM video rental

videoregistra'tore [videoredʒistra'tore] SM (*apparecchio*) video (recorder)

video'teca, -che SF video shop

videote'lefono SM videophone

videotermi'nale SM visual display unit

'vidietc VB *vedi* **vedere**

vidi'mare /**72**/ VT (*Amm*) to authenticate

vidimazi'one [vidimat'tsjone] SF (*Amm*) authentication

Vi'enna SF Vienna

vien'nese AG, SMF Viennese *inv*

vie'tare /**72**/ VT to forbid; (*Amm*) to prohibit; (*libro*) to ban; **~ a qn di fare** to forbid sb to do; to prohibit sb from doing

vie'tato, -a AG (*vedi vb*) forbidden; prohibited; banned; **"~ fumare/l'ingresso"** "no smoking/admittance"; **~ ai minori di 14/18 anni** prohibited to children under 14/18; **"senso ~"** (*Aut*) "no entry"; **"sosta vietata"** (*Aut*) "no parking"

Viet'nam SM: **il ~** Vietnam

vietna'mita, -i, -e AG, SM/F, SM Vietnamese *inv*

vi'eto, -a AG worthless

vi'gente [vi'dʒɛnte] AG in force

'vigere ['vidʒere] VI (*difettivo: si usa solo alla terza persona*) to be in force; **in casa mia vige l'abitudine di ...** at home we are in the habit of ...

vigi'lante [vidʒi'lante] AG vigilant, watchful
vigi'lanza [vidʒi'lantsa] SF vigilance; (*sorveglianza: di operai, alunni*) supervision; (*: di sospetti, criminali*) surveillance; **~ notturna** night-watchman service
vigi'lare [vidʒi'lare] /**72**/ VT to watch over, keep an eye on; **~ che** to make sure that, see to it that
vigi'lato, -a [vidʒi'lato] SM/F (*Dir*) person under police surveillance
vigila'trice [vidʒila'tritʃe] SF: **~ d'infanzia** nursery-school teacher; **~ scolastica** school health officer
'vigile ['vidʒile] AG watchful ► SM (*anche:* **vigile urbano**) policeman (*in towns*); **~ del fuoco** fireman; *see note*

▌ The *vigili urbani* are a municipal police force attached to the *Comune*. Their duties involve everyday aspects of life such as traffic, public works and services, and commerce.

vigi'lessa [vidʒi'lessa] SF (traffic) policewoman
vi'gilia [vi'dʒilja] SF (*giorno antecedente*) eve; **la ~ di Natale** Christmas Eve
vigliacche'ria [viʎʎakke'ria] SF cowardice
vigli'acco, -a, -chi, -che [viʎ'ʎakko] AG cowardly ► SM/F coward
'vigna ['viɲɲa] SF, **vi'gneto** [viɲ'ɲeto] SM vineyard
vi'gnetta [viɲ'ɲetta] SF cartoon; (*Aut: anche:* **vignetta autostradale**: *tassa*) car tax (*for motorways*); (*: adesivo*) *sticker showing that this tax has been paid*
vi'gogna [vi'goɲɲa] SF vicuña
vi'gore SM vigour (*BRIT*), vigor (*US*); (*Dir*): **essere/entrare in ~** to be in/come into force; **non è più in ~** it is no longer in force, it no longer applies
vigo'roso, -a AG vigorous
'vile AG (*spregevole*) low, mean, base; (*codardo*) cowardly
vili'pendere /**8**/ VT to despise, scorn
vili'pendio SM contempt, scorn
vili'peso, -a PP *di* **vilipendere**
'villa SF villa
vil'laggio [vil'laddʒo] SM village; **~ turistico** holiday village
villa'nia SF rudeness, lack of manners; **fare (o dire) una ~ a qn** to be rude to sb
vil'lano, -a AG rude, ill-mannered ► SM/F boor
villeggi'ante [villed'dʒante] SMF holiday-maker (*BRIT*), vacationer (*US*)
villeggi'are [villed'dʒare] /**62**/ VI to holiday, spend one's holidays, vacation (*US*)
villeggia'tura [villeddʒa'tura] SF holiday(s *pl*) (*BRIT*), vacation (*US*); **luogo di ~** (holiday) resort

vil'letta SF, **vil'lino** SM small house (with a garden), cottage
vil'loso, -a AG hairy
viltà SF cowardice *no pl*; (*gesto*) cowardly act
Vimi'nale SM *see note*

▌ The *Viminale*, which takes its name from one of the famous Seven Hills of Rome on which it stands, is home to the Ministry of the Interior.

'vimini SMPL wicker; **mobili di ~** wicker furniture *sg*
vi'naio SM wine merchant
'vincere ['vintʃere] /**129**/ VT (*in guerra, al gioco, a una gara*) to defeat, beat; (*premio, guerra, partita*) to win; (*fig*) to overcome, conquer ► VI to win; **~ qn in** (*abilità, bellezza*) to surpass sb in
'vincita ['vintʃita] SF win; (*denaro vinto*) winnings *pl*
vinci'tore, -'trice [vintʃi'tore] SM/F winner; (*Mil*) victor
vinco'lante AG binding
vinco'lare /**72**/ VT to bind; (*Comm: denaro*) to tie up
vinco'lato, -a AG: **deposito ~** (*Comm*) fixed deposit
'vincolo SM (*fig*) bond, tie; (*Dir*) obligation
vi'nicolo, -a AG wine *cpd*; **regione vinicola** wine-producing area
vinificazi'one [vinifikat'tsjone] SF wine-making
'vino SM wine; **~ bianco/rosato/rosso** white/rosé/red wine; **~ da pasto** table wine
'vinsi *etc* VB *vedi* **vincere**
'vinto, -a PP *di* **vincere** ► AG: **darla vinta a qn** to let sb have his (*o* her) way; **darsi per ~** to give up, give in
vi'ola SF (*Bot*) violet; (*Mus*) viola ► AG, SM INV (*colore*) purple
vio'lare /**72**/ VT (*chiesa*) to desecrate, violate; (*giuramento, legge*) to violate
violazi'one [violat'tsjone] SF desecration; violation; **~ di domicilio** (*Dir*) breaking and entering
violen'tare /**72**/ VT to use violence on; (*donna*) to rape
vio'lento, -a AG violent
vio'lenza [vio'lɛntsa] SF violence; **~ carnale** rape
vio'letto, -a AG, SM (*colore*) violet ► SF (*Bot*) violet
violi'nista, -i, -e SM/F violinist
vio'lino SM violin
violoncel'lista, -i, -e [violontʃel'lista] SM/F cellist, cello player
violon'cello [violon'tʃɛllo] SM cello
vi'ottolo SM path, track
VIP [vip] SM INV/F INV (= *Very Important Person*) VIP

V

'**vipera** SF viper, adder

vi'**raggio** [vi'raddʒo] SM (Naut, Aer) turn; (Fot) toning

vi'**rale** AG viral

vi'**rare** /72/ VI (Naut, Aer) to turn; (Fot) to tone; ~ **di bordo** to change course; (Naut) to tack

vi'**rata** SF coming about; turning; change of course

'**virgola** SF (Ling) comma; (Mat) point

virgo'**lette** SFPL inverted commas, quotation marks

vi'**rile** AG (proprio dell'uomo) masculine; (non puerile, da uomo) manly, virile

viri'**lità** SF masculinity; manliness; (sessuale) virility

vir'**tù** SF INV virtue; **in** o **per ~ di** by virtue of, by

virtu'**ale** AG virtual

virtu'**oso, -a** AG virtuous ▶ SM/F (Mus ecc) virtuoso

viru'**lento, -a** AG virulent

'**virus** SM INV (anche Inform) virus

visa'**gista, -i, -e** [viza'dʒista] SM/F beautician

visce'**rale** [viʃʃe'rale] AG (Med) visceral; (fig) profound, deep-rooted

'**viscere** ['viʃʃere] SM (Anat) internal organ ▶ SFPL (di animale) entrails pl; (fig) depths pl, bowels pl

'**vischio** ['viskjo] SM (Bot) mistletoe; (pania) birdlime

vischi'**oso, -a** [vis'kjoso] AG sticky

visci'**dità** [viʃʃidi'ta] SF sliminess

'**viscido, -a** ['viʃʃido] AG slimy

vis'**conte, -'essa** SM/F viscount (viscountess)

visco'**sità** SF viscosity

vis'**coso, -a** AG viscous

vi'**sibile** AG visible

visi'**bilio** SM: **andare in ~** to go into raptures

visi'**bilità** SF visibility

visi'**era** SF (di elmo) visor; (di berretto) peak

visio'**nare** /72/ VT (gen) to look at, examine; (Cine) to screen

visio'**nario, -a** AG, SM/F visionary

visi'**one** SF vision; **prendere ~ di qc** to examine sth, look sth over; **prima/seconda ~** (Cine) first/second showing

'**visita** SF visit; (Med) visit, call; (: esame) examination; **far ~ a qn, andare in ~ da qn** to visit sb, pay sb a visit; **in ~ ufficiale in Italia** on an official visit to Italy; **orario di visite** (ospedale) visiting hours; **~ di controllo** (Med) checkup; **~ medica** medical examination; **~ a domicilio** house call; **~ guidata** guided tour; **~ sanitaria** sanitary inspection

visi'**tare** /72/ VT to visit; (Med) to visit, call on; (: esaminare) to examine

visita'**tore, -'trice** SM/F visitor

vi'**sivo, -a** AG visual

'**viso** SM face; **fare buon ~ a cattivo gioco** to make the best of things

vi'**sone** SM mink

vi'**sore** SM (Fot) viewer

'**vispo, -a** AG quick, lively

'**vissi** etc VB vedi **vivere**

vis'**suto, -a** PP di **vivere** ▶ AG (aria, modo di fare) experienced

'**vista** SF (facoltà) (eye)sight; (veduta) view; (fatto di vedere): **la ~ di** the sight of; **con ~ sul lago** with a view over the lake; **sparare a ~** to shoot on sight; **pagabile a ~** payable on demand; **in ~** in sight; **avere in ~ qc** to have sth in view; **mettersi in ~** to draw attention to o.s.; (peg) to show off; **perdere qn di ~** to lose sight of sb; (fig) to lose touch with sb; **far ~ di fare** to pretend to do; **a ~ d'occhio** as far as the eye can see; (fig) before one's very eyes

vis'**tare** /72/ VT to approve; (Amm: passaporto) to visa

'**visto, -a** PP di **vedere** ▶ SM visa; **~ che** cong seeing (that); **~ d'ingresso/di transito** entry/transit visa; **~ permanente/di soggiorno** permanent/tourist visa

vis'**toso, -a** AG gaudy, garish; (ingente) considerable

visu'**ale** AG visual

visualiz'**zare** [vizualid'dzare] /72/ VT to visualize

visualizza'**tore** [vizualiddza'tore] SM (Inform) visual display unit, VDU

visualizzazi'**one** [vizualiddzat'tsjone] SF (Inform) display

'**vita** SF life; (Anat) waist; **essere in ~** to be alive; **pieno di ~** full of life; **a ~** for life; **membro a ~** life member

vi'**tale** AG vital

vitali'**tà** SF vitality

vita'**lizio, -a** [vita'littsjo] AG life cpd ▶ SM life annuity

vita'**mina** SF vitamin

'**vite** SF (Bot) vine; (Tecn) screw; **giro di ~** (anche fig) turn of the screw

vi'**tello** SM (Zool) calf; (carne) veal; (pelle) calfskin

vi'**ticcio** [vi'tittʃo] SM (Bot) tendril

viticol'**tore** SM wine grower

viticol'**tura** SF wine growing

'**vitreo, -a** AG vitreous; (occhio, sguardo) glassy

'**vittima** SF victim

vitti'**mismo** SM self-pity

'**vitto** SM food; (in un albergo ecc) board; **~ e alloggio** board and lodging

vit'**toria** SF victory

vittori'**ano, -a** AG Victorian

vittori'**oso, -a** AG victorious

vitupe'**rare** /72/ VT to rail at o against

vi'**uzza** [vi'uttsa] SF (in città) alley

'**viva** ESCL: **~ il re!** long live the king!

vivacchi'are [vivak'kjare] /**19**/ vi to scrape a living

vi'vace [vi'vatʃe] AG (*vivo, animato*) lively; (*mente*) lively, sharp; (*colore*) bright

vivacità [vivatʃi'ta] SF liveliness; brightness

vivaciz'zare [vivatʃid'dzare] /**72**/ VT to liven up

vi'vaio SM (*di pesci*) hatchery; (*Agr*) nursery

viva'mente AV (*commuoversi*) deeply, profoundly; (*ringraziare ecc*) sincerely, warmly

vi'vanda SF food; (*piatto*) dish

viva'voce [viva'votʃe] SM INV (*dispositivo*) loudspeaker ▶ AG INV: **telefono ~** speakerphone; **mettere in ~** to switch on the loudspeaker

vi'vente AG living, alive; **i viventi** the living

'vivere /**130**/ VI to live ▶ VT to live; (*passare: brutto momento*) to live through, go through; (*sentire: gioie, pene di qn*) to share ▶ SM life; (*anche:* **modo di vivere**) way of life; **viveri** SMPL (*cibo*) food sg, provisions; **~ di** to live on

vi'veur [vi'vœr] SM INV pleasure-seeker

'vivido, -a AG (*colore*) vivid, bright

vivifi'care /**20**/ VT to enliven, give life to; (*piante ecc*) to revive

vivisezi'one [viviset'tsjone] SF vivisection

'vivo, -a AG (*vivente*) alive, living; (*: animale*) live; (*fig*) lively; (*: colore*) bright, brilliant ▶ SM: **entrare nel ~ di una questione** to get to the heart of a matter; **i vivi** the living; **esperimenti su animali vivi** experiments on live o living animals; **~ e vegeto** hale and hearty; **farsi ~** (*fig*) to show one's face; to keep in touch; **con ~ rammarico** with deep regret; **congratulazioni vivissime** heartiest congratulations; **con i più vivi ringraziamenti** with deepest o warmest thanks; **ritrarre dal ~** to paint from life; **pungere qn nel ~** (*fig*) to cut sb to the quick

vivrò etc VB vedi **vivere**

vizi'are [vit'tsjare] /**19**/ VT (*bambino*) to spoil; (*corrompere moralmente*) to corrupt; (*Dir*) to invalidate

vizi'ato, -a [vit'tsjato] AG spoilt; (*aria, acqua*) polluted; (*Dir*) invalid, invalidated

'vizio ['vittsjo] SM (*morale*) vice; (*cattiva abitudine*) bad habit; (*imperfezione*) flaw, defect; (*errore*) fault, mistake; **~ di forma** legal flaw o irregularity; **~ procedurale** procedural error

vizi'oso, -a [vit'tsjoso] AG depraved; (*inesatto*) incorrect; **circolo ~** vicious circle

V.le ABBR = **viale**

vocabo'lario SM (*dizionario*) dictionary; (*lessico*) vocabulary

vo'cabolo SM word

vo'cale AG vocal ▶ SF vowel

vocazi'one [vokat'tsjone] SF vocation; (*fig*) natural bent

'voce ['votʃe] SF voice; (*diceria*) rumour (BRIT), rumor (US); (*di un elenco: in bilancio*) item; (*di dizionario*) entry; **parlare a alta/bassa ~** to speak in a loud/low o soft voice; **fare la ~ grossa** to raise one's voice; **dar ~ a qc** to voice sth, give voice to sth; **a gran ~** in a loud voice, loudly; **te lo dico a ~** I'll tell you when I see you; **a una ~** unanimously; **aver ~ in capitolo** (*fig*) to have a say in the matter; **voci di corridoio** rumours

voci'are [vo'tʃare] /**14**/ VI to shout, yell

vocife'rante [votʃife'rante] AG noisy

vo'cio [vo'tʃio] SM shouting

'vodka SF INV vodka

'voga SF (*Naut*) rowing; (*usanza*): **essere in ~** to be in fashion o in vogue

vo'gare /**80**/ VI to row

voga'tore, -'trice SM/F oarsman(-woman) ▶ SM rowing machine

voghe'rò etc [voge'rɔ] VB vedi **vogare**

'voglia ['vɔʎʎa] SF desire, wish; (*macchia*) birthmark; **aver ~ di qc/di fare** to feel like sth/like doing; (*più forte*) to want sth/to do; **di buona ~** willingly

'voglio etc ['vɔʎʎo] VB vedi **volere**

vogli'oso, -a [voʎ'ʎoso] AG (*sguardo ecc*) longing; (*più forte*) full of desire

'voi PRON you; **~ stessi(e)** you yourselves

voi'altri PRON you

vol. ABBR (= *volume*) vol.

vo'lano SM (*Sport*) shuttlecock; (*Tecn*) flywheel

vo'lant [vɔ'lã] SM INV frill

vo'lante AG flying ▶ SM (steering) wheel ▶ SF (*Polizia: anche:* **squadra volante**) flying squad

volanti'naggio [volanti'naddʒo] SM leafleting

volanti'nare /**72**/ VT (*distribuire volantini*) to leaflet, hand out leaflets

volan'tino SM leaflet

vo'lare /**72**/ VI (*uccello, aereo, fig*) to fly; (*cappello*) to blow away o off, fly away o off; **~ via** to fly away o off

vo'lata SF flight; (*d'uccelli*) flock, flight; (*corsa*) rush; (*Sport*) final sprint; **passare di ~ da qn** to drop in on sb briefly

vo'latile AG (*Chim*) volatile ▶ SM (*Zool*) bird

volatiliz'zarsi [volatilid'dzarsi] /**61**/ VPR (*Chim*) to volatilize; (*fig*) to vanish, disappear

vo'lente AG: **verrai ~ o nolente** you'll come whether you like it or not

volente'roso, -a AG willing, keen

volenti'eri AV willingly; **"~"** "with pleasure", "I'd be glad to"

⸢ **PAROLA CHIAVE** ⸥

vo'lere /**131**/ SM will, wish(es); **contro il volere di** against the wishes of; **per volere di qn** in obedience to sb's will o wishes
▶ VT **1** (*esigere, desiderare*) to want; **volere**

fare qc to want to do sth; **volere che qn faccia qc** to want sb to do sth; **vorrei andarmene** I'd like to go; **vorrei che se ne andasse** I'd like him to go; **vorrei questo/fare** I would *o* I'd like this/to do; **volevo parlartene** I meant to talk to you about it; **come vuoi** as you like; **la vogliono al telefono** there's a call for you; **che tu lo voglia o no** whether you like it or not; **vuoi un caffè?** would you like a coffee?; **senza volere** (*inavvertitamente*) without meaning to, unintentionally; **te la sei voluta** you asked for it; **la tradizione vuole che ...** custom requires that ...; **la leggenda vuole che ...** legend has it that ...

2 (*consentire*): **vogliate attendere, per piacere** please wait; **vogliamo andare?** shall we go?; **vuole essere così gentile da ...?** would you be so kind as to ...?; **non ha voluto ricevermi** he wouldn't see me

3: **volerci** (*essere necessario: materiale, attenzione*) to be needed; (*: tempo*) to take; **quanta farina ci vuole per questa torta?** how much flour do you need for this cake?; **ci vuole un'ora per arrivare a Venezia** it takes an hour to get to Venice; **è quel che ci vuole** it's just what is needed

4: **voler bene a qn** (*amore*) to love sb; (*affetto*) to be fond of sb, like sb very much; **voler male a qn** to dislike sb; **volerne a qn** to bear sb a grudge; **voler dire** to mean; **voglio dire ...** I mean ...; **volevo ben dire!** I thought as much!

vol'gare AG vulgar
volgarità SF vulgarity
volgariz'zare [volgarid'dzare] /**72**/ VT to popularize
volgar'mente AV (*in modo volgare*) vulgarly, coarsely; (*del popolo*) commonly, popularly
'volgere ['vɔldʒere] /**96**/ VT to turn ▶ VI to turn; (*tendere*): **~ a: il tempo volge al brutto/al bello** the weather is breaking/is setting fair; **un rosso che volge al viola** a red verging on purple; **volgersi** VPR to turn; **~ al peggio** to take a turn for the worse; **~ al termine** to draw to an end
'volgo SM common people
voli'era SF aviary
voli'tivo, -a AG strong-willed
'volli *etc* VB *vedi* **volere**
'volo SM flight; **ci sono due ore di ~ da Londra a Milano** it's a two-hour flight between London and Milan; **colpire qc al ~** to hit sth as it flies past; **prendere al ~** (*autobus, treno*) to catch at the last possible moment; (*palla*) to catch as it flies past; (*occasione*) to seize; **capire al ~** to understand straight away; **veduta a ~ d'uccello**

bird's-eye view; **~ charter** charter flight; **~ di linea** scheduled flight
volontà SF INV will; **a ~** (*mangiare, bere*) as much as one likes; **buona/cattiva ~** goodwill/lack of goodwill; **le sue ultime ~** (*testamento*) his last will and testament *sg*
volontaria'mente AV voluntarily
volontari'ato SM (*Mil*) voluntary service; (*lavoro*) voluntary work
volon'tario, -a AG voluntary ▶ SM (*Mil*) volunteer
'volpe SF fox
vol'pino, -a AG (*pelo, coda*) fox's; (*aspetto, astuzia*) fox-like ▶ SM (*cane*) Pomeranian
vol'pone, -a SM/F (*fig*) old fox
'volsi *etc* VB *vedi* **volgere**
volt SM INV (*Elettr*) volt
'volta SF (*momento, circostanza*) time; (*turno, giro*) turn; (*curva*) turn, bend; (*Archit*) vault; (*direzione*): **partire alla ~ di** to set off for; **a mia** (*o* **tua** *etc*) **~** in turn; **una ~** once; **una ~ sola** only once; **c'era una ~** once upon a time there was; **le cose di una ~** the things of the past; **due volte** twice; **tre volte** three times; **una cosa per ~** one thing at a time; **una ~ o l'altra** one of these days; **una ~ per tutte** once and for all; **una ~ tanto** just for once; **lo facciamo un'altra ~** we'll do it another time *o* some other time; **a volte** at times, sometimes; **di ~ in ~** from time to time; **una ~ che** (*temporale*) once; (*causale*) since; **3 volte 4** 3 times 4; **ti ha dato di ~ il cervello?** have you gone out of your mind?
volta'faccia [volta'fattʃa] SM INV (*fig*) volte-face
vol'taggio [vol'taddʒo] SM (*Elettr*) voltage
vol'tare /**72**/ VT to turn; (*girare: moneta*) to turn over; (*rigirare*) to turn round ▶ VI to turn; **voltarsi** VPR to turn; to turn over; to turn round
voltas'tomaco SM nausea; (*fig*) disgust
volteggi'are [volted'dʒare] /**62**/ VI (*volare*) to circle; (*in equitazione*) to do trick riding; (*in ginnastica*) to vault
'volto, -a PP *di* **volgere** ▶ AG (*inteso a*): **il mio discorso è ~ a spiegare ...** in my speech I intend to explain ... ▶ SM face
vo'lubile AG changeable, fickle
vo'lume SM volume
volumi'noso, -a AG voluminous, bulky
vo'luta SF (*gen*) spiral; (*Archit*) volute
voluttà SF sensual pleasure *o* delight
voluttu'oso, -a AG voluptuous
vomi'tare /**72**/ VT, VI to vomit
'vomito SM vomiting *no pl*; vomit; **ho il ~** I feel sick
'vongola SF clam
vo'race [vo'ratʃe] AG voracious, greedy

voracità[voratʃi'ta] SF voracity, voraciousness

vo'ragine[vo'radʒine] SF abyss, chasm

vorròetc VB vedi **volere**

'vortice['vɔrtitʃe] SM whirlwind; whirlpool; (fig) whirl

vorti'coso, -aAG whirling

'vostro, -a DET: **il (la) ~(a)** etc your ▶ PRON: **il (la) ~(a)** etc yours ▶ SM: **avete speso del ~?** did you spend your own money? ▶ SF: **la vostra** (opinione) your view; **i vostri** (famiglia) your family; **un ~ amico** a friend of yours; **è dei vostri, è dalla vostra** he's on your side; **l'ultima vostra** (Comm: lettera) your most recent letter; **alla vostra!** (brindisi) here's to you!, your health!

vo'tante SMF voter

vo'tare/72/ VI to vote ▶ VT (sottoporre a votazione) to take a vote on; (approvare) to vote for; (Rel): **~ qc a** to dedicate sth to; **votarsi** VPR to devote o.s. to

votazi'one[votat'tsjone] SF vote, voting; **votazioni**SFPL (Pol) votes; (Ins) marks

'voto SM (Pol) vote; (Ins) mark (BRIT), grade (US); (Rel) vow; (: offerta) votive offering; **aver voti belli/brutti** (Ins) to get good/bad marks o grades; **prendere i voti** to take one's vows; **~ di fiducia** vote of confidence

V.P.ABBR (= vicepresidente) VP

VRSIGLA = **Verona**

v.r.ABBR (= vedi retro) PTO

vs.ABBR (= vostro) yr

v.s.ABBR = **vedi sopra**

VTSIGLA = **Viterbo**

V.U.ABBR = **vigile urbano**

vul'canico, -a, -ci, -cheAG volcanic

vulcanizzazi'one[vulkaniddzat'tsjone] SF vulcanization

vul'canoSM volcano

vulne'rabileAG vulnerable

vulnerabilitàSF vulnerability

vu'oi, vu'oleVB vedi **volere**

vuo'tare/72/ VT, **vuo'tarsi**VPR to empty

vu'oto, -aAG empty; (fig: privo): **~ di** (senso ecc) devoid of ▶ SM empty space, gap; (spazio in bianco) blank; (Fisica) vacuum; (fig: mancanza) gap, void; **a mani vuote** empty-handed; **assegno a ~** dud cheque (BRIT), bad check (US); **~ d'aria** air pocket; **"~ a perdere"** "no deposit"; **"~ a rendere"** "returnable bottle"

V

Ww

W, w ['dɔppjovu] SM O F INV (*lettera*) W, w;
 W come Washington ≈ W for William
W ABBR = **viva, evviva**
'**wafer** ['vafer] SM INV (*Cuc, Elettr*) wafer
wagon-'lit [vagɔ̃'li] SM INV (*Ferr*) sleeping
 car
'**walkman** ® ['wɔːkmən] SM INV Walkman®
'**water** ['wɔːtə'] SM INV toilet
'**water 'closet** ['wɔːtə'klɔzıt] SM INV toilet,
 lavatory
watt [vat] SM INV (*Elettr*) watt
wat'tora [vat'tora] SM INV (*Elettr*) watt-hour
WC SM INV WC
web [ueb] SM: **il** ~ the web ▶ AG INV: **pagina** ~
 webpage; **cercare nel** ~ to search the web

webcam [web'kam] SF INV (*Inform*) webcam
'**webinar** ['wɛbinar] SM INV (*Inform*) webinar
web'mail [wɛb'meil] SF webmail; **delle** ~
 (*Inform*) webmail services
'**weekend** ['wiːkend] SM INV weekend
'**western** ['wɛstern] AG (*Cine*) cowboy *cpd*
 ▶ SM INV western, cowboy film;
 ~ **all'italiana** spaghetti western
'**whisky** ['wiski] SM INV whisky
Wi-Fi [uai'fai] (*Inform*) SM Wi-Fi ▶ AG INV
 Wi-Fi
'**wiki** ['wiki] SM INV (*Internet*) wiki
'**windsurf** ['windsəːf] SM INV (*tavola*)
 windsurfer, sailboard; (*sport*) windsurfing
'**würstel** ['vyrstəl] SM INV frankfurter

Xx

X, x [iks] SM O F INV (*lettera*) X, x; **X come Xeres** ≈ X for Xmas

xenofo'bia [ksenofo'bia] SF xenophobia

xe'nofobo, -a [kse'nɔfobo] AG xenophobic ▸ SM/F xenophobe

'xeres ['ksɛres] SM INV sherry

xero'copia [ksero'kɔpja] SF xerox®, photocopy

xerocopi'are [kseroko'pjare] /**19**/ VT to photocopy

xi'lofono [ksi'lɔfono] SM xylophone

Yy

Y, y ['ipsilon] SM O F INV (*lettera*) Y, y; **Y come Yacht** = Y for Yellow (*BRIT*), ≈ Y for Yoke (*US*)

yacht [jɔt] SM INV yacht

'yankee ['jæŋki] SM INV/F INV Yank, Yankee

Y.C.I. ABBR = **Yacht Club d'Italia**

'Yemen ['jemen] SM: **lo ~** Yemen

yen [jen] SM INV (*moneta*) yen

'yiddish ['jidiʃ] AG INV, SM INV Yiddish

'yoga ['jɔga] AG INV, SM yoga (*cpd*)

yogurt ['jɔgurt] SM INV yog(h)urt

Zz

Z, z ['dzɛta] SM O F INV (*lettera*) Z, z; **Z come Zara** ≈ Z for Zebra

zabai'one [dzaba'jone] SM *dessert made of egg yolks, sugar and marsala*

zaffata [tsaf'fata] SF (*tanfo*) stench

zaffe'rano [dzaffe'rano] SM saffron

zaffiro [dzaf'firo] SM sapphire

'zagara ['dzagara] SF orange blossom

zai'netto [dzai'netto] SM (small) rucksack

'zaino ['dzaino] SM rucksack

Za'ire [dza'ire] SM: **lo ~** Zaire

'Zambia ['dzambja] SM: **lo ~** Zambia

'zampa ['tsampa] SF (*di animale: gamba*) leg; (: *piede*) paw; **a quattro zampe** on all fours; **zampe di gallina** (*calligrafia*) scrawl; (*rughe*) crow's feet

zam'pata [tsam'pata] SF (*di cane, gatto*) blow with a paw

zampet'tare [tsampet'tare] /**72**/ VI to scamper

zampil'lare [tsampil'lare] /**72**/ VI to gush, spurt

zam'pillo [tsam'pillo] SM gush, spurt

zam'pino [tsam'pino] SM paw; **qui c'è sotto il suo ~** (*fig*) he's had a hand in this

zam'pogna [tsam'poɲɲa] SF *instrument similar to bagpipes*

'zanna ['tsanna] SF (*di elefante*) tusk; (*di carnivori*) fang

zan'zara [dzan'dzara] SF mosquito

zanzari'era [dzandza'rjɛra] SF mosquito net

'zappa ['tsappa] SF hoe

zap'pare [tsap'pare] /**72**/ VT to hoe

zappa'tore [tsappa'tore] SM (*Agr*) hoer

zappa'tura [tsappa'tura] SF (*Agr*) hoeing

'zapping ['tsapiŋ] SM (*TV*) channel-hopping

zar, za'rina [tsar, tsa'rina] SM/F tsar (tsarina)

'zattera ['dzattera] SF raft

za'vorra [dza'vɔrra] SF ballast

'zazzera ['tsattsera] SF shock of hair

'zebra ['dzɛbra] SF zebra; **zebre** SFPL (*Aut*) zebra crossing *sg* (BRIT), crosswalk *sg* (US)

ze'brato, -a [dze'brato] AG with black and white stripes; **strisce zebrate,**

attraversamento ~ (*Aut*) zebra crossing (BRIT), crosswalk (US)

'zecca, -che ['tsekka] SF (*Zool*) tick; (*officina di monete*) mint

zec'chino [tsek'kino] SM gold coin; **oro ~** pure gold

ze'lante [dze'lante] AG zealous

'zelo ['dzɛlo] SM zeal

'zenit ['dzɛnit] SM zenith

'zenzero ['dzendzero] SM ginger

'zeppa ['tseppa] SF wedge

'zeppo, -a ['tseppo] AG: **~ di** crammed o packed with

zer'bino [dzer'bino] SM doormat

'zero ['dzɛro] SM zero, nought; **vincere per tre a ~** (*Sport*) to win three-nil

'zeta ['dzɛta] SM O F zed, (the letter) z

'zia ['tsia] SF aunt

zibel'lino [dzibel'lino] SM sable

zi'gano, -a [tsi'gano] AG, SM/F gypsy

'zigomo ['dzigomo] SM cheekbone

zigri'nare [dzigri'nare] /**72**/ VT (*gen*) to knurl; (*pellame*) to grain; (*monete*) to mill

zig'zag [dzig'dzag] SM INV zigzag; **andare a ~** to zigzag

Zim'babwe [tsim'babwe] SM: **lo ~** Zimbabwe

zim'bello [dzim'bɛllo] SM (*oggetto di burle*) laughing-stock

'zinco ['dzinko] SM zinc

zinga'resco, -a, -schi, -sche [dzinga'resko] AG gypsy *cpd*

'zingaro, -a ['dzingaro] SM/F gypsy

'zio ['tsio] (*pl* **zii**) SM uncle; **zii** SMPL (*zio e zia*) uncle and aunt

zip'pare [dzip'pare] /**72**/ VT (*Inform: file*) to zip

zi'tella [dzi'tɛlla] SF spinster; (*peg*) old maid

zit'tire [tsit'tire] /**55**/ VT to silence, hush o shut up ▶ VI to hiss

'zitto, -a ['tsitto] AG quiet, silent; **sta' ~!** be quiet!

ziz'zania [dzid'dzanja] SF (*Bot*) darnel; (*fig*) discord; **gettare** o **seminare ~** to sow discord

z

'**zoccolo** ['tsɔkkolo] SM (*calzatura*) clog; (*di cavallo ecc*) hoof; (*Archit*) plinth; (*di parete*) skirting (board); (*di armadio*) base

zodia'cale [dzodia'kale] AG zodiac *cpd*; **segno** ~ sign of the zodiac

zo'diaco [dzo'diako] SM zodiac

zolfa'nello [tsolfa'nɛllo] SM (sulphur) match

'**zolfo** ['tsolfo] SM sulphur (*BRIT*), sulfur (*US*)

'**zolla** ['dzolla] SF clod (of earth)

zol'letta [dzol'letta] SF sugar lump

'**zona** ['dzɔna] SF zone, area; ~ **di depressione** (*Meteor*) trough of low pressure; ~ **disco** (*Aut*) ≈ meter zone; ~ **industriale** industrial estate; ~ **erogena** erogenous zone; ~ **pedonale** pedestrian precinct; ~ **verde** (*di abitato*) green area

'**zonzo** ['dzondzo]: **a** ~ *av*: **andare a** ~ to wander about, stroll about

'**zoo** ['dzɔo] SM INV zoo

zoolo'gia [dzoolo'dʒia] SF zoology

zoo'logico, -a, -ci, -che [dzoo'lɔdʒiko] AG zoological

zo'ologo, -a, -gi, -ghe [dzo'ɔlogo] SM/F zoologist

zoosa'fari [dzoosa'fari] SM INV safari park

zoo'tecnico, -a, -ci, -che [dzoo'tɛkniko] AG zootechnical; **il patrimonio** ~ **di un paese** a country's livestock resources

zoppi'care [tsoppi'kare] /**20**/ VI to limp; (*fig: mobile*) to be shaky, rickety

'**zoppo, -a** ['tsɔppo] AG lame; (*fig: mobile*) shaky, rickety

zoti'cone [dzoti'kone] SM lout

ZTL [dzetati'ɛlle] SIGLA F (= *Zona a Traffico Limitato*) controlled traffic zone

zu'ava [dzu'ava] SF: **pantaloni alla** ~ knickerbockers

'**zucca, -che** ['tsukka] SF (*Bot*) marrow (*BRIT*), vegetable marrow (*US*); pumpkin; (*scherzoso*) head

zucche'rare [tsukke'rare] /**72**/ VT to put sugar in

zucche'rato, -a [tsukke'rato] AG sweet, sweetened

zuccheri'era [tsukke'rjɛra] SF sugar bowl

zuccheri'ficio [tsukkeri'fitʃo] SM sugar refinery

zucche'rino, -a [tsukke'rino] AG sugary, sweet

'**zucchero** ['tsukkero] SM sugar; ~ **di canna** cane sugar; ~ **caramellato** caramel; ~ **filato** candy floss, cotton candy (*US*); ~ **a velo** icing sugar (*BRIT*), confectioner's sugar (*US*)

zucche'roso, -a [tsukke'roso] AG sugary

zuc'china [tsuk'kina] SF, **zuc'chino** [tsuk'kino] SM courgette (*BRIT*), zucchini (*US*)

zuc'cotto [tsuk'kɔtto] SM ice-cream sponge

'**zuffa** ['tsuffa] SF brawl

zufo'lare [tsufo'lare] /**72**/ VT, VI to whistle

'**zufolo** ['tsufolo] SM (*Mus*) flageolet

'**zuppa** ['tsuppa] SF soup; (*fig*) mixture, muddle; ~ **inglese** (*Cuc*) *dessert made with sponge cake, custard and chocolate*, ≈ trifle (*BRIT*)

zuppi'era [tsup'pjɛra] SF soup tureen

'**zuppo, -a** ['tsuppo] AG: ~ **(di)** drenched (with), soaked (with)

Zu'rigo [dzu'rigo] SF Zurich

ENGLISH–ITALIAN

INGLESE–ITALIANO

Aa

A, a [eɪ] N (*letter*) A, a *f inv* or *m inv*; (*Scol: mark*) ≈ 10 (*ottimo*); (*Mus*): **A** la *m*; **A for Andrew**, (*US*) **A for Able** ≈ A come Ancona; **from A to Z** dall'A alla Z; **A road** *n* (*BRIT Aut*) ≈ strada statale; **A shares** *npl* (*BRIT Stock Exchange*) azioni *fpl* senza diritto di voto; **A to Z**® *n* stradario

(KEYWORD)

a [ə] (*before vowel or silent h: an*) INDEF ART **1** un, uno (+ *s impure, gn, pn, ps, x, z*), una *f*, un' + *vowel*; **a book** un libro; **a mirror** uno specchio; **an apple** una mela; **she's a doctor** è medico **2** (*instead of the number "one"*) un(o), una *f*; **a year ago** un anno fa; **a hundred/thousand pounds** cento/mille sterline **3** (*in expressing ratios, prices etc*) a, per; **3 a day/ week** 3 al giorno/alla settimana; **10 km an hour** 10 km all'ora; **£5 a person** 5 sterline a persona or per persona

a. ABBR = **acre**
A2 N ABBR (*BRIT Scol*) seconda parte del diploma di studi superiori chiamato "A level"
AA N ABBR (*BRIT: = Automobile Association*) ≈ A.C.I. *m* (= Automobile Club d'Italia); (*US: = Associate in/of Arts*) titolo di studio; (= *Alcoholics Anonymous*) A.A. *f* (= *Anonima Alcolisti*); (*Mil*) = **anti-aircraft**
AAA N ABBR (= *American Automobile Association*) ≈ A.C.I. *m* (= Automobile Club d'Italia); (*BRIT*) = **Amateur Athletics Association**
A & R N ABBR (*Mus*) = **artists and repertoire**; **~ man** talent scout *m inv*
AAUP N ABBR (= *American Association of University Professors*) associazione dei professori universitari
AB ABBR (*BRIT*) = **able-bodied seaman**; (*CANADA*) = **Alberta**
aback [ə'bæk] ADV: **to be taken ~** essere sbalordito(-a)
abacus ['æbəkəs] (*pl* **abaci** [-saɪ]) N pallottoliere *m*, abaco
abandon [ə'bændən] VT abbandonare ▶ N abbandono; **to ~ ship** abbandonare la nave;

with ~ sfrenatamente, spensieratamente
abandoned [ə'bændənd] ADJ (*child, house etc*) abbandonato(-a); (*unrestrained: manner*) disinvolto(-a)
abase [ə'beɪs] VT: **to ~ o.s. (so far as to do)** umiliarsi or abbassarsi (al punto di fare)
abashed [ə'bæʃt] ADJ imbarazzato(-a)
abate [ə'beɪt] VI calmarsi
abatement [ə'beɪtmənt] N (*of pollution, noise*) soppressione *f*, eliminazione *f*; **noise ~ society** associazione *f* per la lotta contro i rumori
abattoir ['æbətwɑːʳ] N (*BRIT*) mattatoio
abbey ['æbɪ] N abbazia, badia
abbot ['æbət] N abate *m*
abbreviate [ə'briːvɪeɪt] VT abbreviare
abbreviation [əbriːvɪ'eɪʃən] N abbreviazione *f*
ABC N ABBR (= *American Broadcasting Company*) *rete televisiva americana*
abdicate ['æbdɪkeɪt] VT abdicare a ▶ VI abdicare
abdication [æbdɪ'keɪʃən] N abdicazione *f*
abdomen ['æbdəmən] N addome *m*
abdominal [æb'dɔmɪnl] ADJ addominale
abduct [æb'dʌkt] VT rapire
abduction [æb'dʌkʃən] N rapimento
Aberdonian [æbə'dəunɪən] ADJ di Aberdeen ▶ N abitante *mf* di Aberdeen, originario(-a) di Aberdeen
aberration [æbə'reɪʃən] N aberrazione *f*
abet [ə'bɛt] VT *see* **aid**
abeyance [ə'beɪəns] N: **in ~** in sospeso
abhor [əb'hɔːʳ] VT aborrire
abhorrent [əb'hɔrənt] ADJ odioso(-a)
abide [ə'baɪd] VT sopportare; **I can't ~ it/him** non lo posso soffrire or sopportare ▶ **abide by** VT FUS conformarsi a
abiding [ə'baɪdɪŋ] ADJ (*memory etc*) persistente, duraturo(-a)
ability [ə'bɪlɪtɪ] N abilità *f inv*; **to the best of my ~** con il massimo impegno
abject ['æbdʒɛkt] ADJ (*poverty*) abietto(-a); (*apology*) umiliante; (*coward*) indegno(-a), vile

ablaze ['ə'bleɪz] ADJ in fiamme; **~ with light** risplendente di luce

able ['eɪbl] ADJ capace; **to be ~ to do sth** essere capace di fare qc, poter fare qc

able-bodied ['eɪbl'bɔdɪd] ADJ robusto(-a)

able-bodied seaman N (BRIT) marinaio scelto

ably ['eɪblɪ] ADV abilmente

ABM N ABBR (= *anti-ballistic missile*) ABM *m*

abnormal [æb'nɔ:məl] ADJ anormale

abnormality [æbnɔː'mælɪtɪ] N (*condition*) anormalità; (*instance*) anomalia

aboard [ə'bɔːd] ADV a bordo ▶ PREP a bordo di; **~ the train** in *or* sul treno

abode [ə'bəud] N (*old*) dimora; (*Law*) domicilio, dimora; **of no fixed ~** senza fissa dimora

abolish [ə'bɔlɪʃ] VT abolire

abolition [æbəu'lɪʃən] N abolizione *f*

abominable [ə'bɔmɪnəbl] ADJ abominevole

aborigine [æbə'rɪdʒɪnɪ] N aborigeno(-a)

abort [ə'bɔːt] VT (*Med, fig*) abortire; (*Comput*) interrompere l'esecuzione di

abortion [ə'bɔːʃən] N aborto; **to have an ~** avere un aborto, abortire

abortionist [ə'bɔːʃənɪst] N abortista *mf*

abortive [ə'bɔːtɪv] ADJ abortivo(-a)

abound [ə'baund] VI abbondare; **to ~ in** abbondare di

(KEYWORD)

about [ə'baut] ADV **1** (*approximately*) circa, quasi; **about a hundred/thousand** un centinaio/migliaio, circa cento/mille; **it takes about 10 hours** ci vogliono circa 10 ore; **at about 2 o'clock** verso le 2; **I've just about finished** ho quasi finito; **it's about here** è qui intorno, è qui vicino

2 (*referring to place*) qua e là, in giro; **to leave things lying about** lasciare delle cose in giro; **to run about** correre qua e là; **to walk about** camminare; **is Paul about?** (BRIT) hai visto Paul in giro?; **it's the other way about** (BRIT) è il contrario

3: to be about to do sth stare per fare qc; **I'm not about to do all that for nothing** non ho intenzione di fare tutto questo per niente

▶ PREP **1** (*relating to*) su, di; **a book about London** un libro su Londra; **what is it about?** di che si tratta?; (*book, film etc*) di cosa tratta?; **we talked about it** ne abbiamo parlato; **do something about it!** fai qualcosa!; **what** *or* **how about doing this?** che ne dici di fare questo?

2 (*referring to place*): **to walk about the town** camminare per la città; **her clothes were scattered about the room** i suoi vestiti erano sparsi *or* in giro per tutta la stanza

about-face [ə'baut'feɪs], **about-turn** [ə'baut'tə:n] N (*Mil*) dietro front *m inv*

above [ə'bʌv] ADV, PREP sopra; **mentioned ~** suddetto; **costing ~ £10** più caro di 10 sterline; **he's not ~ a bit of blackmail** non rifuggirebbe dal ricatto; **~ all** soprattutto

aboveboard [ə'bʌv'bɔːd] ADJ aperto(-a); onesto(-a)

abrasion [ə'breɪʒən] N abrasione *f*

abrasive [ə'breɪzɪv] ADJ abrasivo(-a)

abreast [ə'brest] ADV di fianco; **3 ~** per 3 di fronte; **to keep ~ of** tenersi aggiornato su

abridge [ə'brɪdʒ] VT ridurre

abroad [ə'brɔːd] ADV all'estero; **there is a rumour ~ that ...** (*fig*) si sente dire in giro che ..., circola la voce che ...

abrupt [ə'brʌpt] ADJ (*steep*) erto(-a); (*sudden*) improvviso(-a); (*gruff, blunt*) brusco(-a)

abscess ['æbsɪs] N ascesso

abscond [əb'skɔnd] VI scappare

absence ['æbsəns] N assenza; **in the ~ of** (*person*) in assenza di; (*thing*) in mancanza di

absent ['æbsənt] ADJ assente; **to be ~ without leave** (*Mil etc*) essere assente ingiustificato

absentee [æbsən'ti:] N assente *mf*

absenteeism [æbsən'ti:ɪzəm] N assenteismo

absent-minded ['æbsənt'maɪndɪd] ADJ distratto(-a)

absent-mindedness ['æbsənt'maɪndɪdnɪs] N distrazione *f*

absolute ['æbsəlu:t] ADJ assoluto(-a)

absolutely [æbsə'lu:tlɪ] ADV assolutamente

absolve [əb'zɔlv] VT: **to ~ sb (from)** (*sin etc*) assolvere qn (da); **to ~ sb from** (*oath*) sciogliere qn da

absorb [əb'sɔːb] VT assorbire; **to be absorbed in a book** essere immerso(-a) in un libro

absorbent [əb'sɔːbənt] ADJ assorbente

absorbent cotton [əb'zɔːbənt-] N (*US*) cotone *m* idrofilo

absorbing [əb'sɔːbɪŋ] ADJ avvincente, molto interessante

absorption [əb'sɔːpʃən] N assorbimento

abstain [əb'steɪn] VI: **to ~ (from)** astenersi (da)

abstemious [əb'sti:mɪəs] ADJ astemio(-a)

abstention [əb'stenʃən] N astensione *f*

abstinence ['æbstɪnəns] N astinenza

abstract ['æbstrækt] ADJ astratto(-a) ▶ N (*summary*) riassunto ▶ VT [æb'strækt] estrarre

absurd [əb'sə:d] ADJ assurdo(-a)

absurdity [əb'sə:dɪtɪ] N assurdità *f inv*

ABTA ['æbtə] N ABBR = **Association of British Travel Agents**

Abu Dhabi ['æbu:'dɑ:bɪ] N Abu Dhabi *f*

abundance [ə'bʌndəns] N abbondanza

abundant [ə'bʌndənt] ADJ abbondante
abuse N [ə'bjuːs] abuso; (*insults*) ingiurie *fpl*
▶ VT [ə'bjuːz] abusare di; **open to ~** che si
presta ad abusi
abusive [ə'bjuːsɪv] ADJ ingiurioso(-a)
abysmal [ə'bɪzməl] ADJ spaventoso(-a)
abyss [ə'bɪs] N abisso
AC N ABBR (*US*) = **athletic club**
a/c ABBR (*Banking etc*) = **account**; (= *account
current*) c
academic [ækə'dɛmɪk] ADJ accademico(-a);
(*pej: issue*) puramente formale ▶ N
universitario(-a)
academic year N anno accademico
academy [ə'kædəmɪ] N (*learned body*)
accademia; (*school*) scuola privata; **military/
naval ~** scuola militare/navale; **~ of music**
conservatorio
ACAS ['eɪkæs] N ABBR (*BRIT*: = *Advisory,
Conciliation and Arbitration Service*) comitato
governativo per il miglioramento della
contrattazione collettiva
accede [æk'siːd] VI: **to ~ to** (*request*) accedere
a; (*throne*) ascendere a
accelerate [æk'sɛləreɪt] VT, VI accelerare
acceleration [æksɛlə'reɪʃən] N
accelerazione *f*
accelerator [æk'sɛləreɪtəʳ] N acceleratore *m*
accent ['æksɛnt] N accento
accentuate [æk'sɛntjueɪt] VT (*syllable*)
accentuare; (*need, difference etc*) accentuare,
mettere in risalto *or* in evidenza
accept [ək'sɛpt] VT accettare
acceptable [ək'sɛptəbl] ADJ accettabile
acceptance [ək'sɛptəns] N accettazione *f*; **to
meet with general ~** incontrare il favore *or*
il consenso generale
access ['æksɛs] N accesso ▶ VT (*Comput*)
accedere a; **to have ~ to** avere accesso a; **the
burglars gained ~ through a window** i
ladri sono riusciti a penetrare da *or*
attraverso una finestra
accessible [æk'sɛsəbl] ADJ accessibile
accession [æk'sɛʃən] N (*addition*) aggiunta;
(*to library*) accessione *f*, acquisto; (*of king*)
ascesa *or* salita al trono
accessory [æk'sɛsərɪ] N accessorio; (*Law*):
~ to complice *mf* di; **toilet accessories** npl
(*BRIT*) articoli *mpl* da toilette
access road N strada d'accesso; (*to motorway*)
raccordo di entrata
access time N (*Comput*) tempo di accesso
accident ['æksɪdənt] N incidente *m*; (*chance*)
caso; **to meet with** *or* **to have an ~** avere un
incidente; **I've had an ~** ho avuto un
incidente; **accidents at work** infortuni *mpl*
sul lavoro; **by ~** per caso
accidental [æksɪ'dɛntl] ADJ accidentale
accidentally [æksɪ'dɛntəlɪ] ADV per caso

Accident and Emergency Department N
(*BRIT*) pronto soccorso
accident insurance N assicurazione *f* contro
gli infortuni
accident-prone ['æksɪdənt'prəun] ADJ:
he's very ~ è un vero passaguai
acclaim [ə'kleɪm] VT acclamare ▶ N
acclamazione *f*
acclamation [æklə'meɪʃən] N (*approval*)
acclamazione *f*; (*applause*) applauso
acclimatize [ə'klaɪmətaɪz], (*US*) **acclimate**
[ə'klaɪmeɪt] VT: **to become acclimatized**
acclimatarsi
accolade ['ækəleɪd] N encomio
accommodate [ə'kɔmədeɪt] VT alloggiare;
(*oblige, help*) favorire; **this car
accommodates 4 people comfortably**
quest'auto può trasportare comodamente
4 persone
accommodating [ə'kɔmədeɪtɪŋ] ADJ
compiacente
accommodation [əkɔmə'deɪʃən] N, (*US*)
accommodations [əkɔmə'deɪʃənz] NPL
alloggio; **seating ~** (*BRIT*) posti a sedere;
"~ to let" (*BRIT*) "camere in affitto"; **have
you any ~?** avete posto?
accompaniment [ə'kʌmpənɪmənt] N
accompagnamento
accompanist [ə'kʌmpənɪst] N (*Mus*)
accompagnatore(-trice)
accompany [ə'kʌmpənɪ] VT accompagnare
accomplice [ə'kʌmplɪs] N complice *mf*
accomplish [ə'kʌmplɪʃ] VT compiere;
(*achieve*) ottenere; (*goal*) raggiungere
accomplished [ə'kʌmplɪʃt] ADJ (*person*)
esperto(-a)
accomplishment [ə'kʌmplɪʃmənt] N
compimento; realizzazione *f*; (*thing achieved*)
risultato; **accomplishments** NPL (*skills*) doti
fpl
accord [ə'kɔːd] N accordo ▶ VT accordare; **of
his own ~** di propria iniziativa; **with one ~**
all'unanimità, di comune accordo
accordance [ə'kɔːdəns] N: **in ~ with** in
conformità con
according [ə'kɔːdɪŋ]: **~ to** prep secondo; **it
went ~ to plan** è andata secondo il previsto
accordingly [ə'kɔːdɪŋlɪ] ADV in conformità
accordion [ə'kɔːdɪən] N fisarmonica
accost [ə'kɔst] VT avvicinare
account [ə'kaunt] N (*Comm*) conto; (*report*)
descrizione *f*; **accounts** NPL (*Comm*) conti
mpl; **"~ payee only"** (*BRIT*) "assegno non
trasferibile"; **to keep an ~ of** tenere nota di;
**to bring sb to ~ for sth/for having done
sth** chiedere a qn render conto di qc/per
aver fatto qc; **by all accounts** a quanto si
dice; **of little ~** di poca importanza; **on ~** in
acconto; **to buy sth on ~** comprare qc a

credito; **on no ~** per nessun motivo; **on ~ of** a causa di; **to take into ~**, **take ~ of** tener conto di

▶ **account for** VT FUS (*explain*) spiegare; giustificare; **all the children were accounted for** nessun bambino mancava all'appello

accountability [ə'kauntə'bɪlɪtɪ] N responsabilità

accountable [ə'kauntəbl] ADJ responsabile; **to be held ~ for sth** dover rispondere di qc; **~ (to)** responsabile (verso)

accountancy [ə'kauntənsɪ] N ragioneria

accountant [ə'kauntənt] N ragioniere(-a)

accounting [ə'kauntɪŋ] N contabilità

accounting period N esercizio finanziario, periodo contabile

account number N numero di conto

account payable N conto passivo

account receivable N conto da esigere

accredited [ə'krɛdɪtɪd] ADJ accreditato(-a)

accretion [ə'kriːʃən] N accrescimento

accrue [ə'kruː] VI (*mount up*) aumentare; **to ~ to** derivare a; **accrued charges** ratei *mpl* passivi; **accrued interest** interesse *m* maturato

accumulate [ə'kjuːmjuleɪt] VT accumulare ▶ VI accumularsi

accumulation [əkjuːmju'leɪʃən] N accumulazione *f*

accuracy ['ækjurəsɪ] N precisione *f*

accurate ['ækjurɪt] ADJ preciso(-a)

accurately ['ækjurɪtlɪ] ADV precisamente

accusation [ækju'zeɪʃən] N accusa

accusative [ə'kjuːzətɪv] N (*Ling*) accusativo

accuse [ə'kjuːz] VT accusare

accused [ə'kjuːzd] N accusato(-a)

accuser [ə'kjuːzər] N accusatore(-trice)

accustom [ə'kʌstəm] VT abituare; **to ~ o.s. to sth** abituarsi a qc

accustomed [ə'kʌstəmd] ADJ (*usual*) abituale; **~ to** abituato(-a) a

AC/DC ABBR (= *alternating current/direct current*) c.a./c.c.

ACE [eɪs] N ABBR = **American Council on Education**

ace [eɪs] N asso; **within an ~ of** (BRIT) a un pelo da

acerbic [ə'səːbɪk] ADJ (*also fig*) acido(-a)

acetate ['æsɪteɪt] N acetato

ache [eɪk] N male *m*, dolore *m* ▶ VI (*be sore*) far male, dolere; (*yearn*): **to ~ to do sth** morire dalla voglia di fare qc; **I've got stomach ~** or (US) **a stomach ~** ho mal di stomaco; **my head aches** mi fa male la testa; **I'm aching all over** mi duole dappertutto

achieve [ə'tʃiːv] VT (*aim*) raggiungere; (*victory, success*) ottenere; (*task*) compiere

achievement [ə'tʃiːvmənt] N compimento; successo

Achilles heel [ə'kɪliːz-] N tallone *m* d'Achille

acid ['æsɪd] ADJ acido(-a) ▶ N acido

acidity [ə'sɪdɪtɪ] N acidità

acid rain N pioggia acida

acid test N (*fig*) prova del fuoco

acknowledge [ək'nɔlɪdʒ] VT (*fact*) riconoscere; (*letter: also*: **acknowledge receipt of**) accusare ricevuta di

acknowledgement [ək'nɔlɪdʒmənt] N riconoscimento; (*of letter*) conferma; **acknowledgements** NPL (*in book*) ringraziamenti *mpl*

ACLU N ABBR (= *American Civil Liberties Union*) *unione americana per le libertà civili*

acme ['ækmɪ] N culmine *m*, acme *m*

acne ['æknɪ] N acne *f*

acorn ['eɪkɔːn] N ghianda

acoustic [ə'kuːstɪk] ADJ acustico(-a); *see also* **acoustics**

acoustic coupler [-'kʌplər] N (*Comput*) accoppiatore *m* acustico

acoustics [ə'kuːstɪks] N, NPL acustica

acquaint [ə'kweɪnt] VT: **to ~ sb with sth** far sapere qc a qn; **to be acquainted with** (*person*) conoscere

acquaintance [ə'kweɪntəns] N conoscenza; (*person*) conoscente *mf*; **to make sb's ~** fare la conoscenza di qn

acquiesce [ækwɪ'ɛs] VI (*agree*): **to ~ (in)** acconsentire (a)

acquire [ə'kwaɪər] VT acquistare

acquired [ə'kwaɪəd] ADJ acquisito(-a); **it's an ~ taste** è una cosa che si impara ad apprezzare

acquisition [ækwɪ'zɪʃən] N acquisto

acquisitive [ə'kwɪzɪtɪv] ADJ a cui piace accumulare le cose

acquit [ə'kwɪt] VT assolvere; **to ~ o.s. well** comportarsi bene

acquittal [ə'kwɪtl] N assoluzione *f*

acre ['eɪkər] N acro (= 4047 m²)

acreage ['eɪkərɪdʒ] N superficie *f* in acri

acrid ['ækrɪd] ADJ (*smell*) acre, pungente; (*fig*) pungente

acrimonious [ækrɪ'məunɪəs] ADJ astioso(-a)

acrobat ['ækrəbæt] N acrobata *mf*

acrobatic [ækrə'bætɪk] ADJ acrobatico(-a)

acrobatics [ækrə'bætɪks] N acrobatica ▶ NPL acrobazie *fpl*

acronym ['ækrənɪm] N acronimo

Acropolis [ə'krɔpəlɪs] N: **the ~** l'Acropoli *f*

across [ə'krɔs] PREP (*on the other side*) dall'altra parte di; (*crosswise*) attraverso ▶ ADV dall'altra parte; in larghezza; **to walk ~ (the road)** attraversare (la strada); **to run/swim ~** attraversare di corsa/a nuoto; **to take sb ~ the road** far attraversare la strada a qn;

~ **from** di fronte a; **the lake is 12 km** ~ il lago ha una larghezza di 12 km *or* è largo 12 km; **to get sth** ~ **to sb** (*fig*) far capire qc a qn

acrylic [ə'krɪlɪk] ADJ acrilico(-a) ▸ N acrilico

ACT N ABBR (= *American College Test*) *esame di ammissione a college*

act [ækt] N atto; (*in music-hall etc*) numero; (*Law*) decreto ▸ VI agire; (*Theat*) recitare; (*pretend*) fingere ▸ VT (*part*) recitare; **to catch sb in the** ~ cogliere qn in flagrante *or* sul fatto; **it's only an** ~ è tutta scena, è solo una messinscena; ~ **of God** (*Law*) calamità *f inv* naturale; **to** ~ **Hamlet** (BRIT) recitare la parte di Amleto; **to** ~ **the fool** (BRIT) fare lo stupido; **to** ~ **as** agire da; **it acts as a deterrent** serve da deterrente; **acting in my capacity as chairman, I** … in qualità di presidente, io …
▸ **act on** VT: **to** ~ **on sth** agire in base a qc
▸ **act out** VT (*event*) ricostruire; (*fantasies*) dare forma concreta a
▸ **act up** (*col*) VI (*person*) comportarsi male; (*knee, back, injury*) fare male; (*machine*) non funzionare

acting ['æktɪŋ] ADJ che fa le funzioni di ▸ N (*of actor*) recitazione *f*; **to do some** ~ fare del teatro (*or* del cinema); **he is the** ~ **manager** fa le veci del direttore

action ['ækʃən] N azione *f*; (*Mil*) combattimento; (*Law*) processo ▸ VT (*Comm: request*) evadere; (*tasks*) portare a termine; **to take** ~ agire; **to put a plan into** ~ realizzare un piano; **out of** ~ fuori combattimento; (*machine etc*) fuori servizio; **killed in** ~ (*Mil*) ucciso in combattimento; **to bring an** ~ **against sb** (*Law*) intentare causa contro qn

action replay N (BRIT TV) replay *m inv*

activate ['æktɪveɪt] VT (*mechanism*) fare funzionare, attivare; (*Chem, Physics*) rendere attivo(-a)

active ['æktɪv] ADJ attivo(-a); **to play an** ~ **part in** partecipare attivamente a

active duty N (*US Mil*) = **active service**

actively ['æktɪvlɪ] ADV (*participate*) attivamente; (*discourse, dislike*) vivamente

active partner N (*Comm*) socio effettivo

active service N (BRIT Mil): **to be on** ~ prestar servizio in zona di operazioni

activist ['æktɪvɪst] N attivista *mf*

activity [æk'tɪvɪtɪ] N attività *f inv*

activity holiday N vacanza attiva (*in bici, a cavallo, in barca, a vela ecc.*)

actor ['æktər] N attore *m*

actress ['æktrɪs] N attrice *f*

actual ['æktjuəl] ADJ reale, vero(-a)

actually ['æktjuəlɪ] ADV veramente; (*even*) addirittura

actuary ['æktjuərɪ] N attuario(-a)

actuate ['æktjueɪt] VT attivare

acuity [ə'kju:ɪtɪ] N acutezza

acumen ['ækjumən] N acume *m*; **business** ~ fiuto negli affari

acupuncture ['ækjupʌŋktʃər] N agopuntura

acute [ə'kju:t] ADJ acuto(-a); (*mind, person*) perspicace

AD ADV ABBR (= *Anno Domini*) d. C. ▸ N ABBR (*US Mil*) = **active duty**

ad [æd] N ABBR = **advertisement**

adamant ['ædəmənt] ADJ irremovibile

Adam's apple ['ædəmz-] N pomo di Adamo

adapt [ə'dæpt] VT adattare ▸ VI: **to** ~ (**to**) adattarsi (a)

adaptability [ədæptə'bɪlɪtɪ] N adattabilità

adaptable [ə'dæptəbl] ADJ (*device*) adattabile; (*person*) che sa adattarsi

adaptation [ædæp'teɪʃən] N adattamento

adapter, adaptor [ə'dæptər] N (*Elec*) adattatore *m*

ADC N ABBR (*Mil*) = **aide-de-camp**; (*US:* = *Aid to Dependent Children*) *sussidio per figli a carico*

add [æd] VT aggiungere; (*figures*) addizionare ▸ VI: **to** ~ **to** (*increase*) aumentare ▸ N (*Internet*): **thanks for the** ~ grazie per avermi aggiunto (come amico)
▸ **add on** VT aggiungere
▸ **add up** VT (*figures*) addizionare ▸ VI (*fig*): **it doesn't** ~ **up** non ha senso; **it doesn't** ~ **up to much** non è un granché

adder ['ædər] N vipera

addict ['ædɪkt] N tossicomane *mf*; (*fig*) fanatico(-a); **heroin** ~ eroinomane *mf*; **drug** ~ tossicodipendente *mf*, tossicomane *mf*

addicted [ə'dɪktɪd] ADJ: **to be** ~ **to** (*drink etc*) essere dedito(-a) a; (*fig: football etc*) essere tifoso(-a) di

addiction [ə'dɪkʃən] N (*Med*) tossicodipendenza

addictive [ə'dɪktɪv] ADJ che dà assuefazione

adding machine ['ædɪŋ-] N addizionatrice *f*

Addis Ababa ['ædɪs'æbəbə] N Addis Abeba *f*

addition [ə'dɪʃən] N addizione *f*; (*thing added*) aggiunta; **in** ~ inoltre; **in** ~ **to** oltre

additional [ə'dɪʃənl] ADJ supplementare

additive ['ædɪtɪv] N additivo

address [ə'drɛs] N (*gen, Comput*) indirizzo; (*talk*) discorso ▸ VT indirizzare; (*speak to*) fare un discorso a; (*issue*) affrontare; **my** ~ **is** … il mio indirizzo è…; **form of** ~ (*gen*) formula di cortesia; (*in letters*) formula d'indirizzo *or* di intestazione; **to** ~ **o.s. to sth** indirizzare le proprie energie verso qc; **absolute/relative** ~ (*Comput*) indirizzo assoluto/relativo

address book N rubrica

addressee [ædrɛ'si:] N destinatario(-a)

Aden ['eɪdən] N: **the Gulf of** ~ il golfo di Aden

adenoids ['ædɪnɔɪdz] NPL adenoidi *fpl*

adept ['ædɛpt] ADJ: ~ **at** esperto(-a) in

adequate ['ædɪkwɪt] ADJ (*description, reward*)

adeguato(-a); (*amount*) sufficiente; **to feel ~ to a task** sentirsi all'altezza di un compito

adequately ['ædɪkwɪtlɪ] ADV adeguatamente; sufficientemente

adhere [əd'hɪərʳ] VI: **to ~ to** aderire a; (*fig: rule, decision*) seguire

adhesion [əd'hi:ʒən] N adesione *f*

adhesive [əd'hi:zɪv] ADJ adesivo(-a) ▶ N adesivo; **~ tape** (*BRIT: for parcels etc*) nastro adesivo; (*US Med*) cerotto adesivo

ad hoc [æd'hɔk] ADJ (*decision*) ad hoc *inv*; (*committee*) apposito(-a)

ad infinitum ['ædɪnfɪ'naɪtəm] ADV all'infinito

adjacent [ə'dʒeɪsənt] ADJ adiacente; **~ to** accanto a

adjective ['ædʒɛktɪv] N aggettivo

adjoin [ə'dʒɔɪn] VT essere contiguo(-a) *or* attiguo(-a)

adjoining [ə'dʒɔɪnɪŋ] ADJ accanto *inv*, adiacente ▶ PREP accanto a

adjourn [ə'dʒə:n] VT rimandare, aggiornare; (*US: end*) sospendere ▶ VI essere aggiornato(-a); (*Parliament*) sospendere i lavori; (*go*) spostarsi; **to ~ a meeting till the following week** aggiornare *or* rinviare un incontro alla settimana seguente; **they adjourned to the pub** (*col*) si sono trasferiti al pub

adjournment [ə'dʒə:nmənt] N rinvio, aggiornamento; sospensione *f*

Adjt ABBR (*Mil*) = **adjutant**

adjudicate [ə'dʒu:dɪkeɪt] VT (*contest*) giudicare; (*claim*) decidere su

adjudication [ədʒu:dɪ'keɪʃən] N decisione *f*

adjust [ə'dʒʌst] VT aggiustare; (*Comm: change*) rettificare ▶ VI: **to ~ (to)** adattarsi (a)

adjustable [ə'dʒʌstəbl] ADJ regolabile

adjuster [ə'dʒʌstəʳ] N *see* **loss adjuster**

adjustment [ə'dʒʌstmənt] N (*Psych*) adattamento; (*of machine*) regolazione *f*; (*of prices, wages*) aggiustamento

adjutant ['ædʒətənt] N aiutante *m*

ad-lib [æd'lɪb] VT, VI improvvisare ▶ N improvvisazione *f* ▶ ADV: **ad lib** a piacere, a volontà

adman ['ædmæn] N (*irreg*) (*col*) pubblicitario

admin [æd'mɪn] N ABBR (*col*) = **administration**

administer [əd'mɪnɪstəʳ] VT amministrare; (*justice*) somministrare

administration [ədmɪnɪs'treɪʃən] N amministrazione *f*; **the A~** (*US*) il Governo

administrative [əd'mɪnɪstrətɪv] ADJ amministrativo(-a)

administrator [əd'mɪnɪstreɪtəʳ] N amministratore(-trice)

admirable ['ædmərəbl] ADJ ammirevole

admiral ['ædmərəl] N ammiraglio

Admiralty ['ædmərəltɪ] N (*BRIT: also:* **Admiralty Board**) Ministero della Marina

admiration [ædmə'reɪʃən] N ammirazione *f*

admire [əd'maɪəʳ] VT ammirare

admirer [əd'maɪərəʳ] N ammiratore(-trice)

admiring [əd'maɪərɪŋ] ADJ (*glance etc*) di ammirazione

admissible [əd'mɪsəbl] ADJ ammissibile

admission [əd'mɪʃən] N ammissione *f*; (*to exhibition, nightclub etc*) ingresso; (*confession*) confessione *f*; **by his own ~** per sua ammissione; **"~ free"**, **"free ~"** "ingresso gratuito"

admit [əd'mɪt] VT ammettere; far entrare; (*agree*) riconoscere; **"children not admitted"** "vietato l'ingresso ai bambini"; **this ticket admits two** questo biglietto è valido per due persone; **I must ~ that ...** devo ammettere *or* confessare che ...
▶ **admit of** VT FUS lasciare adito a
▶ **admit to** VT FUS riconoscere

admittance [əd'mɪtəns] N ingresso; **"no ~"** "vietato l'ingresso"

admittedly [əd'mɪtɪdlɪ] ADV bisogna pur riconoscere (che)

admonish [əd'mɔnɪʃ] VT ammonire

ad nauseam [æd'nɔ:zɪæm] ADV fino alla nausea, a non finire

ado [ə'du:] N: **without (any) more ~** senza più indugi

adolescence [ædəu'lɛsns] N adolescenza

adolescent [ædəu'lɛsnt] ADJ, N adolescente *mf*

adopt [ə'dɔpt] VT adottare

adopted [ə'dɔptɪd] ADJ adottivo(-a)

adoption [ə'dɔpʃən] N adozione *f*

adore [ə'dɔ:ʳ] VT adorare

adoring [ə'dɔ:rɪŋ] ADJ adorante; **his ~ wife** sua moglie che lo adora

adoringly [ə'dɔ:rɪŋlɪ] ADV con adorazione

adorn [ə'dɔ:n] VT ornare

adornment [ə'dɔ:nmənt] N ornamento

ADP N ABBR = **automatic data processing**

adrenalin [ə'drɛnəlɪn] N adrenalina; **it gets the ~ going** ti dà una carica

Adriatic [eɪdrɪ'ætɪk] N: **the ~ (Sea)** il mare Adriatico, l'Adriatico

adrift [ə'drɪft] ADV alla deriva; **to come ~** (*boat*) andare alla deriva; (*wire, rope etc*) essersi staccato(-a) *or* sciolto(-a)

adroit [ə'drɔɪt] ADJ abile, destro(-a)

ADSL N ABBR (= *asymmetric digital subscriber line*) ADSL *m*

ADT ABBR (*US:* = *Atlantic Daylight Time*) ora legale di New York

adult ['ædʌlt] N adulto(-a) ▶ ADJ adulto(-a); (*work, education*) per adulti

adult education N scuola per adulti

adulterate [ə'dʌltəreɪt] VT adulterare

adulterer [ə'dʌltərəʳ] N adultero
adulteress [ə'dʌltərɪs] N adultera
adultery [ə'dʌltərɪ] N adulterio
adulthood ['ædʌlthud] N età adulta
advance [əd'vɑːns] N avanzamento; (money) anticipo ▶ ADJ (booking etc) in anticipo ▶ VT avanzare; (date, money) anticipare ▶ VI avanzare; **in ~** in anticipo; **to make advances to sb** (gen) fare degli approcci a qn; (amorously) fare delle avances a qn; **do I need to book in ~?** occorre che prenoti in anticipo?
advanced [əd'vɑːnst] ADJ avanzato(-a); (Scol: studies) superiore; **~ in years** avanti negli anni
advancement [əd'vɑːnsmənt] N avanzamento
advance notice N preavviso
advantage [əd'vɑːntɪdʒ] N (also Tennis) vantaggio; **to take ~ of** approfittarsi di; **it's to our ~** è nel nostro interesse, torna a nostro vantaggio
advantageous [ædvən'teɪdʒəs] ADJ vantaggioso(-a)
advent ['ædvənt] N avvento; **A~** (Rel) Avvento
Advent calendar N calendario dell'Avvento
adventure [əd'vɛntʃəʳ] N avventura
adventure playground N area attrezzata di giochi per bambini con funi, strutture in legno ecc
adventurous [əd'vɛntʃərəs] ADJ avventuroso(-a)
adverb ['ædvəːb] N avverbio
adversary ['ædvəsərɪ] N avversario(-a)
adverse ['ædvəːs] ADJ avverso(-a); **in ~ circumstances** nelle avversità; **~ to** contrario(-a) a
adversity [əd'vəːsɪtɪ] N avversità
advert ['ædvəːt] N ABBR (BRIT) = **advertisement**
advertise ['ædvətaɪz] VI, VT fare pubblicità or réclame (a), fare un'inserzione (per vendere); **to ~ for** (staff) cercare tramite annuncio
advertisement [əd'vəːtɪsmənt] N (Comm) réclame f inv, pubblicità f inv; (in classified ads) inserzione f
advertiser ['ædvətaɪzəʳ] N azienda che reclamizza un prodotto; (in newspaper) inserzionista mf
advertising ['ædvətaɪzɪŋ] N pubblicità
advertising agency N agenzia pubblicitaria or di pubblicità
advertising campaign N campagna pubblicitaria
advice [əd'vaɪs] N consigli mpl; (notification) avviso; **piece of ~** consiglio; **to ask (sb) for ~** chiedere il consiglio (di qn), chiedere un consiglio (a qn); **legal ~** consulenza legale; **to take legal ~** consultare un avvocato

advice note N (BRIT) avviso di spedizione
advisable [əd'vaɪzəbl] ADJ consigliabile
advise [əd'vaɪz] VT consigliare; **to ~ sb of sth** informare qn di qc; **to ~ sb against sth/ against doing sth** sconsigliare qc a qn/ a qn di fare qc; **you will be well/ill advised to go** fareste bene/male ad andare
advisedly [əd'vaɪzɪdlɪ] ADV (deliberately) deliberatamente
adviser [əd'vaɪzəʳ] N consigliere(-a); (in business) consulente mf, consigliere(-a)
advisory [-ərɪ, əd'vaɪzərɪ] ADJ consultivo(-a); **in an ~ capacity** in veste di consulente
advocate N ['ædvəkɪt] (upholder) sostenitore(-trice); (Law) avvocato (difensore) ▶ VT ['ædvəkeɪt] propugnare; **to be an ~ of** essere a favore di
advt. ABBR = **advertisement**
AEA N ABBR (BRIT: = Atomic Energy Authority) ente di controllo sulla ricerca e lo sviluppo dell'energia atomica
AEC N ABBR (US: = Atomic Energy Commission) ente di controllo sulla ricerca e lo sviluppo dell'energia atomica
Aegean (Sea) [iː'dʒiːən-] N (mare m) Egeo
aegis ['iːdʒɪs] N: **under the ~ of** sotto gli auspici di
aeon ['iːən] N eternità f inv
aerial ['ɛərɪəl] N antenna ▶ ADJ aereo(-a)
aerobatics ['ɛərəu'bætɪks] NPL acrobazia sg aerea; (stunts) acrobazie fpl aeree
aerobics [ɛə'rəubɪks] N aerobica
aerodrome ['ɛərədrəum] N (BRIT) aerodromo
aerodynamic ['ɛərəudaɪ'næmɪk] ADJ aerodinamico(-a)
aeronautics [ɛərə'nɔːtɪks] N aeronautica
aeroplane ['ɛərəpleɪn] (BRIT) N aeroplano
aerosol ['ɛərəsɔl] (BRIT) N aerosol m inv
aerospace industry ['ɛərəuspeɪs-] N industria aerospaziale
aesthetic [ɪs'θɛtɪk] ADJ estetico(-a)
afar [ə'fɑːʳ] ADV lontano; **from ~** da lontano
AFB N ABBR (US) = **Air Force Base**
AFDC N ABBR (US: = Aid to Families with Dependent Children) ≈ A.F. (= assegni familiari)
affable ['æfəbl] ADJ affabile
affair [ə'fɛəʳ] N affare m; (also: **love affair**) relazione f amorosa; **affairs** NPL (business) affari; **the Watergate ~** il caso Watergate
affect [ə'fɛkt] VT toccare; (influence) influire su, incidere su; (feign) fingere
affectation [æfɛk'teɪʃən] N affettazione f
affected [ə'fɛktɪd] ADJ affettato(-a)
affection [ə'fɛkʃən] N affetto
affectionate [ə'fɛkʃənɪt] ADJ affettuoso(-a)
affectionately [ə'fɛkʃənɪtlɪ] ADV affettuosamente
affidavit [æfɪ'deɪvɪt] N (Law) affidavit m inv

417

affiliated [ə'fɪlɪeɪtɪd] ADJ affiliato(-a);
~ **company** filiale f

affinity [ə'fɪnɪtɪ] N affinità f inv

affirm [ə'fə:m] VT affermare, asserire

affirmation [æfə'meɪʃən] N affermazione f

affirmative [ə'fə:mətɪv] ADJ affermativo(-a)
▶ N: **in the** ~ affermativamente

affix [ə'fɪks] VT apporre; attaccare

afflict [ə'flɪkt] VT affliggere

affliction [ə'flɪkʃən] N afflizione f

affluence ['æfluəns] N ricchezza

affluent ['æfluənt] ADJ ricco(-a); **the ~
society** la società del benessere

afford [ə'fɔ:d] VT permettersi; (provide)
fornire; **I can't ~ the time** non ho
veramente il tempo; **can we ~ a car?**
possiamo permetterci un'automobile?

affordable [ə'fɔ:dəbl] ADJ (che ha un prezzo)
abbordabile

affray [ə'freɪ] N (BRIT Law) rissa

affront [ə'frʌnt] N affronto

affronted [ə'frʌntɪd] ADJ insultato(-a)

Afghan ['æfgæn] ADJ, N afgano(-a)

Afghanistan [æf'gænɪstɑ:n] N Afganistan m

afield [ə'fi:ld] ADV: **far ~** lontano

AFL-CIO N ABBR (= American Federation of Labor
and Congress of Industrial Organizations)
confederazione sindacale

afloat [ə'fləʊt] ADJ, ADV a galla

afoot [ə'fʊt] ADV: **there is something ~** si sta
preparando qualcosa

aforementioned [ə'fɔ:mɛnʃənd] ADJ
suddetto(-a)

aforesaid [ə'fɔ:sɛd] ADJ suddetto(-a),
predetto(-a)

afraid [ə'freɪd] ADJ impaurito(-a); **to be ~ of**
aver paura di; **to be ~ of doing** or **to do** aver
paura di fare; **to be ~ that** aver paura che; **I
am ~ that I'll be late** mi dispiace, ma farò
tardi; **I'm ~ so!** ho paura di sì!, temo proprio
di sì!; **I'm ~ not** no, mi dispiace, purtroppo
no

afresh [ə'frɛʃ] ADV di nuovo

Africa ['æfrɪkə] N Africa

African ['æfrɪkən] ADJ, N africano(-a)

African-American ADJ, N afroamericano(-a)

Afrikaans [æfrɪ'kɑ:ns] N afrikaans m

Afrikaner [æfrɪ'kɑ:nə'] N africaner m inv

Afro-American ['æfrəʊə'mɛrɪkən] ADJ
afroamericano(-a)

Afro-Caribbean ['æfrəʊkærɪ'bɪən] ADJ
afrocaraibico(-a)

AFT N ABBR (= American Federation of Teachers)
sindacato degli insegnanti

aft [ɑːft] ADV a poppa, verso poppa

after ['ɑːftə'] PREP, ADV dopo ▶ CONJ dopo che;
~ **dinner** dopo cena; **the day ~ tomorrow**
dopodomani; **what/who are you ~?** che/chi
cerca?; **the police are ~ him** è ricercato

dalla polizia; ~ **he left/having done** dopo
che se ne fu andato/dopo aver fatto; **to
name sb ~ sb** dare a qn il nome di qn; **it's
twenty ~ eight** (US) sono le otto e venti; **to
ask ~ sb** chiedere di qn; ~ **you!** prima lei!,
dopo di lei!; ~ **all** dopo tutto

afterbirth ['ɑːftəbə:θ] N placenta

aftercare ['ɑːftəkɛə'] N (BRIT Med) assistenza
medica post-degenza

after-effects ['ɑːftərɪfɛkts] NPL conseguenze
fpl; (of illness) postumi mpl

afterlife ['ɑːftəlaɪf] N vita dell'al di là

aftermath ['ɑːftəmæθ] N conseguenze fpl; **in
the ~ of** nel periodo dopo

afternoon ['ɑːftə'nu:n] N pomeriggio; **good
~!** buon giorno!

afterparty ['ɑːftəpɑːtɪ] N after-party m inv

afters ['ɑːftəz] N (BRIT col: dessert) dessert m inv

after-sales service [ɑːftə'seɪlz-] N servizio
assistenza clienti

after-shave ['ɑːftəʃeɪv], **after-shave lotion**
['ɑːftəʃeɪv-] N dopobarba m inv

aftershock ['ɑːftəʃɔk] N scossa di
assestamento

aftersun ['ɑːftəsʌn] ADJ: ~ **(lotion/cream)**
(lozione f/crema) doposole m inv

aftertaste ['ɑːftəteɪst] N retrogusto

afterthought ['ɑːftəθɔ:t] N: **as an ~** come
aggiunta

afterwards ['ɑːftəwədz], (US) **afterward**
ADV dopo

again [ə'gɛn] ADV di nuovo; **to begin/see ~**
ricominciare/rivedere; **he opened it ~** l'ha
aperto di nuovo, l'ha riaperto; **not ... ~** non
... più; ~ **and ~** ripetutamente; **now and ~** di
tanto in tanto, a volte

against [ə'gɛnst] PREP contro; ~ **a blue
background** su uno sfondo azzurro;
leaning ~ the desk appoggiato alla
scrivania; **(as) ~** (BRIT) in confronto a, contro

age [eɪdʒ] N età f inv ▶ VT, VI invecchiare;
what ~ is he? quanti anni ha?; **he is 20
years of ~** ha 20 anni; **aged 10** di 10 anni;
under ~ minorenne; **to come of ~** diventare
maggiorenne; **it's been ages since ...** sono
secoli che ...; **the aged** gli anziani

aged ['eɪdʒd] ADJ: ~ **10** di 10 anni ▶ NPL
['eɪdʒɪd]: **the ~** gli anziani

age group N generazione f; **the 40 to 50 ~** le
persone fra i 40 e i 50 anni

ageing ['eɪdʒɪŋ] ADJ che diventa vecchio(-a);
an ~ film star una diva stagionata

ageless ['eɪdʒlɪs] ADJ senza età

age limit N limite m d'età

agency ['eɪdʒənsɪ] N agenzia; **through** or **by
the ~ of** grazie a

agenda [ə'dʒɛndə] N ordine m del giorno; **on
the ~** all'ordine del giorno

agent ['eɪdʒənt] N agente m

aggravate ['ægrəveɪt] VT aggravare, peggiorare; (annoy) esasperare

aggravation [ægrə'veɪʃən] N peggioramento; esasperazione f

aggregate ['ægrɪgeɪt] N aggregato; **on ~** (Sport) con punteggio complessivo

aggression [ə'grɛʃən] N aggressione f

aggressive [ə'grɛsɪv] ADJ aggressivo(-a)

aggressiveness [ə'grɛsɪvnɪs] N aggressività

aggressor [ə'grɛsər] N aggressore m

aggrieved [ə'gri:vd] ADJ addolorato(-a)

aggro ['ægrəu] N (BRIT col: behaviour) aggressività f inv; (hassle) rottura

aghast [ə'ga:st] ADJ sbigottito(-a)

agile ['ædʒaɪl] ADJ agile

agility [ə'dʒɪlɪtɪ] N agilità f inv

agitate ['ædʒɪteɪt] VT turbare; agitare ▶ VI: **to ~ for** agitarsi per

agitated ['ædʒɪteɪtɪd] ADJ agitato(-a), turbato(-a)

agitator ['ædʒɪteɪtər] N agitatore(-trice)

AGM N ABBR = **annual general meeting**

agnostic [æg'nɔstɪk] ADJ, N agnostico(-a)

ago [ə'gəu] ADV: **2 days ~** 2 giorni fa; **not long ~** poco tempo fa; **as long ~ as 1960** già nel 1960; **how long ~?** quanto tempo fa?

agog [ə'gɔg] ADJ: **(all) ~ (for)** ansioso(-a) (di), impaziente (di)

agonize ['ægənaɪz] VI: **to ~ (over)** angosciarsi (per)

agonizing ['ægənaɪzɪŋ] ADJ straziante

agony ['ægənɪ] N dolore m atroce; **I was in ~** avevo dei dolori atroci

agony aunt N (BRIT col) chi tiene la rubrica della posta del cuore

agony column N posta del cuore

agree [ə'gri:] VT (price) pattuire ▶ VI: **to ~ (with)** essere d'accordo (con); (Ling) concordare (con); **to ~ to sth/to do sth** accettare qc/di fare qc; **to ~ that** (admit) ammettere che; **to ~ on sth** accordarsi su qc; **it was agreed that ...** è stato deciso (di comune accordo) che ...; **garlic doesn't ~ with me** l'aglio non mi va

agreeable [ə'gri:əbl] ADJ gradevole; (willing) disposto(-a); **are you ~ to this?** è d'accordo con questo?

agreed [ə'gri:d] ADJ (time, place) stabilito(-a); **to be ~** essere d'accordo

agreement [ə'gri:mənt] N accordo; **in ~** d'accordo; **by mutual ~** di comune accordo

agricultural [ægrɪ'kʌltʃərəl] ADJ agricolo(-a)

agriculture ['ægrɪkʌltʃər] N agricoltura

aground [ə'graund] ADV: **to run ~** arenarsi

ahead [ə'hɛd] ADV avanti; davanti; **~ of** davanti a; (fig: schedule etc) in anticipo su; **~ of time** in anticipo; **go ~!** avanti!; **go right or straight ~** tiri diritto; **they were (right) ~ of us** erano (proprio) davanti a noi

AI N ABBR = **Amnesty International**; (Comput) = **artificial intelligence**

AIB N ABBR (BRIT: = Accident Investigation Bureau) ufficio d'inchiesta per incidenti aerei e simili

AID N ABBR = **artificial insemination by donor**; (US: = Agency for International Development) A.I.D. f

aid [eɪd] N aiuto ▶ VT aiutare; **with the ~ of** con l'aiuto di; **in ~ of** a favore di; **to ~ and abet** (Law) essere complice di

aide [eɪd] N (person) aiutante mf

aide-de-camp ['eɪddə'kɔŋ] N (Mil) aiutante m di campo

AIDS [eɪdz] N ABBR (= acquired immune deficiency or immunodeficiency syndrome) AIDS f

AIH N ABBR = **artificial insemination by husband**

ailing ['eɪlɪŋ] ADJ sofferente; (fig: economy, industry etc) in difficoltà

ailment ['eɪlmənt] N indisposizione f

aim [eɪm] VT: **to ~ sth at** (gun) mirare qc a, puntare qc a; (camera, remark) rivolgere qc a; (missile) lanciare qc contro; (blow etc) tirare qc a ▶ VI (also: **take aim**) prendere la mira ▶ N mira; **to ~ at** mirare; **to ~ to do** aver l'intenzione di fare

aimless ['eɪmlɪs] ADJ senza scopo

aimlessly ['eɪmlɪslɪ] ADV senza scopo

ain't [eɪnt] (col) = **am not**; **aren't**; **isn't**

air [ɛər] N aria ▶ VT (room, bed) arieggiare; (clothes) far prendere aria a; (idea, grievance) esprimere pubblicamente, manifestare; (views) far conoscere ▶ CPD (currents) d'aria; (attack) aereo(-a); **to throw sth into the ~** lanciare qc in aria; **by ~** (travel) in aereo; **to be on the ~** (Radio, TV: station) trasmettere; (: programme) essere in onda

air bag N airbag m inv

air base N base f aerea

airbed ['ɛəbɛd] N (BRIT) materassino

airborne ['ɛəbɔ:n] ADJ (plane) in volo; (troops) aerotrasportato(-a); **as soon as the plane was ~** appena l'aereo ebbe decollato

air cargo N carico trasportato per via aerea

air-conditioned ['ɛəkən'dɪʃənd] ADJ con or ad aria condizionata

air conditioning N condizionamento d'aria

air-cooled ['ɛəku:ld] ADJ raffreddato(-a) ad aria

aircraft ['ɛəkrɑ:ft] N pl inv apparecchio

aircraft carrier N portaerei f inv

air cushion N cuscino gonfiabile; (Tech) cuscino d'aria

airfield ['ɛəfi:ld] N campo d'aviazione

Air Force N aviazione f militare

air freight N spedizione f di merci per via aerea; (goods) carico spedito per via aerea

airgun ['ɛəgʌn] N fucile m ad aria compressa

air hostess N (BRIT) hostess f inv

airily ['ɛərɪlɪ] ADV con disinvoltura

airing ['ɛərɪŋ] N: **to give an ~ to** (linen) far prendere aria a; (room) arieggiare; (fig: ideas etc) ventilare

airing cupboard ['ɛərɪŋ-] N armadio riscaldato per asciugare panni.

air letter N (BRIT) aerogramma m

airlift ['ɛəlɪft] N ponte m aereo

airline ['ɛəlaɪn] N linea aerea

airliner ['ɛəlaɪnəʳ] N aereo di linea

airlock ['ɛəlɔk] N cassa d'aria

airmail N posta aerea; **by ~** per via or posta aerea

air mattress N materassino gonfiabile

airplane ['ɛəpleɪn] N (US) aeroplano

air pocket N vuoto d'aria

airport ['ɛəpɔːt] N aeroporto

air rage N comportamento aggressivo dei passeggeri di un aereo

air raid N incursione f aerea

air rifle N fucile m ad aria compressa

airsick ['ɛəsɪk] ADJ: **to be ~** soffrire di mal d'aereo

airspace ['ɛəspeɪs] N spazio aereo

airspeed ['ɛəspiːd] N velocità f inv di crociera (Aer)

airstrip ['ɛəstrɪp] N pista d'atterraggio

air terminal N air-terminal m inv

airtight ['ɛətaɪt] ADJ ermetico(-a)

air time N (Radio) spazio radiofonico; (TV) spazio televisivo

air traffic control N controllo del traffico aereo

air traffic controller N controllore m del traffico aereo

airway ['ɛəweɪ] N (Aviat) rotte fpl aeree; (Anat) vie fpl respiratorie

airy ['ɛərɪ] ADJ arioso(-a); (manners) noncurante

aisle [aɪl] N (of church) navata laterale; navata centrale; (of plane) corridoio

aisle seat N (on plane) posto sul corridoio

ajar [ə'dʒɑːʳ] ADJ socchiuso(-a)

AK ABBR (US) = **Alaska**

aka ABBR (= also known as) alias

akin [ə'kɪn] PREP: **~ to** simile a

AL ABBR (US) = **Alabama**

ALA N ABBR = **American Library Association**

Ala. ABBR (US) = **Alabama**

à la carte [ɑːlɑː'kɑːt] ADV alla carta

alacrity [ə'lækrɪtɪ] N: **with ~** con prontezza

alarm [ə'lɑːm] N allarme m ▶ VT allarmare

alarm call N (in hotel etc) sveglia; **could I have an ~ at 7 am, please?** vorrei essere svegliato alle 7, per favore

alarm clock N sveglia

alarmed [ə'lɑːmd] ADJ (person) allarmato(-a); (house, car etc) dotato(-a) di allarme

alarming [ə'lɑːmɪŋ] ADJ allarmante, preoccupante

alarmingly [ə'lɑːmɪŋlɪ] ADV in modo allarmante; **~ close** pericolosamente vicino

alarmist [ə'lɑːmɪst] N allarmista mf

alas [ə'læs] EXCL ohimè!, ahimè!

Alas. ABBR (US) = **Alaska**

Alaska [ə'læskə] N Alasca

Albania [æl'beɪnɪə] N Albania

Albanian [æl'beɪnɪən] ADJ albanese ▶ N albanese mf; (Ling) albanese m

albatross ['ælbətrɔs] N albatro, albatros m inv

albeit [ɔːl'biːɪt] CONJ sebbene + sub, benché + sub

album ['ælbəm] N album m inv; (L.P.) 33 giri m inv, L.P. m inv

albumen ['ælbjumɪn] N albume m

alchemy ['ælkɪmɪ] N alchimia

alcohol ['ælkəhɔl] N alcool m

alcohol-free ['ælkəhɔl'friː] ADJ analcolico(-a)

alcoholic [ælkə'hɔlɪk] ADJ alcolico(-a) ▶ N alcolizzato(-a)

alcoholism ['ælkəhɔlɪzəm] N alcolismo

alcove ['ælkəuv] N alcova

Ald. ABBR = **alderman**

alderman ['ɔːldəmən] N (irreg) consigliere m comunale

ale [eɪl] N birra

alert [ə'ləːt] ADJ vivo(-a); (watchful) vigile ▶ N allarme m ▶ VT: **to ~ sb (to sth)** avvisare qn (di qc), avvertire qn (di qc); **to ~ sb to the dangers of sth** mettere qn in guardia contro qc; **on the ~** all'erta

Aleutian Islands [ə'luːʃən-] NPL isole fpl Aleutine

A level N (BRIT) diploma di studi superiori

Alexandria [ælɪg'zændrɪə] N Alessandria (d'Egitto)

alfresco [æl'freskəu] ADJ, ADV all'aperto

algebra ['ældʒɪbrə] N algebra

Algeria [æl'dʒɪərɪə] N Algeria

Algerian [æl'dʒɪərɪən] ADJ, N algerino(-a)

Algiers [æl'dʒɪəz] N Algeri f

algorithm ['ælgərɪðəm] N algoritmo

alias ['eɪlɪəs] ADV alias ▶ N pseudonimo, falso nome m

alibi ['ælɪbaɪ] N alibi m inv

alien ['eɪlɪən] N straniero(-a); (extraterrestrial) alieno(-a) ▶ ADJ: **~ (to)** estraneo(-a) (a)

alienate ['eɪlɪəneɪt] VT alienare

alienation [eɪlɪə'neɪʃən] N alienazione f

alight [ə'laɪt] ADJ acceso(-a) ▶ VI scendere; (bird) posarsi

align [ə'laɪn] VT allineare

alignment [ə'laɪnmənt] N allineamento; **out of ~ (with)** non allineato (con)

alike [ə'laɪk] ADJ simile ▶ ADV allo stesso modo; **to look ~** assomigliarsi; **winter and summer ~** sia d'estate che d'inverno

alimony ['ælɪmənɪ] N (*payment*) alimenti *mpl*
alive [ə'laɪv] ADJ vivo(-a); (*active*) attivo(-a);
~ **with** pieno(-a) di; ~ **to** conscio(-a) di
alkali ['ælkəlaɪ] N alcali *m inv*

(KEYWORD)

all [ɔːl] ADJ tutto(-a); **all day** tutto il giorno;
all night tutta la notte; **all men** tutti gli
uomini; **all five girls** tutt'e cinque le
ragazze; **all five came** sono venuti tutti e
cinque; **all the books** tutti i libri; **all the
food** tutto il cibo; **all the time** tutto il
tempo; (*always*) sempre; **all his life** tutta la
vita; **for all their efforts** nonostante tutti i
loro sforzi
▶ PRON **1** tutto(-a); **is that all?** non c'è altro?;
(*in shop*) basta così?; **all of them** tutti(-e); **all
of it** tutto(-a); **I ate it all, I ate all of it** l'ho
mangiato tutto; **all of us went** tutti noi
siamo andati; **all of the boys went** tutti i
ragazzi sono andati
2 (*in phrases*): **above all** soprattutto; **after all**
dopotutto; **at all: not at all** (*in answer to
question*) niente affatto; (*in answer to thanks*)
prego!, di niente!, s'immagini!; **I'm not at
all tired** non sono affatto stanco; **anything
at all will do** andrà bene qualsiasi cosa; **all
in all** tutto sommato
▶ ADV: **all alone** tutto(-a) solo(-a); **to be/feel
all in** (*BRIT col*) essere/sentirsi sfinito(-a) *or*
distrutto(-a); **all out** *adv*: **to go all out**
mettercela tutta; **it's not as hard as all
that** non è poi così difficile; **all the more/
the better** tanto più/meglio; **all but** quasi;
the score is two all il punteggio è di due a
due *or* è due pari

Allah ['ælə] N Allah *m*
allay [ə'leɪ] VT (*fears*) dissipare
all clear N (*Mil*) cessato allarme *m inv*; (*fig*)
okay *m*
allegation [ælɪ'geɪʃən] N asserzione *f*
allege [ə'lɛdʒ] VT asserire; **he is alleged to
have said ...** avrebbe detto che ...
alleged [ə'lɛdʒd] ADJ presunto(-a)
allegedly [ə'lɛdʒɪdlɪ] ADV secondo quanto
si asserisce
allegiance [ə'liːdʒəns] N fedeltà
allegory ['ælɪgərɪ] N allegoria
all-embracing ['ɔːlɪm'breɪsɪŋ] ADJ
universale
allergic [ə'ləːdʒɪk] ADJ: ~ **to** allergico(-a) a
allergy ['ælədʒɪ] N allergia
alleviate [ə'liːvɪeɪt] VT alleviare, sollevare
alley ['ælɪ] N vicolo; (*in garden*) vialetto
alleyway ['ælɪweɪ] N vicolo
alliance [ə'laɪəns] N alleanza
allied ['ælaɪd] ADJ alleato(-a)
alligator ['ælɪgeɪtə'] N alligatore *m*

all-important ['ɔːlɪm'pɔːtənt] ADJ
importantissimo(-a)
all-in ['ɔːlɪn] ADJ, ADV (*BRIT: charge*) tutto
compreso
all-in wrestling N (*BRIT*) lotta americana
alliteration [əlɪtə'reɪʃən] N allitterazione *f*
all-night ['ɔːl'naɪt] ADJ aperto(-a) (*or* che dura)
tutta la notte
allocate ['æləkeɪt] VT (*share out*) distribuire;
(*duties, sum, time*): **to ~ sth to** assegnare qc a;
to ~ sth for stanziare qc per
allocation [æləu'keɪʃən] N: ~ (**of money**)
stanziamento
allot [ə'lɔt] VT (*share out*) spartire; **to ~ sth to**
(*time*) dare qc a; (*duties*) assegnare qc a; **in the
allotted time** nel tempo fissato *or*
prestabilito
allotment [ə'lɔtmənt] N (*share*) spartizione *f*;
(*garden*) lotto di terra
all-out ['ɔːlaut] ADJ (*effort etc*) totale ▶ ADV: **to
go all out for** mettercela tutta per
allow [ə'lau] VT (*practice, behaviour*)
permettere; (*sum to spend etc*) accordare; (*sum,
time estimated*) dare; (*concede*): **to ~ that**
ammettere che; **to ~ sb to do** permettere a
qn di fare; **he is allowed to (do it)** lo può
fare; **smoking is not allowed** è vietato
fumare, non è permesso fumare; **we must ~
3 days for the journey** dobbiamo calcolare 3
giorni per il viaggio
▶ **allow for** VT FUS tener conto di
allowance [ə'lauəns] N (*money received*)
assegno; (*for travelling, accommodation*)
indennità *f inv*; (*Tax*) detrazione *f* di imposta;
to make ~(s) for tener conto di; (*person*)
scusare
alloy ['ælɔɪ] N lega
all right ADV (*feel, work*) bene; (*as answer*) va
bene
all-round ['ɔːl'raund] ADJ completo(-a)
all-rounder [ɔːl'raundə'] N (*BRIT*): **to be a
good ~** essere bravo(-a) in tutto
allspice ['ɔːlspaɪs] N pepe *m* della Giamaica
all-time ['ɔːl'taɪm] ADJ (*record*) assoluto(-a)
allude [ə'luːd] VI: **to ~ to** alludere a
alluring [ə'ljuərɪŋ] ADJ seducente
allusion [ə'luːʒən] N allusione *f*
alluvium [ə'luːvɪəm] N materiale *m*
alluvionale
ally N ['ælaɪ] alleato ▶ VT [ə'laɪ]: **to ~ o.s.
with** allearsi con
almighty [ɔːl'maɪtɪ] ADJ onnipotente; (*row
etc*) colossale
almond ['ɑːmənd] N mandorla
almost ['ɔːlməust] ADV quasi; **he ~ fell** per
poco non è caduto
alms [ɑːmz] N elemosina
aloft [ə'lɔft] ADV in alto; (*Naut*)
sull'alberatura

alone [ə'ləun] ADJ, ADV solo(-a); **to leave sb ~** lasciare qn in pace; **to leave sth ~** lasciare stare qc; **let ~ ...** figuriamoci poi ..., tanto meno ...

along [ə'lɒŋ] PREP lungo ▶ ADV: **is he coming ~?** viene con noi?; **he was hopping/limping ~** veniva saltellando/zoppicando; **~ with** insieme con; **all ~** (all the time) sempre, fin dall'inizio

alongside [ə'lɒŋ'saɪd] PREP accanto a; lungo ▶ ADV accanto; (Naut) sottobordo; **we brought our boat ~** (of a pier/shore etc) abbiamo accostato la barca (al molo/alla riva etc)

aloof [ə'luːf] ADJ distaccato(-a) ▶ ADV a distanza, in disparte; **to stand ~** tenersi a distanza or in disparte

aloofness [ə'luːfnɪs] N distacco, riserbo

aloud [ə'laud] ADV ad alta voce

alphabet ['ælfəbet] N alfabeto

alphabetical [ælfə'betɪkəl] ADJ alfabetico(-a); **in ~ order** in ordine alfabetico

alphanumeric [ælfənjuː'mɛrɪk] ADJ alfanumerico(-a)

alpine ['ælpaɪn] ADJ alpino(-a); **~ hut** rifugio alpino; **~ pasture** pascolo alpestre; **~ skiing** sci alpino

Alps [ælps] NPL: **the ~** le Alpi

already [ɔːl'redɪ] ADV già

alright [ɔːl'raɪt] ADV (BRIT) = **all right**

Alsatian [æl'seɪʃən] N (BRIT: dog) pastore m tedesco, (cane m) lupo

also ['ɔːlsəu] ADV anche

Alta. ABBR (CANADA) = **Alberta**

altar ['ɔltər] N altare m

alter ['ɔltər] VT, VI alterare

alteration [ɔltə'reɪʃən] N modificazione f, alterazione f; **alterations** (Sewing, Archit) modifiche fpl; **timetable subject to ~** orario soggetto a variazioni

altercation [ɔːltə'keɪʃən] N alterco, litigio

alternate ADJ [ɔl'təːnɪt] alterno(-a); (US: plan etc) alternativo(-a) ▶ VI ['ɔltəːneɪt] alternare; **to ~ (with)** alternarsi (a); **on ~ days** ogni due giorni

alternately [ɔl'təːnɪtlɪ] ADV alternatamente

alternating current ['ɔltəneɪtɪŋ-] N corrente f alternata

alternative [ɔl'təːnətɪv] ADJ (solutions) alternativo(-a); (solution) altro(-a) ▶ N (choice) alternativa; (other possibility) altra possibilità

alternatively [ɔl'təːnətɪvlɪ] ADV altrimenti, come alternativa

alternative medicine N medicina alternativa

alternator ['ɔltəːneɪtər] N (Aut) alternatore m

although [ɔːl'ðəu] CONJ benché + sub, sebbene + sub

altitude ['æltɪtjuːd] N altitudine f

alto ['æltəu] N contralto

altogether [ɔːltə'gɛðər] ADV del tutto, completamente; (on the whole) tutto considerato; (in all) in tutto; **how much is that ~?** quant'è in tutto?

altruism ['æltruɪzəm] N altruismo

altruistic [æltru'ɪstɪk] ADJ altruistico(-a)

aluminium [ælju'mɪnɪəm], (US) **aluminum** [ə'luːmɪnəm] N alluminio

always ['ɔːlweɪz] ADV sempre

Alzheimer's ['æltshaɪməz] N (also: **Alzheimer's disease**) morbo di Alzheimer

AM ABBR (= amplitude modulation) AM ▶ N ABBR (= Assembly Member) deputato gallese

am [æm] VB see **be**

a.m. ADV ABBR (= ante meridiem) della mattina

AMA N ABBR = **American Medical Association**

amalgam [ə'mælgəm] N amalgama m

amalgamate [ə'mælgəmeɪt] VT amalgamare ▶ VI amalgamarsi

amalgamation [əmælgə'meɪʃən] N amalgamazione f; (Comm) fusione f

amass [ə'mæs] VT ammassare

amateur ['æmətər] N dilettante mf ▶ ADJ (Sport) dilettante; **~ dramatics** n filodrammatica

amateurish ['æmətərɪʃ] ADJ (pej) da dilettante

amaze [ə'meɪz] VT stupire

amazed ADJ sbalordito(-a); **to be ~ (at)** essere sbalordito(-a) (da)

amazement [ə'meɪzmənt] N stupore m

amazing [ə'meɪzɪŋ] ADJ sorprendente, sbalorditivo(-a); (bargain, offer) sensazionale

amazingly [ə'meɪzɪŋlɪ] ADV incredibilmente, sbalorditivamente

Amazon ['æməzən] N (Mythology) Amazzone f; **the ~** il Rio delle Amazzoni ▶ CPD (basin, jungle) amazzonico(-a)

Amazonian [æmə'zəunɪən] ADJ amazzonico(-a)

ambassador [æm'bæsədər] N ambasciatore(-trice)

amber ['æmbər] N ambra; **at ~** (BRIT Aut) giallo

ambidextrous [æmbɪ'dɛkstrəs] ADJ ambidestro(-a)

ambience ['æmbɪəns] N ambiente m

ambiguity [æmbɪ'gjuɪtɪ] N ambiguità f inv

ambiguous [æm'bɪgjuəs] ADJ ambiguo(-a)

ambition [æm'bɪʃən] N ambizione f; **to achieve one's ~** realizzare le proprie aspirazioni or ambizioni

ambitious [æm'bɪʃəs] ADJ ambizioso(-a)

ambivalent [æm'bɪvələnt] ADJ ambivalente

amble ['æmbl] VI (also: **amble along**) camminare tranquillamente

ambulance ['æmbjuləns] N ambulanza

ambush ['æmbʊʃ] N imboscata ▶ VT fare un'imboscata a

ameba [ə'miːbə] N (US) = **amoeba**

ameliorate [ə'miːlɪəreɪt] VT migliorare

amen ['ɑː'mɛn] EXCL così sia, amen

amenable [ə'miːnəbl] ADJ: **~ to** (advice etc) ben disposto(-a) a

amend [ə'mɛnd] VT (law) emendare; (text) correggere ▶ VI emendarsi; **to make amends** fare ammenda

amendment [ə'mɛndmənt] N emendamento; correzione f

amenities [ə'miːnɪtɪz] NPL attrezzature fpl ricreative e culturali

amenity [ə'miːnɪtɪ] N amenità f inv

America [ə'mɛrɪkə] N America

American [ə'mɛrɪkən] ADJ, N americano(-a)

American football N (BRIT) football m americano

americanize [ə'mɛrɪkənaɪz] VT americanizzare

amethyst ['æmɪθɪst] N ametista

Amex ['æmɛks] N ABBR = **American Stock Exchange**

amiable ['eɪmɪəbl] ADJ amabile, gentile

amicable ['æmɪkəbl] ADJ amichevole

amicably ['æmɪkəblɪ] ADV: **to part ~** lasciarsi senza rancori

amid [ə'mɪd], **amidst** [ə'mɪdst] PREP fra, tra, in mezzo a

amiss [ə'mɪs] ADJ, ADV: **there's something ~** c'è qualcosa che non va bene; **don't take it ~** non avertene a male

ammo ['æməʊ] N ABBR (col) = **ammunition**

ammonia [ə'məʊnɪə] N ammoniaca

ammunition [æmjʊ'nɪʃən] N munizioni fpl; (fig) arma

ammunition dump N deposito di munizioni

amnesia [æm'niːzɪə] N amnesia

amnesty ['æmnɪstɪ] N amnistia; **to grant an ~ to** concedere l'amnistia a, amnistiare

Amnesty International N Amnesty International f

amoeba, (US) **ameba** [ə'miːbə] N ameba

amok [ə'mɔk] ADV: **to run ~** diventare pazzo(-a) furioso(-a)

among [ə'mʌŋ], **amongst** [ə'mʌŋst] PREP fra, tra, in mezzo a

amoral [eɪ'mɔrəl] ADJ amorale

amorous ['æmərəs] ADJ amoroso(-a)

amorphous [ə'mɔːfəs] ADJ amorfo(-a)

amortization [əmɔːtaɪ'zeɪʃən] N (Comm) ammortamento

amount [ə'maʊnt] N (sum of money) somma; ammontare m; (of bill etc) importo; (quantity) quantità f inv ▶ VI: **to ~ to** (total) ammontare a; (be same as) essere come; **this amounts to a refusal** questo equivale a un rifiuto

amp ['æmp], **ampère** ['æmpɛər] N ampere m inv; **a 13 ~ plug** una spina con fusibile da 13 ampere

ampersand ['æmpəsænd] N e f commerciale

amphetamine [æm'fɛtəmiːn] N anfetamina

amphibian [æm'fɪbɪən] N anfibio

amphibious [æm'fɪbɪəs] ADJ anfibio(-a)

amphitheatre, (US) **amphitheater** ['æmfɪθɪətər] N anfiteatro

ample ['æmpl] ADJ ampio(-a); spazioso(-a); (enough): **this is ~** questo è più che sufficiente; **to have ~ time/room** avere assai tempo/posto

amplifier ['æmplɪfaɪər] N amplificatore m

amplify ['æmplɪfaɪ] VT amplificare

amply ['æmplɪ] ADV ampiamente

ampoule, (US) **ampule** ['æmpuːl] N (Med) fiala

amputate ['æmpjʊteɪt] VT amputare

amputee [æmpjʊ'tiː] N mutilato(-a), chi ha subito un'amputazione

Amsterdam [æmstə'dæm] N Amsterdam f

amt ABBR = **amount**

Amtrak ['æmtræk] (US) N società ferroviaria americana

amuck [ə'mʌk] ADV = **amok**

amuse [ə'mjuːz] VT divertire; **to ~ o.s. with sth/by doing sth** divertirsi con qc/a fare qc; **to be amused at** essere divertito da; **he was not amused** non l'ha trovato divertente

amusement [ə'mjuːzmənt] N divertimento; **much to my ~** con mio grande spasso

amusement arcade N sala giochi (solo con macchinette a gettoni)

amusement park N luna park m inv

amusing [ə'mjuːzɪŋ] ADJ divertente

an [æn, ən, n] INDEF ART see **a**

ANA N ABBR = **American Newspaper Association**; **American Nurses Association**

anachronism [ə'nækrənɪzəm] N anacronismo

anaemia [ə'niːmɪə] N anemia

anaemic [ə'niːmɪk] ADJ anemico(-a)

anaesthetic [ænɪs'θɛtɪk] ADJ anestetico(-a) ▶ N anestetico; **local/general ~** anestesia locale/totale; **under the ~** sotto anestesia

anaesthetist [æ'niːsθɪtɪst] N anestesista mf

anagram ['ænəgræm] N anagramma m

anal ['eɪnl] ADJ anale

analgesic [ænæl'dʒiːsɪk] ADJ analgesico(-a) ▶ N analgesico

analog, analogue ['ænəlɔg] ADJ (watch, computer) analogico(-a)

analogous [ə'næləgəs] ADJ: **~ to** or **with** analogo(-a) a

analogy [ə'nælədʒɪ] N analogia; **to draw an ~ between** fare un'analogia tra

analyse, (US) **analyze** ['ænəlaɪz] VT analizzare

analysis [ə'næləsɪs] (pl **analyses** [-siːz]) N
analisi f inv; **in the last** ~ in ultima analisi

analyst ['ænəlɪst] N (political analyst etc)
analista mf; (US) (psic)analista mf

analytic [ænə'lɪtɪk], **analytical** [ænə'lɪtɪkl]
ADJ analitico(-a)

analyze ['ænəlaɪz] VT (US) = **analyse**

anarchic [æ'nɑːkɪk] ADJ anarchico(-a)

anarchist ['ænəkɪst] ADJ, N anarchico(-a)

anarchy ['ænəkɪ] N anarchia

anathema [ə'næθɪmə] N: **it is ~ to him** non
ne vuol neanche sentir parlare

anatomical [ænə'tɔmɪkl] ADJ anatomico(-a)

anatomy [ə'nætəmɪ] N anatomia

ANC N ABBR = **African National Congress**

ancestor ['ænsɪstə'] N antenato(-a)

ancestral [æn'sɛstrəl] ADJ avito(-a)

ancestry ['ænsɪstrɪ] N antenati mpl;
ascendenza

anchor ['æŋkə'] N ancora ▶ VI (also: **to drop
anchor**) gettare l'ancora ▶ VT ancorare; **to
weigh** ~ salpare or levare l'ancora

anchorage ['æŋkərɪdʒ] N ancoraggio

anchor man N (irreg) (TV, Radio) anchorman
m inv

anchor woman N (irreg) (TV, Radio)
anchorwoman f inv

anchovy ['æntʃəvɪ] N acciuga

ancient ['eɪnʃənt] ADJ antico(-a); (person, car)
vecchissimo(-a); ~ **monument** monumento
storico

ancillary [æn'sɪlərɪ] ADJ ausiliario(-a)

and [ænd] CONJ e (often 'ed' before vowel); ~ **so
on** e così via; **try ~ do it** prova a farlo; **try ~
come** cerca di venire; **he talked ~ talked**
non la finiva di parlare; **come ~ sit here**
vieni a sedere qui; **better ~ better** sempre
meglio; **more ~ more** sempre di più

Andes ['ændiːz] NPL: **the ~** le Ande

Andorra [æn'dɔːrə] N Andorra

anecdote ['ænɪkdəut] N aneddoto

anemia etc [ə'niːmɪə] (US) = **anaemia** etc

anemone [ə'nɛmənɪ] N (Bot) anemone m;
(sea anemone) anemone m di mare, attinia

anesthetic etc [ænɪs'θɛtɪk] (US) = **anaesthetic**
etc

anew [ə'njuː] ADV di nuovo

angel ['eɪndʒəl] N angelo

angel dust N sedativo usato a scopo
allucinogeno

anger ['æŋgə'] N rabbia ▶ VT arrabbiare

angina [æn'dʒaɪnə] N angina pectoris

angle ['æŋgl] N angolo ▶ VI: **to ~ for** (fig)
cercare di avere; **from their ~** dal loro punto
di vista

angler ['æŋglə'] N pescatore m con la lenza

Anglican ['æŋglɪkən] ADJ, N anglicano(-a)

anglicize ['æŋglɪsaɪz] VT anglicizzare

angling ['æŋglɪŋ] N pesca con la lenza

Anglo- ['æŋgləu] PREFIX, N anglo...; **~Italian**
adj italobritannico(-a)

Anglo-Saxon ['æŋgləu'sæksən] ADJ, N
anglosassone mf

Angola [æŋ'gəulə] N Angola

Angolan [æŋ'gəulən] ADJ, N angolano(-a)

angrily ['æŋgrɪlɪ] ADV con rabbia

angry ['æŋgrɪ] ADJ arrabbiato(-a), furioso(-a);
(wound) infiammato(-a); **to be ~ with sb/at
sth** essere in collera con qn/per qc; **to get ~**
arrabbiarsi; **to make sb ~** fare arrabbiare qn

anguish ['æŋgwɪʃ] N angoscia

anguished ['æŋgwɪʃt] ADJ angosciato(-a),
pieno(-a) d'angoscia

angular ['æŋgjulə'] ADJ angolare

animal ['ænɪməl] ADJ animale ▶ N animale m

animal rights NPL diritti mpl degli animali

animate VT ['ænɪmeɪt] animare ▶ ADJ
['ænɪmɪt] animato(-a)

animated ['ænɪmeɪtɪd] ADJ animato(-a)

animation [ænɪ'meɪʃən] N animazione f

animosity [ænɪ'mɔsɪtɪ] N animosità

aniseed ['ænɪsiːd] N semi mpl di anice

Ankara ['æŋkərə] N Ankara

ankle ['æŋkl] N caviglia

ankle socks NPL calzini mpl

annex N ['ænɛks] (Brit: also: **annexe**) edificio
annesso ▶ VT [ə'nɛks] annettere

annexation [ænɛk'seɪʃən] N annessione f

annihilate [ə'naɪəleɪt] VT annientare

annihilation [ənaɪə'leɪʃən] N
annientamento

anniversary [ænɪ'vəːsərɪ] N anniversario

anniversary dinner N cena commemorativa

annotate ['ænəuteɪt] VT annotare

announce [ə'nauns] VT annunciare; **he
announced that he wasn't going** ha
dichiarato che non (ci) sarebbe andato

announcement [ə'naunsmənt] N annuncio;
(letter, card) partecipazione f; **I'd like to
make an ~** ho una comunicazione da fare

announcer [ə'naunsə'] N (Radio, TV: between
programmes) annunciatore(-trice); (: in a
programme) presentatore(-trice)

annoy [ə'nɔɪ] VT dare fastidio a; **to be
annoyed (at sth/with sb)** essere seccato or
irritato (per qc/con qn); **don't get annoyed!**
non irritarti!

annoyance [ə'nɔɪəns] N fastidio; (cause of
annoyance) noia

annoying [ə'nɔɪɪŋ] ADJ irritante, seccante

annual ['ænjuəl] ADJ annuale ▶ N (Bot)
pianta annua; (book) annuario

annual general meeting N (Brit) assemblea
generale

annually ['ænjuəlɪ] ADV annualmente

annual report N relazione f annuale

annuity [ə'njuːɪtɪ] N annualità f inv; **life ~**
vitalizio

annul [ə'nʌl] VT annullare; (law) rescindere

annulment [ə'nʌlmənt] N annullamento; rescissione f

annum ['ænəm] N see **per annum**

Annunciation [ənʌnsɪ'eɪʃən] N Annunciazione f

anode ['ænəud] N anodo

anoint [ə'nɔɪnt] VT ungere

anomalous [ə'nɔmələs] ADJ anomalo(-a)

anomaly [ə'nɔməlɪ] N anomalia

anon. [ə'nɔn] ABBR = **anonymous**

anonymity [ænə'nɪmɪtɪ] N anonimato

anonymous [ə'nɔnɪməs] ADJ anonimo(-a); **to remain** ~ mantenere l'anonimato

anorak ['ænəræk] N giacca a vento

anorexia [ænə'rɛksɪə] N (Med: also: **anorexia nervosa**) anoressia

anorexic [ænə'rɛksɪk] ADJ, N anoressico(-a)

another [ə'nʌðər] ADJ: ~ **book** (one more) un altro libro, ancora un libro; (a different one) un altro libro ▶ PRON un altro (un'altra), ancora uno(-a); ~ **drink?** ancora qualcosa da bere?; **in** ~ **5 years** fra altri 5 anni; see also **one**

ANSI N ABBR (= American National Standards Institution) Istituto americano di standardizzazione

answer ['ɑːnsər] N risposta; soluzione f ▶ VI rispondere ▶ VT (reply to) rispondere a; (problem) risolvere; (prayer) esaudire; **in** ~ **to your letter** in risposta alla sua lettera; **to** ~ **the phone** rispondere (al telefono); **to** ~ **the bell** rispondere al campanello; **to** ~ **the door** aprire la porta
▶ **answer back** VI ribattere
▶ **answer for** VT FUS essere responsabile di
▶ **answer to** VT FUS (description) corrispondere a

answerable ['ɑːnsərəbl] ADJ: ~ **(to sb/for sth)** responsabile (verso qn/di qc); **I am** ~ **to no-one** non devo rispondere a nessuno

answering machine ['ɑːnsərɪŋ-] N segreteria (telefonica) automatica

answerphone N (esp BRIT) segreteria telefonica

ant [ænt] N formica

ANTA N ABBR = **American National Theater and Academy**

antagonism [æn'tægənɪzəm] N antagonismo

antagonist [æn'tægənɪst] N antagonista mf

antagonistic [æntægə'nɪstɪk] ADJ antagonistico(-a)

antagonize [æn'tægənaɪz] VT provocare l'ostilità di

Antarctic [ænt'ɑːktɪk] N: **the** ~ l'Antartide f ▶ ADJ antartico(-a)

Antarctica [ænt'ɑːktɪkə] N Antartide f

Antarctic Circle N Circolo polare antartico

Antarctic Ocean N Oceano antartico

ante ['æntɪ] N (Cards, fig): **to up the** ~ alzare la posta in palio

ante... ['æntɪ] PREFIX anti..., ante..., pre...

anteater ['æntiːtər] N formichiere m

antecedent [æntɪ'siːdənt] N antecedente m, precedente m

antechamber ['æntɪtʃeɪmbər] N anticamera

antelope ['æntɪləup] N antilope f

antenatal [æntɪ'neɪtl] ADJ prenatale

antenatal clinic N assistenza medica preparto

antenna [æn'tɛnə] (pl **antennae** [-niː]) N antenna

anthem ['ænθəm] N antifona; **national** ~ inno nazionale

ant-hill ['ænthɪl] N formicaio

anthology [æn'θɔlədʒɪ] N antologia

anthrax ['ænθræks] N antrace m

anthropologist [ænθrə'pɔlədʒɪst] N antropologo(-a)

anthropology [ænθrə'pɔlədʒɪ] N antropologia

anti- ['æntɪ] PREFIX anti...

anti-aircraft ['æntɪ'ɛəkrɑːft] ADJ antiaereo(-a)

anti-aircraft defence N difesa antiaerea

antiballistic ['æntɪbə'lɪstɪk] ADJ antibalistico(-a)

antibiotic ['æntɪbaɪ'ɔtɪk] ADJ antibiotico(-a) ▶ N antibiotico

antibody ['æntɪbɔdɪ] N anticorpo

anticipate [æn'tɪsɪpeɪt] VT prevedere; pregustare; (wishes, request) prevenire; **as anticipated** come previsto; **this is worse than I anticipated** è peggio di quel che immaginavo or pensavo

anticipation [æntɪsɪ'peɪʃən] N anticipazione f; (expectation) aspettativa fpl; **thanking you in** ~ vi ringrazio in anticipo

anticlimax ['æntɪ'klaɪmæks] N: **it was an** ~ fu una completa delusione

anticlockwise ['æntɪ'klɔkwaɪz] ADJ, ADV in senso antiorario

antics ['æntɪks] NPL buffonerie fpl

anticyclone ['æntɪ'saɪkləun] N anticiclone m

antidote ['æntɪdəut] N antidoto

antifreeze ['æntɪfriːz] N anticongelante m

anti-globalization [æntɪgləubəlaɪ'zeɪʃən] ADJ antiglobalizzazione inv ▶ N antiglobalizzazione f

antihistamine [æntɪ'hɪstəmɪn] N antistaminico

Antilles [æn'tɪliːz] NPL: **the** ~ le Antille

antipathy [æn'tɪpəθɪ] N antipatia

antiperspirant ['æntɪ'pə:spərənt] ADJ antitraspirante

Antipodean [æntɪpə'diːən] ADJ degli Antipodi

Antipodes [æn'tɪpədiːz] NPL: **the ~** gli Antipodi

antiquarian [æntɪ'kwɛərɪən] ADJ: **~ bookshop** libreria antiquaria ▶ N antiquario(-a)

antiquated ['æntɪkweɪtɪd] ADJ antiquato(-a)

antique [æn'tiːk] N antichità f inv ▶ ADJ antico(-a)

antique dealer N antiquario(-a)

antique shop N negozio d'antichità

antiquity [æn'tɪkwɪtɪ] N antichità f inv

anti-semitic ['æntɪsɪ'mɪtɪk] ADJ antisemitico(-a), antisemita

anti-semitism ['æntɪ'sɛmɪtɪzəm] N antisemitismo

antiseptic [æntɪ'sɛptɪk] ADJ antisettico(-a) ▶ N antisettico

antisocial ['æntɪ'səʊʃəl] ADJ asociale; (against society) antisociale

antitank [æntɪ'tæŋk] ADJ anticarro inv

antithesis [æn'tɪθɪsɪs] (pl **antitheses** [-siːz]) N antitesi f inv; (contrast) carattere m antitetico

anti-trust [æntɪ'trʌst] ADJ (Comm): **~ legislation** legislazione f antitrust inv

antiviral [æntɪ'vaɪərəl] ADJ (Med) antivirale

antivirus [æntɪ'vaɪərəs] ADJ (Comput) antivirus inv; **~ program** antivirus m inv

antivirus software N antivirus m inv

antlers ['æntləz] NPL palchi mpl

Antwerp ['æntwəːp] N Anversa

anus ['eɪnəs] N ano

anvil ['ænvɪl] N incudine f

anxiety [æŋ'zaɪətɪ] N ansia; (keenness): **~ to do** smania di fare

anxious ['æŋkʃəs] ADJ ansioso(-a), inquieto(-a); (worrying) angosciante; (keen): **~ to do/that** impaziente di fare/che +sub; **I'm very ~ about you** sono molto preoccupato or in pensiero per te

anxiously ['æŋkʃəslɪ] ADV ansiosamente, con ansia

(KEYWORD)

any ['ɛnɪ] ADJ **1** (in questions etc): **have you any butter?** hai del burro?, hai un po' di burro?; **have you any children?** hai bambini?; **if there are any tickets left** se ci sono ancora (dei) biglietti, se c'è ancora qualche biglietto

2 (with negative): **I haven't any money/books** non ho soldi/libri; **without any difficulty** senza nessuna or alcuna difficoltà

3 (no matter which) qualsiasi, qualunque; **choose any book you like** scegli un libro qualsiasi

4 (in phrases): **in any case** in ogni caso; **any day now** da un giorno all'altro; **at any moment** in qualsiasi momento, da un momento all'altro; **at any rate** ad ogni modo

▶ PRON **1** (in questions: with negative): **have you got any?** ne hai?; **can any of you sing?** qualcuno di voi sa cantare?; **I haven't any (of them)** non ne ho

2 (no matter which one(s)): **take any of those books (you like)** prendi uno qualsiasi di quei libri

▶ ADV **1** (in questions etc): **do you want any more soup/sandwiches?** vuoi ancora un po' di minestra/degli altri panini?; **are you feeling any better?** ti senti meglio?

2 (with negative): **I can't hear him any more** non lo sento più; **don't wait any longer** non aspettare più

anybody ['ɛnɪbɒdɪ] PRON qualsiasi persona; (in interrogative sentences) qualcuno; (in negative sentences) nessuno; (no matter who) chiunque; **can you see ~?** vedi qualcuno or nessuno?; **if ~ should phone ...** se telefona qualcuno ...; **I don't see ~** non vedo nessuno; **~ could do it** chiunque potrebbe farlo

anyhow ['ɛnɪhaʊ] ADV in qualsiasi modo; (haphazardly) come capita; (at any rate) ad ogni modo, comunque; (haphazard): **do it ~ you like** fallo come ti pare; **I shall go ~** ci andrò lo stesso or comunque; **she leaves things just ~** lascia tutto come capita

anyone ['ɛnɪwʌn] PRON = **anybody**

anyplace ['ɛnɪpleɪs] ADV (US col) = **anywhere**

anything ['ɛnɪθɪŋ] PRON qualsiasi cosa; (in interrogative sentences) qualcosa, niente; (with negative) niente; **you can say ~ you like** (no matter what) puoi dire quello che ti pare; **can you see ~?** vedi niente or qualcosa?; **if ~ happens to me ...** se mi dovesse succedere qualcosa ...; **I can't see ~** non vedo niente; **~ will do** va bene qualsiasi cosa or tutto; **~ else?** (in shop) basta (così)?; **it can cost ~ between £15 and £20** può costare qualcosa come 15 o 20 sterline

anytime ['ɛnɪtaɪm] ADV in qualunque momento; quando vuole

anyway ['ɛnɪweɪ] ADV (at any rate) ad ogni modo, comunque; (besides) ad ogni modo

anywhere ['ɛnɪwɛər] ADV da qualsiasi parte; (in interrogative sentences) da qualche parte; (with negative) da nessuna parte; (no matter where) da qualsiasi or qualunque parte, dovunque; **can you see him ~?** lo vedi da qualche parte?; **I don't see him ~** non lo vedo da nessuna parte; **~ in the world** dovunque nel mondo

Anzac ['ænzæk] N ABBR (= Australia-New Zealand Army Corps) A.N.Z.A.C. m; (soldier) soldato dell'A.N.Z.A.C.

Anzac Day N vedi nota

L' *Anzac Day* è una festa nazionale australiana e neozelandese che cade il 25 aprile e commemora il famoso sbarco delle forze armate congiunte dei due paesi a Gallipoli nel 1915, durante la prima guerra mondiale.

apart [ə'pɑːt] ADV (*to one side*) a parte; (*separately*) separatamente; **with one's legs ~** con le gambe divaricate; **10 miles/a long way ~** a 10 miglia di distanza/molto lontani l'uno dall'altro; **they are living ~** sono separati; **to take ~** smontare; **~ from** *prep* a parte, eccetto

apartheid [ə'pɑːteɪt] N apartheid *f*

apartment [ə'pɑːtmənt] N (*US*) appartamento; (*room*) locale *m*; **apartments** NPL appartamento ammobiliato

apartment building N (*US*) stabile *m*, caseggiato

apathetic [æpə'θetɪk] ADJ apatico(-a)

apathy ['æpəθɪ] N apatia

APB N ABBR (*US: police expression: = all points bulletin*) espressione della polizia che significa "trovate e arrestate il sospetto"

ape [eɪp] N scimmia ▶ VT scimmiottare

Apennines ['æpənaɪnz] NPL: **the ~** gli Apennini

aperitif [ə'perɪtiːf] N aperitivo

aperture ['æpətʃuəʳ] N apertura

APEX ['eɪpɛks] N ABBR (*Aviat: = advance purchase excursion*) APEX *m inv*

apex ['eɪpɛks] N apice *m*

aphid ['æfɪd] N afide *f*

aphrodisiac [æfrəu'dɪzɪæk] ADJ afrodisiaco(-a) ▶ N afrodisiaco

API N ABBR = **American Press Institute**

apiece [ə'piːs] ADV ciascuno(-a)

aplomb [ə'plɔm] N disinvoltura

APO N ABBR (*US: = Army Post Office*) ufficio postale dell'esercito

apocalypse [ə'pɔkəlɪps] N apocalisse *f*

apolitical [eɪpə'lɪtɪkl] ADJ apolitico(-a)

apologetic [əpɔlə'dʒetɪk] ADJ (*tone, letter*) di scusa; **to be very ~ about** scusarsi moltissimo di

apologetically [əpɔlə'dʒetɪkəlɪ] ADV per scusarsi

apologize [ə'pɔlədʒaɪz] VI: **to ~ (for sth to sb)** scusarsi (di qc a qn), chiedere scusa (a qn per qc)

apology [ə'pɔlədʒɪ] N scuse *fpl*; **please accept my apologies** la prego di accettare le mie scuse

apoplectic [æpə'plɛktɪk] ADJ (*Med*) apoplettico(-a); **~ with rage** (*col*) livido(-a) per la rabbia

apoplexy ['æpəplɛksɪ] N apoplessia

apostle [ə'pɔsl] N apostolo

apostrophe [ə'pɔstrəfɪ] N (*sign*) apostrofo

app N ABBR (*col: Comput: = application*) applicazione *f*

appal, (*US*) **appall** [ə'pɔːl] VT atterrire; sconvolgere

Appalachian Mountains [æpə'leɪʃən-] NPL: **the ~** i Monti Appalachi

appalling [ə'pɔːlɪŋ] ADJ spaventoso(-a); **she's an ~ cook** è un disastro come cuoca

apparatus [æpə'reɪtəs] N apparato; (*in gymnasium*) attrezzatura

apparel [ə'pærl] N (*US*) abbigliamento, confezioni *fpl*

apparent [ə'pærənt] ADJ evidente

apparently [ə'pærəntlɪ] ADV evidentemente, a quanto pare

apparition [æpə'rɪʃən] N apparizione *f*

appeal [ə'piːl] VI (*Law*) appellarsi alla legge ▶ N (*Law*) appello; (*request*) richiesta; (*charm*) attrattiva; **to ~ for** chiedere (con insistenza); **to ~ to** (*person*) appellarsi a; (*thing*) piacere a; **to ~ to sb for mercy** chiedere pietà a qn; **it doesn't ~ to me** mi dice poco; **right of ~** diritto d'appello

appealing [ə'piːlɪŋ] ADJ (*moving*) commovente; (*attractive*) attraente

appear [ə'pɪəʳ] VI apparire; (*Law*) comparire; (*publication*) essere pubblicato(-a); (*seem*) sembrare; **it would ~ that** sembra che; **to ~ in Hamlet** recitare nell'Amleto; **to ~ on TV** presentarsi in televisione

appearance [ə'pɪərəns] N apparizione *f*; apparenza; (*look, aspect*) aspetto; **to put in** or **make an ~** fare atto di presenza; **by order of ~** (*Theat*) in ordine di apparizione; **to keep up appearances** salvare le apparenze; **to all appearances** a giudicar dalle apparenze

appease [ə'piːz] VT calmare, appagare

appeasement [ə'piːzmənt] N (*Pol*) appeasement *m inv*

append [ə'pend] VT (*Comput*) aggiungere in coda

appendage [ə'pendɪdʒ] N aggiunta

appendicitis [əpendɪ'saɪtɪs] N appendicite *f*

appendix [ə'pendɪks] (*pl* **appendices** [-siːz]) N appendice *f*; **to have one's ~ out** operarsi or farsi operare di appendicite

appetite ['æpɪtaɪt] N appetito; **that walk has given me an ~** la passeggiata mi ha messo appetito

appetizer ['æpɪtaɪzəʳ] N (*food*) stuzzichino; (*drink*) aperitivo

appetizing ['æpɪtaɪzɪŋ] ADJ appetitoso(-a)

applaud [ə'plɔːd] VT, VI applaudire

applause [ə'plɔːz] N applauso

apple ['æpl] N mela; (*also:* **apple tree**) melo; **the ~ of one's eye** la pupilla dei propri occhi

apple pie N torta di mele

apple turnover N sfogliatella alle mele

appliance [ə'plaɪəns] N apparecchio; **electrical appliances** elettrodomestici mpl

applicable [ə'plɪkəbl] ADJ applicabile; **to be ~ to** essere valido per; **the law is ~ from January** la legge entrerà in vigore in gennaio

applicant ['æplɪkənt] N candidato(-a); (Admin: for benefit etc) chi ha fatto domanda or richiesta

application [æplɪ'keɪʃən] N applicazione f; (for a job, a grant etc) domanda; (Comput) applicazione f; **on ~** su richiesta

application form N modulo per la domanda

application program N (Comput) programma applicativo

applications package N (Comput) software m inv applicativo

applied [ə'plaɪd] ADJ applicato(-a); **~ arts** arti fpl applicate

apply [ə'plaɪ] VT: **to ~ (to)** (paint, ointment) dare (a); (theory, technique) applicare (a) ▶ VI: **to ~ to** (ask) rivolgersi a; (be suitable for, relevant to) riguardare, riferirsi a; **to ~ (for)** (permit, grant, job) fare domanda (per); **to ~ the brakes** frenare; **to ~ o.s. to** dedicarsi a

appoint [ə'pɔɪnt] VT nominare

appointee [əpɔɪn'tiː] N incaricato(-a)

appointment [ə'pɔɪntmənt] N nomina; (arrangement to meet) appuntamento; **by ~** su or per appuntamento; **to make an ~ with sb** prendere un appuntamento con qn; **I have an ~ (with)** ... ho un appuntamento (con) ...; **"appointments (vacant)"** (Press) "offerte fpl di impiego"

apportion [ə'pɔːʃən] VT attribuire

appraisal [ə'preɪzl] N valutazione f

appraise [ə'preɪz] VT (value) valutare, fare una stima di; (situation etc) fare il bilancio di

appreciable [ə'priːʃəbl] ADJ apprezzabile

appreciably [ə'priːʃəblɪ] ADV notevolmente, sensibilmente

appreciate [ə'priːʃɪeɪt] VT (like) apprezzare; (be grateful for) essere riconoscente di; (be aware of) rendersi conto di ▶ VI (Comm) aumentare; **I'd ~ your help** ti sono grato per l'aiuto

appreciation [əpriːʃɪ'eɪʃən] N apprezzamento; (Finance) aumento del valore

appreciative [ə'priːʃɪətɪv] ADJ (person) sensibile; (comment) elogiativo(-a)

apprehend [æprɪ'hɛnd] VT (arrest) arrestare; (understand) comprendere

apprehension [æprɪ'hɛnʃən] N (fear) inquietudine f

apprehensive [æprɪ'hɛnsɪv] ADJ apprensivo(-a)

apprentice [ə'prɛntɪs] N apprendista mf ▶ VT: **to be apprenticed to** lavorare come apprendista presso

apprenticeship [ə'prɛntɪʃɪp] N apprendistato; **to serve one's ~** fare il proprio apprendistato or tirocinio

appro. ['æprəu] ABBR (BRIT Comm: col) **= approval**

approach [ə'prəutʃ] VI avvicinarsi ▶ VT (come near) avvicinarsi a; (ask, apply to) rivolgersi a; (subject, passer-by) avvicinare ▶ N approccio; accesso; (to problem) modo di affrontare; **to ~ sb about sth** rivolgersi a qn per qc

approachable [ə'prəutʃəbl] ADJ accessibile

approach road N strada d'accesso

approbation [æprə'beɪʃən] N approvazione f, benestare m

appropriate VT [ə'prəuprɪeɪt] (take) appropriarsi di ▶ ADJ [ə'prəuprɪɪt] appropriato(-a), adatto(-a); **it would not be ~ for me to comment** non sta a me fare dei commenti

appropriately [ə'prəuprɪɪtlɪ] ADV in modo appropriato

appropriation [əprəuprɪ'eɪʃən] N stanziamento

approval [ə'pruːvəl] N approvazione f; **on ~** (Comm) in prova, in esame; **to meet with sb's ~** soddisfare qn, essere di gradimento di qn

approve [ə'pruːv] VT, VI approvare ▶ **approve of** VT FUS approvare

approved school N (BRIT old) riformatorio

approvingly [ə'pruːvɪŋlɪ] ADV in approvazione

approx. ABBR = **approximately**

approximate ADJ [ə'prɔksɪmɪt] approssimativo(-a) ▶ VT [ə'prɔksɪmeɪt] essere un'approssimazione di, avvicinarsi a

approximately [ə'prɔksɪmətlɪ] ADV circa

approximation [əprɔksɪ'meɪʃən] N approssimazione f

apr N ABBR (= annual percentage rate) tasso di percentuale annuo

Apr. ABBR (= April) apr.

apricot ['eɪprɪkɔt] N albicocca

April ['eɪprəl] N aprile m; **~ fool!** pesce d'aprile!; see also **July**

April Fools' Day N vedi nota

> April Fools' Day è il primo aprile, il giorno degli scherzi e delle burle. Il nome deriva dal fatto che, se una persona cade nella trappola che gli è stata tesa, fa la figura del fool, cioè dello sciocco. Di recente gli scherzi stanno diventando sempre più elaborati, e persino i giornalisti a volte inventano vicende incredibili per burlarsi dei lettori.

apron ['eɪprən] N grembiule m; (Aviat) area di stazionamento

apse [æps] N (*Archit*) abside f
APT N ABBR (*BRIT*: = *advanced passenger train*) treno ad altissima velocità
apt [æpt] ADJ (*suitable*) adatto(-a); (*able*) capace; (*likely*): **to be ~ to do** avere tendenza a fare
Apt. ABBR = **apartment**
aptitude ['æptɪtjuːd] N abilità f inv
aptitude test N test m inv attitudinale
aptly ['æptlɪ] ADV appropriatamente, in modo adatto
aqualung ['ækwəlʌŋ] N autorespiratore m
aquarium [ə'kwɛərɪəm] N acquario
Aquarius [ə'kwɛərɪəs] N Acquario; **to be ~** essere dell'Acquario
aquatic [ə'kwætɪk] ADJ acquatico(-a)
aqueduct ['ækwɪdʌkt] N acquedotto
AR ABBR (*US*) = **Arkansas**
ARA N ABBR (*BRIT*) = **Associate of the Royal Academy**
Arab ['ærəb] ADJ, N arabo(-a)
Arabia [ə'reɪbɪə] N Arabia
Arabian [ə'reɪbɪən] ADJ arabo(-a)
Arabian Desert N Deserto arabico
Arabian Sea N mare m Arabico
Arabic ['ærəbɪk] ADJ arabico(-a), arabo(-a) ▶ N arabo
Arabic numerals NPL numeri mpl arabi, numerazione f araba
arable ['ærəbl] ADJ arabile
ARAM N ABBR (*BRIT*) = **Associate of the Royal Academy of Music**
arbiter ['ɑːbɪtər] N arbitro
arbitrary ['ɑːbɪtrərɪ] ADJ arbitrario(-a)
arbitrate ['ɑːbɪtreɪt] VI arbitrare
arbitration [ɑːbɪ'treɪʃən] N (*Law*) arbitrato; (*Industry*) arbitraggio
arbitrator ['ɑːbɪtreɪtər] N arbitro
ARC N ABBR (= *American Red Cross*) C.R.I. f (= *Croce Rossa Italiana*)
arc [ɑːk] N arco
arcade [ɑː'keɪd] N portico; (*passage with shops*) galleria
arch [ɑːtʃ] N arco; (*of foot*) arco plantare ▶ VT inarcare ▶ PREFIX: **~(-)** grande (*before n*); per eccellenza
archaeological [ɑːkɪə'lɔdʒɪkəl] ADJ archeologico(-a)
archaeologist [ɑːkɪ'ɔlədʒɪst] N archeologo(-a)
archaeology [ɑːkɪ'ɔlədʒɪ] N archeologia
archaic [ɑː'keɪɪk] ADJ arcaico(-a)
archangel ['ɑːkeɪndʒəl] N arcangelo
archbishop [ɑːtʃ'bɪʃəp] N arcivescovo
arched [ɑːtʃt] ADJ arcuato(-a), ad arco
arch-enemy ['ɑːtʃ'ɛnɪmɪ] N arcinemico(-a)
archeology etc [ɑːkɪ'ɔlədʒɪ] = **archaeology** etc
archer ['ɑːtʃər] N arciere m
archery ['ɑːtʃərɪ] N tiro all'arco

archetypal ['ɑːkɪtaɪpəl] ADJ tipico(-a)
archetype ['ɑːkɪtaɪp] N archetipo
archipelago [ɑːkɪ'pɛlɪgəu] N arcipelago
architect ['ɑːkɪtɛkt] N architetto
architectural [ɑːkɪ'tɛktʃərəl] ADJ architettonico(-a)
architecture ['ɑːkɪtɛktʃər] N architettura
archive ['ɑːkaɪv] N (*also Comput*) archivio; **archives** NPL archivi mpl
archive file N (*Comput*) file m inv di archivio
archivist ['ɑːkɪvɪst] N archivista mf
archway ['ɑːtʃweɪ] N arco
ARCM N ABBR (*BRIT*) = **Associate of the Royal College of Music**
Arctic ['ɑːktɪk] ADJ artico(-a) ▶ N: **the ~** l'Artico
Arctic Circle N Circolo polare artico
Arctic Ocean N Oceano artico
ARD N ABBR (*US Med*) = **acute respiratory disease**
ardent ['ɑːdənt] ADJ ardente
ardour, (*US*) **ardor** ['ɑːdər] N ardore m
arduous ['ɑːdjuəs] ADJ arduo(-a)
are [ɑːr] VB see **be**
area ['ɛərɪə] N (*Geom*) area; (*zone*) zona; (: *smaller*) settore m; **dining ~** zona pranzo; **the London ~** la zona di Londra
area code N (*US Tel*) prefisso
arena [ə'riːnə] N arena
aren't [ɑːnt] = **are not**
Argentina [ɑːdʒən'tiːnə] N Argentina
Argentinian [ɑːdʒən'tɪnɪən] ADJ, N argentino(-a)
arguable ['ɑːgjuəbl] ADJ discutibile; **it is ~ whether** ... è una cosa discutibile se ...+ sub
arguably ['ɑːgjuəblɪ] ADV: **it is ~** ... si può sostenere che sia ...
argue ['ɑːgjuː] VI (*quarrel*) litigare; (*reason*) ragionare ▶ VT (*debate: case, matter*) dibattere; **to ~ that** sostenere che; **to ~ about sth (with sb)** litigare per or a proposito di qc (con qn)
argument ['ɑːgjumənt] N (*reasons*) argomento; (*quarrel*) lite f; (*debate*) discussione f; **~ for/against** argomento a or in favore di/contro
argumentative [ɑːgju'mɛntətɪv] ADJ litigioso(-a)
aria ['ɑːrɪə] N aria
ARIBA N ABBR (*BRIT*) = **Associate of the Royal Institute of British Architects**
arid ['ærɪd] ADJ arido(-a)
aridity [ə'rɪdɪtɪ] N aridità
Aries ['ɛərɪz] N Ariete m; **to be ~** essere dell'Ariete
arise [ə'raɪz] (*pt* **arose** [ə'rəuz], *pp* **arisen** [ə'rɪzn]) VI alzarsi; (*opportunity, problem*) presentarsi; **to ~ from** risultare da; **should the need ~** dovesse presentarsi la necessità, in caso di necessità

aristocracy [ærɪsˈtɔkrəsɪ] N aristocrazia
aristocrat [ˈærɪstəkræt] N aristocratico(-a)
aristocratic [ærɪstəˈkrætɪk] ADJ
aristocratico(-a)
arithmetic [əˈrɪθmətɪk] N aritmetica
arithmetical [ærɪθˈmɛtɪkəl] ADJ
aritmetico(-a)
Ariz. ABBR (US) = **Arizona**
ark [ɑːk] N: **Noah's A~** l'arca di Noè
Ark. ABBR (US) = **Arkansas**
arm [ɑːm] N braccio; (Mil: branch) arma ▶ VT
armare; **~ in ~** a braccetto; see also **arms**
armaments [ˈɑːməmənts] NPL (weapons)
armamenti mpl
armband [ˈɑːmbænd] N bracciale m
armchair [ˈɑːmtʃɛəʳ] N poltrona
armed [ɑːmd] ADJ armato(-a)
armed forces NPL forze fpl armate
armed robbery N rapina a mano armata
Armenia [ɑːˈmiːnɪə] N Armenia
Armenian [ɑːˈmiːnɪən] ADJ armeno(-a) ▶ N
armeno(-a); (Ling) armeno
armful [ˈɑːmful] N bracciata
armistice [ˈɑːmɪstɪs] N armistizio
armour, (US) armor [ˈɑːməʳ] N armatura;
(also: **armour-plating**) corazza, blindatura;
(Mil: tanks) mezzi mpl blindati
armoured car, (US) armored car N
autoblinda f inv
armoury, (US) armory [ˈɑːmərɪ] N
arsenale m
armpit [ˈɑːmpɪt] N ascella
armrest [ˈɑːmrɛst] N bracciolo
arms [ɑːmz] NPL (weapons) armi fpl; (Heraldry)
stemma m
arms control N controllo degli armamenti
arms race N corsa agli armamenti
army [ˈɑːmɪ] N esercito
aroma [əˈrəumə] N aroma
aromatherapy [ərəuməˈθɛrəpɪ] N
aromaterapia
aromatic [ærəˈmætɪk] ADJ aromatico(-a)
arose [əˈrəuz] PT of **arise**
around [əˈraund] ADV attorno, intorno ▶ PREP
intorno a; (fig: about): **~ £5/3 o'clock** circa 5
sterline/le 3; **is he ~?** è in giro?
arousal [əˈrauzəl] N (sexual etc) eccitazione f;
(awakening) risveglio
arouse [əˈrauz] VT (sleeper) svegliare; (curiosity,
passions) suscitare
arrange [əˈreɪndʒ] VT sistemare; (programme)
preparare ▶ VI: **we have arranged for a taxi
to pick you up** la faremo venire a prendere
da un taxi; **it was arranged that ...** è stato
deciso or stabilito che ...; **to ~ to do sth**
mettersi d'accordo per fare qc
arrangement [əˈreɪndʒmənt] N
sistemazione f; (agreement) accordo;
arrangements NPL (plans etc) progetti mpl,

piani mpl; **by ~** su richiesta; **to come to an ~
(with sb)** venire ad un accordo (con qn),
mettersi d'accordo or accordarsi (con qn); **I'll
make arrangements for you to be met**
darò disposizioni or istruzioni perché ci sia
qualcuno ad incontrarla
arrant [ˈærənt] ADJ: **~ nonsense** colossali
sciocchezze fpl
array [əˈreɪ] N fila; (Comput) array m inv,
insiemi mpl; (of) fila di
arrears [əˈrɪəz] NPL arretrati mpl; **to be in ~
with one's rent** essere in arretrato con
l'affitto
arrest [əˈrɛst] VT arrestare; (sb's attention)
attirare ▶ N arresto; **under ~** in arresto
arresting [əˈrɛstɪŋ] ADJ (fig) che colpisce
arrival [əˈraɪvəl] N arrivo; (person)
arrivato(-a); **a new ~** un nuovo venuto; (baby)
un neonato
arrive [əˈraɪv] VI arrivare
▶ **arrive at** VT FUS arrivare a
arrogance [ˈærəgəns] N arroganza
arrogant [ˈærəgənt] ADJ arrogante
arrow [ˈærəu] N freccia
arse [ɑːs] N (BRIT col!) culo (!)
arsenal [ˈɑːsɪnl] N arsenale m
arsenic [ˈɑːsnɪk] N arsenico
arson [ˈɑːsn] N incendio doloso
art [ɑːt] N arte f; (craft) mestiere m; **work of ~**
opera d'arte; see also **arts**
art college N scuola di belle arti
artefact, (US) artifact [ˈɑːtɪfækt] N
manufatto
arterial [ɑːˈtɪərɪəl] ADJ (Anat) arterioso(-a);
(road etc) di grande comunicazione; **~ roads**
le (grandi or principali) arterie
artery [ˈɑːtərɪ] N arteria
artful [ˈɑːtful] ADJ furbo(-a)
art gallery N galleria d'arte
arthritis [ɑːˈθraɪtɪs] N artrite f
artichoke [ˈɑːtɪtʃəuk] N carciofo; **Jerusalem
~** topinambur m inv
article [ˈɑːtɪkl] N articolo; **articles** NPL (BRIT
Law: training) contratto di tirocinio; **articles
of clothing** indumenti mpl
articles of association NPL (Comm) statuto
sociale
articulate ADJ [ɑːˈtɪkjulɪt] (person) che si
esprime forbitamente; (speech) articolato(-a)
▶ VI [ɑːˈtɪkjuleɪt] articolare
articulated lorry (BRIT) N autotreno
artifact [ˈɑːtɪfækt] N (US) = **artefact**
artifice [ˈɑːtɪfɪs] N (cunning) abilità, destrezza;
(trick) artificio
artificial [ɑːtɪˈfɪʃəl] ADJ artificiale
artificial insemination [-ɪnsɛmɪˈneɪʃən] N
fecondazione f artificiale
artificial intelligence N intelligenza
artificiale

artificial respiration N respirazione f artificiale

artillery [ɑːˈtɪlərɪ] N artiglieria

artisan [ˈɑːtɪzæn] N artigiano(-a)

artist [ˈɑːtɪst] N artista mf

artistic [ɑːˈtɪstɪk] ADJ artistico(-a)

artistry [ˈɑːtɪstrɪ] N arte f

artless [ˈɑːtlɪs] ADJ semplice, ingenuo(-a)

arts [ɑːts] NPL (Scol) lettere fpl

art school N scuola d'arte

artwork [ˈɑːtwɜːk] N materiale m illustrativo

ARV N ABBR (= American Revised Version) traduzione della Bibbia

AS N ABBR (US Scol: = Associate in Science) titolo di studio

(KEYWORD)

as [æz] CONJ **1** (referring to time) mentre; **as the years went by** col passare degli anni; **he came in as I was leaving** arrivò mentre stavo uscendo; **as from tomorrow** da domani

2 (in comparisons): **as big as** grande come; **twice as big as** due volte più grande di; **as much/many as** tanto quanto/tanti quanti; **as soon as possible** prima possibile

3 (since, because) dal momento che, siccome

4 (referring to manner, way) come; **big as it is** grande com'è; **much as I like them, ...** per quanto mi siano simpatici, ...; **do as you wish** fa' come vuoi; **as she said** come ha detto lei

5 (concerning): **as for** or **to that** per quanto riguarda or quanto a quello

6: **as if** or **though** come se; **he looked as if he was ill** sembrava stare male; see also **long**; **such**; **well**

▶ PREP: **he works as a driver** fa l'autista; **as chairman of the company, he ...** come presidente della compagnia, lui ...; **he gave me it as a present** me lo ha regalato

ASA N ABBR (= American Standards Association) associazione per la normalizzazione; (BRIT: = Advertising Standards Association) ≈ Istituto di Autodisciplina Pubblicitaria

a.s.a.p. ABBR (= as soon as possible) prima possibile

asbestos [æzˈbɛstəs] N asbesto, amianto

ASBO [ˈæzbəʊ] N ABBR (BRIT: = antisocial behaviour order) provvedimento restrittivo per comportamento antisociale

ascend [əˈsɛnd] VT salire

ascendancy [əˈsɛndənsɪ] N ascendente m

ascendant [əˈsɛndənt] N: **to be in the ~** essere in auge

ascension [əˈsɛnʃən] N: **the A~** (Rel) l'Ascensione f

Ascension Island N isola dell'Ascensione

ascent [əˈsɛnt] N salita

ascertain [æsəˈteɪn] VT accertare

ascetic [əˈsɛtɪk] ADJ ascetico(-a)

asceticism [əˈsɛtɪsɪzəm] N ascetismo

ASCII [ˈæskiː] N ABBR (= American Standard Code for Information Interchange) ASCII m

ascribe [əˈskraɪb] VT: **to ~ sth to** attribuire qc a

ASCU N ABBR (US) = **Association of State Colleges and Universities**

ASE N ABBR = **American Stock Exchange**

ASH [æʃ] N ABBR (BRIT: = Action on Smoking and Health) iniziativa contro il fumo

ash [æʃ] N (dust) cenere f; **~ (tree)** frassino

ashamed [əˈʃeɪmd] ADJ vergognoso(-a); **to be ~ of** vergognarsi di; **to be ~ (of o.s.) for having done** vergognarsi di aver fatto

ashen [ˈæʃən] ADJ (pale) livido(-a)

ashore [əˈʃɔːʳ] ADV a terra; **to go ~** sbarcare

ashtray [ˈæʃtreɪ] N portacenere m

Ash Wednesday N Mercoledì m inv delle Ceneri

Asia [ˈeɪʃə] N Asia

Asia Minor N Asia minore

Asian [ˈeɪʃən] ADJ, N asiatico(-a)

Asiatic [eɪsɪˈætɪk] ADJ asiatico(-a)

aside [əˈsaɪd] ADV da parte ▶ N a parte m; **to take sb ~** prendere qn da parte; **~ from** (as well as) oltre a; (except for) a parte

ask [ɑːsk] VT (request) chiedere; (question) domandare; (invite) invitare; **to ~ about sth** informarsi su or di qc; **to ~ sb sth/sb to do sth** chiedere qc a qn/a qn di fare qc; **to ~ sb about sth** chiedere a qn di qc; **to ~ (sb) a question** fare una domanda (a qn); **to ~ sb the time** chiedere l'ora a qn; **to ~ sb out to dinner** invitare qn a mangiare fuori; **you should ~ at the information desk** dovreste rivolgersi all'ufficio informazioni

▶ **ask after** VT FUS chiedere di

▶ **ask for** VT FUS chiedere; **it's just asking for trouble** or **for it** è proprio (come) andarsele a cercare

askance [əˈskɑːns] ADV: **to look ~ at sb** guardare qn di traverso

askew [əˈskjuː] ADV di traverso, storto

asking price [ˈɑːskɪŋ-] N prezzo di partenza

asleep [əˈsliːp] ADJ addormentato(-a); **to be ~** dormire; **to fall ~** addormentarsi

ASLEF [ˈæzlɛf] N ABBR (BRIT: = Associated Society of Locomotive Engineers and Firemen) sindacato dei conducenti dei treni e dei macchinisti

AS level N ABBR (= Advanced Subsidiary level) prima parte del diploma di studi superiori chiamato "A level"

asp [æsp] N cobra m inv egiziano

asparagus [əsˈpærəgəs] N asparagi mpl

asparagus tips NPL punte fpl d'asparagi

431

ASPCA N ABBR (= *American Society for the Prevention of Cruelty to Animals*) ≈ E.N.P.A. *m* (= *Ente Nazionale per la Protezione degli Animali*)

aspect ['æspɛkt] N aspetto

aspersions [əs'pə:ʃənz] NPL: **to cast ~ on** diffamare

asphalt ['æsfælt] N asfalto

asphyxiate [æs'fɪksɪeɪt] VT asfissiare

asphyxiation [æsfɪksɪ'eɪʃən] N asfissia

aspiration [æspə'reɪʃən] N aspirazione *f*; **aspirations** NPL aspirazioni *fpl*

aspire [əs'paɪər] VI: **to ~ to** aspirare a

aspirin ['æsprɪn] N aspirina

aspiring [əs'paɪərɪŋ] ADJ aspirante

ass [æs] N asino; (*col*) scemo(-a); (*US col!*) culo (!)

assail [ə'seɪl] VT assalire

assailant [ə'seɪlənt] N assalitore *m*

assassin [ə'sæsɪn] N assassino

assassinate [ə'sæsɪneɪt] VT assassinare

assassination [əsæsɪ'neɪʃən] N assassinio

assault [ə'sɔ:lt] N (*Mil*) assalto; (*gen: attack*) aggressione *f*; (*Law*): **~ (and battery)** minacce e vie di fatto *fpl* ▶ VT assaltare; aggredire; (*sexually*) violentare

assemble [ə'sɛmbl] VT riunire; (*Tech*) montare ▶ VI riunirsi

assembly [ə'sɛmblɪ] N (*meeting*) assemblea; (*construction*) montaggio

assembly language N (*Comput*) linguaggio assemblativo

assembly line N catena di montaggio

assent [ə'sɛnt] N assenso, consenso ▶ VI assentire; **to ~ (to sth)** approvare (qc)

assert [ə'sə:t] VT asserire; (*insist on*) far valere; **to ~ o.s.** farsi valere

assertion [ə'sə:ʃən] N asserzione *f*

assertive [ə'sə:tɪv] ADJ che sa imporsi

assess [ə'sɛs] VT valutare

assessment [ə'sɛsmənt] N valutazione *f*; (*judgment*): **~ (of)** giudizio (su)

assessor [ə'sɛsər] N perito; funzionario del fisco

asset ['æsɛt] N vantaggio; (*person*) elemento prezioso; **assets** NPL (*Comm: of individual*) beni *mpl*; disponibilità *fpl* (*of company*) attivo

asset-stripping ['æset'strɪpɪŋ] N (*Comm*) acquisto di una società in fallimento con lo scopo di rivenderne le attività

assiduous [ə'sɪdjuəs] ADJ assiduo(-a)

assign [ə'saɪn] VT: **to ~ (to)** (*task*) assegnare (a); (*resources*) riservare (a); (*cause, meaning*) attribuire (a); **to ~ a date to sth** fissare la data di qc

assignment [ə'saɪnmənt] N compito

assimilate [ə'sɪmɪleɪt] VT assimilare

assimilation [əsɪmɪ'leɪʃən] N assimilazione *f*

assist [ə'sɪst] VT assistere, aiutare

assistance [ə'sɪstəns] N assistenza, aiuto

assistant [ə'sɪstənt] N assistente *mf*; (BRIT: *also*: **shop assistant**) commesso(-a)

assistant manager N vicedirettore *m*

assizes [ə'saɪzɪz] NPL assise *fpl*

associate ADJ [ə'səuʃɪɪt] associato(-a); (*member*) aggiunto(-a) ▶ N [ə'səuʃɪɪt] collega *mf*; (*in business*) socio(-a) ▶ VT [ə'səuʃɪeɪt] associare ▶ VI [ə'səuʃɪeɪt]: **to ~ with sb** frequentare qn

associated company [ə'səusɪ'eɪtɪd-] N società collegata

associate director N amministratore *m* aggiunto

association [əsəusɪ'eɪʃən] N associazione *f*; **in ~ with** in collaborazione con

association football N (BRIT) (gioco del) calcio

assorted [ə'sɔ:tɪd] ADJ assortito(-a); **in ~ sizes** in diverse taglie

assortment [ə'sɔ:tmənt] N assortimento

Asst. ABBR = **assistant**

assuage [ə'sweɪdʒ] VT alleviare

assume [ə'sju:m] VT supporre; (*responsibilities etc*) assumere; (*attitude, name*) prendere

assumed name N nome *m* falso

assumption [ə'sʌmpʃən] N supposizione *f*, ipotesi *f inv*; (*of power*) assunzione *f*; **on the ~ that ...** partendo dal presupposto che ...

assurance [ə'ʃuərəns] N assicurazione *f*; (*self-confidence*) fiducia in se stesso; **I can give you no assurances** non posso assicurarle *or* garantirle niente

assure [ə'ʃuər] VT assicurare

assured [ə'ʃuəd] ADJ (*confident*) sicuro(-a); (*certain: promotion etc*) assicurato(-a)

AST ABBR (US: = *Atlantic Standard Time*) ora invernale di New York

asterisk ['æstərɪsk] N asterisco

astern [ə'stə:n] ADV a poppa

asteroid ['æstərɔɪd] N asteroide *m*

asthma ['æsmə] N asma

asthmatic [æs'mætɪk] ADJ, N asmatico(-a)

astigmatism [ə'stɪgmətɪzəm] N astigmatismo

astir [ə'stə:r] ADV in piedi; (*excited*) in fermento

astonish [ə'stɔnɪʃ] VT stupire

astonished [ə'stɔnɪʃt] ADJ stupito(-a), sorpreso(-a); **to be ~ (at)** essere stupito(-a) (da)

astonishing [ə'stɔnɪʃɪŋ] ADJ sorprendente, stupefacente; **I find it ~ that ...** mi stupisce che ...

astonishingly [ə'stɔnɪʃɪŋlɪ] ADV straordinariamente, incredibilmente

astonishment [ə'stɔnɪʃmənt] N stupore *m*; **to my ~** con mia gran meraviglia, con mio grande stupore

astound [ə'staund] VT sbalordire

astray [ə'streɪ] ADV: **to go ~** smarrirsi; (*fig*)

traviarsi; **to lead ~** portare sulla cattiva strada; **to go ~ in one's calculations** sbagliare i calcoli

astride [ə'straɪd] ADV a cavalcioni ▶ PREP a cavalcioni di

astringent [əs'trɪndʒənt] ADJ, N astringente m

astrologer [əs'trɒlədʒə^r] N astrologo(-a)

astrology [əs'trɒlədʒɪ] N astrologia

astronaut ['æstrənɔːt] N astronauta mf

astronomer [əs'trɒnəmə^r] N astronomo(-a)

astronomical [æstrə'nɒmɪkl] ADJ astronomico(-a)

astronomy [əs'trɒnəmɪ] N astronomia

astrophysics ['æstrəʊ'fɪzɪks] N astrofisica

astute [əs'tjuːt] ADJ astuto(-a)

asunder [ə'sʌndə^r] ADV: **to tear ~** strappare

ASV N ABBR (= *American Standard Version*) *traduzione della Bibbia*

asylum [ə'saɪləm] N asilo; (*lunatic asylum*) manicomio; **to seek political ~** chiedere asilo politico

asymmetric [eɪsɪ'mɛtrɪk], **asymmetrical** [eɪsɪ'mɛtrɪkəl] ADJ asimmetrico(-a)

(KEYWORD)

at [æt] PREP **1** (*referring to position, direction*) a; **at the top** in cima; **at the desk** al banco, alla scrivania; **at home/school** a casa/scuola; **at Paolo's** da Paolo; **at the baker's** dal panettiere; **to look at sth** guardare qc; **to throw sth at sb** lanciare qc a qn

2 (*referring to time*) a; **at 4 o'clock** alle 4; **at night** di notte; **at Christmas** a Natale; **at times** a volte

3 (*referring to rates, speed etc*) a; **at £1 a kilo** a 1 sterlina al chilo; **two at a time** due alla volta, due per volta; **at 50 km/h** a 50 km/h; **at full speed** a tutta velocità

4 (*referring to manner*): **at a stroke** d'un solo colpo; **at peace** in pace

5 (*referring to activity*): **to be at work** essere al lavoro; **to play at cowboys** giocare ai cowboy; **to be good at sth/doing sth** essere bravo in qc/a fare qc

6 (*referring to cause*): **shocked/surprised/annoyed at sth** colpito da/sorpreso da/arrabbiato per qc; **I went at his suggestion** ci sono andato dietro suo consiglio

▶ N (*Comput: @ symbol*) chiocciola

ate [eɪt] PT *of* **eat**

atheism ['eɪθɪɪzəm] N ateismo

atheist ['eɪθɪɪst] N ateo(-a)

Athenian [ə'θiːnɪən] ADJ, N ateniese mf

Athens ['æθɪnz] N Atene f

athlete ['æθliːt] N atleta mf

athletic [æθ'lɛtɪk] ADJ atletico(-a)

athletics [æθ'lɛtɪks] N atletica

Atlantic [ət'læntɪk] ADJ atlantico(-a)
▶ N: **the ~ (Ocean)** l'Atlantico, l'Oceano Atlantico

atlas ['ætləs] N atlante m

Atlas Mountains NPL: **the ~** i Monti dell'Atlante

ATM ABBR (= *automated telling machine*) (sportello) Bancomat® m inv

atmosphere ['ætməsfɪə^r] N atmosfera; (*air*) aria

atmospheric [ætməs'fɛrɪk] ADJ atmosferico(-a)

atmospherics [ætməs'fɛrɪks] NPL (*Radio*) scariche fpl

atoll ['ætɒl] N atollo

atom ['ætəm] N atomo

atom bomb, atomic bomb N bomba atomica

atomic [ə'tɒmɪk] ADJ atomico(-a)

atomizer ['ætəmaɪzə^r] N atomizzatore m

atone [ə'təʊn] VI: **to ~ for** espiare

atonement [ə'təʊnmənt] N espiazione f

ATP N ABBR = **Association of Tennis Professionals**

atrocious [ə'trəʊʃəs] ADJ atroce, pessimo(-a)

atrocity [ə'trɒsɪtɪ] N atrocità f inv

atrophy ['ætrəfɪ] N atrofia ▶ VI atrofizzarsi

attach [ə'tætʃ] VT attaccare; (*document, letter*) allegare; (*importance etc*) attribuire; (*Mil: troops*) assegnare; **to be attached to sb/sth** (*to like*) essere affezionato(-a) a qn/qc; **the attached letter** la lettera acclusa *or* allegata

attaché [ə'tæʃeɪ] N addetto

attaché case N valigetta per documenti

attachment [ə'tætʃmənt] N (*tool*) accessorio; (*Comput*) allegato; (*love*): **~ (to)** affetto (per)

attack [ə'tæk] VT attaccare; (*person*) aggredire; (*task etc*) iniziare; (*problem*) affrontare ▶ N attacco; (*also*: **heart attack**) infarto

attacker [ə'tækə^r] N aggressore m, assalitore(-trice)

attain [ə'teɪn] VT (*also*: **attain to**) arrivare a, raggiungere

attainments [ə'teɪnmənts] NPL cognizioni fpl

attempt [ə'tɛmpt] N tentativo ▶ VT tentare; **attempted murder** (*Law*) tentato omicidio; **to make an ~ on sb's life** attentare alla vita di qn; **he made no ~ to help** non ha (neanche) tentato *or* cercato di aiutare

attend [ə'tɛnd] VT frequentare; (*meeting, talk*) andare a; (*patient*) assistere
▶ **attend to** VT FUS (*needs, affairs etc*) prendersi cura di; (*customer*) occuparsi di

attendance [ə'tɛndəns] N (*being present*) presenza; (*people present*) gente f presente

attendant [ə'tɛndənt] N custode mf; persona di servizio ▶ ADJ concomitante

attention [ə'tɛnʃən] N attenzione f;
attentions premure fpl, attenzioni fpl; **~!**
(Mil) attenti!; **at ~** (Mil) sull'attenti; **for the
~ of** (Admin) per l'attenzione di; **it has come
to my ~ that** ... sono venuto a conoscenza
(del fatto) che ...

attentive [ə'tɛntɪv] ADJ attento(-a); (kind)
premuroso(-a)

attentively [ə'tɛntɪvlɪ] ADV attentamente

attenuate [ə'tɛnjueɪt] VT attenuare ▶ VI
attenuarsi

attest [ə'tɛst] VI: **to ~ to** attestare

attic ['ætɪk] N soffitta

attire [ə'taɪəʳ] N abbigliamento

attitude ['ætɪtjuːd] N (behaviour)
atteggiamento; (posture) posa; (view): **~ (to)**
punto di vista (nei confronti di)

attorney [ə'təːnɪ] N (US: lawyer) avvocato;
(having proxy) mandatario; **power of ~**
procura

Attorney General N (BRIT) Procuratore m
Generale; (US) Ministro della Giustizia

attract [ə'trækt] VT attirare

attraction [ə'trækʃən] N (gen pl: pleasant
things) attrattiva; (Physics, fig: towards sth)
attrazione f

attractive [ə'træktɪv] ADJ attraente; (idea,
offer, price) allettante, interessante

attribute N ['ætrɪbjuːt] attributo ▶ VT
[ə'trɪbjuːt]: **to ~ sth to** attribuire qc a

attrition [ə'trɪʃən] N: **war of ~** guerra di
logoramento

Atty. Gen. ABBR = **Attorney General**

atypical [eɪ'tɪpɪkl] ADJ atipico(-a)

AU N ABBR (= African Union) Unione Africana

aubergine ['əubəʒiːn] N melanzana

auburn ['ɔːbən] ADJ tizianesco(-a)

auction ['ɔːkʃən] N (also: **sale by auction**) asta
▶ VT (also: **sell by auction**) vendere all'asta;
(also: **put up for auction**) mettere all'asta

auctioneer [ɔːkʃə'nɪəʳ] N banditore m

auction room N sala dell'asta

audacious [ɔː'deɪʃəs] ADJ (bold) audace;
(impudent) sfrontato(-a)

audacity [ɔː'dæsɪtɪ] N audacia

audible ['ɔːdɪbl] ADJ udibile

audience ['ɔːdɪəns] N (people) pubblico;
spettatori mpl; ascoltatori mpl; (interview)
udienza

audio-typist ['ɔːdɪəu'taɪpɪst] N
dattilografo(-a) che trascrive da nastro

audiovisual [ɔːdɪəu'vɪzjuəl] ADJ
audiovisivo(-a); **~ aids** sussidi mpl
audiovisivi

audit ['ɔːdɪt] N revisione f, verifica ▶ VT
rivedere, verificare

audition [ɔː'dɪʃən] N (Theat) audizione f;
(Cine) provino ▶ VI fare un'audizione (or un
provino)

auditor ['ɔːdɪtəʳ] N revisore m

auditorium [ɔːdɪ'tɔːrɪəm] N sala, auditorio

Aug. ABBR (= August) ago., ag.

augment [ɔːg'mɛnt] VT, VI aumentare

augur ['ɔːgəʳ] VT (be a sign of) predire ▶ VI: **it
augurs well** promette bene

August ['ɔːgəst] N agosto; see also **July**

august [ɔː'gʌst] ADJ augusto(-a)

aunt [ɑːnt] N zia

auntie, aunty ['ɑːntɪ] N zietta

au pair ['əu'pɛəʳ] N (also: **au pair girl**) (ragazza
f) alla pari inv

aura ['ɔːrə] N aura

auspices ['ɔːspɪsɪz] NPL: **under the ~ of** sotto
gli auspici di

auspicious [ɔːs'pɪʃəs] ADJ propizio(-a)

austere [ɔs'tɪəʳ] ADJ austero(-a)

austerity [ɔs'tɛrɪtɪ] N austerità f inv

Australasia [ɔstrə'leɪzɪə] N Australasia

Australia [ɔs'treɪlɪə] N Australia

Australian [ɔs'treɪlɪən] ADJ, N australiano(-a)

Austria ['ɔstrɪə] N Austria

Austrian ['ɔstrɪən] ADJ, N austriaco(-a)

AUT N ABBR (BRIT: = Association of University
Teachers) associazione dei docenti universitari

authentic [ɔː'θɛntɪk] ADJ autentico(-a)

authenticate [ɔː'θɛntɪkeɪt] VT autenticare

authenticity [ɔːθɛn'tɪsɪtɪ] N autenticità

author ['ɔːθəʳ] N autore(-trice)

authoritarian [ɔːθɔrɪ'tɛərɪən] ADJ
autoritario(-a)

authoritative [ɔː'θɔrɪtətɪv] ADJ (account etc)
autorevole; (manner) autoritario(-a)

authority [ɔː'θɔrɪtɪ] N autorità f inv;
(permission) autorizzazione f; **the authorities**
NPL (government etc) le autorità; **to have ~ to
do sth** avere l'autorizzazione a fare or il
diritto di fare qc

authorization [ɔːθəraɪ'zeɪʃən] N
autorizzazione f

authorize ['ɔːθəraɪz] VT autorizzare

authorized capital N capitale m nominale

authorship ['ɔːθəʃɪp] N paternità (letteraria
ecc)

autistic [ɔː'tɪstɪk] ADJ autistico(-a)

auto ['ɔːtəu] N (US) auto f inv

autobiography [ɔːtəbaɪ'ɔgrəfɪ] N
autobiografia

autocratic [ɔːtə'krætɪk] ADJ autocratico(-a)

Autocue® ['ɔːtəukjuː] N (BRIT) gobbo (TV)

autograph ['ɔːtəgrɑːf] N autografo ▶ VT
firmare

autoimmune [ɔːtəu'mjuːn] ADJ
autoimmune

automat ['ɔːtəmæt] N (US) tavola calda fornita
esclusivamente di distributori automatici

automated ['ɔːtəmeɪtɪd] ADJ
automatizzato(-a)

automatic [ɔːtə'mætɪk] ADJ automatico(-a)

▶ N (*gun*) arma automatica; (*car*) automobile f con cambio automatico; (*washing machine*) lavatrice f automatica

automatically [ɔːtə'mætɪklɪ] ADV automaticamente

automatic data processing N elaborazione f automatica dei dati

automation [ɔːtə'meɪʃən] N automazione f

automaton [ɔː'tɔmətən] (*pl* **automata** [-tə]) N automa m

automobile ['ɔːtəməbiːl] N (*US*) automobile f

autonomous [ɔː'tɔnəməs] ADJ autonomo(-a)

autonomy [ɔː'tɔnəmɪ] N autonomia

autopsy ['ɔːtɔpsɪ] N autopsia

autumn ['ɔːtəm] N autunno

auxiliary [ɔːg'zɪlɪərɪ] ADJ ausiliario(-a) ▶ N ausiliare mf

AV N ABBR (= *Authorized Version*) traduzione inglese della Bibbia ▶ ABBR = **audiovisual**

Av. ABBR = **avenue**

avail [ə'veɪl] VT: **to ~ o.s. of** servirsi di; approfittarsi di ▶ N: **to no ~** inutilmente

availability [əveɪlə'bɪlɪtɪ] N disponibilità

available [ə'veɪləbl] ADJ disponibile; **every ~ means** tutti i mezzi disponibili; **to make sth ~ to sb** mettere qc a disposizione di qn; **is the manager ~?** è libero il direttore?

avalanche ['ævəlɑːnʃ] N valanga

avant-garde ['ævɑ̃ː'gɑːd] ADJ d'avanguardia

avarice ['ævərɪs] N avarizia

avaricious [ævə'rɪʃəs] ADJ avaro(-a)

avdp. ABBR (= *avoirdupois*) sistema ponderale anglosassone basato su libbra, oncia e multipli

Ave. ABBR = **avenue**

avenge [ə'vendʒ] VT vendicare

avenue ['ævənjuː] N viale m; (*fig*) strada, via

average ['ævərɪdʒ] N media ▶ ADJ medio(-a) ▶ VT (*also*: **average out at**) aggirarsi in media su, essere in media di; **on ~** in media; **above/below (the) ~** sopra/sotto la media

averse [ə'vəːs] ADJ: **to be ~ to sth/doing** essere contrario(-a) a qc/a fare; **I wouldn't be ~ to a drink** non avrei nulla in contrario a bere qualcosa

aversion [ə'vəːʃən] N avversione f

avert [ə'vəːt] VT evitare, prevenire; (*one's eyes*) distogliere

avian flu ['eɪvɪən-] N influenza aviaria

aviary ['eɪvɪərɪ] N voliera, uccelliera

aviation [eɪvɪ'eɪʃən] N aviazione f

avid ['ævɪd] ADJ avido(-a); (*supporter etc*) accanito(-a)

avidly ['ævɪdlɪ] ADV avidamente

avocado [ævə'kɑːdəu] N (*BRIT*: *also*: **avocado pear**) avocado m inv

avoid [ə'vɔɪd] VT evitare

avoidable [ə'vɔɪdəbl] ADJ evitabile

avoidance [ə'vɔɪdəns] N l'evitare m

avowed [ə'vaud] ADJ dichiarato(-a)

AVP N ABBR (*US*) = **assistant vice-president**

AWACS ['eɪwæks] N ABBR (= *airborne warning and control system*) sistema di allarme e controllo in volo

await [ə'weɪt] VT aspettare; **awaiting attention** (*Comm*: *letter*) in attesa di risposta; (: *order*) in attesa di essere evaso; **long awaited** tanto atteso(-a)

awake [ə'weɪk] (*pt* **awoke**, *pp* **awoken** or **awaked**) VT svegliare ▶ VI svegliarsi ▶ ADJ sveglio(-a); **~ to** consapevole di

awakening [ə'weɪknɪŋ] N risveglio

award [ə'wɔːd] N premio; (*Law*) decreto; (*sum*) risarcimento ▶ VT assegnare; (*Law*: *damages*) decretare

aware [ə'weə^r] ADJ: **~ of** (*conscious*) conscio(-a) di; (*informed*) informato(-a) di; **to become ~ of** accorgersi di; **politically/socially ~** politicamente/socialmente preparato(-a); **I am fully ~ that …** mi rendo perfettamente conto che …

awareness [ə'weənɪs] N consapevolezza; coscienza; **to develop people's ~ (of)** sensibilizzare la gente (a)

awash [ə'wɔʃ] ADJ: **~ (with)** inondato(-a) (da)

away [ə'weɪ] ADV, ADJ via; lontano(-a); **two kilometres ~** a due chilometri di distanza; **two hours ~ by car** a due ore di distanza in macchina; **the holiday was two weeks ~** mancavano due settimane alle vacanze; **~ from** lontano da; **he's ~ for a week** è andato via per una settimana; **he's ~ in Milan** è (andato) a Milano; **to take ~** vt portare via; **he was working/pedalling ~** lavorava/pedalava più che poteva; **to fade ~** scomparire

away game N (*Sport*) partita fuori casa

awe [ɔː] N timore m

awe-inspiring ['ɔːɪnspaɪərɪŋ], **awesome** ['ɔːsəm] ADJ imponente

awestruck ['ɔːstrʌk] ADJ sgomento(-a)

awful ['ɔːfəl] ADJ terribile; **an ~ lot of** (*people, cars, dogs*) un numero incredibile di; (*jam, flowers*) una quantità incredibile di

awfully ['ɔːflɪ] ADV (*very*) terribilmente

awhile [ə'waɪl] ADV (per) un po'

awkward ['ɔːkwəd] ADJ (*clumsy*) goffo(-a); (*inconvenient*) scomodo(-a); (*embarrassing*) imbarazzante; (*difficult*) delicato(-a), difficile

awkwardness ['ɔːkwədnɪs] N goffaggine f; scomodità; imbarazzo; delicatezza, difficoltà

awl ['ɔːl] N punteruolo

awning ['ɔːnɪŋ] N (*of tent*) veranda; (*of shop, hotel etc*) tenda

awoke [ə'wəuk] PT of **awake**

awoken [ə'wəukən] PP of **awake**

AWOL ['eɪwɔl] ABBR (*Mil etc*) = **absent without leave**

awry [ə'raɪ] ADV di traverso ▶ ADJ storto(-a); **to go ~** andare a monte

axe, (*US*)**ax** [æks] N scure *f* ▶ VT (*project etc*) abolire; (*jobs*) sopprimere; **to have an ~ to grind** (*fig*) fare i propri interessi *or* il proprio tornaconto

axiom ['æksɪəm] N assioma *m*

axiomatic [æksɪəu'mætɪk] ADJ assiomatico(-a)

axis ['æksɪs] (*pl* **axes** [-siːz]) N asse *m*

axle ['æksl] N (*also:* **axle-tree**) asse *m*

ay, aye [aɪ] EXCL (*yes*) sì

AYH N ABBR = **American Youth Hostels**

AZ ABBR (*US*) = **Arizona**

azalea [ə'zeɪlɪə] N azalea

Azerbaijan [æzəbaɪ'dʒɑːn] N Azerbaigian *m*

Azerbaijani [æzəbaɪ'dʒɑːnɪ], **Azeri** [ə'zɛərɪ] ADJ, N azerbaigiano(-a), azero(-a)

Azores [ə'zɔːz] NPL: **the ~** le Azzorre

AZT N ABBR (= *azidothymidine*) AZT *m*

Aztec ['æztɛk] ADJ, N azteco(-a)

azure ['eɪʒə^r] ADJ azzurro(-a)

Bb

B, b [biː] N (*letter*) B, b f *inv* or m *inv*; (*Scol: mark*)
≈ 8 (*buono*); (*Mus*): **B** si m; **B for Benjamin**,
(*US*) **B for Baker** ≈ B come Bologna; **B road** n
(*Brit Aut*) ≈ strada secondaria
b. ABBR = **born**
BA N ABBR = **British Academy**; (*Scol*)
= **Bachelor of Arts**
babble ['bæbl] VI cianciare; mormorare ▸ N
ciance fpl mormorio
babe [beɪb] N (*col*): **she's a real ~** è uno
schianto di ragazza
baboon [bə'buːn] N babbuino
baby ['beɪbɪ] N bambino(-a)
baby carriage N (*US*) carrozzina
baby grand N (*also*: **baby grand piano**)
pianoforte m a mezza coda
babyhood ['beɪbɪhud] N prima infanzia
babyish ['beɪbɪɪʃ] ADJ infantile
baby-minder ['beɪbɪ'maɪndə'] N (*Brit*)
bambinaia (*che tiene i bambini mentre la madre
lavora*)
baby-sit ['beɪbɪsɪt] VI fare il (*or* la) babysitter
baby-sitter ['beɪbɪsɪtə'] N baby-sitter mf
baby wipe N salvietta umidificata
bachelor ['bætʃələ'] N scapolo; **B~ of Arts/
Science (BA/BSc)** ≈ laureato(-a) in lettere/
scienze; **B~ of Arts/Science degree (BA/
BSc)** n ≈ laurea in lettere/scienze; *vedi nota*

> Il *Bachelor's degree* è il riconoscimento che
> viene conferito a chi ha completato un
> corso di laurea di tre o quattro anni
> all'università. I *Bachelor's degree* più
> importanti sono il *BA* (*Bachelor of Arts*), il
> *BSc* (*Bachelor of Science*), il *BEd* (*Bachelor of
> Education*), e il *LLB* (*Bachelor of Laws*); *vedi
> anche* **Master's degree, doctorate.**

bachelorhood ['bætʃələhud] N celibato
bachelor party N (*US*) festa di addio al
celibato
back [bæk] N (*of person, horse*) dorso, schiena;
(*as opposed to front*) dietro; (*of hand*) dorso; (*of
house, car*) didietro; (*of train*) coda; (*of chair*)
schienale m; (*of page*) rovescio; (*of book*) retro;
(*Football*) difensore m ▸ VT (*financially*)

finanziare; (*candidate: also*: **back up**)
appoggiare; (*horse: at races*) puntare su; (*car*)
guidare a marcia indietro ▸ VI indietreggiare;
(*car etc*) fare marcia indietro ▸ ADJ (*in
compounds*) posteriore, di dietro; arretrato(-a)
▸ ADV (*not forward*) indietro; (*returned*): **he's ~** è
tornato; **~ to front** all'incontrario; **to break
the ~ of a job** (*Brit*) fare il grosso or il peggio
di un lavoro; **to have one's ~ to the wall** (*fig*)
essere *or* trovarsi con le spalle al muro; **when
will you be ~?** quando torni?; **he ran ~** tornò
indietro di corsa; **throw the ball ~**
(*restitution*) ritira la palla; **can I have it ~?**
posso riaverlo?; **he called ~** (*again*) ha
richiamato; **~ seats/wheels** (*Aut*) sedili mpl/
ruote fpl posteriori; **to take a ~ seat** (*fig*)
restare in secondo piano; **~ payments/rent**
arretrati mpl; **~ garden/room** giardino/
stanza sul retro (della casa)
▸ **back down** VI (*fig*) fare marcia indietro
▸ **back on to** VT FUS: **the house backs on to
the golf course** il retro della casa dà sul
campo da golf
▸ **back out** VI (*of promise*) tirarsi indietro
▸ **back up** VT (*support*) appoggiare, sostenere;
(*Comput*) fare una copia di riserva di
backache ['bækeɪk] N mal m di schiena
backbencher ['bæk'bentʃə'] N (*Brit*)
parlamentare che non ha incarichi né al governo né
all'opposizione
back benches NPL posti in Parlamento occupati
dai backbencher; *vedi nota*

> Nella *House of Commons*, una delle camere
> del Parlamento britannico, sono
> chiamati *back benches* gli scanni dove
> siedono i *backbenchers*, parlamentari che
> non hanno incarichi né al governo né
> all'opposizione. Nelle file davanti ad essi
> siedono i *frontbencher*; *vedi anche* **front
> bench.**

backbiting ['bækbaɪtɪŋ] N maldicenza
backbone ['bækbəun] N spina dorsale; **the ~
of the organization** l'anima
dell'organizzazione

backchat ['bæktʃæt] N (BRIT col)
impertinenza

backcloth ['bækklɔθ] N (BRIT) scena di
sfondo

backcomb ['bækkəum] VT (BRIT) cotonare

backdate [bæk'deɪt] VT (letter) retrodatare;
backdated pay rise aumento retroattivo

back door N porta sul retro

backdrop ['bækdrɔp] N = **backcloth**

backer ['bækər] N sostenitore(-trice); (Comm)
fautore m

backfire ['bæk'faɪər] VI (Aut) dar ritorni di
fiamma; (plans) fallire

backgammon ['bækgæmən] N tavola reale

background ['bækgraund] N sfondo; (of
events, Comput) background m inv; (basic
knowledge) base f; (experience) esperienza ▶ CPD
(noise, music) di fondo; ~ **reading** letture fpl
sull'argomento; **family ~** ambiente m
familiare

backhand ['bækhænd] N (Tennis: also:
backhand stroke) rovescio

backhanded [bæk'hændɪd] ADJ (fig)
ambiguo(-a)

backhander ['bækhændər] N (BRIT: bribe)
bustarella

backing ['bækɪŋ] N (Comm) finanziamento;
(Mus) accompagnamento; (fig) appoggio

backlash ['bæklæʃ] N contraccolpo,
ripercussione f

backlog ['bæklɔg] N: ~ **of work** lavoro
arretrato

back number N (of magazine etc) numero
arretrato

backpack ['bækpæk] N zaino

backpacker ['bækpækər] N chi viaggia con zaino
e sacco a pelo

back pay N arretrato di paga

backpedal ['bækpedl] VI pedalare
all'indietro; (fig) far marcia indietro

backseat driver ['bæksi:t-] N passeggero che
dà consigli non richiesti al guidatore

backside [bæk'saɪd] N (col) sedere m

backslash ['bækslæʃ] N backslash m inv, barra
obliqua inversa

backslide ['bækslaɪd] VI ricadere

backspace ['bækspeɪs] VI (in typing) battere il
tasto di ritorno

backstage [bæk'steɪdʒ] ADV nel retroscena

back street N vicolo

back-street ['bækstri:t] ADJ: ~ **abortionist**
praticante mf di aborti clandestini

backstroke ['bækstrəuk] N nuoto sul dorso

backtrack ['bæktræk] VI = **backpedal**

backup ['bækʌp] ADJ (train, plane)
supplementare; (Comput) di riserva ▶ N
(support) appoggio, sostegno; (Comput: also:
backup file) file m inv di riserva

backward ['bækwəd] ADJ (movement) indietro

inv; (person) tardivo(-a); (country) arretrato(-a);
~ **and forward movement** movimento
avanti e indietro

backwards ['bækwədz] ADV indietro; (fall,
walk) all'indietro; **to know sth ~** or (US) ~
and forwards (col) sapere qc a menadito

backwater ['bækwɔːtər] N (fig) posto morto

back yard N cortile m sul retro

bacon ['beɪkən] N pancetta

bacteria [bæk'tɪərɪə] NPL batteri mpl

bacteriology [bæktɪərɪ'ɔlədʒɪ] N
batteriologia

bad [bæd] ADJ cattivo(-a); (child) cattivello(-a);
(meat, food) andato(-a) a male; **his ~ leg** la sua
gamba malata; **to go ~** (meat, food) andare a
male; **to have a ~ time of it** passarsela
male; **I feel ~ about it** (guilty) mi sento un
po' in colpa; ~ **debt** credito difficile da
recuperare; ~ **faith** malafede f

baddie, baddy ['bædɪ] N (col: Cine etc)
cattivo(-a)

bade [bæd] PT of **bid**

badge [bædʒ] N insegna; (of policeman)
stemma m; (stick-on) adesivo

badger ['bædʒər] N tasso ▶ VT tormentare

badly ['bædlɪ] ADV (work, dress etc) male;
things are going ~ le cose vanno male;
~ **wounded** gravemente ferito; **he needs it ~**
ne ha gran bisogno; ~ **off** adj povero(-a)

bad-mannered [bæd'mænəd] ADJ
maleducato(-a), sgarbato(-a)

badminton ['bædmɪntən] N badminton m

bad-tempered [bæd'tempəd] ADJ irritabile;
(in bad mood) di malumore

baffle ['bæfl] VT (puzzle) confondere

baffling ['bæflɪŋ] ADJ sconcertante

bag [bæg] N sacco; (handbag etc) borsa; (of
hunter) carniere m; bottino ▶ VT (col: take)
mettersi in tasca; prendersi; **bags of** (col: lots
of) un sacco di; **to pack one's bags** fare le
valigie; **bags under the eyes** borse sotto gli
occhi

bagful ['bægful] N sacco (pieno)

baggage ['bægɪdʒ] N bagagli mpl

baggage allowance N peso bagaglio
consentito

baggage car N (US) bagagliaio

baggage claim, baggage reclaim N ritiro
m bagaglio inv

baggy ['bægɪ] ADJ largo(-a), sformato(-a)

Baghdad [bæg'dæd] N Bagdad f

bag lady N (col) stracciona, barbona

bagpipes ['bægpaɪps] NPL cornamusa

bag-snatcher ['bægsnætʃər] N (BRIT)
scippatore(-trice)

bag-snatching ['bægsnætʃɪŋ] N (BRIT) scippo

Bahamas [bə'hɑːməz] NPL: **the ~** le isole
Bahama

Bahrain [bɑː'reɪn] N Bahrein m

b

bail [beɪl] N cauzione f ▶ VT (*prisoner: also:* **grant bail to**) concedere la libertà provvisoria su cauzione a; (*Naut: also:* **bail out**) aggottare; **on** ~ in libertà provvisoria su cauzione; **to be released on** ~ essere rilasciato(-a) su cauzione
▶ **bail out** VT (*prisoner*) ottenere la libertà provvisoria su cauzione di; (*fig*) tirare fuori dai guai ▶ VI *see* **bale out**

bailiff ['beɪlɪf] N usciere m; fattore m

bailout ['beɪlaʊt] N ricapitalizzazione f; **government bailouts of large corporations** ricapitalizzazioni di grosse società da parte del governo

bait [beɪt] N esca ▶ VT (*hook*) innescare; (*trap*) munire di esca; (*fig*) tormentare

bake [beɪk] VT cuocere al forno ▶ VI cuocersi al forno

baked beans [-bi:nz] NPL fagioli mpl in salsa di pomodoro

baked potato N patata (con la buccia) cotta al forno

baker ['beɪkər] N fornaio(-a), panettiere(-a)

bakery ['beɪkərɪ] N panetteria

baking ['beɪkɪŋ] N cottura (al forno)

baking powder N lievito in polvere

baking tin N stampo, tortiera

baking tray N teglia

balaclava [bælə'klɑːvə] N (*also:* **balaclava helmet**) passamontagna m inv

balance ['bæləns] N equilibrio; (*Comm: sum*) bilancio; (*remainder*) resto; (*scales*) bilancia ▶ VT tenere in equilibrio; (*pros and cons*) soppesare; (*budget*) far quadrare; (*account*) pareggiare; (*compensate*) contrappesare; ~ **of trade/payments** bilancia commerciale/dei pagamenti; ~ **brought forward** saldo riportato; ~ **carried forward** saldo da riportare; **to** ~ **the books** fare il bilancio

balanced ['bælənst] ADJ (*personality, diet*) equilibrato(-a)

balance sheet N bilancio

balcony ['bælkənɪ] N balcone m; (*in theatre*) balconata

bald [bɔːld] ADJ calvo(-a); (*tyre*) liscio(-a)

baldness ['bɔːldnɪs] N calvizie f

bale [beɪl] N balla
▶ **bale out** VT (*Naut: water*) vuotare; (*: boat*) aggottare ▶ VI (*of a plane*) gettarsi col paracadute

Balearic Islands NPL: **the Balearics** le Baleari fpl

baleful ['beɪlful] ADJ funesto(-a)

balk [bɔːlk] VI: **to** ~ (**at**) tirarsi indietro (davanti a); (*horse*) recalcitrare (davanti a)

Balkan ['bɔːlkən] ADJ balcanico(-a) ▶ N: **the Balkans** i Balcani

ball [bɔːl] N palla; (*football*) pallone m; (*for golf*) pallina; (*of wool, string*) gomitolo; (*dance*) ballo; **to play** ~ (**with sb**) giocare a palla (con qn); (*fig*) stare al gioco (di qn); **to be on the** ~ (*fig: competent*) essere in gamba (*: alert*) stare all'erta; **to start the** ~ **rolling** (*fig*) fare la prima mossa; **the** ~ **is in your court** (*fig*) a lei la prossima mossa; *see also* **balls**

ballad ['bæləd] N ballata

ballast ['bæləst] N zavorra

ball bearing N cuscinetto a sfere

ball cock N galleggiante m

ballerina [bælə'riːnə] N ballerina

ballet ['bæleɪ] N balletto

ballet dancer N ballerino(-a) classico(-a)

ballistic [bə'lɪstɪk] ADJ balistico(-a)

ballistics [bə'lɪstɪks] N balistica

balloon [bə'luːn] N pallone m; (*in comic strip*) fumetto ▶ VI gonfiarsi

balloonist [bə'luːnɪst] N aeronauta mf

ballot ['bælət] N scrutinio

ballot box N urna (per le schede)

ballot paper N scheda

ballpark ['bɔːlpɑːk] N (*US*) stadio di baseball

ballpark figure N (*col*) cifra approssimativa

ball-point pen ['bɔːlpɔɪnt-] N penna a sfera

ballroom ['bɔːlrum] N sala da ballo

balls [bɔːlz] NPL (*col!*) coglioni mpl (!)

balm [bɑːm] N balsamo

balmy ['bɑːmɪ] ADJ (*breeze, air*) balsamico(-a); (*BRIT col*) = **barmy**

BALPA ['bælpə] N ABBR (= *British Airline Pilots' Association*) sindacato dei piloti

balsa ['bɔːlsə], **balsa wood** N (legno di) balsa

balsam ['bɔːlsəm] N balsamo

Baltic ['bɔːltɪk] ADJ, N: **the** ~ **Sea** il (mar) Baltico

balustrade [bæləs'treɪd] N balaustrata

bamboo [bæm'buː] N bambù m

bamboozle [bæm'buːzl] VT (*col*) infinocchiare

ban [bæn] N interdizione f ▶ VT interdire; **he was banned from driving** (*BRIT*) gli hanno ritirato la patente

banal [bə'nɑːl] ADJ banale

banana [bə'nɑːnə] N banana

band [bænd] N banda; (*at a dance*) orchestra; (*Mil*) fanfara
▶ **band together** VI collegarsi

bandage ['bændɪdʒ] N benda, fascia

Band-Aid® ['bændeɪd] N (*US*) cerotto

B & B N ABBR = **bed and breakfast**

bandit ['bændɪt] N bandito

bandstand ['bændstænd] N palco dell'orchestra

bandwagon ['bændwægən] N: **to jump on the** ~ (*fig*) seguire la corrente

bandy ['bændɪ] VT (*jokes, insults*) scambiare
▶ **bandy about** VT far circolare

bandy-legged ['bændɪ'legɪd] ADJ dalle gambe storte

bane [beɪn] N: **it** (or **he** etc) **is the ~ of my life** è la mia rovina

bang [bæŋ] N botta; (of door) lo sbattere; (blow) colpo ▶ VT battere (violentemente); (door) sbattere ▶ VI scoppiare; sbattere ▶ ADV (BRIT col): **to be ~ on time** spaccare il secondo; **to ~ at the door** picchiare alla porta; **to ~ into sth** sbattere contro qc; see also **bangs**

banger ['bæŋəʳ] N (BRIT col: car: also: **old banger**) macinino; (: sausage) salsiccia; (firework) mortaretto

Bangkok ['bæŋkɔk] N Bangkok f

Bangladesh [bɑːŋglə'deʃ] N Bangladesh m

bangle ['bæŋgl] N braccialetto

bangs [bæŋz] NPL (US: fringe) frangia, frangetta

banish ['bænɪʃ] VT bandire

banister ['bænɪstəʳ] N,**banisters** ['bænɪstəz] NPL ringhiera

banjo ['bændʒəu] (pl **banjoes** or **banjos**) N banjo m inv

bank [bæŋk] N (for money) banca, banco; (of river, lake) riva, sponda; (of earth) banco ▶ VI (Aviat) inclinarsi in virata; (Comm): **they ~ with Pitt's** sono clienti di Pitt's
▶ **bank on** VT FUS contare su

bank account N conto in banca

bank balance N saldo; **a healthy ~** un solido conto in banca

bank card N carta f assegni inv

bank charges NPL (BRIT) spese fpl bancarie

bank draft N assegno circolare or bancario

banker ['bæŋkəʳ] N banchiere m; **~'s card** (BRIT) carta f assegni inv; **~'s order** (BRIT) ordine m di banca

bank giro N bancogiro

bank holiday N (BRIT) giorno di festa; vedi nota

Una bank holiday, in Gran Bretagna, è una giornata in cui le banche e molti negozi sono chiusi. Generalmente le bank holiday cadono di lunedì e molti ne approfittano per fare una breve vacanza fuori città. Di conseguenza, durante questi fine settimana lunghi (bank holiday weekend) si verifica un notevole aumento del traffico sulle strade, negli aeroporti e nelle stazioni e molte località turistiche registrano il tutto esaurito.

banking ['bæŋkɪŋ] N attività bancaria; professione f di banchiere

banking hours NPL orario di sportello

bank loan N prestito bancario

bank manager N direttore m di banca

banknote ['bæŋknəut] N banconota

bank rate N tasso bancario

bankrupt ['bæŋkrʌpt] ADJ, N fallito(-a); **to go ~** fallire

bankruptcy ['bæŋkrʌptsɪ] N fallimento

bank statement N estratto conto

banned substance N sostanza al bando (nello sport)

banner ['bænəʳ] N striscione m

bannister ['bænɪstəʳ] N,**bannisters** ['bænɪstəz] NPL see **banister**

banns [bænz] NPL pubblicazioni fpl di matrimonio

banquet ['bæŋkwɪt] N banchetto

bantam-weight ['bæntəmweɪt] N peso gallo

banter ['bæntəʳ] N scherzi mpl bonari

baptism ['bæptɪzəm] N battesimo

Baptist ['bæptɪst] ADJ, N battista (mf)

baptize [bæp'taɪz] VT battezzare

bar [bɑːʳ] N (rod) barra; (of window etc) sbarra; (of chocolate) tavoletta; (fig) ostacolo; restrizione f; (pub) bar m inv; (counter: in pub) banco; (Mus) battuta ▶ VT (road, window) sbarrare; (person) escludere; (activity) interdire; **~ of soap** saponetta; **the B~** (Law) l'Ordine m degli avvocati; **behind bars** (prisoner) dietro le sbarre; **~ none** senza eccezione

Barbados [bɑː'beɪdɔs] N Barbados fsg

barbaric [bɑː'bærɪk],**barbarous** ['bɑːbərəs] ADJ barbaro(-a), barbarico(-a)

barbecue ['bɑːbɪkjuː] N barbecue m inv

barbed wire ['bɑːbd-] N filo spinato

barber ['bɑːbəʳ] N barbiere m

barber's (shop), (US)**barber shop** N barbiere m

barbiturate [bɑː'bɪtjurɪt] N barbiturico

Barcelona [bɑːsɪ'ləunə] N Barcellona

bar chart N diagramma m di frequenza

bar code N codice m a barre

bare [bɛəʳ] ADJ nudo(-a) ▶ VT scoprire, denudare; (teeth) mostrare; **the ~ essentials**, **the ~ necessities** lo stretto necessario

bareback ['bɛəbæk] ADV senza sella

barefaced ['bɛəfeɪst] ADJ sfacciato(-a)

barefoot ['bɛəfut] ADJ, ADV scalzo(-a)

bareheaded [bɛə'hɛdɪd] ADJ, ADV a capo scoperto

barely ['bɛəlɪ] ADV appena

Barents Sea ['bærənts-] N: **the ~** il mar di Barents

bargain ['bɑːgɪn] N (transaction) contratto; (good buy) affare m ▶ VI (haggle) tirare sul prezzo; (trade) contrattare; **into the ~** per giunta
▶ **bargain for** VT FUS (col): **to ~ for sth** aspettarsi qc; **he got more than he bargained for** gli è andata peggio di quel che si aspettasse

bargaining ['bɑːgənɪŋ] N contrattazione f

bargaining position N: **to be in a weak/ strong ~** non avere/avere potere contrattuale

b

barge [bɑːdʒ] N chiatta
▶ **barge in** VI (walk in) piombare dentro; (interrupt talk) intromettersi a sproposito
▶ **barge into** VT FUS urtare contro
baritone ['bærɪtəʊn] N baritono
barium meal ['bɛərɪəm-] N (pasto di) bario
bark [bɑːk] N (of tree) corteccia; (of dog) abbaio
▶ VI abbaiare
barley ['bɑːlɪ] N orzo
barley sugar N zucchero d'orzo
barmaid ['bɑːmeɪd] N cameriera al banco
barman ['bɑːmən] N (irreg) barista m
barmy ['bɑːmɪ] ADJ (BRIT col) tocco(-a)
barn [bɑːn] N granaio; (for animals) stalla
barnacle ['bɑːnəkl] N cirripede m
barn owl N barbagianni m inv
barometer [bə'rɒmɪtər] N barometro
baron ['bærən] N barone m; (fig) magnate m; **the oil barons** i magnati del petrolio; **the press barons** i baroni della stampa
baroness ['bærənɪs] N baronessa
baronet ['bærənɪt] N baronetto
barrack ['bærək] VT (BRIT): **to ~ sb** subissare qn di grida e fischi
barracking ['bærəkɪŋ] N (BRIT): **to give sb a ~** subissare qn di grida e fischi
barracks ['bærəks] NPL caserma
barrage ['bærɑːʒ] N (Mil, dam) sbarramento; (fig) fiume m; **a ~ of questions** una raffica di or un fuoco di fila di domande
barrel ['bærəl] N barile m; (of gun) canna
barrel organ N organetto a cilindro
barren ['bærən] ADJ sterile; (soil) arido(-a)
barrette [bə'rɛt] N (US) fermaglio per capelli
barricade [bærɪ'keɪd] N barricata ▶ VT barricare
barrier ['bærɪər] N barriera; (BRIT: also: **crash barrier**) guardrail m inv
barrier cream N (BRIT) crema protettiva
barring ['bɑːrɪŋ] PREP salvo
barrister ['bærɪstər] N (BRIT) avvocato(-essa); vedi nota

> Il barrister è un membro della più prestigiosa delle due branche della professione legale (l'altra è quella dei solicitor); la sua funzione è quella di rappresentare i propri clienti in tutte le corti (magistrates' court, crown court e Court of Appeal), generalmente seguendo le istruzioni del caso preparate dai solicitor.

barrow ['bærəʊ] N (cart) carriola
barstool ['bɑːstuːl] N sgabello
Bart. ABBR (BRIT) = **baronet**
bartender ['bɑːtɛndər] N (US) barista m
barter ['bɑːtər] N baratto ▶ VT: **to ~ sth for** barattare qc con
base [beɪs] N base f ▶ ADJ vile ▶ VT: **to ~ sth on** basare qc su; **to ~ at** (troops) mettere di stanza a; **coffee-based** a base di caffè; **a**

Paris-based firm una ditta con sede centrale a Parigi; **I'm based in London** sono di base or ho base a Londra
baseball ['beɪsbɔːl] N baseball m
baseball cap N berretto da baseball
baseboard ['beɪsbɔːd] N (US) zoccolo, battiscopa m inv
base camp N campo m base inv
Basel [bɑːl] N = **Basle**
baseline ['beɪslaɪn] N (Tennis) linea di fondo
basement ['beɪsmənt] N seminterrato; (of shop) piano interrato
base rate N tasso di base
bases ['beɪsiːz] NPL of **basis**
bash [bæʃ] VT (col) picchiare ▶ N: **I'll have a ~ (at it)** (BRIT col) ci proverò; **bashed in** adj sfondato(-a)
▶ **bash up** VT (col: car) sfasciare; (: BRIT: person) riempire di or prendere a botte
bashful ['bæʃful] ADJ timido(-a)
bashing ['bæʃɪŋ] N: **Paki-/queer-~** atti mpl di violenza contro i pachistani/gli omosessuali
BASIC ['beɪsɪk] N (Comput) BASIC m
basic ['beɪsɪk] ADJ (principles, precautions, rules) elementare; (salary) base inv (after n)
basically ['beɪsɪklɪ] ADV fondamentalmente, sostanzialmente
basic rate N (of tax) aliquota minima
basics NPL: **the ~** l'essenziale m
basil ['bæzl] N basilico
basin ['beɪsn] N (vessel, also Geo) bacino; (also: **washbasin**) lavabo; (BRIT: for food) terrina
basis ['beɪsɪs] (pl **bases** [-siːz]) N base f; **on a part-time ~** part-time; **on a trial ~** in prova; **on the ~ of what you've said** in base alle sue asserzioni
bask [bɑːsk] VI: **to ~ in the sun** crogiolarsi al sole
basket ['bɑːskɪt] N cesta; (smaller) cestino; (with handle) paniere m
basketball ['bɑːskɪtbɔːl] N pallacanestro f
basketball player N cestista mf
Basle [bɑːl] N Basilea
basmati rice [bəz'mætɪ-] N riso basmati
Basque [bæsk] ADJ, N basco(-a)
bass [beɪs] N (Mus) basso
bass clef N chiave f di basso
bassoon [bə'suːn] N fagotto
bastard ['bɑːstəd] N bastardo(-a); (col!) stronzo (!)
baste [beɪst] VT (Culin) ungere con grasso; (Sewing) imbastire
bastion ['bæstɪən] N bastione m; (fig) baluardo
bat [bæt] N pipistrello; (for baseball etc) mazza; (BRIT: for table tennis) racchetta; **off one's own ~** di propria iniziativa ▶ VT: **he didn't ~ an eyelid** non battè ciglio

batch [bætʃ] N (of bread) infornata; (of papers) cumulo; (of applicants, letters) gruppo; (of work) sezione f; (of goods) partita, lotto

batch processing N (Comput) elaborazione f a blocchi

bated ['beɪtɪd] ADJ: **with ~ breath** col fiato sospeso

bath [bɑːθ] (pl **baths** [bɑːðz]) N bagno; (bathtub) vasca da bagno ▶ VT far fare il bagno a; **to have a ~** fare un bagno; see also **baths**

bathchair ['bɑːθʃɛəʳ] N (BRIT) poltrona a rotelle

bathe [beɪð] VI fare il bagno ▶ VT bagnare; (wound etc) lavare

bather ['beɪðəʳ] N bagnante mf

bathing ['beɪðɪŋ] N bagni mpl

bathing cap N cuffia da bagno

bathing costume, (US)**bathing suit** N costume m da bagno

bathmat ['bɑːθmæt] N tappetino da bagno

bathrobe ['bɑːθrəub] N accappatoio

bathroom ['bɑːθrum] N stanza da bagno

baths [bɑːðz] NPL bagni mpl pubblici

bath towel N asciugamano da bagno

bathtub ['bɑːθtʌb] N (vasca da) bagno

batman ['bætmən] N (irreg) (BRIT Mil) attendente m

baton ['bætən] N bastone m; (Mus) bacchetta; (Athletics) testimone m; (club) manganello

battalion [bə'tæliən] N battaglione m

batten ['bætən] N (Carpentry) assicella, correntino; (for flooring) tavola per pavimenti; (Naut) serretta; (: on sail) stecca

▶ **batten down** VT (Naut): **to ~ down the hatches** chiudere i boccaporti

batter ['bætəʳ] VT battere ▶ N pastella

battered ['bætəd] ADJ (hat) sformato(-a); (pan) ammaccato(-a); **~ wife/baby** consorte f/bambino(-a) maltrattato(-a)

battering ram ['bætərɪŋ-] N ariete m

battery ['bætərɪ] N batteria; (of torch) pila

battery charger N caricabatterie m inv

battery farming N allevamento in batteria

battle ['bætl] N battaglia ▶ VI battagliare, lottare; **to fight a losing ~** (fig) battersi per una causa persa; **that's half the ~** (col) è già una mezza vittoria

battle dress N uniforme f da combattimento

battlefield ['bætlfiːld] N campo di battaglia

battlements ['bætlmənts] NPL bastioni mpl

battleship ['bætlʃɪp] N nave f da guerra

batty ['bætɪ] ADJ (col: person) svitato(-a), strambo(-a); (behaviour, idea) strampalato(-a)

bauble ['bɔːbl] N ninnolo

baud [bɔːd] N (Comput) baud m inv

baulk [bɔːlk] VI = **balk**

bauxite ['bɔːksaɪt] N bauxite f

Bavaria [bə'vɛərɪə] N Baviera

Bavarian [bə'vɛərɪən] ADJ, N bavarese (mf)

bawdy ['bɔːdɪ] ADJ piccante

bawl [bɔːl] VI urlare

bay [beɪ] N (of sea) baia; (BRIT: for parking) piazzola di sosta; (: for loading) piazzale m di (sosta e) carico; **to hold sb at ~** tenere qn a bada

bay leaf N foglia d'alloro

bayonet ['beɪənɪt] N baionetta

bay tree N alloro

bay window N bovindo

bazaar [bə'zɑːʳ] N bazar m inv; vendita di beneficenza

bazooka [bə'zuːkə] N bazooka m inv

BB N ABBR (BRIT: = Boys' Brigade) organizzazione giovanile a fine educativo

BBB N ABBR (US: = Better Business Bureau) organismo per la difesa dei consumatori

BBC N ABBR (= British Broadcasting Corporation) vedi nota

La BBC è l'azienda statale che fornisce il servizio radiofonico e televisivo in Gran Bretagna. Pur dovendo rispondere al Parlamento del proprio operato, la BBC non è soggetta al controllo dello stato per scelte e programmi, anche perché si autofinanzia con il ricavato dei canoni d'abbonamento. La BBC ha canali televisivi digitali e terrestri, oltre a diverse emittenti radiofoniche nazionali e locali. Fornisce un servizio di informazione internazionale, il BBC World Service, trasmesso in tutto il mondo.

BBE N ABBR (US: = Benevolent and Protective Order of Elks) organizzazione filantropica

BC ADV ABBR (= before Christ) a.C. ▶ ABBR (CANADA) = **British Columbia**

BCG N ABBR (= Bacillus Calmette-Guérin) vaccino antitubercolare

BD N ABBR (= Bachelor of Divinity) titolo di studio

B/D ABBR = **bank draft**

BDS N ABBR (= Bachelor of Dental Surgery) titolo di studio

(KEYWORD)

be [biː] (pt **was, were**, pp **been**) AUX VB **1** (with present participle: forming continuous tenses): **what are you doing?** che fai?, che stai facendo?; **they're coming tomorrow** vengono domani; **I've been waiting for her for hours** sono ore che l'aspetto

2 (with pp: forming passives) essere; **to be killed** essere or venire ucciso(-a); **the box had been opened** la scatola era stata aperta; **the thief was nowhere to be seen** il ladro non si trovava da nessuna parte

3 (in tag questions): **it was fun, wasn't it?** è stato divertente, no?; **he's good-looking, isn't he?** è un bell'uomo, vero?; **she's back, is she?** così è tornata, eh?

4 (+ *to* + *infinitive*): **the house is to be sold** abbiamo (*or* hanno *etc*) intenzione di vendere casa; **you're to be congratulated for all your work** dovremo farvi i complimenti per tutto il vostro lavoro; **am I to understand that ...?** devo dedurre che ...?; **he's not to open it** non deve aprirlo; **he was to have come yesterday** sarebbe dovuto venire ieri

▶ VB + COMPLEMENT **1** (*gen*) essere; **I'm English** sono inglese; **I'm tired** sono stanco(-a); **I'm hot/cold** ho caldo/freddo; **he's a doctor** è medico; **2 and 2 are 4** 2 più 2 fa 4; **be careful!** sta attento(-a)!; **be good** sii buono(-a); **if I were you ...** se fossi in te ...

2 (*of health*) stare; **how are you?** come sta?; **he's very ill** sta molto male

3 (*of age*): **how old are you?** quanti anni hai?; **I'm sixteen (years old)** ho sedici anni

4 (*cost*) costare; **how much was the meal?** quant'era *or* quanto costava il pranzo?; **that'll be £5, please** (sono) 5 sterline, per favore

▶ VI **1** (*exist, occur etc*) essere, esistere; **the best singer that ever was** il migliore cantante mai esistito *or* di tutti i tempi; **be that as it may** comunque sia, sia come sia; **so be it** sia pure, e sia

2 (*referring to place*) essere, trovarsi; **I won't be here tomorrow** non ci sarò domani; **Edinburgh is in Scotland** Edimburgo si trova in Scozia

3 (*referring to movement*): **where have you been?** dove sei stato?; **I've been to China** sono stato in Cina

▶ IMPERS VB **1** (*referring to time, distance*) essere; **it's 5 o'clock** sono le 5; **it's the 28th of April** è il 28 aprile; **it's 10 km to the village** di qui al paese sono 10 km

2 (*referring to the weather*) fare; **it's too hot/cold** fa troppo caldo/freddo; **it's windy** c'è vento

3 (*emphatic*): **it's me** sono io; **it's only me** sono solo io; **it was Maria who paid the bill** è stata Maria che ha pagato il conto

B/E ABBR = **bill of exchange**

beach [biːtʃ] N spiaggia ▶ VT tirare in secco

beach buggy N dune buggy *f inv*

beachcomber ['biːtʃkəʊməʳ] N vagabondo (*che s'aggira sulla spiaggia*)

beachwear ['biːtʃwɛəʳ] N articoli *mpl* da spiaggia

beacon ['biːkən] N (*lighthouse*) faro; (*marker*) segnale *m*; (*also*: **radio beacon**) radiofaro

bead [biːd] N perlina; (*of dew, sweat*) goccia; **beads** NPL (*necklace*) collana

beady ['biːdɪ] ADJ: ~ **eyes** occhi *mpl* piccoli e penetranti

beagle ['biːgl] N cane *m* da lepre

beak [biːk] N becco

beaker ['biːkəʳ] N coppa

beam [biːm] N trave *f*; (*of light*) raggio; (*Radio*) fascio (d'onde) ▶ VI brillare; (*smile*): **to ~ at sb** rivolgere un radioso sorriso a qn; **to drive on full** *or* **main ~** *or* (*US*) **high ~** guidare con gli abbaglianti accesi

beaming ['biːmɪŋ] ADJ (*sun, smile*) raggiante

bean [biːn] N fagiolo; (*coffee bean*) chicco; **runner ~** fagiolino

beanpole ['biːnpəʊl] N (*col*) spilungone(-a)

beansprouts ['biːnsprauts] NPL germogli *mpl* di soia

bear [bɛəʳ] (*pt* **bore** [bɔːʳ], *pp* **borne** [bɔːn]) N orso; (*Stock Exchange*) ribassista *mf* ▶ VT (*gen*) portare; (*produce*) generare; (: *fruit*) produrre, dare; (: *traces, signs*) mostrare; (*Comm*: *interest*) fruttare; (*endure*) sopportare ▶ VI: **to ~ right/left** piegare a destra/sinistra; **to ~ the responsibility of** assumersi la responsabilità di; **to ~ comparison with** reggere al paragone con; **I can't ~ him** non lo posso soffrire *or* sopportare; **to bring pressure to ~ on sb** fare pressione su qn

▶ **bear out** VT (*theory, suspicion*) confermare, convalidare

▶ **bear up** VI farsi coraggio; **he bore up well under the strain** ha sopportato bene lo stress

▶ **bear with** VT FUS (*sb's moods, temper*) sopportare (con pazienza); **~ with me a minute** solo un attimo, prego

bearable ['bɛərəbl] ADJ sopportabile

beard [bɪəd] N barba

bearded ['bɪədɪd] ADJ barbuto(-a)

bearer ['bɛərəʳ] N portatore *m*; (*of passport*) titolare *mf*

bearing ['bɛərɪŋ] N portamento; (*connection*) rapporto; **bearings** NPL (*also*: **ball bearings**) cuscinetti *mpl* a sfere; **to take a ~** fare un rilevamento; **to find one's bearings** orientarsi

beast [biːst] N bestia

beastly ['biːstlɪ] ADJ meschino(-a); (*weather*) da cani

beat [biːt] (*pt* ~, *pp* **beaten**) N colpo; (*of heart*) battito; (*Mus*) tempo; battuta; (*of policeman*) giro ▶ VT battere; (*eggs, cream*) sbattere; **off the beaten track** fuori mano; **to ~ about the bush** menare il cane per l'aia; **to ~ time** battere il tempo; **that beats everything!** (*col*) questo è il colmo!; **~ it!** (*col*) fila!, fuori dai piedi!

▶ **beat down** VT (*door*) abbattere, buttare giù; (*price*) far abbassare; (*seller*) far scendere ▶ VI (*rain*) scrosciare; (*sun*) picchiare

▶ **beat off** VT respingere

▶ **beat up** VT (*col*: *person*) picchiare; (*eggs*) sbattere

beater ['bi:tə'] N (for eggs, cream) frullino
beating ['bi:tɪŋ] N botte fpl; (defeat) batosta;
  to take a ~ prendere una (bella) batosta
beat-up [bi:t'ʌp] ADJ (col) scassato(-a)
beautician [bju:'tɪʃən] N estetista mf
beautiful ['bju:tɪful] ADJ bello(-a)
beautifully ADV splendidamente
beautify ['bju:tɪfaɪ] VT abbellire
beauty ['bju:tɪ] N bellezza; (concept) bello;
  the ~ of it is that ... il bello è che ...
beauty contest N concorso di bellezza
beauty parlour [-'pɑ:lə'], (US) **beauty**
  parlor N salone m di bellezza
beauty queen N miss f inv, reginetta di
  bellezza
beauty salon N istituto di bellezza
beauty sleep N: **to get one's ~** farsi un
  sonno ristoratore
beauty spot N neo; (Brit Tourism) luogo
  pittoresco
beaver ['bi:və'] N castoro
becalmed [bɪ'kɑ:md] ADJ in bonaccia
became [bɪ'keɪm] PT of **become**
because [bɪ'kɔz] CONJ perché; **~ of** prep a
  causa di
beck [bɛk] N: **to be at sb's ~ and call** essere a
  completa disposizione di qn
beckon ['bɛkən] VT (also: **beckon to**)
  chiamare con un cenno
become [bɪ'kʌm] VT (irreg: like **come**)
  diventare; **to ~ fat/thin** ingrassarsi/
  dimagrire; **to ~ angry** arrabbiarsi; **it**
  became known that ... si è venuto a sapere
  che ...; **what has ~ of him?** che gli è
  successo?
becoming [bɪ'kʌmɪŋ] ADJ (behaviour) che si
  conviene; (clothes) grazioso(-a)
BECTU ['bɛktu:] N ABBR (Brit) = Broadcasting
  Entertainment Cinematographic and
  Theatre Union
BEd N ABBR (= Bachelor of Education) laurea con
  abilitazione all'insegnamento
bed [bɛd] N letto; (of flowers) aiuola; (of coal,
  clay) strato; (of sea, lake) fondo; **to go to ~**
  andare a letto
  ▶ **bed down** VI sistemarsi (per dormire)
bed and breakfast N (terms) camera con
  colazione; (place) ≈ pensione f familiare;
  vedi nota

> I bed and breakfasts, anche B & Bs, sono
> piccole pensioni a conduzione familiare,
> in case private o fattorie, dove si affittano
> camere e viene servita al mattino la
> tradizionale colazione all'inglese. Queste
> pensioni offrono un servizio di camera
> con prima colazione, appunto bed and
> breakfast, a prezzi più contenuti rispetto
> agli alberghi.

bedbug ['bɛdbʌg] N cimice f

bedclothes ['bɛdkləuðz] NPL coperte e
  lenzuola fpl
bedcover ['bɛdkʌvə'] N copriletto
bedding ['bɛdɪŋ] N coperte e lenzuola fpl
bedevil [bɪ'dɛvl] VT (person) tormentare;
  (plans) ostacolare continuamente
bedfellow ['bɛdfɛləu] N: **they are strange**
  bedfellows (fig) fanno una coppia ben
  strana
bedlam ['bɛdləm] N baraonda
bed linen N biancheria da letto
bedpan ['bɛdpæn] N padella
bedpost ['bɛdpəust] N colonnina del letto
bedraggled [bɪ'drægld] ADJ sbrindellato(-a);
  (wet) fradicio(-a)
bedridden ['bɛdrɪdən] ADJ costretto(-a) a
  letto
bedrock ['bɛdrɔk] N (Geo) basamento; (fig)
  fatti mpl di base
bedroom ['bɛdrum] N camera da letto
Beds ABBR (Brit) = **Bedfordshire**
bed settee N divano m letto inv
bedside ['bɛdsaɪd] N: **at sb's ~** al capezzale di
  qn
bedside lamp N lampada da comodino
bedside table N comodino
bedsit ['bɛdsɪt], **bedsitter** ['bɛdsɪtə'] N (Brit)
  monolocale m
bedspread ['bɛdsprɛd] N copriletto
bedtime ['bɛdtaɪm] N: **it's ~** è ora di andare a
  letto
bee [bi:] N ape f; **to have a ~ in one's bonnet**
  (**about sth**) avere la fissazione (di qc)
beech [bi:tʃ] N faggio
beef [bi:f] N manzo; **roast ~** arrosto di manzo
  ▶ **beef up** VT (col) rinforzare
beefburger ['bi:fbə:gə'] N hamburger m inv
Beefeater ['bi:fi:tə'] N guardia della Torre di
  Londra
beehive ['bi:haɪv] N alveare m
bee-keeping ['bi:ki:pɪŋ] N apicoltura
beeline ['bi:laɪn] N: **to make a ~ for** buttarsi
  a capo fitto verso
been [bi:n] PP of **be**
beep [bi:p] N (of horn) colpo di clacson; (of
  phone etc) segnale m (acustico), bip m inv ▶ VI
  suonare
beeper ['bi:pə'] N (of doctor etc) cercapersone m
  inv
beer [bɪə'] N birra
beer belly N (col) stomaco da bevitore
beer can N lattina di birra
beer garden N (Brit) giardino (di pub)
beet [bi:t] (US) N (also: **red beet**) barbabietola
  rossa
beetle ['bi:tl] N scarafaggio; coleottero
beetroot ['bi:tru:t] N (Brit) barbabietola
befall [bɪ'fɔ:l] VI, VT (irreg: like **fall**) accadere (a)
befit [bɪ'fɪt] VT addirsi a

before [bɪ'fɔː^r] PREP (*in time*) prima di; (*in space*) davanti a ▶ CONJ prima che + *sub*; prima di ▶ ADV prima; **~ going** prima di andare; **~ she goes** prima che vada; **the week ~** la settimana prima; **I've seen it ~** l'ho già visto; **I've never seen it ~** è la prima volta che lo vedo

beforehand [bɪ'fɔːhænd] ADV in anticipo

befriend [bɪ'frɛnd] VT assistere; mostrarsi amico a

befuddled [bɪ'fʌdld] ADJ confuso(-a)

beg [bɛg] VI chiedere l'elemosina ▶ VT (*also:* **beg for**) chiedere in elemosina; (: *favour*) chiedere; (: *entreat*) pregare; **I ~ your pardon** (*apologising*) mi scusi; (*not hearing*) scusi?; **this begs the question of ...** questo presuppone che sia già risolto il problema di ...; **to ~ sb to do** pregare qn di fare

began [bɪ'gæn] PT *of* **begin**

beggar ['bɛgə^r] N (*also:* **beggarman, beggarwoman**) mendicante *mf*

begin [bɪ'gɪn] (*pt* **began** [bɪ'gæn], *pp* **begun** [bɪ'gʌn]) VT, VI cominciare; **to ~ doing** *or* **to do sth** incominciare *or* iniziare a fare qc; **I can't ~ to thank you** non so proprio come ringraziarla; **to ~ with, I'd like to know ...** tanto per cominciare vorrei sapere ...; **beginning from Monday** a partire da lunedì

beginner [bɪ'gɪnə^r] N principiante *mf*

beginning [bɪ'gɪnɪŋ] N inizio, principio; **right from the ~** fin dall'inizio

begrudge [bɪ'grʌdʒ] VT: **to ~ sb sth** dare qc a qn a malincuore; invidiare qn per qc

beguile [bɪ'gaɪl] VT (*enchant*) incantare

beguiling [bɪ'gaɪlɪŋ] ADJ (*charming*) allettante; (*deluding*) ingannevole

begun [bɪ'gʌn] PP *of* **begin**

behalf [bɪ'hɑːf] N: **on ~ of**, (*US*) **in ~ of** per conto di; a nome di

behave [bɪ'heɪv] VI comportarsi; (*well: also:* **behave o.s.**) comportarsi bene

behaviour, (*US*) **behavior** [bɪ'heɪvjə^r] N comportamento, condotta

behead [bɪ'hɛd] VT decapitare

beheld [bɪ'hɛld] PT, PP *of* **behold**

behind [bɪ'haɪnd] PREP dietro; (*followed by pronoun*) dietro di; (*time*) in ritardo con ▶ ADV dietro; in ritardo; (*leave, stay*) indietro ▶ N didietro; **we're ~ them in technology** siamo più indietro *or* più arretrati di loro nella tecnica; **~ the scenes** dietro le quinte; **to be ~ (schedule) with sth** essere indietro con qc; (*payments*) essere in arretrato con qc; **to leave sth ~** dimenticare di prendere qc

behold [bɪ'həuld] VT (*irreg: like* **hold**) vedere, scorgere

beige [beɪʒ] ADJ beige *inv*

Beijing [beɪ'dʒɪŋ] N Pechino *f*

being ['biːɪŋ] N essere *m*; **to come into ~** cominciare ad esistere

Beirut [beɪ'ruːt] N Beirut *f*

Belarus ['bɛlærus] N Bielorussia

Belarussian [bɛlə'rʌʃən] ADJ bielorusso(-a) ▶ N bielorusso(-a); (*Ling*) bielorusso

belated [bɪ'leɪtɪd] ADJ tardo(-a)

belch [bɛltʃ] VI ruttare ▶ VT (*gen: also:* **belch out**: *smoke etc*) eruttare

beleaguered [bɪ'liːgəd] ADJ (*city*) assediato(-a); (*army*) accerchiato(-a); (*fig*) assillato(-a)

Belfast ['bɛlfɑːst] N Belfast *f*

belfry ['bɛlfrɪ] N campanile *m*

Belgian ['bɛldʒən] ADJ, N belga *mf*

Belgium ['bɛldʒəm] N Belgio

Belgrade [bɛl'greɪd] N Belgrado *f*

belie [bɪ'laɪ] VT smentire; (*give false impression of*) nascondere

belief [bɪ'liːf] N (*opinion*) opinione *f*, convinzione *f*; (*trust, faith*) fede *f*; (*acceptance as true*) credenza; **in the ~ that** nella convinzione che; **it's beyond ~** è incredibile

believe [bɪ'liːv] VT, VI credere; **to ~ in** (*God*) credere in; (*ghosts*) credere a; (*method*) avere fiducia in; **I don't ~ in corporal punishment** sono contrario alle punizioni corporali; **he is believed to be abroad** si pensa che sia all'estero

believer [bɪ'liːvə^r] N (*Rel*) credente *mf*; (*in idea: activity*): **to be a ~ in** credere in

belittle [bɪ'lɪtl] VT sminuire

Belize [bɛ'liːz] N Belize *m*

bell [bɛl] N campana; (*small, on door, electric*) campanello; **that rings a ~** (*fig*) mi ricorda qualcosa

bell-bottoms ['bɛlbɔtəmz] NPL calzoni *mpl* a zampa d'elefante

bellboy ['bɛlbɔɪ], (*US*) **bellhop** ['bɛlhɔp] N ragazzo d'albergo, fattorino d'albergo

belligerent [bɪ'lɪdʒərənt] ADJ (*at war*) belligerante; (*fig*) bellicoso(-a)

bellow ['bɛləu] VI muggire; (*cry*) urlare (a squarciagola) ▶ VT (*orders*) urlare (a squarciagola)

bellows ['bɛləuz] NPL soffietto

bell pepper (*esp US*) N peperone *m*

bell push N (*BRIT*) pulsante *m* del campanello

belly ['bɛlɪ] N pancia

bellyache ['bɛlɪeɪk] N mal *m* di pancia ▶ VI (*col*) mugugnare

bellybutton ['bɛlɪbʌtn] N ombelico

bellyful ['bɛlɪful] N (*col*): **to have had a ~ of** (*fig*) averne piene le tasche

belong [bɪ'lɔŋ] VI: **to ~ to** appartenere a; (*club etc*) essere socio di; **this book belongs here** questo libro va qui

belongings [bɪ'lɔŋɪŋz] NPL cose *fpl*, roba; **personal ~** effetti *mpl* personali

Belorussia [bɛləuˈrʌʃə] N Bielorussia
Belorussian [bɛləuˈrʌʃən] ADJ, N
= **Belarussian**
beloved [bɪˈlʌvɪd] ADJ adorato(-a)
below [bɪˈləu] PREP sotto, al di sotto di ▶ ADV
sotto, di sotto; giù; **see ~** vedi sotto or oltre;
temperatures ~ normal temperature al di
sotto del normale
belt [bɛlt] N cintura; (*Tech*) cinghia ▶ VT
(*thrash*) picchiare ▶ VI (*BRIT col*) filarsela;
industrial ~ zona industriale
▶ **belt out** VT (*song*) cantare a squarciagola
▶ **belt up** VI (*BRIT col*) chiudere la boccaccia
beltway [ˈbɛltweɪ] N (*US: Aut: ring road*)
circonvallazione f; (: *motorway*) autostrada
bemoan [bɪˈməun] VT lamentare
bemused [bɪˈmjuːzd] ADJ perplesso(-a),
stupito(-a)
bench [bɛntʃ] N panca; (*in workshop, Pol*)
banco; **the B~** (*Law*) la Corte
bench mark N banco di prova
bend [bɛnd] (*pt, pp* **bent** [bɛnt]) VT curvare;
(*leg, arm*) piegare ▶ VI curvarsi; piegarsi ▶ N
(*in road*) curva; (*in pipe, river*) gomito
▶ **bend down** VI chinarsi
▶ **bend over** VI piegarsi
bends [bɛndz] NPL (*Med*) embolia
beneath [bɪˈniːθ] PREP sotto, al di sotto di;
(*unworthy of*) indegno(-a) di ▶ ADV sotto, di
sotto
benefactor [ˈbɛnɪfæktəʳ] N benefattore m
benefactress [ˈbɛnɪfæktrɪs] N benefattrice f
beneficial [bɛnɪˈfɪʃəl] ADJ che fa bene;
vantaggioso(-a); **~ to** che giova a
beneficiary [bɛnɪˈfɪʃərɪ] N (*Law*)
beneficiario(-a)
benefit [ˈbɛnɪfɪt] N beneficio, vantaggio;
(*allowance of money*) indennità f inv ▶ VT far
bene a ▶ VI: **he'll ~ from it** ne trarrà
beneficio or profitto
benefit performance N spettacolo di
beneficenza
Benelux [ˈbɛnɪlʌks] N Benelux m
benevolent [bɪˈnɛvələnt] ADJ benevolo(-a)
BEng N ABBR (= *Bachelor of Engineering*) laurea in
ingegneria
benign [bɪˈnaɪn] ADJ (*person, smile*)
benevolo(-a); (*Med*) benigno(-a)
bent [bɛnt] PT, PP *of* **bend** ▶ N inclinazione f
▶ ADJ (*wire, pipe*) piegato(-a), storto(-a); (*col:
dishonest*) losco(-a); **to be ~ on** essere
deciso(-a) a
bequeath [bɪˈkwiːð] VT lasciare in eredità
bequest [bɪˈkwɛst] N lascito
bereaved [bɪˈriːvd] ADJ in lutto ▶ NPL: **the ~** i
familiari in lutto
bereavement [bɪˈriːvmənt] N lutto
beret [ˈbɛreɪ] N berretto
Bering Sea [ˈbɛrɪŋ-] N: **the ~** il mar di Bering

berk [bəːk] N (*BRIT col!*) coglione(-a) (!)
Berks ABBR (*BRIT*) = **Berkshire**
Berlin [bəːˈlɪn] N Berlino f; **East/West ~**
Berlino est/ovest
berm [bəːm] N (*US Aut*) corsia d'emergenza
Bermuda [bəːˈmjuːdə] N le Bermude
Bermuda shorts NPL bermuda mpl
Bern [bəːn] N Berna f
berry [ˈbɛrɪ] N bacca
berserk [bəˈsəːk] ADJ: **to go ~** montare su
tutte le furie
berth [bəːθ] N (*bed*) cuccetta; (*for ship*)
ormeggio ▶ VI (*in harbour*) entrare in porto;
(*at anchor*) gettare l'ancora; **to give sb a wide
~** (*fig*) tenersi alla larga da qn
beseech [bɪˈsiːtʃ] (*pt, pp* **besought** [bɪˈsɔːt]) VT
implorare
beset [bɪˈsɛt] (*pt, pp ~*) VT assalire ▶ ADJ: **a
policy ~ with dangers** una politica irta or
piena di pericoli
besetting [bɪˈsɛtɪŋ] ADJ: **his ~ sin** il suo più
grande difetto
beside [bɪˈsaɪd] PREP accanto a; (*compared
with*) rispetto a, in confronto a; **to be ~ o.s.
(with anger)** essere fuori di sé; **that's ~ the
point** non c'entra
besides [bɪˈsaɪdz] ADV inoltre, per di più
▶ PREP oltre a; (*except*) a parte
besiege [bɪˈsiːdʒ] VT (*town*) assediare; (*fig*)
tempestare
besotted [bɪˈsɔtɪd] ADJ (*BRIT*): **~ with**
infatuato(-a) di
besought [bɪˈsɔːt] PT, PP *of* **beseech**
bespectacled [bɪˈspɛktɪkld] ADJ
occhialuto(-a)
bespoke [bɪˈspəuk] ADJ (*BRIT: garment*) su
misura; **~ tailor** sarto
best [bɛst] ADJ migliore ▶ ADV meglio; **the ~
thing to do is ...** la cosa migliore da fare or
farsi è ...; **the ~ part of** (*quantity*) la maggior
parte di; **at ~** tutt'al più; **to make the ~ of
sth** cavare il meglio possibile da qc; **to do
one's ~** fare del proprio meglio; **to the ~ of
my knowledge** per quel che ne so; **to the ~
of my ability** al massimo delle mie capacità;
he's not exactly patient at the ~ of times
non è mai molto paziente
best-before date N (*Comm*): **"~: ..."** da
consumarsi preferibilmente entro il...
best man N (*irreg*) testimone m dello sposo
bestow [bɪˈstəu] VT: **to ~ sth on sb** conferire
qc a qn
bestseller [ˈbɛstˈsɛləʳ] N bestseller m inv
bet [bɛt] (*pt, pp ~ or* **betted**) N scommessa
▶ VT, VI scommettere; **to ~ sb sth**
scommettere qc con qn; **it's a safe ~** (*fig*) è
molto probabile
Bethlehem [ˈbɛθlɪhɛm] N Betlemme f
betray [bɪˈtreɪ] VT tradire

betrayal [bɪ'treɪəl] N tradimento
better ['bɛtəʳ] ADJ migliore ▶ ADV meglio
▶ VT migliorare ▶ N: **to get the ~ of** avere la
meglio su; **you had ~ do it** è meglio che lo
faccia; **he thought ~ of it** cambiò idea; **to
get ~** migliorare; **a change for the ~** un
cambiamento in meglio; **that's ~!** così va
meglio!; **I had ~ go** dovrei andare; **~ off** adj
più ricco(-a); (fig) **you'd be ~ off this way**
starebbe meglio così
betting ['bɛtɪŋ] N scommesse fpl
betting shop N (BRIT) ufficio dell'allibratore
between [bɪ'twiːn] PREP tra ▶ ADV in mezzo,
nel mezzo; **the road ~ here and London** la
strada da qui a Londra; **we only had £5 ~ us**
fra tutti e due avevamo solo 5 sterline
bevel ['bɛvl] N (also: **bevel(led) edge**) profilo
smussato
beverage ['bɛvərɪdʒ] N bevanda
bevy ['bɛvɪ] N: **a ~ of** una banda di
bewail [bɪ'weɪl] VT lamentare
beware [bɪ'wɛəʳ] VT, VI: **to ~ (of)** stare
attento(-a) (a); **"~ of the dog"** "attenti al
cane"
bewildered [bɪ'wɪldəd] ADJ sconcertato(-a),
confuso(-a)
bewildering [bɪ'wɪldərɪŋ] ADJ sconcertante,
sbalorditivo(-a)
bewitching [bɪ'wɪtʃɪŋ] ADJ affascinante
beyond [bɪ'jɔnd] PREP (in space) oltre;
(exceeding) al di sopra di ▶ ADV di là; **~ doubt**
senza dubbio; **~ repair** irreparabile
b/f ABBR = **brought forward**
BFPO N ABBR (= British Forces Post Office) recapito
delle truppe britanniche all'estero
bhp N ABBR (Aut: = brake horsepower) c.v. (= cavallo
vapore)
bi... [baɪ] PREFIX bi...
biannual [baɪ'ænjuəl] ADJ semestrale
bias ['baɪəs] N (prejudice) pregiudizio;
(preference) preferenza
biased, biassed ['baɪəst] ADJ parziale; **to be
bias(s)ed against** essere prevenuto(-a)
contro
biathlon [baɪ'æθlən] N biathlon m
bib [bɪb] N bavaglino
Bible ['baɪbl] N Bibbia
bibliography [bɪblɪ'ɔgrəfɪ] N bibliografia
bicarbonate of soda [baɪ'kɑːbənɪt-] N
bicarbonato (di sodio)
bicentenary [baɪsɛn'tiːnərɪ], **bicentennial**
[baɪsɛn'tɛnɪəl] N bicentenario
biceps ['baɪsɛps] N bicipite m
bicker ['bɪkəʳ] VI bisticciare
bicycle ['baɪsɪkl] N bicicletta
bicycle path, bicycle track N sentiero
ciclabile
bicycle pump N pompa della bicicletta
bid [bɪd] N offerta; (attempt) tentativo

▶ VI (pt, pp ~) fare un'offerta ▶ VT (pt **bade**
[bæd], pp **bidden** ['bɪdn]) fare un'offerta di;
to ~ sb good day dire buon giorno a qn
bidder ['bɪdəʳ] N: **the highest ~** il maggior
offerente
bidding ['bɪdɪŋ] N offerte fpl
bide [baɪd] VT: **to ~ one's time** aspettare il
momento giusto
bidet ['biːdeɪ] N bidè m inv
bidirectional ['baɪdɪ'rɛkʃənl] ADJ
bidirezionale
biennial [baɪ'ɛnɪəl] ADJ biennale ▶ N (pianta)
biennale f
bier [bɪəʳ] N bara
bifocals [baɪ'fəuklz] NPL occhiali mpl bifocali
big [bɪg] ADJ grande; grosso(-a); **my ~
brother** mio fratello maggiore; **to do
things in a ~ way** fare le cose in grande
bigamy ['bɪgəmɪ] N bigamia
Big Apple N vedi nota

Tutti sanno che *The Big Apple*, la Grande
Mela, è New York ("*apple*" in gergo
significa grande città), ma sicuramente
i soprannomi di altre città americane
non sono così conosciuti. Chicago è
soprannominata *the Windy City* perché è
ventosa, New Orleans si chiama *the Big
Easy* per il modo di vivere tranquillo e
rilassato dei suoi abitanti, e l'industria
automobilistica ha fatto sì che Detroit
fosse soprannominata *Motown*.

big dipper [-'dɪpəʳ] N montagne fpl russe,
otto m inv volante
big end N (Aut) testa di biella
biggish ['bɪgɪʃ] ADJ see **big** piuttosto grande,
piuttosto grosso(-a); **a ~ rent** un affitto
piuttosto alto
bigheaded ['bɪg'hɛdɪd] ADJ presuntuoso(-a)
big-hearted ['bɪg'hɑːtɪd] ADJ generoso(-a)
bigot ['bɪgət] N persona gretta
bigoted ['bɪgətɪd] ADJ gretto(-a)
bigotry ['bɪgətrɪ] N grettezza
big toe N alluce m
big top N tendone m del circo
big wheel N (at fair) ruota (panoramica)
bigwig ['bɪgwɪg] N (col) pezzo grosso
bike [baɪk] N bici f inv
bike lane N pista ciclabile
bikini [bɪ'kiːnɪ] N bikini m inv
bilateral [baɪ'lætərl] ADJ bilaterale
bile [baɪl] N bile f
bilingual [baɪ'lɪŋgwəl] ADJ bilingue
bilious ['bɪlɪəs] ADJ biliare; (fig) bilioso(-a)
bill [bɪl] N (in hotel, restaurant) conto; (Comm)
fattura; (for gas, electricity) bolletta, conto;
(Pol) atto; (US: banknote) banconota; (notice)
avviso; (of bird) becco; (of show) locandina;
(Theat): **on the ~** in cartellone ▶ VT mandare
il conto a; **may I have the ~ please?** posso

avere il conto per piacere?; **"stick** or **post no bills"** "divieto di affissione"; **to fit** or **fill the ~** (fig) fare al caso; **~ of exchange** cambiale f, tratta; **~ of lading** polizza di carico; **~ of sale** atto di vendita

billboard ['bɪlbɔːd] N tabellone m

billet ['bɪlɪt] N alloggio ▶ VT (troops etc) alloggiare

billfold ['bɪlfəuld] N (US) portafoglio

billiards ['bɪljədz] N biliardo

billion ['bɪljən] N (BRIT) bilione m; (US) miliardo

billow ['bɪləu] N (of smoke) nuvola; (of sail) rigonfiamento ▶ VI (smoke) alzarsi in volute; (sail) gonfiarsi

bills payable NPL effetti mpl passivi

bills receivable NPL effetti mpl attivi

billy goat ['bɪlɪgəut] N caprone m, becco

bimbo ['bɪmbəu] N (col) pollastrella, svampitella

bin [bɪn] N (for coal, rubbish) bidone m; (for bread) cassetta; (BRIT: also: **dustbin**) pattumiera; (also: **litter bin**) cestino

binary ['baɪnərɪ] ADJ binario(-a)

bind [baɪnd] (pt, pp **bound** [baund]) VT legare; (oblige) obbligare ▶ N (col) scocciatura ▶ **bind over** VT (Law) dare la condizionale a ▶ **bind up** VT (wound) fasciare, bendare; **to be bound up in** (work, research etc) essere completamente assorbito da; **to be bound up with** (person) dedicarsi completamente a

binder ['baɪndəʳ] N (file) classificatore m

binding ['baɪndɪŋ] N (of book) legatura ▶ ADJ (contract) vincolante

binge [bɪndʒ] N (col): **to go on a ~** fare baldoria

binge drinker N persona che di norma beve troppo

bingo ['bɪŋgəu] N gioco simile alla tombola

bin liner N sacchetto per l'immondizia

binoculars [bɪ'nɔkjuləz] NPL binocolo

bio... [baɪə...] PREFIX bio

biochemistry [baɪəu'kemɪstrɪ] N biochimica

biodegradable ['baɪəudɪ'greɪdəbl] ADJ biodegradabile

biodiesel ['baɪəudiːzl] N biodiesel m

biodiversity ['baɪəudaɪ'vəːsɪtɪ] N biodiversità f inv

biofuel ['baɪəufjuəl] N biocarburante m

biographer [baɪ'ɔgrəfəʳ] N biografo(-a)

biographic [baɪə'græfɪk], **biographical** [baɪə'græfɪkl] ADJ biografico(-a)

biography [baɪ'ɔgrəfɪ] N biografia

biological [baɪə'lɔdʒɪkl] ADJ biologico(-a)

biological clock N orologio biologico

biologist [baɪ'ɔlədʒɪst] N biologo(-a)

biology [baɪ'ɔlədʒɪ] N biologia

biometric [baɪəu'metrɪk] ADJ biometrico(-a)

biophysics [baɪəu'fɪzɪks] N biofisica

biopic ['baɪəupɪk] N film m inv biografia inv

biopsy ['baɪɔpsɪ] N biopsia

biosphere ['baɪəusfɪəʳ] N biosfera

biotechnology [baɪəutek'nɔlədʒɪ] N biotecnologia

bioterrorism [baɪəu'terərɪzəm] N bioterrorismo

birch [bəːtʃ] N betulla

bird [bəːd] N uccello; (BRIT col: girl) bambola

bird flu N influenza aviaria

bird of prey N (uccello) rapace m

bird's-eye view ['bəːdzaɪ-] N veduta a volo d'uccello

bird watcher N ornitologo(-a) dilettante

birdwatching N birdwatching m

Biro® ['baɪrəu] N biro® f inv

birth [bəːθ] N nascita; **to give ~ to** dare alla luce, partorire; (fig) dare inizio a

birth certificate N certificato di nascita

birth control N controllo delle nascite; contraccezione f

birthday ['bəːθdeɪ] N compleanno ▶ CPD di compleanno

birthmark ['bəːθmɑːk] N voglia

birthplace ['bəːθpleɪs] N luogo di nascita

birth rate N indice m di natalità

Biscay ['bɪskeɪ] N: **the Bay of ~** il golfo di Biscaglia

biscuit ['bɪskɪt] N (BRIT) biscotto; (US) panino al latte

bisect [baɪ'sekt] VT tagliare in due (parti); (Math) bisecare

bisexual ['baɪ'seksjuəl] ADJ, N bisessuale (mf)

bishop ['bɪʃəp] N vescovo; (Chess) alfiere m

bistro ['biːstrəu] N bistrò m inv

bit [bɪt] PT of **bite** ▶ N pezzo; (of tool) punta; (of horse) morso; (Comput) bit m inv; (US: coin) ottavo di dollaro; **a ~ of** un po' di; **a ~ mad/dangerous** un po' matto/pericoloso; **~ by ~** a poco a poco; **to do one's ~** fare la propria parte; **to come to bits** (break) andare a pezzi; **bring all your bits and pieces** porta tutte le tue cose

bitch [bɪtʃ] N (dog) cagna; (col!) puttana (!)

bite [baɪt] (pt **bit**, pp **bitten**) VT, VI mordere; (insect) pungere ▶ N morso; (insect bite) puntura; (mouthful) boccone m; **let's have a ~ to eat** mangiamo un boccone; **to ~ one's nails** mangiarsi le unghie

biting ['baɪtɪŋ] ADJ pungente

bit part N (Theat) particina

bitten ['bɪtn] PP of **bite**

bitter ['bɪtəʳ] ADJ amaro(-a); (wind, criticism) pungente; (icy: weather) gelido(-a) ▶ N (BRIT: beer) birra amara; **to the ~ end** a oltranza

bitterly ['bɪtəlɪ] ADV (disappoint, complain, weep) amaramente; (oppose, criticise) aspramente; (jealous) profondamente; **it's ~ cold** fa un freddo gelido

bitterness ['bɪtənɪs] N amarezza; gusto amaro

bittersweet ['bɪtəswi:t] ADJ agrodolce

bitty ['bɪtɪ] ADJ (BRIT col) frammentario(-a)

bitumen ['bɪtjumɪn] N bitume m

bivouac ['bɪvuæk] N bivacco

bizarre [bɪ'zɑ:ʳ] ADJ bizzarro(-a)

bk ABBR = **bank**; **book**

BL N ABBR = **Bachelor of Law(s)**; (= Bachelor of Letters) titolo di studio; (US: = Bachelor of Literature) titolo di studio

B/L ABBR = **bill of lading**

blab [blæb] VI parlare troppo ▶ VT (also: **blab out**) spifferare

black [blæk] ADJ nero(-a) ▶ N nero ▶ VT (BRIT Industry) boicottare; **B~** negro(-a); **~ coffee** caffè m inv nero; **to give sb a ~ eye** fare un occhio nero a qn; **in the ~** (in credit) in attivo; **there it is in ~ and white** (fig) eccolo nero su bianco; **~ and blue** adj tutto(-a) pesto(-a) ▶ **black out** VI (faint) svenire

black belt N (Sport) cintura nera; (US: area): **the ~** zona abitata principalmente da negri

blackberry ['blækbərɪ] N mora

blackbird ['blækbə:d] N merlo

blackboard ['blækbɔ:d] N lavagna

black box N (Aviat) scatola nera

Black Country N (BRIT): **the ~** zona carbonifera del centro dell'Inghilterra

blackcurrant [blæk'kʌrənt] N ribes m inv

black economy N (BRIT) economia sommersa

blacken ['blækn] VT annerire

Black Forest N: **the ~** la Foresta Nera

blackhead ['blækhɛd] N punto nero, comedone m

black hole N (Astron) buco nero

black ice N strato trasparente di ghiaccio

blackjack ['blækdʒæk] N (Cards) ventuno; (US: truncheon) manganello

blackleg ['blæklɛg] N (BRIT) crumiro

blacklist ['blæklɪst] N lista nera ▶ VT mettere sulla lista nera

blackmail ['blækmeɪl] N ricatto ▶ VT ricattare

blackmailer ['blækmeɪləʳ] N ricattatore(-trice)

black market N mercato nero

blackout ['blækaut] N oscuramento; (fainting) svenimento; (TV) interruzione f delle trasmissioni

black pepper N pepe m nero

black pudding N sanguinaccio

Black Sea N: **the ~** il mar Nero

black sheep N pecora nera

blacksmith ['blæksmɪθ] N fabbro ferraio

black spot N (Aut) luogo famigerato per gli incidenti

bladder ['blædəʳ] N vescica

blade [bleɪd] N lama; (of oar) pala; **~ of grass** filo d'erba

blame [bleɪm] N colpa ▶ VT: **to ~ sb/sth for sth** dare la colpa di qc a qn/qc; **who's to ~?** chi è colpevole?; **I'm not to ~** non è colpa mia

blameless ['bleɪmlɪs] ADJ irreprensibile

blanch [blɑ:ntʃ] VI (person) sbiancare in viso ▶ VT (Culin) scottare

bland [blænd] ADJ mite; (taste) blando(-a)

blank [blæŋk] ADJ bianco(-a); (look) distratto(-a) ▶ N spazio vuoto; (cartridge) cartuccia a salve; **to draw a ~** (fig) non aver nessun risultato

blank cheque, (US) **blank check** N assegno in bianco; **to give sb a ~ to do** (fig) dare carta bianca a qn per fare

blanket ['blæŋkɪt] N coperta ▶ ADJ (statement, agreement) globale

blanket cover N: **to give ~** (insurance policy) coprire tutti i rischi

blare [blɛəʳ] VI strombettare; (radio) suonare a tutto volume

blasé ['blɑ:zeɪ] ADJ blasé inv

blasphemous ['blæsfɪməs] ADJ blasfemo(-a)

blasphemy ['blæsfɪmɪ] N bestemmia

blast [blɑ:st] N (of wind) raffica; (of air, steam) getto; (bomb blast) esplosione f ▶ VT far saltare ▶ EXCL (BRIT col) mannaggia!; **(at) full ~** a tutta forza ▶ **blast off** VI (Space) essere lanciato(-a)

blast-off ['blɑ:stɔf] N (Space) lancio

blatant ['bleɪtənt] ADJ flagrante

blatantly ['bleɪtəntlɪ] ADV: **it's ~ obvious** è lampante

blaze [bleɪz] N (fire) incendio; (glow: of fire, sun etc) bagliore m; (fig) vampata; splendore m ▶ VI (fire) ardere, fiammeggiare; (fig) infiammarsi; (guns) sparare senza sosta; (fig: eyes) ardere ▶ VT: **to ~ a trail** (fig) tracciare una via nuova; **in a ~ of publicity** circondato da grande pubblicità

blazer ['bleɪzəʳ] N blazer m inv

bleach [bli:tʃ] N (also: **household bleach**) varechina ▶ VT (material) candeggiare

bleached ['bli:tʃt] ADJ (hair) decolorato(-a)

bleachers ['bli:tʃəz] NPL (US Sport) posti mpl di gradinata

bleak [bli:k] ADJ (prospect, future) tetro(-a); (landscape) desolato(-a); (weather) gelido(-a) e cupo(-a); (smile) pallido(-a)

bleary-eyed ['blɪərɪ'aɪd] ADJ dagli occhi offuscati

bleat [bli:t] VI belare

bled [blɛd] PT, PP of **bleed**

bleed [bli:d] (pt, pp **bled** [blɛd]) VT dissanguare; (brakes, radiator) spurgare ▶ VI sanguinare; **my nose is bleeding** mi viene fuori sangue dal naso

bleep [bli:p] N breve segnale *m* acustico, bip *m inv* ▶ VI suonare ▶ VT (*doctor*) chiamare con il cercapersone

bleeper ['bli:pə'] N (*of doctor etc*) cercapersone *m inv*

blemish ['blɛmɪʃ] N macchia

blend [blɛnd] N miscela ▶ VT mescolare ▶ VI (*colours etc: also:* **blend in**) armonizzare

blender ['blɛndə'] N (*Culin*) frullatore *m*

bless [blɛs] (*pt, pp* **blessed** *or* **blest** [blɛst]) VT benedire; (*sneezing*) salute!; **to be blessed with** godere di

blessed ['blɛsɪd] ADJ (*Rel: holy*) benedetto(-a); (*happy*) beato(-a); **every ~ day** tutti i santi giorni

blessing ['blɛsɪŋ] N benedizione *f*; fortuna; **to count one's blessings** ringraziare Iddio, ritenersi fortunato; **it was a ~ in disguise** in fondo è stato un bene

blest [blɛst] PT, PP *of* **bless**

blew [blu:] PT *of* **blow**

blight [blaɪt] N (*of plants*) golpe *f* ▶ VT (*hopes etc*) deludere; (*life*) rovinare

blimey ['blaɪmɪ] EXCL (*BRIT col*) accidenti!

blind [blaɪnd] ADJ cieco(-a) ▶ N (*for window*) avvolgibile *m*; (*Venetian blind*) veneziana ▶ VT accecare; **the blind** NPL i ciechi; **to turn a ~ eye (on** *or* **to)** chiudere un occhio (su)

blind alley N vicolo cieco

blind corner N (*BRIT*) svolta cieca

blind date N appuntamento combinato (*tra due persone che non si conoscono*)

blinders ['blaɪndəz] NPL (*US*) = **blinkers**

blindfold ['blaɪndfəuld] N benda ▶ ADJ, ADV bendato(-a) ▶ VT bendare gli occhi a

blinding ['blaɪndɪŋ] ADJ (*flash, light*) accecante; (*pain*) atroce

blindly ['blaɪndlɪ] ADV ciecamente

blindness ['blaɪndnɪs] N cecità

blind spot N (*Aut etc*) punto cieco; (*fig*) punto debole

bling [blɪŋ] N *gioielli vistosi*

blink [blɪŋk] VI battere gli occhi; (*light*) lampeggiare ▶ N: **to be on the ~** (*col*) essere scassato(-a)

blinkers ['blɪŋkəz] NPL (*BRIT*) paraocchi *mpl*

blinking ['blɪŋkɪŋ] ADJ (*BRIT col*): **this ~ ...** questo(-a) maledetto(-a) ...

blip [blɪp] N (*on radar etc*) segnale *m* intermittente; (*on graph*) piccola variazione *f*; (*fig*) momentanea battuta d'arresto

bliss [blɪs] N estasi *f*

blissful ['blɪsfəl] ADJ (*event, day*) stupendo(-a), meraviglioso(-a); (*smile*) beato(-a); **in ~ ignorance** nella (più) beata ignoranza

blissfully ['blɪsfəlɪ] ADV (*sigh, smile*) beatamente; **~ happy** magnificamente felice

blister ['blɪstə'] N (*on skin*) vescica; (*on paintwork*) bolla ▶ VI (*paint*) coprirsi di bolle

BLit, BLitt N ABBR (= *Bachelor of Literature*) titolo di studio

blithe [blaɪð] ADJ gioioso(-a), allegro(-a)

blithely ['blaɪðlɪ] ADV allegramente

blithering ['blɪðərɪŋ] ADJ (*col*): **this ~ idiot** questa razza d'idiota

blitz [blɪts] N blitz *m*; **to have a ~ on sth** (*fig*) prendere d'assalto qc

blizzard ['blɪzəd] N bufera di neve

bloated ['bləutɪd] ADJ gonfio(-a)

blob [blɔb] N (*drop*) goccia; (*stain, spot*) macchia

bloc [blɔk] N (*Pol*) blocco

block [blɔk] N (*gen, Comput*) blocco; (*in pipes*) ingombro; (*toy*) cubo; (*of buildings*) isolato ▶ VT (*gen, Comput*) bloccare; **the sink is blocked** il lavandino è otturato; **~ of flats** caseggiato; **3 blocks from here** a 3 isolati di distanza da qui; **mental ~** blocco mentale ▶ **block up** VT bloccare; (*pipe*) ingorgare, intasare

blockade [blɔ'keɪd] N blocco ▶ VT assediare

blockage ['blɔkɪdʒ] N ostacolo

block and tackle N (*Tech*) paranco

block booking N prenotazione *f* in blocco

blockbuster ['blɔkbʌstə'] N grande successo

block capitals NPL stampatello

blockhead ['blɔkhɛd] N testa di legno

block letters NPL stampatello

block release N (*BRIT*) periodo pagato concesso a tirocinante per effettuare studi superiori

block vote N (*BRIT*) voto per delega

blog [blɔg] N blog *m inv* ▶ VI scrivere blog, bloggare

blogger [blɔgə'] N (*Comput*) blogger *mf*

blogging ['blɔgɪŋ] N blogging *m* ▶ ADJ: **~ website** sito di blogging

blogosphere ['blɔgəsfɪə'] N blogosfera *f*

bloke [bləuk] N (*BRIT col*) tizio

blond, blonde [blɔnd] N (*man*) biondo; (*woman*) bionda ▶ ADJ biondo(-a)

blood [blʌd] N sangue *m*; **new ~** (*fig*) nuova linfa

blood bank N banca del sangue

blood count N conteggio di globuli rossi e bianchi

bloodcurdling ['blʌdkə:dlɪŋ] ADJ raccapricciante, da far gelare il sangue

blood donor N donatore(-trice) di sangue

blood group N gruppo sanguigno

bloodhound ['blʌdhaund] N segugio

bloodless ['blʌdlɪs] ADJ (*pale*) smorto(-a), esangue; (*coup*) senza spargimento di sangue

bloodletting ['blʌdlɛtɪŋ] N (*Med*) salasso; (*fig*) spargimento di sangue

blood poisoning N setticemia

blood pressure N pressione f sanguigna; **to have high/low ~** avere la pressione alta/bassa

bloodshed ['blʌdʃɛd] N spargimento di sangue

bloodshot ['blʌdʃɔt] ADJ: **~ eyes** occhi iniettati di sangue

bloodstained ['blʌdsteɪnd] ADJ macchiato(-a) di sangue

bloodstream ['blʌdstri:m] N flusso del sangue

blood test N analisi f inv del sangue

bloodthirsty ['blʌdθə:stɪ] ADJ assetato(-a) di sangue

blood transfusion N trasfusione f di sangue

blood type N gruppo sanguigno

blood vessel N vaso sanguigno

bloody ['blʌdɪ] ADJ (fight) sanguinoso(-a); (nose) sanguinante; (BRIT col!): **this ~ ...** questo maledetto ...; **~ awful/good** (col!) veramente terribile/buono; **a ~ awful day** (col!) una giornata di merda (!)

bloody-minded ['blʌdɪ'maɪndɪd] ADJ (BRIT col) indisponente

bloom [blu:m] N fiore m ▶ VI essere in fiore

blooming ['blu:mɪŋ] ADJ (col): **this ~ ...** questo(-a) dannato(-a) ...

blossom ['blɔsəm] N fiore m; (with pl sense) fiori mpl ▶ VI essere in fiore; **to ~ into** (fig) diventare

blot [blɔt] N macchia ▶ VT macchiare; **to be a ~ on the landscape** rovinare il paesaggio; **to ~ one's copy book** (fig) farla grossa ▶ **blot out** VT (memories) cancellare; (view) nascondere; (nation, city) annientare

blotchy ['blɔtʃɪ] ADJ (complexion) coperto(-a) di macchie

blotter ['blɔtə'] N tampone m (di carta assorbente)

blotting paper ['blɔtɪŋ-] N carta assorbente

blotto ['blɔtəu] ADJ (col) sbronzo(-a)

blouse [blauz] N camicetta

blow [bləu] (pt **blew**, pp **blown**) N colpo ▶ VI soffiare ▶ VT (fuse) far saltare; (wind) spingere; (instrument) suonare; **to come to blows** venire alle mani; **to ~ one's nose** soffiarsi il naso; **to ~ a whistle** fischiare ▶ **blow away** VI volare via ▶ VT portare via ▶ **blow down** VT abbattere ▶ **blow off** VT far volare via; **to ~ off course** far uscire di rotta ▶ **blow out** VI scoppiare ▶ **blow over** VI calmarsi ▶ **blow up** VI saltare in aria ▶ VT far saltare in aria; (tyre) gonfiare; (Phot) ingrandire

blow-dry ['bləudraɪ] N (hairstyle) messa in piega a föhn ▶ VT asciugare con il föhn

blowlamp ['bləulæmp] N (BRIT) lampada a benzina per saldare

blown [bləun] PP of **blow**

blowout ['bləuaut] N (of tyre) scoppio; (col: big meal) abbuffata

blowtorch ['bləutɔ:tʃ] N lampada a benzina per saldare

blowzy ['blauzɪ] ADJ trasandato(-a)

BLS N ABBR (US) = **Bureau of Labor Statistics**

blubber ['blʌbə'] N grasso di balena ▶ VI (pej) piangere forte

bludgeon ['blʌdʒən] VT prendere a randellate

blue [blu:] ADJ azzurro(-a), celeste; (darker) blu inv; (depressed) giù inv; **~ film/joke** film/barzelletta pornografico(a); **(only) once in a ~ moon** a ogni morte di papa; **out of the ~** (fig) all'improvviso; see also **blues**

blue baby N neonato cianotico

bluebell ['blu:bɛl] N giacinto di bosco

blueberry N mirtillo

bluebottle ['blu:bɔtl] N moscone m

blue cheese N formaggio tipo gorgonzola

blue-chip ['blu:tʃɪp] ADJ: **~ investment** investimento sicuro

blue-collar worker ['blu:kɔlə'-] N operaio(-a)

blue jeans NPL blue-jeans mpl

blueprint ['blu:prɪnt] N cianografia; (fig): **~ (for)** formula (di)

blues [blu:z] NPL: **the ~** (Mus) il blues; **to have the ~** (col: feeling) essere a terra

bluetit N cinciarella

bluff [blʌf] VI bluffare ▶ N bluff m inv; (promontory) promontorio scosceso ▶ ADJ (person) brusco(-a); **to call sb's ~** mettere alla prova il bluff di qn

blunder ['blʌndə'] N abbaglio ▶ VI prendere un abbaglio; **to ~ into sb/sth** andare a sbattere contro qn/qc

blunt [blʌnt] ADJ (edge) smussato(-a); (point) spuntato(-a); (knife) che non taglia; (person) brusco(-a) ▶ VT smussare; spuntare; **this pencil is ~** questa matita non ha più la punta; **~ instrument** (Law) corpo contundente

bluntly ['blʌntlɪ] ADV (speak) senza mezzi termini

bluntness ['blʌntnɪs] N (of person) brutale franchezza

blur [blə:'] N forma indistinta ▶ VT offuscare

blurb [blə:b] N trafiletto pubblicitario

blurred [blə:d] ADJ (photo) mosso(-a); (TV) sfuocato(-a)

blurt out [blə:t-] VT lasciarsi sfuggire

blush [blʌʃ] VI arrossire ▶ N rossore m

blusher ['blʌʃə'] N fard m inv

bluster ['blʌstə'] N spacconate fpl; (threats) vuote minacce fpl ▶ VI fare lo spaccone; minacciare a vuoto

blustering ['blʌstərɪŋ] ADJ (tone etc) da spaccone

blustery ['blʌstərɪ] ADJ (*weather*) burrascoso(-a)

Blvd ABBR = **boulevard**

BM N ABBR = **British Museum**; (*Scol*: = *Bachelor of Medicine*) titolo di studio

BMA N ABBR = **British Medical Association**

BMJ N ABBR = **British Medical Journal**

BMus N ABBR (= *Bachelor of Music*) titolo di studio

BMX N ABBR (= *bicycle motocross*) BMX *f inv*; **~ bike** mountain bike *f inv* per cross

bn ABBR = **billion**

BO N ABBR (*col*: = *body odour*) odori *mpl* sgradevoli (del corpo); = **box office**

boar [bɔːʳ] N cinghiale *m*

board [bɔːd] N tavola; (*on wall*) tabellone *m*; (*for chess etc*) scacchiera; (*committee*) consiglio, comitato; (*in firm*) consiglio d'amministrazione; (*Naut, Aviat*): **on ~ a** bordo ▶ VT (*ship*) salire a bordo di; (*train*) salire su; **full ~** (*BRIT*) pensione *f* completa; **half ~** (*BRIT*) mezza pensione; **~ and lodging** vitto e alloggio; **above ~** (*fig*) regolare; **across the ~** (*fig*) *adv* per tutte le categorie; *adj* generale; **to go by the ~** venir messo(-a) da parte

▶ **board up** VT (*door*) chiudere con assi

boarder ['bɔːdəʳ] N pensionante *mf*; (*Scol*) convittore(-trice)

board game N gioco da tavolo

boarding card ['bɔːdɪŋ-] N (*Aviat, Naut*) carta d'imbarco

boarding house N pensione *f*

boarding party N squadra di ispezione (*del carico di una nave*)

boarding pass N (*BRIT*) = **boarding card**

boarding school N collegio

board meeting N riunione *f* di consiglio

board room N sala del consiglio

boardwalk ['bɔːdwɔːk] N (*US*) passeggiata a mare

boast [bəust] VI: **to ~ (about** *or* **of)** vantarsi (di) ▶ VT vantare; ▶ N vanteria; vanto

boastful ['bəustful] ADJ vanaglorioso(-a)

boastfulness ['bəustfulnɪs] N vanagloria

boat [bəut] N nave *f*; (*small*) barca; **to go by ~** andare in barca *or* in nave; **we're all in the same ~** (*fig*) siamo tutti nella stessa barca

boater ['bəutəʳ] N (*hat*) paglietta

boating ['bəutɪŋ] N canottaggio

boat people N boat people *mpl*

boatswain ['bəusn] N nostromo

bob [bɔb] VI (*boat, cork on water: also:* **bob up and down**) andare su e giù ▶ N (*BRIT col*) = **shilling**

▶ **bob up** VI saltare fuori

bobbin ['bɔbɪn] N bobina; (*of sewing machine*) rocchetto

bobby ['bɔbɪ] N (*BRIT col*) ≈ poliziotto

bobby pin ['bɔbɪ-] (*US*) N fermaglio per capelli

bobsleigh ['bɔbsleɪ] N bob *m inv*

bode [bəud] VI: **to ~ well/ill (for)** essere di buon/cattivo auspicio (per)

bodice ['bɔdɪs] N corsetto

bodily ['bɔdɪlɪ] ADJ (*comfort, needs*) materiale; (*pain*) fisico(-a) ▶ ADV (*carry*) in braccio; (*lift*) di peso

body ['bɔdɪ] N corpo; (*of car*) carrozzeria; (*of plane*) fusoliera; (*fig: group*) gruppo; (*: organization*) associazione *f*, organizzazione *f*; (*quantity*) quantità *f inv*; (*of speech, document*) parte *f* principale; (*also:* **body stocking**) body *m inv*; **in a ~** in massa; **ruling ~** direttivo; **a wine with ~** un vino corposo

body blow N (*fig*) duro colpo

body-building ['bɔdɪ'bɪldɪŋ] N culturismo

bodyguard ['bɔdɪgɑːd] N guardia del corpo

body language N linguaggio del corpo

body repairs NPL (*Aut*) lavori *mpl* di carrozzeria

body search N perquisizione *f* personale; **to submit to** *or* **undergo a ~** essere sottoposto(-a) a perquisizione personale

bodywork ['bɔdɪwɜːk] N carrozzeria

boffin ['bɔfɪn] N scienziato

bog [bɔg] N palude *f* ▶ VT: **to get bogged down** (*fig*) impantanarsi

bogey ['bəugɪ] N (*worry*) spauracchio; (*also:* **bogey man**) babau *m inv*

boggle ['bɔgl] VI: **the mind boggles** è incredibile

Bogotá [bəugə'tɑː] N Bogotà *f*

bogus ['bəugəs] ADJ falso(-a); finto(-a)

Bohemia [bəu'hiːmɪə] N Boemia

Bohemian [bəu'hiːmɪən] ADJ, N boemo(-a)

boil [bɔɪl] VT, VI bollire ▶ N (*Med*) foruncolo; **to come to the** *or* (*US*) **a ~** raggiungere l'ebollizione; **to bring to the** *or* (*US*) **a ~** portare a ebollizione; **boiled egg** uovo alla coque; **boiled potatoes** patate *fpl* bollite *or* lesse

▶ **boil down** VI (*fig*): **to ~ down to** ridursi a

▶ **boil over** VI traboccare (bollendo)

boiler ['bɔɪləʳ] N caldaia

boiler suit N (*BRIT*) tuta

boiling ['bɔɪlɪŋ] ADJ bollente; **I'm ~ (hot)** (*col*) sto morendo di caldo

boiling point N punto di ebollizione

boil-in-the-bag [bɔɪlɪnðə'bæg] ADJ (*rice etc*) da bollire nel sacchetto

boisterous ['bɔɪstərəs] ADJ chiassoso(-a)

bold [bəuld] ADJ audace; (*child*) impudente; (*outline*) chiaro(-a); (*colour*) deciso(-a)

boldness ['bəuldnɪs] N audacia; impudenza

bold type N (*Typ*) neretto, grassetto

Bolivia [bə'lɪvɪə] N Bolivia

Bolivian [bə'lɪvɪən] ADJ, N boliviano(-a)

bollard ['bɔləd] N (Naut) bitta; (Brit Aut) colonnina luminosa

Bollywood ['bɔlɪwud] N Bollywood f

bolshy ['bɔlʃɪ] ADJ (Brit col) piantagrane, ribelle; **to be in a ~ mood** essere in vena di piantar grane

bolster ['bəulstər] N capezzale m
▶ **bolster up** VT sostenere

bolt [bəult] N chiavistello; (with nut) bullone m ▶ ADV: **~ upright** diritto(-a) come un fuso ▶ VT serrare; (also: **bolt together**) imbullonare; (food) mangiare in fretta ▶ VI scappare via; **a ~ from the blue** (fig) un fulmine a ciel sereno

bomb [bɔm] N bomba ▶ VT bombardare

bombard [bɔm'bɑːd] VT bombardare

bombardment [bɔm'bɑːdmənt] N bombardamento

bombastic [bɔm'bæstɪk] ADJ ampolloso(-a)

bomb disposal N: **~ expert** artificiere m; **~ unit** corpo degli artificieri

bomber ['bɔmər] N (Aviat) bombardiere m; (terrorist) dinamitardo(-a)

bombing ['bɔmɪŋ] N bombardamento

bomb scare N stato di allarme (per sospetta presenza di una bomba)

bombshell ['bɔmʃel] N (fig) notizia bomba

bomb site N luogo bombardato

bona fide ['bəunə'faɪdɪ] ADJ sincero(-a); (offer) onesto(-a)

bonanza [bə'nænzə] N cuccagna

bond [bɔnd] N legame m; (binding promise, Finance) obbligazione f; (Comm): **in ~** (of goods) in attesa di sdoganamento

bondage ['bɔndɪdʒ] N schiavitù f

bonded warehouse ['bɔndɪd-] N magazzino doganale

bone [bəun] N osso; (of fish) spina, lisca ▶ VT disossare; togliere le spine a

bone china N porcellana fine

bone-dry ['bəun'draɪ] ADJ asciuttissimo(-a)

bone idle ADJ: **to be ~** essere un(a) fannullone(-a)

bone marrow N midollo osseo

boner ['bəunər] N (US) gaffe f inv

bonfire ['bɔnfaɪər] N falò m inv

bonk [bɔŋk] VT, VI (humorous, col) scopare (!)

bonkers ['bɔŋkəz] ADJ (Brit col) suonato(-a)

Bonn [bɔn] N Bonn f

bonnet ['bɔnɪt] N cuffia; (Brit: of car) cofano

bonny ['bɔnɪ] ADJ (esp Scottish) bello(-a), carino(-a)

bonus ['bəunəs] N premio; (on wages) gratifica; (fig) sovrappiù m inv

bony ['bəunɪ] ADJ (thin: person) ossuto(-a), angoloso(-a); (arm, face, Med: tissue) osseo(-a); (meat) pieno(-a) di ossi; (fish) pieno(-a) di spine

boo [buː] EXCL ba! ▶ VT fischiare ▶ N fischio

boob [buːb] N (col: breast) tetta; (: Brit: mistake) gaffe f inv

booby prize ['buːbɪ-] N premio per il peggior contendente

booby trap ['buːbɪ-] N trabocchetto; (bomb) congegno che esplode al contatto

booby-trapped ['buːbɪtræpt] ADJ: **a ~ car** una macchina con dell'esplosivo a bordo

book [buk] N libro; (of stamps etc) blocchetto ▶ VT (ticket, seat, room) prenotare; (driver) multare; (football player) ammonire; **books** NPL (Comm) conti mpl; **to keep the books** (Comm) tenere la contabilità; **by the ~** secondo le regole; **to throw the ~ at sb** incriminare qn seriamente or con tutte le aggravanti
▶ **book in** VI (Brit: at hotel) prendere una camera
▶ **book up** VT riservare, prenotare; **the hotel is booked up** l'albergo è al completo; **all seats are booked up** è tutto esaurito

bookable ['bukəbl] ADJ: **seats are ~** si possono prenotare i posti

bookcase ['bukkeɪs] N libreria

book ends NPL reggilibri mpl

booking ['bukɪŋ] N (Brit) prenotazione f

booking office N (Brit Rail) biglietteria; (Theat) botteghino

book-keeping ['buk'kiːpɪŋ] N contabilità

booklet ['buklɪt] N opuscolo, libriccino

bookmaker ['bukmeɪkər] N allibratore m

bookmark ['bukmɑːk] (also Comput) N segnalibro ▶ VT (Comput) mettere un segnalibro a; (Internet) aggiungere a "Preferiti"

bookseller ['buksɛlər] N libraio

bookshelf ['bukʃelf] N mensola (per libri); **bookshelves** NPL (bookcase) libreria

bookshop ['bukʃɔp] N libreria

bookstall ['bukstɔːl] N bancarella di libri

bookstore ['bukstɔːr] N = **bookshop**

book token N buono m libri inv

book value N valore m contabile

bookworm ['bukwəːm] N (fig) topo di biblioteca

boom [buːm] N (noise) rimbombo; (busy period) boom m inv ▶ VI rimbombare; andare a gonfie vele

boomerang ['buːməræŋ] N boomerang m inv ▶ VI (fig) avere effetto contrario; **to ~ on sb** (fig) ritorcersi contro qn

boom town N città f inv in rapidissima espansione

boon [buːn] N vantaggio

boorish ['buərɪʃ] ADJ maleducato(-a)

boost [buːst] N spinta ▶ VT spingere; (increase: sales, production) incentivare; **to give a ~ to** (morale) tirar su; **it gave a ~ to his**

confidence è stata per lui un'iniezione di fiducia

booster ['buːstər] N (*Elec*) amplificatore *m*; (*TV*) amplificatore *m* di segnale; (*also*: **booster rocket**) razzo vettore; (*Med*) richiamo

booster seat N (*Aut: for children*) seggiolino di sicurezza

boot [buːt] N stivale *m*; (*ankle boot*) stivaletto; (*for hiking*) scarpone *m* da montagna; (*for football etc*) scarpa; (*Brit: of car*) portabagagli *m inv* ▶ VT (*Comput*) inizializzare; **to ~** (*in addition*) per giunta, in più; **to give sb the ~** (*col*) mettere qn alla porta

booth [buːð] N (*at fair*) baraccone *m*; (*of cinema, telephone etc*) cabina; (*also*: **voting booth**) cabina (elettorale)

bootleg ['buːtleg] ADJ di contrabbando; **~ record** registrazione *f* pirata *inv*

booty ['buːtɪ] N bottino

booze [buːz] (*col*) N alcool *m* ▶ VI trincare

boozer ['buːzər] N (*col: person*) beone *m*; (*Brit col: pub*) osteria

border ['bɔːdər] N orlo; margine *m*; (*of a country*) frontiera; (*for flowers*) aiuola (laterale) ▶ VT (*road*) costeggiare; **the B~** *la frontiera tra l'Inghilterra e la Scozia*; **the Borders** *la zona di confine tra l'Inghilterra e la Scozia*
▶ **border on** VT FUS confinare con

borderline ['bɔːdəlaɪn] N (*fig*) linea di demarcazione ▶ ADJ: **~ case** caso limite; **on the ~** incerto(-a)

bore [bɔːr] PT *of* **bear** ▶ VT (*hole*) scavare; (*person*) annoiare ▶ N (*person*) seccatore(-trice); (*of gun*) calibro

bored ADJ annoiato(-a); **to be ~** annoiarsi; **he's ~ to tears** *or* **~ to death** *or* **~ stiff** è annoiato a morte, si annoia da morire

boredom ['bɔːdəm] N noia

boring ['bɔːrɪŋ] ADJ noioso(-a)

born [bɔːn] ADJ: **to be ~** nascere; **I was ~ in 1960** sono nato nel 1960; **~ blind** cieco dalla nascita; **a ~ comedian** un comico nato

born-again [bɔːnə'gɛn] ADJ: **~ Christian** convertito(-a) alla chiesa evangelica

borne [bɔːn] PP *of* **bear**

Borneo ['bɔːnɪəu] N Borneo

borough ['bʌrə] N comune *m*

borrow ['bɔrəu] VT: **to ~ sth (from sb)** prendere in prestito qc (da qn); **may I ~ your car?** può prestarmi la macchina?

borrower ['bɔrəuər] N (*gen*) chi prende a prestito; (*Econ*) mutuatario(-a)

borrowing ['bɔrəuɪŋ] N prestito

borstal ['bɔːstl] N (*Brit*) riformatorio

Bosnia ['bɔznɪə] N Bosnia

Bosnia-Herzegovina
['bɔznɪəhɛrtsə'gəuviːnə] N (*also*: **Bosnia-Hercegovina**) Bosnia-Erzegovina

Bosnian ['bɔznɪən] ADJ, N bosniaco(-a)

bosom ['buzəm] N petto; (*fig*) seno

bosom friend N amico(-a) del cuore

boss [bɔs] N capo ▶ VT (*also*: **boss about** *or* **around**) comandare a bacchetta; **stop bossing everyone about!** smettila di dare ordini a tutti!

bossy ['bɔsɪ] ADJ prepotente

bosun ['bəusn] N nostromo

botanical [bə'tænɪkl] ADJ botanico(-a)

botanist ['bɔtənɪst] N botanico(-a)

botany ['bɔtənɪ] N botanica

botch [bɔtʃ] VT fare un pasticcio di

both [bəuθ] ADJ entrambi(-e), tutt'e due
▶ PRON: **~ of them** entrambi(-e) ▶ ADV: **they sell ~ meat and poultry** vendono insieme la carne ed il pollame; **~ of us went, we ~ went** ci siamo andati tutt'e due

bother ['bɔðər] VT (*worry*) preoccupare; (*annoy*) infastidire ▶ VI (*gen: also*: **bother o.s.**) preoccuparsi ▶ N: **it is a ~ to have to do** è una seccatura dover fare ▶ EXCL uffa!, accidenti!; **it was no ~** non c'era problema; **to ~ doing sth** darsi la pena di fare qc; **I'm sorry to ~ you** mi dispiace disturbarla; **please don't ~** non si scomodi; **it's no ~** non c'è problema

Botswana [bɔt'swɑːnə] N Botswana *m*

bottle ['bɔtl] N bottiglia; (*of perfume, shampoo etc*) flacone *m*; (*baby's*) biberon *m inv* ▶ VT imbottigliare; **~ of wine/milk** bottiglia di vino/latte; **wine/milk ~** bottiglia da vino/del latte
▶ **bottle up** VT contenere

bottle bank N contenitore *m* per la raccolta del vetro

bottle-fed ['bɔtlfɛd] ADJ allattato(-a) artificialmente

bottleneck ['bɔtlnɛk] N ingorgo

bottle-opener ['bɔtləupnər] N apribottiglie *m inv*

bottom ['bɔtəm] N fondo; (*of mountain, tree, hill*) piedi *mpl*; (*buttocks*) sedere *m* ▶ ADJ più basso(-a), ultimo(-a); **at the ~ of** in fondo a; **to get to the ~ of sth** (*fig*) andare al fondo di *or* in fondo a qc

bottomless ['bɔtəmlɪs] ADJ senza fondo

bottom line N: **the ~ is ...** in ultima analisi ....

botulism ['bɔtjulɪzəm] N botulismo

bough [bau] N ramo

bought [bɔːt] PT, PP *of* **buy**

boulder ['bəuldər] N masso (tondeggiante)

boulevard ['buːlvɑːd] N viale *m*

bounce [bauns] VI (*ball*) rimbalzare; (*cheque*) essere restituito(-a) ▶ VT far rimbalzare ▶ N (*rebound*) rimbalzo; **to ~ in** entrare di slancio *or* con foga; **he's got plenty of ~** (*fig*) è molto esuberante

bouncer ['baunsə^r] (col) N buttafuori m inv
bouncy castle® ['baunsɪ-] N grande castello gonfiabile per giocare
bound [baund] PT, PP of **bind** ▶ N (gen pl) limite m; (leap) salto ▶ VI saltare ▶ VT (leap) saltare; (limit) delimitare ▶ ADJ: **~ by law** obbligato(-a) per legge; **to be ~ to do sth** (obliged) essere costretto(-a) a fare qc; **he's ~ to fail** (likely) fallirà di certo; **~ for** diretto(-a) a; **out of bounds** il cui accesso è vietato
boundary ['baundrɪ] N confine m
boundless ['baundlɪs] ADJ illimitato(-a)
bountiful ['bauntɪful] ADJ (person) munifico(-a); (God) misericordioso(-a); (supply) abbondante
bounty ['bauntɪ] N (generosity) liberalità, munificenza; (reward) taglia
bounty hunter N cacciatore m di taglie
bouquet ['bukeɪ] N bouquet m inv
bourbon ['buəbən] N (US: also: **bourbon whiskey**) bourbon m inv
bourgeois ['buəʒwa:] ADJ, N borghese (mf)
bout [baut] N periodo; (of malaria etc) attacco m; (Boxing etc) incontro
boutique [bu:'ti:k] N boutique f inv
bow¹ [bəu] N nodo; (weapon) arco; (Mus) archetto
bow² [bau] N (with body) inchino; (Naut: also: **bows**) prua ▶ VI inchinarsi; (yield): **to ~ to** or **before** sottomettersi a; **to ~ to the inevitable** rassegnarsi all'inevitabile
bowels [bauəlz] NPL intestini mpl; (fig) viscere fpl
bowl [bəul] N (for eating) scodella; (for washing) bacino; (ball) boccia; (of pipe) fornello; (US: stadium) stadio ▶ VI (Cricket) servire (la palla); see also **bowls**
  ▶ **bowl over** VT (fig) sconcertare
bow-legged ['bəu'lɛgɪd] ADJ dalle gambe storte
bowler ['bəulə^r] N giocatore m di bocce; (Cricket) lanciatore m; (BRIT: also: **bowler hat**) bombetta
bowling ['bəulɪŋ] N (game) gioco delle bocce; bowling m
bowling alley N pista da bowling
bowling green N campo di bocce
bowls [bəulz] N gioco delle bocce
bow tie N cravatta a farfalla
box [bɔks] N scatola; (also: **cardboard box**) (scatola di) cartone m; (crate: also for money) cassetta; (Theat) palco; (BRIT Aut) area d'incrocio ▶ VI fare pugilato ▶ VT mettere in (una) scatola, inscatolare; (Sport) combattere contro
boxer ['bɔksə^r] N (person) pugile m; (dog) boxer m inv
boxer shorts ['bɔksəʃɔ:ts] NPL boxer; **a pair of ~** un paio di boxer

boxing ['bɔksɪŋ] N (Sport) pugilato
Boxing Day N (BRIT) ≈ Santo Stefano; vedi nota
  Il Boxing Day è un giorno di festa e cade in genere il 26 dicembre. Prende il nome dall'usanza di donare pacchi regalo natalizi, un tempo chiamati Christmas boxes, a fornitori e dipendenti.
boxing gloves NPL guantoni mpl da pugile
boxing ring N ring m inv
box number N (for advertisements) casella
box office N biglietteria
box room N ripostiglio
boy [bɔɪ] N ragazzo; (small) bambino; (son) figlio; (servant) servo
boy band N gruppo pop di soli ragazzi maschi creato per far presa su un pubblico giovane
boycott ['bɔɪkɔt] N boicottaggio ▶ VT boicottare
boyfriend ['bɔɪfrɛnd] N ragazzo
boyish ['bɔɪɪʃ] ADJ di or da ragazzo
bp ABBR = **bishop**
bra [bra:] N reggipetto, reggiseno
brace [breɪs] N sostegno; (on teeth) apparecchio correttore; (tool) trapano; (Typ: also: **brace bracket**) graffa ▶ VT rinforzare, sostenere; **to ~ o.s.** (fig) farsi coraggio; see also **braces**
bracelet ['breɪslɪt] N braccialetto
braces ['breɪsɪz] NPL (BRIT) bretelle fpl
bracing ['breɪsɪŋ] ADJ invigorante
bracken ['brækən] N felce f
bracket ['brækɪt] N (Tech) mensola; (group) gruppo; (Typ) parentesi f inv ▶ VT mettere fra parentesi; (fig: also: **bracket together**) mettere insieme; **in brackets** tra parentesi; **round/square brackets** parentesi tonde/ quadre; **income ~** fascia di reddito
brackish ['brækɪʃ] ADJ (water) salmastro(-a)
brag [bræg] VI vantarsi
braid [breɪd] N (trimming) passamano; (of hair) treccia
Braille [breɪl] N braille m
brain [breɪn] N cervello; **brains** NPL (intelligence) cervella fpl; **he's got brains** è intelligente
brainchild ['breɪntʃaɪld] N creatura, creazione f
braindead ['breɪndɛd] ADJ (Med) che ha subito morte cerebrale; (col) cerebroleso(-a), deficiente
brainless ['breɪnlɪs] ADJ deficiente, stupido(-a)
brainstorm ['breɪnstɔ:m] N (fig) attacco di pazzia; (US) = **brainwave**
brainwash ['breɪnwɔʃ] VT fare un lavaggio di cervello a
brainwave ['breɪnweɪv] N lampo di genio
brainy ['breɪnɪ] ADJ intelligente
braise [breɪz] VT brasare

455

brake [breɪk] N (*on vehicle*) freno ▶ VT, VI frenare

brake light N (fanalino dello) stop *m inv*

brake pedal N pedale *m* del freno

bramble ['bræmbl] N rovo; (*fruit*) mora

bran [bræn] N crusca

branch [brɑːntʃ] N ramo; (*Comm*) succursale *f*, filiale *f*
  ▶ **branch off** VI diramarsi
  ▶ **branch out** VI: **to ~ out into** intraprendere una nuova attività nel ramo di

branch line N (*Rail*) linea secondaria

branch manager N direttore *m* di filiale

brand [brænd] N marca; (*fig*) tipo ▶ VT (*cattle*) marcare (a ferro rovente); (*fig: pej*): **to ~ sb a communist** *etc* definire qn come comunista *etc*

brandish ['brændɪʃ] VT brandire

brand name N marca

brand-new ['brænd'njuː] ADJ nuovo(-a) di zecca

brandy ['brændɪ] N brandy *m inv*

brash [bræʃ] ADJ sfacciato(-a)

Brasilia [brə'zɪljə] N Brasilia

brass [brɑːs] N ottone *m*; **the ~** (*Mus*) gli ottoni

brass band N fanfara

brassière ['bræsɪəʳ] N reggipetto, reggiseno

brass tacks NPL: **to get down to ~** (*col*) venire al sodo

brat [bræt] N (*pej*) marmocchio, monello(-a)

bravado [brə'vɑːdəu] N spavalderia

brave [breɪv] ADJ coraggioso(-a) ▶ N guerriero *m* pellerossa *inv* ▶ VT affrontare

bravery ['breɪvərɪ] N coraggio

bravo [brɑː'vəu] EXCL bravo!, bene!

brawl [brɔːl] N rissa ▶ VI azzuffarsi

brawn [brɔːn] N muscolo; (*meat*) carne *f* di testa di maiale

brawny ['brɔːnɪ] ADJ muscoloso(-a)

bray [breɪ] N raglio ▶ VI ragliare

brazen ['breɪzn] ADJ svergognato(-a) ▶ VT: **~ it out** fare lo sfacciato

brazier ['breɪzɪəʳ] N braciere *m*

Brazil [brə'zɪl] N Brasile *m*

Brazilian [brə'zɪljən] ADJ, N brasiliano(-a)

Brazil nut N noce *f* del Brasile

breach [briːtʃ] VT aprire una breccia in ▶ N (*gap*) breccia, varco; (*estrangement*) rottura; (*of duty*) abuso; (*breaking*): **~ of contract** rottura di contratto; **~ of the peace** violazione *f* dell'ordine pubblico; **~ of trust** abuso di fiducia

bread [brɛd] N pane *m*; (*col: money*) grana; **to earn one's daily ~** guadagnarsi il pane; **to know which side one's ~ is buttered on** saper fare i propri interessi; **~ and butter** *n* pane e burro; (*fig*) mezzi *mpl* di sussistenza

breadbin ['brɛdbɪn] N (*BRIT*) cassetta *f* portapane *inv*

breadboard ['brɛdbɔːd] N tagliere *m* (*per il pane*); (*Comput*) pannello per esperimenti

breadbox ['brɛdbɔks] N (*US*) cassetta *f* portapane *inv*

breadcrumbs ['brɛdkrʌmz] NPL briciole *fpl*; (*Culin*) pangrattato

breadline ['brɛdlaɪn] N: **to be on the ~** avere appena denaro per vivere

breadth [brɛtθ] N larghezza; (*fig: of knowledge etc*) ampiezza

breadwinner ['brɛdwɪnəʳ] N chi guadagna il pane per tutta la famiglia

break [breɪk] (*pt* **broke**, *pp* **broken**) VT rompere; (*law*) violare; (*promise*) mancare a ▶ VI rompersi; (*storm*) scoppiare; (*weather*) cambiare; (*dawn*) spuntare; (*news*) saltare fuori ▶ N (*gap*) breccia; (*fracture*) rottura; (*rest, also Scol*) intervallo; (*: short*) pausa; (*chance*) possibilità *f inv*; (*holiday*) vacanza; **to ~ one's leg** *etc* rompersi la gamba *etc*; **to ~ a record** battere un primato; **to ~ the news to sb** comunicare per primo la notizia a qn; **to ~ with sb** (*fig*) rompere con qn; **to ~ even** *vi* coprire le spese; **to ~ free** *or* **loose** liberarsi; **without a ~** senza una pausa; **to have** *or* **take a ~** (*few minutes*) fare una pausa; (*holiday*) prendere un po' di riposo; **a lucky ~** un colpo di fortuna
  ▶ **break down** VT (*figures, data*) analizzare; (*door etc*) buttare giù, abbattere; (*resistance*) stroncare ▶ VI crollare; (*Med*) avere un esaurimento (nervoso); (*Aut*) guastarsi
  ▶ **break in** VT (*horse etc*) domare ▶ VI (*burglar*) fare irruzione
  ▶ **break into** VT FUS (*house*) fare irruzione in
  ▶ **break off** VI (*speaker*) interrompersi; (*branch*) troncarsi ▶ VT (*talks, engagement*) rompere
  ▶ **break open** VT (*door etc*) sfondare
  ▶ **break out** VI evadere; **to ~ out in spots** coprirsi di macchie
  ▶ **break through** VI: **the sun broke through** il sole ha fatto capolino tra le nuvole ▶ VT (*defences, barrier*) sfondare, penetrare in; (*crowd*) aprirsi un varco in *or* tra, aprirsi un passaggio in *or* tra
  ▶ **break up** VI (*partnership*) sciogliersi; (*friends*) separarsi; **the line's** *or* **you're breaking up** la linea è disturbata ▶ VT fare in pezzi, spaccare; (*fight etc*) interrompere, far cessare; (*marriage*) finire

breakable ['breɪkəbl] ADJ fragile; **breakables** NPL oggetti *mpl* fragili

breakage ['breɪkɪdʒ] N rottura; **to pay for breakages** pagare i danni

breakaway ['breɪkəweɪ] ADJ (*group etc*) scissionista, dissidente

break-dancing ['breɪkdɑ:nsɪŋ] N breakdance f
breakdown ['breɪkdaun] N (Aut) guasto; (in communications) interruzione f; (of marriage) rottura; (Med: also: **nervous breakdown**) esaurimento nervoso; (of payments, statistics etc) resoconto
breakdown service N (BRIT) servizio riparazioni
breakdown truck, breakdown van N carro m attrezzi inv
breakdown van N see **breakdown truck**
breaker ['breɪkəʳ] N frangente m
breakeven ['breɪk'i:vn] CPD: **~ chart** diagramma m del punto di rottura or pareggio; **~ point** punto di rottura or pareggio
breakfast ['brɛkfəst] N colazione f
breakfast cereal N fiocchi mpl d'avena or di mais etc
break-in ['breɪkɪn] N irruzione f
breaking point ['breɪkɪŋ-] N punto di rottura
breakthrough ['breɪkθru:] N (Mil) breccia; (fig) passo avanti
break-up ['breɪkʌp] N (of partnership, marriage) rottura
break-up value N (Comm) valore m di realizzo
breakwater ['breɪkwɔ:təʳ] N frangiflutti m inv
breast [brɛst] N (of woman) seno; (chest, Culin) petto
breast-feed ['brɛstfi:d] VT, VI (irreg: like **feed**) allattare (al seno)
breast pocket N taschino
breast-stroke ['brɛststrəuk] N nuoto a rana
breath [brɛθ] N respiro; **out of ~** senza fiato; **to go out for a ~ of air** andare a prendere una boccata d'aria
Breathalyser® ['brɛθəlaɪzəʳ] (BRIT) N alcoltest m inv
breathe [bri:ð] VT, VI respirare; **I won't ~ a word about it** non fiaterò
▶ **breathe in** VI inspirare ▶ VT respirare
▶ **breathe out** VT, VI espirare
breather ['bri:ðəʳ] N attimo di respiro
breathing ['bri:ðɪŋ] N respiro, respirazione f
breathing space N (fig) attimo di respiro
breathless ['brɛθlɪs] ADJ senza fiato; (with excitement) con il fiato sospeso
breath-taking ['brɛθteɪkɪŋ] ADJ mozzafiato inv
breath test N ≈ prova del palloncino
bred [brɛd] PT, PP of **breed**
-bred [brɛd] SUFFIX: **to be well-/ill-** essere ben educato(-a)/maleducato(-a)
breed [bri:d] (pt, pp **bred**) VT allevare; (fig: hate, suspicion) generare, provocare ▶ VI riprodursi ▶ N razza; (type, class) varietà f inv
breeder ['bri:dəʳ] N (Physics: also: **breeder**

reactor) reattore m autofertilizzante
breeding ['bri:dɪŋ] N riproduzione f; allevamento
breeze [bri:z] N brezza
breeze block N (BRIT) mattone composto di scorie di coke
breezy ['bri:zɪ] ADJ (day) ventilato(-a); (person) allegro(-a)
Breton ['brɛtən] ADJ, N bretone (mf)
brevity ['brɛvɪtɪ] N brevità
brew [bru:] VT (tea) fare un infuso di; (beer) fare; (plot) tramare ▶ VI (tea) essere in infusione; (beer) essere in fermentazione; (storm, fig: trouble etc) prepararsi
brewer ['bru:əʳ] N birraio
brewery ['bru:ərɪ] N fabbrica di birra
briar ['braɪəʳ] N (thorny bush) rovo; (wild rose) rosa selvatica
bribe [braɪb] N bustarella ▶ VT comprare; **to ~ sb to do sth** pagare qn sottobanco perché faccia qc
bribery ['braɪbərɪ] N corruzione f
bric-a-brac ['brɪkəbræk] N bric-a-brac m
brick [brɪk] N mattone m
bricklayer ['brɪkleɪəʳ] N muratore m
brickwork ['brɪkwə:k] N muratura in mattoni
brickworks ['brɪkwə:ks] N fabbrica di mattoni
bridal ['braɪdl] ADJ nuziale; **~ party** corteo nuziale
bride [braɪd] N sposa
bridegroom ['braɪdgru:m] N sposo
bridesmaid ['braɪdzmeɪd] N damigella d'onore
bridge [brɪdʒ] N ponte m; (Naut) ponte di comando; (of nose) dorso; (Cards, Dentistry) bridge m inv ▶ VT (river) fare un ponte sopra; (fig: gap) colmare
bridging loan ['brɪdʒɪŋ-] N (BRIT) anticipazione f sul mutuo
bridle ['braɪdl] N briglia ▶ VT tenere a freno; (horse) mettere la briglia a ▶ VI (in anger etc) adombrarsi, adontarsi
bridle path N sentiero (per cavalli)
brief [bri:f] ADJ breve ▶ N (Law) comparsa; (gen) istruzioni fpl ▶ VT (Mil etc) dare istruzioni a; **in ~ ...** in breve ..., a farla breve ...; **to ~ sb (about sth)** mettere qn al corrente (di qc); see also **briefs**
briefcase ['bri:fkeɪs] N cartella
briefing ['bri:fɪŋ] N istruzioni fpl, briefing m inv
briefly ['bri:flɪ] ADV (speak, visit, explain, say) brevemente; (glimpse, glance) di sfuggita
briefness ['bri:fnɪs] N brevità
briefs [bri:fs] NPL mutande fpl
Brig. ABBR = **brigadier**
brigade [brɪ'geɪd] N (Mil) brigata

brigadier [brɪgə'dɪəʳ] N generale m di brigata

bright [braɪt] ADJ luminoso(-a); (person) sveglio(-a); (colour) vivace; **to look on the ~ side** vedere il lato positivo delle cose

brighten ['braɪtn], **brighten up** VT (room) rendere luminoso(-a); rallegrare ► VI schiarirsi; (person) rallegrarsi

brightly ['braɪtlɪ] ADV (shine) vivamente, intensamente; (smile) radiosamente; (talk) con animazione

brill [brɪl] EXCL (BRIT col) stupendo!, fantastico!

brilliance ['brɪljəns] N splendore m; (fig: of person) genialità, talento

brilliant ['brɪljənt] ADJ brillante; (sunshine) sfolgorante; (light, smile) radioso(-a); (col) splendido(-a)

brim [brɪm] N orlo

brimful ['brɪm'ful] ADJ pieno(-a) or colmo(-a) fino all'orlo; (fig) pieno(-a)

brine [braɪn] N acqua salmastra; (Culin) salamoia

bring [brɪŋ] (pt, pp **brought** [brɔːt]) VT portare; **to ~ sth to an end** mettere fine a qc; **I can't ~ myself to sack him** non so risolvermi a licenziarlo

► **bring about** VT causare

► **bring back** VT riportare

► **bring down** VT (lower) far scendere; (shoot down) abbattere; (government) far cadere

► **bring forward** VT portare avanti; (in time) anticipare; (Book-keeping) riportare

► **bring in** VT (person) far entrare; (object) portare; (Pol: bill) presentare; (: legislation) introdurre; (Law: verdict) emettere; (produce: income) rendere

► **bring off** VT (task, plan) portare a compimento; (deal) concludere

► **bring on** VT (illness, attack) causare, provocare; (player, substitute) far scendere in campo

► **bring out** VT (meaning) mettere in evidenza; (new product) lanciare; (book) pubblicare, fare uscire

► **bring round**, **bring to** VT (unconscious person) far rinvenire

► **bring up** VT allevare; (question) introdurre

brink [brɪŋk] N orlo; **on the ~ of doing sth** sul punto di fare qc; **she was on the ~ of tears** era lì lì per piangere

brisk [brɪsk] ADJ (person, tone) spiccio(-a), sbrigativo(-a); (: abrupt) brusco(-a); (wind) fresco(-a); (trade etc) vivace, attivo(-a); (pace) svelto(-a); **to go for a ~ walk** fare una camminata di buon passo; **business is ~** gli affari vanno bene

bristle ['brɪsl] N setola ► VI rizzarsi; **bristling with** irto(-a) di

bristly ['brɪslɪ] ADJ (chin) ispido(-a); (beard, hair) irsuto(-a), setoloso(-a)

Brit [brɪt] N ABBR (col: = British person) britannico(-a)

Britain ['brɪtən] N (also: **Great Britain**) Gran Bretagna

British ['brɪtɪʃ] ADJ britannico(-a); **the British** NPL i Britannici; **the ~ Isles** npl le Isole Britanniche

British Summer Time N ora legale (in Gran Bretagna)

Briton ['brɪtən] N britannico(-a)

Brittany ['brɪtənɪ] N Bretagna

brittle ['brɪtl] ADJ fragile

Br(o) ABBR (Rel) = **brother**

broach [brəutʃ] VT (subject) affrontare

broad [brɔːd] ADJ largo(-a); (distinction) generale; (accent) spiccato(-a) ► N (US col) bellona; **~ hint** allusione f esplicita; **in ~ daylight** in pieno giorno; **the ~ outlines** le grandi linee

broadband ['brɔːdbænd] ADJ (Comput) a banda larga, ADSL ► N banda larga, ADSL m inv

broad bean N fava

broadcast ['brɔːdkɑːst] (pt, pp ~) N trasmissione f ► VT trasmettere per radio (or per televisione) ► VI fare una trasmissione

broadcaster ['brɔːdkɑːstəʳ] N annunciatore(-trice) radiotelevisivo(-a) (or radiofonico(-a)

broadcasting ['brɔːdkɑːstɪŋ] N radiodiffusione f; televisione f

broadcasting station N stazione f trasmittente

broaden ['brɔːdn] VT allargare ► VI allargarsi

broadly ['brɔːdlɪ] ADV (fig) in generale

broad-minded ['brɔːd'maɪndɪd] ADJ di mente aperta

broadsheet ['brɔːdʃiːt] N (BRIT) giornale m (si contrappone al tabloid che è di formato più piccolo)

broccoli ['brɔkəlɪ] N (Bot) broccolo; (Culin) broccoli mpl

brochure ['brəuʃjuəʳ] N dépliant m inv

brogue [brəug] N (shoe) scarpa rozza in cuoio; (accent) accento irlandese

broil [brɔɪl] VT cuocere a fuoco vivo

broiler ['brɔɪləʳ] (US) N (grill) griglia

broke [brəuk] PT of **break** ► ADJ (col) squattrinato(-a); **to go ~** fare fallimento

broken ['brəukən] PP of **break** ► ADJ (gen) rotto(-a); (stick, promise, vow) spezzato(-a); (marriage) fallito(-a); **a ~ leg** una gamba rotta; **he comes from a ~ home** i suoi sono divisi; **in ~ French/English** in un francese/ inglese stentato

broken-down ['brəukən'daun] ADJ (car) in panne, rotto(-a); (machine) guasto(-a), fuori uso; (house) abbandonato(-a), in rovina

broken-hearted ['brəukən'hɑ:tɪd] ADJ: **to be ~** avere il cuore spezzato

broker ['brəukə'] N agente m

brokerage ['brəukərɪdʒ] N (Comm) commissione f di intermediazione

brolly ['brɒlɪ] N (BRIT col) ombrello

bronchitis [brɒŋ'kaɪtɪs] N bronchite f

bronze [brɒnz] N bronzo

bronzed [brɒnzd] ADJ abbronzato(-a)

brooch [brəutʃ] N spilla

brood [bru:d] N covata ▶ VI (hen) covare; (person) rimuginare

broody ['bru:dɪ] ADJ (fig) cupo(-a) e taciturno(-a)

brook [bruk] N ruscello

broom [brum] N scopa; (Bot) ginestra

broomstick ['brumstɪk] N manico di scopa

Bros. ABBR (Comm: = brothers) F.lli (= Fratelli)

broth [brɒθ] N brodo

brothel ['brɒθl] N bordello

brother ['brʌðə'] N fratello

brotherhood ['brʌðəhud] N fratellanza; confraternita f inv

brother-in-law ['brʌðərɪnlɔ:] N cognato

brotherly ['brʌðəlɪ] ADJ fraterno(-a)

brought [brɔ:t] PT, PP of **bring**

brought forward ADJ (Comm) riportato(-a)

brow [brau] N fronte f; (rare, gen: also: **eyebrow**) sopracciglio; (of hill) cima

browbeat ['braubi:t] VT (irreg: like **beat**) intimidire

brown [braun] ADJ bruno(-a), marrone; (hair) castano(-a); (tanned) abbronzato(-a) ▶ N (colour) color m bruno or marrone ▶ VT (Culin) rosolare; **to go ~** (person) abbronzarsi; (leaves) ingiallire

brown bread N pane m integrale, pane nero

Brownie ['braunɪ] N giovane esploratrice f

brown paper N carta da pacchi or da imballaggio

brown rice N riso greggio

brown sugar N zucchero greggio

browse [brauz] VI (animal) brucare; (in bookshop etc) curiosare; (Comput) navigare (in Internet); ▶ VT: **to ~ the web** navigare in Internet ▶ N: **to have a ~ (around)** dare un'occhiata (in giro); **to ~ through a book** sfogliare un libro

browser [brauzə'] N (Comput) browser m inv

bruise [bru:z] N ammaccatura; (on person) livido ▶ VT ammaccare; (one's leg etc) farsi un livido a; (fig: feelings) urtare ▶ VI (fruit) ammaccarsi

Brum [brʌm], **Brummagem** ['brʌmədʒəm] N (col) = **Birmingham**

Brummie ['brʌmɪ] N (BRIT col) abitante mf di Birmingham, originario(-a) di Birmingham

brunch [brʌntʃ] N ricca colazione consumata in tarda mattinata

brunette [bru:'nɛt] N bruna

brunt [brʌnt] N: **the ~ of** (attack, criticism etc) il peso maggiore di

brush [brʌʃ] N spazzola; (for painting, shaving) pennello; (quarrel) schermaglia ▶ VT spazzolare; (also: **brush past, brush against**) sfiorare; **to have a ~ with sb** (verbally) avere uno scontro con qn; (physically) venire a diverbio or alle mani con qn; **to have a ~ with the police** avere delle noie con la polizia
▶ **brush aside** VT scostare
▶ **brush up** VT (knowledge) rinfrescare

brushed [brʌʃt] ADJ (Tech: steel, chrome etc) sabbiato(-a); (nylon, denim etc) pettinato(-a)

brush-off ['brʌʃɒf] N: **to give sb the ~** dare il ben servito a qn

brushwood ['brʌʃwud] N macchia

brusque [bru:sk] ADJ (person, manner) brusco(-a); (tone) secco(-a)

Brussels ['brʌslz] N Bruxelles f

Brussels sprout [-spraut] N cavolo di Bruxelles

brutal ['bru:tl] ADJ brutale

brutality [bru:'tælɪtɪ] N brutalità

brutalize ['bru:təlaɪz] VT (harden) abbrutire; (ill-treat) brutalizzare

brute [bru:t] N bestia; **by ~ force** con la forza, a viva forza

brutish ['bru:tɪʃ] ADJ da bruto

BS N ABBR (US: = Bachelor of Science) titolo di studio

bs ABBR = **bill of sale**

BSA N ABBR (US) = **Boy Scouts of America**

BSc N ABBR (Univ) = **Bachelor of Science**

BSE N ABBR (= bovine spongiform encephalopathy) encefalite f bovina spongiforme

BSI N ABBR (= British Standards Institution) associazione per la normalizzazione

BST ABBR (= British Summer Time) ora legale

Bt. ABBR (BRIT) = **baronet**

btu N ABBR (= British thermal unit) Btu m (= 1054.2 joules)

bubble ['bʌbl] N bolla ▶ VI ribollire; (sparkle: fig) essere effervescente

bubble bath N bagno m schiuma inv

bubble gum N gomma americana

bubble jet printer ['bʌbldʒet-] N stampante f a getto d'inchiostro

bubbly ['bʌblɪ] ADJ (also fig) frizzante ▶ N (col: champagne) spumante m

Bucharest [bu:kə'rɛst] N Bucarest f

buck [bʌk] N maschio (di camoscio, caprone, coniglio ecc); (US col) dollaro ▶ VI sgroppare; **to pass the ~ (to sb)** scaricare (su di qn) la propria responsabilità
▶ **buck up** VI (cheer up) rianimarsi ▶ VT: **to ~ one's ideas up** mettere la testa a partito

bucket ['bʌkɪt] N secchio ▶ VI (BRIT col): **the rain is bucketing (down)** piove a catinelle

459

Buckingham Palace ['bʌkɪŋəm-] N *vedi nota*

> Buckingham Palace è la residenza ufficiale a Londra del sovrano britannico. Costruita nel 1703 per il duca di Buckingham, fu acquistata nel 1762 dal re Giorgio III e ricostruita tra il 1821 e il 1838 sotto la guida dell'architetto John Nash. All'inizio del Novecento alcune sue parti sono state ulteriormente modificate.

buckle ['bʌkl] N fibbia ▶ VT allacciare; (*warp*) deformare ▶ VI (*wheel etc*) piegarsi
  ▶ **buckle down** VI mettersi sotto
Bucks [bʌks] ABBR (*BRIT*) = **Buckinghamshire**
bud [bʌd] N gemma; (*of flower*) bocciolo ▶ VI germogliare; (*flower*) sbocciare
Budapest [bju:də'pest] N Budapest f
Buddha ['budə] N Budda m
Buddhism ['budɪzəm] N buddismo
Buddhist ['budɪst] ADJ, N buddista (*mf*)
budding ['bʌdɪŋ] ADJ (*flower*) in boccio; (*poet etc*) in erba
buddy ['bʌdɪ] N (*US*) compagno
budge [bʌdʒ] VT scostare; (*fig*) smuovere
  ▶ VI spostarsi; smuoversi
budgerigar ['bʌdʒərɪgɑ:ʳ] N pappagallino
budget ['bʌdʒɪt] N bilancio preventivo ▶ VI:
  to ~ for sth fare il bilancio per qc; **I'm on a tight ~** devo contare la lira; **she works out her ~ every month** fa il preventivo delle spese ogni mese
budgie ['bʌdʒɪ] N = **budgerigar**
Buenos Aires ['bweɪnɔs'aɪrɪz] N Buenos Aires f
buff [bʌf] ADJ color camoscio *inv* ▶ N (*col: enthusiast*) appassionato(-a)
buffalo ['bʌfələu] (*pl ~ or* **buffaloes**) N bufalo; (*US*) bisonte m
buffer ['bʌfəʳ] N respingente m; (*Comput*) memoria tampone, buffer m *inv* ▶ VI (*Comput*) fare il buffering, trasferire nella memoria tampone
buffering ['bʌfərɪŋ] N buffering m *inv*, trasferimento nella memoria tampone
buffer state N stato cuscinetto
buffer zone N zona f cuscinetto *inv*
buffet N ['bufeɪ] (*food, BRIT: bar*) buffet m *inv*
  ▶ VT ['bʌfɪt] sferzare; urtare
buffet car N (*BRIT Rail*) ≈ servizio ristoro
buffet lunch N pranzo in piedi
buffoon [bə'fu:n] N buffone m
bug [bʌg] N (*insect*) cimice f; (*: gen*) insetto; (*fig: germ*) virus m *inv*; (*spy device*) microfono spia; (*Comput*) bug m *inv*, errore m nel programma ▶ VT mettere sotto controllo; (*room*) installare microfoni spia in; (*annoy*) scocciare; **I've got the travel ~** (*fig*) mi è presa la mania dei viaggi
bugbear ['bʌgbɛəʳ] N spauracchio
bugger ['bʌgəʳ] (*col!*) N bastardo (!)

> ▶ VI: **~ off!** vaffanculo! (!) ▶ VT: **~ (it)!** merda! (!)

buggy ['bʌgɪ] N (*baby buggy*) passeggino
bugle ['bju:gl] N tromba
build [bɪld] (*pt, pp* **built**) N (*of person*) corporatura ▶ VT costruire
  ▶ **build on** VT FUS (*fig*) prendere il via da
  ▶ **build up** VT (*establish: business*) costruire; (*: reputation*) fare, consolidare; (*increase: production*) allargare, incrementare; **don't ~ your hopes up too soon** non sperarci troppo
builder ['bɪldəʳ] N costruttore m
building ['bɪldɪŋ] N costruzione f; edificio; (*also:* **building trade**) edilizia
building contractor N costruttore m, imprenditore m (edile)
building industry N industria edilizia
building site N cantiere m di costruzione
building society N *società immobiliare e finanziaria*; *vedi nota*

> Le *building societies* sono società immobiliari e finanziarie che forniscono anche numerosi servizi bancari ai clienti che vi investono i risparmi, e in particolare concedono mutui per l'acquisto della casa.

building trade N = **building industry**
build-up ['bɪldʌp] N (*of gas etc*) accumulo; (*publicity*): **to give sb/sth a good ~** fare buona pubblicità a qn/qc
built [bɪlt] PT, PP *of* **build**; **well-~** robusto(-a)
built-in ['bɪlt'ɪn] ADJ (*cupboard*) a muro; (*device*) incorporato(-a)
built-up area ['bɪltʌp-] N abitato
bulb [bʌlb] N (*Bot*) bulbo; (*Elec*) lampadina
bulbous ['bʌlbəs] ADJ bulboso(-a)
Bulgaria [bʌl'gɛərɪə] N Bulgaria
Bulgarian [bʌl'gɛərɪən] ADJ bulgaro(-a)
  ▶ N bulgaro(-a); (*Ling*) bulgaro
bulge [bʌldʒ] N rigonfiamento; (*in birth rate, sales*) punta ▶ VI essere protuberante *or* rigonfio(-a); **to be bulging with** essere pieno(-a) *or* zeppo(-a) di
bulimia [bə'lɪmɪə] N bulimia
bulimic [bju:'lɪmɪk] ADJ, N bulimico(-a)
bulk [bʌlk] N massa, volume m; **the ~ of** il grosso di; (**to buy**) **in ~** (comprare) in grande quantità; (*Comm*) (comprare) all'ingrosso
bulk buying N acquisto di merce in grande quantità
bulk carrier N grossa nave f da carico
bulkhead ['bʌlkhɛd] N paratia
bulky ['bʌlkɪ] ADJ grosso(-a); voluminoso(-a)
bull [bul] N toro; (*male elephant, whale*) maschio; (*Stock Exchange*) rialzista *mf*; (*Rel*) bolla (papale)
bulldog ['buldɔg] N bulldog m *inv*

bulldoze ['buldəuz] VT aprire or spianare col bulldozer; **I was bulldozed into doing it** (*fig: col*) mi ci hanno costretto con la prepotenza

bulldozer ['buldəuzə^r] N bulldozer *m inv*

bullet ['bulɪt] N pallottola

bulletin ['bulɪtɪn] N bollettino

bulletin board N (*Comput*) bulletin board *m inv*

bullet point N punto; **bullet points** elenco *sg* puntato

bullet-proof ['bulɪtpruːf] ADJ a prova di proiettile; **~ vest** giubbotto antiproiettile

bullfight ['bulfaɪt] N corrida

bullfighter ['bulfaɪtə^r] N torero

bullfighting ['bulfaɪtɪŋ] N tauromachia

bullion ['buljən] N oro or argento in lingotti

bullock ['bu:lək] N giovenco

bullring ['bulrɪŋ] N arena (per corride)

bull's-eye ['bulzaɪ] N centro del bersaglio

bullshit ['bulʃɪt] (*col!*) EXCL, N stronzate *fpl* (!)
▶ VI raccontare stronzate (!) ▶ VT raccontare stronzate a (!)

bully ['bulɪ] N prepotente *m* ▶ VT angariare; (*frighten*) intimidire

bullying ['bulɪŋ] N prepotenze *fpl*

bum [bʌm] N (*col: backside*) culo; (*tramp*) vagabondo(-a); (*US: idler*) fannullone(-a)
▶ **bum around** VI (*col*) fare il vagabondo

bumblebee ['bʌmblbiː] N (*Zool*) bombo

bumf [bʌmf] N (*col: forms etc*) scartoffie *fpl*

bump [bʌmp] N (*blow*) colpo; (*in car*) piccolo tamponamento; (*jolt*) scossa; (*noise*) botto; (*on road etc*) protuberanza; (*on head*) bernoccolo ▶ VT battere; (*car*) urtare, sbattere
▶ **bump along** VI procedere sobbalzando
▶ **bump into** VT FUS scontrarsi con; (*col: meet*) imbattersi in, incontrare per caso

bumper ['bʌmpə^r] N (*BRIT*) paraurti *m inv*
▶ ADJ: **~ harvest** raccolto eccezionale

bumper cars NPL (*US*) autoscontri *mpl*

bumph [bʌmf] N = **bumf**

bumptious ['bʌmpʃəs] ADJ presuntuoso(-a)

bumpy ['bʌmpɪ] ADJ (*road*) dissestato(-a); (*journey, flight*) movimentato(-a)

bun [bʌn] N focaccia; (*of hair*) crocchia

bunch [bʌntʃ] N (*of flowers, keys*) mazzo; (*of bananas*) casco; (*of people*) gruppo; **~ of grapes** grappolo d'uva; **bunches** NPL (*in hair*) codine *fpl*

bundle ['bʌndl] N fascio ▶ VT (*also: **bundle up***) legare in un fascio; (*put*): **to ~ sth/sb into** spingere qc/qn in
▶ **bundle off** VT (*person*) mandare via in gran fretta
▶ **bundle out** VT far uscire (senza tante cerimonie)

bun fight N (*BRIT col*) tè *m inv* (*ricevimento*)

bung [bʌŋ] N tappo ▶ VT (*BRIT: throw: also:* **bung into**) buttare; (*also:* **bung up***: pipe, hole*) tappare, otturare; **my nose is bunged up** (*col*) ho il naso otturato

bungalow ['bʌŋgələu] N bungalow *m inv*

bungee jumping ['bʌndʒiː'dʒʌmpɪŋ] N salto nel vuoto da ponti, grattacieli ecc con un cavo fissato alla caviglia

bungle ['bʌŋgl] VT abborracciare

bunion ['bʌnjən] N callo (al piede)

bunk [bʌŋk] N cuccetta
▶ **bunk off** VI (*BRIT col*): **to ~ off school** marinare la scuola; **I'll ~ off at 3 this afternoon** oggi me la filo dal lavoro alle 3

bunk beds NPL letti *mpl* a castello

bunker ['bʌŋkə^r] N (*coal store*) ripostiglio per il carbone; (*Mil, Golf*) bunker *m inv*

bunny ['bʌnɪ] N (*also:* **bunny rabbit***) coniglietto

bunny girl N coniglietta

bunny hill N (*US Ski*) pista per principianti

bunting ['bʌntɪŋ] N pavesi *mpl*, bandierine *fpl*

buoy [bɔɪ] N boa
▶ **buoy up** VT tenere a galla; (*fig*) sostenere

buoyancy ['bɔɪənsɪ] N (*of ship*) galleggiabilità

buoyant ['bɔɪənt] ADJ galleggiante; (*fig*) vivace; (*Comm: market*) sostenuto(-a); (*: prices, currency*) stabile

burden ['bəːdn] N carico, fardello ▶ VT caricare; (*oppress*) opprimere; **to ~ sb with** caricare qn di; **to be a ~ to sb** essere di peso a qn

bureau ['bjuərəu] (*pl* **bureaux** [-z]) N (*BRIT: writing desk*) scrivania; (*US: chest of drawers*) cassettone *m*; (*office*) ufficio, agenzia

bureaucracy [bjuə'rɔkrəsɪ] N burocrazia

bureaucrat ['bjuərəkræt] N burocrate *mf*

bureaucratic [bjuərə'krætɪk] ADJ burocratico(-a)

bureau de change [-də'ʃɑʒ] (*pl* **bureaux de change**) N cambiavalute *m inv*

bureaux [bjuə'rəuz] NPL *of* **bureau**

burgeon ['bəːdʒən] VI svilupparsi rapidamente

burger ['bəːgə^r] N hamburger *m inv*

burglar ['bəːglə^r] N scassinatore *m*

burglar alarm N (allarme *m*) antifurto *m inv*

burglarize ['bəːgləraɪz] VT (*US*) svaligiare

burglary ['bəːglərɪ] N furto con scasso

burgle ['bəːgl] VT svaligiare

Burgundy ['bəːgəndɪ] N Borgogna

burial ['berɪəl] N sepoltura

burial ground N cimitero

burly ['bəːlɪ] ADJ robusto(-a)

Burma ['bəːmə] N Birmania; *see* **Myanmar**

Burmese [bəː'miːz] ADJ birmano(-a) ▶ N (*pl inv*) birmano(-a); (*Ling*) birmano

burn [bəːn] (*pt, pp* **burned** *or* **burnt**) VT, VI bruciare ▶ N bruciatura, scottatura; (*Med*)

ustione f; **I've burnt myself!** mi sono
bruciato!; **the cigarette burnt a hole in
her dress** si è fatta un buco nel vestito con la
sigaretta
▸ **burn down** VT distruggere col fuoco
▸ **burn out** VT (writer etc): **to ~ o.s. out**
esaurirsi
burner ['bəːnəʳ] N fornello
burning ['bəːnɪŋ] ADJ (building, forest) in
fiamme; (sand) che scotta; (ambition)
bruciante; (issue, question) scottante
burnish ['bəːnɪʃ] VT brunire
Burns Night N vedi nota

Burns Night è la festa celebrata il 25
gennaio per commemorare il poeta
scozzese Robert Burns (1759–1796). Gli
scozzese festeggiano questa data con una
cena, Burns supper a base de haggis e whisky,
spesso al suono di una cornamusa
durante la cena vengono recitate le
poesie di Robert Burns e vengono letti
discorsi alla sua memoria.

burnt [bəːnt] PT, PP of **burn**
burnt sugar N (BRIT) caramello
burp [bəːp] (col) N rutto ▸ VI ruttare
burrow ['bʌrəu] N tana ▸ VT scavare
bursar ['bəːsəʳ] N economo(-a); (BRIT: student)
borsista mf
bursary ['bəːsərɪ] N (BRIT) borsa di studio
burst [bəːst] (pt, pp **~**) VT far scoppiare or
esplodere ▸ VI esplodere; (tyre) scoppiare ▸ N
scoppio; (also: **burst pipe**) rottura nel tubo,
perdita; **~ of energy/laughter** scoppio
d'energia/di risa; **a ~ of applause** uno
scroscio d'applausi; **a ~ of speed** uno scatto
(di velocità); **~ blood vessel** rottura di un
vaso sanguigno; **the river has ~ its banks** il
fiume ha rotto gli argini or ha straripato; **to
~ into flames/tears** scoppiare in fiamme/
lacrime; **to be bursting with** essere pronto
a scoppiare di; **to ~ out laughing** scoppiare
a ridere; **to ~ open** vi aprirsi
improvvisamente; (door) spalancarsi
▸ **burst into** VT FUS (room etc) irrompere in
▸ **burst out of** VT FUS precipitarsi fuori da
bury ['bɛrɪ] VT seppellire; **to ~ one's face in
one's hands** nascondere la faccia tra le
mani; **to ~ one's head in the sand** (fig) fare
(la politica del)lo struzzo; **to ~ the hatchet**
(fig) seppellire l'ascia di guerra
bus [bʌs] (pl **buses** ['bʌsɪz]) N autobus m inv
bus boy N (US) aiuto inv cameriere(-a)
bus conductor N autista mf (dell'autobus)
bush [buʃ] N cespuglio; (scrub land) macchia;
to beat about the ~ menare il cane per l'aia
bushed [buʃt] ADJ (col) distrutto(-a)
bushel ['buʃl] N staio
bushfire ['buʃfaɪəʳ] N grande incendio in aperta
campagna

bushy ['buʃɪ] ADJ (plant, tail, beard) folto(-a);
(eyebrows) irsuto(-a)
busily ['bɪzɪlɪ] ADV con impegno,
alacremente
business ['bɪznɪs] N (matter) affare m;
(trading) affari mpl; (firm) azienda; (job, duty)
lavoro; **to be away on ~** essere andato via
per affari; **I'm here on ~** sono qui per affari;
to do ~ with sb fare affari con qn; **he's in
the insurance ~** lavora nel campo delle
assicurazioni; **it's none of my ~** questo non
mi riguarda; **he means ~** non scherza
business address N indirizzo di lavoro or
d'ufficio
business card N biglietto da visita della
ditta
business class N (Aviat) business class f
businesslike ['bɪznɪslaɪk] ADJ serio(-a);
efficiente
businessman ['bɪznɪsmən] N (irreg) uomo
d'affari
business trip N viaggio d'affari
businesswoman ['bɪznɪswumən] N (irreg)
donna d'affari
busker ['bʌskəʳ] N (BRIT) suonatore(-trice)
ambulante
bus lane N (BRIT) corsia riservata agli autobus
bus pass N tessera dell'autobus
bus shelter N pensilina (alla fermata
dell'autobus)
bus station N stazione f delle corriere,
autostazione f
bus stop N fermata d'autobus
bust [bʌst] N (Art) busto; (Anat: bosom) seno
▸ ADJ (col: broken) rotto(-a) ▸ VT (col: Police:
arrest) pizzicare, beccare; **to go ~** fallire
bustle ['bʌsl] N movimento, attività ▸ VI
darsi da fare
bustling ['bʌslɪŋ] ADJ (person) indaffarato(-a);
(town) animato(-a)
bust-up ['bʌstʌp] N (BRIT col) lite f
busty ['bʌstɪ] ADJ (col) tettone(-a)
busy ['bɪzɪ] ADJ occupato(-a); (shop, street)
molto frequentato(-a) ▸ VT: **to ~ o.s.** darsi da
fare; **he's a ~ man** (normally) è un uomo
molto occupato; (temporarily) ha molto da
fare, è molto occupato
busybody ['bɪzɪbɔdɪ] N ficcanaso mf
busy signal N (US Tel) segnale m di occupato

(KEYWORD)

but [bʌt] CONJ ma; **I'd love to come, but I'm
busy** vorrei tanto venire, ma ho da fare
▸ PREP (apart from, except) eccetto, tranne,
meno; **nothing but** nient'altro che; **he was
nothing but trouble** non dava altro che
guai; **no-one but him** solo lui; **no-one but
him can do it** nessuno può farlo tranne lui;
the last but one (BRIT) il penultimo(-a);

but for you/your help se non fosse per te/per il tuo aiuto; **anything but that** tutto ma non questo; **anything but finished** tutt'altro che finito

▶ ADV (just, only) solo, soltanto; **she's but a child** è solo una bambina; **had I but known** se solo avessi saputo; **I can but try** tentar non nuoce; **all but finished** quasi finito

butane ['bju:teɪn] N (also: **butane gas**) butano

butch [butʃ] ADJ (col: woman: pej) mascolino(-a); (man) macho inv

butcher ['butʃər] N macellaio ▶ VT macellare; **~'s (shop)** macelleria

butler ['bʌtlər] N maggiordomo

butt [bʌt] N (cask) grossa botte f; (thick end) estremità f inv più grossa; (of gun) calcio; (of cigarette) mozzicone m; (BRIT fig: target) oggetto ▶ VT cozzare
▶ **butt in** VI (interrupt) interrompere

butter ['bʌtər] N burro ▶ VT imburrare

buttercup ['bʌtəkʌp] N ranuncolo

butter dish N burriera

butterfingers ['bʌtəfɪŋgəz] N (col) mani fpl di ricotta

butterfly ['bʌtəflaɪ] N farfalla; (Swimming: also: **butterfly stroke**) (nuoto a) farfalla

buttocks ['bʌtəks] NPL natiche fpl

button ['bʌtn] N bottone m; (US: badge) distintivo ▶ VT (also: **button up**) abbottonare ▶ VI abbottonarsi

buttonhole ['bʌtnhəul] N asola, occhiello
▶ VT (person) attaccar bottone a

buttress ['bʌtrɪs] N contrafforte m

buxom ['bʌksəm] ADJ formoso(-a)

buy [baɪ] (pt, pp **bought**) VT comprare, acquistare ▶ N acquisto; **a good/bad ~** un buon/cattivo acquisto or affare; **to ~ sb sth/sth from sb** comprare qc per qn/qc da qn; **to ~ sb a drink** offrire da bere a qn
▶ **buy back** VT riprendersi, prendersi indietro
▶ **buy in** VT (BRIT: goods) far provvista di
▶ **buy into** VT FUS (BRIT Comm) acquistare delle azioni di
▶ **buy off** VT (col: bribe) comprare
▶ **buy out** VT (business) rilevare
▶ **buy up** VT accaparrare

buyer ['baɪər] N compratore(-trice); **~'s market** mercato favorevole ai compratori

buy-out ['baɪaut] N (Comm) acquisto di una società da parte dei suoi dipendenti

buzz [bʌz] N ronzio; (col: phone call) colpo di telefono ▶ VI ronzare ▶ VT (call on intercom) chiamare al citofono; (: with buzzer) chiamare col cicalino; (Aviat: plane, building) passare rasente; **my head is buzzing** mi gira la testa

▶ **buzz off** VI (BRIT col) filare, levarsi di torno

buzzard ['bʌzəd] N poiana

buzzer ['bʌzər] N cicalino

buzz word N (col) termine m in voga

(KEYWORD)

by [baɪ] PREP **1** (referring to cause, agent) da; **killed by lightning** ucciso da un fulmine; **surrounded by a fence** circondato da uno steccato; **a painting by Picasso** un quadro di Picasso
2 (referring to method: manner: means): **by bus/car/train** in autobus/macchina/treno, con l'autobus/la macchina/il treno; **to pay by cheque** pagare con (un) assegno; **by moonlight** al chiaro di luna; **by saving hard, he ...** risparmiando molto, lui ...
3 (via, through) per; **we came by Dover** siamo venuti via Dover
4 (close to, past) accanto a; **the house by the river** la casa sul fiume; **a holiday by the sea** una vacanza al mare; **she sat by his bed** si sedette accanto al suo letto; **she rushed by me** mi è passata accanto correndo; **I go by the post office every day** passo davanti all'ufficio postale ogni giorno
5 (not later than) per, entro; **by 4 o'clock** per or entro le 4; **by this time tomorrow** domani a quest'ora; **by the time I got here it was too late** quando sono arrivato era ormai troppo tardi
6 (during): **by day/night** di giorno/notte
7 (amount) a; **by the kilo** a chili; **paid by the hour** pagato all'ora; **to increase by the hour** aumentare di ora in ora; **one by one** uno per uno; **little by little** a poco a poco
8 (Math: measure): **to divide/multiply by 3** dividere/moltiplicare per 3; **a room 3 metres by 4** una stanza di 3 metri per 4; **it's broader by a metre** è un metro più largo, è più largo di un metro
9 (according to) per; **to play by the rules** attenersi alle regole; **it's all right by me** per me va bene
10: (all) by oneself (tutto(-a)) solo(-a); **he did it (all) by himself** lo ha fatto (tutto) da solo
11: **by the way** a proposito; **this wasn't my idea by the way** tra l'altro l'idea non è stata mia
▶ ADV **1** see **go**; **pass** etc
2: **by and by** (in past) poco dopo; (in future) fra breve; **by and large** nel complesso

bye ['baɪ], **bye-bye** ['baɪ'baɪ] EXCL ciao!, arrivederci!

bye-law ['baɪlɔ:] N legge f locale

by-election ['baɪɪlɛkʃən] N (BRIT) elezione f straordinaria; vedi nota

Una *by-election* in Gran Bretagna e in alcuni paesi del *Commonwealth* è un'elezione che si tiene per coprire un posto in Parlamento resosi vacante, a governo ancora in carica. é importante in quanto serve a misurare il consenso degli elettori in vista delle successive elezioni politiche.

Byelorussia [bjɛləu'rʌʃə] N Bielorussia, Belorussia

Byelorussian [bjɛləu'rʌʃən] ADJ, N = **Belarussian**

bygone ['baɪɡɔn] ADJ passato(-a) ▶ N: **let bygones be bygones** mettiamoci una pietra sopra

by-law ['baɪlɔ:] N legge *f* locale

bypass ['baɪpɑ:s] N circonvallazione *f*; (*Med*) by-pass *m inv* ▶ VT fare una deviazione intorno a

by-product ['baɪprɔdʌkt] N sottoprodotto; (*fig*) conseguenza secondaria

byre ['baɪəʳ] N (*BRIT*) stalla

bystander ['baɪstændəʳ] N spettatore(-trice)

byte [baɪt] N (*Comput*) byte *m inv*, bicarattere *m*

byway ['baɪweɪ] N strada secondaria

byword ['baɪwə:d] N: **to be a ~ for** essere sinonimo di

by-your-leave ['baɪjɔ:'li:v] N: **without so much as a ~** senza nemmeno chiedere il permesso

Cc

C, c [siː] N (letter) C, c f inv or m inv; (Scol: mark) ≈ 6 (sufficiente); (Mus): **C** do; **C for Charlie** ≈ C come Como

C ABBR = **Celsius**; (= centigrade) C

c. ABBR (= century) sec.; (US etc) = **cent**; (= circa) c

CA ABBR = **Central America**; (US) = **California** ▶ N ABBR (BRIT) = **chartered accountant**

ca. ABBR (= circa) ca

c/a ABBR = **capital account; credit account; current account**

CAA N ABBR BRIT: = **Civil Aviation Authority**; (US: = Civil Aeronautics Authority) organismo di controllo e di sviluppo dell'aviazione civile

CAB N ABBR (BRIT: = Citizens' Advice Bureau) organizzazione per la tutela del consumatore

cab [kæb] N taxi m inv; (of train, truck) cabina; (horsedrawn) carrozza

cabaret ['kæbəreɪ] N cabaret m inv

cabbage ['kæbɪdʒ] N cavolo

cabbie, cabby ['kæbɪ] N (col) tassista mf

cab driver N tassista mf

cabin ['kæbɪn] N capanna; (on ship) cabina

cabin crew N equipaggio

cabin cruiser N cabinato

cabinet ['kæbɪnɪt] N (Pol) consiglio dei ministri; (furniture) armadietto; (also: **display cabinet**) vetrinetta; **cocktail ~** mobile m bar inv

cabinet-maker ['kæbɪnɪt'meɪkə^r] N stipettaio

cabinet minister N ministro (membro del Consiglio)

cable ['keɪbl] N cavo; fune f; (Tel) cablogramma m ▶ VT telegrafare

cable-car ['keɪblkaː^r] N funivia

cablegram ['keɪblgræm] N cablogramma m

cable railway N funicolare f

cable television N televisione f via cavo

cache [kæʃ] N nascondiglio; **a ~ of food** etc un deposito segreto di viveri etc

cackle ['kækl] VI schiamazzare

cactus ['kæktəs] (pl **cacti** [-taɪ]) N cactus m inv

CAD N ABBR (= computer-aided design) progettazione f con l'ausilio dell'elaboratore

caddie ['kædɪ] N caddie m inv

cadet [kə'dɛt] N (Mil) cadetto; **police ~** allievo poliziotto

cadge [kædʒ] VT (col) scroccare; **to ~ a meal (off sb)** scroccare un pranzo (a qn)

cadre ['kædrɪ] N quadro

Caesarean, (US)Cesarean [siː'zɛərɪən] ADJ: **~ (section)** (taglio) cesareo

CAF ABBR (BRIT: = cost and freight) Caf m

café ['kæfeɪ] N caffè m inv

cafeteria [kæfɪ'tɪərɪə] N self-service m inv

caffein, caffeine ['kæfiːn] N caffeina

cage [keɪdʒ] N gabbia ▶ VT mettere in gabbia

cagey ['keɪdʒɪ] ADJ (col) chiuso(-a); guardingo(-a)

cagoule [kə'guːl] N K-way® m inv

cahoots [kə'huːts] N: **to be in ~ (with sb)** essere in combutta (con qn)

CAI N ABBR (= computer-aided instruction) istruzione f assistita dall'elaboratore

Cairo ['kaɪərəu] N il Cairo

cajole [kə'dʒəul] VT allettare

cake [keɪk] N (large) torta; (small) pasticcino; **~ of soap** saponetta; **it's a piece of ~** (col) è una cosa da nulla; **he wants to have his ~ and eat it (too)** (fig) vuole la botte piena e la moglie ubriaca

caked [keɪkt] ADJ: **~ with** incrostato(-a) di

cake shop N pasticceria

Cal. ABBR (US) = **California**

calamitous [kə'læmɪtəs] ADJ disastroso(-a)

calamity [kə'læmɪtɪ] N calamità f inv

calcium ['kælsɪəm] N calcio

calculate ['kælkjuleɪt] VT calcolare; (estimate: chances, effect) valutare
  ▶ **calculate on** VT FUS: **to ~ on sth/on doing sth** contare su qc/di fare qc

calculated ['kælkjuleɪtɪd] ADJ calcolato(-a), intenzionale; **a ~ risk** un rischio calcolato

calculating ['kælkjuleɪtɪŋ] ADJ calcolatore(-trice)

calculation [kælkju'leɪʃən] N calcolo

calculator ['kælkjuleɪtə^r] N calcolatrice f

calculus ['kælkjuləs] N calcolo; **integral/ differential** ~ calcolo integrale/ differenziale

calendar ['kæləndə'] N calendario

calendar year N anno civile

calf [kɑːf] (pl **calves** [kɑːvz]) N (of cow) vitello; (of other animals) piccolo; (also: **calfskin**) (pelle f di) vitello; (Anat) polpaccio

caliber ['kælɪbə'] N (US) = **calibre**

calibrate ['kælɪbreɪt] VT (gun etc) calibrare; (scale of measuring instrument) tarare

calibre, (US) **caliber** ['kælɪbə'] N calibro

calico ['kælɪkəu] N tela grezza, cotone m grezzo; (US) cotonina stampata

Calif. ABBR (US) = **California**

California [kælɪ'fɔːnɪə] N California

calipers ['kælɪpəz] NPL (US) = **callipers**

call [kɔːl] VT (gen, also Tel) chiamare; (announce: flight) annunciare; (: meeting, strike) indire, proclamare ▶ VI chiamare; (visit: also: **call in, call round**) passare ▶ N (shout) grido, urlo; (visit) visita; (summons: for flight etc) chiamata; (fig: lure) richiamo; (also: **telephone call**) telefonata; **to be called** (person, object) chiamarsi; **to be on** ~ essere a disposizione; **to make a** ~ telefonare, fare una telefonata; **please give me a** ~ **at 7** per piacere mi chiami alle 7; **to pay a** ~ **on sb** fare (una) visita a qn; **there's not much** ~ **for these items** non c'è molta richiesta di questi articoli; **she's called Jane** si chiama Jane; **who is calling?** (Tel) chi parla?; **London calling** (Radio) qui Londra

▶ **call at** VT FUS (ship) fare scalo a; (train) fermarsi a

▶ **call back** VI (return) ritornare; (Tel) ritelefonare, richiamare ▶ VT (Tel) ritelefonare a, richiamare; **can you** ~ **back later?** può richiamare più tardi?

▶ **call for** VT FUS (demand: action etc) richiedere; (collect: person) passare a prendere; (: goods) ritirare

▶ **call in** VT (doctor, expert, police) chiamare, far venire

▶ **call off** VT (meeting, race) disdire; (deal) cancellare; (dog) richiamare; **the strike was called off** lo sciopero è stato revocato

▶ **call on** VT FUS (visit) passare da; (request): **to** ~ **on sb to do** chiedere a qn di fare

▶ **call out** VI (in pain) urlare; (to person) chiamare ▶ VT (doctor, police, troops) chiamare

▶ **call up** VT (Mil) richiamare; (Tel) telefonare a

Callanetics® [kælə'nɛtɪks] NSG tipo di ginnastica basata sulla ripetizione di piccoli movimenti

callbox ['kɔːlbɔks] N (BRIT) cabina telefonica

call centre, (US) **call center** N centro informazioni telefoniche

caller ['kɔːlə'] N persona che chiama; visitatore(-trice); **hold the line,** ~**!** (Tel) rimanga in linea, signore (or signora)!

call girl N ragazza f squillo inv

call-in ['kɔːlɪn] N (US) = **phone-in**

calling ['kɔːlɪŋ] N vocazione f

calling card N (US) biglietto da visita

callipers, (US) **calipers** ['kælɪpəz] NPL (Med) gambale m; (Math) calibro

callous ['kæləs] ADJ indurito(-a), insensibile

callousness ['kæləsnɪs] N insensibilità

callow ['kæləu] ADJ immaturo(-a)

calm [kɑːm] ADJ calmo(-a) ▶ N calma ▶ VT calmare

▶ **calm down** VI calmarsi ▶ VT calmare

calmly ['kɑːmlɪ] ADV con calma

calmness ['kɑːmnɪs] N calma

Calor gas® ['kæləs] N (BRIT) butano

calorie ['kælərɪ] N caloria; **low-**~ **product** prodotto a basso contenuto di calorie

calve [kɑːv] VI figliare

calves [kɑːvz] NPL of **calf**

CAM N ABBR (= computer-aided manufacturing) fabbricazione f con l'ausilio dell'elaboratore

camber ['kæmbə'] N (of road) bombatura

Cambodia [kæm'bəudjə] N Cambogia

Cambodian [kæm'bəudɪən] ADJ, N cambogiano(-a)

Cambs ABBR (BRIT) = **Cambridgeshire**

camcorder ['kæmkɔːdə'] N videocamera

came [keɪm] PT of **come**

camel ['kæməl] N cammello

cameo ['kæmɪəu] N cammeo

camera ['kæmərə] N macchina fotografica; (Cine, TV) telecamera; (also: **cinecamera, movie camera**) cinepresa; **in** ~ a porte chiuse

cameraman ['kæmərəmæn] N (irreg) cameraman m inv

camera phone N telefono cellulare con fotocamera integrata

Cameroon, Cameroun ['kæməruːn] N Camerun m

camouflage ['kæməflɑːʒ] N (feeling) camuffamento; (Mil, Zool) mimetizzazione f ▶ VT (feeling) camuffare; mimetizzare

camp [kæmp] N campeggio; (Mil) campo ▶ VI campeggiare; accamparsi; **to go camping** andare in campeggio ▶ ADJ effeminato(-a)

campaign [kæm'peɪn] N (Mil, Pol etc) campagna ▶ VI: **to** ~ **(for/against)** (also fig) fare una campagna (per/contro)

campaigner [kæm'peɪnə'] N: ~ **for** fautore(-trice) di; ~ **against** oppositore(-trice) di

campbed ['kæmp'bɛd] N (BRIT) brandina

camper ['kæmpə'] N campeggiatore(-trice); (vehicle) camper m inv

campground N (US) campeggio

camping ['kæmpɪŋ] N campeggio; **to go ~** andare in campeggio

camp site ['kæmpsaɪt], **camping site** N campeggio

campus ['kæmpəs] N campus *m inv*

camshaft ['kæmʃɑːft] N albero a camme

can¹ [kæn] N (*of milk*) scatola; (*of oil*) bidone *m*; (*of water*) tanica; (*tin*) scatola ▸ VT mettere in scatola; **a ~ of beer** una lattina di birra; **to carry the ~** (*BRIT col*) prendere la colpa

(KEYWORD)

can² [kæn] (*negative* **cannot**, **can't**, *pt*, *conditional* **could**) AUX VB **1** (*be able to*) potere; **I can't go any further** non posso andare oltre; **you can do it if you try** sei in grado di farlo - basta provarci; **I'll help you all I can** ti aiuterò come potrò; **I can't see you** non ti vedo; **can you hear me?** mi senti?, riesci a sentirmi?

2 (*know how to*) sapere, essere capace di; **I can swim** so nuotare; **can you speak French?** parla francese?

3 (*may*) potere; **could I have a word with you?** posso parlarle un momento?

4 (*expressing disbelief: puzzlement etc*): **it can't be true!** non può essere vero!; **what CAN he want?** cosa può mai volere?

5 (*expressing possibility: suggestion etc*): **he could be in the library** può darsi che sia in biblioteca; **they could have forgotten** potrebbero essersene dimenticati; **she could have been delayed** può aver avuto un contrattempo

Canada ['kænədə] N Canada *m*

Canadian [kə'neɪdɪən] ADJ, N canadese (*mf*)

canal [kə'næl] N canale *m*

canary [kə'nɛərɪ] N canarino

Canary Islands, Canaries [kə'nɛərɪz] NPL: **the ~** le (isole) Canarie

Canberra ['kænbərə] N Camberra

cancel ['kænsəl] VT annullare; (*train*) sopprimere; (*cross out*) cancellare ▸ **cancel out** VT (*Math*) semplificare; (*fig*) annullare; **they ~ each other out** (*also fig*) si annullano a vicenda

cancellation [kænsə'leɪʃən] N annullamento; soppressione *f*; cancellazione *f*; (*Tourism*) prenotazione *f* annullata

cancer ['kænsər] N cancro; **C~** (*sign*) Cancro; **to be C~** essere del Cancro

cancerous ['kænsərəs] ADJ canceroso(-a)

cancer patient N malato(-a) di cancro

cancer research N ricerca sul cancro

C and F ABBR (*BRIT*: = *cost and freight*) Caf *m*

candid ['kændɪd] ADJ onesto(-a)

candidacy ['kændɪdəsɪ] N candidatura

candidate ['kændɪdeɪt] N candidato(-a)

candidature ['kændɪdətʃər] N (*BRIT*) = **candidacy**

candied ['kændɪd] ADJ candito(-a); **~ apple** (*US*) mela caramellata

candle ['kændl] N candela; (*in church*) cero

candlelight ['kændl'laɪt] N: **by ~** a lume di candela

candlestick ['kændlstɪk] N (*also*: **candle holder**) bugìa; (*bigger, ornate*) candeliere *m*

candour,(*US*) **candor** ['kændər] N sincerità

C & W N ABBR = **country and western (music)**

candy ['kændɪ] N zucchero candito; (*US*) caramella; caramelle *fpl*

candy bar(*US*) N *lungo biscotto, in genere ricoperto di cioccolata*

candy-floss ['kændɪflɒs] N (*BRIT*) zucchero filato

candy store N (*US*) ≈ pasticceria

cane [keɪn] N canna; (*for baskets, chairs etc*) bambù *m*; (*Scol*) verga; (*for walking*) bastone *m* (da passeggio) ▸ VT (*BRIT Scol*) punire a colpi di verga

canine ['kænaɪn] ADJ canino(-a)

canister ['kænɪstər] N scatola metallica

cannabis ['kænəbɪs] N canapa indiana

canned ['kænd] ADJ (*food*) in scatola; (*col: recorded: music*) registrato(-a); (*BRIT col: drunk*) sbronzo(-a); (*US col: worker*) licenziato(-a)

cannibal ['kænɪbəl] N cannibale *mf*

cannibalism ['kænɪbəlɪzəm] N cannibalismo

cannon ['kænən] (*pl ~ or* **cannons**) N (*gun*) cannone *m*

cannonball ['kænənbɔːl] N palla di cannone

cannon fodder N carne *f* da macello

cannot ['kænɔt] = **can not**

canny ['kænɪ] ADJ furbo(-a)

canoe [kə'nuː] N canoa; (*Sport*) canotto

canoeing [kə'nuːɪŋ] N (*sport*) canottaggio

canoeist [kə'nuːɪst] N canottiere *m*

canon ['kænən] N (*clergyman*) canonico; (*standard*) canone *m*

canonize ['kænənaɪz] VT canonizzare

can opener [-əupnər] N apriscatole *m inv*

canopy ['kænəpɪ] N baldacchino

cant [kænt] N gergo ▸ VT inclinare ▸ VI inclinarsi

can't [kænt] = **can not**

Cantab. ABBR (*BRIT*: = *cantabrigiensis*) *of Cambridge*

cantankerous [kæn'tæŋkərəs] ADJ stizzoso(-a)

canteen [kæn'tiːn] N mensa; (*BRIT: of cutlery*) portaposate *m inv*

canter ['kæntər] N piccolo galoppo ▸ VI andare al piccolo galoppo

cantilever ['kæntɪliːvər] N trave *f* a sbalzo

canvas ['kænvəs] N tela; **under ~** (camping) sotto la tenda; (Naut) sotto la vela

canvass ['kænvəs] VI (Pol): **to ~ for** raccogliere voti per ▶ VT (Comm: district) fare un'indagine di mercato in; (: citizens, opinions) fare un sondaggio di; (Pol: district) fare un giro elettorale di; (: person) fare propaganda elettorale a

canvasser ['kænvəsə'] N (Comm) agente m viaggiatore, piazzista m; (Pol) propagandista mf (elettorale)

canvassing ['kænvəsɪŋ] N sollecitazione f

canyon ['kænjən] N canyon m inv

CAP N ABBR (= Common Agricultural Policy) PAC f

cap [kæp] N (also BRIT Football: hat) berretto; (of pen) coperchio; (of bottle) tappo; (for swimming) cuffia; (BRIT: contraceptive: also: **Dutch cap**) diaframma m ▶ VT tappare; (outdo) superare; (limit) fissare un tetto a; **capped with** ricoperto(-a) di; **and to ~ it all, he ...** (BRIT) e per completare l'opera, lui ...

capability [keɪpə'bɪlɪtɪ] N capacità f inv, abilità f inv

capable ['keɪpəbl] ADJ capace; **~ of** capace di; suscettibile di

capacious [kə'peɪʃəs] ADJ capace

capacity [kə'pæsɪtɪ] N capacità f inv; (of lift etc) capienza; **in his ~ as** nella sua qualità di; **to work at full ~** lavorare al massimo delle proprie capacità; **this work is beyond my ~** questo lavoro supera le mie possibilità; **filled to ~** pieno zeppo; **in an advisory ~** a titolo consultativo

cape [keɪp] N (garment) cappa; (Geo) capo

Cape of Good Hope N Capo di Buona Speranza

caper ['keɪpə'] N (Culin: also: **capers**) cappero; (leap) saltello; (escapade) birichinata; (prank) scherzetto

Cape Town N Città del Capo

capita ['kæpɪtə] see **per capita**

capital ['kæpɪtl] N (also: **capital city**) capitale f; (money) capitale m; (also: **capital letter**) (lettera) maiuscola

capital account N conto capitale

capital allowance N ammortamento fiscale

capital assets NPL capitale m fisso

capital expenditure N spese fpl in capitale

capital gains tax N imposta sulla plusvalenza

capital goods N beni mpl d'investimento, beni mpl capitali

capital-intensive ['kæpɪtlɪn'tensɪv] ADJ ad alta intensità di capitale

capitalism ['kæpɪtəlɪzəm] N capitalismo

capitalist ['kæpɪtəlɪst] ADJ, N capitalista (mf)

capitalize ['kæpɪtəlaɪz] VT (provide with capital) capitalizzare

▶ **capitalize on** VT FUS (fig) trarre vantaggio da

capital punishment N pena capitale

capital transfer tax N (BRIT) imposta sui trasferimenti di capitali

Capitol ['kæpɪtl] N: **the ~** il Campidoglio; vedi nota

> Il Capitol è l'edificio che ospita le riunioni del Congresso degli Stati Uniti. é situato sull'omonimo colle, Capitol Hill, a Washington DC. In molti stati americani il termine Capitol viene usato per indicare l'edificio dove si riuniscono i rappresentanti dello stato.

capitulate [kə'pɪtjuleɪt] VI capitolare

capitulation [kəpɪtju'leɪʃən] N capitolazione f

capricious [kə'prɪʃəs] ADJ capriccioso(-a)

Capricorn ['kæprɪkɔ:n] N Capricorno; **to be ~** essere del Capricorno

caps [kæps] ABBR = **capital letters**

capsize [kæp'saɪz] VT capovolgere ▶ VI capovolgersi

capstan ['kæpstən] N argano

capsule ['kæpsju:l] N capsula

Capt. ABBR (= captain) Cap.

captain ['kæptɪn] N capitano ▶ VT capitanare

caption ['kæpʃən] N leggenda

captivate ['kæptɪveɪt] VT avvincere

captive ['kæptɪv] ADJ, N prigioniero(-a)

captivity [kæp'tɪvɪtɪ] N prigionia; **in ~** (animal) in cattività

captor ['kæptə'] N (lawful) chi ha catturato; (unlawful) rapitore m

capture ['kæptʃə'] VT catturare, prendere; (attention) attirare; (Comput) registrare ▶ N cattura; (data capture) registrazione f or rilevazione f di dati

car [kɑ:'] N macchina, automobile f; (US Rail) vagone m; **by ~** in macchina

Caracas [kə'rækəs] N Caracas f

carafe [kə'ræf] N caraffa

carafe wine N (in restaurant) ≈ vino sfuso

caramel ['kærəməl] N caramello

carat ['kærət] N carato; **18 ~ gold** oro a 18 carati

caravan ['kærəvæn] N (BRIT) roulotte f inv; (of camels) carovana

caravan site N (BRIT) campeggio per roulotte

caraway ['kærəweɪ] N: **~ seed** seme m di cumino

carb [kɑ:b] N (col) cibo m ad alto contenuto di • carboidrati

carbohydrate [kɑ:bəu'haɪdreɪt] N carboidrato

carbolic acid [kɑ:'bɔlɪk-] N acido fenico, fenolo

car bomb N ordigno esplosivo collocato in una macchina; **a ~ went off yesterday** ieri è esplosa un'autobomba

carbon ['kɑ:bən] N carbonio

carbonated ['kɑ:bəneɪtəd] ADJ (drink) gassato(-a)

carbon copy N copia f carbone inv

carbon credit N quota f di emissione

carbon dioxide [-daɪ'ɔksaɪd] N diossido di carbonio

carbon footprint N impronta di carbonio

carbon monoxide [-mɔ'nɔksaɪd] N monossido di carbonio

carbon-neutral ADJ a zero emissioni di gas serra

carbon offset N riduzione f delle emissioni di gas serra

carbon paper N carta carbone

carbon ribbon N nastro carbonato

car boot sale N vedi nota

> Il car boot sale è un mercatino dell'usato molto popolare in Gran Bretagna. Normalmente ha luogo in un parcheggio o in un grande spiazzo, e la merce viene in genere esposta nei bagagliai, in inglese appunto boots, aperti delle macchine.

carburettor, (US) **carburetor** [kɑ:bju'rɛtə^r] N carburatore m

carcass ['kɑ:kəs] N carcassa

carcinogenic [kɑ:sɪnə'dʒɛnɪk] ADJ cancerogeno(-a)

card [kɑ:d] N carta; (thin cardboard) cartoncino; (visiting card etc) biglietto; (membership card) tessera; (Christmas card etc) cartolina; **to play cards** giocare a carte

cardamom ['kɑ:dəməm] N cardamomo

cardboard ['kɑ:dbɔ:d] N cartone m

cardboard box N (scatola di) cartone m

cardboard city N luogo dove dormono in scatole di cartone emarginati senzatetto

card-carrying member ['kɑ:d'kærɪɪŋ-] N tesserato(-a)

card game N gioco di carte

cardiac ['kɑ:dɪæk] ADJ cardiaco(-a)

cardigan ['kɑ:dɪgən] N cardigan m inv

cardinal ['kɑ:dɪnl] ADJ, N cardinale (m)

card index N schedario

cardphone ['kɑ:dfəʊn] N telefono a scheda (magnetica)

cardsharp ['kɑ:dʃɑ:p] N baro

card vote N (BRIT) voto (palese) per delega

CARE [kɛə^r] N ABBR = **Cooperative for American Relief Everywhere**

care [kɛə^r] N cura, attenzione f; (worry) preoccupazione f ▶ VI: **to ~ about** curarsi di; (thing, idea) interessarsi di; **would you ~ to/ for ...?** le piacerebbe ...?; **I wouldn't ~ to do it** non lo vorrei fare; **in sb's ~** alle cure di qn; **to take ~** fare attenzione; **to take ~ of** curarsi di; (details, arrangements, bill, problem) occuparsi di; **I don't ~** non me ne importa; **I couldn't ~ less** non me ne importa un bel

niente; **~ of (c/o)** (on letter) presso; **"with ~"** "fragile"; **the child has been taken into ~** il bambino è stato preso in custodia
> **care for** VT FUS aver cura di; (like) voler bene a

careen [kə'ri:n] VI (ship) sbandare ▶ VT carenare

career [kə'rɪə^r] N carriera; (occupation) professione f ▶ VI (also: **career along**) andare di (gran) carriera

career girl N donna dedita alla carriera

careers officer N consulente mf d'orientamento professionale

carefree ['kɛəfri:] ADJ sgombro(-a) di preoccupazioni

careful ['kɛəful] ADJ attento(-a); (cautious) cauto(-a); **(be) ~!** attenzione!; **he's very ~ with his money** bada molto alle spese

carefully ['kɛəfəlɪ] ADV con cura; cautamente

caregiver (US) N (professional) badante mf; (unpaid) persona che si prende cura di un parente malato o anziano

careless ['kɛəlɪs] ADJ negligente; (remark) privo(-a) di tatto; (heedless) spensierato(-a)

carelessly ['kɛəlɪslɪ] ADV negligentemente; senza tatto; (without thinking) distrattamente

carelessness ['kɛəlɪsnɪs] N negligenza; mancanza di tatto

carer ['kɛərə^r] N chi si occupa di un familiare anziano o invalido

caress [kə'rɛs] N carezza ▶ VT accarezzare

caretaker ['kɛəteɪkə^r] N custode m

caretaker government N (BRIT) governo m ponte inv

car-ferry ['kɑ:fɛrɪ] N traghetto

cargo ['kɑ:gəʊ] (pl **cargoes**) N carico

cargo boat N cargo

cargo plane N aereo di linea da carico

car hire N (BRIT) autonoleggio

Caribbean [kærɪ'bi:ən] ADJ caraibico(-a); **the ~ (Sea)** il Mar dei Caraibi

caricature ['kærɪkətjʊə^r] N caricatura

caring ['kɛərɪŋ] ADJ (person) premuroso(-a); (society, organization) umanitario(-a)

carnage ['kɑ:nɪdʒ] N carneficina

carnal ['kɑ:nl] ADJ carnale

carnation [kɑ:'neɪʃən] N garofano

carnival ['kɑ:nɪvəl] N (public celebration) carnevale m; (US: funfair) luna park m inv

carnivorous [kɑ:'nɪvərəs] ADJ carnivoro(-a)

carol ['kærəl] N: **(Christmas) ~** canto di Natale

carouse [kə'raʊz] VI far baldoria

carousel [kærə'sɛl] N (US) giostra

carp [kɑ:p] N (fish) carpa
> **carp at** VT FUS trovare a ridire su

car park N (BRIT) parcheggio

carpenter ['kɑ:pɪntə^r] N carpentiere m

carpentry ['kɑ:pɪntrɪ] N carpenteria

carpet ['kɑːpɪt] N tappeto; (BRIT: fitted carpet) moquette f inv ▶ VT coprire con tappeto

carpet bombing N bombardamento a tappeto

carpet slippers NPL pantofole fpl

carpet sweeper N scopatappeti m inv

car phone N telefonino per auto

car rental N (US) autonoleggio

carriage ['kærɪdʒ] N vettura; (of goods) trasporto; (of typewriter) carrello; (bearing) portamento; **~ forward** porto assegnato; **~ free** franco di porto; **~ paid** porto pagato

carriage return N (on typewriter etc) leva (or tasto) del ritorno a capo

carriageway ['kærɪdʒweɪ] N (BRIT: part of road) carreggiata

carrier ['kærɪər] N (of disease) portatore(-trice); (Comm) impresa di trasporti; (Naut) portaerei f inv

carrier bag N (BRIT) sacchetto

carrier pigeon N colombo viaggiatore

carrion ['kærɪən] N carogna

carrot ['kærət] N carota

carry ['kærɪ] VT (person) portare; (vehicle) trasportare; (a motion, bill) far passare; (involve: responsibilities etc) comportare; (Med) essere portatore(-trice) di; (Comm: goods) tenere; (: interest) avere; (Math: figure) riportare ▶ VI (sound) farsi sentire; **this loan carries 10% interest** questo prestito è sulla base di un interesse del 10%; **to be** or **get carried away** (fig) farsi trascinare
  ▶ **carry forward** VT (Math, Comm) riportare
  ▶ **carry on** VI: **to ~ on with sth/doing** continuare qc/a fare ▶ VT mandare avanti
  ▶ **carry out** VT (orders) eseguire; (investigation) svolgere; (accomplish etc: plan) realizzare; (perform, implement: idea, threat) mettere in pratica

carrycot ['kærɪkɔt] N (BRIT) culla portabile

carry-on [kærɪ'ɔn] N (col: fuss) casino, confusione f; (: annoying behaviour): **I've had enough of your ~!** mi hai proprio scocciato!

cart [kɑːt] N carro ▶ VT (col) trascinare, scarrozzare

carte blanche ['kɑːt'blɒnʃ] N: **to give sb ~** dare carta bianca a qn

cartel [kɑː'tɛl] N (Comm) cartello

cartilage ['kɑːtɪlɪdʒ] N cartilagine f

cartographer [kɑː'tɔgrəfər] N cartografo(-a)

cartography [kɑː'tɔgrəfɪ] N cartografia

carton ['kɑːtən] N (box) scatola di cartone; (of yogurt) cartone m; (of cigarettes) stecca

cartoon [kɑː'tuːn] N (in newspaper etc) vignetta; (comic strip) fumetto; (Cine, TV) cartone m animato; (Art) cartone

cartoonist [kɑː'tuːnɪst] N vignettista mf; cartonista mf

cartridge ['kɑːtrɪdʒ] N (for gun, pen) cartuccia; (for camera) caricatore m; (music tape) cassetta; (of record player) testina

cartwheel ['kɑːtwiːl] N: **to turn a ~** (Sport etc) fare la ruota

carve [kɑːv] VT (meat) trinciare; (wood, stone) intagliare
  ▶ **carve up** VT (meat) tagliare; (fig: country) suddividere

carving ['kɑːvɪŋ] N (in wood etc) scultura

carving knife N trinciante m

car wash N lavaggio auto

Casablanca [kæsə'blæŋkə] N Casablanca

cascade [kæs'keɪd] N cascata ▶ VI scendere a cascata

case [keɪs] N caso; (Law) causa, processo; (box) scatola; (BRIT: also: **suitcase**) valigia; (Typ): **lower/upper ~** (carattere m) minuscolo/maiuscolo; **to have a good ~** avere pretese legittime; **there's a strong ~ for reform** ci sono validi argomenti a favore della riforma; **in ~ of** in caso di; **in ~ he** caso mai lui; **in any ~** in ogni caso; **just in ~** in caso di bisogno

case history N (Med) cartella clinica

case-sensitive ['keɪs'sɛnsɪtɪv] ADJ (Comput) sensibile alle maiuscole o minuscole

case study N studio di un caso

cash [kæʃ] N (coins, notes) soldi mpl, denaro ▶ VT incassare; **I haven't got any ~** non ho contanti; **to pay (in) ~** pagare in contanti; **to be short of ~** essere a corto di soldi; **~ with order/on delivery (COD)** (Comm) pagamento all'ordinazione/alla consegna
  ▶ **cash in** VT (insurance policy etc) riscuotere, riconvertire
  ▶ **cash in on** VT FUS: **to ~ in on sth** sfruttare qc

cash account N conto m cassa inv

cash-and-carry ['kæʃənd'kærɪ] N cash and carry m inv

cashback N (discount) sconto; (at supermarket etc) anticipo di contanti ottenuto presso la cassa di un negozio tramite una carta di debito

cashbook ['kæʃbuk] N giornale m di cassa

cash box N cassetta per il denaro spicciolo

cash card N (BRIT) carta per prelievi automatici

cash desk N (BRIT) cassa

cash discount N sconto per contanti

cash dispenser N (BRIT) sportello automatico

cashew [kæ'ʃuː] N (also: **cashew nut**) anacardio

cash flow N cash-flow m inv, liquidità f inv

cashier [kæ'ʃɪər] N cassiere(-a) ▶ VT (esp Mil) destituire

cashmere ['kæʃmɪər] N cachemire m

cash payment N pagamento in contanti

cash point N sportello bancario automatico, Bancomat® m inv

cash price N prezzo per contanti
cash register N registratore *m* di cassa
cash sale N vendita per contanti
casing ['keɪsɪŋ] N rivestimento
casino [kə'siːnəu] N casinò *m inv*
cask [kɑːsk] N botte *f*
casket ['kɑːskɪt] N cofanetto; (*US: coffin*) bara
Caspian Sea ['kæspɪən-] N: **the ~** il mar Caspio
casserole ['kæsərəul] N casseruola; **chicken ~** pollo in casseruola
cassette [kæ'sɛt] N cassetta
cassette deck N piastra di registrazione
cassette player N riproduttore *m* a cassette
cassette recorder N registratore *m* a cassette
cast [kɑːst] (*pt, pp ~*) VT (*throw*) gettare; (*shed*) perdere; spogliarsi di; (*metal*) gettare, fondere; (*Theat*): **to ~ sb as Hamlet** scegliere qn per la parte di Amleto ► N (*Theat*) cast *m inv*; (*mould*) forma; (*also*: **plaster cast**) ingessatura; **to ~ one's vote** votare, dare il voto
► **cast aside** VT (*reject*) mettere da parte
► **cast off** VI (*Naut*) salpare ► VT (*Naut*) disormeggiare; (*Knitting*) diminuire, calare
► **cast on** (*Knitting*) VT avviare ► VI avviare (le maglie)
castanets [kæstə'nɛts] NPL castagnette *fpl*
castaway ['kɑːstəwəɪ] N naufrago(-a)
caste [kɑːst] N casta
caster sugar ['kɑːstə-] N (*Brit*) zucchero semolato
casting vote ['kɑːstɪŋ-] N (*Brit*) voto decisivo
cast iron N ghisa ► ADJ: **cast-iron** (*lit*) di ghisa; (*fig: will, alibi*) di ferro, d'acciaio
castle ['kɑːsl] N castello; (*fortified*) rocca
castor ['kɑːstə*ʳ*] N (*wheel*) rotella
castor oil N olio di ricino
castrate [kæs'treɪt] VT castrare
casual ['kæʒjul] ADJ (*chance*) casuale, fortuito(-a); (*irregular: work etc*) avventizio(-a); (*unconcerned*) noncurante, indifferente; **~ wear** casual *m*
casual labour N manodopera avventizia
casually ['kæʒjulɪ] ADV con disinvoltura; (*by chance*) casualmente
casualty ['kæʒjultɪ] N ferito(-a); (*dead*) morto(-a), vittima; (*Med: department*) pronto soccorso; **heavy casualties** grosse perdite *fpl*
casualty ward N (*Brit*) pronto soccorso (*reparto*)
cat [kæt] N gatto
catacombs ['kætəkuːmz] NPL catacombe *fpl*
catalogue, (*US*) **catalog** ['kætələg] N catalogo ► VT catalogare
catalyst ['kætəlɪst] N catalizzatore *m*
catalytic converter [kætə'lɪtɪk kən'vɜːtə*ʳ*] N marmitta catalitica, catalizzatore *m*

catapult ['kætəpʌlt] N catapulta; fionda
cataract ['kætərækt] N (*also Med*) cateratta
catarrh [kə'tɑː*ʳ*] N catarro
catastrophe [kə'tæstrəfɪ] N catastrofe *f*
catastrophic [kætə'strɔfɪk] ADJ catastrofico(-a)
catcall ['kætkɔːl] N (*at meeting etc*) fischio
catch [kætʃ] (*pt, pp* **caught** [kɔːt]) VT prendere; (*train, thief, cold*) acchiappare; (*ball*) afferrare; (*person: by surprise*) sorprendere; (*understand*) comprendere; (*get entangled*) impigliare; (*attention*) attirare; (*comment, whisper*) cogliere; (*person*) raggiungere ► VI (*fire*) prendere ► N (*fish etc caught*) retata; (*of ball*) presa; (*trick*) inganno; (*Tech*) gancio; (*game*) catch *m inv*; **to ~ fire** prendere fuoco; **to ~ sight of** scorgere
► **catch on** VI (*become popular*) affermarsi, far presa; (*understand*): **to ~ on (to sth)** capire (qc)
► **catch out** VT (*Brit fig: with trick question*) cogliere in fallo
► **catch up** VI mettersi in pari ► VT (*also*: **catch up with**) raggiungere
catching ['kætʃɪŋ] ADJ (*Med*) contagioso(-a)
catchment area ['kætʃmənt-] N (*Brit Scol*) circoscrizione *f* scolare; (*Geo*) bacino pluviale
catch phrase N slogan *m inv*; frase *f* fatta
catch-22 ['kætʃtwɛntɪ'tuː] N: **it's a ~ situation** non c'è via d'uscita
catchy ['kætʃɪ] ADJ orecchiabile
catechism ['kætɪkɪzəm] N catechismo
categoric [kætɪ'gɔrɪk], **categorical** [kætɪ'gɔrɪkl] ADJ categorico(-a)
categorize ['kætɪgəraɪz] VT categorizzare
category ['kætɪgərɪ] N categoria
cater ['keɪtə*ʳ*]
► **cater for** VT FUS (*Brit: needs*) provvedere a; (: *readers, consumers*) incontrare i gusti di; (*Comm: provide food*) provvedere alla ristorazione di
caterer ['keɪtərə*ʳ*] N fornitore *m*
catering ['keɪtərɪŋ] N approvvigionamento
catering trade N settore *m* ristoranti
caterpillar ['kætəpɪlə*ʳ*] N (*Zool*) bruco ► CPD (*vehicle*) cingolato(-a); **~ track** cingolo
cat flap N gattaiola
cathedral [kə'θiːdrəl] N cattedrale *f*, duomo
cathode ['kæθəud] N catodo
cathode ray tube N tubo a raggi catodici
Catholic ['kæθəlɪk] ADJ, N (*Rel*) cattolico(-a)
catholic ['kæθəlɪk] ADJ (*wide-ranging*) universale; aperto(-a); eclettico(-a)
CAT scanner [kæt-] N (*Med: = computerized axial tomography scanner*) (rilevatore *m* per la) TAC *f inv*
Catseye® ['kæts'aɪ] N (*Brit Aut*) catarifrangente *m*
catsup ['kætsəp] N (*US*) ketchup *m inv*
cattle ['kætl] NPL bestiame *m*, bestie *fpl*

catty ['kætɪ] ADJ maligno(-a), dispettoso(-a)
catwalk ['kætwɔːk] N passerella
Caucasian [kɔːˈkeɪzɪən] ADJ, N caucasico(-a)
Caucasus ['kɔːkəsəs] N Caucaso
caucus ['kɔːkəs] N (US Pol) (riunione f del) comitato elettorale; (BRIT Pol: group) comitato di dirigenti; *vedi nota*

> *Caucus* è il termine usato, specialmente negli Stati Uniti, per indicare una riunione informale dei rappresentanti di spicco di un partito politico che precede una riunione ufficiale. Con uso estensivo, la parola indica il nucleo direttivo di un partito politico.

caught [kɔːt] PT, PP *of* **catch**
cauliflower ['kɔlɪflauəʳ] N cavolfiore m
cause [kɔːz] N causa ▶ VT causare; **there is no ~ for concern** non c'è ragione di preoccuparsi; **to ~ sb to do sth** far fare qc a qn; **to ~ sth to be done** far fare qc
causeway ['kɔːzweɪ] N strada rialzata
caustic ['kɔːstɪk] ADJ caustico(-a)
caution ['kɔːʃən] N prudenza; (*warning*) avvertimento ▶ VT avvertire; ammonire
cautious ['kɔːʃəs] ADJ cauto(-a), prudente
cautiously ['kɔːʃəslɪ] ADV prudentemente
cautiousness ['kɔːʃəsnɪs] N cautela
cavalier [kævəˈlɪəʳ] N (*knight*) cavaliere m ▶ ADJ (*pej: offhand*) brusco(-a)
cavalry ['kævəlrɪ] N cavalleria
cave [keɪv] N caverna, grotta ▶ VI: **to go caving** fare speleologia
▶ **cave in** VI (*roof etc*) crollare
caveman ['keɪvmæn] N (*irreg*) uomo delle caverne
cavern ['kævən] N caverna
caviar, caviare ['kævɪɑːʳ] N caviale m
cavity ['kævɪtɪ] N cavità f inv
cavity wall insulation N isolamento per pareti a intercapedine
cavort [kəˈvɔːt] VI far capriole
cayenne [keɪˈɛn], **cayenne pepper** [keɪˈɛn-] N pepe m di Caienna
CB N ABBR (BRIT: = Companion (of the Order) of the Bath) titolo; (= Citizens' Band (Radio)) C.B m; **CB radio (set)** baracchino
CBC N ABBR = **Canadian Broadcasting Corporation**
CBE N ABBR (BRIT: = Companion (of the Order) of the British Empire) titolo
CBI N ABBR (= Confederation of British Industry) ≈ CONFINDUSTRIA (= Confederazione Generale dell'Industria Italiana)
CBS N ABBR (US) = **Columbia Broadcasting System**
CC ABBR (BRIT) = **county council**
cc ABBR (= cubic centimetre) cc; (on letter etc) = **carbon copy**
CCA N ABBR (US: = Circuit Court of Appeals) corte f

d'appello itinerante
CCTV N ABBR (= closed-circuit television) televisione f a circuito chiuso
CCTV camera N telecamera f TVCC
CCU N ABBR (US: = coronary care unit) unità coronarica
CD N ABBR (= compact disk) CD m inv; (player) lettore m CD inv; (Mil: BRIT) = **Civil Defence (Corps)**; (: US) = **Civil Defense** ▶ ABBR (BRIT: = Corps Diplomatique) C.D.
CD burner N masterizzatore m (di) CD
CDC N ABBR (US) = **center for disease control**
CD-I ® N CD-I m inv, compact disc m inv interattivo
CD player N lettore m CD
Cdr. ABBR (= commander) Com
CD-ROM ['siːdiːˈrɔm] N ABBR (= compact disc read-only memory) CD-ROM m inv
CDT (US: = Central Daylight Time) ora legale del centro; (BRIT Scol: = Craft, Design and Technology) educazione tecnica
CDW N ABBR = **collision damage waiver**
CD writer N masterizzatore m
cease [siːs] VT, VI cessare
ceasefire ['siːsfaɪəʳ] N cessate il fuoco m inv
ceaseless ['siːslɪs] ADJ incessante, continuo(-a)
CED N ABBR (US) = **Committee for Economic Development**
cedar ['siːdəʳ] N cedro
cede [siːd] VT cedere
CEEB N ABBR (US: = College Entrance Examination Board) commissione per l'esame di ammissione al college
ceilidh ['keɪlɪ] N festa con musiche e danze popolari scozzesi o irlandesi
ceiling ['siːlɪŋ] N soffitto; (fig: upper limit) tetto, limite m massimo
celebrate ['sɛlɪbreɪt] VT, VI celebrare
celebrated ['sɛlɪbreɪtɪd] ADJ celebre
celebration [sɛlɪˈbreɪʃən] N celebrazione f
celebrity [sɪˈlɛbrɪtɪ] N celebrità f inv
celeriac [səˈlɛrɪæk] N sedano m rapa inv
celery ['sɛlərɪ] N sedano
celestial [sɪˈlɛstɪəl] ADJ celeste
celibacy ['sɛlɪbəsɪ] N celibato
cell [sɛl] N cella; (of revolutionaries, Biol) cellula; (Elec) elemento (di batteria)
cellar ['sɛləʳ] N sottosuolo; cantina
cellist ['tʃɛlɪst] N violoncellista mf
cello ['tʃɛləu] N violoncello
cellophane ® ['sɛləfeɪn] N cellophane® m
cellphone ['sɛlfəun] N cellulare m
cell tower N (US Tel) stazione f radio base
cellular ['sɛljuləʳ] ADJ cellulare
celluloid ['sɛljulɔɪd] N celluloide f
cellulose ['sɛljuləus] N cellulosa
Celsius ['sɛlsɪəs] ADJ Celsius inv
Celt [kɛlt, sɛlt] N celta mf

Celtic ['kɛltɪk, 'sɛltɪk] ADJ celtico(-a) ▶ N (*Ling*) celtico

cement [sə'mɛnt] N cemento ▶ VT cementare

cement mixer N betoniera

cemetery ['sɛmɪtrɪ] N cimitero

cenotaph ['sɛnətɑ:f] N cenotafio

censor ['sɛnsə^r] N censore *m* ▶ VT censurare

censorship ['sɛnsəʃɪp] N censura

censure ['sɛnʃə^r] VT censurare

census ['sɛnsəs] N censimento

cent [sɛnt] N (*of dollar, euro*) centesimo; *see also* **per cent**

centenary [sɛn'ti:nərɪ], (*US*) **centennial** [sɛn'tɛnɪəl] N centenario

center ['sɛntə^r] N, VT (*US*) = **centre**

centigrade ['sɛntɪgreɪd] ADJ centigrado(-a)

centilitre, (*US*) **centiliter** ['sɛntɪli:tə^r] N centilitro

centimetre, (*US*) **centimeter** ['sɛntɪmi:tə^r] N centimetro

centipede ['sɛntɪpi:d] N centopiedi *m inv*

central ['sɛntrəl] ADJ centrale

Central African Republic N Repubblica centrafricana

Central America N America centrale

central heating N riscaldamento centrale

centralize ['sɛntrəlaɪz] VT accentrare

central processing unit N (*Comput*) unità *f inv* centrale di elaborazione

central reservation N (*Brit Aut*) banchina *f* spartitraffico *inv*

centre, (*US*) **center** ['sɛntə^r] N centro ▶ VT centrare; (*concentrate*): **to ~ (on)** concentrare (su)

centrefold, (*US*) **centerfold** ['sɛntəfəuld] N (*Press*) poster *m* (all'interno di rivista)

centre-forward ['sɛntə'fɔ:wəd] N (*Sport*) centroavanti *m inv*

centre-half ['sɛntə'hɑ:f] N (*Sport*) centromediano

centrepiece, (*US*) **centerpiece** ['sɛntəpi:s] N centrotavola *m*; (*fig*) punto centrale

centre spread N (*Brit*) pubblicità a doppia pagina

centre-stage [sɛntə'steɪdʒ] N: **to take ~** porsi al centro dell'attenzione

centrifugal [sɛn'trɪfjugəl] ADJ centrifugo(-a)

centrifuge ['sɛntrɪfju:ʒ] N centrifuga

century ['sɛntjurɪ] N secolo; **in the twentieth ~** nel ventesimo secolo

CEO N ABBR = **chief executive officer**

ceramic [sɪ'ræmɪk] ADJ ceramico(-a)

cereal ['si:rɪəl] N cereale *m*

cerebral ['sɛrɪbrəl] ADJ cerebrale

ceremonial [sɛrɪ'məunɪəl] N cerimoniale *m*; (*rite*) rito

ceremony ['sɛrɪmənɪ] N cerimonia; **to stand on ~** fare complimenti

cert [sə:t] N (*Brit col*): **it's a dead ~** non c'è alcun dubbio

certain ['sə:tən] ADJ certo(-a); **to make ~ of** assicurarsi di; **for ~** per certo, di sicuro

certainly ['sə:tənlɪ] ADV certamente, certo

certainty ['sə:təntɪ] N certezza

certificate [sə'tɪfɪkɪt] N certificato; diploma *m*

certified letter ['sə:tɪfaɪd-] N (*US*) lettera raccomandata

certified public accountant ['sə:tɪfaɪd-] N (*US*) ≈ commercialista *mf*

certify ['sə:tɪfaɪ] VT certificare; (*award diploma to*) conferire un diploma a; (*declare insane*) dichiarare pazzo(-a) ▶ VI: **to ~ to** attestare a

cervical ['sə:vɪkl] ADJ: **~ cancer** cancro della cervice, tumore *m* al collo dell'utero; **~ smear** Pap-test *m inv*

cervix ['sə:vɪks] N cervice *f*

Cesarean [si:'zɛərɪən] ADJ, N (*US*) = **Caesarean**

cessation [sə'seɪʃən] N cessazione *f*; arresto

cesspit ['sɛspɪt] N pozzo nero

CET ABBR (= *Central European Time*) fuso orario

Ceylon [sɪ'lɔn] N Ceylon *f*

cf. ABBR (= *compare*) cfr

c/f ABBR (*Comm*) = **carried forward**

CFC N ABBR (= *chlorofluorocarbon*) CFC *m inv*

CG N ABBR (*US*) = **coastguard**

cg ABBR (= *centigram*) cg

CH N ABBR (*Brit*: = *Companion of Honour*) titolo

ch. ABBR (= *chapter*) cap

Chad [tʃæd] N Chad *m*

chafe [tʃeɪf] VT fregare, irritare ▶ VI (*fig*): **to ~ against** scontrarsi con

chaffinch ['tʃæfɪntʃ] N fringuello

chagrin ['ʃægrɪn] N disappunto, dispiacere *m*

chain [tʃeɪn] N catena ▶ VT (*also*: **chain up**) incatenare

chain reaction N reazione *f* a catena

chain-smoke ['tʃeɪnsməuk] VI fumare una sigaretta dopo l'altra

chain store N negozio a catena

chair [tʃɛə^r] N sedia; (*armchair*) poltrona; (*of university*) cattedra; (*of meeting*) presidenza ▶ VT (*meeting*) presiedere; **the ~** (*US: electric chair*) la sedia elettrica

chairlift ['tʃɛəlɪft] N seggiovia

chairman ['tʃɛəmən] N (*irreg*) presidente *m*

chairperson ['tʃɛəpə:sn] N presidente(-essa)

chairwoman ['tʃɛəwumən] N (*irreg*) presidentessa

chalet ['ʃæleɪ] N chalet *m inv*

chalice ['tʃælɪs] N calice *m*

chalk [tʃɔ:k] N gesso ▶ **chalk up** VT scrivere col gesso; (*fig: success*) ottenere; (: *victory*) riportare

chalkboard (*US*) N lavagna

challenge ['tʃælɪndʒ] N sfida ▶ VT sfidare; (*statement, right*) mettere in dubbio; **to ~ sb to**

a fight/game sfidare qn a battersi/ad una partita; **to ~ sb to do** sfidare qn a fare

challenger ['tʃælɪndʒər] N (Sport) sfidante mf

challenging ['tʃælɪndʒɪŋ] ADJ (task) impegnativo(-a); (remark) provocatorio(-a); (look) di sfida

chamber ['tʃeɪmbər] N camera; **~ of commerce** camera di commercio

chambermaid ['tʃeɪmbəmeɪd] N cameriera

chamber music N musica da camera

chamberpot ['tʃeɪmbəpɔt] N vaso da notte

chameleon [kə'miːlɪən] N camaleonte m

chamois ['ʃæmwɑː] N camoscio

chamois leather ['ʃæmɪ-] N pelle f di camoscio

champagne [ʃæm'peɪn] N champagne m inv

champers ['ʃæmpəz] NSG (col) sciampagna

champion ['tʃæmpɪən] N campione(-essa); (of cause) difensore m ▶ vT difendere, lottare per

championship ['tʃæmpɪənʃɪp] N campionato

chance [tʃɑːns] N caso; (opportunity) occasione f; (likelihood) possibilità f inv ▶ vT: **to ~ it** rischiare, provarci ▶ ADJ fortuito(-a); **there is little ~ of his coming** è molto improbabile che venga; **to take a ~** rischiare; **by ~** per caso; **it's the ~ of a lifetime** è un'occasione unica; **the chances are that ...** probabilmente ..., è probabile che ... + sub; **to ~ to do sth** (formal: happen) fare per caso qc
▶ chance (up)on vT FUS (person) incontrare per caso, imbattersi in; (thing) trovare per caso

chancel ['tʃɑːnsəl] N coro

chancellor ['tʃɑːnsələr] N cancelliere m; (of university) rettore m (onorario); **C~ of the Exchequer** (BRIT) Cancelliere m dello Scacchiere

chandelier [ʃændə'lɪər] N lampadario

change [tʃeɪndʒ] vT cambiare; (transform): **to ~ sb into** trasformare qn in ▶ vI cambiare; (change one's clothes) cambiarsi; (be transformed): **to ~ into** trasformarsi in ▶ N cambiamento; (money) resto; **to ~ one's mind** cambiare idea; **to ~ gear** (Aut) cambiare (marcia); **she changed into an old skirt** si è cambiata e ha messo una vecchia gonna; **a ~ of clothes** un cambio (di vestiti); **for a ~** tanto per cambiare; **small ~** spiccioli mpl, moneta; **keep the ~** tenga il resto; **can you give me ~ for £1?** mi può cambiare una sterlina?; **sorry, I don't have any ~** mi dispiace, non ho spiccioli
▶ change over vI (from sth to sth) passare; (players etc) scambiarsi (di posto o di campo) ▶ vT cambiare

changeable ['tʃeɪndʒəbl] ADJ (weather) variabile; (person) mutevole

change machine N distributore m automatico di monete

changeover ['tʃeɪndʒəuvər] N cambiamento, passaggio

changing ['tʃeɪndʒɪŋ] ADJ che cambia; (colours) cangiante

changing room N (BRIT: in shop) camerino; (Sport) spogliatoio

channel ['tʃænl] N canale m; (of river, sea) alveo ▶ vT canalizzare; (fig: interest, energies): **to ~ into** concentrare su, indirizzare verso; **through the usual channels** per le solite vie; **the (English) C~** la Manica; **green/red ~** (Customs) uscita "niente da dichiarare"/"merci da dichiarare"

channel-hopping ['tʃænlhɔpɪŋ] N (TV) zapping m

Channel Islands NPL: **the ~** le Isole Normanne

Channel Tunnel N: **the ~** il tunnel sotto la Manica

chant [tʃɑːnt] N canto; salmodia; (of crowd) slogan m inv ▶ vT cantare; salmodiare; **the demonstrators chanted their disapproval** i dimostranti lanciavano slogan di protesta

chaos ['keɪɔs] N caos m

chaos theory N teoria del caos

chaotic [keɪ'ɔtɪk] ADJ caotico(-a)

chap [tʃæp] N (BRIT col: man) tipo ▶ vT (skin) screpolare; **old ~** vecchio mio

chapel ['tʃæpl] N cappella

chaperone ['ʃæpərəun] N accompagnatore(-trice) ▶ vT accompagnare

chaplain ['tʃæplɪn] N cappellano

chapped [tʃæpt] ADJ (skin, lips) screpolato(-a)

chapter ['tʃæptər] N capitolo

char [tʃɑːr] vT (burn) carbonizzare ▶ vI (BRIT: cleaner) lavorare come domestica (a ore) ▶ N (BRIT) = **charlady**

character ['kærɪktər] N (gen, Comput) carattere m; (in novel, film) personaggio; (eccentric) originale m; **a person of good ~** una persona a modo

character code N (Comput) codice m di carattere

characteristic ['kærɪktə'rɪstɪk] ADJ caratteristico(-a) ▶ N caratteristica; **~ of** tipico(-a) di

characterize ['kærɪktəraɪz] vT caratterizzare; (describe): **to ~ (as)** descrivere (come)

charade [ʃə'rɑːd] N sciarada

charcoal ['tʃɑːkəul] N carbone m di legna

charge [tʃɑːdʒ] N accusa; (cost) prezzo; (of gun, battery, Mil: attack) carica; (responsibility) responsabilità ▶ vT (gun, battery, Mil: enemy) caricare; (customer) fare pagare a; (sum) fare pagare; (Law): **to ~ sb (with)** accusare qn (di)

▶ VI (gen with: up, along etc) lanciarsi; **charges**
NPL: **bank charges** commissioni fpl
bancarie; **labour charges** costi mpl del
lavoro; **to reverse the charges** (Tel) fare una
telefonata a carico del destinatario; **to ~ in/
out** precipitarsi dentro/fuori; **to ~ up/down**
lanciarsi su/giù per; **is there a ~?** c'è da
pagare?; **there's no ~** non c'è niente da
pagare; **extra ~** supplemento; **to take ~ of**
incaricarsi di; **to be in ~ of** essere
responsabile per; **to have ~ of sb** aver cura
di qn; **how much do you ~ for this repair?**
quanto chiede per la riparazione?; **to ~ an
expense (up) to sb** addebitare una spesa a
qn; **~ it to my account** lo metta or addebiti
sul mio conto

charge account N conto
charge card N (of shop) carta f clienti inv
chargé d'affaires [ˈʃɑːʒeɪdæˈfɛəʳ] N
incaricato d'affari
chargehand [ˈtʃɑːdʒhænd] N (BRIT)
caposquadra mf
charger [ˈtʃɑːdʒəʳ] N (also: **battery charger**)
caricabatterie m inv; (old: warhorse) destriero
chariot [ˈtʃærɪət] N carro
charismatic [kærɪzˈmætɪk] ADJ
carismatico(-a)
charitable [ˈtʃærɪtəbl] ADJ caritatevole
charity [ˈtʃærɪtɪ] N carità; (organization) opera
pia
charity shop N (BRIT) negozi che vendono articoli
di seconda mano e devolvono il ricavato in
beneficenza
charlady [ˈtʃɑːleɪdɪ] N (BRIT) domestica a ore
charlatan [ˈʃɑːlətən] N ciarlatano
charm [tʃɑːm] N fascino; (on bracelet) ciondolo
▶ VT affascinare, incantare
charm bracelet N braccialetto con ciondoli
charming [ˈtʃɑːmɪŋ] ADJ affascinante
chart [tʃɑːt] N tabella; grafico; (map) carta
nautica; (weather chart) carta del tempo ▶ VT
fare una carta nautica di; (sales, progress)
tracciare il grafico di; **to be in the charts**
(record, pop group) essere in classifica; **charts**
NPL (Mus) hit parade f
charter [ˈtʃɑːtəʳ] VT (plane) noleggiare ▶ N
(document) carta; **on ~ a** nolo
chartered accountant [ˈtʃɑːtəd-] N (BRIT)
ragioniere(-a) professionista
charter flight N volo m charter inv
charwoman [ˈtʃɑːwumən] N (irreg)
= **charlady**
chase [tʃeɪs] VT inseguire; (also: **chase away**)
cacciare ▶ N caccia
  ▶ **chase down** VT (US) = **chase up**
  ▶ **chase up** VT (BRIT: person) scovare;
(information) scoprire, raccogliere
chasm [ˈkæzəm] N abisso
chassis [ˈʃæsɪ] N telaio

chastened [ˈtʃeɪsnd] ADJ abbattuto(-a),
provato(-a)
chastening [ˈtʃeɪsnɪŋ] ADJ che fa riflettere
chastise [tʃæsˈtaɪz] VT punire, castigare
chastity [ˈtʃæstɪtɪ] N castità
chat [tʃæt] VI (also: **have a chat**)
chiacchierare; (on the internet) chattare
  ▶ N chiacchierata; (on the internet) chat f inv
  ▶ **chat up** VT (BRIT col: girl, boy) abbordare
chatline [ˈtʃætlaɪn] N servizio telefonico che
permette a più utenti di conversare insieme
chat room N (Internet) chat f inv
chat show N (BRIT) talk show m inv,
conversazione f televisiva
chattel [ˈtʃætl] N see **goods**
chatter [ˈtʃætəʳ] VI (person) ciarlare; (bird)
cinguettare; (teeth) battere ▶ N ciarle fpl;
cinguettio; **her teeth were chattering**
batteva i denti
chatterbox [ˈtʃætəbɔks] N chiacchierone(-a)
chattering classes [ˈtʃætərɪŋ-] NPL: **the ~**
(col, pej) ≈ gli intellettuali da salotto
chatty [ˈtʃætɪ] ADJ (style) familiare; (person)
chiacchierino(-a)
chauffeur [ˈʃəufəʳ] N autista m
chauvinism [ˈʃəuvɪnɪzəm] N (also: **male
chauvinism**) maschilismo; (nationalism)
sciovinismo
chauvinist [ˈʃəuvɪnɪst] N (also: **male
chauvinist**) maschilista m; (nationalist)
sciovinista mf
chauvinistic [ʃəuvɪˈnɪstɪk] ADJ
sciovinistico(-a)
chav [tʃæv] N (BRIT pej) giovane della periferia
urbana poco colto che indossa abiti sportivi di
particolari marche
ChE ABBR = **chemical engineer**
cheap [tʃiːp] ADJ a buon mercato,
economico(-a); (reduced: fare, ticket)
ridotto(-a); (joke) grossolano(-a); (poor quality)
di cattiva qualità ▶ ADV a buon mercato;
cheaper meno caro; **~ money** denaro a
basso tasso di interesse
cheap day return N biglietto ridotto di andata e
ritorno valido in giornata
cheapen [ˈtʃiːpn] VT ribassare; (fig) avvilire
cheaply [ˈtʃiːplɪ] ADV a buon prezzo, a buon
mercato
cheat [tʃiːt] VI imbrogliare; (at school) copiare
  ▶ VT ingannare; (rob) defraudare ▶ N
imbroglione m; copione m; (trick) inganno;
to ~ sb out of sth defraudare qn di qc
  ▶ **cheat on** VT FUS (husband, wife) tradire; **he's
been cheating on his wife** ha tradito sua
moglie
cheating [ˈtʃiːtɪŋ] N imbrogliare m; copiare m
Chechnya [tʃɪtʃˈnjɑː] N Cecenia
check [tʃɛk] VT verificare; (passport, ticket)
controllare; (halt) fermare; (restrain)

contenere ▶ VI (official etc) informarsi ▶ N
verifica; controllo; (curb) freno; (US: bill)
conto; (pattern: gen pl) quadretti mpl; (US)
= **cheque** ▶ ADJ (pattern, cloth: also: **checked**) a
scacchi, a quadretti; **to ~ with sb** chiedere a
qn; **to keep a ~ on sb/sth** controllare qn/qc,
fare attenzione a qn/qc

▶ **check in** VI (in hotel) registrare; (at airport)
presentarsi all'accettazione ▶ VT (luggage)
depositare

▶ **check off** VT segnare

▶ **check out** VI (from hotel) saldare il conto
▶ VT (luggage) ritirare; (investigate: story)
controllare, verificare; (: person) prendere
informazioni su

▶ **check up** VI: **to ~ up (on sth)** investigare
(qc); **to ~ up on sb** informarsi sul conto di qn
checkbook ['tʃɛkbʊk] N (US) = **chequebook**
checkered ['tʃɛkəd] ADJ (US) = **chequered**
checkers ['tʃɛkəz] N (US) dama
check guarantee card N (US) carta f assegni
inv
check-in ['tʃɛkɪn] N (at airport: also: **check-in
desk**) check-in m inv, accettazione f (bagagli
inv)
checking account ['tʃɛkɪŋ-] N (US) conto
corrente
checklist ['tʃɛklɪst] N lista di controllo
checkmate ['tʃɛkmeɪt] N scaccomatto
checkout ['tʃɛkaʊt] N (in supermarket) cassa
checkpoint ['tʃɛkpɔɪnt] N posto di blocco
checkroom ['tʃɛkrʊm] N (US) deposito m
bagagli inv
checkup ['tʃɛkʌp] N (Med) controllo medico
cheddar ['tʃɛdər] N formaggio duro di latte di
mucca di colore bianco o arancione
cheek [tʃiːk] N guancia; (impudence) faccia
tosta
cheekbone ['tʃiːkbəʊn] N zigomo
cheeky ['tʃiːkɪ] ADJ sfacciato(-a)
cheep [tʃiːp] N (of bird) pigolio ▶ VI pigolare
cheer [tʃɪər] VT applaudire; (gladden)
rallegrare ▶ VI applaudire ▶ N grido (di
incoraggiamento); **cheers** NPL (of approval,
encouragement) applausi mpl; evviva mpl;
cheers! salute!

▶ **cheer on** VT (person etc) incitare
▶ **cheer up** VI rallegrarsi, farsi animo ▶ VT
rallegrare
cheerful ['tʃɪəful] ADJ allegro(-a)
cheerfulness ['tʃɪəfulnɪs] N allegria
cheerio ['tʃɪərɪ'əʊ] EXCL (BRIT) ciao!
cheerleader ['tʃɪəliːdər] N cheerleader f inv
cheerless ['tʃɪəlɪs] ADJ triste
cheese [tʃiːz] N formaggio
cheeseboard ['tʃiːzbɔːd] N piatto del (or per
il) formaggio
cheeseburger ['tʃiːzbəgər] N cheeseburger m
inv

cheesecake ['tʃiːzkeɪk] N specie di torta di
ricotta, a volte con frutta
cheetah ['tʃiːtə] N ghepardo
chef [ʃɛf] N capocuoco
chemical ['kɛmɪkl] ADJ chimico(-a) ▶ N
prodotto chimico
chemical engineering N ingegneria
chimica
chemist ['kɛmɪst] N (BRIT: pharmacist)
farmacista mf; (scientist) chimico(-a); **~'s
shop** n (BRIT) farmacia
chemistry ['kɛmɪstrɪ] N chimica
chemo [kiːməʊ] N chemio f inv
chemotherapy [kiːməʊ'θɛrəpɪ] N
chemioterapia
cheque, (US) **check** [tʃɛk] N assegno;
to pay by ~ pagare per assegno or con un
assegno
chequebook, (US) **checkbook** ['tʃɛkbʊk] N
libretto degli assegni
cheque card N (BRIT) carta f assegni inv
chequered, (US) **checkered** ['tʃɛkəd] ADJ (fig)
movimentato(-a)
cherish ['tʃɛrɪʃ] VT aver caro; (hope etc) nutrire
cheroot [ʃə'ruːt] N sigaro spuntato
cherry ['tʃɛrɪ] N ciliegia; (also: **cherry tree**)
ciliegio
Ches ABBR (BRIT) = **Cheshire**
chess [tʃɛs] N scacchi mpl
chessboard ['tʃɛsbɔːd] N scacchiera
chessman ['tʃɛsmæn] N (irreg) pezzo degli
scacchi
chessplayer ['tʃɛspleɪər] N scacchista mf
chest [tʃɛst] N petto; (box) cassa; **to get sth
off one's ~** (col) sputare il rospo
chest measurement N giro m torace inv
chestnut ['tʃɛsnʌt] N castagna; (also:
chestnut tree) castagno ▶ ADJ castano(-a)
chest of drawers N cassettone m
chesty ['tʃɛstɪ] ADJ: **~ cough** tosse f bronchiale
chew [tʃuː] VT masticare
chewing gum ['tʃuːɪŋ-] N chewing gum m
chic [ʃiːk] ADJ elegante
chick [tʃɪk] N pulcino; (US col) pollastrella
chicken ['tʃɪkɪn] N pollo; (col: coward) coniglio
▶ **chicken out** VI (col) avere fifa; **to ~ out of
sth** tirarsi indietro da qc per fifa or paura
chicken feed N (fig) miseria
chickenpox ['tʃɪkɪnpɔks] N varicella
chick flick N (col) filmetto rosa
chickpea ['tʃɪkpiː] N cece m
chicory ['tʃɪkərɪ] N cicoria
chide [tʃaɪd] VT rimproverare
chief [tʃiːf] N capo ▶ ADJ principale; **C~ of
Staff** (Mil) Capo di Stato Maggiore
chief constable N (BRIT) ≈ questore m
chief executive, (US) **chief executive
officer** N direttore m generale
chiefly ['tʃiːflɪ] ADV per lo più, soprattutto

chief operating officer N direttore(-trice) operativo(-a)

chiffon ['ʃɪfɔn] N chiffon m inv

chilblain ['tʃɪlbleɪn] N gelone m

child [tʃaɪld] (pl **children** ['tʃɪldrən]) N bambino(-a)

child abuse N molestie fpl a minori

child abuser [-əˈbjuːzəʳ] N molestatore(-trice) di minori

child benefit N (BRIT) ≈ assegni mpl familiari

childbirth ['tʃaɪldbəːθ] N parto

childcare N servizio m di custodia dei bambini

childhood ['tʃaɪldhud] N infanzia

childish ['tʃaɪldɪʃ] ADJ puerile

childless ['tʃaɪldlɪs] ADJ senza figli

childlike ['tʃaɪldlaɪk] ADJ fanciullesco(-a)

child minder [-ˈmaɪndəʳ] N (BRIT) bambinaia

child prodigy N bambino m prodigio inv

children ['tʃɪldrən] NPL of **child**

children's home N istituto per l'infanzia

Chile ['tʃɪlɪ] N Cile m

Chilean ['tʃɪlɪən] ADJ, N cileno(-a)

chill [tʃɪl] N freddo; (Med) infreddatura ▶ ADJ freddo(-a), gelido(-a) ▶ VT raffreddare; (Culin) mettere in fresco; **"serve chilled"** "servire fresco"
  ▶ **chill out** VI (esp US col) darsi una calmata

chilli, (US) **chili** ['tʃɪlɪ] N peperoncino

chilling ['tʃɪlɪŋ] ADJ agghiacciante; (wind) gelido(-a)

chilly ['tʃɪlɪ] ADJ freddo(-a), fresco(-a); (sensitive to cold) freddoloso(-a); **to feel ~** sentirsi infreddolito(-a)

chime [tʃaɪm] N carillon m inv ▶ VI suonare, scampanare

chimney ['tʃɪmnɪ] N camino

chimney sweep N spazzacamino

chimpanzee [tʃɪmpæn'ziː] N scimpanzé m inv

chin [tʃɪn] N mento

China ['tʃaɪnə] N Cina

china ['tʃaɪnə] N porcellana

Chinese [tʃaɪ'niːz] ADJ cinese ▶ N (pl inv) cinese mf; (Ling) cinese m

chink [tʃɪŋk] N (opening) fessura; (noise) tintinnio

chinwag ['tʃɪnwæg] N (col): **to have a ~** fare una chiacchierata

chip [tʃɪp] N (gen pl: Culin) patatina fritta; (: US: also: **potato chip**) patatina; (of wood, glass, stone) scheggia; (in gambling) fiche f inv; (Comput: microchip) chip m inv ▶ VT (cup, plate) scheggiare; **when the chips are down** (fig) al momento critico
  ▶ **chip in** VI (col: contribute) contribuire; (interrupt) intromettersi

chip and PIN N sistema m chip e PIN; **~ machine** lettore m di carte chip e PIN; **~ card** carta chip e PIN

chipboard ['tʃɪpbɔːd] N agglomerato

chipmunk ['tʃɪpmʌŋk] N tamia m striato

chippings ['tʃɪpɪŋz] NPL: **loose ~** brecciame m

chip shop N (BRIT); vedi nota

> I chip shops, anche chiamati fish-and-chip shops, sono friggitorie che vendono principalmente filetti di pesce impanati e patatine fritte che un tempo venivano serviti ai clienti avvolti in carta di giornale.

chiropodist [kɪ'rɔpədɪst] N (BRIT) pedicure mf

chiropody [kɪ'rɔpədɪ] N (BRIT) pedicure f inv

chirp [tʃəːp] N cinguettio; (of crickets) cri cri m ▶ VI cinguettare

chirpy ['tʃəːpɪ] ADJ (col) frizzante

chisel ['tʃɪzl] N cesello

chit [tʃɪt] N biglietto

chitchat ['tʃɪttʃæt] N (col) chiacchiere fpl

chivalrous ['ʃɪvəlrəs] ADJ cavalleresco(-a)

chivalry ['ʃɪvəlrɪ] N cavalleria; cortesia

chives [tʃaɪvz] NPL erba cipollina

chloride ['klɔːraɪd] N cloruro

chlorinate ['klɔrɪneɪt] VT clorare

chlorine ['klɔːriːn] N cloro

choc-ice ['tʃɔkaɪs] N (BRIT) gelato ricoperto al cioccolato

chock [tʃɔk] N zeppa

chock-a-block ['tʃɔkə'blɔk], **chockfull** ['tʃɔk'ful] ADJ pieno(-a) zeppo(-a)

chocolate ['tʃɔklɪt] N (substance) cioccolato, cioccolata; (drink) cioccolata; (a sweet) cioccolatino

choice [tʃɔɪs] N scelta ▶ ADJ scelto(-a); **a wide ~** un'ampia scelta; **I did it by** or **from ~** l'ho fatto di mia volontà or per mia scelta

choir ['kwaɪəʳ] N coro

choirboy ['kwaɪəbɔɪ] N corista m fanciullo

choke [tʃəuk] VI soffocare ▶ VT soffocare; (block) ingombrare ▶ N (Aut) valvola dell'aria; **to be choked with** essere intasato(-a)

cholera ['kɔlərə] N colera m

cholesterol [kə'lɛstərɔl] N colesterolo

chook [tʃuk] N (AUSTRALIA, NEW ZEALAND col) gallina

choose [tʃuːz] (pt **chose** [tʃəuz], pp **chosen** ['tʃəuzn]) VT scegliere; **to ~ to do** decidere di fare; preferire fare; **to ~ between** scegliere tra; **to ~ from** scegliere da or tra

choosy ['tʃuːzɪ] ADJ: **(to be) ~** (fare lo) schizzinoso(-a)

chop [tʃɔp] VT (wood) spaccare; (Culin: also: **chop up**) tritare ▶ N colpo netto; (Culin) costoletta; **to get the ~** (BRIT col: project) essere bocciato(-a); (person: be sacked) essere licenziato(-a); see also **chops**
  ▶ **chop down** VT (tree) abbattere
  ▶ **chop off** VT tagliare

choppy ['tʃɔpɪ] ADJ (sea) mosso(-a)

chops [tʃɔps] NPL (jaws) mascelle fpl

C

chopsticks ['tʃɔpstɪks] NPL bastoncini *mpl* cinesi

choral ['kɔːrəl] ADJ corale

chord [kɔːd] N (*Mus*) accordo

chore [tʃɔːʳ] N faccenda; **household chores** faccende *fpl* domestiche

choreographer [kɔrɪ'ɔgrəfəʳ] N coreografo(-a)

choreography [kɔrɪ'ɔgrəfɪ] N coreografia

chorister ['kɔrɪstəʳ] N corista *mf*

chortle ['tʃɔːtl] VI ridacchiare

chorus ['kɔːrəs] N coro; (*repeated part of song, also fig*) ritornello

chose [tʃəuz] PT *of* **choose**

chosen ['tʃəuzn] PP *of* **choose**

chowder ['tʃaudəʳ] N zuppa di pesce

Christ [kraɪst] N Cristo

christen ['krɪsn] VT battezzare

christening ['krɪsnɪŋ] N battesimo

Christian ['krɪstɪən] ADJ, N cristiano(-a)

Christianity [krɪstɪ'ænɪtɪ] N cristianesimo

Christian name N nome *m* di battesimo

Christmas ['krɪsməs] N Natale *m*; **happy or merry ~!** Buon Natale!

Christmas card N cartolina di Natale

Christmas carol N canto natalizio

Christmas Day N il giorno di Natale

Christmas Eve N la vigilia di Natale

Christmas Island N isola di Christmas

Christmas pudding N (*esp BRIT*) specie di budino con frutta secca, spezie e brandy

Christmas tree N albero di Natale

chrome [krəum] N cromo

chromium ['krəumɪəm] N cromo; (*also*: **chromium plating**) cromatura

chromosome ['krəuməsəum] N cromosoma *m*

chronic ['krɔnɪk] ADJ cronico(-a); (*fig: liar, smoker*) incallito(-a)

chronicle ['krɔnɪkl] N cronaca

chronological [krɔnə'lɔdʒɪkl] ADJ cronologico(-a)

chrysanthemum [krɪ'sænθəməm] N crisantemo

chubby ['tʃʌbɪ] ADJ paffuto(-a)

chuck [tʃʌk] VT buttare, gettare; **to ~ (up or in)** (*BRIT: job, person*) piantare
▶ **chuck out** VT buttar fuori

chuckle ['tʃʌkl] VI ridere sommessamente

chuffed [tʃʌft] ADJ (col): **to be ~ about sth** essere arcicontento(-a) di qc

chug [tʃʌg] VI (*also*: **chug along**: *train*) muoversi sbuffando

chum [tʃʌm] N compagno(-a)

chump [tʃʌmp] N (col) idiota *mf*

chunk [tʃʌŋk] N pezzo; (*of bread*) tocco

chunky ['tʃʌŋkɪ] ADJ (*furniture etc*) basso(-a) e largo(-a); (*person*) ben piantato(-a); (*knitwear*) di lana grossa

Chunnel ['tʃʌnəl] N = **Channel Tunnel**

church [tʃəːtʃ] N chiesa; **the C~ of England** la Chiesa anglicana

churchyard ['tʃəːtʃjɑːd] N sagrato

churlish ['tʃəːlɪʃ] ADJ rozzo(-a), sgarbato(-a)

churn [tʃəːn] N (*for butter*) zangola; (*also*: **milk churn**) bidone *m*
▶ **churn out** VT sfornare

chute [ʃuːt] N cascata; (*also*: **rubbish chute**) canale *m* di scarico; (*BRIT: children's slide*) scivolo

chutney ['tʃʌtnɪ] N salsa piccante (di frutta, zucchero e spezie)

CIA N ABBR (*US*: = *Central Intelligence Agency*) C.I.A. *f*

CID N ABBR (*BRIT*: = *Criminal Investigation Department*) ≈ polizia giudiziaria

cider ['saɪdəʳ] N sidro

CIF ABBR (= *cost, insurance, and freight*) C.I.F. *m*

cigar [sɪ'gɑːʳ] N sigaro

cigarette [sɪgə'rɛt] N sigaretta

cigarette case N portasigarette *m inv*

cigarette end N mozzicone *m*

cigarette holder N bocchino

cigarette lighter N accendino

C-in-C ABBR = **commander-in-chief**

cinch [sɪntʃ] N (col): **it's a ~** è presto fatto; (*sure thing*) è una cosa sicura

cinder ['sɪndəʳ] N cenere *f*

Cinderella [sɪndə'rɛlə] N Cenerentola

cine-camera ['sɪnɪ'kæmərə] N (*BRIT*) cinepresa

cine-film ['sɪnɪfɪlm] N (*BRIT*) pellicola

cinema ['sɪnəmə] N cinema *m inv*

cine-projector ['sɪnɪprə'dʒɛktəʳ] N (*BRIT*) proiettore *m*

cinnamon ['sɪnəmən] N cannella

cipher ['saɪfəʳ] N cifra; (*fig: faceless employee etc*) persona di nessun conto; **in ~** in codice

circa ['səːkə] PREP circa

circle ['səːkl] N cerchio; (*of friends etc*) circolo; (*in cinema*) galleria ▶ VI girare in circolo
▶ VT (*surround*) circondare; (*move round*) girare intorno a

circuit ['səːkɪt] N circuito

circuit board N (*Comput*) tavola dei circuiti

circuitous [səː'kjuɪtəs] ADJ indiretto(-a)

circular ['səːkjuləʳ] ADJ circolare ▶ N (*letter*) circolare *f*; (*as advertisement*) volantino pubblicitario

circulate ['səːkjuleɪt] VI circolare; (*person: socially*) girare e andare un po' da tutti
▶ VT far circolare

circulating capital ['səːkjuleɪtɪŋ-] N (*Comm*) capitale *m* d'esercizio

circulation [səːkju'leɪʃən] N circolazione *f*; (*of newspaper*) tiratura

circumcise ['səːkəmsaɪz] VT circoncidere

circumference [sə'kʌmfərəns] N circonferenza

circumflex ['sə:kəmflɛks] N (also: **circumflex accent**) accento circonflesso

circumscribe ['sə:kəmskraɪb] VT circoscrivere; (fig: limit) limitare

circumspect ['sə:kəmspɛkt] ADJ circospetto(-a)

circumstances ['sə:kəmstənsɪz] NPL circostanze fpl; (financial condition) condizioni fpl finanziarie; **in the ~** date le circostanze; **under no ~** per nessun motivo

circumstantial ['sə:kəm'stænʃəl] ADJ (report, statement) circostanziato(-a), dettagliato(-a); **~ evidence** prova indiretta

circumvent [sə:kəm'vɛnt] VT (rule etc) aggirare

circus ['sə:kəs] N circo; (also: **Circus**: in place names) piazza (di forma circolare)

cirrhosis [sɪ'rəusɪs] N (also: **cirrhosis of the liver**) cirrosi f inv (epatica)

CIS N ABBR (= Commonwealth of Independent States) CSI f

cissy ['sɪsɪ] N = **sissy**

cistern ['sɪstən] N cisterna; (in toilet) serbatoio d'acqua

citation [saɪ'teɪʃən] N citazione f

cite [saɪt] VT citare

citizen ['sɪtɪzn] N (Pol: of country) cittadino(-a); (: of town) abitante mf; **the citizens of this town** gli abitanti di questa città

Citizens' Advice Bureau N (BRIT) organizzazione di volontari che offre gratuitamente assistenza su questioni legali e finanziarie

citizenship ['sɪtɪznʃɪp] N cittadinanza

citric acid ['sɪtrɪk] N acido citrico

citrus fruit ['sɪtrəs-] N agrume m

city ['sɪtɪ] N città f inv; **the C~** la Città di Londra (centro commerciale)

city centre N centro della città

City Hall N (US) ≈ Comune m

City Technology College N (BRIT) istituto tecnico superiore (finanziato dall'industria)

civic ['sɪvɪk] ADJ civico(-a)

civic centre N (BRIT) centro civico

civil ['sɪvɪl] ADJ civile; (polite) educato(-a), gentile

civil disobedience N disubbidienza civile

civil engineer N ingegnere m civile

civil engineering N ingegneria civile

civilian [sɪ'vɪlɪən] ADJ, N borghese (mf)

civilization [sɪvɪlaɪ'zeɪʃən] N civiltà f inv

civilized ['sɪvɪlaɪzd] ADJ civilizzato(-a); (fig) cortese

civil law N codice m civile; (study) diritto civile

civil liberties NPL libertà fpl civili

civil rights NPL diritti mpl civili

civil servant N impiegato(-a) statale

Civil Service N amministrazione f statale

civil war N guerra civile

civvies ['sɪvɪz] NPL (col): **in ~** in borghese

CJD N ABBR (= Creutzfeld-Jakob disease) malattia di Creutzfeldt-Jakob

cl ABBR (= centilitre) cl

clad [klæd] ADJ: **~ (in)** vestito(-a) (di)

claim [kleɪm] VT (rights etc) rivendicare; (damages) richiedere; (assert) sostenere, pretendere ▸ N rivendicazione f; pretesa; richiesta; (right) diritto; **to ~ that/ to be** sostenere che/di essere; **(insurance) ~** domanda d'indennizzo; **to put in a ~ for sth** fare una richiesta di qc

claimant ['kleɪmənt] N (Admin, Law) richiedente mf

claim form N (gen) modulo di richiesta; (for expenses) modulo di rimborso spese

clairvoyant [klɛə'vɔɪənt] N chiaroveggente mf

clam [klæm] N vongola
▸ **clam up** VI (col) azzittirsi

clamber ['klæmbəʳ] VI arrampicarsi

clammy ['klæmɪ] ADJ (weather) caldo(-a) umido(-a); (hands) viscido(-a)

clamour, (US) **clamor** ['klæməʳ] N (noise) clamore m; (protest) protesta ▸ VI: **to ~ for sth** chiedere a gran voce qc

clamp [klæmp] N pinza; morsa ▸ VT stringere con una morsa; (Aut: wheel) applicare le ganasce a
▸ **clamp down** VT FUS (fig): **to ~ down (on)** dare un giro di vite (a)

clampdown ['klæmpdaun] N stretta, giro di vite; **a ~ on sth/sb** un giro di vite a qc/qn

clan [klæn] N clan m inv

clandestine [klæn'dɛstɪn] ADJ clandestino(-a)

clang [klæŋ] N fragore m, suono metallico

clanger ['klæŋəʳ] N: **to drop a ~** (BRIT col) fare una gaffe

clansman ['klænzmən] N (irreg) membro di un clan

clap [klæp] VI applaudire ▸ VT: **to ~ one's hands** battere le mani ▸ N: **a ~ of thunder** un tuono

clapping ['klæpɪŋ] N applausi mpl

claptrap ['klæptræp] N (col) stupidaggini fpl

claret ['klærət] N vino di Bordeaux

clarification [klærɪfɪ'keɪʃən] N (fig) chiarificazione f, chiarimento

clarify ['klærɪfaɪ] VT chiarificare, chiarire

clarinet [klærɪ'nɛt] N clarinetto

clarity ['klærɪtɪ] N chiarezza

clash [klæʃ] N frastuono; (fig) scontro ▸ VI (Mil, fig: have an argument) scontrarsi; cozzare; (colours) stridere; (dates, events) coincidere

clasp [klɑːsp] N (hold) stretta; (of necklace, bag) fermaglio, fibbia ▸ VT stringere

class [klɑːs] N classe f; (group, category) tipo, categoria ▶ VT classificare

class-conscious ['klɑːskɔnʃəs] ADJ che ha coscienza di classe

class consciousness N coscienza di classe

classic ['klæsɪk] ADJ classico(-a) ▶ N classico

classical ['klæsɪkəl] ADJ classico(-a)

classics ['klæsɪks] NPL (Scol) studi mpl umanistici

classification [klæsɪfɪ'keɪʃən] N classificazione f

classified ['klæsɪfaɪd] ADJ (information) segreto(-a), riservato(-a); ~ **ads** annunci economici

classify ['klæsɪfaɪ] VT classificare

classless society ['klɑːslɪs-] N società f inv senza distinzioni di classe

classmate ['klɑːsmeɪt] N compagno(-a) di classe

classroom ['klɑːsrum] N aula

classroom assistant N assistente mf in classe dell'insegnante

classy ['klɑːsɪ] ADJ (col) chic inv, elegante

clatter ['klætə'] N tintinnio; scalpitio ▶ VI tintinnare; scalpitare

clause [klɔːz] N clausola; (Ling) proposizione f

claustrophobia [klɔːstrə'fəubɪə] N claustrofobia

claustrophobic [klɔːstrə'fəubɪk] ADJ claustrofobico(-a)

claw [klɔː] N tenaglia; (of bird of prey) artiglio; (of lobster) pinza ▶ VT graffiare; afferrare

clay [kleɪ] N argilla

clean [kliːn] ADJ pulito(-a); (outline, break, movement) netto(-a) ▶ VT pulire ▶ ADV: **he ~ forgot** si è completamente dimenticato; **to come ~** (col: admit guilt) confessare; **to have a ~ driving licence** or **record** (US) non aver mai preso contravvenzioni; **to ~ one's teeth** (BRIT) lavarsi i denti
▶ **clean off** VT togliere
▶ **clean out** VT ripulire
▶ **clean up** VI far pulizia ▶ VT (also fig) ripulire; (fig: make profit): **to ~ up on** fare una barca di soldi con

clean-cut ['kliːn'kʌt] ADJ (man) curato(-a); (situation etc) ben definito(-a)

cleaner ['kliːnə'] N (person) uomo (donna) delle pulizie; (also: **dry cleaner**) tintore(-a) (product) smacchiatore m

cleaner's N (also: **dry cleaner's**) tintoria

cleaning ['kliːnɪŋ] N pulizia

cleaning lady N donna delle pulizie

cleanliness ['klɛnlɪnɪs] N pulizia

cleanly ['kliːnlɪ] ADV in modo netto

cleanse [klɛnz] VT pulire; purificare

cleanser ['klɛnzə'] N detergente m; (cosmetic) latte m detergente

clean-shaven ['kliːn'ʃeɪvn] ADJ sbarbato(-a)

cleansing department ['klɛnzɪŋ-] N (BRIT) nettezza urbana

clean sweep N: **to make a ~ (of)** fare piazza pulita (di)

clean technology N tecnologie fpl ambientali

clean-up ['kliːnʌp] N pulizia

clear [klɪə'] ADJ chiaro(-a); (glass etc) trasparente; (road, way) libero(-a); (profit, majority) netto(-a); (conscience) pulito(-a) ▶ VT sgombrare; liberare; (table) sparecchiare; (site, woodland) spianare; (Comm: goods) liquidare; (Law: suspect) discolpare; (obstacle) superare; (cheque) fare la compensazione di ▶ VI (weather) rasserenarsi; (fog) andarsene ▶ ADV: ~ **of** distante da ▶ N: **to be in the ~** (out of debt) essere in attivo; (out of suspicion) essere a posto; (out of danger) essere fuori pericolo; **to ~ the table** sparecchiare (la tavola); **to ~ one's throat** schiarirsi la gola; **to ~ a profit** avere un profitto netto; **to make o.s. ~** spiegarsi bene; **to make it ~ to sb that ...** far capire a qn che ...; **I have a ~ day tomorrow** (BRIT) non ho impegni domani; **to keep ~ of sb/sth** tenersi lontano da qn/qc, stare alla larga da qn/qc
▶ **clear away** VT (things, clothes, etc) mettere a posto; **to ~ away the dishes** sparecchiare la tavola
▶ **clear off** VI (col: leave) svignarsela
▶ **clear up** VI schiarirsi ▶ VT mettere in ordine; (mystery) risolvere

clearance ['klɪərəns] N (removal) sgombro; (free space) spazio; (permission) autorizzazione f, permesso

clearance sale N vendita di liquidazione

clear-cut ['klɪə'kʌt] ADJ ben delineato(-a), distinto(-a)

clearing ['klɪərɪŋ] N radura; (BRIT Banking) clearing m

clearing bank N (BRIT) banca che fa uso della camera di compensazione

clearing house N (Comm) camera di compensazione

clearly ['klɪəlɪ] ADV chiaramente

clearway ['klɪəweɪ] N (BRIT) strada con divieto di sosta

cleavage ['kliːvɪdʒ] N (of woman) scollatura

cleaver ['kliːvə'] N mannaia

clef [klɛf] N (Mus) chiave f

cleft [klɛft] N (in rock) crepa, fenditura

clemency ['klɛmənsɪ] N clemenza

clement ['klɛmənt] ADJ (weather) mite, clemente

clench [klɛntʃ] VT stringere

clergy ['kləːdʒɪ] N clero

clergyman ['kləːdʒɪmən] N (irreg) ecclesiastico

clerical ['klɛrɪkl] ADJ d'impiegato; (Rel) clericale

clerk [klɑːk, (US) kləːrk] N (BRIT)
impiegato(-a); (US: salesman/woman)
commesso(-a); **C~ of the Court** (Law)
cancelliere m

clever ['klɛvəʳ] ADJ (mentally) intelligente;
(deft, skilful) abile; (device, arrangement)
ingegnoso(-a)

cleverly ['klɛvəlɪ] ADV abilmente

clew [kluː] N (US) = **clue**

cliché ['kliːʃeɪ] N cliché m inv

click [klɪk] VI scattare ▶ VT: **to ~ one's tongue**
schioccare la lingua; **to ~ one's heels**
battere i tacchi

clickable ['klɪkəbl] ADJ cliccabile

client ['klaɪənt] N cliente mf

clientele [kliːãːnˈtɛl] N clientela

cliff [klɪf] N scogliera scoscesa, rupe f

cliffhanger ['klɪfhæŋəʳ] N (TV, fig) episodio
(or situazione etc) ricco(-a) di suspense

climactic [klaɪˈmæktɪk] ADJ culminante

climate ['klaɪmɪt] N clima m

climate change N cambiamenti mpl
climatici

climax ['klaɪmæks] N culmine m; (of play etc)
momento più emozionante; (sexual) orgasmo

climb [klaɪm] VI salire; (clamber)
arrampicarsi; (plane) prendere quota ▶ VT
salire; (Climbing) scalare ▶ N salita;
arrampicata; scalata; **to ~ over a wall**
scavalcare un muro
▶ **climb down** VI scendere; (BRIT fig) far
marcia indietro

climbdown ['klaɪmdaun] N (BRIT) ritirata

climber ['klaɪməʳ] N (also: **rock climber**)
rocciatore(-trice); alpinista mf

climbing ['klaɪmɪŋ] N (also: **rock climbing**)
alpinismo

clinch [klɪntʃ] VT (deal) concludere

clincher ['klɪntʃəʳ] N (col): **that was the ~**
quello è stato il fattore decisivo

cling [klɪŋ] (pt, pp **clung** [klʌŋ]) VI: **to ~ (to)**
tenersi stretto(-a) (a), aggrapparsi (a);
(clothes) aderire strettamente (a)

clingfilm ® ['klɪŋfɪlm] N pellicola trasparente
(per alimenti)

clinic ['klɪnɪk] N clinica; (session) seduta; serie
f di sedute

clinical ['klɪnɪkəl] ADJ clinico(-a); (fig)
freddo(-a), distaccato(-a)

clink [klɪŋk] VI tintinnare

clip [klɪp] N (for hair) forcina; (also: **paper clip**)
graffetta; (TV, Cine) sequenza; (BRIT: also:
bulldog clip) fermafogli m inv; (holding hose
etc) anello d'attacco ▶ VT (also: **clip together**:
papers) attaccare insieme; (hair, nails) tagliare;
(hedge) tosare

clippers ['klɪpəz] NPL macchinetta per
capelli; (also: **nail clippers**) forbicine fpl per le
unghie

clipping ['klɪpɪŋ] N (from newspaper) ritaglio

clique [kliːk] N cricca

cloak [kləuk] N mantello ▶ VT avvolgere

cloakroom ['kləukrum] N (for coats etc)
guardaroba m inv; (BRIT: W.C.) gabinetti mpl

clock [klɔk] N orologio; (of taxi) tassametro;
around the ~ ventiquattr'ore su
ventiquattro; **to sleep round the ~** or **the ~
round** dormire un giorno intero; **to work
against the ~** lavorare in gara col tempo;
30,000 on the ~ (BRIT Aut) 30.000 sul
contachilometri
▶ **clock in, clock on** VI (BRIT) timbrare il
cartellino (all'entrata)
▶ **clock off, clock out** VI (BRIT) timbrare il
cartellino (all'uscita)
▶ **clock up** VT (miles, hours etc) fare

clockwise ['klɔkwaɪz] ADV in senso orario

clockwork ['klɔkwəːk] N movimento or
meccanismo a orologeria ▶ ADJ (toy, train) a
molla

clog [klɔg] N zoccolo ▶ VT intasare ▶ VI (also:
clog up) intasarsi, bloccarsi

cloister ['klɔɪstəʳ] N chiostro

clone [kləun] N clone m ▶ VT clonare

close¹ [kləus] ADJ vicino(-a); (writing, texture)
fitto(-a); (watch) stretto(-a); (examination)
attento(-a); (contest) combattuto(-a);
(weather) afoso(-a) ▶ ADV vicino, dappresso;
~ to prep vicino a; **~ by**, **~ at hand** qui (or lì)
vicino; **how ~ is Edinburgh to Glasgow?**
quanto dista Edimburgo da Glasgow?; **a ~
friend** un amico intimo; **to have a ~ shave**
(fig) scamparla bella; **at ~ quarters** da vicino

close² [kləuz] VT chiudere; (bargain, deal)
concludere ▶ VI (shop etc) chiudere; (lid, door
etc) chiudersi; (end) finire ▶ N (end) fine f; **to
bring sth to a ~** terminare qc
▶ **close down** VT chiudere (definitivamente)
▶ VI cessare (definitivamente)
▶ **close in** VI (hunters) stringersi attorno;
(evening, night, fog) calare; **to ~ in on sb**
accerchiare qn; **the days are closing in** le
giornate si accorciano
▶ **close off** VT (area) chiudere

closed [kləuzd] ADJ chiuso(-a)

closed-circuit ['kləuzd'səːkɪt] ADJ:
~ television televisione f a circuito chiuso

closed shop N azienda o fabbrica che impiega solo
aderenti ai sindacati

close-knit ['kləus'nɪt] ADJ (family, community)
molto unito(-a)

closely ['kləuslɪ] ADV (examine, watch) da
vicino; **we are ~ related** siamo parenti
stretti; **a ~ guarded secret** un assoluto
segreto

close season ['kləuz-] N (Football) periodo di
vacanza del campionato; (Hunting) stagione f
di chiusura (di caccia, pesca ecc)

closet ['klɔzɪt] N (*cupboard*) armadio
close-up ['kləʊsʌp] N primo piano
closing ['kləʊzɪŋ] ADJ (*stages, remarks*) conclusivo(-a), finale; **~ price** (*Stock Exchange*) prezzo di chiusura
closing time N orario di chiusura
closure ['kləʊʒəʳ] N chiusura
clot [klɔt] N (*also*: **blood clot**) coagulo; (*col: idiot*) scemo(-a) ▶ vi coagularsi
cloth [klɔθ] N (*material*) tessuto, stoffa; (BRIT: *also*: **teacloth**) strofinaccio; (*also*: **tablecloth**) tovaglia
clothe [kləʊð] VT vestire
clothes [kləʊðz] NPL abiti *mpl*, vestiti *mpl*; **to put one's ~ on** vestirsi; **to take one's ~ off** togliersi i vestiti, svestirsi
clothes brush N spazzola per abiti
clothes line N corda (per stendere il bucato)
clothes peg, (US) **clothes pin** N molletta
clothing ['kləʊðɪŋ] N = **clothes**
clotted cream ['klɔtɪd-] N (BRIT) panna rappresa
cloud [klaʊd] N nuvola; (*of dust, smoke, gas*) nube *f* ▶ vT (*liquid*) intorbidire; **to ~ the issue** distogliere dal problema; **every ~ has a silver lining** (*proverb*) non tutto il male vien per nuocere
▶ **cloud over** vi rannuvolarsi; (*fig*) offuscarsi
cloudburst ['klaʊdbəːst] N acquazzone *m*
cloud computing N cloud computing *m inv*
cloud-cuckoo-land ['klaʊd'kuku:'lænd] N (BRIT) mondo dei sogni
cloudy ['klaʊdɪ] ADJ nuvoloso(-a); (*liquid*) torbido(-a)
clout [klaʊt] N (*blow*) colpo; (*fig*) influenza ▶ vT dare un colpo a
clove [kləʊv] N chiodo di garofano
clove of garlic N spicchio d'aglio
clover ['kləʊvəʳ] N trifoglio
cloverleaf ['kləʊvəli:f] N foglia di trifoglio; (*Aut*) raccordo (a quadrifoglio)
clown [klaʊn] N pagliaccio ▶ vi (*also*: **clown about**, **clown around**) fare il pagliaccio
cloying ['klɔɪɪŋ] ADJ (*taste, smell*) nauseabondo(-a)
club [klʌb] N (*society*) club *m inv*, circolo; (*weapon, Golf*) mazza ▶ vT bastonare ▶ vi: **to ~ together** associarsi; **clubs** NPL (*Cards*) fiori *mpl*
club car N (*US Rail*) carrozza *or* vagone *m* ristorante
club class N (*Aviat*) classe *f* club *inv*
clubhouse ['klʌbhaus] N sede *f* del circolo
club soda N (US) = **soda**
cluck [klʌk] vi chiocciare
clue [klu:] N indizio; (*in crosswords*) definizione *f*; **I haven't a ~** non ho la minima idea

clued up, (US) **clued in** [klu:d-] ADJ (*col*) (ben) informato(-a)
clump [klʌmp] N (*of flowers, trees*) gruppo; (*of grass*) ciuffo
clumsy ['klʌmzɪ] ADJ (*person*) goffo(-a), maldestro(-a); (*object*) malfatto(-a), mal costruito(-a)
clung [klʌŋ] PT, PP *of* **cling**
cluster ['klʌstəʳ] N gruppo ▶ vi raggrupparsi
clutch [klʌtʃ] N (*grip, grasp*) presa, stretta; (*Aut*) frizione *f* ▶ vT afferrare, stringere forte; **to ~ at** aggrapparsi a
clutter ['klʌtəʳ] vT (*also*: **clutter up**) ingombrare ▶ N confusione *f*, disordine *m*
cm ABBR (= *centimetre*) cm
CNAA N ABBR (BRIT: = *Council for National Academic Awards*) *organizzazione che conferisce premi accademici*
CND N ABBR (BRIT) = **Campaign for Nuclear Disarmament**
CO N ABBR (= *commanding officer*) Com.; (BRIT) = **Commonwealth Office** ▶ ABBR (US) = **Colorado**
Co. ABBR = **county**; (= *company*) C., C.ia
c/o ABBR (= *care of*) presso
coach [kəʊtʃ] N (*bus*) pullman *m inv*; (*horse-drawn, of train*) carrozza; (*Sport*) allenatore(-trice); (*tutor*) chi dà ripetizioni ▶ vT allenare; dare ripetizioni a
coach station (BRIT) N stazione *f* delle corriere
coach trip N viaggio in pullman
coagulate [kəʊ'ægjuleɪt] vT coagulare ▶ vi coagularsi
coal [kəʊl] N carbone *m*
coalface ['kəʊlfeɪs] N fronte *f*
coalfield ['kəʊlfi:ld] N bacino carbonifero
coalition [kəʊə'lɪʃən] N coalizione *f*
coalman ['kəʊlmən] N (*irreg*) negoziante *m* in carbone
coalmine ['kəʊlmaɪn] N miniera di carbone
coalminer ['kəʊlmaɪnəʳ] N minatore *m*
coalmining ['kəʊlmaɪnɪŋ] N estrazione *f* del carbone
coarse [kɔ:s] ADJ (*salt, sand etc*) grosso(-a); (*cloth, person*) rozzo(-a); (*vulgar: character, laugh*) volgare
coast [kəʊst] N costa ▶ vi (*with cycle etc*) scendere a ruota libera
coastal ['kəʊstəl] ADJ costiero(-a)
coaster ['kəʊstəʳ] N (*Naut*) nave *f* da cabotaggio; (*for glass*) sottobicchiere *m*
coastguard ['kəʊstgɑ:d] N guardia costiera
coastline ['kəʊstlaɪn] N linea costiera
coat [kəʊt] N cappotto; (*of animal*) pelo; (*of paint*) mano *f* ▶ vT coprire; **~ of arms** *n* stemma *m*
coat hanger N attaccapanni *m inv*
coating ['kəʊtɪŋ] N rivestimento

co-author ['kəʊ'ɔ:θəʳ] N coautore(-trice)
coax [kəʊks] VT indurre (con moine)
cob [kɔb] N *see* **corn**
cobbled ['kɔbld] ADJ: ~ **street** strada pavimentata a ciottoli
cobbler ['kɔbləʳ] N calzolaio
cobbles ['kɔblz], **cobblestones** ['kɔblstəʊnz] NPL ciottoli *mpl*
COBOL ['kəʊbɔl] N COBOL *m*
cobra ['kəʊbrə] N cobra *m inv*
cobweb ['kɔbwɛb] N ragnatela
cocaine [kə'keɪn] N cocaina
cock [kɔk] N (*rooster*) gallo; (*male bird*) maschio ▶ VT (*gun*) armare; **to ~ one's ears** (*fig*) drizzare le orecchie
cock-a-hoop [kɔkə'hu:p] ADJ euforico(-a)
cockerel ['kɔkərəl] N galletto
cock-eyed ['kɔkaɪd] ADJ (*fig*) storto(-a); strampalato(-a)
cockle ['kɔkl] N cardio
cockney ['kɔknɪ] N cockney *mf* (*abitante dei quartieri popolari dell'East End di Londra*)
cockpit ['kɔkpɪt] N abitacolo
cockroach ['kɔkrəʊtʃ] N blatta
cocktail ['kɔkteɪl] N cocktail *m inv*; **prawn ~**, (*US*) **shrimp ~** cocktail *m inv* di gamberetti
cocktail cabinet N mobile *m* bar *inv*
cocktail party N cocktail *m inv*
cocktail shaker N shaker *m inv*
cocky ['kɔkɪ] ADJ spavaldo(-a), arrogante
cocoa ['kəʊkəʊ] N cacao
coconut ['kəʊkənʌt] N noce *f* di cocco
cocoon [kə'ku:n] N bozzolo
COD ABBR = **cash on delivery**; (*US*) = **collect on delivery**
cod [kɔd] N merluzzo
C.O.D. ABBR = **cash on delivery**
code [kəʊd] N codice *m*; ~ **of behaviour** regole *fpl* di condotta; ~ **of practice** codice professionale
codeine ['kəʊdi:n] N codeina
codger ['kɔdʒəʳ] N (*BRIT col*): **an old ~** un simpatico nonnetto
codicil ['kɔdɪsɪl] N codicillo
codify ['kəʊdɪfaɪ] VT codificare
cod-liver oil ['kɔdlɪvəʳ-] N olio di fegato di merluzzo
co-driver [kəʊ'draɪvəʳ] N (*in race*) copilota *m*; (*of lorry*) secondo autista *m*
co-ed ['kəʊ'ɛd] ADJ ABBR = **coeducational** ▶ N ABBR (*US: female student*) studentessa presso un'università mista; (*BRIT: school*) scuola mista
coeducational ['kəʊɛdju'keɪʃənl] ADJ misto(-a)
coerce [kəʊ'ə:s] VT costringere
coercion [kəʊ'ə:ʃən] N coercizione *f*
coexistence ['kəʊɪg'zɪstəns] N coesistenza
C. of C. N ABBR = **chamber of commerce**
C of E ABBR = **Church of England**

coffee ['kɔfɪ] N caffè *m inv*; **white ~**, (*US*) **~ with cream** caffellatte *m*
coffee bar N (*BRIT*) caffè *m inv*
coffee bean N grano *or* chicco di caffè
coffee break N pausa per il caffè
coffeecake ['kɔfɪkeɪk] N (*US*) panino dolce all'uva
coffee cup N tazzina da caffè
coffee maker N bollitore *m* per il caffè
coffeepot ['kɔfɪpɔt] N caffettiera
coffee shop N ≈ caffè *m inv*
coffee table N tavolino
coffin ['kɔfɪn] N bara
C of I ABBR = **Church of Ireland**
C of S ABBR = **Church of Scotland**
cog [kɔg] N dente *m*
cogent ['kəʊdʒənt] ADJ convincente
cognac ['kɔnjæk] N cognac *m inv*
cognitive ['kɔgnɪtɪv] ADJ cognitivo(-a)
cogwheel ['kɔgwi:l] N ruota dentata
cohabit [kəʊ'hæbɪt] VI (*formal*): **to ~ (with sb)** coabitare (con qn)
coherent [kəʊ'hɪərənt] ADJ coerente
cohesion [kəʊ'hi:ʒən] N coesione *f*
cohesive [kəʊ'hi:sɪv] ADJ (*fig*) unificante, coesivo(-a)
COI N ABBR (*BRIT*) = **Central Office of Information**
coil [kɔɪl] N rotolo; (*one loop*) anello; (*Aut, Elec*) bobina; (*contraceptive*) spirale *f*; (*of smoke*) filo ▶ VT avvolgere
coin [kɔɪn] N moneta ▶ VT (*word*) coniare
coinage ['kɔɪnɪdʒ] N sistema *m* monetario
coin-box ['kɔɪnbɔks] N (*BRIT*) cabina telefonica
coincide [kəʊɪn'saɪd] VI coincidere
coincidence [kəʊ'ɪnsɪdəns] N combinazione *f*
coin-operated ['kɔɪn'ɔpəreɪtɪd] ADJ (*machine*) (che funziona) a monete
Coke® [kəʊk] N (*Coca-Cola*) coca *f inv*
coke [kəʊk] N coke *m*
Col. ABBR = **colonel**; (*US*) = **Colorado**
COLA N ABBR (*US*: = *cost-of-living adjustment*) ≈ scala mobile
colander ['kɔləndəʳ] N colino
cold [kəʊld] ADJ freddo(-a) ▶ N freddo; (*Med*) raffreddore *m*; **it's ~** fa freddo; **to be ~** (*person*) aver freddo; (*object*) essere freddo(-a); **to catch ~** prendere freddo; **to catch a ~** prendere un raffreddore; **in ~ blood** a sangue freddo; **to have ~ feet** avere i piedi freddi; (*fig*) aver la fifa; **to give sb the ~ shoulder** ignorare qn
cold-blooded [kəʊld'blʌdɪd] ADJ (*Zool*) a sangue freddo
cold call N chiamata pubblicitaria non richiesta
cold cream N crema emolliente

coldly ['kəuldlı] ADV freddamente

cold sore N erpete m

cold sweat N: **to be in a ~ (about sth)** sudare freddo (per qc)

cold turkey N (col): **to go ~** avere la scimmia (drogato)

Cold War N: **the ~** la guerra fredda

coleslaw ['kəulslɔ:] N insalata di cavolo bianco

colic ['kɔlık] N colica

colicky ['kɔlıkı] ADJ che soffre di coliche

collaborate [kə'læbəreıt] vı collaborare

collaboration [kəlæbə'reıʃən] N collaborazione f

collaborator [kə'læbəreıtəʳ] N collaboratore(-trice)

collage [kɔ'lɑ:ʒ] N (Art) collage m inv

collagen ['kɔlədʒən] N collageno

collapse [kə'læps] vı (gen) crollare; (government) cadere; (Med) avere un collasso; (plans) fallire ▶ N crollo; caduta; (Med) collasso; fallimento

collapsible [kə'læpsəbl] ADJ pieghevole

collar ['kɔləʳ] N (of coat, shirt) colletto; (for dog) collare m; (Tech) anello, fascetta ▶ vт (col: person, object) beccare

collarbone ['kɔləbəun] N clavicola

collate [kɔ'leıt] vт collazionare

collateral [kɔ'lætərəl] N garanzia

collation [kɔ'leıʃən] N collazione f

colleague ['kɔli:g] N collega mf

collect [kə'lɛkt] vт (gen) raccogliere; (as a hobby) fare collezione di; (BRIT: call for) prendere; (money owed, pension) riscuotere; (donations, subscriptions) fare una colletta di ▶ vı (people) adunarsi, riunirsi; (rubbish etc) ammucchiarsi ▶ ADV (US Tel): **to call ~** fare una chiamata a carico del destinatario; **to ~ one's thoughts** raccogliere le idee; **~ on delivery** (US Comm) pagamento alla consegna

collected [kə'lɛktıd] ADJ: **~ works** opere fpl raccolte

collection [kə'lɛkʃən] N collezione f; raccolta; (for money) colletta; (Post) levata

collective [kə'lɛktıv] ADJ collettivo(-a) ▶ N collettivo

collective bargaining N trattative fpl (sindacali) collettive

collector [kə'lɛktəʳ] N collezionista mf; (of taxes) esattore m; **~'s item** or **piece** pezzo da collezionista

college ['kɔlıdʒ] N (Scol) college m inv; (of technology, agriculture etc) istituto superiore; (body) collegio; **~ of education** ≈ facoltà f inv di Magistero

collide [kə'laıd] vı: **to ~ (with)** scontrarsi (con)

collie ['kɔlı] N (dog) collie m inv

colliery ['kɔlıərı] N (BRIT) miniera di carbone

collision [kə'lıʒən] N collisione f, scontro; **to be on a ~ course** (also fig) essere in rotta di collisione

collision damage waiver N (Insurance) copertura per i danni alla vettura

colloquial [kə'ləukwıəl] ADJ familiare

collusion [kə'lu:ʒən] N collusione f; **in ~ with** in accordo segreto con

Colo. ABBR (US) = **Colorado**

Cologne [kə'ləun] N Colonia

cologne [kə'ləun] N (also: **eau de cologne**) acqua di colonia

Colombia [kə'lɔmbıə] N Colombia

Colombian [kə'lɔmbıən] ADJ, N colombiano(-a)

colon ['kəulən] N (sign) due punti mpl; (Med) colon m inv

colonel ['kə:nl] N colonnello

colonial [kə'ləunıəl] ADJ coloniale

colonize ['kɔlənaız] vт colonizzare

colony ['kɔlənı] N colonia

color etc ['kʌləʳ] (US) = **colour** etc

Colorado beetle [kɔlə'rɑ:dəu-] N dorifora

colossal [kə'lɔsl] ADJ colossale

colour, (US) **color** ['kʌləʳ] N colore m ▶ vт colorare; (tint, dye) tingere; (fig: affect) influenzare ▶ vı (blush) arrossire ▶ CPD (film, photograph, television) a colori; **colours** NPL (of party, club) emblemi mpl
▶ **colour in** vт colorare

colour bar, (US) **color bar** N discriminazione f razziale (in locali ecc)

colour-blind, (US) **color-blind** ['kʌləblaınd] ADJ daltonico(-a)

coloured, (US) **colored** ['kʌləd] ADJ colorato(-a); (photo) a colori; (person) di colore ▶ N: **colo(u)reds** gente f di colore

colour film, (US) **color film** N (for camera) pellicola a colori

colourful, (US) **colorful** ['kʌləful] ADJ pieno(-a) di colore, a vivaci colori; (personality) colorato(-a)

colouring, (US) **coloring** ['kʌlərıŋ] N colorazione f; (substance) colorante m; (complexion) colorito

colour scheme, (US) **color scheme** N combinazione f di colori

colour supplement N (BRIT Press) supplemento a colori

colour television, (US) **color television** N televisione f a colori

colt [kəult] N puledro

column ['kɔləm] N colonna; (fashion column, sports column etc) rubrica; **the editorial ~** l'articolo di fondo

columnist ['kɔləmnıst] N articolista mf

coma ['kəumə] N coma m inv

comb [kəum] N pettine m ▶ vт (hair) pettinare; (area) battere a tappeto

combat ['kɔmbæt] N combattimento ▶ VT combattere, lottare contro
combination [kɔmbɪ'neɪʃən] N combinazione f
combination lock N serratura a combinazione
combine¹ [kəm'baɪn] VT: **to ~ (with)** combinare (con); (one quality with another) **to ~ sth with sth** unire qc a qc ▶ VI unirsi; (Chem) combinarsi ▶ N ['kɔmbaɪn] lega; (Econ) associazione f; **a combined effort** uno sforzo collettivo
combine², **combine harvester** N mietitrebbia
combo ['kɔmbəu] N (Jazz etc) gruppo
combustible [kəm'bʌstɪbl] ADJ combustibile
combustion [kəm'bʌstʃən] N combustione f
come [kʌm] (pt **came** [keɪm], pp ~ [kʌm]) VI venire; (arrive) venire, arrivare; **~ with me** vieni con me; **we've just ~ from Paris** siamo appena arrivati da Parigi; **nothing came of it** non è saltato fuori niente; **~ into sight** or **view** apparire; **to ~ to** (decision etc) raggiungere; **I've ~ to like him** ha cominciato a piacermi; **to ~ undone/loose** slacciarsi/allentarsi; **coming!** vengo!; **if it comes to it** nella peggiore delle ipotesi
▶ **come about** VI succedere
▶ **come across** VT FUS trovare per caso ▶ VI: **to ~ across well/badly** fare una buona/cattiva impressione
▶ **come along** VI (pupil, work) fare progressi; **~ along!** avanti!, andiamo!, forza!
▶ **come apart** VI andare in pezzi; (become detached) staccarsi
▶ **come away** VI venire via; (become detached) staccarsi
▶ **come back** VI ritornare; (reply: col): **can I ~ back to you on that one?** possiamo riparlarne più tardi?
▶ **come by** VT FUS (acquire) ottenere; procurarsi
▶ **come down** VI scendere; (prices) calare; (buildings) essere demolito(-a)
▶ **come forward** VI farsi avanti; presentarsi
▶ **come from** VT FUS venire da; provenire da
▶ **come in** VI entrare
▶ **come in for** VT FUS (criticism etc) ricevere
▶ **come into** VT FUS (money) ereditare
▶ **come off** VI (button) staccarsi; (stain) andar via; (attempt) riuscire
▶ **come on** VI (lights) accendersi; (electricity) entrare in funzione; (pupil, undertaking) fare progressi; **~ on!** avanti!, andiamo!, forza!
▶ **come out** VI (strike) entrare in sciopero; (stain) andare via
▶ **come over** VT FUS: **I don't know what's ~ over him!** non so cosa gli sia successo!
▶ **come round** VI (after faint, operation) riprendere conoscenza, rinvenire
▶ **come through** VI (survive) sopravvivere, farcela; **the call came through** ci hanno passato la telefonata
▶ **come to** VI rinvenire ▶ VT (add up to: amount): **how much does it ~ to?** quanto costa?, quanto viene?
▶ **come under** VT FUS (heading) trovarsi sotto; (influence) cadere sotto, subire
▶ **come up** VI venire su; (sun) salire; (problem) sorgere; (event) essere in arrivo; (in conversation) saltar fuori
▶ **come up against** VT FUS (resistance, difficulties) urtare contro
▶ **come up to** VT FUS arrivare (fino) a; **the film didn't ~ up to our expectations** il film ci ha delusi
▶ **come up with** VT FUS: **he came up with an idea** venne fuori con un'idea
▶ **come upon** VT FUS trovare per caso
comeback ['kʌmbæk] N (Theat etc) ritorno; (reaction) reazione f; (response) risultato, risposta
comedian [kə'miːdɪən] N comico
comedienne [kəmiːdɪ'ɛn] N attrice f comica
comedown ['kʌmdaun] N rovescio
comedy ['kɔmɪdɪ] N commedia
comet ['kɔmɪt] N cometa
comeuppance [kʌm'ʌpəns] N: **to get one's ~** ricevere ciò che si merita
comfort ['kʌmfət] N comodità f inv, benessere m; (relief) consolazione f, conforto ▶ VT consolare, confortare
comfortable ['kʌmfətəbl] ADJ comodo(-a); (financially) agiato(-a); (income, majority) più che sufficiente; **I don't feel very ~ about it** non mi sento molto tranquillo
comfortably ['kʌmfətəblɪ] ADV (sit) comodamente; (live) bene
comforter ['kʌmfətəʳ] N (US) trapunta
comforts ['kʌmfəts] NPL comforts mpl, comodità fpl
comfort station N (US) gabinetti mpl
comic ['kɔmɪk] ADJ (also: **comical**) comico(-a), divertente ▶ N comico; (BRIT: magazine) giornaletto
comic book N (US) giornalino (a fumetti)
comic strip N fumetto
coming ['kʌmɪŋ] N arrivo ▶ ADJ (next) prossimo(-a); (future) futuro(-a); **in the ~ weeks** nelle prossime settimane
comings and goings NPL, **coming and going** N andirivieni m inv
Comintern ['kɔmɪntəːn] N KOMINTERN m
comma ['kɔmə] N virgola
command [kə'mɑːnd] N ordine m, comando; (Mil: authority) comando; (mastery) padronanza; (Comput) command m inv, comando ▶ VT comandare; **to ~ sb to do**

C

485

ordinare a qn di fare; **to have/take ~ of** avere/prendere il comando di; **to have at one's ~** (*money, resources etc*) avere a propria disposizione

command economy N = **planned economy**

commandeer [kɔmən'dɪə^r] VT requisire

commander [kə'mɑːndə^r] N capo; (*Mil*) comandante *m*

commander-in-chief [kə'mɑːndərɪn'tʃiːf] N (*Mil*) comandante *m* in capo

commanding [kə'mɑːndɪŋ] ADJ (*appearance*) imponente; (*voice, tone*) autorevole; (*lead, position*) dominante

commanding officer N comandante *m*

commandment [kə'mɑːndmənt] N (*Rel*) comandamento

command module N (*Space*) modulo di comando

commando [kə'mɑːndəu] N commando *m inv*; membro di un commando

commemorate [kə'mɛməreɪt] VT commemorare

commemoration [kəmɛmə'reɪʃən] N commemorazione *f*

commemorative [kə'mɛmərətɪv] ADJ commemorativo(-a)

commence [kə'mɛns] VT, VI cominciare

commencement [kə'mɛnsmənt] (*US*) N (*Univ*) cerimonia di consegna dei diplomi

commend [kə'mɛnd] VT lodare; raccomandare

commendable [kə'mɛndəbl] ADJ lodevole

commendation [kɔmɛn'deɪʃən] N lode *f*; raccomandazione *f*; (*for bravery etc*) encomio

commensurate [kə'mɛnʃərɪt] ADJ: **~ with** proporzionato(-a) a

comment ['kɔmɛnt] N commento ▶ VI: **to ~ (on)** fare commenti (su); **to ~ that** osservare che; **"no ~"** "niente da dire"

commentary ['kɔməntəri] N commentario; (*Sport*) radiocronaca; telecronaca

commentator ['kɔmənteɪtə^r] N commentatore(-trice); (*Sport*) radiocronista *mf*; telecronista *mf*

commerce ['kɔmə:s] N commercio

commercial [kə'mə:ʃəl] ADJ commerciale ▶ N (*TV, Radio*) pubblicità *f inv*

commercial bank N banca commerciale

commercial break N intervallo pubblicitario

commercial college N ≈ istituto commerciale

commercialism [kə'mə:ʃəlɪzəm] N affarismo

commercial television N televisione *f* commerciale

commercial traveller N commesso viaggiatore

commercial vehicle N veicolo commerciale

commiserate [kə'mɪzəreɪt] VI: **to ~ with** condolersi con

commission [kə'mɪʃən] N commissione *f*; (*for salesman*) commissione, provvigione *f* ▶ VT (*Mil*) nominare (al comando); (*work of art*) commissionare; **I get 10% ~** ricevo il 10% sulle vendite; **out of ~** (*Naut*) in disarmo; (*machine*) fuori uso; **to ~ sb to do sth** incaricare qn di fare qc; **to ~ sth from sb** (*painting etc*) commissionare qc a qn; **~ of inquiry** (*BRIT*) commissione *f* d'inchiesta

commissionaire [kəmɪʃə'nɛə^r] N (*BRIT: at shop, cinema etc*) portiere *m* in livrea

commissioner [kə'mɪʃənə^r] N commissionario; (*Police*) questore *m*

commit [kə'mɪt] VT (*act*) commettere; (*to sb's care*) affidare; **to ~ o.s. (to do)** impegnarsi (a fare); **to ~ suicide** suicidarsi; **to ~ sb for trial** rinviare qn a giudizio

commitment [kə'mɪtmənt] N impegno; promessa

committed [kə'mɪtɪd] ADJ (*writer*) impegnato(-a); (*Christian*) convinto(-a)

committee [kə'mɪtɪ] N comitato, commissione *f*; **to be on a ~** far parte di un comitato *or* di una commissione

committee meeting N riunione *f* di comitato *or* di commissione

commodity [kə'mɔdɪtɪ] N prodotto, articolo; (*food*) derrata

commodity exchange N borsa *f* merci *inv*

common ['kɔmən] ADJ comune; (*pej*) volgare; (*usual*) normale ▶ N terreno comune; **in ~** in comune; **in ~ use** di uso comune; **it's ~ knowledge that** è di dominio pubblico che; **to the ~ good** nell'interesse generale, per il bene comune; *see also* **Commons**

common cold N: **the ~** il raffreddore

common denominator N denominatore *m* comune

commoner ['kɔmənə^r] N cittadino(-a) (non nobile)

common ground N (*fig*) terreno comune

common land N terreno di uso pubblico

common law N diritto consuetudinario

common-law ['kɔmənlɔː] ADJ: **~ wife** convivente *f* more uxorio

commonly ['kɔmənlɪ] ADV comunemente, usualmente

Common Market N Mercato Comune

commonplace ['kɔmənpleɪs] ADJ banale, ordinario(-a)

common room ['kɔmənrum] N sala di riunione; (*Scol*) sala dei professori

Commons ['kɔmənz] NPL (*BRIT Pol*): **the (House of) ~** la Camera dei Comuni

common sense N buon senso

Commonwealth ['kɔmənwɛlθ] N: **the ~** il Commonwealth; *vedi nota*

Il *Commonwealth* è un'associazione di stati sovrani indipendenti e di alcuni territori annessi che facevano parte dell'antico Impero Britannico. Ancora oggi molti stati del *Commonwealth* riconoscono simbolicamente il sovrano britannico come capo di stato, e i loro rappresentanti si riuniscono per discutere questioni di comune interesse.

commotion [kə'məʊʃən] N confusione *f*, tumulto

communal ['kɔmjuːnl] ADJ (*life*) comunale; (*for common use*) pubblico(-a)

commune N ['kɔmjuːn] (*group*) comune *f* ▶ VI [kə'mjuːn]: **to ~ with** mettersi in comunione con

communicate [kə'mjuːnɪkeɪt] VT comunicare, trasmettere ▶ VI: **to ~ (with)** comunicare (con)

communication [kəmjuːnɪ'keɪʃən] N comunicazione *f*

communication cord N (*BRIT*) segnale *m* d'allarme

communications network N rete *f* delle comunicazioni

communications satellite N satellite *m* per telecomunicazioni

communicative [kə'mjuːnɪkətɪv] ADJ (*gen*) loquace

communion [kə'mjuːnɪən] N (*also:* **Holy Communion**) comunione *f*

communiqué [kə'mjuːnɪkeɪ] N comunicato

communism ['kɔmjunɪzəm] N comunismo

communist ['kɔmjunɪst] ADJ, N comunista (*mf*)

community [kə'mjuːnɪtɪ] N comunità *f inv*

community centre, (*US*) **community center** N circolo ricreativo

community chest N (*US*) fondo di beneficenza

community health centre N centro socio-sanitario

community home N (*BRIT*) riformatorio

community service N (*BRIT*) ≈ lavoro sostitutivo

community spirit N spirito civico

commutation ticket [kɔmju'teɪʃən-] N (*US*) biglietto di abbonamento

commute [kə'mjuːt] VI fare il pendolare ▶ VT (*Law*) commutare

commuter [kə'mjuːtər] N pendolare *mf*

compact ADJ [kəm'pækt] compatto(-a) ▶ N ['kɔmpækt] (*also:* **powder compact**) portacipria *m inv*

compact disc N compact disc *m inv*

compact disc player N lettore *m* CD *inv*

companion [kəm'pænjən] N compagno(-a)

companionship [kəm'pænjənʃɪp] N compagnia

companionway [kəm'pænjənweɪ] N (*Naut*) scala

company ['kʌmpənɪ] N (*also Comm, Mil, Theat*) compagnia; **he's good ~** è di buona compagnia; **we have ~** abbiamo ospiti; **to keep sb ~** tenere compagnia a qn; **to part ~ with** separarsi da; **Smith and C~** Smith e soci

company car N macchina (di proprietà) della ditta

company director N amministratore *m*, consigliere *m* di amministrazione

company secretary N (*BRIT Comm*) segretario(-a) generale

comparable ['kɔmpərəbl] ADJ simile; **~ to** *or* **with** paragonabile a

comparative [kəm'pærətɪv] ADJ (*freedom, cost*) relativo(-a); (*adjective, adverb etc*) comparativo(-a); (*literature*) comparato(-a)

comparatively [kəm'pærətɪvlɪ] ADV relativamente

compare [kəm'pɛər] VT: **to ~ sth/sb with/to** confrontare qc/qn con/a ▶ VI: **to ~ (with)** reggere il confronto (con); **compared with** *or* **to** a paragone di, rispetto a; **how do the prices ~?** che differenza di prezzo c'è?

comparison [kəm'pærɪsn] N confronto; **in ~ with** confronto a

compartment [kəm'pɑːtmənt] N compartimento; (*Rail*) scompartimento

compass ['kʌmpəs] N bussola; (**a pair of**) **compasses** (*Math*) compasso; **within the ~ of** entro i limiti di

compassion [kəm'pæʃən] N compassione *f*

compassionate [kəm'pæʃənɪt] ADJ compassionevole; **on ~ grounds** per motivi personali

compassionate leave N congedo straordinario (*per gravi motivi di famiglia*)

compatibility [kəmpætɪ'bɪlɪtɪ] N compatibilità

compatible [kəm'pætɪbl] ADJ compatibile

compel [kəm'pɛl] VT costringere, obbligare

compelling [kəm'pɛlɪŋ] ADJ (*fig: argument*) irresistibile

compendium [kəm'pɛndɪəm] N compendio

compensate ['kɔmpənseɪt] VT risarcire ▶ VI: **to ~ for** compensare

compensation [kɔmpən'seɪʃən] N compensazione *f*; (*money*) risarcimento

compère ['kɔmpɛər] N presentatore(-trice)

compete [kəm'piːt] VI (*take part*) concorrere; (*vie*): **to ~ (with)** fare concorrenza (a)

competence ['kɔmpɪtəns] N competenza

competent ['kɔmpɪtənt] ADJ competente

competing [kəm'piːtɪŋ] ADJ (*theories, ideas*) opposto(-a); (*companies*) in concorrenza; **three ~ explanations (of)** tre spiegazioni contrastanti tra di loro (di)

competition [kɔmpɪ'tɪʃən] N gara; concorso; (Sport) gara; (Econ) concorrenza; **in ~ with** in concorrenza con

competitive [kəm'pɛtɪtɪv] ADJ (sports) agonistico(-a); (person) che ha spirito di competizione; che ha spirito agonistico; (Econ) concorrenziale

competitive examination N concorso

competitor [kəm'pɛtɪtər] N concorrente mf

compile [kəm'paɪl] VT compilare

complacency [kəm'pleɪsnsɪ] N compiacenza di sé

complacent [kəm'pleɪsnt] ADJ compiaciuto(-a) di sé

complain [kəm'pleɪn] VI lagnarsi, lamentarsi; **to ~ (about)** lagnarsi (di); (in shop etc) reclamare (per)
▶ **complain of** VT FUS (Med) accusare

complaint [kəm'pleɪnt] N lamento; (in shop etc) reclamo; (Med) malattia

complement N ['kɔmplɪmənt] complemento; (especially of ship's crew etc) effettivo ▶ VT ['kɔmplɪmɛnt] (enhance) accompagnarsi bene a

complementary [kɔmplɪ'mɛntərɪ] ADJ complementare

complete [kəm'pliːt] ADJ completo(-a) ▶ VT completare; (form) riempire; **it's a ~ disaster** è un vero disastro

completely [kəm'pliːtlɪ] ADV completamente

completion [kəm'pliːʃən] N completamento; **to be nearing ~** essere in fase di completamento; **on ~ of contract** alla firma del contratto

complex ['kɔmplɛks] ADJ complesso(-a) ▶ N (Psych, buildings etc) complesso

complexion [kəm'plɛkʃən] N (of face) carnagione f; (of event etc) aspetto

complexity [kəm'plɛksɪtɪ] N complessità f inv

compliance [kəm'plaɪəns] N acquiescenza; **in ~ with** (orders, wishes etc) in conformità con

compliant [kəm'plaɪənt] ADJ acquiescente, arrendevole

complicate ['kɔmplɪkeɪt] VT complicare

complicated ['kɔmplɪkeɪtɪd] ADJ complicato(-a)

complication [kɔmplɪ'keɪʃən] N complicazione f

compliment N ['kɔmplɪmənt] complimento ▶ VT ['kɔmplɪmɛnt] fare un complimento a; **compliments** NPL complimenti mpl; rispetti mpl; **to pay sb a ~** fare un complimento a qn; **to ~ sb (on sth/on doing sth)** congratularsi or complimentarsi con qn (per qc/per aver fatto qc)

complimentary [kɔmplɪ'mɛntərɪ] ADJ complimentoso(-a), elogiativo(-a); (free) in omaggio

complimentary ticket N biglietto d'omaggio

compliments slip N cartoncino della società

comply [kəm'plaɪ] VI: **to ~ with** assentire a; conformarsi a

component [kəm'pəunənt] ADJ, N componente (m)

compose [kəm'pəuz] VT (music, poem etc) comporre; **to ~ o.s.** ricomporsi; **composed of** composto(-a) di

composed [kəm'pəuzd] ADJ calmo(-a)

composer [kəm'pəuzər] N (Mus) compositore(-trice)

composite ['kɔmpəzɪt] ADJ composito(-a); (Math) composto(-a)

composition [kɔmpə'zɪʃən] N composizione f

compost ['kɔmpɔst] N composta, concime m

composure [kəm'pəuʒər] N calma

compound ['kɔmpaund] N (Chem, Ling) composto; (enclosure) recinto ▶ ADJ composto(-a) ▶ VT [kəm'paund] (fig: problem, difficulty) peggiorare

compound fracture N frattura esposta

compound interest N interesse m composto

comprehend [kɔmprɪ'hɛnd] VT comprendere, capire

comprehension [kɔmprɪ'hɛnʃən] N comprensione f

comprehensive [kɔmprɪ'hɛnsɪv] ADJ completo(-a) ▶ N (Brit: also: **comprehensive school**) scuola secondaria aperta a tutti

comprehensive insurance policy N polizza multi-rischio inv

compress VT [kəm'prɛs] comprimere ▶ N ['kɔmprɛs] (Med) compressa

compression [kəm'prɛʃən] N compressione f

comprise [kəm'praɪz] VT (also: **be comprised of**) comprendere

compromise ['kɔmprəmaɪz] N compromesso ▶ VT compromettere ▶ VI venire a un compromesso ▶ CPD (decision, solution) di compromesso

compulsion [kəm'pʌlʃən] N costrizione f; **under ~** sotto pressioni

compulsive [kəm'pʌlsɪv] ADJ (Psych) incontrollabile; (liar, gambler) che non riesce a controllarsi; (viewing, reading) cui non si può fare a meno

compulsory [kəm'pʌlsərɪ] ADJ obbligatorio(-a)

compulsory purchase N espropriazione f

compunction [kəm'pʌŋkʃən] N scrupolo; **to have no ~ about doing sth** non farsi scrupoli a fare qc

computer [kəm'pjuːtər] N computer m inv, elaboratore m elettronico

computer game N gioco per computer

computer-generated ADJ realizzato(-a) al computer

computerization [kəmpju:təraɪˈzeɪʃən] N computerizzazione f

computerize [kəmˈpju:təraɪz] VT computerizzare

computer language N linguaggio m macchina inv

computer literate ADJ: **to be ~** essere in grado di usare il computer

computer peripheral N unità periferica

computer program N programma m di computer

computer programmer N programmatore(-trice)

computer programming N programmazione f di computer

computer science N informatica

computer scientist N informatico(-a)

computer studies NPL informatica

computing [kəmˈpju:tɪŋ] N informatica

comrade [ˈkɔmrɪd] N compagno(-a)

comradeship [ˈkɔmrɪdʃɪp] N cameratismo

Comsat® [ˈkɔmsæt] N ABBR
= **communications satellite**

con [kɔn] VT (col) truffare ▶ N truffa; **to ~ sb into doing sth** indurre qn a fare qc con raggiri

concave [ˈkɔnkeɪv] ADJ concavo(-a)

conceal [kənˈsi:l] VT nascondere

concede [kənˈsi:d] VT concedere; (admit) ammettere ▶ VI cedere

conceit [kənˈsi:t] N presunzione f, vanità

conceited [kənˈsi:tɪd] ADJ presuntuoso(-a), vanitoso(-a)

conceivable [kənˈsi:vəbl] ADJ concepibile; **it is ~ that ...** può anche darsi che ...

conceivably [kənˈsi:vəblɪ] ADV: **he may ~ be right** può anche darsi che abbia ragione

conceive [kənˈsi:v] VT concepire ▶ VI concepire un bambino; **to ~ of sth/of doing sth** immaginare qc/di fare qc

concentrate [ˈkɔnsəntreɪt] VI concentrarsi ▶ VT concentrare

concentration [kɔnsənˈtreɪʃən] N concentrazione f

concentration camp N campo di concentramento

concentric [kɔnˈsɛntrɪk] ADJ concentrico(-a)

concept [ˈkɔnsɛpt] N concetto

conception [kənˈsɛpʃən] N concezione f; (idea) idea, concetto

concern [kənˈsə:n] N affare m; (Comm) azienda, ditta; (anxiety) preoccupazione f ▶ VT riguardare; **to be concerned (about)** preoccuparsi (di); **to be concerned with** occuparsi di; **as far as I am concerned** per quanto mi riguarda; **"to whom it may ~"** "a tutti gli interessati"; **the department**

concerned (under discussion) l'ufficio in questione; (relevant) l'ufficio competente

concerning [kənˈsə:nɪŋ] PREP riguardo a, circa

concert [ˈkɔnsət] N concerto; **in ~** di concerto

concerted [kənˈsə:tɪd] ADJ concertato(-a)

concert hall N sala da concerti

concertina [kɔnsəˈti:nə] N piccola fisarmonica ▶ VI ridursi come una fisarmonica

concerto [kənˈtʃə:təu] N concerto

concession [kənˈsɛʃən] N concessione f

concessionaire [kənsɛʃəˈnɛəʳ] N concessionario

concessionary [kənˈsɛʃənərɪ] ADJ (ticket, fare) a prezzo ridotto

conciliation [kənsɪlɪˈeɪʃən] N conciliazione f

conciliatory [kənˈsɪlɪətrɪ] ADJ conciliativo(-a)

concise [kənˈsaɪs] ADJ conciso(-a)

conclave [ˈkɔnkleɪv] N riunione f segreta; (Rel) conclave m

conclude [kənˈklu:d] VT concludere ▶ VI (speaker) concludere; (events): **to ~ (with)** concludersi (con)

concluding [kənˈklu:dɪŋ] ADJ (remarks etc) conclusivo(-a), finale

conclusion [kənˈklu:ʒən] N conclusione f; **to come to the ~ that ...** concludere che ..., arrivare alla conclusione che ...

conclusive [kənˈklu:sɪv] ADJ conclusivo(-a)

concoct [kənˈkɔkt] VT inventare

concoction [kənˈkɔkʃən] N (food, drink) miscuglio

concord [ˈkɔŋkɔ:d] N (harmony) armonia, concordia; (treaty) accordo

concourse [ˈkɔŋkɔ:s] N (hall) atrio

concrete [ˈkɔŋkri:t] N calcestruzzo ▶ ADJ concreto(-a); (Constr) di calcestruzzo

concrete mixer N betoniera

concur [kənˈkə:ʳ] VI concordare

concurrently [kənˈkʌrntlɪ] ADV simultaneamente

concussion [kənˈkʌʃən] N (Med) commozione f cerebrale

condemn [kənˈdɛm] VT condannare; (building) dichiarare pericoloso(-a)

condemnation [kɔndɛmˈneɪʃən] N condanna

condensation [kɔndɛnˈseɪʃən] N condensazione f

condense [kənˈdɛns] VI condensarsi ▶ VT condensare

condensed milk N latte m condensato

condescend [kɔndɪˈsɛnd] VI condiscendere; **to ~ to do sth** degnarsi di fare qc

condescending [kɔndɪˈsɛndɪŋ] ADJ condiscendente

condition [kənˈdɪʃən] N condizione f; (disease)

malattia ► VT condizionare, regolare; **in good/poor** ~ in buone/cattive condizioni; **to have a heart** ~ soffrire di (mal di) cuore; **weather conditions** condizioni meteorologiche; **on** ~ **that** a condizione che +*sub*, a condizione di

conditional [kən'dıʃənl] ADJ condizionale; **to be** ~ **upon** dipendere da

conditioner [kən'dıʃənəʳ] N (*for hair*) balsamo; (*for fabrics*) ammorbidente *m*

condo ['kɔndəu] N ABBR (*US col*) = **condominium**

condolences [kən'dəulənsız] NPL condoglianze *fpl*

condom ['kɔndəm] N preservativo

condominium [kɔndə'mınıəm] N (*US*) condominio

condone [kən'dəun] VT condonare

conducive [kən'dju:sıv] ADJ: ~ **to** favorevole a

conduct N ['kɔndʌkt] condotta ► VT [kən'dʌkt] condurre; (*manage*) dirigere; amministrare; (*Mus*) dirigere; **to** ~ **o.s.** comportarsi

conducted tour [kən'dʌktıd-] N gita accompagnata

conductor [kən'dʌktəʳ] N (*of orchestra*) direttore *m* d'orchestra; (*on bus*) bigliettaio; (*US Rail*) controllore *m*; (*Elec*) conduttore *m*

conductress [kən'dʌktrıs] N (*on bus*) bigliettaia

conduit ['kɔndıt] N condotto; tubo

cone [kəun] N cono; (*Bot*) pigna; (*traffic cone*) birillo

confectioner [kən'fɛkʃənəʳ] N: ~**'s (shop)** = pasticceria

confectionery [kən'fɛkʃənərı] N dolciumi *mpl*

confederate [kən'fɛdərıt] ADJ confederato(-a) ► N (*pej*) complice *mf*; (*US Hist*) confederato

confederation [kənfɛdə'reıʃən] N confederazione *f*

confer [kən'fə:ʳ] VT: **to** ~ **sth on** conferire qc a ► VI conferire; **to** ~ **(with sb about sth)** consultarsi (con qn su qc)

conference ['kɔnfərns] N congresso; **to be in** ~ essere in riunione

conference room N sala *f* conferenze *inv*

confess [kən'fɛs] VT confessare, ammettere ► VI confessarsi

confession [kən'fɛʃən] N confessione *f*

confessional [kən'fɛʃənl] N confessionale *m*

confessor [kən'fɛsəʳ] N confessore *m*

confetti [kən'fɛtı] N coriandoli *mpl*

confide [kən'faıd] VI: **to** ~ **in** confidarsi con

confidence ['kɔnfıdns] N confidenza; (*trust*) fiducia; (*also:* **self-confidence**) sicurezza di sé; **in** ~ (*speak, write*) in confidenza, confidenzialmente; **to tell sb sth in strict**

~ dire qc a qn in via strettamente confidenziale; **to have (every)** ~ **that ...** essere assolutamente certo(-a) che ...; **motion of no** ~ mozione *f* di sfiducia

confidence trick N truffa

confident ['kɔnfıdənt] ADJ sicuro(-a); (*also:* **self-confident**) sicuro(-a) di sé

confidential [kɔnfı'dɛnʃəl] ADJ riservato(-a), confidenziale; (*secretary*) particolare

confidentiality ['kɔnfıdɛnʃı'ælıtı] N riservatezza, carattere *m* confidenziale

configuration [kən'fıgju'reıʃən] N (*Comput*) configurazione *f*

confine [kən'faın] VT limitare; (*shut up*) rinchiudere; **to** ~ **o.s. to doing sth** limitarsi a fare qc; *see also* **confines**

confined [kən'faınd] ADJ (*space*) ristretto(-a)

confinement [kən'faınmənt] N prigionia; (*Mil*) consegna; (*Med*) parto

confines ['kɔnfaınz] NPL confini *mpl*

confirm [kən'fə:m] VT confermare; (*Rel*) cresimare

confirmation [kɔnfə'meıʃən] N conferma; (*Rel*) cresima

confirmed [kən'fə:md] ADJ inveterato(-a)

confiscate ['kɔnfıskeıt] VT confiscare

confiscation [kɔnfıs'keıʃən] N confisca

conflagration [kɔnflə'greıʃən] N conflagrazione *f*

conflict N ['kɔnflıkt] conflitto ► VI [kən'flıkt] essere in conflitto

conflicting [kən'flıktıŋ] ADJ contrastante; (*reports, evidence, opinions*) contraddittorio(-a)

conform [kən'fɔ:m] VI: **to** ~ **(to)** conformarsi (a)

conformist [kən'fɔ:mıst] N conformista *mf*

confound [kən'faund] VT confondere; (*amaze*) sconcertare

confounded [kən'faundıd] ADJ maledetto(-a)

confront [kən'frʌnt] VT confrontare; (*enemy, danger*) affrontare

confrontation [kɔnfrən'teıʃən] N scontro

confrontational [kɔnfrən'teıʃənəl] ADJ polemico(-a), aggressivo(-a)

confuse [kən'fju:z] VT imbrogliare; (*one thing with another*) confondere

confused [kən'fju:zd] ADJ confuso(-a); **to get** ~ confondersi

confusing [kən'fju:zıŋ] ADJ che fa confondere

confusion [kən'fju:ʒən] N confusione *f*

congeal [kən'dʒi:l] VI (*blood*) congelarsi

congenial [kən'dʒi:nıəl] ADJ (*person*) simpatico(-a); (*place, work, company*) piacevole

congenital [kən'dʒɛnıtl] ADJ congenito(-a)

conger eel ['kɔngəʳ-] N grongo

congested [kən'dʒɛstıd] ADJ congestionato(-a); (*telephone lines*) sovraccarico(-a)

congestion [kən'dʒɛstʃən] N congestione f
congestion charge N pedaggio da pagare per poter circolare in automobile nel centro di alcune città, introdotto per la prima volta a Londra nel 2002
conglomerate [kən'glɔmərɪt] N (Comm) conglomerato
conglomeration [kənglɔmə'reɪʃən] N conglomerazione f
Congo ['kɔŋgəu] N Congo
congratulate [kən'grætjuleɪt] VT: **to ~ sb (on)** congratularsi con qn (per or di)
congratulations [kəngrætju'leɪʃənz] NPL auguri mpl; (on success) complimenti mpl; **~ (on)** congratulazioni fpl (per) ▶ EXCL congratulazioni!, rallegramenti!
congregate ['kɔŋgrɪgeɪt] VI congregarsi, riunirsi
congregation [kɔŋgrɪ'geɪʃən] N congregazione f
congress ['kɔŋgrɛs] N congresso; (US Pol): **C~** il Congresso; vedi nota

> Il Congress è l'assemblea statunitense che si riunisce a Washington D.C. nel Capitol per elaborare e discutere le leggi federali. é costituita dalla House of Representatives (435 membri, eletti nei vari stati in base al numero degli abitanti) e dal Senate (100 senatori, due per ogni stato). Sia i membri della House of Representatives che quelli del Senate sono eletti direttamente dal popolo.

congressman ['kɔŋgrɛsmən] N (irreg) (US) membro del Congresso
congresswoman ['kɔŋgrɛswumən] N (irreg) (US) (donna) membro del Congresso
conical ['kɔnɪkl] ADJ conico(-a)
conifer ['kɔnɪfər] N conifero
coniferous [kə'nɪfərəs] ADJ (forest) di conifere
conjecture [kən'dʒɛktʃər] N congettura ▶ VT, VI congetturare
conjoined twin [kən'dʒɔɪnd-] N fratello (or sorella) siamese
conjugal ['kɔndʒugl] ADJ coniugale
conjugate ['kɔndʒugeɪt] VT coniugare
conjugation [kɔndʒə'geɪʃən] N coniugazione f
conjunction [kən'dʒʌŋkʃən] N congiunzione f; **in ~ with** in accordo con, insieme con
conjunctivitis [kəndʒʌŋktɪ'vaɪtɪs] N congiuntivite f
conjure ['kʌndʒər] VI fare giochi di prestigio ▶ **conjure up** VT (ghost, spirit) evocare; (memories) rievocare
conjurer ['kʌndʒərər] N prestigiatore(-trice), prestidigitatore(-trice)
conjuring trick ['kʌndʒərɪŋ-] N gioco di prestigio
conker ['kɔŋkər] N (BRIT col) castagna (d'ippocastano)

conk out [kɔŋk-] VI (col) andare in panne
conman ['kɔnmæn] N (irreg) truffatore m
Conn. ABBR (US) = **Connecticut**
connect [kə'nɛkt] VT connettere, collegare; (Elec) collegare; (fig) associare ▶ VI (train): **to ~ with** essere in coincidenza con; **to be connected with** (associated) aver rapporti con; essere imparentato(-a) con; **I am trying to ~ you** (Tel) sto cercando di darle la linea
connecting flight N volo in coincidenza
connection [kə'nɛkʃən] N relazione f, rapporto; (Elec) connessione f; (Tel) collegamento; (train, plane etc) coincidenza; **in ~ with** con riferimento a, a proposito di; **what is the ~ between them?** in che modo sono legati?; **business connections** rapporti d'affari; **to miss/get one's ~** (train etc) perdere/prendere la coincidenza
connexion [kə'nɛkʃən] N (BRIT) = **connection**
conning tower ['kɔnɪŋ-] N torretta di comando
connive [kə'naɪv] VI: **to ~ at** essere connivente in
connoisseur [kɔnɪ'sə:ʳ] N conoscitore(-trice)
connotation [kɔnə'teɪʃən] N connotazione f
connubial [kə'nju:bɪəl] ADJ coniugale
conquer ['kɔŋkəʳ] VT conquistare; (feelings) vincere
conqueror ['kɔŋkərəʳ] N conquistatore m
conquest ['kɔŋkwɛst] N conquista
cons [kɔnz] NPL see **pro**; **convenience**
conscience ['kɔnʃəns] N coscienza; **in all ~** onestamente, in coscienza
conscientious [kɔnʃɪ'ɛnʃəs] ADJ coscienzioso(-a)
conscientious objector N obiettore m di coscienza
conscious ['kɔnʃəs] ADJ consapevole; (Med) cosciente; (deliberate: insult, error) intenzionale, voluto(-a); **to become ~ of sth/that** rendersi conto di qc/che
consciousness ['kɔnʃəsnɪs] N consapevolezza; (Med) coscienza; **to lose/regain ~** perdere/riprendere coscienza
conscript ['kɔnskrɪpt] N coscritto
conscription [kən'skrɪpʃən] N coscrizione f
consecrate ['kɔnsɪkreɪt] VT consacrare
consecutive [kən'sɛkjutɪv] ADJ consecutivo(-a); **on 3 ~ occasions** 3 volte di fila
consensus [kən'sɛnsəs] N consenso; **the ~ of opinion** l'opinione f unanime or comune
consent [kən'sɛnt] N consenso ▶ VI: **to ~ (to)** acconsentire (a); **age of ~** età legale (per avere rapporti sessuali); **by common ~** di comune accordo
consenting adults [kən'sɛntɪŋ-] NPL adulti mpl consenzienti

491

consequence ['kɔnsɪkwəns] N conseguenza, risultato; importanza; **in ~** di conseguenza

consequently ['kɔnsɪkwəntlɪ] ADV di conseguenza, dunque

conservation [kɔnsə'veɪʃən] N conservazione f; (also: **nature conservation**) tutela dell'ambiente; **energy ~** risparmio energetico

conservationist [kɔnsə'veɪʃənɪst] N fautore(-trice) della tutela dell'ambiente

conservative [kən'sə:vətɪv] ADJ conservatore(-trice); (cautious) cauto(-a); **C~** adj, n (BRIT Pol) conservatore(-trice); **the C~ Party** il partito conservatore

conservatory [kən'sə:vətrɪ] N (greenhouse) serra; (Mus) conservatorio

conserve [kən'sə:v] VT conservare ▶ N conserva

consider [kən'sɪdər] VT considerare; (take into account) tener conto di; **to ~ doing sth** considerare la possibilità di fare qc; **all things considered** tutto sommato or considerato; **~ yourself lucky** puoi dirti fortunato

considerable [kən'sɪdərəbl] ADJ considerevole, notevole

considerably [kən'sɪdərəblɪ] ADV notevolmente, decisamente

considerate [kən'sɪdərɪt] ADJ premuroso(-a)

consideration [kənsɪdə'reɪʃən] N considerazione f; (reward) rimunerazione f; **out of ~ for** per riguardo a; **under ~** in esame; **my first ~ is my family** il mio primo pensiero è per la mia famiglia

considered [kən'sɪdəd] ADJ: **it is my ~ opinion that** ... dopo lunga riflessione il mio parere è che ...

considering [kən'sɪdərɪŋ] PREP in considerazione di; **~ (that)** se si considera (che)

consign [kən'saɪn] VT consegnare; (send: goods) spedire

consignee [kɔnsaɪ'ni:] N consegnatario(-a), destinatario(-a)

consignment [kən'saɪnmənt] N (of goods) consegna; spedizione f

consignment note N (Comm) nota di spedizione

consignor [kən'saɪnər] N mittente mf

consist [kən'sɪst] VI: **to ~ of** constare di, essere composto(-a) di

consistency [kən'sɪstənsɪ] N consistenza; (fig) coerenza

consistent [kən'sɪstənt] ADJ coerente; (constant) costante; **~ with** compatibile con

consolation [kɔnsə'leɪʃən] N consolazione f

console VT [kən'səul] consolare ▶ N ['kɔnsəul] quadro di comando

consolidate [kən'sɔlɪdeɪt] VT consolidare

consols ['kɔnsɔlz] NPL (Stock Exchange) titoli mpl del debito consolidato

consommé [kən'sɔmeɪ] N consommé m inv, brodo ristretto

consonant ['kɔnsənənt] N consonante f

consort ['kɔnsɔ:t] N consorte mf; **prince ~** principe m consorte ▶ VI [kən'sɔ:t] (often pej): **to ~ with sb** frequentare qn

consortium [kən'sɔ:tɪəm] N consorzio

conspicuous [kən'spɪkjuəs] ADJ cospicuo(-a); **to make o.s. ~** farsi notare

conspiracy [kən'spɪrəsɪ] N congiura, cospirazione f

conspiratorial [kənspɪrə'tɔ:rɪəl] ADJ cospiratorio(-a)

conspire [kən'spaɪər] VI congiurare, cospirare

constable ['kʌnstəbl] N (BRIT: also: **police constable**) = poliziotto, agente m di polizia; **chief ~** = questore m

constabulary [kən'stæbjulərɪ] N forze fpl dell'ordine

constant ['kɔnstənt] ADJ costante; continuo(-a)

constantly ['kɔnstəntlɪ] ADV costantemente; continuamente

constellation [kɔnstə'leɪʃən] N costellazione f

consternation [kɔnstə'neɪʃən] N costernazione f

constipated ['kɔnstɪpeɪtɪd] ADJ stitico(-a)

constipation [kɔnstɪ'peɪʃən] N stitichezza

constituency [kən'stɪtjuənsɪ] N collegio elettorale; (people) elettori mpl (del collegio); vedi nota

> Con il termine constituency viene indicato sia un collegio elettorale che i suoi elettori. In Gran Bretagna ogni collegio elegge un rappresentante che in seguito incontra regolarmente i propri elettori in riunioni chiamate surgeries per discutere questioni di interesse locale.

constituency party N sezione f locale (del partito)

constituent [kən'stɪtjuənt] N elettore(-trice); (part) elemento componente

constitute ['kɔnstɪtju:t] VT costituire

constitution [kɔnstɪ'tju:ʃən] N costituzione f

constitutional [kɔnstɪ'tju:ʃənl] ADJ costituzionale

constitutional monarchy N monarchia costituzionale

constrain [kən'streɪn] VT costringere

constrained [kən'streɪnd] ADJ costretto(-a)

constraint [kən'streɪnt] N (restraint) limitazione f, costrizione f; (embarrassment) imbarazzo, soggezione f

constrict [kən'strɪkt] VT comprimere; opprimere

construct [kən'strʌkt] VT costruire
construction [kən'strʌkʃən] N costruzione f;
(fig: interpretation) interpretazione f; **under ~**
in costruzione
construction industry N edilizia, industria
edile
constructive [kən'strʌktɪv] ADJ
costruttivo(-a)
construe [kən'stru:] VT interpretare
consul ['kɔnsl] N console m
consulate ['kɔnsjulɪt] N consolato
consult [kən'sʌlt] VT: **to ~ sb (about sth)**
consultare qn (su or riguardo a qc)
consultancy [kən'sʌltənsɪ] N consulenza
consultancy fee N onorario di consulenza
consultant [kən'sʌltənt] N (Med) consulente
m medico; (other specialist) consulente ▸ CPD:
~ engineer n ingegnere m consulente;
~ paediatrician n specialista mf in pediatria;
legal/management ~ consulente legale/
gestionale
consultation [kɔnsəl'teɪʃən] N (discussion)
consultazione f; (Med, Law) consulto; **in ~**
with consultandosi con
consultative [kən'sʌltətɪv] ADJ di
consulenza
consulting room [kən'sʌltɪŋ-] N (BRIT)
ambulatorio
consume [kən'sju:m] VT consumare
consumer [kən'sju:mə[r]] N
consumatore(-trice); (of electricity, gas etc)
utente mf
consumer credit N credito al consumatore
consumer durables NPL prodotti mpl di
consumo durevole
consumer goods NPL beni mpl di consumo
consumerism [kən'sju:mərɪzəm] N (consumer
protection) tutela del consumatore; (Econ)
consumismo
consumer society N società dei consumi
consumer watchdog N comitato di difesa
dei consumatori
consummate ['kɔnsʌmeɪt] VT consumare
consumption [kən'sʌmpʃən] N consumo;
(Med) consunzione f; **not fit for human ~**
non commestibile
cont. ABBR (= continued) segue
contact ['kɔntækt] N contatto; (person)
conoscenza ▸ VT mettersi in contatto con; **to**
be in ~ with sb/sth essere in contatto con
qn/qc; **business contacts** contatti mpl
d'affari
contact lenses NPL lenti fpl a contatto
contagious [kən'teɪdʒəs] ADJ (also fig)
contagioso(-a)
contain [kən'teɪn] VT contenere; **to ~ o.s.**
contenersi
container [kən'teɪnə[r]] N recipiente m; (for
shipping etc) container m inv

containerize [kən'teɪnəraɪz] VT mettere in
container
container ship N nave f container inv
contaminate [kən'tæmɪneɪt] VT
contaminare
contamination [kəntæmɪ'neɪʃən] N
contaminazione f
cont'd ABBR (= continued) segue
contemplate ['kɔntəmpleɪt] VT
contemplare; (consider) pensare a (or di)
contemplation [kɔntəm'pleɪʃən] N
contemplazione f
contemporary [kən'tɛmpərərɪ] ADJ
contemporaneo(-a); (design) moderno(-a)
▸ N contemporaneo(-a); (of the same age)
coetaneo(-a)
contempt [kən'tɛmpt] N disprezzo; **~ of**
court (Law) oltraggio alla Corte
contemptible [kən'tɛmptəbl] ADJ
spregevole, vergognoso(-a)
contemptuous [kən'tɛmptjuəs] ADJ
sdegnoso(-a)
contend [kən'tɛnd] VT: **to ~ that** sostenere
che ▸ VI: **to ~ with** lottare contro; **he has a**
lot to ~ with ha un sacco di guai
contender [kən'tɛndə[r]] N contendente mf;
concorrente mf
content¹ ['kɔntɛnt] N contenuto; **contents**
NPL (of box, case etc) contenuto; (of barrel etc:
capacity) capacità f inv; **(table of) contents**
indice m
content² [kən'tɛnt] ADJ contento(-a),
soddisfatto(-a) ▸ VT contentare, soddisfare;
to be ~ with essere contento di; **to ~ o.s.**
with sth/with doing sth accontentarsi di
qc/di fare qc
contented [kən'tɛntɪd] ADJ contento(-a),
soddisfatto(-a)
contentedly [kən'tɛntɪdlɪ] ADV con
soddisfazione
contention [kən'tɛnʃən] N contesa;
(assertion) tesi f inv; **bone of ~** pomo della
discordia
contentious [kən'tɛnʃəs] ADJ polemico(-a)
contentment [kən'tɛntmənt] N
contentezza
contest N ['kɔntɛst] lotta; (competition) gara,
concorso ▸ VT [kən'tɛst] contestare; (Law)
impugnare; (compete for) contendersi
contestant [kən'tɛstənt] N concorrente mf;
(in fight) avversario(-a)
context ['kɔntɛkst] N contesto; **in/out of ~**
nel/fuori dal contesto
continent ['kɔntɪnənt] N continente m; **the**
C~ (BRIT) l'Europa continentale; **on the C~**
in Europa
continental [kɔntɪ'nɛntl] ADJ continentale
▸ N (BRIT) abitante mf dell'Europa
continentale

continental breakfast N colazione f
all'europea (senza piatti caldi)
continental quilt N (BRIT) piumino
contingency [kən'tɪndʒənsɪ] N eventualità
f inv
contingency plan N misura d'emergenza
contingent [kən'tɪndʒənt] N contingenza
▶ ADJ: **to be ~ upon** dipendere da
continual [kən'tɪnjuəl] ADJ continuo(-a)
continually [kən'tɪnjuəlɪ] ADV di continuo
continuation [kəntɪnju'eɪʃən] N
continuazione f; (after interruption) ripresa;
(of story) seguito
continue [kən'tɪnju:] VI continuare ▶ VT
continuare; (start again) riprendere; **to be
continued** (story) continua; **continued on
page 10** segue or continua a pagina 10
continuing education [kən'tɪnjuɪŋ-] N
corsi mpl per adulti
continuity [kɔntɪ'nju:ɪtɪ] N continuità;
(Cine) (ordine m della) sceneggiatura
continuity girl N (Cine) segretaria di edizione
continuous [kən'tɪnjuəs] ADJ continuo(-a),
ininterrotto(-a); **~ performance** (Cine)
spettacolo continuato; **~ stationery**
(Comput) carta a moduli continui
continuous assessment N (BRIT)
valutazione f continua
continuously [kən'tɪnjuəslɪ] ADV (repeatedly)
continuamente; (uninterruptedly)
ininterrottamente
contort [kən'tɔ:t] VT contorcere
contortion [kən'tɔ:ʃən] N contorcimento;
(of acrobat) contorsione f
contortionist [kən'tɔ:ʃənɪst] N
contorsionista mf
contour ['kɔntuər] N contorno, profilo;
(also: **contour line**) curva di livello
contraband ['kɔntrəbænd] N contrabbando
▶ ADJ di contrabbando
contraception [kɔntrə'sɛpʃən] N
contraccezione f
contraceptive [kɔntrə'sɛptɪv] ADJ
contraccettivo(-a) ▶ N contraccettivo
contract N ['kɔntrækt] contratto ▶ CPD
['kɔntrækt] (price, date) del contratto; (work) a
contratto ▶ VI [kən'trækt] (become smaller)
contrarsi; (Comm): **to ~ to do sth** fare un
contratto per fare qc ▶ VT [kən'trækt] (illness)
contrarre; **to be under ~ to do sth** aver
stipulato un contratto per fare qc; **~ of
employment** contratto di lavoro
▶ **contract in** VI impegnarsi (con un
contratto); (BRIT Admin) scegliere di pagare i
contributi per una pensione
▶ **contract out** VI: **to ~ out (of)** ritirarsi (da);
(BRIT Admin) (scegliere di) non pagare i contributi
per una pensione
contraction [kən'trækʃən] N contrazione f

contractor [kən'træktər] N imprenditore m
contractual [kən'træktjuəl] ADJ
contrattuale
contradict [kɔntrə'dɪkt] VT contraddire
contradiction [kɔntrə'dɪkʃən] N
contraddizione f; **to be in ~ with** discordare
con
contradictory [kɔntrə'dɪktərɪ] ADJ
contraddittorio(-a)
contralto [kən'træltəu] N contralto
contraption [kən'træpʃən] N (pej) aggeggio
contrary¹ ['kɔntrərɪ] ADJ contrario(-a);
(unfavourable) avverso(-a), contrario(-a) ▶ N
contrario; **on the ~** al contrario; **unless you
hear to the ~** salvo contrordine; **~ to what
we thought** a differenza di or
contrariamente a quanto pensavamo
contrary² [kən'trɛərɪ] ADJ (perverse)
bisbetico(-a)
contrast N ['kɔntrɑːst] contrasto ▶ VT
[kən'trɑːst] mettere in contrasto; **in ~ to** or
with a differenza di, contrariamente a
contrasting [kən'trɑːstɪŋ] ADJ contrastante,
di contrasto
contravene [kɔntrə'viːn] VT contravvenire
contravention [kɔntrə'vɛnʃən] N: **~ (of)**
contravvenzione f (a), infrazione f (di)
contribute [kən'trɪbjuːt] VI contribuire ▶ VT:
to ~ £10/an article to dare 10 sterline/un
articolo a; **to ~ to** contribuire a; (newspaper)
scrivere per; (discussion) partecipare a
contribution [kɔntrɪ'bjuːʃən] N contributo
contributor [kən'trɪbjutər] N (to newspaper)
collaboratore(-trice)
contributory [kən'trɪbjutərɪ] ADJ (cause) che
contribuisce; **it was a ~ factor in ...** quello
ha contribuito a ...
contributory pension scheme N (BRIT)
sistema di pensionamento finanziato
congiuntamente dai contributi del lavoratore e del
datore di lavoro
contrite ['kɔntraɪt] ADJ contrito(-a)
contrivance [kən'traɪvəns] N congegno;
espediente m
contrive [kən'traɪv] VT inventare; escogitare
▶ VI: **to ~ to do** fare in modo di fare
control [kən'trəul] VT dominare; (firm,
operation etc) dirigere; (check) controllare;
(disease, fire) arginare, limitare ▶ N controllo;
controls NPL (of vehicle etc) comandi mpl; **to
take ~ of** assumere il controllo di; **to be in ~
of** avere il controllo di; essere responsabile
di; controllare; **to ~ o.s.** controllarsi;
everything is under ~ tutto è sotto
controllo; **to go out of ~** (car) non rispondere
ai comandi; (situation) sfuggire di mano;
circumstances beyond our ~ circostanze fpl
che non dipendono da noi
control key N (Comput) tasto di controllo

controlled substance [kən'trəuld-] N sostanza stupefacente

controller [kən'trəulər] N controllore m

controlling interest [kən'trəulɪŋ-] N (Comm) maggioranza delle azioni

control panel N (on aircraft, ship, TV etc) quadro dei comandi

control point N punto di controllo

control room N (Naut, Mil) sala di comando; (Radio, TV) sala di regia

control tower N (Aviat) torre f di controllo

control unit N (Comput) unità f inv di controllo

controversial [kɔntrə'və:ʃl] ADJ controverso(-a), polemico(-a)

controversy ['kɔntrəvə:sɪ] N controversia, polemica

conurbation [kɔnə:'beɪʃən] N conurbazione f

convalesce [kɔnvə'lɛs] VI rimettersi in salute

convalescence [kɔnvə'lɛsns] N convalescenza

convalescent [kɔnvə'lɛsnt] ADJ, N convalescente (mf)

convector [kən'vɛktər] N convettore m

convene [kən'vi:n] VT convocare; (meeting) organizzare ▶ VI convenire, adunarsi

convenience [kən'vi:nɪəns] N comodità f inv; **at your ~** a suo comodo; **at your earliest ~** (Comm) appena possibile; **all modern conveniences**, (BRIT) **all mod cons** tutte le comodità moderne

convenience foods NPL cibi mpl precotti

convenient [kən'vi:nɪənt] ADJ comodo(-a); **if it is ~ to you** se per lei va bene, se non la incomoda

conveniently [kən'vi:nɪəntlɪ] ADV (happen) a proposito; (situated) in un posto comodo

convent ['kɔnvənt] N convento

convention [kən'vɛnʃən] N convenzione f; (meeting) convegno

conventional [kən'vɛnʃənl] ADJ convenzionale

convent school N scuola retta da suore

converge [kən'və:dʒ] VI convergere

conversant [kən'və:snt] ADJ: **to be ~ with** essere al corrente di; essere pratico(-a) di

conversation [kɔnvə'seɪʃən] N conversazione f

conversational [kɔnvə'seɪʃənl] ADJ non formale; (Comput) conversazionale; **~ Italian** l'italiano parlato

conversationalist [kɔnvə'seɪʃnəlɪst] N conversatore(-trice)

converse N ['kɔnvə:s] contrario, opposto ▶ VI [kən'və:s]: **to ~ (with sb about sth)** conversare (con qn su qc)

conversely [kɔn'və:slɪ] ADV al contrario, per contro

conversion [kən'və:ʃən] N conversione f; (BRIT: of house) trasformazione f, rimodernamento

conversion table N tavola di equivalenze

convert VT [kən'və:t] (Rel, Comm) convertire; (alter) trasformare ▶ N ['kɔnvə:t] convertito(-a)

convertible [kən'və:təbl] N macchina decappottabile

convex ['kɔnvɛks] ADJ convesso(-a)

convey [kən'veɪ] VT trasportare; (thanks) comunicare; (idea) dare

conveyance [kən'veɪəns] N (of goods) trasporto; (vehicle) mezzo di trasporto

conveyancing [kən'veɪənsɪŋ] N (Law) redazione f di transazioni di proprietà

conveyor belt [kən'veɪər-] N nastro trasportatore

convict VT [kən'vɪkt] dichiarare colpevole ▶ N ['kɔnvɪkt] carcerato(-a)

conviction [kən'vɪkʃən] N condanna; (belief) convinzione f

convince [kən'vɪns] VT: **to ~ sb (of sth/that)** convincere qn (di qc/che), persuadere qn (di qc/che)

convinced ADJ: **~ of/that** convinto(-a) di/che

convincing [kən'vɪnsɪŋ] ADJ convincente

convincingly [kən'vɪnsɪŋlɪ] ADV in modo convincente

convivial [kən'vɪvɪəl] ADJ allegro(-a)

convoluted ['kɔnvəlu:tɪd] ADJ (shape) attorcigliato(-a), avvolto(-a); (argument) involuto(-a)

convoy ['kɔnvɔɪ] N convoglio

convulse [kən'vʌls] VT sconvolgere; **to be convulsed with laughter** contorcersi dalle risa

convulsion [kən'vʌlʃən] N convulsione f

COO N ABBR = **chief operating officer**

coo [ku:] VI tubare

cook [kuk] VT cucinare, cuocere; (meal) preparare ▶ VI cuocere; (person) cucinare ▶ N cuoco(-a)

▶ **cook up** VT (col: excuse, story) improvvisare, inventare

cookbook ['kukbuk] N = **cookery book**

cooker ['kukər] N fornello, cucina

cookery N cucina

cookery book N (BRIT) libro di cucina

cookie ['kukɪ] N (US) biscotto; (Comput) cookie m inv

cooking ['kukɪŋ] N cucina ▶ CPD (apples, chocolate) da cuocere; (utensils, salt, foil) da cucina

cookout ['kukaut] N (US) pranzo (cucinato) all'aperto

cool [ku:l] ADJ fresco(-a); (not afraid) calmo(-a); (unfriendly) freddo(-a); (impertinent) sfacciato(-a) ▶ VT raffreddare; (room)

rinfrescare ▸ vɪ (water) raffreddarsi; (air)
rinfrescarsi; **it's ~** (weather) fa fresco; **to
keep sth ~** or **in a ~ place** tenere qc in fresco
▸ **cool down** vɪ raffreddarsi; (fig: person,
situation) calmarsi
▸ **cool off** vɪ (become calmer) calmarsi; (lose
enthusiasm) perdere interesse

coolant ['ku:lənt] N (liquido) refrigerante m

cool box, (US) **cooler** ['ku:lər] N borsa
termica

cooling ['ku:lɪŋ] ADJ (breeze) fresco(-a)

cooling tower N torre f di raffreddamento

coolly ['ku:lɪ] ADV (calmly) con calma,
tranquillamente; (audaciously) come se
niente fosse; (unenthusiastically) freddamente

coolness ['ku:lnɪs] N freschezza; sangue m
freddo, calma

coop [ku:p] N stia ▸ vT: **to ~ up** (fig)
rinchiudere

co-op ['kəuɔp] N ABBR (= cooperative (society))
coop f

cooperate [kəu'ɔpəreɪt] vɪ cooperare,
collaborare

cooperation [kəuɔpə'reɪʃən] N cooperazione
f, collaborazione f

cooperative [kəu'ɔpərətɪv] ADJ
cooperativo(-a) ▸ N cooperativa

coopt [kəu'ɔpt] vT: **to ~ sb into sth** cooptare
qn per qc

coordinate vT [kəu'ɔ:dɪneɪt] coordinare ▸ N
[kəu'ɔ:dɪnət] (Math) coordinata; **coordinates**
NPL (clothes) coordinati mpl

coordination [kəuɔ:dɪ'neɪʃən] N
coordinazione f

coot [ku:t] N folaga

co-ownership [kəu'əunəʃɪp] N comproprietà

cop [kɔp] N (col) sbirro

cope [kəup] vɪ farcela; **to ~ with** (problems) far
fronte a

Copenhagen [kəupən'heɪgən] N
Copenhagen f

copier ['kɔpɪər] N (also: **photocopier**)
(foto)copiatrice f

co-pilot ['kəupaɪlət] N secondo pilota m

copious ['kəupɪəs] ADJ copioso(-a),
abbondante

copper ['kɔpər] N rame m; (col: policeman)
sbirro; **coppers** NPL spiccioli mpl

coppice ['kɔpɪs], **copse** [kɔps] N bosco ceduo

copulate ['kɔpjuleɪt] vɪ accoppiarsi

copy ['kɔpɪ] N copia; (book etc) esemplare m;
(material: for printing) materiale m, testo ▸ vT
(gen, Comput) copiare; (imitate) imitare;
rough/fair ~ brutta/bella (copia); **to make
good ~** (fig) fare notizia
▸ **copy out** vT ricopiare, trascrivere

copycat ['kɔpɪkæt] N (pej) copione m

copyright ['kɔpɪraɪt] N diritto d'autore;
~ reserved tutti i diritti riservati

copy typist N dattilografo(-a)

copywriter ['kɔpɪraɪtər] N redattore m
pubblicitario

coral ['kɔrəl] N corallo

coral reef N barriera corallina

Coral Sea N: **the ~** il mar dei Coralli

cord [kɔ:d] N corda; (Elec) filo; (fabric) velluto
a coste; **cords** NPL (trousers) calzoni mpl (di
velluto) a coste

cordial ['kɔ:dɪəl] ADJ, N cordiale (m)

cordless ['kɔ:dlɪs] ADJ senza cavo

cordon ['kɔ:dn] N cordone m
▸ **cordon off** vT fare cordone intorno a

corduroy ['kɔ:dərɔɪ] N fustagno

CORE [kɔ:r] N ABBR (US) = **Congress of Racial
Equality**

core [kɔ:r] N (of fruit) torsolo; (Tech) centro; (of
earth, nuclear reactor) nucleo; (of organization etc)
cuore m; (of problem etc) cuore m, nocciolo ▸ vT
estrarre il torsolo da; **rotten to the ~** marcio
fino al midollo

Corfu [kɔ:'fu:] N Corfù f

coriander [kɔrɪ'ændər] N coriandolo

cork [kɔ:k] N sughero; (of bottle) tappo

corkage ['kɔ:kɪdʒ] N somma da pagare se il
cliente porta il proprio vino

corked [kɔ:kt], (US) **corky** ['kɔ:kɪ] ADJ (wine)
che sa di tappo

corkscrew ['kɔ:kskru:] N cavatappi m inv

cormorant ['kɔ:mərnt] N cormorano

corn [kɔ:n] N (BRIT: wheat) grano; (US: maize)
granturco; (on foot) callo; **~ on the cob** (Culin)
pannocchia cotta

cornea ['kɔ:nɪə] N cornea

corned beef ['kɔ:nd-] N carne f di manzo in
scatola

corner ['kɔ:nər] N angolo; (Aut) curva;
(Football: also: **corner kick**) corner m inv, calcio
d'angolo ▸ vT intrappolare; mettere con le
spalle al muro; (Comm: market) accaparrare
▸ vɪ prendere una curva; **to cut corners** (fig)
prendere una scorciatoia

corner flag N (Football) bandierina d'angolo

corner kick N (Football) calcio d'angolo

corner shop N (BRIT) piccolo negozio di
generi alimentari

cornerstone ['kɔ:nəstəun] N pietra angolare

cornet ['kɔ:nɪt] N (Mus) cornetta; (BRIT: of
ice-cream) cono

cornflakes ['kɔ:nfleɪks] NPL fiocchi mpl di
granturco

cornflour ['kɔ:nflauər] N (BRIT) farina
finissima di granturco

cornice ['kɔ:nɪs] N cornicione m; cornice f

Cornish ['kɔ:nɪʃ] ADJ della Cornovaglia

corn oil N olio di mais

cornstarch ['kɔ:nstɑ:tʃ] N (US) = **cornflour**

cornucopia [kɔ:nju'kəupɪə] N grande
abbondanza

Cornwall ['kɔːnwəl] N Cornovaglia
corny ['kɔːnɪ] ADJ (col) trito(-a)
corollary [kə'rɒlərɪ] N corollario
coronary ['kɒrənərɪ] N: **~ (thrombosis)**
trombosi *f* coronaria
coronation [kɒrə'neɪʃən] N incoronazione *f*
coroner ['kɒrənə'] N *magistrato incaricato di
indagare la causa di morte in circostanze sospette*
coronet ['kɒrənɪt] N diadema *m*
Corp. ABBR = **corporation**
corporal ['kɔːprəl] N caporalmaggiore *m*
▶ ADJ: **~ punishment** pena corporale
corporate ['kɔːpərɪt] ADJ comune; (*Comm*)
costituito(-a) (in corporazione)
corporate hospitality N omaggi *mpl* ai
clienti (*come biglietti per spettacoli, cene ecc*)
corporate identity, corporate image N (*of
organization*) immagine *f* di marca
corporation [kɔːpə'reɪʃən] N (*of town*)
consiglio comunale; (*Comm*) ente *m*
corporation tax N ≈ imposta societaria
corps [kɔː] (*pl* ~ [kɔːz]) N corpo; **press ~**
ufficio *m* stampa *inv*
corpse [kɔːps] N cadavere *m*
corpuscle ['kɔːpʌsl] N corpuscolo
corral [kə'rɑːl] N recinto
correct [kə'rɛkt] ADJ (*accurate*) corretto(-a),
esatto(-a); (*proper*) corretto(-a) ▶ VT
correggere; **you are ~** ha ragione
correction [kə'rɛkʃən] N correzione *f*
correlate ['kɒrɪleɪt] VT mettere in
correlazione ▶ VI: **to ~ with** essere in
rapporto con
correlation [kɒrɪ'leɪʃən] N correlazione *f*
correspond [kɒrɪs'pɒnd] VI corrispondere
correspondence [kɒrɪs'pɒndəns] N
corrispondenza
correspondence course N corso per
corrispondenza
correspondent [kɒrɪs'pɒndənt] N
corrispondente *mf*
corresponding ADJ corrispondente
corridor ['kɒrɪdɔː'] N corridoio
corroborate [kə'rɒbəreɪt] VT corroborare,
confermare
corrode [kə'rəud] VT corrodere ▶ VI
corrodersi
corrosion [kə'rəuʒən] N corrosione *f*
corrosive [kə'rəuzɪv] ADJ corrosivo(-a)
corrugated ['kɒrəgeɪtɪd] ADJ increspato(-a),
ondulato(-a)
corrugated iron N lamiera di ferro ondulata
corrupt [kə'rʌpt] ADJ corrotto(-a); (*Comput*)
alterato(-a) ▶ VT corrompere; **~ practices**
(*dishonesty, bribery*) pratiche *fpl* illecite
corruption [kə'rʌpʃən] N corruzione *f*
corset ['kɔːsɪt] N busto
Corsica ['kɔːsɪkə] N Corsica
Corsican ['kɔːsɪkən] ADJ, N corso(-a)

cortège [kɔː'teɪʒ] N corteo
cortisone ['kɔːtɪzəun] N cortisone *m*
coruscating ['kɒrəskeɪtɪŋ] ADJ scintillante
cosh [kɒʃ] N (*BRIT*) randello (corto)
cosignatory [kəu'sɪgnətərɪ] N
cofirmatario(-a)
cosiness ['kəuzɪnɪs] N intimità
cos lettuce ['kɒs-] N lattuga romana
cosmetic [kɒz'mɛtɪk] N cosmetico ▶ ADJ
(*preparation*) cosmetico(-a); (*fig: reforms,
measures*) apparente
cosmetic surgery N chirurgia plastica
cosmic ['kɒzmɪk] ADJ cosmico(-a)
cosmonaut ['kɒzmənɔːt] N cosmonauta *mf*
cosmopolitan [kɒzmə'pɒlɪtn] ADJ
cosmopolita
cosmos ['kɒzmɔs] N cosmo
cosset ['kɒsɪt] VT vezzeggiare
cost [kɒst] (*pt, pp* ~) N costo ▶ VI costare ▶ VT
stabilire il prezzo di; **costs** NPL (*Law*) spese
fpl; **it costs £5/too much** costa 5 sterline/
troppo; **it ~ him his life/job** gli costò la vita/
il suo lavoro; **how much does it ~?** quanto
costa?, quanto viene?; **what will it ~ to have
it repaired?** quanto costerà farlo riparare?;
~ of living costo della vita; **at all costs** a
ogni costo
cost accountant N analizzatore *m* dei costi
co-star ['kəustɑː'] N *attore/trice della stessa
importanza del protagonista*
Costa Rica ['kɒstə'riːkə] N Costa Rica
cost centre N centro di costo
cost control N controllo dei costi
cost-effective ['kɒstɪ'fɛktɪv] ADJ (*gen*)
conveniente, economico(-a); (*Comm*)
redditizio(-a), conveniente
cost-effectiveness ['kɒstɪ'fɛktɪvnɪs] N
convenienza
costing ['kɒstɪŋ] N (determinazione *f* dei)
costi *mpl*
costly ['kɒstlɪ] ADJ costoso(-a), caro(-a)
cost-of-living ['kɒstəv'lɪvɪŋ] ADJ:
~ allowance indennità *f inv* di contingenza;
~ index indice *m* della scala mobile
cost price N (*BRIT*) prezzo all'ingrosso
costume ['kɒstjuːm] N costume *m*; (*lady's suit*)
tailleur *m inv*; (*BRIT: also:* **swimming
costume**) costume da bagno
costume jewellery N bigiotteria
cosy, (*US*) **cozy** ['kəuzɪ] ADJ intimo(-a); (*room,
atmosphere*) accogliente; **I'm very ~ here** sto
proprio bene qui
cot [kɒt] N (*BRIT: child's*) lettino; (*US: folding
bed*) brandina
cot death N improvvisa e inspiegabile morte nel
sonno di un neonato
Cotswolds ['kɒtswəuldz] NPL: **the ~** *zona
collinare del Gloucestershire*
cottage ['kɒtɪdʒ] N cottage *m inv*

cottage cheese N fiocchi *mpl* di latte magro
cottage industry N industria artigianale basata *sul lavoro a cottimo*
cottage pie N piatto a base di carne macinata in *sugo e purè di patate*
cotton ['kɔtn] N cotone *m*; ~ **dress** *etc* vestito *etc* di cotone
　▶ **cotton on** VI (*col*): **to ~ on (to sth)** afferrare (qc)
cotton bud N (*BRIT*) cotton fioc® *m inv*
cotton candy (*US*) N zucchero filato
cotton wool N (*BRIT*) cotone *m* idrofilo
couch [kautʃ] N sofà *m inv*; (*in doctor's surgery*) lettino ▶ VT esprimere
couchette [ku:'ʃɛt] N cuccetta
couch potato N (*col*) pigrone(-a) teledipendente
cough [kɔf] VI tossire ▶ N tosse *f*; **I've got a ~** ho la tosse
cough drop N pasticca per la tosse
cough mixture, cough syrup N sciroppo per la tosse
could [kud] PT *of* **can²**
couldn't ['kudnt] = **could not**
council ['kaunsl] N consiglio; **city** *or* **town ~** consiglio comunale; **C~ of Europe** Consiglio d'Europa
council estate N (*BRIT*) quartiere *m* di case popolari
council house N (*BRIT*) casa popolare
council housing N alloggi *mpl* popolari
councillor ['kaunsələʳ] N consigliere(-a)
council tax N (*BRIT*) tassa comunale sulla *proprietà*
counsel ['kaunsl] N avvocato; consultazione *f* ▶ VT: **to ~ sth/sb to do sth** consigliare qc/a qn di fare qc; ~ **for the defence/the prosecution** avvocato difensore/di parte civile
counselling, (*US*) **counseling** N (*Psych*) assistenza psicologica
counsellor, (*US*) **counselor** ['kaunsləʳ] N consigliere(-a); (*US: lawyer*) avvocato(-essa)
count [kaunt] VT, VI contare ▶ N conto; (*nobleman*) conte *m*; **to ~ (up) to 10** contare fino a 10; **to ~ the cost of** calcolare il costo di; **not counting the children** senza contare i bambini; **10 counting him** 10 compreso lui; ~ **yourself lucky** considerati fortunato; **it counts for very little** non conta molto, non ha molta importanza; **to keep ~ of sth** tenere il conto di qc
　▶ **count in** VT (*col*) includere; ~ **me in** ci sto anch'io
　▶ **count on** VT FUS contare su; **to ~ on doing sth** contare di fare qc
　▶ **count up** VT addizionare
countdown ['kauntdaun] N conto alla rovescia

countenance ['kauntɪnəns] N volto, aspetto ▶ VT approvare
counter ['kauntəʳ] N banco; (*position: in post office, bank*) sportello; (*in game*) gettone *m*; (*Tech*) contatore *m* ▶ VT opporsi a; (*blow*) parare ▶ ADV: ~ **to** contro; in opposizione a; **to buy under the ~** (*fig*) comperare sottobanco; **to ~ sth with sth/by doing sth** rispondere a qc con qc/facendo qc
counteract [kauntər'ækt] VT agire in opposizione a; (*poison etc*) annullare gli effetti di
counterattack ['kauntərətæk] N contrattacco ▶ VI contrattaccare
counterbalance ['kauntəbæləns] VT contrappesare
counter-clockwise ['kauntə'klɔkwaɪz] (*US*) ADV in senso antiorario
counter-espionage [kauntər'ɛspɪənɑ:ʒ] N controspionaggio
counterfeit ['kauntəfɪt] N contraffazione *f*, falso ▶ VT contraffare, falsificare ▶ ADJ falso(-a)
counterfoil ['kauntəfɔɪl] N matrice *f*
counterintelligence ['kauntərɪn'tɛlɪdʒəns] N = **counter-espionage**
countermand ['kauntəmɑ:nd] VT annullare
countermeasure ['kauntəmɛʒəʳ] N contromisura
counteroffensive ['kauntərə'fɛnsɪv] N controffensiva
counterpane ['kauntəpeɪn] N copriletto *m inv*
counterpart ['kauntəpɑ:t] N (*of document etc*) copia; (*of person*) corrispondente *mf*
counterproductive ['kauntəprə'dʌktɪv] ADJ controproducente
counterproposal ['kauntəprə'pəuzl] N controproposta
countersign ['kauntəsaɪn] VT controfirmare
countersink ['kauntəsɪŋk] VT (*hole*) svasare
counterterrorism ['kauntə'terərɪzəm] N antiterrorismo
countess ['kauntɪs] N contessa
countless ['kauntlɪs] ADJ innumerevole
countrified ['kʌntrɪfaɪd] ADJ rustico(-a), campagnolo(-a)
country ['kʌntrɪ] N paese *m*; (*native land*) patria; (*as opposed to town*) campagna; (*region*) regione *f*; **in the ~** in campagna; **mountainous ~** territorio montagnoso
country and western, country and western music N musica country e western, country *m*
country dancing N (*BRIT*) danza popolare
country house N villa in campagna
countryman ['kʌntrɪmən] N (*irreg*) (*national*) compatriota *m*; (*rural*) contadino
countryside ['kʌntrɪsaɪd] N campagna

country-wide ['kʌntrɪ'waɪd] ADJ diffuso(-a) in tutto il paese ▶ ADV in tutto il paese
county ['kauntɪ] N contea
county council N (BRIT) consiglio di contea
county town N (BRIT) capoluogo
coup [ku:] (pl **coups** [ku:z]) N colpo; (also: **coup d'état**) colpo di Stato; (triumph) bel colpo
coupé [ku:'peɪ] N coupé m inv
couple ['kʌpl] N coppia ▶ VT (carriages) agganciare; (Tech) accoppiare; (ideas, names) associare; **a ~ of** un paio di
couplet ['kʌplɪt] N distico
coupling ['kʌplɪŋ] N (Rail) agganciamento
coupon ['ku:pɔn] N (voucher) buono; (Comm) coupon m inv
courage ['kʌrɪdʒ] N coraggio
courageous [kə'reɪdʒəs] ADJ coraggioso(-a)
courgette [kuə'ʒet] N (BRIT) zucchina
courier ['kurɪəʳ] N corriere m; (for tourists) guida
course [kɔ:s] N corso; (of ship) rotta; (for golf) campo; (part of meal) piatto; **first ~** primo piatto; **of ~** adv senz'altro, naturalmente; **(no) of ~ not!** certo che no!, no di certo!; **in the ~ of the next few days** nel corso dei prossimi giorni; **in due ~** a tempo debito; **~ (of action)** modo d'agire; **the best ~ would be to ...** la cosa migliore sarebbe ...; **we have no other ~ but to ...** non possiamo far altro che ...; **~ of lectures** corso di lezioni; **a ~ of treatment** (Med) una cura
court [kɔ:t] N corte f; (Tennis) campo ▶ VT (woman) fare la corte a; (fig: favour, popularity) cercare di conquistare; (: death, disaster) sfiorare, rasentare; **out of ~** (Law: settle) in via amichevole; **to take to ~** citare in tribunale; **C~ of Appeal** corte d'appello
courteous ['kə:tɪəs] ADJ cortese
courtesan [kɔ:tɪ'zæn] N cortigiana
courtesy ['kə:təsɪ] N cortesia; **by ~ of** per gentile concessione di
courtesy bus, courtesy coach N navetta gratuita (di hotel, aeroporto)
courtesy car N vettura sostitutiva
courtesy light N (Aut) luce f interna
court-house ['kɔ:thaus] N (US) palazzo di giustizia
courtier ['kɔ:tɪəʳ] N cortigiano(-a)
court martial (pl **courts martial**) N corte f marziale
courtroom ['kɔ:trum] N tribunale m
court shoe N scarpa f décolleté inv
courtyard ['kɔ:tjɑ:d] N cortile m
cousin ['kʌzn] N cugino(-a); **first ~** cugino di primo grado
cove [kəuv] N piccola baia
covenant ['kʌvənənt] N accordo ▶ VT: **to ~ to do sth** impegnarsi (per iscritto) a fare qc

Coventry ['kɔvəntrɪ] N: **to send sb to ~** (fig) dare l'ostracismo a qn
cover ['kʌvəʳ] VT (gen) coprire; (distance) coprire, percorrere; (book, table) rivestire; (include) comprendere; (Press: report on) fare un servizio su ▶ N (of pan) coperchio; (over furniture) fodera; (of bed) copriletto; (of book) copertina; (shelter) riparo; (Comm, Insurance, of spy) copertura; **covers** NPL (on bed) lenzuola e coperte fpl; **to take ~** mettersi al riparo; **under ~** al riparo; **under ~ of darkness** protetto dall'oscurità; **under separate ~** (Comm) a parte, in plico separato; **£10 will ~ everything** 10 sterline saranno sufficienti ▶ **cover up** VT (hide: truth, facts) nascondere; (child, object): **to ~ up (with)** coprire (di) ▶ VI: **to ~ up for sb** (fig) coprire qn
coverage ['kʌvərɪdʒ] N (Press, TV, Radio): **to give full ~ to** fare un ampio servizio su
coveralls ['kʌvərɔ:lz] NPL (US) tuta
cover charge N coperto
covering ['kʌvərɪŋ] N copertura
covering letter, (US) **cover letter** N lettera d'accompagnamento
cover note N (Insurance) polizza (di assicurazione) provvisoria
cover price N prezzo di copertina
covert ['kʌvət] ADJ nascosto(-a); (glance) di sottecchi, furtivo(-a)
cover-up ['kʌvərʌp] N occultamento (di informazioni)
covet ['kʌvɪt] VT bramare
cow [kau] N vacca ▶ CPD femmina ▶ VT (person) intimidire; **~ elephant** n elefantessa
coward ['kauəd] N vigliacco(-a)
cowardice ['kauədɪs] N vigliaccheria
cowardly ['kauədlɪ] ADJ vigliacco(-a)
cowboy ['kaubɔɪ] N cow-boy m inv
cower ['kauəʳ] VI acquattarsi
cowshed ['kauʃed] N stalla
cowslip ['kauslɪp] N (Bot) primula (odorata)
coxswain ['kɔksn] N (also: **cox**) timoniere m
coy [kɔɪ] ADJ falsamente timido(-a)
coyote [kɔɪ'əutɪ] N coyote m inv
cozy ['kəuzɪ] ADJ (US) = **cosy**
CP N ABBR (= Communist Party) P.C. m
cp. ABBR (= compare) cfr.
CPA N ABBR (US) = **certified public accountant**
CPI N ABBR (US: = Consumer Price Index) indice dei prezzi al consumo
Cpl. ABBR = **corporal**
CP/M N ABBR (= Control Program for Microcomputers) CP/M m
c.p.s. ABBR (= characters per second) c.p.s.
CPSA N ABBR (BRIT: = Civil and Public Services Association) sindacato dei servizi pubblici
CPU N ABBR = **central processing unit**
cr. ABBR = **credit; creditor**
crab [kræb] N granchio

crab apple N mela selvatica

crack [kræk] N (split, slit) fessura, crepa; incrinatura; (noise) schiocco; (: of gun) scoppio; (joke) battuta; (col: attempt): **to have a ~ at sth** tentare qc; (Drugs) crack m inv ▶ VT spaccare; incrinare; (whip) schioccare; (nut) schiacciare; (solve: problem, case) risolvere; (: code) decifrare ▶ CPD (athlete) di prim'ordine; (troops) fuori classe; **to ~ jokes** (col) dire battute, scherzare; **to get cracking** (col) darsi una mossa

▶ **crack down on** VT FUS prendere serie misure contro, porre freno a

▶ **crack up** VI crollare

crackdown ['krækdaun] N repressione f

cracked [krækt] ADJ (col) matto(-a)

cracker ['krækəʳ] N cracker m inv; (fireworks) petardo; (Christmas cracker) mortaretto natalizio (con sorpresa); **a ~ of a ...** (BRIT col) un(-a) ... formidabile; **he's crackers** (BRIT col) è tocco

crackle ['krækl] VI crepitare

crackling ['kræklɪŋ] N crepitio; (on radio, telephone) disturbo; (of pork) cotenna croccante (del maiale)

crackpot ['krækpɒt] N (col) imbecille mf con idee assurde, assurdo(-a)

cradle ['kreɪdl] N culla ▶ VT (child) tenere fra le braccia; (object) reggere tra le braccia

craft [krɑːft] N mestiere m; (cunning) astuzia; (boat) naviglio

craftsman ['krɑːftsmən] N (irreg) artigiano

craftsmanship ['krɑːftsmənʃɪp] N abilità

crafty ['krɑːftɪ] ADJ furbo(-a), astuto(-a)

crag [kræg] N roccia

cram [kræm] VI (for exams) prepararsi (in gran fretta) ▶ VT (fill): **to ~ sth with** riempire qc di; (put): **to ~ sth into** stipare qc in

cramming ['kræmɪŋ] N (fig: pej) sgobbare m

cramp [kræmp] N crampo ▶ VT soffocare, impedire; **I've got ~ in my leg** ho un crampo alla gamba

cramped [kræmpt] ADJ ristretto(-a)

crampon ['kræmpən] N (Climbing) rampone m

cranberry ['krænbərɪ] N mirtillo

crane [kreɪn] N gru f inv ▶ VT, VI: **to ~ forward, to ~ one's neck** allungare il collo

cranium ['kreɪnɪəm] (pl **crania** ['kreɪnɪə]) N cranio

crank [kræŋk] N manovella; (person) persona stramba

crankshaft ['kræŋkʃɑːft] N albero a gomiti

cranky ['kræŋkɪ] ADJ eccentrico(-a); (bad-tempered): **to be ~** avere i nervi

cranny ['krænɪ] N see **nook**

crap [kræp] N (col!) fesserie fpl; **to have a ~** cacare (!)

crappy ['kræpɪ] ADJ (col) di merda (!)

crash [kræʃ] N fragore m; (of car) incidente m; (of plane) caduta; (of business) fallimento; (Stock Exchange) crollo ▶ VT fracassare ▶ VI (plane) fracassarsi; (car) avere un incidente; (two cars) scontrarsi; (fig: business etc) fallire, andare in rovina; **to ~ into** scontrarsi con; **he crashed the car into a wall** andò a sbattere contro un muro con la macchina

crash barrier N (BRIT Aut) guardrail m inv

crash course N corso intensivo

crash helmet N casco

crash landing N atterraggio di fortuna

crass [kræs] ADJ crasso(-a)

crate [kreɪt] N cassa

crater ['kreɪtəʳ] N cratere m

cravat, cravate [krə'væt] N fazzoletto da collo

crave [kreɪv] VT, VI: **to ~ (for)** desiderare ardentemente

craving ['kreɪvɪŋ] N: **~ (for)** (for food, cigarettes etc) (gran) voglia (di)

crawl [krɔːl] VI strisciare carponi; (child) andare a gattoni; (vehicle) avanzare lentamente ▶ N (Swimming) crawl m; **to ~ to sb** (col: suck up) arruffianarsi qn

crawler lane ['krɔːlə-] N (BRIT Aut) corsia riservata al traffico lento

crayfish ['kreɪfɪʃ] N INV (freshwater) gambero (d'acqua dolce); (saltwater) gambero

crayon ['kreɪən] N matita colorata

craze [kreɪz] N mania

crazed [kreɪzd] ADJ (look, person) folle, pazzo(-a); (pottery, glaze) incrinato(-a)

crazy ['kreɪzɪ] ADJ matto(-a); (col: keen): **to be ~ about sb** essere pazzo di qn; : **to be ~ about sth** andare matto per qc; **to go ~** uscir di senno, impazzire

crazy paving N (BRIT) lastricato a mosaico irregolare

creak [kriːk] VI cigolare, scricchiolare

cream [kriːm] N crema; (fresh) panna ▶ ADJ (colour) color crema inv; **whipped ~** panna montata

▶ **cream off** VT (best talents, part of profits) portarsi via

cream cake N torta alla panna

cream cheese N formaggio fresco

creamery ['kriːmərɪ] N (shop) latteria; (factory) caseificio

creamy ['kriːmɪ] ADJ cremoso(-a)

crease [kriːs] N grinza; (deliberate) piega ▶ VT sgualcire ▶ VI sgualcirsi

crease-resistant ['kriːsrɪzɪstənt] ADJ ingualcibile

create [kriː'eɪt] VT creare; (fuss, noise) fare

creation [kriː'eɪʃən] N creazione f

creative [kriː'eɪtɪv] ADJ creativo(-a)

creativity [kriːeɪ'tɪvɪtɪ] N creatività

creator [kriː'eɪtəʳ] N creatore(-trice)

creature ['kriːtʃəʳ] N creatura

crèche, creche [krɛʃ] N asilo infantile
credence ['kri:dns] N credenza, fede f
credentials [krɪ'dɛnʃlz] NPL (papers)
credenziali fpl; (letters of reference) referenze fpl
credibility [krɛdɪ'bɪlɪtɪ] N credibilità
credible ['krɛdɪbl] ADJ credibile; (witness, source) attendibile
credit ['krɛdɪt] N credito; onore m; (Scol: esp US) certificato del compimento di una parte del corso universitario ▶ VT (Comm) accreditare; (believe: also: **give credit to**) credere, prestar fede a; **to ~ £5 to sb** accreditare 5 sterline a qn; **to ~ sb with sth** (fig) attribuire qc a qn; **on ~** a credito; **to one's ~** a proprio onore; **to take the ~ for** farsi il merito di; **to be in ~** (person) essere creditore(-trice); (bank account) essere coperto(-a); **he's a ~ to his family** fa onore alla sua famiglia; see also **credits**
creditable ['krɛdɪtəbl] ADJ che fa onore, degno(-a) di lode
credit account N conto di credito
credit agency N (BRIT) agenzia di analisi di credito
credit balance N saldo attivo
credit bureau N (US) agenzia di analisi di credito
credit card N carta di credito
credit control N controllo dei crediti
credit crunch N improvvisa stretta di credito
credit facilities NPL agevolazioni fpl creditizie
credit limit N limite m di credito
credit note N (BRIT) nota di credito
creditor ['krɛdɪtər] N creditore(-trice)
credits ['krɛdɪts] NPL (Cine) titoli mpl
credit transfer N bancogiro, postagiro
creditworthy ['krɛdɪt'wəːðɪ] ADJ autorizzabile al credito
credulity [krɪ'djuːlɪtɪ] N credulità
creed [kriːd] N credo; dottrina
creek [kriːk] N insenatura; (US) piccolo fiume m
creel [kriːl] N cestino per il pesce; (also: **lobster creel**) nassa
creep [kriːp] (pt, pp **crept** [krɛpt]) VI avanzare furtivamente (or pian piano); (plant) arrampicarsi ▶ N (col): **he's a ~** è un tipo viscido; **it gives me the creeps** (col) mi fa venire la pelle d'oca; **to ~ up on sb** avvicinarsi quatto quatto a qn; (fig: old age etc) cogliere qn alla sprovvista
creeper ['kriːpər] N pianta rampicante
creepers ['kriːpəz] NPL (US: rompers) tutina
creepy ['kriːpɪ] ADJ (frightening) che fa accapponare la pelle
creepy-crawly ['kriːpɪ'krɔːlɪ] N (col) bestiolina, insetto
cremate [krɪ'meɪt] VT cremare
cremation [krɪ'meɪʃən] N cremazione f

crematorium [krɛmə'tɔːrɪəm] (pl **crematoria** [-'tɔːrɪə]) N forno crematorio
creosote ['krɪəsəut] N creosoto
crêpe [kreɪp] N crespo
crêpe bandage N (BRIT) fascia elastica
crêpe paper N carta crespa
crêpe sole N suola di para
crept [krɛpt] PT, PP of **creep**
crescendo [krɪ'ʃɛndəu] N crescendo
crescent ['krɛsnt] N (shape) mezzaluna; (street) strada semicircolare
cress [krɛs] N crescione m
crest [krɛst] N cresta; (of helmet) pennacchiera; (of coat of arms) cimiero
crestfallen ['krɛstfɔːlən] ADJ mortificato(-a)
Crete ['kriːt] N Creta
crevasse [krɪ'væs] N crepaccio
crevice ['krɛvɪs] N fessura, crepa
crew [kruː] N equipaggio; (Cine) troupe f inv; (gang) banda, compagnia
crew-cut ['kruːkʌt] N: **to have a ~** avere i capelli a spazzola
crew-neck ['kruːnɛk] N girocollo
crib [krɪb] N culla; (Rel) presepio ▶ VT (col) copiare
cribbage ['krɪbɪdʒ] N tipo di gioco di carte
crick [krɪk] N crampo; **~ in the neck** torcicollo
cricket ['krɪkɪt] N (insect) grillo; (game) cricket m
cricketer ['krɪkɪtər] N giocatore m di cricket
crime [kraɪm] N (in general) criminalità; (instance) crimine m, delitto
crime wave N ondata di criminalità
criminal ['krɪmɪnl] ADJ, N criminale (mf); **C~ Investigation Department (CID)** ≈ polizia giudiziaria
crimp [krɪmp] VT arricciare
crimson ['krɪmzn] ADJ color cremisi inv
cringe [krɪndʒ] VI acquattarsi; (fig) essere servile; (in embarrassment) sentirsi sprofondare
crinkle ['krɪŋkl] VT arricciare, increspare
cripple ['krɪpl] N zoppo(-a) ▶ VT azzoppare; (ship, plane) avariare; (production, exports) rovinare; **crippled with arthritis** sciancato(-a) per l'artrite
crippling ['krɪplɪŋ] ADJ (taxes, debts) esorbitante; (disease) molto debilitante
crisis ['kraɪsɪs] (pl **crises** [-siːz]) N crisi f inv
crisp [krɪsp] ADJ croccante; (fig) frizzante; vivace; deciso(-a)
crisps [krɪsps] NPL (BRIT) patatine fpl fritte
crispy ADJ croccante
criss-cross ['krɪskrɔs] ADJ incrociato(-a) ▶ VT incrociarsi
criterion [kraɪ'tɪərɪən] (pl **criteria** [-'tɪərɪə]) N criterio
critic ['krɪtɪk] N critico(-a)

critical ['krɪtɪkl] ADJ critico(-a); **to be ~ of sb/ sth** criticare qn/qc, essere critico verso qn/qc

critically ['krɪtɪklɪ] ADV criticamente; **~ ill** gravemente malato

criticism ['krɪtɪsɪzəm] N critica

criticize ['krɪtɪsaɪz] VT criticare

critique [krɪ'tiːk] N critica, saggio critico

croak [krəuk] VI gracchiare

Croat ['krəuæt] ADJ, N = **Croatian**

Croatia [krəu'eɪʃə] N Croazia

Croatian [krəu'eɪʃən] ADJ croato(-a) ▶ N croato(-a); (Ling) croato

crochet ['krəuʃeɪ] N lavoro all'uncinetto

crock [krɔk] N coccio; (col: person: also: **old crock**) rottame m; (car etc) caffettiera, rottame m

crockery ['krɔkərɪ] N vasellame m; (plates, cups etc) stoviglie fpl

crocodile ['krɔkədaɪl] N coccodrillo

crocus ['krəukəs] N croco

croft [krɔft] N (BRIT) piccolo podere m

crofter ['krɔftər] N (BRIT) affittuario di un piccolo podere

croissant ['krwasã] N brioche f inv, croissant m inv

crone [krəun] N strega

crony ['krəunɪ] N (col) amicone(-a)

crook [kruk] N (col) truffatore m; (of shepherd) bastone m

crooked ['krukɪd] ADJ curvo(-a), storto(-a); (person, action) disonesto(-a)

crop [krɔp] N raccolto; (produce) coltivazione f; (amount produced) raccolto; (riding crop) frustino; (of bird) gozzo, ingluvie f ▶ VT (cut: hair) tagliare, rapare; (animals: grass) brucare ▶ **crop up** VI presentarsi

cropper ['krɔpər] N: **to come a ~** (col) fare fiasco

crop spraying N spruzzatura di antiparassitari

croquet ['krəukeɪ] N croquet m

croquette [krə'kɛt] N crocchetta

cross [krɔs] N croce f; (Biol) incrocio ▶ VT (street etc) attraversare; (arms, legs, Biol) incrociare; (cheque) sbarrare; (thwart: person, plan) contrastare, ostacolare ▶ VI: **the boat crosses from ... to ...** la barca fa la traversata da ... a ... ▶ ADJ di cattivo umore; **to ~ o.s.** fare il segno della croce, segnarsi; **we have a crossed line** (BRIT: on telephone) c'è un'interferenza; **they've got their lines crossed** (fig) si sono fraintesi; **to be/get ~ with sb (about sth)** essere arrabbiato(-a)/ arrabbiarsi con qn (per qc)
▶ **cross off** VT cancellare (tirando una riga con la penna)
▶ **cross out** VT cancellare
▶ **cross over** VI attraversare

crossbar ['krɔsbɑːr] N traversa

crossbow ['krɔsbəu] N balestra

crossbreed ['krɔsbriːd] N incrocio

cross-Channel ferry ['krɔs'tʃænl-] N traghetto che attraversa la Manica

cross-check ['krɔstʃɛk] N controprova ▶ VI fare una controprova

crosscountry [krɔs'kʌntrɪ],**crosscountry race** [krɔs'kʌntrɪ-] N cross-country m inv

cross-dressing [krɔs'drɛsɪŋ] N travestitismo

cross-examination ['krɔsɪgzæmɪ'neɪʃən] N (Law) controinterrogatorio

cross-examine ['krɔsɪg'zæmɪn] VT (Law) sottoporre a controinterrogatorio

cross-eyed ['krɔsaɪd] ADJ strabico(-a)

crossfire ['krɔsfaɪər] N fuoco incrociato

crossing ['krɔsɪŋ] N incrocio; (sea-passage) traversata; (also: **pedestrian crossing**) passaggio pedonale

crossing guard (US) N dipendente comunale che aiuta i bambini ad attraversare la strada

crossing point N valico di frontiera

cross-purposes ['krɔs'pəːpəsɪz] NPL: **to be at ~ with sb** (misunderstand) fraintendere qn; **to talk at ~** fraintendersi

cross-question [krɔs'kwɛstʃən] VT (Law) = **cross-examine**; (fig) sottoporre ad un interrogatorio

cross-reference ['krɔs'rɛfərəns] N rinvio, rimando

crossroads ['krɔsrəudz] N incrocio

cross section N (Biol) sezione f trasversale; (in population) settore m rappresentativo

crosswalk ['krɔswɔːk] N (US) strisce fpl pedonali, passaggio pedonale

crosswind ['krɔswɪnd] N vento di traverso

crosswise ['krɔswaɪz] ADV di traverso

crossword ['krɔswəːd] N cruciverba m inv

crotch [krɔtʃ] N (Anat) inforcatura; (of garment) pattina

crotchet ['krɔtʃɪt] N (Mus) semiminima

crotchety ['krɔtʃɪtɪ] ADJ (person) burbero(-a)

crouch [krautʃ] VI acquattarsi; rannicchiarsi

croup [kruːp] N (Med) croup m

crouton ['kruːtɔn] N crostino

crow [krəu] N (bird) cornacchia; (of cock) canto del gallo ▶ VI (cock) cantare; (fig) vantarsi; cantar vittoria

crowbar ['krəubɑːr] N piede m di porco

crowd [kraud] N folla ▶ VT affollare, stipare ▶ VI affollarsi; **crowds of people** un sacco di gente; **to ~ round/in** affollarsi intorno a/in

crowded ['kraudɪd] ADJ affollato(-a); **~ with** stipato(-a) di

crowd scene N (Cine, Theat) scena di massa

crowdsource ['kraudsɔːs] VT ricorrere al crowdsourcing per

crowdsourcing ['kraudsɔːsɪŋ] N crowdsourcing m

crown ['kraʊn] N corona; (*of head*) calotta cranica; (*of hat*) cocuzzolo; (*of hill*) cima ▶ VT incoronare; (*tooth*) incapsulare; (*fig: career*) coronare; **and to ~ it all …** (*fig*) e per giunta …, e come se non bastasse …; *vedi nota*

> Nel sistema legale inglese, la *crown court* è un tribunale penale che si sposta da una città all'altra. È formata da una giuria locale ed è presieduta da un giudice che si sposta assieme alla *court*. Vi si discutono i reati più gravi, mentre dei reati minori si occupano le *magistrates' courts*, presiedute da un giudice di pace, ma senza giuria. è il giudice di pace che decide se passare o meno un caso alla *crown court*.

crowning ['kraʊnɪŋ] ADJ (*achievement, glory*) supremo(-a)
crown jewels NPL gioielli *mpl* della Corona
crown prince N principe *m* ereditario
crow's-feet ['krəʊzfiːt] NPL zampe *fpl* di gallina
crow's-nest ['krəʊznest] N (*on sailing-ship*) coffa
crucial ['kruːʃl] ADJ cruciale, decisivo(-a); **~ to** essenziale per
crucifix ['kruːsɪfɪks] N crocifisso
crucifixion [kruːsɪ'fɪkʃən] N crocifissione *f*
crucify ['kruːsɪfaɪ] VT crocifiggere, mettere in croce; (*fig*) distruggere, fare a pezzi
crude [kruːd] ADJ (*materials*) greggio(-a); non raffinato(-a); (*fig: basic*) crudo(-a), primitivo(-a), (: *vulgar*) rozzo(-a), grossolano(-a) ▶ N (*also*: **crude oil**) (petrolio) greggio
cruel ['kruəl] ADJ crudele
cruelty ['kruəltɪ] N crudeltà *f inv*
cruet ['kruːɪt] N ampolla
cruise [kruːz] N crociera ▶ VI andare a velocità di crociera; (*taxi*) circolare
cruise missile N missile *m* cruise *inv*
cruiser ['kruːzər] N incrociatore *m*
cruising speed ['kruːzɪŋ-] N velocità *f inv* di crociera
crumb [krʌm] N briciola
crumble ['krʌmbl] VT sbriciolare ▶ VI sbriciolarsi; (*plaster etc*) sgretolarsi; (*land, earth*) franare; (*building, fig*) crollare
crumbly ['krʌmblɪ] ADJ friabile
crummy ['krʌmɪ] ADJ (*col: cheap*) di infima categoria; (: *depressed*) giù *inv*
crumpet ['krʌmpɪt] N *specie di frittella*
crumple ['krʌmpl] VT raggrinzare, spiegazzare
crunch [krʌntʃ] VT sgranocchiare; (*underfoot*) scricchiolare ▶ N (*fig*) punto *or* momento cruciale
crunchy ['krʌntʃɪ] ADJ croccante
crusade [kruː'seɪd] N crociata ▶ VI (*fig*): **to ~ for/against** fare una crociata per/contro

crusader [kruː'seɪdər] N crociato; (*fig*): **~ (for)** sostenitore(-trice) (di)
crush [krʌʃ] N folla; (*love*): **to have a ~ on sb** avere una cotta per qn; (*drink*): **lemon ~** spremuta di limone ▶ VT schiacciare; (*crumple*) sgualcire; (*grind, break up: garlic, ice*) tritare; (: *grapes*) pigiare
crush barrier N (BRIT) transenna
crushing ['krʌʃɪŋ] ADJ schiacciante
crust [krʌst] N crosta
crustacean [krʌs'teɪʃən] N crostaceo
crusty ['krʌstɪ] ADJ (*bread*) croccante; (*person*) brontolone(-a); (*remark*) brusco(-a)
crutch [krʌtʃ] N (*Med*) gruccia; (*support*) sostegno; (*also*: **crotch**) pattina
crux [krʌks] N nodo
cry [kraɪ] VI piangere; (*shout: also*: **cry out**) urlare ▶ N urlo, grido; (*of animal*) verso; **to ~ for help** gridare aiuto; **what are you crying about?** perché piangi?; **she had a good ~** si è fatta un bel pianto; **it's a far ~ from …** (*fig*) è tutt'un'altra cosa da …
  ▶ **cry off** VI ritirarsi
  ▶ **cry out** VI, VT gridare
crying ['kraɪɪŋ] ADJ (*fig*) palese; urgente
crypt [krɪpt] N cripta
cryptic ['krɪptɪk] ADJ ermetico(-a)
crystal ['krɪstl] N cristallo
crystal-clear ['krɪstl'klɪər] ADJ cristallino(-a); (*fig*) chiaro(-a) (come il sole)
crystallize ['krɪstəlaɪz] VI cristallizzarsi ▶ VT (*fig*) concretizzare, concretare; **crystallized fruits** (BRIT) frutta candita
CSA N ABBR (US) = **Confederate States of America**; (BRIT: = *Child Support Agency*) *istituto a difesa dei figli di coppie separate, che si adopera affinché venga rispettato l'obbligo del mantenimento*
CSC N ABBR (= *Civil Service Commission*) *commissione per il reclutamento dei funzionari statali*
CS gas N (BRIT) *tipo di gas lacrimogeno*
CST ABBR (US: = *Central Standard Time*) *fuso orario*
CT ABBR (US) = **Connecticut**
ct ABBR = **cent**; **court**
CTC N ABBR (BRIT: = *city technology college*) *istituto tecnico superiore*
cu. ABBR = **cubic**
cub [kʌb] N cucciolo; (*also*: **cub scout**) lupetto
Cuba ['kjuːbə] N Cuba
Cuban ['kjuːbə] ADJ, N cubano(-a)
cubbyhole ['kʌbɪhəʊl] N angolino
cube [kjuːb] N cubo ▶ VT (*Math*) elevare al cubo
cube root N radice *f* cubica
cubic ['kjuːbɪk] ADJ cubico(-a); **~ metre** *etc* metro *etc* cubo; **~ capacity** (*Aut*) cilindrata
cubicle ['kjuːbɪkl] N scompartimento separato; cabina

cuckoo ['kuku:] N cucù m inv
cuckoo clock N orologio a cucù
cucumber ['kju:kʌmbəʳ] N cetriolo
cud [kʌd] N: **to chew the** ~ ruminare
cuddle ['kʌdl] VT abbracciare, coccolare
  ▶ VI abbracciarsi
cuddly ['kʌdlɪ] ADJ (person) coccolone(-a);
  (col) paffuto(-a); ~ **toy** (animale m di)
  peluche m inv
cudgel ['kʌdʒl] N randello ▶ VT: **to** ~ **one's**
  brains scervellarsi, spremere le meningi
cue [kju:] N stecca; (Theat etc) segnale m
cuff [kʌf] N (BRIT: of shirt, coat etc) polsino;
  (US: on trousers) risvolto; (blow) schiaffo
  ▶ VT dare uno schiaffo a; **off the** ~ adv
  improvvisando
cufflink ['kʌflɪŋk] N gemello
cu. ft. ABBR = **cubic feet**
cu. in. ABBR = **cubic inches**
cuisine [kwɪ'zi:n] N cucina
cul-de-sac ['kʌldəsæk] N vicolo cieco
culinary ['kʌlɪnərɪ] ADJ culinario(-a)
cull [kʌl] VT (kill selectively: animals) selezionare
  e abbattere; (: ideas etc) scegliere ▶ N (of
  animals) abbattimento selettivo
culminate ['kʌlmɪneɪt] VI: **to** ~ **in** culminare
  con
culmination [kʌlmɪ'neɪʃən] N culmine m
culottes [kju:'lɔts] NPL gonna f pantalone inv
culpable ['kʌlpəbl] ADJ colpevole
culprit ['kʌlprɪt] N colpevole mf
cult [kʌlt] N culto
cult figure N idolo
cultivate ['kʌltɪveɪt] VT (also fig) coltivare
cultivation [kʌltɪ'veɪʃən] N coltivazione f
cultural ['kʌltʃərəl] ADJ culturale
culture ['kʌltʃəʳ] N (also fig) cultura
cultured ['kʌltʃəd] ADJ colto(-a)
cumbersome ['kʌmbəsəm] ADJ ingombrante
cumin ['kʌmɪn] N (spice) cumino
cumulative ['kju:mjulətɪv] ADJ
  cumulativo(-a)
cunning ['kʌnɪŋ] N astuzia, furberia ▶ ADJ
  astuto(-a), furbo(-a); (clever: device, idea)
  ingegnoso(-a)
cunt [kʌnt] N (col!) figa (!); (insult) stronzo(-a)
  (!)
cup [kʌp] N tazza; (prize, of bra) coppa; **a** ~ **of**
  tea una tazza di tè
cupboard ['kʌbəd] N armadio
cup final N (BRIT Football) finale f di coppa
Cupid ['kju:pɪd] N Cupido; **cupid** cupido
cupidity [kju:'pɪdɪtɪ] N cupidigia
cupola ['kju:pələ] N cupola
cuppa ['kʌpə] N (BRIT col) tazza di tè
cup-tie ['kʌptaɪ] N (BRIT Football) partita di
  coppa
curable ['kjuərəbl] ADJ curabile
curate ['kjuərɪt] N cappellano

curator [kjuə'reɪtəʳ] N direttore m (di museo ecc)
curb [kə:b] VT tenere a freno; (expenditure)
  limitare ▶ N freno; (US) bordo del
  marciapiede
curd cheese [kə:d-] N cagliata
curdle ['kə:dl] VI cagliare
curds [kə:dz] NPL latte m cagliato
cure [kjuəʳ] VT guarire; (Culin) trattare;
  affumicare; essiccare ▶ N rimedio; **to be**
  cured of sth essere guarito(-a) da qc
cure-all ['kjuərɔ:l] N (also fig) panacea,
  toccasana m inv
curfew ['kə:fju:] N coprifuoco
curio ['kjuərɪəu] N curiosità f inv
curiosity [kjuərɪ'ɔsɪtɪ] N curiosità
curious ['kjuərɪəs] ADJ curioso(-a); **I'm** ~
  about him m'incuriosisce
curiously ['kjuərɪəslɪ] ADV con curiosità;
  (strangely) stranamente; ~ **enough, ...** per
  quanto possa sembrare strano, ...
curl [kə:l] N riccio; (of smoke etc) anello ▶ VT
  ondulare; (tightly) arricciare ▶ VI arricciarsi
  ▶ **curl up** VI avvolgersi a spirale;
  rannicchiarsi
curler ['kə:ləʳ] N bigodino; (Sport)
  giocatore(-trice) di curling
curlew ['kə:lu:] N chiurlo
curling ['kə:lɪŋ] N (Sport) curling m
curling tongs, (US) **curling irons** NPL (for
  hair) arricciacapelli m inv
curly ['kə:lɪ] ADJ ricciuto(-a)
currant ['kʌrnt] N (dried) uvetta; (bush, fruit)
  ribes m inv
currency ['kʌrnsɪ] N moneta; **foreign** ~
  divisa estera; **to gain** ~ (fig) acquistare larga
  diffusione
current ['kʌrnt] ADJ corrente; (tendency, price,
  event) attuale ▶ N corrente f; **in** ~ **use** in uso
  corrente, d'uso comune; **the** ~ **issue of a**
  magazine l'ultimo numero di una rivista;
  direct/alternating ~ (Elec) corrente
  continua/alternata
current account N (BRIT) conto corrente
current affairs NPL attualità fpl
current assets NPL (Comm) attivo
  realizzabile e disponibile
current liabilities NPL (Comm) passività fpl
  correnti
currently ['kʌrntlɪ] ADV attualmente
curriculum [kə'rɪkjuləm] (pl **curriculums** or
  curricula [-lə]) N curriculum m inv
curriculum vitae [-'vi:taɪ] N curriculum
  vitae m inv
curry ['kʌrɪ] N curry m inv ▶ VT: **to** ~ **favour**
  with cercare di attirarsi i favori di; **chicken**
  ~ pollo al curry
curry powder N curry m
curse [kə:s] VT maledire ▶ VI bestemmiare
  ▶ N maledizione f; bestemmia

cursor ['kə:sə^r] N (*Comput*) cursore *m*
cursory ['kə:sərɪ] ADJ superficiale
curt [kə:t] ADJ secco(-a)
curtail [kə:'teɪl] VT (*visit etc*) accorciare; (*expenses etc*) ridurre, decurtare
curtain ['kə:tn] N tenda; (*Theat*) sipario; **to draw the curtains** (*together*) chiudere *or* tirare le tende; (*apart*) aprire le tende
curtain call N (*Theat*) chinata alla ribalta
curtsy, curtsey ['kə:tsɪ] N inchino, riverenza ▶ VI fare un inchino *or* una riverenza
curvature ['kə:vətʃə^r] N curvatura
curve [kə:v] N curva ▶ VT curvare ▶ VI curvarsi; (*road*) fare una curva
curved [kə:vd] ADJ curvo(-a)
cushion ['kuʃən] N cuscino ▶ VT (*shock*) fare da cuscinetto a
cushy ['kuʃɪ] ADJ (*col*): **a ~ job** un lavoro di tutto riposo; **to have a ~ time** spassarsela
custard ['kʌstəd] N (*for pouring*) crema
custard powder N (*BRIT*) crema pasticcera in polvere
custodial sentence [kʌs'təudɪəl-] N condanna a pena detentiva
custodian [kʌs'təudɪən] N custode *mf*; (*of museum etc*) soprintendente *mf*
custody ['kʌstədɪ] N (*of child*) custodia; (*for offenders*) arresto; **to take sb into ~** mettere qn in detenzione preventiva; **in the ~ of** alla custodia di
custom ['kʌstəm] N costume *m*, usanza; (*Law*) consuetudine *f*; (*Comm*) clientela; *see also* **customs**
customary ['kʌstəmərɪ] ADJ consueto(-a); **it is ~ to do** è consuetudine fare
custom-built ['kʌstəm'bɪlt] ADJ *see* **custom-made**
customer ['kʌstəmə^r] N cliente *mf*; **he's an awkward ~** (*col*) è un tipo incontentabile
customer profile N profilo del cliente
customize ['kʌstəmaɪz] VT customizzare
customized ['kʌstəmaɪzd] ADJ personalizzato(-a); (*car*) fuoriserie *inv*
custom-made ['kʌstəm'meɪd] ADJ (*clothes*) fatto(-a) su misura; (*other goods: also:* **custom-built**) fatto(-a) su ordinazione
customs ['kʌstəmz] NPL dogana; **to go through (the) ~** passare la dogana
Customs and Excise N (*BRIT*) Ufficio Dazi e Dogana
customs officer N doganiere *m*
cut [kʌt] (*pt, pp ~*) VT tagliare; (*shape, make*) intagliare; (*reduce*) ridurre; (*col: avoid: class, lecture, appointment*) saltare ▶ VI tagliare; (*intersect*) tagliarsi ▶ N taglio; (*in salary etc*) riduzione *f*; **cold cuts** npl (*US*) affettati mpl; **power ~** mancanza di corrente elettrica; **to ~ one's finger** tagliarsi un dito; **I've ~**

myself mi sono tagliato; **to get one's hair ~** farsi tagliare i capelli; **to ~ a tooth** mettere un dente; **to ~ sb/sth short** interrompere qn/qc; **to ~ sb dead** ignorare qn completamente
▶ **cut back** VT (*plants*) tagliare; (*production, expenditure*) ridurre
▶ **cut down** VT (*tree*) abbattere; (*consumption, expenses*) ridurre; **to ~ sb down to size** (*fig*) sgonfiare *or* ridimensionare qn
▶ **cut down on** VT FUS ridurre
▶ **cut in** VI: **to ~ in (on)** (*interrupt conversation*) intromettersi (in); (*Aut*) tagliare la strada (a)
▶ **cut off** VT tagliare; (*fig*) isolare; **we've been ~ off** (*Tel*) è caduta la linea
▶ **cut out** VT tagliare; eliminare; (*picture*) ritagliare
▶ **cut up** VT (*gen*) tagliare a pezzi
cut-and-dried ['kʌtən'draɪd] ADJ (*also:* **cut-and-dry**) assodato(-a)
cutaway ['kʌtəweɪ] ADJ, N: **~ (drawing)** spaccato
cutback ['kʌtbæk] N riduzione *f*
cute [kju:t] ADJ carino(-a); (*clever*) astuto(-a)
cut glass N cristallo
cuticle ['kju:tɪkl] N (*on nail*) pellicina, cuticola
cutlery ['kʌtlərɪ] N posate *fpl*
cutlet ['kʌtlɪt] N costoletta; (*nut cutlet*) cotoletta vegetariana
cutoff ['kʌtɔf] N (*also:* **cutoff point**) limite *m*
cutoff switch N interruttore *m*
cutout ['kʌtaut] N (*switch*) interruttore *m*; (*paper, cardboard figure*) ritaglio
cut-price ['kʌt'praɪs], (*US*) **cut-rate** ['kʌt'reɪt] ADJ a prezzo ridotto
cutthroat ['kʌtθrəut] N assassino ▶ ADJ: **~ competition** concorrenza spietata
cutting ['kʌtɪŋ] ADJ tagliente; (*fig*) pungente ▶ N (*BRIT: Press*) ritaglio (di giornale); (*: Rail*) trincea; (*Cine*) montaggio; (*from plant*) talea
cutting edge N (*of knife*) taglio, filo; **on** *or* **at the ~ of sth** all'avanguardia di qc
cutting-edge [kʌtɪŋ'ɛdʒ] ADJ d'avanguardia
cuttlefish ['kʌtlfɪʃ] N seppia
cut-up ['kʌtʌp] ADJ stravolto(-a)
CV N ABBR = **curriculum vitae**
CWO ABBR = **cash with order**
cwt. ABBR = **hundredweight**
cyanide ['saɪənaɪd] N cianuro
cyber attack N attacco *m* informatico
cyberbullying ['saɪbəbulɪɪŋ] N bullismo informatico
cybercafé ['saɪbəkæfeɪ] N cybercaffè *m inv*
cybercrime ['saɪbəkraɪm] N delinquenza informatica
cybernetics [saɪbə'nɛtɪks] N cibernetica
cybersecurity [saɪbəsɪ'kjurɪtɪ] N sicurezza *f* informatica
cyberspace ['saɪbəspeɪs] N ciberspazio

cyberterrorism [saɪbə'tɛrərɪzəm] N ciberterrorismo

cyclamen ['sɪkləmən] N ciclamino

cycle ['saɪkl] N ciclo; (bicycle) bicicletta ▶ VI andare in bicicletta

cycle hire N noleggio m biciclette inv

cycle lane N pista ciclabile

cycle path N pista ciclabile

cycle race N gara or corsa ciclistica

cycle rack N portabiciclette m inv

cycle track N percorso ciclabile; (in velodrome) pista

cycling ['saɪklɪŋ] N ciclismo; **to go on a ~ holiday** (BRIT) fare una vacanza in bicicletta

cyclist ['saɪklɪst] N ciclista mf

cyclone ['saɪkləun] N ciclone m

cygnet ['sɪgnɪt] N cigno giovane

cylinder ['sɪlɪndər] N cilindro

cylinder capacity N cilindrata

cylinder head N testata

cylinder head gasket N guarnizione f della testata del cilindro

cymbals ['sɪmblz] NPL piatti mpl

cynic ['sɪnɪk] N cinico(-a)

cynical ['sɪnɪkl] ADJ cinico(-a)

cynicism ['sɪnɪsɪzəm] N cinismo

cypress ['saɪprɪs] N cipresso

Cypriot ['sɪprɪət] ADJ, N cipriota (mf)

Cyprus ['saɪprəs] N Cipro

cyst [sɪst] N cisti f inv

cystitis [sɪ'staɪtɪs] N cistite f

CZ N ABBR (US: = Canal Zone) zona del Canale di Panama

czar [zɑːr] N zar m inv

Czech [tʃɛk] ADJ ceco(-a) ▶ N ceco(-a); (Ling) ceco

Czechoslovak [tʃɛkə'sləuvæk] ADJ, N (Hist) = **Czechoslovakian**

Czechoslovakia [tʃɛkəslə'vækɪə] N (Hist) Cecoslovacchia

Czechoslovakian [tʃɛkəslə'vækɪən] (Hist) ADJ, N cecoslovacco(-a)

Czech Republic N: **the ~** la Repubblica Ceca

Dd

D, d [di:] N (letter) D, d f inv or m inv; (Mus):
  D re m; **D for David**, (US) **D for Dog** ≈ D come
  Domodossola
D ABBR (US Pol) = **democrat**
d ABBR (BRIT old) = **penny**
d. ABBR = **died**
DA N ABBR (US) = **district attorney**
dab [dæb] VT (eyes, wound) tamponare;
  (paint, cream) applicare (con leggeri colpetti);
  a ~ of paint un colpetto di vernice
dabble ['dæbl] VI: **to ~ in** occuparsi (da
  dilettante) di
Dacca ['dækə] N Dacca f
dachshund ['dækshund] N bassotto
dad [dæd], **daddy** ['dædɪ] N babbo, papà m inv
daddy-long-legs [dædɪ'lɔŋlɛgz] N tipula,
  zanzarone m
daffodil ['dæfədɪl] N trombone m,
  giunchiglia
daft [dɑːft] ADJ sciocco(-a); **to be ~ about sb**
  perdere la testa per qn; **to be ~ about sth**
  andare pazzo per qc
dagger ['dægər] N pugnale m
dahlia ['deɪljə] N dalia
daily ['deɪlɪ] ADJ quotidiano(-a), giornaliero(-a)
  ► N quotidiano; (BRIT: servant) donna di
  servizio ► ADV tutti i giorni; **twice ~** due
  volte al giorno
dainty ['deɪntɪ] ADJ delicato(-a),
  grazioso(-a)
dairy ['dɛərɪ] N (shop) latteria; (on farm)
  caseificio ► CPD caseario(-a)
dairy cow N mucca da latte
dairy farm N caseificio
dairy produce N latticini mpl
dais ['deɪɪs] N pedana, palco
daisy ['deɪzɪ] N margherita
daisy wheel N (on printer) margherita
daisy-wheel printer ['deɪzɪwiːl-] N
  stampante f a margherita
Dakar ['dækər] N Dakar f
dale [deɪl] N valle f
dally ['dælɪ] VI trastullarsi
dalmatian [dæl'meɪʃən] N (dog) dalmata m

dam [dæm] N diga; (reservoir) bacino
  artificiale ► VT sbarrare; costruire dighe su
damage ['dæmɪdʒ] N danno, danni mpl; (fig)
  danno ► VT danneggiare; (fig) recar danno a;
  ~ to property danni materiali
damages NPL (Law) danni mpl; **to pay £5000
  in** ~ pagare 5000 sterline di indennizzo
damaging ['dæmɪdʒɪŋ] ADJ: **~ (to)** nocivo(-a)
  (a)
Damascus [də'mɑːskəs] N Damasco f
dame [deɪm] N (title, US col) donna; (Theat)
  vecchia signora (ruolo comico di donna recitato da
  un uomo)
damn [dæm] VT condannare; (curse) maledire
  ► N (col): **I don't give a ~** non me ne frega
  niente ► ADJ (col: also: **damned**): **this ~ ...**
  questo maledetto ...; **~ (it)!** accidenti!
damnable ['dæmnəbl] ADJ (col: behaviour)
  vergognoso(-a); (weather) schifoso(-a)
damnation [dæm'neɪʃən] N (Rel) dannazione
  f ► EXCL (col) dannazione!, diavolo!
damning ['dæmɪŋ] ADJ (evidence) schiacciante
damp [dæmp] ADJ umido(-a) ► N umidità,
  umido ► VT (also: **dampen**: cloth, rag)
  inumidire, bagnare; (: enthusiasm etc)
  spegnere
dampcourse ['dæmpkɔːs] N strato m
  isolante antiumido inv
damper ['dæmpər] N (Mus) sordina; (of fire)
  valvola di tiraggio; **to put a ~ on sth** (fig:
  atmosphere) gelare; (enthusiasm) far sbollire
dampness ['dæmpnɪs] N umidità, umido
damson ['dæmzən] N susina damaschina
dance [dɑːns] N danza, ballo; (ball) ballo ► VI
  ballare; **to ~ about** saltellare
dance floor N pista da ballo
dance hall N dancing m inv, sala da ballo
dancer ['dɑːnsər] N danzatore(-trice);
  (professional) ballerino(-a)
dancing ['dɑːnsɪŋ] N danza, ballo
D and C N ABBR (Med: = dilation and curettage)
  raschiamento
dandelion ['dændɪlaɪən] N dente m di leone
dandruff ['dændrəf] N forfora

D & T N ABBR (BRIT Scol) = **design and technology**

dandy ['dændɪ] N dandy m inv, elegantone m ▶ ADJ (US col) fantastico(-a)

Dane [deɪn] N danese mf

danger ['deɪndʒə^r] N pericolo; **there is a ~ of fire** c'è pericolo di incendio; **in ~** in pericolo; **out of ~** fuori pericolo; **he was in ~ of falling** rischiava di cadere

danger list N (Med): **on the ~** in prognosi riservata

dangerous ['deɪndʒrəs] ADJ pericoloso(-a)

dangerously ['deɪndʒrəslɪ] ADV: **~ ill** in pericolo di vita

danger zone N area di pericolo

dangle ['dæŋgl] VT dondolare; (fig) far balenare ▶ VI pendolare

Danish ['deɪnɪʃ] ADJ danese ▶ N (Ling) danese m

Danish pastry N dolce m di pasta sfoglia

dank [dæŋk] ADJ freddo(-a) e umido(-a)

Danube ['dænju:b] N: **the ~** il Danubio

dapper ['dæpə^r] ADJ lindo(-a)

Dardanelles [dɑ:də'nɛlz] NPL Dardanelli mpl

dare [dɛə^r] VT: **to ~ sb to do** sfidare qn a fare ▶ VI: **to ~ (to) do sth** osare fare qc; **I daren't tell him** (BRIT) non oso dirglielo; **I ~ say** (I suppose) immagino (che); **I ~ say he'll turn up** immagino che spunterà

daredevil ['dɛədɛvl] N scavezzacollo mf

Dar-es-Salaam [dɑ:rɛssə'lɑ:m] N Dar-es-Salaam f

daring ['dɛərɪŋ] ADJ audace, ardito(-a) ▶ N audacia

dark [dɑ:k] ADJ (night, room) buio(-a), scuro(-a); (colour, complexion) scuro(-a); (fig) cupo(-a), tetro(-a), nero(-a) ▶ N: **in the ~** al buio; **it is/is getting ~** è/si sta facendo buio; **in the ~ about** (fig) all'oscuro di; **after ~** a notte fatta; **~ chocolate** cioccolata amara

darken ['dɑ:kən] VT (room) oscurare; (photo, painting) far scuro(-a); (colour) scurire ▶ VI (sky, room) oscurarsi; imbrunirsi

dark glasses NPL occhiali mpl scuri

dark horse N (fig) incognita

darkly ['dɑ:klɪ] ADV (gloomily) cupamente, con aria cupa; (in a sinister way) minacciosamente

darkness ['dɑ:knɪs] N oscurità, buio

darkroom ['dɑ:kru:m] N camera oscura

darling ['dɑ:lɪŋ] ADJ caro(-a) ▶ N tesoro

darn [dɑ:n] VT rammendare

dart [dɑ:t] N freccetta; (Sewing) pince f inv ▶ VI: **to ~ towards** (also: **make a dart towards**) precipitarsi verso; **to ~ along** passare come un razzo; **to ~ away/along** sfrecciare via/lungo; see also **darts**

dartboard ['dɑ:tbɔ:d] N bersaglio (per freccette)

darts [dɑ:ts] N tiro al bersaglio (con freccette)

dash [dæʃ] N (sign) lineetta; (small quantity: of liquid) goccio, goccino; (: of soda) spruzzo ▶ VT (missile) gettare; (hopes) infrangere ▶ VI: **to ~ towards** (also: **make a dash towards**) precipitarsi verso
▶ **dash away** VI scappare via

dashboard ['dæʃbɔ:d] N (Aut) cruscotto

dashing ['dæʃɪŋ] ADJ ardito(-a)

dastardly ['dæstədlɪ] ADJ vile

DAT N ABBR (= digital audio tape) cassetta f digitale audio inv

data ['deɪtə] NPL dati mpl

database ['deɪtəbeɪs] N database m inv, base f di dati

data capture N registrazione f or rilevazione f di dati

data processing N elaborazione f (elettronica) dei dati

data transmission N trasmissione f di dati

date [deɪt] N data; (appointment) appuntamento; (fruit) dattero ▶ VT datare; (person) uscire con; **what's the ~ today?** quanti ne abbiamo oggi?; **~ of birth** data di nascita; **closing ~** scadenza, termine m; **to ~** adv (until now) fino a oggi; **out of ~** scaduto(-a); (old-fashioned) passato(-a) di moda; **up to ~** moderno(-a), aggiornato(-a); **to bring up to ~** (correspondence, information) aggiornare; (method) modernizzare; (person) aggiornare, mettere al corrente; **dated the 13th** datato il 13; **thank you for your letter dated 5th July** or **July 5th** (US) la ringrazio per la sua lettera in data 5 luglio

dated ['deɪtɪd] ADJ passato(-a) di moda

dateline ['deɪtlaɪn] N linea del cambiamento di data

date rape N stupro perpetrato da persona conosciuta

date stamp N timbro datario

daub [dɔ:b] VT imbrattare

daughter ['dɔ:tə^r] N figlia

daughter-in-law ['dɔ:tərɪnlɔ:] N nuora

daunt [dɔ:nt] VT intimidire

daunting ['dɔ:ntɪŋ] ADJ non invidiabile

dauntless ['dɔ:ntlɪs] ADJ intrepido(-a)

dawdle ['dɔ:dl] VI bighellonare; **to ~ over one's work** gingillarsi con il lavoro

dawn [dɔ:n] N alba ▶ VI (day) spuntare; (fig) venire in mente; **at ~** all'alba; **from ~ to dusk** dall'alba al tramonto; **it dawned on him that ...** gli è venuto in mente che ...

dawn chorus N (BRIT) coro mattutino degli uccelli

day [deɪ] N giorno; (as duration) giornata; (period of time, age) tempo, epoca; **the ~ before** il giorno avanti or prima; **the ~ after, the following ~** il giorno dopo, il giorno seguente; **the ~ before yesterday** l'altro ieri; **the ~ after tomorrow** dopodomani; **(on) that ~** quel giorno; **(on) the ~ that ...** il

giorno che *or* in cui ...; **to work an 8-hour ~**
avere una giornata lavorativa di 8 ore; **by ~**
di giorno; **~ by ~** giorno per giorno; **paid by
the ~** pagato(-a) a giornata; **these days, in
the present ~** di questi tempi, oggigiorno
daybook ['deɪbuk] N (BRIT) brogliaccio
day boy N (Scol) alunno esterno
daybreak ['deɪbreɪk] N spuntar *m* del giorno
day care centre N scuola materna
daydream ['deɪdriːm] N sogno a occhi aperti
▶ VI sognare a occhi aperti
day girl N (Scol) alunna esterna
daylight ['deɪlaɪt] N luce *f* del giorno
daylight robbery N: **it's ~!** (BRIT col) è un vero
furto!
Daylight Saving Time N (US) ora legale
day release N: **to be on ~** *avere un giorno di
congedo alla settimana per formazione professionale*
day return, day return ticket N (BRIT)
biglietto giornaliero di andata e ritorno
day shift N turno di giorno
daytime ['deɪtaɪm] N giorno
day-to-day ['deɪtə'deɪ] ADJ (routine, life,
organization) quotidiano(-a); (expenses)
giornaliero(-a); **on a ~ basis** a giornata
day trader N (Stock Exchange) day dealer *mf*,
*operatore che compra e vende titoli nel corso della
stessa giornata*
day trip N gita (di un giorno)
day tripper N gitante *mf*
daze [deɪz] VT (drug) inebetire; (blow) stordire
▶ N: **in a ~** inebetito(-a), stordito(-a)
dazed [deɪzd] ADJ stordito(-a)
dazzle ['dæzl] VT abbagliare
dazzling ['dæzlɪŋ] ADJ (light) abbagliante;
(colour) violento(-a); (smile) smagliante
dB ABBR (= decibel) db
DC ABBR (Elec: = direct current) c.c.; (US)
= District of Columbia
DCC® N ABBR **= digital compact cassette**
DD N ABBR (= Doctor of Divinity) titolo di studio
DD ABBR **= direct debit**
dd. ABBR (Comm) **= delivered**
D-day ['diːdeɪ] N giorno dello sbarco alleato in
Normandia
DDS N ABBR US: **= Doctor of Dental Science**;
(= Doctor of Dental Surgery) titoli di studio
DDT N ABBR (= dichlorodiphenyl trichloroethane)
D.D.T. *m*
DE (US) **= Delaware**
deacon ['diːkən] N diacono
dead [dɛd] ADJ morto(-a); (numb)
intirizzito(-a); (telephone) muto(-a); (battery)
scarico(-a) ▶ ADV assolutamente,
perfettamente; **the dead** NPL i morti; **he
was shot ~** fu colpito a morte; **~ on time** in
perfetto orario; **~ tired** stanco(-a) morto(-a);
to stop ~ fermarsi di colpo; **the line has
gone ~** (Tel) è caduta la linea

dead beat ADJ (col) stanco(-a) morto(-a)
deaden ['dɛdn] VT (blow, sound) ammortire;
(make numb) intirizzire
dead end N vicolo cieco
dead-end ['dɛdɛnd] ADJ: **a ~ job** un lavoro
senza sbocchi
dead heat N (Sport): **to finish in a ~** finire
alla pari
dead-letter office [dɛd'lɛtə-] N ufficio
della posta in giacenza
deadline ['dɛdlaɪn] N scadenza; **to work
to a ~** avere una scadenza
deadlock ['dɛdlɔk] N punto morto
dead loss N (col): **to be a ~** (person, thing) non
valere niente
deadly ['dɛdlɪ] ADJ mortale; (weapon, poison)
micidiale ▶ ADV: **~ dull** di una noia micidiale
deadpan ['dɛdpæn] ADJ a faccia impassibile
Dead Sea N: **the ~** il mar Morto
deaf [dɛf] ADJ sordo(-a); **to turn a ~ ear to
sth** fare orecchi da mercante a qc
deaf-aid ['dɛfeɪd] N apparecchio per la
sordità
deaf-and-dumb ['dɛfən'dʌm] ADJ (person)
sordomuto(-a); (alphabet) dei sordomuti
deafen ['dɛfn] VT assordare
deafening ['dɛfnɪŋ] ADJ fragoroso(-a),
assordante
deaf-mute ['dɛfmjuːt] N sordomuto(-a)
deafness ['dɛfnɪs] N sordità
deal [diːl] (pt, pp **dealt** [dɛlt]) N accordo;
(business deal) affare *m* ▶ VT (blow, cards) dare;
to strike a ~ with sb fare un affare con qn;
it's a ~! (col) affare fatto!; **he got a bad/fair ~
from them** l'hanno trattato male/bene; **a
good ~ of, a great ~ of** molto(-a)
▶ **deal in** VT FUS (Comm) occuparsi di
▶ **deal with** VT FUS (Comm) fare affari con,
trattare con; (handle) occuparsi di; (be about:
book etc) trattare di
dealer ['diːləʳ] N commerciante *mf*
dealership ['diːləʃɪp] N rivenditore *m*
dealings ['diːlɪŋz] NPL (Comm) relazioni *fpl*;
(relations) rapporti *mpl*; (in goods, shares)
transazioni *fpl*
dealt [dɛlt] PT, PP *of* **deal**
dean [diːn] N (Rel) decano; (Scol) preside *m* di
facoltà (or di collegio)
dear [dɪəʳ] ADJ caro(-a) ▶ N: **my ~** caro mio/
cara mia ▶ EXCL: **~ me!** Dio mio!; **D~ Sir/
Madam** (in letter) Egregio Signore/Egregia
Signora; **D~ Mr/Mrs X** Gentile Signor/
Signora X
dearly ['dɪəlɪ] ADV (love) moltissimo; (pay) a
caro prezzo
dear money N (Comm) denaro ad alto
interesse
dearth [dəːθ] N scarsità, carestia
death [dɛθ] N morte *f*; (Admin) decesso

deathbed ['dɛθbɛd] N letto di morte
death certificate N atto di decesso
death duty N (BRIT) imposta or tassa di successione
deathly ['dɛθlɪ] ADJ di morte ▶ ADV come un cadavere
death penalty N pena di morte
death rate N indice m di mortalità
death row [-rəu] N (US): **to be on ~** essere nel braccio della morte
death sentence N condanna a morte
death squad N squadra della morte
deathtrap ['dɛθtræp] N trappola mortale
deb [dɛb] N ABBR (col) = **debutante**
debacle [deɪ'bɑːkl] N (defeat) disfatta; (collapse) sfacelo
debar [dɪ'bɑːʳ] VT: **to ~ sb from a club** etc escludere qn da un club etc; **to ~ sb from doing** vietare a qn di fare
debase [dɪ'beɪs] VT (currency) adulterare; (person) degradare
debatable [dɪ'beɪtəbl] ADJ discutibile; **it is ~ whether ...** è in dubbio se ...
debate [dɪ'beɪt] N dibattito ▶ VT dibattere; discutere ▶ VI (consider): **to ~ whether** riflettere se
debauchery [dɪ'bɔːtʃərɪ] N dissolutezza
debenture [dɪ'bɛntʃəʳ] N (Comm) obbligazione f
debilitate [dɪ'bɪlɪteɪt] VT debilitare
debit ['dɛbɪt] N debito ▶ VT: **to ~ a sum to sb** or **to sb's account** addebitare una somma a qn
debit balance N saldo debitore
debit card N carta di debito
debit note N nota di addebito
debonair [dɛbə'nɛəʳ] ADJ gioviale e disinvolto(-a)
debrief [diː'briːf] VT chiamare a rapporto (a operazione ultimata)
debriefing [diː'briːfɪŋ] N rapporto
debris ['dɛbriː] N detriti mpl
debt [dɛt] N debito; **to be in ~** essere indebitato(-a); **debts of £5000** debiti per 5000 sterline; **bad ~** debito insoluto
debt collector N agente m di recupero crediti
debtor ['dɛtəʳ] N debitore(-trice)
debug [diː'bʌg] VT (Comput) localizzare e rimuovere errori in
debunk [diː'bʌŋk] VT (col: theory) demistificare; (claim) smentire; (person, institution) screditare
debut ['deɪbjuː] N debutto
debutante ['dɛbjutɑːnt] N debuttante f
Dec. ABBR (= December) dic.
decade ['dɛkeɪd] N decennio
decadence ['dɛkədəns] N decadenza
decadent ['dɛkədənt] ADJ decadente
de-caff ['diːkæf] N (col) decaffeinato

decaffeinated [dɪ'kæfɪneɪtɪd] ADJ decaffeinato(-a)
decamp [dɪ'kæmp] VI (col) filarsela, levare le tende
decant [dɪ'kænt] VT (wine) travasare
decanter [dɪ'kæntəʳ] N caraffa
decarbonize [diː'kɑːbənaɪz] VT (Aut) decarburare
decathlon [dɪ'kæθlən] N decathlon m
decay [dɪ'keɪ] N decadimento; imputridimento; (fig) rovina; (also: **tooth decay**) carie f ▶ VI (rot) imputridire; (fig) andare in rovina
decease [dɪ'siːs] N decesso
deceased [dɪ'siːst] N: **the ~** il(la) defunto(a)
deceit [dɪ'siːt] N inganno
deceitful [dɪ'siːtful] ADJ ingannevole, perfido(-a)
deceive [dɪ'siːv] VT ingannare; **to ~ o.s.** illudersi, ingannarsi
decelerate [diː'sɛləreɪt] VT, VI rallentare
December [dɪ'sɛmbəʳ] N dicembre m; see also **July**
decency ['diːsənsɪ] N decenza
decent ['diːsənt] ADJ decente; (respectable) per bene; (kind) gentile; **they were very ~ about it** si sono comportati da signori riguardo a ciò
decently ['diːsəntlɪ] ADV (respectably) decentemente, convenientemente; (kindly) gentilmente
decentralization [diːsɛntrəlaɪ'zeɪʃən] N decentramento
decentralize [diː'sɛntrəlaɪz] VT decentrare
deception [dɪ'sɛpʃən] N inganno
deceptive [dɪ'sɛptɪv] ADJ ingannevole
decibel ['dɛsɪbɛl] N decibel m inv
decide [dɪ'saɪd] VT (person) far prendere una decisione a; (question, argument) risolvere, decidere ▶ VI decidere, decidersi; **to ~ to do/ that** decidere di fare/che; **to ~ on** decidere per; **to ~ against doing sth** decidere di non fare qc
decided [dɪ'saɪdɪd] ADJ (resolute) deciso(-a); (clear, definite) netto(-a), chiaro(-a)
decidedly [dɪ'saɪdɪdlɪ] ADV indubbiamente; decisamente
deciding [dɪ'saɪdɪŋ] ADJ decisivo(-a)
deciduous [dɪ'sɪdjuəs] ADJ deciduo(-a)
decimal ['dɛsɪməl] ADJ, N decimale (m); **to 3 ~ places** al terzo decimale
decimalize ['dɛsɪmələɪz] VT (BRIT) convertire al sistema metrico decimale
decimal point N ≈ virgola
decimate ['dɛsɪmeɪt] VT decimare
decipher [dɪ'saɪfəʳ] VT decifrare
decision [dɪ'sɪʒən] N decisione f; **to make a ~** prendere una decisione
decisive [dɪ'saɪsɪv] ADJ (victory, factor) decisivo(-a); (influence) determinante;

(*manner, person*) risoluto(-a), deciso(-a); (*reply*) deciso(-a), categorico(-a)

deck [dɛk] N (*Naut*) ponte *m*; (*of cards*) mazzo; **top ~** imperiale *m*; **to go up on ~** salire in coperta; **below ~** sotto coperta; **cassette ~** piastra (di registrazione); **record ~** piatto (giradischi); (*of cards*) mazzo

deckchair ['dɛktʃɛəʳ] N sedia a sdraio

deck hand N marinaio

declaration [dɛklə'reɪʃən] N dichiarazione *f*

declare [dɪ'klɛəʳ] VT dichiarare

declassify [diː'klæsɪfaɪ] VT rendere accessibile al pubblico

decline [dɪ'klaɪn] N (*decay*) declino; (*lessening*) ribasso ▶ VT declinare; rifiutare ▶ VI declinare; diminuire; **~ in living standards** abbassamento del tenore di vita; **to ~ to do sth** rifiutar(si) di fare qc

declutch [diː'klʌtʃ] VI (*Brit*) premere la frizione

decode [diː'kəud] VT decifrare

decoder [diː'kəudəʳ] N (*Comput, TV*) decodificatore *m*

decompose [diːkəm'pəuz] VI decomporre

decomposition [diːkɔmpə'zɪʃən] N decomposizione *f*

decompression [diːkəm'prɛʃən] N decompressione *f*

decompression chamber N camera di decompressione

decongestant [diːkən'dʒɛstənt] N decongestionante *m*

decontaminate [diːkən'tæmɪneɪt] VT decontaminare

decontrol [diːkən'trəul] VT (*trade*) liberalizzare; (*prices*) togliere il controllo governativo a

decor ['deɪkɔːʳ] N decorazione *f*

decorate ['dɛkəreɪt] VT (*adorn, give a medal to*) decorare; (*paint and paper*) tinteggiare e tappezzare

decoration [dɛkə'reɪʃən] N (*medal etc, adornment*) decorazione *f*

decorative ['dɛkərətɪv] ADJ decorativo(-a)

decorator ['dɛkəreɪtəʳ] N decoratore(-trice)

decorum [dɪ'kɔːrəm] N decoro

decoy ['diːkɔɪ] N zimbello; **they used him as a ~ for the enemy** l'hanno usato come esca per il nemico

decrease N ['diːkriːs] diminuzione *f* ▶ VT, VI [diː'kriːs] diminuire; **to be on the ~** essere in diminuzione

decreasing [diː'kriːsɪŋ] ADJ sempre meno *inv*

decree [dɪ'kriː] N decreto ▶ VT: **to ~ (that)** decretare (che + *sub*); **~ absolute** sentenza di divorzio definitiva; **~ nisi** sentenza provvisoria di divorzio

decrepit [dɪ'krɛpɪt] ADJ decrepito(-a); (*building*) cadente

decry [dɪ'kraɪ] VT condannare, deplorare

decrypt [diː'krɪpt] VT (*Comput, Tel*) decriptare

dedicate ['dɛdɪkeɪt] VT consacrare; (*book etc*) dedicare

dedicated ['dɛdɪkeɪtɪd] ADJ coscienzioso(-a); (*Comput*) specializzato(-a), dedicato(-a)

dedication [dɛdɪ'keɪʃən] N (*devotion*) dedizione *f*; (*in book*) dedica

deduce [dɪ'djuːs] VT dedurre

deduct [dɪ'dʌkt] VT: **to ~ sth (from)** dedurre qc (da); (*from wage etc*) trattenere qc (da)

deduction [dɪ'dʌkʃən] N (*deducting*) deduzione *f*; (*from wage etc*) trattenuta; (*deducing*) deduzione *f*, conclusione *f*

deed [diːd] N azione *f*, atto; (*Law*) atto; **~ of covenant** atto di donazione

deem [diːm] VT (*formal*) giudicare, ritenere; **to ~ it wise to do** ritenere prudente fare

deep [diːp] ADJ profondo(-a) ▶ ADV: **~ in snow** affondato(-a) nella neve; **spectators stood 20 ~** c'erano 20 file di spettatori; **knee-~ in water** in acqua fino alle ginocchia; **4 metres ~** profondo(a) 4 metri; **he took a ~ breath** fece un respiro profondo; **how ~ is the water?** quanto è profonda l'acqua?

deepen ['diːpn] VT (*hole*) approfondire ▶ VI approfondirsi; (*darkness*) farsi più intenso(-a)

deep-freeze [diːp'friːz] N congelatore *m* ▶ VT congelare

deep-fry ['diːp'fraɪ] VT friggere in olio abbondante

deeply ['diːplɪ] ADV profondamente; **to regret sth ~** rammaricarsi sinceramente di qc

deep-rooted ['diːp'ruːtɪd] ADJ (*prejudice*) profondamente radicato(-a); (*affection*) profondo(-a); (*habit*) inveterato(-a)

deep-sea diver ['diːp'siː-] N palombaro

deep-sea diving N immersione *f* in alto mare

deep-sea fishing N pesca d'alto mare

deep-seated ['diːp'siːtɪd] ADJ (*beliefs*) radicato(-a)

deep-set ['diːp'sɛt] ADJ (*eyes*) infossato(-a)

deep-vein thrombosis ['diːp'vəɪn-] N trombosi *f inv* venosa profonda

deer [dɪəʳ] N (*pl inv*): **the ~** i cervidi (*Zool*); **(red) ~** cervo; **(fallow) ~** daino; **(roe) ~** capriolo

deerskin ['dɪəskɪn] N pelle *f* di daino

deerstalker ['dɪəstɔːkəʳ] N berretto da cacciatore

deface [dɪ'feɪs] VT imbrattare

defamation [dɛfə'meɪʃən] N diffamazione *f*

defamatory [dɪ'fæmətərɪ] ADJ diffamatorio(-a)

default [dɪ'fɔːlt] VI (*Law*) essere contumace; (*gen*) essere inadempiente ▶ N (*Comput: also:* **default value**) default *m inv*; **by ~** (*Law*) in

511

contumacia; (*Sport*) per abbandono; **to ~ on a debt** non onorare un debito

defaulter [dɪˈfɔːltər] N (*on debt*) inadempiente *mf*

default option N (*Comput*) opzione *f* di default

defeat [dɪˈfiːt] N sconfitta ▶ VT (*team, opponents*) sconfiggere; (*fig: plans, efforts*) frustrare

defeatism [dɪˈfiːtɪzəm] N disfattismo

defeatist [dɪˈfiːtɪst] ADJ, N disfattista (*mf*)

defecate [ˈdɛfəkeɪt] VI defecare

defect N [ˈdiːfɛkt] difetto ▶ VI [dɪˈfɛkt]: **to ~ to the enemy/the West** passare al nemico/all'Ovest; **physical ~** difetto fisico; **mental ~** anomalia mentale

defective [dɪˈfɛktɪv] ADJ difettoso(-a)

defector [dɪˈfɛktər] N rifugiato(-a) politico(-a)

defence, (*US*) **defense** [dɪˈfɛns] N difesa; **in ~ of** in difesa di; **the Ministry of D~,** (*US*) **the Department of Defense** il Ministero della Difesa; **witness for the ~** teste *mf* a difesa

defenceless [dɪˈfɛnslɪs] ADJ senza difesa

defend [dɪˈfɛnd] VT difendere; (*decision, action*) giustificare; (*opinion*) sostenere

defendant [dɪˈfɛndənt] N imputato(-a)

defender [dɪˈfɛndər] N difensore(-a)

defending champion N (*Sport*) campione(-essa) in carica

defending counsel N (*Law*) avvocato difensore

defense [dɪˈfɛns] N (*US*) = **defence**

defensive [dɪˈfɛnsɪv] ADJ difensivo(-a) ▶ N difensiva; **on the ~** sulla difensiva

defer [dɪˈfəːr] VT (*postpone*) differire, rinviare ▶ VI (*submit*): **to ~ to sb/sth** rimettersi a qn/qc

deference [ˈdɛfərəns] N deferenza; riguardo; **out of** *or* **in ~ to** per riguardo a

defiance [dɪˈfaɪəns] N sfida; **in ~ of** a dispetto di

defiant [dɪˈfaɪənt] ADJ (*attitude*) di sfida; (*person*) ribelle

defiantly [dɪˈfaɪəntlɪ] ADV con aria di sfida

deficiency [dɪˈfɪʃənsɪ] N deficienza; carenza; (*Comm*) ammanco

deficiency disease N malattia da carenza

deficient [dɪˈfɪʃənt] ADJ deficiente; insufficiente; **to be ~ in** mancare di

deficit [ˈdɛfɪsɪt] N disavanzo, deficit *m inv*

defile [dɪˈfaɪl] VT contaminare ▶ VI sfilare ▶ N [ˈdiːfaɪl] gola, stretta

define [dɪˈfaɪn] VT (*gen, Comput*) definire

definite [ˈdɛfɪnɪt] ADJ (*fixed*) definito(-a), preciso(-a); (*clear, obvious*) ben definito(-a), esatto(-a); (*Ling*) determinativo(-a); **he was ~ about it** ne era sicuro

definitely [ˈdɛfɪnɪtlɪ] ADV indubbiamente

definition [dɛfɪˈnɪʃən] N definizione *f*

definitive [dɪˈfɪnɪtɪv] ADJ definitivo(-a)

deflate [diːˈfleɪt] VT sgonfiare; (*Econ*) deflazionare; (*pompous person*) fare abbassare la cresta a

deflation [diːˈfleɪʃən] N (*Econ*) deflazione *f*

deflationary [diːˈfleɪʃənrɪ] ADJ (*Econ*) deflazionistico(-a)

deflect [dɪˈflɛkt] VT deflettere, deviare

defog [ˈdiːˈfɔg] VT (*US Aut*) sbrinare

defogger [ˈdiːˈfɔgər] N (*US Aut*) sbrinatore *m*

deform [dɪˈfɔːm] VT deformare

deformed [dɪˈfɔːmd] ADJ deforme

deformity [dɪˈfɔːmɪtɪ] N deformità *f inv*

Defra N ABBR (*BRIT*) = **Department for Environment, Food and Rural Affairs**

defraud [dɪˈfrɔːd] VT: **to ~ (of)** defraudare (di)

defray [dɪˈfreɪ] VT: **to ~ sb's expenses** sostenere le spese di qn

defriend [diːˈfrɛnd] VT (*Internet*) cancellare dagli amici

defrost [diːˈfrɔst] VT (*fridge*) disgelare; (*frozen food*) scongelare

deft [dɛft] ADJ svelto(-a), destro(-a)

defunct [dɪˈfʌŋkt] ADJ defunto(-a)

defuse [diːˈfjuːz] VT disinnescare; (*fig*) distendere

defy [dɪˈfaɪ] VT sfidare; (*efforts etc*) resistere a; (*refuse to obey: person*) rifiutare di obbedire a; **it defies description** supera ogni descrizione

degenerate VI [dɪˈdʒɛnəreɪt] degenerare ▶ ADJ [dɪˈdʒɛnərɪt] degenere

degradation [dɛgrəˈdeɪʃən] N degradazione *f*

degrade [dɪˈgreɪd] VT degradare

degrading [dɪˈgreɪdɪŋ] ADJ degradante

degree [dɪˈgriː] N grado; (*Scol*) laurea (universitaria); **10 degrees below freezing** 10 gradi sotto zero; **a (first) ~ in maths** una laurea in matematica; **a considerable ~ of risk** una grossa percentuale di rischio; **by degrees** (*gradually*) gradualmente, a poco a poco; **to some ~, to a certain ~** fino a un certo punto, in certa misura

dehydrated [diːhaɪˈdreɪtɪd] ADJ disidratato(-a); (*milk, eggs*) in polvere

dehydration [diːhaɪˈdreɪʃən] N disidratazione *f*

de-ice [diːˈaɪs] VT (*windscreen*) disgelare

de-icer [ˈdiːaɪsər] N sbrinatore *m*

deign [deɪn] VI: **to ~ to do** degnarsi di fare

deity [ˈdiːɪtɪ] N divinità *f inv*; dio (dea)

déjà vu [deɪʒɑːˈvuː] N déjà vu *m inv*

dejected [dɪˈdʒɛktɪd] ADJ abbattuto(-a), avvilito(-a)

dejection [dɪˈdʒɛkʃən] N abbattimento, avvilimento

Del. ABBR (*US*) = **Delaware**

delay [dɪˈleɪ] VT (*journey, operation*) ritardare, rinviare; (*travellers, trains*) ritardare; (*payment*) differire ▶ VI: **to ~ (in doing sth)** ritardare (a fare qc) ▶ N ritardo; **without ~** senza ritardo; **to be delayed** subire un ritardo; (*person*) essere trattenuto(-a)

delayed-action [dɪ'leɪd'ækʃən] ADJ a azione ritardata

delectable [dɪ'lɛktəbl] ADJ delizioso(-a)

delegate N ['dɛlɪgɪt] delegato(-a) ▶ VT ['dɛlɪgeɪt] delegare; **to ~ sth to sb/sb to do sth** delegare qc a qn/qn a fare qc

delegation [dɛlɪ'geɪʃən] N delegazione f; (*of work etc*) delega

delete [dɪ'liːt] VT (*gen, Comput*) cancellare

Delhi ['dɛlɪ] N Delhi f

deli ['dɛlɪ] N = **delicatessen**

deliberate ADJ [dɪ'lɪbərɪt] (*intentional*) intenzionale; (*slow*) misurato(-a) ▶ VI [dɪ'lɪbəreɪt] deliberare, riflettere

deliberately [dɪ'lɪbərɪtlɪ] ADV (*on purpose*) deliberatamente

deliberation [dɪlɪbə'reɪʃən] N (*consideration*) riflessione f; (*discussion*) discussione f, deliberazione f

delicacy ['dɛlɪkəsɪ] N delicatezza

delicate ['dɛlɪkɪt] ADJ delicato(-a)

delicately ['dɛlɪkɪtlɪ] ADV (*gen*) delicatamente; (*act, express*) con delicatezza

delicatessen [dɛlɪkə'tɛsn] N ≈ salumeria

delicious [dɪ'lɪʃəs] ADJ delizioso(-a), squisito(-a)

delight [dɪ'laɪt] N delizia, gran piacere m ▶ VT dilettare; **it is a ~ to the eyes** è un piacere guardarlo; **to take ~ in** divertirsi a; **to be the ~ of** essere la gioia di

delighted [dɪ'laɪtɪd] ADJ: **~ (at or with sth)** contentissimo(-a) (di qc), felice (di qc); **to be ~ to do sth/that** essere felice di fare qc/che + sub; **I'd be ~** con grande piacere

delightful [dɪ'laɪtful] ADJ (*person, place, meal*) delizioso(-a); (*smile, manner*) incantevole

delimit [diː'lɪmɪt] VT delimitare

delineate [dɪ'lɪnɪeɪt] VT delineare

delinquency [dɪ'lɪŋkwənsɪ] N delinquenza

delinquent [dɪ'lɪŋkwənt] ADJ, N delinquente (*mf*)

delirious [dɪ'lɪrɪəs] ADJ (*Med, fig*) delirante, in delirio; **to be ~** delirare; (*fig*) farneticare

delirium [dɪ'lɪrɪəm] N delirio

deliver [dɪ'lɪvə'] VT (*mail*) distribuire; (*goods*) consegnare; (*speech*) pronunciare; (*free*) liberare; (*Med*) far partorire; **to ~ a message** fare un'ambasciata; **to ~ the goods** (*fig*) partorire

deliverance [dɪ'lɪvrəns] N liberazione f

delivery [dɪ'lɪvərɪ] N distribuzione f; consegna; (*of speaker*) dizione f; (*Med*) parto; **to take ~ of** prendere in consegna

delivery note N bolla di consegna

delivery van, (*US*) **delivery truck** N furgoncino (per le consegne)

delta ['dɛltə] N delta m

delude [dɪ'luːd] VT deludere, illudere

deluge ['dɛljuːdʒ] N diluvio ▶ VT (*fig*): **to ~ (with)** subissare (di), inondare (di)

delusion [dɪ'luːʒən] N illusione f

de luxe [də'lʌks] ADJ di lusso

delve [dɛlv] VI: **to ~ into** frugare in; (*subject*) far ricerche in

Dem. ABBR (*US Pol*) = **democrat**

demagogue ['dɛməgɒg] N demagogo

demand [dɪ'mɑːnd] VT richiedere; (*rights*) rivendicare ▶ N richiesta; (*Econ*) domanda; (*claim*) rivendicazione f; **to ~ sth (from or of sb)** pretendere qc (da qn), esigere qc (da qn); **in ~** ricercato(-a), richiesto(-a); **on ~** a richiesta

demand draft N (*Comm*) tratta a vista

demanding [dɪ'mɑːndɪŋ] ADJ (*boss*) esigente; (*work*) impegnativo(-a)

demarcation [diːmɑː'keɪʃən] N demarcazione f

demarcation dispute N (*Industry*) controversia settoriale (*or* di categoria)

demean [dɪ'miːn] VT: **to ~ o.s.** umiliarsi

demeanour, (*US*) **demeanor** [dɪ'miːnə'] N comportamento; contegno

demented [dɪ'mɛntɪd] ADJ demente, impazzito(-a)

demilitarized zone [diː'mɪlɪtəraɪzd-] N zona smilitarizzata

demise [dɪ'maɪz] N decesso

demist [diː'mɪst] VT (*Brit Aut*) sbrinare

demister [diː'mɪstə'] N (*Brit Aut*) sbrinatore m

demo ['dɛməu] N ABBR (*col*: = *demonstration*) manifestazione f

demobilize [diː'məubɪlaɪz] VT smobilitare

democracy [dɪ'mɔkrəsɪ] N democrazia

democrat ['dɛməkræt] N democratico(-a)

democratic [dɛmə'krætɪk] ADJ democratico(-a); **the D~ Party** (*US*) il partito democratico

demography [dɪ'mɔgrəfɪ] N demografia

demolish [dɪ'mɔlɪʃ] VT demolire

demolition [dɛmə'lɪʃən] N demolizione f

demon ['diːmən] N (*also fig*) demonio ▶ CPD: **a ~ squash player** un mago dello squash; **a ~ driver** un guidatore folle

demonstrate ['dɛmənstreɪt] VT dimostrare, provare ▶ VI: **to ~ (for/against)** dimostrare (per/contro), manifestare (per/contro)

demonstration [dɛmən'streɪʃən] N dimostrazione f; (*Pol*) manifestazione f, dimostrazione; **to hold a ~** (*Pol*) tenere una manifestazione, fare una dimostrazione

demonstrative [dɪ'mɔnstrətɪv] ADJ dimostrativo(-a)

demonstrator ['dɛmənstreɪtə'] N (*Pol*) dimostrante mf; (*Comm: sales person*) dimostratore(-trice); (: *car, computer etc*) modello per dimostrazione

demoralize [dɪ'mɔrəlaɪz] VT demoralizzare

demote [dɪ'məʊt] VT far retrocedere

demotion [dɪ'məʊʃən] N retrocessione *f*, degradazione *f*

demur [dɪ'mə:ʳ] VI (*formal*): **to ~ (at)** sollevare obiezioni (a *or* su) ▶ N: **without ~** senza obiezioni

demure [dɪ'mjʊəʳ] ADJ contegnoso(-a)

demurrage [dɪ'mʌrɪdʒ] N diritti *mpl* di immagazzinaggio; spese *fpl* di controstallia

den [dɛn] N tana, covo; (*room*) buco

denationalization ['di:næʃnəlaɪ'zeɪʃən] N denazionalizzazione *f*

denationalize [di:'næʃnəlaɪz] VT snazionalizzare

denial [dɪ'naɪəl] N diniego; rifiuto

denier ['dɛnɪəʳ] N denaro (*di filati, calze*)

denigrate ['dɛnɪgreɪt] VT denigrare

denim ['dɛnɪm] N tessuto di cotone ritorto; *see also* **denims**

denim jacket N giubbotto di jeans

denims ['dɛnɪmz] NPL blue jeans *mpl*

denizen ['dɛnɪzən] N (*inhabitant*) abitante *mf*; (*foreigner*) straniero(-a) naturalizzato(-a)

Denmark ['dɛnmɑːk] N Danimarca

denomination [dɪnɔmɪ'neɪʃən] N (*of money*) valore *m*; (*Rel*) confessione *f*

denominator [dɪ'nɔmɪneɪtəʳ] N denominatore *m*

denote [dɪ'nəʊt] VT denotare

denounce [dɪ'naʊns] VT denunciare

dense [dɛns] ADJ fitto(-a); (*smoke*) denso(-a); (*col: stupid*) ottuso(-a), duro(-a)

densely ['dɛnslɪ] ADV: **~ wooded** fittamente boscoso(-a); **~ populated** densamente popolato(-a)

density ['dɛnsɪtɪ] N densità *f inv*; **single/ double ~ disk** (*Comput*) disco a singola/ doppia densità di registrazione

dent [dɛnt] N ammaccatura ▶ VT (*also*: **make a dent in**) ammaccare; (: *fig*) intaccare

dental ['dɛntl] ADJ dentale

dental floss [-flɔs] N filo interdentale

dental surgeon N medico(-a) dentista

dental surgery N studio dentistico

dentist ['dɛntɪst] N dentista *mf*; **~'s surgery** (*BRIT*) studio dentistico

dentistry ['dɛntɪstrɪ] N odontoiatria

dentures ['dɛntʃəz] NPL dentiera

denunciation [dɪnʌnsɪ'eɪʃən] N denuncia

deny [dɪ'naɪ] VT negare; (*refuse*) rifiutare; **he denies having said it** nega di averlo detto

deodorant [di:'əʊdərənt] N deodorante *m*

depart [dɪ'pɑːt] VI partire; **to ~ from** (*leave*) allontanarsi da, partire da; (*fig*) deviare da

departed [dɪ'pɑːtɪd] ADJ estinto(-a)
▶ N: **the ~** il buon estinto/la cara estinta

department [dɪ'pɑːtmənt] N (*Comm*) reparto; (*Scol*) sezione *f*, dipartimento; (*Pol*) ministero; **that's not my ~** (*also fig*) questo non è di mia competenza; **D~ of State** (*US*) Dipartimento di Stato

departmental [di:pɑːt'mɛntl] ADJ (*dispute*) settoriale; (*meeting*) di sezione; **~ manager** caporeparto *mf*

department store N grande magazzino

departure [dɪ'pɑːtʃəʳ] N partenza; (*fig*): **~ from** deviazione *f* da; **a new ~** una svolta (decisiva)

departure lounge N sala d'attesa

depend [dɪ'pɛnd] VI: **to ~ (up)on** dipendere da; (*rely on*) contare su; (*be dependent on*) dipendere (economicamente) da, essere a carico di; **it depends** dipende; **depending on the result ...** a seconda del risultato ...

dependable [dɪ'pɛndəbl] ADJ fidato(-a); (*car etc*) affidabile

dependant [dɪ'pɛndənt] N persona a carico

dependence [dɪ'pɛndəns] N dipendenza

dependent [dɪ'pɛndənt] ADJ: **to be ~ (on)** (*gen*) dipendere (da); (*child, relative*) essere a carico (di) ▶ N = **dependant**

depict [dɪ'pɪkt] VT (*in picture*) dipingere; (*in words*) descrivere

depilatory [dɪ'pɪlətərɪ] N (*also*: **depilatory cream**) crema depilatoria

depleted [dɪ'pliːtɪd] ADJ diminuito(-a)

deplorable [dɪ'plɔːrəbl] ADJ deplorevole, lamentevole

deplore [dɪ'plɔːʳ] VT deplorare

deploy [dɪ'plɔɪ] VT dispiegare

depopulate [di:'pɔpjuleɪt] VT spopolare

depopulation ['di:pɔpju'leɪʃən] N spopolamento

deport [dɪ'pɔːt] VT deportare; espellere

deportation [di:pɔː'teɪʃən] N deportazione *f*

deportation order N foglio di via obbligatorio

deportee [di:pɔː'tiː] N deportato(-a)

deportment [dɪ'pɔːtmənt] N portamento

depose [dɪ'pəʊz] VT deporre

deposit [dɪ'pɔzɪt] N (*Comm, Geo*) deposito; (*of ore, oil*) giacimento; (*Chem*) sedimento; (*part payment*) acconto; (*for hired goods etc*) cauzione *f* ▶ VT depositare; dare in acconto; (*luggage etc*) mettere *or* lasciare in deposito; **to put down a ~ of £50** versare una caparra di 50 sterline

deposit account N conto vincolato

depositor [dɪ'pɔzɪtəʳ] N depositante *mf*

depository [dɪ'pɔzɪtərɪ] N (*person*) depositario(-a); (*place*) deposito

depot ['dɛpəʊ] N deposito; (*US*) stazione *f* ferroviaria

depraved [dɪ'preɪvd] ADJ depravato(-a)

depravity [dɪ'prævɪtɪ] N depravazione *f*

deprecate ['dɛprɪkeɪt] VT deprecare
deprecating ['dɛprɪkeɪtɪŋ] ADJ (disapproving) di biasimo; (apologetic): **a ~ smile** un sorriso di scusa
depreciate [dɪ'priːʃɪeɪt] VT svalutare ▶ VI svalutarsi
depreciation [dɪpriːʃɪ'eɪʃən] N svalutazione f
depress [dɪ'prɛs] VT deprimere; (price, wages) abbassare; (press down) premere
depressant [dɪ'prɛsnt] N (Med) sedativo
depressed [dɪ'prɛst] ADJ (person) depresso(-a), abbattuto(-a); (area) depresso(-a); (Comm: market, trade) stagnante, in ribasso; (: industry) in crisi; **to get ~** deprimersi
depressing [dɪ'prɛsɪŋ] ADJ deprimente
depression [dɪ'prɛʃən] N depressione f
deprivation [dɛprɪ'veɪʃən] N privazione f; (state) indigenza; (Psych) carenza affettiva
deprive [dɪ'praɪv] VT: **to ~ sb of** privare qn di
deprived [dɪ'praɪvd] ADJ disgraziato(-a)
dept. ABBR = **department**
depth [dɛpθ] N profondità f inv; **at a ~ of 3 metres** a una profondità di 3 metri, a 3 metri di profondità; **in the depths of** nel profondo di; nel cuore di; **in the depths of winter** in pieno inverno; **to study sth in ~** studiare qc in profondità; **to be out of one's ~** (BRIT: swimmer) essere dove non si tocca; (fig) non sentirsi all'altezza della situazione
depth charge N carica di profondità
deputation [dɛpju'teɪʃən] N deputazione f, delegazione f
deputize ['dɛpjutaɪz] VI: **to ~ for** svolgere le funzioni di
deputy ['dɛpjutɪ] N (replacement) supplente mf; (second in command) vice mf; (US: also: **deputy sheriff**) vice-sceriffo ▶ CPD: **~ chairman** vicepresidente m; **~ head** (BRIT: Scol) vicepreside mf; **~ leader** (BRIT Pol) sottosegretario
derail [dɪ'reɪl] VT far deragliare; **to be derailed** deragliare
derailment [dɪ'reɪlmənt] N deragliamento
deranged [dɪ'reɪndʒd] ADJ: **to be (mentally) ~** essere pazzo(a)
derby ['dɑːbɪ] N (US) bombetta
deregulate [diː'rɛgjuleɪt] VT eliminare la regolamentazione di
deregulation ['diːrɛgju'leɪʃən] N eliminazione f della regolamentazione
derelict ['dɛrɪlɪkt] ADJ abbandonato(-a)
deride [dɪ'raɪd] VT deridere
derision [dɪ'rɪʒən] N derisione f
derisive [dɪ'raɪsɪv] ADJ di derisione
derisory [dɪ'raɪsərɪ] ADJ (sum) irrisorio(-a)
derivation [dɛrɪ'veɪʃən] N derivazione f
derivative [dɪ'rɪvətɪv] N derivato ▶ ADJ derivato(-a)

derive [dɪ'raɪv] VT: **to ~ sth from** derivare qc da; trarre qc da ▶ VI: **to ~ from** derivare da
dermatitis [dəːmə'taɪtɪs] N dermatite f
dermatology [dəːmə'tɔlədʒɪ] N dermatologia
derogatory [dɪ'rɔgətərɪ] ADJ denigratorio(-a)
derrick ['dɛrɪk] N gru f inv; (for oil) derrick m inv
derv [dəːv] N (BRIT) gasolio
desalination [diːsælɪ'neɪʃən] N desalinizzazione f, dissalazione f
descend [dɪ'sɛnd] VT, VI discendere, scendere; **to ~ from** discendere da; **to ~ to** (lying, begging) abbassarsi a; **in descending order of importance** in ordine decrescente d'importanza
▶ **descend on** VT FUS (enemy, angry person) assalire, piombare su; (misfortune) arrivare addosso a; (fig: gloom, silence) scendere su; **visitors descended (up)on us** ci sono arrivate visite tra capo e collo
descendant [dɪ'sɛndənt] N discendente mf
descent [dɪ'sɛnt] N discesa; (origin) discendenza, famiglia
describe [dɪs'kraɪb] VT descrivere
description [dɪs'krɪpʃən] N descrizione f; (sort) genere m, specie f; **of every ~** di ogni genere e specie
descriptive [dɪs'krɪptɪv] ADJ descrittivo(-a)
desecrate ['dɛsɪkreɪt] VT profanare
desert N ['dɛzət] deserto ▶ VT [dɪ'zəːt] lasciare, abbandonare ▶ VI [dɪ'zəːt] (Mil) disertare; see also **deserts**
deserted [dɪ'zəːtɪd] ADJ deserto(-a)
deserter [dɪ'zəːtəʳ] N disertore m
desertion [dɪ'zəːʃən] N diserzione f
desert island N isola deserta
deserts [dɪ'zəːts] NPL: **to get one's just ~** avere ciò che si merita
deserve [dɪ'zəːv] VT meritare
deservedly [dɪ'zəːvɪdlɪ] ADV meritatamente, giustamente
deserving [dɪ'zəːvɪŋ] ADJ (person) meritevole, degno(-a); (cause) meritorio(-a)
desiccated ['dɛsɪkeɪtɪd] ADJ essiccato(-a)
design [dɪ'zaɪn] N (sketch) disegno; (: of dress, car) modello; (layout, shape) linea; (pattern) fantasia; (Comm) disegno tecnico; (intention) intenzione f ▶ VT disegnare; progettare; **to have designs on** aver mire su; **well-designed** ben concepito; **industrial ~** disegno industriale
design and technology N (BRIT Scol) progettazione f e tecnologie f pl
designate VT ['dɛzɪgneɪt] designare ▶ ADJ ['dɛzɪgnɪt] designato(-a)
designation [dɛzɪg'neɪʃən] N designazione f
designer [dɪ'zaɪnəʳ] N (Tech) disegnatore(-trice), progettista mf; (of furniture) designer mf; (fashion designer)

designer baby – detox

disegnatore(-trice) di moda; (of theatre sets) scenografo/(-a)

designer baby N bambino progettato geneticamente prima della nascita

desirability [dɪzaɪərə'bɪlɪtɪ] N desiderabilità; vantaggio

desirable [dɪ'zaɪərəbl] ADJ desiderabile; **it is ~ that** è opportuno che + sub

desire [dɪ'zaɪə] N desiderio, voglia ▸ VT desiderare, volere; **to ~ sth/to do sth/that** desiderare qc/di fare qc/che + sub

desirous [dɪ'zaɪərəs] ADJ: **~ of** desideroso(-a) di

desk [dɛsk] N (in office) scrivania; (for pupil) banco; (BRIT: in shop, restaurant) cassa; (in hotel) ricevimento; (at airport) accettazione f

desk job N lavoro d'ufficio

desktop N computer m inv desktop

desktop computer ['dɛsktɒp-] N personal m inv, personal computer m inv

desktop publishing N desktop publishing m

desolate ['dɛsəlɪt] ADJ desolato(-a)

desolation [dɛsə'leɪʃən] N desolazione f

despair [dɪs'pɛə] N disperazione f ▸ VI: **to ~ of** disperare di; **in ~** disperato(-a)

despatch [dɪs'pætʃ] N, VT = **dispatch**

desperate ['dɛspərɪt] ADJ disperato(-a); (measures) estremo(-a); (fugitive) capace di tutto; **to be ~ for sth/to do** volere disperatamente qc/fare; **we are getting ~** siamo sull'orlo della disperazione

desperately ['dɛspərɪtlɪ] ADV disperatamente; (very) terribilmente, estremamente; **~ ill** in pericolo di vita

desperation [dɛspə'reɪʃən] N disperazione f; **in ~** per disperazione

despicable [dɪs'pɪkəbl] ADJ disprezzabile

despise [dɪs'paɪz] VT disprezzare, sdegnare

despite [dɪs'paɪt] PREP malgrado, a dispetto di, nonostante

despondent [dɪs'pɒndənt] ADJ abbattuto(-a), scoraggiato(-a)

despot ['dɛspɒt] N despota m

dessert [dɪ'zə:t] N dolce m; frutta

dessertspoon [dɪ'zə:tspu:n] N cucchiaio da dolci

destabilize [di:'steɪbɪlaɪz] VT privare di stabilità; (fig) destabilizzare

destination [dɛstɪ'neɪʃən] N destinazione f

destine ['dɛstɪn] VT destinare

destined ['dɛstɪnd] ADJ: **to be ~ to do sth** essere destinato(a) a fare qc; **~ for London** diretto a Londra, con destinazione Londra

destiny ['dɛstɪnɪ] N destino

destitute ['dɛstɪtju:t] ADJ indigente, bisognoso(-a); **~ of** privo(a) di

destroy [dɪs'trɔɪ] VT distruggere

destroyer [dɪs'trɔɪə] N (Naut) cacciatorpediniere m

destruction [dɪs'trʌkʃən] N distruzione f

destructive [dɪs'trʌktɪv] ADJ distruttivo(-a)

desultory ['dɛsəltərɪ] ADJ (reading) disordinato(-a); (conversation) sconnesso(-a); (contact) saltuario(-a), irregolare

detach [dɪ'tætʃ] VT staccare, distaccare

detachable [dɪ'tætʃəbl] ADJ staccabile

detached [dɪ'tætʃt] ADJ (attitude) distante

detached house N villa

detachment [dɪ'tætʃmənt] N (Mil) distaccamento; (fig) distacco

detail ['di:teɪl] N particolare m, dettaglio; (Mil) piccolo distaccamento ▸ VT dettagliare, particolareggiare; (Mil): **to ~ sb (for)** assegnare qn (a); **in ~** nei particolari; **to go into ~(s)** scendere nei particolari

detailed ['di:teɪld] ADJ particolareggiato(-a)

detain [dɪ'teɪn] VT trattenere; (in captivity) detenere

detainee [di:teɪ'ni:] N detenuto(-a)

detect [dɪ'tɛkt] VT scoprire, scorgere; (Med, Police, Radar etc) individuare

detection [dɪ'tɛkʃən] N scoperta; individuazione f; **crime ~** indagini fpl criminali; **to escape ~** (criminal) eludere le ricerche; (mistake) passare inosservato(-a)

detective [dɪ'tɛktɪv] N investigatore(-trice); **private ~** investigatore m privato

detective story N giallo

detector [dɪ'tɛktə] N rivelatore m

détente [deɪ'tɑ:nt] N distensione f

detention [dɪ'tɛnʃən] N detenzione f; (Scol) permanenza forzata per punizione

deter [dɪ'tə:] VT dissuadere

detergent [dɪ'tə:dʒənt] N detersivo

deteriorate [dɪ'tɪərɪəreɪt] VI deteriorarsi

deterioration [dɪtɪərɪə'reɪʃən] N deterioramento

determination [dɪtə:mɪ'neɪʃən] N determinazione f

determine [dɪ'tə:mɪn] VT determinare; **to ~ to do sth** decidere di fare qc

determined [dɪ'tə:mɪnd] ADJ (person) risoluto(-a), deciso(-a); **to be ~ to do sth** essere determinato or deciso a fare qc; **a ~ effort** uno sforzo di volontà

deterrence [dɪ'tɛrəns] N deterrenza

deterrent [dɪ'tɛrənt] N deterrente m; **to act as a ~** fungere da deterrente

detest [dɪ'tɛst] VT detestare

detestable [dɪ'tɛstəbl] ADJ detestabile, abominevole

detonate ['dɛtəneɪt] VI detonare ▸ VT far detonare

detonator ['dɛtəneɪtə] N detonatore m

detour ['di:tuə] N deviazione f

detox ['di:tɒks] VT disintossicare ▸ VI disintossicarsi ▸ N disintossicazione f

detoxification [di:tɔksɪfɪ'keɪʃən] N disintossicazione f

detoxify [di:'tɔksɪfaɪ] VT disintossicare ▶ VI disintossicarsi

detract [dɪ'trækt] VI: **to ~ from** detrarre da

detractor [dɪ'træktər] N detrattore(-trice)

detriment ['dɛtrɪmənt] N: **to the ~ of** a detrimento di; **without ~ to** senza danno a

detrimental [dɛtrɪ'mɛntl] ADJ: **~ to** dannoso(-a) a, nocivo(-a) a

deuce [dju:s] N (Tennis) quaranta pari m inv

devaluation [di:vælju'eɪʃən] N svalutazione f

devalue ['di:'vælju:] VT svalutare

devastate ['dɛvəsteɪt] VT devastare; **he was devastated by the news** la notizia fu per lui un colpo terribile

devastating ['dɛvəsteɪtɪŋ] ADJ devastatore(-trice), sconvolgente

devastation [dɛvə'steɪʃən] N devastazione f

develop [dɪ'vɛləp] VT sviluppare; (habit) prendere (gradualmente) ▶ VI svilupparsi; (facts, symptoms: appear) manifestarsi, rivelarsi; **to ~ a taste for sth** imparare a gustare qc; **to ~ into** diventare

developer [dɪ'vɛləpər] N (Phot) sviluppatore m; **property ~** costruttore m (edile)

developing country [dɪ'vɛləpɪŋ-] N paese m in via di sviluppo

development [dɪ'vɛləpmənt] N sviluppo

development area N area di sviluppo industriale

deviant ['di:vɪənt] ADJ deviante

deviate ['di:vɪeɪt] VI: **to ~ (from)** deviare (da)

deviation [di:vɪ'eɪʃən] N deviazione f

device [dɪ'vaɪs] N (apparatus) congegno; (explosive device) ordigno esplosivo

devil ['dɛvl] N diavolo; demonio

devilish ['dɛvlɪʃ] ADJ diabolico(-a)

devil-may-care ['dɛvlmeɪ'kɛər] ADJ impudente

devil's advocate N: **to play ~** fare l'avvocato del diavolo

devious ['di:vɪəs] ADJ (means) indiretto(-a), tortuoso(-a); (person) subdolo(-a)

devise [dɪ'vaɪz] VT escogitare, concepire

devoid [dɪ'vɔɪd] ADJ: **~ of** privo(-a) di

devolution [di:və'lu:ʃən] N (Pol) decentramento

devolve [dɪ'vɔlv] VI: **to ~ (up)on** ricadere su

devote [dɪ'vəut] VT: **to ~ sth to** dedicare qc a

devoted [dɪ'vəutɪd] ADJ devoto(-a); **to be ~ to** essere molto affezionato(-a) a

devotee [dɛvəu'ti:] N (Rel) adepto(-a); (Mus, Sport) appassionato(-a)

devotion [dɪ'vəuʃən] N devozione f, attaccamento; (Rel) atto di devozione, preghiera

devour [dɪ'vauər] VT divorare

devout [dɪ'vaut] ADJ pio(-a), devoto(-a)

dew [dju:] N rugiada

dexterity [dɛks'tɛrɪtɪ] N destrezza

dexterous, dextrous ['dɛkstrəs] ADJ (skilful) destro(-a), abile; (movement) agile

DfEE N ABBR (BRIT: = Department for Education and Employment) Ministero della pubblica istruzione e dell'occupazione

dg ABBR (= decigram) dg

diabetes [daɪə'bi:ti:z] N diabete m

diabetic [daɪə'bɛtɪk] ADJ diabetico(-a); (chocolate, jam) per diabetici ▶ N diabetico(-a)

diabolical [daɪə'bɔlɪkl] ADJ diabolico(-a); (col: dreadful) infernale, atroce

diaeresis [daɪ'ɛrɪsɪs] N dieresi f inv

diagnose [daɪəg'nəuz] VT diagnosticare

diagnosis [daɪəg'nəusɪs] (pl **diagnoses** [-si:z]) N diagnosi f inv

diagonal [daɪ'ægənl] ADJ, N diagonale (f)

diagram ['daɪəgræm] N diagramma m

dial ['daɪəl] N quadrante m; (on radio) lancetta; (on telephone) disco combinatore ▶ VT (number) fare; **to ~ a wrong number** sbagliare numero; **can I ~ London direct?** si può chiamare Londra in teleselezione?

dial. ABBR = **dialect**

dialect ['daɪəlɛkt] N dialetto

dialling code ['daɪəlɪŋ-], (US) **area code** N prefisso

dialling tone ['daɪəlɪŋ-], (US) **dial tone** N segnale m di linea libera

dialogue, (US) **dialog** ['daɪəlɔg] N dialogo

dialysis [daɪ'ælɪsɪs] N dialisi f

diameter [daɪ'æmɪtər] N diametro

diametrically [daɪə'mɛtrɪklɪ] ADV: **~ opposed (to)** diametralmente opposto(-a) (a)

diamond ['daɪəmənd] N diamante m; (shape) rombo; **diamonds** NPL (Cards) quadri mpl

diamond ring N anello di brillanti; (with one diamond) anello con brillante

diaper ['daɪəpər] N (US) pannolino

diaphragm ['daɪəfræm] N diaframma m

diarrhoea, (US) **diarrhea** [daɪə'ri:ə] N diarrea

diary ['daɪərɪ] N (daily account) diario; (book) agenda; **to keep a ~** tenere un diario

diatribe ['daɪətraɪb] N diatriba

dice [daɪs] N (pl inv) dado ▶ VT (Culin) tagliare a dadini

dicey ['daɪsɪ] ADJ (col): **it's a bit ~** è un po' un rischio

dichotomy [daɪ'kɔtəmɪ] N dicotomia

dickhead ['dɪkhɛd] N (BRIT col!) testa m di cazzo (!)

Dictaphone® ['dɪktəfəun] N dittafono

dictate VT [dɪk'teɪt] dettare ▶ VI: **to ~ to** (person) dare ordini a, dettar legge a ▶ N ['dɪkteɪt] dettame m; **I won't be dictated to** non ricevo ordini

d

517

dictation [dɪk'teɪʃən] N (*to secretary etc*) dettatura; (*Scol*) dettato; **at ~ speed** a velocità di dettatura

dictator [dɪk'teɪtəʳ] N dittatore *m*

dictatorship [dɪk'teɪtəʃɪp] N dittatura

diction ['dɪkʃən] N dizione *f*

dictionary ['dɪkʃənrɪ] N dizionario

did [dɪd] PT *of* **do**

didactic [daɪ'dæktɪk] ADJ didattico(-a)

didn't ['dɪdnt] = **did not**

die [daɪ] N (*pl* **dies**) conio; matrice *f*; stampo
▶ VI morire; **to be dying** star morendo; **to be dying for sth/to do sth** morire dalla voglia di qc/di fare qc; **to ~ (of** *or* **from) morire (di)
▶ **die away** VI spegnersi a poco a poco
▶ **die down** VI abbassarsi
▶ **die out** VI estinguersi

diehard ['daɪhɑːd] N reazionario(-a)

diesel ['diːzl] N (*vehicle*) diesel *m inv*

diesel engine N motore *m* diesel *inv*

diesel fuel, diesel oil N gasolio (per motori diesel)

diet ['daɪət] N alimentazione *f*; (*restricted food*) dieta ▶ VI (*also:* **be on a diet**) stare a dieta; **to live on a ~ of** nutrirsi di

dietician [daɪə'tɪʃən] N dietologo(-a)

differ ['dɪfəʳ] VI: **to ~ from sth** differire da qc; essere diverso(-a) da qc; **to ~ from sb over sth** essere in disaccordo con qn su qc

difference ['dɪfrəns] N differenza; (*quarrel*) screzio; **it makes no ~ to me** per me è lo stesso; **to settle one's differences** risolvere la situazione

different ['dɪfrənt] ADJ diverso(-a)

differential [dɪfə'renʃəl] N (*Aut, in wages*) differenziale *m*

differentiate [dɪfə'renʃɪeɪt] VI differenziarsi; **to ~ between** discriminare fra, fare differenza fra

differently ['dɪfrəntlɪ] ADV diversamente

difficult ['dɪfɪkəlt] ADJ difficile; **~ to understand** difficile da capire

difficulty ['dɪfɪkəltɪ] N difficoltà *f inv*; **to have difficulties with** (*police, landlord etc*) avere noie con; **to be in ~** essere *or* trovarsi in difficoltà

diffidence ['dɪfɪdəns] N mancanza di sicurezza

diffident ['dɪfɪdənt] ADJ sfiduciato(-a)

diffuse ADJ [dɪ'fjuːs] diffuso(-a) ▶ VT [dɪ'fjuːz] diffondere, emanare

dig [dɪg] (*pt, pp* **dug** [dʌg]) VT (*hole*) scavare; (*garden*) vangare ▶ VI scavare ▶ N (*prod*) gomitata; (*fig*) frecciata; (*Archaeology*) scavo, scavi *mpl*; **to ~ into** (*snow, soil*) scavare; **to ~ into one's pockets for sth** frugarsi le tasche cercando qc; **to ~ one's nails into** conficcare le unghie in; *see also* **digs**
▶ **dig in** VI (*col: eat*) attaccare a mangiare;

(*also:* **dig o.s. in**: *Mil*) trincerarsi; (: *fig*) insediarsi, installarsi ▶ VT (*compost*) interrare; (*knife, claw*) affondare; **to ~ in one's heels** (*fig*) impuntarsi
▶ **dig out** VT (*survivors, car from snow*) tirar fuori (scavando), estrarre (scavando)
▶ **dig up** VT scavare; (*tree etc*) sradicare; (*information*) scavare fuori

digest VT [daɪ'dʒɛst] digerire ▶ N ['daɪdʒɛst] compendio

digestible [dɪ'dʒɛstəbl] ADJ digeribile

digestion [dɪ'dʒɛstʃən] N digestione *f*

digestive [dɪ'dʒɛstɪv] ADJ digestivo(-a); **~ system** apparato digerente

digit ['dɪdʒɪt] N cifra; (*finger*) dito

digital ['dɪdʒɪtəl] ADJ digitale

digital camera N fotocamera digitale

digital compact cassette N piastra digitale per CD

digital radio N radio digitale

digital TV N televisione *f* digitale

dignified ['dɪgnɪfaɪd] ADJ dignitoso(-a)

dignitary ['dɪgnɪtərɪ] N dignitario

dignity ['dɪgnɪtɪ] N dignità

digress [daɪ'grɛs] VI: **to ~ from** divagare da

digression [daɪ'grɛʃən] N digressione *f*

digs [dɪgz] NPL (*BRIT col*) camera ammobiliata

dilapidated [dɪ'læpɪdeɪtɪd] ADJ cadente

dilate [daɪ'leɪt] VT dilatare ▶ VI dilatarsi

dilatory ['dɪlətərɪ] ADJ dilatorio(-a)

dilemma [daɪ'lɛmə] N dilemma *m*; **to be in a ~** essere di fronte a un dilemma

diligent ['dɪlɪdʒənt] ADJ diligente

dill [dɪl] N aneto

dilly-dally ['dɪlɪdælɪ] VI gingillarsi

dilute [daɪ'luːt] VT diluire; (*with water*) annacquare ▶ ADJ diluito(-a)

dim [dɪm] ADJ (*light, eyesight*) debole; (*memory, outline*) vago(-a); (*room*) in penombra; (*col: stupid*) ottuso(-a), tonto(-a) ▶ VT (*light: also US Aut*) abbassare; **to take a ~ view of sth** non vedere di buon occhio qc

dime [daɪm] N (*US*) = **10 cents**

dimension [dɪ'mɛnʃən] N dimensione *f*

-dimensional [dɪ'mɛnʃənl] ADJ SUFFIX: **two~** bi-dimensionale

diminish [dɪ'mɪnɪʃ] VT, VI diminuire

diminished [dɪ'mɪnɪʃt] ADJ: **~ responsibility** (*Law*) incapacità d'intendere e di volere

diminutive [dɪ'mɪnjutɪv] ADJ minuscolo(-a) ▶ N (*Ling*) diminutivo

dimly ['dɪmlɪ] ADV debolmente; indistintamente

dimmer ['dɪməʳ] N (*also:* **dimmer switch**) dimmer *m inv*, interruttore *m* a reostato; **dimmers** NPL (*US Aut*) anabbaglianti *mpl*; (*parking lights*) luci *fpl* di posizione

dimple ['dɪmpl] N fossetta

dim-witted ['dɪm'wɪtɪd] ADJ (col) sciocco(-a), stupido(-a)

din [dɪn] N chiasso, fracasso ▸ VT: **to ~ sth into sb** (col) ficcare qc in testa a qn

dine [daɪn] VI pranzare

diner ['daɪnə^r] N (person: in restaurant) cliente mf; (Rail) carrozza or vagone m ristorante; (US: eating place) tavola calda

dinghy ['dɪŋgɪ] N gommone m; (also: **sailing dinghy**) dinghy m inv

dingy ['dɪndʒɪ] ADJ grigio(-a)

dining area ['daɪnɪŋ-] N zona pranzo inv

dining car ['daɪnɪŋ-] (BRIT) N vagone m ristorante

dining room N sala da pranzo

dining table N tavolo da pranzo

dinkum ['dɪŋkʌm] ADJ (AUSTRALIA, NEW ZEALAND col) genuino(-a)

dinner ['dɪnə^r] N (lunch) pranzo; (evening meal) cena; (public) banchetto; **~'s ready!** a tavola!

dinner jacket N smoking m inv

dinner party N cena

dinner service N servizio da tavola

dinner time N ora di pranzo (or cena)

dinosaur ['daɪnəsɔː^r] N dinosauro

dint [dɪnt] N: **by ~ of (doing) sth** a forza di (fare) qc

diocese ['daɪəsɪs] N diocesi f inv

dioxide [daɪ'ɔksaɪd] N biossido

dip [dɪp] N (slope) discesa; (in sea) bagno; (Culin) salsetta ▸ VT immergere; bagnare; (BRIT Aut: lights) abbassare ▸ VI (road) essere in pendenza; (bird, plane) abbassarsi

Dip. ABBR (BRIT) = **diploma**

diphtheria [dɪf'θɪərɪə] N difterite f

diphthong ['dɪfθɔŋ] N dittongo

diploma [dɪ'pləumə] N diploma m

diplomacy [dɪ'pləuməsɪ] N diplomazia

diplomat ['dɪpləmæt] N diplomatico

diplomatic [dɪplə'mætɪk] ADJ diplomatico(-a); **to break off ~ relations** rompere le relazioni diplomatiche

diplomatic corps N corpo diplomatico

diplomatic immunity N immunità f inv diplomatica

dipstick ['dɪpstɪk] N (Aut) indicatore m di livello dell'olio

dipswitch ['dɪpswɪtʃ] N (BRIT Aut) levetta dei fari

dire [daɪə^r] ADJ terribile; estremo(-a)

direct [daɪ'rɛkt] ADJ diretto(-a); (manner, person) franco(-a), esplicito(-a) ▸ VT dirigere; (order): **to ~ sb to do sth** dare direttive a qn di fare qc ▸ ADV direttamente; **can you ~ me to …?** mi può indicare la strada per …?

direct cost N (Comm) costo diretto

direct current N (Elec) corrente f continua

direct debit N (Banking) addebito effettuato per ordine di un cliente di banca

direct dialling N (Tel) = teleselezione f

direct hit N (Mil) colpo diretto

direction [dɪ'rɛkʃən] N direzione f; (of play, film, programme) regia; **directions**NPL (advice) chiarimenti mpl; (instructions: to a place) indicazioni fpl; **directions for use** istruzioni fpl; **to ask for directions** chiedere la strada; **sense of ~** senso dell'orientamento; **in the ~ of** in direzione di

directive [dɪ'rɛktɪv] N direttiva, ordine m; **a government ~** una disposizione governativa

direct labour N manodopera diretta

directly [dɪ'rɛktlɪ] ADV (in straight line) direttamente; (at once) subito

direct mail N pubblicità diretta

direct mailshot N (BRIT) materiale m pubblicitario ad approccio diretto

directness [daɪ'rɛktnɪs] N (of person, speech) franchezza

director [dɪ'rɛktə^r] N direttore(-trice), amministratore(-trice); (Theat, Cine, TV) regista mf; **D~ of Public Prosecutions** (BRIT) = Procuratore m della Repubblica

directory [dɪ'rɛktərɪ] N elenco; (street directory) stradario; (trade directory) repertorio del commercio; (Comput) directory m inv

directory enquiries, (US) **directory assistance** N (Tel) servizio informazioni, informazioni fpl elenco abbonati

dirt [də:t] N sporcizia; immondizia; (earth) terra; **to treat sb like ~** trattare qn come uno straccio

dirt-cheap ['də:t'tʃiːp] ADJ da due soldi

dirt road N strada non asfaltata

dirty ['də:tɪ] ADJ sporco(-a) ▸ VT sporcare; **~ bomb** bomba convenzionale contenente materiale radioattivo; **~ story** storia oscena; **~ trick** brutto scherzo

disability [dɪsə'bɪlɪtɪ] N invalidità f inv; (Law) incapacità f inv

disability allowance N pensione f d'invalidità

disable [dɪs'eɪbl] VT (illness, accident) rendere invalido(-a); (tank, gun) mettere fuori uso

disabled [dɪs'eɪbld] ADJ invalido(-a); (maimed) mutilato(-a); (mentally) ritardato(-a); (through illness, old age) inabile ▸ NPL: **the ~** gli invalidi

disadvantage [dɪsəd'vɑːntɪdʒ] N svantaggio

disadvantaged [dɪsəd'vɑːntɪdʒd] ADJ (person) svantaggiato(-a)

disadvantageous [dɪsædvɑːn'teɪdʒəs] ADJ svantaggioso(-a)

disaffected [dɪsə'fɛktɪd] ADJ: **~ (to or towards)** scontento(-a) di, insoddisfatto(-a) di

disaffection [dɪsə'fɛkʃən] N malcontento, insoddisfazione f

d

disagree [dɪsə'griː] VI (differ) discordare; (be against, think otherwise): **to ~ (with)** essere in disaccordo (con), dissentire (da); **I ~ with you** non sono d'accordo con lei; **garlic disagrees with me** l'aglio non mi va

disagreeable [dɪsə'griːəbl] ADJ sgradevole; (person) antipatico(-a)

disagreement [dɪsə'griːmənt] N disaccordo; (quarrel) dissapore m; **to have a ~ with sb** litigare con qn

disallow ['dɪsə'lau] VT respingere; (BRIT Football: goal) annullare

disappear [dɪsə'pɪəʳ] VI scomparire

disappearance [dɪsə'pɪərəns] N scomparsa

disappoint [dɪsə'pɔɪnt] VT deludere

disappointed [dɪsə'pɔɪntɪd] ADJ deluso(-a)

disappointing [dɪsə'pɔɪntɪŋ] ADJ deludente

disappointment [dɪsə'pɔɪntmənt] N delusione f

disapproval [dɪsə'pruːvəl] N disapprovazione f

disapprove [dɪsə'pruːv] VI: **to ~ of** disapprovare

disapproving [dɪsə'pruːvɪŋ] ADJ di disapprovazione

disarm [dɪs'ɑːm] VT disarmare

disarmament [dɪs'ɑːməmənt] N disarmo

disarming [dɪs'ɑːmɪŋ] ADJ (smile) disarmante

disarray [dɪsə'reɪ] N: **in ~** (troops) in rotta; (thoughts) confuso(-a); (clothes) in disordine; **to throw into ~** buttare all'aria

disaster [dɪ'zɑːstəʳ] N disastro

disaster area N zona disastrata

disastrous [dɪ'zɑːstrəs] ADJ disastroso(-a)

disband [dɪs'bænd] VT sbandare; (Mil) congedare ▶ VI sciogliersi

disbelief ['dɪsbə'liːf] N incredulità; **in ~** incredulo(-a)

disbelieve ['dɪsbə'liːv] VT (person, story) non credere a, mettere in dubbio; **I don't ~ you** vorrei poterle credere

disc [dɪsk] N disco; (Comput) = **disk**

disc. ABBR (Comm) = **discount**

discard [dɪs'kɑːd] VT (old things) scartare; (fig) abbandonare

disc brake N freno a disco

discern [dɪ'səːn] VT discernere, distinguere

discernible [dɪ'səːnəbl] ADJ percepibile

discerning [dɪ'səːnɪŋ] ADJ perspicace

discharge VT [dɪs'tʃɑːdʒ] (duties) compiere; (settle: debt) pagare, estinguere; (Elec, waste etc) scaricare; (Med) emettere; (patient) dimettere; (employee) licenziare; (soldier) congedare; (defendant) liberare ▶ N ['dɪstʃɑːdʒ] (Elec) scarica; (Med, of gas, chemicals) emissione f; (vaginal discharge) perdite fpl (bianche); (dismissal) licenziamento; congedo; liberazione f; **to ~ one's gun** fare fuoco

discharged bankrupt [dɪs'tʃɑːdʒd-] N fallito cui il tribunale ha concesso la riabilitazione

disciple [dɪ'saɪpl] N discepolo

disciplinary ['dɪsɪplɪnərɪ] ADJ disciplinare; **to take ~ action against sb** prendere un provvedimento disciplinare contro qn

discipline ['dɪsɪplɪn] N disciplina ▶ VT disciplinare; (punish) punire; **to ~ o.s. to do sth** imporsi di fare qc

disc jockey N disc jockey m inv

disclaim [dɪs'kleɪm] VT negare, smentire

disclaimer [dɪs'kleɪməʳ] N smentita; **to issue a ~** pubblicare una smentita

disclose [dɪs'kləuz] VT rivelare, svelare

disclosure [dɪs'kləuʒəʳ] N rivelazione f

disco ['dɪskəu] N ABBR discoteca

discolour, (US) **discolor** [dɪs'kʌləʳ] VT scolorire; (sth white) ingiallire ▶ VI sbiadire, scolorirsi; (sth white) ingiallire

discolouration, (US) **discoloration** [dɪskʌlə'reɪʃən] N scolorimento

discoloured, (US) **discolored** [dɪs'kʌləd] ADJ scolorito(-a), ingiallito(-a)

discomfort [dɪs'kʌmfət] N disagio; (lack of comfort) scomodità f inv

disconcert [dɪskən'səːt] VT sconcertare

disconnect [dɪskə'nɛkt] VT sconnettere, staccare; (Elec, Radio) staccare; (gas, water) chiudere

disconnected [dɪskə'nɛktɪd] ADJ (speech, thought) sconnesso(-a)

disconsolate [dɪs'kɔnsəlɪt] ADJ sconsolato(-a)

discontent [dɪskən'tɛnt] N scontentezza

discontented [dɪskən'tɛntɪd] ADJ scontento(-a)

discontinue [dɪskən'tɪnjuː] VT smettere, cessare; **"discontinued"** (Comm) "fuori produzione"

discord ['dɪskɔːd] N disaccordo; (Mus) dissonanza

discordant [dɪs'kɔːdənt] ADJ discordante; dissonante

discothèque ['dɪskəutɛk] N discoteca

discount N ['dɪskaunt] sconto ▶ VT [dɪs'kaunt] scontare; (report, idea etc) non badare a; **at a ~** con uno sconto; **to give sb a ~ on sth** fare uno sconto a qn su qc; **~ for cash** sconto m cassa inv

discount house N (Finance) casa di sconto, discount house f inv; (Comm: also: **discount store**) discount m inv

discount rate N tasso di sconto

discourage [dɪs'kʌrɪdʒ] VT scoraggiare; (dissuade, deter) tentare di dissuadere

discouragement [dɪs'kʌrɪdʒmənt] N (dissuasion) disapprovazione f; (depression) scoraggiamento; **to act as a ~ to** ostacolare

discouraging [dɪs'kʌrɪdʒɪŋ] ADJ scoraggiante

discourteous [dɪs'kə:tɪəs] ADJ scortese

discover [dɪs'kʌvəʳ] VT scoprire

discovery [dɪs'kʌvərɪ] N scoperta

discredit [dɪs'krɛdɪt] VT screditare; mettere in dubbio ► N discredito

discreet [dɪ'skri:t] ADJ discreto(-a)

discreetly [dɪ'skri:tlɪ] ADV con discrezione

discrepancy [dɪ'skrɛpənsɪ] N discrepanza

discretion [dɪ'skrɛʃən] N discrezione f; **use your own ~** giudichi lei

discretionary [dɪs'krɛʃənərɪ] ADJ (*powers*) discrezionale

discriminate [dɪ'skrɪmɪneɪt] VI: **to ~ between** distinguere tra; **to ~ against** discriminare contro

discriminating [dɪs'krɪmɪneɪtɪŋ] ADJ (*ear, taste*) fine, giudizioso(-a); (*person*) esigente; (*tax, duty*) discriminante

discrimination [dɪskrɪmɪ'neɪʃən] N discriminazione f; (*judgement*) discernimento; **racial/sexual ~** discriminazione razziale/sessuale

discus ['dɪskəs] N disco

discuss [dɪ'skʌs] VT discutere; (*debate*) dibattere

discussion [dɪ'skʌʃən] N discussione f; **under ~** in discussione

discussion forum N (*Comput*) forum m inv di discussione

disdain [dɪs'deɪn] N disdegno

disease [dɪ'zi:z] N malattia

diseased [dɪ'zi:zd] ADJ malato(-a)

disembark [dɪsɪm'bɑ:k] VT, VI sbarcare

disembarkation [dɪsɛmbɑ:'keɪʃən] N sbarco

disembodied [dɪsɪm'bɔdɪd] ADJ disincarnato(-a)

disembowel [dɪsɪm'bauəl] VT sbudellare, sventrare

disenchanted [dɪsɪn'tʃɑ:ntɪd] ADJ disincantato(-a); **~ (with)** deluso(-a) (da)

disenfranchise [dɪsɪn'fræntʃaɪz] VT privare del diritto di voto; (*Comm*) revocare una condizione di privilegio commerciale a

disengage [dɪsɪn'geɪdʒ] VT disimpegnare; (*Tech*) distaccare; (*Aut*) disinnestare

disentangle [dɪsɪn'tæŋgl] VT sbrogliare

disfavour, (US) **disfavor** [dɪs'feɪvəʳ] N sfavore m; disgrazia

disfigure [dɪs'fɪgəʳ] VT sfigurare

disgorge [dɪs'gɔ:dʒ] VT (*river*) riversare

disgrace [dɪs'greɪs] N vergogna; (*disfavour*) disgrazia ► VT disonorare, far cadere in disgrazia

disgraceful [dɪs'greɪsful] ADJ scandaloso(-a), vergognoso(-a)

disgruntled [dɪs'grʌntld] ADJ scontento(-a), di cattivo umore

disguise [dɪs'gaɪz] N travestimento ► VT travestire; (*voice*) contraffare; (*feelings etc*) mascherare; **to ~ o.s. as** travestirsi da; **in ~** travestito(-a); **there's no disguising the fact that …** non si può nascondere (il fatto) che …

disgust [dɪs'gʌst] N disgusto, nausea ► VT disgustare, far schifo a

disgusted [dɪs'gʌstɪd] ADJ indignato(-a)

disgusting [dɪs'gʌstɪŋ] ADJ disgustoso(-a), ripugnante

dish [dɪʃ] N piatto; **to do** or **wash the dishes** fare i piatti
  ► **dish out** VT (*food*) servire; (*advice*) elargire; (*money*) tirare fuori; (*exam papers*) distribuire
  ► **dish up** VT (*food*) servire; (*facts, statistics*) presentare

dishcloth ['dɪʃklɔθ] N strofinaccio dei piatti

dishearten [dɪs'hɑ:tn] VT scoraggiare

dishevelled, (US) **disheveled** [dɪ'ʃɛvəld] ADJ arruffato(-a), scapigliato(-a)

dishonest [dɪs'ɔnɪst] ADJ disonesto(-a)

dishonesty [dɪs'ɔnɪstɪ] N disonestà

dishonour, (US) **dishonor** [dɪs'ɔnəʳ] N disonore m

dishonourable, (US) **dishonorable** [dɪs'ɔnərəbl] ADJ disonorevole

dish soap N (US) detersivo liquido (per stoviglie)

dishtowel ['dɪʃtauəl] N strofinaccio dei piatti

dishwasher ['dɪʃwɔʃəʳ] N lavastoviglie f inv; (*person*) sguattero(-a)

dishy ['dɪʃɪ] ADJ (BRIT col) figo(-a)

disillusion [dɪsɪ'lu:ʒən] VT disilludere, disingannare ► N disillusione f; **to become disillusioned (with)** perdere le illusioni (su)

disillusionment [dɪsɪ'lu:ʒənmənt] N disillusione f

disincentive [dɪsɪn'sɛntɪv] N: **to act as a ~ (to)** agire da freno (su); **to be a ~ to** scoraggiare

disinclined [dɪsɪn'klaɪnd] ADJ: **to be ~ to do sth** essere poco propenso(-a) a fare qc

disinfect [dɪsɪn'fɛkt] VT disinfettare

disinfectant [dɪsɪn'fɛktənt] N disinfettante m

disinflation [dɪsɪn'fleɪʃən] N disinflazione f

disinformation [dɪsɪnfə'meɪʃən] N disinformazione f

disinherit [dɪsɪn'hɛrɪt] VT diseredare

disintegrate [dɪs'ɪntɪgreɪt] VI disintegrarsi

disinterested [dɪs'ɪntrəstɪd] ADJ disinteressato(-a)

disjointed [dɪs'dʒɔɪntɪd] ADJ sconnesso(-a)

disk [dɪsk] N (*Comput*) disco; **double-sided ~** disco a doppia faccia

disk drive N disk drive m inv

diskette [dɪs'kɛt] N (*Comput*) dischetto

disk operating system N sistema m operativo a disco

dislike [dɪs'laɪk] N antipatia, avversione f; (gen pl) cosa che non piace ▶ VT: **he dislikes it** non gli piace; **I ~ the idea** l'idea non mi va; **to take a ~ to sb/sth** prendere in antipatia qn/qc

dislocate ['dɪsləkeɪt] VT (Med) slogare; (fig) disorganizzare; **he dislocated his shoulder** si è lussato una spalla

dislodge [dɪs'lɔdʒ] VT rimuovere, staccare; (enemy) sloggiare

disloyal [dɪs'lɔɪəl] ADJ sleale

dismal ['dɪzml] ADJ triste, cupo(-a)

dismantle [dɪs'mæntl] VT (machine) smantellare, smontare; (fort, warship) disarmare

dismast [dɪs'mɑ:st] VT disalberare

dismay [dɪs'meɪ] N costernazione f ▶ VT sgomentare; **much to my ~** con mio gran stupore

dismiss [dɪs'mɪs] VT congedare; (employee) licenziare; (idea) scacciare; (Law) respingere ▶ VI (Mil) rompere i ranghi

dismissal [dɪs'mɪsəl] N congedo; licenziamento

dismount [dɪs'maunt] VI scendere ▶ VT (rider) disarcionare

disobedience [dɪsə'bi:dɪəns] N disubbidienza

disobedient [dɪsə'bi:dɪənt] ADJ disubbidiente

disobey [dɪsə'beɪ] VT disubbidire a; (rule) trasgredire a

disorder [dɪs'ɔ:dəʳ] N disordine m; (rioting) tumulto; (Med) disturbo; **civil ~** disordini mpl interni

disorderly [dɪs'ɔ:dəlɪ] ADJ disordinato(-a), tumultuoso(-a)

disorderly conduct N (Law) comportamento atto a turbare l'ordine pubblico

disorganize [dɪs'ɔ:gənaɪz] VT disorganizzare

disorganized [dɪs'ɔ:gənaɪzd] ADJ (person, life) disorganizzato(-a); (system, meeting) male organizzato(-a)

disorientated [dɪs'ɔ:rɪenteɪtɪd] ADJ disorientato(-a)

disown [dɪs'əun] VT rinnegare, disconoscere

disparaging [dɪs'pærɪdʒɪŋ] ADJ spregiativo(-a), sprezzante; **to be ~ about sb/sth** denigrare qn/qc

disparate ['dɪspərɪt] ADJ disparato(-a)

disparity [dɪs'pærɪtɪ] N disparità f inv

dispassionate [dɪs'pæʃənət] ADJ calmo(-a), freddo(-a); imparziale

dispatch [dɪs'pætʃ] VT spedire, inviare; (deal with: business) sbrigare ▶ N spedizione f, invio; (Mil, Press) dispaccio

dispatch department N reparto spedizioni

dispatch rider N (Mil) corriere m, portaordini m inv

dispel [dɪs'pɛl] VT dissipare, scacciare

dispensary [dɪs'pɛnsərɪ] N farmacia; (in chemist's) dispensario

dispense [dɪs'pɛns] VT distribuire, amministrare; (medicine) preparare e dare; **to ~ sb from** dispensare qn da
▶ **dispense with** VT FUS fare a meno di; (make unnecessary) rendere superfluo(-a)

dispenser [dɪs'pɛnsəʳ] N (container) distributore m

dispensing chemist N (BRIT) farmacista mf

dispersal [dɪs'pə:sl] N dispersione f

disperse [dɪs'pə:s] VT disperdere; (knowledge) disseminare ▶ VI disperdersi

dispirited [dɪs'pɪrɪtɪd] ADJ scoraggiato(-a), abbattuto(-a)

displace [dɪs'pleɪs] VT spostare

displaced person N (Pol) profugo(-a)

displacement [dɪs'pleɪsmənt] N spostamento

display [dɪs'pleɪ] N mostra; esposizione f; (of feeling etc) manifestazione f; (military display) parata (militare); (computer display) display m inv; (pej) ostentazione f; (screen) schermo ▶ VT mostrare; (goods) esporre; (pej) ostentare; (results) affiggere; (departure times) indicare; **on ~** (gen) in mostra; (goods) in vetrina

display advertising N pubblicità tabellare

displease [dɪs'pli:z] VT dispiacere a, scontentare; **displeased with** scontento(-a) di

displeasure [dɪs'plɛʒəʳ] N dispiacere m

disposable [dɪs'pəuzəbl] ADJ (pack etc) a perdere; (income) disponibile; **~ nappy** (BRIT) pannolino di carta

disposal [dɪs'pəuzl] N (of rubbish) smaltimento; (of property etc: by selling) vendita; (: by giving away) cessione f; **at one's ~** alla sua disposizione; **to put sth at sb's ~** mettere qc a disposizione di qn

dispose [dɪs'pəuz] VT disporre
▶ **dispose of** VT FUS (time, money) disporre di; (Comm: sell) vendere; (unwanted goods) sbarazzarsi di; (problem) eliminare

disposed [dɪs'pəuzd] ADJ: **~ to do** disposto(-a) a fare

disposition [dɪspə'zɪʃən] N disposizione f; (temperament) carattere m

dispossess ['dɪspə'zɛs] VT: **to ~ sb (of)** spossessare qn (di)

disproportion [dɪsprə'pɔ:ʃən] N sproporzione f

disproportionate [dɪsprə'pɔ:ʃənət] ADJ sproporzionato(-a)

disprove [dɪs'pru:v] VT confutare

dispute [dɪs'pju:t] N disputa; (also: **industrial dispute**) controversia (sindacale) ▶ VT contestare; (matter) discutere; (victory) disputare; **to be in** or **under ~** (matter) essere in discussione; (*territory*) essere oggetto di contesa

disqualification [dɪskwɔlɪfɪ'keɪʃən] N squalifica; ~ **(from driving)** (BRIT) ritiro della patente

disqualify [dɪs'kwɔlɪfaɪ] VT (*Sport*) squalificare; **to ~ sb from sth/from doing** rendere qn incapace a qc/a fare; squalificare qn da qc/da fare; **to ~ sb from driving** (BRIT) ritirare la patente a qn

disquiet [dɪs'kwaɪət] N inquietudine f

disquieting [dɪs'kwaɪətɪŋ] ADJ inquietante, allarmante

disregard [dɪsrɪ'gɑːd] VT non far caso a, non badare a ▶ N (*indifference*): ~ **(for)** (*feelings*) insensibilità (a), indifferenza (verso); (*danger*) noncuranza (di); (*money*) disprezzo (di)

disrepair [dɪsrɪ'pɛəʳ] N cattivo stato; **to fall into ~** (*building*) andare in rovina; (*street*) deteriorarsi

disreputable [dɪs'rɛpjutəbl] ADJ (*person*) di cattiva fama; (*area*) malfamato(-a), poco raccomandabile

disrepute ['dɪsrɪ'pjuːt] N disonore m, vergogna; **to bring into ~** rovinare la reputazione di

disrespectful [dɪsrɪ'spɛktful] ADJ che manca di rispetto

disrupt [dɪs'rʌpt] VT (*meeting, lesson*) disturbare, interrompere; (*public transport*) creare scompiglio in; (*plans*) scombussolare

disruption [dɪs'rʌpʃən] N disordine m; interruzione f

disruptive [dɪs'rʌptɪv] ADJ (*influence*) negativo(-a), deleterio(-a); (*strike action*) paralizzante

dissatisfaction [dɪssætɪs'fækʃən] N scontentezza, insoddisfazione f

dissatisfied [dɪs'sætɪsfaɪd] ADJ: ~ **(with)** scontento(a) *or* insoddisfatto(a) (di)

dissect [dɪ'sɛkt] VT sezionare; (*fig*) sviscerare

disseminate [dɪ'sɛmɪneɪt] VT disseminare

dissent [dɪ'sɛnt] N dissenso

dissenter [dɪ'sɛntəʳ] N (*Rel, Pol etc*) dissidente mf

dissertation [dɪsə'teɪʃən] N (*Scol*) tesi f inv, dissertazione f

disservice [dɪs'sə:vɪs] N: **to do sb a ~** fare un cattivo servizio a qn

dissident ['dɪsɪdnt] ADJ dissidente; (*speech, voice*) di dissenso ▶ N dissidente mf

dissimilar [dɪ'sɪmɪləʳ] ADJ: ~ **(to)** dissimile *or* diverso(a) (da)

dissipate ['dɪsɪpeɪt] VT dissipare

dissipated ['dɪsɪpeɪtɪd] ADJ dissipato(-a)

dissociate [dɪ'səuʃɪeɪt] VT dissociare; **to ~ o.s. from** dichiarare di non avere niente a che fare con

dissolute ['dɪsəluːt] ADJ dissoluto(-a), licenzioso(-a)

dissolve [dɪ'zɔlv] VT dissolvere, sciogliere; (*Comm, Pol, marriage*) sciogliere ▶ VI dissolversi, sciogliersi; (*fig*) svanire

dissuade [dɪ'sweɪd] VT: **to ~ sb (from)** dissuadere qn (da)

distaff side ['dɪstɑːf-] N ramo femminile di una famiglia

distance ['dɪstns] N distanza; **in the ~** in lontananza; **what's the ~ to London?** quanto dista Londra?; **it's within walking ~** ci si arriva a piedi; **at a ~ of 2 metres** a 2 metri di distanza

distant ['dɪstnt] ADJ lontano(-a), distante; (*manner*) riservato(-a), freddo(-a)

distaste [dɪs'teɪst] N ripugnanza

distasteful [dɪs'teɪstful] ADJ ripugnante, sgradevole

Dist. Atty. ABBR (US) = **district attorney**

distemper [dɪs'tɛmpəʳ] N (*paint*) tempera; (*of dogs*) cimurro

distend [dɪs'tɛnd] VT dilatare ▶ VI dilatarsi

distended [dɪs'tɛndɪd] ADJ (*stomach*) dilatato(-a)

distil, (US)**distill** [dɪs'tɪl] VT distillare

distillery [dɪs'tɪləri] N distilleria

distinct [dɪs'tɪŋkt] ADJ distinto(-a); (*preference, progress*) definito(-a); **as ~ from** a differenza di

distinction [dɪs'tɪŋkʃən] N distinzione f; (*in exam*) lode f; **to draw a ~ between** fare distinzione tra; **a writer of ~** uno scrittore di notevoli qualità

distinctive [dɪs'tɪŋktɪv] ADJ distintivo(-a)

distinctly [dɪs'tɪŋktlɪ] ADV distintamente; (*remember*) chiaramente; (*unhappy, better*) decisamente

distinguish [dɪs'tɪŋgwɪʃ] VT distinguere; discernere ▶ VI: **to ~ (between)** distinguere (tra); **to ~ o.s.** distinguersi

distinguished [dɪs'tɪŋgwɪʃt] ADJ (*eminent*) eminente; (*career*) brillante; (*refined*) distinto(-a), signorile

distinguishing [dɪs'tɪŋgwɪʃɪŋ] ADJ (*feature*) distinto(-a), caratteristico(-a)

distort [dɪs'tɔːt] VT (*also fig*) distorcere; (*account, news*) falsare; (*Tech*) deformare

distortion [dɪs'tɔːʃən] N (*gen*) distorsione f; (*of truth etc*) alterazione f; (*of facts*) travisamento; (*Tech*) deformazione f

distract [dɪs'trækt] VT distrarre

distracted [dɪs'træktɪd] ADJ distratto(-a)

distraction [dɪs'trækʃən] N distrazione f; **to drive sb to ~** spingere qn alla pazzia

distraught [dɪs'trɔːt] ADJ stravolto(-a)

distress [dɪs'trɛs] N angoscia; (*pain*) dolore m ▶ VT affliggere; **in ~** (*ship etc*) in pericolo, in difficoltà; **distressed area** (BRIT) zona sinistrata

distressing [dɪs'trɛsɪŋ] ADJ doloroso(-a), penoso(-a)

distress signal N segnale m di pericolo

distribute [dɪs'trɪbjuːt] VT distribuire

distribution [dɪstrɪ'bjuːʃən] N distribuzione f

distribution cost N costo di distribuzione

distributor [dɪs'trɪbjutəʳ] N distributore m; (Comm) concessionario

district ['dɪstrɪkt] N (of country) regione f; (of town) quartiere m; (Admin) distretto

district attorney N (US) ≈ sostituto procuratore m della Repubblica

district council N organo di amministrazione regionale; vedi nota

In Inghilterra e in Galles, il district council è l'organo responsabile dell'amministrazione dei paesi più piccoli e dei distretti di campagna. È finanziato tramite una tassa locale e riceve un contributo da parte del governo. I district councils vengono eletti a livello locale ogni quattro anni. L'organo amministrativo nelle città è invece il city council.

district nurse N (BRIT) infermiera di quartiere

distrust [dɪs'trʌst] N diffidenza, sfiducia ▶ VT non aver fiducia in

distrustful [dɪs'trʌstful] ADJ diffidente

disturb [dɪs'təːb] VT disturbare; (inconvenience) scomodare; **sorry to ~ you** scusi se la disturbo

disturbance [dɪs'təːbəns] N disturbo; (political etc) tumulto; (by drunks etc) disordini mpl; **~ of the peace** disturbo della quiete pubblica; **to cause a ~** provocare disordini

disturbed [dɪs'təːbd] ADJ (worried, upset) turbato(-a); **to be emotionally ~** avere turbe emotive; **to be mentally ~** essere malato(-a) di mente

disturbing [dɪs'təːbɪŋ] ADJ sconvolgente

disuse [dɪs'juːs] N: **to fall into ~** cadere in disuso

disused [dɪs'juːzd] ADJ abbandonato(-a)

ditch [dɪtʃ] N fossa ▶ VT (col) piantare in asso

dither ['dɪðəʳ] VI vacillare

ditto ['dɪtəu] ADV idem

divan [dɪ'væn] N divano

divan bed N divano letto inv

dive [daɪv] N tuffo; (of submarine) immersione f; (Aviat) picchiata; (pej) buco ▶ VI tuffarsi; immergersi

diver ['daɪvəʳ] N tuffatore(-trice); (deep-sea diver) palombaro

diverge [daɪ'vəːdʒ] VI divergere

divergent [daɪ'vəːdʒənt] ADJ divergente

diverse [daɪ'vəːs] ADJ vario(-a)

diversification [daɪvəːsɪfɪ'keɪʃən] N diversificazione f

diversify [daɪ'vəːsɪfaɪ] VT diversificare

diversion [daɪ'vəːʃən] N (BRIT Aut) deviazione f; (distraction) divertimento

diversionary tactics [daɪ'vəːʃənrɪ-] NPL tattica fsg diversiva

diversity [daɪ'vəːsɪtɪ] N diversità f inv, varietà f inv

divert [daɪ'vəːt] VT (traffic, river) deviare; (train, plane) dirottare; (amuse) divertire

divest [daɪ'vɛst] VT: **to ~ sb of** spogliare qn di

divide [dɪ'vaɪd] VT dividere; (separate) separare ▶ VI dividersi; **to ~** (**between** or **among**) dividere (tra), ripartire (tra); **40 divided by 5** 40 diviso 5
▶ **divide out** VT: **to ~ out** (**between** or **among**) (sweets etc) distribuire (tra); (tasks) distribuire or ripartire (tra)

divided [dɪ'vaɪdɪd] ADJ (country) diviso(-a); (opinions) discordi

divided highway N (US) strada a doppia carreggiata

divided skirt N gonna f pantalone inv

dividend ['dɪvɪdɛnd] N dividendo

dividend cover N rapporto dividendo profitti

dividers [dɪ'vaɪdəz] NPL compasso a punte fisse

divine [dɪ'vaɪn] ADJ divino(-a) ▶ VT (future) divinare, predire; (truth) indovinare; (water, metal) individuare tramite radioestesia

diving ['daɪvɪŋ] N tuffo

diving board N trampolino

diving suit N scafandro

divinity [dɪ'vɪnɪtɪ] N divinità f inv; teologia

division [dɪ'vɪʒən] N divisione f; separazione f; (BRIT Football) serie f inv; **~ of labour** divisione f del lavoro

divisive [dɪ'vaɪsɪv] ADJ che è causa di discordia

divorce [dɪ'vɔːs] N divorzio ▶ VT divorziare da; (dissociate) separare

divorced [dɪ'vɔːst] ADJ divorziato(-a)

divorcee [dɪvɔː'siː] N divorziato(-a)

divot ['dɪvət] N (Golf) zolla di terra (sollevata accidentalmente)

divulge [daɪ'vʌldʒ] VT divulgare, rivelare

D.I.Y. ADJ, N ABBR (BRIT) = **do-it-yourself**

dizziness ['dɪzɪnɪs] N vertigini fpl

dizzy ['dɪzɪ] ADJ (height) vertiginoso(-a); **to feel ~** avere il capogiro; **I feel ~** mi gira la testa, ho il capogiro; **to make sb ~** far girare la testa a qn

DJ N ABBR = **disc jockey**

dj N ABBR = **dinner jacket**

Djakarta [dʒə'kɑːtə] N Giakarta

DJIA N ABBR (US Stock Exchange: = Dow-Jones Industrial Average) indice m Dow-Jones

dl ABBR (= decilitre) dl

DLit, DLitt N ABBR = **Doctor of Literature**; **Doctor of Letters**

dm ABBR (= *decimetre*) dm

DMus N ABBR = **Doctor of Music**

DMZ N ABBR (= *demilitarized zone*) zona smilitarizzata

DNA N ABBR (= *deoxyribonucleic acid*) DNA *m*

DNA test N test *m inv* del DNA

(KEYWORD)

do [duː] (*pt* **did**, *pp* **done**) AUX VB **1** (*in negative constructions*) *non tradotto*; **I don't understand** non capisco

2 (*to form questions*) *non tradotto*; **didn't you know?** non lo sapevi?; **why didn't you come?** perché non sei venuto?

3 (*for emphasis: in polite expressions*): **she does seem rather late** sembra essere piuttosto in ritardo; **I DO wish I could …** magari potessi …; **but I DO like it!** sì che mi piace!; **do sit down** si accomodi la prego, prego si sieda; **do take care!** mi raccomando, stai attento!

4 (*used to avoid repeating vb*): **she swims better than I do** lei nuota meglio di me; **do you agree? — yes, I do/no, I don't** sei d'accordo? — sì/no; **she lives in Glasgow — so do I** lei vive a Glasgow — anch'io; **he asked me to help him and I did** mi ha chiesto di aiutarlo ed io l'ho fatto; **they come here often — do they?** vengono qui spesso — ah sì?, davvero?

5 (*in question tags*): **you like him, don't you?** ti piace, vero?; **I don't know him, do I?** non lo conosco, vero?

▶ VT (*gen: carry out, perform etc*) fare; **what are you doing tonight?** che fai stasera?; **what can I do for you?** (*in shop*) desidera?; **I'll do all I can** farò tutto il possibile; **to do the cooking** cucinare; **to do the washing-up** fare i piatti; **to do one's teeth** lavarsi i denti; **to do one's hair/nails** farsi i capelli/ le unghie; **the car was doing 100** la macchina faceva i 100 all'ora; **how do you like your steak done?** come preferisce la bistecca?; **well done** ben cotto(-a)

▶ VI **1** (*act, behave*) fare; **do as I do** faccia come me, faccia come faccio io; **what did he do with the cat?** che ne ha fatto del gatto?

2 (*get on, fare*) andare; **he's doing well/badly at school** va bene/male a scuola; **how do you do?** piacere!

3 (*suit*) andare bene; **this room will do** questa stanza va bene

4 (*be sufficient*) bastare; **will £10 do?** basteranno 10 sterline?; **that'll do** basta così; **that'll do!** (*in annoyance*) ora basta!; **to make do (with)** arrangiarsi (con)

▶ N (*col: party etc*) festa; **it was rather a grand do** è stato un ricevimento piuttosto importante

▶ **do away with** VT FUS (*col: kill*) far fuori; (*abolish*) abolire

▶ **do for** VT FUS (BRIT *col: clean for*) fare i servizi per

▶ **do out of** VT FUS: **to do sb out of sth** fregare qc a qn

▶ **do up** VT (*laces*) allacciare; (*dress, buttons*) abbottonare; (*renovate: room, house*) rimettere a nuovo, rifare; **to do o.s. up** farsi bello(-a)

▶ **do with** VT FUS (*need*) aver bisogno di; **I could do with some help/a drink** un aiuto/un bicchierino non guasterebbe; **it could do with a wash** una lavata non gli farebbe male; (*be connected*): **what has it got to do with you?** e tu che c'entri?; **I won't have anything to do with it** non voglio avere niente a che farci; **it has to do with money** si tratta di soldi

▶ **do without** VI fare senza ▶ VT FUS fare a meno di

do. ABBR = **ditto**

DOA ABBR (= *dead on arrival*) morto(a) durante il trasporto

d.o.b. ABBR = **date of birth**

doc [dɔk] N (*col*) dottore(-essa)

docile ['dəusaɪl] ADJ docile

dock [dɔk] N (*Naut*) bacino; (*wharf*) molo; (*Law*) banco degli imputati ▶ VI (*Naut*) entrare in bacino; (*Space*) agganciarsi; **docks** NPL, VT (*Naut*) dock *m inv*; (*pay etc*) decurtare

dock dues NPL diritti *mpl* di banchina

docker ['dɔkəʳ] N scaricatore *m*

docket ['dɔkɪt] N (*on parcel etc*) etichetta, cartellino

dockyard ['dɔkjɑːd] N cantiere *m* navale

doctor ['dɔktəʳ] N medico(-a), dottore(-essa); (*PhD etc*) dottore(-essa) ▶ VT (*interfere with: food, drink*) adulterare; (: *text, document*) alterare, manipolare; **~'s office** (*US*) gabinetto medico, ambulatorio

doctorate ['dɔktərɪt] N dottorato di ricerca; *vedi nota*

Il *doctorate* è il riconoscimento accademico più prestigioso in tutti i campi del sapere e viene conferito in seguito alla presentazione di una tesi originale di fronte ad una commissione di esperti. Generalmente tale tesi è un compendio del lavoro svolto durante più anni di studi; *vedi anche* **Bachelor's degree**, **Master's degree**.

Doctor of Philosophy, PhD N dottorato di ricerca; (*person*) titolare *mf* di un dottorato di ricerca

doctrine ['dɔktrɪn] N dottrina

docudrama [dɔkju'drɑːmə] N (*TV*) ricostruzione *f* filmata

d

525

document N ['dɔkjumənt] documento ▶ VT ['dɔkjumɛnt] documentare

documentary [dɔkju'mɛntərɪ] ADJ documentario(-a); (*evidence*) documentato(-a) ▶ N documentario

documentation [dɔkjumən'teɪʃən] N documentazione *f*

DOD N ABBR (*US*) = **Department of Defense**

doddering ['dɔdərɪŋ] ADJ traballante

doddery ['dɔdərɪ] ADJ malfermo(-a)

doddle ['dɔdl] N: **it's a ~** (*col*) è un gioco da ragazzi

Dodecanese Islands [dəudɪkə'niːz-] NPL Isole *fpl* del Dodecanneso

dodge [dɔdʒ] N trucco; schivata ▶ VT schivare, eludere ▶ VI scansarsi; (*Sport*) fare una schivata; **to ~ out of the way** scansarsi; **to ~ through the traffic** destreggiarsi nel traffico

Dodgems® ['dɔdʒəmz] NPL (*BRIT*) autoscontri *mpl*

dodgy ['dɔdʒɪ] ADJ (*BRIT col*: *uncertain*) rischioso(-a); (*untrustworthy*) sospetto(-a)

DOE N ABBR (*US*) = **Department of Energy**

doe [dəu] N (*deer*) femmina di daino; (*rabbit*) coniglia

does [dʌz] *see* **do**

doesn't ['dʌznt] = **does not**

dog [dɔg] N cane *m* ▶ VT (*follow closely*) pedinare; (*fig: memory etc*) perseguitare; **to go to the dogs** (*person*) ridursi male, lasciarsi andare; (*nation etc*) andare in malora

dog biscuits NPL biscotti *mpl* per cani

dog collar N collare *m* di cane; (*fig*) collarino

dog-eared ['dɔgɪəd] ADJ (*book*) con orecchie

dog food N cibo per cani

dogged ['dɔgɪd] ADJ ostinato(-a), tenace

doggie, doggy ['dɔgɪ] N (*col*) cane *m*, cagnolino

doggy bag N sacchetto per gli avanzi (*da portare a casa*)

dogma ['dɔgmə] N dogma *m*

dogmatic [dɔg'mætɪk] ADJ dogmatico(-a)

do-gooder [duː'gudəʳ] N (*col, pej*): **to be a ~** fare il filantropo

dogsbody ['dɔgzbɔdɪ] N (*BRIT*) factotum *m inv*

doily ['dɔɪlɪ] N centrino di carta sottopiatto

doing ['duːɪŋ] N: **this is your ~** è opera tua, sei stato tu

doings ['duːɪŋz] NPL attività *fpl*

do-it-yourself ['duːɪtjɔː'sɛlf] N il far da sé

doldrums ['dɔldrəmz] NPL (*fig*): **to be in the ~** essere giù; (*business*) attraversare un momento difficile

dole [dəul] N (*BRIT*) sussidio di disoccupazione; **to be on the ~** vivere del sussidio

▶ **dole out** VT distribuire

doleful ['dəulful] ADJ triste, doloroso(-a)

doll [dɔl] N bambola

▶ **doll up** VT: **to ~ o.s. up** farsi bello(a)

dollar ['dɔləʳ] N dollaro

dollop ['dɔləp] N (*of food*) cucchiaiata

dolly ['dɔlɪ] N bambola

dolphin ['dɔlfɪn] N delfino

domain [də'meɪn] N dominio; (*fig*) campo, sfera

dome [dəum] N cupola

domestic [də'mɛstɪk] ADJ (*duty, happiness, animal*) domestico(-a); (*policy, affairs, flights*) nazionale; (*news*) dall'interno

domestic appliance N elettrodomestico

domesticated [də'mɛstɪkeɪtɪd] ADJ addomesticato(-a); (*person*) casalingo(-a)

domesticity [dəumɛs'tɪsɪtɪ] N vita di famiglia

domestic servant N domestico(-a)

domicile ['dɔmɪsaɪl] N domicilio

dominant ['dɔmɪnənt] ADJ dominante

dominate ['dɔmɪneɪt] VT dominare

domination [dɔmɪ'neɪʃən] N dominazione *f*

domineering [dɔmɪ'nɪərɪŋ] ADJ dispotico(-a), autoritario(-a)

Dominican Republic [də'mɪnɪkən-] N Repubblica Dominicana

dominion [də'mɪnɪən] N dominio; sovranità; (*BRIT Pol*) dominion *m inv*

domino ['dɔmɪnəu] (*pl* **dominoes**) N domino; **dominoes** NPL (*game*) gioco del domino

don [dɔn] N (*BRIT*) docente *mf* universitario(-a) ▶ VT indossare

donate [də'neɪt] VT donare

donation [də'neɪʃən] N donazione *f*

done [dʌn] PP *of* **do**

dongle ['dɔŋgl] N (*Comput*) dongle *m inv*; chiave *f* hardware

donkey ['dɔŋkɪ] N asino

donkey-work ['dɔŋkɪwəːk] N (*BRIT col*) lavoro ingrato

donor ['dəunəʳ] N donatore(-trice)

donor card N tessera di donatore di organi

don't [dəunt] = **do not**

donut ['dəunʌt] N (*US*) = **doughnut**

doodle ['duːdl] N scarabocchio ▶ VI scarabocchiare

doom [duːm] N destino; rovina ▶ VT: **to be doomed (to failure)** essere predestinato(-a) (a fallire)

doomsday ['duːmzdeɪ] N il giorno del Giudizio

door [dɔːʳ] N porta; (*of vehicle*) sportello, portiera; **from ~ to ~** di porta in porta

doorbell ['dɔːbɛl] N campanello

door handle N maniglia

doorknob ['dɔːnɔb] N pomello, maniglia

doorman ['dɔːmæn] N (*irreg*) (*in hotel*) portiere *m* in livrea; (*in block of flats*) portinaio

doormat ['dɔːmæt] N stuoia della porta

doorstep ['dɔ:stɛp] N gradino della porta

door-to-door ['dɔ:təˈdɔːʳ] ADJ: ~ **selling** vendita porta a porta

doorway ['dɔ:weɪ] N porta; **in the** ~ nel vano della porta

dope [dəup] N (col: drugs) roba; (: information) dati mpl ▶ VT (horse etc) drogare

dopey ['dəupɪ] ADJ (col) inebetito(-a)

dormant ['dɔ:mənt] ADJ inattivo(-a); (fig) latente

dormer ['dɔ:məʳ] N (also: **dormer window**) abbaino

dormice ['dɔ:maɪs] NPL of **dormouse**

dormitory ['dɔ:mɪtrɪ] N dormitorio; (US: hall of residence) casa dello studente

dormouse ['dɔ:maus] (pl **dormice** [-maɪs]) N ghiro

DOS [dɔs] N ABBR (= disk operating system) DOS m

dosage ['dəusɪdʒ] N (on medicine bottle) posologia

dose [dəus] N dose f; (BRIT: bout) attacco ▶ VT: **to** ~ **sb with sth** somministrare qc a qn; **a** ~ **of flu** una bella influenza

dosser ['dɔsəʳ] N (BRIT col) barbone(-a)

doss house ['dɔs-] N (BRIT) asilo notturno

dossier ['dɔsɪeɪ] N dossier m inv

DOT N ABBR (US) = **Department of Transportation**

dot [dɔt] N punto; macchiolina ▶ VT: **dotted with** punteggiato(a) di; **on the** ~ in punto

dotcom [dɔtˈkɔm] N azienda che opera in Internet

dot command N (Comput) dot command m inv

dote [dəut]: **to** ~ **on** vt fus essere infatuato(a) di

dot-matrix printer [dɔtˈmeɪtrɪks-] N stampante f a matrice a punti

dotted line ['dɔtɪd-] N linea punteggiata; **to sign on the** ~ firmare (nell'apposito spazio); (fig) accettare

dotty ['dɔtɪ] ADJ (col) strambo(-a)

double ['dʌbl] ADJ doppio(-a) ▶ ADV (fold) in due, doppio; (twice): **to cost** ~ **sth** costare il doppio (di qc) ▶ N sosia m inv; (Cine) controfigura ▶ VT raddoppiare; (fold) piegare doppio or in due ▶ VI raddoppiarsi; **spelt with a** ~ **"l"** scritto con due elle or con doppia elle; ~ **five two six (5526)** (BRIT Tel) cinque cinque due sei; **on the** ~, (BRIT) **at the** ~ a passo di corsa; **to** ~ **as** (have two uses etc) funzionare or servire anche da; see also **doubles**

▶ **double back** VI (person) tornare sui propri passi

▶ **double up** VI (bend over) piegarsi in due; (share room) dividere la stanza

double bass N contrabbasso

double bed N letto matrimoniale

double-breasted ['dʌblˈbrɛstɪd] ADJ a doppio petto

double-check ['dʌblˈtʃɛk] VT, VI ricontrollare

double-click VI (Comput) fare doppio click

double-clutch ['dʌblˈklʌtʃ] VI (US) fare la doppietta

double cream N (BRIT) doppia panna

double-cross ['dʌblˈkrɔs] VT fare il doppio gioco con

doubledecker ['dʌblˈdɛkəʳ] N autobus m inv a due piani

double declutch VI (BRIT) fare la doppietta

double exposure N (Phot) sovrimpressione f

double glazing N (BRIT) doppi vetri mpl

double-page ['dʌblpeɪdʒ] ADJ: ~ **spread** pubblicità a doppia pagina

double parking N parcheggio in doppia fila

double room N camera matrimoniale

doubles ['dʌblz] N (Tennis) doppio

double time N tariffa doppia per lavoro straordinario

double whammy [-'wæmɪ] N doppia mazzata (fig)

double yellow lines NPL (BRIT Aut) linea gialla doppia continua che segnala il divieto di sosta

doubly ['dʌblɪ] ADV doppiamente

doubt [daut] N dubbio ▶ VT dubitare di; **to** ~ **that** dubitare che + sub; **without (a)** ~ senza dubbio; **beyond** ~ fuor di dubbio; **I** ~ **it very much** ho i miei dubbi, nutro seri dubbi in proposito

doubtful ['dautful] ADJ dubbioso(-a), incerto(-a); (person) equivoco(-a); **to be** ~ **about sth** avere dei dubbi su qc, non essere convinto di qc; **I'm a bit** ~ non ne sono sicuro

doubtless ['dautlɪs] ADV indubbiamente

dough [dəu] N pasta, impasto; (col: money) grana

doughnut, (US)**donut** ['dəunʌt] N bombolone m

dour [duəʳ] ADJ arcigno(-a)

douse [daus] VT (with water) infradiciare; (flames) spegnere

dove [dʌv] N colombo(-a)

Dover ['dəuvəʳ] N Dover f

dovetail ['dʌvteɪl] N: ~ **joint** incastro a coda di rondine ▶ VI (fig) combaciare

dowager ['dauədʒəʳ] N vedova titolata

dowdy ['daudɪ] ADJ trasandato(-a), malvestito(-a)

Dow-Jones average ['dauˈdʒəunz-] N (US) indice m Dow-Jones

down [daun] N (fluff) piumino; (hill) collina, colle m ▶ ADV giù, di sotto ▶ PREP giù per ▶ VT (col: drink) scolarsi; ~ **there** laggiù, là in fondo; ~ **here** quaggiù; **I'll be** ~ **in a minute** scendo tra un minuto; **the price of meat is** ~ il prezzo della carne è sceso; **I've got it** ~ **in**

my diary ce l'ho sulla mia agenda; **to pay £2
~** dare 2 sterline in acconto or di anticipo;
I've been ~ with flu sono stato a letto con
l'influenza; **England is two goals ~**
l'Inghilterra sta perdendo per due goal; **to ~
tools** (BRIT) incrociare le braccia; **~ with X!**
abbasso X!

down-and-out ['daunəndaut] N (tramp)
barbone m

down-at-heel ['daunət'hi:l] ADJ
scalcagnato(-a); (fig) trasandato(-a)

downbeat ['daunbi:t] N (Mus) tempo in
battere ▶ ADJ (col) volutamente distaccato(-a)

downcast ['daunka:st] ADJ abbattuto(-a)

downer ['daunəᴿ] N (col: drug) farmaco
depressivo; **to be on a ~** (depressed) essere giù

downfall ['daunfɔ:l] N caduta; rovina

downgrade ['daungreid] VT (job, hotel)
declassare; (employee) degradare

downhearted [daun'ha:tid] ADJ
scoraggiato(-a)

downhill [daun'hil] ADV verso il basso; **to go
~** andare in discesa; (business) lasciarsi
andare; andare a rotoli ▶ N (Ski: also:
downhill race) discesa libera

Downing Street ['daunin-] N: **10 ~** residenza
del primo ministro inglese; vedi nota

> Downing Street è la via di Westminster che
> porta da Whitehall al parco di St James
> dove, al numero 10, si trova la residenza
> del primo ministro inglese. Nella stessa
> via, al numero 11, si trova la residenza del
> Cancelliere dello Scacchiere. Spesso si usa
> Downing Street per indicare il governo
> britannico.

download ['daunləud] VT (Comput) scaricare
▶ N (Comput) file m inv da scaricare

downloadable ADJ (Comput) scaricabile

down-market ['daun'ma:kit] ADJ rivolto(-a)
ad una fascia di mercato inferiore

down payment N acconto

downplay ['daunplei] VT (US) minimizzare

downpour ['daunpɔ:ᴿ] N scroscio di pioggia

downright ['daunrait] ADJ franco(-a);
(refusal) assoluto(-a)

Downs [daunz] NPL (BRIT): **the ~** colline ricche
di gesso nel sud-est dell'Inghilterra

downsize ['daunsaiz] VT (workforce) ridurre

Down's syndrome N sindrome f di Down

downstairs ['daun'stɛəz] ADV di sotto; al
piano inferiore; **to come ~, go ~** scendere
giù

downstream ['daun'stri:m] ADV a valle

downtime ['dauntaim] N (Comm) tempi mpl
morti

down-to-earth ['dauntu'ə:θ] ADJ pratico(-a)

downtown ['daun'taun] ADV in città ▶ ADJ
(US): **~ Chicago** il centro di Chicago

downtrodden ['dauntrɔdn] ADJ oppresso(-a)

down under ADV (Australia etc) agli antipodi

downward ['daunwəd] ADJ in giù, in discesa;
a ~ trend una diminuzione progressiva
▶ ADV in giù, in discesa

downwards ['daunwədz] ADV in giù, in
discesa

dowry ['dauri] N dote f

doz. ABBR = **dozen**

doze [dəuz] VI sonnecchiare
▶ **doze off** VI appisolarsi

dozen ['dʌzn] N dozzina; **a ~ books** una
dozzina di libri; **80p a ~** 80 pence la dozzina;
dozens of times centinaia or migliaia di
volte

DPh, DPhil N ABBR (= Doctor of Philosophy)
≈ dottorato di ricerca

DPP N ABBR (BRIT) = **Director of Public
Prosecutions**

DPT N ABBR (Med: = diphtheria, pertussis, tetanus)
vaccino

Dr, Dr. ABBR (= doctor) Dr, Dott./Dott.ssa;
(in street names) = **drive**

dr ABBR (Comm) = **debtor**

drab [dræb] ADJ tetro(-a), grigio(-a)

draft [dra:ft] N abbozzo; (Pol) bozza; (Comm)
tratta; (US Mil) contingente m; (: call-up) leva
▶ VT abbozzare; (document, report) stendere (in
versione preliminare); see also **draught**

drag [dræg] VT trascinare; (river) dragare
▶ VI trascinarsi ▶ N (Aviat, Naut) resistenza
(aerodinamica); (col: person) noioso(-a);
(: task) noia; (women's clothing): **in ~** travestito
(da donna)
▶ **drag away** VT: **to ~ away (from)**
tirare via (da)
▶ **drag on** VI tirar avanti lentamente

dragnet ['drægnɛt] N giacchio; (fig)
rastrellamento

dragon ['drægən] N drago

dragonfly ['drægənflai] N libellula

dragoon [drə'gu:n] N (cavalryman) dragone m
▶ VT: **to ~ sb into doing sth** (BRIT)
costringere qn a fare qc

drain [drein] N canale m di scolo;
(for sewage) fogna; (on resources) salasso
▶ VT (land, marshes) prosciugare; (vegetables)
scolare; (reservoir etc) vuotare ▶ VI (water)
defluire; **to feel drained** sentirsi
svuotato(-a), sentirsi sfinito(-a)

drainage ['dreinidʒ] N prosciugamento;
fognatura

draining board ['dreinin-], (US) **drainboard**
['dreinbɔ:d] N piano del lavello

drainpipe ['dreinpaip] N tubo di scarico

drake [dreik] N maschio dell'anatra

dram [dræm] N bicchierino (di whisky etc)

drama ['dra:mə] N (art) dramma m, teatro;
(play) commedia; (event) dramma

dramatic [drə'mætik] ADJ drammatico(-a)

dramatically [drə'mætɪklɪ] ADV in modo spettacolare

dramatist ['dræmətɪst] N drammaturgo(-a)

dramatize ['dræmətaɪz] VT (events etc) drammatizzare; (adapt: novel: for TV) ridurre or adattare per la televisione; (: for cinema) ridurre or adattare per lo schermo

drank [dræŋk] PT of **drink**

drape [dreɪp] VT drappeggiare; see also **drapes**

draper ['dreɪpər] N (BRIT) negoziante mf di stoffe

drapes [dreɪps] NPL (US: curtains) tende fpl

drastic ['dræstɪk] ADJ drastico(-a)

drastically ['dræstɪklɪ] ADV drasticamente

draught, (US)**draft** [drɑːft] N corrente f d'aria; (Naut) pescaggio; **on ~** (beer) alla spina; see also **draughts**

draught beer N birra alla spina

draughtboard ['drɑːftbɔːd] N scacchiera

draughts [drɑːfts] N (BRIT) (gioco della) dama

draughtsman, (US)**draftsman** ['drɑːftsmən] N (irreg) disegnatore m

draughtsmanship, (US)**draftsmanship** ['drɑːftsmənʃɪp] N disegno tecnico; (skill) arte f del disegno

draw [drɔː] (pt **drew** [druː], pp **drawn** [drɔːn]) VT tirare; (take out) estrarre; (attract) attirare; (picture) disegnare; (line, circle) tracciare; (money) ritirare; (formulate: conclusion) trarre, ricavare; (: comparison, distinction): **to ~ (between)** fare (tra) ▶ VI (Sport) pareggiare ▶ N (Sport) pareggio; (in lottery) estrazione f; (attraction) attrazione f; **to ~ to a close** avvicinarsi alla conclusione; **to ~ near** vi avvicinarsi

▶ **draw back** VI: **to ~ back (from)** indietreggiare (di fronte a), tirarsi indietro (di fronte a)

▶ **draw in** VI (BRIT: car) accostarsi; (train) entrare in stazione

▶ **draw on** VT (resources) attingere a; (imagination, person) far ricorso a

▶ **draw out** VI (lengthen) allungarsi ▶ VT (money) ritirare

▶ **draw up** VI (stop) arrestarsi, fermarsi ▶ VT (chair) avvicinare; (document) compilare; (plans) formulare

drawback ['drɔːbæk] N svantaggio, inconveniente m

drawbridge ['drɔːbrɪdʒ] N ponte m levatoio

drawee [drɔː'iː] N trattario

drawer [drɔːr] N cassetto ['drɔːər]; (of cheque) riscuotitore(-trice)

drawing ['drɔːɪŋ] N disegno

drawing board N tavola da disegno

drawing pin N (BRIT) puntina da disegno

drawing room N salotto

drawl [drɔːl] N pronuncia strascicata

drawn [drɔːn] PP of **draw** ▶ ADJ (haggard: with tiredness) tirato(-a); (: with pain) contratto(-a) (dal dolore)

drawstring ['drɔːstrɪŋ] N laccio (per stringere maglie, sacche ecc)

dread [drɛd] N terrore m ▶ VT tremare all'idea di

dreadful ['drɛdful] ADJ terribile; **I feel ~!** (ill) mi sento uno straccio!; (ashamed) vorrei scomparire (dalla vergogna)!

dream [driːm] (pt, pp **dreamed** or **dreamt** [drɛmt]) N sogno ▶ VT, VI sognare; **to have a ~ about sb/sth** fare un sogno su qn/qc; **sweet dreams!** sogni d'oro!

▶ **dream up** VT (reason, excuse) inventare; (plan, idea) escogitare

dreamer ['driːmər] N sognatore(-trice)

dreamt [drɛmt] PT, PP of **dream**

dreamy ['driːmɪ] ADJ (look, voice) sognante; (person) distratto(-a), sognatore(-trice)

dreary ['drɪərɪ] ADJ tetro(-a); monotono(-a)

dredge [drɛdʒ] VT dragare

▶ **dredge up** VT tirare alla superficie; (fig: unpleasant facts) rivangare

dredger ['drɛdʒər] N draga; (BRIT: also: **sugar dredger**) spargizucchero m inv

dregs [drɛgz] NPL feccia

drench [drɛntʃ] VT inzuppare; **drenched to the skin** bagnato(a) fino all'osso, bagnato(a) fradicio(a)

dress [drɛs] N vestito; (no pl: clothing) abbigliamento ▶ VT vestire; (wound) fasciare; (food) condire; preparare; (shop window) allestire ▶ VI vestirsi; **to ~ o.s., to get dressed** vestirsi; **she dresses very well** veste molto bene

▶ **dress up** VI vestirsi a festa; (in fancy dress) vestirsi in costume

dress circle (BRIT) N prima galleria

dress designer N disegnatore(-trice) di moda

dresser ['drɛsər] N (Theat) assistente mf del camerino; (also: **window dresser**) vetrinista mf (furniture) credenza; (US) cassettone m

dressing ['drɛsɪŋ] N (Med) benda; (Culin) condimento

dressing gown N (BRIT) vestaglia

dressing room N (Theat) camerino; (Sport) spogliatoio

dressing table N toilette f inv

dressmaker ['drɛsmeɪkər] N sarta

dressmaking ['drɛsmeɪkɪŋ] N sartoria; confezioni fpl per donna

dress rehearsal N prova generale

dress shirt N camicia da sera

dressy ['drɛsɪ] ADJ (col) elegante

drew [druː] PT of **draw**

dribble ['drɪbl] VI gocciolare; (baby) sbavare; (Football) dribblare ▶ VT (ball) dribblare

dried[draɪd] ADJ (*fruit, beans*) secco(-a); (*eggs, milk*) in polvere

drier['draɪəʳ] N = **dryer**

drift[drɪft] N (*of current etc*) direzione *f*; forza; (*of sand, snow*) cumulo; turbine *m*; (*general meaning*) senso ▶ VI (*boat*) essere trasportato(-a) dalla corrente; (*sand, snow*) ammucchiarsi; **to catch sb's ~** capire dove qn vuole arrivare; **to let things ~** lasciare che le cose vadano come vogliono; **to ~ apart** (*friends*) perdersi di vista; (*lovers*) allontanarsi l'uno dall'altro

drifter['drɪftəʳ] N *persona che fa una vita da zingaro*

driftwood['drɪftwud] N resti *mpl* della mareggiata

drill[drɪl] N trapano; (*Mil*) esercitazione *f* ▶ VT trapanare; (*soldiers*) esercitare, addestrare; (*pupils: in grammar*) fare esercitare ▶ VI (*for oil*) fare trivellazioni

drilling['drɪlɪŋ] N (*for oil*) trivellazione *f*

drilling rig N (*on land*) torre *f* di perforazione; (*at sea*) piattaforma (per trivellazioni subacquee)

drily['draɪlɪ] ADV = **dryly**

drink[drɪŋk] (*pt* **drank** [dræŋk], *pp* **drunk** [drʌŋk]) N bevanda, bibita; (*alcoholic drink*) bicchierino; (*sip*) sorso ▶ VT, VI bere; **to have a ~** bere qualcosa; **a ~ of water** un po' d'acqua; **would you like something to ~?** vuole qualcosa da bere?; **we had drinks before lunch** abbiamo preso l'aperitivo

▶ **drink in** VT (*person: fresh air*) aspirare; (*: story*) ascoltare avidamente; (*: sight*) ammirare, bersi con gli occhi

drinkable['drɪŋkəbl] ADJ (*not poisonous*) potabile; (*palatable*) bevibile

drink-driving['drɪŋk'draɪvɪŋ] N guida in stato di ebbrezza

drinker['drɪŋkəʳ] N bevitore(-trice)

drinking['drɪŋkɪŋ] N (*drunkenness*) il bere, alcoolismo

drinking fountain N fontanella

drinking water N acqua potabile

drip[drɪp] N goccia; (*dripping*) sgocciolio; (*Med*) fleboclisi *f inv*; (*col: spineless person*) lavativo ▶ VI gocciolare; (*washing, tap*) sgocciolare; (*wall*) trasudare

drip-dry['drɪp'draɪ] ADJ (*shirt*) che non si stira

drip-feed['drɪpfiːd] VT alimentare mediante fleboclisi

dripping['drɪpɪŋ] N (*Culin*) grasso d'arrosto ▶ ADJ: **~ wet** fradicio(a)

drive[draɪv] (*pt* **drove** [drəuv], *pp* **driven** ['drɪvn]) N passeggiata *or* giro in macchina; (*also:* **driveway**) viale *m* d'accesso; (*energy*) energia; (*Psych*) impulso; bisogno; (*push*) sforzo eccezionale; (*campaign*) campagna; (*Sport*) drive *m inv*; (*Tech*) trasmissione *f*;

(*Comput: also:* **disk drive**) disk drive *m inv* ▶ VT (*vehicle*) guidare; (*nail*) piantare; (*push*) cacciare, spingere; (*Tech: motor*) azionare; far funzionare ▶ VI (*Aut: at controls*) guidare; (*: travel*) andare in macchina; **to go for a ~** andare a fare un giro in macchina; **it's 3 hours' ~ from London** è a 3 ore di macchina da Londra; **left-/right-hand ~** (*Aut*) guida a sinistra/destra; **front-/rear-wheel ~** (*Aut*) trazione *f* anteriore/posteriore; **to ~ sb to (do) sth** spingere qn a (fare) qc; **to ~ sb mad** far impazzire qn; **he drives a taxi** fa il tassista; **to ~ at 50 km an hour** guidare *or* andare a 50 km all'ora

▶ **drive at** VT FUS (*fig: intend, mean*) mirare a, voler dire

▶ **drive on** VI proseguire, andare (più) avanti ▶ VT (*incite, encourage*) sospingere, spingere

▶ **drive out** VT (*force out*) cacciare, mandare via

drive-by['draɪvbaɪ] N (*also:* **drive-by shooting**) sparatoria dalla macchina; **he was killed in a ~ shooting** lo hanno ammazzato sparandogli da una macchina in corsa

drive-in['draɪvɪn] ADJ, N (*esp US*) drive-in (*m inv*)

drive-in window N (*US*) sportello di drive-in

drivel['drɪvl] N (*col: nonsense*) ciance *fpl*

driven['drɪvn] PP *of* **drive**

driver['draɪvəʳ] N conducente *mf*; (*of taxi*) tassista *m*; (*chauffeur: of bus*) autista *mf*; (*Comput*) driver *m inv*

driver's license N (*US*) patente *f* di guida

driveway['draɪvweɪ] N viale *m* d'accesso

driving['draɪvɪŋ] ADJ: **~ rain** pioggia sferzante ▶ N guida

driving force N forza trainante

driving instructor N istruttore(-trice) di scuola guida

driving lesson N lezione *f* di guida

driving licence N (*BRIT*) patente *f* di guida

driving school N scuola *f* guida *inv*

driving test N esame *m* di guida

drizzle['drɪzl] N pioggerella ▶ VI piovigginare

droll[drəul] ADJ buffo(-a)

dromedary['drɒmədərɪ] N dromedario

drone[drəun] N ronzio; (*male bee*) fuco ▶ VI (*bee, aircraft, engine*) ronzare; (*also:* **drone on**: *person*) continuare a parlare (in modo monotono); (*: voice*) continuare a ronzare

drool[druːl] VI sbavare; **to ~ over sb/sth** (*fig*) andare in estasi per qn/qc

droop[druːp] VI abbassarsi; languire; (*flower*) appassire; (*head, shoulders*) chinarsi

drop[drɒp] N (*of water*) goccia; (*lessening*) diminuzione *f*; (*fall*) caduta; (*: in price*) calo, ribasso; (*: in salary*) riduzione *f*, taglio; (*also:*

parachute drop) lancio; (*steep incline*) salto
▶ VT lasciar cadere; (*voice, eyes, price*)
abbassare; (*set down from car*) far scendere;
(*name from list*) lasciare fuori ▶ VI cascare;
(*decrease: wind, temperature, price*) calare,
abbassarsi; (: *numbers, attendance*) diminuire;
(*voice*) abbassarsi; **drops**N PL (*Med*) gocce *fpl*;
cough drops pastiglie *fpl* per la tosse; **a ~ of
10%** un calo del 10%; **to ~ sb a line** mandare
due righe a qn; **to ~ anchor** gettare l'ancora
▶ **drop in**VI (*col: visit*): **to ~ in (on)** fare un
salto (da), passare (da)
▶ **drop off**VI (*sleep*) addormentarsi ▶ VT: **to ~
sb off** far scendere qn
▶ **drop out**VI (*withdraw*) ritirarsi; (*student etc*)
smettere di studiare
droplet['drɔplɪt] N gocciolina
dropout['drɔpaut] N (*from society/university*)
chi ha abbandonato (la società/gli studi)
dropper['drɔpəʳ] N (*Med*) contagocce *m inv*
droppings['drɔpɪŋz] N PL sterco
dross[drɔs] N scoria; scarto
drought[draut] N siccità *f inv*
drove[drəuv] PT *of* **drive** ▶ N: **droves of
people** una moltitudine di persone
drown[draun] VT affogare; (*fig: noise*)
soffocare; (*also:* **drown out**: *sound*) coprire
▶ VI affogare
drowse[drauz] VI sonnecchiare
drowsy['drauzɪ] ADJ sonnolento(-a),
assonnato(-a)
drudge[drʌdʒ] N (*person*) uomo (donna) di
fatica; (*job*) faticaccia
drudgery['drʌdʒərɪ] N fatica improba;
housework is sheer ~ le faccende
domestiche sono alienanti
drug[drʌg] N farmaco; (*narcotic*) droga ▶ VT
drogare; **to be on drugs** drogarsi; (*Med*)
prendere medicinali; **hard/soft drugs**
droghe pesanti/leggere
drug abuser[-ə'bjuːzəʳ] N chi fa uso di
droghe
drug addictN tossicomane *mf*
drug dealerN trafficante *mf* di droga
drug drivingN guida *f* sotto l'effetto di
droghe
druggist['drʌgɪst] N (*US*) farmacista *mf*
drug peddlerN spacciatore(-trice) di droga
drugstore['drʌgstɔːʳ] N (*US*) *negozio di generi
vari e di articoli di farmacia con un bar*
drum[drʌm] N tamburo; (*for oil, petrol*) fusto
▶ VT: **to ~ one's fingers on the table**
tamburellare con le dita sulla tavola ▶ VI
tamburellare; **drums**N PL (*Mus: set of drums*)
batteria
▶ **drum up**VT (*enthusiasm, support*)
conquistarsi
drummer['drʌməʳ] N batterista *mf*
drum rollN rullio di tamburi

drumstick['drʌmstɪk] N (*Mus*) bacchetta;
(*chicken leg*) coscia di pollo
drunk[drʌŋk] PP *of* **drink** ▶ ADJ ubriaco(-a),
ebbro(-a) ▶ N ubriacone(-a); **to get ~**
ubriacarsi, prendere una sbornia
drunkard['drʌŋkəd] N ubriacone(-a)
drunken['drʌŋkən] ADJ ubriaco(-a), da
ubriaco; **~ driving** guida in stato di ebbrezza
drunkenness['drʌŋkənnɪs] N ubriachezza;
ebbrezza
dry[draɪ] ADJ secco(-a); (*day, clothes: fig:
humour*) asciutto(-a); (*uninteresting: lecture,
subject*) poco avvincente ▶ VT seccare; (*clothes,
hair, hands*) asciugare ▶ VI asciugarsi; **on ~
land** sulla terraferma; **to ~ one's hands/
hair/eyes** asciugarsi le mani/i capelli/gli
occhi
▶ **dry off**VI asciugarsi ▶ VT asciugare
▶ **dry up**VI seccarsi; (*source of supply*)
esaurirsi; (*fig: imagination etc*) inaridirsi;
(*fall silent: speaker*) azzittirsi
dry-clean[draɪ'kliːn] VT pulire *or* lavare a
secco
dry-cleaner's[draɪ'kliːnəz] N lavasecco *m inv*
dry-cleaning[draɪ'kliːnɪŋ] N pulitura a
secco
dry dockN (*Naut*) bacino di carenaggio
dryer['draɪəʳ] N (*for hair*) föhn *m inv*,
asciugacapelli *m inv*; (*for clothes*)
asciugabiancheria *m inv*; (*US: spin-dryer*)
centrifuga
dry goodsN PL (*Comm*) tessuti *mpl* e mercerie
fpl
dry goods storeN (*US*) negozio di stoffe
dry iceN ghiaccio secco
dryly['draɪlɪ] ADV con fare asciutto
dryness['draɪnɪs] N secchezza; (*of ground*)
aridità
dry rotN fungo del legno
dry runN (*fig*) prova
dry ski slopeN pista artificiale
DScN ABBR (= *Doctor of Science*) titolo di studio
DSSN ABBR (*BRIT*: = *Department of Social Security*)
ministero della Previdenza sociale
DSTABBR = **Daylight Saving Time**
DTIN ABBR (*BRIT*) = **Department of Trade and
Industry**; *see* **trade**
DTPN ABBR (= *desk-top publishing*) desktop
publishing *m inv*; (*Med*: = *diphtheria, tetanus,
pertussis*) vaccino
DT'sN ABBR (*col*) = **delirium tremens**
dual['djuəl] ADJ doppio(-a)
dual carriagewayN (*BRIT*) strada a doppia
carreggiata
dual-control['djuəlkən'trəul] ADJ con doppi
comandi
dual nationalityN doppia nazionalità
dual-purpose['djuəl'pəːpəs] ADJ
a doppio uso

d

dubbed [dʌbd] ADJ (Cine) doppiato(-a); (nicknamed) soprannominato(-a)

dubious ['dju:bɪəs] ADJ dubbio(-a); (character, manner) ambiguo(-a), equivoco(-a); **I'm very ~ about it** ho i miei dubbi in proposito

Dublin ['dʌblɪn] N Dublino f

Dubliner ['dʌblɪnə^r] N dublinese mf

duchess ['dʌtʃɪs] N duchessa

duck [dʌk] N anatra ▶ VI abbassare la testa ▶ VT spingere sotto (acqua)

duckling ['dʌklɪŋ] N anatroccolo

duct [dʌkt] N condotto; (Anat) canale m

dud [dʌd] N (shell) proiettile m che fa cilecca; (object, tool): **it's a ~** è inutile, non funziona ▶ ADJ (cheque) a vuoto; (note, coin) falso(-a)

due [dju:] ADJ dovuto(-a); (expected) atteso(-a); (fitting) giusto(-a) ▶ N dovuto ▶ ADV: **~ north** diritto verso nord; **dues** NPL (for club, union) quota; (in harbour) diritti mpl di porto; **in ~ course** a tempo debito; finalmente; **~ to** dovuto a; a causa di; **the rent's ~ on the 30th** l'affitto scade il 30; **the train is ~ at 8** il treno è atteso per le 8; **she is ~ back tomorrow** dovrebbe essere di ritorno domani; **I am ~ 6 days' leave** mi spettano 6 giorni di ferie

due date N data di scadenza

duel ['djuəl] N duello

duet [dju:'ɛt] N duetto

duff [dʌf] ADJ (BRIT col) barboso(-a)

duffelbag, duffle bag ['dʌflbæg] N sacca da viaggio di tela

duffelcoat, duffle coat ['dʌflkəut] N montgomery m inv

duffer ['dʌfə^r] N (col) schiappa

dug [dʌg] PT, PP of **dig**

dugout ['dʌgaut] N (Football) panchina

duke [dju:k] N duca m

dull [dʌl] ADJ (light) debole; (boring) noioso(-a); (slow-witted) ottuso(-a); (sound, pain) sordo(-a); (weather, day) fosco(-a), scuro(-a); (blade) smussato(-a) ▶ VT (pain, grief) attutire; (mind, senses) intorpidire

duly ['dju:lɪ] ADV (on time) a tempo debito; (as expected) debitamente

dumb [dʌm] ADJ muto(-a); (stupid) stupido(-a); **to be struck ~** (fig) ammutolire, restare senza parole

dumbbell ['dʌmbɛl] N (Sport) manubrio, peso

dumbfounded [dʌm'faundɪd] ADJ stupito(-a), stordito(-a)

dummy ['dʌmɪ] N (tailor's model) manichino; (Sport) finto; (Tech, Comm) riproduzione f; (BRIT: for baby) tettarella ▶ ADJ falso(-a), finto(-a)

dummy run N giro di prova

dump [dʌmp] N (also: **rubbish dump**) mucchio di rifiuti (place) discarica; (Mil) deposito; (Comput) scaricamento, dump m inv

▶ VT (put down) scaricare; mettere giù; (get rid of) buttar via; (Comm: goods) svendere; (Comput) scaricare; **to be (down) in the dumps** (col) essere giù di corda

dumping ['dʌmpɪŋ] N (Econ) dumping m; **"no ~"** "vietato lo scarico"

dumpling ['dʌmplɪŋ] N specie di gnocco

dumpy ['dʌmpɪ] ADJ tracagnotto(-a)

dunce [dʌns] N asino

dune [dju:n] N duna

dung [dʌŋ] N concime m

dungarees [dʌŋgə'ri:z] NPL tuta

dungeon ['dʌndʒən] N prigione f sotterranea

dunk [dʌŋk] VT inzuppare

duo ['dju:əu] N (gen, Mus) duo m inv

duodenal [dju:əu'di:nl] ADJ (ulcer) duodenale

duodenum [dju:əu'di:nəm] N duodeno

dupe [dju:p] VT gabbare, ingannare

duplex ['dju:plɛks] N (US: house) casa con muro divisorio in comune con un'altra; (also: **duplex apartment**) appartamento su due piani

duplicate [n 'dju:plɪkət] doppio; (copy of letter etc) duplicato ▶ VT ['dju:plɪkeɪt] duplicare; (on machine) ciclostilare ▶ ADJ (copy) conforme, esattamente uguale; **in ~** in duplice copia; **~ key** duplicato (della chiave)

duplicity [dju:'plɪsɪtɪ] N doppiezza, duplicità

Dur. ABBR (BRIT) = **Durham**

durability [djuərə'bɪlɪtɪ] N durevolezza; resistenza

durable ['djuərəbl] ADJ durevole; (clothes, metal) resistente

duration [djuə'reɪʃən] N durata

duress [djuə'rɛs] N: **under ~** sotto costrizione

Durex ® ['djuərɛks] N (BRIT) preservativo

during ['djuərɪŋ] PREP durante, nel corso di

dusk [dʌsk] N crepuscolo

dusky ['dʌskɪ] ADJ scuro(-a)

dust [dʌst] N polvere f ▶ VT (furniture) spolverare; (cake etc): **to ~ with** cospargere con

▶ **dust off** VT rispolverare

dustbin ['dʌstbɪn] N (BRIT) pattumiera

duster ['dʌstə^r] N straccio per la polvere

dust jacket N sopraccoperta

dustman ['dʌstmən] N (irreg) (BRIT) netturbino

dustpan ['dʌstpæn] N pattumiera

dusty ['dʌstɪ] ADJ polveroso(-a)

Dutch [dʌtʃ] ADJ olandese ▶ N (Ling) olandese m ▶ ADV: **to go ~** or **dutch** (col) fare alla romana; **the ~** gli Olandesi

Dutch auction N asta all'olandese

Dutchman ['dʌtʃmən], **Dutchwoman** ['dʌtʃwumən] N (irreg) olandese mf

dutiable ['dju:tɪəbl] ADJ soggetto(-a) a dazio

dutiful ['dju:tɪful] ADJ (child) rispettoso(-a); (husband) premuroso(-a); (employee) coscienzioso(-a)

duty ['djuːtɪ] N dovere m; (tax) dazio, tassa; **duties** NPL mansioni fpl; **on** ~ di servizio; (Med: in hospital) di guardia; **off** ~ libero(a), fuori servizio; **to make it one's** ~ **to do sth** assumersi l'obbligo di fare qc; **to pay** ~ **on sth** pagare il dazio su qc

duty-free ['djuːtɪ'friː] ADJ esente da dazio; ~ **shop** duty free m inv

duty officer N (Mil etc) ufficiale m di servizio

duvet ['duːveɪ] (BRIT) N piumino, piumone m

DV ABBR (= Deo volente) D.V.

DVD N ABBR (= digital versatile or video disc) DVD m inv

DVD burner N masterizzatore m (di) DVD

DVD player N lettore m DVD

DVD writer N masterizzatore m (di) DVD

DVLA N ABBR (BRIT: = Driver and Vehicle Licensing Agency) ≈ I.M.C.T.C. m (= Ispettorato Generale della Motorizzazione Civile e dei Trasporti in Concessione)

DVM N ABBR (US: = Doctor of Veterinary Medicine) titolo di studio

DVT N ABBR = **deep-vein thrombosis**

dwarf [dwɔːf] N nano(-a) ▶ VT far apparire piccolo

dwell [dwɛl] (pt, pp **dwelt** [dwɛlt]) VI dimorare ▶ **dwell on** VT FUS indugiare su

dweller ['dwɛlər] N abitante mf; **city** ~ cittadino(-a)

dwelling ['dwɛlɪŋ] N dimora

dwelt [dwɛlt] PT, PP of **dwell**

dwindle ['dwɪndl] VI diminuire, decrescere

dwindling ['dwɪndlɪŋ] ADJ (strength, interest) che si affievolisce; (resources, supplies) in diminuzione

dye [daɪ] N colore m; (chemical) colorante m, tintura ▶ VT tingere; **hair** ~ tinta per capelli

dyestuffs ['daɪstʌfs] NPL coloranti mpl

dying ['daɪɪŋ] ADJ morente, moribondo(-a)

dyke [daɪk] N diga; (channel) canale m di scolo; (causeway) sentiero rialzato

dynamic [daɪ'næmɪk] ADJ dinamico(-a)

dynamics [daɪ'næmɪks] N, NPL dinamica

dynamite ['daɪnəmaɪt] N dinamite f ▶ VT far saltare con la dinamite

dynamo ['daɪnəməu] N dinamo f inv

dynasty ['dɪnəstɪ] N dinastia

dysentery ['dɪsntrɪ] N dissenteria

dyslexia [dɪs'lɛksɪə] N dislessia

dyslexic [dɪs'lɛksɪk] ADJ, N dislessico(-a)

dyspepsia [dɪs'pɛpsɪə] N dispepsia

dystrophy ['dɪstrəfɪ] N distrofia; **muscular** ~ distrofia muscolare

d

Ee

E, e [iː] N (letter) E, e f inv or m inv; (Mus): **E** mi m; **E for Edward**, (US) **E for Easy** ≈ E come Empoli

E ABBR (= east) E ▶ N ABBR (= Ecstasy) ecstasy f inv

e- [iː] PREFIX e-

E111 N ABBR (formerly: also: **form E111**) E111 (modulo UE per rimborso spese mediche)

ea. ABBR = **each**

each [iːtʃ] ADJ ogni, ciascuno(-a) ▶ PRON ciascuno(-a), ognuno(-a); **~ one** ognuno(a); **~ other** si (or ci etc); **they hate ~ other** si odiano (l'un l'altro); **you are jealous of ~ other** siete gelosi l'uno dell'altro; **~ day** ogni giorno; **they have 2 books ~** hanno 2 libri ciascuno; **they cost £5 ~** costano 5 sterline l'uno; **~ of us** ciascuno or ognuno di noi

eager ['iːgəʳ] ADJ impaziente; desideroso(-a); ardente; (keen: pupil) appassionato(-a), attento(-a); **to be ~ to do sth** non veder l'ora di fare qc; essere desideroso di fare qc; **to be ~ for** essere desideroso di, aver gran voglia di

eagle ['iːgl] N aquila

E & OE ABBR (= errors and omissions excepted) S.E.O.

ear [ɪəʳ] N orecchio; (of corn) pannocchia; **up to the ears in debt** nei debiti fino al collo

earache ['ɪəreɪk] N mal m d'orecchi

eardrum ['ɪədrʌm] N timpano

earful ['ɪəful] N: **to give sb an ~** fare una ramanzina a qn

earl [əːl] (BRIT) N conte m

earlier ['əːlɪəʳ] ADJ (date etc) anteriore; (edition etc) precedente, anteriore ▶ ADV prima; **I can't come any ~** non posso venire prima

early ['əːlɪ] ADV presto, di buon'ora; (ahead of time) in anticipo ▶ ADJ primo(-a); anticipato(-a); (man) primitivo(-a); (quick: reply) veloce; **~ in the morning/afternoon** nelle prime ore del mattino/del pomeriggio; **you're ~!** sei in anticipo!; **at an ~ hour** di buon'ora; **have an ~ night/start** vada a letto/parta presto; **in the ~** or **~ in the**

spring/19th century all'inizio della primavera/dell'Ottocento; **she's in her ~ forties** ha appena passato la quarantina; **at your earliest convenience** (Comm) non appena possibile

early retirement N prepensionamento

early warning system N sistema m di preallarme

earmark ['ɪəmɑːk] VT: **to ~ sth for** destinare qc a

earn [əːn] VT guadagnare; (rest, reward) meritare; (Comm: yield) maturare; **to ~ one's living** guadagnarsi da vivere; **this earned him much praise, he earned much praise for this** si è attirato grandi lodi per questo

earned income N reddito da lavoro

earnest ['əːnɪst] ADJ serio(-a) ▶ N (also: **earnest money**) caparra; **in ~** adv sul serio

earnings ['əːnɪŋz] NPL guadagni mpl; (of company etc) proventi mpl; (salary) stipendio

ear, nose and throat specialist N otorinolaringoiatra mf

earphones ['ɪəfəunz] NPL cuffia

earplugs ['ɪəplʌgz] NPL tappi mpl per le orecchie

earring ['ɪərɪŋ] N orecchino

earshot ['ɪəʃɔt] N: **out of/within ~** fuori portata/a portata d'orecchio

earth [əːθ] N (gen: also BRIT Elec) terra; (of fox etc) tana ▶ VT (BRIT Elec) mettere a terra

earthenware ['əːθənwɛəʳ] N terracotta; stoviglie fpl di terracotta ▶ ADJ di terracotta

earthly ['əːθlɪ] ADJ terreno(-a); **~ paradise** paradiso terrestre; **there is no ~ reason to think ...** non vi è ragione di pensare ...

earthquake ['əːθkweɪk] N terremoto

earth-shattering ['əːθʃætərɪŋ] ADJ stupefacente

earth tremor N scossa sismica

earthworks ['əːθwəːks] NPL lavori mpl di sterro

earthworm ['əːθwəːm] N lombrico

earthy ['əːθɪ] ADJ (fig) grossolano(-a)

earwax ['ɪəwæks] N cerume m

earwig ['ɪəwɪg] N forbicina
ease [iːz] N agio, comodo ▶ VT (soothe)
calmare; (loosen) allentare ▶ VI (situation)
allentarsi, distendersi; **life of ~** vita comoda;
with ~ senza difficoltà; **at ~** a proprio agio;
(Mil) a riposo; **to feel at ~/ill at ~** sentirsi a
proprio agio/a disagio; **to ~ sth out/in** tirare
fuori/infilare qc con delicatezza; facilitare
l'uscita/l'entrata di qc
  ▶ **ease off, ease up** VI diminuire; (slow down)
  rallentarsi; (fig) rilassarsi
easel ['iːzl] N cavalletto
easily ['iːzɪlɪ] ADV facilmente
easiness ['iːzɪnɪs] N facilità, semplicità;
(of manners) disinvoltura
east [iːst] N est m ▶ ADJ dell'est ▶ ADV a
oriente; **the E~** l'Oriente m; (Pol) i Paesi
dell'Est
eastbound ['iːstbaʊnd] ADJ (traffic)
diretto(-a) a est; (carriageway) che porta
a est
Easter ['iːstə'] N Pasqua ▶ ADJ (holidays)
pasquale, di Pasqua
Easter egg N uovo di Pasqua
Easter Island N isola di Pasqua
easterly ['iːstəlɪ] ADJ dell'est, d'oriente
Easter Monday N Pasquetta
eastern ['iːstən] ADJ orientale, d'oriente;
(Pol) dell'est; **E~ Europe** l'Europa orientale;
the E~ bloc (Pol) i Paesi dell'Est
Easter Sunday N domenica di Pasqua
East Germany N (formerly) Germania dell'Est
eastward ['iːstwəd], **eastwards** ['iːstwədz]
ADV verso est, verso levante
easy ['iːzɪ] ADJ facile; (manner) disinvolto(-a);
(carefree: life) agiato(-a), tranquillo(-a) ▶ ADV:
to take it or **things ~** prendersela con calma;
I'm ~ (col) non ho problemi; **easier said
than done** tra il dire e il fare c'è di mezzo il
mare; **payment on ~ terms** (Comm)
facilitazioni fpl di pagamento
easy chair N poltrona
easy-going ['iːzɪ'gəʊɪŋ] ADJ accomodante
eat [iːt] (pt **ate** [eɪt], pp **eaten** ['iːtn]) VT
mangiare
  ▶ **eat away** VT (sea) erodere; (acid) corrodere
  ▶ **eat away at, eat into** VT FUS rodere
  ▶ **eat out** VI mangiare fuori
  ▶ **eat up** VT (meal etc) finire di mangiare; **it
  eats up electricity** consuma un sacco di
  corrente
eatable ['iːtəbl] ADJ mangiabile; (safe to eat)
commestibile
eaten ['iːtn] PP of **eat**
eau de Cologne ['əʊdəkə'ləʊn] N acqua di
colonia
eaves [iːvz] NPL gronda
eavesdrop ['iːvzdrɔp] VI: **to ~ (on a
conversation)** origliare (una conversazione)

ebb [ɛb] N riflusso ▶ VI rifluire; (fig: also: **ebb
away**) declinare; **~ and flow** flusso e
riflusso; **to be at a low ~** (fig: person, spirits)
avere il morale a terra; (: business) andar male
ebb tide N marea discendente
ebony ['ɛbənɪ] N ebano
e-book ['iːbuk] N libro elettronico
ebullient [ɪ'bʌlɪənt] ADJ esuberante
e-business ['iːbɪznɪs] N (company) azienda
che opera in Internet; (commerce) commercio
elettronico
EC N ABBR (= European Community) CE f
e-card ['iːkɑːd] N e-card f inv, cartolina
virtuale
ECB N ABBR (= European Central Bank) BCE f
eccentric [ɪk'sɛntrɪk] ADJ, N eccentrico(-a)
ecclesiastic [ɪkliːzɪ'æstɪk] N ecclesiastico
▶ ADJ ecclesiastico(-a)
ecclesiastical [ɪkliːzɪ'æstɪkəl] ADJ
ecclesiastico(-a)
ECG N ABBR = **electrocardiogram**
echo ['ɛkəʊ] (pl **echoes**) N eco m or f ▶ VT
ripetere; fare eco a ▶ VI echeggiare; dare
un eco
éclair ['eɪklɛə'] N ≈ bignè m inv
eclipse [ɪ'klɪps] N eclissi f inv ▶ VT eclissare
eco... ['iːkəʊ] PREFIX eco...
eco-friendly [iːkəʊ'frɛndlɪ] ADJ ecologico(-a)
ecological [iːkə'lɔdʒɪkəl] ADJ ecologico(-a)
ecologist [ɪ'kɔlədʒɪst] N ecologo(-a)
ecology [ɪ'kɔlədʒɪ] N ecologia
e-commerce [iːˈkɔmɜːs] N commercio
elettronico, e-commerce m inv
economic [iːkə'nɔmɪk] ADJ economico(-a);
(profitable: price) vantaggioso(-a); (: business)
che rende
economical [iːkə'nɔmɪkəl] ADJ
economico(-a); (person) economo(-a)
economically [iːkə'nɔmɪklɪ] ADV con
economia; (regarding economics) dal punto di
vista economico
economics [iːkə'nɔmɪks] N economia ▶ NPL
(financial aspect) lato finanziario
economist [ɪ'kɔnəmɪst] N economista mf
economize [ɪ'kɔnəmaɪz] VI risparmiare, fare
economia
economy [ɪ'kɔnəmɪ] N economia;
economies of scale (Comm) economie fpl di
scala
economy class N (Aviat etc) classe f
turistica
economy class syndrome N sindrome f
della classe economica
economy size N confezione f economica
ecosystem ['iːkəʊsɪstəm] N ecosistema m
eco-tourism [iːkəʊ'tuərɪzəm] N ecoturismo
ECSC N ABBR (= European Coal & Steel Community)
C.E.C.A. f (= Comunità Europea del Carbone e
dell'Acciaio)

ecstasy ['ɛkstəsɪ] N estasi f inv; **to go into ecstasies over** andare in estasi davanti a; **E-** (drug) ecstasy f inv

ecstatic [ɛks'tætɪk] ADJ estatico(-a), in estasi

ECT N ABBR = **electroconvulsive therapy**

ECU, ecu ['eɪkjuː] N ABBR (= European Currency Unit) ECU f inv, ecu f inv

Ecuador ['ɛkwədɔːʳ] N Ecuador m

ecumenical [iːkjuː'mɛnɪkl] ADJ ecumenico(-a)

eczema ['ɛksɪmə] N eczema m

eddy ['ɛdɪ] N mulinello

edge [ɛdʒ] N margine m; (of table, plate, cup) orlo; (of knife etc) taglio ▶ VT bordare ▶ VI: **to ~ away from** sgattaiolare da; **to ~ past** passar rasente; **to ~ forward** avanzare a poco a poco; **on ~** (fig) = **edgy; to have the ~ on** essere in vantaggio su; **to ~ away from** sgattaiolare da

edgeways ['ɛdʒweɪz] ADV di fianco; **he couldn't get a word in ~** non riuscì a dire una parola

edging ['ɛdʒɪŋ] N bordo

edgy ['ɛdʒɪ] ADJ nervoso(-a)

edible ['ɛdɪbl] ADJ commestibile; (meal) mangiabile

edict ['iːdɪkt] N editto

edifice ['ɛdɪfɪs] N edificio

edifying ['ɛdɪfaɪɪŋ] ADJ edificante

Edinburgh ['ɛdɪnbərə] N Edimburgo f

edit ['ɛdɪt] VT curare; (newspaper, magazine) dirigere; (Comput) correggere e modificare, editare

edition [ɪ'dɪʃən] N edizione f

editor ['ɛdɪtəʳ] N (in newspaper) redattore(-trice); redattore(-trice) capo; (of sb's work) curatore(-trice); (film editor) responsabile mf del montaggio

editorial [ɛdɪ'tɔːrɪəl] ADJ redazionale, editoriale ▶ N editoriale m; **the ~ staff** la redazione

EDP N ABBR = **electronic data processing**

EDT ABBR (US: = Eastern Daylight Time) ora legale di New York

educate ['ɛdjukeɪt] VT istruire; educare

educated ADJ istruito(-a)

educated guess ['ɛdjukeɪtɪd-] N ipotesi f ben fondata

education [ɛdju'keɪʃən] N (teaching) insegnamento; (schooling) istruzione f; (knowledge, culture) cultura; (Scol: subject etc) pedagogia; **primary** or (US) **elementary/secondary ~** scuola primaria/secondaria

educational [ɛdju'keɪʃənl] ADJ pedagogico(-a); scolastico(-a); istruttivo(-a); **~ technology** tecnologie fpl applicate alla didattica

Edwardian [ɛd'wɔːdɪən] ADJ edoardiano(-a)

EE ABBR = **electrical engineer**

EEG N ABBR = **electroencephalogram**

eel [iːl] N anguilla

EENT N ABBR (US Med) = **eye, ear, nose and throat**

EEOC N ABBR (US) = **Equal Employment Opportunity Commission**

eerie ['ɪərɪ] ADJ che fa accapponare la pelle

EET ABBR (= Eastern European Time) fuso orario

effect [ɪ'fɛkt] N effetto ▶ VT effettuare; **to take ~** (law) entrare in vigore; (drug) fare effetto; **to have an ~ on sb/sth** avere or produrre un effetto su qn/qc; **to put into ~** (plan) attuare; **in ~** effettivamente; **his letter is to the ~ that ...** il contenuto della sua lettera è che ...; see also **effects**

effective [ɪ'fɛktɪv] ADJ efficace; (actual) effettivo(-a); (striking: display, outfit) che fa colpo; **~ date** data d'entrata in vigore; **to become ~** (law) entrare in vigore

effectively [ɪ'fɛktɪvlɪ] ADV (efficiently) efficacemente; effettivamente; (strikingly) ad effetto; (in reality) di fatto; (in effect) in effetti

effectiveness [ɪ'fɛktɪvnɪs] N efficacia

effects [ɪ'fɛkts] NPL (Theat) effetti mpl scenici; (property) effetti mpl

effeminate [ɪ'fɛmɪnɪt] ADJ effeminato(-a)

effervescent [ɛfə'vɛsnt] ADJ effervescente

efficacy ['ɛfɪkəsɪ] N efficacia

efficiency [ɪ'fɪʃənsɪ] N efficienza; rendimento effettivo

efficiency apartment N (US) miniappartamento

efficient [ɪ'fɪʃənt] ADJ efficiente; (remedy, product, system) efficace; (machine, car) che ha un buon rendimento

efficiently [ɪ'fɪʃəntlɪ] ADV efficientemente; efficacemente

effigy ['ɛfɪdʒɪ] N effigie f

effluent ['ɛfluənt] N effluente m

effort ['ɛfət] N sforzo; **to make an ~ to do sth** sforzarsi di fare qc

effortless ['ɛfətlɪs] ADJ senza sforzo, facile

effrontery [ɪ'frʌntərɪ] N sfrontatezza

effusive [ɪ'fjuːsɪv] ADJ (person) espansivo(-a); (welcome, letter) caloroso(-a); (thanks, apologies) interminabile

EFL N ABBR (Scol) = **English as a foreign language**

EFTA ['ɛftə] N ABBR (= European Free Trade Association) E.F.T.A. f

e.g. ADV ABBR (= exempli gratia) per esempio, p.es.

egalitarian [ɪgælɪ'tɛərɪən] ADJ egualitario(-a)

egg [ɛg] N uovo; **hard-boiled/soft-boiled ~** uovo sodo/alla coque
▶ **egg on** VT incitare

eggcup ['ɛgkʌp] N portauovo m inv

eggplant ['ɛgplɑːnt] N (esp US) melanzana

eggshell ['εgʃεl] N guscio d'uovo ▶ADJ (colour) guscio d'uovo inv

egg-timer ['εgtaɪmə^r] N clessidra (per misurare il tempo di cottura delle uova)

egg white N albume m, bianco d'uovo

egg yolk N tuorlo, rosso (d'uovo)

ego ['i:gəu] N ego m inv

egoism ['εgəuɪzəm] N egoismo

egoist ['εgəuɪst] N egoista mf

egotism ['εgəutɪzəm] N egotismo

egotist ['εgəutɪst] N egotista mf

ego trip N: **to be on an ~** gasarsi

Egypt ['i:dʒɪpt] N Egitto

Egyptian [ɪ'dʒɪpʃən] ADJ, N egiziano(-a)

eiderdown ['aɪdədaun] N piumino

eight [eɪt] NUM otto

eighteen ['eɪ'ti:n] NUM diciotto

eighteenth NUM diciottesimo(-a)

eighth [eɪtθ] NUM ottavo(-a)

eightieth ['eɪtɪɪθ] NUM ottantesimo(-a)

eighty [eɪtɪ] NUM ottanta

Eire ['εərə] N Repubblica d'Irlanda

EIS N ABBR (= Educational Institute of Scotland) principale sindacato degli insegnanti in Scozia

either ['aɪðə^r] ADJ l'uno(-a) o l'altro(-a); (both, each) ciascuno(-a); **on ~ side** su ciascun lato ▶PRON: **~ (of them)** (o) l'uno(a) o l'altro(a); **I don't like ~** non mi piace né l'uno né l'altro ▶ADV neanche; **no, I don't ~** no, neanch'io ▶CONJ: **~ good or bad** o buono o cattivo; **I haven't seen ~ one or the other** non ho visto né l'uno né l'altro

ejaculation [ɪdʒækju'leɪʃən] N (Physiol) eiaculazione f

eject [ɪ'dʒεkt] VT espellere; lanciare ▶VI (pilot) catapultarsi

ejector seat [ɪ'dʒεktə-] N sedile m eiettabile

eke [i:k]: **to ~ out** vt far durare; aumentare

EKG N ABBR (US) = **electrocardiogram**

el [εl] N ABBR (US col) = **elevated railroad**

elaborate ADJ [ɪ'læbərɪt] elaborato(-a), minuzioso(-a) ▶VT [ɪ'læbəreɪt] elaborare ▶VI [ɪ'læbəreɪt] fornire i dettagli

elapse [ɪ'læps] VI trascorrere, passare

elastic [ɪ'læstɪk] ADJ elastico(-a) ▶N elastico

elastic band N (BRIT) elastico

elasticity [ɪlæs'tɪsɪtɪ] N elasticità

elated [ɪ'leɪtɪd] ADJ pieno(-a) di gioia

elation [ɪ'leɪʃən] N gioia

elbow ['εlbəu] N gomito ▶VT: **to ~ one's way through the crowd** farsi largo tra la folla a gomitate

elbow grease N: **to use a bit of ~** usare un po' di olio di gomiti

elbowroom ['εlbəurum] N spazio

elder ['εldə^r] ADJ maggiore, più vecchio(-a) ▶N (tree) sambuco; **one's elders** i più anziani

elderly ['εldəlɪ] ADJ anziano(-a) ▶NPL: **the ~** gli anziani

elder statesman N (irreg) anziano uomo politico in pensione, ma ancora influente; (of company) anziano(-a) consigliere(-a)

eldest ['εldɪst] ADJ, N: **the ~ (child)** il(la) maggiore (dei bambini)

elect [ɪ'lεkt] VT eleggere; (choose): **to ~ to do** decidere di fare ▶ADJ: **the president ~** il presidente designato

election [ɪ'lεkʃən] N elezione f; **to hold an ~** indire un'elezione

election campaign N campagna elettorale

electioneering [ɪlεkʃə'nɪərɪŋ] N propaganda elettorale

elector [ɪ'lεktə^r] N elettore(-trice)

electoral [ɪ'lεktərəl] ADJ elettorale

electoral college N collegio elettorale

electoral roll N (BRIT) registro elettorale

electoral system N sistema m elettorale

electorate [ɪ'lεktərɪt] N elettorato

electric [ɪ'lεktrɪk] ADJ elettrico(-a)

electrical [ɪ'lεktrɪkəl] ADJ elettrico(-a)

electrical engineer N ingegnere m elettrotecnico

electrical failure N guasto all'impianto elettrico

electric blanket N coperta elettrica

electric chair N sedia elettrica

electric cooker N cucina elettrica

electric current N corrente f elettrica

electric fire N (BRIT) stufa elettrica

electrician [ɪlεk'trɪʃən] N elettricista m

electricity [ɪlεk'trɪsɪtɪ] N elettricità; **to switch on/off the ~** attaccare/staccare la corrente

electricity board N (BRIT) ente m regionale per l'energia elettrica

electric light N luce f elettrica

electric shock N scossa (elettrica)

electrify [ɪ'lεktrɪfaɪ] VT (Rail) elettrificare; (audience) elettrizzare

electro... [ɪ'lεktrəu] PREFIX elettro...

electrocardiogram [ɪ'lεktrə'ka:dɪəgræm] N elettrocardiogramma m

electroconvulsive therapy [ɪ'lεktrəkən'vʌlsɪv-] N elettroshockterapia

electrocute [ɪ'lεktrəkju:t] VT fulminare

electrode [ɪ'lεktrəud] N elettrodo

electroencephalogram [ɪ'lεktrəuen'sεfələgræm] N (Med) elettroencefalogramma m

electrolysis [ɪlεk'trɒlɪsɪs] N elettrolisi f

electromagnetic [ɪ'lεktrəumæg'nεtɪk] N elettromagnetico(-a)

electron [ɪ'lεktrɒn] N elettrone m

electronic [ɪlεk'trɒnɪk] ADJ elettronico(-a); see also **electronics**

electronic data processing N elaborazione f elettronica di dati

electronic mail N posta elettronica

electronics [ɪlɛk'trɒnɪks] N elettronica

electron microscope N microscopio elettronico

electroplated [ɪ'lɛktrəʊ'pleɪtɪd] ADJ galvanizzato(-a)

electrotherapy [ɪ'lɛktrəʊ'θɛrəpɪ] N elettroterapia

elegance ['ɛlɪgəns] N eleganza

elegant ['ɛlɪgənt] ADJ elegante

element ['ɛlɪmənt] N elemento; (of heater, kettle etc) resistenza

elementary [ɛlɪ'mɛntərɪ] ADJ elementare

elementary school N (US) scuola elementare; vedi nota

> Negli Stati Uniti e in Canada, i bambini frequentano la *elementary school* per almeno sei anni, a volte anche per otto. Negli Stati Uniti si chiama anche *grade school* o *grammar school*.

elephant ['ɛlɪfənt] N elefante(-essa)

elevate ['ɛlɪveɪt] VT elevare

elevated railroad, el N (US) (ferrovia) soprelevata

elevation [ɛlɪ'veɪʃən] N elevazione f; (height) altitudine f

elevator ['ɛlɪveɪtər] N elevatore m; (US: lift) ascensore m

eleven [ɪ'lɛvn] NUM undici

elevenses [ɪ'lɛvnzɪz] NPL (BRIT) caffè m a metà mattina

eleventh [ɪ'lɛvnθ] ADJ undicesimo(-a); **at the ~ hour** (fig) all'ultimo minuto

elf [ɛlf] (pl **elves** [ɛlvz]) N elfo

elicit [ɪ'lɪsɪt] VT: **to ~ (from)** trarre (da), cavare fuori (da); **to ~ sth (from sb)** strappare qc (a qn)

eligible ['ɛlɪdʒəbl] ADJ eleggibile; (for membership) che ha i requisiti; **to be ~ for a pension** essere pensionabile

eliminate [ɪ'lɪmɪneɪt] VT eliminare

elimination [ɪlɪmɪ'neɪʃən] N eliminazione f; **by process of ~** per eliminazione

élite [eɪ'liːt] N élite f inv

elitist [eɪ'liːtɪst] ADJ (pej) elitario(-a)

elixir [ɪ'lɪksər] N elisir m inv

Elizabethan [ɪlɪzə'biːθən] N elisabettiano(-a)

ellipse [ɪ'lɪps] N ellisse f

elliptical [ɪ'lɪptɪkl] ADJ ellittico(-a)

elm [ɛlm] N olmo

elocution [ɛlə'kjuːʃən] N elocuzione f

elongated ['iːlɒŋgeɪtɪd] ADJ allungato(-a)

elope [ɪ'ləʊp] VI (lovers) scappare

elopement [ɪ'ləʊpmənt] N fuga romantica

eloquence ['ɛləkwəns] N eloquenza

eloquent ['ɛləkwənt] ADJ eloquente

else [ɛls] ADV altro; **something ~** qualcos'altro; **somewhere ~** altrove; **everywhere ~** in qualsiasi altro luogo; **nobody ~** nessun altro; **where ~?** in quale

altro luogo?; **little ~** poco altro; **everyone ~** tutti gli altri; **nothing ~** nient'altro; **or ~** (otherwise) altrimenti; **is there anything ~ I can do?** posso fare qualcos'altro?

elsewhere [ɛls'wɛər] ADV altrove

ELT N ABBR (Scol) = **English Language Teaching**

elucidate [ɪ'luːsɪdeɪt] VT delucidare

elude [ɪ'luːd] VT eludere

elusive [ɪ'luːsɪv] ADJ elusivo(-a); (answer) evasivo(-a); **he is very ~** è proprio inafferrabile or irraggiungibile

elves [ɛlvz] NPL of **elf**

emaciated [ɪ'meɪsɪeɪtɪd] ADJ emaciato(-a)

email ['iːmeɪl] N ABBR (= electronic mail) posta elettronica, e-mail m inv ▶ VT mandare un messaggio di posta elettronica or un e-mail a; **to ~ sb** comunicare con qn mediante posta elettronica; **~ account** account m inv di posta elettronica

email address N indirizzo di posta elettronica

emanate ['ɛməneɪt] VI: **to ~ from** emanare da

emancipate [ɪ'mænsɪpeɪt] VT emancipare

emancipation [ɪmænsɪ'peɪʃən] N emancipazione f

emasculate [ɪ'mæskjuleɪt] VT (fig) rendere impotente

embalm [ɪm'bɑːm] VT imbalsamare

embankment [ɪm'bæŋkmənt] N (of road, railway) massicciata; (riverside) argine m; (dyke) diga

embargo [ɪm'bɑːgəʊ] (pl **embargoes**) N (Comm, Naut) embargo ▶ VT mettere l'embargo su; **to put an ~ on sth** mettere l'embargo su qc

embark [ɪm'bɑːk] VI: **to ~ (on)** imbarcarsi (su) ▶ VT imbarcare; **to ~ on** (fig) imbarcarsi in; (journey) intraprendere

embarkation [ɛmbɑː'keɪʃən] N imbarco

embarkation card N carta d'imbarco

embarrass [ɪm'bærəs] VT imbarazzare

embarrassed ADJ imbarazzato(-a); **to be ~** essere imbarazzato(-a)

embarrassing [ɪm'bærəsɪŋ] ADJ imbarazzante

embarrassment [ɪm'bærəsmənt] N imbarazzo

embassy ['ɛmbəsɪ] N ambasciata; **the Italian E~** l'ambasciata d'Italia

embed [ɪm'bɛd] VT conficcare; incastrare

embellish [ɪm'bɛlɪʃ] VT abbellire; **to ~ (with)** (fig: story, truth) infiorare (con)

embers ['ɛmbəz] NPL braci fpl

embezzle [ɪm'bɛzl] VT appropriarsi indebitamente di

embezzlement [ɪm'bɛzlmənt] N appropriazione f indebita, malversazione f

embezzler [ɪm'bɛzlə^r] N malversatore(-trice)
embitter [ɪm'bɪtə^r] VT amareggiare; inasprire
emblem ['ɛmbləm] N emblema *m*
embodiment [ɪm'bɔdɪmənt] N personificazione *f*, incarnazione *f*
embody [ɪm'bɔdɪ] VT (*features*) racchiudere, comprendere; (*ideas*) dar forma concreta a, esprimere
embolden [ɪm'bəuldn] VT incitare
embolism ['ɛmbəlɪzəm] N embolia
embossed [ɪm'bɔst] ADJ in rilievo; goffrato(-a); **~ with ...** con in rilievo ...
embrace [ɪm'breɪs] VT abbracciare; (*include*) comprendere ▶ VI abbracciarsi ▶ N abbraccio
embroider [ɪm'brɔɪdə^r] VT ricamare; (*fig: story*) abbellire
embroidery [ɪm'brɔɪdərɪ] N ricamo
embroil [ɪm'brɔɪl] VT: **to become embroiled (in sth)** restare invischiato(a) (in qc)
embryo ['ɛmbrɪəu] N (*also fig*) embrione *m*
emcee [ɛm'si:] N ABBR = **master of ceremonies**
emend [ɪ'mɛnd] VT (*text*) correggere, emendare
emerald ['ɛmərəld] N smeraldo
emerge [ɪ'mə:dʒ] VI apparire, emergere; **it emerges that** (*BRIT*) risulta che
emergence [ɪ'mə:dʒəns] N apparizione *f*; (*of nation*) nascita
emergency [ɪ'mə:dʒənsɪ] N emergenza; **in an ~** in caso di emergenza; **to declare a state of ~** dichiarare lo stato di emergenza
emergency brake (*US*) N freno a mano
emergency exit N uscita di sicurezza
emergency landing N atterraggio forzato
emergency lane N (*US Aut*) corsia d'emergenza
emergency road service N (*US*) servizio riparazioni
emergency room (*US Med*) N pronto soccorso
emergency service N servizio di pronto intervento
emergency stop N (*BRIT Aut*) frenata improvvisa
emergent [ɪ'mə:dʒənt] ADJ: **~ nation** paese *m* in via di sviluppo
emery board ['ɛmərɪ-] N limetta di carta smerigliata
emery paper N carta smerigliata
emetic [ɪ'mɛtɪk] N emetico
emigrant ['ɛmɪɡrənt] N emigrante *mf*
emigrate ['ɛmɪɡreɪt] VI emigrare
emigration [ɛmɪ'ɡreɪʃən] N emigrazione *f*
émigré ['ɛmɪɡreɪ] N emigrato(-a)
eminence ['ɛmɪnəns] N eminenza
eminent ['ɛmɪnənt] ADJ eminente
eminently ['ɛmɪnəntlɪ] ADV assolutamente, perfettamente

emirate [ɛ'mɪərɪt] N emirato
emission [ɪ'mɪʃən] N (*of gas, radiation*) emissione *f*
emit [ɪ'mɪt] VT emettere
emolument [ɪ'mɔljumənt] N (*often pl: formal*) emolumento
emoticon [ɪ'məutɪkən] N (*Comput*) faccina
emotion [ɪ'məuʃən] N emozione *f*; (*love, jealousy etc*) sentimento
emotional [ɪ'məuʃənl] ADJ (*person*) emotivo(-a); (*scene*) commovente; (*tone, speech*) carico(-a) d'emozione
emotionally [ɪ'məuʃnəlɪ] ADV (*behave, be involved*) sentimentalmente; (*speak*) con emozione; **~ disturbed** con turbe emotive
emotive [ɪ'məutɪv] ADJ emotivo(-a); **~ power** capacità di commuovere
empathy ['ɛmpəθɪ] N immedesimazione *f*; **to feel ~ with sb** immedesimarsi con i sentimenti di qn
emperor ['ɛmpərə^r] N imperatore *m*
emphasis ['ɛmfəsɪs] (*pl* **emphases** [-si:z]) N enfasi *f inv*; importanza; **to lay** *or* **place ~ on sth** (*fig*) mettere in risalto *or* in evidenza qc; **the ~ is on sport** si dà molta importanza allo sport
emphasize ['ɛmfəsaɪz] VT (*word, point*) sottolineare; (*feature*) mettere in evidenza
emphatic [ɪm'fætɪk] ADJ (*strong*) vigoroso(-a); (*unambiguous, clear*) netto(-a), categorico(-a)
emphatically [ɪm'fætɪkəlɪ] ADV vigorosamente; nettamente
emphysema [ɛmfɪ'si:mə] N (*Med*) enfisema *m*
empire ['ɛmpaɪə^r] N impero
empirical [ɛm'pɪrɪkl] ADJ empirico(-a)
employ [ɪm'plɔɪ] VT (*make use of: thing, method, person*) impiegare, servirsi di; (*give job to*) dare lavoro a, impiegare; **he's employed in a bank** lavora in banca
employee [ɪmplɔɪ'i:] N impiegato(-a)
employer [ɪm'plɔɪə^r] N principale *mf*, datore *m* di lavoro
employment [ɪm'plɔɪmənt] N impiego; **to find ~** trovare impiego *or* lavoro; **without ~** disoccupato(a); **place of ~** posto di lavoro
employment agency N agenzia di collocamento
employment exchange N (*BRIT*) ufficio *m* collocamento *inv*
empower [ɪm'pauə^r] VT: **to ~ sb to do** concedere autorità a qn di fare
empress ['ɛmprɪs] N imperatrice *f*
emptiness ['ɛmptɪnɪs] N vuoto
empty ['ɛmptɪ] ADJ vuoto(-a); (*street, area*) deserto(-a); (*threat, promise*) vano(-a) ▶ N (*bottle*) vuoto ▶ VT vuotare ▶ VI vuotarsi; (*liquid*) scaricarsi; **on an ~ stomach** a stomaco vuoto; **to ~ into** (*river*) gettarsi in

empty-handed [ɛmptɪˈhændɪd] ADJ a mani vuote

empty-headed [ɛmptɪˈhɛdɪd] ADJ sciocco(-a)

EMS N ABBR (= European Monetary System) S.M.E. m

EMT N ABBR (US) = **emergency medical technician**

EMU N ABBR (= European Monetary Union) Unità f monetaria europea; (= economic and monetary union) UEM f

emulate [ˈɛmjuleɪt] VT emulare

emulsion [ɪˈmʌlʃən] N emulsione f; (also: **emulsion paint**) colore m a tempera

enable [ɪˈneɪbl] VT: **to ~ sb to do** permettere a qn di fare

enact [ɪnˈækt] VT (law) emanare; (play, scene) rappresentare

enamel [ɪˈnæməl] N smalto

enamel paint N vernice f a smalto

enamoured [ɪˈnæməd] ADJ: **~ of** innamorato(a) di

enc. ABBR (on letters etc: = enclosed, enclosure) all., alleg.

encampment [ɪnˈkæmpmənt] N accampamento

encased [ɪnˈkeɪst] ADJ: **~ in** racchiuso(a) in, rivestito(a) di

enchant [ɪnˈtʃɑːnt] VT incantare; (magic spell) catturare

enchanting [ɪnˈtʃɑːntɪŋ] ADJ incantevole, affascinante

encircle [ɪnˈsəːkl] VT accerchiare

encl. ABBR (on letters etc: = enclosed, enclosure) all., alleg.

enclose [ɪnˈkləuz] VT (land) circondare, recingere; (letter etc) **to ~ (with)** allegare (con); **please find enclosed** trovi qui accluso

enclosure [ɪnˈkləuʒər] N recinto; (Comm) allegato

encoder [ɪnˈkəudər] N (Comput) codificatore m

encompass [ɪnˈkʌmpəs] VT comprendere

encore [ɔŋˈkɔːr] EXCL, N bis (m inv)

encounter [ɪnˈkauntər] N incontro ▶ VT incontrare

encourage [ɪnˈkʌrɪdʒ] VT incoraggiare; (industry, growth etc) favorire; **to ~ sb to do sth** incoraggiare qn a fare qc

encouragement [ɪnˈkʌrɪdʒmənt] N incoraggiamento

encouraging [ɪnˈkʌrɪdʒɪŋ] ADJ incoraggiante

encroach [ɪnˈkrəutʃ] VI: **to ~ (up)on** (rights) usurpare; (time) abusare di; (land) oltrepassare i limiti di

encrusted [ɪnˈkrʌstɪd] ADJ: **~ with** incrostato(a) di

encrypt [ɪnˈkrɪpt] VT (Comput, Tel) criptare

encumbered [ɪnˈkʌmbəd] ADJ: **to be ~ (with)** essere carico(a) di

encyclopedia, encyclopaedia [ɛnsaɪkləuˈpiːdɪə] N enciclopedia

end [ɛnd] N fine f; (aim) fine m; (of table) bordo estremo; (of line, rope etc) estremità f inv; (of pointed object) punta; (of town) parte f ▶ VT finire; (also: **bring to an end, put an end to**) mettere fine a ▶ VI finire; **from ~ to ~** da un'estremità all'altra; **to come to an ~** arrivare alla fine, finire; **to be at an ~** essere finito; **in the ~** alla fine; **at the ~ of the street** in fondo alla strada; **at the ~ of the day** (BRIT fig) in fin dei conti; **on ~** (object) ritto(a); **to stand on ~** (hair) rizzarsi; **for 5 hours on ~** per 5 ore di fila; **for hours on ~** per ore e ore; **to this ~, with this ~ in view** a questo fine; **to ~ (with)** concludere (con) ▶ **end up** VI: **to ~ up in** finire in

endanger [ɪnˈdeɪndʒər] VT mettere in pericolo; **an endangered species** una specie in via di estinzione

endear [ɪnˈdɪər] VT: **to ~ o.s. to sb** accattivarsi le simpatie di qn

endearing [ɪnˈdɪərɪŋ] ADJ accattivante

endearment [ɪnˈdɪəmənt] N: **to whisper endearments** sussurrare tenerezze; **term of ~** vezzeggiativo, parola affettuosa

endeavour, (US) **endeavor** [ɪnˈdɛvər] N sforzo, tentativo ▶ VI: **to ~ to do** cercare or sforzarsi di fare

endemic [ɛnˈdɛmɪk] ADJ endemico(-a)

ending [ˈɛndɪŋ] N fine f, conclusione f; (Ling) desinenza

endive [ˈɛndaɪv] N (curly) indivia (riccia); (smooth, flat) indivia belga

endless [ˈɛndlɪs] ADJ senza fine; (patience, resources) infinito(-a); (possibilities) illimitato(-a)

endorse [ɪnˈdɔːs] VT (cheque) girare; (approve) approvare, appoggiare

endorsee [ɪndɔːˈsiː] N giratario(-a)

endorsement [ɪnˈdɔːsmənt] N (approval) approvazione f; (signature) firma; (BRIT: on driving licence) contravvenzione registrata sulla patente

endorser [ɪnˈdɔːsər] N girante mf

endow [ɪnˈdau] VT (prize) istituire; (hospital) fondare; (provide with money) devolvere denaro a; (equip) **to ~ with** fornire di, dotare di

endowment [ɪnˈdaumənt] N istituzione f; fondazione f; (amount) donazione f

endowment mortgage N mutuo che viene ripagato sotto forma di un'assicurazione a vita

endowment policy N polizza-vita mista

end product N (Industry) prodotto finito; (fig) risultato

end result N risultato finale

endurable [ɪnˈdjuərəbl] ADJ sopportabile

endurance [ɪnˈdjuərəns] N resistenza; pazienza

endurance test N prova di resistenza

endure [ɪn'djuə^r] VT sopportare, resistere a ▸ VI durare

enduring [ɪn'djuərɪŋ] ADJ duraturo(-a)

end user N (*Comput*) consumatore(-trice) effettivo(-a)

enema ['ɛnɪmə] N (*Med*) clistere *m*

enemy ['ɛnəmɪ] ADJ, N nemico(-a); **to make an ~ of sb** inimicarsi qn

energetic [ɛnə'dʒɛtɪk] ADJ energico(-a), attivo(-a)

energy ['ɛnədʒɪ] N energia; **Department of E~** (*US*) Ministero dell'Energia

energy crisis N crisi *f* energetica

energy drink N bevanda energetica

energy-saving ['ɛnədʒɪ'seɪvɪŋ] ADJ (*policy*) del risparmio energetico; (*device*) che risparmia energia

enervating ['ɛnə:veɪtɪŋ] ADJ debilitante

enforce [ɪn'fɔːs] VT (*Law*) applicare, far osservare

enforced [ɪn'fɔːst] ADJ forzato(-a)

enfranchise [ɪn'fræntʃaɪz] VT (*give vote to*) concedere il diritto di voto a; (*set free*) affrancare

engage [ɪn'geɪdʒ] VT (*hire*) assumere; (*lawyer*) incaricare; (*attention, interest*) assorbire; (*Mil*) attaccare; (*Tech*): **to ~ gear/the clutch** innestare la marcia/la frizione ▸ VI (*Tech*) ingranare; **to ~ in** impegnarsi in; **he is engaged in research/a survey** si occupa di ricerca/di un'inchiesta; **to ~ sb in conversation** attaccare conversazione con qn

engaged [ɪn'geɪdʒd] ADJ (*BRIT: busy, in use*) occupato(-a); (*betrothed*) fidanzato(-a); **the line's ~** (*BRIT*) la linea è occupata; **to get ~** fidanzarsi

engaged tone N (*BRIT Tel*) segnale *m* di occupato

engagement [ɪn'geɪdʒmənt] N impegno, obbligo; appuntamento; (*to marry*) fidanzamento; (*Mil*) combattimento; **I have a previous ~** ho già un impegno

engagement ring N anello di fidanzamento

engaging [ɪn'geɪdʒɪŋ] ADJ attraente

engender [ɪn'dʒɛndə^r] VT produrre, causare

engine ['ɛndʒɪn] N (*Aut*) motore *m*; (*Rail*) locomotiva

engine driver N (*BRIT: of train*) macchinista *m*

engineer [ɛndʒɪ'nɪə^r] N ingegnere *m*; (*BRIT: for domestic appliances*) tecnico; (*US Rail*) macchinista *m*; **civil/mechanical ~** ingegnere civile/meccanico

engineering [ɛndʒɪ'nɪərɪŋ] N ingegneria ▸ CPD (*works, factory, worker etc*) metalmeccanico(-a)

engine failure N guasto al motore

engine trouble N panne *f*

England ['ɪŋglənd] N Inghilterra

English ['ɪŋglɪʃ] ADJ inglese ▸ N (*Ling*) inglese *m*; **the English** NPL gli Inglesi; **to be an ~ speaker** essere anglofono(-a)

English Channel N: **the ~** il Canale della Manica

Englishman ['ɪŋglɪʃmən] N (*irreg*) inglese *m*

English-speaking ['ɪŋglɪʃspiːkɪŋ] ADJ di lingua inglese

Englishwoman ['ɪŋglɪʃwumən] N (*irreg*) inglese *f*

engrave [ɪn'greɪv] VT incidere

engraving [ɪn'greɪvɪŋ] N incisione *f*

engrossed [ɪn'grəust] ADJ: **~ in** assorbito(-a) da, preso(a) da

engulf [ɪn'gʌlf] VT inghiottire

enhance [ɪn'hɑːns] VT accrescere; (*position, reputation*) migliorare

enigma [ɪ'nɪgmə] N enigma *m*

enigmatic [ɛnɪg'mætɪk] ADJ enigmatico(-a)

enjoy [ɪn'dʒɔɪ] VT godere; (*have: success, fortune*) avere; (*have benefit of: health*) godere (di); **I ~ dancing** mi piace ballare; **to ~ o.s.** godersela, divertirsi

enjoyable [ɪn'dʒɔɪəbl] ADJ piacevole

enjoyment [ɪn'dʒɔɪmənt] N piacere *m*, godimento

enlarge [ɪn'lɑːdʒ] VT ingrandire ▸ VI: **to ~ on** (*subject*) dilungarsi su

enlarged [ɪn'lɑːdʒd] ADJ (*edition*) ampliato(-a); (*Med: organ, gland*) ingrossato(-a)

enlargement [ɪn'lɑːdʒmənt] N (*Phot*) ingrandimento

enlighten [ɪn'laɪtn] VT illuminare; dare chiarimenti a

enlightened [ɪn'laɪtnd] ADJ illuminato(-a)

enlightening [ɪn'laɪtnɪŋ] ADJ istruttivo(-a)

enlightenment [ɪn'laɪtnmənt] N progresso culturale; chiarimenti *mpl*; (*Hist*): **the E~** l'Illuminismo

enlist [ɪn'lɪst] VT arruolare; (*support*) procurare ▸ VI arruolarsi; **enlisted man** (*US Mil*) soldato semplice

enliven [ɪn'laɪvn] VT (*people*) rallegrare; (*events*) ravvivare

enmity ['ɛnmɪtɪ] N inimicizia

ennoble [ɪ'nəubl] VT nobilitare; (*with title*) conferire un titolo nobiliare a

enormity [ɪ'nɔːmɪtɪ] N enormità *f inv*

enormous [ɪ'nɔːməs] ADJ enorme

enormously [ɪ'nɔːməslɪ] ADV enormemente

enough [ɪ'nʌf] ADJ, N: **~ time/books** assai tempo/libri; **have you got ~?** ne ha abbastanza *or* a sufficienza? ▸ ADV: **big ~** abbastanza grande; **he has not worked ~** non ha lavorato abbastanza; **~!** basta!; **it's hot ~ (as it is)!** fa abbastanza caldo così!; **will £5 be ~?** bastano 5 sterline?; **that's ~, thanks** basta così, grazie; **I've had ~!** non ne posso più!; **I've had ~ of him** ne ho abbastanza di lui; **he was kind ~ to lend me the money** è stato così gentile da prestarmi i soldi; **… which, funnily ~** … che, strano a dirsi

enquire [ɪnˈkwaɪəʳ] VT, VI (*esp BRIT*) = **inquire**
enquiry [ɪnˈkwaɪərɪ] N (*esp BRIT*) = **inquiry**
enrage [ɪnˈreɪdʒ] VT fare arrabbiare
enrich [ɪnˈrɪtʃ] VT arricchire
enrol, (*US*) **enroll** [ɪnˈrəul] VT iscrivere; (*at university*) immatricolare ▶ VI iscriversi
enrolment, (*US*) **enrollment** [ɪnˈrəulmənt] N iscrizione *f*
en route [ɔnˈruːt] ADV: **~ for/from/to** in viaggio per/da/a
ensconced [ɪnˈskɔnst] ADJ: **~ in** ben sistemato(a) in
ensemble [ãːnˈsãːmbl] N (*Mus*) ensemble *m inv*
enshrine [ɪnˈʃraɪn] VT conservare come una reliquia
ensign N (*Naut*) [ˈɛnsən] bandiera; (*Mil*) [ˈɛnsaɪn] portabandiera *m inv*
enslave [ɪnˈsleɪv] VT fare schiavo
ensue [ɪnˈsjuː] VI seguire, risultare
en suite [ɔnˈswiːt] ADJ: **room with ~ bathroom** camera con bagno
ensure [ɪnˈʃuəʳ] VT assicurare; garantire; **to ~ that** assicurarsi che
ENT N ABBR (*Med: = ear, nose and throat*) O.R.L.
entail [ɪnˈteɪl] VT comportare
entangle [ɪnˈtæŋgl] VT (*thread etc*) impigliare; **to become entangled in sth** (*fig*) rimanere impegolato in qc
enter [ˈɛntəʳ] VT (*gen*) entrare in; (*club*) associarsi a; (*profession*) intraprendere; (*army*) arruolarsi in; (*competition*) partecipare a; (*sb for a competition*) iscrivere; (*write down*) registrare; (*Comput: data*) introdurre, inserire ▶ VI entrare
▶ **enter for** VT FUS iscriversi a
▶ **enter into** VT FUS (*explanation*) cominciare a dare; (*debate*) partecipare a; (*agreement*) concludere; (*negotiations*) prendere parte a
▶ **enter (up)on** VT FUS cominciare
enteritis [ɛntəˈraɪtɪs] N enterite *f*
enterprise [ˈɛntəpraɪz] N (*undertaking, company*) impresa; (*spirit*) iniziativa; **free ~** liberalismo economico; **private ~** iniziativa privata
enterprising [ˈɛntəpraɪzɪŋ] ADJ intraprendente
entertain [ɛntəˈteɪn] VT divertire; (*invite*) ricevere; (*idea, plan*) nutrire
entertainer [ɛntəˈteɪnəʳ] N comico(-a)
entertaining [ɛntəˈteɪnɪŋ] ADJ divertente ▶ N: **to do a lot of ~** avere molti ospiti
entertainment [ɛntəˈteɪnmənt] N (*amusement*) divertimento; (*show*) spettacolo

entertainment allowance N spese *fpl* di rappresentanza
enthral [ɪnˈθrɔːl] VT affascinare, avvincere
enthralled [ɪnˈθrɔːld] ADJ affascinato(-a)
enthralling [ɪnˈθrɔːlɪŋ] ADJ avvincente
enthuse [ɪnˈθuːz] VI: **to ~ (about** or **over)** entusiasmarsi (per)
enthusiasm [ɪnˈθuːzɪæzəm] N entusiasmo
enthusiast [ɪnˈθuːzɪæst] N entusiasta *mf*; **a jazz** etc **~** un appassionato di jazz *etc*
enthusiastic [ɪnθuːzɪˈæstɪk] ADJ entusiasta, entusiastico(-a); **to be ~ about sth/sb** essere appassionato di qc/entusiasta di qn
entice [ɪnˈtaɪs] VT allettare, sedurre
enticing [ɪnˈtaɪsɪŋ] ADJ allettante
entire [ɪnˈtaɪəʳ] ADJ intero(-a)
entirely [ɪnˈtaɪəlɪ] ADV completamente, interamente
entirety [ɪnˈtaɪərətɪ] N: **in its ~** nel suo complesso
entitle [ɪnˈtaɪtl] VT (*give right*): **to ~ sb to sth/ to do** dare diritto a qn a qc/a fare
entitled [ɪnˈtaɪtld] ADJ (*book*) che si intitola; **to be ~ to sth** avere diritto a qc; **to be ~ to do sth** avere il diritto di fare qc
entity [ˈɛntɪtɪ] N entità *f inv*
entrails [ˈɛntreɪlz] NPL interiora *fpl*
entrance N [ˈɛntrns] entrata, ingresso; (*of person*) entrata ▶ VT [ɪnˈtrɑːns] incantare, rapire; **to gain ~ to** (*university etc*) essere ammesso a
entrance examination N (*to school*) esame *m* di ammissione
entrance fee N tassa d'iscrizione; (*to museum etc*) prezzo d'ingresso
entrance ramp N (*US Aut*) rampa di accesso
entrancing [ɪnˈtrɑːnsɪŋ] ADJ incantevole
entrant [ˈɛntrnt] N partecipante *mf*; concorrente *mf*; (*BRIT: in exam*) candidato(-a)
entreat [ɛnˈtriːt] VT supplicare
entreaty [ɪnˈtriːtɪ] N supplica, preghiera
entrée [ˈɔntreɪ] N (*Culin*) prima portata
entrenched [ɛnˈtrɛntʃt] ADJ radicato(-a)
entrepreneur [ˈɔntrəprəˈnəːʳ] N imprenditore *m*
entrepreneurial [ˈɔntrəprəˈnəːrɪəl] ADJ imprenditoriale
entrust [ɪnˈtrʌst] VT: **to ~ sth to** affidare qc a
entry [ˈɛntrɪ] N entrata; (*way in*) entrata, ingresso; (*item: on list*) iscrizione *f*; (*in dictionary*) voce *f*; (*in diary, ship's log*) annotazione *f*, registrazione *f*; (*in account book, ledger, list*) registrazione *f*; **"no ~"** "vietato l'ingresso"; (*Aut*) "divieto di accesso"; **single/double ~ book-keeping** partita semplice/doppia
entry form N modulo d'iscrizione
entry phone N (*BRIT*) citofono
entwine [ɪnˈtwaɪn] VT intrecciare
E number N sigla di additivo alimentare

enumerate [ɪ'nju:məreɪt] VT enumerare
enunciate [ɪ'nʌnsɪeɪt] VT enunciare;
pronunciare
envelop [ɪn'vɛləp] VT avvolgere, avviluppare
envelope ['ɛnvələup] N busta
enviable ['ɛnvɪəbl] ADJ invidiabile
envious ['ɛnvɪəs] ADJ invidioso(-a)
environment [ɪn'vaɪərənmənt] N ambiente
m; **Department of the E~** (BRIT) ≈ Ministero
dell'Ambiente
environmental [ɪnvaɪərən'mɛntl] ADJ
ecologico(-a); ambientale; **~ studies** (*in
school etc*) ecologia
environmentalist [ɪn'vaɪərən'mɛntəlɪst] N
studioso(-a) della protezione dell'ambiente
environmentally [ɪnvaɪərən'mɛntəlɪ] ADV:
~ sound/friendly che rispetta l'ambiente
Environmental Protection Agency N (US)
≈ Ministero dell'Ambiente
envisage [ɪn'vɪzɪdʒ] VT immaginare;
prevedere
envision [ɪn'vɪʒən] VT concepire, prevedere
envoy ['ɛnvɔɪ] N inviato(-a)
envy ['ɛnvɪ] N invidia ▶ VT invidiare; **to ~ sb
sth** invidiare qn per qc
enzyme ['ɛnzaɪm] N enzima *m*
EPA N ABBR (US) = **Environmental Protection
Agency**
ephemeral [ɪ'fɛmərəl] ADJ effimero(-a)
epic ['ɛpɪk] N poema *m* epico ▶ ADJ epico(-a)
epicentre, (US)**epicenter** ['ɛpɪsɛntə^r] N
epicentro
epidemic [ɛpɪ'dɛmɪk] N epidemia
epilepsy ['ɛpɪlɛpsɪ] N epilessia
epileptic [ɛpɪ'lɛptɪk] ADJ, N epilettico(-a)
epileptic fit N attacco epilettico
epilogue ['ɛpɪlɔg] N epilogo
Epiphany [ɪ'pɪfənɪ] N Epifania
episcopal [ɪ'pɪskəpəl] ADJ episcopale
episode ['ɛpɪsəud] N episodio
epistle [ɪ'pɪsl] N epistola
epitaph ['ɛpɪtɑːf] N epitaffio
epithet ['ɛpɪθɛt] N epiteto
epitome [ɪ'pɪtəmɪ] N epitome *f*;
quintessenza
epitomize [ɪ'pɪtəmaɪz] VT (*fig*) incarnare
epoch ['iːpɔk] N epoca
epoch-making ['iːpɔkmeɪkɪŋ] ADJ che fa
epoca
eponymous [ɪ'pɒnɪməs] ADJ dello stesso
nome
equable ['ɛkwəbl] ADJ uniforme; (*climate*)
costante; (*character*) equilibrato(-a)
equal ['iːkwl] ADJ, N pari (*mf*) ▶ VT uguagliare;
~ to (*task*) all'altezza di
equality [iː'kwɔlɪtɪ] N uguaglianza
equalize ['iːkwəlaɪz] VT, VI pareggiare
equalizer ['iːkwəlaɪzə^r] N punto del pareggio
equally ['iːkwəlɪ] ADV ugualmente; **they are**

~ clever sono intelligenti allo stesso modo
Equal Opportunities Commission, (US)
**Equal Employment Opportunity
Commission** N *commissione contro
discriminazioni sessuali o razziali nel mondo del
lavoro*
equal sign, equals sign N segno
d'uguaglianza
equanimity [ɛkwə'nɪmɪtɪ] N serenità
equate [ɪ'kweɪt] VT: **to ~ sth with**
considerare qc uguale a; (*compare*)
paragonare qc con; **to ~ A to B** mettere in
equazione A e B
equation [ɪ'kweɪʃən] N (*Math*) equazione *f*
equator [ɪ'kweɪtə^r] N equatore *m*
Equatorial Guinea [ɛkwə'tɔːrɪəl-] N Guinea
Equatoriale
equestrian [ɪ'kwɛstrɪən] ADJ equestre ▶ N
cavaliere (amazzone)
equilibrium [iːkwɪ'lɪbrɪəm] N equilibrio
equinox ['iːkwɪnɔks] N equinozio
equip [ɪ'kwɪp] VT equipaggiare, attrezzare;
to ~ sb/sth with fornire qn/qc di; **equipped
with** (*machinery etc*) dotato(a) di; **to be well
equipped** (*office etc*) essere ben attrezzato(-a);
he is well equipped for the job ha i
requisiti necessari per quel lavoro
equipment [ɪ'kwɪpmənt] N attrezzatura;
(*electrical etc*) apparecchiatura
equitable ['ɛkwɪtəbl] ADJ equo(-a), giusto(-a)
equities ['ɛkwɪtɪz] NPL (*BRIT Comm*) azioni *fpl*
ordinarie
equity ['ɛkwɪtɪ] N equità
equity capital N capitale *m* azionario
equivalent [ɪ'kwɪvələnt] ADJ, N equivalente
(*m*); **to be ~ to** equivalere a
equivocal [ɪ'kwɪvəkl] ADJ equivoco(-a); (*open
to suspicion*) dubbio(-a)
equivocate [ɪ'kwɪvəkeɪt] VI esprimersi in
modo equivoco
equivocation [ɪkwɪvə'keɪʃən] N parole *fpl*
equivoche
ER ABBR BRIT: = **Elizabeth Regina**; (*US Med*)
= **emergency room**
ERA N ABBR (*US Pol*) = **Equal Rights
Amendment**
era ['ɪərə] N era, età *f inv*
eradicate [ɪ'rædɪkeɪt] VT sradicare
erase [ɪ'reɪz] VT cancellare
eraser [ɪ'reɪzə^r] N gomma
e-reader ['iː'riːdə^r] N lettore *m* di e-book
erect [ɪ'rɛkt] ADJ eretto(-a) ▶ VT costruire;
(*assemble*) montare; (*monument, tent*) alzare
erection [ɪ'rɛkʃən] N (*also Physiol*) erezione *f*;
(*of building*) costruzione *f*; (*of machinery*)
montaggio
ergonomics [əːgə'nɔmɪks] N ergonomia
ERISA N ABBR (*US*: = *Employee Retirement Income
Security Act*) *legge relativa al pensionamento statale*

e

543

Eritrea [ɛrɪ'treɪə] N Eritrea

ERM N ABBR (= *Exchange Rate Mechanism*)
ERM *m*, meccanismo dei tassi di cambio

ermine ['ə:mɪn] N ermellino

ERNIE ['ə:nɪ] N ABBR (*BRIT*: = *Electronic Random Number Indicator Equipment*) *sistema che seleziona i numeri vincenti di buoni del Tesoro*

erode [ɪ'rəud] VT erodere; (*metal*) corrodere

erogenous zone [ɪ'rɔdʒənəs–] N zona erogena

erosion [ɪ'rəuʒən] N erosione *f*

erotic [ɪ'rɔtɪk] ADJ erotico(-a)

eroticism [ɪ'rɔtɪsɪzəm] N erotismo

err [ə:ʳ] VI errare; (*Rel*) peccare

errand ['ɛrənd] N commissione *f*; (*also*: **run errands**) fare commissioni; **~ of mercy** atto di carità

errand boy N fattorino

erratic [ɪ'rætɪk] ADJ imprevedibile; (*person, mood*) incostante

erroneous [ɪ'rəunɪəs] ADJ erroneo(-a)

error ['ɛrəʳ] N errore *m*; **typing/spelling ~** errore di battitura/di ortografia; **in ~** per errore; **errors and omissions excepted** salvo errori ed omissioni

error message N (*Comput*) messaggio di errore

erstwhile ['ə:stwaɪl] ADV allora, un tempo ▶ ADJ di allora

erudite ['ɛrjudaɪt] ADJ erudito(-a)

erupt [ɪ'rʌpt] VI erompere; (*volcano*) mettersi (*or* essere) in eruzione; (*war, crisis*) scoppiare

eruption [ɪ'rʌpʃən] N eruzione *f*; (*of anger, violence*) esplosione *f*; scoppio

ESA N ABBR (= *European Space Agency*) ESA *f*

escalate ['ɛskəleɪt] VI intensificarsi; (*costs*) salire

escalation [ɛskə'leɪʃən] N escalation *f*; (*of prices*) aumento

escalation clause N clausola di revisione

escalator ['ɛskəleɪtəʳ] N scala mobile

escapade [ɛskə'peɪd] N scappatella; avventura

escape [ɪ'skeɪp] N evasione *f*; fuga; (*of gas etc*) fuga, fuoriuscita ▶ VI fuggire; (*from jail*) evadere, scappare; (*fig*) sfuggire; (*leak*) uscire ▶ VT sfuggire a; **to ~ from** (*place*) fuggire da; (*person*) sfuggire a; **to ~ to** (*another place*) fuggire in; (*freedom, safety*) fuggire verso; **to ~ notice** passare inosservato(a)

escape artist N mago della fuga

escape clause N clausola scappatoia

escapee [ɪskeɪ'pi:] N evaso(-a)

escape hatch N (*in submarine, space rocket*) portello di sicurezza

escape key N (*Comput*) tasto di escape, tasto per cambio di codice

escape route N percorso della fuga

escapism [ɪs'keɪpɪzəm] N evasione *f* (dalla realtà)

escapist [ɪs'keɪpɪst] ADJ d'evasione ▶ N persona che cerca di evadere dalla realtà

escapologist [ɛskə'pɔlədʒɪst] N (*BRIT*) = **escape artist**

escarpment [ɪs'kɑ:pmənt] N scarpata

eschew [ɪs'tʃu:] VT evitare

escort N ['ɛskɔ:t] scorta; (*to dance etc*): **her ~** il suo cavaliere; **his ~** la sua dama ▶ VT [ɪ'skɔ:t] scortare; accompagnare

escort agency N agenzia di hostess

Eskimo ['ɛskɪməu] ADJ eschimese ▶ N eschimese *mf*; (*Ling*) eschimese *m*

ESL N ABBR (*Scol*) = **English as a Second Language**

esophagus [i:'sɔfəgəs] N (*US*) = **oesophagus**

esoteric [ɛsəu'tɛrɪk] ADJ esoterico(-a)

ESP N ABBR = **extrasensory perception**; (*Scol*) = **English for Specific Purposes**; = **English for Special Purposes**

esp. ABBR (= *especially*) spec.

especially [ɪ'spɛʃlɪ] ADV specialmente; (*above all*) soprattutto; (*specifically*) espressamente; (*particularly*) particolarmente

espionage ['ɛspɪənɑ:ʒ] N spionaggio

esplanade [ɛsplə'neɪd] N lungomare *m*

espouse [ɪ'spauz] VT abbracciare

Esquire [ɪ'skwaɪəʳ] N (*BRIT*): **J. Brown, ~** Signor J. Brown

essay ['ɛseɪ] N (*Scol*) composizione *f*; (*Literature*) saggio

essence ['ɛsns] N essenza; **in ~** in sostanza; **speed is of the ~** la velocità è di estrema importanza

essential [ɪ'sɛnʃəl] ADJ essenziale; (*basic*) fondamentale ▶ N elemento essenziale; **it is ~ that** è essenziale che + *sub*

essentially [ɪ'sɛnʃəlɪ] ADV essenzialmente

essentials NPL: **the ~** l'essenziale *msg*

EST ABBR (*US*: = *Eastern Standard Time*) fuso orario

est. ABBR (= *established*) = **estimate**

establish [ɪ'stæblɪʃ] VT stabilire; (*business*) mettere su; (*one's power etc*) affermare; (*prove: fact, identity, sb's innocence*) dimostrare

establishment [ɪs'tæblɪʃmənt] N stabilimento; (*business*) azienda; **the E~** la classe dirigente; l'establishment *m*; **a teaching ~** un istituto d'istruzione

estate [ɪ'steɪt] N proprietà *f* inv; (*Law*) beni *mpl*, patrimonio; (*BRIT: also*: **housing estate**) complesso edilizio

estate agency N (*BRIT*) agenzia immobiliare

estate agent N (*BRIT*) agente *m* immobiliare

estate car N (*BRIT*) giardiniera

esteem [ɪ'sti:m] N stima ▶ VT considerare; stimare; **I hold him in high ~** gode di tutta la mia stima

esthetic [ɪs'θɛtɪk] ADJ (*US*) = **aesthetic**

estimate N ['ɛstɪmət] stima; (*Comm*) preventivo ▶ VT ['ɛstɪmeɪt] stimare, valutare

▶ VI (*BRIT Comm*): **to ~ for** fare il preventivo per; **to give sb an ~ of** fare a qn una valutazione approssimativa (*or* un preventivo) di; **at a rough ~** approssimativamente

estimation [ɛstɪ'meɪʃən] N stima; opinione *f*; **in my ~** a mio giudizio, a mio avviso

Estonia [ɛ'stəunɪə] N Estonia

Estonian [ɛ'stəunɪən] ADJ estone *inv* ▶ N estone *mf*; (*Ling*) estone *m*

estranged [ɪ'streɪndʒd] ADJ separato(-a)

estrangement [ɪs'treɪndʒmənt] N alienazione *f*

estrogen ['iːstrəudʒən] N (*US*) = **oestrogen**

estuary ['ɛstjuərɪ] N estuario

ET ABBR (= *Eastern Time*) fuso orario; (*BRIT*: = *Employment Training*) corso di formazione professionale per disoccupati

ETA N ABBR (= *estimated time of arrival*) ora di arrivo prevista

e-tailer ['iːteɪlə'] N venditore(-trice) in Internet

e-tailing ['iːteɪlɪŋ] N commercio in Internet

et al. ABBR (= *et alii: and others*) ed altri

etc. ABBR (= *et cetera*) ecc., etc.

etch [ɛtʃ] VT incidere all'acquaforte

etching ['ɛtʃɪŋ] N acquaforte *f*

ETD N ABBR (= *estimated time of departure*) ora di partenza prevista

eternal [ɪ'təːnl] ADJ eterno(-a)

eternity [ɪ'təːnɪtɪ] N eternità

ether ['iːθə'] N etere *m*

ethereal [ɪ'θɪərɪəl] ADJ etereo(-a)

ethical ['ɛθɪkl] ADJ etico(-a), morale

ethics ['ɛθɪks] N etica ▶ NPL morale *f*

Ethiopia [iːθɪ'əupɪə] N Etiopia

Ethiopian [iːθɪ'əupɪən] ADJ, N etiope (*mf*)

ethnic ['ɛθnɪk] ADJ etnico(-a)

ethnic cleansing [-'klɛnzɪŋ] N pulizia etnica

ethnic minority N minoranza etnica

ethnology [ɛθ'nɔlədʒɪ] N etnologia

ethos ['iːθɔs] N (*of culture, group*) norma di vita

e-ticket ['iːtɪkɪt] N e-ticket *m inv*, biglietto elettronico

etiquette ['ɛtɪkɛt] N etichetta

ETV N ABBR (*US*) = **Educational Television**

etymology [ɛtɪ'mɔlədʒɪ] N etimologia

EU N ABBR (= *European Union*) UE *f*

eucalyptus [juːkə'lɪptəs] N eucalipto

eulogy ['juːlədʒɪ] N elogio

euphemism ['juːfəmɪzəm] N eufemismo

euphemistic [juːfə'mɪstɪk] ADJ eufemistico(-a)

euphoria [juː'fɔːrɪə] N euforia

Eurasia [juə'reɪʃə] N Eurasia

Eurasian [juə'reɪʃən] ADJ, N eurasiano(-a)

Euratom [juə'rætəm] N ABBR (= *European Atomic Energy Community*) EURATOM *f*

euro ['juərəu] N (*currency*) euro *m inv*

Euro- ['juərəu] PREFIX euro-

Eurocheque ['juərəutʃɛk] N eurochèque *m inv*

Eurocrat ['juərəukræt] N eurocrate *mf*

Eurodollar ['juərəudɔlə'] N eurodollaro

Euroland ['juərəulænd] N Eurolandia

Europe ['juərəp] N Europa

European [juərə'piːən] ADJ, N europeo(-a)

European Community N Comunità Europea

European Court of Justice N Corte *f* di Giustizia della Comunità Europea

European Union N Unione *f* europea

Europol ['juərəupɔl] N Europol *f*

Euro-sceptic ['juərəuskɛptɪk] N euroscettico(-a)

Eurostar® ['juərəustɑːʳ] N Eurostar® *m inv*

Eurozone ['juərəuzəun] N zona euro

euthanasia [juːθə'neɪzɪə] N eutanasia

evacuate [ɪ'vækjueɪt] VT evacuare

evacuation [ɪvækju'eɪʃən] N evacuazione *f*

evacuee [ɪvækju'iː] N sfollato(-a)

evade [ɪ'veɪd] VT eludere; (*tax*) evadere; (*duties etc*) sottrarsi a; (*person*) schivare

evaluate [ɪ'væljueɪt] VT valutare

evangelist [ɪ'vændʒəlɪst] N evangelista *m*

evangelize [ɪ'vændʒəlaɪz] VT evangelizzare

evaporate [ɪ'væpəreɪt] VI evaporare ▶ VT far evaporare

evaporated milk N latte *m* concentrato

evaporation [ɪvæpə'reɪʃən] N evaporazione *f*

evasion [ɪ'veɪʒən] N evasione *f*

evasive [ɪ'veɪsɪv] ADJ evasivo(-a)

eve [iːv] N: **on the ~ of** alla vigilia di

even- ['iːvn] ADJ regolare; (*number*) pari *inv* ▶ ADV anche, perfino; **~ if**, **~ though** anche se; **~ more** ancora di più; **he loves her ~ more** la ama anche di più; **~ faster** ancora più veloce; **~ so** ciò nonostante; **not ~ ...** nemmeno ...; **to break ~** finire in pari *or* alla pari; **to get ~ with sb** dare la pari a qn ▶ **even out** VI pareggiare

even-handed ['iːvn'hændɪd] ADJ imparziale, equo(-a)

evening ['iːvnɪŋ] N sera; (*as duration, event*) serata; **in the ~** la sera; **this ~** stasera, questa sera; **tomorrow/yesterday ~** domani/ieri sera

evening class N corso serale

evening dress N (*woman's*) abito da sera; **in ~** (*man*) in abito scuro; (*woman*) in abito lungo

evenly ['iːvənlɪ] ADV (*distribute, space, spread*) uniformemente; (*divide*) in parti uguali

evensong ['iːvnsɔŋ] N = vespro

event [ɪ'vɛnt] N avvenimento; (*Sport*) gara; **in the ~ of** in caso di; **at all events**, (*BRIT*) **in any ~** in ogni caso; **in the ~** in realtà, di fatto; **in the course of events** nel corso degli eventi

eventful [ɪ'vɛntful] ADJ denso(-a) di eventi

eventing [ɪ'vɛntɪŋ] N (*Horseriding*) concorso ippico

eventual [ɪ'vɛntʃuəl] ADJ finale

eventuality [ɪvɛntʃu'ælɪtɪ] N possibilità *f inv*, eventualità *f inv*

eventually [ɪ'vɛntʃuəlɪ] ADV alla fine

ever ['ɛvə^r] ADV mai; (*at all times*) sempre; **for ~** per sempre; **the best ~** il migliore che ci sia mai stato; **hardly ~** non ... quasi mai; **have you ~ seen it?** l'ha mai visto?; **have you ~ been there?** c'è mai stato?; **~ so pretty** così bello(a); **thank you ~ so much** grazie mille; **yours ~** (BRIT: *in letters*) sempre tuo; **~ since** *adv* da allora; *conj* sin da quando

Everest ['ɛvərɪst] N (*also:* **Mount Everest**) Everest *m*

evergreen ['ɛvəgriːn] N sempreverde *m*

everlasting [ɛvə'lɑːstɪŋ] ADJ eterno(-a)

every ['ɛvrɪ] ADJ ogni; **~ day** tutti i giorni, ogni giorno; **~ other/third day** ogni due/tre giorni; **~ other car** una macchina su due; **~ now and then** ogni tanto, di quando in quando; **I have ~ confidence in him** ho piena fiducia in lui

everybody ['ɛvrɪbɔdɪ] PRON ognuno, tutti *pl*; **~ else** tutti gli altri; **~ knows about it** lo sanno tutti

everyday ['ɛvrɪdeɪ] ADJ quotidiano(-a); di ogni giorno; (*use, occurrence, experience*) comune; (*expression*) di uso corrente

everyone ['ɛvrɪwʌn] = **everybody**

everything ['ɛvrɪθɪŋ] PRON tutto, ogni cosa; **~ is ready** è tutto pronto; **he did ~ possible** ha fatto tutto il possibile

everywhere ['ɛvrɪwɛə^r] ADV in ogni luogo, dappertutto; (*wherever*) ovunque; **~ you go you meet ...** ovunque si vada si trova ...

evict [ɪ'vɪkt] VT sfrattare

eviction [ɪ'vɪkʃən] N sfratto

eviction notice N avviso di sfratto

evidence ['ɛvɪdəns] N (*proof*) prova; (*of witness*) testimonianza; **to show ~ of** (*sign*) dare segni di; **to give ~** deporre; **in ~** (*obvious*) in evidenza; in vista

evident ['ɛvɪdənt] ADJ evidente

evidently ['ɛvɪdəntlɪ] ADV evidentemente

evil ['iːvl] ADJ cattivo(-a), maligno(-a) ▶ N male *m*

evince [ɪ'vɪns] VT manifestare

evocative [ɪ'vɔkətɪv] ADJ evocativo(-a)

evoke [ɪ'vəuk] VT evocare; (*admiration*) suscitare

evolution [iːvə'luːʃən] N evoluzione *f*

evolve [ɪ'vɔlv] VT elaborare ▶ VI svilupparsi, evolversi

ewe [juː] N pecora

ex [ɛks] N (*col*): **my ex** il mio(-a) ex

ex- [ɛks] PREFIX ex; (*out of*): **the price ~works** il prezzo franco fabbrica

exacerbate [ɪk'sæsəbeɪt] VT (*pain*) aggravare; (*fig: relations, situation*) esacerbare, esasperare

exact [ɪg'zækt] ADJ esatto(-a) ▶ VT: **to ~ sth (from)** estorcere qc (da); esigere qc (da)

exacting [ɪg'zæktɪŋ] ADJ esigente; (*work*) faticoso(-a)

exactitude [ɪg'zæktɪtjuːd] N esattezza, precisione *f*

exactly [ɪg'zæktlɪ] ADV esattamente; **~!** esatto!

exaggerate [ɪg'zædʒəreɪt] VT, VI esagerare

exaggeration [ɪgzædʒə'reɪʃən] N esagerazione *f*

exalt [ɪg'zɔːlt] VT esaltare; elevare

exalted [ɪg'zɔːltɪd] ADJ (*rank, person*) elevato(-a); (*elated*) esaltato(-a)

exam [ɪg'zæm] N ABBR (*Scol*) = **examination**

examination [ɪgzæmɪ'neɪʃən] N (*Scol*) esame *m*; (*Med*) controllo; **to take** *or* **sit an ~** (BRIT) sostenere *or* dare un esame; **the matter is under ~** la questione è all'esame

examine [ɪg'zæmɪn] VT esaminare; (*Scol: orally, Law: person*) interrogare; (*inspect: machine, premises*) ispezionare; (: *luggage, passport*) controllare; (*Med*) visitare

examiner [ɪg'zæmɪnə^r] N esaminatore(-trice)

example [ɪg'zɑːmpl] N esempio; **for ~** ad *or* per esempio; **to set a good/bad ~** dare il buon/cattivo esempio

exasperate [ɪg'zɑːspəreɪt] VT esasperare; **exasperated by** (*or* **at** *or* **with**) esasperato da

exasperated [ɪg'zɑːspəreɪtɪd] ADJ esasperato(-a)

exasperating [ɪg'zɑːspəreɪtɪŋ] ADJ esasperante

exasperation [ɪgzɑːspə'reɪʃən] N esasperazione *f*

excavate ['ɛkskəveɪt] VT scavare

excavation [ɛkskə'veɪʃən] N escavazione *f*

excavator ['ɛkskəveɪtə^r] N scavatore *m*, scavatrice *f*

exceed [ɪk'siːd] VT superare; (*one's powers, time limit*) oltrepassare

exceedingly [ɪk'siːdɪŋlɪ] ADV eccessivamente

excel [ɪk'sɛl] VI eccellere ▶ VT sorpassare; **to ~ o.s.** (BRIT) superare se stesso

excellence ['ɛksələns] N eccellenza

Excellency ['ɛksələnsɪ] N: **His ~** Sua Eccellenza

excellent ['ɛksələnt] ADJ eccellente

except [ɪk'sɛpt] PREP (*also:* **except for, excepting**) salvo, all'infuori di, eccetto ▶ VT escludere; **~ if/when** salvo se/quando; **~ that** salvo che

exception [ɪk'sɛpʃən] N eccezione *f*; **to take ~ to** trovare a ridire su; **with the ~ of** ad eccezione di

exceptional [ɪk'sɛpʃənl] ADJ eccezionale

exceptionally [ɪk'sepʃənəlɪ] ADV eccezionalmente

excerpt ['ɛksəːpt] N estratto

excess [ɪk'sɛs] N eccesso; **in ~ of** al di sopra di

excess baggage N bagaglio in eccedenza

excess fare N supplemento

excessive [ɪk'sɛsɪv] ADJ eccessivo(-a)

excess supply N eccesso di offerta

exchange [ɪks'tʃeɪndʒ] N scambio; (*also:* **telephone exchange**) centralino ▶ VT: **to ~ (for)** scambiare (con); **in ~ for** in cambio di; **foreign ~** (*Comm*) cambio

exchange control N controllo sui cambi

exchange market N mercato dei cambi

exchange rate N tasso di cambio

Exchequer [ɪks'tʃekəʳ] N: **the ~** (*Brit*) lo Scacchiere, ≈ il ministero delle Finanze

excisable [ɪk'saɪzəbl] ADJ soggetto(-a) a dazio

excise N ['ɛksaɪz] imposta, dazio ▶ VT [ɛk'saɪz] recidere

excise duties NPL dazi *mpl*

excitable [ɪk'saɪtəbl] ADJ eccitabile

excite [ɪk'saɪt] VT eccitare; **to get excited** eccitarsi

excited ADJ: **to get ~** essere elettrizzato(-a)

excitement [ɪk'saɪtmənt] N eccitazione *f*; agitazione *f*

exciting [ɪk'saɪtɪŋ] ADJ avventuroso(-a); (*film, book*) appassionante

excl. ABBR (= *excluding, exclusive (of)*) escl.

exclaim [ɪk'skleɪm] VI esclamare

exclamation [ɛksklə'meɪʃən] N esclamazione *f*

exclamation mark, (*US*) **exclamation point** N punto esclamativo

exclude [ɪk'skluːd] VT escludere

excluding [ɪk'skluːdɪŋ] PREP: **~ VAT** IVA esclusa

exclusion [ɪk'skluːʒən] N esclusione *f*; **to the ~ of** escludendo

exclusion clause N clausola di esclusione

exclusion zone N area interdetta

exclusive [ɪk'skluːsɪv] ADJ esclusivo(-a); (*club*) selettivo(-a); (*district*) snob *inv* ▶ ADV (*Comm*) non compreso; **~ of VAT** IVA esclusa; **~ of postage** spese postali escluse; **~ of service** servizio escluso; **from 1st to 15th March ~** dal 1º al 15 marzo esclusi; **~ rights** *npl* (*Comm*) diritti *mpl* esclusivi

exclusively [ɪk'skluːsɪvlɪ] ADV esclusivamente

excommunicate [ɛkskə'mjuːnɪkeɪt] VT scomunicare

excrement ['ɛkskrəmənt] N escremento

excruciating [ɪk'skruːʃɪeɪtɪŋ] ADJ straziante, atroce

excursion [ɪk'skəːʃən] N escursione *f*, gita

excursion ticket N biglietto a tariffa escursionistica

excusable [ɪk'skjuːzəbl] ADJ scusabile

excuse N [ɪk'skjuːs] scusa ▶ VT [ɪk'skjuːz] scusare; (*justify*) giustificare; **to make excuses for sb** trovare giustificazioni per qn; **to ~ sb from** (*activity*) dispensare qn da; **~ me!** mi scusi!; **now if you will ~ me, ...** ora, mi scusi ma ...; **to ~ o.s. (for (doing) sth)** giustificarsi (per (aver fatto) qc)

ex-directory ['ɛksdɪ'rɛktərɪ] ADJ (*Brit*): **to be ~** non essere sull'elenco; **~ (phone) number** numero non compreso nell'elenco telefonico

execrable ['ɛksɪkrəbl] ADJ (*gen*) pessimo(-a); (*manners*) esecrabile

execute ['ɛksɪkjuːt] VT (*prisoner*) giustiziare; (*plan etc*) eseguire

execution [ɛksɪ'kjuːʃən] N esecuzione *f*

executioner [ɛksɪ'kjuːʃnəʳ] N boia *m inv*

executive [ɪg'zɛkjutɪv] N (*Comm*) dirigente *m*; (*Pol*) esecutivo *m* ▶ ADJ esecutivo(-a); (*secretary*) di direzione; (*offices, suite*) della direzione; (*car, plane*) dirigenziale; (*position, job, duties*) direttivo(-a)

executive director N amministratore(-trice)

executor [ɪg'zɛkjutəʳ] N esecutore(-trice) testamentario(-a)

exemplary [ɪg'zɛmplərɪ] ADJ esemplare

exemplify [ɪg'zɛmplɪfaɪ] VT esemplificare

exempt [ɪg'zɛmpt] ADJ: **~ (from)** (*person: from tax*) esentato(-a) (da); (*: from military service etc*) esonerato(-a) (da); (*goods*) esente (da) ▶ VT: **to ~ sb from** esentare qn da

exemption [ɪg'zɛmpʃən] N esenzione *f*

exercise ['ɛksəsaɪz] N (*keep fit*) moto; (*Scol, Mil etc*) esercizio ▶ VT esercitare; (*patience*) usare; (*dog*) portar fuori ▶ VI (*also:* **take exercise**) fare del movimento *or* moto

exercise bike N cyclette® *f inv*

exercise book N quaderno

exert [ɪg'zəːt] VT esercitare; (*strength, force*) impiegare; **to ~ o.s.** sforzarsi

exertion [ɪg'zəːʃən] N sforzo

ex gratia ['ɛks'greɪʃə] ADJ: **~ payment** gratifica

exhale [ɛks'heɪl] VT, VI espirare

exhaust [ɪg'zɔːst] N (*also:* **exhaust fumes**) scappamento; (*also:* **exhaust pipe**) tubo di scappamento ▶ VT esaurire; **to ~ o.s.** sfiancarsi

exhausted [ɪg'zɔːstɪd] ADJ esaurito(-a)

exhausting [ɪg'zɔːstɪŋ] ADJ estenuante

exhaustion [ɪg'zɔːstʃən] N esaurimento; **nervous ~** sovraffaticamento mentale

exhaustive [ɪg'zɔːstɪv] ADJ esauriente

exhibit [ɪg'zɪbɪt] N (*Art*) oggetto esposto; (*Law*) documento *or* oggetto esibito ▶ VT esporre; (*courage, skill*) dimostrare

exhibition [ɛksɪ'bɪʃən] N mostra, esposizione *f*; (*of rudeness etc*) spettacolo; **to make an ~ of o.s.** dare spettacolo di sé

exhibitionist [ɛksɪ'bɪʃənɪst] N esibizionista *mf*

exhibitor [ɪg'zɪbɪtə^r] N espositore(-trice)

exhilarating [ɪg'zɪləreɪtɪŋ] ADJ esilarante; stimolante

exhilaration [ɪgzɪlə'reɪʃən] N esaltazione *f*, ebbrezza

exhort [ɪg'zɔːt] VT esortare

exile ['ɛksaɪl] N esilio; *(person)* esiliato(-a) ▶ VT esiliare; **in ~** in esilio

exist [ɪg'zɪst] VI esistere

existence [ɪg'zɪstəns] N esistenza; **to be in ~** esistere

existentialism [ɛgzɪs'tɛnʃəlɪzəm] N esistenzialismo

existing [ɪg'zɪstɪŋ] ADJ esistente; *(laws, regime)* attuale

exit ['ɛksɪt] N uscita ▶ VI *(Comput, Theat)* uscire

exit poll N exit poll *m inv*, sondaggio all'uscita dei seggi

exit ramp N *(US Aut)* rampa di uscita

exit visa N visto d'uscita

exodus ['ɛksədəs] N esodo

ex officio ['ɛksə'fɪʃɪəu] ADJ, ADV d'ufficio

exonerate [ɪg'zɔnəreɪt] VT: **to ~ from** discolpare da

exorbitant [ɪg'zɔːbɪtənt] ADJ *(price)* esorbitante; *(demands)* spropositato(-a)

exorcize ['ɛksɔːsaɪz] VT esorcizzare

exotic [ɪg'zɔtɪk] ADJ esotico(-a)

expand [ɪk'spænd] VT *(chest, economy etc)* sviluppare; *(market, operations)* espandere; *(influence)* estendere; *(horizons)* allargare ▶ VI svilupparsi; *(gas)* espandersi; *(metal)* dilatarsi; **to ~ on** *(notes, story etc)* ampliare

expanse [ɪk'spæns] N distesa, estensione *f*

expansion [ɪk'spænʃən] N *(gen)* espansione *f*; *(of town, economy)* sviluppo; *(of metal)* dilatazione *f*

expansionism [ɪk'spænʃənɪzəm] N espansionismo

expansionist [ɪk'spænʃənɪst] ADJ espansionistico(-a)

expatriate N [ɛks'pætrɪət] espatriato(-a) ▶ VT [ɛks'pætrɪeɪt] espatriare

expect [ɪk'spɛkt] VT *(anticipate)* prevedere, aspettarsi, prevedere *or* aspettarsi che + *sub*; *(count on)* contare su; *(hope for)* sperare; *(require)* richiedere, esigere; *(suppose)* supporre; *(await, also baby)* aspettare ▶ VI: **to be expecting** essere in stato interessante; **to ~ sb to do** aspettarsi che qn faccia; **to ~ to do sth** pensare *or* contare di fare qc; **as expected** come previsto; **I ~ so** credo di sì

expectancy [ɪk'spɛktənsɪ] N attesa; **life ~** probabilità *fpl* di vita

expectant [ɪk'spɛktənt] ADJ pieno(-a) di aspettative

expectantly [ɪk'spɛktəntlɪ] ADV *(look, listen)* con un'aria d'attesa

expectant mother N gestante *f*

expectation [ɛkspɛk'teɪʃən] N aspettativa; speranza; **in ~ of** in previsione di; **against** *or* **contrary to all ~(s)** contro ogni aspettativa; **to come** *or* **live up to sb's expectations** rispondere alle attese di qn

expedience [ɪk'spiːdɪəns], **expediency** [ɪk'spiːdɪənsɪ] N convenienza; **for the sake of ~** per una questione di comodità

expedient [ɪk'spiːdɪənt] ADJ conveniente; vantaggioso(-a) ▶ N espediente *m*

expedite ['ɛkspədaɪt] VT sbrigare; facilitare

expedition [ɛkspə'dɪʃən] N spedizione *f*

expeditionary force [ɛkspə'dɪʃənərɪ-] N corpo di spedizione

expeditious [ɛkspə'dɪʃəs] ADJ sollecito(-a), rapido(-a)

expel [ɪk'spɛl] VT espellere

expend [ɪk'spɛnd] VT spendere; *(use up)* consumare

expendable [ɪk'spɛndəbl] ADJ sacrificabile

expenditure [ɪk'spɛndɪtʃə^r] N spesa; *(of time, effort)* dispendio

expense [ɪk'spɛns] N spesa; *(high cost)* costo; **expenses** NPL *(Comm)* spese *fpl*, indennità *fpl*; **to go to the ~ of** sobbarcarsi la spesa di; **at great ~** con grande impiego di mezzi; **at the ~ of** a spese di

expense account N conto *m* spese *inv*

expensive [ɪk'spɛnsɪv] ADJ caro(-a), costoso(-a); **she has ~ tastes** le piacciono le cose costose

experience [ɪk'spɪərɪəns] N esperienza ▶ VT *(pleasure)* provare; *(hardship)* soffrire; **to learn by ~** imparare per esperienza

experienced [ɪk'spɪərɪənst] ADJ esperto(-a)

experiment N [ɪk'spɛrɪmənt] esperimento, esperienza ▶ VI [ɪk'spɛrɪmɛnt] fare esperimenti; **to perform** *or* **carry out an ~** fare un esperimento; **as an ~** a titolo di esperimento; **to ~ with a new vaccine** sperimentare un nuovo vaccino

experimental [ɪkspɛrɪ'mɛntl] ADJ sperimentale; **at the ~ stage** in via di sperimentazione

expert ['ɛkspəːt] ADJ, N esperto(-a); **~ witness** *(Law)* esperto(-a); **~ in** *or* **at doing sth** esperto nel fare qc; **an ~ on sth** un esperto di qc

expertise [ɛkspəː'tiːz] N competenza

expire [ɪk'spaɪə^r] VI *(period of time, licence)* scadere

expiry [ɪk'spaɪərɪ] N scadenza

expiry date N *(of medicine, food item)* data di scadenza

explain [ɪk'spleɪn] VT spiegare ▶ **explain away** VT dar ragione di

explanation [ɛksplə'neɪʃən] N spiegazione f;
to find an ~ for sth trovare la spiegazione
di qc
explanatory [ɪk'splænətrɪ] ADJ
esplicativo(-a)
expletive [ɪk'spliːtɪv] N imprecazione f
explicit [ɪk'splɪsɪt] ADJ esplicito(-a); (*definite*)
netto(-a)
explode [ɪk'spləʊd] VI esplodere ▸ VT (*fig:
theory*) demolire; **to ~ a myth** distruggere un
mito
exploit N ['ɛksplɔɪt] impresa ▸ VT [ɪk'splɔɪt]
sfruttare
exploitation [ɛksplɔɪ'teɪʃən] N sfruttamento
exploration [ɛksplə'reɪʃən] N esplorazione f
exploratory [ɪk'splɔrətrɪ] ADJ (*fig: talks*)
esplorativo(-a); **~ operation** (*Med*)
intervento d'esplorazione
explore [ɪk'splɔːʳ] VT esplorare; (*possibilities*)
esaminare
explorer [ɪk'splɔːrəʳ] N esploratore(-trice)
explosion [ɪk'spləʊʒən] N esplosione f
explosive [ɪk'spləʊsɪv] ADJ esplosivo(-a) ▸ N
esplosivo
exponent [ɪk'spəʊnənt] N esponente mf
export VT [ɛk'spɔːt] esportare ▸ N ['ɛkspɔːt]
esportazione f; articolo di esportazione
▸ CPD d'esportazione
exportation [ɛkspɔː'teɪʃən] N esportazione f
exporter [ɪk'spɔːtəʳ] N esportatore m
export licence N licenza d'esportazione
expose [ɪk'spəʊz] VT esporre; (*unmask*)
smascherare; **to ~ o.s.** (*Law*) oltraggiare il
pudore
exposed [ɪk'spəʊzd] ADJ (*land, house*)
esposto(-a); (*Elec: wire*) scoperto(-a); (: *pipe,
beam*) a vista
exposition [ɛkspə'zɪʃən] N esposizione f
exposure [ɪk'spəʊʒəʳ] N esposizione f; (*Phot*)
posa; (*Med*) assideramento; **to die of ~**
morire assiderato(-a)
exposure meter N esposimetro
expound [ɪk'spaʊnd] VT esporre; (*theory, text*)
spiegare
express [ɪk'sprɛs] ADJ (*definite*) chiaro(-a),
espresso(-a); (*Brit: letter etc*) espresso inv ▸ N
(*train*) espresso ▸ ADV: **to send sth ~** spedire
qc per espresso ▸ VT esprimere; **to ~ o.s.**
esprimersi
expression [ɪk'sprɛʃən] N espressione f
expressionism [ɪk'sprɛʃənɪzəm] N
espressionismo
expressive [ɪk'sprɛsɪv] ADJ espressivo(-a)
expressly [ɪk'sprɛslɪ] ADV espressamente
expressway [ɪk'sprɛsweɪ] N (*US: urban
motorway*) autostrada che attraversa la città
expropriate [ɛks'prəʊprɪeɪt] VT espropriare
expulsion [ɪk'spʌlʃən] N espulsione f
exquisite [ɛk'skwɪzɪt] ADJ squisito(-a)

ex-serviceman ['ɛks'səːvɪsmən] N (*irreg*) ex
combattente m
ext. ABBR (*Tel: = extension*) int. (= *interno*)
extemporize [ɪk'stɛmpəraɪz] VI
improvvisare
extend [ɪk'stɛnd] VT (*visit*) protrarre; (*road,
deadline*) prolungare; (*building*) ampliare;
(*offer*) offrire, porgere; (*Comm: credit*)
accordare ▸ VI (*land*) estendersi
extension [ɪk'stɛnʃən] N (*of road, term*)
prolungamento; (*of contract, deadline*)
proroga; (*building*) annesso; (*to wire, table*)
prolunga; (*telephone*) interno; (: *in private
house*) apparecchio supplementare; **~ 3718**
(*Tel*) interno 3718
extension cable, extension lead N (*Elec*)
prolunga
extensive [ɪk'stɛnsɪv] ADJ esteso(-a),
ampio(-a); (*damage*) su larga scala;
(*alterations*) notevole; (*inquiries, coverage,
discussion*) esauriente; (*use*) grande
extensively [ɪk'stɛnsɪvlɪ] ADV (*altered,
damaged etc*) radicalmente; **he's travelled ~**
ha viaggiato molto
extent [ɪk'stɛnt] N estensione f; (*of knowledge,
activities, power*) portata; (*degree: of damage, loss*)
proporzioni fpl; **to some ~** fino a un certo
punto; **to a certain/large ~** in certa/larga
misura; **to what ~?** fino a che punto?; **to
such an ~ that ...** a tal punto che ...; **to the ~
of ...** fino al punto di ...
extenuating [ɪk'stɛnjueɪtɪŋ] ADJ:
~ circumstances attenuanti fpl
exterior [ɛk'stɪərɪəʳ] ADJ esteriore, esterno(-a)
▸ N esteriore m, esterno; aspetto (esteriore)
exterminate [ɪk'stəːmɪneɪt] VT sterminare
extermination [ɪkstəːmɪ'neɪʃən] N
sterminio
external [ɛk'stəːnl] ADJ esterno(-a), esteriore
▸ N: **the externals** le apparenze; **for ~ use
only** (*Med*) solo per uso esterno; **~ affairs**
(*Pol*) affari mpl esteri
externally [ɛk'stəːnəlɪ] ADV esternamente
extinct [ɪk'stɪŋkt] ADJ estinto(-a)
extinction [ɪk'stɪŋkʃən] N estinzione f
extinguish [ɪk'stɪŋgwɪʃ] VT estinguere
extinguisher [ɪk'stɪŋgwɪʃəʳ] N estintore m
extol, (*US*) **extoll** [ɪk'stəʊl] VT (*merits, virtues*)
magnificare; (*person*) celebrare
extort [ɪk'stɔːt] VT: **to ~ sth from** estorcere
qc (da)
extortion [ɪk'stɔːʃən] N estorsione f
extortionate [ɪk'stɔːʃənɪt] ADJ esorbitante
extra ['ɛkstrə] ADJ extra inv, supplementare
▸ ADV (*in addition*) di più ▸ N extra m inv;
(*surcharge*) supplemento; (*Theat*) comparso;
wine will cost ~ il vino è extra; **~ large sizes**
taglie fpl forti
extra... ['ɛkstrə] PREFIX extra...

extract VT [ɪk'strækt] estrarre; (*money, promise*) strappare ▶ N ['εkstrækt] estratto; (*passage*) brano

extraction [ɪk'strækʃən] N estrazione f; (*descent*) origine f

extractor fan [ɪk'stræktər-] N aspiratore m

extracurricular [εkstrəkə'rɪkjulər] ADJ (*Scol*) parascolastico(-a)

extradite ['εkstrədaɪt] VT estradare

extradition [εkstrə'dɪʃən] N estradizione f

extramarital [εkstrə'mærɪtl] ADJ extraconiugale

extramural [εkstrə'mjuərl] ADJ fuori dell'università

extraneous [εk'streɪnɪəs] ADJ: ~ **to** estraneo(a) a

extraordinary [ɪk'strɔːdnrɪ] ADJ straordinario(-a); **the ~ thing is that ...** la cosa strana è che ...

extraordinary general meeting N assemblea straordinaria

extrapolation [ɪkstræpə'leɪʃən] N estrapolazione f

extrasensory perception [εkstrə'sεnsərɪ-] N percezione f extrasensoriale

extra time N (*Football*) tempo supplementare

extravagance [ɪk'strævəgəns] N (*excessive spending*) sperpero; (*thing bought*) stravaganza

extravagant [ɪk'strævəgənt] ADJ (*in spending: person*) prodigo(-a); (: *tastes*) dispendioso(-a); (*behaviour*) esagerato(-a)

extreme [ɪk'striːm] ADJ estremo(-a) ▶ N estremo; **extremes of temperature** eccessivi sbalzi mpl di temperatura; **the ~ left/right** (*Pol*) l'estrema sinistra/destra

extremely [ɪk'striːmlɪ] ADV estremamente

extremist [ɪk'striːmɪst] ADJ, N estremista (*mf*)

extremity [ɪk'strεmɪtɪ] N estremità f inv

extricate ['εkstrɪkeɪt] VT: **to ~ sth from** districare qc (da)

extrovert ['εkstrəvəːt] N estroverso(-a)

exuberance [ɪg'zuːbərəns] N esuberanza

exuberant [ɪg'zjuːbərənt] ADJ esuberante

exude [ɪg'zjuːd] VT trasudare; (*fig*) emanare

exult [ɪg'zʌlt] VI esultare, gioire

exultant [ɪg'zʌltənt] ADJ (*person, smile*) esultante; (*shout, expression*) di giubilo

exultation [εgzʌl'teɪʃən] N giubilo; **in ~** per la gioia

eye [aɪ] N occhio; (*of needle*) cruna ▶ VT osservare; **to keep an ~ on** tenere d'occhio; **in the public ~** esposto(a) al pubblico; **as far as the ~ can see** a perdita d'occhio; **with an ~ to doing sth** (*BRIT*) con l'idea di far qc; **to have an ~ for sth** avere occhio per qc; **there's more to this than meets the ~** non è così semplice come sembra

eyeball ['aɪbɔːl] N globo dell'occhio

eyebath ['aɪbɑːθ] N occhino

eyebrow ['aɪbrau] N sopracciglio

eyebrow pencil N matita per le sopracciglia

eye-catching ['aɪkætʃɪŋ] ADJ che colpisce l'occhio

eye cup N (*US*) = **eyebath**

eyedrops ['aɪdrɔps] NPL gocce fpl oculari, collirio

eyeful ['aɪful] N: **to get an ~ (of sth)** (*col*) avere l'occasione di dare una bella sbirciata (a qc)

eyeglass ['aɪglɑːs] N monocolo

eyelash ['aɪlæʃ] N ciglio

eyelet ['aɪlɪt] N occhiello

eye-level ['aɪlεvl] ADJ all'altezza degli occhi

eyelid ['aɪlɪd] N palpebra

eyeliner ['aɪlaɪnər] N eye-liner m inv

eye-opener ['aɪəupnər] N rivelazione f

eyeshadow ['aɪʃædəu] N ombretto

eyesight ['aɪsaɪt] N vista

eyesore ['aɪsɔːr] N pugno nell'occhio

eyestrain ['aɪstreɪn] N: **to get ~** stancarsi gli occhi

eye-tooth ['aɪtuːθ] (*pl* **eye-teeth** [-tiːθ]) N canino superiore; **to give one's eye-teeth for sth/to do sth** (*fig*) dare non so che cosa per qc/per fare qc

eyewash ['aɪwɔʃ] N collirio; (*fig*) sciocchezze fpl

eye witness N testimone mf oculare

eyrie ['ɪərɪ] N nido (d'aquila)

Ff

F, f [ɛf] N (letter) F, f inv or m inv; (Mus): **F** fa m; **F for Frederick**, (US) **F for Fox** = F come Firenze

F. ABBR (= Fahrenheit) F

FA N ABBR (BRIT) = **Football Association**

FAA N ABBR (US) = **Federal Aviation Administration**

fable ['feɪbl] N favola

fabric ['fæbrɪk] N stoffa, tessuto; (Archit) struttura

fabricate ['fæbrɪkeɪt] VT fabbricare

fabrication [fæbrɪ'keɪʃən] N fabbricazione f

fabric ribbon N (for typewriter) dattilonastro di tessuto

fabulous ['fæbjuləs] ADJ favoloso(-a); (col: super) favoloso(-a), fantastico(-a)

façade [fə'sɑːd] N facciata; (fig) apparenza

face [feɪs] N faccia, viso, volto; (expression) faccia; (grimace) smorfia; (of clock) quadrante m; (of building) facciata; (side, surface) faccia; (of mountain, cliff) parete f ▶ VT fronteggiare; (fig) affrontare; **~ down** (person) bocconi; (object) a faccia in giù; **to lose/save ~** perdere/salvare la faccia; **to pull a ~** fare una smorfia; **in the ~ of** (difficulties etc) di fronte a; **on the ~ of it** a prima vista; **~ to ~** faccia a faccia; **to ~ the fact that …** riconoscere or ammettere che …
▶ **face up to** VT FUS affrontare, far fronte a

Facebook® ['feɪsˌbʊk] N Facebook® m

facebook® ['feɪsˌbʊk] VB messaggiare vt su Facebook/facebook

face cloth N (BRIT) guanto di spugna

face cream N crema per il viso

faceless ['feɪslɪs] ADJ anonimo(-a)

face lift N lifting m inv; (of façade etc) ripulita

face pack N (BRIT) maschera di bellezza

face powder N cipria

face-saving ['feɪs'seɪvɪŋ] ADJ che salva la faccia

facet ['fæsɪt] N faccetta, sfaccettatura; (fig) sfaccettatura

facetious [fə'siːʃəs] ADJ faceto(-a)

face-to-face ['feɪstə'feɪs] ADV faccia a faccia

face value ['feɪs'vælju:] N (of coin) valore m facciale or nominale; **to take sth at ~** (fig) giudicare qc dalle apparenze

facia ['feɪʃɪə] N = **fascia**

facial ['feɪʃəl] ADJ facciale, del viso ▶ N trattamento del viso

facile ['fæsaɪl] ADJ facile; superficiale

facilitate [fə'sɪlɪteɪt] VT facilitare

facility [fə'sɪlɪtɪ] N facilità; **facilities** NPL attrezzature fpl; **credit facilities** facilitazioni fpl di credito

facing ['feɪsɪŋ] N (of wall etc) rivestimento; (Sewing) paramontura

facsimile [fæk'sɪmɪlɪ] N facsimile m inv

facsimile machine N telecopiatrice f

fact [fækt] N fatto; **in ~** in effetti; **to know for a ~ that …** sapere per certo che …; **the ~ (of the matter) is that …** la verità è che …; **the facts of life** (sex) i fatti riguardanti la vita sessuale; (fig) le realtà della vita

fact-finding ['fæktfaɪndɪŋ] ADJ: **a ~ tour/mission** un viaggio/una missione d'inchiesta

faction ['fækʃən] N fazione f

factional ['fækʃənl] ADJ: **~ fighting** scontri mpl tra fazioni

factor ['fæktə'] N fattore m; (Comm: company) organizzazione specializzata nell'incasso di crediti per conto terzi; (: agent) agente m depositario
▶ VI incassare crediti per conto terzi; **human ~** elemento umano; **safety ~** coefficiente m di sicurezza

factory ['fæktərɪ] N fabbrica, stabilimento

factory farming N (BRIT) allevamento su scala industriale

factory floor N: **the ~** (workers) gli operai; (area) il reparto produzione; **on the ~** nel reparto produzione

factory ship N nave f fattoria inv

factual ['fæktjuəl] ADJ che si attiene ai fatti

faculty ['fækəltɪ] N facoltà f inv; (US: teaching staff) corpo insegnante

fad [fæd] N mania; capriccio

fade [feɪd] VI sbiadire, sbiadirsi; (*light, sound, hope*) attenuarsi, affievolirsi; (*flower*) appassire
▶ **fade away** VI (*sound*) affievolirsi
▶ **fade in** VT (*picture*) aprire in dissolvenza; (*sound*) aumentare gradualmente d'intensità
▶ **fade out** VT (*picture*) chiudere in dissolvenza; (*sound*) diminuire gradualmente d'intensità
faeces, (*US*) **feces** ['fiːsiːz] NPL feci *fpl*
fag [fæg] N (*BRIT: col: cigarette*) cicca; (: *chore*) sfacchinata; (*US col: homosexual*) frocio
fag end N (*BRIT col*) mozzicone *m*
fagged out ['fægd-] ADJ (*BRIT col*) stanco(-a) morto(-a)
Fahrenheit ['fɑːrənhaɪt] N Fahrenheit *m inv*
fail [feɪl] VT (*exam*) non superare; (*candidate*) bocciare; (*courage, memory*) mancare a ▶ VI fallire; (*student*) essere respinto(-a); (*supplies*) mancare; (*eyesight, health, light: also:* **be failing**) venire a mancare; (: *brakes*) non funzionare; **to ~ to do sth** (*neglect*) mancare di fare qc; (*be unable*) non riuscire a fare qc; **without ~** senza fallo; certamente
failing ['feɪlɪŋ] N difetto ▶ PREP in mancanza di; **~ that** se questo non è possibile
failsafe ['feɪlseɪf] ADJ (*device etc*) di sicurezza
failure ['feɪljəʳ] N fallimento; (*person*) fallito(-a); (*mechanical etc*) guasto; (*in exam*) insuccesso, bocciatura; (*of crops*) perdita; **his ~ to come** il fatto che non sia venuto; **it was a complete ~** è stato un vero fiasco
faint [feɪnt] ADJ debole; (*recollection*) vago(-a); (*mark*) indistinto(-a); (*smell, breeze, trace*) leggero(-a) ▶ N (*Med*) svenimento ▶ VI svenire; **to feel ~** sentirsi svenire
faintest ['feɪntɪst] ADJ: **I haven't the ~ idea** non ho la più pallida idea
faint-hearted [feɪnt'hɑːtɪd] ADJ pusillanime
faintly ['feɪntlɪ] ADV debolmente; vagamente
faintness ['feɪntnɪs] N debolezza
fair [fɛəʳ] ADJ (*person, decision*) giusto(-a), equo(-a); (*quite large, quite good*) discreto(-a); (*hair etc*) biondo(-a); (*skin, complexion*) chiaro(-a); (*weather*) bello(-a), clemente; (*good enough*) assai buono(-a); (*sizeable*) bello(-a) ▶ ADV: **to play ~** giocare correttamente ▶ N fiera; (*BRIT: funfair*) luna park *m inv*; (*also:* **trade fair**) fiera campionaria; **it's not ~!** non è giusto!; **a ~ amount of** un bel po' di
fair copy N bella copia
fair game N: **to be ~** (*person*) essere bersaglio legittimo
fairground ['fɛəɡraʊnd] N luna park *m inv*
fair-haired [fɛə'hɛəd] ADJ (*person*) biondo(-a)
fairly ['fɛəlɪ] ADV equamente; (*quite*) abbastanza

fairness ['fɛənɪs] N equità, giustizia; **in all ~** per essere giusti, a dire il vero
fair play N correttezza
fair trade N commercio equo e solidale
fairway N (*Golf*) fairway *m inv*
fairy ['fɛərɪ] N fata
fairy godmother N fata buona
fairy lights NPL (*BRIT*) lanternine *fpl* colorate
fairy tale N fiaba
faith [feɪθ] N fede *f*; (*trust*) fiducia; (*sect*) religione *f*, fede *f*; **to have ~ in sb/sth** avere fiducia in qn/qc
faithful ['feɪθful] ADJ fedele
faithfully ['feɪθfəlɪ] ADV fedelmente; **yours ~** (*BRIT: in letters*) distinti saluti
faith healer N guaritore(-trice)
fake [feɪk] N imitazione *f*; (*picture*) falso; (*person*) impostore(-a) ▶ ADJ falso(-a) ▶ VT (*accounts*) falsificare; (*illness*) fingere; (*painting*) contraffare; **his illness is a ~** fa finta di essere malato
falcon ['fɔːlkən] N falco, falcone *m*
Falkland Islands ['fɔːlklənd-] NPL: **the ~** le isole Falkland
fall [fɔːl] (*pt* **fell** [fɛl], *pp* **fallen** ['fɔːlən]) N caduta; (*decrease*) diminuzione *f*, calo; (*in temperature*) abbassamento; (*in price*) ribasso; (*US: autumn*) autunno ▶ VI cadere; (*temperature, price*) scendere; **a ~ of earth** uno smottamento; **a ~ of snow** (*BRIT*) una nevicata; **to ~ in love (with sb/sth)** innamorarsi (di qn/qc); **to ~ short of** (*sb's expectations*) non corrispondere a; **to ~ flat** VI (*on one's face*) cadere bocconi; (*joke*) fare cilecca; (*plan*) fallire; *see also* **falls**
▶ **fall apart** VI cadere a pezzi
▶ **fall back** VI indietreggiare; (*Mil*) ritirarsi
▶ **fall back on** VT FUS ripiegare su; **to have sth to ~ back on** avere qc di riserva
▶ **fall behind** VI rimanere indietro; (*fig: with payments*) essere in arretrato
▶ **fall down** VI (*person*) cadere; (*building, hopes*) crollare
▶ **fall for** VT FUS (*person*) prendere una cotta per; **to ~ for a trick** (*or* **a story** *etc*) cascarci
▶ **fall in** VI crollare; (*Mil*) mettersi in riga
▶ **fall in with** VT FUS (*sb's plans etc*) trovarsi d'accordo con
▶ **fall off** VI cadere; (*diminish*) diminuire, abbassarsi
▶ **fall out** VI (*hair, teeth*) cadere; (*friends etc*) litigare
▶ **fall over** VI cadere
▶ **fall through** VI (*plan, project*) fallire
fallacy ['fæləsɪ] N errore *m*
fallback ['fɔːlbæk] ADJ: **~ position** posizione *f* di ripiego
fallen ['fɔːlən] PP *of* **fall**
fallible ['fælɪbl] ADJ fallibile

falling ['fɔːlɪŋ] ADJ: ~ **market** (Comm) mercato in ribasso

falling-off ['fɔːlɪŋ'ɔf] N calo

fallopian tube [fə'ləupɪən-] N (Anat) tuba di Falloppio

fallout ['fɔːlaut] N fall-out m

fallout shelter N rifugio antiatomico

fallow ['fæləu] ADJ incolto(-a); a maggese

falls [fɔːlz] NPL (waterfall) cascate fpl

false [fɔːls] ADJ falso(-a); **under ~ pretences** con l'inganno

false alarm N falso allarme m

falsehood ['fɔːlshud] N menzogna

falsely ['fɔːlslɪ] ADV (accuse) a torto

false teeth NPL (BRIT) denti mpl finti

falsify ['fɔːlsɪfaɪ] VT falsificare; (figures) alterare

falter ['fɔːltə^r] VI esitare, vacillare

fame [feɪm] N fama, celebrità

familiar [fə'mɪlɪə^r] ADJ familiare; (common) comune; (close) intimo(-a); **to be ~ with** (subject) conoscere; **to make o.s. ~ with** familiarizzarsi con; **to be on ~ terms with** essere in confidenza con

familiarity [fəmɪlɪ'ærɪtɪ] N familiarità; intimità

familiarize [fə'mɪlɪəraɪz] VT: **to ~ sb with sth** far conoscere qc a qn; **to ~ o.s. with** familiarizzare con

family ['fæmɪlɪ] N famiglia

family allowance N (BRIT) assegni mpl familiari

family business N impresa familiare

family credit N (BRIT) ≈ assegni mpl familiari

family doctor N medico di famiglia

family life N vita familiare

family man N (irreg) padre m di famiglia

family planning N pianificazione f familiare

family planning clinic N consultorio familiare

family tree N albergo genealogico

famine ['fæmɪn] N carestia

famished ['fæmɪʃt] ADJ affamato(-a); **I'm ~!** (col) ho una fame da lupo!

famous ['feɪməs] ADJ famoso(-a)

famously ['feɪməslɪ] ADV (get on) a meraviglia

fan [fæn] N (folding) ventaglio; (machine) ventilatore m; (person) ammiratore(-trice); (Sport) tifoso(-a) ▶ VT far vento a; (fire, quarrel) alimentare

▶ **fan out** VI spargersi (a ventaglio)

fanatic [fə'nætɪk] N fanatico(-a)

fanatical [fə'nætɪkl] ADJ fanatico(-a)

fan belt N cinghia del ventilatore

fancied ['fænsɪd] ADJ immaginario(-a)

fanciful ['fænsɪful] ADJ fantasioso(-a); (object) di fantasia

fan club N fan club m inv

fancy ['fænsɪ] N immaginazione f, fantasia; (whim) capriccio ▶ CPD (di) fantasia inv

▶ ADJ (hat) stravagante; (hotel, food) speciale

▶ VT (feel like, want) aver voglia di; (imagine) immaginare, credere; **to take a ~ to** incapricciarsi di; **it took** or **caught my ~** mi è piaciuto; **when the ~ takes him** quando ne ha voglia; **to ~ that** immaginare che; **he fancies her** gli piace

fancy dress N costume m (per maschera)

fancy-dress ball N ballo in maschera

fancy goods NPL articoli mpl di ogni genere

fanfare ['fænfeə^r] N fanfara

fanfold paper ['fænfəuld-] N carta a moduli continui

fang [fæŋ] N zanna; (of snake) dente m

fan heater N (BRIT) stufa ad aria calda

fanlight ['fænlaɪt] N lunetta

fanny ['fænɪ] N (BRIT col!) figa (!); (US col) culo (!)

fantasize ['fæntəsaɪz] VI fantasticare, sognare

fantastic [fæn'tæstɪk] ADJ fantastico(-a)

fantasy ['fæntəsɪ] N fantasia, immaginazione f; fantasticheria; chimera

fanzine ['fænziːn] N rivista specialistica (per appassionati)

FAO N ABBR (= Food and Agriculture Organization) FAO f

FAQ ABBR (= free alongside quay) franco lungo banchina; (Comput: = frequently asked question(s)) FAQ

far [fɑː^r] ADJ lontano(-a) ▶ ADV lontano; (much, greatly) molto; **is it ~ from here?** è molto lontano da qui?; **it's not ~ (from here)** non è lontano (da qui); **how ~?** quanto lontano?; (referring to activity etc) fino a dove?; **how ~ is the town centre?** quanto dista il centro da qui?; **~ away, ~ off** lontano, distante; **the ~ side/end** l'altra parte/l'altro capo; **the ~ left/right** (Pol) l'estrema sinistra/destra; **~ better** assai migliore; **~ from** lontano da; **by ~** di gran lunga; **as ~ back as the 13th century** già nel duecento; **go as ~ as the farm** vada fino alla fattoria; **as ~ as I know** per quel che so; **as ~ as possible** nei limiti del possibile; **how ~ have you got with your work?** dov'è arrivato con il suo lavoro?

faraway ['fɑːrəweɪ] ADJ lontano(-a); (voice, look) assente

farce [fɑːs] N farsa

farcical ['fɑːsɪkəl] ADJ farsesco(-a)

fare [feə^r] N (on trains, buses) tariffa; (in taxi) prezzo della corsa; (food) vitto, cibo ▶ VI passarsela; **half ~** metà tariffa; **full ~** tariffa intera

Far East N: **the ~** l'Estremo Oriente m

farewell [feə'wɛl] EXCL, N addio ▶ CPD (party etc) d'addio

far-fetched ['fɑː'fɛtʃt] ADJ (explanation) stiracchiato(-a), forzato(-a); (idea, scheme, story) inverosimile
farm [fɑːm] N fattoria, podere m ▶ VT coltivare
▶ **farm out** VT (work) dare in consegna
farmer ['fɑːmə'] N coltivatore(-trice), agricoltore(-trice)
farmhand ['fɑːmhænd] N bracciante m agricolo
farmhouse ['fɑːmhaus] N fattoria
farming ['fɑːmɪŋ] N (gen) agricoltura; (of crops) coltivazione f; (of animals) allevamento; **intensive ~** coltura intensiva; **sheep ~** allevamento di pecore
farm labourer N = **farmhand**
farmland ['fɑːmlænd] N terreno da coltivare
farm produce N prodotti mpl agricoli
farm worker N = **farmhand**
farmyard ['fɑːmjɑːd] N aia
Faroe Islands ['fɛərəu-], **Faroes** ['fɛərəuz] NPL: **the ~** le isole Faeroer
far-reaching ['fɑː'riːtʃɪŋ] ADJ di vasta portata
far-sighted ['fɑː'saɪtɪd] ADJ presbite; (fig) lungimirante
fart [fɑːt] (col!) N scoreggia (!) ▶ VI scoreggiare (!)
farther ['fɑːðə'] ADV più lontano ▶ ADJ più lontano(-a)
farthest ['fɑːðɪst] ADV SUPERLATIVE of **far**
FAS ABBR (BRIT: = free alongside ship) franco banchina nave
fascia ['feɪʃɪə] N (Aut) cruscotto; (of mobile phone) cover f inv
fascinate ['fæsɪneɪt] VT affascinare
fascinated ADJ affascinato(-a)
fascinating ['fæsɪneɪtɪŋ] ADJ affascinante
fascination [fæsɪ'neɪʃən] N fascino
fascism ['fæʃɪzəm] N fascismo
fascist ['fæʃɪst] ADJ, N fascista (mf)
fashion ['fæʃən] N moda; (manner) maniera, modo ▶ VT foggiare, formare; **in ~** alla moda; **out of ~** passato(a) di moda; **after a ~** (finish, manage etc) così così; **in the Greek ~** alla greca
fashionable ['fæʃənəbl] ADJ alla moda, di moda; (writer) di grido
fashion designer N disegnatore(-trice) di moda
fashionista [fæʃə'nɪstə] N fashionista mf, maniaco(-a) della moda
fashion show N sfilata di moda
fast [fɑːst] ADJ rapido(-a), svelto(-a), veloce; (clock): **to be ~** andare avanti; (dye, colour) solido(-a) ▶ ADV rapidamente; (stuck, held) saldamente ▶ N digiuno ▶ VI digiunare; **~ asleep** profondamente addormentato; **as ~ as I can** più in fretta possibile; **my watch is 5 minutes ~** il mio orologio va avanti di 5

minuti; **to make a boat ~** (BRIT) ormeggiare una barca
fasten ['fɑːsn] VT chiudere, fissare; (coat) abbottonare, allacciare ▶ VI chiudersi, fissarsi; abbottonarsi, allacciarsi
▶ **fasten (up)on** VT FUS (idea) cogliere al volo
fastener ['fɑːsnə'], **fastening** ['fɑːsnɪŋ] N fermaglio, chiusura; (BRIT: zip fastener) chiusura lampo
fast food N fast food m inv
fastidious [fæs'tɪdɪəs] ADJ esigente, difficile
fast lane N (Aut) ≈ corsia di sorpasso
fat [fæt] ADJ grasso(-a); (book, profit etc) grosso(-a) ▶ N grasso; **to live off the ~ of the land** vivere nel lusso, avere ogni ben di Dio
fatal ['feɪtl] ADJ fatale; mortale; disastroso(-a)
fatalism ['feɪtəlɪzəm] N fatalismo
fatality [fə'tælɪtɪ] N (road death etc) morto(-a), vittima
fatally ['feɪtəlɪ] ADV a morte
fate [feɪt] N destino; (of person) sorte f; **to meet one's ~** trovare la morte
fated ['feɪtɪd] ADJ (governed by fate) destinato(-a); (person, project etc) destinato(-a) a finire male
fateful ['feɪtful] ADJ fatidico(-a)
fat-free ['fæt'friː] ADJ senza grassi
father ['fɑːðə'] N padre m
Father Christmas N Babbo Natale
fatherhood ['fɑːðəhuːd] N paternità
father-in-law ['fɑːðərɪnlɔː] N suocero
fatherland ['fɑːðəlænd] N patria
fatherly ['fɑːðəlɪ] ADJ paterno(-a)
fathom ['fæðəm] N braccio (= 1828 mm) ▶ VT (mystery) penetrare, sondare
fatigue [fə'tiːg] N stanchezza; (Mil) corvé f; **metal ~** fatica del metallo
fatness ['fætnɪs] N grassezza
fatten ['fætn] VT, VI ingrassare; **chocolate is fattening** la cioccolata fa ingrassare
fattening ['fætnɪŋ] ADJ (food) che fa ingrassare
fatty ['fætɪ] ADJ (food) grasso(-a) ▶ N (col) ciccione(-a)
fatuous ['fætjuəs] ADJ fatuo(-a)
faucet ['fɔːsɪt] N (US) rubinetto
fault [fɔːlt] N colpa; (Tennis) fallo; (defect) difetto; (Geo) faglia ▶ VT criticare; **it's my ~** è colpa mia; **to find ~ with** trovare da ridire su; **at ~** in fallo; **generous to a ~** eccessivamente generoso
faultless ['fɔːltlɪs] ADJ perfetto(-a); senza difetto; impeccabile
faulty ['fɔːltɪ] ADJ difettoso(-a)
fauna ['fɔːnə] N fauna
faux pas [fəu'pɑː] N gaffe f inv
favour, (US) **favor** ['feɪvə'] N favore m ▶ VT (proposition) favorire, essere favorevole a;

(*pupil etc*) favorire; (*team, horse*) dare per vincente; **to do sb a ~** fare un favore *or* una cortesia a qn; **in ~ of** in favore di; **to be in ~ of sth/of doing sth** essere favorevole a qc/a fare qc; **to find ~ with sb** (*person*) entrare nelle buone grazie di qn; (*suggestion*) avere l'approvazione di qn

favourable, (*US*)**favorable** ['feɪvərəbl] ADJ favorevole

favourably, (*US*)**favorably** ['feɪvərəblɪ] ADV favorevolmente

favourite, (*US*)**favorite** ['feɪvrɪt] ADJ, N favorito(-a)

favouritism, (*US*)**favoritism** ['feɪvrɪtɪzəm] N favoritismo

fawn [fɔːn] N daino ▶ ADJ (*also:* **fawn-coloured**) marrone chiaro *inv* ▶ VI: **to ~ (up)on** adulare servilmente

fax [fæks] N (*document, machine*) facsimile *m inv*, telecopia; (*machine*) telecopiatrice *f* ▶ VT teletrasmettere, spedire via fax

FBI N ABBR (*US*: = *Federal Bureau of Investigation*) FBI *f*

FCC N ABBR (*US*) = **Federal Communications Commission**

FCO N ABBR (*BRIT*: = *Foreign and Commonwealth Office*) ≈ Ufficio affari esteri

FD N ABBR (*US*) = **fire department**

FDA N ABBR (*US*) = **Food and Drug Administration**

FE N ABBR = **further education**

fear [fɪər] N paura, timore *m* ▶ VT aver paura di, temere ▶ VI: **to ~ for** temere per, essere in ansia per; **~ of heights** vertigini *fpl*; **for ~ of** per paura di; **to ~ that** avere paura di (*or* che + *sub*), temere di (*or* che + *sub*)

fearful ['fɪəful] ADJ pauroso(-a); (*sight, noise*) terribile, spaventoso(-a); (*frightened*): **to be ~ of** temere

fearfully ['fɪəfəlɪ] ADV (*timidly*) timorosamente; (*col: very*) terribilmente, spaventosamente

fearless ['fɪəlɪs] ADJ intrepido(-a), senza paura

fearsome ['fɪəsəm] ADJ (*opponent*) formidabile, terribile; (*sight*) terrificante

feasibility [fiːzə'bɪlɪtɪ] N praticabilità

feasibility study N studio delle possibilità di realizzazione

feasible ['fiːzəbl] ADJ fattibile, realizzabile

feast [fiːst] N festa, banchetto; (*Rel: also:* **feast day**) festa ▶ VI banchettare; **to ~ on** godersi, gustare

feat [fiːt] N impresa, fatto insigne

feather ['fɛðər] N penna ▶ CPD (*mattress, bed, pillow*) di piume ▶ VT: **to ~ one's nest** (*fig*) arricchirsi

feather-weight ['fɛðəweɪt] N peso *m* piuma *inv*

feature ['fiːtʃər] N caratteristica; (*article*) articolo ▶ VT (*film*) avere come protagonista ▶ VI figurare; **features** NPL (*of face*) fisionomia; **a (special) ~ on sth/sb** un servizio speciale su qc/qn; **it featured prominently in ...** ha avuto un posto di prima importanza in ...

feature film N film *m inv* principale

featureless ['fiːtʃəlɪs] ADJ anonimo(-a), senza caratteri distinti

Feb. [fɛb] ABBR (= *February*) feb.

February ['fɛbruərɪ] N febbraio; *see also* **July**

feces ['fiːsiːz] NPL (*US*) = **faeces**

feckless ['fɛklɪs] ADJ irresponsabile, incosciente

Fed [fɛd] ABBR (*US*) = **federal; federation**

fed [fɛd] PT, PP *of* **feed**

Fed. [fɛd] N ABBR (*US col*) = **Federal Reserve Board**

federal ['fɛdərəl] ADJ federale

Federal Republic of Germany N Repubblica Federale Tedesca

Federal Reserve Board N (*US*) *organo di controllo del sistema bancario statunitense*

Federal Trade Commission N (*US*) *organismo di protezione contro le pratiche commerciali abusive*

federation [fɛdə'reɪʃən] N federazione *f*

fed up ADJ: **to be ~** essere stufo(-a)

fee [fiː] N pagamento; (*of doctor, lawyer*) onorario; (*for examination*) tassa d'esame; **school fees** tasse *fpl* scolastiche; **entrance ~, membership ~** quota d'iscrizione; **for a small ~** per una somma modesta

feeble ['fiːbl] ADJ debole

feeble-minded [fiːbl'maɪndɪd] ADJ deficiente

feed [fiːd] (*pt, pp* **fed**) N (*of baby*) pappa; (*of animal*) mangime *m*; (*on printer*) meccanismo di alimentazione ▶ VT nutrire; (*baby*) allattare; (*horse etc*) dare da mangiare a; (*fire, machine*) alimentare ▶ VI (*baby, animal*) mangiare; **to ~ material into sth** introdurre materiale in qc; **to ~ data/ information into sth** inserire dati/ informazioni in qc
  ▶ **feed back** VT (*results*) riferire
  ▶ **feed on** VT FUS nutrirsi di

feedback ['fiːdbæk] N feed-back *m*; (*from person*) reazioni *fpl*

feeder ['fiːdər] N (*bib*) bavaglino

feeding bottle ['fiːdɪŋ-] N (*BRIT*) biberon *m inv*

feel [fiːl] (*pt, pp* **felt**) N sensazione *f*; (*sense of touch*) tatto; (*of substance*) consistenza ▶ VT toccare; palpare; tastare; (*cold, pain, anger*) sentire; (*grief*) provare; (*think, believe*): **to ~ that** pensare che; **I ~ that you ought to do it** penso che dovreste farlo; **to ~ hungry/ cold** aver fame/freddo; **to ~ lonely/better**

sentirsi solo/meglio; **I don't ~ well** non mi sento bene; **to ~ sorry for** dispiacersi per; **it feels soft** è morbido al tatto; **it feels colder out here** sembra più freddo qui fuori; **it feels like velvet** sembra velluto (al tatto); **to ~ like** (want) aver voglia di; **to ~ about** or **around for** cercare a tastoni; **to ~ about** or **around in one's pocket for** frugarsi in tasca per cercare; **I'm still feeling my way** (fig) sto ancora tastando il terreno; **to get the ~ of sth** (fig) abituarsi a qc

feeler ['fi:lə'] N (of insect) antenna; **to put out feelers** (fig) fare un sondaggio

feelgood ['fi:lgud] ADJ (film, song) allegro(-a) e a lieto fine

feeling ['fi:lɪŋ] N sensazione f; (emotion) sentimento; (impression) senso, impressione f; **to hurt sb's feelings** offendere qn; **what are your feelings about the matter?** che cosa ne pensa?; **my ~ is that ...** ho l'impressione che ...; **I got the ~ that ...** ho avuto l'impressione che ...; **feelings ran high about it** la cosa aveva provocato grande eccitazione

fee-paying school ['fi:peɪɪŋ-] N scuola privata

feet [fi:t] NPL of **foot**

feign [feɪn] VT fingere, simulare

felicitous [fɪ'lɪsɪtəs] ADJ felice

fell [fɛl] PT of **fall** ▶ VT (tree) abbattere; (person) atterrare ▶ ADJ: **with one ~ blow** con un colpo terribile; **at one ~ swoop** in un colpo solo ▶ N (Brit: mountain) monte m; (: moorland): **the fells** la brughiera

fellow ['fɛləu] N individuo, tipo; (comrade) compagno; (of learned society) membro cpd; (of university) ≈ docente mf ▶ CPD: **their ~ prisoners/students** i loro compagni di prigione/studio

fellow citizen N concittadino(-a)

fellow countryman N (irreg) compatriota m

fellow feeling N simpatia

fellow men NPL simili mpl

fellowship ['fɛləuʃɪp] N associazione f; compagnia; (Scol) specie di borsa di studio universitaria

fellow traveller N compagno(-a) di viaggio; (Pol) simpatizzante mf

fell-walking ['fɛlwɔːkɪŋ] N (Brit) passeggiate fpl in montagna

felon ['fɛlən] N (Law) criminale mf

felony ['fɛlənɪ] N (Law) reato, crimine m

felt [fɛlt] PT, PP of **feel** ▶ N feltro

felt-tip pen ['fɛlttɪp-] N pennarello

female ['fi:meɪl] N (Zool) femmina; (pej: woman) donna, femmina ▶ ADJ (sex, character) femminile; (Biol, Elec) femmina inv; (vote etc) di donne; **male and ~ students** studenti e studentesse

female impersonator N (Theat) attore comico che fa parti da donna

feminine ['fɛmɪnɪn] ADJ, N femminile (m)

femininity [fɛmɪ'nɪnɪtɪ] N femminilità

feminism ['fɛmɪnɪzəm] N femminismo

feminist ['fɛmɪnɪst] N femminista mf

fen [fɛn] N (Brit): **the Fens** la regione delle Fen

fence [fɛns] N recinto; (Sport) ostacolo; (col: person) ricettatore(-trice) ▶ VT (also: **fence in**) recingere ▶ VI schermire; **to sit on the ~** (fig) rimanere neutrale; (Sport) tirare di scherma

fencing ['fɛnsɪŋ] N (Sport) scherma

fend [fɛnd] VI: **to ~ for o.s.** arrangiarsi ▶ **fend off** VT (attack, attacker) respingere, difendersi da; (blow) parare; (awkward question) eludere

fender ['fɛndə'] N parafuoco; (on boat) parabordo; (US) parafango; paraurti m inv

fennel ['fɛnl] N finocchio

ferment VI [fə'mɛnt] fermentare ▶ N ['fə:mɛnt] (fig) agitazione f, eccitazione f

fermentation [fə:mɛn'teɪʃən] N fermentazione f

fern [fə:n] N felce f

ferocious [fə'rəuʃəs] ADJ feroce

ferocity [fə'rɒsɪtɪ] N ferocità

ferret ['fɛrɪt] N furetto
▶ **ferret about, ferret around** VI frugare
▶ **ferret out** VT (person) scovare, scoprire; (secret, truth) scoprire

ferry ['fɛrɪ] N (small) traghetto; (large: also: **ferryboat**) nave f traghetto inv ▶ VT traghettare; **to ~ sth/sb across** or **over** traghettare qc/qn da una parte all'altra

ferryman ['fɛrɪmən] N (irreg) traghettatore m

fertile ['fə:taɪl] ADJ fertile; (Biol) fecondo(-a); **~ period** periodo di fecondità

fertility [fə'tɪlɪtɪ] N fertilità; fecondità

fertility drug N farmaco fecondativo

fertilize ['fə:tɪlaɪz] VT fertilizzare; fecondare

fertilizer ['fə:tɪlaɪzə'] N fertilizzante m

fervent ['fə:vənt] ADJ ardente, fervente

fervour, (US) **fervor** ['fə:və'] N fervore m, ardore m

fester ['fɛstə'] VI suppurare

festival ['fɛstɪvəl] N (Rel) festa; (Art, Mus) festival m inv

festive ['fɛstɪv] ADJ di festa; **the ~ season** (Brit: Christmas) il periodo delle feste

festivities [fɛs'tɪvɪtɪz] NPL festeggiamenti mpl

festoon [fɛ'stu:n] VT: **to ~ with** ornare di; decorare con

fetch [fɛtʃ] VT andare a prendere; (sell for) essere venduto(-a) per; **how much did it ~?** a or per quanto lo ha venduto?
▶ **fetch up** VI (Brit) andare a finire

fetching ['fɛtʃɪŋ] ADJ attraente

fête [feɪt] N festa

fetid ['fɛtɪd] ADJ fetido(-a)

fetish ['fɛtɪʃ] N feticcio

fetter ['fɛtə^r] VT (*person*) incatenare; (*horse*) legare; (*fig*) ostacolare

fetters ['fɛtəz] NPL catene *fpl*

fettle ['fɛtl] N (*BRIT*): **in fine ~** in gran forma

fetus ['fi:təs] N (*US*) = **foetus**

feud [fju:d] N contesa, lotta ▶ VI essere in lotta; **a family ~** una lite in famiglia

feudal ['fju:dl] ADJ feudale

feudalism ['fju:dəlɪzəm] N feudalesimo

fever ['fi:və^r] N febbre *f*; **he has a ~** ha la febbre

feverish ['fi:vərɪʃ] ADJ (*also fig*) febbrile; (*person*) febbricitante

few [fju:] ADJ pochi(-e) ▶ PRON alcuni(-e); **~ succeed** pochi ci riescono; **they were ~** erano pochi; **a ~ ...** qualche ...; **I know a ~** ne conosco alcuni; **a good ~**, **quite a ~** parecchi; **in the next ~ days** nei prossimi giorni; **in the past ~ days** negli ultimi giorni, in questi ultimi giorni; **every ~ days/ months** ogni due o tre giorni/mesi; **a ~ more days** qualche altro giorno

fewer ['fju:ə^r] ADJ meno *inv*; meno numerosi(-e) ▶ PRON meno; **they are ~ now** adesso ce ne sono di meno

fewest ['fju:ɪst] ADJ il minor numero di

FFA N ABBR = **Future Farmers of America**

FH ABBR (*BRIT*) = **fire hydrant**

FHA N ABBR (*US*) = **Federal Housing Administration**

fiancé [fɪ'ɑ̃:ŋseɪ] N fidanzato

fiancée [fɪ'ɑ̃:ŋseɪ] N fidanzata

fiasco [fɪ'æskəu] N fiasco

fib [fɪb] N piccola bugia

fibre, (*US*) **fiber** ['faɪbə^r] N fibra

fibreboard, (*US*) **fiberboard** ['faɪbəbɔ:d] N pannello di fibre

fibreglass, (*US*) **fiberglass** N fibra di vetro

fibrositis [faɪbrə'saɪtɪs] N cellulite *f*

FICA N ABBR (*US*) = **Federal Insurance Contributions Act**

fickle ['fɪkl] ADJ incostante, capriccioso(-a)

fiction ['fɪkʃən] N narrativa, romanzi *mpl*; (*sth made up*) finzione *f*

fictional ['fɪkʃənl] ADJ immaginario(-a)

fictionalize ['fɪkʃənəlaɪz] VT romanzare

fictitious [fɪk'tɪʃəs] ADJ fittizio(-a)

fiddle ['fɪdl] N (*Mus*) violino; (*cheating*) imbroglio; truffa ▶ VT (*BRIT*: *accounts*) falsificare, falsare; **tax ~** frode *f* fiscale; **to work a ~** fare un imbroglio
▶ **fiddle with** VT FUS gingillarsi con

fiddler ['fɪdlə^r] N violinista *mf*

fiddly ['fɪdlɪ] ADJ (*task*) da certosino; (*object*) complesso(-a)

fidelity [fɪ'dɛlɪtɪ] N fedeltà; (*accuracy*) esattezza

fidget ['fɪdʒɪt] VI agitarsi

fidgety ['fɪdʒɪtɪ] ADJ agitato(-a)

fiduciary [fɪ'du:ʃɪərɪ] N fiduciario

field [fi:ld] N (*gen*, *Comput*) campo; **to lead the ~** (*Sport*, *Comm*) essere in testa, essere al primo posto; **to have a ~ day** (*fig*) divertirsi, spassarsela

field glasses NPL binocolo (da campagna)

field hospital N ospedale *m* da campo

field marshal N feldmaresciallo

fieldwork ['fi:ldwə:k] N ricerche *fpl* esterne; (*Archaeology*, *Geo*) lavoro sul campo

fiend [fi:nd] N demonio

fiendish ['fi:ndɪʃ] ADJ demoniaco(-a)

fierce [fɪəs] ADJ (*look*) fiero(-a); (*fighting*) accanito(-a); (*wind*) furioso(-a); (*heat*) intenso(-a); (*animal*, *person*, *attack*) feroce; (*enemy*) acerrimo(-a)

fiery ['faɪərɪ] ADJ ardente; infocato(-a)

FIFA ['fi:fə] N ABBR (= *Fédération Internationale de Football Association*) F.I.F.A. *f*

fifteen [fɪf'ti:n] NUM quindici

fifteenth NUM quindicesimo(-a)

fifth [fɪfθ] NUM quinto(-a)

fiftieth ['fɪftɪɪθ] NUM cinquantesimo(-a)

fifty ['fɪftɪ] NUM cinquanta

fifty-fifty ['fɪftɪ'fɪftɪ] ADJ: **a ~ chance** una possibilità su due ▶ ADV: **to go ~ with sb** fare a metà con qn

fig [fɪg] N fico

fight [faɪt] (*pt*, *pp* **fought** [fɔ:t]) N zuffa, rissa; (*Mil*) battaglia, combattimento; (*against cancer etc*) lotta ▶ VT (*person*) azzuffarsi con; (*enemy*: *also Mil*) combattere; (*cancer*, *alcoholism*, *emotion*) lottare contro, combattere; (*election*) partecipare a; (*Law*: *case*) difendere ▶ VI battersi, combattere; (*quarrel*): **to ~ (with sb)** litigare (con qn); (*fig*): **to ~ (for/against)** lottare (per/contro)
▶ **fight back** VI difendersi; (*Sport*, *after illness*) riprendersi ▶ VT (*tears*) ricacciare
▶ **fight down** VT (*anger*, *anxiety*) vincere; (*urge*) reprimere
▶ **fight off** VT (*attack*, *attacker*) respingere; (*disease*, *sleep*, *urge*) lottare contro
▶ **fight out** VT: **to ~ it out** risolvere la questione a pugni

fighter ['faɪtə^r] N combattente *m*; (*plane*) aeroplano da caccia

fighter-bomber ['faɪtəbɔmə^r] N cacciabombardiere *m*

fighter pilot N pilota *m* di caccia

fighting ['faɪtɪŋ] N combattimento; (*in streets*) scontri *mpl*

figment ['fɪgmənt] N: **a ~ of the imagination** un parto della fantasia

figurative ['fɪgjurətɪv] ADJ figurato(-a)

figure ['fɪɡəʳ] N (Drawing, Geom, person) figura; (number, cipher) cifra; (body, outline) forma ▶ VT (think: esp US) pensare ▶ VI (appear) figurare; (US: make sense) spiegarsi; essere logico(-a) ▶ VT (US: think, calculate) pensare, immaginare; **public ~** personaggio pubblico; **~ of speech** figura retorica
▶ **figure on** VT FUS (US) contare su
▶ **figure out** VT riuscire a capire; calcolare
figurehead ['fɪɡəhed] N (Naut) polena; (pej) prestanome mf
figure skating N pattinaggio artistico
Fiji ['fiːdʒiː] N, **Fiji Islands** NPL le (isole) Figi
filament ['fɪləmənt] N filamento
filch [fɪltʃ] VT (col: steal) grattare
file [faɪl] N (tool) lima; (for nails) limetta; (dossier) incartamento; (in cabinet) scheda; (folder) cartellina; (for loose leaf) raccoglitore m; (row) fila; (Comput) archivio, file m inv ▶ VT (nails, wood) limare; (papers) archiviare; (Law: claim) presentare; passare agli atti ▶ VI: **to ~ in/out** entrare/uscire in fila; **to ~ past** marciare in fila davanti a; **to ~ a suit against sb** intentare causa contro qn
file name N (Comput) nome m del file
file sharing [-ʃeərɪŋ] N (Comput) file sharing m, condivisione f di file
filibuster ['fɪlɪbʌstəʳ] (esp US Pol) N (also: **filibusterer**) ostruzionista mf ▶ VI fare ostruzionismo
filing ['faɪlɪŋ] N archiviare m; see also **filings**
filing cabinet ['faɪlɪŋ-] N casellario
filing clerk N archivista mf
filings ['faɪlɪŋz] NPL limatura
Filipino [fɪlɪ'piːnəu] N filippino(-a); (Ling) tagal m
fill [fɪl] VT riempire; (tooth) otturare; (job) coprire; (supply: order, requirements, need) soddisfare ▶ N: **to eat one's ~** mangiare a sazietà; **we've already filled that vacancy** abbiamo già assunto qualcuno per quel posto
▶ **fill in** VT (hole) riempire; (form) compilare; (details, report) completare ▶ VI: **to ~ in for sb** sostituire qn; **to ~ sb in on sth** (col) mettere qn al corrente di qc
▶ **fill out** VT (form, receipt) riempire
▶ **fill up** VT riempire ▶ VI (Aut) fare il pieno; **~ it up, please** (Aut) il pieno, per favore
fillet ['fɪlɪt] N filetto
fillet steak N bistecca di filetto
filling ['fɪlɪŋ] N (Culin) impasto, ripieno; (for tooth) otturazione f
filling station N stazione f di rifornimento
fillip ['fɪlɪp] N incentivo, stimolo
filly ['fɪlɪ] N puledra
film [fɪlm] N (Cine) film m inv; (Phot) pellicola, rullino; (of powder, liquid) sottile strato; (thin layer) velo ▶ VT (scene) filmare ▶ VI girare

film script N copione m
film star N divo(-a) dello schermo
filmstrip ['fɪlmstrɪp] N filmina
film studio N studio cinematografico
Filofax® ['faɪləufæks] N agenda ad anelli
filter ['fɪltəʳ] N filtro ▶ VT filtrare
▶ **filter in, filter through** VI (news) trapelare
filter coffee N caffè m da passare al filtro
filter lane N (Brit Aut) corsia di svincolo
filter tip N filtro
filth [fɪlθ] N sporcizia; (fig) oscenità
filthy ['fɪlθɪ] ADJ lordo(-a), sozzo(-a); (language) osceno(-a)
fin [fɪn] N (of fish) pinna
final ['faɪnl] ADJ finale, ultimo(-a); definitivo(-a) ▶ N (Sport) finale f; **finals** NPL (Scol) esami mpl finali; **~ demand** ingiunzione f di pagamento
finale [fɪ'nɑːlɪ] N finale m
finalist ['faɪnəlɪst] N (Sport) finalista mf
finality [faɪ'nælɪtɪ] N irrevocabilità; **with an air of ~** con risolutezza
finalize ['faɪnəlaɪz] VT mettere a punto
finally ['faɪnəlɪ] ADV (lastly) alla fine; (eventually) finalmente; (once and for all) definitivamente
finance [faɪ'næns] N finanza; (funds) fondi mpl; (capital) capitale m ▶ VT finanziare; **finances** NPL (funds) finanze fpl
financial [faɪ'nænʃəl] ADJ finanziario(-a); **~ statement** estratto conto finanziario
financial adviser N consulente mf finanziario(-a)
financially [faɪ'nænʃəlɪ] ADV finanziariamente
financial year N anno finanziario, esercizio finanziario
financier [faɪ'nænsɪəʳ] N finanziatore m
find [faɪnd] (pt, pp **found** [faund]) VT trovare; (lost object) ritrovare ▶ N trovata, scoperta; **to ~ (some) difficulty in doing sth** trovare delle difficoltà nel fare qc; **to ~ sb guilty** (Law) giudicare qn colpevole
▶ **find out** VT informarsi di; (truth, secret) scoprire; (person) cogliere in fallo ▶ VI: **to ~ out about** informarsi su; (by chance) venire a sapere
findings ['faɪndɪŋz] NPL (Law) sentenza, conclusioni fpl; (of report) conclusioni
fine [faɪn] ADJ bello(-a); ottimo(-a); (thin, subtle) fine ▶ ADV (well) molto bene; (small) finemente ▶ N (Law) multa ▶ VT (Law) multare; **to be ~** (person) stare bene; (weather) far bello; **you're doing ~** te la cavi benissimo; **to cut it ~** (with time, money) farcela per un pelo
fine arts NPL belle arti fpl
finely ['faɪnlɪ] ADV (splendidly) in modo stupendo; (chop) finemente; (adjust) con precisione

fine print N: **the ~** i caratteri minuti
finery ['faɪnərɪ] N abiti mpl eleganti
finesse [fɪ'nɛs] N finezza
fine-tooth comb ['faɪntu:θ-] N: **to go through sth with a ~** (fig) passare qc al setaccio
finger ['fɪŋgəʳ] N dito ▶ VT toccare, tastare; **little/index ~** mignolo/(dito) indice m
fingernail ['fɪŋgəneɪl] N unghia
fingerprint ['fɪŋgəprɪnt] N impronta digitale ▶ VT (person) prendere le impronte digitali di
fingerstall ['fɪŋgəstɔ:l] N ditale m
fingertip ['fɪŋgətɪp] N punta del dito; **to have sth at one's fingertips** (fig) avere qc sulla punta delle dita
finicky ['fɪnɪkɪ] ADJ esigente, pignolo(-a); minuziosoa(-a)
finish ['fɪnɪʃ] N fine f; (Sport: place) traguardo; (: polish etc) finitura ▶ VT finire; (use up) esaurire ▶ VI finire; (session) terminare; **to ~ doing sth** finire di fare qc; **to ~ first/second** (Sport) arrivare primo/secondo; **she's finished with him** ha chiuso con lui
▶ **finish off** VT compiere; (kill) uccidere
▶ **finish up** VI, VT finire
finished ['fɪnɪʃt] ADJ (product) finito(-a); (performance) perfetto(-a); (col: tired) sfinito(-a)
finishing line ['fɪnɪʃɪŋ-] N linea d'arrivo
finishing school N scuola privata di perfezionamento (per signorine)
finishing touches NPL ultimi ritocchi mpl
finite ['faɪnaɪt] ADJ limitato(-a); (verb) finito(-a)
Finland ['fɪnlənd] N Finlandia
Finn [fɪn] N finlandese mf
Finnish ['fɪnɪʃ] ADJ finlandese ▶ N (Ling) finlandese m
fiord [fjɔ:d] N fiordo
fir [fə:ʳ] N abete m
fire [faɪəʳ] N fuoco; (destructive) incendio; (gas fire, electric fire) stufa ▶ VT (discharge): **to ~ a gun** fare fuoco; (arrow) sparare; (fig) infiammare; (dismiss) licenziare ▶ VI sparare, far fuoco; **~!** al fuoco!; **on ~** in fiamme; **insured against ~** assicurato contro gli incendi; **electric/gas ~** stufa elettrica/a gas; **to set ~ to sth, set sth on ~** dar fuoco a qc, incendiare qc; **to be/come under ~ (from)** essere/finire sotto il fuoco or il tiro (di)
fire alarm N allarme m d'incendio
firearm ['faɪəra:m] N arma da fuoco
fire brigade [-brɪ'geɪd], (US)**fire department** N (BRIT) (corpo dei) pompieri mpl
fire chief N (US) = **fire master**
fire department N = **fire brigade**
fire door N porta f rompifuoco inv
fire drill N esercitazione f antincendio
fire engine N autopompa

fire escape N scala di sicurezza
fire exit N uscita di sicurezza
fire extinguisher [-ɪk'stɪŋgwɪʃəʳ] N estintore m
fireguard ['faɪəga:d] N (BRIT) parafuoco
fire hazard N: **that's a ~** comporta rischi in caso d'incendio
fire hydrant N idrante m
fire insurance N assicurazione f contro gli incendi
fireman ['faɪəmən] N (irreg) pompiere m
fire master N (BRIT) comandante m dei vigili del fuoco
fireplace ['faɪəpleɪs] N focolare m
fireplug ['faɪəplʌg] N (US) = **fire hydrant**
fire practice N = **fire drill**
fireproof ['faɪəpru:f] ADJ resistente al fuoco
fire regulations NPL norme fpl antincendio
fire screen N parafuoco
fireside ['faɪəsaɪd] N angolo del focolare
fire station N caserma dei pompieri
firetruck (US) N = **fire engine**
firewall ['faɪəwɔ:l] N (Internet) firewall m inv
firewood ['faɪəwud] N legna
fireworks NPL fuochi mpl d'artificio
firing ['faɪərɪŋ] N (Mil) spari mpl, tiro
firing line N linea del fuoco; **to be in the ~** (fig) essere sotto tiro
firing squad N plotone m d'esecuzione
firm [fə:m] ADJ fermo(-a); (offer, decision) definitivo(-a) ▶ N ditta, azienda; **to be a ~ believer in sth** credere fermamente in qc
firmly ['fə:mlɪ] ADV fermamente
firmness ['fə:mnɪs] N fermezza
first [fə:st] ADJ primo(-a) ▶ ADV (before others) il primo, la prima; (before other things) per primo; (for the first time) per la prima volta; (when listing reasons etc) per prima cosa ▶ N (person: in race) primo(-a); (BRIT Scol) laurea con lode; (Aut) prima; **at ~** dapprima, all'inizio; **~ of all** prima di tutto; **in the ~ instance** prima di tutto, in primo luogo; **I'll do it ~ thing tomorrow** lo farò per prima cosa domani; **from the (very) ~** fin dall'inizio, fin dal primo momento; **the ~ of January** il primo (di) gennaio
first aid N pronto soccorso
first-aid kit ['fə:st'eɪd-] N cassetta pronto soccorso
first-class ['fə:st'kla:s] ADJ di prima classe
first-class mail N ≈ espresso
first-hand ['fə:st'hænd] ADJ di prima mano; diretto(-a)
first lady N (US) moglie f del presidente
firstly ['fə:stlɪ] ADV in primo luogo
first name N prenome m
first night N (Theat) prima
first-rate ['fə:st'reɪt] ADJ di prima qualità, ottimo(-a)

559

first-time buyer ['fə:sttaɪm-] N acquirente *mf* di prima casa

First World War N: **the ~** la prima guerra mondiale

fir tree N abete *m*

fiscal ['fɪskəl] ADJ fiscale; **~ year** anno fiscale

fish [fɪʃ] N (pl *inv*) pesce *m* ▶ VT (*river, area*) pescare in ▶ VI pescare; **to go fishing** andare a pesca
▶ **fish out** VT (*from water*) ripescare; (*from box etc*) tirare fuori

fish-and-chip shop [fɪʃən'tʃɪp-] N ≈ friggitoria; *see* **chip shop**

fishbone ['fɪʃbəun] N lisca, spina

fisherman ['fɪʃəmən] N (*irreg*) pescatore *m*

fishery ['fɪʃərɪ] N zona da pesca

fish factory N (*BRIT*) fabbrica per la lavorazione del pesce

fish farm N vivaio

fish fingers NPL (*BRIT*) bastoncini *mpl* di pesce (surgelati)

fish hook N amo

fishing N pesca

fishing boat ['fɪʃɪŋ-] N barca da pesca

fishing industry N industria della pesca

fishing line N lenza

fishing net N rete *f* da pesca

fishing rod N canna da pesca

fishing tackle N attrezzatura da pesca

fish market N mercato del pesce

fishmonger ['fɪʃmʌŋɡəʳ] N pescivendolo; **~'s (shop)** pescheria

fish slice N (*BRIT*) posata per servire il pesce

fish sticks NPL (*US*) = **fish fingers**

fishy ['fɪʃɪ] ADJ (*fig: tale, story*) sospetto(-a)

fission ['fɪʃən] N fissione *f*; **atomic/nuclear ~** fissione atomica/nucleare

fissure ['fɪʃəʳ] N fessura

fist [fɪst] N pugno

fistfight ['fɪstfaɪt] N scazzottata

fit [fɪt] ADJ (*Med, Sport*) in forma; (*proper*) adatto(-a), appropriato(-a); conveniente ▶ VT (*clothes*) stare bene a; (*match: facts etc*) concordare con; (: *description*) corrispondere a; (*adjust*) aggiustare; (*put in, attach*) mettere; installare; (*equip*) fornire, equipaggiare ▶ VI (*clothes*) stare bene; (*parts*) andare bene, adattarsi; (*in space, gap*) entrare ▶ N (*Med*) accesso, attacco; **~ to** in grado di; **~ for** adatto(-a) a; degno(-a) di; **to keep ~** tenersi in forma; **~ for work** (*after illness*) in grado di riprendere il lavoro; **do as you think** or **see ~** faccia come meglio crede; **this dress is a tight/good ~** questo vestito è stretto/sta bene; **~ of anger/enthusiasm** accesso d'ira/d'entusiasmo; **to have a ~** (*Med*) avere un attacco di convulsioni; (*col*) andare su tutte le furie; **by fits and starts** a sbalzi
▶ **fit in** VI accordarsi; adattarsi ▶ VT (*object*)

far entrare; (*fig: appointment, visitor*) trovare il tempo per; **to ~ in with sb's plans** adattarsi ai progetti di qn
▶ **fit out** VT (*BRIT: also:* **fit up**) equipaggiare

fitful ['fɪtful] ADJ saltuario(-a)

fitment ['fɪtmənt] N componibile *m*

fitness ['fɪtnɪs] N (*Med*) forma fisica; (*of remark*) appropriatezza

fitness instructor N instruttore(-trice) di fitness

fitted ['fɪtɪd] ADJ: **~ carpet** moquette *f inv*; **~ cupboards** armadi *mpl* a muro; **~ kitchen** (*BRIT*) cucina componibile

fitter ['fɪtəʳ] N aggiustatore *m* or montatore *m* meccanico; (*Dress*) sarto(-a)

fitting ['fɪtɪŋ] ADJ appropriato(-a) ▶ N (*of dress*) prova; (*of piece of equipment*) montaggio, aggiustaggio; *see also* **fittings**

fitting room N (*in shop*) camerino

fittings ['fɪtɪŋz] NPL (*in building*) impianti *mpl*

five [faɪv] NUM cinque

five-day week ['faɪvdeɪ-] N settimana di 5 giorni (lavorativi)

fiver ['faɪvəʳ] N (*col: BRIT*) biglietto da cinque sterline; (: *US*) biglietto da cinque dollari

fix [fɪks] VT fissare; (*mend*) riparare; (*make ready: meal, drink*) preparare ▶ N: **to be in a ~** essere nei guai; **the fight was a ~** (*col*) l'incontro è stato truccato
▶ **fix up** VT (*arrange: date, meeting*) fissare, stabilire; **to ~ sb up with sth** procurare qc a qn

fixation [fɪk'seɪʃən] N (*Psych, fig*) fissazione *f*, ossessione *f*

fixed [fɪkst] ADJ (*prices etc*) fisso(-a); **there's a ~ charge** c'è una quota fissa; **how are you ~ for money?** (*col*) a soldi come stai?

fixed assets NPL beni *mpl* patrimoniali

fixed penalty, fixed penalty fine N contravvenzione *f* a importo fisso

fixture ['fɪkstʃəʳ] N impianto (fisso); (*Sport*) incontro (del calendario sportivo)

fizz [fɪz] VI frizzare

fizzle ['fɪzl] VI frizzare; (*also:* **fizzle out**: *enthusiasm, interest*) smorzarsi, svanire; (: *plan*) fallire

fizzy ['fɪzɪ] ADJ frizzante; gassato(-a)

fjord [fjɔːd] N = **fiord**

FL, Fla. ABBR (*US*) = **Florida**

flabbergasted ['flæbəgɑːstɪd] ADJ sbalordito(-a)

flabby ['flæbɪ] ADJ flaccido(-a)

flag [flæɡ] N bandiera; (*also:* **flagstone**) pietra da lastricare ▶ VI stancarsi; affievolirsi; **~ of convenience** bandiera di convenienza
▶ **flag down** VT fare segno (di fermarsi) a

flagon ['flæɡən] N bottiglione *m*

flagpole ['flæɡpəul] N albero

flagrant ['fleɪɡrənt] ADJ flagrante

flag stop N (US: for bus) fermata facoltativa, fermata a richiesta

flair [flɛəʳ] N (for business etc) fiuto; (for languages etc) facilità; (style) stile m

flak [flæk] N (Mil) fuoco d'artiglieria; (col: criticism) critiche fpl

flake [fleɪk] N (of rust, paint) scaglia; (of snow, soap powder) fiocco ▶ VI (also: **flake off**) sfaldarsi

flaky ['fleɪkɪ] ADJ (paintwork) scrostato(-a); (skin) squamoso(-a); ~ **pastry** (Culin) pasta sfoglia

flamboyant [flæm'bɔɪənt] ADJ sgargiante

flame [fleɪm] N fiamma; **old** ~ (col) vecchia fiamma

flamingo [flə'mɪŋɡəʊ] N fenicottero, fiammingo

flammable ['flæməbl] ADJ infiammabile

flan [flæn] N (BRIT) flan m inv

Flanders ['flɑːndəz] N Fiandre fpl

flange [flændʒ] N flangia; (on wheel) suola

flank [flæŋk] N fianco ▶ VT fiancheggiare

flannel ['flænl] N (BRIT: also: **face flannel**) guanto di spugna; (fabric) flanella; **flannels** NPL pantaloni mpl di flanella

flannelette [flænə'lɛt] N flanella di cotone

flap [flæp] N (of pocket) patta; (of envelope) lembo; (Aviat) flap m inv ▶ VT (wings) battere ▶ VI (sail, flag) sbattere; (col: also: **be in a flap**) essere in agitazione

flapjack ['flæpdʒæk] N (US: pancake) frittella; (BRIT: biscuit) biscotto di avena

flare [flɛəʳ] N razzo; (in skirt etc) svasatura; **flares** (trousers) pantaloni mpl a zampa d'elefante
▶ **flare up** VI andare in fiamme; (fig: person) infiammarsi di rabbia; (: revolt) scoppiare

flared ['flɛəd] ADJ (trousers) svasato(-a)

flash [flæʃ] N vampata; (also: **news flash**) notizia f lampo inv; (: Phot) flash m inv; (: US: torch) torcia elettrica, lampadina tascabile ▶ VT accendere e spegnere; (send: message) trasmettere; (: look, smile) lanciare; (flaunt) ostentare ▶ VI brillare; (light on ambulance, eyes etc) lampeggiare; **in a** ~ in un lampo; ~ **of inspiration** lampo di genio; **to** ~ **one's headlights** lampeggiare; **he flashed by** or **past** ci passò davanti come un lampo

flashback ['flæʃbæk] N flashback m inv

flashbulb ['flæʃbʌlb] N cubo m flash m inv

flash card N (Scol) scheda didattica

flashcube ['flæʃkjuːb] N flash m inv

flash drive N (Comput) chiavetta USB

flasher ['flæʃəʳ] N (Aut) lampeggiatore m

flashlight ['flæʃlaɪt] N (torch) lampadina tascabile

flashpoint ['flæʃpɔɪnt] N punto di infiammabilità; (fig) livello critico

flashy ['flæʃɪ] ADJ (pej) vistoso(-a)

flask [flɑːsk] N fiasco; (Chem) beuta; (also: **vacuum flask**) thermos® m inv

flat [flæt] ADJ piatto(-a); (tyre) sgonfio(-a), a terra; (battery) scarico(-a); (beer) svampito(-a); (denial) netto(-a); (Mus) bemolle inv; (: voice) stonato(-a); (: instrument) scordato(-a) ▶ N (BRIT: rooms) appartamento; (Mus) bemolle m; (Aut) pneumatico sgonfio ▶ ADV: **(to work)** ~ **out** (lavorare) a più non posso; ~ **rate of pay** tariffa unica di pagamento

flat-footed ['flæt'fʊtɪd] ADJ: **to be** ~ avere i piedi piatti

flatly ['flætlɪ] ADV categoricamente, nettamente

flatmate ['flætmeɪt] N (BRIT): **he's my** ~ divide l'appartamento con me

flatness ['flætnɪs] N (of land) assenza di rilievi

flat-pack ['flætpæk] ADJ: ~ **furniture** mobili mpl in kit ▶ N: **flat pack** kit m inv

flat-screen ['flætskriːn] ADJ a schermo piatto

flatten ['flætn] VT (also: **flatten out**) appiattire; (: house, city) abbattere, radere al suolo

flatter ['flætəʳ] VT lusingare; (show to advantage) donare a

flatterer ['flætərəʳ] N adulatore(-trice)

flattering ['flætərɪŋ] ADJ lusinghiero(-a); (clothes etc) che dona, che abbellisce

flattery ['flætərɪ] N adulazione f

flatulence ['flætjʊləns] N flatulenza

flaunt [flɔːnt] VT fare mostra di

flavour, (US) **flavor** ['fleɪvəʳ] N gusto, sapore m ▶ VT insaporire, aggiungere sapore a; **what flavours do you have?** che gusti avete?; **vanilla-flavoured** al gusto di vaniglia

flavouring, (US) **flavoring** ['fleɪvərɪŋ] N essenza (artificiale)

flaw [flɔː] N difetto

flawless ['flɔːlɪs] ADJ senza difetti

flax [flæks] N lino

flaxen ['flæksən] ADJ biondo(-a)

flea [fliː] N pulce f

flea market N mercato delle pulci

fleck [flɛk] N (of mud, paint, colour) macchiolina; (of dust) granello ▶ VT (with blood, mud etc) macchiettare; **brown flecked with white** marrone screziato di bianco

fled [flɛd] PT, PP of **flee**

fledgeling, fledgling ['flɛdʒlɪŋ] N uccellino

flee [fliː] (pt, pp **fled** [flɛd]) VT fuggire da ▶ VI fuggire, scappare

fleece [fliːs] N vello; (garment) pile m inv ▶ VT (col) pelare

fleecy ['fliːsɪ] ADJ (blanket) soffice; (cloud) come ovatta

fleet [fliːt] N flotta; (of lorries etc) convoglio; (of cars) parco

fleeting ['fli:tɪŋ] ADJ fugace, fuggitivo(-a); (*visit*) volante

Flemish ['flɛmɪʃ] ADJ fiammingo(-a) ▸ N (*Ling*) fiammingo; **the Flemish** NPL i Fiamminghi

flesh [flɛʃ] N carne *f*; (*of fruit*) polpa

flesh wound N ferita superficiale

flew [flu:] PT *of* **fly**

flex [flɛks] N filo (flessibile) ▸ VT flettere; (*muscles*) contrarre

flexibility [flɛksɪ'bɪlɪtɪ] N flessibilità

flexible ['flɛksəbl] ADJ flessibile

flexitime ['flɛksɪtaɪm] N orario flessibile

flick [flɪk] N colpetto; scarto ▸ VT dare un colpetto a; *see also* **flicks**
   ▸ **flick through** VT FUS sfogliare

flicker ['flɪkə'] VI tremolare ▸ N tremolio; **a ~ of light** un breve bagliore

flick knife N (*BRIT*) coltello a serramanico

flicks NPL: **the ~** (*col*) il cine

flier ['flaɪə'] N aviatore *m*

flies [flaɪz] NPL *of* **fly**

flight [flaɪt] N volo; (*escape*) fuga; (*also:* **flight of steps**) scalinata; **to take ~** darsi alla fuga; **to put to ~** mettere in fuga

flight attendant N (*US*) steward *m*, hostess *f inv*

flight crew N equipaggio

flight deck N (*Aviat*) cabina di controllo; (*Naut*) ponte *m* di comando

flight path N (*of aircraft*) rotta di volo; (*of rocket, projectile*) traiettoria

flight recorder N registratore *m* di volo

flimsy ['flɪmzɪ] ADJ (*fabric*) leggero(-a); (*building*) poco solido(-a); (*excuse*) debole

flinch [flɪntʃ] VI ritirarsi; **to ~ from** tirarsi indietro di fronte a

fling [flɪŋ] (*pt, pp* **flung** [flʌŋ]) VT lanciare, gettare ▸ N (*love affair*) avventura

flint [flɪnt] N selce *f*; (*in lighter*) pietrina

flip [flɪp] N colpetto ▸ VT dare un colpetto a; (*switch*) far scattare; (*coin*) lanciare in aria; (*US: pancake*) far saltare (in aria) ▸ VI: **to ~ for sth** (*US*) fare a testa e croce per qc
   ▸ **flip through** VT FUS (*book, records*) dare una scorsa a

flip-flops ['flɪpflɔps] NPL (*esp BRIT: sandals*) infradito *mpl*

flippant ['flɪpənt] ADJ senza rispetto, irriverente

flipper ['flɪpə'] N pinna

flip side N (*of record*) retro

flirt [flə:t] VI flirtare ▸ N civetta

flirtation [flə:'teɪʃən] N flirt *m inv*

flit [flɪt] VI svolazzare

float [fləut] N galleggiante *m*; (*in procession*) carro; (*sum of money*) somma ▸ VI galleggiare; (*bather*) fare il morto; (*Comm: currency*) fluttuare ▸ VT far galleggiare; (*loan, business*) lanciare; **to ~ an idea** ventilare un'idea

floating ['fləutɪŋ] ADJ a galla; **~ vote** voto oscillante; **~ voter** elettore *m* indeciso

flock [flɔk] N (*of sheep, Rel*) gregge *m*; (*of people*) folla; (*of birds*) stormo ▸ VI: **to ~ to** accorrere in massa a

floe [fləu] N (*also:* **ice floe**) banchisa

flog [flɔg] VT flagellare

flood [flʌd] N alluvione *f*; (*of words, tears etc*) diluvio; (*of letters etc*) marea ▸ VT inondare, allagare; (*people*) invadere; (*Aut: carburettor*) ingolfare ▸ VI (*place*) allagarsi; (*people*): **to ~ into** riversarsi in; **in ~** in pieno; **to ~ the market** (*Comm*) inondare il mercato

flooding ['flʌdɪŋ] N inondazione *f*

floodlight ['flʌdlaɪt] N riflettore *m* ▸ VT (*irreg: like* **light**) illuminare a giorno

floodlit ['flʌdlɪt] PT, PP *of* **floodlight** ▸ ADJ illuminato(-a) a giorno

flood tide N alta marea, marea crescente

floodwater ['flʌdwɔ:tə'] N acque *fpl* (*di inondazione*)

floor [flɔ:'] N pavimento; (*storey*) piano; (*of sea, valley*) fondo; (*fig: at meeting*): **the ~** il pubblico ▸ VT pavimentare; (*knock down*) atterrare; (*baffle*) confondere; (*silence*) far tacere; **on the ~** sul pavimento, per terra; **ground ~**, (*US*) **first ~** pianterreno; **first ~**, (*US*) **second ~** primo piano; **top ~** ultimo piano; **to have the ~** (*speaker*) prendere la parola

floorboard ['flɔ:bɔ:d] N tavellone *m* di legno

flooring ['flɔ:rɪŋ] N (*floor*) pavimento; (*material*) materiale *m* per pavimentazioni

floor lamp N (*US*) lampada a stelo

floor show N spettacolo di varietà

floorwalker ['flɔ:wɔ:kə'] N (*esp US*) ispettore *m* di reparto

flop [flɔp] N fiasco ▸ VI (*fail*) far fiasco; (*fall*) lasciarsi cadere

floppy ['flɔpɪ] ADJ floscio(-a), molle ▸ N (*Comput*) = **floppy disk**; **~ hat** cappello floscio

floppy disk N floppy disk *m inv*

flora ['flɔ:rə] N flora

floral ['flɔ:rl] ADJ floreale

Florence ['flɔrəns] N Firenze *f*

Florentine ['flɔrəntaɪn] ADJ fiorentino(-a)

florid ['flɔrɪd] ADJ (*complexion*) florido(-a); (*style*) fiorito(-a)

florist ['flɔrɪst] N fioraio(-a)

florist's, florist's shop N fioraio(-a); **at the ~ (shop)** dal fioraio

flotation [fləu'teɪʃən] N (*Comm*) lancio

flounce [flauns] N balzo
   ▸ **flounce out** VI uscire stizzito(-a)

flounder ['flaundə'] VI annaspare ▸ N (*Zool*) passera di mare

flour ['flauə'] N farina

flourish ['flʌrɪʃ] VI fiorire ▸ VT brandire ▸ N

abbellimento; svolazzo; (of trumpets) fanfara; (bold gesture): **with a ~** con ostentazione

flourishing ['flʌrɪʃɪŋ] ADJ prosperoso(-a), fiorente

flout [flaut] VT (order) contravvenire a; (convention) sfidare

flow [fləu] N flusso; circolazione f; (of river, also Elec) corrente f ▶ VI fluire; (traffic, blood in veins) circolare; (hair) scendere

flow chart N schema m di flusso

flow diagram N organigramma m

flower ['flauə'] N fiore m ▶ VI fiorire; **in ~** in fiore

flower bed N aiuola

flowerpot ['flauəpɔt] N vaso da fiori

flowery ['flauərɪ] ADJ fiorito(-a)

flown [fləun] PP of **fly**

fl. oz. ABBR = **fluid ounce**

flu [flu:] N influenza

fluctuate ['flʌktjueɪt] VI fluttuare, oscillare

fluctuation [flʌktju'eɪʃən] N fluttuazione f, oscillazione f

flue [flu:] N canna fumaria

fluency ['flu:ənsɪ] N facilità, scioltezza; **his ~ in English** la sua scioltezza nel parlare l'inglese

fluent ['flu:ənt] ADJ (speech) facile, sciolto(-a); corrente; **he's a ~ speaker/reader** si esprime/legge senza difficoltà; **he speaks ~ Italian, he's ~ in Italian** parla l'italiano correntemente

fluently ['flu:əntlɪ] ADV con facilità; correntemente

fluff [flʌf] N lanugine f

fluffy ['flʌfɪ] ADJ lanuginoso(-a); (toy) di peluche

fluid ['flu:ɪd] ADJ fluido(-a) ▶ N fluido; (in diet) liquido

fluid ounce N (BRIT) = 0.028 l; 0.05 pints

fluke [flu:k] N (col) colpo di fortuna

flummox ['flʌməks] VT rendere perplesso(-a)

flung [flʌŋ] PT, PP of **fling**

flunky ['flʌŋkɪ] N tirapiedi mf

fluorescent [fluə'rɛsnt] ADJ fluorescente

fluoride ['fluəraɪd] N fluoruro

fluorine ['fluəri:n] N fluoro

flurry ['flʌrɪ] N (of snow) tempesta; **a ~ of activity/excitement** un'intensa attività/un'improvvisa agitazione

flush [flʌʃ] N rossore m; (fig) ebbrezza; (fig: of youth, beauty etc) rigoglio, pieno vigore ▶ VT ripulire con un getto d'acqua; (also: **flush out**: birds) far alzare in volo; (: animals, fig: criminal) stanare ▶ VI arrossire ▶ ADJ: **~ with** a livello di, pari a; **~ against** aderente a; **hot flushes** (Med) vampate fpl di calore; **to ~ the toilet** tirare l'acqua

flushed [flʌʃt] ADJ tutto(-a) rosso(-a)

fluster ['flʌstə'] N agitazione f

flustered ['flʌstəd] ADJ sconvolto(-a)

flute [flu:t] N flauto

flutter ['flʌtə'] N agitazione f; (of wings) battito ▶ VI (bird) battere le ali

flux [flʌks] N: **in a state of ~** in continuo mutamento

fly [flaɪ] (pt **flew** [flu:], pp **flown** [fləun]) N (insect) mosca; (on trousers: also: **flies**) patta ▶ VT pilotare; (passengers, cargo) trasportare (in aereo); (distances) percorrere ▶ VI volare; (passengers) andare in aereo; (escape) fuggire; (flag) sventolare; **to ~ open** spalancarsi all'improvviso; **to ~ off the handle** perdere le staffe, uscire dai gangheri

▶ **fly away** VI volar via

▶ **fly in** VI (plane) arrivare; (person) arrivare in aereo

▶ **fly off** VI volare via

▶ **fly out** VI (plane) partire; (person) partire in aereo

fly-drive N: **~ holiday** fly and drive m inv

fly-fishing ['flaɪfɪʃɪŋ] N pesca con la mosca

flying ['flaɪɪŋ] N (activity) aviazione f; (action) volo ▶ ADJ: **~ visit** visita volante; **with ~ colours** con risultati brillanti; **he doesn't like ~** non gli piace viaggiare in aereo

flying buttress N arco rampante

flying picket N picchetto (proveniente da fabbriche non direttamente coinvolte nello sciopero)

flying saucer N disco volante

flying squad N (Police) (squadra) volante f

flying start N: **to get off to a ~** partire come un razzo

flyleaf ['flaɪli:f] N risguardo

flyover ['flaɪəuvə'] N (BRIT: bridge) cavalcavia m inv

flypast ['flaɪpɑ:st] N esibizione f della pattuglia aerea

flysheet ['flaɪʃi:t] N (for tent) sopratetto

flyweight ['flaɪweɪt] N (Sport) peso m mosca inv

flywheel ['flaɪwi:l] N volano

FM ABBR = **frequency modulation**; (BRIT Mil) = **Field Marshal**

FMB N ABBR (US) = **Federal Maritime Board**

FMCS N ABBR (US: = Federal Mediation and Conciliation Services) organismo di conciliazione in caso di conflitti sul lavoro

FO N ABBR (BRIT) = **Foreign Office**

foal [fəul] N puledro

foam [fəum] N schiuma; (also: **foam rubber**) gommapiuma® ▶ VI schiumare; (soapy water) fare la schiuma

foam rubber N gommapiuma®

FOB ABBR (= free on board) franco a bordo

fob [fɔb] VT: **to ~ sb off with** appioppare qn con; sbarazzarsi di qn con ▶ N (also: **watch fob**: chain) catena per orologio; (: band of cloth) nastro per orologio

foc ABBR (BRIT) = **free of charge**

focal ['fəʊkəl] ADJ focale

focal point N punto focale

focus ['fəʊkəs] N (pl **focuses**) fuoco; (of interest) centro ▶ VT (field glasses etc) mettere a fuoco; (light rays) far convergere ▶ VI: **to ~ on** (with camera) mettere a fuoco; (person) fissare lo sguardo su; **in ~** a fuoco; **out of ~** sfocato(-a)

focus group N (Pol) gruppo di discussione, focus group m inv

fodder ['fɒdər] N foraggio

FOE N ABBR (= Friends of the Earth) Amici mpl della Terra; (US: = Fraternal Order of Eagles) organizzazione filantropica

foe [fəʊ] N nemico

foetus, (US)**fetus** ['fiːtəs] N feto

fog [fɒg] N nebbia

fogbound ['fɒgbaʊnd] ADJ fermo(-a) a causa della nebbia

foggy ['fɒgɪ] ADJ nebbioso(-a); **it's ~** c'è nebbia

fog lamp, (US)**fog light** N (Aut) faro m antinebbia inv

foible ['fɔɪbl] N debolezza, punto debole

foil [fɔɪl] VT confondere, frustrare ▶ N lamina di metallo; (also: **kitchen foil**) foglio di alluminio; (: Fencing) fioretto; **to act as a ~ to** (fig) far risaltare

foist [fɔɪst] VT: **to ~ sth on sb** rifilare qc a qn

fold [fəʊld] N (bend, crease) piega; (Agr) ovile m; (fig) gregge m ▶ VT piegare; **to ~ one's arms** incrociare le braccia

▶ **fold up** VI (map etc) piegarsi; (business) crollare ▶ VT (map etc) piegare, ripiegare

folder ['fəʊldər] N (for papers) cartella; cartellina; (binder) raccoglitore m

folding ['fəʊldɪŋ] ADJ (chair, bed) pieghevole

foliage ['fəʊlɪɪdʒ] N fogliame m

folk [fəʊk] NPL gente f ▶ CPD popolare; **folks** NPL: **my folks** i miei

folklore ['fəʊklɔːr] N folclore m

folk music N musica folk inv

folk singer N cantante mf folk inv

folksong ['fəʊksɒŋ] N canto popolare

follow ['fɒləʊ] VT seguire ▶ VI seguire; (result) conseguire, risultare; **to ~ sb's advice** seguire il consiglio di qn; **I don't quite ~ you** non ti capisco or seguo affatto; **to ~ in sb's footsteps** seguire le orme di qn; **it follows that …** ne consegue che …; **he followed suit** lui ha fatto lo stesso

▶ **follow on** VI (continue): **to ~ on from** seguire

▶ **follow out** VT (implement: idea, plan) eseguire, portare a termine

▶ **follow through** VT = **follow out**

▶ **follow up** VT (victory) sfruttare; (letter, offer) fare seguito a; (case) seguire

follower ['fɒləʊər] N seguace mf, discepolo(-a)

following ['fɒləʊɪŋ] ADJ seguente, successivo(-a) ▶ N seguito, discepoli mpl

follow-up ['fɒləʊʌp] N seguito

folly ['fɒlɪ] N pazzia, follia

fond [fɒnd] ADJ (memory, look) tenero(-a), affettuoso(-a); **to be ~ of** volere bene a; **she's ~ of swimming** le piace nuotare

fondle ['fɒndl] VT accarezzare

fondly ['fɒndlɪ] ADV (lovingly) affettuosamente; (naïvely): **he ~ believed that …** ha avuto l'ingenuità di credere che …

fondness ['fɒndnɪs] N affetto; ~ **(for sth)** predilezione f (per qc)

font [fɒnt] N (Rel) fonte m (battesimale); (Typ) stile m di carattere

food [fuːd] N cibo

food chain N catena alimentare

food mixer N frullatore m

food poisoning N intossicazione f alimentare

food processor [-'prəʊsɛsə] N tritatutto m inv elettrico

food stamp N (US) buono alimentare dato agli indigenti

foodstuffs ['fuːdstʌfs] NPL generi fpl alimentari

fool [fuːl] N sciocco(-a); (Hist: of king) buffone m; (Culin) frullato ▶ VT ingannare ▶ VI (gen): ~ **around** fare lo sciocco; **to make a ~ of sb** prendere in giro qn; **to make a ~ of o.s.** coprirsi di ridicolo; **you can't ~ me** non mi inganna

▶ **fool about, fool around** VI (waste time) perdere tempo

foolhardy ['fuːlhɑːdɪ] ADJ avventato(-a)

foolish ['fuːlɪʃ] ADJ scemo(-a), stupido(-a); imprudente

foolishly ['fuːlɪʃlɪ] ADV stupidamente

foolishness ['fuːlɪʃnɪs] N stupidità

foolproof ['fuːlpruːf] ADJ (plan etc) sicurissimo(-a)

foolscap ['fuːlskæp] N carta protocollo

foot [fʊt] N (pl **feet** [fiːt]) piede m; (measure) piede (= 304 mm; = 12 inches); (of animal) zampa; (of page, stairs etc) fondo ▶ VT (bill) pagare; **on ~** a piedi; **to put one's ~ down** (Aut) schiacciare l'acceleratore; (say no) imporsi; **to find one's feet** ambientarsi

footage ['fʊtɪdʒ] N (Cine: length) ≈ metraggio; (: material) sequenza

foot and mouth, foot and mouth disease N afta epizootica

football ['fʊtbɔːl] N pallone m; (sport: BRIT) calcio; (: US) football m americano

footballer ['fʊtbɔːlər] N (BRIT) = **football player**

football ground N campo di calcio

football match N (BRIT) partita di calcio
football player N (BRIT: *also*: **footballer**) calciatore *m*; (*US*) giocatore *m* di football americano
footbrake ['fu:tbreɪk] N freno a pedale
footbridge ['fu:tbrɪdʒ] N passerella
foothills ['fu:thɪlz] NPL contrafforti *fpl*
foothold ['futhəuld] N punto d'appoggio
footing ['futɪŋ] N (*fig*) posizione *f*; **to lose one's ~** mettere un piede in fallo; **on an equal ~** in condizioni di parità
footlights ['futlaɪts] NPL luci *fpl* della ribalta
footman ['futmən] N (*irreg*) lacchè *m inv*
footnote ['futnəut] N nota (a piè di pagina)
footpath ['futpɑ:θ] N sentiero; (*in street*) marciapiede *m*
footprint ['futprɪnt] N orma, impronta
footrest ['futrɛst] N poggiapiedi *m inv*
Footsie ['futsɪ], **Footsie index** ['futsɪ-] N (*col*) = **Financial Times Stock Exchange 100 Index**
footsie ['futsɪ] N (*col*): **to play ~ with sb** fare piedino a qn
footsore ['futsɔ:ʳ] ADJ: **to be ~** avere mal di piedi
footstep ['futstɛp] N passo
footwear ['futwɛəʳ] N calzatura
FOR ABBR (= *free on rail*) franco vagone

(KEYWORD)

for [fɔ:ʳ] PREP **1** (*indicating destination, intention, purpose*) per; **the train for London** il treno per Londra; **he went for the paper** è andato a prendere il giornale; **it's time for lunch** è ora di pranzo; **what's it for?** a che serve?; **what for?** (*why*) perché?
2 (*on behalf of, representing*) per; **to work for sb/sth** lavorare per qn/qc; **I'll ask him for you** glielo chiederò a nome tuo; **G for George** ≈ G come George
3 (*because of*) per, a causa di; **for this reason** per questo motivo
4 (*with regard to*) per; **it's cold for July** è freddo per luglio; **for everyone who voted yes, 50 voted no** per ogni voto a favore ce n'erano 50 contro
5 (*in exchange for*) per; **I sold it for £5** l'ho venduto per 5 sterline
6 (*in favour of*) per, a favore di; **are you for or against us?** sei con noi o contro di noi?; **I'm all for it** sono completamente a favore
7 (*referring to distance, time*) per; **there are roadworks for 5 km** ci sono lavori in corso per 5 km; **he was away for 2 years** è stato via per 2 anni; **she will be away for a month** starà via un mese; **it hasn't rained for 3 weeks** non piove da 3 settimane; **can you do it for tomorrow?** può farlo per domani?
8 (*with infinitive clauses*): **it is not for me to decide** non sta a me decidere; **it would be best for you to leave** sarebbe meglio che lei se ne andasse; **there is still time for you to do it** ha ancora tempo per farlo; **for this to be possible ...** perché ciò sia possibile ...
9 (*in spite of*) nonostante; **for all his complaints, he's very fond of her** nonostante tutte le sue lamentele, le vuole molto bene
  ► CONJ (*since, as: formal*) dal momento che, poiché

forage ['fɔrɪdʒ] VI foraggiare
forage cap N bustina
foray ['fɔreɪ] N incursione *f*
forbad, forbade [fə'bæd] PT *of* **forbid**
forbearing [fɔ:'bɛərɪŋ] ADJ paziente, tollerante
forbid [fə'bɪd] (*pt* **forbad(e)** [-'bæd], *pp* **forbidden** [-'bɪdn]) VT vietare, interdire; **to ~ sb to do sth** proibire a qn di fare qc
forbidden PT *of* **forbid** ► ADJ (*food*) proibito(-a); (*area, territory*) vietato(-a); (*word, subject*) tabù *inv*
forbidding [fə'bɪdɪŋ] ADJ arcigno(-a), d'aspetto minaccioso
force [fɔ:s] N forza ► VT forzare; (*obtain by force: smile, confession*) strappare; **the Forces** NPL (BRIT) le forze armate; **in ~** (*in large numbers*) in gran numero; (*law*) in vigore; **to come into ~** entrare in vigore; **a ~ 5 wind** un vento forza 5; **to join forces** unire le forze; **the sales ~** (*Comm*) l'effettivo dei rappresentanti; **to ~ sb to do sth** costringere qn a fare qc
  ► **force back** VT (*crowd, enemy*) respingere; (*tears*) ingoiare
  ► **force down** VT (*food*) sforzarsi di mangiare
forced [fɔ:st] ADJ forzato(-a)
force-feed ['fɔ:sfi:d] VT sottoporre ad alimentazione forzata
forceful ['fɔ:sful] ADJ forte, vigoroso(-a)
forcemeat ['fɔ:smi:t] N (BRIT Culin) ripieno
forceps ['fɔ:sɪps] NPL forcipe *m*
forcibly ['fɔ:səblɪ] ADV con la forza; (*vigorously*) vigorosamente
ford [fɔ:d] N guado ► VT guadare
fore [fɔ:ʳ] N: **to the ~** in prima linea; **to come to the ~** mettersi in evidenza
forearm ['fɔ:rɑ:m] N avambraccio
forebear ['fɔ:bɛəʳ] N antenato
foreboding [fɔ:'bəudɪŋ] N presagio di male
forecast ['fɔ:kɑ:st] N (*irreg: like* **cast**) previsione *f*; (*weather forecast*) previsioni *fpl* del tempo ► VT (*irreg: like* **cast**) prevedere
foreclose [fɔ:'kləuz] VT (*Law: also*: **foreclose on**) sequestrare l'immobile ipotecato di
foreclosure [fɔ:'kləuʒəʳ] N sequestro di immobile ipotecato

forecourt ['fɔːkɔːt] N (of garage) corte f esterna
forefathers ['fɔːfɑːðəz] NPL antenati mpl, avi mpl
forefinger ['fɔːfɪŋgəʳ] N (dito) indice m
forefront ['fɔːfrʌnt] N: **in the ~ of** all'avanguardia di
forego [fɔːˈgəu] VT = **forgo**
foregoing ['fɔːgəuɪŋ] ADJ precedente
foregone ['fɔːgɔn] PP of **forego** ▶ ADJ: **it's a ~ conclusion** è una conclusione scontata
foreground ['fɔːgraund] N primo piano ▶ CPD (Comput) foreground inv, di primo piano
forehand ['fɔːhænd] N (Tennis) diritto
forehead ['fɔrɪd] N fronte f
foreign ['fɔrən] ADJ straniero(-a); (trade) estero(-a); (object, matter) estraneo(-a)
foreign body N corpo estraneo
foreign currency N valuta estera
foreigner ['fɔrənəʳ] N straniero(-a)
foreign exchange N cambio di valuta; (currency) valuta estera
foreign exchange market N mercato delle valute
foreign exchange rate N cambio
foreign investment N investimento all'estero
foreign minister N ministro degli Affari esteri
Foreign Office N (BRIT) Ministero degli Esteri
foreign secretary N (BRIT) ministro degli Affari esteri
foreleg ['fɔːlɛg] N zampa anteriore
foreman ['fɔːmən] N (irreg) caposquadra m; (Law: of jury) portavoce m della giuria
foremost ['fɔːməust] ADJ principale; più in vista ▶ ADV: **first and ~** innanzitutto
forename ['fɔːneɪm] N nome m di battesimo
forensic [fəˈrɛnsɪk] ADJ: **~ medicine** medicina legale; **~ expert** esperto della (polizia) scientifica
foreplay ['fɔːpleɪ] N preliminari mpl
forerunner ['fɔːrʌnəʳ] N precursore m
foresee [fɔːˈsiː] (pt **foresaw** [-ˈsɔː], pp **foreseen** [-ˈsiːn]) VT (irreg: like **see**) prevedere
foreseeable [fɔːˈsiːəbl] ADJ prevedibile
foreseen [fɔːˈsiːn] PP of **foresee**
foreshadow [fɔːˈʃædəu] VT presagire, far prevedere
foreshorten [fɔːˈʃɔːtn] VT (figure, scene) rappresentare in scorcio
foresight ['fɔːsaɪt] N previdenza
foreskin ['fɔːskɪn] N (Anat) prepuzio
forest ['fɔrɪst] N foresta
forestall [fɔːˈstɔːl] VT prevenire
forestry ['fɔrɪstrɪ] N silvicoltura
foretaste ['fɔːteɪst] N pregustazione f
foretell [fɔːˈtɛl] VT (irreg: like **tell**) predire
forethought ['fɔːθɔːt] N previdenza

foretold [fɔːˈtəuld] PT, PP of **foretell**
forever [fəˈrɛvəʳ] ADV per sempre; (fig: endlessly) sempre, di continuo
forewarn [fɔːˈwɔːn] VT avvisare in precedenza
forewent [fɔːˈwɛnt] PT of **forego**
foreword ['fɔːwəːd] N prefazione f
forfeit ['fɔːfɪt] N ammenda, pena ▶ VT perdere; (one's happiness, health) giocarsi
forgave [fəˈgeɪv] PT of **forgive**
forge [fɔːdʒ] N fucina ▶ VT falsificare; (signature) contraffare, falsificare; (wrought iron) fucinare, foggiare
▶ **forge ahead** VI tirare avanti
forger ['fɔːdʒəʳ] N contraffattore m
forgery ['fɔːdʒərɪ] N falso; (activity) contraffazione f
forget [fəˈgɛt] (pt **forgot** [-ˈgɔt], pp **forgotten** [-ˈgɔtn]) VT, VI dimenticare
forgetful [fəˈgɛtful] ADJ di corta memoria; **~ of** dimentico(a) di
forgetfulness [fəˈgɛtfulnɪs] N smemoratezza; (oblivion) oblio
forget-me-not [fəˈgɛtmɪnɔt] N nontiscordardimé m inv
forgive [fəˈgɪv] (pt **forgave** [-ˈgeɪv], pp **forgiven** [-ˈgɪvn]) VT perdonare; **to ~ sb for sth/for doing sth** perdonare qc a qn/a qn di aver fatto qc
forgiveness [fəˈgɪvnɪs] N perdono
forgiving [fəˈgɪvɪŋ] ADJ indulgente
forgo [fɔːˈgəu] (pt **forwent** [-ˈwɛnt], pp **forgone** [-ˈgɔn]) VT rinunciare a
forgot [fəˈgɔt] PT of **forget**
forgotten [fəˈgɔtn] PP of **forget**
fork [fɔːk] N (for eating) forchetta; (for gardening) forca; (of roads, railways) bivio, biforcazione f ▶ VI (road) biforcarsi
▶ **fork out** (col: pay) VT sborsare ▶ VI pagare
forked [fɔːkt] ADJ (lightning) a zigzag
fork-lift truck ['fɔːklɪft-] N carrello elevatore
forlorn [fəˈlɔːn] ADJ (person) sconsolato(-a); (deserted: cottage) abbandonato(-a); (desperate: attempt) disperato(-a); (: hope) vano(-a)
form [fɔːm] N forma; (Scol) classe f; (questionnaire) modulo ▶ VT formare; (circle, queue etc) fare; **in the ~ of** a forma di, sotto forma di; **to be in good ~** (Sport, fig) essere in forma; **in top ~** in gran forma; **to ~ part of sth** far parte di qc
formal ['fɔːməl] ADJ formale; (gardens) simmetrico(-a), regolare; (offer, receipt) vero(-a) e proprio(-a); (person) cerimonioso(-a); (occasion, dinner) formale, ufficiale; (Art, Philosophy) formale; **~ dress** abito da cerimonia; (evening dress) abito da sera
formality [fɔːˈmælɪtɪ] N formalità f inv
formalize ['fɔːməlaɪz] VT rendere ufficiale

formally ['fɔːməlɪ] ADV ufficialmente; formalmente; cerimoniosamente; **to be ~ invited** ricevere un invito ufficiale

format ['fɔːmæt] N formato ▶ VT (Comput) formattare

formation [fɔː'meɪʃən] N formazione f

formative ['fɔːmətɪv] ADJ: ~ **years** anni mpl formativi

former ['fɔːməʳ] ADJ vecchio(-a) (before n), ex inv (before n); **the ~ president** l'ex presidente; **the ~ ... the latter** quello ... questo; **the ~ Yugoslavia/Soviet Union** l'ex Jugoslavia/ Unione Sovietica

formerly ['fɔːməlɪ] ADV in passato

form feed N (on printer) alimentazione f modulo

formidable ['fɔːmɪdəbl] ADJ formidabile

formula ['fɔːmjulə] N formula; **F~ One** (Aut) formula uno

formulate ['fɔːmjuleɪt] VT formulare

fornicate ['fɔːnɪkeɪt] VI fornicare

forsake [fə'seɪk] (pt **forsook** [-'suk], pp **forsaken** [-'seɪkən]) VT abbandonare

fort [fɔːt] N forte m; **to hold the ~** (fig) prendere le redini (della situazione)

forte ['fɔːtɪ] N forte m

forth [fɔːθ] ADV in avanti; **to go back and ~** andare avanti e indietro; **and so ~** e così via

forthcoming [fɔːθ'kʌmɪŋ] ADJ (event) prossimo(-a); (help) disponibile; (character) aperto(-a), comunicativo(-a)

forthright ['fɔːθraɪt] ADJ franco(-a), schietto(-a)

forthwith [fɔːθ'wɪθ] ADV immediatamente, subito

fortieth ['fɔːtɪɪθ] NUM quarantesimo(-a)

fortification [fɔːtɪfɪ'keɪʃən] N fortificazione f

fortified wine N vino ad alta gradazione alcolica

fortify ['fɔːtɪfaɪ] VT (city) fortificare; (person) armare

fortitude ['fɔːtɪtjuːd] N forza d'animo

fortnight ['fɔːtnaɪt] N (BRIT) quindici giorni mpl, due settimane fpl; **it's a ~ since ...** sono due settimane da quando ...

fortnightly ['fɔːtnaɪtlɪ] ADJ bimensile ▶ ADV ogni quindici giorni

FORTRAN ['fɔːtræn] N FORTRAN m

fortress ['fɔːtrɪs] N fortezza, rocca

fortuitous [fɔː'tjuːɪtəs] ADJ fortuito(-a)

fortunate ['fɔːtʃənɪt] ADJ fortunato(-a); **he is ~ to have ...** ha la fortuna di avere ...; **it is ~ that** è una fortuna che + sub

fortunately ['fɔːtʃənɪtlɪ] ADV fortunatamente

fortune ['fɔːtʃən] N fortuna; **to make a ~** farsi una fortuna

fortune-teller ['fɔːtʃəntɛləʳ] N indovino(-a)

forty ['fɔːtɪ] NUM quaranta

forum ['fɔːrəm] N foro; (fig) luogo di pubblica discussione

forward ['fɔːwəd] ADJ (ahead of schedule) in anticipo; (movement, position) in avanti; (not shy) sfacciato(-a); (Comm: delivery, sales, exchange) a termine ▶ ADV avanti ▶ N (Sport) avanti m inv ▶ VT (letter) inoltrare; (parcel, goods) spedire; (fig: career, plans) promuovere, appoggiare; **to move ~** avanzare; **"please ~"** "si prega di inoltrare"; ~ **planning** programmazione f in anticipo

forwarding address N nuovo recapito cui spedire la posta

forwards ['fɔːwədz] ADV avanti

forward slash N barra obliqua

forwent [fɔː'wɛnt] PT of **forgo**

fossick ['fɔsɪk] VI (AUSTRALIA, NEW ZEALAND col) cercare; **to ~ in a drawer** rovistare in un cassetto

fossil ['fɔsl] ADJ, N fossile (m); ~ **fuel** combustibile m fossile

foster ['fɔstəʳ] VT incoraggiare, nutrire; (child) avere in affidamento

foster brother N fratello addottivo (in affidamento temporaneo presso la propria famiglia)

foster child N (irreg) bambino(-a) preso(-a) in affidamento

foster mother N madre f affidataria

foster sister N sorella addottiva (in affidamento temporaneo presso la propria famiglia)

fought [fɔːt] PT, PP of **fight**

foul [faul] ADJ (smell, food) cattivo(-a); (weather) brutto(-a), orribile; (language) osceno(-a); (deed) infame ▶ N (Football) fallo ▶ VT sporcare; (football player) commettere un fallo su; (entangle: anchor, propeller) impigliarsi in

foul play N (Sport) gioco scorretto; ~ **is not suspected** si è scartata l'ipotesi dell'atto criminale

found [faund] PT, PP of **find** ▶ VT (establish) fondare

foundation [faun'deɪʃən] N (act) fondazione f; (base) base f; (also: **foundation cream**) fondo tinta; **foundations** NPL (of building) fondamenta fpl; **to lay the foundations** gettare le fondamenta

foundation stone N prima pietra

founder ['faundəʳ] N fondatore(-trice) ▶ VI affondare

founding ['faundɪŋ] ADJ: ~ **fathers** (US) padri mpl fondatori; ~ **member** socio fondatore

foundry ['faundrɪ] N fonderia

fount [faunt] N fonte f; (Typ) stile m di carattere

fountain ['fauntɪn] N fontana

fountain pen N penna stilografica

four [fɔːʳ] NUM quattro; **on all fours** a carponi

four-by-four [fɔːbaɪ'fɔːʳ] N quattro per quattro f inv

four-letter word ['fɔ:lɛtə-] N parolaccia
four-poster ['fɔ:'pəustə'] N (also: **four-poster bed**) letto a quattro colonne
foursome ['fɔ:səm] N partita a quattro; uscita in quattro
fourteen ['fɔ:ti:n] NUM quattordici
fourteenth NUM quattordicesimo(-a)
fourth [fɔ:θ] NUM quarto(-a) ▶ N (Aut: also: **fourth gear**) quarta
four-wheel drive ['fɔ:wi:l-] N (Aut): **with ~** con quattro ruote motrici
fowl [faul] N pollame m; volatile m
fox [fɔks] N volpe f ▶ VT confondere
fox fur N volpe f, pelliccia di volpe
foxglove ['fɔksglʌv] N (Bot) digitale f
fox-hunting ['fɔkshʌntɪŋ] N caccia alla volpe
foyer ['fɔɪeɪ] N atrio; (Theat) ridotto
FPA N ABBR (BRIT: = Family Planning Association) ≈ A.I.E.D. f (= Associazione Italiana Educazione Demografica)
Fr. ABBR (Rel) = **father; friar**
fr. ABBR (= franc) fr.
fracas ['fræka:] N rissa, lite f
fraction ['frækʃən] N frazione f
fractionally ['frækʃnəlɪ] ADV un tantino, minimamente
fractious ['frækʃəs] ADJ irritabile
fracture ['fræktʃə'] N frattura ▶ VT fratturare
fragile ['frædʒaɪl] ADJ fragile
fragment ['frægmənt] N frammento
fragmentary ['frægməntərɪ] ADJ frammentario(-a)
fragrance ['freɪɡrəns] N fragranza, profumo
fragrant ['freɪɡrənt] ADJ fragrante, profumato(-a)
frail [freɪl] ADJ debole, delicato(-a)
frame [freɪm] N (of building) armatura; (of human, animal) ossatura, corpo; (of picture) cornice f; (of door, window) telaio; (of spectacles: also: **frames**) montatura ▶ VT (picture) incorniciare; **to ~ sb** (col) incastrare qn; **~ of mind** stato d'animo
framework ['freɪmwə:k] N struttura
France [frɑ:ns] N Francia
franchise ['fræntʃaɪz] N (Pol) diritto di voto; (Comm) concessione f
franchisee [fræntʃaɪ'zi:] N concessionaria
franchiser ['fræntʃaɪzə'] N concedente m
frank [fræŋk] ADJ franco(-a), aperto(-a) ▶ VT (letter) affrancare
Frankfurt ['fræŋkfə:t] N Francoforte f
frankfurter ['fræŋkfə:tə'] N würstel m inv
franking machine ['fræŋkɪŋ-] N macchina affrancatrice
frankly ['fræŋklɪ] ADV francamente, sinceramente
frankness ['fræŋknɪs] N franchezza
frantic ['fræntɪk] ADJ (activity, pace) frenetico(-a); (desperate: need, desire) pazzo(-a),

sfrenato(-a); (: search) affannoso(-a); (person) fuori di sé
frantically ['fræntɪklɪ] ADV freneticamente; affannosamente
fraternal [frə'tə:nl] ADJ fraterno(-a)
fraternity [frə'tə:nɪtɪ] N (club) associazione f; (spirit) fratellanza
fraternize ['frætənaɪz] VI fraternizzare
fraud [frɔ:d] N truffa; (Law) frode f; (person) impostore(-a)
fraudulent ['frɔ:djulənt] ADJ fraudolento(-a)
fraught [frɔ:t] ADJ (tense) teso(-a); **~ with** pieno(a) di, intriso(a) da
fray [freɪ] N baruffa ▶ VT logorare ▶ VI logorarsi; **to return to the ~** tornare nella mischia; **tempers were getting frayed** cominciavano a innervosirsi; **her nerves were frayed** aveva i nervi a pezzi
FRB N ABBR (US) = **Federal Reserve Board**
FRCM N ABBR (BRIT) = **Fellow of the Royal College of Music**
FRCO N ABBR (BRIT) = **Fellow of the Royal College of Organists**
FRCP N ABBR (BRIT) = **Fellow of the Royal College of Physicians**
FRCS N ABBR (BRIT) = **Fellow of the Royal College of Surgeons**
freak [fri:k] N fenomeno, mostro; (col: enthusiast) fanatico(-a) ▶ ADJ (storm, conditions) anormale; (victory) inatteso(-a)
▶ **freak out** VI (col) andare fuori di testa
freakish ['fri:kɪʃ] ADJ (result, appearance) strano(-a), bizzarro(-a); (weather) anormale
freckle ['frekl] N lentiggine f
free [fri:] ADJ libero(-a); (gratis) gratuito(-a); (liberal) generoso(-a) ▶ VT (prisoner, jammed person) liberare; (jammed object) districare; **~ (of charge)** gratuitamente; **admission ~** entrata libera; **to give sb a ~ hand** dare carta bianca a qn; **~ and easy** rilassato
freebie ['fri:bɪ] N (col): **it's a ~** è in omaggio
freedom ['fri:dəm] N libertà
freedom fighter N combattente mf per la libertà
free enterprise N liberalismo economico
Freefone® ['fri:fəun] N (BRIT) ≈ numero verde
free-for-all ['fri:fərɔ:l] N parapiglia m generale
free gift N regalo, omaggio
freehold ['fri:həuld] N proprietà assoluta
free kick N (Sport) calcio libero
freelance ['fri:lɑ:ns] ADJ indipendente; **~ work** collaborazione f esterna
freeloader ['fri:ləudə'] N (pej) scroccone(-a)
freely ['fri:lɪ] ADV liberamente; (liberally) liberalmente
free-market economy [fri:'mɑ:kɪt-] N economia di libero mercato
freemason ['fri:meɪsn] N massone m

freemasonry ['fri:meɪsnrɪ] N massoneria
Freepost® ['fri:pəust] N affrancatura a carica del destinatario
free-range ['fri:'reɪndʒ] ADJ (*hen*) ruspante; (*eggs*) di gallina ruspante
free sample N campione *m* gratuito
free speech N libertà di parola
freestyle ['fri:staɪl] N (*in swimming*) stile *m* libero
free trade N libero scambio
freeway ['fri:weɪ] N (*US*) superstrada
freewheel [fri:'wi:l] VI andare a ruota libera
freewheeling [fri:'wi:lɪŋ] ADJ a ruota libera
free will N libero arbitrio; **of one's own ~** di spontanea volontà
freeze [fri:z] (*pt* **froze** [frəuz], *pp* **frozen** ['frəuzn]) VI gelare ▶ VT gelare; (*food*) congelare; (*prices, salaries*) bloccare ▶ N gelo; blocco
  ▶ **freeze over** VI (*lake, river*) ghiacciarsi; (*windows, windscreen*) coprirsi di ghiaccio
  ▶ **freeze up** VI gelarsi
freeze-dried ['fri:zdraɪd] ADJ liofilizzato(-a)
freezer ['fri:zəʳ] N congelatore *m*
freezing ['fri:zɪŋ] ADJ (*wind, weather*) gelido(-a); **I'm ~** mi sto congelando ▶ N (*also:* **freezing point**) punto di congelamento; **3 degrees below ~** 3 gradi sotto zero
freight [freɪt] N (*goods*) merce *f*, merci *fpl*; (*money charged*) spese *fpl* di trasporto; **~ forward** spese a carico del destinatario; **~ inward** spese di trasporto sulla merce in entrata
freight car N (*US*) carro *m* merci *inv*
freighter ['freɪtəʳ] N (*Naut*) nave *f* da carico
freight forwarder [-'fɔ:wədəʳ] N spedizioniere *m*
freight train N (*US*) treno *m* merci *inv*
French [frɛntʃ] ADJ francese ▶ N (*Ling*) francese *m*; **the French** NPL i Francesi
French bean N fagiolino
French bread N baguette *f inv*
French Canadian ADJ, N franco-canadese (*mf*)
French dressing N (*Culin*) condimento per insalata
French fried potatoes, (*US*) **French fries** NPL patate *fpl* fritte
French Guiana [-gaɪ'ænə] N Guiana francese
French loaf N ≈ filoncino
Frenchman ['frɛntʃmən] N (*irreg*) francese *m*
French Riviera N: **the ~** la Costa Azzurra
French stick N baguette *f inv*
French window N portafinestra
Frenchwoman ['frɛntʃwumən] N (*irreg*) francese *f*
frenetic [frə'nɛtɪk] ADJ frenetico(-a)
frenzy ['frɛnzɪ] N frenesia
frequency ['fri:kwənsɪ] N frequenza

frequency modulation N modulazione *f* di frequenza
frequent ADJ ['fri:kwənt] frequente ▶ VT [frɪ'kwɛnt] frequentare
frequently ['fri:kwəntlɪ] ADV frequentemente, spesso
fresco ['frɛskəu] N affresco
fresh [frɛʃ] ADJ fresco(-a); (*new*) nuovo(-a); (*cheeky*) sfacciato(-a); **to make a ~ start** cominciare da capo
freshen ['frɛʃən] VI (*wind, air*) rinfrescare ▶ **freshen up** VI rinfrescarsi
freshener ['frɛʃnəʳ] N: **skin ~** tonico rinfrescante; **air ~** deodorante *m* per ambienti
fresher ['frɛʃəʳ] N (*Brit Scol: col*) = **freshman**
freshly ['frɛʃlɪ] ADV di recente, di fresco
freshman ['frɛʃmən] N (*irreg*) (*Scol*) matricola
freshness ['frɛʃnɪs] N freschezza
freshwater ['frɛʃwɔ:təʳ] ADJ (*fish*) d'acqua dolce
fret [frɛt] VI agitarsi, affliggersi
fretful ['frɛtful] ADJ (*child*) irritabile
Freudian ['frɔɪdɪən] ADJ freudiano(-a); **~ slip** lapsus *m inv* freudiano
FRG N ABBR = **Federal Republic of Germany**
Fri. ABBR (= *Friday*) ven.
friar ['fraɪəʳ] N frate *m*
friction ['frɪkʃən] N frizione *f*, attrito
friction feed N (*on printer*) trascinamento ad attrito
Friday ['fraɪdɪ] N venerdì *m inv*; *see also* **Tuesday**
fridge [frɪdʒ] N (*Brit*) frigo, frigorifero
fridge-freezer ['frɪdʒ'fri:zəʳ] N freezer *m inv*
fried [fraɪd] PT, PP *of* **fry** ▶ ADJ fritto(-a); **~ egg** uovo fritto
friend [frɛnd] N amico(-a); **to make friends with** fare amicizia con ▶ VT (*Internet*) aggiungere tra gli amici
friendliness ['frɛndlɪnɪs] N amichevolezza
friendly ['frɛndlɪ] ADJ amichevole ▶ N (*also:* **friendly match**) partita amichevole; **to be ~ with** essere amico di; **to be ~ to** essere cordiale con
friendly fire N fuoco amico
friendly society N società *f inv* di mutuo soccorso
friendship ['frɛndʃɪp] N amicizia
fries [fraɪz] NPL (*esp US*) patate *fpl* fritte
frieze [fri:z] N fregio
frigate ['frɪgɪt] N (*Naut: modern*) fregata
fright [fraɪt] N paura, spavento; **to take ~** spaventarsi; **she looks a ~!** guarda com'è conciata!
frighten ['fraɪtn] VT spaventare, far paura a ▶ **frighten away, frighten off** VT (*birds, children etc*) scacciare (facendogli paura)
frightened ['fraɪtnd] ADJ spaventato(-a); **to be ~ (of)** avere paura (di)

frightening ['fraɪtnɪŋ] ADJ spaventoso(-a), pauroso(-a)

frightful ['fraɪtful] ADJ orribile

frightfully ['fraɪtfulɪ] ADV terribilmente; **I'm ~ sorry** mi dispiace moltissimo

frigid ['frɪdʒɪd] ADJ (woman) frigido(-a)

frigidity [frɪ'dʒɪdɪtɪ] N frigidità

frill [frɪl] N balza; **without frills** (fig) senza fronzoli

frilly ['frɪlɪ] ADJ (clothes, lampshade) pieno(-a) di fronzoli

fringe [frɪndʒ] N (BRIT: of hair) frangia; (edge: of forest etc) margine m; (fig): **on the ~** al margine

fringe benefits NPL vantaggi mpl

fringe theatre N teatro d'avanguardia

Frisbee ® ['frɪzbɪ] N frisbee® m inv

frisk [frɪsk] VT perquisire

frisky ['frɪskɪ] ADJ vivace, vispo(-a)

fritter ['frɪtər] N frittella
  ▶ **fritter away** VT sprecare

frivolity [frɪ'vɔlɪtɪ] N frivolezza

frivolous ['frɪvələs] ADJ frivolo(-a)

frizzy ['frɪzɪ] ADJ crespo(-a)

fro [frəu] ADV: **to and ~** avanti e indietro

frock [frɔk] N vestito

frog [frɔg] N rana; **to have a ~ in one's throat** avere la voce rauca

frogman ['frɔgmən] N (irreg) uomo m rana inv

frogmarch ['frɔgmɑːtʃ] VT (BRIT): **to ~ sb in/out** portar qn dentro/fuori con la forza

frolic ['frɔlɪk] VI sgambettare

(KEYWORD)

from [frɔm] PREP **1** (indicating starting place, origin etc) da; **where do you come from?**, **where are you from?** da dove viene?, di dov'è?; **where has he come from?** da dove arriva?; **from London to Glasgow** da Londra a Glasgow; **a letter from my sister** una lettera da mia sorella; **tell him from me that ...** gli dica da parte mia che ...
2 (indicating time) da; **from one o'clock to** or **until** or **till two** dall'una alle due; **(as) from Friday** a partire da venerdì; **from January (on)** da gennaio, a partire da gennaio
3 (indicating distance) da; **the hotel is 1 km from the beach** l'albergo è a 1 km dalla spiaggia
4 (indicating price, number etc) da; **from a pound** da una sterlina in su; **prices range from £10 to £50** i prezzi vanno dalle 10 alle 50 sterline
5 (indicating difference) da; **he can't tell red from green** non sa distinguere il rosso dal verde
6 (because of, on the basis of): **from what he says** da quanto dice lui; **weak from hunger** debole per la fame

frond [frɔnd] N fronda

front [frʌnt] N (of house, dress) davanti m inv; (of train) testa; (of book) copertina; (promenade: also: **sea front**) lungomare m; (Mil, Pol, Meteor) fronte m; (fig: appearances) fronte f
  ▶ ADJ primo(-a); anteriore, davanti inv ▶ VI: **to ~ onto sth** dare su qc, guardare verso qc; **in ~ (of)** davanti (a)

frontage ['frʌntɪdʒ] N facciata

frontal ['frʌntl] ADJ frontale

front bench N posti in Parlamento occupati dai frontbencher; vedi nota

> Nel Parlamento britannico, si chiamano front bench gli scanni della House of Commons che si trovano alla sinistra e alla destra dello Speaker davanti ai backbenches. I front bench sono occupati dai frontbenchers, parlamentari che ricoprono una carica di governo o che fanno parte dello shadow cabinet dell'opposizione.

frontbencher ['frʌnt'bɛntʃər] N (BRIT) parlamentare con carica al governo o all'opposizione

front desk N (US: in hotel) reception f inv; (: at doctor's) accettazione f

front door N porta d'entrata; (of car) sportello anteriore

frontier ['frʌntɪər] N frontiera

frontispiece ['frʌntɪspiːs] N frontespizio

front page N prima pagina

front room N (BRIT) salotto

front runner N (fig) favorito(-a)

front-wheel drive ['frʌntwiːl-] N trasmissione f anteriore

frost [frɔst] N gelo; (also: **hoarfrost**) brina

frostbite ['frɔstbaɪt] N congelamento

frosted ['frɔstɪd] ADJ (glass) smerigliato(-a); (US: cake) glassato(-a)

frosting ['frɔstɪŋ] N (US: on cake) glassa

frosty ['frɔstɪ] ADJ (window) coperto(-a) di ghiaccio; (weather, look, welcome) gelido(-a)

froth [frɔθ] N spuma; schiuma

frown [fraun] N cipiglio ▶ VI accigliarsi
  ▶ **frown on** VT FUS (fig) disapprovare

froze [frəuz] PT of **freeze**

frozen ['frəuzn] PP of **freeze** ▶ ADJ (food) congelato(-a); (Comm: assets) bloccato(-a)

FRS N ABBR (BRIT) = **Fellow of the Royal Society**; (US: = Federal Reserve System) sistema bancario degli Stati Uniti

frugal ['fruːgəl] ADJ frugale; (person) economo(-a)

fruit [fruːt] N (pl inv) frutto; (collectively) frutta

fruiterer ['fruːtərər] N fruttivendolo; **at the ~'s (shop)** dal fruttivendolo

fruit fly N mosca della frutta

fruitful ['fruːtful] ADJ fruttuoso(-a); (plant) fruttifero(-a); (soil) fertile

fruition [fruː'ɪʃən] N: **to come to ~** realizzarsi

fruit juice N succo di frutta

fruitless ['fru:tlɪs] ADJ (fig) vano(-a), inutile
fruit machine N (BRIT) macchina f
mangiasoldi inv
fruit salad N macedonia
frump [frʌmp] N: **to feel a ~** sentirsi
infagottato (a)
frustrate [frʌs'treɪt] VT frustrare
frustrated [frʌs'treɪtɪd] ADJ frustrato(-a)
frustrating [frʌs'treɪtɪŋ] ADJ (job) frustrante;
(day) disastroso(-a)
frustration [frʌs'treɪʃən] N frustrazione f
fry [fraɪ] (pt, pp **fried** [-d]) VT friggere ▶ NPL:
the small ~ i pesci piccoli
frying pan N ['fraɪɪŋ-] N padella
FT N ABBR (BRIT: = Financial Times) giornale
finanziario; **the FT index** l'indice FT
ft. ABBR = **foot; feet**
FTC N ABBR (US) = **Federal Trade Commission**
FT-SE 100 Index N ABBR = **Financial Times
Stock Exchange 100 Index**
fuchsia ['fju:ʃə] N fucsia
fuck [fʌk] VT, VI (col!) fottere (!); **~ off!**
vaffanculo! (!)
fuddled ['fʌdld] ADJ (muddled) confuso(-a);
(col: tipsy) brillo(-a)
fuddy-duddy ['fʌdɪdʌdɪ] N (pej) parruccone m
fudge [fʌdʒ] N (Culin) specie di caramella a base di
latte, burro e zucchero ▶ VT (issue, problem) evitare
fuel [fjuəl] N (for heating) combustibile m; (for
propelling) carburante m ▶ VT (furnace etc)
alimentare; (aircraft, ship etc) rifornire di
carburante
fuel oil N nafta
fuel poverty N povertà energetica
fuel pump N (Aut) pompa del carburante
fuel tank N deposito m nafta inv; (on vehicle)
serbatoio (della benzina)
fug [fʌg] N (BRIT) aria viziata
fugitive ['fju:dʒɪtɪv] N fuggitivo(-a),
profugo(-a); (from prison) evaso(-a)
fulfil, (US) **fulfill** [ful'fɪl] VT (function)
compiere; (order) eseguire; (wish, desire)
soddisfare, appagare
fulfilled [ful'fɪld] ADJ (person) realizzato(-a),
soddisfatto(-a)
fulfilment, (US) **fulfillment** [ful'fɪlmənt] N
(of wishes) soddisfazione f, appagamento
full [ful] ADJ pieno(-a); (details, skirt)
ampio(-a); (price) intero(-a) ▶ ADV: **to know ~
well that** sapere benissimo che; **~ (up)** (hotel
etc) al completo; **I'm ~ (up)** sono sazio; **a ~
two hours** due ore intere; **at ~ speed** a tutta
velocità; **in ~** per intero; **to pay in ~** pagare
tutto; **~ name** nome m e cognome m;
~ employment piena occupazione; **~ fare**
tariffa completa
fullback ['fulbæk] N (Rugby, Football) terzino
full-blooded ['ful'blʌdɪd] ADJ (vigorous: attack)
energico(-a); (virile: male) virile

full-cream ['ful'kri:m] ADJ: **~ milk** (BRIT) latte
m intero
full-grown ['ful'grəun] ADJ maturo(-a)
full-length ['ful'lɛŋθ] ADJ (portrait) in piedi;
(film) a lungometraggio; (coat, novel)
lungo(-a)
full moon N luna piena
full-scale ['fulskeɪl] ADJ (plan, model) in
grandezza naturale; (attack, search, retreat) su
vasta scala
full-sized ['ful'saɪzd] ADJ (portrait etc) a
grandezza naturale
full stop N punto
full-time ['ful'taɪm] ADJ, ADV (work) a tempo
pieno ▶ N (Sport) fine f partita
fully ['fulɪ] ADV interamente, pienamente,
completamente; (at least): **~ as big** almeno
così grosso
fully-fledged ['fulɪ'flɛdʒd] ADJ (bird)
adulto(-a); (fig: teacher, member etc) a tutti gli
effetti
fulsome ['fulsəm] ADJ (pej: praise)
esagerato(-a), eccessivo(-a); (manner)
insincero
fumble ['fʌmbl] VI brancolare, andare a
tentoni ▶ VT (ball) lasciarsi sfuggire
▶ **fumble with** VT FUS trafficare con
fume [fju:m] VI essere furioso(-a); **fumes** NPL
esalazioni fpl, vapori mpl
fumigate ['fju:mɪgeɪt] VT suffumicare
fun [fʌn] N divertimento, spasso; **to have ~**
divertirsi; **for ~** per scherzo; **it's not much
~** non è molto divertente; **to make ~ of**
prendersi gioco di
function ['fʌŋkʃən] N funzione f; cerimonia,
ricevimento ▶ VI funzionare; **to ~ as** fungere
da, funzionare da
functional ['fʌŋkʃənl] ADJ funzionale
function key N (Comput) tasto di funzioni
fund [fʌnd] N fondo, cassa; (source) fondo;
(store) riserva; **funds** NPL (money) fondi mpl
fundamental [fʌndə'mɛntl] ADJ
fondamentale; **fundamentals** NPL basi fpl
fundamentalism [fʌndə'mɛntəlɪzəm] N
fondamentalismo
fundamentalist [fʌndə'mɛntəlɪst] N
fondamentalista mf
fundamentally [fʌndə'mɛntəlɪ] ADV
essenzialmente, fondamentalmente
funding ['fʌndɪŋ] N finanziamento
fund-raising ['fʌndreɪzɪŋ] N raccolta di fondi
funeral ['fju:nərəl] N funerale m
funeral director N impresario di pompe
funebri
funeral parlour [-'pɑ:ləʳ] N impresa di
pompe funebri
funeral service N ufficio funebre
funereal [fju:'nɪərɪəl] ADJ funereo(-a),
lugubre

fun fair ['fʌnfɛər] N luna park m inv
fungus ['fʌŋgəs] (pl **fungi** [-gaɪ]) N fungo; (mould) muffa
funicular [fjuː'nɪkjulər] ADJ (also: **funicular railway**) funicolare f
funky ['fʌŋkɪ] ADJ (music) funky inv; (col: excellent) figo(-a)
funnel ['fʌnl] N imbuto; (of ship) ciminiera
funnily ['fʌnɪlɪ] ADV in modo divertente; (oddly) stranamente
funny ['fʌnɪ] ADJ divertente, buffo(-a); (strange) strano(-a), bizzarro(-a)
funny bone N osso cubitale
fun run N marcia non competitiva
fur [fəːr] N pelo; pelliccia; pelle f; (BRIT: in kettle etc) deposito calcare
fur coat N pelliccia
furious ['fjuərɪəs] ADJ furioso(-a); (effort) accanito(-a); (argument) violento(-a)
furiously ['fjuərɪəslɪ] ADV furiosamente; accanitamente
furl [fəːl] VT (sail) piegare
furlong ['fəːlɔŋ] N 201.17 m (termine ippico)
furlough ['fəːləu] N (US) congedo, permesso
furnace ['fəːnɪs] N fornace f
furnish ['fəːnɪʃ] VT ammobiliare; (supply) fornire; **furnished flat** or (US) **apartment** appartamento ammobiliato
furnishings ['fəːnɪʃɪŋz] NPL mobili mpl, mobilia
furniture ['fəːnɪtʃər] N mobili mpl; **piece of ~** mobile m
furore [fjuə'rɔːrɪ] N (protests) scalpore m; (enthusiasm) entusiasmo
furrier ['fʌrɪər] N pellicciaio(-a)
furrow ['fʌrəu] N solco ▶ VT (forehead) segnare di rughe
furry ['fəːrɪ] ADJ (animal) peloso(-a); (toy) di peluche
further ['fəːðər] ADJ supplementare, altro(-a); nuovo(-a); più lontano(-a) ▶ ADV più lontano; (more) di più; (moreover) inoltre ▶ VT favorire, promuovere; **until ~ notice** fino a nuovo avviso; **how much ~ is it?** quanto manca or dista?; **~ to your letter of ...** (Comm) con riferimento alla vostra lettera del ...; **to ~ one's interests** fare i propri interessi
further education N ≈ corsi mpl di formazione; **college of ~** istituto statale con corsi specializzati (di formazione professionale, aggiornamento professionale ecc)
furthermore [fəːðə'mɔːr] ADV inoltre, per di più
furthermost ['fəːðəməust] ADJ più lontano(-a)
furthest ['fəːðɪst] ADV SUPERLATIVE of **far**
furtive ['fəːtɪv] ADJ furtivo(-a)
fury ['fjuərɪ] N furore m
fuse, (US) **fuze** [fjuːz] N fusibile m; (for bomb etc) miccia, spoletta ▶ VT fondere; (Elec): **to ~ the lights** far saltare i fusibili ▶ VI fondersi; **a ~ has blown** è saltato un fusibile
fuse box N cassetta dei fusibili
fuselage ['fjuːzəlɑːʒ] N fusoliera
fuse wire N filo (di fusibile)
fusillade [fjuːzɪ'leɪd] N scarica di fucileria; (fig) fuoco di fila, serie f inv incalzante
fusion ['fjuːʒən] N fusione f
fuss [fʌs] N agitazione f, trambusto, confusione f; (complaining) storie fpl ▶ VT (person) infastidire, scocciare ▶ VI agitarsi; **to make a ~** fare delle storie; **to make a ~ of sb** coprire qn di attenzioni
▶ **fuss over** VT FUS (person) circondare di premure
fusspot ['fʌspɔt] N (col): **he's such a ~** fa sempre tante storie
fussy ['fʌsɪ] ADJ (person) puntiglioso(-a), esigente; che fa le storie; (dress) carico(-a) di fronzoli; (style) elaborato(-a); **I'm not ~** (col) per me è lo stesso
fusty ['fʌstɪ] ADJ (pej: archaic) stantio(-a); (: smell) che sa di stantio
futile ['fjuːtaɪl] ADJ futile
futility [fjuː'tɪlɪtɪ] N futilità
futon ['fuːtɔn] N futon m inv, letto giapponese
future ['fjuːtʃər] ADJ futuro(-a) ▶ N futuro, avvenire m; (Ling) futuro; **futures** NPL (Comm) operazioni fpl a termine; **in ~** in futuro; **in the near ~** in un prossimo futuro; **in the immediate ~** nell'immediato futuro
futuristic [fjuːtʃə'rɪstɪk] ADJ futuristico(-a)
fuze [fjuːz] N, VT, VI (US) = **fuse**
fuzzy ['fʌzɪ] ADJ (Phot) indistinto(-a), sfocato(-a); (hair) crespo(-a)
fwd. ABBR = **forward**
fwy ABBR (US) = **freeway**
FY ABBR = **fiscal year**
FYI ABBR = **for your information**

Gg

G, g [dʒiː] N (letter) G, g f inv or m inv; (Mus): **G**
sol m; **G for George** ≈ G come Genova

G N ABBR (BRIT Scol: mark: = good) ≈ buono; (US
Cine: = general audience) per tutti

g ABBR (= gram, gravity) g

G7 N ABBR (Pol: = Group of Seven) G7 mpl

G8 N ABBR (Pol: = Group of Eight) G8 m

G20 N ABBR (Pol: = Group of Twenty) G20 m

GA ABBR (US Post) = **Georgia**

gab [gæb] N (col): **to have the gift of the ~**
avere parlantina

gabble ['gæbl] VI borbottare; farfugliare

gaberdine [gæbə'diːn] N gabardine m inv

gable ['geɪbl] N frontone m

Gabon [gə'bɔn] N Gabon m

gad about [gæd-] VI (col) svolazzare (qua e là)

gadget ['gædʒɪt] N aggeggio

Gaelic ['geɪlɪk] ADJ gaelico(-a) ▶ N (language)
gaelico

gaffe [gæf] N gaffe f inv

gaffer ['gæfə'] N (BRIT col) capo

gag [gæg] N bavaglio; (joke) facezia, scherzo
▶ VT (prisoner etc) imbavagliare ▶ VI (choke)
soffocare

gaga ['gɑːgɑː] ADJ: **to go ~** rimbambirsi

gage [geɪdʒ] N, VT (US) = **gauge**

gaiety ['geɪɪtɪ] N gaiezza

gaily ['geɪlɪ] ADV allegramente

gain [geɪn] N guadagno, profitto ▶ VT
guadagnare ▶ VI (watch) andare avanti;
(benefit): **to ~ (from)** trarre beneficio (da); **to
~ in/by** aumentare di/con; **to ~3lbs (in
weight)** aumentare di 3 libbre; **to ~ ground**
guadagnare terreno
▶ **gain (up)on** VT FUS guadagnare terreno su,
accorciare le distanze da

gainful ['geɪnful] ADJ profittevole,
lucrativo(-a)

gainfully ['geɪnfəlɪ] ADV: **to be ~ employed**
avere un lavoro retribuito

gainsay [geɪn'seɪ] VT (irreg: like **say**)
contraddire; negare

gait [geɪt] N andatura

gal. ABBR = **gallon**

gala ['gɑːlə] N gala; **swimming ~**
manifestazione f di nuoto

Galapagos Islands [gə'læpəgəs-] NPL: **the ~**
le isole Galapagos

galaxy ['gæləksɪ] N galassia

gale [geɪl] N vento forte; burrasca; **~ force 10**
vento forza 10

gall [gɔːl] N (Anat) bile f; (fig: impudence) fegato,
faccia ▶ VT urtare (i nervi a)

gall. ABBR = **gallon**

gallant ['gælənt] ADJ valoroso(-a); (towards
ladies) galante, cortese

gallantry ['gæləntrɪ] N valore m militare;
galanteria, cortesia

gall bladder ['gɔːl-] N cistifellea

galleon ['gælɪən] N galeone m

gallery ['gælərɪ] N galleria; loggia; (for
spectators) tribuna; (in theatre) loggione m,
balconata; (also: **art gallery**: state-owned)
museo; (: private) galleria

galley ['gælɪ] N (ship's kitchen) cambusa; (ship)
galea; (also: **galley proof**) bozza in colonna

Gallic ['gælɪk] ADJ gallico(-a); (French) francese

galling ['gɔːlɪŋ] ADJ irritante

gallon ['gælən] N gallone m (Brit = 4.543 l; 8
pints; US = 3.785 l)

gallop ['gæləp] N galoppo ▶ VI galoppare;
galloping inflation inflazione f galoppante

gallows ['gæləuz] N forca

gallstone ['gɔːlstəun] N calcolo biliare

Gallup Poll ['gæləp-] N sondaggio a
campione

galore [gə'lɔː'] ADV a iosa, a profusione

galvanize ['gælvənaɪz] VT galvanizzare; **to ~
sb into action** (fig) galvanizzare qn,
spronare qn all'azione

Gambia ['gæmbɪə] N Gambia m

gambit ['gæmbɪt] N (fig): (**opening**) ~ prima
mossa

gamble ['gæmbl] N azzardo, rischio calcolato
▶ VT, VI giocare; **to ~ on** (fig) giocare su; **to ~
on the Stock Exchange** giocare in Borsa

gambler ['gæmblə'] N giocatore(-trice)
d'azzardo

gambling ['gæmblɪŋ] N gioco d'azzardo
gambol ['gæmbəl] vɪ saltellare
game [geɪm] N gioco; (event) partita; (Tennis) game m inv; (Hunting, Culin) selvaggina ▶ ADJ coraggioso(-a); (ready): **to be ~ (for sth/to do)** essere pronto(-a) (a qc/a fare); **games** NPL (Scol) attività fpl sportive; **big ~** selvaggina grossa
game bird N uccello selvatico
gamekeeper ['geɪmki:pəʳ] N guardacaccia m inv
gamely ['geɪmlɪ] ADV coraggiosamente
gamer ['geɪməʳ] N chi gioca con i videogame
game reserve N riserva di caccia
games console [geɪmz-] N console f inv dei videogame
gameshow ['geɪmʃəu] N gioco a premi
gamesmanship ['geɪmzmənʃɪp] N abilità
gaming ['geɪmɪŋ] N gioco d'azzardo; (Comput) il giocare con i videogame
gammon ['gæmən] N (bacon) quarto di maiale; (ham) prosciutto affumicato
gamut ['gæmət] N gamma
gang [gæŋ] N banda, squadra ▶ vɪ: **to ~ up on sb** far combutta contro qn
Ganges ['gændʒi:z] N: **the ~** il Gange
gangland ['gæŋlænd] ADJ della malavita; **~ killer** sicario
gangling ['gæŋglɪŋ] ADJ allampanato(-a)
gangly ['gæŋglɪ] ADJ = **gangling**
gangplank ['gæŋplæŋk] N passerella
gangrene ['gæŋgri:n] N cancrena
gangster ['gæŋstəʳ] N gangster m inv
gangway ['gæŋweɪ] N passerella; (BRIT: of bus) passaggio
gantry ['gæntrɪ] N (for crane, railway signal) cavalletto; (for rocket) torre f di lancio
GAO N ABBR (US: = General Accounting Office) ≈ Corte f dei Conti
gaol [dʒeɪl] N, vт (BRIT) = **jail**
gap [gæp] N (space) buco; (in time) intervallo; (fig) lacuna; vuoto; (difference): **~ (between)** divario (tra)
gape [geɪp] vɪ (person) restare a bocca aperta; (shirt, hole) essere spalancato(-a)
gaping ['geɪpɪŋ] ADJ (hole) squarciato(-a)
gap year N (Scol) anno di pausa preso prima di iniziare l'università, per lavorare o viaggiare
garage ['gæra:ʒ] N garage m inv
garage sale N vendita di oggetti usati nel garage di un privato
garb [gɑ:b] N abiti mpl, veste f
garbage ['gɑ:bɪdʒ] (US) N immondizie fpl, rifiuti mpl; (col) sciocchezze fpl; (fig: film, book) porcheria, robaccia; (: nonsense) fesserie fpl
garbage can N (US) bidone m della spazzatura
garbage collector N (US) spazzino(-a)
garbage disposal unit N tritarifiuti m inv

garbage truck N (US) camion m inv della spazzatura
garbled ['gɑ:bld] ADJ deformato(-a); ingarbugliato(-a)
garden ['gɑ:dn] N giardino ▶ vɪ lavorare nel giardino; **gardens** NPL (public) giardini pubblici; (private) parco
garden centre N vivaio
garden city N (BRIT) città f inv giardino inv
gardener ['gɑ:dnəʳ] N giardiniere(-a)
gardening ['gɑ:dnɪŋ] N giardinaggio
gargle ['gɑ:gl] vɪ fare gargarismi ▶ N gargarismo
gargoyle ['gɑ:gɔɪl] N gargouille f inv
garish ['gɛərɪʃ] ADJ vistoso(-a)
garland ['gɑ:lənd] N ghirlanda; corona
garlic ['gɑ:lɪk] N aglio
garment ['gɑ:mənt] N indumento
garner ['gɑ:nəʳ] vт ammucchiare, raccogliere
garnish ['gɑ:nɪʃ] vт (food) guarnire
garret ['gærɪt] N soffitta
garrison ['gærɪsn] N guarnigione f ▶ vт guarnire
garrulous ['gærjuləs] ADJ ciarliero(-a), loquace
garter ['gɑ:təʳ] N giarrettiera; (US: suspender) gancio (di reggicalze)
garter belt N (US) reggicalze m inv
gas [gæs] N gas m inv; (used as anaesthetic) etere m; (US: gasoline) benzina ▶ vт asfissiare con il gas; (Mil) gasare
gas cooker N (BRIT) cucina a gas
gas cylinder N bombola del gas
gaseous ['gæsɪəs] ADJ gassoso(-a)
gas fire N (BRIT) radiatore m a gas
gas-fired ['gæsfaɪəd] ADJ (alimentato(-a)) a gas
gash [gæʃ] N sfregio ▶ vт sfregiare
gasket ['gæskɪt] N (Aut) guarnizione f
gas mask N maschera f antigas inv
gas meter N contatore m del gas
gasoline ['gæsəli:n] N (US) benzina
gasp [gɑ:sp] N respiro affannoso, ansito ▶ vɪ ansimare, boccheggiare; (in surprise) restare senza fiato
▶ **gasp out** vт dire affannosamente
gas pedal (esp US) N pedale m dell'acceleratore
gas ring N fornello a gas
gas station N (US) distributore m di benzina
gas stove N cucina a gas
gassy ['gæsɪ] ADJ gassoso(-a)
gas tank N (US Aut) serbatoio (di benzina)
gas tap N (on cooker) manopola del gas; (on pipe) rubinetto del gas
gastric ['gæstrɪk] ADJ gastrico(-a)
gastric band N (Med) sistema m di bendaggio gastrico

gastric ulcer N ulcera gastrica
gastroenteritis ['gæstrəʊɛntə'raɪtɪs] N gastroenterite f
gastronomy [gæs'trɔnəmɪ] N gastronomia
gasworks ['gæswə:ks] N, NPL impianto di produzione del gas
gate [geɪt] N cancello; (of castle, town) porta; (at airport) uscita; (at level crossing) barriera
gâteau ['gætəu] (pl **gâteaux** [-z]) N torta
gatecrash ['geɪtkræʃ] (BRIT) VT partecipare senza invito a
gatecrasher ['geɪtkræʃə'] N intruso(-a), ospite mf non invitato(-a)
gated community ['geɪtɪd-] N quartiere residenziale autonomo, recintato e sorvegliato, con accesso limitato
gatehouse ['geɪthaus] N casetta del custode (all'entrata di un parco)
gateway ['geɪtweɪ] N porta
gather ['gæðə'] VT (flowers, fruit) cogliere; (pick up) raccogliere; (assemble) radunare; raccogliere; (understand) capire; (Sewing) increspare ▶ VI (assemble) radunarsi; (dust) accumularsi; (clouds) addensarsi; **to ~ speed** acquistare velocità; **to ~ (from/that)** comprendere (da/che), dedurre (da/che); **as far as I can ~** da quel che ho potuto capire
gathering ['gæðərɪŋ] N adunanza
GATT [gæt] N ABBR (= General Agreement on Tariffs and Trade) G.A.T.T m
gauche [gəuʃ] ADJ goffo(-a), maldestro(-a)
gaudy ['gɔ:dɪ] ADJ vistoso(-a)
gauge [geɪdʒ] N (standard measure) calibro; (Rail) scartamento; (instrument) indicatore m ▶ VT misurare; (fig: sb's capabilities, character) valutare, stimare; **to ~ the right moment** calcolare il momento giusto; **petrol ~**, (US) **gas ~** indicatore m or spia della benzina
gaunt [gɔ:nt] ADJ scarno(-a); (grim, desolate) desolato(-a)
gauntlet ['gɔ:ntlɪt] N (fig): **to run the ~ through an angry crowd** passare sotto il fuoco di una folla ostile; **to throw down the ~** gettare il guanto
gauze [gɔ:z] N garza
gave [geɪv] PT of **give**
gawky ['gɔ:kɪ] ADJ goffo(-a), sgraziato(-a)
gawp [gɔ:p] VI: **to ~ at** guardare a bocca aperta
gay [geɪ] ADJ (homosexual) omosessuale; (cheerful) gaio(-a), allegro(-a); (colour) vivace, vivo(-a)
gaze [geɪz] N sguardo fisso ▶ VI: **to ~ at** guardare fisso
gazelle [gə'zɛl] N gazzella
gazette [gə'zɛt] N (newspaper) gazzetta; (official publication) gazzetta ufficiale
gazetteer [gæzə'tɪə'] N (book) dizionario dei nomi geografici; (section of book) indice m dei nomi geografici

gazump [gə'zʌmp] VT (BRIT): **to ~ sb** nella compravendita di immobili, venire meno all'impegno preso con un acquirente accettando un'offerta migliore fatta da altri
GB ABBR (= Great Britain) GB
GBH N ABBR (BRIT Law: col) = **grievous bodily harm**
GC N ABBR (BRIT: = George Cross) decorazione al valore
GCE N ABBR (BRIT: = General Certificate of Education) ≈ diploma m di maturità
GCHQ N ABBR (BRIT: = Government Communications Headquarters) centro per l'intercettazione delle telecomunicazioni straniere
GCSE N ABBR (BRIT: = General Certificate of Secondary Education) diploma di istruzione secondaria conseguito a 16 anni in Inghilterra e Galles
Gdns. ABBR = **gardens**
GDP N ABBR = **gross domestic product**
GDR N ABBR (Hist) = **German Democratic Republic**
gear [gɪə'] N attrezzi mpl, equipaggiamento; (belongings) roba; (Tech) ingranaggio; (Aut) marcia ▶ VT (fig: adapt): **to ~ sth to** adattare qc a; **top** or **high/low/bottom ~** (US) quinta (or sesta)/seconda/prima; **in ~** in marcia; **out of ~** in folle; **our service is geared to meet the needs of the disabled** la nostra organizzazione risponde espressamente alle esigenze degli handicappati
▶ **gear up** VI: **to ~ up (to do)** prepararsi (a fare)
gear box N scatola del cambio
gear lever, (US) **gear shift** N leva del cambio
GED N ABBR (US Scol) = **general educational development**
geese [gi:s] NPL of **goose**
geezer ['gi:zə'] N (BRIT col) tizio
Geiger counter ['gaɪgə-] N geiger m inv
gel [dʒɛl] N gel m inv
gelatin, gelatine ['dʒɛləti:n] N gelatina
gelignite ['dʒɛlɪgnaɪt] N nitroglicerina
gem [dʒɛm] N gemma
Gemini ['dʒɛmɪnaɪ] N Gemelli mpl; **to be ~** essere dei Gemelli
gen [dʒɛn] N (BRIT col): **to give sb the ~ on sth** mettere qn al corrente di qc
Gen. ABBR (Mil: = General) Gen.
gen. ABBR = **general**; (= generally) gen.
gender ['dʒɛndə'] N genere m
gene [dʒi:n] N (Biol) gene m
genealogy [dʒi:nɪ'ælədʒɪ] N genealogia
general ['dʒɛnərl] N generale m ▶ ADJ generale; **in ~** in genere; **the ~ public** il grande pubblico
general anaesthetic, (US) **general anesthetic** N anestesia totale
general delivery N (US) fermo posta m

general election N elezioni *fpl* generali
generalization ['dʒɛnrəlaɪ'zeɪʃən] N
generalizzazione *f*
generalize ['dʒɛnrəlaɪz] VI generalizzare
generally ['dʒɛnrəlɪ] ADV generalmente
general manager N direttore *m* generale
general practitioner N medico generico
general store N emporio
general strike N sciopero generale
generate ['dʒɛnəreɪt] VT generare
generation [dʒɛnə'reɪʃən] N generazione *f*;
(*of electricity etc*) produzione *f*
generator ['dʒɛnəreɪtəʳ] N generatore *m*
generic [dʒɪ'nɛrɪk] ADJ generico(-a)
generosity [dʒɛnə'rɔsɪtɪ] N generosità
generous ['dʒɛnərəs] ADJ generoso(-a);
(*copious*) abbondante
genesis ['dʒɛnɪsɪs] N genesi *f*
genetic [dʒɪ'nɛtɪk] ADJ genetico(-a);
~ engineering ingegneria genetica
genetically modified [dʒɪ'nɛtɪklɪ'mɔdɪfaɪd]
ADJ geneticamente modificato(-a),
transgenico(-a); **~ organism** organismo
geneticamente modificato
genetic fingerprinting [-fɪŋɡəprɪntɪŋ] N
rilevamento delle impronte genetiche
genetics [dʒɪ'nɛtɪks] N genetica
Geneva [dʒɪ'ni:və] N Ginevra; **Lake ~** il lago
di Ginevra
genial ['dʒi:nɪəl] ADJ geniale, cordiale
genitals ['dʒɛnɪtlz] NPL genitali *mpl*
genitive ['dʒɛnɪtɪv] N genitivo
genius ['dʒi:nɪəs] N genio
Genoa ['dʒɛnəuə] N Genova
genocide ['dʒɛnəusaɪd] N genocidio
Genoese [dʒɛnəu'i:z] ADJ, N (*pl inv*) genovese
(*mf*)
genome ['dʒi:nəum] N (*Biol*) genoma *m*
gent [dʒɛnt] N ABBR (*BRIT col*) = **gentleman**
genteel [dʒɛn'ti:l] ADJ raffinato(-a),
distinto(-a)
gentle ['dʒɛntl] ADJ delicato(-a); (*person*) dolce
gentleman ['dʒɛntlmən] N (*irreg*) signore *m*;
(*well-bred man*) gentiluomo; **~'s agreement**
impegno sulla parola
gentlemanly ['dʒɛntlmənlɪ] ADJ da
gentiluomo
gentleness ['dʒɛntlnɪs] N delicatezza;
dolcezza
gently ['dʒɛntlɪ] ADV delicatamente
gentry ['dʒɛntrɪ] N nobiltà minore
gents [dʒɛnts] N W.C. *m* (per signori)
genuine ['dʒɛnjuɪn] ADJ autentico(-a);
sincero(-a)
genuinely ['dʒɛnjuɪnlɪ] ADV genuinamente
geographer [dʒɪ'ɔɡrəfəʳ] N geografo(-a)
geographic [dʒɪə'ɡræfɪk], **geographical**
[dʒɪə'ɡræfɪkl] ADJ geografico(-a)
geography [dʒɪ'ɔɡrəfɪ] N geografia

geological [dʒɪə'lɔdʒɪkl] ADJ geologico(-a)
geologist [dʒɪ'ɔlədʒɪst] N geologo(-a)
geology [dʒɪ'ɔlədʒɪ] N geologia
geometric [dʒɪə'mɛtrɪk], **geometrical**
[dʒɪə'mɛtrɪkl] ADJ geometrico(-a)
geometry [dʒɪ'ɔmətrɪ] N geometria
Geordie [dʒɔ:dɪ] N (*col*) abitante *mf* del
Tyneside; originario(-a) del Tyneside
Georgia ['dʒɔ:dʒə] N Georgia
Georgian ['dʒɔ:dʒən] ADJ georgiano(-a) ▶ N
georgiano(-a); (*Ling*) georgiano
geranium [dʒɪ'reɪnɪəm] N geranio
geriatric [dʒɛrɪ'ætrɪk] ADJ geriatrico(-a)
germ [dʒə:m] N (*Med*) microbo; (*Biol*, *fig*)
germe *m*
German ['dʒə:mən] ADJ tedesco(-a) ▶ N
tedesco(-a); (*Ling*) tedesco
German Democratic Republic N
Repubblica Democratica Tedesca
germane [dʒə:'meɪn] ADJ (*formal*): **to be ~ to**
sth essere attinente a qc
German measles (*BRIT*) N rosolia
Germany ['dʒə:mənɪ] N Germania
germination [dʒə:mɪ'neɪʃən] N
germinazione *f*
germ warfare N guerra batteriologica
gerrymandering ['dʒɛrɪmændərɪŋ] N
manipolazione *f* dei distretti elettorali.
gestation [dʒɛs'teɪʃən] N gestazione *f*
gesticulate [dʒɛs'tɪkjuleɪt] VI gesticolare
gesture ['dʒɛstjəʳ] N gesto; **as a ~ of**
friendship in segno d'amicizia

(KEYWORD)

get [ɡɛt] (*pt, pp* **got**, *US pp* **gotten**) VI **1** (*become,
be*) diventare, farsi; **to get drunk** ubriacarsi;
to get killed venire *or* rimanere ucciso(-a);
it's getting late si sta facendo tardi; **to get
old** invecchiare; **to get paid** venire
pagato(-a); **when do I get paid?** quando mi
pagate?; **to get ready** prepararsi; **to get
shaved** farsi la barba; **to get tired** stancarsi;
to get washed lavarsi
2 (*go*): **to get to/from** andare a/da; **to get
home** arrivare *or* tornare a casa; **how did
you get here?** come sei venuto?; **he got
across the bridge** ha attraversato il ponte;
he got under the fence è passato sotto il
recinto
3 (*begin*) mettersi a, cominciare a; **to get to
know sb** incominciare a conoscere qn; **let's
get going** *or* **started** muoviamoci
4 (*modal aux vb*): **you've got to do it** devi farlo
▶ VT **1**: **to get sth done** (*do*) fare qc; (*have done*)
far fare qc; **to get sth/sb ready** preparare
qc/qn; **to get one's hair cut** tagliarsi *or* farsi
tagliare i capelli; **to get sb to do sth** far fare
qc a qn
2 (*obtain: money, permission, results*) ottenere;

(find: job, flat) trovare; (fetch: person, doctor) chiamare; **get me Mr Jones, please** (Tel) mi passi il signor Jones, per favore; (: object) prendere; **to get sth for sb** prendere or procurare qc a qn; **can I get you a drink?** le posso offrire da bere?

3 (receive: present, letter, prize) ricevere; (: acquire: reputation) farsi; **how much did you get for the painting?** quanto le hanno dato per il quadro?

4 (catch) prendere; **to get sb by the arm/throat** afferrare qn per un braccio/alla gola; **get him!** prendetelo!; **he really gets me** (fig: annoy) mi dà proprio sui nervi

5 (hit: target etc) colpire

6 (take, move) portare; **to get sth to sb** far avere qc a qn; **do you think we'll get it through the door?** pensi che riusciremo a farlo passare per la porta?

7 (catch, take: plane, bus etc) prendere; **he got the last bus** ha preso l'ultimo autobus; **she got the morning flight to Milan** ha preso il volo per Milano del mattino; **where do we get the ferry to …?** dove si prende il traghetto per …?

8 (understand) afferrare; **I've got it!** ci sono arrivato!, ci sono!

9 (hear) sentire; **I'm sorry, I didn't get your name** scusi, non ho capito (or sentito) come si chiama

10 (have, possess): **to have got** avere; **how many have you got?** quanti ne ha?

▶ **get about** vi muoversi; (news) diffondersi
▶ **get across** vt: **to get across (to)** (message, meaning) comunicare (a) ▶ vi: **to get across to** (speaker) comunicare con
▶ **get along** vi (agree) andare d'accordo; (depart) andarsene; (manage) = **get by**
▶ **get at** vt fus (attack) prendersela con; (reach) raggiungere, arrivare a; **what are you getting at?** dove vuoi arrivare?
▶ **get away** vi partire, andarsene; (escape) scappare
▶ **get away with** vt fus cavarsela; farla franca; **he'll never get away with it!** non riuscirà a farla franca!
▶ **get back** vi (return) ritornare, tornare ▶ vt riottenere, riavere; **to get back to** (start again) ritornare a; (contact again) rimettersi in contatto con; **when do we get back?** quando ritorniamo?
▶ **get back at** vt fus (col): **to get back at sb (for sth)** rendere pan per focaccia a qn (per qc)
▶ **get by** vi (pass) passare; (manage) farcela; **I can get by in Dutch** mi arrangio in olandese
▶ **get down** vi, vt fus scendere ▶ vt far scendere; (depress) buttare giù

▶ **get down to** vt fus (work) mettersi a (fare); **to get down to business** venire al dunque
▶ **get in** vi entrare; (train) arrivare; (arrive home) ritornare, tornare ▶ vt (bring in: harvest) raccogliere; (: coal, shopping, supplies) fare provvista di; (insert) far entrare, infilare
▶ **get into** vt fus entrare in; **to get into a rage** incavolarsi; **to get into bed** mettersi a letto
▶ **get off** vi (from train etc) scendere; (depart: person, car) andare via; (escape) cavarsela ▶ vt (remove: clothes, stain) levare; (send off) spedire; (have as leave: days, time): **we got 2 days off** abbiamo avuto 2 giorni liberi ▶ vt fus (train, bus) scendere da; **to get off to a good start** (fig) cominciare bene
▶ **get on** vi: **how did you get on?** com'è andata?; **he got on quite well** ha fatto bene, (gli) è andata bene; **to get on (with sb)** andare d'accordo (con qn); **how are you getting on?** come va la vita? ▶ vt fus montare in; (horse) montare su
▶ **get on to** vt fus (BRIT col: contact: on phone etc) contattare, rintracciare; (deal with) occuparsi di
▶ **get out** vi uscire; (of vehicle) scendere ▶ vt tirar fuori, far uscire; **to get out (of)** (money from bank etc) ritirare (da)
▶ **get out of** vt fus uscire da; (duty etc) evitare; **what will you get out of it?** cosa ci guadagni?
▶ **get over** vt fus (illness) riaversi da; (communicate: idea etc) comunicare, passare; **let's get it over (with)** togliamoci il pensiero
▶ **get round** vt fus aggirare; (fig: person) rigirare ▶ vi: **to get round to doing sth** trovare il tempo di fare qc
▶ **get through** vi (Tel) avere la linea ▶ vt fus (finish: work) sbrigare; (: book) finire
▶ **get through to** vt fus (Tel) parlare a
▶ **get together** vi riunirsi ▶ vt raccogliere; (people) adunare
▶ **get up** vi (rise) alzarsi ▶ vt fus salire su per
▶ **get up to** vt fus (reach) raggiungere; (prank etc) fare

getaway ['gɛtəweɪ] N fuga
getaway car N macchina per la fuga
get-together ['gɛttəgɛðəʳ] N (piccola) riunione f; (party) festicciola
get-up ['gɛtʌp] N (col: outfit) tenuta
get-well card [gɛt'wɛl-] N cartolina di auguri di pronta guarigione
geyser ['giːzəʳ] N scaldabagno; (Geo) geyser m inv
Ghana ['gɑːnə] N Ghana m
Ghanaian [gɑː'neɪən] ADJ, N ganaense (mf)
ghastly ['gɑːstlɪ] ADJ orribile, orrendo(-a); (pale) spettrale

gherkin ['gə:kɪn] N cetriolino
ghetto ['gɛtəu] N ghetto
ghetto blaster [-'blɑːstər] N maxistereo portatile
ghost [gəust] N fantasma *m*, spettro ▶ VT (*book*) fare lo scrittore ombra per
ghostly ['gəustlɪ] ADJ spettrale
ghostwriter ['gəustraɪtər] N scrittore(-trice) ombra *inv*
ghoul [guːl] N vampiro che si nutre di cadaveri
ghoulish ['guːlɪʃ] ADJ (*tastes etc*) macabro(-a)
GHQ N ABBR (*Mil:* = *general headquarters*) ≈ comando di Stato maggiore
GI N ABBR (*US: col:* = *government issue*) G.I. *m*, soldato americano
giant ['dʒaɪənt] N gigante(-essa) ▶ ADJ gigantesco(-a), enorme; ~ **(size) packet** confezione *f* gigante
giant killer N (*Sport*) piccola squadra che riesce a batterne una importante
gibber ['dʒɪbər] VI (*monkey*) squittire confusamente; (*idiot*) farfugliare
gibberish ['dʒɪbərɪʃ] N parole *fpl* senza senso
gibe [dʒaɪb] N frecciata ▶ VI: **to ~ at** lanciare frecciate a
giblets ['dʒɪblɪts] NPL frattaglie *fpl*
Gibraltar [dʒɪ'brɔːltər] N Gibilterra
giddiness ['gɪdɪnɪs] N vertigine *f*
giddy ['gɪdɪ] ADJ (*dizzy*): **to be ~** aver le vertigini; (*height*) vertiginoso(-a); **I feel ~** mi gira la testa
gift [gɪft] N regalo; (*donation, ability*) dono; (*Comm: also:* **free gift**) omaggio; **to have a ~ for sth** (*talent*) avere il dono di qc
gifted ['gɪftɪd] ADJ dotato(-a)
gift shop, (*US*) **gift store** N negozio di souvenir
gift token, gift voucher N buono (acquisto)
gig [gɪg] N (*col: of musician*) serata
gigabyte [gi:gəbaɪt] N gigabyte *m inv*
gigantic [dʒaɪ'gæntɪk] ADJ gigantesco(-a)
giggle ['gɪgl] VI ridere scioccamente ▶ N risolino (sciocco)
GIGO ['gaɪgəu] ABBR (*Comput: col:* = *garbage in, garbage out*) qualità di input = qualità di output
gild [gɪld] VT dorare
gill [dʒɪl] N (*measure*) = 0.25 pints (*Brit* = 0.148 *l*; *US* = 0.118 *l*)
gills [gɪlz] NPL (*of fish*) branchie *fpl*
gilt [gɪlt] N doratura ▶ ADJ dorato(-a)
gilt-edged ['gɪltɛdʒd] ADJ (*stocks, securities*) della massima sicurezza
gimlet ['gɪmlɪt] N succhiello
gimmick ['gɪmɪk] N trucco; **sales ~** trovata commerciale
gin [dʒɪn] N (*liquor*) gin *m inv*
ginger ['dʒɪndʒər] N zenzero

▶ **ginger up** VT scuotere; animare
ginger ale, ginger beer N bibita gassosa allo zenzero
gingerbread ['dʒɪndʒəbrɛd] N pan *m* di zenzero
ginger group N (*BRIT*) gruppo di pressione
ginger-haired ['dʒɪndʒə'hɛəd] ADJ rossiccio(-a)
gingerly ['dʒɪndʒəlɪ] ADV cautamente
gingham ['gɪŋəm] N percalle *m* a righe (*or* quadretti)
ginseng ['dʒɪnsɛŋ] N ginseng *m*
gipsy ['dʒɪpsɪ] N zingaro(-a) ▶ ADJ degli zingari
giraffe [dʒɪ'rɑːf] N giraffa
girder ['gə:dər] N trave *f*
girdle ['gə:dl] N (*corset*) guaina
girl [gə:l] N ragazza; (*young unmarried woman*) signorina; (*daughter*) figlia, figliola; **a little ~** una bambina
girl band N gruppo pop di sole ragazze creato per far presa su un pubblico giovane
girlfriend ['gə:lfrɛnd] N (*of girl*) amica; (*of boy*) ragazza
girlish ['gə:lɪʃ] ADJ da ragazza
Girl Scout N (*US*) Giovane Esploratrice *f*
Giro ['dʒaɪrəu] N: **the National ~** (*BRIT*) ≈ la *or* il Bancoposta
giro ['dʒaɪrəu] N (*bank giro*) versamento bancario; (*post office giro*) postagiro
girth [gə:θ] N circonferenza; (*of horse*) cinghia
gist [dʒɪst] N succo
give [gɪv] (*pt* **gave** [geɪv], *pp* **given** ['gɪvn]) N (*of fabric*) elasticità ▶ VT dare ▶ VI cedere; **to ~ sb sth, ~ sth to sb** dare qc a qn; **I'll ~ you £5 for it** te lo pago 5 sterline; **to ~ a cry/sigh** emettere un grido/sospiro; **to ~ a speech** fare un discorso; **how much did you ~ for it?** quanto (l')hai pagato?; **12 o'clock, ~ or take a few minutes** mezzogiorno, minuto più minuto meno; **to ~ way** vi cedere; (*BRIT Aut*) dare la precedenza
▶ **give away** VT dare via; (*give free*) fare dono di; (*betray*) tradire; (*disclose*) rivelare; (*bride*) condurre all'altare
▶ **give back** VT rendere
▶ **give in** VI cedere ▶ VT consegnare
▶ **give off** VT emettere
▶ **give out** VT distribuire; annunciare ▶ VI (*be exhausted: supplies*) esaurirsi, venir meno; (*fail: engine*) fermarsi; (*: strength*) mancare
▶ **give up** VI rinunciare ▶ VT rinunciare a; **to ~ up smoking** smettere di fumare; **to ~ o.s. up** arrendersi
give-and-take [gɪvən'teɪk] N (*col*) elasticità (da ambo le parti), concessioni *fpl* reciproche
giveaway ['gɪvəweɪ] N (*col*): **her expression was a ~** le si leggeva tutto in volto; **the exam was a ~!** l'esame è stato uno scherzo! ▶ CPD:

~ **prices** prezzi stracciati

given ['gɪvn] PP of **give** ▸ ADJ (*fixed: time, amount*) dato(-a), determinato(-a) ▸ CONJ: ~ **(that)** ... dato che ...; ~ **the circumstances** ... date le circostanze ...

glacial ['gleɪsɪəl] ADJ glaciale

glacier ['glæsɪər] N ghiacciaio

glad [glæd] ADJ lieto(-a), contento(-a); **to be ~ about sth/that** essere contento or lieto di qc/che + sub; **I was ~ of his help** gli sono stato grato del suo aiuto

gladden ['glædn] VT rallegrare, allietare

glade [gleɪd] N radura

gladioli [glædɪ'əʊlaɪ] NPL gladioli mpl

gladly ['glædlɪ] ADV volentieri

glamorous ['glæmərəs] ADJ (*gen*) favoloso(-a); (*person*) affascinante, seducente; (*occasion*) brillante, elegante

glamour, (*US*) **glamor** ['glæmər] N fascino

glance [glɑːns] N occhiata, sguardo ▸ VI: **to ~ at** dare un'occhiata a

▸ **glance off** VT FUS (*bullet*) rimbalzare su

glancing ['glɑːnsɪŋ] ADJ (*blow*) che colpisce di striscio

gland [glænd] N ghiandola

glandular ['glændjʊlər] ADJ: ~ **fever** (*BRIT*) mononucleosi f

glare [gleər] N (*of anger*) sguardo furioso; (*of light*) riverbero, luce f abbagliante; (*of publicity*) chiasso ▸ VI abbagliare; **to ~ at** guardare male

glaring ['gleərɪŋ] ADJ (*mistake*) madornale

glasnost ['glæznɔst] N glasnost f

glass [glɑːs] N (*substance*) vetro; (*tumbler*) bicchiere m; (*also*: **looking glass**) specchio; *see also* **glasses**

glass-blowing ['glɑːsbləʊɪŋ] N soffiatura del vetro

glass ceiling N (*fig*) barriera invisibile

glasses ['glɑːsɪz] NPL (*spectacles*) occhiali mpl

glass fibre N fibra di vetro

glasshouse ['glɑːshaʊs] N serra

glassware ['glɑːsweər] N vetrame m

glassy ['glɑːsɪ] ADJ (*eyes*) vitreo(-a)

Glaswegian [glæs'wiːdʒən] ADJ di Glasgow ▸ N abitante mf di Glasgow, originario(-a) di Glasgow

glaze [gleɪz] VT (*door*) fornire di vetri; (*pottery*) smaltare; (*Culin*) glassare ▸ N smalto; glassa

glazed ['gleɪzd] ADJ (*eye*) vitreo(-a); (*tiles, pottery*) smaltato(-a)

glazier ['gleɪzɪər] N vetraio

gleam [gliːm] N barlume m; raggio ▸ VI luccicare; **a ~ of hope** un barlume di speranza

gleaming ['gliːmɪŋ] ADJ lucente

glean [gliːn] VT (*information*) racimolare

glee [gliː] N allegrezza, gioia

gleeful ['gliːful] ADJ allegro(-a), gioioso(-a)

glen [glɛn] N valletta

glib [glɪb] ADJ dalla parola facile; facile

glide [glaɪd] VI scivolare; (*Aviat, birds*) planare ▸ N scivolata; planata

glider ['glaɪdər] N (*Aviat*) aliante m

gliding ['glaɪdɪŋ] N (*Aviat*) volo a vela

glimmer ['glɪmər] VI luccicare ▸ N barlume m

glimpse [glɪmps] N impressione f fugace ▸ VT vedere di sfuggita; **to catch a ~ of** vedere di sfuggita

glint [glɪnt] N luccichio ▸ VI luccicare

glisten ['glɪsn] VI luccicare

glitter ['glɪtər] VI scintillare ▸ N scintillio

glitz [glɪts] N (*col*) vistosità, chiassosità

gloat [gləʊt] VI: **to ~ (over)** gongolare di piacere (per)

global ['gləʊbl] ADJ globale; (*world-wide*) mondiale

globalization [gləʊbəlaɪ'zeɪʃən] N globalizzazione f

global warming N riscaldamento globale

globe [gləʊb] N globo, sfera

globetrotter ['gləʊbtrɔtər] N giramondo mf

globule ['glɔbjuːl] N (*Anat*) globulo; (*of water etc*) gocciolina

gloom [gluːm] N oscurità, buio; (*sadness*) tristezza, malinconia

gloomy ['gluːmɪ] ADJ scuro(-a), fosco(-a), triste; **to feel ~** sentirsi giù or depresso

glorification [glɔːrɪfɪ'keɪʃən] N glorificazione f

glorify ['glɔːrɪfaɪ] VT glorificare; celebrare, esaltare

glorious ['glɔːrɪəs] ADJ glorioso(-a), magnifico(-a)

glory ['glɔːrɪ] N gloria; splendore m ▸ VI: **to ~ in** gloriarsi di or in

glory hole N (*col*) ripostiglio

Glos ABBR (*BRIT*) = **Gloucestershire**

gloss [glɔs] N (*shine*) lucentezza; (*also*: **gloss paint**) vernice f a olio

▸ **gloss over** VT FUS scivolare su

glossary ['glɔsərɪ] N glossario

glossy ['glɔsɪ] ADJ lucente ▸ N (*also*: **glossy magazine**) rivista di lusso

glove [glʌv] N guanto

glove compartment N (*Aut*) vano portaoggetti

glow [gləʊ] VI ardere; (*face*) essere luminoso(-a) ▸ N bagliore m; (*of face*) colorito acceso

glower ['glaʊər] VI: **to ~ (at sb)** guardare (qn) in cagnesco

glowing ['gləʊɪŋ] ADJ (*fire*) ardente; (*complexion*) luminoso(-a); (*fig: report, description etc*) entusiasta

glow-worm ['gləʊwəːm] N lucciola

glucose ['gluːkəʊs] N glucosio

glue [gluː] N colla ▸ VT incollare

glue-sniffing ['glu:snɪfɪŋ] N sniffare m
(colla)

glum [glʌm] ADJ abbattuto(-a)

glut [glʌt] N eccesso ▸ VT saziare; (market)
saturare

glutinous ['glu:tɪnəs] ADJ colloso(-a),
appiccicoso(-a)

glutton ['glʌtn] N ghiottone(-a); **a ~ for
work** un(-a) patito(-a) del lavoro

gluttonous ['glʌtənəs] ADJ ghiotto(-a),
goloso(-a)

gluttony ['glʌtənɪ] N ghiottoneria; (sin) gola

glycerin, glycerine ['glɪsəri:n] N glicerina

GM ADJ ABBR (= genetically modified)
geneticamente modificato(-a)

gm ABBR = **gram**

GMAT N ABBR (US: = Graduate Management
Admissions Test) esame di ammissione all'ultimo
biennio di scuola superiore

GMB N ABBR (BRIT) = **General, Municipal, and
Boilermakers (Union)**

GM crop N pianta transgenica

GM food N cibo transgenico

GM-free [dʒi:ɛm'fri:] ADJ privo(-a) di OGM

GMO N ABBR (= genetically modified organism)
OGM m inv

GMT ABBR (= Greenwich Mean Time) T.M.G.

gnarled [nɑ:ld] ADJ nodoso(-a)

gnash [næʃ] VT: **to ~ one's teeth** digrignare i
denti

gnat [næt] N moscerino

gnaw [nɔ:] VT rodere

gnome [nəum] N gnomo

GNP N ABBR = **gross national product**

go [gəu] VI (pt **went** [wɛnt], pp **gone** [gɔn])
andare; (depart) partire, andarsene; (work)
funzionare; (time) passare; (break etc) cedere;
(be sold): **to go for £10** essere venduto per 10
sterline; (fit, suit): **to go with** andare bene
con; (become): **to go pale** diventare
pallido(-a); **to go mouldy** ammuffire ▸ N (pl
goes): **to have a go (at)** provare; **to be on
the go** essere in moto; **whose go is it?** a chi
tocca?; **to go by car/on foot** andare in
macchina/a piedi; **he's going to do** sta per
fare; **to go for a walk** andare a fare una
passeggiata; **to go dancing/shopping**
andare a ballare/fare la spesa; **just then the
bell went** proprio allora suonò il
campanello; **to go looking for sb/sth**
andare in cerca di qn/qc; **to go to sleep**
addormentarsi; **to go and see sb, to go to
see sb** andare a trovare qn; **how is it going?**
come va (la vita)?; **how did it go?** com'è
andato?; **to go round the back/by the shop**
passare da dietro/davanti al negozio; **my
voice has gone** m'è andata via la voce; **the
cake is all gone** il dolce è finito tutto; **I'll
take whatever is going** (BRIT) prendo quello

che c'è; ... **to go** (US: food) ... da portar via;
the money will go towards our holiday
questi soldi li mettiamo per la vacanza

▸ **go about** VI (also: **go around**) aggirarsi;
(: rumour) correre, circolare ▸ VT FUS: **how do I
go about this?** qual è la prassi per questo?;
to go about one's business occuparsi delle
proprie faccende

▸ **go after** VT FUS (pursue) correr dietro a,
rincorrere; (job, record etc) mirare a

▸ **go against** VT FUS (be unfavourable to) essere
contro; (be contrary to) andare contro

▸ **go ahead** VI andare avanti; **go ahead!**
faccia pure!

▸ **go along** VI andare, avanzare ▸ VT FUS
percorrere; **to go along with** (accompany)
andare con, accompagnare; (agree with: idea)
sottoscrivere, appoggiare

▸ **go away** VI partire, andarsene

▸ **go back** VI tornare, ritornare; (go again)
andare di nuovo

▸ **go back on** VT FUS (promise) non mantenere

▸ **go by** VI (years, time) scorrere ▸ VT FUS
attenersi a, seguire (alla lettera); prestar
fede a

▸ **go down** VI scendere; (ship) affondare;
(sun) tramontare ▸ VT FUS scendere; **that
should go down well with him** dovrebbe
incontrare la sua approvazione

▸ **go for** VT FUS (fetch) andare a prendere;
(like) andare matto(-a) per; (attack) attaccare;
saltare addosso a

▸ **go in** VI entrare

▸ **go in for** VT FUS (competition) iscriversi a; (be
interested in) interessarsi di

▸ **go into** VT FUS entrare in; (investigate)
indagare, esaminare; (embark on) lanciarsi in

▸ **go off** VI partire, andar via; (food)
guastarsi; (explode) esplodere, scoppiare;
(lights etc) spegnersi; (event) passare ▸ VT FUS:
I've gone off chocolate la cioccolata non mi
piace più; **the gun went off** il fucile si
scaricò; **the party went off well** la festa è
andata or è riuscita bene; **to go off to sleep**
addormentarsi

▸ **go on** VI continuare; (happen) succedere;
(lights) accendersi ▸ VT FUS (be guided by:
evidence etc) basarsi su, fondarsi su; **to go on
doing** continuare a fare; **what's going on
here?** che succede or che sta succedendo qui?

▸ **go on at** VT FUS (nag) assillare

▸ **go on with** VT FUS continuare, proseguire

▸ **go out** VI uscire; (fire, light) spegnersi; (ebb:
tide) calare; **to go out with sb** uscire con qn;
they went out for 3 years (couple) sono stati
insieme per 3 anni

▸ **go over** VI (ship) ribaltarsi ▸ VT FUS (check)
esaminare; **to go over sth in one's mind**
pensare bene a qc

▶ **go past** VI passare ▶ VT FUS passare davanti a

▶ **go round** VI (*circulate: news, rumour*) circolare; (*revolve*) girare; (*suffice*) bastare (per tutti); **to go round (to sb's)** (*visit*) passare (da qn); **to go round (by)** (*make a detour*) passare (per)

▶ **go through** VT FUS (*town etc*) attraversare; (*search through: files, papers*) vagliare attentamente; (*examine: list, book*) leggere da cima a fondo; (*perform*) fare

▶ **go through with** VT FUS (*plan, crime*) mettere in atto, eseguire; **I couldn't go through with it** non sono riuscito ad andare fino in fondo

▶ **go under** VI (*sink: ship*) affondare, colare a picco; (*: person*) andare sotto; (*fig: business, firm*) fallire

▶ **go up** VI salire ▶ VT FUS salire su per; **to go up in flames** andare in fiamme

▶ **go with** VT FUS (*accompany*) accompagnare

▶ **go without** VT FUS fare a meno di

goad [gəud] VT spronare

go-ahead ['gəuəhɛd] ADJ intraprendente
▶ N: **to give sb/sth the ~** dare il via libera a qn/qc

goal [gəul] N (*Sport*) gol *m*, rete *f*; (*: place*) porta; (*fig: aim*) fine *m*, scopo

goal difference N differenza *f* reti *inv*

goalie ['gəulɪ] N (*col*) portiere *m*

goalkeeper ['gəulki:pə^r] N portiere *m*

goalpost ['gəulpəust] N palo (della porta)

goat [gəut] N capra

gobble ['gɔbl] VT (*also*: **gobble down, gobble up**) ingoiare

go-between ['gəubɪtwi:n] N intermediario(-a)

Gobi Desert ['gəubɪ-] N: **the ~** il Deserto dei Gobi

goblet ['gɔblɪt] N calice *m*, coppa

goblin ['gɔblɪn] N folletto

go-cart ['gəuka:t] N go-kart *m inv* ▶ CPD: **~ racing** *n* kartismo

god [gɔd] N dio; **G~** Dio

god-awful [gɔd'ɔ:fəl] ADJ (*col*) di merda (*!*)

godchild ['gɔdtʃaɪld] N (*irreg*) figlioccio(-a)

goddamn ['gɔddæm], (*US*) **goddamned** ['gɔddæmd] (*esp col*) EXCL: **~!** porca miseria! ▶ ADJ fottuto(-a) (*!*), maledetto(-a) ▶ ADV maledettamente

goddaughter ['gɔddɔ:tə^r] N figlioccia

goddess ['gɔdɪs] N dea

godfather ['gɔdfa:ðə^r] N padrino

god-fearing ['gɔdfɪərɪŋ] ADJ timorato(-a) di Dio

god-forsaken ['gɔdfəseɪkən] ADJ desolato(-a), sperduto(-a)

godmother ['gɔdmʌðə^r] N madrina

godparents ['gɔdpɛərənts] NPL: **the ~** il padrino e la madrina

godsend ['gɔdsɛnd] N dono del cielo

godson ['gɔdsʌn] N figlioccio

goes [gəuz] *see* **go**

gofer ['gəufə^r] N (*col*) tuttofare *mf*, tirapiedi *mf*

go-getter ['gəugɛtə^r] N arrivista *mf*

goggle ['gɔgl] VI: **to ~ (at)** stare con gli occhi incollati *or* appiccicati (a *or* addosso a)

goggles ['gɔglz] NPL occhiali *mpl* (di protezione)

going ['gəuɪŋ] N (*conditions*) andare *m*, stato del terreno ▶ ADJ: **the ~ rate** la tariffa in vigore; **a ~ concern** un'azienda avviata; **it was slow ~** si andava a rilento

going-over [gəuɪŋ'əuvə^r] N (*col*) controllata; (*violent attack*) pestaggio

goings-on ['gəuɪŋz'ɔn] NPL (*col*) fatti *mpl* strani, cose *fpl* strane

go-kart ['gəuka:t] N = **go-cart**

gold [gəuld] N oro ▶ ADJ d'oro; (*reserves*) aureo(-a)

golden ['gəuldən] ADJ (*made of gold*) d'oro; (*gold in colour*) dorato(-a)

golden age N età d'oro

golden handshake N (*BRIT*) gratifica di fine servizio

golden rule N regola principale

goldfish ['gəuldfɪʃ] N pesce *m* dorato *or* rosso

gold leaf N lamina d'oro

gold medal N (*Sport*) medaglia d'oro

goldmine ['gəuldmaɪn] N (*also fig*) miniera d'oro

gold-plated ['gəuld'pleɪtɪd] ADJ placcato(-a) oro *inv*

goldsmith ['gəuldsmɪθ] N orefice *m*, orafo

gold standard N tallone aureo

golf [gɔlf] N golf *m*

golf ball N (*for game*) pallina da golf; (*on typewriter*) pallina

golf club N circolo di golf; (*stick*) bastone *m or* mazza da golf

golf course N campo di golf

golfer ['gɔlfə^r] N giocatore(-trice) di golf

golfing ['gɔlfɪŋ] N il gioco a golf

gondola ['gɔndələ] N gondola

gondolier [gɔndə'lɪə^r] N gondoliere *m*

gone [gɔn] PP *of* **go** ▶ ADJ partito(-a)

goner ['gɔnə^r] N (*col*): **I thought you were a ~** pensavo che ormai fossi spacciato

gong [gɔŋ] N gong *m inv*

good [gud] ADJ buono(-a); (*kind*) buono(-a), gentile; (*child*) bravo(-a) ▶ N bene *m*; **~!** bene!, ottimo!; **to be ~ at** essere bravo(-a) in; **to be ~ for** andare bene per; **it's ~ for you** fa bene; **it's a ~ thing you were there** meno male che c'era; **she is ~ with children/her hands** ci sa fare coi bambini/è abile nei lavori manuali; **to feel ~** sentirsi bene; **it's ~ to see you** che piacere vederla; **to make ~**

(loss, damage) compensare; **he's up to no ~** ne sta combinando qualcuna; **it's no ~ complaining** brontolare non serve a niente; **for the common ~** nell'interesse generale, per il bene comune; **for ~** (for ever) per sempre, definitivamente; **would you be ~ enough to ...?** avrebbe la gentilezza di ...?; **that's very ~ of you** è molto gentile da parte sua; **is this any ~?** (will it do?) va bene questo?; (what's it like?) com'è?; **a ~ deal (of)** molto(-a), una buona quantità (di); **a ~ many** molti(-e); **~ morning!** buon giorno!; **~ afternoon/evening!** buona sera!; **~ night!** buona notte!; see also **goods**

goodbye [gud'baɪ] EXCL arrivederci!; **to say ~ to** (person) salutare

good faith N buona fede

good-for-nothing ['gudfənʌθɪŋ] N buono(-a) a nulla, vagabondo(-a)

Good Friday N Venerdì Santo

good-humoured [gud'hju:məd] ADJ (person) di buon umore; (remark, joke) bonario(-a)

good-looking [gud'lukɪŋ] ADJ bello(-a)

good-natured [gud'neɪtʃəd] ADJ (person) affabile; (discussion) amichevole, cordiale

goodness ['gudnɪs] N (of person) bontà; **for ~ sake!** per amor di Dio!; **~ gracious!** santo cielo!, mamma mia!

goods [gudz] NPL (Comm etc) merci fpl, articoli mpl; **~ and chattels** beni mpl e effetti mpl

goods train N (BRIT) treno m merci inv

goodwill [gud'wɪl] N amicizia, benevolenza; (Comm) avviamento

goody-goody ['gudɪgudɪ] N (pej) santarellino(-a)

gooey ['gu:ɪ] ADJ (col: sticky) appiccicoso(-a); (cake, dessert) troppo zuccherato(-a)

Google® ['gu:gl] VT, VI cercare su Google®

goose [gu:s] (pl **geese** [gi:s]) N oca

gooseberry ['guzbərɪ] N uva spina; **to play ~** (BRIT) tenere la candela

goose bumps ['gu:sbʌmpz] NPL, **gooseflesh** ['gu:sfleʃ] N, **goosepimples** ['gu:spɪmplz] NPL pelle f d'oca

goose step N (Mil) passo dell'oca

GOP N ABBR (US Pol: col: = Grand Old Party) partito repubblicano

gopher ['gəufər] N = **gofer**

gore [gɔːr] VT incornare ▶ N sangue m (coagulato)

gorge [gɔːdʒ] N gola ▶ VT: **to ~ o.s. (on)** ingozzarsi (di)

gorgeous ['gɔːdʒəs] ADJ magnifico(-a)

gorilla [gə'rɪlə] N gorilla m inv

gormless ['gɔːmlɪs] ADJ (BRIT: col) tonto(-a); (: stronger) deficiente

gorse [gɔːs] N ginestrone m

gory ['gɔːrɪ] ADJ sanguinoso(-a)

gosh [gɔʃ] EXCL (col) perdinci!

go-slow ['gəu'sləu] N (BRIT) rallentamento dei lavori (per agitazione sindacale)

gospel ['gɔspl] N vangelo

gossamer ['gɔsəmər] N (cobweb) fili mpl della Madonna or di ragnatela; (light fabric) stoffa sottilissima

gossip ['gɔsɪp] N chiacchiere fpl; pettegolezzi mpl; (person) pettegolo(-a) ▶ VI chiacchierare; (maliciously) pettegolare; **a piece of ~** un pettegolezzo

gossip column N cronaca mondana

got [gɔt] PT, PP of **get**

Gothic ['gɔθɪk] ADJ gotico(-a)

gotten ['gɔtn] (US) PP of **get**

gouge [gaudʒ] VT (also: **gouge out**: hole etc) scavare; (: initials) scolpire; (: sb's eyes) cavare

gourd [guəd] N zucca

gourmet ['guəmeɪ] N buongustaio(-a)

gout [gaut] N gotta

govern ['gʌvən] VT governare; (Ling) reggere

governess ['gʌvənɪs] N governante f

governing ['gʌvənɪŋ] ADJ (Pol) al potere, al governo; **~ body** consiglio di amministrazione

government ['gʌvnmənt] N governo; (BRIT: ministers) ministero ▶ CPD statale; **local ~** amministrazione f locale

governmental [gʌvn'mɛntl] ADJ governativo(-a)

government housing N (US) alloggi mpl popolari

government stock N titoli mpl di stato

governor ['gʌvənər] N (of state, bank) governatore m; (of school, hospital) amministratore m; (BRIT: of prison) direttore(-trice)

Govt ABBR = **government**

gown [gaun] N vestito lungo; (of teacher, judge: BRIT) toga

GP N ABBR (Med) = **general practitioner**; **who's your GP?** qual è il suo medico di fiducia?

GPMU N ABBR (BRIT) = **Graphical, Paper and Media Union**

GPO N ABBR (BRIT old) = **General Post Office**; (US: = Government Printing Office) ≈ Poligrafici dello Stato

GPS N ABBR (= global positioning system) GPS m

gr. ABBR (Comm) = **gross**

grab [græb] VT afferrare, arraffare; (property, power) impadronirsi di ▶ VI: **to ~ at** cercare di afferrare

grace [greɪs] N grazia; (graciousness) garbo, cortesia ▶ VT onorare; **5 days' ~** dilazione f di 5 giorni; **to say ~** dire il benedicite; **with a good/bad ~** volentieri/malvolentieri; **his sense of humour is his saving ~** il suo senso dell'umorismo è quello che lo salva

graceful ['greɪsful] ADJ elegante, aggraziato(-a)

gracious ['greɪʃəs] ADJ grazioso(-a), misericordioso(-a) ▶ EXCL: **(good) ~!** madonna (mia)!

gradation [grə'deɪʃən] N gradazione f

grade [greɪd] N (Comm) qualità f inv; classe f; categoria; (in hierarchy) grado; (US Scol: mark) voto; classe; (gradient) pendenza, gradiente m ▶ VT classificare; ordinare; graduare; **to make the ~** (fig) farcela

grade crossing N (US) passaggio a livello

grade school N (US) scuola elementare or primaria

gradient ['greɪdɪənt] N pendenza, inclinazione m

gradual ['grædjuəl] ADJ graduale

gradually ['grædjuəlɪ] ADV man mano, a poco a poco

graduate N ['grædjuɪt] laureato(-a); (US Scol) diplomato(-a), licenziato(-a) ▶ VI ['grædjueɪt] laurearsi; diplomarsi

graduated pension ['grædjueɪtɪd-] N pensione calcolata sugli ultimi stipendi

graduation [grædju'eɪʃən] N cerimonia del conferimento della laurea; (US Scol) consegna dei diplomi

graffiti [grə'fi:tɪ] NPL graffiti mpl

graft [grɑ:ft] N (Agr, Med) innesto; (col: bribery) corruzione f; (Brit col): **hard ~** duro lavoro ▶ VT innestare; **it's hard ~** (Brit col) è un lavoraccio

grain [greɪn] N (no pl: cereals) cereali mpl; (US: corn) grano; (of sand) granello; (of wood) venatura; **it goes against the ~** (fig) va contro la mia (or la sua etc) natura

gram [græm] N grammo

grammar ['græmər] N grammatica

grammar school N (Brit) ≈ liceo; (US) ≈ scuola elementare

grammatical [grə'mætɪkl] ADJ grammaticale

gramme [græm] N = **gram**

gramophone ['græməfəun] N (Brit) grammofono

gran [græn] N (col: Brit) nonna

granary ['grænərɪ] N granaio

grand [grænd] ADJ grande, magnifico(-a); grandioso(-a) ▶ N (col: thousand) mille dollari mpl (or sterline fpl)

grandad ['grændæd] N (col) = **granddad**

grandchild ['græntʃaɪld] (pl **-children** [-tʃɪldrən]) N nipote m

granddad ['grændæd] N (col) nonno

granddaughter ['grændɔ:tər] N nipote f

grandeur ['grændjər] N (of style, house) splendore m; (of occasion, scenery etc) grandiosità, maestà

grandfather ['grændfɑ:ðər] N nonno

grandiose ['grændɪəus] ADJ grandioso(-a); (pej) pomposo(-a)

grand jury N (US) giuria (formata da 12 a 23 membri)

grandma ['grænmɑ:] N (col) nonna

grandmother ['grænmʌðər] N nonna

grandpa ['grænpɑ:] N (col) = **granddad**

grandparent ['grænpɛərənt] N nonno(-a)

grand piano N pianoforte m a coda

Grand Prix ['grɑ̃:'pri:] N (Aut) Gran Premio, Grand Prix m inv

grandson ['grænsʌn] N nipote m

grandstand ['grændstænd] N (Sport) tribuna

grand total N somma complessiva

granite ['grænɪt] N granito

granny ['grænɪ] N (col) nonna

grant [grɑ:nt] VT accordare; (a request) accogliere; (admit) ammettere, concedere ▶ N (Scol) borsa; (Admin) sussidio, sovvenzione f; **to take sth for granted** dare qc per scontato; **to take sb for granted** dare per scontata la presenza di qn

granulated ['grænjuleɪtɪd] ADJ: **~ sugar** zucchero cristallizzato

granule ['grænju:l] N granello

grape [greɪp] N chicco d'uva, acino; **a bunch of grapes** un grappolo d'uva

grapefruit ['greɪpfru:t] N pompelmo

grapevine ['greɪpvaɪn] N vite f; **I heard it on the ~** (fig) me l'ha detto l'uccellino

graph [grɑ:f] N grafico

graphic ['græfɪk] ADJ grafico(-a); (vivid) vivido(-a); see also **graphics**

graphic designer N grafico(-a)

graphic equalizer N equalizzatore m grafico

graphics ['græfɪks] N (art, process) grafica ▶ NPL (drawings) illustrazioni fpl

graphite ['græfaɪt] N grafite f

graph paper N carta millimetrata

grapple ['græpl] VI: **to ~ with** essere alle prese con

grappling iron ['græplɪŋ-] N (Naut) grappino

grasp [grɑ:sp] VT afferrare ▶ N (grip) presa; (fig) potere m; comprensione f; **to have sth within one's ~** avere qc a portata di mano; **to have a good ~ of** (subject) avere una buona padronanza di
▶ **grasp at** VT FUS (rope etc) afferrarsi a, aggrapparsi a; (fig: opportunity) non farsi sfuggire, approfittare di

grasping ['grɑ:spɪŋ] ADJ avido(-a)

grass [grɑ:s] N erba; (pasture) pascolo, prato; (Brit col: informer) informatore(-trice); (ex-terrorist) pentito(-a)

grasshopper ['grɑ:ʃɔpər] N cavalletta

grassland ['grɑ:slænd] N prateria

grass roots NPL (fig) base f

grass snake N natrice f

grassy ['grɑ:sɪ] ADJ erboso(-a)

grate [greɪt] N graticola (del focolare) ▶ VI cigolare, stridere ▶ VT (Culin) grattugiare

grateful ['greɪtful] ADJ grato(-a), riconoscente

gratefully ['greɪtfulɪ] ADV con gratitudine

grater ['greɪtəʳ] N grattugia

gratification [grætɪfɪ'keɪʃən] N soddisfazione f

gratify ['grætɪfaɪ] VT appagare; (whim) soddisfare

gratifying ['grætɪfaɪɪŋ] ADJ gradito(-a), soddisfacente

grating ['greɪtɪŋ] N (iron bars) grata ▶ ADJ (noise) stridente, stridulo(-a)

gratitude ['grætɪtjuːd] N gratitudine f

gratuitous [grə'tjuːɪtəs] ADJ gratuito(-a)

gratuity [grə'tjuːɪtɪ] N mancia

grave [greɪv] N tomba ▶ ADJ grave, serio(-a)

gravedigger ['greɪvdɪgəʳ] N becchino

gravel ['grævl] N ghiaia

gravely ['greɪvlɪ] ADV gravemente, solennemente; ~ **ill** in pericolo di vita

gravestone ['greɪvstəun] N pietra tombale

graveyard ['greɪvjɑːd] N cimitero

gravitate ['grævɪteɪt] VI gravitare

gravity ['grævɪtɪ] N (Physics) gravità; pesantezza; (seriousness) gravità, serietà

gravy ['greɪvɪ] N intingolo della carne; salsa

gravy boat N salsiera

gravy train N: **the ~** (col) l'albero della cuccagna

gray [greɪ] ADJ (US) = **grey**

graze [greɪz] VI pascolare, pascere ▶ VT (touch lightly) sfiorare; (scrape) escoriare ▶ N (Med) escoriazione f

grazing ['greɪzɪŋ] N pascolo

grease [griːs] N (fat) grasso; (lubricant) lubrificante m ▶ VT ingrassare; lubrificare; **to ~ the skids** (US fig) spianare la strada

grease gun N ingrassatore m

greasepaint ['griːspeɪnt] N cerone m

greaseproof paper ['griːspruːf-] N (BRIT) carta oleata

greasy ['griːsɪ] ADJ grasso(-a), untuoso(-a); (BRIT: road, surface) scivoloso(-a); (hands, clothes) unto(-a)

great [greɪt] ADJ grande; (pain, heat) forte, intenso(-a); (col) magnifico(-a), meraviglioso(-a); **they're ~ friends** sono grandi amici; **the ~ thing is that …** il bello è che …; **it was ~!** è stato fantastico!; **we had a ~ time** ci siamo divertiti un mondo

Great Barrier Reef N: **the ~** la Grande Barriera Corallina

Great Britain N Gran Bretagna

great-grandchild [greɪt'græntʃaɪld] (pl **-children** [-tʃɪldrən]) N pronipote mf

great-grandfather [greɪt'grændfɑːðəʳ] N bisnonno

great-grandmother [greɪt'grænmʌðəʳ] N bisnonna

Great Lakes NPL: **the ~** i Grandi Laghi

greatly ['greɪtlɪ] ADV molto

greatness ['greɪtnɪs] N grandezza

Grecian ['griːʃən] ADJ greco(-a)

Greece [griːs] N Grecia

greed [griːd] N (also: **greediness**) avarizia; (: for food) golosità, ghiottoneria

greedily ['griːdɪlɪ] ADV avidamente; golosamente

greedy ['griːdɪ] ADJ avido(-a); goloso(-a), ghiotto(-a)

Greek [griːk] ADJ greco(-a) ▶ N greco(-a); (Ling) greco; **ancient/modern** ~ greco antico/moderno

green [griːn] ADJ (also Pol) verde; (inexperienced) inesperto(-a), ingenuo(-a) ▶ N verde m; (stretch of grass) prato; (also: **village green**) ≈ piazza del paese (of golf course) green m inv; **greens** NPL (vegetables) verdura; **to have ~ fingers** or (US) **a ~ thumb** (fig) avere il pollice verde; **the G~ Party** (BRIT Pol) i Verdi

green belt N (round town) cintura di verde

green card N (BRIT Aut) carta verde; (US Admin) permesso di soggiorno e di lavoro

greenery ['griːnərɪ] N verde m

greenfly ['griːnflaɪ] N afide f

greengage ['griːngeɪdʒ] N susina Regina Claudia

greengrocer ['griːngrəusəʳ] N (BRIT) fruttivendolo(-a), erbivendolo(-a)

greenhouse ['griːnhaus] N serra

greenhouse effect N: **the ~** l'effetto serra

greenhouse gas N gas m inv responsabile dell'effetto serra

greenish ['griːnɪʃ] ADJ verdastro(-a)

Greenland ['griːnlənd] N Groenlandia

Greenlander ['griːnləndəʳ] N groenlandese mf

green light N: **to give sb the ~** dare via libera a qn

green pepper N peperone m verde

green salad N insalata verde

green tax N ecotassa

greet [griːt] VT salutare

greeting ['griːtɪŋ] N saluto; **Christmas/ birthday greetings** auguri mpl di Natale/di compleanno; **Season's greetings** Buone Feste

greetings card N cartolina d'auguri

gregarious [grə'gɛərɪəs] ADJ gregario(-a), socievole

grenade [grə'neɪd] N (also: **hand grenade**) granata

grew [gruː] PT of **grow**

grey, (US) **gray** [greɪ] ADJ grigio(-a); **to go ~** diventar grigio

grey-haired ADJ dai capelli grigi

greyhound ['greɪhaund] N levriere m
grey vote N elettori mpl senior
grid [grɪd] N grata; (Elec) rete f; (US Aut) area d'incrocio
griddle ['grɪdl] N piastra
gridiron ['grɪdaɪən] N graticola
gridlock ['grɪdlɔk] N (traffic jam) paralisi f inv del traffico; **gridlocked** adj paralizzato(-a) dal traffico; (talks etc) in fase di stallo
grief [griːf] N dolore m; **to come to ~** (plan) naufragare; (person) finire male
grievance ['griːvəns] N doglianza, lagnanza; (cause for complaint) motivo di risentimento
grieve [griːv] VI affliggersi ▶ VT addolorare; **to ~ for sb** compiangere qn; (dead person) piangere qn
grievous bodily harm ['griːvəs-] N (Law) aggressione f
grill [grɪl] N (on cooker) griglia; (also: **mixed grill**) grigliata mista ▶ VT (BRIT) cuocere ai ferri; (col: question) interrogare senza sosta; **grilled meat** (BRIT) carne f ai ferri or alla griglia; see **grillroom**
grille [grɪl] N grata; (Aut) griglia
grillroom ['grɪlrum], **grill** ['grɪl] N rosticceria
grim [grɪm] ADJ sinistro(-a), brutto(-a)
grimace [grɪ'meɪs] N smorfia ▶ VI fare smorfie
grime [graɪm] N sudiciume m
grimy ['graɪmɪ] ADJ sudicio(-a)
grin [grɪn] N sorriso smagliante ▶ VI: **to ~ (at)** sorridere (a), fare un gran sorriso (a)
grind [graɪnd] (pt, pp **ground** [graund]) VT macinare; (US: meat) tritare, macinare; (make sharp) arrotare; (polish: gem, lens) molare ▶ VI (car gears) grattare ▶ N (work) sgobbata; **to ~ one's teeth** digrignare i denti; **to ~ to a halt** (vehicle) arrestarsi con uno stridio di freni; (fig: talks, scheme) insabbiarsi (: work, production) cessare del tutto; **the daily ~** (col) il tran tran quotidiano
grinder ['graɪndər] N (machine: for coffee) macinino
grindstone ['graɪndstəun] N: **to keep one's nose to the ~** darci sotto
grip [grɪp] N impugnatura; presa; (holdall) borsa da viaggio ▶ VT (object) afferrare; (attention) catturare; **to come to grips with** affrontare; cercare di risolvere; **to ~ the road** (tyres) far presa sulla strada; (car) tenere bene la strada; **to lose one's ~** perdere or allentare la presa; (fig) perdere la grinta
gripe [graɪp] N (Med) colica; (col: complaint) lagna ▶ VI (col) brontolare
gripping ['grɪpɪŋ] ADJ avvincente
grisly ['grɪzlɪ] ADJ macabro(-a), orrido(-a)
grist [grɪst] N (fig): **it's (all) ~ to the mill** tutto aiuta
gristle ['grɪsl] N cartilagine f

grit [grɪt] N ghiaia; (courage) fegato ▶ VT (road) coprire di sabbia; **to ~ one's teeth** stringere i denti; **I've got a piece of ~ in my eye** ho un bruscolino nell'occhio
grits [grɪts] NPL (US) macinato grosso (di avena etc)
grizzle ['grɪzl] VI (BRIT) piagnucolare
grizzly ['grɪzlɪ] N (also: **grizzly bear**) orso grigio, grizzly m inv
groan [grəun] N gemito ▶ VI gemere
grocer ['grəusər] N negoziante m di generi alimentari; **~'s (shop)** negozio di alimentari
groceries ['grəusərɪz] NPL provviste fpl
grocery ['grəusərɪ] N (shop) (negozio di) alimentari
grog [grɔg] N grog m inv
groggy ['grɔgɪ] ADJ barcollante
groin [grɔɪn] N inguine m
groom [gruːm] N palafreniere m; (also: **bridegroom**) sposo ▶ VT (horse) strigliare; (fig): **to ~ sb for** avviare qn a; **well-groomed** (person) curato(-a)
groove [gruːv] N scanalatura, solco
grope [grəup] VI andare a tentoni; **to ~ for sth** cercare qc a tastoni
gross [grəus] ADJ grossolano(-a); (Comm) lordo(-a) ▶ N (pl inv: twelve dozen) grossa ▶ VT (Comm) incassare, avere un incasso lordo di
gross domestic product N prodotto interno lordo
grossly ['grəuslɪ] ADV (greatly) molto
gross national product N prodotto nazionale lordo
grotesque [grəu'tɛsk] ADJ grottesco(-a)
grotto ['grɔtəu] N grotta
grotty ['grɔtɪ] ADJ (BRIT col) squallido(-a)
grouch [grautʃ] (col) VI brontolare ▶ N (person) brontolone(-a)
ground [graund] PT, PP of **grind** ▶ ADJ (coffee etc) macinato(-a) ▶ N suolo, terra; (land) terreno; (Sport) campo; (reason: gen pl) ragione f; (US: also: **ground wire**) (presa a) terra ▶ VT (plane) tenere a terra; (US Elec) mettere la presa a terra a ▶ VI (ship) arenarsi; **grounds** NPL (of coffee etc) fondi mpl; (gardens etc) terreno, giardini mpl; **on/to the ~** per/a terra; **below ~** sottoterra; **common ~** terreno comune; **to gain/lose ~** guadagnare/perdere terreno; **he covered a lot of ~ in his lecture** ha toccato molti argomenti nel corso della conferenza
ground cloth N (US) = **groundsheet**
ground control N (Aviat, Space) base f di controllo
ground floor N pianterreno
grounding ['graundɪŋ] N (in education) basi fpl
groundless ['graundlɪs] ADJ infondato(-a)
groundnut ['graundnʌt] N arachide f

g

585

ground rent N (*Brit*) canone *m* di affitto di un terreno

ground rules NPL regole *fpl* fondamentali

groundsheet ['graundʃiːt] N (*Brit*) telone *m* impermeabile

groundsman ['graundzmən] (*irreg*), (*US*) **groundskeeper** ['graundzkiːpəʳ] N (*Sport*) custode *m* (di campo sportivo)

ground staff N personale *m* di terra

groundswell ['graundswɛl] N maremoto; (*fig*) movimento

ground-to-air ['graundtu'ɛəʳ] ADJ terra-aria *inv*

ground-to-ground ['grauntə'graund] ADJ: **~ missile** missile *m* terra-terra

groundwork ['graundwəːk] N preparazione *f*

group [gruːp] N gruppo; (*Mus: pop group*) complesso, gruppo ▶ VT (*also:* **group together**) raggruppare ▶ VI (*also:* **group together**) raggrupparsi

groupie ['gruːpɪ] N groupie *mf*, fan *m inv f inv* scatenato(-a)

group therapy N terapia di gruppo

grouse [graus] N (*pl inv: bird*) tetraone *m* ▶ VI (*complain*) brontolare

grove [grəuv] N boschetto

grovel ['grɔvl] VI (*fig*): **to ~ (before)** strisciare (di fronte a)

grow [grəu] (*pt* **grew** [gruː], *pp* **grown** [grəun]) VI crescere; (*increase*) aumentare; (*develop*) svilupparsi; (*become*) **to ~ rich/weak** arricchirsi/indebolirsi ▶ VT coltivare, far crescere; **to ~ tired of waiting** stancarsi di aspettare

▶ **grow apart** VI (*fig*) estraniarsi

▶ **grow away from** VT FUS (*fig*) allontanarsi da, staccarsi da

▶ **grow on** VT FUS: **that painting is growing on me** quel quadro più lo guardo più mi piace

▶ **grow out of** VT FUS (*clothes*) diventare troppo grande per indossare; (*habit*) perdere (col tempo); **he'll ~ out of it** gli passerà

▶ **grow up** VI farsi grande, crescere

grower ['grəuəʳ] N coltivatore(-trice)

growing ['grəuɪŋ] ADJ (*fear, amount*) crescente; **~ pains** (*also fig*) problemi *mpl* di crescita

growl [graul] VI ringhiare

grown [grəun] PP *of* **grow** ▶ ADJ adulto(-a), maturo(-a)

grown-up [grəun'ʌp] N adulto(-a), grande *mf*

growth [grəuθ] N crescita, sviluppo; (*what has grown*) crescita; (*Med*) escrescenza, tumore *m*

growth rate N tasso di crescita

grub [grʌb] N larva; (*col: food*) roba (da mangiare)

grubby ['grʌbɪ] ADJ sporco(-a)

grudge [grʌdʒ] N rancore *m* ▶ VT: **to ~ sb sth** dare qc a qn di malavoglia; invidiare qc a qn; **to bear sb a ~ (for)** serbar rancore a qn (per)

grudgingly ['grʌdʒɪŋlɪ] ADV di malavoglia, di malincuore

gruelling, (*US*) **grueling** ['gruəlɪŋ] ADJ estenuante

gruesome ['gruːsəm] ADJ orribile

gruff [grʌf] ADJ rozzo(-a)

grumble ['grʌmbl] VI brontolare, lagnarsi

grumpy ['grʌmpɪ] ADJ scorbutico(-a)

grunge [grʌndʒ] N (*Mus*) grunge *m inv*; (*style*) moda *f* grunge *inv*

grunt [grʌnt] VI grugnire ▶ N grugnito

G-string ['dʒiːstrɪŋ] N (*garment*) tanga *m inv*

GT ABBR (*Aut: = gran turismo*) GT

GU ABBR (*US Post*) = **Guam**

guarantee [gærən'tiː] N garanzia ▶ VT garantire; **he can't ~ (that) he'll come** non può garantire che verrà

guarantor [gærən'tɔːʳ] N garante *mf*

guard [gɑːd] N guardia; (*protection*) riparo, protezione *f*; (*Boxing*) difesa; (*one man*) guardia, sentinella; (*Brit Rail*) capotreno; (*safety device: on machine*) schermo protettivo; (*also:* **fire guard**) parafuoco ▶ VT fare la guardia a; **to ~ (against** *or* **from)** proteggere (da), salvaguardare (da); **to be on one's ~** (*fig*) stare in guardia

▶ **guard against** VI: **to ~ against doing sth** guardarsi dal fare qc

guard dog N cane *m* da guardia

guarded ['gɑːdɪd] ADJ (*fig*) cauto(-a), guardingo(-a)

guardian ['gɑːdɪən] N custode *m*; (*of minor*) tutore(-trice)

guard's van N (*Brit Rail*) vagone *m* di servizio

Guatemala [gwɑːtə'mɑːlə] N Guatemala *m*

Guernsey ['gəːnzɪ] N Guernsey *f*

guerrilla [gə'rɪlə] N guerrigliero

guerrilla warfare N guerriglia

guess [gɛs] VI indovinare ▶ VT indovinare; (*US*) credere, pensare ▶ N congettura; **to take** *or* **have a ~** provare a indovinare; **my ~ is that ...** suppongo che ...; **to keep sb guessing** tenere qn in sospeso *or* sulla corda; **I ~ you're right** mi sa che hai ragione

guesstimate ['gɛstɪmɪt] N (*col*) stima approssimativa

guesswork ['gɛswəːk] N: **I got the answer by ~** ho azzeccato la risposta

guest [gɛst] N ospite *mf*; (*in hotel*) cliente *mf*; **be my ~** (*col*) fai come (se fossi) a casa tua

guest-house ['gɛsthaus] N pensione *f*

guest room N camera degli ospiti

guff [gʌf] N (*col*) stupidaggini *fpl*, assurdità *fpl*

guffaw [gʌ'fɔː] N risata sonora ▶ VI scoppiare di una risata sonora

guidance ['gaɪdəns] N guida, direzione f; **marriage/vocational ~** consulenza matrimoniale/per l'avviamento professionale

guide [gaɪd] N (person, book etc) guida; (BRIT: also: **girl guide**) giovane esploratrice f ▸ VT guidare; **to be guided by sb/sth** farsi or lasciarsi guidare da qn/qc

guidebook ['gaɪdbʊk] N guida

guided missile N missile m telecomandato

guide dog N (BRIT) cane m guida inv

guided tour N visita guidata; **what time does the ~ start?** a che ora comincia la visita guidata?

guidelines ['gaɪdlaɪnz] NPL (fig) indicazioni fpl, linee fpl direttive

guild [gɪld] N arte f, corporazione f; associazione f

guildhall ['gɪldhɔ:l] N (BRIT) palazzo municipale

guile [gaɪl] N astuzia

guileless ['gaɪllɪs] ADJ candido(-a)

guillotine ['gɪləti:n] N ghigliottina

guilt [gɪlt] N colpevolezza

guilty ['gɪltɪ] ADJ colpevole; **to feel ~ (about)** sentirsi in colpa (per); **to plead ~/not ~** dichiararsi colpevole/innocente

Guinea ['gɪnɪ] N: **Republic of ~** Repubblica di Guinea

guinea ['gɪnɪ] N (BRIT) ghinea (= 21 shillings: valuta ora fuori uso)

guinea pig ['gɪnɪ-] N cavia

guise [gaɪz] N maschera

guitar [gɪ'ta:ʳ] N chitarra

guitarist [gɪ'ta:rɪst] N chitarrista mf

gulch [gʌltʃ] N (US) burrone m

gulf [gʌlf] N golfo; (abyss) abisso; **the (Persian) G~** il Golfo Persico

Gulf States NPL: **the ~** i paesi del Golfo Persico

Gulf Stream N: **the ~** la corrente del Golfo

gull [gʌl] N gabbiano

gullet ['gʌlɪt] N gola

gullibility [gʌlɪ'bɪlɪtɪ] N semplicioneria

gullible ['gʌlɪbl] ADJ credulo(-a)

gully ['gʌlɪ] N burrone m; gola; canale m

gulp [gʌlp] VI deglutire; (from emotion) avere il nodo in gola ▸ VT (also: **gulp down**) tracannare, inghiottire ▸ N (of liquid) sorso; (of food) boccone m; **in** or **at one ~** in un sorso, d'un fiato

gum [gʌm] N (Anat) gengiva; (glue) colla; (sweet) caramella gommosa; (also: **chewing-gum**) chewing-gum m ▸ VT incollare ▸ **gum up** VT: **to ~ up the works** (col) mettere il bastone tra le ruote

gumboil ['gʌmbɔɪl] N ascesso (dentario)

gumboots ['gʌmbu:ts] NPL (BRIT) stivali mpl di gomma

gumption ['gʌmpʃən] N buon senso, senso pratico

gun [gʌn] N fucile m; (small) pistola, rivoltella; (rifle) carabina; (shotgun) fucile da caccia; (cannon) cannone m ▸ VT (also: **gun down**) abbattere a colpi di pistola or fucile; **to stick to one's guns** (fig) tener duro

gunboat ['gʌnbəʊt] N cannoniera

gun dog N cane m da caccia

gunfire ['gʌnfaɪəʳ] N spari mpl

gung-ho ['gʌŋ'həʊ] ADJ (col) stupidamente entusiasta

gunk [gʌŋk] N porcherie fpl

gunman ['gʌnmən] N (irreg) bandito armato

gunner ['gʌnəʳ] N artigliere m

gunpoint ['gʌnpɔɪnt] N: **at ~** sotto minaccia di fucile

gunpowder ['gʌnpaʊdəʳ] N polvere f da sparo

gunrunner ['gʌnrʌnəʳ] N contrabbandiere d'armi

gunrunning ['gʌnrʌnɪŋ] N contrabbando d'armi

gunshot ['gʌnʃɒt] N sparo; **within ~** a portata di fucile

gunsmith ['gʌnsmɪθ] N armaiolo

gurgle ['gə:gl] N gorgoglio ▸ VI gorgogliare

guru ['gʊru:] N guru m inv

gush [gʌʃ] N fiotto, getto ▸ VI sgorgare; (fig) abbandonarsi ad effusioni

gushing ['gʌʃɪŋ] ADJ che fa smancerie, smorfioso(-a)

gusset ['gʌsɪt] N gherone m; (in tights, pants) rinforzo

gust [gʌst] N (of wind) raffica; (of smoke) buffata

gusto ['gʌstəʊ] N entusiasmo

gusty ['gʌstɪ] ADJ (wind) a raffiche; (day) tempestoso(-a)

gut [gʌt] N intestino, budello; (Mus etc) minugia ▸ VT (poultry, fish) levare le interiora a, sventrare; (building) svuotare; (: fire) divorare l'interno di; **guts** NPL (col: innards) budella fpl; (: of animals) interiora fpl; (courage) fegato; **to hate sb's guts** odiare qn a morte

gut reaction N reazione f istintiva

gutsy ['gʌtsɪ] ADJ (col, style) che ha mordente; (plucky) coraggioso(-a)

gutted ['gʌtɪd] ADV (col: upset) scioccato(-a)

gutter ['gʌtəʳ] N (of roof) grondaia; (in street) cunetta

gutter press N: **the ~** la stampa scandalistica

guttural ['gʌtərl] ADJ gutturale

guy [gaɪ] N (also: **guyrope**) cavo or corda di fissaggio; (: col: man) tipo, elemento; (: figure) effigie di Guy Fawkes

Guyana [gaɪ'ænə] N Guayana f

Guy Fawkes Night [-'fɔ:ks-] N (BRIT); vedi nota

> La sera del 5 novembre, in occasione della *Guy Fawkes Night*, altrimenti chiamata *Bonfire Night*, viene commemorato con falò e fuochi d'artificio il fallimento della Congiura delle Polveri contro Giacomo I nel 1605. La festa prende il nome dal principale congiurato della cospirazione, Guy Fawkes, la cui effigie viene bruciata durante i festeggiamenti.

guzzle ['gʌzl] vɪ gozzovigliare ▶ vᴛ trangugiare

gym [dʒɪm] ɴ (*also*: **gymnasium**) palestra; (*also*: **gymnastics**) ginnastica

gymkhana [dʒɪm'kɑːnə] ɴ gimkana

gymnasium [dʒɪm'neɪzɪəm] ɴ palestra

gymnast ['dʒɪmnæst] ɴ ginnasta *mf*

gymnastics [dʒɪm'næstɪks] ɴ, ɴᴘʟ ginnastica

gym shoes ɴᴘʟ scarpe *fpl* da ginnastica

gym slip ɴ (*Bʀɪᴛ*) grembiule *m* da scuola (*per ragazze*)

gynaecologist, (*US*) **gynecologist** [gaɪnɪ'kɔlədʒɪst] ɴ ginecologo(-a)

gynaecology, (*US*) **gynecology** [gaɪnə'kɔlədʒɪ] ɴ ginecologia

gypsy ['dʒɪpsɪ] ɴ = **gipsy**

gyrate [dʒaɪ'reɪt] vɪ girare

gyroscope ['dʒaɪərəskəup] ɴ giroscopio

H h

H, h [eɪtʃ] N (letter) H, h f inv or m inv; **H for Harry**, (US) **H for How** ≈ H come Hotel

habeas corpus ['heɪbɪəs'kɔ:pəs] N (Law) habeas corpus m inv

haberdashery ['hæbədæʃərɪ] (BRIT) N merceria

habit ['hæbɪt] N abitudine f; (costume) abito; (Rel) tonaca; **to get out of/into the ~ of doing sth** perdere/prendere l'abitudine di fare qc

habitable ['hæbɪtəbl] ADJ abitabile

habitat ['hæbɪtæt] N habitat m inv

habitation [hæbɪ'teɪʃən] N abitazione f

habitual [hə'bɪtjuəl] ADJ abituale; (drinker, liar) inveterato(-a)

habitually [hə'bɪtjuəlɪ] ADV abitualmente, di solito

hack [hæk] VT tagliare, fare a pezzi ▶ N (cut) taglio; (blow) colpo; (old horse) ronzino; (pej: writer) scribacchino(-a)

hacker ['hækə^r] N (Comput) pirata m informatico

hackles ['hæklz] NPL: **to make sb's ~ rise** (fig) rendere qn furioso

hackney cab ['hæknɪ-] N carrozza a nolo

hackneyed ['hæknɪd] ADJ comune, trito(-a)

hacksaw ['hæksɔ:] N seghetto (per metallo)

had [hæd] PT, PP of **have**

haddock ['hædək] (pl ~ or **haddocks**) N eglefino

hadn't ['hædnt]= **had not**

haematology, (US) **hematology** [hi:mə'tɔlədʒɪ] N ematologia

haemoglobin, (US) **hemoglobin** [hi:məu'ɡləubɪn] N emoglobina

haemophilia, (US) **hemophilia** [hi:məu'fɪlɪə] N emofilia

haemorrhage, (US) **hemorrhage** ['hɛmərɪdʒ] N emorragia

haemorrhoids, (US) **hemorrhoids** ['hɛmərɔɪdz] NPL emorroidi fpl

hag [hæg] N (ugly) befana; (nasty) megera; (witch) strega

haggard ['hægəd] ADJ smunto(-a)

haggis ['hægɪs] N (SCOTTISH) insaccato a base di frattaglie di pecora e avena

haggle ['hægl] VI mercanteggiare; **to ~ (over)** contrattare (su); (argue) discutere (su)

haggling ['hæglɪŋ] N contrattazioni fpl

Hague [heɪɡ] N: **The ~** L'Aia

hail [heɪl] N grandine f; (of criticism etc) pioggia ▶ VT (call) chiamare; (flag down: taxi) fermare; (greet) salutare ▶ VI grandinare; **to ~ (as)** acclamare (come); **he hails from Scotland** viene dalla Scozia

hailstone ['heɪlstəun] N chicco di grandine

hailstorm ['heɪlstɔ:m] N grandinata

hair [hɛə^r] N capelli mpl; (single hair: on head) capello; (: on body) pelo; **to do one's ~** pettinarsi

hairband ['hɛəbænd] N (elastic) fascia per i capelli; (rigid) cerchietto

hairbrush ['hɛəbrʌʃ] N spazzola per capelli

haircut ['hɛəkʌt] N taglio di capelli; **I need a ~** devo tagliarmi i capelli

hairdo ['hɛədu:] N acconciatura, pettinatura

hairdresser ['hɛədrɛsə^r] N parrucchiere(-a)

hairdresser's N parrucchiere(-a)

hair-dryer ['hɛədraɪə^r] N asciugacapelli m inv

-haired [hɛəd] SUFFIX: **fair/long~** dai capelli biondi/lunghi

hair gel N gel m inv per capelli

hairgrip ['hɛəɡrɪp] N forcina

hairline ['hɛəlaɪn] N attaccatura dei capelli

hairline fracture N incrinatura

hairnet ['hɛənɛt] N retina (per capelli)

hair oil N brillantina

hairpiece ['hɛəpi:s] N toupet m inv

hairpin ['hɛəpɪn] N forcina

hairpin bend, (US) **hairpin curve** N tornante m

hair-raising ['hɛəreɪzɪŋ] ADJ orripilante

hair remover N crema depilatoria

hair spray N lacca per capelli

hairstyle ['hɛəstaɪl] N pettinatura, acconciatura

hairy ['hɛərɪ] ADJ irsuto(-a); peloso(-a); (col: frightening) spaventoso(-a)

Haiti ['heɪtɪ] N Haiti f

haka ['hɑːkə] N (NEW ZEALAND) danza eseguita dai giocatori prima di una partita

hake [heɪk] (pl ~ or **hakes**) N nasello

halal [hə'lɑːl] N: ~ **meat** carne macellata secondo la legge mussulmana

halcyon ['hælsɪən] ADJ sereno(-a)

hale [heɪl] ADJ: ~ **and hearty** che scoppia di salute

half [hɑːf] N (pl **halves** [hɑːvz]) mezzo, metà f inv; (Sport: of match) tempo; (: of ground) metà campo ▶ ADJ mezzo(-a) ▶ ADV a mezzo, a metà; ~ **an hour** mezz'ora; ~ **a dozen** mezza dozzina; ~ **a pound** mezza libbra; **two and a** ~ due e mezzo; **a week and a** ~ una settimana e mezza; ~ **(of it)** la metà; ~ **(of)** la metà di; ~ **the amount of** la metà di; **to cut sth in** ~ tagliare qc in due; ~ **empty/closed** mezzo vuoto/chiuso, semivuoto/semichiuso; ~ **past 3** le 3 e mezza; **to go halves (with sb)** fare a metà (con qn); ~ **asleep** mezzo(-a) addormentato(-a)

half-back ['hɑːfbæk] N (Sport) mediano

half-baked [hɑːf'beɪkt] ADJ (col: idea, scheme) mal combinato(-a), che non sta in piedi

half board (BRIT) N mezza pensione

half-breed ['hɑːfbriːd] N = **half-caste**

half-brother ['hɑːfbrʌðə*] N fratellastro

half-caste ['hɑːfkɑːst] N (pej) meticcio(-a)

half day N mezza giornata

half fare N tariffa a metà prezzo

half-hearted [hɑːf'hɑːtɪd] ADJ tiepido(-a)

half-hour [hɑːf'auə*] N mezz'ora

half-mast ['hɑːfmɑːst] N: **at** ~ (flag) a mezz'asta

halfpenny ['heɪpnɪ] N mezzo penny m inv

half-price ['hɑːf'praɪs] ADJ a metà prezzo ▶ ADV (also: **at half-price**) a metà prezzo

half-sister ['hɑːfsɪstə*] N sorellastra

half term N (BRIT Scol) vacanza a or di metà trimestre

half-time [hɑːf'taɪm] N (Sport) intervallo

halfway [hɑːf'weɪ] ADV a metà strada; **to meet sb** ~ (fig) arrivare a un compromesso con qn

halfway house N (hostel) ostello dove possono alloggiare temporaneamente ex detenuti; (fig) via di mezzo

half-wit ['hɑːfwɪt] N (col) idiota mf

half-yearly [hɑːf'jɪəlɪ] ADV semestralmente, ogni sei mesi ▶ ADJ semestrale

halibut ['hælɪbət] N (pl inv) ippoglosso

halitosis [hælɪ'təusɪs] N alitosi f

hall [hɔːl] N sala, salone m; (entrance way) entrata; (corridor) corridoio; (mansion) grande villa, maniero; ~ **of residence** n (BRIT) casa dello studente

hallmark ['hɔːlmɑːk] N marchio di garanzia; (fig) caratteristica

hallo [hə'ləu] EXCL = **hello**

hall of residence (BRIT) N casa dello studente

Halloween ['hæləu'iːn] N vigilia d'Ognissanti

Secondo la tradizione anglosassone, durante la notte di Halloween, il 31 di ottobre, è possibile vedere le streghe e i fantasmi. I bambini, travestiti da fantasmi, streghe, mostri o simili, vanno di porta in porta e raccolgono dolci e piccoli doni.

hallucination [həluːsɪ'neɪʃən] N allucinazione f

hallucinogenic [həluːsɪnəu'dʒɛnɪk] ADJ allucinogeno(-a)

hallway ['hɔːlweɪ] N ingresso; corridoio

halo ['heɪləu] N (of saint etc) aureola; (of sun) alone m

halt [hɔːlt] N fermata ▶ VT fermare ▶ VI fermarsi; **to call a** ~ **(to sth)** (fig) mettere or porre fine (a qc)

halter ['hɔːltə*] N (for horse) cavezza

halterneck ['hɔːltənɛk] ADJ allacciato(-a) dietro il collo

halve [hɑːv] VT (apple etc) dividere a metà; (expense) ridurre di metà

halves [hɑːvz] NPL of **half**

ham [hæm] N prosciutto; (col: also: **radio ham**) radioamatore(-trice); (also: **ham actor**) attore(-trice) senza talento

Hamburg ['hæmbəːg] N Amburgo f

hamburger ['hæmbəːgə*] N hamburger m inv

ham-fisted ['hæm'fɪstɪd], (US) **ham-handed** ['hæm'hændɪd] ADJ maldestro(-a)

hamlet ['hæmlɪt] N paesetto

hammer ['hæmə*] N martello ▶ VT martellare; (fig) sconfiggere duramente ▶ VI (at door) picchiare; **to** ~ **a point home to sb** cacciare un'idea in testa a qn; **to** ~ **on** or **at the door** picchiare alla porta ▶ **hammer out** VT (metal) spianare (a martellate); (fig: solution, agreement) mettere a punto

hammock ['hæmək] N amaca

hamper ['hæmpə*] VT impedire ▶ N cesta

hamster ['hæmstə*] N criceto

hamstring ['hæmstrɪŋ] N (Anat) tendine m del ginocchio

hand [hænd] N mano f; (of clock) lancetta; (handwriting) scrittura; (at cards) mano; (: game) partita; (worker) operaio(-a); (measurement: of horse) ≈ dieci centimetri ▶ VT dare, passare; **to give sb a** ~ dare una mano a qn; **at** ~ a portata di mano; **in** ~ a disposizione; (work) in corso; **we have the matter in** ~ ci stiamo occupando della cosa; **we have the situation in** ~ abbiamo la situazione sotto controllo; **to be on** ~ (person) essere disponibile; (emergency services) essere pronto(-a) a intervenire; **to** ~ (information etc)

a portata di mano; **to force sb's** ~ forzare la mano a qn; **to have a free** ~ avere carta bianca; **to have in one's** ~ *(also fig)* avere in mano *or* in pugno; **on the one** ~ **..., on the other** ~ da un lato ..., dall'altro
▶ **hand down** VT passare giù; *(tradition, heirloom)* tramandare; *(US: sentence, verdict)* emettere
▶ **hand in** VT consegnare
▶ **hand out** VT *(leaflets)* distribuire; *(advice)* elargire
▶ **hand over** VT passare; cedere
▶ **hand round** VT *(BRIT: information, papers)* far passare; *(distribute: chocolates etc)* far girare; *(hostess)* offrire
handbag ['hændbæg] N borsetta
hand baggage N bagaglio a mano
handball ['hændbɔːl] N pallamano *f*
handbasin ['hændbeɪsn] N lavandino
handbook ['hændbʊk] N manuale *m*
handbrake ['hændbreɪk] N freno a mano
h & c ABBR *(BRIT)* = **hot and cold (water)**
hand cream N crema per le mani
handcuffs ['hændkʌfs] NPL manette *fpl*
handful ['hændfʊl] N manciata, pugno
hand-held ['hænd'held] ADJ portatile
handicap ['hændɪkæp] N handicap *m inv* ▶ VT handicappare; **to be mentally handicapped** essere un handicappato mentale; **to be physically handicapped** essere handicappato
handicraft ['hændɪkrɑːft] N lavoro d'artigiano
handiwork ['hændɪwəːk] N lavorazione *f* a mano; **this looks like his** ~ *(pej)* qui c'è il suo zampino
handkerchief ['hæŋkətʃɪf] N fazzoletto
handle ['hændl] N *(of door etc)* maniglia; *(of cup etc)* ansa; *(of knife etc)* impugnatura; *(of saucepan)* manico; *(for winding)* manovella ▶ VT toccare, maneggiare; manovrare; *(deal with)* occuparsi di; *(treat: people)* trattare; **"~ with care"** "fragile"; **to fly off the** ~ *(fig)* perdere le staffe, uscire dai gangheri
handlebar ['hændlbɑːʳ] N, **handlebars** ['hændlbɑːz] NPL manubrio
handling ['hændlɪŋ] N *(Aut)* maneggevolezza; *(of issue)* modo di affrontare
handling charges NPL commissione *f* per la prestazione; *(for goods)* spese *fpl* di trasporto; *(Banking)* spese *fpl* bancarie
hand luggage ['hændlʌgɪdʒ] N bagagli *mpl* a mano
handmade [hænd'meɪd] ADJ fatto(-a) a mano; *(biscuits etc)* fatto(-a) in casa
handout ['hændaut] N *(money, food)* elemosina; *(leaflet)* volantino; *(at lecture)* prospetto; *(press handout)* comunicato stampa

hand-picked [hænd'pɪkt] ADJ *(produce)* scelto(-a), selezionato(-a); *(staff etc)* scelto(-a)
handrail ['hændreɪl] N *(on staircase etc)* corrimano
handset ['hændset] N *(Tel)* ricevitore *m*
hands-free ['hændzfriː] N, ADJ *(telephone)* con auricolare; *(microphone)* vivavoce *inv*
handshake ['hændʃeɪk] N stretta di mano; *(Comput)* colloquio
handsome ['hænsəm] ADJ bello(-a); *(reward)* generoso(-a); *(profit, fortune)* considerevole
hands-on ['hændz'ɔn] ADJ: ~ **experience** esperienza diretta *or* pratica
handstand ['hændstænd] N: **to do a** ~ fare la verticale
hand-to-mouth ['hændtə'mauθ] ADJ *(existence)* precario(-a)
handwriting ['hændraɪtɪŋ] N scrittura
handwritten ['hændrɪtn] ADJ scritto(-a) a mano, manoscritto(-a)
handy ['hændɪ] ADJ *(person)* bravo(-a); *(close at hand)* a portata di mano; *(convenient)* comodo(-a); *(useful: machine etc)* pratico(-a), utile; **to come in** ~ servire
handyman ['hændɪmæn] N *(irreg)* tuttofare *m inv*; **tools for the** ~ arnesi per il fatelo-da-voi
hang [hæŋ] *(pt, pp* **hung** [hʌŋ]*)* VT appendere; *(pt, pp* **hanged**: *criminal)* impiccare ▶ VI pendere; *(painting)* essere appeso(-a); *(hair)* scendere; *(drapery)* cadere; **to get the** ~ **of (doing) sth** *(col)* cominiciare a capire (come si fa) qc
▶ **hang about** VI bighellonare, ciondolare
▶ **hang back** VI *(hesitate)*: **to** ~ **back (from doing)** essere riluttante (a fare)
▶ **hang down** VI ricadere
▶ **hang on** VI *(wait)* aspettare ▶ VT FUS *(depend on: decision etc)* dipendere da; **to** ~ **on to** *(keep hold of)* aggrapparsi a, attaccarsi a; *(keep)* tenere
▶ **hang out** VT *(washing)* stendere (fuori); *(col: live)* stare ▶ VI penzolare, pendere
▶ **hang round** VI = **hang around**
▶ **hang together** VI *(argument etc)* stare in piedi
▶ **hang up** VI *(Tel)* riattaccare ▶ VT appendere; **to** ~ **up on sb** *(Tel)* metter giù il ricevitore a qn
hangar ['hæŋəʳ] N hangar *m inv*
hangdog ['hæŋdɔg] ADJ *(guilty: look, expression)* da cane bastonato
hanger ['hæŋəʳ] N gruccia
hanger-on [hæŋər'ɔn] N parassita *m*
hang-glider ['hæŋglaɪdəʳ] N deltaplano
hang-gliding ['hæŋglaɪdɪŋ] N volo col deltaplano
hanging ['hæŋɪŋ] N *(execution)* impiccagione *f*
hangman ['hæŋmən] N *(irreg)* boia *m*, carnefice *m*

hangover ['hæŋəuvə^r] N (*after drinking*) postumi *mpl* di sbornia

hang-up ['hæŋʌp] N complesso

hank [hæŋk] N matassa

hanker ['hæŋkə^r] VI: **to ~ after** bramare

hankering ['hæŋkərɪŋ] N: **to have a ~ for sth/to do sth** avere una gran voglia di qc/di fare qc

hankie, hanky ['hæŋkɪ] N ABBR = **handkerchief**

Hants ABBR (*BRIT*) = **Hampshire**

haphazard [hæp'hæzəd] ADJ a casaccio, alla carlona

hapless ['hæplɪs] ADJ disgraziato(-a); (*unfortunate*) sventurato(-a)

happen ['hæpən] VI accadere, succedere; **she happened to be free** per caso era libera; **to ~ to do sth** fare qc per caso; **if anything happened to him** se dovesse succedergli qualcosa; **as it happens** guarda caso; **what's happening?** cosa succede?, cosa sta succedendo?
▸ **happen (up)on** VT FUS capitare su

happening ['hæpnɪŋ] N avvenimento

happily ['hæpɪlɪ] ADV felicemente; fortunatamente

happiness ['hæpɪnɪs] N felicità, contentezza

happy ['hæpɪ] ADJ felice, contento(-a); **~ with** (*arrangements etc*) soddisfatto(-a) di; **to be ~ to do** (*willing*) fare volentieri; **yes, I'd be ~ to** (certo,) con piacere, (ben) volentieri; **~ birthday!** buon compleanno!; **~ Christmas/New Year!** buon Natale/anno!

happy-go-lucky ['hæpɪgəu'lʌkɪ] ADJ spensierato(-a)

happy hour N *orario in cui i pub hanno prezzi ridotti*

harangue [hə'ræŋ] VT arringare

harass ['hærəs] VT molestare

harassed ['hærəst] ADJ assillato(-a)

harassment ['hærəsmənt] N molestia

harbour, (*US*) **harbor** ['hɑːbə^r] N porto ▸ VT (*hope*) nutrire; (*fear*) avere; (*grudge*) covare; (*criminal*) dare rifugio a

harbour dues, (*US*) **harbor dues** NPL diritti *mpl* portuali

harbour master, (*US*) **harbor master** N capitano di porto

hard [hɑːd] ADJ duro(-a) ▸ ADV (*work*) sodo; (*think, try*) bene; **to look ~ at** guardare fissamente; esaminare attentamente; **to drink ~** bere forte; **~ luck!** peccato!; **no ~ feelings!** senza rancore!; **to be ~ of hearing** essere duro(-a) d'orecchio; **to be ~ on sb** essere severo con qn; **to be ~ done by** essere trattato(-a) ingiustamente; **I find it ~ to believe that ...** stento *or* faccio fatica a credere che ... + *sub*

hard-and-fast ['hɑːdən'fɑːst] ADJ ferreo(-a)

hardback ['hɑːdbæk] N libro rilegato

hardboard ['hɑːdbɔːd] N legno precompresso

hard-boiled egg ['hɑːd'bɔɪld-] N uovo sodo

hard cash N denaro in contanti

hard copy N (*Comput*) hard copy *f inv*, terminale *m* di stampa

hard-core ['hɑːd'kɔː^r] ADJ (*pornography*) hardcore *inv*; (*supporters*) irriducibile

hard court N (*Tennis*) campo in terra battuta

hard disk N (*Comput*) hard disk *m inv*, disco rigido

hard drive N (*Comput*) hard drive *m inv*

harden ['hɑːdn] VT indurire; (*steel*) temprare; (*fig: determination*) rafforzare ▸ VI (*substance*) indurirsi

hardened ['hɑːdnd] ADJ (*criminal*) incallito(-a); **to be ~ to sth** essere (diventato) insensibile a qc

hard graft N: **by sheer ~** lavorando da matti

hard-headed ['hɑːd'hɛdɪd] ADJ pratico(-a)

hard-hearted ['hɑːd'hɑːtɪd] ADJ che non si lascia commuovere, dal cuore duro

hard-hitting ['hɑːd'hɪtɪŋ] ADJ molto duro(-a); **a ~ documentary** un documentario *m* verità *inv*

hard labour N lavori forzati *mpl*

hardliner [hɑːd'laɪnə^r] N fautore(-trice) della linea dura

hard-luck story [hɑːd'lʌk-] N storia lacrimosa (*con un fine ben preciso*)

hardly ['hɑːdlɪ] ADV (*scarcely*) appena, a mala pena; **it's ~ the case** non è proprio il caso; **~ anyone/anywhere** quasi nessuno/da nessuna parte; **~ ever** quasi mai; **I can ~ believe it** stento a crederci

hardness ['hɑːdnɪs] N durezza

hard-nosed ['hɑːd'nəuzd] ADJ (*people*) con i piedi per terra

hard-pressed ['hɑːd'prɛst] ADJ in difficoltà

hard sell N (*Comm*) intensa campagna promozionale

hardship ['hɑːdʃɪp] N avversità *f inv*; privazioni *fpl*

hard shoulder N (*BRIT Aut*) corsia d'emergenza

hard-up [hɑːd'ʌp] ADJ (*col*) al verde

hardware ['hɑːdwɛə^r] N ferramenta *fpl*; (*Comput*) hardware *m*; (*Mil*) armamenti *mpl*

hardware shop, (*US*) **hardware store** N (negozio di) ferramenta *fpl*

hard-wearing [hɑːd'wɛərɪŋ] ADJ resistente, robusto(-a)

hard-won ['hɑːd'wʌn] ADJ sudato(-a)

hard-working [hɑːd'wəːkɪŋ] ADJ lavoratore(-trice)

hardy ['hɑːdɪ] ADJ robusto(-a); (*plant*) resistente al gelo

hare [hɛə^r] N lepre *f*

hare-brained ['hɛəbreɪnd] ADJ folle; scervellato(-a)

harelip ['hɛəlɪp] N (Med) labbro leporino
harem [hɑːˈriːm] N harem m inv
hark back [hɑːk-] VI: **to ~ to** (former days) rievocare; (earlier occasion) ritornare a or su
harm [hɑːm] N male m; (wrong) danno ▶ VT (person) fare male a; (thing) danneggiare; **to mean no ~** non avere l'intenzione d'offendere; **out of ~'s way** al sicuro; **there's no ~ in trying** tentar non nuoce
harmful ['hɑːmful] ADJ dannoso(-a)
harmless ['hɑːmlɪs] ADJ innocuo(-a); inoffensivo(-a)
harmonic [hɑːˈmɔnɪk] ADJ armonico(-a)
harmonica [hɑːˈmɔnɪkə] N armonica
harmonics [hɑːˈmɔnɪks] NPL armonia
harmonious [hɑːˈməunɪəs] ADJ armonioso(-a)
harmonium [hɑːˈməunɪəm] N armonium m inv
harmonize ['hɑːmənaɪz] VT, VI armonizzare
harmony ['hɑːmənɪ] N armonia
harness ['hɑːnɪs] N (for horse) bardatura, finimenti mpl; (for child) briglie fpl; (safety harness) imbracatura ▶ VT (horse) bardare; (resources) sfruttare
harp [hɑːp] N arpa ▶ VI: **to ~ on about** insistere tediosamente su
harpist ['hɑːpɪst] N arpista mf
harpoon [hɑːˈpuːn] N arpione m
harpsichord ['hɑːpsɪkɔːd] N clavicembalo
harrow ['hærəu] N (Agr) erpice m
harrowing ['hærəuɪŋ] ADJ straziante
harry ['hærɪ] VT (Mil) saccheggiare; (person) assillare
harsh [hɑːʃ] ADJ (life, winter) duro(-a); (judge, criticism) severo(-a); (sound) rauco(-a); (colour) chiassoso(-a); (light) violento(-a)
harshly ['hɑːʃlɪ] ADV duramente; severamente
harshness ['hɑːʃnɪs] N durezza; severità
harvest ['hɑːvɪst] N raccolto; (of grapes) vendemmia ▶ VT fare il raccolto di, raccogliere; vendemmiare ▶ VI fare il raccolto; vendemmiare
harvester ['hɑːvɪstəʳ] N (machine) mietitrice f; (also: **combine harvester**) mietitrebbia (person) mietitore(-trice)
has [hæz] see **have**
has-been ['hæzbiːn] N (col: person): **he's/she's a ~** ha fatto il suo tempo
hash [hæʃ] N (Culin) specie di spezzatino fatto con carne già cotta; (fig: mess) pasticcio ▶ N ABBR (col) = **hashish**
hashish ['hæʃɪʃ] N hascisc m
hashtag ['hæʃtæg] N (on Twitter) hashtag m inv; cancelletto
hasn't ['hæznt] = **has not**
hassle ['hæsl] N (col) sacco di problemi
haste [heɪst] N fretta; precipitazione f

hasten ['heɪsn] VT affrettare ▶ VI: **to ~ (to)** affrettarsi (a); **I ~ to add that ...** mi preme di aggiungere che ...
hastily ['heɪstɪlɪ] ADV in fretta, precipitosamente
hasty ['heɪstɪ] ADJ affrettato(-a), precipitoso(-a)
hat [hæt] N cappello
hatbox ['hætbɔks] N cappelliera
hatch [hætʃ] N (Naut: also: **hatchway**) boccaporto; (BRIT: also: **service hatch**) portello di servizio ▶ VI (bird) uscire dal guscio; (egg) schiudersi ▶ VT covare; (fig: scheme, plot) elaborare, mettere a punto
hatchback ['hætʃbæk] N (Aut) tre (or cinque) porte f inv
hatchet ['hætʃɪt] N accetta
hatchet job N (col) attacco spietato; **to do a ~ on sb** fare a pezzi qn
hatchet man N (irreg) (col) tirapiedi m inv, scagnozzo
hate [heɪt] VT odiare, detestare ▶ N odio; **to ~ to do** or **doing** detestare fare; **I ~ to trouble you, but ...** mi dispiace disturbarla, ma ...
hateful ['heɪtful] ADJ odioso(-a), detestabile
hater ['heɪtəʳ] N: **cop-~** persona che odia i poliziotti; **woman-~** misogino(-a)
hatred ['heɪtrɪd] N odio
hat trick N (BRIT Sport, also fig): **to get a ~** segnare tre punti consecutivi (or vincere per tre volte consecutive)
haughty ['hɔːtɪ] ADJ altero(-a), arrogante
haul [hɔːl] VT trascinare, tirare ▶ N (of fish) pescata; (of stolen goods etc) bottino
haulage ['hɔːlɪdʒ] N trasporto; autotrasporto
haulage contractor N (BRIT: firm) impresa di trasporti; (: person) autotrasportatore m
haulier ['hɔːlɪəʳ], (US) **hauler** ['hɔːləʳ] N autotrasportatore m
haunch [hɔːntʃ] N anca; **a ~ of venison** una coscia di cervo
haunt [hɔːnt] VT (fear) pervadere; (person) frequentare ▶ N rifugio; **this house is haunted** questa casa è abitata da un fantasma
haunted ['hɔːntɪd] ADJ (castle etc) abitato(-a) dai fantasmi or dagli spiriti; (look) ossessionato(-a), tormentato(-a)
haunting ['hɔːntɪŋ] ADJ (sight, music) ossessionante, che perseguita
Havana [həˈvænə] N l'Avana

(KEYWORD)

have [hæv] (pt, pp **had**) AUX VB **1** (gen) avere; essere; **to have arrived/gone** essere arrivato(-a)/andato(-a); **to have eaten/slept** avere mangiato/dormito; **he has been kind/promoted** è stato gentile/promosso; **having finished** or **when he had finished,**

h

he left dopo aver finito, se n'è andato
2 (*in tag questions*): **you've done it, haven't
you?** l'hai fatto, (non è) vero?; **he hasn't
done it, has he?** non l'ha fatto, vero?
3 (*in short answers and questions*): **you've made a
mistake — no I haven't/so I have** ha fatto
un errore — ma no, niente affatto/sì, è vero;
we haven't paid — yes we have! non
abbiamo pagato — ma sì che abbiamo
pagato!; **I've been there before, have you?**
ci sono già stato, e lei?
▶ MODAL AUX VB (*be obliged*): **to have (got) to
do sth** dover fare qc; **I haven't got** *or* **I don't
have to wear glasses** non ho bisogno di
portare gli occhiali; **I had better leave** è
meglio che io vada
▶ VT **1** (*possess, obtain*) avere; **he has (got)
blue eyes/dark hair** ha gli occhi azzurri/i
capelli scuri; **have you got** *or* **do you have a
car/phone?** ha la macchina/il telefono?;
may I have your address? potrebbe darmi il
suo indirizzo?; **you can have it for £5** te lo
do per 5 sterline
2 (+ *noun: take, hold etc*): **to have breakfast/a
swim/a bath** fare colazione/una nuotata/un
bagno; **to have a cigarette** fumare una
sigaretta; **to have dinner** cenare; **to have a
drink** bere qualcosa; **to have lunch**
pranzare; **to have a party** dare *or* fare una
festa; **to have an operation** avere *or* subire
un'operazione; **I'll have a coffee** prendo un
caffè; **let me have a try** fammi *or* lasciami
provare
3: **to have sth done** far fare qc; **to have
one's hair cut** tagliarsi *or* farsi tagliare i
capelli; **he had a suit made** si fece fare un
abito; **to have sb do sth** far fare qc a qn; **he
had me phone his boss** mi ha fatto
telefonare al suo capo
4 (*experience, suffer*) avere; **to have a cold/flu**
avere il raffreddore/l'influenza; **she had
her bag stolen** le hanno rubato la borsa
5 (*phrases*): (*col*) **you've been had!** ci sei
cascato!; **I won't have it!** (*accept*) non mi sta
affatto bene!; *see also* **haves**
▶ **have in** VT: **to have it in for sb** (*col*)
avercela con qn
▶ **have on** VT (*garment*) avere addosso; (*be busy
with*) avere da fare; **I don't have any money
on me** non ho soldi con me; **have you
anything on tomorrow?** (*BRIT*) ha qualcosa
in programma per domani?; **to have sb on**
(*BRIT col*) prendere in giro qn
▶ **have out** VT: **to have it out with sb** (*settle a
problem etc*) mettere le cose in chiaro con qn

haven ['heɪvn] N porto; (*fig*) rifugio
haven't ['hævnt] = **have not**
haversack ['hævəsæk] N zaino

haves [hævz] NPL (*col*): **the ~ and the
have-nots** gli abbienti e i non abbienti
havoc ['hævək] N gran subbuglio; **to play ~
with sth** scombussolare qc; **to wreak ~ on
sth** mettere in subbuglio qc
Hawaii [hə'waɪ:] N le Hawaii
Hawaiian [hə'waɪjən] ADJ hawaiano(-a)
▶ N hawaiano(-a); (*Ling*) lingua hawaiana
hawk [hɔ:k] N falco ▶ VT (*goods for sale*)
vendere per strada
hawker ['hɔ:kəʳ] N venditore *m* ambulante
hawkish ['hɔ:kɪʃ] ADJ violento(-a)
hawthorn ['hɔ:θɔ:n] N biancospino
hay [heɪ] N fieno
hay fever N febbre *f* da fieno
haystack ['heɪstæk] N pagliaio
haywire ['heɪwaɪəʳ] ADJ (*col*): **to go ~** perdere
la testa; impazzire
hazard ['hæzəd] N (*chance*) azzardo, ventura;
(: *risk*) pericolo, rischio ▶ VT (*one's life*)
rischiare, mettere a repentaglio; (*guess,
remark*) azzardare; **to be a health/fire ~**
essere pericoloso per la salute/in caso
d'incendio; **to ~ a guess** tirare a indovinare
hazardous ['hæzədəs] ADJ pericoloso(-a),
rischioso(-a)
hazard pay N (*US*) indennità di rischio
hazard warning lights NPL (*Aut*) luci *fpl* di
emergenza
haze [heɪz] N foschia
hazel ['heɪzl] N (*tree*) nocciolo ▶ ADJ (*eyes*)
(*color*) nocciola *inv*
hazelnut ['heɪzlnʌt] N nocciola
hazy ['heɪzɪ] ADJ fosco(-a); (*idea*) vago(-a);
(*photograph*) indistinto(-a)
H-bomb ['eɪtʃbɔm] N bomba H
HD ABBR (= *high definition*) HD, alta definizione
HDTV N ABBR (= *high definition television*)
televisore *m* HD, TV *f inv* ad alta definizione
HE ABBR = **high explosive**; (*Rel, Diplomacy*: = *His
(or Her) Excellency*) S.E.
he [hi:] PRON lui, egli; **it is he who ...** è lui
che ...; **here he is** eccolo; **he-bear** *etc* orso *etc*
maschio
head [hɛd] N testa, capo; (*leader*) capo; (*of
school*) preside *mf*; (*on tape recorder, computer etc*)
testina ▶ VT (*list*) essere in testa a; (*group*)
essere a capo di; **heads (or tails)** testa (o
croce), pari (o dispari); **~ first** a capofitto, di
testa; **~ over heels in love** pazzamente
innamorato(-a); **£10 a** *or* **per ~** 10 sterline a
testa; **to sit at the ~ of the table** sedersi a
capotavola; **to have a ~ for business** essere
tagliato per gli affari; **to have no ~ for
heights** soffrire di vertigini; **to lose/keep
one's ~** perdere/non perdere la testa; **to
come to a ~** (*fig: situation etc*) precipitare; **to ~
the ball** (*Sport*) dare di testa alla palla
▶ **head for** VT FUS dirigersi verso

▶ **head off** VT (*threat, danger*) sventare
headache ['hɛdeɪk] N mal *m* di testa;
  to have a ~ aver mal di testa
headband ['hɛdbænd] N fascia per i capelli
headboard ['hɛdbɔːd] N testiera (del letto)
head cold N raffreddore *m* di testa
headdress ['hɛddrɛs] N (*of Indian etc*)
  copricapo; (*of bride*) acconciatura
headed notepaper ['hɛdɪd-] N carta
  intestata
header ['hɛdəʳ] N (BRIT: *col*: *Football*) colpo di
  testa; (: *fall*) caduta di testa
head-first ['hɛd'fəːst] ADV a testa in giù;
  (*fig*) senza pensare
headhunt ['hɛdhʌnt] VT: **to be headhunted**
  avere un'offerta di lavoro da un cacciatore di
  teste
headhunter ['hɛdhʌntəʳ] N cacciatore *m*
  di teste
heading ['hɛdɪŋ] N titolo; intestazione *f*
headlamp ['hɛdlæmp] N (BRIT) = **headlight**
headland ['hɛdlənd] N promontorio
headlight ['hɛdlaɪt] N fanale *m*
headline ['hɛdlaɪn] N titolo
headlong ['hɛdlɔŋ] ADV (*fall*) a capofitto;
  (*rush*) precipitosamente
headmaster [hɛd'mɑːstəʳ] N preside *m*
headmistress [hɛd'mɪstrɪs] N preside *f*
head office N sede *f* (centrale)
head-on [hɛd'ɔn] ADJ (*collision*) frontale
headphones ['hɛdfəunz] NPL cuffia
headquarters [hɛd'kwɔːtəz] NPL ufficio
  centrale; (*Mil*) quartiere *m* generale
head-rest ['hɛdrɛst] N poggiacapo
headroom ['hɛdrum] N (*in car*) altezza
  dell'abitacolo; (*under bridge*) altezza limite
headscarf ['hɛdskɑːf] N foulard *m inv*
headset ['hɛdsɛt] N = **headphones**
headstone ['hɛdstəun] N (*on grave*) lapide *f*,
  pietra tombale
headstrong ['hɛdstrɔŋ] ADJ testardo(-a)
headteacher N (*of primary school*)
  direttore(-trice); (*of secondary school*) preside
  mf
head waiter N capocameriere *m*
headway ['hɛdweɪ] N: **to make ~** fare
  progressi *or* passi avanti
headwind ['hɛdwɪnd] N controvento
heady ['hɛdɪ] ADJ che dà alla testa; inebriante
heal [hiːl] VT, VI guarire
health [hɛlθ] N salute *f*; **Department of H~**
  = Ministero della Sanità
health care N assistenza sanitaria
health centre N (BRIT) poliambulatorio
health food N, **health foods** NPL alimenti
  mpl macrobiotici
health hazard N pericolo per la salute
Health Service N: **the ~** (BRIT) ≈ il Servizio
  Sanitario Statale

healthy ['hɛlθɪ] ADJ (*person*) sano(-a), in
  buona salute; (*climate*) salubre; (*food*)
  salutare; (*appetite, attitude etc*) sano(-a);
  (*economy*) florido(-a); (*bank balance*) solido(-a)
heap [hiːp] N mucchio ▶ VT (*stones, sand*): **to ~**
  (**up**) ammucchiare; **heaps** (**of**) (*col*: *lots*) un
  sacco (di), un mucchio (di); **to ~ favours/**
  praise/gifts etc **on sb** ricolmare qn di favori/
  lodi/regali *etc*
hear [hɪəʳ] (*pt, pp* **heard** [həːd]) VT sentire;
  (*news*) ascoltare; (*lecture*) assistere a; (*Law*:
  case) esaminare ▶ VI sentire; **to ~ about**
  avere notizie di; sentire parlare di; (*have news
  of*) avere notizie di; **did you ~ about the
  move?** ha sentito del trasloco?; **to ~ from sb**
  ricevere notizie da qn
  ▶ **hear out** VT ascoltare senza interrompere
hearing ['hɪərɪŋ] N (*sense*) udito; (*of witnesses*)
  audizione *f*; (*of a case*) udienza; **to give sb a ~**
  dare ascolto a qn
hearing aid N apparecchio acustico
hearsay ['hɪəseɪ] N dicerie *fpl*, chiacchiere *fpl*;
  by ~ *adv* per sentito dire
hearse [həːs] N carro funebre
heart [hɑːt] N cuore *m*; **hearts** NPL (*Cards*)
  cuori *mpl*; **at ~** in fondo; **by ~** (*learn, know*) a
  memoria; **to take ~** farsi coraggio *or* animo;
  to lose ~ perdere coraggio, scoraggiarsi; **to
  have a weak ~** avere il cuore debole; **to set
  one's ~ on sth/on doing sth** tenere molto a
  qc/a fare qc; **the ~ of the matter** il nocciolo
  della questione
heartache ['hɑːteɪk] N pene *fpl*, dolori *mpl* .
heart attack N attacco di cuore
heartbeat ['hɑːtbiːt] N battito del cuore
heartbreak ['hɑːtbreɪk] N immenso dolore *m*
heartbreaking ['hɑːtbreɪkɪŋ] ADJ straziante
heartbroken ['hɑːtbrəukən] ADJ affranto(-a);
  to be ~ avere il cuore spezzato
heartburn ['hɑːtbəːn] N bruciore *m* di stomaco
heart disease N malattia di cuore
-hearted ['hɑːtɪd] SUFFIX: **a kind~ person**
  una persona molto gentile
heartening ['hɑːtnɪŋ] ADJ incoraggiante
heart failure N (*Med*) arresto cardiaco
heartfelt ['hɑːtfɛlt] ADJ sincero(-a)
hearth [hɑːθ] N focolare *m*
heartily ['hɑːtɪlɪ] ADV (*laugh*) di cuore; (*eat*) di
  buon appetito; (*agree*) in pieno,
  completamente; **to be ~ sick of** (BRIT) essere
  veramente stufo di, essere arcistufo di
heartland ['hɑːtlænd] N zona centrale;
  Italy's industrial ~ il cuore dell'industria
  italiana
heartless ['hɑːtlɪs] ADJ senza cuore,
  insensibile; crudele
heartstrings ['hɑːtstrɪŋz] NPL: **to tug at sb's
  ~** toccare il cuore a qn, toccare qn nel
  profondo

h

heart-throb ['hɑ:tθrɔb] N rubacuori m inv
heart-to-heart ['hɑ:ttə'hɑ:t] ADJ, ADV a cuore aperto
heart transplant N trapianto del cuore
heartwarming ['hɑ:twɔ:mɪŋ] ADJ confortante, che scalda il cuore
hearty ['hɑ:tɪ] ADJ caloroso(-a); robusto(-a), sano(-a); vigoroso(-a)
heat [hi:t] N calore m; (fig) ardore m; fuoco; (Sport: also: **qualifying heat**) prova eliminatoria ▶ VT scaldare; **in** or (BRIT) **on ~** in calore
 ▶ **heat up** VI (liquids) scaldarsi; (room) riscaldarsi ▶ VT riscaldare
heated ['hi:tɪd] ADJ riscaldato(-a); (fig) appassionato(-a); (argument) acceso(-a)
heater ['hi:tə'] N radiatore m; (stove) stufa
heath [hi:θ] N (BRIT) landa
heathen ['hi:ðn] ADJ, N pagano(-a)
heather ['hɛðə'] N erica
heating ['hi:tɪŋ] N riscaldamento
heat-resistant ['hi:trɪzɪstənt] ADJ termoresistente
heat-seeking ['hi:tsi:kɪŋ] ADJ che cerca fonti di calore
heatstroke ['hi:tstrəuk] N colpo di sole
heatwave ['hi:tweɪv] N ondata di caldo
heave [hi:v] VT sollevare (con forza) ▶ VI sollevarsi ▶ N (push) grande spinta; **to ~ a sigh** emettere or mandare un sospiro
 ▶ **heave to** (pt, pp **hove**) VI (Naut) mettersi in cappa
heaven ['hɛvn] N paradiso, cielo; **~ forbid!** Dio ce ne guardi!; **for ~'s sake!** (pleading) per amor del cielo!, per carità!; (protesting) santo cielo!, in nome del cielo!; **thank ~!** grazie al cielo!
heavenly ['hɛvnlɪ] ADJ divino(-a), celeste
heavily ['hɛvɪlɪ] ADV pesantemente; (drink, smoke) molto
heavy ['hɛvɪ] ADJ pesante; (sea) grosso(-a); (rain) forte; (weather) afoso(-a); (drinker, smoker) gran (before noun); **it's ~ going** è una gran fatica; **~ industry** industria pesante
heavy cream N (US) doppia panna
heavy-duty ['hɛvɪ'dju:tɪ] ADJ molto resistente
heavy goods vehicle N (BRIT) veicolo per trasporti pesanti
heavy-handed ['hɛvɪ'hændɪd] ADJ (clumsy, tactless) pesante
heavy metal N (Mus) heavy metal m
heavy-set ['hɛvɪ'sɛt] ADJ (esp US) tarchiato(-a)
heavyweight ['hɛvɪweɪt] N (Sport) peso massimo
Hebrew ['hi:bru:] ADJ ebreo(-a) ▶ N (Ling) ebraico
Hebrides ['hɛbrɪdi:z] NPL: **the ~** le Ebridi
heck [hɛk] (col) EXCL: **oh ~!** oh no!

 ▶ N: **a ~ of a lot of** un gran bel po' di
heckle ['hɛkl] VT interpellare e dare noia a (un oratore)
heckler ['hɛklə'] N agitatore(-trice)
hectare ['hɛktɑ:'] N (BRIT) ettaro
hectic ['hɛktɪk] ADJ movimentato(-a); (busy) frenetico(-a)
hector ['hɛktə'] VT usare le maniere forti con
he'd [hi:d] = **he would**; **he had**
hedge [hɛdʒ] N siepe f ▶ VI essere elusivo(-a); **as a ~ against inflation** per cautelarsi contro l'inflazione; **to ~ one's bets** (fig) coprirsi dai rischi
 ▶ **hedge in** VT recintare con una siepe
hedgehog ['hɛdʒhɔg] N riccio
hedgerow ['hɛdʒrəu] N siepe f
hedonism ['hi:dənɪzəm] N edonismo
heed [hi:d] VT (also: **take heed of**) badare a, far conto di ▶ N: **to pay (no) ~ to, to take (no) ~ of** (non) ascoltare, (non) tener conto di
heedless ['hi:dlɪs] ADJ sbadato(-a)
heel [hi:l] N (Anat) calcagno; (of shoe) tacco ▶ VT (shoe) rifare i tacchi a; **to bring to ~** addomesticare; **to take to one's heels** (col) darsela a gambe, alzare i tacchi
hefty ['hɛftɪ] ADJ (person) solido(-a); (parcel) pesante; (piece, price, profit) grosso(-a)
heifer ['hɛfə'] N giovenca
height [haɪt] N altezza; (high ground) altura; (fig: of glory) apice m; (: of stupidity) colmo; **what ~ are you?** quanto sei alto?; **of average ~** di statura media; **to be afraid of heights** soffrire di vertigini; **it's the ~ of fashion** è l'ultimo grido della moda
heighten ['haɪtn] VT innalzare; (fig) accrescere
heinous ['heɪnəs] ADJ nefando(-a), atroce
heir [ɛə'] N erede m
heir apparent N erede mf legittimo(-a)
heiress ['ɛərɛs] N erede f
heirloom ['ɛəlu:m] N mobile m (or gioiello or quadro) di famiglia
heist [haɪst] N (US col) rapina
held [hɛld] PT, PP of **hold**
helicopter ['hɛlɪkɔptə'] N elicottero
heliport ['hɛlɪpɔ:t] N eliporto
helium ['hi:lɪəm] N elio
hell [hɛl] N inferno; **a ~ of a ...** (col) un(-a) maledetto(-a) ...; **oh ~!** (col) porca miseria!, accidenti!
he'll [hi:l] = **he will**; **he shall**
hell-bent [hɛl'bɛnt] ADJ (col): **to be ~ on doing sth** voler fare qc a tutti i costi
hellish ['hɛlɪʃ] ADJ infernale
hello [hə'ləu] EXCL buon giorno!; ciao! (to sb one addresses as "tu"); (surprise) ma guarda!
helm [hɛlm] N (Naut) timone m
helmet ['hɛlmɪt] N casco
helmsman ['hɛlmzmən] N (irreg) timoniere m

help [hɛlp] N aiuto; (*charwoman*) donna di servizio; (*assistant etc*) impiegato(-a) ▶ VT aiutare; **~!** aiuto!; **with the ~ of** con l'aiuto di; **to be of ~ to sb** essere di aiuto *or* essere utile a qn; **to ~ sb (to) do sth** aiutare qn a far qc; **can you ~ me?** può aiutarmi?; **can I ~ you?** (*in shop*) desidera?; **~ yourself (to bread)** si serva (del pane); **I can't ~ saying** non posso evitare di dire; **he can't ~ it** non ci può far niente
▶ **help out** VI aiutare ▶ VT: **to ~ sb out** aiutare qn

help desk N (*esp Comput*) help desk *m inv*
helper ['hɛlpə^r] N aiutante *mf*, assistente *mf*
helpful ['hɛlpful] ADJ di grande aiuto; (*useful*) utile
helping ['hɛlpɪŋ] N porzione *f*
helping hand N: **to give sb a ~** dare una mano a qn
helpless ['hɛlplɪs] ADJ impotente; debole; (*baby*) indifeso(-a)
helplessly ['hɛlplɪslɪ] ADV (*watch*) senza poter fare nulla
helpline ['hɛlplaɪn] N ≈ telefono amico; (*Comm*) servizio *m* informazioni *inv* (*a pagamento*)
Helsinki ['hɛlsɪŋkɪ] N Helsinki *f*
helter-skelter ['hɛltə'skɛltə^r] N (*BRIT: in funfair*) scivolo (a spirale)
hem [hɛm] N orlo ▶ VT fare l'orlo a
▶ **hem in** VT cingere; **to feel hemmed in** (*fig*) sentirsi soffocare
he-man ['hi:mæn] N (*irreg*) (*col*) fusto
hematology [hi:mə'tɔlədʒɪ] N (*US*)
= **haematology**
hemisphere ['hɛmɪsfɪə^r] N emisfero
hemlock ['hɛmlɔk] N cicuta
hemoglobin [hi:məu'gləubɪn] N (*US*)
= **haemoglobin**
hemophilia [hi:məu'fɪlɪə] N (*US*)
= **haemophilia**
hemorrhage ['hɛmərɪdʒ] N (*US*)
= **haemorrhage**
hemorrhoids ['hɛmərɔɪdz] NPL (*US*)
= **haemorrhoids**
hemp [hɛmp] N canapa
hen [hɛn] N gallina; (*female bird*) femmina
hence [hɛns] ADV (*therefore*) dunque; **2 years ~** di qui a 2 anni
henceforth [hɛns'fɔ:θ] ADV d'ora in poi
henchman ['hɛntʃmən] N (*irreg*) (*pej*) caudatario
henna ['hɛnə] N henna
hen night N (*col*) addio al nubilato
hen party N (*col*) festa di sole donne
henpecked ['hɛnpɛkt] ADJ dominato dalla moglie
hepatitis [hɛpə'taɪtɪs] N epatite *f*
her [hə:^r] PRON (*direct*) la, l' + *vowel*; (*indirect*) le;

(*stressed, after prep*) lei ▶ ADJ il (la) suo(-a), i (le) suoi (sue); **I see ~** la vedo; **give ~ a book** le dia un libro; **after ~** dopo (di) lei; *see also* **me**; **my**

herald ['hɛrəld] N araldo ▶ VT annunciare
heraldic [hɛ'rældɪk] ADJ araldico(-a)
heraldry ['hɛrəldrɪ] N araldica
herb [hə:b] N erba; **herbs** NPL (*Culin*) erbette *fpl*
herbaceous [hə:'beɪʃəs] ADJ erbaceo(-a)
herbal ['hə:bəl] ADJ di erbe; **~ tea** tisana
herbicide ['hə:bɪsaɪd] N erbicida *m*
herd [hə:d] N mandria; (*of wild animals, swine*) branco ▶ VT (*drive, gather: animals*) guidare; (: *people*) radunare; **herded together** ammassati (come bestie)
here [hɪə^r] ADV qui, qua ▶ EXCL ehi!; **~!** (*at roll call*) presente!; **~ is, ~ are** ecco; **~'s my sister** ecco mia sorella; **~ he/she is** eccolo/eccola; **~ she comes** eccola che viene; **come ~!** vieni qui!; **~ and there** qua e là
hereabouts ['hɪərəbauts] ADV da queste parti
hereafter [hɪər'ɑ:ftə^r] ADV in futuro; dopo questo ▶ N: **the ~** l'al di là *m*
hereby [hɪə'baɪ] ADV (*in letter*) con la presente
hereditary [hɪ'rɛdɪtrɪ] ADJ ereditario(-a)
heredity [hɪ'rɛdɪtɪ] N eredità
heresy ['hɛrəsɪ] N eresia
heretic ['hɛrətɪk] N eretico(-a)
heretical [hɪ'rɛtɪkl] ADJ eretico(-a)
herewith [hɪə'wɪð] ADV qui accluso
heritage ['hɛrɪtɪdʒ] N eredità; (*of country, nation*) retaggio; **our national ~** il nostro patrimonio nazionale
hermetically [hə:'mɛtɪklɪ] ADV ermeticamente; **~ sealed** ermeticamente chiuso
hermit ['hə:mɪt] N eremita *m*
hernia ['hə:nɪə] N ernia
hero ['hɪərəu] (*pl* **heroes**) N eroe *m*
heroic [hɪ'rəuɪk] ADJ eroico(-a)
heroin ['hɛrəuɪn] N eroina (*droga*)
heroin addict N eroinomane *mf*
heroine ['hɛrəuɪn] N eroina (*donna*)
heroism ['hɛrəuɪzəm] N eroismo
heron ['hɛrən] N airone *m*
hero worship N divismo
herring ['hɛrɪŋ] N aringa
hers [hə:z] PRON il (la) suo(-a), i (le) suoi (sue); **a friend of ~** un suo amico; **this is ~** questo è (il) suo; *see also* **mine**¹
herself [hə:'sɛlf] PRON (*reflexive*) si; (*emphatic*) lei stessa; (*after prep*) se stessa, sé; *see also* **oneself**
Herts ABBR (*BRIT*) = **Hertfordshire**
he's [hi:z] = **he is; he has**
hesitant ['hɛzɪtənt] ADJ esitante, indeciso(-a); **to be ~ about doing sth** esitare a fare qc

597

hesitate ['hɛzɪteɪt] VI: **to ~ (about/to do)** esitare (su/a fare); **don't ~ to ask (me)** non aver timore or paura di chiedermelo

hesitation [hɛzɪ'teɪʃən] N esitazione f; **I have no ~ in saying (that)** ... non esito a dire che ...

hessian ['hɛsɪən] N tela di canapa

heterogeneous [hɛtərəu'dʒiːnɪəs] ADJ eterogeneo(-a)

heterosexual [hɛtərəu'sɛksjuəl] ADJ, N eterosessuale (mf)

het up [hɛt'ʌp] ADJ agitato(-a)

HEW N ABBR (US: = Department of Health, Education, and Welfare) ministero della sanità, della pubblica istruzione e della previdenza sociale

hew [hjuː] VT tagliare (con l'accetta)

hex [hɛks] (US) N stregoneria ▶ VT stregare

hexagon ['hɛksəgən] N esagono

hexagonal [hɛk'sægənl] ADJ esagonale

hey [heɪ] EXCL ehi!

heyday ['heɪdeɪ] N: **the ~ of** i bei giorni di, l'età d'oro di

HF N ABBR (= high frequency) AF

HGV N ABBR = **heavy goods vehicle**

HI ABBR (US) = **Hawaii**

hi [haɪ] EXCL ciao!

hiatus [haɪ'eɪtəs] N vuoto; (Ling) iato

hibernate ['haɪbəneɪt] VI ibernare

hibernation [haɪbə'neɪʃən] N letargo, ibernazione f

hiccough, hiccup ['hɪkʌp] VI singhiozzare ▶ N singhiozzo; **to have (the) hiccoughs** avere il singhiozzo

hick [hɪk] N (US col) buzzurro(-a)

hid [hɪd] PT of **hide**

hidden ['hɪdn] PP of **hide** ▶ ADJ nascosto(-a); **there are no ~ extras** è veramente tutto compreso nel prezzo; **~ agenda** programma m occulto

hide [haɪd] (pt **hid**, pp **hidden**) N (skin) pelle f ▶ VT: **to ~ sth (from sb)** nascondere qc (a qn) ▶ VI: **to ~ (from sb)** nascondersi (da qn)

hide-and-seek ['haɪdən'siːk] N rimpiattino

hideaway ['haɪdəweɪ] N nascondiglio

hideous ['hɪdɪəs] ADJ laido(-a); orribile

hide-out ['haɪdaut] N nascondiglio

hiding ['haɪdɪŋ] N (beating) bastonata; **to be in ~** (concealed) tenersi nascosto(-a)

hiding place N nascondiglio

hierarchy ['haɪərɑːkɪ] N gerarchia

hieroglyphic [haɪərə'glɪfɪk] ADJ geroglifico(-a); **hieroglyphics** NPL geroglifici mpl

hi-fi ['haɪfaɪ] ADJ, N ABBR (= high fidelity) hi-fi (m) inv

higgledy-piggledy ['hɪgldɪ'pɪgldɪ] ADV alla rinfusa

high [haɪ] ADJ alto(-a); (speed, respect, number) grande; (wind) forte; (voice) acuto(-a); (BRIT: Culin: meat, game) frollato(-a); (: spoilt)

andato(-a) a male; (col: on drugs) fatto(-a); (: on drink) su di giri ▶ ADV alto, in alto ▶ N: **exports have reached a new ~** le esportazioni hanno toccato un nuovo record; **20m ~** alto(-a) 20m; **to pay a ~ price for sth** pagare (molto) caro qc

highball ['haɪbɔːl] N (US: drink) whisky (or brandy) e soda con ghiaccio

highboy ['haɪbɔɪ] N (US) cassettone m

highbrow ['haɪbrau] ADJ, N intellettuale (mf)

highchair ['haɪtʃɛəʳ] N seggiolone m

high-class ['haɪ'klɑːs] ADJ (neighbourhood) elegante; (hotel) di prim'ordine; (person) di gran classe; (food) raffinato(-a)

High Court N alta corte f; vedi nota

> Nel sistema legale inglese e gallese, la High Court e la Court of Appeal compongono la Supreme Court of Judicature, e si occupa di casi più importanti e complessi. In Scozia, invece, la High Court è la corte che si occupa dei reati più gravi e corrisponde alla crown court inglese.

higher ['haɪəʳ] ADJ (form of life, study etc) superiore ▶ ADV più in alto, più in su

higher education N istruzione f superiore or universitaria

highfalutin [haɪfə'luːtɪn] ADJ (col) pretenzioso(-a)

high finance N alta finanza

high-flier, high-flyer [haɪ'flaɪəʳ] N (giovane) promessa (fig)

high-flying [haɪ'flaɪɪŋ] ADJ (fig) promettente

high-handed [haɪ'hændɪd] ADJ prepotente

high-heeled [haɪ'hiːld] ADJ a tacchi alti

high heels NPL (heels) tacchi mpl alti; (shoes) scarpe fpl con i tacchi alti

highjack ['haɪdʒæk] VT, N = **hijack**

high jump N (Sport) salto in alto

highlands ['haɪləndz] NPL zona montuosa; **the H~** le Highlands scozzesi

high-level ['haɪlɛvl] ADJ (talks etc, Comput) ad alto livello

highlight ['haɪlaɪt] N (fig: of event) momento culminante; (in hair) colpo di sole ▶ VT mettere in evidenza; **highlights** NPL (in hair) colpi mpl di sole

highlighter ['haɪlaɪtəʳ] N (pen) evidenziatore m

highly ['haɪlɪ] ADV molto; **~ paid** pagato molto bene; **to speak ~ of** parlare molto bene di

highly-strung ['haɪlɪ'strʌn] ADJ teso(-a) di nervi, eccitabile

High Mass N messa cantata or solenne

highness ['haɪnɪs] N altezza; **Her H~** Sua Altezza

high-pitched [haɪ'pɪtʃt] ADJ acuto(-a)

high point N: **the ~** il momento più importante

high-powered ['haɪ'pauəd] ADJ (engine) molto potente, ad alta potenza; (fig: person) di prestigio

high-pressure ['haɪprɛʃər] ADJ ad alta pressione; (fig) aggressivo(-a)

high-rise N (also: **high-rise block**, **high-rise building**) palazzone m

high-rise block ['haɪraɪz-] N palazzone m

high school N (BRIT) scuola secondaria; (US) istituto d'istruzione secondaria; vedi nota

> Negli Stati Uniti la high school è un istituto di istruzione secondaria. Si suddivide in junior high school (dal settimo al nono anno di corso) e senior high school (dal decimo al dodicesimo), dove vengono impartiti sia insegnamenti scolastici che di formazione professionale. In Gran Bretagna molte scuole secondarie si chiamano high school.

high season N (BRIT) alta stagione

high spirits NPL buonumore m, euforia; **to be in ~** essere euforico(-a)

high street N (BRIT) strada principale

high-tech ADJ (col) high-tech inv

highway ['haɪweɪ] N strada maestra; **the information ~** l'autostrada telematica

Highway Code N (BRIT) codice m della strada

highwayman ['haɪweɪmən] N (irreg) bandito

hijack ['haɪdʒæk] VT dirottare ▶ N dirottamento; (also: **hijacking**) pirateria aerea

hijacker ['haɪdʒækər] N dirottatore(-trice)

hike [haɪk] VI fare un'escursione a piedi ▶ N escursione f a piedi; (col: in prices etc) aumento ▶ VT (col) aumentare

hiker ['haɪkər] N escursionista mf

hiking ['haɪkɪŋ] N escursioni fpl a piedi

hilarious [hɪ'lɛərɪəs] ADJ che fa schiantare dal ridere; (behaviour, event) spassosissimo(-a)

hilarity [hɪ'lærɪtɪ] N ilarità

hill [hɪl] N collina, colle m; (fairly high) montagna; (on road) salita

hillbilly ['hɪlbɪlɪ] N (US) montanaro(-a) dal sud degli Stati Uniti; (pej) zotico(-a)

hillock ['hɪlək] N collinetta, poggio

hillside ['hɪlsaɪd] N fianco della collina

hill start N (Aut) partenza in salita

hill walking N escursioni fpl in collina

hilly ['hɪlɪ] ADJ collinoso(-a)

hilt [hɪlt] N (of sword) elsa; **to the ~** (fig: support) fino in fondo

him [hɪm] PRON (direct) lo, l' + vowel; (indirect) gli; (stressed, after prep) lui; **I see ~** lo vedo; **give ~ a book** gli dia un libro; **after ~** dopo (di) lui

Himalayas [hɪmə'leɪəz] NPL: **the ~** l'Himalaia m

himself [hɪm'sɛlf] PRON (reflexive) si; (emphatic) lui stesso; (after prep) se stesso, sé; see also **oneself**

hind [haɪnd] ADJ posteriore ▶ N cerva

hinder ['haɪndər] VT ostacolare; (delay) tardare; (prevent): **to ~ sb from doing** impedire a qn di fare

hindquarters ['haɪndkwɔːtəz] NPL (Zool) posteriore m

hindrance ['hɪndrəns] N ostacolo, impedimento

hindsight ['haɪndsaɪt] N senno di poi; **with (the benefit of) ~** con il senno di poi

Hindu ['hɪnduː] N indù mf

Hinduism N (Rel) induismo

hinge [hɪndʒ] N cardine m ▶ VI (fig): **to ~ on** dipendere da

hint [hɪnt] N (suggestion) allusione f; (advice) consiglio; (sign) accenno ▶ VT: **to ~ that** lasciar capire che ▶ VI: **to ~ at** accennare a, alludere a; **to drop a ~** lasciar capire; **give me a ~** (clue) dammi almeno un'idea, dammi un'indicazione

hip [hɪp] N anca, fianco; (Bot) frutto della rosa canina

hip flask N fiaschetta da liquore tascabile

hip hop N hip-hop m

hippie ['hɪpɪ] N hippy mf

hippo ['hɪpəu] (pl **hippos**) N ippopotamo

hip pocket N tasca posteriore dei calzoni

hippopotamus [hɪpə'pɔtəməs] (pl **hippopotamuses** or **hippopotami** [-'pɔtəmaɪ]) N ippopotamo

hippy ['hɪpɪ] N = **hippie**

hire ['haɪər] VT (BRIT: car, equipment) noleggiare; (worker) assumere, dare lavoro a ▶ N nolo, noleggio; **for ~** da nolo; (taxi) libero(-a); **on ~** a nolo

▶ **hire out** VT noleggiare, dare a nolo or noleggio, affittare

hire car, **hired car** N (BRIT) macchina a nolo

hire purchase N (BRIT) acquisto (or vendita) rateale; **to buy sth on ~** comprare qc a rate

his [hɪz] ADJ, PRON il (la) suo (sua), i (le) suoi (sue); **this is ~** questo è (il) suo; see also **my**; **mine**[1]

Hispanic [hɪs'pænɪk] ADJ ispanico(-a)

hiss [hɪs] VI fischiare; (cat, snake) sibilare ▶ N fischio, sibilo

histogram ['hɪstəgræm] N istogramma m

historian [hɪ'stɔːrɪən] N storico(-a)

historic [hɪ'stɔrɪk], **historical** [hɪ'stɔrɪkl] ADJ storico(-a)

history ['hɪstərɪ] N storia; **there's a long ~ of that illness in his family** ci sono molti precedenti (della malattia) nella sua famiglia

histrionics [hɪstrɪ'ɔnɪks] N istrionismo

hit [hɪt] (pt, pp **~**) VT colpire, picchiare; (knock against) battere; (reach: target) raggiungere; (collide with: car) urtare contro; (fig: affect) colpire; (find: problem) incontrare ▶ N colpo;

h

599

(*success, song*) successo; **to ~ the headlines** far titolo; **to ~ the road** (*col*) mettersi in cammino; **to ~ it off with sb** andare molto d'accordo con qn; **to get a ~/10,000 hits** (*Comput*) trovare una pagina Web/10.000 pagine Web; **our web page had 10,000 hits last month** lo scorso mese il nostro sito ha avuto 10.000 visitatori

▶ **hit back** VI: **to ~ back at sb** restituire il colpo a qn

▶ **hit out at** VT FUS sferrare dei colpi contro; (*fig*) attaccare

▶ **hit (up)on** VT FUS (*answer*) imbroccare, azzeccare; (*solution*) trovare (per caso)

hit-and-run driver ['hɪtænd'rʌn-] N pirata *m* della strada

hitch [hɪtʃ] VT (*fasten*) attaccare; (*also*: **hitch up**) tirare su ▶ N (*difficulty*) intoppo, difficoltà *f inv*; **technical ~** difficoltà tecnica; **to ~ a lift** fare l'autostop

▶ **hitch up** VT (*horse, cart*) attaccare

hitch-hike ['hɪtʃhaɪk] VI fare l'autostop

hitch-hiker ['hɪtʃhaɪkə'] N autostoppista *mf*

hitch-hiking N autostop *m*

hi-tech ['haɪ'tek] ADJ high-tech *inv*, a tecnologia avanzata

hitherto ['hɪðə'tu:] ADV finora

hit list N libro nero

hitman ['hɪtmæn] N (*irreg*) (*col*) sicario

hit-or-miss ['hɪtə'mɪs] ADJ casuale; **it's ~ whether ...** è in dubbio se ...; **the service in this hotel is very ~** il servizio dell'albergo lascia a desiderare

hit parade N hit-parade *f*

HIV N ABBR (= *human immunodeficiency virus*) virus *m inv* di immunodeficienza; **~-negative/-positive** adj sieronegativo(-a)/sieropositivo(-a)

hive [haɪv] N alveare *m*; **the shop was a ~ of activity** (*fig*) c'era una grande attività nel negozio

▶ **hive off** VT (*col*) separare

hl ABBR (= *hectolitre*) hl

HM ABBR (= *His (or Her) Majesty*) S.M. (= *Sua Maestà*)

HMG ABBR (*BRIT*) = **Her Majesty's Government; His Majesty's Government**

HMI N ABBR (*BRIT Scol*: = *His (or Her) Majesty's Inspector*) ≈ ispettore *m* scolastico

HMO N ABBR (*US*: = *Health Maintenance Organization*) organo per la salvaguardia della salute pubblica

HMS ABBR (*BRIT*) = **His Majesty's Ship; Her Majesty's Ship**

HNC N ABBR (*BRIT*: = *Higher National Certificate*) diploma di istituto tecnico o professionale

HND N ABBR (*BRIT*: = *Higher National Diploma*) diploma in materie tecniche equivalente ad una laurea

hoard [hɔ:d] N (*of food*) provviste *fpl*; (*of money*) gruzzolo ▶ VT ammassare

hoarding ['hɔ:dɪŋ] N (*BRIT*) tabellone *m* per affissioni

hoarfrost ['hɔ:frɔst] N brina

hoarse [hɔ:s] ADJ rauco(-a)

hoax [həʊks] N scherzo; falso allarme

hob [hɔb] N piastra (con fornelli)

hobble ['hɔbl] VI zoppicare

hobby ['hɔbɪ] N hobby *m inv*, passatempo

hobby-horse ['hɔbɪhɔ:s] N cavallo a dondolo; (*fig*) chiodo fisso

hobnail boots ['hɔbneɪl-], **hobnailed boots** ['hɔbneɪld-] N scarponi *mpl* chiodati

hobnob ['hɔbnɔb] VI: **to ~ (with)** mescolarsi (con)

hobo ['həʊbəʊ] N (*US*) vagabondo

hock [hɔk] N (*BRIT*: *wine*) vino del Reno; (*of animal, Culin*) garretto; (*col*): **to be in ~** avere debiti

hockey ['hɔkɪ] N hockey *m*

hockey stick N bastone *m* da hockey

hocus-pocus ['həʊkəs'pəʊkəs] N (*trickery*) trucco; (*words: of magician*) abracadabra *m inv*; (: *jargon*) parolone *fpl*

hod [hɔd] N (*Tech*) cassetta per portare i mattoni

hodgepodge ['hɔdʒpɔdʒ] N = **hotchpotch**

hoe [həʊ] N zappa ▶ VT (*ground*) zappare

hog [hɔg] N maiale *m* ▶ VT (*fig*) arraffare; **to go the whole ~** farlo fino in fondo

Hogmanay [hɔgmə'neɪ] N (*SCOTTISH*) ≈ San Silvestro

hogwash ['hɔgwɔʃ] N (*col*) stupidaggini *fpl*

hoist [hɔɪst] N paranco ▶ VT issare

hoity-toity [hɔɪtɪ'tɔɪtɪ] ADJ (*col*) altezzoso(-a)

hold [həʊld] (*pt, pp* **held**) VT tenere; (*contain*) contenere; (*keep back*) trattenere; (*believe*) mantenere; considerare; (*possess*) avere, possedere; detenere ▶ VI (*withstand pressure*) tenere; (*be valid*) essere valido(-a) ▶ N presa; (*fig*) potere *m*; (*control*): **to have a ~ over** avere controllo su; (*Naut*) stiva; **~ the line!** (*Tel*) resti in linea!; **to ~ office** (*Pol*) essere in carica; **to ~ sb responsible for sth** considerare *or* ritenere qn responsabile di qc; **to ~ one's own** (*fig*) difendersi bene; **he holds the view that ...** è del parere che ...; **to ~ firm** *or* **fast** resistere bene, tenere; **to catch** *or* **get (a) ~ of** afferrare; **to get ~ of** (*fig*) trovare; **to get ~ of o.s.** trattenersi

▶ **hold back** VT trattenere; (*secret*) tenere celato(-a); **to ~ sb back from doing sth** impedire a qn di fare qc

▶ **hold down** VT (*person*) tenere a terra; (*job*) tenere

▶ **hold forth** VI fare *or* tenere una concione

▶ **hold off** VT tener lontano ▶ VI (*rain*): **if the rain holds off** se continua a non piovere

▶ **hold on** VI tener fermo; (*wait*) aspettare;
~ **on!** (*Tel*) resti in linea!
▶ **hold on to** VT FUS tenersi stretto(-a) a;
(*keep*) conservare
▶ **hold out** VT offrire ▶ VI (*resist*): **to ~ out
(against)** resistere (a)
▶ **hold over** VT (*meeting etc*) rimandare,
rinviare
▶ **hold up** VT (*raise*) alzare; (*support*) sostenere;
(*delay*) ritardare; (*traffic*) rallentare; (*rob: bank*)
assaltare

holdall ['həuldɔːl] N (*BRIT*) borsone *m*
holder ['həuldəʳ] N (*container*) contenitore *m*;
(*of ticket, title*) possessore (posseditrice); (*of
office etc*) incaricato(-a); (*of passport, post*)
titolare; (*of record*) detentore(-trice)
holding ['həuldɪŋ] N (*share*) azioni *fpl*, titoli
mpl; (*farm*) podere *m*, tenuta
holding company N holding *f inv*
holdup ['həuldʌp] N (*robbery*) rapina a mano
armata; (*delay*) ritardo; (*BRIT: in traffic*) blocco
hole [həul] N buco, buca ▶ VT bucare; ~ **in
the heart** (*Med*) morbo blu; **to pick holes in**
(*fig*) trovare da ridire su
▶ **hole up** VI nascondersi, rifugiarsi
holiday ['hɔlədɪ] N vacanza; (*from work*) ferie
fpl; (*day off*) giorno di vacanza; (*public*) giorno
festivo; **to be on ~** essere in vacanza;
tomorrow is a ~ domani è festa
holiday camp N (*BRIT: for children*) colonia (di
villeggiatura); (*also:* **holiday centre**)
≈ villaggio (di vacanze)
holiday home N seconda casa (*per le vacanze*)
holiday job N (*BRIT*) ≈ lavoro estivo
holiday-maker ['hɔlədɪmeɪkəʳ] N (*BRIT*)
villeggiante *mf*
holiday pay N stipendio delle ferie
holiday resort N luogo di villeggiatura
holiday season N stagione *f* delle vacanze
holiness ['həulɪnɪs] N santità
holistic [həu'lɪstɪk] ADJ olistico(-a)
Holland ['hɔlənd] N Olanda
holler ['hɔləʳ] VI gridare, urlare
hollow ['hɔləu] ADJ cavo(-a); (*container, claim*)
vuoto(-a); (*laugh*) forzato(-a), falso(-a);
(*sound*) cavernoso(-a) ▶ N cavità *f inv*; (*in land*)
valletta, depressione *f*
▶ **hollow out** VT scavare
holly ['hɔlɪ] N agrifoglio
hollyhock ['hɔlɪhɔk] N malvone *m*
Hollywood ['hɔlɪwud] N Hollywood *f*
holocaust ['hɔləkɔːst] N olocausto
hologram ['hɔləgræm] N ologramma *m*
hols [hɔlz] NPL: **the ~** le vacanze
holster ['həulstəʳ] N fondina (di pistola)
holy ['həulɪ] ADJ santo(-a); (*bread*)
benedetto(-a), consacrato(-a); (*ground*)
consacrato(-a); **the H~ Father** il Santo Padre
Holy Communion N la Santa Comunione

Holy Ghost, Holy Spirit N Spirito Santo
Holy Land N: **the ~** la Terra Santa
holy orders NPL ordini *mpl* (sacri)
homage ['hɔmɪdʒ] N omaggio; **to pay ~ to**
rendere omaggio a
home [həum] N casa; (*country*) patria;
(*institution*) casa, ricovero ▶ CPD (*life*)
familiare; (*cooking etc*) casalingo(-a); (*Econ,
Pol*) nazionale, interno(-a); (*Sport: team*) di
casa; (*: match, win*) in casa ▶ ADV a casa; in
patria; (*right in: nail etc*) fino in fondo; **at ~** a
casa; (*in situation*) a proprio agio; **to go** (*or
come*) ~ tornare a casa (*or* in patria); **it's
near my ~** è vicino a casa mia; **make
yourself at ~** si metta a suo agio
▶ **home in on** VT FUS (*missiles*) dirigersi
(automaticamente) verso
home address N indirizzo di casa
home-brew [həum'bruː] N birra *or* vino
fatto(-a) in casa
homecoming ['həumkʌmɪŋ] N ritorno
home computer N home computer *m inv*
Home Counties NPL contee *fpl* intorno a
Londra
home economics N economia domestica
home ground N (*fig*): **to be on ~** essere sul
proprio terreno
home-grown [həum'grəun] ADJ
nostrano(-a), di produzione locale
home help N (*BRIT*) collaboratore familiare per
persone bisognose stipendiato dal comune
homeland ['həumlænd] N patria
homeless ['həumlɪs] ADJ senza tetto;
spatriato(-a); **the homeless** NPL i senzatetto
home loan N prestito con garanzia
immobiliare
homely ['həumlɪ] ADJ semplice, alla buona;
accogliente
home-made [həum'meɪd] ADJ casalingo(-a)
home match N partita in casa
Home Office N (*BRIT*) ministero degli Interni
homeopathy *etc* [həumɪ'ɔpəθɪ] (*US*)
= **homoeopathy** *etc*
home owner N proprietario(-a) di casa
home page N (*Comput*) home page *f inv*
home rule N autogoverno
Home Secretary N (*BRIT*) ministro degli
Interni
homesick ['həumsɪk] ADJ: **to be ~** avere la
nostalgia
homestead ['həumstɛd] N fattoria e terreni
home town N città *f inv* natale
home truth N: **to tell sb a few home truths**
dire a qn qualche amara verità
homeward ['həumwəd] ADJ (*journey*) di
ritorno ▶ ADV verso casa
homewards ['həumwədz] ADV verso casa
homework ['həumwəːk] N compiti *mpl*
(per casa)

homicidal [hɔmɪ'saɪdl] ADJ omicida

homicide ['hɔmɪsaɪd] N (US) omicidio

homily ['hɔmɪlɪ] N omelia

homing ['həumɪŋ] ADJ (device, missile) autocercante; ~ **pigeon** piccione m viaggiatore

homoeopath, (US) **homeopath** ['həumɪəupæθ] N omeopatico

homoeopathic, (US) **homeopathic** ['həumɪəu'pæθɪk] ADJ omeopatico(-a)

homoeopathy, (US) **homeopathy** [həumɪ'ɔpəθɪ] N omeopatia

homogeneous [hɔməu'dʒiːnɪəs] ADJ omogeneo(-a)

homogenize [hə'mɔdʒənaɪz] VT omogenizzare

homosexual [hɔməu'sɛksjuəl] ADJ, N omosessuale (mf)

Hon. ABBR = **honourable; honorary**

Honduras [hɔn'djuərəs] N Honduras m

hone [həun] VT (sharpen) affilare; (fig) affinare

honest ['ɔnɪst] ADJ onesto(-a); sincero(-a); **to be quite ~ with you** ... se devo dirle la verità ...

honestly ['ɔnɪstlɪ] ADV onestamente; sinceramente

honesty ['ɔnɪstɪ] N onestà

honey ['hʌnɪ] N miele m; (US col) tesoro, amore m

honeycomb ['hʌnɪkəum] N favo ▶ VT (fig): **honeycombed with tunnels** etc pieno(-a) di gallerie etc

honeymoon ['hʌnɪmuːn] N luna di miele, viaggio di nozze

honeysuckle ['hʌnɪsʌkl] N (Bot) caprifoglio

Hong Kong ['hɔŋ'kɔŋ] N Hong Kong f

honk [hɔŋk] N (Aut) colpo di clacson ▶ VI suonare il clacson

Honolulu [hɔnə'luːluː] N Honolulu f

honorary ['ɔnərərɪ] ADJ onorario(-a); (duty, title) onorifico(-a)

honour, (US) **honor** ['ɔnər] VT onorare ▶ N onore m; **in ~ of** in onore di

honourable, (US) **honorable** ['ɔnərəbl] ADJ onorevole

honour-bound, (US) **honor-bound** ['ɔnə'baund] ADJ: **to be hono(u)r-bound to do** dover fare per una questione di onore

honours degree N (Scol) laurea (con corso di studi di 4 o 5 anni); vedi nota

> In Gran Bretagna esistono titoli universitari di diverso livello. Gli studenti che conseguono ottimi risultati e che approfondiscono una o più materie possono ottenere l' honours degree. Questo titolo, abbreviato in Hons., viene posto dopo il titolo ottenuto (ad esempio BA Hons); vedi anche **ordinary degree**.

honours list N (BRIT) elenco ufficiale dei destinati al conferimento di onorificenze; vedi nota

> La honours list è un elenco di cittadini britannici e del Commonwealth che si sono distinti in campo imprenditoriale, militare, sportivo ecc, meritando il conferimento di un titolo o di una decorazione da parte del sovrano. Ogni anno vengono redatte dal primo ministro due honours lists, una a Capodanno e una in occasione del compleanno del sovrano.

Hons. [ɔnz] ABBR (Scol) = **hono(u)rs degree**

hood [hud] N cappuccio; (on cooker) cappa; (BRIT Aut) capote f; (US Aut) cofano; (col) malvivente mf

hooded ['hudɪd] ADJ (robber) mascherato(-a)

hoodie ['hudɪ] N felpa con cappuccio

hoodlum ['huːdləm] N malvivente mf

hoodwink ['hudwɪŋk] VT infinocchiare

hoof [huːf] (pl **hoofs** or **hooves** [huːvz]) N zoccolo

hook [huk] N gancio; (for fishing) amo ▶ VT uncinare; (dress) agganciare; **to be hooked on** (col) essere fanatico di; **hooks and eyes** gancetti; **by ~ or by crook** in un modo o nell'altro

▶ **hook up** VT (Radio, TV etc) allacciare, collegare

hooligan ['huːlɪgən] N giovinastro, teppista m

hooliganism ['huːlɪgənɪzəm] N teppismo

hoop [huːp] N cerchio

hooray [huː'reɪ] EXCL = **hurrah**

hoot [huːt] VI (Aut) suonare il clacson; (siren) ululare; (owl) gufare ▶ N colpo di clacson; **to ~ with laughter** farsi una gran risata

hooter ['huːtər] N (Aut) clacson m inv; (Naut, at factory) sirena

hoover® ['huːvər] N (BRIT) aspirapolvere m inv ▶ VT pulire con l'aspirapolvere

hooves [huːvz] NPL of **hoof**

hop [hɔp] VI saltellare, saltare; (on one foot) saltare su una gamba ▶ N salto; **hops** npl luppoli mpl

hope [həup] VT: **to ~ that/to do** sperare che/di fare ▶ VI sperare ▶ N speranza; **I ~ so/not** spero di sì/no

hopeful ['həupful] ADJ (person) pieno(-a) di speranza; (situation) promettente; **I'm ~ that she'll manage to come** ho buone speranze che venga

hopefully ['həupfulɪ] ADV con speranza; ~ **he will recover** speriamo che si riprenda

hopeless ['həuplɪs] ADJ senza speranza, disperato(-a); (useless) inutile

hopelessly ['həuplɪslɪ] ADV (live etc) senza speranza; (involved, complicated) spaventosamente; (late) disperatamente, irrimediabilmente; **I'm ~ confused/lost**

sono completamente confuso/perso
hopper ['hɔpə'] N (*chute*) tramoggia
hops [hɔps] NPL luppoli *mpl*
horde [hɔːd] N orda
horizon [hə'raɪzn] N orizzonte *m*
horizontal [hɔrɪ'zɔntl] ADJ orizzontale
hormone ['hɔːməun] N ormone *m*
hormone replacement therapy N terapia
ormonale (*usata in menopausa*)
horn [hɔːn] N (*Zool, Mus*) corno; (*Aut*) clacson
m inv
horned [hɔːnd] ADJ (*animal*) cornuto(-a)
hornet ['hɔːnɪt] N calabrone *m*
horny ['hɔːnɪ] ADJ corneo(-a); (*hands*)
calloso(-a)
horoscope ['hɔrəskəup] N oroscopo
horrendous [hɔ'rɛndəs] ADJ orrendo(-a)
horrible ['hɔrɪbl] ADJ orribile, tremendo(-a)
horrid ['hɔrɪd] ADJ orrido(-a); (*person*)
odioso(-a)
horrific [hɔ'rɪfɪk] ADJ (*accident*)
spaventoso(-a); (*film*) orripilante
horrify ['hɔrɪfaɪ] VT lasciare inorridito(-a)
horrifying ['hɔrɪfaɪɪŋ] ADJ terrificante
horror ['hɔrə'] N orrore *m*
horror film N film *m inv* dell'orrore
horror-struck ['hɔrəstrʌk], **horror-stricken**
['hɔrəstrɪkn] ADJ inorridito(-a)
hors d'œuvre [ɔː'dəːvrə] N antipasto
horse [hɔːs] N cavallo
horseback ['hɔːsbæk]: **on ~** *adj, adv* a cavallo
horsebox ['hɔːsbɔks] N carro *or* furgone *m* per
il trasporto dei cavalli
horse chestnut N ippocastano
horse-drawn ['hɔːsdrɔːn] ADJ tirato(-a) da
cavallo
horsefly ['hɔːsflaɪ] N tafano, mosca cavallina
horseman ['hɔːsmən] N (*irreg*) cavaliere *m*
horsemanship ['hɔːsmənʃɪp] N equitazione *f*
horseplay ['hɔːspleɪ] N giochi *mpl* scatenati
horsepower ['hɔːspauə'] N cavallo (vapore),
c/v
horse-racing ['hɔːsreɪsɪŋ] N ippica
horseradish ['hɔːsrædɪʃ] N rafano
horse riding N (*BRIT*) equitazione *f*
horseshoe ['hɔːsʃuː] N ferro di cavallo
horse show N concorso ippico, gare *fpl*
ippiche
horse-trading ['hɔːstreɪdɪŋ] N
mercanteggiamento
horse trials NPL = **horse show**
horsewhip ['hɔːswɪp] VT frustare
horsewoman ['hɔːswumən] N (*irreg*)
amazzone *f*
horsey ['hɔːsɪ] ADJ (*col: person*) che adora i
cavalli; (*appearance*) cavallino(-a), da cavallo
horticulture ['hɔːtɪkʌltʃə'] N orticoltura
hose [həuz] N (*also:* **hosepipe**) tubo; (*also:*
garden hose) tubo per annaffiare

▶ **hose down** VT lavare con un getto d'acqua
hosepipe ['həuzpaɪp] N *see* **hose**
hosiery ['həuzɪərɪ] N (*in shop*) (reparto di)
calze *fpl* e calzini *mpl*
hospice ['hɔspɪs] N ricovero, ospizio
hospitable [hɔ'spɪtəbl] ADJ ospitale
hospital ['hɔspɪtl] N ospedale *m*; **in ~**, (*US*) **in
the ~** all'ospedale
hospitality [hɔspɪ'tælɪtɪ] N ospitalità
hospitalize ['hɔspɪtəlaɪz] VT ricoverare (in *or*
all'ospedale)
host [həust] N ospite *m*; (*TV, Radio*)
presentatore(-trice); (*Rel*) ostia; (*large
number*): **a ~ of** una schiera di ▶ VT (*TV
programme, games*) presentare
hostage ['hɔstɪdʒ] N ostaggio(-a)
host country N paese *m* ospite, paese che
ospita
hostel ['hɔstl] N ostello; (*for students, nurses etc*)
pensionato; (*for homeless people*) ospizio,
ricovero; (*also:* **youth hostel**) ostello della
gioventù
hostelling ['hɔstəlɪŋ] N: **to go (youth) ~**
passare le vacanze negli ostelli della
gioventù
hostess ['həustɪs] N ospite *f*; (*BRIT Aviat*)
hostess *f inv*; (*in nightclub*) entraineuse *f inv*
hostile ['hɔstaɪl] ADJ ostile
hostility [hɔ'stɪlɪtɪ] N ostilità *f inv*
hot [hɔt] ADJ caldo(-a); (*as opposed to only warm*)
molto caldo(-a); (*spicy*) piccante; (*fig*)
accanito(-a); ardente; violento(-a),
focoso(-a); **to be ~** (*person*) aver caldo; (*thing*)
essere caldo(-a); (*Meteor*) far caldo
▶ **hot up** (*BRIT col*) VI (*situation*) farsi più
teso(-a); (*party*) scaldarsi ▶ VT (*pace*)
affrettare; (*engine*) truccare
hot-air balloon [hɔt'ɛə-] N mongolfiera
hotbed ['hɔtbɛd] N (*fig*) focolaio
hotchpotch ['hɔtʃpɔtʃ] N (*BRIT*) pot-pourri *m*
hot dog N hot dog *m inv*
hotel [həu'tɛl] N albergo
hotelier [həu'tɛljeɪ] N albergatore(-trice)
hotel industry N industria alberghiera
hotel room N camera d'albergo
hot flush N (*BRIT*) scalmana, caldana
hotfoot ['hɔtfut] ADV di gran carriera
hothead ['hɔthɛd] N (*fig*) testa calda
hotheaded [hɔt'hɛdɪd] ADJ focoso(-a),
eccitabile
hothouse ['hɔthaus] N serra
hot line N (*Pol*) telefono rosso
hotly ['hɔtlɪ] ADV violentemente
hotplate ['hɔtpleɪt] N fornello; piastra
riscaldante
hotpot ['hɔtpɔt] N (*BRIT Culin*) stufato
hot potato N (*BRIT col*) patata bollente; **to
drop sb/sth like a ~** mollare subito qn/qc
hot seat N (*fig*) posto che scotta

h

hotspot ['hɔtspɔt] N (*Comput: also:* **wireless hotspot**) hotspot *m inv* Wi-Fi

hot spot N (*fig*) zona calda

hot spring N sorgente *f* termale

hot-tempered [hɔt'tɛmpəd] ADJ irascibile

hot-water bottle [hɔt'wɔ:tə-] N borsa dell'acqua calda

hot-wire ['hɔtwaɪəʳ] VT (*col: car*) avviare mettendo in contatto i fili dell'accensione

hound [haund] VT perseguitare ▶ N segugio; **the hounds** la muta

hour ['auəʳ] N ora; **at 30 miles an ~** a 30 miglia all'ora; **lunch ~** intervallo di pranzo; **to pay sb by the ~** pagare qn a ore

hourly ['auəlɪ] ADJ (*ad*) ogni ora; (*rate*) orario(-a) ▶ ADV ogni ora; **~ paid** *adj* pagato(-a) a ore

house (*pl* **houses** ['hauzɪz]) N [haus] casa; (*Pol*) camera; (*Theat*) sala; pubblico; spettacolo ▶ VT [hauz] (*person*) ospitare, alloggiare; **at** (*or* **to**) **my ~** a casa mia; **the H~ (of Commons/Lords)** (*BRIT*) la Camera dei Comuni/Lords; **the H~ (of Representatives)** (*US*) ≈ la Camera dei Deputati; **on the ~** (*fig*) offerto(-a) dalla casa

house arrest N arresti *mpl* domiciliari

houseboat ['hausbəut] N house boat *f inv*

housebound ['hausbaund] ADJ confinato(-a) in casa

housebreaking ['hausbreɪkɪŋ] N furto con scasso

house-broken ['hausbrəukn] ADJ (*US*) = **house-trained**

housecoat ['hauskəut] N vestaglia

household ['haushəuld] N famiglia; casa

householder ['haushəuldəʳ] N padrone(-a) di casa; (*head of house*) capofamiglia *mf*

household name N nome *m* che tutti conoscono

househunting ['haushʌntɪŋ] N: **to go ~** mettersi a cercar casa

housekeeper ['hauski:pəʳ] N governante *f*

housekeeping ['hauski:pɪŋ] N (*work*) governo della casa; (*also:* **housekeeping money**) soldi *mpl* per le spese di casa; (*: Comput*) ausilio

houseman ['hausmən] N (*irreg*) (*BRIT Med*) ≈ interno

house-owner ['hausəunəʳ] N possessore *mf* di casa

house plant N pianta da appartamento

house-proud ['hauspraud] ADJ che è maniaco(-a) della pulizia

house-to-house ['haustə'haus] ADJ (*collection*) di porta in porta; (*search*) casa per casa

house-train ['haustreɪn] VT (*BRIT: pet animal*) addestrare a non sporcare in casa

house-trained ['haustreɪnd] ADJ (*BRIT: animal*) che non sporca in casa

house-warming party ['hauswɔ:mɪŋ-] N festa per inaugurare la casa nuova

housewife ['hauswaɪf] N (*irreg*) massaia, casalinga

house wine N vino della casa

housework ['hauswə:k] N faccende *fpl* domestiche

housing ['hauzɪŋ] N alloggio ▶ CPD (*problem, shortage*) degli alloggi

housing association N cooperativa edilizia

housing benefit N (*BRIT*) contributo abitativo (*ad affittuari e a coloro che comprano una casa*)

housing conditions NPL condizioni *fpl* di abitazione

housing development, (*BRIT*) **housing estate** N zona residenziale con case popolari e/o private

hovel ['hɔvl] N casupola

hover ['hɔvəʳ] VI (*bird*) librarsi; (*helicopter*) volare a punto fisso; **to ~ round sb** aggirarsi intorno a qn

hovercraft ['hɔvəkrɑ:ft] N hovercraft *m inv*

hoverport ['hɔvəpɔ:t] N porto per hovercraft

how [hau] ADV come; **~ are you?** come sta?; **~ do you do?** piacere!, molto lieto!; **~ far is it to ...?** quanto è lontano ...?; **~ long have you been here?** da quanto tempo è qui?; **~ lovely!** che bello!; **~ many?** quanti(-e)?; **~ much?** quanto(-a)?; **~ many people/much milk?** quante persone/quanto latte?; **~ old are you?** quanti anni ha?; **~'s life?** (*col*) come va (la vita)?; **~ about a drink?** che ne diresti di andare a bere qualcosa?; **~ is it that ...?** com'è che ...? + *sub*

however [hau'ɛvəʳ] ADV in qualsiasi modo *or* maniera che; (*+ adjective*) per quanto + *sub*; (*in questions*) come ▶ CONJ comunque, però

howitzer ['hauɪtsəʳ] N (*Mil*) obice *m*

howl [haul] N ululato ▶ VI ululare; (*baby, person*) urlare

howler ['hauləʳ] N marronata

howling ['haulɪŋ] ADJ: **a ~ wind** *or* **gale** un vento terribile

HP N ABBR (*BRIT*) = **hire purchase**

hp ABBR (*Aut*) = **horsepower**

HQ N ABBR (= *headquarters*) Q.G.

HR N ABBR (*US*) = **House of Representatives**; (*human resources: department*) ufficio personale; (*: staff*) isorse umane

hr ABBR (= *hour*) h

HRH ABBR (= *His (or Her) Royal Highness*) S.A.R.

hrs ABBR (= *hours*) h

HRT N ABBR = **hormone replacement therapy**

HS ABBR (*US*) = **high school** .

HST ABBR (= *Hawaiian Standard Time*) fuso orario

HT ABBR (= *high tension*) A.T.

HTML N ABBR (*Comput:* = *hypertext markup language*) HTML *m inv*

hub [hʌb] N (of wheel) mozzo; (fig) fulcro

hubbub ['hʌbʌb] N baccano

hubcap ['hʌbkæp] N (Aut) coprimozzo

HUD N ABBR (US) = **Department of Housing and Urban Development**

huddle ['hʌdl] VI: **to ~ together** rannicchiarsi l'uno contro l'altro

hue [hju:] N tinta; **~ and cry** n clamore m

huff [hʌf] N: **in a ~** stizzito(-a); **to take the ~** mettere il broncio

huffy ['hʌfɪ] ADJ (col) stizzito(-a), indispettito(-a)

hug [hʌg] VT abbracciare; (shore, kerb) stringere ▶ N abbraccio, stretta; **to give sb a ~** abbracciare qn

huge [hju:dʒ] ADJ enorme, immenso(-a)

hulk [hʌlk] N carcassa

hulking ['hʌlkɪŋ] ADJ: **~ (great)** grosso(-a) e goffo(-a)

hull [hʌl] N (of ship) scafo

hullabaloo [hʌləbə'lu:] N (col: noise) fracasso

hullo [hə'ləu] EXCL = **hello**

hum [hʌm] VT (tune) canticchiare ▶ VI canticchiare; (insect, plane, tool) ronzare ▶ N (also Elec) ronzio; (of traffic, machines) rumore m; (of voices etc) mormorio, brusio

human ['hju:mən] ADJ (irreg) umano(-a) ▶ N (also: **human being**) essere m umano

humane [hju:'meɪn] ADJ umanitario(-a)

humanism ['hju:mənɪzəm] N umanesimo

humanitarian [hju:mænɪ'tɛərɪən] ADJ umanitario(-a)

humanity [hju:'mænɪtɪ] N umanità; **the humanities** gli studi umanistici

humanly ['hju:mənlɪ] ADV umanamente

humanoid ['hju:mənɔɪd] ADJ che sembra umano(-a) ▶ N umanoide mf

human rights NPL diritti mpl dell'uomo

humble ['hʌmbl] ADJ umile, modesto(-a) ▶ VT umiliare

humbly ['hʌmblɪ] ADV umilmente, modestamente

humbug ['hʌmbʌg] N inganno; sciocchezze fpl; (BRIT: sweet) caramella alla menta

humdrum ['hʌmdrʌm] ADJ monotono(-a), tedioso(-a)

humid ['hju:mɪd] ADJ umido(-a)

humidifier [hju:'mɪdɪfaɪər] N umidificatore m

humidity [hju:'mɪdɪtɪ] N umidità

humiliate [hju:'mɪlɪeɪt] VT umiliare

humiliating ADJ umiliante

humiliation [hju:mɪlɪ'eɪʃən] N umiliazione f

humility [hju:'mɪlɪtɪ] N umiltà

hummus ['huməs] N purè di ceci

humorist ['hju:mərɪst] N umorista mf

humorous ['hju:mərəs] ADJ umoristico(-a); (person) buffo(-a)

humour, (US) **humor** ['hju:mər] N umore m

▶ VT (person) assecondare; **sense of ~** senso dell'umorismo; **to be in a good/bad ~** essere di buon/cattivo umore

humourless, (US) **humorless** ['hju:məlɪs] ADJ privo(-a) di umorismo

hump [hʌmp] N gobba

humpback ['hʌmpbæk] N schiena d'asino; (BRIT: also: **humpback bridge**) ponte m a schiena d'asino

humus ['hju:məs] N humus m

hunch [hʌntʃ] N gobba; (premonition) intuizione f; **I have a ~ that** ho la vaga impressione che

hunchback ['hʌntʃbæk] N gobbo(-a)

hunched [hʌntʃt] ADJ incurvato(-a)

hundred ['hʌndrəd] NUM cento; **about a ~ people** un centinaio di persone; **hundreds of people** centinaia fpl di persone; **I'm a ~ per cent sure** sono sicuro al cento per cento

hundredth [-ɪdθ] NUM centesimo(-a)

hundredweight ['hʌndrɪdweɪt] N (BRIT) = 50.8 kg; = 112 lb; (US) = 45.3 kg; = 100 lb

hung [hʌŋ] PT, PP of **hang**

Hungarian [hʌŋ'gɛərɪən] ADJ ungherese ▶ N ungherese mf; (Ling) ungherese m

Hungary ['hʌŋgərɪ] N Ungheria

hunger ['hʌŋgər] N fame f ▶ VI: **to ~ for** desiderare ardentemente

hunger strike N sciopero della fame

hungover [hʌŋ'əuvər] ADJ (col): **to be ~** avere i postumi della sbornia

hungrily ['hʌŋgrəlɪ] ADV voracemente; (fig) avidamente

hungry ['hʌŋgrɪ] ADJ affamato(-a); **to be ~** aver fame; **~ for** (fig) assetato di

hung up ADJ (col) complessato(-a)

hunk [hʌŋk] N bel pezzo

hunt [hʌnt] VT (seek) cercare; (Sport) cacciare ▶ VI: **to ~ (for)** andare a caccia (di) ▶ N caccia ▶ **hunt down** VT scovare

hunter ['hʌntər] N cacciatore m; (BRIT: horse) cavallo da caccia

hunting ['hʌntɪŋ] N caccia

hurdle ['hə:dl] N (Sport, fig) ostacolo

hurl [hə:l] VT lanciare con violenza

hurling ['hə:lɪŋ] N (Sport) hurling m

hurly-burly ['hə:lɪ'bə:lɪ] N chiasso, baccano

hurrah [hu'rɑ:], **hurray** [hu'reɪ] EXCL urra!, evviva!

hurricane ['hʌrɪkən] N uragano

hurried ['hʌrɪd] ADJ affrettato(-a); (work) fatto(-a) in fretta

hurriedly ['hʌrɪdlɪ] ADV in fretta

hurry ['hʌrɪ] N fretta ▶ VI (also: **hurry up**) affrettarsi ▶ VT (also: **hurry up**: person) affrettare; (: work) far in fretta; **to be in a ~** aver fretta; **to do sth in a ~** fare qc in fretta; **to ~ in/out** entrare/uscire in fretta; **to ~ back/ home** affrettarsi a tornare indietro/a casa

▶ **hurry along** VI camminare in fretta
▶ **hurry away, hurry off** VI andarsene in fretta
▶ **hurry up** VI sbrigarsi
hurt [həːt] (*pt, pp* ~) VT (*cause pain to*) far male a; (*injure, fig*) ferire; (*business, interests etc*) colpire, danneggiare ▶ VI far male ▶ ADJ ferito(-a); **I ~ my arm** mi sono fatto male al braccio; **where does it ~?** dove ti fa male?
hurtful ['həːtful] ADJ (*remark*) che ferisce
hurtle ['həːtl] VT scagliare ▶ VI: **to ~ past/down** passare/scendere a razzo
husband ['hʌzbənd] N marito
hush [hʌʃ] N silenzio, calma ▶ VT zittire; ~! zitto(-a)!
▶ **hush up** VT (*fact*) cercare di far passare sotto silenzio
hush-hush ['hʌʃ'hʌʃ] ADJ (*col*) segretissimo(-a)
husk [hʌsk] N (*of wheat*) cartoccio; (*of rice, maize*) buccia
husky ['hʌskɪ] ADJ roco(-a) ▶ N cane *m* eschimese
hustings ['hʌstɪŋz] NPL (*BRIT Pol*) comizi *mpl* elettorali
hustle ['hʌsl] VT spingere, incalzare ▶ N pigia pigia *m inv*; **~ and bustle** trambusto
hut [hʌt] N rifugio; (*shed*) ripostiglio
hutch [hʌtʃ] N gabbia
hyacinth ['haɪəsɪnθ] N giacinto
hybrid ['haɪbrɪd] ADJ ibrido(-a) ▶ N ibrido
hydrangea [haɪ'dreɪnʒə] N ortensia
hydrant ['haɪdrənt] N (*also:* **fire hydrant**) idrante *m*
hydraulic [haɪ'drɔlɪk] ADJ idraulico(-a)
hydraulics [haɪ'drɔlɪks] N idraulica
hydrochloric [haɪdrə'klɔrɪk] ADJ: ~ **acid** acido cloridrico
hydroelectric [haɪdrəʊɪ'lɛktrɪk] ADJ idroelettrico(-a)
hydrofoil ['haɪdrəfɔɪl] N aliscafo
hydrogen ['haɪdrədʒən] N idrogeno
hydrogen bomb N bomba all'idrogeno
hydrophobia [haɪdrə'fəʊbɪə] N idrofobia
hydroplane ['haɪdrəʊpleɪn] N idrovolante *m*
hyena [haɪ'iːnə] N iena
hygiene ['haɪdʒiːn] N igiene *f*
hygienic [haɪ'dʒiːnɪk] ADJ igienico(-a)
hymn [hɪm] N inno; cantica
hype [haɪp] N (*col*) battage *m inv* pubblicitario
hyperactive [haɪpər'æktɪv] ADJ iperattivo(-a)
hyperlink ['haɪpəlɪŋk] N link *m inv* ipertestuale
hypermarket ['haɪpəmɑːkɪt] N (*BRIT*) ipermercato
hypertension [haɪpə'tɛnʃən] N (*Med*) ipertensione *f*
hypertext ['haɪpətɛkst] N (*Comput*) ipertesto
hyphen ['haɪfn] N trattino
hypnosis [hɪp'nəʊsɪs] N ipnosi *f*
hypnotic [hɪp'nɔtɪk] ADJ ipnotico(-a)
hypnotism ['hɪpnətɪzəm] N ipnotismo
hypnotist ['hɪpnətɪst] N ipnotizzatore(-trice)
hypnotize ['hɪpnətaɪz] VT ipnotizzare
hypoallergenic [haɪpəʊælə'dʒɛnɪk] ADJ ipoallergico(-a)
hypochondriac [haɪpə'kɔndrɪæk] N ipocondriaco(-a)
hypocrisy [hɪ'pɔkrɪsɪ] N ipocrisia
hypocrite ['hɪpəkrɪt] N ipocrita *mf*
hypocritical [hɪpə'krɪtɪkl] ADJ ipocrita
hypodermic [haɪpə'dəːmɪk] ADJ ipodermico(-a) ▶ N (*syringe*) siringa ipodermica
hypotenuse [haɪ'pɔtɪnjuːz] N ipotenusa
hypothermia [haɪpəʊ'θəːmɪə] N ipotermia
hypothesis [haɪ'pɔθɪsɪs] (*pl* **hypotheses** [-siːz]) N ipotesi *f inv*
hypothetical [haɪpəʊ'θɛtɪkl] ADJ ipotetico(-a)
hysterectomy [hɪstə'rɛktəmɪ] N isterectomia
hysteria [hɪ'stɪərɪə] N isteria
hysterical [hɪ'stɛrɪkl] ADJ isterico(-a); **to become ~** avere una crisi isterica
hysterics [hɪ'stɛrɪks] NPL accesso di isteria; (*laughter*) attacco di riso; **to have ~** avere una crisi isterica

I i

I, i [aɪ] N (letter) I, i f inv or m inv; **I for Isaac**, (US) **I for Item** ≈ I come Imola

I [aɪ] PRON io ▶ ABBR (= island, isle) Is.

IA ABBR (US) = **Iowa**

IAEA N ABBR = **International Atomic Energy Agency**

ib. ['ɪb] ABBR (= ibidem: from the same source) ibid

Iberian [aɪ'bɪərɪən] ADJ iberico(-a)

Iberian Peninsula N: **the ~** la Penisola iberica

IBEW N ABBR (US: = International Brotherhood of Electrical Workers) associazione internazionale degli elettrotecnici

ibid. ['ɪbɪd] ABBR (= ibidem: from the same source) ibid

i/c ABBR (BRIT) = **in charge**

ICBM N ABBR (= intercontinental ballistic missile) ICBM m inv

ICC N ABBR (= International Chamber of Commerce) C.C.I. f; (US: = Interstate Commerce Commission) commissione per il commercio tra gli stati degli USA

ice [aɪs] N ghiaccio; (on road) gelo ▶ VT (cake) glassare; (drink) mettere in fresco ▶ VI (also: **ice over**) ghiacciare; (also: **ice up**) gelare; **to keep sth on ~** (fig: plan, project) mettere da parte (per il momento), accantonare

Ice Age N era glaciale

ice axe N piccozza da ghiaccio

iceberg ['aɪsbəːg] N iceberg m inv; **tip of the ~** (also fig) punta dell'iceberg

icebox ['aɪsbɔks] N (US) frigorifero; (BRIT) reparto ghiaccio; (insulated box) frigo portatile

icebreaker ['aɪsbreɪkə'] N rompighiaccio m inv

ice bucket N secchiello del ghiaccio

ice-cap ['aɪskæp] N calotta polare

ice-cold [aɪs'kəuld] ADJ gelato(-a)

ice cream N gelato

ice-cream soda N (gelato) affogato al seltz

ice cube N cubetto di ghiaccio

iced [aɪst] ADJ (drink) ghiacciato(-a); (coffee, tea) freddo(-a); (cake) glassato(-a)

ice hockey N hockey m su ghiaccio

Iceland ['aɪslənd] N Islanda

Icelander ['aɪsləndə'] N islandese mf

Icelandic [aɪs'lændɪk] ADJ islandese ▶ N (Ling) islandese m

ice lolly N (BRIT) ghiacciolo

ice pick N piccone m per ghiaccio

ice rink N pista di pattinaggio

ice-skate ['aɪsskeɪt] N pattino da ghiaccio ▶ VI pattinare sul ghiaccio

ice skating ['aɪsskeɪtɪŋ] N pattinaggio sul ghiaccio

icicle ['aɪsɪkl] N ghiacciolo

icing ['aɪsɪŋ] N (Aviat etc) patina di ghiaccio; (Culin) glassa

icing sugar (BRIT) N zucchero a velo

ICJ N ABBR = **International Court of Justice**

icon ['aɪkɔn] N icona; (Comput) immagine f

ICR N ABBR (US) = **Institute for Cancer Research**

ICRC N ABBR (= International Committee of the Red Cross) CICR m

ICT N ABBR (BRIT Scol: = Information and Communications Technology) informatica

ICU N ABBR = **intensive care unit**

icy ['aɪsɪ] ADJ ghiacciato(-a); (weather, temperature) gelido(-a)

ID ABBR = **identification document**; (US) = **Idaho**

I'd [aɪd] = **I would**; **I had**

Ida. ABBR (US) = **Idaho**

ID card N = **identity card**

IDD N ABBR (BRIT Tel: = International direct dialling) teleselezione f internazionale

idea [aɪ'dɪə] N idea; **good ~!** buon'idea!; **to have an ~ that ...** aver l'impressione che ...; **I haven't the least ~** non ne ho la minima idea

ideal [aɪ'dɪəl] ADJ, N ideale (m)

idealist [aɪ'dɪəlɪst] N idealista mf

ideally [aɪ'dɪəlɪ] ADV perfettamente, assolutamente; **~ the book should have ...** l'ideale sarebbe che il libro avesse ...

identical [aɪ'dɛntɪkl] ADJ identico(-a)

identification [aɪdɛntɪfɪ'keɪʃən] N identificazione f; **means of ~** carta d'identità

identify [aɪ'dɛntɪfaɪ] ᴠᴛ identificare ▶ ᴠɪ: **to ~ with** identificarsi con

Identikit® [aɪ'dɛntɪkɪt] ɴ: **~ (picture)** identikit *m inv*

identity [aɪ'dɛntɪtɪ] ɴ identità *f inv*

identity card ɴ carta d'identità

identity parade ɴ (Bʀɪᴛ) confronto all'americana

identity theft ɴ furto d'identità

ideological [aɪdɪə'lɔdʒɪkəl] ᴀᴅJ ideologico(-a)

ideology [aɪdɪ'ɔlədʒɪ] ɴ ideologia

idiocy ['ɪdɪəsɪ] ɴ idiozia

idiom ['ɪdɪəm] ɴ idioma *m*; (*phrase*) espressione *f* idiomatica

idiomatic [ɪdɪə'mætɪk] ᴀᴅJ idiomatico(-a)

idiosyncrasy [ɪdɪəu'sɪŋkrəsɪ] ɴ idiosincrasia

idiot ['ɪdɪət] ɴ idiota *mf*

idiotic [ɪdɪ'ɔtɪk] ᴀᴅJ idiota

idle ['aɪdl] ᴀᴅJ inattivo(-a); (*lazy*) pigro(-a), ozioso(-a); (*unemployed*) disoccupato(-a); (*question, pleasures*) ozioso(-a) ▶ ᴠɪ (*engine*) girare al minimo; **to lie ~** stare fermo, non funzionare

▶ **idle away** ᴠᴛ (*time*) sprecare, buttar via

idleness ['aɪdlnɪs] ɴ ozio; pigrizia

idler ['aɪdləʳ] ɴ ozioso(-a), fannullone(-a)

idle time ɴ tempi *mpl* morti

idol ['aɪdl] ɴ idolo

idolize ['aɪdəlaɪz] ᴠᴛ idoleggiare

idyllic [ɪ'dɪlɪk] ᴀᴅJ idillico(-a)

i.e. ᴀʙʙʀ = **id est** (*that is*) cioè

IED [aɪiː'diː] ɴ (= *Improvised Explosive Device*) ordigno esplosivo improvvisato; IED *m inv*

if [ɪf] ᴄᴏɴJ se ▶ ɴ: **there are a lot of ifs and buts** ci sono molti se e ma; **I'd be pleased if you could do it** sarei molto contento se potesse farlo; **if I were you ...** se fossi in te ..., io al tuo posto ...; **if so** se è così; **if not** se no; **if necessary** se (è) necessario; **if only** se solo *or* soltanto; **if only he were here** se solo fosse qui; **if only to show him my gratitude** se non altro per esprimergli la mia gratitudine

iffy ['ɪfɪ] ᴀᴅJ (*col*) incerto(-a)

igloo ['ɪgluː] ɴ igloo *m inv*

ignite [ɪg'naɪt] ᴠᴛ accendere ▶ ᴠɪ accendersi

ignition [ɪg'nɪʃən] ɴ (Aut) accensione *f*; **to switch on/off the ~** accendere/spegnere il motore

ignition key ɴ (Aut) chiave *f* dell'accensione

ignoble [ɪg'nəubl] ᴀᴅJ ignobile

ignominious [ɪgnə'mɪnɪəs] ᴀᴅJ vergognoso(-a), ignominioso(-a)

ignoramus [ɪgnə'reɪməs] ɴ ignorante *mf*

ignorance ['ɪgnərəns] ɴ ignoranza; **to keep sb in ~ of sth** tenere qn all'oscuro di qc

ignorant ['ɪgnərənt] ᴀᴅJ ignorante; **to be ~ of** (*subject*) essere ignorante in; (*events*) essere ignaro(-a) di

ignore [ɪg'nɔːʳ] ᴠᴛ non tener conto di; (*person, fact*) ignorare

ikon ['aɪkɔn] ɴ = **icon**

IL ᴀʙʙʀ (*US*) = **Illinois**

ILA ɴ ᴀʙʙʀ (*US*: = *International Longshoremen's Association*) associazione internazionale degli scaricatori di porto

ill [ɪl] ᴀᴅJ (*sick*) malato(-a); (*bad*) cattivo(-a) ▶ ɴ male *m*; **to take** *or* **be taken ~** ammalarsi; **to feel ~** star male; **to speak/think ~ of sb** parlar/pensar male di qn

Ill. ᴀʙʙʀ (*US*) = **Illinois**

I'll [aɪl] = **I will; I shall**

ill-advised [ɪləd'vaɪzd] ᴀᴅJ (*decision*) poco giudizioso(-a); (*person*) mal consigliato(-a)

ill-at-ease [ɪlət'iːz] ᴀᴅJ a disagio

ill-considered [ɪlkən'sɪdəd] ᴀᴅJ (*plan*) avventato(-a)

ill-disposed [ɪldɪs'pəuzd] ᴀᴅJ: **to be ~ towards sb/sth** essere maldisposto(-a) verso qn/qc *or* nei riguardi di qn/qc

illegal [ɪ'liːgl] ᴀᴅJ illegale

illegally [ɪ'liːgəlɪ] ᴀᴅᴠ illegalmente

illegible [ɪ'lɛdʒɪbl] ᴀᴅJ illeggibile

illegitimate [ɪlɪ'dʒɪtɪmət] ᴀᴅJ illegittimo(-a)

ill-fated [ɪl'feɪtɪd] ᴀᴅJ nefasto(-a)

ill-favoured, (*US*) **ill-favored** [ɪl'feɪvəd] ᴀᴅJ sgraziato(-a), brutto(-a)

ill feeling ɴ rancore *m*

ill-gotten ['ɪlgɔtn] ᴀᴅJ: **~ gains** maltolto

ill health ɴ problemi *mpl* di salute

illicit [ɪ'lɪsɪt] ᴀᴅJ illecito(-a)

ill-informed [ɪlɪn'fɔːmd] ᴀᴅJ (*judgement, speech*) pieno(-a) di inesattezze; (*person*) male informato(-a)

illiterate [ɪ'lɪtərət] ᴀᴅJ analfabeta, illetterato(-a); (*letter*) scorretto(-a)

ill-mannered [ɪl'mænəd] ᴀᴅJ maleducato(-a), sgarbato(-a)

illness ['ɪlnɪs] ɴ malattia

illogical [ɪ'lɔdʒɪkl] ᴀᴅJ illogico(-a)

ill-suited [ɪl'suːtɪd] ᴀᴅJ (*couple*) mal assortito(-a); **he is ~ to the job** è inadatto a quel lavoro

ill-timed [ɪl'taɪmd] ᴀᴅJ intempestivo(-a), inopportuno(-a)

ill-treat [ɪl'triːt] ᴠᴛ maltrattare

ill-treatment [ɪl'triːtmənt] ɴ maltrattamenti *mpl*

illuminate [ɪ'luːmɪneɪt] ᴠᴛ illuminare; **illuminated sign** insegna luminosa

illuminating [ɪ'luːmɪneɪtɪŋ] ᴀᴅJ chiarificatore(-trice)

illumination [ɪluːmɪ'neɪʃən] ɴ illuminazione *f*

illusion [ɪ'luːʒən] ɴ illusione *f*; **to be under the ~ that** avere l'impressione che

illusive [ɪ'luːsɪv], **illusory** [ɪ'luːsərɪ] ᴀᴅJ illusorio(-a)

illustrate ['ɪləstreɪt] VT illustrare
illustration [ɪlə'streɪʃən] N illustrazione f
illustrator ['ɪləstreɪtə^r] N illustratore(-trice)
illustrious [ɪ'lʌstrɪəs] ADJ illustre
ill will N cattiva volontà
ILO N ABBR (= International Labour Organization) OIL f
IM N (= instant messaging) messaggeria istantanea
I'm [aɪm] = **I am**
image ['ɪmɪdʒ] N immagine f; (public face) immagine (pubblica)
imagery ['ɪmɪdʒərɪ] N immagini fpl
imaginable [ɪ'mædʒɪnəbl] ADJ immaginabile, che si possa immaginare
imaginary [ɪ'mædʒɪnərɪ] ADJ immaginario(-a)
imagination [ɪmædʒɪ'neɪʃən] N immaginazione f, fantasia
imaginative [ɪ'mædʒɪnətɪv] ADJ immaginoso(-a)
imagine [ɪ'mædʒɪn] VT immaginare
imbalance [ɪm'bæləns] N squilibrio
imbecile ['ɪmbəsi:l] N imbecille mf
imbue [ɪm'bju:] VT: **to ~ sth with** impregnare qc di
IMF N ABBR = **International Monetary Fund**
imitate ['ɪmɪteɪt] VT imitare
imitation [ɪmɪ'teɪʃən] N imitazione f
imitator ['ɪmɪteɪtə^r] N imitatore(-trice)
immaculate [ɪ'mækjulət] ADJ immacolato(-a); (dress, appearance) impeccabile
immaterial [ɪmə'tɪərɪəl] ADJ immateriale, indifferente; **it is ~ whether** poco importa se or che + sub
immature [ɪmə'tjʊə^r] ADJ immaturo(-a)
immaturity [ɪmə'tjʊərɪtɪ] N immaturità, mancanza di maturità
immeasurable [ɪ'mɛʒərəbl] ADJ incommensurabile
immediacy [ɪ'mi:dɪəsɪ] N immediatezza
immediate [ɪ'mi:dɪət] ADJ immediato(-a)
immediately [ɪ'mi:dɪətlɪ] ADV (at once) subito, immediatamente; **~ next to** proprio accanto a
immense [ɪ'mɛns] ADJ immenso(-a); enorme
immensely ADV immensamente
immensity [ɪ'mɛnsɪtɪ] N (of size, difference) enormità; (of problem etc) vastità
immerse [ɪ'mə:s] VT immergere
immersion heater [ɪ'mə:ʃən-] N (BRIT) scaldaacqua m inv a immersione
immigrant ['ɪmɪgrənt] N immigrante mf; (already established) immigrato(-a)
immigration [ɪmɪ'greɪʃən] N immigrazione f
immigration authorities NPL ufficio stranieri
immigration laws NPL leggi fpl relative all'immigrazione

imminent ['ɪmɪnənt] ADJ imminente
immobile [ɪ'məubaɪl] ADJ immobile
immobilize [ɪ'məubɪlaɪz] VT immobilizzare
immobilizer [ɪ'məubɪlaɪzə^r] N (Aut) immobilizer m inv, dispositivo di bloccaggio del motore
immoderate [ɪ'mɔdərɪt] ADJ (person) smodato(-a), sregolato(-a); (opinion, reaction, demand) eccessivo(-a)
immodest [ɪ'mɔdɪst] ADJ (indecent) indecente, impudico(-a); (boasting) presuntuoso(-a)
immoral [ɪ'mɔrl] ADJ immorale
immorality [ɪmɔ'rælɪtɪ] N immoralità
immortal [ɪ'mɔ:tl] ADJ, N immortale (mf)
immortalize [ɪ'mɔ:təlaɪz] VT rendere immortale
immovable [ɪ'mu:vəbl] ADJ (object) non movibile; (person) irremovibile
immune [ɪ'mju:n] ADJ: **~ (to)** immune (da)
immune system N sistema m immunitario
immunity [ɪ'mju:nɪtɪ] N (also fig: of diplomat) immunità; **diplomatic ~** immunità diplomatica
immunization [ɪmjunaɪ'zeɪʃən] N immunizzazione f
immunize ['ɪmjunaɪz] VT immunizzare
imp [ɪmp] N folletto, diavoletto; (child) diavoletto
impact ['ɪmpækt] N impatto
impair [ɪm'pɛə^r] VT danneggiare
impaired [ɪm'pɛəd] ADJ indebolito(-a)
-impaired [ɪm'pɛəd] SUFFIX: **visually~** videoleso(-a)
impale [ɪm'peɪl] VT impalare
impart [ɪm'pɑ:t] VT (make known) comunicare; (bestow) impartire
impartial [ɪm'pɑ:ʃl] ADJ imparziale
impartiality [ɪmpɑ:ʃɪ'ælɪtɪ] N imparzialità
impassable [ɪm'pɑ:səbl] ADJ insuperabile; (road) impraticabile
impasse [æm'pɑ:s] N impasse f inv
impassioned [ɪm'pæʃənd] ADJ appassionato(-a)
impassive [ɪm'pæsɪv] ADJ impassibile
impatience [ɪm'peɪʃəns] N impazienza
impatient [ɪm'peɪʃənt] ADJ impaziente; **to get** or **grow ~** perdere la pazienza
impeach [ɪm'pi:tʃ] VT accusare, attaccare; (public official) mettere sotto accusa
impeachment [ɪm'pi:tʃmənt] N (Law) imputazione f
impeccable [ɪm'pɛkəbl] ADJ impeccabile
impecunious [ɪmpɪ'kju:nɪəs] ADJ povero(-a)
impede [ɪm'pi:d] VT impedire
impediment [ɪm'pɛdɪmənt] N impedimento; (also: **speech impediment**) difetto di pronuncia
impel [ɪm'pɛl] VT (force): **to ~ sb (to do sth)** costringere or obbligare qn (a fare qc)

impending [ɪm'pɛndɪŋ] ADJ imminente

impenetrable [ɪm'pɛnɪtrəbl] ADJ impenetrabile

imperative [ɪm'pɛrətɪv] ADJ imperativo(-a); necessario(-a), urgente; (voice) imperioso(-a) ▶ N (Ling) imperativo

imperceptible [ɪmpə'sɛptɪbl] ADJ impercettibile

imperfect [ɪm'pə:fɪkt] ADJ imperfetto(-a); (goods etc) difettoso(-a) ▶ N (Ling: also: **imperfect tense**) imperfetto

imperfection [ɪmpə:'fɛkʃən] N imperfezione f; (flaw) difetto

imperial [ɪm'pɪərɪəl] ADJ imperiale; (measure) legale

imperialism [ɪm'pɪərɪəlɪzəm] N imperialismo

imperil [ɪm'pɛrɪl] VT mettere in pericolo

imperious [ɪm'pɪərɪəs] ADJ imperioso(-a)

impersonal [ɪm'pə:sənl] ADJ impersonale

impersonate [ɪm'pə:səneɪt] VT spacciarsi per, fingersi; (Theat) imitare

impersonation [ɪmpə:sə'neɪʃən] N (Law) usurpazione f d'identità; (Theat) imitazione f

impersonator [ɪm'pə:səneɪtər] N (gen, Theat) imitatore(-trice)

impertinence [ɪm'pə:tɪnəns] N impertinenza

impertinent [ɪm'pə:tɪnənt] ADJ impertinente

imperturbable [ɪmpə'tə:bəbl] ADJ imperturbabile

impervious [ɪm'pə:vɪəs] ADJ impermeabile; **~ to** (fig) insensibile a; impassibile di fronte a

impetuous [ɪm'pɛtjuəs] ADJ impetuoso(-a), precipitoso(-a)

impetus ['ɪmpətəs] N impeto

impinge [ɪm'pɪndʒ]: **to ~ on** vt fus (person) colpire; (rights) ledere

impish ['ɪmpɪʃ] ADJ malizioso(-a), birichino(-a)

implacable [ɪm'plækəbl] ADJ implacabile

implant [ɪm'plɑ:nt] VT (Med) innestare; (fig: idea, principle) inculcare

implausible [ɪm'plɔ:zɪbl] ADJ non plausibile

implement N ['ɪmplɪmənt] attrezzo; (for cooking) utensile m ▶ VT ['ɪmplɪmɛnt] effettuare

implicate ['ɪmplɪkeɪt] VT implicare

implication [ɪmplɪ'keɪʃən] N implicazione f; **by ~** implicitamente

implicit [ɪm'plɪsɪt] ADJ implicito(-a); (complete) completo(-a)

implicitly [ɪm'plɪsɪtlɪ] ADV implicitamente

implore [ɪm'plɔ:r] VT implorare

imply [ɪm'plaɪ] VT insinuare; suggerire

impolite [ɪmpə'laɪt] ADJ scortese

imponderable [ɪm'pɔndərəbl] ADJ imponderabile

import VT [ɪm'pɔ:t] importare ▶ N ['ɪmpɔ:t] (Comm) importazione f; (meaning) significato, senso ▶ CPD (duty, licence etc) d'importazione

importance [ɪm'pɔ:tns] N importanza; **to be of great/little ~** importare molto/poco, essere molto/poco importante

important [ɪm'pɔ:tnt] ADJ importante; **it's not ~** non ha importanza; **it is ~ that** è importante che + sub

importantly [ɪm'pɔ:təntlɪ] ADV (pej) con (un'aria d')importanza; **but, more ~, ...** ma, quel che più conta or importa, ...

importation [ɪmpɔ:'teɪʃən] N importazione f

imported [ɪm'pɔ:tɪd] ADJ importato(-a)

importer [ɪm'pɔ:tər] N importatore(-trice)

impose [ɪm'pəuz] VT imporre ▶ VI: **to ~ on sb** sfruttare la bontà di qn

imposing [ɪm'pəuzɪŋ] ADJ imponente

imposition [ɪmpə'zɪʃən] N imposizione f; **to be an ~ on** (person) abusare della gentilezza di

impossibility [ɪmpɔsə'bɪlɪtɪ] N impossibilità

impossible [ɪm'pɔsɪbl] ADJ impossibile; **it is ~ for me to leave now** mi è impossibile venir via adesso

impostor [ɪm'pɔstər] N impostore(-a)

impotence ['ɪmpətns] N impotenza

impotent ['ɪmpətnt] ADJ impotente

impound [ɪm'paund] VT confiscare

impoverished [ɪm'pɔvərɪʃt] ADJ impoverito(-a)

impracticable [ɪm'præktɪkəbl] ADJ impraticabile

impractical [ɪm'præktɪkl] ADJ non pratico(-a)

imprecise [ɪmprɪ'saɪs] ADJ impreciso(-a)

impregnable [ɪm'prɛgnəbl] ADJ (fortress) inespugnabile; (fig) inoppugnabile; irrefutabile

impregnate ['ɪmprɛgneɪt] VT impregnare; (fertilize) fecondare

impresario [ɪmprɪ'sɑ:rɪəu] N impresario(-a)

impress [ɪm'prɛs] VT impressionare; (mark) imprimere, stampare; **to ~ sth on sb** far capire qc a qn

impression [ɪm'prɛʃən] N impressione f; **to be under the ~ that** avere l'impressione che; **to make a good/bad ~ on sb** fare una buona/cattiva impressione a or su qn

impressionable [ɪm'prɛʃnəbl] ADJ impressionabile

impressionist [ɪm'prɛʃənɪst] N impressionista mf

impressive [ɪm'prɛsɪv] ADJ notevole

imprint ['ɪmprɪnt] N (Publishing) sigla editoriale

imprinted [ɪm'prɪntɪd] ADJ: **~ on** impresso(-a) in

imprison [ɪm'prɪzn] VT imprigionare

imprisonment [ɪm'prɪznmənt] N
imprigionamento
improbable [ɪm'prɔbəbl] ADJ improbabile;
(*excuse*) inverosimile
impromptu [ɪm'prɔmptjuː] ADJ
improvvisato(-a) ▶ ADV improvvisando, così
su due piedi
improper [ɪm'prɔpər] ADJ scorretto(-a);
(*unsuitable*) inadatto(-a), improprio(-a);
sconveniente, indecente
impropriety [ɪmprə'praɪətɪ] N sconvenienza;
(*of expression*) improprietà
improve [ɪm'pruːv] VT migliorare ▶ VI
migliorare; (*pupil etc*) fare progressi
▶ **improve (up)on** VT FUS (*offer*) aumentare
improvement [ɪm'pruːvmənt] N
miglioramento; progresso; **to make
improvements to** migliorare, apportare dei
miglioramenti a
improvisation [ɪmprəvaɪ'zeɪʃən] N
improvvisazione f
improvise ['ɪmprəvaɪz] VT, VI improvvisare
imprudence [ɪm'pruːdns] N imprudenza
imprudent [ɪm'pruːdnt] ADJ imprudente
impudence ['ɪmpjudns] N impudenza
impudent ['ɪmpjudnt] ADJ impudente,
sfacciato(-a)
impugn [ɪm'pjuːn] VT impugnare
impulse ['ɪmpʌls] N impulso; **to act on ~**
agire d'impulso *or* impulsivamente
impulse buy N acquisto fatto d'impulso
impulsive [ɪm'pʌlsɪv] ADJ impulsivo(-a)
impunity [ɪm'pjuːnɪtɪ] N: **with ~**
impunemente
impure [ɪm'pjuər] ADJ impuro(-a)
impurity [ɪm'pjuərɪtɪ] N impurità f inv
IN ABBR (*US*) = **Indiana**

(KEYWORD)

in [ɪn] PREP **1** (*indicating place, position*) in; **in
the house/garden** in casa/giardino; **in the
box** nella scatola; **in the fridge** nel
frigorifero; **I have it in my hand** ce l'ho in
mano; **in town/the country** in città/
campagna; **in school** a scuola; **in here/
there** qui/lì dentro
2 (*with place names: of town: region: country*): **in
London** a Londra; **in England** in
Inghilterra; **in the United States** negli
Stati Uniti; **in Yorkshire** nello Yorkshire
3 (*indicating time: during, in the space of*) in; **in
spring/summer** in primavera/estate; **in
1988** nel 1988; **in May** in *or* a maggio; **I'll see
you in July** ci vediamo a luglio; **in the
afternoon** nel pomeriggio; **at 4 o'clock in
the afternoon** alle 4 del pomeriggio; **I did
it in 3 hours/days** l'ho fatto in 3 ore/giorni;
I'll see you in 2 weeks *or* **in 2 weeks' time** ci
vediamo tra 2 settimane; **once in a**

hundred years una volta ogni cento anni
4 (*indicating manner etc*) a; **in a loud/soft voice**
a voce alta/bassa; **in pencil** a matita; **in
English/French** in inglese/francese; **in
writing** per iscritto; **the boy in the blue
shirt** il ragazzo con la camicia blu
5 (*indicating circumstances*): **in the sun** al sole;
in the shade all'ombra; **in the rain** sotto la
pioggia; **a rise in prices** un aumento dei
prezzi
6 (*indicating mood: state*): **in tears** in lacrime;
in anger per la rabbia; **in despair**
disperato(-a); **in good condition** in buono
stato, in buone condizioni; **to live in luxury**
vivere nel lusso
7 (*with ratios: numbers*): **1 in 10** 1 su 10; **20
pence in the pound** 20 pence per sterlina;
they lined up in twos si misero in fila per
due; **in hundreds** a centinaia
8 (*referring to people, works*) in; **the disease is
common in children** la malattia è comune
nei bambini; **in (the works of) Dickens** in
Dickens, nelle opere di Dickens
9 (*indicating profession etc*) in; **to be in
teaching** fare l'insegnante, insegnare; **to
be in publishing** lavorare nell'editoria
10 (*after superlative*) di; **the best in the class**
il migliore della classe
11 (*with present participle*): **in saying this**
dicendo questo, nel dire questo
12: **in that** *conj* poiché
▶ ADV: **to be in** (*person: at home, work*) esserci;
(*train, ship, plane*) essere arrivato(-a); (*in fashion*)
essere di moda; **their party is in** il loro
partito è al potere; **to ask sb in** invitare qn
ad entrare; **to run/limp etc in** entrare di
corsa/zoppicando *etc*
▶ N: **the ins and outs of the problem** tutti
gli aspetti del problema

in., ins ABBR = **inch**
inability [ɪnə'bɪlɪtɪ] N inabilità, incapacità;
~ to pay impossibilità di pagare
inaccessible [ɪnək'sɛsɪbl] ADJ inaccessibile
inaccuracy [ɪn'ækjurəsɪ] N inaccuratezza;
inesattezza; imprecisione f
inaccurate [ɪn'ækjurət] ADJ inaccurato(-a);
(*figures*) inesatto(-a); (*translation*)
impreciso(-a)
inaction [ɪn'ækʃən] N inazione f
inactivity [ɪnæk'tɪvɪtɪ] N inattività
inadequacy [ɪn'ædɪkwəsɪ] N insufficienza
inadequate [ɪn'ædɪkwət] ADJ insufficiente
inadmissible [ɪnəd'mɪsəbl] ADJ
inammissibile
inadvertent [ɪnəd'vəːtənt] ADJ
involontario(-a)
inadvertently [ɪnəd'vəːtntlɪ] ADV senza
volerlo

inadvisable [ɪnəd'vaɪzəbl] ADJ sconsigliabile

inane [ɪ'neɪn] ADJ vacuo(-a), stupido(-a)

inanimate [ɪn'ænɪmət] ADJ inanimato(-a)

inapplicable [ɪn'æplɪkəbl] ADJ inapplicabile

inappropriate [ɪnə'prəʊprɪət] ADJ non adatto(-a); (word, expression) improprio(-a)

inapt [ɪn'æpt] ADJ maldestro(-a); fuori luogo

inaptitude [ɪn'æptɪtjuːd] N improprietà

inarticulate [ɪnɑː'tɪkjulət] ADJ (person) che si esprime male; (speech) inarticolato(-a)

inasmuch as [ɪnəz'mʌtʃæz] ADV in quanto che; (seeing that) poiché

inattention [ɪnə'tɛnʃən] N mancanza di attenzione

inattentive [ɪnə'tɛntɪv] ADJ disattento(-a), distratto(-a); negligente

inaudible [ɪn'ɔːdɪbl] ADJ che non si riesce a sentire

inaugural [ɪ'nɔːgjurəl] ADJ inaugurale

inaugurate [ɪ'nɔːgjureɪt] VT inaugurare; (president, official) insediare

inauguration [ɪnɔːgju'reɪʃən] N inaugurazione f; insediamento in carica

inauspicious [ɪnɔːs'pɪʃəs] ADJ poco propizio(-a)

in-between [ɪnbɪ'twiːn] ADJ fra i (or le) due

inborn [ɪn'bɔːn] ADJ (feeling) innato(-a); (defect) congenito(-a)

inbox ['ɪnbɔks] N (Comput) posta in arrivo; (US: intray) vaschetta della corrispondenza in arrivo

inbred [ɪn'brɛd] ADJ innato(-a); (family) connaturato(-a)

inbreeding [ɪn'briːdɪŋ] N incrocio ripetuto di animali consanguinei; unioni fpl fra consanguinei

Inc. ABBR (US: = incorporated) S.A.

Inca ['ɪŋkə] ADJ (also: **Incan**) inca inv
▶ N inca mf

incalculable [ɪn'kælkjuləbl] ADJ incalcolabile

incapability [ɪnkeɪpə'bɪlɪtɪ] N incapacità

incapable [ɪn'keɪpəbl] ADJ: ~ **(of doing sth)** incapace (di fare qc)

incapacitate [ɪnkə'pæsɪteɪt] VT: **to ~ sb from doing** rendere qn incapace di fare

incapacitated [ɪnkə'pæsɪteɪtɪd] ADJ (Law) inabilitato(-a)

incapacity [ɪnkə'pæsɪtɪ] N incapacità

incarcerate [ɪn'kɑːsəreɪt] VT imprigionare

incarnate ADJ [ɪn'kɑːnɪt] incarnato(-a) ▶ VT ['ɪnkɑːneɪt] incarnare

incarnation [ɪnkɑː'neɪʃən] N incarnazione f

incendiary [ɪn'sɛndɪərɪ] ADJ incendiario(-a) ▶ N (bomb) bomba incendiaria

incense N ['ɪnsɛns] incenso ▶ VT [ɪn'sɛns] (anger) infuriare

incense burner N incensiere m

incentive [ɪn'sɛntɪv] N incentivo

incentive scheme N piano di incentivazione

inception [ɪn'sɛpʃən] N inizio, principio

incessant [ɪn'sɛsnt] ADJ incessante

incessantly [ɪn'sɛsntlɪ] ADV di continuo, senza sosta

incest ['ɪnsɛst] N incesto

inch [ɪntʃ] N pollice m (= 25 mm; 12 in a foot); **within an ~ of** a un pelo da; **he wouldn't give an ~** (fig) non ha ceduto di un millimetro
▶ **inch forward** VI avanzare pian piano

inch tape N (BRIT) metro a nastro (da sarto)

incidence ['ɪnsɪdns] N (of crime, disease) incidenza

incident ['ɪnsɪdnt] N incidente m; (in book) episodio

incidental [ɪnsɪ'dɛntl] ADJ accessorio(-a), d'accompagnamento; (unplanned) incidentale; ~ **to** marginale a; ~ **expenses** npl spese fpl accessorie

incidentally [ɪnsɪ'dɛntəlɪ] ADV (by the way) a proposito

incidental music N sottofondo (musicale), musica di sottofondo

incident room N (Police) centrale f delle operazioni (per indagini)

incinerate [ɪn'sɪnəreɪt] VT incenerire

incinerator [ɪn'sɪnəreɪtəʳ] N inceneritore m

incipient [ɪn'sɪpɪənt] ADJ incipiente

incision [ɪn'sɪʒən] N incisione f

incisive [ɪn'saɪsɪv] ADJ incisivo(-a); tagliante; acuto(-a)

incisor [ɪn'saɪzəʳ] N incisivo

incite [ɪn'saɪt] VT incitare

incl. ABBR = **including**; **inclusive (of)**

inclement [ɪn'klɛmənt] ADJ inclemente

inclination [ɪnklɪ'neɪʃən] N inclinazione f

incline N ['ɪnklaɪn] pendenza, pendio ▶ VT [ɪn'klaɪn] inclinare ▶ VI (surface) essere inclinato(-a); **to ~ to** tendere a; **to be inclined to do** tendere a fare; essere propenso(-a) a fare; **to be well inclined towards sb** essere ben disposto(-a) verso qn

include [ɪn'kluːd] VT includere, comprendere; **the tip is/is not included** la mancia è compresa/esclusa

including [ɪn'kluːdɪŋ] PREP compreso(-a), incluso(-a); ~ **tip** mancia compresa, compresa la mancia

inclusion [ɪn'kluːʒən] N inclusione f

inclusive [ɪn'kluːsɪv] ADJ incluso(-a), compreso(-a); **£50, ~ of all surcharges** 50 sterline, incluse tutte le soprattasse; ~ **of tax** etc tasse etc comprese

inclusive terms NPL (BRIT) prezzo tutto compreso

incognito [ɪnkɔg'niːtəʊ] ADV in incognito

incoherent [ɪnkəʊ'hɪərənt] ADJ incoerente

income ['ɪnkʌm] N reddito; **gross/net ~**

reddito lordo/netto; ~ **and expenditure account** conto entrate ed uscite

income support N (BRIT) sussidio di indigenza or povertà

income tax N imposta sul reddito

income tax inspector N ispettore m delle imposte dirette

income tax return N dichiarazione f annuale dei redditi

incoming ['ɪnkʌmɪŋ] ADJ (passengers, flight, mail) in arrivo; (government, tenant) subentrante; ~ **tide** marea montante

incommunicado [ɪnkəmjunɪ'kɑːdəu] ADJ: **to hold sb** ~ tenere qn in segregazione

incomparable [ɪn'kɔmpərəbl] ADJ incomparabile

incompatible [ɪnkəm'pætɪbl] ADJ incompatibile

incompetence [ɪn'kɔmpɪtns] N incompetenza, incapacità

incompetent [ɪn'kɔmpɪtnt] ADJ incompetente, incapace

incomplete [ɪnkəm'pliːt] ADJ incompleto(-a)

incomprehensible [ɪnkɔmprɪ'hɛnsɪbl] ADJ incomprensibile

inconceivable [ɪnkən'siːvəbl] ADJ inimmaginabile

inconclusive [ɪnkən'kluːsɪv] ADJ improduttivo(-a); (argument) poco convincente

incongruous [ɪn'kɔŋgruəs] ADJ poco appropriato(-a); (remark, act) incongruo(-a)

inconsequential [ɪnkɔnsɪ'kwɛnʃl] ADJ senza importanza

inconsiderable [ɪnkən'sɪdərəbl] ADJ: **not ~** non trascurabile

inconsiderate [ɪnkən'sɪdərət] ADJ sconsiderato(-a)

inconsistency [ɪnkən'sɪstənsɪ] N (of actions etc) incongruenza; (of work) irregolarità; (of statement etc) contraddizione f

inconsistent [ɪnkən'sɪstnt] ADJ incoerente; poco logico(-a); contraddittorio(-a); ~ **with** in contraddizione con

inconsolable [ɪnkən'səuləbl] ADJ inconsolabile

inconspicuous [ɪnkən'spɪkjuəs] ADJ incospicuo(-a); (colour) poco appariscente; (dress) dimesso(-a); **to make o.s.** ~ cercare di passare inosservato(-a)

inconstant [ɪn'kɔnstnt] ADJ incostante; mutevole

incontinence [ɪn'kɔntɪnəns] N incontinenza

incontinent [ɪn'kɔntɪnənt] ADJ incontinente

incontrovertible [ɪnkɔntrə'vəːtəbl] ADJ incontrovertibile

inconvenience [ɪnkən'viːnjəns] N inconveniente m; (trouble) disturbo ▶ VT disturbare; **to put sb to great** ~ creare degli inconvenienti a qn; **don't** ~ **yourself** non si disturbi

inconvenient [ɪnkən'viːnjənt] ADJ scomodo(-a); **that time is very ~ for me** quell'ora mi è molto scomoda, non è un'ora adatta per me

incorporate [ɪn'kɔːpəreɪt] VT incorporare; (contain) contenere

incorporated [ɪn'kɔːpəreɪtɪd] ADJ: ~ **company** (US) società f inv registrata

incorrect [ɪnkə'rɛkt] ADJ scorretto(-a); (statement) inesatto(-a)

incorrigible [ɪn'kɔrɪdʒəbl] ADJ incorreggibile

incorruptible [ɪnkə'rʌptɪbl] ADJ incorruttibile

increase N ['ɪnkriːs] aumento ▶ VI [ɪn'kriːs] aumentare; **to be on the** ~ essere in aumento; **an ~ of £5/10%** un aumento di 5 sterline/del 10%

increasing [ɪn'kriːsɪŋ] ADJ (number) crescente

increasingly [ɪn'kriːsɪŋlɪ] ADV sempre più

incredible [ɪn'krɛdɪbl] ADJ incredibile

incredibly ADV incredibilmente

incredulous [ɪn'krɛdjuləs] ADJ incredulo(-a)

increment ['ɪnkrɪmənt] N aumento, incremento

incriminate [ɪn'krɪmɪneɪt] VT compromettere

incriminating [ɪn'krɪmɪneɪtɪŋ] ADJ incriminante

incubate ['ɪnkjubeɪt] VT (eggs) covare ▶ VI (egg) essere in incubazione; (disease) avere un'incubazione

incubation [ɪnkju'beɪʃən] N incubazione f

incubation period N (periodo di) incubazione f

incubator ['ɪnkjubeɪtər] N incubatrice f

inculcate ['ɪnkʌlkeɪt] VT: **to ~ sth in sb** inculcare qc a qn, instillare qc a qn

incumbent [ɪn'kʌmbənt] ADJ: **it is ~ on him to do ...** è suo dovere fare ... ▶ N titolare mf

incur [ɪn'kəːr] VT (expenses) incorrere; (debt) contrarre; (loss) subire; (anger, risk) esporsi a

incurable [ɪn'kjuərəbl] ADJ incurabile

incursion [ɪn'kəːʃən] N incursione f

Ind. ABBR (US) = **Indiana**

indebted [ɪn'dɛtɪd] ADJ: **to be ~ to sb (for)** essere obbligato(-a) verso qn (per)

indecency [ɪn'diːsnsɪ] N indecenza

indecent [ɪn'diːsnt] ADJ indecente

indecent assault N (BRIT) aggressione f a scopo di violenza sessuale

indecent exposure N atti mpl osceni in luogo pubblico

indecipherable [ɪndɪ'saɪfərəbl] ADJ indecifrabile

indecision [ɪndɪ'sɪʒən] N indecisione f

indecisive [ɪndɪ'saɪsɪv] ADJ indeciso(-a); (discussion) non decisivo(-a)

indeed [ɪn'diːd] ADV infatti; veramente;
yes ~! certamente!

indefatigable [ɪndɪ'fætɪgəbl] ADJ
infaticabile, instancabile

indefensible [ɪndɪ'fɛnsəbl] ADJ (conduct)
ingiustificabile

indefinable [ɪndɪ'faɪnəbl] ADJ indefinibile

indefinite [ɪn'dɛfɪnɪt] ADJ indefinito(-a);
(answer) vago(-a); (period, number)
indeterminato(-a)

indefinitely [ɪn'dɛfɪnɪtlɪ] ADV (wait)
indefinitamente

indelible [ɪn'dɛlɪbl] ADJ indelebile

indelicate [ɪn'dɛlɪkɪt] ADJ (tactless)
indelicato(-a), privo(-a) di tatto; (not polite)
sconveniente

indemnify [ɪn'dɛmnɪfaɪ] VT indennizzare

indemnity [ɪn'dɛmnɪtɪ] N (insurance)
assicurazione f; (compensation) indennità,
indennizzo

indent [ɪn'dɛnt] VT (Typ: text) far rientrare dal
margine

indentation [ɪndɛn'teɪʃən] N dentellatura;
(Typ) rientranza; (dent) tacca

indented [ɪn'dɛntɪd] ADJ (Typ) rientrante

indenture [ɪn'dɛntʃəʳ] N contratto m
formazione inv

independence [ɪndɪ'pɛndns] N
indipendenza

Independence Day N (US); vedi nota

> Negli Stati Uniti il 4 luglio si festeggia l'
> Independence Day, il giorno in cui è stata
> firmata, nel 1776, la Dichiarazione di
> Indipendenza con la quale quante tredici colonie
> britanniche dichiaravano la propria
> indipendenza dalla Gran Bretagna e la
> propria appartenenza agli Stati Uniti
> d'America.

independent [ɪndɪ'pɛndnt] ADJ
indipendente

independently [ɪndɪ'pɛndntlɪ] ADV
indipendentemente; separatamente; **~ of**
indipendentemente da

independent school N (BRIT) istituto
scolastico indipendente che si autofinanzia

in-depth ['ɪn'dɛpθ] ADJ approfondito(-a)

indescribable [ɪndɪ'skraɪbəbl] ADJ
indescrivibile

indestructible [ɪndɪ'strʌktəbl] ADJ
indistruttibile

indeterminate [ɪndɪ'təːmɪnɪt] ADJ
indeterminato(-a)

index ['ɪndɛks] N (pl **indexes**) (in book) indice
m; (in library etc) catalogo; (pl **indices**: ratio,
sign) indice m

index card N scheda

index finger N (dito) indice m

index-linked ['ɪndɛks'lɪŋkt], (US) **indexed**
['ɪndɛkst] ADJ legato(-a) al costo della vita

India ['ɪndɪə] N India

Indian ['ɪndɪən] ADJ, N indiano(-a)

Indian ink N inchiostro di china

Indian Ocean N: **the ~** l'Oceano Indiano

Indian Summer N (fig) estate f di San
Martino

India paper N carta d'India, carta bibbia

India rubber N caucciù m

indicate ['ɪndɪkeɪt] VT indicare ▸ VI (BRIT Aut):
to ~ left/right mettere la freccia a sinistra/a
destra

indication [ɪndɪ'keɪʃən] N indicazione f, segno

indicative [ɪn'dɪkətɪv] ADJ: **~ of** indicativo(-a)
di ▸ N (Ling) indicativo; **to be ~ of sth** essere
indicativo(-a) or un indice di qc

indicator ['ɪndɪkeɪtəʳ] N (sign) segno; (Aut)
indicatore m di direzione, freccia

indices ['ɪndɪsiːz] NPL of **index**

indict [ɪn'daɪt] VT accusare

indictable [ɪn'daɪtəbl] ADJ passibile di pena;
~ offence atto che costituisce reato

indictment [ɪn'daɪtmənt] N accusa

indifference [ɪn'dɪfrəns] N indifferenza

indifferent [ɪn'dɪfrənt] ADJ indifferente;
(poor) mediocre

indigenous [ɪn'dɪdʒɪnəs] ADJ indigeno(-a)

indigestible [ɪndɪ'dʒɛstɪbl] ADJ indigeribile

indigestion [ɪndɪ'dʒɛstʃən] N indigestione f

indignant [ɪn'dɪgnənt] ADJ: **~ (at sth/with sb)**
indignato(-a) (per qc/contro qn)

indignation [ɪndɪg'neɪʃən] N indignazione f

indignity [ɪn'dɪgnɪtɪ] N umiliazione f

indigo ['ɪndɪgəu] ADJ, N indaco (inv)

indirect [ɪndɪ'rɛkt] ADJ indiretto(-a)

indirectly [ɪndɪ'rɛktlɪ] ADV indirettamente

indiscreet [ɪndɪ'skriːt] ADJ indiscreto(-a);
(rash) imprudente

indiscretion [ɪndɪ'skrɛʃən] N indiscrezione f;
imprudenza

indiscriminate [ɪndɪ'skrɪmɪnət] ADJ (person)
che non sa discernere; (admiration) cieco(-a);
(killings) indiscriminato(-a)

indispensable [ɪndɪ'spɛnsəbl] ADJ
indispensabile

indisposed [ɪndɪ'spəuzd] ADJ (unwell)
indisposto(-a)

indisposition [ɪndɪspə'zɪʃən] N (illness)
indisposizione f

indisputable [ɪndɪ'spjuːtəbl] ADJ
incontestabile, indiscutibile

indistinct [ɪndɪ'stɪŋkt] ADJ indistinto(-a);
(memory, noise) vago(-a)

indistinguishable [ɪndɪ'stɪŋgwɪʃəbl] ADJ
indistinguibile

individual [ɪndɪ'vɪdjuəl] N individuo ▸ ADJ
individuale; (characteristic) particolare,
originale

individualist [ɪndɪ'vɪdjuəlɪst] N
individualista mf

individuality [ɪndɪvɪdjuˈælɪtɪ] N individualità

individually [ɪndɪˈvɪdjuəlɪ] ADV singolarmente, uno(-a) per uno(-a)

indivisible [ɪndɪˈvɪzɪbl] ADJ indivisibile

Indochina [ˈɪndəuˈtʃaɪnə] N Indocina

indoctrinate [ɪnˈdɔktrɪneɪt] VT indottrinare

indoctrination [ɪndɔktrɪˈneɪʃən] N indottrinamento

indolent [ˈɪndələnt] ADJ indolente

Indonesia [ɪndəuˈniːzɪə] N Indonesia

Indonesian [ɪndəuˈniːzɪən] ADJ, N indonesiano(-a); (Ling) indonesiano

indoor [ˈɪndɔːʳ] ADJ da interno; (plant) d'appartamento; (swimming pool) coperto(-a); (sport, games) fatto(-a) al coperto

indoors [ɪnˈdɔːz] ADV all'interno; (at home) in casa

indubitable [ɪnˈdjuːbɪtəbl] ADJ indubitabile

induce [ɪnˈdjuːs] VT persuadere; (bring about, Med) provocare; **to ~ sb to do sth** persuadere qn a fare qc

inducement [ɪnˈdjuːsmənt] N incitamento; (incentive) stimolo, incentivo

induct [ɪnˈdʌkt] VT insediare; (fig) iniziare

induction [ɪnˈdʌkʃən] N (Med: of birth) parto indotto

induction course N (BRIT) corso di avviamento

indulge [ɪnˈdʌldʒ] VT (whim) compiacere, soddisfare; (child) viziare ▶ VI: **to ~ in sth** concedersi qc; abbandonarsi a qc

indulgence [ɪnˈdʌldʒəns] N lusso (che uno si permette); (leniency) indulgenza

indulgent [ɪnˈdʌldʒənt] ADJ indulgente

industrial [ɪnˈdʌstrɪəl] ADJ industriale; (injury) sul lavoro; (dispute) di lavoro

industrial action N azione f rivendicativa

industrial estate N (BRIT) N zona industriale

industrialist [ɪnˈdʌstrɪəlɪst] N industriale m

industrialize [ɪnˈdʌstrɪəlaɪz] VT industrializzare

industrial park N (US) zona industriale

industrial relations NPL relazioni fpl industriali

industrial tribunal N (BRIT) = Tribunale m Amministrativo Regionale

industrial unrest N (BRIT) agitazione f (sindacale)

industrious [ɪnˈdʌstrɪəs] ADJ industrioso(-a), assiduo(-a)

industry [ˈɪndəstrɪ] N industria; (diligence) operosità

inebriated [ɪˈniːbrɪeɪtɪd] ADJ ubriaco(-a)

inedible [ɪnˈedɪbl] ADJ immangiabile; non commestibile

ineffective [ɪnɪˈfektɪv] ADJ inefficace

ineffectual [ɪnɪˈfektʃuəl] ADJ inefficace; incompetente

inefficiency [ɪnɪˈfɪʃənsɪ] N inefficienza

inefficient [ɪnɪˈfɪʃənt] ADJ inefficiente

inelegant [ɪnˈelɪgənt] ADJ poco elegante

ineligible [ɪnˈelɪdʒɪbl] ADJ (candidate) ineleggibile; **to be ~ for sth** non avere il diritto a qc

inept [ɪˈnept] ADJ inetto(-a)

ineptitude [ɪˈneptɪtjuːd] N inettitudine f, stupidità

inequality [ɪnɪˈkwɔlɪtɪ] N ineguaglianza

inequitable [ɪnˈekwɪtəbl] ADJ iniquo(-a)

ineradicable [ɪnɪˈrædɪkəbl] ADJ inestirpabile

inert [ɪˈnəːt] ADJ inerte

inertia [ɪˈnəːʃə] N inerzia

inertia-reel seat belt [ɪˈnəːʃəˈriːl-] N cintura di sicurezza con arrotolatore

inescapable [ɪnɪˈskeɪpəbl] ADJ inevitabile

inessential [ɪnɪˈsenʃl] ADJ non essenziale

inestimable [ɪnˈestɪməbl] ADJ inestimabile, incalcolabile

inevitable [ɪnˈevɪtəbl] ADJ inevitabile

inevitably [ɪnˈevɪtəblɪ] ADV inevitabilmente; **as ~ happens ...** come immancabilmente succede ...

inexact [ɪnɪgˈzækt] ADJ inesatto(-a)

inexcusable [ɪnɪksˈkjuːzəbl] ADJ imperdonabile

inexhaustible [ɪnɪgˈzɔːstɪbl] ADJ inesauribile; (person) instancabile

inexorable [ɪnˈeksərəbl] ADJ inesorabile

inexpensive [ɪnɪkˈspensɪv] ADJ poco costoso(-a)

inexperience [ɪnɪkˈspɪərɪəns] N inesperienza

inexperienced [ɪnɪkˈspɪərɪənst] ADJ inesperto(-a), senza esperienza; **to be ~ in sth** essere poco pratico di qc

inexplicable [ɪnɪkˈsplɪkəbl] ADJ inesplicabile

inexpressible [ɪnɪkˈspresəbl] ADJ inesprimibile

inextricable [ɪnɪkˈstrɪkəbl] ADJ inestricabile

infallibility [ɪnfæləˈbɪlɪtɪ] N infallibilità

infallible [ɪnˈfælɪbl] ADJ infallibile

infamous [ˈɪnfəməs] ADJ infame

infamy [ˈɪnfəmɪ] N infamia

infancy [ˈɪnfənsɪ] N infanzia

infant [ˈɪnfənt] N bambino(-a)

infantile [ˈɪnfəntaɪl] ADJ infantile

infant mortality N mortalità infantile

infantry [ˈɪnfəntrɪ] N fanteria

infantryman [ˈɪnfəntrɪmən] N (irreg) fante m

infant school N (BRIT) scuola elementare (per bambini dall'età di 5 a 7 anni)

infatuated [ɪnˈfætjueɪtɪd] ADJ: **~ with** infatuato(-a) di; **to become ~ (with sb)** infatuarsi (di qn)

infatuation [ɪnfætjuˈeɪʃən] N infatuazione f

infect [ɪnˈfekt] VT infettare; **infected with** (illness) affetto(-a) da; **to become infected** (wound) infettarsi

615

infection [ɪnˈfɛkʃən] N infezione f
infectious [ɪnˈfɛkʃəs] ADJ (disease) infettivo(-a), contagioso(-a); (person, laughter, enthusiasm) contagioso(-a)
infer [ɪnˈfəːʳ] VT: **to ~ (from)** dedurre (da), concludere (da)
inference [ˈɪnfərəns] N deduzione f, conclusione f
inferior [ɪnˈfɪərɪəʳ] ADJ inferiore; (goods) di qualità scadente ▶ N inferiore mf; (in rank) subalterno(-a); **to feel ~** sentirsi inferiore
inferiority [ɪnfɪərɪˈɔrətɪ] N inferiorità
inferiority complex N complesso di inferiorità
infernal [ɪnˈfəːnl] ADJ infernale
inferno [ɪnˈfəːnəu] N inferno
infertile [ɪnˈfəːtaɪl] ADJ sterile
infertility [ɪnfəːˈtɪlɪtɪ] N sterilità
infested [ɪnˈfɛstɪd] ADJ: **~ (with)** infestato(-a) (di)
infidelity [ɪnfɪˈdɛlɪtɪ] N infedeltà
in-fighting [ˈɪnfaɪtɪŋ] N lotte fpl intestine
infiltrate [ˈɪnfɪltreɪt] VT (troops etc) far penetrare; (enemy line etc) infiltrare ▶ VI infiltrarsi
infinite [ˈɪnfɪnɪt] ADJ infinito(-a); **an ~ amount of time/money** un'illimitata quantità di tempo/denaro
infinitely [ˈɪnfɪnɪtlɪ] ADV infinitamente
infinitesimal [ɪnfɪnɪˈtɛsɪməl] ADJ infinitesimale
infinitive [ɪnˈfɪnɪtɪv] N infinito
infinity [ɪnˈfɪnɪtɪ] N infinità; (also Math) infinito
infirm [ɪnˈfəːm] ADJ infermo(-a)
infirmary [ɪnˈfəːmərɪ] N ospedale m; (in school, factory) infermeria
infirmity [ɪnˈfəːmɪtɪ] N infermità f inv
inflamed [ɪnˈfleɪmd] ADJ infiammato(-a)
inflammable [ɪnˈflæməbl] ADJ infiammabile
inflammation [ɪnfləˈmeɪʃən] N infiammazione f
inflammatory [ɪnˈflæmətərɪ] ADJ (speech) incendiario(-a)
inflatable [ɪnˈfleɪtəbl] ADJ gonfiabile
inflate [ɪnˈfleɪt] VT (tyre, balloon) gonfiare; (fig) esagerare; gonfiare; **to ~ the currency** far ricorso all'inflazione
inflated [ɪnˈfleɪtɪd] ADJ (style) gonfio(-a); (value) esagerato(-a)
inflation [ɪnˈfleɪʃən] N (Econ) inflazione f
inflationary [ɪnˈfleɪʃənərɪ] ADJ inflazionistico(-a)
inflexible [ɪnˈflɛksɪbl] ADJ inflessibile, rigido(-a)
inflict [ɪnˈflɪkt] VT: **to ~ on** infliggere a
infliction [ɪnˈflɪkʃən] N inflizione f; afflizione f
in-flight [ˈɪnflaɪt] ADJ a bordo

inflow [ˈɪnfləu] N afflusso
influence [ˈɪnfluəns] N influenza ▶ VT influenzare; **under the ~ of** sotto l'influenza di; **under the ~ of alcohol** sotto l'influenza or l'effetto dell'alcool
influential [ɪnfluˈɛnʃl] ADJ influente
influenza [ɪnfluˈɛnzə] N (Med) influenza
influx [ˈɪnflʌks] N afflusso
info [ˈɪnfəu] N (col) = **information**
inform [ɪnˈfɔːm] VT: **to ~ sb (of)** informare qn (di) ▶ VI: **to ~ on sb** denunciare qn; **to ~ sb about** mettere qn al corrente di
informal [ɪnˈfɔːml] ADJ (person, manner) alla buona, semplice; (visit, discussion) informale; (announcement, invitation) non ufficiale; **"dress ~"** "non è richiesto l'abito scuro"; **~ language** linguaggio colloquiale
informality [ɪnfɔːˈmælɪtɪ] N semplicità, informalità; carattere m non ufficiale
informally [ɪnˈfɔːməlɪ] ADV senza cerimonie; (invite) in modo non ufficiale
informant [ɪnˈfɔːmənt] N informatore(-trice)
informatics [ɪnfəˈmætɪks] N informatica
information [ɪnfəˈmeɪʃən] N informazioni fpl; particolari mpl; **to get ~ on** informarsi su; **a piece of ~** un'informazione; **for your ~** a titolo d'informazione, per sua informazione
information bureau N ufficio m informazioni inv
information office N ufficio m informazioni inv
information processing N elaborazione f delle informazioni
information retrieval N ricupero delle informazioni
information superhighway N autostrada informatica
information technology N informatica
informative [ɪnˈfɔːmətɪv] ADJ istruttivo(-a)
informed [ɪnˈfɔːmd] ADJ (observer) (ben) informato(-a); **an ~ guess** un'ipotesi fondata
informer [ɪnˈfɔːməʳ] N informatore(-trice)
infra dig [ˈɪnfrəˈdɪg] ADJ ABBR (col: = infra dignitatem: beneath one's dignity) indecoroso(-a)
infra-red [ɪnfrəˈrɛd] ADJ infrarosso(-a)
infrastructure [ˈɪnfrəstrʌktʃəʳ] N infrastruttura
infrequent [ɪnˈfriːkwənt] ADJ infrequente, raro(-a)
infringe [ɪnˈfrɪndʒ] VT infrangere ▶ VI: **to ~ on** calpestare
infringement [ɪnˈfrɪndʒmənt] N: **~ (of)** infrazione f (di)
infuriate [ɪnˈfjuərɪeɪt] VT rendere furioso(-a)
infuriating [ɪnˈfjuərɪeɪtɪŋ] ADJ molto irritante

infuse [ɪn'fjuːz] vt (*with courage, enthusiasm*): **to ~ sb with sth** infondere qc a qn, riempire qn di qc

infusion [ɪn'fjuːʒən] N (*tea etc*) infuso, infusione f

ingenious [ɪn'dʒiːnjəs] ADJ ingegnoso(-a)

ingenuity [ɪndʒɪ'njuːɪtɪ] N ingegnosità

ingenuous [ɪn'dʒɛnjuəs] ADJ ingenuo(-a)

ingot ['ɪŋgət] N lingotto

ingrained [ɪn'greɪnd] ADJ radicato(-a)

ingratiate [ɪn'greɪʃɪeɪt] vt: **to ~ o.s. with sb** ingraziarsi qn

ingratiating [ɪn'greɪʃɪeɪtɪŋ] ADJ (*smile, speech*) suadente, cattivante; (*person*) compiacente

ingratitude [ɪn'grætɪtjuːd] N ingratitudine f

ingredient [ɪn'griːdɪənt] N ingrediente m; elemento

ingrowing ['ɪngrəuɪŋ], **ingrown** ['ɪngrəun] ADJ: **~ (toe)nail** unghia incarnita

inhabit [ɪn'hæbɪt] vt abitare

inhabitable [ɪn'hæbɪtəbl] ADJ abitabile

inhabitant [ɪn'hæbɪtnt] N abitante mf

inhale [ɪn'heɪl] vt inalare ▶ vi (*in smoking*) aspirare

inhaler [ɪn'heɪləʳ] N inalatore m

inherent [ɪn'hɪərənt] ADJ: **~ (in or to)** inerente (a)

inherently [ɪn'hɪərəntlɪ] ADV (*easy, difficult*) di per sé, di per se stesso(-a); **~ lazy** pigro di natura

inherit [ɪn'hɛrɪt] vt ereditare

inheritance [ɪn'hɛrɪtəns] N eredità

inhibit [ɪn'hɪbɪt] vt (*Psych*) inibire; **to ~ sb from doing** impedire a qn di fare

inhibited [ɪn'hɪbɪtɪd] ADJ (*person*) inibito(-a)

inhibiting [ɪn'hɪbɪtɪŋ] ADJ che inibisce

inhibition [ɪnhɪ'bɪʃən] N inibizione f

inhospitable [ɪnhɔs'pɪtəbl] ADJ inospitale

in-house ['ɪn'haus] ADJ effettuato(-a) da personale interno, interno(-a) ▶ ADV (*training*) all'interno dell'azienda

inhuman [ɪn'hjuːmən] ADJ inumano(-a), disumano(-a)

inhumane [ɪnhjuː'meɪn] ADJ inumano(-a), disumano(-a)

inimitable [ɪ'nɪmɪtəbl] ADJ inimitabile

iniquity [ɪ'nɪkwɪtɪ] N iniquità f inv

initial [ɪ'nɪʃl] ADJ iniziale ▶ N iniziale f ▶ vt siglare; **initials** NPL (*of name*) iniziali fpl; (*as signature*) sigla

initialize [ɪ'nɪʃəlaɪz] vt (*Comput*) inizializzare

initially [ɪ'nɪʃəlɪ] ADV inizialmente, all'inizio

initiate [ɪ'nɪʃɪeɪt] vt (*start*) avviare; intraprendere; iniziare; (*person*) iniziare; **to ~ sb into sth** iniziare qn a qc; **to ~ sb into a secret** mettere qn a parte di un segreto; **to ~ proceedings against sb** (*Law*) intentare causa a or contro qn

initiation [ɪnɪʃɪ'eɪʃən] N iniziazione f

initiative [ɪ'nɪʃətɪv] N iniziativa; **to take the ~** prendere l'iniziativa

inject [ɪn'dʒɛkt] vt (*liquid*) iniettare; (*person*) fare un'iniezione a; (*fig: money*): **to ~ sb with sth** fare a qn un'iniezione di qc; **to ~ into** immettere in

injection [ɪn'dʒɛkʃən] N iniezione f, puntura; **to have an ~** farsi fare un'iniezione or una puntura

injudicious [ɪndʒu'dɪʃəs] ADJ poco saggio(-a)

injunction [ɪn'dʒʌŋkʃən] N (*Law*) ingiunzione f, intimazione f

injure ['ɪndʒəʳ] vt ferire; (*wrong*) fare male or torto a; (*damage: reputation etc*) nuocere a; (: *feelings*) offendere; **to ~ o.s.** farsi male

injured ['ɪndʒəd] ADJ (*person, leg etc*) ferito(-a); (*tone, feelings*) offeso(-a); **~ party** (*Law*) parte f lesa

injurious [ɪn'dʒuərɪəs] ADJ: **~ (to)** nocivo(-a) (a), pregiudizievole (per)

injury ['ɪndʒərɪ] N ferita; (*wrong*) torto; **to escape without ~** rimanere illeso

injury time N (*Sport*) tempo di ricupero

injustice [ɪn'dʒʌstɪs] N ingiustizia; **you do me an ~** mi fa un torto, è ingiusto verso di me

ink [ɪŋk] N inchiostro

ink-jet printer ['ɪŋkdʒɛt-] N stampante f a getto d'inchiostro

inkling ['ɪŋklɪŋ] N sentore m, vaga idea

inkpad ['ɪŋkpæd] N tampone m, cuscinetto per timbri

inky ['ɪŋkɪ] ADJ macchiato(-a) or sporco(-a) d'inchiostro

inlaid ['ɪnleɪd] ADJ incrostato(-a); (*table etc*) intarsiato(-a)

inland ADJ ['ɪnlənd] interno(-a) ▶ ADV [ɪn'lænd] all'interno; **~ waterways** canali e fiumi mpl navigabili

Inland Revenue N (*BRIT*) Fisco

in-laws ['ɪnlɔːz] NPL suoceri mpl; famiglia del marito (*or* della moglie)

inlet ['ɪnlɛt] N (*Geo*) insenatura, baia

inlet pipe N (*Tech*) tubo d'immissione

inmate ['ɪnmeɪt] N (*in prison*) carcerato(-a); (*in asylum*) ricoverato(-a)

inmost ['ɪnməust] ADJ più profondo(-a), più intimo(-a)

inn [ɪn] N locanda

innards ['ɪnədz] NPL (*col*) interiora fpl, budella fpl

innate [ɪ'neɪt] ADJ innato(-a)

inner ['ɪnəʳ] ADJ interno(-a), interiore

inner city N centro di una zona urbana

innermost ['ɪnəməust] ADJ = **inmost**

inner tube N camera d'aria

inning ['ɪnɪŋ] N (*US Baseball*) ripresa; **innings** (*Cricket*) turno di battuta; (*BRIT fig*) **he has had a good innings** ha avuto molto dalla vita

innocence ['ɪnəsns] N innocenza

innocent ['ɪnəsnt] ADJ innocente

innocuous [ɪ'nɔkjuəs] ADJ innocuo(-a)

innovation [ɪnəu'veɪʃən] N innovazione f

innovative ['ɪnəu'veɪtɪv] ADJ innovativo(-a)

innuendo [ɪnju'ɛndəu] (pl **innuendoes**) N insinuazione f

innumerable [ɪ'nju:mrəbl] ADJ innumerevole

inoculate [ɪ'nɔkjuleɪt] VT: **to ~ sb with sth/against sth** inoculare qc a qn/qn contro qc

inoculation [ɪnɔkju'leɪʃən] N inoculazione f

inoffensive [ɪnə'fɛnsɪv] ADJ inoffensivo(-a), innocuo(-a)

inopportune [ɪn'ɔpətju:n] ADJ inopportuno(-a)

inordinate [ɪ'nɔ:dɪnɪt] ADJ eccessivo(-a)

inordinately [ɪ'nɔ:dɪnətlɪ] ADV smoderatamente

inorganic [ɪnɔ:'gænɪk] ADJ inorganico(-a)

in-patient ['ɪnpeɪʃənt] N ricoverato(-a)

input ['ɪnput] N (Elec) energia, potenza; (of machine) alimentazione f; (of computer) input m ▶ VT (Comput) inserire, introdurre

inquest ['ɪnkwɛst] N inchiesta

inquire [ɪn'kwaɪəʳ] VI informarsi ▶ VT domandare, informarsi di or su; **to ~ about** informarsi di or su, chiedere informazioni su; **to ~ when/where/whether** informarsi di quando/su dove/se
  ▶ **inquire after** VT FUS (person) chiedere di; (sb's health) informarsi di
  ▶ **inquire into** VT FUS indagare su, fare delle indagini or ricerche su

inquiring [ɪn'kwaɪərɪŋ] ADJ (mind) inquisitivo(-a)

inquiry [ɪn'kwaɪərɪ] N domanda; (Law) indagine f, investigazione f; **"inquiries"** "informazioni"; **to hold an ~ into sth** fare un'inchiesta su qc

inquiry desk N (BRIT) banco delle informazioni

inquiry office N (BRIT) ufficio m informazioni inv

inquisition [ɪnkwɪ'zɪʃən] N inquisizione f, inchiesta; (Rel): **the I~** l'Inquisizione

inquisitive [ɪn'kwɪzɪtɪv] ADJ curioso(-a)

inroads ['ɪnrəudz] NPL: **to make ~ into** (savings, supplies) intaccare (seriamente)

ins. ABBR = **inches**

insane [ɪn'seɪn] ADJ matto(-a), pazzo(-a); (Med) alienato(-a)

insanitary [ɪn'sænɪtərɪ] ADJ insalubre

insanity [ɪn'sænɪtɪ] N follia; (Med) alienazione f mentale

insatiable [ɪn'seɪʃəbl] ADJ insaziabile

inscribe [ɪn'skraɪb] VT iscrivere; (book etc): **to ~ (to sb)** dedicare (a qn)

inscription [ɪn'skrɪpʃən] N iscrizione f; (in book) dedica

inscrutable [ɪn'skru:təbl] ADJ imperscrutabile

inseam ['ɪnsi:m] N (US): **~ measurement** lunghezza interna

insect ['ɪnsɛkt] N insetto

insect bite N puntura or morsicatura di insetto

insecticide [ɪn'sɛktɪsaɪd] N insetticida m

insect repellent N insettifugo

insecure [ɪnsɪ'kjuəʳ] ADJ malsicuro(-a); (person) insicuro(-a)

insecurity [ɪnsɪ'kjuərɪtɪ] N mancanza di sicurezza

insensible [ɪn'sɛnsɪbl] ADJ insensibile; (unconscious) privo(-a) di sensi

insensitive [ɪn'sɛnsɪtɪv] ADJ insensibile

insensitivity [ɪnsɛnsɪ'tɪvɪtɪ] N mancanza di sensibilità

inseparable [ɪn'sɛprəbl] ADJ inseparabile

insert VT [ɪn'sə:t] inserire, introdurre ▶ N ['ɪnsə:t] inserto

insertion [ɪn'sə:ʃən] N inserzione f

in-service ['ɪn'sə:vɪs] ADJ (course, training) dopo l'assunzione

inshore [ɪn'ʃɔ:ʳ] ADJ costiero(-a) ▶ ADV presso la riva; verso la riva

inside ['ɪn'saɪd] N interno, parte f interiore; (of road: BRIT) sinistra; (: US, in Europe etc) destra ▶ ADJ interno(-a), interiore ▶ ADV dentro, all'interno ▶ PREP dentro, all'interno di; (of time): **~ 10 minutes** entro 10 minuti; **insides** NPL (col) ventre m; **~ out** adv alla rovescia; **to turn sth ~ out** rivoltare qc; **to know sth ~ out** conoscere qc a fondo; **~ information** informazioni fpl riservate; **~ story** storia segreta

inside forward N (Sport) mezzala, interno

inside lane N (Aut) corsia di marcia

inside leg measurement N (BRIT) lunghezza interna

insider [ɪn'saɪdəʳ] N uno(-a) che ha le mani in pasta

insider dealing, insider trading N (Stock Exchange) insider trading m inv

insidious [ɪn'sɪdɪəs] ADJ insidioso(-a)

insight ['ɪnsaɪt] N acume m, perspicacia; (glimpse, idea) percezione f; **to gain** or **get an ~ into sth** potersi render conto di qc

insignia [ɪn'sɪgnɪə] NPL insegne fpl

insignificant [ɪnsɪg'nɪfɪknt] ADJ insignificante

insincere [ɪnsɪn'sɪəʳ] ADJ insincero(-a)

insincerity [ɪnsɪn'sɛrɪtɪ] N falsità, insincerità

insinuate [ɪn'sɪnjueɪt] VT insinuare

insinuation [ɪnsɪnju'eɪʃən] N insinuazione f

insipid [ɪn'sɪpɪd] ADJ insipido(-a), insulso(-a)

insist [ɪn'sɪst] VI insistere; **to ~ on doing** insistere per fare; **to ~ that** insistere perché + sub; (claim) sostenere che

insistence [ɪn'sɪstəns] N insistenza
insistent [ɪn'sɪstənt] ADJ insistente
insofar [ɪnsəu'fɑː^r] CONJ: ~ **as** in quanto
insole ['ɪnsəul] N soletta; (fixed part of shoe) tramezza
insolence ['ɪnsələns] N insolenza
insolent ['ɪnsələnt] ADJ insolente
insoluble [ɪn'sɔljubl] ADJ insolubile
insolvency [ɪn'sɔlvənsɪ] N insolvenza
insolvent [ɪn'sɔlvənt] ADJ insolvente
insomnia [ɪn'sɔmnɪə] N insonnia
insomniac [ɪn'sɔmnɪæk] N chi soffre di insonnia
inspect [ɪn'spɛkt] VT ispezionare; (BRIT: ticket) controllare
inspection [ɪn'spɛkʃən] N ispezione f; controllo
inspector [ɪn'spɛktə^r] N ispettore(-trice); (BRIT: on buses, trains) controllore m
inspiration [ɪnspə'reɪʃən] N ispirazione f
inspire [ɪn'spaɪə^r] VT ispirare
inspired [ɪn'spaɪəd] ADJ (writer, book etc) ispirato(-a); **in an ~ moment** in un momento d'ispirazione
inspiring [ɪn'spaɪərɪŋ] ADJ stimolante
inst. [ɪnst] ABBR (BRIT Comm: = instant) c.m. (= corrente mese)
instability [ɪnstə'bɪlɪtɪ] N instabilità
install [ɪn'stɔːl], (US) **instal** VT installare
installation [ɪnstə'leɪʃən] N installazione f
installment plan N (US) acquisto a rate
instalment, (US) **installment** [ɪn'stɔːlmənt] N rata; (of TV serial etc) puntata; **in instalments** (pay) a rate; (receive) una parte per volta (: publication) a fascicoli
instance ['ɪnstəns] N esempio, caso; **for ~** per or ad esempio; **in that ~** in quel caso; **in the first ~** in primo luogo
instant ['ɪnstənt] N istante m, attimo ▶ ADJ immediato(-a); urgente; (coffee, food) in polvere; **the 10th ~** il 10 corrente (mese)
instantaneous [ɪnstən'teɪnɪəs] ADJ istantaneo(-a)
instantly ['ɪnstəntlɪ] ADV immediatamente, subito
instant message N messaggio istantaneo
instant messaging N messaggeria istantanea
instant replay N (US TV) replay m inv
instead [ɪn'stɛd] ADV invece; ~ **of** invece di; ~ **of sb** al posto di qn
instep ['ɪnstɛp] N collo del piede; (of shoe) collo della scarpa
instigate ['ɪnstɪgeɪt] VT (rebellion, strike, crime) istigare a; (new ideas etc) promuovere
instigation [ɪnstɪ'geɪʃən] N istigazione f; **at sb's ~** per or in seguito al suggerimento di qn
instil [ɪn'stɪl] VT: **to ~ (into)** inculcare (in)
instinct ['ɪnstɪŋkt] N istinto

instinctive [ɪn'stɪŋktɪv] ADJ istintivo(-a)
instinctively [ɪn'stɪŋktɪvlɪ] ADV per istinto
institute ['ɪnstɪtjuːt] N istituto ▶ VT istituire, stabilire; (inquiry) avviare; (proceedings) iniziare
institution [ɪnstɪ'tjuːʃən] N istituzione f; istituto (d'istruzione); istituto (psichiatrico)
institutional [ɪnstɪ'tjuːʃnl] ADJ istituzionale; ~ **care** assistenza presso un istituto
instruct [ɪn'strʌkt] VT istruire; **to ~ sb in sth** insegnare qc a qn; **to ~ sb to do** dare ordini a qn di fare
instruction [ɪn'strʌkʃən] N istruzione f; **instructions (for use)** istruzioni per l'uso
instruction book N libretto di istruzioni
instructive [ɪn'strʌktɪv] ADJ istruttivo(-a)
instructor [ɪn'strʌktə^r] N istruttore(-trice); (for skiing) maestro(-a)
instrument ['ɪnstrumənt] N strumento
instrumental [ɪnstru'mɛntl] ADJ (Mus) strumentale; **to be ~ in sth/in doing sth** contribuire fattivamente a qc/a fare qc
instrumentalist [ɪnstru'mɛntəlɪst] N strumentista mf
instrument panel N quadro m, portastrumenti inv
insubordinate [ɪnsə'bɔːdənɪt] ADJ insubordinato(-a)
insubordination [ɪnsəbɔːdə'neɪʃən] N insubordinazione f
insufferable [ɪn'sʌfrəbl] ADJ insopportabile
insufficient [ɪnsə'fɪʃənt] ADJ insufficiente
insufficiently [ɪnsə'fɪʃəntlɪ] ADV in modo insufficiente
insular ['ɪnsjulə^r] ADJ insulare; (person) di mente ristretta
insulate ['ɪnsjuleɪt] VT isolare
insulating tape ['ɪnsjuleɪtɪŋ-] N nastro isolante
insulation [ɪnsju'leɪʃən] N isolamento
insulin ['ɪnsjulɪn] N insulina
insult N ['ɪnsʌlt] insulto, affronto ▶ VT [ɪn'sʌlt] insultare
insulting [ɪn'sʌltɪŋ] ADJ offensivo(-a), ingiurioso(-a)
insuperable [ɪn'sjuːprəbl] ADJ insormontabile, insuperabile
insurance [ɪn'ʃuərəns] N assicurazione f; **fire/life ~** assicurazione contro gli incendi/sulla vita; **to take out ~ (against)** fare un'assicurazione (contro), assicurarsi (contro)
insurance agent N agente m d'assicurazioni
insurance broker N broker m inv d'assicurazioni
insurance company N società di assicurazioni
insurance policy N polizza d'assicurazione

insurance premium N premio assicurativo
insure [ɪnˈʃʊəʳ] VT assicurare; **to ~ sb** or **sb's life** assicurare qn sulla vita; **to be insured for £5000** essere assicurato per 5000 sterline
insured [ɪnˈʃʊəd] N: **the ~** l'assicurato(-a)
insurer [ɪnˈʃʊərəʳ] N assicuratore(-trice)
insurgent [ɪnˈsəːdʒənt] ADJ ribelle ▶ N insorto(-a), rivoltoso(-a)
insurmountable [ɪnsəˈmauntəbl] ADJ insormontabile
insurrection [ɪnsəˈrɛkʃən] N insurrezione f
intact [ɪnˈtækt] ADJ intatto(-a)
intake [ˈɪnteɪk] N (Tech) immissione f; (of food) consumo; (BRIT: of pupils etc) afflusso
intangible [ɪnˈtændʒɪbl] ADJ intangibile
integral [ˈɪntɪɡrəl] ADJ integrale; (part) integrante
integrate [ˈɪntɪɡreɪt] VT integrare ▶ VI integrarsi
integrated circuit N (Comput) circuito integrato
integration [ɪntɪˈɡreɪʃən] N integrazione f; **racial ~** integrazione razziale
integrity [ɪnˈtɛɡrɪtɪ] N integrità
intellect [ˈɪntəlɛkt] N intelletto
intellectual [ɪntəˈlɛktjuəl] ADJ, N intellettuale (mf)
intelligence [ɪnˈtɛlɪdʒəns] N intelligenza; (Mil etc) informazioni fpl
intelligence quotient N quoziente m d'intelligenza
Intelligence Service N servizio segreto
intelligence test N test m inv d'intelligenza
intelligent [ɪnˈtɛlɪdʒənt] ADJ intelligente
intelligible [ɪnˈtɛlɪdʒɪbl] ADJ intelligibile
intemperate [ɪnˈtɛmpərət] ADJ immoderato(-a); (drinking too much) intemperante nel bere
intend [ɪnˈtɛnd] VT (gift etc): **to ~ sth for** destinare qc a; **to ~ to do** aver l'intenzione di fare
intended [ɪnˈtɛndɪd] ADJ (insult) intenzionale; (effect) voluto(-a); (journey, route) progettato(-a)
intense [ɪnˈtɛns] ADJ intenso(-a); (person) di forti sentimenti
intensely [ɪnˈtɛnslɪ] ADV intensamente; profondamente
intensify [ɪnˈtɛnsɪfaɪ] VT intensificare
intensity [ɪnˈtɛnsɪtɪ] N intensità
intensive [ɪnˈtɛnsɪv] ADJ intensivo(-a)
intensive care N terapia intensiva; **~ unit** reparto terapia intensiva
intent [ɪnˈtɛnt] N intenzione f ▶ ADJ: **~ (on)** intento(-a) (a), immerso(-a) (in); **to all intents and purposes** a tutti gli effetti; **to be ~ on doing sth** essere deciso a fare qc
intention [ɪnˈtɛnʃən] N intenzione f

intentional [ɪnˈtɛnʃənl] ADJ intenzionale, deliberato(-a)
intentionally [ɪnˈtɛnʃənəlɪ] ADV apposta
intently [ɪnˈtɛntlɪ] ADV attentamente
inter [ɪnˈtəːʳ] VT sotterrare
interact [ɪntərˈækt] VI agire reciprocamente, interagire
interaction [ɪntərˈækʃən] N azione f reciproca, interazione f
interactive [ɪntərˈæktɪv] ADJ (Comput) interattivo(-a)
intercede [ɪntəˈsiːd] VI: **to ~ (with sb/on behalf of sb)** intercedere (presso qn/a favore di qn)
intercept [ɪntəˈsɛpt] VT intercettare; (person) fermare
interception [ɪntəˈsɛpʃən] N intercettamento
interchange N [ˈɪntətʃeɪndʒ] (exchange) scambio; (on motorway) incrocio pluridirezionale ▶ VT [ɪntəˈtʃeɪndʒ] scambiare; sostituire l'uno(-a) per l'altro(-a)
interchangeable [ɪntəˈtʃeɪndʒəbl] ADJ intercambiabile
intercity [ɪntəˈsɪtɪ] ADJ: **~ (train)** = (treno) rapido
intercom [ˈɪntəkɔm] N interfono
interconnect [ɪntəkəˈnɛkt] VI (rooms) essere in comunicazione
intercontinental [ˈɪntəkɔntɪˈnɛntl] ADJ intercontinentale
intercourse [ˈɪntəkɔːs] N rapporti mpl; (sexual intercourse) rapporti sessuali
interdependent [ɪntədɪˈpɛndənt] ADJ interdipendente
interest [ˈɪntrɪst] N interesse m; (Comm: stake, share) interessi mpl ▶ VT interessare; **compound/simple ~** interesse composto/semplice; **business interests** attività fpl commerciali; **British interests in the Middle East** gli interessi (commerciali) britannici nel Medio Oriente
interested [ˈɪntrɪstɪd] ADJ interessato(-a); **to be ~ in** interessarsi di
interest-free [ˈɪntrɪstˈfriː] ADJ senza interesse
interesting [ˈɪntrɪstɪŋ] ADJ interessante
interest rate N tasso di interesse
interface [ˈɪntəfeɪs] N (Comput) interfaccia
interfere [ɪntəˈfɪəʳ] VI: **to ~ (in)** (quarrel, other people's business) immischiarsi (in); **to ~ with** (object) toccare; (plans, duty) interferire con
interference [ɪntəˈfɪərəns] N interferenza
interfering [ɪntəˈfɪərɪŋ] ADJ invadente
interim [ˈɪntərɪm] ADJ provvisorio(-a) ▶ N: **in the ~** nel frattempo; **~ dividend** (Comm) acconto di dividendo
interior [ɪnˈtɪərɪəʳ] N interno; (of country) entroterra ▶ ADJ interiore, interno(-a); (minister) degli Interni

interior decorator, interior designer N decoratore(-trice) (d'interni)

interior design N architettura d'interni

interjection [ɪntə'dʒɛkʃən] N interiezione f

interlock [ɪntə'lɔk] VI ingranarsi ▶ VT ingranare

interloper ['ɪntələupə'] N intruso(-a)

interlude ['ɪntəlu:d] N intervallo; (Theat) intermezzo

intermarry [ɪntə'mærɪ] VI imparentarsi per mezzo di matrimonio; sposarsi tra parenti

intermediary [ɪntə'mi:dɪərɪ] N intermediario(-a)

intermediate [ɪntə'mi:dɪət] ADJ intermedio(-a); (Scol: course, level) medio(-a)

interment [ɪn'tə:mənt] N (formal) inumazione f

interminable [ɪn'tə:mɪnəbl] ADJ interminabile

intermission [ɪntə'mɪʃən] N pausa; (Theat, Cine) intermissione f, intervallo

intermittent [ɪntə'mɪtnt] ADJ intermittente

intermittently [ɪntə'mɪtntlɪ] ADV a intermittenza

intern VT [ɪn'tə:n] internare ▶ N ['ɪntə:n] (US) medico interno

internal [ɪn'tə:nl] ADJ interno(-a); **~ injuries** lesioni fpl interne

internally [ɪn'tə:nəlɪ] ADV all'interno; "**not to be taken ~**" "per uso esterno"

Internal Revenue, Internal Revenue Service N (US) Fisco

international [ɪntə'næʃənl] ADJ internazionale ▶ N (Brit Sport) incontro internazionale

International Atomic Energy Agency N Agenzia Internazionale per l'Energia Atomica

International Court of Justice N Corte f Internazionale di Giustizia

international date line N linea del cambiamento di data

internationally [ɪntə'næʃnəlɪ] ADV a livello internazionale

International Monetary Fund N Fondo monetario internazionale

international relations NPL rapporti mpl internazionali

internecine [ɪntə'ni:saɪn] ADJ sanguinoso(-a)

internee [ɪntə:'ni:] N internato(-a)

Internet ['ɪntənɛt] N: **the ~** Internet f

Internet café N cybercaffè m inv

Internet Service Provider N Provider m inv

Internet user N utente mf Internet

internment [ɪn'tə:nmənt] N internamento

interplay ['ɪntəpleɪ] N azione e reazione f

Interpol ['ɪntəpɔl] N Interpol f

interpret [ɪn'tə:prɪt] VT interpretare ▶ VI fare da interprete

interpretation [ɪntə:prɪ'teɪʃən] N interpretazione f

interpreter [ɪn'tə:prɪtə'] N interprete mf

interpreting [ɪn'tə:prɪtɪŋ] N (profession) interpretariato

interrelated [ɪntərɪ'leɪtɪd] ADJ correlato(-a)

interrogate [ɪn'tɛrəugeɪt] VT interrogare

interrogation [ɪntɛrəu'geɪʃən] N interrogazione f; (of suspect etc) interrogatorio

interrogative [ɪntə'rɔgətɪv] ADJ interrogativo(-a) ▶ N (Ling) interrogativo

interrogator [ɪn'tɛrəgeɪtə'] N interrogante mf

interrupt [ɪntə'rʌpt] VT, VI interrompere

interruption [ɪntə'rʌpʃən] N interruzione f

intersect [ɪntə'sɛkt] VT intersecare ▶ VI (roads) intersecarsi

intersection [ɪntə'sɛkʃən] N intersezione f; (of roads) incrocio

intersperse [ɪntə'spə:s] VT: **to ~ with** costellare di

interstate ['ɪntəsteɪt] (US) N fra stati

intertwine [ɪntə'twaɪn] VT intrecciare ▶ VI intrecciarsi

interval ['ɪntəvl] N intervallo; (Brit Scol) ricreazione f, intervallo; **bright intervals** (in weather) schiarite fpl; **at intervals** a intervalli

intervene [ɪntə'vi:n] VI (time) intercorrere; (event, person) intervenire

intervention [ɪntə'vɛnʃən] N intervento

interview ['ɪntəvju:] N (Radio, TV etc) intervista; (for job) colloquio ▶ VT intervistare; avere un colloquio con

interviewee [ɪntəvju'i:] N (TV) intervistato(-a); (for job) chi si presenta ad un colloquio di lavoro

interviewer ['ɪntəvju:ə'] N intervistatore(-trice)

intestate [ɪn'tɛsteɪt] ADJ intestato(-a)

intestinal [ɪn'tɛstɪnl] ADJ intestinale

intestine [ɪn'tɛstɪn] N intestino; **large/ small ~** intestino crasso/tenue

intimacy ['ɪntɪməsɪ] N intimità

intimate ADJ ['ɪntɪmət] intimo(-a); (knowledge) profondo(-a) ▶ VT ['ɪntɪmeɪt] lasciar capire

intimately ['ɪntɪmɪtlɪ] ADV intimamente

intimation [ɪntɪ'meɪʃən] N annuncio

intimidate [ɪn'tɪmɪdeɪt] VT intimidire, intimorire

intimidating [ɪn'tɪmɪdeɪtɪŋ] ADJ (sight) spaventoso(-a); (appearance, figure) minaccioso(-a)

intimidation [ɪntɪmɪ'deɪʃən] N intimidazione f

into ['ɪntu] PREP dentro, in; **come ~ the house** entra in casa; **he worked late ~ the night** lavorò fino a tarda notte; **~ pieces**

a pezzi; ~ **Italian** in italiano; **to change pounds ~ dollars** cambiare delle sterline in dollari

intolerable [ɪn'tɔlərəbl] ADJ intollerabile

intolerance [ɪn'tɔlərns] N intolleranza

intolerant [ɪn'tɔlərnt] ADJ: **~ (of)** intollerante (di)

intonation [ɪntəu'neɪʃən] N intonazione f

intoxicate [ɪn'tɔksɪkeɪt] VT inebriare

intoxicated [ɪn'tɔksɪkeɪtɪd] ADJ inebriato(-a)

intoxication [ɪntɔksɪ'keɪʃən] N ebbrezza

intractable [ɪn'træktəbl] ADJ intrattabile; (*illness*) difficile da curare; (*problem*) insolubile

intranet ['ɪntrənɛt] N Intranet f

intransigence [ɪn'trænsɪdʒəns] N intransigenza

intransigent [ɪn'trænsɪdʒənt] ADJ intransigente

intransitive [ɪn'trænsɪtɪv] ADJ intransitivo(-a)

intra-uterine device [ɪntrə'juːtəraɪn-] N dispositivo intrauterino

intravenous [ɪntrə'viːnəs] ADJ endovenoso(-a)

in-tray ['ɪntreɪ] N raccoglitore m per le carte in arrivo

intrepid [ɪn'trɛpɪd] ADJ intrepido(-a)

intricacy ['ɪntrɪkəsɪ] N complessità f inv

intricate ['ɪntrɪkət] ADJ intricato(-a), complicato(-a)

intrigue [ɪn'triːg] N intrigo ▶ VT affascinare ▶ VI complottare, tramare

intriguing [ɪn'triːgɪŋ] ADJ affascinante

intrinsic [ɪn'trɪnsɪk] ADJ intrinseco(-a)

introduce [ɪntrə'djuːs] VT introdurre; **to ~ sb (to sb)** presentare qn (a qn); **to ~ sb to** (*pastime, technique*) iniziare qn a; **may I ~ ...?** permette che le presenti ...?

introduction [ɪntrə'dʌkʃən] N introduzione f; (*of person*) presentazione f; (*to new experience*) iniziazione f; **a letter of ~** una lettera di presentazione

introductory [ɪntrə'dʌktərɪ] ADJ introduttivo(-a); **an ~ offer** un'offerta di lancio; **~ remarks** osservazioni fpl preliminari

introspection [ɪntrəu'spɛkʃən] N introspezione f

introspective [ɪntrəu'spɛktɪv] ADJ introspettivo(-a)

introvert ['ɪntrəuvəːt] ADJ, N introverso(-a)

intrude [ɪn'truːd] VI (*person*) intromettersi; **to ~ on** (*person*) importunare; **~ on** or **into** (*conversation*) intromettersi in; **am I intruding?** disturbo?

intruder [ɪn'truːdər] N intruso(-a)

intrusion [ɪn'truːʒən] N intrusione f

intrusive [ɪn'truːsɪv] ADJ importuno(-a)

intuition [ɪntjuː'ɪʃən] N intuizione f

intuitive [ɪn'tjuːɪtɪv] ADJ intuitivo(-a); dotato(-a) di intuito

inundate ['ɪnʌndeɪt] VT: **to ~ with** inondare di

inure [ɪn'juər] VT: **to ~ (to)** assuefare (a)

invade [ɪn'veɪd] VT invadere

invader [ɪn'veɪdər] N invasore m

invalid N ['ɪnvəlɪd] malato(-a); (*with disability*) invalido(-a) ▶ ADJ [ɪn'vælɪd] (*not valid*) invalido(-a), non valido(-a)

invalidate [ɪn'vælɪdeɪt] VT invalidare

invalid chair N (BRIT) sedia a rotelle

invaluable [ɪn'væljuəbl] ADJ prezioso(-a); inestimabile

invariable [ɪn'vɛərɪəbl] ADJ costante, invariabile

invariably [ɪn'vɛərɪəblɪ] ADV invariabilmente; sempre; **she is ~ late** è immancabilmente in ritardo

invasion [ɪn'veɪʒən] N invasione f

invective [ɪn'vɛktɪv] N invettiva

inveigle [ɪn'viːgl] VT: **to ~ sb into (doing) sth** circuire qn per (fargli fare) qc

invent [ɪn'vɛnt] VT inventare

invention [ɪn'vɛnʃən] N invenzione f

inventive [ɪn'vɛntɪv] ADJ inventivo(-a)

inventiveness [ɪn'vɛntɪvnɪs] N inventiva

inventor [ɪn'vɛntər] N inventore m

inventory ['ɪnvəntrɪ] N inventario

inventory control N (*Comm*) controllo delle giacenze

inverse [ɪn'vəːs] ADJ inverso(-a) ▶ N inverso, contrario; **in ~ proportion (to)** in modo inversamente proporzionale (a)

inversely [ɪn'vəːslɪ] ADV inversamente

invert [ɪn'vəːt] VT invertire; (*object*) rovesciare

invertebrate [ɪn'vəːtɪbrɪt] N invertebrato

inverted commas [ɪn'vəːtɪd-] NPL (BRIT) virgolette fpl

invest [ɪn'vɛst] VT investire; (*fig: time, effort*) impiegare; (*endow*): **to ~ sb with sth** investire qn di qc ▶ VI fare investimenti; **to ~ in** investire in, fare (degli) investimenti in; (*acquire*) comprarsi

investigate [ɪn'vɛstɪgeɪt] VT investigare, indagare; (*crime*) fare indagini su

investigation [ɪnvɛstɪ'geɪʃən] N investigazione f; (*of crime*) indagine f

investigative [ɪn'vɛstɪgətɪv] ADJ: **~ journalism** giornalismo investigativo

investigator [ɪn'vɛstɪgeɪtər] N investigatore(-trice); **a private ~** un investigatore privato, un detective

investiture [ɪn'vɛstɪtʃər] N investitura

investment [ɪn'vɛstmənt] N investimento

investment income N reddito da investimenti

investment trust N fondo comune di investimento

investor [ɪn'vɛstə'] N investitore(-trice); (*shareholder*) azionista *mf*

inveterate [ɪn'vɛtərət] ADJ inveterato(-a)

invidious [ɪn'vɪdɪəs] ADJ odioso(-a); (*task*) spiacevole

invigilate [ɪn'vɪdʒɪleɪt] VT, VI (*BRIT Scol*) sorvegliare

invigilator [ɪn'vɪdʒɪleɪtə'] N (*BRIT*) chi sorveglia agli esami

invigorating [ɪn'vɪgəreɪtɪŋ] ADJ stimolante; vivificante

invincible [ɪn'vɪnsɪbl] ADJ invincibile

inviolate [ɪn'vaɪələt] ADJ inviolato(-a)

invisible [ɪn'vɪzɪbl] ADJ invisibile

invisible assets NPL (*BRIT*) beni *mpl* immateriali

invisible ink N inchiostro simpatico

invisible mending N rammendo invisibile

invitation [ɪnvɪ'teɪʃən] N invito; **by ~ only** esclusivamente su *or* per invito; **at sb's ~** dietro invito di qn

invite [ɪn'vaɪt] VT invitare; (*opinions etc*) sollecitare; (*trouble*) provocare; **to ~ sb (to do)** invitare qn (a fare); **to ~ sb to dinner** invitare qn a cena
▶ **invite out** VT invitare fuori
▶ **invite over** VT invitare (a casa)

inviting [ɪn'vaɪtɪŋ] ADJ invitante, attraente

invoice ['ɪnvɔɪs] N fattura ▶ VT fatturare; **to ~ sb for goods** inviare a qn la fattura per le *or* delle merci

invoke [ɪn'vəuk] VT invocare

involuntary [ɪn'vɔləntrɪ] ADJ involontario(-a)

involve [ɪn'vɔlv] VT (*entail*) richiedere, comportare; (*associate*): **to ~ sb (in)** implicare qn (in); coinvolgere qn (in); **to ~ o.s. in sth** (*politics etc*) impegnarsi in qc

involved [ɪn'vɔlvd] ADJ involuto(-a), complesso(-a); **to feel ~** sentirsi coinvolto(-a); **to be ~ in** essere coinvolto(-a) in; **to become ~ with sb** (*socially*) legarsi a qn; (*emotionally*) legarsi sentimentalmente a qn

involvement [ɪn'vɔlvmənt] N implicazione *f*; coinvolgimento; impegno; partecipazione *f*

invulnerable [ɪn'vʌlnərəbl] ADJ invulnerabile

inward ['ɪnwəd] ADJ (*movement*) verso l'interno; (*thought, feeling*) interiore, intimo(-a) ▶ ADV verso l'interno

inwardly ['ɪnwədlɪ] ADV (*feel, think etc*) nell'intimo, entro di sé

inwards ['ɪnwədz] ADV verso l'interno

I/O ABBR (*Comput*: = *input/output*) I/O

IOC N ABBR (= *International Olympic Committee*) CIO *m* (= *Comitato Internazionale Olimpico*)

iodine ['aɪəudi:n] N iodio

IOM ABBR (*BRIT*) = **Isle of Man**

ion ['aɪən] N ione *m*

Ionian Sea [aɪ'əunɪən-] N: **the ~** il mare Ionio

ioniser ['aɪənaɪzə'] N ionizzatore *m*

iota [aɪ'əutə] N (*fig*) briciolo

IOU N ABBR (= *I owe you*) pagherò *m inv*

IOW ABBR (*BRIT*) = **Isle of Wight**

IPA N ABBR (= *International Phonetic Alphabet*) I.P.A. *m*

iPad® ['aɪˌpæd] N iPad® *m inv*

IP address N (*Comput*) indirizzo IP

iPhone® ['aɪˌfəun] N iPhone® *m inv*

iPod® ['aɪpɔd] N iPod® *m inv*, lettore *m* MP3

IQ N ABBR (= *intelligence quotient*) quoziente *m* d'intelligenza

IRA N ABBR (= *Irish Republican Army*) I.R.A. *f*; (*US*) = **individual retirement account**

Iran [ɪ'rɑ:n] N Iran *m*

Iranian [ɪ'reɪnɪən] ADJ iraniano(-a) ▶ N iraniano(-a); (*Ling*) iranico

Iraq [ɪ'rɑ:k] N Iraq *m*

Iraqi [ɪ'rɑ:kɪ] ADJ iracheno(-a) ▶ N iracheno(-a)

irascible [ɪ'ræsɪbl] ADJ irascibile

irate [aɪ'reɪt] ADJ irato(-a)

Ireland ['aɪələnd] N Irlanda; **Republic of ~** Repubblica d'Irlanda, Eire *f*

iris ['aɪrɪs] (*pl* **irises** [-ɪz]) N iride *f*; (*Bot*) giaggiolo, iride

Irish ['aɪrɪʃ] ADJ irlandese ▶ NPL: **the ~** gli Irlandesi

Irishman ['aɪrɪʃmən] N (*irreg*) irlandese *m*

Irish Sea N: **the ~** il mar d'Irlanda

Irishwoman ['aɪrɪʃwumən] N (*irreg*) irlandese *f*

irk [ə:k] VT seccare

irksome ['ə:ksəm] ADJ seccante

IRN N ABBR (= *Independent Radio News*) agenzia d'informazioni per la radio

IRO N ABBR (= *International Refugee Organization*) O.I.R. *f* (= *Organizzazione Internazionale per i Rifugiati*)

iron ['aɪən] N ferro; (*for clothes*) ferro da stiro ▶ ADJ di *or* in ferro ▶ VT (*clothes*) stirare; *see also* **irons**
▶ **iron out** VT (*crease*) appianare; (*fig*) spianare; far sparire

Iron Curtain N: **the ~** la cortina di ferro

iron foundry N fonderia

ironic [aɪ'rɔnɪk], **ironical** [aɪ'rɔnɪkl] ADJ ironico(-a)

ironically [aɪ'rɔnɪklɪ] ADV ironicamente

ironing ['aɪənɪŋ] N (*act*) stirare *m*; (*clothes*) roba da stirare

ironing board N asse *f* da stiro

iron lung N (*Med*) polmone *m* d'acciaio

ironmonger ['aɪənmʌŋgəʳ] N (BRIT)
negoziante m in ferramenta; **~'s (shop)** n
negozio di ferramenta
iron ore N minerale m di ferro
irons ['aɪənz] NPL (chains) catene fpl
ironworks ['aɪənwəːks] N ferriera
irony ['aɪrənɪ] N ironia
irrational [ɪ'ræʃənl] ADJ irrazionale;
irragionevole; illogico(-a)
irreconcilable [ɪrekən'saɪləbl] ADJ
irreconciliabile; (opinion): **~ with**
inconciliabile con
irredeemable [ɪrɪ'diːməbl] ADJ (Comm)
irredimibile
irrefutable [ɪrɪ'fjuːtəbl] ADJ irrefutabile
irregular [ɪ'regjuləʳ] ADJ irregolare
irregularity [ɪregju'lærɪtɪ] N irregolarità f inv
irrelevance [ɪ'reləvəns] N inappropriatezza
irrelevant [ɪ'reləvənt] ADJ non pertinente
irreligious [ɪrɪ'lɪdʒəs] ADJ irreligioso(-a)
irreparable [ɪ'reprəbl] ADJ irreparabile
irreplaceable [ɪrɪ'pleɪsəbl] ADJ insostituibile
irrepressible [ɪrɪ'presəbl] ADJ irrefrenabile
irreproachable [ɪrɪ'prəutʃəbl] ADJ
irreprensibile
irresistible [ɪrɪ'zɪstɪbl] ADJ irresistibile
irresolute [ɪ'rezəluːt] ADJ irresoluto(-a),
indeciso(-a)
irrespective [ɪrɪ'spektɪv]: **~ of** prep senza
riguardo a
irresponsible [ɪrɪ'spɔnsɪbl] ADJ
irresponsabile
irretrievable [ɪrɪ'triːvəbl] ADJ (object)
irrecuperabile; (loss, damage) irreparabile
irreverent [ɪ'revərnt] ADJ irriverente
irrevocable [ɪ'revəkəbl] ADJ irrevocabile
irrigate ['ɪrɪgeɪt] VT irrigare
irrigation [ɪrɪ'geɪʃən] N irrigazione f
irritable ['ɪrɪtəbl] ADJ irritabile
irritant ['ɪrɪtənt] N sostanza irritante
irritate ['ɪrɪteɪt] VT irritare
irritating ADJ (person, sound etc) irritante
irritation [ɪrɪ'teɪʃən] N irritazione f
IRS N ABBR (US) = **Internal Revenue Service**
is [ɪz] VB see **be**
ISA ['aɪsə] N ABBR (= individual savings account)
forma di investimento detassata
ISBN N ABBR (= International Standard Book
Number) ISBN m
ISDN N ABBR (= Integrated Services Digital
Network) ISDN f
Islam ['ɪzlɑːm] N Islam m
Islamic [ɪz'læmɪk] ADJ islamico(-a)
island ['aɪlənd] N isola; (also: **traffic island**)
salvagente m
islander ['aɪləndəʳ] N isolano(-a)
isle [aɪl] N isola
isn't ['ɪznt] = **is not**
isolate ['aɪsəleɪt] VT isolare

isolated ['aɪsəleɪtɪd] ADJ isolato(-a)
isolation [aɪsə'leɪʃən] N isolamento
isolationism [aɪsə'leɪʃənɪzəm] N
isolazionismo
isotope ['aɪsəutəup] N isotopo
ISP N ABBR (Comput: = internet service provider)
provider m inv
Israel ['ɪzreɪl] N Israele m
Israeli [ɪz'reɪlɪ] ADJ, N israeliano(-a)
issue ['ɪʃuː] N questione f, problema m;
(outcome) esito, risultato; (of banknotes etc)
emissione f; (of newspaper etc) numero;
(offspring) discendenza ▸ VT (statement)
rilasciare; (rations, equipment) distribuire;
(orders) dare; (book) pubblicare; (banknotes,
cheques, stamps) emettere ▸ VI: **to ~ (from)**
uscire (da), venir fuori (da); **at ~** in gioco, in
discussione; **to avoid the ~** evitare la
discussione; **to take ~ with sb (over sth)**
prendere posizione contro qn (riguardo a
qc); **to confuse** or **obscure the ~** confondere
le cose; **to make an ~ of sth** fare un
problema di qc; **to ~ sth to sb, ~ sb with sth**
consegnare qc a qn
Istanbul [ɪstæn'buːl] N Istanbul f
isthmus ['ɪsməs] N istmo
IT N ABBR = **information technology**

(KEYWORD)

it [ɪt] PRON **1** (specific: subject) esso(-a) (mostly
omitted in Italian); (: direct object) lo (la), l';
(: indirect object) gli (le); **where's my book?
— it's on the table** dov'è il mio libro? — è
sulla tavola; **what is it?** che cos'è?; (what's the
matter?) cosa c'è?; **where is it?** dov'è?; **I can't
find it** non lo (or la) trovo; **give it to me**
dammelo (or dammela); **about/from/of it**
ne; **I spoke to him about it** gliene ho
parlato; **what did you learn from it?** quale
insegnamento ne hai tratto?; **I'm proud of
it** ne sono fiero; **in/to/at it** ci; **put the book
in it** mettici il libro; **did you go to it?** ci sei
andato?; **I wasn't at it** non c'ero; **above/
over it** sopra; **below/under it** sotto; **in
front of/behind it** lì davanti/dietro
2 (impers): **it's raining** piove; **it's Friday
tomorrow** domani è venerdì; **it's 6 o'clock**
sono le 6; **it's 2 hours on the train** sono or ci
vogliono 2 ore di treno; **who is it? — it's me**
chi è? — sono io

ITA N ABBR (BRIT: = initial teaching alphabet)
alfabeto fonetico semplificato per insegnare a
leggere
Italian [ɪ'tæljən] ADJ italiano(-a) ▸ N
italiano(-a); (Ling) italiano; **the Italians** gli
Italiani
italic [ɪ'tælɪk] ADJ corsivo(-a); **italics** NPL
corsivo

Italy ['ɪtəlɪ] N Italia

ITC N ABBR (*Brit*: = *Independent Television Commission*) *organo di controllo sulle reti televisive*

itch [ɪtʃ] N prurito ▶ VI (*person*) avere il prurito; (*part of body*) prudere; **to be itching to do** avere una gran voglia di fare

itchy ['ɪtʃɪ] ADJ che prude; **my back is** ~ ho prurito alla schiena

it'd ['ɪtd] = **it would**; **it had**

item ['aɪtəm] N articolo; (*on agenda*) punto; (*in programme*) numero; (*also*: **news item**) notizia; **items of clothing** capi *mpl* di abbigliamento

itemize ['aɪtəmaɪz] VT specificare, dettagliare

itemized bill ['aɪtəmaɪzd-] N conto dettagliato

itinerant [ɪ'tɪnərənt] ADJ ambulante

itinerary [aɪ'tɪnərərɪ] N itinerario

it'll ['ɪtl] = **it will**; **it shall**

ITN N ABBR (*Brit*: = *Independent Television News*) *agenzia d'informazioni per la televisione*

its [ɪts] ADJ, PRON il (la) suo(-a), i (le) suoi (sue)

it's [ɪts] = **it is**; **it has**

itself [ɪt'sɛlf] PRON (*emphatic*) esso(-a) stesso(-a); (*reflexive*) si

ITV N ABBR (*Brit*: = *Independent Television*) *rete televisiva indipendente*; *vedi nota*

> La ITV è un'azienda televisiva privata che comprende una serie di emittenti regionali, la prima delle quali è stata aperta nel 1955. Si autofinanzia tramite la pubblicità ed è sottoposta al controllo di un ente ufficiale, la Ofcom; *vedi anche* **BBC**.

IUD N ABBR = **intra-uterine device**

I've [aɪv] = **I have**

ivory ['aɪvərɪ] N avorio

Ivory Coast N Costa d'Avorio

ivory tower N torre *f* d'avorio

ivy ['aɪvɪ] N edera

Ivy League N (*US*); *vedi nota*

> *Ivy League* è il termine usato per indicare le otto università più prestigiose degli Stati Uniti nordorientali (Brown, Columbia, Cornell, Dartmouth College, Harvard, Princeton, University of Pennsylvania e Yale).

Jj

J, j [dʒeɪ] N *(letter)* J, j *f inv or m inv;* **J for Jack,** *(US)* **J for Jig** = J come Jersey
JA N ABBR = **judge advocate**
J/A ABBR = **joint account**
jab [dʒæb] VT dare colpetti a; **to ~ sth into** affondare *or* piantare qc dentro ▶ VI: **to ~ at** dare colpi a ▶ N colpo; *(Med: col)* puntura
jabber ['dʒæbə^r] VT, VI borbottare
jack [dʒæk] N *(Aut)* cricco; *(Bowls)* boccino, pallino; *(Cards)* fante *m*
  ▶ **jack in** VT *(col)* mollare
  ▶ **jack up** VT sollevare sul cricco; *(raise: prices etc)* alzare
jackal ['dʒækl] N sciacallo
jackass ['dʒækæs] N *(also fig)* asino, somaro
jackdaw ['dʒækdɔ:] N taccola
jacket ['dʒækɪt] N giacca; *(of book)* copertura; **potatoes in their jackets** *(BRIT)* patate *fpl* con la buccia
jacket potato N *patata cotta al forno con la buccia*
jack-in-the-box ['dʒækɪnðəbɔks] N scatola a sorpresa (con pupazzo a molla)
jack-knife ['dʒæknaɪf] VI: **the lorry jack-knifed** l'autotreno si è piegato su se stesso
jack-of-all-trades [dʒækəv'ɔ:ltreɪdz] N uno che fa un po' di tutto
jack plug N *(BRIT)* jack plug *f inv*
jackpot ['dʒækpɔt] N primo premio (in denaro)
Jacuzzi® [dʒə'ku:zɪ] N vasca per idromassaggio Jacuzzi®
jade [dʒeɪd] N *(stone)* giada
jaded ['dʒeɪdɪd] ADJ sfinito(-a), spossato(-a)
jagged ['dʒægɪd] ADJ seghettato(-a); *(cliffs etc)* frastagliato(-a)
jaguar ['dʒægjuə^r] N giaguaro
jail [dʒeɪl] N prigione *f* ▶ VT mandare in prigione
jailbird ['dʒeɪlbə:d] N avanzo di galera
jailbreak ['dʒeɪlbreɪk] N evasione *f*
jailer ['dʒeɪlə^r] N custode *m* del carcere
jail sentence N condanna al carcere

jalopy [dʒə'lɔpɪ] N *(col)* macinino
jam [dʒæm] N marmellata; *(of shoppers etc)* ressa; *(also:* **traffic jam***)* ingorgo; *(: col)* pasticcio ▶ VT *(passage etc)* ingombrare, ostacolare; *(mechanism, drawer etc)* bloccare; *(Radio)* disturbare con interferenze ▶ VI *(mechanism, sliding part)* incepparsi, bloccarsi; *(gun)* incepparsi; **to get sb out of a ~** tirare qn fuori dai pasticci; **to ~ sth into** forzare qc dentro; infilare qc a forza dentro; **the telephone lines are jammed** le linee sono sovraccariche
Jamaica [dʒə'meɪkə] N Giamaica
Jamaican [dʒə'meɪkən] ADJ, N giamaicano(-a)
jamb [dʒæm] N stipite *m*
jammed [dʒæmd] ADJ *(door)* bloccato(-a); *(rifle, printer)* inceppato(-a)
jam-packed [dʒæm'pækt] ADJ: **~ (with)** pieno(-a) zeppo(-a) (di), strapieno(-a) (di)
jam session N improvvisazione *f* jazzistica
Jan. ABBR *(= January)* gen., genn.
jangle ['dʒæŋgl] VI risuonare; *(bracelet)* tintinnare
janitor ['dʒænɪtə^r] N *(caretaker)* portiere *m*; *(: Scol)* bidello
January ['dʒænjuərɪ] N gennaio; *see also* **July**
Japan [dʒə'pæn] N Giappone *m*
Japanese [dʒæpə'ni:z] ADJ giapponese ▶ N *(pl inv)* giapponese *mf;* *(Ling)* giapponese *m*
jar [dʒɑ:^r] N *(container)* barattolo, vasetto ▶ VI *(sound)* stridere; *(colours etc)* stonare ▶ VT *(shake)* scuotere
jargon ['dʒɑ:gən] N gergo
jarring ['dʒɑ:rɪŋ] ADJ *(sound, colour)* stonato(-a)
Jas. ABBR = **James**
jasmin, jasmine ['dʒæzmɪn] N gelsomino
jaundice ['dʒɔ:ndɪs] N itterizia
jaundiced ['dʒɔ:ndɪst] ADJ *(fig)* invidioso(-a) e critico(-a)
jaunt [dʒɔ:nt] N gita
jaunty ['dʒɔ:ntɪ] ADJ vivace; disinvolto(-a), spigliato(-a)
Java ['dʒɑ:və] N Giava

javelin['dʒævlɪn] N giavellotto
jaw[dʒɔ:] N mascella; **jaws**NPL (*Tech: of vice etc*) morsa
jawbone['dʒɔ:bəʊn] N mandibola
jay[dʒeɪ] N ghiandaia
jaywalker['dʒeɪwɔ:kər] N pedone(-a) indisciplinato(-a)
jazz[dʒæz] N jazz *m*
 ▶ **jazz up**VT rendere vivace
jazz bandN banda *f* jazz *inv*
jazzy['dʒæzɪ] ADJ vistoso(-a), chiassoso(-a)
JCB® N scavatrice *f*
JCSN ABBR (*US*) = **Joint Chiefs of Staff**
JDN ABBR (*US: = Doctor of Laws*) titolo di studio; (*= Justice Department*) ministero della Giustizia
jealous['dʒɛləs] ADJ geloso(-a)
jealously['dʒɛləslɪ] ADV (*enviously*) con gelosia; (*watchfully*) gelosamente
jealousy['dʒɛləsɪ] N gelosia
jeans[dʒi:nz] NPL (blue-)jeans *mpl*
Jeep® [dʒi:p] N jeep *m inv*
jeer[dʒɪər] VI: **to ~ (at)** fischiare; beffeggiare; *see also* **jeers**
jeering['dʒɪərɪŋ] ADJ (*crowd*) che urla e fischia
 ▶ N fischi *mpl*; parole *fpl* di scherno
jeers['dʒɪəz] NPL fischi *mpl*
Jello® ['dʒɛləʊ] N (*US*) gelatina di frutta
jelly['dʒɛlɪ] N gelatina
jellyfish['dʒɛlɪfɪʃ] N medusa
jeopardize['dʒɛpədaɪz] VT mettere in pericolo
jeopardy['dʒɛpədɪ] N: **in ~** in pericolo
jerk[dʒə:k] N sobbalzo, scossa; sussulto; (*col*) povero(-a) scemo(-a) ▶ VT dare una scossa a
 ▶ VI (*vehicles*) sobbalzare
jerkin['dʒə:kɪn] N giubbotto
jerky['dʒə:kɪ] ADJ a scatti; a sobbalzi
jerry-built['dʒɛrɪbɪlt] ADJ fatto(-a) di cartapesta
jerry can['dʒɛrɪ-] N tanica
Jersey['dʒə:zɪ] N Jersey *m*
jersey['dʒə:zɪ] N maglia; (*fabric*) jersey *m*
Jerusalem[dʒə'ru:sələm] N Gerusalemme *f*
jest[dʒɛst] N scherzo; **in ~** per scherzo
jester['dʒɛstər] N (*Hist*) buffone *m*
Jesus['dʒi:zəs] N Gesù *m*; **~ Christ** Gesù Cristo
jet[dʒɛt] N (*of gas, liquid*) getto; (*Aut*) spruzzatore *m*; (*Aviat*) aviogetto
jet-black['dʒɛt'blæk] ADJ nero(-a) come l'ebano, corvino(-a)
jet engineN motore *m* a reazione
jet lagN (problemi *mpl* dovuti allo) sbalzo dei fusi orari
jetsam['dʒɛtsəm] N relitti *mpl* di mare
jet-setter['dʒɛtsɛtər] N membro del jet set
jet-skiVI acquascooter *m inv*
jettison['dʒɛtɪsn] VT gettare in mare
jetty['dʒɛtɪ] N molo

Jew[dʒu:] N ebreo
jewel['dʒu:əl] N gioiello
jeweller,(*US*) **jeweler**['dʒu:ələr] N orefice *m*, gioielliere(-a); **~'s shop** oreficeria, gioielleria
jewellery,(*US*) **jewelry**['dʒu:əlrɪ] N gioielli *mpl*; **jewelry store** (*US*) oreficeria, gioielleria
Jewess['dʒu:ɪs] N ebrea
Jewish['dʒu:ɪʃ] ADJ ebreo(-a), ebraico(-a)
JFKN ABBR (*US*) = **John Fitzgerald Kennedy International Airport**
jib[dʒɪb] N (*Naut*) fiocco; (*of crane*) braccio ▶ VI (*horse*) impennarsi; **to ~ at doing sth** essere restio a fare qc
jibe[dʒaɪb] N beffa
jiffy['dʒɪfɪ] N (*col*): **in a ~** in un batter d'occhio
jig[dʒɪg] N (*dance, tune*) giga
jigsaw['dʒɪgsɔ:] N (*tool*) sega da traforo; (*also:* **jigsaw puzzle**) puzzle *m inv*
jilt[dʒɪlt] VT piantare in asso
jingle['dʒɪŋgl] N (*advert*) sigla pubblicitaria
 ▶ VI tintinnare, scampanellare
jingoism['dʒɪŋgəʊɪzəm] N sciovinismo
jinx[dʒɪŋks] N (*col*) iettatura; (*person*) iettatore(-trice)
jitters['dʒɪtəz] NPL (*col*): **to get the ~** aver fifa
jittery['dʒɪtərɪ] ADJ (*col*) teso(-a), agitato(-a); **to be ~** aver fifa
jiujitsu[dʒu:'dʒɪtsu:] N jujitsu *m*
job[dʒɔb] N lavoro; (*employment*) impiego, posto; **a part-time/full-time ~** un lavoro a mezza giornata/a tempo pieno; **that's not my ~** non è compito mio; **he's only doing his ~** non fa che il suo dovere; **it's a good ~ that ...** meno male che ...; **just the ~!** proprio quello che ci vuole!
jobber['dʒɔbər] N (*BRIT Stock Exchange*) intermediario tra agenti di cambio
jobbing['dʒɔbɪŋ] ADJ (*BRIT: workman*) a ore, a giornata
job centre(*BRIT*) N ufficio di collocamento
job creation schemeN progetto per la creazione di nuovi posti di lavoro
job descriptionN caratteristiche *fpl* (di un lavoro)
jobless['dʒɔblɪs] ADJ senza lavoro, disoccupato(-a) ▶ NPL: **the ~** i senza lavoro
job lotN partita di articoli disparati
job satisfactionN soddisfazione *f* nel lavoro
job securityN sicurezza del posto di lavoro
job shareVI fare un lavoro ripartito ▶ N lavoro ripartito
job specificationN caratteristiche *fpl* (di un lavoro)
jock[dʒɔk] N (*col*) *termine colloquiale per chiamare uno scozzese*
jockey['dʒɔkɪ] N fantino, jockey *m inv* ▶ VI: **to ~ for position** manovrare per una posizione di vantaggio

jockey box N (US Aut) vano portaoggetti
jockstrap ['dʒɔkstræp] N conchiglia (per atleti)
jocular ['dʒɔkjuləʳ] ADJ gioviale; scherzoso(-a)
jog [dʒɔg] VT urtare ▶ VI (Sport) fare footing, fare jogging; **to ~ along** trottare; (fig) andare avanti pian piano; **to ~ sb's memory** rinfrescare la memoria di qn
jogger ['dʒɔgəʳ] N persona che fa footing or jogging
jogging ['dʒɔgɪŋ] N footing m, jogging m
john [dʒɔn] N (US col): **the ~** il gabinetto
join [dʒɔɪn] VT unire, congiungere; (become member of) iscriversi a; (meet) raggiungere; riunirsi a ▶ VI (roads, rivers) confluire ▶ N giuntura; **to ~ forces (with)** allearsi (con or a); (fig) mettersi insieme (a); **will you ~ us for dinner?** viene a cena con noi?; **I'll ~ you later** vi raggiungo più tardi
 ▶ **join in** VT FUS unirsi a, prendere parte a, partecipare a ▶ VI partecipare
 ▶ **join up** VI incontrarsi; (Mil) arruolarsi
joiner ['dʒɔɪnəʳ] N (BRIT) falegname m
joinery ['dʒɔɪnərɪ] N falegnameria
joint [dʒɔɪnt] N (Tech) giuntura; giunto; (Anat) articolazione f, giuntura; (Brit Culin) arrosto; (col: place) locale m; (: of cannabis) spinello ▶ ADJ comune; (responsibility) collettivo(-a); (committee) misto(-a)
joint account N (at bank etc) conto comune
jointly ['dʒɔɪntlɪ] ADV in comune, insieme
joint ownership N comproprietà
joint-stock company ['dʒɔɪntstɔk-] N società f inv per azioni
joist [dʒɔɪst] N trave f
joke [dʒəuk] N scherzo; (funny story) barzelletta; (also: **practical joke**) beffa ▶ VI scherzare; **to play a ~ on** fare uno scherzo a
joker ['dʒəukəʳ] N buffone(-a), burlone(-a); (Cards) matta, jolly m inv
joking ['dʒəukɪŋ] N scherzi mpl
jollity ['dʒɔlɪtɪ] N allegria
jolly ['dʒɔlɪ] ADJ allegro(-a), gioioso(-a) ▶ ADV (BRIT col) veramente, proprio ▶ VT (BRIT): **to ~ sb along** cercare di tenere qn su (di morale); **~ good!** (BRIT) benissimo!
jolt [dʒəult] N scossa, sobbalzo ▶ VT urtare
Jordan ['dʒɔːdən] N (country) Giordania; (river) Giordano
Jordanian [dʒɔːˈdeɪnɪən] ADJ, N giordano(-a)
joss stick [dʒɔs-] N bastoncino d'incenso
jostle ['dʒɔsl] VT spingere coi gomiti ▶ VI farsi spazio coi gomiti
jot [dʒɔt] N: **not one ~** nemmeno un po'
 ▶ **jot down** VT annotare in fretta, buttare giù
jotter ['dʒɔtəʳ] N (BRIT) quaderno; blocco
journal ['dʒɜːnl] N (newspaper) giornale m; (periodical) rivista; (diary) diario

journalese [dʒɜːnəˈliːz] N (pej) stile m giornalistico
journalism ['dʒɜːnəlɪzəm] N giornalismo
journalist ['dʒɜːnəlɪst] N giornalista mf
journey ['dʒɜːnɪ] N viaggio; (distance covered) tragitto; **how was your ~?** com'è andato il viaggio?; **the ~ takes two hours** il viaggio dura due ore; **a 5-hour ~** un viaggio or un tragitto di 5 ore
jovial ['dʒəuvɪəl] ADJ gioviale, allegro(-a)
jowl [dʒaul] N mandibola; guancia
joy [dʒɔɪ] N gioia
joyful ['dʒɔɪful] **joyous** ['dʒɔɪəs] ADJ gioioso(-a), allegro(-a)
joyride ['dʒɔɪraɪd] N: **to go for a ~** rubare una macchina per farsi un giro
joyrider ['dʒɔɪraɪdəʳ] N chi ruba una macchina per andare a farsi un giro
joy stick ['dʒɔɪstɪk] N (Aviat) barra di comando; (Comput) joystick m inv
JP N ABBR = **Justice of the Peace**
Jr. ABBR = **junior**
jubilant ['dʒuːbɪlnt] ADJ giubilante; trionfante
jubilation [dʒuːbɪˈleɪʃən] N giubilo
jubilee ['dʒuːbɪliː] N giubileo; **silver ~** venticinquesimo anniversario
judge [dʒʌdʒ] N giudice mf ▶ VT giudicare; (consider) ritenere; (estimate: weight, size etc) calcolare, valutare ▶ VI: **judging** or **to ~ by his expression** a giudicare dalla sua espressione; **as far as I can ~** a mio giudizio; **I judged it necessary to inform him** ho ritenuto necessario informarlo
judge advocate N (Mil) magistrato militare
judgment, judgement ['dʒʌdʒmənt] N giudizio; (punishment) punizione f; **in my judg(e)ment** a mio giudizio; **to pass judg(e)ment (on)** (Law) pronunciare un giudizio (su); (fig) dare giudizi affrettati (su)
judicial [dʒuːˈdɪʃl] ADJ giudiziale, giudiziario(-a)
judiciary [dʒuːˈdɪʃɪərɪ] N magistratura
judicious [dʒuːˈdɪʃəs] ADJ giudizioso(-a)
judo ['dʒuːdəu] N judo
jug [dʒʌg] N brocca, bricco
jugged hare [dʒʌgd-] N (BRIT) lepre f in salmì
juggernaut ['dʒʌgənɔːt] N (BRIT: huge truck) bestione m
juggle ['dʒʌgl] VI fare giochi di destrezza
juggler ['dʒʌgləʳ] N giocoliere(-a)
Jugoslav ['juːgəuˈslɑːv] ADJ, N = **Yugoslav**
jugular ['dʒʌgjuləʳ] ADJ: **~ (vein)** vena giugulare
juice [dʒuːs] N succo; (of meat) sugo; **we've run out of ~** (col: petrol) siamo rimasti a secco
juicy ['dʒuːsɪ] ADJ succoso(-a)
jukebox ['dʒuːkbɔks] N juke-box m inv
Jul. ABBR (= July) lug., lu.

July [dʒuː'laɪ] N luglio; **the first of ~** il primo luglio; **(on) the eleventh of ~** l'undici luglio; **in the month of ~** nel mese di luglio; **at the beginning/end of ~** all'inizio/alla fine di luglio; **in the middle of ~** a metà luglio; **during ~** durante (il mese di) luglio; **in ~ of next year** a luglio dell'anno prossimo; **each** or **every ~** ogni anno a luglio; **~ was wet this year** ha piovuto molto a luglio quest'anno

jumble ['dʒʌmbl] N miscuglio ▶ VT (also: **jumble up, jumble together**) mischiare, mettere alla rinfusa

jumble sale (BRIT) N ≈ vendita di beneficenza; vedi nota

La jumble sale è un mercatino dove vengono venduti vari oggetti, per lo più di seconda mano; viene organizzata in chiese, scuole o circoli ricreativi. I proventi delle vendite vengono devoluti in beneficenza o usati per una giusta causa.

jumbo ['dʒʌmbəʊ] ADJ: **~ jet** jumbo-jet m inv; **~ size** formato gigante

jump [dʒʌmp] VI saltare, balzare; (start) sobbalzare; (increase) rincarare ▶ VT saltare ▶ N salto, balzo; sobbalzo; (Showjumping) salto; (fence) ostacolo; **to ~ the queue** (BRIT) passare davanti agli altri (in una coda)
 ▶ **jump about** VI fare salti, saltellare
 ▶ **jump at** VT FUS (fig) cogliere or afferrare al volo; **he jumped at the offer** si affrettò ad accettare l'offerta
 ▶ **jump down** VI saltare giù
 ▶ **jump up** VI saltare in piedi

jumped-up ['dʒʌmptʌp] ADJ (BRIT pej) presuntuoso(-a)

jumper ['dʒʌmpəʳ] N (BRIT: pullover) maglione m; (US: pinafore dress) scamiciato; (Sport) saltatore(-trice)

jump leads, (US) **jumper cables** NPL cavi mpl per batteria

jump-start ['dʒʌmpstɑːt] VT (car) far partire spingendo; (fig) dare una spinta a, rimettere in moto

jump suit N tuta

jumpy ['dʒʌmpɪ] ADJ nervoso(-a), agitato(-a)

Jun. ABBR (= June) giu.

Jun., Junr ABBR = **junior**

junction ['dʒʌŋkʃən] N (BRIT: of roads) incrocio; (of rails) nodo ferroviario

juncture ['dʒʌŋktʃəʳ] N: **at this ~** in questa congiuntura

June [dʒuːn] N giugno; see also **July**

jungle ['dʒʌŋgl] N giungla

junior ['dʒuːnɪəʳ] ADJ, N: **he's ~ to me (by 2 years), he's my ~ (by 2 years)** è più giovane di me (di 2 anni); **he's ~ to me** (seniority) è al di sotto di me, ho più anzianità di lui

junior executive N giovane dirigente m

junior high school N (US) scuola media (da 12 a 15 anni)

junior minister N (BRIT Pol) ministro che non fa parte del Cabinet

junior partner N socio meno anziano

junior school N (BRIT) scuola elementare (da 8 a 11 anni)

junior sizes NPL (Comm) taglie fpl per ragazzi

juniper ['dʒuːnɪpəʳ] N: **~ berry** bacca di ginepro

junk [dʒʌŋk] N (rubbish) cianfrusaglie fpl; (cheap goods) robaccia; (ship) giunca ▶ VT disfarsi di

junk bond N (Comm) titolo m spazzatura inv

junk dealer N rigattiere m

junket ['dʒʌŋkɪt] N (Culin) giuncata; (BRIT col): **to go on a ~** fare bisboccia

junk food N porcherie fpl, cibo a scarso valore nutritivo

junkie ['dʒʌŋkɪ] N (col) drogato(-a)

junk mail N pubblicità f inv in cassetta

junk room N (US) ripostiglio

junk shop N chincaglieria

junta ['dʒʌntə] N giunta

Jupiter ['dʒuːpɪtəʳ] N (planet) Giove m

jurisdiction [dʒuərɪs'dɪkʃən] N giurisdizione f; **it falls** or **comes within/outside our ~** è/ non è di nostra competenza

jurisprudence [dʒuərɪs'pruːdəns] N giurisprudenza

juror ['dʒuərəʳ] N giurato(-a)

jury ['dʒuərɪ] N giuria

jury box N banco della giuria

juryman ['dʒuərɪmən] N (irreg) = **juror**

just [dʒʌst] ADJ giusto(-a) ▶ ADV: **he's ~ done it/left** lo ha appena fatto/è appena partito; **~ as I expected** proprio come me lo aspettavo; **~ right** proprio giusto; **~ 2 o'clock** le 2 precise; **she's ~ as clever as you** è in gamba proprio quanto te; **~ as I arrived** proprio mentre arrivavo; **we were ~ going** stavamo uscendo; **I was ~ about to phone** stavo proprio per telefonare; **~ as he was leaving** proprio mentre se ne stava andando; **it was ~ before/enough/here** era poco prima/appena assai/proprio qui; **it's ~ me** sono solo io; **it's ~ a mistake** non è che uno sbaglio; **~ missed/caught** appena perso/ preso; **~ listen to this!** senta un po' questo!; **~ ask someone the way** basta che tu chieda la strada a qualcuno; **it's ~ as good** è altrettanto buono; **it's ~ as well you didn't go** meno male che non ci sei andato; **not ~ now** non proprio adesso; **~ a minute!, ~ one moment!** un attimo!

justice ['dʒʌstɪs] N giustizia; **Lord Chief J~** (BRIT) presidente m della Corte d'Appello; **this photo doesn't do you ~** questa foto non ti fa giustizia

Justice of the Peace N giudice *m* conciliatore

justifiable [dʒʌstɪˈfaɪəbl] ADJ giustificabile

justifiably [dʒʌstɪˈfaɪəblɪ] ADV legittimamente, con ragione

justification [dʒʌstɪfɪˈkeɪʃən] N giustificazione *f*; (*Typ*) giustezza

justify [ˈdʒʌstɪfaɪ] VT giustificare; (*Typ etc*) allineare, giustificare; **to be justified in doing sth** avere ragione di fare qc

justly [ˈdʒʌstlɪ] ADV giustamente

justness [ˈdʒʌstnɪs] N giustezza

jut [dʒʌt] VI (*also*: **jut out**) sporgersi

jute [dʒuːt] N iuta

juvenile [ˈdʒuːvənaɪl] ADJ giovane, giovanile; (*court*) dei minorenni; (*books*) per ragazzi ▶ N giovane *mf*, minorenne *mf*

juvenile delinquency N delinquenza minorile

juvenile delinquent N delinquente *mf* minorenne

juxtapose [ˈdʒʌkstəpəuz] VT giustapporre

juxtaposition [dʒʌkstəpəˈzɪʃən] N giustapposizione *f*

Kk

K, k [keɪ] N (*letter*) K, k f *inv or m inv*; **K for King** ≈ K come Kursaal

K N ABBR (= *one thousand*) mille ▶ ABBR (*BRIT*: = *Knight*) *titolo*; (= *kilobyte*) K

kaftan ['kæftæn] N caffettano

Kalahari Desert [kælə'hɑːrɪ-] N Deserto di Calahari

kale [keɪl] N cavolo verde

kaleidoscope [kə'laɪdəskəup] N caleidoscopio

kamikaze [kæmɪ'kɑːzɪ] ADJ da kamikaze

Kampala [kæm'pɑːlə] N Kampala f

Kampuchea [kæmpu'tʃɪə] N Kampuchea f

kangaroo [kæŋɡə'ruː] N canguro

Kans. ABBR (*US*) = **Kansas**

kaput [kə'put] ADJ (*col*) kaputt *inv*

karaoke [kɑːrə'əukɪ] N karaoke m *inv*

karate [kə'rɑːtɪ] N karate m

Kashmir [kæʃ'mɪər] N Kashmir m

Kazakhstan [kæzæk'stɑːn] N Kazakistan m

KC N ABBR (*BRIT Law*: = *King's Counsel*) avvocato della Corona; *see also* **QC**

kebab [kə'bæb] N spiedino

keel [kiːl] N chiglia; **on an even ~** (*fig*) in uno stato normale
▶ **keel over** VI (*Naut*) capovolgersi; (*person*) crollare

keen [kiːn] ADJ (*interest, desire*) vivo(-a); (*eye, intelligence*) acuto(-a); (*competition*) serrato(-a); (*edge*) affilato(-a); (*eager*) entusiasta; **to be ~ to do** *or* **on doing sth** avere una gran voglia di fare qc; **to be ~ on sth** essere appassionato(-a) di qc; **to be ~ on sb** avere un debole per qn; **I'm not ~ on going** non mi va di andare

keenly ['kiːnlɪ] ADV (*enthusiastically*) con entusiasmo; (*acutely*) vivamente; in modo penetrante

keenness ['kiːnnɪs] N (*eagerness*) entusiasmo

keep [kiːp] (*pt, pp* **kept** [kept]) VT tenere; (*hold back*) trattenere; (*feed: one's family etc*) mantenere, sostentare; (*a promise*) mantenere; (*chickens, bees, pigs etc*) allevare
▶ VI (*food*) mantenersi; (*remain: in a certain state or place*) restare ▶ N (*of castle*) maschio; (*food etc*): **enough for his ~** abbastanza per vitto e alloggio; **to ~ doing sth** continuare a fare qc; fare qc di continuo; **to ~ sb from doing/ sth from happening** impedire a qn di fare/ che qc succeda; **to ~ sb busy/a place tidy** tenere qn occupato(-a)/un luogo in ordine; **to ~ sb waiting** far aspettare qn; **to ~ an appointment** andare ad un appuntamento; **to ~ a record** *or* **note of sth** prendere nota di qc; **to ~ sth to o.s.** tenere qc per sé; **to ~ sth (back) from sb** celare qc a qn; **to ~ time** (*clock*) andar bene; **~ the change** tenga il resto; *see also* **keeps**
▶ **keep away** VT: **to ~ sth/sb away from sb** tenere qc/qn lontano da qn ▶ VI: **to ~ away (from)** stare lontano (da)
▶ **keep back** VT (*crowds, tears, money*) trattenere ▶ VI tenersi indietro
▶ **keep down** VT (*control: prices, spending*) contenere, ridurre; (*retain: food*) trattenere, ritenere ▶ VI tenersi giù, stare giù
▶ **keep in** VT (*invalid, child*) tenere a casa; (*Scol*) trattenere a scuola ▶ VI (*col*): **to ~ in with sb** tenersi buono qn
▶ **keep off** VT (*dog, person*) tenere lontano da ▶ VI stare alla larga; **~ your hands off!** non toccare!, giù le mani!; **"~ off the grass"** "non calpestare l'erba"
▶ **keep on** VI continuare; **to ~ on doing** continuare a fare; **to ~ on (about sth)** continuare a insistere (su qc)
▶ **keep out** VT tener fuori ▶ VI restare fuori; **"~ out"** "vietato l'accesso"
▶ **keep up** VT continuare, mantenere ▶ VI mantenersi; **to ~ up with** tener dietro a, andare di pari passo con; (*work etc*) farcela a seguire; **to ~ up with sb** (*in race etc*) mantenersi al passo con qn

keeper ['kiːpər] N custode mf, guardiano(-a)

keep-fit [kiːp'fɪt] N ginnastica

keeping ['kiːpɪŋ] N (*care*) custodia; **in ~ with** in armonia con; in accordo con

keeps [kiːps] N: **for ~** (*col*) per sempre

keepsake ['ki:pseɪk] N ricordo
keg [kɛg] N barilotto
Ken. ABBR (US) = **Kentucky**
kennel ['kɛnl] N canile m; **kennels** NPL canile m; **to put a dog in kennels** mettere un cane al canile
Kenya ['kɛnjə] N Kenia m
Kenyan ['kɛnjən] ADJ, N Keniano(-a), Keniota (mf)
kept [kɛpt] PT, PP of **keep**
kerb [kə:b] N (BRIT) orlo del marciapiede
kerb crawler [-'krɔ:lər] N chi va in macchina in cerca di una prostituta
kernel ['kə:nl] N nocciolo
kerosene ['kɛrəsi:n] N cherosene m
ketchup ['kɛtʃəp] N ketchup m inv
kettle ['kɛtl] N bollitore m
kettle drum N timpano
kettling ['kɛtəlɪŋ] N tecnica di contenimento forzato impiegata dalla polizia per accerchiare i manifestanti
key [ki:] N (gen, Mus) chiave f; (of piano, typewriter) tasto; (on map) leg(g)enda ▶ CPD (vital: position, industry etc) chiave inv
  ▶ **key in** VT (text) digitare
keyboard ['ki:bɔ:d] N tastiera ▶ VT (text) comporre su tastiera
keyboarder ['ki:bɔ:dər] N dattilografo(-a)
keyed up [ki:d'ʌp] ADJ: **to be ~** essere agitato(-a)
keyhole ['ki:həul] N buco della serratura
keyhole surgery N chirurgia mininvasiva
keynote ['ki:nəut] N (Mus) tonica; (fig) nota dominante
keypad ['ki:pæd] N tastierino numerico
key ring N portachiavi m inv
keystroke ['ki:strəuk] N battuta (di un tasto)
kg ABBR (= kilogram) Kg
KGB N ABBR KGB m
khaki ['kɑ:kɪ] ADJ, N cachi (m)
kibbutz [kɪ'buts] N kibbutz m inv
kick [kɪk] VT calciare, dare calci a; (col: habit etc) liberarsi di ▶ VI (horse) tirar calci
  ▶ N calcio; (of rifle) contraccolpo; (col: thrill): **he does it for kicks** lo fa giusto per il piacere di farlo
  ▶ **kick around** VI (col) essere in giro
  ▶ **kick off** VI (Sport) dare il primo calcio
kick-off ['kɪkɔf] N (Sport) calcio d'inizio
kick-start ['kɪkstɑːt] N (also: **kick-starter**) pedale m d'avviamento
kid [kɪd] N (col: child) ragazzino(-a); (animal, leather) capretto ▶ VI (col) scherzare ▶ VT (col) prendere in giro
kid gloves NPL: **to treat sb with ~** trattare qn coi guanti
kidnap ['kɪdnæp] VT rapire, sequestrare
kidnapper ['kɪdnæpər] N rapitore(-trice)

kidnapping ['kɪdnæpɪŋ] N sequestro (di persona)
kidney ['kɪdnɪ] N (Anat) rene m; (Culin) rognone m
kidney bean N fagiolo borlotto
kidney machine N rene m artificiale
Kilimanjaro [kɪlɪmən'dʒɑ:rəu] N: **Mount ~** il monte Kilimangiaro
kill [kɪl] VT uccidere, ammazzare; (fig) sopprimere; sopraffare; ammazzare ▶ N uccisione f; **to ~ time** ammazzare il tempo
  ▶ **kill off** VT sterminare; (fig) eliminare, soffocare
killer ['kɪlər] N uccisore m, killer m inv; assassino(-a)
killer instinct N: **to have a/the ~** essere spietato(-a)
killing ['kɪlɪŋ] N assassinio; (massacre) strage f; (col): **to make a ~** fare un bel colpo
kill-joy ['kɪldʒɔɪ] N guastafeste mf
kiln [kɪln] N forno
kilo ['ki:ləu] N ABBR (= kilogram) chilo
kilobyte ['kɪləbaɪt] N (Comput) kilobyte m inv
kilogram, kilogramme ['kɪləugræm] N chilogrammo
kilometre, (US)kilometer ['kɪləmi:tər] N chilometro
kilowatt ['kɪləuwɔt] N chilowatt m inv
kilt [kɪlt] N gonnellino scozzese
kilter ['kɪltər] N: **out of ~** fuori fase
kimono [kɪ'məunəu] N chimono
kin [kɪn] N see **next of kin**; **kith**
kind [kaɪnd] ADJ gentile, buono(-a) ▶ N sorta, specie f; (species) genere m; **what ~ of ...?** che tipo di ...?; **to be two of a ~** essere molto simili; **would you be ~ enough to ...?**, **would you be so ~ as to ...?** sarebbe così gentile da ...?; **it's very ~ of you (to do)** è molto gentile da parte sua (di fare); **in ~** (Comm) in natura; (fig) **to repay sb in ~** ripagare qn della stessa moneta
kindergarten ['kɪndəgɑ:tn] N giardino d'infanzia
kind-hearted [kaɪnd'hɑ:tɪd] ADJ di buon cuore
Kindle ® ['kɪndl] N Kindle® m inv
kindle ['kɪndl] VT accendere, infiammare
kindling ['kɪndlɪŋ] N frasche fpl, ramoscelli mpl
kindly ['kaɪndlɪ] ADJ pieno(-a) di bontà, benevolo(-a) ▶ ADV con bontà, gentilmente; **will you ~ ...** per favore; **he didn't take it ~** se l'è presa a male
kindness ['kaɪndnɪs] N bontà, gentilezza
kindred ['kɪndrɪd] ADJ imparentato(-a); **~ spirit** spirito affine
kinetic [kɪ'nɛtɪk] ADJ cinetico(-a)
king [kɪŋ] N re m inv
kingdom ['kɪŋdəm] N regno, reame m

kingfisher ['kɪŋfɪʃəʳ] N martin m inv pescatore
kingpin ['kɪŋpɪn] N (Tech, fig) perno
king-size ['kɪŋsaɪz], **king-sized** ['kɪŋsaɪzd] ADJ super inv; gigante; (cigarette) extra lungo(-a)
king-size bed, king-sized bed N letto king-size
kink [kɪŋk] N (of rope) attorcigliamento; (in hair) ondina; (fig) aberrazione f
kinky ['kɪŋkɪ] ADJ (fig) eccentrico(-a); dai gusti particolari
kinship ['kɪnʃɪp] N parentela
kinsman ['kɪnzmən] N (irreg) parente m
kinswoman ['kɪnzwumən] N (irreg) parente f
kiosk ['kiːɔsk] N edicola, chiosco; (BRIT: also: **telephone kiosk**) cabina (telefonica); (also: **newspaper kiosk**) edicola
kipper ['kɪpəʳ] N aringa affumicata
Kirghizia [kəːˈɡɪzɪə] N Kirghizistan
kiss [kɪs] N bacio ▶ VT baciare; **to ~ (each other)** baciarsi; **to ~ sb goodbye** congedarsi da qn con un bacio; **~ of life** (BRIT) respirazione f bocca a bocca
kissagram ['kɪsəɡræm] N servizio di recapito a domicilio di messaggi e baci augurali
kit [kɪt] N equipaggiamento, corredo; (set of tools etc) attrezzi mpl; (for assembly) scatola di montaggio; **tool ~** cassetta or borsa degli attrezzi
  ▶ **kit out** VT (BRIT) attrezzare, equipaggiare
kitbag ['kɪtbæg] N zaino; sacco militare
kitchen ['kɪtʃɪn] N cucina
kitchen garden N orto
kitchen sink N acquaio
kitchen unit N (BRIT) elemento da cucina
kitchenware ['kɪtʃɪnwɛəʳ] N stoviglie fpl; utensili mpl da cucina
kite [kaɪt] N (toy) aquilone m; (Zool) nibbio
kith [kɪθ] N: **~ and kin** amici e parenti mpl
kitten ['kɪtn] N gattino(-a), micino(-a)
kitty ['kɪtɪ] N (money) fondo comune
kiwi ['kiːwiː], **kiwi fruit** N kiwi m inv
KKK N ABBR (US) = **Ku Klux Klan**
Kleenex® ['kliːnɛks] N fazzolettino di carta
kleptomaniac [klɛptəʊˈmeɪnɪæk] N cleptomane mf
km ABBR (= kilometre) km
km/h ABBR (= kilometres per hour) km/h
knack [næk] N: **to have a ~ (for doing)** avere una pratica (per fare); **to have the ~ of** avere l'abilità di; **there's a ~ to doing this** c'è un trucco per fare questo
knackered ['nækəd] ADJ (col) fuso(-a)
knapsack ['næpsæk] N zaino, sacco da montagna
knave [neɪv] N (Cards) fante m
knead [niːd] VT impastare
knee [niː] N ginocchio
kneecap ['niːkæp] N rotula ▶ VT gambizzare

knee-deep ['niːˈdiːp] ADJ: **the water was ~** l'acqua ci arrivava alle ginocchia
kneel [niːl] (pt, pp **knelt** [nɛlt]) VI (also: **kneel down**) inginocchiarsi
kneepad ['niːpæd] N ginocchiera
knell [nɛl] N rintocco
knelt [nɛlt] PT, PP of **kneel**
knew [njuː] PT of **know**
knickers ['nɪkəz] NPL (BRIT) mutandine fpl
knick-knack ['nɪknæk] N ninnolo
knife [naɪf] (pl **knives**) N coltello ▶ VT accoltellare, dare una coltellata a; **~, fork and spoon** coperto
knife edge N: **to be on a ~** (fig) essere appeso(-a) a un filo
knight [naɪt] N cavaliere m; (Chess) cavallo
knighthood ['naɪthud] N cavalleria; (title): **to get a ~** essere fatto cavaliere
knit [nɪt] VT fare a maglia; (fig): **to ~ together** unire ▶ VI lavorare a maglia; (broken bones) saldarsi; **to ~ one's brows** aggrottare le sopracciglia
knitted ['nɪtɪd] ADJ lavorato(-a) a maglia
knitting ['nɪtɪŋ] N lavoro a maglia
knitting machine N macchina per maglieria
knitting needle N ferro (da calza)
knitting pattern N modello (per maglia)
knitwear ['nɪtwɛəʳ] N maglieria
knives [naɪvz] NPL of **knife**
knob [nɔb] N bottone m; manopola; (BRIT): **a ~ of butter** una noce di burro
knobbly ['nɔblɪ], (US) **knobby** ['nɔbɪ] ADJ (wood, surface) nodoso(-a); (knee) ossuto(-a)
knock [nɔk] VT (strike) colpire; urtare; (fig: col) criticare ▶ VI (engine) battere; (at door etc): **to ~ at/on** bussare a ▶ N bussata; colpo, botta; **he knocked at the door** ha bussato alla porta; **to ~ a nail into sth** conficcare un chiodo in qc
  ▶ **knock down** VT abbattere; (pedestrian) investire; (price) abbassare
  ▶ **knock off** VI (col: finish) smettere (di lavorare) ▶ VT (strike off) far cadere; (from price) far abbassare; (col: steal) sgraffignare, grattare; **to ~ off £10** fare uno sconto di 10 sterline
  ▶ **knock out** VT stendere; (Boxing) mettere K.O., mettere fuori combattimento; (defeat) battere
  ▶ **knock over** VT (object) far cadere; (pedestrian) investire
knockdown ['nɔkdaun] ADJ (price) fortemente scontato(-a)
knocker ['nɔkəʳ] N (on door) battente m
knocking ['nɔkɪŋ] N colpi mpl
knock-kneed [nɔkˈniːd] ADJ che ha le gambe ad x
knockout ['nɔkaut] N (Boxing) knock out m inv
  ▶ CPD a eliminazione

k

knockout competition N (BRIT) gara ad eliminazione

knock-up ['nɔkʌp] N (Tennis etc) palleggio; **to have a ~** palleggiare

knot [nɔt] N nodo ▶ VT annodare; **to tie a ~** fare un nodo

knotty ['nɔtɪ] ADJ (fig) spinoso(-a)

know [nəu] (pt **knew** [njuː], pp **known** [nəun]) VT sapere; (person, author, place) conoscere ▶ VI sapere; **to ~ that ...** sapere che ...; **to ~ how to do** sapere fare; **to get to ~ sth** venire a sapere qc; **I ~ nothing about it** non ne so niente; **I don't ~ him** non lo conosco; **to ~ right from wrong** distinguere il bene dal male; **as far as I ~ ...** che io sappia ..., per quanto io ne sappia ...; **yes, I ~** sì, lo so; **I don't ~** non lo so; **to ~ about** or **of sth/sb** conoscere qc/qn

know-all ['nəuɔːl] N (BRIT pej) sapientone(-a)

know-how ['nəuhau] N tecnica; pratica

knowing ['nəuɪŋ] ADJ (look etc) d'intesa

knowingly ['nəuɪŋlɪ] ADV (purposely) consapevolmente; di complicità; (smile, look) con aria d'intesa

know-it-all ['nəuɪtɔːl] N (US) = **know-all**

knowledge ['nɔlɪdʒ] N consapevolezza; (learning) conoscenza, sapere m; **to have no ~ of** ignorare, non sapere; **not to my ~** che io sappia, no; **to have a working ~ of Italian** avere una conoscenza pratica dell'italiano; **without my ~** a mia insaputa; **it is common ~ that ...** è risaputo che ...; **it has come to my ~ that ...** sono venuto a sapere che ...

knowledgeable ['nɔlɪdʒəbl] ADJ ben informato(-a)

known [nəun] PP of **know** ▶ ADJ (thief, facts) noto(-a); (expert) riconosciuto(-a)

knuckle ['nʌkl] N nocca
▶ **knuckle down** VI (col): **to ~ down to some hard work** mettersi sotto a lavorare
▶ **knuckle under** VI (col) cedere

knuckleduster ['nʌkldʌstər] N tirapugni m inv

KO ABBR = **knock out** ▶ N K.O. m ▶ VT mettere K.O.

koala [kəuˈɑːlə] N (also: **koala bear**) koala m inv

kook [kuːk] N (US col) svitato(-a)

Koran [kɔˈrɑːn] N Corano

Korea [kəˈriːə] N Corea; **North/South ~** Corea del Nord/Sud

Korean [kəˈriːən] ADJ, N coreano(-a)

kosher ['kəuʃər] ADJ kasher inv

Kosovar, Kosovan ['kɔsəvɑːr, 'kɔsəvən] ADJ kosovaro(-a)

Kosovo ['kusəvəu] N Kosovo

kowtow ['kau'tau] VI: **to ~ to sb** mostrarsi ossequioso(-a) verso qn

Kremlin ['kremlɪn] N: **the ~** il Cremlino

KS ABBR (US) = **Kansas**

Kt ABBR (BRIT: = Knight) titolo

Kuala Lumpur ['kwɑːlə'lumpuər] N Kuala Lumpur f

kudos ['kjuːdɔs] N gloria, fama

Kurd [kəːd] N curdo(-a)

Kuwait [ku'weɪt] N Kuwait m

Kuwaiti [ku'weɪtɪ] ADJ, N kuwaitiano(-a)

kW ABBR (= kilowatt) kw

KY, Ky. ABBR (US) = **Kentucky**

L l

L, l [ɛl] N (letter) L, l f inv or m inv; **L for Lucy,** (US) **L for Love** ≈ L come Livorno

L ABBR (= lake) l; (= large) taglia grande; (= left) sin.; (BRIT Aut) = **learner**

l ABBR (= litre) l

LA N ABBR (US) = **Los Angeles** ▸ ABBR (US) = **Louisiana**

La. ABBR (US) = **Louisiana**

lab [læb] N ABBR (= laboratory) laboratorio

Lab. ABBR (CANADA) = **Labrador**

label ['leɪbl] N etichetta, cartellino; (brand: of record) casa ▸ VT etichettare; classificare

labor etc ['leɪbə^r] (US) = **labour** etc

laboratory [lə'bɔrətərɪ] N laboratorio

Labor Day N (US) festa del lavoro; vedi nota

> Negli Stati Uniti e nel Canada il Labor Day, la festa del lavoro, cade il primo lunedì di settembre, contrariamente a quanto accade nella maggior parte dei paesi europei dove tale celebrazione ha luogo il primo maggio.

laborious [lə'bɔːrɪəs] ADJ laborioso(-a)

labor union N (US) sindacato

Labour ['leɪbə^r] N (BRIT Pol: also: **the Labour Party**) il partito laburista, i laburisti

labour, (US) **labor** ['leɪbə^r] N (task) lavoro; (workmen) manodopera; (Med) travaglio del parto, doglie fpl ▸ VI: **to ~ (at)** lavorare duro(a); **to be in ~** (Med) avere le doglie; **hard ~** lavori mpl forzati

labour camp, (US) **labor camp** N campo dei lavori forzati

labour cost, (US) **labor cost** N costo del lavoro

labour dispute, (US) **labor dispute** N conflitto tra lavoratori e datori di lavoro

laboured, (US) **labored** ['leɪbəd] ADJ (breathing) affaticato(-a), affannoso(-a); (style) elaborato(-a), pesante

labourer, (US) **laborer** ['leɪbərə^r] N manovale m; **farm ~** lavoratore m agricolo

labour force, (US) **labor force** N manodopera

labour-intensive, (US) **labor-intensive** [leɪbərɪn'tɛnsɪv] ADJ che assorbe molta manodopera

labour market, (US) **labor market** N mercato del lavoro

labour pains, (US) **labor pains** NPL doglie fpl

labour relations, (US) **labor relations** NPL relazioni fpl industriali

labour-saving, (US) **labor-saving** ['leɪbəseɪvɪŋ] ADJ che fa risparmiare fatica or lavoro

labour unrest, (US) **labor unrest** N agitazioni fpl degli operai

labyrinth ['læbɪrɪnθ] N labirinto

lace [leɪs] N merletto, pizzo; (of shoe etc) laccio ▸ VT (shoe: also: **lace up**) allacciare; (: drink: fortify with spirits) correggere

lacemaking ['leɪsmeɪkɪŋ] N fabbricazione f dei pizzi or dei merletti

laceration [læsə'reɪʃən] N lacerazione f

lace-up ['leɪsʌp] ADJ (shoes etc) con i lacci, con le stringhe

lack [læk] N mancanza, scarsità ▸ VT mancare di; **through or for ~ of** per mancanza di; **to be lacking** mancare; **to be lacking in** mancare di

lackadaisical [lækə'deɪzɪkl] ADJ disinteressato(-a), noncurante

lackey ['lækɪ] N (also fig) lacchè m inv

lacklustre, (US) **lackluster** ['læklʌstə^r] ADJ (surface) opaco(-a); (style) scialbo(-a); (eyes) spento(-a)

laconic [lə'kɔnɪk] ADJ laconico(-a)

lacquer ['lækə^r] N lacca; **hair ~** lacca per (i) capelli

lacy ['leɪsɪ] ADJ (like lace) che sembra un pizzo

lad [læd] N ragazzo, giovanotto; (BRIT: in stable etc) mozzo or garzone m di stalla

ladder ['lædə^r] N scala; (BRIT: in tights) smagliatura ▸ VT smagliare ▸ VI smagliarsi

laden ['leɪdn] ADJ: **~ (with)** carico(-a) or caricato(-a) (di); **fully ~** (truck, ship) a pieno carico

ladle ['leɪdl] N mestolo

lady ['leɪdɪ] N signora; dama; **L~ Smith**

lady Smith; **the ladies' (toilets)** i gabinetti per signore; **a ~ doctor** una dottoressa

ladybird ['leɪdɪbəːd], (US) **ladybug** ['leɪdɪbʌg] N coccinella

lady-in-waiting ['leɪdɪɪn'weɪtɪŋ] N dama di compagnia

ladykiller ['leɪdɪkɪlər] N dongiovanni m inv

ladylike ['leɪdɪlaɪk] ADJ da signora, distinto(-a)

ladyship ['leɪdɪʃɪp] N: **your L~** signora contessa etc

lag [læg] N (of time) lasso, intervallo ▶ VI (also: **lag behind**) trascinarsi ▶ VT (pipes) rivestire di materiale isolante

lager ['lɑːgər] N lager m inv

lager lout N (BRIT col) giovinastro ubriaco

lagging ['lægɪŋ] N rivestimento di materiale isolante

lagoon [lə'guːn] N laguna

Lagos ['leɪgɔs] N Lagos f

laid [leɪd] PT, PP of **lay**

laid-back [leɪd'bæk] ADJ (col) rilassato(-a), tranquillo(-a)

lain [leɪn] PP of **lie**

lair [lɛər] N covo, tana

laissez-faire [lɛseɪ'fɛər] N liberismo

laity ['leɪətɪ] N laici mpl

lake [leɪk] N lago

Lake District N: **the ~** (BRIT) la regione dei laghi

lamb [læm] N agnello

lamb chop N cotoletta d'agnello

lambskin ['læmskɪn] N (pelle f d')agnello

lambswool ['læmzwuːl] N lamb's wool m

lame [leɪm] ADJ zoppo(-a), (excuse etc) zoppicante; **~ duck** (fig: person) persona inetta; (firm) azienda traballante

lamely ['leɪmlɪ] ADV (fig) in modo poco convincente

lament [lə'mɛnt] N lamento ▶ VT lamentare, piangere

lamentable ['læməntəbl] ADJ doloroso(-a); deplorevole

laminated ['læmɪneɪtɪd] ADJ laminato(-a)

lamp [læmp] N lampada

lamplight ['læmplaɪt] N: **by ~** a lume della lampada

lampoon [læm'puːn] N satira

lamppost ['læmppəust] (BRIT) N lampione m

lampshade ['læmpʃeɪd] N paralume m

lance [lɑːns] N lancia ▶ VT (Med) incidere

lance corporal N (BRIT) caporale m

lancet ['lɑːnsɪt] N (Med) bisturi m inv

Lancs [læŋks] ABBR (BRIT) = **Lancashire**

land [lænd] N (as opposed to sea) terra (ferma); (country) paese m; (soil) terreno; suolo; (estate) terreni mpl, terre fpl ▶ VI (from ship) sbarcare; (Aviat) atterrare; (fig: fall) cadere ▶ VT (obtain) acchiappare; (passengers) sbarcare; (goods)

scaricare; **to go/travel by ~** andare/ viaggiare per via di terra; **to own ~** possedere dei terreni, avere delle proprietà (terriere); **to ~ sb with sth** affibbiare qc a qn; **to ~ on one's feet** cadere in piedi; (fig: to be lucky) cascar bene

▶ **land up** VI andare a finire

landed gentry ['lændɪd-] N proprietari mpl terrieri

landfill site ['lændfɪl-] N discarica dove i rifiuti vengono sepolti

landing ['lændɪŋ] N (from ship) sbarco; (Aviat) atterraggio; (of staircase) pianerottolo

landing card N carta di sbarco

landing craft N mezzo da sbarco

landing gear N (Aviat) carrello d'atterraggio

landing stage N pontile m da sbarco

landing strip N pista d'atterraggio

landlady ['lændleɪdɪ] N padrona or proprietaria di casa

landline ['lændlaɪn] N telefono fisso

landlocked ['lændlɔkt] ADJ senza sbocco sul mare

landlord ['lændlɔːd] N padrone m or proprietario di casa; (of pub etc) padrone m

landlubber ['lændlʌbər] N marinaio d'acqua dolce

landmark ['lændmɑːk] N punto di riferimento; (fig) pietra miliare

landowner ['lændəunər] N proprietario(-a) terriero(-a)

landscape ['lænskeɪp] N paesaggio

landscape architect, landscape gardener N paesaggista mf

landscape painting N (Art) paesaggistica

landslide ['lændslaɪd] N (Geo) frana; (fig: Pol) valanga

lane [leɪn] N (in country) viottolo; (in town) stradina; (Aut, in race) corsia; **shipping ~** rotta (marittima); **"get in ~"** "immettersi in corsia"

language ['læŋgwɪdʒ] N lingua; (way one speaks) linguaggio; **bad ~** linguaggio volgare

language laboratory N laboratorio linguistico

language school N scuola di lingue

languid ['læŋgwɪd] ADJ languente, languido(-a)

languish ['læŋgwɪʃ] VI languire

lank [læŋk] ADJ (hair) liscio(-a) e opaco(-a)

lanky ['læŋkɪ] ADJ allampanato(-a)

lanolin, lanoline ['lænəlɪn] N lanolina

lantern ['læntn] N lanterna

Laos [lauz] N Laos m

lap [læp] N (of track) giro; **in** or **on one's ~** in grembo ▶ VT (also: **lap up**) papparsi, leccare ▶ VI (waves) sciabordare

▶ **lap up** VT (fig: compliments, attention) bearsi di

La Paz [læˈpæz] N La Paz f

lapdog [ˈlæpdɔg] N cane m da grembo

lapel [ləˈpɛl] N risvolto

Lapland [ˈlæplænd] N Lapponia

Lapp [læp] ADJ lappone ▶ N lappone mf; (Ling) lappone m

lapse [læps] N lapsus m inv; (longer) caduta; (fault) mancanza; (in behaviour) scorrettezza ▶ VI (law, act) cadere; (ticket, passport, membership, contract) scadere; **to ~ into bad habits** pigliare cattive abitudini; **~ of time** spazio di tempo; **a ~ of memory** un vuoto di memoria

laptop [ˈlæptɔp] N (also: **laptop computer**) laptop m inv

larceny [ˈlɑːsənɪ] N furto

lard [lɑːd] N lardo

larder [ˈlɑːdəʳ] N dispensa

large [lɑːdʒ] ADJ grande; (person, animal) grosso(-a) ▶ ADV: **by and ~** generalmente; **at ~** (free) in libertà; (generally) in generale; nell'insieme; **to make larger** ingrandire; **a ~ number of people** molta gente; **on a ~ scale** su vasta scala

largely [ˈlɑːdʒlɪ] ADV in gran parte

large-scale [ˈlɑːdʒˈskeɪl] ADJ (map, drawing etc) in grande scala; (reforms, business activities) su vasta scala

lark [lɑːk] N (bird) allodola; (joke) scherzo, gioco
▶ **lark about** VI fare lo stupido

larrikin [ˈlærɪkɪn] N (AUSTRALIA, NEW ZEALAND col) furfante mf

larva [ˈlɑːvə] (pl **larvae** [-iː]) N larva

laryngitis [lærɪnˈdʒaɪtɪs] N laringite f

larynx [ˈlærɪŋks] N laringe f

lasagne [ləˈzænjə] N lasagne fpl

lascivious [ləˈsɪvɪəs] ADJ lascivo(-a)

laser [ˈleɪzəʳ] N laser m

laser beam N raggio m laser inv

laser printer N stampante f laser inv

lash [læʃ] N frustata; (also: **eyelash**) ciglio
▶ VT frustare; (tie) legare; **to ~ to/together** legare a insieme
▶ **lash down** VT assicurare (con corde) ▶ VI (rain) scrosciare
▶ **lash out** VI: **to ~ out (at or against sb/sth)** attaccare violentemente (qn/qc); **to ~ out (on sth)** (col: spend) spendere un sacco di soldi (per qc)

lashing [ˈlæʃɪŋ] N (beating) frustata, sferzata; **lashings of** (BRIT col) un mucchio di, una montagna di

lass [læs] N ragazza

lasso [læˈsuː] N laccio ▶ VT acchiappare con il laccio

last [lɑːst] ADJ ultimo(-a); (week, month, year) scorso(-a), passato(-a) ▶ ADV per ultimo ▶ VI durare; **~ week** la settimana scorsa; **~ night** ieri sera, la notte scorsa; **at ~** finalmente, alla fine; **~ but one** penultimo(-a); **the ~ time** l'ultima volta; **it lasts (for) 2 hours** dura 2 ore

last-ditch [ˈlɑːstˈdɪtʃ] ADJ ultimo(-a) e disperato(-a)

lasting [ˈlɑːstɪŋ] ADJ durevole

lastly [ˈlɑːstlɪ] ADV infine, per finire, per ultimo

last-minute [ˈlɑːstmɪnɪt] ADJ fatto(-a) (or preso(-a) etc) all'ultimo momento

latch [lætʃ] N chiavistello; (automatic lock) serratura a scatto
▶ **latch on to** VT FUS (cling to: person) attaccarsi a, appiccicarsi a; (: idea) afferrare, capire

latchkey [ˈlætʃkiː] N chiave f di casa

late [leɪt] ADJ (not on time) in ritardo; (far on in day etc) tardi inv; tardo(-a); (recent) recente, ultimo(-a); (former) ex; (dead) defunto(-a) ▶ ADV tardi; (behind time, schedule) in ritardo; **to be (10 minutes) ~** essere in ritardo (di 10 minuti); **to work ~** lavorare fino a tardi; **~ in life** in età avanzata; **sorry I'm ~** scusi il ritardo; **the flight is two hours ~** il volo ha due ore di ritardo; **it's too ~** è troppo tardi; **of ~** di recente; **in the ~ afternoon** nel tardo pomeriggio; **in ~ May** verso la fine di maggio; **the ~ Mr X** il defunto Signor X

latecomer [ˈleɪtkʌməʳ] N ritardatario(-a)

lately [ˈleɪtlɪ] ADV recentemente

lateness [ˈleɪtnɪs] N (of person) ritardo; (of event) tardezza, ora tarda

latent [ˈleɪtnt] ADJ latente; **~ defect** vizio occulto

later [ˈleɪtəʳ] ADJ (date etc) posteriore; (version etc) successivo(-a) ▶ ADV più tardi; **~ on today** oggi più tardi

lateral [ˈlætərl] ADJ laterale

latest [ˈleɪtɪst] ADJ ultimo(-a), più recente; **at the ~** al più tardi; **the ~ news** le ultime notizie

latex [ˈleɪtɛks] N latice m

lath [læθ] N (pl **laths** [læðz]) assicella

lathe [leɪð] N tornio

lather [ˈlɑːðəʳ] N schiuma di sapone ▶ VT insaponare ▶ VI far schiuma

Latin [ˈlætɪn] N latino ▶ ADJ latino(-a)

Latin America N America Latina

Latin American ADJ sudamericano(-a)

latitude [ˈlætɪtjuːd] N latitudine f; (fig: freedom) libertà d'azione

latrine [ləˈtriːn] N latrina

latter [ˈlætəʳ] ADJ secondo(-a); più recente
▶ N: **the ~** quest'ultimo, il secondo

latterly [ˈlætəlɪ] ADV recentemente, negli ultimi tempi

lattice [ˈlætɪs] N traliccio; graticolato

lattice window N finestra con vetrata a losanghe

Latvia ['lætvɪə] N Lettonia
Latvian ['lætvɪən] ADJ lettone *inv* ▶ N lettone *mf*; (*Ling*) lettone *m*
laudable ['lɔ:dəbl] ADJ lodevole
laudatory ['lɔ:dətrɪ] ADJ elogiativo(-a)
laugh [lɑ:f] N risata ▶ VI ridere
  ▶ **laugh at** VT FUS (*misfortune etc*) ridere di; **I laughed at his joke** la sua barzelletta mi fece ridere
  ▶ **laugh off** VT prendere alla leggera
laughable ['lɑ:fəbl] ADJ ridicolo(-a)
laughing ['lɑ:fɪŋ] ADJ (*face*) ridente; **this is no ~ matter** non è una cosa da ridere
laughing gas N gas *m* esilarante
laughing stock N: **the ~ of** lo zimbello di
laughter ['lɑ:ftə^r] N riso; risate *fpl*
launch [lɔ:ntʃ] N (*of rocket, product etc*) lancio; (*of new ship*) varo; (*boat*) scialuppa; (*also*: **motor launch**) lancia ▶ VT (*rocket, product*) lanciare; (*ship, plan*) varare
  ▶ **launch into** VT FUS lanciarsi in
  ▶ **launch out** VI: **to ~ out (into)** lanciarsi (in)
launching ['lɔ:ntʃɪŋ] N lancio; varo
launch pad, launching pad N rampa di lancio
launder ['lɔ:ndə^r] VT lavare e stirare
Launderette® [lɔ:n'drɛt] (*US*), **Laundromat**® ['lɔ:ndrəmæt] N lavanderia (automatica)
laundry ['lɔ:ndrɪ] N lavanderia; (*clothes*) biancheria; (: *dirty*) panni *mpl* da lavare; **to do the ~** fare il bucato
laureate ['lɔ:rɪət] ADJ *see* **poet laureate**
laurel ['lɔrl] N lauro, alloro; **to rest on one's laurels** riposare *or* dormire sugli allori
Lausanne [ləu'zæn] N Losanna
lava ['lɑ:və] N lava
lavatory ['lævətərɪ] N gabinetto
lavatory paper N (*BRIT*) carta igienica
lavender ['lævndə^r] N lavanda
lavish ['lævɪʃ] ADJ copioso(-a), abbondante; sontuoso(-a); (*giving freely*): **~ with** prodigo(-a) di, largo(-a) in ▶ VT: **to ~ sth on sb/sth** colmare qn/qc di qc
lavishly ['lævɪʃlɪ] ADV (*give, spend*) generosamente; (*furnished*) sontuosamente, lussuosamente
law [lɔ:] N legge *f*; **against the ~** contro la legge; **to study ~** studiare diritto; **to go to ~** (*BRIT*) ricorrere alle vie legali; **civil/criminal ~** diritto civile/penale
law-abiding ['lɔ:əbaɪdɪŋ] ADJ ubbidiente alla legge
law and order N l'ordine *m* pubblico
lawbreaker ['lɔ:breɪkə^r] N violatore(-trice) della legge
law court N tribunale *m*, corte *f* di giustizia
lawful ['lɔ:ful] ADJ legale, lecito(-a)
lawfully ['lɔ:fəlɪ] ADV legalmente

lawless ['lɔ:lɪs] ADJ senza legge; illegale
Law Lords NPL ≈ Corte *f* Suprema
lawmaker ['lɔ:meɪkə^r] N legislatore *m*
lawn [lɔ:n] N tappeto erboso
lawnmower ['lɔ:nməuə^r] N tosaerba *m inv or f inv*
lawn tennis N tennis *m* su prato
law school N facoltà *f inv* di legge
law student N studente(-essa) di legge
lawsuit ['lɔ:su:t] N processo, causa; **to bring a ~ against** intentare causa a
lawyer ['lɔ:jə^r] N (*consultant, with company*) giurista *mf*; (*for sales, wills etc*) ≈ notaio; (*partner, in court*) ≈ avvocato(-essa)
lax [læks] ADJ (*conduct*) rilassato(-a); (*person: careless*) negligente; (: *on discipline*) permissivo(-a)
laxative ['læksətɪv] N lassativo
laxity ['læksɪtɪ] N rilassatezza; negligenza
lay [leɪ] PT *of* **lie** ▶ ADJ laico(-a); secolare; (*not expert*) profano(-a) ▶ VT (*pt, pp* **laid** [leɪd]) posare, mettere; (*eggs*) fare; (*trap*) tendere; (*plans*) fare, elaborare; **to ~ the table** apparecchiare la tavola; **to ~ the facts/one's proposals before sb** presentare i fatti/delle proposte a qn; **to get laid** (*col!*) scopare (!), essere scopato(-a) (!)
  ▶ **lay aside, lay by** VT mettere da parte
  ▶ **lay down** VT mettere giù; (*rules etc*) formulare, fissare; **to ~ down the law** (*fig*) dettar legge; **to ~ down one's life** dare la propria vita
  ▶ **lay in** VT fare una scorta di
  ▶ **lay into** VT FUS (*col: attack, scold*) aggredire
  ▶ **lay off** VT (*workers*) licenziare
  ▶ **lay on** VT (*water, gas*) installare, mettere; (*provide: meal etc*) fornire; (: *paint*) applicare
  ▶ **lay out** VT (*design*) progettare; (*display*) presentare; (*spend*) sborsare
  ▶ **lay up** VT (*to store*) accumulare; (*ship*) mettere in disarmo; (*illness*) costringere a letto
layabout ['leɪəbaut] N sfaccendato(-a), fannullone(-a)
lay-by ['leɪbaɪ] N (*BRIT*) piazzola (di sosta)
lay days NPL (*Naut*) stallie *fpl*
layer ['leɪə^r] N strato
layette [leɪ'ɛt] N corredino (per neonato)
layman ['leɪmən] N (*irreg*) laico; profano
lay-off ['leɪɔf] N sospensione *f*, licenziamento
layout ['leɪaut] N lay-out *m inv*, disposizione *f*; (*Press*) impaginazione *f*
laze [leɪz] VI oziare
laziness ['leɪzɪnɪs] N pigrizia
lazy ['leɪzɪ] ADJ pigro(-a)
lb. ABBR (*pound: = pound (weight)*) lb.
lbw ABBR (*Cricket: = leg before wicket*) fallo dovuto al fatto che il giocatore ha la gamba davanti alla porta

LC N ABBR (US) = **Library of Congress**

lc ABBR (Typ) = **lower case**

L/C ABBR = **letter of credit**

LCD N ABBR = **liquid crystal display**

Ld ABBR (BRIT: = lord) titolo

LDS N ABBR (BRIT: = Licentiate in Dental Surgery) specializzazione dopo la laurea; (= Latter-day Saints) Chiesa di Gesù Cristo dei Santi dell'Ultimo Giorno

LEA N ABBR (BRIT: = local education authority) ≈ Provveditorato degli Studi

lead¹ [liːd] (pt, pp **led** [lɛd]) N (front position) posizione f di testa; (distance, time ahead) vantaggio; (clue) indizio; (Elec) filo (elettrico); (for dog) guinzaglio; (Theat) parte f principale ▶ VT menare, guidare, condurre; (induce) indurre; (be leader of) essere a capo di; (: orchestra: BRIT) essere il primo violino di; (: US) dirigere; (Sport) essere in testa a ▶ VI condurre; (Sport) essere in testa; **in the** ~ in testa; **to** ~ **the way** fare strada; **to take the** ~ (Sport) passare in testa; (fig) prendere l'iniziativa; **to** ~ **to** menare a; condurre a; portare a; **to** ~ **astray** sviare; **to** ~ **sb to believe that ...** far credere a qn che ...; **to** ~ **sb to do sth** portare qn a fare qc

▶ **lead away** VT condurre via

▶ **lead back** VT riportare, ricondurre

▶ **lead off** VT portare ▶ VI partire da

▶ **lead on** VT (tease) tenere sulla corda

▶ **lead on to** VT (induce) portare a

▶ **lead up to** VT FUS portare a; (fig) preparare la strada per

lead² [lɛd] N (metal) piombo; (in pencil) mina

leaded ['lɛdɪd] ADJ (petrol) con piombo; ~ **windows** vetrate fpl (artistiche)

leaden ['lɛdn] ADJ di piombo

leader ['liːdər] N capo; leader m inv; (in newspaper) articolo di fondo; (Sport) chi è in testa; **they are leaders in their field** (fig) sono all'avanguardia nel loro campo; **the L~ of the House** (BRIT) il capo della maggioranza ministeriale

leadership ['liːdəʃɪp] N direzione f; capacità di comando; **under the** ~ **of ...** sotto la direzione or guida di ...; **qualities of** ~ qualità fpl di un capo

lead-free ['lɛdfriː] ADJ senza piombo

leading ['liːdɪŋ] ADJ primo(-a), principale; **a** ~ **question** una domanda tendenziosa; ~ **role** ruolo principale

leading lady N (Theat) prima attrice

leading light N (person) personaggio di primo piano

leading man N (irreg) (Theat) primo attore

lead pencil [lɛd-] N matita con la mina di grafite

lead poisoning [lɛd-] N saturnismo

lead singer N cantante alla testa di un gruppo

lead time [liːd-] N (Comm) tempo di consegna

lead weight [lɛd-] N piombino, piombo

leaf [liːf] (pl **leaves**) N foglia; (of table) ribalta; **to turn over a new** ~ (fig) cambiar vita; **to take a** ~ **out of sb's book** (fig) prendere esempio da qn

▶ **leaf through** VT (book) sfogliare

leaflet ['liːflɪt] N dépliant m inv; (Pol, Rel) volantino

leafy ['liːfɪ] ADJ ricco(-a) di foglie

league [liːg] N lega; (Football) campionato; **to be in** ~ **with** essere in lega con

league table N classifica

leak [liːk] N (out) fuga; (in) infiltrazione f; (fig: of information) fuga di notizie; (security leak) fuga d'informazioni ▶ VI (roof, bucket) perdere; (liquid) uscire; (shoes) lasciar passare l'acqua ▶ VT (liquid) spandere; (information) divulgare

▶ **leak out** VI uscire; (information) trapelare

leakage ['liːkɪdʒ] N (of water, gas etc) perdita

leaky ['liːkɪ] ADJ (pipe, bucket, roof) che perde; (shoe) che lascia passare l'acqua; (boat) che fa acqua

lean [liːn] (pt, pp **leaned**, **leant** [lɛnt]) ADJ magro(-a) ▶ N (of meat) carne f magra ▶ VT: **to** ~ **sth on** appoggiare qc su ▶ VI (slope) pendere; (rest): **to** ~ **against** appoggiarsi contro; essere appoggiato(-a) a; **to** ~ **on** appoggiarsi a

▶ **lean back** VT sporgersi indietro

▶ **lean forward** VI sporgersi in avanti

▶ **lean out** VI: **to** ~ **out (of)** sporgersi (da)

▶ **lean over** VI inclinarsi

leaning ['liːnɪŋ] N: ~ **(towards)** propensione f (per) ▶ ADJ inclinato(-a), pendente; **the L~ Tower of Pisa** la torre (pendente) di Pisa

leant [lɛnt] PT, PP of **lean**

lean-to ['liːntuː] N (roof) tettoia; (building) edificio con tetto appoggiato ad altro edificio

leap [liːp] (pt, pp **leaped** or **leapt** [lɛpt]) N salto, balzo ▶ VI saltare, balzare; **to** ~ **at an offer** afferrare al volo una proposta

▶ **leap up** VI (person) alzarsi d'un balzo, balzare su

leapfrog ['liːpfrɒg] N gioco della cavallina

▶ VI: **to** ~ **over sb/sth** saltare (alla cavallina) qn/qc

leapt [lɛpt] PT, PP of **leap**

leap year N anno bisestile

learn [ləːn] (pt, pp **learned**, **learnt** [-t]) VT, VI imparare; **to** ~ **(how) to do sth** imparare a fare qc; **to** ~ **that ...** apprendere che ...; **to** ~ **about sth** (Scol) studiare qc; (hear) apprendere qc; **we were sorry to** ~ **that it was closing down** ci ha fatto dispiacere la notizia della chiusura

learned ['ləːnɪd] ADJ erudito(-a), dotto(-a)

learner ['ləːnər] N principiante mf;

apprendista *mf*; **he's a ~ (driver)** (BRIT) sta imparando a guidare

learning ['lə:nıŋ] N erudizione *f*, sapienza

learnt [lə:nt] PT, PP *of* **learn**

lease [li:s] N contratto d'affitto ▸ VT affittare; **on ~** in affitto
  ▸ **lease back** VT effettuare un lease-back *inv*

leaseback ['li:sbæk] N lease-back *m inv*

leasehold ['li:shəuld] N (*contract*) contratto di affitto (*a lungo termine con responsabilità simili a quelle di un proprietario*) ▸ ADJ in affitto

leash [li:ʃ] N guinzaglio

least [li:st] ADJ: **the ~** (*+ noun*) il (la) più piccolo(-a), il (la) minimo(-a); (*smallest amount of*) il (la) meno ▸ ADV (*+ verb*) meno; **the ~** (*+ adjective*): **the ~ beautiful girl** la ragazza meno bella; **the ~ expensive** il (la) meno caro(-a); **the ~ possible effort** il minimo sforzo possibile; **I have the ~ money** ho meno denaro di tutti; **at ~** almeno; **not in the ~** affatto, per nulla

leather ['lɛðər] N (*soft*) pelle *f*; (*hard*) cuoio
  ▸ CPD di *or* in pelle; di cuoio; **~ goods** pelletteria, pelletterie *fpl*

leave [li:v] (*pt, pp* **left** [lɛft]) VT lasciare; (*go away from*) partire da ▸ VI partire, andarsene; (*bus, train*) partire ▸ N (*time off*) congedo; (*Mil, consent*) licenza; **to be left** rimanere; **there's some milk left over** c'è rimasto del latte; **to take one's ~ of** congedarsi di; **he's already left for the airport** è già uscito per andare all'aeroporto; **to ~ school** finire la scuola; **~ it to me!** ci penso io!, lascia fare a me!; **on ~** in congedo; **on ~ of absence** in permesso; (*public employee*) in congedo; (*Mil*) in licenza
  ▸ **leave behind** VT (*also fig*) lasciare; (*forget*) dimenticare
  ▸ **leave off** VT non mettere; (BRIT col: *stop*): **to ~ off doing sth** smetterla *or* piantarla di fare qc
  ▸ **leave on** VT lasciare su; (*light, fire, cooker*) lasciare acceso(-a)
  ▸ **leave out** VT omettere, tralasciare

leaves [li:vz] NPL *of* **leaf**

leavetaking ['li:vteıkıŋ] N commiato, addio

Lebanese [lɛbə'ni:z] ADJ, N (*pl inv*) libanese (*mf*)

Lebanon ['lɛbənən] N Libano

lecherous ['lɛtʃərəs] ADJ lascivo(-a), lubrico(-a)

lectern ['lɛktə:n] N leggio

lecture ['lɛktʃər] N conferenza; (*Scol*) lezione *f*
  ▸ VI fare conferenze; fare lezioni; (*reprove*) rimproverare, fare una ramanzina a ▸ VT (*scold*): **to ~ sb on** *or* **about sth** rimproverare qn *or* fare una ramanzina a qn per qc; **to ~ on** fare una conferenza su; **to give a ~ (on)** (BRIT) fare una conferenza (su); fare lezione (su)

lecture hall N aula magna

lecturer ['lɛktʃərər] N (*speaker*) conferenziere(-a); (BRIT: *at university*) professore(-essa), docente *mf*; **assistant ~** (BRIT) ≈ professore(-essa) associato(-a); **senior ~** (BRIT) ≈ professore(-essa) ordinario(-a)

lecture theatre N = **lecture hall**

LED N ABBR (*Elec: = light-emitting diode*) diodo a emissione luminosa

led [lɛd] PT, PP *of* **lead¹**

ledge [lɛdʒ] N (*of window*) davanzale *m*; (*on wall etc*) sporgenza; (*of mountain*) cornice *f*, cengia

ledger ['lɛdʒər] N libro maestro, registro

lee [li:] N lato sottovento; **in the ~ of** a ridosso di, al riparo di

leech [li:tʃ] N sanguisuga

leek [li:k] N porro

leer [lıər] VI: **to ~ at sb** gettare uno sguardo voglioso (*or* maligno) su qn

leeward ['li:wəd] ADJ sottovento *inv* ▸ N lato sottovento; **to ~** sottovento

leeway ['li:weı] N (*fig*): **to have some ~** avere una certa libertà di agire

left [lɛft] PT, PP *of* **leave** ▸ ADJ sinistro(-a)
  ▸ ADV a sinistra ▸ N sinistra; **on the ~**, **to the ~** a sinistra; **the L~** (*Pol*) la sinistra

left-click ['lɛftklık] VI (*Comput*): **to ~ on** cliccare con il pulsante sinistro del mouse su

left-hand ADJ: **the ~ side** il lato sinistro

left-hand drive ['lɛfthænd-] N, ADJ (BRIT) guida a sinistra

left-handed [lɛft'hændıd] ADJ mancino(-a); **~ scissors** forbici *fpl* per mancini

left-hand side ['lɛfthænd-] N lato *or* fianco sinistro

leftie ['lɛftı] N: **a ~** (*col*) uno(-a) di sinistra

leftist ['lɛftıst] ADJ (*Pol*) di sinistra

left-luggage [lɛft'lʌgıdʒ], (BRIT) **left-luggage office** [lɛft'lʌgıdʒ-] N deposito *m* bagagli *inv*

left-luggage locker N armadietto per deposito bagagli

left-overs ['lɛftəuvəz] NPL avanzi *mpl*, resti *mpl*

left wing N (*Mil, Sport*) ala sinistra; (*Pol*) sinistra ▸ ADJ: **left-wing** (*Pol*) di sinistra

left-winger [lɛft'wıŋər] N (*Pol*) uno(-a) di sinistra; (*Sport*) ala sinistra

lefty ['lɛftı] N = **leftie**

leg [lɛg] N gamba; (*of animal*) zampa; (*of furniture*) piede *m*; (*Culin: of chicken*) coscia; (*of journey*) tappa; **1st/2nd ~** (*Sport*) partita di andata/ritorno; **~ of lamb** (*Culin*) cosciotto d'agnello; **to stretch one's legs** sgranchirsi le gambe

legacy ['lɛgəsı] N eredità *f inv*; (*fig*) retaggio

legal ['li:gl] ADJ legale; **to take ~ action** *or* **proceedings against sb** intentare

un'azione legale contro qn, far causa a qn
legal adviser N consulente *mf* legale
legal holiday N (*US*) giorno festivo, festa
nazionale
legality [lɪˈgælɪtɪ] N legalità
legalize [ˈliːgəlaɪz] VT legalizzare
legally [ˈliːgəlɪ] ADV legalmente; ~ **binding**
legalmente vincolante
legal tender N moneta legale
legation [lɪˈgeɪʃən] N legazione *f*
legend [ˈlɛdʒənd] N leggenda
legendary [ˈlɛdʒəndərɪ] ADJ leggendario(-a)
-legged [ˈlɛgɪd] SUFFIX: **two-** a due gambe (*or*
zampe), bipede
leggings [ˈlɛgɪŋz] NPL ghette *fpl*
leggy [ˈlɛgɪ] ADJ dalle gambe lunghe
legibility [lɛdʒɪˈbɪlɪtɪ] N leggibilità
legible [ˈlɛdʒəbl] ADJ leggibile
legibly [ˈlɛdʒəblɪ] ADV in modo leggibile
legion [ˈliːdʒən] N legione *f*
legionnaire [liːdʒəˈnɛəʳ] N legionario; **~'s**
disease morbo del legionario
legislate [ˈlɛdʒɪsleɪt] VI legiferare
legislation [lɛdʒɪsˈleɪʃən] N legislazione *f*; **a**
piece of ~ una legge
legislative [ˈlɛdʒɪslətɪv] ADJ legislativo(-a)
legislator [ˈlɛdʒɪsleɪtəʳ] N legislatore(-trice)
legislature [ˈlɛdʒɪslətʃəʳ] N corpo legislativo
legitimacy [lɪˈdʒɪtɪməsɪ] N legittimità
legitimate [lɪˈdʒɪtɪmət] ADJ legittimo(-a)
legitimize [lɪˈdʒɪtɪmaɪz] VT (*gen*) legalizzare,
rendere legale; (*child*) legittimare
legless [ˈlɛglɪs] ADJ (*BRIT col*) sbronzo(-a),
fatto(-a)
leg-room [ˈlɛgruːm] N spazio per le gambe
Leics ABBR (*BRIT*) = **Leicestershire**
leisure [ˈlɛʒəʳ] N agio, tempo libero;
ricreazioni *fpl*; **at ~** con comodo
leisure centre N centro di ricreazione
leisurely [ˈlɛʒəlɪ] ADJ tranquillo(-a), fatto(-a)
con comodo *or* senza fretta
leisure suit N (*BRIT*) tuta (da ginnastica)
lemon [ˈlɛmən] N limone *m*
lemonade [lɛməˈneɪd] N limonata
lemon cheese, lemon curd N crema di
limone (*che si spalma sul pane ecc*)
lemon juice N succo di limone
lemon squeezer N spremiagrumi *m inv*
lemon tea N tè *m inv* al limone
lend [lɛnd] (*pt, pp* **lent** [lɛnt]) VT: **to ~ sth (to**
sb) prestare qc (a qn); **to ~ a hand** dare una
mano
lender [ˈlɛndəʳ] N prestatore(-trice)
lending library [ˈlɛndɪŋ-] N biblioteca
circolante
length [lɛŋθ] N lunghezza; (*distance*)
distanza; (*section: of road, pipe etc*) pezzo,
tratto; ~ **of time** periodo (di tempo); **what ~**
is it? quant'è lungo?; **it is 2 metres in ~** è

lungo 2 metri; **to fall full ~** cadere lungo
disteso; **at ~** (*at last*) finalmente, alla fine;
(*lengthily*) a lungo; **to go to any ~(s) to do sth**
fare qualsiasi cosa pur di *or* per fare qc
lengthen [ˈlɛŋθən] VT allungare, prolungare
▶ VI allungarsi
lengthways [ˈlɛŋθweɪz] ADV per il lungo
lengthy [ˈlɛŋθɪ] ADJ molto lungo(-a)
leniency [ˈliːnɪənsɪ] N indulgenza, clemenza
lenient [ˈliːnɪənt] ADJ indulgente, clemente
leniently [ˈliːnɪəntlɪ] ADV con indulgenza
lens [lɛnz] N lente *f*; (*of camera*) obiettivo
Lent [lɛnt] N Quaresima
lent [lɛnt] PT, PP *of* **lend**
lentil [ˈlɛntl] N lenticchia
Leo [ˈliːəu] N Leone *m*; **to be ~** essere del
Leone
leopard [ˈlɛpəd] N leopardo
leotard [ˈliːətɑːd] N calzamaglia
leper [ˈlɛpəʳ] N lebbroso(-a)
leper colony N lebbrosario
leprosy [ˈlɛprəsɪ] N lebbra
lesbian [ˈlɛzbɪən] N lesbica ▶ ADJ lesbico(-a)
lesion [ˈliːʒən] N (*Med*) lesione *f*
Lesotho [lɪˈsuːtu] N Lesotho *m*
less [lɛs] ADJ, PRON, ADV, PREP meno;
~ **tax/10% discount** meno tasse/il 10% di
sconto; ~ **than you/ever** meno di lei/che
mai; ~ **than half** meno della metà; ~ **and ~**
sempre meno; **the ~ he works ...** meno
lavora ...; ~ **than £1/a kilo/3 metres** meno
di una sterlina/un chilo/3 metri
lessee [lɛˈsiː] N affittuario(-a), locatario(-a)
lessen [ˈlɛsn] VI diminuire, attenuarsi ▶ VT
diminuire, ridurre
lesser [ˈlɛsəʳ] ADJ minore, più piccolo(-a); **to a**
~ **extent** *or* **degree** in grado *or* misura
minore
lesson [ˈlɛsn] N lezione *f*; **a maths ~** una
lezione di matematica; **to give lessons in**
dare *or* impartire lezioni di; **to teach sb a ~**
dare una lezione a qn; **it taught him a ~** (*fig*)
gli è servito di lezione
lessor [ˈlɛsɔːʳ, lɛˈsɔːʳ] N locatore(-trice)
lest [lɛst] CONJ per paura di + *infinitive*, per
paura che + *sub*
let [lɛt] VT (*pt, pp* **~**) lasciare; (*BRIT*: *lease*) dare
in affitto; **to ~ sb do sth** lasciar fare qc a qn,
lasciare che qn faccia qc; **to ~ sb know sth**
far sapere qc a qn; **to ~ sb have sth** dare qc a
qn; **he ~ me go** mi ha lasciato andare; **the ~**
water boil and ... fate bollire l'acqua e ...;
~'s go andiamo; ~ **him come** lo lasci venire;
"to ~" "affittasi"
▶ **let down** VT (*lower*) abbassare; (*dress*)
allungare; (*hair*) sciogliere; (*disappoint*)
deludere; (*BRIT*: *tyre*) sgonfiare
▶ **let go** VI mollare ▶ VT mollare; (*allow to go*)
lasciare andare

▶ **let in** VT lasciare entrare; (visitor etc) far entrare; **what have you ~ yourself in for?** in che guai or pasticci sei andato a cacciarti?

▶ **let off** VT (allow to go) lasciare andare; (firework etc) far partire; (smell etc) emettere; (taxi driver, bus driver) far scendere; **to ~ off steam** (fig: col) sfogarsi, scaricarsi

▶ **let on** VI (col): **to ~ on that ...** lasciar capire che ...

▶ **let out** VT lasciare uscire; (dress) allargare; (scream) emettere; (rent out) affittare, dare in affitto

▶ **let up** VI diminuire

let-down ['lɛtdaun] N (disappointment) delusione f

lethal ['liːθl] ADJ letale, mortale

lethargic [lɛ'θɑːdʒɪk] ADJ letargico(-a)

lethargy ['lɛθədʒɪ] N letargia

letter ['lɛtə'] N lettera; **letters** NPL (Literature) lettere; **small/capital ~** lettera minuscola/maiuscola; **~ of credit** lettera di credito; **documentary ~ of credit** lettera di credito documentata

letter bomb N lettera esplosiva

letterbox ['lɛtəbɔks] (BRIT) N buca delle lettere

letterhead ['lɛtəhɛd] N intestazione f

lettering ['lɛtərɪŋ] N iscrizione f; caratteri mpl

letter-opener ['lɛtərəupnə'] N tagliacarte m inv

letterpress ['lɛtəprɛs] N (method) rilievografia

letter quality N (of printer) qualità di stampa

letters patent NPL brevetto di invenzione

lettuce ['lɛtɪs] N lattuga, insalata

let-up ['lɛtʌp] N (col) interruzione f

leukaemia, (US) **leukemia** [luːˈkiːmɪə] N leucemia

level ['lɛvl] ADJ piatto(-a), piano(-a); orizzontale ▶ N livello; (also: **spirit level**) livella (a bolla d'aria) ▶ VT livellare, spianare; (gun) puntare (verso); (accusation): **to ~ (against)** lanciare (a or contro) ▶ VI (col): **to ~ with sb** essere franco(-a) con qn; **to be ~ with** essere alla pari di; **a ~ spoonful** (Culin) un cucchiaio raso; **to draw ~ with** (team) mettersi alla pari di; (runner, car) affiancarsi a; **A levels** npl (BRIT) ≈ esami mpl di maturità; **O levels** npl (BRIT formerly) diploma di istruzione secondaria conseguito a 16 anni in Inghilterra e Galles, ora sostituito dal GCSE; **on the ~** piatto(-a); (fig) onesto(-a)

▶ **level off, level out** VI (prices etc) stabilizzarsi; (ground) diventare pianeggiante; (aircraft) volare in quota

level crossing N (BRIT) passaggio a livello

level-headed [lɛvl'hɛdɪd] ADJ equilibrato(-a)

levelling, (US) **leveling** ['lɛvlɪŋ] ADJ (process, effect) di livellamento

level playing field N: **to compete on a ~** (fig) competere ad armi pari

lever ['liːvə'] N leva ▶ VT: **to ~ up/out** sollevare/estrarre con una leva

leverage ['liːvərɪdʒ] N: **~ (on or with)** forza (su); (fig) ascendente m (su)

levity ['lɛvɪtɪ] N leggerezza, frivolità

levy ['lɛvɪ] N tassa, imposta ▶ VT imporre

lewd [luːd] ADJ osceno(-a), lascivo(-a)

lexicographer [lɛksɪ'kɔɡrəfə'] N lessicografo(-a)

lexicography [lɛksɪ'kɔɡrəfɪ] N lessicografia

LGBT N LGBT mpl, persone lesbiche, gay, bisessuali e transessuali

LGV N ABBR (BRIT: = Large Goods Vehicle) automezzo pesante

LI ABBR (US) = **Long Island**

liabilities [laɪə'bɪlətɪz] NPL debiti mpl; (on balance sheet) passivo

liability [laɪə'bɪlətɪ] N responsabilità f inv; (handicap) peso

liable ['laɪəbl] ADJ (subject): **~ to** soggetto(-a) a; passibile di; (responsible) **~ (for)** responsabile (di); (likely) **~ to do** propenso(-a) a fare; **to be ~ to a fine** essere passibile di multa

liaise [liːˈeɪz] VI: **to ~ (with)** mantenere i contatti (con)

liaison [liːˈeɪzɔn] N relazione f; (Mil) collegamento

liar ['laɪə'] N bugiardo(-a)

libel ['laɪbl] N libello, diffamazione f ▶ VT diffamare

libellous, (US) **libelous** ['laɪbləs] ADJ diffamatorio(-a)

liberal ['lɪbərl] ADJ liberale; (generous): **to be ~ with** distribuire liberalmente ▶ N (Pol): **L~** liberale mf

Liberal Democrat N liberaldemocratico(-a)

liberality [lɪbə'rælɪtɪ] N (generosity) generosità, liberalità

liberalize ['lɪbərəlaɪz] VT liberalizzare

liberal-minded [lɪbərl'maɪndɪd] ADJ tollerante

liberate ['lɪbəreɪt] VT liberare

liberation [lɪbə'reɪʃən] N liberazione f

liberation theology N teologia della liberazione

Liberia [laɪ'bɪərɪə] N Liberia

Liberian [laɪ'bɪərɪən] ADJ, N liberiano(-a)

liberty ['lɪbətɪ] N libertà f inv; **at ~** (criminal) in libertà; **at ~ to do** libero(-a) di fare; **to take the ~ of** prendersi la libertà di, permettersi di

libido [lɪ'biːdəu] N libido f

Libra ['liːbrə] N Bilancia; **to be ~** essere della Bilancia

librarian [laɪ'brɛərɪən] N bibliotecario(-a)

library ['laɪbrərɪ] N biblioteca

library book N libro della biblioteca

libretto [lɪˈbrɛtəu] N libretto
Libya [ˈlɪbɪə] N Libia
Libyan [ˈlɪbɪən] ADJ, N libico(-a)
lice [laɪs] NPL *of* **louse**
licence, (US) **license** [ˈlaɪsns] N
  autorizzazione f, permesso; (*Comm*) licenza;
  (*Radio, TV*) canone m, abbonamento; (*also:*
  driving licence, US **driver's license**) patente f
  di guida; (*excessive freedom*) licenza; **import ~**
  licenza di importazione; **produced under ~**
  prodotto su licenza
licence number N (*Brit Aut*) numero di targa
license [ˈlaɪsns] N (*US*) = **licence** ► VT dare una
  licenza a; (*car*) pagare la tassa di circolazione
  or il bollo di
licensed [ˈlaɪsnst] ADJ (*for alcohol*) che ha la
  licenza di vendere bibite alcoliche
licensed trade N commercio di bevande
  alcoliche con licenza speciale
licensee [laɪsənˈsiː] N (*Brit: of pub*)
  detentore(-trice) di autorizzazione alla
  vendita di bevande alcoliche
license plate N (*esp US Aut*) targa
  (automobilistica)
licensing hours (*Brit*) NPL orario d'apertura
  (*di un pub*)
licentious [laɪˈsɛnʃəs] ADJ licenzioso(-a)
lichen [ˈlaɪkən] N lichene m
lick [lɪk] VT leccare; (*col: defeat*) suonarle a,
  stracciare ► N leccata; **a ~ of paint** una
  passata di vernice; **to ~ one's lips** (*fig*)
  leccarsi i baffi
licorice [ˈlɪkərɪs] N = **liquorice**
lid [lɪd] N coperchio; (*eyelid*) palpebra; **to take
  the ~ off sth** (*fig*) smascherare qc
lido [ˈlaɪdəu] N piscina all'aperto; (*part of the
  beach*) lido, stabilimento balneare
lie [laɪ] N bugia, menzogna ► VI (*pt, pp* **lied**)
  mentire, dire bugie; (*pt* **lay** [leɪ], *pp* **lain**
  [leɪn]: *rest*) giacere, star disteso(-a); (*in grave*)
  giacere, riposare; (*object: be situated*) trovarsi,
  essere; **to tell lies** raccontare *or* dire bugie;
  to ~ low (*fig*) latitare
  ► **lie about, lie around** VI (*things*) essere in
  giro; (*person*) bighellonare
  ► **lie back** VI stendersi
  ► **lie down** VI stendersi, sdraiarsi
  ► **lie up** VI (*hide*) nascondersi
Liechtenstein [ˈlɪktənstaɪn] N
  Liechtenstein m
lie detector N macchina della verità
lie-down [ˈlaɪdaun] N (*Brit*): **to have a ~**
  sdraiarsi, riposarsi
lie-in [ˈlaɪɪn] N (*Brit*): **to have a ~** rimanere a
  letto
lieu [luː] N: **in ~ of** invece di, al posto di
Lieut. ABBR (= *lieutenant*) Ten.
lieutenant [lɛfˈtɛnənt, (*US*) luːˈtɛnənt] N
  tenente m

lieutenant-colonel [lɛfˈtɛnəntˈkəːnl, (*US*)
  luːˈtɛnəntˈkəːnl] N tenente colonnello
life [laɪf] N (*pl* **lives**) vita ► CPD di vita; della
  vita; a vita; **to come to ~** rianimarsi;
  country/city ~ vita di campagna/di città;
  to be sent to prison for ~ essere condannato
  all'ergastolo; **true to ~** fedele alla realtà;
  to paint from ~ dipingere dal vero
life annuity N rendita vitalizia
life assurance N (*Brit*) = **life insurance**
lifebelt [ˈlaɪfbɛlt] N (*Brit*) salvagente m
lifeblood [ˈlaɪfblʌd] N (*fig*) linfa vitale
lifeboat [ˈlaɪfbəut] N scialuppa di
  salvataggio
life expectancy N durata media della vita
lifeguard [ˈlaɪfgɑːd] N bagnino
life imprisonment N ergastolo
life insurance N assicurazione f sulla vita
life jacket N giubbotto di salvataggio
lifeless [ˈlaɪflɪs] ADJ senza vita
lifelike [ˈlaɪflaɪk] ADJ che sembra vero(-a);
  rassomigliante
lifeline [ˈlaɪflaɪn] N cavo di salvataggio
lifelong [ˈlaɪflɔŋ] ADJ per tutta la vita
life preserver [-prɪˈzəːvəʳ] N (*US*)
  salvagente m; giubbotto di salvataggio;
  (*Brit*) sfollagente m
lifer [ˈlaɪfəʳ] N (*col*) ergastolano(-a)
life-raft [ˈlaɪfrɑːft] N zattera di salvataggio
life-saver [ˈlaɪfseɪvəʳ] N bagnino
life sentence N (*condanna all'*)ergastolo
life-sized [ˈlaɪfsaɪzd] ADJ a grandezza
  naturale
life span N (durata della) vita
life style N stile m di vita
life support system N (*Med*) respiratore m
  automatico
lifetime [ˈlaɪftaɪm] N: **in his ~** durante la sua
  vita; **in a ~** nell'arco della vita, in tutta la
  vita; **the chance of a ~** un'occasione unica
lift [lɪft] VT sollevare; (*ban, rule*) levare; (*steal*)
  prendere, rubare ► VI (*fog*) alzarsi ► N (*Brit:*
  elevator) ascensore m; **to give sb a ~** (*Brit*)
  dare un passaggio a qn
  ► **lift off** VT togliere ► VI (*rocket*) partire;
  (*helicopter*) decollare
  ► **lift out** VT tirar fuori; (*troops, evacuees etc*) far
  evacuare per mezzo di elicotteri (*or* aerei)
  ► **lift up** VT sollevare, alzare
lift-off [ˈlɪftɔf] N decollo
ligament [ˈlɪgəmənt] N legamento
light [laɪt] (*pt, pp* **lighted**, *pt, pp* **lit** [lɪt]) N luce
  f, lume m; (*daylight*) luce, giorno; (*lamp*)
  lampada; (*Aut: rear light*) luce f di posizione;
  (: *headlamp*) fanale m; (*for cigarette etc*): **have
  you got a ~?** ha da accendere? ► VT (*candle,
  cigarette, fire*) accendere; (*room*) illuminare
  ► ADJ (*room, colour*) chiaro(-a); (*not heavy, also fig*)
  leggero(-a) ► ADV (*travel*) con poco bagaglio;

lights NPL (*Aut: traffic lights*) semaforo; **in the ~ of** alla luce di; **to turn the ~ on/off** accendere/spegnere la luce; **to come to ~** venire alla luce, emergere; **to cast** *or* **shed** *or* **throw ~ on** gettare luce su; **to make ~ of sth** (*fig*) prendere alla leggera qc, non dar peso a qc; **to be lit by** essere illuminato(-a) da
▶ **light up** VI illuminarsi ▶ VT illuminare
light bulb N lampadina
lighten ['laɪtn] VI schiarirsi ▶ VT (*give light to*) illuminare; (*make lighter*) schiarire; (*make less heavy*) alleggerire
lighter ['laɪtəʳ] N (*also:* **cigarette lighter**) accendino (*boat*) chiatta
light-fingered [laɪt'fɪŋgəd] ADJ lesto(-a) di mano
light-headed ['laɪt'hɛdɪd] ADJ stordito(-a)
light-hearted ['laɪt'hɑːtɪd] ADJ gioioso(-a), gaio(-a)
lighthouse ['laɪthaus] N faro
lighting ['laɪtɪŋ] N illuminazione f
lighting-up time ['laɪtɪŋʌp-] N (*BRIT*) orario per l'accensione delle luci
lightly ['laɪtlɪ] ADV leggermente; **to get off ~** cavarsela a buon mercato
light meter N (*Phot*) esposimetro
lightness ['laɪtnɪs] N chiarezza; (*in weight*) leggerezza
lightning ['laɪtnɪŋ] N lampo, fulmine m; **a flash of ~** un lampo, un fulmine
lightning conductor, (US)lightning rod N parafulmine m
lightning strike N (*BRIT*) sciopero m lampo *inv*
light pen N penna luminosa
lightship ['laɪtʃɪp] N battello m faro *inv*
lightweight ['laɪtweɪt] ADJ (*suit*) leggero(-a)
▶ N (*Boxing*) peso leggero
light year ['laɪtjɪəʳ] N anno m luce *inv*
Ligurian [lɪ'gjuərɪən] ADJ, N ligure (*mf*)
like [laɪk] VT (*person*) volere bene a; (*activity, object, food*): **I ~ swimming/that book/ chocolate** mi piace nuotare/quel libro/il cioccolato ▶ PREP come ▶ ADJ simile, uguale
▶ N: **the ~** uno(-a) uguale; **I would ~, I'd ~** mi piacerebbe, vorrei; **would you ~ a coffee?** gradirebbe un caffè?; **if you ~** se vuoi; **to be/ look ~ sb/sth** somigliare a qn/qc; **what does it look/taste ~?** che aspetto/gusto ha?; **what does it sound ~?** come fa?; **what's he ~?** che tipo è?, com'è?; **what's the weather ~?** che tempo fa?; **that's just ~ him** è proprio da lui; **something ~ that** qualcosa del genere; **do it ~ this** fallo così; **I feel ~ a drink** avrei voglia di bere qualcosa; **there's nothing ~ …** non c'è niente di meglio di *or* niente come …; **it is nothing ~ …** non è affatto come …; **his likes and dislikes** i suoi gusti

likeable ['laɪkəbl] ADJ simpatico(-a)
likelihood ['laɪklɪhud] N probabilità; **in all ~** con ogni probabilità, molto probabilmente
likely ['laɪklɪ] ADJ probabile; plausibile; **he's ~ to leave** probabilmente partirà, è probabile che parta; **not ~!** (*col*) neanche per sogno!
like-minded ['laɪk'maɪndɪd] ADJ che pensa allo stesso modo
liken ['laɪkən] VT: **to ~ sth to** paragonare qc a
likeness ['laɪknɪs] N (*similarity*) somiglianza
likewise ['laɪkwaɪz] ADV similmente, nello stesso modo
liking ['laɪkɪŋ] N: **~ (for)** simpatia (per); debole m (per); **to be to sb's ~** piacere a qn; **to take a ~ to sb** prendere qn in simpatia
lilac ['laɪlək] N lilla m *inv* ▶ ADJ lilla *inv*
Lilo ® ['laɪləu] N materassino gonfiabile
lilt [lɪlt] N cadenza
lilting ['lɪltɪŋ] ADJ melodioso(-a)
lily ['lɪlɪ] N giglio; **~ of the valley** mughetto
Lima ['liːmə] N Lima
limb [lɪm] N arto; **to be out on a ~** (*fig*) sentirsi spaesato(-a) *or* tagliato(-a) fuori
limber ['lɪmbəʳ]: **to ~ up** VI riscaldarsi i muscoli
limbo ['lɪmbəu] N: **to be in ~** (*fig*) essere lasciato(-a) nel dimenticatoio
lime [laɪm] N (*tree*) tiglio; (*fruit*) limetta; (*Geo*) calce f
lime juice N succo di limetta
limelight ['laɪmlaɪt] N: **in the ~** (*fig*) alla ribalta, in vista
limerick ['lɪmərɪk] N *poesiola umoristica di cinque versi*
limestone ['laɪmstəun] N pietra calcarea; (*Geo*) calcare m
limit ['lɪmɪt] N limite m ▶ VT limitare; **weight/speed ~** limite di peso/di velocità; **within limits** entro certi limiti
limitation [lɪmɪ'teɪʃən] N limitazione f, limite m
limited ['lɪmɪtɪd] ADJ limitato(-a), ristretto(-a); **~ edition** edizione f a bassa tiratura; **to be ~ to** limitarsi a
limited company, limited liability company N (*BRIT*) ≈ società f *inv* a responsabilità limitata (S.r.l.)
limitless ['lɪmɪtlɪs] ADJ illimitato(-a)
limousine ['lɪməziːn] N limousine f *inv*
limp [lɪmp] N: **to have a ~** zoppicare ▶ VI zoppicare ▶ ADJ floscio(-a), flaccido(-a)
limpet ['lɪmpɪt] N patella
limpid ['lɪmpɪd] ADJ (*poet*) limpido(-a)
linchpin ['lɪntʃpɪn] N acciarino, bietta; (*fig*) perno
Lincs ABBR (*BRIT*) = **Lincolnshire**
line [laɪn] N (*gen, Comm*) linea; (*rope*) corda; (*for fishing*) lenza; (*wire*) filo; (*of poem*) verso;

(*row, series*) fila, riga; coda; (*on face*) ruga ▶ vt (*trees, crowd*) fiancheggiare; **to ~ (with)** (*clothes*) foderare (di); (*box*) rivestire *or* foderare (di); **to cut in ~** (*US*) passare avanti; **in his ~ of business** nel suo ramo; **on the right lines** sulla buona strada; **a new ~ in cosmetics** una nuova linea di cosmetici; **hold the ~ please** (*Brit Tel*) resti in linea per cortesia; **to be in ~ for sth** (*fig*) essere in lista per qc; **in ~ with** d'accordo con, in linea con; **to bring sth into ~ with sth** mettere qc al passo con qc; **to draw the ~ at (doing) sth** (*fig*) rifiutarsi di fare qc; **to take the ~ that** ... essere del parere che ...
▶ **line up** vi allinearsi, mettersi in fila ▶ vt mettere in fila; (*event, celebration*) preparare; **to have sth lined up** avere qc in programma; **to have sb lined up** avere qn in mente

linear ['lɪnɪə^r] adj lineare

lined [laɪnd] adj (*paper*) a righe, rigato(-a); (*face*) rugoso(-a); (*clothes*) foderato(-a)

line feed n (*Comput*) avanzamento di una interlinea

linen ['lɪnɪn] n biancheria, panni *mpl*; (*cloth*) tela di lino

line printer n stampante *f* parallela

liner ['laɪnə^r] n nave *f* di linea; **dustbin ~** sacchetto per la pattumiera

linesman ['laɪnzmən] n (*irreg*) guardalinee *m inv*, segnalinee *m inv*

line-up ['laɪnʌp] n allineamento, fila; (*also:* **police line-up**) confronto all'americana; (*: Sport*) formazione *f* di gioco

linger ['lɪŋgə^r] vi attardarsi; indugiare; (*smell, tradition*) persistere

lingerie ['lænʒəriː] n biancheria intima (femminile)

lingering ['lɪŋgərɪŋ] adj lungo(-a), persistente; (*death*) lento(-a)

lingo ['lɪŋgəu] n (*pl* **lingoes**) (*pej*) gergo

linguist ['lɪŋgwɪst] n linguista *mf*; poliglotta *mf*

linguistic [lɪŋ'gwɪstɪk] adj linguistico(-a)

linguistics [lɪŋ'gwɪstɪks] n linguistica

lining ['laɪnɪŋ] n fodera, (*Tech*) rivestimento (interno); (*of brake*) guarnizione *f*

link [lɪŋk] n (*of a chain*) anello; (*relationship*) legame *m*; (*connection*) legame *m*, collegamento; (*Comput*) link, collegamento ▶ vt collegare, unire, congiungere; (*Comput*) creare un collegamento con; (*associate*): **to ~ with** *or* **to** collegare a ▶ vi (*Comput*): **to ~ to a site** creare un collegamento con un sitio; **rail ~** collegamento ferroviario; *see also* **links**
▶ **link up** vt collegare, unire ▶ vi riunirsi; associarsi

links [lɪŋks] npl pista *or* terreno da golf

link-up ['lɪŋkʌp] n legame *m*; (*of roads*) nodo;

(*of spaceships*) aggancio; (*Radio, TV*) collegamento

linoleum [lɪ'nəulɪəm] n linoleum *m inv*

linseed oil ['lɪnsiːd-] n olio di semi di lino

lint [lɪnt] n garza

lintel ['lɪntl] n architrave *f*

lion ['laɪən] n leone *m*

lion cub n leoncino

lioness ['laɪənɪs] n leonessa

lip [lɪp] n labbro; (*of cup etc*) orlo; (*insolence*) sfacciataggine *f*

liposuction ['lɪpəusʌkʃən] n liposuzione *f*

lipread ['lɪpriːd] vi leggere sulle labbra

lip salve [-sælv] n burro di cacao

lip service n: **to pay ~ to sth** essere favorevole a qc solo a parole

lipstick ['lɪpstɪk] n rossetto

liquefy ['lɪkwɪfaɪ] vt liquefare ▶ vi liquefarsi

liqueur [lɪ'kjuə^r] n liquore *m*

liquid ['lɪkwɪd] n liquido ▶ adj liquido(-a)

liquid assets npl attività *fpl* liquide, crediti *mpl* liquidi

liquidate ['lɪkwɪdeɪt] vt liquidare

liquidation [lɪkwɪ'deɪʃən] n liquidazione *f*; **to go into ~** andare in liquidazione

liquidator ['lɪkwɪdeɪtə^r] n liquidatore *m*

liquid crystal display n visualizzazione *f* a cristalli liquidi

liquidity [lɪ'kwɪdɪtɪ] n (*Comm*) liquidità

liquidize ['lɪkwɪdaɪz] vt (*Brit Culin*) passare al frullatore

liquidizer ['lɪkwɪdaɪzə^r] n (*Brit Culin*) frullatore *m* (a brocca)

liquor ['lɪkə^r] n alcool *m*

liquorice ['lɪkərɪs] n liquirizia

liquor store n (*US*) negozio di liquori

Lisbon ['lɪzbən] n Lisbona

lisp [lɪsp] n pronuncia blesa della "s"

lissom ['lɪsəm] adj leggiadro(-a)

list [lɪst] n lista, elenco; (*of ship*) sbandamento ▶ vt (*write down*) mettere in lista; fare una lista di; (*enumerate*) elencare; (*Comput*) stampare (un prospetto di) ▶ vi (*ship*) sbandare; **shopping ~** lista *or* nota della spesa

listed building ['lɪstəd-] n (*Archit*) edificio sotto la protezione delle Belle Arti

listed company n società quotata in Borsa

listen ['lɪsn] vi ascoltare; **to ~ to** ascoltare

listener ['lɪsnə^r] n ascoltatore(-trice)

listeria [lɪs'tɪərɪə] n listeria

listing ['lɪstɪŋ] n (*Comput*) lista stampata

listless ['lɪstlɪs] adj svogliato(-a); apatico(-a)

listlessly ['lɪstlɪslɪ] adv svogliatamente; apaticamente

list price n prezzo di listino

lit [lɪt] pt, pp *of* **light**

litany ['lɪtənɪ] n litania

liter ['liːtə^r] n (*US*) = **litre**

literacy ['lɪtərəsɪ] N il sapere leggere e scrivere

literacy campaign N lotta contro l'analfabetismo

literal ['lɪtərl] ADJ letterale

literally ['lɪtərəlɪ] ADV alla lettera, letteralmente

literary ['lɪtərərɪ] ADJ letterario(-a)

literate ['lɪtərɪt] ADJ che sa leggere e scrivere

literature ['lɪtərɪtʃəʳ] N letteratura; (*brochures etc*) materiale *m*

lithe [laɪð] ADJ agile, snello(-a)

lithography [lɪ'θɒɡrəfɪ] N litografia

Lithuania [lɪθju'eɪnɪə] N Lituania

Lithuanian [lɪθju'eɪnɪən] ADJ lituano(-a) ▸ N lituano(-a); (*Ling*) lituano

litigate ['lɪtɪɡeɪt] VT muovere causa a ▸ VI litigare

litigation [lɪtɪ'ɡeɪʃən] N causa

litmus ['lɪtməs] N: ~ **paper** cartina di tornasole

litre, (*US*)**liter** ['liːtəʳ] N litro

litter ['lɪtəʳ] N (*rubbish*) rifiuti *mpl*; (*young animals*) figliata ▸ VT sparpagliare; lasciare rifiuti in; **littered with** coperto(-a) di

litter bin N (*BRIT*) cestino per rifiuti

littered ADJ: ~ **with** coperto(-a) di

litter lout, (*US*)**litterbug** ['lɪtəbʌɡ] N *persona che butta per terra le cartacce o i rifiuti*

little ['lɪtl] ADJ (*small*) piccolo(-a); (*not much*) poco(-a) ▸ ADV poco; **a ~** un po' (di); **a ~ milk** un po' di latte; **a ~ bit** un pochino; **with ~ difficulty** senza fatica *or* difficoltà; **~ by ~** a poco a poco; **as ~ as possible** il meno possibile; **for a ~ while** per un po'; **to make ~ of** dare poca importanza a

little finger N mignolo

little-known ['lɪtl'nəun] ADJ poco noto(-a)

liturgy ['lɪtədʒɪ] N liturgia

live¹ [lɪv] VI vivere; (*reside*) vivere, abitare; **where do you ~?** dove abita?; **to ~ in London** abitare a Londra
▸ **live down** VT far dimenticare (alla gente)
▸ **live in** VI essere interno(-a); avere vitto e alloggio
▸ **live off** VI (*land, fish etc*) vivere di; (*pej: parents etc*) vivere alle spalle *or* a spese di
▸ **live on** VT FUS (*food*) vivere di ▸ VI sopravvivere, continuare a vivere; **to ~ on £50 a week** vivere con 50 sterline la settimana
▸ **live out** VI (*BRIT: students*) essere esterno(-a)
▸ VT: **to ~ out one's days** *or* **life** trascorrere gli ultimi anni
▸ **live together** VI vivere insieme, convivere
▸ **live up** VT: **to ~ it up** (*col*) fare la bella vita
▸ **live up to** VT FUS tener fede a, non venir meno a

live² [laɪv] ADJ (*animal*) vivo(-a); (*issue*) scottante, d'attualità; (*wire*) sotto tensione; (*broadcast*) diretto(-a); (*ammunition: not blank*) carico(-a); (: *unexploded*) inesploso(-a); (*performance*) dal vivo

live-in ['lɪvɪn] ADJ (*partner*) convivente; (*servant*) che vive in casa; **he has a ~ girlfriend** la sua ragazza vive con lui

livelihood ['laɪvlɪhud] N mezzi *mpl* di sostentamento

liveliness ['laɪvlɪnəs] N vivacità

lively ['laɪvlɪ] ADJ vivace, vivo(-a)

liven up ['laɪvn-] VT (*room etc*) ravvivare; (*discussion, evening*) animare ▸ VI ravvivarsi

liver ['lɪvəʳ] N fegato

liverish ['lɪvərɪʃ] ADJ che soffre di mal di fegato; (*fig*) scontroso(-a)

Liverpudlian [lɪvə'pʌdlɪən] ADJ di Liverpool ▸ N abitante *mf* di Liverpool; originario(-a) di Liverpool

livery ['lɪvərɪ] N livrea

lives [laɪvz] NPL *of* **life**

livestock ['laɪvstɔk] N bestiame *m*

live wire [laɪv-] N (*col: fig*): **to be a ~** essere pieno(-a) di vitalità

livid ['lɪvɪd] ADJ livido(-a); (*furious*) livido(-a) di rabbia, furibondo(-a)

living ['lɪvɪŋ] ADJ vivo(-a), vivente ▸ N: **to earn** *or* **make a ~** guadagnarsi la vita; **cost of ~** costo della vita, carovita *m*; **within ~ memory** a memoria d'uomo

living conditions NPL condizioni *fpl* di vita

living expenses NPL spese *fpl* di mantenimento

living room N soggiorno

living standards NPL tenore *m* di vita

living wage N salario sufficiente per vivere

living will N testamento biologico

lizard ['lɪzəd] N lucertola

llama ['lɑːmə] N lama *m inv*

LLB N ABBR (= *Bachelor of Laws*) ≈ laurea in legge

LLD N ABBR (= *Doctor of Laws*) titolo di studio

LMT ABBR (*US: = Local Mean Time*) tempo medio locale

load [ləud] N (*weight*) peso; (*Elec, Tech, thing carried*) carico ▸ VT (*also:* **load up**): **to ~ (with)** (*lorry, ship*) caricare (di); (*gun, camera*) caricare (con); **a ~ of, loads of** (*fig*) un sacco di; **to ~ a program** (*Comput*) caricare un programma

loaded ['ləudɪd] ADJ (*dice*) falsato(-a); (*question, word*) capzioso(-a); (*col: rich*) pieno(-a) di soldi; **~ (with)** (*vehicle*) carico(-a) (di)

loading bay ['ləudɪŋ-] N piazzola di carico

loaf [ləuf] (*pl* **loaves**) N pane *m*, pagnotta ▸ VI (*also:* **loaf about, loaf around**) bighellonare

loam [ləum] N terra di marna

loan [ləun] N prestito ▸ VT dare in prestito; **on ~** in prestito

loan account N conto dei prestiti

loan capital N capitale *m* di prestito
loan shark N (*col, pej*) strozzino(-a)
loath [ləuθ] ADJ: **to be ~ to do** essere restio(-a) a fare
loathe [ləuð] VT detestare, aborrire
loathing ['ləuðɪŋ] N aborrimento, disgusto
loathsome ['ləuðsəm] ADJ (*gen*) ripugnante; (*person*) detestabile, odioso(-a)
loaves [ləuvz] NPL *of* **loaf**
lob [lɔb] VT (*ball*) lanciare
lobby ['lɔbɪ] N atrio, vestibolo; (*Pol: pressure group*) gruppo di pressione ▶ VT fare pressione su
lobbyist ['lɔbɪɪst] N appartenente *mf* ad un gruppo di pressione
lobe [ləub] N lobo
lobster ['lɔbstər] N aragosta
lobster pot N nassa per aragoste
local ['ləukl] ADJ locale ▶ N (*BRIT: pub*) ≈ bar *m inv* all'angolo; **the locals** NPL la gente della zona
local anaesthetic N anestesia locale
local authority N ente *m* locale
local call N (*Tel*) telefonata urbana
local government N amministrazione *f* locale
locality [ləu'kælɪtɪ] N località *f inv*; (*position*) posto, luogo
localize ['ləukəlaɪz] VT localizzare
locally ['ləukəlɪ] ADV da queste parti; nel vicinato
locate [ləu'keɪt] VT (*find*) trovare; (*situate*) collocare; situare
location [ləu'keɪʃən] N posizione *f*; **on ~** (*Cine*) all'esterno
loch [lɔx] N lago
lock [lɔk] N (*of door, box*) serratura; (*of canal*) chiusa; (*of hair*) ciocca, riccio ▶ VT (*with key*) chiudere a chiave; (*immobilize*) bloccare ▶ VI (*door etc*) chiudersi; (*wheels*) bloccarsi, incepparsi; **~ stock and barrel** (*fig*) in blocco; **on full ~** (*BRIT Aut*) a tutto sterzo
▶ **lock away** VT (*valuables*) tenere (rinchiuso(-a)) al sicuro; (*criminal*) metter dentro
▶ **lock in** VT chiudere dentro (a chiave)
▶ **lock out** VT chiudere fuori; **to ~ workers out** fare una serrata
▶ **lock up** VT (*criminal, mental patient*) rinchiudere; (*house*) chiudere (a chiave) ▶ VI chiudere tutto (a chiave)
locker ['lɔkər] N armadietto
locker-room N (*US Sport*) spogliatoio
locket ['lɔkɪt] N medaglione *m*
lockjaw ['lɔkdʒɔ:] N tetano
lockout ['lɔkaut] N (*Industry*) serrata
locksmith ['lɔksmɪθ] N magnano
lock-up ['lɔkʌp] N (*prison*) prigione *f*; (*cell*) guardina; (*also:* **lock-up garage**) box *m inv*

locomotive [ləukə'məutɪv] N locomotiva
locum ['ləukəm] N (*Med*) medico sostituto
locust ['ləukəst] N locusta
lodge [lɔdʒ] N casetta, portineria; (*hunting lodge*) casino di caccia; (*Freemasonry*) loggia ▶ VI (*person*): **to ~ (with)** essere a pensione (*presso or* da); (*bullet etc*) conficcarsi ▶ VT (*appeal etc*) presentare, fare; **to ~ a complaint** presentare un reclamo; **to ~ (itself) in/between** piantarsi dentro/fra
lodger ['lɔdʒər] N affittuario(-a); (*with room and meals*) pensionante *mf*
lodging ['lɔdʒɪŋ] N alloggio; *see also* **board**; **lodgings**
lodging house N (*BRIT*) casa con camere in affitto
lodgings ['lɔdʒɪŋz] NPL camera d'affitto; camera ammobiliata
loft [lɔft] N solaio, soffitta; (*Agr*) granaio; (*US*) appartamento ricavato da solaio (*or* granaio *etc*)
lofty ['lɔftɪ] ADJ alto(-a); (*haughty*) altezzoso(-a); (*sentiments, aims*) nobile
log [lɔg] N (*of wood*) ceppo; (*also:* **logbook**: *Naut, Aviat*) diario di bordo; (*Aut*) libretto di circolazione ▶ N ABBR = **logarithm** ▶ VT registrare
▶ **log in, log on** VI (*Comput*) aprire una sessione (*con codice di riconoscimento*)
▶ **log off, log out** VI (*Comput*) terminare una sessione
logarithm ['lɔgərɪðm] N logaritmo
logbook ['lɔgbuk] N (*Naut, Aviat*) diario di bordo; (*Aut*) libretto di circolazione; (*of lorry driver*) registro di viaggio; (*of events, movement of goods etc*) registro
log cabin N capanna di tronchi
log fire N fuoco di legna
logger ['lɔgər] N boscaiolo, taglialegna *m inv*
loggerheads ['lɔgəhɛdz] NPL: **at ~ (with)** ai ferri corti (con)
logic ['lɔdʒɪk] N logica
logical ['lɔdʒɪkəl] ADJ logico(-a)
logically ['lɔdʒɪkəlɪ] ADV logicamente
login ['lɔgɪn] N (*Comput*) nome *m* utente *inv*
logistics [lɔ'dʒɪstɪks] N logistica
logjam ['lɔgdʒæm] N: **to break the ~** superare l'impasse
logo ['ləugəu] N logo *m inv*
loin [lɔɪn] N (*Culin*) lombata; **loins** NPL reni *fpl*
loin cloth N perizoma *m*
loiter ['lɔɪtər] VI attardarsi; **to ~ (about)** indugiare, bighellonare
LOL ABBR (*col:* = *laugh out loud*) LOL, grandi risate (*nel gergo di Internet*)
loll [lɔl] VI (*also:* **loll about**) essere stravaccato(-a)
lollipop ['lɔlɪpɔp] N lecca lecca *m inv*

lollipop man, lollipop lady N (*irreg*) (BRIT); *vedi nota*

In Gran Bretagna il *lollipop man* e la *lollipop lady* sono persone incaricate di regolare il traffico in prossimità delle scuole e di aiutare i bambini ad attraversare la strada usano una paletta la cui forma ricorda quella di un lecca lecca, in inglese, appunto, *lollipop*.

lollop ['lɔləp] VI (BRIT) camminare (*or* correre) goffamente
lolly ['lɔlɪ] N (*col*) lecca lecca *m inv*; (*also:* **ice lolly**) ghiacciolo; (: *money*) grana
Lombardy ['lɔmbədɪ] N Lombardia
London ['lʌndən] N Londra
Londoner ['lʌndənəʳ] N londinese *mf*
lone [ləun] ADJ solitario(-a)
loneliness ['ləunlɪnɪs] N solitudine *f*, isolamento
lonely ['ləunlɪ] ADJ solo(-a); solitario(-a); (*place*) isolato(-a); **to feel** ~ sentirsi solo(-a)
lonely hearts ADJ: ~ **ads**, ~ **column** messaggi *mpl* personali; ~ **club** club *m inv* dei cuori solitari
lone parent N (*unmarried: mother*) ragazza madre; (: *father*) ragazzo padre; (*divorced*) genitore *m* divorziato(-a); (*widowed*) genitore rimasto vedovo
loner ['ləunəʳ] N solitario(-a)
lonesome ['ləunsəm] ADJ solo(-a)
long [lɔŋ] ADJ lungo(-a) ▶ ADV a lungo, per molto tempo ▶ N: **the ~ and the short of it is that ...** (*fig*) a farla breve ... ▶ VI: **to ~ for sth/to do** desiderare qc/di fare; non veder l'ora di aver qc/di fare; **he had ~ understood that ...** aveva capito da molto tempo che ...; **how ~ is this river/course?** quanto è lungo questo fiume/corso?; **6 metres ~** lungo 6 metri; **6 months ~** che dura 6 mesi, di 6 mesi; **all night ~** tutta la notte; **he no longer comes** non viene più; ~ **before** molto tempo prima; **before ~** (+*future*) presto, fra poco; (+*past*) poco tempo dopo; ~ **ago** molto tempo fa; **don't be ~!** faccia presto!; **I shan't be ~** non ne avrò per molto; **at ~ last** finalmente; **in the ~ run** alla fin fine; **so *or* as ~ as** (*while*) finché; (*provided that*) sempre che +*sub*
long-distance [lɔŋ'dɪstəns] ADJ (*race*) di fondo; (*call*) interurbano(-a)
long-haired ['lɔŋ'hɛəd] ADJ (*person*) dai capelli lunghi; (*animal*) dal pelo lungo
longhand ['lɔŋhænd] N scrittura normale
long-haul ['lɔŋhɔ:l] ADJ (*flight*) a lunga percorrenza *inv*
longing ['lɔŋɪŋ] N desiderio, voglia, brama ▶ ADJ di desiderio; pieno(-a) di nostalgia
longingly ['lɔŋɪŋlɪ] ADV con desiderio (*or* nostalgia)

longitude ['lɔŋgɪtju:d] N longitudine *f*
long johns [-dʒɔnz] NPL mutande *fpl* lunghe
long jump N salto in lungo
long-life ADJ (*milk*) a lunga conservazione; (*batteries*) di lunga durata
long-lost ['lɔŋlɔst] ADJ perduto(-a) da tempo
long-playing ['lɔŋpleɪɪŋ] ADJ: ~ **record (LP)** (*disco*) 33 giri *m inv*
long-range [lɔŋ'reɪndʒ] ADJ a lunga portata; (*weather forecast*) a lungo termine
longshoreman ['lɔŋʃɔ:mən] N (*irreg*) (US) scaricatore *m* (di porto), portuale *m*
long-sighted [lɔŋ'saɪtɪd] ADJ (BRIT) presbite; (*fig*) lungimirante
long-standing ['lɔŋstændɪŋ] ADJ di vecchia data
long-suffering [lɔŋ'sʌfərɪŋ] ADJ estremamente paziente; infinitamente tollerante
long-term ['lɔŋtə:m] ADJ a lungo termine
long wave N (*Radio*) onde *fpl* lunghe
long-winded [lɔŋ'wɪndɪd] ADJ prolisso(-a), interminabile
loo [lu:] N (BRIT *col*) W.C. *m inv*, cesso
loofah ['lu:fə] N luffa
look [luk] VI guardare; (*seem*) sembrare, parere; (*building etc*): **to ~ south/on to the sea** dare a sud/sul mare ▶ N sguardo; (*appearance*) aspetto, aria; **looks** NPL aspetto; (*good looks*) bellezza; **to ~ like** assomigliare a; **to ~ ahead** guardare avanti; **it looks about 4 metres long** sarà lungo un 4 metri; **it looks all right to me** a me pare che vada bene; **to have a ~ at sth** dare un'occhiata a qc; **to have a ~ for sth** cercare qc
▶ **look after** VT FUS occuparsi di, prendersi cura di; (*keep an eye on*) guardare, badare a
▶ **look around** VI guardarsi intorno
▶ **look at** VT FUS guardare
▶ **look back** VI: **to ~ back at sth/sb** voltarsi a guardare qc/qn; **to ~ back on** (*event, period*) ripensare a
▶ **look down on** VT FUS (*fig*) guardare dall'alto, disprezzare
▶ **look for** VT FUS cercare
▶ **look forward to** VT FUS non veder l'ora di; **I'm not looking forward to it** non ne ho nessuna voglia; **looking forward to hearing from you** (*in letter: to a friend*); aspettando tue notizie; (: *more formal*) in attesa di una vostra gentile risposta
▶ **look in** VI: **to ~ in on sb** (*visit*) fare un salto da qn
▶ **look into** VT FUS (*matter, possibility*) esaminare
▶ **look on** VI fare da spettatore
▶ **look out** VI (*beware*): **to ~ out (for)** stare in guardia (per)
▶ **look out for** VT FUS cercare; (*watch out for*):

to ~ out for sb/sth guardare se arriva qn/qc
► **look over** VT (*essay*) dare un'occhiata a, riguardare; (*town, building*) vedere; (*person*) esaminare
► **look round** VI (*turn*) girarsi, voltarsi; (*in shops*) dare un'occhiata a; **to ~ round for sth** guardarsi intorno cercando qc
► **look through** VT FUS (*papers, book*) scorrere; (*telescope*) guardare attraverso
► **look to** VT FUS stare attento(-a) a; (*rely on*) contare su
► **look up** VI alzare gli occhi; (*improve*) migliorare ► VT (*word*) cercare; (*friend*) andare a trovare
► **look up to** VT FUS avere rispetto per
lookout ['lukaut] N posto d'osservazione; guardia; **to be on the look-out (for)** stare in guardia (per)
look-up table ['lukʌp-] N (*Comput*) tabella di consultazione
loom [lu:m] N telaio ► VI sorgere; (*fig*) incombere
loony ['lu:nɪ] ADJ, N (*col*) pazzo(-a)
loop [lu:p] N cappio; (*Comput*) anello ► VT: **to ~ sth round sth** passare qc intorno a qc
loophole ['lu:phəul] N via d'uscita; scappatoia
loose [lu:s] ADJ (*knot*) sciolto(-a); (*screw*) allentato(-a); (*stone*) cadente; (*clothes*) ampio(-a), largo(-a); (*animal*) in libertà, scappato(-a); (*life, morals*) dissoluto(-a); (*discipline*) allentato(-a); (*thinking*) poco rigoroso(-a), vago(-a) ► N: **to be on the ~** essere in libertà ► VT (*untie*) sciogliere; (*slacken*) allentare; (*free*) liberare; (*BRIT: arrow*) scoccare; **~ connection** (*Elec*) filo che fa contatto; **to be at a ~ end** or (*US*) **at ~ ends** (*fig*) non saper che fare; **to tie up ~ ends** (*fig*) avere ancora qualcosa da sistemare
loose change N spiccioli *mpl*, moneta
loose-fitting ['lu:sfɪtɪŋ] ADJ ampio(-a)
loose-leaf ['lu:sli:f] ADJ: **~ binder** or **folder** raccoglitore *m*
loose-limbed [lu:s'lɪmd] ADJ snodato(-a), agile
loosely ['lu:slɪ] ADV senza stringere; approssimativamente
loosely-knit ['lu:slɪ'nɪt] ADJ non rigidamente strutturato(-a)
loosen ['lu:sn] VT sciogliere; (*belt etc*) allentare
► **loosen up** VI (*before game*) sciogliere i muscoli, scaldarsi; (*col: relax*) rilassarsi
loot [lu:t] N bottino ► VT saccheggiare
looter ['lu:tər] N saccheggiatore(-trice)
looting ['lu:tɪŋ] N saccheggio
lop [lɔp] VT (*also*: **lop off**) tagliare via, recidere
lop-sided ['lɔp'saɪdɪd] ADJ non equilibrato(-a), asimmetrico(-a)

lord [lɔ:d] N signore *m*; **L~ Smith** lord Smith; **the L~** (*Rel*) il Signore; **good L~!** buon Dio!; **the (House of) Lords** (*BRIT*) la Camera dei Lord
lordly ['lɔ:dlɪ] ADJ nobile, maestoso(-a); (*arrogant*) altero(-a)
lordship ['lɔ:dʃɪp] N (*BRIT*): **your L~** Sua Eccellenza
lore [lɔ:ʳ] N tradizioni *fpl*
lorry ['lɔrɪ] N (*BRIT*) camion *m inv*
lorry driver N (*BRIT*) camionista *m*
lose [lu:z] (*pt, pp* **lost** [lɔst]) VT perdere; (*pursuers*) distanziare ► VI perdere; **to ~ (time)** (*clock*) ritardare; **to ~ no time (in doing sth)** non perdere tempo (a fare qc); **to get lost** (*person*) perdersi, smarrirsi; (*object*) andare perso or perduto
► **lose out** VI rimetterci
loser ['lu:zəʳ] N perdente *mf*; **to be a good/bad ~** saper/non saper perdere
loss [lɔs] N perdita; **to cut one's losses** rimetterci il meno possibile; **to make a ~** subire una perdita; **to sell sth at a ~** vendere qc in perdita; **to be at a ~** essere perplesso(-a); **to be at a ~ to explain sth** non saper come fare a spiegare qc
loss adjuster N (*Insurance*) responsabile *mf* della valutazione dei danni
loss leader N (*Comm*) articolo a prezzo ridottissimo per attirare la clientela
lost [lɔst] PT, PP *of* **lose** ► ADJ perduto(-a); **~ in thought** immerso or perso nei propri pensieri; **~ and found property** *n* (*US*) oggetti *mpl* smarriti; **~ and found** *n* (*US*) ufficio oggetti smarriti
lost property, (*US*) **lost and found** N (*BRIT*) oggetti *mpl* smarriti; **~ office** or **department** ufficio oggetti smarriti
lot [lɔt] N (*at auctions*) lotto; (*destiny*) destino, sorte *f*; **the ~** tutto(-a) quanto(-a); tutti(-e) quanti(-e); **a ~** molto; **a ~ of** una gran quantità di, un sacco di; **lots of** molto(-a); **to draw lots (for sth)** tirare a sorte (per qc)
lotion ['ləuʃən] N lozione *f*
lottery ['lɔtərɪ] N lotteria
loud [laud] ADJ forte, alto(-a); (*gaudy*) vistoso(-a), sgargiante ► ADV (*speak etc*) forte; **out ~** (*read etc*) ad alta voce
loudhailer [laud'heɪləʳ] N (*BRIT*) portavoce *m inv*
loudly ['laudlɪ] ADV fortemente, ad alta voce
loudspeaker [laud'spi:kəʳ] N altoparlante *m*
lounge [laundʒ] N salotto, soggiorno; (*of hotel*) salone *m*; (*of airport*) sala d'attesa; (*BRIT: also*: **lounge bar**) bar *m inv* con servizio a tavolino ► VI oziare; starsene colle mani in mano
lounge bar N bar *m inv* con servizio a tavolino
lounge suit N (*BRIT*) completo da uomo

louse [laus] (*pl* **lice**) N pidocchio
▶ **louse up** VT (*col*) rovinare
lousy ['lauzı] ADJ (*col: fig*) orrendo(-a),
schifoso(-a); **to feel ~** stare da cani
lout [laut] N zoticone *m*
louvre, (*US*) **louver** ['luːvə'] ADJ (*door, window*)
con apertura a gelosia
lovable ['lʌvəbl] ADJ simpatico(-a), carino(-a);
amabile
love [lʌv] N amore *m* ▶ VT amare; voler bene
a; **I ~ you** ti amo; **to ~ to do: I ~ to do** mi
piace fare; **I'd ~ to come** mi piacerebbe
molto venire; **to be in ~ with** essere
innamorato(-a) di; **to fall in ~ with**
innamorarsi di; **to make ~** fare l'amore;
~ at first sight amore a prima vista, colpo di
fulmine; **to send one's ~ to sb** mandare i
propri saluti a qn; **~ from Anne, ~, Anne**
con affetto, Anne; **"15 ~"** (*Tennis*) "15 a zero"
love affair N relazione *f*
love child N (*irreg*) figlio(-a) dell'amore
loved ones [lʌvd-] NPL: **my ~** i miei cari
love-hate relationship ['lʌv'heɪt-] N
rapporto amore-odio *inv*
love letter N lettera d'amore
love life N vita sentimentale
lovely ['lʌvlı] ADJ bello(-a); (*delicious: smell,
meal*) buono(-a); **we had a ~ time** ci siamo
divertiti molto
lover ['lʌvə'] N amante *mf*; (*person in love*)
innamorato(-a); (*amateur*): **a ~ of** un (un')
amante di; un (un') appassionato(-a) di
lovesick ['lʌvsɪk] ADJ malato(-a) d'amore
lovesong ['lʌvsɔŋ] N canzone *f* d'amore
loving ['lʌvɪŋ] ADJ affettuoso(-a),
amoroso(-a), tenero(-a)
low [ləu] ADJ basso(-a) ▶ ADV in basso ▶ N
(*Meteor*) depressione *f* ▶ VI (*cow*) muggire; **to
be ~ on** (*supplies etc*) avere scarsità di; **to feel
~** sentirsi giù; **he's very ~** (*ill*) è molto debole;
to reach a new *or* **an all-time ~** toccare il
livello più basso *or* il minimo; **to turn
(down)** ~ *vt* abbassare
low-alcohol [ləu'ælkəhɔl] ADJ a basso
contenuto alcolico
lowbrow ['ləubrau] ADJ (*person*) senza pretese
intellettuali
low-calorie ['ləu'kælərı] ADJ a basso
contenuto calorico
low-carb [ləu'kɑːb] ADJ (*col*) a basso
contenuto di carboidrati
low-cut ['ləukʌt] ADJ (*dress*) scollato(-a)
low-down ['ləudaun] ADJ (*mean*) ignobile ▶ N
(*col*): **he gave me the ~ on it** mi ha messo al
corrente dei fatti
lower ['ləuə'] ADJ, ADV COMPARATIVE (*bottom: of
2 things*) più basso; (*less important*) meno
importante ▶ VT (*gen*) calare; (*reduce: price,
eyes, voice*) abbassare, ridurre; (: *resistance*)

indebolire ▶ VI ['lauə'] (*sky*) minacciare; **to ~
(at sb)** (*person*) dare un'occhiataccia (a qn)
lower case N minuscolo
low-fat ['ləu'fæt] ADJ magro(-a)
low-key ['ləu'kiː] ADJ moderato(-a); (*operation*)
condotto(-a) con discrezione
lowland ['ləulənd] N bassopiano, pianura
low-level ['ləulɛvl] ADJ a basso livello; (*flying*)
a bassa quota
low-loader ['ləuləudə'] N camion *m* a
pianale basso
lowly ['ləulı] ADJ umile, modesto(-a)
low-lying [ləu'laııŋ] ADJ a basso livello
low-paid [ləu'peɪd] ADJ mal pagato(-a)
low-rise ['ləuraɪz] ADJ di altezza contenuta
low-tech ['ləu'tɛk] ADJ a basso contenuto
tecnologico
loyal ['lɔɪəl] ADJ fedele, leale
loyalist ['lɔɪəlɪst] N lealista *mf*
loyalty ['lɔɪəltı] N fedeltà, lealtà
loyalty card N *carta che offre sconti a clienti
abituali*
lozenge ['lɔzɪndʒ] N (*Med*) pastiglia; (*Geom*)
losanga
LP N ABBR (= *long-playing record*) LP *m*
LPG N ABBR (= *liquefied petroleum gas*) GPL *m*
(= *gas di petrolio liquefatto*)
L-plate ['ɛlpleɪt] (*BRIT*) N ≈ contrassegno P
principiante; *vedi nota*

> Le *L-plates* sono delle tabelle bianche con
> una L rossa che in Gran Bretagna i
> guidatori principianti, *learners*, in
> possesso di una *provisional licence*, che
> corrisponde al nostro foglio rosa, devono
> applicare davanti e dietro alla loro
> autovettura finché non ottengono la
> patente.

L-plates ['ɛlpleɪts] NPL *targhette con la lettera L
(per 'learner') da esporre davanti e dietro ai veicoli
guidati da principianti*
LPN N ABBR (*US*: = *Licensed Practical Nurse*)
≈ infermiera diplomata
LRAM N ABBR (*BRIT*: = *Licentiate of the Royal
Academy of Music*) *specializzazione dopo la laurea*
LSD N ABBR (= *lysergic acid diethylamide*) L.S.D. *m*;
(*BRIT*: = *pounds, shillings and pence*) *sistema
monetario in vigore in Gran Bretagna fino al 1971*
LSE N ABBR = **London School of Economics**
LT ABBR (*Elec*: = *low tension*) B.T.
Lt. ABBR (= *lieutenant*) Ten.
Ltd ABBR (*Comm*: = *limited*) ≈ S.r.l.
lubricant ['luːbrɪkənt] N lubrificante *m*
lubricate ['luːbrɪkeɪt] VT lubrificare
lucid ['luːsɪd] ADJ lucido(-a)
lucidity [luːˈsɪdɪtɪ] N lucidità
luck [lʌk] N fortuna, sorte *f*; **bad ~** sfortuna,
mala sorte; **good ~** (buona) fortuna; **to be in
~** essere fortunato(-a); **to be out of ~** essere
sfortunato(-a)

luckily ['lʌkɪlɪ] ADV fortunatamente, per
fortuna
luckless ['lʌklɪs] ADJ sventurato(-a)
lucky ['lʌkɪ] ADJ fortunato(-a); (number etc)
che porta fortuna
lucrative ['lu:krətɪv] ADJ lucrativo(-a),
lucroso(-a), profittevole
ludicrous ['lu:dɪkrəs] ADJ ridicolo(-a),
assurdo(-a)
ludo ['lu:dəu] N ≈ gioco dell'oca
lug [lʌg] VT trascinare
luggage ['lʌgɪdʒ] N bagagli mpl
luggage rack N portabagagli m inv
luggage van, (US) **luggage car** N (Rail)
bagagliaio
lugubrious [lu'gu:brɪəs] ADJ lugubre
lukewarm ['lu:kwɔ:m] ADJ tiepido(-a)
lull [lʌl] N intervallo di calma ▶ VT (child)
cullare; (person, fear) acquietare, calmare;
to ~ sb to sleep cullare qn finché si
addormenta
lullaby ['lʌləbaɪ] N ninnananna
lumbago [lʌm'beɪgəu] N lombaggine f
lumber ['lʌmbəʳ] N (wood) legname m; (junk)
roba vecchia ▶ VT (BRIT col): **to ~ sb with sth/
sb** affibbiare or rifilare qc/qn a qn ▶ VI (also:
lumber about, lumber along) muoversi
pesantemente
lumberjack ['lʌmbədʒæk] N boscaiolo
lumber room N (BRIT) sgabuzzino
lumber yard N segheria
luminous ['lu:mɪnəs] ADJ luminoso(-a)
lump [lʌmp] N pezzo; (in sauce) grumo;
(swelling) gonfiore m; (also: **sugar lump**)
zolletta ▶ VT (also: **lump together**) riunire,
mettere insieme
lump sum N somma globale
lumpy ['lʌmpɪ] ADJ (sauce) pieno(-a) di grumi;
(bed) bitorzoluto(-a)
lunacy ['lu:nəsɪ] N demenza, follia, pazzia
lunar ['lu:nəʳ] ADJ lunare
lunatic ['lu:nətɪk] ADJ, N pazzo(-a), matto(-a)
lunatic asylum N manicomio
lunch [lʌntʃ] N pranzo, colazione f; **to invite
sb to or for ~** invitare qn a pranzo or a colazione
lunch break N intervallo del pranzo
luncheon ['lʌntʃən] N pranzo
luncheon meat N ≈ mortadella

luncheon voucher N buono m pasto inv
lunch hour N = **lunch break**
lunchtime ['lʌntʃtaɪm] N ora di pranzo
lung [lʌŋ] N polmone m
lung cancer N cancro del polmone
lunge [lʌndʒ] VI (also: **lunge forward**) fare un
balzo in avanti; **to ~ at sb** balzare su qn
lupin ['lu:pɪn] N lupino
lurch [lə:tʃ] VI vacillare, barcollare ▶ N scatto
improvviso; **to leave sb in the ~** piantare in
asso qn
lure [luəʳ] N richiamo; lusinga ▶ VT attirare
(con l'inganno)
lurid ['luərɪd] ADJ sgargiante; (details etc)
impressionante
lurk [lə:k] VI stare in agguato
luscious ['lʌʃəs] ADJ succulento(-a);
delizioso(-a)
lush [lʌʃ] ADJ lussureggiante
lust [lʌst] N lussuria; cupidigia; desiderio;
(fig): **~ for** sete f di
▶ **lust after** VT FUS bramare, desiderare
luster ['lʌstəʳ] N (US) = **lustre**
lustful ['lʌstful] ADJ lascivo(-a), voglioso(-a)
lustre, (US) **luster** ['lʌstəʳ] N lustro,
splendore m
lusty ['lʌstɪ] ADJ vigoroso(-a), robusto(-a)
lute [lu:t] N liuto
Luxembourg ['lʌksəmbə:g] N (state)
Lussemburgo m; (city) Lussemburgo f
luxuriant [lʌg'zjuərɪənt] ADJ lussureggiante
luxurious [lʌg'zjuərɪəs] ADJ sontuoso(-a), di
lusso
luxury ['lʌkʃərɪ] N lusso ▶ CPD di lusso
LV N ABBR (BRIT) = **luncheon voucher**
LW ABBR (Radio: = long wave) O.L.
Lycra® ['laɪkrə] N lycra® f inv
lying ['laɪɪŋ] N bugie fpl, menzogne fpl;
▶ ADJ (statement, story) falso(-a); (person)
bugiardo(-a)
lynch [lɪntʃ] VT linciare
lynx [lɪŋks] N lince f
Lyons ['laɪənz] N Lione f
lyre ['laɪəʳ] N lira
lyric ['lɪrɪk] ADJ lirico(-a); **lyrics** NPL (of song)
parole fpl
lyrical ['lɪrɪkl] ADJ lirico(-a)
lyricism ['lɪrɪsɪzəm] N lirismo

Mm

M, m [ɛm] N (*letter*) M, m *f inv or m inv*; **M for Mary,** (*US*) **M for Mike** ≈ M come Milano

M N ABBR (*BRIT*) = **motorway** ▶ ABBR (= *medium*) taglia media; **the M8** ≈ l'A8

m ABBR (= *metre*) m; ≈ **mile; million**

MA N ABBR (*Scol*) = **Master of Arts**; (*US*) = **military academy** ▶ ABBR (*US*) = **Massachusetts**

ma [mɑ:] N (*col*) mamma

mac [mæk] N (*BRIT*) impermeabile *m*

macabre [mə'kɑ:brə] ADJ macabro(-a)

macaroni [mækə'rəʊnɪ] N maccheroni *mpl*

macaroon [mækə'ru:n] N amaretto (*biscotto*)

mace [meɪs] N mazza; (*spice*) macis *m or f*

Macedonia [mæsɪ'dəʊnɪə] N Macedonia

Macedonian [mæsɪ'dəʊnɪən] ADJ macedone ▶ N macedone *mf*; (*Ling*) macedone *m*

machinations [mækɪ'neɪʃənz] NPL macchinazioni *fpl*, intrighi *mpl*

machine [mə'ʃi:n] N macchina ▶ VT (*dress etc*) cucire a macchina; (*Tech*) lavorare (a macchina)

machine code N (*Comput*) codice *m* di macchina, codice assoluto

machine gun N mitragliatrice *f*

machine language N (*Comput*) linguaggio *m* macchina *inv*

machine-readable [mə'ʃi:nri:dəbl] ADJ (*Comput*) leggibile dalla macchina

machinery [mə'ʃi:nərɪ] N macchinario, macchine *fpl*; (*fig*) macchina

machine shop N officina meccanica

machine tool N macchina utensile

machine washable ADJ lavabile in lavatrice

machinist [mə'ʃi:nɪst] N macchinista *mf*

macho ['mætʃəʊ] ADJ macho *inv*

mackerel ['mækrəl] N (*pl inv*) sgombro

mackintosh ['mækɪntɔʃ] N (*BRIT*) impermeabile *m*

macro... ['mækrəʊ] PREFIX macro...

macroeconomics ['mækrəʊi:kə'nɔmɪks] N macroeconomia

mad [mæd] ADJ matto(-a), pazzo(-a); (*foolish*) sciocco(-a); (*angry*) furioso(-a); **to go ~**

impazzire, diventar matto; **~ (at or with sb)** furibondo(-a) (con qn); **to be ~ (keen) about** *or* **on sth** (*col*) andar matto(-a) per qc

Madagascar [mædə'gæskəʳ] N Madagascar *m*

madam ['mædəm] N signora; **M~ Chairman** Signora Presidentessa

madcap ['mædkæp] ADJ (*col*) senza senso, assurdo(-a)

mad cow disease N encefalite *f* bovina spongiforme

madden ['mædn] VT fare infuriare

maddening ['mædnɪŋ] ADJ esasperante

made [meɪd] PT, PP *of* **make**

Madeira [mə'dɪərə] N (*Geo*) Madera; (*wine*) madera *m*

made-to-measure ['meɪdtə'mɛʒəʳ] ADJ (*BRIT*) fatto(-a) su misura

made-up ['meɪdʌp] ADJ (*story*) inventato(-a)

madhouse ['mædhaʊs] N (*also fig*) manicomio

madly ['mædlɪ] ADV follemente; (*love*) alla follia

madman ['mædmən] N (*irreg*) pazzo, alienato

madness ['mædnɪs] N pazzia

Madrid [mə'drɪd] N Madrid *f*

Mafia ['mæfɪə] N mafia *f*

mag. [mæg] N ABBR (*BRIT col: Press*) = **magazine**

magazine [mægə'zi:n] N (*Press*) rivista; (*Radio, TV*) rubrica; (*Mil: store*) magazzino, deposito; (*of firearm*) caricatore *m*

maggot ['mægət] N baco, verme *m*

magic ['mædʒɪk] N magia ▶ ADJ magico(-a)

magical ['mædʒɪkəl] ADJ magico(-a)

magician [mə'dʒɪʃən] N mago(-a)

magistrate ['mædʒɪstreɪt] N magistrato; giudice *mf*

magistrates' court N *see* **crown**

magnanimous [mæg'nænɪməs] ADJ magnanimo(-a)

magnate ['mægneɪt] N magnate *m*

magnesium [mæg'ni:zɪəm] N magnesio

magnet ['mægnɪt] N magnete *m*, calamita

magnetic [mæg'nɛtɪk] ADJ magnetico(-a)
magnetic disk N (*Comput*) disco magnetico
magnetic tape N nastro magnetico
magnetism ['mægnɪtɪzəm] N magnetismo
magnification [mægnɪfɪ'keɪʃən] N
ingrandimento
magnificence [mæg'nɪfɪsns] N magnificenza
magnificent [mæg'nɪfɪsnt] ADJ
magnifico(-a)
magnify ['mægnɪfaɪ] VT ingrandire
magnifying glass ['mægnɪfaɪɪŋ-] N lente *f*
d'ingrandimento
magnitude ['mægnɪtjuːd] N grandezza;
importanza
magnolia [mæg'nəʊlɪə] N magnolia
magpie ['mægpaɪ] N gazza
mahogany [mə'hɔgənɪ] N mogano ▶ CPD di
or in mogano
maid [meɪd] N domestica; (*in hotel*)
cameriera; **old ~** (*pej*) vecchia zitella
maiden ['meɪdn] N fanciulla ▶ ADJ (*aunt etc*)
nubile; (*speech, voyage*) inaugurale
maiden name ['meɪdn-] N nome da *m* nubile
or da ragazza
mail [meɪl] N posta ▶ VT spedire (per posta);
by ~ per posta
mailbox ['meɪlbɔks] N (*US*) cassetta delle
lettere; (*Comput*) mailbox *f inv*
mailing list ['meɪlɪŋ-] N elenco d'indirizzi
mailman ['meɪlmæn] N (*irreg*) (*US*)
portalettere *m inv*, postino
mail-order ['meɪlɔːdə'] N vendita (*or*
acquisto) per corrispondenza ▶ CPD: **~ firm**
or **house** ditta di vendita per corrispondenza
mailshot ['meɪlʃɔt] N mailing *m inv*
mail train N treno postale
mail truck N (*US Aut*) = **mail van**
mail van N (*BRIT: Aut*) furgone *m* postale;
(: *Rail*) vagone *m* postale
maim [meɪm] VT mutilare
main [meɪn] ADJ principale ▶ N (*pipe*)
conduttura principale; **the mains** (*Elec*) la
linea principale; **mains operated** *adj* che
funziona a elettricità; **in the ~** nel
complesso, nell'insieme
main course N (*Culin*) piatto principale,
piatto forte
mainframe ['meɪnfreɪm] N (*also*: **mainframe
computer**) mainframe *m inv*
mainland ['meɪnlənd] N continente *m*
mainline ['meɪnlaɪn] ADJ (*Rail*) della linea
principale ▶ VT (*drugs slang*) bucarsi di ▶ VI
(*drugs slang*) bucarsi
main line N (*Rail*) linea principale
mainly ['meɪnlɪ] ADV principalmente,
soprattutto
main road N strada principale
mainstay ['meɪnsteɪ] N (*fig*) sostegno
principale

mainstream ['meɪnstriːm] N (*fig*) corrente *f*
principale
main street N strada principale
maintain [meɪn'teɪn] VT mantenere;
(*affirm*) sostenere; **to ~ that …** sostenere
che …
maintenance ['meɪntənəns] N
manutenzione *f*; (*alimony*) alimenti *mpl*
maintenance contract N contratto di
manutenzione
maintenance order N (*Law*) obbligo degli
alimenti
maisonette [meɪzə'nɛt] N (*BRIT*)
appartamento a due piani
maize [meɪz] N granturco, mais *m*
Maj. ABBR (*Mil*) = **major**
majestic [mə'dʒɛstɪk] ADJ maestoso(-a)
majesty ['mædʒɪstɪ] N maestà *f inv*
major ['meɪdʒə'] N (*Mil*) maggiore *m* ▶ ADJ
(*greater, Mus*) maggiore; (*in importance*)
principale, importante ▶ VI (*US Scol*): **to ~ (in)**
specializzarsi (in); **a ~ operation** (*Med*) una
grossa operazione
Majorca [mə'jɔːkə] N Maiorca
major general N (*Mil*) generale *m* di
divisione
majority [mə'dʒɔrɪtɪ] N maggioranza ▶ CPD
(*verdict*) maggioritario(-a)
majority holding N (*Comm*): **to have a ~**
essere maggiore azionista
make [meɪk] (*pt, pp* **made** [meɪd]) VT fare;
(*manufacture*) fare, fabbricare; (*cause to be*): **to
~ sb sad** *etc* rendere qn triste *etc*; (*force*): **to ~
sb do sth** costringere qn a fare qc, far fare qc
a qn; (*equal*): **2 and 2 ~ 4** 2 più 2 fa 4 ▶ N
fabbricazione *f*; (*brand*) marca; **to ~ a fool of
sb** far fare a qn la figura dello scemo; **to ~ a
profit** realizzare un profitto; **to ~ a loss**
subire una perdita; **to ~ it** (*in time etc*)
arrivare; (*succeed*) farcela; **what time do you
~ it?** che ora fai?; **to ~ good** *vi* (*succeed*) aver
successo; *vt* (*deficit*) colmare; (*losses*)
compensare; **to ~ do with** arrangiarsi con
▶ **make for** VT FUS (*place*) avviarsi verso
▶ **make off** VI svignarsela
▶ **make out** VT (*write out*) scrivere; (: *cheque*)
emettere; (*understand*) capire; (*see*)
distinguere; (: *numbers*) decifrare; (*claim,
imply*): **to ~ out (that)** voler far credere (che);
to ~ out a case for sth presentare delle
valide ragioni in favore di qc
▶ **make over** VT (*assign*): **to ~ over (to)**
passare (a), trasferire (a)
▶ **make up** VT (*constitute*) formare; (*invent*)
inventare; (*parcel*) fare ▶ VI conciliarsi; (*with
cosmetics*) truccarsi; **to be made up of** essere
composto di *or* formato da
▶ **make up for** VT FUS compensare;
ricuperare

make-believe ['meɪkbɪliːv] N: **a world of ~** un mondo di favole; **it's just ~** è tutta un'invenzione

makeover ['meɪkəʊvəʳ] N cambio di immagine; **to give sb a ~** far cambiare immagine a qn

maker ['meɪkəʳ] N (of programme etc) creatore(-trice); (manufacturer) fabbricante m

makeshift ['meɪkʃɪft] ADJ improvvisato(-a)

make-up ['meɪkʌp] N trucco

make-up bag N borsa del trucco

make-up remover N struccatore m

making ['meɪkɪŋ] N (fig): **in the ~** in formazione; **he has the makings of an actor** ha la stoffa dell'attore

maladjusted [mælə'dʒʌstɪd] ADJ disadattato(-a)

maladroit [mælə'drɔɪt] ADJ maldestro(-a)

malaise [mæ'leɪz] N malessere m

malaria [mə'lɛərɪə] N malaria

Malawi [mə'lɑːwɪ] N Malawi m

Malay [mə'leɪ] ADJ malese ▶ N malese mf; (Ling) malese m

Malaya [mə'leɪə] N Malesia

Malayan [mə'leɪən] ADJ, N = **Malay**

Malaysia [mə'leɪzɪə] N Malaysia

Malaysian [mə'leɪzɪən] ADJ, N malaysiano(-a)

Maldives ['mɔːldaɪvz] NPL: **the ~** le (isole) Maldive

male [meɪl] N (Biol, Elec) maschio ▶ ADJ (gen, sex) maschile; (animal, child) maschio(-a); **~ and female students** studenti e studentesse

male chauvinist N maschilista m

male nurse N infermiere m

malevolence [mə'lɛvələns] N malevolenza

malevolent [mə'lɛvələnt] ADJ malevolo(-a)

malfunction [mæl'fʌŋkʃən] N funzione f difettosa

malice ['mælɪs] N malevolenza

malicious [mə'lɪʃəs] ADJ malevolo(-a); (Law) doloso(-a)

malign [mə'laɪn] VT malignare su; calunniare

malignant [mə'lɪgnənt] ADJ (Med) maligno(-a)

malingerer [mə'lɪŋgərəʳ] N scansafatiche mf

mall [mɔːl] N (also: **shopping mall**) centro commerciale

malleable ['mælɪəbl] ADJ malleabile

mallet ['mælɪt] N maglio

malnutrition [mælnjuː'trɪʃən] N denutrizione f

malpractice [mæl'præktɪs] N prevaricazione f; negligenza

malt [mɔːlt] N malto ▶ CPD (whisky) di malto

Malta ['mɔːltə] N Malta

Maltese [mɔːl'tiːz] ADJ, N (pl inv) maltese (mf); (Ling) maltese m

maltreat [mæl'triːt] VT maltrattare

malware ['mælwɛəʳ] N (Comput) malware mpl, software mpl maligni

mammal ['mæml] N mammifero

mammoth ['mæməθ] N mammut m inv ▶ ADJ enorme, gigantesco(-a)

man [mæn] (pl **men**) N uomo; (Chess) pezzo; (Draughts) pedina ▶ VT fornire d'uomini; stare a; essere di servizio a; **an old ~** un vecchio; **~ and wife** marito e moglie

Man. ABBR (CANADA) = **Manitoba**

manacles ['mænəklz] NPL manette fpl

manage ['mænɪdʒ] VI farcela ▶ VT (be in charge of) occuparsi di; (shop, restaurant) gestire; **to ~ without sth/sb** fare a meno di qc/qn; **to ~ to do sth** riuscire a far qc

manageable ['mænɪdʒəbl] ADJ maneggevole; (task etc) fattibile

management ['mænɪdʒmənt] N amministrazione f, direzione f; gestione f; (persons: of business, firm) dirigenti mpl; (: of hotel, shop, theatre) direzione f; **"under new ~"** "sotto nuova gestione"

management accounting N contabilità di gestione

management buyout N acquisto di una società da parte dei suoi dirigenti

management consultant N consulente mf aziendale

manager ['mænɪdʒəʳ] N direttore m; (of shop, restaurant) gerente m; (of artist, Sport) manager m inv; **sales ~** direttore m delle vendite

manageress [mænɪdʒə'rɛs] N direttrice f; gerente f

managerial [mænə'dʒɪərɪəl] ADJ dirigenziale

managing director ['mænɪdʒɪŋ-] N amministratore m delegato

Mancunian [mæŋ'kjuːnɪən] ADJ di Manchester ▶ N abitante mf di Manchester; originario(-a) di Manchester

mandarin ['mændərɪn] N (person, fruit) mandarino

mandate ['mændeɪt] N mandato

mandatory ['mændətərɪ] ADJ obbligatorio(-a); ingiuntivo(-a)

mandolin, mandoline ['mændəlɪn] N mandolino

mane [meɪn] N criniera

maneuver etc [mə'nuːvəʳ] (US) = **manoeuvre** etc

manful ['mænful] ADJ coraggioso(-a), valoroso(-a)

manfully ['mænfəlɪ] ADV valorosamente

manganese [mæŋgə'niːz] N manganese m

mangetout ['mɔnʒ'tuː] N pisello dolce, taccola

mangle ['mæŋgl] VT straziare; mutilare ▶ N strizzatoio

mango ['mæŋgəu] (pl **mangoes**) N mango

mangrove ['mæŋgrəuv] N mangrovia

mangy ['meɪndʒɪ] ADJ rognoso(-a)
manhandle ['mænhændl] VT (*treat roughly*)
malmenare; (*move by hand: goods*) spostare a
mano
manhole ['mænhəul] N botola stradale
manhood ['mænhud] N età virile; virilità
man-hour ['mænauəʳ] N ora di lavoro
manhunt ['mænhʌnt] N caccia all'uomo
mania ['meɪnɪə] N mania
maniac ['meɪnɪæk] N maniaco(-a)
manic ['mænɪk] ADJ (*behaviour, activity*)
maniacale
manic-depressive ['mænɪkdɪ'presɪv] ADJ
maniaco-depressivo(-a) ▶ N persona affetta
da mania depressiva
manicure ['mænɪkjuəʳ] N manicure *f inv*
manicure set N trousse *f inv* della manicure
manifest ['mænɪfest] VT manifestare ▶ ADJ
manifesto(-a), palese ▶ N (*Aviat, Naut*)
manifesto
manifestation [mænɪfes'teɪʃən] N
manifestazione *f*
manifesto [mænɪ'festəu] N manifesto
manifold ['mænɪfəuld] ADJ molteplice ▶ N
(*Aut etc*): **exhaust ~** collettore *m* di scarico
Manila [mə'nɪlə] N Manila
manila, manilla [mə'nɪlə] ADJ (*paper, envelope*)
manilla *inv*
manipulate [mə'nɪpjuleɪt] VT (*tool*)
maneggiare; (*controls*) azionare; (*limb, facts*)
manipolare
manipulation [mənɪpju'leɪʃən] N
maneggiare *m*; capacità di azionare;
manipolazione *f*
mankind [mæn'kaɪnd] N umanità, genere *m*
umano
manliness ['mænlɪnɪs] N virilità
manly ['mænlɪ] ADJ virile; coraggioso(-a)
man-made ['mæn'meɪd] ADJ sintetico(-a);
artificiale
manna ['mænə] N manna
mannequin ['mænɪkɪn] N (*dummy*)
manichino; (*fashion model*) indossatrice *f*
manner ['mænəʳ] N maniera, modo;
(*behaviour*) modo di fare; (*type, sort*): **all ~ of
things** ogni genere di cosa; **manners** NPL
(*conduct*) maniere *fpl*; **(good) manners**
buona educazione *f*, buone maniere; **bad
manners** maleducazione *f*; **all ~ of** ogni
sorta di
mannerism ['mænərɪzəm] N vezzo, tic *m inv*
mannerly ['mænəlɪ] ADJ educato(-a), civile
manoeuvrable, (*US*)**maneuverable**
[mə'nu:vrəbl] ADJ facile da manovrare; (*car*)
maneggevole
manoeuvre, (*US*)**maneuver** [mə'nu:vəʳ] VT
manovrare ▶ VI far manovre ▶ N manovra;
to ~ sb into doing sth costringere
abilmente qn a fare qc

manor ['mænəʳ] N (*also*: **manor house**)
maniero
manpower ['mænpauəʳ] N manodopera
Manpower Services Commission N (*BRIT*)
ente nazionale per l'occupazione
manservant ['mænsə:vənt] (*pl* **menservants**
['men-]) N domestico
mansion ['mænʃən] N casa signorile
manslaughter ['mænslɔ:təʳ] N omicidio
preterintenzionale
mantelpiece ['mæntlpi:s] N mensola del
caminetto
mantle ['mæntl] N mantello
man-to-man ['mæntə'mæn] ADJ, ADV da
uomo a uomo
Mantua ['mæntjuə] N Mantova
manual ['mænjuəl] ADJ, N manuale (*m*)
manual worker N manovale *m*
manufacture [mænju'fæktʃəʳ] VT fabbricare
▶ N fabbricazione *f*, manifattura
manufactured goods NPL manufatti *mpl*
manufacturer [mænju'fæktʃərəʳ] N
fabbricante *m*
manufacturing industries
[mænju'fæktʃərɪŋ-] NPL industrie *fpl*
manifatturiere
manure [mə'njuəʳ] N concime *m*
manuscript ['mænjuskrɪpt] N manoscritto
many ['menɪ] ADJ molti(-e) ▶ PRON molti(-e),
un gran numero; **a great ~** moltissimi(-e),
un gran numero (di); **~ a ...** molti(-e) ..., più
di un(-a) ...; **too ~ difficulties** troppe
difficoltà; **twice as ~** due volte tanto; **how
~?** quanti(-e)?
Maori ['maurɪ] ADJ, N maori (*mf*) inv
map [mæp] N carta (geografica); (*of city*)
cartina ▶ VT fare una carta di
▶ **map out** VT tracciare un piano di; (*fig:
career, holiday, essay*) pianificare
maple ['meɪpl] N acero
mar [mɑːʳ] VT sciupare
Mar. ABBR (= *March*) mar.
marathon ['mærəθən] N maratona ▶ ADJ: **a ~
session** una seduta fiume
marathon runner N maratoneta *mf*
marauder [mə'rɔ:dəʳ] N saccheggiatore *m*;
predatore *m*
marble ['mɑ:bl] N marmo; (*toy*) pallina, bilia;
marbles N (*game*) palline, bilie
March [mɑ:tʃ] N marzo; *see also* **July**
march [mɑ:tʃ] VI marciare; sfilare ▶ N
marcia; (*demonstration*) dimostrazione *f*; **to ~
into a room** entrare a passo deciso in una
stanza
marcher ['mɑ:tʃəʳ] N dimostrante *mf*
marching ['mɑ:tʃɪŋ] N: **to give sb his ~
orders** (*fig*) dare il benservito a qn
march-past ['mɑ:tʃpɑ:st] N sfilata
mare [mɛəʳ] N giumenta

m

marg [mɑːdʒ] N ABBR (col) = **margarine**
margarine [mɑːdʒəˈriːn] N margarina
marge [mɑːdʒ] N ABBR (col) = **margarine**
margin ['mɑːdʒɪn] N margine m
marginal ['mɑːdʒɪnl] ADJ marginale; ~ **seat**
  (Pol) seggio elettorale ottenuto con una stretta
  maggioranza
marginally ['mɑːdʒɪnəlɪ] ADV (bigger, better)
  lievemente, di poco; (different) un po'
marigold ['mærɪɡəʊld] N calendola
marijuana [mærɪˈwɑːnə] N marijuana
marina [məˈriːnə] N marina
marinade N [mærɪˈneɪd] marinata ▶ VT
  ['mærɪneɪd] = **marinate**
marinate ['mærɪneɪt] VT marinare
marine [məˈriːn] ADJ (animal, plant)
  marino(-a); (forces, engineering) marittimo(-a)
  ▶ N (BRIT) fante m di marina; (US) marine
  m inv
marine insurance N assicurazione f
  marittima
marital ['mærɪtl] ADJ maritale, coniugale;
  ~ **status** stato coniugale
maritime ['mærɪtaɪm] ADJ marittimo(-a)
maritime law N diritto marittimo
marjoram ['mɑːdʒərəm] N maggiorana
mark [mɑːk] N segno; (stain) macchia; (of skid
  etc) traccia; (BRIT Scol) voto; (Sport) bersaglio;
  (Hist: currency) marco; (BRIT Tech): **M~ 2/3** 1a/2a
  serie f ▶ VT segnare; (stain) macchiare;
  (indicate) indicare; (BRIT Scol) dare un voto a;
  correggere; (Sport: player) marcare;
  punctuation marks segni di
  punteggiatura; **to be quick off the ~ (in
  doing)** (fig) non perdere tempo (per fare); **up
  to the ~** (in efficiency) all'altezza; **to ~ time**
  segnare il passo
  ▶ **mark down** VT (reduce: prices, goods)
  ribassare, ridurre
  ▶ **mark off** VT (tick off) spuntare, cancellare
  ▶ **mark out** VT delimitare
  ▶ **mark up** VT (price) aumentare
marked ['mɑːkt] ADJ spiccato(-a), chiaro(-a)
markedly ['mɑːkɪdlɪ] ADV visibilmente,
  notevolmente
marker ['mɑːkər] N (sign) segno; (bookmark)
  segnalibro
market ['mɑːkɪt] N mercato ▶ VT (Comm)
  mettere in vendita; (promote) lanciare sul
  mercato; **to play the ~** giocare or speculare
  in borsa; **to be on the ~** essere (messo) in
  vendita or in commercio; **open ~** mercato
  libero
marketable ['mɑːkɪtəbl] ADJ
  commercializzabile
market analysis N analisi f di mercato
market day N giorno di mercato
market demand N domanda del mercato
market economy N economia di mercato

market forces NPL forze fpl di mercato
market garden N (BRIT) orto industriale
marketing ['mɑːkɪtɪŋ] N marketing m
marketplace ['mɑːkɪtpleɪs] N (piazza del)
  mercato; (world of trade) piazza, mercato
market price N prezzo di mercato
market research N indagine f or ricerca di
  mercato
market value N valore m di mercato
marking ['mɑːkɪŋ] N (on animal) marcatura di
  colore; (on road) segnaletica orizzontale
marksman ['mɑːksmən] N (irreg) tiratore m
  scelto
marksmanship ['mɑːksmənʃɪp] N abilità nel
  tiro
mark-up ['mɑːkʌp] N (Comm: margin) margine
  m di vendita; (: increase) aumento
marmalade ['mɑːməleɪd] N marmellata
  d'arance
maroon [məˈruːn] VT (fig): **to be marooned
  (in** or **at)** essere abbandonato(-a) (in) ▶ ADJ
  bordeaux inv
marquee [mɑːˈkiː] N padiglione m
marquess, marquis ['mɑːkwɪs] N
  marchese m
Marrakech, Marrakesh [mærəˈkeʃ] N
  Marrakesh f
marriage ['mærɪdʒ] N matrimonio
marriage bureau N agenzia matrimoniale
marriage certificate N certificato di
  matrimonio
marriage guidance, (US) **marriage
  counseling** N consulenza matrimoniale
marriage of convenience N matrimonio di
  convenienza
married ['mærɪd] ADJ sposato(-a); (life, love)
  coniugale, matrimoniale
marrow ['mærəʊ] N midollo; (vegetable)
  zucca
marry ['mærɪ] VT sposare, sposarsi con;
  (father, priest etc) dare in matrimonio ▶ VI (also:
  get married) sposarsi
Mars [mɑːz] N (planet) Marte m
Marseilles [mɑːˈseɪlz] N Marsiglia
marsh [mɑːʃ] N palude f
marshal ['mɑːʃl] N maresciallo; (US: fire
  marshal) capo; (: police marshal) capitano; (for
  demonstration, meeting) membro del servizio
  d'ordine ▶ VT (thoughts, support) ordinare;
  (soldiers) adunare
marshalling yard ['mɑːʃlɪŋ-] N scalo
  smistamento
marshmallow [mɑːʃˈmæləʊ] N (Bot) altea;
  (sweet) caramella soffice e gommosa
marshy ['mɑːʃɪ] ADJ paludoso(-a)
marsupial [mɑːˈsuːpɪəl] ADJ, N marsupiale (m)
martial ['mɑːʃl] ADJ marziale
martial arts NPL arti fpl marziali
martial law N legge f marziale

Martian ['mɑːʃən] N marziano(-a)

martin ['mɑːtɪn] N (*also:* **house martin**) balestruccio

martyr ['mɑːtər] N martire *mf* ▶ VT martirizzare

martyrdom ['mɑːtədəm] N martirio

marvel ['mɑːvl] N meraviglia ▶ VI: **to ~ (at)** meravigliarsi (di)

marvellous, (*US*)**marvelous** ['mɑːvələs] ADJ meraviglioso(-a)

Marxism ['mɑːksɪzəm] N marxismo

Marxist ['mɑːksɪst] ADJ, N marxista (*mf*)

marzipan ['mɑːzɪpæn] N marzapane *m*

mascara [mæs'kɑːrə] N mascara *m inv*

mascot ['mæskət] N mascotte *f inv*

masculine ['mæskjulɪn] ADJ maschile; (*woman*) mascolino(-a) ▶ N genere *m* maschile

masculinity [mæskju'lɪnɪtɪ] N mascolinità

MASH [mæʃ] N ABBR (*US Mil*: = *mobile army surgical hospital*) ospedale di campo di unità mobile dell'esercito

mash [mæʃ] VT (*Culin*) passare, schiacciare

mashed [mæʃt] ADJ: **~ potatoes** purè *m* di patate

mask [mɑːsk] N (*gen*, *Elec*) maschera ▶ VT mascherare

masochism ['mæsəkɪzəm] N masochismo

masochist ['mæsəkɪst] N masochista *mf*

mason ['meɪsn] N (*also:* **stonemason**) scalpellino; (*also:* **freemason**) massone *m*

masonic [mə'sɔnɪk] ADJ massonico(-a)

masonry ['meɪsnrɪ] N muratura

masquerade [mæskə'reɪd] N ballo in maschera; (*fig*) mascherata ▶ VI: **to ~ as** farsi passare per

mass [mæs] N moltitudine *f*, massa; (*Physics*) massa; (*Rel*) messa ▶ CPD di massa ▶ VI ammassarsi; **the masses** (*ordinary people*) le masse; **masses of** (*col*) una montagna di; **to go to ~** andare a *or* alla messa

Mass. ABBR (*US*) = **Massachusetts**

massacre ['mæsəkər] N massacro ▶ VT massacrare

massage ['mæsɑːʒ] N massaggio ▶ VT massaggiare

masseur [mæ'səːr] N massaggiatore *m*

masseuse [mæ'səːz] N massaggiatrice *f*

massive ['mæsɪv] ADJ enorme, massiccio(-a)

mass market N mercato di massa

mass media NPL mass media *mpl*

mass meeting N (*of everyone concerned*) riunione *f* generale; (*huge*) adunata popolare

mass-produce ['mæsprə'djuːs] VT produrre in serie

mass production N produzione *f* in serie

mast [mɑːst] N albero; (*Radio*, *TV*) pilone *m* (a traliccio)

mastectomy [mæs'tɛktəmɪ] N mastectomia

master ['mɑːstər] N padrone *m*; (*teacher: in primary school*, *Art etc*) maestro; (: *in secondary school*) professore *m*; (*title for boys*): **M~ X** Signorino X ▶ VT domare; (*learn*) imparare a fondo; (*understand*) conoscere a fondo; **~ of ceremonies** *n* maestro di cerimonie; **M~'s degree** *n vedi nota*

> Il *Master's degree* è il riconoscimento che viene conferito a chi segue un corso di specializzazione dopo aver conseguito un *Bachelor's degree*. Vi sono diversi tipi di *Master's Degree*; i più comuni sono il *Master of Arts* (*MA*) e il *Master of Science* (*MSc*) che si ottengono dopo aver seguito un corso e aver presentato una tesi originale. Per il *Master of Letters* (*MLitt*) e il *Master of Philosophy* (*MPhil*) è invece sufficiente presentare la tesi; *vedi anche* **doctorate**.

master disk N (*Comput*) disco *m* master *inv*, disco principale

masterful ['mɑːstəful] ADJ autoritario(-a), imperioso(-a)

master key N chiave *f* maestra

masterly ['mɑːstəlɪ] ADJ magistrale

mastermind ['mɑːstəmaɪnd] N mente *f* superiore ▶ VT essere il cervello di

Master of Arts/Science N Master *m inv* in lettere/scienze

masterpiece ['mɑːstəpiːs] N capolavoro

master plan N piano generale

master stroke N colpo maestro

mastery ['mɑːstərɪ] N dominio; padronanza

mastiff ['mæstɪf] N mastino inglese

masturbate ['mæstəbeɪt] VI masturbare

masturbation [mæstə'beɪʃən] N masturbazione *f*

mat [mæt] N stuoia; (*also:* **doormat**) stoino, zerbino; (*also:* **table mat**) sottopiatto ▶ ADJ = **matt**

match [mætʃ] N fiammifero; (*game*) partita, incontro; (*fig*) uguale *mf*; matrimonio; partito ▶ VT intonare; (*go well with*) andare benissimo con; (*equal*) uguagliare; (*correspond to*) corrispondere a; (*pair: also:* **match up**) accoppiare ▶ VI intonarsi; **to be a good ~** andare bene

▶ **match up** VT intonare

matchbox ['mætʃbɔks] N scatola per fiammiferi

matching ['mætʃɪŋ] ADJ ben assortito(-a)

matchless ['mætʃlɪs] ADJ senza pari

mate [meɪt] N compagno(-a) di lavoro; (*col: friend*) amico(-a); (*animal*) compagno(-a); (*in merchant navy*) secondo ▶ VI accoppiarsi ▶ VT accoppiare

material [mə'tɪərɪəl] N (*substance*) materiale *m*, materia; (*cloth*) stoffa ▶ ADJ materiale; (*important*) essenziale; **materials** NPL (*equipment etc*) materiali *mpl*; occorrente *m*

m

materialistic [mətɪərɪə'lɪstɪk] ADJ materialistico(-a)

materialize [mə'tɪərɪəlaɪz] VI materializzarsi, realizzarsi

materially [mə'tɪərɪəlɪ] ADV dal punto di vista materiale; sostanzialmente

maternal [mə'tə:nl] ADJ materno(-a)

maternity [mə'tə:nɪtɪ] N maternità ▸ CPD di maternità; (clothes) pre-maman inv

maternity benefit N sussidio di maternità

maternity hospital N ≈ clinica ostetrica

maternity leave N congedo di maternità

matey ['meɪtɪ] ADJ (BRIT col) amicone(-a)

math [mæθ] N ABBR (US) = **mathematics**

mathematical [mæθə'mætɪkl] ADJ matematico(-a)

mathematician [mæθəmə'tɪʃən] N matematico(-a)

mathematics [mæθə'mætɪks] N matematica

maths [mæθs] N ABBR (BRIT) = **mathematics**

matinée ['mætɪneɪ] N matinée f inv

mating ['meɪtɪŋ] N accoppiamento

mating call N chiamata all'accoppiamento

mating season N stagione f degli amori

matriarchal [meɪtrɪ'ɑ:kl] ADJ matriarcale

matrices ['meɪtrisi:z] NPL of **matrix**

matriculation [mətrɪkju'leɪʃən] N immatricolazione f

matrimonial [mætrɪ'məunɪəl] ADJ matrimoniale, coniugale

matrimony ['mætrɪmənɪ] N matrimonio

matrix ['meɪtrɪks] (pl **matrices** ['meɪtrisi:z]) N matrice f

matron ['meɪtrən] N (in hospital) capoinfermiera; (in school) infermiera

matronly ['meɪtrənlɪ] ADJ da matrona

matt [mæt] ADJ opaco(-a)

matted ['mætɪd] ADJ ingarbugliato(-a)

matter ['mætə'] N questione f; (Physics) materia, sostanza; (content) contenuto; (Med: pus) pus m ▸ VI importare; **matters** NPL (affairs) questioni; **it doesn't** ~ non importa; (I don't mind) non fa niente; **what's the** ~? che cosa c'è?; **no** ~ **what** qualsiasi cosa accada; **that's another** ~ quello è un altro affare; **as a** ~ **of course** come cosa naturale; **as a** ~ **of fact** in verità; **it's a** ~ **of habit** è una questione di abitudine; **printed** ~ stampe fpl; **reading** ~ (BRIT) qualcosa da leggere

matter-of-fact [mætərəv'fækt] ADJ prosaico(-a)

matting ['mætɪŋ] N stuoia

mattress ['mætrɪs] N materasso

mature [mə'tjuə'] ADJ maturo(-a); (cheese) stagionato(-a) ▸ VI maturare; stagionare; (Comm) scadere

mature student N studente universitario che ha più di 25 anni

maturity [mə'tjuərɪtɪ] N maturità

maudlin ['mɔ:dlɪn] ADJ lacrimoso(-a)

maul [mɔ:l] VT lacerare

Mauritania [mɔrɪ'teɪnɪə] N Mauritania

Mauritius [mə'rɪʃəs] N Maurizio

mausoleum [mɔ:sə'lɪəm] N mausoleo

mauve [məuv] ADJ malva inv

maverick ['mævərɪk] N (fig) chi sta fuori del branco

mawkish ['mɔ:kɪʃ] ADJ sdolcinato(-a); insipido(-a)

max. ABBR = **maximum**

maxim ['mæksɪm] N massima

maxima ['mæksɪmə] NPL of **maximum**

maximize ['mæksɪmaɪz] VT (profits etc) massimizzare; (chances) aumentare al massimo

maximum ['mæksɪməm] (pl **maxima**) ADJ massimo(-a) ▸ N massimo

May [meɪ] N maggio; see also **July**

may [meɪ] (conditional **might**) VI (indicating possibility): **he** ~ **come** può darsi che venga; (be allowed to) ~ **I smoke?** posso fumare?; ~ **I sit here?** le dispiace se mi siedo qua?; (wishes) ~ **God bless you!** Dio la benedica!; **he might be there** può darsi che ci sia; **he might come** potrebbe venire, può anche darsi che venga; **I might as well go** potrei anche andarmene; **you might like to try** forse le piacerebbe provare

maybe ['meɪbi:] ADV forse, può darsi; ~ **he'll** ... può darsi che lui ... + sub, forse lui ...; ~ **not** forse no, può darsi di no

mayday ['meɪdeɪ] N S.O.S. m, mayday m inv

May Day N il primo maggio

mayhem ['meɪhɛm] N cagnara

mayonnaise [meɪə'neɪz] N maionese f

mayor [mɛə'] N sindaco

mayoress ['mɛərɛs] N sindaco (donna); moglie f del sindaco

maypole ['meɪpəul] N palo ornato di fiori attorno a cui si danza durante la festa di maggio

maze [meɪz] N labirinto, dedalo

MB ABBR (Comput) = megabyte; (CANADA) = **Manitoba**

MBA N ABBR (= Master of Business Administration) titolo di studio

MBE N ABBR (BRIT: = Member of the Order of the British Empire) titolo

MBO N ABBR = **management buyout**

MC N ABBR = **master of ceremonies**; (US: = Member of Congress) membro del Congresso

MCAT N ABBR (US: = Medical College Admissions Test) esame di ammissione a studi superiori di medicina

MD N ABBR (= Doctor of Medicine) titolo di studio; (Comm) = **managing director** ▸ ABBR (US) = **Maryland**

Md. ABBR (US) = **Maryland**

MDT ABBR (*US*: = *Mountain Daylight Time*) ora legale delle Montagne Rocciose

ME ABBR (*US*) = **Maine** ▶ N ABBR (*Med*: = *myalgic encephalomyelitis*) sindrome *f* da affaticamento cronico; (*US*) = **medical examiner**

me [mi:] PRON mi, m' + *vowel or silent "h"*; (*stressed, after prep*) me; **he heard me** mi ha *or* m'ha sentito; **give me a book** dammi (*or* mi dia) un libro; **it's me** sono io; **it's for me** è per me; **with me** con me; **without me** senza di me

meadow ['mɛdəu] N prato

meagre,(*US*) **meager** ['mi:gə^r] ADJ magro(-a)

meal [mi:l] N pasto; (*flour*) farina; **to go out for a ~** mangiare fuori

meals on wheels N (*BRIT*) distribuzione *f* di pasti caldi a domicilio (*per persone malate o anziane*)

mealtime ['mi:ltaɪm] N l'ora di mangiare

mealy-mouthed ['mi:lɪmauðd] ADJ che parla attraverso eufemismi

mean [mi:n] (*pt, pp* **meant** [mɛnt]) ADJ (*with money*) avaro(-a), gretto(-a); (*unkind*) meschino(-a), maligno(-a); (*US: vicious: animal*) cattivo(-a); (: *person*) perfido(-a); (*shabby*) misero(-a); (*average*) medio(-a) ▶ VT (*signify*) significare, voler dire; (*intend*): **to ~ to do** aver l'intenzione di fare ▶ N mezzo; (*Math*) media; **to be meant for** essere destinato(-a) a; **do you ~ it?** dice sul serio?; **what do you ~?** che cosa vuol dire?; *see also* **means**

meander [mɪ'ændə^r] VI far meandri; (*fig*) divagare

meaning ['mi:nɪŋ] N significato, senso

meaningful ['mi:nɪŋful] ADJ significativo(-a); (*relationship*) valido(-a)

meaningless ['mi:nɪŋlɪs] ADJ senza senso

meanness ['mi:nnɪs] N avarizia; meschinità

means [mi:nz] NPL (*way, money*) mezzi *mpl*; **by ~ of** per mezzo di; (*person*) a mezzo di; **by all ~** ma certo, prego

means test N (*Admin*) accertamento dei redditi (*per una persona che ha chiesto un aiuto finanziario*)

meant [mɛnt] PT, PP *of* **mean**

meantime ['mi:ntaɪm], **meanwhile** ['mi:nwaɪl] ADV (*also*: **in the meantime**) nel frattempo

measles ['mi:zlz] N morbillo

measly ['mi:zlɪ] ADJ (*col*) miserabile

measurable ['mɛʒərəbl] ADJ misurabile

measure ['mɛʒə^r] VT, VI misurare ▶ N misura; (*ruler*) metro; **a litre ~** una misura da un litro; **some ~ of success** un certo successo; **to take measures to do sth** prendere provvedimenti per fare qc

 ▶ **measure up** VI: **to ~ up (to)** dimostrarsi *or* essere all'altezza (di)

measured ['mɛʒəd] ADJ misurato(-a)

measurement ['mɛʒəmənt] N (*act*) misurazione *f*; (*measure*) misura; **chest/hip ~** giro petto/fianchi; **to take sb's measurements** prendere le misure di qn

meat [mi:t] N carne *f*; **cold meats** (*BRIT*) affettati *mpl*; **crab ~** polpa di granchio

meatball ['mi:tbɔ:l] N polpetta di carne

meat pie N torta salata in pasta frolla con ripieno di carne

meaty ['mi:tɪ] ADJ che sa di carne; (*fig*) sostanzioso(-a); (*person*) corpulento(-a); (*part of body*) carnoso(-a); **~ meal** pasto a base di carne

. **Mecca** ['mɛkə] N La Mecca; (*fig*): **a ~ (for)** la Mecca (di)

mechanic [mɪ'kænɪk] N meccanico; *see also* **mechanics**

mechanical [mɪ'kænɪkəl] ADJ meccanico(-a)

mechanical engineering N (*science*) ingegneria meccanica; (*industry*) costruzioni *fpl* meccaniche

mechanics [mə'kænɪks] N meccanica ▶ NPL meccanismo

mechanism ['mɛkənɪzəm] N meccanismo

mechanization [mɛkənaɪ'zeɪʃən] N meccanizzazione *f*

MEd N ABBR (= *Master of Education*) titolo di studio

medal ['mɛdl] N medaglia

medallion [mɪ'dælɪən] N medaglione *m*

medallist,(*US*) **medalist** ['mɛdəlɪst] N (*Sport*) vincitore(-trice) di medaglia; **to be a gold ~** essere medaglia d'oro

meddle ['mɛdl] VI: **to ~ in** immischiarsi in, mettere le mani in; **to ~ with** toccare

meddlesome ['mɛdlsəm], **meddling** ['mɛdlɪŋ] ADJ (*interfering*) che mette il naso dappertutto; (*touching things*) che tocca tutto

media ['mi:dɪə] NPL (*Press, Radio, TV*) media *mpl*

media circus N carrozzone *m* dell'informazione

mediaeval [mɛdɪ'i:vl] ADJ = **medieval**

median ['mi:dɪən] N (*US: also*: **median strip**) banchina *f* spartitraffico *inv*

media research N sondaggio tra gli utenti dei mass media

mediate ['mi:dɪeɪt] VI interporsi; fare da mediatore(-trice)

mediation [mi:dɪ'eɪʃən] N mediazione *f*

mediator ['mi:dɪeɪtə^r] N mediatore(-trice)

Medicaid ['mɛdɪkeɪd] N (*US*) assistenza medica ai poveri

medical ['mɛdɪkl] ADJ medico(-a); **~ (examination)** *n* visita medica

medical certificate N certificato medico

medical examiner N (*US*) medico incaricato di indagare la causa di morte in circostanze sospette

medical student N studente(-essa) di medicina

Medicare ['mɛdɪkeəʳ] N (US) assistenza medica agli anziani
medicated ['mɛdɪkeɪtɪd] ADJ medicato(-a)
medication [mɛdɪ'keɪʃən] N (drugs etc) medicinali mpl, farmaci mpl
medicinal [mɛ'dɪsɪnl] ADJ medicinale
medicine ['mɛdsɪn] N medicina
medicine chest N armadietto farmaceutico
medicine man N (irreg) stregone m
medieval [mɛdɪ'iːvl] ADJ medievale
mediocre [miːdɪ'əukəʳ] ADJ mediocre
mediocrity [miːdɪ'ɔkrɪtɪ] N mediocrità
meditate ['mɛdɪteɪt] VI: **to ~ (on)** meditare (su)
meditation [mɛdɪ'teɪʃən] N meditazione f
Mediterranean [mɛdɪtə'reɪnɪən] ADJ mediterraneo(-a); **the ~ (Sea)** il (mare) Mediterraneo
medium ['miːdɪəm] ADJ medio(-a) ► N (pl **media**: means) mezzo; (pl **mediums**: person) medium m inv; **the happy ~** una giusta via di mezzo; see also **media**
medium-dry ['miːdɪəm'draɪ] ADJ demisec inv
medium-sized ['miːdɪəmsaɪzd] ADJ (tin etc) di grandezza media; (clothes) di taglia media
medium wave N (Radio) onde fpl medie
medley ['mɛdlɪ] N selezione f
meek [miːk] ADJ dolce, umile
meet [miːt] (pt, pp **met** [mɛt]) VT incontrare; (for the first time) fare la conoscenza di; (go and fetch) andare a prendere; (fig) affrontare; far fronte a; soddisfare; raggiungere ► VI incontrarsi; (in session) riunirsi; (join: objects) unirsi ► N (BRIT Hunting) raduno (dei partecipanti alla caccia alla volpe); (US Sport) raduno (sportivo); **I'll ~ you at the station** verrò a prenderla alla stazione; **pleased to ~ you!** piacere (di conoscerla)!
► **meet up** VI: **to ~ up with sb** incontrare qn
► **meet with** VT FUS incontrare; **he met with an accident** ha avuto un incidente
meeting ['miːtɪŋ] N incontro, (session: of club etc) riunione f; (interview) intervista; (formal) colloquio; (Sport: rally) raduno; **she's at a ~** (Comm) è in riunione; **to call a ~** convocare una riunione
meeting place N luogo d'incontro
megabyte ['mɛgəbaɪt] N (Comput) megabyte m inv
megalomaniac [mɛgələu'meɪnɪæk] N megalomane mf
megaphone ['mɛgəfəun] N megafono
megapixel ['mɛgəpɪksl] N megapixel m inv
megawatt ['mɛgəwɔt] N megawatt m inv
melancholy ['mɛlənkəlɪ] N malinconia ► ADJ malinconico(-a)
mellow ['mɛləu] ADJ (wine, sound) ricco(-a); (person, light) dolce; (colour) caldo(-a); (fruit) maturo(-a) ► VI (person) addolcirsi

melodious [mɪ'ləudɪəs] ADJ melodioso(-a)
melodrama ['mɛləudrɑːmə] N melodramma m
melodramatic [mɛlədrə'mætɪk] ADJ melodrammatico(-a)
melody ['mɛlədɪ] N melodia
melon ['mɛlən] N melone m
melt [mɛlt] VI (gen) sciogliersi, struggersi; (metals) fondersi; (fig) intenerirsi ► VT sciogliere, struggere; fondere; (person) commuovere; **melted butter** burro fuso
► **melt away** VI sciogliersi completamente
► **melt down** VT fondere
meltdown ['mɛltdaun] N melt-down m inv
melting point ['mɛltɪŋ-] N punto di fusione
melting pot ['mɛltɪŋ-] N (fig) crogiolo; **to be in the ~** essere ancora in discussione
member ['mɛmbəʳ] N membro; (of club) socio(-a), iscritto(-a); (of political party) iscritto(-a); **~ country/state** n paese m/stato membro
Member of Congress (US) N membro del Congresso
Member of Parliament (BRIT) N deputato(-a)
Member of the European Parliament (BRIT) N eurodeputato(-a)
Member of the House of Representatives (US) N membro della Camera dei Rappresentanti
Member of the Scottish Parliament (BRIT) N deputato(-a) del Parlamento scozzese
membership ['mɛmbəʃɪp] N iscrizione f; (number d')iscritti mpl, membri mpl
membership card N tessera (di iscrizione)
membrane ['mɛmbreɪn] N membrana
memento [mə'mɛntəu] N ricordo, souvenir m inv
memo ['mɛməu] N appunto; (Comm etc) comunicazione f di servizio
memoir ['mɛmwɑːʳ] N memoria; **memoirs** NPL memorie fpl, ricordi mpl
memo pad N bloccchetto per appunti
memorable ['mɛmərəbl] ADJ memorabile
memorandum [mɛmə'rændəm] (pl **memoranda** [-də]) N appunto; (Comm etc) comunicazione f di servizio; (Diplomacy) memorandum m inv
memorial [mɪ'mɔːrɪəl] N monumento commemorativo ► ADJ commemorativo(-a)
Memorial Day N (US); vedi nota

> Negli Stati Uniti il Memorial Day è una festa nazionale per la commemorazione di tutti i soldati americani caduti in guerra. Le celebrazioni sono tenute ogni anno l'ultimo lunedì di maggio.

memorize ['mɛməraɪz] VT memorizzare
memory ['mɛmərɪ] N (gen, Comput) memoria; (recollection) ricordo; **in ~ of** in memoria di;

to have a good/bad ~ aver buona/cattiva memoria; **loss of ~** amnesia

memory card N (*for digital camera*) scheda di memoria

memory stick N (*Comput*) stick *m inv* di memoria

men [mɛn] NPL *of* **man**

menace ['mɛnɪs] N minaccia; (*col: nuisance*) peste *f* ▶ VT minacciare; **a public ~** un pericolo pubblico

menacing ['mɛnɪsɪŋ] ADJ minaccioso(-a)

menagerie [mɪ'nædʒərɪ] N serraglio

mend [mɛnd] VT aggiustare, riparare; (*darn*) rammendare ▶ N rammendo; **on the ~** in via di guarigione

mending ['mɛndɪŋ] N rammendo; (*items to be mended*) roba da rammendare

menial ['miːnɪəl] ADJ da servo, domestico(-a); umile

meningitis [mɛnɪn'dʒaɪtɪs] N meningite *f*

menopause ['mɛnəupɔːz] N menopausa

menservants ['mɛnsəːvənts] NPL *of* **manservant**

men's room N: **the ~** (*esp US*) la toilette degli uomini

menstruate ['mɛnstrueɪt] VI mestruare

menstruation [mɛnstru'eɪʃən] N mestruazione *f*

menswear ['mɛnzwɛər] N abbigliamento maschile

mental ['mɛntl] ADJ mentale; **~ illness** malattia mentale

mental hospital N ospedale *m* psichiatrico

mentality [mɛn'tælɪtɪ] N mentalità *f inv*

mentally ['mɛntlɪ] ADV: **to be ~ handicapped** essere minorato psichico

menthol ['mɛnθɒl] N mentolo

mention ['mɛnʃən] N menzione *f* ▶ VT menzionare, far menzione di; **don't ~ it!** non c'è di che!, prego!; **I need hardly ~ that ...** inutile dire che ...; **not to ~, without mentioning** per non parlare di, senza contare

mentor ['mɛntɔːʳ] N mentore *m*

menu ['mɛnjuː] N (*set menu, Comput*) menù *m inv*; (*printed*) carta

menu-driven ['mɛnjuːdrɪvn] ADJ (*Comput*) guidato(-a) da menù

MEP N ABBR = **Member of the European Parliament**

mercantile ['məːkəntaɪl] ADJ mercantile; (*law*) commerciale

mercenary ['məːsɪnərɪ] ADJ venale ▶ N mercenario

merchandise ['məːtʃəndaɪz] N merci *fpl* ▶ VT commercializzare

merchandiser ['məːtʃəndaɪzəʳ] N merchandiser *m inv*

merchant ['məːtʃənt] N (*trader*) mercante *m*, commerciante *m*; (*shopkeeper*) negoziante *m*; **timber/wine ~** negoziante di legno/vino

merchant bank N (*BRIT*) banca d'affari

merchantman ['məːtʃəntmən] N (*irreg*) mercantile *m*

merchant navy, (*US*) **merchant marine** N marina mercantile

merciful ['məːsɪful] ADJ pietoso(-a), clemente

mercifully ['məːsɪflɪ] ADV con clemenza; (*fortunately*) per fortuna

merciless ['məːsɪlɪs] ADJ spietato(-a)

mercurial [məː'kjuərɪəl] ADJ (*unpredictable*) volubile

mercury ['məːkjurɪ] N mercurio

mercy ['məːsɪ] N pietà; (*Rel*) misericordia; **to have ~ on sb** aver pietà di qn; **at the ~ of** alla mercé di

mercy killing N eutanasia

mere [mɪəʳ] ADJ semplice; **by a ~ chance** per mero caso

merely ['mɪəlɪ] ADV semplicemente, non ... che

merge [məːdʒ] VT unire; (*Comput: files, text*) fondere ▶ VI fondersi, unirsi; (*Comm*) fondersi

merger ['məːdʒəʳ] N (*Comm*) fusione *f*

meridian [mə'rɪdɪən] N meridiano

meringue [mə'ræŋ] N meringa

merit ['mɛrɪt] N merito, valore *m* ▶ VT meritare

meritocracy [mɛrɪ'tɔkrəsɪ] N meritocrazia

mermaid ['məːmeɪd] N sirena

merriment ['mɛrɪmənt] N gaiezza, allegria

merry ['mɛrɪ] ADJ gaio(-a), allegro(-a); **M~ Christmas!** Buon Natale!

merry-go-round ['mɛrɪɡəuraund] N carosello

mesh [mɛʃ] N maglia; rete *f* ▶ VI (*gears*) ingranarsi; **wire ~** rete metallica

mesmerize ['mɛzməraɪz] VT ipnotizzare; affascinare

mess [mɛs] N confusione *f*, disordine *m*; (*fig*) pasticcio; (*dirt*) sporcizia; (*Mil*) mensa; **to be (in) a ~** (*house, room*) essere in disordine (*or* molto sporco); (*fig: marriage, life*) essere un caos; **to be/get o.s. in a ~** (*fig*) essere/cacciarsi in un pasticcio

  ▶ **mess about, mess around** VI (*col*) trastullarsi

  ▶ **mess about with, mess around with, mess with** VT FUS (*col*) gingillarsi con; (*: plans*) fare un pasticcio di; (*: challenge, confront*) litigare con (*col*); (*: drugs, drinks*) abusare di

  ▶ **mess up** VT sporcare; fare un pasticcio di; rovinare

message ['mɛsɪdʒ] N messaggio ▶ VT messaggiare; (*col*) messaggiare; **to get the ~** (*fig: col*) capire l'antifona; **she messaged me on Facebook®** mi ha messaggiato su Facebook®

message board N (*Comput*) bacheca elettronica

message switching N (*Comput*) smistamento messaggi

messenger ['mɛsɪndʒəʳ] N messaggero(-a)

Messiah [mɪ'saɪə] N Messia *m*

Messrs, Messrs. ['mɛsəz] ABBR (*on letters:* = *messieurs*) Spett.

messy ['mɛsɪ] ADJ sporco(-a); disordinato(-a); (*confused: situation etc*) ingarbugliato(-a)

Met [mɛt] N ABBR (*US*) = **Metropolitan Opera**

met [mɛt] PT, PP *of* **meet** ▶ ADJ ABBR = **meteorological**; **the M~ Office** l'Ufficio Meteorologico

metabolism [mɛ'tæbəlɪzəm] N metabolismo

metal ['mɛtl] N metallo ▶ VT massicciare

metallic [mɛ'tælɪk] ADJ metallico(-a)

metallurgy [mɛ'tælədʒɪ] N metallurgia

metalwork ['mɛtlwəːk] N (*craft*) lavorazione *f* del metallo

metamorphosis [mɛtə'mɔːfəsɪs] (*pl* **-phoses** [-iːz]) N metamorfosi *f inv*

metaphor ['mɛtəfəʳ] N metafora

metaphysics [mɛtə'fɪzɪks] N metafisica

mete [miːt]: **to ~ out** *vt fus* infliggere

meteor ['miːtɪəʳ] N meteora

meteoric [miːtɪ'ɔrɪk] ADJ (*fig*) fulmineo(-a)

meteorite ['miːtɪəraɪt] N meteorite *m*

meteorological [miːtɪərə'lɔdʒɪkl] ADJ meteorologico(-a)

meteorology [miːtɪə'rɔlədʒɪ] N meteorologia

meter ['miːtəʳ] N (*instrument*) contatore *m*; (*parking meter*) parchimetro; (*US: unit*) = **metre**

methane ['miːθeɪn] N metano

method ['mɛθəd] N metodo; **~ of payment** modo *or* modalità *f inv* di pagamento

methodical [mɪ'θɔdɪkl] ADJ metodico(-a)

Methodist ['mɛθədɪst] ADJ, N metodista (*mf*)

meths [mɛθs] (*BRIT*) N = **methylated spirit**

methylated spirits ['mɛθɪleɪtɪd-] N (*BRIT: also:* **meths**) alcool *m* denaturato

meticulous [mɛ'tɪkjuləs] ADJ meticoloso(-a)

metre, (*US***)meter** ['miːtəʳ] N metro

metric ['mɛtrɪk] ADJ metrico(-a); **to go ~** adottare il sistema metrico decimale

metrical ['mɛtrɪkl] ADJ metrico(-a)

metrication [mɛtrɪ'keɪʃən] N conversione *f* al sistema metrico

metric system N sistema *m* metrico decimale

metric ton N tonnellata

metro ['mɛtrəu] N metro *m inv*

metronome ['mɛtrənəum] N metronomo

metropolis [mɪ'trɔpəlɪs] N metropoli *f inv*

metropolitan [mɛtrə'pɔlɪtən] ADJ metropolitano(-a)

Metropolitan Police N (*BRIT*): **the ~** la polizia di Londra

mettle ['mɛtl] N coraggio

mew [mjuː] VI (*cat*) miagolare

mews [mjuːz] N (*BRIT*): **~ flat** appartamentino ricavato da una vecchia scuderia

Mexican ['mɛksɪkən] ADJ, N messicano(-a)

Mexico ['mɛksɪkəu] N Messico

Mexico City N Città del Messico

mezzanine ['mɛtsəniːn] N mezzanino

MFA N ABBR (*US*: = *Master of Fine Arts*) titolo di studio

mfr ABBR = **manufacture; manufacturer**

mg ABBR (= *milligram*) mg

Mgr ABBR (= *Monseigneur; Monsignor*) mons.; (*Comm*) = **manager**

MHR N ABBR (*US*) = **Member of the House of Representatives**

MHz ABBR (= *megahertz*) MHz

MI ABBR (*US*) = **Michigan**

MI5 N ABBR (*BRIT*: = *Military Intelligence, section five*) agenzia di controspionaggio

MI6 N ABBR (*BRIT*: = *Military Intelligence, section six*) agenzia di spionaggio

MIA ABBR = **missing in action**

miaow [miː'au] VI miagolare

mice [maɪs] NPL *of* **mouse**

Mich. ABBR (*US*) = **Michigan**

micro... ['maɪkrəu] PREFIX micro...

microbe ['maɪkrəub] N microbio

microbiology [maɪkrəubaɪ'ɔlədʒɪ] N microbiologia

microblog ['maɪkrəublɔg] N microblog *m inv*

microchip ['maɪkrəutʃɪp] N microcircuito integrato, chip *m inv*

microcomputer [maɪkrəukəm'pjuːtəʳ] N microcomputer *m inv*

microcosm ['maɪkrəukɔzəm] N microcosmo

microeconomics [maɪkrəuiːkə'nɔmɪks] N microeconomia

microfiche ['maɪkrəufiːʃ] N microfiche *f inv*

microfilm ['maɪkrəufɪlm] N microfilm *m inv* ▶ VT microfilmare

microlight ['maɪkrəulaɪt] N aereo *m* biposto *inv*

micrometer [maɪ'krɔmɪtəʳ] N micrometro, palmer *m inv*

microphone ['maɪkrəfəun] N microfono

microprocessor [maɪkrəu'prəusɛsəʳ] N microprocessore *m*

micro-scooter ['maɪkrəuskuːtəʳ] N monopattino

microscope ['maɪkrəskəup] N microscopio; **under the ~** al microscopio

microscopic [maɪkrə'skɔpɪk] ADJ microscopico(-a)

microwavable, microwaveable ['maɪkrəuweɪvəbl] ADJ adatto(-a) al forno a microonde

microwave ['maɪkrəuweɪv] N (*also:* **microwave oven**) forno a microonde

mid [mɪd] ADJ: ~ **May** metà maggio;
~ **afternoon** metà pomeriggio; **in ~ air** a
mezz'aria; **he's in his ~ thirties** avrà circa
trentacinque anni

midday [mɪd'deɪ] N mezzogiorno

middle ['mɪdl] N mezzo; centro; (waist) vita
▶ ADJ di mezzo; **I'm in the ~ of reading it** sto
proprio leggendolo ora; **in the ~ of the
night** nel cuore della notte

middle age N mezza età

middle-aged [mɪdl'eɪdʒd] ADJ di mezza età

Middle Ages NPL: **the ~** il Medioevo

middle class ADJ (also: **middle-class**)
≈ borghese ▶ N: **the ~(es)** ≈ la borghesia

Middle East N: **the ~** il Medio Oriente

middleman ['mɪdlmæn] N (irreg)
intermediario; agente m rivenditore

middle management N quadri mpl
intermedi

middle name N secondo nome m

middle-of-the-road ['mɪdləvðə'rəʊd] ADJ
moderato(-a)

middle school N (US) scuola media per ragazzi
dagli 11 ai 14 anni; (BRIT) scuola media per ragazzi
dagli 8 o 9 ai 12 o 13 anni

middleweight ['mɪdlweɪt] N (Boxing) peso
medio

middling ['mɪdlɪŋ] ADJ medio(-a)

midge [mɪdʒ] N moscerino

midget ['mɪdʒɪt] N nano(-a)

midi system ['mɪdɪ-] N (hi-fi) compatto

Midlands ['mɪdləndz] NPL contee del centro
dell'Inghilterra

midnight ['mɪdnaɪt] N mezzanotte f; **at ~** a
mezzanotte

midriff ['mɪdrɪf] N diaframma m

midst [mɪdst] N: **in the ~ of** in mezzo a

midsummer [mɪd'sʌmər] N mezza or piena
estate f

midway [mɪd'weɪ] ADJ, ADV: ~ **(between)** a
mezza strada (fra); ~ **(through)** a metà (di)

midweek [mɪd'wiːk] ADV, ADJ a metà
settimana

midwife ['mɪdwaɪf] (pl **midwives** [-vz]) N
levatrice f

midwifery ['mɪdwɪfərɪ] N ostetrica

midwinter [mɪd'wɪntər] N pieno inverno

miffed [mɪft] ADJ (col) seccato(-a), stizzito(-a)

might [maɪt] VB see **may** ▶ N potere m, forza

mighty ['maɪtɪ] ADJ forte, potente ▶ ADV (col)
molto

migraine ['miːgreɪn] N emicrania

migrant ['maɪgrənt] N (bird, animal)
migratore m; (person) migrante mf; nomade
mf ▶ ADJ (bird) migratore(-trice), nomade;
(worker) emigrato(-a)

migrate [maɪ'greɪt] VI (bird) migrare; (person)
emigrare

migration [maɪ'greɪʃən] N migrazione f

mike [maɪk] N ABBR (= microphone) microfono

Milan [mɪ'læn] N Milano f

mild [maɪld] ADJ mite; (person, voice) dolce;
(flavour) delicato(-a); (illness) leggero(-a);
(interest) blando(-a) ▶ N (beer) birra leggera

mildew ['mɪldjuː] N muffa

mildly ['maɪldlɪ] ADV mitemente;
dolcemente; delicatamente; leggermente;
blandamente; **to put it ~** a dire poco

mildness ['maɪldnɪs] N mitezza; dolcezza;
delicatezza; non gravità

mile [maɪl] N miglio; **to do 20 miles per
gallon** ≈ usare 14 litri per cento chilometri

mileage ['maɪlɪdʒ] N distanza in miglia,
≈ chilometraggio

mileage allowance N rimborso per miglio

mileometer [maɪ'lɒmɪtər] N (BRIT)
= **milometer**

milestone ['maɪlstəʊn] N pietra miliare

milieu ['miːljɜː] N ambiente m

militant ['mɪlɪtnt] ADJ, N militante (mf)

militarism ['mɪlɪtərɪzəm] N militarismo

militaristic [mɪlɪtə'rɪstɪk] ADJ
militaristico(-a)

military ['mɪlɪtərɪ] ADJ militare ▶ N: **the ~**
i militari, l'esercito

military service N servizio militare

militate ['mɪlɪteɪt] VI: **to ~ against** essere
d'ostacolo a

militia [mɪ'lɪʃə] N milizia

milk [mɪlk] N latte m ▶ VT (cow) mungere;
(fig) sfruttare

milk chocolate N cioccolato al latte

milk float N (BRIT) furgone m del lattaio

milking ['mɪlkɪŋ] N mungitura

milkman ['mɪlkmən] N (irreg) lattaio

milk shake N frappé m inv

milk tooth N dente m di latte

milk truck N (US) = **milk float**

milky ['mɪlkɪ] ADJ lattiginoso(-a); (colour)
latteo(-a)

Milky Way N Via Lattea

mill [mɪl] N mulino; (small: for coffee, pepper etc)
macinino; (factory) fabbrica; (spinning mill)
filatura ▶ VT macinare ▶ VI (also: **mill about**)
brulicare

millennium [mɪ'lɛnɪəm] (pl **millenniums** or
millennia [-'lɛnɪə]) N millennio

millennium bug N baco di fine millennio

miller ['mɪlər] N mugnaio

millet ['mɪlɪt] N miglio

milli… ['mɪlɪ] PREFIX milli…

milligram, milligramme ['mɪlɪgræm] N
milligrammo

millilitre, (US) **milliliter** ['mɪlɪliːtər] N
millilitro

millimetre, (US) **millimeter** ['mɪlɪmiːtər] N
millimetro

milliner ['mɪlɪnər] N modista

millinery ['mɪlɪnərɪ] N modisteria
million ['mɪljən] NUM milione m
millionaire [mɪljə'nɛəʳ] N milionario,
≈ miliardario
millionth NUM milionesimo(-a)
millipede ['mɪlɪpiːd] N millepiedi m inv
millstone ['mɪlstəʊn] N macina
millwheel ['mɪlwiːl] N ruota di mulino
milometer [maɪ'lɔmɪtəʳ] N
≈ contachilometri m inv
mime [maɪm] N mimo ▶ VT, VI mimare
mimic ['mɪmɪk] N imitatore(-trice)
▶ VT (comedian) imitare; (animal, person)
scimmiottare
mimicry ['mɪmɪkrɪ] N imitazioni fpl; (Zool)
mimetismo
Min. ABBR (BRIT Pol: = ministry) Min.
min. ABBR = **minute**; (= minimum) min.
minaret [mɪnə'rɛt] N minareto
mince [mɪns] VT tritare, macinare ▶ VI (in
walking) camminare a passettini ▶ N (BRIT
Culin) carne f tritata or macinata; **he does
not ~ (his) words** parla chiaro e tondo
mincemeat ['mɪnsmiːt] N frutta secca tritata
per uso in pasticceria; (US) carne f tritata or
macinata
mince pie N specie di torta con frutta secca
mincer ['mɪnsəʳ] N tritacarne m inv
mincing ['mɪnsɪŋ] ADJ lezioso(-a)
mind [maɪnd] N mente f ▶ VT (attend to, look
after) badare a, occuparsi di; (be careful) fare
attenzione a, stare attento(-a) a; (object to):
I don't ~ the noise il rumore non mi dà
alcun fastidio; **do you ~ if ...?** le dispiace se
...?; **I don't ~** non m'importa; **~ you, ...** sì,
però va detto che ...; **never ~** non importa,
non fa niente; (don't worry) non preoccuparti;
it is on my ~ mi preoccupa; **to change one's
~** cambiare idea; **to be in two minds about
sth** essere incerto su qc; **to my ~** secondo
me, a mio parere; **to be out of one's ~** essere
uscito(-a) di mente; **to keep sth in ~** non
dimenticare qc; **to bear sth in ~** tener
presente qc; **to have sb/sth in ~** avere in
mente qn/qc; **to have in ~ to do** aver
l'intenzione di fare; **it went right out of
my ~** mi è completamente passato di mente,
me ne sono completamente dimenticato;
to bring or **call sth to ~** riportare or
richiamare qc alla mente; **to make up
one's ~** decidersi; **"~ the step"** "attenzione
allo scalino"
mind-boggling ['maɪndbɔglɪŋ] ADJ (col)
sconcertante
-minded ['maɪndɪd] ADJ: **fair~** imparziale;
an industrially~ nation una nazione
orientata verso l'industria
minder ['maɪndəʳ] N (child minder) bambinaia;
(bodyguard) guardia del corpo

mindful ['maɪndful] ADJ: **~ of** attento(-a) a;
memore di
mindless ['maɪndlɪs] ADJ idiota; (violence,
crime) insensato(-a)
mine¹ [maɪn] PRON il (la) mio(-a); (pl) i (le)
miei (mie); **this book is ~** questo libro è mio;
yours is red, ~ is green il tuo è rosso, il mio
è verde; **a friend of ~** un mio amico
mine² [maɪn] N miniera; (explosive) mina
▶ VT (coal) estrarre; (ship, beach) minare
mine detector N rivelatore m di mine
minefield ['maɪnfiːld] N campo minato
miner ['maɪnəʳ] N minatore m
mineral ['mɪnərəl] ADJ minerale ▶ N
minerale m; **minerals** NPL (BRIT: soft drinks)
bevande fpl gasate
mineralogy [mɪnə'rælədʒɪ] N mineralogia
mineral water N acqua minerale
minesweeper ['maɪnswiːpəʳ] N dragamine
m inv
mingle ['mɪŋgl] VT mescolare, mischiare
▶ VI: **to ~ with** mescolarsi a, mischiarsi con
mingy ['mɪndʒɪ] ADJ (col: amount) misero(-a);
(: person) spilorcio(-a)
miniature ['mɪnətʃəʳ] ADJ in miniatura
▶ N miniatura
minibar ['mɪnɪbɑːʳ] N minibar m inv
minibus ['mɪnɪbʌs] N minibus m inv
minicab ['mɪnɪkæb] N (BRIT) ≈ taxi m inv
minicomputer ['mɪnɪkəm'pjuːtəʳ] N
minicomputer m inv
Minidisc ® ['mɪnɪdɪsk] N minidisc m inv
minim ['mɪnɪm] N (Mus) minima
minima ['mɪnɪmə] NPL of **minimum**
minimal ['mɪnɪml] ADJ minimo(-a)
minimalist ['mɪnɪməlɪst] ADJ, N minimalista
(mf)
minimize ['mɪnɪmaɪz] VT minimizzare
minimum ['mɪnɪməm] (pl **minima**) N
minimo ▶ ADJ minimo(-a); **to reduce to a ~**
ridurre al minimo; **~ wage** salario minimo
garantito
minimum lending rate N (BRIT) ≈ tasso
ufficiale di sconto
mining ['maɪnɪŋ] N industria mineraria
▶ ADJ minerario(-a); di minatori
minion ['mɪnjən] N (pej) caudatario;
favorito(-a)
mini-series ['mɪnɪsɪəriːz] N miniserie f inv
miniskirt ['mɪnɪskəːt] N minigonna
minister ['mɪnɪstəʳ] N (BRIT Pol) ministro;
(Rel) pastore m ▶ VI: **to ~ to sb** assistere qn;
to ~ to sb's needs provvedere ai bisogni
di qn
ministerial [mɪnɪs'tɪərɪəl] ADJ (BRIT Pol)
ministeriale
ministry ['mɪnɪstrɪ] N (BRIT Pol) ministero;
(Rel): **to go into the ~** diventare pastore
mink [mɪŋk] N visone m

mink coat N pelliccia di visone
Minn. ABBR (US) = **Minnesota**
minnow ['mɪnəu] N pesciolino d'acqua dolce
minor ['maɪnə'] ADJ minore, di poca
importanza; (Mus) minore ▶ N (Law)
minorenne mf
Minorca [mɪ'nɔ:kə] N Minorca
minority [maɪ'nɔrɪtɪ] N minoranza; **to be
in a ~** essere in minoranza
minster ['mɪnstə'] N cattedrale f (annessa a
monastero)
minstrel ['mɪnstrəl] N giullare m, menestrello
mint [mɪnt] N (plant) menta; (sweet) pasticca
di menta ▶ VT (coins) battere; **the (Royal) M~**
(BRIT), **the (US) M~** (US) la Zecca; **in ~
condition** come nuovo(-a) di zecca
mint sauce N salsa di menta
minuet [mɪnju'ɛt] N minuetto
minus ['maɪnəs] N (also: **minus sign**) segno
meno ▶ PREP meno
minuscule ['mɪnəskju:l] ADJ minuscolo(-a)
minute¹ ['mɪnɪt] N minuto; (official record)
processo verbale, resoconto sommario;
minutesNPL (of meeting) verbale m, verbali
mpl; **it is 5 minutes past 3** sono le 3 e 5
(minuti); **wait a ~!** (aspetta) un momento!;
at the last ~ all'ultimo momento; **up to
the ~** ultimissimo; modernissimo
minute² [maɪ'nju:t] ADJ minuscolo(-a);
(detail) minuzioso(-a); **in ~ detail**
minuziosamente
minute book N libro dei verbali
minute hand N lancetta dei minuti
minutely [maɪ'nju:tlɪ] ADV (by a small amount)
di poco; (in detail) minuziosamente
minutiae [mɪ'nju:ʃiɪ:] NPL minuzie fpl
miracle ['mɪrəkl] N miracolo
miraculous [mɪ'rækjuləs] ADJ miracoloso(-a)
mirage ['mɪrɑ:ʒ] N miraggio
mire ['maɪə'] N pantano, melma
mirror ['mɪrə'] N specchio; (in car) specchietto
▶ VT rispecchiare, riflettere
mirror image N immagine f speculare
mirth [mə:θ] N gaiezza
misadventure [mɪsəd'vɛntʃə'] N
disavventura; **death by ~** (BRIT) morte f
accidentale
misanthropist [mɪ'zænθrəpɪst] N
misantropo(-a)
misapply [mɪsə'plaɪ] VT impiegare male
misapprehension ['mɪsæprɪ'hɛnʃən] N
malinteso
misappropriate [mɪsə'prəuprɪeɪt] VT
appropriarsi indebitamente di
misappropriation ['mɪsəprəuprɪ'eɪʃən] N
appropriazione f indebita
misbehave [mɪsbɪ'heɪv] VI comportarsi male
misbehaviour,(US) **misbehavior**
[mɪsbɪ'heɪvjə'] N comportamento scorretto

misc. ABBR = **miscellaneous**
miscalculate [mɪs'kælkjuleɪt] VT calcolare
male
miscalculation ['mɪskælkju'leɪʃən] N errore
m di calcolo
miscarriage ['mɪskærɪdʒ] N (Med) aborto
spontaneo; **~ of justice** errore m giudiziario
miscarry [mɪs'kærɪ] VI (Med) abortire; (fail:
plans) andare a monte, fallire
miscellaneous [mɪsɪ'leɪnɪəs] ADJ (items)
vario(-a); (selection) misto(-a); **~ expenses**
spese varie
miscellany [mɪ'sɛlənɪ] N raccolta
mischance [mɪs'tʃɑ:ns] N: **by (some) ~** per
sfortuna
mischief ['mɪstʃɪf] N (naughtiness)
birichineria; (harm) male m, danno;
(maliciousness) malizia
mischievous ['mɪstʃɪvəs] ADJ (naughty)
birichino(-a); (harmful) dannoso(-a)
misconception [mɪskən'sɛpʃən] N idea
sbagliata
misconduct [mɪs'kɔndʌkt] N cattiva
condotta; **professional ~** reato
professionale
misconstrue [mɪskən'stru:] VT
interpretare male
miscount [mɪs'kaunt] VT, VI contare male
misdeed [mɪs'di:d] N (old) misfatto
misdemeanour,(US) **misdemeanor**
[mɪsdɪ'mi:nə'] N misfatto; infrazione f
misdirect [mɪsdɪ'rɛkt] VT mal indirizzare
miser ['maɪzə'] N avaro
miserable ['mɪzərəbl] ADJ infelice; (wretched)
miserabile; (weather) deprimente; (offer,
failure) misero(-a); **to feel ~** sentirsi avvilito
or giù di morale
miserably ['mɪzərəblɪ] ADV (fail, live, pay)
miseramente; (smile, answer) tristemente
miserly ['maɪzəlɪ] ADJ avaro(-a)
misery ['mɪzərɪ] N (unhappiness) tristezza;
(pain) sofferenza; (wretchedness) miseria
misfire [mɪs'faɪə'] VI far cilecca; (car engine)
perdere colpi
misfit ['mɪsfɪt] N (person) spostato(-a)
misfortune [mɪs'fɔ:tʃən] N sfortuna
misgiving [mɪs'gɪvɪŋ] N, **misgivings**
[mɪs'gɪvɪŋz] NPL dubbi mpl; **to have
misgivings about sth** essere diffidente or
avere dei dubbi per quanto riguarda qc
misguided [mɪs'gaɪdɪd] ADJ sbagliato(-a);
poco giudizioso(-a)
mishandle [mɪs'hændl] VT (treat roughly)
maltrattare; (mismanage) trattare male
mishap ['mɪshæp] N disgrazia
mishear [mɪs'hɪə'] VT, VI (irreg: like **hear**)
capire male
mishmash ['mɪʃmæʃ] N (col) minestrone m,
guazzabuglio

m

misinform [mɪsɪn'fɔ:m] vt informare male

misinterpret [mɪsɪn'tə:prɪt] vt interpretare male

misinterpretation ['mɪsɪntə:prɪ'teɪʃən] N errata interpretazione f

misjudge [mɪs'dʒʌdʒ] vt giudicare male

mislay [mɪs'leɪ] vt (irreg: like **lay**) smarrire

mislead [mɪs'li:d] vt (irreg: like **lead¹**) sviare

misleading [mɪs'li:dɪŋ] ADJ ingannevole

misled [mɪs'lɛd] PT, PP of **mislead**

mismanage [mɪs'mænɪdʒ] vt gestire male; trattare male

mismanagement [mɪs'mænɪdʒmənt] N cattiva amministrazione f

misnomer [mɪs'nəumə'] N termine m sbagliato or improprio

misogynist [mɪ'sɔdʒɪnɪst] N misogino

misplace [mɪs'pleɪs] vt smarrire; collocare fuori posto; **to be misplaced** (trust etc) essere malriposto(-a)

misprint ['mɪsprɪnt] N errore m di stampa

mispronounce [mɪsprə'naʊns] vt pronunziare male

misquote [mɪs'kwəʊt] vt citare erroneamente

misread [mɪs'ri:d] vt (irreg: like **read**) leggere male

misrepresent [mɪsrɛprɪ'zɛnt] vt travisare

Miss [mɪs] N Signorina; **Dear ~ Smith** Cara Signorina; (formal) Gentile Signorina

miss [mɪs] vt (fail to get) perdere; (fail to hit) mancare; (appointment, class) mancare a; (escape, notice) evitare; (notice loss of: money etc) accorgersi di non avere più; (fail to see): **you can't ~ it** non puoi non vederlo; (regret the absence of): **I ~ him/it** sento la sua mancanza, lui/esso mi manca ▶ vi mancare ▶ N (shot) colpo mancato; (fig): **that was a near ~** c'è mancato poco; **the bus just missed the wall** l'autobus per un pelo non è andato a finire contro il muro; **we missed our train** abbiamo perso il treno; **you're missing the point** non capisce
  ▶ **miss out** vt (Brit) omettere
  ▶ **miss out on** vt fus (fun, party) perdersi; (chance, bargain) lasciarsi sfuggire

Miss. ABBR (US) = **Mississippi**

missal ['mɪsl] N messale m

misshapen [mɪs'ʃeɪpən] ADJ deforme

missile ['mɪsaɪl] N (Aviat) missile m; (object thrown) proiettile m

missile base N base f missilistica

missile launcher N lancia-missili m inv

missing ['mɪsɪŋ] ADJ perso(-a), smarrito(-a); (removed) mancante; **to go ~** sparire; **~ person** scomparso(-a); (after disaster) disperso(-a); **~ in action** (Mil) disperso(-a); **to be ~** mancare

mission ['mɪʃən] N missione f; **on a ~ to sb** in missione da qn

missionary ['mɪʃənrɪ] N missionario(-a)

misspell [mɪs'spɛl] vt (irreg: like **spell**) sbagliare l'ortografia di

misspent [mɪs'spɛnt] ADJ: **his ~ youth** la sua gioventù sciupata

mist [mɪst] N nebbia, foschia ▶ vi (also: **mist over, mist up**) annebbiarsi; (: Brit: windows) appannarsi

mistake [mɪs'teɪk] N sbaglio, errore m ▶ vt (irreg: like **take**) sbagliarsi di; fraintendere; **to ~ for** prendere per; **by ~** per sbaglio; **to make a ~** (in writing, calculating etc) fare uno sbaglio or un errore, sbagliare; **to make a ~ about sb/sth** sbagliarsi sul conto di qn/su qc; **there must be some ~** ci dev'essere un errore

mistaken [mɪs'teɪkən] PP of **mistake** ▶ ADJ (idea etc) sbagliato(-a); **to be ~** sbagliarsi

mistaken identity N errore m di persona

mistakenly [mɪs'teɪkənlɪ] ADV per errore

mister ['mɪstə'] N (col) signore m; see **Mr**

mistletoe ['mɪsltəʊ] N vischio

mistook [mɪs'tʊk] PT of **mistake**

mistranslation [mɪstræns'leɪʃən] N traduzione f errata

mistreat [mɪs'tri:t] vt maltrattare

mistress ['mɪstrɪs] N padrona; (lover) amante f; (Brit Scol) insegnante f

mistrust [mɪs'trʌst] vt diffidare di ▶ N: **~ (of)** diffidenza (nei confronti di)

mistrustful [mɪs'trʌstful] ADJ: **~ (of)** diffidente (nei confronti di)

misty ['mɪstɪ] ADJ nebbioso(-a), brumoso(-a)

misty-eyed ['mɪstɪ'aɪd] ADJ trasognato(-a)

misunderstand [mɪsʌndə'stænd] vt, vi (irreg: like **stand**) capire male, fraintendere

misunderstanding [mɪsʌndə'stændɪŋ] N malinteso, equivoco; **there's been a ~** c'è stato un malinteso

misunderstood [mɪsʌndə'stʊd] PT, PP of **misunderstand**

misuse N [mɪs'ju:s] cattivo uso; (of power) abuso ▶ vt [mɪs'ju:z] far cattivo uso di; abusare di

MIT N ABBR (US) = **Massachusetts Institute of Technology**

mite [maɪt] N (small quantity) briciolo; (Brit: small child): **poor ~!** povera creaturina!

miter ['maɪtə'] N (US) = **mitre**

mitigate ['mɪtɪgeɪt] vt mitigare; (suffering) alleviare; **mitigating circumstances** circostanze fpl attenuanti

mitigation [mɪtɪ'geɪʃən] N mitigazione f; alleviamento

mitre, (US) miter ['maɪtə'] N mitra; (Carpentry) giunto ad angolo retto

mitt ['mɪt], **mitten** ['mɪtn] N mezzo guanto; manopola

mix [mɪks] VT mescolare ▶ VI mescolarsi;
(*people*): **to ~ with** avere a che fare con ▶ N
mescolanza; preparato; **to ~ sth with sth**
mischiare qc a qc; **to ~ business with
pleasure** unire l'utile al dilettevole; **cake ~**
preparato per torta
▶ **mix in** VT (*eggs etc*) incorporare
▶ **mix up** VT mescolare; (*confuse*) confondere;
to be mixed up in sth essere coinvolto in qc
mixed [mɪkst] ADJ misto(-a)
mixed-ability ['mɪkstə'bɪlɪtɪ] ADJ (*class etc*)
con alunni di capacità diverse
mixed bag N miscuglio, accozzaglia; **it's a ~**
c'è un po' di tutto
mixed blessing N: **it's a ~** ha i suoi lati
positivi e negativi
mixed doubles NPL (*Sport*) doppio misto
mixed economy N economia mista
mixed grill N (*BRIT*) misto alla griglia
mixed marriage N matrimonio misto
mixed salad N insalata mista
mixed-up [mɪkst'ʌp] ADJ (*confused*)
confuso(-a)
mixer ['mɪksə^r] N (*for food: electric*) frullatore *m*;
(: *hand*) frullino; **he is a good ~** è molto
socievole
mixer tap N miscelatore *m*
mixture ['mɪkstʃə^r] N mescolanza; (*blend: of
tobacco etc*) miscela; (*Med*) sciroppo
mix-up ['mɪksʌp] N confusione *f*
MK ABBR (*BRIT Tech*) = **mark**
mk ABBR (*Hist: currency*) = **mark**
mkt ABBR = **market**
ml ABBR (= *millilitre(s)*) ml
MLitt N ABBR = **Master of Literature**;
(= *Master of Letters*) titolo di studio
MLR N ABBR (*BRIT*) = **minimum lending rate**
mm ABBR (= *millimetre*) mm
MMS N ABBR (= *multimedia messaging service*)
mms *m inv* (*servizio*); ~ **message** mms *m inv*
MN ABBR (*BRIT*) = **merchant navy**; (*US*)
= **Minnesota**
MO N ABBR = **medical officer**; (*US: col*: = *modus
operandi*) modo d'agire ▶ ABBR (*US*) = **Missouri**
m.o. ABBR = **money order**
moan [məun] N gemito ▶ VI gemere; (*col:
complain*): **to ~ (about)** lamentarsi (di)
moaner ['məunə^r] N (*col*) uno(-a) che si
lamenta sempre
moaning ['məunɪŋ] N gemiti *mpl*
moat [məut] N fossato
mob [mɔb] N folla; (*disorderly*) calca; (*pej*): **the
~** la plebaglia ▶ VT accalcarsi intorno a
mobile ['məubaɪl] ADJ mobile ▶ N (*phone*)
telefonino, cellulare *m*; (*Art*) mobile *m inv*;
applicants must be ~ (*BRIT*) i candidati
devono essere disposti a viaggiare
mobile home N grande roulotte *f inv*
(*utilizzata come domicilio*)

mobile phone N telefono portatile,
telefonino
mobile shop N (*BRIT*) negozio ambulante
mobility [məu'bɪlɪtɪ] N mobilità; (*of applicant*)
disponibilità a viaggiare
mobilize ['məubɪlaɪz] VT mobilitare ▶ VI
mobilitarsi
moccasin ['mɔkəsɪn] N mocassino
mock [mɔk] VT deridere, burlarsi di ▶ ADJ
falso(-a); **mocks** NPL (*BRIT col: Scol*)
simulazione *f* degli esami
mockery ['mɔkərɪ] N derisione *f*; **to make
a ~ of** burlarsi di; (*exam*) rendere una farsa
mocking ['mɔkɪŋ] ADJ derisorio(-a)
mockingbird ['mɔkɪŋbə:d] N mimo
(*uccello*)
mock-up ['mɔkʌp] N modello dimostrativo;
abbozzo
MOD N ABBR (*BRIT*) = **Ministry of Defence**; *see*
defence
mod cons ['mɔd'kɔnz] NPL ABBR (*BRIT*)
= **modern conveniences**
mode [məud] N modo; (*of transport*) mezzo;
(*Comput*) modalità *f inv*
model ['mɔdl] N modello; (*person: for fashion*)
indossatore(-trice); (: *for artist*) modello(-a)
▶ VT modellare ▶ VI fare l'indossatore (*or
l'indossatrice*) ▶ ADJ (*small-scale: railway etc*) in
miniatura; (*child, factory*) modello *inv*; **to ~
clothes** presentare degli abiti; **to ~ sb/sth
on** modellare qn/qc su
modem ['məudɛm] N modem *m inv*
moderate ADJ ['mɔdərɪt] moderato(-a)
▶ N (*Pol*) moderato(-a) ▶ VI ['mɔdəreɪt]
moderarsi, placarsi ▶ VT moderare
moderately ['mɔdərɪtlɪ] ADV (*act*) con
moderazione; (*expensive, difficult*) non troppo;
(*pleased, happy*) abbastanza, discretamente;
~ priced a prezzo modico
moderation [mɔdə'reɪʃən] N moderazione *f*,
misura; **in ~** in quantità moderata, con
moderazione
moderator ['mɔdəreɪtə^r] N
moderatore(-trice); (*Rel*) moderatore in
importanti riunioni ecclesiastiche
modern ['mɔdən] ADJ moderno(-a);
~ conveniences comodità *fpl* moderne;
~ languages lingue *fpl* moderne
modernization [mɔdənaɪ'zeɪʃən] N
rimodernamento, modernizzazione *f*
modernize ['mɔdənaɪz] VT modernizzare
modest ['mɔdɪst] ADJ modesto(-a)
modesty ['mɔdɪstɪ] N modestia
modicum ['mɔdɪkəm] N: **a ~ of** un minimo di
modification [mɔdɪfɪ'keɪʃən] N
modificazione *f*; **to make modifications**
fare *or* apportare delle modifiche
modify ['mɔdɪfaɪ] VT modificare
modish ['məudɪʃ] ADJ (*literary*) à la page *inv*

Mods [mɔdz] N ABBR (BRIT: = (Honour) Moderations) esame all'università di Oxford
modular ['mɔdjuləʳ] ADJ (filing, unit) modulare
modulate ['mɔdjuleɪt] VT modulare
modulation [mɔdju'leɪʃən] N modulazione f
module ['mɔdjuːl] N modulo
Mogadishu [mɔgə'dɪʃuː] N Mogadiscio f
mogul ['məugl] N (fig) magnate m, pezzo grosso; (Ski) cunetta
MOH N ABBR (BRIT: = Medical Officer of Health) = ufficiale m sanitario
mohair ['məuhɛəʳ] N mohair m
Mohammed [məu'hæmɪd] N Maometto
moist [mɔɪst] ADJ umido(-a)
moisten ['mɔɪsn] VT inumidire
moisture ['mɔɪstʃəʳ] N umidità; (on glass) goccioline fpl di vapore
moisturize ['mɔɪstʃəraɪz] VT (skin) idratare
moisturizer ['mɔɪstʃəraɪzəʳ] N idratante f
molar ['məuləʳ] N molare m
molasses [məu'læsɪz] N molassa
mold etc [məuld] (US) = **mould** etc
Moldavia [mɔl'deɪvɪə], **Moldova** [mɔl'dəuvə] N Moldavia
Moldavian [mɔl'deɪvɪən], **Moldovan** [mɔl'dəuvən] ADJ moldavo(-a)
mole [məul] N (animal, fig) talpa; (spot) neo
molecule ['mɔlɪkjuːl] N molecola
molehill ['məulhɪl] N cumulo di terra sulla tana di una talpa •
molest [məu'lɛst] VT molestare
mollusc, (US) **mollusk** ['mɔləsk] N mollusco
mollycoddle ['mɔlɪkɔdl] VT coccolare, vezzeggiare
Molotov cocktail ['mɔlətɔf-] N (bottiglia) Molotov f inv
molt [məult] VI (US) = **moult**
molten ['məultən] ADJ fuso(-a)
mom [mɔm] N (US) = **mum**
moment ['məumənt] N momento, istante m; importanza; **at that ~** in quel momento; **at the ~** al momento, in questo momento; **for the ~** per il momento, per ora; **in a ~** tra un momento; **"one ~ please"** (Tel) "attenda, prego"
momentarily ['məuməntərɪlɪ] ADV per un momento; (US: very soon) da un momento all'altro
momentary ['məuməntərɪ] ADJ momentaneo(-a), passeggero(-a)
momentous [məu'mɛntəs] ADJ di grande importanza
momentum [məu'mɛntəm] N velocità acquisita, slancio; (Physics) momento; (fig) impeto; **to gather ~** aumentare di velocità; (fig) prendere or guadagnare terreno
mommy ['mɔmɪ] N (US) mamma
Mon. ABBR (= Monday) lun.
Monaco ['mɔnəkəu] N Monaco f

monarch ['mɔnək] N monarca m
monarchist ['mɔnəkɪst] N monarchico(-a)
monarchy ['mɔnəkɪ] N monarchia
monastery ['mɔnəstərɪ] N monastero
monastic [mə'næstɪk] ADJ monastico(-a)
Monday ['mʌndɪ] N lunedì m inv; see also **Tuesday**
Monegasque [mɔnə'gæsk] ADJ, N monegasco(-a)
monetarist ['mʌnɪtərɪst] N monetarista mf
monetary ['mʌnɪtərɪ] ADJ monetario(-a)
money ['mʌnɪ] N denaro, soldi mpl; **to make ~** (person) fare (i) soldi; (business) rendere; **danger ~** (BRIT) indennità di rischio; **I've got no ~ left** non ho più neanche una lira
money belt N marsupio (per soldi)
moneyed ['mʌnɪd] ADJ ricco(-a)
moneylender ['mʌnɪlɛndəʳ] N prestatore m di denaro
moneymaker ['mʌnɪmeɪkəʳ] N (BRIT col: business) affare m d'oro
moneymaking ['mʌnɪmeɪkɪŋ] ADJ che rende (bene or molto), lucrativo(-a)
money market N mercato monetario
money order N vaglia m inv
money-spinner ['mʌnɪspɪnəʳ] N (col) miniera d'oro (fig)
money supply N liquidità monetaria
Mongol ['mɔŋgəl] N mongolo(-a); (Ling) mongolo
mongol ['mɔŋgəl] ADJ, N (Med) mongoloide (mf)
Mongolia [mɔŋ'gəulɪə] N Mongolia
Mongolian [mɔŋ'gəulɪən] ADJ mongolico(-a) ▶ N mongolo(-a); (Ling) mongolo
mongoose ['mɔŋguːs] N mangusta
mongrel ['mʌŋgrəl] N (dog) cane m bastardo
monitor ['mɔnɪtəʳ] N (BRIT Scol) capoclasse mf; (US Scol) chi sorveglia agli esami; (TV, Comput) monitor m inv ▶ VT controllare; (foreign station) ascoltare le trasmissioni di
monk [mʌŋk] N monaco
monkey ['mʌŋkɪ] N scimmia
monkey business N (col) scherzi mpl
monkey nut N (BRIT) nocciolina americana
monkey wrench N chiave f a rullino
mono ['mɔnəu] ADJ mono inv; (broadcast) in mono
mono... ['mɔnəu] PREFIX mono...
monochrome ['mɔnəkrəum] ADJ monocromo(-a)
monocle ['mɔnəkl] N monocolo
monogamous [mə'nɔgəməs] ADJ monogamo(-a)
monogamy [mə'nɔgəmɪ] N monogamia
monogram ['mɔnəgræm] N monogramma m
monolith ['mɔnəlɪθ] N monolito
monologue ['mɔnəlɔg] N monologo

monoplane ['mɔnəupleɪn] N monoplano
monopolize [mə'nɔpəlaɪz] VT monopolizzare
monopoly [mə'nɔpəlɪ] N monopolio; **Monopolies and Mergers Commission** (BRIT) commissione f antimonopoli
monorail ['mɔnəureɪl] N monorotaia
monosodium glutamate [mɔnə'səudɪəm'glu:təmeɪt] N glutammato di sodio
monosyllabic [mɔnəsɪ'læbɪk] ADJ monosillabico(-a); (person) che parla a monosillabi
monosyllable ['mɔnəsɪləbl] N monosillabo
monotone ['mɔnətəun] N pronunzia (or voce f) monotona; **to speak in a** ~ parlare con voce monotona
monotonous [mə'nɔtənəs] ADJ monotono(-a)
monotony [mə'nɔtənɪ] N monotonia
monoxide [mɔ'nɔksaɪd] N: **carbon** ~ ossido di carbonio
monsoon [mɔn'su:n] N monsone m
monster ['mɔnstə'] N mostro
monstrosity [mɔn'strɔsɪtɪ] N mostruosità f inv
monstrous ['mɔnstrəs] ADJ mostruoso(-a)
Mont. ABBR (US) = **Montana**
montage [mɔn'tɑ:ʒ] N montaggio
Mont Blanc [mɔ̃blɑ̃] N Monte m Bianco
month [mʌnθ] N mese m; **300 dollars a** ~ 300 dollari al mese; **every** ~ (happen) tutti i mesi; (pay) mensilmente, ogni mese
monthly ['mʌnθlɪ] ADJ mensile ▶ ADV al mese; ogni mese ▶ N (magazine) rivista mensile; **twice** ~ due volte al mese
monument ['mɔnjumənt] N monumento
monumental [mɔnju'mɛntl] ADJ monumentale; (fig) colossale
monumental mason N lapidario
moo [mu:] VI muggire, mugghiare
mood ~ [mu:d] N umore m; **to be in a good/bad** ~ essere di buon/cattivo umore; **to be in the** ~ **for** essere disposto(-a) a, aver voglia di
moody ['mu:dɪ] ADJ (variable) capriccioso(-a), lunatico(-a); (sullen) imbronciato(-a)
moon [mu:n] N luna
moonbeam ['mu:nbi:m] N raggio di luna
moon landing N allunaggio
moonlight ['mu:nlaɪt] N chiaro di luna ▶ VI fare del lavoro nero
moonlighting ['mu:nlaɪtɪŋ] N lavoro nero
moonlit ['mu:nlɪt] ADJ illuminato(-a) dalla luna; **a** ~ **night** una notte rischiarata dalla luna
moonshot ['mu:nʃɔt] N lancio sulla luna
moonstruck ['mu:nstrʌk] ADJ lunatico(-a)
moony ['mu:nɪ] ADJ (eyes) sognante
Moor [muə'] N moro(-a)

moor [muə'] N brughiera ▶ VT (ship) ormeggiare ▶ VI ormeggiarsi
moorings ['muərɪŋz] NPL (chains) ormeggi mpl; (place) ormeggio
Moorish ['muərɪʃ] ADJ moresco(-a)
moorland ['muələnd] N brughiera
moose [mu:s] N (pl inv) alce m
moot [mu:t] VT sollevare ▶ ADJ: ~ **point** punto discutibile
mop [mɔp] N lavapavimenti m inv; (also: **mop of hair**) zazzera ▶ VT lavare con lo straccio; (face) asciugare; **to** ~ **one's brow** asciugarsi la fronte
▶ **mop up** VT asciugare con uno straccio
mope [məup] VI fare il broncio
▶ **mope about, mope around** VI trascinarsi or aggirarsi con aria avvilita
moped ['məuped] N (BRIT) ciclomotore m
MOR ADJ ABBR (Mus) = **middle-of-the-road**; ~ **music** musica leggera
moral ['mɔrəl] ADJ morale ▶ N morale f; **morals** NPL (principles) moralità
morale [mɔ'rɑ:l] N morale m
morality [mə'rælɪtɪ] N moralità
moralize ['mɔrəlaɪz] VI: **to** ~ **(about)** fare il (or la) moralista (riguardo), moraleggiare (riguardo)
morally ['mɔrəlɪ] ADV moralmente
moral victory N vittoria morale
morass [mə'ræs] N palude f, pantano
moratorium [mɔrə'tɔ:rɪəm] N moratoria
morbid ['mɔ:bɪd] ADJ morboso(-a)

(KEYWORD)

more [mɔ:'] ADJ **1** (greater in number etc) più; **more people/letters than we expected** più persone/lettere di quante ne aspettavamo; **I have more wine/money than you** ho più vino/soldi di te; **I have more wine than beer** ho più vino che birra
2 (additional) altro(-a), ancora; **do you want (some) more tea?** vuole dell'altro tè?, vuole ancora del tè?; **I have no** or **I don't have any more money** non ho più soldi
▶ PRON **1** (greater amount) più; **more than 10** più di 10; **it cost more than we expected** è costato più di quanto ci aspettassimo; **and what's more ...** e per di più ...
2 (further or additional amount) ancora; **is there any more?** ce n'è ancora?; **there's no more** non ce n'è più; **a little more** ancora un po'; **many/much more** molti(-e)/molto(-a) di più
▶ ADV: **more dangerous/easily (than)** più pericoloso/facilmente (di); **more and more** sempre di più; **more and more difficult** sempre più difficile; **more or less** più o meno; **more than ever** più che mai; **once more** ancora (una volta), un'altra volta; **no**

more, not any more non ... più; **I have no more money, I haven't any more money** non ho più soldi

moreover [mɔːˈrəuvəʳ] ADV inoltre, di più

morgue [mɔːg] N obitorio

MORI [ˈmɔːrɪ] N ABBR (BRIT: = Market & Opinion Research Institute) istituto di sondaggio

moribund [ˈmɔrɪbʌnd] ADJ moribondo(-a)

morning [ˈmɔːnɪŋ] N mattina, mattino; (duration) mattinata ► CPD del mattino; **in the ~** la mattina; **this ~** stamattina; **7 o'clock in the ~** le 7 di or della mattina

morning-after pill [ˈmɔːnɪŋˈɑːftə-] N pillola del giorno dopo

morning sickness N nausee fpl mattutine

Moroccan [məˈrɔkən] ADJ, N marocchino(-a)

Morocco [məˈrɔkəu] N Marocco

moron [ˈmɔːrɔn] N (col) deficiente mf

moronic [məˈrɔnɪk] ADJ deficiente

morose [məˈrəus] ADJ cupo(-a), tetro(-a)

morphine [ˈmɔːfiːn] N morfina

morris dancing [ˈmɔrɪs-] N vedi nota

> Il morris dancing è una danza folcloristica inglese tradizionale riservata agli uomini. Vestiti di bianco e con dei campanelli attaccati alle caviglie, i ballerini eseguono una danza tenendo in mano dei fazzoletti bianchi e lunghi bastoni. Questa danza è molto popolare nelle feste paesane.

Morse [mɔːs] N (also: **Morse code**) alfabeto Morse

morsel [ˈmɔːsl] N boccone m

mortal [ˈmɔːtl] ADJ, N mortale (m)

mortality [mɔːˈtælɪtɪ] N mortalità

mortality rate N tasso di mortalità

mortar [ˈmɔːtəʳ] N (Constr) malta; (dish) mortaio

mortgage [ˈmɔːgɪdʒ] N ipoteca; (loan) prestito ipotecario ► VT ipotecare; **to take out a ~** contrarre un mutuo (or un'ipoteca)

mortgage company N (US) società f inv immobiliare

mortgagee [mɔːgɪˈdʒiː] N creditore m ipotecario

mortgagor [ˈmɔːgɪdʒəʳ] N debitore m ipotecario

mortician [mɔːˈtɪʃən] N (US) impresario di pompe funebri

mortified [ˈmɔːtɪfaɪd] ADJ umiliato(-a)

mortise lock [ˈmɔːtɪs-] N serratura incastrata

mortuary [ˈmɔːtjuərɪ] N camera mortuaria; obitorio

mosaic [məuˈzeɪɪk] N mosaico

Moscow [ˈmɔskəu] N Mosca

Moslem [ˈmɔzləm] ADJ, N = **Muslim**

mosque [mɔsk] N moschea

mosquito [mɔsˈkiːtəu] (pl **mosquitoes**) N zanzara

mosquito net N zanzariera

moss [mɔs] N muschio

mossy [ˈmɔsɪ] ADJ muscoso(-a)

most [məust] ADJ (almost all) la maggior parte di; il più di; (largest, greatest): **who has (the) ~ money?** chi ha più soldi di tutti? ► PRON la maggior parte ► ADV più; (work, sleep etc) di più; (very) molto, estremamente; **the ~** (also: + adjective) il (la) più; **~ fish** la maggior parte dei pesci; **~ of** la maggior parte di; **~ of them** quasi tutti; **I saw ~** ho visto più io; **at the (very) ~** al massimo; **to make the ~ of** trarre il massimo vantaggio da; **a ~ interesting book** un libro estremamente interessante

mostly [ˈməustlɪ] ADV per lo più

MOT N ABBR (BRIT) = **Ministry of Transport**; **the ~ (test)** revisione obbligatoria degli autoveicoli

motel [məuˈtɛl] N motel m inv

moth [mɔθ] N farfalla notturna; tarma

mothball [ˈmɔθbɔːl] N pallina di naftalina

moth-eaten [ˈmɔθiːtn] ADJ tarmato(-a)

mother [ˈmʌðəʳ] N madre f ► VT (care for) fare da madre a

mother board N (Comput) scheda madre

motherhood [ˈmʌðəhud] N maternità

mother-in-law [ˈmʌðərɪnlɔː] N suocera

mother-of-pearl [mʌðərəvˈpəːl] N madreperla

Mother's Day N la festa della mamma

mother's help N bambinaia

mother-to-be [mʌðətəˈbiː] N futura mamma

mother tongue N madrelingua

mothproof [ˈmɔθpruːf] ADJ antitarmico(-a)

motif [məuˈtiːf] N motivo

motion [ˈməuʃən] N movimento, moto; (gesture) gesto; (at meeting) mozione f; (BRIT: also: **bowel motion**) evacuazione f ► VT, VI: **to ~ (to) sb to do** fare cenno a qn di fare; **to be in ~** (vehicle) essere in moto; **to set in ~** avviare; **to go through the motions of doing sth** (fig) fare qc pro forma

motionless [ˈməuʃənlɪs] ADJ immobile

motion picture N film m inv

motivate [ˈməutɪveɪt] VT (act, decision) dare origine a, motivare; (person) spingere

motivated [ˈməutɪveɪtɪd] ADJ motivato(-a)

motivation [məutɪˈveɪʃən] N motivazione f

motive [ˈməutɪv] N motivo ► ADJ motore(-trice); **from the best motives** con le migliori intenzioni

motley [ˈmɔtlɪ] ADJ eterogeneo(-a), molto vario(-a)

motor [ˈməutəʳ] N motore m; (BRIT col: vehicle) macchina ► ADJ (industry, accident) automobilistico(-a); **~ vehicle** autoveicolo

motorbike ['məutəbaɪk] N moto f inv
motorboat ['məutəbəut] N motoscafo
motorcade ['məutəkeɪd] N corteo di macchine
motorcar ['məutəkɑ:] N (BRIT) automobile f
motorcoach ['məutəkəutʃ] N (BRIT) pullman m inv
motorcycle ['məutəsaɪkl] N motocicletta
motorcyclist ['məutəsaɪklɪst] N motociclista mf
motoring ['məutərɪŋ] N (BRIT) turismo automobilistico ▶ ADJ (accident) d'auto, automobilistico(-a); (offence) di guida; ~ **holiday** vacanza in macchina
motorist ['məutərɪst] N automobilista mf
motorize ['məutəraɪz] VT motorizzare
motor oil N olio lubrificante
motor racing N (BRIT) corse fpl automobilistiche
motor scooter N motorscooter m inv
motor vehicle N autoveicolo
motorway ['məutəweɪ] N (BRIT) autostrada
mottled ['mɔtld] ADJ chiazzato(-a), marezzato(-a)
motto ['mɔtəu] (pl **mottoes**) N motto
mould, (US) **mold** [məuld] N forma, stampo; (mildew) muffa ▶ VT formare; (fig) foggiare
moulder, (US) **molder** ['məuldə'] VI (decay) ammuffire
moulding, (US) **molding** ['məuldɪŋ] N (Archit) modanatura
mouldy, (US) **moldy** ['məuldɪ] ADJ ammuffito(-a); (smell) di muffa
moult, (US) **molt** [məult] VI far la muta
mound [maund] N rialzo, collinetta; (heap) mucchio
mount [maunt] N (Geo) monte m, montagna; (horse) cavalcatura; (for jewel etc) montatura ▶ VT montare; (horse) montare a; (exhibition) organizzare; (attack) sferrare, condurre; (picture, stamp) sistemare ▶ VI salire; (get on a horse) montare a cavallo
▶ **mount up** VI (build up) accumularsi
mountain ['mauntɪn] N montagna ▶ CPD di montagna; **to make a ~ out of a molehill** fare di una mosca un elefante
mountain bike N mountain bike f inv
mountaineer [mauntɪ'nɪə'] N alpinista mf
mountaineering [mauntɪ'nɪərɪŋ] N alpinismo; **to go ~** fare dell'alpinismo
mountainous ['mauntɪnəs] ADJ montagnoso(-a)
mountain range N catena montuosa
mountain rescue team N ≈ squadra di soccorso alpino
mountainside ['mauntɪnsaɪd] N fianco della montagna
mounted ['mauntɪd] ADJ a cavallo

mourn [mɔ:n] VT piangere, lamentare
▶ VI: **to ~ (for sb)** piangere (la morte di qn)
mourner ['mɔ:nə'] N parente mf (or amico(-a)) del defunto
mourning ['mɔ:nɪŋ] N lutto ▶ CPD (dress) da lutto; **in ~** in lutto
mouse [maus] (pl **mice** [maɪs]) N topo; (Comput) mouse m inv
mouse mat, mouse pad N (Comput) tappetino del mouse
mousetrap ['maustræp] N trappola per i topi
moussaka [mu'sɑ:kə] N moussaka
mousse [mu:s] N mousse f inv
moustache, (US) **mustache** [məs'tɑ:ʃ] N baffi mpl
mousy ['mausɪ] ADJ (person) timido(-a); (hair) né chiaro(-a) né scuro(-a)
mouth [mauθ] (pl **mouths** [-ðz]) N bocca; (of river) bocca, foce f; (opening) orifizio
mouthful ['mauθful] N boccata
mouth organ N armonica
mouthpiece ['mauθpi:s] N (Mus) imboccatura, bocchino; (Tel) microfono; (of breathing apparatus) boccaglio; (person) portavoce mf
mouth-to-mouth ['mauθtə'mauθ] ADJ: ~ **resuscitation** respirazione f bocca a bocca
mouthwash ['mauθwɔʃ] N collutorio
mouth-watering ['mauθwɔ:tərɪŋ] ADJ che fa venire l'acquolina in bocca
movable ['mu:vəbl] ADJ mobile
move [mu:v] N (movement) movimento; (in game) mossa; (: turn to play) turno; (change: of house) trasloco; (: of job) cambiamento ▶ VT muovere; (change position of) spostare; (emotionally) commuovere; (Pol: resolution etc) proporre ▶ VI (gen) muoversi, spostarsi; (traffic) circolare; (also: **move house**) cambiar casa, traslocare; **to ~ towards** andare verso; **to ~ sb to do sth** indurre or spingere qn a fare qc; **to get a ~ on** affrettarsi, sbrigarsi; **to be moved** (emotionally) essere commosso(-a)
▶ **move about, move around** VI (fidget) agitarsi; (travel) viaggiare
▶ **move along** VI muoversi avanti
▶ **move away** VI allontanarsi, andarsene
▶ **move back** VI indietreggiare; (return) ritornare
▶ **move forward** VI avanzare ▶ VT avanzare, spostare in avanti; (people) far avanzare
▶ **move in** VI (to a house) entrare (in una nuova casa); (police etc) intervenire
▶ **move off** VI partire
▶ **move on** VI riprendere la strada ▶ VT (onlookers) far circolare
▶ **move out** VI (of house) sgombrare
▶ **move over** VI spostarsi
▶ **move up** VI avanzare

movement ['muːvmənt] N (gen) movimento; (gesture) gesto; (of stars, water, physical) moto; ~ **(of the bowels)** (Med) evacuazione f

mover ['muːvə^r] N proponente mf

movie ['muːvɪ] N film m inv; **the movies** il cinema

movie camera N cinepresa

moviegoer ['muːvɪɡəʊə^r] N (US) frequentatore(-trice) di cinema

movie theater (US) N cinema m inv

moving ['muːvɪŋ] ADJ mobile; (causing emotion) commovente; (instigating) animatore(-trice)

mow [məʊ] (pt **mowed**, pp **mowed** or **mown** [məʊn]) VT falciare; (grass) tagliare; (corn) mietere
  ▶ **mow down** VT falciare

mower ['məʊə^r] N (also: **lawn mower**) tagliaerba m inv

mown [məʊn] PP of **mow**

Mozambique [məʊzəm'biːk] N Mozambico

MP N ABBR = **Military Police**; (BRIT) = **Member of Parliament**; (CANADA) = **Mounted Police**

MP3 N MP3 m inv

MP3 player N lettore m MP3

mpg N ABBR = **miles per gallon**

mph N ABBR = **miles per hour**

MPhil N ABBR (= Master of Philosophy) titolo di studio

MPS N ABBR (BRIT) = **Member of the Pharmaceutical Society**

Mr, (US) **Mr.** ['mɪstə^r] N: **Mr X** Signor X, Sig. X

MRC N ABBR (BRIT: = Medical Research Council) ufficio governativo per la ricerca medica in Gran Bretagna e nel Commonwealth

MRCP N ABBR (BRIT) = **Member of the Royal College of Physicians**

MRCS N ABBR (BRIT) = **Member of the Royal College of Surgeons**

MRCVS N ABBR (BRIT) = **Member of the Royal College of Veterinary Surgeons**

Mrs, (US) **Mrs.** ['mɪsɪz] N: ~ **X** Signora X, Sig. ra X

MS N ABBR (US: = Master of Science) titolo di studio; (Med) = **multiple sclerosis**; (= manuscript) ms
  ▶ ABBR (US) = **Mississippi**

Ms, (US) **Ms.** [mɪz] N = **Miss**; **Mrs**; **Ms X** ≈ Signora X, ≈ Sig.ra X

  In inglese si usa Ms al posto di Mrs (Signora) o Miss (Signorina) per evitare la distinzione tradizionale tra le donne sposate e quelle nubili.

MSA N ABBR (US: = Master of Science in Agriculture) titolo di studio

MSc N ABBR = **Master of Science**

MSG ABBR = **monosodium glutamate**

MSP N ABBR (BRIT) = **Member of the Scottish Parliament**

MST ABBR (US: = Mountain Standard Time) ora invernale delle Montagne Rocciose

MSW N ABBR (US: = Master of Social Work) titolo di studio

MT N ABBR = **machine translation** ▶ ABBR (US) = **Montana**

Mt ABBR (Geo: = mount) M

mth ABBR (= month) m

MTV N ABBR = **music television**

(KEYWORD)

much [mʌtʃ] ADJ, PRON molto(-a); **he's done so much work** ha lavorato così tanto; **I have as much money as you** ho tanti soldi quanti ne hai tu; **how much is it?** quant'è?; **it's not much** non è tanto; **it costs too much** costa troppo; **as much as you want** quanto vuoi
  ▶ ADV **1** (greatly) molto, tanto; **thank you very much** molte grazie; **I like it very/so much** mi piace moltissimo/così tanto; **much to my amazement** con mio enorme stupore; **he's very much the gentleman** è il vero gentiluomo; **I read as much as I can** leggo quanto posso; **as much as you** tanto quanto te
  2 (by far) molto; **it's much the biggest company in Europe** è di gran lunga la più grossa società in Europa
  3 (almost) grossomodo, praticamente; **they're much the same** sono praticamente uguali

muck [mʌk] N (mud) fango; (dirt) sporcizia
  ▶ **muck about, muck around** VI (col) fare lo stupido; (waste time) gingillarsi; (tinker) armeggiare
  ▶ **muck in** VI (BRIT col) mettersi insieme
  ▶ **muck out** VT (stable) pulire
  ▶ **muck up** VT (col: dirty) sporcare; (spoil) rovinare

muckraking ['mʌkreɪkɪŋ] N (fig: col) caccia agli scandali ▶ ADJ scandalistico(-a)

mucky ['mʌkɪ] ADJ (dirty) sporco(-a), lordo(-a)

mucus ['mjuːkəs] N muco

mud [mʌd] N fango

muddle ['mʌdl] N confusione f, disordine m; pasticcio ▶ VT (also: **muddle up**) mettere sottosopra; confondere; **to be in a ~** (person) non riuscire a raccapezzarsi; **to get in a ~** (while explaining etc) imbrogliarsi
  ▶ **muddle along** VI andare avanti a casaccio
  ▶ **muddle through** VI cavarsela alla meno peggio

muddle-headed [mʌdl'hɛdɪd] ADJ (person) confusionario(-a)

muddy ['mʌdɪ] ADJ fangoso(-a)

mud flats NPL distesa fangosa

mudguard ['mʌdɡɑːd] N parafango

mudpack ['mʌdpæk] N maschera di fango

mud-slinging ['mʌdslɪŋɪŋ] N (fig) infangamento

muesli ['mju:zlɪ] N muesli m inv

muff [mʌf] N manicotto ▶ VT (shot, catch etc) mancare, sbagliare; **to ~ it** sbagliare tutto

muffin ['mʌfɪn] N specie di pasticcino soffice da tè

muffle ['mʌfl] VT (sound) smorzare, attutire; (against cold) imbacuccare

muffled ['mʌfld] ADJ smorzato(-a), attutito(-a)

muffler ['mʌflər] N (scarf) sciarpa (pesante); (US: Aut) marmitta; (: on motorbike) silenziatore m

mufti ['mʌftɪ] N: **in** ~ in borghese

mug [mʌg] N (cup) tazzone m; (for beer) boccale m; (col: face) muso; (: fool) scemo(-a) ▶ VT (assault) assalire; **it's a ~'s game** (BRIT) è proprio (una cosa) da fessi
▶ **mug up** VT (BRIT col: also: **mug up on**) studiare bene

mugger ['mʌgər] N aggressore m

mugging ['mʌgɪŋ] N aggressione f (a scopo di rapina)

muggins ['mʌgɪnz] N (col) semplicione(-a), sprovveduto(-a)

muggy ['mʌgɪ] ADJ afoso(-a)

mug shot N (col) foto f inv segnaletica

mulatto [mju:'lætəu] (pl **mulattoes**) N mulatto(-a)

mulberry ['mʌlbərɪ] N (fruit) mora (di gelso); (tree) gelso, moro

mule [mju:l] N mulo

mull [mʌl]: **to ~ over** vt rimuginare

mulled [mʌld] ADJ: ~ **wine** vino caldo

multi... ['mʌltɪ] PREFIX multi...

multi-access [mʌltɪ'æksɛs] ADJ (Comput) ad accesso multiplo

multicoloured, (US) multicolored ['mʌltɪkʌləd] ADJ multicolore, variopinto(-a)

multifarious [mʌltɪ'fɛərɪəs] ADJ molteplice, svariato(-a)

multilateral [mʌltɪ'lætərəl] ADJ (Pol) multilaterale

multi-level ['mʌltɪlɛvl] ADJ (US) = **multistorey**

multimedia ['mʌltɪ'mi:dɪə] ADJ multimedia inv

multimillionaire [mʌltɪmɪljə'nɛər] N multimiliardario(-a)

multinational [mʌltɪ'næʃənl] ADJ, N multinazionale (f)

multiple ['mʌltɪpl] ADJ multiplo(-a); molteplice ▶ N multiplo; (BRIT: also: **multiple store**) grande magazzino che fa parte di una catena

multiple choice (test) N esercizi mpl a scelta multipla

multiple crash N serie f inv di incidenti a catena

multiple sclerosis [-sklɪ'rəusɪs] N sclerosi f a placche

multiplex ['mʌltɪplɛks] N (also: **multiplex cinema**) cinema m inv multisale inv

multiplication [mʌltɪplɪ'keɪʃən] N moltiplicazione f

multiplication table N tavola pitagorica

multiplicity [mʌltɪ'plɪsɪtɪ] N molteplicità

multiply ['mʌltɪplaɪ] VT moltiplicare ▶ VI moltiplicarsi

multiracial [mʌltɪ'reɪʃəl] ADJ multirazziale

multistorey ['mʌltɪ'stɔ:rɪ] ADJ (BRIT: building, car park) a più piani

multitude ['mʌltɪtju:d] N moltitudine f

mum [mʌm] N (BRIT col) mamma ▶ ADJ: **to keep** ~ non aprire bocca; **~'s the word!** acqua in bocca!

mumble ['mʌmbl] VT, VI borbottare

mumbo jumbo ['mʌmbəu-] N (col) parole fpl incomprensibili

mummify ['mʌmɪfaɪ] VT mummificare

mummy ['mʌmɪ] N (BRIT: mother) mamma; (embalmed) mummia

mumps [mʌmps] N orecchioni mpl

munch [mʌntʃ] VT, VI sgranocchiare

mundane [mʌn'deɪn] ADJ terra a terra inv

Munich ['mju:nɪk] N Monaco f (di Baviera)

municipal [mju:'nɪsɪpl] ADJ municipale

municipality [mju:nɪsɪ'pælɪtɪ] N municipio

munitions [mju:'nɪʃənz] NPL munizioni fpl

mural ['mjuərəl] N dipinto murale

murder ['mə:dər] N assassinio, omicidio ▶ VT assassinare; **to commit** ~ commettere un omicidio

murderer ['mə:dərər] N omicida m, assassino

murderess ['mə:dərɪs] N omicida f, assassina

murderous ['mə:dərəs] ADJ micidiale

murk [mə:k] N oscurità, buio

murky ['mə:kɪ] ADJ tenebroso(-a), buio(-a)

murmur ['mə:mər] N mormorio ▶ VT, VI mormorare; **heart** ~ (Med) soffio al cuore

MusB, MusBac N ABBR (= Bachelor of Music) titolo di studio

muscle ['mʌsl] N muscolo; (fig) forza
▶ **muscle in** VI immischiarsi

muscular ['mʌskjulər] ADJ muscolare; (person, arm) muscoloso(-a)

muscular dystrophy N distrofia muscolare

MusD, MusDoc N ABBR (= Doctor of Music) titolo di studio

muse [mju:z] VI meditare, sognare ▶ N musa

museum [mju:'zɪəm] N museo

mush [mʌʃ] N pappa

mushroom ['mʌʃrum] N fungo ▶ VI (fig) svilupparsi rapidamente

mushy ['mʌʃɪ] ADJ (food) spappolato(-a); (sentimental) sdolcinato(-a)

music ['mju:zɪk] N musica

musical ['mju:zɪkəl] ADJ musicale; (person) portato(-a) per la musica ▶ N (show) commedia musicale

musical box N carillon *m inv*
musical chairs N gioco delle sedie (*in cui bisogna sedersi non appena cessa la musica*); (*fig*) scambio delle poltrone
musical instrument N strumento musicale
music box N carillon *m inv*
music centre N impianto *m* stereo *inv* monoblocco *inv*
music hall N teatro di varietà
musician [mjuːˈzɪʃən] N musicista *mf*
music stand N leggio
musk [mʌsk] N muschio
musket [ˈmʌskɪt] N moschetto
muskrat [ˈmʌskræt] N topo muschiato
musk rose N (*Bot*) rosa muschiata
Muslim [ˈmʌzlɪm] ADJ, N musulmano(-a)
muslin [ˈmʌzlɪn] N mussola
musquash [ˈmʌskwɔʃ] N (*fur*) rat musqué *m inv*
mussel [ˈmʌsl] N cozza
must [mʌst] AUX VB (*obligation*): **I ~ do it** devo farlo; (*probability*): **he ~ be there by now** dovrebbe essere arrivato ormai; **I ~ have made a mistake** devo essermi sbagliato ▸ N: **this programme/trip is a ~** è un programma/viaggio da non perdersi
mustache [ˈmʌstæʃ] N (*US*) = **moustache**
mustard [ˈmʌstəd] N senape *f*, mostarda
mustard gas N iprite *f*
muster [ˈmʌstəʳ] VT radunare; (*also:* **muster up:** *strength, courage*) fare appello a
mustiness [ˈmʌstɪnɪs] N odor di muffa *or* di stantio
mustn't [ˈmʌsnt]= **must not**
musty [ˈmʌstɪ] ADJ che sa di muffa *or* di rinchiuso
mutant [ˈmjuːtənt] ADJ, N mutante (*m*)
mutate [mjuːˈteɪt] VI subire una mutazione
mutation [mjuːˈteɪʃən] N mutazione *f*
mute [mjuːt] ADJ, N muto(-a)
muted [ˈmjuːtɪd] ADJ (*noise*) attutito(-a), smorzato(-a); (*criticism*) attenuato(-a); (*Mus*) in sordina; (: *trumpet*) con sordina
mutilate [ˈmjuːtɪleɪt] VT mutilare

mutilation [mjuːtɪˈleɪʃən] N mutilazione *f*
mutinous [ˈmjuːtɪnəs] ADJ (*troops*) ammutinato(-a); (*attitude*) ribelle
mutiny [ˈmjuːtɪnɪ] N ammutinamento ▸ VI ammutinarsi
mutter [ˈmʌtəʳ] VT, VI borbottare, brontolare
mutton [ˈmʌtn] N carne *f* di montone
mutual [ˈmjuːtʃuəl] ADJ mutuo(-a), reciproco(-a)
mutually [ˈmjuːtʃuəlɪ] ADV reciprocamente
Muzak® [ˈmjuːzæk] N (*often pej*) musica di sottofondo
muzzle [ˈmʌzl] N muso; (*protective device*) museruola; (*of gun*) bocca ▸ VT mettere la museruola a
MV ABBR (= *motor vessel*) M/N, m/n
MVP N ABBR (*US Sport:* = *most valuable player*) titolo ottenuto da sportivo
MW (*Radio:* = *medium wave*) O.M.; = **megawatt**
my [maɪ] ADJ il (la) mio(-a); (*pl*) i (le) miei (mie); **my house** la mia casa; **my books** i miei libri; **my brother** mio fratello; **I've washed my hair/cut my finger** mi sono lavato i capelli/tagliato
Myanmar [ˈmaɪænmɑːʳ] N Myanma
myopic [maɪˈɔpɪk] ADJ miope
myriad [ˈmɪrɪəd] N miriade *f*
myself [maɪˈsɛlf] PRON (*reflexive*) mi; (*emphatic*) io stesso(-a); (*after prep*) me; *see also* **oneself**
mysterious [mɪsˈtɪərɪəs] ADJ misterioso(-a)
mystery [ˈmɪstərɪ] N mistero
mystery story N racconto del mistero
mystic [ˈmɪstɪk] ADJ, N mistico(-a)
mystical [ˈmɪstɪkəl] ADJ mistico(-a)
mystify [ˈmɪstɪfaɪ] VT mistificare; (*puzzle*) confondere
mystique [mɪsˈtiːk] N fascino
myth [mɪθ] N mito
mythical [ˈmɪθɪkl] ADJ mitico(-a)
mythological [mɪθəˈlɔdʒɪkl] ADJ mitologico(-a)
mythology [mɪˈθɔlədʒɪ] N mitologia

Nn

N, n [ɛn] N (letter) N, n f inv or m inv; **N for Nellie**, (US) **N for Nan** = N come Napoli

N ABBR (= north) N

NA N ABBR (US: = Narcotics Anonymous) associazione in aiuto dei tossicodipendenti; (US) = **National Academy**

n/a ABBR (= not applicable) non pertinente

NAACP N ABBR (US) = **National Association for the Advancement of Colored People**

NAAFI ['næfɪ] N ABBR (BRIT: = Navy, Army, & Air Force Institutes) organizzazione che gestisce negozi, mense ecc. per il personale militare

nab [næb] VT (col) beccare, acchiappare

NACU N ABBR (US) = **National Association of Colleges and Universities**

nadir ['neɪdɪəʳ] N (Astron) nadir m; (fig) punto più basso

nag [næg] N (pej: horse) ronzino; (person) brontolone(-a) ▶ VT tormentare ▶ VI brontolare in continuazione

nagging ['nægɪŋ] ADJ (doubt, pain) persistente ▶ N brontolii mpl, osservazioni fpl continue

nail [neɪl] N (human) unghia; (metal) chiodo ▶ VT inchiodare; **to ~ sb down to a date/price** costringere qn a un appuntamento/ad accettare un prezzo; **to pay cash on the ~** (BRIT) pagare a tamburo battente

nailbrush ['neɪlbrʌʃ] N spazzolino da or per unghie

nailfile ['neɪlfaɪl] N lima da or per unghie

nail polish N smalto da or per unghie

nail polish remover N acetone m, solvente m

nail scissors NPL forbici fpl da or per unghie

nail varnish N (BRIT) = **nail polish**

Nairobi [naɪ'rəʊbɪ] N Nairobi f

naïve [naɪ'iːv] ADJ ingenuo(-a)

naïveté [naːiːv'teɪ], **naivety** [naɪ'iːvtɪ] N ingenuità f inv

naked ['neɪkɪd] ADJ nudo(-a); **with the ~ eye** a occhio nudo

nakedness ['neɪkɪdnɪs] N nudità

NAM N ABBR (US) = **National Association of Manufacturers**

name [neɪm] N nome m; (reputation) nome, reputazione f ▶ VT (baby etc) chiamare; (plant, illness) nominare; (person, object) identificare; (price, date) fissare; **by ~** di nome; **she knows them all by ~** li conosce tutti per nome; **in the ~ of** in nome di; **what's your ~?** come si chiama?; **my ~ is Peter** mi chiamo Peter; **to take sb's ~ and address** prendere nome e indirizzo di qn; **to make a ~ for o.s.** farsi un nome; **to get (o.s.) a bad ~** farsi una cattiva fama or una brutta reputazione; **to call sb names** insultare qn

name dropping N menzionare qualcuno per fare bella figura

nameless ['neɪmlɪs] ADJ senza nome

namely ['neɪmlɪ] ADV cioè

nameplate ['neɪmpleɪt] N (on door etc) targa

namesake ['neɪmseɪk] N omonimo

nan bread [naːn-] N tipo di pane indiano poco lievitato di forma allungata

nanny ['nænɪ] N bambinaia

nanny goat N capra

nap [næp] N (sleep) pisolino; (of cloth) peluria ▶ VI: **to be caught napping** essere preso alla sprovvista; **to have a ~** schiacciare un pisolino

NAPA N ABBR (US: = National Association of Performing Artists) associazione nazionale degli artisti di palcoscenico

napalm ['neɪpaːm] N napalm m

nape [neɪp] N: **~ of the neck** nuca

napkin ['næpkɪn] N tovagliolo; (BRIT: for baby) pannolino

Naples ['neɪplz] N Napoli f

Napoleonic [nəpəʊlɪ'ɔnɪk] ADJ napoleonico(-a)

nappy ['næpɪ] N (BRIT) pannolino

nappy liner N (BRIT) fogliettino igienico

narcissistic [naːsɪ'sɪstɪk] ADJ narcisistico(-a)

narcissus [naː'sɪsəs] (pl **narcissi** [-saɪ]) N narciso

narcotic [naː'kɔtɪk] N (Med) narcotico; **narcotics** NPL (drugs) narcotici, stupefacenti mpl

nark [naːk] VT (BRIT col) scocciare

narrate [nə'reɪt] VT raccontare, narrare
narration [nə'reɪʃən] N narrazione f
narrative ['nærətɪv] N narrativa ▸ ADJ narrativo(-a)
narrator [nə'reɪtə'] N narratore(-trice)
narrow ['nærəu] ADJ stretto(-a); (resources, means) limitato(-a), modesto(-a); (fig): **to take a ~ view of** avere una visione limitata di ▸ VI restringersi; **to have a ~ escape** farcela per un pelo
▸ **narrow down** VT (search, investigation, possibilities) restringere; (list) ridurre; **to ~ sth down to** ridurre qc a
narrow gauge ADJ (Rail) a scartamento ridotto
narrowly ['nærəulɪ] ADV per un pelo; (time) per poco; **Maria ~ escaped drowning** per un pelo Maria non è affogata; **he ~ missed hitting the cyclist** per poco non ha investito il ciclista
narrow-minded [nærəu'maɪndɪd] ADJ meschino(-a)
NAS N ABBR (US) = **National Academy of Sciences**
NASA ['næsə] N ABBR (US: = National Aeronautics and Space Administration) N.A.S.A. f
nasal ['neɪzl] ADJ nasale
Nassau ['næsɔ:] N Nassau f
nastily ['nɑ:stɪlɪ] ADV con cattiveria
nastiness ['nɑ:stɪnɪs] N (of person, remark) cattiveria; (: spitefulness) malignità
nasturtium [nəs'tə:ʃəm] N cappuccina, nasturzio (indiano)
nasty ['nɑ:stɪ] ADJ (unpleasant: person, remark) cattivo(-a); (: spiteful) maligno(-a); (rude) villano(-a); (smell, wound, situation) brutto(-a); **to turn ~** (situation) mettersi male; (weather) guastarsi; (person) incattivirsi; **it's a ~ business** è una brutta faccenda, è un brutto affare
NAS/UWT N ABBR (BRIT: = National Association of Schoolmasters/Union of Women Teachers) sindacato di insegnanti in Inghilterra e Galles
nation ['neɪʃən] N nazione f
national ['næʃnl] ADJ nazionale ▸ N cittadino(-a)
national anthem N inno nazionale
National Curriculum N (BRIT) ≈ programma m scolastico ministeriale (in Inghilterra e Galles)
national debt N debito pubblico
national dress N costume m nazionale
National Guard N (US) milizia nazionale (volontaria, in ogni stato)
National Health Service N (BRIT) ≈ Servizio sanitario nazionale
National Insurance N (BRIT) ≈ Previdenza Sociale
nationalism ['næʃnəlɪzəm] N nazionalismo

nationalist ['næʃnəlɪst] ADJ, N nazionalista (mf)
nationality [næʃə'nælɪtɪ] N nazionalità f inv
nationalization [næʃnəlaɪ'zeɪʃən] N nazionalizzazione f
nationalize ['næʃnəlaɪz] VT nazionalizzare
nationally ['næʃnəlɪ] ADV a livello nazionale
national park N parco nazionale
national press N stampa a diffusione nazionale
National Security Council N (US) consiglio nazionale di sicurezza
national service N (Mil) servizio militare
National Trust N sovrintendenza ai beni culturali e ambientali; vedi nota

Fondato nel 1895, il National Trust è un'organizzazione che si occupa della tutela e salvaguardia di edifici e monumenti di interesse storico e di territori di interesse ambientale nel Regno Unito.

nationwide ['neɪʃənwaɪd] ADJ diffuso(-a) in tutto il paese ▸ ADV in tutto il paese
native ['neɪtɪv] N abitante mf del paese; (in colonies) indigeno(-a) ▸ ADJ indigeno(-a); (country) natio(-a); (ability) innato(-a); **a ~ of Russia** un nativo della Russia; **a ~ speaker of French** una persona di madrelingua francese; **~ language** madrelingua
Native American N discendente di tribù dell'America settentrionale
Nativity [nə'tɪvɪtɪ] N (Rel): **the ~** la Natività
nativity play N recita sulla Natività
NATO ['neɪtəu] N ABBR (= North Atlantic Treaty Organization) N.A.T.O. f
natter ['nætə'] (BRIT col) VI chiacchierare ▸ N chiacchierata
natural ['nætʃrəl] ADJ naturale; (ability) innato(-a); (manner) semplice; **death from ~ causes** (Law) morte f per cause naturali
natural childbirth N parto indolore
natural gas N gas m metano
natural history N storia naturale
naturalist ['nætʃrəlɪst] N naturalista mf
naturalization [nætʃrəlaɪ'zeɪʃən] N naturalizzazione f; acclimatazione f
naturalize ['nætʃrəlaɪz] VT: **to be naturalized** (person) naturalizzarsi; **to become naturalized** (animal, plant) acclimatarsi
naturally ['nætʃrəlɪ] ADV naturalmente; (by nature: gifted) di natura
naturalness ['nætʃrəlnɪs] N naturalezza
natural resources NPL risorse fpl naturali
natural selection N selezione f naturale
natural wastage N (Industry) diminuzione f di manodopera (per pensionamento decesso ecc)
nature ['neɪtʃə'] N natura; (character) natura, indole f; **by ~** di natura; **documents of a**

confidential ~ documenti *mpl* di natura privata
-natured ['neɪtʃəd] SUFFIX: **ill~** maldisposto(-a)
nature reserve N (BRIT) parco naturale
nature trail N *percorso tracciato in parchi nazionali ecc con scopi educativi*
naturist ['neɪtʃərɪst] N naturista *mf*, nudista *mf*
naught [nɔːt] N = **nought**
naughtiness ['nɔːtɪnɪs] N cattiveria
naughty ['nɔːtɪ] ADJ (*child*) birichino(-a), cattivello(-a); (*story, film*) spinto(-a)
nausea ['nɔːsɪə] N (*Med*) nausea; (*fig: disgust*) schifo
nauseate ['nɔːsɪeɪt] VT nauseare; far schifo a
nauseating ['nɔːsɪeɪtɪŋ] ADJ nauseante; (*fig*) disgustoso(-a)
nauseous ['nɔːsɪəs] ADJ nauseabondo(-a); (*feeling sick*): **to be** ~ avere la nausea
nautical ['nɔːtɪkl] ADJ nautico(-a)
nautical mile N miglio nautico *or* marino
naval ['neɪvl] ADJ navale
naval officer N ufficiale *m* di marina
nave [neɪv] N navata centrale
navel ['neɪvl] N ombelico
navigable ['nævɪgəbl] ADJ navigabile
navigate ['nævɪgeɪt] VT percorrere navigando ▶ VI navigare; (*Aut*) fare da navigatore
navigation [nævɪ'geɪʃən] N navigazione *f*
navigator ['nævɪgeɪtə'] N (*Naut, Aviat*) ufficiale *m* di rotta; (*explorer*) navigatore *m*; (*Aut*) copilota *mf*
navvy ['nævɪ] N manovale *m*
navy ['neɪvɪ] N marina; **Department of the N~** (*US*) Ministero della Marina ▶ ADJ blu scuro *inv*
navy-blue ['neɪvɪ'bluː] ADJ blu scuro *inv*
Nazareth ['næzərɪθ] N Nazareth *f*
Nazi ['nɑːtsɪ] ADJ, N nazista (*mf*)
NB ABBR (= *nota bene*) N.B.; (CANADA) = **New Brunswick**
NBA N ABBR (*US*: = *National Basketball Association*) ≈ F.I.P. *f* (= *Federazione Italiana Pallacanestro*); = **National Boxing Association**
NBC N ABBR (*US*: = *National Broadcasting Company*) compagnia nazionale di radiodiffusione
NBS N ABBR (*US*: = *National Bureau of Standards*) ufficio per la normalizzazione
NC ABBR (*Comm etc*: = *no charge*) gratis; (*US*) = **North Carolina**
NCC N ABBR (*US*) = **National Council of Churches**
NCO N ABBR = **non-commissioned officer**
ND, N. Dak. ABBR (*US*) = **North Dakota**
NE ABBR (*US*) = **Nebraska; New England**
NEA N ABBR (*US*) = **National Education Association**

neap [niːp] N (*also*: **neaptide**) marea di quadratura
Neapolitan [nɪə'pɔlɪtən] ADJ, N napoletano(-a)
near [nɪə'] ADJ vicino(-a); (*relation*) prossimo(-a) ▶ ADV vicino ▶ PREP (*also*: **near to**) vicino a, presso; (: *in time*) verso ▶ VT avvicinarsi a; **to come** ~ avvicinarsi; ~ **here/there** qui/lì vicino; **£25,000 or nearest offer** (BRIT) 25.000 sterline trattabili; **in the** ~ **future** in un prossimo futuro; **the building is nearing completion** il palazzo è quasi terminato *or* ultimato
nearby [nɪə'baɪ] ADJ vicino(-a) ▶ ADV vicino
Near East N: **the** ~ il Medio Oriente
nearer ['nɪərə'] ADJ più vicino(-a) ▶ ADV più vicino
nearly ['nɪəlɪ] ADV quasi; **not** ~ non … affatto; **I** ~ **lost it** per poco non lo perdevo; **she was** ~ **crying** era lì lì per piangere
near miss N: **that was a** ~ c'è mancato poco
nearness ['nɪənɪs] N vicinanza
nearside ['nɪəsaɪd] N (*right-hand drive*) lato sinistro; (*left-hand drive*) lato destro ▶ ADJ sinistro(-a); destro(-a)
near-sighted [nɪə'saɪtɪd] ADJ miope
neat [niːt] ADJ (*person, room*) ordinato(-a); (*work*) pulito(-a); (*solution, plan*) ben indovinato(-a), azzeccato(-a); (*spirits*) liscio(-a)
neatly ['niːtlɪ] ADV con ordine; (*skilfully*) abilmente
neatness ['niːtnɪs] N (*tidiness*) ordine *m*; (*skilfulness*) abilità
Nebr. ABBR (*US*) = **Nebraska**
nebulous ['nɛbjuləs] ADJ nebuloso(-a); (*fig*) vago(-a)
necessarily ['nɛsɪsrɪlɪ] ADV necessariamente; **not** ~ non è detto, non necessariamente
necessary ['nɛsɪsrɪ] ADJ necessario(-a); **if** ~ se necessario
necessitate [nɪ'sɛsɪteɪt] VT rendere necessario(-a)
necessity [nɪ'sɛsɪtɪ] N necessità *f inv*; **in case of** ~ in caso di necessità
neck [nɛk] N collo; (*of garment*) colletto ▶ VI (*col*) pomiciare, sbaciucchiarsi; ~ **and** ~ testa a testa; **to stick one's** ~ **out** (*col*) rischiare (forte)
necklace ['nɛklɪs] N collana
neckline ['nɛklaɪn] N scollatura
necktie ['nɛktaɪ] N (*esp US*) cravatta
nectar ['nɛktə'] N nettare *m*
nectarine ['nɛktərɪn] N nocepesca
née [neɪ] ADJ: ~ **Scott** nata Scott
need [niːd] N bisogno ▶ VT aver bisogno di; **do you** ~ **anything?** ha bisogno di qualcosa?; **I** ~ **to do it** lo devo fare, bisogna che io lo faccia; **you don't** ~ **to go** non deve andare,

n

677

non c'è bisogno che lei vada; **a signature is needed** occorre or ci vuole una firma; **to be in ~ of, have ~ of** aver bisogno di; **£10 will meet my immediate needs** 10 sterline mi basteranno per le necessità più urgenti; **in case of ~** in caso di bisogno or necessità; **there's no ~ for ...** non c'è bisogno or non occorre che ...; **there's no ~ to do ...** non occorre fare ...; **the needs of industry** le esigenze dell'industria

needle ['ni:dl] N ago; (on record player) puntina ▶ VT punzecchiare

needlecord ['ni:dlkɔ:d] N (BRIT) velluto a coste sottili

needless ['ni:dlɪs] ADJ inutile; **~ to say, ...** inutile dire che ...

needlessly ['ni:dlɪslɪ] ADV inutilmente

needlework ['ni:dlwə:k] N cucito

needn't ['ni:dnt]= **need not**

needy ['ni:dɪ] ADJ bisognoso(-a)

negation [nɪ'geɪʃən] N negazione f

negative ['nɛgətɪv] N (Phot) negativa, negativo; (Elec) polo negativo; (Ling) negazione f ▶ ADJ negativo(-a); **to answer in the ~** rispondere negativamente or di no

negative equity N situazione in cui l'ammontare del mutuo su un immobile supera il suo valore sul mercato

neglect [nɪ'glɛkt] VT trascurare ▶ N (of person, duty) negligenza; (of child, house etc) scarsa cura; **state of ~** stato di abbandono; **to ~ to do sth** trascurare or tralasciare di fare qc

neglected [nɪ'glɛktɪd] ADJ trascurato(-a)

neglectful [nɪ'glɛktful] ADJ (gen) negligente; **to be ~ of sb/sth** trascurare qn/qc

negligee ['nɛglɪʒeɪ] N négligé m inv

negligence ['nɛglɪdʒəns] N negligenza

negligent ['nɛglɪdʒənt] ADJ negligente

negligently ['nɛglɪdʒəntlɪ] ADV con negligenza

negligible ['nɛglɪdʒɪbl] ADJ insignificante, trascurabile

negotiable [nɪ'gəuʃɪəbl] ADJ negoziabile; (cheque) trasferibile; (road) transitabile

negotiate [nɪ'gəuʃɪeɪt] VI negoziare ▶ VT (Comm) negoziare; (obstacle) superare; (bend in road) prendere; **to ~ with sb for sth** trattare con qn per ottenere qc

negotiating table [nɪ'gəuʃɪeɪtɪŋ-] N tavolo delle trattative

negotiation [nɪgəuʃɪ'eɪʃən] N trattativa; (Pol) negoziato; **to enter into negotiations with sb** entrare in trattative (or intavolare i negoziati) con qn

negotiator [nɪ'gəuʃɪeɪtəʳ] N negoziatore(-trice)

Negress ['ni:grɪs] N negra

Negro ['ni:grəu] (pl **Negroes**) ADJ, N negro(-a)

neigh [neɪ] VI nitrire

neighbour, (US) **neighbor** ['neɪbəʳ] N vicino(-a)

neighbourhood, (US) **neighborhood** ['neɪbəhud] N vicinato

neighbourhood watch N (BRIT: also: **neighbourhood watch scheme**) sistema di vigilanza reciproca in un quartiere

neighbouring, (US) **neighboring** ['neɪbərɪŋ] ADJ vicino(-a)

neighbourly, (US) **neighborly** ['neɪbəlɪ] ADJ: **he is a neighbo(u)rly person** è un buon vicino

neither ['naɪðəʳ] ADJ, PRON né l'uno(-a) né l'altro(-a), nessuno(-a) dei due ▶ CONJ neanche, nemmeno, neppure ▶ ADV: **~ good nor bad** né buono né cattivo; **I didn't move and ~ did Claude** io non mi mossi e nemmeno Claude; **... ~ did I refuse ...**, ma non ho nemmeno rifiutato

neo... ['ni:əu] PREFIX neo...

neolithic [ni:əu'lɪθɪk] ADJ neolitico(-a)

neologism [nɪ'ɔlədʒɪzəm] N neologismo

neon ['ni:ɔn] N neon m

neon light N luce f al neon

neon sign N insegna al neon

Nepal [nɪ'pɔ:l] N Nepal m

nephew ['nɛvju:] N nipote m

nepotism ['nɛpətɪzəm] N nepotismo

nerd [nə:d] N (col) sfigato(-a), povero(-a) fesso(-a)

nerve [nə:v] N nervo; (fig) coraggio; (impudence) faccia tosta; **he gets on my nerves** mi dà ai nervi, mi fa venire i nervi; **a fit of nerves** una crisi di nervi; **to lose one's ~** (self-confidence) perdere fiducia in se stesso; **I lost my ~** (courage) mi è mancato il coraggio

nerve centre N (Anat) centro nervoso; (fig) cervello, centro vitale

nerve gas N gas m nervino

nerve-racking ['nə:vrækɪŋ] ADJ che spezza i nervi

nervous ['nə:vəs] ADJ nervoso(-a); (anxious) agitato(-a), in apprensione

nervous breakdown N esaurimento nervoso

nervously ['nə:vəslɪ] ADV nervosamente

nervousness ['nə:vəsnɪs] N nervosismo

nervous wreck N: **to be a ~** (col) essere nevrastenico(-a)

nervy ['nə:vɪ] ADJ agitato(-a), nervoso(-a)

nest [nɛst] N nido; **~ of tables** tavolini mpl cicogna inv ▶ VI fare il nido, nidificare

nest egg N (fig) gruzzolo

nestle ['nɛsl] VI accoccolarsi

nestling ['nɛslɪŋ] N uccellino di nido

net [nɛt] N rete f; (fabric) tulle m ▶ ADJ netto(-a) ▶ VT (person, profit) ricavare un utile netto di; (fish etc) prendere con la rete; (deal, *sale*) dare un utile netto di; **the N~** (*Internet*) Internet *f*; **~ of tax** netto, al netto di tasse; **he earns £10,000 ~ per year** guadagna 10.000 sterline nette all'anno

netball ['nɛtbɔ:l] N *specie di pallacanestro*

net curtains NPL tende *fpl* di tulle

Netherlands ['nɛðələndz] NPL: **the ~** i Paesi Bassi

netiquette ['nɛtɪkɛt] N netiquette *f inv*

net profit N utile *m* netto

netsurfer ['nɛtsə:fə'] N navigatore(-trice) in Internet

nett [nɛt] ADJ = **net**

netting ['nɛtɪŋ] N (*for fence etc*) reticolato; (*fabric*) tulle *m*

nettle ['nɛtl] N ortica

network ['nɛtwə:k] N rete *f*

neuralgia [njuə'rældʒə] N nevralgia

neurological [njuərə'lɔdʒɪkl] ADJ neurologico(-a)

neurosis [njuə'rəusɪs] (*pl* **neuroses** [-si:z]) N nevrosi *f inv*

neurotic [njuə'rɔtɪk] ADJ, N nevrotico(-a)

neuter ['nju:tə'] ADJ neutro(-a) ► N neutro ► VT (*cat etc*) castrare

neutral ['nju:trəl] ADJ neutro(-a); (*person, nation*) neutrale ► N (*Aut*): **in ~** in folle

neutrality [nju:'trælɪtɪ] N neutralità

neutralize ['nju:trəlaɪz] VT neutralizzare

neutron bomb ['nju:trɔn-] N bomba al neutrone

Nev. ABBR (*US*) = **Nevada**

never ['nɛvə'] ADV (non...) mai; **~ again** mai più; **I'll ~ go there again** non ci vado più; **~ in my life** mai in vita mia; *see also* **mind**

never-ending [nɛvər'ɛndɪŋ] ADJ interminabile

nevertheless [nɛvəðə'lɛs] ADV tuttavia, ciò nonostante, ciò nondimeno

new [nju:] ADJ nuovo(-a); (*brand new*) nuovo(-a) di zecca; **as good as ~** come nuovo

New Age ADJ, N New Age *f inv*

newbie ['nju:bɪ] N (*Comput, Tech*) utilizzatore(-trice) inesperto(-a); (*to a job or group*) nuovo(-a) arrivato(-a); (*to a hobby or experience*) neofita *mf*

newborn ['nju:bɔ:n] ADJ neonato(-a)

newcomer ['nju:kʌmə'] N nuovo(-a) venuto(-a)

new-fangled ['nju:fæŋgld] ADJ (*pej*) stramoderno(-a)

new-found ['nju:faund] ADJ nuovo(-a)

Newfoundland ['nju:fənlənd] N Terranova

New Guinea N Nuova Guinea

newly ['nju:lɪ] ADV di recente

newly-weds ['nju:lɪwɛdz] NPL sposini *mpl*, sposi *mpl* novelli

new moon N luna nuova

newness ['nju:nɪs] N novità

news [nju:z] N notizie *fpl*; (*Radio*) giornale *m* radio; (*TV*) telegiornale *m*; **a piece of ~** una notizia; **good/bad ~** buone/cattive notizie; **financial ~** (*Press*) pagina economica e finanziaria; (*Radio, TV*) notiziario economico

news agency N agenzia di stampa

newsagent ['nju:zeɪdʒənt] N (*BRIT*) giornalaio

news bulletin N (*Radio, TV*) notiziario

newscaster ['nju:zkɑ:stə'] N (*Radio, TV*) annunciatore(-trice)

newsdealer ['nju:zdi:lə'] N (*US*) = **newsagent**

newsflash ['nju:zflæʃ] N notizia *f* lampo *inv*

newsletter ['nju:zlɛtə'] N bollettino (*di ditta, associazione*)

newspaper ['nju:zpeɪpə'] N giornale *m*; **daily ~** quotidiano; **weekly ~** settimanale *m*

newsprint ['nju:zprɪnt] N carta da giornale

newsreader ['nju:zri:də'] N = **newscaster**

newsreel ['nju:zri:l] N cinegiornale *m*

newsroom ['nju:zrum] N (*Press*) redazione *f*; (*Radio, TV*) studio

news stand N edicola

newsworthy ['nju:zwə:ðɪ] ADJ degno(-a) di menzione (*per radio, TV ecc*); **to be ~** fare notizia

newt [nju:t] N tritone *m*

new town N (*BRIT*) nuovo centro urbano creato con fondi pubblici

New Year N Anno Nuovo; **Happy ~!** Buon Anno!; **to wish sb a happy ~** augurare Buon Anno a qn

New Year's Day N il Capodanno

New Year's Eve N la vigilia di Capodanno

New York [-'jɔ:k] N New York *f*, Nuova York *f*; (*also*: **New York State**) stato di New York

New Zealand [-'zi:lənd] N Nuova Zelanda ► ADJ neozelandese

New Zealander [-'zi:ləndə'] N neozelandese *mf*

next [nɛkst] ADJ prossimo(-a) ► ADV accanto; (*in time*) dopo; **~ to** prep accanto a; **~ to nothing** quasi niente; **~ please!** (*avanti*) il prossimo!; **~ time** *adv* la prossima volta; **~ week** la settimana prossima; **the ~ week** la settimana dopo *or* seguente; **the week after ~** fra due settimane; **the ~ day** il giorno dopo, l'indomani; **~ year** l'anno prossimo *or* venturo; **"turn to the ~ page"** "vedi pagina seguente"; **who's ~?** a chi tocca?; **when do we meet ~?** quando ci rincontriamo?

next door ADV, ADJ accanto *inv*

next of kin N parente *mf* prossimo(-a)

NF N ABBR (*BRIT Pol*: = *National Front*) partito di estrema destra ► ABBR (*CANADA*) = **Newfoundland**

NFL N ABBR (*US*) = **National Football League**

Nfld. ABBR (*CANADA*) = **Newfoundland**

n

NG ABBR (US) = **National Guard**
NGO N ABBR = **non-governmental organization**
NH ABBR (US) = **New Hampshire**
NHL N ABBR (US: = National Hockey League) ≈ F.I.H.P. f (= Federazione Italiana Hockey e Pattinaggio)
NHS N ABBR (BRIT) = **National Health Service**
NI ABBR = **Northern Ireland**; (BRIT) = **National Insurance**
Niagara Falls [naɪˈægərə-] NPL: **the ~** le cascate del Niagara
nib [nɪb] N (of pen) pennino
nibble [ˈnɪbl] VT mordicchiare
Nicaragua [nɪkəˈrægjuə] N Nicaragua m
Nicaraguan [nɪkəˈrægjuən] ADJ, N nicaraguense (mf)
Nice [niːs] N Nizza
nice [naɪs] ADJ (holiday, trip) piacevole; (flat, picture) bello(-a); (person) simpatico(-a), gentile; (taste, smell, meal) buono(-a); (distinction, point) sottile
nice-looking [ˈnaɪslʊkɪŋ] ADJ bello(-a)
nicely [ˈnaɪslɪ] ADV bene; **that will do ~** andrà benissimo
niceties [ˈnaɪsɪtɪz] NPL finezze fpl
niche [niːʃ] N (Archit) nicchia
nick [nɪk] N taglietto; tacca ▶ VT intaccare; tagliare; (col: steal) rubare; (: BRIT: arrest) beccare; **in the ~ of time** appena in tempo; **in good ~** (BRIT col) decente, in buono stato; **to ~ o.s.** farsi un taglietto
nickel [ˈnɪkl] N nichel m; (US) moneta da cinque centesimi di dollaro
nickname [ˈnɪkneɪm] N soprannome m ▶ VT soprannominare
Nicosia [nɪkəˈsiːə] N Nicosia
nicotine [ˈnɪkətiːn] N nicotina
nicotine patch N cerotto antifumo (a base di nicotina)
niece [niːs] N nipote f
nifty [ˈnɪftɪ] ADJ (col: car, jacket) chic inv; (: gadget, tool) ingegnoso(-a)
Niger [ˈnaɪdʒəʳ] N Niger m
Nigeria [naɪˈdʒɪərɪə] N Nigeria
Nigerian [naɪˈdʒɪərɪən] ADJ, N nigeriano(-a)
niggardly [ˈnɪgədlɪ] ADJ (person) tirchio(-a), spilorcio(-a); (allowance, amount) misero(-a)
nigger [ˈnɪgəʳ] N (col!) negro(-a)
niggle [ˈnɪgl] VT assillare ▶ VI fare il pignolo(-a)
niggling [ˈnɪglɪŋ] ADJ pignolo(-a); (detail) insignificante; (doubt, pain) persistente
night [naɪt] N notte f; (evening) sera; **at ~** la notte, la sera; **by ~** di notte; **in the ~**, **during the ~** durante la notte; **the ~ before last** l'altro ieri notte; l'altro ieri sera
night-bird [ˈnaɪtbəːd] N uccello notturno; (fig) nottambulo(-a)

nightcap [ˈnaɪtkæp] N bicchierino prima di andare a letto
night club N locale m notturno
nightdress [ˈnaɪtdrɛs] N camicia da notte
nightfall [ˈnaɪtfɔːl] N crepuscolo
nightie [ˈnaɪtɪ] N camicia da notte
nightingale [ˈnaɪtɪŋgeɪl] N usignolo
night life [ˈnaɪtlaɪf] N vita notturna
nightly [ˈnaɪtlɪ] ADJ di ogni notte or sera; (by night) notturno(-a) ▶ ADV ogni notte or sera
nightmare [ˈnaɪtmɛəʳ] N incubo
night porter N portiere m di notte
night safe N cassa continua
night school N scuola serale
nightshade [ˈnaɪtʃeɪd] N: **deadly ~** (Bot) belladonna
nightshift [ˈnaɪtʃɪft] N turno di notte
night-time [ˈnaɪttaɪm] N notte f
night watchman N (irreg) guardiano notturno
nihilism [ˈnaɪɪlɪzəm] N nichilismo
nil [nɪl] N nulla m; (BRIT Sport) zero
Nile [naɪl] N: **the ~** il Nilo
nimble [ˈnɪmbl] ADJ agile
nine [naɪn] NUM nove
9-11 N 11 settembre
nineteen [naɪnˈtiːn] NUM diciannove
nineteenth [naɪnˈtiːnθ] NUM diciannovesimo(-a)
ninetieth [ˈnaɪntɪɪθ] NUM novantesimo(-a)
ninety [ˈnaɪntɪ] NUM novanta
ninth [naɪnθ] NUM nono(-a)
nip [nɪp] VT pizzicare; (bite) mordere ▶ VI (BRIT col): **to ~ out/down/up** fare un salto fuori/giù/di sopra ▶ N (pinch) pizzico; (drink) goccio, bicchierino
nipple [ˈnɪpl] N (Anat) capezzolo
nippy [ˈnɪpɪ] ADJ (weather) pungente; (BRIT: car, person) svelto(-a)
nit [nɪt] N (of louse) lendine m; (col: idiot) cretino(-a), scemo(-a)
nit-pick [ˈnɪtpɪk] VI (col) cercare il pelo nell'uovo
nitrogen [ˈnaɪtrədʒən] N azoto
nitroglycerin, nitroglycerine [naɪtrəʊˈglɪsəriːn] N nitroglicerina
nitty-gritty [ˈnɪtɪˈgrɪtɪ] N (col): **to get down to the ~** venire al sodo
nitwit [ˈnɪtwɪt] N (col) scemo(-a)
NJ ABBR (US) = **New Jersey**
NLF N ABBR (= National Liberation Front) ≈ F.L.N. m
NLRB N ABBR (US: = National Labor Relations Board) organismo per la tutela dei lavoratori
NM, N. Mex. ABBR (US) = **New Mexico**

(KEYWORD)

no [nəʊ] ADV (opposite of "yes") no; **are you coming? — no (I'm not)** viene? — no (non

vengo); **would you like some more? — no
thank you** ne vuole ancora un po'? — no,
grazie; **I have no more wine** non ho più
vino
▶ ADJ *(not any)* nessuno(-a); **I have no money/
time/books** non ho soldi/tempo/libri; **no
student would have done it** nessuno
studente lo avrebbe fatto; **there is no
reason to believe ...** non c'è nessuna
ragione per credere ...; **"no parking"**
"divieto di sosta"; **"no smoking"** "vietato
fumare"; **"no entry"** "ingresso vietato";
"no dogs" "vietato l'accesso ai cani"
▶ N *(pl* **noes)** no *m inv*; **I won't take no for an
answer** non accetterò un rifiuto

no. ABBR *(= number)* n.
nobble ['nɔbl] VT *(BRIT col: bribe: person)*
comprare, corrompere; *(person to speak to,
criminal)* bloccare, beccare; *(Racing: horse, dog)*
drogare
Nobel prize [nəu'bɛl-] N premio Nobel
nobility [nəu'bɪlɪtɪ] N nobiltà
noble ['nəubl] ADJ, N nobile *m*
nobleman ['nəublmən] N *(irreg)* nobile *m*,
nobiluomo
nobly ['nəublɪ] ADV *(selflessly)* generosamente
nobody ['nəubədɪ] PRON nessuno
no-claims bonus ['nəukleɪmz-] N bonus
malus *m inv*
nocturnal [nɔk'tə:nl] ADJ notturno(-a)
nod [nɔd] VI accennare col capo, fare un
cenno; *(in agreement)* annuire con un cenno
del capo; *(sleep)* sonnecchiare ▶ VT: **to ~
one's head** fare di sì col capo ▶ N cenno;
they nodded their agreement
accennarono di sì (col capo)
▶ **nod off** VI assopirsi
no-fly zone [nəu'flaɪ-] N zona di
interdizione aerea
noise [nɔɪz] N rumore *m*; *(din, racket)* chiasso
noiseless ['nɔɪzlɪs] ADJ silenzioso(-a)
noisily ['nɔɪzɪlɪ] ADV rumorosamente
noisy ['nɔɪzɪ] ADJ *(street, car)* rumoroso(-a);
(person) chiassoso(-a)
nomad ['nəumæd] N nomade *mf*
nomadic [nəu'mædɪk] ADJ nomade
no man's land N terra di nessuno
nominal ['nɔmɪnl] ADJ nominale; *(rent)*
simbolico(-a)
nominate ['nɔmɪneɪt] VT *(propose)* proporre
come candidato; *(elect)* nominare
nomination [nɔmɪ'neɪʃən] N nomina;
candidatura
nominee [nɔmɪ'ni:] N persona nominata;
candidato(-a)
non... [nɔn] PREFIX non...
non-alcoholic ['nɔnælkə'hɔlɪk] ADJ
analcolico(-a)

non-breakable [nɔn'breɪkəbl] ADJ
infrangibile
nonce word ['nɔns-] N parola coniata per
l'occasione
nonchalant ['nɔnʃələnt] ADJ incurante,
indifferente
non-commissioned [nɔnkə'mɪʃnd] ADJ:
~ officer sottufficiale *m*
non-committal [nɔnkə'mɪtl] ADJ evasivo(-a)
nonconformist [nɔnkən'fɔ:mɪst] N
anticonformista *mf*; *(BRIT Rel)* dissidente *mf*
▶ ADJ anticonformista
non-contributory [nɔnkən'trɪbjutərɪ] ADJ:
~ pension scheme *or* (US) **plan** *sistema di
pensionamento con i contributi interamente a carico
del datore di lavoro*
non-cooperation ['nɔnkəuɔpə'reɪʃən] N non
cooperazione *f*, non collaborazione *f*
nondescript ['nɔndɪskrɪpt] ADJ qualunque
inv
none [nʌn] PRON *(not one thing)* niente; *(not one
person)* nessuno(-a); **~ of you** nessuno(-a) di
voi; **I have ~** non ne ho nemmeno uno; **I
have ~ left** non ne ho più; **~ at all** proprio
niente; *(not one)* nemmeno uno; **he's ~ the
worse for it** non ne ha risentito
nonentity [nɔ'nɛntɪtɪ] N persona
insignificante
non-essential [nɔnɪ'sɛnʃl] ADJ non
essenziale ▶ N: **non-essentials** superfluo,
cose *fpl* superflue
nonetheless ['nʌnðə'lɛs] ADV nondimeno
non-event [nɔnɪ'vɛnt] N delusione *f*
non-executive [nɔnɪg'zɛkjutɪv] ADJ:
~ director direttore *m* senza potere esecutivo
non-existent [nɔnɪg'zɪstənt] ADJ inesistente
non-fiction [nɔn'fɪkʃən] N saggistica
non-flammable [nɔn'flæməbl] ADJ
ininfiammabile
non-intervention ['nɔnɪntə'vɛnʃən] N non
intervento
no-no ['nəunəu] N: **it's a ~!** *(undesirable)* è
inaccettabile!; *(forbidden)* non si può fare!
non obst. ABBR *(notwithstanding: = non obstante)*
nonostante
no-nonsense [nəu'nɔnsəns] ADJ che va al
sodo
non-payment [nɔn'peɪmənt] N mancato
pagamento
nonplussed [nɔn'plʌst] ADJ sconcertato(-a)
non-profit-making [nɔn'prɔfɪtmeɪkɪŋ] ADJ
senza scopo di lucro
nonsense ['nɔnsəns] N sciocchezze *fpl*; **~!** che
sciocchezze!, che assurdità!; **it is ~ to say
that ...** è un'assurdità *or* non ha senso dire
che ...
nonsensical [nɔn'sɛnsɪkl] ADJ assurdo(-a),
ridicolo(-a)
non-shrink [nɔn'ʃrɪŋk] ADJ *(BRIT)* irrestringibile

non-skid [nɔn'skɪd] ADJ antisdrucciolo(-a)
non-smoker ['nɔn'sməukə^r] N non
fumatore(-trice)
non-smoking ADJ (*person*) che non fuma;
(*area, section*) per non fumatori
non-starter [nɔn'stɑːtə^r] N: **it's a ~** è fallito
in partenza
non-stick ['nɔn'stɪk] ADJ antiaderente,
antiadesivo(-a)
non-stop ['nɔn'stɔp] ADJ continuo(-a); (*train*,
bus) direttissimo(-a) ▶ ADV senza sosta
non-taxable [nɔn'tæksəbl] ADJ: **~ income**
reddito non imponibile
non-U [nɔn'juː] ADJ ABBR (*BRIT col*) = **non-upper class**
non-volatile [nɔn'vɔlətaɪl] ADJ: **~ memory**
(*Comput*) memoria permanente
non-voting [nɔn'vəutɪŋ] ADJ: **~ shares** azioni
fpl senza diritto di voto
non-white ['nɔn'waɪt] ADJ di colore ▶ N
persona di colore
noodles ['nuːdlz] NPL taglierini *mpl*
nook [nuk] N: **nooks and crannies**
angoli *mpl*
noon [nuːn] N mezzogiorno
no one ['nəuwʌn] PRON = **nobody**
noose [nuːs] N nodo scorsoio, cappio;
(*hangman's*) cappio
nor [nɔː^r] CONJ = **neither** ▶ ADV *see* **neither**
norm [nɔːm] N norma
normal ['nɔːml] ADJ normale ▶ N: **to return
to ~** tornare alla normalità
normality [nɔː'mælɪtɪ] N normalità
normally ['nɔːməlɪ] ADV normalmente
Normandy ['nɔːməndɪ] N Normandia
north [nɔːθ] N nord *m*, settentrione *m* ▶ ADJ
nord *inv*, del nord, settentrionale ▶ ADV verso
nord
North Africa N Africa del Nord
North African ADJ, N nordafricano(-a)
North America N America del Nord
North American ADJ, N nordamericano(-a)
Northants [nɔː'θænts] ABBR (*BRIT*)
= **Northamptonshire**
northbound ['nɔːθbaund] ADJ (*traffic*)
diretto(-a) a nord; (*carriageway*) nord *inv*
north-east [nɔːθ'iːst] N nord-est *m*
northeastern ADJ nordorientale
northerly ['nɔːðəlɪ] ADJ (*wind*) del nord;
(*direction*) verso nord
northern ['nɔːðən] ADJ del nord,
settentrionale
Northern Ireland N Irlanda del Nord
North Korea N Corea del Nord
North Pole N: **the ~** il Polo Nord
North Sea N: **the ~** il mare del Nord
North Sea oil N petrolio del mare del Nord
northward ['nɔːθwəd], **northwards**
['nɔːθwədz] ADV verso nord

north-west [nɔːθ'wɛst] N nord-ovest *m*
northwestern ADJ nordoccidentale
Norway ['nɔːweɪ] N Norvegia
Norwegian [nɔː'wiːdʒən] ADJ norvegese
▶ N norvegese *mf*; (*Ling*) norvegese *m*
nos. ABBR (= *numbers*) nn.
nose [nəuz] N naso; (*of animal*) muso ▶ VI
(*also*: **nose one's way**) avanzare cautamente;
to pay through the ~ (for sth) (*col*) pagare
(qc) un occhio della testa
▶ **nose about, nose around** VI aggirarsi
nosebleed ['nəuzbliːd] N emorragia nasale
nose-dive ['nəuzdaɪv] N picchiata
nose drops NPL gocce *fpl* per il naso
nosey ['nəuzɪ] ADJ curioso(-a)
nostalgia [nɔs'tældʒɪə] N nostalgia
nostalgic [nɔs'tældʒɪk] ADJ nostalgico(-a)
nostril ['nɔstrɪl] N narice *f*; (*of horse*) frogia
nosy ['nəuzɪ] ADJ = **nosey**
not [nɔt] ADV non; **~ at all** niente affatto;
(*after thanks*) prego, s'immagini; **you must ~**
or **mustn't do this** non deve fare questo;
it's too late, isn't it or **is it ~?** è troppo tardi,
vero?; **he is ~** or **isn't here** non è qui, non c'è;
I hope ~ spero di no; **~ that I don't like him**
non che (lui) non mi piaccia; **~ yet/now** non
ancora/ora
notable ['nəutəbl] ADJ notevole
notably ['nəutəblɪ] ADV notevolmente;
(*in particular*) in particolare
notary ['nəutərɪ] N (*also*: **notary public**)
notaio
notation [nəu'teɪʃən] N notazione *f*
notch [nɔtʃ] N tacca; (*in saw*) dente *m*
▶ **notch up** VT (*score, victory*) marcare, segnare
note [nəut] N nota; (*letter, banknote*) biglietto
▶ VT prendere nota di; **to take ~ of** prendere
nota di; **to take notes** prendere appunti;
to compare notes (*fig*) scambiarsi le
impressioni; **of ~** eminente, importante;
just a quick ~ to let you know ... ti scrivo
solo due righe per informarti ...
notebook ['nəutbuk] N taccuino; (*for
shorthand*) bloc-notes *m inv*
note-case ['nəutkeɪs] N (*BRIT*) portafoglio
noted ['nəutɪd] ADJ celebre
notepad ['nəutpæd] N bloc-notes *m inv*,
blocchetto
notepaper ['nəutpeɪpə^r] N carta da lettere
noteworthy ['nəutwəːðɪ] ADJ degno(-a) di
nota, importante
nothing ['nʌθɪŋ] N nulla *m*, niente *m*; (*zero*)
zero; **he does ~** non fa niente; **~ new** niente
di nuovo; **for ~** (*free*) per niente; **~ at all**
proprio niente
notice ['nəutɪs] N avviso; (*of leaving*)
preavviso; (*BRIT*: *review: of play etc*) critica,
recensione *f* ▶ VT notare, accorgersi di; **to
take ~ of** fare attenzione a; **to bring sth to**

sb's ~ far notare qc a qn; **to give sb** ~ **of sth** avvisare qn di qc; **to hand in one's** ~, **give** ~ (*employee*) licenziarsi; **without** ~ senza preavviso; **at short** ~ con un breve preavviso; **until further** ~ fino a nuovo avviso; **advance** ~ preavviso; **to escape** *or* **avoid** ~ passare inosservato; **it has come to my** ~ **that** ... sono venuto a sapere che ...

noticeable ['nəʊtɪsəbl] ADJ evidente

notice board N (*BRIT*) tabellone *m* per affissi

notification [nəʊtɪfɪ'keɪʃən] N annuncio; notifica; denuncia

notify ['nəʊtɪfaɪ] VT: **to** ~ **sth to sb** notificare qc a qn; **to** ~ **sb of sth** avvisare qn di qc; (*police*) denunciare qc a qn

notion ['nəʊʃən] N idea; (*concept*) nozione *f*

notions ['nəʊʃənz] NPL (*US: haberdashery*) merceria

notoriety [nəʊtə'raɪətɪ] N notorietà

notorious [nəʊ'tɔ:rɪəs] ADJ famigerato(-a)

notoriously [nəʊ'tɔ:rɪəslɪ] ADV notoriamente

Notts [nɔts] ABBR (*BRIT*) = **Nottinghamshire**

notwithstanding [nɔtwɪθ'stændɪŋ] ADV nondimeno ▶ PREP nonostante, malgrado

nougat ['nu:gɑ:] N torrone *m*

nought [nɔ:t] N zero

noun [naʊn] N nome *m*, sostantivo

nourish ['nʌrɪʃ] VT nutrire

nourishing ['nʌrɪʃɪŋ] ADJ nutriente

nourishment ['nʌrɪʃmənt] N nutrimento

Nov. ABBR (= *November*) nov.

Nova Scotia ['nəʊvə'skəʊʃə] N Nuova Scozia

novel ['nɔvl] N romanzo ▶ ADJ nuovo(-a)

novelist ['nɔvəlɪst] N romanziere(-a)

novelty ['nɔvəltɪ] N novità *f inv*

November [nəʊ'vɛmbə'] N novembre *m*; *see also* **July**

novice ['nɔvɪs] N principiante *mf*; (*Rel*) novizio(-a)

NOW [naʊ] N ABBR (*US: = National Organization for Women*) ≈ U.D.I. *f* (= *Unione Donne Italiane*)

now [naʊ] ADV ora, adesso ▶ CONJ: ~ **(that)** adesso che, ora che; **right** ~ subito; **by** ~ ormai; **just** ~ proprio ora; **that's the fashion just** ~ è la moda del momento; **I saw her just** ~ l'ho vista proprio adesso; **I'll read it just** ~ lo leggo subito; ~ **and then**, ~ **and again** ogni tanto; **from** ~ **on** da ora in poi; **in 3 days from** ~ fra 3 giorni; **between** ~ **and Monday** da qui a lunedì, entro lunedì; **that's all for** ~ per ora basta

nowadays ['naʊədeɪz] ADV oggidì

nowhere ['nəʊwɛə'] ADV in nessun luogo, da nessuna parte; ~ **else** in nessun altro posto

no-win situation [nəʊ'wɪn-] N: **to be in a** ~ aver perso in partenza

noxious ['nɔkʃəs] ADJ nocivo(-a)

nozzle ['nɔzl] N (*of hose etc*) boccaglio; (*of fire extinguisher*) lancia

NP N ABBR = **notary public**

nr ABBR (*BRIT*) = **near**

NS ABBR (*CANADA*) = **Nova Scotia**

NSC N ABBR (*US*) = **National Security Council**

NSF N ABBR (*US*) = **National Science Foundation**

NSPCC N ABBR (*BRIT*) = **National Society for the Prevention of Cruelty to Children**

NSW ABBR (*AUSTRALIA*) = **New South Wales**

NT N ABBR (= *New Testament*) N.T. ▶ ABBR (*CANADA*) = **Northwest Territories**

nth [ɛnθ] ADJ: **for the** ~ **time** (*col*) per l'ennesima volta

nuance ['nju:ɑ:ns] N sfumatura

nubile ['nju:baɪl] ADJ nubile; (*attractive*) giovane e desiderabile

nuclear ['nju:klɪə'] ADJ nucleare; (*warfare*) atomico(-a)

nuclear disarmament N disarmo nucleare

nuclear family N famiglia nucleare

nuclear-free zone ['nju:klɪə'fri:-] N zona denuclearizzata

nucleus ['nju:klɪəs] (*pl* **nuclei** ['nju:klɪaɪ]) N nucleo

NUCPS N ABBR (*BRIT*) = **National Union of Civil and Public Servants**

nude [nju:d] ADJ nudo(-a) ▶ N (*Art*) nudo; **in the** ~ tutto(-a) nudo(-a)

nudge [nʌdʒ] VT dare una gomitata a

nudist ['nju:dɪst] N nudista *mf*

nudity ['nju:dɪtɪ] N nudità

nugget ['nʌgɪt] N pepita

nuisance ['nju:sns] N: **it's a** ~ è una seccatura; **he's a** ~ dà fastidio; **what a ~!** che seccatura!

NUJ N ABBR (*BRIT*: = *National Union of Journalists*) sindacato nazionale dei giornalisti

nuke [nju:k] N (*col*) bomba atomica

null [nʌl] ADJ: ~ **and void** nullo(-a)

nullify ['nʌlɪfaɪ] VT annullare

NUM N ABBR (*BRIT*: = *National Union of Mineworkers*) sindacato nazionale dei dipendenti delle miniere

numb [nʌm] ADJ intorpidito(-a) ▶ VT intorpidire; ~ **with** (*fear, grief*) paralizzato(-a) da, impietrito(-a) da; ~ **with cold** intirizzito(-a) (dal freddo)

number ['nʌmbə'] N numero ▶ VT numerare; (*include*) contare; **a** ~ **of** un certo numero di; **to be numbered among** venire annoverato(-a) tra; **telephone** ~ numero di telefono; **wrong** ~ (*Tel*) numero sbagliato; **the staff numbers 20** gli impiegati sono in 20; **they were 10 in** ~ erano in tutto 10

numbered account ['nʌmbəd-] N (*in bank*) conto numerato

number plate N (*BRIT Aut*) targa

Number Ten N (BRIT: = 10 Downing Street)
residenza del Primo Ministro del Regno Unito
numbness ['nʌmnɪs] N intorpidimento;
(due to cold) intirizzimento
numbskull ['nʌmskʌl] N (col) imbecille mf,
idiota mf
numeral ['njuːmərəl] N numero, cifra
numerate ['njuːmərɪt] ADJ (BRIT): **to be ~**
saper far di conto
numerical [njuː'mɛrɪkl] ADJ numerico(-a)
numerous ['njuːmərəs] ADJ numeroso(-a)
nun [nʌn] N suora, monaca
nunnery ['nʌnərɪ] N convento
nuptial ['nʌpʃəl] ADJ nuziale
nurse [nəːs] N infermiere(-a); (also:
nursemaid) bambinaia ▶ VT (patient, cold)
curare; (baby: BRIT) cullare; (: US) allattare,
dare il latte a; (hope) nutrire
nursery ['nəːsərɪ] N (room) camera dei
bambini; (institution) asilo; (for plants) vivaio
nursery rhyme N filastrocca
nursery school N scuola materna
nursery slope N (BRIT Ski) pista per
principianti
nursing ['nəːsɪŋ] N (profession) professione f
di infermiere (or di infermiera); (care) cura
▶ ADJ (mother) che allatta
nursing home N casa di cura
nurture ['nəːtʃəʳ] VT allevare; nutrire
NUS N ABBR (BRIT: = National Union of Students)
sindacato nazionale degli studenti
NUT N ABBR (BRIT: = National Union of Teachers)
sindacato nazionale degli insegnanti
nut [nʌt] N (of metal) dado; (fruit) noce f (or
nocciola or mandorla etc) ▶ ADJ (chocolate etc)
alla nocciola etc; **he's nuts** (col) è matto
nutcase ['nʌtkeɪs] N (col) mattarello(-a)
nutcrackers ['nʌtkrækəz] NPL schiaccianoci
m inv
nutmeg ['nʌtmɛg] N noce f moscata
nutrient ['njuːtrɪənt] ADJ nutriente ▶ N
sostanza nutritiva
nutrition [njuː'trɪʃən] N nutrizione f
nutritionist [njuː'trɪʃənɪst] N
nutrizionista mf
nutritious [njuː'trɪʃəs] ADJ nutriente
nutshell ['nʌtʃɛl] N guscio di noce; **in a ~**
in poche parole
nutty ['nʌtɪ] ADJ di noce (or nocciola or
mandorla etc); (BRIT col) tocco(-a), matto(-a)
nuzzle ['nʌzl] VI: **to ~ up to** strofinare il
muso contro
NV ABBR (US) = **Nevada**
NVQ N ABBR BRIT: = **National Vocational
Qualification**
NWT ABBR (CANADA) = **Northwest Territories**
NY ABBR (US) = **New York**
NYC ABBR (US) = **New York City**
nylon ['naɪlɔn] N nailon m ▶ ADJ di nailon;
nylons NPL calze fpl di nailon
nymph [nɪmf] N ninfa
nymphomaniac [nɪmfəu'meɪnɪæk] ADJ, N
ninfomane (f)
NYSE ABBR (US) = **New York Stock Exchange**

Oo

O, o [əu] N (letter) O, o f inv or m inv; (US Scol:
= outstanding) ≈ ottimo; (number: Tel etc) zero;
O for Oliver, (US) **O for Oboe** ≈ O come
Otranto

oaf [əuf] N zoticone m

oak [əuk] N quercia ▶ CPD di quercia

OAP N ABBR (BRIT) = **old-age pensioner**

oar [ɔːʳ] N remo; **to put** or **shove one's ~ in**
(fig: col) intromettersi

oarsman ['ɔːzmən], **oarswoman**
['ɔːzwumən] N (irreg) rematore(-trice)

OAS N ABBR (= Organization of American States)
O.S.A. f (= Organizzazione degli Stati Americani)

oasis [əu'eisis] (pl **oases** [əu'eisiːz]) N oasi f inv

oath [əuθ] N giuramento; (swear word)
bestemmia; **to take the ~** giurare; **on ~**
(BRIT) or **under ~** sotto giuramento

oatmeal ['əutmiːl] N farina d'avena

oats [əuts] NPL avena

obdurate ['ɔbdjurit] ADJ testardo(-a);
incallito(-a); ostinato(-a), irremovibile

OBE N ABBR (BRIT: = Order of the British Empire)
titolo

obedience [ə'biːdiəns] N ubbidienza;
in ~ to conformemente a

obedient [ə'biːdiənt] ADJ ubbidiente;
to be ~ to sb/sth ubbidire a qn/qc

obelisk ['ɔbilisk] N obelisco

obese [əu'biːs] ADJ obeso(-a)

obesity [əu'biːsiti] N obesità

obey [ə'bei] VT ubbidire a; (instructions,
regulations) osservare ▶ VI ubbidire

obituary [ə'bitjuəri] N necrologia

object N ['ɔbdʒikt] oggetto; (purpose) scopo,
intento; (Ling) complemento oggetto ▶ VI
[əb'dʒɛkt]: **to ~ to** (attitude) disapprovare;
(proposal) protestare contro, sollevare delle
obiezioni contro; **I ~!** mi oppongo!; **he
objected that ...** obiettò che ...; **do you ~ to
my smoking?** la disturba se fumo?; **what's
the ~ of doing that?** a che serve farlo?;
expense is no ~ non si bada a spese

objection [əb'dʒɛkʃən] N obiezione f;
(drawback) inconveniente m; **if you have no ~**
se non ha obiezioni; **to make** or **raise an ~**
sollevare un'obiezione

objectionable [əb'dʒɛkʃənəbl] ADJ
antipatico(-a); (smell) sgradevole; (language)
scostumato(-a)

objective [əb'dʒɛktiv] N obiettivo ▶ ADJ
obiettivo(-a)

objectivity [ɔbdʒik'tiviti] N obiettività

object lesson N: ~ **(in)** dimostrazione f (di)

objector [əb'dʒɛktəʳ] N oppositore(-trice)

obligation [ɔbli'geiʃən] N obbligo, dovere m;
(debt) obbligo (di riconoscenza); **"without
~"** "senza impegno"; **to be under an ~ to
sb/to do sth** essere in dovere verso qn/di
fare qc

obligatory [ə'bligətəri] ADJ obbligatorio(-a)

oblige [ə'blaidʒ] VT (do a favour) fare una
cortesia a; (force): **to ~ sb to do** costringere
qn a fare; **to be obliged to sb for sth** essere
grato a qn per qc; **anything to ~!** (col) questo
e altro!

obliging [ə'blaidʒiŋ] ADJ servizievole,
compiacente

oblique [ə'bliːk] ADJ obliquo(-a); (allusion)
indiretto(-a) ▶ N (BRIT Typ): ~ **(stroke)** barra

obliterate [ə'blitəreit] VT cancellare

oblivion [ə'bliviən] N oblio

oblivious [ə'bliviəs] ADJ: ~ **of** incurante di;
inconscio(-a) di

oblong ['ɔblɔŋ] ADJ oblungo(-a) ▶ N
rettangolo

obnoxious [əb'nɔkʃəs] ADJ odioso(-a); (smell)
disgustoso(-a), ripugnante

oboe ['əubəu] N oboe m

obscene [əb'siːn] ADJ osceno(-a)

obscenity [əb'sɛniti] N oscenità f inv

obscure [əb'skjuəʳ] ADJ oscuro(-a) ▶ VT
oscurare; (hide: sun) nascondere

obscurity [əb'skjuəriti] N oscurità;
(obscure point) punto oscuro; (lack of fame)
anonimato

obsequious [əb'siːkwiəs] ADJ ossequioso(-a)

observable [əb'zəːvəbl] ADJ osservabile;
(appreciable) notevole

observance [əb'zə:vns] N osservanza;
religious observances pratiche *fpl* religiose
observant [əb'zə:vnt] ADJ attento(-a)
observation [ɔbzə'veɪʃən] N osservazione *f*;
(*by police etc*) sorveglianza
observation post N (*Mil*) osservatorio
observatory [əb'zə:vətrɪ] N osservatorio
observe [əb'zə:v] VT osservare; (*remark*) fare
osservare
observer [əb'zə:və'] N osservatore(-trice)
obsess [əb'sɛs] VT ossessionare; **to be**
obsessed by *or* **with sb/sth** essere
ossessionato da qn/qc
obsession [əb'sɛʃən] N ossessione *f*
obsessive [əb'sɛsɪv] ADJ ossessivo(-a)
obsolescence [ɔbsə'lɛsns] N obsolescenza;
built-in *or* **planned ~** (*Comm*) obsolescenza
programmata
obsolescent [ɔbsə'lɛsnt] ADJ obsolescente
obsolete ['ɔbsəli:t] ADJ obsoleto(-a); (*word*)
desueto(-a)
obstacle ['ɔbstəkl] N ostacolo
obstacle race N corsa agli ostacoli
obstetrician [ɔbstə'trɪʃən] N ostetrico(-a)
obstetrics [ɔb'stɛtrɪks] N ostetrica
obstinacy ['ɔbstɪnəsɪ] N ostinatezza
obstinate ['ɔbstɪnɪt] ADJ ostinato(-a)
obstreperous [əb'strɛpərəs] ADJ
turbolento(-a)
obstruct [əb'strʌkt] VT (*block*) ostruire,
ostacolare; (*halt*) fermare; (*hinder*) impedire
obstruction [əb'strʌkʃən] N ostruzione *f*;
ostacolo
obstructive [əb'strʌktɪv] ADJ ostruttivo(-a);
che crea impedimenti
obtain [əb'teɪn] VT ottenere ▶ VI essere in
uso; **to ~ sth (for o.s.)** procurarsi qc
obtainable [əb'teɪnəbl] ADJ ottenibile
obtrusive [əb'tru:sɪv] ADJ (*person*)
importuno(-a); (*smell*) invadente; (*building*
etc) imponente e invadente
obtuse [əb'tju:s] ADJ ottuso(-a)
obverse ['ɔbvə:s] N opposto, inverso
obviate ['ɔbvɪeɪt] VT ovviare a, evitare
obvious ['ɔbvɪəs] ADJ ovvio(-a), evidente
obviously ['ɔbvɪəslɪ] ADV ovviamente; **~!**
certo!; **~ not!** certo che no!; **he was ~ not**
drunk si vedeva che non era ubriaco; **he**
was not ~ drunk non si vedeva che era
ubriaco
OCAS N ABBR = **Organization of Central**
American States
occasion [ə'keɪʒən] N occasione *f*; (*event*)
avvenimento ▶ VT cagionare; **on that ~** in
quell'occasione, quella volta; **to rise to the**
~ mostrarsi all'altezza della situazione
occasional [ə'keɪʒənl] ADJ occasionale; **I**
smoke an ~ cigarette ogni tanto fumo una
sigaretta

occasionally [ə'keɪʒənlɪ] ADV ogni tanto;
very ~ molto raramente
occasional table N tavolino
occult [ɔ'kʌlt] ADJ occulto(-a) ▶ N: **the ~**
l'occulto
occupancy ['ɔkjupənsɪ] N occupazione *f*
occupant ['ɔkjupənt] N occupante *mf*; (*of*
boat, car etc) persona a bordo
occupation [ɔkju'peɪʃən] N occupazione *f*;
(*job*) mestiere *m*, professione *f*; **unfit for ~**
(*house*) inabitabile
occupational [ɔkju'peɪʃənl] ADJ (*disease*)
professionale; (*hazard*) del mestiere;
~ accident infortunio sul lavoro
occupational guidance N (*Brit*)
orientamento professionale
occupational pension scheme N sistema
pensionistico programmato dal datore di lavoro
occupational therapy N ergoterapia
occupier ['ɔkjupaɪə'] N occupante *mf*
occupy ['ɔkjupaɪ] VT occupare; **to ~ o.s. by**
doing occuparsi a fare; **to be occupied with**
sth/in doing sth essere preso da qc/
occupato a fare qc
occur [ə'kə:'] VI accadere; (*difficulty,*
opportunity) capitare; (*phenomenon, error*)
trovarsi; **to ~ to sb** venire in mente a qn
occurrence [ə'kʌrəns] N caso, fatto; presenza
ocean ['əuʃən] N oceano; **oceans of** (*col*) un
sacco di
ocean bed N fondale *m* oceanico
ocean-going ['əuʃəngəuɪŋ] ADJ d'alto mare
Oceania [əuʃɪ'ɑ:nɪə] N Oceania
ocean liner N transatlantico
ochre, (*US*) **ocher** ['əukə'] ADJ ocra *inv*
o'clock [ə'klɔk] ADV: **it is one ~** è l'una; **it is**
5 ~ sono le 5
OCR N ABBR = **optical character reader;**
optical character recognition
Oct. ABBR (= *October*) ott.
octagonal [ɔk'tægənl] ADJ ottagonale
octane ['ɔkteɪn] N ottano; **high-~ petrol** *or*
(*US*) **gas** benzina ad alto numero di ottani
octave ['ɔktɪv] N ottava
October [ɔk'təubə'] N ottobre *m*; *see also* **July**
octogenarian [ɔktəudʒɪ'nɛərɪən] N
ottuagenario(-a)
octopus ['ɔktəpəs] N polpo, piovra
odd [ɔd] ADJ (*strange*) strano(-a), bizzarro(-a);
(*number*) dispari *inv*; (*left over*) in più; (*not of a*
set) spaiato(-a); **60-~** 60 e oltre; **at ~ times** di
tanto in tanto; **the ~ one out** l'eccezione *f*
oddball ['ɔdbɔ:l] N (*col*) eccentrico(-a)
oddity ['ɔdɪtɪ] N bizzarria; (*person*) originale
mf
odd-job man [ɔd'dʒɔb-] N (*irreg*) tuttofare *m*
inv
odd jobs NPL lavori *mpl* occasionali
oddly ['ɔdlɪ] ADV stranamente

oddments ['ɔdmənts] NPL (BRIT Comm) rimanenze fpl

odds [ɔdz] NPL (in betting) quota; **the ~ are against his coming** c'è poca probabilità che venga; **it makes no ~** non importa; **at ~** in contesa; **to succeed against all the ~** riuscire contro ogni aspettativa; **~ and ends** avanzi mpl

odds-on [ɔdz'ɔn] ADJ (col) probabile; **~ favourite** (Racing) favorito(-a)

ode [əud] N ode f

odious ['əudɪəs] ADJ odioso(-a), ripugnante

odometer [ɔ'dɔmɪtər] N odometro

odour, (US)**odor** ['əudər] N odore m; (unpleasant) cattivo odore

odourless, (US)**odorless** ['əudəlɪs] ADJ inodoro(-a)

OECD N ABBR (= Organization for Economic Cooperation and Development) O.C.S.E. f (= Organizzazione per la Cooperazione e lo Sviluppo Economico)

oesophagus, (US)**esophagus** [iː'sɔfəgəs] N esofago

oestrogen, (US)**estrogen** ['iːstrəudʒən] N estrogeno

(KEYWORD)

of [ɔv, əv] PREP **1** (gen) di; **a boy of 10** un ragazzo di 10 anni; **a friend of ours** un nostro amico; **that was kind of you** è stato molto gentile da parte sua
2 (expressing quantity, amount, dates etc) di; **a kilo of flour** un chilo di farina; **how much of this do you need?** quanto gliene serve?; **there were four of them** (people) erano in quattro; (objects) ce n'erano quattro; **three of us went** tre di noi sono andati; **the 5th of July** il 5 luglio; **a quarter of 4** (US) le 4 meno un quarto
3 (from, out of) di, in; **made of wood** (fatto) di or in legno

Ofcom ['ɔfkɔm] N ABBR (BRIT: = Office of Communications) organismo di regolamentazione delle telecomunicazioni

---

(KEYWORD)

off [ɔf] ADV **1** (distance: time): **it's a long way off** è lontano; **the game is 3 days off** la partita è tra 3 giorni
2 (departure, removal) via; **to go off to Paris** andarsene a Parigi; **I must be off** devo andare via; **to take off one's coat** togliersi il cappotto; **the button came off** il bottone è venuto via or si è staccato; **10% off** con lo sconto del 10%
3 (not at work): **to have a day off** avere un giorno libero; **to be off sick** essere assente per malattia

▶ ADJ (engine) spento(-a); (tap) chiuso(-a); (cancelled) sospeso(-a); (BRIT: food) andato(-a) a male; **to be well/badly off** essere/non essere benestante; **the lid was off** non c'era il coperchio; **I'm afraid the chicken is off** (BRIT: not available) purtroppo il pollo è finito; **on the off chance** nel caso; **to have an off day** non essere in forma; **that's a bit off, isn't it?** (fig: col) non è molto carino, vero?
▶ PREP **1** (motion, removal etc) da; (: distant from) a poca distanza da; **a street off the square** una strada che parte dalla piazza; **5km off the road** a 5km dalla strada; **off the coast** al largo della costa; **a house off the main road** una casa che non è sulla strada principale
2: **to be off meat** non mangiare più la carne

offal ['ɔfl] N (Culin) frattaglie fpl

offbeat ['ɔfbiːt] ADJ eccentrico(-a)

off-centre, (US)**off-center** [ɔf'sɛntər] ADJ storto(-a), fuori centro

off-colour ['ɔf'kʌlər] ADJ (BRIT: ill) malato(-a), indisposto(-a); **to feel ~** sentirsi poco bene

offence, (US)**offense** [ə'fɛns] N (Law) contravvenzione f; (: more serious) reato; **to give ~ to** offendere; **to take ~ at** offendersi per; **to commit an ~** commettere un reato

offend [ə'fɛnd] VT (person) offendere ▶ VI: **to ~ against** (law, rule) trasgredire

offender [ə'fɛndər] N delinquente mf; (against regulations) contravventore(-trice)

offending [ə'fɛndɪŋ] ADJ (often humorous): **the ~ word/object** la parola incriminata/l'oggetto incriminato

offense [ə'fɛns] N (US) = **offence**

offensive [ə'fɛnsɪv] ADJ offensivo(-a); (smell etc) sgradevole, ripugnante ▶ N (Mil) offensiva

offer ['ɔfər] N offerta, proposta ▶ VT offrire; **"on ~"** (Comm) "in offerta speciale"; **to make an ~ for sth** fare un'offerta per qc; **to ~ sth to sb, ~ sb sth** offrire qc a qn; **to ~ to do sth** offrirsi di fare qc

offering ['ɔfərɪŋ] N offerta

off-grid [ɔf'grɪd] ADJ autonomo non allacciato alla rete elettrica (o dell'acqua, del gas, ecc.)

offhand [ɔf'hænd] ADJ disinvolto(-a), noncurante ▶ ADV all'improvviso; **I can't tell you ~** non posso dirglielo su due piedi

office ['ɔfɪs] N (place) ufficio; (position) carica; **doctor's ~** (US) ambulatorio; **to take ~** entrare in carica; **through his good offices** con il suo prezioso aiuto; **O~ of Fair Trading** (BRIT) organismo di protezione contro le pratiche commerciali abusive

office automation N automazione f d'ufficio, burotica

office bearer N (of club etc) membro dell'amministrazione

office block, (US) **office building** N complesso di uffici

office boy N garzone m

office hours NPL orario d'ufficio; (US Med) orario di visite

office manager N capoufficio mf

officer [ˈɒfɪsəʳ] N (Mil etc) ufficiale m; (of organization) funzionario; (also: **police officer**) agente m di polizia

office work N lavoro d'ufficio

office worker N impiegato(-a) d'ufficio

official [əˈfɪʃl] ADJ (authorized) ufficiale ▶ N ufficiale m; (civil servant) impiegato(-a) statale; funzionario

officialdom [əˈfɪʃəldəm] N burocrazia

officially [əˈfɪʃəlɪ] ADV ufficialmente

official receiver N curatore m fallimentare

officiate [əˈfɪʃɪeɪt] VI (Rel) ufficiare; **to ~ as Mayor** esplicare le funzioni di sindaco; **to ~ at a marriage** celebrare un matrimonio

officious [əˈfɪʃəs] ADJ invadente

offing [ˈɒfɪŋ] N: **in the ~** (fig) in vista

off-key [ɒfˈkiː] ADJ stonato(-a) ▶ ADV fuori tono

off-licence [ˈɒflaɪsns] N (BRIT) spaccio di bevande alcoliche; vedi nota

> In Gran Bretagna e in Irlanda, gli *off-licences* sono esercizi pubblici specializzati nella vendita strettamente regolamentata di bevande alcoliche, per la quale è necessario avere un'apposita licenza. In genere sono aperti fino a tarda sera.

off-limits [ɒfˈlɪmɪts] ADJ (esp US) in cui vige il divieto d'accesso

off-line ADJ, ADV (Comput) off-line inv, non in linea; (: switched off) spento(-a)

off-load [ˈɒfləud] VT scaricare

off-peak [ˈɒfpiːk] ADJ (ticket etc) a tariffa ridotta; (time) non di punta

off-putting [ˈɒfputɪŋ] ADJ (BRIT) sgradevole

off-season [ˈɒfsiːzn] ADJ, ADV fuori stagione

offset [ˈɒfsɛt] VT (irreg: like **set**) (counteract) controbilanciare, compensare ▶ N (also: **offset printing**) offset m

offshoot [ˈɒfʃuːt] N (fig) diramazione f

offshore [ɒfˈʃɔːʳ] ADJ (breeze) di terra; (island) vicino alla costa; (fishing) costiero(-a); **~ oilfield** giacimento petrolifero in mare aperto

offside [ˈɒfsaɪd] ADJ (Sport) fuori gioco; (Aut: with right-hand drive) destro(-a); (: with left-hand drive) sinistro(-a) ▶ N destra; sinistra

offspring [ˈɒfsprɪŋ] N prole f, discendenza

offstage [ɒfˈsteɪdʒ] ADV dietro le quinte

off-the-cuff [ɒfðəˈkʌf] ADV improvvisando

off-the-job [ɒfðəˈdʒɔb] ADJ: **~ training** addestramento fuori sede

off-the-peg [ˈɒfðəˈpɛg], (US) **off-the-rack** [ˈɒfðəˈræk] ADV prêt-à-porter

off-the-record [ˈɒfðəˈrɛkɔːd] ADJ ufficioso(-a) ▶ ADV in via ufficiosa

off-white [ˈɒfwaɪt] ADJ bianco sporco inv

Ofgem [ˈɒfdʒɛm] N ABBR (BRIT: = Office of Gas and Electricity Markets) organo indipendente di controllo per la tutela dei consumatori

often [ˈɒfn] ADV spesso; **how ~ do you go?** quanto spesso ci va?; **as ~ as not** quasi sempre

Ofwat [ˈɒfwɔt] N ABBR (BRIT: = Office of Water Services) in Inghilterra e Galles, organo indipendente di controllo per la tutela dei consumatori

ogle [ˈəugl] VT occhieggiare

ogre [ˈəugəʳ] N orco

OH ABBR (US) = Ohio

oh [əu] EXCL oh!

OHMS ABBR (BRIT) = **On His Majesty's Service**; **On Her Majesty's Service**

oil [ɔɪl] N olio; (petroleum) petrolio; (for central heating) nafta ▶ VT (machine) lubrificare

oilcan [ˈɔɪlkæn] N oliatore m a mano; (for storing) latta da olio

oil change N cambio dell'olio

oilfield [ˈɔɪlfiːld] N giacimento, petrolifero

oil filter N (Aut) filtro dell'olio

oil-fired [ˈɔɪlfaɪəd] ADJ a nafta

oil gauge N indicatore m del livello dell'olio

oil industry N industria del petrolio

oil level N livello dell'olio

oil painting N quadro a olio

oil refinery N raffineria di petrolio

oil rig N derrick m inv; (at sea) piattaforma per trivellazioni subacquee

oilskins [ˈɔɪlskɪnz] NPL indumenti mpl di tela cerata

oil slick N chiazza d'olio

oil tanker N (ship) petroliera; (truck) autocisterna per petrolio

oil well N pozzo petrolifero

oily [ˈɔɪlɪ] ADJ unto(-a), oleoso(-a); (food) grasso(-a)

ointment [ˈɔɪntmənt] N unguento

OK ABBR (US) = **Oklahoma**

O.K., okay [əuˈkeɪ] EXCL d'accordo! ▶ VT approvare ▶ N: **to give sth one's O.K.** approvare qc ▶ ADJ non male inv; **is it O.K.?**, **are you O.K.?** tutto bene?; **it's O.K. with** or **by me** per me va bene; **are you O.K. for money?** sei a posto coi soldi?

Okla. ABBR (US) = **Oklahoma**

old [əuld] ADJ vecchio(-a); (ancient) antico(-a), vecchio(-a); (person) vecchio(-a), anziano(-a); **how ~ are you?** quanti anni ha?; **he's 10 years ~** ha 10 anni; **older brother/sister** fratello/sorella maggiore; **any ~ thing will do** va bene qualsiasi cosa

old age N vecchiaia

old-age pension [ˈəuldeɪdʒ-] N (BRIT) pensione f di vecchiaia

old-age pensioner [ˈəuldeɪdʒ-] N (BRIT)
pensionato(-a)

old-fashioned [ˈəuldˈfæʃnd] ADJ
antiquato(-a), fuori moda; (*person*) all'antica

old maid N zitella

old people's home N ricovero per anziani

old-style [ˈəuldstaɪl] ADJ (di) vecchio stampo
inv

old-time [ˈəuldtaɪm] ADJ di una volta

old-timer [əuldˈtaɪməʳ] N veterano(-a)

old wives' tale N vecchia superstizione f

O levels NPL (BRIT *formerly*) diploma di istruzione
secondaria conseguito a 16 anni in Inghilterra e
Galles, ora sostituito dal GCSE

olive [ˈɒlɪv] N (*fruit*) oliva; (*tree*) olivo ▶ ADJ
(*also*: **olive-green**) verde oliva *inv*

olive oil N olio d'oliva

Olympic [əuˈlɪmpɪk] ADJ olimpico(-a); **the ~**
Games, the Olympics i giochi olimpici, le
Olimpiadi

OM N ABBR (BRIT: = *Order of Merit*) titolo

Oman [əuˈmɑːn] N Oman *m*

OMB N ABBR (US: = *Office of Management and*
Budget) *servizio di consulenza al Presidente in*
materia di bilancio

omelet, omelette [ˈɒmlɪt] N omelette f *inv*;
ham/cheese ~(te) omelette al prosciutto/al
formaggio

omen [ˈəumən] N presagio, augurio

OMG ABBR (*col*) *nel linguaggio degli SMS, esprime*
sorpresa o entusiasmo

ominous [ˈɒmɪnəs] ADJ minaccioso(-a);
(*event*) di malaugurio

omission [əuˈmɪʃən] N omissione f

omit [əuˈmɪt] VT omettere; **to ~ to do sth**
tralasciare *or* trascurare di fare qc

omnivorous [ɒmˈnɪvərəs] ADJ onnivoro(-a)

ON ABBR (CANADA) = **Ontario**

⸻ KEYWORD ⸻

on [ɒn] PREP **1** (*indicating position*) su; **on the**
wall sulla parete; **on the left** a *or* sulla
sinistra; **I haven't any money on me** non
ho soldi con me

2 (*indicating means: method: condition etc*): **on**
foot a piedi; **on the train/plane** in treno/
aereo; **on the telephone** al telefono; **on the**
radio/television alla radio/televisione; **to**
be on drugs drogarsi; **he's on £16,000 a year** guadagna
16.000 sterline all'anno; **this round's on**
me questo giro lo offro io

3 (*referring to time*): **on Friday** venerdì; **on**
Fridays il *or* di venerdì; **on June 20th** il 20
giugno; **on Friday, June 20th** venerdì, 20
giugno; **a week on Friday** venerdì a otto;
on his arrival al suo arrivo; **on seeing this**
vedendo ciò

4 (*about, concerning*) su, di; **information on**

train services informazioni sui
collegamenti ferroviari; **a book on**
Goldoni/physics un libro su Goldoni/di *or*
sulla fisica

▶ ADV **1** (*referring to dress: covering*): **to have**
one's coat on avere indosso il cappotto; **to**
put one's coat on mettersi il cappotto;
what's she got on? cosa indossa?; **she put**
her boots/gloves/hat on si mise gli stivali/i
guanti/il cappello; **screw the lid on tightly**
avvita bene il coperchio

2 (*further, continuously*): **to walk on, go on** *etc*
continuare, proseguire; **to read on**
continuare a leggere; **on and off** ogni tanto;
from that day on da quel giorno in poi; **it**
was well on in the evening era sera
inoltrata

▶ ADJ **1** (*in operation: machine, TV, light*)
acceso(-a); (*tap*) aperto(-a); (*brake*)
inserito(-a); **is the meeting still on?** (*in*
progress) la riunione è ancora in corso?; (*not*
cancelled) è confermato l'incontro?; **there's a**
good film on at the cinema danno un buon
film al cinema; **when is the film on?**
quando c'è questo film?; **my father's**
always on at me to get a job (*col*) mio padre
mi tormenta sempre perché trovi un lavoro

2 (*col*): **that's not on!** (*not acceptable*) non si fa
così!; (*not possible*) non se ne parla neanche!

once [wʌns] ADV una volta ▶ CONJ non
appena, quando; **~ he had left/it was done**
dopo che se n'era andato/fu fatto; **at ~**
subito; (*simultaneously*) a un tempo; **all at**
~ (*tutto*) ad un tratto; **~ a week** una volta alla
settimana; **~ more** ancora una volta; **I**
knew him ~ un tempo *or* in passato lo
conoscevo; **~ and for all** una volta per
sempre; **~ upon a time there was …** c'era
una volta …

oncoming [ˈɒnkʌmɪŋ] ADJ (*traffic*) che viene
in senso opposto

⸻ KEYWORD ⸻

one [wʌn] NUM uno(-a); **one hundred and**
fifty centocinquanta; **one day** un giorno;
it's one (o'clock) è l'una; **to be one up on**
sb essere avvantaggiato(-a) rispetto a qn; **to**
be at one (with sb) andare d'accordo (con qn)

▶ ADJ **1** (*sole*) unico(-a); **the one book which**
l'unico libro che; **the one man who** l'unico
che

2 (*same*) stesso(-a); **they came in the one**
car sono venuti nella stessa macchina

▶ PRON **1**: **this one** questo(-a); **that one**
quello(-a); **which one do you want?**
quale vuole?; **I've already got one/a red**
one ne ho già uno/uno rosso; **one by one**
uno per uno

2: **one another** l'un l'altro; **to look at one another** guardarsi; **to help one another** aiutarsi l'un l'altro *or* a vicenda
3 (*impersonal*) si; **one never knows** non si sa mai; **to cut one's finger** tagliarsi un dito; **to express one's opinion** esprimere la propria opinione; **one needs to eat** bisogna mangiare

one-armed bandit ['wʌnɑːmd-] N slot-machine *f inv*
one-day excursion ['wʌndeɪ-] N (*US*) biglietto giornaliero di andata e ritorno
One-hundred share index ['wʌnhʌndrəd-] N *indice borsistico del Financial Times*
one-man ['wʌn'mæn] ADJ (*business*) diretto(-a) *etc* da un solo uomo
one-man band N *suonatore ambulante con vari strumenti*
one-off [wʌn'ɔf] (*BRIT col*) N fatto eccezionale
▶ ADJ eccezionale
one-parent family ['wʌnpɛərənt-] N famiglia monogenitore
one-piece ['wʌnpiːs] ADJ (*bathing suit*) intero(-a)
onerous ['ɔnərəs] ADJ (*task, duty*) gravoso(-a); (*responsibility*) pesante
oneself [wʌn'sɛlf] PRON (*reflexive*) si; (*after prep*) sé, se stesso(-a); **to do sth (by)** ~ fare qc da sé; **to hurt** ~ farsi male; **to keep sth for** ~ tenere qc per sé; **to talk to** ~ parlare da solo
one-shot [wʌn'ʃɔt] N (*US*) = **one-off**
one-sided [wʌn'saɪdɪd] ADJ (*decision, view, argument*) unilaterale; (*judgement, account*) parziale; (*game, contest*) impari *inv*
one-time ['wʌntaɪm] ADJ *ex inv*
one-to-one ['wʌntəwʌn] ADJ (*relationship*) univoco(-a)
one-upmanship [wʌn'ʌpmənʃɪp] N: **the art of** ~ l'arte *f* di primeggiare
one-way ['wʌnweɪ] ADJ (*street, traffic*) a senso unico
ongoing ['ɔngəuɪŋ] ADJ in corso; in attuazione
onion ['ʌnjən] N cipolla
on-line ['ɔnlaɪn] ADJ, ADV (*Comput*) on-line *inv*, in linea; (: *switched on*) acceso(-a)
onlooker ['ɔnlukər] N spettatore(-trice)
only ['əunlɪ] ADV solo, soltanto ▶ ADJ solo(-a), unico(-a) ▶ CONJ solo che, ma; **an** ~ **child** un figlio unico; **not** ~ non solo; **I** ~ **took one** ne ho preso soltanto uno, non ne ho preso che uno; **I saw her** ~ **yesterday** l'ho vista appena ieri; **I'd be** ~ **too pleased to help** sarei proprio felice di essere d'aiuto; **I would come,** ~ **I'm very busy** verrei volentieri, solo che sono molto occupato
ono ABBR = **or nearest offer**; *see* near
on-screen [ɔn'skriːn] ADJ sullo schermo *inv*
onset ['ɔnsɛt] N inizio; (*of winter*) arrivo

onshore ['ɔnʃɔːr] ADJ (*wind*) di mare
onslaught ['ɔnslɔːt] N attacco, assalto
Ont. ABBR (CANADA) = **Ontario**
on-the-job ['ɔnðə'dʒɔb] ADJ: ~ **training** addestramento in sede
onto ['ɔntu] PREP su, sopra
onus ['əunəs] N onere *m*, peso; **the** ~ **is upon him to prove it** sta a lui dimostrarlo
onward ['ɔnwəd], **onwards** ['ɔnwədz] ADV (*move*) in avanti; **from this time** ~(s) d'ora in poi
onyx ['ɔnɪks] N onice *f*
oops [ups] EXCL ops! (*esprime rincrescimento per un piccolo contrattempo*); ~-**a-daisy!** oplà!
ooze [uːz] VI stillare
opacity [əu'pæsɪtɪ] N opacità
opal ['əupl] N opale *m or f*
opaque [əu'peɪk] ADJ opaco(-a)
OPEC ['əupɛk] N ABBR (= *Organization of Petroleum-Exporting Countries*) O.P.E.C. *f*
open ['əupn] ADJ aperto(-a); (*road*) libero(-a); (*meeting*) pubblico(-a); (*admiration*) evidente, franco(-a); (*question*) insoluto(-a); (*enemy*) dichiarato(-a) ▶ VT aprire ▶ VI (*eyes, door, debate*) aprirsi; (*flower*) sbocciare; (*shop, bank, museum*) aprire; (*book etc*: *commence*) cominciare; **in the** ~ (**air**) all'aperto; **the** ~ **sea** il mare aperto, l'alto mare; ~ **ground** (*among trees*) radura; (*waste ground*) terreno non edificato; **to have an** ~ **mind (on sth)** non avere ancora deciso (su qc); **is it** ~ **to the public?** è aperto al pubblico?; **what time do you** ~? a che ora aprite?
▶ **open on to** VT FUS (*room, door*) dare su
▶ **open out** VT aprire ▶ VI aprirsi
▶ **open up** VT aprire; (*blocked road*) sgombrare
▶ VI aprirsi; (*shop, business*) aprire
open-air [əupn'ɛər] ADJ all'aperto
open-and-shut ['əupnən'ʃʌt] ADJ: ~ **case** caso indubbio
open day N (BRIT) giornata di apertura al pubblico
open-ended [əupn'ɛndɪd] ADJ (*fig*) aperto(-a), senza limiti
opener ['əupnər] N (*also*: **can opener, tin opener**) apriscatole *m inv*
open-heart [əupn'hɑːt] ADJ: ~ **surgery** chirurgia a cuore aperto
opening ['əupnɪŋ] N apertura; (*opportunity*) occasione *f*, opportunità *f inv*; sbocco; (*job*) posto vacante ▶ ADJ (*speech*) di apertura
opening hours NPL orario d'apertura
opening night N (*Theat*) prima
open learning N *sistema educativo secondo il quale lo studente ha maggior controllo e gestione delle modalità di apprendimento*
openly ['əupnlɪ] ADV apertamente
open-minded [əupn'maɪndɪd] ADJ che ha la mente aperta

open-necked ['əupnnɛkt] ADJ col collo slacciato

openness ['əupnnɪs] N *(frankness)* franchezza, sincerità

open-plan ['əupn'plæn] ADJ senza pareti divisorie

open prison N *istituto di pena dove viene data maggiore libertà ai detenuti*

open sandwich N canapè *m inv*

open shop N *fabbrica o ditta dove sono accolti anche operai non iscritti ai sindacati*

Open University N (BRIT); *vedi nota*

> La *Open University* (OU), fondata in Gran Bretagna nel 1969, organizza corsi universitari per corrispondenza o via Internet, basati anche su lezioni che vengono trasmesse dalla BBC per radio e per televisione e su corsi estivi.

opera ['ɔpərə] N opera

opera glasses NPL binocolo da teatro

opera house N opera

opera singer N cantante *mf* d'opera *or* lirico(-a)

operate ['ɔpəreɪt] VT *(machine)* azionare, far funzionare; *(system)* usare ▶ VI funzionare; *(drug, person)* agire; **to ~ on sb (for)** *(Med)* operare qn (di)

operatic [ɔpə'rætɪk] ADJ dell'opera, lirico(-a)

operating ['ɔpəreɪtɪŋ] ADJ *(Comm: costs etc)* di gestione; *(Med)* operatorio(-a)

operating room N *(US)* = **operating theatre**

operating system N *(Comput)* sistema *m* operativo

operating theatre N *(Med)* sala operatoria

operation [ɔpə'reɪʃən] N operazione *f*; **to be in ~** *(machine)* essere in azione *or* funzionamento; *(system)* essere in vigore; **to have an ~ (for)** *(Med)* essere operato(-a) (di)

operational [ɔpə'reɪʃənl] ADJ operativo(-a); *(Comm)* di gestione, d'esercizio; *(ready for use or action)* in attività, in funzione; **when the service is fully ~** quando il servizio sarà completamente in funzione

operative ['ɔpərətɪv] ADJ *(measure)* operativo(-a) ▶ N *(in factory)* operaio(-a); **the ~ word** la parola chiave

operator ['ɔpəreɪtəʳ] N *(of machine)* operatore(-trice); *(Tel)* centralinista *mf*

operetta [ɔpə'rɛtə] N operetta

ophthalmologist [ɔfθæl'mɔlədʒɪst] N oftalmologo(-a)

opinion [ə'pɪnjən] N opinione *f*, parere *m*; **in my ~** secondo me, a mio avviso; **to seek a second ~** *(Med etc)* consultarsi con un altro medico *etc*

opinionated [ə'pɪnjəneɪtɪd] ADJ dogmatico(-a)

opinion poll N sondaggio di opinioni

opium ['əupɪəm] N oppio

opponent [ə'pəunənt] N avversario(-a)

opportune ['ɔpətjuːn] ADJ opportuno(-a)

opportunist [ɔpə'tjuːnɪst] N opportunista *mf*

opportunity [ɔpə'tjuːnɪtɪ] N opportunità *f inv*, occasione *f*; **to take the ~ to do** *or* **of doing** cogliere l'occasione per fare

oppose [ə'pəuz] VT opporsi a; **opposed to** contrario(-a) a; **as opposed to** in contrasto con

opposing [ə'pəuzɪŋ] ADJ opposto(-a); *(team)* avversario(-a)

opposite ['ɔpəzɪt] ADJ opposto(-a); *(house etc)* di fronte ▶ ADV di fronte, dirimpetto ▶ PREP di fronte a ▶ N opposto, contrario; *(of word)* contrario; **"see ~ page"** "vedere pagina a fronte"; **the ~ sex** l'altro sesso

opposite number N controparte *f*, corrispondente *mf*

opposite sex N: **the ~** l'altro sesso

opposition [ɔpə'zɪʃən] N opposizione *f*

oppress [ə'prɛs] VT opprimere

oppression [ə'prɛʃən] N oppressione *f*

oppressive [ə'prɛsɪv] ADJ oppressivo(-a)

opprobrium [ə'prəubrɪəm] N *(formal)* obbrobrio

opt [ɔpt] VI: **to ~ for** optare per; **to ~ to do** scegliere di fare

> **opt out** VI: **to ~ out of** ritirarsi da; *(of NHS)* scegliere di non far più parte di; *(of agreement, arrangement)* scegliere di non partecipare a

optical ['ɔptɪkl] ADJ ottico(-a)

optical character reader N lettore *m* ottico

optical character recognition N lettura ottica di caratteri

optical fibre N fibra ottica

optician [ɔp'tɪʃən] N ottico

optics ['ɔptɪks] N ottica

optimism ['ɔptɪmɪzəm] N ottimismo

optimist ['ɔptɪmɪst] N ottimista *mf*

optimistic [ɔptɪ'mɪstɪk] ADJ ottimistico(-a)

optimum ['ɔptɪməm] ADJ ottimale

option ['ɔpʃən] N scelta; *(Scol)* materia facoltativa; *(Comm)* opzione *f*; **to keep one's options open** *(fig)* non impegnarsi; **I have no ~** non ho scelta

optional ['ɔpʃənl] ADJ facoltativo(-a); *(Comm)* a scelta; **~ extra** optional *m inv*

opulence ['ɔpjuləns] N opulenza

opulent ['ɔpjulənt] ADJ opulento(-a)

OR ABBR *(US)* = **Oregon**

or [ɔːʳ] CONJ o, oppure; *(with negative)*: **he hasn't seen or heard anything** non ha visto né sentito niente; **or else** se no, altrimenti; oppure

oracle ['ɔrəkl] N oracolo

oral ['ɔːrəl] ADJ orale ▶ N esame *m* orale

orange ['ɔrɪndʒ] N *(fruit)* arancia ▶ ADJ arancione

orangeade [ɔrɪndʒ'eɪd] N aranciata

orange juice N succo d'arancia

orange squash N succo d'arancia (*da diluire con l'acqua*)

oration [ɔːˈreɪʃən] N orazione f

orator [ˈɔrətəʳ] N oratore(-trice)

oratorio [ɔrəˈtɔːrɪəu] N oratorio

orb [ɔːb] N orbe m

orbit [ˈɔːbɪt] N orbita ▸ VT orbitare intorno a; **to be in/go into ~ (round)** essere/entrare in orbita (attorno a)

orbital [ˈɔːbɪtl] N (*also:* **orbital motorway**) raccordo anulare

orchard [ˈɔːtʃəd] N frutteto; **apple ~** meleto

orchestra [ˈɔːkɪstrə] N orchestra; (*US: seating*) platea

orchestral [ɔːˈkɛstrəl] ADJ orchestrale; (*concert*) sinfonico(-a)

orchestrate [ˈɔːkɪstreɪt] VT (*Mus: fig*) orchestrare

orchid [ˈɔːkɪd] N orchidea

ordain [ɔːˈdeɪn] VT (*Rel*) ordinare; (*decide*) decretare

ordeal [ɔːˈdiːl] N prova, travaglio

order [ˈɔːdəʳ] N ordine m; (*Comm*) ordinazione f ▸ VT ordinare; **to ~ sb to do** ordinare a qn di fare; **in ~** in ordine; (*document*) in regola; **in ~ of size** in ordine di grandezza; **in ~ to do** per fare; **in ~ that** affinché + *sub*; **a machine in working ~** una macchina che funziona bene; **out of ~** non in ordine; **to be out of ~** (*machine, toilets*) essere guasto(-a); (*telephone*) essere fuori servizio; **to place an ~ for sth with sb** ordinare qc a qn; **to the ~ of** (*Banking*) all'ordine di; **to be under orders to do sth** avere l'ordine di fare qc; **a point of ~** una questione di procedura; **to be on ~** essere stato ordinato; **made to ~** fatto su commissione; **the lower orders** (*pej*) i ceti inferiori

order book N copiacommissioni m inv

order form N modulo d'ordinazione

orderly [ˈɔːdəlɪ] N (*Mil*) attendente m; (*Med*) inserviente m ▸ ADJ (*room*) in ordine; (*mind*) metodico(-a); (*person*) ordinato(-a), metodico(-a)

order number N numero di ordinazione

ordinal [ˈɔːdɪnl] ADJ (*number*) ordinale

ordinary [ˈɔːdnrɪ] ADJ normale, comune; (*pej*) mediocre ▸ N: **out of the ~** diverso dal solito, fuori dell'ordinario

ordinary degree N laurea; *vedi nota*

> Il corso universitario di studi che porta al conferimento del *Bachelor's degree* può avere una durata diversa, a seconda del profitto dello studente. Chi non è interessato a proseguire gli studi oltre tre anni di corso può optare per l' *ordinary degree*; *vedi anche* **honours degree**.

ordinary seaman N (*irreg*) (*BRIT*) marinaio semplice

ordinary shares NPL azioni fpl ordinarie

ordination [ɔːdɪˈneɪʃən] N ordinazione f

ordnance [ˈɔːdnəns] N (*Mil: unit*) (reparto di) sussistenza

Ordnance Survey map N (*BRIT*) ≈ carta topografica dell'IGM

ore [ɔːʳ] N minerale m grezzo

Ore., Oreg. ABBR (*US*) = **Oregon**

oregano [ɔrɪˈgɑːnəu] N origano

organ [ˈɔːgən] N organo

organic [ɔːˈgænɪk] ADJ organico(-a); (*food, produce*) biologico(-a)

organism [ˈɔːgənɪzəm] N organismo

organist [ˈɔːgənɪst] N organista mf

organization [ɔːgənaɪˈzeɪʃən] N organizzazione f

organization chart N organigramma m

organize [ˈɔːgənaɪz] VT organizzare; **to get organized** organizzarsi

organized [ˈɔːgənaɪzd] ADJ organizzato(-a)

organized crime [ˈɔːgənaɪzd-] N criminalità organizzata

organized labour [ˈɔːgənaɪzd-] N manodopera organizzata

organizer [ˈɔːgənaɪzəʳ] N organizzatore(-trice)

orgasm [ˈɔːgæzəm] N orgasmo

orgy [ˈɔːdʒɪ] N orgia

Orient [ˈɔːrɪənt] N: **the ~** l'Oriente m

oriental [ɔːrɪˈɛntl] ADJ, N orientale (mf)

orientate [ˈɔːrɪənteɪt] VT orientare

orientation [ɔːrɪenˈteɪʃən] N orientamento

orifice [ˈɔrɪfɪs] N orifizio

origin [ˈɔrɪdʒɪn] N origine f; **country of ~** paese m d'origine

original [əˈrɪdʒɪnl] ADJ originale; (*earliest*) originario(-a) ▸ N originale m

originality [ərɪdʒɪˈnælɪtɪ] N originalità

originally [əˈrɪdʒɪnəlɪ] ADV (*at first*) all'inizio

originate [əˈrɪdʒɪneɪt] VI: **to ~ from** venire da, essere originario(-a) di; (*suggestion*) provenire da; **to ~ in** nascere in; (*custom*) avere origine in

originator [əˈrɪdʒɪneɪtəʳ] N iniziatore(-trice)

Orkneys [ˈɔːknɪz] NPL: **the ~** (*also:* **the Orkney Islands**) le (isole) Orcadi

ornament [ˈɔːnəmənt] N ornamento; (*trinket*) ninnolo

ornamental [ɔːnəˈmɛntl] ADJ ornamentale

ornamentation [ɔːnəmɛnˈteɪʃən] N decorazione f, ornamento

ornate [ɔːˈneɪt] ADJ molto ornato(-a)

ornithologist [ɔːnɪˈθɔlədʒɪst] N ornitologo(-a)

ornithology [ɔːnɪˈθɔlədʒɪ] N ornitologia

orphan [ˈɔːfn] N orfano(-a) ▸ VT: **to be orphaned** diventare orfano

orphanage [ˈɔːfənɪdʒ] N orfanotrofio

orthodox [ˈɔːθədɔks] ADJ ortodosso(-a)

orthopaedic,(US) **orthopedic** [ɔːθə'piːdɪk]
ADJ ortopedico(-a)
OS ABBR (BRIT: = *Ordnance Survey*) ≈ IGM *m*
= **Istituto Geografico Militare;** (*Naut*)
= **ordinary seaman;** (*Dress*) = **outsize**
O.S. ABBR = **out of stock**
Oscar ['ɔskə^r] N Oscar *m inv*
oscillate ['ɔsɪleɪt] VI oscillare
OSHA N ABBR (US: = *Occupational Safety and
Health Administration*) amministrazione per la
sicurezza e la salute sul lavoro
Oslo ['ɔzləu] N Oslo *f*
ostensible [ɔs'tɛnsɪbl] ADJ preteso(-a);
apparente
ostensibly [ɔs'tɛnsɪblɪ] ADV all'apparenza
ostentation [ɔstɛn'teɪʃən] N
ostentazione *f*
ostentatious [ɔstɛn'teɪʃəs] ADJ
pretenzioso(-a); ostentato(-a)
osteopath ['ɔstɪəpæθ] N specialista *mf* di
osteopatia
ostracize ['ɔstrəsaɪz] VT dare l'ostracismo a
ostrich ['ɔstrɪtʃ] N struzzo
OT ABBR (= *Old Testament*) V.T.
OTB N ABBR (US: = *off-track betting*) puntate
effettuate fuori dagli ippodromi
OTE ABBR (= *on-target earnings*) stipendio compreso
le commissioni
other ['ʌðə^r] ADJ altro(-a) ▶ PRON: **the ~**
l'altro(-a); **the others** gli altri; **the ~ day**
l'altro giorno; **some ~ people have still to
arrive** (alcuni) altri devono ancora arrivare;
some actor or ~ un certo attore; **somebody
or ~** qualcuno; **~ than** altro che; a parte; **the
car was none ~ than Roberta's** la
macchina era proprio di Roberta
otherwise ['ʌðəwaɪz] ADV, CONJ altrimenti;
an ~ good piece of work un lavoro
comunque buono
OTT ABBR (*col*) = **over the top;** *see* **top**
otter ['ɔtə^r] N lontra
OU N ABBR (BRIT) = **Open University**
ouch [autʃ] EXCL ohi!, ahi!
ought [ɔːt] AUX VB: **I ~ to do it** dovrei farlo;
this ~ to have been corrected questo
avrebbe dovuto essere corretto; **he ~ to win**
dovrebbe vincere; **you ~ to go and see it**
dovreste andare a vederlo, fareste bene ad
andarlo a vedere
ounce [auns] N oncia (= *28.35 g; 16 in a
pound*)
our [auə^r] ADJ il nostro(-a); (*pl*) i nostri(-e)
ours [auəz] PRON il nostro(-a); (*pl*) i
nostri(-e); *see also* **mine**¹
ourselves [auə'sɛlvz] PL PRON (*reflexive*) ci;
(*after preposition*) noi; (*emphatic*) noi stessi(-e);
we did it (all) by ~ l'abbiamo fatto (tutto) da
soli; *see also* **oneself**
oust [aust] VT cacciare, espellere

(KEYWORD)

out [aut] ADV (*gen*) fuori; **out here/there** qui/
là fuori; **to speak out loud** parlare forte; **to
have a night out** uscire una sera; **to be out
and about** *or* (US) **around again** essere di
nuovo in piedi; **the boat was 10 km out** la
barca era a 10 km dalla costa; **the journey
out** l'andata; **3 days out from Plymouth** a
3 giorni da Plymouth
▶ ADJ: **to be out** (*gen*) essere fuori; (*unconscious*)
aver perso i sensi; (*style, singer*) essere fuori
moda; **before the week was out** prima che
la settimana fosse finita; **to be out to do
sth** avere intenzione di fare qc; **he's out for
all he can get** sta cercando di trarne il
massimo profitto; **to be out in one's
calculations** aver sbagliato i calcoli
▶ PREP: **out of** (*outside, beyond*) fuori di; (*because
of*) per; (*origin*) da; (*without*) senza; **out of 10**
(*from among*) su 10; **to go out of the house**
uscire di casa; **to look out of the window**
guardare fuori dalla finestra; **out of pity**
per pietà; **out of boredom** per noia; **made
out of wood** (fatto) di *or* in legno; **to drink
out of a cup** bere da una tazza; **out of
petrol** senza benzina; **it's out of stock**
(*Comm*) è esaurito

outage ['autɪdʒ] N (*esp US: power failure*)
interruzione *f or* mancanza di corrente
elettrica
out-and-out ['autəndaut] ADJ vero(-a) e
proprio(-a)
outback ['autbæk] N zona isolata; (*in
Australia*) interno, entroterra
outbid [aut'bɪd] (*pt, pp* ~) VT fare un'offerta
più alta di
outboard ['autbɔːd] N: **~ (motor)** (motore *m*)
fuoribordo
outbound ['autbaund] ADJ: **~ (for *or* from)** in
partenza (per *or* da)
outbox ['autbɔks] N (*Comput*) posta in uscita;
(*US: out-tray*) vaschetta della corrispondenza
in uscita
outbreak ['autbreɪk] N scoppio; epidemia
outbuilding ['autbɪldɪŋ] N dipendenza
outburst ['autbəːst] N scoppio
outcast ['autkɑːst] N esule *mf*; (*socially*) paria
m inv
outclass [aut'klɑːs] VT surclassare
outcome ['autkʌm] N esito, risultato
outcrop ['autkrɔp] N affioramento
outcry ['autkraɪ] N protesta, clamore *m*
outdated [aut'deɪtɪd] ADJ (*custom, clothes*)
fuori moda; (*idea*) sorpassato(-a)
outdistance [aut'dɪstəns] VT distanziare
outdo [aut'duː] VT (*irreg: like* **do**) sorpassare
outdoor [aut'dɔː^r] ADJ all'aperto
outdoors [aut'dɔːz] ADV fuori; all'aria aperta

o

outer ['autər] ADJ esteriore; ~ **suburbs** estrema periferia

outer space N spazio cosmico

outfit ['autfɪt] N equipaggiamento; (clothes) completo; (: for sport) tenuta; (col: organization) organizzazione f

outfitter ['autfɪtər] N (BRIT): **"(gent's) outfitters"** "confezioni da uomo"

outgoing ['autgəuɪŋ] ADJ (president, tenant) uscente; (means of transport) in partenza; (character) socievole

outgoings ['autgəuɪŋz] NPL (BRIT: expenses) spese fpl, uscite fpl

outgrow [aut'grəu] VT (irreg: like **grow**) (clothes) diventare troppo grande per

outhouse ['authaus] N costruzione f annessa

outing ['autɪŋ] N gita; escursione f

outlandish [aut'lændɪʃ] ADJ strano(-a)

outlast [aut'la:st] VT sopravvivere a

outlaw ['autlɔ:] N fuorilegge mf ▶ VT (person) mettere fuori della legge; (practice) bandire

outlay ['autleɪ] N spese fpl; (investment) sborsa, spesa

outlet ['autlɛt] N (for liquid etc) sbocco, scarico; (for emotion) sfogo; (for goods) sbocco, mercato; (also: **retail outlet**) punto di vendita; (: US Elec) presa di corrente

outline ['autlaɪn] N contorno, profilo; (summary) abbozzo, grandi linee fpl ▶ VT (fig) descrivere a grandi linee

outlive [aut'lɪv] VT sopravvivere a

outlook ['autluk] N prospettiva, vista

outlying ['autlaɪɪŋ] ADJ periferico(-a)

outmanoeuvre, (US)**outmaneuver** [autmə'nu:vər] VT (rival etc) superare in strategia

outmoded [aut'məudɪd] ADJ passato(-a) di moda; antiquato(-a)

outnumber [aut'nʌmbər] VT superare in numero

out-of-court [autəv'kɔ:t] ADJ extragiudiziale ▶ ADV (settle) senza ricorrere al tribunale

out-of-date [autəv'deɪt] ADJ (passport, ticket) scaduto(-a); (theory, idea) sorpassato(-a), superato(-a); (custom) antiquato(-a); (clothes) fuori moda inv

out-of-doors [autəv'dɔ:z] ADV all'aperto

out-of-the-way ['autəvðə'weɪ] ADJ (remote) fuori mano; (unusual) originale, insolito(-a)

out-of-town [ˌautəv'taun] ADJ (shopping centre etc) inv uori città

outpatient ['autpeɪʃənt] N paziente mf esterno(-a)

outpost ['autpəust] N avamposto

outpouring ['autpɔ:rɪŋ] N (fig) torrente m

output ['autput] N produzione f; (Comput) output m inv ▶ VT emettere

outrage ['autreɪdʒ] N oltraggio; scandalo ▶ VT oltraggiare

outrageous [aut'reɪdʒəs] ADJ oltraggioso(-a); scandaloso(-a)

outrider ['autraɪdər] N (on motorcycle) battistrada m inv

outright ADV [aut'raɪt] completamente; schiettamente; apertamente; sul colpo ▶ ADJ ['autraɪt] completo(-a); schietto(-a) e netto(-a)

outrun [aut'rʌn] VT (irreg: like **run**) superare (nella corsa)

outset ['autsɛt] N inizio

outshine [aut'ʃaɪn] VT (irreg: like **shine**) (fig) eclissare

outside [aut'saɪd] N esterno, esteriore m ▶ ADJ esterno(-a), esteriore; (remote, unlikely): **an ~ chance** una vaga possibilità ▶ ADV fuori, all'esterno ▶ PREP fuori di, all'esterno di; **at the ~** (fig) al massimo; ~ **left/right** n (Football) ala sinistra/destra

outside broadcast N (Radio, TV) trasmissione f in esterno

outside lane N (Aut) corsia di sorpasso

outside line N (Tel) linea esterna

outsider [aut'saɪdər] N (in race etc) outsider m inv; (stranger) straniero(-a)

outsize ['autsaɪz] ADJ enorme; (clothes) per taglie forti

outskirts ['autskə:ts] NPL sobborghi mpl

outsmart [aut'sma:t] VT superare in astuzia

outspoken [aut'spəukən] ADJ molto franco(-a)

outspread ['autspred] ADJ (wings) aperto(-a), spiegato(-a)

outstanding [aut'stændɪŋ] ADJ eccezionale, di rilievo; (unfinished) non completo(-a); non evaso(-a); non regolato(-a); **your account is still ~** deve ancora saldare il conto

outstay [aut'steɪ] VT: **to ~ one's welcome** diventare un ospite sgradito

outstretched [aut'strɛtʃt] ADJ (hand) teso(-a); (body) disteso(-a)

outstrip [aut'strɪp] VT (also fig) superare

out-tray ['auttreɪ] N raccoglitore m per le carte da spedire

outvote [aut'vəut] VT: **to ~ sb (by)** avere la maggioranza rispetto a qn (per); **to ~ sth (by)** respingere qc (per)

outward ['autwəd] ADJ (sign, appearances) esteriore; (journey) d'andata

outwardly ['autwədlɪ] ADV esteriormente; in apparenza

outwards ['autwədz] ADV (esp BRIT) = **outward**

outweigh [aut'weɪ] VT avere maggior peso di

outwit [aut'wɪt] VT superare in astuzia

oval ['əuvl] ADJ ovale (m)

Oval Office N (US); vedi nota

L' *Oval Office* è una grande stanza di forma ovale nella *White House*, la Casa Bianca, dove ha sede l'ufficio del Presidente degli Stati Uniti. Spesso il termine è usato per indicare la stessa presidenza degli Stati Uniti.

ovarian [əu'vɛərɪən] ADJ ovarico(-a)

ovary ['əuvərɪ] N ovaia

ovation [əu'veɪʃən] N ovazione f

oven ['ʌvn] N forno

oven glove N guanto da forno

ovenproof ['ʌvnpruːf] ADJ da forno

oven-ready ['ʌvnrɛdɪ] ADJ pronto(-a) da infornare

ovenware ['ʌvnwɛəʳ] N vasellame m da mettere in forno

over ['əuvəʳ] ADV al di sopra; (excessively) molto, troppo ▶ ADJ, ADV (finished) finito(-a), terminato(-a); (too much) troppo; (remaining) che avanza ▶ PREP su; sopra; (above) al di sopra di; (on the other side of) di là di; (more than) più di; (during) durante; ~ **here** qui; ~ **there** là; **all** ~ (everywhere) dappertutto; (finished) tutto(-a) finito(-a); ~ **and** ~ (again) più e più volte; ~ **and above** oltre (a); **to ask** ~ invitare qn (a passare); **now** ~ **to our Rome correspondent** diamo ora la linea al nostro corrispondente da Roma; **the world** ~ in tutto il mondo; **she's not** ~ -**intelligent** (BRIT) non è troppo intelligente; **they fell out** ~ **money** litigarono per una questione di denaro

over... ['əuvəʳ] PREFIX: **overabundant** sovrabbondante

overact [əuvər'ækt] VI (Theat) esagerare or strafare la propria parte

overall ADJ ['əuvərɔːl] totale ▶ N ['əuvərɔːl] (BRIT) grembiule m ▶ ADV [əuvər'ɔːl] nell'insieme, complessivamente; **overalls** NPL tuta (da lavoro)

overall majority N maggioranza assoluta

overanxious [əuvər'æŋkʃəs] ADJ troppo ansioso(-a)

overawe [əuvər'ɔː] VT intimidire

overbalance [əuvə'bæləns] VI perdere l'equilibrio

overbearing [əuvə'bɛərɪŋ] ADJ imperioso(-a), prepotente

overboard ['əuvəbɔːd] ADV (Naut) fuori bordo, in acqua; **to go** ~ **for sth** (fig) impazzire per qc

overbook [əuvə'buk] VT sovrapprenotare

overcame [əuvə'keɪm] PT of **overcome**

overcapitalize [əuvə'kæpɪtəlaɪz] VT sovraccapitalizzare

overcast ['əuvəkɑːst] ADJ (sky) coperto(-a)

overcharge [əuvə'tʃɑːdʒ] VT: **to** ~ **sb for sth** far pagare troppo caro a qn per qc

overcoat ['əuvəkəut] N soprabito, cappotto

overcome [əuvə'kʌm] VT (irreg: like **come**) superare; sopraffare; ~ **with grief** sopraffatto(-a) dal dolore

overconfident [əuvə'kɒnfɪdənt] ADJ troppo sicuro(-a) (di sé), presuntuoso(-a)

overcrowded [əuvə'kraudɪd] ADJ sovraffollato(-a)

overcrowding [əuvə'kraudɪŋ] N sovraffollamento; (in bus) calca

overdo [əuvə'duː] VT (irreg: like **do**) esagerare; (overcook) cuocere troppo; **to** ~ **it**, **to** ~ **things** (work too hard) lavorare troppo

overdone [əuvə'dʌn] ADJ troppo cotto(-a)

overdose ['əuvədəus] N dose f eccessiva

overdraft ['əuvədrɑːft] N scoperto (di conto)

overdrawn [əuvə'drɔːn] ADJ (account) scoperto(-a)

overdrive ['əuvədraɪv] N (Aut) overdrive m inv

overdue [əuvə'djuː] ADJ in ritardo; (recognition) tardivo(-a); (bill) insoluto(-a); **that change was long** ~ quel cambiamento ci voleva da tempo

overemphasis [əuvər'ɛmfəsɪs] N: ~ **on sth** importanza eccessiva data a qc

overemphasize [əuvər'ɛmfəsaɪz] VT dare un'importanza eccessiva a

overestimate [əuvər'ɛstɪmeɪt] VT sopravvalutare

overexcited [əuvərɪk'saɪtɪd] ADJ sovraeccitato(-a)

overexertion [əuvərɪg'zəːʃən] N logorio (fisico)

overexpose [əuvərɪk'spəuz] VT (Phot) sovraesporre

overflow VI [əuvə'fləu] traboccare ▶ N ['əuvəfləu] eccesso; (also: **overflow pipe**) troppopieno

overfly [əuvə'flaɪ] VT (irreg: like **fly**) sorvolare

overgenerous [əuvə'dʒənərəs] ADJ troppo generoso(-a)

overgrown [əuvə'grəun] ADJ (garden) ricoperto(-a) di vegetazione; **he's just an** ~ **schoolboy** è proprio un bambinone

overhang [əuvə'hæŋ] VT (irreg: like **hang**) sporgere da ▶ VI sporgere

overhaul VT [əuvə'hɔːl] revisionare ▶ N ['əuvəhɔːl] revisione f

overhead ADV [əuvə'hɛd] di sopra ▶ ADJ ['əuvəhɛd] aereo(-a); (lighting) verticale ▶ N ['əuvəhɛd] (US) = **overheads**

overhead projector N lavagna luminosa

overheads ['əuvəhɛdz] NPL (BRIT) spese fpl generali

overhear [əuvə'hɪəʳ] VT (irreg: like **hear**) sentire (per caso)

overheat [əuvə'hiːt] VI surriscaldarsi

overjoyed [əuvə'dʒɔɪd] ADJ pazzo(-a) di gioia

overkill ['əuvəkɪl] N (fig) strafare m

overland ['əuvəlænd] ADJ, ADV per via di terra

overlap VI [əuvə'læp] sovrapporsi ▶ N ['əuvəlæp] sovrapposizione f

overleaf [əuvə'liːf] ADV a tergo

overload [əuvə'ləud] VT sovraccaricare

overlook [əuvə'luk] VT (have view of) dare su; (miss) trascurare; (forgive) passare sopra a

overlord ['əuvəlɔːd] N capo supremo

O

overmanning [əuvə'mænɪŋ] N eccedenza di manodopera

overnight [əuvə'naɪt] (*happen*) durante la notte; (*fig*) tutto ad un tratto ▶ ADJ ['əuvənaɪt] di notte; fulmineo(-a); **he stayed there ~** ci ha passato la notte; **if you travel ~ ...** se viaggia di notte ...; **he'll be away ~** passerà la notte fuori

overnight bag N borsa da viaggio

overpass ['əuvəpɑːs] N cavalcavia *m inv*

overpay [əuvə'peɪ] VT (*irreg: like* **pay**): **to ~ sb by £50** pagare 50 sterline in più a qn

overplay [əuvə'pleɪ] VT dare troppa importanza a; **to ~ one's hand** sopravvalutare la propria posizione

overpower [əuvə'pauəʳ] VT sopraffare

overpowering [əuvə'pauərɪŋ] ADJ irresistibile; (*heat, stench*) soffocante

overproduction ['əuvəprə'dʌkʃən] N sovrapproduzione *f*

overrate [əuvə'reɪt] VT sopravvalutare

overreach [əuvə'riːtʃ] VT: **to ~ o.s.** volere strafare

overreact [əuvəriː'ækt] VI reagire in modo esagerato

override [əuvə'raɪd] VT (*irreg: like* **ride**) (*order, objection*) passar sopra a; (*decision*) annullare

overriding [əuvə'raɪdɪŋ] ADJ preponderante

overrule [əuvə'ruːl] VT (*decision*) annullare; (*claim*) respingere

overrun [əuvə'rʌn] VT (*irreg: like* **run**) (*Mil: country etc*) invadere; (: *time limit etc*) superare, andare al di là di ▶ VI protrarsi; **the town is ~ with tourists** la città è invasa dai turisti

overseas [əuvə'siːz] ADV oltremare; (*abroad*) all'estero ▶ ADJ (*trade*) estero(-a); (*visitor*) straniero(-a)

oversee [əuvə'siː] VT (*irreg: like* **see**) sorvegliare

overseer ['əuvəsiəʳ] N (*in factory*) caposquadra *m*

overshadow [əuvə'ʃædəu] VT far ombra su; (*fig*) eclissare

overshoot [əuvə'ʃuːt] VT (*irreg: like* **shoot**) superare

oversight ['əuvəsaɪt] N omissione *f*, svista; **due to an ~** per una svista

oversimplify [əuvə'sɪmplɪfaɪ] VT rendere troppo semplice

oversleep [əuvə'sliːp] VI (*irreg: like* **sleep**) dormire troppo a lungo

overspend [əuvə'spend] VI (*irreg: like* **spend**) spendere troppo; **we have overspent by 5000 dollars** abbiamo speso 5000 dollari di troppo

overspill ['əuvəspɪl] N eccedenza di popolazione

overstaffed [əuvə'stɑːft] ADJ: **to be ~** avere troppo personale

overstate [əuvə'steɪt] VT esagerare

overstatement [əuvə'steɪtmənt] N esagerazione *f*

overstay [əuvə'steɪ] VT: **to ~ one's welcome** trattenersi troppo a lungo (come ospite)

overstep [əuvə'step] VT: **to ~ the mark** superare ogni limite

overstock [əuvə'stɔk] VT sovrapprovvigionare, sovraimmagazzinare

overstretched [əuvə'stretʃt] ADJ sovraccarico(-a); (*budget*) arrivato(-a) al limite

overstrike N ['əuvəstraɪk] (*on printer*) sovrapposizione *f* (di caratteri) ▶ VT [əuvə'straɪk] (*irreg: like* **strike**) sovrapporre

overt [əu'vəːt] ADJ palese

overtake [əuvə'teɪk] VT (*irreg: like* **take**) sorpassare

overtaking [əuvə'teɪkɪŋ] N (*Aut*) sorpasso

overtax [əuvə'tæks] VT (*Econ*) imporre tasse eccessive a, tassare eccessivamente; (*fig: strength, patience*) mettere alla prova, abusare di; **to ~ o.s.** chiedere troppo alle proprie forze

overthrow [əuvə'θrəu] VT (*irreg: like* **throw**) (*government*) rovesciare

overtime ['əuvətaɪm] N (*lavoro*) straordinario; **to do** *or* **work ~** fare lo straordinario

overtime ban N rifiuto sindacale a fare gli straordinari

overtone ['əuvətəun] N (*also:* **overtones**) sfumatura

overtook [əuvə'tuk] PT *of* **overtake**

overture ['əuvətʃuəʳ] N (*Mus*) ouverture *f inv*; (*fig*) approccio

overturn [əuvə'təːn] VT rovesciare ▶ VI rovesciarsi

overview ['əuvəvjuː] N visione *f* d'insieme

overweight [əuvə'weɪt] ADJ (*person*) troppo grasso(-a); (*luggage*) troppo pesante

overwhelm [əuvə'welm] VT sopraffare; sommergere; schiacciare

overwhelming [əuvə'welmɪŋ] ADJ (*victory, defeat*) schiacciante; (*heat, desire*) intenso(-a); **one's ~ impression is of heat** l'impressione dominante è quella di caldo

overwhelmingly [əuvə'welmɪŋlɪ] ADV in massa

overwork [əuvə'wəːk] VT far lavorare troppo ▶ VI lavorare troppo, strapazzarsi

overwrite [əuvə'raɪt] VT (*irreg: like* **write**) (*Comput*) ricoprire

overwrought [əuvə'rɔːt] ADJ molto agitato(-a)

ovulation [ɔvjuˈleɪʃən] N ovulazione *f*

ow [au] EXCL ahi!

owe [əu] VT dovere; **to ~ sb sth, to ~ sth to sb** dovere qc a qn

owing to ['əuɪŋtuː] PREP a causa di

owl [aul] N gufo

own [əun] ADJ proprio(-a) ▶ VT possedere ▶ VI (*BRIT*): **to ~ to sth** ammettere qc; **to ~ to**

having done sth ammettere di aver fatto qc; **a room of my** ~ la mia propria camera; **to get one's ~ back** vendicarsi; **on one's ~** tutto(-a) solo(-a); **can I have it for my (very) ~?** posso averlo tutto per me?; **to come into one's ~** mostrare le proprie qualità
▶ **own up** VI confessare
own brand N (*Comm*) etichetta propria
owner ['əunər] N proprietario(-a)
owner-occupier ['əunər'ɔkjupaɪər] N proprietario/a della casa in cui abita
ownership ['əunəʃɪp] N possesso; **it's under new ~** ha un nuovo proprietario
own goal N (*also fig*) autogol *m inv*
ox [ɔks] (*pl* **oxen** ['ɔksn]) N bue *m*
Oxbridge ['ɔksbrɪdʒ] N *le università di Oxford e/o Cambridge; vedi nota*

La parola *Oxbridge* deriva dalla fusione dei nomi Ox(ford) e (Cam)bridge e fa riferimento a queste due antiche università.

oxen ['ɔksn] NPL *of* **ox**
Oxfam ['ɔksfæm] N ABBR (*BRIT*: = *Oxford Committee for Famine Relief*) *organizzazione per aiuti al terzo mondo*
oxide ['ɔksaɪd] N ossido
Oxon. ['ɔksn] ABBR (*BRIT*: *of Oxford*) = **Oxoniensis**
oxtail ['ɔksteɪl] N: ~ **soup** minestra di coda di bue
oxyacetylene ['ɔksɪə'sɛtɪliːn] ADJ ossiacetilenico(-a); ~ **burner**, ~ **lamp** cannello ossiacetilenico
oxygen ['ɔksɪdʒən] N ossigeno
oxygen mask N maschera ad ossigeno
oxygen tent N tenda ad ossigeno
oyster ['ɔɪstər] N ostrica
oz. ABBR = **ounce**
ozone ['əuzəun] N ozono
ozone-friendly ['əuzəun'frɛndlɪ] ADJ che non danneggia lo strato d'ozono
ozone layer N fascia d'ozono

o

Pp

P, p [piː] N (letter) P, p f inv or m inv; **P for Peter**
≈ P come Padova

P ABBR = **president; prince**

p [piː] ABBR (= page) p; (BRIT) = **penny; pence**

PA N ABBR = **personal assistant; public
address system** ▶ ABBR (US) = **Pennsylvania**

pa [pɑː] N (col) papà m inv, babbo

p.a. ABBR = **per annum**

PAC N ABBR (US) = **political action committee**

pace [peɪs] N passo; (speed) passo; velocità
▶ VI: **to ~ up and down** camminare su e giù;
to keep ~ with camminare di pari passo a;
(events) tenersi al corrente di; **to put sb
through his paces** (fig) mettere qn alla
prova; **to set the ~** (running) fare l'andatura;
(fig) dare il la or il tono

pacemaker ['peɪsmeɪkə^r] N (Med) pacemaker
m inv, stimolatore m cardiaco; (Sport) chi fa
l'andatura

Pacific [pə'sɪfɪk] ADJ pacifico(-a) ▶ N: **the ~
(Ocean)** il Pacifico, l'Oceano Pacifico

pacification [pæsɪfɪ'keɪʃən] N pacificazione f

pacifier ['pæsɪfaɪə^r] N (US: dummy) succhiotto,
ciuccio (col)

pacifist ['pæsɪfɪst] N pacifista mf

pacify ['pæsɪfaɪ] VT pacificare; (soothe)
calmare

pack [pæk] N (packet) pacco; (Comm)
confezione f; (US: of cigarettes) pacchetto;
(of goods) balla; (of hounds) muta; (of wolves)
branco; (of thieves etc) banda; (of cards) mazzo
▶ VT (goods) impaccare, imballare; (in suitcase
etc) mettere; (box) riempire; (cram) stipare,
pigiare; (press down) tamponare; turare;
(Comput) comprimere, impaccare ▶ VI: **to ~
one's bags** fare la valigia; **to send sb
packing** (col) spedire via qn
▶ **pack in** (BRIT col) VI (watch, car) guastarsi
▶ VT mollare, piantare; **~ it in!** piantala!,
dacci un taglio!
▶ **pack off** VT (col: person) spedire; **to ~ sb off**
spedire via qn
▶ **pack up** VI (BRIT col: machine) guastarsi;
(person) far fagotto ▶ VT (belongings, clothes)
mettere in una valigia; (goods, presents)
imballare

package ['pækɪdʒ] N pacco; balla; (also:
package deal) pacchetto; forfait m inv ▶ VT
(goods) confezionare

package holiday N (BRIT) vacanza
organizzata

package tour N viaggio organizzato

packaging ['pækɪdʒɪŋ] N confezione f,
imballo

packed [pækt] ADJ (crowded) affollato(-a);
~ lunch (BRIT) pranzo al sacco

packer ['pækə^r] N (person) imballatore(-trice)

packet ['pækɪt] N pacchetto

packet switching [-swɪtʃɪŋ] N (Comput)
commutazione f di pacchetto

pack ice ['pækaɪs] N banchisa

packing ['pækɪŋ] N imballaggio

packing case N cassa da imballaggio

pact [pækt] N patto, accordo; trattato

pad [pæd] N blocco; (for inking) tampone m;
(to prevent friction) cuscinetto; (col: flat)
appartamentino ▶ VT imbottire ▶ VI: **to ~
about/in** etc camminare/entrare etc a passi
felpati

padded ADJ imbottito(-a)

padded cell ['pædɪd-] N cella imbottita

padding ['pædɪŋ] N imbottitura; (fig)
riempitivo

paddle ['pædl] N (oar) pagaia; (US: for table
tennis) racchetta da ping-pong ▶ VI sguazzare
▶ VT (boat) fare andare a colpi di pagaia

paddle steamer N battello a ruote

paddling pool ['pædlɪŋ-] N (BRIT) piscina per
bambini

paddock ['pædək] N prato recintato; (at
racecourse) paddock m inv

paddy ['pædɪ] N (also: **paddy field**) risaia

padlock ['pædlɒk] N lucchetto ▶ VT chiudere
con il lucchetto

padre ['pɑːdrɪ] N cappellano

Padua ['pædʒuə] N Padova

paediatrician, (US) **pediatrician**
[piːdɪə'trɪʃən] N pediatra mf

paediatrics, (US) **pediatrics** [piːdɪˈætrɪks] N pediatria

paedophile, (US) **pedophile** ['piːdəufaɪl] ADJ, N pedofilo(-a)

pagan ['peɪgən] ADJ, N pagano(-a)

page [peɪdʒ] N pagina; (also: **page boy**) fattorino; (: at wedding) paggio ▶ VT (in hotel etc) (far) chiamare

pageant ['pædʒənt] N spettacolo storico; grande cerimonia

pageantry ['pædʒəntrɪ] N pompa

page break N interruzione f di pagina

pager ['peɪdʒəʳ] N (Tel) cicalino, cercapersone m inv

paginate ['pædʒɪneɪt] VT impaginare

pagination [pædʒɪ'neɪʃən] N impaginazione f

pagoda [pə'gəudə] N pagoda

paid [peɪd] PT, PP of **pay** ▶ ADJ (work, official) rimunerato(-a); **to put ~ to** (BRIT) mettere fine a

paid-up ['peɪdʌp], (US) **paid in** ['peɪdɪn] ADJ (member) che ha pagato la sua quota; (share) interamente pagato(-a); **~ capital** capitale m interamente versato

pail [peɪl] N secchio

pain [peɪn] N dolore m; **to be in ~** soffrire, aver male; **to have a ~ in** aver male or un dolore a; **to take pains to do** mettercela tutta per fare; **on ~ of death** sotto pena di morte

pained [peɪnd] ADJ addolorato(-a), afflitto(-a)

painful ['peɪnful] ADJ doloroso(-a), che fa male; (difficult) difficile, penoso(-a)

painfully ['peɪnfəlɪ] ADV (fig: very) fin troppo

painkiller ['peɪnkɪləʳ] N antalgico, antidolorifico

painstaking ['peɪnzteɪkɪŋ] ADJ (person) sollecito(-a); (work) accurato(-a)

paint [peɪnt] N (for house etc) tinta, vernice f; (Art) colore m ▶ VT (Art: walls) dipingere; (: door etc) verniciare; **a tin of ~** un barattolo di tinta or vernice; **to ~ the door blue** verniciare la porta di azzurro; **to ~ in oils** dipingere a olio

paintbox ['peɪntbɔks] N scatola di colori

paintbrush ['peɪntbrʌʃ] N pennello

painter ['peɪntəʳ] N (artist) pittore m; (decorator) imbianchino

painting ['peɪntɪŋ] N (activity: of artist) pittura; (: of decorator) imbiancatura; verniciatura; (picture) dipinto, quadro

paint-stripper ['peɪntstrɪpəʳ] N prodotto sverniciante

paintwork ['peɪntwəːk] N (BRIT) tinta; (: of car) vernice f

pair [pɛəʳ] N (of shoes, gloves etc) paio; (of people) coppia; duo m inv; **a ~ of scissors/trousers** un paio di forbici/pantaloni

▶ **pair off** VI: **to ~ off (with sb)** fare coppia (con qn)

pajamas [pə'dʒɑːməz] NPL (US) pigiama m

Pakistan [pɑːkɪ'stɑːn] N Pakistan m

Pakistani [pɑːkɪ'stɑːnɪ] ADJ, N pakistano(-a)

PAL [pæl] N ABBR (TV: = phase alternation line) PAL m

pal [pæl] N (col) amico(-a), compagno(-a)

palace ['pæləs] N palazzo

palatable ['pælɪtəbl] ADJ gustoso(-a)

palate ['pælɪt] N palato

palatial [pə'leɪʃəl] ADJ sontuoso(-a), sfarzoso(-a)

palaver [pə'lɑːvəʳ] N chiacchiere fpl; storie fpl

pale [peɪl] ADJ pallido(-a) ▶ VI impallidire
▶ N: **to be beyond the ~** aver oltrepassato ogni limite; **to grow** or **turn ~** (person) diventare pallido(-a), impallidire; **to ~ into insignificance (beside)** perdere d'importanza (nei confronti di); **~ blue** azzurro or blu pallido inv

paleness ['peɪlnɪs] N pallore m

Palestine ['pælɪstaɪn] N Palestina

Palestinian [pælɪs'tɪnɪən] ADJ, N palestinese (mf)

palette ['pælɪt] N tavolozza

paling ['peɪlɪŋ] N (stake) palo; (fence) palizzata

palisade [pælɪ'seɪd] N palizzata

pall [pɔːl] N (of smoke) cappa ▶ VI: **to ~ (on)** diventare noioso(-a) (a)

pallet ['pælɪt] N (for goods) paletta

pallid ['pælɪd] ADJ pallido(-a), smorto(-a)

pallor ['pæləʳ] N pallore m

pally ['pælɪ] ADJ (col) amichevole

palm [pɑːm] N (Anat) palma, palmo; (also: **palm tree**) palma ▶ VT: **to ~ sth off on sb** (col) rifilare qc a qn

palmist ['pɑːmɪst] N chiromante mf

Palm Sunday N Domenica delle Palme

palpable ['pælpəbl] ADJ palpabile

palpitation [pælpɪ'teɪʃən] N palpitazione f; **to have palpitations** avere le palpitazioni

paltry ['pɔːltrɪ] ADJ derisorio(-a), insignificante

pamper ['pæmpəʳ] VT viziare, coccolare

pamphlet ['pæmflət] N dépliant m inv; (political etc) volantino, manifestino

pan [pæn] N (also: **saucepan**) casseruola; (also: **frying pan**) padella ▶ VI (Cine) fare una panoramica; **to ~ for gold** (lavare le sabbie aurifere per) cercare l'oro

panacea [pænə'sɪə] N panacea

panache [pə'næʃ] N stile m

Panama ['pænəmɑː] N Panama m

Panama Canal N canale m di Panama

Panamanian [pænə'meɪnɪən] ADJ, N panamense (mf)

pancake ['pænkeɪk] N frittella

Pancake Day N (BRIT) martedì m grasso

pancake roll N crêpe ripiena di verdure alla cinese
pancreas ['pæŋkrɪəs] N pancreas *m inv*
panda ['pændə] N panda *m inv*
panda car N (*BRIT*) auto *f* della polizia
pandemic [pæn'dɛmɪk] N pandemia
pandemonium [pændɪ'məʊnɪəm] N pandemonio
pander ['pændər] VI: **to ~ to** lusingare; concedere tutto a
p & h ABBR (*US*: = *postage and handling*) affrancatura e trasporto
P & L ABBR (= *profit and loss*) P.P.
p & p ABBR (*BRIT*: = *postage and packing*) affrancatura ed imballaggio
pane [peɪn] N vetro
panel ['pænl] N (*of wood, cloth etc*) pannello; (*Radio, TV*) giuria
panel game N (*BRIT*) quiz *m inv* a squadre
panelling, (*US*) **paneling** ['pænəlɪŋ] N rivestimento a pannelli
panellist, (*US*) **panelist** ['pænəlɪst] N partecipante *mf* (al quiz, alla tavola rotonda *etc*)
pang [pæŋ] N: **to feel pangs of remorse** essere torturato(-a) dal rimorso; **pangs of hunger** spasimi *mpl* della fame; **pangs of conscience** morsi *mpl* di coscienza
panhandler ['pænhændlər] N (*US col*) accattone(-a)
panic ['pænɪk] N panico ▶ VI perdere il sangue freddo
panic buying [-baɪɪŋ] N accaparramento (*di generi alimentari ecc*)
panicky ['pænɪkɪ] ADJ (*person*) pauroso(-a)
panic-stricken ['pænɪkstrɪkən] ADJ (*person*) preso(-a) dal panico, in preda al panico; (*look*) terrorizzato(-a)
pannier ['pænɪər] N (*on animal*) bisaccia; (*on bicycle*) borsa
panorama [pænə'rɑːmə] N panorama *m*
panoramic [pænə'ræmɪk] ADJ panoramico(-a)
pansy ['pænzɪ] N (*Bot*) viola del pensiero, pensée *f inv*; (*col, pej*) femminuccia
pant [pænt] VI ansare
pantechnicon [pæn'tɛknɪkən] N (*BRIT*) grosso furgone *m* per traslochi
panther ['pænθər] N pantera
panties ['pæntɪz] NPL slip *m*, mutandine *fpl*
pantihose ['pæntɪhəʊz] N (*US*) collant *m inv*
panto ['pæntəʊ] N (*BRIT col*) *see* **pantomime**
pantomime ['pæntəmaɪm] N (*BRIT*: *at Christmas*) spettacolo natalizio; (*tecnica*) pantomima; *vedi nota*

> In Gran Bretagna la *pantomime* (abbreviata in *panto*) è una sorta di libera interpretazione delle favole più conosciute che vengono messe in scena nei teatri durante il periodo natalizio.

Gli attori principali sono la dama, *dame*, che è un uomo vestito da donna, il protagonista, *principal boy*, che è una donna travestita da uomo, e il cattivo, *villain*. È uno spettacolo per tutta la famiglia, che prevede la partecipazione del pubblico.

pantry ['pæntrɪ] N dispensa
pants [pænts] NPL (*BRIT*) mutande *fpl*, slip *m*; (*US: trousers*) pantaloni *mpl*
pantsuit ['pæntsuːt] N (*US*) completo *m or* tailleur *m inv* pantalone *inv*
papacy ['peɪpəsɪ] N papato
papal ['peɪpəl] ADJ papale, pontificio(-a)
paparazzi [pæpə'rætsiː] NPL paparazzi *mpl*
paper ['peɪpər] N carta; (*also:* **wallpaper**) carta da parati, tappezzeria; (*also:* **newspaper**) giornale *m*; (*: study, article*) saggio; (*: exam*) prova scritta ▶ ADJ di carta ▶ VT tappezzare; **a piece of ~** (*odd bit*) un pezzo di carta; (*sheet*) un foglio (di carta); **to put sth down on ~** mettere qc per iscritto; *see also* **papers**
paper advance N (*on printer*) avanzamento della carta
paperback ['peɪpəbæk] N tascabile *m*; edizione *f* economica ▶ ADJ: **~ edition** edizione *f* tascabile
paper bag N sacchetto di carta
paperboy ['peɪpəbɔɪ] N (*selling*) strillone *m*; (*delivering*) ragazzo che recapita i giornali
paper clip N graffetta, clip *f inv*
paper handkerchief N fazzolettino di carta
paper mill N cartiera
paper money N cartamoneta, moneta cartacea
paper profit N utile *m* teorico
papers ['peɪpəz] NPL (*also:* **identity papers**) carte *fpl*, documenti *mpl*
paper shop N (*BRIT*) giornalaio (*negozio*)
paperweight ['peɪpəweɪt] N fermacarte *m inv*
paperwork ['peɪpəwəːk] N lavoro amministrativo
papier-mâché ['pæpɪeɪ'mæʃeɪ] N cartapesta
paprika ['pæprɪkə] N paprica
Pap test, Pap smear ['pæp-] N (*Med*) pap-test *m inv*
par [pɑːr] N parità, pari *f*; (*Golf*) norma; **on a ~ with** alla pari con; **at/above/below ~** (*Comm*) alla/sopra la/sotto la pari; **above/below ~** (*gen, Golf*) al di sopra/al di sotto della norma; **to feel below** *or* **under** *or* **not up to ~** non sentirsi in forma
parable ['pærəbl] N parabola (*Rel*)
parabola [pə'ræbələ] N parabola (*Math*)
paracetamol [pærə'siːtəmɔl] N (*BRIT*) paracetamolo
parachute ['pærəʃuːt] N paracadute *m inv* ▶ VI scendere col paracadute

parachute jump N lancio col paracadute
parachutist ['pærəʃuːtɪst] N paracadutista
mf
parade [pə'reɪd] N parata; (*inspection*) rivista,
rassegna ▶ VT (*fig*) fare sfoggio di ▶ VI sfilare
in parata; **a fashion ~** (*BRIT*) una sfilata di
moda
parade ground N piazza d'armi
paradise ['pærədaɪs] N paradiso
paradox ['pærədɔks] N paradosso
paradoxical [pærə'dɔksɪkl] ADJ paradossale
paradoxically [pærə'dɔksɪklɪ] ADV
paradossalmente
paraffin ['pærəfɪn] N (*BRIT*): ~ **(oil)** paraffina;
liquid ~ olio di paraffina
paraffin heater N (*BRIT*) stufa al cherosene
paraffin lamp N (*BRIT*) lampada al cherosene
paragon ['pærəgən] N modello di perfezione
or di virtù
paragraph ['pærəgrɑːf] N paragrafo; **to
begin a new ~** andare a capo
Paraguay ['pærəgwaɪ] N Paraguay *m*
Paraguayan [pærə'gwaɪən] ADJ, N
paraguaiano(-a)
parallel ['pærəlɛl] ADJ (*also Comput*)
parallelo(-a); (*fig*) analogo(-a) ▶ N (*line*)
parallela; (*fig, Geo*) parallelo; ~ **(with** *or* **to)**
parallelo(-a) (a)
paralysed ['pærəlaɪzd] ADJ paralizzato(-a)
paralysis [pə'rælɪsɪs] (*pl* **paralyses** [-siːz]) N
paralisi *f inv*
paralytic [pærə'lɪtɪk] ADJ paralitico(-a); (*BRIT
col: drunk*) ubriaco(-a) fradicio(-a)
paralyze ['pærəlaɪz] VT paralizzare
paramedic [pærə'mɛdɪk] N paramedico
parameter [pə'ræmɪtə] N parametro
paramilitary [pærə'mɪlɪtərɪ] ADJ
paramilitare
paramount ['pærəmaunt] ADJ: **of ~
importance** di capitale importanza
paranoia [pærə'nɔɪə] N paranoia
paranoid ['pærənɔɪd] ADJ paranoico(-a)
paranormal [pærə'nɔːml] ADJ paranormale
paraphernalia [pærəfə'neɪlɪə] N attrezzi
mpl, roba
paraphrase ['pærəfreɪz] VT parafrasare
paraplegic [pærə'pliːdʒɪk] N paraplegico(-a)
parapsychology [pærəsaɪ'kɔlədʒɪ] N
parapsicologia
parasite ['pærəsaɪt] N parassita *m*
parasol ['pærəsɔl] N parasole *m inv*
paratrooper ['pærətruːpə] N paracadutista
m (soldato)
parcel ['pɑːsl] N pacco, pacchetto ▶ VT (*also:
parcel up) impaccare
▶ **parcel out** VT spartire
parcel bomb N (*BRIT*) pacchetto esplosivo
parcel post N servizio pacchi
parch [pɑːtʃ] VT riardere

parched ['pɑːtʃt] ADJ (*person*) assetato(-a)
parchment ['pɑːtʃmənt] N pergamena
pardon ['pɑːdn] N perdono; grazia ▶ VT
perdonare; (*Law*) graziare; ~! scusi!; ~ **me!**
mi scusi!; **I beg your ~!** scusi!; **(I beg your)
~?**, (*US*) ~ **me?** prego?
pare [pɛə] VT (*BRIT: nails*) tagliarsi; (: *fruit etc*)
sbucciare, pelare
parent ['pɛərənt] N padre *m (or* madre *f)*;
parents NPL genitori *mpl*
parentage ['pɛərəntɪdʒ] N natali *mpl*; **of
unknown ~** di genitori sconosciuti
parental [pə'rɛntl] ADJ dei genitori
parent company N società madre *f inv*
parenthesis [pə'rɛnθɪsɪs] (*pl* **parentheses**
[-siːz]) N parentesi *f inv*; **in parentheses**
fra parentesi
parenthood ['pɛərənthud] N paternità *or*
maternità
parenting ['pɛərəntɪŋ] N mestiere *m* di
genitore
Paris ['pærɪs] N Parigi *f*
parish ['pærɪʃ] N parrocchia; (*BRIT: civil*)
≈ municipio ▶ ADJ parrocchiale
parish council N (*BRIT*) ≈ consiglio comunale
parishioner [pə'rɪʃənə] N parrocchiano(-a)
Parisian [pə'rɪzɪən] ADJ, N parigino(-a)
parity ['pærɪtɪ] N parità
park [pɑːk] N parco; (*public*) giardino
pubblico ▶ VT, VI parcheggiare
parka ['pɑːkə] N eskimo
park and ride N parcheggio di interscambio
parking ['pɑːkɪŋ] N parcheggio; **"no ~"**
"sosta vietata"
parking lights NPL luci *fpl* di posizione
parking lot N (*US*) posteggio, parcheggio
parking meter N parchimetro
parking offence N (*BRIT*) infrazione *f* al
divieto di sosta
parking place N posto di parcheggio
parking ticket N multa per sosta vietata
parking violation N (*US*) = **parking offence**
Parkinson's ['pɑːkɪnsənz] N (*also:
Parkinson's disease) morbo di Parkinson
parkway ['pɑːkweɪ] N (*US*) viale *m*
parlance ['pɑːləns] N: **in common/modern
~** nel gergo *or* linguaggio comune/moderno
parliament ['pɑːləmənt] N parlamento;
vedi nota

> Nel Regno Unito il Parlamento, *Parliament*,
> è formato da due camere: la *House of
> Commons*, e la *House of Lords*. Nella *House
> of Commons* siedono 650 parlamentari,
> chiamati *MPs*, eletti per votazione diretta
> del popolo nelle rispettive circoscrizioni
> elettorali, le *constituencies*. Le sessioni del
> Parlamento sono presiedute e moderate
> dal presidente della Camera, lo *Speaker*.
> Alla *House of Lords*, i cui poteri sono più

P

limitati, in passato si accedeva per nomina o per carica ereditaria mentre ora le cariche ereditarie sono state ridotte e in futuro verranno abolite.

parliamentary [pɑːləˈmɛntərɪ] ADJ parlamentare

parlour, (US) **parlor** [ˈpɑːləʳ] N salotto

parlous [ˈpɑːləs] ADJ periglioso(-a)

Parmesan [pɑːmɪˈzæn] N (also: **Parmesan cheese**) parmigiano

parochial [pəˈrəukɪəl] ADJ parrocchiale; (pej) provinciale

parody [ˈpærədɪ] N parodia

parole [pəˈrəul] N: **on ~** in libertà per buona condotta

paroxysm [ˈpærəksɪzəm] N (Med) parossismo; (of anger, laughter, coughing) convulso; (of grief) attacco

parquet [ˈpɑːkeɪ] N: **~ floor(ing)** parquet m

parrot [ˈpærət] N pappagallo

parrot fashion ADV in modo pappagallesco

parry [ˈpærɪ] VT parare

parsimonious [pɑːsɪˈməunɪəs] ADJ parsimonioso(-a)

parsley [ˈpɑːslɪ] N prezzemolo

parsnip [ˈpɑːsnɪp] N pastinaca

parson [ˈpɑːsn] N prete m; (Church of England) parroco

part [pɑːt] N parte f; (of machine) pezzo; (Theat etc) parte, ruolo; (Mus) voce f; parte; (US: in hair) scriminatura ▶ ADJ in parte ▶ ADV = **partly** ▶ VT separare ▶ VI (people) separarsi; (roads) dividersi; **to take ~ in** prendere parte a; **to take sb's ~** parteggiare per qn, prendere le parti di qn; **on his ~** da parte sua; **for my ~** per parte mia; **for the most ~** in generale; nella maggior parte dei casi; **for the better ~ of the day** per la maggior parte della giornata; **to be ~ and parcel of** essere parte integrante di; **to take sth in good/bad ~** prendere bene/male qc; **~ of speech** (Ling) parte del discorso

▶ **part with** VT FUS separarsi da; rinunciare a

partake [pɑːˈteɪk] VI (irreg: like **take**) (formal): **to ~ of sth** consumare qc, prendere qc

part exchange N (Brit): **in ~** in pagamento parziale

partial [ˈpɑːʃl] ADJ parziale; **to be ~ to** avere un debole per

partially [ˈpɑːʃəlɪ] ADV in parte, parzialmente

participant [pɑːˈtɪsɪpənt] N: **~ (in)** partecipante mf (a)

participate [pɑːˈtɪsɪpeɪt] VI: **to ~ (in)** prendere parte (a), partecipare (a)

participation [pɑːtɪsɪˈpeɪʃən] N partecipazione f

participle [ˈpɑːtɪsɪpl] N participio

particle [ˈpɑːtɪkl] N particella

particular [pəˈtɪkjuləʳ] ADJ particolare; speciale; (fussy) difficile; meticoloso(-a);

particulars NPL particolari mpl, dettagli mpl; (information) informazioni fpl; **in ~** in particolare, particolarmente; **to be very ~ about** essere molto pignolo(-a) su; **I'm not ~** per me va bene tutto

particularly [pəˈtɪkjuləlɪ] ADV particolarmente; in particolare

parting [ˈpɑːtɪŋ] N separazione f; (Brit: in hair) scriminatura ▶ ADJ d'addio; **~ shot** (fig) battuta finale

partisan [pɑːtɪˈzæn] N partigiano(-a) ▶ ADJ partigiano(-a); di parte

partition [pɑːˈtɪʃən] N (Pol) partizione f; (wall) tramezzo

partly [ˈpɑːtlɪ] ADV parzialmente; in parte

partner [ˈpɑːtnəʳ] N (Comm) socio(-a); (wife, husband etc, Sport) compagno(-a); (at dance) cavaliere (dama)

partnership [ˈpɑːtnəʃɪp] N associazione f; (Comm) società f inv; **to go into ~ (with)**, **form a ~ (with)** mettersi in società (con), associarsi (a)

part payment N acconto

partridge [ˈpɑːtrɪdʒ] N pernice f

part-time [pɑːtˈtaɪm] ADJ, ADV a orario ridotto, part-time (inv)

part-timer [ˈpɑːtˈtaɪməʳ] N (also: **part-time worker**) lavoratore(-trice) part-time

party [ˈpɑːtɪ] N (Pol) partito; (team) squadra; gruppo; (Law) parte f; (celebration) ricevimento; serata; festa ▶ ADJ (Pol) del partito, di partito; **dinner ~** cena; **to give** or **throw a ~** dare una festa or un party; **to be a ~ to a crime** essere coinvolto in un reato

party line N (Pol) linea del partito; (Tel) duplex m inv

party piece N: **to do one's ~** (Brit col) esibirsi nel proprio pezzo forte a una festa, cena ecc

party political broadcast N comunicato radiotelevisivo di propaganda

pass [pɑːs] VT (gen) sorpassare; (place) passare davanti a; (exam) passare, superare; (candidate) promuovere; (overtake, surpass) sorpassare, superare; (approve) approvare ▶ VI passare; (Scol) essere promosso(-a) ▶ N (permit) lasciapassare m inv; permesso; (in mountains) passo, gola; (Sport) passaggio; (Scol: also: **pass mark**): **to get a ~** prendere la sufficienza; **to ~ for** passare per; **could you ~ the vegetables round?** potrebbe far passare i contorni?; **to ~ sth through a hole** etc far passare qc attraverso un buco etc; **to make a ~ at sb** (col) fare delle proposte or delle avances a qn; **things have come to a pretty ~** (Brit) ecco a cosa siamo arrivati

▶ **pass away** VI morire

▶ **pass by** VI passare ▶ VT trascurare

▶ **pass down** VT (customs, inheritance)

tramandare, trasmettere

▶ **pass on** vi (*die*) spegnersi, mancare ▶ vt (*hand on*): **to ~ on (to)** (*news, information, object*) passare (a); (*cold, illness*) attaccare (a); (*benefits*) trasmettere (a); (*price rises*) riversare (su)

▶ **pass out** vi svenire; (*BRIT Mil*) uscire dall'accademia

▶ **pass over** vi (*die*) spirare ▶ vt lasciare da parte

▶ **pass up** vt (*opportunity*) lasciarsi sfuggire, perdere

passable ['pɑ:səbl] ADJ (*road*) praticabile; (*work*) accettabile

passage ['pæsɪdʒ] N (*gen*) passaggio; (*also*: **passageway**) corridoio; (: *in book*) brano, passo; (: *by boat*) traversata

passenger ['pæsɪndʒəʳ] N passeggero(-a)

passer-by [pɑ:sə'baɪ] N passante *mf*

passing ['pɑ:sɪŋ] ADJ (*fig*) fuggevole; **to mention sth in ~** accennare a qc di sfuggita

passing place N (*Aut*) piazzola (di sosta)

passion ['pæʃən] N passione *f*; amore *m*; **to have a ~ for sth** aver la passione di *or* per qc

passionate ['pæʃənɪt] ADJ appassionato(-a)

passion fruit N frutto della passione

passion play N rappresentazione *f* della Passione di Cristo

passive ['pæsɪv] ADJ (*also Ling*) passivo(-a)

passive smoking N fumo passivo

passkey ['pɑ:ski:] N passe-partout *m inv*

Passover ['pɑ:səʊvəʳ] N Pasqua ebraica

passport ['pɑ:spɔ:t] N passaporto

passport control N controllo *m* passaporti *inv*

passport office N ufficio *m* passaporti *inv*

password ['pɑ:swɜ:d] N parola d'ordine

past [pɑ:st] PREP (*further than*) oltre, di là di; dopo; (*later than*) dopo ▶ ADV: **to run ~** passare di corsa; **to walk ~** passare ▶ ADJ passato(-a); (*president etc*) ex *inv* ▶ N passato; **quarter/half ~ four** le quattro e un quarto/e mezzo; **ten/twenty ~ four** le quattro e dieci/venti; **he's ~ forty** ha più di quarant'anni; **it's ~ midnight** è mezzanotte passata; **ten ~ eight** le otto e dieci; **for the ~ few days** da qualche giorno; in questi ultimi giorni; **for the ~ 3 days** negli ultimi 3 giorni; **in the ~** in *or* nel passato; (*Ling*) al passato; **I'm ~ caring** non me ne importa più nulla; **to be ~ it** (*BRIT col: person*) essere finito(-a)

pasta ['pæstə] N pasta

paste [peɪst] N (*glue*) colla; (*Culin*) pâté *m inv*; pasta ▶ vt collare; **tomato ~** concentrato di pomodoro

pastel ['pæstl] ADJ pastello *inv*

pasteurized ['pæstəraɪzd] ADJ pastorizzato(-a)

pastille ['pæstl] N pastiglia

pastime ['pɑ:staɪm] N passatempo

past master N (*BRIT*): **to be a ~ at** essere molto esperto(-a) in

pastor ['pɑ:stəʳ] N pastore *m*

pastoral ['pɑ:stərl] ADJ pastorale

past participle [-'pɑ:tɪsɪpl] N (*Ling*) participio passato

pastry ['peɪstrɪ] N pasta

pasture ['pɑ:stʃəʳ] N pascolo

pasty¹ ['pæstɪ] N pasticcio di carne

pasty² ['peɪstɪ] ADJ pastoso(-a); (*complexion*) pallido(-a), smorto(-a)

pat [pæt] vt accarezzare, dare un colpetto (affettuoso) a ▶ N: **a ~ of butter** un panetto di burro; **to give sb/o.s. a ~ on the back** (*fig*) congratularsi *or* compiacersi con qn/se stesso; **he knows it (off) ~**, (*US*) **he has it down ~** lo conosce *or* sa a menadito

patch [pætʃ] N (*of material*) toppa; (*eye patch*) benda; (*spot*) macchia; (*of land*) pezzo ▶ vt (*clothes*) rattoppare; **a bad ~** (*BRIT*) un brutto periodo

▶ **patch up** vt rappezzare

patchwork ['pætʃwə:k] N patchwork *m*

patchy ['pætʃɪ] ADJ irregolare

pate [peɪt] N: **a bald ~** una testa pelata

pâté ['pæteɪ] N pâté *m inv*

patent ['peɪtnt] N brevetto ▶ vt brevettare ▶ ADJ patente, manifesto(-a)

patent leather N cuoio verniciato

patently ['peɪtntlɪ] ADV palesemente

patent medicine N specialità *f inv* medicinale

patent office N ufficio brevetti

paternal [pə'tə:nl] ADJ paterno(-a)

paternity [pə'tə:nɪtɪ] N paternità

paternity leave [pə'tə:nɪtɪ-] N congedo di paternità

paternity suit N (*Law*) causa di riconoscimento della paternità

path [pɑ:θ] N sentiero, viottolo; viale *m*; (*fig*) via, strada; (*of planet, missile*) traiettoria

pathetic [pə'θetɪk] ADJ (*pitiful*) patetico(-a); (*very bad*) penoso(-a)

pathological [pæθə'lɔdʒɪkl] ADJ patologico(-a)

pathologist [pə'θɔlədʒɪst] N patologo(-a)

pathology [pə'θɔlədʒɪ] N patologia

pathos ['peɪθɔs] N pathos *m*

pathway ['pɑ:θweɪ] N sentiero, viottolo

patience ['peɪʃns] N pazienza; (*BRIT Cards*) solitario; **to lose one's ~** spazientirsi

patient ['peɪʃnt] N paziente *mf*; malato(-a) ▶ ADJ paziente; **to be ~ with sb** essere paziente *or* aver pazienza con qn

patiently ['peɪʃntlɪ] ADV pazientemente

patio ['pætɪəu] N terrazza

patriot ['peɪtrɪət] N patriota *mf*

patriotic [pætrɪ'ɔtɪk] ADJ patriottico(-a)

patriotism ['pætrɪətɪzəm] N patriottismo

P

patrol [pə'trəul] N pattuglia ▶ VT pattugliare; **to be on ~** fare la ronda; essere in ricognizione; essere in perlustrazione

patrol boat N guardacoste *m inv*

patrol car N autoradio *f inv* (della polizia)

patrolman [pə'trəulmən] N (*irreg*) (*US*) poliziotto

patron ['peɪtrən] N (*in shop*) cliente *mf*; (*of charity*) benefattore(-trice); **~ of the arts** mecenate *mf*

patronage ['pætrənɪdʒ] N patronato

patronize ['pætrənaɪz] VT essere cliente abituale di; (*fig*) trattare con condiscendenza

patronizing ['pætrənaɪzɪŋ] ADJ condiscendente

patron saint N patrono

patter ['pætər] N picchiettio; (*sales talk*) propaganda di vendita ▶ VI picchiettare

pattern ['pætən] N modello; (*Sewing etc*) modello (di carta), cartamodello; (*design*) disegno, motivo; (*sample*) campione *m*; **behaviour patterns** tipi *mpl* di comportamento

patterned ['pætənd] ADJ a disegni, a motivi; (*material*) fantasia *inv*

paucity ['pɔːsɪtɪ] N scarsità

paunch [pɔːntʃ] N pancione *m*

pauper ['pɔːpər] N indigente *mf*; **~'s grave** fossa comune

pause [pɔːz] N pausa ▶ VI fare una pausa, arrestarsi; **to ~ for breath** fermarsi un attimo per riprender fiato

pave [peɪv] VT pavimentare; **to ~ the way for** aprire la via a

pavement ['peɪvmənt] N (*BRIT*) marciapiede *m*; (*US*) pavimentazione *f* stradale

pavilion [pə'vɪlɪən] N padiglione *m*; tendone *m*; (*Sport*) edificio annesso a un campo sportivo

paving ['peɪvɪŋ] N pavimentazione *f*

paving stone N lastra di pietra

paw [pɔː] N zampa ▶ VT dare una zampata a; (*person: pej*) palpare

pawn [pɔːn] N pegno; (*Chess*) pedone *m*; (*fig*) pedina ▶ VT dare in pegno

pawnbroker ['pɔːnbrəukər] N prestatore *m* su pegno

pawnshop ['pɔːnʃɔp] N monte *m* di pietà

pay [peɪ] (*pt, pp* **paid** [peɪd]) N stipendio; paga ▶ VT pagare; (*be profitable to: also fig*) convenire a ▶ VI pagare; (*be profitable*) rendere; **to ~ attention (to)** fare attenzione (a); **to ~ sb a visit** far visita a qn; **to ~ one's respects to sb** porgere i propri rispetti a qn; **I paid £5 for that record** quel disco l'ho pagato 5 sterline; **how much did you ~ for it?** quanto l'ha pagato?; **to ~ one's way** pagare la propria parte; (*company*) coprire le spese; **to ~ dividends** (*fig*) dare buoni frutti

▶ **pay back** VT rimborsare

▶ **pay for** VT FUS pagare

▶ **pay in** VT versare

▶ **pay off** VT (*debts*) saldare; (*creditor*) pagare; (*mortgage*) estinguere; (*workers*) licenziare ▶ VI (*scheme*) funzionare; (*patience*) dare dei frutti; **to ~ sth off in instalments** pagare qc a rate

▶ **pay out** VT (*money*) sborsare, tirar fuori; (*rope*) far allentare

▶ **pay up** VT saldare

payable ['peɪəbl] ADJ pagabile; **to make a cheque ~ to sb** intestare un assegno a (nome di) qn

pay-as-you-go ['peɪəzjə'gəu] ADJ (*mobile phone*) con scheda prepagata

pay award N aumento salariale

pay day N giorno di paga

PAYE N ABBR (*BRIT: = pay as you earn*) pagamento di imposte tramite ritenute alla fonte

payee [peɪ'iː] N beneficiario(-a)

pay envelope N (*US*) busta *f* paga *inv*

paying ['peɪɪŋ] ADJ: **~ guest** ospite *mf* pagante, pensionante *mf*

payload ['peɪləud] N carico utile

payment ['peɪmənt] N pagamento; versamento; saldo; **advance ~** (*part sum*) anticipo, acconto; (*total sum*) pagamento anticipato; **deferred ~, ~ by instalments** pagamento dilazionato *or* a rate; **in ~ for, in ~ of** in pagamento di; **on ~ of £5** dietro pagamento di 5 sterline

payout N pagamento; (*in competition*) premio

pay packet N (*BRIT*) busta *f* paga *inv*

payphone ['peɪfəun] N cabina telefonica

payroll ['peɪrəul] N ruolo (organico); **to be on a firm's ~** far parte del personale di una ditta

pay slip N (*BRIT*) foglio *m* paga *inv*

pay station N (*US*) cabina telefonica

pay television N televisione *f* a pagamento, pay-tv *f inv*

paywall ['peɪwɔːl] N (*Comput*) paywall *m inv*

PBS N ABBR (*US: = Public Broadcasting Service*) servizio che collabora alla realizzazione di programmi per la rete televisiva nazionale

PBX ABBR (*= private branch exchange*) sistema telefonico con centralino

PC N ABBR = **personal computer**; (*BRIT*) = **police constable** ▶ ABBR (*BRIT*) = **Privy Councillor** ▶ ADJ ABBR = **politically correct**

pc ABBR = **per cent**; (*= postcard*) C.P.

p/c ABBR = **petty cash**

PCB N ABBR = **printed circuit board**

pcm ABBR = **per calendar month**

PD N ABBR (*US*) = **police department**

pd ABBR = **paid**

PDA N ABBR (*= personal digital assistant*) PDA *m inv*

PDQ ABBR (*col*) = **pretty damn quick**

PDSA N ABBR (*BRIT: = People's Dispensary for Sick*

Animals) assistenza veterinaria gratuita

PDT ABBR (*US:* = *Pacific Daylight Time*) ora legale del Pacifico

PE N ABBR (= *physical education*) ed. fisica ▶ ABBR (*CANADA*) = **Prince Edward Island**

pea [pi:] N pisello

peace [pi:s] N pace *f*; (*calm*) calma, tranquillità; **to be at ~ with sb/sth** essere in pace con qn/qc; **to keep the ~** (*policeman*) mantenere l'ordine pubblico; (*citizen*) rispettare l'ordine pubblico

peaceable ['pi:səbl] ADJ pacifico(-a)

peaceful ['pi:sful] ADJ pacifico(-a), calmo(-a)

peacekeeping ['pi:ski:piŋ] N mantenimento della pace; **~ force** forza di pace

peace offering N (*fig*) dono in segno di riconciliazione

peach [pi:tʃ] N pesca

peacock ['pi:kɔk] N pavone *m*

peak [pi:k] N (*of mountain*) cima, vetta; (*mountain itself*) picco; (*of cap*) visiera; (*fig*) massimo; (: *of career*) apice *m*

peak-hour ['pi:kauəʳ] ADJ (*traffic etc*) delle ore di punta

peak hours NPL ore *fpl* di punta

peak period N periodo di punta

peak rate N tariffa massima

peaky ['pi:kɪ] ADJ (*BRIT col*) sbattuto(-a)

peal [pi:l] N (*of bells*) scampanio, carillon *m inv*; **peals of laughter** scoppi *mpl* di risa

peanut ['pi:nʌt] N arachide *f*, nocciolina americana

peanut butter N burro di arachidi

pear [pɛəʳ] N pera

pearl [pə:l] N perla

peasant ['pɛznt] N contadino(-a)

peat [pi:t] N torba

pebble ['pɛbl] N ciottolo

peck [pɛk] VT (*also:* **peck at**) beccare; (: *food*) mangiucchiare ▶ N colpo di becco; (*kiss*) bacetto

pecking order ['pɛkɪŋ-] N (*fig*) ordine *m* gerarchico

peckish ['pɛkɪʃ] ADJ (*BRIT col*): **I feel ~** ho un languorino

peculiar [pɪ'kju:lɪəʳ] ADJ strano(-a), bizzarro(-a); (*particular: importance, qualities*) particolare; **~ to** tipico(-a) di, caratteristico(-a) di

peculiarity [pɪkju:lɪ'ærɪtɪ] N peculiarità *f inv*; (*oddity*) bizzarria

pecuniary [pɪ'kju:nɪərɪ] ADJ pecuniario(-a)

pedal ['pɛdl] N pedale *m* ▶ VI pedalare

pedal bin N (*BRIT*) pattumiera a pedale

pedalo ['pɛdələu] N pedalò *m inv*

pedantic [pɪ'dæntɪk] ADJ pedantesco(-a)

peddle ['pɛdl] VT (*goods*) andare in giro a vendere; (*drugs*) spacciare; (*gossip*) mettere in giro

peddler ['pɛdləʳ] N venditore *m* ambulante

pedestal ['pɛdəstl] N piedestallo

pedestrian [pɪ'dɛstrɪən] N pedone(-a) ▶ ADJ pedonale; (*fig*) prosaico(-a), pedestre

pedestrian crossing N (*BRIT*) passaggio pedonale

pedestrianized ADJ: **a ~ street** una zona pedonalizzata

pedestrian mall N (*US*) zona pedonale

pedestrian precinct, (*US*) **pedestrian zone** N zona pedonale

pediatrics [pi:dɪ'ætrɪks] N (*US*) = **paediatrics**

pedigree ['pɛdɪgri:] N stirpe *f*; (*of animal*) pedigree *m inv*; (*fig*) background *m inv* ▶ CPD (*animal*) di razza

pedlar ['pɛdləʳ] N = **peddler**

pedophile ['pi:dəufaɪl] (*US*) N = **paedophile**

pee [pi:] VI (*col*) pisciare

peek [pi:k] VI guardare furtivamente

peel [pi:l] N buccia; (*of orange, lemon*) scorza ▶ VT sbucciare ▶ VI (*paint etc*) staccarsi ▶ **peel back** VT togliere, levare

peeler [pi:ləʳ] N: **potato ~** sbucciapatate *m inv*

peelings ['pi:lɪŋz] NPL bucce *fpl*

peep [pi:p] N (*look*) sguardo furtivo, sbirciata; (*sound*) pigolio ▶ VI guardare furtivamente ▶ **peep out** VI mostrarsi furtivamente

peephole ['pi:phəul] N spioncino

peer [pɪəʳ] VI: **to ~ at** scrutare ▶ N (*noble*) pari *m inv*; (*equal*) pari *mf*, uguale *mf*; (*contemporary*) contemporaneo(-a)

peerage ['pɪərɪdʒ] N dignità di pari; pari *mpl*

peerless ['pɪəlɪs] ADJ impareggiabile, senza pari

peeved [pi:vd] ADJ stizzito(-a)

peevish ['pi:vɪʃ] ADJ stizzoso(-a)

peg [pɛg] N caviglia; (*tent peg*) picchetto; (*for coat etc*) attaccapanni *m inv*; (*BRIT: also:* **clothes peg**) molletta ▶ VT (*clothes*) appendere con le mollette; (*BRIT: groundsheet*) fissare con i picchetti; (*fig: prices, wages*) fissare, stabilizzare; **off the ~** confezionato(-a)

pejorative [pɪ'dʒɔrətɪv] ADJ peggiorativo(-a)

Pekin [pi:'kɪn], **Peking** [pi:'kɪŋ] N Pechino *f*

pekinese, pekingese [pi:kɪ'ni:z] N pechinese *m*

pelican ['pɛlɪkən] N pellicano

pelican crossing N (*BRIT Aut*) attraversamento pedonale con semaforo a controllo manuale

pellet ['pɛlɪt] N pallottola, pallina

pell-mell ['pɛl'mɛl] ADV disordinatamente, alla rinfusa

pelmet ['pɛlmɪt] N mantovana; cassonetto

pelt [pɛlt] VT: **to ~ sb (with)** bombardare qn (con) ▶ VI (*rain*) piovere a dirotto; (*col: run*) filare ▶ N pelle *f*

pelvis ['pɛlvɪs] N pelvi *f inv*, bacino

pen [pɛn] N penna; (*for sheep*) recinto; (*US col:*

prison) galera; **to put ~ to paper** prendere la penna in mano

penal ['piːnl] ADJ penale

penalize ['piːnəlaɪz] VT punire; (*Sport*) penalizzare; (*fig*) svantaggiare

penal servitude [-'səːvɪtjuːd] N lavori *mpl* forzati

penalty ['pɛnltɪ] N penalità *f inv*; sanzione *f* penale; (*fine*) ammenda; (*Sport*) penalizzazione *f*; (*Football: also:* **penalty kick**) calcio di rigore

penalty area N (*BRIT Sport*) area di rigore

penalty clause N penale *f*

penalty kick N (*Football*) calcio di rigore

penalty shoot-out [-'ʃuːtaut] N (*Football*) rigori *mpl*; **to beat a team in a ~** battere una squadra ai rigori

penance ['pɛnəns] N penitenza

pence [pɛns] NPL (*BRIT*) *of* **penny**

penchant ['pɑ̃ːʃɑ̃ːŋ] N debole *m*

pencil ['pɛnsl] N matita ▶ VT (*also:* **pencil in**) scrivere a matita

pencil case N astuccio per matite

pencil sharpener N temperamatite *m inv*

pendant ['pɛndnt] N pendaglio

pending ['pɛndɪŋ] PREP in attesa di ▶ ADJ in sospeso

pendulum ['pɛndjuləm] N pendolo

penetrate ['pɛnɪtreɪt] VT penetrare

penetrating ['pɛnɪtreɪtɪŋ] ADJ penetrante

penetration [pɛnɪ'treɪʃən] N penetrazione *f*

penfriend ['pɛnfrɛnd] N (*BRIT*) corrispondente *mf*

penguin ['pɛŋgwɪn] N pinguino

penicillin [pɛnɪ'sɪlɪn] N penicillina

peninsula [pə'nɪnsjulə] N penisola

penis ['piːnɪs] N pene *m*

penitence ['pɛnɪtns] N penitenza

penitent ['pɛnɪtnt] ADJ penitente

penitentiary [pɛnɪ'tɛnʃərɪ] N (*US*) carcere *m*

penknife ['pɛnnaɪf] N temperino

Penn., Penna. ABBR (*US*) = **Pennsylvania**

pen name N pseudonimo

pennant ['pɛnənt] N banderuola

penniless ['pɛnɪlɪs] ADJ senza un soldo

Pennines ['pɛnaɪnz] NPL: **the ~** i Pennini

penny ['pɛnɪ] (*pl* **pennies** ['pɛnɪz] *or* **pence** [pɛns]) N (*BRIT*) penny *m* (*pl* = *pence*); (*US*) centesimo

penpal ['pɛnpæl] N corrispondente *mf*

penpusher ['pɛnpuʃəʳ] N (*pej*) scribacchino(-a)

pension ['pɛnʃən] N pensione *f*
  ▶ **pension off** VT mandare in pensione

pensionable ['pɛnʃənəbl] ADJ (*person*) che ha diritto a una pensione, pensionabile; (*age*) pensionabile

pensioner ['pɛnʃənəʳ] N (*BRIT*) pensionato(-a)

pension fund N fondo pensioni

pensive ['pɛnsɪv] ADJ pensoso(-a)

pentagon ['pɛntəgən] N pentagono; **the P~** (*US Pol*) il Pentagono; *vedi nota*

> Il *Pentagon* è un edificio a pianta pentagonale che si trova ad Arlington, in Virginia, nel quale hanno sede gli uffici del Ministero della Difesa degli Stati Uniti. Il termine *Pentagon* è usato anche per indicare la dirigenza militare del paese.

Pentecost ['pɛntɪkɔst] N Pentecoste *f*

penthouse ['pɛnthaus] N appartamento (di lusso) nell'attico

pent-up ['pɛntʌp] ADJ (*feelings*) represso(-a)

penultimate [pɪ'nʌltɪmət] ADJ penultimo(-a)

penury ['pɛnjurɪ] N indigenza

people ['piːpl] NPL gente *f*; persone *fpl*; (*citizens*) popolo ▶ N (*nation, race*) popolo ▶ VT popolare; **old ~** i vecchi; **young ~** i giovani; **~ at large** il grande pubblico; **a man of the ~** un uomo del popolo; **4/several ~ came** 4/parecchie persone sono venute; **the room was full of ~** la stanza era piena di gente; **~ say that ...** si dice *or* la gente dice che ...

PEP [pɛp] N ABBR = **personal equity plan**

pep [pɛp] N (*col*) dinamismo
  ▶ **pep up** VT vivacizzare; (*food*) rendere più gustoso(-a)

pepper ['pɛpəʳ] N pepe *m*; (*vegetable*) peperone *m* ▶ VT pepare; (*fig*): **to ~ with** spruzzare di

peppermint ['pɛpəmɪnt] N (*plant*) menta peperita; (*sweet*) pasticca di menta

pepperoni [pɛpə'rəunɪ] N salsiccia piccante

pepperpot ['pɛpəpɔt] N pepaiola

peptalk ['pɛptɔːk] N (*col*) discorso di incoraggiamento

per [pəːʳ] PREP per; a; **~ hour** all'ora; **~ kilo** *etc* il chilo *etc*; **~ day** al giorno; **~ week** alla settimana; **~ person** a testa, a *or* per persona; **as ~ your instructions** secondo le vostre istruzioni

per annum ADV all'anno

per capita ADJ, ADV pro capite

perceive [pə'siːv] VT percepire; (*notice*) accorgersi di

per cent ADV per cento; **a 20 ~ discount** uno sconto del 20 per cento

percentage [pə'sɛntɪdʒ] N percentuale *f*; **on a ~ basis** a percentuale

percentage point N punto percentuale

perceptible [pə'sɛptɪbl] ADJ percettibile

perception [pə'sɛpʃən] N percezione *f*; sensibilità; perspicacia

perceptive [pə'sɛptɪv] ADJ percettivo(-a); perspicace

perch [pəːtʃ] N (*fish*) pesce *m* persico; (*for bird*) sostegno, ramo ▶ VI appollaiarsi

percolate ['pəːkəleɪt] VT filtrare

percolator ['pəːkəleɪtəʳ] N caffettiera a

pressione; caffettiera elettrica

percussion [pə'kʌʃən] N percussione f; (Mus)
strumenti mpl a percussione

peremptory [pə'rɛmptəri] ADJ perentorio(-a)

perennial [pə'rɛnɪəl] ADJ perenne ▶ N pianta
perenne

perfect ['pə:fɪkt] ADJ perfetto(-a) ▶ N (also:
perfect tense) perfetto, passato prossimo
▶ VT [pə'fɛkt] perfezionare; mettere a punto;
he's a ~ stranger to me mi è
completamente sconosciuto

perfection [pə'fɛkʃən] N perfezione f

perfectionist [pə'fɛkʃənɪst] N perfezionista
mf

perfectly ['pə:fɪktlɪ] ADV perfettamente, alla
perfezione; **I'm ~ happy with the situation**
sono completamente soddisfatta della
situazione; **you know ~ well** sa benissimo

perforate ['pə:fəreɪt] VT perforare

perforated ulcer ['pə:fəreɪtɪd-] N (Med)
ulcera perforata

perforation [pə:fə'reɪʃən] N perforazione f;
(line of holes) dentellatura

perform [pə'fɔ:m] VT (carry out) eseguire, fare;
(symphony etc) suonare; (play, ballet) dare;
(opera) fare ▶ VI suonare; recitare

performance [pə'fɔ:məns] N esecuzione f;
(at theatre etc) rappresentazione f, spettacolo;
(of an artist) interpretazione f; (of player etc)
performance f; (of car, engine) prestazione f;
the team put up a good ~ la squadra ha
giocato una bella partita

performer [pə'fɔ:mə'] N artista mf

performing [pə'fɔ:mɪŋ] ADJ (animal)
ammaestrato(-a)

performing arts NPL: **the ~** le arti dello
spettacolo

perfume ['pə:fju:m] N profumo ▶ VT
profumare

perfunctory [pə'fʌŋktərɪ] ADJ superficiale,
per la forma

perhaps [pə'hæps] ADV forse; **~ he'll come**
forse verrà, può darsi che venga; **~ so/not**
forse sì/no, può darsi di sì/di no

peril ['pɛrɪl] N pericolo

perilous ['pɛrɪləs] ADJ pericoloso(-a)

perilously ['pɛrɪləslɪ] ADV: **they came ~ close
to being caught** sono stati a un pelo
dall'esser presi

perimeter [pə'rɪmɪtə'] N perimetro

perimeter wall N muro di cinta

period ['pɪərɪəd] N periodo; (Hist) epoca;
(Scol) lezione f; (full stop) punto; (US Football)
tempo; (Med) mestruazioni fpl ▶ ADJ (costume,
furniture) d'epoca; **for a ~ of three weeks** per
un periodo di or per la durata di tre
settimane; **the holiday ~** (BRIT) il periodo
delle vacanze

periodic [pɪərɪ'ɔdɪk] ADJ periodico(-a)

periodical [pɪərɪ'ɔdɪkl] ADJ periodico(-a) ▶ N
periodico

periodically [pɪərɪ'ɔdɪklɪ] ADV
periodicamente

period pains NPL (BRIT) dolori mpl mestruali

peripatetic [pɛrɪpə'tɛtɪk] ADJ (salesman)
ambulante; (BRIT: teacher) peripatetico(-a)

peripheral [pə'rɪfərəl] ADJ periferico(-a) ▶ N
(Comput) unità f inv periferica

periphery [pə'rɪfərɪ] N periferia

periscope ['pɛrɪskəup] N periscopio

perish ['pɛrɪʃ] VI perire, morire; (decay)
deteriorarsi

perishable ['pɛrɪʃəbl] ADJ deperibile

perishables ['pɛrɪʃəblz] NPL merci fpl deperibili

perishing ['pɛrɪʃɪŋ] ADJ (BRIT col): **it's ~ (cold)**
fa un freddo da morire

peritonitis [pɛrɪtə'naɪtɪs] N peritonite f

perjure ['pə:dʒə'] VT: **to ~ o.s.** spergiurare

perjury ['pə:dʒərɪ] N (Law: in court) falso
giuramento; (breach of oath) spergiuro

perk [pə:k] N (col) vantaggio
▶ **perk up** VI (cheer up) rianimarsi

perky ['pə:kɪ] ADJ (cheerful) vivace, allegro(-a)

perm [pə:m] N (for hair) permanente f ▶ VT: **to
have one's hair permed** farsi fare la
permanente

permanence ['pə:mənəns] N permanenza

permanent ['pə:mənənt] ADJ permanente;
(job, position) fisso(-a); (dye, ink) indelebile;
~ address residenza fissa; **I'm not ~ here**
non sono fisso qui

permanently ['pə:mənəntlɪ] ADV
definitivamente

permeable ['pə:mɪəbl] ADJ permeabile

permeate ['pə:mɪeɪt] VI penetrare ▶ VT
permeare

permissible [pə'mɪsɪbl] ADJ permissibile,
ammissibile

permission [pə'mɪʃən] N permesso; **to give
sb ~ to do sth** dare a qn il permesso di fare qc

permissive [pə'mɪsɪv] ADJ tollerante; **the ~
society** la società permissiva

permit N ['pə:mɪt] permesso; (entrance pass)
lasciapassare m ▶ VT, VI [pə'mɪt] permettere;
fishing ~ licenza di pesca; **to ~ sb to do**
permettere a qn di fare, dare il permesso a
qn di fare; **weather permitting** tempo
permettendo

permutation [pə:mju'teɪʃən] N
permutazione f

pernicious [pə:'nɪʃəs] ADJ pernicioso(-a),
nocivo(-a)

pernickety [pə'nɪkɪtɪ] ADJ (col: person)
pignolo(-a); (task) da certosino

perpendicular [pə:pən'dɪkjulə'] ADJ, N
perpendicolare (f)

perpetrate ['pə:pɪtreɪt] VT perpetrare,
commettere

perpetual [pə'pɛtjuəl] ADJ perpetuo(-a)
perpetuate [pə'pɛtjueɪt] VT perpetuare
perpetuity [pə:pɪ'tju:ɪtɪ] N: **in ~** in perpetuo
perplex [pə'plɛks] VT lasciare perplesso(-a)
perplexing [pə'plɛksɪŋ] ADJ che lascia
  perplesso(-a)
perquisites ['pə:kwɪzɪts] NPL (also: **perks**)
  benefici mpl collaterali
persecute ['pə:sɪkju:t] VT perseguitare
persecution [pə:sɪ'kju:ʃən] N persecuzione f
perseverance [pə:sɪ'vɪərəns] N perseveranza
persevere [pə:sɪ'vɪəʳ] VI perseverare
Persia ['pə:ʃə] N Persia
Persian ['pə:ʃən] ADJ persiano(-a) ▶ N (Ling)
  persiano; **the ~ Gulf** n il Golfo Persico
Persian cat N gatto persiano
persist [pə'sɪst] VI: **to ~ (in doing)** persistere
  (nel fare); ostinarsi (a fare)
persistence [pə'sɪstəns] N persistenza;
  ostinazione f
persistent [pə'sɪstənt] ADJ persistente;
  ostinato(-a); (lateness, rain) continuo(-a);
  ~ offender (Law) delinquente mf abituale
persnickety [pə'snɪkɪtɪ] ADJ (US col)
  = **pernickety**
person ['pə:sn] N persona; **in ~** di or in
  persona, personalmente; **on** or **about one's
  ~** (weapon) su di sé; (money) con sé; **a ~ to ~ call**
  (Tel) una chiamata con preavviso
personable ['pə:snəbl] ADJ di bell'aspetto
personal ['pə:snl] ADJ personale;
  individuale; **~ belongings, ~ effects** oggetti
  mpl d'uso personale; **a ~ interview** un
  incontro privato
personal allowance N (Tax) quota del
  reddito non imponibile
personal assistant N segretaria personale
personal call N (Tel) chiamata con preavviso
personal column N messaggi mpl personali
personal computer N personal computer
  m inv
personal details NPL dati mpl personali
personal equity plan N (Finance) fondo di
  investimento azionario con agevolazioni fiscali
  destinato al piccolo risparmiatore
personal identification number N (Comput,
  Banking) numero di codice segreto
personality [pə:sə'nælɪtɪ] N personalità f inv
personally ['pə:snlɪ] ADV personalmente;
  to take sth ~ prendere qc come una critica
  personale
personal organizer N agenda; (electronic)
  agenda elettronica
personal property N beni mpl personali
personal stereo N walkman® m inv
personify [pə:'sɔnɪfaɪ] VT personificare
personnel [pə:sə'nɛl] N personale m
personnel department N ufficio
  del personale

personnel manager N direttore(-trice) del
  personale
perspective [pə'spɛktɪv] N prospettiva; **to
  get sth into ~** ridimensionare qc
Perspex® ['pə:spɛks] N (BRIT) tipo di resina
  termoplastica
perspicacity [pə:spɪ'kæsɪtɪ] N perspicacia
perspiration [pə:spɪ'reɪʃən] N traspirazione f,
  sudore m
perspire [pə'spaɪəʳ] VI traspirare
persuade [pə'sweɪd] VT: **to ~ sb to do sth**
  persuadere qn a fare qc; **to ~ sb of sth/that**
  persuadere qn di qc/che
persuasion [pə'sweɪʒən] N persuasione f;
  (creed) convinzione f, credo
persuasive [pə'sweɪsɪv] ADJ persuasivo(-a)
pert [pə:t] ADJ (bold) sfacciato(-a),
  impertinente; (hat) spiritoso(-a)
pertaining [pə:'teɪnɪŋ]: **~ to** prep che riguarda
pertinent ['pə:tɪnənt] ADJ pertinente
perturb [pə'tə:b] VT turbare
perturbing [pə'tə:bɪŋ] ADJ inquietante
Peru [pə'ru:] N Perù m
perusal [pə'ru:zl] N attenta lettura
Peruvian [pə'ru:vjən] ADJ, N peruviano(-a)
pervade [pə'veɪd] VT pervadere
pervasive [pə:'veɪsɪv] ADJ (smell) penetrante;
  (influence) dilagante; (gloom, feelings) diffuso(-a)
perverse [pə'və:s] ADJ perverso(-a)
perversion [pə'və:ʃən] N pervertimento,
  perversione f
perversity [pə'və:sɪtɪ] N perversità
pervert N ['pə:və:t] pervertito(-a) ▶ VT
  [pə'və:t] pervertire
pessimism ['pɛsɪmɪzəm] N pessimismo
pessimist ['pɛsɪmɪst] N pessimista mf
pessimistic [pɛsɪ'mɪstɪk] ADJ
  pessimistico(-a)
pest [pɛst] N animale m (or insetto) pestifero;
  (fig) peste f
pest control N disinfestazione f
pester ['pɛstəʳ] VT tormentare, molestare
pesticide ['pɛstɪsaɪd] N pesticida m
pestilence ['pɛstɪləns] N pestilenza
pestle ['pɛsl] N pestello
pet [pɛt] N animale m domestico; (favourite)
  favorito(-a) ▶ VT accarezzare ▶ VI (col) fare il
  petting; **~ lion** etc leone m etc ammaestrato;
  teacher's ~ favorito(-a) del maestro
petal ['pɛtl] N petalo
peter ['pi:təʳ]: **to ~ out** vi esaurirsi;
  estinguersi
petite [pə'ti:t] ADJ piccolo(-a) e aggraziato(-a)
petition [pə'tɪʃən] N petizione f ▶ VI
  richiedere; **to ~ for divorce** presentare
  un'istanza di divorzio
pet name N (BRIT) nomignolo
petrified ['pɛtrɪfaɪd] ADJ (fig) morto(-a)
  di paura

petrify ['pɛtrɪfaɪ] VT pietrificare; (*fig*) terrorizzare

petrochemical [pɛtrə'kɛmɪkl] ADJ petrolchimico(-a)

petrodollars ['pɛtrəudɔləz] NPL petrodollari *mpl*

petrol ['pɛtrəl] N (BRIT) benzina; **two/four-star** ~ ≈ benzina normale/super

petrol bomb N (BRIT) (bottiglia) molotov *f inv*

petrol can N (BRIT) tanica per benzina

petrol engine N (BRIT) motore *m* a benzina

petroleum [pə'trəuliəm] N petrolio

petroleum jelly N vaselina

petrol pump N (BRIT: *in car, at garage*) pompa di benzina

petrol station N (BRIT) stazione *f* di rifornimento

petrol tank N (BRIT) serbatoio della benzina

petticoat ['pɛtɪkəut] N sottana

pettifogging ['pɛtɪfɔgɪŋ] ADJ cavilloso(-a)

pettiness ['pɛtɪnɪs] N meschinità

petty ['pɛtɪ] ADJ (*mean*) meschino(-a); (*unimportant*) insignificante

petty cash N piccola cassa

petty officer N sottufficiale *m* di marina

petulant ['pɛtjulənt] ADJ irritabile

pew [pju:] N panca (di chiesa)

pewter ['pju:təʳ] N peltro

Pfc ABBR (*US Mil*) = **private first class**

PG N ABBR (*Cine*: = *parental guidance*) consenso dei genitori richiesto

PG 13 ABBR (*US Cine*: = *Parental Guidance 13*) vietato ai minori di 13 anni non accompagnati dai genitori

PGA N ABBR (= *Professional Golfers Association*) associazione dei giocatori di golf professionisti

PH N ABBR (*US Mil*: = *Purple Heart*) decorazione per ferite riportate in guerra

PHA N ABBR (*US*: = *Public Housing Administration*) amministrazione per l'edilizia pubblica

phallic ['fælɪk] ADJ fallico(-a)

phantom ['fæntəm] N fantasma *m*

Pharaoh ['fɛərəu] N faraone *m*

pharmaceutical [fɑ:mə'sju:tɪkl] ADJ farmaceutico(-a) ▶ N: **pharmaceuticals** prodotti *mpl* farmaceutici

pharmacist ['fɑ:məsɪst] N farmacista *mf*

pharmacy ['fɑ:məsɪ] N farmacia

phase [feɪz] N fase *f*, periodo
▶ **phase in** VT introdurre gradualmente
▶ **phase out** VT (*machinery*) eliminare gradualmente; (*product*) ritirare gradualmente; (*job, subsidy*) abolire gradualmente

PhD N ABBR = **Doctor of Philosophy**

pheasant ['fɛznt] N fagiano

phenomena [fə'nɔmɪnə] NPL *of* **phenomenon**

phenomenal [fɪ'nɔmɪnl] ADJ fenomenale

phenomenon [fə'nɔmɪnən] (*pl* **phenomena** [-nə]) N fenomeno

phew [fju:] EXCL uff!

phial ['faɪəl] N fiala

philanderer [fɪ'lændərəʳ] N donnaiolo

philanthropic [fɪlən'θrɔpɪk] ADJ filantropico(-a)

philanthropist [fɪ'lænθrəpɪst] N filantropo

philatelist [fɪ'lætəlɪst] N filatelico(-a)

philately [fɪ'lætəlɪ] N filatelia

Philippines ['fɪlɪpi:nz] NPL (*also*: **Philippine Islands**): **the** ~ le Filippine

philosopher [fɪ'lɔsəfəʳ] N filosofo(-a)

philosophical [fɪlə'sɔfɪkl] ADJ filosofico(-a)

philosophy [fɪ'lɔsəfɪ] N filosofia

phlegm [flɛm] N flemma

phlegmatic [flɛg'mætɪk] ADJ flemmatico(-a)

phobia ['fəubjə] N fobia

phone [fəun] N telefono ▶ VT telefonare a
▶ VI telefonare; **to be on the** ~ avere il telefono; (*be calling*) essere al telefono
▶ **phone back** VT, VI richiamare
▶ **phone up** VT telefonare a ▶ VI telefonare

phone book N guida del telefono, elenco telefonico

phone box, (*US*) **phone booth** N cabina telefonica

phone call N telefonata

phonecard ['fəunkɑ:d] N scheda telefonica

phone-in ['fəunɪn] N (BRIT *Radio*, *TV*) *trasmissione radiofonica o televisiva con intervento telefonico degli ascoltatori*

phone number N numero di telefono

phone tapping [-tæpɪŋ] N intercettazioni *fpl* telefoniche

phonetics [fə'nɛtɪks] N fonetica

phoney ['fəunɪ] ADJ falso(-a), fasullo(-a) ▶ N (*person*) ciarlatano

phonograph ['fəunəgrɑ:f] N (*US*) giradischi *m inv*

phony ['fəunɪ] ADJ, N = **phoney**

phosphate ['fɔsfeɪt] N fosfato

phosphorus ['fɔsfərəs] N fosforo

photo... ['fəutəu] N foto *f inv*

photo... ['fəutəu] PREFIX foto...

photo album N (*new*) album *m inv* per fotografie; (*containing photos*) album *m inv* delle fotografie

photocall ['fəutəukɔ:l] N *convocazione di fotoreporter a scopo pubblicitario*

photocopier ['fəutəukɔpɪəʳ] N fotocopiatrice *f*

photocopy ['fəutəukɔpɪ] N fotocopia ▶ VT fotocopiare

photoelectric [fəutəuɪ'lɛktrɪk] ADJ: ~ **cell** cellula fotoelettrica

Photofit® ['fəutəufɪt] N photofit *m inv*

photogenic [fəutəu'dʒɛnɪk] ADJ fotogenico(-a)

photograph ['fəutəgræf] N fotografia ▶ VT fotografare; **to take a** ~ **of sb** fare una fotografia a *or* fotografare qn

P

photographer [fə'tɔgrəfə^r] N fotografo
photographic [fəutə'græfɪk] ADJ fotografico(-a)
photography [fə'tɔgrəfɪ] N fotografia
photo opportunity N opportunità di scattare delle foto ad un personaggio importante
Photoshop® ['fəutəuʃɔp] N Photoshop® m
Photostat® ['fəutəustæt] N fotocopia
photosynthesis [fəutəu'sɪnθəsɪs] N fotosintesi f
phrase [freɪz] N espressione f; (Ling) locuzione f; (Mus) frase f ▶ VT esprimere; (letter) redigere
phrasebook ['freɪzbuk] N vocabolarietto
physical ['fɪzɪkl] ADJ fisico(-a);
~ **examination** visita medica; ~ **education** educazione f fisica; ~ **exercises** ginnastica
physically ['fɪzɪklɪ] ADV fisicamente
physician [fɪ'zɪʃən] N medico
physicist ['fɪzɪsɪst] N fisico
physics ['fɪzɪks] N fisica
physiological [fɪzɪə'lɔdʒɪkəl] ADJ fisiologico(-a)
physiology [fɪzɪ'ɔlədʒɪ] N fisiologia
physiotherapist [fɪzɪəu'θerəpɪst] N fisioterapista mf
physiotherapy [fɪzɪəu'θerəpɪ] N fisioterapia
physique [fɪ'ziːk] N fisico; costituzione f
pianist ['piːənɪst] N pianista mf
piano [pɪ'ænəu] N pianoforte m
piano accordion N (BRIT) fisarmonica (a tastiera)
piccolo ['pɪkələu] N ottavino
pick [pɪk] N (tool: also: **pick-axe**) piccone m ▶ VT scegliere; (gather) cogliere; (remove) togliere; (lock) far scattare; (scab, spot) grattarsi ▶ VI: **to ~ and choose** scegliere con cura; **take your ~** scelga; **the ~ of** il fior fiore di; **to ~ one's nose** mettersi le dita nel naso; **to ~ one's teeth** pulirsi i denti con lo stuzzicadenti; **to ~ sb's brains** farsi dare dei suggerimenti da qn; **to ~ pockets** borseggiare; **to ~ a fight/quarrel with sb** attaccar rissa/briga con qn; **to ~ one's way through** attraversare stando ben attento a dove mettere i piedi
▶ **pick off** VT (kill) abbattere
▶ **pick on** VT FUS (person) avercela con
▶ **pick out** VT scegliere; (distinguish) distinguere
▶ **pick up** VI (improve) migliorarsi ▶ VT raccogliere; (Police) prendere; (collect) passare a prendere; (Aut: give lift to) far salire; (person: for sexual encounter) rimorchiare; (learn) imparare; (Radio, TV, Tel) ricevere; **to ~ o.s. up** rialzarsi; **to ~ up where one left off** riprendere dal punto in cui ci si era fermati; **to ~ up speed** acquistare velocità
pickaxe, (US) pickax ['pɪkæks] N piccone m

picket ['pɪkɪt] N (in strike) scioperante mf che fa parte di un picchetto; picchetto ▶ VT picchettare
picket line N cordone m degli scioperanti
pickings ['pɪkɪŋz] NPL (pilferings): **there are good ~ to be had here** qui ci sono buone possibilità di intascare qualcosa sottobanco
pickle ['pɪkl] N (as condiment: also: **pickles**) sottaceti mpl; (fig): **in a ~** nei pasticci ▶ VT mettere sottaceto; mettere in salamoia
pick-me-up ['pɪkmiːʌp] N tiramisù m inv
pickpocket ['pɪkpɔkɪt] N borsaiolo
pickup ['pɪkʌp] N (BRIT: on record player) pick-up m inv; (small truck: also: **pickup truck, pickup van**) camioncino
picnic ['pɪknɪk] N picnic m inv ▶ VI fare un picnic
picnic area N area per il picnic
picnicker ['pɪknɪkə^r] N chi partecipa a un picnic
pictorial [pɪk'tɔːrɪəl] ADJ illustrato(-a)
picture ['pɪktʃə^r] N quadro; (painting) pittura; (photograph) foto(grafia); (drawing) disegno; (TV) immagine f; (film) film m inv ▶ VT raffigurarsi; **the pictures** (BRIT) il cinema; **to take a ~ of sb/sth** fare una foto a qn/di qc; **we get a good ~ here** (TV) la ricezione qui è buona; **the overall ~** il quadro generale; **to put sb in the ~** mettere qn al corrente
picture book N libro illustrato
picture frame N cornice m inv
picture messaging N picture messaging m, invio di messaggini con immagini
picturesque [pɪktʃə'resk] ADJ pittoresco(-a)
picture window N finestra panoramica
piddling ['pɪdlɪŋ] ADJ (col) insignificante
pidgin English ['pɪdʒɪn-] N inglese semplificato misto ad elementi indigeni
pie [paɪ] N torta; (of meat) pasticcio
piebald ['paɪbɔːld] ADJ pezzato(-a)
piece [piːs] N pezzo; (of land) appezzamento; (Draughts etc) pedina; (item): **a ~ of furniture/advice** un mobile/consiglio ▶ VT: **to ~ together** mettere insieme; **in pieces** (broken) in pezzi; (not yet assembled) smontato(-a); **to take to pieces** smontare; **~ by ~** poco alla volta; **a 10p ~** (BRIT) una moneta da 10 pence; **a six-~ band** un complesso di sei strumentisti; **in one ~** (object) intatto; **to get back all in one ~** (person) tornare a casa incolume or sano e salvo; **to say one's ~** dire la propria
piecemeal ['piːsmiːl] ADV pezzo a pezzo, a spizzico
piece rate N tariffa a cottimo
piecework ['piːswəːk] N (lavoro a) cottimo
pie chart N grafico a torta
Piedmont ['piːdmɔnt] N Piemonte m
pier [pɪə^r] N molo; (of bridge etc) pila

pierce [pɪəs] VT forare; (with arrow etc) trafiggere; **to have one's ears pierced** farsi fare i buchi per gli orecchini
pierced ADJ: **I've got ~ ears** ho i buchi per gli orecchini
piercing ['pɪəsɪŋ] ADJ (cry) acuto(-a)
piety ['paɪətɪ] N pietà, devozione f
piffling ['pɪflɪŋ] ADJ insignificante
pig [pɪg] N maiale m, porco
pigeon ['pɪdʒən] N piccione m
pigeonhole ['pɪdʒənhəul] N casella ▶ VT classificare
pigeon-toed ['pɪdʒən'təud] ADJ che cammina con i piedi in dentro
piggy bank ['pɪgɪ-] N salvadanaio
pigheaded ['pɪg'hɛdɪd] ADJ caparbio(-a), cocciuto(-a)
piglet ['pɪglɪt] N porcellino
pigment ['pɪgmənt] N pigmento
pigmentation [pɪgmən'teɪʃən] N pigmentazione f
pigmy ['pɪgmɪ] N = **pygmy**
pigskin ['pɪgskɪn] N cinghiale m
pigsty ['pɪgstaɪ] N porcile m
pigtail ['pɪgteɪl] N treccina
pike [paɪk] N (spear) picca; (fish) luccio
pilchard ['pɪltʃəd] N specie di sardina
pile [paɪl] N (pillar, of books) pila; (heap) mucchio; (of carpet) pelo; **to ~ into** (car) stiparsi or ammucchiarsi in
 ▶ **pile up** VT ammucchiare ▶ VI ammucchiarsi; **in a ~** ammucchiato; see also **piles**
 ▶ **pile on** VT: **to ~ it on** (col) esagerare, drammatizzare
piles [paɪlz] NPL (Med) emorroidi fpl
pileup ['paɪlʌp] N (Aut) tamponamento a catena
pilfer ['pɪlfə^r] VT rubacchiare ▶ VI fare dei furtarelli
pilfering ['pɪlfərɪŋ] N rubacchiare m
pilgrim ['pɪlgrɪm] N pellegrino(-a)
pilgrimage ['pɪlgrɪmɪdʒ] N pellegrinaggio
pill [pɪl] N pillola; **to be on the ~** prendere la pillola
pillage ['pɪlɪdʒ] VT saccheggiare
pillar ['pɪlə^r] N colonna
pillar box N (BRIT) cassetta delle lettere (a colonnina)
pillion ['pɪljən] N (of motor cycle) sellino posteriore; **to ride ~** viaggiare dietro
pillory ['pɪlərɪ] N berlina ▶ VT mettere alla berlina
pillow ['pɪləu] N guanciale m
pillowcase ['pɪləukeɪs], **pillowslip** ['pɪləuslɪp] N federa
pilot ['paɪlət] N pilota mf ▶ CPD (scheme etc) pilota inv ▶ VT pilotare
pilot boat N pilotina

pilot light N fiamma pilota
pimento [pɪ'mɛntəu] N peperoncino
pimp [pɪmp] N mezzano
pimple ['pɪmpl] N foruncolo
pimply ['pɪmplɪ] ADJ foruncoloso(-a)
PIN N ABBR (= personal identification number) codice m segreto, PIN m inv
pin [pɪn] N spillo; (Tech) perno; (BRIT: drawing pin) puntina da disegno; (BRIT Elec: of plug) spinotto ▶ VT attaccare con uno spillo; **pins and needles** formicolio; **to ~ sb against/to** inchiodare qn contro/a; **to ~ sth on sb** (fig) addossare la colpa di qc a qn
 ▶ **pin down** VT (fig): **to ~ sb down** obbligare qn a pronunziarsi; **there's something strange here but I can't quite ~ it down** c'è qualcosa di strano qua ma non riesco a capire cos'è
pinafore ['pɪnəfɔː^r] N (also: **pinafore dress**) scamiciato
pinball ['pɪnbɔːl] N flipper m inv
pincers ['pɪnsəz] NPL pinzette fpl
pinch [pɪntʃ] N pizzicotto, pizzico ▶ VT pizzicare; (col: steal) grattare ▶ VI (shoe) stringere; **at a ~** in caso di bisogno; **to feel the ~** (fig) trovarsi nelle ristrettezze
pinched [pɪntʃt] ADJ (drawn) dai lineamenti tirati; (short): **~ for money/space** a corto di soldi/di spazio; **~ with cold** raggrinzito dal freddo
pincushion ['pɪnkuʃən] N puntaspilli m inv
pine [paɪn] N (also: **pine tree**) pino ▶ VI: **to ~ for** struggersi dal desiderio di
 ▶ **pine away** VI languire
pineapple ['paɪnæpl] N ananas m inv
pine cone N pigna
pine needles NPL aghi mpl di pino
ping [pɪŋ] N (noise) tintinnio
Ping-Pong® ['pɪŋpɔŋ] N ping-pong® m
pink [pɪŋk] ADJ rosa inv ▶ N (colour) rosa m inv; (Bot) garofano
pinking shears ['pɪŋkɪŋ-] N forbici fpl a zigzag
pin money N (BRIT) denaro per le piccole spese
pinnacle ['pɪnəkl] N pinnacolo
pinpoint ['pɪnpɔɪnt] VT indicare con precisione
pinstripe ['pɪnstraɪp] N stoffa gessata; (also: **pinstripe suit**) gessato
pint [paɪnt] N pinta (Brit = 0.57 l; US = 0.47 l); (BRIT col: of beer) ≈ birra grande
pinup ['pɪnʌp] N pin-up girl f inv
pioneer [paɪə'nɪə^r] N pioniere(-a) ▶ VT essere un pioniere in
pious ['paɪəs] ADJ pio(-a)
pip [pɪp] N (seed) seme m; (BRIT: time signal on radio) segnale m orario
pipe [paɪp] N tubo; (for smoking) pipa; (Mus) piffero ▶ VT portare per mezzo di tubazione;

pipes NPL (*also*: **bagpipes**) cornamusa (scozzese)
  ▶ **pipe down** VI (*col*) calmarsi
pipe cleaner N scovolino
piped music [paɪpt-] N musica di sottofondo
pipe dream N vana speranza
pipeline ['paɪplaɪn] N conduttura; (*for oil*) oleodotto; (*for natural gas*) metanodotto; **it is in the ~** (*fig*) è in arrivo
piper ['paɪpər] N piffero; suonatore(-trice) di cornamusa
pipe tobacco N tabacco da pipa
piping ['paɪpɪŋ] ADV: **~ hot** bollente
piquant ['piːkənt] ADJ (*sauce*) piccante; (*conversation*) stimolante
pique [piːk] N picca
piracy ['paɪərəsɪ] N pirateria
pirate ['paɪərət] N pirata *m* ▶ VT (*record, video, book*) riprodurre abusivamente
pirate radio N (BRIT) radio pirata *f inv*
pirouette [pɪru'ɛt] N piroetta ▶ VI piroettare
Pisces ['paɪsiːz] N Pesci *mpl*; **to be ~** essere dei Pesci
piss [pɪs] VI (*col!*) pisciare; **~ off!** vaffanculo! (!)
pissed [pɪst] ADJ (BRIT col: *drunk*) ubriaco(-a) fradicio(-a)
pistol ['pɪstl] N pistola
piston ['pɪstən] N pistone *m*
pit [pɪt] N buca, fossa; (*also*: **coal pit**) miniera; (*also*: **orchestra pit**) orchestra; (: *quarry*) cava
  ▶ VT: **to ~ sb against sb** opporre qn a qn; **pits** NPL (*Aut*) box *m*; **to ~ o.s. against** opporsi a
pitapat ['pɪtə'pæt] ADV (BRIT): **to go ~** (*heart*) palpitare, battere forte; (*rain*) picchiettare
pitch [pɪtʃ] N (*throw*) lancia; (*Mus*) tono; (*of voice*) altezza; (*fig: degree*) grado, punto; (*also*: **sales pitch**) discorso di vendita, imbonimento; (: BRIT *Sport*) campo; (: *Naut*) beccheggio; (: *tar*) pece *f* ▶ VT (*throw*) lanciare ▶ VI (*fall*) cascare; (*Naut*) beccheggiare; **to ~ a tent** piantare una tenda; **at this ~** a questo ritmo
pitch-black [pɪtʃ'blæk] ADJ nero(-a) come la pece
pitched battle [pɪtʃt-] N battaglia campale
pitcher ['pɪtʃər] N brocca
pitchfork ['pɪtʃfɔːk] N forcone *m*
piteous ['pɪtɪəs] ADJ pietoso(-a)
pitfall ['pɪtfɔːl] N trappola
pith [pɪθ] N (*of plant*) midollo; (*of orange*) parte *f* interna della scorza; (*fig*) essenza, succo; vigore *m*
pithead ['pɪthɛd] N (BRIT) imbocco della miniera
pithy ['pɪθɪ] ADJ conciso(-a); vigoroso(-a)
pitiable ['pɪtɪəbl] ADJ pietoso(-a)
pitiful ['pɪtɪful] ADJ (*touching*) pietoso(-a); (*contemptible*) miserabile

pitifully ['pɪtɪfəlɪ] ADV pietosamente; **it's ~ obvious** è penosamente chiaro
pitiless ['pɪtɪlɪs] ADJ spietato(-a)
pittance ['pɪtns] N miseria, magro salario
pitted ['pɪtɪd] ADJ: **~ with** (*potholes*) pieno(-a) di; (*chickenpox*) butterato(-a) da
pity ['pɪtɪ] N pietà ▶ VT aver pietà di, compatire, commiserare; **to have** *or* **take ~ on sb** aver pietà di qn; **it is a ~ that you can't come** è un peccato che non possa venire; **what a ~!** che peccato!
pitying ['pɪtɪɪŋ] ADJ compassionevole
pivot ['pɪvət] N perno ▶ VI imperniarsi
pixel ['pɪksl] N (*Comput*) pixel *m inv*
pixie ['pɪksɪ] N folletto
pizza ['piːtsə] N pizza
placard ['plækɑːd] N affisso
placate [plə'keɪt] VT placare, calmare
placatory [plə'keɪtərɪ] ADJ conciliante
place [pleɪs] N posto, luogo; (*proper position, rank, seat*) posto; (*house*) casa, alloggio; (*home*): **at/to his ~** a casa sua; (*in street names*): **Laurel P~** via dei Lauri ▶ VT (*object*) posare, mettere; (*identify*) riconoscere; individuare; (*goods*) piazzare; **to take ~** aver luogo; succedere; **out of ~** (*not suitable*) inopportuno(-a); **I feel rather out of ~ here** qui mi sento un po' fuori posto; **in the first ~** in primo luogo; **to change places with sb** scambiare il posto con qn; **to put sb in his ~** (*fig*) mettere a posto qn, mettere qn al suo posto; **from ~ to ~** da un posto all'altro; **all over the ~** dappertutto; **he's going places** (*fig: col*) si sta facendo strada; **it is not my ~ to do it** non sta a me farlo; **how are you placed next week?** com'è messo la settimana prossima?; **to ~ an order with sb (for)** (*Comm*) fare un'ordinazione a qn (di); **to be placed** (*in race, exam*) classificarsi
placebo [plə'siːbəu] N placebo *m inv*
place mat N sottopiatto; (*in linen etc*) tovaglietta
placement ['pleɪsmənt] N collocamento; (*job*) lavoro
place name N toponimo
placenta [plə'sɛntə] N placenta
placid ['plæsɪd] ADJ placido(-a), calmo(-a)
placidity [plə'sɪdɪtɪ] N placidità
plagiarism ['pleɪdʒərɪzəm] N plagio
plagiarist ['pleɪdʒərɪst] N plagiario(-a)
plagiarize ['pleɪdʒəraɪz] VT plagiare
plague [pleɪg] N peste *f* ▶ VT tormentare; **to ~ sb with questions** assillare qn di domande
plaice [pleɪs] N (*pl inv*) pianuzza
plaid [plæd] N plaid *m inv*
plain [pleɪn] ADJ (*clear*) chiaro(-a), palese; (*simple*) semplice; (*frank*) franco(-a), aperto(-a); (*not handsome*) bruttino(-a); (*without seasoning etc*) scondito(-a); naturale;

(*in one colour*) tinta unita *inv* ▶ ADV
francamente, chiaramente ▶ N pianura; **to
make sth ~ to sb** far capire chiaramente qc
a qn; **in ~ clothes** (*police*) in borghese
plain chocolate N cioccolato fondente
plainly ['pleɪnlɪ] ADV chiaramente; (*frankly*)
francamente
plainness ['pleɪnnɪs] N semplicità
plain speaking N: **there has been some ~
between the two leaders** i due leader si
sono parlati chiaro
plaintiff ['pleɪntɪf] N attore(-trice)
plaintive ['pleɪntɪv] ADJ (*voice, song*)
lamentoso(-a); (*look*) struggente
plait [plæt] N treccia ▶ VT intrecciare; **to ~
one's hair** farsi una treccia (*or* le trecce)
plan [plæn] N pianta; (*scheme*) progetto,
piano ▶ VT (*think in advance*) progettare;
(*prepare*) organizzare; (*intend*) avere in
progetto ▶ VI: **to ~ (for)** far piani *or* progetti
(per); **to ~ to do** progettare di fare, avere
l'intenzione di fare; **how long do you ~ to
stay?** quanto conta di restare?
plane [pleɪn] N (*Aviat*) aereo; (*tree*) platano;
(*tool*) pialla; (*Art, Math etc*) piano ▶ ADJ
piano(-a), piatto(-a) ▶ VT (*with tool*) piallare
planet ['plænɪt] N pianeta *m*
planetarium [plænɪ'tɛərɪəm] N planetario
plank [plæŋk] N tavola, asse *f*
plankton ['plæŋktən] N plancton *m*
planned economy [plænd-] N economia
pianificata
planner ['plænər] N pianificatore(-trice);
(*chart*) calendario; **town** *or* (US) **city ~**
urbanista *mf*
planning ['plænɪŋ] N progettazione *f*; (*Pol,
Econ*) pianificazione *f*; **family ~**
pianificazione delle nascite
planning permission N (BRIT) permesso di
costruzione
plant [plɑ:nt] N pianta; (*machinery*) impianto;
(*factory*) fabbrica ▶ VT piantare; (*bomb*)
mettere
plantation [plæn'teɪʃən] N piantagione *f*
plant pot N (BRIT) vaso (di fiori)
plaque [plæk] N placca
plasma ['plæzmə] N plasma *m*
plasma TV N TV *f inv* al plasma
plaster ['plɑ:stər] N intonaco; (*also:* **plaster
of Paris**) gesso; (BRIT: *also:* **sticking plaster**)
cerotto ▶ VT intonacare; ingessare; (*col: mud
etc*) impiastricciare; (*cover*): **to ~ with** coprire
di; **in ~** (BRIT: *leg etc*) ingessato(-a)
plasterboard ['plɑ:stəbɔ:d] N lastra di
cartone ingessato
plaster cast N (*Med*) ingessatura, gesso;
(*model, statue*) modello in gesso
plastered ['plɑ:stəd] ADJ (*col*) ubriaco(-a)
fradicio(-a)

plasterer ['plɑ:stərər] N intonacatore *m*
plastic ['plæstɪk] N plastica ▶ ADJ (*made of
plastic*) di *or* in plastica; (*flexible*) plastico(-a),
malleabile; (*art*) plastico(-a)
plastic bag N sacchetto di plastica
plastic bullet N pallottola di plastica
plastic explosive N esplosivo al plastico
plasticine® ['plæstɪsi:n] N plastilina®
plastic surgery N chirurgia plastica
plate [pleɪt] N (*dish*) piatto; (*sheet of metal*)
lamiera; (*Phot*) lastra; (*Typ*) cliché *m inv*; (*in
book*) tavola; (*on door*) targa, targhetta; (*Aut:
number plate*) targa; (*dental plate*) dentiera;
(*dishes*): **gold/silver ~** vasellame *m*
d'oro/d'argento
plateau ['plætəu] (*pl* **plateaus** *or* **plateaux**
[-z]) N altipiano
plateful ['pleɪtful] N piatto
plate glass N vetro piano
platen ['plætən] N (*on typewriter, printer*) rullo
plate rack N scolapiatti *m inv*
platform ['plætfɔ:m] N (*stage, at meeting*)
palco; (BRIT: *on bus*) piattaforma; (*Rail*)
marciapiede *m*; **the train leaves from ~ 7**
il treno parte dal binario 7
platform ticket N (BRIT) biglietto d'ingresso
ai binari
platinum ['plætɪnəm] N platino
platitude ['plætɪtju:d] N luogo comune
platoon [plə'tu:n] N plotone *m*
platter ['plætər] N piatto
plaudits ['plɔ:dɪts] NPL plauso
plausible ['plɔ:zɪbl] ADJ plausibile, credibile;
(*person*) convincente
play [pleɪ] N gioco; (*Theat*) commedia ▶ VT
(*game*) giocare a; (*team, opponent*) giocare
contro; (*instrument, piece of music*) suonare;
(*record, tape*) ascoltare; (*play, part*) interpretare
▶ VI giocare; suonare; recitare; **to ~ safe**
giocare sul sicuro; **to bring** *or* **call into ~**
(*plan*) mettere in azione; (*emotions*) esprimere;
~ on words gioco di parole; **to ~ a trick on
sb** fare uno scherzo a qn; **they're playing at
soldiers** stanno giocando ai soldati; **to ~ for
time** (*fig*) cercare di guadagnar tempo; **to ~
into sb's hands** (*fig*) fare il gioco di qn
▶ **play about, play around** VI (*person*)
divertirsi; **to ~ about** *or* **around with** (*fiddle
with*) giocherellare con; (*idea*) accarezzare
▶ **play along** VI: **to ~ along with** (*fig: person*)
stare al gioco di; (*plan, idea*) fingere di
assecondare ▶ VT (*fig*): **to ~ sb along** tenere
qn in sospeso
▶ **play back** VT riascoltare, risentire
▶ **play down** VT minimizzare
▶ **play on** VT FUS (*sb's feelings, credulity*) giocare
su; **to ~ on sb's nerves** dare sui nervi a qn
▶ **play up** VI (*cause trouble*) fare i capricci
playact ['pleɪækt] VI fare la commedia

playboy ['pleɪbɔɪ] N playboy *m inv*
played-out ['pleɪd'aut] ADJ spossato(-a)
player ['pleɪəʳ] N giocatore(-trice); *(Theat)* attore(-trice); *(Mus)* musicista *mf*
playful ['pleɪful] ADJ giocoso(-a)
playgoer ['pleɪɡəuəʳ] N assiduo(-a) frequentatore(-a) di teatri
playground ['pleɪɡraund] N *(in school)* cortile *m* per la ricreazione; *(in park)* parco *m* giochi *inv*
playgroup ['pleɪɡruːp] N giardino d'infanzia
playing card ['pleɪɪŋ-] N carta da gioco
playing field ['pleɪɪŋ-] N campo sportivo
playmaker ['pleɪmeɪkəʳ] N *(Sport)* playmaker *m inv*
playmate ['pleɪmeɪt] N compagno(-a) di gioco
play-off ['pleɪɔf] N *(Sport)* bella
playpen ['pleɪpɛn] N box *m inv*
playroom ['pleɪruːm] N stanza dei giochi
playschool N = **playgroup**
plaything ['pleɪθɪŋ] N giocattolo
playtime ['pleɪtaɪm] N *(Scol)* ricreazione *f*
playwright ['pleɪraɪt] N drammaturgo(-a)
plc ABBR *(BRIT: = public limited company) società per azioni a responsabilità limitata quotata in borsa*
plea [pliː] N *(request)* preghiera, domanda; *(excuse)* scusa; *(Law)* (argomento di) difesa
plea bargaining N *(Law)* patteggiamento
plead [pliːd] VT patrocinare; *(give as excuse)* addurre a pretesto ▶ VI *(Law)* perorare la causa; *(beg)*: **to ~ with sb** implorare qn; **to ~ for sth** implorare qc; **to ~ guilty/not guilty** *(defendant)* dichiararsi colpevole/innocente
pleasant ['plɛznt] ADJ piacevole, gradevole
pleasantly ['plɛzntlɪ] ADV piacevolmente
pleasantry ['plɛzntrɪ] N *(joke)* scherzo; *(polite remark)*: **to exchange pleasantries** scambiarsi i convenevoli
please [pliːz] VT piacere a ▶ VI *(think fit)*: **do as you ~** faccia come le pare; **~!** per piacere!, per favore!; *(acceptance)* **yes, ~** sì, grazie; **my bill, ~** il conto, per piacere; **~ yourself!** come ti (*or* le) pare!; **~ don't cry!** ti prego, non piangere!
pleased [pliːzd] ADJ *(happy)* felice, lieto(-a); **~ (with)** *(satisfied)* contento(-a) (di); **we are ~ to inform you that ...** abbiamo il piacere di informarla che ...; **~ to meet you!** piacere!
pleasing ['pliːzɪŋ] ADJ piacevole, che fa piacere
pleasurable ['plɛʒərəbl] ADJ molto piacevole, molto gradevole
pleasure ['plɛʒəʳ] N piacere *m*; **with ~** con piacere, volentieri; **"it's a ~"** "prego"; **is this trip for business or ~?** è un viaggio d'affari o di piacere?
pleasure cruise N crociera
pleat [pliːt] N piega
plebiscite ['plɛbɪsɪt] N plebiscito

plebs [plɛbz] NPL *(pej)* plebe *f*
plectrum ['plɛktrəm] N plettro
pledge [plɛdʒ] N pegno; *(promise)* promessa ▶ VT impegnare; promettere; **to ~ support for sb** impegnarsi a sostenere qn; **to ~ sb to secrecy** far promettere a qn di mantenere il segreto
plenary ['pliːnərɪ] ADJ plenario(-a); **in ~ session** in seduta plenaria
plentiful ['plɛntɪful] ADJ abbondante, copioso(-a)
plenty ['plɛntɪ] N abbondanza; **~ of** tanto(-a), molto(-a); un'abbondanza di; **we've got ~ of time to get there** abbiamo un sacco di tempo per arrivarci
pleurisy ['pluərɪsɪ] N pleurite *f*
Plexiglas® ['plɛksɪɡlɑːs] N *(US)* plexiglas® *m*
pliable ['plaɪəbl] ADJ flessibile; *(person)* malleabile
pliers ['plaɪəz] NPL pinza
plight [plaɪt] N situazione *f* critica
plimsolls ['plɪmsəlz] NPL *(BRIT)* scarpe *fpl* da tennis
plinth [plɪnθ] N plinto; piedistallo
PLO N ABBR *(= Palestine Liberation Organization)* O.L.P. *f*
plod [plɔd] VI camminare a stento; *(fig)* sgobbare
plodder ['plɔdəʳ] N sgobbone *m*
plodding ['plɔdɪŋ] ADJ lento(-a) e pesante
plonk [plɔŋk] *(col)* N *(BRIT: wine)* vino da poco ▶ VT: **to ~ sth down** buttare giù qc bruscamente
plot [plɔt] N congiura, cospirazione *f*; *(of story, play)* trama; *(of land)* lotto ▶ VT *(mark out)* fare la pianta di; rilevare; *(: diagram etc)* tracciare; *(conspire)* congiurare, cospirare ▶ VI congiurare; **a vegetable ~** *(BRIT)* un orticello
plotter ['plɔtəʳ] N cospiratore(-trice); *(Comput)* plotter *m inv*, tracciatore *m* di curve
plough, *(US)* **plow** [plau] N aratro ▶ VT *(earth)* arare; **to ~ money into** *(company etc)* investire danaro in
▶ **plough back** VT *(Comm)* reinvestire
▶ **plough through** VT FUS *(snow etc)* procedere a fatica in
ploughing, *(US)* **plowing** ['plauɪŋ] N aratura
ploughman, *(US)* **plowman** ['plaumən] N *(irreg)* aratore *m*; **~'s lunch** *n* *(BRIT)* semplice pasto a base di pane e formaggio
plow *etc* [plau] *(US)* = **plough** *etc*
ploy [plɔɪ] N stratagemma *m*
pls ABBR = **please**
pluck [plʌk] VT *(fruit)* cogliere; *(musical instrument)* pizzicare; *(bird)* spennare; *(hairs)* togliere ▶ N coraggio, fegato; **to ~ one's eyebrows** depilarsi le sopracciglia; **to ~ up courage** farsi coraggio
plucky ['plʌkɪ] ADJ coraggioso(-a)

plug [plʌg] N tappo; (*Elec*) spina; (*Aut: also:* **spark(ing) plug**) candela ▶ VT (*hole*) tappare; (*col: advertise*) spingere; **to give sb/sth a ~** fare pubblicità a qn/qc
▶ **plug in** (*Elec*) VI inserire la spina ▶ VT attaccare a una presa

plughole ['plʌghəul] N (*BRIT*) scarico

plug-in ['plʌgɪn] N (*Comput*) plug-in *m inv*

plum [plʌm] N (*fruit*) susina ▶ CPD: **~ job** (*col*) impiego ottimo *or* favoloso

plumage ['pluːmɪdʒ] N piume *fpl*, piumaggio

plumb [plʌm] ADJ verticale ▶ N piombo ▶ ADV (*exactly*) esattamente ▶ VT sondare
▶ **plumb in** VT (*washing machine*) collegare all'impianto idraulico

plumber ['plʌmə^r] N idraulico

plumbing ['plʌmɪŋ] N (*trade*) lavoro di idraulico; (*piping*) tubature *fpl*

plumbline ['plʌmlaɪn] N filo a piombo

plume [pluːm] N piuma, penna; (*decorative*) pennacchio

plummet ['plʌmɪt] VI: **to ~ (down)** cadere a piombo

plump [plʌmp] ADJ grassoccio(-a) ▶ VT: **to ~ sth (down) on** lasciar cadere qc di peso su
▶ **plump for** VT FUS (*col: choose*) decidersi per
▶ **plump up** VT sprimacciare

plunder ['plʌndə^r] N saccheggio ▶ VT saccheggiare

plunge [plʌndʒ] N tuffo; (*fig*) caduta ▶ VT immergere ▶ VI (*dive*) tuffarsi; (*fall*) cadere, precipitare; **to take the ~** (*fig*) saltare il fosso; **to ~ a room into darkness** far piombare una stanza nel buio

plunger ['plʌndʒə^r] N (*for blocked sink*) sturalavandini *m inv*

plunging ['plʌndʒɪŋ] ADJ (*neckline*) profondo(-a)

pluperfect [pluːˈpəːfɪkt] N piuccheperfetto

plural ['pluərl] ADJ, N plurale (*m*)

plus [plʌs] N (*also:* **plus sign**) segno più ▶ PREP più ▶ ADJ (*Math, Elec*) positivo(-a); **ten/twenty ~** più di dieci/venti; **it's a ~** (*fig*) è un vantaggio

plus fours NPL calzoni *mpl* alla zuava

plush [plʌʃ] ADJ lussuoso(-a) ▶ N felpa

plus-one ['plʌsˈwʌn] N accompagnatore(-trice)

plutonium [pluːˈtəunɪəm] N plutonio

ply [plaɪ] N (*of wool*) capo; (*of wood*) strato ▶ VT (*tool*) maneggiare; (*a trade*) esercitare ▶ VI (*ship*) fare il servizio; **three-~ (wool)** lana a tre capi; **to ~ sb with drink** dare da bere continuamente a qn

plywood ['plaɪwud] N legno compensato

PM N ABBR (*BRIT*) = **prime minister**

p.m. ADV ABBR (= *post meridiem*) del pomeriggio

PMS N ABBR (= *premenstrual syndrome*) sindrome *f* premestruale

PMT N ABBR (= *premenstrual tension*) sindrome *f* premestruale

pneumatic [njuːˈmætɪk] ADJ pneumatico(-a); **~ drill** martello pneumatico

pneumonia [njuːˈməunɪə] N polmonite *f*

PO N ABBR (= *Post Office*) ≈ P.T. (= *Poste e Telegrafi*)
▶ ABBR (*Naut*) = **petty officer**

po ABBR = **postal order**

POA N ABBR (*BRIT*: = *Prison Officers' Association*) sindacato delle guardie carcerarie

poach [pəutʃ] VT (*cook: egg*) affogare; (: *fish*) cuocere in bianco; (*steal*) cacciare (*or* pescare) di frodo ▶ VI fare il bracconiere

poached [pəutʃt] ADJ (*egg*) affogato(-a)

poacher ['pəutʃə^r] N bracconiere *m*

poaching ['pəutʃɪŋ] N caccia (*or* pesca) di frodo

PO box N ABBR = **post office box**

pocket ['pɔkɪt] N tasca ▶ VT intascare; **to be out of ~** (*BRIT*) rimetterci; **to be £5 in/out of ~** (*BRIT*) trovarsi con 5 sterline in più/in meno; **air ~** vuoto d'aria

pocketbook ['pɔkɪtbuk] N (*US: wallet*) portafoglio; (*notebook*) taccuino; (*handbag*) busta

pocket knife N temperino

pocket money N paghetta, settimana

pockmarked ['pɔkmɑːkt] ADJ (*face*) butterato(-a)

pod [pɔd] N guscio ▶ VT sgusciare

podcast ['pɔdkɑːst] N podcast *m inv*

podgy ['pɔdʒɪ] ADJ grassoccio(-a)

podiatrist [pɔˈdiːətrɪst] N (*US*) callista *mf*, pedicure *mf*

podiatry [pɔˈdiːətrɪ] N (*US*) mestiere *m* di callista

podium ['pəudɪəm] N podio

POE N ABBR = **port of embarkation**; **port of entry**

poem ['pəuɪm] N poesia

poet ['pəuɪt] N poeta(-essa)

poetic [pəuˈɛtɪk] ADJ poetico(-a)

poet laureate N (*BRIT*) poeta *m* laureato; *vedi nota*

In Gran Bretagna il *poet laureate* è un poeta che riceve un vitalizio dalla casa reale britannica e che ha l'incarico di scrivere delle poesie commemorative in occasione delle festività ufficiali.

poetry ['pəuɪtrɪ] N poesia

poignant ['pɔɪnjənt] ADJ struggente

point [pɔɪnt] N (*gen*) punto; (*tip: of needle etc*) punta; (*BRIT Elec: also:* **power point**) presa (di corrente); (*in time*) punto, momento; (*Scol*) voto; (*main idea, important part*) nocciolo; (*also:* **decimal point**): **2 ~ 3 (2.3)** 2 virgola 3 (2,3) ▶ VT (*show*) indicare; (*gun etc*): **to ~ sth at** puntare qc contro ▶ VI: **to ~ at** mostrare a dito; **to ~ to**

indicare; (*fig*) dimostrare; **points** NPL (*Aut*)
puntine *fpl*; (*Rail*) scambio; **to make a ~** fare
un'osservazione; **to get/miss the ~** capire/
non capire; **to come to the ~** venire al fatto;
when it comes to the ~ quando si arriva al
dunque; **to be on the ~ of doing sth** essere
sul punto di *or* stare (proprio) per fare qc; **to
be beside the ~** non entrarci; **to make a ~ of
doing sth** non mancare di fare qc; **there's
no ~ (in doing)** è inutile (fare); **in ~ of fact** a
dire il vero; **that's the whole ~!**
precisamente!, sta tutto lì!; **you've got a ~
there!** giusto!, ha ragione!; **the train stops
at Carlisle and all points south** il treno
ferma a Carlisle e in tutte le stazioni a sud di
Carlisle; **good points** vantaggi *mpl*; (*of person*)
qualità *fpl*; **~ of departure** (*also fig*) punto di
partenza; **~ of order** mozione *f* d'ordine;
~ of sale (*Comm*) punto di vendita; **~ of view**
punto di vista
▸ **point out** VT far notare

point-blank ['pɔɪnt'blæŋk] ADV (*also:* **at
point-blank range**) a bruciapelo; (: *fig*)
categoricamente

point duty N (*Brit*): **to be on ~** dirigere il
traffico

pointed ['pɔɪntɪd] ADJ (*shape*) aguzzo(-a),
appuntito(-a); (*remark*) specifico(-a)

pointedly ['pɔɪntɪdlɪ] ADV in maniera
inequivocabile

pointer ['pɔɪntəʳ] N (*stick*) bacchetta; (*needle*)
lancetta; (*clue*) indicazione *f*; (*advice*)
consiglio; (*dog*) pointer *m*, cane *m* da punta

pointless ['pɔɪntlɪs] ADJ inutile, vano(-a)

poise [pɔɪz] N (*balance*) equilibrio; (*of head,
body*) portamento; (*calmness*) calma ▸ VT
tenere in equilibrio; **to be poised for** (*fig*)
essere pronto(-a) a

poison ['pɔɪzn] N veleno ▸ VT avvelenare

poisoning ['pɔɪznɪŋ] N avvelenamento

poisonous ['pɔɪznəs] ADJ velenoso(-a);
(*fumes*) venefico(-a), tossico(-a); (*ideas,
literature*) pernicioso(-a); (*rumours, individual*)
perfido(-a)

poke [pəuk] VT (*fire*) attizzare; (*jab with finger,
stick etc*) punzecchiare; (*put*): **to ~ sth in(to)**
spingere qc dentro ▸ N (*jab*) colpetto; (*with
elbow*) gomitata; **to ~ one's head out of the
window** mettere la testa fuori dalla finestra;
to ~ fun at sb prendere in giro qn
▸ **poke about, poke around** VI frugare
▸ **poke out** VI (*stick out*) sporgere fuori

poker ['pəukəʳ] N attizzatoio; (*Cards*) poker *m*

poker-faced ['pəukə'feɪst] ADJ dal viso
impassibile

poky ['pəukɪ] ADJ piccolo(-a) e stretto(-a)

Poland ['pəulənd] N Polonia

polar ['pəuləʳ] ADJ polare

polar bear N orso bianco

polarize ['pəuləraɪz] VT polarizzare

Pole [pəul] N polacco(-a)

pole [pəul] N (*of wood*) palo; (*Elec, Geo*) polo

poleaxe, (*US*) **poleax** ['pəulæks] VT (*fig*)
stendere

pole bean N (*US: runner bean*) fagiolino

polecat ['pəulkæt] N puzzola; (*US*) moffetta

Pol. Econ. ['pɔlɪkɔn] N ABBR = **political
economy**

polemic [pɔ'lɛmɪk] N polemica

pole star N stella polare

pole vault N salto con l'asta

police [pə'li:s] N polizia ▸ VT mantenere
l'ordine in; (*streets, city, frontier*) presidiare; **a
large number of ~ were hurt** molti
poliziotti sono rimasti feriti

police car N macchina della polizia

police constable N (*Brit*) agente *m* di polizia

police department N (*US*) dipartimento di
polizia

police force N corpo di polizia, polizia

policeman [pə'li:smən] N (*irreg*) poliziotto,
agente *m* di polizia

police officer N = **police constable**

police record N: **to have a ~** avere precedenti
penali

police state N stato di polizia

police station N posto di polizia

policewoman [pə'li:swumən] N (*irreg*) donna
f poliziotto *inv*

policy ['pɔlɪsɪ] N politica; (*of newspaper,
company*) linea di condotta, prassi *f inv*; (*also:*
insurance policy) polizza (d'assicurazione);
to take out a ~ (*Insurance*) stipulare una
polizza di assicurazione

policy holder N assicurato(-a)

policy-making ['pɔlɪsɪmeɪkɪŋ] N messa a
punto di programmi

polio ['pəulɪəu] N polio *f*

Polish ['pəulɪʃ] ADJ polacco(-a) ▸ N (*Ling*)
polacco

polish ['pɔlɪʃ] N (*for shoes*) lucido; (*for floor*)
cera; (*for nails*) smalto; (*shine*) lucentezza,
lustro; (*fig: refinement*) raffinatezza ▸ VT
lucidare; (*fig: improve*) raffinare
▸ **polish off** VT (*work*) sbrigare; (*food*)
mangiarsi

polished ['pɔlɪʃt] ADJ (*fig*) raffinato(-a)

polite [pə'laɪt] ADJ cortese; **it's not ~ to do
that** non è educato *or* buona educazione fare
questo

politely [pə'laɪtlɪ] ADV cortesemente

politeness [pə'laɪtnɪs] N cortesia

politic ['pɔlɪtɪk] ADJ diplomatico(-a)

political [pə'lɪtɪkl] ADJ politico(-a)

political asylum N asilo politico

politically [pə'lɪtɪklɪ] ADV politicamente

politically correct ADJ politicamente
corretto(-a)

politician [pɒlɪ'tɪʃən] N politico
politics ['pɒlɪtɪks] N politica ▸ NPL (*views, policies*) idee *fpl* politiche
polka ['pɒlkə] N polca
polka dot N pois *m inv*
poll [pəul] N scrutinio; (*votes cast*) voti *mpl*; (*also:* **opinion poll**) sondaggio (d'opinioni) ▸ VT ottenere; **to go to the polls** (*voters*) andare alle urne; (*government*) indire le elezioni
pollen ['pɒlən] N polline *m*
pollen count N tasso di polline nell'aria
pollination [pɒlɪ'neɪʃən] N impollinazione *f*
polling ['pəulɪŋ] N (*Pol*) votazione *f*, votazioni *fpl*; (*Tel*) interrogazione *f* ciclica
polling booth N (*BRIT*) cabina elettorale
polling day N (*BRIT*) giorno delle elezioni
polling station ['pəulɪŋ-] N (*BRIT*) sezione *f* elettorale
pollster ['pəulstər] N chi esegue sondaggi d'opinione
poll tax N (*BRIT*) *imposta locale sulla persona fisica (non più in vigore)*
pollutant [pə'lu:tənt] N sostanza inquinante
pollute [pə'lu:t] VT inquinare
pollution [pə'lu:ʃən] N inquinamento
polo ['pəuləu] N polo
polo neck N collo alto; (*also:* **polo neck sweater**) dolcevita ▸ ADJ a collo alto
polo shirt N polo *f inv*
poly ['pɒlɪ] N ABBR (*BRIT*) = **polytechnic**
poly bag N (*BRIT col*) borsa di plastica
polyester [pɒlɪ'ɛstər] N poliestere *m*
polygamy [pə'lɪgəmɪ] N poligamia
polygraph ['pɒlɪgrɑ:f] N macchina della verità
Polynesia [pɒlɪ'ni:zɪə] N Polinesia
Polynesian [pɒlɪ'ni:zɪən] ADJ, N polinesiano(-a)
polyp ['pɒlɪp] N (*Med*) polipo
polystyrene [pɒlɪ'staɪri:n] N polistirolo
polytechnic [pɒlɪ'tɛknɪk] N (*college*) istituto superiore ad indirizzo tecnologico
polythene ['pɒlɪθi:n] N politene *m*
polythene bag N sacchetto di plastica
polyurethane ['pɒlɪ'juərɪθeɪn] N poliuretano
pomegranate ['pɒmɪgrænɪt] N melagrana
pommel ['pɒml] N pomo ▸ VT = **pummel**
pomp [pɒmp] N pompa, fasto
pompom ['pɒmpɒm] N pompon *m inv*
pompous ['pɒmpəs] ADJ pomposo(-a); (*person*) pieno(-a) di boria
pond [pɒnd] N pozza; stagno; (*in park*) laghetto
ponder ['pɒndər] VI riflettere, meditare ▸ VT ponderare, riflettere su
ponderous ['pɒndərəs] ADJ ponderoso(-a), pesante
pong [pɒŋ] N (*BRIT col*) puzzo ▸ VI puzzare

pontiff ['pɒntɪf] N pontefice *m*
pontificate [pɒn'tɪfɪkeɪt] VI (*fig*): **to ~ (about)** pontificare (su)
pontoon [pɒn'tu:n] N pontone *m*; (*BRIT Cards*) ventuno
pony ['pəunɪ] N pony *m inv*
ponytail ['pəunɪteɪl] N coda di cavallo
pony trekking [-trɛkɪŋ] N (*BRIT*) escursione *f* a cavallo
poodle ['pu:dl] N barboncino, barbone *m*
pooh-pooh [pu:'pu:] VT deridere
pool [pu:l] N (*of rain*) pozza; (*pond*) stagno; (*artificial*) vasca; (*also:* **swimming pool**) piscina; (*fig: of light*) cerchio; (*sth shared*) fondo comune; (*Comm: consortium*) pool *m inv*; (*US: monopoly trust*) trust *m inv*; (*billiards*) specie di biliardo a buca ▸ VT mettere in comune; **typing ~**, (*US*) **secretary ~** servizio comune di dattilografia; **to do the (football) pools** ≈ fare la schedina, ≈ giocare al totocalcio
poor [puər] ADJ povero(-a); (*mediocre*) mediocre, cattivo(-a) ▸ NPL: **the ~** i poveri; **~ in** povero(-a) di
poorly ['puəlɪ] ADV poveramente; (*badly*) male ▸ ADJ indisposto(-a), malato(-a)
pop [pɒp] N (*noise*) schiocco; (*Mus*) musica pop; (*US col: father*) babbo; (*col: drink*) bevanda gasata ▸ VT (*put*) mettere (in fretta) ▸ VI scoppiare; (*cork*) schioccare; **she popped her head out** (*of the window*) sporse fuori la testa
▸ **pop in** VI passare
▸ **pop out** VI fare un salto fuori
▸ **pop up** VI apparire, sorgere
pop concert N concerto *m* pop *inv*
popcorn ['pɒpkɔ:n] N pop-corn *m*
pope [pəup] N papa *m*
poplar ['pɒplər] N pioppo
poplin ['pɒplɪn] N popeline *f*
popper ['pɒpər] N (*BRIT*) bottone *m* a pressione, bottone *m* automatico
poppy ['pɒpɪ] N papavero
poppycock ['pɒpɪkɒk] N (*col*) scempiaggini *fpl*
Popsicle® ['pɒpsɪkl] N (*US: ice lolly*) ghiacciolo
pop star N pop star *f inv*
populace ['pɒpjuləs] N popolo
popular ['pɒpjulər] ADJ popolare; (*fashionable*) in voga; **to be ~ (with)** (*person*) essere benvoluto(-a) *or* ben visto(-a) (da); (*decision*) essere gradito(-a); **a ~ song** una canzone di successo
popularity [pɒpju'lærɪtɪ] N popolarità
popularize ['pɒpjuləraɪz] VT divulgare; (*science*) volgarizzare
populate ['pɒpjuleɪt] VT popolare
population [pɒpju'leɪʃən] N popolazione *f*
population explosion N forte espansione *f* demografica

P

populous ['pɔpjuləs] ADJ popolato(-a)

pop-up ADJ (*Comput: menu, window*) a comparsa

porcelain ['pɔːslɪn] N porcellana

porch [pɔːtʃ] N veranda

porcupine ['pɔːkjupaɪn] N porcospino

pore [pɔːʳ] N poro ▶ VI: **to ~ over** essere immerso(-a) in

pork [pɔːk] N carne *f* di maiale

pork chop N braciola *or* costoletta di maiale

pork pie N (*Brit Culin*) pasticcio di maiale in crosta

porn [pɔːn] (*col*) N pornografia ▶ ADJ porno *inv*

pornographic [pɔːnə'græfɪk] ADJ pornografico(-a)

pornography [pɔː'nɔgrəfɪ] N pornografia

porous ['pɔːrəs] ADJ poroso(-a)

porpoise ['pɔːpəs] N focena

porridge ['pɔrɪdʒ] N porridge *m*

port¹ [pɔːt] N porto; (*opening in ship*) portello; (*Naut: left side*) babordo; (*Comput*) porta; **to ~** (*Naut*) a babordo; **~ of call** (porto di) scalo

port² [pɔːt] N (*wine*) porto

portable ['pɔːtəbl] ADJ portatile

portal ['pɔːtl] N portale *m*

portcullis [pɔːt'kʌlɪs] N saracinesca

portent ['pɔːtɛnt] N presagio

porter ['pɔːtəʳ] N (*for luggage*) facchino, portabagagli *m inv*; (*doorkeeper*) portiere *m*, portinaio; (*US Rail*) addetto ai vagoni letto

portfolio [pɔːt'fəulɪəu] N (*case*) cartella; (*Pol: office: Econ*) portafoglio; (*of artist*) raccolta dei propri lavori

porthole ['pɔːthəul] N oblò *m inv*

portico ['pɔːtɪkəu] N portico

portion ['pɔːʃən] N porzione *f*

portly ['pɔːtlɪ] ADJ corpulento(-a)

portrait ['pɔːtreɪt] N ritratto

portray [pɔː'treɪ] VT fare il ritratto di; (*character on stage*) rappresentare; (*in writing*) ritrarre

portrayal ['pɔːtreɪəl] N ritratto; rappresentazione *f*

Portugal ['pɔːtjugl] N Portogallo

Portuguese [pɔːtju'giːz] ADJ portoghese ▶ N (*pl inv*) portoghese *mf*; (*Ling*) portoghese *m*

Portuguese man-of-war [-mænəv'wɔːʳ] N (*jellyfish*) medusa

pose [pəuz] N posa ▶ VI posare; (*pretend*): **to ~ as** atteggiarsi a, posare a ▶ VT porre; **to strike a ~** mettersi in posa

poser ['pəuzəʳ] N (*person*) domanda difficile; = **poseur**

poseur [pəu'zəːʳ] N (*pej*) persona affettata

posh [pɔʃ] ADJ (*col*) elegante; (*family*) per bene ▶ ADV (*col*): **to talk ~** parlare in modo snob

position [pə'zɪʃən] N posizione *f*; (*job*) posto ▶ VT sistemare, collocare; **to be in a ~ to do sth** essere nella posizione di fare qc

positive ['pɔzɪtɪv] ADJ positivo(-a); (*certain*) sicuro(-a), certo(-a); (*definite*) preciso(-a); definitivo(-a)

positively ADV (*affirmatively, enthusiastically*) positivamente; (*decisively*) decisamente; (*really*) assolutamente

posse ['pɔsɪ] N (*US*) drappello

possess [pə'zɛs] VT possedere; **like one possessed** come un ossesso; **whatever can have possessed you?** cosa ti ha preso?

possession [pə'zɛʃən] N possesso; (*object*) bene *m*; **to take ~ of sth** impossessarsi *or* impadronirsi di qc; **possessions** NPL (*belongings*) beni *mpl*

possessive [pə'zɛsɪv] ADJ possessivo(-a)

possessiveness [pə'zɛsɪvnɪs] N possessività

possessor [pə'zɛsəʳ] N possessore (posseditrice)

possibility [pɔsɪ'bɪlɪtɪ] N possibilità *f inv*; **he's a ~ for the part** è uno dei candidati per la parte

possible ['pɔsɪbl] ADJ possibile; **it is ~ to do it** è possibile farlo; **if ~** se possibile; **as big as ~** il più grande possibile; **as far as ~** nei limiti del possibile

possibly ['pɔsɪblɪ] ADV (*perhaps*) forse; **if you ~ can** se le è possibile; **I cannot ~ come** proprio non posso venire

post [pəust] N (*Brit: mail, letters, delivery*) posta; (*: collection*) levata; (*job, situation*) posto; (*Mil*) postazione *f*; (*pole*) palo; (*trading post*) stazione *f* commerciale; (*on blog, social network*) post *m inv*, commento ▶ VT (*Brit: send by post*) impostare; (*Mil*) appostare; (*notice*) affiggere; (*to internet: video*) caricare; (*: comment*) mandare; (*Brit*): (*appoint*) **to ~ to** assegnare a; **by ~** (*Brit*) per posta; **by return of ~** (*Brit*) a giro di posta; **to keep sb posted** tenere qn al corrente

post... [pəust] PREFIX post...; **post-1990** dopo il 1990

postage ['pəustɪdʒ] N affrancatura

postage stamp N francobollo

postal ['pəustəl] ADJ postale

postal order N vaglia *m inv* postale

postbag ['pəustbæg] N (*Brit*) sacco postale, sacco della posta

postbox ['pəustbɔks] (*Brit*) N cassetta delle lettere

postcard ['pəustkɑːd] N cartolina

postcode ['pəustkəud] N (*Brit*) codice *m* (di avviamento) postale

postdate ['pəust'deɪt] VT (*cheque*) postdatare

poster ['pəustəʳ] N manifesto, affisso

poste restante [pəust'rɛstɑ̃ːnt] N (*Brit*) fermo posta *m*

posterior [pɔs'tɪərɪəʳ] N (*col*) deretano, didietro

posterity [pɔs'tɛrɪtɪ] N posterità

poster paint N tempera

post exchange N (*US Mil*) spaccio militare

post-free [pəust'fri:] ADJ, ADV (*BRIT*) franco di porto

postgraduate ['pəust'grædjuət] N *laureato/a che continua gli studi*

posthumous ['pɔstjuməs] ADJ postumo(-a)

posthumously ['pɔstjuməslɪ] ADV dopo la mia (*or* sua *etc*) morte

posting ['pəustɪŋ] N (*BRIT*) incarico

postman ['pəustmən] N (*irrég*) postino

postmark ['pəustmɑ:k] N bollo *or* timbro postale

postmaster ['pəustmɑ:stə^r] N direttore *m* di un ufficio postale

Postmaster General N ≈ ministro delle Poste

postmistress ['pəustmɪstrɪs] N direttrice *f* di un ufficio postale

post-mortem [pəust'mɔ:təm] N autopsia; (*fig*) analisi *f inv* a posteriori

postnatal ['pəust'neɪtl] ADJ post-parto *inv*

post office N (*building*) ufficio postale; (*organization*) poste *fpl*; **the Post Office** ≈ le Poste e Telecomunicazioni

post office box N casella postale

post-paid ['pəust'peɪd] ADJ già affrancato(-a)

postpone [pəust'pəun] VT rinviare

postponement [pəust'pəunmənt] N rinvio

postscript ['pəustskrɪpt] N poscritto

postulate ['pɔstjuleɪt] VT postulare

posture ['pɔstʃə^r] N portamento; (*pose*) posa, atteggiamento ▶ VI posare

postwar ['pəust'wɔ:^r] ADJ del dopoguerra

postwoman ['pəustwumən] N (*irrég*) (*BRIT*) postina

posy ['pəuzɪ] N mazzetto di fiori

pot [pɔt] N (*for cooking*) pentola; casseruola; (*teapot*) teiera; (*coffeepot*) caffettiera; (*for plants, jam*) vaso; (*piece of pottery*) ceramica; (*col: marijuana*) erba ▶ VT (*plant*) piantare in vaso; **a ~ of tea for two** tè per due; **to go to ~** (*col: work, performance*) andare in malora; **pots of** (*BRIT col*) un sacco di

potash ['pɔtæʃ] N potassa

potassium [pə'tæsɪəm] N potassio

potato [pə'teɪtəu] (*pl* **potatoes**) N patata

potato crisps, (*US*)**potato chips** NPL patatine *fpl*

potato flour N fecola di patate

potato peeler N sbucciapatate *m inv*

potbellied ['pɔtbɛlɪd] ADJ (*from overeating*) panciuto(-a); (*from malnutrition*) dal ventre gonfio

potency ['pəutnsɪ] N potenza; (*of drink*) forza

potent ['pəutnt] ADJ potente, forte

potentate ['pəutnteɪt] N potentato

potential [pə'tɛnʃl] ADJ potenziale ▶ N possibilità *fpl*; **to have ~** essere promettente

potentially [pə'tɛnʃəlɪ] ADV potenzialmente

pothole ['pɔthəul] N (*in road*) buca; (*BRIT: underground*) caverna

potholer ['pɔthəulə^r] N (*BRIT*) speleologo(-a)

potholing ['pɔthəulɪŋ] N (*BRIT*): **to go ~** fare la speleologia

potion ['pəuʃən] N pozione *f*

potluck [pɔt'lʌk] N: **to take ~** tentare la sorte

pot plant N pianta in vaso

potpourri [pəu'puri:] N (*dried petals etc*) miscuglio di petali essiccati profumati; (*fig*) pot-pourri *m inv*

pot roast N brasato

potshot ['pɔtʃɔt] N: **to take potshots at** tirare a casaccio contro

potted ['pɔtɪd] ADJ (*food*) in conserva; (*plant*) in vaso; (*fig: shortened*) condensato(-a)

potter ['pɔtə^r] N vasaio ▶ VI (*BRIT*): **to ~ around, ~ about** lavoracchiare; **to ~ round the house** sbrigare con calma le faccende di casa; **~'s wheel** tornio (da vasaio)

pottery ['pɔtərɪ] N ceramiche *fpl*; (*factory*) fabbrica di ceramiche; **a piece of ~** una ceramica

potty ['pɔtɪ] ADJ (*BRIT col: mad*) tocco(-a) ▶ N (*child's*) vasino

potty-trained ['pɔtɪtreɪnd] ADJ che ha imparato a farla nel vasino

pouch [pautʃ] N borsa; (*Zool*) marsupio

pouf, pouffe [pu:f] N (*stool*) pouf *m inv*

poultice ['pəultɪs] N impiastro, cataplasma *m*

poultry ['pəultrɪ] N pollame *m*

poultry farm N azienda avicola

poultry farmer N pollicoltore(-trice)

pounce [pauns] VI: **to ~ (on)** balzare addosso (a), piombare (su) ▶ N balzo

pound [paund] N (*weight*) libbra (= 453g, 16 ounces); (*money*) (lira) sterlina (= 100 pence); (*for dogs*) canile *m* municipale ▶ VT (*beat*) battere; (*crush*) pestare, polverizzare ▶ VI (*beat*) battere, martellare; **half a ~** mezza libbra; **a five-~ note** una banconota da cinque sterline

pounding ['paundɪŋ] N: **to take a ~** (*fig*) prendere una batosta

pound sterling N sterlina

pour [pɔ:^r] VT versare ▶ VI riversarsi; (*rain*) piovere a dirotto

▶ **pour away, pour off** VT vuotare

▶ **pour in** VI (*people*) entrare in fiotto; **to come pouring in** (*water*) entrare a fiotti; (*letters*) arrivare a valanghe; (*cars, people*) affluire in gran quantità

▶ **pour out** VI (*people*) riversarsi fuori ▶ VT vuotare; versare; (*fig*) sfogare

pouring ['pɔ:rɪŋ] ADJ: **~ rain** pioggia torrenziale

pout [paut] VI sporgere le labbra; fare il broncio

poverty ['pɔvətɪ] N povertà, miseria

p

poverty line N soglia di povertà
poverty-stricken ['povətɪstrɪkən] ADJ molto
povero(-a), misero(-a)
poverty trap N (*BRIT*) circolo vizioso della
povertà
POW N ABBR = **prisoner of war**
powder ['paudə'] N polvere *f* ▶ VT
spolverizzare; (*face*) incipriare; **powdered
milk** latte *m* in polvere; **to ~ one's nose**
incipriarsi il naso; (*euphemism*) andare alla
toilette
powder compact N portacipria *m inv*
powder keg N (*fig: area*) polveriera; (*: situation*)
situazione *f* esplosiva
powder puff N piumino della cipria
powder room N toilette *f inv* (per signore)
powdery ['paudərɪ] ADJ polveroso(-a)
power ['pauə'] N (*strength*) potenza, forza,
(*ability, Pol: of party, leader*) potere *m*; (*Math*)
potenza; (*Elec*) corrente *f* ▶ VT fornire di
energia; azionare; **to be in ~** essere al
potere; **to do all in one's ~ to help sb** fare
tutto quello che si può per aiutare qn; **the
world powers** le grandi potenze; **mental
powers** capacità *fpl* mentali
powerboat ['pauəbəut] N (*BRIT*) motobarca,
imbarcazione *f* a motore
power cut N (*BRIT*) interruzione *f or*
mancanza di corrente
powered ['pauəd] ADJ: **~ by** azionato(-a) da;
nuclear-~ submarine sottomarino a
propulsione atomica
power failure N interruzione *f* della corrente
elettrica
powerful ['pauəful] ADJ potente, forte
powerhouse ['pauəhaus] N (*fig: person*)
persona molto dinamica; **a ~ of ideas** una
miniera di idee
powerless ['pauəlɪs] ADJ impotente,
senza potere; **~ to do** impossibilitato(-a)
a fare
power line N linea elettrica
power of attorney N procura
power point N (*BRIT*) presa di corrente
power station N centrale *f* elettrica
power steering N (*Aut: also:* **power-assisted
steering**) servosterzo
powwow ['pauwau] N riunione *f*
pp ABBR (= *pages*) pp; (*per procurationem*): **pp J.
Smith** per il Signor J. Smith
PPE N ABBR (*BRIT Scol:* = *philosophy, politics, and
economics*) corso di laurea
PPS N ABBR (*BRIT:* = *parliamentary private
secretary*) parlamentare che assiste un ministro;
= **post postscriptum**
PQ ABBR (*CANADA*) = **Province of Quebec**
PR N ABBR = **proportional representation**;
public relations ▶ ABBR (*US*) = **Puerto Rico**
Pr. ABBR = **prince**

practicability [præktɪkə'bɪlɪtɪ] N
praticabilità
practicable ['præktɪkəbl] ADJ (*scheme*)
praticabile
practical ['præktɪkl] ADJ pratico(-a)
practicality [præktɪ'kælɪtɪ] N (*of plan*)
fattibilità; (*of person*) senso pratico;
practicalities NPL dettagli *mpl* pratici
practical joke N beffa
practically ['præktɪklɪ] ADV (*almost*) quasi,
praticamente
practice ['præktɪs] N pratica; (*of profession*)
esercizio; (*at football etc*) allenamento;
(*business*) gabinetto; clientela ▶ VT, VI (*US*)
= **practise**; **in ~** (*in reality*) in pratica; **out of ~**
fuori esercizio; **2 hours' piano ~** 2 ore di
esercizio al pianoforte; **it's common ~** è
d'uso; **to put sth into ~** mettere qc in
pratica; **target ~** pratica di tiro
practice match N partita di allenamento
practise, (*US*) **practice** ['præktɪs] VT (*work at:
piano, one's backhand etc*) esercitarsi a; (*train for:
skiing, running etc*) allenarsi a; (*a sport, religion*)
praticare; (*method*) usare; (*profession*)
esercitare ▶ VI esercitarsi; (*train*) allenarsi;
(*lawyer, doctor*) esercitare; **to ~ for a match**
allenarsi per una partita
practised ['præktɪst] ADJ (*BRIT: person*)
esperto(-a); (*: performance*) da virtuoso(-a);
(*: liar*) matricolato(-a); **with a ~ eye** con
occhio esperto
practising ['præktɪsɪŋ] ADJ (*Christian etc*)
praticante; (*lawyer*) che esercita la
professione; (*homosexual*) attivo(-a)
practitioner [præk'tɪʃənə'] N professionista
mf; (*Med*) medico
pragmatic [præg'mætɪk] ADJ pragmatico(-a)
Prague [prɑːɡ] N Praga
prairie ['prɛərɪ] N prateria
praise [preɪz] N elogio, lode *f* ▶ VT elogiare,
lodare
praiseworthy ['preɪzwə:ðɪ] ADJ lodevole
pram [præm] N (*BRIT*) carrozzina
prance [prɑːns] VI (*horse*) impennarsi
prank [præŋk] N burla
prat [præt] N (*BRIT col*) cretino(-a)
prattle ['prætl] VI cinguettare
prawn [prɔːn] N gamberetto
prawn cocktail N cocktail *m inv* di gamberetti
pray [preɪ] VI pregare
prayer [prɛə'] N preghiera
prayer book N libro di preghiere
pre... [priː] PREFIX pre...; **pre-1970** prima del
1970
preach [priːtʃ] VT, VI predicare; **to ~ at sb** fare
la predica a qn
preacher ['priːtʃə'] N predicatore(-trice); (*US:
minister*) pastore *m*
preamble [prɪ'æmbl] N preambolo

prearranged [pri:ə'reɪndʒd] ADJ
organizzato(-a) in anticipo

precarious [prɪ'kɛərɪəs] ADJ precario(-a)

precaution [prɪ'kɔ:ʃən] N precauzione f

precautionary [prɪ'kɔ:ʃənərɪ] ADJ (measure)
precauzionale

precede [prɪ'si:d] VT, VI precedere

precedence ['prɛsɪdəns] N precedenza; **to
take ~ over** avere la precedenza su

precedent ['prɛsɪdənt] N precedente m; **to
establish** or **set a ~** creare un precedente

preceding [prɪ'si:dɪŋ] ADJ precedente

precept ['pri:sɛpt] N precetto

precinct ['pri:sɪŋkt] N (round cathedral)
recinto; (US: district) circoscrizione f;
precincts NPL (neighbourhood) dintorni mpl,
vicinanze fpl; **pedestrian ~** zona pedonale;
shopping ~ (BRIT) centro commerciale

precious ['prɛʃəs] ADJ prezioso(-a) ▶ ADV (col):
~ little/few ben poco/pochi; **your ~ dog**
(ironic) il suo amatissimo cane

precipice ['prɛsɪpɪs] N precipizio

precipitate ADJ [prɪ'sɪpɪtɪt] (hasty)
precipitoso(-a) ▶ VT [prɪ'sɪpɪteɪt] accelerare

precipitation [prɪsɪpɪ'teɪʃən] N
precipitazione f

precipitous [prɪ'sɪpɪtəs] ADJ (steep) erto(-a),
ripido(-a)

précis ['preɪsi:] (pl ~ [-z]) N riassunto

precise [prɪ'saɪs] ADJ preciso(-a)

precisely [prɪ'saɪslɪ] ADV precisamente; **~!**
appunto!

precision [prɪ'sɪʒən] N precisione f

preclude [prɪ'klu:d] VT precludere, impedire;
to ~ sb from doing impedire a qn di fare

precocious [prɪ'kəʊʃəs] ADJ precoce

preconceived [pri:kən'si:vd] ADJ (idea)
preconcetto(-a)

preconception [pri:kən'sɛpʃən] N
preconcetto

precondition [pri:kən'dɪʃən] N condizione f
necessaria

precursor [pri:'kə:sər] N precursore m

predate [pri:'deɪt] VT (precede) precedere

predator ['prɛdətər] N predatore m

predatory ['prɛdətərɪ] ADJ predatore(-trice)

predecessor ['pri:dɪsɛsər] N predecessore(-a)

predestination [pri:dɛstɪ'neɪʃən] N
predestinazione f

predetermine [pri:dɪ'tə:mɪn] VT
predeterminare

predicament [prɪ'dɪkəmənt] N situazione f
difficile

predicate ['prɛdɪkɪt] N (Ling) predicativo

predict [prɪ'dɪkt] VT predire

predictable [prɪ'dɪktəbl] ADJ prevedibile

predictably [prɪ'dɪktəblɪ] ADV (behave, react) in
modo prevedibile; **~ she didn't arrive** come
era da prevedere, non è arrivata

prediction [prɪ'dɪkʃən] N predizione f

predispose [pri:dɪs'pəʊz] VT predisporre

predominance [prɪ'dɔmɪnəns] N
predominanza

predominant [prɪ'dɔmɪnənt] ADJ
predominante

predominantly [prɪ'dɔmɪnəntlɪ] ADV in
maggior parte; soprattutto

predominate [prɪ'dɔmɪneɪt] VI predominare

pre-eminent [pri:'ɛmɪnənt] ADJ preminente

pre-empt [prɪ'ɛmpt] VT acquistare per
diritto di prelazione; (fig) anticipare

pre-emptive [prɪ'ɛmptɪv] ADJ: **~ strike**
azione f preventiva

preen [pri:n] VT: **to ~ itself** (bird) lisciarsi le
penne; **to ~ o.s.** agghindarsi

prefab ['pri:fæb] N casa prefabbricata

prefabricated [pri:'fæbrikeɪtɪd] ADJ
prefabbricato(-a)

preface ['prɛfəs] N prefazione f

prefect ['pri:fɛkt] N (BRIT: in school) studente/
essa con funzioni disciplinari; (Admin: in Italy)
prefetto

prefer [prɪ'fə:r] VT preferire; (Law: charges,
complaint) sporgere; (: action) intentare; **to ~
coffee to tea** preferire il caffè al tè; **to ~
doing** or **to do** preferire fare

preferable ['prɛfrəbl] ADJ preferibile

preferably ['prɛfrəblɪ] ADV preferibilmente

preference ['prɛfrəns] N preferenza; **in ~
to sth** piuttosto che qc

preference shares NPL (BRIT) azioni fpl
privilegiate

preferential [prɛfə'rɛnʃəl] ADJ preferenziale;
~ treatment trattamento di favore

preferred stock [prɪ'fə:d-] NPL (US)
= preference shares

prefix ['pri:fɪks] N prefisso

pregnancy ['prɛgnənsɪ] N gravidanza

pregnancy test N test m inv di gravidanza

pregnant ['prɛgnənt] ADJ incinta adj f;
(animal) gravido(-a); (fig: remark, pause)
significativo(-a); **3 months ~** incinta di 3
mesi

prehistoric ['pri:hɪs'tɔrɪk] ADJ preistorico(-a)

prehistory [pri:'hɪstərɪ] N preistoria

prejudge [pri:'dʒʌdʒ] VT pregiudicare

prejudice ['prɛdʒudɪs] N pregiudizio; (harm)
torto, danno ▶ VT pregiudicare, ledere; (bias):
to ~ sb in favour of/against disporre bene/
male qn verso

prejudiced ['prɛdʒudɪst] ADJ (person) pieno(-a)
di pregiudizi; (view) prevenuto(-a); **to be ~
against sb/sth** essere prevenuto contro qn/
qc; **~ (in favour of)** ben disposto(-a) (verso)

prelate ['prɛlət] N prelato

preliminaries [prɪ'lɪmɪnərɪz] NPL
preliminari mpl

preliminary [prɪ'lɪmɪnərɪ] ADJ preliminare

p

prelude ['prɛljuːd] N preludio
premarital ['priːˈmærɪtl] ADJ prematrimoniale
premature ['prɛmətʃuər] ADJ prematuro(-a); *(arrival)* (molto) anticipato(-a); **you are being a little ~** è un po' troppo precipitoso
premeditated [priːˈmɛdɪteɪtɪd] ADJ premeditato(-a)
premeditation [priːmɛdɪˈteɪʃən] N premeditazione f
premenstrual tension [priːˈmɛnstruəl-] N *(Med)* tensione f premestruale
premier ['prɛmɪər] ADJ primo(-a) ▶ N *(Pol)* primo ministro
première ['prɛmɪɛər] N prima
Premier League [prɛmɪəˈliːg] N ≈ serie A
premise ['prɛmɪs] N premessa
premises ['prɛmɪsɪz] NPL locale m; **on the ~** sul posto; **business ~** locali commerciali
premium ['priːmɪəm] N premio; **to be at a ~** *(fig: housing etc)* essere ricercatissimo; **to sell at a ~** *(shares)* vendere sopra la pari
premium bond N *(BRIT)* obbligazione f a premio
premium deal N *(Comm)* offerta speciale
premium gasoline N *(US)* super f
premonition [prɛməˈnɪʃən] N premonizione f
preoccupation [priːɔkjuˈpeɪʃən] N preoccupazione f
preoccupied [priːˈɔkjupaɪd] ADJ preoccupato(-a)
pre-owned [priːˈəund] ADJ di seconda mano
prepackaged [priːˈpækɪdʒd] ADJ già impacchettato(-a)
prepaid [priːˈpeɪd] ADJ pagato(-a) in anticipo; *(envelope)* affrancato(-a)
preparation [prɛpəˈreɪʃən] N preparazione f; **preparations** NPL *(for trip, war)* preparativi mpl; **in ~ for sth** in vista di qc
preparatory [prɪˈpærətərɪ] ADJ preparatorio(-a); **~ to sth/to doing sth** prima di qc/di fare qc
preparatory school [prɪˈpærətərɪ-] N *(BRIT)* scuola elementare privata; *(US)* scuola superiore privata; *vedi nota*

> In Gran Bretagna, la *prep(aratory) school* è una scuola privata frequentata da bambini dai 7 ai 13 anni in vista dell'iscrizione alla *public school*. Negli Stati Uniti, invece, è una scuola superiore privata che prepara i ragazzi che si iscriveranno al *college*.

prepare [prɪˈpɛər] VT preparare ▶ VI: **to ~ for** prepararsi a
prepared [prɪˈpɛəd] ADJ: **~ for** preparato(-a) a; **~ to** pronto(-a) a; **to be ~ to help sb** *(willing)* essere disposto or pronto ad aiutare qn

preponderance [prɪˈpɔndərns] N preponderanza
preposition [prɛpəˈzɪʃən] N preposizione f
prepossessing [priːpəˈzɛsɪŋ] ADJ simpatico(-a), attraente
preposterous [prɪˈpɔstərəs] ADJ assurdo(-a)
prep school [prɛp-] N = **preparatory school**
prerecord ['priːrɪˈkɔːd] VT registrare in anticipo; **prerecorded broadcast** trasmissione f registrata; **prerecorded cassette** (musi)cassetta
prerequisite [priːˈrɛkwɪzɪt] N requisito indispensabile
prerogative [prɪˈrɔgətɪv] N prerogativa
presbyterian [prɛzbɪˈtɪərɪən] ADJ, N presbiteriano(-a)
presbytery ['prɛzbɪtərɪ] N presbiterio
preschool ['priːˈskuːl] ADJ *(age)* prescolastico(-a); *(child)* in età prescolastica
prescribe [prɪˈskraɪb] VT *(Med)* prescrivere, ordinare; **prescribed books** *(BRIT Scol)* testi mpl in programma
prescription [prɪˈskrɪpʃən] N prescrizione f; *(Med)* ricetta; **to make up** or *(US)* **fill a ~** preparare or fare una ricetta; **"only available on ~"** "ottenibile solo dietro presentazione di ricetta medica"
prescription charges NPL *(BRIT)* ticket m inv
prescriptive [prɪˈskrɪptɪv] ADJ normativo(-a)
presence ['prɛzns] N presenza; **~ of mind** presenza di spirito
present ['prɛznt] ADJ presente; *(wife, residence, job)* attuale ▶ N *(gift)* regalo; *(also:* **present tense)** tempo presente; **the ~** il presente ▶ VT [prɪˈzɛnt] presentare; *(give)*: **to ~ sb with sth** offrire qc a qn; **to be ~ at** essere presente a; **those ~** i presenti; **at ~** al momento; **to give sb a ~** fare un regalo a qn; **to make sb a ~ of sth** regalare qc a qn
presentable [prɪˈzɛntəbl] ADJ presentabile
presentation [prɛznˈteɪʃən] N presentazione f; *(gift)* regalo, dono; *(ceremony)* consegna ufficiale; **on ~ of the voucher** dietro presentazione del buono
present-day ['prɛzntdeɪ] ADJ attuale, d'oggigiorno
presenter [prɪˈzɛntər] N *(BRIT Radio, TV)* presentatore(-trice)
presently ['prɛzntlɪ] ADV *(soon)* fra poco, presto; *(at present)* al momento; *(US: now)* adesso, ora
present participle N participio presente
preservation [prɛzəˈveɪʃən] N preservazione f, conservazione f
preservative [prɪˈzəːvətɪv] N conservante m
preserve [prɪˈzəːv] VT *(keep safe)* preservare, proteggere; *(maintain)* conservare; *(food)* mettere in conserva ▶ N *(for game, fish)*

riserva; (*often pl: jam*) marmellata; (: *fruit*)
frutta sciroppata
preshrunk [priːˈʃrʌŋk] ADJ irrestringibile
preside [prɪˈzaɪd] VI: **to ~ (over)** presiedere (a)
presidency [ˈprezɪdənsɪ] N presidenza; (*US: of company*) direzione f
president [ˈprezɪdənt] N presidente m; (*US: of company*) direttore(-trice) generale
presidential [prezɪˈdɛnʃl] ADJ presidenziale
press [prɛs] N (*tool, machine*) pressa; (*for wine*) torchio; (*newspapers*) stampa; (*crowd*) folla
▶ VT (*push*) premere, pigiare; (*doorbell*) suonare; (*squeeze*) spremere; (: *hand*) stringere; (*clothes: iron*) stirare; (*pursue*) incalzare; (*insist*): **to ~ sth on sb** far accettare qc da qn; (*urge, entreat*): **to ~ sb to do** or **into doing sth** fare pressione su qn affinché faccia qc ▶ VI premere; accalcare; **to go to ~** (*newspaper*) andare in macchina; **to be in the ~** (*in the newspapers*) essere sui giornali; **we are pressed for time** ci manca il tempo; **to ~ for sth** insistere per avere qc; **to ~ sb for an answer** insistere perché qn risponda; **to ~ charges against sb** (*Law*) sporgere una denuncia contro qn
▶ **press ahead** VI: **to ~ ahead (with)** andare avanti (con)
▶ **press on** VI continuare
press agency N agenzia di stampa
press clipping N ritaglio di giornale
press conference N conferenza stampa
press cutting N = **press clipping**
press-gang [ˈprɛsgæŋ] VT: **to ~ sb into doing sth** costringere qn a viva forza a fare qc
pressing [ˈprɛsɪŋ] ADJ urgente ▶ N stiratura
press officer N addetto(-a) stampa *inv*
press release N comunicato stampa
press stud N (*BRIT*) bottone m a pressione
press-up [ˈprɛsʌp] N (*BRIT*) flessione f sulle braccia
pressure [ˈprɛʃə^r] N pressione f ▶ VT: **to put ~ on sb (to do)** mettere qn sotto pressione (affinché faccia); **high/low ~** alta/bassa pressione; **to put ~ on sb** fare pressione su qn
pressure cooker N pentola a pressione
pressure gauge N manometro
pressure group N gruppo di pressione
pressurize [ˈprɛʃəraɪz] VT pressurizzare; (*fig*): **to ~ sb (into doing sth)** fare delle pressioni su qn (per costringerlo a fare qc)
pressurized [ˈprɛʃəraɪzd] ADJ pressurizzato(-a)
Prestel® [ˈprɛstɛl] N Videotel® m inv
prestige [prɛsˈtiːʒ] N prestigio
prestigious [prɛsˈtɪdʒəs] ADJ prestigioso(-a)
presumably [prɪˈzjuːməblɪ] ADV presumibilmente; **~ he did it** penso or presumo che l'abbia fatto

presume [prɪˈzjuːm] VT supporre; **to ~ to do** (*dare*) permettersi di fare
presumption [prɪˈzʌmpʃən] N presunzione f; (*boldness*) audacia
presumptuous [prɪˈzʌmpʃəs] ADJ presuntuoso(-a)
presuppose [priːsəˈpəuz] VT presupporre
pre-tax [priːˈtæks] ADJ al lordo d'imposta
pretence, (*US*) **pretense** [prɪˈtɛns] N (*claim*) pretesa; (*pretext*) pretesto, scusa; **to make a ~ of doing** far finta di fare; **on** or **under the ~ of doing sth** con il pretesto or la scusa di fare qc; **she is devoid of all ~** non si nasconde dietro false apparenze; **under false pretences** con l'inganno
pretend [prɪˈtɛnd] VT (*feign*) fingere ▶ VI far finta; (*claim*): **to ~ to sth** pretendere a qc; **to ~ to do** far finta di fare
pretense [prɪˈtɛns] N (*US*) = **pretence**
pretension [prɪˈtɛnʃən] N (*claim*) pretesa; **to have no pretensions to sth/to being sth** non avere la pretesa di avere qc/di essere qc
pretentious [prɪˈtɛnʃəs] ADJ pretenzioso(-a)
preterite [ˈprɛtərɪt] N preterito
pretext [ˈpriːtɛkst] N pretesto; **on** or **under the ~ of doing sth** col pretesto di fare qc
pretty [ˈprɪtɪ] ADJ grazioso(-a), carino(-a)
▶ ADV abbastanza, assai
prevail [prɪˈveɪl] VI (*win, be usual*) prevalere; (*persuade*): **to ~ (up)on sb to do** persuadere qn a fare
prevailing [prɪˈveɪlɪŋ] ADJ dominante
prevalent [ˈprɛvələnt] ADJ (*belief*) predominante; (*customs*) diffuso(-a); (*fashion*) corrente; (*disease*) comune
prevarication [prɪværɪˈkeɪʃən] N tergiversazione f
prevent [prɪˈvɛnt] VT prevenire; **to ~ sb from doing** impedire a qn di fare; **to ~ sth from happening** impedire che qc succeda
preventable [prɪˈvɛntəbl] ADJ evitabile
preventative [prɪˈvɛntətɪv] ADJ preventivo(-a)
prevention [prɪˈvɛnʃən] N prevenzione f
preventive [prɪˈvɛntɪv] ADJ preventivo(-a)
preview [ˈpriːvjuː] N (*of film*) anteprima
previous [ˈpriːvɪəs] ADJ precedente; anteriore; **I have a ~ engagement** ho già (preso) un impegno; **~ to doing** prima di fare
previously [ˈpriːvɪəslɪ] ADV prima
prewar [ˈpriːˈwɔː^r] ADJ anteguerra *inv*
prey [preɪ] N preda ▶ VI: **to ~ on** far preda di; **it was preying on his mind** lo stava ossessionando
price [praɪs] N prezzo; (*Betting: odds*) quotazione f ▶ VT (*goods*) fissare il prezzo di; valutare; **what is the ~ of …?** quanto costa …?; **to go up** or **rise in ~** salire or aumentare

p

di prezzo; **to put a ~ on sth** valutare *or* stimare qc; **he regained his freedom, but at a ~** ha riconquistato la sua libertà, ma a caro prezzo; **what ~ his promises now?** (BRIT) a che valgono ora le sue promesse?; **to be priced out of the market** (*article*) essere così caro da diventare invendibile; (*producer, nation*) non poter sostenere la concorrenza

price control N controllo dei prezzi

price-cutting ['praɪskʌtɪŋ] N riduzione *f* dei prezzi

priceless ['praɪslɪs] ADJ di valore inestimabile; (*col: amusing*) impagabile, spassosissimo(-a)

price list N listino (dei) prezzi

price range N gamma di prezzi; **it's within my ~** rientra nelle mie possibilità

price tag N cartellino del prezzo

price war N guerra dei prezzi

pricey ['praɪsɪ] ADJ (*col*) caruccio(-a)

prick [prɪk] N puntura ▶ VT pungere; **to ~ up one's ears** drizzare gli orecchi

prickle ['prɪkl] N (*of plant*) spina; (*sensation*) pizzicore *m*

prickly ['prɪklɪ] ADJ spinoso(-a); (*fig: person*) permaloso(-a)

prickly heat N sudamina

prickly pear N fico d'India

pride [praɪd] N orgoglio; superbia ▶ VT: **to ~ o.s. on** essere orgoglioso(-a) di; vantarsi di; **to take (a) ~ in** tenere molto a; essere orgoglioso di; **to take a ~ in doing** andare orgoglioso di fare; **to have ~ of place** (BRIT) essere al primo posto

priest [priːst] N prete *m*, sacerdote *m*

priestess ['priːstɪs] N sacerdotessa

priesthood ['priːsthud] N sacerdozio

prig [prɪg] N: **he's a ~** è compiaciuto di se stesso

prim [prɪm] ADJ pudico(-a); contegnoso(-a)

primacy ['praɪməsɪ] N primato

prima facie ['praɪmə'feɪʃɪ] ADJ: **to have a ~ case** (*Law*) presentare una causa in apparenza fondata

primal ['praɪməl] ADJ primitivo(-a), originario(-a)

primarily ['praɪmərɪlɪ] ADV principalmente, essenzialmente

primary ['praɪmərɪ] ADJ primario(-a); (*first in importance*) primo(-a) ▶ N (*US: election*) primarie *fpl*; *vedi nota*

Negli Stati Uniti, attraverso le *primaries* viene fatta una prima scrematura dei candidati dei partiti alle elezioni presidenziali. La scelta definitiva del candidato da presentare alla presidenza si basa sui risultati delle *primaries* e ha luogo durante le *Conventions* dei partiti, che si tengono in luglio e in agosto.

primary colour N colore *m* fondamentale

primary school N (BRIT) scuola elementare; *vedi nota*

In Gran Bretagna la *primary school* è la scuola elementare, frequentata dai bambini dai 5 agli 11 anni di età. È suddivisa in *infant school* (5-7 anni) e *junior school* (7-11 anni); *vedi anche* **secondary school**.

primate N (*Rel*) ['praɪmɪt] primate *m*; (*Zool*) ['praɪmeɪt] primate *m*

prime [praɪm] ADJ primario(-a), fondamentale; (*excellent*) di prima qualità ▶ N: **in the ~ of life** nel fiore della vita ▶ VT (*gun*) innescare; (*pump*) adescare; (*wood*) preparare; (*fig*) mettere al corrente

prime minister N primo ministro

primer ['praɪmə^r] N (*book*) testo elementare; (*paint*) vernice *f* base *inv*

prime time N (*Radio, TV*) fascia di massimo ascolto

primeval [praɪ'miːvl] ADJ primitivo(-a)

primitive ['prɪmɪtɪv] ADJ primitivo(-a)

primrose ['prɪmrəuz] N primavera

primus ® ['praɪməs], **primus stove** ® N (BRIT) fornello a petrolio

prince [prɪns] N principe *m*

prince charming N principe *m* azzurro

princess [prɪn'sɛs] N principessa

principal ['prɪnsɪpl] ADJ principale ▶ N (*of school, college etc*) preside *mf*; (*money*) capitale *m*; (*in play*) protagonista *mf*

principality [prɪnsɪ'pælɪtɪ] N principato

principally ['prɪnsɪplɪ] ADV principalmente

principle ['prɪnsɪpl] N principio; **in ~** in linea di principio; **on ~** per principio

print [prɪnt] N (*mark*) impronta; (*letters*) caratteri *mpl*; (*fabric*) tessuto stampato; (*Art, Phot*) stampa ▶ VT imprimere; (*publish*) stampare, pubblicare; (*write in capitals*) scrivere in stampatello; **out of ~** esaurito(-a) ▶ **print out** VT (*Comput*) stampare

printed circuit board [prɪntɪd-] N circuito stampato

printed matter [prɪntɪd-] N stampe *fpl*

printer ['prɪntə^r] N tipografo; (*machine*) stampante *f*

printhead ['prɪnthɛd] N testa di stampa

printing ['prɪntɪŋ] N stampa

printing press N macchina tipografica

print-out ['prɪntaut] N tabulato

print wheel N margherita

prior ['praɪə^r] ADJ precedente; (*claim etc*) più importante ▶ N (*Rel*) priore *m*; **~ to doing** prima di fare; **without ~ notice** senza preavviso; **to have a ~ claim to sth** avere un diritto di precedenza su qc

priority [praɪ'ɔrɪtɪ] N priorità *f inv*; precedenza; **to have** *or* **take ~ over sth**

avere la precedenza su qc
priory ['praɪərɪ] N monastero
prise [praɪz] VT: **to ~ open** forzare
prism ['prɪzəm] N prisma *m*
prison ['prɪzn] N prigione *f* ▶ CPD *(system)*
carcerario(-a); *(conditions, food)* nelle *or* delle
prigioni
prison camp N campo di prigionia
prisoner ['prɪznə'] N prigioniero(-a); **to take**
sb ~ far prigioniero qn; **the ~ at the bar**
l'accusato, l'imputato; **~ of war**
prigioniero(-a) di guerra
prissy ['prɪsɪ] ADJ per benino
pristine ['prɪstiːn] ADJ originario(-a);
intatto(-a); immacolato(-a)
privacy ['prɪvəsɪ] N solitudine *f*, intimità
private ['praɪvɪt] ADJ privato(-a); personale
▶ N soldato semplice; **"~"** *(on envelope)*
"riservata"; *(on door)* "privato"; **in ~** in
privato; **in (his) ~ life** nella vita privata; **he**
is a very ~ person è una persona molto
riservata; **~ hearing** *(Law)* udienza a porte
chiuse; **to be in ~ practice** essere medico
non convenzionato (con la mutua)
private enterprise N iniziativa privata
private eye N investigatore *m* privato
private limited company N (BRIT) *società per*
azioni non quotata in Borsa
privately ['praɪvɪtlɪ] ADV in privato; *(within*
o.s.) dentro di sé
private parts NPL *(Anat)* parti *fpl* intime
private property N proprietà privata
private school N scuola privata
privation [praɪ'veɪʃən] N *(state)* privazione *f*;
(hardship) privazioni *fpl*, stenti *mpl*
privatize ['praɪvɪtaɪz] VT privatizzare
privet ['prɪvɪt] N ligustro
privilege ['prɪvɪlɪdʒ] N privilegio
privileged ['prɪvɪlɪdʒd] ADJ privilegiato(-a);
to be ~ to do sth avere il privilegio *or* l'onore
di fare qc
privy ['prɪvɪ] ADJ: **to be ~ to** essere al corrente
di
Privy Council N (BRIT) Consiglio della
Corona; *vedi nota*

> Il *Privy Council*, un gruppo di consiglieri del
> re, era il principale organo di governo
> durante il regno dei Tudor e degli Stuart.
> Col tempo ha perso la sua importanza e
> oggi è un organo senza potere effettivo
> formato da ministri e altre personalità
> politiche ed ecclesiastiche.

Privy Councillor N (BRIT) Consigliere *m* della
Corona
prize [praɪz] N premio ▶ ADJ *(example, idiot)*
perfetto(-a); *(bull, novel)* premiato(-a) ▶ VT
apprezzare, pregiare
prize-fighter ['praɪzfaɪtə'] N pugile *m* (*che si*
batte per conquistare un premio)

prize giving N premiazione *f*
prize money N soldi *mpl* del premio
prizewinner ['praɪzwɪnə'] N premiato(-a)
prizewinning ['praɪzwɪnɪŋ] ADJ vincente;
(novel, essay etc) premiato(-a)
PRO N ABBR = **public relations officer**
pro [prəu] N *(Sport)* professionista *mf* ▶ PREP
pro; **the pros and cons** il pro e il contro
pro- [prəu] PREFIX *(in favour of)* filo...; **~Soviet**
adj filosovietico(-a)
pro-active [prəu'æktɪv] ADJ: **to be ~** agire
d'iniziativa
probability [prɔbə'bɪlɪtɪ] N probabilità *f inv*;
in all ~ con ogni probabilità
probable ['prɔbəbl] ADJ probabile; **it is ~/**
hardly ~ that ... è probabile/poco probabile
che ... + *sub*
probably ['prɔbəblɪ] ADV probabilmente
probate ['prəubɪt] N *(Law)* omologazione *f (di*
un testamento)
probation [prə'beɪʃən] N *(in employment)*
periodo di prova; *(Law)* libertà vigilata; *(Rel)*
probandato; **on ~** *(employee)* in prova; *(Law)* in
libertà vigilata
probationary [prəu'beɪʃənərɪ] ADJ: **~ period**
periodo di prova
probe [prəub] N *(Med, Space)* sonda; *(enquiry)*
indagine *f*, investigazione *f* ▶ VT sondare,
esplorare; indagare
probity ['prəubɪtɪ] N probità
problem ['prɔbləm] N problema *m*; **to have**
problems with the car avere dei problemi
con la macchina; **what's the ~?** che cosa
c'è?; **I had no ~ in finding her** non mi è
stato difficile trovarla; **no ~!** ma
certamente!, non c'è problema!
problematic [prɔblə'mætɪk] ADJ
problematico(-a)
problem-solving ['prɔbləmsɔlvɪŋ] N
risoluzione *f* di problemi
procedure [prə'siːdʒə'] N *(Admin, Law)*
procedura; *(method)* metodo, procedimento
proceed [prə'siːd] VI *(go forward)* avanzare,
andare avanti; *(go about it)* procedere;
(continue): **to ~ (with)** continuare; **to ~ to**
andare a; passare a; **to ~ to do** mettersi a
fare; **to ~ against sb** *(Law)* procedere contro
qn; **I am not sure how to ~** non so bene
come fare
proceedings [prə'siːdɪŋz] NPL misure *fpl*;
(Law) procedimento; *(meeting)* riunione *f*;
(records) rendiconti *mpl*; atti *mpl*
proceeds ['prəusiːdz] NPL profitto, incasso
process ['prəuses] N processo; *(method)*
metodo, sistema *m* ▶ VT trattare; *(information)*
elaborare ▶ VI [prə'ses] (BRIT *formal: go in*
procession) sfilare, procedere in corteo; **we are**
in the ~ of moving to ... stiamo per
trasferirci a ...

p

processed cheese, (US)**process cheese** N formaggio fuso

processing ['prəʊsesɪŋ] N trattamento; elaborazione f

procession [prə'sɛʃən] N processione f, corteo; **funeral ~** corteo funebre

pro-choice [prəʊ'tʃɔɪs] ADJ per la libertà di scelta di gravidanza

proclaim [prə'kleɪm] VT proclamare, dichiarare

proclamation [prɔklə'meɪʃən] N proclamazione f

proclivity [prə'klɪvɪtɪ] N tendenza, propensione f

procrastination [prəʊkræstɪ'neɪʃən] N procrastinazione f

procreation [prəʊkrɪ'eɪʃən] N procreazione f

Procurator Fiscal ['prɔkjʊreɪtə-] N (SCOTTISH) procuratore m

procure [prə'kjʊə'] VT (for o.s.) procurarsi; (for sb) procurare

procurement [prə'kjuəmənt] N approvvigionamento

prod [prɔd] VT dare un colpetto a; pungolare ▶ N (push, jab) colpetto

prodigal ['prɔdɪgl] ADJ prodigo(-a)

prodigious [prə'dɪdʒəs] ADJ prodigioso(-a)

prodigy ['prɔdɪdʒɪ] N prodigio

produce N ['prɔdjuːs] (Agr) prodotto, prodotti mpl ▶ VT [prə'djuːs] produrre; (show) esibire, mostrare; (proof of identity) produrre, fornire; (cause) cagionare, causare; (Theat) mettere in scena

producer [prə'djuːsə'] N (Theat, Cine, Agr) produttore m

product ['prɔdʌkt] N prodotto

production [prə'dʌkʃən] N produzione f; (Theat) messa in scena; **to put into ~** mettere in produzione

production agreement N (US) accordo sui tempi di produzione

production line N catena di lavorazione

production manager N production manager m inv, direttore m della produzione

productive [prə'dʌktɪv] ADJ produttivo(-a)

productivity [prɔdʌk'tɪvɪtɪ] N produttività

productivity agreement N (BRIT) accordo sui tempi di produzione

productivity bonus N premio di produzione

Prof. ABBR (= professor) Prof.

profane [prə'feɪn] ADJ profano(-a); (language) empio(-a)

profess [prə'fɛs] VT professare; **I do not ~ to be an expert** non pretendo di essere un esperto

professed [prə'fɛst] ADJ (self-declared) dichiarato(-a)

profession [prə'fɛʃən] N professione f; **the professions** le professioni liberali

professional [prə'fɛʃənl] N (Sport) professionista mf ▶ ADJ professionale; (work) da professionista; **he's a ~ man** è un professionista; **to take ~ advice** consultare un esperto

professionalism [prə'fɛʃnəlɪzəm] N professionismo

professionally [prə'fɛʃnəlɪ] ADV professionalmente, in modo professionale; (Sport) come professionista; **I only know him ~** con lui ho solo rapporti di lavoro

professor [prə'fɛsə'] N professore m (titolare di una cattedra); (US: teacher) professore(-essa)

professorship [prə'fɛsəʃɪp] N cattedra

proffer ['prɔfə'] VT (remark) profferire; (apologies) porgere, presentare; (one's hand) porgere

proficiency [prə'fɪʃənsɪ] N competenza, abilità

proficient [prə'fɪʃənt] ADJ competente, abile

profile ['prəʊfaɪl] N profilo; **to keep a low ~** (fig) cercare di passare inosservato or di non farsi notare troppo; **to maintain a high ~** mettersi in mostra

profit ['prɔfɪt] N profitto; beneficio ▶ VI: **to ~ (by** or **from)** approfittare (di); **~ and loss account** conto perdite e profitti; **to make a ~** realizzare un profitto; **to sell sth at a ~** vendere qc con un utile

profitability [prɔfɪtə'bɪlɪtɪ] N redditività

profitable ['prɔfɪtəbl] ADJ redditizio(-a); (fig: beneficial) vantaggioso(-a); (: meeting, visit) fruttuoso(-a)

profit centre N centro di profitto

profiteering [prɔfɪ'tɪərɪŋ] N (pej) affarismo

profit-making ['prɔfɪtmeɪkɪŋ] ADJ a scopo di lucro

profit margin N margine m di profitto

profit-sharing ['prɔfɪtʃɛərɪŋ] N compartecipazione f agli utili

profits tax N (BRIT) imposta sugli utili

profligate ['prɔflɪgɪt] ADJ (dissolute: behaviour) dissipato(-a); (: person) debosciato(-a); (extravagant): **he's very ~ with his money** è uno che sperpera i suoi soldi

pro forma ['prəʊ'fɔ:mə] ADV: **~ invoice** fattura proforma

profound [prə'faʊnd] ADJ profondo(-a)

profuse [prə'fjuːs] ADJ infinito(-a), abbondante

profusely [prə'fjuːslɪ] ADV con grande effusione

profusion [prə'fjuːʒən] N profusione f, abbondanza

progeny ['prɔdʒɪnɪ] N progenie f; discendenti mpl

programme, (US)**program** ['prəʊgræm] N programma m ▶ VT programmare

programmer, (US) **programer** ['prəʊgræməʳ] N programmatore(-trice)
programming, (US) **programing** ['prəʊgræmɪŋ] N programmazione f
programming language, programing language N linguaggio di programmazione
progress N ['prəʊgrɛs] progresso ▶ VI [prə'grɛs] (go forward) avanzare, procedere; (in time) procedere; (also: **make progress**) far progressi; **in** ~ in corso
progression [prə'grɛʃən] N progressione f
progressive [prə'grɛsɪv] ADJ progressivo(-a); (person) progressista
progressively [prə'grɛsɪvlɪ] ADV progressivamente
progress report N (Med) bollettino medico; (Admin) rendiconto dei lavori
prohibit [prə'hɪbɪt] VT proibire, vietare; **to** ~ **sb from doing sth** vietare or proibire a qn di fare qc; **"smoking prohibited"** "vietato fumare"
prohibition [prəʊɪ'bɪʃən] N (US) proibizionismo
prohibitive [prə'hɪbɪtɪv] ADJ (price etc) proibitivo(-a)
project N ['prɔdʒɛkt] (plan) piano; (venture) progetto; (Scol) studio, ricerca ▶ VT [prə'dʒɛkt] proiettare ▶ VI (stick out) sporgere
projectile [prə'dʒɛktaɪl] N proiettile m
projection [prə'dʒɛkʃən] N proiezione f; sporgenza
projectionist [prə'dʒɛkʃənɪst] N (Cine) proiezionista mf
projection room N (Cine) cabina or sala di proiezione
projector [prə'dʒɛktəʳ] N proiettore m
proletarian [prəʊlɪ'tɛərɪən] ADJ, N proletario(-a)
proletariat [prəʊlɪ'tɛərɪət] N proletariato
pro-life [prəʊ'laɪf] ADJ per il diritto alla, vita
proliferate [prə'lɪfəreɪt] VI proliferare
proliferation [prəlɪfə'reɪʃən] N proliferazione f
prolific [prə'lɪfɪk] ADJ prolifico(-a); (artist etc) fecondo(-a)
prologue, (US) **prolog** ['prəʊlɔg] N prologo
prolong [prə'lɔŋ] VT prolungare
prom [prɔm] N ABBR = **promenade**; **promenade concert**; (US: ball) ballo studentesco; vedi nota

In Gran Bretagna i Proms (= promenade concerts) sono concerti di musica classica, i più noti dei quali sono quelli eseguiti nella Royal Albert Hall a Londra. Prendono il nome dal fatto che in origine il pubblico li ascoltava stando in piedi o passeggiando. Negli Stati Uniti, invece, con prom si intende il ballo studentesco di un'università o di un college.

promenade [prɔmə'nɑːd] N (by sea) lungomare m
promenade concert N concerto (con posti in piedi)
promenade deck N (Naut) ponte m di passeggiata
prominence ['prɔmɪnəns] N prominenza; importanza
prominent ['prɔmɪnənt] ADJ (standing out) prominente; (important) importante; **he is** ~ **in the field of** ... è un'autorità nel campo di ...
prominently ['prɔmɪnəntlɪ] ADV (display, set) ben in vista; **he figured** ~ **in the case** ha avuto una parte di primo piano nella faccenda
promiscuity [prɔmɪs'kjuːɪtɪ] N (sexual) rapporti mpl multipli
promiscuous [prə'mɪskjuəs] ADJ (sexually) di facili costumi
promise ['prɔmɪs] N promessa ▶ VT, VI promettere; **to make sb a** ~ fare una promessa a qn; **to** ~ **sb sth, to** ~ **sth to sb** promettere qc a qn; **a young man of** ~ un giovane promettente; **to** ~ **(sb) that/to do sth** promettere (a qn) che/di fare qc
promising ['prɔmɪsɪŋ] ADJ promettente
promissory note ['prɔmɪsərɪ-] N pagherò m inv
promontory ['prɔməntrɪ] N promontorio
promote [prə'məʊt] VT promuovere; (venture, event) organizzare; (product) lanciare, reclamizzare; **the team was promoted to the second division** (Brit Football) la squadra è stata promossa in serie B
promoter [prə'məʊtəʳ] N (of sporting event) organizzatore(-trice); (of cause etc) sostenitore(-trice)
promotion [prə'məʊʃən] N promozione f
prompt [prɔmpt] ADJ rapido(-a), svelto(-a); puntuale; (reply) sollecito(-a) ▶ ADV (punctually) in punto ▶ N (Comput) prompt m inv ▶ VT incitare; provocare; (Theat) suggerire a; **at 8 o'clock** ~ alle 8 in punto; **to be** ~ **to do sth** essere sollecito nel fare qc; **to** ~ **sb to do** spingere qn a fare
prompter ['prɔmptəʳ] N (Theat) suggeritore m
promptly ['prɔmptlɪ] ADV prontamente; puntualmente
promptness ['prɔmptnɪs] N prontezza; puntualità
prone [prəʊn] ADJ (lying) prono(-a); ~ **to** propenso(-a) a, incline a; **to be** ~ **to illness** essere soggetto(-a) a malattie; **she is** ~ **to burst into tears if** ... può facilmente scoppiare in lacrime se ...
prong [prɔŋ] N rebbio, punta
pronoun ['prəʊnaun] N pronome m
pronounce [prə'nauns] VT pronunciare

▶ vi: **to ~ (up)on** pronunciare su; **they pronounced him unfit to drive** lo hanno dichiarato inabile alla guida; **how do you ~ it?** come si pronuncia?

pronounced [prə'naʊnst] ADJ (*marked*) spiccato(-a)

pronouncement [prə'naʊnsmənt] N dichiarazione *f*

pronunciation [prənʌnsɪ'eɪʃən] N pronuncia

proof [pruːf] N prova; (*of book*) bozza; (*Phot*) provino; **70% ~ ≈ 40°** in volume ▶ vt (*tent, anorak*) impermeabilizzare ▶ ADJ: **~ against** a prova di

proofreader ['pruːfriːdər] N correttore(-trice) di bozze

prop [prɒp] N sostegno, appoggio ▶ vt (*also:* **prop up**) sostenere, appoggiare; (*lean*): **to ~ sth against** appoggiare qc contro *or* a; **props** oggetti *m inv* di scena

Prop. ABBR (*Comm*) = **proprietor**

propaganda [prɒpə'gændə] N propaganda

propagation [prɒpə'geɪʃən] N propagazione *f*

propel [prə'pɛl] vt spingere (in avanti), muovere

propeller [prə'pɛlər] N elica

propelling pencil [prə'pɛlɪŋ-] N (*BRIT*) matita a mina

propensity [prə'pɛnsɪtɪ] N tendenza

proper ['prɒpər] ADJ (*suited, right*) adatto(-a), appropriato(-a); (*seemly*) decente; (*authentic*) vero(-a); (*col: real*) 'n' + vero(-a) e proprio(-a); **to go through the ~ channels** (*Admin*) seguire la regolare procedura

properly ['prɒpəlɪ] ADV decentemente; (*really, thoroughly*) veramente; (*eat, study*) bene; (*behave*) come si deve

proper noun N nome *m* proprio

property ['prɒpətɪ] N (*things owned*) beni *mpl*; (*land, building, Chem etc: quality*) proprietà *f inv*

property developer N (*BRIT*) costruttore *m* edile

property owner N proprietario(-a)

property tax N imposta patrimoniale

prophecy ['prɒfɪsɪ] N profezia

prophesy ['prɒfɪsaɪ] vt predire, profetizzare

prophet ['prɒfɪt] N profeta *m*

prophetic [prə'fɛtɪk] ADJ profetico(-a)

proportion [prə'pɔːʃən] N proporzione *f*; (*share*) parte *f* ▶ vt proporzionare, commisurare; **proportions** NPL (*size*) proporzioni *fpl*; **to be in/out of ~ to** *or* **with sth** essere in proporzione/sproporzionato rispetto a qc; **to see sth in ~** (*fig*) dare il giusto peso a qc

proportional [prə'pɔːʃənl] ADJ proporzionale

proportional representation N rappresentanza proporzionale

proportionate [prə'pɔːʃənɪt] ADJ proporzionato(-a)

proposal [prə'pəʊzl] N proposta; (*plan*) progetto; (*of marriage*) proposta di matrimonio

propose [prə'pəʊz] vt proporre, suggerire ▶ vi fare una proposta di matrimonio; **to ~ to do** proporsi di fare, aver l'intenzione di fare

proposer [prə'pəʊzər] N (*BRIT: of motion*) proponente *mf*

proposition [prɒpə'zɪʃən] N proposizione *f*; (*proposal*) proposta; **to make sb a ~** proporre qualcosa a qn

propound [prə'paʊnd] vt proporre, presentare

proprietary [prə'praɪətərɪ] ADJ: **~ article** prodotto con marchio depositato; **~ brand** marchio di fabbrica

proprietor [prə'praɪətər] N proprietario(-a)

propriety [prə'praɪətɪ] N (*seemliness*) decoro, rispetto delle convenienze sociali

propulsion [prə'pʌlʃən] N propulsione *f*

pro rata [prəʊ'rɑːtə] ADV in proporzione

prosaic [prəʊ'zeɪɪk] ADJ prosaico(-a)

Pros. Atty. ABBR (*US*) = **prosecuting attorney**

proscribe [prə'skraɪb] vt proscrivere

prose [prəʊz] N prosa; (*Scol: translation*) traduzione *f* dalla madrelingua

prosecute ['prɒsɪkjuːt] vt (*Law*) perseguire

prosecuting attorney ['prɒsɪkjuːtɪŋ-] N (*US*) ≈ procuratore *m*

prosecution [prɒsɪ'kjuːʃən] N (*Law*) procedimento giudiziario; (*accusing side*) accusa

prosecutor ['prɒsɪkjuːtər] N (*also:* **public prosecutor**) ≈ procuratore *m* della Repubblica

prospect N ['prɒspɛkt] prospettiva; (*hope*) speranza ▶ vt [prə'spɛkt] esplorare ▶ vi: **to ~ for gold** cercare l'oro; **there is every ~ of an early victory** tutto lascia prevedere una rapida vittoria; *see also* **prospects**

prospecting [prə'spɛktɪŋ] N prospezione *f*

prospective [prə'spɛktɪv] ADJ (*buyer*) potenziale; (*legislation, son-in-law*) futuro(-a)

prospector [prə'spɛktər] N prospettore *m*; **gold ~** cercatore *m* d'oro

prospects ['prɒspɛkts] NPL (*for work etc*) prospettive *fpl*

prospectus [prə'spɛktəs] N prospetto, programma *m*

prosper ['prɒspər] vi prosperare

prosperity [prɒ'spɛrɪtɪ] N prosperità

prosperous ['prɒspərəs] ADJ prospero(-a)

prostate ['prɒsteɪt] N (*also:* **prostate gland**) prostata, ghiandola prostatica

prostitute ['prɒstɪtjuːt] N prostituta; **male ~** uomo che si prostituisce

prostitution [prɒstɪ'tjuːʃən] N prostituzione *f*

prostrate ADJ ['prɔstreɪt] prostrato(-a) ▶ VT [prə'streɪt]: **to ~ o.s.** (*before sb*) prostrarsi

protagonist [prə'tægənɪst] N protagonista *mf*

protect [prə'tɛkt] VT proteggere, salvaguardare

protection [prə'tɛkʃən] N protezione *f*; **to be under sb's ~** essere sotto la protezione di qn

protectionism [prə'tɛkʃənɪzəm] N protezionismo

protection racket N racket *m inv*

protective [prə'tɛktɪv] ADJ protettivo(-a); **~ custody** (*Law*) protezione *f*

protector [prə'tɛktər] N protettore(-trice)

protégé ['prəutɪʒeɪ] N protetto

protégée ['prəutɪʒeɪ] N protetta

protein ['prəuti:n] N proteina

pro tem [prəu'tɛm] ADV ABBR (*for the time being*: = *pro tempore*) pro tempore

protest N ['prəutɛst] protesta ▶ VT, VI [prə'tɛst] protestare; **to do sth under ~** fare qc protestando; **to ~ against/about** protestare contro/per

Protestant ['prɔtɪstənt] ADJ, N protestante (*mf*)

protester, protestor [prə'tɛstər] N (*in demonstration*) dimostrante *mf*

protest march N marcia di protesta

protocol ['prəutəkɔl] N protocollo

prototype ['prəutətaɪp] N prototipo

protracted [prə'træktɪd] ADJ tirato(-a) per le lunghe

protractor [prə'træktər] N (*Geom*) goniometro

protrude [prə'tru:d] VI sporgere

protuberance [prə'tju:bərəns] N sporgenza

proud [praud] ADJ fiero(-a), orgoglioso(-a); (*pej*) superbo(-a); **to be ~ to do sth** essere onorato(-a) di fare qc; **to do sb ~** non far mancare nulla a qn; **to do o.s. ~** trattarsi bene

proudly ['praudlɪ] ADV con orgoglio, fieramente

prove [pru:v] VT provare, dimostrare ▶ VI: **to ~ (to be) correct** *etc* risultare vero(-a) *etc*; **to ~ o.s.** mostrare le proprie capacità; **to ~ o.s./itself (to be) useful** *etc* mostrarsi *or* rivelarsi utile *etc*; **he was proved right in the end** alla fine i fatti gli hanno dato ragione

Provence [prɔvɑ̃s] N Provenza

proverb ['prɔvəːb] N proverbio

proverbial [prə'vəːbɪəl] ADJ proverbiale

provide [prə'vaɪd] VT fornire, provvedere; **to ~ sb with sth** fornire *or* provvedere qn di qc; **to be provided with** essere dotato *or* munito di

▶ **provide for** VT FUS provvedere a; (*future event*) prevedere

provided [prə'vaɪdɪd] CONJ: **~ (that)** purché + *sub*, a condizione che + *sub*

Providence ['prɔvɪdəns] N Provvidenza

providing [prə'vaɪdɪŋ] CONJ purché + *sub*, a condizione che + *sub*

province ['prɔvɪns] N provincia

provincial [prə'vɪnʃəl] ADJ provinciale

provision [prə'vɪʒən] N (*supply*) riserva; (*supplying*) provvista; rifornimento; (*stipulation*) condizione *f*; **provisions** NPL (*food*) provviste *fpl*; **to make ~ for** (*one's family, future*) pensare a; **there's no ~ for this in the contract** il contratto non lo prevede

provisional [prə'vɪʒənl] ADJ provvisorio(-a) ▶ N: **P~** (*IRISH Pol*) provisional *m inv*

provisional licence N (*BRIT Aut*) ≈ foglio *m* rosa *inv*

provisionally [prə'vɪʒnəlɪ] ADV provvisoriamente; (*appoint*) a titolo provvisorio

proviso [prə'vaɪzəu] N condizione *f*; **with the ~ that** a condizione che + *sub*, a patto che + *sub*

Provo ['prɔvəu] N ABBR (*col*) = **Provisional**

provocation [prɔvə'keɪʃən] N provocazione *f*

provocative [prə'vɔkətɪv] ADJ (*aggressive*) provocatorio(-a); (*thought-provoking*) stimolante; (*seductive*) provocante

provoke [prə'vəuk] VT provocare; incitare; **to ~ sb to sth/to do** *or* **into doing sth** spingere qn a qc/a fare qc

provoking [prə'vəukɪŋ] ADJ irritante, esasperante

provost ['prɔvəst] N (*BRIT: of university*) rettore *m*; (*SCOTTISH*) sindaco

prow [prau] N prua

prowess ['prauɪs] N prodezza; **his ~ as a footballer** le sue capacità di calciatore

prowl [praul] VI (*also*: **prowl about, prowl around**) aggirarsi furtivamente ▶ N: **on the ~** in caccia

prowler ['praulər] N tipo sospetto (*che s'aggira con l'intenzione di rubare, aggredire ecc*)

proximity [prɔk'sɪmɪtɪ] N prossimità

proxy ['prɔksɪ] N procura; **by ~** per procura

PRP N ABBR (= *performance related pay*) retribuzione *f* commensurata al rendimento

prude [pru:d] N puritano(-a)

prudence ['pru:dns] N prudenza

prudent ['pru:dnt] ADJ prudente

prudish ['pru:dɪʃ] ADJ puritano(-a)

prune [pru:n] N prugna secca ▶ VT potare

pry [praɪ] VI: **to ~ into** ficcare il naso in

PS N ABBR (= *postscript*) P.S.

psalm [sɑ:m] N salmo

PSAT® N ABBR (*US*) = **Preliminary Scholastic Aptitude Test**

PSBR N ABBR (*BRIT*: = *public sector borrowing requirement*) fabbisogno di prestiti per il settore pubblico

pseud ['sjuːd] N (BRIT: col: intellectually) intellettualoide mf; (: socially) snob mf
pseudo- ['sjuːdəu] PREFIX pseudo...
pseudonym ['sjuːdənɪm] N pseudonimo
PSHE N ABBR (BRIT Scol: = personal, social and health education) formazione di formazione sociale e sanitaria
PST ABBR (US: = Pacific Standard Time) ora invernale del Pacifico
psyche ['saɪkɪ] N psiche f
psychedelic [saɪkɪ'dɛlɪk] ADJ psichedelico(-a)
psychiatric [saɪkɪ'ætrɪk] ADJ psichiatrico(-a)
psychiatrist [saɪ'kaɪətrɪst] N psichiatra mf
psychiatry [saɪ'kaɪətrɪ] N psichiatria
psychic ['saɪkɪk] ADJ (also: **psychical**) psichico(-a); (: person) dotato(-a) di qualità telepatiche
psycho ['saɪkəu] N (col) folle mf, psicopatico(-a)
psychoanalyse [saɪkəu'ænəlaɪz] VT psicanalizzare
psychoanalysis [saɪkəuə'nælɪsɪs] (pl **-ses** [-siːz]) N psicanalisi f inv
psychoanalyst [saɪkəu'ænəlɪst] N psicanalista mf
psychological [saɪkə'lɔdʒɪkl] ADJ psicologico(-a)
psychologist [saɪ'kɔlədʒɪst] N psicologo(-a)
psychology [saɪ'kɔlədʒɪ] N psicologia
psychopath ['saɪkəupæθ] N psicopatico(-a)
psychosis [saɪ'kəusɪs] (pl **psychoses** [-siːz]) N psicosi f inv
psychosomatic [saɪkəusə'mætɪk] ADJ psicosomatico(-a)
psychotherapy [saɪkəu'θɛrəpɪ] N psicoterapia
psychotic [saɪ'kɔtɪk] ADJ, N psicotico(-a)
PT N ABBR (BRIT: = physical training) ed. fisica
pt ABBR = **pint**; (= point) pt
Pt. ABBR (in place names: = Point) Pt.
PTA N ABBR (= Parent-Teacher Association) associazione genitori e insegnanti
Pte. ABBR (BRIT Mil) = **private**
PTO ABBR (= please turn over) v.r. (= vedi retro)
PTV N ABBR (US) = **pay television; public television**
pub [pʌb] N ABBR (= public house) pub m inv; vedi nota

> In Gran Bretagna e in Irlanda i pubs sono locali dove vengono servite bibite alcoliche ed analcoliche e dove è anche possibile mangiare. Sono punti di ritrovo dove spesso si può giocare a biliardo, a freccette o guardare la televisione. Le leggi che regolano la vendita degli alcolici sono molto severe in Gran Bretagna e quindi gli orari di apertura e di chiusura vengono osservati scrupolosamente.

pub crawl N: **to go on a ~** (BRIT col) fare il giro dei pub
puberty ['pjuːbətɪ] N pubertà
pubic ['pjuːbɪk] ADJ pubico(-a), del pube
public ['pʌblɪk] ADJ pubblico(-a) ▸ N pubblico; **in ~** in pubblico; **the general ~** il pubblico; **to make sth ~** render noto or di pubblico dominio qc; **to be ~ knowledge** essere di dominio pubblico; **to go ~** (Comm) emettere le azioni sul mercato
public address system N impianto di amplificazione
publican ['pʌblɪkən] N (BRIT) gestore m (or proprietario) di un pub
publication [pʌblɪ'keɪʃən] N pubblicazione f
public company N ≈ società f inv per azioni (costituita tramite pubblica sottoscrizione)
public convenience N (BRIT) gabinetti mpl
public holiday N (BRIT) giorno festivo, festa nazionale
public house N (BRIT) pub m inv
publicity [pʌb'lɪsɪtɪ] N pubblicità
publicize ['pʌblɪsaɪz] VT rendere pubblico(-a), pubblicizzare
public limited company N ≈ società per azioni a responsabilità limitata (quotata in Borsa)
publicly ['pʌblɪklɪ] ADV pubblicamente
public opinion N opinione f pubblica
public ownership N proprietà pubblica or sociale; **to be taken into ~** essere statalizzato(-a)
public prosecutor N pubblico ministero; **~'s office** ufficio del pubblico ministero
public relations N pubbliche relazioni fpl
public relations officer N addetto(-a) alle pubbliche relazioni
public school N (BRIT) scuola privata; (US) scuola statale; vedi nota

> In Inghilterra le public schools sono scuole o collegi privati di istruzione secondaria, spesso di un certo prestigio. In Scozia e negli Stati Uniti, invece, le public schools sono scuole pubbliche gratuite amministrate dallo stato.

public sector N settore m pubblico
public service vehicle N (BRIT) mezzo pubblico
public-spirited [pʌblɪk'spɪrɪtɪd] ADJ che ha senso civico
public transport, (US) public transportation N mezzi mpl pubblici
public utility N servizio pubblico
public works NPL lavori mpl pubblici
publish ['pʌblɪʃ] VT pubblicare
publisher ['pʌblɪʃər] N editore m; (firm) casa editrice
publishing ['pʌblɪʃɪŋ] N (industry) editoria; (of a book) pubblicazione f

publishing company N casa or società editrice
pub lunch N: **to go for a ~** andare a mangiare al pub
puce [pju:s] ADJ color pulce inv
puck [pʌk] N (Ice Hockey) disco
pucker ['pʌkəʳ] VT corrugare
pudding ['pudɪŋ] N budino; (BRIT: dessert) dolce m; **black ~,** (US) **blood ~** sanguinaccio; **rice ~** budino di riso
puddle ['pʌdl] N pozza, pozzanghera
puerile ['pjuəraɪl] ADJ puerile
Puerto Rico ['pwə:təu'ri:kəu] N Portorico
puff [pʌf] N sbuffo; (also: **powder puff**) piumino ► VT (also: **puff out**: sails, cheeks) gonfiare ► VI uscire a sbuffi; (pant) ansare; **to ~ out smoke** mandar fuori sbuffi di fumo; **to ~ one's pipe** tirare sboccate di fumo
puffed [pʌft] ADJ (col: out of breath) senza fiato
puffin ['pʌfɪn] N puffino
puff pastry, (US) **puff paste** N pasta sfoglia
puffy ['pʌfɪ] ADJ gonfio(-a)
pugnacious [pʌg'neɪʃəs] ADJ combattivo(-a)
pull [pul] N (tug) strattone m, tirata; (of moon, magnet, the sea etc) attrazione f; (fig) influenza ► VT tirare; (muscle) strappare, farsi uno strappo a; (trigger) premere ► VI tirare; **to give sth a ~** tirare su qc; **to ~ a face** fare una smorfia; **to ~ to pieces** fare a pezzi; **to ~ one's punches** (Boxing) risparmiare l'avversario; **not to ~ one's punches** (fig) non avere peli sulla lingua; **to ~ one's weight** dare il proprio contributo; **to ~ o.s. together** ricomporsi, riprendersi; **to ~ sb's leg** prendere in giro qn; **to ~ strings (for sb)** muovere qualche pedina (per qn)
 ► **pull about** VT (BRIT: handle roughly: object) strapazzare; (: person) malmenare
 ► **pull apart** VT (break) fare a pezzi
 ► **pull away** VI (move off: vehicle) muoversi, partire; (: boat) staccarsi dal molo, salpare; (draw back: person) indietreggiare
 ► **pull back** VT (lever etc) tirare indietro; (curtains) aprire ► VI (from confrontation etc) tirarsi indietro; (Mil: withdraw) ritirarsi
 ► **pull down** VT (house) demolire; (tree) abbattere
 ► **pull in** VI (Aut: at the kerb) accostarsi; (Rail) entrare in stazione
 ► **pull off** VT (clothes) togliere; (deal etc) portare a compimento
 ► **pull out** VI partire; (withdraw) ritirarsi; (Aut: come out of line) spostarsi sulla mezzeria ► VT staccare; far uscire; (withdraw) ritirare
 ► **pull over** VI (Aut) accostare
 ► **pull round** VI (unconscious person) rinvenire; (sick person) ristabilirsi
 ► **pull through** VI farcela

 ► **pull up** VI (stop) fermarsi ► VT (uproot) sradicare; (stop) fermare; (raise) sollevare
pulley ['pulɪ] N puleggia, carrucola
pull-out ['pulaut] N inserto ► CPD staccabile
pullover ['puləuvəʳ] N pullover m inv
pulp [pʌlp] N (of fruit) polpa; (for paper) pasta per carta; (magazines, books) stampa di qualità e di tono scadenti; **to reduce sth to ~** spappolare qc
pulpit ['pulpɪt] N pulpito
pulsate [pʌl'seɪt] VI battere, palpitare
pulse [pʌls] N polso; (Bot) legume m; **to feel** or **take sb's ~** sentire or tastare il polso a qn
pulses ['pʌlsəz] NPL (Culin) legumi mpl
pulverize ['pʌlvəraɪz] VT polverizzare
puma ['pju:mə] N puma m inv
pumice ['pʌmɪs], **pumice stone** ['pʌmɪs-] N (pietra) pomice f
pummel ['pʌml] VT dare pugni a
pump [pʌmp] N pompa; (shoe) scarpetta ► VT pompare; (fig: col) far parlare; **to ~ sb for information** cercare di strappare delle informazioni a qn
 ► **pump up** VT gonfiare
pumpkin ['pʌmpkɪn] N zucca
pun [pʌn] N gioco di parole
punch [pʌntʃ] N (blow) pugno; (fig: force) forza; (tool) punzone m; (drink) ponce m ► VT (hit): **to ~ sb/sth** dare un pugno a qn/qc; **to ~ a hole (in)** fare un buco (in)
 ► **punch in** VI (US) timbrare il cartellino (all'entrata)
 ► **punch out** VI (US) timbrare il cortellino (all'uscita)
punch card, punched card ['pʌntʃt-] N scheda perforata
punch-drunk ['pʌntʃdrʌŋk] ADJ (BRIT) stordito(-a)
punch line N (of joke) battuta finale
punch-up ['pʌntʃʌp] N (BRIT col) rissa
punctual ['pʌŋktjuəl] ADJ puntuale
punctuality [pʌŋktju'ælɪtɪ] N puntualità
punctually ['pʌŋktjuəlɪ] ADV puntualmente; **it will start ~ at 6** comincerà alle 6 precise or in punto
punctuate ['pʌŋktjueɪt] VT punteggiare
punctuation [pʌŋktju'eɪʃən] N interpunzione f, punteggiatura
punctuation mark N segno d'interpunzione
puncture ['pʌŋktʃəʳ] N (BRIT) foratura ► VT forare; **to have a ~** (Aut) forare (una gomma)
pundit ['pʌndɪt] N sapientone(-a)
pungent ['pʌndʒənt] ADJ piccante; (fig) mordace, caustico(-a)
punish ['pʌnɪʃ] VT punire; **to ~ sb for sth/for doing sth** punire qn per qc/per aver fatto qc
punishable ['pʌnɪʃəbl] ADJ punibile
punishing ['pʌnɪʃɪŋ] ADJ (fig: exhausting) sfiancante

p

punishment ['pʌnɪʃmənt] N punizione f; **to take a lot of ~** (col: boxer) incassare parecchi colpi; (car) essere messo(-a) a dura prova

punk [pʌŋk] N (person: also: **punk rocker**) punk mf; (music: also: **punk rock**) musica punk, punk rock m; (US col: hoodlum) teppista m

punt [pʌnt] N (boat) barchino; (Football) colpo a volo; (IRISH) sterlina irlandese ▶ VI (BRIT: bet) scommettere

punter ['pʌntəʳ] N (BRIT: gambler) scommettitore(-trice)

puny ['pjuːnɪ] ADJ gracile

pup [pʌp] N cucciolo(-a)

pupil ['pjuːpl] N allievo(-a); (Anat) pupilla

puppet ['pʌpɪt] N burattino

puppet government N governo fantoccio

puppy ['pʌpɪ] N cucciolo(-a), cagnolino(-a)

purchase ['pəːtʃɪs] N acquisto, compera; (grip) presa ▶ VT comprare; **to get a ~ on** (grip) trovare un appoggio su

purchase order N ordine m d'acquisto, ordinazione f

purchase price N prezzo d'acquisto

purchaser ['pəːtʃɪsəʳ] N compratore(-trice)

purchase tax N (BRIT) tassa d'acquisto

purchasing power ['pəːtʃɪsɪŋ-] N potere m d'acquisto

pure [pjuəʳ] ADJ puro(-a); **a ~ wool jumper** un golf di pura lana; **it's laziness ~ and simple** è pura pigrizia

purebred ['pjuəbrɛd] ADJ di razza pura

purée ['pjuəreɪ] N purè m inv

purely ['pjuəlɪ] ADV puramente

purge [pəːdʒ] N (Med) purga; (Pol) epurazione f ▶ VT purgare; (fig) epurare

purification [pjuərɪfɪ'keɪʃən] N purificazione f

purify ['pjuərɪfaɪ] VT purificare

purist ['pjuərɪst] N purista mf

puritan ['pjuərɪtən] ADJ, N puritano(-a)

puritanical [pjuərɪ'tænɪkl] ADJ puritano(-a)

purity ['pjuərɪtɪ] N purezza

purl [pəːl] N punto rovescio ▶ VT lavorare a rovescio

purloin [pəː'lɔɪn] VT rubare

purple ['pəːpl] ADJ di porpora; viola inv

purport [pəː'pɔːt] VI: **to ~ to be/do** pretendere di essere/fare

purpose ['pəːpəs] N intenzione f, scopo; **on ~** apposta, di proposito; **for illustrative purposes** a titolo illustrativo; **for teaching purposes** per l'insegnamento; **for the purposes of this meeting** agli effetti di questa riunione; **to no ~** senza nessun risultato, inutilmente

purpose-built ['pəːpəs'bɪlt] ADJ (BRIT) costruito(-a) allo scopo

purposeful ['pəːpəsful] ADJ deciso(-a), risoluto(-a)

purposely ['pəːpəslɪ] ADV apposta

purr [pəːʳ] N fusa fpl ▶ VI fare le fusa

purse [pəːs] N (BRIT) borsellino; (US: handbag) borsetta, borsa ▶ VT contrarre

purser ['pəːsəʳ] N (Naut) commissario di bordo

purse snatcher [-'snætʃəʳ] N (US) scippatore m

pursue [pə'sjuː] VT inseguire; essere alla ricerca di; (inquiry, matter) approfondire; (fig: activity etc) continuare con; (: aim etc) perseguire

pursuer [pə'sjuːəʳ] N inseguitore(-trice)

pursuit [pə'sjuːt] N inseguimento; (occupation) occupazione f, attività f inv; (fig) ricerca; (pastime) passatempo; **in (the) ~ of sth** alla ricerca di qc; **scientific pursuits** ricerche fpl scientifiche

purveyor [pə'veɪəʳ] N fornitore(-trice)

pus [pʌs] N pus m

push [puʃ] N spinta; (effort) grande sforzo; (drive) energia ▶ VT spingere; (button) premere; (fig) fare pubblicità a; (thrust): **to ~ sth (into)** ficcare qc (in) ▶ VI spingere; premere; **to ~ a door open/shut** aprire/chiudere una porta con una spinta or spingendola; **to be pushed for time/money** essere a corto di tempo/soldi; **she is pushing 50** (col) va per i 50; **to ~ for** (better pay, conditions etc) insistere per ottenere; **"~"** (on door) "spingere"; (on bell) "suonare"; **at a ~** (BRIT col) in caso di necessità

▶ **push aside** VT scostare

▶ **push in** VI introdursi a forza

▶ **push off** VI (col) filare

▶ **push on** VI (continue) continuare

▶ **push over** VT far cadere

▶ **push through** VI farsi largo spingendo ▶ VT (measure) far approvare

▶ **push up** VT (total, prices) far salire

push-bike ['puʃbaɪk] N (BRIT) bicicletta

push-button ['puʃbʌtn] ADJ a pulsante

pushchair ['puʃtʃɛəʳ] (BRIT) N passeggino

pusher ['puʃəʳ] N (also: **drug pusher**) spacciatore(-trice) (di droga)

pushover ['puʃəuvəʳ] N (col): **it's a ~** è un lavoro da bambini

push-up ['puʃʌp] N (US: press-up) flessione f sulle braccia

pushy ['puʃɪ] ADJ (pej) troppo intraprendente

puss [pus], **pussy(-cat)** ['pusɪ-] N micio

put [put] (pt, pp ~) VT mettere, porre; (say) dire, esprimere; (a question) fare; (estimate) stimare ▶ ADV: **to stay ~** non muoversi; **to ~ sb to bed** mettere qn a letto; **to ~ sb in a good/bad mood** mettere qn di buon/cattivo umore; **to ~ sb to a lot of trouble** scomodare qn; **to ~ a lot of time into sth** dedicare molto tempo a qc; **to ~ money on a horse** scommettere su un cavallo; **how**

shall I ~ it? come dire?; **I ~ it to you that ...** (BRIT) io sostengo che ...

▸ **put about** VI (Naut) virare di bordo ▸ VT (rumour) diffondere

▸ **put across** VT (ideas etc) comunicare, far capire

▸ **put aside** VT (lay down: book etc) mettere da una parte, posare; (save) mettere da parte; (in shop) tenere da parte

▸ **put away** VT (clothes, toys etc) mettere via; (return) mettere a posto

▸ **put back** VT (replace) rimettere (a posto); (postpone) rinviare; (delay) ritardare; (set back: watch, clock) mettere indietro; **this will ~ us back 10 years** questo ci farà tornare indietro di 10 anni

▸ **put by** VT (money) mettere da parte

▸ **put down** VT (parcel etc) posare, mettere giù; (pay) versare; (in writing) mettere per iscritto; (suppress: revolt etc) reprimere, sopprimere; (attribute) attribuire

▸ **put forward** VT (ideas) avanzare, proporre; (date) anticipare

▸ **put in** VT (application, complaint) presentare; (time, effort) mettere

▸ **put in for** VT FUS (job) far domanda per; (promotion) far domanda di

▸ **put off** VT (postpone) rimandare, rinviare; (discourage) dissuadere

▸ **put on** VT (clothes, lipstick etc) mettere; (light etc) accendere; (play etc) mettere in scena; (concert, exhibition etc) allestire, organizzare; (extra bus, train etc) mettere in servizio; (food, meal) mettere su; (brake) mettere; (assume: accent, manner) affettare; (col: tease) prendere in giro; (inform, indicate): **to ~ sb on to sb/sth** indicare qn/qc a qn; **to ~ on weight** ingrassare; **to ~ on airs** darsi delle arie

▸ **put out** VT mettere fuori; (one's hand) porgere; (light etc) spegnere; (inconvenience: person) scomodare; (dislocate: shoulder, knee) lussarsi; (: back) farsi uno strappo a ▸ VI (Naut): **to ~ out to sea** prendere il largo; **to ~ out from Plymouth** partire da Plymouth

▸ **put through** VT (Tel: caller) mettere in comunicazione; (: call) passare; (plan) far approvare; **~ me through to Miss Blair** mi passi la signorina Blair

▸ **put together** VT mettere insieme, riunire; (assemble: furniture) montare; (: meal) improvvisare

▸ **put up** VT (raise) sollevare, alzare; (: umbrella) aprire; (: tent) montare; (pin up) affiggere; (hang) appendere; (build) costruire, erigere; (increase) aumentare; (accommodate) alloggiare; (incite): **to ~ sb up to doing sth** istigare qn a fare qc; **to ~ sth up for sale** mettere in vendita qc

▸ **put upon** VT FUS: **to be ~ upon** (imposed on) farsi mettere sotto i piedi

▸ **put up with** VT FUS sopportare

putrid ['pjuːtrɪd] ADJ putrido(-a)

putt [pʌt] VT (ball) colpire leggermente ▸ N colpo leggero

putter ['pʌtəʳ] N (Golf) putter m inv ▸ VI (US) = **potter**

putting green ['pʌtɪŋ-] N green m inv; campo da putting

putty ['pʌtɪ] N stucco

put-up ['pʊtʌp] ADJ: **~ job** montatura

puzzle ['pʌzl] N enigma m, mistero; (jigsaw) puzzle m; (also: **crossword puzzle**) parole fpl incrociate, cruciverba m inv ▸ VT confondere, rendere perplesso(-a) ▸ VI scervellarsi; **to ~ over** (sb's actions) cercare di capire; (mystery, problem) cercare di risolvere

puzzled ADJ perplesso(-a); **to be ~ about sth** domandarsi il perché di qc

puzzling ['pʌzlɪŋ] ADJ (question) poco chiaro(-a); (attitude, set of instructions) incomprensibile

PVC N ABBR (= polyvinyl chloride) P.V.C. m

Pvt. ABBR (US Mil) = **private**

PW N ABBR (US) = **prisoner of war**

pw ABBR = **per week**

PX N ABBR (US Mil) = **post exchange**

pygmy ['pɪgmɪ] N pigmeo(-a)

pyjamas (BRIT), (US) **pajamas** [pə'dʒɑːməz] NPL pigiama m; **a pair of ~** un pigiama

pylon ['paɪlən] N pilone m

pyramid ['pɪrəmɪd] N piramide f

Pyrenean [pɪrə'niːən] ADJ pirenaico(-a)

Pyrenees [pɪrə'niːz] NPL: **the ~** i Pirenei

Pyrex® ['paɪrɛks] N Pirex® m inv ▸ CPD: **~ dish** pirofila

python ['paɪθən] N pitone m

Qq

Q, q [kju:] N (*letter*) Q, q *f inv or m inv*; **Q for Queen** ≈ Q come Quarto

Qatar [kæ'tɑːʳ] N Qatar *m*

QC N ABBR (*BRIT*: = *Queen's Counsel*) *avvocato della Corona*

QED ABBR (= *quod erat demonstrandum*) qed

QM N ABBR = **quartermaster**

q.t. N ABBR *col*: = **quiet**; **on the q.t.** di nascosto

qty ABBR = **quantity**

quack [kwæk] N (*of duck*) qua qua *m inv*; (*pej: doctor*) ciarlatano(-a)

quad [kwɔd] N ABBR = **quadrangle**; **quadruple**; **quadruplet**

quadrangle ['kwɔdræŋgl] N (*Math*) quadrilatero; (*courtyard*) cortile *m*

quadruped ['kwɔdrupɛd] N quadrupede *m*

quadruple [kwɔ'drupl] ADJ quadruplo(-a) ▶ N quadruplo ▶ VT quadruplicare ▶ VI quadruplicarsi

quadruplet [kwɔ'druːplɪt] N uno(-a) di quattro gemelli

quagmire ['kwægmaɪəʳ] N pantano

quail [kweɪl] N (*Zool*) quaglia ▶ VI (*person*): **to ~ at** *or* **before** perdersi d'animo davanti a

quaint [kweɪnt] ADJ bizzarro(-a); (*old-fashioned*) antiquato(-a) e pittoresco(-a)

quake [kweɪk] VI tremare ▶ N ABBR = **earthquake**

Quaker ['kweɪkəʳ] N quacchero(-a)

qualification [kwɔlɪfɪ'keɪʃən] N (*degree etc*) qualifica, titolo; (*ability*) competenza, qualificazione *f*; (*limitation*) riserva, restrizione *f*; **what are your qualifications?** quali sono le sue qualifiche?

qualified ['kwɔlɪfaɪd] ADJ qualificato(-a); (*able*) competente, qualificato(-a); (*limited*) condizionato(-a); **~ for/to do** qualificato(-a) per/per fare; **he's not ~ for the job** non ha i requisiti necessari per questo lavoro; **it was a ~ success** è stato un successo parziale

qualify ['kwɔlɪfaɪ] VT abilitare; (*limit: statement*) modificare, precisare ▶ VI: **to ~ (as)** qualificarsi (come); **to ~ (for)** acquistare i requisiti necessari (per); (*Sport*) qualificarsi (per *or* a); **to ~ as an engineer** diventare un perito tecnico

qualifying ['kwɔlɪfaɪɪŋ] ADJ (*exam*) di ammissione; (*round*) eliminatorio(-a)

qualitative ['kwɔlɪtətɪv] ADJ qualitativo(-a)

quality ['kwɔlɪtɪ] N qualità *f inv* ▶ CPD di qualità; **of good ~** di buona qualità; **of poor ~** scadente; **~ of life** qualità della vita

quality control N controllo di qualità

quality papers NPL, **quality press** N (*BRIT*): **the ~** la stampa d'informazione; *vedi nota*

> Il termine *quality press* si riferisce ai quotidiani o ai settimanali che offrono un'informazione seria ed approfondita. Questi giornali si differenziano da quelli popolari, i *tabloid*, per formato e contenuti. Questa divisione tra tipi di giornali riflette il tradizionale divario tra classi sociali nella società britannica; *vedi anche* **tabloid press**.

qualm [kwɑːm] N dubbio; scrupolo; **to have qualms about sth** avere degli scrupoli per qc

quandary ['kwɔndrɪ] N: **in a ~** in un dilemma

quango ['kwæŋgəu] N ABBR (*BRIT*: = *quasi-autonomous non-governmental organization*) *commissione consultiva di nomina governativa*

quantifiable ['kwɔntɪfaɪəbl] ADJ quantificabile

quantify ['kwɔntɪfaɪ] VT quantificare

quantitative ['kwɔntɪtətɪv] ADJ quantitativo(-a)

quantity ['kwɔntɪtɪ] N quantità *f inv*; **in ~** in grande quantità

quantity surveyor N (*BRIT*) geometra *m* (*specializzato nel calcolare la quantità e il costo del materiale da costruzione*)

quantum leap ['kwɔntəm-] N (*fig*) enorme cambiamento

quarantine ['kwɔrntiːn] N quarantena

quark [kwɑːk] N quark *m inv*

quarrel ['kwɔrl] N lite *f*, disputa ▶ VI litigare; **to have a ~ with sb** litigare con qn; **I've no ~**

with him non ho niente contro di lui; **I can't ~ with that** non ho niente da ridire su questo

quarrelsome ['kwɔrəlsəm] ADJ litigioso(-a)

quarry ['kwɔrɪ] N (*for stone*) cava; (*animal*) preda ▶ VT (*marble etc*) estrarre

quart [kwɔ:t] N due pinte *fpl*, ≈ litro

quarter ['kwɔ:tə*ʳ*] N quarto; (*of year*) trimestre *m*; (*district*) quartiere *m*; (US, CANADA: *25 cents*) quarto di dollaro, 25 centesimi ▶ VT dividere in quattro; (*Mil*) alloggiare; **quarters** NPL (*living quarters*) alloggio; (*Mil*) alloggi *mpl*, quadrato; **to pay by the ~** pagare trimestralmente; **a ~ of an hour** un quarto d'ora; **it's a ~ to 3**, (US) **it's a ~ of 3** sono le 3 meno un quarto, manca un quarto alle 3; **it's a ~ past 3**, (US) **it's a ~ after 3** sono le 3 e un quarto; **from all quarters** da tutte le parti *or* direzioni; **at close quarters** a distanza ravvicinata

quarterback ['kwɔ:təbæk] N (*US Football*) quarterback *m inv*

quarter-deck ['kwɔ:tədɛk] N (*Naut*) cassero

quarter final N quarto di finale

quarterly ['kwɔ:təlɪ] ADJ trimestrale ▶ ADV trimestralmente ▶ N periodico trimestrale

quartermaster ['kwɔ:təmɑ:stə*ʳ*] N (*Mil*) furiere *m*

quartet, quartette [kwɔ:'tɛt] N quartetto

quarto ['kwɔ:təu] ADJ, N in quarto *m inv*

quartz [kwɔ:ts] N quarzo ▶ CPD di quarzo; (*watch, clock*) al quarzo

quash [kwɔʃ] VT (*verdict*) annullare

quasi- ['kweɪzaɪ] PREFIX quasi + *noun*; quasi, pressoché + *adjective*

quaver ['kweɪvə*ʳ*] N (*BRIT Mus*) croma ▶ VI tremolare

quay [ki:] N (*also*: **quayside**) banchina

Que. ABBR (CANADA) = **Quebec**

queasy ['kwi:zɪ] ADJ (*stomach*) delicato(-a); **to feel ~** aver la nausea

Quebec [kwɪ'bɛk] N Quebec *m*

queen [kwi:n] N (*gen*) regina; (*Cards etc*) regina, donna

queen mother N regina madre

Queen's speech N (BRIT); *vedi nota*

Durante la sessione di apertura del Parlamento britannico il sovrano legge un discorso redatto dal primo ministro, il *Queen's speech* (se si tratta della regina), che contiene le linee generali del nuovo programma politico.

queer [kwɪə*ʳ*] ADJ strano(-a), curioso(-a); (*suspicious*) dubbio(-a), sospetto(-a); (BRIT: *sick*): **I feel ~** mi sento poco bene ▶ N (*col*) finocchio

quell [kwɛl] VT domare

quench [kwɛntʃ] VT (*flames*) spegnere; **to ~ one's thirst** dissetarsi

querulous ['kwɛrələs] ADJ querulo(-a)

query ['kwɪərɪ] N domanda, questione *f*; (*doubt*) dubbio ▶ VT mettere in questione; (*disagree with, dispute*) contestare

quest [kwɛst] N cerca, ricerca

question ['kwɛstʃən] N domanda, questione *f* ▶ VT (*person*) interrogare; (*plan, idea*) mettere in questione *or* in dubbio; **to ask sb a ~**, **put a ~ to sb** fare una domanda a qn; **to bring** *or* **call sth into ~** mettere in dubbio qc; **the ~ is** ... il problema è ...; **it's a ~ of doing** si tratta di fare; **there's some ~ of doing** c'è chi suggerisce di fare; **beyond ~** fuori di dubbio; **out of the ~** fuori discussione, impossibile

questionable ['kwɛstʃənəbl] ADJ discutibile

questioner ['kwɛstʃənə*ʳ*] N interrogante *mf*

questioning ['kwɛstʃənɪŋ] ADJ interrogativo(-a) ▶ N interrogatorio

question mark N punto interrogativo

questionnaire [kwɛstʃə'nɛə*ʳ*] N questionario

queue [kju:] N (BRIT) coda, fila ▶ VI fare la coda; **to jump the ~** passare davanti agli altri (in una coda)

quibble ['kwɪbl] VI cavillare

quiche [ki:ʃ] N *torta salata a base di uova, formaggio, prosciutto o altro*

quick [kwɪk] ADJ rapido(-a), veloce; (*reply*) pronto(-a); (*mind*) pronto(-a), acuto(-a) ▶ ADV rapidamente, presto ▶ N: **cut to the ~** (*fig*) toccato(-a) sul vivo; **be ~!** fa presto!; **to be ~ to act** agire prontamente; **she was ~ to see that ...** ha visto subito che ...

quicken ['kwɪkn] VT accelerare, affrettare; (*rouse*) animare, stimolare ▶ VI accelerare, affrettarsi

quick fix N soluzione *f* tampone *inv*

quicklime ['kwɪklaɪm] N calce *f* viva

quickly ['kwɪklɪ] ADV rapidamente, velocemente; **we must act ~** dobbiamo agire tempestivamente

quickness ['kwɪknɪs] N rapidità; prontezza; acutezza

quicksand ['kwɪksænd] N sabbie *fpl* mobili

quickstep ['kwɪkstɛp] N *tipo di ballo simile al fox-trot*

quick-tempered [kwɪk'tɛmpəd] ADJ che si arrabbia facilmente

quick-witted [kwɪk'wɪtɪd] ADJ pronto(-a) d'ingegno

quid [kwɪd] N (*pl inv*: BRIT *col*) sterlina

quid pro quo ['kwɪdprəu'kwəu] N contraccambio

quiet ['kwaɪət] ADJ tranquillo(-a), quieto(-a); (*reserved*) quieto(-a), taciturno(-a); (*ceremony*) semplice; (*not noisy: engine*) silenzioso(-a); (*not busy: day*) calmo(-a), tranquillo(-a); (: *colour*) discreto(-a) ▶ N tranquillità, calma ▶ VT, VI (US) = **quieten**; **keep ~!** sta zitto!; **on the ~** di nascosto; **I'll have a ~ word with**

him gli dirò due parole in privato; **business is ~ at this time of year** questa è la stagione morta

quieten ['kwaɪətn] vɪ (Brɪt: *also*: **quieten down**) calmarsi, chetarsi ▸ vт calmare, chetare

quietly ['kwaɪətlɪ] adv tranquillamente, calmamente; silenziosamente

quietness ['kwaɪətnɪs] N tranquillità, calma; silenzio

quill [kwɪl] N penna d'oca

quilt [kwɪlt] N trapunta; **continental ~** piumino

quin [kwɪn] N abbr = **quintuplet**

quince [kwɪns] N (mela) cotogna; (*tree*) cotogno

quinine [kwɪ'niːn] N chinino

quintet, quintette [kwɪn'tɛt] N quintetto

quintuplet [kwɪn'tjuːplɪt] N uno(-a) di cinque gemelli

quip [kwɪp] N battuta di spirito

quire ['kwaɪəʳ] N ventesima parte di una risma

quirk [kwəːk] N ghiribizzo; **by some ~ of fate** per un capriccio della sorte

quirky ['kwəːkɪ] adj stravagante

quit [kwɪt] (*pt, pp ~ or* **quitted**) vт mollare; (*premises*) lasciare, partire da ▸ vɪ (*give up*) mollare; (*resign*) dimettersi; **to ~ doing** smettere di fare; **~ stalling!** (*US col*) non tirarla per le lunghe!; **notice to ~** (*Brɪt*) preavviso (*dato all'inquilino*)

quite [kwaɪt] adv (*rather*) assai; (*entirely*) completamente, del tutto; **I ~ understand** capisco perfettamente; **~ a few of them** non pochi di loro; **~ (so)!** esatto!; **~ new** proprio nuovo; **that's not ~ right** non è proprio esatto; **she's ~ pretty** è piuttosto carina

Quito ['kiːtəu] N Quito *m*

quits [kwɪts] adj: **~ (with)** pari (con); **let's call it ~** adesso siamo pari

quiver ['kwɪvəʳ] vɪ tremare, fremere ▸ N (*for arrows*) faretra

quiz [kwɪz] N (*game*) quiz *m inv*; indovinello ▸ vт interrogare

quizzical ['kwɪzɪkəl] adj enigmatico(-a)

quoits [kwɔɪts] npl gioco degli anelli

quorum ['kwɔːrəm] N quorum *m*

quota ['kwəutə] N quota

quotation [kwəu'teɪʃən] N citazione *f*; (*of shares etc*) quotazione *f*; (*estimate*) preventivo

quotation marks npl virgolette *fpl*

quote [kwəut] N citazione *f* ▸ vт (*sentence*) citare; (*price*) dare, indicare, fissare; (*shares*) quotare ▸ vɪ: **to ~ from** citare; **to ~ for a job** dare un preventivo per un lavoro; **quotes** npl (*col*) = **quotation marks**; **in quotes** tra virgolette; **~ ... unquote** (*in dictation*) aprire le virgolette ... chiudere le virgolette

quotient ['kwəuʃənt] N quoziente *m*

qv abbr (= *quod vide: which see*) v

qwerty keyboard ['kwəːtɪ-] N tastiera qwerty *inv*

Rr

R, r [ɑːʳ] N (*letter*) R, r f *inv or m inv*; **R for Robert**, (*US*) **R for Roger** ≈ R come Roma

R ABBR (= *Réaumur (scale)*) R; (= *river*) F; (= *right*) D; (*US Cine*: = *restricted*) ≈ vietato; (*US Pol*) = **republican**; (*BRIT*) = **Rex**; **Regina**

RA N ABBR (*BRIT*) = **Royal Academy**; **Royal Academician** ▶ ABBR = **rear admiral**

RAAF N ABBR = **Royal Australian Air Force**

Rabat [rə'bɑːt] N Rabat f

rabbi ['ræbaɪ] N rabbino

rabbit ['ræbɪt] N coniglio ▶ VI: **to ~ (on)** (*BRIT*) blaterare

rabbit hole N tana di coniglio

rabbit hutch N conigliera

rabble ['ræbl] N (*pej*) canaglia, plebaglia

rabid ['ræbɪd] ADJ rabbioso(-a); (*fig*) fanatico(-a)

rabies ['reɪbiːz] N rabbia

RAC N ABBR (*BRIT*: = *Royal Automobile Club*) ≈ A.C.I. m (= *Automobile Club d'Italia*)

raccoon, racoon [rə'kuːn] N procione m

race [reɪs] N razza; (*competition, rush*) corsa ▶ VT (*person*) gareggiare (in corsa) con; (*horse*) far correre; (*engine*) imballare ▶ VI correre; (*engine*) imballarsi; **the human ~** la razza umana; **he raced across the road** ha attraversato la strada di corsa; **to ~ in/out** *etc* precipitarsi dentro/fuori *etc*

race car N (*US*) = **racing car**

race car driver N (*US*) = **racing driver**

racecourse ['reɪskɔːs] N campo di corse, ippodromo

racehorse ['reɪshɔːs] N cavallo da corsa

race relations NPL rapporti razziali

racetrack ['reɪstræk] N pista

racial ['reɪʃl] ADJ razziale

racial discrimination N discriminazione f razziale

racialism ['reɪʃəlɪzəm] N razzismo

racialist ['reɪʃəlɪst] ADJ, N razzista *mf*

racing ['reɪsɪŋ] N corsa

racing car N (*BRIT*) macchina da corsa

racing driver N (*BRIT*) corridore m automobilista

racism ['reɪsɪzəm] N razzismo

racist ['reɪsɪst] ADJ, N (*pej*) razzista *mf*

rack [ræk] N rastrelliera; (*also*: **luggage rack**) rete f, portabagagli m *inv*; (*also*: **roof rack**) portabagagli; (: *dish rack*) scolapiatti m *inv* ▶ VT torturare, tormentare; **magazine ~** portariviste m *inv*; **shoe ~** scarpiera; **toast ~** portatoast m *inv*; **to go to ~ and ruin** (*building*) andare in rovina; (*business*) andare in malora *or* a catafascio; **to ~ one's brains** scervellarsi; **racked by** torturato(-a) da ▶ **rack up** VT accumulare

racket ['rækɪt] N (*for tennis*) racchetta; (*noise*) fracasso; baccano; (*swindle*) imbroglio, truffa; (*organized crime*) racket m *inv*

racketeer [rækɪ'tɪəʳ] N (*US*) trafficante *mf*

racoon [rə'kuːn] N = **raccoon**

racquet ['rækɪt] N racchetta

racy ['reɪsɪ] ADJ brioso(-a); piccante

RADA ['rɑːdə] N ABBR (*BRIT*) = **Royal Academy of Dramatic Art**

radar ['reɪdɑːʳ] N radar m ▶ CPD radar *inv*

radar trap N controllo della velocità con radar

radial ['reɪdɪəl] ADJ (*also*: **radial-ply**) radiale

radiance ['reɪdɪəns] N splendore m, radiosità

radiant ['reɪdɪənt] ADJ raggiante; (*Physics*) radiante

radiate ['reɪdɪeɪt] VT (*heat*) irraggiare, irradiare ▶ VI (*lines*) irradiarsi

radiation [reɪdɪ'eɪʃən] N irradiamento; (*radioactive*) radiazione f

radiation sickness N malattia da radiazioni

radiator ['reɪdɪeɪtəʳ] N radiatore m

radiator cap N tappo del radiatore

radiator grill N (*Aut*) mascherina, calandra

radical ['rædɪkl] ADJ radicale

radii ['reɪdɪaɪ] NPL *of* **radius**

radio ['reɪdɪəu] N radio f *inv* ▶ VT (*information*) trasmettere per radio; (*one's position*) comunicare via radio; (*person*) chiamare via radio ▶ VI: **to ~ to sb** comunicare via radio con qn; **on the ~** alla radio

radio... ['reɪdɪəu] PREFIX radio...

r

radioactive ['reɪdɪəʊ'æktɪv] ADJ radioattivo(-a)

radioactivity ['reɪdɪəʊæk'tɪvɪtɪ] N radioattività

radio announcer N annunciatore/trice della radio

radio-controlled ['reɪdɪəʊkən'trəʊld] ADJ radiocomandato(-a), radioguidato(-a)

radiographer [reɪdɪ'ɒgrəfə^r] N (*tecnico*) radiologo(-a)

radiography [reɪdɪ'ɒgrəfɪ] N radiografia

radiologist [reɪdɪ'ɒlədʒɪst] N (*medico*) radiologo(-a)

radiology [reɪdɪ'ɒlədʒɪ] N radiologia

radio station N stazione *f* radio *inv*

radio taxi N radiotaxi *m inv*

radiotelephone ['reɪdɪəʊ'tɛlɪfəʊn] N radiotelefono

radiotherapist ['reɪdɪəʊ'θɛrəpɪst] N radioterapista *mf*

radiotherapy ['reɪdɪəʊ'θɛrəpɪ] N radioterapia

radish ['rædɪʃ] N ravanello

radium ['reɪdɪəm] N radio

radius ['reɪdɪəs] (*pl* **radii** [-ɪaɪ]) N raggio; (*Anat*) radio; **within a ~ of 50 miles** in un raggio di 50 miglia

RAF N ABBR (*BRIT*) = **Royal Air Force**

raffia ['ræfɪə] N rafia

raffish ['ræfɪʃ] ADJ dal look trasandato

raffle ['ræfl] N lotteria ▶ VT (*object*) mettere in palio

raft [rɑːft] N zattera; (*also*: **life raft**) zattera di salvataggio

rafter ['rɑːftə^r] N trave *f*

rag [ræg] N straccio, cencio; (*pej: newspaper*) giornalaccio, bandiera; (*for charity*) *iniziativa studentesca a scopo benefico* ▶ VT (*BRIT*) prendere in giro; **rags** NPL (*torn clothes*) stracci *mpl*, brandelli *mpl*; **in rags** stracciato

rag-and-bone man ['rægən'bəʊn-] N (*irreg*) straccivendolo

ragbag ['rægbæg] N (*fig*) guazzabuglio

rag doll N bambola di pezza

rage [reɪdʒ] N (*fury*) collera, furia ▶ VI (*person*) andare su tutte le furie; (*storm*) infuriare; **it's all the ~** fa furore; **to fly into a ~** andare *or* montare su tutte le furie

ragged ['rægɪd] ADJ (*edge*) irregolare; (*cuff*) logoro(-a); (*appearance*) pezzente

raging ['reɪdʒɪŋ] ADJ (*all senses*) furioso(-a); **in a ~ temper** su tutte le furie

rag trade N (*col*): **the ~** l'abbigliamento

rag week N (*BRIT*); *vedi nota*

Durante il *rag week*, gli studenti universitari organizzano vari spettacoli e manifestazioni i cui proventi vengono devoluti in beneficenza.

raid [reɪd] N (*Mil*) incursione *f*; (*criminal*) rapina; (*by police*) irruzione *f* ▶ VT fare un'incursione in; rapinare; fare irruzione in

raider ['reɪdə^r] N rapinatore(-trice); (*plane*) aeroplano da incursione

rail [reɪl] N (*on stair*) ringhiera; (*on bridge, balcony*) parapetto; (*of ship*) battagliola; (*for train*) rotaia; **rails** NPL binario, rotaie *fpl*; **by ~** per ferrovia, in treno

railcard ['reɪlkɑːd] N (*BRIT*) tessera di riduzione ferroviaria

railing ['reɪlɪŋ] N, **railings** ['reɪlɪŋz] NPL ringhiere *fpl*

railroad (*US*) N = **railway**

railway (*BRIT*) ['reɪlweɪ], (*US*) **railroad** ['reɪlrəʊd] N ferrovia

railway engine N (*BRIT*) locomotiva

railway line N (*BRIT*) linea ferroviaria

railwayman ['reɪlweɪmən] N (*irreg*) (*BRIT*) ferroviere *m*

railway station N (*BRIT*) stazione *f* ferroviaria

rain [reɪn] N pioggia ▶ VI piovere; **in the ~** sotto la pioggia; **it's raining** piove; **it's raining cats and dogs** piove a catinelle

rainbow ['reɪnbəʊ] N arcobaleno

raincoat ['reɪnkəʊt] N impermeabile *m*

raindrop ['reɪndrɒp] N goccia di pioggia

rainfall ['reɪnfɔːl] N pioggia; (*measurement*) piovosità

rainforest ['reɪnfɒrɪst] N foresta pluviale *or* equatoriale

rainproof ['reɪnpruːf] ADJ impermeabile

rainstorm ['reɪnstɔːm] N pioggia torrenziale

rainwater ['reɪnwɔːtə^r] N acqua piovana

rainy ['reɪnɪ] ADJ piovoso(-a)

raise [reɪz] N aumento ▶ VT (*lift*) alzare; sollevare; (*build*) erigere; (*increase*) aumentare; (*a debate, doubt, question*) sollevare; (*cattle, family*) allevare; (*crop*) coltivare; (*army, funds*) raccogliere; (*loan*) ottenere; (*end: siege, embargo*) togliere; **to ~ one's voice** alzare la voce; **to ~ sb's hopes** accendere le speranze di qn; **to ~ one's glass to sb/sth** brindare a qn/qc; **to ~ a laugh/a smile** far ridere/sorridere

raisin ['reɪzn] N uva secca

Raj [rɑːdʒ] N: **the ~** l'impero britannico (*in India*)

rajah ['rɑːdʒə] N ragià *m inv*

rake [reɪk] N (*tool*) rastrello; (*person*) libertino ▶ VT (*garden*) rastrellare; (*with machine gun*) spazzare ▶ VI: **to ~ through** (*fig: search*) frugare tra

rake-off ['reɪkɔf] N (*col*) parte *f* percentuale, fetta

rakish ['reɪkɪʃ] ADJ dissoluto(-a); disinvolto(-a)

rally ['rælɪ] N (*Pol etc*) riunione *f*; (*Aut*) rally

m inv; (*Tennis*) scambio ▶ VT riunire, radunare ▶ VI raccogliersi, radunarsi; (*sick person, Stock Exchange*) riprendersi

▶ **rally round** VT FUS raggrupparsi intorno a; venire in aiuto di

rallying point ['ræliɪŋ-] N (*Pol, Mil*) punto di riunione, punto di raduno

RAM [ræm] N ABBR (*Comput:* = *random access memory*) RAM *f*

ram [ræm] N montone *m*, ariete *m*; (*device*) ariete ▶ VT conficcare; (*crash into*) cozzare, sbattere contro; percuotere; speronare

Ramadan [ræmə'dæn] N Ramadan *m inv*

ramble ['ræmbl] N escursione *f* ▶ VI (*pej: also:* **ramble on**) divagare

rambler ['ræmblə'] N escursionista *mf*; (*Bot*) rosa rampicante

rambling ['ræmblɪŋ] ADJ (*speech*) sconnesso(-a); (*Bot*) rampicante; (*house*) tutto(-a) nicchie e corridoi

rambunctious [ræm'bʌŋkʃəs] ADJ (*US*) = **rumbustious**

RAMC N ABBR (*Brit*) = **Royal Army Medical Corps**

ramification [ræmɪfɪ'keɪʃən] N ramificazione *f*

ramp [ræmp] N rampa; **on/off** ~ (*US Aut*) raccordo di entrata/uscita

rampage [ræm'peɪdʒ] N: **to go on the** ~ scatenarsi in modo violento ▶ VI: **they went rampaging through the town** si sono scatenati in modo violento per la città

rampant ['ræmpənt] ADJ (*disease etc*) che infierisce

rampart ['ræmpɑːt] N bastione *m*

ram raiding [-reɪdɪŋ] N *il rapinare un negozio sfondandone la vetrina con un veicolo rubato*

ramshackle ['ræmʃækl] ADJ (*house*) cadente; (*car etc*) sgangherato(-a)

RAN N ABBR = **Royal Australian Navy**

ran [ræn] PT *of* **run**

ranch [rɑːntʃ] N ranch *m inv*

rancher ['rɑːntʃə'] N (*owner*) proprietario di un ranch; (*ranch hand*) cowboy *m inv*

rancid ['rænsɪd] ADJ rancido(-a)

rancour, (*US*) **rancor** ['ræŋkə'] N rancore *m*

R & B N ABBR = **rhythm and blues**

R & D N ABBR = **research and development**

random ['rændəm] ADJ fatto(-a) *or* detto(-a) per caso; (*Comput, Math*) casuale ▶ N: **at** ~ a casaccio

random access N (*Comput*) accesso casuale

R & R N ABBR (= *rest and recreation*) ricreazione *f*; (*US Mil*) *permesso per militari*

randy ['rændɪ] ADJ (*col*) arrapato(-a); lascivo(-a)

rang [ræŋ] PT *of* **ring**

range [reɪndʒ] N (*of mountains*) catena; (*of missile, voice*) portata; (*of products*) gamma;

(*Mil: also:* **shooting range**) campo di tiro; (*also:* **kitchen range**) fornello, cucina economica ▶ VT (*place*) disporre, allineare; (*roam*) vagare per ▶ VI: **to** ~ **over** coprire; **to** ~ **from ... to** andare da ... a; **price** ~ gamma di prezzi; **do you have anything else in this price** ~? ha nient'altro su *or* di questo prezzo?; **within (firing)** ~ a portata di tiro; **ranged left/right** (*text*) allineato(-a) a destra/sinistra

ranger ['reɪndʒə'] N guardia forestale

Rangoon [ræŋ'guːn] N Rangun *f*

rank [ræŋk] N fila; (*status, Mil*) grado; (*Brit: also:* **taxi rank**) posteggio di taxi ▶ VI: **to** ~ **among** essere tra ▶ ADJ (*smell*) puzzolente; (*hypocrisy, injustice*) vero(-a) e proprio(-a); **the ranks** (*Mil*) la truppa; **the** ~ **and file** (*fig*) la gran massa; **to close ranks** (*Mil: fig*) serrare i ranghi; **I** ~ **him sixth** gli do il sesto posto, lo metto al sesto posto

rankle ['ræŋkl] VI: **to** ~ **with sb** bruciare (a qn)

rank outsider N outsider *mf*

ransack ['rænsæk] VT rovistare; (*plunder*) saccheggiare

ransom ['rænsəm] N riscatto; **to hold sb to** ~ (*fig*) esercitare pressione su qn

rant [rænt] VI vociare

ranting ['ræntɪŋ] N vociare *m*

rap [ræp] N (*noise*) colpetti *mpl*; (*at a door*) bussata; (*music*) rap *m inv* ▶ VT dare dei colpetti a; bussare a

rape [reɪp] N violenza carnale, stupro; (*Bot*) ravizzone *m* ▶ VT violentare

rape oil, rapeseed oil ['reɪpsiːd-] N olio di ravizzone

rapid ['ræpɪd] ADJ rapido(-a)

rapidity [rə'pɪdɪtɪ] N rapidità

rapidly ['ræpɪdlɪ] ADV rapidamente

rapids ['ræpɪdz] NPL (*Geo*) rapida

rapist ['reɪpɪst] N violentatore *m*

rapport [ræ'pɔː'] N rapporto

rapt [ræpt] ADJ (*attention*) rapito(-a), profondo(-a); **to be** ~ **in contemplation** essere in estatica contemplazione

rapture ['ræptʃə'] N estasi *f inv*; **to go into raptures over** andare in sollucchero per

rapturous ['ræptʃərəs] ADJ estatico(-a)

rare [rɛə'] ADJ raro(-a); (*Culin: steak*) al sangue; **it is** ~ **to find that ...** capita di rado *or* raramente che ... + *sub*

rarebit ['rɛəbɪt] N *see* **Welsh rarebit**

rarefied ['rɛərɪfaɪd] ADJ (*air, atmosphere*) rarefatto(-a)

rarely ['rɛəlɪ] ADV raramente

raring ['rɛərɪŋ] ADJ: **to be** ~ **to go** (*col*) non veder l'ora di cominciare

rarity ['rɛərɪtɪ] N rarità *f inv*

rascal ['rɑːskl] N mascalzone *m*

r

rash [ræʃ] ADJ imprudente, sconsiderato(-a) ▶ N (*Med*) eruzione *f*; (*of events etc*) scoppio; **to come out in a ~** avere uno sfogo

rasher ['ræʃəʳ] N fetta sottile (di lardo *or* prosciutto)

rasp [rɑːsp] N (*tool*) lima ▶ VT (*speak: also*: **rasp out**) gracchiare

raspberry ['rɑːzbərɪ] N lampone *m*

raspberry bush N lampone *m* (*pianta*)

rasping ['rɑːspɪŋ] ADJ stridulo(-a)

Rastafarian [ræstə'fɛərɪən] ADJ, N rastafariano(-a)

rat [ræt] N ratto

ratable ['reɪtəbl] ADJ = **rateable**

ratchet ['rætʃɪt] N: **~ wheel** ruota dentata

rate [reɪt] N (*proportion*) tasso, percentuale *f*; (*speed*) velocità *f inv*; (*price*) tariffa ▶ VT valutare; stimare; **to ~ sb/sth as** valutare qn/qc come; **to ~ sb/sth among** annoverare qn/qc tra; **to ~ sb/sth highly** stimare molto qn/qc; **at a ~ of 60 kph** alla velocità di 60 km all'ora; **~ of exchange** tasso di cambio; **~ of flow** flusso medio; **~ of growth** tasso di crescita; **~ of return** tasso di rendimento; **pulse ~** frequenza delle pulsazioni; *see also* **rates**

rateable value ['reɪtəbl-] N (*BRIT*) valore *m* imponibile (agli effetti delle imposte comunali)

ratepayer ['reɪtpeɪəʳ] N (*BRIT*) contribuente *mf* (che paga le imposte comunali)

rates [reɪts] NPL (*BRIT: property tax*) imposte *fpl* comunali; (*fees*) tariffe *fpl*

rather ['rɑːðəʳ] ADV piuttosto; (*somewhat*) abbastanza; (*to some extent*) un po'; **it's ~ expensive** è piuttosto caro; (*too much*) è un po' caro; **there's ~ a lot** ce n'è parecchio; **I would** *or* **I'd ~ go** preferirei andare; **I had ~ go** farei meglio ad andare; **I'd ~ not leave** preferirei non partire; **or ~** (*more accurately*) anzi, per essere (più) precisi; **I ~ think he won't come** credo proprio che non verrà

ratification [rætɪfɪ'keɪʃən] N ratificazione *f*

ratify ['rætɪfaɪ] VT ratificare

rating ['reɪtɪŋ] N classificazione *f*; (*assessment*) valutazione *f*; (*score*) punteggio di merito; (*Naut: category*) classe *f*; (: *BRIT: sailor*) marinaio semplice

ratings ['reɪtɪŋz] NPL (*Radio, TV*) indice *m* di ascolto

ratio ['reɪʃɪəu] N proporzione *f*; **in the ~ of 2 to 1** in rapporto di 2 a 1

ration ['ræʃən] N razione *f* ▶ VT razionare; **rations** NPL razioni *fpl*

rational ['ræʃənl] ADJ razionale, ragionevole; (*solution, reasoning*) logico(-a)

rationale [ræʃə'nɑːl] N fondamento logico; giustificazione *f*

rationalization [ræʃnəlaɪ'zeɪʃən] N razionalizzazione *f*

rationalize ['ræʃnəlaɪz] VT razionalizzare

rationally ['ræʃnəlɪ] ADV razionalmente; logicamente

rationing ['ræʃnɪŋ] N razionamento

ratpack ['rætpæk] N (*BRIT col*) stampa scandalistica

rat poison N veleno per topi

rat race N carrierismo, corsa al successo

rattan [ræ'tæn] N malacca

rattle ['rætl] N tintinnio; (*louder*) rumore *m* di ferraglia; (*object: of baby*) sonaglino; (: *of sports fan*) raganella ▶ VI risuonare, tintinnare; fare un rumore di ferraglia ▶ VT far tintinnare; (*col: disconcert*) sconcertare

rattlesnake ['rætlsneɪk] N serpente *m* a sonagli

ratty ['rætɪ] ADJ (*col*) incavolato(-a)

raucous ['rɔːkəs] ADJ sguaiato(-a)

raucously ['rɔːkəslɪ] ADV sguaiatamente

raunchy ['rɔːntʃɪ] ADJ (*col: person*) allupato(-a); (*voice, song*) libidinoso(-a)

ravage ['rævɪdʒ] VT devastare

ravages ['rævɪdʒɪz] NPL danni *mpl*

rave [reɪv] VI (*in anger*) infuriarsi; (*with enthusiasm*) andare in estasi; (*Med*) delirare ▶ N (*BRIT*): **a ~ (party)** un rave ▶ ADJ (*scene, culture, music*) del fenomeno rave ▶ CPD: **~ review** (*col*) critica entusiastica

raven ['reɪvən] N corvo

ravenous ['rævənəs] ADJ affamato(-a)

ravine [rə'viːn] N burrone *m*

raving ['reɪvɪŋ] ADJ: **~ lunatic** pazzo(-a) furioso(-a)

ravings ['reɪvɪŋz] NPL vaneggiamenti *mpl*

ravioli [rævɪ'əulɪ] N ravioli *mpl*

ravish ['rævɪʃ] VT (*delight*) estasiare

ravishing ['rævɪʃɪŋ] ADJ incantevole

raw [rɔː] ADJ (*uncooked*) crudo(-a); (*not processed*) greggio(-a); (*sore*) vivo(-a); (*inexperienced*) inesperto(-a); (*weather, day*) gelido(-a); **to get a ~ deal** (*col: bad bargain*) prendere un bidone; (: *harsh treatment*) venire trattato ingiustamente

Rawalpindi [rɔːl'pɪndɪ] N Rawalpindi *f*

raw material N materia prima

ray [reɪ] N raggio; **a ~ of hope** un barlume di speranza

rayon ['reɪɔn] N raion *m*

raze [reɪz] VT radere, distruggere; (*also*: **raze to the ground**) radere al suolo

razor ['reɪzəʳ] N rasoio

razor blade N lama di rasoio

razzle ['ræzl], **razzle-dazzle** ['ræzl'dæzl] N (*BRIT col*): **to be/go on the ~(-dazzle)** darsi alla pazza gioia

razzmatazz ['ræzmə'tæz] N (*col*) clamore *m*

RC ABBR = **Roman Catholic**

RCAF N ABBR = **Royal Canadian Air Force**
RCMP N ABBR = **Royal Canadian Mounted Police**
RCN N ABBR = **Royal Canadian Navy**
RD ABBR (*US Post*) = **rural delivery**
Rd ABBR = **road**
RDC N ABBR (*BRIT*) = **rural district council**
RE N ABBR (*BRIT Mil*: = *Royal Engineers*) ≈ G.M.
(= *Genio Militare*); (*BRIT*) = **religious education**
re [ri:] PREP con riferimento a
reach [ri:tʃ] N portata; (*of river etc*) tratto ▶ VT
raggiungere; arrivare a ▶ VI stendersi;
(*stretch out hand: also*: **reach down, reach over, reach across** *etc*) allungare una mano; **out of/within ~** (*object*) fuori/a portata di mano; **within easy ~ (of)** (*place*) a breve distanza
(di), vicino (a); **to ~ sb by phone** contattare
qn per telefono; **can I ~ you at your hotel?**
la posso contattare al suo albergo?
▶ **reach out** VT (*hand*) allungare ▶ VI: **to ~ out for** stendere la mano per prendere
react [ri:'ækt] VI reagire
reaction [ri:'ækʃən] N reazione *f*
reactionary [ri:'ækʃənrɪ] ADJ, N
reazionario(-a)
reactor [ri:'æktə ʳ] N reattore *m*
read [ri:d] (*pt, pp* ~ [rɛd]) VI leggere ▶ VT
leggere; (*understand*) intendere, interpretare;
(*study*) studiare; **do you ~ me?** (*Tel*) mi
ricevete?; **to take sth as ~** (*fig*) dare qc per
scontato
▶ **read out** VT leggere ad alta voce
▶ **read over** VT rileggere attentamente
▶ **read through** VT (*quickly*) dare una scorsa a;
(*thoroughly*) leggere da cima a fondo
▶ **read up, read up on** VT studiare bene
readable ['ri:dəbl] ADJ leggibile; che si legge
volentieri
reader ['ri:dəʳ] N lettore(-trice); (*book*) libro di
lettura; (*BRIT: at university*) professore con
funzioni preminenti di ricerca
readership ['ri:dəʃɪp] N (*of paper etc*) numero
di lettori
readily ['rɛdɪlɪ] ADV volentieri; (*easily*)
facilmente; (*quickly*) prontamente
readiness ['rɛdɪnɪs] N prontezza; **in ~**
(*prepared*) pronto(-a)
reading ['ri:dɪŋ] N lettura; (*understanding*)
interpretazione *f*; (*on instrument*)
indicazione *f*
reading lamp N lampada da studio
reading room N sala di lettura
readjust [ri:ə'dʒʌst] VT raggiustare ▶ VI
(*person*): **to ~ (to)** riadattarsi (a)
ready ['rɛdɪ] ADJ pronto(-a); (*willing*)
pronto(-a), disposto(-a); (*quick*) rapido(-a);
(*available*) disponibile ▶ N: **at the ~** (*Mil*)
pronto a sparare; (*fig*) tutto(-a) pronto(-a)
▶ VT preparare; **~ for use** pronto per l'uso; **to**

be ~ to do sth essere pronto a fare qc; **to get ~** VI prepararsi
ready cash N denaro in contanti
ready-cooked [rɛdɪ'kukt] ADJ già cotto(-a)
ready-made [rɛdɪ'meɪd] ADJ
prefabbricato(-a); (*clothes*) confezionato(-a)
ready reckoner [-'rɛkənəʳ] N (*BRIT*)
prontuario di calcolo
ready-to-wear [rɛdɪtə'wɛəʳ] ADJ prêt-à-
porter *inv*
reagent [ri:'eɪdʒənt] N: **chemical ~** reagente
m chimico
real [rɪəl] ADJ reale; vero(-a) ▶ ADV (*US col: very*)
veramente, proprio; **in ~ terms** in realtà; **in
~ life** nella realtà
real ale N birra ad effervescenza naturale
real estate N beni *mpl* immobili
realism ['rɪəlɪzəm] N (*Art*) realismo
realist ['rɪəlɪst] N realista *mf*
realistic [rɪə'lɪstɪk] ADJ realistico(-a)
reality [ri:'ælɪtɪ] N realtà *f inv*; **in ~** in realtà,
in effetti
reality TV N reality TV *f*
realization [rɪəlaɪ'zeɪʃən] N (*awareness*) presa
di coscienza; (*of hopes, project etc*)
realizzazione *f*
realize ['rɪəlaɪz] VT (*understand*) rendersi conto
di; (*a project, Comm: asset*) realizzare; **I ~ that
…** mi rendo conto *or* capisco che …
really ['rɪəlɪ] ADV veramente, davvero; **~!**
(*indicating annoyance*) oh, insomma!
realm [rɛlm] N reame *m*, regno
real time N (*Comput*) tempo reale
Realtor® ['rɪəltɔːʳ] N (*US*) agente *m*
immobiliare
ream [ri:m] N risma; **reams** (*fig: col*) pagine
e pagine *fpl*
reap [ri:p] VT mietere; (*fig*) raccogliere
reaper ['ri:pəʳ] N (*machine*) mietitrice *f*
reappear [ri:ə'pɪəʳ] VI ricomparire,
riapparire
reappearance [ri:ə'pɪərəns] N
riapparizione *f*
reapply [ri:ə'plaɪ] VI: **to ~ for** fare un'altra
domanda per
reappraisal [ri:ə'preɪzl] N riesame *m*
rear [rɪəʳ] ADJ di dietro; (*Aut: wheel etc*)
posteriore ▶ N didietro, parte *f* posteriore
▶ VT (*cattle, family*) allevare ▶ VI (*also:* **rear up**:
animal) impennarsi
rear admiral N contrammiraglio
rear-engined ['rɪər'ɛndʒɪnd] ADJ (*Aut*) con
motore posteriore
rearguard ['rɪəɡɑːd] N retroguardia
rearm [ri:'ɑːm] VT, VI riarmare
rearmament [ri:'ɑːməmənt] N riarmo
rearrange [ri:ə'reɪndʒ] VT riordinare
rear-view mirror ['rɪəvju:-] N (*Aut*) specchio
retrovisivo

r

rear-wheel drive N trazione fpl posteriore

reason ['ri:zn] N ragione f; (cause, motive) ragione, motivo ▶ VI: **to ~ with sb** far ragionare qn; **to have ~ to think** avere motivi per pensare; **it stands to ~ that** è ovvio che; **the ~ for/why** la ragione or il motivo di/per cui; **with good ~** a ragione; **all the more ~ why you should not sell it** ragione di più per non venderlo

reasonable ['ri:znəbl] ADJ ragionevole; (not bad) accettabile

reasonably ['ri:znəblɪ] ADV ragionevolmente; **one can ~ assume that ...** uno può facilmente supporre che ...

reasoned ['ri:znd] ADJ (argument) ponderato(-a)

reasoning ['ri:znɪŋ] N ragionamento

reassemble [ri:ə'sɛmbl] VT riunire; (machine) rimontare

reassert [ri:ə'sə:t] VT riaffermare

reassurance [ri:ə'ʃuərəns] N rassicurazione f

reassure [ri:ə'ʃuəʳ] VT rassicurare; **to ~ sb of** rassicurare qn di or su

reassuring [ri:ə'ʃuərɪŋ] ADJ rassicurante

reawakening [ri:ə'weɪknɪŋ] N risveglio

rebate ['ri:beɪt] N rimborso; (on tax etc) sgravio

rebel N ['rɛbl] ribelle mf ▶ VI [rɪ'bɛl] ribellarsi

rebellion [rɪ'bɛljən] N ribellione f

rebellious [rɪ'bɛljəs] ADJ ribelle

rebirth [ri:'bə:θ] N rinascita

rebound VI [rɪ'baund] (ball) rimbalzare ▶ N ['ri:baund] rimbalzo

rebuff [rɪ'bʌf] N secco rifiuto ▶ VT respingere

rebuild [ri:'bɪld] VT (irreg: like **build**) ricostruire

rebuke [rɪ'bju:k] N rimprovero ▶ VT rimproverare

rebut [rɪ'bʌt] VT rifiutare

rebuttal [rɪ'bʌtl] N rifiuto

recalcitrant [rɪ'kælsɪtrənt] ADJ recalcitrante

recall [rɪ'kɔ:l] VT (gen, Comput) richiamare; (remember) ricordare, richiamare alla mente ▶ N ['ri:kɔl] richiamo; **beyond ~** irrevocabile

recant [rɪ'kænt] VI ritrattarsi; (Rel) fare abiura

recap ['ri:kæp] N ricapitolazione f ▶ VT ricapitolare ▶ VI riassumere

recapture [ri:'kæptʃəʳ] VT riprendere; (atmosphere) ricreare

recd. ABBR = **received**

recede [rɪ'si:d] VI allontanarsi; ritirarsi; calare

receding [rɪ'si:dɪŋ] ADJ (forehead, chin) sfuggente; **he's got a ~ hairline** è stempiato

receipt [rɪ'si:t] N (document) ricevuta; (act of receiving) ricevimento; **to acknowledge ~ of** accusare ricevuta di; **we are in ~ of ...** abbiamo ricevuto ...

receipts [rɪ'si:ts] NPL (Comm) introiti mpl

receivable [rɪ'si:vəbl] ADJ (Comm) esigibile; (: owed) dovuto(-a)

receive [rɪ'si:v] VT ricevere; (guest) ricevere, accogliere; **"received with thanks"** (Comm) "per quietanza"

Received Pronunciation N (BRIT); vedi nota

Si chiama Received Pronunciation (RP) l'accento dell'inglese parlato in alcune parti del sud-est dell'Inghilterra. In esso si identifica l'inglese standard delle classi colte, privo di inflessioni regionali e adottato tradizionalmente dagli annunciatori della BBC. È anche l'accento standard dell'inglese insegnato come lingua straniera.

receiver [rɪ'si:vəʳ] N (Tel) ricevitore m; (Radio) apparecchio ricevente; (of stolen goods) ricettatore(-trice); (Law, Comm) curatore m fallimentare

receivership [rɪ'si:vəʃɪp] N curatela; **to go into ~** andare in amministrazione controllata

recent ['ri:snt] ADJ recente; **in ~ years** negli ultimi anni

recently ['ri:sntlɪ] ADV recentemente; **as ~ as ...** soltanto ...; **until ~** fino a poco tempo fa

receptacle [rɪ'sɛptɪkl] N recipiente m

reception [rɪ'sɛpʃən] N (gen) ricevimento; (welcome) accoglienza; (TV etc) ricezione f

reception centre N (BRIT) centro di raccolta

reception desk N (in hotel) reception f inv; (in hospital, at doctor's) accettazione f; (in large building, offices) portineria

receptionist [rɪ'sɛpʃənɪst] N receptionist mf

receptive [rɪ'sɛptɪv] ADJ ricettivo(-a)

recess [rɪ'sɛs] N (in room) alcova; (Pol etc: holiday) vacanze fpl; (US Law: short break) sospensione f; (US Scol) intervallo

recession [rɪ'sɛʃən] N (Econ) recessione f

recessionista [rɪsɛʃə'nɪstə] N recessionista mf

recharge [ri:'tʃɑ:dʒ] VT (battery) ricaricare

rechargeable ['ri:'tʃɑ:dʒəbl] ADJ ricaricabile

recipe ['rɛsɪpɪ] N ricetta

recipient [rɪ'sɪpɪənt] N beneficiario(-a); (of letter) destinatario(-a)

reciprocal [rɪ'sɪprəkl] ADJ reciproco(-a)

reciprocate [rɪ'sɪprəkeɪt] VT ricambiare, contraccambiare

recital [rɪ'saɪtl] N recital m inv; concerto (di solista)

recite [rɪ'saɪt] VT (poem) recitare

reckless ['rɛkləs] ADJ (driver etc) spericolato(-a); (spender) incosciente; (spending) folle

recklessly ['rɛkləslɪ] ADV in modo spericolato; da incosciente

reckon ['rɛkən] VT (count) calcolare; (consider) considerare, stimare; (think): **I ~ that ...**

penso che .. ▶ vɪ contare, calcolare; **to ~ without sb/sth** non tener conto di qn/qc; **he is somebody to be reckoned with** è uno da non sottovalutare

▶ **reckon on** vt ғus contare su

reckoning ['rɛknɪŋ] ɴ conto; stima; **the day of ~** il giorno del giudizio

reclaim [rɪ'kleɪm] vt (land) bonificare; (demand back) richiedere, reclamare; (materials) recuperare

reclamation [rɛklə'meɪʃən] ɴ bonifica

recline [rɪ'klaɪn] vɪ stare sdraiato(-a)

reclining [rɪ'klaɪnɪŋ] ADJ (seat) ribaltabile

recluse [rɪ'klu:s] ɴ eremita m, recluso(-a)

recognition [rɛkəg'nɪʃən] ɴ riconoscimento; **to gain ~** essere riconosciuto(-a); **in ~ of** in or come segno di riconoscimento per; **transformed beyond ~** irriconoscibile

recognizable ['rɛkəgnaɪzəbl] ADJ: **~ (by)** riconoscibile (a or da)

recognize ['rɛkəgnaɪz] vt: **to ~ (by/as)** riconoscere (a or da/come)

recoil [rɪ'kɔɪl] vɪ (gun) rinculare; (spring) balzare indietro; (person): **to ~ (from)** indietreggiare (davanti a) ▶ ɴ (gun) rinculo

recollect [rɛkə'lɛkt] vt ricordare

recollection [rɛkə'lɛkʃən] ɴ ricordo; **to the best of my ~** per quello che mi ricordo

recommend [rɛkə'mɛnd] vt raccomandare; (advise) consigliare; **she has a lot to ~ her** ha molti elementi a suo favore

recommendation [rɛkəmɛn'deɪʃən] ɴ raccomandazione f; consiglio

recommended retail price [rɛkə'mɛndɪd-] ɴ (Bʀɪт) prezzo raccomandato al dettaglio

recompense ['rɛkəmpɛns] vt ricompensare; (compensate) risarcire ▶ ɴ ricompensa; risarcimento

reconcilable ['rɛkənsaɪləbl] ADJ conciliabile

reconcile ['rɛkənsaɪl] vt (two people) riconciliare; (two facts) conciliare, quadrare; **to ~ o.s. to** rassegnarsi a

reconciliation [rɛkənsɪlɪ'eɪʃən] ɴ riconciliazione f; conciliazione f

recondite [rɪ'kɔndaɪt] ADJ recondito(-a)

recondition [ri:kən'dɪʃən] vt rimettere a nuovo; rifare

reconnaissance [rɪ'kɔnɪsns] ɴ (Mil) ricognizione f

reconnoitre, (US**) reconnoiter** (Mil) [rɛkə'nɔɪtəʳ] vt fare una ricognizione di ▶ vɪ fare una ricognizione

reconsider [ri:kən'sɪdəʳ] vt riconsiderare

reconstitute [ri:'kɔnstɪtju:t] vt ricostituire

reconstruct [ri:kən'strʌkt] vt ricostruire

reconstruction [ri:kən'strʌkʃən] ɴ ricostruzione f

reconvene [ri:kən'vi:n] vt riconvocare ▶ vɪ radunarsi

record ɴ ['rɛkɔ:d] ricordo, documento; (of meeting etc) nota, verbale m; (register) registro; (file) pratica, dossier m inv; (Comput) record m inv, registrazione f; (also: **police record**) fedina penale sporca; (Mus: disc) disco; (Sport) record m inv, primato ▶ vt [rɪ'kɔ:d] (set down) prendere nota di, registrare; (relate) raccontare; (Comput, Mus: song etc) registrare; **off the ~** adj ufficioso(-a); adv ufficiosamente; **public records** archivi mpl; **Italy's excellent ~** i brillanti successi italiani; **in ~ time** a tempo di record; **to keep a ~ of** tener nota di; **to set the ~ straight** mettere le cose in chiaro; **he is on ~ as saying that ...** ha dichiarato pubblicamente che ...

record card ɴ (in file) scheda

recorded delivery letter [rɪ'kɔ:dɪd-] ɴ (Bʀɪт Post) lettera raccomandata

recorder [rɪ'kɔ:dəʳ] ɴ (Law) avvocato che funge da giudice; (Mus) flauto diritto

record holder ɴ (Sport) primatista mf

recording [rɪ'kɔ:dɪŋ] ɴ (Mus) registrazione f

recording studio ɴ studio di registrazione

record library ɴ discoteca

record player ɴ giradischi m inv

recount [rɪ'kaunt] vt raccontare, narrare

re-count ɴ ['ri:kaunt] (Pol: of votes) nuovo conteggio ▶ vt [ri:'kaunt] ricontare

recoup [rɪ'ku:p] vt ricuperare; **to ~ one's losses** ricuperare le perdite, rifarsi

recourse [rɪ'kɔ:s] ɴ: **to have ~ to** ricorrere a

recover [rɪ'kʌvəʳ] vt ricuperare ▶ vɪ (from illness) rimettersi (in salute), ristabilirsi; **to ~ (from)** (country, person: from shock) riprendersi (da)

re-cover [ri:'kʌvəʳ] vt (chair etc) ricoprire

recovery [rɪ'kʌvərɪ] ɴ ricupero; ristabilimento; ripresa

recreate [ri:krɪ'eɪt] vt ricreare

recreation [rɛkrɪ'eɪʃən] ɴ ricreazione f; svago

recreational [rɛkrɪ'eɪʃənəl] ADJ ricreativo(-a)

recreational drug [rɛkrɪ'eɪʃənl-] ɴ droga usata saltuariamente

recreational vehicle ɴ (US) camper m inv

recrimination [rɪkrɪmɪ'neɪʃən] ɴ recriminazione f

recruit [rɪ'kru:t] ɴ recluta; (in company) nuovo(-a) assunto(-a) ▶ vt reclutare

recruiting office [rɪ'kru:tɪŋ-] ɴ ufficio di reclutamento

recruitment [rɪ'kru:tmənt] ɴ reclutamento

rectangle ['rɛktæŋgl] ɴ rettangolo

rectangular [rɛk'tæŋgjuləʳ] ADJ rettangolare

rectify ['rɛktɪfaɪ] vt (error) rettificare; (omission) riparare

rector ['rɛktəʳ] ɴ (Rel) parroco (anglicano); (in Scottish universities) personalità eletta dagli studenti per rappresentarli

r

rectory ['rɛktərɪ] N presbiterio
rectum ['rɛktəm] N (*Anat*) retto
recuperate [rɪ'kjuːpəreɪt] vɪ ristabilirsi
recur [rɪ'kəːʳ] vɪ riaccadere; (*idea, opportunity*) riapparire; (*symptoms*) ripresentarsi
recurrence [rɪ'kʌrəns] N ripresentarsi *m*; riapparizione *f*
recurrent [rɪ'kʌrənt] ADJ ricorrente, periodico(-a)
recurring [rɪ'kʌrɪŋ] ADJ (*Math*) periodico(-a)
recyclable [riː'saɪkləbl] ADJ riciclabile
recycle [riː'saɪkl] vᴛ riciclare
recycling [riː'saɪklɪŋ] N riciclaggio
red [rɛd] N rosso; (*Pol: pej*) rosso(-a) ▶ ADJ rosso(-a); **in the ~** (*account*) scoperto; (*business*) in deficit
red alert N allarme *m* rosso
red-blooded ['rɛd'blʌdɪd] ADJ (*col*) gagliardo(-a)
red-brick university ['rɛdbrɪk-] N (*Brɪᴛ*) *università di recente formazione; vedi nota*

> In Gran Bretagna, con *red-brick university* (letteralmente, università di mattoni rossi) si indicano le università istituite tra la fine dell'Ottocento e i primi del Novecento, per contraddistinguerle dalle università più antiche, i cui edifici sono di pietra; *vedi anche* **Oxbridge**.

red carpet treatment N cerimonia col gran pavese
Red Cross N Croce *f* Rossa
redcurrant ['rɛdkʌrənt] N ribes *m inv*
redden ['rɛdn] vᴛ arrossare ▶ vɪ arrossire
reddish ['rɛdɪʃ] ADJ rossiccio(-a)
redecorate [riː'dɛkəreɪt] vᴛ tinteggiare (e tappezzare) di nuovo
redeem [rɪ'diːm] vᴛ (*debt*) riscattare; (*sth in pawn*) ritirare; (*fig, also Rel*) redimere
redeemable [rɪ'diːməbl] ADJ con diritto di riscatto; redimibile
redeeming [rɪ'diːmɪŋ] ADJ (*feature*) che salva
redefine [riː'dɪ'faɪn] vᴛ ridefinire
redemption [rɪ'dɛmpʃən] N (*Rel*) redenzione *f*; (*also*: **past** *or* **beyond redemption**) irrecuperabile
redeploy [riː'dɪ'plɔɪ] vᴛ (*Mil*) riorganizzare lo schieramento di; (*resources*) riorganizzare
redeployment [riː'dɪ'plɔɪmənt] N riorganizzazione *f*
redevelop [riː'dɪ'vɛləp] vᴛ ristrutturare
redevelopment [riː'dɪ'vɛləpmənt] N ristrutturazione *f*
red-haired [-'hɛəd] ADJ dai capelli rossi
red-handed [rɛd'hændɪd] ADJ: **to be caught ~** essere preso(-a) in flagrante *or* con le mani nel sacco
redhead ['rɛdhɛd] N rosso(-a)
red herring N (*fig*) falsa pista
red-hot [rɛd'hɔt] ADJ arroventato(-a)

redirect [riːdaɪ'rɛkt] vᴛ (*mail*) far seguire
redistribute [riːdɪ'strɪbjuːt] vᴛ ridistribuire
red-letter day ['rɛdlɛtə-] N giorno memorabile
red light N: **to go through a ~** (*Aut*) passare col rosso
red-light district [rɛd'laɪt-] N quartiere *m* a luci rosse
red meat N carne *f* rossa
redness ['rɛdnɪs] N rossore *m*; (*of hair*) rosso
redo [riː'duː] vᴛ (*irreg: like* **do**) rifare
redolent ['rɛdələnt] ADJ: **~ of** che sa di; (*fig*) che ricorda
redouble [riː'dʌbl] vᴛ: **to ~ one's efforts** raddoppiare gli sforzi
redraft [riː'drɑːft] vᴛ fare una nuova stesura di
redress [rɪ'drɛs] N riparazione *f* ▶ vᴛ riparare; **to ~ the balance** ristabilire l'equilibrio
Red Sea N: **the ~** il mar Rosso
redskin ['rɛdskɪn] N pellerossa *mf*
red tape N (*fig*) burocrazia
reduce [rɪ'djuːs] vᴛ ridurre; (*lower*) ridurre, abbassare; **"~ speed now"** (*Aut*) "rallentare"; **to ~ sth by/to** ridurre qc di/a; **to ~ sb to silence/despair/tears** ridurre qn al silenzio/alla disperazione/in lacrime; **at a reduced price** scontato(-a)
reduced [rɪ'djuːst] ADJ (*decreased*) ridotto(-a); **at a ~ price** a prezzo ribassato *or* ridotto; **"greatly ~ prices"** "grandi ribassi"
reduction [rɪ'dʌkʃən] N riduzione *f*; (*of price*) ribasso; (*discount*) sconto
redundancy [rɪ'dʌndənsɪ] N licenziamento (per eccesso di personale); **compulsory ~** licenziamento; **voluntary ~** *forma di cassa integrazione volontaria*
redundancy payment N (*Brɪᴛ*) indennità *f inv* di licenziamento
redundant [rɪ'dʌndnt] ADJ (*Brɪᴛ: worker*) licenziato(-a); (*detail, object*) superfluo(-a); **to be made ~** (*Brɪᴛ*) essere licenziato (per eccesso di personale)
reed [riːd] N (*Bot*) canna; (*Mus: of clarinet etc*) ancia
re-educate [riː'edjukeɪt] vᴛ rieducare
reedy ['riːdɪ] ADJ (*voice, instrument*) acuto(-a)
reef [riːf] N (*at sea*) scogliera; **coral ~** barriera corallina
reek [riːk] vɪ: **to ~ (of)** puzzare (di)
reel [riːl] N bobina, rocchetto; (*Tech*) aspo; (*Fishing*) mulinello; (*Cine*) rotolo; (*dance*) *danza veloce scozzese* ▶ vᴛ (*Tech*) annaspare; (*also*: **reel up**) avvolgere ▶ vɪ (*sway*) barcollare, vacillare; **my head is reeling** mi gira la testa
  ▶ **reel off** vᴛ snocciolare
re-election [riːɪ'lɛkʃən] N rielezione *f*
re-enter [riː'ɛntəʳ] vᴛ rientrare in

re-entry [riː'ɛntrɪ] N rientro
re-export VT [riːɪk'spɔːt] riesportare ▶ N [riː'ɛkspɔːt] merce f riesportata, riesportazione f
ref [rɛf] N ABBR (col: = referee) arbitro
ref. ABBR (Comm: = with reference to) sogg
refectory [rɪ'fɛktərɪ] N refettorio
refer [rɪ'fəːʳ] VT: **to ~ sth to** (dispute, decision) deferire qc a; **to ~ sb to** (inquirer, Med: patient) indirizzare qn a; (: reader: to text) rimandare qn a; **he referred me to the manager** mi ha detto di rivolgermi al direttore
▶ **refer to** VT FUS (allude to) accennare a; (apply to) riferire a; (consult) rivolgersi a; **referring to your letter** (Comm) in riferimento alla Vostra lettera
referee [rɛfə'riː] N arbitro; (Tennis) giudice m di gara; (BRIT: for job application) referenza ▶ VT arbitrare
reference ['rɛfrəns] N riferimento; (mention) menzione f, allusione f; (for job application: letter) referenza; lettera di raccomandazione; (: person) referenza; (in book) rimando; **with ~ to** riguardo a; (Comm: in letter) in or con riferimento a; **"please quote this ~"** (Comm) "si prega di far riferimento al numero di protocollo"
reference book N libro di consultazione
reference library N biblioteca per la consultazione
reference number N (Comm) numero di riferimento
referendum [rɛfə'rɛndəm] (pl **referenda** [-də]) N referendum m inv
referral [rɪ'fəːrəl] N deferimento; (Med) richiesta (di visita specialistica)
refill VT [riː'fɪl] riempire di nuovo; (pen, lighter etc) ricaricare ▶ N ['riːfɪl] (for pen etc) ricambio
refine [rɪ'faɪn] VT raffinare
refined [rɪ'faɪnd] ADJ (person, taste) raffinato(-a)
refinement [rɪ'faɪnmənt] N (of person) raffinatezza
refinery [rɪ'faɪnərɪ] N raffineria
refit N ['riːfɪt] (Naut) raddobbo ▶ VT [riː'fɪt] (ship) raddobbare
reflate [riː'fleɪt] VT (economy) rilanciare
reflation [riː'fleɪʃən] N rilancio
reflationary [riː'fleɪʃənərɪ] ADJ nuovamente inflazionario(-a)
reflect [rɪ'flɛkt] VT (light, image) riflettere; (fig) rispecchiare ▶ VI (think) riflettere, considerare; **it reflects badly/well on him** si ripercuote su di lui in senso negativo/positivo
▶ **reflect on** VT FUS (discredit) rispecchiarsi su
reflection [rɪ'flɛkʃən] N riflessione f; (image) riflesso; (criticism): **~ on** giudizio su; attacco a; **on ~** pensandoci sopra

reflector [rɪ'flɛktəʳ] N (also Aut) catarifrangente m
reflex ['riːflɛks] ADJ riflesso(-a) ▶ N riflesso
reflexive [rɪ'flɛksɪv] ADJ (Ling) riflessivo(-a)
reform [rɪ'fɔːm] N (of sinner etc) correzione f; (of law etc) riforma ▶ VT correggere; riformare
reformat [rɪ'fɔːmæt] VT (Comput) riformattare
Reformation [rɛfə'meɪʃən] N: **the ~** la Riforma
reformatory [rɪ'fɔːmətərɪ] N (US) riformatorio
reformed [rɪ'fɔːmd] ADJ cambiato(-a) (per il meglio)
reformer [rɪ'fɔːməʳ] N riformatore(-trice)
refrain [rɪ'freɪn] VI: **to ~ from doing** trattenersi dal fare ▶ N ritornello
refresh [rɪ'frɛʃ] VT rinfrescare; (food, sleep) ristorare
refresher course [rɪ'frɛʃə-] N (BRIT) corso di aggiornamento
refreshing [rɪ'frɛʃɪŋ] ADJ (drink) rinfrescante; (sleep) riposante, ristoratore(-trice); (change etc) piacevole; (idea, point of view) originale
refreshment [rɪ'frɛʃmənt] N (eating, resting etc) ristoro; **~(s)** rinfreschi mpl
refrigeration [rɪfrɪdʒə'reɪʃən] N refrigerazione f
refrigerator [rɪ'frɪdʒəreɪtəʳ] N frigorifero
refuel [riː'fjuəl] VT rifornire (di carburante) ▶ VI far rifornimento (di carburante)
refuge ['rɛfjuːdʒ] N rifugio; **to take ~ in** rifugiarsi in
refugee [rɛfju'dʒiː] N rifugiato(-a), profugo(-a)
refugee camp N campo (di) profughi
refund N ['riːfʌnd] rimborso ▶ VT [rɪ'fʌnd] rimborsare
refurbish [riː'fəːbɪʃ] VT rimettere a nuovo
refurnish [riː'fəːnɪʃ] VT ammobiliare di nuovo
refusal [rɪ'fjuːzəl] N rifiuto; **to have first ~ on sth** avere il diritto d'opzione su qc
refuse¹ ['rɛfjuːs] N rifiuti mpl
refuse² [rɪ'fjuːz] VT, VI rifiutare; **to ~ to do sth** rifiutare or rifiutarsi di fare qc
refuse collection N raccolta di rifiuti
refuse disposal N sistema m di scarico dei rifiuti
refusenik [rɪ'fjuːznɪk] N ebreo a cui il governo sovietico impediva di lasciare il paese
refute [rɪ'fjuːt] VT confutare
regain [rɪ'geɪn] VT riguadagnare; riacquistare, ricuperare
regal ['riːgl] ADJ regale
regale [rɪ'geɪl] VT: **to ~ sb with sth** intrattenere qn con qc
regalia [rɪ'geɪlɪə] N insegne fpl reali

regard [rɪ'gɑːd] N riguardo, stima ▶ VT considerare, stimare; **to give one's regards to** porgere i suoi saluti a; **(kind) regards** cordiali saluti; **as regards, with ~ to** riguardo a

regarding [rɪ'gɑːdɪŋ] PREP riguardo a, per quanto riguarda

regardless [rɪ'gɑːdlɪs] ADV lo stesso; **~ of** a dispetto di, nonostante

regatta [rɪ'gætə] N regata

regency ['riːdʒənsɪ] N reggenza

regenerate [rɪ'dʒɛnəreɪt] VT rigenerare; (feelings, enthusiasm) far rinascere ▶ VI rigenerarsi; rinascere

regent ['riːdʒənt] N reggente m

reggae ['rɛgeɪ] N reggae m

régime [reɪ'ʒiːm] N regime m

regiment N ['rɛdʒɪmənt] reggimento ▶ VT ['rɛdʒɪmɛnt] irreggimentare

regimental [rɛdʒɪ'mɛntl] ADJ reggimentale

regimentation [rɛdʒɪmɛn'teɪʃən] N irreggimentazione f

region ['riːdʒən] N regione f; **in the ~ of** (fig) all'incirca di

regional ['riːdʒənl] ADJ regionale

regional development N sviluppo regionale

register ['rɛdʒɪstə^r] N registro; (also: **electoral register**) lista elettorale ▶ VT registrare; (vehicle) immatricolare; (luggage) spedire assicurato(-a); (letter) assicurare; (instrument) segnare ▶ VI iscriversi; (at hotel) firmare il registro; (make impression) entrare in testa; **to ~ a protest** fare un esposto; **to ~ for a course** iscriversi a un corso

registered ['rɛdʒɪstəd] ADJ (design) depositato(-a); (BRIT: letter) assicurato(-a); (student, voter) iscritto(-a)

registered company N società iscritta al registro

registered nurse N (US) infermiere(-a) diplomato(-a)

registered office N sede f legale

registered trademark N marchio depositato

registrar ['rɛdʒɪstrɑː^r] N ufficiale m di stato civile; segretario

registration [rɛdʒɪs'treɪʃən] N (act) registrazione f; iscrizione f; (Aut: also: **registration number**) numero di targa

registry ['rɛdʒɪstrɪ] N ufficio del registro

registry office N (BRIT) anagrafe f; **to get married in a ~** ≈ sposarsi in municipio

regret [rɪ'grɛt] N rimpianto, rincrescimento ▶ VT rimpiangere; **I ~ that I/he cannot help** mi rincresce di non poter aiutare/che lui non possa aiutare; **we ~ to inform you that ...** siamo spiacenti di informarla che ...

regretfully [rɪ'grɛtfəlɪ] ADV con rincrescimento

regrettable [rɪ'grɛtəbl] ADJ deplorevole

regrettably [rɪ'grɛtəblɪ] ADV purtroppo, sfortunatamente

regroup [riː'gruːp] VT raggruppare ▶ VI raggrupparsi

regt ABBR (= regiment) Reg

regular ['rɛgjulə^r] ADJ regolare; (usual) abituale, normale; (listener, reader) fedele; (soldier) dell'esercito regolare; (Comm: size) normale ▶ N (client etc) cliente mf abituale

regularity [rɛgju'lærɪtɪ] N regolarità f inv

regularly ['rɛgjuləlɪ] ADV regolarmente

regulate ['rɛgjuleɪt] VT regolare

regulation [rɛgju'leɪʃən] N (rule) regola, regolamento; (adjustment) regolazione f ▶ CPD (Mil) di ordinanza

rehabilitate [riːə'bɪlɪteɪt] VT (criminal, drug addict, invalid) ricuperare, reinserire

rehabilitation ['riːəbɪlɪ'teɪʃən] N (see vb) ricupero, reinserimento; (of offender) riabilitazione f; (of disabled) riadattamento

rehash [riː'hæʃ] VT (col) rimaneggiare

rehearsal [rɪ'həːsəl] N prova; **dress ~** prova generale

rehearse [rɪ'həːs] VT provare

rehouse [riː'hauz] VT rialloggiare

reign [reɪn] N regno ▶ VI regnare

reigning ['reɪnɪŋ] ADJ (monarch) regnante; (champion) attuale

reimburse [riːɪm'bəːs] VT rimborsare

rein [reɪn] N (for horse) briglia; **to give sb free ~** (fig) lasciare completa libertà a qn

reincarnation [riːɪnkɑː'neɪʃən] N reincarnazione f

reindeer ['reɪndɪə^r] N pl inv renna

reinforce [riːɪn'fɔːs] VT rinforzare

reinforced concrete [riːɪn'fɔːst-] N cemento armato

reinforcement [riːɪn'fɔːsmənt] N (action) rinforzamento; **reinforcements** NPL (Mil) rinforzi mpl

reinstate [riːɪn'steɪt] VT reintegrare

reinstatement [riːɪn'steɪtmənt] N reintegrazione f

reissue [riː'ɪʃjuː] VT (book) ristampare, ripubblicare; (film) distribuire di nuovo

reiterate [riː'ɪtəreɪt] VT reiterare, ripetere

reject N ['riːdʒɛkt] (Comm) scarto ▶ VT [rɪ'dʒɛkt] rifiutare, respingere; (Comm: goods) scartare

rejection [rɪ'dʒɛkʃən] N rifiuto

rejoice [rɪ'dʒɔɪs] VI: **to ~ (at or over)** provare diletto (in)

rejoinder [rɪ'dʒɔɪndə^r] N (retort) replica

rejuvenate [rɪ'dʒuːvəneɪt] VT ringiovanire

rekindle [riː'kɪndl] VT riaccendere

relapse [rɪ'læps] N (Med) ricaduta

relate [rɪ'leɪt] VT (tell) raccontare; (connect) collegare ▶ VI: **to ~ to** (refer to) riferirsi a; (get

on with) stabilire un rapporto con;
relating to che riguarda, rispetto a
related [rɪˈleɪtɪd] ADJ imparentato(-a);
collegato(-a), connesso(-a); **~ to**
imparentato(-a) con; collegato(-a) *or*
connesso(-a) con
relating [rɪˈleɪtɪŋ]: **~ to** prep che riguarda,
rispetto a
relation [rɪˈleɪʃən] N (*person*) parente *mf*;
(*link*) rapporto, relazione *f*; **relations** NPL
(*relatives*) parenti *mpl*; **in ~ to** con riferimento
a; **diplomatic/international relations**
rapporti diplomatici/internazionali;
to bear a ~ to corrispondere a
relationship [rɪˈleɪʃənʃɪp] N rapporto;
(*personal ties*) rapporti *mpl*, relazioni *fpl*;
(*also*: **family relationship**) legami *mpl* di
parentela; (*: affair*) relazione *f*; **they have
a good ~** vanno molto d'accordo
relative [ˈrɛlətɪv] N parente *mf* ▶ ADJ
relativo(-a); (*respective*) rispettivo(-a)
relatively [ˈrɛlətɪvlɪ] ADV relativamente;
(*fairly, rather*) abbastanza
relax [rɪˈlæks] VI rilasciarsi; (*person: unwind*)
rilassarsi ▶ VT rilasciare; (*mind, person*)
rilassare; **~!** (*calm down*) calma!
relaxation [riːlækˈseɪʃən] N rilasciamento;
rilassamento; (*entertainment*) ricreazione *f*,
svago
relaxed [rɪˈlækst] ADJ rilasciato(-a);
rilassato(-a)
relaxing [rɪˈlæksɪŋ] ADJ rilassante
relay [ˈriːleɪ] N (*Sport*) corsa a staffetta ▶ VT
(*message*) trasmettere
release [rɪˈliːs] N (*from prison*) rilascio; (*from
obligation*) liberazione *f*; (*of gas etc*) emissione
f; (*of film etc*) distribuzione *f*; (*record*) disco;
(*device*) disinnesto ▶ VT (*prisoner*) rilasciare;
(*from obligation, wreckage etc*) liberare; (*book,
film*) fare uscire; (*news*) rendere pubblico(-a);
(*gas etc*) emettere; (*Tech: catch, spring etc*)
disinnestare; (*let go*) rilasciare; lasciar
andare; sciogliere; **to ~ one's grip** mollare
la presa; **to ~ the clutch** (*Aut*) staccare la
frizione
relegate [ˈrɛləɡeɪt] VT relegare; (*BRIT Sport*):
to be relegated essere retrocesso(-a)
relent [rɪˈlɛnt] VI cedere
relentless [rɪˈlɛntlɪs] ADJ implacabile
relevance [ˈrɛləvəns] N pertinenza; **~ of sth
to sth** rapporto tra qc e qc
relevant [ˈrɛləvənt] ADJ pertinente; (*chapter*)
in questione; **~ to** pertinente a
reliability [rɪlaɪəˈbɪlɪtɪ] N (*of person*) serietà;
(*of machine*) affidabilità
reliable [rɪˈlaɪəbl] ADJ (*person, firm*) fidato(-a),
che dà affidamento; (*method*) sicuro(-a);
(*machine*) affidabile
reliably [rɪˈlaɪəblɪ] ADV: **to be ~ informed**

sapere da fonti sicure
reliance [rɪˈlaɪəns] N: **~ (on)** dipendenza (da)
reliant [rɪˈlaɪənt] ADJ: **to be ~ on sth/sb**
dipendere da qc/qn
relic [ˈrɛlɪk] N (*Rel*) reliquia; (*of the past*) resto
relief [rɪˈliːf] N (*from pain, anxiety*) sollievo;
(*help, supplies*) soccorsi *mpl*; (*of guard*) cambio;
(*Art, Geo*) rilievo; **by way of light ~** come
diversivo
relief map N carta in rilievo
relief road N (*BRIT*) circonvallazione *f*
relieve [rɪˈliːv] VT (*pain, patient*) sollevare;
(*bring help*) soccorrere; (*take over from: gen*)
sostituire; (*: guard*) rilevare; **to ~ sb of sth**
(*load*) alleggerire qn di qc; **to ~ sb of his
command** (*Mil*) esonerare qn dal comando;
to ~ o.s. (*euphemism*) fare i propri bisogni
relieved [rɪˈliːvd] ADJ sollevato(-a); **to be ~
that ...** essere sollevato(-a) (dal fatto) che ...;
I'm ~ to hear it mi hai tolto un peso con
questa notizia
religion [rɪˈlɪdʒən] N religione *f*
religious [rɪˈlɪdʒəs] ADJ religioso(-a)
religious education N religione *f*
relinquish [rɪˈlɪŋkwɪʃ] VT abbandonare;
(*plan, habit*) rinunziare a
relish [ˈrɛlɪʃ] N (*Culin*) condimento; (*enjoyment*)
gran piacere *m* ▶ VT (*food etc*) godere; **to ~
doing** adorare fare
relive [riːˈlɪv] VT rivivere
reload [riːˈləud] VT ricaricare
relocate [riːləuˈkeɪt] VT (*business*) trasferire
▶ VI trasferirsi; **to ~ in** trasferire la propria
sede a
reluctance [rɪˈlʌktəns] N riluttanza
reluctant [rɪˈlʌktənt] ADJ riluttante, mal
disposto(-a); **to be ~ to do sth** essere restio a
fare qc
reluctantly [rɪˈlʌktəntlɪ] ADV di mala voglia,
a malincuore
rely [rɪˈlaɪ]: **to ~ on** vt fus contare su; (*be
dependent*) dipendere da
remain [rɪˈmeɪn] VI restare, rimanere;
to ~ silent restare in silenzio; **I ~, yours
faithfully** (*BRIT: in letters*) distinti saluti
remainder [rɪˈmeɪndəʳ] N resto; (*Comm*)
rimanenza
remaining [rɪˈmeɪnɪŋ] ADJ che rimane
remains [rɪˈmeɪnz] NPL resti *mpl*
remand [rɪˈmɑːnd] N: **on ~** in detenzione
preventiva ▶ VT: **to ~ in custody** rinviare in
carcere; trattenere a disposizione della legge
remand home N (*BRIT*) riformatorio, casa di
correzione
remark [rɪˈmɑːk] N osservazione *f* ▶ VT
osservare, dire; (*notice*) notare ▶ VI: **to ~ on
sth** fare dei commenti su qc
remarkable [rɪˈmɑːkəbl] ADJ notevole;
eccezionale

remarry [riːˈmærɪ] VI risposarsi
remedial [rɪˈmiːdɪəl] ADJ (*tuition, classes*) di riparazione
remedy [ˈrɛmədɪ] N: ~ **(for)** rimedio (per) ▶ VT rimediare a
remember [rɪˈmɛmbəʳ] VT ricordare, ricordarsi di; **I ~ seeing it, I ~ having seen it** (mi) ricordo di averlo visto; **she remembered to do it** si è ricordata di farlo; ~ **me to your wife and children!** saluti sua moglie e i bambini da parte mia!
remembrance [rɪˈmɛmbrəns] N memoria; ricordo
Remembrance Day, (BRIT) **Remembrance Sunday** N; *vedi nota*

> Nel Regno Unito, la domenica più vicina all'11 di novembre, data in cui fu firmato l'armistizio con la Germania nel 1918, ricorre il *Remembrance Day* o *Remembrance Sunday*, giorno in cui vengono commemorati i caduti in guerra. In questa occasione molti portano un papavero di carta appuntato al petto in segno di rispetto.

remind [rɪˈmaɪnd] VT: **to ~ sb of sth** ricordare qc a qn; **to ~ sb to do** ricordare a qn di fare; **that reminds me!** a proposito!
reminder [rɪˈmaɪndəʳ] N richiamo; (*note etc*) promemoria *m inv*
reminisce [rɛmɪˈnɪs] VI: **to ~ (about)** abbandonarsi ai ricordi (di)
reminiscences [rɛmɪˈnɪsnsɪz] NPL reminiscenze *fpl*, memorie *fpl*
reminiscent [rɛmɪˈnɪsnt] ADJ: ~ **of** che fa pensare a, che richiama
remiss [rɪˈmɪs] ADJ negligente; **it was ~ of me** è stata una negligenza da parte mia
remission [rɪˈmɪʃən] N remissione *f*; (*of fee*) esonero
remit [rɪˈmɪt] VT rimettere
remittance [rɪˈmɪtəns] N rimessa
remnant [ˈrɛmnənt] N resto, avanzo; **remnants** NPL (*Comm*) scampoli *mpl*; fine *f* serie
remonstrate [ˈrɛmənstreɪt] VI protestare; **to ~ with sb about sth** fare le proprie rimostranze a qn circa qc
remorse [rɪˈmɔːs] N rimorso
remorseful [rɪˈmɔːsful] ADJ pieno(-a) di rimorsi
remorseless [rɪˈmɔːslɪs] ADJ (*fig*) spietato(-a)
remote [rɪˈməut] ADJ remoto(-a), lontano(-a); (*person*) distaccato(-a); **there is a ~ possibility that ...** c'è una vaga possibilità che ... +*sub*
remote control N telecomando
remote-controlled [rɪˈməutkənˈtrəuld] ADJ telecomandato(-a)

remotely [rɪˈməutlɪ] ADV remotamente; (*slightly*) vagamente
remoteness [rɪˈməutnɪs] N lontananza
remould [ˈriːməuld] N (BRIT: *tyre*) gomma rivestita
removable [rɪˈmuːvbl] ADJ (*detachable*) staccabile
removal [rɪˈmuːvəl] N (*taking away*) rimozione *f*; soppressione *f*; (BRIT: *from house*) trasloco; (*from office: sacking*) destituzione *f*; (*Med*) ablazione *f*
removal man N (*irreg*) (BRIT) addetto ai traslochi
removal van N (BRIT) furgone *m* per traslochi
remove [rɪˈmuːv] VT togliere, rimuovere; (*employee*) destituire; (*stain*) far sparire; (*doubt, abuse*) sopprimere, eliminare; **first cousin once removed** cugino di secondo grado
remover [rɪˈmuːvəʳ] N (*for paint*) prodotto sverniciante; (*for varnish*) solvente *m*; **make-up ~** struccatore *m*
remunerate [rɪˈmjuːnəreɪt] VT rimunerare
remuneration [rɪmjuːnəˈreɪʃən] N rimunerazione *f*
Renaissance [rəˈneɪsəns] N: **the ~** il Rinascimento
rename [riːˈneɪm] VT ribattezzare
rend [rɛnd] (*pt, pp* **rent** [rɛnt]) VT lacerare
render [ˈrɛndəʳ] VT rendere; (*Culin: fat*) struggere
rendering [ˈrɛndərɪŋ] N (*Mus etc*) interpretazione *f*
rendez-vous [ˈrɔndɪvuː] N appuntamento; (*place*) luogo d'incontro; (*meeting*) incontro ▶ VI ritrovarsi; (*spaceship*) effettuare un rendez-vous
rendition [rɛnˈdɪʃən] N (*Mus*) interpretazione *f*
renegade [ˈrɛnɪgeɪd] N rinnegato(-a)
renew [rɪˈnjuː] VT rinnovare; (*negotiations*) riprendere
renewable [rɪˈnjuːəbl] ADJ riutilizzabile; (*contract*) rinnovabile; ~ **energy, renewables** fonti *mpl* di energia rinnovabile
renewal [rɪˈnjuːəl] N rinnovamento; ripresa
renounce [rɪˈnauns] VT rinunziare a; (*disown*) ripudiare
renovate [ˈrɛnəveɪt] VT rinnovare; (*art work*) restaurare
renovation [rɛnəˈveɪʃən] N rinnovamento; restauro
renown [rɪˈnaun] N rinomanza
renowned [rɪˈnaund] ADJ rinomato(-a)
rent [rɛnt] PT, PP of **rend** ▶ N affitto ▶ VT (*take for rent*) prendere in affitto; (*car, TV*) noleggiare, prendere a noleggio; (*also:* **rent out**) dare in affitto; (: *car, TV*) noleggiare, dare a noleggio

rental ['rɛntl] N (cost: on TV, telephone) abbonamento; (on car) noleggio

rent boy N (BRIT col) giovane prostituto

renunciation [rɪnʌnsɪ'eɪʃən] N rinnegamento; (self-denial) rinunzia

reopen [ri:'əupən] VT riaprire

reopening [ri:'əupnɪŋ] N riapertura

reorder [ri:'ɔ:də'] VT ordinare di nuovo; (rearrange) riorganizzare

reorganize [ri:'ɔ:gənaɪz] VT riorganizzare

Rep ABBR (US Pol) = **representative**; **republican**

rep [rɛp] N ABBR (Comm: = representative) rappresentante mf; (Theat: repertory) teatro di repertorio

repair [rɪ'pɛə'] N riparazione f ▶ VT riparare; **in good/bad ~** in buono/cattivo stato; **under ~** in riparazione

repair kit N kit m inv per riparazioni

repair man N (irreg) riparatore m

repair shop N (Aut etc) officina

repartee [rɛpɑ:'ti:] N risposta pronta

repast [rɪ'pɑ:st] N (formal) pranzo

repatriate [ri:'pætrɪeɪt] VT rimpatriare

repay [ri:'peɪ] VT (irreg: like **pay**) (money, creditor) rimborsare, ripagare; (sb's efforts) ricompensare; (favour) ricambiare

repayment [ri:'peɪmənt] N rimborso

repeal [rɪ'pi:l] N (of law) abrogazione f; (of sentence) annullamento ▶ VT abrogare; annullare

repeat [rɪ'pi:t] N (Radio, TV) replica ▶ VT ripetere; (pattern) riprodurre; (promise, attack, also Comm: order) rinnovare ▶ VI ripetere

repeatedly [rɪ'pi:tɪdlɪ] ADV ripetutamente, spesso

repeat order N (Comm): **to place a ~ (for)** rinnovare l'ordinazione (di)

repeat prescription N (BRIT) ricetta ripetibile

repel [rɪ'pɛl] VT respingere

repellent [rɪ'pɛlənt] ADJ repellente ▶ N: **insect ~** prodotto m anti-insetti inv; **moth ~** anti-tarmico

repent [rɪ'pɛnt] VI: **to ~ (of)** pentirsi (di)

repentance [rɪ'pɛntəns] N pentimento

repercussion [ri:pə'kʌʃən] N (consequence) ripercussione f

repertoire ['rɛpətwɑ:'] N repertorio

repertory ['rɛpətərɪ] N (also: **repertory theatre**) teatro di repertorio

repertory company N compagnia di repertorio

repetition [rɛpɪ'tɪʃən] N ripetizione f; (Comm: of order etc) rinnovo

repetitious [rɛpɪ'tɪʃəs] ADJ (speech) pieno(-a) di ripetizioni

repetitive [rɪ'pɛtɪtɪv] ADJ (movement) che si ripete; (work) monotono(-a); (speech) pieno(-a) di ripetizioni

replace [rɪ'pleɪs] VT (put back) rimettere a posto; (take the place of) sostituire; (Tel): "**~ the receiver**" "riattaccare"

replacement [rɪ'pleɪsmənt] N rimessa; sostituzione f; (person) sostituto(-a)

replacement part N pezzo di ricambio

replay ['ri:pleɪ] N (of match) partita ripetuta; (of tape, film) replay m inv

replenish [rɪ'plɛnɪʃ] VT (glass) riempire; (stock etc) rifornire

replete [rɪ'pli:t] ADJ: **~ (with)** ripieno(-a) (di); (well-fed) sazio(-a) (di)

replica ['rɛplɪkə] N replica, copia

reply [rɪ'plaɪ] N risposta ▶ VI rispondere; **in ~** in risposta; **there's no ~** (Tel) non risponde (nessuno)

reply coupon N buono di risposta

report [rɪ'pɔ:t] N rapporto; (Press etc) cronaca; (BRIT: also: **school report**) pagella; (of gun) sparo ▶ VT riportare; (Press etc) fare una cronaca su; (bring to notice: occurrence) segnalare; (: person) denunciare ▶ VI (make a report) fare un rapporto (or una cronaca); (present o.s.): **to ~ (to sb)** presentarsi (a qn); **to ~ (on)** fare un rapporto (su); **it is reported that** si dice che; **it is reported from Berlin that ...** ci è stato riferito da Berlino che ...

report card N (US, SCOTTISH) pagella

reportedly [rɪ'pɔ:tɪdlɪ] ADV stando a quanto si dice; **he ~ told them to ...** avrebbe detto loro di ...; **she is ~ living in Spain** si dice che vive in Spagna

reported speech [rɪ'pɔ:tɪd-] N (Ling) discorso indiretto

reporter [rɪ'pɔ:tə'] N (Press) cronista mf, reporter m inv; (Radio) radiocronista mf; (TV) telecronista mf

repose [rɪ'pəuz] N: **in ~** in riposo

repossess [ri:pə'zɛs] VT rientrare in possesso di

repossession order [ri:pə'zɛʃən-] N ordine m di espropriazione

reprehensible [rɛprɪ'hɛnsɪbl] ADJ riprensibile

represent [rɛprɪ'zɛnt] VT rappresentare

representation [rɛprɪzɛn'teɪʃən] N rappresentazione f; (petition) rappresentanza; **representations** NPL (protest) protesta

representative [rɛprɪ'zɛntətɪv] N rappresentativo(-a); (Comm) rappresentante m (di commercio); (US Pol) deputato(-a) ▶ ADJ: **~ (of)** rappresentativo(-a) (di)

repress [rɪ'prɛs] VT reprimere

repression [rɪ'prɛʃən] N repressione f

repressive [rɪ'prɛsɪv] ADJ repressivo(-a)

reprieve [rɪ'pri:v] N (Law) sospensione f

r

dell'esecuzione della condanna; (*fig*)
dilazione *f* ▶ vt sospendere l'esecuzione
della condanna a; accordare una dilazione a
reprimand ['rɛprɪmɑːnd] N rimprovero ▶ vt
rimproverare, redarguire
reprint ['riːprɪnt] N ristampa ▶ vt
ristampare
reprisal [rɪ'praɪzl] N rappresaglia; **to take
reprisals** fare delle rappresaglie
reproach [rɪ'prəutʃ] N rimprovero ▶ vt: **to ~
sb with sth** rimproverare qn di qc; **beyond ~**
irreprensibile
reproachful [rɪ'prəutʃful] ADJ di rimprovero
reproduce [riːprə'djuːs] vt riprodurre ▶ vi
riprodursi
reproduction [riːprə'dʌkʃən] N
riproduzione *f*
reproductive [riːprə'dʌktɪv] ADJ
riproduttore(-trice); riproduttivo(-a)
reproof [rɪ'pruːf] N riprovazione *f*
reprove [rɪ'pruːv] vt (*action*) disapprovare;
(*person*): **to ~ (for)** biasimare (per)
reproving [rɪ'pruːvɪŋ] ADJ di disapprovazione
reptile ['rɛptaɪl] N rettile *m*
Repub. ABBR (*US Pol*) = **republican**
republic [rɪ'pʌblɪk] N repubblica
republican [rɪ'pʌblɪkən] ADJ, N
repubblicano(-a)
repudiate [rɪ'pjuːdɪeɪt] vt ripudiare
repugnant [rɪ'pʌgnənt] ADJ ripugnante
repulse [rɪ'pʌls] vt respingere
repulsion [rɪ'pʌlʃən] N ripulsione *f*
repulsive [rɪ'pʌlsɪv] ADJ ripugnante,
ripulsivo(-a)
reputable ['rɛpjutəbl] ADJ di buona
reputazione; (*occupation*) rispettabile
reputation [rɛpju'teɪʃən] N reputazione *f*; **he
has a ~ for being awkward** ha la fama di
essere un tipo difficile
repute [rɪ'pjuːt] N reputazione *f*
reputed [rɪ'pjuːtɪd] ADJ reputato(-a); **to be ~
to be rich/intelligent** *etc* essere ritenuto(-a)
ricco(-a)/intelligente *etc*
reputedly [rɪ'pjuːtɪdlɪ] ADV secondo quanto
si dice
request [rɪ'kwɛst] N domanda; (*formal*)
richiesta ▶ vt: **to ~ (of** or **from sb)** chiedere
(a qn); **at the ~ of** su richiesta di; **"you are
requested not to smoke"** "si prega di non
fumare"
request stop N (*Brit: for bus*) fermata
facoltativa or a richiesta
requiem ['rɛkwɪəm] N requiem *m inv* or *f inv*
require [rɪ'kwaɪər] vt (*need: person*) aver
bisogno di; (*: thing, situation*) richiedere;
(*want*) volere; esigere; (*order*) obbligare; **to ~
sb to do sth/sth of sb** esigere che qn faccia
qc/qc da qn; **what qualifications are
required?** che requisiti ci vogliono?;

required by law prescritto dalla legge; **if
required** in caso di bisogno
required [rɪ'kwaɪəd] ADJ richiesto(-a)
requirement [rɪ'kwaɪəmənt] N (*need*)
esigenza; bisogno; (*condition*) requisito; **to
meet sb's requirements** soddisfare le
esigenze di qn
requisite ['rɛkwɪzɪt] N cosa necessaria ▶ ADJ
necessario(-a); **toilet requisites** articoli *mpl*
da toletta
requisition [rɛkwɪ'zɪʃən] N: **~ (for)** richiesta
(di) ▶ vt (*Mil*) requisire
reroute [riː'ruːt] vt (*train etc*) deviare
resale ['riː'seɪl] N rivendita
resale price maintenance N prezzo
minimo di vendita imposto
resat [riː'sæt] PT, PP of **resit**
rescind [rɪ'sɪnd] vt annullare; (*law*)
abrogare; (*judgement*) rescindere
rescue ['rɛskjuː] N salvataggio; (*help*)
soccorso ▶ vt salvare; **to come/go to sb's ~**
venire/andare in aiuto a or di qn
rescue party N squadra di salvataggio
rescuer ['rɛskjuər] N salvatore(-trice)
research [rɪ'səːtʃ] N ricerca, ricerche *fpl* ▶ vt
fare ricerche su ▶ vi: **to ~ (into sth)** fare
ricerca (su qc); **a piece of ~** un lavoro di
ricerca; **~ and development** ricerca e
sviluppo
researcher [rɪ'səːtʃər] N ricercatore(-trice)
research work N ricerche *fpl*
resell [riː'sɛl] vt (*irreg: like* **sell**) rivendere
resemblance [rɪ'zɛmbləns] N somiglianza;
to bear a strong ~ to somigliare
moltissimo a
resemble [rɪ'zɛmbl] vt assomigliare a
resent [rɪ'zɛnt] vt risentirsi di
resentful [rɪ'zɛntful] ADJ pieno(-a) di
risentimento
resentment [rɪ'zɛntmənt] N risentimento
reservation [rɛzə'veɪʃən] N (*booking*)
prenotazione *f*; (*doubt*) dubbio; (*protected area*)
riserva; (*Brit Aut: also:* **central reservation**)
spartitraffico *m inv*; **to make a ~ (in an
hotel/a restaurant/on a plane)** prenotare
(una camera/una tavola/un posto); **with
reservations** (*doubts*) con le dovute riserve
reservation desk N (*US: in hotel*) reception
f inv
reserve [rɪ'zəːv] N riserva ▶ vt (*seats etc*)
prenotare; **reserves** NPL (*Mil*) riserve *fpl*; **in ~**
in serbo
reserve currency N valuta di riserva
reserved [rɪ'zəːvd] ADJ (*shy*) riservato(-a);
(*seat*) prenotato(-a)
reserve price N (*Brit*) prezzo di riserva,
prezzo *m* base *inv*
reserve team N (*Brit Sport*) seconda squadra
reservist [rɪ'zəːvɪst] N (*Mil*) riservista *m*

reservoir ['rɛzəvwɑː^r] N serbatoio; (*artificial lake*) bacino idrico
reset [riː'sɛt] VT (*irreg: like* **set**) (*Comput*) azzerare
reshape [riː'ʃeɪp] VT (*policy*) ristrutturare
reshuffle [riː'ʃʌfl] N: **Cabinet ~** (*Pol*) rimpasto governativo
reside [rɪ'zaɪd] VI risiedere
residence ['rɛzɪdəns] N residenza; **to take up ~** prendere residenza; **in ~** (*queen etc*) in sede; (*doctor*) fisso
residence permit N (*BRIT*) permesso di soggiorno
resident ['rɛzɪdənt] N (*gen, Comput*) residente *mf*; (*in hotel*) cliente *mf* fisso(-a) ▶ ADJ residente; (*doctor*) fisso(-a); (*course, college*) a tempo pieno con pernottamento
residential [rɛzɪ'dɛnʃəl] ADJ di residenza; (*area*) residenziale
residue ['rɛzɪdjuː] N resto; (*Chem, Physics*) residuo
resign [rɪ'zaɪn] VT (*one's post*) dimettersi da ▶ VI: **to ~ (from)** dimettersi (da), dare le dimissioni (da); **to ~ o.s. to** rassegnarsi a
resignation [rɛzɪg'neɪʃən] N dimissioni *fpl*; rassegnazione *f*; **to tender one's ~** dare le dimissioni
resilience [rɪ'zɪlɪəns] N (*of material*) elasticità, resilienza; (*of person*) capacità di recupero
resilient [rɪ'zɪlɪənt] ADJ elastico(-a); (*person*) che si riprende facilmente
resin ['rɛzɪn] N resina
resist [rɪ'zɪst] VT resistere a
resistance [rɪ'zɪstəns] N resistenza
resistant [rɪ'zɪstənt] ADJ: **~ (to)** resistente (a)
resit ['riː'sɪt] (*BRIT*) VT (*irreg: like* **sit**) (*exam*) ripresentarsi a; (*subject*) ridare l'esame di ▶ N: **he's got his French ~ on Friday** deve ridare l'esame di francese venerdì
resolute ['rɛzəluːt] ADJ risoluto(-a)
resolution [rɛzə'luːʃən] N (*resolve*) fermo proposito, risoluzione *f*; (*determination*) risolutezza; (*on screen*) risoluzione *f*; **to make a ~** fare un proposito
resolve [rɪ'zɔlv] N risoluzione *f* ▶ VI (*decide*): **to ~ to do** decidere di fare ▶ VT (*problem*) risolvere
resolved [rɪ'zɔlvd] ADJ risoluto(-a)
resonance ['rɛzənəns] N risonanza
resonant ['rɛzənənt] ADJ risonante
resort [rɪ'zɔːt] N (*town*) stazione *f*; (*place*) località *f inv*; (*recourse*) ricorso ▶ VI: **to ~ to** far ricorso a; **seaside/winter sports ~** stazione *f* balneare/di sport invernali; **as a last ~** come ultima risorsa
resound [rɪ'zaund] VI: **to ~ (with)** risonare (di)
resounding [rɪ'zaundɪŋ] ADJ risonante
resource [rɪ'sɔːs] N risorsa; **resources** NPL risorse *fpl*; **natural resources** risorse naturali; **to leave sb to his** (*or* **her**) **own resources** (*fig*) lasciare che qn si arrangi (per conto suo)
resourceful [rɪ'sɔːsful] ADJ pieno(-a) di risorse, intraprendente
resourcefulness [rɪ'sɔːsfəlnɪs] N intraprendenza
respect [rɪs'pɛkt] N rispetto; (*point, detail*): **in some respects** sotto certi aspetti ▶ VT rispettare; **respects** NPL ossequi *mpl*; **to have** *or* **show ~ for** aver rispetto per; **out of ~ for** per rispetto *or* riguardo a; **with ~ to** rispetto a, riguardo a; **in ~ of** quanto a; **in this ~** per questo riguardo; **with (all) due ~ I ...** con rispetto parlando, io ...
respectability [rɪspɛktə'bɪlɪtɪ] N rispettabilità
respectable [rɪs'pɛktəbl] ADJ rispettabile; (*quite big: amount etc*) considerevole; (*quite good: player, result etc*) niente male *inv*
respectful [rɪs'pɛktful] ADJ rispettoso(-a)
respective [rɪs'pɛktɪv] ADJ rispettivo(-a)
respectively [rɪs'pɛktɪvlɪ] ADV rispettivamente
respiration [rɛspɪ'reɪʃən] N respirazione *f*
respirator ['rɛspɪreɪtə*] N respiratore *m*
respiratory ['rɛspərətərɪ] ADJ respiratorio(-a)
respite ['rɛspaɪt] N respiro, tregua
resplendent [rɪs'plɛndənt] ADJ risplendente
respond [rɪs'pɔnd] VI rispondere
respondent [rɪs'pɔndənt] N (*Law*) convenuto(-a)
response [rɪs'pɔns] N risposta; **in ~ to** in risposta a
responsibility [rɪspɔnsɪ'bɪlɪtɪ] N responsabilità *f inv*; **to take ~ for sth/sb** assumersi *or* prendersi la responsabilità di qc/per qn
responsible [rɪs'pɔnsɪbl] ADJ (*liable*): **~ (for)** responsabile (di); (*trustworthy*) fidato(-a); (*job*) di (grande) responsabilità; **to be ~ to sb (for sth)** dover rispondere a qn (di qc)
responsibly [rɪs'pɔnsəblɪ] ADV responsabilmente
responsive [rɪs'pɔnsɪv] ADJ che reagisce
rest [rɛst] N riposo; (*stop*) sosta, pausa; (*Mus*) pausa; (*support*) appoggio, sostegno; (*remainder*) resto, avanzi *mpl* ▶ VI riposarsi; (*remain*) rimanere, restare; (*be supported*): **to ~ on** appoggiarsi su ▶ VT (far) riposare; (*lean*): **to ~ sth on/against** appoggiare qc su/contro; **to set sb's mind at ~** tranquillizzare qn; **the ~ of them** gli altri; **to ~ one's eyes** *or* **gaze on** posare lo sguardo su; **~ assured that ...** stia tranquillo che ...; **it rests with him to decide** sta a lui decidere
restart [riː'stɑːt] VT (*engine*) rimettere in marcia; (*work*) ricominciare

restaurant ['rɛstərɔŋ] N ristorante *m*
restaurant car N (*BRIT*) vagone *m* ristorante
rest cure N cura del riposo
restful ['rɛstful] ADJ riposante
rest home N casa di riposo
restitution [rɛstɪ'tjuːʃən] N (*act*) restituzione *f*; (*reparation*) riparazione *f*
restive ['rɛstɪv] ADJ agitato(-a), impaziente; (*horse*) restio(-a)
restless ['rɛstlɪs] ADJ agitato(-a), irrequieto(-a); **to get ~** spazientirsi
restlessly ['rɛstlɪslɪ] ADV in preda all'agitazione
restock [riː'stɔk] VT rifornire
restoration [rɛstə'reɪʃən] N restauro; restituzione *f*
restorative [rɪ'stɔrətɪv] ADJ corroborante, ristorativo(-a) ▶ N ricostituente *m*
restore [rɪ'stɔːʳ] VT (*building*) restaurare; (*sth stolen*) restituire; (*peace, health*) ristorare
restorer [rɪs'tɔːrəʳ] N (*Art etc*) restauratore(-trice)
restrain [rɪs'treɪn] VT (*feeling*) contenere, frenare; (*person*): **to ~ (from doing)** trattenere (dal fare)
restrained [rɪs'treɪnd] ADJ (*style*) contenuto(-a), sobrio(-a); (*manner*) riservato(-a)
restraint [rɪs'treɪnt] N (*restriction*) limitazione *f*; (*moderation*) ritegno; (*of style*) contenutezza; **wage ~** restrizioni *fpl* salariali
restrict [rɪs'trɪkt] VT restringere, limitare
restricted area [rɪs'trɪktɪd-] N (*Aut*) zona a velocità limitata
restriction [rɪs'trɪkʃən] N: **~ (on)** restrizione *f* (di), limitazione *f* (di)
restrictive [rɪs'trɪktɪv] ADJ restrittivo(-a)
restrictive practices NPL (*Industry*) pratiche restrittive di produzione
rest room N (*US*) toletta
restructure [riː'strʌktʃəʳ] VT ristrutturare
result [rɪ'zʌlt] N risultato ▶ VI: **to ~ in** avere per risultato; **as a ~ (of)** in *or* di conseguenza (a), in seguito (a); **to ~ (from)** essere una conseguenza (di), essere causato(-a) (da)
resultant [rɪ'zʌltənt] ADJ risultante, conseguente
resume [rɪ'zjuːm] VT, VI (*work, journey*) riprendere; (*sum up*) riassumere
résumé ['reɪzjuːmeɪ] N riassunto; (*US*: *curriculum vitae*) curriculum vitae *m inv*
resumption [rɪ'zʌmpʃən] N ripresa
resurgence [rɪ'səːdʒəns] N rinascita
resurrection [rɛzə'rɛkʃən] N risurrezione *f*
resuscitate [rɪ'sʌsɪteɪt] VT (*Med*) risuscitare
resuscitation [rɪsʌsɪ'teɪʃən] N rianimazione *f*
retail ['riːteɪl] N (vendita al) minuto ▶ CPD al minuto ▶ VT vendere al minuto ▶ VI: **to ~ at**

essere in vendita al pubblico al prezzo di
retailer ['riːteɪləʳ] N commerciante *mf* al minuto, dettagliante *mf*
retail outlet N punto di vendita al dettaglio
retail price N prezzo al minuto
retail price index N indice *m* dei prezzi al consumo
retain [rɪ'teɪn] VT (*keep*) tenere, serbare
retainer [rɪ'teɪnəʳ] N (*servant*) servitore *m*; (*fee*) onorario
retaliate [rɪ'tælɪeɪt] VI: **to ~ (against)** vendicarsi (di); **to ~ on sb** fare una rappresaglia contro qn
retaliation [rɪtælɪ'eɪʃən] N rappresaglie *fpl*; **in ~ for** per vendicarsi di
retaliatory [rɪ'tælɪətərɪ] ADJ di rappresaglia, di ritorsione
retarded [rɪ'tɑːdɪd] ADJ ritardato(-a); (*also:* **mentally retarded**) tardo(-a) (di mente)
retch [rɛtʃ] VI aver conati di vomito
retentive [rɪ'tɛntɪv] ADJ ritentivo(-a)
rethink ['riː'θɪŋk] VT ripensare
reticence ['rɛtɪsns] N reticenza
reticent ['rɛtɪsnt] ADJ reticente
retina ['rɛtɪnə] N retina
retinue ['rɛtɪnjuː] N seguito, scorta
retire [rɪ'taɪəʳ] VI (*give up work*) andare in pensione; (*withdraw*) ritirarsi, andarsene; (*go to bed*) andare a letto, ritirarsi
retired [rɪ'taɪəd] ADJ (*person*) pensionato(-a)
retirement [rɪ'taɪəmənt] N pensione *f*; (*act*) pensionamento
retirement age N età del pensionamento
retiring [rɪ'taɪərɪŋ] ADJ (*person*) riservato(-a); (*departing: chairman*) uscente
retort [rɪ'tɔːt] N (*reply*) rimbecco; (*container*) storta ▶ VI rimbeccare
retrace [riː'treɪs] VT ricostruire; **to ~ one's steps** tornare sui propri passi
retract [rɪ'trækt] VT (*statement*) ritrattare; (*claws, undercarriage, aerial*) ritrarre, ritirare ▶ VI ritrarsi
retractable [rɪ'træktəbl] ADJ retrattile
retrain [riː'treɪn] VT (*worker*) riaddestrare
retraining [riː'treɪnɪŋ] N riaddestramento
retread VT [riː'trɛd] (*Aut: tyre*) rigenerare ▶ N ['riːtrɛd] gomma rigenerata
retreat [rɪ'triːt] N ritirata; (*place*) rifugio ▶ VI battere in ritirata; (*flood*) ritirarsi; **to beat a hasty ~** (*fig*) battersela
retrial [riː'traɪəl] N nuovo processo
retribution [rɛtrɪ'bjuːʃən] N castigo
retrieval [rɪ'triːvəl] N ricupero
retrieve [rɪ'triːv] VT (*sth lost*) ricuperare, ritrovare; (*situation, honour*) salvare; (*error, loss*) rimediare a; (*Comput*) ricuperare
retriever [rɪ'triːvəʳ] N cane *m* da riporto
retroactive [rɛtrəu'æktɪv] ADJ retroattivo(-a)
retrograde ['rɛtrəugreɪd] ADJ retrogrado(-a)

retrospect ['rɛtrəspɛkt] N: **in ~** guardando indietro

retrospective [rɛtrə'spɛktɪv] ADJ retrospettivo(-a); (law) retroattivo(-a) ▶ N (Art) retrospettiva

return [rɪ'tə:n] N (going or coming back) ritorno; (of sth stolen etc) restituzione f; (Comm: from land, shares) profitto, reddito, (: of merchandise) resa; (report) rapporto; (reward): **in ~ (for)** in cambio (di) ▶ CPD (journey, match) di ritorno; (BRIT: ticket) di andata e ritorno ▶ VI tornare, ritornare ▶ VT rendere, restituire; (bring back) riportare; (send back) mandare indietro; (put back) rimettere; (Pol: candidate) eleggere; **returns** NPL (Comm) incassi mpl; profitti mpl; **by ~ of post** a stretto giro di posta; **many happy returns (of the day)!** cento di questi giorni!

returnable [rɪ'tə:nəbl] ADJ: **~ bottle** vuoto a rendere

returner [rɪ'tə:nər] N donna che ritorna al lavoro dopo la maternità

returning officer [rɪ'tə:nɪŋ-] N (BRIT Pol) funzionario addetto all'organizzazione delle elezioni in un distretto

return key N (Comput) tasto di ritorno

return ticket N (esp BRIT) biglietto di andata e ritorno

retweet [ri:'twi:t] N (on Twitter) retweet m inv ▶ VT ritwittare

reunion [ri:'ju:nɪən] N riunione f

reunite [ri:ju:'naɪt] VT riunire

rev [rɛv] N ABBR (Aut: = revolution) giro ▶ VT (also: **rev up**) imballare ▶ VI (also: **rev up**) imballarsi

Rev., Revd. ABBR = **Reverend**

revaluation [ri:væljuˈeɪʃən] N rivalutazione f

revamp ['ri:'væmp] VT rinnovare; (firm) riorganizzare

rev counter N contagiri m inv

reveal [rɪ'vi:l] VT (make known) rivelare, svelare; (display) rivelare, mostrare

revealing [rɪ'vi:lɪŋ] ADJ rivelatore(-trice); (dress) scollato(-a)

reveille [rɪ'vælɪ] N (Mil) sveglia

revel ['rɛvl] VI: **to ~ in sth/in doing** dilettarsi di qc/a fare

revelation [rɛvə'leɪʃən] N rivelazione f

reveller ['rɛvlər] N festaiolo(-a)

revelry ['rɛvlrɪ] N baldoria

revenge [rɪ'vɛndʒ] N vendetta; (in game etc) rivincita ▶ VT vendicare; **to ~ on** vendicarsi di; **to get one's ~ (for sth)** vendicarsi (di qc)

revengeful [rɪ'vɛndʒful] ADJ vendicatore(-trice); vendicativo(-a)

revenue ['rɛvənju:] N reddito

reverberate [rɪ'və:bəreɪt] VI (sound) rimbombare; (light) riverberarsi

reverberation [rɪvə:bə'reɪʃən] N (of light, sound) riverberazione f

revere [rɪ'vɪər] VT venerare

reverence ['rɛvərəns] N venerazione f, riverenza

Reverend ['rɛvərənd] ADJ (in titles) reverendo(-a)

reverent ['rɛvərənt] ADJ riverente

reverie ['rɛvərɪ] N fantasticheria

reversal [rɪ'və:sl] N capovolgimento

reverse [rɪ'və:s] N contrario, opposto; (back) rovescio; (Aut: also: **reverse gear**) marcia indietro ▶ ADJ (order) inverso(-a); (direction) opposto(-a) ▶ VT (turn) invertire, rivoltare; (change) capovolgere, rovesciare; (Law: judgement) cassare; (car) fare marcia indietro con ▶ VI (BRIT Aut, person etc) fare marcia indietro; **in ~ order** in ordine inverso; **to go into ~** fare marcia indietro

reverse-charge call [rɪ'və:stʃɑ:dʒ-] N (BRIT Tel) telefonata con addebito al ricevente

reverse video N reverse video m

reversible [rɪ'və:səbl] ADJ (garment) double-face inv; (procedure) reversibile

reversing lights [rɪ'və:sɪŋ-] NPL (BRIT Aut) luci fpl per la retromarcia

reversion [rɪ'və:ʃən] N ritorno

revert [rɪ'və:t] VI: **to ~ to** tornare a

review [rɪ'vju:] N rivista; (of book, film) recensione f; (of situation) esame m ▶ VT passare in rivista; fare la recensione di; fare il punto di; **to come under ~** essere preso in esame

reviewer [rɪ'vju:ər] N recensore(-a)

revile [rɪ'vaɪl] VT insultare

revise [rɪ'vaɪz] VT (manuscript) rivedere, correggere; (opinion) emendare, modificare; (study: subject, notes) ripassare; **revised edition** edizione riveduta

revision [rɪ'vɪʒən] N revisione f; ripasso; (revised version) versione riveduta e corretta

revitalize [ri:'vaɪtəlaɪz] VT ravvivare

revival [rɪ'vaɪvəl] N ripresa; ristabilimento; (of faith) risveglio

revive [rɪ'vaɪv] VT (person) rianimare; (custom) far rivivere; (hope, courage, economy) ravvivare; (play, fashion) riesumare ▶ VI (person) rianimarsi; (hope) ravvivarsi; (activity) riprendersi

revoke [rɪ'vəuk] VT revocare; (promise, decision) rinvenire su

revolt [rɪ'vəult] N rivolta, ribellione f ▶ VI rivoltarsi, ribellarsi; **to ~ (against sb/sth)** ribellarsi (a qn/qc) ▶ VT (far) rivoltare

revolting [rɪ'vəultɪŋ] ADJ ripugnante

revolution [rɛvə'lu:ʃən] N rivoluzione f; (of wheel etc) rivoluzione, giro

revolutionary [rɛvə'lu:ʃənrɪ] ADJ, N rivoluzionario(-a)

revolutionize [rɛvə'luːʃənaɪz] VT
rivoluzionare

revolve [rɪ'vɔlv] VI girare

revolver [rɪ'vɔlvəʳ] N rivoltella

revolving [rɪ'vɔlvɪŋ] ADJ girevole

revolving door N porta girevole

revue [rɪ'vjuː] N (Theat) rivista

revulsion [rɪ'vʌlʃən] N ripugnanza

reward [rɪ'wɔːd] N ricompensa, premio ▸ VT:
to ~ (for) ricompensare (per)

rewarding [rɪ'wɔːdɪŋ] ADJ (fig) soddisfacente;
financially ~ conveniente dal punto di vista
economico

rewind [riː'waɪnd] VT (irreg: like **wind²**) (watch)
ricaricare; (ribbon etc) riavvolgere

rewire [riː'waɪəʳ] VT (house) rifare l'impianto
elettrico di

reword [riː'wəːd] VT formulare or esprimere
con altre parole

rewritable [riː'raɪtəbl] ADJ (CD, DVD)
riscrivibile

rewrite [riː'raɪt] VT (irreg: like **write**) riscrivere

Reykjavik ['reɪkjəviːk] N Reykjavik f

RFD ABBR (US Post) = **rural free delivery**

RGN N ABBR (BRIT: = Registered General Nurse)
infermiera diplomata (dopo corso triennale)

Rh ABBR (= rhesus) Rh

rhapsody ['ræpsədɪ] N (Mus) rapsodia; (fig)
elogio stravagante

rhesus negative ['riːsəs-] ADJ (Med)
Rh-negativo(-a)

rhesus positive ADJ (Med) Rh-positivo(-a)

rhetoric ['rɛtərɪk] N retorica

rhetorical [rɪ'tɔrɪkl] ADJ retorico(-a)

rheumatic [ruː'mætɪk] ADJ reumatico(-a)

rheumatism ['ruːmətɪzəm] N reumatismo

rheumatoid arthritis ['ruːmətɔɪd-] N
artrite f reumatoide

Rhine [raɪn] N: **the ~** il Reno

rhinestone ['raɪnstəun] N diamante m falso

rhinoceros [raɪ'nɔsərəs] N rinoceronte m

Rhodes [rəudz] N Rodi f

Rhodesia [rəu'diːʒə] N Rhodesia

Rhodesian [rəu'diːʒən] ADJ, N
Rhodesiano(-a)

rhododendron [rəudə'dɛndrn] N
rododendro

Rhone [rəun] N: **the ~** il Rodano

rhubarb ['ruːbɑːb] N rabarbaro

rhyme [raɪm] N rima; (verse) poesia ▸ VI: **to ~
(with)** fare rima (con); **without ~ or reason**
senza capo né coda

rhythm ['rɪðm] N ritmo

rhythmic ['rɪðmɪk], **rhythmical** ['rɪðmɪkəl]
ADJ ritmico(-a)

rhythmically ['rɪðmɪkəlɪ] ADV con ritmo

rhythm method N metodo Ogino-Knauss

RI ABBR (US) = **Rhode Island** ▸ N ABBR (BRIT)
= **religious instruction**

rib [rɪb] N (Anat) costola ▸ VT (tease)
punzecchiare

ribald ['rɪbəld] ADJ licenzioso(-a), volgare

ribbed [rɪbd] ADJ (knitting) a coste

ribbon ['rɪbən] N nastro; **in ribbons** (torn) a
brandelli

rice [raɪs] N riso

ricefield ['raɪsfiːld] N risaia

rice pudding N budino di riso

rich [rɪtʃ] ADJ ricco(-a); (clothes) sontuoso(-a);
the ~ npl i ricchi; **riches** NPL ricchezze fpl; **to
be ~ in sth** essere ricco di qc

richly ['rɪtʃlɪ] ADV riccamente; (dressed)
sontuosamente; (deserved) pienamente

rickets ['rɪkɪts] N rachitismo

rickety ['rɪkɪtɪ] ADJ zoppicante

rickshaw ['rɪkʃɔː] N risciò m inv

ricochet ['rɪkəʃeɪ] N rimbalzo ▸ VI rimbalzare

rid [rɪd] (pt, pp ~) VT: **to ~ sb of** sbarazzare or
liberare qn di; **to get ~ of** sbarazzarsi di

riddance ['rɪdns] N: **good ~!** che liberazione!

ridden ['rɪdn] PP of **ride**

riddle ['rɪdl] N (puzzle) indovinello ▸ VT: **to be
riddled with** (holes) essere crivellato(-a) di;
(doubts) essere pieno(-a) di

ride [raɪd] (pt **rode** [rəud], pp **ridden** ['rɪdn])
(on horse) cavalcata; (outing) passeggiata;
(distance covered) cavalcata; corsa ▸ VI (as sport)
cavalcare; (go somewhere: on horse, bicycle)
andare (a cavallo or in bicicletta etc); (journey:
on bicycle, motorcycle, bus) andare, viaggiare
▸ VT (a horse) montare, cavalcare; **to go for a
~** andare a fare una cavalcata; andare a fare
un giro; **can you ~ a bike?** sai andare in
bicicletta?; **we rode all day/all the way**
abbiamo cavalcato tutto il giorno/per tutto il
tragitto; **to ~ a horse/bicycle/camel**
montare a cavallo/in bicicletta/in groppa a
un cammello; **to ~ at anchor** (Naut) essere
alla fonda; **horse ~** cavalcata; **car ~**
passeggiata in macchina; **to take sb for a ~**
(fig) prendere in giro qn; fregare qn
▸ **ride out** VT: **to ~ out the storm** (fig)
mantenersi a galla

rider ['raɪdəʳ] N cavalcatore(-trice); (jockey)
fantino; (on bicycle) ciclista mf; (on motorcycle)
motociclista mf; (in document) clausola
addizionale, aggiunta

ridge [rɪdʒ] N (of hill) cresta; (of roof) colmo;
(of mountain) giogo; (on object) riga (in rilievo)

ridicule ['rɪdɪkjuːl] N ridicolo; scherno ▸ VT
mettere in ridicolo; **to hold sb/sth up to ~**
mettere in ridicolo qn/qc

ridiculous [rɪ'dɪkjuləs] ADJ ridicolo(-a)

riding ['raɪdɪŋ] N equitazione f

riding school N scuola di equitazione

rife [raɪf] ADJ diffuso(-a); **to be ~ with**
abbondare di

riffraff ['rɪfræf] N canaglia, gentaglia

rifle ['raɪfl] N carabina ▸ VT vuotare
  ▸ **rifle through** VT FUS frugare
rifle range N campo di tiro; (*at fair*) tiro a
  segno
rift [rɪft] N fessura, crepatura; (*fig:
  disagreement*) incrinatura, disaccordo
rig [rɪg] N (*also*: **oil rig**: *on land*) derrick *m inv*;
  (: *at sea*) piattaforma di trivellazione ▸ VT
  (*election etc*) truccare
  ▸ **rig out** VT (*BRIT*) attrezzare; (*pej*) abbigliare,
    agghindare
  ▸ **rig up** VT allestire
rigging ['rɪgɪŋ] N (*Naut*) attrezzatura
right [raɪt] ADJ giusto(-a); (*suitable*)
  appropriato(-a); (*not left*) destro(-a) ▸ N
  giusto; (*title, claim*) diritto; (*not left*) destra
  ▸ ADV (*answer*) correttamente; (*not on the left*) a
  destra ▸ VT raddrizzare; (*fig*) riparare ▸ EXCL
  bene!; **the ~ time** l'ora esatta; **to be ~**
  (*person*) aver ragione; (*answer*) essere
  giusto(-a) *or* corretto(-a); **to get sth ~** far
  giusto qc; **you did the ~ thing** ha fatto bene;
  let's get it ~ this time! cerchiamo di farlo
  bene stavolta!; **to put a mistake ~** (*BRIT*)
  correggere un errore; **~ now** proprio adesso;
  subito; **~ away** subito; **~ before/after** subito
  prima/dopo; **to go ~ to the end of sth**
  andare fino in fondo a qc; **~ against the
  wall** proprio contro il muro; **~ ahead** sempre
  diritto; proprio davanti; **~ in the middle**
  proprio nel mezzo; **by rights** di diritto; **on
  the ~**, **to the ~** a destra; **to be in the ~** aver
  ragione, essere nel giusto; **~ and wrong** il
  bene e il male; **to have a ~ to sth** aver diritto
  a qc; **film rights** diritti di riproduzione
  cinematografica
right angle N angolo retto
right-click ['raɪtklɪk] VI (*Comput*): **to ~ on**
  cliccare con il pulsante destro del mouse su
righteous ['raɪtʃəs] ADJ retto(-a), virtuoso(-a);
  (*anger*) giusto(-a), giustificato(-a)
righteousness ['raɪtʃəsnɪs] N rettitudine *f*,
  virtù *f*
rightful ['raɪtful] ADJ (*heir*) legittimo(-a)
rightfully ['raɪtfəlɪ] ADV legittimamente
right-hand ADJ: **~ drive** guida a destra; **the ~
  side** il lato destro; **~ man** braccio destro (*fig*)
right-handed [raɪt'hændɪd] ADJ (*person*) che
  adopera la mano destra
rightly ['raɪtlɪ] ADV bene, correttamente;
  (*with reason*) a ragione; **if I remember ~** se mi
  ricordo bene
right-minded [raɪt'maɪndɪd] ADJ sensato(-a)
right of way N diritto di passaggio; (*Aut*)
  precedenza
rights issue N (*Stock Exchange*) emissione *f* di
  azioni riservate agli azionisti
right wing N (*Mil*, *Sport*) ala destra; (*Pol*)
  destra ▸ ADJ: **right-wing** (*Pol*) di destra

right-winger [raɪt'wɪŋə^r] N (*Pol*) uno(-a) di
  destra; (*Sport*) ala destra
rigid ['rɪdʒɪd] ADJ rigido(-a); (*principle*)
  rigoroso(-a)
rigidity [rɪ'dʒɪdɪtɪ] N rigidità
rigidly ['rɪdʒɪdlɪ] ADV rigidamente
rigmarole ['rɪgmərəul] N tiritera; commedia
rigor ['rɪgə^r] N (*US*) = **rigour**
rigor mortis ['rɪgə'mɔːtɪs] N rigidità
  cadaverica
rigorous ['rɪgərəs] ADJ rigoroso(-a)
rigorously ['rɪgərəslɪ] ADV rigorosamente
rigour,(*US*) **rigor** ['rɪgə^r] N rigore *m*
rig-out ['rɪgaut] N (*BRIT col*) tenuta
rile [raɪl] VT irritare, seccare
rim [rɪm] N orlo; (*of spectacles*) montatura;
  (*of wheel*) cerchione *m*
rimless ['rɪmlɪs] ADJ (*spectacles*) senza
  montatura
rimmed [rɪmd] ADJ bordato(-a); cerchiato(-a)
rind [raɪnd] N (*of bacon*) cotenna; (*of lemon etc*)
  scorza
ring [rɪŋ] (*pt* **rang**, *pp* **rung**) N anello;
  (*also*: **wedding ring**) fede *f*; (*of people, objects*)
  cerchio; (*of spies*) giro; (*of smoke etc*) spirale *f*;
  (*arena*) pista, arena; (*for boxing*) ring *m inv*; (*sound
  of bell*) scampanio; (*telephone call*) colpo di
  telefono ▸ VI (*person, bell, telephone*) suonare;
  (*also*: **ring out**: *voice, words*) risuonare; (*Tel*)
  telefonare; (*ears*) fischiare ▸ VT (*BRIT Tel*: *also*:
  ring up) telefonare a; (*bell, doorbell*) suonare; **to
  give sb a ~** (*BRIT Tel*) dare un colpo di telefono a
  qn; **that has the ~ of truth about it** questo
  ha l'aria d'essere vero; **to ~ the bell** suonare
  il campanello; **the name doesn't ~ a bell
  (with me)** questo nome non mi dice niente
  ▸ **ring back** VT, VI (*BRIT Tel*) richiamare
  ▸ **ring off** VI (*BRIT Tel*) mettere giù, riattaccare
ring binder N classificatore *m* a anelli
ring-fence [rɪŋ'fɛns] VT isolare
ring finger N anulare *m*
ringing ['rɪŋɪŋ] N (*of bell*) scampanio; (: *louder*)
  scampanellata; (*of telephone*) squillo; (*in ears*)
  fischio, ronzio
ringing tone N (*BRIT Tel*) segnale *m* di libero
ringleader ['rɪŋliːdə^r] N (*of gang*) capobanda *m*
ringlets ['rɪŋlɪts] NPL boccoli *mpl*
ring road N (*BRIT*) raccordo anulare
ringtone N (*Tel*) suoneria
rink [rɪŋk] N (*also*: **ice rink**) pista di
  pattinaggio; (: *for roller-skating*) pista di
  pattinaggio (a rotelle)
rinse [rɪns] N risciacquatura; (*hair tint*) cachet
  m inv ▸ VT sciacquare
Rio ['riːəu], **Rio de Janeiro**
  ['riːəudədʒə'nɪərəu] N Rio de Janeiro *f*
riot ['raɪət] N sommossa, tumulto ▸ VI
  tumultuare; **a ~ of colours** un'orgia di
  colori; **to run ~** creare disordine

r

rioter ['raɪətəʳ] N dimostrante *mf* (*durante dei disordini*)

riot gear N: **in ~** in assetto di guerra

riotous ['raɪətəs] ADJ tumultuoso(-a); che fa crepare dal ridere

riotously ['raɪətəslɪ] ADV: **~ funny** che fa crepare dal ridere

riot police N ≈ la Celere

RIP ABBR (= *requiescat or requiescant in pace*) R.I.P.

rip [rɪp] N strappo ▶ VT strappare ▶ VI strapparsi
  ▶ **rip off** VT (*col: cheat*) fregare
  ▶ **rip up** VT stracciare

ripcord ['rɪpkɔːd] N cavo di spiegamento

ripe [raɪp] ADJ (*fruit, grain*) maturo(-a); (*cheese*) stagionato(-a)

ripen ['raɪpən] VT maturare ▶ VI maturarsi; stagionarsi

ripeness ['raɪpnɪs] N maturità

rip-off ['rɪpɔf] N (*col*): **it's a ~!** è un furto!

riposte [rɪ'pɔst] N risposta per le rime

ripple ['rɪpl] N increspamento, ondulazione *f*; mormorio ▶ VI incresparsi ▶ VT increspare

rise [raɪz] (*pt* **rose** [rəuz], *pp* **risen** ['rɪzn]) N (*slope*) salita, pendio; (*hill*) altura; (*increase: in wages: BRIT*) aumento; (: *in prices, temperature*) rialzo, aumento; (*fig: to power etc*) ascesa ▶ VI alzarsi, levarsi; (*prices*) aumentare; (*waters, river*) crescere; (*sun, wind, person: from chair, bed*) levarsi; (*building: also*: **rise up**) ergersi; (*rebel*) insorgere; ribellarsi; (*in rank*) salire; **to give ~ to** provocare, dare origine a; **to ~ to the occasion** dimostrarsi all'altezza della situazione

risen ['rɪzn] PP *of* **rise**

rising ['raɪzɪŋ] ADJ (*increasing: number*) sempre crescente; (: *prices*) in aumento; (*tide*) montante; (*sun, moon*) nascente, che sorge ▶ N (*uprising*) sommossa

rising damp N infiltrazioni *fpl* d'umidità

rising star N (*also fig*) astro nascente

risk [rɪsk] N rischio; pericolo ▶ VT rischiare; **to take** *or* **run the ~ of doing** correre il rischio di fare; **at ~** in pericolo; **at one's own ~** a proprio rischio e pericolo; **fire/health ~** rischio d'incendio/per la salute; **I'll ~ it** ci proverò lo stesso

risk capital N capitale *m* di rischio

risky ['rɪskɪ] ADJ rischioso(-a)

risqué ['riːskeɪ] ADJ (*joke*) spinto(-a)

rissole ['rɪsəul] N crocchetta

rite [raɪt] N rito; **last rites** l'estrema unzione

ritual ['rɪtjuəl] ADJ, N rituale (*m*)

rival ['raɪvl] N rivale *mf*; (*in business*) concorrente *mf* ▶ ADJ rivale; che fa concorrenza ▶ VT essere in concorrenza con; **to ~ sb/sth in** competere con qn/qc in

rivalry ['raɪvəlrɪ] N rivalità; concorrenza

river ['rɪvəʳ] N fiume *m* ▶ CPD (*port, traffic*) fluviale; **up/down ~** a monte/valle

riverbank ['rɪvəbæŋk] N argine *m*

riverbed ['rɪvəbɛd] N alveo (fluviale)

riverside ['rɪvəsaɪd] N sponda del fiume

rivet ['rɪvɪt] N ribattino, rivetto ▶ VT ribadire; (*fig*) concentrare, fissare

riveting ['rɪvɪtɪŋ] ADJ (*fig*) avvincente

Riviera [rɪvɪ'ɛərə] N: **the (French) ~** la Costa Azzurra; **the Italian ~** la Riviera

Riyadh [rɪ'jɑːd] N Riad *f*

RMT N ABBR (= *National Union of Rail, Maritime and Transport Workers*) sindacato dei Ferrovieri, Marittimi e Trasportatori

RN N ABBR (*BRIT*) = **Royal Navy**; (*US*) = **registered nurse**

RNA N ABBR (= *ribonucleic acid*) R.N.A. *m*

RNLI N ABBR (*BRIT*: = *Royal National Lifeboat Institution*) associazione volontaria che organizza e dispone di scialuppe di salvataggio

RNZAF N ABBR = **Royal New Zealand Air Force**

RNZN N ABBR = **Royal New Zealand Navy**

road [rəud] N strada; (*small*) cammino; (*in town*) via ▶ CPD stradale; **main ~** strada principale; **major/minor ~** strada con/senza diritto di precedenza; **it takes 4 hours by ~** sono 4 ore di macchina (*or* in camion *etc*); **on the ~ to success** sulla via del successo; **"~ up"** (*BRIT*) "attenzione: lavori in corso"

road accident N incidente *m* stradale

roadblock ['rəudblɔk] N blocco stradale

road haulage N autotrasporti *mpl*

roadhog ['rəudhɔg] N pirata *m* della strada

road map N carta stradale

road rage N comportamento aggressivo al volante

road safety N sicurezza sulle strade

roadside ['rəudsaɪd] N margine *m* della strada; **by the ~** a lato della strada

roadsign ['rəudsaɪn] N cartello stradale

roadsweeper ['rəudswiːpəʳ] N (*BRIT: person*) spazzino

road tax N (*BRIT*) tassa di circolazione

road user N utente *mf* della strada

roadway ['rəudweɪ] N carreggiata

roadworks ['rəudwəːks] NPL lavori *mpl* stradali

roadworthy ['rəudwəːðɪ] ADJ in buono stato di marcia

roam [rəum] VI errare, vagabondare ▶ VT vagare per

roar [rɔːʳ] N ruggito; (*of crowd*) tumulto; (*of thunder, storm*) muggito; (*of laughter*) scoppio ▶ VI ruggire; tumultuare; muggire; **to ~ with laughter** scoppiare dalle risa; **to do a roaring trade** fare affari d'oro

roaring ['rɔːrɪŋ] ADJ: **a ~ fire** un bel fuoco; **to do a ~ trade** fare affari d'oro; **a ~ success** un successo strepitoso

roast [rəust] N arrosto ▸ VT (*meat*) arrostire; (*coffee*) tostare, torrefare
roast beef N arrosto di manzo
roasting ['rəustɪŋ] N (*col*): **to give sb a ~** dare una lavata di capo a qn
rob [rɔb] VT (*person*) rubare; (*bank*) svaligiare; **to ~ sb of sth** derubare qn di qc; (*fig: deprive*) privare qn di qc
robber ['rɔbəʳ] N ladro; (*armed*) rapinatore m
robbery ['rɔbərɪ] N furto; rapina
robe [rəub] N (*for ceremony etc*) abito; (*also:* **bathrobe**) accappatoio; (*US: also:* **lap robe**) coperta ▸ VT vestire
robin ['rɔbɪn] N pettirosso
robot ['rəubɔt] N robot m inv
robotics ['rəubɔtɪks] N robotica
robust [rəu'bʌst] ADJ robusto(-a); (*material, economy*) solido(-a)
rock [rɔk] N (*substance*) roccia; (*boulder*) masso; roccia; (*in sea*) scoglio; (*US: pebble*) ciottolo; (BRIT: *sweet*) zucchero candito ▸ VT (*swing gently: cradle*) dondolare; (*: child*) cullare; (*shake*) scrollare, far tremare ▸ VI dondolarsi; oscillare; **on the rocks** (*drink*) col ghiaccio; (*ship*) sugli scogli; (*marriage etc*) in crisi; **to ~ the boat** (*fig*) piantare grane
rock and roll N rock and roll m
rock-bottom ['rɔk'bɔtəm] N (*fig*) stremo; **to reach** or **touch ~** (*price*) raggiungere il livello più basso; (*person*) toccare il fondo
rock climber N rocciatore(-trice), scalatore(-trice)
rock climbing N roccia
rockery ['rɔkərɪ] N giardino roccioso
rocket ['rɔkɪt] N razzo; (*Mil*) razzo, missile m ▸ VI (*prices*) salire alle stelle
rocket launcher [-lɔ:ntʃəʳ] N lanciarazzi m inv
rock face N parete f della roccia
rock fall N caduta di massi
rocking chair ['rɔkɪŋ-] N sedia a dondolo
rocking horse N cavallo a dondolo
rocky ['rɔkɪ] ADJ (*hill*) roccioso(-a); (*path*) sassoso(-a); (*unsteady: table*) traballante; (*: marriage etc*) instabile
Rocky Mountains NPL: **the ~** le Montagne Rocciose
rod [rɔd] N (*metallic, Tech*) asta; (*wooden*) bacchetta; (*also:* **fishing rod**) canna da pesca
rode [rəud] PT of **ride**
rodent ['rəudnt] N roditore m
rodeo ['rəudɪəu] N rodeo
roe [rəu] N (*species: also:* **roe deer**) capriolo; (*of fish: also:* **hard roe**) uova fpl di pesce; **soft ~** latte m di pesce
roe deer N (*species*) capriolo; (*female deer: pl inv*) capriolo femmina
rogue [rəug] N mascalzone m
roguish ['rəugɪʃ] ADJ birbantesco(-a)

role [rəul] N ruolo
role model N modello (di comportamento)
role-play ['rəulpleɪ], **role-playing** ['rəulpleɪɪŋ] N il recitare un ruolo, role-playing m inv
roll [rəul] N rotolo; (*of banknotes*) mazzo; (*also:* **bread roll**) panino; (*register*) lista; (*sound, of drums etc*) rullo; (*movement, of ship*) rullio ▸ VT rotolare; (*also:* **roll up:** *string*) aggomitolare; (*: sleeves*) rimboccare; (*cigarettes*) arrotolare; (*eyes*) roteare; (*pastry: also:* **roll out**) stendere; (*lawn, road etc*) spianare ▸ VI rotolare; (*wheel*) girare; (*drum*) rullare; (*vehicle: also:* **roll along**) avanzare; (*ship*) rollare; **cheese ~** panino al formaggio
▸ **roll about, roll around** VI rotolare qua e là; (*person*) rotolarsi
▸ **roll by** VI (*time*) passare
▸ **roll in** VI (*mail, cash*) arrivare a bizzeffe
▸ **roll over** VI rivoltarsi
▸ **roll up** VI (*col: arrive*) arrivare ▸ VT (*carpet, cloth, map*) arrotolare; (*sleeves*) rimboccare; **to ~ o.s. up into a ball** raggomitolarsi
roll call N appello
rolled gold [rəuld-] ADJ d'oro laminato
roller ['rəuləʳ] N rullo; (*wheel*) rotella; (*for hair*) bigodino
rollerblades® ['rəuləbleɪdz] NPL pattini mpl in linea
roller blind N (BRIT) avvolgibile m
roller coaster [-'kəustəʳ] N montagne fpl russe
roller skates NPL pattini mpl a rotelle
roller-skating N pattinaggio a rotelle; **to go ~** andare a pattinare (*con i pattini a rotelle*)
rollicking ['rɔlɪkɪŋ] ADJ allegro(-a) e chiassoso(-a); **to have a ~ time** divertirsi pazzamente
rolling ['rəulɪŋ] ADJ (*landscape*) ondulato(-a)
rolling mill N fabbrica di laminati
rolling pin N matterello
rolling stock N (*Rail*) materiale m rotabile
roll-on-roll-off ['rəulɔn'rəulɔf] ADJ (BRIT: *ferry*) roll-on roll-off inv
roly-poly ['rəulɪ'pəulɪ] N (BRIT Culin) rotolo di pasta con ripieno di marmellata
ROM [rɔm] N ABBR (*Comput:* = read-only memory) ROM f
Roman ['rəumən] ADJ, N romano(-a)
Roman Catholic ADJ, N cattolico(-a)
romance [rə'mæns] N storia (*or avventura or film m inv*) romantico(-a); (*charm*) poesia; (*love affair*) idillio
Romanesque [rəumə'nɛsk] ADJ romanico(-a)
Romania [rəu'meɪnɪə] N Romania
Romanian [rəu'meɪnɪən] ADJ romeno(-a) ▸ N romeno(-a); (*Ling*) romeno
Roman numeral N numero romano

romantic [rə'mæntɪk] ADJ romantico(-a); sentimentale

romanticism [rə'mæntɪsɪzəm] N romanticismo

Romany ['rɔmənɪ] ADJ zingaresco(-a) ▶ N (*person*) zingaro(-a); (*Ling*) lingua degli zingari

Rome [rəum] N Roma

romp [rɔmp] N gioco chiassoso ▶ VI (*also:* **romp about**) giocare chiassosamente; **to ~ home** (*horse*) vincere senza difficoltà, stravincere

rompers ['rɔmpəz] NPL pagliaccetto

rondo ['rɔndəu] N (*Mus*) rondò *m inv*

roof [ru:f] N tetto; (*of tunnel, cave*) volta ▶ VT coprire (con un tetto); **~ of the mouth** palato

roof garden N giardino pensile

roofing ['ru:fɪŋ] N materiale *m* per copertura

roof rack N (*Aut*) portabagagli *m inv*

rook [ruk] N (*bird*) corvo nero; (*Chess*) torre *f* ▶ VT (*cheat*) truffare, spennare

rookie ['rukɪ] N (*col: esp Mil*) pivellino(-a)

room [ru:m] N (*in house*) stanza; (*bedroom, in hotel*) camera; (*in school etc*) sala; (*space*) posto, spazio; **rooms** NPL (*lodging*) alloggio; **rooms to let**", (*US*) "**rooms for rent**" "si affittano camere"; **is there ~ for this?** c'è spazio per questo?, ci sta anche questo?; **to make ~ for sb** far posto a qn; **there is ~ for improvement** si potrebbe migliorare

rooming house ['ru:mɪŋ-] N (*US*) *casa in cui si affittano camere o appartamentini ammobiliati*

roommate ['ru:mmeɪt] N compagno(-a) di stanza

room service N servizio da camera

room temperature N temperatura ambiente

roomy ['ru:mɪ] ADJ spazioso(-a); (*garment*) ampio(-a)

roost [ru:st] N appollaiato ▶ VI appollaiarsi

rooster ['ru:stə^r] N gallo

root [ru:t] N radice *f* ▶ VI (*plant, belief*) attecchire ▶ VT (*plant, belief*) far radicare; **to take ~** (*plant*) attecchire, prendere; (*idea*) far presa; **the ~ of the problem is that ...** il problema deriva dal fatto che ...
▶ **root about** VI (*fig*) frugare
▶ **root for** VT FUS (*col*) fare il tifo per
▶ **root out** VT estirpare

root beer N (*US*) *bibita dolce a base di estratti di erbe e radici*

rope [rəup] N corda, fune *f*; (*Naut*) cavo ▶ VT (*box*) legare; (*climbers*) legare in cordata; **to ~ sb in** (*fig*) coinvolgere qn; **to know the ropes** (*fig*) conoscere i trucchi del mestiere

rope ladder N scala di corda

ropey ['rəupɪ] ADJ (*col*) scadente, da quattro soldi; **to feel ~** (*ill*) sentirsi male

rort [rɔ:t] N (*AUSTRALIA, NEW ZEALAND col*) truffa ▶ VT fregare

rosary ['rəuzərɪ] N rosario; roseto

rose [rəuz] PT *of* **rise** ▶ N rosa; (*also:* **rose bush**) rosaio; (: *on watering can*) rosetta ▶ ADJ rosa *inv*

rosé ['rəuzeɪ] N vino rosato

rosebed ['rəuzbɛd] N roseto

rosebud ['rəuzbʌd] N bocciolo di rosa

rosebush ['rəuzbuʃ] N rosaio

rosemary ['rəuzmərɪ] N rosmarino

rosette [rəu'zɛt] N coccarda

ROSPA ['rɔspə] N ABBR (*BRIT:* = *Royal Society for the Prevention of Accidents*) ≈ E.N.P.I. *m* (= *Ente Nazionale Prevenzione Infortuni*)

roster ['rɔstə^r] N: **duty ~** ruolino di servizio

rostrum ['rɔstrəm] N tribuna

rosy ['rəuzɪ] ADJ roseo(-a)

rot [rɔt] N (*decay*) putrefazione *f*; (*col: nonsense*) stupidaggini *fpl* ▶ VT, VI imputridire, marcire; **dry/wet ~** funghi parassiti del legno; **to stop the ~** (*BRIT fig*) salvare la situazione

rota ['rəutə] N tabella dei turni; **on a ~ basis** a turno

rotary ['rəutərɪ] ADJ rotante

rotate [rəu'teɪt] VT (*revolve*) far girare; (*change round: jobs*) fare a turno; (: *crops*) avvicendare ▶ VI (*revolve*) girare

rotating [rəu'teɪtɪŋ] ADJ (*movement*) rotante

rotation [rəu'teɪʃən] N rotazione *f*; **in ~** a turno, in rotazione

rote [rəut] N: **to learn sth by ~** imparare qc a memoria

rotor ['rəutə^r] N rotore *m*

rotten ['rɔtn] ADJ (*decayed*) putrido(-a), marcio(-a); (: *teeth*) cariato(-a); (*dishonest*) corrotto(-a); (*col: bad*) brutto(-a); (: *action*) vigliacco(-a); **to feel ~** (*ill*) sentirsi a pezzi

rotting ['rɔtɪŋ] ADJ in putrefazione

rotund [rəu'tʌnd] ADJ grassoccio(-a); tondo(-a)

rouble, (*US*)**ruble** ['ru:bl] N rublo

rouge [ru:ʒ] N belletto

rough [rʌf] ADJ (*skin, surface*) ruvido(-a); (*terrain, road*) accidentato(-a); (*voice*) rauco(-a); (*person, manner: coarse*) rozzo(-a), aspro(-a); (: *violent*) brutale; (*district*) malfamato(-a); (*weather*) cattivo(-a); (*sea*) mosso(-a); (*plan*) abbozzato(-a); (*guess*) approssimativo(-a) ▶ N (*Golf*) macchia; **~ estimate** approssimazione *f*; **to ~ it** far vita dura; **to play ~** far il gioco pesante; **to sleep ~** (*BRIT*) dormire all'addiaccio; **to feel ~** (*BRIT*) sentirsi male; **to have a ~ time (of it)** passare un periodaccio; **the sea is ~ today** c'è mare grosso oggi
▶ **rough out** VT (*draft*) abbozzare

roughage ['rʌfɪdʒ] N alimenti *mpl* ricchi di cellulosa

rough-and-ready ['rʌfən'rɛdɪ] ADJ rudimentale

rough-and-tumble ['rʌfən'tʌmbl] N zuffa

roughcast ['rʌfkɑːst] N intonaco grezzo

rough copy, rough draft N brutta copia

roughen ['rʌfn] VT (a surface) rendere ruvido(-a)

rough justice N giustizia sommaria

roughly ['rʌflɪ] ADV (handle) rudemente, brutalmente; (make) grossolanamente; (speak) bruscamente; (approximately) approssimativamente; **~ speaking** grosso modo, ad occhio e croce

roughness ['rʌfnɪs] N asprezza; rozzezza; brutalità

roughshod ['rʌfʃɔd] ADV: **to ride ~ over** (person) mettere sotto i piedi; (objection) passare sopra a

rough work N (at school etc) brutta copia

roulette [ruː'lɛt] N roulette f

Roumaniaetc [ruː'meɪnɪə] = **Romania** etc

round [raund] ADJ rotondo(-a) ▶ N tondo, cerchio; (BRIT: of toast) fetta; (duty: of policeman, milkman etc) giro; (: of doctor) visite fpl; (game: of cards, golf, in competition) partita; (Boxing) round m inv; (of talks) serie f inv ▶ VT (corner) girare; (bend) prendere; (cape) doppiare ▶ PREP intorno a ▶ ADV: **right ~, all ~** tutt'attorno; **the long way ~** il giro più lungo; **all the year ~** tutto l'anno; **in ~ figures** in cifra tonda; **it's just ~ the corner** (also fig) è dietro l'angolo; **to ask sb ~** invitare qn (a casa propria); **I'll be ~ at 6 o'clock** ci sarò alle 6; **to go ~** fare il giro; **to go ~ to sb's (house)** andare da qn; **to go ~ an obstacle** aggirare un ostacolo; **go ~ the back** passi da dietro; **to go ~ a house** visitare una casa; **enough to go ~** abbastanza per tutti; **she arrived ~ (about) noon** è arrivata intorno a mezzogiorno; **~ the clock** 24 ore su 24, ininterrottamente; **to go the rounds** (illness) diffondersi; (story) circolare, passare di bocca in bocca; **the daily ~** (fig) la routine quotidiana; **~ of ammunition** cartuccia; **~ of applause** applausi mpl; **~ of drinks** giro di bibite; **~ of sandwiches** (BRIT) sandwich m inv
  ▶ **round off** VT (speech etc) finire
  ▶ **round up** VT radunare; (criminals) fare una retata di; (prices) arrotondare

roundabout ['raundəbaut] N (BRIT: Aut) rotatoria; (: at fair) giostra ▶ ADJ (route, means) indiretto(-a)

rounded ['raundɪd] ADJ arrotondato(-a); (style) armonioso(-a)

rounders ['raundəz] NPL (game) gioco simile al baseball

roundly ['raundlɪ] ADV (fig) chiaro e tondo

round robin N (Sport: also: **round robin** tournament**) ≈ torneo all'italiana

round-shouldered [raund'ʃəuldəd] ADJ dalle spalle tonde

round trip N (viaggio di) andata e ritorno

roundup ['raundʌp] N raduno; (of criminals) retata; **a ~ of the latest news** un sommario or riepilogo delle ultime notizie

rouse [rauz] VT (wake up) svegliare; (stir up) destare; provocare; risvegliare

rousing ['rauzɪŋ] ADJ (speech, applause) entusiastico(-a)

rout [raut] N (Mil) rotta ▶ VT mettere in rotta

route [ruːt] N itinerario; (of bus) percorso; (of trade, shipping) rotta; **"all routes"** (Aut) "tutte le direzioni"; **the best ~ to London** la strada migliore per andare a Londra; **en ~ for** in viaggio verso; **en ~ from ... to** viaggiando da ... a

route map N (BRIT: for journey) cartina di itinerario; (for trains etc) pianta dei collegamenti

routine [ruː'tiːn] ADJ (work) corrente, abituale; (procedure) solito(-a) ▶ N (pej) routine f, tran tran m; (Theat) numero; (Comput) sottoprogramma m; **daily ~** orario quotidiano; **~ procedure** prassi f

roving ['rəuvɪŋ] ADJ (life) itinerante

roving reporter N reporter m inv volante

row¹ [rəu] N (line) riga, fila; (Knitting) ferro; (behind one another: of cars, people) fila; (in boat) remata ▶ VI (in boat) remare; (as sport) vogare ▶ VT (boat) manovrare a remi; **in a ~** (fig) di fila

row² [rau] N (noise) baccano, chiasso; (dispute) lite f; (scolding) sgridata ▶ VI (argue) litigare; **to make a ~** far baccano; **to have a ~** litigare

rowboat ['rəubəut] N (US) barca a remi

rowdiness ['raudɪnɪs] N baccano; (fighting) zuffa

rowdy ['raudɪ] ADJ chiassoso(-a), turbolento(-a) ▶ N teppista mf

rowdyism ['raudɪɪzəm] N teppismo

rowing ['rəuɪŋ] N canottaggio

rowing boat N (BRIT) barca a remi

rowlock ['rɔlək] N scalmo

royal ['rɔɪəl] ADJ reale

Royal Academy N (BRIT); vedi nota

L'Accademia Reale d'Arte britannica, Royal Academy (of the Arts), è un'istituzione fondata nel 1768 al fine di incoraggiare la pittura, la scultura e l'architettura. Ogni anno organizza una mostra estiva d'arte contemporanea.

Royal Air Force N (BRIT) aeronautica militare britannica

royal blue ADJ blu reale inv

royalist ['rɔɪəlɪst] ADJ, N realista mf

Royal Navy N (BRIT) marina militare britannica

royalty ['rɔɪəltɪ] N (royal persons) (membri mpl della) famiglia reale; (payment: to author)

r

diritti *mpl* d'autore; (: *to inventor*) diritti di brevetto

RP N ABBR (*Brit*: = *received pronunciation*) pronuncia standard

RPI ABBR (*Brit*) = **retail price index**

rpm ABBR (= *revolutions per minute*) giri/min

RR ABBR (*US*: = *railroad*) Ferr

RRP N ABBR (*Brit*) = **recommended retail price**

RSA N ABBR (*Brit*) = **Royal Society of Arts**; **Royal Scottish Academy**

RSI N ABBR (*Med*: = *repetitive strain injury*) lesione al braccio tipica di violinisti e terminalisti

RSPB N ABBR (*Brit*: = *Royal Society for the Protection of Birds*) ≈ L.I.P.U. *f* (= *Lega Italiana Protezione Uccelli*)

RSPCA N ABBR (*Brit*: = *Royal Society for the Prevention of Cruelty to Animals*) ≈ E.N.P.A. *m* (= *Ente Nazionale per la Protezione degli Animali*)

RSVP ABBR (= *répondez s'il vous plaît*) R.S.V.P.

RTA N ABBR (= *road traffic accident*) incidente *m* stradale

Rt. Hon. ABBR (*Brit*: = *Right Honourable*) ≈ On. (= *Onorevole*)

Rt Rev. ABBR (= *Right Reverend*) Rev.

rub [rʌb] N (*with cloth*) fregata, strofinata; (*on person*) frizione *f*, massaggio; **to give sth a ~** strofinare qc; (*sore place*) massaggiare qc ▶ VT fregare, strofinare; frizionare; massaggiare; (*hands: also*:) sfregarsi; **to ~ sb up** *or* (*US*) **~ sb the wrong way** lisciare qn contro pelo

▶ **rub down** VT (*body*) strofinare, frizionare; (*horse*) strigliare

▶ **rub in** VT (*ointment*) far penetrare (massaggiando *or* frizionando)

▶ **rub off** VI andare via; **to ~ off on** lasciare una traccia su

▶ **rub out** VT cancellare ▶ VI cancellarsi

rubber ['rʌbə^r] N gomma

rubber band N elastico

rubber bullet N pallottola di gomma

rubber gloves NPL guanti *mpl* di gomma

rubber plant N ficus *m inv*

rubber ring N (*for swimming*) ciambella

rubber stamp N timbro di gomma

rubber-stamp [rʌbə'stæmp] VT (*fig*) approvare senza discussione

rubbery ['rʌbərɪ] ADJ gommoso(-a)

rubbish ['rʌbɪʃ] N (*from household*) immondizie *fpl*, rifiuti *mpl*; (*fig, pej*) cose *fpl* senza valore; robaccia; (*nonsense*) sciocchezze *fpl* ▶ VT (*col*) sputtanare; **what you've just said is ~** quello che ha appena detto è una sciocchezza

rubbish bin N (*Brit*) pattumiera

rubbish dump N discarica

rubbishy ['rʌbɪʃɪ] ADJ (*Brit col*) scadente, che non vale niente

rubble ['rʌbl] N macerie *fpl*; (*smaller*) pietrisco

ruble ['ru:bl] N (*US*) = **rouble**

ruby ['ru:bɪ] N rubino

RUC N ABBR (*Brit*: = *Royal Ulster Constabulary*) *forza di polizia dell'Irlanda del Nord*

rucksack ['rʌksæk] N zaino

ructions ['rʌkʃənz] NPL putiferio, finimondo

rudder ['rʌdə^r] N timone *m*

ruddy ['rʌdɪ] ADJ (*face*) fresco(-a); (*col: damned*) maledetto(-a)

rude [ru:d] ADJ (*impolite: person*) scortese, rozzo(-a); (: *word, manners*) grossolano(-a), rozzo(-a); (*shocking*) indecente; **to be ~ to sb** essere maleducato con qn

rudely ['ru:dlɪ] ADV scortesemente; grossolanamente

rudeness ['ru:dnɪs] N scortesia; grossolanità

rudiment ['ru:dɪmənt] N rudimento

rudimentary [ru:dɪ'mɛntərɪ] ADJ rudimentale

rue [ru:] VT pentirsi amaramente di

rueful ['ru:ful] ADJ mesto(-a), triste

ruff [rʌf] N gorgiera

ruffian ['rʌfɪən] N briccone *m*, furfante *m*

ruffle ['rʌfl] VT (*hair*) scompigliare; (*clothes, water*) increspare; (*fig: person*) turbare

rug [rʌg] N tappeto; (*Brit: for knees*) coperta

rugby ['rʌgbɪ] N (*also*: **rugby football**) rugby *m*

rugged ['rʌgɪd] ADJ (*landscape*) aspro(-a); (*features, determination*) duro(-a); (*character*) brusco(-a)

rugger ['rʌgə^r] N (*col*) rugby *m*

ruin ['ru:ɪn] N rovina ▶ VT rovinare; (*spoil: clothes*) sciupare; **ruins** NPL (*of building, castle etc*) rovine *fpl*, ruderi *mpl*; **in ruins** in rovina

ruination [ru:ɪ'neɪʃən] N rovina

ruinous ['ru:ɪnəs] ADJ rovinoso(-a); (*expenditure*) inverosimile

rule [ru:l] N (*gen*) regola; (*regulation*) regolamento, regola; (*government*) governo; (*ruler*) riga; (*dominion etc*) **under British ~** sotto la sovranità britannica ▶ VT (*country*) governare; (*person*) dominare; (*decide*) decidere ▶ VI regnare; decidere; (*Law*) dichiarare; **to ~ against/in favour of/on** (*Law*) pronunciarsi a sfavore di/in favore di/ su; **it's against the rules** è contro le regole or il regolamento; **by ~ of thumb** a lume di naso; **as a ~** normalmente, di regola

▶ **rule out** VT escludere; **murder cannot be ruled out** non si esclude che si tratti di omicidio

ruled [ru:ld] ADJ (*paper*) vergato(-a)

ruler ['ru:lə^r] N (*sovereign*) sovrano(-a); (*leader*) capo (dello Stato); (*for measuring*) regolo, riga

ruling ['ru:lɪŋ] ADJ (*party*) al potere; (*class*) dirigente ▶ N (*Law*) decisione *f*

rum [rʌm] N rum *m* ▶ ADJ (*Brit col*) strano(-a)

Rumania *etc* [ru:'meɪnɪə] = **Romania** *etc*

rumble ['rʌmbl] N rimbombo; brontolio ▶ VI rimbombare; (stomach, pipe) brontolare

rumbustious [rʌm'bʌstʃəs] ADJ (person): **to be ~** essere un terremoto

rummage ['rʌmɪdʒ] VI frugare

rumour, (US) **rumor** ['ruːməʳ] N voce f ▶ VT: **it is rumoured that** corre voce che

rump [rʌmp] N (of animal) groppa

rumple ['rʌmpl] VT (hair) arruffare, scompigliare; (clothes) spiegazzare, sgualcire

rump steak [rʌmp-] N bistecca di girello

rumpus ['rʌmpəs] N (col) baccano; (quarrel) rissa; **to kick up a ~** fare un putiferio

run [rʌn] (pt **ran**, pp **~**) N corsa; (outing) gita (in macchina); (distance travelled) percorso, tragitto; (series) serie f inv; (Theat) periodo di rappresentazione; (Ski) pista; (Cricket, Baseball) meta; (in tights, stockings) smagliatura ▶ VT (distance) correre; (operate: business) gestire, dirigere; (: competition, course) organizzare; (: hotel) gestire; (: house) governare; (Comput: program) eseguire; (water, bath) far scorrere; (force through): (rope, pipe) **to ~ sth through** far passare qc attraverso; (pass): (hand, finger) **to ~ sth over** passare qc su; (Press: feature) presentare ▶ VI correre; (flee) scappare; (pass: road etc) passare; (work: machine, factory) funzionare, andare; (bus, train: operate) far servizio; (: travel) circolare; (continue: play, contract) durare; (slide: drawer: flow: river, bath) scorrere; (colours, washing) stemperarsi; (in election) presentarsi come candidato; (nose) colare; **to go for a ~** andare a correre; (in car) fare un giro (in macchina); **to break into a ~** mettersi a correre; **a ~ of luck** un periodo di fortuna; **to have the ~ of sb's house** essere libero di andare e venire in casa di qn; **there was a ~ on ...** c'era una corsa a ...; **in the long ~** a lungo andare; in fin dei conti; **in the short ~** sulle prime; **on the ~** in fuga; **to make a ~ for it** scappare, tagliare la corda; **to ~ a race** partecipare ad una gara; **I'll ~ you to the station** la porto alla stazione; **to ~ a risk** correre un rischio; **to ~ errands** andare a fare commissioni; **the train runs between Gatwick and Victoria** il treno collega Gatwick alla stazione Victoria; **the bus runs every 20 minutes** c'è un autobus ogni 20 minuti; **it's very cheap to ~** comporta poche spese; **to ~ on petrol** or (US) **gas/on diesel/off batteries** andare a benzina/a diesel/a batterie; **to ~ for the bus** fare una corsa per prendere l'autobus; **to ~ for president** presentarsi come candidato per la presidenza; **their losses ran into millions** le loro perdite hanno raggiunto i milioni; **to be ~ off one's feet** (Brit) doversi fare in quattro

▶ **run about** VI (children) correre qua e là

▶ **run across** VT FUS (find) trovare per caso

▶ **run after** VT FUS (to catch up) rincorrere; (chase) correre dietro a

▶ **run away** VI fuggire

▶ **run down** VI (clock) scaricarsi ▶ VT (Aut) investire; (criticize) criticare; (Brit: reduce: production) ridurre gradualmente; (: factory, shop) rallentare l'attività di; **to be ~ down** (battery) essere scarico(-a); (person) essere spossato(-a)

▶ **run in** VT (Brit: car) rodare, fare il rodaggio di

▶ **run into** VT FUS (meet: person) incontrare per caso; (: trouble) incontrare, trovare; (collide with) andare a sbattere contro; **to ~ into debt** trovarsi nei debiti

▶ **run off** VI fuggire ▶ VT (water) far defluire; (copies) fare

▶ **run out** VI (person) uscire di corsa; (liquid) colare; (lease) scadere; (money) esaurirsi

▶ **run out of** VT FUS rimanere a corto di; **I've ~ out of petrol** or (US) **gas** sono rimasto senza benzina

▶ **run over** VT (Aut) investire, mettere sotto ▶ VT FUS (revise) rivedere

▶ **run through** VT FUS (instructions) dare una scorsa a; (rehearse: play) riprovare, ripetere

▶ **run up** VT (debt) lasciar accumulare; **to ~ up against** (difficulties) incontrare

runaround ['rʌnəraund] N (col): **to give sb the ~** far girare a vuoto qn

runaway ['rʌnəweɪ] ADJ (person) fuggiasco(-a); (horse) in libertà; (truck) fuori controllo; (inflation) galoppante

rundown ['rʌndaun] N (Brit: of industry etc) riduzione f graduale dell'attività di

rung [rʌŋ] PP of **ring** ▶ N (of ladder) piolo

run-in ['rʌnɪn] N (col) scontro

runner ['rʌnəʳ] N (in race) corridore m; (: horse) partente mf; (on sledge) pattino; (for drawer etc, carpet) guida

runner bean N (Brit) fagiolino

runner-up [rʌnər'ʌp] N secondo(-a) arrivato(-a)

running ['rʌnɪŋ] N corsa; direzione f; organizzazione f; funzionamento ▶ ADJ (water) corrente; (commentary) simultaneo(-a); **6 days ~** 6 giorni di seguito; **to be in/out of the ~ for sth** essere/non essere più in lizza per qc

running costs NPL (of business) costi mpl d'esercizio; (of car) spese fpl di mantenimento

running head N (Typ) testata, titolo corrente

running mate N (US Pol) candidato alla vicepresidenza

runny ['rʌnɪ] ADJ che cola

run-off ['rʌnɔf] N (in contest, election) confronto

r

definitivo; (*extra race*) spareggio

run-of-the-mill ['rʌnəvðə'mɪl] ADJ solito(-a), banale

runt [rʌnt] N omuncolo; (*Zool*) animale *m* più piccolo del normale

run-through ['rʌnθru:] N prova

run-up ['rʌnʌp] N (*BRIT*): ~ **to sth** (*election etc*) periodo che precede qc

runway ['rʌnweɪ] N (*Aviat*) pista (di decollo)

rupture ['rʌptʃəʳ] N (*Med*) ernia ▶ VT: **to ~ o.s.** farsi venire un'ernia

rural ['ruərl] ADJ rurale

rural district council N (*BRIT*) consiglio (amministrativo) di distretto rurale

ruse [ru:z] N trucco

rush [rʌʃ] N corsa precipitosa; (*of crowd*) afflusso; (*hurry*) furia, fretta; (*of emotion*) impeto; (*Bot*) giunco; (*sudden demand*): ~ **for** corsa a; (*current*) flusso ▶ VT mandare *or* spedire velocemente; (*attack: town etc*) prendere d'assalto ▶ VI precipitarsi; **is there any ~ for this?** è urgente?; **we've had a ~ of orders** abbiamo avuto una valanga di ordinazioni; **I'm in a ~ (to do)** ho fretta *or* premura (di fare); **gold ~** corsa all'oro; **to ~ sth off** spedire con urgenza qc; **don't ~ me!** non farmi fretta!

▶ **rush through** VT (*meal*) mangiare in fretta; (*book*) dare una scorsa frettolosa a; (*town*) attraversare in fretta; (*Comm: order*) eseguire d'urgenza ▶ VT FUS (*work*) sbrigare frettolosamente

rush hour N ora di punta

rush job N (*urgent*) lavoro urgente

rush matting N stuoia

rusk [rʌsk] N fetta biscottata

Russia ['rʌʃə] N Russia

Russian ['rʌʃən] ADJ russo(-a) ▶ N russo(-a); (*Ling*) russo

rust [rʌst] N ruggine *f* ▶ VI arrugginirsi

rustic ['rʌstɪk] ADJ rustico(-a) ▶ N (*pej*) cafone(-a)

rustle ['rʌsl] VI frusciare ▶ VT (*paper*) far frusciare; (*US: cattle*) rubare

rustproof ['rʌstpru:f] ADJ inossidabile

rustproofing ['rʌstpru:fɪŋ] N trattamento antiruggine

rusty ['rʌstɪ] ADJ arrugginito(-a)

rut [rʌt] N solco; (*Zool*) fregola; **to be in a ~** (*fig*) essersi fossilizzato(-a)

rutabaga [ru:tə'beɪgə] N (*US*) rapa svedese

ruthless ['ru:θlɪs] ADJ spietato(-a)

ruthlessness ['ru:θlɪsnɪs] N spietatezza

RV ABBR (= *revised version*) *versione riveduta della Bibbia* ▶ N ABBR (*US*) = **recreational vehicle**

rye [raɪ] N segale *f*

Ss

S, s [ɛs] N (letter) S, s f inv or m inv; (US Scol:
= satisfactory) ≈ sufficiente; **S for Sugar** ≈ S
come Savona

S ABBR (= saint) S.; (on clothes) = **small**; (= south) S

SA ABBR = **South Africa**; **South America**

Sabbath ['sæbəθ] N (Jewish) sabato; (Christian)
domenica

sabbatical [sə'bætɪkl] ADJ: ~ **year** anno
sabbatico

sabotage ['sæbətɑːʒ] N sabotaggio ▶ VT
sabotare

saccharin, saccharine ['sækərɪn] N
saccarina

sachet ['sæʃeɪ] N bustina

sack [sæk] N (bag) sacco ▶ VT (dismiss)
licenziare, mandare a spasso; (plunder)
saccheggiare; **to get the** ~ essere mandato
a spasso; **to give sb the** ~ licenziare qn,
mandare qn a spasso

sackful ['sækful] N: **a ~ of** un sacco di

sacking ['sækɪŋ] N tela di sacco; (dismissal)
licenziamento

sacrament ['sækrəmənt] N sacramento

sacred ['seɪkrɪd] ADJ sacro(-a)

sacred cow N (fig: person) intoccabile mf;
(: institution) caposaldo; (: idea, belief) dogma m

sacrifice ['sækrɪfaɪs] N sacrificio ▶ VT
sacrificare; **to make sacrifices (for sb)** fare
(dei) sacrifici (per qn)

sacrilege ['sækrɪlɪdʒ] N sacrilegio

sacrosanct ['sækrəʊsæŋkt] ADJ sacrosanto(-a)

sad [sæd] ADJ triste; (deplorable) deplorevole

sadden ['sædn] VT rattristare

saddle ['sædl] N sella ▶ VT (horse) sellare;
to be saddled with sth (col) avere qc sulle
spalle

saddlebag ['sædlbæg] N bisaccia; (on bicycle)
borsa

sadism ['seɪdɪzəm] N sadismo

sadist ['seɪdɪst] N sadico(-a)

sadistic [sə'dɪstɪk] ADJ sadico(-a)

sadly ['sædlɪ] ADV tristemente; (regrettably)
sfortunatamente; ~ **lacking in**
penosamente privo di

sadness ['sædnɪs] N tristezza

sadomasochism [seɪdəʊ'mæsəkɪzəm] N
sadomasochismo

sae ABBR (BRIT: = stamped addressed envelope)
busta affrancata e con indirizzo

safari [sə'fɑːrɪ] N safari m inv

safari park N zoosafari m inv

safe [seɪf] ADJ sicuro(-a); (out of danger)
salvo(-a), al sicuro; (cautious) prudente
▶ N cassaforte f; ~ **from** al sicuro da; ~ **and
sound** sano(-a) e salvo(-a); ~ **journey!** buon
viaggio!; (just) **to be on the** ~ **side** per non
correre rischi; **to play** ~ giocare sul sicuro;
it is ~ **to say that ...** si può affermare con
sicurezza che ...

safe bet N: **it's a** ~ è una cosa sicura

safe-breaker ['seɪfbreɪkəʳ] N (BRIT)
scassinatore m

safe-conduct [seɪf'kɔndʌkt] N
salvacondotto

safe-cracker ['seɪfkrækəʳ] N = **safe-breaker**

safe-deposit ['seɪfdɪpɔzɪt] N (vault) caveau
m inv; (box) cassetta di sicurezza

safeguard ['seɪfgɑːd] N salvaguardia ▶ VT
salvaguardare

safe haven N zona sicura or protetta

safekeeping ['seɪf'kiːpɪŋ] N custodia

safely ['seɪflɪ] ADV sicuramente; sano(-a) e
salvo(-a) prudentemente; prudentemente;
I can ~ **say ...** posso tranquillamente
asserire ...

safe passage N passaggio sicuro

safe sex N sesso sicuro

safety ['seɪftɪ] N sicurezza; ~ **first!** la
prudenza innanzitutto!

safety belt N cintura di sicurezza

safety catch N sicura

safety net N rete f di protezione

safety pin N spilla di sicurezza

safety valve N valvola di sicurezza

saffron ['sæfrən] N zafferano

sag [sæg] VI incurvarsi; afflosciarsi

saga ['sɑːgə] N saga; (fig) odissea

sage [seɪdʒ] N (herb) salvia; (man) saggio

S

Sagittarius [sædʒɪ'tɛərɪəs] N Sagittario;
to be ~ essere del Sagittario

sago ['seɪɡəu] N sagù m

Sahara [sə'hɑːrə] N: **the ~ Desert** il Deserto del Sahara

Sahel [sæ'hɛl] N Sahel m

said [sɛd] PT, PP of **say**

Saigon [saɪ'ɡɔn] N Saigon f

sail [seɪl] N (on boat) vela; (trip): **to go for a ~** fare un giro in barca a vela ▶ VT (boat) condurre, governare ▶ VI (travel: ship) navigare; (: passenger) viaggiare per mare; (set off) salpare; (Sport) fare della vela; **they sailed into Genoa** entrarono nel porto di Genova
▶ **sail through** VT FUS (fig) superare senza difficoltà ▶ VI farcela senza difficoltà

sailboat ['seɪlbəut] N (US) barca a vela

sailing ['seɪlɪŋ] N (sport) vela; **to go ~** fare della vela

sailing boat N barca a vela

sailing ship N veliero

sailor ['seɪlər] N marinaio

saint [seɪnt] N santo(-a)

saintly ['seɪntlɪ] ADJ da santo(-a); santo(-a)

sake [seɪk] N: **for the ~ of** per, per amore di; **for pity's ~** per pietà; **for the ~ of argument** tanto per fare un esempio; **art for art's ~** l'arte per l'arte

salad ['sæləd] N insalata; **tomato ~** insalata di pomodori

salad bowl N insalatiera

salad cream N (BRIT) (tipo di) maionese f

salad dressing N condimento per insalata

salad oil N olio da tavola

salami [sə'lɑːmɪ] N salame m

salaried ['sælərɪd] ADJ stipendiato(-a)

salary ['sælərɪ] N stipendio

salary scale N scala dei salari

sale [seɪl] N vendita; (at reduced prices) svendita, liquidazione f; (auction) vendita all'asta; **sales** NPL (total amount sold) vendite fpl; **"for ~"** "in vendita"; **on ~** in vendita; **on ~ or return** da vendere o rimandare; **a closing-down** or (US) **liquidation ~** una liquidazione; **~ and lease back** n lease back m inv

saleroom ['seɪlrum] N sala delle aste

sales assistant, (US) **sales clerk** N commesso(-a)

sales clerk N (US) commesso(-a)

sales conference N riunione f marketing e vendite

sales drive N campagna di vendita, sforzo promozionale

sales force N personale m addetto alle vendite

salesman ['seɪlzmən] N (irreg) commesso; (representative) rappresentante m

sales manager N direttore m commerciale

salesmanship ['seɪlzmənʃɪp] N arte f del vendere

salesperson N (irreg) (in shop) commesso(-a); (representative) rappresentante mf di commercio

sales rep N rappresentante mf di commercio

sales tax N (US) imposta sulle vendite

saleswoman ['seɪlzwumən] N (irreg) commessa; (representative) rappresentante f

salient ['seɪlɪənt] ADJ saliente

saline ['seɪlaɪn] ADJ salino(-a)

saliva [sə'laɪvə] N saliva

sallow ['sæləu] ADJ giallastro(-a)

sally forth, sally out ['sælɪ-] VI uscire di gran carriera

salmon ['sæmən] N (pl inv) salmone m

salmon trout N trota (di mare)

salon ['sælɔn] N (hairdressing salon) parrucchiere(-a); (beauty salon) salone m di bellezza

saloon [sə'luːn] N (US) saloon m inv, bar m inv; (BRIT Aut) berlina; (ship's lounge) salone m

SALT [sɔːlt] N ABBR (= Strategic Arms Limitation Talks/Treaty) S.A.L.T. m

salt [sɔːlt] N sale m ▶ VT salare ▶ CPD di sale; (Culin) salato(-a); **an old ~** un lupo di mare
▶ **salt away** VT ammucchiare, mettere via

salt cellar N saliera

salt-free ['sɔːlt'friː] ADJ senza sale

saltwater ['sɔːltwɔːtər] ADJ (fish etc) di mare

salty ['sɔːltɪ] ADJ salato(-a)

salubrious [sə'luːbrɪəs] ADJ salubre; (fig: district etc) raccomandabile

salutary ['sæljutərɪ] ADJ salutare

salute [sə'luːt] N saluto ▶ VT salutare

salvage ['sælvɪdʒ] N (saving) salvataggio; (things saved) beni mpl salvati or recuperati ▶ VT salvare, mettere in salvo

salvage vessel N scialuppa di salvataggio

salvation [sæl'veɪʃən] N salvezza

Salvation Army [sæl'veɪʃən-] N Esercito della Salvezza

salver ['sælvər] N vassoio

salvo, salvoes ['sælvəu] N salva

Samaritan [sə'mærɪtən] N: **the Samaritans** (organization) ≈ telefono amico

same [seɪm] ADJ stesso(-a), medesimo(-a)
▶ PRON: **the ~** lo (la) stesso(-a), gli (le) stessi(-e); **the ~ book as** lo stesso libro di (or che); **on the ~ day** lo stesso giorno; **at the ~ time** allo stesso tempo; **all** or **just the ~** tuttavia; **to do the ~** fare la stessa cosa; **to do the ~ as sb** fare come qn; **the ~ again** (in bar etc) un altro; **they're one and the ~** (person/thing) sono la stessa persona/cosa; **and the ~ to you!** altrettanto a lei!; **~ here!** anch'io!

sample ['sɑːmpl] N campione m ▶ VT (food) assaggiare; (wine) degustare; **to take a ~**

prelevare un campione; **free ~** campione omaggio

sanatorium [sænəˈtɔːrɪəm] (pl **sanatoria** [-rɪə]) N sanatorio

sanctify [ˈsæŋktɪfaɪ] VT santificare

sanctimonious [sæŋktɪˈməʊnɪəs] ADJ bigotto(-a), bacchettone(-a)

sanction [ˈsæŋkʃən] N sanzione f ▶ VT sancire, sanzionare; **sanctions** NPL (Pol) sanzioni fpl; **to impose economic sanctions on** or **against** adottare sanzioni economiche contro

sanctity [ˈsæŋktɪtɪ] N santità

sanctuary [ˈsæŋktjʊərɪ] N (holy place) santuario; (refuge) rifugio; (for wildlife) riserva

sand [sænd] N sabbia ▶ VT cospargere di sabbia; (also: **sand down**: wood etc) cartavetrare; see also **sands**

sandal [ˈsændl] N sandalo

sandbag [ˈsændbæg] N sacco di sabbia

sandblast [ˈsændblɑːst] VT sabbiare

sandbox [ˈsændbɔks] N (US: for children) buca di sabbia

sandcastle [ˈsændkɑːsl] N castello di sabbia

sand dune N duna di sabbia

sander [ˈsændəʳ] N levigatrice f

sandpaper [ˈsændpeɪpəʳ] N carta vetrata

sandpit [ˈsændpɪt] N (BRIT: for children) buca di sabbia

sands [sændz] NPL spiaggia

sandstone [ˈsændstəʊn] N arenaria

sandstorm [ˈsændstɔːm] N tempesta di sabbia

sandwich [ˈsændwɪtʃ] N tramezzino, panino, sandwich m inv ▶ VT (also: **sandwich in**) infilare; **cheese/ham ~** sandwich al formaggio/prosciutto; **to be sandwiched between** essere incastrato(-a) fra

sandwich board N cartello pubblicitario (portato da un uomo sandwich)

sandwich course N (BRIT) corso di formazione professionale

sandwich man N uomo m sandwich inv

sandy [ˈsændɪ] ADJ sabbioso(-a); (colour) color sabbia inv, biondo(-a) rossiccio(-a)

sane [seɪn] ADJ (person) sano(-a) di mente; (outlook) sensato(-a)

sang [sæŋ] PT of **sing**

sanguine [ˈsæŋgwɪn] ADJ ottimista

sanitarium [sænɪˈtɛərɪəm] (pl **sanitaria** [-rɪə]) N (US) = **sanatorium**

sanitary [ˈsænɪtərɪ] ADJ (system, arrangements) sanitario(-a); (clean) igienico(-a)

sanitary towel [ˈsænɪtərɪ-], (US) **sanitary napkin** N assorbente m (igienico)

sanitation [sænɪˈteɪʃən] N (in house) impianti mpl sanitari; (in town) fognature fpl

sanitation department N (US) nettezza urbana

sanity [ˈsænɪtɪ] N sanità mentale; (common sense) buon senso

sank [sæŋk] PT of **sink**

San Marino [sænməˈriːnəʊ] N San Marino f

Santa Claus [sæntəˈklɔːz] N Babbo Natale

Santiago [sæntɪˈɑːgəʊ] N (also: **Santiago de Chile**) Santiago (del Cile) f

sap [sæp] N (of plants) linfa ▶ VT (strength) fiaccare

sapling [ˈsæplɪŋ] N alberello

sapphire [ˈsæfaɪəʳ] N zaffiro

sarcasm [ˈsɑːkæzm] N sarcasmo

sarcastic [sɑːˈkæstɪk] ADJ sarcastico(-a); **to be ~** fare del sarcasmo

sarcophagus [sɑːˈkɔfəgəs] (pl **sarcophagi** [-gaɪ]) N sarcofago

sardine [sɑːˈdiːn] N sardina

Sardinia [sɑːˈdɪnɪə] N Sardegna

Sardinian [sɑːˈdɪnɪən] ADJ, N sardo(-a)

sardonic [sɑːˈdɔnɪk] ADJ sardonico(-a)

sari [ˈsɑːrɪ] N sari m inv

SARS [sɑːz] N ABBR (= severe acute respiratory syndrome) SARS f, polmonite atipica

sartorial [sɑːˈtɔːrɪəl] ADJ di sartoria

SAS N ABBR (BRIT Mil: = Special Air Service) reparto dell'esercito britannico specializzato in operazioni clandestine

SASE N ABBR (US: = self-addressed stamped envelope) busta affrancata e con indirizzo

sash [sæʃ] N fascia

sash window N finestra a ghigliottina

Sask. ABBR (CANADA) = **Saskatchewan**

SAT N ABBR (US) = **Scholastic Aptitude Test**

sat [sæt] PT, PP of **sit**

Sat. ABBR (= Saturday) sab.

Satan [ˈseɪtən] N Satana m

satanic [səˈtænɪk] ADJ satanico(-a)

satchel [ˈsætʃl] N cartella

sated [ˈseɪtɪd] ADJ soddisfatto(-a); sazio(-a)

satellite [ˈsætəlaɪt] ADJ, N satellite m

satellite dish N antenna parabolica

satellite television N televisione f via satellite

satiate [ˈseɪʃɪeɪt] VT saziare

satin [ˈsætɪn] N raso, satin m ▶ ADJ di or in raso, di or in satin; **with a ~ finish** satinato(-a)

satire [ˈsætaɪəʳ] N satira

satirical [səˈtɪrɪkl] ADJ satirico(-a)

satirist [ˈsætərɪst] N (writer etc) scrittore(-trice) etc satirico(-a); (cartoonist) caricaturista mf

satirize [ˈsætɪraɪz] VT satireggiare

satisfaction [sætɪsˈfækʃən] N soddisfazione f; **has it been done to your ~?** ne è rimasto soddisfatto?

satisfactory [sætɪsˈfæktərɪ] ADJ soddisfacente

satisfied [ˈsætɪsfaɪd] ADJ (customer)

S

soddisfatto(-a); **to be ~ (with sth)** essere soddisfatto(-a) (di qc)

satisfy ['sætɪsfaɪ] ᴠᴛ soddisfare; (*convince*) convincere; **to ~ the requirements** rispondere ai requisiti; **to ~ sb (that)** convincere qn (che), persuadere qn (che); **to ~ o.s. of sth** accertarsi di qc

satisfying ['sætɪsfaɪɪŋ] ADJ soddisfacente

satnav ['sætnæv] ɴ ᴀʙʙʀ (= *satellite navigation*) navigatore *m* satellitare

SATs ɴ ᴀʙʙʀ (Bʀɪᴛ: = *standard assessment tasks or tests*) esame di fine anno sostenuto dagli allievi delle scuole pubbliche inglesi a 7, 11 o 14 anni

satsuma [sæt'suːmə] ɴ agrume di provenienza giapponese

saturate ['sætʃəreɪt] ᴠᴛ: **to ~ (with)** saturare (di)

saturated fat ['sætʃəreɪtɪd-] ɴ grassi *mpl* saturi

saturation [sætʃə'reɪʃən] ɴ saturazione *f*

Saturday ['sætədɪ] ɴ sabato; *see also* **Tuesday**

sauce [sɔːs] ɴ salsa; (*containing meat, fish*) sugo

saucepan ['sɔːspən] ɴ casseruola

saucer ['sɔːsəʳ] ɴ sottocoppa *m*, piattino

saucy ['sɔːsɪ] ADJ impertinente

Saudi ['saudɪ], **Saudi Arabian** ['saudɪ-] ADJ, ɴ saudita *mf*

Saudi Arabia ['saudɪ-] ɴ Arabia Saudita

sauna ['sɔːnə] ɴ sauna

saunter ['sɔːntəʳ] ᴠɪ andare a zonzo, bighellonare

sausage ['sɔsɪdʒ] ɴ salsiccia; (*salami etc*) salame *m*

sausage roll ɴ rotolo di pasta sfoglia ripieno di salsiccia

sauté ['səuteɪ] ADJ (*Culin: potatoes*) saltato(-a); (: *onions*) soffritto(-a) ▶ ᴠᴛ far saltare; far soffriggere

sautéed ['səuteɪd] ADJ saltato(-a)

savage ['sævɪdʒ] ADJ (*cruel, fierce*) selvaggio(-a), feroce; (*primitive*) primitivo(-a) ▶ ɴ selvaggio(-a) ▶ ᴠᴛ attaccare selvaggiamente

savagery ['sævɪdʒrɪ] ɴ crudeltà, ferocia

save [seɪv] ᴠᴛ (*person, belongings, Comput*) salvare; (*money*) risparmiare, mettere da parte; (*time*) risparmiare; (*food*) conservare; (*avoid: trouble*) evitare; (*Sport*) parare ▶ ᴠɪ (*also:* **save up**) economizzare ▶ ɴ (*Sport*) parata ▶ ᴘʀᴇᴘ salvo, a eccezione di; **it will ~ me an hour** mi farà risparmiare un'ora; **to ~ face** salvare la faccia; **God ~ the Queen!** Dio salvi la Regina!

saving ['seɪvɪŋ] ɴ risparmio ▶ ADJ: **the ~ grace of** l'unica cosa buona di; **savings** ɴᴘʟ risparmi *mpl*; **to make savings** fare economia

savings account ɴ (US) libretto di risparmio

savings and loan association ɴ (US)

≈ società di credito immobiliare

savings bank ɴ cassa di risparmio

saviour, (US) **savior** ['seɪvjəʳ] ɴ salvatore *m*

savour, (US) **savor** ['seɪvəʳ] ɴ sapore *m*, gusto ▶ ᴠᴛ gustare

savoury, (US) **savory** ['seɪvərɪ] ADJ saporito(-a); (*dish: not sweet*) salato(-a)

savvy ['sævɪ] ɴ (*col*) arguzia

saw [sɔː] ᴘᴛ *of* **see** ▶ ɴ (*tool*) sega ▶ ᴠᴛ (*pt* **sawed**, *pp* **sawed** *or* **sawn** [sɔːn]) segare; **to ~ sth up** fare a pezzi qc con la sega

sawdust ['sɔːdʌst] ɴ segatura

sawmill ['sɔːmɪl] ɴ segheria

sawn [sɔːn] ᴘᴘ *of* **saw**

sawn-off ['sɔːnɔf], (US) **sawed-off** ['sɔːdɔf] ADJ: **~ shotgun** fucile *m* a canne mozze

saxophone ['sæksəfəun] ɴ sassofono

say [seɪ] (*pt, pp* **said** [sed]) ɴ: **to have one's ~** fare sentire il proprio parere; **to have a** *or* **some ~** avere voce in capitolo ▶ ᴠᴛ dire; **could you ~ that again?** potrebbe ripeterlo?; **to ~ yes/no** dire di sì/di no; **she said (that) I was to give you this** ha detto di darle questo; **my watch says 3 o'clock** il mio orologio fa le 3; **shall we ~ Tuesday?** facciamo martedì?; **that doesn't ~ much for him** non torna a suo credito; **when all is said and done** a conti fatti; **there is something** *or* **a lot to be said for it** ha i suoi lati positivi; **that is to ~** cioè, vale a dire; **to ~ nothing of** per non parlare di; **~ that ...** mettiamo *or* diciamo che ...; **that goes without saying** va da sé

saying ['seɪɪŋ] ɴ proverbio, detto

SBA ɴ ᴀʙʙʀ (US: = *Small Business Administration*) organismo ausiliario per piccole imprese

SC ɴ ᴀʙʙʀ (US) = **supreme court** ▶ ᴀʙʙʀ (US) = **South Carolina**

s/c ᴀʙʙʀ (= *self-contained*) indipendente

scab [skæb] ɴ crosta; (*pej*) crumiro(-a)

scabby ['skæbɪ] ADJ crostoso(-a)

scaffold ['skæfəuld] ɴ impalcatura; (*gallows*) patibolo

scaffolding ['skæfəldɪŋ] ɴ impalcatura

scald [skɔːld] ɴ scottatura ▶ ᴠᴛ scottare

scalding ['skɔːldɪŋ] ADJ (*also:* **scalding hot**) bollente

scale [skeɪl] ɴ scala; (*of fish*) squama ▶ ᴠᴛ (*mountain*) scalare; **pay ~** scala dei salari; **~ of charges** tariffa; **on a large ~** su vasta scala; **to draw sth to ~** disegnare qc in scala; **small-~ model** modello in scala ridotta; *see also* **scales**
▶ **scale down** ᴠᴛ ridurre (proporzionalmente)

scaled-down [skeɪld'daun] ADJ su scala ridotta

scale drawing ɴ disegno in scala

scale model ɴ modello in scala

scales [skeɪlz] NPL (*for weighing*) bilancia

scallion ['skæljən] N cipolla; (*US: shallot*) scalogna; (: *leek*) porro

scallop ['skɔləp] N (*Zool*) pettine *m*; (*Sewing*) smerlo

scalp [skælp] N cuoio capelluto ▶ VT scotennare

scalpel ['skælpl] N bisturi *m inv*

scalper ['skælpə^r] N (*US col: of tickets*) bagarino

scam [skæm] N (*col*) truffa

scamp [skæmp] N (*col: child*) peste *f*

scamper ['skæmpə^r] VI: **to ~ away, ~ off** darsela a gambe

scampi ['skæmpɪ] NPL scampi *mpl*

scan [skæn] VT scrutare; (*glance at quickly*) scorrere, dare un'occhiata a; (*poetry*) scandire; (*TV*) analizzare; (*Radar*) esplorare ▶ N (*Med*) ecografia

scandal ['skændl] N scandalo; (*gossip*) pettegolezzi *mpl*

scandalize ['skændəlaɪz] VT scandalizzare

scandalous ['skændələs] ADJ scandaloso(-a)

Scandinavia [skændɪ'neɪvɪə] N Scandinavia

Scandinavian [skændɪ'neɪvɪən] ADJ, N scandinavo(-a)

scanner ['skænə^r] N (*Radar, Med*) scanner *m inv*

scant [skænt] ADJ scarso(-a)

scantily ['skæntɪlɪ] ADV: **~ clad** or **dressed** succintamente vestito(-a)

scanty ['skæntɪ] ADJ insufficiente; (*swimsuit*) ridotto(-a)

scapegoat ['skeɪpgəut] N capro espiatorio

scar [skɑː^r] N cicatrice *f* ▶ VT sfregiare

scarce [skɛəs] ADJ scarso(-a); (*copy, edition*) raro(-a); **to make o.s. ~** (*col*) squagliarsela

scarcely ['skɛəslɪ] ADV appena; **~ anybody** quasi nessuno; **I can ~ believe it** faccio fatica a crederci

scarcity ['skɛəsɪtɪ] N scarsità, mancanza

scarcity value N valore *m* di rarità

scare [skɛə^r] N spavento, paura; panico ▶ VT spaventare, atterrire; **to ~ sb stiff** spaventare a morte qn; **bomb ~** evacuazione *f* per sospetta presenza di un ordigno esplosivo; **there was a bomb ~ at the bank** hanno evacuato la banca per paura di un attentato dinamitardo

▶ **scare away, scare off** VT mettere in fuga

scarecrow ['skɛəkrəu] N spaventapasseri *m inv*

scared [skɛəd] ADJ: **to be ~** aver paura

scaremonger ['skɛəmʌŋgə^r] N allarmista *mf*

scarf [skɑːf] (*pl* **scarves** [skɑːvz]) N (*long*) sciarpa; (*square*) fazzoletto da testa, foulard *m inv*

scarlet ['skɑːlɪt] ADJ scarlatto(-a)

scarlet fever N scarlattina

scarper ['skɑːpə^r] VI (*BRIT col*) darsela a gambe

SCART socket ['skɑː-] N presa *f* SCART *inv*

scarves [skɑːvz] NPL *of* **scarf**

scary ['skɛərɪ] ADJ (*col*) che fa paura

scathing ['skeɪðɪŋ] ADJ aspro(-a); **to be ~ about sth** essere molto critico rispetto a qc

scatter ['skætə^r] VT spargere; (*crowd*) disperdere ▶ VI disperdersi

scatterbrained ['skætəbreɪnd] ADJ scervellato(-a), sbadato(-a)

scattered ['skætəd] ADJ sparso(-a), sparpagliato(-a)

scatty ['skætɪ] ADJ (*col*) scervellato(-a), sbadato(-a)

scavenge ['skævɪndʒ] VI (*person*): **to ~ (for)** frugare tra i rifiuti (alla ricerca di); (*hyenas etc*) nutrirsi di carogne

scavenger ['skævəndʒə^r] N spazzino

SCE N ABBR = **Scottish Certificate of Education**

scenario [sɪ'nɑːrɪəu] N (*Theat, Cine*) copione *m*; (*fig*) situazione *f*

scene [siːn] N (*Theat, fig etc*) scena; (*of crime, accident*) scena, luogo; (*sight, view*) vista, veduta; **behind the scenes** (*also fig*) dietro le quinte; **to appear** or **come on the ~** (*also fig*) entrare in scena; **the political ~ in Italy** il quadro politico in Italia; **to make a ~** (*col: fuss*) fare una scenata

scenery ['siːnərɪ] N (*Theat*) scenario; (*landscape*) panorama *m*

scenic ['siːnɪk] ADJ scenico(-a); panoramico(-a)

scent [sɛnt] N odore *m*, profumo; (*sense of smell*) olfatto, odorato; (*fig: track*) pista; **to put** or **throw sb off the ~** (*fig*) far perdere le tracce a qn, sviare qn

sceptic, (*US*) **skeptic** ['skɛptɪk] N scettico(-a)

sceptical, (*US*) **skeptical** ['skɛptɪkl] ADJ scettico(-a)

scepticism, (*US*) **skepticism** ['skɛptɪsɪzm] N scetticismo

sceptre, (*US*) **scepter** ['sɛptə^r] N scettro

schedule ['ʃɛdjuːl, (*US*) 'skɛdjuːl] N programma *m*, piano; (*of trains*) orario; (*of prices etc*) lista, tabella ▶ VT fissare; **as scheduled** come stabilito; **on ~** in orario; **to be ahead of/behind ~** essere in anticipo/ ritardo sul previsto; **we are working to a very tight ~** il nostro programma di lavoro è molto intenso; **everything went according to ~** tutto è andato secondo i piani *or* secondo il previsto

scheduled flight ['ʃɛdjuːld, (*US*) 'skɛdjuːld] N (*date, time*) fissato(-a); (*visit, event*) programmato(-a); (*train, bus, stop*) previsto(-a) (sull'orario); **~** volo di linea

schematic [skɪ'mætɪk] ADJ schematico(-a)

scheme [skiːm] N piano, progetto; (*method*) sistema *m*; (*dishonest plan, plot*) intrigo, trama;

S

(*arrangement*) disposizione f, sistemazione f; (*pension scheme etc*) programma m ▶ VT progettare; (*plot*) ordire ▶ VI fare progetti; (*intrigue*) complottare; **colour ~** combinazione f di colori

scheming ['ski:mɪŋ] ADJ intrigante ▶ N intrighi mpl, macchinazioni fpl

schism ['skɪzəm] N scisma m

schizophrenia [skɪtsəˈfriːnɪə] N schizofrenia

schizophrenic [skɪtsəˈfrɛnɪk] ADJ, N schizofrenico(-a)

scholar ['skɔlər] N studioso(-a)

scholarly ['skɔləlɪ] ADJ dotto(-a), erudito(-a)

scholarship ['skɔləʃɪp] N erudizione f; (*grant*) borsa di studio

school [sku:l] N (*primary, secondary*) scuola; (*in university: US*) scuola, facoltà f inv ▶ CPD scolare, scolastico(-a) ▶ VT (*animal*) addestrare

school age N età scolare

schoolbook ['sku:lbʊk] N libro scolastico

schoolboy ['sku:lbɔɪ] N scolaro

schoolchild ['sku:ltʃaɪld] (*pl* **-children** [-ˈtʃɪldrən]) N scolaro(-a)

schooldays ['sku:ldeɪz] NPL giorni mpl di scuola

schoolgirl ['sku:lgə:l] N scolara

schooling ['sku:lɪŋ] N istruzione f

school-leaver ['sku:lli:vər] N (*BRIT*) ≈ neodiplomato(-a)

schoolmaster ['sku:lmɑ:stər] N (*primary*) maestro; (*secondary*) insegnante m

schoolmistress ['sku:lmɪstrɪs] N (*primary*) maestra; (*secondary*) insegnante f

school report N (*BRIT*) pagella

schoolroom ['sku:lru:m] N classe f, aula

schoolteacher ['sku:lti:tʃər] N insegnante mf, docente mf; (*primary*) maestro(-a)

schoolyard ['sku:ljɑ:d] N (*US*) cortile m della scuola

schooner ['sku:nər] N (*ship*) goletta, schooner m inv; (*glass*) bicchiere m alto da sherry

sciatica [saɪˈætɪkə] N sciatica

science ['saɪəns] N scienza; **the sciences** le scienze; (*Scol*) le materie scientifiche

science fiction N fantascienza

scientific [saɪənˈtɪfɪk] ADJ scientifico(-a)

scientist ['saɪəntɪst] N scienziato(-a)

sci-fi ['saɪfaɪ] N ABBR (*col*) = **science fiction**

Scilly Isles ['sɪlɪˈaɪlz] NPL, **Scillies** ['sɪlɪz] NPL: **the ~** le isole Scilly

scintillating ['sɪntɪleɪtɪŋ] ADJ scintillante; (*wit, conversation, company*) brillante

scissors ['sɪzəz] NPL forbici fpl; **a pair of ~** un paio di forbici

sclerosis [sklɪˈrəʊsɪs] N sclerosi f

scoff [skɔf] VT (*BRIT col: eat*) trangugiare, ingozzare ▶ VI: **to ~ (at)** (*mock*) farsi beffe (di)

scold [skəʊld] VT rimproverare

scolding ['skəʊldɪŋ] N lavata di capo, sgridata

scone [skɔn] N focaccina da tè

scoop [sku:p] N mestolo; (*for ice cream*) cucchiaio dosatore; (*Press*) colpo giornalistico, notizia (in) esclusiva
  ▶ **scoop out** VT scavare
  ▶ **scoop up** VT tirare su, sollevare

scooter ['sku:tər] N (*motorcycle*) motoretta, scooter m inv; (*toy*) monopattino

scope [skəʊp] N (*capacity: of plan, undertaking*) portata; (*: of person*) capacità fpl; (*opportunity*) possibilità fpl; **to be within the ~ of** rientrare nei limiti di; **it's well within his ~ to ...** è perfettamente in grado di ...; **there is plenty of ~ for improvement** (*BRIT*) ci sono notevoli possibilità di miglioramento

scorch [skɔ:tʃ] VT (*clothes*) strinare, bruciacchiare; (*earth, grass*) seccare, bruciare

scorched earth policy [skɔ:tʃt-] N tattica della terra bruciata

scorcher ['skɔ:tʃər] N (*col: hot day*) giornata torrida

scorching ['skɔ:tʃɪŋ] ADJ cocente, scottante

score [skɔ:r] N punti mpl, punteggio; (*Mus*) partitura, spartito; (*twenty*): **a ~** venti ▶ VT (*goal, point*) segnare, fare; (*success*) ottenere; (*cut: leather, wood, card*) incidere ▶ VI segnare; (*Football*) fare un goal; (*keep score*) segnare i punti; **on that ~** a questo riguardo; **to have an old ~ to settle with sb** (*fig*) avere un vecchio conto da saldare con qn; **scores of people** (*fig*) un sacco di gente; **to ~ 6 out of 10** prendere 6 su 10
  ▶ **score out** VT cancellare con un segno

scoreboard ['skɔ:bɔ:d] N tabellone m segnapunti

scorecard ['skɔ:kɑ:d] N cartoncino segnapunti

scoreline ['skɔ:laɪn] N (*Sport*) risultato

scorer ['skɔ:rər] N marcatore(-trice); (*keeping score*) segnapunti m inv

scorn [skɔ:n] N disprezzo ▶ VT disprezzare

scornful ['skɔ:nful] ADJ sprezzante

Scorpio ['skɔ:pɪəʊ] N Scorpione m; **to be ~** essere dello Scorpione

scorpion ['skɔ:pɪən] N scorpione m

Scot [skɔt] N scozzese mf

Scotch [skɔtʃ] N whisky m scozzese, scotch m

scotch [skɔtʃ] VT (*rumour etc*) soffocare

Scotch tape® [skɔtʃ-] N scotch® m

scot-free ['skɔt'fri:] ADJ impunito(-a); **to get off ~** (*unpunished*) farla franca; (*unhurt*) uscire illeso(-a)

Scotland ['skɔtlənd] N Scozia

Scots [skɔts] ADJ scozzese

Scotsman ['skɔtsmən] N (*irreg*) scozzese m

Scotswoman ['skɔtswʊmən] N (*irreg*) scozzese f

Scottish ['skɔtɪʃ] ADJ scozzese; **the ~ National Party** il partito nazionalista scozzese; **the ~ Parliament** il Parlamento scozzese

scoundrel ['skaundrl] N farabutto(-a); (*child*) furfantello(-a)

scour ['skauə^r] VT (*clean*) pulire strofinando; raschiare via; ripulire; (*search*) battere, perlustrare

scourer ['skauərə^r] N (*pad*) paglietta; (*powder*) (detersivo) abrasivo

scourge [skə:dʒ] N flagello

scout [skaut] N (*Mil*) esploratore m; (*also:* **boy scout**) giovane esploratore, scout m inv
▶ **scout around** VI cercare in giro

scowl [skaul] VI acciglarsi, aggrottare le sopracciglia; **to ~ at** guardare torvo

scrabble ['skræbl] VI (*claw*): **to ~ (at)** graffiare, grattare; **to ~ about** or **around for sth** cercare affannosamente qc ▶ N: **S-®** Scarabeo®

scraggy ['skrægɪ] ADJ scarno(-a), molto magro(-a)

scram [skræm] VI (*col*) filare via

scramble ['skræmbl] N arrampicata ▶ VI inerpicarsi; **to ~ out** *etc* uscire *etc* in fretta; **to ~ for** azzuffarsi per; **to go scrambling** (*Sport*) fare il motocross

scrambled eggs NPL uova fpl strapazzate

scrap [skræp] N pezzo, pezzetto; (*fight*) zuffa; (*also:* **scrap iron**) rottami mpl di ferro, ferraglia ▶ VT demolire; (*fig*) scartare ▶ VI: **to ~ (with sb)** fare a botte (con qn); **scraps** NPL (*waste*) scarti mpl; **to sell sth for ~** vendere qc come ferro vecchio

scrapbook ['skræpbuk] N album m inv di ritagli

scrap dealer N commerciante m di ferraglia

scrape [skreɪp] VT, VI raschiare, grattare ▶ N: **to get into a ~** cacciarsi in un guaio
▶ **scrape through** VI (*succeed*) farcela per un pelo, cavarsela ▶ VT FUS (*exam*) passare per miracolo, passare per il rotto della cuffia

scraper ['skreɪpə^r] N raschietto

scrap heap N mucchio di rottami; **to throw sth on the ~** (*fig*) mettere qc nel dimenticatoio

scrap merchant N (*BRIT*) commerciante m di ferraglia

scrap metal N ferraglia

scrap paper N cartaccia

scrappy ['skræpɪ] ADJ frammentario(-a), sconnesso(-a)

scrap yard N deposito di rottami; (*for cars*) cimitero delle macchine

scratch [skrætʃ] N graffio ▶ CPD: **~ team** squadra raccogliticcia ▶ VT graffiare, rigare; (*Comput*) cancellare ▶ VI grattare; (*paint, car*) graffiare; **to start from ~** cominciare or partire da zero; **to be up to ~** essere all'altezza

scratch card N (*BRIT*) cartolina f gratta e vinci

scratch pad N (*US*) notes m inv, blocchetto

scrawl [skrɔ:l] N scarabocchio ▶ VI scarabocchiare

scrawny ['skrɔ:nɪ] ADJ scarno(-a), pelle e ossa inv

scream [skri:m] N grido, urlo ▶ VI urlare, gridare; **to ~ at sb (to do sth)** gridare a qn (di fare qc); **it was a ~** (*fig: col*) era da crepar dal ridere; **he's a ~** (*fig: col*) è una sagoma, è uno spasso

scree [skri:] N ghiaione m

screech [skri:tʃ] N strido; (*of tyres, brakes*) stridore m ▶ VI stridere

screen [skri:n] N schermo; (*fig*) muro, cortina, velo ▶ VT schermare, fare schermo a; (*from the wind etc*) riparare; (*film*) proiettare; (*book*) adattare per lo schermo; (*candidates etc*) passare al vaglio; (*for illness*) sottoporre a controlli medici

screen editing [-ɛdɪtɪŋ] N (*Comput*) correzione f e modifica su schermo

screening ['skri:nɪŋ] N (*Med*) dépistage m inv; (*of film*) proiezione f; (*for security*) controlli mpl (di sicurezza)

screen memory N (*Comput*) memoria di schermo

screenplay ['skri:npleɪ] N sceneggiatura

screensaver N (*Comput*) screen saver m inv

screenshot ['skri:nʃɔt] N (*Comput*) schermata

screen test N provino (cinematografico)

screw [skru:] N vite f; (*propeller*) elica ▶ VT avvitare; **to ~ sth to the wall** fissare qc al muro con viti
▶ **screw up** VT (*paper, material*) spiegazzare; (*col: ruin*) mandare a monte; **to ~ up one's face** fare una smorfia; **to ~ up one's eyes** strizzare gli occhi

screwdriver ['skru:draɪvə^r] N cacciavite m

screwed-up ['skru:d'ʌp] ADJ (*col*): **she's totally ~** è nel pallone

screwy ['skru:ɪ] ADJ (*col*) svitato(-a)

scribble ['skrɪbl] N scarabocchio ▶ VT scribacchiare ▶ VI scarabocchiare; **to ~ sth down** scribacchiare qc

scribe [skraɪb] N scriba m

script [skrɪpt] N (*Cine etc*) copione m; (*in exam*) elaborato or compito d'esame; (*writing*) scrittura

scripted ['skrɪptɪd] ADJ (*Radio, TV*) preparato(-a)

Scripture ['skrɪptʃə^r] N Sacre Scritture fpl

scriptwriter ['skrɪptraɪtə^r] N soggettista mf

scroll [skrəul] N rotolo di carta ▶ VT (*Comput*) scorrere

S

scroll bar N (*Comput*) barra di scorrimento

scrotum ['skrəutəm] N scroto

scrounge [skraundʒ] VT (*col*): **to ~ sth (off** *or* **from sb)** scroccare qc (a qn) ▶ VI: **to ~ on sb** vivere alle spalle di qn

scrounger ['skraundʒər] N scroccone(-a)

scrub [skrʌb] N (*clean*) strofinata; (*land*) boscaglia ▶ VT pulire strofinando; (*reject*) annullare

scrubbing brush ['skrʌbɪŋ-] N spazzolone m

scruff [skrʌf] N: **by the ~ of the neck** per la collottola

scruffy ['skrʌfɪ] ADJ sciatto(-a)

scrum ['skrʌm], **scrummage** ['skrʌmɪdʒ] N mischia

scruple ['skru:pl] N scrupolo; **to have no scruples about doing sth** non avere scrupoli a fare qc

scrupulous ['skru:pjuləs] ADJ scrupoloso(-a)

scrupulously ['skru:pjuəslɪ] ADV scrupolosamente; **he tries to be ~ fair/ honest** cerca di essere più imparziale/ onesto che può

scrutinize ['skru:tɪnaɪz] VT scrutare, esaminare attentamente

scrutiny ['skru:tɪnɪ] N esame m accurato; **under the ~ of sb** sotto la sorveglianza di qn

scuba ['sku:bə] N autorespiratore m

scuba diving ['sku:bə-] N immersioni fpl subacquee

scuff [skʌf] VT (*shoes*) consumare strascicando

scuffle ['skʌfl] N baruffa, tafferuglio

scullery ['skʌlərɪ] N retrocucina m or f

sculptor ['skʌlptər] N scultore m

sculpture ['skʌlptʃər] N scultura

scum [skʌm] N schiuma; (*pej: people*) feccia

scupper ['skʌpər] VT autoaffondare; (*BRIT fig*) far naufragare

scurrilous ['skʌrɪləs] ADJ scurrile, volgare

scurry ['skʌrɪ] VI sgambare, affrettarsi

scurvy ['skə:vɪ] N scorbuto

scuttle ['skʌtl] N (*Naut*) portellino; (*also:* **coal scuttle**) secchio del carbone ▶ VT (*ship*) autoaffondare ▶ VI (*scamper*): **to ~ away, ~ off** darsela a gambe, scappare

scythe [saɪð] N falce f

SD, S. Dak. ABBR (*US*) = **South Dakota**

SDI N ABBR (= *Strategic Defense Initiative*) S.D.I. f

SDLP N ABBR (*BRIT Pol*) = **Social Democratic and Labour Party**

sea [si:] N mare m ▶ CPD marino(-a), del mare; (*ship, port, route, transport*) marittimo(-a); (*bird, fish*) di mare; **on the ~** (*boat*) in mare; (*town*) di mare; **to go by ~** andare per mare; **by** *or* **beside the ~** (*holiday*) al mare; (*village*) sul mare; **to look out to ~** guardare il mare; **out to ~** al largo; **(out) at ~** in mare; **heavy** *or* **rough ~(s)** mare grosso

or agitato; **a ~ of faces** (*fig*) una marea di gente; **to be all at ~** (*fig*) non sapere che pesci pigliare

sea bed N fondo marino

sea bird N uccello di mare

seaboard ['si:bɔ:d] N costa

sea breeze N brezza di mare

seafarer ['si:fɛərər] N navigante m

seafaring ['si:fɛərɪŋ] ADJ (*community*) marinaro(-a); (*life*) da marinaio

seafood ['si:fu:d] N frutti mpl di mare

sea front N lungomare m

seagoing ['si:gəuɪŋ] ADJ (*ship*) d'alto mare

seagull ['si:gʌl] N gabbiano

seal [si:l] N (*animal*) foca; (*stamp*) sigillo; (*impression*) impronta del sigillo ▶ VT sigillare; (*decide: sb's fate*) segnare; (: *bargain*) concludere; **~ of approval** beneplacito ▶ **seal off** VT (*close*) sigillare; (*forbid entry to*) bloccare l'accesso a

sea level N livello del mare

sealing wax ['si:lɪŋ-] N ceralacca

sea lion N leone m marino

sealskin ['si:lskɪn] N pelle f di foca

seam [si:m] N cucitura; (*of coal*) filone m; **the hall was bursting at the seams** l'aula era piena zeppa

seaman ['si:mən] N (*irreg*) marinaio

seamanship ['si:mənʃɪp] N tecnica di navigazione

seamless ['si:mlɪs] ADJ senza cucitura

seamy ['si:mɪ] ADJ malfamato(-a); squallido(-a)

seance ['seɪɔns] N seduta spiritica

seaplane ['si:pleɪn] N idrovolante m

seaport ['si:pɔ:t] N porto di mare

search [sə:tʃ] N (*for person, thing*) ricerca; (*of drawer, pockets*) esame m accurato; (*Law: at sb's home*) perquisizione f ▶ VT perlustrare, frugare; (*scan, examine*) esaminare minuziosamente; (*Comput*) ricercare ▶ VI: **to ~ for** ricercare; **in ~ of** alla ricerca di; **"~ and replace"** (*Comput*) "ricercare e sostituire" ▶ **search through** VT FUS frugare

search engine N (*Comput*) motore m di ricerca

searcher ['sə:tʃər] N chi cerca

searching ['sə:tʃɪŋ] ADJ minuzioso(-a); penetrante; (*question*) pressante

searchlight ['sə:tʃlaɪt] N proiettore m

search party N squadra di soccorso

search warrant N mandato di perquisizione

searing ['sɪərɪŋ] ADJ (*heat*) rovente; (*pain*) acuto(-a)

seashore ['si:ʃɔ:r] N spiaggia; **on the ~** sulla riva del mare

seasick ['si:sɪk] ADJ che soffre il mal di mare; **to be ~** avere il mal di mare

seaside ['si:saɪd] N spiaggia; **to go to the ~** andare al mare

seaside resort N stazione f balneare
season ['si:zn] N stagione f ▶ VT condire,
insaporire; **to be in/out of ~** essere di/fuori
stagione; **the busy ~** (for shops) il periodo di
punta; (for hotels etc) l'alta stagione; **the
open ~** (Hunting) la stagione della caccia
seasonal ['si:zənl] ADJ stagionale
seasoned ['si:znd] ADJ (wood) stagionato(-a);
(fig: worker, actor, troops) con esperienza; **a ~
campaigner** un veterano
seasoning ['si:znɪŋ] N condimento
season ticket N abbonamento
seat [si:t] N sedile m; (in bus, train: place) posto;
(Parliament) seggio; (centre: of government etc, of
infection) sede f; (buttocks) didietro; (of trousers)
fondo ▶ VT far sedere; (have room for) avere or
essere fornito(-a) di posti a sedere per; **are
there any seats left?** ci sono posti?; **to take
one's ~** prendere posto; **to be seated** essere
seduto(-a); **please be seated** accomodatevi
per favore
seat belt N cintura di sicurezza
seating N posti mpl a sedere
seating arrangements ['si:tɪŋ-] NPL
sistemazione f or disposizione f dei posti
seating capacity N posti mpl a sedere
SEATO ['si:təu] N ABBR (= Southeast Asia Treaty
Organization) SEATO f
sea water N acqua di mare
seaweed ['si:wi:d] N alghe fpl
seaworthy ['si:wə:ði] ADJ atto(-a) alla
navigazione
SEC N ABBR (US: = Securities and Exchange
Commission) commissione di controllo sulle
operazioni in Borsa
sec. ABBR = **second¹**
secateurs [sɛkə'tə:z] NPL forbici fpl per
potare
secede [sɪ'si:d] VI: **to ~ (from)** ritirarsi (da)
secluded [sɪ'klu:dɪd] ADJ isolato(-a),
appartato(-a)
seclusion [sɪ'klu:ʒən] N isolamento
second¹ ['sɛkənd] NUM secondo(-a) ▶ ADV (in
race etc) al secondo posto; (Rail) in seconda
▶ N (unit of time) secondo; (in series, position)
secondo(-a); (Brit Scol: degree) laurea con
punteggio discreto; (Aut: also: **second gear**)
seconda; (Comm: imperfect) scarto ▶ VT (motion)
appoggiare; **Charles the S~** Carlo Secondo;
just a ~! un attimo!; **~ floor** (Brit) secondo
piano; (US) primo piano; **to ask for a ~
opinion** (Med) chiedere un altro or ulteriore
parere; **~ thoughts** ripensamenti mpl; **to
have ~ thoughts (about doing sth)** avere
dei ripensamenti (quanto a fare qc); **on ~
thoughts** (Brit) or **thought** (US) a
ripensarci, ripensandoci bene
second² [sɪ'kɔnd] VT (employee) distaccare
secondary ['sɛkəndərɪ] ADJ secondario(-a)

secondary school N scuola secondaria;
vedi nota

> In Gran Bretagna la secondary school è la
> scuola frequentata dai ragazzi dagli 11 ai
> 18 anni. Nel paese è obbligatorio andare a
> scuola fino a 16 anni; vedi anche **primary
> school**.

second-best [sɛkənd'bɛst] N ripiego; **as a ~**
in mancanza di meglio
second-class [sɛkənd'klɑ:s] ADJ di seconda
classe ▶ ADV: **to travel ~** viaggiare in
seconda (classe); **to send sth ~** spedire qc
per posta ordinaria; **~ citizen** cittadino di
second'ordine
second cousin N cugino di secondo grado
seconder ['sɛkəndər] N sostenitore(-trice)
second-guess ['sɛkənd'gɛs] VT (predict)
anticipare; (after the event) giudicare col
senno di poi
second hand N (on clock) lancetta dei secondi
second-hand [sɛkənd'hænd] ADJ di seconda
mano, usato(-a) ▶ ADV (buy) di seconda mano;
to hear sth ~ venire a sapere qc da terze
persone
second-in-command ['sɛkəndɪnkə'mɑ:nd]
N (Mil) comandante m in seconda; (Admin)
aggiunto
secondly ['sɛkəndlɪ] ADV in secondo luogo
secondment [sɪ'kɔndmənt] N (Brit)
distaccamento
second-rate [sɛkənd'reɪt] ADJ scadente
Second World War N: **the ~** la seconda
guerra mondiale
secrecy ['si:krəsɪ] N segretezza
secret ['si:krɪt] ADJ segreto(-a) ▶ N segreto;
in ~ in segreto, segretamente; **to keep sth ~
(from sb)** tenere qc segreto (a qn), tenere qc
nascosto (a qn); **keep it ~** che rimanga un
segreto; **to make no ~ of sth** non far
mistero di qc
secret agent N agente m segreto
secretarial [sɛkrɪ'tɛərɪəl] ADJ (work) da
segretario(-a); (college, course) di segretariato
secretariat [sɛkrɪ'tɛərɪət] N segretariato
secretary ['sɛkrətrɪ] N segretario(-a); **S~ of
State** (US Pol) ≈ Ministro degli Esteri; **S~ of
State (for)** (Brit Pol) ministro (di)
secretary-general ['sɛkrətrɪ'dʒɛnərl] N
segretario generale
secrete [sɪ'kri:t] VT (Med, Anat, Biol) secernere;
(hide) nascondere
secretion [sɪ'kri:ʃən] N secrezione f
secretive ['si:krətɪv] ADJ riservato(-a)
secretly ['si:krɪtlɪ] ADV in segreto,
segretamente
secret police N polizia segreta
secret service N servizi mpl segreti
sect [sɛkt] N setta
sectarian [sɛk'tɛərɪən] ADJ settario(-a)

S

section ['sɛkʃən] N sezione f; (of document) articolo ▶ VT sezionare, dividere in sezioni; **the business ~** (Press) la pagina economica
sector ['sɛktəʳ] N settore m
secular ['sɛkjuləʳ] ADJ secolare
secure [sɪ'kjuəʳ] ADJ (free from anxiety) sicuro(-a); (firmly fixed) assicurato(-a), ben fermato(-a); (in safe place) al sicuro ▶ VT (fix) fissare, assicurare; (get) ottenere, assicurarsi; (Comm: loan) garantire; **to make sth ~** fissare bene qc; **to ~ sth for sb** procurare qc per or a qn
secured creditor [sɪ'kjuəd-] N creditore m privilegiato
security [sɪ'kjuərɪtɪ] N sicurezza; (for loan) garanzia; **securities** NPL (Stock Exchange) titoli mpl; **to increase/tighten ~** aumentare/intensificare la sorveglianza; **~ of tenure** garanzia del posto di lavoro, garanzia di titolo or di godimento
Security Council N: **the ~** il Consiglio di Sicurezza
security forces NPL forze fpl dell'ordine
security guard N guardia giurata
security risk N rischio per la sicurezza
secy. ABBR = **secretary**
sedan [sə'dæn] N (US Aut) berlina
sedate [sɪ'deɪt] ADJ posato(-a); calmo(-a) ▶ VT calmare
sedation [sɪ'deɪʃən] N (Med): **to be under ~** essere sotto l'azione di sedativi
sedative ['sɛdɪtɪv] N sedativo, calmante m
sedentary ['sɛdntrɪ] ADJ sedentario(-a)
sediment ['sɛdɪmənt] N sedimento
sedition [sɪ'dɪʃən] N sedizione f
seduce [sɪ'dju:s] VT sedurre
seduction [sɪ'dʌkʃən] N seduzione f
seductive [sɪ'dʌktɪv] ADJ seducente
see [si:] (pt **saw**, pp **seen**) VT vedere; (accompany): **to ~ sb to the door** accompagnare qn alla porta ▶ VI vedere; (understand) capire ▶ N sede f vescovile; **to ~ that** (ensure) badare che + sub, fare in modo che + sub; **to go and ~ sb** andare a trovare qn; **~ you soon/later/tomorrow!** a presto/più tardi/domani!; **as far as I can ~** da quanto posso vedere; **there was nobody to be seen** non c'era anima viva; **let me ~** (show me) fammi vedere; (let me think) vediamo (un po'); **~ for yourself** vai a vedere con i tuoi occhi; **I don't know what she sees in him** non so che cosa ci trovi in lui
▶ **see about** VT FUS (deal with) occuparsi di
▶ **see off** VT salutare alla partenza
▶ **see out** VT (take to the door) accompagnare alla porta
▶ **see through** VT portare a termine ▶ VT FUS non lasciarsi ingannare da
▶ **see to** VT FUS occuparsi di

seed [si:d] N seme m; (fig) germe m; (Tennis) testa di serie; **to go to ~** fare seme; (fig) scadere
seedless ['si:dlɪs] ADJ senza semi
seedling ['si:dlɪŋ] N piantina di semenzaio
seedy ['si:dɪ] ADJ (shabby: person) sciatto(-a); (: place) cadente
seeing ['si:ɪŋ] CONJ: **~ (that)** visto che
seek [si:k] (pt, pp **sought**) VT cercare; **to ~ advice/help from sb** chiedere consiglio/aiuto a qn
▶ **seek out** VT (person) andare a cercare
seem [si:m] VI sembrare, parere; **there seems to be ...** sembra che ci sia ...; **it seems (that) ...** sembra or pare che ... + sub; **what seems to be the trouble?** cosa c'è che non va?
seemingly ['si:mɪŋlɪ] ADV apparentemente
seen [si:n] PP of **see**
seep [si:p] VI filtrare, trapelare
seer [sɪəʳ] N profeta(-essa), veggente mf
seersucker ['sɪəsʌkəʳ] N cotone m indiano
seesaw ['si:sɔ:] N altalena a bilico
seethe [si:ð] VI ribollire; **to ~ with anger** fremere di rabbia
see-through ['si:θru:] ADJ trasparente
segment ['sɛgmənt] N segmento
segregate ['sɛgrɪgeɪt] VT segregare, isolare
segregation [sɛgrɪ'geɪʃən] N segregazione f
Seine [seɪn] N Senna
seismic ['saɪzmɪk] ADJ sismico(-a)
seize [si:z] VT (grasp) afferrare; (take possession of) impadronirsi di; (Law) sequestrare
▶ **seize up** VI (Tech) grippare
▶ **seize (up)on** VT FUS ricorrere a
seizure ['si:ʒəʳ] N (Med) attacco; (Law) confisca, sequestro
seldom ['sɛldəm] ADV raramente
select [sɪ'lɛkt] ADJ scelto(-a); (hotel, restaurant) chic inv; (club) esclusivo(-a) ▶ VT scegliere, selezionare; **a ~ few** pochi eletti mpl
selection [sɪ'lɛkʃən] N selezione f, scelta
selection committee N comitato di selezione
selective [sɪ'lɛktɪv] ADJ selettivo(-a)
selector [sɪ'lɛktəʳ] N (person) selezionatore(-trice); (Tech) selettore m
self [sɛlf] (pl **selves** [sɛlvz]) N: **the ~** l'io m
▶ PREFIX auto...
self-addressed ['sɛlfə'drɛst] ADJ: **~ envelope** busta col proprio nome e indirizzo
self-adhesive [sɛlfəd'hi:zɪv] ADJ autoadesivo(-a)
self-assertive [sɛlfə'sə:tɪv] ADJ autoritario(-a)
self-assurance [sɛlfə'ʃuərəns] N sicurezza di sé
self-assured [sɛlfə'ʃuəd] ADJ sicuro(-a) di sé

self-catering [sɛlfˈkeɪtərɪŋ] ADJ (BRIT) in cui ci si cucina da sé; **~ apartment** appartamento (per le vacanze)

self-centred, (US) **self-centered** [sɛlfˈsɛntəd] ADJ egocentrico(-a)

self-cleaning [sɛlfˈkliːnɪŋ] ADJ autopulente

self-confessed [sɛlfkənˈfɛst] ADJ (alcoholic etc) dichiarato(-a)

self-confidence [sɛlfˈkɒnfɪdəns] N sicurezza di sé

self-confident ADJ sicuro(-a) di sé

self-conscious [sɛlfˈkɒnʃəs] ADJ timido(-a)

self-contained [sɛlfkənˈteɪnd] ADJ (BRIT: flat) indipendente

self-control [sɛlfkənˈtrəʊl] N autocontrollo

self-defeating [sɛlfdɪˈfiːtɪŋ] ADJ futile

self-defence, (US) **self-defense** [sɛlfdɪˈfɛns] N autodifesa; (Law) legittima difesa

self-discipline [sɛlfˈdɪsɪplɪn] N autodisciplina

self-drive ADJ (BRIT: rented car) senza autista

self-employed [sɛlfɪmˈplɔɪd] ADJ che lavora in proprio

self-esteem [sɛlfɪˈstiːm] N amor proprio m

self-evident [sɛlfˈɛvɪdənt] ADJ evidente

self-explanatory [sɛlfɪkˈsplænətərɪ] ADJ ovvio(-a)

self-governing [sɛlfˈgʌvənɪŋ] ADJ autonomo(-a)

self-harm [sɛlfˈhɑːm] N autolesionismo ▶ VI farsi del male intenzionalmente

self-help [ˈsɛlfˈhɛlp] N iniziativa individuale

self-importance [sɛlfɪmˈpɔːtns] N sufficienza

self-indulgent [sɛlfɪnˈdʌldʒənt] ADJ indulgente verso se stesso(-a)

self-inflicted [sɛlfɪnˈflɪktɪd] ADJ autoinflitto(-a)

self-interest [sɛlfˈɪntrɪst] N interesse m personale

selfish [ˈsɛlfɪʃ] ADJ egoista

selfishly [ˈsɛlfɪʃlɪ] ADV egoisticamente

selfishness [ˈsɛlfɪʃnɪs] N egoismo

selfless [ˈsɛlflɪs] ADJ altruista

selflessly [ˈsɛlflɪslɪ] ADV altruisticamente

selflessness [ˈsɛlflɪsnɪs] N altruismo

self-made man [ˈsɛlfmeɪd-] N (irreg) self-made man m inv, uomo che si è fatto da sé

self-pity [sɛlfˈpɪtɪ] N autocommiserazione f

self-portrait [sɛlfˈpɔːtrɪt] N autoritratto

self-possessed [sɛlfpəˈzɛst] ADJ controllato(-a)

self-preservation [ˈsɛlfprɛzəˈveɪʃən] N istinto di conservazione

self-raising [sɛlfˈreɪzɪŋ], (US) **self-rising** [sɛlfˈraɪzɪŋ] ADJ: **~ flour** miscela di farina e lievito

self-reliant [sɛlfrɪˈlaɪənt] ADJ indipendente

self-respect [sɛlfrɪsˈpɛkt] N rispetto di sé, amor proprio

self-respecting [sɛlfrɪsˈpɛktɪŋ] ADJ che ha rispetto di sé

self-righteous [sɛlfˈraɪtʃəs] ADJ soddisfatto(-a) di sé

self-rising [sɛlfˈraɪzɪŋ] ADJ (US) = **self-raising**

self-sacrifice [sɛlfˈsækrɪfaɪs] N abnegazione f

self-same [ˈsɛlfseɪm] ADJ stesso(-a)

self-satisfied [sɛlfˈsætɪsfaɪd] ADJ compiaciuto(-a) di sé

self-sealing [sɛlfˈsiːlɪŋ] ADJ autosigillante

self-service [sɛlfˈsəːvɪs] N autoservizio, self-service m

self-styled [sɛlfˈstaɪld] ADJ sedicente

self-sufficient [sɛlfsəˈfɪʃənt] ADJ autosufficiente

self-supporting [sɛlfsəˈpɔːtɪŋ] ADJ economicamente indipendente

self-taught [sɛlfˈtɔːt] ADJ autodidatta

self-test [ˈsɛlftɛst] N (Comput) autoverifica

sell [sɛl] (pt, pp **sold** [səʊld]) VT vendere ▶ VI vendersi; **to ~ at** or **for 100 euros** essere in vendita a 100 euro; **to ~ sb an idea** (fig) far accettare un'idea a qn
 ▶ **sell off** VT svendere, liquidare
 ▶ **sell out** VI: **to ~ out (to sb/sth)** (Comm) vendere (tutto) (a qn/qc) ▶ VT esaurire; **the tickets are all sold out** i biglietti sono esauriti
 ▶ **sell up** VI vendere (tutto)

sell-by date [ˈsɛlbaɪ-] N data di scadenza

seller [ˈsɛlə*] N venditore(-trice); **~'s market** mercato favorevole ai venditori

selling price [ˈsɛlɪŋ-] N prezzo di vendita

Sellotape® [ˈsɛləʊteɪp] N (BRIT) nastro adesivo, scotch® m

sellout [ˈsɛlaʊt] N (betrayal) tradimento; **it was a ~** registrò un tutto esaurito

selves [sɛlvz] NPL of **self**

semantic [sɪˈmæntɪk] ADJ semantico(-a)

semantics [sɪˈmæntɪks] N semantica

semaphore [ˈsɛməfɔː*] N segnali mpl con bandiere; (Rail) semaforo

semblance [ˈsɛmbləns] N parvenza, apparenza

semen [ˈsiːmən] N sperma m

semester [sɪˈmɛstə*] N (US) semestre m

semi... [ˈsɛmɪ] PREFIX semi... ▶ N: **semi** = **semidetached (house)**

semi-breve [ˈsɛmɪbriːv] N (BRIT) semibreve f

semicircle [ˈsɛmɪsəːkl] N semicerchio

semicircular [ˈsɛmɪˈsəːkjulə*] ADJ semicircolare

semicolon [sɛmɪˈkəʊlən] N punto e virgola

semiconductor [sɛmɪkənˈdʌktə*] N semiconduttore m

semiconscious [sɛmɪˈkɒnʃəs] ADJ parzialmente cosciente

semidetached (house) [sɛmɪdɪˈtætʃt-] N (BRIT) casa gemella

semifinal [sɛmɪˈfaɪnl] N semifinale f

seminar [ˈsɛmɪnɑːʳ] N seminario

seminary [ˈsɛmɪnərɪ] N (Rel: for priests) seminario

semiprecious [sɛmɪˈprɛʃəs] ADJ semiprezioso(-a)

semiquaver [ˈsɛmɪkweɪvəʳ] N (BRIT) semicroma

semiskilled [ˈsɛmɪˈskɪld] ADJ: ~ **worker** operaio(-a) non specializzato(-a)

semi-skimmed [ˈsɛmɪˈskɪmd] ADJ (milk) parzialmente scremato(-a)

semitone [ˈsɛmɪtəun] N (Mus) semitono

semolina [sɛməˈliːnə] N semolino

Sen., sen. ABBR = **senator; senior**

senate [ˈsɛnɪt] N senato

senator [ˈsɛnɪtəʳ] N senatore(-trice)

send [sɛnd] (pt, pp **sent**) VT mandare; **to ~ by post** or (US) **mail** spedire per posta; **to ~ sb for sth** mandare qn a prendere qc; **to ~ word that …** mandare a dire che …; **she sends (you) her love** ti saluta affettuosamente; **to ~ sb to Coventry** (BRIT) dare l'ostracismo a qn; **to ~ sb to sleep/into fits of laughter** far addormentare/scoppiare dal ridere qn; **to ~ sth flying** far volare via qc
  ▶ **send away** VT (letter, goods) spedire; (person) mandare via
  ▶ **send away for** VT FUS richiedere per posta, farsi spedire
  ▶ **send back** VT rimandare
  ▶ **send for** VT FUS mandare a chiamare, far venire; (by post) ordinare per posta
  ▶ **send in** VT (report, application, resignation) presentare
  ▶ **send off** VT (goods) spedire; (BRIT Sport: player) espellere
  ▶ **send on** VT (BRIT: letter) inoltrare; (luggage etc: in advance) spedire in anticipo
  ▶ **send out** VT (invitation) diramare; (emit: light, heat) mandare, emanare; (: signals) emettere
  ▶ **send round** VT (letter, document etc) far circolare
  ▶ **send up** VT (person, price) far salire; (BRIT: parody) mettere in ridicolo

sender [ˈsɛndəʳ] N mittente mf

send-off [ˈsɛndɔf] N: **to give sb a good ~** festeggiare la partenza di qn

Senegal [sɛnɪˈɡɔːl] N Senegal m

Senegalese [sɛnɪɡəˈliːz] ADJ, N senegalese mf

senile [ˈsiːnaɪl] ADJ senile

senility [sɪˈnɪlɪtɪ] N senilità f

senior [ˈsiːnɪəʳ] ADJ (older) più vecchio(-a); (of higher rank) di grado più elevato ▶ N persona più anziana; (in service) persona con maggiore anzianità; **P. Jones ~** P. Jones senior, P. Jones padre

senior citizen N persona anziana

senior high school N (US) ≈ liceo

seniority [siːnɪˈɔrɪtɪ] N anzianità; (in rank) superiorità

sensation [sɛnˈseɪʃən] N sensazione f; **to create a ~** fare scalpore

sensational [sɛnˈseɪʃənl] ADJ sensazionale; (marvellous) eccezionale

sense [sɛns] N senso; (feeling) sensazione f, senso; (meaning) senso, significato; (wisdom) buonsenso ▶ VT sentire, percepire; **senses** NPL (sanity) ragione f; **it makes ~** ha senso; **there is no ~ in (doing) that** non ha senso (farlo); **~ of humour** (senso dell')umorismo; **to come to one's senses** (regain consciousness) riprendere i sensi; (become reasonable) tornare in sé; **to take leave of one's senses** perdere il lume or l'uso della ragione

senseless [ˈsɛnslɪs] ADJ sciocco(-a); (unconscious) privo(-a) di sensi

sensibilities [sɛnsɪˈbɪlɪtɪz] NPL sensibilità fsg

sensible [ˈsɛnsɪbl] ADJ sensato(-a), ragionevole

sensitive [ˈsɛnsɪtɪv] ADJ sensibile; (skin, question) delicato(-a); **~ (to)** sensibile (a); **he is very ~ about it** è un tasto che è meglio non toccare con lui

sensitivity [sɛnsɪˈtɪvɪtɪ] N sensibilità

sensual [ˈsɛnsjuəl] ADJ sensuale

sensuous [ˈsɛnsjuəs] ADJ sensuale

sent [sɛnt] PT, PP of **send**

sentence [ˈsɛntns] N (Ling) frase f; (Law: judgement) sentenza; (: punishment) condanna
  ▶ VT: **to ~ sb to death/to 5 years** condannare qn a morte/a 5 anni; **to pass ~ on sb** condannare qn

sentiment [ˈsɛntɪmənt] N sentimento; (opinion) opinione f

sentimental [sɛntɪˈmɛntl] ADJ sentimentale

sentimentality [sɛntɪmɛnˈtælɪtɪ] N sentimentalità, sentimentalismo

sentry [ˈsɛntrɪ] N sentinella

sentry duty N: **to be on ~** essere di sentinella

Seoul [səul] N Seul f

Sep. ABBR (= September) Sett.

separable [ˈsɛprəbl] ADJ separabile

separate ADJ [ˈsɛprɪt] separato(-a) ▶ VT [ˈsɛpəreɪt] separare ▶ VI [ˈsɛpəreɪt] separarsi; **~ from** separato da; **under ~ cover** (Comm) in plico a parte; **to ~ into** dividere in; see also **separates**

separately [ˈsɛprɪtlɪ] ADV separatamente

separates [ˈsɛprɪts] NPL (clothes) coordinati mpl

separation [sɛpəˈreɪʃən] N separazione f

Sept. ABBR (= September) sett., set.

September [sɛpˈtɛmbəʳ] N settembre m; see also **July**

septic ['sɛptɪk] ADJ settico(-a); (wound)
infettato(-a); **to go** ~ infettarsi
septicaemia, (US) **septicemia** [sɛptɪ'siːmɪə]
N setticemia
septic tank N fossa settica
sequel ['siːkwl] N conseguenza; (of story)
seguito; (of film) sequenza
sequence ['siːkwəns] N (series) serie f inv;
(order) ordine m; **in** ~ in ordine, di seguito;
~ **of tenses** concordanza dei tempi
sequential [sɪ'kwɛnʃəl] ADJ: ~ **access** (Comput)
accesso sequenziale
sequin ['siːkwɪn] N lustrino, paillette f inv
Serb [səːb] ADJ, N = **Serbian**
Serbia ['səːbɪə] N Serbia
Serbian ['səːbɪən] ADJ serbo(-a) ▶ N serbo(-a);
(Ling) serbo
Serbo-Croat ['səːbəu'krəuæt] N (Ling)
serbocroato
serenade [sɛrə'neɪd] N serenata ▶ VT fare la
serenata a
serene [sɪ'riːn] ADJ sereno(-a), calmo(-a)
serenity [sɪ'rɛnɪtɪ] N serenità, tranquillità
sergeant ['saːdʒənt] N sergente m; (Police)
brigadiere m
sergeant major N maresciallo
serial ['sɪərɪəl] N (Press) romanzo a puntate;
(Radio, TV) trasmissione f a puntate, serial m
inv ▶ CPD (number) di serie; (Comput) seriale
serialize ['sɪərɪəlaɪz] VT pubblicare a puntate;
trasmettere a puntate
serial killer N serial killer mf
serial number N numero di serie
series ['sɪəriːz] N (pl inv) serie f inv; (Publishing)
collana
serious ['sɪərɪəs] ADJ serio(-a), grave; **are you**
~ **(about it)?** parla sul serio?
seriously ['sɪərɪəslɪ] ADV seriamente; **he's** ~
rich (col: extremely) ha un casino di soldi; **to**
take sth/sb ~ prendere qc/qn sul serio
seriousness ['sɪərɪəsnɪs] N serietà, gravità
sermon ['səːmən] N sermone m
serrated [sɪ'reɪtɪd] ADJ seghettato(-a)
serum ['sɪərəm] N siero
servant ['səːvənt] N domestico(-a)
serve [səːv] VT (employer etc) servire, essere a
servizio di; (purpose) servire a; (customer, food,
meal) servire; (apprenticeship) fare; (prison term)
scontare ▶ VI (also Tennis) servire; (soldier etc)
prestare servizio; (be useful): **to** ~ **as/for/to do**
servire da/per/per fare ▶ N (Tennis) servizio;
are you being served? la stanno servendo?;
to ~ **on a committee/jury** far parte di un
comitato/una giuria; **it serves him right**
ben gli sta, se l'è meritata; **it serves my**
purpose fa al caso mio, serve al mio scopo
▶ **serve out, serve up** VT (food) servire
server ['səːvəʳ] N (Comput) server m inv
service ['səːvɪs] N servizio; (Aut: maintenance)

assistenza, revisione f; (Rel) funzione f ▶ VT
(car, washing machine) revisionare; **services**
NPL (BRIT: on motorway) stazione f di servizio;
(Mil): **the Services** le forze armate; **to be of**
~ **to sb, to do sb a** ~ essere d'aiuto a qn; **to**
put one's car in for (a) ~ portare la
macchina in officina per una revisione;
dinner ~ servizio da tavola; ~ **included/not**
included servizio compreso/escluso
serviceable ['səːvɪsəbl] ADJ pratico(-a), utile;
(usable, working) usabile
service area N (on motorway) area di servizio
service charge N (BRIT) servizio
service industries NPL settore m terziario
serviceman ['səːvɪsmən] N (irreg) militare m
service provider N (Comput) provider m inv
service station N stazione f di servizio
serviette [səːvɪ'ɛt] N (BRIT) tovagliolo
servile ['səːvaɪl] ADJ servile
session ['sɛʃən] N (sitting) seduta, sessione f;
(Scol) anno scolastico (or accademico); **to be**
in ~ essere in seduta
session musician N musicista mf di studio
set [sɛt] (pt, pp ~) N serie f inv; (of cutlery etc)
servizio; (Radio, TV) apparecchio; (Tennis) set
m inv; (group of people) mondo, ambiente m;
(Cine) scenario; (Theat: stage) scene fpl;
(: scenery) scenario; (Math) insieme m;
(Hairdressing) messa in piega ▶ ADJ (fixed)
stabilito(-a), determinato(-a); (ready)
pronto(-a) ▶ VT (place) posare, mettere;
(arrange) sistemare; (fix) fissare; (assign: task,
homework) dare, assegnare; (adjust) regolare;
(decide: rules etc) stabilire, fissare; (Typ)
comporre ▶ VI (sun) tramontare; (jam, jelly)
rapprendersi; (concrete) fare presa; **to be** ~
on doing essere deciso a fare; **to be all** ~ **to**
do sth essere pronto fare qc; **to be (dead)** ~
against essere completamente contrario a;
~ **in one's ways** abitudinario; **a novel** ~ **in**
Rome un romanzo ambientato a Roma; **to** ~
to music mettere in musica; **to** ~ **on fire**
dare fuoco a; **to** ~ **free** liberare; **to** ~ **sth**
going mettere in moto qc; **to** ~ **sail** prendere
il mare; **a** ~ **phrase** una frase fatta; **a** ~ **of**
false teeth una dentiera; **a** ~ **of dining-**
room furniture una camera da pranzo
▶ **set about** VT FUS (task) intraprendere,
mettersi a; **to** ~ **about doing sth** mettersi a
fare qc
▶ **set aside** VT mettere da parte
▶ **set back** VT (progress) ritardare; **to** ~ **back**
(by) (in time) mettere indietro (di); **a house** ~
back from the road una casa a una certa
distanza dalla strada
▶ **set down** VT (bus, train) lasciare
▶ **set in** VI (infection) svilupparsi;
(complications) intervenire; **the rain has** ~ **in**
for the day ormai pioverà tutto il giorno

S

▶ **set off** VI partire ▶ VT (*bomb*) far scoppiare; (*cause to start*) mettere in moto; (*show up well*) dare risalto a

▶ **set out** VI partire; (*aim*): **to ~ out to do** proporsi di fare ▶ VT (*arrange*) disporre; (*state*) esporre, presentare

▶ **set up** VT (*organization*) fondare, costituire; (*record*) stabilire; (*monument*) innalzare

setback ['sɛtbæk] N (*hitch*) contrattempo, inconveniente *m*; (*in health*) ricaduta

set menu N menù *m inv* fisso

set square N squadra

settee [sɛ'ti:] N divano, sofà *m inv*

setting ['sɛtɪŋ] N (*background*) ambiente *m*; (*of controls*) posizione *f*; (*of sun*) tramonto; (*scenery*) sfondo; (*of jewel*) montatura

setting lotion N fissatore *m*

settle ['sɛtl] VT (*argument, matter*) appianare; (*problem*) risolvere; (*pay: bill, account*) regolare, saldare; (*Med: calm*) calmare; (*: colonize: land*) colonizzare ▶ VI (*bird, dust etc*) posarsi; (*sediment*) depositarsi; (*also*: **settle down**) sistemarsi, stabilirsi; (*: become calmer*) calmarsi; **to ~ to sth** applicarsi a qc; **to ~ for sth** accontentarsi di qc; **to ~ on sth** decidersi per qc; **that's settled then** allora è deciso; **to ~ one's stomach** calmare il mal di stomaco

▶ **settle in** VI sistemarsi

▶ **settle up** VI: **to ~ up with sb** regolare i conti con qn

settlement ['sɛtlmənt] N (*payment*) pagamento, saldo; (*agreement*) accordo; (*colony*) colonia; (*village etc*) villaggio, comunità *f inv*; **in ~ of our account** (*Comm*) a saldo del nostro conto

settler ['sɛtləʳ] N colonizzatore(-trice)

setup ['sɛtʌp] N (*arrangement*) sistemazione *f*; (*situation*) situazione *f*; (*Comput*) setup *m inv*, installazione *f*

seven ['sɛvn] NUM sette

seventeen [sɛvn'ti:n] NUM diciassette

seventeenth [sɛvn'ti:nθ] NUM diciassettesimo(-a)

seventh ['sɛvnθ] NUM settimo(-a)

seventieth ['sɛvntɪɪθ] NUM settantesimo(-a)

seventy ['sɛvntɪ] NUM settanta

sever ['sɛvəʳ] VT recidere, tagliare; (*relations*) troncare

several ['sɛvərl] ADJ, PRON alcuni(-e), diversi(-e); **~ of us** alcuni di noi; **~ times** diverse volte

severance ['sɛvərəns] N (*of relations*) rottura

severance pay N indennità di licenziamento

severe [sɪ'vɪəʳ] ADJ severo(-a); (*serious*) serio(-a), grave; (*hard*) duro(-a); (*plain*) semplice, sobrio(-a)

severely [sɪ'vɪəlɪ] ADV (*gen*) severamente; (*wounded, ill*) gravemente

severity [sɪ'vɛrɪtɪ] N severità; gravità; (*of weather*) rigore *m*

sew [səu] (*pt* **sewed**, *pp* **sewn**) VT, VI cucire

▶ **sew up** VT ricucire; **it is all sewn up** (*fig*) è tutto apposto

sewage ['su:ɪdʒ] N acque *fpl* di scolo

sewage works N stabilimento per la depurazione dei liquami

sewer ['su:əʳ] N fogna

sewing ['səuɪŋ] N cucitura; cucito

sewing machine N macchina da cucire

sewn [səun] PP *of* **sew**

sex [sɛks] N sesso; **to have ~ with** avere rapporti sessuali con

sex act N atto sessuale

sex appeal N sex appeal *m inv*

sex education N educazione *f* sessuale

sexism ['sɛksɪzəm] N sessismo

sexist ['sɛksɪst] ADJ, N sessista (*mf*)

sex life N vita sessuale

sex object N oggetto sessuale; **to be treated like a ~** (*woman*) essere trattata da donna oggetto

sextet [sɛks'tɛt] N sestetto

sexual ['sɛksjuəl] ADJ sessuale; **~ assault** violenza carnale; **~ harassment** molestie *fpl* sessuali; **~ intercourse** rapporti *mpl* sessuali

sexuality [sɛksju'ælɪtɪ] N sessualità

sexy ['sɛksɪ] ADJ provocante, sexy *inv*

Seychelles [seɪ'ʃɛlz] NPL: **the ~** le Seicelle

SF N ABBR = **science fiction**

SG N ABBR (*US*) = **Surgeon General**

Sgt. ABBR (= *sergeant*) serg.

shabbiness ['ʃæbɪnɪs] N trasandatezza; squallore *m*; meschinità

shabby ['ʃæbɪ] ADJ trasandato(-a); (*building*) squallido(-a), malandato(-a); (*behaviour*) meschino(-a)

shack [ʃæk] N baracca, capanna

shackles ['ʃæklz] NPL ferri *mpl*, catene *fpl*

shade [ʃeɪd] N ombra; (*for lamp*) paralume *m*; (*of colour*) tonalità *f inv*; (*US: window shade*) veneziana; (*small quantity*): **a ~ (more/too large)** un po' (di più/troppo grande); **a ~ smaller** un tantino più piccolo ▶ VT ombreggiare, fare ombra a; **shades** NPL (*US: sunglasses*) occhiali *mpl* da sole; **in the ~** all'ombra

shadow ['ʃædəu] N ombra ▶ VT (*follow*) pedinare; **without** *or* **beyond a ~ of doubt** senz'ombra di dubbio

shadow cabinet N (*Brit Pol*) governo *m* ombra *inv*

shadowy ['ʃædəuɪ] ADJ ombreggiato(-a), ombroso(-a); (*dim*) vago(-a), indistinto(-a)

shady ['ʃeɪdɪ] ADJ ombroso(-a); (*fig: dishonest*) losco(-a), equivoco(-a)

shaft [ʃɑ:ft] N (*of arrow, spear*) asta; (*Aut, Tech*)

albero; (of mine) pozzo; (of lift) tromba; (of light) raggio; **ventilator** ~ condotto di ventilazione

shaggy ['ʃægɪ] ADJ ispido(-a)

shake [ʃeɪk] (pt **shook**, pp **shaken**) VT scuotere; (bottle, cocktail) agitare ▶ VI tremare ▶ N scossa; **to ~ one's head** (in refusal, dismay) scuotere la testa; **to ~ hands with sb** stringere or dare la mano a qn
▶ **shake off** VT scrollare (via); (fig) sbarazzarsi di
▶ **shake up** VT scuotere

shake-up ['ʃeɪkʌp] N riorganizzazione f drastica

shakily ['ʃeɪkɪlɪ] ADV (reply) con voce tremante; (walk) con passo malfermo; (write) con mano tremante

shaky ['ʃeɪkɪ] ADJ (hand, voice) tremante; (memory) labile; (knowledge) incerto(-a); (building) traballante

shale [ʃeɪl] N roccia scistosa

shall [ʃæl] AUX VB: **I ~ go** andrò; **~ I open the door?** apro io la porta?; **I'll get some, ~ I?** ne prendo un po', va bene?

shallot [ʃə'lɔt] N (BRIT) scalogna

shallow ['ʃæləu] ADJ poco profondo(-a); (fig) superficiale

sham [ʃæm] N finzione f, messinscena; (jewellery, furniture) imitazione f ▶ ADJ finto(-a) ▶ VT fingere, simulare

shambles ['ʃæmblz] N confusione f, baraonda, scompiglio; **the economy is (in) a complete** ~ l'economia è nel caos più totale

shambolic [ʃæm'bɔlɪk] ADJ (col) incasinato(-a)

shame [ʃeɪm] N vergogna ▶ VT far vergognare; **it is a ~ (that/to do)** è un peccato (che + sub/fare); **what a ~!** che peccato!; **to put sb/sth to ~** (fig) far sfigurare qn/qc

shamefaced ['ʃeɪmfeɪst] ADJ vergognoso(-a)

shameful ['ʃeɪmful] ADJ vergognoso(-a)

shameless ['ʃeɪmlɪs] ADJ sfrontato(-a); (immodest) spudorato(-a)

shampoo [ʃæm'pu:] N shampoo m inv ▶ VT fare lo shampoo a; ~ **and set** shampoo e messa in piega

shamrock ['ʃæmrɔk] N trifoglio (simbolo nazionale dell'Irlanda)

shandy ['ʃændɪ] N birra con gassosa

shan't [ʃɑ:nt] = **shall not**

shanty town ['ʃæntɪ-] N bidonville f inv

SHAPE [ʃeɪp] N ABBR (= Supreme Headquarters Allied Powers, Europe) supremo quartier generale delle Potenze Alleate in Europa

shape [ʃeɪp] N forma ▶ VT (clay, stone) dar forma a; (fig: ideas, character) formare; (: course of events) determinare, condizionare;

(statement) formulare; (sb's ideas) condizionare ▶ VI (also: **shape up**: events) andare, mettersi; (: person) cavarsela; **to take** ~ prendere forma; **in the ~ of a heart** a forma di cuore; **to get s.o. into** ~ rimettersi in forma; **I can't bear gardening in any ~ or form** detesto il giardinaggio d'ogni genere e specie

-shaped [ʃeɪpt] SUFFIX: **heart~** a forma di cuore

shapeless ['ʃeɪplɪs] ADJ senza forma, informe

shapely ['ʃeɪplɪ] ADJ ben proporzionato(-a)

share [ʃɛə'] N (thing received, contribution) parte f; (Comm) azione f ▶ VT dividere; (have in common) condividere, avere in comune; **to ~ out (among** or **between)** dividere (tra); **to ~ in** partecipare a

share capital N capitale m azionario

share certificate N certificato azionario

shareholder ['ʃɛəhəuldə'] N azionista mf

share index N listino di Borsa

shark [ʃɑːk] N squalo, pescecane m

sharp [ʃɑːp] ADJ (razor, knife) affilato(-a); (point) acuto(-a), acuminato(-a); (nose, chin) aguzzo(-a); (outline) netto(-a); (curve, bend) stretto(-a), accentuato(-a); (cold, pain) pungente; (voice) stridulo(-a); (person: quick-witted) sveglio(-a); (: unscrupulous) disonesto(-a); (Mus): **C** ~ do diesis ▶ N (Mus) diesis m inv ▶ ADV: **at 2 o'clock** ~ alle due in punto; **turn ~ left** giri tutto a sinistra; **to be ~ with sb** rimproverare qn; **look ~!** sbrigati!

sharpen ['ʃɑːpən] VT affilare; (pencil) fare la punta a; (fig) acuire

sharpener ['ʃɑːpnə'] N (also: **pencil sharpener**) temperamatite m inv; (also: **knife sharpener**) affilacoltelli m inv

sharp-eyed [ʃɑːp'aɪd] ADJ dalla vista acuta

sharpish ['ʃɑːpɪʃ] ADV (BRIT col: quickly) subito

sharply ['ʃɑːplɪ] ADV (abruptly) bruscamente; (clearly) nettamente; (harshly) duramente, aspramente

sharp-tempered [ʃɑːp'tempəd] ADJ irascibile

shatter ['ʃætə'] VT mandare in frantumi, frantumare; (fig: upset) distruggere; (: ruin) rovinare ▶ VI frantumarsi, andare in pezzi

shattered ['ʃætəd] ADJ (grief-stricken) sconvolto(-a); (exhausted) a pezzi, distrutto(-a)

shatterproof ['ʃætəpruːf] ADJ infrangibile

shave [ʃeɪv] VT radere, rasare ▶ VI radersi, farsi la barba ▶ N: **to have a** ~ farsi la barba

shaven ['ʃeɪvn] ADJ (head) rasato(-a), tonsurato(-a)

shaver ['ʃeɪvə'] N (also: **electric shaver**) rasoio elettrico

shaving ['ʃeɪvɪŋ] N (action) rasatura; **shavings** NPL (of wood etc) trucioli mpl

shaving brush N pennello da barba

shaving cream N crema da barba
shaving foam N = **shaving cream**
shaving soap N sapone *m* da barba
shawl [ʃɔːl] N scialle *m*
she [ʃiː] PRON ella, lei; **there ~ is** eccola;
~-**bear** orsa; ~-**cat** gatta; ~-**elephant**
elefantessa, *for ships, countries follow the gender
of your translation*
sheaf [ʃiːf] (*pl* **sheaves**) N covone *m*
shear [ʃɪəʳ] (*pt* **sheared**, *pp* **sheared** *or* **shorn**
[ʃɔːn]) VT (*sheep*) tosare
▶ **shear off** VI (*break off*) spezzarsi
shears [ʃɪəz] NPL (*for hedge*) cesoie *fpl*
sheath [ʃiːθ] N fodero, guaina; (*contraceptive*)
preservativo
sheathe [ʃiːð] VT rivestire; (*sword*)
rinfoderare
sheath knife N coltello (con fodero)
sheaves [ʃiːvz] NPL *of* **sheaf**
shed [ʃɛd] (*pt, pp* ~) N capannone *m* ▶ VT
(*leaves, fur etc*) perdere; (*tears, blood*) versare;
(*workers*) liberarsi di; **to ~ light on** (*problem,
mystery*) far luce su
she'd [ʃiːd] = **she had; she would**
sheen [ʃiːn] N lucentezza
sheep [ʃiːp] N (*pl inv*) pecora
sheepdog [ˈʃiːpdɔg] N cane *m* da pastore
sheep farmer N allevatore *m* di pecore
sheepish [ˈʃiːpɪʃ] ADJ vergognoso(-a),
timido(-a)
sheepskin [ˈʃiːpskɪn] N pelle *f* di pecora
sheepskin jacket N (giacca di) montone *m*
sheer [ʃɪəʳ] ADJ (*utter*) vero(-a) (e proprio(-a));
(*steep*) a picco, perpendicolare; (*transparent*)
trasparente; (*almost transparent*) sottile ▶ ADV
a picco; **by ~ chance** per puro caso
sheet [ʃiːt] N (*on bed*) lenzuolo; (*of paper*)
foglio; (*of glass*) lastra; (*of metal*) foglio,
lamina
sheet feed N (*on printer*) alimentazione *f* di
fogli
sheet lightning N lampo diffuso
sheet metal N lamiera
sheet music N fogli *mpl* di musica
sheik, sheikh [ʃeɪk] N sceicco
shelf [ʃɛlf] (*pl* **shelves** [ʃɛlvz]) N scaffale *m*,
mensola
shelf life N (*Comm*) durata di conservazione
shell [ʃɛl] N (*on beach*) conchiglia; (*of egg, nut
etc*) guscio; (*explosive*) granata; (*of building*)
scheletro, struttura ▶ VT (*peas*) sgranare;
(*Mil*) bombardare, cannoneggiare
▶ **shell out** VI (*col*): **to ~ out (for)** sganciare
soldi (per)
she'll [ʃiːl] = **she will; she shall**
shellfish [ˈʃɛlfɪʃ] N (*pl inv: crab etc*) crostaceo;
(*scallop etc*) mollusco; (*pl: as food*) crostacei;
molluschi
shellsuit [ˈʃɛlsuːt] N tuta di acetato

shelter [ˈʃɛltəʳ] N riparo, rifugio ▶ VT
riparare, proteggere; (*give lodging to*) dare
rifugio *or* asilo a ▶ VI ripararsi, mettersi al
riparo; **to take ~ (from)** mettersi al
riparo (da)
sheltered [ˈʃɛltəd] ADJ (*life*) ritirato(-a); (*spot*)
riparato(-a), protetto(-a)
shelve [ʃɛlv] VT (*fig*) accantonare, rimandare
shelves [ʃɛlvz] NPL *of* **shelf**
shelving [ˈʃɛlvɪŋ] N scaffalature *fpl*
shepherd [ˈʃɛpəd] N pastore *m* ▶ VT (*guide*)
guidare
shepherdess [ˈʃɛpədɪs] N pastora
shepherd's pie (BRIT) N timballo di carne
macinata e purè di patate
sherbet [ˈʃəːbət] N (BRIT: *powder*) polvere
effervescente al gusto di frutta; (US: *water ice*)
sorbetto
sheriff [ˈʃɛrɪf] (US) N sceriffo
sherry [ˈʃɛrɪ] N sherry *m inv*
she's [ʃiːz] = **she is; she has**
Shetland [ˈʃɛtlənd] N (*also*: **the Shetlands,
the Shetland Isles**) le (isole) Shetland
Shetland pony N pony *m inv* delle Shetland
shield [ʃiːld] N scudo; (*trophy*) scudetto;
(*protection*) schermo ▶ VT: **to ~ (from)**
riparare (da), proteggere (da *or* contro)
shift [ʃɪft] N (*change*) cambiamento; (*of
workers*) turno ▶ VT spostare, muovere;
(*remove*) rimuovere ▶ VI spostarsi, muoversi;
~ in demand (*Comm*) variazione *f* della
domanda; **the wind has shifted to the
south** il vento si è girato e soffia da sud
shift key N (*on typewriter*) tasto delle
maiuscole
shiftless [ˈʃɪftlɪs] ADJ fannullone(-a)
shift work N lavoro a squadre; **to do ~** fare i
turni
shifty [ˈʃɪftɪ] ADJ ambiguo(-a); (*eyes*)
sfuggente
Shiite [ˈʃiːaɪt] ADJ, N sciita *mf*
shilling [ˈʃɪlɪŋ] N (BRIT) scellino (*12 old pence; 20
in a pound*)
shilly-shally [ˈʃɪlɪʃælɪ] VI tentennare, esitare
shimmer [ˈʃɪməʳ] VI brillare, luccicare
shimmering [ˈʃɪmərɪŋ] ADJ (*gen*) luccicante,
scintillante; (*haze*) tremolante; (*satin etc*)
cangiante
shin [ʃɪn] N tibia ▶ VI: **to ~ up/down a tree**
arrampicarsi in cima a/scivolare giù da un
albero
shindig [ˈʃɪndɪg] N (*col*) festa chiassosa
shine [ʃaɪn] (*pt, pp* **shone**) N splendore *m*,
lucentezza ▶ VI (ri)splendere, brillare ▶ VT
far brillare, far risplendere; (*torch*): **to ~ sth
on** puntare qc verso
shingle [ˈʃɪŋgl] N (*on beach*) ciottoli *mpl*; (*on
roof*) assicella di copertura
shingles [ˈʃɪŋglz] N (*Med*) herpes zoster *m*

shining ['ʃaɪnɪŋ] ADJ (*surface, hair*) lucente; (*light*) brillante

shiny ['ʃaɪnɪ] ADJ lucente, lucido(-a)

ship [ʃɪp] N nave f ▶ VT trasportare (via mare); (*send*) spedire (via mare); (*load*) imbarcare, caricare; **on board ~** a bordo

shipbuilder ['ʃɪpbɪldə^r] N costruttore m navale

shipbuilding ['ʃɪpbɪldɪŋ] N costruzione f navale

ship chandler [-'tʃɑ:ndlə^r] N fornitore m marittimo

shipment ['ʃɪpmənt] N carico

shipowner ['ʃɪpəunə^r] N armatore m

shipper ['ʃɪpə^r] N spedizioniere m (marittimo)

shipping ['ʃɪpɪŋ] N (*ships*) naviglio; (*traffic*) navigazione f

shipping agent N agente m marittimo

shipping company N compagnia di navigazione

shipping lane N rotta (di navigazione)

shipping line N = **shipping company**

shipshape ['ʃɪpʃeɪp] ADJ in perfetto ordine

shipwreck ['ʃɪprɛk] N relitto m; (*event*) naufragio ▶ VT: **to be shipwrecked** naufragare, fare naufragio

shipyard ['ʃɪpjɑ:d] N cantiere m navale

shire ['ʃaɪə^r] N (BRIT) contea

shirk [ʃə:k] VT sottrarsi a, evitare

shirt [ʃə:t] N (*man's*) camicia; **in ~ sleeves** in maniche di camicia

shirty ['ʃə:tɪ] ADJ (BRIT col) incavolato(-a)

shit [ʃɪt] EXCL (col!) merda (!)

shiver ['ʃɪvə^r] N brivido ▶ VI rabbrividire, tremare

shoal [ʃəul] N (*of fish*) banco

shock [ʃɔk] N (*impact*) urto, colpo; (*Elec*) scossa; (*emotional*) colpo, shock m inv; (*Med*) shock ▶ VT colpire, scioccare; scandalizzare; **to give sb a ~** far venire un colpo a qn; **to be suffering from ~** essere in stato di shock; **it came as a ~ to hear that ...** è stata una grossa sorpresa sentire che ...

shock absorber N ammortizzatore m

shocker ['ʃɔkə^r] N: **it was a real ~** (col) è stata una vera bomba

shocking ['ʃɔkɪŋ] ADJ scioccante, traumatizzante; (*scandalous*) scandaloso(-a); (*very bad: weather, handwriting*) orribile; (: *results*) disastroso(-a)

shockproof ['ʃɔkpru:f] ADJ antiurto inv

shock therapy, shock treatment N (*Med*) shockterapia

shock wave N onda d'urto; (*fig: usually pl*) impatto *msg*

shod [ʃɔd] PT, PP of **shoe**

shoddy ['ʃɔdɪ] ADJ scadente

shoe [ʃu:] N scarpa; (*pt, pp* **shod** [ʃɔd]) N scarpa;

(*also:* **horseshoe**) ferro di cavallo; (: *brake shoe*) ganascia (del freno) ▶ VT (*horse*) ferrare

shoebrush ['ʃu:brʌʃ] N spazzola per le scarpe

shoehorn ['ʃu:hɔ:n] N calzante m

shoelace ['ʃu:leɪs] N stringa

shoemaker ['ʃu:meɪkə^r] N calzolaio

shoe polish N lucido per scarpe

shoeshop ['ʃu:ʃɔp] N calzoleria

shoestring ['ʃu:strɪŋ] N stringa (delle scarpe); **on a ~** (*fig: do sth*) con quattro soldi

shoetree ['ʃu:tri:] N forma per scarpe

shone [ʃɔn] PT, PP of **shine**

shonky ['ʃɔŋkɪ] ADJ (AUSTRALIA, NEW ZEALAND col: *untrustworthy*) sospetto(-a)

shoo [ʃu:] EXCL sciò!, via! ▶ VT (*also:* **shoo away, shoo off**) cacciare (via)

shook [ʃuk] PT of **shake**

shoot [ʃu:t] (*pt, pp* **shot** [ʃɔt]) N (*on branch, seedling*) germoglio; (*shooting party*) partita di caccia; (*competition*) gara di tiro ▶ VT (*game:* BRIT) cacciare, andare a caccia di; (*person*) sparare a; (*execute*) fucilare; (*film*) girare ▶ VI (*Football*) sparare, tirare (forte); **to ~ (at)** (*with gun*) sparare (a), fare fuoco (su); (*with bow*) tirare (su); **to ~ past sb** passare vicino a qn come un fulmine; **to ~ in/out** entrare/uscire come una freccia

▶ **shoot down** VT (*plane*) abbattere

▶ **shoot up** VI (*fig*) salire alle stelle

shooting ['ʃu:tɪŋ] N (*shots*) sparatoria; (*murder*) uccisione f (a colpi d'arma da fuoco); (*Hunting*) caccia; (*Cine*) riprese fpl

shooting range N poligono (di tiro), tirassegno

shooting star N stella cadente

shop [ʃɔp] N negozio; (*workshop*) officina ▶ VI (*also:* **go shopping**) fare spese; **repair ~** officina di riparazione; **to talk ~** (*fig*) parlare di lavoro

▶ **shop around** VI fare il giro dei negozi

shopaholic ['ʃɔpə'hɔlɪk] N (col) maniaco(-a) dello shopping

shop assistant N (BRIT) commesso(-a)

shop floor N (BRIT fig) operai mpl, maestranze fpl

shopkeeper ['ʃɔpki:pə^r] N negoziante mf, bottegaio(-a)

shoplift ['ʃɔplɪft] VI taccheggiare

shoplifter ['ʃɔplɪftə^r] N taccheggiatore(-trice)

shoplifting ['ʃɔplɪftɪŋ] N taccheggio

shopper ['ʃɔpə^r] N compratore(-trice)

shopping ['ʃɔpɪŋ] N (*goods*) spesa, acquisti mpl

shopping bag N borsa per la spesa

shopping cart N (US Comput: *shopping trolley*) carrello

shopping centre, (US) shopping center N centro commerciale

shopping mall N centro commerciale

shopping trolley N (BRIT) carrello del supermercato
shop-soiled ['ʃɒpsɔɪld] ADJ sciupato(-a) a forza di stare in vetrina
shop steward N (BRIT Industry) rappresentante m sindacale
shop window N vetrina
shore [ʃɔːʳ] N (of sea) riva, spiaggia; (of lake) riva ▶ VT: **to ~ (up)** puntellare; **on ~** a riva
shore leave N (Naut) franchigia
shorn [ʃɔːn] PP of **shear**
short [ʃɔːt] ADJ (not long) corto(-a); (soon finished) breve; (person) basso(-a); (curt) brusco(-a), secco(-a); (insufficient) insufficiente ▶ N (also: **short film**) cortometraggio; **it is ~ for** è l'abbreviazione or il diminutivo di; **a ~ time ago** poco tempo fa; **in the ~ term** nell'immediato futuro; **to be ~ of sth** essere a corto di or mancare di qc; **to run ~ of sth** rimanere senza qc; **to be in ~ supply** scarseggiare; **I'm 3 ~** me ne mancano 3; **in ~** in breve; **~ of doing** a meno che non si faccia; **everything ~ of** tutto fuorché; **to cut ~** (speech, visit) accorciare, abbreviare; (person) interrompere; **to fall ~ of** venire meno a; non soddisfare; **to stop ~** fermarsi di colpo; **to stop ~ of** non arrivare fino a; see also **shorts**
shortage ['ʃɔːtɪdʒ] N scarsezza, carenza
shortbread ['ʃɔːtbred] N biscotto di pasta frolla
short-change [ʃɔːt'tʃeɪndʒ] VT: **to ~ sb** imbrogliare qn sul resto
short-circuit [ʃɔːt'səːkɪt] N cortocircuito ▶ VT cortocircuitare ▶ VI fare cortocircuito
shortcoming ['ʃɔːtkʌmɪŋ] N difetto
shortcrust pastry ['ʃɔːtkrʌst-], **short pastry** ['ʃɔːt-] N (BRIT) pasta frolla
shortcut ['ʃɔːtkʌt] N scorciatoia
shorten ['ʃɔːtn] VT accorciare, ridurre
shortening ['ʃɔːtnɪŋ] N grasso per pasticceria
shortfall ['ʃɔːtfɔːl] N deficit m inv
shorthand ['ʃɔːthænd] N (BRIT) stenografia; **to take sth down in ~** stenografare qc
shorthand notebook N (BRIT) bloc-notes m inv per stenografia
shorthand typist N (BRIT) stenodattilografo(-a)
short list N (BRIT: for job) rosa dei candidati
short-lived ['ʃɔːt'lɪvd] ADJ effimero(-a), di breve durata
shortly ['ʃɔːtlɪ] ADV fra poco
shortness ['ʃɔːtnɪs] N brevità; insufficienza
shorts [ʃɔːts] NPL (also: **a pair of shorts**) i calzoncini
short-sighted [ʃɔːt'saɪtɪd] ADJ (BRIT) miope; (fig) poco avveduto(-a)
short-sleeved ['ʃɔːtsliːvd] ADJ a maniche corte

short-staffed [ʃɔːt'stɑːft] ADJ a corto di personale
short story N racconto, novella
short-tempered [ʃɔːt'tempəd] ADJ irascibile
short-term ['ʃɔːttəːm] ADJ (effect) di or a breve durata; (borrowing) a breve scadenza
short time N (Industry): **to work ~, be on ~** essere or lavorare a orario ridotto
short wave N (Radio) onde fpl corte
shot [ʃɒt] PT, PP of **shoot** ▶ N sparo, colpo; (shotgun pellets) pallottole fpl; (person) tiratore m; (try) prova; (Football) tiro; (injection) iniezione f; (Phot) foto f inv; **like a ~** come un razzo; (very readily) immediatamente; **to fire a ~ at sb/sth** sparare un colpo a qn/qc; **to have a ~ at sth/doing sth** provarci con qc/a fare qc; **a big ~** (col) un pezzo grosso, un papavero; **to get ~ of sb/sth** (col) sbarazzarsi di qn/qc
shotgun ['ʃɒtɡʌn] N fucile m da caccia
should [ʃud] AUX VB: **I ~ go now** dovrei andare ora; **he ~ be there now** dovrebbe essere arrivato ora; **I ~ go if I were you** se fossi in lei andrei; **I ~ like to** mi piacerebbe; **~ he phone ...** se telefonasse ...
shoulder ['ʃəuldəʳ] N spalla; **hard ~** corsia d'emergenza ▶ VT (fig) addossarsi, prendere sulle proprie spalle; **to look over one's ~** guardarsi alle spalle; **to rub shoulders with sb** (fig) essere a contatto con qn; **to give sb the cold ~** (fig) trattare qn con freddezza
shoulder bag N borsa a tracolla
shoulder blade N scapola
shoulder strap N bretella, spallina
shouldn't ['ʃudnt]= **should not**
shout [ʃaut] N urlo, grido ▶ VT gridare ▶ VI (also: **shout out**) urlare, gridare; **to give sb a ~** chiamare qn gridando
▶ **shout down** VT zittire gridando
shouting ['ʃautɪŋ] N urli mpl
shouting match N (col) vivace scambio di opinioni
shove [ʃʌv] VT spingere; (col: put): **to ~ sth in** ficcare qc in ▶ N spintone m; **he shoved me out of the way** mi ha spinto da parte
▶ **shove off** VI (Naut) scostarsi
shovel ['ʃʌvl] N pala ▶ VT spalare
show [ʃəu] (pt **showed**, pp **shown** [ʃəun]) N (of emotion) dimostrazione f, manifestazione f; (semblance) apparenza; (exhibition) mostra, esposizione f; (Theat, Cine) spettacolo; (Comm, Tech) salone m, fiera ▶ VT far vedere, mostrare; (courage etc) dimostrare, dar prova di; (exhibit) esporre ▶ VI vedersi, essere visibile; **to ~ sb to his seat/to the door** accompagnare qn al suo posto/alla porta; **to ~ a profit/loss** (Comm) registrare un utile/una perdita; **it just goes to ~ that ...** il che sta a dimostrare che ...; **to ask for a ~ of**

hands chiedere che si voti per alzata di mano; **to be on** ~ essere esposto; **it's just for** ~ è solo per far scena; **who's running the** ~ **here?** (col) chi è il padrone qui?
▶ **show in** VT (person) far entrare
▶ **show off** VI (pej) esibirsi, mettersi in mostra ▶ VT (display) mettere in risalto; (pej) mettere in mostra
▶ **show out** VT (person) accompagnare alla porta
▶ **show up** VI (stand out) essere ben visibile; (col: turn up) farsi vedere ▶ VT mettere in risalto; (unmask) smascherare
showbiz ['ʃəubɪz] N (col) = **show business**
show business N industria dello spettacolo
showcase ['ʃəukeɪs] N vetrina, bacheca
showdown ['ʃəudaun] N prova di forza
shower ['ʃauəʳ] N doccia; (rain) acquazzone m; (of stones etc) pioggia; (US: party) festa in cui si fanno regali alla persona festeggiata (di fidanzamento ecc) ▶ VI fare la doccia ▶ VT: **to ~ sb with** (gifts, abuse etc) coprire qn di; (missiles) lanciare contro qn una pioggia di; **to have** or **take a** ~ fare la doccia
shower cap N cuffia da doccia
shower gel N gel m doccia inv
showerproof ['ʃauəpruːf] ADJ impermeabile
showery ['ʃauərɪ] ADJ (weather) con piogge intermittenti
showground ['ʃəugraund] N terreno d'esposizione
showing ['ʃəuɪŋ] N (of film) proiezione f
show jumping N concorso ippico (di salto ad ostacoli)
showman ['ʃəumən] N (irreg) (at fair, circus) impresario; (fig) attore m
showmanship ['ʃəumənʃɪp] N abilità d'impresario
shown [ʃəun] PP of **show**
show-off ['ʃəuɔf] N (col: person) esibizionista mf
showpiece ['ʃəupiːs] N (of exhibition) pezzo forte; **that hospital is a** ~ è un ospedale modello
showroom ['ʃəurum] N sala d'esposizione
show trial N processo a scopo dimostrativo (spesso ideologico)
showy ['ʃəuɪ] ADJ vistoso(-a), appariscente
shrank [ʃræŋk] PT of **shrink**
shrapnel ['ʃræpnl] N shrapnel m
shred [ʃred] N (gen pl) brandello; (fig: of truth, evidence) briciolo ▶ VT fare a brandelli; (Culin) sminuzzare, tagliuzzare; (documents) distruggere, sminuzzare
shredder ['ʃredəʳ] N (for documents, papers) distruttore m di documenti, sminuzzatrice f
shrew [ʃruː] N (Zool) toporagno; (fig: pej: woman) strega
shrewd [ʃruːd] ADJ astuto(-a), scaltro(-a)

shrewdness ['ʃruːdnɪs] N astuzia
shriek [ʃriːk] N strillo ▶ VT, VI strillare
shrift [ʃrɪft] N: **to give sb short** ~ sbrigare qn
shrill [ʃrɪl] ADJ acuto(-a), stridulo(-a), stridente
shrimp [ʃrɪmp] N gamberetto
shrine [ʃraɪn] N reliquario; (place) santuario
shrink [ʃrɪŋk] (pt **shrank** [ʃræŋk], pp **shrunk** [ʃrʌŋk]) VI restringersi; (fig) ridursi; (also: **shrink away**) ritrarsi ▶ VT (wool) far restringere ▶ N (col, pej) psicanalista mf; **to ~ from doing sth** rifuggire dal fare qc
shrinkage ['ʃrɪŋkɪdʒ] N restringimento
shrink-wrap ['ʃrɪŋkræp] VT confezionare con plastica sottile
shrivel ['ʃrɪvl], **shrivel up** VT raggrinzare, avvizzire ▶ VI raggrinzirsi, avvizzire
shroud [ʃraud] N lenzuolo funebre ▶ VT: **shrouded in mystery** avvolto(-a) nel mistero
Shrove Tuesday ['ʃrəuv-] N martedì m grasso
shrub [ʃrʌb] N arbusto
shrubbery ['ʃrʌbərɪ] N arbusti mpl
shrug [ʃrʌg] N scrollata di spalle ▶ VT, VI: **to ~ (one's shoulders)** alzare le spalle, fare spallucce
▶ **shrug off** VT passare sopra a; (cold, illness) sbarazzarsi di
shrunk [ʃrʌŋk] PP of **shrink**
shrunken ['ʃrʌŋkən] ADJ rattrappito(-a)
shudder ['ʃʌdəʳ] N brivido ▶ VI rabbrividire
shuffle ['ʃʌfl] VT (cards) mescolare; **to ~ (one's feet)** strascicare i piedi
shun [ʃʌn] VT sfuggire, evitare
shunt [ʃʌnt] VT (Rail: direct) smistare; (: divert) deviare ▶ VI: **to ~ (to and fro)** fare la spola
shunting yard N fascio di smistamento
shush [ʃuʃ] EXCL zitto(-a)!
shut [ʃʌt] (pt, pp ~) VT chiudere ▶ VI chiudersi, chiudere
▶ **shut down** VT, VI chiudere definitivamente
▶ **shut off** VT (stop: power) staccare; (: water) chiudere; (: engine) spegnere; (isolate) isolare
▶ **shut out** VT (person, noise, cold) non far entrare; (block: view) impedire, bloccare; (: memory) scacciare
▶ **shut up** VI (col: keep quiet) stare zitto(-a), fare silenzio ▶ VT (close) chiudere; (silence) far tacere
shutdown ['ʃʌtdaun] N chiusura
shutter ['ʃʌtəʳ] N imposta; (Phot) otturatore m
shuttle ['ʃʌtl] N spola, navetta; (space shuttle) navetta (spaziale); (also: **shuttle service**) servizio m navetta inv ▶ VI (vehicle, person) fare la spola ▶ VT (to and fro: passengers) portare (avanti e indietro)
shuttlecock ['ʃʌtlkɔk] N volano
shuttle diplomacy N frequenti mediazioni fpl diplomatiche

S

shy [ʃaɪ] ADJ timido(-a) ▶ VI: **to ~ away from doing sth** (fig) rifuggire dal fare qc; **to fight ~ of** tenersi alla larga da; **to be ~ of doing sth** essere restio a fare qc

shyness ['ʃaɪnɪs] N timidezza

Siam [saɪˈæm] N Siam m

Siamese [saɪəˈmiːz] ADJ: **~ cat** gatto siamese; **~ twins** fratelli mpl (or sorelle fpl) siamesi

Siberia [saɪˈbɪərɪə] N Siberia

sibling ['sɪblɪŋ] N (formal) fratello/sorella

Sicilian [sɪˈsɪlɪən] ADJ, N siciliano(-a)

Sicily ['sɪsɪlɪ] N Sicilia

sick [sɪk] ADJ (ill) malato(-a); (humour) macabro(-a); **to be ~** (vomiting) vomitare; **to feel ~** avere la nausea; **to be ~ of** (fig) averne abbastanza di; **a ~ person** un malato; **to be (off) ~** essere assente perché malato; **to fall** or **take ~** ammalarsi

sickbag ['sɪkbæg] N sacchetto (da usarsi in caso di malessere)

sick bay N infermeria

sick building syndrome N malattia causata da mancanza di ventilazione e luce naturale

sicken ['sɪkn] VT nauseare ▶ VI: **to be sickening for sth** (cold, flu etc) covare qc

sickening ['sɪknɪŋ] ADJ (fig) disgustoso(-a), rivoltante

sickle ['sɪkl] N falcetto

sick leave N congedo per malattia

sickle-cell anaemia ['sɪklsɛl-] N anemia drepanocitica

sickly ['sɪklɪ] ADJ malaticcio(-a); (causing nausea) nauseante

sickness ['sɪknɪs] N malattia; (vomiting) vomito

sickness benefit N indennità di malattia

sick pay N sussidio per malattia

sickroom ['sɪkruːm] N stanza di malato

side [saɪd] N (gen) lato; (of person, animal) fianco; (of lake) riva; (face, surface: gen) faccia; (: of paper) facciata; (fig: aspect) aspetto, lato; (team: Sport) squadra; (: Pol etc) parte f ▶ CPD (door, entrance) laterale ▶ VI: **to ~ with sb** parteggiare per qn, prendere le parti di qn; **by the ~ of** a fianco di; (road) sul ciglio di; **~ by ~** fianco a fianco; **to take sides (with)** schierarsi (con); **the right/wrong ~** il dritto/rovescio; **from ~ to ~** da una parte all'altra; **~ of beef** quarto di bue

sideboard ['saɪdbɔːd] N credenza

sideboards ['saɪdbɔːdz], (US) **sideburns** ['saɪdbəːnz] NPL (whiskers) basette fpl

sidecar ['saɪdkɑːʳ] N sidecar m inv

side dish N contorno

side drum N (Mus) piccolo tamburo

side effect N (Med) effetto collaterale

sidekick ['saɪdkɪk] N (col) compagno(-a)

sidelight ['saɪdlaɪt] N (Aut) luce f di posizione

sideline ['saɪdlaɪn] N (Sport) linea laterale;

(fig) attività secondaria

sidelong ['saɪdlɔŋ] ADJ obliquo(-a); **to give a ~ glance at sth** guardare qc con la coda dell'occhio

side order N contorno (pietanza)

side plate N piattino

side road N strada secondaria

sidesaddle ['saɪdsædl] ADV all'amazzone

side show N attrazione f

sidestep ['saɪdstɛp] VT (question) eludere; (problem) scavalcare ▶ VI (Boxing etc) spostarsi di lato

side street N traversa

sidetrack ['saɪdtræk] VT (fig) distrarre

sidewalk ['saɪdwɔːk] N (US) marciapiede m

sideways ['saɪdweɪz] ADV (move) di lato, di fianco; (look) con la coda dell'occhio

siding ['saɪdɪŋ] N (Rail) binario di raccordo

sidle ['saɪdl] VI: **to ~ up (to)** avvicinarsi furtivamente (a)

SIDS N (= sudden infant death syndrome) = **cot death**

siege [siːdʒ] N assedio; **to lay ~ to** porre l'assedio a

siege economy N economia da stato d'assedio

Sierra Leone [sɪˈɛrəliˈəun] N Sierra Leone f

sieve [sɪv] N setaccio ▶ VT setacciare

sift [sɪft] VT passare al crivello; (fig) vagliare ▶ VI: **to ~ through** esaminare minuziosamente

sigh [saɪ] N sospiro ▶ VI sospirare

sight [saɪt] N (faculty) vista; (spectacle) spettacolo; (on gun) mira ▶ VT avvistare; **in ~** in vista; **on ~** a vista; **out of ~** non visibile; **at first ~** a prima vista; **to catch ~ of sth/sb** scorgere qc/qn; **to lose ~ of sb/sth** perdere di vista qn/qc; **to set one's sights on sth/on doing sth** mirare a qc/a fare qc; **at ~** a vista; **I know her by ~** la conosco di vista

sighted ['saɪtɪd] ADJ che ha il dono della vista; **partially ~** parzialmente cieco

sightseeing ['saɪtsiːɪŋ] N giro turistico; **to go ~** visitare una località

sightseer ['saɪtsiːəʳ] N turista mf

sign [saɪn] N segno; (with hand etc) segno, gesto; (notice) insegna, cartello; (road sign) segnale m ▶ VT firmare; (player) ingaggiare; **as a ~ of** in segno di; **it's a good/bad ~** è buon/brutto segno; **to show signs/no ~ of doing sth** accennare/non accennare a fare qc; **plus/minus ~** segno del più/meno; **to ~ one's name** firmare, apporre la propria firma

▶ **sign away** VT (rights etc) cedere (con una firma)

▶ **sign for** VT FUS (item) firmare per l'accettazione di

▶ **sign in** VI firmare il registro (all'arrivo)

▶ **sign off** VI (*Radio*, *TV*) chiudere le trasmissioni

▶ **sign on** VI (*Mil etc*: *enlist*) arruolarsi; (*as unemployed*) iscriversi sulla lista (dell'ufficio di collocamento); (*begin work*) prendere servizio; (*enrol*): **to ~ on for a course** iscriversi a un corso ▶ VT (*Mil*) arruolare; (*employee*) assumere

▶ **sign out** VI firmare il registro (alla partenza)

▶ **sign over** VT: **to ~ sth over to sb** cedere qc con scrittura legale a qn

▶ **sign up** (*Mil*) VT arruolare; (*player*) ingaggiare; (*recruits*) reclutare ▶ VI arruolarsi; (*for course*) iscriversi

signal ['sɪɡnl] N segnale *m* ▶ VT (*person*) fare segno a; (*message*) comunicare per mezzo di segnali ▶ VI (*Aut*) segnalare, mettere la freccia; **to ~ to sb (to do sth)** far segno a qn (di fare qc); **to ~ a left/right turn** (*Aut*) segnalare un cambiamento di direzione a sinistra/destra

signal box N (*Rail*) cabina di manovra

signalman ['sɪɡnlmən] N (*irreg*) (*Rail*) deviatore *m*

signatory ['sɪɡnətərɪ] N firmatario(-a)

signature ['sɪɡnətʃəʳ] N firma

signature tune N sigla musicale

signet ring ['sɪɡnət-] N anello con sigillo

significance [sɪɡ'nɪfɪkəns] N (*of remark*) significato; (*of event*) importanza; **that is of no ~** ciò non ha importanza

significant [sɪɡ'nɪfɪkənt] ADJ (*improvement, amount*) notevole; (*discovery, event*) importante; (*evidence, smile*) significativo(-a); **it is ~ that ...** è significativo che ...

significantly [sɪɡ'nɪfɪkəntlɪ] ADV (*smile*) in modo eloquente; (*improve, increase*) considerevolmente, decisamente

signify ['sɪɡnɪfaɪ] VT significare

sign language N linguaggio dei muti

signpost ['saɪnpəust] N cartello indicatore

Sikh [siːk] ADJ, N sikh *mf*

silage ['saɪlɪdʒ] N insilato

silence ['saɪlns] N silenzio ▶ VT far tacere, ridurre al silenzio

silencer ['saɪlənsəʳ] N (*on gun*, BRIT *Aut*) silenziatore *m*

silent ['saɪlnt] ADJ silenzioso(-a); (*film*) muto(-a); **to keep** *or* **remain ~** tacere, stare zitto(-a)

silently ['saɪlntlɪ] ADV silenziosamente, in silenzio

silent partner N (*Comm*) socio accomandante

silhouette [sɪluːˈɛt] N silhouette *f inv* ▶ VT: **to be silhouetted against** stagliarsi contro

silicon ['sɪlɪkən] N silicio

silicon chip ['sɪlɪkən-] N chip *m inv* (al silicio)

silicone ['sɪlɪkəun] N silicone *m*

silk [sɪlk] N seta ▶ CPD di seta

silky ['sɪlkɪ] ADJ di seta, come la seta

sill [sɪl] N (*windowsill*) davanzale *m*; (*Aut*) predellino

silly ['sɪlɪ] ADJ stupido(-a), sciocco(-a); **to do something ~** fare una sciocchezza

silo ['saɪləu] N silo

silt [sɪlt] N limo

silver ['sɪlvəʳ] N argento; (*money*) monete da 5, 10, 20 o 50 pence; (*also*: **silverware**) argenteria ▶ CPD d'argento

silver foil, (BRIT) **silver paper** N carta argentata, (carta) stagnola

silver-plated [sɪlvəˈpleɪtɪd] ADJ argentato(-a)

silversmith ['sɪlvəsmɪθ] N argentiere *m*

silverware ['sɪlvəwɛəʳ] N argenteria, argento

silvery ['sɪlvərɪ] ADJ (*colour*) argenteo(-a); (*sound*) argentino(-a)

SIM card ['sɪm-] N (*Tel*: = *Subscriber Identity Module card*) SIM card *f inv*

similar ['sɪmɪləʳ] ADJ: **~ (to)** simile (a)

similarity [sɪmɪˈlærɪtɪ] N somiglianza, rassomiglianza

similarly ['sɪmɪləlɪ] ADV (*in a similar way*) allo stesso modo; (*as is similar*) così pure

simile ['sɪmɪlɪ] N similitudine *f*

simmer ['sɪməʳ] VI cuocere a fuoco lento

▶ **simmer down** VI (*fig*: *col*) calmarsi

simper ['sɪmpəʳ] VI fare lo(la) smorfioso(-a)

simpering ['sɪmpərɪŋ] ADJ lezioso(-a), smorfioso(-a)

simple ['sɪmpl] ADJ semplice; **the ~ truth** la pura verità

simple interest N (*Math*, *Comm*) interesse *m* semplice

simple-minded [sɪmplˈmaɪndɪd] ADJ sempliciotto(-a)

simpleton ['sɪmpltən] N semplicione(-a), sempliciotto(-a)

simplicity [sɪmˈplɪsɪtɪ] N semplicità

simplification [sɪmplɪfɪˈkeɪʃən] N semplificazione *f*

simplify ['sɪmplɪfaɪ] VT semplificare

simply ['sɪmplɪ] ADV semplicemente

simulate ['sɪmjuleɪt] VT fingere, simulare

simulation [sɪmjuˈleɪʃən] N simulazione *f*

simultaneous [sɪmələˈteɪnɪəs] ADJ simultaneo(-a)

simultaneously [sɪmələˈteɪnɪəslɪ] ADV simultaneamente, contemporaneamente

sin [sɪn] N peccato ▶ VI peccare

Sinai ['saɪnaɪ] N Sinai *m*

since [sɪns] ADV da allora ▶ PREP da ▶ CONJ (*time*) da quando; (*because*) poiché, dato che; **~ then, ever ~** da allora; **~ Monday** da lunedì; **(ever) ~ I arrived** (fin) da quando sono arrivato

sincere [sɪnˈsɪəʳ] ADJ sincero(-a)

sincerely [sɪnˈsɪəlɪ] ADV sinceramente;

S

Yours ~ (*at end of letter*) distinti saluti
sincerity [sɪn'sɛrɪtɪ] N sincerità
sine [saɪn] N (*Math*) seno
sinew ['sɪnju:] N tendine *m*; **sinews** NPL
(*muscles*) muscoli *mpl*
sinful ['sɪnful] ADJ peccaminoso(-a)
sing [sɪŋ] (*pt* **sang**, *pp* **sung**) VT, VI cantare
Singapore [sɪŋgə'pɔːʳ] N Singapore *f*
singe [sɪndʒ] VT bruciacchiare
singer ['sɪŋəʳ] N cantante *mf*
Singhalese [sɪŋə'liːz] ADJ = **Sinhalese**
singing ['sɪŋɪŋ] N (*of person, bird*) canto; (*of
kettle, bullet, in ears*) fischio
single ['sɪŋgl] ADJ solo(-a), unico(-a);
(*unmarried: man*) celibe; (: *woman*) nubile; (*not
double*) semplice ▶ N (*BRIT: also:* **single ticket**)
biglietto di (sola) andata; (*record*) 45 giri *m inv*;
not a ~ one was left non ne è rimasto
nemmeno uno; **every ~ day** tutti i santi
giorni; *see also* **singles**
▶ **single out** VT scegliere; (*distinguish*)
distinguere
single bed N letto a una piazza
single-breasted ['sɪŋglbrɛstɪd] ADJ a un
petto
Single European Market N: **the ~** il Mercato
Unico
single file N: **in ~** in fila indiana
single-handed [sɪŋgl'hændɪd] ADV senza
aiuto, da solo(-a)
single-minded [sɪŋgl'maɪndɪd] ADJ tenace,
risoluto(-a)
single parent N ragazzo padre/ragazza
madre; genitore *m* separato; **~ family**
famiglia monoparentale
single room N camera singola
singles ['sɪŋglz] NPL (*Tennis*) singolo; (*US:
single people*) single *mf*
singles bar N (*esp US*) bar *m inv* per single
single-sex school ['sɪŋgl'sɛks-] N (*for boys*)
scuola maschile; (*for girls*) scuola femminile
singlet ['sɪŋglɪt] N canottiera
singly ['sɪŋglɪ] ADV separatamente
singsong ['sɪŋsɔŋ] ADJ (*tone*) cantilenante
▶ N (*songs*): **to have a ~** farsi una cantata
singular ['sɪŋgjuləʳ] ADJ (*Ling*) singolare;
(*unusual*) strano(-a), singolare ▶ N (*Ling*)
singolare *m*; **in the feminine ~** al
femminile singolare
singularly ['sɪŋgjuləlɪ] ADV stranamente
Sinhalese [sɪnhə'liːz] ADJ singalese
sinister ['sɪnɪstəʳ] ADJ sinistro(-a)
sink [sɪŋk] (*pt* **sank**, *pp* **sunk**) N lavandino,
acquaio ▶ VT (*ship*) (fare) affondare, colare a
picco; (*foundations*) scavare; (*piles etc*): **to ~ sth
into** conficcare qc in ▶ VI affondare, andare
a fondo; (*ground etc*) cedere, avvallarsi; **my
heart sank** mi sentii venir meno; **he sank
into a chair/the mud** sprofondò in una

poltrona/nel fango
▶ **sink in** VI penetrare; **it took a long time
to ~ in** ci ho (*or* ha *etc*) messo molto a capirlo
sinking ['sɪŋkɪŋ] ADJ: **that ~ feeling** una
stretta allo stomaco
sinking fund N (*Comm*) fondo
d'ammortamento
sink unit N blocco lavello
sinner ['sɪnəʳ] N peccatore(-trice)
Sinn Féin [ʃɪn'feɪn] N *movimento separatista
irlandese*
sinuous ['sɪnjuəs] ADJ sinuoso(-a)
sinus ['saɪnəs] N (*Anat*) seno
sip [sɪp] N sorso ▶ VT sorseggiare
siphon ['saɪfən] N sifone *m* ▶ VT (*funds*)
trasferire
▶ **siphon off** VT travasare (con un sifone)
sir [səʳ] N signore *m*; **S~ John Smith** Sir John
Smith; **yes ~** sì, signore; **Dear S~** (*in letter*)
Egregio signor (*followed by name*); **Dear Sirs**
Spettabile ditta
siren ['saɪərn] N sirena
sirloin ['səːlɔɪn] N controfiletto
sirloin steak N bistecca di controfiletto
sirocco [sɪ'rɔkəu] N scirocco
sisal ['saɪsəl] N sisal *f inv*
sissy ['sɪsɪ] N (*col*) femminuccia
sister ['sɪstəʳ] N sorella; (*nun*) suora; (*BRIT:
nurse*) infermiera *f* caposala *inv* ▶ CPD:
~ organization organizzazione *f* affine;
~ ship nave *f* gemella
sister-in-law ['sɪstərɪnlɔː] N cognata
sit [sɪt] (*pt, pp* **sat**) VI sedere, sedersi; (*dress etc*)
cadere; (*assembly*) essere in seduta; (*for
painter*) posare ▶ VT (*exam*) sostenere, dare; **to
~ on a committee** far parte di una
commissione
▶ **sit about, sit around** VI star seduto(-a)
(senza far nulla)
▶ **sit back** VI (*in seat*) appoggiarsi allo
schienale
▶ **sit down** VI sedersi; **to be sitting down**
essere seduto(-a)
▶ **sit in** VI: **to ~ in on a discussion** assistere
ad una discussione
▶ **sit on** VT FUS (*jury, committee*) far parte di
▶ **sit up** VI tirarsi su a sedere; (*not go to bed*)
stare alzato(-a) fino a tardi
sitcom ['sɪtkɔm] N ABBR (*TV: = situation comedy*)
sceneggiato a episodi (*comico*)
sit-down ['sɪtdaun] ADJ: **~ strike** sciopero
bianco (con occupazione della fabbrica); **a ~
meal** un pranzo
site [saɪt] N posto; (*also:* **building site**)
cantiere *m*; (: *Comput*) sito ▶ VT situare
sit-in ['sɪtɪn] N (*demonstration*) sit-in *m inv*
siting ['saɪtɪŋ] N ubicazione *f*
sitter ['sɪtəʳ] N (*for painter*) modello(-a); (*also:*
baby sitter) babysitter *mf*

sitting ['sɪtɪŋ] N (of assembly etc) seduta; (in canteen) turno

sitting member N (Pol) deputato(-a) in carica

sitting room N soggiorno

sitting tenant N (BRIT) attuale affittuario

situate ['sɪtjueɪt] VT collocare

situated ['sɪtjueɪtɪd] ADJ situato(-a)

situation [sɪtju'eɪʃən] N situazione f; (job) lavoro; (location) posizione f; **"situations vacant/wanted"** (BRIT) "offerte/domande di impiego"

situation comedy N (Theat) commedia di situazione

six [sɪks] NUM sei

six-pack ['sɪkspæk] N (esp US) confezione f da sei

sixteen [sɪks'ti:n] NUM sedici

sixteenth [sɪks'ti:nθ] NUM sedicesimo(-a)

sixth [sɪksθ] NUM sesto(-a) ▶ N: **the upper/ lower ~** (BRIT Scol) l'ultimo/il penultimo anno di scuola superiore

sixth form N (BRIT) ultimo biennio delle scuole superiori

sixth-form college N istituto che offre corsi di preparazione all'esame di maturità per ragazzi dai 16 ai 18 anni

sixtieth ['sɪkstɪɪθ] NUM sessantesimo(-a) ▶ PRON (in series) sessantesimo(-a); (fraction) sessantesimo

sixty ['sɪkstɪ] NUM sessanta

size [saɪz] N dimensioni fpl; (of clothing) taglia, misura; (of shoes) numero; (glue) colla; **I take ~ 14 in a dress** = porto la 44 di vestiti; **I'd like the small/large ~** (of soap powder etc) vorrei la confezione piccola/grande
▶ **size up** VT giudicare, farsi un'idea di

sizeable ['saɪzəbl] ADJ considerevole

sizzle ['sɪzl] VI sfrigolare

SK ABBR (CANADA) = **Saskatchewan**

skate [skeɪt] N pattino; (fish: pl inv) razza ▶ VI pattinare
▶ **skate over, skate around** VT (problem, issue) prendere alla leggera, prendere sottogamba

skateboard ['skeɪtbɔ:d] N skateboard m inv

skateboarding N skateboard m inv

skater ['skeɪtə^r] N pattinatore(-trice)

skating ['skeɪtɪŋ] N pattinaggio

skating rink N pista di pattinaggio

skeleton ['skɛlɪtn] N scheletro

skeleton key N passe-partout m inv

skeleton staff N personale m ridotto

skeptic etc ['skɛptɪk] (US) = **sceptic** etc

skeptical ['skɛptɪkl] (US) ADJ = **sceptical**

sketch [skɛtʃ] N (drawing) schizzo, abbozzo; (Theat etc) scenetta comica, sketch m inv ▶ VT abbozzare, schizzare

sketch book N album m inv per schizzi

sketch pad N blocco per schizzi

sketchy ['skɛtʃɪ] ADJ incompleto(-a), lacunoso(-a)

skew [skju:] N (BRIT): **on the ~** di traverso

skewer ['skju:ə^r] N spiedo

ski [ski:] N sci m inv ▶ VI sciare

ski boot N scarpone m da sci

skid [skɪd] N slittamento; (sideways slip) sbandamento ▶ VI slittare; sbandare; **to go into a ~** slittare; sbandare

skid mark N segno della frenata

skier ['ski:ə^r] N sciatore(-trice)

skiing ['ski:ɪŋ] N sci m

ski instructor N maestro(-a) di sci

ski jump N (ramp) trampolino; (event) salto con gli sci

skilful, (US)**skillful** ['skɪlful] ADJ abile

skilfully, (US)**skillfully** ['skɪlfəlɪ] ADV abilmente

ski lift N sciovia

skill [skɪl] N abilità f inv, capacità f inv; (technique) tecnica

skilled [skɪld] ADJ esperto(-a); (worker) qualificato(-a), specializzato(-a)

skillet ['skɪlɪt] N padella

skillful ['skɪlful] ADJ (US) = **skilful**

skillfully ['skɪlfəlɪ] ADV (US) = **skilfully**

skim [skɪm] VT (milk) scremare; (soup) schiumare; (glide over) sfiorare ▶ VI: **to ~ through** (fig) scorrere, dare una scorsa a

skimmed milk, (US)**skim milk** N latte m scremato

skimp [skɪmp] VI: **to ~ on** (work) fare alla carlona; (cloth etc) lesinare su

skimpy ['skɪmpɪ] ADJ misero(-a); striminzito(-a); frugale

skin [skɪn] N pelle f; (of fruit, vegetable) buccia; (on pudding, paint) crosta ▶ VT (fruit etc) sbucciare; (animal) scuoiare, spellare; **wet** or **soaked to the ~** bagnato fino al midollo

skin cancer N cancro alla pelle

skin-deep [skɪn'di:p] ADJ superficiale

skin diver N subacqueo

skin diving N nuoto subacqueo

skinflint ['skɪnflɪnt] N taccagno(-a), tirchio(-a)

skin graft N innesto epidermico

skinhead ['skɪnhɛd] N skinhead mf

skinny ['skɪnɪ] ADJ molto magro(-a), pelle e ossa inv

skin test N prova di reazione cutanea

skintight ['skɪntaɪt] ADJ aderente

skip [skɪp] N saltello; (BRIT) balzo; (container) benna ▶ VI saltare; (with rope) saltare la corda ▶ VT (pass over) saltare; **to ~ school** (US) marinare la scuola

ski pants NPL pantaloni mpl da sci

ski pass N ski pass m inv

ski pole N racchetta (da sci)

skipper ['skɪpə^r] N (Naut, Sport) capitano

S

skipping rope ['skɪpɪŋ-], (US) **skip rope** N corda per saltare

ski resort N località f inv sciistica

skirmish ['skə:mɪʃ] N scaramuccia

skirt [skə:t] N gonna, sottana ▶ VT fiancheggiare, costeggiare

skirting board ['skə:tɪŋ-] N (BRIT) zoccolo

ski run N pista (da sci)

ski slope N pista da sci

ski suit N tuta da sci

skit [skɪt] N parodia; scenetta satirica

ski tow N = **ski lift**

skittle ['skɪtl] N birillo; **skittles** N (game) (gioco dei) birilli mpl

skive [skaɪv] VI (BRIT col) fare il lavativo

skulk [skʌlk] VI muoversi furtivamente

skull [skʌl] N cranio, teschio

skullcap ['skʌlkæp] N (worn by Jews) zucchetto; (worn by Pope) papalina

skunk [skʌŋk] N moffetta

sky [skaɪ] N cielo; **to praise sb to the skies** portare alle stelle qn

sky-blue [skaɪ'blu:] ADJ azzurro(-a), celeste

sky-diving ['skaɪdaɪvɪŋ] N caduta libera, paracadutismo acrobatico

sky-high [skaɪ'haɪ] ADV (throw) molto in alto ▶ ADJ (col) esorbitante; **prices have gone ~** (col) i prezzi sono saliti alle stelle

skylark ['skaɪlɑ:k] N allodola

skylight ['skaɪlaɪt] N lucernario

skyline ['skaɪlaɪn] N (horizon) orizzonte m; (of city) profilo

sky marshal N agente mf a bordo

Skype® [skaɪp] (Internet, Tel) N Skype® m ▶ VT: **to ~ sb** chiamare qn su Skype

skyscraper ['skaɪskreɪpəʳ] N grattacielo

slab [slæb] N lastra; (of wood) tavola; (of meat, cheese) fetta

slack [slæk] ADJ (loose) allentato(-a); (slow) lento(-a); (careless) negligente; (Comm: market) stagnante; (: demand) scarso(-a); (period) morto(-a) ▶ N (in rope etc) parte f non tesa; **business is ~** l'attività commerciale è scarsa; see also **slacks**

slacken ['slækn], **slacken off** VI rallentare, diminuire ▶ VT allentare; (pressure) diminuire

slacks [slæks] NPL (trousers) pantaloni mpl

slag [slæg] N scorie fpl

slag heap N ammasso di scorie

slain [sleɪn] PP of **slay**

slake [sleɪk] VT (one's thirst) spegnere

slalom ['slɑ:ləm] N slalom m

slam [slæm] VT (door) sbattere; (throw) scaraventare; (criticize) stroncare ▶ VI sbattere

slammer ['slæməʳ] N: **the ~** (col) la gattabuia

slander ['slɑ:ndəʳ] N calunnia; (Law) diffamazione f ▶ VT calunniare; diffamare

slanderous ['slɑ:ndrəs] ADJ calunnioso(-a); diffamatorio(-a)

slang [slæŋ] N gergo, slang m

slanging match ['slæŋɪŋ-] N (BRIT col) rissa verbale

slant [slɑ:nt] N pendenza, inclinazione f; (fig) angolazione f, punto di vista

slanted ['slɑ:ntɪd] ADJ tendenzioso(-a)

slanting ['slɑ:ntɪŋ] ADJ in pendenza, inclinato(-a)

slap [slæp] N manata, pacca; (on face) schiaffo ▶ VT dare una manata a; schiaffeggiare ▶ ADV (directly) in pieno; **it fell ~ in the middle** cadde proprio nel mezzo; **~ a coat of paint on it** dagli una mano di vernice

slapdash ['slæpdæʃ] ADJ abborracciato(-a)

slaphead ['slæphɛd] N (BRIT col) imbecille mf

slapstick ['slæpstɪk] N (comedy) farsa grossolana

slap-up ['slæpʌp] ADJ (BRIT): **a ~ meal** un pranzo (or una cena) coi fiocchi

slash [slæʃ] VT tagliare; (face) sfregiare; (fig: prices) ridurre drasticamente, tagliare

slat [slæt] N (of wood) stecca

slate [sleɪt] N ardesia; (piece) lastra di ardesia ▶ VT (fig: criticize) stroncare, distruggere

slaughter ['slɔ:təʳ] N (of animals) macellazione f; (of people) strage f, massacro ▶ VT (animal) macellare; (people) trucidare, massacrare

slaughterhouse ['slɔ:təhaus] N macello, mattatoio

Slav [slɑ:v] ADJ, N slavo(-a)

slave [sleɪv] N schiavo(-a) ▶ VI (also: **slave away**) lavorare come uno schiavo; **to ~ (away) at sth/at doing sth** ammazzarsi di fatica or sgobbare per qc/per fare qc

slave driver N (col, pej) schiavista mf

slave labour N lavoro degli schiavi; (fig): **we're just ~ here** siamo solamente sfruttati qui dentro

slaver ['slævəʳ] VI (dribble) sbavare

slavery ['sleɪvərɪ] N schiavitù f

Slavic ['slævɪk] ADJ slavo(-a)

slavish ['sleɪvɪʃ] ADJ servile; pedissequo(-a)

slavishly ['sleɪvɪʃlɪ] ADV (copy) pedissequamente

Slavonic [slə'vɔnɪk] ADJ slavo(-a)

slay [sleɪ] (pt **slew** [slu:], pp **slain** [sleɪn]) VT (formal) uccidere

sleazy ['sli:zɪ] ADJ trasandato(-a)

sled [slɛd] (US) = **sledge**

sledge [slɛdʒ] N slitta

sledgehammer ['slɛdʒhæməʳ] N martello da fabbro

sleek [sli:k] ADJ (hair, fur) lucido(-a), lucente; (car, boat) slanciato(-a), affusolato(-a)

sleep [sli:p] (pt, pp **slept** [slɛpt]) N sonno ▶ VI dormire ▶ VT: **we can ~ 4** abbiamo 4 posti

letto, possiamo alloggiare 4 persone;
to have a good night's ~ farsi una bella
dormita; **to go to** ~ addormentarsi; **to ~
lightly** avere il sonno leggero; **to put to ~**
(*patient*) far addormentare; (*animal:
euphemism: kill*) abbattere; **to ~ with sb**
(*euphemism: have sex*) andare a letto con qn
  ▶ **sleep in** VI (*lie late*) alzarsi tardi; (*oversleep*)
  dormire fino a tardi
  ▶ **sleep together** VI (*have sex*) andare a letto
  insieme
sleeper ['sli:pə^r] N (*person*) dormiente *mf*;
(*BRIT: Rail: on track*) traversina; (: *train*) treno di
vagoni letto
sleepily ['sli:pɪlɪ] ADV con aria assonnata
sleeping ['sli:pɪŋ] ADJ addormentato(-a)
sleeping bag N sacco a pelo
sleeping car N vagone *m* letto *inv*, carrozza *f*
letto *inv*
sleeping partner N (*BRIT Comm*) = **silent
partner**
sleeping pill N sonnifero
sleeping sickness N malattia del sonno
sleepless ['sli:plɪs] ADJ (*person*) insonne;
a ~ night una notte in bianco
sleeplessness ['sli:plɪsnɪs] N insonnia
sleepover ['sli:pəʊvə^r] N *il dormire a casa di
amici, usato in riferimento a bambini*
sleepwalk ['sli:pwɔ:k] VI camminare nel
sonno; (*as a habit*) essere sonnambulo(-a)
sleepwalker ['sli:pwɔ:kə^r] N sonnambulo(-a)
sleepy ['sli:pɪ] ADJ assonnato(-a),
sonnolento(-a); (*fig*) addormentato(-a);
to be *or* **feel** ~ avere sonno
sleet [sli:t] N nevischio
sleeve [sli:v] N manica; (*of record*) copertina
sleeveless ['sli:vlɪs] ADJ (*garment*) senza
maniche
sleigh [sleɪ] N slitta
sleight [slaɪt] N: ~ **of hand** gioco di destrezza
slender ['slɛndə^r] ADJ snello(-a), sottile; (*not
enough*) scarso(-a), esiguo(-a)
slept [slɛpt] PT, PP of **sleep**
sleuth [slu:θ] N (*col*) segugio
slew [slu:] VI (*BRIT: also:* **slew round**) girare
  ▶ PT *of* **slay**
slice [slaɪs] N fetta ▶ VT affettare, tagliare a
fette; **sliced bread** pane *m* a cassetta
slick [slɪk] ADJ (*skilful*) brillante; (*insincere*)
untuoso(-a), falso(-a) ▶ N (*also:* **oil slick**)
chiazza di petrolio
slid [slɪd] PT, PP of **slide**
slide [slaɪd] (*pt, pp* **slid** [slɪd]) N scivolone *m*;
(*in playground*) scivolo; (*Phot*) diapositiva;
(*microscope slide*) vetrino; (*BRIT: also:* **hair slide**)
fermaglio (per capelli); (*in prices*) caduta ▶ VT
far scivolare ▶ VI scivolare; **to let things ~**
(*fig*) lasciare andare tutto, trascurare tutto
slide projector N proiettore *m* per diapositive

slide rule N regolo calcolatore
slide show N (*Comput*) diaporama *m*
sliding ['slaɪdɪŋ] ADJ (*door*) scorrevole; ~ **roof**
(*Aut*) capotte *f inv*
sliding scale N scala mobile
slight [slaɪt] ADJ (*slim*) snello(-a), sottile; (*frail*)
delicato(-a), fragile; (*trivial*) insignificante;
(*small*) piccolo(-a) ▶ N offesa, affronto ▶ VT
(*offend*) offendere, fare un affronto a; **the
slightest** il minimo (*or* la minima); **not in
the slightest** affatto, neppure per sogno
slightly ['slaɪtlɪ] ADV lievemente, un po';
~ **built** esile
slim [slɪm] ADJ magro(-a), snello(-a) ▶ VI
dimagrire; fare *or* seguire) una dieta
dimagrante
slime [slaɪm] N limo, melma; viscidume *m*
slimming ['slɪmɪŋ] ADJ (*diet, pills*) dimagrante;
(*food*) ipocalorico(-a)
slimy ['slaɪmɪ] ADJ (*also fig: person*) viscido(-a);
(*covered with mud*) melmoso(-a)
sling [slɪŋ] (*pt, pp* **slung** [slʌŋ]) N (*Med*) fascia
al collo; (*for baby*) marsupio ▶ VT lanciare,
tirare; **to have one's arm in a** ~ avere un
braccio al collo
slink [slɪŋk] (*pt, pp* **slunk**) VI: **to ~ away, ~ off**
svignarsela
slinky ['slɪŋkɪ] ADJ (*clothing*) aderente,
attillato(-a)
slip [slɪp] N scivolata, scivolone *m*; (*mistake*)
errore *m*, sbaglio; (*underskirt*) sottoveste *f*;
(*paper*) foglietto, tagliando, scontrino ▶ VT
(*slide*) far scivolare ▶ VI (*slide*) scivolare;
(*decline*) declinare; **to ~ into/out of** (*move
smoothly*) scivolare in/fuori da; **to give sb the
~** sfuggire qn; **a ~ of paper** un foglietto; **a ~
of the tongue** un lapsus linguae; **to ~ sth
on/off** infilarsi/togliersi qc; **to let a chance
~ by** lasciarsi scappare un'occasione; **it
slipped from her hand** le sfuggì di mano
  ▶ **slip away** VI svignarsela
  ▶ **slip in** VT introdurre casualmente
  ▶ **slip out** VI uscire furtivamente
  ▶ **slip up** VI sbagliarsi
slip-on ['slɪpɔn] ADJ (*gen*) comodo(-a) da
mettere; (*shoes*) senza allacciatura
slipped disc ['slɪpt-] N spostamento delle
vertebre
slipper ['slɪpə^r] N pantofola
slippery ['slɪpərɪ] ADJ scivoloso(-a); **it's** ~ si
scivola
slip road N (*BRIT: to motorway*) rampa di accesso
slipshod ['slɪpʃɔd] ADJ sciatto(-a),
trasandato(-a)
slip-up ['slɪpʌp] N granchio (*fig*)
slipway ['slɪpweɪ] N scalo di costruzione
slit [slɪt] (*pt, pp* ~) N fessura, fenditura; (*cut*)
taglio; (*tear*) strappo ▶ VT fendere; tagliare;
to ~ sb's throat tagliare la gola a qn

S

787

slither ['slɪðəʳ] vɪ scivolare, sdrucciolare

sliver ['slɪvəʳ] ɴ (of glass, wood) scheggia; (of cheese, sausage) fettina

slob [slɒb] ɴ (col) sciattone(-a)

slog [slɒg] (Bʀɪᴛ) ɴ faticata ▶ vɪ lavorare con accanimento, sgobbare

slogan ['sləʊgən] ɴ motto, slogan m inv

slop [slɒp] vɪ (also: **slop over**) traboccare; versarsi ▶ vᴛ spandere; versare ▶ ɴᴘʟ: **slops** acqua sporca; sbobba

slope [sləʊp] ɴ pendio; (side of mountain) versante m; (ski slope) pista; (of roof) pendenza; (of floor) inclinazione f ▶ vɪ: **to ~ down** declinare; **to ~ up** essere in salita

sloping ['sləʊpɪŋ] ᴀᴅᴊ inclinato(-a)

sloppy ['slɒpɪ] ᴀᴅᴊ (work) tirato(-a) via; (appearance) sciatto(-a); (film etc) sdolcinato(-a)

slosh [slɒʃ] vɪ (col): **to ~ about** or **around** (person) sguazzare; (liquid) guazzare

sloshed [slɒʃt] ᴀᴅᴊ (col: drunk) sbronzo(-a)

slot [slɒt] ɴ fessura; (fig: in timetable, Radio, TV) spazio ▶ vᴛ: **to ~ into** infilare in

sloth [sləʊθ] ɴ (vice) pigrizia, accidia; (Zool) bradipo

slot machine ɴ (Bʀɪᴛ: vending machine) distributore m automatico; (for amusement) slot-machine f inv

slot meter ɴ contatore m a gettoni

slouch [slaʊtʃ] vɪ (when walking) camminare dinoccolato(-a); **she was slouched in a chair** era sprofondata in una poltrona ▶ **slouch about, slouch around** vɪ (laze) oziare

Slovak ['sləʊvæk] ᴀᴅᴊ slovacco(-a) ▶ ɴ slovacco(-a); (Ling) slovacco; **the ~ Republic** la Repubblica Slovacca

Slovakia [sləʊ'vækɪə] ɴ Slovacchia

Slovakian [sləʊ'vækɪən] ᴀᴅᴊ, ɴ = **Slovak**

Slovene ['sləʊviːn] ᴀᴅᴊ sloveno(-a) ▶ ɴ sloveno(-a); (Ling) sloveno

Slovenia [sləʊ'viːnɪə] ɴ Slovenia

Slovenian [sləʊ'viːnɪən] ᴀᴅᴊ, ɴ = **Slovene**

slovenly ['slʌvənlɪ] ᴀᴅᴊ sciatto(-a), trasandato(-a)

slow [sləʊ] ᴀᴅᴊ lento(-a); (watch): **to be ~** essere indietro ▶ ᴀᴅᴠ lentamente ▶ vᴛ, vɪ (also: **slow down**, **slow up**) rallentare; **"~"** (road sign) "rallentare"; **at a ~ speed** a bassa velocità; **to be ~ to act/decide** essere lento ad agire/a decidere; **my watch is 20 minutes ~** il mio orologio è indietro di 20 minuti; **business is ~** (Comm) gli affari procedono a rilento; **to go ~** (driver) andare piano; (in industrial dispute) fare uno sciopero bianco

slow-acting ['sləʊ'æktɪŋ] ᴀᴅᴊ che agisce lentamente, ad azione lenta

slowly ['sləʊlɪ] ᴀᴅᴠ lentamente; **to drive ~** andare piano

slow motion ɴ: **in ~** al rallentatore

slowness ['sləʊnɪs] ɴ lentezza

sludge [slʌdʒ] ɴ fanghiglia

slug [slʌg] ɴ lumaca; (bullet) pallottola

sluggish ['slʌgɪʃ] ᴀᴅᴊ lento(-a); (business, market, sales) stagnante, fiacco(-a)

sluice [sluːs] ɴ chiusa ▶ vᴛ: **to ~ down** or **out** lavare (con abbondante acqua)

slum [slʌm] ɴ catapecchia

slumber ['slʌmbəʳ] ɴ sonno

slump [slʌmp] ɴ crollo, caduta; (economic) depressione f, crisi f inv ▶ vɪ crollare; **he was slumped over the wheel** era curvo sul volante

slung [slʌŋ] ᴘᴛ, ᴘᴘ of **sling**

slunk [slʌŋk] ᴘᴛ, ᴘᴘ of **slink**

slur [sləːʳ] ɴ pronuncia indistinta; (stigma) diffamazione f, calunnia; (Mus) legatura; (smear): **~ (on)** macchia (su) ▶ vᴛ pronunciare in modo indistinto; **to cast a ~ on sb** calunniare qn

slurp [sləːp] vᴛ, vɪ bere rumorosamente ▶ ɴ rumore fatto bevendo

slurred [sləːd] ᴀᴅᴊ (pronunciation) inarticolato(-a), disarticolato(-a)

slush [slʌʃ] ɴ neve f mista a fango

slush fund ɴ fondi mpl neri

slushy ['slʌʃɪ] ᴀᴅᴊ (snow) che si scioglie; (Bʀɪᴛ fig) sdolcinato(-a)

slut [slʌt] ɴ donna trasandata, sciattona

sly [slaɪ] ᴀᴅᴊ (smile, remark) sornione(-a); (person) furbo(-a), scaltro(-a); **on the ~** di soppiatto

SM ɴ ᴀʙʙʀ (= sadomasochism) sadomasochismo

smack [smæk] ɴ (slap) pacca; (on face) schiaffo ▶ vᴛ schiaffeggiare; (child) picchiare ▶ vɪ: **to ~ of** puzzare di; **to ~ one's lips** fare uno schiocco con le labbra

smacker ['smækəʳ] ɴ (col: kiss) bacio; (: Bʀɪᴛ: pound note) sterlina; (: US: dollar bill) dollaro

small [smɔːl] ᴀᴅᴊ piccolo(-a); (in height) basso(-a); (letter) minuscolo(-a) ▶ ɴ: **the ~ of the back** le reni; **to get** or **grow smaller** (stain, town) rimpicciolire; (debt, organization, numbers) ridursi; **to make smaller** (amount, income) ridurre; (garden, object, garment) rimpicciolire; **in the ~ hours** alle ore piccole; **a ~ shopkeeper** un piccolo negoziante

small ads ɴᴘʟ (Bʀɪᴛ) piccoli annunci mpl

small arms ɴᴘʟ armi fpl portatili or leggere

small business ɴ piccola impresa

small change ɴ moneta, spiccioli mpl

smallholder ['smɔːlhəʊldəʳ] ɴ (Bʀɪᴛ) piccolo proprietario

smallholding ['smɔːlhəʊldɪŋ] ɴ (Bʀɪᴛ) piccola tenuta

smallish ['smɔːlɪʃ] ᴀᴅᴊ piccolino(-a)

small-minded [smɔːl'maɪndɪd] ᴀᴅᴊ meschino(-a)

smallpox ['smɔːlpɔks] N vaiolo
small print N caratteri mpl piccoli; (on document) parte scritta in piccolo
small-scale ['smɔːlskeɪl] ADJ (map, model) in scala ridotta; (business, farming) modesto(-a)
small talk N chiacchiere fpl
small-time ['smɔːltaɪm] ADJ (col) da poco; **a ~ thief** un ladro di polli
small-town ['smɔːltaun] ADJ (pej) provinciale, di paese
smarmy ['smɑːmɪ] ADJ (BRIT pej) untuoso(-a), strisciante
smart [smɑːt] ADJ elegante; (fashionable) alla moda; (clever) intelligente; (quick) sveglio(-a) ▶ VI bruciare; **the ~ set** il bel mondo; **to look ~** essere elegante; **my eyes are smarting** mi bruciano gli occhi
smartcard ['smɑːtkɑːd] N smartcard f inv, carta intelligente
smarten up ['smɑːtn-] VI farsi bello(-a) ▶ VT (people) fare bello(-a); (things) abbellire
smash [smæʃ] N (also: **smash-up**) scontro, collisione f; (: sound) fracasso; (: smash hit) successone m ▶ VT frantumare, fracassare; (opponent) annientare, schiacciare; (hopes) distruggere; (Sport: record) battere ▶ VI frantumarsi, andare in pezzi
  ▶ **smash up** VT (car) sfasciare; (room) distruggere
smash-hit [smæʃˈhɪt] N successone m
smashing ['smæʃɪŋ] ADJ (col) favoloso(-a), formidabile
smattering ['smætərɪŋ] N: **a ~ of** un'infarinatura di
SME N PL ABBR (= small and medium-sized enterprises) PMI fpl inv (= Piccole e Medie Imprese)
smear [smɪər] N macchia; (Med) striscio; (insult) calunnia ▶ VT ungere; (make dirty) sporcare; (fig) denigrare, diffamare; **his hands were smeared with oil/ink** aveva le mani sporche di olio/inchiostro
smear campaign N campagna diffamatoria
smear test N (BRIT Med) Pap-test m inv
smell [smɛl] (pt, pp smelt [smɛlt], smelled [smɛld]) N odore m; (sense) olfatto, odorato ▶ VT sentire (l')odore di ▶ VI (food etc): **to ~ (of)** avere odore (di); (pej) puzzare, avere un cattivo odore; **it smells good** ha un buon odore
smelly ['smɛlɪ] ADJ puzzolente
smelt [smɛlt] PT, PP of **smell** ▶ VT (ore) fondere
smile [smaɪl] N sorriso ▶ VI sorridere
smiling ['smaɪlɪŋ] ADJ sorridente
smirk [smɜːk] N sorriso furbo; sorriso compiaciuto
smith [smɪθ] N fabbro
smithy ['smɪðɪ] N fucina
smitten ['smɪtn] ADJ: **~ with** colpito(-a) da
smock [smɔk] N grembiule m, camice m

smog [smɔg] N smog m
smoke [sməuk] N fumo ▶ VT, VI fumare; **to have a ~** fumarsi una sigaretta; **do you ~?** fumi?; **to go up in ~** (house etc) bruciare, andare distrutto dalle fiamme; (fig) andare in fumo
smoke alarm N rivelatore f di fumo
smoked [sməukt] ADJ (bacon, glass) affumicato(-a)
smokeless fuel ['sməuklɪs-] N carburante m che non da fumo
smokeless zone N (BRIT) zona dove sono vietati gli scarichi di fumo
smoker ['sməukər] N (person) fumatore(-trice); (Rail) carrozza per fumatori
smoke screen N cortina fumogena or di fumo; (fig) copertura
smoke shop N (US) tabaccheria
smoking ['sməukɪŋ] N fumo; **"no ~"** (sign) "vietato fumare"; **he's given up ~** ha smesso di fumare
smoking compartment,(US) **smoking car** N carrozza (per) fumatori
smoky ['sməukɪ] ADJ fumoso(-a); (taste, surface) affumicato(-a)
smolder ['sməuldər] VI (US) = **smoulder**
smoochy ['smuːtʃɪ] ADJ (col) romantico(-a)
smooth [smuːð] ADJ liscio(-a); (sauce) omogeneo(-a); (flavour, whisky) amabile; (cigarette) leggero(-a); (movement) regolare; (person) melliflu(o)(-a); (landing, takeoff, flight) senza scosse ▶ VT lisciare, spianare; (also: **smooth out**: difficulties) appianare
  ▶ **smooth over** VT: **to ~ things over** (fig) sistemare le cose
smoothly ['smuːðlɪ] ADV (easily) liscio; **everything went ~** tutto andò liscio
smother ['smʌðər] VT soffocare
smoulder,(US) **smolder** ['sməuldər] VI covare sotto la cenere
SMS N ABBR (= short message service) SMS m (servizio)
SMS message N SMS m inv, messaggino
smudge [smʌdʒ] N macchia; sbavatura ▶ VT imbrattare, sporcare
smug [smʌg] ADJ soddisfatto(-a), compiaciuto(-a)
smuggle ['smʌgl] VT contrabbandare; **to ~ in/out** (goods etc) far entrare/uscire di contrabbando
smuggler ['smʌglər] N contrabbandiere(-a)
smuggling ['smʌglɪŋ] N contrabbando
smut [smʌt] N (grain of soot) granello di fuliggine; (mark) segno nero; (in conversation etc) sconcezze fpl
smutty ['smʌtɪ] ADJ (fig) osceno(-a), indecente
snack [snæk] N spuntino; **to have a ~** fare uno spuntino

S

snack bar N tavola calda, snack bar *m inv*

snag [snæg] N intoppo, ostacolo imprevisto

snail [sneɪl] N chiocciola

snake [sneɪk] N serpente *m*

snap [snæp] N (*sound*) schianto, colpo secco; (*photograph*) istantanea; (*game*) rubamazzo ▶ ADJ improvviso(-a) ▶ VT (*far*) schioccare; (*break*) spezzare di netto; (*photograph*) scattare un'istantanea di ▶ VI spezzarsi con un rumore secco; (*fig: person*) crollare; **to ~ at sb** rivolgersi a qn con tono brusco; (*dog*) cercare di mordere qn; **to ~ open/shut** aprirsi/chiudersi di scatto; **to ~ one's fingers at** (*fig*) infischiarsi di; **a cold ~** (*of weather*) un'improvvisa ondata di freddo
  ▶ **snap off** VT (*break*) schiantare
  ▶ **snap up** VT afferrare

snap fastener N bottone *m* automatico

snappy ['snæpɪ] ADJ rapido(-a); **make it ~!** (*col: hurry up*) sbrigati!, svelto!

snapshot ['snæpʃɒt] N istantanea

snare [snɛəʳ] N trappola

snarl [snɑːl] VI ringhiare ▶ VT: **to get snarled up** (*wool, plans*) ingarbugliarsi; (*traffic*) intasarsi

snatch [snætʃ] N (*fig*) furto; (*BRIT: small amount*): **snatches of** frammenti *mpl* di ▶ VT strappare (con violenza); (*steal*) rubare ▶ VI: **don't ~!** non strappare le cose di mano!; **to ~ a sandwich** mangiarsi in fretta un panino; **to ~ some sleep** riuscire a dormire un po'
  ▶ **snatch up** VT raccogliere in fretta

snazzy ['snæzɪ] ADJ (*col: clothes*) sciccoso(-a)

sneak [sniːk] (*US pt* **snuck**) VI: **to ~ in/out** entrare/uscire di nascosto ▶ N spione(-a); **to ~ up on sb** avvicinarsi quatto quatto a qn ▶ VT: **to ~ a look at sth** guardare di sottecchi qc

sneakers ['sniːkəz] NPL scarpe *fpl* da ginnastica

sneaking ['sniːkɪŋ] ADJ: **to have a ~ feeling/ suspicion that ...** avere la vaga impressione/il vago sospetto che ...

sneaky ['sniːkɪ] ADJ falso(-a), disonesto(-a)

sneer [snɪəʳ] N ghigno, sogghigno ▶ VI ghignare, sogghignare; **to ~ at sb/sth** farsi beffe di qn/qc

sneeze [sniːz] N starnuto ▶ VI starnutire

snide [snaɪd] ADJ maligno(-a)

sniff [snɪf] N fiutata, annusata ▶ VI fiutare, annusare; tirare su col naso; (*in contempt*) arricciare il naso ▶ VT fiutare, annusare; (*glue, drug*) sniffare
  ▶ **sniff at** VT FUS: **it's not to be sniffed at** non è da disprezzare

sniffer dog ['snɪfə-] N cane *m* poliziotto (*per stupefacenti o esplosivi*)

snigger ['snɪgəʳ] N riso represso ▶ VI ridacchiare, ridere sotto i baffi

snip [snɪp] N pezzetto; (*bargain*) (*buon*) affare *m*, occasione *f* ▶ VT tagliare

sniper ['snaɪpəʳ] N (*marksman*) franco tiratore *m*, cecchino

snippet ['snɪpɪt] N frammento

snivelling ['snɪvlɪŋ] ADJ piagnucoloso(-a)

snob [snɒb] N snob *mf*

snobbery ['snɒbərɪ] N snobismo

snobbish ['snɒbɪʃ] ADJ snob *inv*

snog [snɒg] VI (*col*) pomiciare

snooker ['snuːkəʳ] N *tipo di gioco del biliardo*

snoop [snuːp] VI: **to ~ on sb** spiare qn; **to ~ about** curiosare

snooper ['snuːpəʳ] N ficcanaso *mf*

snooty ['snuːtɪ] ADJ borioso(-a), snob *inv*

snooze [snuːz] N sonnellino, pisolino ▶ VI fare un sonnellino

snore [snɔːʳ] VI russare

snoring ['snɔːrɪŋ] N russare *m*

snorkel ['snɔːkl] N (*of swimmer*) respiratore *m* a tubo

snort [snɔːt] N sbuffo ▶ VI sbuffare ▶ VT (*drugs slang*) sniffare

snotty ['snɒtɪ] ADJ moccioso(-a)

snout [snaut] N muso

snow [snəu] N neve *f* ▶ VI nevicare ▶ VT: **to be snowed under with work** essere sommerso di lavoro

snowball ['snəubɔːl] N palla di neve ▶ VI (*fig*) crescere a vista d'occhio

snowboard ['snəubɔːd] N snowboard *m inv*; **to go snowboarding** fare snowboard

snowbound ['snəubaund] ADJ bloccato(-a) dalla neve

snow-capped ['snəukæpt] ADJ (*mountain*) con la cima coperta di neve; (*peak*) coperto(-a) di neve

snowdrift ['snəudrɪft] N cumulo di neve (*ammucchiato dal vento*)

snowdrop ['snəudrɒp] N bucaneve *m inv*

snowfall ['snəufɔːl] N nevicata

snowflake ['snəufleɪk] N fiocco di neve

snowman ['snəumæn] N (*irreg*) pupazzo di neve

snowplough, **(*US*)snowplow** ['snəuplau] N spazzaneve *m inv*

snowshoe ['snəuʃuː] N racchetta da neve

snowstorm ['snəustɔːm] N tormenta

snowy ['snəuɪ] ADJ nevoso(-a)

SNP N ABBR (*BRIT Pol*) = **Scottish National Party**

snub [snʌb] VT snobbare ▶ N offesa, affronto

snub-nosed [snʌb'nəuzd] ADJ dal naso camuso

snuff [snʌf] N tabacco da fiuto ▶ VT (*also*: **snuff out**: *candle*) spegnere

snuff movie N (*col*) *film porno dove una persona viene uccisa realmente*

snug [snʌg] ADJ comodo(-a); (*room, house*)

accogliente, comodo(-a); **it's a ~ fit** è attillato

snuggle ['snʌgl] VI: **to ~ down in bed** accovacciarsi a letto; **to ~ up to sb** stringersi a qn

snugly ['snʌglɪ] ADV comodamente; **it fits ~** (object in pocket etc) entra giusto giusto; (garment) sta ben attillato

SO ABBR (Banking) = **standing order**

(KEYWORD)

so [səu] ADV **1** (thus, likewise) così; **if so** se è così, quand'è così; **I didn't do it — you did so!** non l'ho fatto io — sì che l'hai fatto!; **so do I, so am I** anch'io; **it's 5 o'clock — so it is!** sono le 5 — davvero!; **I hope so** lo spero; **I think so** penso di sì; **quite so!** esattamente!; **even so** comunque; **so far** finora, fin qui; (in past) fino ad allora

2 (in comparisons etc: to such a degree) così; **so big (that)** così grande (che); **she's not so clever as her brother** lei non è (così) intelligente come suo fratello

3: **so much** adj tanto(-a); adv tanto; **I've got so much work/money** ho tanto lavoro/tanti soldi; **I love you so much** ti amo tanto; **so many** tanti(-e)

4 (phrases): **10 or so** circa 10; **so long!** (col: goodbye) ciao!, ci vediamo!; **so to speak** per così dire; **so what?** (col) e allora?, e con questo?

▶ CONJ **1** (expressing purpose): **so as to do** in modo or così da fare; **we hurried so as not to be late** ci affrettammo per non fare tardi; **so (that)** affinché + sub, perché + sub

2 (expressing result): **he didn't arrive so I left** non è venuto così me ne sono andata; **so you see, I could have gone** vedi, sarei potuto andare; **so that's the reason!** allora è questo il motivo!, ecco perché!

soak [səuk] VT inzuppare; (clothes) mettere a mollo ▶ VI inzupparsi; (clothes) essere a mollo; **to be soaked through** essere fradicio
▶ **soak in** VI penetrare
▶ **soak up** VT assorbire

soaking ['səukɪŋ] ADJ (also: **soaking wet**) fradicio(-a)

so-and-so ['səuənsəu] N (somebody) un tale; **Mr/Mrs ~** signor/signora tal dei tali

soap [səup] N sapone m

soapbox ['səupbɒks] N palco improvvisato (per orazioni pubbliche)

soapflakes ['səupfleɪks] NPL sapone m in scaglie

soap opera N soap opera f inv

soap powder N detersivo

soapsuds ['səupsʌdz] NPL saponata

soapy ['səupɪ] ADJ insaponato(-a)

soar [sɔːʳ] VI volare in alto; (price, morale, spirits) salire alle stelle; (building) ergersi

sob [sɒb] N singhiozzo ▶ VI singhiozzare

s.o.b. N ABBR (US: col!: = son of a bitch) figlio di puttana (!)

sober ['səubəʳ] ADJ non ubriaco(-a); (sedate) serio(-a); (moderate) moderato(-a); (colour, style) sobrio(-a)
▶ **sober up** VT far passare la sbornia a ▶ VI farsi passare la sbornia

sobriety [səu'braɪətɪ] N (not being drunk) sobrietà; (seriousness, sedateness) sobrietà, pacatezza

sob story N (col, pej) storia lacrimosa

Soc. ABBR (= society) Soc

so-called ['səu'kɔːld] ADJ cosiddetto(-a)

soccer ['sɒkəʳ] N calcio

soccer pitch N campo di calcio

soccer player N calciatore m

sociable ['səuʃəbl] ADJ socievole

social ['səuʃl] ADJ sociale ▶ N festa, serata

social climber N arrampicatore(-trice) sociale, arrivista mf

social club N club m inv sociale

Social Democrat N socialdemocratico(-a)

social insurance N (US) assicurazione f sociale

socialism ['səuʃəlɪzəm] N socialismo

socialist ['səuʃəlɪst] ADJ, N socialista mf

socialite ['səuʃəlaɪt] N persona in vista nel bel mondo

socialize ['səuʃəlaɪz] VI frequentare la gente; farsi degli amici; **to ~ with** socializzare con

social life N vita sociale

socially ['səuʃəlɪ] ADV socialmente, in società

social media NPL social media mpl

social network ['səʃəl 'nɛtwəːk] N social network m inv, rete f sociale

social networking N il comunicare tramite social network

social networking site N social network m

social science N scienze fpl sociali

social security N previdenza sociale; **Department of Social Security** (BRIT) ≈ Istituto di Previdenza Sociale

social services NPL servizi mpl sociali

social welfare N assistenza sociale

social work N servizio sociale

social worker N assistente mf sociale

society [sə'saɪətɪ] N società f inv; (club) società, associazione f; (also: **high society**) alta società ▶ CPD (party, column) mondano(-a)

socioeconomic ['səusɪəui:kə'nɒmɪk] ADJ socio-economico(-a)

sociological [səusɪə'lɒdʒɪkl] ADJ sociologico(-a)

sociologist [səusɪ'ɒlədʒɪst] N sociologo(-a)

sociology [səusɪ'ɒlədʒɪ] N sociologia

S

sock [sɔk] N calzino ▸ VT (*hit*) dare un pugno a; **to pull one's socks up** (*fig*) darsi una regolata

socket ['sɔkɪt] N cavità *f inv*; (*of eye*) orbita; (*BRIT Elec: also:* **wall socket**) presa di corrente; (*: for light bulb*) portalampada *m inv*

sod [sɔd] N (*of earth*) zolla erbosa; (*BRIT col!*) bastardo(-a) (*!*)
▸ **sod off** VI: **~ off!** (*BRIT col!*) levati dalle palle! (*!*)

soda ['səudə] N (*Chem*) soda; (*also:* **soda water**) acqua di seltz; (*US: also:* **soda pop**) gassosa

sodden ['sɔdn] ADJ fradicio(-a)

sodium ['səudɪəm] N sodio

sodium chloride N cloruro di sodio

sofa ['səufə] N sofà *m inv*

sofa bed N divano *m* letto *inv*

Sofia ['səufɪə] N Sofia

soft [sɔft] ADJ (*not rough*) morbido(-a); (*not hard*) soffice; (*not loud*) sommesso(-a); (*not bright*) tenue; (*kind*) gentile; (*: look, smile*) dolce; (*not strict*) indulgente; (*weak*) debole; (*stupid*) stupido(-a)

soft-boiled ['sɔftbɔɪld] ADJ (*egg*) alla coque

soft drink N analcolico

soft drugs NPL droghe *fpl* leggere

soften ['sɔfn] VT ammorbidire; addolcire; attenuare ▸ VI ammorbidirsi; addolcirsi; attenuarsi

softener ['sɔfnər] N ammorbidente *m*

soft fruit N (*BRIT*) ≈ frutti *mpl* di bosco

soft furnishings NPL tessuti *mpl* d'arredo

soft-hearted [sɔft'hɑːtɪd] ADJ sensibile

softly ['sɔftlɪ] ADV dolcemente; morbidamente

softness ['sɔftnɪs] N dolcezza; morbidezza

soft option N soluzione *f* (più) facile

soft sell N persuasione *f* all'acquisto

soft target N obiettivo civile (*e quindi facile da colpire*)

soft touch N (*col*): **to be a ~** lasciarsi spillare facilmente denaro

soft toy N giocattolo di peluche

software ['sɔftwɛər] N (*Comput*) software *m*

software package N pacchetto di software

soft water N acqua non calcarea

soggy ['sɔgɪ] ADJ inzuppato(-a)

soil [sɔɪl] N (*earth*) terreno, suolo ▸ VT sporcare; (*fig*) macchiare

soiled [sɔɪld] ADJ sporco(-a), sudicio(-a)

sojourn ['sɔdʒəːn] N (*formal*) soggiorno

solace ['sɔlɪs] N consolazione *f*

solar ['səulər] ADJ solare

solarium [sə'lɛərɪəm] (*pl* **solaria** [-rɪə]) N solarium *m inv*

solar panel N pannello solare

solar plexus [-'plɛksəs] N (*Anat*) plesso solare

solar power N energia solare

solar system N sistema *m* solare

sold [səuld] PT, PP *of* **sell**

solder ['səuldər] VT saldare ▸ N saldatura

soldier ['səuldʒər] N soldato, militare *m* ▸ VI: **to ~ on** perseverare; **toy ~** soldatino

sold out ADJ (*Comm*) esaurito(-a)

sole [səul] N (*of foot*) pianta (del piede); (*of shoe*) suola; (*fish: pl inv*) sogliola ▸ ADJ solo(-a), unico(-a); (*exclusive*) esclusivo(-a)

solely ['səullɪ] ADV solamente, unicamente; **I will hold you ~ responsible** la considererò il solo responsabile

solemn ['sɔləm] ADJ solenne; grave; serio(-a)

sole trader N (*Comm*) commerciante *m* in proprio

solicit [sə'lɪsɪt] VT (*request*) richiedere, sollecitare ▸ VI (*prostitute*) adescare i passanti

solicitor [sə'lɪsɪtər] N (*BRIT: for wills etc*) ≈ notaio; (*in court*) ≈ avvocato; *vedi nota*

> Il *solicitor* appartiene a una delle due branche della professione legale britannica (*vedi anche* **barrister**). È compito dei *solicitors* agire come consulenti in materia legale, redarre documenti legali, preparare i casi per i *barristers*. Contrariamente a questi ultimi, i *solicitors* non sono qualificati a rappresentare una parte nelle corti investite della potestà di decidere sui reati più gravi.

solid ['sɔlɪd] ADJ (*not hollow*) pieno(-a); (*strong, sound, reliable, not liquid*) solido(-a); (*meal*) sostanzioso(-a); (*line*) ininterrotto(-a); (*vote*) unanime ▸ N solido; **to be on ~ ground** essere su terraferma; (*fig*) muoversi su terreno sicuro; **we waited 2 ~ hours** abbiamo aspettato due ore buone

solidarity [sɔlɪ'dærɪtɪ] N solidarietà

solid fuel N combustibile *m* solido

solidify [sə'lɪdɪfaɪ] VI solidificarsi ▸ VT solidificare

solidity [sə'lɪdɪtɪ] N solidità

solid-state ['sɔlɪdsteɪt] ADJ (*Elec*) a transistor

soliloquy [sə'lɪləkwɪ] N soliloquio

solitaire [sɔlɪ'tɛər] N (*game, gem*) solitario

solitary ['sɔlɪtərɪ] ADJ solitario(-a)

solitary confinement N (*Law*): **to be in ~** essere in cella d'isolamento

solitude ['sɔlɪtjuːd] N solitudine *f*

solo ['səuləu] N (*Mus*) assolo

soloist ['səuləuɪst] N solista *mf*

Solomon Islands ['sɔləmən-] N: **the ~** le isole Salomone

solstice ['sɔlstɪs] N solstizio

soluble ['sɔljubl] ADJ solubile

solution [sə'luːʃən] N soluzione *f*

solve [sɔlv] VT risolvere

solvency ['sɔlvənsɪ] N (*Comm*) solvenza, solvibilità

solvent ['sɔlvənt] ADJ (*Comm*) solvibile
  ▶ N (*Chem*) solvente *m*
solvent abuse N abuso di colle e, solventi
Somali [sə'mɑːlɪ] ADJ somalo(-a)
Somalia [səu'mɑːlɪə] N Somalia
Somaliland [səu'mɑːlɪlænd] N paesi *mpl* del
  corno d'Africa
sombre, (*US*) **somber** ['sɔmbə^r] ADJ scuro(-a);
  (*mood, person*) triste

(KEYWORD)

some [sʌm] ADJ 1 (*a certain amount or number of*):
  some tea/water/cream del tè/dell'acqua/
  della panna; **there's some milk in the**
  fridge c'è (del) latte nel frigo; **some**
  children/apples dei bambini/delle mele;
  after some time dopo un po'; **at some**
  length a lungo
  2 (*certain: in contrasts*) certo(-a); **some people**
  say that … alcuni dicono che …, certa gente
  dice che …
  3 (*unspecified*) un(-a) certo(-a), qualche; **some**
  woman was asking for you una tale
  chiedeva di lei; **some day** un giorno; **some**
  day next week un giorno della prossima
  settimana; **in some form or other** in una
  forma o nell'altra
  ▶ PRON 1 (*a certain number*) alcuni(-e), certi(-e);
  I've got some (*books etc*) ne ho alcuni; **some**
  (of them) have been sold alcuni sono stati
  venduti
  2 (*a certain amount*) un po'; **I've got some**
  (*money, milk*) ne ho un po'; **I've read some of**
  the book ho letto parte del libro; **some (of**
  it) was left ne è rimasto un po'; **could I**
  have some of that cheese? potrei avere un
  po' di quel formaggio?
  ▶ ADV: **some 10 people** circa 10 persone

somebody ['sʌmbədɪ] PRON qualcuno;
  ~ or other qualcuno
someday ['sʌmdeɪ] ADV uno di questi giorni,
  un giorno o l'altro
somehow ['sʌmhau] ADV in un modo o
  nell'altro, in qualche modo; (*for some reason*)
  per qualche ragione
someone ['sʌmwʌn] PRON = **somebody**
someplace ['sʌmpleɪs] ADV (*US*)
  = **somewhere**
somersault ['sʌməsɔːlt] N capriola; (*in air*)
  salto mortale ▶ VI fare una capriola (*or un*
  salto mortale); (*car*) cappottare
something ['sʌmθɪŋ] PRON qualcosa,
  qualche cosa; **~ nice** qualcosa di bello;
  ~ to do qualcosa da fare; **he's ~ like me** mi
  assomiglia un po'; **it's ~ of a problem** è un
  bel problema
sometime ['sʌmtaɪm] ADV (*in future*) una
  volta o l'altra; (*in past*): **~ last month**

durante il mese scorso; **I'll finish it ~** lo
  finirò prima o poi
sometimes ['sʌmtaɪmz] ADV qualche volta
somewhat ['sʌmwɔt] ADV piuttosto
somewhere ['sʌmwɛə^r] ADV in *or* da qualche
  parte; **~ else** da qualche altra parte
son [sʌn] N figlio
sonar ['səunɑː^r] N sonar *m*
sonata [sə'nɑːtə] N sonata
song [sɔŋ] N canzone *f*
songbook ['sɔŋbuk] N canzoniere *m*
songwriter ['sɔŋraɪtə^r] N compositore(-trice)
  di canzoni
sonic ['sɔnɪk] ADJ (*boom*) sonico(-a)
son-in-law ['sʌnɪnlɔː] N genero
sonnet ['sɔnɪt] N sonetto
sonny ['sʌnɪ] N (*col*) ragazzo mio
soon [suːn] ADV presto, fra poco; (*early*)
  presto; **~ afterwards** poco dopo; **very/quite**
  ~ molto/abbastanza presto; **as ~ as possible**
  prima possibile; **I'll do it as ~ as I can** lo
  farò appena posso; **how ~ can you be ready?**
  fra quanto tempo sarà pronto?; **see you ~!** a
  presto!
sooner ['suːnə^r] ADV (*time*) prima; (*preference*):
  I would ~ do preferirei fare; **~ or later** prima
  o poi; **no ~ said than done** detto fatto; **the ~**
  the better prima è meglio è; **no ~ had we**
  left than … eravamo appena partiti,
  quando …
soot [sut] N fuliggine *f*
soothe [suːð] VT calmare
soothing ['suːðɪŋ] ADJ (*ointment etc*) calmante;
  (*tone, words etc*) rassicurante
SOP N ABBR = **standard operating procedure**
sop [sɔp] N: **that's only a ~** è soltanto un
  contentino
sophisticated [sə'fɪstɪkeɪtɪd] ADJ
  sofisticato(-a); raffinato(-a); complesso(-a);
  (*film, mind*) sottile
sophistication [səfɪstɪ'keɪʃən] N
  raffinatezza; (*of machine*) complessità;
  (*of argument etc*) sottigliezza
sophomore ['sɔfəmɔː^r] N (*US*)
  studente(-essa) del secondo anno
soporific [sɔpə'rɪfɪk] ADJ soporifero(-a)
sopping ['sɔpɪŋ] ADJ (*also*: **sopping wet**)
  bagnato(-a) fradicio(-a)
soppy ['sɔpɪ] ADJ (*pej*) sentimentale
soprano [sə'prɑːnəu] N (*voice*) soprano *m*;
  (*singer*) soprano *mf*
sorbet ['sɔːbeɪ] N sorbetto
sorcerer ['sɔːsərə^r] N stregone *m*, mago
sordid ['sɔːdɪd] ADJ sordido(-a)
sore [sɔː^r] ADJ (*painful*) dolorante; (*col: offended*)
  offeso(-a) ▶ N piaga; **my eyes are ~, I have ~**
  eyes mi fanno male gli occhi; **~ throat** mal
  m di gola; **it's a ~ point** (*fig*) è un punto
  delicato

S

sorely ['sɔːlɪ] ADV (*tempted*) fortemente
sorrel ['sɔrəl] N acetosa
sorrow ['sɔrəu] N dolore *m*
sorrowful ['sɔrəuful] ADJ triste
sorry ['sɔrɪ] ADJ spiacente; (*condition, excuse*) misero(-a), pietoso(-a); (*sight, failure*) triste; ~! scusa! (*or* scusi! *or* scusate!); **to feel ~ for sb** rincrescersi per qn; **I'm ~ to hear that …** mi dispiace (sentire) che …; **to be ~ about sth** essere dispiaciuto *or* spiacente di qc
sort [sɔːt] N specie *f*, genere *m*; (*make: of coffee, car etc*) tipo ▸ VT (*also:* **sort out:** *papers*) classificare; ordinare; (: *letters etc*) smistare; (: *problems*) risolvere; (*Comput*) ordinare; **what ~ of car?** che tipo di macchina?; **I shall do nothing of the ~!** nemmeno per sogno!; **it's ~ of awkward** (*col*) è piuttosto difficile
sortie ['sɔːtɪ] N sortita
sorting office ['sɔːtɪŋ-] N ufficio *m* smistamento *inv*
SOS N S.O.S. *m inv*
so-so ['səusəu] ADV così così
soufflé ['suːfleɪ] N soufflé *m inv*
sought [sɔːt] PT, PP *of* **seek**
sought-after ['sɔːtɑːftə⁻] ADJ richiesto(-a)
soul [səul] N anima; **the poor ~ had nowhere to sleep** il poveraccio non aveva dove dormire; **I didn't see a ~** non ho visto anima viva
soul-destroying ['səuldɪ'strɔɪɪŋ] ADJ demoralizzante
soulful ['səulful] ADJ pieno(-a) di sentimento
soulless ['səullɪs] ADJ senz'anima, inumano(-a)
soul mate N anima gemella
soul-searching ['səulsəːtʃɪŋ] N: **after much ~** dopo un profondo esame di coscienza
sound [saund] ADJ (*healthy*) sano(-a); (*safe, not damaged*) solido(-a), in buono stato; (*reliable, not superficial*) solido(-a); (*sensible*) giudizioso(-a), di buon senso; (*valid: argument, policy, claim*) valido(-a) ▸ ADV: **~ asleep** profondamente addormentato ▸ N (*noise*) suono; rumore *m*; (*Geo*) stretto ▸ VT (*alarm*) suonare; (*also:* **sound out:** *opinions*) sondare ▸ VI suonare; (*fig: seem*) sembrare; **to ~ like** rassomigliare a; **to be of ~ mind** essere sano di mente; **I don't like the ~ of it** (*fig: film etc*) non mi dice niente (: *news*) è preoccupante; **it sounds as if …** ho l'impressione che …; **it sounds like French** somiglia al francese; **that sounds like them arriving** mi sembra di sentirli arrivare
▸ **sound off** VI (*col*): **to ~ off (about)** (*give one's opinions*) fare dei grandi discorsi (su)
sound barrier N muro del suono
soundbite ['saundbaɪt] N frase *f* incisiva
sound effects NPL effetti *mpl* sonori

sound engineer N tecnico del suono
sounding ['saundɪŋ] N (*Naut etc*) scandagliamento
sounding board N (*Mus*) cassa di risonanza; (*fig*): **to use sb as a ~ for one's ideas** provare le proprie idee su qn
soundly ['saundlɪ] ADV (*sleep*) profondamente; (*beat*) duramente
soundproof ['saundpruːf] VT insonorizzare, isolare acusticamente ▸ ADJ insonorizzato(-a), isolato(-a) acusticamente
sound system N impianto *m*, audio *inv*
soundtrack ['saundtræk] N (*of film*) colonna sonora
soup [suːp] N minestra; (*clear*) brodo; (*thick*) zuppa; **in the ~** (*fig*) nei guai
soup course N minestra
soup kitchen N mensa per i poveri
soup plate N piatto fondo
soupspoon ['suːpspuːn] N cucchiaio da minestra
sour ['sauə⁻] ADJ aspro(-a); (*fruit*) acerbo(-a); (*milk*) acido(-a), fermentato(-a); (*fig*) arcigno(-a), acido(-a); **to go** *or* **turn ~** (*milk, wine*) inacidirsi; (*fig: relationship, plans*) guastarsi; **it's ~ grapes** (*fig*) è soltanto invidia
source [sɔːs] N fonte *f*, sorgente *f*; (*fig*) fonte; **I have it from a reliable ~ that …** ho saputo da fonte sicura che …
south [sauθ] N sud *m*, meridione *m*, mezzogiorno ▸ ADJ del sud, sud *inv*, meridionale ▸ ADV verso sud; **(to the) ~ of** a sud di; **the S~ of France** il sud della Francia; **to travel ~** viaggiare verso sud
South Africa N Sudafrica *m*
South African ADJ, N sudafricano(-a)
South America N Sudamerica *m*, America del sud
South American ADJ, N sudamericano(-a)
southbound ['sauθbaund] ADJ (*gen*) diretto(-a) a sud; (*carriageway*) sud *inv*
south-east [sauθ'iːst] N sud-est *m*
South-East Asia N Asia sudorientale
southeastern [sauθ'iːstən] ADJ sudorientale
southerly ['sʌðəlɪ] ADJ del sud
southern ['sʌðən] ADJ del sud, meridionale; (*wall*) esposto(-a) a sud; **the ~ hemisphere** l'emisfero australe
South Korea N Corea *f* del Sud
South Pole N Polo Sud
South Sea Islands NPL: **the ~** le isole dei Mari del Sud
South Seas NPL: **the ~** i Mari del Sud
South Vietnam N Vietnam *m* del Sud
southward ['sauθwəd], **southwards** ['sauθwədz] ADV verso sud
south-west [sauθ'wɛst] N sud-ovest *m*
southwestern [sauθ'wɛstən] ADJ sudoccidentale

souvenir [suːvəˈnɪəʳ] N ricordo, souvenir m inv

sovereign [ˈsɔvrɪn] ADJ, N sovrano(-a)

sovereignty [ˈsɔvrəntɪ] N sovranità

soviet [ˈsəuvɪət] ADJ sovietico(-a)

Soviet Union N: **the ~** l'Unione f Sovietica

sow¹ [səu] (pt **sowed**, pp **sown** [səun]) VT seminare

sow² [sau] N scrofa

soya [ˈsɔɪə], (US) **soy** [sɔɪ] N: **~ bean** seme m di soia; **~ sauce** salsa di soia

sozzled [ˈsɔzld] ADJ (BRIT col) sbronzo(-a)

spa [spɑː] N (resort) stazione f termale; (US: also: **health spa**) centro di cure estetiche

space [speɪs] N spazio; (room) posto; spazio; (length of time) intervallo ▶ CPD spaziale ▶ VT (also: **space out**) distanziare; **in a confined ~** in un luogo chiuso; **to clear a ~ for sth** fare posto per qc; **in a short ~ of time** in breve tempo; **(with)in the ~ of an hour/three generations** nell'arco di un'ora/di tre generazioni

space bar N (on typewriter) barra spaziatrice

spacecraft [ˈspeɪskrɑːft] N (pl inv) veicolo spaziale

spaceman [ˈspeɪsmæn] N (irreg) astronauta m, cosmonauta m

spaceship [ˈspeɪsʃɪp] N astronave f, navicella spaziale

space shuttle N shuttle m inv

spacesuit [ˈspeɪssuːt] N tuta spaziale

spacewoman [ˈspeɪswumən] N (irreg) astronauta f, cosmonauta f

spacing [ˈspeɪsɪŋ] N spaziatura; **single/ double ~** (Typ etc) spaziatura singola/doppia

spacious [ˈspeɪʃəs] ADJ spazioso(-a), ampio(-a)

spade [speɪd] N (tool) vanga; pala; (child's) paletta; **spades** NPL (Cards) picche fpl

spadework [ˈspeɪdwəːk] N (fig) duro lavoro preparatorio

spaghetti [spəˈgɛtɪ] N spaghetti mpl

Spain [speɪn] N Spagna

spam [spæm] (Comput) N spamming m ▶ VT: **to ~ sb** inviare a qn messaggi pubblicitari non richiesti via email

span [spæn] N (of bird, plane) apertura alare; (of arch) campata; (in time) periodo; durata ▶ VT attraversare; (fig) abbracciare

Spaniard [ˈspænjəd] N spagnolo(-a)

spaniel [ˈspænjəl] N spaniel m inv

Spanish [ˈspænɪʃ] ADJ spagnolo(-a) ▶ N (Ling) spagnolo; **the ~** npl gli Spagnoli; **~ omelette** frittata di cipolle, pomodori e peperoni

spank [spæŋk] VT sculacciare

spanner [ˈspænəʳ] N (BRIT) chiave f inglese

spar [spɑːʳ] N asta, palo ▶ VI (Boxing) allenarsi

spare [spɛəʳ] ADJ di riserva, di scorta; (surplus) in più, d'avanzo ▶ N (part) pezzo di ricambio ▶ VT (do without) fare a meno di; (afford to give) concedere; (refrain from hurting, using) risparmiare; **to ~** (surplus) d'avanzo; **there are 2 going ~** (BRIT) ce ne sono 2 in più; **to ~ no expense** non badare a spese; **can you ~ the time?** ha tempo?; **I've a few minutes to ~** ho un attimino di tempo; **there is no time to ~** non c'è tempo da perdere; **can you ~ (me) £10?** puoi prestarmi 10 sterline?

spare part N pezzo di ricambio

spare room N stanza degli ospiti

spare time N tempo libero

spare tyre, (US) **spare tire** N (Aut) gomma di scorta

spare wheel N (Aut) ruota di scorta

sparing [ˈspɛərɪŋ] ADJ (amount) scarso(-a); (use) parsimonioso(-a); **to be ~ with** essere avaro(-a) di

sparingly [ˈspɛərɪŋlɪ] ADV moderatamente

spark [spɑːk] N scintilla

sparkle [ˈspɑːkl] N scintillio, sfavillio ▶ VI scintillare, sfavillare; (bubble) spumeggiare, frizzare

sparkler [ˈspɑːkləʳ] N fuoco d'artificio

sparkling [ˈspɑːklɪŋ] ADJ scintillante, sfavillante; (wine) spumante

spark plug N candela

sparring partner [ˈspɑːrɪŋ-] N sparring partner m inv; (fig) interlocutore abituale in discussioni, dibattiti, tavole rotonde ecc

sparrow [ˈspærəu] N passero

sparse [spɑːs] ADJ sparso(-a), rado(-a)

spartan [ˈspɑːtən] ADJ (fig) spartano(-a)

spasm [ˈspæzəm] N (Med) spasmo; (fig) accesso, attacco

spasmodic [spæzˈmɔdɪk] ADJ spasmodico(-a); (fig) intermittente

spastic [ˈspæstɪk] N spastico(-a)

spat [spæt] PT, PP of **spit** ▶ N (US) battibecco

spate [speɪt] N (fig): **~ of** diluvio or fiume m di; **in ~** (river) in piena

spatial [ˈspeɪʃəl] ADJ spaziale

spatter [ˈspætəʳ] VT, VI schizzare

spatula [ˈspætjulə] N spatola

spawn [spɔːn] VT deporre; (pej) produrre ▶ VI deporre le uova ▶ N uova fpl

SPCA N ABBR (US: = Society for the Prevention of Cruelty to Animals) ≈ E.N.P.A. m (= Ente Nazionale per la Protezione degli Animali)

SPCC N ABBR (US) = **Society for the Prevention of Cruelty to Children**

speak [spiːk] (pt **spoke** [spəuk], pp **spoken** [ˈspəukn]) VT (language) parlare; (truth) dire ▶ VI parlare; **to ~ to sb/of** or **about sth** parlare a qn/di qc; **~ up!** parli più forte!; **to ~ at a conference/in a debate** partecipare ad una conferenza/ad un dibattito; **speaking!** (on telephone) sono io!; **to ~ one's mind** dire quello che si pensa; **he has no money to ~ of** non si può proprio dire che sia ricco

S

▶ **speak for** VT FUS: **to ~ for sb** parlare a nome di qn; **that picture is already spoken for** (*in shop*) quel quadro è già stato venduto

speaker ['spiːkəʳ] N (*in public*) oratore(-trice); (*also:* **loudspeaker**) altoparlante *m*; (*Pol*) **the S~** *il presidente della Camera dei Comuni or* (*US*) *dei Rappresentanti;* **are you a Welsh ~?** parla gallese?

speaking ['spiːkɪŋ] ADJ parlante; **Italian-~ people** persone che parlano italiano; **to be on ~ terms** parlarsi

spear [spɪəʳ] N lancia ▶ VT infilzare

spearhead ['spɪəhɛd] N punta di lancia; (*Mil*) reparto d'assalto ▶ VT (*attack etc*) condurre

spearmint ['spɪəmɪnt] N (*Bot etc*) menta verde

spec [spɛk] N (*BRIT col*): **on ~** sperando bene; **to buy sth on ~** comprare qc sperando di fare un affare

special ['spɛʃl] ADJ speciale ▶ N (*train*) treno supplementare; **nothing ~** niente di speciale; **take ~ care** siate particolarmente prudenti

special agent N agente *m* segreto

special correspondent N inviato speciale

special delivery N (*Post*): **by ~** per espresso

special effects NPL (*Cine*) effetti *mpl* speciali

specialist ['spɛʃəlɪst] N specialista *mf*; **a heart ~** (*Med*) un cardiologo

speciality [spɛʃɪˈælɪtɪ], (*esp US*) **specialty** ['spɛʃəltɪ] N specialità *f inv*

specialize ['spɛʃəlaɪz] VI: **to ~ (in)** specializzarsi (in)

specially ['spɛʃəlɪ] ADV specialmente, particolarmente

special needs ADJ: **~ children** bambini *mpl* con difficoltà di apprendimento

special offer N (*Comm*) offerta speciale

special school N (*BRIT*) scuola speciale (*per portatori di handicap*)

specialty ['spɛʃəltɪ] N (*esp US*) = **speciality**

species ['spiːʃiːz] N (*pl inv*) specie *f inv*

specific [spəˈsɪfɪk] ADJ specifico(-a); preciso(-a); **to be ~ to** avere un legame specifico con

specifically [spəˈsɪfɪklɪ] ADV (*explicitly: state, warn*) chiaramente, esplicitamente; (*especially: design, intend*) appositamente

specification [spɛsɪfɪˈkeɪʃən] N specificazione *f*; **specifications** NPL (*of car, machine*) dati *mpl* caratteristici; (*for building*) dettagli *mpl*

specify ['spɛsɪfaɪ] VT specificare, precisare; **unless otherwise specified** salvo indicazioni contrarie

specimen ['spɛsɪmən] N esemplare *m*, modello; (*Med*) campione *m*

specimen copy N campione *m*

specimen signature N firma depositata

speck [spɛk] N puntino, macchiolina; (*particle*) granello

speckled ['spɛkld] ADJ macchiettato(-a)

specs [spɛks] NPL (*col*) occhiali *mpl*

spectacle ['spɛktəkl] N spettacolo; *see also* **spectacles**

spectacle case N (*BRIT*) fodero per gli occhiali

spectacles ['spɛktəklz] NPL (*BRIT*) occhiali *mpl*

spectacular [spɛkˈtækjuləʳ] ADJ spettacolare ▶ N (*Cine etc*) film *m inv etc* spettacolare

spectator [spɛkˈteɪtəʳ] N spettatore(-trice)

spectator sport N sport *m inv* come spettacolo

spectra ['spɛktrə] NPL *of* **spectrum**

spectre, (*US*) **specter** ['spɛktəʳ] N spettro

spectrum ['spɛktrəm] (*pl* **spectra** [-rə]) N spettro; (*fig*) gamma

speculate ['spɛkjuleɪt] VI speculare; (*try to guess*): **to ~ about** fare ipotesi su

speculation [spɛkjuˈleɪʃən] N speculazione *f*; congetture *fpl*

speculative ['spɛkjulətɪv] ADJ speculativo(-a)

speculator ['spɛkjuleɪtəʳ] N speculatore(-trice)

sped [spɛd] PT, PP *of* **speed**

speech [spiːtʃ] N (*faculty*) parola; (*talk, Theat*) discorso; (*manner of speaking*) parlata; (*language*) linguaggio; (*enunciation*) elocuzione *f*

speech day N (*BRIT Scol*) giorno della premiazione

speech impediment N difetto di pronuncia

speechless ['spiːtʃlɪs] ADJ ammutolito(-a), muto(-a)

speech therapy N cura dei disturbi del linguaggio

speed [spiːd] (*pt, pp* **sped** [spɛd]) N velocità *f inv*; (*promptness*) prontezza; (*Aut: gear*) marcia ▶ VI: **to ~ along** procedere velocemente; **the years sped by** gli anni sono volati; (*Aut: exceed speed limit*) andare a velocità eccessiva; **at ~** (*BRIT*) velocemente; **at full** *or* **top ~** a tutta velocità; **at a ~ of 70 km/h** a una velocità di 70 km l'ora; **shorthand/typing speeds** numero di parole al minuto in stenografia/dattilografia; **a five-~ gearbox** un cambio a cinque marce

▶ **speed up** (*pt, pp* **speeded up**) VI, VT accelerare

speedboat ['spiːdbəut] N motoscafo; fuoribordo *m inv*

speed camera N Autovelox *m inv*

speed dating [-deɪtɪŋ] N *sistema di appuntamenti grazie al quale si possono incontrare in pochissimo tempo diverse persone e scegliere eventualmente chi frequentare*

speedily ['spiːdɪlɪ] ADV velocemente; prontamente

speeding ['spiːdɪŋ] N (Aut) eccesso di velocità

speed limit N limite m di velocità

speedometer [spɪ'dɔmɪtəʳ] N tachimetro

speed trap N (Aut) tratto di strada sul quale la polizia controlla la velocità dei veicoli

speedway ['spiːdweɪ] N (Sport) pista per motociclismo

speedy ['spiːdɪ] ADJ veloce, rapido(-a); (reply) pronto(-a)

speleologist [spɛlɪ'ɔlədʒɪst] N speleologo(-a)

spell [spɛl] (pt, pp **spelt** [spɛlt] or **spelled** [spɛld]) N (also: **magic spell**) incantesimo; (period of time) (breve) periodo ▶ VT (in writing) scrivere (lettera per lettera); (aloud) dire lettera per lettera; (fig) significare; **to cast a ~ on sb** fare un incantesimo a qn; **he can't ~** fa errori di ortografia; **how do you ~ your name?** come si scrive il suo nome?; **can you ~ it for me?** me lo può dettare lettera per lettera?
▶ **spell out** VT (letter by letter) dettare lettera per lettera; (explain): **to ~ sth out for sb** spiegare qc a qn per filo e per segno

spellbound ['spɛlbaʊnd] ADJ incantato(-a), affascinato(-a)

spellchecker ['spɛltʃɛkəʳ] N correttore m ortografico

spelling ['spɛlɪŋ] N ortografia

spelt [spɛlt] PT, PP of **spell**

spend [spɛnd] (pt, pp **spent** [spɛnt]) VT (money) spendere; (time, life) passare; **to ~ time/money/effort on sth** dedicare tempo/soldi/energie a qc

spending ['spɛndɪŋ] N: **government ~** spesa pubblica

spending money N denaro per le piccole spese

spending power N potere m d'acquisto

spendthrift ['spɛndθrɪft] N spendaccione(-a)

spent [spɛnt] PT, PP of **spend** ▶ ADJ (patience) esaurito(-a); (cartridge, bullets, match) usato(-a)

sperm [spəːm] N sperma m

sperm bank N banca dello sperma

sperm whale N capodoglio

spew [spjuː] VT vomitare

sphere [sfɪəʳ] N sfera

spherical ['sfɛrɪkl] ADJ sferico(-a)

sphinx [sfɪŋks] N sfinge f

spice [spaɪs] N spezia ▶ VT aromatizzare

spick-and-span ['spɪkən'spæn] ADJ impeccabile

spicy ['spaɪsɪ] ADJ piccante

spider ['spaɪdəʳ] N ragno; **~'s web** ragnatela

spiel [spiːl] N (col) tiritera

spike [spaɪk] N punta; **spikes** NPL (Sport) scarpe fpl chiodate

spike heel N (US) tacco a spillo

spiky ['spaɪkɪ] ADJ (bush, branch) spinoso(-a); (animal) ricoperto(-a) di aculei

spill [spɪl] (pt, pp **spilt** [-t], **spilled** [-d]) VT versare, rovesciare ▶ VI versarsi, rovesciarsi; **to ~ the beans** (col) vuotare il sacco
▶ **spill out** VI riversarsi fuori
▶ **spill over** VI: **to ~ over (into)** (liquid) versarsi (in); (crowd) riversarsi (in)

spillage ['spɪlɪdʒ] N (event) fuoriuscita; (substance) sostanza fuoriuscita

spin [spɪn] (pt, pp **spun** [spʌn]) N (revolution of wheel) rotazione f; (Aviat) avvitamento; (trip in car) giretto ▶ VT (wool etc) filare; (wheel) far girare; (BRIT: clothes) mettere nella centrifuga ▶ VI girare; **to ~ a yarn** raccontare una storia; **to ~ a coin** (BRIT) lanciare in aria una moneta
▶ **spin out** VT far durare

spina bifida ['spaɪnə'bɪfɪdə] N spina bifida

spinach ['spɪnɪtʃ] N spinacio; (as food) spinaci mpl

spinal ['spaɪnl] ADJ spinale

spinal column N colonna vertebrale, spina dorsale

spinal cord N midollo spinale

spindly ['spɪndlɪ] ADJ lungo(-a) e sottile, filiforme

spin doctor N (col) esperto di comunicazioni responsabile dell'immagine di un partito politico

spin-dry ['spɪn'draɪ] VT asciugare con la centrifuga

spin-dryer [spɪn'draɪəʳ] N (BRIT) centrifuga

spine [spaɪn] N spina dorsale; (thorn) spina

spine-chilling ['spaɪntʃɪlɪŋ] ADJ agghiacciante

spineless ['spaɪnlɪs] ADJ invertebrato(-a), senza spina dorsale; (fig) smidollato(-a)

spinner ['spɪnəʳ] N (of thread) tessitore(-trice)

spinning ['spɪnɪŋ] N filatura

spinning top N trottola

spinning wheel N filatoio

spin-off ['spɪnɔf] N applicazione f secondaria

spinster ['spɪnstəʳ] N nubile f; zitella

spiral ['spaɪərl] N spirale f ▶ ADJ a spirale ▶ VI (prices) salire vertiginosamente; **the inflationary ~** la spirale dell'inflazione

spiral staircase N scala a chiocciola

spire ['spaɪəʳ] N guglia

spirit ['spɪrɪt] N (soul) spirito, anima; (ghost) spirito, fantasma m; (mood) stato d'animo, umore m; (courage) coraggio; **spirits** NPL (drink) alcolici mpl; **in good spirits** di buon umore; **in low spirits** triste, abbattuto(-a); **community ~**, **public ~** senso civico

spirit duplicator N duplicatore m a spirito

spirited ['spɪrɪtɪd] ADJ vivace, vigoroso(-a); (horse) focoso(-a)

spirit level N livella a bolla (d'aria)

spiritual ['spɪrɪtjuəl] ADJ spirituale ▶ N (also: **Negro spiritual**) spiritual m inv

spiritualism ['spɪrɪtjuəlɪzəm] N spiritismo

spit [spɪt] (pt, pp **spat** [spæt]) N (for roasting) spiedo; (spittle) sputo; (saliva) saliva ▶ vi sputare; (fire, fat) scoppiettare

spite [spaɪt] N dispetto ▶ vt contrariare, far dispetto a; **in ~ of** nonostante, malgrado

spiteful ['spaɪtful] ADJ dispettoso(-a); (tongue, remark) maligno(-a), velenoso(-a)

spitroast ['spɪt'rəust] vt cuocere allo spiedo

spitting ['spɪtɪŋ] N: **"~ prohibited"** "vietato sputare" ▶ ADJ: **to be the ~ image of sb** essere il ritratto vivente or sputato di qn

spittle ['spɪtl] N saliva; sputo

spiv [spɪv] N (Brit col) imbroglione m

splash [splæʃ] N spruzzo; (sound) tonfo; (of colour) schizzo ▶ vt spruzzare ▶ vi (also: **splash about**) sguazzare; **to ~ paint on the floor** schizzare il pavimento di vernice ▶ **splash out** vi (col: Brit) fare spese folli

splashdown ['splæʃdaun] N ammaraggio

splay [spleɪ] ADJ: **~ footed** che ha i piedi piatti

spleen [spli:n] N (Anat) milza

splendid ['splɛndɪd] ADJ splendido(-a), magnifico(-a)

splendour, (US) **splendor** ['splɛndər] N splendore m

splice [splaɪs] vt (rope) impiombare; (wood) calettare

splint [splɪnt] N (Med) stecca

splinter ['splɪntər] N scheggia ▶ vi scheggiarsi

splinter group N gruppo dissidente

split [splɪt] (pt, pp **~**) N spaccatura; (fig: division, quarrel) scissione f ▶ vt spaccare; (party) dividere; (work, profits) spartire, ripartire ▶ vi (divide) dividersi; **to do the splits** fare la spaccata; **to ~ the difference** dividersi la differenza
▶ **split up** vi (couple) separarsi, rompere; (meeting) sciogliersi

split-level ['splɪtlɛvl] ADJ (house) a piani sfalsati

split peas NPL piselli mpl secchi spaccati

split personality N doppia personalità

split second N frazione f di secondo

splitting ['splɪtɪŋ] ADJ: **a ~ headache** un mal di testa da impazzire

splutter ['splʌtər] vi farfugliare; sputacchiare

spoil [spɔɪl] (pt, pp **spoilt** [-t], **spoiled** [-d]) vt (damage) rovinare, guastare; (mar) sciupare; (child) viziare; (ballot paper) rendere nullo(-a), invalidare; **to be spoiling for a fight** morire dalla voglia di litigare

spoils [spɔɪlz] NPL bottino

spoilsport ['spɔɪlspɔːt] N guastafeste mf

spoilt [spɔɪlt] PT, PP of **spoil** ▶ ADJ (child) viziato(-a); (ballot paper) nullo(-a)

spoke [spəuk] PT of **speak** ▶ N raggio

spoken ['spəukn] PP of **speak**

spokesman ['spəuksmən] N (irreg) portavoce m inv

spokesperson ['spəukspəːsn] N portavoce mf

spokeswoman ['spəukswumən] N (irreg) portavoce f inv

sponge [spʌndʒ] N spugna; (Culin: also: **sponge cake**) pan m di Spagna ▶ vt spugnare, pulire con una spugna ▶ vi: **to ~ on** or **off** scroccare a

sponge bag N (Brit) nécessaire m inv

sponge cake N pan m di Spagna

sponger ['spʌndʒər] N (pej) parassita mf, scroccone(-a)

spongy ['spʌndʒɪ] ADJ spugnoso(-a)

sponsor ['spɔnsər] N (Radio, TV, Sport etc) sponsor m inv; (of enterprise, bill, for fund-raising) promotore(-trice) ▶ vt sponsorizzare; patrocinare; (Pol: bill) presentare; **I sponsored him at 3p a mile** (in fund-raising race) ho offerto in beneficenza 3 penny per ogni miglio che fa

sponsorship ['spɔnsəʃɪp] N sponsorizzazione f; patrocinio

spontaneity [spɔntə'neɪɪtɪ] N spontaneità

spontaneous [spɔn'teɪnɪəs] ADJ spontaneo(-a)

spoof [spu:f] N presa in giro, parodia

spooky ['spu:kɪ] ADJ (col) che fa accapponare la pelle

spool [spu:l] N bobina

spoon [spu:n] N cucchiaio

spoon-feed ['spu:nfi:d] vt nutrire con il cucchiaio; (fig) imboccare

spoonful ['spu:nful] N cucchiaiata

sporadic [spə'rædɪk] ADJ sporadico(-a)

sport [spɔːt] N sport m inv; (person) persona di spirito; (amusement) divertimento ▶ vt sfoggiare; **indoor/outdoor sports** sport mpl al chiuso/all'aria aperta; **to say sth in ~** dire qc per scherzo

sporting ['spɔːtɪŋ] ADJ sportivo(-a); **to give sb a ~ chance** dare a qn una possibilità (di vincere)

sport jacket N (US) = **sports jacket**

sports car N automobile f sportiva

sports centre N (Brit) centro sportivo

sports drink N sport drink m inv

sports ground N campo sportivo

sports jacket N (Brit) giacca sportiva

sportsman ['spɔːtsmən] N (irreg) sportivo

sportsmanship ['spɔːtsmənʃɪp] N spirito sportivo

sports page N pagina sportiva

sports utility vehicle N (esp US) SUV m inv

sportswear ['spɔːtsweər] N abiti mpl sportivi

sportswoman ['spɔːtswumən] N (irreg) sportiva

sporty ['spɔːtɪ] ADJ sportivo(-a)

spot [spɔt] N punto; (*mark*) macchia; (*dot: on pattern*) pallino; (*pimple*) foruncolo; (*place*) posto; (*Radio, TV: also*: **spot advertisement**) spot *m inv*; (*small amount*): **a ~ of** un po' di ▶ VT (*notice*) individuare, distinguere; **on the ~** sul posto; **to do sth on the ~** fare qc immediatamente *or* su due piedi; **to put sb on the ~** mettere qn in difficoltà; **to come out in spots** coprirsi di foruncoli

spot check N controllo senza preavviso
spotless ['spɔtlɪs] ADJ immacolato(-a)
spotlight ['spɔtlaɪt] N proiettore *m*; (*Aut*) faro ausiliario
spot-on [spɔt'ɔn] ADJ (BRIT) esatto(-a)
spot price N (*Comm*) prezzo del pronto
spotted ['spɔtɪd] ADJ macchiato(-a); a puntini, a pallini; **~ with** punteggiato(-a) di
spotty ['spɔtɪ] ADJ (*face*) foruncoloso(-a)
spouse [spauz] N sposo(-a)
spout [spaut] N (*of jug*) beccuccio; (*of liquid*) zampillo, getto ▶ VI zampillare
sprain [spreɪn] N storta, distorsione *f* ▶ VT: **to ~ one's ankle** storcersi una caviglia
sprang [spræŋ] PT *of* **spring**
sprawl [sprɔ:l] VI sdraiarsi (in modo scomposto); (*place*) estendersi (disordinatamente) ▶ N: **urban ~** sviluppo urbanistico incontrollato; **to send sb sprawling** mandare qn a gambe all'aria
spray [spreɪ] N spruzzo; (*container*) nebulizzatore *m*, spray *m inv*; (*of flowers*) mazzetto ▶ CPD (*deodorant*) spray *inv* ▶ VT spruzzare; (*crops*) irrorare
spread [sprɛd] (*pt, pp* **~**) N diffusione *f*; (*distribution*) distribuzione *f*; (*Press, Typ: two pages*) doppia pagina; (: *across columns*) articolo a più colonne; (*Culin*) pasta (da spalmare); (*col: food*) banchetto ▶ VT (*cloth*) stendere, distendere; (*butter etc*) spalmare; (*disease, knowledge*) propagare, diffondere ▶ VI stendersi, distendersi; spalmarsi; propagarsi, diffondersi; **middle-age ~** pancetta; **repayments will be ~ over 18 months** i versamenti saranno scaglionati lungo un periodo di 18 mesi
▶ **spread out** VI (*move apart*) separarsi
spread-eagled ['sprɛdi:gld] ADJ: **to be** *or* **lie ~** essere disteso(-a) a gambe e braccia aperte
spreadsheet ['sprɛdʃi:t] N (*Comput*) foglio elettronico
spree [spri:] N: **to go on a ~** fare baldoria
sprig [sprɪg] N ramoscello
sprightly ['spraɪtlɪ] ADJ vivace
spring [sprɪŋ] (*pt* **sprang** [spræŋ], *pp* **sprung** [sprʌŋ]) N (*leap*) salto, balzo; (*bounciness*) elasticità; (*coiled metal*) molla; (*season*) primavera; (*of water*) sorgente *f* ▶ VI saltare, balzare ▶ VT: **to ~ a leak** (*pipe etc*) cominciare a perdere; **to walk with a ~ in one's step**

camminare con passo elastico; **in ~**, **in the ~** in primavera; **to ~ from** provenire da; **to ~ into action** entrare (rapidamente) in azione; **he sprang the news on me** mi ha sorpreso con quella notizia
▶ **spring up** VI (*problem*) presentarsi
springboard ['sprɪŋbɔ:d] N trampolino
spring-clean [sprɪŋ'kli:n] N (*also*: **spring-cleaning**) grandi pulizie *fpl* di primavera
spring onion N (BRIT) cipollina
spring roll N *involtino fritto di verdure o carne tipico della cucina cinese*
springtime ['sprɪŋtaɪm] N primavera
springy ['sprɪŋɪ] ADJ elastico(-a)
sprinkle ['sprɪŋkl] VT spruzzare; spargere; **to ~ water** *etc* **on, ~ with water** *etc* spruzzare dell'acqua *etc* su; **to ~ sugar** *etc* **on, ~ with sugar** *etc* spolverizzare di zucchero *etc*; **sprinkled with** (*fig*) cosparso(-a) di
sprinkler ['sprɪŋklə'] N (*for lawn etc*) irrigatore *m*; (*for fire-fighting*) sprinkler *m inv*
sprinkling ['sprɪŋklɪŋ] N (*of water*) qualche goccia; (*of salt, sugar*) pizzico
sprint [sprɪnt] N scatto ▶ VI scattare; **the 200-metres ~** i 200 metri piani
sprinter ['sprɪntə'] N velocista *mf*
sprite [spraɪt] N elfo, folletto
spritzer ['sprɪtsə'] N spritz *m inv*
sprocket ['sprɔkɪt] N (*on printer etc*) dente *m*, rocchetto
sprout [spraut] VI germogliare
sprouts [sprauts] NPL (*also*: **Brussels sprouts**) cavolini *mpl* di Bruxelles
spruce [spru:s] N abete *m* rosso ▶ ADJ lindo(-a); azzimato(-a)
▶ **spruce up** VT (*tidy*) mettere in ordine; (*smarten up: room etc*) abbellire; **to ~ o.s. up** farsi bello(-a)
sprung [sprʌŋ] PP *of* **spring**
spry [spraɪ] ADJ arzillo(-a), sveglio(-a)
SPUC N ABBR (= *Society for the Protection of Unborn Children*) *associazione anti-abortista*
spun [spʌn] PT, PP *of* **spin**
spur [spə:'] N sperone *m*; (*fig*) sprone *m*, incentivo ▶ VT (*also*: **spur on**) spronare; **on the ~ of the moment** lì per lì
spurious ['spjuərɪəs] ADJ falso(-a)
spurn [spə:n] VT rifiutare con disprezzo, sdegnare
spurt [spə:t] N (*of water*) getto; (*of energy*) esplosione *f* ▶ VI sgorgare; zampillare; **to put in** *or* **on a ~** (*runner*) fare uno scatto; (*fig: in work etc*) affrettarsi, sbrigarsi
sputter ['spʌtə'] VI = **splutter**
spy [spaɪ] N spia ▶ CPD (*film, story*) di spionaggio ▶ VI: **to ~ on** spiare ▶ VT (*see*) scorgere
spying ['spaɪɪŋ] N spionaggio
spyware ['spaɪwɛə'] N (*Comput*) spyware *mpl*

799

Sq. ABBR (*in address*) = **square**

sq. ABBR (*Math etc*) = **square**

squabble ['skwɔbl] N battibecco ▶ VI bisticciarsi

squad [skwɔd] N (*Mil*) plotone *m*; (*Police*) squadra; **flying ~** (*Police*) volante *f*

squad car 'N (*BRIT Police*) automobile *f* della polizia

squaddie ['skwɔdɪ] N (*Mil: col*) burba

squadron ['skwɔdrn] N (*Mil*) squadrone *m*; (*Aviat*, *Naut*) squadriglia

squalid ['skwɔlɪd] ADJ sordido(-a)

squall [skwɔ:l] N burrasca

squalor ['skwɔlə'] N squallore *m*

squander ['skwɔndə'] VT dissipare

square [skwεə'] N quadrato; (*in town*) piazza; (*US: block of houses*) blocco, isolato; (*instrument*) squadra ▶ ADJ quadrato(-a); (*honest*) onesto(-a); (*col: ideas, person*) di vecchio stampo ▶ VT (*arrange*) regolare; (*Math*) elevare al quadrato; (*reconcile*) conciliare ▶ VI (*agree*) accordarsi; **a ~ meal** un pasto abbondante; **2 metres ~** di 2 metri per 2; **1 ~ metre** 1 metro quadrato; **we're back to ~ one** (*fig*) siamo al punto di partenza; **all ~** pari; **to get one's accounts ~** mettere in ordine i propri conti; **I'll ~ it with him** (*col*) sistemo io le cose con lui; **can you ~ it with your conscience?** (*reconcile*) puoi conciliarlo con la tua coscienza?

▶ **square up** VI (*BRIT: settle*) saldare, pagare; **to ~ up with sb** regolare i conti con qn

square bracket N (*Typ*) parentesi *f inv* quadra

squarely ['skwεəlɪ] ADV (*directly*) direttamente; (*honestly, fairly*) onestamente

square root N radice *f* quadrata

squash [skwɔʃ] N (*vegetable*) zucca; (*Sport*) squash *m*; **lemon/orange ~** (*BRIT*) sciroppo di limone/arancia ▶ VT schiacciare

squat [skwɔt] ADJ tarchiato(-a), tozzo(-a) ▶ VI accovacciarsi; (*on property*) occupare abusivamente

squatter ['skwɔtə'] N occupante *mf* abusivo(-a)

squawk [skwɔ:k] VI emettere strida rauche

squeak [skwi:k] VI squittire ▶ N (*of hinge, wheel etc*) cigolio; (*of shoes*) scricchiolio; (*of mouse etc*) squittio

squeaky ['skwi:kɪ] ADJ (*col*) cigolante; **to be ~ clean** (*fig*) avere un'immagine pulita

squeal [skwi:l] VI strillare

squeamish ['skwi:mɪʃ] ADJ schizzinoso(-a); disgustato(-a)

squeeze [skwi:z] N pressione *f*; (*also Econ*) stretta; (*credit squeeze*) stretta creditizia ▶ VT premere; (*hand, arm*) stringere ▶ VI (*also*: **squeeze in**) infilarsi; **to ~ past/under sth** passare vicino/sotto a qc con difficoltà; **a ~ of lemon** una spruzzata di limone

▶ **squeeze out** VT spremere

squelch [skwεltʃ] VI fare ciac; sguazzare

squib [skwɪb] N petardo

squid [skwɪd] N calamaro

squint [skwɪnt] VI essere strabico(-a); (*in the sunlight*) strizzare gli occhi ▶ N: **he has a ~** è strabico; **to ~ at sth** guardare qc di traverso; (*quickly*) dare un'occhiata a qc

squire ['skwaɪə'] N (*BRIT*) proprietario terriero

squirm [skwə:m] VI contorcersi

squirrel ['skwɪrəl] N scoiattolo

squirt [skwə:t] N schizzo ▶ VI schizzare; zampillare ▶ VT spruzzare

Sr ABBR = **senior**; **sister**

SRC N ABBR (*BRIT*: = *Students' Representative Council*) comitato di rappresentanza studenti

Sri Lanka [srɪ'læŋkə] N Sri Lanka *m*

SRO ABBR (*US*: = *standing room only*) solo posti in piedi

SS ABBR = **steamship**

SSA N ABBR (*US*: = *Social Security Administration*) ≈ Previdenza Sociale

SST N ABBR (*US*) = **supersonic transport**

ST ABBR (*US*: = *Standard Time*) ora ufficiale

St ABBR = **saint**; **street**

stab [stæb] N (*with knife etc*) pugnalata; (*of pain*) fitta; (*col: try*): **to have a ~ at (doing) sth** provare a fare qc ▶ VT pugnalare; **to ~ sb to death** uccidere qn a coltellate

stabbing ['stæbɪŋ] N: **there's been a ~** qualcuno è stato pugnalato ▶ ADJ (*pain, ache*) lancinante

stability [stə'bɪlɪtɪ] N stabilità

stabilization [steɪbəlaɪ'zeɪʃən] N stabilizzazione *f*

stabilize ['steɪbəlaɪz] VT stabilizzare ▶ VI stabilizzarsi

stabilizer ['steɪbəlaɪzə'] N (*Aviat*, *Naut*) stabilizzatore *m*

stable ['steɪbl] N (*for horses*) scuderia; (*for cattle*) stalla ▶ ADJ stabile; **riding stables** maneggio

staccato [stə'kɑ:təu] ADV in modo staccato ▶ ADJ (*Mus*) staccato(-a); (*sound*) scandito(-a)

stack [stæk] N catasta, pila; (*col*) mucchio, sacco ▶ VT accatastare, ammucchiare; **there's stacks of time to finish it** (*BRIT col*) abbiamo un sacco di tempo per finirlo

stadium ['steɪdɪəm] N stadio

staff [stɑ:f] N (*work force: gen*) personale *m*; (*: BRIT Scol*) personale insegnante; (*: servants*) personale di servizio; (*Mil*) stato maggiore; (*stick*) bastone *m* ▶ VT fornire di personale

staffroom ['stɑ:fru:m] N sala dei professori

Staffs ABBR (*BRIT*) = **Staffordshire**

stag [stæg] N cervo; (*BRIT Stock Exchange*) rialzista *mf* su nuove emissioni

stage [steɪdʒ] N (*platform*) palco; (*in theatre*)

palcoscenico; **the ~** il teatro, la scena; (point) fase f, stadio ▶ vt (play) allestire, mettere in scena; (demonstration) organizzare; (fig: perform: recovery etc) effettuare; **in stages** per gradi; a tappe; **in the early/final stages** negli stadi iniziali/finali; **to go through a difficult ~** attraversare un periodo difficile

stagecoach ['steɪdʒkəʊtʃ] N diligenza

stage door N ingresso degli artisti

stage fright N paura del pubblico

stagehand ['steɪdʒhænd] N macchinista m

stage-manage ['steɪdʒmænɪdʒ] vt allestire le scene per; montare

stage manager N direttore m di scena

stagger ['stægər] vi barcollare ▶ vt (person) sbalordire; (hours, holidays) scaglionare

staggering ['stægərɪŋ] ADJ (amazing) incredibile, sbalorditivo(-a)

staging post ['steɪdʒɪŋ-] N passaggio obbligato

stagnant ['stægnənt] ADJ stagnante

stagnate [stæg'neɪt] vi (also fig) stagnare

stagnation [stæg'neɪʃən] N stagnazione f, ristagno

stag night, stag party N festa di addio al celibato

staid [steɪd] ADJ posato(-a), serio(-a)

stain [steɪn] N macchia; (colouring) colorante m ▶ vt macchiare; (wood) tingere

stained glass [ˌsteɪnd'glɑːs] N vetro colorato

stained glass window ['steɪnd-] N vetrata

stainless ['steɪnlɪs] ADJ (steel) inossidabile

stain remover N smacchiatore m

stair [steər] N (step) gradino; **stairs** NPL (flight of stairs) scale fpl, scala

staircase ['steəkeɪs], **stairway** ['steəweɪ] N scale fpl, scala

stairwell ['steəwel] N tromba delle scale

stake [steɪk] N palo, piolo; (Comm) interesse m; (Betting) puntata, scommessa ▶ vt (bet) scommettere; (risk) rischiare; (also: **stake out**: area) delimitare con paletti; **to be at ~** essere in gioco; **to have a ~ in sth** avere un interesse in qc; **to ~ a claim (to sth)** rivendicare (qc)

stakeout ['steɪkaʊt] N sorveglianza

stalactite ['stæləktaɪt] N stalattite f

stalagmite ['stæləgmaɪt] N stalagmite f

stale [steɪl] ADJ (bread) raffermo(-a); (food) stantio(-a); (air) viziato(-a); (beer) svaporato(-a); (smell) di chiuso

stalemate ['steɪlmeɪt] N stallo; (fig) punto morto

stalk [stɔːk] N gambo, stelo ▶ vt inseguire ▶ vi camminare impettito(-a)

stall [stɔːl] N (in street, market etc) bancarella; (in stable) box m inv di stalla ▶ vt (Aut) far spegnere; (fig) bloccare ▶ vi (Aut) spegnersi, fermarsi; (fig) temporeggiare; **stalls** NPL (BRIT: in cinema, theatre) platea; **newspaper/flower ~** chiosco del giornalaio/del fioraio

stallholder ['stɔːlhəʊldər] N (BRIT) bancarellista mf

stallion ['stæljən] N stallone m

stalwart ['stɔːlwət] N membro fidato

stamen ['steɪmen] N stame m

stamina ['stæmɪnə] N vigore m, resistenza

stammer ['stæmər] N balbuzie f ▶ vi balbettare

stamp [stæmp] N (postage stamp) francobollo; (implement) timbro; (mark, also fig) marchio, impronta; (on document) bollo; timbro ▶ vi (also: **stamp one's foot**) battere il piede ▶ vt battere; (letter) affrancare; (mark with a stamp) timbrare; **stamped addressed envelope** busta affrancata per la risposta

▶ **stamp out** vt (fire) estinguere; (crime) eliminare; (opposition) soffocare

stamp album N album m inv per francobolli

stamp collecting N filatelia

stamp duty N (BRIT) bollo

stampede [stæm'piːd] N fuggi fuggi m inv; (of cattle) fuga precipitosa

stamp machine N distributore m automatico di francobolli

stance [stæns] N posizione f

stand [stænd] (pt, pp **stood** [stʊd]) N (position) posizione f; (Mil) resistenza; (for taxis) posteggio; (structure) supporto, sostegno; (at exhibition) stand m inv; (in shop) banco; (at market) bancarella; (booth) chiosco; (Sport) tribuna; (also: **music stand**) leggio m ▶ vi stare in piedi; (rise) alzarsi in piedi; (be placed) trovarsi ▶ vt (place) mettere, porre; (tolerate, withstand) resistere, sopportare; **to make a ~** prendere posizione; **to take a ~ on an issue** prendere posizione su un problema; **to ~ for parliament** (BRIT) presentarsi come candidato (per il parlamento); **to ~ guard or watch** (Mil) essere di guardia; **it stands to reason** è logico; **as things ~** stando così le cose; **to ~ sb a drink/meal** offrire da bere/un pranzo a qn; **I can't ~ him** non lo sopporto

▶ **stand aside** vi farsi da parte, scostarsi

▶ **stand back** vi prendere le distanze

▶ **stand by** vi (be ready) tenersi pronto(-a) ▶ vt fus (opinion) sostenere

▶ **stand down** vi (withdraw) ritirarsi; (Law) lasciare il banco dei testimoni

▶ **stand for** vt fus (signify) rappresentare, significare; (tolerate) sopportare, tollerare

▶ **stand in for** vt fus sostituire

▶ **stand out** vi (be prominent) spiccare

▶ **stand up** vi (rise) alzarsi in piedi

▶ **stand up for** vt fus difendere

▶ **stand up to** vt fus tener testa a, resistere a

stand-alone ['stændələʊn] ADJ (Comput) stand-alone inv

801

standard ['stændəd] N modello, standard m
inv; (level) livello; (flag) stendardo ▶ ADJ (size
etc) normale, standard inv; (practice) normale;
(model) di serie; **standards** NPL (morals)
principi mpl, valori mpl; **to be** or **come up to**
~ rispondere ai requisiti; **below** or **not up to**
~ (work) mediocre; **to apply a double** ~ usare
metri diversi (nel giudicare or fare etc); ~ **of
living** livello di vita

standardization [stændədaɪˈzeɪʃən] N
standardizzazione f

standardize ['stændədaɪz] VT normalizzare,
standardizzare

standard lamp N (BRIT) lampada a stelo

standard time N ora ufficiale

stand-by ['stændbaɪ] N riserva, sostituto; **to
be on** ~ (gen) tenersi pronto(-a); (doctor) essere
di guardia; **a** ~ **ticket** un biglietto standby;
to fly ~ essere in lista d'attesa per un volo

stand-by generator N generatore m
d'emergenza

stand-by passenger N (Aviat) passeggero(-a)
in lista d'attesa

stand-by ticket N (Aviat) biglietto senza
garanzia

stand-in ['stændɪn] N sostituto(-a); (Cine)
controfigura

standing ['stændɪŋ] ADJ diritto(-a), in piedi;
(permanent: committee) permanente; (: rule)
fisso(-a); (: army) regolare; (grievance)
continuo(-a) ▶ N rango, condizione f,
posizione f; (duration): **of 6 months'** ~ che
dura da 6 mesi; **of many years'** ~ che esiste
da molti anni; **it's a** ~ **joke** è diventato
proverbiale; **he was given a** ~ **ovation** tutti
si alzarono per applaudirlo; **a man of some**
~ un uomo di una certa importanza

standing committee N commissione f
permanente

standing order N (BRIT: at bank) ordine m di
pagamento (permanente); **standing orders**
NPL (Mil) regolamento

standing room N posto all'impiedi

stand-off ['stændɔf] N (esp US: stalemate)
situazione f di stallo

standoffish [stændˈɔfɪʃ] ADJ scostante,
freddo(-a)

standpat ['stændpæt] ADJ (US) irremovibile

standpipe ['stændpaɪp] N fontanella

standpoint ['stændpɔɪnt] N punto di vista

standstill ['stændstɪl] N: **at a** ~ fermo(-a);
(fig) a un punto morto; **to come to a** ~
fermarsi; giungere a un punto morto

stank [stæŋk] PT of **stink**

stanza ['stænzə] N stanza (poesia)

staple ['steɪpl] N (for papers) graffetta; (chief
product) prodotto principale ▶ ADJ (food etc) di
base; (crop, industry) principale ▶ VT cucire

stapler ['steɪplər] N cucitrice f

star [stɑːr] N stella; (celebrity) divo(-a);
(principal actor) vedette f inv ▶ VI: **to** ~ **(in)**
essere il (or la) protagonista (di) ▶ VT (Cine)
essere interpretato(-a) da; **the stars** NPL
(Astrology) le stelle; **four-** ~ **hotel** ≈ albergo di
prima categoria; **2-** ~ **petrol** (BRIT) ≈ benzina
normale; **4-** ~ **petrol** (BRIT) ≈ super f

star attraction N numero principale

starboard ['stɑːbəd] N dritta; **to** ~ a dritta

starch [stɑːtʃ] N amido

starched [stɑːtʃt] ADJ (collar) inamidato(-a)

starchy ['stɑːtʃɪ] ADJ (food) ricco(-a) di amido

stardom ['stɑːdəm] N celebrità

stare [stɛər] N sguardo fisso ▶ VI: **to** ~ **at**
fissare

starfish ['stɑːfɪʃ] N stella di mare

stark [stɑːk] ADJ (bleak) desolato(-a);
(simplicity, colour) austero(-a); (reality, poverty,
truth) crudo(-a) ▶ ADV: ~ **naked**
completamente nudo(-a)

starkers ['stɑːkəz] ADJ: **to be** ~ (BRIT col) essere
nudo(-a) come un verme

starlet ['stɑːlɪt] N (Cine) stellina

starlight ['stɑːlaɪt] N: **by** ~ alla luce delle
stelle

starling ['stɑːlɪŋ] N storno

starlit ['stɑːlɪt] ADJ stellato(-a)

starry ['stɑːrɪ] ADJ stellato(-a)

starry-eyed [stɑːrɪˈaɪd] ADJ (idealistic, gullible)
ingenuo(-a); (from wonder) meravigliato(-a)

Stars and Stripes NPL: **the** ~ la bandiera a
stelle e strisce

star sign N segno zodiacale

star-studded ['stɑːstʌdɪd] ADJ: **a** ~ **cast** un
cast di attori famosi

start [stɑːt] N inizio; (of race) partenza;
(sudden movement) sobbalzo; (advantage)
vantaggio ▶ VT cominciare, iniziare; (found:
business, newspaper) fondare, creare; (: car)
mettere in moto ▶ VI cominciare; (on journey)
partire, mettersi in viaggio; (jump)
sobbalzare; **to** ~ **doing sth** (in)cominciare a
fare qc; **at the** ~ all'inizio; **for a** ~ tanto per
cominciare; **to make an early** ~ partire di
buon'ora; **to** ~ **(off) with ...** (firstly) per
prima cosa ...; (at the beginning) all'inizio; **to** ~
a fire provocare un incendio
▶ **start off** VI cominciare; (leave) partire
▶ **start out** VI (begin) cominciare; (set out)
partire
▶ **start over** VI (US) ricominciare
▶ **start up** VI cominciare; (car) avviarsi ▶ VT
iniziare; (car) avviare

starter ['stɑːtər] N (Aut) motorino
d'avviamento; (Sport: official) starter m inv;
(: runner, horse) partente mf; (BRIT Culin) primo
piatto

starting handle ['stɑːtɪŋ-] N (BRIT)
manovella d'avviamento

starting point N punto di partenza
starting price N prezzo m base *inv*
startle ['stɑːtl] VT far trasalire
startling ['stɑːtlɪŋ] ADJ sorprendente, sbalorditivo(-a)
star turn N (BRIT) attrazione f principale
starvation [stɑːˈveɪʃən] N fame f, inedia; **to die of** ~ morire d'inedia
starve [stɑːv] VI morire di fame; soffrire la fame ▶ VT far morire di fame, affamare; **I'm starving** muoio di fame
stash [stæʃ] VT: **to** ~ **sth away** (*col*) nascondere qc
state [steɪt] N stato; (*pomp*): **in** ~ in pompa ▶ VT dichiarare, affermare; annunciare; **to be in a** ~ essere agitato(-a); **the** ~ **of the art** il livello di tecnologia (*or* cultura *etc*); ~ **of emergency** stato di emergenza; ~ **of mind** stato d'animo
state control N controllo statale
stated ['steɪtɪd] ADJ fissato(-a), stabilito(-a)
State Department N (US) Dipartimento di Stato, = Ministero degli Esteri
state education N (BRIT) istruzione f pubblica *or* statale
stateless ['steɪtlɪs] ADJ apolide
stately ['steɪtlɪ] ADJ maestoso(-a), imponente
stately home N residenza nobiliare (*d'interesse storico o artistico spesso aperta al pubblico*)
statement ['steɪtmənt] N dichiarazione f; (*Law*) deposizione f; (*Finance*) rendiconto; **official** ~ comunicato ufficiale; ~ **of account, bank** ~ estratto conto
state-owned ['steɪt'əund] ADJ statalizzato(-a)
States [steɪts] NPL: **the** ~ (*USA*) gli Stati Uniti
state school N scuola statale
statesman ['steɪtsmən] N (*irreg*) statista m
statesmanship ['steɪtsmənʃɪp] N abilità politica
static ['stætɪk] N (*Radio*) scariche fpl ▶ ADJ statico(-a); ~ **electricity** elettricità statica
station ['steɪʃən] N stazione f; (*rank*) rango, condizione f ▶ VT collocare, disporre; **action stations** posti mpl di combattimento; **to be stationed in** (*Mil*) essere di stanza in
stationary ['steɪʃənərɪ] ADJ fermo(-a), immobile
stationer ['steɪʃənəʳ] N cartolaio(-a); ~**'s shop** cartoleria
stationery ['steɪʃənərɪ] N articoli mpl di cancelleria; (*writing paper*) carta da lettere
station master N (*Rail*) capostazione m
station wagon N (US) giardinetta
statistic [stəˈtɪstɪk] N statistica; *see also* **statistics**
statistical [stəˈtɪstɪkəl] ADJ statistico(-a)
statistics [stəˈtɪstɪks] N (*science*) statistica

statue ['stætjuː] N statua
statuesque [stætjuˈɛsk] ADJ statuario(-a)
statuette [stætjuˈɛt] N statuetta
stature ['stætʃəʳ] N statura
status ['steɪtəs] N posizione f, condizione f sociale; (*prestige*) prestigio; (*legal, marital*) stato
status quo [-ˈkwəu] N: **the** ~ lo statu quo
status symbol N simbolo di prestigio
statute ['stætjuːt] N legge f; **statutes** NPL (*of club etc*) statuto
statute book N codice m
statutory ['stætjutərɪ] ADJ stabilito(-a) dalla legge, statutario(-a); ~ **meeting** (*Comm*) assemblea ordinaria
staunch [stɔːntʃ] ADJ fidato(-a), leale ▶ VT (*flow*) arrestare; (*blood*) arrestare il flusso di
stave [steɪv] N (*Mus*) rigo ▶ VT: **to** ~ **off** (*attack*) respingere; (*threat*) evitare
stay [steɪ] N (*period of time*) soggiorno, permanenza ▶ VI rimanere; (*reside*) alloggiare, stare; (*spend some time*) trattenersi, soggiornare; ~ **of execution** (*Law*) sospensione f dell'esecuzione; **to** ~ **put** non muoversi; **to** ~ **with friends** stare presso amici; **to** ~ **the night** passare la notte
   ▶ **stay away** VI (*from person, building*) stare lontano (*from event*) non andare
   ▶ **stay behind** VI restare indietro
   ▶ **stay in** VI (*at home*) stare in casa
   ▶ **stay on** VI restare, rimanere
   ▶ **stay out** VI (*of house*) rimanere fuori (di casa); (*strikers*) continuare lo sciopero
   ▶ **stay up** VI (*at night*) rimanere alzato(-a)
staying power ['steɪɪŋ-] N capacità di resistenza
STD N ABBR (BRIT: = *subscriber trunk dialling*) teleselezione f; (= *sexually transmitted disease*) malattia venerea
stead [stɛd] N (BRIT): **in sb's** ~ al posto di qn; **to stand sb in good** ~ essere utile a qn
steadfast ['stɛdfɑːst] ADJ fermo(-a), risoluto(-a)
steadily ['stɛdɪlɪ] ADV (*firmly*) saldamente; (*constantly*) continuamente; (*fixedly*) fisso; (*walk*) con passo sicuro
steady ['stɛdɪ] ADJ (*not wobbling*) stabile, solido(-a), fermo(-a); (*regular*) costante; (*boyfriend etc*) fisso(-a); (*person, character*) serio(-a); (: *calm*) calmo(-a), tranquillo(-a)
   ▶ VT stabilizzare; calmare; **to** ~ **o.s.** ritrovare l'equilibrio
steak [steɪk] N (*meat*) bistecca; (*fish*) trancia
steakhouse ['steɪkhaus] N *ristorante specializzato in bistecche*
steal [stiːl] (*pt* **stole** [stəul], *pp* **stolen** ['stəuln]) VT rubare ▶ VI (*thieve*) rubare; (*move*) muoversi furtivamente
   ▶ **steal away, steal off** VI svignarsela, andarsene alla chetichella

S

stealth [stɛlθ] N: **by ~** furtivamente

stealthy ['stɛlθɪ] ADJ furtivo(-a)

steam [sti:m] N vapore m ▶ VT trattare con vapore; (Culin) cuocere a vapore ▶ VI fumare; (ship): **to ~ along** filare; **to let off ~** (fig) sfogarsi; **under one's own ~** (fig) da solo, con i propri mezzi; **to run out of ~** (fig: person) non farcela più
  ▶ **steam up** VI (window) appannarsi; **to get steamed up about sth** (fig) andare in bestia per qc

steam engine N macchina a vapore; (Rail) locomotiva a vapore

steamer ['sti:mə^r] N piroscafo, vapore m; (Culin) pentola a vapore

steam iron N ferro a vapore

steamroller ['sti:mrəulə^r] N rullo compressore

steamship ['sti:mʃɪp] N piroscafo, vapore m

steamy ['sti:mɪ] ADJ (room) pieno(-a) di vapore; (window) appannato(-a)

steed [sti:d] N (literary) corsiero, destriero

steel [sti:l] N acciaio ▶ CPD di acciaio

steel band N banda di strumenti a percussione (tipica dei Caribi)

steel industry N industria dell'acciaio

steel mill N acciaieria

steelworks ['sti:lwə:ks] N acciaieria

steely ['sti:lɪ] ADJ (determination) inflessibile; (gaze) duro(-a); (eyes) freddo(-a) come l'acciaio

steep [sti:p] ADJ ripido(-a), scosceso(-a); (price) eccessivo(-a) ▶ VT inzuppare; (washing) mettere a mollo

steeple ['sti:pl] N campanile m

steeplechase ['sti:pltʃeɪs] N corsa a ostacoli, steeplechase m inv

steeplejack ['sti:pldʒæk] N chi ripara campanili e ciminiere

steer [stɪə^r] N manzo ▶ VT (ship) governare; (car) guidare ▶ VI (Naut: person) governare; (: ship) rispondere al timone; (car) guidarsi; **to ~ clear of sb/sth** (fig) tenersi alla larga da qn/qc

steering ['stɪərɪŋ] N (Aut) sterzo

steering column N piantone m dello sterzo

steering committee N comitato direttivo

steering wheel N volante m

stem [stɛm] N (of flower, plant) stelo; (of tree) fusto; (of glass) gambo; (of fruit, leaf) picciolo ▶ VT contenere, arginare
  ▶ **stem from** VT FUS provenire da, derivare da

stem cell N cellula staminale

stench [stɛntʃ] N puzzo, fetore m

stencil ['stɛnsl] N (of metal, cardboard) stampino, mascherina; (in typing) matrice f

stenographer [stɛ'nɔgrəfə^r] N (US) stenografo(-a)

stenography [stɛ'nɔgrəfɪ] N (US) stenografia

step [stɛp] N passo; (stair) gradino, scalino; (action) mossa, azione f ▶ VI: **to ~ forward/back** fare un passo avanti/indietro; **steps** NPL (BRIT) = **stepladder**; **~ by ~** un passo dietro l'altro; (fig) poco a poco; **to be in/out of ~ with** (also fig) stare/non stare al passo con
  ▶ **step down** VI (fig) ritirarsi
  ▶ **step in** VI fare il proprio ingresso
  ▶ **step off** VT FUS scendere da
  ▶ **step over** VT FUS scavalcare
  ▶ **step up** VT aumentare; intensificare

step aerobics N step m inv

stepbrother ['stɛpbrʌðə^r] N fratellastro

stepchild ['stɛptʃaɪld] N (irreg) figliastro(-a)

stepdaughter ['stɛpdɔ:tə^r] N figliastra

stepfather ['stɛpfɑ:ðə^r] N patrigno

stepladder ['stɛplædə^r] N scala a libretto

stepmother ['stɛpmʌðə^r] N matrigna

stepping stone ['stɛpɪŋ-] N pietra di un guado; (fig) trampolino

step Reebok® [-'ri:bɔk] N step m inv

stepsister ['stɛpsɪstə^r] N sorellastra

stepson ['stɛpsʌn] N figliastro

stereo ['stɛrɪəu] N (system) sistema m stereofonico; (record player) stereo m inv ▶ ADJ (also: **stereophonic**) stereofonico(-a); **in ~** in stereofonia

stereotype ['stɪərɪətaɪp] N stereotipo

sterile ['stɛraɪl] ADJ sterile

sterility [stɛ'rɪlɪtɪ] N sterilità

sterilization [stɛrɪlaɪ'zeɪʃən] N sterilizzazione f

sterilize ['stɛrɪlaɪz] VT sterilizzare

sterling ['stə:lɪŋ] ADJ (gold, silver) di buona lega; (fig) autentico(-a), genuino(-a) ▶ N (Econ) (lira) sterlina; **a pound ~** una lira sterlina

sterling area N area della sterlina

stern [stə:n] ADJ severo(-a) ▶ N (Naut) poppa

sternum ['stə:nəm] N sterno

steroid ['stɛrɔɪd] N steroide m

stethoscope ['stɛθəskəup] N stetoscopio

stevedore ['sti:vɪdɔ:^r] N scaricatore m di porto

stew [stju:] N stufato ▶ VT, VI cuocere in umido; **stewed tea** tè lasciato troppo in infusione; **stewed fruit** frutta cotta

steward ['stju:əd] N (Aviat, Naut, Rail) steward m inv; (in club etc) dispensiere m; (shop steward) rappresentante mf sindacale

stewardess ['stju:ədɛs] N assistente f di volo, hostess f inv

stewardship ['stju:ədʃɪp] N amministrazione f

stewing steak ['stju:ɪŋ-], (US) **stew meat** N carne f (di manzo) per stufato

St. Ex. ABBR = **stock exchange**

stg ABBR = **sterling**

stick [stɪk] (*pt, pp* **stuck** [stʌk]) N bastone *m*; (*of rhubarb, celery*) gambo; (*of dynamite*) candelotto ▶ VT (*glue*) attaccare; (*thrust*): **to ~ sth into** conficcare *or* piantare *or* infiggere qc in; (*col: put*) ficcare; (: *tolerate*) sopportare ▶ VI attaccarsi; tenere; (*remain*) restare, rimanere; (*get jammed: door, lift*) bloccarsi; **to ~ to** (*one's word, promise*) mantenere; (*principles*) tener fede a; **to get hold of the wrong end of the ~** (*fig*) capire male; **it stuck in my mind** mi è rimasto in mente
  ▶ **stick around** VI (*col*) restare, fermarsi
  ▶ **stick out** VI sporgere, spuntare ▶ VT: **to ~ it out** (*col*) tener duro
  ▶ **stick up** VI sporgere, spuntare
  ▶ **stick up for** VT FUS difendere
sticker ['stɪkər] N cartellino adesivo
sticking plaster ['stɪkɪŋ-] N cerotto adesivo
sticking point N (*fig*) punto di stallo, impasse *f inv*
stick insect N insetto *m* stecco *inv*
stickleback ['stɪklbæk] N spinarello
stickler ['stɪklər] N: **to be a ~ for** essere pignolo(-a) su, tenere molto a
stick-on ['stɪkɔn] ADJ (*label*) adesivo(-a)
stick shift N (*US Aut*) cambio manuale
stick-up ['stɪkʌp] N (*col*) rapina a mano armata
sticky ['stɪkɪ] ADJ attaccaticcio(-a), vischioso(-a); (*label*) adesivo(-a); (*fig: situation*) difficile
stiff [stɪf] ADJ rigido(-a), duro(-a); (*muscle*) legato(-a), indolenzito(-a); (*difficult*) difficile, arduo(-a); (*cold: manner etc*) freddo(-a), formale; (*strong*) forte; (*high: price*) molto alto(-a) ▶ ADV: **bored ~** annoiato(-a) a morte; **to be** *or* **feel ~** (*person*) essere *or* sentirsi indolenzito; **to have a ~ neck/back** avere il torcicollo/mal di schiena; **to keep a ~ upper lip** (*BRIT fig*) conservare il sangue freddo
stiffen ['stɪfn] VT irrigidire; rinforzare ▶ VI irrigidirsi; indurirsi
stiffness ['stɪfnɪs] N rigidità; indolenzimento; difficoltà; freddezza
stifle ['staɪfl] VT soffocare
stifling ['staɪflɪŋ] ADJ (*heat*) soffocante
stigma ['stɪgmə] N (*pl* (*Bot, Med*) **stigmata** [stɪg'mɑːtə], *pl* (*fig*) **stigmas**) stigma *m*
stigmata [stɪg'mɑːtə] NPL (*Rel*) stigmate *fpl*
stile [staɪl] N cavalcasiepe *m*; cavalcasteccato
stiletto [stɪ'letəu] N (*BRIT: also:* **stiletto heel**) tacco a spillo
still [stɪl] ADJ fermo(-a); (*quiet*) silenzioso(-a); (*orange juice etc*) non gassato(-a) ▶ ADV (*up to this time, even*) ancora; (*nonetheless*) tuttavia, ciò nonostante ▶ N (*Cine*) fotogramma *m*; **keep ~!** stai fermo!; **he ~ hasn't arrived** non è ancora arrivato
stillborn ['stɪlbɔːn] ADJ nato(-a) morto(-a)

still life N natura morta
stilt [stɪlt] N trampolo; (*pile*) palo
stilted ['stɪltɪd] ADJ freddo(-a), formale; artificiale
stimulant ['stɪmjulənt] N stimolante *m*
stimulate ['stɪmjuleɪt] VT stimolare
stimulating ['stɪmjuleɪtɪŋ] ADJ stimolante
stimulation [stɪmju'leɪʃən] N stimolazione *f*
stimulus ['stɪmjuləs] (*pl* **stimuli** ['stɪmjulaɪ]) N stimolo
sting [stɪŋ] (*pt, pp* **stung**) N puntura; (*organ*) pungiglione *m*; (*col*) trucco ▶ VT pungere ▶ VI bruciare; **my eyes are stinging** mi bruciano gli occhi
stingy ['stɪndʒɪ] ADJ spilorcio(-a), tirchio(-a)
stink [stɪŋk] (*pt* **stank** [stæŋk], *pp* **stunk** [stʌŋk]) N fetore *m*, puzzo ▶ VI puzzare
stinker ['stɪŋkər] N (*col*) porcheria; (*person*) fetente *mf*
stinking ['stɪŋkɪŋ] ADJ (*col*): **a ~ ...** uno schifo di ..., un(-a) maledetto(-a) ...; **~ rich** ricco(-a) da far paura
stint [stɪnt] N lavoro, compito ▶ VI: **to ~ on** lesinare su
stipend ['staɪpend] N stipendio, congrua
stipendiary [staɪ'pendɪərɪ] ADJ: **~ magistrate** magistrato stipendiato
stipulate ['stɪpjuleɪt] VT stipulare
stipulation [stɪpju'leɪʃən] N stipulazione *f*
stir [stəːr] N agitazione *f*, clamore *m* ▶ VT mescolare; (*move*) smuovere, agitare; (*fig*) risvegliare ▶ VI muoversi; **to give sth a ~** mescolare qc; **to cause a ~** fare scalpore
  ▶ **stir up** VT provocare, suscitare
stir-fry ['stəː'fraɪ] VT saltare in padella ▶ N pietanza al salto
stirring ['stəːrɪŋ] ADJ eccitante; commovente
stirrup ['stɪrəp] N staffa
stitch [stɪtʃ] N (*Sewing*) punto; (*Knitting*) maglia; (*Med*) punto (di sutura); (*pain*) fitta ▶ VT cucire, attaccare; suturare
stoat [stəut] N ermellino
stock [stɔk] N riserva, provvista; (*Comm*) giacenza, stock *m inv*; (*Agr*) bestiame *m*; (*Culin*) brodo; (*Finance*) titoli *mpl*, azioni *fpl*; (*Rail: also:* **rolling stock**) materiale *m* rotabile; (: *descent, origin*) stirpe *f* ▶ ADJ (*fig: reply etc*) consueto(-a), solito(-a), classico(-a); (*greeting*) usuale; (*Comm: goods, size*) standard *inv* ▶ VT (*have in stock*) avere, vendere; **well-stocked** ben fornito(-a); **to have sth in ~** avere qc in magazzino; **out of ~** esaurito(-a); **to take ~** (*fig*) fare il punto; **stocks and shares** valori *mpl* di borsa; **government ~** titoli di Stato
  ▶ **stock up** VI: **to ~ up (with)** fare provvista (di)
stockade [stɔ'keɪd] N palizzata
stockbroker ['stɔkbrəukər] N agente *m* di cambio

S

stock control N gestione f magazzino
stock cube N (BRIT Culin) dado
stock exchange N Borsa (valori)
stockholder ['stɔkhəuldə'] N (Finance) azionista mf
Stockholm ['stɔkhəum] N Stoccolma
stocking ['stɔkɪŋ] N calza
stock-in-trade ['stɔkɪn'treɪd] N (fig): **it's his ~** è la sua specialità
stockist ['stɔkɪst] N (BRIT) fornitore m
stock market N (BRIT) Borsa, mercato finanziario
stock phrase N cliché m inv
stockpile ['stɔkpaɪl] N riserva ▶ VT accumulare riserve di
stockroom ['stɔkrum] N magazzino
stocktaking ['stɔkteɪkɪŋ] N (BRIT Comm) inventario
stocky ['stɔkɪ] ADJ tarchiato(-a), tozzo(-a)
stodgy ['stɔdʒɪ] ADJ pesante, indigesto(-a)
stoic ['stəuɪk] N stoico(-a)
stoical ['stəuɪkəl] ADJ stoico(-a)
stoke [stəuk] VT alimentare
stoker ['stəukə'] N fochista m
stole [stəul] PT of **steal** ▶ N stola
stolen ['stəuln] PP of **steal**
stolid ['stɔlɪd] ADJ impassibile
stomach ['stʌmək] N stomaco; (abdomen) ventre m; (belly) pancia ▶ VT sopportare, digerire
stomach ache N mal m di stomaco
stomach pump N pompa gastrica
stomach ulcer N ulcera allo stomaco
stomp [stɔmp] VI: **to ~ in/out** etc entrare/uscire etc con passo pesante
stone [stəun] N pietra; (pebble) sasso, ciottolo; (in fruit) nocciolo; (Med) calcolo; (BRIT: weight) 6.348 kg., 14 libbre ▶ CPD di pietra ▶ VT lapidare; (fruit) togliere il nocciolo a; **within a ~'s throw of the station** a due passi dalla stazione
Stone Age N: **the ~** l'età della pietra
stone-cold [stəun'kəuld] ADJ gelido(-a)
stoned [stəund] ADJ (col: drunk) sbronzo(-a); (on drugs) fuori inv
stone-deaf [stəun'dɛf] ADJ sordo(-a) come una campana
stonemason ['stəunmeɪsn] N scalpellino
stonewall [stəun'wɔːl] VI fare ostruzionismo ▶ VT ostacolare
stonework ['stəunwəːk] N muratura
stony ['stəunɪ] ADJ pietroso(-a), sassoso(-a)
stood [stud] PT, PP of **stand**
stooge [stuːdʒ] N (col) tirapiedi mf
stool [stuːl] N sgabello
stoop [stuːp] VI (also: **have a stoop**) avere una curvatura; (also: **stoop down**: bend) chinarsi, curvarsi; **to ~ to sth/doing sth** abbassarsi a qc/a fare qc

stop [stɔp] N arresto; (stopping place) fermata; (in punctuation) punto ▶ VT arrestare, fermare; (break off) interrompere; (also: **put a stop to**) porre fine a; (: prevent) impedire ▶ VI fermarsi; (rain, noise etc) cessare, finire; **to ~ doing sth** cessare or finire di fare qc; **to ~ sb (from) doing sth** impedire a qn di fare qc; **to ~ dead** fermarsi di colpo; **~ it!** smettila!, basta!
▶ **stop by** VI passare, fare un salto
▶ **stop off** VI sostare brevemente
▶ **stop up** VT (hole) chiudere, turare
stopcock ['stɔpkɔk] N rubinetto di arresto
stopgap ['stɔpgæp] N (person) tappabuchi mf; (measure) ripiego ▶ CPD (measures, solution) di fortuna
stoplights ['stɔplaɪts] NPL (Aut) stop mpl
stopover ['stɔpəuvə'] N breve sosta; (Aviat) scalo
stoppage ['stɔpɪdʒ] N arresto, fermata; (of pay) trattenuta; (strike) interruzione f del lavoro
stopper ['stɔpə'] N tappo
stop press N ultimissime fpl
stopwatch ['stɔpwɔtʃ] N cronometro
storage ['stɔːrɪdʒ] N immagazzinamento; (Comput) memoria
storage heater N (BRIT) radiatore m elettrico che accumula calore
store [stɔː'] N provvista, riserva; (depot) deposito; (BRIT: department store) grande magazzino; (US: shop) negozio ▶ VT mettere da parte; conservare; (grain, goods) immagazzinare; (Comput) registrare; **to set great/little ~ by sth** dare molta/poca importanza a qc; **in ~** di riserva; in serbo; **who knows what is in ~ for us?** chissà cosa ci riserva il futuro?
▶ **store up** VT mettere in serbo, conservare
storehouse ['stɔːhaus] N magazzino, deposito
storekeeper ['stɔːkiːpə'] N (US) negoziante mf
storeroom ['stɔːrum] N dispensa
storey, (US) **story** ['stɔːrɪ] N piano
stork [stɔːk] N cicogna
storm [stɔːm] N tempesta; (also: **thunderstorm**) temporale m, burrasca; uragano; (fig) infuriarsi ▶ VT prendere d'assalto
storm cloud N nube f temporalesca
storm door N controporta
stormy ['stɔːmɪ] ADJ tempestoso(-a), burrascoso(-a)
story ['stɔːrɪ] N storia; favola; racconto; (Press) articolo; (US) = **storey**
storybook ['stɔːrɪbuk] N libro di racconti
storyteller ['stɔːrɪtɛlə'] N narratore(-trice)
stout [staut] ADJ solido(-a), robusto(-a); (brave) coraggioso(-a); (supporter) tenace; (fat)

corpulento(-a), grasso(-a) ▶ N birra scura

stove [stəʊv] N (for cooking) fornello; (: small) fornelletto; (for heating) stufa; **gas/electric ~** cucina a gas/elettrica

stow [stəʊ] VT mettere via

stowaway ['stəʊəweɪ] N passeggero(-a) clandestino(-a)

straddle ['strædl] VT stare a cavalcioni di

strafe [strɑːf] VT mitragliare

straggle ['strægl] VI crescere (or estendersi) disordinatamente; trascinarsi; rimanere indietro; **straggled along the coast** disseminati(-e) lungo la costa

straggler ['stræglə^r] N sbandato(-a)

straggling ['stræglɪŋ], **straggly** ['stræglɪ] ADJ (hair) in disordine

straight [streɪt] ADJ (continuous, direct) dritto(-a); (frank) onesto(-a), franco(-a); (plain, uncomplicated) semplice; (Theat: part, play) serio(-a); (col: heterosexual) eterosessuale ▶ ADV diritto; (drink) liscio ▶ N: **the ~** la linea retta; (Rail) il rettilineo; (Sport) la dirittura d'arrivo; **to put** or **get ~** mettere in ordine, mettere ordine in; **to be (all) ~** (tidy) essere a posto, essere sistemato; (clarified) essere chiaro; **ten ~ wins** dieci vittorie di fila; **~ away, ~ off** (at once) immediatamente; **~ off, ~ out** senza esitare; **I went ~ home** sono andato direttamente a casa

straighten ['streɪtn] VT (also: **straighten out**) raddrizzare; **to ~ things out** mettere le cose a posto

straighteners ['streɪtnəz] NPL (for hair) piastra f per capelli

straight-faced [streɪt'feɪst] ADJ impassibile, imperturbabile ▶ ADV con il viso serio

straightforward [streɪt'fɔːwəd] ADJ semplice; (frank) onesto(-a), franco(-a)

strain [streɪn] N (Tech) sollecitazione f; (physical) sforzo; (mental) tensione f; (Med) strappo; distorsione f; (streak, trace) tendenza; elemento; (breed) razza; (of virus) tipo ▶ VT tendere; (muscle) stirare; (ankle) slogar; (friendship, marriage) mettere a dura prova; (filter) colare, filtrare; (resources) pesare su; (food) colare; passare ▶ VI sforzarsi; **strains** NPL (Mus) note fpl; **she's under a lot of ~** è molto tesa, è sotto pressione

strained [streɪnd] ADJ (muscle) stirato(-a); (laugh etc) forzato(-a); (relations) teso(-a)

strainer ['streɪnə^r] N passino, colino

strait [streɪt] N (Geo) stretto; **straits** NPL: **to be in dire straits** (fig) essere nei guai

straitjacket ['streɪtdʒækɪt] N camicia di forza

strait-laced [streɪt'leɪst] ADJ puritano(-a)

strand [strænd] N (of thread) filo

stranded ADJ nei guai; senza mezzi di trasporto

strange [streɪndʒ] ADJ (not known) sconosciuto(-a); (odd) strano(-a), bizzarro(-a)

strangely ['streɪndʒlɪ] ADV stranamente

stranger ['streɪndʒə^r] N (unknown) sconosciuto(-a); (from another place) estraneo(-a); **I'm a ~ here** non sono del posto

strangle ['stræŋgl] VT strangolare

stranglehold ['stræŋglhəʊld] N (fig) stretta (mortale)

strangulation [stræŋgju'leɪʃən] N strangolamento

strap [stræp] N cinghia; (of slip, dress) spallina, bretella ▶ VT legare con una cinghia; (child etc) punire con una cinghia)

straphanging ['stræphæŋɪŋ] N viaggiare m in piedi (su mezzi pubblici reggendosi a un sostegno)

strapless ['stræplɪs] ADJ (bra, dress) senza spalline

strapped [stræpt] ADJ: **~ for cash** a corto di soldi; **financially ~** finanziariamente a terra

strapping ['stræpɪŋ] ADJ ben piantato(-a)

Strasbourg ['stræzbəːg] N Strasburgo f

strata ['strɑːtə] NPL of **stratum**

stratagem ['strætɪdʒəm] N stratagemma m

strategic [strə'tiːdʒɪk] ADJ strategico(-a)

strategist ['strætɪdʒɪst] N stratega m

strategy ['strætɪdʒɪ] N strategia

stratosphere ['strætəsfɪə^r] N stratosfera

stratum ['strɑːtəm] (pl **strata** ['strɑːtə]) N strato

straw [strɔː] N paglia; (drinking straw) cannuccia; **that's the last ~!** è la goccia che fa traboccare il vaso!

strawberry ['strɔːbərɪ] N fragola

stray [streɪ] ADJ (animal) randagio(-a); (bullet) vagante; (scattered) sparso(-a) ▶ VI perdersi; allontanarsi, staccarsi (dal gruppo); **~ bullet** proiettile m vagante

streak [striːk] N striscia; (of hair) mèche f inv; **a ~ of** una vena di ▶ VT striare, screziare ▶ VI: **to ~ past** passare come un fulmine; **to have streaks in one's hair** avere le mèche nei capelli; **a winning/losing ~** un periodo fortunato/sfortunato

streaker ['striːkə^r] N streaker mf

streaky ['striːkɪ] ADJ screziato(-a), striato(-a)

streaky bacon N (BRIT) ≈ pancetta

stream [striːm] N ruscello; corrente f; (of people, smoke etc) fiume m ▶ VT (Scol) dividere in livelli di rendimento ▶ VI scorrere; **to ~ in/out** entrare/uscire a fiotti; **against the ~** controcorrente; **on ~** (new power plant etc) in funzione, in produzione

streamer ['striːmə^r] N (of paper) stella filante

stream feed N (on photocopier etc) alimentazione f continua

streamline ['striːmlaɪn] VT dare una linea aerodinamica a; (fig) razionalizzare

streamlined ['stri:mlaɪnd] ADJ
aerodinamico(-a), affusolato(-a); (fig)
razionalizzato(-a)

street [stri:t] N strada, via; **the back streets**
le strade secondarie; **to be on the streets**
(homeless) essere senza tetto; (as prostitute)
battere il marciapiede

streetcar ['stri:tkɑ:ʳ] N (US) tram m inv

street cred [-krɛd] N (col) credibilità presso i
giovani

street lamp N lampione m

street light N lampione m

street lighting N illuminazione f stradale

street map N pianta (di una città)

street market N mercato all'aperto

street plan N pianta (di una città)

streetwise ['stri:twaɪz] ADJ (col) esperto(-a)
dei bassifondi

strength [strɛŋθ] N forza; (of girder, knot etc)
resistenza, solidità; (of chemical solution)
concentrazione f; (of wine) gradazione f
alcolica; **on the ~ of** sulla base di, in virtù di;
below/at full ~ con gli effettivi ridotti/al
completo

strengthen ['strɛŋθən] VT rinforzare;
(muscles) irrobustire; fortificare; (economy,
currency) consolidare

strenuous ['strɛnjuəs] ADJ vigoroso(-a),
energico(-a); (tiring) duro(-a), pesante

stress [strɛs] N (force, pressure) pressione f;
(mental strain) tensione f; (accent) accento;
(emphasis) enfasi f ▶ VT insistere su,
sottolineare; accentare; **to be under ~**
essere sotto tensione; **to lay great ~ on sth**
dare grande importanza a qc

stressed ADJ (tense: person) stressato(-a); (Ling,
Poetry: syllable) accentato(-a)

stressful ['strɛsful] ADJ (job) difficile,
stressante

stretch [strɛtʃ] N (of sand etc) distesa; (of time)
periodo ▶ VI stirarsi; (extend): **to ~ to or as far
as** estendersi fino a; (be enough: money, food):
to ~ (to) bastare (per) ▶ VT tendere,
allungare; (spread) distendere; (fig) spingere
(al massimo); **at a ~** ininterrottamente; **to ~
a muscle** tendere un muscolo; **to ~ one's
legs** sgranchirsi le gambe

▶ **stretch out** VI allungarsi, estendersi ▶ VT
(arm etc) allungare, tendere; (spread)
distendere; **to ~ out for sth** allungare la
mano per prendere qc

stretcher ['strɛtʃəʳ] N barella, lettiga

stretcher-bearer ['strɛtʃəbɛərəʳ] N
barelliere m

stretch marks NPL smagliature fpl

strewn [stru:n] ADJ: **~ with** cosparso(-a) di

stricken ['strɪkən] ADJ provato(-a),
affranto(-a); **~ with** colpito(-a) da

strict [strɪkt] ADJ (severe) rigido(-a), severo(-a);
(: order, rule) rigoroso(-a); (: supervision)
stretto(-a); (: precise) preciso(-a), stretto(-a);
in ~ confidence in assoluta confidenza

strictly ['strɪktlɪ] ADV severamente;
rigorosamente; strettamente;
~ confidential strettamente confidenziale;
~ speaking a rigor di termini; **~ between
ourselves ...** detto fra noi ...

stride [straɪd] (pt **strode** [strəud], pp **stridden**
['strɪdn]) N passo lungo ▶ VI camminare a
grandi passi; **to take in one's ~** (fig: changes
etc) prendere con tranquillità

strident ['straɪdnt] ADJ stridente

strife [straɪf] N conflitto; litigi mpl

strike [straɪk] (pt, pp **struck** [strʌk]) N
sciopero; (of oil etc) scoperta; (attack) attacco
▶ VT colpire; (oil etc) scoprire, trovare;
(produce, make: coin, medal) coniare; (: agreement,
deal) concludere; (bargain) fare; (fig): **the
thought or it strikes me that ...** mi viene
in mente che ... ▶ VI far sciopero, scioperare;
(attack) attaccare; (clock) suonare; **on ~**
(workers) in sciopero; **to go on or come out
on ~** mettersi in sciopero; **to ~ a match**
accendere un fiammifero; **to ~ a balance**
(fig) trovare il giusto mezzo

▶ **strike back** VI (Mil) fare rappresaglie; (fig)
reagire

▶ **strike down** VT (fig) atterrare

▶ **strike off** VT (from list) cancellare; (: doctor
etc) radiare

▶ **strike out** VT depennare

▶ **strike up** VT (Mus) attaccare; **to ~ up a
friendship with** fare amicizia con

strikebreaker ['straɪkbreɪkəʳ] N crumiro(-a)

striker ['straɪkəʳ] N scioperante mf; (Sport)
attaccante m

striking ['straɪkɪŋ] ADJ impressionante

Strimmer® ['strɪməʳ] N tagliabordi m inv

string [strɪŋ] (pt, pp **strung** [strʌŋ]) N spago;
(row) fila; sequenza; catena; (Comput) stringa,
sequenza; (Mus) corda ▶ VT: **to ~ out** disporre
di fianco; **to ~ together** (words, ideas) mettere
insieme; **the strings** NPL (Mus) gli archi; **~ of
pearls** filo di perle; **with no strings
attached** (fig) senza vincoli, senza obblighi;
to pull strings for sb (fig) raccomandare qn

string bean N fagiolino

stringed instrument, string instrument
N (Mus) strumento a corda

stringent ['strɪndʒənt] ADJ rigoroso(-a);
(reasons, arguments) stringente, impellente

string quartet N quartetto d'archi

strip [strɪp] N striscia; (Sport): **wearing the
Celtic ~** con la divisa del Celtic ▶ VT
spogliare; (paint) togliere; (also: **strip down**:
machine) smontare ▶ VI spogliarsi

▶ **strip off** VT (paint etc) staccare ▶ VI (person)
spogliarsi

strip cartoon N fumetto
stripe [straip] N striscia, riga; (Mil, Police) gallone m
striped ['straipt] ADJ a strisce or righe
strip light N (BRIT) tubo al neon
stripper ['strɪpəʳ] N spogliarellista mf
strip-search ['strɪpsəːtʃ] VT: **to ~ sb** perquisire qn facendolo(-a) spogliare ▶ N perquisizione f (facendo spogliare il perquisito)
striptease ['strɪptiːz] N spogliarello
strive [straiv] (pt **strove** [strəuv], pp **striven** ['strɪvn]) VI: **to ~ to do** sforzarsi di fare
strobe [strəub] N (also: **strobe light**) luce f stroboscopica
strode [strəud] PT of **stride**
stroke [strəuk] N colpo; (of piston) corsa; (Med) colpo apoplettico; (Swimming) bracciata; (: style) stile m; (caress) carezza ▶ VT accarezzare; **at a ~** in un attimo; **on the ~ of 5** alle 5 in punto, allo scoccare delle 5; **a ~ of luck** un colpo di fortuna; **two-~ engine** motore a due tempi
stroll [strəul] N giretto, passeggiatina ▶ VI andare a spasso; **to go for a ~, have** or **take a ~** andare a fare un giretto or due passi
stroller ['strəuləʳ] N (US) passeggino
strong [strɔŋ] ADJ (gen) forte; (sturdy: table, fabric etc) robusto(-a); (concentrated, intense: bleach, acid) concentrato(-a); (: protest, letter, measures) energico(-a) ▶ ADV: **to be going ~** (company) andare a gonfie vele; (person) essere attivo(-a); **they are 50 ~** sono in 50; **~ language** (swearing) linguaggio volgare
strong-arm ['strɔŋɑːm] ADJ (tactics, methods) energico(-a)
strongbox ['strɔŋbɔks] N cassaforte f
stronghold ['strɔŋhəuld] N fortezza; (also fig) roccaforte f
strongly ['strɔŋlɪ] ADV fortemente, con forza; solidamente; energicamente; **to feel ~ about sth** avere molto a cuore qc
strongman ['strɔŋmæn] N (irreg) personaggio di spicco
strongroom ['strɔŋrum] N camera di sicurezza
stroppy ['strɔpɪ] ADJ (BRIT col) scontroso(-a), indisponente
strove [strəuv] PT of **strive**
struck [strʌk] PT, PP of **strike**
structural ['strʌktʃərəl] ADJ strutturale; (Constr) di costruzione; di struttura
structurally ['strʌktʃrəlɪ] ADV dal punto di vista della struttura
structure ['strʌktʃəʳ] N struttura; (building) costruzione f, fabbricato
struggle ['strʌgl] N lotta ▶ VI lottare; **to have a ~ to do sth** avere dei problemi per fare qc
strum [strʌm] VT (guitar) strimpellare
strung [strʌŋ] PT, PP of **string**

strut [strʌt] N sostegno, supporto ▶ VI pavoneggiarsi
strychnine ['strɪkniːn] N stricnina
stub [stʌb] N mozzicone m; (of ticket etc) matrice f, talloncino ▶ VT: **to ~ one's toe (on sth)** urtare or sbattere il dito del piede (contro qc)
  ▶ **stub out** VT schiacciare; **to ~ out a cigarette** spegnere una sigaretta
stubble ['stʌbl] N stoppia; (on chin) barba ispida
stubborn ['stʌbən] ADJ testardo(-a), ostinato(-a)
stubby ['stʌbɪ] ADJ tozzo(-a)
stucco ['stʌkəu] N stucco
stuck [stʌk] PT, PP of **stick** ▶ ADJ (jammed) bloccato(-a)
stuck-up [stʌk'ʌp] ADJ presuntuoso(-a)
stud [stʌd] N bottoncino; borchia; (also: **stud earring**) orecchino a pressione (of horses) scuderia, allevamento di cavalli; (also: **stud horse**) stallone m ▶ VT (fig): **studded with** tempestato(-a) di
student ['stjuːdənt] N studente(-essa) ▶ CPD studentesco(-a); universitario(-a); degli studenti; **a law/medical ~** uno studente di legge/di medicina
student driver N (US) conducente mf principiante
students' union N (BRIT: association) circolo universitario; (: building) sede f del circolo universitario
studied ['stʌdɪd] ADJ studiato(-a), calcolato(-a)
studio ['stjuːdɪəu] N studio
studio flat, (US) **studio apartment** N monolocale m
studious ['stjuːdɪəs] ADJ studioso(-a); (studied) studiato(-a), voluto(-a)
studiously ['stjuːdɪəslɪ] ADV (carefully) deliberatamente, di proposito
study ['stʌdɪ] N studio ▶ VT studiare; esaminare ▶ VI studiare; **to make a ~ of sth** fare uno studio su qc; **to ~ for an exam** prepararsi a un esame
stuff [stʌf] N (substance) materiale m; (belongings) cose fpl, roba ▶ VT imbottire; (animal: for exhibition) impagliare; (Culin) farcire; (col: push) ficcare; **my nose is stuffed up** ho il naso chiuso; **get stuffed!** (col!) va' a farti fottere! (!); **stuffed toy** giocattolo di peluche
stuffing ['stʌfɪŋ] N imbottitura; (Culin) ripieno
stuffy ['stʌfɪ] ADJ (room) mal ventilato(-a), senz'aria; (ideas) antiquato(-a)
stumble ['stʌmbl] VI inciampare; **to ~ across** (fig) imbattersi in
stumbling block ['stʌmblɪŋ-] N ostacolo, scoglio

S

stump [stʌmp] N ceppo; *(of limb)* moncone *m*
  ▸ VT: **to be stumped** essere sconcertato(-a);
  to be stumped for an answer essere
  incapace di rispondere
stun [stʌn] VT stordire; *(amaze)* sbalordire
stung [stʌŋ] PT, PP *of* **sting**
stunk [stʌŋk] PP *of* **stink**
stunned [stʌnd] ADJ *(from blow)* stordito(-a);
  (amazed, shocked) sbalordito(-a)
stunning ['stʌnɪŋ] ADJ *(piece of news etc)*
  sbalorditivo(-a); *(girl, dress)* stupendo(-a),
  favoloso(-a)
stunt [stʌnt] N bravata; trucco pubblicitario;
  (Aviat) acrobazia ▸ VT arrestare
stunted ['stʌntɪd] ADJ stentato(-a),
  rachitico(-a)
stuntman ['stʌntmæn] N *(irreg)* cascatore *m*
stupefaction [stju:pɪ'fækʃən] N
  stupefazione *f*, stupore *m*
stupefy ['stju:pɪfaɪ] VT stordire; intontire;
  (fig) stupire
stupendous [stju:'pɛndəs] ADJ stupendo(-a),
  meraviglioso(-a)
stupid ['stju:pɪd] ADJ stupido(-a)
stupidity [stju:'pɪdɪtɪ] N stupidità *f inv*,
  stupidaggine *f*
stupidly ['stju:pɪdlɪ] ADV stupidamente
stupor ['stju:pə^r] N torpore *m*
sturdy ['stə:dɪ] ADJ robusto(-a), vigoroso(-a);
  solido(-a)
sturgeon ['stə:dʒən] N storione *m*
stutter ['stʌtə^r] N balbuzie *f* ▸ VI balbettare
Stuttgart ['ʃtutgart] N Stoccarda
sty [staɪ] N *(of pigs)* porcile *m*
stye [staɪ] N *(Med)* orzaiolo
style [staɪl] N stile *m*; *(distinction)* eleganza,
  classe *f*; *(hair style)* pettinatura; *(of dress etc)*
  modello, linea; **in the latest ~** all'ultima
  moda
styli ['staɪlaɪ] NPL *of* **stylus**
stylish ['staɪlɪʃ] ADJ elegante
stylist ['staɪlɪst] N: **hair ~** parrucchiere(-a)
stylized ['staɪlaɪzd] ADJ stilizzato(-a)
stylus ['staɪləs] *(pl* **styluses** *or* **styli** [-laɪ]*)* N *(of
  record player)* puntina
Styrofoam® ['staɪrəfəum] N *(US)*
  = **polystyrene** ▸ ADJ *(cup)* di polistirene
suave [swɑ:v] ADJ untuoso(-a)
sub [sʌb] N ABBR = **submarine; subscription**
sub... [sʌb] PREFIX sub..., sotto...
subcommittee ['sʌbkəmɪtɪ] N sottocomitato
subconscious [sʌb'kɔnʃəs] ADJ, N
  subcosciente *m*
subcontinent [sʌb'kɔntɪnənt] N: **the
  (Indian) ~** il subcontinente (indiano)
subcontract N [sʌb'kɔntrækt] subappalto
  ▸ VT [sʌbkən'trækt] subappaltare
subcontractor ['sʌbkən'træktə^r] N
  subappaltatore(-trice)

subdivide [sʌbdɪ'vaɪd] VT suddividere
subdivision ['sʌbdɪvɪʒən] N suddivisione *f*
subdue [səb'dju:] VT sottomettere,
  soggiogare
subdued [səb'dju:d] ADJ pacato(-a); *(light)*
  attenuato(-a); *(person)* poco esuberante
sub-editor ['sʌb'ɛdɪtə^r] N *(Brit)* redattore(-a)
  aggiunto(-a)
subject N ['sʌbdʒɪkt] soggetto; *(citizen etc)*
  cittadino(-a); *(Scol)* materia ▸ VT [səb'dʒɛkt]:
  to ~ to sottomettere a; esporre a; **to be ~ to**
  (law) essere sottomesso(-a) a; *(disease)* essere
  soggetto(-a) a; **~ to confirmation in
  writing** a condizione di ricevere conferma
  scritta; **to change the ~** cambiare discorso
subjection [səb'dʒɛkʃən] N sottomissione *f*,
  soggezione *f*
subjective [səb'dʒɛktɪv] ADJ soggettivo(-a)
subject matter N argomento; contenuto
sub judice [sʌb'dʒu:dɪsɪ] ADJ *(Law)* sub iudice
subjugate ['sʌbdʒugeɪt] VT sottomettere,
  soggiogare
subjunctive [səb'dʒʌŋktɪv] ADJ
  congiuntivo(-a) ▸ N congiuntivo
sublet [sʌb'lɛt] VT, VI *(irreg)* subaffittare
sublime [sə'blaɪm] ADJ sublime
subliminal [sʌb'lɪmɪnl] ADJ subliminale
submachine gun ['sʌbmə'ʃi:n-] N mitra *m inv*
submarine [sʌbmə'ri:n] N sommergibile *m*
submerge [səb'mə:dʒ] VT sommergere;
  immergere ▸ VI immergersi
submersion [səb'mə:ʃən] N sommersione *f*;
  immersione *f*
submission [səb'mɪʃən] N sottomissione *f*;
  (to committee etc) richiesta, domanda
submissive [səb'mɪsɪv] ADJ remissivo(-a)
submit [səb'mɪt] VT sottomettere; *(proposal,
  claim)* presentare ▸ VI sottomettersi
subnormal [sʌb'nɔ:məl] ADJ subnormale
subordinate [sə'bɔ:dɪnət] ADJ, N
  subordinato(-a)
subpoena [səb'pi:nə] N *(Law)* citazione *f*,
  mandato di comparizione ▸ VT *(Law)* citare
  in giudizio
subprime ['sʌbpraɪm] ADJ *(Finance)* subprime
  inv; **~ mortgage** mutuo subprime
subroutine ['sʌbru:ti:n] N *(Comput)*
  sottoprogramma *m*
subscribe [səb'skraɪb] VI contribuire; **to ~ to**
  (opinion) approvare, condividere; *(fund)*
  sottoscrivere a; *(newspaper)* abbonarsi a;
  essere abbonato(-a) a
subscriber [səb'skraɪbə^r] N *(to periodical,
  telephone)* abbonato(-a)
subscript ['sʌbskrɪpt] N deponente *m*
subscription [səb'skrɪpʃən] N sottoscrizione
  f; abbonamento; **to take out a ~ to**
  abbonarsi a
subsequent ['sʌbsɪkwənt] ADJ *(later)*

successivo(-a), seguente; conseguente;
(*further*) ulteriore; **~ to** in seguito a
subsequently ['sʌbsɪkwəntlɪ] ADV in
seguito, successivamente
subservient [səb'sə:vɪənt] ADJ: **~ (to)**
remissivo(-a) (a), sottomesso(-a) (a)
subside [səb'saɪd] VI cedere, abbassarsi;
(*flood*) decrescere; (*wind*) calmarsi
subsidence [səb'saɪdns] N cedimento,
abbassamento
subsidiarity [səbsɪdɪ'ærɪtɪ] N (*Pol*) *principio del
decentramento del potere*
subsidiary [səb'sɪdɪərɪ] ADJ sussidiario(-a);
accessorio(-a); (*Brit Scol: subject*)
complementare ▶ N filiale *f*
subsidize ['sʌbsɪdaɪz] VT sovvenzionare
subsidy ['sʌbsɪdɪ] N sovvenzione *f*
subsist [səb'sɪst] VI: **to ~ on sth** vivere di qc
subsistence [səb'sɪstəns] N esistenza; mezzi
mpl di sostentamento
subsistence allowance N indennità *f inv* di
trasferta
subsistence level N livello minimo di vita
substance ['sʌbstəns] N sostanza; (*fig*)
essenza; **to lack ~** (*argument*) essere debole
substance abuse N abuso di sostanze
tossiche
substandard [sʌb'stændəd] ADJ (*goods,
housing*) di qualità scadente
substantial [səb'stænʃl] ADJ solido(-a);
(*amount, progress etc*) notevole; (*meal*)
sostanzioso(-a)
substantially [səb'stænʃəlɪ] ADV
sostanzialmente; **~ bigger** molto più grande
substantiate [səb'stænʃɪeɪt] VT comprovare
substitute ['sʌbstɪtju:t] N (*person*)
sostituto(-a); (*thing*) succedaneo, surrogato
▶ VT: **to ~ sth/sb for** sostituire qc/qn a
substitute teacher N (*US*) supplente *mf*
substitution [sʌbstɪ'tju:ʃən] N sostituzione *f*
subterfuge ['sʌbtəfju:dʒ] N sotterfugio
subterranean [sʌbtə'reɪnɪən] ADJ
sotterraneo(-a)
subtitle ['sʌbtaɪtl] N (*Cine*) sottotitolo
subtle ['sʌtl] ADJ sottile; (*flavour, perfume*)
delicato(-a)
subtlety ['sʌtltɪ] N sottigliezza
subtly ['sʌtlɪ] ADV sottilmente;
delicatamente
subtotal [sʌb'təutl] N somma parziale
subtract [səb'trækt] VT sottrarre
subtraction [səb'trækʃən] N sottrazione *f*
suburb ['sʌbə:b] N sobborgo; **the suburbs** la
periferia
suburban [sə'bə:bən] ADJ suburbano(-a)
suburbia [sə'bə:bɪə] N periferia, sobborghi
mpl
subversion [səb'və:ʃən] N sovversione *f*
subversive [səb'və:sɪv] ADJ sovversivo(-a)

subway ['sʌbweɪ] N (*US: underground*)
metropolitana; (*Brit: underpass*)
sottopassaggio
subzero [sʌb'zɪərəu] ADJ: **~ temperatures**
temperature *fpl* sotto zero
succeed [sək'si:d] VI riuscire; avere successo
▶ VT succedere a; **to ~ in doing** riuscire a fare
succeeding [sək'si:dɪŋ] ADJ (*following*)
successivo(-a); **~ generations** generazioni
fpl future
success [sək'sɛs] N successo
successful [sək'sɛsful] ADJ (*venture*)
coronato(-a) da successo, riuscito(-a); **to be ~
(in doing)** riuscire (a fare)
successfully [sək'sɛsfəlɪ] ADV con successo
succession [sək'sɛʃən] N successione *f*; **in ~**
di seguito
successive [sək'sɛsɪv] ADJ successivo(-a);
consecutivo(-a); **on 3 ~ days** per 3 giorni
consecutivi *or* di seguito
successor [sək'sɛsə'] N successore *m*
succinct [sək'sɪŋkt] ADJ succinto(-a), breve
succulent ['sʌkjulənt] ADJ succulento(-a) ▶ N
(*Bot*): **succulents** piante *fpl* grasse
succumb [sə'kʌm] VI soccombere
such [sʌtʃ] ADJ tale; **~ books** tali libri, libri del
genere; (*so much*): **~ courage** tanto coraggio;
(*of that kind*): **~ a book** un tale libro, un libro
del genere ▶ ADV talmente, così; **~ a long
trip** un viaggio così lungo; **~ good books**
libri così buoni; **~ a lot of** talmente *or* così
tanto(-a); **making ~ a noise that** facendo
un rumore tale che; **~ a long time ago** tanto
tempo fa; **~ as** (*like*) come; **a noise ~ as to** un
rumore tale da; **~ books as I have** quei pochi
libri che ho; **as ~** come *or* in quanto tale;
I said no ~ thing non ho detto niente del
genere
such-and-such ['sʌtʃənsʌtʃ] ADJ tale (*after
noun*)
suchlike ['sʌtʃlaɪk] PRON (*col*): **and ~** e così via
suck [sʌk] VT succhiare; (*baby*) poppare;
(*pump, machine*) aspirare
sucker ['sʌkə'] N (*Zool, Tech*) ventosa; (*Bot*)
pollone *m*; (*col*) gonzo(-a), babbeo(-a)
suckle ['sʌkl] VT allattare
sucrose ['su:krəuz] N saccarosio
suction ['sʌkʃən] N succhiamento; (*Tech*)
aspirazione *f*
suction pump N pompa aspirante
Sudan [su:'dɑ:n] N Sudan *m*
Sudanese [su:də'ni:z] ADJ, N sudanese *mf*
sudden ['sʌdn] ADJ improvviso(-a); **all of a ~**
improvvisamente, all'improvviso
sudden-death [sʌdn'dɛθ] N (*also:* **sudden-
death playoff**: *Sport*) spareggio, bella
suddenly ['sʌdnlɪ] ADV bruscamente,
improvvisamente, di colpo
sudoku [su'dəuku:] N sudoku *m inv*

S

suds [sʌdz] NPL schiuma (di sapone)

sue [su:] VT citare in giudizio ▶ VI: **to ~ (for)** intentare causa (per); **to ~ for divorce** intentare causa di divorzio; **to ~ sb for damages** citare qn per danni

suede [sweɪd] N pelle f scamosciata ▶ CPD scamosciato(-a)

suet ['suɪt] N grasso di rognone

Suez ['su:ɪz] N: **the ~ Canal** il Canale di Suez

suffer ['sʌfər] VT soffrire, patire; (bear) sopportare, tollerare; (undergo: loss, setback) subire ▶ VI soffrire; **to ~ from** soffrire di; **to ~ from the effects of alcohol/a fall** risentire degli effetti dell'alcool/di una caduta

sufferance ['sʌfərəns] N: **he was only there on ~** era più che altro sopportato lì

sufferer ['sʌfərər] N (Med): **~ (from)** malato(-a) (di)

suffering ['sʌfərɪŋ] N sofferenza; (hardship, deprivation) privazione f

suffice [sə'faɪs] VI essere sufficiente, bastare

sufficient [sə'fɪʃənt] ADJ sufficiente; **~ money** abbastanza soldi

sufficiently [sə'fɪʃəntlɪ] ADV sufficientemente, abbastanza

suffix ['sʌfɪks] N suffisso

suffocate ['sʌfəkeɪt] VI (have difficulty breathing) soffocare; (die through lack of air) asfissiare

suffocation [sʌfə'keɪʃən] N soffocamento; (Med) asfissia

suffrage ['sʌfrɪdʒ] N suffragio

suffuse [sə'fju:z] VT: **to ~ (with)** (colour) tingere (di); (light) soffondere (di); **her face was suffused with joy** la gioia si dipingeva sul suo volto

sugar ['ʃugər] N zucchero ▶ VT zuccherare

sugar beet N barbabietola da zucchero

sugar bowl N zuccheriera

sugar cane N canna da zucchero

sugar-coated ['ʃugəkəutɪd] ADJ ricoperto(-a) di zucchero

sugar lump N zolletta di zucchero

sugar refinery N raffineria di zucchero

sugary ['ʃugərɪ] ADJ zuccherino(-a), dolce; (fig) sdolcinato(-a)

suggest [sə'dʒɛst] VT proporre, suggerire; (indicate) indicare; **what do you ~ I do?** cosa mi suggerisce di fare?

suggestion [sə'dʒɛstʃən] N suggerimento, proposta; indicazione f

suggestive [sə'dʒɛstɪv] ADJ suggestivo(-a); (indecent) spinto(-a), indecente

suicidal [suɪ'saɪdl] ADJ suicida inv; (fig) fatale, disastroso(-a)

suicide ['suɪsaɪd] N (person) suicida mf; (act) suicidio; **to commit ~** suicidarsi

suicide attempt, suicide bid N tentato suicidio

suicide bomber N kamikaze mf, attentatore(-trice) suicida

suicide bombing N attentato suicida

suit [su:t] N (man's) vestito; (woman's) completo, tailleur m inv; (lawsuit) causa; (Cards) seme m, colore m ▶ VT andar bene a or per; essere adatto(-a) a or per; (adapt): **to ~ sth to** adattare qc a; **to be suited to sth** (suitable for) essere adatto a qc; **well suited** (couple) ben assortito(-a); **to bring a ~ against sb** intentare causa a qn; **to follow ~** (fig) fare altrettanto

suitable ['su:təbl] ADJ adatto(-a); appropriato(-a); **would tomorrow be ~?** andrebbe bene domani?; **we found somebody ~** abbiamo trovato la persona adatta

suitably ['su:təblɪ] ADV (dress) in modo adatto; (thank) adeguatamente

suitcase ['su:tkeɪs] N valigia

suite [swi:t] N (of rooms) appartamento; (Mus) suite f inv; (furniture): **bedroom/dining room ~** arredo or mobilia per la camera da letto/ sala da pranzo; **a three-piece ~** un salotto comprendente un divano e due poltrone

suitor ['su:tər] N corteggiatore m, spasimante m

sulfate ['sʌlfeɪt] N (US) = **sulphate**

sulfur etc ['sʌlfər] (US) = **sulphur** etc

sulk [sʌlk] VI fare il broncio

sulky ['sʌlkɪ] ADJ imbronciato(-a)

sullen ['sʌlən] ADJ scontroso(-a); cupo(-a)

sulphate, (US) **sulfate** ['sʌlfeɪt] N solfato; **copper ~** solfato di rame

sulphur, (US) **sulfur** ['sʌlfər] N zolfo

sulphur dioxide N biossido di zolfo

sulphuric, (US) **sulfuric** [sʌl'fjuərɪk] ADJ: **~ acid** acido solforico

sultan ['sʌltən] N sultano

sultana [sʌl'tɑ:nə] N (fruit) uva (secca) sultanina

sultry ['sʌltrɪ] ADJ afoso(-a)

sum [sʌm] N somma; (Scol etc) addizione f ▶ **sum up** VT riassumere; (evaluate rapidly) valutare, giudicare ▶ VI riassumere

Sumatra [su'mɑ:trə] N Sumatra

summarize ['sʌməraɪz] VT riassumere, riepilogare

summary ['sʌmərɪ] N riassunto ▶ ADJ (justice) sommario(-a)

summer ['sʌmər] N estate f ▶ CPD d'estate, estivo(-a); **in (the) ~** d'estate

summer camp N (US) colonia (estiva)

summer holidays NPL vacanze fpl estive

summerhouse ['sʌməhaus] N (in garden) padiglione m

summertime ['sʌmətaɪm] N (season) estate f

summer time N (*by clock*) ora legale (estiva)
summery ['sʌmərɪ] ADJ estivo(-a)
summing-up [sʌmɪŋ'ʌp] N (*Law*) ricapitolazione f del processo
summit ['sʌmɪt] N cima, sommità; (*Pol*) vertice m
summit conference N conferenza al vertice
summon ['sʌmən] VT chiamare, convocare; **to ~ a witness** citare un testimone
▶ **summon up** VT raccogliere, fare appello a
summons N ordine m di comparizione ▶ VT citare; **to serve a ~ on sb** notificare una citazione a qn
sumo ['su:məʊ] N (*also:* **sumo wrestling**) sumo
sump [sʌmp] N (*Aut*) coppa dell'olio
sumptuous ['sʌmptjʊəs] ADJ sontuoso(-a)
sun [sʌn] N sole m; **in the ~** al sole; **to catch the ~** prendere sole; **they have everything under the ~** hanno tutto ciò che possono desiderare
Sun. ABBR (= *Sunday*) dom.
sunbathe ['sʌnbeɪð] VI prendere un bagno di sole
sunbeam ['sʌnbi:m] N raggio di sole
sunbed ['sʌnbɛd] N lettino solare
sunblock ['sʌnblɔk] N crema solare a protezione totale
sunburn ['sʌnbə:n] N (*tan*) abbronzatura; (*painful*) scottatura
sunburnt ['sʌnbə:nt], **sunburned** ['sʌnbə:nd] ADJ abbronzato(-a); (*painfully*) scottato(-a) dal sole
sun cream N crema solare
sundae ['sʌndeɪ] N coppa di gelato guarnita
Sunday ['sʌndɪ] N domenica; *see also* **Tuesday**
Sunday paper N giornale m della domenica; *vedi nota*

I *Sunday papers* sono i giornali che escono di domenica. Sono generalmente corredati da supplementi e riviste di argomento culturale, sportivo e di attualità ed hanno un'alta tiratura.

Sunday school N ≈ scuola di catechismo
sundial ['sʌndaɪəl] N meridiana
sundown ['sʌndaʊn] N tramonto
sundries ['sʌndrɪz] NPL articoli diversi, cose diverse
sundry ['sʌndrɪ] ADJ vari(-e), diversi(-e); **all and ~** tutti quanti
sunflower ['sʌnflaʊəʳ] N girasole m
sung [sʌŋ] PP *of* **sing**
sunglasses ['sʌnglɑ:sɪz] NPL occhiali mpl da sole
sunk [sʌŋk] PP *of* **sink**
sunken ['sʌŋkən] ADJ sommerso(-a); (*eyes, cheeks*) infossato(-a); (*bath*) incassato(-a)
sunlamp ['sʌnlæmp] N lampada a raggi ultravioletti

sunlight ['sʌnlaɪt] N (luce f del) sole m
sunlit ['sʌnlɪt] ADJ assolato(-a), soleggiato(-a)
sun lounger N sedia a sdraio
sunny ['sʌnɪ] ADJ assolato(-a), soleggiato(-a); (*fig*) allegro(-a), felice; **it is ~** c'è il sole
sunrise ['sʌnraɪz] N levata del sole, alba
sunroof ['sʌnru:f] N (*on building*) tetto a terrazzo; (*Aut*) tetto apribile
sunscreen ['sʌnskri:n] N (*protective ingredient*) filtro solare; (*cream*) crema solare protettiva
sunset ['sʌnsɛt] N tramonto
sunshade ['sʌnʃeɪd] N parasole m
sunshine ['sʌnʃaɪn] N (luce f del) sole m
sunspot ['sʌnspɔt] N macchia solare
sunstroke ['sʌnstrəʊk] N insolazione f, colpo di sole
suntan ['sʌntæn] N abbronzatura
suntan lotion N lozione f solare
suntanned ['sʌntænd] ADJ abbronzato(-a)
suntan oil N olio solare
suntrap ['sʌntræp] N luogo molto assolato, angolo pieno di sole
super ['su:pəʳ] ADJ (*col*) fantastico(-a)
superannuation [su:pərænju'eɪʃən] N contributi mpl pensionistici, pensione f
superb [su:'pə:b] ADJ magnifico(-a)
Super Bowl N (*US Sport*) Super Bowl m inv
supercilious [su:pə'sɪlɪəs] ADJ sprezzante, sdegnoso(-a)
superconductor [su:pəkən'dʌktəʳ] N superconduttore m
superficial [su:pə'fɪʃəl] ADJ superficiale
superficially [su:pə'fɪʃəlɪ] ADV superficialmente
superfluous [su'pə:fluəs] ADJ superfluo(-a)
superglue ['su:pəglu:] N colla a presa rapida
superhighway ['su:pəhaɪweɪ] N (*US*) autostrada; **the information ~** l'autostrada telematica
superhuman [su:pə'hju:mən] ADJ sovrumano(-a)
superimpose ['su:pərɪm'pəʊz] VT sovrapporre
superintend [su:pərɪn'tɛnd] VT dirigere, sovraintendere
superintendent [su:pərɪn'tɛndənt] N direttore(-trice); (*Police*) ≈ commissario (capo)
superior [su'pɪərɪəʳ] ADJ superiore; (*Comm: goods, quality*) di prim'ordine, superiore; (*smug: person*) che fa il superiore ▶ N superiore mf; **Mother S~** (*Rel*) Madre f Superiora, Superiora
superiority [supɪərɪ'ɔrɪtɪ] N superiorità
superlative [su'pə:lətɪv] ADJ superlativo(-a), supremo(-a) ▶ N (*Ling*) superlativo
superman ['su:pəmæn] N (*irreg*) superuomo
supermarket ['su:pəmɑ:kɪt] N supermercato
supermodel ['su:pəmɔdl] N top model mf

S

supernatural [suːpəˈnætʃərəl] ADJ, N soprannaturale m

supernova [suːpəˈnəʊvə] N supernova

superpower ['suːpəpaʊəʳ] N (Pol) superpotenza

superscript ['suːpəskrɪpt] N esponente m

supersede [suːpəˈsiːd] VT sostituire, soppiantare

supersonic ['suːpəˈsɒnɪk] ADJ supersonico(-a)

superstar ['suːpəstɑːʳ] ADJ, N superstar f inv

superstition [suːpəˈstɪʃən] N superstizione f

superstitious [suːpəˈstɪʃəs] ADJ superstizioso(-a) -

superstore ['suːpəstɔːʳ] N (BRIT) grande supermercato

supertanker ['suːpətæŋkəʳ] N superpetroliera

supertax ['suːpətæks] N soprattassa

supervise ['suːpəvaɪz] VT (person etc) sorvegliare; (organization) soprintendere a

supervision [suːpəˈvɪʒən] N sorveglianza; supervisione f; **under medical ~** sotto controllo medico

supervisor ['suːpəvaɪzəʳ] N sorvegliante mf; soprintendente mf; (in shop) capocommesso(-a); (at university) relatore(-trice)

supervisory ['suːpəvaɪzərɪ] ADJ di sorveglianza

supine ['suːpaɪn] ADJ supino(-a)

supper ['sʌpəʳ] N cena; **to have ~** cenare

supplant [səˈplɑːnt] VT soppiantare

supple ['sʌpl] ADJ flessibile; agile

supplement N ['sʌplɪmənt] supplemento ▶ VT [sʌplɪˈmɛnt] completare, integrare

supplementary [sʌplɪˈmɛntərɪ] ADJ supplementare

supplementary benefit N (BRIT) forma di indennità assistenziale

supplier [səˈplaɪəʳ] N fornitore m

supply [səˈplaɪ] VT (a need) soddisfare; **to ~ sth (to sb)** (goods) fornire qc (a qn); **to ~ sb (with sth)** (people, organization) fornire a qn (qc); **to ~ sth (with sth)** (system, machine) alimentare qc (con qc) ▶ N riserva, provvista; (supplying) approvvigionamento; (Tech) alimentazione f; **supplies** NPL (food) viveri mpl; (Mil) sussistenza; **office supplies** forniture fpl per ufficio; **to be in short ~** scarseggiare, essere scarso(-a); **the electricity/water/gas ~** l'erogazione f di corrente/d'acqua/di gas; **~ and demand** la domanda e l'offerta; **the car comes supplied with a radio** l'auto viene fornita completa di radio

supply teacher N (BRIT) supplente mf

support [səˈpɔːt] N (moral, financial etc) sostegno, appoggio; (Tech) supporto ▶ VT sostenere; (financially) mantenere; (uphold) sostenere, difendere; (Sport: team) fare il tifo per; **they stopped work in ~ (of)** hanno smesso di lavorare per solidarietà (con); **to ~ o.s.** (financially) mantenersi

supporter [səˈpɔːtəʳ] N (Pol etc) sostenitore(-trice), fautore(-trice); (Sport) tifoso(-a)

supporting [səˈpɔːtɪŋ] ADJ (wall) di sostegno

supporting actor N attore m non protagonista

supporting actress N attrice f non protagonista

supporting role N ruolo non protagonista

supportive [səˈpɔːtɪv] ADJ d'appoggio; **I have a ~ wife/family** mia moglie/la mia famiglia mi appoggia

suppose [səˈpəʊz] VT, VI supporre; immaginare; **to be supposed to do** essere tenuto(-a) a fare; **always supposing (that) he comes** ammesso e non concesso che venga; **I don't ~ she'll come** non credo che venga; **he's supposed to be an expert** dicono che sia un esperto, passa per un esperto

supposedly [səˈpəʊzɪdlɪ] ADV presumibilmente; (seemingly) apparentemente

supposing [səˈpəʊzɪŋ] CONJ se, ammesso che + sub

supposition [sʌpəˈzɪʃən] N supposizione f, ipotesi f inv

suppository [səˈpɒzɪtərɪ] N supposta/ suppositorio

suppress [səˈprɛs] VT reprimere; sopprimere; tenere segreto(-a); occultare

suppression [səˈprɛʃən] N repressione f; soppressione f

suppressor [səˈprɛsəʳ] N (Elec etc) soppressore m

supremacy [suˈprɛməsɪ] N supremazia

supreme [suˈpriːm] ADJ supremo(-a)

Supreme Court N (US) Corte f suprema; **~ of Judicature** corte di giudizio suprema dell'Inghilterra e del Galles

supremo [suˈpriːməʊ] N autorità f inv massima

Supt. ABBR (Police) = **superintendent**

surcharge ['səːtʃɑːdʒ] N supplemento; (extra tax) soprattassa

sure [ʃʊəʳ] ADJ sicuro(-a); (definite, convinced) sicuro(-a), certo(-a) ▶ ADV (col: US): **that ~ is pretty, that's ~ pretty** è veramente or davvero carino; **~!** (of course) senz'altro!, certo!; **~ enough** infatti; **to make ~ of** assicurarsi di; **to be ~ of sth** essere sicuro di qc; **to be ~ of o.s.** essere sicuro di sé; **I'm not ~ how/why/when** non so bene come/perché/ quando + sub

sure-fire ['ʃʊəfaɪəʳ] ADJ (col) infallibile

sure-footed [ʃuə'futɪd] ADJ dal passo sicuro

surely ['ʃuəlɪ] ADV sicuramente; certamente; **~ you don't mean that!** non parlerà sul serio!

surety ['ʃuərətɪ] N garanzia; **to go** or **stand ~ for sb** farsi garante per qn

surf [səːf] N (waves) cavalloni mpl; (foam) spuma ▶ VT: **to ~ the Net** navigare in Internet

surface ['səːfɪs] N superficie f ▶ VT (road) asfaltare ▶ VI risalire alla superficie; (fig: person, news, feeling) venire a galla, farsi vivo(-a); **on the ~ it seems that …** (fig) superficialmente sembra che …

surface area N superficie f

surface mail N posta ordinaria

surface-to-surface ['səːfɪstə'səːfɪs] ADJ (Mil) terra-terra inv

surfboard ['səːfbɔːd] N tavola per surfing

surfeit ['səːfɪt] N: **a ~ of** un eccesso di; un'indigestione di

surfer ['səːfər] N (in sea) surfista mf; (on the Internet) navigatore(-trice)

surfing ['səːfɪŋ] N surfing m

surge [səːdʒ] N (strong movement) ondata; (of feeling) impeto; (Elec) sovracorrente f transitoria ▶ VI (waves) gonfiarsi; (people) riversarsi; (Elec: power) aumentare improvvisamente; **to ~ forward** buttarsi avanti

surgeon ['səːdʒən] N chirurgo

Surgeon General N (US) ≈ Ministro della Sanità

surgery ['səːdʒərɪ] N chirurgia; (BRIT Med: room) studio or gabinetto medico, ambulatorio; (: session) visita ambulatoriale; (BRIT: of MP etc) incontri mpl con gli elettori; (also: **surgery hours**) orario delle visite or di consultazione; **to undergo ~** subire un intervento chirurgico

surgery hours NPL (BRIT) orario delle visite or di consultazione

surgical ['səːdʒɪkl] ADJ chirurgico(-a)

surgical spirit N (BRIT) alcool denaturato

surly ['səːlɪ] ADJ scontroso(-a), burbero(-a)

surmise [səː'maɪz] VT supporre, congetturare

surmount [səː'maunt] VT sormontare

surname ['səːneɪm] N cognome m

surpass [səː'pɑːs] VT superare

surplus ['səːpləs] N eccedenza; (Econ) surplus m inv ▶ ADJ eccedente, d'avanzo; **it is ~ to our requirements** eccede i nostri bisogni; **~ stock** merce f in sovrappiù

surprise [sə'praɪz] N sorpresa; (astonishment) stupore m ▶ VT sorprendere; stupire; **to take by ~** (person) cogliere di sorpresa; (Mil: town, fort) attaccare di sorpresa

surprised [sə'praɪzd] ADJ (look, smile) sorpreso(-a); **to be ~** essere sorpreso, sorprendersi

surprising [sə'praɪzɪŋ] ADJ sorprendente, stupefacente

surprisingly [sə'praɪzɪŋlɪ] ADV (easy, helpful) sorprendentemente; **(somewhat) ~, he agreed** cosa (alquanto) sorprendente, ha accettato

surrealism [sə'rɪəlɪzəm] N surrealismo

surrealist [sə'rɪəlɪst] ADJ, N surrealista mf

surrender [sə'rɛndər] N resa, capitolazione f ▶ VI arrendersi ▶ VT (claim, right) rinunciare a

surrender value N (Comm) valore m di riscatto

surreptitious [sʌrəp'tɪʃəs] ADJ furtivo(-a)

surrogate ['sʌrəgɪt] N (BRIT: substitute) surrogato ▶ ADJ surrogato(-a)

surrogate mother N madre f sostitutiva

surround [sə'raund] VT circondare; (Mil etc) accerchiare

surrounding [sə'raundɪŋ] ADJ circostante

surroundings [sə'raundɪŋz] NPL dintorni mpl; (fig) ambiente m

surtax ['səːtæks] N soprattassa

surveillance [səː'veɪləns] N sorveglianza, controllo

survey N ['səːveɪ] (comprehensive view: of situation, development) quadro generale; (study) indagine f, studio; (in housebuying etc) perizia; (of land) rilevamento, rilievo topografico ▶ VT [səː'veɪ] osservare; esaminare; (Surveying: building) fare una perizia di; (: land) fare il rilevamento di

surveying [sə'veɪɪŋ] N (of land) agrimensura

surveyor [sə'veɪər] N perito; geometra m; (of land) agrimensore m

survival [sə'vaɪvl] N sopravvivenza; (relic) reliquia, vestigio

survival course N corso di sopravvivenza

survival kit N equipaggiamento di prima necessità

survive [sə'vaɪv] VI sopravvivere ▶ VT sopravvivere a

survivor [sə'vaɪvər] N superstite mf, sopravvissuto(-a)

susceptible [sə'sɛptəbl] ADJ: **~ (to)** sensibile (a); (disease) predisposto(-a) (a)

suspect ADJ ['sʌspɛkt] sospetto(-a) ▶ N ['sʌspɛkt] persona sospetta ▶ VT [səs'pɛkt] sospettare; (think likely) supporre; (doubt) dubitare di

suspected [səs'pɛktɪd] ADJ presunto(-a); **to have a ~ facture** avere una sospetta frattura

suspend [səs'pɛnd] VT sospendere

suspended animation N: **in a state of ~** in stato comatoso

suspended sentence N condanna con la condizionale

suspender belt [səs'pɛndər-] N (BRIT) reggicalze m inv

suspenders [sə'spɛndəz] NPL (BRIT) giarrettiere fpl; (US) bretelle fpl

suspense [səs'pɛns] N apprensione f; (in film etc) suspense m; **to keep sb in ~** tenere qn in sospeso

suspension [səs'pɛnʃən] N (gen, Aut) sospensione f; (of driving licence) ritiro temporaneo

suspension bridge N ponte m sospeso

suspicion [səs'pɪʃən] N sospetto; **to be under ~** essere sospettato; **arrested on ~ of murder** arrestato come presunto omicida

suspicious [səs'pɪʃəs] ADJ (suspecting) sospettoso(-a); (causing suspicion) sospetto(-a); **to be ~ of** or **about sb/sth** nutrire sospetti nei riguardi di qn/qc

suss out VT (BRIT col): **I've sussed it/him out** ho capito come stanno le cose/che tipo è

sustain [səs'teɪn] VT sostenere; sopportare; (Law: charge) confermare; (suffer) subire

sustainable [səs'teɪnəbl] ADJ sostenibile

sustained [sə'steɪnd] ADJ (effort) prolungato(-a)

sustenance ['sʌstɪnəns] N nutrimento; mezzi mpl di sostentamento

suture ['suːtʃə'] N sutura

SUV N ABBR (= sports utility vehicle) SUV m inv

SW ABBR (Radio: = short wave) O.C.

swab [swɔb] N (Med) tampone m ▶ VT (Naut: also: **swab down**) radazzare

swagger ['swægə'] VI pavoneggiarsi

swallow ['swɔləu] N (bird) rondine f; (of food) boccone m; (of drink) sorso ▶ VT inghiottire; (fig: story) bere
▶ **swallow up** VT inghiottire

swam [swæm] PT of **swim**

swamp [swɔmp] N palude f ▶ VT sommergere

swampy ['swɔmpɪ] ADJ palludoso(-a), pantanoso(-a)

swan [swɔn] N cigno

swank [swæŋk] VI (col: talk boastfully) fare lo spaccone; (: show off) mettersi in mostra

swan song N (fig) canto del cigno

swap [swɔp] N scambio ▶ VT: **to ~ (for)** scambiare (con)

SWAPO ['swɑːpəu] N ABBR = **South-West Africa People's Organization**

swarm [swɔːm] N sciame m ▶ VI formicolare; (bees) sciamare; (people) brulicare; (place): **to be swarming with** brulicare di

swarthy ['swɔːðɪ] ADJ di carnagione scura

swashbuckling ['swɔʃbʌklɪŋ] ADJ (role, hero) spericolato(-a)

swastika ['swɔstɪkə] N croce f uncinata, svastica

SWAT [swɔt] N ABBR (US: = Special Weapons and Tactics) reparto speciale di polizia; (= a SWAT team) uno squadrone del reparto speciale (di polizia)

swat [swɔt] VT schiacciare ▶ N (BRIT: also: **fly swat**) ammazzamosche m inv

swathe [sweɪð] N fascio ▶ VT: **to ~ in** (bandages, blankets) avvolgere in

swatter ['swɔtə'] N (also: **fly swatter**) ammazzamosche m inv

sway [sweɪ] VI (building) oscillare; (tree) ondeggiare; (person) barcollare ▶ VT (influence) influenzare, dominare ▶ N (rule, power): **~ (over)** influenza (su); **to hold ~ over sb** dominare qn

Swaziland ['swɑːzɪlænd] N Swaziland m

swear [swɛə'] (pt **swore**, pp **sworn**) VI (witness etc) giurare; (curse) bestemmiare, imprecare ▶ VT: **to ~ an oath** prestare giuramento; **to ~ to sth** giurare qc
▶ **swear in** VT prestare giuramento a

swearword ['swɛəwə:d] N parolaccia

sweat [swɛt] N sudore m, traspirazione f ▶ VI sudare; **in a ~** in un bagno di sudore

sweatband ['swɛtbænd] N (Sport) fascia elastica (per assorbire il sudore)

sweater ['swɛtə'] N maglione m

sweatshirt ['swɛtʃə:t] N felpa f

sweatshop ['swɛtʃɔp] N azienda o fabbrica dove i dipendenti sono sfruttati

sweaty ['swɛtɪ] ADJ sudato(-a); bagnato(-a) di sudore

Swede [swiːd] N svedese mf

swede [swiːd] N (BRIT) rapa svedese

Sweden ['swiːdn] N Svezia

Swedish ['swiːdɪʃ] ADJ svedese ▶ N (Ling) svedese m

sweep [swiːp] (pt, pp **swept**) N spazzata; (curve) curva; (expanse) distesa; (range) portata; (also: **chimney sweep**) spazzacamino ▶ VT spazzare, scopare; (fashion, craze) invadere; (current) spazzare ▶ VI camminare maestosamente; precipitarsi, lanciarsi; (e)stendersi; (hand) muoversi con gesto ampio; (wind) infuriare
▶ **sweep away** VT spazzare via; trascinare via
▶ **sweep past** VI sfrecciare accanto; passare accanto maestosamente
▶ **sweep up** VT, VI spazzare

sweeper ['swiːpə'] N (person) spazzino(-a); (machine) spazzatrice f; (Football) libero

sweeping ['swiːpɪŋ] ADJ (gesture) ampio(-a); (changes, reforms) ampio(-a), radicale; **a ~ statement** un'affermazione generica

sweepstake ['swiːpsteɪk] N lotteria (spesso abbinata alle corse dei cavalli)

sweet [swiːt] N (BRIT: pudding) dolce m; (candy) caramella ▶ ADJ dolce; (fresh) fresco(-a); (fig) piacevole; delicato(-a), grazioso(-a); (kind) gentile; (cute) carino(-a) ▶ ADV: **to smell/ taste ~** avere un odore/sapore dolce; **~ and sour** adj agrodolce

sweetbread ['swiːtbrɛd] N animella

sweetcorn ['swiːtkɔːn] N granturco dolce

sweeten ['swi:tn] VT addolcire; zuccherare
sweetener ['swi:tnə^r] N (*Culin*) dolcificante *m*
sweetheart ['swi:thɑ:t] N innamorato(-a)
sweetly ['swi:tlɪ] ADV dolcemente
sweetness ['swi:tnɪs] N sapore *m* dolce; dolcezza
sweet pea N pisello odoroso
sweet potato N patata americana, patata dolce
sweetshop ['swi:tʃɔp] N (*BRIT*) ≈ pasticceria
sweet tooth N: **to have a ~** avere un debole per i dolci
swell [swɛl] (*pt* **swelled**, *pp* **swollen** ['swəulən] *or* **swelled**) N (*of sea*) mare *m* lungo ▸ ADJ (*US col: excellent*) favoloso(-a) ▸ VT gonfiare, ingrossare; (*numbers, sales etc*) aumentare ▸ VI gonfiarsi, ingrossarsi; (*sound*) crescere; (*Med: also*: **swell up**) gonfiarsi
swelling ['swɛlɪŋ] N (*Med*) tumefazione *f*, gonfiore *m*
sweltering ['swɛltərɪŋ] ADJ soffocante
swept [swɛpt] PT, PP *of* **sweep**
swerve [swə:v] VI deviare; (*driver*) sterzare; (*boxer*) scartare
swift [swɪft] N (*bird*) rondone *m* ▸ ADJ rapido(-a), veloce
swiftly ['swɪftlɪ] ADV rapidamente, velocemente
swiftness ['swɪftnɪs] N rapidità, velocità
swig [swɪg] N (*col: drink*) sorsata
swill [swɪl] N broda ▸ VT (*also*: **swill out, swill down**) risciacquare
swim [swɪm] (*pt* **swam** [swæm], *pp* **swum** [swʌm]) N: **to go for a ~** andare a fare una nuotata ▸ VI nuotare; (*Sport*) fare del nuoto; (*head, room*) girare ▸ VT (*river, channel*) attraversare *or* percorrere a nuoto; (*length*) nuotare; **to go swimming** andare a nuotare; **to ~ a length** fare una vasca (a nuoto)
swimmer ['swɪmə^r] N nuotatore(-trice)
swimming ['swɪmɪŋ] N nuoto
swimming baths NPL (*BRIT*) piscina
swimming cap N cuffia
swimming costume N (*BRIT*) costume *m* da bagno
swimmingly ['swɪmɪŋlɪ] ADV: **to go ~** (*wonderfully*) andare a gonfie vele
swimming pool N piscina
swimming trunks NPL costume *m* da bagno (da uomo)
swimsuit ['swɪmsu:t] N costume *m* da bagno
swindle ['swɪndl] N truffa ▸ VT truffare
swindler ['swɪndlə^r] N truffatore(-trice)
swine [swaɪn] N (*pl inv*) maiale *m*, porco; (*col!*) porco (!)
swine flu N influenza suina
swing [swɪŋ] (*pt, pp* **swung** [swʌŋ]) N altalena; (*movement*) oscillazione *f*; (*Mus*)

ritmo; (*also*: **swing music**) swing *m* ▸ VT dondolare, far oscillare; (*also*: **swing round**) far girare ▸ VI oscillare, dondolare; (*also*: **swing round**: *object*) roteare; (: *person*) girarsi, voltarsi; **to be in full ~** (*activity*) essere in piena attività; (*party etc*) essere nel pieno; **a ~ to the left** (*Pol*) una svolta a sinistra; **to get into the ~ of things** entrare nel pieno delle cose; **the road swings south** la strada prende la direzione sud
swing bridge N ponte *m* girevole
swing door N (*BRIT*) porta battente
swingeing ['swɪndʒɪŋ] ADJ (*BRIT: defeat*) violento(-a); (: *price increase*) enorme
swinging ['swɪŋɪŋ] ADJ (*step*) cadenzato(-a), ritmico(-a); (*rhythm, music*) trascinante; **~ door** (*US*) porta battente
swipe [swaɪp] N forte colpo; schiaffo ▸ VT (*hit*) colpire con forza; dare uno schiaffo a; (*col: steal*) sgraffignare; (*credit card etc*) far passare (nell'apposita macchinetta)
swipe card N tessera magnetica
swirl [swə:l] N turbine *m*, mulinello ▸ VI turbinare, far mulinello
swish [swɪʃ] ADJ (*col: smart*) all'ultimo grido, alla moda ▸ N (*sound, of whip*) sibilo; (: *of skirts, grass*) fruscio ▸ VI sibilare
Swiss [swɪs] ADJ, N (*pl inv*) svizzero(-a)
Swiss French ADJ svizzero(-a) francese
Swiss German ADJ svizzero(-a) tedesco(-a)
switch [swɪtʃ] N (*for light, radio etc*) interruttore *m*; (*change*) cambiamento ▸ VT (*also*: **switch round, switch over**) cambiare; scambiare
▸ **switch off** VT spegnere
▸ **switch on** VT accendere; (*engine, machine*) mettere in moto, avviare; (*Aut: ignition*) inserire; (*BRIT: water supply*) aprire
switchback ['swɪtʃbæk] N (*BRIT*) montagne *fpl* russe
switchblade ['swɪtʃbleɪd] N (*also*: **switchblade knife**) coltello a scatto
switchboard ['swɪtʃbɔ:d] N (*Tel*) centralino
switchboard operator N centralinista *mf*
Switzerland ['swɪtsələnd] N Svizzera
swivel ['swɪvl] VI (*also*: **swivel round**) girare
swollen ['swəulən] PP *of* **swell** ▸ ADJ (*ankle etc*) gonfio(-a)
swoon [swu:n] VI svenire
swoop [swu:p] N (*by police etc*) incursione *f*; (*of bird etc*) picchiata ▸ VI (*also*: **swoop down**) scendere in picchiata, piombare; (*police*) **to ~ (on)** fare un'incursione (in)
swop [swɔp] N, VT = **swap**
sword [sɔ:d] N spada
swordfish ['sɔ:dfɪʃ] N pesce *m* spada *inv*
swore [swɔ:^r] PT *of* **swear**
sworn [swɔ:n] PP *of* **swear** ▸ ADJ giurato(-a)
swot [swɔt] VT sgobbare su ▸ VI sgobbare
swum [swʌm] PP *of* **swim**

S

817

swung [swʌŋ] PT, PP *of* **swing**

sycamore ['sɪkəmɔːʳ] N sicomoro

sycophant ['sɪkəfənt] N leccapiedi *mf*

sycophantic [sɪkə'fæntɪk] ADJ ossequioso(-a), adulatore(-trice)

Sydney ['sɪdnɪ] N Sydney *f*

syllable ['sɪləbl] N sillaba

syllabus ['sɪləbəs] N programma *m*; **on the ~** in programma d'esame

symbol ['sɪmbl] N simbolo ADJ simbolico(-a); **to be ~ of sth** simboleggiare qc

symbolism ['sɪmbəlɪzəm] N simbolismo

symbolize ['sɪmbəlaɪz] VT simbolizzare

symmetrical [sɪ'mɛtrɪkl] ADJ simmetrico(-a)

symmetry ['sɪmɪtrɪ] N simmetria

sympathetic [sɪmpə'θɛtɪk] ADJ (*showing pity*) compassionevole; (*kind*) comprensivo(-a); **~ towards** ben disposto(-a) verso; **to be ~ to a cause** (*well-disposed*) simpatizzare per una causa

sympathetically [sɪmpə'θɛtɪklɪ] ADV in modo compassionevole; con comprensione

sympathize ['sɪmpəθaɪz] VI: **to ~ with sb** compatire qn; partecipare al dolore di qn; (*understand*) capire qn; **to ~ with a cause** simpatizzare per una causa

sympathizer ['sɪmpəθaɪzəʳ] N (*Pol*) simpatizzante *mf*

sympathy ['sɪmpəθɪ] N compassione *f*; **in ~ with** d'accordo con; (*strike*) per solidarietà con; **with our deepest ~** con le nostre più sincere condoglianze

symphonic [sɪm'fɒnɪk] ADJ sinfonico(-a)

symphony ['sɪmfənɪ] N sinfonia

symphony orchestra N orchestra sinfonica

symposium [sɪm'pəuzɪəm] N simposio

symptom ['sɪmptəm] N sintomo; indizio

symptomatic [sɪmptə'mætɪk] ADJ: **~ (of)** sintomatico(-a) (di)

synagogue ['sɪnəgɒg] N sinagoga

sync [sɪŋk] N (*col*): **in/out of ~** in/fuori sincronia; (*fig: people*): **they are in ~** sono in sintonia

synchromesh [sɪŋkrəu'mɛʃ] N cambio sincronizzato

synchronize ['sɪŋkrənaɪz] VT sincronizzare ▶ VI: **to ~ with** essere contemporaneo(-a) a

synchronized swimming N nuoto sincronizzato

syncopated ['sɪŋkəpeɪtɪd] ADJ sincopato(-a)

syndicate ['sɪndɪkɪt] N sindacato; (*Press*) agenzia di stampa

syndrome ['sɪndrəum] N sindrome *f*

synonym ['sɪnənɪm] N sinonimo

synonymous [sɪ'nɒnɪməs] ADJ: **~ (with)** sinonimo(-a) (di)

synopsis [sɪ'nɒpsɪs] (*pl* **synopses** [-siːz]) N sommario, sinossi *f inv*

syntax ['sɪntæks] N sintassi *f inv*

synthesis ['sɪnθəsɪs] (*pl* **syntheses** [-siːz]) N sintesi *f inv*

synthesizer ['sɪnθəsaɪzəʳ] N (*Mus*) sintetizzatore *m*

synthetic [sɪn'θɛtɪk] ADJ sintetico(-a) ▶ N prodotto sintetico; (*Textiles*) fibra sintetica

syphilis ['sɪfɪlɪs] N sifilide *f*

syphon ['saɪfən] = **siphon**

Syria ['sɪrɪə] N Siria

Syrian ['sɪrɪən] ADJ, N siriano(-a)

syringe [sɪ'rɪndʒ] N siringa

syrup ['sɪrəp] N sciroppo; (*also:* **golden syrup**) melassa raffinata

syrupy ['sɪrəpɪ] ADJ sciropposo(-a)

system ['sɪstəm] N sistema *m*; (*network*) rete *f*; (*order*) metodo; (*Anat*) apparato; **it was a shock to his ~** è stato uno shock per il suo organismo

systematic [sɪstə'mætɪk] ADJ sistematico(-a); metodico(-a)

system disk N (*Comput*) disco del sistema

systems analyst N analista *mf* di sistemi

Tt

T, t [tiː] N (*letter*) T, t *m inv or f inv*; **T for Tommy** ≈ T come Taranto

TA N ABBR (*BRIT*) = **Territorial Army**

ta [tɑː] EXCL (*BRIT col*) grazie!

tab [tæb] N ABBR = **tabulator** ▶ N (*loop: on coat etc*) laccetto; (*label*) etichetta; **to keep tabs on** (*fig*) tenere d'occhio

tabby ['tæbɪ] N (*also:* **tabby cat**) (gatto) soriano, gatto tigrato

tabernacle ['tæbənækl] N tabernacolo

table ['teɪbl] N tavolo, tavola; (*Math, Chem etc*) tavola; (*chart*) tabella ▶ VT (*BRIT: motion etc*) presentare; **to lay** *or* **set the** ~ apparecchiare *or* preparare la tavola; **to clear the** ~ sparecchiare; **league** ~ (*Football, Rugby*) classifica; ~ **of contents** indice *m*

tablecloth ['teɪblklɔθ] N tovaglia

table d'hôte [tɑːbl'dəut] ADJ (*meal*) a prezzo fisso

table lamp N lampada da tavolo

tablemat ['teɪblmæt] N sottopiatto

table salt N sale *m* fino *or* da tavola

tablespoon ['teɪblspuːn] N cucchiaio da tavola; (*also:* **tablespoonful**: *as measurement*) cucchiaiata

tablet ['tæblɪt] N (*Med*) compressa; (: *for sucking*) pastiglia; (*for writing*) blocco; (*of stone*) targa; ~ **of soap** (*BRIT*) saponetta

table tennis N tennis *m* da tavolo, ping-pong® *m*

table wine N vino da tavola

tabloid ['tæblɔɪd] N (*newspaper*) tabloid *m inv* (*giornale illustrato di formato ridotto*); **the tabloids, the** ~ **press** i giornali popolari; *vedi nota*

> Il termine *tabloid press* si riferisce ai quotidiani o ai settimanali popolari che, rispetto ai *quality papers* hanno un formato ridotto e presentano le notizie in modo più sensazionalistico e meno approfondito; *vedi anche* **quality press**.

taboo [tə'buː] ADJ, N tabù *m inv*

tabulate ['tæbjuleɪt] VT (*data, figures*) tabulare, disporre in tabelle

tabulator ['tæbjuleɪtər] N tabulatore *m*

tachograph ['tækəgrɑːf] N tachigrafo

tachometer [tæ'kɔmɪtər] N tachimetro

tacit ['tæsɪt] ADJ tacito(-a)

taciturn ['tæsɪtəːn] ADJ taciturno(-a)

tack [tæk] N (*nail*) bulletta; (*stitch*) punto d'imbastitura; (*Naut*) bordo, bordata; (*fig*) approccio ▶ VT imbullettare; imbastire ▶ VI bordeggiare; **to change** ~ virare di bordo; **on the wrong** ~ (*fig*) sulla strada sbagliata; **to** ~ **sth on to (the end of) sth** (*of letter, book*) aggiungere qc alla fine di qc

tackle ['tækl] N (*equipment*) attrezzatura, equipaggiamento; (*for lifting*) paranco; (*Rugby*) placcaggio; (*Football*) contrasto ▶ VT (*difficulty*) affrontare; (*Rugby*) placcare; (*Football*) contrastare

tacky ['tækɪ] ADJ colloso(-a), appiccicaticcio(-a); ancora bagnato(-a); (*pej: shabby*) scadente

tact [tækt] N tatto

tactful ['tæktful] ADJ delicato(-a), discreto(-a); **to be** ~ avere tatto

tactfully ['tæktfəlɪ] ADV con tatto

tactical ['tæktɪkl] ADJ tattico(-a)

tactical voting N voto tattico

tactician [tæk'tɪʃən] N tattico(-a)

tactics ['tæktɪks] N, NPL tattica

tactless ['tæktlɪs] ADJ che manca di tatto

tactlessly ['tæktlɪslɪ] ADV senza tatto

tadpole ['tædpəul] N girino

taffy ['tæfɪ] N (*US*) caramella *f* mou *inv*

tag [tæg] N etichetta; **price/name** ~ etichetta del prezzo/con il nome
▶ **tag along** VI seguire

Tahiti [tə'hiːtɪ] N Tahiti *f*

tail [teɪl] N coda; (*of shirt*) falda ▶ VT (*follow*) seguire, pedinare; **to turn** ~ voltare la schiena; **tails** NPL (*formal suit*) frac *m inv*; *see also* **head**
▶ **tail away, tail off** VI (*in size, quality etc*) diminuire gradatamente

tailback ['teɪlbæk] N (*BRIT*) ingorgo

tail coat N marsina

tail end N (*of train, procession etc*) coda; (*of meeting etc*) fine *f*

tailgate ['teɪlgeɪt] N (*Aut*) portellone *m* posteriore

tail light N (*Aut*) fanalino di coda

tailor ['teɪləʳ] N sarto ▶ VT: **to ~ sth (to)** adattare qc (alle esigenze di); **~'s (shop)** sartoria (da uomo)

tailoring ['teɪlərɪŋ] N (*cut*) taglio

tailor-made ['teɪlə'meɪd] ADJ (*also fig*) fatto(-a) su misura

tailwind ['teɪlwɪnd] N vento di coda

taint [teɪnt] VT (*meat, food*) far avariare; (*fig: reputation*) infangare

tainted ['teɪntɪd] ADJ (*food*) guasto(-a); (*water, air*) infetto(-a); (*fig*) corrotto(-a)

Taiwan [taɪ'wɑːn] N Taiwan *m*

Taiwanese [taɪwə'niːz] ADJ, N taiwanese

Tajikistan [tɑːdʒɪkɪ'stɑːn] N Tagikistan *m*

take [teɪk] (*pt* **took**, *pp* **taken**) VT prendere; (*gain: prize*) ottenere, vincere; (*require: effort, courage*) occorrere, volerci; (*tolerate*) accettare, sopportare; (*hold: passengers etc*) contenere; (*accompany*) accompagnare; (*bring, carry*) portare; (*conduct: meeting*) condurre; (*exam*) sostenere, presentarsi a; **to ~ a photo/a shower** fare una fotografia/una doccia ▶ VI (*dye, fire etc*) prendere; (*injection*) fare effetto; (*plant*) attecchire ▶ N (*Cine*) ripresa; **I ~ it that** suppongo che; **to ~ for a walk** (*child, dog*) portare a fare una passeggiata; **to ~ sb's hand** prendere qn per mano; **to ~ it upon o.s. to do sth** prendersi la responsabilità di fare qc; **to be taken ill** avere un malore; **be taken with sb/sth** (*attracted*) essere tutto preso da qn/qc; **it won't ~ long** non ci vorrà molto tempo; **it takes a lot of time/courage** occorre *or* ci vuole molto tempo/coraggio; **it will ~ at least 5 litres** contiene almeno 5 litri; **~ the first on the left** prenda la prima a sinistra; **to ~ Russian at university** fare russo all'università; **I took him for a doctor** l'ho preso per un dottore

▶ **take after** VT FUS assomigliare a

▶ **take apart** VT smontare

▶ **take away** VT portare via; togliere; **to ~ away (from)** sottrarre (da)

▶ **take back** VT (*return*) restituire; riportare; (*one's words*) ritirare

▶ **take down** VT (*building*) demolire; (*dismantle: scaffolding*) smontare; (: *letter etc*) scrivere

▶ **take in** VT (*lodger*) prendere, ospitare; (*orphan*) accogliere; (*stray dog*) raccogliere; (*Sewing*) stringere; (*deceive*) imbrogliare, abbindolare; (*understand*) capire; (*include*) comprendere, includere

▶ **take off** VI (*Aviat*) decollare; (*go away*) andarsene ▶ VT (*remove*) togliere; (*imitate*) imitare

▶ **take on** VT (*work*) accettare, intraprendere; (*employee*) assumere; (*opponent*) sfidare, affrontare

▶ **take out** VT portare fuori; (*remove*) togliere; (*licence*) prendere, ottenere; **to ~ sth out of** (*drawer, pocket etc*) tirare qc fuori da; estrarre qc da; **don't ~ it out on me!** non prendertela con me!

▶ **take over** VT (*business*) rilevare ▶ VI: **to ~ over from sb** prendere le consegne *or* il controllo da qn

▶ **take to** VT FUS (*person*) prendere in simpatia; (*activity*) prendere gusto a; (*form habit of*): **to ~ to doing sth** prendere *or* cominciare a fare qc

▶ **take up** VT (*one's story*) riprendere; (*dress*) accorciare; (*absorb: liquids*) assorbire; (*accept: offer, challenge*) accettare; (*occupy: time, space*) occupare; (*engage in: hobby etc*) mettersi a; **to ~ up with sb** fare amicizia con qn; **to ~ sb up on sth** accettare qc da qn

takeaway ['teɪkəweɪ] (BRIT) ADJ (*food*) da portar via ▶ N (*shop etc*) ≈ rosticceria; (*food*) pasto per asporto

take-home pay ['teɪkhəum-] N stipendio netto

taken ['teɪkn] PP *of* **take**

takeoff ['teɪkɔf] N (*Aviat*) decollo

takeout ['teɪkaut] ADJ, N (*US*) = **takeaway**

takeover ['teɪkəuvəʳ] N (*Comm*) assorbimento

takeover bid N offerta di assorbimento

takings ['teɪkɪŋz] NPL (*Comm*) incasso

talc [tælk] N (*also*: **talcum powder**) talco

tale [teɪl] N racconto, storia; (*pej*) fandonia; **to tell tales** (*fig: to teacher, parent etc*) fare la spia

talent ['tælənt] N talento

talented ['tæləntɪd] ADJ di talento

talent scout N talent scout *mf*

talisman ['tælɪzmən] N talismano

talk [tɔːk] N discorso; (*gossip*) chiacchiere *fpl*; (*conversation*) conversazione *f*; (*interview*) discussione *f* ▶ VI parlare; (*chatter*) chiacchierare; **talks** NPL (*Pol etc*) colloqui *mpl*; **to give a ~** tenere una conferenza; **to ~ about** parlare di; (*converse*) discorrere *or* conversare su; **to ~ sb out of/into doing** dissuadere qn da/convincere qn a fare; **to ~ shop** parlare di lavoro *or* di affari; **talking of films, have you seen ...?** a proposito di film, ha visto ...?

▶ **talk over** VT discutere

talkative ['tɔːkətɪv] ADJ loquace, ciarliero(-a)

talking point ['tɔːkɪŋ-] N argomento di conversazione

talking-to ['tɔːkɪŋtuː] N: **to give sb a good ~** fare una bella paternale a qn

talk show N (TV, Radio) talk show m inv

tall [tɔ:l] ADJ alto(-a); **to be 6 feet ~** = essere alto 1 metro e 80; **how ~ are you?** quanto è alto?

tallboy ['tɔ:lbɔɪ] N (BRIT) cassettone m alto

tallness ['tɔ:lnɪs] N altezza

tall story N panzana, frottola

tally ['tælɪ] N conto, conteggio ▶ VI: **to ~ (with)** corrispondere (a); **to keep a ~ of sth** tener il conto di qc

talon ['tælən] N artiglio

tambourine [tæmbə'ri:n] N tamburello

tame [teɪm] ADJ addomesticato(-a); (fig: story, style) insipido(-a), scialbo(-a)

Tamil ['tæmɪl] ADJ tamil inv ▶ N tamil mf; (Ling) tamil m

tamper ['tæmpər] VI: **to ~ with** manomettere

tampon ['tæmpɔn] N tampone m

tan [tæn] N (also: **suntan**) abbronzatura ▶ VT abbronzare ▶ VI abbronzarsi ▶ ADJ (colour) marrone rossiccio inv; **to get a ~** abbronzarsi

tandem ['tændəm] N tandem m inv

tandoori [tæn'duərɪ] ADJ nella cucina indiana, detto di carni o verdure cucinate allo spiedo in particolari forni

tang [tæŋ] N odore m penetrante; sapore m piccante

tangent ['tændʒənt] N (Math) tangente f; **to go off at a ~** (fig) partire per la tangente

tangerine [tændʒə'ri:n] N mandarino

tangible ['tændʒəbl] ADJ tangibile; **~ assets** patrimonio reale

Tangier [tæn'dʒɪər] N Tangeri f

tangle ['tæŋgl] N groviglio ▶ VT aggrovigliare; **to get in(to) a ~** aggrovigliarsi; (fig) combinare un pasticcio

tango ['tæŋgəu] N tango

tank [tæŋk] N serbatoio; (for processing) vasca; (for fish) acquario; (Mil) carro armato

tankard ['tæŋkəd] N boccale m

tanker ['tæŋkər] N (ship) nave f cisterna inv; (for oil) petroliera; (truck) autobotte f, autocisterna

tankini [tæn'ki:nɪ] N tankini m inv

tanned [tænd] ADJ abbronzato(-a)

tannin ['tænɪn] N tannino

tanning ['tænɪŋ] N (of leather) conciatura

tannoy® ['tænɔɪ] N (BRIT) altoparlante m; **over the ~** per altoparlante

tantalizing ['tæntəlaɪzɪŋ] ADJ allettante

tantamount ['tæntəmaunt] ADJ: **~ to** equivalente a

tantrum ['tæntrəm] N accesso di collera; **to throw a ~** fare le bizze

Tanzania [tænzə'nɪə] N Tanzania

Tanzanian [tænzə'nɪən] ADJ, N tanzaniano(-a)

tap [tæp] N (on sink etc) rubinetto; (gentle blow) colpetto ▶ VT dare un colpetto a; (resources) sfruttare, utilizzare; (telephone conversation) intercettare; (telephone) mettere sotto controllo; **on ~** (beer) alla spina; (fig: resources) a disposizione

tap-dancing ['tæpdɑ:nsɪŋ] N tip tap m

tape [teɪp] N nastro; (also: **magnetic tape**) nastro (magnetico); (: sticky tape) nastro adesivo ▶ VT (record) registrare (su nastro); (stick) attaccare con nastro adesivo; **on ~** (song etc) su nastro

tape deck N piastra di registrazione

tape measure N metro a nastro

taper ['teɪpər] N candelina ▶ VI assottigliarsi

tape-record ['teɪprɪkɔ:d] VT registrare (su nastro)

tape recorder N registratore m (a nastro)

tape recording N registrazione f

tapered ['teɪpəd], **tapering** ['teɪpərɪŋ] ADJ affusolato(-a)

tapestry ['tæpɪstrɪ] N arazzo; tappezzeria

tape-worm ['teɪpwə:m] N tenia, verme m solitario

tapioca [tæpɪ'əukə] N tapioca

tappet ['tæpɪt] N punteria

tar [tɑ:r] N catrame m; **low-/middle-~ cigarettes** sigarette a basso/medio contenuto di nicotina

tarantula [tə'ræntjulə] N tarantola

tardy ['tɑ:dɪ] ADJ tardo(-a); tardivo(-a)

target ['tɑ:gɪt] N bersaglio; (fig: objective) obiettivo; **to be on ~** (project) essere nei tempi (di lavorazione)

target practice N tiro al bersaglio

tariff ['tærɪf] N tariffa

tarmac ['tɑ:mæk] N (BRIT: on road) macadam m al catrame; (Aviat) pista di decollo ▶ VT (BRIT) macadamizzare

tarnish ['tɑ:nɪʃ] VT offuscare, annerire; (fig) macchiare

tarot ['tærəu] N tarocco

tarpaulin [tɑ:'pɔ:lɪn] N tela incatramata

tarragon ['tærəgən] N dragoncello

tart [tɑ:t] N (Culin) crostata; (BRIT col, pej: woman) sgualdrina ▶ ADJ (flavour) aspro(-a), agro(-a)

▶ **tart up** VT (col): **to ~ o.s. up** farsi bello(-a); (pej) agghindarsi

tartan ['tɑ:tn] N tartan m inv

tartar ['tɑ:tər] N (on teeth) tartaro

tartar sauce, tartare sauce N salsa tartara

task [tɑ:sk] N compito; **to take to ~** rimproverare

task force N (Mil, Police) unità operativa

taskmaster ['tɑ:skmɑ:stər] N: **he's a hard ~** è un vero tiranno

Tasmania [tæz'meɪnɪə] N Tasmania

tassel ['tæsl] N fiocco

taste [teɪst] N gusto; (flavour) sapore m, gusto; (sample) assaggio; (fig: glimpse, idea) idea ▶ VT gustare; (*sample*) assaggiare ► vɪ: **to ~ of** or **like** (*fish etc*) sapere di, avere sapore di; **what does it ~ like?** che sapore or gusto ha?; **it tastes like fish** sa di pesce; **in good/bad ~** di buon/cattivo gusto; **you can ~ the garlic (in it)** (ci) si sente il sapore dell'aglio; **can I have a ~?** posso assaggiarlo?; **can I have a ~ of this wine?** posso assaggiare un po' di questo vino?; **to have a ~ of sth** assaggiare qc; **to have a ~ for sth** avere un'inclinazione per qc; **to be in bad** or **poor ~** essere di cattivo gusto

taste bud N papilla gustativa

tasteful ['teɪstful] ADJ di buon gusto

tastefully ['teɪstfəlɪ] ADV con gusto

tasteless ['teɪstlɪs] ADJ (*food*) insipido(-a); (*remark*) di cattivo gusto

tasty ['teɪstɪ] ADJ saporito(-a), gustoso(-a)

tattered ['tætəd] ADJ *see* **tatters**

tatters ['tætəz] NPL: **in ~** (*also*: **tattered**) a brandelli, sbrindellato(-a)

tattoo [tə'tu:] N tatuaggio; (*spectacle*) parata militare ► vᴛ tatuare

tatty ['tætɪ] ADJ (*Bʀɪᴛ col*) malandato(-a)

taught [tɔ:t] ᴘᴛ, ᴘᴘ *of* **teach**

taunt [tɔ:nt] N scherno ► vᴛ schernire

Taurus ['tɔ:rəs] N Toro; **to be ~** essere del Toro

taut [tɔ:t] ADJ teso(-a)

tavern ['tævən] N taverna

tawdry ['tɔ:drɪ] ADJ pacchiano(-a)

tawny ['tɔ:nɪ] ADJ fulvo(-a)

tax [tæks] N (*on goods*) imposta; (*on services*) tassa; (*on income*) imposte *fpl*, tasse *fpl* ► vᴛ tassare; (*fig: strain: patience etc*) mettere alla prova; **free of ~** esentasse *inv*, esente da imposte; **before/after ~** al lordo/netto delle tasse

taxable ['tæksəbl] ADJ imponibile

tax allowance N detrazione *f* d'imposta

taxation [tæk'seɪʃən] N tassazione *f*; tasse *fpl*, imposte *fpl*; **system of ~** sistema *m* fiscale

tax avoidance N *l'evitare legalmente il pagamento di imposte*

tax collector N esattore *m* delle imposte

tax disc N (*Bʀɪᴛ Aut*) ≈ bollo

tax evasion N evasione *f* fiscale

tax exemption N esenzione *f* fiscale

tax exile N *chi ripara all'estero per evadere le imposte*

tax-free [tæks'fri:] ADJ esente da imposte

tax haven N paradiso fiscale

taxi ['tæksɪ] N taxi *m inv* ► vɪ (*Aviat*) rullare

taxidermist ['tæksɪdə:mɪst] N tassidermista *mf*

taxi driver N tassista *mf*

tax inspector N (*Bʀɪᴛ*) ispettore *m* delle tasse

taxi rank, (*US*)**taxi stand** N posteggio dei taxi

taxi stand (*US*) N = **taxi rank**

tax payer N contribuente *mf*

tax rebate N rimborso fiscale

tax relief N sgravio fiscale

tax return N dichiarazione *f* dei redditi

tax shelter N paradiso fiscale

tax year N anno fiscale

TB N ABBR (= *tuberculosis*) TBC *f*

tbc ABBR (= *to be confirmed*) da confermarsi

TD N ABBR (*US*) = **Treasury Department**; (*Football*) = **touchdown**

tea [ti:] N tè *m inv*; (*Bʀɪᴛ: snack: for children*) merenda; **high ~** (*Bʀɪᴛ*) cena leggera (*presa nel tardo pomeriggio*)

tea bag N bustina di tè

tea break N (*Bʀɪᴛ*) intervallo per il tè

teacake ['ti:keɪk] N (*Bʀɪᴛ*) panino dolce all'uva

teach [ti:tʃ] (*pt, pp* **taught** [tɔ:t]) vᴛ: **to ~ sb sth, ~ sth to sb** insegnare qc a qn ► vɪ insegnare; **it taught him a lesson** (*fig*) gli è servito da lezione

teacher ['ti:tʃəʳ] N (*gen*) insegnante *mf*; (*in secondary school*) professore(-essa); (*in primary school*) maestro(-a); **French ~** insegnante di francese

teacher training college N (*for primary schools*) ≈ istituto magistrale; (*for secondary schools*) *scuola universitaria per l'abilitazione all'insegnamento nelle medie superiori*

teaching ['ti:tʃɪŋ] N insegnamento

teaching aids NPL materiali *mpl* per l'insegnamento

teaching hospital N (*Bʀɪᴛ*) clinica universitaria

teaching staff N (*Bʀɪᴛ*) insegnanti *mpl*, personale *m* insegnante

tea cloth N (*for dishes*) strofinaccio; (*Bʀɪᴛ: for trolley*) tovaglietta da tè

tea cosy N copriteiera *m inv*

teacup ['ti:kʌp] N tazza da tè

teak [ti:k] N teak *m*

tea leaves NPL foglie *fpl* di tè

team [ti:m] N squadra; (*of animals*) tiro
 ► **team up** vɪ: **to ~ up (with)** mettersi insieme (a)

team games NPL giochi *mpl* di squadra

teamwork ['ti:mwə:k] N lavoro di squadra

tea party N tè *m inv* (*ricevimento*)

teapot ['ti:pɔt] N teiera

tear¹ [tɪəʳ] N lacrima; **in tears** in lacrime; **to burst into tears** scoppiare in lacrime

tear² [tɛəʳ] (*pt* **tore** [tɔ:ʳ], *pp* **torn** [tɔ:n]) N strappo ► vᴛ strappare ► vɪ strapparsi; **to ~ to pieces** or **to bits** or **to shreds** (*also fig*) fare a pezzi or a brandelli
 ► **tear along** vɪ (*rush*) correre all'impazzata
 ► **tear apart** vᴛ (*also fig*) distruggere
 ► **tear away** vᴛ: **to ~ o.s. away (from sth)**

(fig) staccarsi (da qc)
▶ **tear down** VT *(building, statue)* demolire;
(poster, flag) tirare giù
▶ **tear off** VT *(sheet of paper etc)* strappare;
(one's clothes) togliersi di dosso
▶ **tear out** VT *(sheet of paper, cheque)* staccare
▶ **tear up** VT *(sheet of paper etc)* strappare
tearaway ['tɛərəweɪ] N *(col)* monello(-a)
teardrop ['tɪədrɔp] N lacrima
tearful ['tɪəful] ADJ piangente, lacrimoso(-a)
tear gas N gas *m* lacrimogeno
tearoom ['tiːruːm] N sala da tè
tease [tiːz] VT canzonare; *(unkindly)*
tormentare
tea set N servizio da tè
teashop ['tiːʃɔp] N *(BRIT)* sala da tè
Teasmaid® ['tiːzmeɪd] N macchinetta per
fare il tè
teaspoon ['tiːspuːn] N cucchiaino da tè;
(also: **teaspoonful:** *as measurement)* cucchiaino
tea strainer N colino da tè
teat [tiːt] N capezzolo; *(of bottle)* tettarella
teatime ['tiːtaɪm] N ora del tè
tea towel N *(BRIT)* strofinaccio (per i piatti)
tea urn N bollitore *m* per il tè
tech [tɛk] N ABBR *(col)* (= *technical college)*
= **technical college**; **technology**
technical ['tɛknɪkl] ADJ tecnico(-a)
technical college N ≈ istituto tecnico
technicality [tɛknɪ'kælɪtɪ] N tecnicità;
(detail) dettaglio tecnico; **on a legal ~** grazie
a un cavillo legale
technically ['tɛknɪklɪ] ADV dal punto di vista
tecnico
technician [tɛk'nɪʃən] N tecnico(-a)
technique [tɛk'niːk] N tecnica
techno ['tɛknəu] N *(Mus)* techno *f* inv
technocrat ['tɛknəkræt] N tecnocrate *mf*
technological [tɛknə'lɔdʒɪkl] ADJ
tecnologico(-a)
technologist [tɛk'nɔlədʒɪst] N tecnologo(-a)
technology [tɛk'nɔlədʒɪ] N tecnologia
teddy ['tɛdɪ], **teddy bear** ['tɛdɪ-] N
orsacchiotto
tedious ['tiːdɪəs] ADJ noioso(-a), tedioso(-a)
tedium ['tiːdɪəm] N noia, tedio
tee [tiː] N *(Golf)* tee *m* inv
teem [tiːm] VI abbondare, brulicare; **to ~**
with brulicare di; **it is teeming (with rain)**
piove a dirotto
teen [tiːn] ADJ = **teenage** ▶ N *(US)* = **teenager**
teenage ['tiːneɪdʒ] ADJ *(fashions etc)* per
giovani, per adolescenti
teenager ['tiːneɪdʒər] N adolescente *mf*
teens [tiːnz] NPL: **to be in one's ~** essere
adolescente
tee-shirt ['tiːʃəːt] N = **T-shirt**
teeter ['tiːtər] VI barcollare, vacillare
teeth [tiːθ] NPL *of* **tooth**

teethe [tiːð] VI mettere i denti
teething ring ['tiːðɪŋ-] N dentaruolo
teething troubles NPL *(fig)* difficoltà *fpl*
iniziali
teetotal ['tiː'təutl] ADJ astemio(-a)
teetotaller, *(US)* **teetotaler** ['tiː'təutlər] N
astemio(-a)
TEFL ['tɛfl] N ABBR = **Teaching of English as a**
Foreign Language
Teflon® ['tɛflɔn] N teflon® *m*
Tehran [tɛə'rɑːn] N Tehran *f*
tel. ABBR (= *telephone)* tel
Tel Aviv ['tɛlə'viːv] N Tel Aviv *f*
telecast ['tɛlɪkɑːst] VT, VI teletrasmettere
telecommunications
['tɛlɪkəmjuːnɪ'keɪʃənz] N telecomunicazioni
fpl
teleconferencing ['tɛlɪkɔnfərnsɪŋ] N
teleconferenza
telegram ['tɛlɪgræm] N telegramma *m*
telegraph ['tɛlɪgrɑːf] N telegrafo
telegraphic [tɛlɪ'græfɪk] ADJ telegrafico(-a)
telegraph pole N palo del telegrafo
telegraph wire N filo del telegrafo
telepathic [tɛlɪ'pæθɪk] ADJ telepatico(-a)
telepathy [tə'lɛpəθɪ] N telepatia
telephone ['tɛlɪfəun] N telefono ▶ VT *(person)*
telefonare a; *(message)* comunicare per
telefono; **to have a ~,** *(BRIT)* **to be on the ~**
(subscriber) avere il telefono; **to be on the ~**
(be speaking) essere al telefono
telephone book N elenco telefonico
telephone box, *(US)* **telephone booth** N
cabina telefonica
telephone call N telefonata
telephone directory N elenco telefonico
telephone exchange N centralino
telefonico
telephone number N numero di telefono
telephone operator N centralinista *mf*
telephone tapping N intercettazione *f*
telefonica
telephonist [tə'lɛfənɪst] N *(BRIT)* telefonista
mf
telephoto lens ['tɛlɪfəutəu-] N teleobiettivo
teleprinter ['tɛlɪprɪntər] N telescrivente *f*
Teleprompter® ['tɛlɪprɔmptər] N *(US)* gobbo
telesales ['tɛlɪseɪlz] N vendita per telefono
telescope ['tɛlɪskəup] N telescopio ▶ VI
chiudersi a telescopio; *(fig: vehicles)*
accartocciarsi
telescopic [tɛlɪs'kɔpɪk] ADJ telescopico(-a);
(umbrella) pieghevole
Teletext® ['tɛlɪtɛkst] N *(system)* teletext *m* inv;
(in Italy) televideo
telethon ['tɛlɪθɔn] N maratona televisiva
televise ['tɛlɪvaɪz] VT teletrasmettere
television ['tɛlɪvɪʒən] N televisione *f*; **on ~**
alla televisione

television licence N (BRIT) abbonamento alla televisione

television programme N programma m televisivo

television set N televisore m

teleworking ['tɛlɪwəːkɪŋ] N telelavoro

telex ['tɛlɛks] N telex m inv ▶ VT trasmettere per telex ▶ VI mandare un telex; **to ~ sb (about sth)** informare qn via telex (di qc)

tell [tɛl] (pt, pp **told**) VT dire; (relate: story) raccontare; (distinguish): **to ~ sth from** distinguere qc da ▶ VI (talk): **to ~ (of)** parlare (di); (have effect) farsi sentire, avere effetto; **to ~ sb to do** dire a qn di fare; **to ~ sb about sth** dire a qn di qc; raccontare qc a qn; **to ~ the time** leggere l'ora; **can you ~ me the time?** può dirmi l'ora?; **(I) ~ you what …** so io che cosa fare …; **I couldn't ~ them apart** non riuscivo a distinguerli
▶ **tell off** VT rimproverare, sgridare
▶ **tell on** VT FUS (inform against) denunciare

teller ['tɛləʳ] N (in bank) cassiere(-a)

telling ['tɛlɪŋ] ADJ (remark, detail) rivelatore(-trice)

telltale ['tɛlteɪl] ADJ (sign) rivelatore(-trice) ▶ N malalingua, pettegolo(-a)

telly ['tɛlɪ] N ABBR (BRIT: col: = television) tivù f inv

temerity [tə'mɛrɪtɪ] N temerarietà

temp [tɛmp] ABBR (BRIT col) = **temporary** ▶ N impiegato(-a) interinale ▶ VI lavorare come impiegato(-a) interinale

temper ['tɛmpəʳ] N (nature) carattere m; (mood) umore m; (fit of anger) collera ▶ VT (moderate) temperare, moderare; **to be in a ~** essere in collera; **to keep one's ~** restare calmo; **to lose one's ~** andare in collera

temperament ['tɛmprəmənt] N (nature) temperamento

temperamental [tɛmprə'mɛntl] ADJ capriccioso(-a)

temperance ['tɛmpərns] N moderazione f; (in drinking) temperanza nel bere

temperate ['tɛmprət] ADJ moderato(-a); (climate) temperato(-a)

temperature ['tɛmprətʃəʳ] N temperatura; **to have** or **run a ~** avere la febbre

tempered ['tɛmpəd] ADJ (steel) temprato(-a)

tempest ['tɛmpɪst] N tempesta

tempestuous [tɛm'pɛstjuəs] ADJ (relationship, meeting) burrascoso(-a)

tempi ['tɛmpiː] NPL of **tempo**

template, (US)templet ['tɛmplɪt] N sagoma

temple ['tɛmpl] N (building) tempio; (Anat) tempia

templet ['tɛmplɪt] N (US) = **template**

tempo ['tɛmpəu] (pl **tempos, tempi**) N tempo; (fig: of life etc) ritmo

temporal ['tɛmpərl] ADJ temporale

temporarily ['tɛmpərərɪlɪ] ADV temporaneamente

temporary ['tɛmpərərɪ] ADJ temporaneo(-a); (job, worker) avventizio(-a), temporaneo(-a); **~ secretary** segretaria temporanea; **~ teacher** supplente mf

temporize ['tɛmpəraɪz] VI temporeggiare

tempt [tɛmpt] VT tentare; **to ~ sb into doing** indurre qn a fare; **to be tempted to do sth** essere tentato di/a fare qc

temptation [tɛmp'teɪʃən] N tentazione f

tempting ['tɛmptɪŋ] ADJ allettante, seducente

ten [tɛn] NUM dieci ▶ N dieci; **tens of thousands** decine di migliaia

tenable ['tɛnəbl] ADJ sostenibile

tenacious [tə'neɪʃəs] ADJ tenace

tenacity [tə'næsɪtɪ] N tenacia

tenancy ['tɛnənsɪ] N affitto; condizione f di inquilino

tenant ['tɛnənt] N inquilino(-a)

tend [tɛnd] VT badare a, occuparsi di; (sick etc) prendersi cura di ▶ VI: **to ~ to do** tendere a fare; **to ~ to** (colour) tendere a

tendency ['tɛndənsɪ] N tendenza

tender ['tɛndəʳ] ADJ tenero(-a); (sore) dolorante; (fig: subject) delicato(-a) ▶ N (Comm: offer) offerta; (money): **legal ~** moneta in corso legale ▶ VT offrire; **to put in a ~ (for)** fare un'offerta (per); **to put work out to ~** (BRIT) dare lavoro in appalto; **to ~ one's resignation** presentare le proprie dimissioni

tenderize ['tɛndəraɪz] VT (Culin) far intenerire

tenderly ['tɛndəlɪ] ADV teneramente

tenderness ['tɛndənɪs] N tenerezza; sensibilità

tendon ['tɛndən] N tendine m

tenement ['tɛnəmənt] N casamento

Tenerife [tɛnə'riːf] N Tenerife f

tenet ['tɛnət] N principio

Tenn. ABBR (US) = **Tennessee**

tenner ['tɛnəʳ] N (BRIT col) (banconota da) dieci sterline fpl

tennis ['tɛnɪs] N tennis m

tennis ball N palla da tennis

tennis court N campo da tennis

tennis elbow N (Med) gomito del tennista

tennis match N partita di tennis

tennis player N tennista mf

tennis racket N racchetta da tennis

tennis shoes NPL scarpe fpl da tennis

tenor ['tɛnəʳ] N (Mus, of speech etc) tenore m

tenpin bowling ['tɛnpɪn-] N (BRIT) bowling m

tense [tɛns] ADJ teso(-a) ▶ N (Ling) tempo ▶ VT (tighten: muscles) tendere

tenseness ['tɛnsnɪs] N tensione f

tension ['tɛnʃən] N tensione f
tent [tɛnt] N tenda
tentacle ['tɛntəkl] N tentacolo
tentative ['tɛntətɪv] ADJ esitante, incerto(-a); (*conclusion*) provvisorio(-a)
tenterhooks ['tɛntəhuks] NPL: **on ~** sulle spine
tenth [tɛnθ] NUM decimo(-a)
tent peg N picchetto da tenda
tent pole N palo da tenda, montante m
tenuous ['tɛnjuəs] ADJ tenue
tenure ['tɛnjuəʳ] N (*of property*) possesso; (*of job*) incarico; (*guaranteed employment*): **to have ~** essere di ruolo
tepid ['tɛpɪd] ADJ tiepido(-a)
Ter. ABBR = **terrace**
term [təːm] N (*limit*) termine m; (*word*) vocabolo, termine; (*Scol*) trimestre m; (*Law*) sessione f ▶ VT chiamare, definire; **terms** NPL (*conditions*) condizioni fpl; (*Comm*) prezzi mpl, tariffe fpl; **~ of imprisonment** periodo di prigionia; **during his ~ of office** durante il suo incarico; **in the short/long ~** a breve/lunga scadenza; **"easy terms"** (*Comm*) "facilitazioni di pagamento"; **to be on good terms with** essere in buoni rapporti con; **to come to terms with** (*person*) arrivare a un accordo con; (*problem*) affrontare
terminal ['təːmɪnl] ADJ finale, terminale; (*disease*) terminale ▶ N (*Elec, Comput*) morsetto; (*Aviat, for oil, ore etc*) terminal m inv; (*BRIT: also:* **coach terminal**) capolinea m
terminate ['təːmɪneɪt] VT mettere fine a ▶ VI: **to ~ in** finire in or con
termination [təːmɪ'neɪʃən] N fine f; (*of contract*) rescissione f; **~ of pregnancy** (*Med*) interruzione f della gravidanza
termini ['təːmɪnaɪ] NPL of **terminus**
terminology [təːmɪ'nɔlədʒɪ] N terminologia
terminus ['təːmɪnəs] (*pl* **termini** ['təːmɪnaɪ]) N (*for buses*) capolinea m; (*for trains*) stazione f terminale
termite ['təːmaɪt] N termite f
term paper N (*US Univ*) saggio scritto da consegnare a fine trimestre
Terr. ABBR = **terrace**
terrace ['tɛrəs] N terrazza; (*BRIT: row of houses*) fila di case a schiera; **the terraces** NPL (*BRIT Sport*) le gradinate
terraced ['tɛrɪst] ADJ (*garden*) a terrazze; (*in a row: house, cottage etc*) a schiera
terrain [tɛ'reɪn] N terreno
terrestrial [tɪ'rɛstrɪəl] ADJ (*life*) terrestre; (*BRIT: channel*) terrestre
terrible ['tɛrɪbl] ADJ terribile; (*weather*) bruttissimo(-a); (*performance, report*) pessimo(-a)
terribly ['tɛrəblɪ] ADV terribilmente; (*very badly*) malissimo

terrier ['tɛrɪəʳ] N terrier m inv
terrific [tə'rɪfɪk] ADJ incredibile, fantastico(-a); (*wonderful*) formidabile, eccezionale
terrified ['tɛrɪfaɪd] ADJ atterrito(-a)
terrify ['tɛrɪfaɪ] VT terrorizzare; **to be terrified** essere atterrito(-a)
terrifying ADJ terrificante
territorial [tɛrɪ'tɔːrɪəl] ADJ territoriale
territorial waters NPL acque fpl territoriali
territory ['tɛrɪtərɪ] N territorio
terror ['tɛrəʳ] N terrore m
terror attack N attentato terroristico
terrorism ['tɛrərɪzəm] N terrorismo
terrorist ['tɛrərɪst] N terrorista mf
terrorize ['tɛrəraɪz] VT terrorizzare
terse [təːs] ADJ (*style*) conciso(-a); (*reply*) laconico(-a)
tertiary ['təːʃərɪ] ADJ (*gen*) terziario(-a); **~ education** (*BRIT*) educazione f superiore post-scolastica
Terylene® ['tɛrəliːn] N (*BRIT*) terital® m, terilene® m
TESL ['tɛsl] N ABBR = **Teaching of English as a Second Language**
TESSA ['tɛsə] N ABBR (*BRIT*: = *Tax Exempt Special Savings Account*) deposito a risparmio esente da tasse
test [tɛst] N (*trial, check: of courage etc*) prova; (: *of goods in factory*) controllo, collaudo; (*Med*) esame m; (*Chem*) analisi f inv; (*exam: of intelligence etc*) test m inv; (: *in school*) compito in classe; (*also:* **driving test**) esame m di guida ▶ VT provare; controllare, collaudare; esaminare; analizzare; sottoporre ad esame; **to put sth to the ~** mettere qc alla prova; **to ~ sth for sth** analizzare qc alla ricerca di qc; **to ~ sb in history** esaminare qn in storia
testament ['tɛstəmənt] N testamento; **the Old/New T~** il Vecchio/Nuovo testamento
test ban N (*also:* **nuclear test ban**) divieto di esperimenti nucleari
test case N (*Law, fig*) caso che farà testo
testes ['tɛstiːz] NPL testicoli mpl
test flight N volo di prova
testicle ['tɛstɪkl] N testicolo
testify ['tɛstɪfaɪ] VI (*Law*) testimoniare, deporre; **to ~ to sth** (*Law*) testimoniare qc; (*gen*) comprovare or dimostrare qc; (*be sign of*) essere una prova di qc
testimonial [tɛstɪ'məunɪəl] N (*reference*) benservito; (*gift*) testimonianza di stima
testimony ['tɛstɪmənɪ] N (*Law*) testimonianza, deposizione f
testing ['tɛstɪŋ] ADJ (*difficult: time*) duro(-a)
test match N (*Cricket, Rugby*) partita internazionale
testosterone [tɛs'tɔstərəun] N testosterone m

t

test paper N (*Scol*) interrogazione *f* scritta
test pilot N pilota *m* collaudatore
test tube N provetta
test-tube baby ['tɛsttjuːb-] N bambino(-a) concepito(-a) in provetta
testy ['tɛstɪ] ADJ irritabile
tetanus ['tɛtənəs] N tetano
tetchy ['tɛtʃɪ] ADJ irritabile, irascibile
tether ['tɛðəʳ] VT legare ▶ N: **at the end of one's ~** al limite (della pazienza)
Tex. ABBR (*US*) = **Texas**
text [tɛkst] N testo; (*Tel*) sms *m inv*, messaggino ▶ VT: **to ~ sb** (*col*) mandare un sms a ▶ VI messaggiarsi
textbook ['tɛkstbʊk] N libro di testo
textile ['tɛkstaɪl] N tessile *m*; **textiles** NPL tessuti *mpl*
texting ['tɛkstɪŋ] N invio di sms
text message N (*Tel*) sms *m inv*, messaggino
text messaging [-'mɛsɪdʒɪŋ] N il mandarsi sms
textual ['tɛkstjʊəl] ADJ testuale, del testo
texture ['tɛkstʃəʳ] N tessitura; (*of skin, paper etc*) struttura
TGIF ABBR (*col*) = **thank God it's Friday**
TGWU N ABBR (*Brit*: = *Transport and General Workers' Union*) sindacato degli operai dei trasporti e non specializzati
Thai [taɪ] ADJ tailandese ▶ N tailandese *mf*; (*Ling*) tailandese *m*
Thailand ['taɪlænd] N Tailandia
thalidomide® [θəˈlɪdəmaɪd] N talidomide® *m*
Thames [tɛmz] N: **the ~** il Tamigi
than [ðæn, ðən] CONJ (*in comparisons*) che; (*with numerals, pronouns, proper names*) di; **more ~ 10/Maria/once** più di 10/Maria/una volta; **I have more/less ~ you** ne ho più/meno di te; **you know her better ~ I do** la conosce meglio di me *or* di quanto non la conosca io; **she has more apples ~ pears** ha più mele che pere; **it is better to phone ~ to write** è meglio telefonare che scrivere; **no sooner did he leave ~ the phone rang** non appena uscì il telefono suonò; **she is older ~ you think** è più vecchia di quanto tu (non) pensi
thank [θæŋk] VT ringraziare; **~ you (very much)** grazie (tante); **~ heavens/God!** grazie al cielo/a Dio!; *see also* **thanks**
thankful ['θæŋkful] ADJ: **~ (for)** riconoscente (per); **~ for/that** (*relieved*) sollevato(a) da/dal fatto che
thankfully ['θæŋkfəlɪ] ADV con riconoscenza; con sollievo; **~ there were few victims** grazie al cielo ci sono state poche vittime
thankless ['θæŋklɪs] ADJ ingrato(-a)
thanks [θæŋks] NPL ringraziamenti *mpl*, grazie *fpl* ▶ EXCL grazie!; **~ to** *prep* grazie a
Thanksgiving (Day) ['θæŋksɡɪvɪŋ-] N (*US*) giorno del ringraziamento; *vedi nota*

Negli Stati Uniti il quarto giovedì di novembre ricorre il *Thanksgiving (Day)*, festa nazionale in ricordo della celebrazione con cui i Padri Pellegrini, i puritani inglesi che fondarono la colonia di Plymouth nel Massachusetts, ringraziarono Dio del buon raccolto del 1621.

⸢KEYWORD⸣

that [ðæt] (*pl* **those**) ADJ (*demonstrative*) quel (quell', quello) *m*; quella (quell') *f*; **that man/woman/book** quell'uomo/quella donna/quel libro; (*not "this"*) quell'uomo/quella donna/quel libro là; **that one** quello(-a) là
▶ PRON **1** (*demonstrative*) ciò; (: *not "this one"*) quello(-a); **who's that?** chi è?; **what's that?** cos'è quello?; **is that you?** sei tu?; **I prefer this to that** preferisco questo a quello; **that's what he said** questo è ciò che ha detto; **after that** dopo; **what happened after that?** che è successo dopo?; **that is (to say)** cioè; **at** *or* **with that she ...** con ciò lei ...; **do it like that** fallo così
2 (*relative: direct*) che; (: *indirect*) cui; **the book (that) I read** il libro che ho letto; **the box (that) I put it in** la scatola in cui l'ho messo; **the people (that) I spoke to** le persone con cui *or* con le quali ho parlato; **not that I know of** non che io sappia
3 (*relative: of time*) in cui; **the day (that) he came** il giorno in cui è venuto
▶ CONJ che; **he thought that I was ill** pensava che io fossi malato
▶ ADV (*demonstrative*) così; **I can't work that much** non posso lavorare (così) tanto; **that high** così alto; **the wall's about that high and that thick** il muro è alto circa così e spesso circa così

thatched [θætʃt] ADJ (*roof*) di paglia; **~ cottage** cottage *m inv* col tetto di paglia
Thatcherism ['θætʃərɪzəm] N thatcherismo
thaw [θɔː] N disgelo ▶ VI (*ice*) sciogliersi; (*food*) scongelarsi ▶ VT (*food*) (fare) scongelare; **it's thawing** (*weather*) sta sgelando

⸢KEYWORD⸣

the [ðiː, ðə] DEF ART **1** (*gen*) il (lo, l') *m*; la (l') *f*; i (gli) *mpl*; le *fpl*; **the boy/girl/ink** il ragazzo/la ragazza/l'inchiostro; **the books/pencils** i libri/le matite; **the history of the world** la storia del mondo; **give it to the postman** dallo al postino; **I haven't the time/money** non ho tempo/soldi; **the rich and the poor** i ricchi e i poveri; **1.5 euros to the dollar** 1.5 euro per un dollaro; **paid by the hour** pagato a ore

2 (*in titles*): **Elizabeth the First** Elisabetta prima; **Peter the Great** Pietro il Grande **3** (*in comparisons*): **the more he works, the more he earns** più lavora più guadagna; **the sooner the better** prima è meglio è

theatre, (*US*) **theater** ['θɪətə^r] N teatro; (*also:* **lecture theatre**) aula magna; (*also:* **operating theatre**) sala operatoria
theatre-goer ['θɪətəɡəʊə^r] N frequentatore(-trice) di teatri
theatrical [θɪ'ætrɪkl] ADJ teatrale
theft [θeft] N furto
their [ðɛə^r] ADJ il (la) loro *pl* i (le) loro
theirs [ðɛəz] PRON il (la) loro *pl* i (le) loro; **it is ~** è loro; **a friend of ~** un loro amico; *see also* **my**; **mine**[1]
them [ðɛm, ðəm] PRON (*direct*) li(le); (*indirect*) gli, loro (*after vb*); (*stressed, after prep: people*) loro; (: *people, things*) essi(-e); **I see ~** li vedo; **give ~ the book** dà loro *or* dagli il libro; **give me a few of ~** dammene un po' *or* qualcuno; *see also* **me**
theme [θiːm] N tema *m*
theme park N parco a tema
theme song, theme tune N tema musicale
themselves [ðəm'sɛlvz] PL PRON (*reflexive*) si; (*emphatic*) loro stessi(-e); (*after prep*) se stessi(-e); **between ~** tra (di) loro
then [ðɛn] ADV (*at that time*) allora; (*next*) poi, dopo; (*and also*) e poi ▶ CONJ (*therefore*) perciò, dunque, quindi ▶ ADJ: **the ~ president** il presidente di allora; **by ~** allora; **from ~ on** da allora in poi; **until ~** fino ad allora; **and ~ what?** e poi?, e allora?; **what do you want me to do ~?** allora cosa vuole che faccia?
theologian [θɪə'ləʊdʒən] N teologo(-a)
theological [θɪə'lɒdʒɪkl] ADJ teologico(-a)
theology [θɪ'ɒlədʒɪ] N teologia
theorem ['θɪərəm] N teorema *m*
theoretical [θɪə'rɛtɪkl] ADJ teorico(-a)
theorize ['θɪəraɪz] VI teorizzare
theory ['θɪərɪ] N teoria; **in ~** in teoria
therapeutic [θɛrə'pjuːtɪk], **therapeutical** [θɛrə'pjuːtɪkl] ADJ terapeutico(-a)
therapist ['θɛrəpɪst] N terapista *mf*
therapy ['θɛrəpɪ] N terapia

(KEYWORD)

there [ðɛə^r] ADV **1**: **there is** c'è; **there are** ci sono; **there 3 of them** (*people*) sono in 3; (*things*) ce ne sono 3; **there is no-one here** non c'è nessuno qui; **there has been an accident** c'è stato un incidente
2 (*referring to place*) là, lì; **it's there** è là *or* lì; **up/in/down there** lassù/là dentro/laggiù; **back there** là dietro; **on there** lassù; **over there** là; **through there** di là; **he went there on Friday** ci è andato venerdì; **it**

takes two hours to go there and back ci vogliono due ore per andare e tornare; **I want that book there** voglio quel libro là *or* lì; **there he is!** eccolo!
3: **there, there** (*esp to child*) su, su

thereabouts ['ðɛərəbauts] ADV (*place*) nei pressi, da quelle parti; (*amount*) giù di lì, all'incirca
thereafter [ðɛər'ɑːftə^r] ADV da allora in poi
thereby [ðɛə'baɪ] ADV con ciò
therefore ['ðɛəfɔː^r] ADV perciò, quindi
there's [ðɛəz] = **there is**; **there has**
thereupon [ðɛərə'pɒn] ADV (*at that point*) a quel punto; (*formal: on that subject*) in merito
thermal ['θəːml] ADJ (*currents, spring*) termale; (*underwear, printer*) termico(-a); (*paper*) termosensibile
thermodynamics [θəːməʊdaɪ'næmɪks] N termodinamica
thermometer [θə'mɒmɪtə^r] N termometro
thermonuclear ['θəːməʊ'njuːklɪə^r] ADJ termonucleare
Thermos® ['θəːməs] N (*also:* **Thermos flask**) thermos® *m inv*
thermostat ['θəːməstæt] N termostato
thesaurus [θɪ'sɔːrəs] N dizionario dei sinonimi
these [ðiːz] PL PRON, ADJ questi(-e)
thesis ['θiːsɪs] (*pl* **theses** ['θiːsiːz]) N tesi *f inv*
they [ðeɪ] PL PRON essi(esse); (*people only*) loro; **~ say that ...** (*it is said that*) si dice che ...
they'd [ðeɪd] = **they would**; **they had**
they'll [ðeɪl] = **they will**; **they shall**
they're [ðɛə^r] = **they are**
they've [ðeɪv] = **they have**
thick [θɪk] ADJ spesso(-a); (*crowd*) compatto(-a); (*stupid*) ottuso(-a), lento(-a) ▶ N: **in the ~ of** nel folto di; **it's 20 cm ~** ha uno spessore di 20 cm
thicken ['θɪkən] VI ispessire ▶ VT (*sauce etc*) ispessire, rendere più denso(-a)
thicket ['θɪkɪt] N boscaglia
thickly ['θɪklɪ] ADV (*spread*) a strati spessi; (*cut*) a fette grosse; (*populated*) densamente
thickness ['θɪknɪs] N spessore *m*
thickset [θɪk'sɛt] ADJ tarchiato(-a), tozzo(-a)
thickskinned [θɪk'skɪnd] ADJ (*fig*) insensibile
thief [θiːf] (*pl* **thieves** [θiːvz]) N ladro(-a)
thieving ['θiːvɪŋ] N furti *mpl*
thigh [θaɪ] N coscia
thighbone ['θaɪbəʊn] N femore *m*
thimble ['θɪmbl] N ditale *m*
thin [θɪn] ADJ sottile; (*person*) magro(-a); (*soup*) poco denso(-a); (*hair, crowd*) rado(-a); (*fog*) leggero(-a) ▶ VT (*hair*) sfoltire ▶ VI (*fog*) diradarsi; (*also:* **thin out**: *crowd*) disperdersi; **to ~ (down)** (*sauce, paint*) diluire; **his hair is thinning** sta perdendo i capelli

t

thing [θɪŋ] N cosa; (object) oggetto; (contraption) aggeggio; (mania): **to have a ~ about** essere fissato(-a) con; **things** NPL (belongings) cose fpl; **for one ~** tanto per cominciare; **the best ~ would be to** la cosa migliore sarebbe di; **the ~ is …** il fatto è che …; **the main ~ is to …** la cosa più importante è di …; **first ~ (in the morning)** come or per prima cosa (di mattina); **last ~ (at night)** come or per ultima cosa (di sera); **poor ~** poveretto(-a); **she's got a ~ about mice** è terrorizzata dai topi; **how are things?** come va?

think [θɪŋk] (pt, pp **thought** [θɔ:t]) VI pensare, riflettere ▶ VT pensare, credere; (imagine) immaginare; **to ~ of** pensare a; **what did you ~ of them?** cosa ne ha pensato?; **to ~ about sth/sb** pensare a qc/qn; **I'll ~ about it** ci penserò; **to ~ of doing** pensare di fare; **I ~ so/not** penso or credo di sì/no; **to ~ well of** avere una buona opinione di; **to ~ aloud** pensare ad alta voce; **~ again!** rifletti!, pensaci su!
   ▶ **think out** VT (plan) elaborare; (solution) trovare
   ▶ **think over** VT riflettere su; **I'd like to ~ things over** vorrei pensarci su
   ▶ **think through** VT riflettere a fondo su
   ▶ **think up** VT ideare

thinking ['θɪŋkɪŋ] N: **to my (way of) ~** a mio parere

think tank N gruppo di esperti

thinly ['θɪnlɪ] ADV (cut) a fette sottili; (spread) in uno strato sottile

thinness ['θɪnnɪs] N sottigliezza; magrezza

third [θə:d] N terzo(-a) ▶ N terzo(-a); (fraction) terzo, terza parte f; (Aut) terza; (Brit Scol: degree) laurea col minimo dei voti

third-degree burns ['θə:ddɪ'gri:-] NPL ustioni fpl di terzo grado

thirdly ['θə:dlɪ] ADV in terzo luogo

third party insurance N (Brit) assicurazione f contro terzi

third-rate [θə:d'reɪt] ADJ di qualità scadente

Third World N: **the ~** il Terzo Mondo

thirst [θə:st] N sete f

thirsty ['θə:stɪ] ADJ (person) assetato(-a), che ha sete; **to be ~** aver sete

thirteen [θə:'ti:n] NUM tredici

thirteenth [-'ti:nθ] NUM tredicesmo(-a)

thirtieth ['θə:tɪɪθ] NUM trentesimo(-a)

thirty ['θə:tɪ] NUM trenta

<u>(KEYWORD)</u>

this [ðɪs ʃ] (pl **these**) ADJ (demonstrative) questo(-a); **this man/woman/book** quest'uomo/questa donna/questo libro; (not "that") quest'uomo/questa donna/questo libro qui; **this one** questo(-a) qui; **this time** questa volta; **this time last year** l'anno scorso in questo periodo; **this way** (in this direction) da questa parte; (in this fashion) così
   ▶ PRON (demonstrative) questo(-a); (: not "that one") questo(-a) qui; **who/what is this?** chi è/che cos'è questo?; **I prefer this to that** preferisco questo a quello; **this is where I live** io abito qui; **this is what he said** questo è ciò che ha detto; **they were talking of this and that** stavano parlando del più e del meno; **this is Mr Brown** (in introductions, photo) questo è il signor Brown; (on telephone) sono il signor Brown
   ▶ ADV (demonstrative): **this high/long** etc alto/lungo etc così; **it's about this high** è alto circa così; **I didn't know things were this bad** non sapevo andasse così male

thistle ['θɪsl] N cardo

thong [θɒŋ] N cinghia

thorn [θɔ:n] N spina

thorny ['θɔ:nɪ] ADJ spinoso(-a)

thorough ['θʌrə] ADJ (person) preciso(-a), accurato(-a); (search) minuzioso(-a); (knowledge, research) approfondito(-a), profondo(-a); (person) coscienzioso(-a); (cleaning) a fondo

thoroughbred ['θʌrəbrɛd] N (horse) purosangue mf

thoroughfare ['θʌrəfɛəʳ] N strada transitabile; **"no ~"** (Brit) "divieto di transito"

thoroughgoing ['θʌrəgəuɪŋ] ADJ (analysis) approfondito(-a); (reform) totale

thoroughly ['θʌrəlɪ] ADV accuratamente; (search) minuziosamente, in profondità; (wash, study) a fondo; (very) assolutamente; **he ~ agreed** fu completamente d'accordo

thoroughness ['θʌrənɪs] N precisione f

those [ðəuz] PL PRON quelli(-e) ▶ PL ADJ quei (quegli) mpl; quelle fpl

though [ðəu] CONJ benché, sebbene ▶ ADV comunque, tuttavia; **even ~** anche se; **it's not so easy, ~** tuttavia non è così facile

thought [θɔ:t] PT, PP of **think** ▶ N pensiero; (opinion) opinione f; (intention) intenzione f; **after much ~** dopo molti ripensamenti; **I've just had a ~** mi è appena venuta un'idea; **to give sth some ~** prendere qc in considerazione, riflettere su qc

thoughtful ['θɔ:tful] ADJ pensieroso(-a), pensoso(-a); ponderato(-a); (considerate) premuroso(-a)

thoughtfully ['θɔ:tfəlɪ] ADV (pensively) con aria pensierosa

thoughtless ['θɔ:tlɪs] ADJ sconsiderato(-a); (behaviour) scortese

thoughtlessly ['θɔ:tlɪslɪ] ADV sconsideratamente; scortesemente

thought-provoking ['θɔːtprəvəukɪŋ] ADJ stimolante

thousand ['θauzənd] NUM mille; **one ~** mille; **thousands of** migliaia di

thousandth ['θauzəntθ] NUM millesimo(-a)

thrash [θræʃ] VT picchiare; bastonare; (defeat) battere
  ▶ **thrash about** VI dibattersi
  ▶ **thrash out** VT dibattere, sviscerare

thrashing ['θræʃɪŋ] N: **to give sb a ~** picchiare qn di santa ragione

thread [θrɛd] N filo; (of screw) filetto ▶ VT (needle) infilare; **to ~ one's way between** infilarsi tra

threadbare ['θrɛdbɛəʳ] ADJ consumato(-a), logoro(-a)

threat [θrɛt] N minaccia; **to be under ~ of** (closure, extinction) rischiare di; (exposure) essere minacciato(-a) di

threaten ['θrɛtn] VI (storm) minacciare ▶ VT: **to ~ sb with sth/to do** minacciare qn con qc/di fare

threatening ['θrɛtnɪŋ] ADJ minaccioso(-a)

three [θriː] NUM tre

three-dimensional [θriːdaɪ'mɛnʃənl] ADJ tridimensionale; (film) stereoscopico(-a)

three-piece ['θriːpiːs] CPD: **~ suit** n completo (con gilè); **~ suite** n salotto comprendente un divano e due poltrone

three-ply [θriː'plaɪ] ADJ (wood) a tre strati; (wool) a tre fili

three-quarters [θriː'kwɔːtəz] NPL tre quarti mpl; **~ full** pieno per tre quarti

three-wheeler [θriː'wiːləʳ] N (car) veicolo a tre ruote

thresh [θrɛʃ] VT (Agr) trebbiare

threshing machine ['θrɛʃɪŋ-] N trebbiatrice f

threshold ['θrɛʃhəuld] N soglia; **to be on the ~ of** (fig) essere sulla soglia di

threshold agreement N (Econ) ≈ scala mobile

threw [θruː] PT of **throw**

thrift [θrɪft] N parsimonia

thrifty ['θrɪftɪ] ADJ economico(-a), parsimonioso(-a)

thrill [θrɪl] N brivido ▶ VI eccitarsi, tremare ▶ VT (audience) elettrizzare; **to be thrilled** (with gift etc) essere elettrizzato(-a)

thrilled ADJ: **I was ~ to get your letter** la tua lettera mi ha fatto veramente piacere

thriller ['θrɪləʳ] N thriller m inv

thrilling ['θrɪlɪŋ] ADJ (book, play etc) pieno(-a) di suspense; (news, discovery) elettrizzante

thrive [θraɪv] (pt **thrived** or **throve** [θrəuv], pp **thrived** or **thriven** ['θrɪvn]) VI crescere or svilupparsi bene; (business) prosperare; **he thrives on it** gli fa bene, ne gode

thriving ['θraɪvɪŋ] ADJ (industry etc) fiorente

throat [θrəut] N gola; **to have a sore ~** avere (un or il) mal di gola

throb [θrɔb] N (of heart) battito; (of engine) vibrazione f; (of pain) fitta ▶ VI (heart) palpitare; (engine) vibrare; (with pain) pulsare; **my head is throbbing** mi martellano le tempie

throes [θrəuz] NPL: **in the ~ of** alle prese con; in preda a; **in the ~ of death** in agonia

thrombosis [θrɔm'bəusɪs] N trombosi f

throne [θrəun] N trono

throng [θrɔŋ] N moltitudine f ▶ VT affollare

throttle ['θrɔtl] N (Aut) valvola a farfalla; (on motorcycle) (manopola del) gas ▶ VT strangolare

through [θruː] PREP attraverso; (time) per, durante; (by means of) per mezzo di; (owing to) a causa di ▶ ADJ (ticket, train, passage) diretto(-a) ▶ ADV attraverso; **(from) Monday ~ Friday** (US) da lunedì a venerdì; **I am halfway ~ the book** sono a metà libro; **to let sb ~** lasciar passare qn; **to put sb ~ to sb** (Tel) passare qn a qn; **to be ~** (Tel) ottenere la comunicazione; (have finished) avere finito; **"no ~ traffic"** (US) "divieto d'accesso"; **"no ~ road"** (BRIT) "strada senza sbocco"

throughout [θruː'aut] PREP (place) dappertutto in; (time) per or durante tutto(-a) ▶ ADV dappertutto; sempre

throughput ['θruːput] N (of goods, materials) materiale m in lavorazione; (Comput) volume m di dati immessi

throve [θrəuv] PT of **thrive**

throw [θrəu] (pt **threw**, pp **thrown**) N tiro, getto; (Sport) lancio ▶ VT tirare, gettare; (Sport) lanciare; (rider) disarcionare; (fig) confondere; (pottery) formare al tornio; **to ~ a party** dare una festa; **to ~ open** (doors, windows) spalancare; (house, gardens etc) aprire al pubblico; (competition, race) aprire a tutti
  ▶ **throw about, throw around** VT (litter etc) spargere
  ▶ **throw away** VT gettare or buttare via
  ▶ **throw in** VT (Sport: ball) rimettere in gioco; (include) aggiungere
  ▶ **throw off** VT sbarazzarsi di
  ▶ **throw out** VT buttare fuori; (reject) respingere
  ▶ **throw together** VT (clothes, meal etc) mettere insieme; (essay) buttar giù
  ▶ **throw up** VI vomitare

throwaway ['θrəuəweɪ] ADJ da buttare

throwback ['θrəubæk] N: **it's a ~ to** (fig) ciò risale a

throw-in ['θrəuɪn] N (Sport) rimessa in gioco

thrown [θrəun] PP of **throw**

thru [θruː] PREP, ADJ, ADV (US) = **through**

thrush [θrʌʃ] N (Zool) tordo; (Med: esp in children) mughetto; (: BRIT: in women) candida

thrust [θrʌst] (pt, pp ~) N (Tech) spinta ▶ VT spingere con forza; (push in) conficcare

t

thrusting ['θrʌstɪŋ] ADJ (troppo) intraprendente
thud [θʌd] N tonfo
thug [θʌg] N delinquente *m*
thumb [θʌm] N (*Anat*) pollice *m* ▶ VT (*book*) sfogliare; **to ~ a lift** fare l'autostop; **to give sb/sth the thumbs up/down** approvare/disapprovare qn/qc
thumb index N indice *m* a rubrica
thumbnail ['θʌmneɪl] N unghia del pollice
thumbnail sketch N descrizione *f* breve
thumbtack ['θʌmtæk] N (*US*) puntina da disegno
thump [θʌmp] N colpo forte; (*sound*) tonfo ▶ VT (*person*) picchiare; (*object*) battere su ▶ VI picchiare; battere
thunder ['θʌndə*r*] N tuono ▶ VI tuonare; (*train etc*): **to ~ past** passare con un rombo
thunderbolt ['θʌndəbəult] N fulmine *m*
thunderclap ['θʌndəklæp] N rombo di tuono
thunderous ['θʌndərəs] ADJ fragoroso(-a)
thunderstorm ['θʌndəstɔːm] N temporale *m*
thunderstruck ['θʌndəstrʌk] ADJ (*fig*) sbigottito(-a)
thundery ['θʌndərɪ] ADJ temporalesco(-a)
Thur(s). ABBR (= *Thursday*) gio.
Thursday ['θəːzdɪ] N giovedì *m inv*; *see also* **Tuesday**
thus [ðʌs] ADV così
thwart [θwɔːt] VT contrastare
thyme [taɪm] N timo
thyroid ['θaɪrɔɪd] N tiroide *f*
tiara [tɪ'ɑːrə] N (*woman's*) diadema *m*
Tiber ['taɪbə*r*] N: **the ~** il Tevere
Tibet [tɪ'bɛt] N Tibet *m*
Tibetan [tɪ'bɛtən] ADJ tibetano(-a) ▶ N (*person*) tibetano(-a); (*Ling*) tibetano
tibia ['tɪbɪə] N tibia
tic [tɪk] N tic *m inv*
tick [tɪk] N (*sound, of clock*) tic tac *m inv*; (*mark*) segno; spunta; (*Zool*) zecca; (*BRIT col*): **in a ~** in un attimo; (: *credit*): **to buy sth on ~** comprare qc a credito ▶ VI fare tic tac ▶ VT spuntare; **to put a ~ against sth** fare un segno di fianco a qc
  ▶ **tick off** VT spuntare; (*person*) sgridare
  ▶ **tick over** VI (*BRIT: engine*) andare al minimo
ticker tape ['tɪkə-] N nastro di telescrivente; (*US: in celebrations*) stelle *fpl* filanti
ticket ['tɪkɪt] N biglietto; (*in shop: on goods*) etichetta; (: *from cash register*) scontrino; (*for library*) scheda; (*US Pol*) lista dei candidati; **to get a (parking) ~** (*Aut*) prendere una multa (per sosta vietata); **a single/return ~ to ...** un biglietto di sola andata/di andata e ritorno per...
ticket agency N (*Theat*) agenzia di vendita di biglietti
ticket barrier N (*BRIT Rail*) cancelletto d'ingresso

ticket collector N bigliettaio
ticket holder N persona munita di biglietto
ticket inspector N controllore *m*
ticket machine N distributore *m* di biglietti
ticket office N biglietteria
tickle ['tɪkl] N solletico ▶ VT fare il solletico a; (*fig*) stuzzicare; piacere a; far ridere ▶ VI: **it tickles mi** (*or* gli *etc*) fa il solletico
ticklish ['tɪklɪʃ] ADJ che soffre il solletico; (*which tickles: blanket, cough*) che provoca prurito; (*problem*) delicato(-a)
tidal ['taɪdl] ADJ di marea
tidal wave N onda anomala
tidbit ['tɪdbɪt] N (*US*) = **titbit**
tiddlywinks ['tɪdlɪwɪŋks] N gioco della pulce
tide [taɪd] N marea; (*fig: of events*) corso ▶ VT: **will £20 ~ you over till Monday?** ti basteranno 20 sterline fino a lunedì?; **high/low ~** alta/bassa marea; **the ~ of public opinion** l'orientamento dell'opinione pubblica
tidily ['taɪdɪlɪ] ADV in modo ordinato; **to arrange ~** sistemare; **to dress ~** vestirsi per benino
tidiness ['taɪdɪnɪs] N ordine *m*
tidy ['taɪdɪ] ADJ (*room*) ordinato(-a), lindo(-a); (*dress, work*) curato(-a), in ordine; (*person*) ordinato(-a); (*mind*) organizzato(-a) ▶ VT (*also:* **tidy up**) riordinare, mettere in ordine; **to ~ o.s. up** rassettarsi
tie [taɪ] N (*string etc*) legaccio; (*BRIT: also:* **necktie**) cravatta; (*fig: link*) legame *m*; (*Sport: match*) incontro; (: *draw*) pareggio; (*US Rail*) traversina ▶ VT (*parcel*) legare; (*ribbon*) annodare ▶ VI (*Sport*) pareggiare; **"black/white ~"** "smoking/abito di rigore"; **family ties** legami familiari; **to ~ sth in a bow** annodare qc; **to ~ a knot in sth** fare un nodo a qc
  ▶ **tie down** VT legare, assicurare con una corda; (*fig*): **to ~ sb down to** (*price etc*) costringere qn ad accettare
  ▶ **tie in** VI: **to ~ in (with)** (*correspond*) corrispondere (a)
  ▶ **tie on** VT (*BRIT: label etc*) attaccare
  ▶ **tie up** VT (*parcel, dog*) legare; (*boat*) ormeggiare; (*arrangements*) concludere; **to be tied up** (*busy*) essere occupato *or* preso
tie-break ['taɪbreɪk], **tie-breaker** ['taɪbreɪkə*r*] N (*Tennis*) tie-break *m inv*; (*in quiz*) spareggio
tie-on ['taɪɔn] ADJ (*BRIT: label*) volante
tie-pin ['taɪpɪn] N (*BRIT*) fermacravatta *m inv*
tier [tɪə*r*] N fila; (*of cake*) piano, strato
Tierra del Fuego [tɪ'ɛrədɛl'fweɪgəu] N Terra del Fuoco
tie tack N (*US*) fermacravatta *m inv*
tiff [tɪf] N battibecco
tiger ['taɪgə*r*] N tigre *f*

tight [taɪt] ADJ (*rope*) teso(-a), tirato(-a); (*money*) poco(-a); (*clothes, budget, programme, bend*) stretto(-a); (*control*) severo(-a), fermo(-a); (*col: drunk*) sbronzo(-a) ▶ ADV (*squeeze*) fortemente; (*shut*) ermeticamente; **to be packed ~** (*suitcase*) essere pieno zeppo; (*people*) essere pigiati; **everybody hold ~!** tenetevi stretti!; *see also* **tights**

tighten ['taɪtn] VT (*rope*) tendere; (*screw*) stringere; (*control*) rinforzare ▶ VI tendersi; stringersi

tight-fisted [taɪt'fɪstɪd] ADJ avaro(-a)

tight-lipped ['taɪt'lɪpt] ADJ: **to be ~** essere reticente; (*angry*) tenere le labbra serrate

tightly ['taɪtlɪ] ADV (*grasp*) bene, saldamente

tightrope ['taɪtrəup] N corda (da acrobata)

tightrope walker N funambolo(-a)

tights [taɪts] NPL (BRIT) collant *m inv*

tigress ['taɪgrɪs] N tigre *f* (femmina)

tilde ['tɪldə] N tilde *f*

tile [taɪl] N (*on roof*) tegola; (*on floor, wall*) mattonella, piastrella ▶ VT (*floor, bathroom etc*) piastrellare

tiled [taɪld] ADJ rivestito(-a) di tegole; a mattonelle; a piastrelle

till [tɪl] N registratore *m* di cassa ▶ VT (*land*) coltivare ▶ PREP, CONJ = **until**

tiller ['tɪlə^r] N (*Naut*) barra del timone

tilt [tɪlt] VT inclinare, far pendere ▶ VI inclinarsi, pendere ▶ N (*slope*) pendio; **to wear one's hat at a ~** portare il cappello sulle ventitré; **(at) full ~** a tutta velocità

timber ['tɪmbə^r] N (*material*) legname *m*; (*trees*) alberi *mpl* da legname

time [taɪm] N tempo; (*epoch: often pl*) epoca, tempo; (*by clock*) ora; (*moment*) momento; (*occasion, also Math*) volta; (*Mus*) tempo ▶ VT (*race*) cronometrare; (*programme*) calcolare la durata di; (*fix moment for*) programmare; (*remark etc*): **to ~ sth well/badly** scegliere il momento più/meno opportuno per qc; **a long ~** molto tempo; **for the ~ being** per il momento; **4 at a ~** 4 per or alla volta; **from ~ to ~** ogni tanto; **~ after ~, ~ and again** mille volte; **in ~** (*soon enough*) in tempo; (*after some time*) col tempo; (*Mus*) a tempo; **at times** a volte; **to take one's ~** prenderla con calma; **in a week's ~** fra una settimana; **in no ~** in un attimo; **any ~** in qualsiasi momento; **on ~** puntualmente; **to be 30 minutes behind/ahead of ~** avere 30 minuti di ritardo/anticipo; **by the ~ he arrived** quando è arrivato; **5 times 5** 5 volte 5, 5 per 5; **what ~ is it?** che ora è?, che ore sono?; **what ~ do you make it?** che ora fa?; **to have a good ~** divertirsi; **they had a hard ~ of it** è stato duro per loro; **~'s up!** è (l')ora!; **to be behind the times** vivere nel passato; **I've no ~ for it** (*fig*) non ho tempo da perdere con cose del genere; **he'll do it in his own (good) ~** (*without being hurried*) lo farà quando avrà (un minuto di) tempo; **he'll do it in** *or* (US) **on his own ~** (*out of working hours*) lo farà nel suo tempo libero; **the bomb was timed to explode 5 minutes later** la bomba era stata regolata in modo da esplodere 5 minuti più tardi

time-and-motion study ['taɪmənd'məuʃən-] N analisi *f inv* dei tempi e dei movimenti

time bomb N bomba a orologeria

time card N cartellino (da timbrare)

time clock N orologio *m* marcatempo *inv*

time-consuming ['taɪmkənsju:mɪŋ] ADJ che richiede molto tempo

time difference N differenza di fuso orario

time frame N tempi *mpl*

time-honoured, (US) **time-honored** ['taɪmɔnəd] ADJ consacrato(-a) dal tempo

timekeeper ['taɪmki:pə^r] N (*Sport*) cronometrista *mf*

time lag N intervallo, ritardo; (*in travel*) differenza di fuso orario

timeless ['taɪmlɪs] ADJ eterno(-a)

time limit N limite *m* di tempo

timely ['taɪmlɪ] ADJ opportuno(-a)

time off N tempo libero

timer ['taɪmə^r] N (*in kitchen*) contaminuti *m inv*; (*Tech: time switch*) timer *m inv*, temporizzatore *m*

time-saving ['taɪmseɪvɪŋ] ADJ che fa risparmiare tempo

time scale N tempi *mpl* d'esecuzione

time-share ADJ: **~ apartment/villa** appartamento/villa in multiproprietà

time-sharing ['taɪmʃɛərɪŋ] N (*Comput*) divisione *f* di tempo

time sheet N = **time card**

time signal N segnale *m* orario

time switch N interruttore *m* a tempo

timetable ['taɪmteɪbl] N orario; (*programme of events etc*) programma *m*

time zone N fuso orario

timid ['tɪmɪd] ADJ timido(-a); (*easily scared*) pauroso(-a)

timidity [tɪ'mɪdɪtɪ] N timidezza

timing ['taɪmɪŋ] N sincronizzazione *f*; (*fig*) scelta del momento opportuno, tempismo; (*Sport*) cronometraggio

timing device N (*on bomb*) timer *m inv*

timpani ['tɪmpənɪ] NPL timpani *mpl*

tin [tɪn] N stagno; (*also:* **tin plate**) latta; (BRIT: *can*) barattolo (di latta), lattina; (*container*) scatola; (*for baking*) teglia; **a ~ of paint** un barattolo di tinta *or* vernice

tin foil N stagnola

tinge [tɪndʒ] N sfumatura ▶ VT: **tinged with** tinto(-a) di

t

tingle ['tɪŋgl] vi (cheeks, skin: from cold) pungere, pizzicare; (: from bad circulation) formicolare

tinker ['tɪŋkə'] N stagnino ambulante; (gipsy) zingaro(-a)
▶ **tinker with** vt fus armeggiare intorno a; cercare di riparare

tinkle ['tɪŋkl] vi tintinnare ▶ N (col): **to give sb a ~** dare un colpo di telefono a qn

tin mine N miniera di stagno

tinned [tɪnd] ADJ (BRIT: food) in scatola

tinnitus [tɪ'naɪtəs] N (Med) ronzio auricolare

tinny ['tɪnɪ] ADJ metallico(-a)

tin-opener ['tɪnəupnə'] N (BRIT) apriscatole m inv

tinsel ['tɪnsl] N decorazioni fpl natalizie (argentate)

tint [tɪnt] N tinta; (for hair) shampoo m inv colorante ▶ vt (hair) fare uno shampoo colorante a

tinted ['tɪntɪd] ADJ (hair) tinto(-a); (spectacles, glass) colorato(-a)

tiny ['taɪnɪ] ADJ minuscolo(-a)

tip [tɪp] N (end) punta; (protective: on umbrella etc) puntale m; (gratuity) mancia; (for coal) discarica; (BRIT: for rubbish) immondezzaio; (advice) suggerimento ▶ vt (waiter) dare la mancia a; (tilt) inclinare; (overturn: also: **tip over**) capovolgere; (empty: also: **tip out**) scaricare; (predict: winner) pronosticare; (: horse) dare vincente; **he tipped out the contents of the box** ha rovesciato il contenuto della scatola
▶ **tip off** vt fare una soffiata a

tip-off ['tɪpɔf] N (hint) soffiata

tipped ['tɪpt] ADJ (BRIT: cigarette) col filtro; **steel-~** con la punta d'acciaio

Tipp-Ex® ['tɪpɛks] N (BRIT) liquido correttore

tipple ['tɪpl] (BRIT) vi sbevazzare ▶ N: **to have a ~** prendere un bicchierino

tipster ['tɪpstə'] N (Racing) chi vende informazioni sulle corse e altre manifestazioni oggetto di scommessa

tipsy ['tɪpsɪ] ADJ brillo(-a)

tiptoe ['tɪptəu] N: **on ~** in punta di piedi

tiptop ['tɪptɔp] ADJ: **in ~ condition** in ottime condizioni

tirade [taɪ'reɪd] N filippica

tire ['taɪə'] vt stancare ▶ vi stancarsi ▶ N (US) = **tyre**
▶ **tire out** vt sfinire, spossare

tired ['taɪəd] ADJ stanco(-a); **to be/feel/look ~** essere/sentirsi/sembrare stanco; **to be ~ of** essere stanco or stufo di

tiredness ['taɪədnɪs] N stanchezza

tireless ['taɪəlɪs] ADJ instancabile

tire pressure N (US) = **tyre pressure**

tiresome ['taɪəsəm] ADJ noioso(-a)

tiring ['taɪərɪŋ] ADJ faticoso(-a)

tissue ['tɪʃu:] N tessuto; (paper handkerchief)

fazzoletto di carta

tissue paper N carta velina

tit [tɪt] N (bird) cinciallegra; (col: breast) tetta; **to give ~ for tat** rendere pan per focaccia

titanium [tɪ'teɪnɪəm] N titanio

titbit ['tɪtbɪt], (US) **tidbit** ['tɪdbɪt] N (food) leccornia; (news) notizia, ghiotta

titillate ['tɪtɪleɪt] vt titillare

titivate ['tɪtɪveɪt] vt agghindare

title ['taɪtl] N titolo; (Law: right): **~ (to)** diritto (a)

title deed N (Law) titolo di proprietà

title page N frontespizio

title role N ruolo or parte f principale

titter ['tɪtə'] vi ridere scioccamente

tittle-tattle ['tɪtltætl] N chiacchiere fpl, pettegolezzi mpl

titular ['tɪtjulə'] ADJ (in name only) nominale

tizzy ['tɪzɪ] N (col): **to be in a ~** essere in agitazione

T-junction ['ti:'dʒʌŋkʃən] N incrocio a T

TM N ABBR (= transcendental meditation) M.T. f; (Comm) = **trademark**

TN ABBR (US) = **Tennessee**

TNT N ABBR (= trinitrotoluene) T.N.T. m

(KEYWORD)

to [tu:, tə] PREP **1** (direction) a; **to go to France/London/school** andare in Francia/a Londra/a scuola; **to go to town** andare in città; **to go to Paul's/the doctor's** andare da Paul/dal dottore; **the road to Edinburgh** la strada per Edimburgo; **to the left/right** a sinistra/destra

2 (as far as) (fino) a; **from here to London** da qui a Londra; **to count to 10** contare fino a 10; **from 40 to 50 people** da 40 a 50 persone

3 (with expressions of time): **a quarter to 5** le 5 meno un quarto; **it's twenty to 3** sono le 3 meno venti

4 (for, of): **the key to the front door** la chiave della porta d'ingresso; **a letter to his wife** una lettera per la moglie

5 (expressing indirect object) a; **to give sth to sb** dare qc a qn; **give it to me** dammelo; **to talk to sb** parlare a qn; **it belongs to him** gli appartiene, è suo; **to be a danger to sb/ sth** rappresentare un pericolo per qn/qc

6 (in relation to) a; **3 goals to 2** 3 goal a 2; **30 miles to the gallon** ≈ 11 chilometri con un litro; **4 apples to the kilo** 4 mele in un chilo

7 (purpose, result): **to come to sb's aid** venire in aiuto a qn; **to sentence sb to death** condannare a morte qn; **to my surprise** con mia sorpresa

▶ WITH VB **1** (simple infinitive): **to go/eat** etc andare/mangiare etc

2 (following another vb): **to want/try/start to do** volere/cercare di/cominciare a fare

3 (*with vb omitted*): **I don't want to** non voglio (farlo); **you ought to** devi (farlo)
4 (*purpose, result*) per; **I did it to help you** l'ho fatto per aiutarti
5 (*equivalent to relative clause*): **I have things to do** ho da fare; **the main thing is to try** la cosa più importante è provare
6 (*after adjective etc*): **ready to go** pronto(-a) a partire; **too old/young to ...** troppo vecchio(-a)/giovane per ...
▶ ADV: **to push the door to** accostare la porta; **to go to and fro** andare e tornare

toad [təud] N rospo
toadstool ['təudstu:l] N fungo (velenoso)
toady ['təudɪ] VI adulare
toast [təust] N (*Culin*) pane m tostato; (*drink, speech*) brindisi m inv ▶ VT (*Culin*) tostare; (*drink to*) brindare a; **a piece** or **slice of** ~ una fetta di pane tostato
toaster ['təustə^r] N tostapane m inv
toastmaster ['təustmɑ:stə^r] N direttore m dei brindisi
toast rack N portatoast m inv
tobacco [tə'bækəu] N tabacco; **pipe** ~ tabacco da pipa
tobacconist [tə'bækənɪst] N tabaccaio(-a); **~'s (shop)** tabaccheria
Tobago [tə'beɪgəu] N *see* **Trinidad and Tobago**
toboggan [tə'bɔgən] N toboga m inv; (*child's*) slitta
today [tə'deɪ] ADV, N (*also fig*) oggi m inv; **what day is it** ~? che giorno è oggi?; **what date is it** ~? quanti ne abbiamo oggi?; **~ the 4th of March** (oggi) è il 4 di marzo; **~'s paper** il giornale di oggi; **a fortnight** ~ quindici giorni a oggi
toddler ['tɔdlə^r] N bambino(-a) che impara a camminare
toddy ['tɔdɪ] N grog m inv
to-do [tə'du:] N (*fuss*) storie fpl
toe [təu] N dito del piede; (*of shoe*) punta ▶ VT: **to** ~ **the line** (*fig*) stare in riga, conformarsi; **big** ~ alluce m; **little** ~ mignolino
TOEFL ['təufl] N ABBR = **Test(ing) of English as a Foreign Language**
toehold ['təuhəuld] N punto d'appoggio
toenail ['təuneɪl] N unghia del piede
toffee ['tɔfɪ] N caramella
toffee apple N (*BRIT*) mela caramellata
tofu ['təufu:] N tofu m (*latte di soia non fermentato*)
toga ['təugə] N toga
together [tə'gɛðə^r] ADV insieme; (*at same time*) allo stesso tempo; ~ **with** insieme a
togetherness [tə'gɛðənɪs] N solidarietà; intimità
toggle switch ['tɔgl-] N (*Comput*) tasto bistabile

Togo ['təugəu] N Togo
togs [tɔgz] NPL (*col: clothes*) vestiti mpl
toil [tɔɪl] N travaglio, fatica ▶ VI affannarsi; sgobbare
toilet ['tɔɪlət] N (*BRIT: lavatory*) gabinetto ▶ CPD (*soap etc*) da toletta; **to go to the** ~ andare al gabinetto or al bagno
toilet bag N (*BRIT*) nécessaire m inv da toilette
toilet bowl N vaso or tazza del gabinetto
toilet paper N carta igienica
toiletries ['tɔɪlɪtrɪz] NPL articoli mpl da toletta
toilet roll N rotolo di carta igienica
toilet water N acqua di colonia
to-ing and fro-ing ['tu:ɪŋən'frəuɪŋ] N (*BRIT*) andirivieni m inv
token ['təukən] N (*sign*) segno; (*voucher*) buono ▶ CPD (*fee, strike*) simbolico(-a); (*substitute coin*) gettone m; **book/record/gift** ~ (*BRIT*) buono-libro/-disco/-regalo; **by the same** ~ (*fig*) per lo stesso motivo
tokenism ['təukənɪzəm] N (*Pol*) concessione f pro forma inv
Tokyo ['təukjəu] N Tokyo f
told [təuld] PT, PP *of* **tell**
tolerable ['tɔlərəbl] ADJ (*bearable*) tollerabile; (*fairly good*) passabile
tolerably ['tɔlərəblɪ] ADV (*good, comfortable*) abbastanza
tolerance ['tɔlərns] N (*also Tech*) tolleranza
tolerant ['tɔlərnt] ADJ: ~ **(of)** tollerante (nei confronti di)
tolerate ['tɔləreɪt] VT sopportare; (*Med, Tech*) tollerare
toleration [tɔlə'reɪʃən] N tolleranza
toll [təul] N (*tax, charge*) pedaggio ▶ VI (*bell*) suonare; **the accident** ~ **on the roads** il numero delle vittime della strada
tollbridge ['təulbrɪdʒ] N ponte m a pedaggio
toll call N (*US Tel*) (telefonata) interurbana
toll-free ['təul'fri:] (*US*) ADJ senza addebito, gratuito(-a) ▶ ADV gratuitamente; ~ **number** = numero verde
tomato [tə'mɑ:təu] (*pl* **tomatoes**) N pomodoro
tomato sauce N salsa di pomodoro
tomb [tu:m] N tomba
tombola [tɔm'bəulə] N tombola
tomboy ['tɔmbɔɪ] N maschiaccio
tombstone ['tu:mstəun] N pietra tombale
tomcat ['tɔmkæt] N gatto
tomorrow [tə'mɔrəu] ADV, N (*also fig*) domani m inv; **the day after** ~ dopodomani; **a week** ~ domani a otto; ~ **morning** domani mattina
ton [tʌn] N tonnellata (*Brit = 1016 kg; 20 cwt; US = 907 kg; metric = 1000 kg*); (*Naut: also: **register ton***) tonnellata di stazza (= 2.83 cu.m; 100 cu.ft); **tons of** (*col*) un mucchio or sacco di
tonal ['təunl] ADJ tonale

t

833

tone [təʊn] N tono; (*of musical instrument*) timbro ▶ vi (*also*: **tone in**) intonarsi
▶ **tone down** vт (*colour, criticism, sound*) attenuare
▶ **tone up** vт (*muscles*) tonificare

tone-deaf [təʊn'dɛf] ADJ che non ha orecchio (musicale)

toner ['təʊnəʳ] N (*for photocopier*) colorante *m* organico, toner *m*

Tonga ['tɔŋgə] N isole *fpl* Tonga

tongs [tɔŋz] NPL tenaglie *fpl*; (*for coal*) molle *fpl*; (*for hair*) arricciacapelli *m inv*

tongue [tʌŋ] N lingua; ~ **in cheek** (*fig: say, speak*) ironicamente

tongue-tied ['tʌŋtaɪd] ADJ (*fig*) muto(-a)

tongue-twister ['tʌŋtwɪstəʳ] N scioglilingua *m inv*

tonic ['tɔnɪk] N (*Med*) ricostituente *m*; (*skin tonic*) tonico; (*Mus*) nota tonica; (*also*: **tonic water**) acqua tonica

tonight [tə'naɪt] ADV stanotte; (*this evening*) stasera ▶ N questa notte; questa sera; **I'll see you** ~ ci vediamo stasera

tonnage ['tʌnɪdʒ] N (*Naut*) tonnellaggio, stazza

tonne [tʌn] N (*BRIT: metric ton*) tonnellata

tonsil ['tɔnsl] N tonsilla; **to have one's tonsils out** farsi operare di tonsille

tonsillitis [tɔnsɪ'laɪtɪs] N tonsillite *f*; **to have** ~ avere la tonsillite

too [tu:] ADV (*excessively*) troppo; (*also*) anche; **it's** ~ **sweet** è troppo dolce; **I went** ~ ci sono andato anch'io; ~ **much** *adv* troppo; *adj* troppo(-a); ~ **many** *adj* troppi(-e); ~ **bad!** tanto peggio!; peggio così!

took [tʊk] PT *of* **take**

tool [tu:l] N utensile *m*, attrezzo; (*fig: person*) strumento ▶ vт lavorare con un attrezzo

tool box N cassetta *f* portautensili *inv*

tool kit N cassetta di attrezzi

toot [tu:t] vi suonare; (*with car horn*) suonare il clacson

tooth [tu:θ] (*pl* **teeth** [ti:θ]) N (*Anat, Tech*) dente *m*; **to clean one's teeth** lavarsi i denti; **to have a ~ out** *or* (*US*) **pulled** farsi togliere un dente; **by the skin of one's teeth** per il rotto della cuffia

toothache ['tu:θeɪk] N mal *m* di denti; **to have** ~ avere il mal di denti

toothbrush N spazzolino da denti

tooth fairy N: **the** ~ *fatina che porta soldini in regalo a un bimbo quando perde un dentino di latte*, ≈ topolino

toothpaste ['tu:θpeɪst] N dentifricio

toothpick ['tu:θpɪk] N stuzzicadenti *m inv*

tooth powder N dentifricio in polvere

top [tɔp] N (*of mountain, page, ladder*) cima; (*of box, cupboard, table*) sopra *m inv*, parte *f* superiore; (*lid: of box, jar*) coperchio; (: *of bottle*)

tappo; (*toy*) trottola; (*Dress: blouse etc*) camicia (*or maglietta etc*); (*of pyjamas etc*) giacca ▶ ADJ più alto(-a); (*in rank*) primo(-a); (*best*) migliore ▶ vт (*exceed*) superare; (*be first in*) essere in testa a; **on** ~ **of** sopra, in cima a; (*in addition to*) oltre a; **from** ~ **to toe** (*BRIT*) dalla testa ai piedi; **from** ~ **to bottom** da cima a fond; **at the** ~ **of the stairs/page/street** in cima alle scale/alla pagina/alla strada; **the** ~ **of the milk** (*BRIT*) la panna; **at** ~ **speed** a tutta velocità; **at the** ~ **of one's voice** (*fig*) a squarciagola; **over the** ~ (*col: behaviour etc*) eccessivo(-a); **to go over the** ~ esagerare
▶ **top up**, (*US*) **top off** vт riempire; (*salary*) integrare

topaz ['təʊpæz] N topazio

top-class ['tɔp'klɑ:s] ADJ di prim'ordine

topcoat ['tɔpkəʊt] N soprabito

topflight ['tɔpflaɪt] ADJ di primaria importanza

top floor N ultimo piano

top hat N cilindro

top-heavy [tɔp'hɛvɪ] ADJ (*object*) con la parte superiore troppo pesante

topic ['tɔpɪk] N argomento

topical ['tɔpɪkəl] ADJ d'attualità

topless ['tɔplɪs] ADJ (*bather etc*) col seno scoperto; ~ **swimsuit** topless *m inv*

top-level ['tɔplɛvl] ADJ (*talks*) ad alto livello

topmost ['tɔpməʊst] ADJ il(la) più alto(-a)

top-notch ['tɔp'nɔtʃ] ADJ (*col: player, performer*) di razza; (: *school, car*) eccellente

topography [tə'pɔgrəfɪ] N topografia

topping ['tɔpɪŋ] N (*Culin*) guarnizione *f*

topple ['tɔpl] vт rovesciare, far cadere ▶ vi cadere; traballare

top-ranking ['tɔp'ræŋkɪŋ] ADJ di massimo grado

top-secret ['tɔp'si:krɪt] ADJ segretissimo(-a)

top-security ['tɔpsɪ'kjʊərɪtɪ] ADJ (*BRIT*) di massima sicurezza

topsy-turvy ['tɔpsɪ'tə:vɪ] ADJ, ADV sottosopra *inv*

top-up ['tɔpʌp] N (*for mobile phone: also*: **top-up card**) ricarica; **would you like a ~?** vuole che le riempia il bicchiere (*or* la tazza *etc*)?

top-up loan N (*BRIT*) prestito integrativo

torch [tɔ:tʃ] N torcia; (*BRIT: electric*) lampadina tascabile

tore [tɔ:ʳ] PT *of* **tear²**

torment N ['tɔ:mɛnt] tormento ▶ vт [tɔ:'mɛnt] tormentare; (*fig: annoy*) infastidire

torn [tɔ:n] PP *of* **tear²** ▶ ADJ: ~ **between** (*fig*) combattuto(-a) tra

tornado [tɔ:'neɪdəʊ] (*pl* **tornadoes**) N tornado

torpedo [tɔ:'pi:dəʊ] (*pl* **torpedoes**) N siluro

torpedo boat N motosilurante *f*

torpor ['tɔ:pəʳ] N torpore *m*

torrent ['tɔrnt] N torrente m
torrential [tɔ'rɛnʃl] ADJ torrenziale
torrid ['tɔrɪd] ADJ torrido(-a); (fig) denso(-a) di passione
torso ['tɔ:səu] N torso
tortoise ['tɔ:təs] N tartaruga
tortoiseshell ['tɔ:təʃɛl] ADJ di tartaruga
tortuous ['tɔ:tjuəs] ADJ tortuoso(-a)
torture ['tɔ:tʃər] N tortura ▶ VT torturare
torturer ['tɔ:tʃərər] N torturatore(-trice)
Tory ['tɔ:rɪ] ADJ, N (BRIT Pol) tory mf, conservatore(-trice)
toss [tɔs] VT gettare, lanciare; (BRIT: pancake) far saltare; (head) scuotere ▶ N (movement, of head etc) movimento brusco; (of coin) lancio; **to win/lose the ~** vincere/perdere a testa o croce; (Sport) vincere/perdere il sorteggio; **to ~ a coin** fare a testa o croce; **to ~ up for sth** fare a testa o croce per qc; **to ~ and turn** (in bed) girarsi e rigirarsi
tot [tɔt] N (BRIT: drink) bicchierino; (child) bimbo(-a)
 ▶ **tot up** VT (BRIT: figures) sommare
total ['təutl] ADJ totale ▶ N totale m ▶ VT (add up) sommare; (amount to) ammontare a; **in ~** in tutto
totalitarian [təutælɪ'tɛərɪən] ADJ totalitario(-a)
totality [təu'tælɪtɪ] N totalità
totally ['təutəlɪ] ADV completamente
tote bag ['təut-] N sporta
totem pole ['təutəm-] N totem m inv
totter ['tɔtər] VI barcollare; (object, government) vacillare
touch [tʌtʃ] N tocco; (sense) tatto; (contact) contatto; (Football) fuori gioco m ▶ VT toccare; **a ~ of** (fig) un tocco di; un pizzico di; **to get in ~ with** mettersi in contatto con; **to lose ~** (friends) perdersi di vista; **I'll be in ~** mi farò sentire; **to be out of ~ with events** essere tagliato fuori; **the personal ~** una nota personale; **to put the finishing touches to sth** dare gli ultimi ritocchi a qc
 ▶ **touch down** VI (on land) atterrare
 ▶ **touch on** VT FUS (topic) sfiorare, accennare a
 ▶ **touch up** VT (improve) ritoccare
touch-and-go ['tʌtʃən'gəu] ADJ incerto(-a); **it was ~ with the sick man** il malato era tra la vita e la morte
touchdown ['tʌtʃdaun] N atterraggio; (on sea) ammaraggio; (US Football) meta
touched [tʌtʃt] ADJ commosso(-a); (col) tocco(-a), toccato(-a)
touching ['tʌtʃɪŋ] ADJ commovente
touchline ['tʌtʃlaɪn] N (Sport) linea laterale
touch screen N (Tech) schermo touch screen; **touch-screen mobile** telefono touch screen; **touch-screen technology** tecnologia touch screen
touch-sensitive ['tʌtʃ'sɛnsɪtɪv] ADJ sensibile al tatto
touch-type ['tʌtʃtaɪp] VI dattilografare (senza guardare i tasti)
touchy ['tʌtʃɪ] ADJ (person) suscettibile
tough [tʌf] ADJ duro(-a); (resistant) resistente; (meat) duro(-a), tiglioso(-a); (journey) faticoso(-a), duro(-a); (person: rough) violento(-a), brutale ▶ N (gangster etc) delinquente mf; **~ luck!** che sfortuna!
toughen ['tʌfn] VT indurire, rendere più resistente
toughness ['tʌfnɪs] N durezza; resistenza
toupee ['tu:peɪ] N parrucchino
tour [tuər] N viaggio; (also: **package tour**) viaggio organizzato or tutto compreso (of town, museum) visita; (by artist) tournée f inv ▶ VT visitare; **to go on a ~ of** (region, country) fare il giro di; (museum, castle) visitare; **to go on ~** andare in tournée
tour guide N guida turistica
touring ['tuərɪŋ] N turismo
tourism ['tuərɪzəm] N turismo
tourist ['tuərɪst] N turista mf ▶ ADV (travel) in classe turistica ▶ CPD turistico(-a); **the ~ trade** il turismo
tourist class N (Aviat) classe f turistica
tourist office N pro loco f inv
tournament ['tuənəmənt] N torneo
tourniquet ['tuənɪkeɪ] N (Med) laccio emostatico, pinza emostatica
tour operator N (BRIT) operatore m turistico
tousled ['tauzld] ADJ (hair) arruffato(-a)
tout [taut] VI: **to ~ for** procacciare, raccogliere; cercare clienti per ▶ N (BRIT: also: **ticket tout**) bagarino; **to ~ sth (around)** (BRIT) cercare di (ri)vendere qc
tow [təu] VT rimorchiare ▶ N rimorchio; **"on ~"**, (US) **"in ~"** (Aut) "veicolo rimorchiato"; **to give sb a ~** rimorchiare qn
toward [tə'wɔ:d], **towards** [tə'wɔ:dz] PREP verso; (of attitude) nei confronti di; (of purpose) per; **~(s) noon/the end of the year** verso mezzogiorno/la fine dell'anno; **to feel friendly ~(s) sb** provare un sentimento d'amicizia per qn
towel ['tauəl] N asciugamano; (also: **tea towel**) strofinaccio; **to throw in the ~** (fig) gettare la spugna
towelling ['tauəlɪŋ] N (fabric) spugna
towel rail, (US) **towel rack** N portasciugamano
tower ['tauər] N torre f ▶ VI (building, mountain) innalzarsi; **to ~ above** or **over sb/sth** sovrastare qn/qc
tower block N (BRIT) palazzone m
towering ['tauərɪŋ] ADJ altissimo(-a), imponente

towline ['təʊlaɪn] N (cavo da) rimorchio
town [taʊn] N città *f inv*; **to go to ~** andare in
città; *(fig)* mettercela tutta; **in (the) ~** in
città; **to be out of ~** essere fuori città
town centre N centro (città)
town clerk N segretario comunale
town council N consiglio comunale
town crier [-'kraɪə'] N *(Brit)* banditore(-trice)
town hall N ≈ municipio
townie ['taʊnɪ] N *(Brit col)* uno(-a) di città
town plan N pianta della città
town planner N urbanista *mf*
town planning N urbanistica
township ['taʊnʃɪp] N township *f inv*
townspeople ['taʊnzpiːpl] NPL
cittadinanza, cittadini *mpl*
towpath ['təʊpɑːθ] N alzaia
towrope ['təʊrəʊp] N (cavo da) rimorchio
tow truck N *(US)* carro *m* attrezzi *inv*
toxic ['tɒksɪk] ADJ tossico(-a)
toxic asset N *(Econ)* titolo tossico
toxic bank N *(Econ)* banca cattiva *(che investe in
titoli tossici)*
toxin ['tɒksɪn] N tossina
toy [tɔɪ] N giocattolo
▶ **toy with** VT FUS giocare con; *(idea)*
accarezzare, trastullarsi con
toyshop ['tɔɪʃɒp] N negozio di giocattoli
trace [treɪs] N traccia ▶ VT *(draw)* tracciare;
(follow) seguire; *(locate)* rintracciare;
without ~ *(disappear)* senza lasciare traccia;
there was no ~ of it non ne restava traccia
trace element N oligoelemento
trachea [trə'kɪə] N *(Anat)* trachea
tracing paper ['treɪsɪŋ-] N carta da ricalco
track [træk] N *(mark: of person, animal)* traccia;
(on tape, Sport: path: gen) pista; *(: of bullet etc)*
traiettoria; *(: of suspect, animal)* pista, tracce
fpl; *(Rail)* binario, rotaie *fpl*; *(Comput)* traccia,
pista ▶ VT seguire le tracce di; **to keep ~ of**
seguire; **to be on the right ~** *(fig)* essere
sulla buona strada
▶ **track down** VT *(prey)* scovare; snidare; *(sth
lost)* rintracciare
tracker dog ['trækə-] N *(Brit)* cane *m*
poliziotto *inv*
track events NPL *(Sport)* prove *fpl* su pista
tracking station ['trækɪŋ-] N *(Space)*
osservatorio spaziale
track meet N *(US)* meeting *m inv* di atletica
track record N: **to have a good ~** *(fig)* avere
un buon curriculum
tracksuit ['træksuːt] N tuta sportiva
tract [trækt] N *(Geo)* tratto, estensione *f*;
(pamphlet) opuscolo, libretto; **respiratory ~**
(Anat) apparato respiratorio
traction ['trækʃən] N trazione *f*
tractor ['træktə'] N trattore *m*
trade [treɪd] N commercio; *(skill, job)*
mestiere *m*; *(industry)* industria, settore *m*
▶ VI commerciare; **to ~ with/in**
commerciare con/in ▶ VT: **to ~ sth (for sth)**
barattare qc (con qc); **foreign ~** commercio
estero; **Department of T~ and Industry**
(Brit) ≈ Ministero del Commercio
▶ **trade in** VT *(old car etc)* dare come
pagamento parziale
trade barrier N barriera commerciale
trade deficit N bilancio commerciale in
deficit
Trade Descriptions Act N *(Brit)* legge *f* a
tutela del consumatore
trade discount N sconto sul listino
trade fair N fiera campionaria
trade-in ['treɪdɪn] N: **to take as a ~** accettare
in permuta
trade-in price N prezzo di permuta
trademark ['treɪdmɑːk] N marchio di
fabbrica
trade mission N missione *f* commerciale
trade name N marca, nome *m* depositato
trade-off ['treɪdɔf] N compromesso,
accomodamento
trader ['treɪdə'] N commerciante *mf*
trade secret N segreto di fabbricazione
tradesman ['treɪdzmən] N *(irreg)* fornitore *m*;
(shopkeeper) negoziante *m*
trade union N sindacato
trade unionist [-'juːnjənɪst] N sindacalista *mf*
trade wind N aliseo
trading ['treɪdɪŋ] N commercio
trading estate N *(Brit)* zona industriale
trading stamp N bollo premio
tradition [trə'dɪʃən] N tradizione *f*;
traditions NPL tradizioni, usanze *fpl*
traditional [trə'dɪʃənl] ADJ tradizionale
traffic ['træfɪk] N traffico ▶ VI: **to ~ in** *(pej:
liquor, drugs)* trafficare in
traffic calming [-'kɑːmɪŋ] N *uso di
accorgimenti per rallentare il traffico in zone abitate*
traffic circle N *(US)* isola rotatoria
traffic island N salvagente *m*, isola *f*,
spartitraffico *inv*
traffic jam N ingorgo (del traffico)
trafficker ['træfɪkə'] N trafficante *mf*
traffic lights NPL semaforo
traffic offence N *(Brit)* infrazione *f* al codice
stradale
traffic sign N cartello stradale
traffic violation N *(US)* = **traffic offence**
traffic warden N addetto(-a) al controllo del
traffico e del parcheggio
tragedy ['trædʒədɪ] N tragedia
tragic ['trædʒɪk] ADJ tragico(-a)
trail [treɪl] N *(tracks)* tracce *fpl*, pista; *(path)*
sentiero; *(of smoke etc)* scia ▶ VT trascinare,
strascicare; *(follow)* seguire ▶ VI essere al
traino; *(dress etc)* strusciare; *(plant)*

arrampicarsi; strusciare; (*in game*) essere in svantaggio; **to be on sb's** ~ essere sulle orme di qn
▶ **trail away, trail off** VI (*sound*) affievolirsi; (*interest, voice*) spegnersi a poco a poco
▶ **trail behind** VI essere al traino
trailer ['treɪləʳ] N (*Aut*) rimorchio; (*US*) roulotte *f inv*; (*Cine*) prossimamente *m inv*
trailer truck N (*US*) autoarticolato
train [treɪn] N treno; (*of dress*) coda, strascico; (*BRIT: series*): ~ **of events** serie *f* di avvenimenti a catena ▶ VT (*apprentice, doctor etc*) formare; (*sportsman*) allenare; (*dog*) addestrare; (*memory*) esercitare; (*point: gun etc*): **to** ~ **sth on** puntare qc contro ▶ VI formarsi; allenarsi; (*learn a skill*) fare pratica, fare tirocinio; **to go by** ~ andare in *or* col treno; **one's** ~ **of thought** il filo dei propri pensieri; **to** ~ **sb to do sth** preparare qn a fare qc
train attendant N (*US*) addetto(-a) ai vagoni letto
trained [treɪnd] ADJ qualificato(-a); allenato(-a), addestrato(-a)
trainee [treɪˈniː] N allievo(-a); (*in trade*) apprendista *mf*; **he's a ~ teacher** sta facendo tirocinio come insegnante
trainer ['treɪnəʳ] N (*Sport*) allenatore(-trice); (*of dogs etc*) addestratore(-trice); **trainers** NPL (*shoes*) scarpe *fpl* da ginnastica
training ['treɪnɪŋ] N formazione *f*; allenamento; addestramento; **in** ~ (*Sport*) in allenamento; (*fit*) in forma
training college N istituto professionale
training course N corso di formazione professionale
training shoes NPL scarpe *fpl* da ginnastica
train wreck N (*fig*) persona distrutta; (: *pej*) rottame *m*; **he's a complete** ~ è completamente distrutto, è un rottame
traipse [treɪps] VI: **to** ~ **in/out** *etc* entrare/ uscire *etc* trascinandosi
trait [treɪt] N tratto
traitor ['treɪtəʳ] N traditore(-trice)
trajectory [trəˈdʒɛktərɪ] N traiettoria
tram [træm] N (*BRIT: also*: **tramcar**) tram *m inv*
tramline ['træmlaɪn] N linea tranviaria
tramp [træmp] N (*person*) vagabondo(-a); (*col, pej: woman*) sgualdrina ▶ VI camminare con passo pesante ▶ VT (*walk through: town, streets*) percorrere a piedi
trample ['træmpl] VT: **to** ~ **(underfoot)** calpestare
trampoline ['træmpəliːn] N trampolino
trance [trɑːns] N trance *f inv*; (*Med*) catalessi *f inv*; **to go into a** ~ cadere in trance
tranquil ['træŋkwɪl] ADJ tranquillo(-a)
tranquillity, (*US*) **tranquility** [træŋˈkwɪlɪtɪ] N tranquillità

tranquillizer, (*US*) **tranquilizer** ['træŋkwɪlaɪzəʳ] N (*Med*) tranquillante *m*
transact [trænˈzækt] VT (*business*) trattare
transaction [trænˈzækʃən] N transazione *f*; **transactions** NPL (*minutes*) atti *mpl*; **cash** ~ operazione *f* in contanti
transatlantic ['trænzətˈlæntɪk] ADJ transatlantico(-a)
transcend [trænˈsɛnd] VT trascendere; (*excel over*) superare
transcendental [trænsɛnˈdɛntl] ADJ: ~ **meditation** meditazione *f* trascendentale
transcribe [trænˈskraɪb] VT trascrivere
transcript ['trænskrɪpt] N trascrizione *f*
transcription [trænˈskrɪpʃən] N trascrizione *f*
transept ['trænsɛpt] N transetto
transfer N ['trænsfəʳ] (*gen, also Sport*) trasferimento; (*Pol: of power*) passaggio; (*picture, design*) decalcomania; (: *stick-on*) autoadesivo ▶ VT [trænsˈfəːʳ] trasferire; passare; decalcare; **by bank** ~ tramite trasferimento bancario; **to** ~ **the charges** (*BRIT Tel*) fare una chiamata a carico del destinatario
transferable [trænsˈfəːrəbl] ADJ trasferibile; **not** ~ non cedibile, personale
transfix [trænsˈfɪks] VT trafiggere; (*fig*): **transfixed with fear** paralizzato dalla paura
transform [trænsˈfɔːm] VT trasformare
transformation [trænsfəˈmeɪʃən] N trasformazione *f*
transformer [trænsˈfɔːməʳ] N (*Elec*) trasformatore *m*
transfusion [trænsˈfjuːʒən] N trasfusione *f*
transgress [trænsˈɡrɛs] VT (*go beyond*) infrangere; (*violate*) trasgredire, infrangere
tranship [trænˈʃɪp] VT trasbordare
transient ['trænzɪənt] ADJ transitorio(-a), fugace
transistor [trænˈzɪstəʳ] N (*Elec*) transistor *m inv*; (*also*: **transistor radio**) radio *f inv* a transistor
transit ['trænzɪt] N: **in** ~ in transito
transit camp N campo (di raccolta) profughi
transition [trænˈzɪʃən] N passaggio, transizione *f*
transitional [trænˈzɪʃənl] ADJ di transizione
transitive ['trænzɪtɪv] ADJ (*Ling*) transitivo(-a)
transit lounge N (*Aviat*) sala di transito
transitory ['trænzɪtərɪ] ADJ transitorio(-a)
translate [trænzˈleɪt] VT tradurre; **to** ~ **(from/into)** tradurre (da/in)
translation [trænzˈleɪʃən] N traduzione *f*; (*Scol: as opposed to prose*) versione *f*
translator [trænzˈleɪtəʳ] N traduttore(-trice)
translucent [trænzˈluːsnt] ADJ traslucido(-a)

t

transmission [trænz'mɪʃən] N trasmissione f
transmit [trænz'mɪt] VT trasmettere
transmitter [trænz'mɪtər] N trasmettitore m
transparency [træns'pɛərnsɪ] N (Phot) diapositiva
transparent [træns'pærnt] ADJ trasparente
transpire [træns'paɪər] VI (happen) succedere; **it finally transpired that ...** alla fine si è venuto a sapere che ...
transplant VT [træns'plɑːnt] trapiantare ▶ N ['trænsplɑːnt] (Med) trapianto; **to have a heart ~** subire un trapianto cardiaco
transport N ['trænspɔːt] trasporto ▶ VT [træns'pɔːt] trasportare; **public ~** mezzi mpl pubblici; **Department of T~** (BRIT) Ministero dei Trasporti
transportation ['trænspɔː'teɪʃən] N (mezzo di) trasporto; (of prisoners) deportazione f; **Department of T~** (US) Ministero dei Trasporti
transport café N (BRIT) trattoria per camionisti
transpose [træns'pəʊz] VT trasporre
transsexual [trænz'sɛksjuəl] ADJ, N transessuale mf
transverse ['trænzvəːs] ADJ trasversale
transvestite [trænz'vɛstaɪt] N travestito(-a)
trap [træp] N (snare, trick) trappola; (carriage) calesse m ▶ VT prendere in trappola, intrappolare; (immobilize) bloccare; (jam) chiudere, schiacciare; **to set** or **lay a ~ (for sb)** tendere una trappola (a qn); **to ~ one's finger in the door** chiudersi il dito nella porta; **shut your ~!** (col) chiudi quella boccaccia!
trap door N botola
trapeze [trə'piːz] N trapezio
trapper ['træpər] N cacciatore m di animali da pelliccia
trappings ['træpɪŋz] NPL ornamenti mpl; indoratura, sfarzo
trash [træʃ] N (col: goods) ciarpame m; (: nonsense) sciocchezze fpl; (US: rubbish) rifiuti mpl, spazzatura
trash can N (US) secchio della spazzatura
trashy ['træʃɪ] ADJ (col) scadente
trauma ['trɔːmə] N trauma m
traumatic [trɔː'mætɪk] ADJ (Psych: fig) traumatico(-a), traumatizzante
travel ['trævl] N viaggio; viaggi mpl ▶ VI viaggiare; (move) andare, spostarsi ▶ VT (distance) percorrere; **this wine doesn't ~ well** questo vino non resiste agli spostamenti
travel agency N agenzia (di) viaggi
travel agent N agente m di viaggio
travel brochure N dépliant m di viaggi
travel insurance N assicurazione f di viaggio

traveller, (US)**traveler** ['trævlər] N viaggiatore(-trice); (Comm) commesso viaggiatore
traveller's cheque, (US)**traveler's check** N assegno turistico
travelling, (US)**traveling** ['trævlɪŋ] N viaggi mpl ▶ ADJ (circus, exhibition) itinerante ▶ CPD (bag, clock) da viaggio; (expenses) di viaggio
travelling salesman, (US)**traveling salesman** N (irreg) commesso viaggiatore
travelogue ['trævəlɔg] N (book, film) diario or documentario di viaggio; (talk) conferenza sui viaggi
travel-sick ADJ: **to get ~** (in vehicle) soffrire di mal d'auto; (in aeroplane) soffrire di mal d'aria; (in boat) soffrire di mal di mare
travel sickness N mal m d'auto (or di mare or d'aria)
traverse ['trævəs] VT traversare, attraversare
travesty ['trævəstɪ] N parodia
trawler ['trɔːlər] N peschereccio (a strascico)
tray [treɪ] N (for carrying) vassoio; (on desk) vaschetta
treacherous ['trɛtʃərəs] ADJ infido(-a); **road conditions today are ~** oggi il fondo stradale è pericoloso
treachery ['trɛtʃərɪ] N tradimento
treacle ['triːkl] N melassa
tread [trɛd] (pt **trod,** pp **trodden**) N passo; (sound) rumore m di passi; (of stairs) pedata; (of tyre) battistrada m inv ▶ VI camminare ▶ **tread on** VT FUS calpestare
treadle ['trɛdl] N pedale m
treas. ABBR = **treasurer**
treason ['triːzn] N tradimento
treasure ['trɛʒər] N tesoro ▶ VT (value) tenere in gran conto, apprezzare molto; (store) custodire gelosamente
treasure hunt N caccia al tesoro
treasurer [trɛʒərər] N tesoriere(-a)
treasury ['trɛʒərɪ] N tesoreria; (Pol): **the T~** (BRIT), **the T~ Department** (US) ≈ il Ministero del Tesoro
treasury bill N buono del tesoro
treat [triːt] N regalo ▶ VT trattare; (Med) curare; (consider) considerare; **it was a ~** mi (or ci etc) ha fatto veramente piacere; **to ~ sb to sth** offrire qc a qn; **to ~ sth as a joke** considerare qc uno scherzo
treatise ['triːtɪz] N trattato
treatment ['triːtmənt] N trattamento; **to have ~ for sth** (Med) farsi curare qc
treaty ['triːtɪ] N patto, trattato
treble [trɛbl] ADJ triplo(-a), triplice ▶ N (Mus) soprano mf ▶ VT triplicare ▶ VI triplicarsi
treble clef N chiave f di violino
tree [triː] N albero
tree-lined ['triːlaɪnd] ADJ fiancheggiato(-a) da alberi

treetop ['tri:tɔp] N cima di un albero
tree trunk N tronco d'albero
trek [trɛk] N (hike) escursione f a piedi; (in car) escursione f in macchina; (tiring walk) camminata sfiancante ▶ vi (as holiday) fare dell'escursionismo
trellis ['trɛlɪs] N graticcio, pergola
tremble ['trɛmbl] vi tremare; (machine) vibrare
trembling ['trɛmblɪŋ] N tremito ▶ ADJ tremante
tremendous [trɪ'mɛndəs] ADJ (enormous) enorme; (excellent) meraviglioso(-a), formidabile
tremendously [trɪ'mɛndəslɪ] ADV incredibilmente; **he enjoyed it** ~ gli è piaciuto da morire
tremor [trɛmə^r] N tremore m, tremito m; (also: **earth tremor**) scossa sismica
trench [trɛntʃ] N trincea
trench coat N trench m inv
trench warfare N guerra di trincea
trend [trɛnd] N (tendency) tendenza; (of events) corso; (fashion) moda; ~ **towards/away from** tendenza a/ad allontanarsi da; **to set the** ~ essere all'avanguardia; **to set a** ~ lanciare una moda
trendy ['trɛndɪ] ADJ (idea) di moda; (clothes) all'ultima moda
trepidation [trɛpɪ'deɪʃən] N trepidazione f, agitazione f
trespass ['trɛspəs] vi: **to** ~ **on** entrare abusivamente in; (fig) abusare di; **"no trespassing"** "proprietà privata", "vietato l'accesso"
trespasser ['trɛspəsə^r] N trasgressore m; **"trespassers will be prosecuted"** "i trasgressori saranno puniti secondo i termini di legge"
trestle ['trɛsl] N cavalletto
trestle table N tavola su cavalletti
trial ['traɪəl] N (Law) processo; (test: of machine etc) collaudo; (hardship) prova, difficoltà f inv; (worry) cruccio; **trials** NPL (Athletics) prove fpl di qualificazione; **horse trials** concorso ippico; **to be on** ~ (Law) essere sotto processo; ~ **by jury** processo penale con giuria; **to be sent for** ~ essere rinviato a giudizio; **to bring sb to** ~ **(for a crime)** portare qn in giudizio (per un reato); **by** ~ **and error** a tentoni
trial balance N (Comm) bilancio di verifica
trial basis N: **on a** ~ in prova
trial period N periodo di prova
trial run N periodo di prova
triangle ['traɪæŋgl] N (Math, Mus) triangolo
triangular [traɪ'æŋgjulə^r] ADJ triangolare
triathlon [traɪ'æθlən] N triathlon m inv
tribal ['traɪbəl] ADJ tribale

tribe [traɪb] N tribù f inv
tribesman ['traɪbzmən] N (irreg) membro della tribù
tribulation [trɪbju'leɪʃən] N tribolazione f
tribunal [traɪ'bju:nl] N tribunale m
tributary ['trɪbjutərɪ] N (river) tributario, affluente m
tribute ['trɪbju:t] N tributo, omaggio; **to pay** ~ **to** rendere omaggio a
trice [traɪs] N: **in a** ~ in un attimo
trick [trɪk] N trucco; (clever act) stratagemma m; (joke) tiro; (Cards) presa ▶ vt imbrogliare, ingannare; **to play a** ~ **on sb** giocare un tiro a qn; **it's a** ~ **of the light** è un effetto ottico; **that should do the** ~ (col) vedrai che funziona; **to** ~ **sb into doing sth** convincere qn a fare qc con l'inganno; **to** ~ **sb out of sth** fregare qc a qn
trickery ['trɪkərɪ] N inganno
trickle ['trɪkl] N (of water etc) rivolo; gocciolio ▶ vi gocciolare; **to** ~ **in/out** (people) entrare/uscire alla spicciolata
trick question N domanda f trabocchetto inv
trickster ['trɪkstə^r] N imbroglione(-a)
tricky ['trɪkɪ] ADJ difficile, delicato(-a)
tricycle ['traɪsɪkl] N triciclo
trifle ['traɪfl] N sciocchezza; (BRIT Culin) ≈ zuppa inglese ▶ ADV: **a** ~ **long** un po' lungo ▶ vi: **to** ~ **with** prendere alla leggera
trifling ['traɪflɪŋ] ADJ insignificante
trigger ['trɪgə^r] N (of gun) grilletto
▶ **trigger off** vt dare l'avvio a
trigonometry [trɪgə'nɔmətrɪ] N trigonometria
trilby ['trɪlbɪ] N (BRIT: also: **trilby hat**) cappello floscio di feltro
trill [trɪl] N (of bird, Mus) trillo
trilogy ['trɪlədʒɪ] N trilogia
trim [trɪm] ADJ ordinato(-a); (house, garden) ben tenuto(-a); (figure) snello(-a) ▶ N (haircut etc) spuntata, regolata; (embellishment) finiture fpl; (on car) guarnizioni fpl ▶ vt spuntare; (Naut: a sail) orientare; (decorate): **to** ~ **(with)** decorare (con); **to keep in (good)** ~ mantenersi in forma
trimmings ['trɪmɪŋz] NPL decorazioni fpl; (extras: gen: Culin) guarnizione f
Trinidad and Tobago ['trɪnɪdæd-] N Trinidad e Tobago m
Trinity ['trɪnɪtɪ] N: **the** ~ la Trinità
trinket ['trɪŋkɪt] N gingillo; (piece of jewellery) ciondolo
trio ['tri:əu] N trio
trip [trɪp] N viaggio; (excursion) gita, escursione f; (stumble) passo falso ▶ vi inciampare; (go lightly) camminare con passo leggero; **on a** ~ in viaggio
▶ **trip up** vi inciampare ▶ vt fare lo sgambetto a

t

tripartite [traɪˈpɑːtaɪt] ADJ (*agreement*) tripartito(-a); (*talks*) a tre

tripe [traɪp] N (*Culin*) trippa; (*pej: rubbish*) sciocchezze *fpl*, fesserie *fpl*

triple [ˈtrɪpl] ADJ triplo(-a) ▶ ADV: ~ **the distance/the speed** tre volte più lontano/ più veloce

triple jump N triplo salto

triplets [ˈtrɪplɪts] NPL bambini(-e) trigemini(-e)

triplicate [ˈtrɪplɪkət] N: **in** ~ in triplice copia

tripod [ˈtraɪpɒd] N treppiede *m*

Tripoli [ˈtrɪpəlɪ] N Tripoli *f*

tripper [ˈtrɪpəʳ] N (*BRIT*) gitante *mf*

tripwire [ˈtrɪpwaɪəʳ] N filo in tensione che fa scattare una trappola, allarme ecc

trite [traɪt] ADJ banale, trito(-a)

triumph [ˈtraɪʌmf] N trionfo ▶ VI: **to ~ (over)** trionfare (su)

triumphal [traɪˈʌmfl] ADJ trionfale

triumphant [traɪˈʌmfənt] ADJ trionfante

trivia [ˈtrɪvɪə] NPL banalità *fpl*

trivial [ˈtrɪvɪəl] ADJ insignificante; (*matter*) futile; (*excuse, comment*) banale; (*amount*) irrisorio(-a); (*mistake*) di poco conto

triviality [trɪvɪˈælɪtɪ] N frivolezza; (*trivial detail*) futilità

trivialize [ˈtrɪvɪəlaɪz] VT sminuire

trod [trɒd] PT *of* **tread**

trodden [ˈtrɒdn] PP *of* **tread**

troll [trɒl] N (*also Comput*) troll *m inv*

trolley [ˈtrɒlɪ] N carrello; (*in hospital*) lettiga

trolley bus N filobus *m inv*

trollop [ˈtrɒləp] N prostituta

trombone [trɒmˈbəʊn] N trombone *m*

troop [truːp] N gruppo; (*Mil*) squadrone *m*; **troops** NPL (*Mil*) truppe *fpl*; **trooping the colour** (*BRIT: ceremony*) sfilata della bandiera
   ▶ **troop in** VI entrare a frotte
   ▶ **troop out** VI uscire a frotte

troop carrier N (*plane*) aereo per il trasporto (di) truppe; (*Naut: also:* **troopship**) nave *f* per il trasporto (di) truppe

trooper [ˈtruːpəʳ] N (*Mil*) soldato di cavalleria; (*US: policeman*) poliziotto (della polizia di stato)

troopship [ˈtruːpʃɪp] N nave *f* per il trasporto (di) truppe

trophy [ˈtrəʊfɪ] N trofeo

tropic [ˈtrɒpɪk] N tropico; **in the tropics** ai tropici; **T~ of Cancer/Capricorn** tropico del Cancro/Capricorno

tropical [ˈtrɒpɪkəl] ADJ tropicale

trot [trɒt] N trotto ▶ VI trottare; **on the ~** (*BRIT fig*) di fila, uno(-a) dopo l'altro(-a)
   ▶ **trot out** VT (*excuse, reason*) tirar fuori; (*names, facts*) recitare di fila

trouble [ˈtrʌbl] N difficoltà *f inv*, problema *m*; (*problems*) difficoltà *fpl*, problemi *mpl*; (*worry*) preoccupazione *f*; (*bother, effort*) sforzo; (*with sth mechanical*) noie *fpl*; (*Pol*) conflitti *mpl*, disordine *m*; (*Med*): **stomach** *etc* ~ disturbi *mpl* gastrici *etc* ▶ VT disturbare; (*worry*) preoccupare ▶ VI: **to ~ to do** disturbarsi a fare; **troubles** NPL (*Pol etc*) disordini *mpl*; **to be in** ~ avere dei problemi; (*for doing wrong*) essere nei guai; **to go to the ~ of doing** darsi la pena di fare; **it's no ~!** di niente!; **what's the ~?** cosa c'è che non va?; **the ~ is …** c'è che …, il guaio è che …; **to have ~ doing sth** avere delle difficoltà a fare qc; **please don't ~ yourself** non si disturbi

troubled [ˈtrʌbld] ADJ (*person*) preoccupato(-a), inquieto(-a); (*epoch, life*) agitato(-a), difficile

trouble-free [ˈtrʌblfriː] ADJ senza problemi

troublemaker [ˈtrʌblmeɪkəʳ] N elemento disturbatore, agitatore(-trice); (*child*) disloco(-a)

troubleshooter [ˈtrʌblʃuːtəʳ] N (*in conflict*) conciliatore *m*

troublesome [ˈtrʌblsəm] ADJ fastidioso(-a), seccante

trouble spot N zona calda

troubling [ˈtrʌblɪŋ] ADJ (*thought*) preoccupante; **these are ~ times** questi sono tempi difficili

trough [trɒf] N (*also:* **drinking trough**) abbeveratoio; (*also:* **feeding trough**) trogolo, mangiatoia; (: *channel*) canale *m*; ~ **of low pressure** (*Meteor*) depressione *f*

trounce [traʊns] VT (*defeat*) sgominare

troupe [truːp] N troupe *f inv*

trouser press N stirapantaloni *m inv*

trousers [ˈtraʊzəz] NPL pantaloni *mpl*, calzoni *mpl*; **short ~** (*BRIT*) calzoncini *mpl*

trouser suit N (*BRIT*) completo *m or* tailleur *m inv* pantalone *inv*

trousseau [ˈtruːsəʊ] (*pl* **trousseaux** *or* **trousseaus** [-z]) N corredo da sposa

trout [traʊt] N (*pl inv*) trota

trowel [ˈtraʊəl] N cazzuola

truant [ˈtruːənt] N: **to play ~** (*BRIT*) marinare la scuola

truce [truːs] N tregua

truck [trʌk] N autocarro, camion *m inv*; (*Rail*) carro merci aperto; (*for luggage*) carrello *m* portabagagli *inv*

truck driver, (*US*) **trucker** [ˈtrʌkəʳ] N camionista *mf*

truck farm N (*US*) orto industriale

trucking [ˈtrʌkɪŋ] N (*esp US*) autotrasporto

trucking company N (*esp US*) impresa di trasporti

truculent [ˈtrʌkjulənt] ADJ aggressivo(-a), brutale

trudge [trʌdʒ] VI trascinarsi pesantemente

true [truː] ADJ vero(-a); (*accurate*) accurato(-a),

esatto(-a); (*genuine*) reale; (*faithful*) fedele; (*wall, beam*) a piombo; (*wheel*) centrato(-a); **to come ~** avverarsi; **~ to life** verosimile

truffle ['trʌfl] N tartufo

truly ['truːlɪ] ADV veramente; (*truthfully*) sinceramente; (*faithfully*) fedelmente; **yours ~** (*in letter-writing*) distinti saluti

trump [trʌmp] N (*Cards*) atout *m inv*; **to turn up trumps** (*fig*) fare miracoli

trump card N atout *m inv*; (*fig*) asso nella manica

trumped-up [trʌmpt'ʌp] ADJ inventato(-a)

trumpet ['trʌmpɪt] N tromba

truncated [trʌŋ'keɪtɪd] ADJ tronco(-a)

truncheon ['trʌntʃən] N sfollagente *m inv*

trundle ['trʌndl] VT, VI: **to ~ along** rotolare rumorosamente

trunk [trʌŋk] N (*of tree, person*) tronco (*of elephant*) proboscide *f*; (*case*) baule *m*; (*US Aut*) bagagliaio

trunk call N (*Brit Tel*) (telefonata) interurbana

trunk road N (*Brit*) strada principale

trunks [trʌŋks] NPL (*also*: **swimming trunks**) calzoncini *mpl* da bagno

truss [trʌs] N (*Med*) cinto erniario ▶ VT: **to ~ (up)** (*Culin*) legare

trust [trʌst] N fiducia; (*Law*) amministrazione *f* fiduciaria; (*Comm*) trust *m inv* ▶ VT (*have confidence in*) fidarsi di; (*rely on*) contare su; (*entrust*): **to ~ sth to sb** affidare qc a qn; (*hope*): **to ~ (that)** sperare (che); **you'll have to take it on ~** deve credermi sulla parola; **in ~** (*Law*) in amministrazione fiduciaria

trust company N trust *m inv*

trusted ['trʌstɪd] ADJ fidato(-a)

trustee [trʌs'tiː] N (*Law*) amministratore(-a) fiduciario(-a); (*of school etc*) amministratore(-trice)

trustful ['trʌstful] ADJ fiducioso(-a)

trust fund N fondo fiduciario

trusting ['trʌstɪŋ] ADJ = **trustful**

trustworthy ['trʌstwəːðɪ] ADJ fidato(-a), degno(-a) di fiducia

trusty ['trʌstɪ] ADJ fidato(-a)

truth [truːθ] (*pl* **truths** [truːðz]) N verità *f inv*

truthful ['truːθful] ADJ (*person*) sincero(-a); (*description*) veritiero(-a), esatto(-a)

truthfully ['truːθfəlɪ] ADV sinceramente

truthfulness ['truːθfəlnɪs] N veracità

try [traɪ] N prova, tentativo; (*Rugby*) meta ▶ VT (*Law*) giudicare; (*test: also*: **try out**: *sth new*) provare; (*strain: patience, person*) mettere alla prova ▶ VI provare; **to have a ~** fare un tentativo; **to ~ to do** provare a fare; (*seek*) cercare di fare; **to give sth a ~** provare qc; **to ~ one's (very) best** *or* **one's (very) hardest** mettercela tutta

▶ **try on** VT (*clothes*) provare, mettere alla prova; **to ~ it on** (*fig*) cercare di farla

▶ **try out** VT provare, mettere alla prova

trying ['traɪɪŋ] ADJ (*day, experience*) logorante, pesante; (*child*) difficile, insopportabile

tsar [zɑːʳ] N zar *m inv*

T-shirt ['tiːʃəːt] N maglietta

TSO N ABBR (*Brit*: = *The Stationery Office*) ≈ Poligrafici *mpl* dello Stato

T-square ['tiːskwɛəʳ] N riga a T

tsunami [tsuˈnɑːmɪ] N tsunami *m inv*

TT ADJ ABBR (*Brit col*) = **teetotal** ▶ ABBR (*US*) = **Trust Territory**

tub [tʌb] N tinozza; mastello; (*bath*) bagno

tuba ['tjuːbə] N tuba

tubby ['tʌbɪ] ADJ grassoccio(-a)

tube [tjuːb] N tubo; (*Brit*: *underground*) metropolitana, metrò *m inv*; (*for tyre*) camera d'aria; (*col*: *television*): **the ~** la tele

tubeless ['tjuːblɪs] ADJ (*tyre*) senza camera d'aria

tuber ['tjuːbəʳ] N (*Bot*) tubero

tuberculosis [tjubəːkjuˈləʊsɪs] N tubercolosi *f inv*

tube station N (*Brit*) stazione *f* della metropolitana

tubing ['tjuːbɪŋ] N tubazione *f*; **a piece of ~** un tubo

tubular ['tjuːbjuləʳ] ADJ tubolare

TUC N ABBR (*Brit*: = *Trades Union Congress*) confederazione *f* dei sindacati britannici

tuck [tʌk] N (*Sewing*) piega ▶ VT (*put*) mettere

▶ **tuck away** VT riporre; (*building*): **to be tucked away** essere in un luogo isolato

▶ **tuck in** VT mettere dentro; (*child*) rimboccare ▶ VI (*eat*) mangiare di buon appetito; abbuffarsi

▶ **tuck up** VT (*child*) rimboccare

tucker ['tʌkəʳ] N (*Australia, New Zealand col*) cibo

tuck shop N negozio di pasticceria (*in una scuola*)

Tue(s)., Tues. ABBR (= *Tuesday*) mar.

Tuesday ['tjuːzdɪ] N martedì *m inv*; (**the date**) **today is ~ 23 March** oggi è martedì 23 marzo; **on ~** martedì; **on Tuesdays** di martedì; **every ~** tutti i martedì; **every other ~** ogni due martedì; **last/next ~** martedì scorso/prossimo; **~ next** martedì prossimo; **the following ~** (*in past*) il martedì successivo; (*in future*) il martedì dopo; **a week/fortnight on ~**, **~ week/fortnight** martedì fra una settimana/quindici giorni; **the ~ before last** martedì di due settimane fa; **the ~ after next** non questo martedì ma il prossimo; **~ morning/lunchtime/ afternoon/evening** martedì mattina/ all'ora di pranzo/pomeriggio/sera; **~ night** martedì sera; (*overnight*) martedì notte; **~'s newspaper** il giornale di martedì

t

tuft [tʌft] N ciuffo

tug [tʌg] N (*ship*) rimorchiatore *m* ▶ VT tirare con forza

tug-of-love [tʌgəv'lʌv] N contesa per la custodia dei figli; **~ children** bambini *mpl* coinvolti nella contesa per la custodia

tug-of-war [tʌgəv'wɔːʳ] N tiro alla fune

tuition [tjuː'ɪʃən] N (*BRIT: lessons*) lezioni *fpl*; (: *private tuition*) lezioni *fpl* private; (*US: fees*) tasse *fpl* scolastiche (*or* universitarie)

tulip ['tjuːlɪp] N tulipano

tumble ['tʌmbl] N (*fall*) capitombolo ▶ VI capitombolare, ruzzolare; (*somersault*) fare capriole ▶ VT far cadere; **to ~ to sth** (*col*) realizzare qc

tumbledown ['tʌmbldaun] N cadente, diroccato(-a)

tumble dryer N (*BRIT*) asciugatrice *f*

tumbler ['tʌmbləʳ] N bicchiere *m* senza stelo

tummy ['tʌmɪ] N (*col*) pancia

tumour, (US)tumor ['tjuːməʳ] N tumore *m*

tumult ['tjuːmʌlt] N tumulto

tumultuous [tjuː'mʌltjuəs] ADJ tumultuoso(-a)

tuna ['tjuːnə] N (*pl inv: also:* **tuna fish**) tonno

tune [tjuːn] N (*melody*) melodia, aria ▶ VT (*Mus*) accordare; (*Radio, TV, Aut*) regolare, mettere a punto; **to be in/out of ~** (*instrument*) essere accordato(-a)/scordato(-a); (*singer*) essere intonato(-a)/stonato(-a); **to the ~ of** (*fig: amount*) per la modesta somma di; **in ~ with** (*fig*) in accordo con
  ▶ **tune in** VI (*Radio, TV*): **to ~ in (to)** sintonizzarsi (su)
  ▶ **tune up** VI (*musician*) accordare lo strumento

tuneful ['tjuːnful] ADJ melodioso(-a)

tuner ['tjuːnəʳ] N (*radio set*) sintonizzatore *m*; **piano ~** accordatore(-trice) di pianoforte

tuner amplifier N amplificatore *m* di sintonia

tungsten ['tʌŋstn] N tungsteno

tunic ['tjuːnɪk] N tunica

tuning ['tjuːnɪŋ] N messa a punto

tuning fork N diapason *m inv*

Tunis ['tjuːnɪs] N Tunisi *f*

Tunisia [tjuː'nɪzɪə] N Tunisia

Tunisian [tjuː'nɪzɪən] ADJ, N tunisino(-a)

tunnel ['tʌnl] N galleria ▶ VI scavare una galleria

tunnel vision N (*Med*) riduzione *f* del campo visivo; (*fig*) visuale *f* ristretta

tunny ['tʌnɪ] N tonno

turban ['təːbən] N turbante *m*

turbid ['təːbɪd] ADJ torbido(-a)

turbine ['təːbaɪn] N turbina

turbo ['təːbəu] N turbo *m inv*

turbojet ['təːbəu'dʒɛt] N turboreattore *m*

turboprop ['təːbəu'prɔp] N turboelica *m inv*

turbot ['təːbət] N (*pl inv*) rombo gigante

turbulence ['təːbjuləns] N (*Aviat*) turbolenza

turbulent ['təːbjulənt] ADJ turbolento(-a); (*sea*) agitato(-a)

tureen [tə'riːn] N zuppiera

turf [təːf] N terreno erboso; (*clod*) zolla ▶ VT coprire di zolle erbose; **the T~** l'ippodromo
  ▶ **turf out** VT (*col*) buttar fuori

turf accountant N (*BRIT*) allibratore *m*

turgid ['təːdʒɪd] ADJ (*speech*) ampolloso(-a), pomposo(-a)

Turin [tjuə'rɪn] N Torino *f*

Turk [təːk] N turco(-a)

Turkey ['təːkɪ] N Turchia

turkey ['təːkɪ] N tacchino

Turkish ['təːkɪʃ] ADJ turco(-a) ▶ N (*Ling*) turco

Turkish bath N bagno turco

Turkish delight N gelatine ricoperte di zucchero a velo

turmeric ['təːmərɪk] N curcuma

turmoil ['təːmɔɪl] N confusione *f*, tumulto

turn [təːn] N giro; (*change*) cambiamento; (*in road*) curva; (*tendency: of mind, events*) tendenza; (*performance*) numero; (*chance*) turno; (*Med*) crisi *f inv*, attacco ▶ VT girare, voltare; (*milk*) far andare a male; (*shape: wood, metal*) tornire; (*change*): **to ~ sth into** trasformare qc in ▶ VI girare; (*person: look back*) girarsi, voltarsi; (*reverse direction*) girarsi indietro; (*change*) cambiare; (*milk*) andare a male; (*become*) diventare; **to ~ into** trasformarsi in; **a good ~** un buon servizio; **a bad ~** un brutto tiro; **it gave me quite a ~** mi ha fatto prendere un bello spavento; **"no left ~"** (*Aut*) "divieto di svolta a sinistra"; **it's your ~** tocca a lei; **in ~** a sua volta; a turno; **to take turns (at sth)** fare (qc) a turno; **at the ~ of the year/century** alla fine dell'anno/del secolo; **to take a ~ for the worse** (*situation, events*) volgere al peggio; (*patient, health*) peggiorare; **to ~ left/right** girare a sinistra/destra
  ▶ **turn about** VI girarsi indietro
  ▶ **turn away** VI girarsi (dall'altra parte) ▶ VT (*reject: person*) mandar via; (: *business*) rifiutare
  ▶ **turn back** VI ritornare, tornare indietro
  ▶ VT far tornare indietro; (*clock*) spostare indietro
  ▶ **turn down** VT (*refuse*) rifiutare; (*reduce*) abbassare; (*fold*) ripiegare
  ▶ **turn in** VI (*col: go to bed*) andare a letto ▶ VT (*fold*) voltare in dentro
  ▶ **turn off** VI (*from road*) girare, voltare ▶ VT (*light, radio, engine etc*) spegnere
  ▶ **turn on** VI (*light, radio etc*) accendere; (*engine*) avviare
  ▶ **turn out** VT (*light, gas*) chiudere; spegnere; (*produce: goods*) produrre; (: *novel, good pupils*) creare ▶ VI (*appear, attend: troops, doctor, voters etc*)

presentarsi; **to ~ out to be ...** rivelarsi ..., risultare ...

▶ **turn over** vi (*person*) girarsi; (*car etc*) capovolgersi ▶ vt girare

▶ **turn round** vi girare; (*person*) girarsi

▶ **turn to** vt fus: **to ~ to sb** girarsi verso qn; **to ~ to sb for help** rivolgersi a qn per aiuto

▶ **turn up** vi (*person*) arrivare, presentarsi; (*lost object*) saltar fuori ▶ vt (*collar, sound, gas etc*) alzare

turnabout ['təːnəbaut], **turnaround** ['təːnəraund] N (*fig*) dietrofront *m inv*

turncoat ['təːnkəut] N voltagabbana *mf*

turned-up ['təːndʌp] ADJ (*nose*) all'insù

turning ['təːnɪŋ] N (*in road*) curva; (*side road*) strada laterale; **the first ~ on the right** la prima a destra

turning circle N (*BRIT*) diametro di sterzata

turning point N (*fig*) svolta decisiva

turning radius N (*US*) = **turning circle**

turnip ['təːnɪp] N rapa

turnout ['təːnaut] N presenza, affluenza

turnover ['təːnəuvəʳ] N (*Comm: amount of money*) giro di affari; (*: of goods*) smercio; (*Culin*): **apple** *etc* ~ sfogliatella alle mele *etc*; **there is a rapid ~ in staff** c'è un ricambio molto rapido di personale

turnpike ['təːnpaɪk] N (*US*) autostrada a pedaggio

turnstile ['təːnstaɪl] N tornella

turntable ['təːnteɪbl] N (*on record player*) piatto

turn-up ['təːnʌp] N (*BRIT: on trousers*) risvolto

turpentine ['təːpəntaɪn] N (*also*: **turps**) acqua ragia

turquoise [təːkwɔɪz] N (*stone*) turchese *m* ▶ ADJ turchese; di turchese

turret ['tʌrɪt] N torretta

turtle ['təːtl] N testuggine *f*

turtleneck (sweater) ['təːtlnɛk-] N maglione *m* con il collo alto

Tuscan ['tʌskən] ADJ, N toscano(-a)

Tuscany ['tʌskənɪ] N Toscana

tusk [tʌsk] N zanna

tussle ['tʌsl] N baruffa, mischia

tutor ['tjuːtəʳ] N (*in college*) docente *mf* (*responsabile di un gruppo di studenti*); (*private teacher*) precettore *m*

tutorial [tjuːˈtɔːrɪəl] N (*Scol*) lezione *f* con discussione (*a un gruppo limitato*)

tuxedo [tʌkˈsiːdəu] N (*US*) smoking *m inv*

TV [tiːˈviː] N ABBR (= *television*) tivù *f inv*

TV dinner N pasto surgelato pronto in due minuti

twaddle ['twɔdl] N scemenze *fpl*

twang [twæŋ] N (*of instrument*) suono vibrante; (*of voice*) accento nasale ▶ vi vibrare ▶ vt (*guitar*) pizzicare le corde di

tweak [twiːk] vt (*nose*) pizzicare; (*ear, hair*) tirare

tweed [twiːd] N tweed *m inv*

tweet [twiːt] N (*on Twitter*) post *m* su Twitter ▶ vt, vi (*on Twitter*) scrivere su Twitter

tweezers ['twiːzəz] NPL pinzette *fpl*

twelfth [twɛlfθ] NUM dodicesimo(-a)

Twelfth Night N la notte dell'Epifania

twelve [twɛlv] NUM dodici; **at ~** alle dodici, a mezzogiorno; (*midnight*) a mezzanotte

twentieth ['twɛntɪɪθ] NUM ventesimo(-a)

twenty ['twɛntɪ] NUM venti; **in ~ fourteen** nel duemilaquattordici

twerp [twəːp] N (*col*) idiota *mf*

twice [twaɪs] ADV due volte; **~ as much** due volte tanto; **~ a week** due volte alla settimana; **she is ~ your age** ha il doppio dei suoi anni

twiddle ['twɪdl] vt, vi: **to ~ (with) sth** giocherellare con qc; **to ~ one's thumbs** (*fig*) girarsi i pollici

twig [twɪg] N ramoscello ▶ vt, vi (*col*) capire

twilight ['twaɪlaɪt] N (*evening*) crepuscolo; (*morning*) alba; **in the ~** nella penombra

twill [twɪl] N spigato

twin [twɪn] ADJ, N gemello(-a) ▶ vt: **to ~ one town with another** fare il gemellaggio di una città con un'altra

twin-bedded room ['twɪnbɛdɪd-] N stanza con letti gemelli

twin beds NPL letti *mpl* gemelli

twin-carburettor ['twɪnkɑːbjuˈrɛtəʳ] ADJ a doppio carburatore

twine [twaɪn] N spago, cordicella ▶ vi (*plant*) attorcigliarsi; (*road*) serpeggiare

twin-engined ['twɪnˈɛndʒɪnd] ADJ a due motori; **~ aircraft** bimotore *m*

twinge [twɪndʒ] N (*of pain*) fitta; **a ~ of conscience/regret** un rimorso/rimpianto

twinkle ['twɪŋkl] N scintillio ▶ vi scintillare; (*eyes*) brillare

twin room N stanza con letti gemelli

twin town N città *f inv* gemella

twirl [twəːl] N piroetta ▶ vt far roteare ▶ vi roteare

twist [twɪst] N torsione *f*; (*in wire, flex*) piega; (*in story*) colpo di scena; (*bend*) svolta, piega; (*in road*) curva ▶ vt attorcigliare; (*ankle*) slogare; (*weave*) intrecciare; (*roll around*) arrotolare; (*fig*) distorcere ▶ vi attorcigliarsi; arrotolarsi; (*road*) serpeggiare; **to ~ one's ankle/wrist** (*Med*) slogarsi la caviglia/il polso

twisted ['twɪstɪd] ADJ (*wire, rope*) attorcigliato(-a); (*ankle, wrist*) slogato(-a); (*fig: logic, mind*) contorto(-a)

twit [twɪt] N (*col*) cretino(-a)

twitch [twɪtʃ] N tiratina; (*nervous*) tic *m inv* ▶ vi contrarsi; avere un tic

Twitter® ['twɪtəʳ] N Twitter® *m*

two [tuː] NUM due; **~ by ~, in twos** a due a due; **to put ~ and ~ together** (*fig*) fare uno più uno

t

two-bit [tuːˈbɪt] ADJ (*esp US col, pej*) da quattro soldi

two-door [tuːˈdɔːʳ] ADJ (*Aut*) a due porte

two-faced [ˈtuːfeɪst] ADJ (*pej: person*) falso(-a)

twofold [ˈtuːfəuld] ADV: **to increase ~** aumentare del doppio ▶ ADJ (*increase*) doppio(-a); (*reply*) in due punti

two-piece [ˈtuːpiːs] N (*also:* **two-piece suit**) due pezzi *m inv*; (*also:* **two-piece swimsuit**) (costume *m* da bagno a) due pezzi *m inv*

two-seater [ˈtuːsiːtəʳ] N (*plane*) biposto; (*car*) macchina a due posti

twosome [ˈtuːsəm] N (*people*) coppia

two-stroke [ˈtuːstrəuk] N (*engine*) due tempi *m inv* ▶ ADJ a due tempi

two-tone [ˈtuːtəun] ADJ (*colour*) bicolore

two-way [ˈtuːweɪ] ADJ (*traffic*) a due sensi; **~ radio** radio *f inv* ricetrasmittente

TX ABBR (*US*) = **Texas**

tycoon [taɪˈkuːn] N: (**business**) ~ magnate *m*

type [taɪp] N (*category*) genere *m*; (*model*) modello; (*example*) tipo; (*Typ*) tipo, carattere *m* ▶ VT (*letter etc*) battere (a macchina), dattilografare; **what ~ do you want?** che tipo vuole?; **in bold/italic ~** in grassetto/corsivo

type-cast [ˈtaɪpkɑːst] ADJ (*actor*) a ruolo fisso

typeface [ˈtaɪpfeɪs] N carattere *m* tipografico

typescript [ˈtaɪpskrɪpt] N dattiloscritto

typeset [ˈtaɪpsɛt] VT (*irreg: like* **set**) comporre

typesetter [ˈtaɪpsɛtəʳ] N compositore *m*

typewriter [ˈtaɪpraɪtəʳ] N macchina da scrivere

typewritten [ˈtaɪprɪtn] ADJ dattiloscritto(-a), battuto(-a) a macchina

typhoid [ˈtaɪfɔɪd] N tifoidea

typhoon [taɪˈfuːn] N tifone *m*

typhus [ˈtaɪfəs] N tifo

typical [ˈtɪpɪkl] ADJ tipico(-a)

typically ADV tipicamente; **~, he arrived late** come al solito è arrivato tardi

typify [ˈtɪpɪfaɪ] VT essere tipico(-a) di

typing [ˈtaɪpɪŋ] N dattilografia

typing error N errore *m* di battitura

typing pool N ufficio *m*, dattilografia *inv*

typist [ˈtaɪpɪst] N dattilografo(-a)

typo [ˈtaɪpəu] N ABBR (*col:* = *typographical error*) refuso

typography [taɪˈpɔgrəfɪ] N tipografia

tyranny [ˈtɪrənɪ] N tirannia

tyrant [ˈtaɪərnt] N tiranno

tyre, (*US*) **tire** [ˈtaɪəʳ] N pneumatico, gomma; **I've got a flat ~** ho una gomma a terra

tyre pressure N pressione *f* (delle gomme)

Tyrol [tɪˈrəul] N Tirolo

Tyrolean [tɪrəˈliːən], **Tyrolese** [tɪrəˈliːz] ADJ, N tirolese *mf*

Tyrrhenian Sea [tɪˈriːnɪən-] N: **the ~** il mar Tirreno

Uu

U, u [juː] N (letter) U, u m inv or f inv; **U for Uncle** ≈ U come Udine

U N ABBR (BRIT Cine: = universal) per tutti

UAW N ABBR (US: = United Automobile Workers) sindacato degli operai automobilistici

UB40 N ABBR (BRIT: = unemployment benefit form 40) modulo per la richiesta del sussidio di disoccupazione

U-bend ['juːbɛnd] N (in pipe) sifone m

ubiquitous [juːˈbɪkwɪtəs] ADJ onnipresente

UCAS ['juːkæs] N ABBR (BRIT) = **Universities and Colleges Admissions Service**

UDA N ABBR (BRIT: = Ulster Defence Association) organizzazione paramilitare protestante

UDC N ABBR (BRIT) = **Urban District Council**

udder ['ʌdəʳ] N mammella

UDI ABBR (BRIT Pol) = **unilateral declaration of independence**

UDR N ABBR (BRIT: = Ulster Defence Regiment) reggimento dell'esercito britannico in Irlanda del Nord

UEFA [juːˈeɪfə] N ABBR (= Union of European Football Associations) UEFA f

UFO ['juːfəu] N ABBR (= unidentified flying object) UFO m inv

Uganda [juːˈgændə] N Uganda

Ugandan [juːˈgændən] ADJ, N ugandese mf

UGC N ABBR (BRIT: = University Grants Committee) organo che autorizza sovvenzioni alle università

ugh [əːh] EXCL puah!

ugliness ['ʌglɪnɪs] N bruttezza

ugly ['ʌglɪ] ADJ brutto(-a)

UHF ABBR = **ultra-high frequency**

UHT ADJ ABBR (= ultra heat treated) UHT inv, a lunga conservazione; **~ milk** latte m UHT

UK N ABBR = **United Kingdom**

Ukraine [juːˈkreɪn] N Ucraina

Ukrainian [juːˈkreɪnɪən] ADJ ucraino(-a) ▶ N (person) ucraino(-a); (Ling) ucraino

ulcer ['ʌlsəʳ] N ulcera; **mouth ~** afta

Ulster ['ʌlstəʳ] N Ulster m

ulterior [ʌlˈtɪərɪəʳ] ADJ ulteriore; **~ motive** secondo fine m

ultimata [ʌltɪˈmeɪtə] NPL of **ultimatum**

ultimate ['ʌltɪmɪt] ADJ ultimo(-a), finale; (authority) massimo(-a), supremo(-a) ▶ N: **the ~ in luxury** il non plus ultra del lusso

ultimately ['ʌltɪmɪtlɪ] ADV alla fine; in definitiva, in fin dei conti

ultimatum [ʌltɪˈmeɪtəm] (pl **ultimatums** or **ultimata** [-tə]) N ultimatum m inv

ultrasonic [ʌltrəˈsɔnɪk] ADJ ultrasonico(-a)

ultrasound [ʌltrəˈsaund] N ultrasuono; (Med) ecografia

ultraviolet ['ʌltrəvaɪəlɪt] ADJ ultravioletto(-a)

umbilical [ʌmˈbɪlɪkl] ADJ: **~ cord** cordone m ombelicale

umbrage ['ʌmbrɪdʒ] N: **to take ~** offendersi, impermalirsi

umbrella [ʌmˈbrɛlə] N ombrello; **under the ~ of** (fig) sotto l'egida di

umlaut ['umlaut] N Umlaut m inv

umpire ['ʌmpaɪəʳ] N arbitro

umpteen [ʌmpˈtiːn] ADJ non so quanti(-e); **for the umpteenth time** per l'ennesima volta

UMW N ABBR (= United Mineworkers of America) unione dei minatori d'America

UN N ABBR (= United Nations) ONU f

unabashed [ʌnəˈbæʃt] ADJ imperturbato(-a)

unabated [ʌnəˈbeɪtɪd] ADJ non diminuito(-a)

unable [ʌnˈeɪbl] ADJ: **to be ~ to** non potere, essere nell'impossibilità di; (not to know how to) essere incapace di, non sapere

unabridged [ʌnəˈbrɪdʒd] ADJ integrale

unacceptable [ʌnəkˈsɛptəbl] ADJ (proposal, behaviour) inaccettabile; (price) impossibile

unaccompanied [ʌnəˈkʌmpənɪd] ADJ (child, lady) non accompagnato(-a); (singing, song) senza accompagnamento

unaccountably [ʌnəˈkauntəblɪ] ADV inesplicabilmente

unaccounted [ʌnəˈkauntɪd] ADJ: **two passengers are ~ for** due passeggeri mancano all'appello

unaccustomed [ʌnəˈkʌstəmd] ADJ insolito(-a); **to be ~ to sth** non essere abituato(-a) a qc

unacquainted [ʌnəˈkweɪntɪd] ADJ: **to be ~ with** (*facts*) ignorare, non essere al corrente di

unadulterated [ʌnəˈdʌltəreɪtɪd] ADJ (*gen*) puro(-a); (*wine*) non sofisticato(-a)

unaffected [ʌnəˈfɛktɪd] ADJ (*person, behaviour*) naturale, spontaneo(-a); (*emotionally*): **to be ~ by** non essere toccato(-a) da

unafraid [ʌnəˈfreɪd] ADJ: **to be ~** non aver paura

unaided [ʌnˈeɪdɪd] ADV senza aiuto

unanimity [juːnəˈnɪmɪtɪ] N unanimità

unanimous [juːˈnænɪməs] ADJ unanime

unanimously [juːˈnænɪməslɪ] ADV all'unanimità

unanswered [ʌnˈɑːnsəd] ADJ (*question, letter*) senza risposta; (*criticism*) non confutato(-a)

unappetizing [ʌnˈæpɪtaɪzɪŋ] ADJ poco appetitoso(-a)

unappreciative [ʌnəˈpriːʃɪətɪv] ADJ che non apprezza

unarmed [ʌnˈɑːmd] ADJ (*person*) disarmato(-a); (*combat*) senz'armi

unashamed [ʌnəˈʃeɪmd] ADJ sfacciato(-a), senza vergogna

unassisted [ʌnəˈsɪstɪd] ADJ, ADV senza nessun aiuto

unassuming [ʌnəˈsjuːmɪŋ] ADJ modesto(-a), senza pretese

unattached [ʌnəˈtætʃt] ADJ senza legami, libero(-a)

unattended [ʌnəˈtɛndɪd] ADJ (*car, child, luggage*) incustodito(-a)

unattractive [ʌnəˈtræktɪv] ADJ privo(-a) di attrattiva, poco attraente

unauthorized [ʌnˈɔːθəraɪzd] ADJ non autorizzato(-a)

unavailable [ʌnəˈveɪləbl] ADJ (*article, room, book*) non disponibile; (*person*) impegnato(-a)

unavoidable [ʌnəˈvɔɪdəbl] ADJ inevitabile

unavoidably [ʌnəˈvɔɪdəblɪ] ADV (*detained*) per cause di forza maggiore

unaware [ʌnəˈwɛəʳ] ADJ: **to be ~ of** non sapere, ignorare

unawares [ʌnəˈwɛəz] ADV di sorpresa, alla sprovvista

unbalanced [ʌnˈbælənst] ADJ squilibrato(-a)

unbearable [ʌnˈbɛərəbl] ADJ insopportabile

unbeatable [ʌnˈbiːtəbl] ADJ imbattibile

unbeaten [ʌnˈbiːtn] ADJ (*team, army*) imbattuto(-a); (*record*) insuperato(-a)

unbecoming [ʌnbɪˈkʌmɪŋ] ADJ (*unseemly: language, behaviour*) sconveniente; (*unflattering: garment*) che non dona

unbeknown [ʌnbɪˈnəun], **unbeknownst** [ʌnbɪˈnəunst] ADV: **~(st) to** all'insaputa di

unbelief [ʌnbɪˈliːf] N incredulità

unbelievable [ʌnbɪˈliːvəbl] ADJ incredibile

unbelievingly [ʌnbɪˈliːvɪŋlɪ] ADV con aria incredula

unbend [ʌnˈbɛnd] VI (*irreg: like* **bend**) distendersi ▶ VT (*wire*) raddrizzare

unbending [ʌnˈbɛndɪŋ] ADJ (*fig*) inflessibile, rigido(-a)

unbiased, unbiassed [ʌnˈbaɪəst] ADJ obiettivo(-a), imparziale

unblemished [ʌnˈblɛmɪʃt] ADJ senza macchia

unblock [ʌnˈblɔk] VT (*pipe, road*) sbloccare

unborn [ʌnˈbɔːn] ADJ non ancora nato(-a)

unbounded [ʌnˈbaundɪd] ADJ sconfinato(-a), senza limite

unbreakable [ʌnˈbreɪkəbl] ADJ infrangibile

unbridled [ʌnˈbraɪdld] ADJ sbrigliato(-a)

unbroken [ʌnˈbrəukən] ADJ (*intact*) intero(-a); (*continuous*) continuo(-a); (*record*) insuperato(-a)

unbuckle [ʌnˈbʌkl] VT slacciare

unburden [ʌnˈbəːdn] VT: **to ~ o.s.** sfogarsi

unbutton [ʌnˈbʌtn] VT sbottonare

uncalled-for [ʌnˈkɔːldfɔːʳ] ADJ (*remark*) fuori luogo *inv*; (*action*) ingiustificato(-a)

uncanny [ʌnˈkænɪ] ADJ misterioso(-a), strano(-a)

unceasing [ʌnˈsiːsɪŋ] ADJ incessante

unceremonious [ʌnsɛrɪˈməunɪəs] ADJ (*abrupt, rude*) senza tante cerimonie

uncertain [ʌnˈsəːtn] ADJ incerto(-a); dubbio(-a); **it's ~ whether ...** non è sicuro se ...; **in no ~ terms** chiaro e tondo, senza mezzi termini

uncertainty [ʌnˈsəːtntɪ] N incertezza

unchallenged [ʌnˈtʃælɪndʒd] ADJ incontestato(-a); **to go ~** non venire contestato, non trovare opposizione

unchanged [ʌnˈtʃeɪndʒd] ADJ immutato(-a)

uncharitable [ʌnˈtʃærɪtəbl] ADJ duro(-a), severo(-a)

uncharted [ʌnˈtʃɑːtɪd] ADJ inesplorato(-a)

unchecked [ʌnˈtʃɛkt] ADJ incontrollato(-a)

uncivilized [ʌnˈsɪvɪlaɪzd] ADJ (*gen*) selvaggio(-a); (*fig*) incivile, barbaro(-a)

uncle [ˈʌŋkl] N zio

unclear [ʌnˈklɪəʳ] ADJ non chiaro(-a); **I'm still ~ about what I'm supposed to do** non ho ancora ben capito cosa dovrei fare

uncoil [ʌnˈkɔɪl] VT srotolare ▶ VI srotolarsi, svolgersi

uncomfortable [ʌnˈkʌmfətəbl] ADJ scomodo(-a); (*uneasy*) a disagio, agitato(-a); (*unpleasant*) fastidioso(-a); (*situation*) sgradevole

uncomfortably [ʌnˈkʌmfətəblɪ] ADV scomodamente; (*uneasily: say*) con voce inquieta; (: *think*) con inquietudine

uncommitted [ʌnkəˈmɪtɪd] ADJ (*attitude, country*) neutrale

uncommon [ʌnˈkɔmən] ADJ raro(-a), insolito(-a), non comune

uncommunicative [ˌʌnkə'mjuːnɪkətɪv] ADJ poco comunicativo(-a), chiuso(-a)

uncomplicated [ʌn'kɒmplɪkeɪtɪd] ADJ semplice, poco complicato(-a)

uncompromising [ʌn'kɒmprəmaɪzɪŋ] ADJ intransigente, inflessibile

unconcerned [ʌnkən'səːnd] ADJ (*unworried*) tranquillo(-a); **to be ~ about** non darsi pensiero di, non preoccuparsi di *or* per

unconditional [ʌn'kən'dɪʃənl] ADJ incondizionato(-a), senza condizioni

uncongenial [ʌnkən'dʒiːnɪəl] ADJ (*work, surroundings*) poco piacevole

unconnected [ʌnkə'nɛktɪd] ADJ (*unrelated*) senza connessione, senza rapporto; **to be ~ with** essere estraneo(-a) a

unconscious [ʌn'kɒnʃəs] ADJ privo(-a) di sensi, svenuto(-a); (*unaware*) inconsapevole, inconscio(-a) ▶ N: **the ~** l'inconscio; **to knock sb ~** far perdere i sensi a qn con un pugno

unconsciously [ʌn'kɒnʃəslɪ] ADV inconsciamente

unconstitutional [ʌnkɒnstɪ'tjuːʃənl] ADJ incostituzionale

uncontested [ʌnkən'tɛstɪd] ADJ (*champion*) incontestato(-a); (*Pol: seat*) non disputato(-a)

uncontrollable [ʌnkən'trəuləbl] ADJ incontrollabile; indisciplinato(-a)

uncontrolled [ʌnkən'trəuld] ADJ (*child, dog, emotion*) sfrenato(-a); (*inflation, price rises*) che sfugge al controllo

unconventional [ʌnkən'vɛnʃənl] ADJ poco convenzionale

unconvinced [ʌnkən'vɪnst] ADJ: **to be** *or* **remain ~** non essere convinto(-a)

unconvincing [ʌnkən'vɪnsɪŋ] ADJ non convincente, poco persuasivo(-a)

uncork [ʌn'kɔːk] VT stappare

uncorroborated [ʌnkə'rɒbəreɪtɪd] ADJ non convalidato(-a)

uncouth [ʌn'kuːθ] ADJ maleducato(-a), grossolano(-a)

uncover [ʌn'kʌvər] VT scoprire

unctuous ['ʌŋktjuəs] ADJ untuoso(-a)

undamaged [ʌn'dæmɪdʒd] ADJ (*goods*) in buono stato; (*fig: reputation*) intatto(-a)

undaunted [ʌn'dɔːntɪd] ADJ intrepido(-a)

undecided [ʌndɪ'saɪdɪd] ADJ indeciso(-a)

undelivered [ʌndɪ'lɪvəd] ADJ non recapitato(-a); **if ~ return to sender** in caso di mancato recapito rispedire al mittente

undeniable [ʌndɪ'naɪəbl] ADJ innegabile, indiscutibile

under ['ʌndər] PREP sotto; (*less than*) meno di; al disotto di; (*according to*) secondo, in conformità a ▶ ADV (al) disotto; **from ~ sth** da sotto a *or* dal disotto di qc; **~ there** là sotto; **in ~ 2 hours** in meno di 2 ore;

~ anaesthetic sotto anestesia; **~ discussion** in discussione; **~ repair** in riparazione; **~ the circumstances** date le circostanze

under ... ['ʌndər] PREFIX sotto..., sub...

under-age [ʌndər'eɪdʒ] ADJ minorenne

underarm ['ʌndərɑːm] N ascella ▶ ADJ ascellare ▶ ADV da sotto in su

undercapitalized [ʌndə'kæpɪtəlaɪzd] ADJ carente di capitali

undercarriage ['ʌndəkærɪdʒ] N (BRIT Aviat) carrello (d'atterraggio)

undercharge [ʌndə'tʃɑːdʒ] VT far pagare di meno a

underclass ['ʌndəklɑːs] N sottoproletariato

underclothes ['ʌndəkləuðz] NPL biancheria (intima)

undercover ['ʌndəkʌvər] ADJ segreto(-a), clandestino(-a)

undercurrent ['ʌndəkʌrənt] N corrente f sottomarina

undercut [ʌndə'kʌt] VT (*irreg: like* **cut**) vendere a prezzo minore di

underdeveloped ['ʌndədɪ'vɛləpt] ADJ sottosviluppato(-a)

underdog ['ʌndədɒg] N oppresso(-a)

underdone [ʌndə'dʌn] ADJ (*Culin*) al sangue; (*pej*) poco cotto(-a)

under-employment [ʌndərɪm'plɔɪmənt] N sottoccupazione f

underestimate [ʌndər'ɛstɪmeɪt] VT sottovalutare

underexposed [ʌndərɪks'pəuzd] ADJ (*Phot*) sottoesposto(-a)

underfed [ʌndə'fɛd] ADJ denutrito(-a)

underfoot [ʌndə'fut] ADV sotto i piedi

under-funded ['ʌndə'fʌndɪd] ADJ insufficientemente sovvenzionato(-a)

undergo [ʌndə'gəu] VT (*irreg: like* **go**) subire; (*treatment*) sottoporsi a; **the car is undergoing repairs** la macchina è in riparazione

undergraduate [ʌndə'grædjuɪt] N studente(-essa) universitario(-a) ▶ CPD: **~ courses** corsi mpl di laurea

underground ['ʌndəgraund] N (BRIT: *railway*) metropolitana; (*Pol*) movimento clandestino ▶ ADJ sotterraneo(-a); (*fig*) clandestino(-a); (*Art, Cine*) underground *inv* ▶ ADV sottoterra; clandestinamente; **to go ~** (*fig*) darsi alla macchia

undergrowth ['ʌndəgrəuθ] N sottobosco

underhand [ʌndə'hænd], **underhanded** [ʌndə'hændɪd] ADJ (*fig*) furtivo(-a), subdolo(-a)

underinsured [ʌndərɪn'ʃuəd] ADJ non sufficientemente assicurato(-a)

underlie [ʌndə'laɪ] VT (*irreg: like* **lie**) essere alla base di; **the underlying cause** il motivo di fondo

u

underline [ʌndə'laɪn] VT sottolineare

underling ['ʌndəlɪŋ] N (*pej*) subalterno(-a), tirapiedi *mf*

undermanning [ʌndə'mænɪŋ] N carenza di personale

undermentioned [ʌndə'mɛnʃənd] ADJ (riportato(-a)) qui sotto *or* qui di seguito

undermine [ʌndə'maɪn] VT minare

underneath [ʌndə'ni:θ] ADV sotto, disotto
▶ PREP sotto, al di sotto di

undernourished [ʌndə'nʌrɪʃt] ADJ denutrito(-a)

underpaid [ʌndə'peɪd] ADJ mal pagato(-a)

underpants ['ʌndəpænts] NPL (*BRIT*) mutande *fpl*, slip *m inv*

underpass ['ʌndəpɑ:s] N (*BRIT*) sottopassaggio

underpin [ʌndə'pɪn] VT puntellare; (*argument, case*) corroborare

underplay [ʌndə'pleɪ] VT minimizzare

underpopulated [ʌndə'pɔpjuleɪtɪd] ADJ scarsamente popolato(-a), sottopopolato(-a)

underprice [ʌndə'praɪs] VT vendere a un prezzo inferiore al dovuto

underprivileged [ʌndə'prɪvɪlɪdʒd] ADJ svantaggiato(-a)

underrate [ʌndə'reɪt] VT sottovalutare

underscore [ʌndə'skɔ:ʳ] VT sottolineare

underseal ['ʌndəsi:l] VT rendere stagno il fondo di

undersecretary [ʌndə'sɛkrətrɪ] N sottosegretario

undersell ['ʌndə'sɛl] VT (*irreg: like* **sell**) (*competitors*) vendere a prezzi più bassi di

undershirt ['ʌndəʃə:t] N (*US*) maglietta

undershorts ['ʌndəʃɔ:ts] NPL (*US*) mutande *fpl*, slip *m inv*

underside ['ʌndəsaɪd] N disotto

undersigned ['ʌndəsaɪnd] ADJ, N sottoscritto(-a)

underskirt ['ʌndəskə:t] (*BRIT*) N sottoveste *f*

understaffed [ʌndə'stɑ:ft] ADJ a corto di personale

understand [ʌndə'stænd] VT, VI (*irreg: like* **stand**) capire, comprendere; **I don't ~** non capisco; **I ~ that ...** sento che ...; credo di capire che ...; **to make o.s. understood** farsi capire

understandable [ʌndə'stændəbl] ADJ comprensibile

understanding [ʌndə'stændɪŋ] ADJ comprensivo(-a) ▶ N comprensione *f*; (*agreement*) accordo; **on the ~ that ...** a patto che *or* a condizione che ...; **to come to an ~ with sb** giungere ad un accordo con qn

understate [ʌndə'steɪt] VT minimizzare, sminuire

understatement [ʌndə'steɪtmənt] N: **that's an ~!** a dire poco!

understood [ʌndə'stud] PT, PP *of* **understand**
▶ ADJ inteso(-a); (*implied*) sottinteso(-a)

understudy ['ʌndəstʌdɪ] N sostituto(-a), attore(-trice) supplente

undertake [ʌndə'teɪk] VT (*irreg: like* **take**) intraprendere; **to ~ to do sth** impegnarsi a fare qc

undertaker ['ʌndəteɪkəʳ] N impresario di pompe funebri

undertaking [ʌndə'teɪkɪŋ] N impresa; (*promise*) promessa

undertone ['ʌndətəun] N (*low voice*) tono sommesso; (*of criticism etc*) vena, sottofondo; **in an ~** sottovoce

undervalue [ʌndə'vælju:] VT svalutare, sottovalutare

underwater [ʌndə'wɔ:təʳ] ADV sott'acqua
▶ ADJ subacqueo(-a)

underway [ˌʌndə'weɪ] ADJ: **to be ~** essere in corso

underwear ['ʌndəwɛəʳ] N biancheria (intima)

underweight [ʌndə'weɪt] ADJ al di sotto del giusto peso; (*person*) sottopeso *inv*

underwent [ʌndə'wɛnt] VB *see* **undergo**

underworld ['ʌndəwə:ld] N (*of crime*) malavita

underwrite ['ʌndəraɪt] VT (*irreg: like* **write**) (*Finance*) sottoscrivere; (*Insurance*) assicurare

underwriter ['ʌndəraɪtəʳ] N sottoscrittore(-trice); assicuratore(-trice)

undeserving [ʌndɪ'zə:vɪŋ] ADJ: **to be ~ of** non meritare, non essere degno di

undesirable [ʌndɪ'zaɪərəbl] ADJ indesiderato(-a)

undeveloped [ʌndɪ'vɛləpt] ADJ (*land, resources*) non sfruttato(-a)

undies ['ʌndɪz] NPL (*col*) robina, biancheria intima da donna

undiluted [ʌndaɪ'lu:tɪd] ADJ non diluito(-a)

undiplomatic [ʌndɪplə'mætɪk] ADJ poco diplomatico(-a)

undischarged ['ʌndɪs'tʃɑ:dʒd] ADJ: **~ bankrupt** fallito non riabilitato

undisciplined [ʌn'dɪsɪplɪnd] ADJ indisciplinato(-a)

undisguised [ʌndɪs'gaɪzd] ADJ (*dislike, amusement etc*) palese

undisputed [ʌndɪs'pju:tɪd] ADJ indiscusso(-a)

undistinguished [ʌndɪs'tɪŋgwɪʃt] ADJ mediocre, qualunque

undisturbed [ʌndɪs'tə:bd] ADJ tranquillo(-a); **to leave sth ~** lasciare qc così com'è

undivided [ʌndɪ'vaɪdɪd] ADJ: **I want your ~ attention** esigo tutta la sua attenzione

undo [ʌn'du:] VT (*irreg: like* **do**) disfare

undoing [ʌn'du:ɪŋ] N rovina, perdita

undone [ʌn'dʌn] PP *of* **undo**; **to come ~** slacciarsi

undoubted [ʌn'dautɪd] ADJ sicuro(-a), certo(-a)

undoubtedly [ʌn'dautɪdlɪ] ADV senza alcun dubbio

undress [ʌn'drɛs] VI spogliarsi

undrinkable [ʌn'drɪŋkəbl] ADJ (unpalatable) imbevibile; (poisonous) non potabile

undue [ʌn'djuː] ADJ eccessivo(-a)

undulating ['ʌndjuleɪtɪŋ] ADJ ondeggiante, ondulato(-a)

unduly [ʌn'djuːlɪ] ADV eccessivamente

undying [ʌn'daɪɪŋ] ADJ imperituro(-a)

unearned [ʌn'əːnd] ADJ (praise, respect) immeritato(-a); **~ income** rendita

unearth [ʌn'əːθ] VT dissotterrare; (fig) scoprire

unearthly [ʌn'əːθlɪ] ADJ soprannaturale; (hour) impossibile

uneasy [ʌn'iːzɪ] ADJ a disagio; (worried) preoccupato(-a); (peace) precario(-a); **to feel ~ about doing sth** non sentirsela di fare qc

uneconomic ['ʌniːkə'nɔmɪk],
uneconomical ['ʌniːkə'nɔmɪkl] ADJ non economico(-a), antieconomico(-a)

uneducated [ʌn'ɛdjukeɪtɪd] ADJ senza istruzione, incolto(-a)

unemployed [ʌnɪm'plɔɪd] ADJ disoccupato(-a) ▶ NPL: **the ~** i disoccupati

unemployment [ʌnɪm'plɔɪmənt] N disoccupazione f

unemployment benefit, (US)
unemployment compensation N sussidio di disoccupazione

unending [ʌn'ɛndɪŋ] ADJ senza fine

unenviable [ʌn'ɛnvɪəbl] ADJ poco invidiabile

unequal [ʌn'iːkwəl] ADJ (length, objects) disuguale; (amounts) diverso(-a); (division of labour) ineguale

unequalled, (US)**unequaled** [ʌn'iːkwəld] ADJ senza pari, insuperato(-a)

unequivocal [ʌnɪ'kwɪvəkəl] ADJ (answer) inequivocabile; (person) esplicito(-a), chiaro(-a).

unerring [ʌn'əːrɪŋ] ADJ infallibile

UNESCO [juː'nɛskəu] N ABBR (= United Nations Educational, Scientific and Cultural Organization) U.N.E.S.C.O f

unethical [ʌn'ɛθɪkəl] ADJ (methods) poco ortodosso(-a), non moralmente accettabile; (doctor's behaviour) contrario(-a) all'etica professionale

uneven [ʌn'iːvn] ADJ ineguale; (ground) disuguale, accidentato(-a); (heartbeat) irregolare

uneventful [ʌnɪ'vɛntful] ADJ senza sorprese, tranquillo(-a)

unexceptional [ʌnɪk'sɛpʃənl] ADJ che non ha niente d'eccezionale

unexciting [ʌnɪk'saɪtɪŋ] ADJ (news) poco emozionante; (film, evening) poco interessante

unexpected [ʌnɪk'spɛktɪd] ADJ inatteso(-a), imprevisto(-a)

unexpectedly [ʌnɪk'spɛktɪdlɪ] ADV inaspettatamente

unexplained [ʌnɪk'spleɪnd] ADJ inspiegato(-a)

unexploded [ʌnɪk'spləudɪd] ADJ inesploso(-a)

unfailing [ʌn'feɪlɪŋ] ADJ (supply, energy) inesauribile; (remedy) infallibile

unfair [ʌn'fɛəʳ] ADJ: **~ (to)** ingiusto(-a) (nei confronti di); **it's ~ that ...** non è giusto che ...+ sub

unfair dismissal N licenziamento ingiustificato

unfairly [ʌn'fɛəlɪ] ADV ingiustamente

unfaithful [ʌn'feɪθful] ADJ infedele

unfamiliar [ʌnfə'mɪlɪəʳ] ADJ sconosciuto(-a), strano(-a); **to be ~ with sth** non essere pratico di qc, non avere familiarità con qc

unfashionable [ʌn'fæʃnəbl] ADJ (clothes) fuori moda inv; (district) non alla moda

unfasten [ʌn'fɑːsn] VT slacciare; sciogliere

unfathomable [ʌn'fæðəməbl] ADJ insondabile

unfavourable, (US)**unfavorable** [ʌn'feɪvərəbl] ADJ sfavorevole

unfavourably, (US)**unfavorably** [ʌn'feɪvərəblɪ] ADV: **to look ~ upon** vedere di malocchio

unfeeling [ʌn'fiːlɪŋ] ADJ insensibile, duro(-a)

unfinished [ʌn'fɪnɪʃt] ADJ incompiuto(-a)

unfit [ʌn'fɪt] ADJ inadatto(-a); (ill) non in forma; (incompetent): **~ (for)** incompetente (in) (work, Mil) inabile (a); **~ for habitation** inabitabile

unflagging [ʌn'flægɪŋ] ADJ instancabile

unflappable [ʌn'flæpəbl] ADJ calmo(-a), composto(-a)

unflattering [ʌn'flætərɪŋ] ADJ (dress, hairstyle) che non dona

unflinching [ʌn'flɪntʃɪŋ] ADJ che non indietreggia, risoluto(-a)

unfold [ʌn'fəuld] VT spiegare; (fig) rivelare ▶ VI (view) distendersi; (story) svelarsi

unforeseeable ['ʌnfɔː'siːəbl] ADJ imprevedibile

unforeseen [ʌnfɔː'siːn] ADJ imprevisto(-a)

unforgettable [ʌnfə'gɛtəbl] ADJ indimenticabile

unforgivable [ʌnfə'gɪvəbl] ADJ imperdonabile

unformatted [ʌn'fɔːmætɪd] ADJ (disk, text) non formattato(-a)

unfortunate [ʌn'fɔːtʃnɪt] ADJ sfortunato(-a); (event, remark) infelice

unfortunately [ʌn'fɔːtʃnɪtlɪ] ADV sfortunatamente, purtroppo

u

unfounded [ʌn'faundɪd] ADJ infondato(-a)

unfriend [ʌn'frɛnd] VT (*Internet*) cancellare dagli amici

unfriendly [ʌn'frɛndlɪ] ADJ poco amichevole, freddo(-a)

unfulfilled [ʌnful'fɪld] ADJ (*ambition*) non realizzato(-a); (*prophecy*) che non si è avverato(-a); (*desire*) insoddisfatto(-a); (*promise*) non mantenuto(-a); (*terms of contract*) non rispettato(-a); (*person*) frustrato(-a)

unfurl [ʌn'fəːl] VT spiegare

unfurnished [ʌn'fəːnɪʃt] ADJ non ammobiliato(-a)

ungainly [ʌn'geɪnlɪ] ADJ goffo(-a), impacciato(-a)

ungodly [ʌn'gɔdlɪ] ADJ empio(-a); **at an ~ hour** a un'ora impossibile

ungrateful [ʌn'greɪtful] ADJ ingrato(-a)

unguarded [ʌn'gɑːdɪd] ADJ: **in an ~ moment** in un momento di distrazione

unhappily [ʌn'hæpɪlɪ] ADV (*unfortunately*) purtroppo, sfortunatamente

unhappiness [ʌn'hæpɪnɪs] N infelicità

unhappy [ʌn'hæpɪ] ADJ infelice; **~ about/ with** (*arrangements etc*) insoddisfatto(-a) di

unharmed [ʌn'hɑːmd] ADJ incolume, sano(-a) e salvo(-a)

UNHCR N ABBR (= *United Nations High Commission for Refugees*) Alto Commissariato delle Nazioni Unite per Rifugiati

unhealthy [ʌn'hɛlθɪ] ADJ (*gen*) malsano(-a); (*person*) malaticcio(-a)

unheard-of [ʌn'həːdɔv] ADJ inaudito(-a), senza precedenti

unhelpful [ʌn'hɛlpful] ADJ poco disponibile

unhesitating [ʌn'hɛzɪteɪtɪŋ] ADJ (*loyalty*) che non vacilla; (*reply, offer*) pronto(-a), immediato(-a)

unholy [ʌn'həulɪ] ADJ: **an ~ alliance** un'alleanza nefasta; **he returned at an ~ hour** è tornato ad un'ora indecente

unhook [ʌn'huk] VT sganciare; sfibbiare

unhurt [ʌn'həːt] ADJ incolume, illeso(-a)

unhygienic [ʌnhaɪ'dʒiːnɪk] ADJ non igienico(-a)

UNICEF ['juːnɪsɛf] N ABBR (= *United Nations International Children's Emergency Fund*) UNICEF *m*

unicorn ['juːnɪkɔːn] N unicorno

unidentified [ʌnaɪ'dɛntɪfaɪd] ADJ non identificato(-a)

uniform ['juːnɪfɔːm] N uniforme *f*, divisa ▶ ADJ uniforme

uniformity [juːnɪ'fɔːmɪtɪ] N uniformità

unify ['juːnɪfaɪ] VT unificare

unilateral [juːnɪ'lætərəl] ADJ unilaterale

unimaginable [ʌnɪ'mædʒɪnəbl] ADJ inimmaginabile, inconcepibile

unimaginative [ʌnɪ'mædʒɪnətɪv] ADJ privo(-a) di fantasia, a corto di idee

unimpaired [ʌnɪm'pɛəd] ADJ intatto(-a), non danneggiato(-a)

unimportant [ʌnɪm'pɔːtənt] ADJ senza importanza, di scarsa importanza

unimpressed [ʌnɪm'prɛst] ADJ niente affatto impressionato(-a)

uninhabited [ʌnɪn'hæbɪtɪd] ADJ disabitato(-a)

uninhibited [ʌnɪn'hɪbɪtɪd] ADJ senza inibizioni; senza ritegno

uninjured [ʌn'ɪndʒəd] ADJ incolume

uninspiring [ʌnɪn'spaɪərɪŋ] ADJ banale

uninstall [ʌnɪn'stɔːl] VT (*Comput*) disinstallare

unintelligent [ʌnɪn'tɛlɪdʒənt] ADJ poco intelligente

unintentional [ʌnɪn'tɛnʃənəl] ADJ involontario(-a)

unintentionally [ʌnɪn'tɛnʃnəlɪ] ADV senza volerlo, involontariamente

uninvited [ʌnɪn'vaɪtɪd] ADJ non invitato(-a)

uninviting [ʌnɪn'vaɪtɪŋ] ADJ (*place, food*) non invitante, poco invitante; (*offer*) poco allettante

union ['juːnjən] N unione *f*; (*also*: **trade union**) sindacato ▶ CPD sindacale, dei sindacati; **the U~** (*US*) gli stati dell'Unione

unionize ['juːnjənaɪz] VT sindacalizzare, organizzare in sindacato

Union Jack N *bandiera nazionale britannica*

Union of Soviet Socialist Republics N (*Hist*) Unione *f* delle Repubbliche Socialiste Sovietiche

union shop N *stabilimento in cui tutti gli operai sono tenuti ad aderire ad un sindacato*

unique [juːˈniːk] ADJ unico(-a)

unisex ['juːnɪsɛks] ADJ unisex *inv*

Unison ['juːnɪsn] N (*trade union*) *sindacato generale dei funzionari*

unison ['juːnɪsn] N: **in ~** all'unisono

unit ['juːnɪt] N unità *f inv*; (*section: of furniture etc*) elemento; (*team, squad*) reparto, squadra; **production ~** reparto *m*, produzione *inv*; **sink ~** blocco *m* lavello *inv*

unit cost N costo unitario

unite [juːˈnaɪt] VT unire ▶ VI unirsi

united [juːˈnaɪtɪd] ADJ unito(-a); unificato(-a); (*efforts*) congiunto(-a)

United Arab Emirates NPL Emirati *mpl* Arabi Uniti

United Kingdom N Regno Unito

United Nations (Organization) N (Organizzazione *f* delle) Nazioni Unite

United States (of America) N Stati *mpl* Uniti (d'America)

unit price N prezzo unitario

unit trust N (*BRIT Comm*) fondo d'investimento

unity ['juːnɪtɪ] N unità

Univ. ABBR = **university**

universal [juːnɪ'vəːsl] ADJ universale

universe ['juːnɪvəːs] N universo

university [juːnɪ'vəːsɪtɪ] N università *f inv*
▶ CPD (*student, professor, education*)
universitario(-a); (*year*) accademico(-a)

university degree N laurea

unjust [ʌn'dʒʌst] ADJ ingiusto(-a)

unjustifiable ['ʌndʒʌstɪ'faɪəbl] ADJ
ingiustificabile

unjustified [ʌn'dʒʌstɪfaɪd] ADJ
ingiustificato(-a); (*Typ*) non allineato(-a)

unkempt [ʌn'kɛmpt] ADJ trasandato(-a);
spettinato(-a)

unkind [ʌn'kaɪnd] ADJ poco gentile, scortese

unkindly [ʌn'kaɪndlɪ] ADV (*speak*) in modo
sgarbato(-a); (*treat*) male

unknown [ʌn'nəun] ADJ sconosciuto(-a); ~ **to
me ...** a mia insaputa ...; ~ **quantity** (*Math:
fig*) incognita

unladen [ʌn'leɪdn] ADJ (*ship, weight*) a vuoto

unlawful [ʌn'lɔːful] ADJ illecito(-a), illegale

unleaded ['ʌn'lɛdɪd] ADJ senza piombo;
~ **petrol** benzina verde *or* senza piombo

unleash [ʌn'liːʃ] VT sguinzagliare; (*fig*)
scatenare

unleavened [ʌn'lɛvnd] ADJ non lievitato(-a),
azzimo(-a)

unless [ʌn'lɛs] CONJ a meno che (non) + *sub*;
~ **otherwise stated** salvo indicazione
contraria; ~ **I am mistaken** se non mi
sbaglio

unlicensed [ʌn'laɪsənst] ADJ (*BRIT*) senza
licenza per la vendita di alcolici

unlike [ʌn'laɪk] ADJ diverso(-a) ▶ PREP a
differenza di, contrariamente a

unlikelihood [ʌn'laɪklɪhud] N improbabilità

unlikely [ʌn'laɪklɪ] ADJ improbabile;
(*explanation*) inverosimile

unlimited [ʌn'lɪmɪtɪd] ADJ illimitato(-a)

unlisted [ʌn'lɪstɪd] ADJ (*US Tel*): **to be ~** non
essere sull'elenco; (*Stock Exchange*) non
quotato(-a)

unlit [ʌn'lɪt] ADJ (*room*) senza luce; (*road*) non
illuminato(-a)

unload [ʌn'ləud] VT scaricare

unlock [ʌn'lɔk] VT aprire

unlucky [ʌn'lʌkɪ] ADJ sfortunato(-a); (*object,
number*) che porta sfortuna, di malaugurio;
to be ~ (*person*) essere sfortunato, non avere
fortuna

unmanageable [ʌn'mænɪdʒəbl] ADJ (*tool,
vehicle*) poco maneggevole; (*situation*)
impossibile

unmanned [ʌn'mænd] ADJ (*spacecraft*) senza
equipaggio

unmannerly [ʌn'mænəlɪ] ADJ
maleducato(-a)

unmarked [ʌn'mɑːkt] ADJ (*unstained*)
pulito(-a), senza macchie; ~ **police car**
civetta della polizia

unmarried [ʌn'mærɪd] ADJ non sposato(-a);
(*man only*) scapolo, celibe; (*woman only*) nubile

unmarried mother N ragazza *f* madre *inv*

unmask [ʌn'mɑːsk] VT smascherare

unmatched [ʌn'mætʃt] ADJ senza uguali

unmentionable [ʌn'mɛnʃnəbl] ADJ (*vice,
topic*) innominabile; (*word*) irripetibile

unmerciful [ʌn'məːsɪful] ADJ spietato(-a)

unmistakable, unmistakeable
[ʌnmɪs'teɪkəbl] ADJ inconfondibile

unmitigated [ʌn'mɪtɪgeɪtɪd] ADJ (*disaster etc*)
totale, assoluto(-a)

unnamed [ʌn'neɪmd] ADJ (*nameless*) senza
nome; (*anonymous*) anonimo(-a)

unnatural [ʌn'nætʃrəl] ADJ innaturale;
contro natura

unnecessary [ʌn'nɛsəsərɪ] ADJ inutile,
superfluo(-a)

unnerve [ʌn'nəːv] VT (*accident*) sgomentare;
(*hostile attitude*) bloccare; (*long wait, interview*)
snervare

unnoticed [ʌn'nəutɪst] ADJ: **to go** *or* **pass ~**
passare inosservato(-a)

UNO ['juːnəu] N ABBR (= *United Nations
Organization*) ONU *f*

unobservant [ʌnəb'zəːvənt] ADJ: **to be ~** non
avere spirito di osservazione

unobtainable [ʌnəb'teɪnəbl] ADJ (*Tel*) non
ottenibile

unobtrusive [ʌnəb'truːsɪv] ADJ discreto(-a)

unoccupied [ʌn'ɔkjupaɪd] ADJ (*house*)
vuoto(-a); (*seat, Mil: zone*) libero(-a), non
occupato(-a)

unofficial [ʌnə'fɪʃl] ADJ non ufficiale; (*strike*)
non dichiarato(-a) dal sindacato

unopened [ʌn'əupənd] ADJ (*letter*) non
aperto(-a); (*present*) ancora incartato(-a)

unopposed [ʌnə'pəuzd] ADJ senza
incontrare opposizione

unorthodox [ʌn'ɔːθədɔks] ADJ non
ortodosso(-a)

unpack [ʌn'pæk] VI disfare la valigia (*or* le
valigie) ▶ VT disfare

unpaid [ʌn'peɪd] ADJ (*holiday*) non pagato(-a);
(*work*) non retribuito(-a); (*bill, debt*) da pagare

unpalatable [ʌn'pælətəbl] ADJ (*food*)
immangiabile; (*drink*) imbevibile; (*truth*)
sgradevole

unparalleled [ʌn'pærəlɛld] ADJ
incomparabile, impareggiabile

unpatriotic ['ʌnpætrɪ'ɔtɪk] ADJ (*person*) poco
patriottico(-a); (*speech, attitude*)
antipatriottico(-a)

unplanned [ʌn'plænd] ADJ (*visit*)
imprevisto(-a); (*baby*) non previsto(-a)

unpleasant [ʌn'plɛznt] ADJ spiacevole;

u

(*person, remark*) antipatico(-a); (*day, experience*)
brutto(-a)

unplug [ʌn'plʌg] VT staccare

unpolluted [ʌnpə'luːtɪd] ADJ non
inquinato(-a)

unpopular [ʌn'pɔpjulə^r] ADJ impopolare; **to
make o.s. ~ (with)** rendersi antipatico (a);
(*politician etc*) alienarsi le simpatie (di)

unprecedented [ʌn'prɛsɪdəntɪd] ADJ senza
precedenti

unpredictable [ʌnprɪ'dɪktəbl] ADJ
imprevedibile

unprejudiced [ʌn'prɛdʒudɪst] ADJ (*not biased*)
obiettivo(-a), imparziale; (*having no prejudices*)
senza pregiudizi

unprepared [ʌnprɪ'pɛəd] ADJ (*person*)
impreparato(-a); (*speech*) improvvisato(-a)

unprepossessing [ʌnpriː.pə'zɛsɪŋ] ADJ
insulso(-a)

unpretentious [ʌnprɪ'tɛnʃəs] ADJ senza
pretese

unprincipled [ʌn'prɪnsɪpld] ADJ senza
scrupoli

unproductive [ʌnprə'dʌktɪv] ADJ
improduttivo(-a); (*discussion*) sterile

unprofessional [ʌnprə'fɛʃənl] ADJ:
~ conduct scorrettezza professionale

unprofitable [ʌn'prɔfɪtəbl] ADJ (*financially*)
non redditizio(-a); (*job, deal*) poco
lucrativo(-a)

UNPROFOR ['ʌnprəfɔː^r] N ABBR (= *United
Nations Protection Force*) UNPROFOR *m*

unprotected ['ʌnprə'tɛktɪd] ADJ (*sex*) non
protetto(-a)

unprovoked [ʌnprə'vəukt] ADJ non
provocato(-a)

unpunished [ʌn'pʌnɪʃt] ADJ: **to go ~** restare
impunito(-a)

unqualified [ʌn'kwɔlɪfaɪd] ADJ (*worker*) non
qualificato(-a); (*in professions*) non abilitato(-a);
(*success*) assoluto(-a), senza riserve

unquestionably [ʌn'kwɛstʃənəblɪ] ADV
indiscutibilmente

unquestioning [ʌn'kwɛstʃənɪŋ] ADJ
(*obedience, acceptance*) cieco(-a)

unravel [ʌn'rævl] VT dipanare, districare

unreal [ʌn'rɪəl] ADJ irreale

unrealistic [ʌnrɪə'lɪstɪk] ADJ (*idea*)
illusorio(-a); (*estimate*) non realistico(-a)

unreasonable [ʌn'riːznəbl] ADJ
irragionevole; **to make ~ demands on sb**
voler troppo da qn

unrecognizable [ʌn'rɛkəgnaɪzəbl] ADJ
irriconoscibile

unrecognized [ʌn'rɛkəgnaɪzd] ADJ (*talent,
genius*) misconosciuto(-a); (*Pol: regime*) non
ufficialmente riconosciuto(-a)

unrecorded [ʌnrɪ'kɔːdɪd] ADJ non
documentato(-a), non registrato(-a)

unrefined [ʌnrɪ'faɪnd] ADJ (*sugar, petroleum*)
greggio(-a); (*person*) rozzo(-a)

unrehearsed [ʌnrɪ'həːst] ADJ (*Theat etc*)
improvvisato(-a); (*spontaneous*)
imprevisto(-a)

unrelated [ʌnrɪ'leɪtɪd] ADJ: **~ (to)** senza
rapporto (con); (*by family*) non
imparentato(-a) (con)

unrelenting [ʌnrɪ'lɛntɪŋ] ADJ implacabile;
accanito(-a)

unreliable [ʌnrɪ'laɪəbl] ADJ (*person, machine*)
che non dà affidamento; (*news, source of
information*) inattendibile

unrelieved [ʌnrɪ'liːvd] ADJ (*monotony*)
uniforme

unremitting [ʌnrɪ'mɪtɪŋ] ADJ incessante,
infaticabile

unrepeatable [ʌnrɪ'piːtəbl] ADJ (*offer*)
unico(-a)

unrepentant [ʌnrɪ'pɛntənt] ADJ
impenitente

unrepresentative [ʌnrɛprɪ'zɛntətɪv] ADJ
atipico(-a), poco rappresentativo(-a)

unreserved [ʌnrɪ'zəːvd] ADJ (*seat*) non
prenotato(-a), non riservato(-a); (*approval,
admiration*) senza riserve

unresponsive [ʌnrɪs'pɔnsɪv] ADJ che non
reagisce

unrest [ʌn'rɛst] N agitazione *f*

unrestricted [ʌnrɪ'strɪktɪd] ADJ (*power, time*)
illimitato(-a); (*access*) libero(-a)

unrewarded [ʌnrɪ'wɔːdɪd] ADJ non
ricompensato(-a)

unripe [ʌn'raɪp] ADJ acerbo(-a)

unrivalled, (*US*)**unrivaled** [ʌn'raɪvəld] ADJ
senza pari

unroll [ʌn'rəul] VT srotolare

unruffled [ʌn'rʌfld] ADJ (*person*) calmo(-a) e
tranquillo(-a), imperturbato(-a); (*hair*) a
posto

unruly [ʌn'ruːlɪ] ADJ indisciplinato(-a)

unsafe [ʌn'seɪf] ADJ pericoloso(-a),
rischioso(-a); **~ to drink** non potabile; **~ to
eat** non commestibile

unsaid [ʌn'sɛd] ADJ: **to leave sth ~** passare qc
sotto silenzio

unsaleable, (*US*)**unsalable** [ʌn'seɪləbl] ADJ
invendibile

unsatisfactory ['ʌnsætɪs'fæktərɪ] ADJ che
lascia a desiderare, insufficiente

unsavoury, (*US*)**unsavory** [ʌn'seɪvərɪ] ADJ
(*fig: person*) losco(-a); (: *reputation, subject*)
disgustoso(-a), ripugnante

unscathed [ʌn'skeɪðd] ADJ incolume

unscientific ['ʌnsaɪən'tɪfɪk] ADJ poco
scientifico(-a)

unscrew [ʌn'skruː] VT svitare

unscrupulous [ʌn'skruːpjuləs] ADJ senza
scrupoli

unseat [ʌn'siːt] VT (*rider*) disarcionare; (*fig: an official*) spodestare

unsecured [ʌnsɪ'kjuəd] ADJ: **~ creditor** creditore m chirografario

unseeded [ʌn'siːdɪd] ADJ (*Sport*) che non è una testa di serie

unseemly [ʌn'siːmlɪ] ADJ sconveniente

unseen [ʌn'siːn] ADJ (*person*) inosservato(-a); (*danger*) nascosto(-a)

unselfish [ʌn'sɛlfɪʃ] ADJ (*person*) altruista; (*act*) disinteressato(-a)

unsettled [ʌn'sɛtld] ADJ (*person, future*) incerto(-a); indeciso(-a); turbato(-a); (*question*) non risolto(-a); (*weather, market*) instabile; **to feel ~** sentirsi disorientato(-a)

unsettling [ʌn'sɛtlɪŋ] ADJ inquietante

unshakable, unshakeable [ʌn'ʃeɪkəbl] ADJ irremovibile

unshaven [ʌn'ʃeɪvn] ADJ non rasato(-a)

unsightly [ʌn'saɪtlɪ] ADJ brutto(-a), sgradevole a vedersi

unskilled [ʌn'skɪld] ADJ: **~ worker** operaio(-a) specializzato(-a)

unsociable [ʌn'səuʃəbl] ADJ (*person*) poco socievole; (*behaviour*) antipatico(-a)

unsocial [ʌn'səuʃəl] ADJ: **~ hours** orario sconveniente

unsold [ʌn'səuld] ADJ invenduto(-a)

unsolicited [ʌnsə'lɪsɪtɪd] ADJ non richiesto(-a)

unsophisticated [ʌnsə'fɪstɪkeɪtɪd] ADJ semplice, naturale

unsound [ʌn'saund] ADJ (*health*) debole, cagionevole; (*in construction: floor, foundations*) debole, malsicuro(-a); (: *policy, advice*) poco sensato(-a); (: *judgment, investment*) poco sicuro(-a)

unspeakable [ʌn'spiːkəbl] ADJ (*bad*) abominevole

unspoiled ['ʌn'spɔɪld], **unspoilt** ['ʌn'spɔɪlt] ADJ (*place*) non deturpato(-a)

unspoken [ʌn'spəukən] ADJ (*words*) non detto(-a); (*agreement, approval*) tacito(-a)

unstable [ʌn'steɪbl] ADJ (*gen*) instabile; (*mentally*) squilibrato(-a)

unsteady [ʌn'stɛdɪ] ADJ instabile, malsicuro(-a)

unstinting [ʌn'stɪntɪŋ] ADJ (*support*) incondizionato(-a); (*generosity*) illimitato(-a); (*praise*) senza riserve

unstuck [ʌn'stʌk] ADJ: **to come ~** scollarsi; (*fig*) fare fiasco

unsubscribe [ʌnsʌb'skraɪb] VI (*Comput*) disdire l'abbonamento

unsubstantiated [ʌnsəb'stænʃieɪtɪd] ADJ (*rumour, accusation*) infondato(-a)

unsuccessful [ʌnsək'sɛsful] ADJ (*writer, proposal*) che non ha successo; (*marriage, attempt*) mal riuscito(-a), fallito(-a); **to be ~** (*in attempting sth*) non riuscire;

non avere successo; (*application*) non essere considerato(-a)

unsuccessfully [ʌnsək'sɛsfəlɪ] ADV senza successo

unsuitable [ʌn'suːtəbl] ADJ inadatto(-a); (*moment*) inopportuno(-a); sconveniente

unsuited [ʌn'suːtɪd] ADJ: **to be ~ for** *or* **to** non essere fatto(-a) per

unsung ['ʌn'sʌŋ] ADJ: **an ~ hero** un eroe misconosciuto

unsupported [ʌnsə'pɔːtɪd] ADJ (*claim*) senza fondamento; (*theory*) non dimostrato(-a)

unsure [ʌn'ʃuəʳ] ADJ: **~ (of** *or* **about)** incerto(-a) (su); **to be ~ of o.s.** essere insicuro(-a)

unsuspecting [ʌnsə'spɛktɪŋ] ADJ che non sospetta niente

unsweetened [ʌn'swiːtnd] ADJ senza zucchero

unswerving [ʌn'swəːvɪŋ] ADJ fermo(-a)

unsympathetic ['ʌnsɪmpə'θɛtɪk] ADJ (*attitude*) poco incoraggiante; (*person*) antipatico(-a); **~ (to)** non solidale (verso)

untangle [ʌn'tæŋgl] VT sbrogliare

untapped [ʌn'tæpt] ADJ (*resources*) non sfruttato(-a)

untaxed [ʌn'tækst] ADJ (*goods*) esente da imposte; (*income*) non imponibile

unthinkable [ʌn'θɪŋkəbl] ADJ impensabile, inconcepibile

unthinkingly ['ʌn'θɪŋkɪŋlɪ] ADV senza pensare

untidy [ʌn'taɪdɪ] ADJ (*room*) in disordine; (*appearance, work*) trascurato(-a); (*person, writing*) disordinato(-a)

untie [ʌn'taɪ] VT (*knot, parcel*) disfare; (*prisoner, dog*) slegare

until [ʌn'tɪl] PREP fino a; (*after negative*) prima di ▸ CONJ finché, fino a quando; (*in past, after negative*) prima che + *sub*, prima di + *infinitive*; **~ he comes** finché *or* fino a quando non arriva; **~ now** finora; **~ then** fino ad allora; **from morning ~ night** dalla mattina alla sera

untimely [ʌn'taɪmlɪ] ADJ intempestivo(-a), inopportuno(-a); (*death*) prematuro(-a)

untold [ʌn'təuld] ADJ incalcolabile; indescrivibile

untouched [ʌn'tʌtʃt] ADJ (*not used etc*) non toccato(-a), intatto(-a); (*safe: person*) incolume; (*unaffected*): **~ by** insensibile a

untoward [ʌntə'wɔːd] ADJ sfortunato(-a), sconveniente

untrained ['ʌn'treɪnd] ADJ (*worker*) privo(-a) di formazione professionale; (*troops*) privo(-a) di addestramento; **to the ~ eye** ad un occhio inesperto

untrammelled [ʌn'træmld] ADJ illimitato(-a)

untranslatable [ʌntrænz'leɪtəbl] ADJ intraducibile

untrue [ʌn'tru:] ADJ (*statement*) falso(-a), non vero(-a)

untrustworthy [ʌn'trʌstwə:ðɪ] ADJ di cui non ci si può fidare

unusable [ʌn'ju:zəbl] ADJ inservibile, inutilizzabile

unused¹ [ʌn'ju:zd] ADJ (*new*) nuovo(-a); (*not made use of*) non usato(-a), non utilizzato(-a)

unused² [ʌn'ju:st] ADJ: **to be ~ to sth/to doing sth** non essere abituato(-a) a qc/a fare qc

unusual [ʌn'ju:ʒuəl] ADJ insolito(-a), eccezionale raro(-a)

unusually [ʌn'ju:ʒuəlɪ] ADV insolitamente

unveil [ʌn'veɪl] VT scoprire; svelare

unwanted [ʌn'wɒntɪd] ADJ (*clothing*) smesso(-a); (*child*) non desiderato(-a)

unwarranted [ʌn'wɒrəntɪd] ADJ ingiustificato(-a)

unwary [ʌn'wɛərɪ] ADJ incauto(-a)

unwavering [ʌn'weɪvərɪŋ] ADJ fermo(-a), incrollabile

unwelcome [ʌn'wɛlkəm] ADJ (*gen*) non gradito(-a); **to feel ~** sentire che la propria presenza non è gradita

unwell [ʌn'wɛl] ADJ indisposto(-a); **to feel ~** non sentirsi bene

unwieldy [ʌn'wi:ldɪ] ADJ poco maneggevole

unwilling [ʌn'wɪlɪŋ] ADJ: **to be ~ to do** non voler fare

unwillingly [ʌn'wɪlɪŋlɪ] ADV malvolentieri

unwind [ʌn'waɪnd] VT (*irreg: like* **wind²**) svolgere, srotolare ▶ VI (*relax*) rilassarsi

unwise [ʌn'waɪz] ADJ (*decision, act*) poco saggio(-a)

unwitting [ʌn'wɪtɪŋ] ADJ involontario(-a)

unwittingly [ʌn'wɪtɪŋlɪ] ADV senza volerlo

unworkable [ʌn'wə:kəbl] ADJ (*plan etc*) inattuabile

unworthy [ʌn'wə:ðɪ] ADJ indegno(-a); **to be ~ of sth/to do sth** non essere degno di qc/di fare qc

unwrap [ʌn'ræp] VT disfare; (*present*) aprire

unwritten [ʌn'rɪtn] ADJ (*agreement*) tacito(-a)

unzip [ʌn'zɪp] VT aprire (la chiusura lampo di); (*Comput*) dezippare

(KEYWORD)

up [ʌp] PREP su; **he went up the stairs/the hill** è salito su per le scale/sulla collina; **the cat was up a tree** il gatto era su un albero; **they live further up the street** vivono un po' più su nella stessa strada
▶ ADV **1** (*upwards, higher*) su, in alto; **up in the sky/the mountains** su nel cielo/in montagna; **up there** lassù; **up above** su in alto; **up with Leeds United!** viva il Leeds United!

2: **to be up** (*out of bed*) essere alzato(-a); (*prices, level*) essere salito(-a); (*building*) essere terminato(-a); (*tent*) essere piantato(-a); (*curtains, shutters, wallpaper*) essere su; **"this side up"** "alto"; **to be up (by)** (*in price, value*) essere salito(-a) or aumentato(-a) (di); **when the year was up** (*finished*) finito l'anno; **time's up** il tempo è scaduto; **he's well up in** or **on politics** (BRIT) è molto informato di or sulla politica

3: **up to** (*as far as*) fino a; **up to now** finora

4: **to be up to** (*depending on*): **it's up to you** sta a lei, dipende da lei; (*equal to*): **he's not up to it** (*job, task etc*) non ne è all'altezza; (*be doing: col*): **what is he up to?** cosa sta combinando?; **what's up?** (*col: wrong*) che c'è?; **what's up with him?** che ha?, che gli prende?

▶ N: **ups and downs** alti e bassi *mpl*
▶ VI (*col*): **she upped and left** improvvisamente se ne andò

up-and-coming [ʌpənd'kʌmɪŋ] ADJ pieno(-a) di promesse, promettente

upbeat ['ʌpbi:t] N (*Mus*) tempo in levare; (*in economy, prosperity*) incremento ▶ ADJ (*col*) ottimistico(-a)

upbraid [ʌp'breɪd] VT rimproverare

upbringing ['ʌpbrɪŋɪŋ] N educazione *f*

upcoming ['ʌpkʌmɪŋ] ADJ imminente, prossimo(-a)

update [ʌp'deɪt] VT aggiornare

upend [ʌp'ɛnd] VT rovesciare

upfront [ʌp'frʌnt] ADJ (*col*) franco(-a), aperto(-a) ▶ ADV (*pay*) subito

upgrade [ʌp'greɪd] VT promuovere; (*job*) rivalutare; (*house*) rimodernare; (*employee*) avanzare di grado; (*Comput*) fare un upgrade di

upheaval [ʌp'hi:vl] N sconvolgimento; tumulto

uphill [ʌp'hɪl] ADJ in salita; (*fig: task*) difficile
▶ ADV: **to go ~** andare in salita, salire

uphold [ʌp'həuld] VT (*irreg: like* **hold**) approvare; sostenere

upholstery [ʌp'həulstərɪ] N tappezzeria

upkeep ['ʌpki:p] N manutenzione *f*

upload ['ʌpləud] VT caricare

up-market [ʌp'mɑ:kɪt] ADJ (*product*) che si rivolge ad una fascia di mercato superiore

upon [ə'pɒn] PREP su

upper ['ʌpər] ADJ superiore ▶ N (*of shoe*) tomaia; **the ~ class** ≈ l'alta borghesia

upper case N maiuscolo

upper-class [ʌpə'klɑ:s] ADJ dell'alta borghesia; (*district*) signorile; (*accent*) aristocratico(-a); (*attitude*) snob *inv*

uppercut ['ʌpəkʌt] N uppercut *m inv*, montante *m*

upper hand N: **to have the ~** avere il coltello dalla parte del manico

Upper House N: **the ~** (in Britain) la Camera Alta, la Camera dei Lords; (in US etc) il Senato

uppermost ['ʌpəməust] ADJ il(la) più alto(-a); predominante; **it was ~ in my mind** è stata la mia prima preoccupazione

Upper Volta [-'vɔltə] N Alto Volta m

upright ['ʌpraɪt] ADJ diritto(-a); verticale; (fig) diritto(-a), onesto(-a) ▶ N montante m

uprising ['ʌpraɪzɪŋ] N insurrezione f, rivolta

uproar ['ʌprɔːr] N tumulto, clamore m

uproarious [ʌp'rɔːrɪəs] ADJ clamoroso(-a); (hilarious) esilarante; **~ laughter** risata sonora

uproot [ʌp'ruːt] VT sradicare

upset N ['ʌpsɛt] turbamento; (to plan etc) contrattempo ▶ VT [ʌp'sɛt] (irreg: like **set**) (glass etc) rovesciare; (plan, stomach) scombussolare; (person: offend) contrariare; (: grieve) addolorare; sconvolgere ▶ ADJ [ʌp'sɛt] contrariato(-a), addolorato(-a); (stomach) scombussolato(-a), disturbato(-a); **to have a stomach ~** (BRIT) avere lo stomaco in disordine or scombussolato; **to get ~** contrariarsi; addolorarsi

upset price N (US, SCOTTISH) prezzo di riserva

upsetting [ʌp'sɛtɪŋ] ADJ (saddening) sconvolgente; (offending) offensivo(-a); (annoying) fastidioso(-a)

upshot ['ʌpʃɔt] N risultato; **the ~ of it all was that …** la conclusione è stata che …

upside down ['ʌpsaɪd-] ADV sottosopra; **to turn ~** capovolgere; (fig) mettere sottosopra

upstage ['ʌp'steɪdʒ] VT: **to ~ sb** rubare la scena a qn

upstairs [ʌp'stɛəz] ADV, ADJ di sopra, al piano superiore ▶ N piano di sopra

upstart ['ʌpstɑːt] N parvenu m inv

upstream [ʌp'striːm] ADV a monte

upsurge ['ʌpsəːdʒ] N (of enthusiasm etc) ondata

uptake ['ʌpteɪk] N: **he is quick/slow on the ~** è pronto/lento di comprendonio

uptight [ʌp'taɪt] ADJ (col) teso(-a)

up-to-date ['ʌptə'deɪt] ADJ moderno(-a); aggiornato(-a)

uptown ['ʌptaun] (US) ADV verso i quartieri residenziali ▶ ADJ dei quartieri residenziali

upturn ['ʌptəːn] N (in luck) svolta favorevole; (in value of currency) rialzo

upturned ['ʌptəːnd] ADJ (nose) all'insù

upward ['ʌpwəd] ADJ ascendente; verso l'alto ▶ ADV = **upwards**

upwardly-mobile ['ʌpwədlɪ'məubaɪl] N: **to be ~** salire nella scala sociale

upwards ['ʌpwədz] ADV in su, verso l'alto

URA N ABBR (US: = Urban Renewal Administration) amministrazione per il rinnovamento urbano

Ural Mountains ['juərəl-] NPL: **the ~** (also:

the Urals) gli Urali, i Monti Urali

uranium [juə'reɪnɪəm] N uranio

Uranus [juə'reɪnəs] N (planet) Urano

urban ['əːbən] ADJ urbano(-a)

urbane [əː'beɪn] ADJ civile, urbano(-a), educato(-a)

urbanization [əːbənaɪ'zeɪʃən] N urbanizzazione f

urchin ['əːtʃɪn] N monello; **sea ~** riccio di mare

Urdu ['uədu:] N urdu m inv

urge [əːdʒ] N impulso; stimolo; forte desiderio ▶ VT (caution etc) raccomandare vivamente; **to ~ sb to do** esortare qn a fare, spingere qn a fare; raccomandare a qn di fare

▶ **urge on** VT spronare

urgency ['əːdʒənsɪ] N urgenza; (of tone) insistenza

urgent ['əːdʒənt] ADJ urgente; (earnest, persistent: plea) pressante; (: tone, voice) insistente, incalzante

urgently ['əːdʒəntlɪ] ADV d'urgenza; urgentemente; con insistenza

urinal ['juərɪnl] N (BRIT: building) vespasiano; (: vessel) orinale m, pappagallo

urinate ['juərɪneɪt] VI orinare

urine ['juərɪn] N orina

URL N ABBR (= uniform resource locator) URL m inv, indirizzo Internet

urn [əːn] N urna; (also: **tea urn**) bollitore m per il tè

Uruguay ['juərəgwaɪ] N Uruguay m

Uruguayan [juərə'gwaɪən] ADJ, N uruguaiano(-a)

US N ABBR = **United States**

us [ʌs] PRON ci; (stressed, after prep) noi; see also **me**

USA N ABBR (Geo) = **United States of America**; (Mil) = **United States Army**

usable ['juːzəbl] ADJ utilizzabile, usabile

USAF N ABBR = **United States Air Force**

usage ['juːzɪdʒ] N uso

USB stick N pennetta USB

USCG N ABBR = **United States Coast Guard**

USDA N ABBR = **United States Department of Agriculture**

USDAW ['ʌzdɔː] N ABBR (BRIT: = Union of Shop, Distributive and Allied Workers) sindacato dei dipendenti di negozi, reti di distribuzione e simili

USDI N ABBR = **United States Department of the Interior**

use N [juːs] uso; impiego, utilizzazione f ▶ VT [juːz] usare, utilizzare, servirsi di; **she used to do it** lo faceva (una volta), era solita farlo; **in ~** in uso; **out of ~** fuori uso; **to be of ~** essere utile, servire; **to make ~ of sth** far uso di qc, utilizzare qc; **ready for ~** pronto per l'uso; **it's no ~** non serve, è inutile; **to**

855

u

have the ~ of poter usare; **what's this used for?** a che serve?; **to be used to** avere l'abitudine di; **to get used to** abituarsi a, fare l'abitudine a

▶ **use up** vt finire; (supplies) dare fondo a; (left-overs) consumare

used [juːzd] ADJ (car, object) usato(-a)

useful ['juːsful] ADJ utile; **to come in** ~ fare comodo, tornare utile

usefulness ['juːsfəlnɪs] N utilità

useless ['juːslɪs] ADJ inutile; (unusable: object) inservibile; (: person) inetto(-a)

user ['juːzər] N utente mf; (of petrol, gas etc) consumatore(-trice)

user-friendly ['juːzə'frɛndlɪ] ADJ orientato(-a) all'utente; (computer) di facile uso

username ['juːzəneɪm] N username m inv

USES N ABBR = **United States Employment Service**

usher ['ʌʃər] N usciere m; (in cinema) maschera ▶ VT: **to ~ sb in** far entrare qn

usherette [ʌʃə'rɛt] N (in cinema) maschera

USIA N ABBR = **United States Information Agency**

USM N ABBR = **United States Mint; United States Mail**

USN N ABBR = **United States Navy**

USP N ABBR = **unique selling point; unique selling proposition**

USPHS N ABBR = **United States Public Health Service**

USPO N ABBR = **United States Post Office**

USS ABBR = **United States Ship; United States Steamer**

USSR N ABBR (Hist) = **Union of Soviet Socialist Republics**

usu. ABBR = **usually**

usual ['juːʒuəl] ADJ solito(-a); **as ~** come al solito, come d'abitudine

usually ['juːʒuəlɪ] ADV di solito

usurer ['juːʒərər] N usuraio(-a)

usurp [juː'zəːp] VT usurpare

UT ABBR (US) = **Utah**

ute [juːt] N (Australia, New Zealand) pick-up m inv

utensil [juː'tɛnsl] N utensile m; **kitchen utensils** utensili da cucina

uterus ['juːtərəs] N utero

utilitarian [juːtɪlɪ'tɛərɪən] ADJ utilitario(-a)

utility [juː'tɪlɪtɪ] N utilità; (also: **public utility**) servizio pubblico

utility room N locale adibito alla stiratura dei panni ecc

utilization [juːtɪlaɪ'zeɪʃən] N utilizzazione f

utilize ['juːtɪlaɪz] VT utilizzare; sfruttare

utmost ['ʌtməust] ADJ estremo(-a) ▶ N: **to do one's ~** fare il possibile or di tutto; **of the ~ importance** della massima importanza; **it is of the ~ importance that …** è estremamente importante che … + sub

utter ['ʌtər] ADJ assoluto(-a), totale ▶ VT pronunciare, proferire; emettere

utterance ['ʌtərəns] N espressione f; parole fpl

utterly ['ʌtəlɪ] ADV completamente, del tutto

U-turn ['juːtəːn] N inversione f a U; (fig) voltafaccia m inv

Uzbekistan [ʌzbɛkɪ'stɑːn] N Uzbekistan

Vv

V, v [viː] N (letter) V, v m inv or f inv; **V for Victor** ≈ V come Venezia

v ABBR (= verse) v.; (= vide) v., vedi; (= volt) V.; (= versus) contro

VA, Va. ABBR (US) = **Virginia**

vac [væk] N ABBR (BRIT col) = **vacation**

vacancy ['veɪkənsɪ] N (job) posto libero; (room) stanza libera; **"no vacancies"** "completo"; **have you any vacancies?** (office) avete bisogno di personale?; (hotel) avete una stanza?

vacant ['veɪkənt] ADJ (job, seat etc) libero(-a); (expression) assente

vacant lot N terreno non occupato; (for sale) terreno in vendita

vacate [və'keɪt] VT lasciare libero(-a)

vacation [və'keɪʃən] N (esp US) vacanze fpl; **to take a ~** prendere una vacanza, prendere le ferie; **on ~** in vacanza, in ferie

vacation course N corso estivo

vacationer, (US) vacationist N vacanziere(-a)

vaccinate ['væksɪneɪt] VT vaccinare

vaccination [væksɪ'neɪʃən] N vaccinazione f

vaccine ['væksiːn] N vaccino

vacuum ['vækjum] N vuoto

vacuum bottle N (US) = **vacuum flask**

vacuum cleaner N aspirapolvere m inv

vacuum flask N (BRIT) thermos® m inv

vacuum-packed ['vækjum'pækt] ADJ confezionato(-a) sottovuoto

vagabond ['vægəbɔnd] N vagabondo(-a)

vagary ['veɪgərɪ] N capriccio

vagina [və'dʒaɪnə] N vagina

vagrancy ['veɪgrənsɪ] N vagabondaggio

vagrant ['veɪgrənt] N vagabondo(-a)

vague [veɪg] ADJ vago(-a); (blurred: photo, memory) sfocato(-a); **I haven't the vaguest idea** non ho la minima or più pallida idea

vaguely ['veɪglɪ] ADV vagamente

vain [veɪn] ADJ (useless) inutile, vano(-a); (conceited) vanitoso(-a); **in ~** inutilmente, invano

valance ['væləns] N volant m inv, balza

valedictory [vælɪ'dɪktərɪ] ADJ di commiato

valentine ['væləntaɪn] N (also: **valentine card**) cartolina or biglietto di San Valentino

Valentine's Day ['væləntaɪnzdeɪ] N San Valentino m

valet ['vælɪt] N cameriere m personale

valet parking N parcheggio effettuato da un dipendente (dell'albergo ecc)

valet service N (for clothes) servizio di lavanderia; (for car) servizio completo di lavaggio

valiant ['væliənt] ADJ valoroso(-a), coraggioso(-a)

valid ['vælɪd] ADJ valido(-a), valevole; (excuse) valido(-a)

validate ['vælɪdeɪt] VT (contract, document) convalidare; (argument, claim) comprovare

validity [və'lɪdɪtɪ] N validità

valise [və'liːz] N borsa da viaggio

valley ['vælɪ] N valle f

valour, (US) valor ['vælər] N valore m

valuable ['væljuəbl] ADJ (jewel) di (grande) valore; (time, help) prezioso(-a); **valuables** NPL oggetti mpl di valore

valuation [vælju'eɪʃən] N valutazione f, stima

value ['væljuː] N valore m ▶ VT (fix price) valutare, dare un prezzo a; (cherish) apprezzare, tenere a; **values** NPL (principles) valori mpl; **to be of great ~ to sb** avere molta importanza per qn; **to lose (in) ~** (currency) svalutarsi; (property) perdere (di) valore; **to gain (in) ~** (currency) guadagnare; (property) aumentare di valore; **you get good ~ (for money) in that shop** si compra bene in quel negozio

value added tax N (BRIT) imposta sul valore aggiunto

valued ['væljuːd] ADJ (appreciated) stimato(-a), apprezzato(-a)

valuer ['væljuər] N stimatore(-trice)

valve [vælv] N valvola

vampire ['væmpaɪər] N vampiro

van [væn] N (Aut) furgone m; (BRIT Rail) vagone m

V and A N ABBR (*BRIT*) = **Victoria and Albert Museum**

vandal ['vændl] N vandalo(-a)

vandalism ['vændəlɪzəm] N vandalismo

vandalize ['vændəlaɪz] VT vandalizzare

vanguard ['vænɡɑːd] N avanguardia

vanilla [və'nɪlə] N vaniglia ▶ CPD (*ice cream*) alla vaniglia

vanish ['vænɪʃ] VI svanire, scomparire

vanity ['vænɪtɪ] N vanità

vanity case N valigetta per cosmetici

vantage ['vɑːntɪdʒ] N: ~ **point** posizione *f or* punto di osservazione; (*fig*) posizione vantaggiosa

vaporize ['veɪpəraɪz] VT vaporizzare ▶ VI vaporizzarsi

vapour, (*US*)**vapor** ['veɪpə'] N vapore *m*

variable ['vεərɪəbl] ADJ variabile; (*mood*) mutevole ▶ N fattore *m* variabile, variabile *f*

variance ['vεərɪəns] N: **to be at ~ (with)** essere in disaccordo (con); (*facts*) essere in contraddizione (con)

variant ['vεərɪənt] N variante *f*

variation [vεərɪ'eɪʃən] N variazione *f*; (*in opinion*) cambiamento

varicose ['værɪkəʊs] ADJ: ~ **veins** varici *fpl*

varied ['vεərɪd] ADJ vario(-a), diverso(-a)

variety [və'raɪətɪ] N varietà *f inv*; (*quantity*) quantità, numero; **a wide ~ of ...** una vasta gamma di ...; **for a ~ of reasons** per una serie di motivi

variety show N spettacolo di varietà

various ['vεərɪəs] ADJ vario(-a), diverso(-a); (*several*) parecchi(-e), molti(-e); **at ~ times** in momenti diversi; (*several*) diverse volte

varnish ['vɑːnɪʃ] N vernice *f*; (*nail varnish*) smalto ▶ VT verniciare; mettere lo smalto su; **to ~ one's nails** mettersi lo smalto sulle unghie

vary ['vεərɪ] VT, VI variare, mutare; **to ~ (with** *or* **according to)** variare (con *or* a seconda di)

varying ['vεərɪɪŋ] ADJ variabile

vase [vɑːz] N vaso

vasectomy [væ'sεktəmɪ] N vasectomia

Vaseline ® ['væsɪliːn] N vaselina

vast [vɑːst] ADJ vasto(-a); (*amount, success*) enorme

vastly ['vɑːstlɪ] ADV enormemente

vastness ['vɑːstnɪs] N vastità

VAT [væt] N ABBR (*BRIT*: = *value added tax*) I.V.A. *f*

vat [væt] N tino

Vatican ['vætɪkən] N: **the ~** il Vaticano

vatman ['vætmæn] N (*irreg*) (*BRIT col*): **the ~** = l'ispettore *m* dell'IVA

vault [vɔːlt] N (*of roof*) volta; (*tomb*) tomba; (*in bank*) camera blindata; (*jump*) salto ▶ VT (*also*: **vault over**) saltare (d'un balzo)

vaunted ['vɔːntɪd] ADJ: **much-~** tanto celebrato(-a)

VC N ABBR (*BRIT*: = *Victoria Cross*) medaglia al coraggio; = **vice-chairman**

VCR N ABBR = **video cassette recorder**

VD N ABBR = **venereal disease**

VDU N ABBR = **visual display unit**

veal [viːl] N vitello

veer [vɪə'] VI girare; virare

veg. [vεdʒ] N ABBR (*BRIT*: *col*: = *vegetable(s)*) = contorno

vegan ['viːɡən] N (*BRIT*) vegetaliano(-a)

vegeburger, veggieburger ['vεdʒɪbəːɡə'] N hamburger *m inv* vegetariano

vegetable ['vεdʒtəbl] N verdura, ortaggio ▶ ADJ vegetale

vegetable garden N orto

vegetarian [vεdʒɪ'tεərɪən] ADJ, N vegetariano(-a)

vegetate ['vεdʒɪteɪt] VI vegetare

vegetation [vεdʒɪ'teɪʃən] N vegetazione *f*

vegetative ['vεdʒɪtətɪv] ADJ (*also Bot*) vegetativo(-a)

vehemence ['viːɪməns] N veemenza, violenza

vehement ['viːɪmənt] ADJ veemente, violento(-a); profondo(-a)

vehicle ['viːɪkl] N veicolo; (*fig*) mezzo

vehicular [vɪ'hɪkjulə'] ADJ: **"no ~ traffic"** "chiuso al traffico di veicoli"

veil [veɪl] N velo ▶ VT velare; **under a ~ of secrecy** (*fig*) protetto da una cortina di segretezza

veiled [veɪld] ADJ (*also fig*) velato(-a)

vein [veɪn] N vena; (*on leaf*) nervatura; (*fig: mood*) vena, umore *m*

Velcro ® ['vεlkrəʊ] N velcro® *m inv*

vellum ['vεləm] N (*writing paper*) carta patinata

velocity [vɪ'lɔsɪtɪ] N velocità *f inv*

velour [və'luə'] N velours *m inv*

velvet ['vεlvɪt] N velluto ▶ ADJ di velluto

vending machine ['vεndɪŋ-] N distributore *m* automatico

vendor ['vεndə'] N venditore(-trice); **street ~** venditore ambulante

veneer [və'nɪə'] N impiallacciatura; (*fig*) vernice *f*

venerable ['vεnərəbl] ADJ venerabile

venereal disease [vɪ'nɪərɪəl-] N malattia venerea

Venetian [vɪ'niːʃən] ADJ, N veneziano(-a)

Venetian blind N (tenda alla) veneziana

Venezuela [vεnɪ'zweɪlə] N Venezuela *m*

Venezuelan [vεnɪ'zweɪlən] ADJ, N venezuelano(-a)

vengeance ['vεndʒəns] N vendetta; **with a ~** (*fig*) davvero; furiosamente

vengeful ['vεndʒful] ADJ vendicativo(-a)

Venice ['vεnɪs] N Venezia

venison ['vɛnɪsn] N carne f di cervo
venom ['vɛnəm] N veleno
venomous ['vɛnəməs] ADJ velenoso(-a)
vent [vɛnt] N foro, apertura; (in dress, jacket) spacco ▶ VT (fig: one's feelings) sfogare, dare sfogo a
ventilate ['vɛntɪleɪt] VT (room) dare aria a, arieggiare
ventilation [vɛntɪ'leɪʃən] N ventilazione f
ventilation shaft N condotto di aerazione
ventilator ['vɛntɪleɪtə'] N ventilatore m
ventriloquist [vɛn'trɪləkwɪst] N ventriloquo(-a)
venture ['vɛntʃə'] N impresa (rischiosa) ▶ VT rischiare, azzardare ▶ VI arrischiarsi, azzardarsi; **a business ~** un'iniziativa commerciale; **to ~ to do sth** azzardarsi a fare qc
venture capital N capitale m di rischio
venue ['vɛnjuː] N luogo di incontro; (Sport) luogo (designato) per l'incontro
Venus ['viːnəs] N (planet) Venere m
veracity [və'ræsɪtɪ] N veridicità
veranda, verandah [və'rændə] N veranda
verb [vəːb] N verbo
verbal ['vəːbəl] ADJ verbale; (translation) orale
verbally ['vəːbəlɪ] ADV a voce
verbatim [vəː'beɪtɪm] ADV, ADJ parola per parola
verbose [vəː'bəus] ADJ verboso(-a)
verdict ['vəːdɪkt] N verdetto; (opinion) giudizio, parere m; **~ of guilty/not guilty** verdetto di colpevolezza/non colpevolezza
verge [vəːdʒ] N bordo, orlo; **"soft verges"** (BRIT) "banchina cedevole"; **on the ~ of doing** sul punto di fare
▶ **verge on** VT FUS rasentare
verger ['vəːdʒə'] N (Rel) sagrestano
verification [vɛrɪfɪ'keɪʃən] N verifica
verify ['vɛrɪfaɪ] VT verificare; (prove the truth of) confermare
veritable ['vɛrɪtəbl] ADJ vero(-a)
vermin ['vəːmɪn] NPL animali mpl nocivi; (insects) insetti mpl parassiti
vermouth ['vəːməθ] N vermut m inv
vernacular [və'nækjulə'] N vernacolo
versatile ['vəːsətaɪl] ADJ (person) versatile; (machine, tool etc) (che si presta) a molti usi
verse [vəːs] N (of poem) verso; (stanza) stanza, strofa; (in bible) versetto; (no pl: poetry) versi mpl; **in ~** in versi
versed [vəːst] ADJ: **(well-)~ in** versato(-a) in
version ['vəːʃən] N versione f
versus ['vəːsəs] PREP contro
vertebra ['vəːtɪbrə] (pl **vertebrae** [-briː]) N vertebra
vertebrate ['vəːtɪbrɪt] N vertebrato
vertical ['vəːtɪkl] ADJ, N verticale (m)
vertically ['vəːtɪklɪ] ADV verticalmente

vertigo ['vəːtɪgəu] N vertigine f; **to suffer from ~** soffrire di vertigini
verve [vəːv] N brio; entusiasmo
very ['vɛrɪ] ADV molto ▶ ADJ: **the ~ book which** proprio il libro che; **~ much** moltissimo; **~ well** molto bene; **~ little** molto poco; **at the ~ end** proprio alla fine; **the ~ last** proprio l'ultimo; **at the ~ least** almeno; **the ~ thought (of it) alarms me** il solo pensiero mi spaventa, sono spaventato solo al pensiero
vespers ['vɛspəz] NPL vespro
vessel ['vɛsl] N (Anat) vaso; (Naut) nave f; (container) recipiente m
vest [vɛst] N (BRIT) maglia; (: sleeveless) canottiera; (US: waistcoat) gilè m inv ▶ VT: **to ~ sb with sth, to ~ sth in sb** conferire qc a qn
vested interest N: **to have a ~ in doing** avere tutto l'interesse a fare; **vested interests** NPL (Comm) diritti mpl acquisiti
vestibule ['vɛstɪbjuːl] N vestibolo
vestige ['vɛstɪdʒ] N vestigio
vestment ['vɛstmənt] N (Rel) paramento liturgico
vestry ['vɛstrɪ] N sagrestia
Vesuvius [vɪ'suːvɪəs] N Vesuvio
vet [vɛt] N ABBR (BRIT: = veterinary surgeon) veterinario; (US col) = **veteran** ▶ VT esaminare minuziosamente; (text) rivedere; **to ~ sb for a job** raccogliere delle informazioni dettagliate su qn prima di offrirgli un posto
veteran ['vɛtərn] N veterano; (also: **war veteran**) veterano, reduce m ▶ ADJ: **she's a ~ campaigner for ...** lotta da sempre per ...
veteran car N auto f inv d'epoca (anteriore al 1919)
veterinarian [vɛtrɪ'nɛərɪən] N (US) = **veterinary surgeon**
veterinary ['vɛtrɪnərɪ] ADJ veterinario(-a)
veterinary surgeon, (US) **veterinarian** [vɛtrɪ'nɛərɪən] N veterinario
veto ['viːtəu] (pl **vetoes**) N veto ▶ VT opporre il veto a; **to put a ~ on** opporre il veto a
vetting ['vɛtɪŋ] N: **positive ~** indagine per accertare l'idoneità di un aspirante a una carica ufficiale
vex [vɛks] VT irritare, contrariare
vexed [vɛkst] ADJ (question) controverso(-a), dibattuto(-a)
VFD N ABBR (US) = **voluntary fire department**
VG ABBR (BRIT Scol etc: = very good) ottimo
VHF ABBR (= very high frequency) VHF
VI ABBR (US) = **Virgin Islands**
via ['vaɪə] PREP (by way of) via; (by means of) tramite
viability [vaɪə'bɪlɪtɪ] N attuabilità
viable ['vaɪəbl] ADJ attuabile; vitale
viaduct ['vaɪədʌkt] N viadotto

V

vial ['vaɪəl] N fiala

vibes [vaɪbz] NPL (col): **I got good/bad ~** ho trovato simpatica/antipatica l'atmosfera

vibrant ['vaɪbrənt] ADJ (sound) vibrante; (colour) vivace, vivo(-a)

vibraphone ['vaɪbrəfəun] N vibrafono

vibrate [vaɪ'breɪt] VI: **to ~ (with)** vibrare (di); (resound) risonare (di)

vibration [vaɪ'breɪʃən] N vibrazione f

vibrator [vaɪ'breɪtər] N vibratore m

vicar ['vɪkər] N pastore m

vicarage ['vɪkərɪdʒ] N presbiterio

vicarious [vɪ'kɛərɪəs] ADJ sofferto(-a) al posto di un altro; **to get ~ pleasure out of sth** trarre piacere indirettamente da qc

vice [vaɪs] N (evil) vizio; (Tech) morsa

vice- [vaɪs] PREFIX vice ...

vice-chairman [vaɪs'tʃɛəmən] N (irreg) vicepresidente m

vice-chancellor [vaɪs'tʃɑːnsələr] N (BRIT Scol) rettore m (per elezione)

vice-president [vaɪs'prɛzɪdənt] N vicepresidente m

viceroy ['vaɪsrɔɪ] N viceré m inv

vice squad N (squadra del) buon costume f

vice versa ['vaɪsɪ'vəːsə] ADV viceversa

vicinity [vɪ'sɪnɪtɪ] N vicinanze fpl

vicious ['vɪʃəs] ADJ (remark) maligno(-a), cattivo(-a); (dog) cattivo(-a); (blow) violento(-a); **a ~ circle** un circolo vizioso

viciousness ['vɪʃəsnɪs] N malignità, cattiveria; ferocia

vicissitudes [vɪ'sɪsɪtjuːdz] NPL vicissitudini fpl

victim ['vɪktɪm] N vittima; **to be the ~ of** essere vittima di

victimization [vɪktɪmaɪ'zeɪʃən] N persecuzione f; rappresaglie fpl

victimize ['vɪktɪmaɪz] VT perseguitare; compiere delle rappresaglie contro

victor ['vɪktər] N vincitore m

Victorian [vɪk'tɔːrɪən] ADJ vittoriano(-a)

victorious [vɪk'tɔːrɪəs] ADJ vittorioso(-a)

victory ['vɪktərɪ] N vittoria; **to win a ~ over sb** riportare una vittoria su qn

video ['vɪdɪəu] CPD video... ▶ N (video film) video m inv; (also: **video cassette**) videocassetta; (also: **video recorder**) videoregistratore m

video call N videochiamata

video camera N videocamera

video cassette N videocassetta

video cassette recorder N videoregistratore m

videodisc ['vɪdɪəudɪsk] N disco ottico

video game N videogioco

video nasty N video estremamente violento o porno

videophone ['vɪdɪəufəun] N videotelefono

video recorder N videoregistratore m

video recording N registrazione f su video

video shop N videonoleggio

video tape N videotape m inv

video wall N schermo m multivideo inv

vie [vaɪ] VI: **to ~ with** competere con, rivaleggiare con

Vienna [vɪ'ɛnə] N Vienna

Vietnam, Viet Nam [vjɛt'næm] N Vietnam m

Vietnamese [vjɛtnə'miːz] ADJ vietnamita ▶ N vietnamita mf; (Ling) vietnamita m

view [vjuː] N vista, veduta; (opinion) opinione f ▶ VT (also fig: situation) considerare; (house) visitare; **on ~** (in museum etc) esposto(-a); **to be in** or **within ~ (of sth)** essere in vista (di qc); **in full ~ of sb** sotto gli occhi di qn; **an overall ~ of the situation** una visione globale della situazione; **in my ~** a mio parere, secondo me; **in ~ of the fact that** considerato che; **to take** or **hold the ~ that ...** essere dell'opinione che ...; **with a ~ to doing sth** con l'intenzione di fare qc

viewdata ['vjuːdeɪtə] N (BRIT) sistema di televideo

viewer ['vjuːər] N (viewfinder) mirino; (small projector) visore m; (TV) telespettatore(-trice)

viewfinder ['vjuːfaɪndər] N mirino

viewpoint ['vjuːpɔɪnt] N punto di vista; (place) posizione f

vigil ['vɪdʒɪl] N veglia; **to keep ~** vegliare

vigilance ['vɪdʒɪləns] N vigilanza

vigilant ['vɪdʒɪlənt] ADJ vigile

vigilante [vɪdʒɪ'læntɪ] N cittadino che si fa giustizia da solo

vigorous ['vɪgərəs] ADJ vigoroso(-a)

vigour, (US) vigor [vɪgər] N vigore m

vile [vaɪl] ADJ (action) vile; (smell) disgustoso(-a), nauseante; (temper) pessimo(-a)

vilify ['vɪlɪfaɪ] VT diffamare

villa ['vɪlə] N villa

village ['vɪlɪdʒ] N villaggio

villager ['vɪlɪdʒər] N abitante mf di villaggio

villain ['vɪlən] N (scoundrel) canaglia; (BRIT: criminal) criminale m; (in novel etc) cattivo

VIN N ABBR (US) = **vehicle identification number**

vinaigrette [vɪneɪ'grɛt] N vinaigrette f inv

vindicate ['vɪndɪkeɪt] VT comprovare; giustificare

vindication [vɪndɪ'keɪʃən] N: **in ~ of** per giustificare; a discolpa di

vindictive [vɪn'dɪktɪv] ADJ vendicativo(-a)

vine [vaɪn] N vite f; (climbing plant) rampicante m

vinegar ['vɪnɪgər] N aceto

vine grower N viticoltore m

vine-growing ['vaɪngrəuɪŋ] ADJ viticolo(-a) ▶ N viticoltura

vineyard ['vɪnjɑːd] N vigna, vigneto
vintage ['vɪntɪdʒ] N (year) annata, produzione f; **the 1970 ~** il vino del 1970 ▶ CPD d'annata
vintage car N auto f inv d'epoca
vintage wine N vino d'annata
vinyl ['vaɪnl] N vinile m
viola [vɪ'əʊlə] N viola
violate ['vaɪəleɪt] VT violare
violation [vaɪə'leɪʃən] N violazione f; **in ~ of sth** violando qc
violence ['vaɪələns] N violenza; (Pol etc) incidenti mpl violenti
violent [vaɪələnt] ADJ violento(-a); **a ~ dislike of sb/sth** una violenta avversione per qn/qc
violently ['vaɪələntlɪ] ADV violentemente; (ill, angry) terribilmente
violet ['vaɪələt] ADJ (colour) viola inv, violetto(-a) ▶ N (plant) violetta; (colour) violetto
violin [vaɪə'lɪn] N violino
violinist [vaɪə'lɪnɪst] N violinista mf
VIP N ABBR (= very important person) V.I.P. mf
viper ['vaɪpər] N vipera
viral ['vaɪərəl] ADJ virale
virgin ['vəːdʒɪn] N vergine f ▶ ADJ vergine inv; **she is a ~** lei è vergine; **the Blessed V~** la Beatissima Vergine
virginity [vəː'dʒɪnɪtɪ] N verginità
Virgo ['vəːgəʊ] N (sign) Vergine f; **to be ~** essere della Vergine
virile ['vɪraɪl] ADJ virile
virility [vɪ'rɪlɪtɪ] N virilità
virtual ['vəːtjuəl] ADJ effettivo(-a), vero(-a); (Comput, Physics) virtuale; (in effect): **it's a ~ impossibility** è praticamente impossibile; **the ~ leader** il capo all'atto pratico
virtually ['vəːtjuəlɪ] ADV (almost) praticamente; **it is ~ impossible** è praticamente impossibile
virtual reality N (Comput) realtà f inv virtuale
virtue ['vəːtjuː] N virtù f inv; (advantage) pregio, vantaggio; **by ~ of** grazie a
virtuosity [vəːtju'ɔsɪtɪ] N virtuosismo
virtuoso [vəːtju'əʊzəʊ] N virtuoso
virtuous ['vəːtjuəs] ADJ virtuoso(-a)
virulent ['vɪrulənt] ADJ virulento(-a)
virus ['vaɪərəs] N (also Comput) virus m inv
visa ['viːzə] N visto
vis-à-vis [viːzə'viː] PREP rispetto a, nei riguardi di
viscount ['vaɪkaunt] N visconte m
viscous ['vɪskəs] ADJ viscoso(-a)
vise [vaɪs] N (US Tech) = **vice**
visibility [vɪzɪ'bɪlɪtɪ] N visibilità
visible ['vɪzəbl] ADJ visibile; **~ exports/ imports** esportazioni fpl/importazioni fpl visibili

visibly ['vɪzəblɪ] ADV visibilmente
vision ['vɪʒən] N (sight) vista; (foresight, in dream) visione f
visionary ['vɪʒənərɪ] N visionario(-a)
visit ['vɪzɪt] N visita; (stay) soggiorno ▶ VT (person: US: also: **visit with**) andare a trovare; (place) visitare; **to pay a ~ to** (person) fare una visita a; (place) andare a visitare; **on a private/official ~** in visita privata/ufficiale
visiting ['vɪzɪtɪŋ] ADJ (speaker, professor, team) ospite
visiting card N biglietto da visita
visiting hours NPL (in hospital etc) orario delle visite
visitor ['vɪzɪtər] N visitatore(-trice); (guest) ospite mf
visitor centre, (US) **visitor center** N centro informazioni per visitatori di museo, zoo, parco ecc
visitors' book N libro d'oro; (in hotel) registro
visor ['vaɪzər] N visiera
VISTA ['vɪstə] N ABBR (= Volunteers in Service to America) volontariato in zone depresse degli Stati Uniti
vista ['vɪstə] N vista, prospettiva
visual ['vɪzjuəl] ADJ visivo(-a); visuale; ottico(-a)
visual aid N sussidio visivo
visual arts NPL arti fpl figurative
visual display unit N unità f inv di visualizzazione
visualize ['vɪzjuəlaɪz] VT immaginare, figurarsi; (foresee) prevedere
visually ['vɪzjuəlɪ] ADV: **~ appealing** piacevole a vedersi; **~ handicapped** con una menomazione della vista
vital ['vaɪtl] ADJ vitale; **of ~ importance (to sb/sth)** di vitale importanza (per qn/qc)
vitality [vaɪ'tælɪtɪ] N vitalità
vitally ['vaɪtəlɪ] ADV estremamente
vital statistics NPL (of population) statistica demografica; (col: woman's) misure fpl
vitamin ['vɪtəmɪn] N vitamina
vitiate ['vɪʃɪeɪt] VT viziare
vitreous ['vɪtrɪəs] ADJ (rock) vetroso(-a); (china, enamel) vetrificato(-a)
vitriolic [vɪtrɪ'ɔlɪk] ADJ (fig) caustico(-a)
viva ['vaɪvə] N (also: **viva voce**) (esame m) orale
vivacious [vɪ'veɪʃəs] ADJ vivace
vivacity [vɪ'væsɪtɪ] N vivacità
vivid ['vɪvɪd] ADJ vivido(-a)
vividly ['vɪvɪdlɪ] ADV (describe) vividamente; (remember) con precisione
vivisection [vɪvɪ'sɛkʃən] N vivisezione f
vixen ['vɪksn] N volpe f femmina; (pej: woman) bisbetica
viz ABBR (= vide licet: namely) cioè
VLF ABBR (= very low frequency) bassissima frequenza

V

V-neck ['viːnɛk] N maglione *m* con lo scollo a V

VOA N ABBR (= *Voice of America*) voce *f* dell'America (*alla radio*)

vocabulary [vəu'kæbjuləri] N vocabolario

vocal ['vəukl] ADJ (*Mus*) vocale; (*communication*) verbale; (*noisy*) rumoroso(-a)

vocal cords NPL corde *fpl* vocali

vocalist ['vəukəlist] N cantante *mf* (*in un gruppo*)

vocation [vəu'keɪʃən] N vocazione *f*

vocational [vəu'keɪʃənl] ADJ professionale; **~ guidance** orientamento professionale; **~ training** formazione *f* professionale

vociferous [və'sɪfərəs] ADJ rumoroso(-a)

vodka ['vɔdkə] N vodka *f inv*

vogue [vəug] N moda; (*popularity*) popolarità, voga; **to be in ~, be the ~** essere di moda

voice [vɔɪs] N voce *f* ▸ VT (*opinion*) esprimere; **in a loud/soft ~** a voce alta/bassa; **to give ~ to** esprimere

voice mail N servizio di segreteria telefonica

voice-over ['vɔɪsəuvəʳ] N voce *f* fuori campo

void [vɔɪd] N vuoto ▸ ADJ (*invalid*) nullo(-a); (*empty*): **~ of** privo(-a) di

voile [vɔɪl] N voile *m*

vol. ABBR (= *volume*) vol.

volatile ['vɔlətaɪl] ADJ volatile; (*fig*) volubile

volcanic [vɔl'kænɪk] ADJ vulcanico(-a)

volcano [vɔl'keɪnəu] (*pl* **volcanoes**) N vulcano

volition [və'lɪʃən] N: **of one's own ~** di propria volontà

volley ['vɔlɪ] N (*of gunfire*) salva; (*of stones etc*) raffica, gragnola; (*Tennis etc*) volata

volleyball ['vɔlɪbɔːl] N pallavolo *f*

volt [vəult] N volt *m inv*

voltage ['vəultɪdʒ] N tensione *f*, voltaggio; **high/low ~** alta/bassa tensione

voluble ['vɔljubl] ADJ loquace, ciarliero(-a)

volume ['vɔljuːm] N volume *m*; (*of tank*) capacità *f inv*; **~ one/two** (*of book*) volume primo/secondo; **his expression spoke volumes** la sua espressione lasciava capire tutto

volume control N (*Radio, TV*) regolatore *m or* manopola del volume

volume discount N (*Comm*) vantaggio sul volume di vendita

voluminous [və'luːmɪnəs] ADJ voluminoso(-a); (*notes etc*) abbondante

voluntarily ['vɔləntrɪlɪ] ADV volontariamente; gratuitamente

voluntary ['vɔləntərɪ] ADJ volontario(-a); (*unpaid*) gratuito(-a), non retribuito(-a)

voluntary liquidation N (*Comm*) liquidazione *f* volontaria

volunteer [vɔlən'tɪəʳ] N volontario(-a) ▸ VT offrire volontariamente ▸ VI (*Mil*) arruolarsi volontario; **to ~ to do** offrire (volontariamente) di fare

voluptuous [və'lʌptjuəs] ADJ voluttuoso(-a)

vomit ['vɔmɪt] N vomito ▸ VT, VI vomitare

voracious [və'reɪʃəs] ADJ (*appetite*) smisurato(-a); (*reader*) avido(-a)

vote [vəut] N voto, suffragio; (*cast*) voto; (*franchise*) diritto di voto ▸ VI votare ▸ VT (*gen*) votare; (*sum of money etc*) votare a favore di; (*propose*): **to ~ that** approvare la proposta che; **to ~ to do sth** votare a favore di fare qc; **he was voted secretary** è stato eletto segretario; **to put sth to the ~, to take a ~ on sth** mettere qc ai voti; **~ for/against** voto a favore/contrario; **to pass a ~ of confidence/no confidence** dare il voto di fiducia/sfiducia; **~ of thanks** discorso di ringraziamento

voter ['vəutəʳ] N elettore(-trice)

voting ['vəutɪŋ] N scrutinio

voting paper N (*Brit*) scheda elettorale

voting right N diritto di voto

vouch [vautʃ]: **to ~ for** *vt fus* farsi garante di

voucher ['vautʃəʳ] N (*for meal, petrol*) buono; (*receipt*) ricevuta; **travel ~** voucher *m inv*, tagliando

vow [vau] N voto, promessa solenne ▸ VI giurare; **to take** *or* **make a ~ to do sth** fare voto di fare qc ▸ VT: **to ~ to do/that** giurare di fare/che

vowel ['vauəl] N vocale *f*

voyage ['vɔɪɪdʒ] N viaggio per mare, traversata

voyeur [vwɑː'jəːʳ] N guardone(-a)

VP N ABBR (= *vice-president*) V.P.

vs ABBR (= *versus*) contro

VSO N ABBR (*Brit*: = *Voluntary Service Overseas*) *servizio volontario in paesi sottosviluppati*

VT, Vt. ABBR (*US*) = **Vermont**

vulgar ['vʌlgəʳ] ADJ volgare

vulgarity [vʌl'gærɪtɪ] N volgarità

vulnerability [vʌlnərə'bɪlɪtɪ] N vulnerabilità

vulnerable ['vʌlnərəbl] ADJ vulnerabile

vulture ['vʌltʃəʳ] N avvoltoio

Ww

W, w ['dʌblju:] N (letter) W, w m inv or f inv;
W for William ≈ W come Washington

W ABBR (= west) O; (Elec: = watt) w

WA ABBR (US) = **Washington**

wad [wɔd] N (of cotton wool, paper) tampone m;
(of banknotes etc) fascio

wadding ['wɔdɪŋ] N imbottitura

waddle ['wɔdl] VI camminare come una
papera

wade [weɪd] VI: **to ~ through** camminare a
stento in; (fig: book) leggere con fatica ▶ VT
guadare

wafer ['weɪfər] N (Culin) cialda; (Rel) ostia;
(Comput) wafer m inv

wafer-thin ['weɪfə'θɪn] ADJ molto sottile

waffle ['wɔfl] N (Culin) cialda; (col) ciance fpl;
riempitivo ▶ VI cianciare; parlare a vuoto

waffle iron N stampo per cialde

waft [wɔft] VT portare ▶ VI diffondersi

wag [wæg] VT agitare, muovere ▶ VI agitarsi;
the dog wagged its tail il cane scodinzolò

wage [weɪdʒ] N (also: **wages**) salario, paga
▶ VT: **to ~ war** fare la guerra; **a day's wages**
un giorno di paga

wage claim N rivendicazione f salariale

wage differential N differenza di salario

wage earner N salariato(-a)

wage freeze N blocco dei salari

wage packet N (BRIT) busta f paga inv

wager ['weɪdʒər] N scommessa

waggle ['wægl] VT dimenare, agitare ▶ VI
dimenarsi, agitarsi

wagon, waggon ['wægən] N (horse-drawn)
carro; (truck) furgone m; (BRIT Rail) vagone m
(merci)

wail [weɪl] N gemito; (of siren) urlo ▶ VI
gemere; urlare

waist [weɪst] N vita, cintola

waistcoat ['weɪskəut] N (BRIT) panciotto,
gilè m inv

waistline ['weɪstlaɪn] N (giro di) vita

wait [weɪt] N attesa ▶ VI aspettare, attendere;
to ~ for aspettare; **~ for me, please**
aspettami, per favore; **to keep sb waiting**
far aspettare qn; **~ a moment!** (aspetti) un
momento!; **"repairs while you ~"**
"riparazioni lampo"; **I can't ~ to ...** (fig) non
vedo l'ora di ...; **to lie in ~ for** stare in
agguato a

▶ **wait behind** VI rimanere (ad aspettare)

▶ **wait on** VT FUS servire

▶ **wait up** VI restare alzato(-a) (ad aspettare);
don't ~ up for me non rimanere alzato per
me

waiter ['weɪtər] N cameriere m

waiting ['weɪtɪŋ] N: **"no ~"** (BRIT Aut) "divieto
di sosta"

waiting list N lista d'attesa

waiting room N sala d'aspetto or d'attesa

waitress ['weɪtrɪs] N cameriera

waive [weɪv] VT rinunciare a, abbandonare

waiver ['weɪvər] N rinuncia

wake [weɪk] (pt **woke** [wəuk] or **waked**, pp
woken ['wəukn] or **waked**) VT (also: **wake up**)
svegliare ▶ VI (also: **wake up**) svegliarsi ▶ N
(for dead person) veglia funebre; (Naut) scia; **to**
~ up to sth (fig) rendersi conto di qc; **in the ~**
of sulla scia di; **to follow in sb's ~** (fig)
seguire le tracce di qn

waken ['weɪkn] VT, VI = **wake**

Wales [weɪlz] N Galles m

walk [wɔːk] N passeggiata; (short) giretto;
(gait) passo, andatura; (path) sentiero;
(in park etc) sentiero, vialetto ▶ VI camminare;
(for pleasure, exercise) passeggiare ▶ VT
(distance) fare or percorrere a piedi; (dog)
accompagnare, portare a passeggiare;
10 minutes' ~ from 10 minuti di cammino
or a piedi da; **to go for a ~** andare a fare
quattro passi; andare a fare una passeggiata;
from all walks of life di tutte le condizioni
sociali; **to ~ in one's sleep** essere
sonnambulo(-a); **I'll ~ you home** ti
accompagno a casa

▶ **walk out** VI (go out) uscire; (as protest) uscire
(in segno di protesta); (audience) andarsene;
(strike) scendere in sciopero; **to ~ out on sb**
piantare in asso qn

walkabout ['wɔːkəbaut] N: **to go (on a) ~**
avere incontri informali col pubblico (*durante
una visita ufficiale*)

walker ['wɔːkə^r] N (*person*)
camminatore(-trice)

walkie-talkie ['wɔːkɪ'tɔːkɪ] N walkie-talkie
m inv

walking ['wɔːkɪŋ] N camminare *m*; **it's
within ~ distance** ci si arriva a piedi

walking holiday N vacanza fatta di lunghe
camminate

walking shoes NPL scarpe *fpl* da passeggio

walking stick N bastone *m* da passeggio

Walkman® ['wɔːkmən] N walkman® *m inv*

walk-on ['wɔːkɔn] ADJ (*Theat: part*) da
comparsa

walkout ['wɔːkaut] N (*of workers*) sciopero
senza preavviso *or* a sorpresa

walkover ['wɔːkəuvə^r] N (*col*) vittoria facile,
gioco da ragazzi

walkway ['wɔːkweɪ] N passaggio pedonale

wall [wɔːl] N muro; (*internal, of tunnel, cave*)
parete *f*; **to go to the ~** (*fig: firm etc*) fallire
▶ **wall in** VT (*garden etc*) circondare con un
muro

wall cupboard N pensile *m*

walled [wɔːld] ADJ (*city*) fortificato(-a)

wallet ['wɔlɪt] N portafoglio

wallflower ['wɔːlflauə^r] N violacciocca; **to
be a ~** (*fig*) fare da tappezzeria

wall hanging N tappezzeria

wallop ['wɔləp] VT (*col*) pestare

wallow ['wɔləu] VI sguazzare, rotolarsi; **to ~
in one's grief** crogiolarsi nel proprio dolore

wallpaper ['wɔːlpeɪpə^r] N carta da parati;
(*Comput*) sfondo ▶ VT (*room*) mettere la carta
da parati in

wall-to-wall ['wɔːltə'wɔːl] ADJ: **~ carpeting**
moquette *f*

walnut ['wɔːlnʌt] N noce *f*; (*tree*) noce *m*

walrus ['wɔːlrəs] (*pl ~ or* **walruses**) N tricheco

waltz [wɔːlts] N valzer *m inv* ▶ VI ballare il
valzer

wan [wɔn] ADJ pallido(-a), smorto(-a); triste

wand [wɔnd] N (*also:* **magic wand**) bacchetta
(*magica*)

wander ['wɔndə^r] VI (*person*) girare senza
meta, girovagare; (*thoughts*) vagare; (*river*)
serpeggiare ▶ VT girovagare per

wanderer ['wɔndərə^r] N vagabondo(-a)

wandering ['wɔndrɪŋ] ADJ (*tribe*) nomade;
(*minstrel, actor*) girovago(-a); (*path, river*)
tortuoso(-a); (*glance, mind*) distratto(-a)

wane [weɪn] VI (*moon*) calare; (*reputation*)
declinare

wangle ['wæŋgl] (*BRIT col*) VT procurare (con
l'astuzia) ▶ N astuzia

wanker ['wæŋkə^r] N (*col!*) segaiolo (!); (*as
insult*) coglione (!) *m*

want [wɔnt] VT volere; (*need*) aver bisogno di;
(*lack*) mancare di ▶ N (*poverty*) miseria,
povertà; **wants** NPL (*needs*) bisogni *mpl*; **for ~
of** per mancanza di; **to ~ to do** volere fare;
to ~ sb to do volere che qn faccia; **you're
wanted on the phone** la vogliono al
telefono; **"cook wanted"** "cercasi cuoco"

want ads NPL (*US*) piccoli annunci *mpl*

wanted ADJ (*criminal*) ricercato(-a); **"~"** (*in
adverts*) "cercasi"

wanting ['wɔntɪŋ] ADJ: **to be ~ (in)** mancare
(di); **to be found ~** non risultare all'altezza

wanton ['wɔntn] ADJ sfrenato(-a); senza
motivo

war [wɔː^r] N guerra; **to go to ~** entrare in
guerra; **to make ~ (on)** far guerra (a)

warble ['wɔːbl] N (*of bird*) trillo ▶ VI trillare

war cry N grido di guerra

ward [wɔːd] N (*in hospital: room*) corsia;
(*: section*) reparto; (*Pol*) circoscrizione *f*; (*Law:
child: also:* **ward of court**) pupillo(-a)
▶ **ward off** VT parare, schivare

warden ['wɔːdn] N (*of institution*)
direttore(-trice); (*of park, game reserve*)
guardiano(-a); (*BRIT: also:* **traffic warden**)
addetto(-a) al controllo del traffico e del
parcheggio

warder ['wɔːdə^r] N (*BRIT*) guardia carceraria

wardrobe ['wɔːdrəub] N (*cupboard*)
guardaroba *m inv*, armadio; (*clothes*)
guardaroba; (*Theat*) costumi *mpl*

warehouse ['wɛəhaus] N magazzino

wares [wɛəz] NPL merci *fpl*

warfare ['wɔːfɛə^r] N guerra

war game N war game *m inv*

warhead ['wɔːhɛd] N (*Mil*) testata, ogiva

warily ['wɛərɪlɪ] ADV cautamente, con
prudenza

warlike ['wɔːlaɪk] ADJ guerriero(-a)

warm [wɔːm] ADJ caldo(-a); (*welcome, applause*)
caloroso(-a); (*person, greeting*) cordiale; (*heart*)
d'oro; (*supporter*) convinto(-a); **it's ~** fa caldo;
I'm ~ ho caldo; **to keep sth ~** tenere qc al
caldo; **with my warmest thanks** con i miei
più sentiti ringraziamenti
▶ **warm up** VI scaldarsi, riscaldarsi; (*athlete,
discussion*) riscaldarsi ▶ VT scaldare,
riscaldare; (*engine*) far scaldare

warm-blooded ['wɔːm'blʌdɪd] ADJ a sangue
caldo

war memorial N monumento ai caduti

warm-hearted [wɔːm'hɑːtɪd] ADJ
affettuoso(-a)

warmly ['wɔːmlɪ] ADV caldamente; (*applaud,
welcome*) calorosamente; vivamente; (*dress*)
con abiti pesanti

warmonger ['wɔːmʌŋgə^r] N guerrafondaio

warmongering ['wɔːmʌŋgrɪŋ] N bellicismo

warmth [wɔːmθ] N calore *m*

warm-up ['wɔ:mʌp] N (*Sport*) riscaldamento

warn [wɔ:n] VT avvertire, avvisare; **to ~ sb not to do sth** *or* **against doing sth** avvertire *or* avvisare qn di non fare qc; **to ~ sb that** avvertire *or* avvisare qn che

warning ['wɔ:nɪŋ] N avvertimento; (*notice*) avviso; (*signal*) segnalazione f; **without (any) ~** senza preavviso; **gale ~** avviso di burrasca

warning light N spia luminosa

warning triangle N (*Aut*) triangolo

warp [wɔ:p] N (*Textiles*) ordito ▶ VI deformarsi ▶ VT deformare; (*fig*) corrompere

warpath ['wɔ:pɑ:θ] N: **to be on the ~** (*fig*) essere sul sentiero di guerra

warped [wɔ:pt] ADJ (*wood*) curvo(-a); (*fig: character, sense of humour etc*) contorto(-a)

warrant ['wɔrnt] N (*voucher*) buono; (*Law: to arrest*) mandato di cattura; (: *to search*) mandato di perquisizione ▶ VT (*justify, merit*) giustificare

warrant officer N sottufficiale m

warranty ['wɔrəntɪ] N garanzia; **under ~** (*Comm*) in garanzia

warren ['wɔrən] N (*of rabbits*) tana

warring ['wɔ:rɪŋ] ADJ (*interests etc*) opposto(-a), in lotta; (*nations*) in guerra

warrior ['wɔrɪə'] N guerriero(-a)

Warsaw ['wɔ:sɔ:] N Varsavia

warship ['wɔ:ʃɪp] N nave f da guerra

wart [wɔ:t] N verruca

wartime ['wɔ:taɪm] N: **in ~** in tempo di guerra

wary ['wɛərɪ] ADJ prudente; **to be ~ about** *or* **of doing sth** andare cauto nel fare qc

was [wɔz] PT *of* **be**

wash [wɔʃ] VT lavare; (*sweep, carry: sea etc*) portare, trascinare ▶ VI lavarsi; (*sea*): **to ~ over/against sth** infrangersi su/contro qc ▶ N lavaggio; (*of ship*) scia; **to give sth a ~** lavare qc, dare una lavata a qc; **to have a ~** lavarsi; **he was washed overboard** fu trascinato in mare (dalle onde)

▶ **wash away** VT (*stain*) togliere lavando; (*river etc*) trascinare via

▶ **wash down** VT lavare

▶ **wash off** VI andare via con il lavaggio

▶ **wash up** VI (*BRIT*) lavare i piatti; (*US: have a wash*) lavarsi

Wash. ABBR (*US*) = **Washington**

washable ['wɔʃəbl] ADJ lavabile

washbasin ['wɔʃbeɪsn], (*US*) **washbowl** N lavabo

washcloth ['wɔʃklɔθ] N (*US*) pezzuola (per lavarsi)

washer ['wɔʃə'] N (*Tech*) rondella

washing ['wɔʃɪŋ] N (*BRIT: linen etc*) bucato; **dirty ~** biancheria da lavare

washing line N (*BRIT*) corda del bucato

washing machine N lavatrice f

washing powder N (*BRIT*) detersivo (in polvere)

Washington ['wɔʃɪŋtən] N Washington f

washing-up [wɔʃɪŋ'ʌp] N (*dishes*) piatti mpl sporchi; **to do the ~** lavare i piatti

washing-up liquid N (*BRIT*) detersivo liquido (per stoviglie)

wash-out ['wɔʃaut] N (*col*) disastro

washroom ['wɔʃrum] N gabinetto

wasn't ['wɔznt] = **was not**

Wasp, WASP [wɔsp] N ABBR (*US*: = *White Anglo-Saxon Protestant*) W.A.S.P. m (*protestante bianco anglosassone*)

wasp [wɔsp] N vespa

waspish ['wɔspɪʃ] ADJ litigioso(-a)

wastage ['weɪstɪdʒ] N spreco; (*in manufacturing*) scarti mpl

waste [weɪst] N spreco; (*of time*) perdita; (*rubbish*) rifiuti mpl; (*also:* **household waste**) immondizie fpl ▶ ADJ (*material*) di scarto; (*food*) avanzato(-a); (*energy, heat*) sprecato(-a); (*land, ground: in city*) abbandonato(-a); (: *in country*) incolto(-a) ▶ VT sprecare; (*time, opportunity*) perdere; **wastes** NPL distesa desolata; **it's a ~ of money** sono soldi sprecati; **to go to ~** andare sprecato; **to lay ~** devastare

▶ **waste away** VI deperire

wastebasket ['weɪstbɑ:skɪt] N = **wastepaper basket**

waste disposal, waste disposal unit N (*BRIT*) eliminatore m di rifiuti

wasteful ['weɪstful] ADJ sprecone(-a); (*process*) dispendioso(-a)

waste ground N (*BRIT*) terreno incolto *or* abbandonato

wasteland ['weɪstlænd] N terra desolata

wastepaper basket ['weɪstpeɪpə-] N cestino per la carta straccia

waste pipe N tubo di scarico

waste products NPL (*Industry*) materiali mpl di scarto

waster ['weɪstə'] N (*col*) buono(-a) a nulla

watch [wɔtʃ] N (*wristwatch*) orologio (da polso); (*act of watching, vigilance*) sorveglianza; (*guard: Mil, Naut*) guardia; (: *Naut: spell of duty*) quarto ▶ VT (*look at*) osservare; (: *match, programme*) guardare; (*spy on, guard*) sorvegliare, tenere d'occhio; (*be careful of*) fare attenzione a ▶ VI osservare, guardare; (*keep guard*) fare *or* montare la guardia; **to keep a close ~ on sb/sth** tener bene d'occhio qn/qc; **~ how you drive/what you're doing** attento a come guidi/quel che fai

▶ **watch out** VI fare attenzione

watchband ['wɔtʃbænd] N (*US*) cinturino da orologio

W

watchdog ['wɒtʃdɒg] N cane m da guardia; (fig) sorvegliante mf

watchful ['wɒtʃful] ADJ attento(-a), vigile

watchmaker ['wɒtʃmeɪkəʳ] N orologiaio(-a)

watchman ['wɒtʃmən] N (irreg) guardiano; (also: **night watchman**) guardiano notturno

watch stem N (US) corona di carica

watch strap N cinturino da orologio

watchword ['wɒtʃwɜːd] N parola d'ordine

water ['wɔːtəʳ] N acqua ▶ VT (plant) annaffiare ▶ VI (eyes) lacrimare; **in British waters** nelle acque territoriali britanniche; **I'd like a drink of** ~ vorrei un bicchier d'acqua; **to pass** ~ orinare; **to make sb's mouth** ~ far venire l'acquolina in bocca a qn

▶ **water down** VT (milk) diluire; (fig: story) edulcorare

water closet N (BRIT) W.C. m inv, gabinetto

watercolour, (US) **watercolor** ['wɔːtəkʌləʳ] N (picture) acquerello; **watercolours** NPL colori mpl per acquerelli

water-cooled ['wɔːtəkuːld] ADJ raffreddato(-a) ad acqua

watercress ['wɔːtəkrɛs] N crescione m

waterfall ['wɔːtəfɔːl] N cascata

waterfront ['wɔːtəfrʌnt] N (seafront) lungomare m; (at docks) banchina

water heater N scaldabagno

water hole N pozza d'acqua

water ice N (BRIT) sorbetto

watering can ['wɔːtərɪŋ-] N annaffiatoio

water level N livello dell'acqua; (of flood) livello delle acque

water lily N ninfea

waterline ['wɔːtəlaɪn] N (Naut) linea di galleggiamento

waterlogged ['wɔːtəlɒgd] ADJ saturo(-a) d'acqua; imbevuto(-a) d'acqua; (football pitch etc) allagato(-a)

watermark ['wɔːtəmɑːk] N (on paper) filigrana

watermelon ['wɔːtəmɛlən] N anguria, cocomero

water polo N pallanuoto f

waterproof ['wɔːtəpruːf] ADJ impermeabile

water-repellent ['wɔːtərɪ'pɛlənt] ADJ idrorepellente

watershed ['wɔːtəʃɛd] N (Geo, fig) spartiacque m

water-skiing ['wɔːtəskiːɪŋ] N sci m acquatico

water softener N addolcitore m; (substance) anti-calcare m

water tank N serbatoio d'acqua

watertight ['wɔːtətaɪt] ADJ stagno(-a)

water vapour N vapore m acqueo

waterway ['wɔːtəweɪ] N corso d'acqua navigabile

waterworks ['wɔːtəwɜːks] NPL impianto idrico

watery ['wɔːtərɪ] ADJ (colour) slavato(-a); (coffee) acquoso(-a)

watt [wɒt] N watt m inv

wattage ['wɒtɪdʒ] N wattaggio

wattle ['wɒtl] N graticcio

wave [weɪv] N onda; (of hand) gesto, segno; (in hair) ondulazione f; (fig: of enthusiasm, strikes etc) ondata ▶ VI fare un cenno con la mano; (branches, grass) ondeggiare; (flag) sventolare ▶ VT (hand) fare un gesto con; (handkerchief) sventolare; (stick) brandire; (hair) ondulare; **short/medium/long** ~ (Radio) onde corte/medie/lunghe; **the new** ~ (Cine, Mus) la new wave; **to** ~ **sb goodbye, to** ~ **goodbye to sb** fare un cenno d'addio a qn; **he waved us over to his table** ci invitò con un cenno al suo tavolo

▶ **wave aside, wave away** VT (person): **to** ~ **sb aside** fare cenno a qn di spostarsi; (fig: suggestion, objection) respingere, rifiutare (: doubts) scacciare

waveband ['weɪvbænd] N gamma di lunghezze d'onda

wavelength ['weɪvlɛŋθ] N lunghezza d'onda

waver ['weɪvəʳ] VI esitare; (voice) tremolare

wavy ['weɪvɪ] ADJ ondulato(-a); ondeggiante

wax [wæks] N cera ▶ VT dare la cera a; (car) lucidare ▶ VI (moon) crescere

waxworks ['wækswɜːks] NPL cere fpl; museo delle cere

way [weɪ] N via, strada; (path, access) passaggio; (distance) distanza; (direction) parte f, direzione f; (manner) modo, stile m; (habit) abitudine f; (condition) condizione f; **which** ~? — **this** ~ da che parte or in quale direzione? — da questa parte or per di qua; **to crawl one's** ~ **to ...** raggiungere ... strisciando; **he lied his** ~ **out of it** se l'è cavata mentendo; **to lose one's** ~ perdere la strada; **on the** ~ (en route) per strada; (expected) in arrivo; **you pass it on your** ~ **home** ci passi davanti andando a casa; **to be on one's** ~ essere in cammino or sulla strada; **to be in the** ~ bloccare il passaggio; (fig) essere tra i piedi or d'impiccio; **to keep out of sb's** ~ evitare qn; **it's a long** ~ **away** è molto lontano da qui; **the village is rather out of the** ~ il villaggio è abbastanza fuori mano; **to go out of one's** ~ **to do** (fig) mettercela tutta or fare di tutto per fare; **to be under** ~ (work, project) essere in corso; **to lose one's** ~ perdere la strada; **to make** ~ **(for sb/sth)** far strada (a qn/qc); (fig) lasciare il posto or far largo (a qn/qc); **to get one's own** ~ fare come si vuole; **put it the right** ~ **up** (BRIT) mettilo in piedi dalla parte giusta; **to be the wrong** ~ **round** essere al contrario; **he's in a bad** ~ è ridotto male; **in a** ~ in un certo senso; **in some ways** sotto certi aspetti; **in the ~ of** come; **by ~ of** (*through*) attraverso; (*as a sort of*) come; **"~ in"** (BRIT) "entrata", "ingresso"; **"~ out"** (BRIT) "uscita"; **the ~ back** la via del ritorno; **this ~ and that** di qua e di là; **"give ~"** (BRIT *Aut*) "dare la precedenza"; **no ~!** (*col*) neanche per idea!; **by the ~ ...** a proposito ...

waybill ['weɪbɪl] N (*Comm*) bolla di accompagnamento

waylay [weɪ'leɪ] VT (*irreg: like* **lay**) tendere un agguato a; attendere al passaggio; (*fig*): **I got waylaid** ho avuto un contrattempo

wayside ['weɪsaɪd] N bordo della strada; **to fall by the ~** (*fig*) perdersi lungo la strada

way station N (*US Rail*) stazione *f* secondaria; (*fig*) tappa

wayward ['weɪwəd] ADJ capriccioso(-a); testardo(-a)

WC ['dʌblju'si:] N ABBR (BRIT: = *water closet*) W.C. *m inv*, gabinetto

WCC N ABBR (= *World Council of Churches*) Consiglio Ecumenico delle Chiese

we [wi:] PL PRON noi; **here we are** eccoci

weak [wi:k] ADJ debole; (*health*) precario(-a); (*beam etc*) fragile; (*tea, coffee*) leggero(-a); **to grow ~(er)** indebolirsi

weaken ['wi:kən] VI indebolirsi ▶ VT indebolire

weak-kneed ['wi:k'ni:d] ADJ (*fig*) debole, codardo(-a)

weakling ['wi:klɪŋ] N smidollato(-a); debole *mf*

weakly ['wi:klɪ] ADJ deboluccio(-a), gracile ▶ ADV debolmente

weakness ['wi:knɪs] N debolezza; (*fault*) punto debole, difetto; **to have a ~ for** avere un debole per

wealth [wɛlθ] N (*money, resources*) ricchezza, ricchezze *fpl*; (*of details*) abbondanza, profusione *f*

wealth tax N imposta sul patrimonio

wealthy ['wɛlθɪ] ADJ ricco(-a)

wean [wi:n] VT svezzare

weapon ['wɛpən] N arma; **weapons of mass destruction** armi di distruzione di massa

wear [wɛəʳ] (*pt* **wore** [wɔːʳ], *pp* **worn** [wɔːn]) N (*use*) uso; (*deterioration through use*) logorio, usura; (*clothing*): **sports/baby ~** abbigliamento sportivo/per neonati ▶ VT (*clothes*) portare; (*put on*) mettersi; (*look, smile, beard etc*) avere; (*damage: through use*) consumare ▶ VI (*last*) durare; (*rub etc through*) consumarsi; **~ and tear** usura, consumo; **town/evening ~** abiti *mpl* or tenuta da città/ sera; **to ~ a hole in sth** bucare qc a furia di usarlo

▶ **wear away** VT consumare; erodere ▶ VI consumarsi; essere eroso(-a)

▶ **wear down** VT consumare; (*strength*) esaurire

▶ **wear off** VI sparire lentamente

▶ **wear on** VI passare

▶ **wear out** VT consumare; (*person, strength*) esaurire

wearable ['wɛərəbl] ADJ indossabile

wearily ['wɪərɪlɪ] ADV stancamente

weariness ['wɪərɪnɪs] N stanchezza

wearisome ['wɪərɪsəm] ADJ (*tiring*) estenuante; (*boring*) noioso(-a)

weary ['wɪərɪ] ADJ stanco(-a); (*tiring*) faticoso(-a) ▶ VT stancare ▶ VI: **to ~ of** stancarsi di

weasel ['wi:zl] N (*Zool*) donnola

weather ['wɛðəʳ] N tempo ▶ VT (*wood*) stagionare; (*storm, crisis*) superare; **what's the ~ like?** che tempo fa?; **under the ~** (*fig: ill*) poco bene

weather-beaten ['wɛðəbi:tn] ADJ (*person*) segnato(-a) dalle intemperie; (*building*) logorato(-a) dalle intemperie

weather forecast N previsioni *fpl* del tempo, bollettino meteorologico

weatherman ['wɛðəmæn] N (*irreg*) meteorologo

weatherproof ['wɛðəpru:f] ADJ (*garment*) impermeabile

weather report N bollettino meteorologico

weather vane N = **weather cock**

weave [wi:v] (*pt* **wove** [wəuv], *pp* **woven** ['wəuvn]) VT (*cloth*) tessere; (*basket*) intrecciare ▶ VI (*pt, pp* **weaved**) (*fig: move in and out*) zigzagare

weaver ['wi:vəʳ] N tessitore(-trice)

weaving ['wi:vɪŋ] N tessitura

web [wɛb] N (*of spider*) ragnatela; (*on foot*) palma; (*fabric, also fig*) tessuto; **the (World Wide) W~** la Rete

web address N indirizzo Internet

webbed [wɛbd] ADJ (*foot*) palmato(-a)

webbing ['wɛbɪŋ] N (*on chair*) cinghie *fpl*

webcam ['wɛbkæm] N webcam *f inv*

webinar ['wɛbɪnaːʳ] N (*Comput*) webinar *m inv*

webmail ['wɛbmeɪl] N (*Comput*) webmail *f*

web page N (*Comput*) pagina *f* web *inv*

website ['wɛbsaɪt] N (*Comput*) sito (Internet)

wed [wɛd] (*pt, pp* **wedded**) VT sposare ▶ VI sposarsi ▶ N: **the newly-weds** gli sposi novelli

Wed. ABBR (= *Wednesday*) mer.

we'd [wi:d] = **we had**; **we would**

wedded ['wɛdɪd] PT, PP *of* **wed**

wedding ['wɛdɪŋ] N matrimonio; **silver/ golden ~** nozze *fpl* d'argento/d'oro

wedding anniversary N anniversario di matrimonio

wedding day N giorno delle nozze or del matrimonio

wedding dress N abito nuziale
wedding present N regalo di nozze
wedding ring N fede f
wedge [wɛdʒ] N (of wood etc) cuneo; (under door etc) zeppa; (of cake) spicchio, fetta ▶ VT mettere una zeppa sotto (or in); (fix) fissare con zeppe; (pack tightly) incastrare; **to ~ a door open** tenere aperta una porta con un fermo
wedge-heeled shoes ['wɛdʒhi:ld-] NPL scarpe fpl con tacco a zeppa
wedlock ['wɛdlɔk] N vincolo matrimoniale
Wednesday ['wɛnzdɪ] N mercoledì m inv; see also **Tuesday**
wee [wi:] ADJ (SCOTTISH) piccolo(-a)
weed [wi:d] N erbaccia ▶ VT diserbare
▶ **weed out** VT fare lo spoglio di
weed-killer ['wi:dkɪlə^r] N diserbante m
weedy ['wi:dɪ] ADJ (man) allampanato
week [wi:k] N settimana; **once/twice a ~** una volta/due volte alla settimana; **in 2 weeks' time** fra 2 settimane, fra 15 giorni; **Tuesday ~, a ~ on Tuesday** martedì a otto; **a ~ today** oggi a otto
weekday ['wi:kdeɪ] N giorno feriale; (Comm) giornata lavorativa; **on weekdays** durante la settimana
weekend [wi:k'ɛnd] N fine settimana m inv or f inv, weekend m inv
weekend case N borsa da viaggio
weekly ['wi:klɪ] ADV ogni settimana, settimanalmente ▶ ADJ, N settimanale (m)
weep [wi:p] (pt, pp **wept** [wɛpt]) VI (person) piangere; (Med: wound etc) essudare
weeping willow ['wi:pɪŋ-] N salice m piangente
weepy ['wi:pɪ] N (col) film m inv or storia strappalacrime
weft [wɛft] N (Textiles) trama
weigh [weɪ] VT, VI pesare; **to ~ anchor** salpare or levare l'ancora; **to ~ the pros and cons** valutare i pro e i contro
▶ **weigh down** VT (branch) piegare; (fig: with worry) opprimere, caricare
▶ **weigh out** VT (goods) pesare
▶ **weigh up** VT valutare
weighbridge ['weɪbrɪdʒ] N bascula
weighing machine ['weɪɪŋ-] N pesa
weight [weɪt] N peso; **sold by ~** venduto(-a) a peso; **weights and measures** pesi e misure; **to put on/lose ~** ingrassare/dimagrire
weighting ['weɪtɪŋ] N: **~ allowance** indennità f inv speciale (per carovita ecc)
weightlessness ['weɪtlɪsnɪs] N mancanza di peso
weightlifter ['weɪtlɪftə^r] N pesista m
weightlifting N sollevamento pesi
weight training N: **to do ~** allenarsi con i pesi

weighty ['weɪtɪ] ADJ pesante; (fig) importante, grave
weir [wɪə^r] N diga
weird [wɪəd] ADJ strano(-a), bizzarro(-a); (eerie) soprannaturale
weirdo ['wɪədəu] N (col) tipo(-a) allucinante
welcome ['wɛlkəm] ADJ benvenuto(-a) ▶ N accoglienza, benvenuto ▶ VT accogliere cordialmente; (also: **bid welcome**) dare il benvenuto a; (: be glad of) rallegrarsi di; **to be ~** essere il benvenuto(-a); **to make sb ~** accogliere bene qn; **you're ~** (after thanks) prego; **you're ~ to try** provi pure
welcoming ['wɛlkəmɪŋ] ADJ accogliente
weld [wɛld] N saldatura ▶ VT saldare
welder ['wɛldə^r] N (person) saldatore m
welding ['wɛldɪŋ] N saldatura (autogena)
welfare ['wɛlfɛə^r] N benessere m
welfare state N stato sociale
welfare work N assistenza sociale
well [wɛl] N pozzo ▶ ADV bene ▶ ADJ: **to be ~** (person) stare bene ▶ EXCL allora!; ma!; ebbene!; **~ done!** bravo(-a)!; **get ~ soon!** guarisci presto!; **to do ~** andare bene; **to do ~ in sth** riuscire in qc; **to be doing ~** stare bene; **to think ~ of sb** avere una buona opinione di qn; **I don't feel ~** non mi sento bene; **as ~** (in addition) anche; **X as ~ as Y** sia X che Y; **he did as ~ as he could** ha fatto come meglio poteva; **you might as ~ tell me** potresti anche dirmelo; **it would be as ~ to ask** sarebbe bene chiedere; **~, as I was saying …** dunque, come stavo dicendo …
▶ **well up** VI (tears, emotions) sgorgare
we'll [wi:l] = **we will; we shall**
well-behaved ['wɛlbɪ'heɪvd] ADJ ubbidiente
well-being ['wɛl'bi:ɪŋ] N benessere m
well-bred ['wɛl'brɛd] ADJ educato(-a), beneducato(-a)
well-built ['wɛl'bɪlt] ADJ (person) ben fatto(-a)
well-chosen ['wɛl'tʃəuzn] ADJ (remarks, words) ben scelto(-a), appropriato(-a)
well-developed ['wɛldɪ'vɛləpt] ADJ sviluppato(-a)
well-disposed ['wɛldɪs'pəuzd] ADJ: **~ to(wards)** bendisposto(-a) verso
well-dressed ['wɛl'drɛst] ADJ ben vestito(-a), vestito(-a) bene
well-earned ['wɛl'ə:nd] ADJ (rest) meritato(-a)
well-groomed ['wɛl'gru:md] ADJ curato(-a), azzimato(-a)
well-heeled ['wɛl'hi:ld] ADJ (col: wealthy) agiato(-a), facoltoso(-a)
wellies ['wɛlɪz] NPL (BRIT col) stivali mpl di gomma
well-informed ['wɛlɪn'fɔ:md] ADJ ben informato(-a)

Wellington ['wɛlɪŋtən] N Wellington f
wellingtons ['wɛlɪŋtənz] NPL (also:
wellington boots) stivali mpl di gomma
well-kept ['wɛl'kɛpt] ADJ (house, grounds,
secret) ben tenuto(-a); (hair, hands) ben
curato(-a)
well-known ['wɛl'nəun] ADJ noto(-a),
famoso(-a)
well-mannered ['wɛl'mænəd] ADJ ben
educato(-a)
well-meaning ['wɛl'mi:nɪŋ] ADJ ben
intenzionato(-a)
well-nigh ['wɛl'naɪ] ADV: ~ **impossible**
quasi impossibile
well-off ['wɛl'ɔf] ADJ benestante,
danaroso(-a)
well-paid [wel'peɪd] ADJ ben pagato(-a)
well-read ['wɛl'rɛd] ADJ colto(-a)
well-spoken ['wɛl'spəukn] ADJ che parla
bene
well-stocked ['wɛl'stɔkt] ADJ (shop, larder)
ben fornito(-a)
well-timed ['wɛl'taɪmd] ADJ opportuno(-a)
well-to-do ['wɛltə'du:] ADJ abbiente,
benestante
well-wisher ['wɛlwɪʃəʳ] N
ammiratore(-trice); **letters from
well-wishers** lettere fpl di incoraggiamento
well-woman clinic ['wɛlwumən-] N
≈ consultorio (familiare)
Welsh [wɛlʃ] ADJ gallese ▸ N (Ling) gallese m;
the ~ npl i gallesi; **the ~ National Assembly**
il Parlamento gallese
Welshman ['wɛlʃmən] N (irreg) gallese m
Welsh rarebit N crostino al formaggio
Welshwoman ['wɛlʃwumən] N (irreg)
gallese f
welter ['wɛltəʳ] N massa, mucchio
went [wɛnt] PT of **go**
wept [wɛpt] PT, PP of **weep**
were [wəːʳ] PT of **be**
we're [wɪəʳ] = **we are**
weren't [wəːnt] = **were not**
werewolf ['wɪəwulf] (pl **-wolves** [-wulvz]) N
licantropo, lupo mannaro (col)
west [wɛst] N ovest m, occidente m, ponente
m ▸ ADJ (a) ovest inv, occidentale ▸ ADV verso
ovest; **the W~** l'Occidente
westbound ['wɛstbaund] ADJ (traffic)
diretto(-a) a ovest; (carriageway) ovest inv
West Country N: **the** ~ il sud-ovest
dell'Inghilterra
westerly ['wɛstəlɪ] ADJ (wind) occidentale,
da ovest
western ['wɛstən] ADJ occidentale, dell'ovest
▸ N (Cine) western m inv
westerner ['wɛstənəʳ] N occidentale mf
westernized ['wɛstənaɪzd] ADJ
occidentalizzato(-a)

West German ADJ, N (formerly) tedesco(-a)
occidentale
West Germany N (formerly) Germania
Occidentale
West Indian ADJ delle Indie Occidentali
▸ N abitante mf (or originario(-a)) delle Indie
Occidentali
West Indies [-'ɪndɪz] NPL: **the** ~ le Indie
Occidentali
Westminster ['wɛstmɪnstəʳ] N il
parlamento (britannico)
westward ['wɛstwəd], **westwards**
['wɛstwədz] ADV verso ovest
wet [wɛt] ADJ umido(-a), bagnato(-a); (soaked)
fradicio(-a); (rainy) piovoso(-a) ▸ N (BRIT Pol)
politico moderato ▸ VT: **to ~ one's pants** or
o.s. farsi la pipì addosso; **to get ~** bagnarsi;
"~ paint" "vernice fresca"
wet blanket N (fig) guastafeste mf
wetness ['wɛtnɪs] N umidità
wet suit N tuta da sub
we've [wi:v] = **we have**
whack [wæk] VT picchiare, battere
whacked [wækt] ADJ (col: tired) sfinito(-a),
a pezzi
whale [weɪl] N (Zool) balena
whaler ['weɪləʳ] N (ship) baleniera
whaling ['weɪlɪŋ] N caccia alla balena
wharf [wɔːf] (pl **wharves** [wɔːvz]) N banchina

(KEYWORD)

what [wɔt] ADJ **1** (in direct/indirect questions) che;
quale; **what size is it?** che taglia è?; **what
colour is it?** di che colore è?; **what books do
you want?** quali or che libri vuole?; **for what
reason?** per quale motivo?
2 (in exclamations) che; **what a mess!** che
disordine!
▸ PRON **1** (interrogative) che cosa, cosa, che;
what's in there? cosa c'è lì dentro?; **what is
his address?** qual è il suo indirizzo?; **what
will it cost?** quanto costerà?; **what are you
doing?** che or (che) cosa fai?; **what are you
talking about?** di che cosa parli?; **what's
happening?** che or (che) cosa succede?;
what is it called? come si chiama?; **what
about me?** e io?; **what about doing ...?** e se
facessimo ...?
2 (relative) ciò che, quello che; **I saw what
you did** ho visto quello che hai fatto; **I saw
what was on the table** ho visto cosa c'era
sul tavolo; **what I want is a cup of tea** ciò
che voglio adesso è una tazza di tè
3 (indirect use) (che) cosa; **he asked me what
she had said** mi ha chiesto che cosa avesse
detto; **tell me what you're thinking about**
dimmi a cosa stai pensando; **I don't know
what to do** non so cosa fare
▸ EXCL (disbelieving) cosa!, come!

W

whatever [wɔt'ɛvəʳ] ADJ: ~ **book** qualunque or qualsiasi libro + sub ▶ PRON: **do ~ is necessary/you want** faccia qualunque or qualsiasi cosa sia necessaria/lei voglia; ~ **happens** qualunque cosa accada; **no reason ~** or **whatsoever** nessuna ragione affatto or al mondo; ~ **it costs** costi quello che costi; **nothing ~** proprio niente

whatsoever [wɔtsəu'ɛvəʳ] ADJ, PRON = **whatever**

wheat [wi:t] N grano, frumento

wheatgerm ['wi:tdʒə:m] N germe m di grano

wheatmeal ['wi:tmi:l] N farina integrale di frumento

wheedle ['wi:dl] VT: **to ~ sb into doing sth** convincere qn a fare qc (con lusinghe); **to ~ sth out of sb** ottenere qc da qn (con lusinghe)

wheel [wi:l] N ruota; (Aut: also: **steering wheel**) volante m; (Naut) (ruota del) timone m ▶ VT spingere ▶ VI (birds) roteare; (also: **wheel round**) girare

wheelbarrow ['wi:lbærəu] N carriola

wheelbase ['wi:lbeɪs] N interasse m

wheelchair ['wi:ltʃɛəʳ] N sedia a rotelle

wheel clamp N (Aut): **wheel clamps** ganasce fpl (per vetture in sosta vietata)

wheeler-dealer ['wi:lə'di:ləʳ] N trafficone m, maneggione m

wheelie-bin ['wi:lɪbɪn] N (BRIT) bidone m (della spazzatura) a rotelle

wheeling ['wi:lɪŋ] N: ~ **and dealing** maneggi mpl

wheeze [wi:z] N respiro affannoso ▶ VI ansimare

wheezy ['wi:zɪ] ADJ (person) che respira con affanno; (breath) sibilante

WHEN | KEYWORD

when [wɛn] ADV quando; **when did it happen?** quando è successo?
▶ CONJ **1** (at, during, after the time that) quando; **she was reading when I came in** quando sono entrato lei leggeva; **that was when I needed you** era allora che avevo bisogno di te
2 (on, at which): **on the day when I met him** il giorno in cui l'ho incontrato; **one day when it was raining** un giorno che pioveva
3 (whereas) quando, mentre; **you said I was wrong when in fact I was right** mi hai detto che avevo torto, quando in realtà avevo ragione

whenever [wɛn'ɛvəʳ] ADV quando mai ▶ CONJ quando; (every time that) ogni volta che; **I go ~ I can** ci vado ogni volta che posso

where [wɛəʳ] ADV, CONJ dove; **this is ~** è qui che; ~ **are you from?** di dov'è?; ~ **possible** quando è possibile, se possibile

whereabouts [wɛərə'bauts] ADV dove
▶ N: **sb's ~** luogo dove qn si trova

whereas [wɛər'æz] CONJ mentre

whereby [wɛə'baɪ] ADV (formal) per cui

whereupon [wɛərə'pɔn] ADV al che

wherever [wɛər'ɛvəʳ] ADV dove mai ▶ CONJ dovunque + sub; (interrogative) dove mai; **sit ~ you like** si sieda dove vuole

wherewithal ['wɛərwɪðɔ:l] N: **the ~ (to do sth)** i mezzi (per fare qc)

whet [wɛt] VT (tool) affilare; (appetite etc) stimolare

whether ['wɛðəʳ] CONJ se; **I don't know ~ to accept or not** non so se accettare o no; **it's doubtful ~** è poco probabile che; ~ **you go or not** che lei vada o no

whey [weɪ] N siero

KEYWORD

which [wɪtʃ] ADJ **1** (interrogative: direct, indirect) quale; **which picture do you want?** quale quadro vuole?; **which one?** quale?; **which one of you did it?** chi di voi lo ha fatto?; **tell me which one you want** mi dica quale vuole
2: **in which case** nel qual caso; **by which time** e a quel punto
▶ PRON **1** (interrogative) quale; **which (of these) are yours?** quali di questi sono suoi?; **which of you are coming?** chi di voi viene?
2 (relative) che; (: indirect) cui, il (la) quale; **the apple which you ate/which is on the table** la mela che hai mangiato/che è sul tavolo; **the chair on which you are sitting** la sedia sulla quale or su cui sei seduto; **the book of which we were speaking** il libro del quale stavamo parlando; **he said he knew, which is true** ha detto che lo sapeva, il che è vero; **I don't mind which** non mi importa quale; **after which** dopo di che

whichever [wɪtʃ'ɛvəʳ] ADJ: **take ~ book you prefer** prenda qualsiasi libro che preferisce; ~ **book you take** qualsiasi libro prenda; ~ **way you ...** in qualunque modo lei ... + sub

whiff [wɪf] N odore m; **to catch a ~ of sth** sentire l'odore di qc

while [waɪl] N momento ▶ CONJ mentre; (as long as) finché; (although) sebbene + sub; per quanto + sub; **for a ~** per un po'; **in a ~** tra poco; **all the ~** tutto il tempo; **we'll make it worth your ~** faremo in modo che le valga la pena
▶ **while away** VT (time) far passare

whilst [waɪlst] CONJ = **while**

whim [wɪm] N capriccio

whimper ['wɪmpəʳ] N piagnucolio ▶ VI piagnucolare

whimsical ['wɪmzɪkl] ADJ (*person*) capriccioso(-a); (*look*) strano(-a)

whine [waɪn] N gemito ▶ VI gemere; uggiolare; piagnucolare

whip [wɪp] N frusta; (*for riding*) frustino; (*Pol: person*) capogruppo (*che sovrintende alla disciplina dei colleghi di partito*); *vedi nota* ▶ VT frustare; (*Culin: cream, eggs etc*) sbattere; (*snatch*) sollevare (*or* estrarre) bruscamente

▶ **whip up** VT (*cream*) montare, sbattere; (*col: meal*) improvvisare; (*: stir up: support, feeling*) suscitare, stimolare

> Nel Parlamento britannico i *whips* sono parlamentari incaricati di mantenere la disciplina tra i deputati del loro partito durante le votazioni e di verificare la loro presenza in aula.

whiplash ['wɪplæʃ] N (*Med: also:* **whiplash injury**) colpo di frusta

whipped cream ['wɪpt-] N panna montata

whipping boy ['wɪpɪŋ-] N (*fig*) capro espiatorio

whip-round ['wɪpraund] N (*BRIT*) colletta

whirl [wə:l] N turbine *m* ▶ VT (*far*) girare rapidamente; (*far*) turbinare ▶ VI turbinare; (*dancers*) volteggiare; (*leaves, water, dust*) sollevarsi in un vortice

whirlpool ['wə:lpu:l] N mulinello

whirlwind ['wə:lwɪnd] N turbine *m*

whirr [wə:ʳ] VI ronzare

whisk [wɪsk] N (*Culin*) frusta; frullino ▶ VT sbattere, frullare; **to ~ sb away** *or* **off** portar via qn a tutta velocità

whiskers ['wɪskəz] NPL (*of animal*) baffi *mpl*; (*of man*) favoriti *mpl*

whisky, (*IRISH, US*) **whiskey** ['wɪskɪ] N whisky *m inv*

whisper ['wɪspəʳ] N bisbiglio, sussurro; (*rumour*) voce *f* ▶ VT, VI bisbigliare, sussurrare; **to ~ sth to sb** bisbigliare qc a qn

whispering ['wɪspərɪŋ] N bisbiglio

whist [wɪst] N (*BRIT*) whist *m*

whistle ['wɪsl] N (*sound*) fischio; (*object*) fischietto ▶ VI, VT fischiare; **to ~ a tune** fischiettare un motivetto

whistle-stop ['wɪslstɔp] ADJ: **~ tour** (*Pol, fig*) rapido giro

Whit [wɪt] N Pentecoste *f*

white [waɪt] ADJ bianco(-a); (*with fear*) pallido(-a) ▶ N bianco; (*person*) bianco(-a); **to turn** *or* **go ~** (*person*) sbiancare; (*hair*) diventare bianco; **the whites** (*washing*) i capi bianchi; **tennis whites** completo da tennis

whitebait ['waɪtbeɪt] N bianchetti *mpl*

whiteboard ['waɪtbɔ:d] N lavagna bianca; **interactive ~** lavagna interattiva

white-collar worker ['waɪtkɔlə-] N impiegato(-a)

white elephant N (*fig*) oggetto (*or* progetto) costoso ma inutile

white goods NPL (*appliances*) elettrodomestici *mpl*; (*linens*) biancheria per la casa

white-hot [waɪt'hɔt] ADJ (*metal*) incandescente

White House N: **the ~** la Casa Bianca; *vedi nota*

> La *White House* è la residenza ufficiale del presidente degli Stati Uniti e ha sede a Washington DC. Spesso il termine viene usato per indicare l'esecutivo del governo statunitense.

white lie N bugia pietosa

whiteness ['waɪtnɪs] N bianchezza

white noise N rumore *m* bianco

white paper N (*Pol*) libro bianco

whitewash ['waɪtwɔʃ] N (*paint*) bianco di calce ▶ VT imbiancare; (*fig*) coprire

whiting ['waɪtɪŋ] N (*pl inv: fish*) merlango

Whit Monday N lunedì *m inv* di Pentecoste

Whitsun ['wɪtsn] N Pentecoste *f*

whittle ['wɪtl] VT: **to ~ away, ~ down** ridurre, tagliare

whizz [wɪz] VI: **to ~ past** *or* **by** passare sfrecciando

whizz kid N (*col*) prodigio

WHO N ABBR (= *World Health Organization*) O.M.S. *f* (= *Organizzazione mondiale della sanità*)

(KEYWORD)

who [hu:] PRON **1** (*interrogative*) chi; **who is it?, who's there?** chi è?

2 (*relative*) che; **the man who spoke to me** l'uomo che ha parlato con me; **those who can swim** quelli che sanno nuotare

whodunit [hu:'dʌnɪt] N (*col*) giallo

whoever [hu:'ɛvəʳ] PRON: **~ finds it** chiunque lo trovi; **ask ~ you like** lo chieda a chiunque vuole; **~ she marries** chiunque sposerà, non importa chi sposerà; **~ told you that?** chi mai gliel'ha detto?

whole [həul] ADJ (*complete*) tutto(-a), completo(-a); (*not broken*) intero(-a), intatto(-a) ▶ N (*all*): **the ~ of** tutto(-a) il; (*not broken*) tutto; **the ~ lot (of it)** tutto; **the ~ lot (of them)** tutti; **the ~ of the time** tutto il tempo; **the ~ of the town** tutta la città, la città intera; **on the ~, as a ~** nel complesso, nell'insieme; **~ villages were destroyed** interi paesi furono distrutti

wholefood N, **wholefoods** NPL cibo integrale

wholehearted [həul'hɑ:tɪd] ADJ sincero(-a)

wholeheartedly [həul'hɑ:tɪdlɪ] ADV sentitamente, di tutto cuore

wholemeal ['həulmi:l] ADJ (*BRIT: flour, bread*) integrale

w

whole note N (US) semibreve f
wholesale ['həulseɪl] N commercio or vendita all'ingrosso ▶ ADJ all'ingrosso; (*destruction*) totale
wholesaler ['həulseɪlə'] N grossista mf
wholesome ['həulsəm] ADJ sano(-a); (*climate*) salubre
wholewheat ['həulwi:t] ADJ = **wholemeal**
wholly ['həulɪ] ADV completamente, del tutto

(KEYWORD)

whom [hu:m] PRON **1** (*interrogative*) chi; **whom did you see?** chi hai visto?; **to whom did you give it?** a chi lo hai dato?
2 (*relative*) che, prep + il (la) quale; **the man whom I saw** l'uomo che ho visto; **the man to whom I spoke** l'uomo al or con il quale ho parlato; **those to whom I spoke** le persone alle or con le quali ho parlato

whooping cough ['hu:pɪŋ-] N pertosse f
whoops [wu:ps] EXCL: **~-a-daisy!** ops!
whoosh [wuʃ] N: **it came out with a ~** (*sauce etc*) è uscito di getto; (*air*) è uscito con un sibilo
whopper ['wɔpə'] N (*col: lie*) balla; (: *large thing*) cosa enorme
whopping ['wɔpɪŋ] ADJ (*col: big*) enorme
whore [hɔ:'] N (*col, pej*) puttana

(KEYWORD)

whose [hu:z] ADJ **1** (*possessive: interrogative*) di chi; **whose book is this?**, **whose is this book?** di chi è questo libro?; **whose daughter are you?** di chi sei figlia?; **whose pencil have you taken?** di chi è la matita che hai preso?
2 (*possessive: relative*): **the man whose son you rescued** l'uomo il cui figlio hai salvato or a cui hai salvato il figlio; **the girl whose sister you were speaking to** la ragazza alla cui sorella stavi parlando
▶ PRON di chi; **whose is this?** di chi è questo?; **I know whose it is** so di chi è

Who's Who ['hu:z'hu:] N *elenco di personalità*

(KEYWORD)

why [waɪ] ADV perché; **why not?** perché no?; **why not do it now?** perché non farlo adesso?
▶ CONJ perché; **I wonder why he said that** mi chiedo perché l'abbia detto; **that's not why I'm here** non è questo il motivo per cui sono qui; **the reason why** il motivo per cui
▶ EXCL (*surprise*) ma guarda un po'!; (*remonstrating*) ma (via)!; (*explaining*) ebbene!

whyever [waɪ'ɛvə'] ADV perché mai

WI N ABBR (BRIT: = *Women's Institute*) circolo femminile ▶ ABBR (*Geo*) = **West Indies**; (US) = **Wisconsin**
wick [wɪk] N lucignolo, stoppino
wicked ['wɪkɪd] ADJ cattivo(-a), malvagio(-a); (*mischievous*) malizioso(-a); (*terrible: prices, weather*) terribile
wicker ['wɪkə'] N vimine m; (*also:* **wickerwork**) articoli mpl di vimini
wicket ['wɪkɪt] N (*Cricket*) porta; area tra le due porte
wicket keeper N (*Cricket*) ≈ portiere m
wide [waɪd] ADJ largo(-a); (*region, knowledge*) vasto(-a); (*choice*) ampio(-a) ▶ ADV: **to open ~** spalancare; **to shoot ~** tirare a vuoto or fuori bersaglio; **it is 3 metres ~** è largo 3 metri
wide-angle lens ['waɪdæŋgl-] N grandangolare m
wide-awake [waɪdə'weɪk] ADJ completamente sveglio(-a)
wide-eyed [waɪd'aɪd] ADJ con gli occhi spalancati
widely ['waɪdlɪ] ADV (*different*) molto, completamente; (*believed*) generalmente; **~ spaced** molto distanziati(-e); **to be ~ read** (*author*) essere molto letto; (*reader*) essere molto colto
widen ['waɪdn] VT allargare, ampliare
wideness ['waɪdnɪs] N larghezza; vastità; ampiezza
wide open ADJ spalancato(-a)
wide-ranging [waɪd'reɪndʒɪŋ] ADJ (*survey, report*) vasto(-a); (*interests*) svariato(-a)
widescreen ['waɪdskri:n] ADJ (*television, TV*) a schermo panoramico
widespread ['waɪdsprɛd] ADJ (*belief etc*) molto or assai diffuso(-a)
widget ['wɪdʒɪt] N (*Comput*) widget m inv
widow ['wɪdəu] N vedova
widowed ['wɪdəud] ADJ (che è rimasto(-a)) vedovo(-a)
widower ['wɪdəuə'] N vedovo
width [wɪdθ] N larghezza; **it's 7 metres in ~** è largo 7 metri
widthways ['wɪdθweɪz] ADV trasversalmente
wield [wi:ld] VT (*sword*) maneggiare; (*power*) esercitare
wife [waɪf] (*pl* **wives** [waɪvz]) N moglie f
Wi-Fi ['waɪfaɪ] N WiFi m
wig [wɪg] N parrucca
wigging ['wɪgɪŋ] N (BRIT col) lavata di capo
wiggle ['wɪgl] VT dimenare, agitare ▶ VI (*loose screw etc*) traballare; (*worm*) torcersi
wiggly ['wɪglɪ] ADJ (*line*) ondulato(-a), sinuoso(-a)
wiki ['wɪkɪ] N (*Internet*) wiki m inv
wild [waɪld] ADJ (*animal, plant*) selvatico(-a); (*countryside, appearance*) selvaggio(-a); (*sea, weather*) tempestoso(-a); (*idea, life*) folle;

stravagante; (*applause*) frenetico(-a); (*col: angry*) arrabbiato(-a), furibondo(-a); (*enthusiastic*): **to be ~ about** andar pazzo(-a) per ▶ N: **the ~** la natura; **wilds** NPL regione f selvaggia

wild card N (*Comput*) carattere m jolly *inv*

wildcat ['waɪldkæt] N gatto(-a) selvatico(-a)

wildcat strike N ≈ sciopero selvaggio

wilderness ['wɪldənɪs] N deserto

wildfire ['waɪldfaɪə^r] N: **to spread like ~** propagarsi rapidamente

wild-goose chase [waɪld'guːs-] N (*fig*) pista falsa

wildlife ['waɪldlaɪf] N natura

wildly ['waɪldlɪ] ADV selvaggiamente; (*applaud*) freneticamente; (*hit, guess*) a casaccio; (*happy*) follemente

wiles [waɪlz] NPL astuzie *fpl*

wilful, (*US*) **willful** ['wɪlful] ADJ (*person*) testardo(-a); ostinato(-a); (*action*) intenzionale; (*crime*) premeditato(-a)

⸤KEYWORD⸥

will [wɪl] AUX VB **1** (*forming future tense*): **I will finish it tomorrow** lo finirò domani; **I will have finished it by tomorrow** lo finirò entro domani; **will you do it? — yes I will/ no I won't** lo farai? — sì (lo farò)/no (non lo farò); **the car won't start** la macchina non parte

2 (*in conjectures: predictions*): **he will** *or* **he'll be there by now** a quest'ora dovrebbe essere arrivato; **that will be the postman** sarà il postino

3 (*in commands: requests: offers*): **will you be quiet!** vuoi stare zitto?; **will you sit down?** (*politely*) prego, si accomodi; (*angrily*) vuoi metterti seduto?; **will you come?** vieni anche tu?; **will you help me?** mi aiuti?, mi puoi aiutare?; **you won't lose it, will you?** non lo perderai, vero?; **will you have a cup of tea?** vorrebbe una tazza di tè?; **I won't put up with it!** non lo accetterò!

▶ VT (*pt, pp* **willed**): **to will sb to do** volere che qn faccia; **he willed himself to go on** continuò grazie a un grande sforzo di volontà

▶ N **1** (*desire*) volontà; **against sb's will** contro la volontà *or* il volere di qn; **to do sth of one's own free will** fare qc di propria volontà

2 (*Law*) testamento; **to make a/one's will** fare testamento

willful ['wɪlful] ADJ (*US*) = **wilful**

willing ['wɪlɪŋ] ADJ volonteroso(-a) ▶ N: **to show ~** dare prova di buona volontà; **~ to do** disposto(-a) a fare

willingly ['wɪlɪŋlɪ] ADV volentieri

willingness ['wɪlɪŋnɪs] N buona volontà

will-o'-the-wisp [wɪləðə'wɪsp] N (*also fig*) fuoco fatuo

willow ['wɪləu] N salice m

willpower ['wɪlpauə^r] N forza di volontà

willy-nilly ['wɪlɪ'nɪlɪ] ADV volente o nolente

wilt [wɪlt] VI appassire

Wilts [wɪlts] ABBR (*BRIT*) = **Wiltshire**

wily ['waɪlɪ] ADJ furbo(-a)

wimp [wɪmp] N (*col*) mezza calzetta

win [wɪn] (*pt, pp* **won** [wʌn]) N (*in sports etc*) vittoria ▶ VT (*battle, prize, money*) vincere; (*popularity*) guadagnare; (*contract*) aggiudicarsi ▶ VI vincere
▶ **win over,** (*BRIT*) **win round** VT convincere

wince [wɪns] N trasalimento, sussulto ▶ VI trasalire

winch [wɪntʃ] N verricello, argano

Winchester disk ['wɪntʃɪstə-] N (*Comput*) disco Winchester

wind¹ [wɪnd] N vento; (*Med*) flatulenza, ventosità; (*breath*) respiro, fiato ▶ VT (*take breath away*) far restare senza fiato; **the ~(s)** (*Mus*) i fiati; **into** *or* **against the ~** controvento; **to get ~ of sth** venire a sapere qc; **to break ~** scoreggiare (*col*)

wind² [waɪnd] (*pt, pp* **wound** [waund]) VT attorcigliare; (*wrap*) avvolgere; (*clock, toy*) caricare ▶ VI (*road, river*) serpeggiare
▶ **wind down** VT (*car window*) abbassare; (*fig: production, business*) diminuire
▶ **wind up** VT (*clock*) caricare; (*debate*) concludere

windbreak ['wɪndbreɪk] N frangivento

windcheater ['wɪndtʃiːtə^r], (*US*) **windbreaker** ['wɪndbreɪkə^r] N giacca a vento

winder ['waɪndə^r] N (*BRIT: on watch*) corona di carica

windfall ['wɪndfɔːl] N (*money*) guadagno insperato

wind farm N centrale f eolica

winding ['waɪndɪŋ] ADJ (*road*) serpeggiante; (*staircase*) a chiocciola

wind instrument N (*Mus*) strumento a fiato

windmill ['wɪndmɪl] N mulino a vento

window ['wɪndəu] N (*gen, Comput*) finestra; (*in car, train, plane*) finestrino; (*in shop etc*) vetrina; (*also*: **window pane**) vetro

window box N cassetta da fiori

window cleaner N (*person*) pulitore m di finestre

window dressing N allestimento della vetrina

window envelope N busta a finestra

window frame N telaio di finestra

window ledge N davanzale m

window pane N vetro

window seat N posto finestrino

W

window-shopping ['wɪndəuʃɔpɪŋ] N: **to go ~** andare a vedere le vetrine

windowsill ['wɪndəusɪl] N davanzale m

windpipe ['wɪndpaɪp] N trachea

wind power N energia eolica

windscreen ['wɪndskriːn], (US) **windshield** ['wɪndʃiːld] N parabrezza m inv

windscreen washer N lavacristallo

windscreen wiper, (US) **windshield wiper** N tergicristallo

windshield ['wɪndʃiːld] N (US) = **windscreen**

windsurfing ['wɪndsəːfɪŋ] N windsurf m inv

windswept ['wɪndswɛpt] ADJ spazzato(-a) dal vento

wind tunnel N galleria aerodinamica or del vento

wind turbine ['wɪndtəːbaɪn] N pala eolica

windy ['wɪndɪ] ADJ ventoso(-a); **it's ~** c'è vento

wine [waɪn] N vino ▶ VT: **to ~ and dine sb** offrire un ottimo pranzo a qn

wine bar N enoteca (per degustazione)

wine cellar N cantina

wine glass N bicchiere m da vino

wine list N lista dei vini

wine merchant N commerciante m di vino

wine tasting N degustazione f dei vini

wine waiter N sommelier m inv

wing [wɪŋ] N ala; (Aut) fiancata; **wings** NPL (Theat) quinte fpl

winger ['wɪŋər] N (Sport) ala

wing mirror N (BRIT) specchietto retrovisore esterno

wing nut N galletto

wingspan ['wɪŋspæn], **wingspread** ['wɪŋsprɛd] N apertura alare, apertura d'ali

wink [wɪŋk] N occhiolino, strizzatina d'occhi ▶ VI ammiccare, fare l'occhiolino; (light) balluginare

winkle ['wɪŋkl] N litorina

winner ['wɪnər] N vincitore(-trice)

winning ['wɪnɪŋ] ADJ (team) vincente; (goal) decisivo(-a); (charming) affascinante; see also **winnings**

winning post N traguardo

winnings ['wɪnɪŋz] NPL vincite fpl

winsome ['wɪnsəm] ADJ accattivante

winter ['wɪntər] N inverno; **in ~** d'inverno, in inverno

winter sports NPL sport mpl invernali

wintertime N inverno, stagione f invernale

wintry ['wɪntrɪ] ADJ invernale

wipe [waɪp] N pulita, passata ▶ VT pulire (strofinando); (erase: tape) cancellare; (: dishes) asciugare; **to give sth a ~** dare una pulita or una passata a qc; **to ~ one's nose** soffiarsi il naso

▶ **wipe off** VT cancellare; (stains) togliere strofinando

▶ **wipe out** VT (debt) pagare, liquidare; (memory) cancellare; (destroy) annientare

▶ **wipe up** VT asciugare

wire ['waɪər] N filo; (Elec) filo elettrico; (Tel) telegramma m ▶ VT (Elec: house) fare l'impianto elettrico di; (: circuit) installare; (also: **wire up**) collegare, allacciare; (: person) telegrafare a

wire brush N spazzola metallica

wire cutters ['-kʌtəz] NPL tronchese m or f

wireless ['waɪəlɪs] N (BRIT: set) (apparecchio m) radio f inv ▶ ADJ wireless inv, senza fili

wireless technology N tecnologia wireless

wire netting N rete f metallica

wire service N (US) = **news agency**

wire-tapping ['waɪətæpɪŋ] N intercettazione f telefonica

wiring ['waɪərɪŋ] N (Elec) impianto elettrico

wiry ['waɪərɪ] ADJ magro(-a) e nerboruto(-a)

Wis., Wisc. ABBR (US) = **Wisconsin**

wisdom ['wɪzdəm] N saggezza; (of action) prudenza

wisdom tooth N dente m del giudizio

wise [waɪz] ADJ saggio(-a); (advice, remark) prudente; giudizioso(-a); **I'm none the wiser** ne so come prima

▶ **wise up** VI (col): **to ~ up to** divenire più consapevole di

...wise [waɪz] SUFFIX: **timewise** per quanto riguarda il tempo, in termini di tempo

wisecrack ['waɪzkræk] N battuta spiritosa

wish [wɪʃ] N (desire) desiderio; (specific desire) richiesta ▶ VT desiderare, volere; **best wishes** (on birthday etc) i migliori auguri; **with best wishes** (in letter) cordiali saluti, con i migliori saluti; **give her my best wishes** le faccia i migliori auguri da parte mia; **to ~ sb goodbye** dire arrivederci a qn; **he wished me well** mi augurò di riuscire; **to ~ to do/sb to do** desiderare or volere fare/ che qn faccia; **to ~ for** desiderare; **to ~ sth on sb** rifilare qc a qn

wishbone ['wɪʃbəun] N forcella

wishful ['wɪʃful] ADJ: **it's ~ thinking** è prendere i desideri per realtà

wishy-washy ['wɪʃɪwɔʃɪ] ADJ insulso(-a)

wisp [wɪsp] N ciuffo, ciocca; (of smoke, straw) filo

wistful ['wɪstful] ADJ malinconico(-a); (nostalgic) nostalgico(-a)

wit [wɪt] N (gen pl) intelligenza; presenza di spirito; (wittiness) spirito, arguzia; (person) bello spirito; **to be at one's wits' end** (fig) non sapere più cosa fare; **to have** or **keep one's wits about one** avere presenza di spirito; **to ~** adv cioè

witch [wɪtʃ] N strega

witchcraft ['wɪtʃkrɑːft] N stregoneria

witch doctor N stregone m

witch-hunt ['wɪtʃhʌnt] N (*fig*) caccia alle streghe

(KEYWORD)

with [wɪð, wɪθ] PREP **1** (*in the company of*) con; **I was with him** ero con lui; **we stayed with friends** siamo stati da amici; **I'll be with you in a minute** vengo subito

2 (*descriptive*) con; **a room with a view** una camera con vista (sul mare *or* sulle montagne *etc*); **the man with the grey hat/ blue eyes** l'uomo con il cappello grigio/gli occhi blu

3 (*indicating manner: means: cause*): **with tears in her eyes** con le lacrime agli occhi; **red with anger** rosso(-a) dalla rabbia; **to shake with fear** tremare di paura; **covered with snow** coperto(-a) di neve

4: **I'm with you** (*I understand*) la seguo; **to be with it** (*col: up-to-date*) essere alla moda; (*: alert*) essere sveglio(-a); **I'm not really with it today** (*col*) oggi sono un po' fuori

withdraw [wɪθ'drɔ:] VT (*irreg: like* **draw**) ritirare; (*money from bank*) ritirare; prelevare ▶ VI ritirarsi; **to ~ into o.s.** chiudersi in se stesso

withdrawal [wɪθ'drɔ:əl] N ritiro; prelievo; (*of army*) ritirata; (*Med*) stato di privazione

withdrawal symptoms NPL (*Med*) crisi f di astinenza

withdrawn [wɪθ'drɔ:n] PP *of* **withdraw** ▶ ADJ (*person*) distaccato(-a)

withdrew [wɪθ'dru:] PT *of* **withdraw**

wither ['wɪðəʳ] VI appassire

withered ['wɪðəd] ADJ appassito(-a); (*limb*) atrofizzato(-a)

withhold [wɪθ'həuld] VT (*irreg: like* **hold**) (*money*) trattenere; (*permission*): **to ~ (from)** rifiutare (a); (*information*) nascondere (a)

within [wɪð'ɪn] PREP all'interno di; (*in time, distances*) entro ▶ ADV all'interno, dentro; **~ reach (of)** alla portata (di); **~ sight (of)** in vista (di); **~ a mile of** entro un miglio da; **~ the week** prima della fine della settimana; **~ an hour from now** da qui a un'ora; **to be ~ the law** restare nei limiti della legge

without [wɪð'aut] PREP senza; **to go** *or* **do ~ sth** fare a meno di qc; **~ anybody knowing** senza che nessuno lo sappia

withstand [wɪθ'stænd] VT (*irreg: like* **stand**) resistere a

witness ['wɪtnɪs] N (*person, also Law*) testimone *mf* ▶ VT (*event*) essere testimone di; (*document*) attestare l'autenticità di ▶ VI: **to ~ to sth/having seen sth** testimoniare qc/di aver visto qc; **to bear ~ to sth** testimoniare qc; **~ for the prosecution/defence** testimone a carico/discarico

witness box, (*US*) **witness stand** N banco dei testimoni

witticism ['wɪtɪsɪzəm] N spiritosaggine f

witty ['wɪtɪ] ADJ spiritoso(-a)

wives [waɪvz] NPL *of* **wife**

wizard ['wɪzəd] N mago

wizened ['wɪznd] ADJ raggrinzito(-a)

wk ABBR = **week**

Wm. ABBR = **William**

WMD N ABBR *see* **weapons of mass destruction**

WO N ABBR *see* **warrant officer**

wobble ['wɔbl] VI tremare; (*chair*) traballare

wobbly ['wɔblɪ] ADJ (*hand, voice*) tremante; (*table, chair*) traballante; (*object about to fall*) che oscilla pericolosamente

woe [wəu] N dolore *m*; disgrazia

woeful ['wəuful] ADJ (*sad*) triste; (*deplorable*) deplorevole

wok [wɔk] N wok *m inv* (*padella concava usata nella cucina cinese*)

woke [wəuk] PT *of* **wake**

woken ['wəukn] PP *of* **wake**

wolf [wulf] (*pl* **wolves** [wulvz]) N lupo

woman ['wumən] (*pl* **women** ['wɪmɪn]) N donna ▶ CPD: **~ doctor** n dottoressa; **~ friend** n amica; **~ teacher** n insegnante f; **women's page** n (*Press*) rubrica femminile

womanize ['wumənaɪz] VI essere un donnaiolo

womanly ['wumənlɪ] ADJ femminile

womb [wu:m] N (*Anat*) utero

women ['wɪmɪn] NPL *of* **woman**

Women's Movement, Women's Liberation Movement N (*also:* **Women's Lib**) Movimento per la Liberazione della Donna

won [wʌn] PT, PP *of* **win**

wonder ['wʌndəʳ] N meraviglia ▶ VI: **to ~ whether/why** domandarsi se/perché; **to ~ at** essere sorpreso(-a) di; meravigliarsi di; **to ~ about** domandarsi di; pensare a; **it's no ~ that** c'è poco *or* non c'è da meravigliarsi che +*sub*

wonderful ['wʌndəful] ADJ meraviglioso(-a)

wonderfully ['wʌndəfəlɪ] ADV (+ *adjective*) meravigliosamente; (+ *verb*) a meraviglia

wonky ['wɔŋkɪ] ADJ (*BRIT col*) traballante

wont [wəunt] N: **as is his/her ~** com'è solito/a fare

won't [wəunt] = **will not**

woo [wu:] VT (*woman*) fare la corte a

wood [wud] N legno; (*timber*) legname *m*; (*forest*) bosco ▶ CPD di bosco, silvestre

wood carving N scultura in legno, intaglio

wooded ['wudɪd] ADJ boschivo(-a); boscoso(-a)

wooden ['wudn] ADJ di legno; (*fig*) rigido(-a); inespressivo(-a)

w

woodland ['wudlənd] N zona boscosa
woodpecker ['wudpɛkəʳ] N picchio
wood pigeon N colombaccio, palomba
woodwind ['wudwɪnd] NPL (Mus): **the ~** i legni
woodwork ['wudwə:k] N parti fpl in legno; (craft, subject) falegnameria
woodworm ['wudwə:m] N tarlo del legno
woof [wuf] N (of dog) bau bau m ▶ vi abbaiare; **~, ~!** bau bau!
wool [wul] N lana; **to pull the ~ over sb's eyes** (fig) gettare fumo negli occhi a qn
woollen, (US) **woolen** ['wulən] ADJ di lana; (industry) laniero(-a) ▶ N: **woollens** indumenti mpl di lana
woolly, (US) **wooly** ['wulɪ] ADJ di lana; (fig: ideas) confuso(-a)
woozy ['wu:zɪ] ADJ (col) stordito(-a)
word [wə:d] N parola; (news) notizie fpl ▶ vt esprimere, formulare; **~ for ~** parola per parola, testualmente; **what's the ~ for "pen" in Italian?** come si dice "pen" in italiano?; **to put sth into words** esprimere qc a parole; **in other words** in altre parole; **to have a ~ with sb** scambiare due parole con qn; **to have words with sb** (quarrel with) avere un diverbio con qn; **to break/keep one's ~** non mantenere/mantenere la propria parola; **I'll take your ~ for it** la crederò sulla parola; **to send ~ of** avvisare di; **to leave ~ (with or for sb) that ...** lasciare detto (a qn) che ...
wording ['wə:dɪŋ] N formulazione f
word of mouth N passaparola m; **I learned it by or through** lo so per sentito dire
word-perfect ['wə:d'pəfɪkt] ADJ (speech etc) imparato(-a) a memoria
word processing N word processing m, elaborazione f testi
word processor N word processor m inv
wordwrap ['wə:dræp] N (Comput) ritorno carrello automatico
wordy ['wə:dɪ] ADJ verboso(-a), prolisso(-a)
wore [wɔ:ʳ] PT of **wear**
work [wə:k] N lavoro; (Art, Literature) opera ▶ vi lavorare; (mechanism, plan etc) funzionare; (medicine) essere efficace ▶ vt (clay, wood etc) lavorare; (mine etc) sfruttare; (machine) far funzionare; (cause: effect, miracle) fare; **to be at ~ (on sth)** lavorare (a qc); **to set to ~, to start ~** mettersi al lavoro; **to go to ~** andare al lavoro; **to be out of ~** essere disoccupato(-a); **to ~ one's way through a book** riuscire a leggersi tutto un libro; **to ~ one's way through college** lavorare per pagarsi gli studi; **how does this ~?** come funziona?; **the TV isn't working** la TV non funziona; **to ~ hard** lavorare sodo; **to ~ loose** allentarsi; see also **works**

▶ **work on** vt fus lavorare a; (principle) basarsi su; **he's working on the car** sta facendo dei lavori alla macchina

▶ **work out** vi (plans etc) riuscire, andare bene; (Sport) allenarsi ▶ vt (problem) risolvere; (plan) elaborare; **it works out at £100** fa 100 sterline

workable ['wə:kəbl] ADJ (solution) realizzabile
workaholic [wə:kə'hɔlɪk] N stacanovista mf
workbench ['wə:kbɛntʃ] N banco (da lavoro)
worked up ADJ: **to get ~** andare su tutte le furie; eccitarsi
worker ['wə:kəʳ] N lavoratore(-trice); (esp Agr, Industry) operaio(-a); **office ~** impiegato(-a)
work experience ['wə:kɪkspɪərɪəns] N (previous jobs) esperienze fpl lavorative; (student training placement) tirocinio
work force N forza lavoro
work-in ['wə:kɪn] N (Brit) sciopero alla rovescia
working ['wə:kɪŋ] ADJ (day) feriale; (tools, conditions) di lavoro; (clothes) da lavoro; (wife) che lavora; (partner) attivo(-a); **in ~ order** funzionante; **~ knowledge** conoscenza pratica
working capital N (Comm) capitale m d'esercizio
working class N classe f operaia or lavoratrice ▶ ADJ: **working-class** operaio(-a)
working man N (irreg) lavoratore m
working party N (Brit) commissione f
working week N settimana lavorativa
work-in-progress ['wə:kɪn'prəugres] N (products) lavoro in corso; (value) valore m del manufatto in lavorazione
workload ['wə:kləud] N carico di lavoro
workman ['wə:kmən] N (irreg) operaio
workmanship ['wə:kmənʃɪp] N (of worker) abilità; (of thing) fattura
workmate ['wə:kmeɪt] N collega mf
work of art N opera d'arte
workout ['wə:kaut] N (Sport) allenamento
work permit N permesso di lavoro
workplace N posto di lavoro
works [wə:ks] N (Brit: factory) fabbrica ▶ NPL (of clock, machine) meccanismo; **road ~** opere stradali
works council N consiglio aziendale
work sheet N (Comput) foglio col programma di lavoro
workshop ['wə:kʃɔp] N officina; (practical session) gruppo di lavoro
work station N stazione f di lavoro
work study N studio di organizzazione del lavoro
work surface N piano di lavoro
worktop ['wə:ktɔp] N piano di lavoro
work-to-rule ['wə:ktə'ru:l] N (Brit) sciopero bianco

world [wəːld] N mondo ▶ CPD (*tour, champion*) del mondo; (*record, power, war*) mondiale; **all over the ~** in tutto il mondo; **to think the ~ of sb** (*fig*) pensare un gran bene di qn; **out of this ~** (*fig*) formidabile; **what in the ~ is he doing?** che cavolo sta facendo?; **to do sb a ~ of good** fare un gran bene a qn; **W~ War One/Two** la prima/seconda guerra mondiale

world champion N campione(-essa) mondiale

World Cup N (*Football*) Coppa del Mondo

world-famous [wəːldˈfeɪməs] ADJ di fama mondiale

worldly [ˈwəːldlɪ] ADJ di questo mondo

world music N musica etnica

World Series N: **the ~** (*US Baseball*) la finalissima di baseball

world-wide [ˈwəːldˈwaɪd] ADJ universale

World-Wide Web N World Wide Web *m*

worm [wəːm] N (*also:* **earthworm**) verme *m*

worn [wɔːn] PP *of* **wear** ▶ ADJ usato(-a)

worn-out [ˈwɔːnaut] ADJ (*object*) consumato(-a), logoro(-a); (*person*) sfinito(-a)

worried [ˈwʌrɪd] ADJ preoccupato(-a); **to be ~ about sth** essere preoccupato per qc

worrier [ˈwʌrɪər] N ansioso(-a)

worrisome [ˈwʌrɪsəm] ADJ preoccupante

worry [ˈwʌrɪ] N preoccupazione *f* ▶ VT preoccupare ▶ VI preoccuparsi; **to ~ about** *or* **over sth/sb** preoccuparsi di qc/per qn

worrying [ˈwʌrɪɪŋ] ADJ preoccupante

worse [wəːs] ADJ peggiore ▶ ADV, N peggio; **a change for the ~** un peggioramento; **to get ~, to grow ~** peggiorare; **he is none the ~ for it** non ha avuto brutte conseguenze; **so much the ~ for you!** tanto peggio per te!

worsen [ˈwəːsn] VT, VI peggiorare

worse off ADJ in condizioni (economiche) peggiori; (*fig*): **you'll be ~ this way** così sarà peggio per lei; **he is now ~ than before** ora è in condizioni peggiori di prima

worship [ˈwəːʃɪp] N culto ▶ VT (*God*) adorare, venerare; (*person*) adorare; **Your W~** (*BRIT: to mayor*) signor sindaco; (*: to judge*) signor giudice

worshipper [ˈwəːʃɪpər] N adoratore(-trice); (*in church*) fedele *mf*, devoto(-a)

worst [wəːst] ADJ il (la) peggiore ▶ ADV, N peggio; **at ~** al peggio, per male che vada; **to come off ~** avere la peggio; **if the ~ comes to the ~** nel peggior dei casi

worst-case [ˈwəːstˈkeɪs] ADJ: **the ~ scenario** la peggiore delle ipotesi

worsted [ˈwustɪd] N: (**wool**) **~** lana pettinata

worth [wəːθ] N valore *m* ▶ ADJ: **to be ~** valere; **how much is it ~?** quanto vale?; **it's ~ it** ne vale la pena; **it's not ~ the trouble** non ne

vale la pena; **50 pence ~ of apples** 50 pence di mele

worthless [ˈwəːθlɪs] ADJ di nessun valore

worthwhile [ˈwəːθˈwaɪl] ADJ (*activity*) utile; (*cause*) lodevole; **a ~ book** un libro che vale la pena leggere

worthy [ˈwəːðɪ] ADJ (*person*) degno(-a); (*motive*) lodevole; **~ of** degno di

(KEYWORD)

would [wud] AUX VB **1** (*conditional tense*): **if you asked him he would do it** se glielo chiedesse lo farebbe; **if you had asked him he would have done it** se glielo avesse chiesto lo avrebbe fatto

2 (*in offers: invitations: requests*): **would you like a biscuit?** vorrebbe *or* vuole un biscotto?; **would you ask him to come in?** lo faccia entrare, per cortesia; **would you open the window please?** apra la finestra, per favore

3 (*in indirect speech*): **I said I would do it** ho detto che l'avrei fatto

4 (*emphatic*): **it WOULD have to snow today!** doveva proprio nevicare oggi!

5 (*insistence*): **she wouldn't do it** non ha voluto farlo

6 (*conjecture*): **it would have been midnight** sarà stata mezzanotte; **it would seem so** sembrerebbe proprio di sì

7 (*indicating habit*): **he would go there on Mondays** andava lì ogni lunedì

would-be [ˈwudbiː] ADJ (*pej*) sedicente

wouldn't [ˈwudnt]= **would not**

wound¹ [wuːnd] N ferita ▶ VT ferire; **wounded in the leg** ferito(-a) alla gamba

wound² [waund] PT, PP *of* **wind²**

wove [wəuv] PT *of* **weave**

woven [ˈwəuvn] PP *of* **weave**

WP ABBR (*BRIT: col: = weather permitting*) tempo permettendo ▶ N ABBR = **word processing**; **word processor**

WPC N ABBR (*BRIT: = woman police constable*) donna poliziotto

wpm ABBR (= *words per minute*) p.p.m.

WRAC N ABBR (*BRIT: = Women's Royal Army Corps*) ausiliarie dell'esercito

WRAF N ABBR (*BRIT: = Women's Royal Air Force*) ausiliarie dell'aeronautica militare

wrangle [ˈræŋgl] N litigio ▶ VI litigare

wrap [ræp] N (*stole*) scialle *m*; (*cape*) mantellina ▶ VT (*also:* **wrap up**) avvolgere; (*: parcel*) incartare; **under wraps** segreto

wrapper [ˈræpər] N (*on chocolate*) carta; (*BRIT: of book*) copertina

wrapping [ˈræpɪŋ] N carta

wrapping paper [ˈræpɪŋ-] N carta da pacchi; (*for gift*) carta da regali

wrath [rɔθ] N collera, ira

w

wreak [riːk] VT (*destruction*) portare, causare; **to ~ vengeance on** vendicarsi su; **to ~ havoc on** portare scompiglio in

wreath [riːθ] (*pl* **wreaths** [riːðz]) N corona

wreck [rɛk] N (*sea disaster*) naufragio; (*ship*) relitto; (*pej: person*) rottame *m* ▸ VT demolire; (*ship*) far naufragare; (*fig*) rovinare

wreckage ['rɛkɪdʒ] N rottami *mpl*; (*of building*) macerie *fpl*; (*of ship*) relitti *mpl*

wrecker ['rɛkə^r] N (*US: breakdown van*) carro *m* attrezzi *inv*

WREN [rɛn] N ABBR (*BRIT*) membro del WRNS

wren [rɛn] N (*Zool*) scricciolo

wrench [rɛntʃ] N (*Tech*) chiave *f*; (*tug*) torsione *f* brusca; (*fig*) strazio ▸ VT strappare; storcere; **to ~ sth from** strappare qc a *or* da

wrest [rɛst] VT: **to ~ sth from sb** strappare qc a qn

wrestle ['rɛsl] VI: **to ~ (with sb)** lottare (con qn); **to ~ with** (*fig*) combattere *or* lottare contro

wrestler ['rɛslə^r] N lottatore(-trice)

wrestling ['rɛslɪŋ] N lotta; (*also:* **all-in wrestling**: *BRIT*) catch *m*, lotta libera

wrestling match N incontro di lotta (*or* lotta libera)

wretch [rɛtʃ] N disgraziato(-a), sciagurato(-a); **little ~!** (*often humorous*) birbante!

wretched ['rɛtʃɪd] ADJ disgraziato(-a); (*col: weather, holiday*) orrendo(-a), orribile; (*: child, dog*) pestifero(-a)

wriggle ['rɪgl] N contorsione *f* ▸ VI (*also:* **wriggle about**) dimenarsi; (*: snake, worm*) serpeggiare, muoversi serpeggiando

wring [rɪŋ] (*pt, pp* **wrung** [rʌŋ]) VT torcere; (*wet clothes*) strizzare; (*fig*): **to ~ sth out of** strappare qc a

wringer ['rɪŋə^r] N strizzatoio (manuale)

wringing ['rɪŋɪŋ] ADJ (*also:* **wringing wet**) bagnato(-a) fradicio(-a)

wrinkle ['rɪŋkl] N (*on skin*) ruga; (*on paper etc*) grinza ▸ VT (*nose*) torcere; (*forehead*) corrugare; raggrinzire ▸ VI corrugarsi; (*skin, paint*) raggrinzirsi

wrinkled ['rɪŋkld], **wrinkly** ['rɪŋklɪ] ADJ (*fabric, paper*) stropicciato(-a); (*surface*) corrugato(-a), increspato(-a); (*skin*) rugoso(-a)

wrist [rɪst] N polso

wristband ['rɪstbænd] N (*of shirt*) polsino; (*of watch*) cinturino

wrist watch N orologio da polso

writ [rɪt] N ordine *m*; mandato; **to issue a ~ against sb, serve a ~ on sb** notificare un mandato di comparizione a qn

write [raɪt] (*pt* **wrote** [rəut], *pp* **written** ['rɪtn]) VT, VI scrivere; **to ~ sb a letter** scrivere una lettera a qn

▸ **write away** VI: **to ~ away for** (*information*) richiedere per posta; (*goods*) ordinare per posta

▸ **write down** VT annotare; (*put in writing*) mettere per iscritto

▸ **write off** VT (*debt, plan*) cancellare; (*depreciate*) deprezzare; (*smash up: car*) distruggere

▸ **write out** VT mettere per iscritto; (*cheque, receipt*) scrivere; (*copy*) ricopiare

▸ **write up** VT redigere

write-off ['raɪtɔf] N perdita completa; **the car is a ~** la macchina va bene per il demolitore

write-protect ['raɪtprə'tɛkt] VT (*Comput*) proteggere contro scrittura

writer ['raɪtə^r] N autore(-trice), scrittore(-trice)

write-up ['raɪtʌp] N (*review*) recensione *f*

writhe [raɪð] VI contorcersi

writing ['raɪtɪŋ] N scrittura; (*of author*) scritto, opera; **in ~** per iscritto; **in my own ~** scritto di mio pugno

writing case N nécessaire *m inv* per la corrispondenza

writing desk N scrivania, scrittoio

writing paper N carta da lettere

written ['rɪtn] PP *of* **write**

WRNS N ABBR (*BRIT:* = *Women's Royal Naval Service*) ausiliarie della marina militare

wrong [rɔŋ] ADJ sbagliato(-a); (*not suitable*) inadatto(-a); (*wicked*) cattivo(-a); (*unfair*) ingiusto(-a) ▸ ADV in modo sbagliato, erroneamente ▸ N (*evil*) male *m*; (*injustice*) torto ▸ VT fare torto a; **to be ~** (*answer*) essere sbagliato; (*in doing, saying*) avere torto; **you are ~ to do it** ha torto a farlo; **you are ~ about that, you've got it ~** si sbaglia; **to be in the ~** avere torto; **what's ~?** cosa c'è che non va?; **there's nothing ~** va tutto bene; **what's ~ with the car?** cos'ha la macchina che non va?; **to go ~** (*person*) sbagliarsi; (*plan*) fallire, non riuscire; (*machine*) guastarsi; **it's ~ to steal, stealing is ~** è male rubare

wrongdoer ['rɔŋduːə^r] N malfattore(-trice)

wrong-foot [rɔŋ'fut] VT (*Sport: also fig*) prendere in contropiede

wrongful ['rɔŋful] ADJ illegittimo(-a); ingiusto(-a); **~ dismissal** licenziamento ingiustificato

wrongly ['rɔŋlɪ] ADV (*incorrectly, by mistake*) in modo sbagliato; (*accuse, dismiss*) a torto; (*answer, do, count*) erroneamente; (*treat*) ingiustamente

wrong number N: **you have the ~** (*Tel*) ha sbagliato numero

wrong side N (*of cloth*) rovescio

wrote [rəut] PT *of* **write**

wrought [rɔːt] ADJ: **~ iron** ferro battuto
wrung [rʌŋ] PT, PP *of* **wring**
WRVS N ABBR (*BRIT*) = **Women's Royal Voluntary Service**
wry [raɪ] ADJ storto(-a)
wt. ABBR = **weight**

WV, W. Va. ABBR (*US*) = **West Virginia**
WWW N ABBR = **World Wide Web; the ~** la Rete
WY, Wyo. ABBR (*US*) = **Wyoming**
WYSIWYG ['wɪzɪwɪg] ABBR (*Comput*) = **what you see is what you get**

w

X, x [ɛks] N (*letter*) X, x *f inv or m inv*; (BRIT *Cine*: *old*) ≈ film vietato ai minori di 18 anni; **X for Xmas** ≈ X come Xeres

Xerox® ['zɪərɔks] N (*also*: **Xerox machine**) fotocopiatrice *f*; (: *photocopy*) fotocopia ▶ VT fotocopiare

XL ABBR = **extra large**

Xmas ['ɛksməs] N ABBR = **Christmas**

X-rated ['ɛks'reɪtɪd] ADJ (*US*: *film*) ≈ vietato ai minori di 18 anni

X-ray ['ɛks'reɪ] N raggio X; (*photograph*) radiografia ▶ VT radiografare; **to have an ~** farsi fare una radiografia

xylophone ['zaɪləfəun] N xilofono

Yy

Y, y [waɪ] N (letter) Y, y f inv or m inv; **Y for Yellow**, (US) **Y for Yoke** ≈ Y come Yacht

yacht [jɔt] N panfilo, yacht m inv

yachting ['jɔtɪŋ] N yachting m, sport m della vela

yachtsman ['jɔtsmən] N (irreg) yachtsman m inv

yam [jæm] N igname m; (sweet potato) patata dolce

Yank [jæŋk], **Yankee** ['jæŋkɪ] N (pej) yankee mf, nordamericano(-a)

yank [jæŋk] N strattone m ▶ VT tirare, dare uno strattone a

yap [jæp] VI (dog) guaire

yard [jɑːd] N (of house etc) cortile m; (US: garden) giardino; (measure) iarda (= 914 mm; 3 feet); **builder's** ~ deposito di materiale da costruzione

yard sale (US) N vendita di oggetti usati nel cortile di una casa privata

yardstick ['jɑːdstɪk] N (fig) misura, criterio

yarn [jɑːn] N filato; (tale) lunga storia

yawn [jɔːn] N sbadiglio ▶ VI sbadigliare

yawning ['jɔːnɪŋ] ADJ (gap) spalancato(-a)

yd. ABBR = **yard**

yeah [jɛə] ADV (col) sì

year [jɪəʳ] N (gen, Scol) anno; (referring to harvest, wine etc) annata; **every** ~ ogni anno, tutti gli anni; **this** ~ quest'anno; ~ **in**, ~ **out** anno dopo anno; **she's three years old** ha tre anni; **an eight-~-old child** un(a) bambino(-a) di otto anni; **a** or **per** ~ all'anno

yearbook ['jɪəbuk] N annuario

yearly ['jɪəlɪ] ADJ annuale ▶ ADV annualmente; **twice-~** semestrale

yearn [jəːn] VI: **to** ~ **for sth/to do** desiderare ardentemente qc/di fare

yearning ['jəːnɪŋ] N desiderio intenso

yeast [jiːst] N lievito

yell [jɛl] N urlo ▶ VI urlare

yellow ['jɛləu] ADJ giallo(-a)

yellow fever N febbre f gialla

yellowish ['jɛləuɪʃ] ADJ giallastro(-a), giallognolo(-a)

Yellow Pages ® NPL pagine fpl gialle

Yellow Sea N: **the** ~ il mar Giallo

yelp [jɛlp] N guaito, uggiolio ▶ VI guaire, uggiolare

Yemen ['jɛmən] N Yemen m

yen [jɛn] N (currency) yen m inv; (craving): ~ **for/ to do** gran voglia di/di fare

yeoman ['jəumən] N (irreg): **Y~ of the Guard** guardiano della Torre di Londra

yes [jɛs] ADV, N sì (m inv); **to say** ~ **(to)** dire di sì (a)

yesterday ['jɛstədɪ] ADV, N ieri (m inv); ~ **morning/evening** ieri mattina/sera; **the day before** ~ l'altro ieri; **all day** ~ ieri per tutta la giornata

yet [jɛt] ADV ancora; già ▶ CONJ ma, tuttavia; **it is not finished** ~ non è ancora finito; **the best** ~ finora il migliore finora; **as** ~ finora; ~ **again** di nuovo; **must you go just** ~? deve andarsene di già?; **a few days** ~ ancora qualche giorno

yew [juː] N tasso (albero)

Y-fronts ® ['waɪfrʌnts] NPL (BRIT) slip m inv da uomo

YHA N ABBR (BRIT: = Youth Hostels Association) Y.H.A. f

Yiddish ['jɪdɪʃ] N yiddish m

yield [jiːld] N produzione f, resa; reddito; (of crops etc) raccolto ▶ VT produrre, rendere; (surrender) cedere ▶ VI cedere; (US Aut) dare la precedenza; **a** ~ **of 5%** un profitto or un interesse del 5%

YMCA N ABBR (= Young Men's Christian Association) Y.M.C.A. m

yob ['jɔb], **yobbo** ['jɔbəu] N (BRIT col) bullo

yodel ['jəudl] VI cantare lo jodel or alla tirolese

yoga ['jəugə] N yoga m

yoghurt, yogurt ['jəugət] N iogurt m inv

yoke [jəuk] N giogo ▶ VT (also: **yoke together**: oxen) aggiogare

yolk [jəuk] N tuorlo, rosso d'uovo

yonder ['jɔndəʳ] ADV là

yonks [jɔŋks] NPL: **for** ~ (col) da una vita

y

Yorks [jɔːks] ABBR (BRIT) = **Yorkshire**

(KEYWORD)

you [juː] PRON **1** (subject) tu; (: polite form) lei; (: pl) voi; (: formal) loro; **you Italians enjoy your food** a voi italiani piace mangiare bene; **you and I will go** andiamo io e te (or lei ed io); **if I was** or **were you** se fossi in te (or lei etc)

2 (object: direct) ti; la; vi; loro (after vb); (: indirect) ti; le; vi; loro (after vb); **I know you** ti (or la or vi) conosco; **I'll see you tomorrow** ci vediamo domani; **I gave it to you** te l'ho dato; gliel'ho dato; ve l'ho dato; l'ho dato loro

3 (stressed, after prep, in comparisons) te; lei; voi; loro; **I told YOU to do it** ho detto a TE (or a LEI etc) di farlo; **she's younger than you** è più giovane di te (or lei etc)

4 (impers: one) si; **fresh air does you good** l'aria fresca fa bene; **you never know** non si sa mai

you'd [juːd] = **you had**; **you would**
you'll [juːl] = **you will**; **you shall**
young [jʌŋ] ADJ giovane ▶ NPL (of animal) piccoli mpl; **the ~** i giovani, la gioventù; **a ~ man** un giovanotto; **a ~ lady** una signorina; **a ~ woman** una giovane donna; **the younger generation** la nuova generazione; **my younger brother** il mio fratello minore
youngish ['jʌŋɪʃ] ADJ abbastanza giovane
youngster ['jʌŋstəʳ] N giovanotto(-a), ragazzo(-a); (child) bambino(-a)
your [jɔːʳ] ADJ il (la) tuo(-a); (pl) i (le) tuoi (tue); (polite form) il (la) suo(-a); (pl) i (le) suoi (sue); (pl) il (la) vostro(-a); (pl) i (le) vostri(-e); (: formal) il (la) loro; (pl) i (le) loro
you're [juəʳ] = **you are**

yours [jɔːz] PRON il (la) tuo(-a); (pl) i (le) tuoi (tue); (pl) il (la) suo(-a); (pl) i (le) suoi (sue); (pl) il (la) vostro(-a); (pl) i (le) vostri(-e); (: formal) il (la) loro; (pl) i (le) loro; **~ sincerely/faithfully** (in letter) cordiali/distinti saluti; **a friend of ~** un tuo (or suo etc) amico; **is it ~?** è tuo (or suo etc)?; see also **mine¹**
yourself [jɔːˈsɛlf] PRON (reflexive) ti; (: polite form) si; (after prep) te; sé; (emphatic) tu stesso(-a); lei stesso(-a); **you ~ told me** me l'hai detto proprio tu, tu stesso me l'hai detto
yourselves [jɔːˈsɛlvz] PL PRON (reflexive) vi; (: polite form) si; (after prep) voi; loro; (emphatic) voi stessi(-e); loro stessi(-e); see also **oneself**
youth [juːθ] N gioventù f; (pl **youths** [juːðz]: young man) giovane m, ragazzo; **in my ~** da giovane, quando ero giovane
youth club N centro giovanile
youthful ['juːθful] ADJ giovane; da giovane; giovanile
youthfulness ['juːθfəlnɪs] N giovinezza
youth hostel N ostello della gioventù
youth movement N movimento giovanile
you've [juːv] = **you have**
yowl [jaul] N (of dog, person) urlo; (of cat) miagolio ▶ VI urlare; miagolare
yr ABBR = **year**
YT ABBR (CANADA) = **Yukon Territory**
Yugoslav ['juːgəuslɑːv] ADJ, N (formerly) jugoslavo(-a)
Yugoslavia [juːgəuˈslɑːvɪə] N (formerly) Jugoslavia
Yugoslavian [juːgəuˈslɑːvɪən] ADJ, N (formerly) jugoslavo(-a)
Yule log [juːl-] N ceppo nel caminetto a Natale
yuppie ['jʌpɪ] ADJ, N (col) yuppie mf inv
YWCA N ABBR (= Young Women's Christian Association) Y.W.C.A. m

Zz

Z, z [zɛd, (US) ziː] N (letter) Z, z f inv or m inv;
  Z for Zebra ≈ Z come Zara
Zaire [zɑːˈɪəʳ] N Zaire m
Zambia [ˈzæmbɪə] N Zambia m
Zambian [ˈzæmbɪən] ADJ, N zambiano(-a)
zany [ˈzeɪnɪ] ADJ un po' pazzo(-a)
zap [zæp] VT (Comput) cancellare
zeal [ziːl] N zelo; entusiasmo
zealot [ˈzɛlət] N zelota mf
zealous [ˈzɛləs] ADJ zelante; premuroso(-a)
zebra [ˈziːbrə] N zebra
zebra crossing N (BRIT) (passaggio pedonale
  a) strisce fpl, zebre fpl
zenith [ˈzɛnɪθ] N zenit m inv; (fig) culmine m
zero [ˈzɪərəu] N zero; **5° below ~** 5° sotto zero
zero hour N l'ora zero
zero option N (Pol) opzione f zero
zero-rated [ˈzɪərəuˈreɪtɪd] ADJ (BRIT) ad
  aliquota zero
zest [zɛst] N gusto; (Culin) buccia
zigzag [ˈzɪgzæg] N zigzag m inv ▸ VI zigzagare
Zimbabwe [zɪmˈbɑːbwɪ] N Zimbabwe m
Zimbabwean [zɪmˈbɑːbwɪən] ADJ dello
  Zimbabwe
Zimmer® [ˈzɪməʳ] N (also: **Zimmer frame**)
  deambulatore m
zinc [zɪŋk] N zinco

Zionism [ˈzaɪənɪzəm] N sionismo
Zionist [ˈzaɪənɪst] ADJ sionistico(-a) ▸ N
  sionista mf
zip [zɪp] N (also: **zip fastener**) chiusura f or
  cerniera f lampo inv; (: energy) energia, forza
  ▸ VT (Comput) zippare; (also: **zip up**) chiudere
  con una cerniera lampo
zip code N (US) codice m di avviamento
  postale
zipper(US) N cerniera f lampo inv
zit [zɪt] N brufolo
zither [ˈzɪðəʳ] N cetra
zodiac [ˈzəudɪæk] N zodiaco
zombie [ˈzɔmbɪ] N (fig): **like a ~** come un
  morto che cammina
zone [zəun] N (also Mil) zona
zoo [zuː] N zoo m inv
zoological [zuəˈlɔdʒɪkl] ADJ zoologico(-a)
zoologist [zuːˈɔlədʒɪst] N zoologo(-a)
zoology [zuːˈɔlədʒɪ] N zoologia
zoom [zuːm] VI: **to ~ past** sfrecciare; **to ~ in
  (on sb/sth)** (Phot, Cine) zumare (su qn/qc)
zoom lens N zoom m inv, obiettivo a focale
  variabile
zucchini [zuːˈkiːnɪ] N (pl inv: US) zucchina
Zulu [ˈzuːluː] ADJ, N zulù mf
Zürich [ˈzjuərɪk] N Zurigo f

Grammar
Grammatica

Using the grammar

The Grammar section deals systematically and comprehensively with all the information you will need in order to communicate accurately in Italian. The user-friendly layout explains the grammar point on a left-hand page, leaving the facing page free for illustrative examples. The numbers, → ❶ etc, direct you to the relevant example in every case.

The Grammar section also provides invaluable guidance on the danger of translating English structures by identical structures in Italian. Use of Numbers and Punctuation are important areas covered towards the end of the section. Finally, the index lists the main words and grammatical terms in both English and Italian.

Italic letters in Italian words show where stress does not follow the usual rules.

Abbreviations

fem.	*feminine*
infin.	*infinitive*
masc.	*masculine*
perf.	*perfect*
plur.	*plural*
sing.	*singular*
qc	qualcosa
qn	qualcuno
sb	somebody
sth	something

Contents

Simple Tenses: Formation

In English, tenses are either simple, which means they consist of one word, e.g. *I work*, or compound, which means they consist of more than one word, e.g. *I have worked, I have been working*. The same is true in Italian.

In Italian the simple tenses are:

> Present → ❶
> Imperfect → ❷
> Future → ❸
> Present Conditional → ❹
> Past Historic → ❺
> Present Subjunctive → ❻
> Imperfect Subjunctive → ❼

They are formed by adding endings to a verb stem. The endings show the number and person of the subject of the verb → ❽

The stem and endings of regular verbs are totally predictable. The following sections show all the patterns for regular verbs. For irregular verbs see page 80 onwards.

Regular Verbs

There are three regular verb patterns (called conjugations), each identifiable by the ending of the infinitive:

> First conjugation verbs end in **-are** e.g. **parlare** to speak

> Second conjugation verbs end in **-ere** e.g. **credere** to believe

> Third conjugation verbs end in **-ire** e.g. **finire** to finish

These three conjugations are treated in order on the following pages.

Examples

1 parlo

    I speak
    I am speaking

  parlo?

    do I speak?

2 parlavo

    I spoke
    I was speaking
    I used to speak

3 parlerò

    I shall/will/'ll speak

4 parlerei

    I should/would/'d speak

5 parlai

    I spoke

6 (che) parli

    that I speak

7 (che) parlassi

    that I should speak

8 parlo
parliamo
parlerei
parleremmo

    I speak
we speak
I'd speak
we'd speak

Simple Tenses: First Conjugation

The stem is formed by taking the -are ending off the infinitive. The stem of parlare is parl- .

Add the following endings to the stem:

		① PRESENT	② IMPERFECT	③ FUTURE
	1st person	-o	-avo	-erò
sing.	2nd person	-i	-avi	-erai
	3rd person	-a	-ava	-erà
	1st person	-iamo	-avamo	-eremo
plur.	2nd person	-ate	-avate	-erete
	3rd person	-ano	-avano	-eranno

		④ PRESENT CONDITIONAL	⑤ PAST HISTORIC
	1st person	-erei	-ai
sing.	2nd person	-eresti	-asti
	3rd person	-erebbe	-ò
	1st person	-eremmo	-ammo
plur.	2nd person	-ereste	-aste
	3rd person	-erebbero	-arono

		⑥ PRESENT SUBJUNCTIVE	⑦ IMPERFECT SUBJUNCTIVE
sing.	1st, 2nd person	-i	-assi
	3rd person	-i	-asse
	1st person	-iamo	-assimmo
plur.	2nd person	-iate	-aste
	3rd person	-ino	-assero

Examples

1 PRESENT

parlo
parli
parla
parliamo
parlate
parlano

2 IMPERFECT

parlavo
parlavi
parlava
parlavamo
parlavate
parlavano

3 FUTURE

parlerò
parlerai
parlerà
parleremo
parlerete
parleranno

4 PRESENT CONDITIONAL

parlerei
parleresti
parlerebbe
parleremmo
parlereste
parlerebbero

5 PAST HISTORIC

parlai
parlasti
parlò
parlammo
parlaste
parlarono

6 PRESENT SUBJUNCTIVE

parli
parli
parli
parliamo
parliate
parlino

7 IMPERFECT SUBJUNCTIVE

parlassi
parlassi
parlasse
parlassimo
parlaste
parlassero

Simple Tenses: Second Conjugation

The stem is formed by taking the -ere ending off the infinitive. The stem of credere is cred- .

Add the following endings to the stem:

		① PRESENT	② IMPERFECT	③ FUTURE
	1ˢᵗ person	-o	-evo	-erò
sing.	2ⁿᵈ person	-i	-evi	-erai
	3ʳᵈ person	-e	-eva	-erà
	1ˢᵗ person	-iamo	-evamo	-eremo
plur.	2ⁿᵈ person	-ete	-evate	-erete
	3ʳᵈ person	-ono	-evano	-eranno

		④ PRESENT CONDITIONAL	⑤ PAST HISTORIC
	1ˢᵗ person	-erei	-ei or -etti
sing.	2ⁿᵈ person	-eresti	-esti
	3ʳᵈ person	-erebbe	-ette
	1ˢᵗ person	-eremmo	-emmo
plur.	2ⁿᵈ person	-ereste	-este
	3ʳᵈ person	-erebbero	-ettero

		⑥ PRESENT SUBJUNCTIVE	⑦ IMPERFECT SUBJUNCTIVE
sing.	1ˢᵗ, 2ⁿᵈ persons	-a	-essi
	3ʳᵈ person	-a	-esse
	1ˢᵗ person	-iamo	-essimmo
plur.	2ⁿᵈ person	-iate	-este
	3ʳᵈ person	-ano	-essero

Examples

1 PRESENT
credo
credi
crede
crediamo
credete
credono

2 IMPERFECT
credevo
credevi
credeva
credevamo
credevate
credevano

3 FUTURE
crederò
crederai
crederà
crederemo
crederete
crederanno

4 PRESENT CONDITIONAL
crederei
crederesti
crederebbe
crederemmo
credereste
crederebbero

5 PAST HISTORIC
credei *or* credetti
credesti
credette
credemmo
credeste
credettero

6 PRESENT SUBJUNCTIVE
creda
creda
creda
crediamo
crediate
credano

7 IMPERFECT SUBJUNCTIVE
credessi
credessi
credesse
credessimo
credeste
credessero

Simple Tenses: Third Conjugation

Generally, the stem is formed by taking the -ire ending off the infinitive. The stem for most tenses of **finire** is **fin-**.

However, in the present tense and present subjunctive, -**isc**- is added to the basic stem (except for the 1st and 2nd person plural):

EXCEPTIONS: **servire** to serve, **dormire** to sleep, **soffrire** to suffer, **coprire** to cover, **sentire** to feel, **partire** to leave, **offrire** to offer, **aprire** to offer

The present tenses of **finire** and **dormire** are as follows:

sing.	1st person	finisco	dormo
	2nd person	finisci	dormi
	3rd person	finisce	dorme
plur.	1st person	finiamo	dormiamo
	2nd person	finite	dormite
	3rd person	finiscono	dormono

Both types of verb take the following endings:

		➊ PRESENT	➋ IMPERFECT	➌ FUTURE
sing.	1st person	-o	-ivo	-irò
	2nd person	-i	-ivi	-irai
	3rd person	-e	-iva	-irà
plur.	1st person	-iamo	-ivamo	-iremo
	2nd person	-ite	-ivate	-irete
	3rd person	-ono	-ivano	-iranno

		➍ PRESENT CONDITIONAL	➎ PAST HISTORIC
sing.	1st person	-irei	-i
	2nd person	-iresti	-isti
	3rd person	-irebbe	-ì
plur.	1st person	-iremmo	-immo
	2nd person	-ireste	-iste
	3rd person	-irebbero	-irono

	⑥ PRESENT SUBJUNCTIVE	⑦ IMPERFECT SUBJUNCTIVE
sing. 1st, 2nd persons	-a	-issi
3rd person	-a	-isse
1st person	-iamo	-issimmo
plur. 2nd person	-iate	-iste
3rd person	-ano	-issero

① PRESENT
finisc**o**
finisc**i**
finisc**e**
fin**iamo**
fin**ite**
finisc**ono**

② IMPERFECT
fin**ivo**
fin**ivi**
fin**iva**
fin**ivamo**
fin**ivate**
fin**ivano**

③ FUTURE
fin**irò**
fin**irai**
fin**irà**
fin**iremo**
fin**irete**
fin**iranno**

④ PRESENT SUBJUNCTIVE
fin**irei**
fin**iresti**
fin**irebbe**
fin**iremmo**
fin**ireste**
fin**irebbero**

⑤ PAST HISTORIC
fin**ii**
fin**isti**
fin**ì**
fin**immo**
fin**iste**
fin**irono**

⑥ PRESENT SUBJUNCTIVE
finisc**a**
finisc**a**
finisc**a**
fin**iamo**
fin**iate**
fin**iscano**

⑦ IMPERFECT SUBJUNCTIVE
fin**issi**
fin**issi**
fin**isse**
fin**issimo**
fin**iste**
fin**issero**

First Conjugation Spelling Irregularities

Before certain endings, the stems of some -are verbs may change slightly.

Verbs ending:	-care
Change:	c becomes ch before e or i
Tenses affected:	Present, Future, Conditional, Present Subjunctive
Model:	cercare to look for → ❶

Why the change occurs: h is added to keep the c sound hard k.

Verbs ending:	-gare
Change:	g becomes gh before e or i
Tenses affected:	Present, Future, Conditional, Present Subjunctive
Model:	pagare to pay → ❷

Why the change occurs: h is added to keep the g sound hard g.

❶ INFINITIVE
cercare

PRESENT	FUTURE
cerco	**cercherò**
cerchi	**cercherai**
cerca	**cercherà**
cerchiamo	**cercheremo**
cercate	**cercherete**
cercano	**cercheranno**

CONDITIONAL	PRESENT SUBJUNCTIVE
cercherei	**cerchi**
cercheresti	**cerchi**
cercherebbe	**cerchi**
cercheremmo	**cerchiamo**
cerchereste	**cerchiate**
cercherebbero	**cerchino**

❷ INFINITIVE
pagare

PRESENT	FUTURE
pago	**pagherò**
paghi	**pagherai**
paga	**pagherà**
paghiamo	**pagheremo**
pagate	**pagherete**
pagano	**pagheranno**

CONDITIONAL	PRESENT SUBJUNCTIVE
pagherei	**paghi**
pagheresti	**paghi**
pagherebbe	**paghi**
pagheremmo	**paghiamo**
paghereste	**paghiate**
pagherebbero	**paghino**

First Conjugation Spelling Irregularities *continued*

Verbs ending: -ciare
Change: i is dropped before e or i
Tenses affected: Present, Future, Conditional, Present Subjunctive
Model: **annunciare** to announce → ❶

Why the change occurs: the i of the infinitive is needed to keep c soft
                         tʃ before a (before e and i, c is soft, so the i is
                         unnecessary).

Verbs ending: -giare
Change: i is dropped before e or i
Tenses affected: Present, Future, Conditional, Present Subjunctive
Model: **mangiare** to eat → ❷

Why the change occurs: the i of the infinitive is needed to keep g soft
                         dʒ before a (before e and i, g is soft, so the i is
                         unnecessary).

Examples

1 INFINITIVE
annunciare

PRESENT	FUTURE
annuncio	**annuncerò**
annunci	**annuncerai**
annuncia	**annuncerà**
annunciamo	**annunceremo**
annunciate	**annuncerete**
annunciano	**annunceranno**

CONDITIONAL	PRESENT SUBJUNCTIVE
annuncerei	**annunci**
annunceresti	**annunci**
annuncerebbe	**annunci**
annunceremmo	**annunciamo**
annuncereste	**annunciate**
annuncerebbero	**annuncino**

2 INFINITIVE
mangiare

PRESENT	FUTURE
mangio	**mangerò**
mangi	**mangerai**
mangia	**mangerà**
mangiamo	**mangeremo**
mangiate	**mangerete**
mangiano	**mangeranno**

CONDITIONAL	PRESENT SUBJUNCTIVE
mangerei	**mangi**
mangeresti	**mangi**
mangerebbe	**mangi**
mangeremmo	**mangiamo**
mangereste	**mangiate**
mangerebbero	**mangino**

First Conjugation Spelling Irregularities *continued*

Verbs ending: -iare
Change: i is not dropped before another i, which is what usually happens
Tenses affected: Present, Present Subjunctive
Model: **inviare** to send, **sciare** to ski → **❶**

Why the change occurs: The i has to be retained in forms where it is the stressed vowel.

Verbs ending: -gliare
Change: i is dropped before endings beginning with -i
Tenses affected: Present, Present subjunctive, Imperfect Subjunctive, Imperative
Model: **consigliare** to advise, **svegliare** to wake up → **❷**

Why the change occurs: There is no need to retain the i.

Examples

1 INFINITIVE
inviare

PRESENT
invio
invii
invia
inviamo
inviate
inviano

2 INFINITIVE
svegliare

PRESENT
sveglio
svegli
sveglia
svegliamo
svegliate
svegliano

The Imperative

The imperative is the form of the verb used to give commands or instructions. It can be used politely, as in English 'Please take a seat'. In Italian, the polite imperative is the 3rd person form, either singular or plural. The 1st person plural (we) is used to make suggestions, as in 'Let's go'.

The imperative is formed by adding endings to the stem of the verb. The endings for the 1st and 2nd persons plural are the same as those for the present tense, the others are different. → ❶

			FIRST	SECOND	THIRD
sing.	2nd	person	-a	-i	-i
	3rd	person	-i	-a	-a
plur.	1st	person	-iamo	-iamo	-iamo
	2nd	person	-ate	-ete	-ite
	3rd	person	-ino	-ano	-ano

NB Third conjugation verbs which add **isc** to the stem in the present tense also do so in the imperative → ❷

The imperative of irregular verbs is given in the verb tables page 80.

Position of object and reflexive pronouns with the imperative:
- they follow imperatives in the 2nd person and the **-iamo** form, and are joined on to make one word → ❸
- they precede 3rd person polite imperatives, and are not joined on to them → ❹

Changes to pronouns following the imperative:
- the first letter of the pronoun is doubled when the imperative is one syllable: **mi** becomes **mmi**, **ti** becomes **tti**, **lo** becomes **llo** etc → ❺
- When the pronouns **mi**, **ti**, **ci** and **vi** are followed by another pronoun they become **-me**, **-te**, **-ce** and **-ve**, and **gli** and **le** become **glie-** → ❻

Negative imperatives:
- **non** precedes the imperative to make it negative (except in the 2nd person singular) → ❼
- **non** precedes the infinitive in the 2nd person singular) → ❽
- in 2nd person singular negative commands, **non** is used with the infinitive instead of the imperative. Pronouns may be joined onto the infinitive, or precede it → ❽

Examples

1 Compare:

Aspetti, Maria?	Are you waiting, Maria?
and: Aspetta Maria!	Wait Maria!
Prende l'autobus	He gets the bus
and: Prenda l'autobus, signora!	Get the bus, madam!

2

Finisci l'esercizio, Marco!	Finish the exercise, Marco!
Finisca tutto, signore!	Finish it all, sir!
Finiamo tutto	Let's finish it all
Finite i compiti, ragazzi!	Finish your homework, children!
Finiscano tutto signori!	Finish it all, ladies and gentlemen!

3

Guardami, mamma!	Look at me, mum!
Aspettateli!	Wait for them!
Proviamolo!	Let's try it!

4

Mi dia un chilo d'uva, per favore	Give me a kilo of grapes please
Si accomodi!	Take a seat!
La prenda, signore	Take it, sir

5

Dimmi!	Tell me!
Fallo subito!	Do it immediately!

6

Mandameli	Send me them
Daglielo	Give it to him
Mandiamogliela!	Let's send it to them!

7

Non dimentichiamo	Don't let's forget
Non si preoccupi, signore	Don't worry, sir

8

Non dire bugie Andrea!	Don't tell lies Andrea!
Non dimenticare!	Don't forget!
Non toccarlo! or Non lo toccare!	Don't touch it!
Non glielo dire! or Non dirglielo	Don't tell him about it!
Non preoccuparti! or Non ti preoccupare!	Don't worry!

Compound Tenses

Continuous tenses

The simple tense of an Italian verb, e.g. **piove**, can have two meanings: 'it rains', or 'it's raining'; the continuous tense, **sta piovendo** is an alternative way of expressing the English present continuous (it's raining).

The Present Continuous is used less in Italian than in English. It is formed with the present tense of the verb **stare**, plus the gerund → ●

The Past Continuous is formed with the imperfect tense of **stare**, and the gerund → ●

For information on how to form the gerund, see page 52.

The Past Continuous is also less used in Italian than in English, as the imperfect tense can be used to express this meaning.

Examples

1   Ci sto pensando   I'm thinking about it
Stanno arrivando   They're coming
Cosa stai facendo?   What are you doing?

2   Stavo studiando   I was studying
Stava morendo   He was dying
Stavano lavorando   They were working

Compound Tenses *continued*

Formed with the past participle

These are:

> Perfect → **1**
> Pluperfect → **2**
> Future Perfect → **3**
> Perfect Conditional → **4**
> Past Anterior → **5**
> Perfect Subjunctive → **6**
> Pluperfect Subjunctive → **7**

They consist of the past past participle and an auxiliary verb. Most verbs take the auxiliary **avere**, but some take *essere* (see page 30).

These tenses are formed in the same way for regular and irregular verbs, the only difference being that an irregular verb may have an irregular past participle.

The Past Participle

The past participle of regular verbs is formed as follows:

> First conjugation: replace the **-are** of the infinitive with **-ato** → **8**

> Second conjugation: replace the **-ere** of the infinitive with **-uto** → **9**

> Third conjugation: replace the **-ire** of the infinitive with **-ito** → **10**

Examples

with **avere**		with **essere**	
1 ho parlato	I spoke, have spoken	sono andato	I went, have gone
2 avevo parlato	I had spoken	ero andato	I had gone
3 avrò parlato	I will have spoken	sarò andato	I will have gone
4 avrei parlato	I would have spoken	sarei andato	I would have gone
5 ebbi parlato	I had spoken	fui andato	I had gone
6 *a*bbia parlato	I spoke, have spoken	sia andato	I went, have gone
7 avessi parlato	I had spoken	fossi andato	I had gone
8 parlare to speak → parlato spoken			
9 credere to believe → creduto believed			
10 finire to finish → finito finished			

Compound Tenses *continued*

Verbs taking the auxiliary avere

PERFECT TENSE
The present tense of **avere** plus the past participle → ❶

PLUPERFECT TENSE
The imperfect tense of **avere** plus the past participle → ❷

FUTURE PERFECT
The future tense of **avere** plus the past participle → ❸

PERFECT CONDITIONAL
The conditional of **avere** plus the past participle → ❹

PAST ANTERIOR
The past historic of **avere** plus the past participle → ❺

PERFECT SUBJUNCTIVE
The present subjunctive of **avere** plus the past participle → ❻

PLUPERFECT SUBJUNCTIVE
The imperfect subjunctive of **avere** plus the past participle → ❼

For how to form the past participle of regular verbs see page 24. The past participle of irregular verbs is given for each verb in the verb tables, page 80 onwards.

The past participle agrees in number and gender with a preceding direct object when it is **lo, la, li** or **le**, e.g.

Le matite? Le ho comprate ieri   The pencils? I bought them yesterday

Examples

① PERFECT

ho parlato	abbiamo parlato
hai parlato	avete parlato
ha parlato	hanno parlato

② PLUPERFECT

avevo parlato	avevamo parlato
avevi parlato	avevate parlato
aveva parlato	avevano parlato

③ FUTURE PERFECT

avrò parlato	avremo parlato
avrai parlato	avrete parlato
avrà parlato	avranno parlato

④ PERFECT CONDITIONAL

avrei parlato	avremmo parlato
avresti parlato	avreste parlato
avrebbe parlato	avrebbero parlato

⑤ PAST ANTERIOR

ebbi parlato	avemmo parlato
avesti parlato	aveste parlato
ebbe parlato	ebbero parlato

⑥ PERFECT SUBJUNCTIVE

abbia parlato	abbiamo parlato
abbia parlato	abbiate parlato
abbia parlato	abbiano parlato

⑦ PLUPERFECT SUBJUNCTIVE

avessi parlato	avessimo parlato
avessi parlato	aveste parlato
avesse parlato	avessero parlato

Compound Tenses *continued*

Verbs taking the auxiliary *essere*

PERFECT TENSE
The present tense of *essere* plus the past participle → ❶

PLUPERFECT TENSE
The imperfect tense of *essere* plus the past participle → ❷

FUTURE PERFECT
The future tense of *essere* plus the past participle → ❸

PERFECT CONDITIONAL
The conditional of *essere* plus the past participle → ❹

PAST ANTERIOR
The past historic of *essere* plus the past participle → ❺

PERFECT SUBJUNCTIVE
The present subjunctive of *essere* plus the past participle → ❻

PLUPERFECT SUBJUNCTIVE
The imperfect subjunctive of *essere* plus the past participle → ❼

For how to form the past participle of regular verbs see page 24. The past participle of irregular verbs is given for each verb in the verb tables, page 80 onwards.

For agreement of past participles see page 56.

For a list of verbs and verb types that take the auxiliary *essere*, see page 30.

Examples

❶ PERFECT

sono andato(a)	siamo andati(e)
sei andato(a)	siete andati(e)
è andato(a)	sono andati(e)

❷ PLUPERFECT

ero andato(a)	eravamo andati(e)
eri andato(a)	eravate andati(e)
era andato(a)	erano andati(e)

❸ FUTURE PERFECT

sarò andato(a)	saremo andati(e)
sarai andato(a)	sarete andati(e)
sarà andato(a)	saranno andati(e)

❹ PERFECT CONDITIONAL

sarei andato(a)	saremmo andati(e)
saresti andato(a)	sareste andati(e)
sarebbe andato(a)	sarebbero andati(e)

❺ PAST ANTERIOR

fui andato(a)	fummo andati(e)
fosti andato(a)	foste andati(e)
fu andato(a)	furono andati(e)

❻ PERFECT SUBJUNCTIVE

sia andato(a)	siamo andati(e)
sia andato(a)	siate andati(e)
sia andato(a)	siano andati(e)

❼ PLUPERFECT SUBJUNCTIVE

fossi andato(a)	fossimo andati(e)
fossi andato(a)	foste andati(e)
fosse andato(a)	fossero andati(e)

Compound Tenses *continued*

The following verbs take the auxiliary *essere*

Reflexive verbs (see page 32) → ❶

Many intransitive verbs (i.e. verbs not taking a direct object), including the following:

andare to go	**partire** to leave
apparire to appear	**restare** to stay
arrivare to arrive → ❷	**rimanere** to stay
bastare to be enough	**ritornare** to return → ❹
cadere to fall	**riuscire** to succeed/manage → ❺
costare to cost → ❸	**salire** to go up/get on
dipendere to depend	**scadere** to expire
divenire to become	**scappare** to get away
diventare to become	**scendere** to go down
durare to last	**scivolare** to slip
entrare to come in	**sparire** to disappear → ❻
esistere to exist	**stare** to be/stay
essere to be	**succedere** to happen
fuggire to escape	**tornare** to come back
intervenire to intervene	**venire** to come
morire to die	**uscire** to go out
nascere to be born	

The following verbs, often used in impersonal constructions:

bisognare	**occorrere**
convenire	**parere** → ❽
dispiacere	**piacere** → ❾
importare	**sembrare**
mancare → ❼	

Verbs that can be used both transitively and intransitively take the auxiliary *essere* when intransitive and **avere** when transitive → ❿

Impersonal verbs which describe the weather are used with both *essere* and **avere** → ⓫

ⓘ Note that the past participle agrees in gender and number with the subject of verbs conjugated with *essere*.

Examples

1. Mi sono fatto male — I've hurt or I hurt myself
   Si è rotta la gamba — She's broken or She broke her leg
   Vi siete divertiti? — Did you have or Have you had a nice time?
   Si sono addormentati — They've gone or They went to sleep

2. È arrivata — She's arrived or She arrived

3. È costato parecchio — It cost a lot or It has cost a lot

4. Siamo ritornati — We've returned or We returned

5. Sei riuscito? — Did you succeed? or Have you succeeded?

6. Sono spariti — They've disappeared

7. Ti sono mancata? — Did you miss me?

8. Mi è parso strano — It seemed strange to me

9. Vi è piaciuta la musica? — Did you like the music?

10. **passare**
    Intransitive
    Sono passati molti anni — Many years have passed
    Transitive
    Ho passato l'esame — I've passed the exam
    saltare
    Intransitive
    Il gatto è saltato sul tavolo — The cat jumped on the table
    Transitive
    Ho saltato il pranzo — I skipped lunch

11. Ha piovuto or
    È piovuto molto — It rained a lot
    Ha nevicato! or
    È nevicato! — It's snowed!

31

Verbs

Reflexive Verbs

A reflexive verb is one accompanied by a reflexive pronoun, e.g. **divertirsi** to enjoy oneself; **annoiarsi** to get bored.
The reflexive pronouns are:

	SINGULAR	PLURAL
1st person	mi	ci
2nd person	ti	vi
3rd person	si	si

The Italian reflexive pronoun is often not translated in English → ❶

Plural reflexive pronouns can sometimes be translated as 'each other' → ❷

Simple tenses of reflexive verbs are conjugated in exactly the same way as other verbs, except that the reflexive pronoun is always used. Compound tenses are conjugated with the auxiliary **essere**. A sample reflexive verb is conjugated in full on pages 36 and 37.

Position of Reflexive Pronouns

The pronoun generally comes before the verb → ❸

However, in positive 2nd person commands the pronoun is joined onto the end of the imperative → ❹

In the infinitive, the final **e** is dropped and replaced by the reflexive pronoun → ❺

When the infinitive is used with **non** in negative commands, the reflexive pronoun **ti** either comes first, as a separate word, or is joined on at the end → ❻

Two alternatives also exist
- when the infinitive is used after another verb, the pronoun either goes before the main verb or joins onto the infinitive → ❼
- in continuous tenses the pronoun either goes before the main verb or joins onto the gerund → ❽

1
Mi annoio	I'm getting bored
Ti fidi di lui?	Do you trust him?
Si vergogna	He's embarrassed
Non vi preoccupate!	Don't worry!

2
Si odiano	They hate each other

3
Mi diverto	I'm enjoying myself
Ci prepariamo	We're getting ready
Si accomodi!	Take a seat!

4
Svegliati!	Wake up!
Divertitevi!	Enjoy yourselves!

5 Compare:

ordinary infinitive	reflexive infinitive
lavare to wash	lavarsi to get washed, wash oneself
divertire to amuse	divertirsi to enjoy oneself

6
Non ti bruciare! or	
Non bruciarti!	Don't burn yourself!
Non ti preoccupare! or	
Non preoccuparti!	Don't worry!

Mi voglio abbronzare or	
Voglio abbronzarmi	I want to get a tan
Ti devi alzare or	
Devi alzarti	You must get up
Vi dovreste preparare or	
Dovreste prepararvi	You ought to get ready

7
Ti stai annoiando? or	
Stai annoiandoti?	Are you getting bored?
Si stanno alzando? or	
Stanno alzandosi?	Are they getting up?

Reflexive Verbs *continued*

Past Participle Agreement

The past participle used in compound tenses of reflexive verbs generally agrees with the subject of the verb → **1**

Here are some common reflexive verbs:

accomodarsi to sit down/take a seat
addormentarsi to go to sleep
alzarsi to get up
annoiarsi to get bored/be bored
arrabbiarsi to get angry
cambiarsi to get changed
chiamarsi to be called
chiedersi to wonder
divertirsi to enjoy oneself/have fun
farsi male to hurt oneself
fermarsi to stop
lavarsi to wash/get washed
perdersi to get lost
pettinarsi to comb one's hair
preoccuparsi to worry
prepararsi to get ready
ricordarsi to remember
sbrigarsi to hurry
sedersi to sit
svegliarsi to wake up
vestirsi to dress/get dressed

Examples

1 Si è lavato le mani   He washed his hands
Si è lavata le mani   She washed her hands
I ragazzi si sono lavati le mani   The boys washed their hands
Le ragazze si sono lavate le mani   The girls washed their hands

Reflexive Verbs *continued*

Conjugation of: **divertirsi** to enjoy oneself – SIMPLE TENSES

PRESENT

mi diverto
ti diverti
si diverte

ci divertiamo
vi divertite
si divertono

IMPERFECT

mi divertivo
ti divertivi
si divertiva

ci divertivamo
vi divertivate
si divertivano

FUTURE

mi divertirò
ti divertirai
si divertirà

ci divertiremo
vi divertirete
si divertiranno

CONDITIONAL

mi divertirei
ti divertiresti
si divertirebbe

ci divertiremmo
vi divertireste
si divertirebbero

PAST HISTORIC

mi divertii
ti divertisti
si divertì

ci divertimmo
vi divertiste
si divertirono

PRESENT SUBJUNCTIVE

mi diverta
ti diverta
si diverta

ci divertiamo
vi divertiate
si divertano

IMPERFECT SUBJUNCTIVE

mi divertissi
ti divertissi
si divertisse

ci divertissimo
vi divertiste
si divertissero

Verbs

Conjugation of: **divertirsi** to enjoy oneself – COMPOUND TENSES

PRESENT CONTINUOUS
mi sto divertendo*or*
sto divertendomi
ti stai divertendo*or*
stai divertendoti
si sta divertendo*or*
sta divertendosi

ci stiamo divertendo*or*
stiamo divertendoci
vi state divertendo*or*
state divertendovi
si stanno divertendo*or*
stanno divertendosi

PERFECT
mi sono divertito(a)
ti sei divertito(a)
si è divertito(a)

ci siamo divertiti(e)
vi siete divertiti(e)
si sono divertiti(e)

PLUPERFECT
mi ero divertito(a)
ti eri divertito(a)
si era divertito(a)

ci eravamo divertiti(e)
vi eravate divertiti(e)
si erano divertiti(e)

FUTURE PERFECT
mi sarò divertito(a)
ti sarai divertito(a)
si sarà divertito(a)

ci saremo divertiti(e)
vi sarete divertiti(e)
si saranno divertiti(e)

PERFECT CONDITIONAL
mi sarei divertito(a)
ti saresti divertito(a)
si sarebbe divertito(a)

ci saremmo divertiti(e)
vi sareste divertiti(e)
si sarebbero divertiti(e)

PAST ANTERIOR
mi fui divertito(a)
ti fosti divertito(a)
si fu divertito(a)

ci fummo divertiti(e)
vi foste divertiti(e)
si furono divertiti(e)

PERFECT SUBJUNCTIVE
mi sia divertito(a)
ti sia divertito(a)
si sia divertito(a)

ci siamo divertiti(e)
vi siate divertiti(e)
si siano divertiti(e)

PLUPERFECT SUBJUNCTIVE
mi fossi divertito(a)
ti fossi divertito(a)
si fosse divertito(a)

ci fossimo divertiti(e)
vi foste divertiti(e)
si fossero divertiti(e)

The Passive

In the passive, the subject *receives* the action (e.g. I was hit) as opposed to *performing* it (e.g. I hit him). In English the passive is formed with the verb 'to be' and the past participle, and in Italian the passive is formed in exactly the same way, i.e. a tense of **essere** + *past participle*.

The past participle agrees in gender and number with the subject → ❶

A sample verb is conjugated in the passive on pages 40 and 41.

In English it is possible to make the indirect object of an active sentence into the subject of a passive sentence, e.g. Someone told me → I was told.

This is not possible in Italian; instead a 3ʳᵈ person plural can be used → ❷

The passive is used less overall in Italian. The following alternatives are used:
- active constructions → ❸
- the **si passivante** (preceding an active verb with **si** , to make it passive → ❹
- an impersonal construction with **si** → ❺

Examples

1 È stato costretto a ritirarsi dalla gara — He was forced to withdraw from the competition

L'elettricità è stata tagliata ieri — The electricity was cut off yesterday

La partita è stata rinviata — The match has been postponed

Siamo invitati ad una festa a casa loro — We're invited to a party at their house

I ladri sono stati catturati — The thieves have been caught

Le finestre saranno riparate domani — The windows will be repaired tomorrow

2 Mi hanno dato una chiave — I've been given a key

Gli diranno tutto — He'll be told everything

3 Due persone sono morte — Two people were killed

Mi hanno rubato la macchina la settimana scorsa — My car was stolen last week

C'erano delle microspie nella stanza — The room was bugged

Dicono che sia molto ambizioso — He's said to be very ambitious

4 Dove si trovano i vini migliori? — Where are the best wines to be found?

Non si accettano assegni — Cheques are not accepted

Queste parole non si usano più — These words are no longer used

Questo vino si beve a temperatura ambiente — This wine should be drunk at room temperature

5 Non si fa così — That's not how it's done

Si raccomanda la massima discrezione — The utmost discretion is called for

The Passive *continued*

Conjugation of: **invitare** to invite

PRESENT

sono invitato(a)	siamo invitati(e)
sei invitato(a)	siete invitati(e)
è invitato(a)	sono invitati(e)

IMPERFECT

ero invitato(a)	ervamo invitati(e)
eri invitato(a)	eravate invitati(e)
era invitato(a)	erano invitati(e)

FUTURE

sarò invitato(a)	saremo invitati(e)
sarai invitato(a)	sarete invitati(e)
sarà invitato(a)	saranno invitati(e)

CONDITIONAL

sarei invitato(a)	saremmo invitati(e)
saresti invitato(a)	sareste invitati(e)
sarebbe invitato(a)	sarebbero invitati(e)

PAST HISTORIC

fui invitato(a)	fummo invitati(e)
fosti invitato(a)	foste invitati(e)
fu invitato(a)	furono invitati(e)

PRESENT SUBJUNCTIVE

sia invitato(a)	siamo invitati(e)
sia invitato(a)	siate invitati(e)
sia invitato(a)	siano invitati(e)

IMPERFECT SUBJUNCTIVE

fossi invitato(a)	fossimo invitati(e)
fossi invitato(a)	foste invitati(e)
fosse invitato(a)	fossero invitati(e)

The Passive *continued*

Conjugation of: **invitare** to invite

PERFECT

sono stato(a) invitato(a)	siamo stati(e) invitati(e)
sei stato(a) invitato(a)	siete stati(e) invitati(e)
è stato(a) invitato(a)	sono stati(e) invitati(e)

PLUPERFECT

ero stato(a) invitato(a)	eravamo stati(e) invitati(e)
eri stato(a) invitato(a)	eravate stati(e) invitati(e)
era stato(a) invitato(a)	erano stati(e) invitati(e)

FUTURE PERFECT

sarò stato(a) invitato(a)	saremo stati(e) invitati(e)
sarai stato(a) invitato(a)	sarete stati(e) invitati(e)
sarà stato(a) invitato(a)	saranno stati(e) invitati(e)

PERFECT CONDITIONAL

sarei stato(a) invitato(a)	saremmo stati(e) invitati(e)
saresti stato(a) invitato(a)	sareste stati(e) invitati(e)
sarebbe stato(a) invitato(a)	sarebbero stati(e) invitati(e)

PAST ANTERIOR

fui stato(a) invitato(a)	fummo stati(e) invitati(e)
fosti stato(a) invitato(a)	foste stati(e) invitati(e)
fu stato(a) invitato(a)	furono stati(e) invitati(e)

PERFECT SUBJUNCTIVE

sia stato(a) invitato(a)	siamo stati(e) invitati(e)
sia stato(a) invitato(a)	siate stati(e) invitati(e)
sia stato(a) invitato(a)	siano stati(e) invitati(e)

PLUPERFECT SUBJUNCTIVE

fossi stato(a) invitato(a)	fossimo stati(e) invitati(e)
fossi stato(a) invitato(a)	foste stati(e) invitati(e)
fosse stato(a) invitato(a)	fossero stati(e) invitati(e)

Impersonal Verbs

Any verb can be made impersonal by the use of **si** → ➊

si is often used to make the following verbs impersonal:

dire	**si dice che** → ➋ it's said that
potere	**si può** → ➌ it's possible to/you can
trattarsi	**si tratta di** → ➍ it's about/it's a matter of

Impersonal verbs are used only in the infinitive, with a gerund and in third person singular simple tenses. No pronoun is used in Italian.

e.g.
Ha iniziato a piovere.	It started to rain.
Sta piovendo?	Is it raining?
Nevicava da due giorni.	It had been snowing for two days.
È facile capire che...	It's easy to see that...

Common impersonal verbs are:

diluviare	diluvia	it's pouring
gelare	gela	it's freezing
grandinare	grandina	it's hailing
nevicare	nevica	it's snowing
piovere	piove	it's raining
tuonare	tuona	it's thundering

Other verbs are often used impersonally:

bastare	basta	that's enough
importare	non importa	it doesn't matter

Examples

1 In quel ristorante si mangia bene e si spende poco

In that restaurant the food's good and it doesn't cost much

2 Si dice che sia una persona strana

It's said that he's a strange person

3 Si può visitare il castello tutti i giorni dell'anno

You can visit the castle every day of the year

4 Di cosa si tratta?
Si tratta di poche ore

What's it about?
It's a matter of a few hours

Impersonal Verbs *continued*

The following verbs are used in impersonal constructions:

INFINITIVE	CONSTRUCTIONS
bastare	**basta** + *infinitive* → ❶ you just have to
bisognare	**bisogna** + *infinitive* → ❷ you have to
convenire	*indirect pronoun* + **conviene** + *infinitive* → ❸ it's best to
essere	**è** + *noun to do with time/season* → ❹
sono	+ *plural times of the clock* → ❺ it is **è** + *adjective* + *infinitive* → ❻ **è** + *adjective* + **che** → ❼ it is
fare	**fa** + *adjective describing weather* → ❽ it is **fa** + *noun to do with weather, time of day*
occorrere	**occorre** + *infinitive* → ❾ it would be best to
parere	**pare** + **di** + **sì/no** → ❿ it seems so/not **pare** + **che** → ⓫ it seems/apparently
sembrare	**sembra** + **che** → ⓬ it seems

Examples

1. Basta chiedere a qualcuno — You just have to ask someone

2. Bisogna prenotare? — Do you have to book?
   Bisogna arrivare un'ora prima — You have to get there an hour before

3. Conviene partire presto — It's best to set off early

4. È tardi. — It's late
   Era presto — It was early
   Era Pasqua — It was Easter
   È mezzogiorno — It's midday

5. Sono le otto — It's eight o'clock

6. È stato stupido buttarli via — It was stupid to throw them away
   Sarebbe bello andarci — It would be nice to go there

7. È vero che sono stato impaziente — It's true that I've been impatient
   È possibile che abbia sbagliato tu — Maybe you made a mistake

8. Fa caldo — It's hot
   Fa freddo — It's cold
   Faceva bel tempo — It was good weather or The weather was good

   Fa sempre brutto tempo — The weather's always bad
   Si sta facendo buio — It's getting dark

9. Occorre farlo subito — It would be best to do it immediately

10. Sono contenti? — Pare di sì. — Are they happy? — It seems so.
    L'ha creduto? — Pare di no. — Did he believe it? — Apparently not.

11. Pare che sia stato lui — Apparently it was him

12. Sembra che tu abbia ragione — It seems you're right

The Infinitive

The infinitive is the form of the verb found in dictionary entries, e.g.
parlare to speak; **finire** to finish. The infinitive sometimes drops its final -e.

All regular verbs have infinitives ending in **-are**, **-ere**, or **-ire**.

A few irregular verbs have infinitives ending in **-rre**, e.g.

comporre	to compose	**condurre**	to lead
porre	to put	**produrre**	to produce
proporre	to propose	**ridurre**	to reduce
supporre	to suppose	**tradurre**	to translate

In Italian the infinitive is used in the following ways:
- after adjectives and nouns that are followed by **di** → ❶
- after another verb → ❷
- to give instructions and orders → ❸
- in 2nd person negative imperatives → ❹

See page 20 for negative imperatives

- after prepositions → ❺

See pages 190-197 for prepositions

- as the subject or object of a sentence → ❻

There are three main types of constructions when the infinitive follows
another verb:
- no linking preposition → ❼
- linking preposition **a** (see also pages 70-78) → ❽
- linking preposition **di** (see also pages 70-78) → ❾

Examples

1   Sono contento di vederti   I'm glad to see you
Sono sorpreso di vederti qui   I'm surprised to see you here
Sono stufo di studiare   I'm fed up of studying
Non c'è bisogno di prenotare   There's no need to book

2   Non devi mangiare se non vuoi   You don't have to eat if you don't want to

Posso entrare?   Can I come in?
Cosa ti piacerebbe fare?   What would you like to do?

3   Rallentare   Slow down
Spingere   Push

4   Non fare sciocchezze!   Don't do anything silly!
Non toccarlo!   Don't touch it!

5   È andato via senza dire niente   He went away without saying anything

6   Camminare fa bene   Walking is good for you
Mi piace cavalcare   I like riding

7   Devi aspettare   You must wait

8   Hanno cominciato a ridere   They started to laugh

9   Quando sono entrato hanno smesso di parlare   When I came in they stopped talking

The Infinitive *continued*

Verbs followed by the infinitive with no linking preposition

dovere, potere, sapere, volere (i.e. modal auxiliary verbs: page 58).

verbs of seeing and hearing, e.g. vedere to see; sentire to hear → ❶

Verbs used impersonally such as piacere, dispiacere, occorrere and convenire → ❷

fare → ❸

lasciare to let, allow → ❹

The following common verbs:

bisognare → ❺	to be necessary
detestare	to hate
desiderare → ❻	to want
odiare → ❼	to hate
preferire → ❽	to prefer

1	Ci ha visto arrivare	He saw us arriving
	Ti ho sentito cantare	I heard you singing
2	Mi piace andare in bici	I like cycling
	Ci dispiace andar via	We're sorry to be leaving
	Occorre farlo subito	It should be done immediately
	Ti conviene partire presto	You'd best set off early
3	Non mi far ridere!	Don't make me laugh!
4	Lascia fare a me	Let me do it
5	Bisogna prenotare	You need to book
6	Desiderava migliorare il suo inglese	He wanted to improve his English
7	Odio alzarmi presto al mattino	I hate getting up early in the morning
8	Preferisco non parlarne	I prefer not to talk about it

The Infinitive *continued*

Set expressions

The following are set in Italian with the meaning shown:

> far entrare to let in → ①
> far sapere to inform/let someone know → ②
> far fare to have done → ③
> farsi fare to have done → ④
> lasciare stare to leave alone → ⑤
> sentir dire che to hear that → ⑥
> sentir parlare di to hear about → ⑦
> voler dire to mean → ⑧

The Perfect Infinitive

The perfect infinitive is formed using the auxiliary verb avere or *essere* (as appropriate) with the past participle of the verb → ⑨

The perfect infinitive is found:
- after modal verbs → ⑩
- after prepositions → ⑪

Examples

①	Non mi hanno fatto entrare	They wouldn't let me in
②	Ti farò sapere prima possibile	I'll let you know as soon as possible
③	Ho fatto riparare la macchina	I had the car repaired
④	Mi sono fatta tagliare i capelli	I had my hair cut
⑤	Lascia stare mia sorella!	Leave my sister alone!
⑥	Ho sentito dire che è stato licenziato	I heard he's been sacked
⑦	Non ho più sentito parlare di loro	I haven't heard any more about them
⑧	Non so che cosa vuol dire	I don't know what it means
⑨	aver(e) visto	to have seen
	essere partito	to have gone
	essersi fatto male	to have hurt oneself
⑩	Può aver avuto un incidente	He may have had an accident
	Dev'essere successo ieri	It must have happened yesterday
⑪	senza aver dato un esame	without having done an exam
	dopo essere rimasto chiuso	after having been closed

The Gerund

Formation

First conjugation:

Replace the -are of the infinitive with -ando → ❶

Second and Third conjugations:

Replace the -ere, or -ire of the infinitive with -endo → ❷

Exceptions to these rules are:

fare and verbs made by adding a prefix to fare → ❸
dire and verbs made by adding a prefix to dire → ❹
porre and verbs made by adding a prefix to porre → ❺
verbs with infinitives ending in -durre → ❻

The gerund is invariable.*

*A word that is invariable never changes its ending.

Examples

1. parlare to speak → parlando speaking
   andare to go → andando going
   dare to give → dando giving

2. credere to believe → credendo believing
   essere to be → essendo being
   dovere to have to → dovendo having to
   finire to finish → finendo finishing
   dormire to sleep → dormendo sleeping

3. fare to do → facendo doing
   rifare to redo → rifacendo redoing

4. dire to say → dicendo saying
   contraddire to contradict → contraddicendo contradicting

5. porre to put → ponendo putting
   comporre to compose → componendo composing
   supporre to suppose → supponendo supposing

6. condurre to lead → conducendo leading
   produrre to produce → producendo producing
   ridurre to reduce → riducendo reducing

The Gerund *continued*

Uses

The gerund is used with the present tense of **stare** to make the present continuous tense → ❶

The gerund is used with the imperfect tense of **stare** to make the past continuous tense → ❷

ⓘ Note that the Italian past participle is sometimes used with the verbs *stare* or *essere* to make a continuous tense, e.g.

essere or stare disteso	to be lying → ❸
essere or stare seduto	to be sitting → ❸
essere or stare appoggiato	to be leaning → ❸

The gerund can used adverbially, to indicate when or why something happens → ❹

Pronouns are usually joined onto the end of the gerund → ❺

When the gerund is part of a continuous tense the pronoun can either come before **stare** or be joined onto the gerund → ❻

Examples

1   Sto lavorando   I'm working
    Cosa stai facendo?   What are you doing?

2   Il bambino stava piangendo   The little boy was crying
    Stavo lavando i piatti   I was washing the dishes

3   Era disteso sul divano   He was lying on the sofa
    Stava seduta accanto a me   She was sitting next to me
    La scala era appoggiata al muro   The ladder was leaning against the wall

4   Entrando ho sentito odore di pesce   When I came in I could smell fish
    Ripensandoci, credo che non fosse colpa sua   Thinking back on it, I reckon it wasn't his fault
    Vedendolo solo, è venuta a parlargli   Seeing that he was on his own, she came to speak to him
    Sentendomi male, sono andato a letto   Because I felt ill I went to bed
    Volendo, potremmo comprarne un altro   If we wanted to, we could buy another

5   Vedendoli è scoppiata in lacrime   When she saw them she burst into tears
    Mi sono addormentato ascoltandolo   As I listened to him I fell asleep
    Sbagliando si impara   You learn by making mistakes

6   Ti sto parlando *or*
    Sto parlandoti   I'm talking to you
    Si sta vestendo *or*
    Sta vestendosi   He's getting dressed
    Me lo stavano mostrando *or*
    Stavano mostrandomelo   They were showing me it

Past Participle Agreement

For the formation of the past participle, see page 24.

Note that many Italian verbs have irregular past participles → ①

Past participles are sometimes like adjectives, and change their endings. For the rules of agreement, see below:

		MASCULINE	FEMININE
SING.	1st conj	andato	andata
SING.	2nd conj	caduto	caduta
SING.	3rd conj	uscito	uscita
PLUR.	1st conj	andati	andate
PLUR.	2nd conj	caduti	cadute
PLUR.	3rd conj	usciti	uscite

Rules of Agreement in Compound Tenses

When the auxiliary verb is **avere**:

> The past participle generally remains in the masculine singular form → ②

EXCEPTION: When the object of the verb is **la** (*feminine*: her/it), **li** (*masculine plural*: them) or **le** (*feminine plural*: them), the participle agrees with **la**, **li** or **le** → ③

When the auxiliary verb is **essere**:

> The past participle agrees in number and gender with the subject → ④

For the agreement of the past participle with reflexive verbs, see page 34.

The Past Participle as an adjective

When a past participles is used as an adjective it agrees in the normal way → ⑤

Examples

1 crescere to grow   cresciuto **grown**
dire **to say**   detto **said**
fare **to do**   fatto **done**
porre **to put**   posto **put**

2 Mio fratello ha comprato una macchina   My brother has bought a car
Mia sorella ha comprato una macchina   My sister has bought a car
I ragazzi hanno comprato dei gelati   The children bought ice creams

3 Dov'è Marco? L'hai visto?   Where's Marco? Have you seen him?
Dov'è Silvia? L'hai vista?   Where's Silvia? Have you seen her?
Dove sono i ragazzi? Li hai visti?   Where are the boys? Have you seen them?
Dove sono le ragazze? Le hai viste?   Where are the girls? Have you seen them?

4 È andato a casa   He's gone home
È andata a casa   She's gone home
I ragazzi sono usciti   The boys have gone out
Le ragazze sono uscite   The girls have gone out
Si è fatto male?   Has he hurt himself?
Si è fatta male?   Has she hurt herself?
Vi siete fatti male, ragazzi?   Have you hurt yourselves, boys?
Vi siete fatte male, ragazze?   Have you hurt yourselves, girls?

5 È chiuso il supermercato?   Is the supermarket closed?
È chiusa la banca?   Is the bank closed?
Sono chiuse le finestre?   Are the windows closed?

Modal Auxiliary Verbs

In Italian, the modal auxiliary verbs (i verbi servili) are: dovere, potere, sapere and volere.

They are followed by the infinitive (without a connecting preposition) and have the following meanings:

dovere	to have to, must → ❶
	to be going to, to be supposed to → ❷
	in the present conditional/perfect conditional:
	should/should have, ought/ought to have → ❸
potere	to be able to, can → ❹
	to be allowed to, can, may → ❺
	indicating possibility: may/might/could → ❻
sapere	to know how to, can → ❼
volere	to want/wish to → ❽
	with negative won't/wouldn't → ❾
	in polite phrases → ❿

Compound Tenses of dovere and potere

dovere and potere are conjugated with avere if the following verb is conjugated with avere, e.g. dare, risolvere → ⓫

dovere and potere are generally conjugated with essere if the following verb is conjugated with essere, e.g. andare, partire, alzarsi → ⓬

EXCEPTION:	avere is used in compound tenses of dovere and potere when followed by essere, e.g. Avrebbe dovuto essere più freddo It should have been colder

Examples

1. Devi farlo proprio adesso? — Do you have to do it right now?
   È dovuta partire — She had to leave
   Dev'essere caro — It must be expensive

2. Deve scendere qui? — Are you going to get off here?
   Dovevo venire, ma poi non ho avuto tempo — I was going to come, but then I didn't have time
   Dovevano arrivare ieri sera — They were supposed to arrive yesterday evening

3. Dovresti parlargli — You should speak to him
   Avrei dovuto stare più attento — I should have been more careful

4. Non potrò venire domani — I won't be able to come tomorrow
   Cosa posso dire? — What can I say?

5. Posso entrare? — May I come in?
   Non si può parcheggiare qui — You can't park here

6. Può anche essere vero — It may/might even be true
   Potrebbe piovere — It may/might/could rain

7. Sai guidare? — Can you drive?
   Non so fare gli gnocchi — I don't know how to make gnocchi

8. Vuole rimanere ancora un giorno — He wants to stay another day

9. Non vuole aiutarci — She won't help us
   Non voleva ascoltarmi — He wouldn't listen to me

10. Vuole bere qualcosa? — Would you like something to drink?

11. Ho dovuto darglielo — I had to give it to him
    Ho potuto risolvere il problema — I was able to sort out the problem

12. È dovuta partire subito — She had to leave immediately
    Ci siamo dovuti alzare presto — We had to get up early
    Lara è potuta venire — Lara was able to come
    Non si sono potuti decidere — They couldn't decide
    Si sarebbero potuti sbagliare — They could have been mistaken

Verbs

Use of Tenses

The Present

The Italian simple present can be used to translate both the English simple present, e.g. I work, and the English present continuous, e.g. I'm working → ❶

The Italian present continuous tense is also used for continuous actions → ❷

Italian uses the present tense with the preposition **da** to describe an action that *has been continuing for* some time, or *has continued since* some time in the past → ❸

The Italian present is also used
- for the immediate future → ❹
- for offers → ❺
- for arrangements → ❻
- for predictions → ❼
- when asking for suggestions → ❽

The Future

The future is generally used as in English, but note the following:

the future tense is used after **quando**, if the verb in the main clause is in the future → ❾

The Future Perfect

It is used as in English to mean 'shall/will have done' → ❿

It is also used in time clauses relating to the future, where English uses the perfect → ⓫

Examples

① Dove abitano? — Where do they live?
Dove abitano adesso? — Where are they living now?
Piove molto qui — It rains a lot here
Ora piove — It's raining now

② Cosa stai facendo? *or* Cosa fai? — What are you doing?
Sta piovendo *or* Piove — It's raining

③ Studio italiano da due anni — I've been learning Italian for two years

Aspettiamo da un'ora — We've been waiting for an hour
Lavora qui da settembre — She's been working here since September

Non lo vedo da un pezzo — I haven't seen him for a while
Vivono qui dal 2006 — They've lived here since 2006

④ Prendo un espresso — I'll have an espresso
È rotto, lo butto via — It's broken, I'm going to throw it away

⑤ Pago io! — I'll pay!
Devo tornare a casa — Ti porto io! — I need to go home — I'll take you!

⑥ Parto alle due — I'm leaving at two
Domani gioco a tennis — I'm playing tennis tomorrow

⑦ Se fai così lo rompi — If you do that you'll break it
Se piove non viene nessuno — If it rains nobody will come

⑧ Dove lo metto? — Where shall I put it?
Cosa facciamo? — What shall we do?

⑨ Quando finirò, verrò da te *or* Quando finisco, vengo da te — When I finish I'll come to yours
Lo comprerò quando avrò abbastanza soldi — I'll buy it when I've got enough money
Quando verrà saremo già in vacanza — When he comes we'll be on holiday

⑩ Avrò finito fra un'ora — I'll have finished in an hour

⑪ Quando l'avrai letto ritornamelo — When you've read it let me have it back

Partirò quando avrò finito — I'll leave when I've finished

Use of Tenses *continued*

The Imperfect

The imperfect describes:
- an action (or state) in the past without definite time limits → ❶
- habitual action(s) in the past (often translated by 'would' or 'used to') → ❷

Italian uses the imperfect tense with the preposition **da** to describe an action that *had been continuing for* some time, or *had continued since* some time in the past → ❸

The Perfect

The Italian perfect tense corresponds to both the English perfect tense and the English simple past → ❹

The Past Historic

The past historic, used mainly in written Italian, and in the south of Italy, corresponds to the English simple past → ❺

The Past Anterior

This tense is used instead of the pluperfect when a verb in another part of the sentence is in the past historic → ❻

The Perfect Conditional

The perfect conditional, not the present conditional, is used in reported speech → ❼

Examples

1. Avevo la febbre — I had a temperature
   Non ne sapeva niente — He didn't know anything about it
   Guardavo la tivù — I was watching TV

2. Ti prendevano in giro, vero? — They used to tease you, didn't they?

   Facevamo lunghissime passeggiate — We would go for very long walks

   Mi raccontava delle belle storie — She used to tell me lovely stories

3. Studiavo italiano da due anni — I had been learning Italian for two years

   Aspettavamo da molto tempo — We had been waiting for a long time

   Lavorava a Roma dal 2010 — She'd been working in Rome since 2010

   Non lo vedevo da un pezzo — I hadn't seen him for a while

4. Non l'ho mai visto — I've never seen it
   Non l'ho visto ieri — I didn't see it yesterday
   Sono stata in città — I've been to town
   Stamattina sono stata in città — I went to town this morning

5. Dormimmo profondamente e ci svegliammo riposati — We slept soundly and awoke refreshed

6. Mi addormentai dopo che se ne furono andati — I went to sleep after they had gone

7. Ha detto che mi avrebbe aiutato — He said he would help me
   Ho detto che avrei pagato la metà — I said I'd pay half
   Hanno promesso che sarebbero venuti — They promised they would come

The Subjunctive

When to use it

For how to form the subjunctive see page 8 onwards.

The subjunctive follows the conjunction **che**:

- when used with verbs expressing belief or hope, such as **credere**, **pensare** and **sperare** → ①
- when used with verbs and expressions expressing uncertainty → ②
- when it is used with **volere**. The Italian subjunctive + **che** corresponds to the infinitive construction in English → ③
- following impersonal verbs → ④
- after impersonal constructions which express necessity, possibility etc:

è meglio che	it's better (that) → ⑤
è possibile che	it's possible (that) → ⑥
è facile che	it's likely (that) → ⑦
può darsi che	it's possible (that) → ⑧
non è che	it's not that → ⑨
sembra che	it seems (that) → ⑩

Examples

1. Penso che sia giusto — I think it's fair
   Credo che partano domani — I think they're leaving tomorrow
   Spero che Luca arrivi in tempo — I hope Luca arrives in time

2. Non so se sia la risposta giusta — I don't know if it's the right answer
   Non sono sicura che tu abbia ragione — I'm not sure you're right

3. Voglio che i miei ragazzi siano felici — I want my children to be happy
   Vuole che la aiuti — She wants me to help her
   Non voglio che mi parlino — I don't want them to speak to me

4. Mi dispiace che non siano qui — I'm sorry they're not here

5. È meglio che tu te ne vada — You'd better leave

6. È possibile che siano stranieri — It's possible they're foreigners

7. È facile che scelgano quelli rossi — They'll probably choose those red ones

8. Può darsi che non venga — It's possible that he won't come

9. Non è che si debba sempre dire la verità — You don't always have to tell the truth

10. Sembra che abbiano vinto — It seems they've won

The Subjunctive *continued*

The subjunctive is used:

- after the following conjunctions:

prima che	before → ❶
affinché	so that → ❷
a meno che	unless → ❸
benché	although → ❹
nel caso che	in case → ❺
nonostante	even though → ❻
perché	so (that) → ❼
per quanto	however → ❽
purché	as long as → ❾
sebbene	even though → ❿

- after superlatives → ⓫

  la più grande che ci sia   the biggest there is

- after:

  chiunque whoever → ⓬
  qualunque + *noun* whatever → ⓭
  per quanto however → ⓮

Note that che is not always followed by the subjunctive.

The indicative follows che when it is used with positive uses of sapere to know, and with other expressions indicating certainty, such as Sono sicuro *I'm sure* → ⓯

Examples

1. Vuoi parlargli prima che parta? — Do you want to speak to him before he goes?

2. Ti do venti euro affinché tu possa comprarlo — I'll give you twenty euros so that you can buy it

3. Lo prendo io, a meno che lo voglia tu — I'll take it, unless you want it

4. Mi aiutò a fare i compiti benché fosse molto stanca — She helped me do my homework although she was very tired

5. Vi do il mio numero di telefono nel caso che veniate a Roma — I'll give you my phone number in case you come to Rome

6. Vuole alzarsi, nonostante sia ancora malato — He wants to get up even though he's still ill

7. Lo metto qui perché tutti possano usarlo — I'll put it here so everyone can use it

8. Per quanto mi sforzi non riesco a capire — I can't understand, however hard I try

9. Vengo anch'io, purché possa pagare la mia parte — I'll come too as long as I can pay my share

10. Mi prestò il denaro sebbene non ne avesse molto — She lent me the money even though she hadn't got much

11. È la persona più simpatica che conosca — He's the nicest person I know

12. Chiunque sia, digli che non ci sono — Whoever it is, tell them I'm not here

13. qualunque cosa accada — whatever happens

14. per quanto bello sia — however nice it may be

15. So che non è suo — I know it's not hers
    Sai che ti piace — You know you like it
    Sono sicura che l'ha preso lui — I'm sure he took it
    Sei sicuro che verranno? — Are you sure they're coming?

The Subjunctive *continued*

The Perfect Subjunctive

The perfect subjunctive follows the conjunction **che**
- when it follows verbs such as **credere**, **pensare** and **sperare** relating to something in the past → ❶
- when it follows an impersonal expression → ❷
- when it follows a superlative → ❸
- when it follows a conjunction ending in **che** → ❹

The Imperfect Subjunctive

The imperfect subjunctive is used:
- following **che**, and other conjunctions, as above → ❺
- with past tenses of **volere** +**che** → ❻
- following **se** in conditional clauses describing hypothetical situations → ❼

The Pluperfect Subjunctive

The pluperfect subjunctive is used:
- after **che**, in the same way as other tenses of the subjunctive → ❽
- after other conjunctions → ❾
- following **se** in conditional clauses describing past hypothetical situations → ❿

Examples

① Penso che sia stata una buona idea — I think it was a good idea
Spero che non si sia fatta male — I hope she didn't hurt herself
Spero che *abbia* detto la verit*à* — I hope you told the truth

② È possibile che *abbiano* cambiato idea — It's possible they've changed their minds
Mi dispiace che *abbia* fatto brutto tempo — I'm sorry the weather was bad

③ la più bella che *abbia* mai visto — the most beautiful one I've ever seen

④ Sarà qui fra poco, a meno che *abbia* perso l'*autobus* — He'll be here soon, unless he's missed the bus

⑤ Voleva alzarsi nonostante fosse ancora malato — He wanted to get up, even though he was still ill

⑥ Voleva che fossimo pronti alle otto — He wanted us to be ready at eight
Vole*v*ano che tutto fosse in ordine — They wanted everything to be tidy
Volevo che andasse più veloce — I wanted him to go faster
Non volevo che mi parl*a*ssero — I didn't want them to speak to me

⑦ Se tu ne avessi bisogno, te lo darei — If you needed it I'd give it to you
Se potessi dormirei fino a tardi — If I could I'd have a lie-in
Se lo sapesse sarebbe molto deluso — If he knew he'd be very disappointed

Se solo avessi più denaro! — If only I had more money!

⑧ Non pensavo che l'avesse fatto — I didn't think he'd done it
Credevo che fossero partiti — I thought they had left
Ero sicuro che avesse perso il treno — I was sure he'd missed the train
la più bella che avessi mai visto — the most beautiful one I had ever seen

⑨ Non ha detto niente nonostante si fosse fatto male — He didn't say anything even though he'd hurt himself

⑩ Se l'avessi saputo non l'avrei mai fatto — If I had known, I'd never have done it
Se fosse stato più furbo non avrebbe detto niente — If he'd had more sense he wouldn't have said anything
Se l'avessi visto mi crederesti — If you'd seen, it you'd believe me
Se solo mi avessi creduto! — If only you'd believed me!

Verbs

Verbs governing a and di

The following list (pages 70 to 78) contain common verbal constructions using the prepositions a and di

Note the following abbreviations:

infin.	infinitive
perf. infin.	perfect infinitive
qc	qualcosa
qn	qualcuno
sb	somebody
sth	something

Verbs governing a may be followed by the stressed pronouns me, te, lui, lei, noi, voi and loro → ①

More often, however, they are preceded by an unstressed indirect pronoun, without a → ②

For stressed and unstressed pronouns see page 162.

abituarse qn a qc/a + *infin.*	to accustom sb to sth/to doing
abituarsi a + *infin.*	to get used to doing → ③
acconsentire a qc/a + *infin.*	to agree to sth/to do → ④
accorgersi di qc	to notice sth → ⑤
accusare qn di qc/di + *(perf.) infin.*	to accuse sb of sth/of doing, having done → ⑥
affrettarsi a + *infin.*	to hurry to do
aiutare qn a + *infin.*	to help sb to do → ⑦
andare a + *infin.*	to go to do
approfittare di qc/di + *infin.*	to take advantage of sth/of doing
aspettarsi di + *infin.*	to expect to do → ⑧
assistere a qc	to attend sth, be at sth
assomigliare a qn/qc	to look/be like sb/sth → ⑨
aver bisogno di qc /di + *infin.*	to need sth/to do sth
aver paura di qc/di + *infin.*	to be afraid to do/of doing
aver voglia di qc/di + *infin.*	to want sth/to do
avvicinarsi a qn/qc	to approach sb/sth → ⑩
badare a qc/qn	to look after sth/sb
cambiarsi di qc	to change sth → ⑪
cercare di + *infin.*	to try to do → ⑫

Examples

1. Assomigli a lui, non a lei — You look like him, not like her

2. Gli ho chiesto i soldi — I asked him for the money

3. Si è abituato a bere di meno — He got used to drinking less

4. Non hanno acconsentito a venderlo — They haven't agreed to sell it

5. Non si è accorto del mio errore — He didn't notice my mistake

6. Mi ha accusato d'aver mentito — He accused me of lying

7. Aiutatemi a portare queste valigie — Help me to carry these cases

8. Si aspettava di vederlo? — Was she expecting to see him?

9. Sara assomiglia molto a sua madre — Sara looks very like her mother

10. Si è avvicinata a me — She came up to me

11. Mi sono cambiato d'abito — I changed my clothes

12. Ho cercato di capirla — I tried to understand her

Verbs governing a and di *continued*

cessare di + *infin.*	to stop doing → ①
chiedere qc a qn	to ask sb sth/for sth → ②
chiedere a qn di + *infin.*	to ask sb to do → ③
cominciare a + *infin.*	to begin to do, to start to do → ④
comprare qc a qn	to buy sth from sb/for sb → ⑤
consentire qc a qn	to allow sb sth
consentire a qn di + *infin.*	to allow sb to do
consigliare a qn di+ *infin.*	to advise sb to do → ⑥
continuare a + *infin.*	to continue to do
convincere qn a + *infin.*	to persuade sb to do → ⑦
dare la colpa a qn di qc	to blame sb for sth
decidere di + *infin.*	to decide to → ⑧
decidersi a + *infin.*	to resolve to do, to make up one's mind to do
diffidare di qn	to distrust sb
dimenticare di + *infin.*	to forget to do → ⑨
dire a qn di + *infin.*	to tell sb to do → ⑩
discutere di qc	to discuss sth
disobbedire a qn	to disobey sb → ⑪
dispiacere a qn	to displease sb → ⑫
divertirsi a + *infin.*	to enjoy doing
domandare qc a qn	to ask sb sth/for sth
dubitare di qc	to doubt sth
esitare a + *infin.*	to hesitate to do
evitare di + *infin.*	to avoid doing → ⑬
far male a qn	to hurt sb
farcela a + *infin.*	to manage to do
fare a meno di qc	to do/go without sth → ⑭
fare finta di + *infin.*	to pretend to do → ⑮
fidarsi di qn	to trust sb → ⑯
fingere di + *infin.*	to pretend to do → ⑰
finire di + *infin.*	to finish doing → ⑱
forzare qn a + *infin.*	to force sb to do
giocare a (+ *sports, games*)	to play → ⑲
giurare di + *infin.*	to swear to do
godere di qc	to enjoy sth → ⑳

1	Ha cessato di piovere?	Has it stopped raining?
2	Ho chiesto a Paola che ora fosse	I asked Paola what time it was
3	Chiedi a Francesca di farlo	Ask Francesca to do it
4	Comincia a nevicare	It's starting to snow
5	Cristina ha comprato a Paolo due biglietti	Cristina bought two tickets for Paolo
6	Ha consigliato a Paolo di aspettare	He advised Paolo to wait
7	Ci ha convinti a restare	She persuaded us to stay
8	Cosa avete deciso di fare?	What have you decided to do?
9	Non dimenticarti di prendere l'ombrello	Don't forget to take your umbrella
10	Dì a Gigi di stare zitto	Tell Gigi to be quiet
11	Disobbediscono spesso ai genitori	They often disobey their parents
12	A me non dispiace il loro modo di fare	I quite like their attitude
13	Evita di parlarle	He avoids speaking to her
14	Ho fatto a meno dell'elettricità per diversi giorni	I did without electricity for several days
15	Ho fatto finta di non vederlo	I pretended not to see him
16	Non mi fido di quella gente	I don't trust those people
17	Finge di dormire	She's pretending to be asleep
18	Ha finito di leggere questo giornale?	Have you finished reading this newspaper?
19	Gioca a tennis	She plays tennis
20	Gode di buona salute	He enjoys good health

Verbs governing a and di *continued*

imparare a + *infin.*	to learn to do → ①
impedire a qn di + *infin.*	to prevent sb from doing → ②
impegnarsi a + *infin.*	to undertake to do
incaricarsi di qc/di + *infin.*	to see to sth/undertake to do
incoraggiare qn a + *infin.*	to encourage sb to do → ③
iniziare a + *infin.*	to begin to do
insegnare qc a qn	to teach sb sth
insegnare a qn a + *infin.*	to teach sb to do → ④
intendersi di qc	to know about sth
interessarsi a qn/qc	to be interested in sb/sth → ⑤
invitare qn a + *infin.*	to invite sb to do → ⑥
lagnarsi di qc	to complain about sth
lamentarsi di qc	to complain about sth
mancare a qn	to be missed by sb → ⑦
mancare di qc	to lack sth
mancare di + *infin.*	to fail to do → ⑧
meritare di + *infin.*	to deserve to do → ⑨
mettersi a + *infin.*	to begin to do
minacciare di + *infin.*	to threaten to do → ⑩
nascondere qc a qn	to hide sth from sb → ⑪
nuocere a qc	to harm sth, to damage sth → ⑫
obbligare qn a + *infin.*	to oblige/force sb to do → ⑬
occuparsi di qc/qn	to look after sth/sb → ⑭
offrirsi di + *infin.*	to offer to do → ⑮
omettere di + *infin.*	to fail to do
ordinare a qn di + *infin.*	to order sb to do → ⑯
partecipare a qc	to take part in sth
pensare a qn/qc	to think about sb/sth → ⑰
pentirsi di + *(perf.) infin.*	to regret doing, having done → ⑱
perdonare qc a qn	to forgive sb for sth
perdonare a qn di + *perf. infin.*	to forgive sb for doing → ⑲
permettere qc a qn	to allow sb sth
permettere a qn di + *infin.*	to allow sb to do → ⑳

Examples

1. Sta imparando a leggere — She's learning to read

2. Il rumore mi impedisce di lavorare — The noise is preventing me from working

3. Incoraggia i figli ad essere indipendenti — She encourages her children to be independent

4. Gli sto insegnando a nuotare — I'm teaching him to swim

5. Si interessa molto di sport — She's very interested in sport

6. Mi ha invitato a cenare da lui — He invited me for dinner at his house

7. Manchi molto ai tuoi genitori — Your parents miss you very much

8. Non mancherò di dirglielo — I'll be sure to tell him about it

9. Meritano di avere la promozione — They deserve to be promoted

10. Ha minacciato di dare le dimissioni — She threatened to resign

11. Nascondile il regalo! — Hide the present from her!

12. Il fumo nuoce alla salute di tutti — Smoking damages everybody's health

13. Li ha obbligati a farlo — He forced them to do it

14. Mi occupo di mia nipote — I'm looking after my niece

15. Marco si è offerto di venire con noi — Marco has offered to go with us

16. Ha ordinato loro di sparare — He ordered them to shoot

17. Penso spesso a te — I often think about you

18. Mi pento di averglielo detto — I'm sorry I told him

19. Hai perdonato Carlo di averti mentito? — Have you forgiven Carlo for lying to you?

20. Permettetemi di continuare, per favore — Allow me to go on, please

Verbs governing a and di *continued*

persuadere qn a + *infin.*	to persuade sb to do
piacere a qn	to please sb → ①
portare via qc a qn	to take sth away from sb
pregare qn a + *infin.*	to beg sb to do
prendere qc a qn	to take sth from sb → ②
prendersi gioco di qn/qc	to make fun of sb/sth
preparare qn a + *infin.*	to prepare sb to do
prepararsi a + *infin.*	to get ready to do
proibire a qn di + *infin.*	to forbid sb to do → ③
promettere qc a qn	to promise sb sth
promettere a qn di + *infin.*	to promise sb to do → ④
proporre di + *infin.*	to suggest doing → ⑤
provare a + *infin.*	to try to do
rammaricarsi di + *(perf.) infin.*	to regret doing, having done
resistere a qc	to resist sth → ⑥
ricordarsi di qn/qc/di + *(perf.) infin.*	to remember sb/sth/doing, having done → ⑦
ridere di qn/qc	to laugh at sb/sth
rifiutarsi di + *infin.*	to refuse to do → ⑧
rimpiangere di + *(perf.) infin.*	to regret doing, having done
rimproverare qc a qn	to reproach sb with/for sth → ⑨
ringraziare qn di qc/di + *(perf.) infin.*	to thank sb for sth/for doing, having done → ⑩
rinunciare a qc/a + *infin.*	to give up sth /give up doing
rischiare di + *infin.*	to risk doing → ⑪
rispondere a qn	to answer sb
riuscire a + *infin.*	to manage to do → ⑫
rivolgersi a qn	to ask sb
rubare qc a qn	to steal sth from sb
scordare di + *infin.*	to forget to do
scordarsi di + *infin.*	to forget to do
scusarsi di qc/di + *(perf.) infin.*	to apologize for sth/for doing, having done → ⑬
servire a qc/a + *infin.*	to be used for sth/for doing → ⑭
servirsi di qc	to use sth → ⑮
sforzarsi di + *infin.*	to make an effort to do
smettere di + *infin.*	to stop doing → ⑯
sognare di + *infin.*	to dream of doing

Examples

1. A lui piace questo genere di film — He likes this kind of film

2. Gli ho preso il cellulare — I took his mobile phone from him

3. Ho proibito loro di uscire — I've forbidden them to go out

4. Hanno promesso a Luca di venire — They promised Luca they would come

5. Ho proposto a mio fratello di invitarli — I suggested to my brother that he should invite them

6. Come riesci a resistere alla tentazione? — How do you manage to resist the temptation?

7. Vi ricordate di Luciana? Non si ricorda di averlo perso — Do you remember Luciana? He doesn't remember losing it

8. Si è rifiutato di cooperare — He has refused to cooperate

9. Rimproverano alla figlia la sua mancanza d'entusiasmo — They reproach their daughter for her lack of enthusiasm

10. Li abbiamo ringraziati della loro gentilezza — We thanked them for their kindness

11. Rischiate di perdere soldi — You risk losing money

12. Siete riusciti a convincermi — You've managed to convince me

13. Mi scuso del ritardo — I'm sorry I'm late

14. Questo pulsante serve a regolare il volume — This button is for adjusting the volume

15. Si è servito di un cacciavite per aprirlo — He used a screwdriver to open it

16. Smettete di fare rumore! — Stop making so much noise!

Verbs governing a and di *continued*

somigliare a qn/qc	to look/be like sb/sth
sopravvivere a qn	to outlive sb → ❶
spicciarsi a + *infin.*	to hurry to do
spingere qn a + *infin.*	to urge sb to do
strappare via qc a qn	to snatch sth from sb → ❷
stufarsi di qc/qn	to be fed up with sth/sb
stupirsi di qc	to be amazed at sth
succedere a qn	to succeed sb
tardare a + *infin.*	to delay doing → ❸
telefonare a qn	to phone sb
tendere a + *infin.*	to tend to do
tenere a + *infin.*	to be keen to do → ❹
tentare di + *infin.*	to try to do → ❺
togliere qc a qn	to take sth away from sb
trattare di qc	to be about sth
ubbidire a qn	to obey sb
vantarsi di qc	to boast about sth
venire a + *infin.*	to come to do
vietare a qn di + *infin.*	to forbid sb to do → ❻
vivere di qc	to live on sth

Verbs followed by a preposition in Engish but not in Italian.

ascoltare qc/qn	to listen to sth/sb → ❼
aspettare qc/qn	to wait for sth/sb → ❽
cercare qc/qn	to look for sth/sb → ❾
chiedere qc	to ask for sth → ❿
guardare qc/qn	to look at sth/sb → ⓫
pagare qc/qn	to pay for sth/sb → ⓬

Examples

1. È sopravvissuta a suo marito — She outlived her husband

2. Il ladro le ha strappato via la borsa — The thief snatched her bag

3. Non ha tardato a prendere una decisione — He didn't take long to make a decision

4. Ci tiene a farlo da sola — She's keen to do it by herself

5. Ho tentato di darlo ad Alessia — I tried to give it to Alessia

6. Ha vietato ai bambini di giocare con i fiammiferi — He's forbidden the children to play with matches

7. Mi stai ascoltando? — Are you listening to me?

8. Aspettami! — Wait for me!

9. Sto cercando la chiave — I'm looking for my key

10. Ha chiesto qualcosa da mangiare — He asked for something to eat

11. Guarda la sua faccia — Look at his face

12. Ho già pagato il biglietto — I've already paid for my ticket

Introduction

The Verb Tables in the following section contain tables of Italian verbs (some regular and some irregular) in alphabetical order. Each table shows you the following forms: Present, Present Subjunctive, Perfect, Imperfect, Future, Conditional, Past Historic, Pluperfect, Imperative and the Past Participle and Gerund.

In Italian there are regular verbs (their forms follow the regular patterns of -are ,-ere or-ire verbs), and irregular verbs (their forms do not follow the normal rules). Examples of regular verbs in these tables are:

parlare (regular-are verb)
credere (regular-ere verb)
capire (regular-ire verb)

Some irregular verbs are irregular in most of their forms, while others may only have a couple of irregular forms.

accorgersi (to realize)

	PRESENT			IMPERFECT
io	mi accorgo		io	mi accorgevo
tu	ti accorgi		tu	ti accorgevi
lui/lei/Lei	si accorge		lui/lei/Lei	si accorgeva
noi	ci accorgiamo		noi	ci accorgevamo
voi	vi accorgete		voi	vi accorgevate
loro	si accorgono		loro	si accorgevano

	FUTURE			CONDITIONAL
io	mi accorgerò		io	mi accorgerei
tu	ti accorgerai		tu	ti accorgeresti
lui/lei/Lei	si accorgerà		lui/lei/Lei	si accorgerebbe
noi	ci accorgeremo		noi	ci accorgeremmo
voi	vi accorgerete		voi	vi accorgereste
loro	si accorgeranno		loro	si accorgerebbero

	PRESENT SUBJUNCTIVE			PAST HISTORIC
io	mi accorga		io	mi accorsi
tu	ti accorga		tu	ti accorgesti
lui/lei/Lei	si accorga		lui/lei/Lei	si accorse
noi	ci accorgiamo		noi	ci accorgemmo
voi	vi accorgiate		voi	vi accorgeste
loro	si accorgano		loro	si accorsero

PAST PARTICIPLE
accorto

IMPERATIVE
accorgiti
accorgiamoci
accorgetevi

GERUND
accorgendosi

AUXILIARY
essere

addormentarsi (to go to sleep)

	PRESENT		IMPERFECT
io	mi addormento	io	mi addormentavo
tu	ti addormenti	tu	ti addormentavi
lui/lei/Lei	si addormenta	lui/lei/Lei	si addormentava
noi	ci addormentiamo	noi	ci addormentavamo
voi	vi addormentate	voi	vi addormentavate
loro	si addormentano	loro	si addormentavano

	FUTURE		CONDITIONAL
io	mi addormenterò	io	mi addormenterei
tu	ti addormenterai	tu	ti addormenteresti
lui/lei/Lei	si addormenterà	lui/lei/Lei	si addormenterebbe
noi	ci addormenteremo	noi	ci addormenteremmo
voi	vi addormenterete	voi	vi addormentereste
loro	si addormenteranno	loro	si addormenterebbero

	PRESENT SUBJUNCTIVE		PAST HISTORIC
io	mi addormenti	io	mi addormentai
tu	ti addormenti	tu	ti addormentasti
lui/lei/Lei	si addormenti	lui/lei/Lei	si addormentò
noi	ci addormentiamo	noi	ci addormentammo
voi	vi addormentiate	voi	vi addormentaste
loro	si addormentino	loro	si addormentarono

PAST PARTICIPLE
addormentato

IMPERATIVE
addormentati
addormentiamoci
addormentatevi

GERUND
addormentandosi

AUXILIARY
essere

andare (to go)

	PRESENT		IMPERFECT
io	vado	io	andavo
tu	vai	tu	andavi
lui/lei/Lei	va	lui/lei/Lei	andava
noi	andiamo	noi	andavamo
voi	andate	voi	andavate
loro	vanno	loro	andavano

	FUTURE		CONDITIONAL
io	andrò	io	andrei
tu	andrai	tu	andresti
lui/lei/Lei	andrà	lui/lei/Lei	andrebbe
noi	andremo	noi	andremmo
voi	andrete	voi	andreste
loro	andranno	loro	andrebbero

	PRESENT SUBJUNCTIVE		PAST HISTORIC
io	vada	io	andai
tu	vada	tu	andasti
lui/lei/Lei	vada	lui/lei/Lei	andò
noi	andiamo	noi	andammo
voi	andiate	voi	andaste
loro	vadano	loro	andarono

PAST PARTICIPLE	IMPERATIVE
andato	vai
	andiamo
	andate

GERUND	AUXILIARY
andando	essere

aprire (to open)

	PRESENT		IMPERFECT
io	apro	io	aprivo
tu	apri	tu	aprivi
lui/lei/Lei	apre	lui/lei/Lei	apriva
noi	apriamo	noi	aprivamo
voi	aprite	voi	aprivate
loro	aprono	loro	aprivano

	FUTURE		CONDITIONAL
io	aprirò	io	aprirei
tu	aprirai	tu	apriresti
lui/lei/Lei	aprirà	lui/lei/Lei	aprirebbe
noi	apriremo	noi	apriremmo
voi	aprirete	voi	aprireste
loro	apriranno	loro	aprirebbero

	PRESENT SUBJUNCTIVE		PAST HISTORIC
io	apra	io	aprii
tu	apra	tu	apristi
lui/lei/Lei	apra	lui/lei/Lei	aprì
noi	apriamo	noi	aprimmo
voi	apriate	voi	apriste
loro	aprano	loro	aprirono

PAST PARTICIPLE
aperto

IMPERATIVE
apri
apriamo
aprite

GERUND
aprendo

AUXILIARY
avere

assumere (to take on, to employ)

	PRESENT		IMPERFECT
io	assumo	io	assumevo
tu	assumi	tu	assumevi
lui/lei/Lei	assume	lui/lei/Lei	assumeva
noi	assumiamo	noi	assumevamo
voi	assumete	voi	assumevate
loro	assumono	loro	assumevano

	FUTURE		CONDITIONAL
io	assumerò	io	assumerei
tu	assumerai	tu	assumeresti
lui/lei/Lei	assumerà	lui/lei/Lei	assumerebbe
noi	assumeremo	noi	assumeremmo
voi	assumerete	voi	assumereste
loro	assumeranno	loro	assumerebbero

	PRESENT SUBJUNCTIVE		PAST HISTORIC
io	assuma	io	assunsi
tu	assuma	tu	assumesti
lui/lei/Lei	assuma	lui/lei/Lei	assunse
noi	assumiamo	noi	assumemmo
voi	assumiate	voi	assumeste
loro	assumano	loro	assunsero

PAST PARTICIPLE
assunto

IMPERATIVE
assumi
assumiamo
assumete

GERUND
assumendo

AUXILIARY
avere

avere (to have)

	PRESENT			IMPERFECT
io	ho		io	avevo
tu	hai		tu	avevi
lui/lei/Lei	ha		lui/lei/Lei	aveva
noi	abbiamo		noi	avevamo
voi	avete		voi	avevate
loro	hanno		loro	avevano

	FUTURE			CONDITIONAL
io	avrò		io	avrei
tu	avrai		tu	avresti
lui/lei/Lei	avrà		lui/lei/Lei	avrebbe
noi	avremo		noi	avremmo
voi	avrete		voi	avreste
loro	avranno		loro	avrebbero

	PRESENT SUBJUNCTIVE			PAST HISTORIC
io	abbia		io	ebbi
tu	abbia		tu	avesti
lui/lei/Lei	abbia		lui/lei/Lei	ebbe
noi	abbiamo		noi	avemmo
voi	abbiate		voi	aveste
loro	abbiano		loro	ebbero

PAST PARTICIPLE	IMPERATIVE
avuto	abbi
	abbiamo
	abbiate

GERUND	AUXILIARY
avendo	avere

bere (to drink)

	PRESENT		**IMPERFECT**
io	bevo	io	bevevo
tu	bevi	tu	bevevi
lui/lei/Lei	beve	lui/lei/Lei	beveva
noi	beviamo	noi	bevevamo
voi	bevete	voi	bevevate
loro	bevono	loro	bevevano

	FUTURE		**CONDITIONAL**
io	berrò	io	berrei
tu	berrai	tu	berresti
lui/lei/Lei	berrà	lui/lei/Lei	berrebbe
noi	berremo	noi	berremmo
voi	berrete	voi	berreste
loro	berranno	loro	berrebbero

	PRESENT SUBJUNCTIVE		**PAST HISTORIC**
io	beva	io	bevvi
tu	beva	tu	bevesti
lui/lei/Lei	beva	lui/lei/Lei	bevve
noi	beviamo	noi	bevemmo
voi	beviate	voi	beveste
loro	bevano	loro	bevvero

PAST PARTICIPLE
bevuto

IMPERATIVE
bevi
beviamo
bevete

GERUND
bevendo

AUXILIARY
avere

cadere (to fall)

	PRESENT		IMPERFECT
io	cado	io	cadevo
tu	cadi	tu	cadevi
lui/lei/Lei	cade	lui/lei/Lei	cadeva
noi	cadiamo	noi	cadevamo
voi	cadete	voi	cadevate
loro	cadono	loro	cadevano

	FUTURE		CONDITIONAL
io	cadrò	io	cadrei
tu	cadrai	tu	cadresti
lui/lei/Lei	cadrà	lui/lei/Lei	cadrebbe
noi	cadremo	noi	cadremmo
voi	cadrete	voi	cadreste
loro	cadranno	loro	cadrebbero

	PRESENT SUBJUNCTIVE		PAST HISTORIC
io	cada	io	caddi
tu	cada	tu	cadesti
lui/lei/Lei	cada	lui/lei/Lei	cadde
noi	cadiamo	noi	cademmo
voi	cadiate	voi	cadeste
loro	cadano	loro	caddero

PAST PARTICIPLE
caduto

IMPERATIVE
cadi
cadiamo
cadete

GERUND
cadendo

AUXILIARY
essere

capire (to understand)

	PRESENT			IMPERFECT
io	capisco		io	capivo
tu	capisci		tu	capivi
lui/lei/Lei	capisce		lui/lei/Lei	capiva
noi	capiamo		noi	capivamo
voi	capite		voi	capivate
loro	capiscono		loro	capivano

	FUTURE			CONDITIONAL
io	capirò		io	capirei
tu	capirai		tu	capiresti
lui/lei/Lei	capirà		lui/lei/Lei	capirebbe
noi	capiremo		noi	capiremmo
voi	capirete		voi	capireste
loro	capiranno		loro	capirebbero

	PRESENT SUBJUNCTIVE			PAST HISTORIC
io	capisca		io	capii
tu	capisca		tu	capisti
lui/lei/Lei	capisca		lui/lei/Lei	capì
noi	capiamo		noi	capimmo
voi	capiate		voi	capiste
loro	capiscano		loro	capirono

PAST PARTICIPLE	IMPERATIVE
capito	capisci
	capiamo
	capite

GERUND	AUXILIARY
capendo	avere

cercare (to look for)

	PRESENT		**IMPERFECT**
io	cerco	io	cercavo
tu	cerchi	tu	cercavi
lui/lei/Lei	cerca	lui/lei/Lei	cercava
noi	cerchiamo	noi	cercavamo
voi	cercate	voi	cercavate
loro	cercano	loro	cercavano

	FUTURE		**CONDITIONAL**
io	cercherò	io	cercherei
tu	cercherai	tu	cercheresti
lui/lei/Lei	cercherà	lui/lei/Lei	cercherebbe
noi	cercheremo	noi	cercheremmo
voi	cercherete	voi	cerchereste
loro	cercheranno	loro	cercherebbero

	PRESENT SUBJUNCTIVE		**PAST HISTORIC**
io	cerchi	io	cercai
tu	cerchi	tu	cercasti
lui/lei/Lei	cerchi	lui/lei/Lei	cercò
noi	cerchiamo	noi	cercammo
voi	cerchiate	voi	cercaste
loro	cerchino	loro	cercarono

PAST PARTICIPLE	**IMPERATIVE**
cercato	cerca
	cerchiamo
	cercate

GERUND	**AUXILIARY**
cercando	avere

chiudere (to close)

	PRESENT		IMPERFECT
io	chiudo	io	chiudevo
tu	chiudi	tu	chiudevi
lui/lei/Lei	chiude	lui/lei/Lei	chiudeva
noi	chiudiamo	noi	chiudevamo
voi	chiudete	voi	chiudevate
loro	chiudono	loro	chiudevano

	FUTURE		CONDITIONAL
io	chiuderò	io	chiuderei
tu	chiuderai	tu	chiuderesti
lui/lei/Lei	chiuderà	lui/lei/Lei	chiuderebbe
noi	chiuderemo	noi	chiuderemmo
voi	chiuderete	voi	chiudereste
loro	chiuderanno	loro	chiuderebbero

	PRESENT SUBJUNCTIVE		PAST HISTORIC
io	chiuda	io	chiusi
tu	chiuda	tu	chiudesti
lui/lei/Lei	chiuda	lui/lei/Lei	chiuse
noi	chiudiamo	noi	chiudemmo
voi	chiudiate	voi	chiudeste
loro	chiudano	loro	chiusero

PAST PARTICIPLE	IMPERATIVE
chiuso	chiudi
	chiudiamo
	chiudete

GERUND	AUXILIARY
chiudendo	avere

correre (to run)

	PRESENT		IMPERFECT
io	corro	io	correvo
tu	corri	tu	correvi
lui/lei/Lei	corre	lui/lei/Lei	correva
noi	corriamo	noi	correvamo
voi	correte	voi	correvate
loro	corrono	loro	correvano

	FUTURE		CONDITIONAL
io	correrò	io	correrei
tu	correrai	tu	correresti
lui/lei/Lei	correrà	lui/lei/Lei	correrebbe
noi	correremo	noi	correremmo
voi	correrete	voi	correreste
loro	correranno	loro	correrebbero

	PRESENT SUBJUNCTIVE		PAST HISTORIC
io	corra	io	corsi
tu	corra	tu	corresti
lui/lei/Lei	corra	lui/lei/Lei	corse
noi	corriamo	noi	corremmo
voi	corriate	voi	correste
loro	corrano	loro	corsero

PAST PARTICIPLE
corso

IMPERATIVE
corri
corriamo
correte

GERUND
correndo

AUXILIARY
avere

credere (to believe)

	PRESENT			IMPERFECT
io	credo		io	credevo
tu	credi		tu	credevi
lui/lei/Lei	crede		lui/lei/Lei	credeva
noi	crediamo		noi	credevamo
voi	credete		voi	credevate
loro	credono		loro	credevano

	FUTURE			CONDITIONAL
io	crederò		io	crederei
tu	crederai		tu	crederesti
lui/lei/Lei	crederà		lui/lei/Lei	crederebbe
noi	crederemo		noi	crederemmo
voi	crederete		voi	credereste
loro	crederanno		loro	crederebbero

	PRESENT SUBJUNCTIVE			PAST HISTORIC
io	creda		io	credetti *or* credei
tu	creda		tu	credesti
lui/lei/Lei	creda		lui/lei/Lei	credette
noi	crediamo		noi	credemmo
voi	crediate		voi	credeste
loro	credano		loro	credettero

PAST PARTICIPLE	IMPERATIVE
creduto	credi
	crediamo
	credete

GERUND	AUXILIARY
credendo	avere

crescere (to grow)

	PRESENT			IMPERFECT
io	cresco		io	crescevo
tu	cresci		tu	crescevi
lui/lei/Lei	cresce		lui/lei/Lei	cresceva
noi	cresciamo		noi	crescevamo
voi	crescete		voi	crescevate
loro	crescono		loro	crescevano

	FUTURE			CONDITIONAL
io	crescerò		io	crescerei
tu	crescerai		tu	cresceresti
lui/lei/Lei	crescerà		lui/lei/Lei	crescerebbe
noi	cresceremo		noi	cresceremmo
voi	crescerete		voi	crescereste
loro	cresceranno		loro	crescerebbero

	PRESENT SUBJUNCTIVE			PAST HISTORIC
io	cresca		io	crebbi
tu	cresca		tu	crescesti
lui/lei/Lei	cresca		lui/lei/Lei	crebbe
noi	cresciamo		noi	crescemmo
voi	cresciate		voi	cresceste
loro	crescano		loro	crebbero

PAST PARTICIPLE	IMPERATIVE
cresciuto	cresci
	cresciamo
	crescete

GERUND	AUXILIARY
crescendo	essere

dare (to give)

	PRESENT			IMPERFECT
io	do		io	davo
tu	dai		tu	davi
lui/lei/Lei	dà		lui/lei/Lei	dava
noi	diamo		noi	davamo
voi	date		voi	davate
loro	danno		loro	davano

	FUTURE			CONDITIONAL
io	darò		io	darei
tu	darai		tu	daresti
lui/lei/Lei	darà		lui/lei/Lei	darebbe
noi	daremo		noi	daremmo
voi	darete		voi	dareste
loro	daranno		loro	darebbero

	PRESENT SUBJUNCTIVE			PAST HISTORIC
io	dia		io	dette
tu	dia		tu	desti
lui/lei/Lei	dia		lui/lei/Lei	diede *or* detti
noi	diamo		noi	demmo
voi	diate		voi	deste
loro	diano		loro	diedero *or* dettero

PAST PARTICIPLE	IMPERATIVE
dato	dai *or* da'
	diamo
	date

GERUND	AUXILIARY
dando	avere

dire (to say)

	PRESENT			IMPERFECT
io	dico		io	dicevo
tu	dici		tu	dicevi
lui/lei/Lei	dice		lui/lei/Lei	diceva
noi	diciamo		noi	dicevamo
voi	dite		voi	dicevate
loro	dicono		loro	dicevano

	FUTURE			CONDITIONAL
io	dirò		io	direi
tu	dirai		tu	diresti
lui/lei/Lei	dirà		lui/lei/Lei	direbbe
noi	diremo		noi	diremmo
voi	direte		voi	direste
loro	diranno		loro	direbbero

	PRESENT SUBJUNCTIVE			PAST HISTORIC
io	dica		io	dissi
tu	dica		tu	dicesti
lui/lei/Lei	dica		lui/lei/Lei	disse
noi	diciamo		noi	dicemmo
voi	diciate		voi	diceste
loro	dicano		loro	dissero

PAST PARTICIPLE
detto

IMPERATIVE
di'
diciamo
dite

GERUND
dicendo

AUXILIARY
avere

dirigere (to direct)

	PRESENT		IMPERFECT
io	dirigo	io	dirigevo
tu	dirigi	tu	dirigevi
lui/lei/Lei	dirige	lui/lei/Lei	dirigeva
noi	dirigiamo	noi	dirigevamo
voi	dirigete	voi	dirigevate
loro	dirigono	loro	dirigevano

	FUTURE		CONDITIONAL
io	dirigerò	io	dirigerei
tu	dirigerai	tu	dirigeresti
lui/lei/Lei	dirigerà	lui/lei/Lei	dirigerebbe
noi	dirigeremo	noi	dirigeremmo
voi	dirigerete	voi	dirigereste
loro	dirigeranno	loro	dirigerebbero

	PRESENT SUBJUNCTIVE		PAST HISTORIC
io	diriga	io	diressi
tu	diriga	tu	dirigesti
lui/lei/Lei	diriga	lui/lei/Lei	diresse
noi	dirigiamo	noi	dirigemmo
voi	dirigiate	voi	dirigeste
loro	dirigano	loro	diressero

PAST PARTICIPLE
diretto

IMPERATIVE
dirigi
dirigiamo
dirigete

GERUND
dirigendo

AUXILIARY
avere

dormire (to sleep)

	PRESENT			IMPERFECT
io	dormo		io	dormivo
tu	dormi		tu	dormivi
lui/lei/Lei	dorme		lui/lei/Lei	dormiva
noi	dormiamo		noi	dormivamo
voi	dormite		voi	dormivate
loro	dormono		loro	dormivano

	FUTURE			CONDITIONAL
io	dormirò		io	dormirei
tu	dormirai		tu	dormiresti
lui/lei/Lei	dormirà		lui/lei/Lei	dormirebbe
noi	dormiremo		noi	dormiremmo
voi	dormirete		voi	dormireste
loro	dormiranno		loro	dormirebbero

	PRESENT SUBJUNCTIVE			PAST HISTORIC
io	dorma		io	dormii
tu	dorma		tu	dormisti
lui/lei/Lei	dorma		lui/lei/Lei	dormì
noi	dormiamo		noi	dormimmo
voi	dormiate		voi	dormiste
loro	dormano		loro	dormirono

PAST PARTICIPLE
dormito

IMPERATIVE
dormi
dormiamo
dormite

GERUND
dormendo

AUXILIARY
avere

dovere (to have to)

	PRESENT			IMPERFECT
io	devo		io	dovevo
tu	devi		tu	dovevi
lui/lei/Lei	deve		lui/lei/Lei	doveva
noi	dobbiamo		noi	dovevamo
voi	dovete		voi	dovevate
loro	devono		loro	dovevano

	FUTURE			CONDITIONAL
io	dovrò		io	dovrei
tu	dovrai		tu	dovresti
lui/lei/Lei	dovrà		lui/lei/Lei	dovrebbe
noi	dovremo		noi	dovremmo
voi	dovrete		voi	dovreste
loro	dovranno		loro	dovrebbero

	PRESENT SUBJUNCTIVE			PAST HISTORIC
io	debba		io	dovetti
tu	debba		tu	dovesti
lui/lei/Lei	debba		lui/lei/Lei	dovette
noi	dobbiamo		noi	dovemmo
voi	dobbiate		voi	doveste
loro	debbano		loro	dovettero

PAST PARTICIPLE	IMPERATIVE
dovuto	—

GERUND	AUXILIARY
dovendo	avere

essere (to be)

	PRESENT			**IMPERFECT**
io	sono		io	ero
tu	sei		tu	eri
lui/lei/Lei	è		lui/lei/Lei	era
noi	siamo		noi	eravamo
voi	siete		voi	eravate
loro	sono		loro	erano

	FUTURE			**CONDITIONAL**
io	sarò		io	sarei
tu	sarai		tu	saresti
lui/lei/Lei	sarà		lui/lei/Lei	sarebbe
noi	saremo		noi	saremmo
voi	sarete		voi	sareste
loro	saranno		loro	sarebbero

	PRESENT SUBJUNCTIVE			**PAST HISTORIC**
io	sia		io	fui
tu	sia		tu	fosti
lui/lei/Lei	sia		lui/lei/Lei	fu
noi	siamo		noi	fummo
voi	siate		voi	foste
loro	siano		loro	furono

PAST PARTICIPLE
stato

IMPERATIVE
sii
siamo
siate

GERUND
essendo

AUXILIARY
essere

fare (to do, to make)

	PRESENT		IMPERFECT
io	faccio	io	facevo
tu	fai	tu	facevi
lui/lei/Lei	fa	lui/lei/Lei	faceva
noi	facciamo	noi	facevamo
voi	fate	voi	facevate
loro	fanno	loro	facevano

	FUTURE		CONDITIONAL
io	farò	io	farei
tu	farai	tu	faresti
lui/lei/Lei	farà	lui/lei/Lei	farebbe
noi	faremo	noi	faremmo
voi	farete	voi	fareste
loro	faranno	loro	farebbero

	PRESENT SUBJUNCTIVE		PAST HISTORIC
io	faccia	io	feci
tu	faccia	tu	facesti
lui/lei/Lei	faccia	lui/lei/Lei	fece
noi	facciamo	noi	facemmo
voi	facciate	voi	faceste
loro	facciano	loro	fecero

PAST PARTICIPLE
fatto

IMPERATIVE
fai *or* fa'
facciamo
fate

GERUND
facendo

AUXILIARY
avere

leggere (to read)

	PRESENT		IMPERFECT
io	leggo	io	leggevo
tu	leggi	tu	leggevi
lui/lei/Lei	legge	lui/lei/Lei	leggeva
noi	leggiamo	noi	leggevamo
voi	leggete	voi	leggevate
loro	leggono	loro	leggevano

	FUTURE		CONDITIONAL
io	leggerò	io	leggerei
tu	leggerai	tu	leggeresti
lui/lei/Lei	leggerà	lui/lei/Lei	leggerebbe
noi	leggeremo	noi	leggeremmo
voi	leggerete	voi	leggereste
loro	leggeranno	loro	leggerebbero

	PRESENT SUBJUNCTIVE		PAST HISTORIC
io	legga	io	lessi
tu	legga	tu	leggesti
lui/lei/Lei	legga	lui/lei/Lei	lesse
noi	leggiamo	noi	leggemmo
voi	leggiate	voi	leggeste
loro	leggano	loro	lessero

	PAST PARTICIPLE		IMPERATIVE
	letto		leggi
			leggiamo
			leggete

	GERUND		AUXILIARY
	leggendo		avere

mettere (to put)

	PRESENT		IMPERFECT
io	metto	io	mettevo
tu	metti	tu	mettevi
lui/lei/Lei	mette	lui/lei/Lei	metteva
noi	mettiamo	noi	mettevamo
voi	mettete	voi	mettevate
loro	mettono	loro	mettevano

	FUTURE		CONDITIONAL
io	metterò	io	metterei
tu	metterai	tu	metteresti
lui/lei/Lei	metterà	lui/lei/Lei	metterebbe
noi	metteremo	noi	metteremmo
voi	metterete	voi	mettereste
loro	metteranno	loro	metterebbero

	PRESENT SUBJUNCTIVE		PAST HISTORIC
io	metta	io	misi
tu	metta	tu	mettesti
lui/lei/Lei	metta	lui/lei/Lei	mise
noi	mettiamo	noi	mettemmo
voi	mettiate	voi	metteste
loro	mettano	loro	misero

PAST PARTICIPLE	IMPERATIVE
messo	metti
	mettiamo
	mettete

GERUND	AUXILIARY
mettendo	avere

morire (to die)

	PRESENT		IMPERFECT
io	muoio	io	morivo
tu	muori	tu	morivi
lui/lei/Lei	muore	lui/lei/Lei	moriva
noi	moriamo	noi	morivamo
voi	morite	voi	morivate
loro	muoiono	loro	morivano

	FUTURE		CONDITIONAL
io	morirò	io	morirei
tu	morirai	tu	moriresti
lui/lei/Lei	morirà	lui/lei/Lei	morirebbe
noi	moriremo	noi	moriremmo
voi	morirete	voi	morireste
loro	moriranno	loro	morirebbero

	PRESENT SUBJUNCTIVE		PAST HISTORIC
io	muoia	io	morii
tu	muoia	tu	moristi
lui/lei/Lei	muoia	lui/lei/Lei	morì
noi	moriamo	noi	morimmo
voi	moriate	voi	moriste
loro	muoiano	loro	morirono

PAST PARTICIPLE
morto

IMPERATIVE
muori
moriamo
morite

GERUND
morendo

AUXILIARY
essere

muovere (to move)

	PRESENT		IMPERFECT
io	muovo	io	muovevo
tu	muovi	tu	muovevi
lui/lei/Lei	muove	lui/lei/Lei	muoveva
noi	muoviamo	noi	muovevamo
voi	muovete	voi	muovevate
loro	muovono	loro	muovevano

	FUTURE		CONDITIONAL
io	muoverò	io	muoverei
tu	muoverai	tu	muoveresti
lui/lei/Lei	muoverà	lui/lei/Lei	muoverebbe
noi	muoveremo	noi	muoveremmo
voi	muoverete	voi	muovereste
loro	muoveranno	loro	muoverebbero

	PRESENT SUBJUNCTIVE		PAST HISTORIC
io	muova	io	mossi
tu	muova	tu	muovesti
lui/lei/Lei	muova	lui/lei/Lei	mosse
noi	muoviamo	noi	muovemmo
voi	muoviate	voi	muoveste
loro	muovano	loro	mossero

PAST PARTICIPLE
mosso

IMPERATIVE
muovi
muoviamo
muovete

GERUND
muovendo

AUXILIARY
avere

nascere (to be born)

	PRESENT		IMPERFECT
io	nasco	io	nascevo
tu	nasci	tu	nascevi
lui/lei/Lei	nasce	lui/lei/Lei	nasceva
noi	nasciamo	noi	nascevamo
voi	nascete	voi	nascevate
loro	nascono	loro	nascevano

	FUTURE		CONDITIONAL
io	nascerò	io	nascerei
tu	nascerai	tu	nasceresti
lui/lei/Lei	nascerà	lui/lei/Lei	nascerebbe
noi	nasceremo	noi	nasceremmo
voi	nascerete	voi	nascereste
loro	nasceranno	loro	nascerebbero

	PRESENT SUBJUNCTIVE		PAST HISTORIC
io	nasca	io	nacqui
tu	nasca	tu	nascesti
lui/lei/Lei	nasca	lui/lei/Lei	nacque
noi	nasciamo	noi	nascemmo
voi	nasciate	voi	nasceste
loro	nascano	loro	nacquero

PAST PARTICIPLE	IMPERATIVE
nato	nasci
	nasciamo
	nascete

GERUND	AUXILIARY
nascendo	essere

parlare (to speak)

	PRESENT		IMPERFECT
io	parlo	io	parlavo
tu	parli	tu	parlavi
lui/lei/Lei	parla	lui/lei/Lei	parlava
noi	parliamo	noi	parlavamo
voi	parlate	voi	parlavate
loro	parlano	loro	parlavano

	FUTURE		CONDITIONAL
io	parlerò	io	parlerei
tu	parlerai	tu	parleresti
lui/lei/Lei	parlerà	lui/lei/Lei	parlerebbe
noi	parleremo	noi	parleremmo
voi	parlerete	voi	parlereste
loro	parleranno	loro	parlerebbero

	PRESENT SUBJUNCTIVE		PAST HISTORIC
io	parli	io	parlai
tu	parli	tu	parlasti
lui/lei/Lei	parli	lui/lei/Lei	parlò
noi	parliamo	noi	parlammo
voi	parliate	voi	parlaste
loro	parlino	loro	parlarono

PAST PARTICIPLE	IMPERATIVE
parlato	parla
	parliamo
	parlate

GERUND	AUXILIARY
parlando	avere

piacere (to be pleasing)

	PRESENT			IMPERFECT
io	piaccio		io	piacevo
tu	piaci		tu	piacevi
lui/lei/Lei	piace		lui/lei/Lei	piaceva
noi	piacciamo		noi	piacevamo
voi	piacete		voi	piacevate
loro	piacciono		loro	piacevano

	FUTURE			CONDITIONAL
io	piacerò		io	piacerei
tu	piacerai		tu	piaceresti
lui/lei/Lei	piacerà		lui/lei/Lei	piacerebbe
noi	piaceremo		noi	piaceremmo
voi	piacerete		voi	piacereste
loro	piaceranno		loro	piacerebbero

	PRESENT SUBJUNCTIVE			PAST HISTORIC
io	piaccia		io	piacqui
tu	piaccia		tu	piacesti
lui/lei/Lei	piaccia		lui/lei/Lei	piacque
noi	piacciamo		noi	piacemmo
voi	piacciate		voi	piaceste
loro	piacciano		loro	piacquero

PAST PARTICIPLE	IMPERATIVE
piaciuto	piaci
	piacciamo
	piacciate

GERUND	AUXILIARY
piacendo	essere

piovere (to rain)

PRESENT	IMPERFECT
piove	pioveva

FUTURE	CONDITIONAL
pioverà	pioverebbe

PRESENT SUBJUNCTIVE	PAST HISTORIC
piova	piovve

PAST PARTICIPLE	IMPERATIVE
piovuto	–

GERUND	AUXILIARY
piovendo	essere

potere (to be able)

	PRESENT		IMPERFECT
io	posso	io	potevo
tu	puoi	tu	potevi
lui/lei/Lei	può	lui/lei/Lei	poteva
noi	possiamo	noi	potevamo
voi	potete	voi	potevate
loro	possono	loro	potevano

	FUTURE		CONDITIONAL
io	potrò	io	potrei
tu	potrai	tu	potresti
lui/lei/Lei	potrà	lui/lei/Lei	potrebbe
noi	potremo	noi	potremmo
voi	potrete	voi	potreste
loro	potranno	loro	potrebbero

	PRESENT SUBJUNCTIVE		PAST HISTORIC
io	possa	io	potei
tu	possa	tu	potesti
lui/lei/Lei	possa	lui/lei/Lei	poté
noi	possiamo	noi	potemmo
voi	possiate	voi	poteste
loro	possano	loro	poterono

PAST PARTICIPLE	IMPERATIVE
potuto	—

GERUND	AUXILIARY
potendo	avere

prendere (to take)

	PRESENT		IMPERFECT
io	prendo	io	prendevo
tu	prendi	tu	prendevi
lui/lei/Lei	prende	lui/lei/Lei	prendeva
noi	prendiamo	noi	prendevamo
voi	prendete	voi	prendevate
loro	prendono	loro	prendevano

	FUTURE		CONDITIONAL
io	prenderò	io	prenderei
tu	prenderai	tu	prenderesti
lui/lei/Lei	prenderà	lui/lei/Lei	prenderebbe
noi	prenderemo	noi	prenderemmo
voi	prenderete	voi	prendereste
loro	prenderanno	loro	prenderebbero

	PRESENT SUBJUNCTIVE		PAST HISTORIC
io	prenda	io	presi
tu	prenda	tu	prendesti
lui/lei/Lei	prenda	lui/lei/Lei	prese
noi	prendiamo	noi	prendemmo
voi	prendiate	voi	prendeste
loro	prendano	loro	presero

PAST PARTICIPLE

preso

IMPERATIVE

prendi
prendiamo
prendete

GERUND

prendendo

AUXILIARY

avere

rompere (to break)

	PRESENT			IMPERFECT
io	rompo		io	rompevo
tu	rompi		tu	rompevi
lui/lei/Lei	rompe		lui/lei/Lei	rompeva
noi	rompiamo		noi	rompevamo
voi	rompete		voi	rompevate
loro	rompono		loro	rompevano

	FUTURE			CONDITIONAL
io	romperò		io	romperei
tu	romperai		tu	romperesti
lui/lei/Lei	romperà		lui/lei/Lei	romperebbe
noi	romperemo		noi	romperemmo
voi	romperete		voi	rompereste
loro	romperanno		loro	romperebbero

	PRESENT SUBJUNCTIVE			PAST HISTORIC
io	rompa		io	ruppi
tu	rompa		tu	rompesti
lui/lei/Lei	rompa		lui/lei/Lei	ruppe
noi	rompiamo		noi	rompemmo
voi	rompiate		voi	rompeste
loro	rompano		loro	ruppero

PAST PARTICIPLE	IMPERATIVE
rotto	rompi
	rompiamo
	rompete

GERUND	AUXILIARY
rompendo	avere

salire (to go up)

	PRESENT			IMPERFECT
io	salgo		io	salivo
tu	sali		tu	salivi
lui/lei/Lei	sale		lui/lei/Lei	saliva
noi	saliamo		noi	salivamo
voi	salite		voi	salivate
loro	salgono		loro	salivano

	FUTURE			CONDITIONAL
io	salirò		io	salirei
tu	salirai		tu	saliresti
lui/lei/Lei	salirà		lui/lei/Lei	salirebbe
noi	saliremo		noi	saliremmo
voi	salirete		voi	salireste
loro	saliranno		loro	salirebbero

	PRESENT SUBJUNCTIVE			PAST HISTORIC
io	salga		io	salii
tu	salga		tu	salisti
lui/lei/Lei	salga		lui/lei/Lei	salì
noi	saliamo		noi	salimmo
voi	saliate		voi	saliste
loro	salgano		loro	salirono

PAST PARTICIPLE	IMPERATIVE
salito	sali
	saliamo
	salite

GERUND	AUXILIARY
salendo	essere

sapere (to know)

	PRESENT			IMPERFECT
io	so		io	sapevo
tu	sai		tu	sapevi
lui/lei/Lei	sa		lui/lei/Lei	sapeva
noi	sappiamo		noi	sapevamo
voi	sapete		voi	sapevate
loro	sanno		loro	sapevano

	FUTURE			CONDITIONAL
io	saprò		io	saprei
tu	saprai		tu	sapresti
lui/lei/Lei	saprà		lui/lei/Lei	saprebbe
noi	sapremo		noi	sapremmo
voi	saprete		voi	sapreste
loro	sapranno		loro	saprebbero

	PRESENT SUBJUNCTIVE			PAST HISTORIC
io	sappia		io	seppi
tu	sappia		tu	sapesti
lui/lei/Lei	sappia		lui/lei/Lei	seppe
noi	sappiamo		noi	sapemmo
voi	sappiate		voi	sapeste
loro	sappiano		loro	seppero

PAST PARTICIPLE	IMPERATIVE
saputo	sappi
	sappiamo
	sappiate

GERUND	AUXILIARY
sapendo	avere

scrivere (to write)

	PRESENT			IMPERFECT
io	scrivo		io	scrivevo
tu	scrivi		tu	scrivevi
lui/lei/Lei	scrive		lui/lei/Lei	scriveva
noi	scriviamo		noi	scrivevamo
voi	scrivete		voi	scrivevate
loro	scrivono		loro	scrivevano

	FUTURE			CONDITIONAL
io	scriverò		io	scriverei
tu	scriverai		tu	scriveresti
lui/lei/Lei	scriverà		lui/lei/Lei	scriverebbe
noi	scriveremo		noi	scriveremmo
voi	scriverete		voi	scrivereste
loro	scriveranno		loro	scriverebbero

	PRESENT SUBJUNCTIVE			PAST HISTORIC
io	scriva		io	scrissi
tu	scriva		tu	scrivesti
lui/lei/Lei	scriva		lui/lei/Lei	scrisse
noi	scriviamo		noi	scrivemmo
voi	scriviate		voi	scriveste
loro	scrivano		loro	scrissero

PAST PARTICIPLE	IMPERATIVE
scritto	scrivi
	scriviamo
	scrivete

GERUND	AUXILIARY
scrivendo	avere

sedere (to sit)

	PRESENT		IMPERFECT
io	siedo	io	sedevo
tu	siedi	tu	sedevi
lui/lei/Lei	siede	lui/lei/Lei	sedeva
noi	sediamo	noi	sedevamo
voi	sedete	voi	sedevate
loro	siedono	loro	sedevano

	FUTURE		CONDITIONAL
io	sederò	io	sederei
tu	sederai	tu	sederesti
lui/lei/Lei	sederà	lui/lei/Lei	sederebbe
noi	sederemo	noi	sederemmo
voi	sederete	voi	sedereste
loro	sederanno	loro	sederebbero

	PRESENT SUBJUNCTIVE		PAST HISTORIC
io	sieda	io	sedetti
tu	sieda	tu	sedesti
lui/lei/Lei	sieda	lui/lei/Lei	sedette
noi	sediamo	noi	sedemmo
voi	sediate	voi	sedeste
loro	siedano	loro	sedettero

PAST PARTICIPLE	IMPERATIVE
seduto	siedi
	sediamo
	sedete

GERUND	AUXILIARY
sedendo	essere

stare (to be)

	PRESENT			IMPERFECT
io	sto		io	stavo
tu	stai		tu	stavi
lui/lei/Lei	sta		lui/lei/Lei	stava
noi	stiamo		noi	stavamo
voi	state		voi	stavate
loro	stanno		loro	stavano

	FUTURE			CONDITIONAL
io	starò		io	starei
tu	starai		tu	staresti
lui/lei/Lei	starà		lui/lei/Lei	starebbe
noi	staremo		noi	staremmo
voi	starete		voi	stareste
loro	staranno		loro	starebbero

	PRESENT SUBJUNCTIVE			PAST HISTORIC
io	stia		io	stetti
tu	stia		tu	stesti
lui/lei/Lei	stia		lui/lei/Lei	stette
noi	stiamo		noi	stemmo
voi	stiate		voi	steste
loro	stiano		loro	stettero

PAST PARTICIPLE	IMPERATIVE
stato	stai
	stiamo
	state

GERUND	AUXILIARY
stando	essere

succedere (to happen)

	PRESENT		**IMPERFECT**
sing.	succede	*sing.*	succedeva
plur.	succedono	*plur.*	succedevano

	FUTURE		**CONDITIONAL**
sing.	succederà	*sing.*	succederebbe
plur.	succederanno	*plur.*	succederebbero

	PRESENT SUBJUNCTIVE		**PAST HISTORIC**
sing.	succeda	*sing.*	successe
plur.	succedano	*plur.*	successero

PAST PARTICIPLE	**IMPERATIVE**
successo	–

GERUND	**AUXILIARY**
succedendo	essere

tenere (to hold)

	PRESENT			IMPERFECT
io	tengo		io	tenevo
tu	tieni		tu	tenevi
lui/lei/Lei	tiene		lui/lei/Lei	teneva
noi	teniamo		noi	tenevamo
voi	tenete		voi	tenevate
loro	tengono		loro	tenevano

	FUTURE			CONDITIONAL
io	terrò		io	terrei
tu	terrai		tu	terresti
lui/lei/Lei	terrà		lui/lei/Lei	terrebbe
noi	terremo		noi	terremmo
voi	terrete		voi	terreste
loro	terranno		loro	terrebbero

	PRESENT SUBJUNCTIVE			PAST HISTORIC
io	tenga		io	tenni
tu	tenga		tu	tenesti
lui/lei/Lei	tenga		lui/lei/Lei	tenne
noi	teniamo		noi	tenemmo
voi	teniate		voi	teneste
loro	tengano		loro	tennero

PAST PARTICIPLE
tenuto

IMPERATIVE
tieni
teniamo
tenete

GERUND
tenendo

AUXILIARY
avere

uscire (to go out)

	PRESENT		IMPERFECT
io	esco	io	uscivo
tu	esci	tu	uscivi
lui/lei/Lei	esce	lui/lei/Lei	usciva
noi	usciamo	noi	uscivamo
voi	uscite	voi	uscivate
loro	escono	loro	uscivano

	FUTURE		CONDITIONAL
io	uscirò	io	uscirei
tu	uscirai	tu	usciresti
lui/lei/Lei	uscirà	lui/lei/Lei	uscirebbe
noi	usciremo	noi	usciremmo
voi	uscirete	voi	uscireste
loro	usciranno	loro	uscirebbero

	PRESENT SUBJUNCTIVE		PAST HISTORIC
io	esca	io	uscii
tu	esca	tu	uscisti
lui/lei/Lei	esca	lui/lei/Lei	uscì
noi	usciamo	noi	uscimmo
voi	usciate	voi	usciste
loro	escano	loro	uscirono

PAST PARTICIPLE
uscito

IMPERATIVE
esci
usciamo
uscite

GERUND
uscendo

AUXILIARY
essere

vedere (to see)

	PRESENT		IMPERFECT
io	vedo	io	vedevo
tu	vedi	tu	vedevi
lui/lei/Lei	vede	lui/lei/Lei	vedeva
noi	vediamo	noi	vedevamo
voi	vedete	voi	vedevate
loro	vedono	loro	vedevano

	FUTURE		CONDITIONAL
io	vedrò	io	vedrei
tu	vedrai	tu	vedresti
lui/lei/Lei	vedrà	lui/lei/Lei	vedrebbe
noi	vedremo	noi	vedremmo
voi	vedrete	voi	vedreste
loro	vedranno	loro	vedrebbero

	PRESENT SUBJUNCTIVE		PAST HISTORIC
io	veda	io	vidi
tu	veda	tu	vedesti
lui/lei/Lei	veda	lui/lei/Lei	vide
noi	vediamo	noi	vedemmo
voi	vediate	voi	vedeste
loro	vedano	loro	videro

	PAST PARTICIPLE		IMPERATIVE
	visto		vedi
			vediamo
			vedete

	GERUND		AUXILIARY
	vedendo		avere

venire (to come)

	PRESENT		IMPERFECT
io	vengo	io	venivo
tu	vieni	tu	venivi
lui/lei/Lei	viene	lui/lei/Lei	veniva
noi	veniamo	noi	venivamo
voi	venite	voi	venivate
loro	vengono	loro	venivano

	FUTURE		CONDITIONAL
io	verrò	io	verrei
tu	verrai	tu	verresti
lui/lei/Lei	verrà	lui/lei/Lei	verrebbe
noi	verremo	noi	verremmo
voi	verrete	voi	verreste
loro	verranno	loro	verrebbero

	PRESENT SUBJUNCTIVE		PAST HISTORIC
io	venga	io	venni
tu	venga	tu	venisti
lui/lei/Lei	venga	lui/lei/Lei	venne
noi	veniamo	noi	venimmo
voi	veniate	voi	veniste
loro	vengano	loro	vennero

PAST PARTICIPLE
venuto

IMPERATIVE
vieni
veniamo
venite

GERUND
venendo

AUXILIARY
essere

vincere (to defeat)

	PRESENT			IMPERFECT
io	vinco		io	vincevo
tu	vinci		tu	vincevi
lui/lei/Lei	vince		lui/lei/Lei	vinceva
noi	vinciamo		noi	vincevamo
voi	vincete		voi	vincevate
loro	vincono		loro	vincevano

	FUTURE			CONDITIONAL
io	vincerò		io	vincerei
tu	vincerai		tu	vinceresti
lui/lei/Lei	vincerà		lui/lei/Lei	vincerebbe
noi	vinceremo		noi	vinceremmo
voi	vincerete		voi	vincereste
loro	vinceranno		loro	vincerebbero

	PRESENT SUBJUNCTIVE			PAST HISTORIC
io	vinca		io	vinsi
tu	vinca		tu	vincesti
lui/lei/Lei	vinca		lui/lei/Lei	vinse
noi	vinciamo		noi	vincemmo
voi	vinciate		voi	vinceste
loro	vincano		loro	vinsero

PAST PARTICIPLE
vinto

IMPERATIVE
vinci
vinciamo
vincete

GERUND
vincendo

AUXILIARY
avere

vivere (to live)

	PRESENT		**IMPERFECT**
io	vivo	io	vivevo
tu	vivi	tu	vivevi
lui/lei/Lei	vive	lui/lei/Lei	viveva
noi	viviamo	noi	vivevamo
voi	vivete	voi	vivevate
loro	vivono	loro	vivevano

	FUTURE		**CONDITIONAL**
io	vivrò	io	vivrei
tu	vivrai	tu	vivresti
lui/lei/Lei	vivrà	lui/lei/Lei	vivrebbe
noi	vivremo	noi	vivremmo
voi	vivrete	voi	vivreste
loro	vivranno	loro	vivrebbero

	PRESENT SUBJUNCTIVE		**PAST HISTORIC**
io	viva	io	vissi
tu	viva	tu	vivesti
lui/lei/Lei	viva	lui/lei/Lei	visse
noi	viviamo	noi	vivemmo
voi	viviate	voi	viveste
loro	vivano	loro	vissero

PAST PARTICIPLE	**IMPERATIVE**
vissuto	vivi
	viviamo
	vivete

GERUND	**AUXILIARY**
vivendo	avere

volere (to want)

PRESENT

io	voglio
tu	vuoi
lui/lei/Lei	vuole
noi	vogliamo
voi	volete
loro	vogliono

IMPERFECT

io	volevo
tu	volevi
lui/lei/Lei	voleva
noi	volevamo
voi	volevate
loro	volevano

FUTURE

io	vorrò
tu	vorrai
lui/lei/Lei	vorrà
noi	vorremo
voi	vorrete
loro	vorranno

CONDITIONAL

io	vorrei
tu	vorresti
lui/lei/Lei	vorrebbe
noi	vorremmo
voi	vorreste
loro	vorrebbero

PRESENT SUBJUNCTIVE

io	voglia
tu	voglia
lui/lei/Lei	voglia
noi	vogliamo
voi	vogliate
loro	vogliano

PAST HISTORIC

io	volli
tu	volesti
lui/lei/Lei	volle
noi	volemmo
voi	voleste
loro	vollero

PAST PARTICIPLE

voluto

IMPERATIVE

—

GERUND

volendo

AUXILIARY

avere

The Gender of Nouns

In Italian, all nouns are either masculine or feminine, whether they denote people, animals or things.

The gender of a noun is often indicated by its final letter. Here are some guidelines to help you determine what gender a noun is:

Nearly all nouns ending in -o are masculine, e.g.
il treno the train
l'uomo the man
un topo a mouse
un gatto a (tom)cat
un italiano an Italian (man)

EXCEPTIONS:
la mano the hand
una foto a photo
la radio the radio
una moto a motorbike

Very many nouns ending in -a are feminine, e.g.
la casa the house
una donna a woman
una gatta a (she) cat
un'italiana an Italian woman

There are, however, numerous exceptions, e.g.
il dramma the drama
il papa the pope
il problema the problem

A few nouns ending in -a are feminine, but can refer to a man or a woman, e.g.
una guida a guide (male or female)
una persona a person (male or female)
una vittima a victim (male or female)

Nouns ending in -ista denoting people, can be masculine or feminine, e.g.
un giornalista a (male) journalist
una giornalista a (female) journalist

The Gender of Nouns *continued*

un pessimista a (male) pessimist
una pessimista a (female) pessimist

Nearly all words ending in –à, –sione and –zione are feminine, e.g.
una difficoltà a difficulty
un'occasione an opportunity
una conversazione a conversation

Nouns ending in a consonant are nearly always masculine, e.g.
un film a film
un computer a computer
un box a garage

EXCEPTIONS:
una jeep a jeep
una star a star

Nouns ending in –e or –i can be masculine or feminine, e.g.
un mese a month
la mente the mind
un brindisi a toast
una crisi a crisis

The names of languages, and all months, are masculine, whether they
end in –o or –e, e.g.
il tedesco German
il francese French
lo scorso febbraio last February
il prossimo dicembre next December

Suffixes that differentiate between male and female are shown on page 128.

Some words have different meanings depending on their gender, e.g.

il fine the objective	la fine the end
un posto a place	la posta the mail
il manico the handle	la manica the sleeve
un modo a way	la moda the fashion
un mostro a monster	una mostra an exhibition
il capitale capital (money)	una capitale a capital city

Nouns

The Formation of Feminines

As in English, male and female are sometimes differentiated by the use of quite different words, e.g.

>**un fratello** a brother
>**una sorella** a sister
>**un toro** a bull
>**una mucca** a cow

More often, however, words in Italian show gender by their ending:

>Many Italian nouns ending in **-o** can be made feminine by changing the ending to **-a** → ❶

>Some nouns ending in **-e** also change the ending to **-a** for the feminine → ❷

>Some nouns ending in **-a** or **-e** have no change of ending for the feminine → ❸

>Nouns ending in **-ese** that describe nationality are the same for masculine and feminine → ❹

>Nouns ending in **-ante** are the same for masculine and feminine → ❺

>Nouns ending in **-tore** make the the feminine by substituting the ending **-trice** → ❻

>Some nouns ending in **-e** have feminine forms ending in **-essa** → ❼

Examples

1
un cuoco	a (*male*) cook
una cuoca	a (*female*) cook
uno zio	an uncle
una zia	an aunt
una ragazzo	a boy
una ragazza	a girl
un italiano	an Italian (man)
un'italiana	an Italian (woman)

2
un signore	a gentleman
una signora	a lady
un infermiere	a (*male*) nurse
un'infermiera	a (*female*) nurse
un parrucchiere	a (*male*) hairdresser
una parrucchiera	a (*female*) hairdresser

3
un collega	a (*male*) colleague
una collega	a (*female*) colleague
il mio dentista	my dentist (*male*)
la mia dentista	my dentist (*female*)
un nipote	a grandson
una nipote	a granddaughter

4
un irlandese	an Irishman
un'irlandese	an Irishwoman
uno scozzese	a Scotsman
una scozzese	a Scotswoman

5
un cantante	a (*male*) singer
una cantante	a (*female*) singer
un amante	a (*male*) lover
un'amante	a (*female*) lover
un principiante	a (*male*) beginner
una principiante	a (*female*) beginner

6
un attore	an actor
un'attrice	a (*female*) actor
un pittore	a (*male*) painter
una pittrice	a (*female*) painter

7
il professore	the (*male*) teacher
la professoressa	the (*female*) teacher
uno studente	a (*male*) student
una studentessa	a (*female*) student

The Formation of Plurals

Masculine nouns, whether they end in -o, -a or -e, nearly always take the ending -i in the plural → ❶

Feminine nouns ending in -a take the ending -e in the plural → ❷

Feminine nouns ending in -e take the ending -i in the plural → ❸

Nouns that have no change of ending in the plural

Nouns ending in an accented vowel do not change the ending in the plural → ❹

Nouns ending in -i and -ie do not change in the plural → ❺

Words ending with a consonant remain unchanged in the plural → ❻

Other common words that do not change in the plural are:

il cinema	cinema	i cinema
la radio	radio	le radio
la moto	motorbike	le moto
l'auto	car	le auto
la foto	photo	le foto

Examples

①

un anno	one year
due anni	two years
un ragazzo	a boy
i ragazzi	the boys
un ciclista	a (*male*) cyclist
due ciclisti	two cyclists
un problema	a problem
molti problemi	lots of problems
un mese	one month
due mesi	two months
un francese	a Frenchman
due francesi	two Frenchmen

②

una settimana	one week
due settimane	two weeks
una ragazza	one girl
due ragazze	two girls

③

un'inglese	an Englishwoman
due inglesi	two Englishwomen
la vite	the vine
le viti	the vines

④

la città	the city
le città	the cities
la loro università	their university
le loro università	their universities
un caffè	a coffee
due caffè	two coffees
una virtù	a virtue
le sue virtù	her virtues

⑤

un'analisi	an analysis
delle analisi	analyses
una serie	a series
due serie	two series
una specie	a sort
varie specie	various sorts

⑥

il film	the film
i film	the films
il manager	the manager
i manager	the managers
il computer	the computer
i computer	the computers
la jeep	the jeep
le jeep	the jeeps

Irregular Plural Forms

Some masculine nouns become feminine in the plural, and take the ending -a → ❶

The plural of **uomo** man is **uomini**. The plural of **la mano** hand is **le mani**.

Nouns ending in -**ca** and -**ga** add an **h** before the plural ending, to keep the sound of the **c** and **g** hard → ❷

Some nouns ending in -**co** and -**go** also add an **h** before the plural ending, to keep the sound of the **c** and **g** hard → ❸

There are numerous exceptions. You can check the plural of such nouns in the dictionary.

> EXCEPTIONS:
> **amico** friend (*plural* **amici**)
> **nemico** enemy (*plural* **nemici**)
> **psicologo** psychologist (*plural* **psicologi**)
> **geologo** geologist (*plural* **geologi**)

The plurals of compound nouns such as **pescespada** (*swordfish*), **capolavoro** (*masterpiece*), or **apriscatole** (*tin opener*) do not always follow the usual rules. You can find them in the dictionary.

Examples

1

il dito	the finger
le dita	the fingers
un uovo	an egg
le uova	the eggs
il lenzuolo	the sheet
le lenzuola	the sheets

2

amica	(*female*) friend
amiche	(*female*) friends
buca	hole
buche	holes
riga	line
righe	lines
casalinga	housewife
casalinghe	housewives

3

gioco	game
giochi	games
fuoco	fire
fuochi	fires
luogo	place
luoghi	places
borgo	district
borghi	districts

The Definite Article

il (l')/lo, la(l'), i/gli;le

	MASCULINE	FEMININE
SING.	il	la
	lo	
	l'	l'
PLUR.	i	le
	gli	

The form of the Italian article depends on the gender and number of the noun it accompanies. It also depends on the letter the noun starts with.

il is used with masculine nouns starting with most consonants, except for z, gn, pn, ps, x, y and impure s*; lo is used with these. l' is used before vowels → ①

i is used with masculine plural nouns starting with most consonants; gli is used before vowels and z, gn, pn, ps, x, y and impure s*. → ②

la is used before feminine singular nouns beginning with a consonant, and l' is used before a vowel → ③

le is used with all feminine plural nouns → ④

If the article is separated from the noun by an adjective, the first letter of the adjective determines the choice of article → ⑤

For uses of the definite article see page 138.

*Impure s means s + another consonant.

1
il ragazzo	the boy
il cellulare	the mobile phone
lo zio	the uncle
lo studente	the student
lo pneumatico	the tyre
lo psichiatra	the psychiatrist
lo yogurt	the yoghurt
l'ospedale	the hospital
l'albergo	the hotel

2
i fratelli	the brothers
i cellulari	the mobile phones
gli studenti	the students
gli zii	the uncles
gli gnocchi	the gnocchi
gli pneumatici	the tyres
gli yogurt	the yoghurts
gli amici	the friends
gli orari	the timetables

3
la ragazza	the girl
la macchina	the car
l'amica	the (girl) friend
l'arancia	the orange

4
le ragazze	the girls
le amiche	the (girl) friends

5
l'amico the friend	il migliore amico the best friend
lo studente the student	il migliore studente the best student
gli studenti the students	i migliori studenti the best students

The Definite Article *continued*

The prepositions **a, da, di, in** and **su** combine with the article to form one word.

a + article → ❶

SING.	a + il = al	a + la = alla
	a + l' = all'	a + l' = all'
	a + lo = allo	
PLUR.	a + i = ai	a+ le = alle
	a + gli = agli	

da + article → ❷

SING.	da + il = dal	da + la = dalla
	da + l' = dall'	da + l' = dall'
	da + lo = dallo	
PLUR.	da + i = dai	da+ le = dalle
	da + gli = dagli	

di + article → ❸

SING.	di + il = del	di + la = della
	di + l' = dell'	di + l' = dell'
	di + lo = dello	
PLUR.	di + i = dei	di+ le = delle
	di + gli = degli	

in + article → ❹

SING.	in + il = nel	in + la = nella
	in + l' = nell'	in + l' = nell'
	in + lo = nello	
PLUR.	in + i = nei	in+ le = nelle
	in + gli = negli	

su + article → ❺

SING.	su + il = sul	su + la = sulla
	su + l' = sull'	su + l' = sull'
	su + lo = sullo	
PLUR.	su + i = sui	su + le = sulle
	su + gli = sugli	

Examples

1 al cinema — to the cinema
allo stadio — at *or* to the stadium
ai concerti — at *or* to the concerts
alle partite — at *or* to the matches

2 dall'albergo — from the hotel
dalla stazione — from the station
dagli aeroporti — from the airports
della squadra — of the team
degli studenti — of the students

3 nel giardino — in the garden
nell'appartamento — in the flat

4 nei dintorni — in the surroundings

5 sullo scoglio — on the rock
sulla spiaggia — on the beach

The Definite Article *continued*

Uses of the Definite Article

The definite article is used much more in Italian than it is in English. It generally translates the English definite article, but is also used in many contexts where English has no article:

> with possessive pronouns → ①
>
> with plurals and uncountable* nouns → ②
>
> in generalizations → ③
>
> with the names of regions and countries → ④
> EXCEPTIONS: no article with countries following the Italian preposition in *in/to* → ⑤
>
> with parts of the body, replacing the English possessive adjective → ⑥
>
> 'Ownership' of parts of the body, and of clothes, is often indicated by an indirect object pronoun or a reflexive pronoun → ⑦
>
> with the time, dates and years → ⑧
>
> in expressions of quantity/rate/price → ⑨
>
> with titles, ranks, professions followed by a proper name, and colloquially, with female names → ⑩

* An uncountable noun is one which cannot be used in the plural or with an indefinite article, e.g. *milk*.

Examples

1
la mia casa — my house
le sue figlie — her daughters
i vostri amici — your friends

2
I bambini soffrono — Children are suffering
Mi piacciono gli animali — I like animals
Le cose vanno meglio — Things are going better
Il nuoto è il mio sport preferito — Swimming is my favourite sport
Non mi piace il riso — I don't like rice

3
Lo zucchero non fa bene — Sugar isn't good for you
La povertà è un grande problema — Poverty is a big problem

4
L'Australia è molto grande — Australia is very big
La Calabria è bella — Calabria is beautiful

5
Vado in Francia a giugno — I'm going to France in June
Lavorano in Germania — They work in Germany

6
Dammi la mano — Give me your hand
Attento alla testa! — Mind your head!

7
Mi fa male il piede — My foot is hurting
Soffiati il naso! — Blow your nose!
Si è tolto il cappotto — He took off his coat
Mettiti le scarpe — Put your shoes on

8
all'una — at one o'clock
alle due — at two o'clock
Era l'una — It was one o'clock
Sono le due — It's two o'clock
Sono nata il primo maggio 1990 — I was born on May 1, 1990
Verranno nel 2015 — They're coming in 2015

9
Costano 3 euro al chilo — They cost 3 euro a kilo
70 km all'ora — 70 km an hour
50.000 dollari al mese — 50,000 dollars per month
due volte alla settimana — twice a week

10
La signora Rossi è qui — Mrs. Rossi is here
Il dottor Gentile — Doctor Gentile
la regina Elisabetta — Queen Elizabeth
Ecco la Silvia! — Here's Silvia!

Articles

The Partitive Article

The partitive article has the sense of 'some' or 'any', although the Italian is not always translated in English.

Forms of the partitive

	WITH MASC. NOUN	WITH FEM. NOUN
SING.	del	della
	dell'	dell'
	dello	
PLUR.	dei	delle
	degli	

del burro	some butter
dell'olio	some oil
della carta	some paper
dei fiammiferi	some matches
delle uova	some eggs
Hanno rotto dei bicchieri	They broke some glasses
Mi ha fatto vedere delle foto	He showed me some photos
Ci vuole del sale	It needs (some) salt
Aggiungi della farina	Add (some) flour

Articles

The Indefinite Article

MASCULINE	FEMININE
un	una
uno	un'

The form of the indefinite article depends on the gender of the noun it accompanies. It also depends on the letter the noun starts with.

un is used with masculine nouns starting with vowels and most consonants, except for **z**, **gn**, **pn**, **ps**, **x**, **y** and impure **s*** → **①**

uno is used with these → **②**

una is used before feminine nouns beginning with a consonant, and **un'** is used before a vowel → **③**

If the article is separated from the noun by an adjective, the first letter of the adjective determines the choice of article → **④**

The indefinite article is used in Italian largely as it is in English except: → **⑤**

- with the words **cento** and **mille**
- when translating *a few* or *a lot*
- in exclamations with **che**

The indefinite article is not used when speaking of someone's profession – either the verb **essere** is used, with no article, or **fare** is used with the definite article → **⑥**

* impure **s** means **s** + another consonant.

Examples

❶ un cellulare   a mobile phone
un uomo   a man

❷ uno studente   a student
uno zio   an uncle
uno psichiatra   a psychiatrist

❸ una ragazza   a girl
una mela   an apple
un'ora   an hour
un'amica   a (girl) friend
un albergo   a hotel

❹ uno splendido albergo   a magnificent hotel
uno scultore   a sculptor
un bravo scultore   a good sculptor

❺ cento volte   a hundred times
mille sterline   a thousand pounds
qualche parola   a few words
molti soldi   a lot of money
Che sorpresa!   What a surprise!
Che peccato!   What a pity!

❻ È medico   He's a doctor
Sono professori   They're teachers
Faccio l'ingegnere   I'm an engineer
Fa l'avvocato   She's a lawyer

Adjectives

The formation of feminines and plurals

Most adjectives agree in number and gender with the noun or pronoun.

The formation of feminines

If the masculine singular form of the adjective ends in -o, the feminine
ends in -a → ①

If the adjective ends in -e, the ending does not change for the feminine
→ ②

The formation of plurals

If the masculine singular of the adjective ends in -o, the ending changes
to -i for the masculine plural, and to -e for the feminine plural → ③

If the adjective ends in -e, the ending changes to -i for both masculine and
feminine plural → ④

Invariable adjectives

Some adjectives have no change of ending either for the feminine or the
plural → ⑤

Examples

❶ un ragazzo alto — a tall boy
una ragazza alta — a tall girl
un film italiano — an Italian film
una squadra italiana — an Italian team

❷ un libro inglese — an English book
una famiglia inglese — an English family
un treno veloce — a fast train
una macchina veloce — a fast car

❸ un fiore rosso — a red flower
dei fiori rossi — red flowers
un computer nuovo — a new computer
dei computer nuovi — new computers
una strada pericolosa — a dangerous road
delle strade pericolose — dangerous roads
una moto nera — a black motorbike
delle moto nere — black motorbikes

❹ un esercizio difficile — a difficult exercise
degli esercizi difficili — difficult exercises
un sito web interessante — an interesting website
dei siti web interessanti — interesting websites
una storia triste — a sad story
delle storie tristi — sad stories
una valigia pesante — a heavy case
delle valigie pesanti — heavy cases

❺ un calzino rosa — a pink sock
una maglietta rosa — a pink T-shirt
un paio di guanti rosa — a pair of pink gloves

un tappeto blu — a blue rug
una macchina blu — a blue car
delle tende blu — blue curtains

un gruppo pop — a pop group
la musica pop — pop music
dei gruppi pop — pop groups

Irregular Adjectives

When **bello** *beautiful* is used in front of a masculine noun it has different forms depending on which letter follows it.

MASC. SING.	MASC. PLUR.	EXAMPLES
bel	bei	before most consonants → ❶
bell'	begli	before vowels → ❷
bello	begli	before z, gn, pn, ps, x and impure s* → ❸

When used after a verb, **bello** has the same endings as any other adjective ending in -o → ❹

buono good is becomes **buon** when used before a masculine singular noun, unless the noun starts with z, gn, pn, ps, x or impure s* → ❺

grande big, great is often shortened to **gran** when it comes before a singular noun starting with a consonant → ❻

*Impure s means s + another consonant.

Examples

① bel tempo   beautiful weather
    bei nomi   beautiful names

② un bell'albero   a beautiful tree
    dei begli alberi   beautiful trees

③ un bello strumento   a beautiful instrument
    dei begli strumenti   beautiful instruments

④ Il tempo era bello   The weather was beautiful
    I fiori sono belli   The flowers are beautiful

⑤ Buon viaggio!   Have a good journey!
    un buon uomo   a good man
    un buono studente   a good student

⑥ la Gran Bretagna   Great Britain
    un gran numero di macchine   a large number of cars

Adjectives

Comparatives and Superlatives

Comparatives are formed using the following constructions:

      più ... (di) more ... (than) → ❶

      meno ... (di) less ... (than) → ❷

      (così) .... come as ... as → ❸

      (tanto) .... quanto as ... as → ❹

Superlatives are formed using the following constructions:

      il/la/i/le più ... (che) the most ... (that) → ❺

      il/la/i/le meno ... (che) the least ... (that) → ❻

After a superlative the preposition **di** is often translated as 'in' → ❼

If a clause follows a superlative the verb is in the subjunctive → ❽

Adjectives with irregular comparatives/superlatives

ADJECTIVE	COMPARATIVE	SUPERLATIVE
buono	**migliore**	**il migliore**
good	better	the best
cattivo	**peggiore**	**il peggiore**
bad	worse	worst
grande	**maggiore**	**il maggiore**
big	bigger/older	the biggest/oldest
piccolo	**minore**	**il minore**
small	smaller/younger	the smallest/youngest
alto	**superiore**	**il superiore**
high	higher	the highest
basso	**inferiore**	**l'inferiore**
low	lower	the lowest

The above words also have regular comparatives/superlatives → ❾

Emphatic adjectives

For added emphasis, the final vowel of an adjective can be replaced with the ending **-issimo**, or **-issima** → ❿

Examples

1 una macchina più grande   a bigger car
Sono più alto di te   I'm taller than you

2 un computer meno caro   a less expensive computer
i suoi film meno interessanti   his less interesting films
Quello verde è meno caro del nero   The green one is less expensive than the black one

3 È alta come sua sorella   She's as tall as her sister
La mia borsa non è pesante come la tua   My bag's not as heavy as yours
Non è così lontano come credi   It's not as far as you think

4 Sono stanca quanto te   I'm just as tired as you are
Ha tanto lavoro quanto ne hai tu   He's got as much work as you have
Non ho tanti soldi quanti ne hai tu   I haven't got as much money as you

5 il più alto   the tallest
Queste sono le scarpe più comode   These shoes are the most comfortable

6 il meno interessante   the least interesting
Gianni è il meno ambizioso   Gianni is the least ambitious

7 lo stadio più grande d'Italia   the biggest stadium in Italy
il ristorante più caro della città   the most expensive restaurant in the town

8 la persona più pigra che conosca   the laziest person I know
È una delle cose più belle che ci siano   It's one of the nicest things there is

9 Il libro è migliore del film   The book is better than the film
Questo è più buono   This one's better
la loro sorella minore   their younger sister
il loro fratello più piccolo   their younger brother

10 Il tempo era bellissimo   The weather was really beautiful
Anna è sempre elegantissima   Anna is always terribly smart
Sono educatissimi   They're extremely polite

Demonstrative Adjectives

questo/questa/questi/queste → **❶**

	MASCULINE	FEMININE	
SING.	questo	questa	this
PLUR.	questi	queste	these

quello has different forms, depending on the gender of the following noun, and the letter it starts with.

	MASCULINE	FEMININE	
SING.	quel	quella	that
	quello		
	quell'	quell'	
PLUR.	quei	quelle	those
	quegli		

quel is used before most consonants, except for **z**, **gn**, **pn**, **ps**, **x** and impure **s**. **quello** is used before these letters. **quell'** is used before vowels. **quei** is used before most consonants; **quegli** is used before vowels and **z**, **gn**, **pn**, **ps**, **x** and impure **s***.

quella is used before feminine singular nouns beginning with a consonant, with **quell'** used before a vowel → **❷**

*Impure **s** means **s** + another consonant.

Examples

1

Questa gonna è troppo stretta	This skirt is too tight
Questi pantaloni mi piacciono	I like these trousers
Queste scarpe sono comode	These shoes are comfortable

2

quel ragazzo	that boy
quello zaino	that rucksack
quello studente	that student
quell'albero	that tree
quei cani	those dogs
quegli uomini	those men
quegli studenti	those students
quella ragazza	that girl
quell'amica	that friend
quelle macchine	those cars

Interrogative Adjectives

che? what?

che is invariable → ❶

quale/quali? → ❷

	MASCULINE/FEMININE	
SING.	**quale**	what?; which?
PLUR.	**quali**	what?; which?

quanto/quanta/quanti/quante? → ❸

	MASCULINE	FEMININE	
SING.	**quanto**	**quanta**	how much?
PLUR.	**quanti**	**quante**	how many?

Interrogative adjectives are often preceded by prepositions → ❹

Exclamatory Adjectives

che and **quanto** are used with nouns in exclamations → ❺

che is also used with other adjectives → ❻

Examples

1
Che giorno è oggi?	What day is it today?
Che ore sono?	What time is it?
Che gusto preferisci?	Which flavour do you like best?
Che film hai visto?	Which film did you see?
Che programmi hai?	What plans have you got?

2
Quale tipo vuoi?	What kind do you want?

3
Quanto pane hai comprato?	How much bread did you buy?
Quanta minestra vuoi?	How much soup do you want?
Quanti bicchieri ci sono?	How many glasses are there?
Quante uova vuoi?	How many eggs do you want?

4
A che ora ti alzi?	What time do you get up?
Di che colore è?	What colour is it?
Per quale squadra tifi?	Which team do you support?

5
Che peccato!	What a pity!
Che disordine!	What a mess!
Che bella giornata!	What a lovely day!
Che brutto tempo!	What awful weather!
Quanto tempo sprecato!	What a waste of time!
Quanta gente!	What a lot of people!
Quanti soldi!	What a lot of money!
Quante storie!	What a fuss!

6
Che carino!	Isn't he sweet!
Che brutti!	They're horrible!

Adjectives

Possessive Adjectives

WITH SING. NOUN		WITH PLUR. NOUN		
MASC.	FEM.	MASC.	FEM.	
il mio	la mia	i miei	le mie	my
il tuo	la tua	i tuoi	le tue	your
il suo	la sua	i suoi	le sue	his; her; its; your
il nostro	la nostra	i nostri	le nostre	our
il vostro	la vostra	i vostri	le vostre	your
il loro	la loro	i loro	le loro	their

Possessive adjectives are generally preceded by the article → ❶

Possessive adjectives agree in number and gender with the noun they describe (i.e. the thing which is owned), not with the owner → ❷

il suo/la sua/i suoi/le sue can mean either 'his' or 'her'. To make clear which is meant, **di lui** can be used for 'his', and **di lei** for 'her' → ❸

The article is not used with any possessive adjective except loro when referring to singular family members → ❹

EXCEPTIONS: **mamma**, **babbo** and **papà**

Examples

1. Dove sono le mie chiavi? — Where are my keys?
   Luca ha perso il suo portafoglio — Luca has lost his wallet
   Ecco i nostri passaporti — Here are our passports
   Qual è la vostra camera? — Which is your room?
   Il tuo amico ti aspetta — Your friend is waiting for you

2. Anna ha perso il suo cellulare — Anna has lost her mobile phone
   Le ragazze hanno i loro biglietti — The girls have got their tickets

3. Le scarpe di lui sono eleganti — His shoes are smart
   Le scarpe di lei non mi piacciono — I don't like her shoes

4. con mia madre — with my mother
   Dov'è tuo padre? — Where's your father?
   lei e suo marito — she and her husband
   È sua moglie — She's his wife
   mia sorella ed io — my sister and I
   Non è il loro padre — He's not their father
   Maria e il suo papà — Maria and her dad

Adjectives

Position of Adjectives

Italian adjectives usually follow the noun → **❶**

Adjectives of colour or nationality *always* follow the noun → **❷**

As in English, demonstrative, possessive, numerical and interrogative adjectives precede the noun → **❸**

The adjectives **ogni**, **qualche** and **nessuno** always precede the noun → **❹**

The following common adjectives can precede the noun:

ottimo very good	**pessimo** very bad
bello beautiful	**brutto** bad, ugly
bravo good	**buono** good
prossimo next	**ultimo** last
povero poor	**grande** big, great
nuovo new	**vecchio** old
breve short	**piccolo** small

The meaning of the following adjectives can be affected by their position:

	AFTER NOUN	BEFORE NOUN
grande	big	great → **❺**
povero	poor	unfortunate → **❻**
vecchio	old	long-standing → **❼**

Adjectives following the noun are linked by **e** → **❽**

Examples

1. un gesto spontaneo   a spontaneous gesture
   una partita importante   an important match

2. capelli biondi   blonde hair
   pantaloni neri   black trousers
   una parola italiana   an Italian word

3. questo cellulare   this mobile phone
   la mia mamma   my mum
   il primo piano   the first floor
   Quale gusto?   What flavour?

4. ogni giorno   every day
   qualche volta   some times
   Non c'è nessun bisogno di andarci   There's no need to go

5. un uomo grande   a big man
   una grande sorpresa   a great surprise

6. gente povera   poor people
   Povera Anna!   Poor Anna!

7. una casa vecchia   an old house
   un mio vecchio amico   an old friend of mine

8. un libro lungo e noioso   a long, boring book
   ragazze antipatiche e maleducate   nasty rude girls

Pronouns

Personal Pronouns

	SUBJECT PRONOUNS	
	SINGULAR	PLURAL
1st person	**io** I	**noi** we
2nd person	**tu** you	**voi** you
3rd person (*masc.*)	**lui** he	**loro** they
(*fem.*)	**lei** she	
(*used as polite 'you'*)	**lei/Lei** you	

Italian verbs are frequently used without subject pronouns → **1**

tu/lei
Lei, as well as being the 3rd person singular feminine, is used when addressing someone politely. As a general rule, use **tu** only when addressing a friend, a child, a fellow student, someone you know very well, or when invited to do so. In other cases use **lei,** which is occasionally spelled with a capital when used to mean *you* **2**

loro
Loro is used only to refer to people, not to things → **3**

Loro is occasionally used as a very formal alternative to **voi** → **4**

Examples

1. Conosci Paolo?   •   Do you know Paul?
   Parlo italiano   I speak Italian
   Costa troppo   It costs too much

2. Tu cara, cosa prendi?   What are you going to have, dear?

   Lei, signora, cosa prende?   What are you going to have, madam?

3. Loro chi sono?   Who are they?
   Cosa sono? — Sono noci.   What are they? — They're walnuts.

4. Loro cosa prendono?   What will you have, ladies and gentlemen?

Personal Pronouns *continued*

3rd Person Pronouns

lui, **lei** and **loro** are the subject pronouns normally used in spoken Italian. In older written Italian you may find **egli** (masc. sing.), **ella** (fem. sing.), **essi** (masc. plur.) and **esse** (fem. plur.).

esso and **essa** are subject pronouns meaning *it*, but they are very rarely used. In Italian there is normally no pronoun corresponding to *it* at the start of a sentence → **1**

Subject pronouns often follow the verb → **2**

Subject pronouns are used:
- to add emphasis, for clarity, or to attract someone's attention → **3**
- after **anche** *too*, **neanche** *neither* and **pure** *as well* → **4**
- when the verb in Italian is understood → **5**

	UNSTRESSED DIRECT OBJECT PRONOUNS	
	SINGULAR	PLURAL
1st person	mi me	ci us
2nd person	ti you	vi you
3rd person (*masc.*)	lo (l') him; it	li them
(*fem.*)	la (l') her; it	le them
(*used as polite 'you'*)	la/La (l') you	le you

mi, **ti**, **ci** and **vi** can (but do not have to) become **m'**, **t'**, **c'** and **v'** before a vowel or mute **h** → **6**

lo and **la** change to **l'** before a vowel or mute **h** → **7**

For information on past participle agreement see page 56.

lo/la /li/le

lo means *him*, or *it*, when the object referred to is masculine → **8**

la means *her*, or *it*, when the object referred to is feminine → **9**

li refers to people, or objects that are masculine → **10**

le refers to females, or objects that are feminine → **11**

Examples

1 Fa caldo — It's hot
Sono le tre — It's three o'clock
È tardi — It's late

2 Pago io — I'll pay
Ci pensiamo noi — We'll see to it

3 Tu cosa dici? — What do _you_ think?
No, l'ha fatto lui — No, _he_ did it
Lei, signore, cosa prende? — And you sir, what will you have?

4 Prendi un gelato anche tu? — Are you going to have an ice cream too?

Non so perché. — Neanch'io — I don't know why. — Neither do I
È venuto pure lui — He came as well

5 Chi è il più bravo? — Lui. — Who's the best? — He is.
Viene lui, ma lei no — He's coming, but she isn't

6 Non c'hanno visto _or_ — They didn't see us
Non ci hanno visto

7 Non l'ho visto più — I didn't see him again
L'ho incontrata ieri — I met her yesterday

8 Gianni? Non lo vedo mai — Gianni? I never see him
Dov'è il mio cellulare? Non lo vedo — Where's my mobile phone? I can't see it

9 Chiara? Non la vedo mai — Chiara? I never see her
La birra? Non la bevo mai. — Beer? I never drink it.

10 Marco e Sara — li conosci? — Marco and Sara — do you know them?

Hai i biglietti? Sì, li ho nel portafoglio — Have you got the tickets? Yes, I've got them in my wallet

11 Le sue sorelle? Non le conosco — His sisters? I don't know them
Hai le chiavi? Sì, le ho in tasca — Have you got the keys? Yes, I've got them in my pocket

Personal Pronouns *continued*

Position of unstressed direct object pronouns

The pronoun generally comes before the verb → ❶

Unstressed direct pronouns come after the verb

- in imperatives, with the pronoun joined onto the verb → ❷

ⓘ If the verb consists of a single syllable, the initial consonant of the pronoun is doubled, except in the case of **gli** → ❸

- in infinitive constructions, when the final-**e** of the infinitive is dropped, and replaced by the pronoun → ❹

Stressed direct object pronouns

	STRESSED DIRECT OBJECT PRONOUNS	
	SINGULAR	PLURAL
1st person	me	noi
2nd person	te	voi
3rd person (*masc.*)	lui	loro
(*fem.*)	lei	loro
(*used as polite 'you'*)	lei/Lei	loro

Stressed direct object pronouns are used:
- for emphasis or contrast → ❺
- after prepositions → ❻
- in comparisons → ❼

For further information, see Order of Object Pronouns, page 166.

Reflexive Pronouns

These are dealt with under reflexive verbs, page 32.

Examples

1 Ti amo
Lo invito alla festa
Non lo mangio
La guardava
Vi cercavo
Li conosciamo

I love you
I'm inviting him to the party
I'm not going to eat it
He was looking at her
I was looking for you
We know them

2 Aiutami!
Lasciala stare

Help me!
Leave her alone

3 Fallo subito!

Do it right away!

4 Potresti venire a prendermi?
Non posso aiutarvi
Devo proprio farlo?

Could you come and get me?
I can't help you
Do I really have to do it?

5 Amo solo te
Invito lui alla festa, ma lei no

Non guardava me, guardava lei

I love only you
I'm inviting him to the party but not her

He wasn't looking at me, he was looking at her

6 Vengo con te
Sono arrivati dopo di noi

I'll come with you
They arrived after us

7 Sei più alto di me
Sono più ricchi di lui

You're taller than me
They're richer than him

Personal Pronouns *continued*

		UNSTRESSED INDIRECT OBJECT PRONOUNS	
		SINGULAR	PLURAL
1st	person	mi	ci
2nd	person	ti	vi
3rd	person (*masc.*)	gli	gli *or* loro
	(*fem.*)	le	gli *or* loro
(*used as polite 'you'*)		le	loro

The pronouns in the above table replace the preposition **a** + *noun*,
where the noun is a person or an animal → ❶

Indirect object pronouns are used with verbs governing **a** → ❷

Unstressed indirect pronouns are also used with impersonal verbs which
govern **a** → ❸

Position of unstressed indirect object pronouns

Unstressed indirect pronouns generally come before the verb → ❹

Unstressed indirect pronouns come after the verb:
- in imperatives, with the pronoun joined onto the verb → ❺

ⓘ If the verb consists of a single syllable, the initial consonant of the
pronoun is doubled, except in the case of **gli** → ❻

- in infinitive constructions. The final **-e** of the infinitive is dropped,
and replaced by the pronoun → ❼

1 Ho detto la verità a Paola — I told Paola the truth
Le ho detto la verità — I told her the truth
Hai dato del latte al gatto? — Have you given the cat some milk?

Gli hai dato del latte? — Have you given him some milk?
Potresti dare qualche consiglio ai signori? — Could you give the lady and gentleman some advice?
Potresti dar loro *or* dargli qualche consiglio? — Could you give them some advice?

2 telefonare a qn — to phone sb
Non le ho telefonato — I didn't phone her
promettere qc a qn — to promise sb sth
Mi ha promesso un regalo — He promised me a present
consigliare a qn di fare qc — to advise sb to do sth
Ci ha consigliato di aspettare — He advised us to wait

3 Le piacciono i gatti — She likes cats
Non gli importa il prezzo, sono ricchi — They don't care about the price, they're rich
Se gli interessa può venire con me — If he's interested he can come with me

4 Mi assomiglia? — Does she look like me?
Ti piace? — Do you like it?

5 Rispondigli! — Answer him!
Mandami un SMS — Send me a text

6 Dimmi dov'è — Tell me where it is
Dacci una mano — Give us a hand

7 Dovresti scriverle — You ought to write to her
Luigi? Non voglio parlargli — Luigi? I don't want to talk to him

Personal Pronouns *continued*

Stressed Indirect Pronouns

		STRESSED INDIRECT OBJECT PRONOUNS	
		SINGULAR	PLURAL
1st	person	a me	a noi
2nd	person	a te	a voi
3rd	person (*masc.*)	a lui	a loro
	(*fem.*)	a lei	a loro
	(*used as polite 'you'*)	a lei	a loro

The above forms are used for special emphasis, either before or after the verb → ①

For further information, see Order of Object Pronouns, below.

Reflexive Pronouns

These are dealt with under reflexive verbs, page 32.

Order of Object Pronouns

If direct and indirect unstressed pronouns occur together, the indirect pronoun always comes first.

mi/ti/ci/vi when followed by a direct object pronoun become **me, te, ce** and **ve** → ②

gli and **le** when followed by a direct object pronoun both become **glie-**, and add the pronoun to make one word: **glielo, gliela, glieli** or **gliele** → ③

When an indirect pronoun and a direct pronoun follow an imperative, or an infinitive, they join on to it to make one word → ④

When a stressed indirect object pronoun and an unstressed direct object pronoun occur together the above rules do not apply → ⑤

Examples

1 Ho scritto a lei, a lui no
   A me piace, ma Luca preferisce
    l'altro

I wrote to her, but not to him
   I like it, but Luca would rather
    have the other one

2 Me la dai?
   È mia – non te la do

Will you give me it?
   It's mine, I'm not going to give it
    to you

   Ce l'hanno promesso
   Ve lo mando domani

They promised it to us
I'll send it to you tomorrow

3 Glieli hai promessi
   Gliel'ha spedite
   Carlo? Glielo dirò domani

You promised them to her
He sent them to them
Carlo? I'll tell him tomorrow

4 Mi piacciono, ma non vuole
    comprarmeli
   Ecco la lettera di Rita, puoi
    dargliela?
   Ecco le chiavi. Dagliele

I like them but she won't buy me
    them
Here's Rita's letter, can you give it
    to her?
Here are the keys. Give them
    to her.

   Non abbiamo i biglietti – può
    mandarceli?

We haven't got the tickets – can
    you send us them?

5 Mandale a lui, non a me

Send them to him, not to me

The pronoun ne

ne replaces the preposition **di** + *noun* → ❶

There may be no preposition in the English translation of verbal constructions with **di/ne** → ❷

ne also replaces the partitive article (English = some, any) + *noun* → ❸

When used with amounts or numbers, **ne** represents the noun → ❹

Position: **ne** always follows another pronoun and comes before all verbs except imperatives and infinitives → ❺

Pronouns which precede **ne** change their form:
mi/ti/si/ci/vi before **ne** become **me/te/se/ce/ve** → ❻

ne follows the imperative and joins onto to it to make one word → ❼

ne joins onto the infinitive, which drops the final -e → ❽

Pronouns which come between the imperative or infinitive and **ne** change their form: **mi**, **ti**, **ci**, **vi** become **me**, **te**, **ce** and **ve**.
gli and **le** become **glie** → ❾

Examples

1 Sono conscio del pericolo — I'm aware of the danger
Ne sono conscio — I'm aware of it
Sono sicura del fatto — I'm sure of the fact
Ne sono sicura — I'm sure of it
Ha scritto della guerra sul giornale — She's written about the war in the paper

Ne ha scritto sul giornale — She's written about it in the paper
Parliamo del futuro. — Sì, parliamone. — Let's talk about the future. — Yes, let's talk about it.

2 accorgersi di qc — to realize sth
Non se ne accorge — He doesn't realize it
aver bisogno di qc — to need sth
Hai bisogno della chiave? — No, non ne ho più bisogno. — Do you need the key? — No, I don't need it any more.

3 Perché non prendi delle fragole? — Why aren't you having any strawberries?

Perché non ne prendi? — Why aren't you having any?
Vuoi del pane? — Would you like some bread?
Ne vuoi? — Would you like some?

4 Hai due figli? — No, ne ho tre. — Have you got two children? — No, I've got three.

Hai dello zucchero? — Ne ho un poco. — Have you got any sugar? — I've got a bit.

5 Ne hai paura? — Are you afraid of it?

6 Ti ricordi di quel giorno? — Do you remember that day?
Te ne ricordi? — Do you remember it?
Non si accorge degli errori — He doesn't notice mistakes
Non se ne accorge — He doesn't notice them

7 Assaggiane un po' — Try a bit

8 Non voglio parlarne — I don't want to talk about it

9 Dammene uno per favore — Give me one of them please
Dagliene due rossi — Give him two red ones
Non posso dartene uno — I can't give you one
Non posso dargliene due rossi — I can't give him two red ones

Pronouns

The pronoun ci

ci replaces the preposition **a** + *noun* → **1**

There may be no preposition in the English translation of verbal constructions with **a/ci** → **2**

Position: like **ne**, **ci** comes before the verb, unless it is an imperative, infinitive, or the gerund → **3**

For **ci** as a personal pronoun see page 164.

Note that **ci** is also an adverb meaning 'there' → **4**

Examples

1   Credi ai fantasmi?   Do you believe in ghosts?
Ci credi?   Do you believe in them?
Non pensa al futuro   She doesn't think about the future

Non ci pensa   She doesn't think about it

2   far caso a qc   to notice sth
Non ci ho fatto caso   I didn't notice it
avvicinarsi a qc   to approach sth
Ci si avvicinò   He approached it

3   Ci penso io   I'll see to it
BUT
Pensaci un po'   Think about it a bit
Non so che farci   I don't know what to do about it
Ripensandoci mi sono pentito   When I thought it over I was sorry

4   Non voglio andarci   I don't want to go there
Ci sono molti turisti   There are a lot of tourists

Indefinite Pronouns

The following are indefinite pronouns:

alcuni(e) some → ❶

altro(a, i, e) the other one; another one; other people → ❷

chiunque anyone → ❸

ciascuno(a) each → ❹

molto(a, i, e) a lot, lots → ❺

nessuno(a) nobody, anybody; none → ❻

niente nothing → ❼

nulla nothing → ❽

ognuno(a) each → ❾

parecchio, parecchia, parecchi, parecchie quite a lot → ❿

poco, poca, pochi, poche not much, not many → ⓫

qualcosa something, anything → ⓬

qualcuno(a) somebody; any → ⓭

tanto(a, i, e) lots, so much, so many → ⓮

troppo(a, i, e) too much, too many → ⓯

tutti(e) everybody, all → ⓰

tutto everything, all → ⓱

uno(a) somebody → ⓲

Examples

1. Ci sono posti liberi? — Sì, alcuni.   Are there any empty seats?
   — Yes, some.

   Ci sono ancora delle fragole?   Are there any strawberries left?
   — Sì, alcune.   — Yes, some.

2. L'altro è meno caro   The other one is cheaper
   Non m'interessa quello che   I don't care what other people
   dicono gli altri   say
   Prendine un altro   Take another one

3. Attacca discorso con chiunque   She'll talk to anyone

4. Ne avevamo uno per ciascuno   We had one each
   Le torte costano due euro ciascuna   The cakes cost two euros each

5. Ne ha molto   He's got lots
   molti di noi   a lot of us

6. Non è venuto nessuno   Nobody came
   Nessuna delle ragazze è venuta   None of the girls came

7. Cosa c'è? — Niente.   What's wrong? — Nothing.

8. Che cos'hai comprato? — Nulla.   What did you buy? — Nothing.

9. ognuno di voi   each of you

10. C'è ancora del pane? — Sì,   Is there any bread left? — Yes,
    parecchio.   quite a lot.
    Avete avuto problemi?   Did you have problems?
    — Sì, parecchi.   — Yes, a lot.

11. C'è pane? — Poco.   Is there any bread? — Not much.
    Ci sono turisti? — Pochi.   Are there any tourists? —
    Not many.

12. Ho qualcosa da dirti   I've got something to tell you
    Ha bisogno di qualcosa?   Do you need anything?

13. Ha telefonato qualcuno   Somebody phoned
    Conosci qualcuna delle ragazze?   Do you know any of the girls?

14. Hai mangiato? — Sì, tanto!   Have you eaten? — Yes, lots!

15. Ci sono errori? — Sì, troppi.   Are there any mistakes? — Yes,
    too many.

16. Vengono tutti   Everybody is coming
    Sono arrivate tutte   They've all arrived

17. Va tutto bene?   Is everything okay?
    L'ho finito tutto   I've finished it all

18. Ho incontrato uno che ti conosce   I met somebody who knows you

Relative Pronouns

che who; whom; which; that
che is an invariable pronoun that can be the subject or object of a relative clause, and can refer to people or things → ❶

The Italian object pronoun cannot be omitted, though it need not be translated in English → ❷

After a preposition use **cui** → ❸

il che which
This is used to refer to a fact or situation that's just been mentioned → ❹

il quale, la quale, i quali, le quali who; whom; which; that
These are more formal relative pronouns, which agree in number and gender with the noun → ❺

il quale, la quale, i quali and **le quali** are used most often with prepositions.
The prepositions **di, da, a, in** and **su** combine with the articles **il, la, i** and **le** → ❻

Article + preposition combinations are dealt with on page 136

il cui, la cui, i cui, le cui whose
These agree in number and gender with the thing possessed → ❼

Use **cui** instead of **che** with a preposition → ❽

quello che, ciò che what, the thing which

These can be used as the subject or object of a relative clause. Literally they mean 'that which' → ❾

In combination with **di**, **quello** or ciò che become **quello di cui** or **ciò di cui** → ❿

Examples

1 quella signora che ha un piccolo cane nero — that lady who has a little black dog

una persona che detesto — a person whom I detest

l'uomo che hanno arrestato — the man that they've arrested

la squadra che ha vinto — the team which won

2 la persona che ammiro di più — the person (whom) I admire most

il dolce che hai fatto — the pudding (that) you made

3 la ragazza di cui ti ho parlato — the girl that I told you about

gli amici con cui andiamo in vacanza — the friends we go on holiday with

la persona a cui si riferiva — the person he was referring to

il quartiere in cui abito — the area in which I live

4 Non pagano nulla, il che non mi sembra giusto — They don't pay anything, which doesn't seem fair to me

Dice che non è colpa sua, il che è vero — She says it's not her fault, which is true

5 suo padre, il quale è avvocato — his father, who is a lawyer

le sue sorelle, le quali studiano a Roma — his sisters, who study in Rome

6 l'albergo nel quale ci siamo fermati — the hotel that we stayed at

la borsa di studio sulla quale contava — the grant he was counting on

gli amici dai quali ho avuto questo regalo — the friends I had this present from

la medicina della quale ho bisogno — the medicine I need

7 una persona il cui nome mi sfugge — a person whose name escapes me

la persona i cui bagagli sono qui — the person whose bags are here

8 È quello con cui parlavo — He's the one I was talking to

9 Ho visto quello or ciò che c'era sul tavolo — I saw what was on the table

Quello or ciò che mi preoccupa è che... — The thing which worries me is that...

Quello or ciò che dici non ha senso — What you say doesn't make sense

Ho fatto quello or ciò che potevo — I did what I could

10 Non è quello or ciò di cui si tratta — That's not what it's about

Non è quello or ciò che mi aspettavo — That's not what I was expecting

Interrogative Pronouns

These pronouns are used in direct questions:
 chi? who? whom?
 che? what?
 cosa? what?
 che cosa? what?

These pronouns are invariable, and can be the subject or object of the verb → **1**

che cos'è/cos'è? what is it?
This is used to ask for something to be explained or identified → **2**

Prepositions come before the interrogative pronoun, and never at the end of the question → **3**

di chi? whose → **4**

quale? which? which one? what?
quale is the singular form (qual before a vowel), and quali the plural → **5**

qual è?/quali sono? what is/what are?
These are used to ask about a particular detail, name, number etc → **6**

quanto(a)? How much? → **7**

quanti(e)? How many? → **8**

All the pronouns used in direct questions can be used in indirect questions → **9**

Examples

① Chi è?
Chi cerca?
Che vuoi?
Cosa vuole?
Che cosa vogliono?

Who is it?
Who(m) are you looking for?
What do you want?
What does he want?
What do they want?

② Che cos'è? — È un regalo.

What is it? — It's a present.

③ A chi l'hai dato?
Con chi parlavi?
Di che cosa hai bisogno?
Cosa ti aspettavi?

Who did you give it to?
Who were you talking to?
What do you need?
What were you expecting?

④ Di chi è questa borsa?
Di chi sono queste chiavi?

Whose is this bag?
Whose are these keys?

⑤ Conosco sua sorella. — Quale?
Ho rotto dei bicchieri. — Quali?

I know his sister. — Which one?
I broke some glasses. — Which ones?

⑥ Qual è il suo indirizzo?
Qual è la capitale della Finlandia?
Quali sono i loro nomi?

What's her address?
What's the capital of Finland?
What are their names?

⑦ Farina? Quanta ce ne vuole?

Flour? How much is needed?

⑧ Quante di loro passano la sera a leggere?

How many of them spend the evening reading?

⑨ Dimmi chi è
Non so cosa vuol dire
Ho chiesto di chi era
Può dirmi di che cosa si tratta?

Tell me who it is
I don't know what it means
I asked whose it was
Can you tell me what it's about?

Possessive Pronouns

Singular:

MASCULINE	FEMININE	
il mio	la mia	mine
il tuo	la tua	yours
il suo	la sua	his; hers; its; yours
il nostro	la nostra	ours
il vostro	la vostra	yours
il loro	la loro	theirs

Plural:

MASCULINE	FEMININE	
i miei	le mie	mine
i tuoi	le tue	yours
i suoi	le sue	his; hers; its; yours
i nostri	le nostre	ours
i vostri	le vostre	yours
i loro	le loro	theirs

The pronoun agrees in number and gender with the noun it replaces, not with the owner → ❶

di/da/a/su/in + *possessive pronoun*
These prepositions combine with the article → ❷

Examples

❶ Paolo, questa borsa non è la mia, è la tua

Paolo, this bag's not mine, it's yours

La nostra casa è piccola, la vostra è grande

Our house is small, yours is big

I miei genitori e i suoi si conoscono

My parents and hers know each other

❷ La mia macchina è più vecchia della sua

My car is older than his

Preferisco il nostro giardino al loro

I prefer our garden to theirs

Demonstrative Pronouns

questo/questa/questi/queste
quello/quella/quelli/quelle

	MASCULINE	FEMININE	
SING.	questo	questa	this, this one
	quello	quella	that, that one, that man/that woman
PLUR.	questi	queste	these, these ones
	quelli	quelle	those, those ones, those people

The pronoun agrees in number and gender with the noun it replaces → ➊

quello/a used to mean that man/woman is pejorative → ➋

quello(a, i, e) che the one(s) who/which → ➌

quello(a, i, e) di the one(s) belonging to/the one(s) of
This use is often translated by apostrophe s ('s), or s apostrophe (s') → ➍

questo(a, i, e) qui/qua
qui or **qua** can be used with **questo** for emphasis or to distinguish between two things → ➎

quello(a, i, e) lì/là
lì or **là** can be used with **quello** for emphasis or to distinguish between two things → ➏

Examples

① Questo è mio marito — This is my husband
Questa è camera mia — This is my bedroom
Questi sono i miei fratelli — These are my brothers
Quali scarpe ti metti? — Queste — Which shoes are you going to wear? — These ones

Qual è la sua borsa? — Quella — Which bag is yours? — That one
Quelli quanto costano? — How much do those cost?

② Dice sempre bugie quello — That man is always telling lies
Quelle non sono mai contente — Those women are never happy

③ È quello che preferisco — That's the one (that) I prefer
È quella che parla di più — She's the one who talks most
Sono quelli che sono partiti senza pagare — They're the ones who left without paying
Queste scarpe sono quelle che ha ordinato — These shoes are the ones (that) you ordered

④ Questo giardino è più grande di quello di Giulia — This garden is bigger than Giulia's
Preferisco la mia macchina a quella di mio marito — I prefer my car to my husband's
Le mie scarpe sono più belle di quelle di Lucia — My shoes are nicer than Lucia's
i miei genitori e quelli delle mie amiche — my parents and those of my friends
le montagne della Svizzera e quelle della Scozia — the mountains of Switzerland and those of Scotland

⑤ Non quello, questo qui — Not that one, this one here
Voglio queste qua — I want these ones here

⑥ Questa gonna non ti sta bene, prova quella là — This skirt doesn't look good on you, try that one
Quali prendi? — Quelli lì — Which ones are you going to have? — Those over there

Adverbs

Formation

Some adverbs are formed by adding **-mente** to an adjective.

-mente is added to the feminine form, (which ends in **-a**) of an adjective ending in **-o** → ❶

-mente is added to the basic form when an adjective ends in **-e** for both masculine and feminine → ❷

Adjectives ending in **-le** and **-re** drop the final e → ❸

Irregular Adverbs

ADJECTIVE	ADVERB
buono good	**bene** well → ❹
cattivo bad	**male** badly → ❺
migliore better	**meglio** better → ❻
peggiore worse	**peggio** worse → ❼

Adjectives used as adverbs

Certain adjectives are used adverbially. These include: **giusto**, **vicino**, **diritto**, **certo**, **solo**, **forte**, **molto**, **poco** → ❽

Examples

1 MASC./FEM. ADJECTIVE

lento/lenta slow

fortunato/fortunata lucky

ADVERB

lentamente slowly

fortunatamente luckily

2 MASC./FEM. ADJECTIVE

veloce quick, fast

corrente fluent

ADVERB

velocemente quickly, fast

correntemente fluently

3 -le/-re ADJECTIVE

facile easy

particolare particular

ADVERB

facilmente easily

particolarmente particularly

4 Parlano bene l'italiano — They speak Italian well

5 Ho giocato male — I played badly

6 Sto meglio — I'm better

7 Mi sento peggio — I'm feeling worse

8 Ha risposto giusto — She answered correctly

Abitano vicino — They live nearby

Siamo andati sempre diritto — We kept straight on

Vieni stasera? — Certo! — Are you coming tonight?
— Of course!

L'ho incontrata solo due volte — I've only met her twice

Correva forte — He was running fast

Quel quadro mi piace molto — I like that picture a lot

Vengo in ufficio poco spesso — I don't come into the office very
often

Position of Adverbs

When the adverb accompanies a verb in a simple tense, it generally follows the verb → ①

For emphasis the adverb can come at the beginning of the sentence → ②

When adverbs such as **mai**, **sempre**, **già** and **appena** accompany a verb in a compound tense, they come between the auxilary verb and the past participle → ③

When the adverb accompanies an adjective or another adverb it generally precedes the adjective/adverb → ④

Comparatives of Adverbs

These are formed as follows:
>   **più ... (di)** more ... (than) → ⑤
>   **meno ... (di)** less ... (than) → ⑥

sempre più is used with the adjective to mean *more and more* → ⑦

Superlatives of Adverbs

più ... and **meno ...** are also used to express the superlative → ⑧
più ... di tutti/meno di tutti can be used to emphasize the superlative → ⑨

Examples

1 Viene sempre — He always comes
Parli bene l'italiano — You speak Italian well

2 Ora non posso — I can't do it just now
Prima non lo sapevo — I didn't know that before

3 Non sono mai stata a Milano — I've never been to Milan
È sempre venuto con me — He always came with me
L'ho già letto — I've already read it
Se n'è appena andato — He's just left

4 Fa troppo freddo — It's too cold
Vai più piano — Go more slowly

5 più spesso — more often
più lentamente — more slowly
Correva più forte di me — He was running faster than me

6 meno velocemente — less quickly
Costa meno — It costs less
Vengo meno spesso di lui — I come less often than he does

7 Le cose vanno sempre meglio — Things are going better and better

Mio nonno sta sempre peggio — My grandfather's getting worse and worse

Cammina sempre più lento — He's walking slower and slower

8 È Carlo che viene più spesso — It's Carlo who comes most often
Sono loro che lavorano meno volontieri — They're the ones who work least willingly

9 Cammina più piano di tutti — She walks the slowest (of all)
L'ha fatto meno volontieri di tutti — He did it the least willingly

Adverbs with irregular comparatives/superlatives

ADVERB	COMPARATIVE/SUPERLATIVE
bene well	meglio better/best
male badly	peggio worse/worst
molto a lot	più more/most
poco not much	meno less/least

Emphatic Adverbs

For added emphasis the ending -issimamente can be used. It replaces the endings -amente, -emente or -mente → **①**

bene and male have irregular emphatic forms: benissimo and malissimo → **②**

Adverbial phrases

di più and di meno are used to say what you do most/least → **③**

Examples

1 lentamente

slowly

lentissimamente

very slowly

velocemente

quickly

velocissimamente

very quickly

2 Hai fatto benissimo

You did very well

3 la cosa che temeva di più

the thing she feared most

quello che mi piace di meno

the one I like least

Sono quelli che guadagnano di
   meno

They're the ones who earn least

Some common adverbs and their usage

Some common adverbs:

> **abbastanza** quite; enough → ①
>
> **anche** too → ②
>
> **ancora** still; yet → ③
>
> **appena** just; only just → ④
>
> **certo** certainly; of course → ⑤
>
> **così** so; like this; like that → ⑥
>
> **ecco** here → ⑦
>
> **forse** perhaps, maybe → ⑧
>
> **già** already → ⑨
>
> **mai** never; ever → ⑩
>
> **molto** very; very much; much → ⑪
>
> **piuttosto** quite; rather → ⑫
>
> **poco** not very; not at all → ⑬
>
> **presto** soon; early → ⑭
>
> **quasi** nearly → ⑮
>
> **spesso** often → ⑯
>
> **tanto** so; so much → ⑰
>
> **troppo** too; too much → ⑱

Examples

1. È abbastanza alta — She's quite tall
   Non studia abbastanza — He doesn't study enough

2. È venuta anche mia sorella — My sister came too

3. Sei ancora a letto? — Are you still in bed?
   Silvia non è ancora arrivata — Silvia's not here yet

4. L'ho appena fatto — I've just done it
   L'indirizzo era appena leggibile — The address was only just legible

5. Certo che puoi — Of course you can
   Certo che sì — Certainly

6. È così simpatica! — She's so nice!
   Si apre così — It opens like this
   Non si fa così — You don't do it like that

7. Ecco l'autobus! — Here's the bus!
   Dov'è Carla? — Eccola! — Where's Carla? — Here she is!

8. Forse hanno ragione — Maybe they're right

9. Te l'ho già detto — I've already told you

10. Non sono mai stato in America — I've never been to America
    Sei mai stato in America? — Have you ever been to America?

11. Sono molto stanca — I'm very tired
    Ti piace? — Sì, molto. — Do you like it? — Yes, very much
    Ora mi sento molto meglio — I feel much better now

12. Fa piuttosto caldo oggi — It's quite warm today
    È piuttosto lontano — It's rather a long way

13. Mi sento poco bene — I don't feel at all well
    Mi piacciono poco — I don't like them at all

14. Arriverà presto — He'll be here soon
    Mi alzo sempre presto — I always get up early

15. Sono quasi pronta — I'm nearly ready

16. Vanno spesso in centro — They often go into town

17. Questo libro è tanto noioso — This book is so boring
    Mi manchi tanto — I miss you so much

18. È troppo caro — It's too expensive
    Parlano troppo — They talk too much

Prepositions

On the following pages you will find some of the most frequent uses of prepositions in Italian. Particular attention is paid to cases where usage differs greatly from English. It is often difficult to give an English equivalent for Italian prepositions, since usage varies so much between the two languages.

In the list below, the broad meaning of the preposition is given on the left, with examples of usage following.

Prepositions are given in alphabetical order, except for a, di, da and in. These prepositions, shown first, combine with the definite article to make one word.

For combinations of a, di, da, in and su with the definite article, see page 136.

a

at	**alla porta** at the door
	a casa at home
	alla prossima fermata at the next stop
	a 50 chilometri all'ora at 50 km an hour
in	**a Londra** in London
	al sole in the sun
	Sta a letto He's in bed
on	**al terzo piano** on the third floor
	alla radio on the radio
to	**Andiamo al cinema?** Shall we go to the cinema?
	Vai a letto? Are you going to bed?
	Sei mai stato a New York? Have you ever been to New York?
	dare qc a qn to give sth to sb
	A chi l'hai dato? Who did you give it to?
	promettere qc a qn to promise sth to sb
	il primo/l'ultimo a fare qc the first/last to do sth
from	**comprare qc a qn** to buy sth from sb

	nascondere qc a qn to hide sth from sb
	prendere qc a qn to take sth from sb
	rubare qc a qn to steal sth from sb

see you	**a presto** see you soon
	a domani see you tomorrow

manner	**a piedi** on foot
	a mano by hand
	a poco a poco little by little
	all'antica in the old-fashioned way
	alla milanese in the Milanese way

(made) with	**un gelato alla fragola** a strawberry ice cream
	una torta al cioccolato a chocolate cake
	gli spaghetti al pomodoro spaghetti with tomato sauce

time: at	**alle due** at two o'clock
	a mezzanotte at midnight
	a Pasqua at Easter

with month: in	**a maggio** in May

distance	**a tre chilometri da qui** three kilometres from here
	a due ore di distanza in macchina two hours away by car

purpose	**Sono uscita a fare due passi** I went out for a little walk
	Sono andati a fare il bagno They've gone to have a swim

after certain verbs	See pages 70-79

Prepositions

di

of, belonging to	**un amico di famiglia** a friend of the family
	il padre di Marco Marco's father
	la casa dei miei amici my friends' house
	Di chi è? Whose is it?
	il periodo delle vacanze the holiday season
	il professore di francese the French teacher
	il campione del mondo the world champion
(made) by	**un quadro di Picasso** a picture by Picasso
	una commedia di Shakespeare
	a play by Shakespeare
from	**È di Firenze** He's from Florence
	Di dove sei? Where are you from?
comparisons	**È più alto di me** He's taller than me
	È più brava di lui She's better than him
in (after superlative)	**il più grande del mondo** the biggest in the world
	il migliore d'Italia the best in Italy
time	**di domenica** on Sundays
	di notte at night
	d'inverno in winter
contents, composition, material, colour	**una bottiglia di vino** a bottle of wine
	un gruppo di turisti a group of tourists
	una maglietta di cotone a cotton T-shirt
	Di che colore è? What colour is it?
manner	**di rado** rarely
	di solito usually
after certain numbers	**un milione di dollari** a million dollars
	un migliaio di persone about a thousand people
	una ventina di macchine about twenty cars

Prepositions

after certain adjectives	**Le arance sono ricche di vitamina C** Oranges are rich in vitamin C **Era pieno di gente** It was full of people
after certain verbs	see pages 70-79

da

from	**a tre chilometri da qui** three kilometres from here **Viene da Roma** He comes from Rome **da cima a fondo** from top to bottom
off, out of	*Isobel* **è scesa dal treno** Isobel got off the train **È scesa dalla macchina** She got out of the car
at/to the home of	**Sono da Anna** I'm at Anna's house **Andiamo da Gabriele?** Shall we go to Gabriele's house?
at/to (*shop, workplace*)	**Laura è dal parrucchiere** Laura's at the hairdresser's **È andato dal dentista** He's gone to the dentist's
for	**Vivo qui da un anno** I've been living here for a year (*note tense*)
since	**da allora** since then **Ti aspetto dalle tre** I've been waiting for you since three o'clock (*note tense*)
by (*with passive agent*)	**dipinto da un grande artista** painted by a great artist **Sono stati catturati dalla polizia** They were caught by the police
to (*with infinitive*)	**C'è molto da fare** There's lots to do **È un film da vedere** It's a film that you've got to see
as	**Da bambino avevo paura del buio** As a child I was afraid of the dark

Prepositions

descriptive	**una ragazza dagli occhi azzurri** a girl with blue eyes
	un vestito da cento euro
	a dress costing a hundred euros
purpose/use	**un nuovo paio di scarpe da corsa**
	a new pair of running shoes
	Non ho il costume da bagno
	I haven't got my swimming costume

in

to, in (*place*)	**in centro** in/to the town centre
	in Italia in/to Italy
into	**Su! Sali in macchina** Come on! get into the car
on, at (*state*)	**in vacanza** on holiday
	in pace at peace
in (*years, seasons, months*)	**nel duemilasei** in two thousand and six
	in estate in summer
	in ottobre in October
in (*time taken*)	**L'ha fatto in sei mesi** He did it in six months
transport	**in treno** by train
	in bici by bike
language	**in italiano** in Italian

con

with	**Con chi sei stata?** Who were you with?
to	**Hai parlato con lui?** Have you spoken to him?
manner	**con calma** without hurrying
	con la forza by force

Prepositions

davanti a

in front of	Erano seduti davanti a me nell' autobus
	They were sitting in front of me in the bus
opposite	la casa davanti alla mia the house opposite mine

dopo

after	dopo cena after dinner
+ *pronoun* (add di)	dopo di loro after them

fra/tra

in (*time*)	Torno fra or tra un'ora I'll be back in an hour
between	fra or tra la cucina ed il soggiorno
	between the kitchen and the living room
+ *pronoun* (add di)	fra or tra di noi between/among us

per

for	Questo è per te This is for you
	È troppo difficile per lui It's too difficult for him
	L'ho comprato per trenta centesimi
	I bought it for thirty cents
	Ho guidato per trecento chilometri
	I drove for three hundred kilometres
	una camera per due notti a room for two nights
	Parte per Milano She's leaving for Milan
(going) to	il volo per Londra the flight to London
	il treno per Roma the train to Rome
through	I ladri sono entrati per la finestra
	The burglars got in through the window
	Siamo passati per Crewe We went through Crewe

Prepositions

by (means of)	**per posta** by post **per via aerea** by airmail **per posta elettronica** by email **per ferrovia** by rail **per telefono** by phone **per errore** by mistake
(so as) to	**L'ho fatto per aiutarti** I did it to help you **Si è chinato per prenderlo** He bent down to get it
out of	**Ci sono andato per abitudine** I went out of habit **Non l'ho fatto per pigrizia** I didn't do it out of laziness
distribution	**uno per uno** one by one **giorno per giorno** day by day **una per volta** one at a time **due per tre** two times three

prima di

before (+*noun,* *pronoun*)	**prima delle sette** before seven **prima di me** before me
+ *infin*	**prima di cominciare** before starting
until	**Non sarà pronto prima delle otto** It won't be ready until eight o'clock

senza

without	**Esci senza cappotto?** Are you going out without a coat?
+ *pronoun* (add**di**)	**senza di te** without you
+ *infinitive*	**È uscito senza dire niente** He went out without saying anything

Prepositions

sopra

over   **le donne sopra i sessant'anni** women over sixty

above   **cento metri sopra il livello del mare**
                  a hundred metres above sea level

on top of   **sopra l'armadio** on top of the cupboard

su*

on   **sul pavimento** on the floor
            sulla sinistra on the left
            un libro sugli animali a book on animals

in   **sul giornale** in the paper

out of (*ratio*)   **in tre casi su dieci** in three cases out of ten
            due giorni su tre two days out of three

approximation   **sui cinquecento euro** around five hundred euros
            È sulla trentina She's about thirty

* **su** combines with the definite article to make one word

verso

towards (*place*)   **Correva verso l'uscita**
            He was running towards the exit

about   **Arriverò verso le sette** I'll arrive about seven

Conjunctions

Some conjunctions introduce a main clause, e.g. e (and), ma (but), o (or). Others introduce subordinate clauses, e.g. perché (because), mentre (while), quando (when), se (if). Conjunctions also link single words. Most are used in much the same way as in English, but note the following:

e and
When followed by a vowel, e often becomes ed → ❶

> Some Italian conjunctions have to be followed by the subjunctive, see page 66
>
> Some conjunctions are split in Italian, like 'both ... and', 'either ... or' in English.
> o ... o   either ... or → ❷
> né ... né   neither ... nor, either ... or → ❸
> sia ... che both ... and → ❹

In Italian, sentences with split conjunctions can have a singular or a plural verb → ❺

che that
  • is followed by the indicative in statements → ❻
  • is followed by the subjunctive after verbs expressing uncertainty, see page 64

perché because, so that
When perché means 'because' it is followed by the indicative → ❼
When it means 'so that', it is followed by the subjunctive → ❽

Note that perché? can also be used as an adverb with the meaning 'why?'

se if, whether
When used in conditional clauses se is followed by the subjunctive → ❾
Followed by the infinitive, se means 'whether to' → ❿
Followed by the indicative se expresses doubt → ⓫

Conjunctions are sometimes used in phrases where a verb is understood → ⓬

Examples

1. mia sorella ed io
   È venuto qui ed è rimasto mezzora

   my sister and I
   He came here and stayed for half an hour

2. o oggi o domani

   either today or tomorrow

3. Non mi hanno chiamato né Claudio né Luca
   Non avevo né guanti né scarponi

   Neither Claudio nor Luca has phoned me
   I didn't have either gloves or boots

4. Verranno sia Luigi che suo fratello

   Both Luigi and his brother are coming

5. Non vengono or Non viene né lui né sua moglie

   Neither he nor his wife is coming

6. Ha detto che farà tardi

   He said that he'll be late

7. Sono uscita perché faceva bel tempo

   I went out because it was nice weather

8. Gliel'ho dato perché lo leggesse

   I gave it him so that he could read it

9. se fosse qui
   Se avessi studiato avresti passato l'esame

   if he was here
   If you'd worked you would have passed the exam

10. Non so se andarci o no

    I don't know whether to go or not

11. Mi chiedo se avresti accettato

    I wonder if you would have accepted

12. Ti dispiace? — Ma no!
    Ho fame. — Anch'io!
    Sì, lo so — strano però

    Do you mind? — Of course I don't!
    I'm hungry. — So am I!
    Yes, I know — it's odd though

Sentence structure

Word Order

Word order in Italian is very flexible, but:

- unstressed object pronouns always come before the verb, except when attached to the end of an infinitive or an imperative → **1**
  For details see pages 166

- most adjectives come after the noun → **2**
  For details see pages 156

- Adverbs of frequency accompanying verbs in a simple tense usually follow the verb, and those used with a compound tense follow the auxiliary verb → **3**
  For details see pages 184

Other parts of speech, however, may be positioned to give emphasis, or make a contrast:

- the noun which is the object of a verb generally follows the verb, but for emphasis it may come first → **4**

- a question word generally comes first, but for emphasis, a noun subject or object can precede it → **5**

- adjectives generally follow the verb essere, but may precede it for emphasis → **6**

- unstressed object pronouns generally precede the verb, but stressed pronouns can be used instead, and these follow the verb → **7**
  For details see pages 166

- subject pronouns are not normally used, but when added for emphasis they may come before or after the verb → **8**

Examples

1 Li vedo!   I can see them!
Me l'ha dato   He gave it to me

2 la squadra italiana   the Italian team
un vino rosso   a red wine

3 Ci vado spesso   I often go there
Non ci sono mai stato   I've never been there

4 Normal order:
Non posso soffrire quel cane   I can't stand that dog
Emphatic order:
Quel cane non lo posso soffrire
note object pronoun added before the verb

5 Normal order:
Dov'è Lidia?   Where's Lidia?
Di chi sono queste scarpe?   Whose are these shoes?
Dove metto questa borsa?   Where shall I put this bag?
Emphatic order:
Lidia, dov'è?
Queste scarpe di chi sono?
Questa borsa dove la metto?
note added object pronoun

6 Normal order
Sono belli   They're lovely
Sei pazza   You're mad
Emphatic order:
Belli sono!   They're lovely!
Pazza sei!   You're mad!

7 Order with unstressed pronoun:
Me l'ha dato   He gave it to me
Order with stressed pronoun:
L'ha dato a me (non a te)   He gave it to me (not to you)

8 Unemphatic:
Cosa pensi?   What do you think?
Emphatic:
Tu cosa pensi?/Cosa pensi tu?

Negatives

In Italian, sentences are generally made negative by adding **non** before the verb → ①

di no is used after verbs such as **dire**, **credere**, **pensare** and **sperare** → ②

o no? is used to mean 'or not' → ③

noun/pronoun + **no**
no is used when making a distinction between people or things → ④

non is used in combination with other negative words such as **niente** *nothing*, **nessuno** *nobody*, **mai** *never* → ⑤

When **mai** is used with a compound tense, it usually comes between the auxiliary verb and the past participle → ⑥

When **niente** or **nessuno** are the subject of the verb they can come first, or they can follow the verb. If they come first, **non** is not used → ⑦

More than one negative word can follow a negative verb → ⑧

nessuno, nessuna *no*
These negative adjectives change their endings according to the letter that follows them, like the indefinite article **uno** → ⑨

non ... né .... né *neither ... nor/not ... either ... or*
A plural verb is required if there are two subjects → ⑩

Examples

1 Non posso venire — I can't come
Non l'ho visto — I didn't see it
Non è qui — It's not here

2 Ha detto di no — He said not
Credo di no — I don't think so
Pensa di no — He doesn't think so
Speriamo di no — Let's hope not

3 Vieni o no? — Are you coming or not?
che ti piaccia o no — whether you like it or not

4 Invito lui, lei no — I'm going to invite him, but not her
Loro hanno finito, noi no — They've finished, but we haven't
Lei è brava, io no — She's good, but I'm not
Prendo un dolce, il caffè no — I'll have a sweet, but not a coffee

5 Non ho niente — I haven't got anything/I've got nothing

Non l'ho detto a nessuno — I haven't told anyone/I've told nobody

Non ci vado mai — I never go there

6 Non l'ho mai vista — I've never seen her
Non ci siamo mai stati — We've never been there

7 Niente è cambiato — Nothing has changed
BUT
Non è cambiato niente
Nessuno vuole andarci — Nobody wants to go
BUT
Non vuole andarci nessuno

8 Non fanno mai niente — They never do anything
Non si confida mai con nessuno — He never confides in anyone
Non vendiamo più niente — We no longer sell anything

9 Nessun tipo di pianta può viverci — No type of plant can live there
Non ho nessuna voglia di farlo — I have no desire to do it
Non hanno fatto nessuno sforzo — They didn't make any effort

10 Non verranno né Anna né Maria — Neither Anna nor Maria is coming
BUT
Non invito né Anna né Maria — I'm not inviting either Anna or Maria

Sentence structure

Question Forms

In Italian, questions differ from statements in intonation, or the use of a question mark in writing. Unlike in English, the verb forms in questions are no different from those in statements → **1**

Word order

When the subject of the question is a noun, it comes either before or after the verb → **2**

When the object of the question is a noun, it either comes after the verb, or comes first. In this case an object pronoun agreeing with the noun is added before the verb → **3**

A subject pronoun may also be added at the end of a question, for special emphasis → **4**

When answering a question, either say **sì** or **no**, or **sì** or **no** with a full statement. There is no Italian equivalent for short answers such as Yes I do, or No I don't → **5**

Question words such as **dove?** *where?*, **chi?** *who?* **cosa?** *what?* generally come first → **6**

However, note the following:
- a noun subject can either follow the verb, or precede the question word → **7**
- a noun object can follow the verb, or precede the question word. In this case an object pronoun agreeing with the noun is added before the verb → **8**
- prepositions such as **di**, **con** and **a**, must precede question words → **9**

Examples

<table>
<tr><td></td><td>**STATEMENT**</td><td>**QUESTION**</td></tr>
</table>

① STATEMENT

Basta That's enough

Sono di qui They're from here

L'ha fatto lui He did it

Va bene That's okay

QUESTION

Basta? Is that enough?

Sono di qui? Are they from here?

L'ha fatto lui? Did he do it?

Va bene? Is that okay?

② Tua sorella è partita? *or*

È partita tua sorella?   Has your sister gone?

La Calabria è bella? *or*

È bella la Calabria?   Is Calabria beautiful?

Gli spaghetti sono buoni? *or*

Sono buoni gli spaghetti?   Is the spaghetti nice?

③ Vuoi un gelato? *or*

  Un gelato lo vuoi?   Do you want an ice cream?

Vuoi del latte *or*

  Un po' di latte lo vuoi?   Do you want some milk?

④ Contrast

Fai il bucato?   Are you doing the washing?

with

Il bucato lo fai tu?   Will you do the washing?

⑤ Piove? Sì, piove   Is it raining? Yes *or* Yes, it's raining

Capisci? No *or* No, non capisco   Do you understand? No *or*
                                           No, I don't

⑥ Dove vai?   Where are you going?

Chi parla?   Who's speaking?

⑦ Quanto costano queste scarpe? *or*

Queste scarpe, quanto costano?   How much are these shoes?

Chi è quella signora? *or*

Quella signora, chi è?   Who is that lady?

⑧ Chi pagherà il conto? *or*   Who will pay the bill?

Il conto, chi lo pagherà?

⑨ Di che colore è?   What colour is it?

Con chi parlavi?   Who were you talking to?

A cosa stai pensando?   What are you thinking about?

Question Forms *continued*

no?, vero?

no? or **vero?** is used to check that what you've said is correct, like 'isn't it?' or 'haven't you?' in English → ❶

vero is used to check a negative statement → ❷

Indirect Questions

Word order in Italian indirect questions is no different from that of statements → ❸

Tenses in indirect questions are generally the same as in English, except for the use of the perfect conditional where the present conditional is used in English → ❹

Examples

1   Hai finito, no?   You've finished, haven't you?
       Questa è la tua macchina, vero?   This is your car, isn't it?

2   Non sono partiti, vero?   They haven't gone, have they?
       Non fa molto male, vero?   It doesn't hurt much, does it?

3   Vorrei sapere quanto costa   I'd like to know how much it
                                      costs

       Mi domando cosa pensano   I wonder what they think

4   Ha detto che non era colpa sua   He said it wasn't his fault
       Ha detto che verrà   He said he'll come
       Aveva detto che sarebbe venuto   He'd said he'd come

Use of numbers

Cardinal (one, two etc)		Ordinal (first, second etc)	
zero	0		
uno (una, un)	1	primo	1°
due	2	secondo	2°
tre	3	terzo	3°
quattro	4	quarto	4°
cinque	5	quinto	5°
sei	6	sesto	6°
sette	7	settimo	7°
otto	8	ottavo	8°
nove	9	nono	9°
dieci	10	decimo	10°
undici	11	undicesimo	11°
dodici	12	dodicesimo	12°
tredici	13	tredicesimo	13°
quattordici	14	quattordicesimo	14°
quindici	15	quindicesimo	15°
sedici	16	sedicesimo	16°
diciassette	17	diciassettesimo	17°
diciotto	18	diciottesimo	18°
diciannove	19	diciannovesimo	19°
venti	20	ventesimo	20°
ventuno	21	ventunesimo	21°
ventidue	22	ventiduesimo	22°
ventitré	23	ventitreesimo	23°
trenta	30	trentesimo	30°
quaranta	40	quarantesimo	40°
cinquanta	50	cinquantesimo	50°
sessanta	60	sessantesimo	60°
settanta	70	settantesimo	70°
ottanta	80	ottantesimo	80°
novanta	90	novantesimo	90°
novantanove	99	novantanovesimo	99°

Use of numbers

Cardinal		Ordinal	
cento	100	centesimo	100°
centouno	101	centunesimo	101°
(centouna, centoun)			
centodue	102	centoduesimo	102°
centotré	103	centotreesimo	103°
centodieci	110	centodecimo	110°
centoquarantadue	142	centoquarantaduesimo	142°
duecento	200	duecentesimo	200°
duecentouno	201	duecentunesimo	201°
duecentotré	203	duecentotreesimo	203°
trecento	300	trecentesimo	300°
quattrocento	400	quattrocentesimo	400°
cinquecento	500	cinquecentesimo	500°
seicento	600	seicentesimo	600°
settecento	700	settecentesimo	700°
ottocento	800	ottocentesimo	800°
novecento	900	novecentesimo	900°
mille	1000	millesimo	1000°
milleuno	1001	millunesimo	1001°
milleduecentodue	1202	milleduecentoduesimo	1202°
duemila	2000	duemillesimo	2000°
cinquemilatrecento	5300	cinquemilatrecentesimo	5300°
un milione	1.000.000	milionesimo	1.000.000°
due milioni	2.000.000	duemilionesimo	2.000.000°

Ordinal numbers are adjectives which tell you the order in which the noun occurs (first, third, etc). They end with either o, or a, depending on whether the noun is masculine or feminine:

il 15° piano	the 15th floor	la 24ª giornata	the 24th day

Fractions		Other numerical expressions	
un mezzo	a half	zero virgola cinque (0,5)	0.5
un terzo	a third	uno virgola tre (1,3)	1.3
due terzi	two thirds	dieci per cento	10%
un quarto	a quarter	sei più due	6 + 2
tre quarti	three quarters	sei meno due	6 − 2
un quinto	a fifth	due volte sei	2 × 6
un sesto	a sixth	sei diviso due	6 ÷ 2

ⓘ Note the use of commas in decimal numbers, and full stops with millions.

Other Uses

Approximate numbers
- ending in -ina

una ventina di DVD	about twenty DVDs
Eravamo una trentina	There were about thirty of us
È sulla quarantina	He's about forty
gente sulla cinquantina	people of around fifty

- ending in -aio

un centinaio di persone	about a hundred people
centinaia di volte	hundreds of times
un migliaio di casi	about a thousand cases
due migliaia di macchine	about two thousand cars

Measurements

venti metri quadri	20 square metres
venti metri cubi	20 cubic metres
un ponte lungo cento metri	a bridge 100 metres long
essere largo/alto tre metri	to be 3 metres wide/long

Miscellaneous

Abitano al numero dieci	They live at number 10
nel capitolo sei	in chapter 6
Sono a pagina tre	They're on page 3
Abitano al terzo piano	They live on the 3rd floor
Sono arrivata seconda nella gara	I came second in the competition
su una scala da uno a dieci	on a scale of one to ten

Telephone numbers

The digits in a telephone number are spoken individually:

zero zero tre nove zero sei quattro due otto uno sette sei zero due
(0039 0642817602)

tre quattro sette sette zero tre quattro nove zero cinque
(3477034905)

Calendar

Che data è oggi?/ Quanti ne abbiamo oggi?	What's the date today?
È il primo maggio	It's May 1st
È il due maggio	It's May 2nd
È il ventotto febbraio	It's February 28th
Arrivano il diciannove luglio	They're arriving on July 19th

ⓘ Use cardinal numbers except for the first of the month.

Years

È nata nel 1993	She was born in 1993
il dodici febbraio duemilatredici	(on) 12th February 2013

Other expressions

negli anni sessanta	in the sixties
nel ventunesimo secolo	in the twenty-first century
in *or* a maggio	in May
lunedì (quindici)	on Monday (the fifteenth)
di lunedì	on Mondays
fra *or* tra dieci giorni	in 10 days' time
otto giorni fa	8 days ago

211

The time

Che ore sono?	What time is it?
È l'una	It's one o'clock
Sono le due	It's two o'clock

ⓘ Use **sono** for all times except one o'clock.

00.00	mezzanotte midnight, twelve o'clock
00.10	mezzanotte e dieci ten past midnight
00.15	mezzanotte e un quarto, mezzanotte e quindici
00.30	mezzanotte e mezza, mezzanotte e trenta
00.45	l'una meno un quarto, l'una meno quindici, mezzanotte e quarantacinque
01.00	l'una di mattina one a.m., one o'clock in the morning
01.10	l'una e dieci (di mattina)
01.15	l'una e un quarto, l'una e quindici
01.30	l'una e mezza, l'una e trenta
01.45	l'una e quarantacinque; le due meno un quarto, le due meno quindici
01.50	l'una e cinquanta, le due meno dieci
01.59	l'una e cinquantanove, le due meno un minuto
12.00	mezzogiorno, le dodici noon, twelve o'clock
12.30	mezzogiorno e mezza, mezzogiorno e trenta, le dododici e mezza
13.00	l'una (del pomeriggio), le tredici, le ore tredici
01.30	l'una e mezza/trenta (del pomeriggio), le tredici e trenta, le ore tredici e trenta
19.00	le sette (di sera), le diciannove, le ore diciannove
19.30	le sette e mezza/trenta, le diciannove e trenta, le ore diciannove e trenta

ⓘ The twenty-four hour clock is widely used in Italy.

alle diciannove *or*	at nineteen hours
alle ore diciannove	at nineteen hundred hours

A che ora venite? — Alle sette	What time are you coming? — At seven
L'ufficio è chiuso da mezzogiorno alle due	The office is closed from twelve to two
alle due di notte/del pomeriggio	at two o'clock in the morning/afternoon; at two a.m./p.m.
alle otto di sera	at eight in the evening; at eight p.m.
alle cinque in punto	at five o'clock sharp
verso le nove	at around nine
poco dopo mezzogiorno	shortly after noon
fra le otto e le nove	between eight and nine o'clock
Erano le tre e mezza passate	It was after half past three
Devi esserci entro le nove	You have to be there by nine
Ci vogliono tre ore	It takes three hours
Ci metto una mezz'ora	It takes me half an hour
È rimasta in bagno per un'ora	She was in the bathroom for an hour
Li aspetto da quaranta minuti	I've been waiting for them for forty minutes
Sono partiti qualche minuto fa	They left a few minutes ago
L'ho fatto in venti minuti	I did it in twenty minutes
Il treno arriva fra un quarto d'ora	The train arrives in a quarter of an hour
Per quanto tempo dovremo aspettare?	How long will we have to wait?

Translation problems

Beware of translating word for word. The following are examples of where Italian tends to differ from English:

English phrasal verbs (i.e. verbs such as 'to look for'; 'to fall down') are often translated by one word in Italian → **1**

English verbs often require a preposition where there is none in Italian, or vice versa → **2**

Different English prepositions may be translated by the one Italian preposition → **3**

A word which is singular in English may be plural in Italian, or vice versa → **4**

There is no Italian equivalent for the apostrophe s and s apostrophe possessive → **5**

See also at/in/to, page 220.

The following pages look at some specific problems.

Examples

① scappare — to run away
cadere — to fall down
rendere — to give back

② pagare qc — to pay for sth
guardare qc/qn — to look at sth/sb
ascoltare qc/qn — to listen to sth/sb
dire a qn — to tell sb
ubbedire a qn — to obey sb
ricordarsi di qc/qn — to remember sth/sb

③ meravigliarsi di — to be surprised at
stufo di — fed up of/with
rubare qc a — to steal sth from
restio a — reluctant to

④ gli affari — business
i suoi capelli — his/her hair
Le lasagne sono ... — Lasagne is...
i bagagli — luggage

⑤ la macchina di mia sorella — my sister's car
(*literally*: ....of my sister)

la camera delle ragazze — the girls' bedroom
(*literally*... of the girls)

-ing

This is translated by the gerund in Italian:

> 'to be ...-ing' is sometimes translated by **stare** + *gerund*, when the verb describes something at the moment, but a simple tense is often used. A simple tense must be used when the verb refers to the future. → ❶

The past participle, not the gerund, is used for physical positions such as lying and sitting → ❷

> to see/hear sb ...-ing, use an infinitive or **che** + *verb* → ❸

'-ing' can also be translated by:

- an infinitive, see page 46 → ❹
- a perfect infinitive, see page 50 → ❺
- the gerund, when used abverbially, see page 52 → ❻
- a noun → ❼

to be

'to be' is generally translated by **essere** → ❽

Examples

1 Che fai *or* stai facendo? — What are you doing?
Che fai domani sera? — What are you doing tomorrow evening?

Partono *or* Stanno partendo — They're leaving
Partono alle sette — They're leaving at seven

2 Erano seduti in prima fila — They were sitting in the front row
Era sdraiata sulla sabbia — She was lying on the sand

3 L'ho visto partire — I saw him leaving
L'ho visto che partiva
L'ho sentita piangere — I heard her crying
L'ho sentita che piangeva

4 Mi piace cucinare — I like cooking
invece di rispondere — instead of answering
prima di partire — before leaving
Iniziò a piovere — It started raining

5 dopo aver perso molti soldi — after losing a lot of money

6 Essendo più timida di me, — Being shyer than me, she didn't
non ha gli ha parlato — speak to him

7 Il fumo fa molto male — Smoking is very bad for you

8 È tardi — It's late
Sono loro — It's them
Siamo stanchi — We're tired

stare is used

- with the gerund to make continuous tenses → **1**
- in perfect and pluperfect tenses of **essere**, which consist of the present/imperfect tense of **essere** + past participle of **stare** → **2**
- interchangeably with **essere** when talking about locations → **3**
- when talking about health → **4**

In various set expressions **avere** is used (with the final **e** dropped):

aver caldo/freddo	to be hot/cold
aver fame/sete	to be hungry/thirsty
aver paura	to be afraid
aver torto/ragione	to be wrong/right

fare is used to talk about the weather → **5**

avere is used for ages → **6**

it is, it's

These are never translated by a pronoun in Italian → **7**

In expressions of time, use **sono**, except for one o'clock → **8**

To describe the weather, see above.

When 'it's' is followed by a pronoun, such as 'me', 'her' or 'them', the form of **essere** agrees with the person referred to → **9**

can, be able

Ability is generally expressed by **potere** → **10**

If the meaning is 'to know how to' use **sapere** → **11**

'can' with verbs of seeing and hearing is not translated in Italian → **12**

Examples

1. Ci sto pensando — I'm thinking about it
   Stavano chiacchierando — They were chatting

2. Non ci sono mai stata — I've never been there
   Ero stato malato — I had been ill

3. La casa sta *orè* sulla collina — The house is on the hill
   Sta *orè* fuori — It's outside

4. Sto bene, grazie — I'm fine thanks
   Sta male — He's not well

5. Che tempo fa? — What's the weather like?
   Fa caldo/freddo — It's hot/cold
   Fa bel/brutto tempo — It's nice/bad weather

6. Quanti anni hai? — How old are you?
   Ho quindici anni — I'm fifteen

7. Dammelo, è mio — Give it me, it's mine
   È molto lontano — It's a long way

8. Sono le nove — It's nine o'clock
   È l'una meno un quarto — It's a quarter to one

9. Sono io — It's me
   È lei — It's her
   Sono loro — It's them

10. Puoi venire? — Can you come?

11. Non so come spiegarlo — I can't explain it

12. Si vede il mare — You can see the sea
    Non ti sento — I can't hear you

Translation problems

to like

piacere, the Italian verb used to translate 'to like', means 'to be pleasing', so **Mi piace l'Italia** literally means 'Italy is pleasing to me', and **Gli animali piacciono ai bambini** means 'Animals are pleasing to children'.

Remember the following when using **piacere**:
- the thing(s) liked is/are the subject of the Italian verb → ①
- if the thing liked is singular, the verb is singular (**piace/è piaciuto** etc): if the things liked are plural, the verb is plural (**piacciono/sono piaciuti** etc) → ②
- **piacere** is used with **a**, or an indirect object pronoun → ③

to

'to' is often translated by **a**, see page 190 → ④

When telling the time, e.g. ten to six, use **meno** → ⑤

When the meaning is 'in order to' use **per** → ⑥

When 'to' is part of the infinitive following an adjective such as 'easy', 'difficult', 'impossible', use the Italian infinitive with **da** → ⑦

unless the infinitive has an object → ⑧

at/in/to

For 'in' or 'to' + a country, use the Italian preposition **in** → ⑨

For 'in' or 'to' + a town, use the Italian preposition **a** → ⑩

When the meaning is 'to'/'at' + someone's house/place of business use **da** → ⑪

1 Il cane piace a mio figlio
   I cani piacciono a mio figlio

My son likes the dog
My son likes dogs

2 Il concerto è piaciuto a tutti
   I cioccolatini piaceranno a tutti

Everyone liked the concert
Everyone will like the chocolates

3 A mia madre piace molto il
   giardinaggio
   Ti piace questa canzone?
   Non gli piacciono i pomodori

My mother likes gardening very
   much
Do you like this song?
He doesn't like tomatoes

4 Dallo a Patrizia

Give it to Patrizia

5 le sei meno un quarto
   l'una meno tre minuti

a quarter to six
three minutes to one

6 L'ho fatto per rassicurarti
   Si è fermato per guardarlo

I did it to reassure you
He stopped to look at it

7 facile da capire
   impossibile da dimenticare

easy to understand
impossible to forget

8 È facile capirlo
   È impossibile crederci

It's easy to understand it
It's impossible to believe it

9 Abitano negli Stati Uniti
   Andiamo in Germania il quattro
   maggio
   una città in Cina

They live in the United States
We're going to Germany on
   May 4
a city in China

10 È andato a Parigi
   Vive a Bologna

He's gone to Paris
He lives in Bologna

11 Andiamo da Anna
   È dal parucchiere

Let's go to Anna's house
She's at the hairdresser's

General Points

Vowels and consonants are always clearly pronounced in Italian, and each syllable of a word is audible, unlike in English, where letters, and sometimes whole syllables, are often not pronounced. Compare, for example:

lettera (both **e**s are equally clear, audible **r**)
letter (2nd **e** indistinct, **r** usually not pronounced)
interessante, (5 syllables)
interesting (3 syllables)

Diphthongs

A diphthong is a glide between two vowel sounds in the same syllable. The vowels in 'say', 'go' and 'might' are diphthongs. Diphthongs are very common in English, but much less so in Italian, where most vowels are a single sound, as they are in English words such as 'top', 'back' and 'set' The diphthongs found in Italian are vowels preceded by a **y**, or a **w** sound:

ia[ja] - **chiaro**   **ua**[wa] - **sguardo**
ie[je] - **pieno**   **ue**[we] - **guerra**
io[jo] - **pioggia**   **ui**[wi] - **guidare**
iu[ju] - **chiuso**   **uo**[wo] - **fuoco**

Stress

Italian words are generally stressed on the next to the last syllable, (so two-syllable words are stressed on the first syllable, three-syllable words on the second syllable, and so on):

ca sa   set ti **ma** na
ra **gaz** zo   ge ne ral **men** te

For more details see page 180.

If the stress comes on the last vowel of a word with more than one syllable, the vowel is always written with an accent:

per **ché**
par le **rò**
un i ver si **tà**

For more details see page 180.

Pronunciation of Consonants

Most consonants are pronounced as in English, except that they are always clear, and double consonants are audible. Thus, in **sabbia** sand, for example, the **b** sound ending the first syllable carries on to start the second syllable: sab-bya.

Note the following:

		PRONOUNCED	EXAMPLES
c before a, o, u	[k]	like k in kiss	camera, come, cubo
c before e or i	[tʃ]	like ch in China	certo, cinese
ch	[k]	like k in kiss	chiesa
g before a, o, u	[g]	like g in good	gara, largo, gusto
g before e or i	[dʒ]	like g in rage	gelato, giro
gh	[g]	like g in good	laghi, ghiaccio
gl before i	[ʎ]	like ll in million	meglio, gli
gl before other vowels	[gl]	like gl in piglet	sigla
gn	[ɲ]	like ny in canyon	gnocchi, ragno
h is not pronounced		like h in honest	hanno
r	[r]	like r in zero	raro, rapido
sc before e or i	[ʃ]	like sh in ship	scena, sci
z	[dz]	like ds in lids	zanzara
z	[ts]	like ts in bits	ragazzo

Pronunciation of Vowels

		PRONOUNCED	EXAMPLES
a	[a]	like a in apple	animale
e	[ɛ]	like e in set	schema
e	[e]	like ay in day	stella
i	[i]	like ee in sheep	clima
i before a vowel often	[j]	like y in yoghurt	Lidia, negozio
o	[o]	like o in pot	ora
u	[u]	like oo in soot	puro
u before a vowel often	[w]	like w in win	usuale

Stress: Cases where the normal rule does not apply

In cases where the last syllable of a word is stressed, this is shown by an accent. Most of these are:

- nouns ending in -**tà**, many of which have counterparts in English ending in -ty, such as 'reality' and 'university'

re al tà	reality	u ni ver si tà	university
fe li ci tà	happiness, felicity	fe del tà	fidelity
cu rio si tà	curiosity	fa col tà	faculty
bon tà	goodness	cit tà	city
cru del tà	cruelty	e tà	age
me tà	half		

- 1st and 3rd person singular future verbs, and 3rd person singular past historics:

sa rò	I will be
fi ni rà	it will finish
as pet te rà	she'll wait
par lò	he spoke
an dò	she went

- adverbs and conjunctions such as

perché	why
però	however
così	so

In cases where the stress is on an unexpected syllable other than the last, there is no accent to show this. In this book, such vowels are shown in italics, e.g.

m*a*cchina	car
*u*tile	useful
port*a*tile	laptop

Pronunciation

Stress in present tense verb forms

All present tense forms except the 3rd person plural follow the rule, and stress the next to the last syllable, e.g. *parlo* I speak; *considera* he considers

In the 3rd person plural form the stress is not on the next to the last syllable, but matches that of the 1st person singular:

1st person singular		3rd person plural	
par lo	I speak	*par* la no	they speak
con *si* de ro	I consider	con *si* de ra no	they consider
mi al *le* no	I'm training	si al *le* na no	they're training

Stress in 2nd conjugation infinitives

Stress is regular for the infinitives of all 1st and 3rd. and many 2nd conjugation verbs, e.g. **parlare** *to speak*, **finire** *to finish*, **vedere** *to see*. However, there are also many 2nd conjugation infinitives which do not stress the 1st e of the **-ere** ending, eg:

essere *to be*, **vendere** *to sell*, **permettere** *to allow*, **dividere** *to divide*.

When learning 2nd conjugation verbs, note which syllable of the infinitive is stressed.

Pronunciation

From Sounds to Spelling

Apart from the occasional problem of unexpected stress, the way Italian is spelled is a good guide to how it should be pronounced. See page 180.

It is also easy to know how to spell words, if the following points are remembered:

-care/-gare verbs

Verbs with infinitives ending -care, or -gare, for example cercare and pagare, add an h to keep the c or g hard in front of endings starting with e or i:

Vowel that follows c/g	Present of cercare		Present of pagare	
o	cerco	I look for	pago	I pay
i	cerchi	you look for	paghi	you pay
a	cerca	he/she looks for	paga	he/she pays
i	cerchiamo	we look for	paghiamo	we pay
a	cercate	you look for	pagate	you pay
a	cercano	they look for	pagano	they pay

Vowel that follows c/g	Future of cercare		Future of pagare	
e	cercherò	I'll look for	pagherò	I'll pay
e	cercherai	you'll look for	pagherai	you'll pay
e	cercherà	he/she will look for	pagherà	he/she will pay
e	cercheremo	we'll look for	pagheremo	we'll pay
e	cercherete	you'll look for	pagherete	you'll pay
e	cercheranno	they'll look for	pagheranno	they'll pay

-ca/-ga nouns and adjectives

Nouns and adjectives ending in -ca and -ga always keep the hard sound of the consonant in the plural, so h is added before the plural ending -e:

Singular		Plural	
amica	friend	amiche	friends
riga	line	righe	lines
ricca	rich	ricche	rich
lunga	long	lunghe	long

-co/-go nouns and adjectives

Some nouns and adjectives ending in -co and -go keep the hard sound of the consonant in the plural, so h is added before the plural ending -i, e.g.:

Singular		Plural	
fuoco	fire	fuochi	fires
albergo	hotel	alberghi	hotels
ricco	rich	ricchi	rich
lungo	long	lunghi	long

Other nouns nouns and adjectives ending in -co and -go change the sound of the consonant in the plural from hard [k] or [g] to soft [tʃ] or [dʒ], so no h is added, e.g.:

Singular		Plural	
amico	friend	amici	friends
astrologo	astrologer	astrologi	astrologers
greco	Greek	greci	Greek
psicologico	psychological	psicologici	psychological

-io nouns

The plural of nouns ending -io is spelled -ii if the i of the -io ending is a stressed vowel, e.g. zio *uncle* plural: zii, and invio *dispatch* plural: invii.

In cases where the i of the -io is not a stressed vowel, but is pronounced [j], the plural is spelled with a single i, e.g. occhio *eye* plural occhi; figlio *son* plural: figli.

-cia/-gia nouns

Generally, if the i of the -cia/-gia ending of a noun is a stressed vowel, the i is retained in the plural, eg farma*cia* chemist plural: farma*cie*; bu*gia* lie plural: bu*gie*. If the i of the ending serves to keep the c/g soft, and is not pronounced as a vowel, there is no i in the plural: fac*cia* face, plural: fac*ce*; spiag*gia* beach, plural: spiag*ge*.

Accents

Use an accent when a word is stressed on the final syllable, e.g. città, cercherò, università. See page 180.

Accents are also used on certain one-syllable words to distinguish them from words that are spelled the same (homophones):

da	from		dà	he/she gives
e	and		è	is
la	the/it		là	there
li	them		lì	there
ne	of it/them		né	neither
se	if		sé	himself
si	himself/herself/one		sì	yes
te	you		tè	tea

The grave accent (à, è, ì, ò ,ù) is used on most words. The acute accent is used to spell conjunctions ending in che, such as benché although, and perché because. It is also used on né and sé (except in the phrases se stesso and se stessa himself; herself).

può, già, ciò, più and giù are spelled with an accent, for no obvious reason.

Alphabet

The Alphabet

A,a	a	J,j	[i'lunga]	S,s	['ɛsse]
B,b	[bi]	K,k	['kappa]	T,t	[ti]
C,c	[tʃi]	L,l	['ɛlle]	U,u	u
D,d	[di]	M,m	['ɛmme]	V,v	[vi, vu]
E,e	e	N,n	['ɛnne]	W,w	['dɔppjovu]
F,f	['ɛffe]	O,o	[ɔ]	X,x	[iks]
G,g	[dʒi]	P,p	[pi]	Y,y	['ipsilon]
H,h	['akka]	Q,q	[ku]	Z,z	[dzɛta]
I,i	i	R,r	['ɛrre]		

Capital letters are used as in English except for the following:

adjectives of nationality
e.g. una città tedesca   a German town
      una scrittrice italiana   an Italian writer

languages
e.g. Parla inglese?   Do you speak English?
      Parlo francese ed italiano   I speak French and Italian

days of the week:
     lunedì Monday
     martedì Tuesday
     mercoledì Wednesday
     giovedì Thursday
     venerdì Friday
     sabato Saturday
     domenica Sunday

months of the year:
     gennaio January   luglio July
     febbraio February   agosto August
     marzo March   settembre September
     aprile April   ottobre October
     maggio May   novembre November
     giugno June   dicembre December

Index

The following index lists comprehensively both grammatical terms and key words in English and Italian.

Index

Index

Index

Index

Index